JAPAN

ENCYCLOPEDIA

HARVARD
UNIVERSITY
PRESS
REFERENCE
LIBRARY

JAPAN
ENCYCLOPEDIA

LOUIS FRÉDÉRIC

Translated by Käthe Roth

THE BELKNAP PRESS OF
HARVARD UNIVERSITY PRESS
Cambridge, Massachusetts
London, England
2002

First published as *Le Japon: Dictionnaire et Civilisation,*
© 1996 Éditions Robert Laffont S.A., Paris

Published with the assistance of the French Ministry of Culture–CNL

Library of Congress Cataloging-in-Publication Data

Frédéric, Louis, 1923–
    [Japon, dictionnaire et civilisation. English]
    Japan encyclopedia / Louis Frédéric ; translated by Käthe Roth.
      p.   cm.
    Includes bibliographical references and index.
    ISBN 0-674-00770-0
    1. Japan—Civilization—Dictionaries.   I. Roth, Käthe.   II. Title.

  DS821 .F73   2002   2001052570

CONTENTS

INTRODUCTION

To my wife, Yōko, and my son, Nao

Although for the last several decades it has been second only to the United States in economic power, at least for the volume of its exports, and in spite of innumerable articles published in newspapers and cultural events periodically organized in the West, Japan is still largely a mystery to most Westerners. We may have only vague ideas about subjects such as Noh and Kabuki theater, but we are very familiar with Japanese technical prowess in the automotive, electronics, and computer industries. Mention "Japan" and the brand names Toyota, Mazda, Honda, Sony, and Canon immediately spring to mind. However, this media culture is very superficial. It is important to know and understand Japan in its entirety, so that we may judge this small country (small in area only!) with complete impartiality.

Japan is not just the items we import; it is also a history, a people, art and literature, towns and countryside, climates, families, and more. It would be both illusory and vain to try to understand the essence of Japan through the clichéd images of Sumo wrestlers, martial-arts combatants, geisha, women in kimono, and Zen monks. The reality of Japan also includes crafts and traditional industries, and is based on religions, customs, beliefs—an entire way of life—that are foreign to us. Although it is evolved from an ancient civilization, we must not lose sight of the fact that throughout its history, Japan has been resolutely turned toward the future—a future that concerns that country, of course, but also all of us. Not that Japan should necessarily serve as a model—its society is so different in nature to ours—but it can give us a different view of current problems and propose solutions and food for thought. A fairer and more realistic approach to Japan, placing it in its current context (which is in fact the result of a long evolution), is thus needed. The idea is not to make comparisons, which is always risky and generally accentuates differences, but to explain these differences, and therefore better to understand them.

The Japanese have a profound knowledge of every aspect and detail of Western societies. Unfortunately, we Westerners cannot say the same thing about Japan; for us, Europe and America are still the center of the world, and we look at distant countries only as "tourist" or "business" opportunities. Improving our relations with Japan will require us to know that country as well as the Japanese know ours.

A little more than 120 years ago, Japan opened to the West, and in less than one generation—unique in the annals of world civilization—it went from a stratified medieval society to the modern era. Two major upheavals totally transformed both Japanese relations with the West and internal relations: the Meiji revolution in 1868 and the defeat of 1945. Both events shocked the Japanese consciousness and inspired people to make a supreme effort to adapt to new physical and spiritual conditions.

In spite of more than 100 years of close contact with foreigners, publication of huge numbers of travel books and accounts, and numerous scholarly studies, Japan, it is safe to say, is still largely unfamiliar to the general public in the West. Is it because of distance? It is true that we know more about things closer to us; what happens in distant countries affects us only when it might have a direct influence on our lives. Is it lack of interest? I don't think so, since the exoticism of Asian countries, including Japan, has always played an important part in our fantasies about foreign lands. In fact, it may be that, subconsciously, we want to retain a rather stereotyped image of the country, a dream image. Perhaps we do not want to know that Japan has considerably changed in the last 50 years and that the "romantic exoticism" no longer exists there any more than it does in Paris or London. The mind seems to balk at trading this old dream against a sense, much simpler and more prosaic, of a new environment.

One can no longer say, as a traveler in the sixteenth century would have, that the Japanese have forked feet because their shoes separate the big toe from the other toes. Nevertheless, a recent survey made by a group of researchers under the aegis of UNESCO shows that the erroneous views that persist regarding Japan are due essentially to obsolete information in the schoolbooks that our parents used. We may be perfectly aware of the latest Japanese technical achievements, but we remain deliberately ignorant of the history, beliefs, customs (except, perhaps, those that seem bizarre), and people who have made the country what it is. Geographic, climatic, economic, and cultural errors are still rife.

It is commonly thought that Japan is a tropical country, perhaps because rice and bamboo grow there. In reality, even though Tokyo's latitude is around the same as that of Algiers, Japan has a temperate climate: snow falls almost throughout the country in winter, there are four distinct seasons, and it rains as much as it does in France, though with different distribution.

We also have a mistaken tendency to associate Japan with China. Most history and art books lump the countries together under the heading "East Asia," helping to perpetuate in Western minds an association that is far from accurate. Although Japan's civilization owes much to ancient China (just as France owes much to Renaissance Italy), it nevertheless evolved independently of China: its population, language (if not writing), geography, and philosophies are essentially distinct from those of its large mainland neighbor. Buddhism, for example, practically disappeared from China after the thirteenth century, but continued to develop in Japan, modified to fit that society. Similar differences go for economics, agriculture, food, and other sectors.

Most films that Japan exports to the West, some of which are remarkable masterpieces, deal with ancient wars, such as Kurosawa's, or intimate scenes, such as Ozu's. Among the best in their genre, they portray a Japan in transition that no longer exists today.

So, it is time to get up to speed. We know the Japanese only summarily because, most of the time, we do not make the effort to know them—or, worse, we compare our own ways of life to theirs. And why should they be similar? For example, something that strikes the educated traveler in Japan is the extreme rarity of statues of great men. A few effigies in bronze, in European mode, have been erected here and there, but they portray "characters," not statesmen or sovereigns. The Japanese do not admire the man himself, but the virtue he symbolizes; thus, these statues personify a quality of courage, loyalty, or sometimes knowledge, just as statues of Buddhist divinities embody moral or religious principles. The individual, in Japan, exists only through the will of others, the anonymous crowd, and must never lose sight of the fact that a person is just a temporary phenomenon, while the mass of the Japanese people is a continuing entity.

Too many travelers who have gone to Japan have seen the country only through the warped vision imposed on them by tourist agencies that cater to the taste of their customers. One cannot judge the spirit of a country only through the beauties of a landscape or a moss garden; one can at best form an idea of what it once was. In fact, one of the essential characteristics of Japan is change: it is a living society, always in the process of improving and transforming. This perpetual evolution in Japanese thought and behavior, found in a myriad of seemingly innocuous facts of daily life, is where the Japanese nation finds its profound uniqueness. It remains to be seen whether, in the next few years, customs and habits specific to the Japanese will end up disappearing, drowned in the huge wave of homogenization sweeping the modern world.

But the spirit that gave birth to them will survive, in spite of the current international trend toward "equalization," in a certain way of being, thinking, and conceiving of the relationship between human beings and nature that is the very essence of the Japanese people and affects their spiritual survival.

People naturally study their past to draw lessons and reasons to hope for a future. The Japanese, inured to the Buddhist idea of impermanence of everything, know very well that change is inevitable, and they always accept it as a positive thing. Based on the only criteria for permanence that they know, the continuity of all things and the all-powerful spirit, they have a remarkable ability to adapt to new circumstances, constantly attempting to reconcile what seems to us to be irreconcilable—the past and the present, the spirit and the material—for this is the essential element of their existence. They have never seen opposition between two extremes, but complementarity. In Japan and a number of other Asian countries, life is made of perpetual motion between one extreme and another, for these extremes are viewed as fleeting, necessarily transitory aspects of a sort of current that is alternating and continuous at the same time. It is a way of thinking radically different from the Western outlook, which oscillates between extremes by seeing them as opposites.

Thus, the twentieth-century Japanese sometimes observe customs of very ancient origins without being considered strange. In Japan, people can live in the present while following ways of being or customs whose origin is sometimes very ancient. To say that all Japanese are aware of this would be an exaggeration; they usually act from instinct or conform with a consensus considered self-evident, which gives them a sense of sufficiency and continuity. One might almost say that in Japan a number of societies coexist in a unique combination: that of modern labor, similar in all ways to that everywhere in today's world, with its demands, schedules, specialization, uniformity, and despair; that of artisanal labor, where a concern with beautiful materials, constant improvement, and achievement is traditional; that of relationships, public and private, in which a concern with "face"—"what will be said"—is primordial; that of the continuity of names; and, especially, that of behavior, perhaps the most important, since it affects all the others: all individuals are supposed to behave according to their place in society and their "duty" (*see* GIRI, ON, OYABUN-KOBUN). Unlike Western people, who are born with "rights," the Japanese come into the world with duties that they must fulfill scrupulously. They acquire rights (and relative ones at that) only by conforming with the tacit rules that govern their society.

Modern Japanese writers sometimes complain that Japan's too-rapid development is destroying this sense of duty by making ways of being and living homogeneous and not to Japanese standards. But the Japanese are deliberately pessimistic, for fear of being too optimistic. In reality, customs and behaviors do not disappear so easily; they simply become more hidden, overwhelmed by modern life. The "Japan-ness" of inhabitants of the Land of the Rising Sun still underlies all their thoughts and acts, since it is inherited from their parents, their teachers, their history. It is difficult to separate a people from its geographical or social environment. One cannot know a Japanese person unless one sees him or her as a distinct entity that is part of a defined group. A Japanese person alone is a lost person: he or she exists only if he or she is aware of being part of a group, being an integral part of a community, and thus acting in conformity with the other individuals in this group.

Japanese people are deeply individualistic—but individualists who are able to lose themselves in the community. In the West, we act mainly by reacting: we act more willingly "against" than "for" something, and we can easily unite for this purpose; we are, in Pierre Dac's famous words, "against him who is for and for him who is against." In Japan, action, not reaction, incites people to act; they group together with the goal of accomplishing something. Reaction finds them always divided, action always united. This is perhaps the secret to their vitality and success, and to the durability of their thought.

Knowing Japan and the Japanese better is one of the necessities of modern life. To do this, we must know something about their geography, history, struggles, beliefs, arts and literature, and a myriad of other things that form the basis of a civilization, which is made not of monuments and works of art, but of people who lived, struggled, worked, and died for an ideal. It is important, therefore, to learn about the great people who shaped the history and fate of the country, who infused it with a spirit and enabled it to endure. We must gain a fairer and more precise view of their religions and beliefs, probe their thought by studying their literature and poetry, appreciate their art and architecture, and look more deeply at their customs and ways of life.

What book could teach us better than an encyclopedia? As an indispensable complement to general works, it puts within our grasp notions that might be hard to find elsewhere. It gives names and dates and links facts and information. Users can go from one article to another, following corollaries or complements, and thus discover a world within a single subject.

Although this encyclopedia is devoted mainly to Japanese people, Westerners who helped to develop Japan in one way or another, or who influenced its future or thought, are included. General headings such as "History," "Geography," "Literature," and "Painting" refer readers to more specific entries and link the articles to each other. In this work, I have tried systematically to give preference to cultural, religious, literary, artistic, and historical facts and to biographies, without neglecting other areas that are more subject to constant change, such as economics and politics.

One does not read an encyclopedia; one consults it. To make research easier, the articles are in strictly alphabetical order. An index of names and terms used in the articles but not the subject of individual entries enables readers to find other information more easily. The volume also includes a chronology and a bibliography.

The encyclopedic nature of this book covers the entire Japanese territory (though it excludes its ancient and temporary "colonies" and, for lack of space, purely geographic sites) and its entire history—political, literary, religious, scientific, and other—from the dawn of its prehistory to today. It may also, I hope, become a useful companion for students and travelers, and a valuable source of information for those interested in Japan and its civilization—teachers, journalists, writers, art lovers, collectors, artists, and the simply curious. Its first vocation is to be a practical reference. There are, of course, many books on Japan, many of them published in that country. Few of them, however, are written in a Western language, and most are devoted to a particular subject—history, literature, or art. This encyclopedic work was one of the first to be published in French, and it is the result of many years of research in France and Japan. I obtained much information from Japanese and French friends who encouraged me in this research, including Ōtani Chōjun in Kyoto; Bernard Frank, professor at Collège de France in Paris; Bernard Faure, professor at Stanford University; Christine Shimizu, curator of national museums; and others, too numerous to mention here. I would like in particular to thank my editor, Guy Schoeller, and especially Paul Quesson, who so skillfully published the book—they both have my warm gratitude.

Louis Frédéric
Paris, 1996

CHRONOLOGY

Date	Cultural Events	Historical Events
1000 BC(?)–ca. 10th century AD		Jōmon prehistoric period
660 BC		Traditional date of the foundation of the Japanese empire. Mythical emperor Jimmu
300 BC–300 AD		Yayoi period. Yamato kingdoms
Late 3rd century		Arrival of the "archers on horseback" (kibaminzoku) from Korea
Late 4th–early 5th century		First political establishments. Emperor Ōjin. Jingū Kōgō. Conquest of southern Korea
4th–7th century	Period of the large kofun burial sites	
538	Official introduction of Buddhism	Beginning of the Asuka period
562	Arrival of Buddhist sculptures	Defeat of Japan in Korea
587	Foundation of the Hōryū-ji	
592		Shōtoku Taishi, regent
610	First cremations	
645		Reform of the Taika era, regulating public life, law, and protocol. Beginning of the Nara period
670	Reconstruction of the Hōryū-ji	
672	Reconstruction of the Ise sanctuaries every 20 years begins.	
690	Yakushi-ji pagoda	
700	Poems by Kakinomoto no Hitomaro	
701		Taihō Code
700–710	The kondō of the Hōryū-ji is painted	710: transfer of the capital to Heijō-kyō (Nara)
712	The Kojiki is written	
720	The Nihon shoki is written	
731	Izumo fudoki	
735	Sutra of the Kako genzai inga-kyō	
736	Yume-dono of the Hōryū-ji	

Date	Cultural Events	Historical Events
741	Construction of provincial temples (Kokubun-ji)	
745–749	Casting of the Daibutsu of the Tōdai-ji in Nara	
753	Arrival of the monk Ganjin from China	
756	Creation of the Shōsō-in "museum"	
759	Beginning of poems in the *Man'yōshū*	
763	Ganjin dies	
784		Foundation of Nagaoka
794		Beginning of the Heian period. Transfer of the capital to Heian-kyō (Kyoto)
797	Shoku Nihongi	
799	Introduction of cotton	
800–803		Fights against the Emishi in the north
805	Saichō returns from China and founds the Tendai sect on Mt. Heiei	
806	Kūkai returns from China (Shingon sect)	
808	First medical treatise, *Daidō-ruijūhō*	
814	*Ryōun-shū*	
ca. 822	*Nihon ryōiki*, attributed to Keikai	
824–833	Murō-ji pagoda, near Nara	
835	Kūkai dies	
840	*Nihon-kōki* is written	
858	Kagura, Saibara, Fūzoku poems	
879	First history compilation, *Montoku jitsuroku*	
880	Poet Ariwara no Narihira dies	
ca. 890	Shinto statues of the Yakushi-ji. "Red" Fudō (Aka-Fudō) of the Kōya-san	
894	Sugawara no Michizane refuses to go on a mission to China	End of official missions to Tang-dynasty China
ca. 900	*Taketori monogatari*	
903	Sugawara no Michizane dies in Dazaifu (Kyushu)	
904	*Ise monogatari*	
905	*Kōkin waka-shū*	
927	*Engi-shiki*	
935	*Tosa-nikki* by Ki no Tsurayuki	
939–940		Revolt by Taira no Masakado, first evidence of the existence of a warrior class
ca. 950	Active period of painters Hirotaka and Kose Kintada	First Fujiwara regents
947–956	*Ise monogatari emaki*	
951	*Gosen waka-shū*, *Yamato monogatari*	
ca. 970	*Utsubo monogatari*, *Kagerō Nikki*	

Date	Cultural Events	Historical Events
985	*Ōjōyō-shū* by Eshin	
988	*Ochikubo monogatari*	
1000	*Makura no sōshi* by Sei Shōnagon	
1004	*Izumi Shikibu nikki.* Sei Shōnagon dies	
1005 (?)	Beginning of *Genji monogatari. Shūi waka-shū*	
1008–1010	*Murasaki Shikibu nikki*	
1013	*Rōei waka-shū*	
1052	Byōdō-in villa in Uji	
1053	"Amida" by Jōchō at the Byōdō-in	
1050–1060	*Tsutsumi chūnagon monogatari, Sagoromo monogatari,* various novels	
1077	*Konjaku monogatari*	
1078	"Kichijō-ten" and "Bishamon-ten" in the Kondō of the Hōryū-ji	
1069–1134	*Ōkagami*	
1086		The "Retired Emperor" (Insei) regime begins with Shirakawa
ca. 1092	*Eiga monogatari*	
ca. 1100	Toba Sōjō (Kakuyū). "Shigisan engi emaki"	
1127	*Kin'yō waka-shū.* Paintings of the "Celestial Kings" at the Tō-ji in Kyoto	
ca. 1130	"Genji monogatari emaki"	
1140	The "Jūni-shinshō" of the Kōfuku-ji, Nara	
1151	*Shika waka-shū*	
1156		Beginning of the Taira hegemony
ca. 1160	The Taira offer the Lotus Sutra to the Utsukushima-jinja	
1170	*Ima-kagami*	
1178	*Mizu-kagami*	
1180	*Meigetsu-ki* by Fujiwara Teika	Civil wars between the Taira and the Minamoto begin
1185	Sanju-no-tō of the Kōfuku-ji, Nara	Decisive victory by the Minamoto at Dan no Ura
1187	*Senzai waka-shū* by Fujiwara Shunzei	
1192		Foundation of the Kamakura *bakufu*
1194	Tahōtō of the Ishiyama-dera, in Shiga	
ca. 1195	*Mizu-kagami* by Nakayama Tadachika	
1199	"Nandai-mon" of the Tōdai-ji	Minamoto no Yoritomo, first shogun, dies
1203	"Kongō Rikishi" of the Nandai-mon	
1204	Fujiwara Shunzei dies	
1205	*Shin kokin waka-shū*	
1208	Statues of monks by Unkei at the Kōfuku-ji in Nara	
ca. 1210	*Mumyō-shō,* poetry anthology	

Date	Cultural Events	Historical Events
1211	*Hōjō-ki* by Kamo no Chōmei	
1215	*Ujishūi monogatari. Uta-awase* become popular. Minamoto Sanetomo dies	
1220	*Heiji monogatari, Hōgen monogatari*	
1224	Shinran founds the Jodō Shin-shu sect	
1227	Dōgen founds the Zen Sōtō-shū	
1234	*Shin chokusen waka-shū*	
1235	*Ogura hyakunin ishhū. Heike monogatari*	
ca. 1240	*Tōkan kikō*	
1252	Casting of the Daibutsu of Kamakura	
1253	Foundation of the Kenchō-ji in Kamakura	
1254	"Senju Kannon" by Tankei (?) at the Renge-ō-in in Kyoto	
1265	*Gempei seisui-ki*	
1274		First Mongol attack
1281		Second Mongol attack
1282	"Shari-den" of the Engaku-ji in Kamakura	
1299	*Ippen Shōnin emaki*	
1301	*Azuma-kagami*	
1326	*Tsurezure-gusa*	
1333		Destruction of Kamakura
1336		Beginning of the civil war between the Northern and Southern Courts
1338		Ashikaga shogunate in Muromachi
1339	Jinnō shōtō-ki by Kitabatake Chikafusa	
1340	Tenryū-ji garden, Kyoto	
1346	*Fūga waka-shū*	
ca. 1350	Saihō-ji garden, Kyoto	
1356	*Tsukuba-shū*	
ca. 1370	*Taihei-ki*	
1376	*Masu-kagami*	
1392		Reuniting of the Northern and Southern Courts (Nambokuchō)
ca. 1400	First "Otogi-zōshi." *Gigei-ki, Soga monogatari, Kadenshō* by Zeami (beginning of Noh). The Kinkaku-ji	
1423	Development of printing	
1443	Shūbun dies. The *Yōkyoku* are completed. Zeami dies	
1466	Beginning of popular theater (Kōwaka-mai dances)	
1467–1477		Ōnin War
1468	Sesshū travels in China	
1470	*Azuma mondo*, Renga treatise	
ca. 1480	The Ginkaku-ji in Kyoto	

Date	Cultural Events	Historical Events
ca. 1500	Zen garden of the Ryōan-ji in Kyoto	Beginning of the Sengoku (Warring States) period and self-defense leagues
1506	Sesshū (b. 1420) dies	
1510	Zen garden of the Daisen-in (Daitoku-ji, Kyoto)	
1540	First *haikai* poems	
1543	Introduction of firearms	
1549	Francis Xavier arrives in Japan	
ca. 1550	Zō-ami sculpts Noh masks	
1559	Kanō Motonobu dies	
1565	Jesuits banished from Kyoto	Ashikaga Yoshiteru assassinated
1568		Oda Nobunaga occupies Kyoto on the pretext of protecting the emperor and the shogun
1571	Reconstruction of the Honden of the Istukushima-jinja	War against the Buddhist monasteries
1573		Oda Nobunaga becomes shogun
1576	Azuchi castle built	
1582	Seven Christian envoys leave for Rome	Oda Nobunaga dies. Toyotomi Hideyoshi succeeds him
1583–1584	Construction of the Osaka castle begins	
1589	Sesson (b. 1504) dies	
1590	Kanō Eitoku (b. 1543) dies	
1591	Sen no Rikyū is forced to commit suicide	
1592	*Isoho monogatari*	Hideyoshi invades Korea
ca. 1596	First Kana-zōshi in Hiragana	
1597	Hideyoshi persecutes the Jesuits	
1598	Gardens and Shoin style of the Daigo-ji in Kyoto	Hideyoshi dies. Troops withdraw from Korea
1600	William Adams arrives	Battle of Sekigahara. Tokugawa Ieyasu takes on Hideyoshi's political heritage
1602	Nijō castle in Kyoto	
1603	Kabuki theater founded by Okuni	Ieyasu founds the Edo shogunate
1604	Honden of the Ôsaki Hachiman-jinja in Sendai	
1608	Himeji castle expanded	
1610	Hasegawa Tōhaku (b. 1539) dies	
1613	Date Masamune's Christian envoys travel to Acapulco and Rome. Tokugawa Ieyasu bans Christianity	
1614		Winter siege of the Osaka castle
1615	*Buke-shohatto*. Himeji castle is completed	Summer siege of the Osaka castle
1616		Tokugawa Ieyasu dies. A long period of peace and prosperity begins
1621	Kanō Tan'yū becomes chief of official painters	
1624	Katsura pavilions and garden, Kyoto	

Date	Cultural Events	Historical Events
1633	Kiyomizu-dera in Kyoto	
1634–1636	Tōshōgū in Nikkō	Daimyo are obliged to stay at the court one year out of two
1637–1638		Peasant revolt in Shimabara
1639		Closing of foreign relations
1659	Shūgaku-in, Kyoto	
ca. 1675	First akahon and *ukiyo-zōshi*	
1680		Shogunate of Tokugawa Tsunayoshi, "shogun of the dogs"
1684	First of Chimamatsu Monzaemon's plays	
1685–1694	Poems *(haiku)* by Bashō	
1688–1703		Genroku period flourishes
1694	Basho (b. 1644) dies	
1701–1703	Vengeance of the Akō-Gishi	
1716	Ogata Kōrin and Chikamatsu Monzaemon die	Tokugawa Yoshimune, reformist and enlightened shogun
ca. 1738	First *kurohon* and *ao-byōshi* and *kokkei-bon*	
ca. 1741	*Sharebon* become popular	
ca. 1744	*Yomihon* become popular	
ca. 1764	*Senryū* become popular	
1770	Suzuki Harunobu dies	
1774	Sugita Gempaku translates Dutch works on anatomy. First *rangaku* studies	
ca. 1775	First *kibyōshi*	
ca. 1781	*Kyōka* poems	
1783	Yosa Buson dies	
1786		Tokugawa Ienari, "freethinking" shogun. Last Ainu revolt
1791	Utamaro updates his ukiyo-e style	
1792		Russia demands opening of diplomatic relations
1794–1795	Tōshusai Sharaku active in Osaka	
1795	Maruyama Ōkyo dies	
ca. 1805	First *gōkan,* following the *kibyōshi.* Utamaro dies	
ca. 1818	First *ninjō-bon*	
1823	Franz von Siebold in Nagasaki	
ca. 1830	"Thirty-Six Views of Mt. Fuji" by Hokusai	
1832	"Fifty-Three Stages of the Tōkaidō" by Hiroshige	
1849	Hokusai dies	
1853		Arrival of Commodore Perry. Putianin in Nagasaki
1854		Friendship treaty with the United States
1858	Hiroshige dies	
1861	Kuniyoshi dies	

Date	Cultural Events	Historical Events
1868		Beginning of the Meiji period. Restoration of imperial power
1871	Abolition of feudal clans	Establishment of prefectures
1873	Creation of the "Meirokusha"	
1875		Sakhalin exchanged for the Kuril Islands (Chishima Rettō)
1876	Creation of the Tokyo School of Fine Arts (Tokyo Bijutsu Gakkō)	
1877		Satsuma rebellion (Saigō Takamori)
1889		Promulgation of the Constitution
1890	Imperial Rescript on Education (Kiōikuchokugo)	
1894–1895		Sino-Japanese War
1902		Anglo-Japanese alliance
1904–1905		Russo-Japanese War. Portsmouth Treaty, 1905
1910		Annexation of Korea
1912		Emperor Meiji dies. Taishō era begins
1914		Japan declares war on Germany
1915	*Rashōmon* by Akutagawa Ryūnosuke	
1890–1920	Literary movements flourish	
1920–1945	Cultural stagnation. "Japanese" (Nihonga) style in painting	
1923		Earthquake in Tokyo
1924	*Chijin no ai* by Tanizaki Jun'ichirō	
1926		Yoshihito dies. Hirohito accedes to the throne. Shōwa era begins
1928		First elections with universal suffrage
1932		Manchuria incidents. Japan leaves the League of Nations
1937	*Yukiguni* by Kawabata Yasunari	
1940		Japan forms alliance with the Axis (Tripartite Pact)
1941		Pact of neutrality with the USSR. December 7: Pearl Harbor attacked and war on the United States declared
1942		Japan captures the islands of the Pacific and Southeast Asia
1943–1945		Americans recapture the Pacific
1945		Atom bombs fall on Hiroshima and Nagasaki. USSR declares war on Japan. The war ends
1945	Literary revival and creation of awards. Rise of architecture (Tange Kenzō)	Higashikuni, Shigehara cabinets
1946	Emperor Hirohito renounces the myth of imperial divinity	Promulgation of the new Constitution
1948		Liberal Democratic party (Jiyu Minshutō) formed. Verdicts in the war-crimes trials

Date	Cultural Events	Historical Events
1949	Yukawa Hideki wins Nobel Prize for physics. Architect Tange Kenzō begins a successful career with the Peace Center in Hiroshima	
1950–1953		Korean War. Creation of a reserve police force
1951	Kurosawa Akira wins the Gold Lion in Venice for his film Rashōmon	Treaty of San Francisco. Japan admitted into UNESCO
1952	Creation of modern-art museums	American Occupation of Japan ends
1953		Richard Nixon visits Japan
1956	Japan is admitted to the United Nations	Negotiations start with the USSR
1960		Beginning of the "economic miracle"
1964	Olympic Games in Tokyo	
1968	Kawabata Yasunari wins Nobel Prize for literature	
1970	Osaka World's Fair. Mishima Yukio's spectacular suicide	
1974		*Nikuson shokku*
1976		Lockheed Affair: senior executives convicted of corruption
1980		Beginning of international "trade friction"
1985	International Science and Technical Exposition in Tsukuba	
1989		Emperor Hirohito dies. Akihito succeeds him, inaugurating the Heisei era
1994	Ōe Kenzaburō wins Nobel Prize for literature	
1995		Kobe earthquake; Sarin gas attack in subways of Tokyo and Yokohama by members of Aum Shinri-kyō sect

NOTE ON USAGE

Spelling of Japanese terms follows the Hepburn system of romanization. Persons' names are given in Japanese order, with family name preceding the given name: Mishima Yukio. Alphabetical ordering of entries includes the genitive particle *no:*

    Abe Nobuyuki

    Abe no Yoritoki

    Abe Shigetaka

Subentries and related entries are indicated by a bullet (•). Alphabetical ordering of these entries does not include the particle *no:*

- Ise Kōdaijingū
- Ise no Kuni
- Ise Monogatari

Dates are approximate to within one year, because of differences between calendars. Eras are designated with months and years; reigns are given in angle brackets within birth and death dates (1523<1542–1545>1550).

JAPAN
ENCYCLOPEDIA

A. First letter of the hiragana and katakana syllabaries. In Japanese Esoteric Buddhism, the sound represented by this vowel has special significance: Meikaku, an eleventh-century monk, considered it symbolic of the "harmony of all essences." It is associated with various Buddhist divinities worshiped in Japan, including Dainichi Nyorai and Ashuku Nyorai, and with certain eminent monks who were masters of Buddhist doctrine. It also expresses the active divine nature, in opposition (and in complement) to the sound *un* (the Sanskrit *hum*), which represents latent power. Using the Greek analogy, if *a* is alpha, *un* is omega. Together, they form *a-un,* the equivalent of Sanskrit Aum (Om). Japanese Buddhism has portrayed these two fundamental sounds in the form of two "defenders of the Law," the Ni-ō (two kings), one with an open mouth *(a),* the other with a closed mouth *(un),* usually placed on each side of a temple entrance. Their association thus represented the cosmic power of Buddhist law and the totality of the universe. *See* NI-Ō.

Abashiri. Fishing port on the northeast coast of Hokkaido, on the Sea of Okhotsk, active since the early nineteenth century. It is closed every year from January to March, icebergs making navigation dangerous. The main catches are crab, salmon, and, until recently, whales. The Jōmon-period prehistoric site of Moyoro and a small museum are located nearby. *Pop.:* approx. 50,000. *See* MOYORO.

• **Abashiri-ko.** Saltwater lake near the city of Abashiri, with an area of 34 km² and depth of approx. 16 m. Tourist site in Abashiri National Park. *See* NATIONAL PARKS.

Abe. Old Japanese family *(uji)* originally from the province of Iga (Mie prefecture), claiming to be descended from a son of Emperor Kōgen (according to *Nihon shoki,* 720). Many families in the Iga region and in Yamato with the patronymic name Abe are descended from Abi, a legendary character who, according to ancient accounts, was opposed to the conquest of Yamato by the first emperor, Jimmu. These families took refuge in northern Honshu, where they became prominent toward the end of the Heian period (794–1185), mainly in the province of Mutsu (northern Honshu) and in the province of Musashi (Kanto) starting in the eighteenth century.

Abe Akira. Writer, born in 1934 in Hiroshima. A graduate of the University of Tokyo in French literature, he published autobiographical novels. His best-known works are *Miseinen* (The Adolescent, 1968), a collection of short stories; *Shirei no kyūka* (The Commandant's Departure, 1970); and *Momo* (Peaches, 1972). He also writes for radio and television.

Abe Isoo. Christian Socialist politician (1865–1949), born in Fukuoka. After studying with Niijima Jō in Kyoto, he went to the United States in 1891. Upon his return he founded the Shakai Minshutō (Socialist Democratic party) with, notably, Katayama Sen. A professor at Waseda University in Tokyo from 1895 to 1928, he was a proponent of pacifism during the Russo-Japanese War (1904–05) and began publishing a Christian socialist review, *Shinkigen* (The New Era), in 1905. After a number of dissolutions and mergers with other parties, the socialist movement of which he was president was banned in 1940 and he retired from public life. He was elected a deputy four times and was a municipal councillor for Tokyo. *See* KATA-

Abe Jirō. Philosopher and art critic (1883–1959), born in Yamagata prefecture, student of Natsume Sōseki, then professor at various universities, notably Tohoku University in Sendai. Strongly influenced by German idealism, he introduced the principles of neo-Kantian philosophy to Japan. His works, profoundly influential among young people between 1912 and 1930, during the rise of nationalism, included *Santarō no nikki* (Santarō's Journal, 1912–14), *Sekai-bunka to Nihon-bunka* (World Civilization and Japanese Civilization), and *Tokugawa-jidai no geijutsu to shakai* (Art and Society in the Edo Period, 1931). He was the founder of Nihon Bunka Kenkyūjo (Japan Culture Institute).

Abe Kōbō. Writer (Abe Kimifusa, 1924–93), born in Tokyo. Until the age of 16, he lived in Mukden, Manchuria, where his father was a physician. He returned to Tokyo to perform his military service, an experience that left him profoundly antimilitarist. He studied medicine from 1943 to 1948, while writing short stories, then left school to devote himself totally to literature. His wife, Machi, a well-known designer, illustrated his work. In addition to being a prolific novelist, Abe Kōbō was a playwright, and his work is unique for both its writing style and its subject matter. His recurring theme is the loss of individual identity in the incomprehensible world of modern Japan with its totalitarian environment of factories, hospitals, and inhuman cities. In his novels, he described in great detail his characters' emotions when they were put in specific psychological situations that were often improbable but that enabled him to plumb the depths of the human spirit with unusual acuity. A number of his books were adapted for the screen. The work that brought him international fame, *Suna no onna* (The Woman in the Dunes, 1964), was translated into Western languages and made into a film directed by Teshigahara Hiroshi. A member of the Communist party since 1945, he was expelled after the publication of this work, whose theme—loss of identity—was out of step with Communist ideology. He dealt with this theme again in *Tanin no kao* (The Face of Another, 1964). He then published *Mukankeina shi* (An Ill-Timed Death, 1964), *Tomodachi* (Friends, 1967, a play), *Moetsukita chizu* (The Ruined Map, 1967), *Bō ni natta otoko* (The Man Who Turned into a Stick, 1969), *Hako otoko* (The Box Man, 1973), *Mikkai* (Secret Rendezvous, 1977), and *Hakobune Sakuramaru* (The Ark Sakura, 1984).

Among his earlier works are *Akai mayu* (The Red Cocoon, 1950), *Kabe* (The Wall, 1951), which received the Akutagawa Prize, *Seifuku* (Uniform, 1955), *Doreigari* (Slave Hunt, 1955), *Kemonotachi wa kokyō o mezasu* (The Beasts Going Toward the Country of Their Birth, 1957), *Daiyon kampyōki* (Inter Ice Age 4, 1959), *Enomoto buyō* (1965), and *Omae ni mo tsumi ga aru* (You Too Are Guilty, 1965, a play). He left an unfinished novel, *Tobu otoko* (The Flying Man), which was published in the journal *Shinchō* in April 1993 by his wife.

Abe Masahiro. Politician (1819–57), daimyo of Fukuyama and governor of the province of Ise. In 1840, he was appointed to the position of *jisha bugyō* (commissioner of temples and shrines); in 1843, he was elected *rōjū* (senior councillor). He decided to open Japan to the West despite opposition from the shogun and signed a friendship treaty with the United States in 1854, followed by similar treaties with England, Russia, and Holland. His foreign policy raised strong opposition; amid demands to "expel the barbarians," he resigned. He was replaced by Hotta Masayoshi, who favored closing Japan. He continued to exert strong influence on domestic policy, encouraging the teaching of Western sciences and the creation of an effective navy and army. He advocated using all men of talent, no matter what their family background.

Abe Masakatsu. Daimyo (1541–1600) allied with the shogun Tokugawa Ieyasu. He fought at Tokugawa Ieyasu's side at the Battle of Sekigahara, where he died. His son, Abe Masatsugu (1569–1647), succeeded him, remaining in the service of the Tokugawa shogunate, and was appointed a *rōjū* (senior councillor) in 1622.

Abe Masao. Philosopher, born in 1915, a disciple of Nishida Kitarō. A member of the second generation of philosophers of the Kyoto school, he attempted to compare Zen principles with Western thought via the axiom "Without being, there is no knowledge; without knowledge, being does not exist."

Abeno. Plain in the province of Settsu, near the Tennō-ji temple, where many famous battles took place. In 1338, Kitabatake Akiie defeated Kō Moronao; in 1585, Oda Nobunaga cornered and massacred the rebel monks of Ishiyama-dera; and in 1615, Toyotomi Hideyoshi attacked the castle of these same rebels, Ishiyama-jō, razing it.

Abe Nobuya (Yoshibumi). Western-style painter and photographer (1913–71), born in Niigata prefecture. A surrealist, he was a founder of Bijutsu Bunka Kyōkai, an association of surrealist painters and poets who were followers of Fukuzawa Ichirō, in 1939. During the Second World War, he was a newspaper correspondent; afterward, he wrote on art and poetry, including *Adamu to Ibu* (Adam and Eve, 1949) and *Ue* (Fast, 1950). Abe Nobuya's work was exhibited around the world. He died in Rome.

Abe Nobuyuki. General and politician (1875–1953), born in Ishikawa prefecture. After graduating from military academy, he became head of the Bureau of Military Affairs and was then appointed minister of war, replacing Ugaki Issei, who was ill. In August 1939, he succeeded Hiranuma Kiichirō as prime minister. He then tried to end the Sino-Japanese War and to preserve Japan's neutrality in the world war. However, the militarists repudiated him and he resigned in January 1940. He was then sent to Nanjing, China, to provide Japanese support to Chinese general Wang Jingwei in the negotiation of a treaty that would seal Japanese preeminence in economic and military matters. In 1944, he was appointed governor-general of Korea. Placed on the list of war criminals by the Allies in 1945, he was never put on trial and retired from public life.

Abe no Hirafu. Military commander (ca. 575–ca. 664?) and governor of the province of Koshi (he was called Abe no Ōmi at this time). He was best known for leading three maritime campaigns against the Ezo (Ainu) tribes of northern Honshu between 558 and 560, for which he had a fleet of 180 ships built. In 663, he led an expeditionary force to Korea to rescue the Paekche government, which had been attacked by the Silla (Shiragi), but he was defeated in the naval battle of Hakusuki-noe by the Silla forces in combination with Tang Chinese forces. He was then appointed military governor of Dazaifu on the island of Kyushu. His story is told in the *Nihon shoki*.

Abe no Kurahashimaro. Minister of the left *(sadaijin),* died in 649; probably one of the promoters of the Taika Reform (645).

Abe no Manao. Physician (eighth–ninth century) who wrote the first Japanese medical treatise, *Daidō ruijūhō,* in collaboration with Izumo Hirosada, circa 808–811.

Abe no Munetō. Warrior (eleventh century) of the province of Mutsu, son of Abe no Yoritoki. He rebelled against the court during the first Nine-Year War (1051–62, won the battle of the Palisade of Torinomi in 1061, and surrendered his weapons after the death of his brother, Abe no Sadatō. He was exiled to the province of Iyo, then to Dazaifu in Kyushu.

Abe no Nakamaro. Noble of the imperial court (698/701–779), born in Abe, near Nara. In 717, he went to Chang'an, capital of Tang-dynasty China, to study; he was part of the same mission as Kibi no Makibi and the Buddhist monk Gembō. He stayed in China and took the Chinese name Chao Heng *(Jap.:* Chōkō). In 766, he became grand counselor *(dainagon)* to Emperor Daizong, thanks to his talents as an administrator and a poet. He later wanted to return to Japan, but his ship was unable to negotiate the currents on the Vietnam coast and he returned to Chang'an. Appointed governor of Annam, he was charged with pacifying the Manzi tribes. He befriended major Chinese poets such as Li Bai (Li Po), Wang Wei, Zhao Hua, Bao Xin, and Chu Guangxi. In Japan, a *waka* poem of his was included in *Hyakunin isshu.* In it he expresses his regret over not being able to return to the country of his birth: *Ama no hara furisake mireba . . .* (When I lift my eyes to the plains of the sky . . .).

Abe no Sadatō. Warrior (1019–62) of the province of Mutsu, son of Abe no Yoritoki and brother of Abe no Munetō. He fought with them against the court but was killed by Minamoto no Yoriyoshi, which provoked the surrender of his brother. *See* ABE NO MUNETŌ, ABE NO YORITOKI.

Abe no Seimei. Astrologer (921–1005) in the court of Emperor Ichijō, famous in his time for his accurate predictions. He observed the principles of On'yōdō. According to the *Ōkagami* and *Konjaku monogatari,* he also predicted, through observation of celestial phenomena, the abdication of Emperor Kazan. *See* OMMYŌDŌ.

Abe no Yoritoki. Nobleman (?–1057) of the province of Mutsu (northern Honshu). In an attempt to regain his independence, he refused to pay taxes to the court in Kyoto, which responded by sending the troops of Fujiwara no Noritō, then officially governor, to do battle with him and his sons, Munetō and Sadatō. Although he submitted, he rebelled a second time. He was killed by an arrow in combat with

Minamoto no Yoriyoshi. *See* ABE NO MUNETŌ, ABE NO SADATŌ, ZENKUNEN NO EKI.

Abe Shigetaka. Educator (1890–1939), born in Niigata prefecture. He began teaching at the University of Tokyo in 1934, introducing modern American educational methods to Japan. In *Kyōiku kaikaku-ron* (Educational Reform, 1937), he presented his proposed reforms to the Japanese educational system.

Abe Shinnosuke. Writer, journalist, and literary critic (1884–1964), born in Saitama prefecture. He became editor of the newspaper *Osaka Mainichi Shimbun,* which later became *Mainichi Shimbun.* In 1960, he was appointed director of NHK. Among his best-known works are *Kindai seijika-ron* (Modern Politicians) and *Shin jinbutsu-ron* (A New Study of Political Figures), in which he bluntly criticizes the politicians of his time.

Abe Shintarō. Politician (1924–91), minister of foreign affairs from 1982 to 1986, and head of a majority faction of the Liberal Democratic party. Involved in a financial scandal in 1988, he lost all hope of becoming prime minister.

Abe Shōō. Physician and botanist (ca. 1653–1753), born in Morioka. He devoted himself to the study of traditional medicine *(honzōgaku)* and is best known for having encouraged the cultivation of important crops, such as sugar cane, cotton, carrots, and sweet potatoes, and of medicinal plants in the Edo (Tokyo) region. He wrote several works on his research, including *Saiyaku shiki* and *Sambyaku shuroku.*

Abe Shumpō. Modern-style painter who studied in Paris (1925–30), where there was a major exhibition of his work in 1929.

Abe Tadaaki. *Fudai-daimyō* (1602–75) in the service of Tokugawa Iemitsu. Appointed a *wakadoshiyori* (junior councillor) in 1663, then a *rōjū* (senior councillor), he was promoted to the rank of daimyo of the castle of Ōshi (Saitama) with an annual income of 50,000 *koku,* later 80,000 *koku.* He was popular for his integrity and also because he tried to find employment for the masterless samurai *(rōnin)* who had revolted in 1651 (*see* KEIAN JIKEN), under shogun Tokugawa Ietsuna.

Abe Takeo. Historian and professor at the University of Kyoto (1903–59). He was known for his work on the later Uighurs.

Abe Tomoji. Writer and literary critic (1903–73), born in Okayama. He studied English literature at the University of Tokyo. He took a stand against the proletarian literature movement then in style. His first work, a collection of short stories titled *Koi to Afurika,* published in 1930, was quite a popular success. Also in 1930, he wrote a major work of literary criticism, *Shuchiteki bungaku-ron* (Subjective Literary Criticism), and in 1936 he published a major novel, *Fuyu no yado* (Winter Quarters, 1931). After 1945, he traveled to Java, China, and Europe, translating Melville and the Brontë sisters while continuing to write short stories and criticisms such as *Jitsu no mado* (Time Spent Behind Windows, 1959), in which he denounced the militarism and political skepticism of his contemporaries. He was a member of the Shin Kankaku literary society.

Abe Yasukuni. Mathematician and astrologer (eighteenth century). In 1754, with the collaboration of Shibukawa Kōkyō and Nishiyama Seikyū, he modified the Jōkyo-reki calendar, which was renamed Hōriki Kōjutsu Genreki. The errors in the new calendar were corrected in 1798, then in 1844 and 1872. It was abolished in 1872 in favor of the Western calendar.

Abe Yoshishige. Philosopher and educator (1883–1966), born in Ehime prefecture. A disciple of Natsume Sōseki, he wrote many critical texts on the idealist movement and introduced Kantian philosophy to Japan after having studied it in Heidelberg. He then taught in Seoul, Korea, starting in 1926. After the Second World War, he was minister of education in Shidehara Kijūrō's cabinet, and he proved to be a firm proponent of modern educational methods. He was also fiercely opposed to the rearmament of Japan. In 1947, he was appointed rector of the Gakushūin (Peers' School) and founded a university by this name in 1949. He wrote an important work on Western philosophy, *Seiyō kodai chūsei tetsugaku-shi* (History of Ancient and Medieval European Philosophy, 1917), and *Seiyō dōtoku shisō-shi* (History of European Ethics).

Abuna-e. Ukiyo-e printmaking technique, in use in the seventeenth and eighteenth centuries, used mostly to portray beautiful women *(bijin)* and erotic images *(shunga).*

Abutsu-ni. The "Abutsu nun" (?–1283), a poet who was a lady in the court of Empress Ankamon-in, wife of Emperor Juntoku. As a young lady in the court, she was called Shijō and Uemon no Suke. Some historians think that she may have been a daughter of Taira no Norishige, but this is not certain. She was one of the concubines of Fujiwara no Tameie, a famous poet. After he died, she became a Buddhist nun and took the name Abutsu-ni. Unable to obtain a ruling on a dispute over her property, she went to Kamakura to arrange for the transfer of her possessions to her son, Reizei Tamesuke, but she died before the judgment was rendered. She became known for her account of the trip from Kyoto to Kamakura in *Izayoi nikki* (1277). This account, which included 166 poems written by herself or others, finishes with a 151-verse poem *(chōka)*. She is also credited with the authorship of *Utatane no ki* (Account of a Nap), describing the events of the year 1238, and *Yoru no tsuru* (Night Crane), a collection of letters on poetics that she sent to her son Tamesuke, who lived in Kyoto. Most of her poems were included in anthologies collected by imperial order, notably in *Shoku kokinshū*, *Gyokuyō-shū*, and *Fūga-shū*. All of her work is imbued with a profound melancholy and, though she is not one of the great poets, her writings are interesting from a historical perspective.

Accessories. Men and women in Japan have always liked to accent their clothing, hair styles, and even shoes with utilitarian and ornamental accessories, which have varied, of course, according to sex, social position, and period. Notably, however, ornamental jewelry such as rings, earrings, necklaces, and bracelets, so highly valued in other cultures, were never in style and almost never worn. Only since the beginning of the twentieth century, influenced by Western styles, have women adopted such ornamentation. Nor have cosmetics been widely used (*see* BENI-BANA, DETSUSHI, KUMADORI).

Men's accessories traditionally included a *gyoku-hai,* a sort of rosary hung from the belt—though with no religious connotation—which made a sound when they walked. It was made of mother-of-pearl beads or shells, strung on a cord. Also considered ornamental were *tachi* swords and *tosu* daggers, which, according to the rules of *engi-shiki* (early tenth century), could not be more than 18 cm long, at least for nobles below the fifth rank (*see* I). Both men and women sometimes wore a decorated cloth pouch *(hako-seko)* to hold sheets of paper *(tatō-gami).* The women also carried in the folds of their garments a small box called a *hakufun-ho* that contained rice powder. The fan was an accessory for both men and women. Especially during the Heian period, the *sokutai* garment worn by the aristocracy was closed with a leather belt *(sekitai)* decorated with semiprecious stones. The women's obi sash was sometimes ornamented with a small brooch *(obidome),* sometimes with an over-ribbon. During the Edo period, the most important accessory for both sexes was the *inrō,* with its inseparable pieces, the *ojime* and *netsuke.* The fob watch appeared only at the beginning of the Meiji era.

Women used simple or double hairpins, made of precious metal or other material and called *kanzashi,* in their hairdos (*see* MAGE). Such hairpins were also used in the court by high-ranking nobles to secure their headpieces *(kammuri).* Ornamental combs *(kushi)* of tortoiseshell, wood, or metal were women's accessories. Although rings were known in Japan, they were rarely used except as seals. The wedding ring has been adopted only very recently by the Japanese, as have such Western jewelry as pearl necklaces and earrings. *See* CLOTHING, FANS, HAIRSTYLES, KASA (parasols, umbrellas), SHOES.

Achiki. This Korean messenger delivered to the court of Yamato (under the reign of Ōjin) two horses, gifts from the king of Paekche, around 284. Because Achiki had an extensive knowledge of Chinese and Confucianism, he was charged with the education of Prince Uji no Waki-iratsuko. He had another scholar, Wani, sent from Korea, and he introduced to Japan the rudiments of Confucian philosophy. Some texts claim that he arrived in Japan about 400, at the same time as other Chinese and Korean immigrants. Their story is told in the *Kojiki* and the *Nihon shoki. See* ACHI NO ŌMI, YUZUKI NO KIMI.

Achi no Ōmi. Chinese immigrant who arrived at the court of Yamato at the beginning of the fifth century, according to the *Nihon shoki* (ca. 306–10, according to the *Kojiki*). He was accompanied by his son, Tsuka no Ōmi, and other immigrants from China and Korea. According to the *Shoku Nihongi,* he was the grandson of Emperor Lingdi (168–89) of the later Han dynasty, but this ancestry cannot be confirmed. Women from the state of Wu accompanied them, introducing to the islands the art of embroidery on silk. Also called Achi no Atae, Ku-Rando. *See* ACHIKI, AYAHATORI, YUZUKI NO KIMI.

Acupuncture. Chinese acupuncture, called *hari* (needles) in Japan, was probably introduced to the islands in the sixth century, at the same time as the practice of moxa (*kyū* in Japanese) and traditional Chinese medicine *(kampō)*. These techniques spread very rapidly; today, acupuncture is still extremely popular in Japan, where it is the object of scientific study. The meridian points are called *keiketsu. See* HANAWA HOKIICHI, SHIATSU.

Adachi Buntarō. Physician and anthropologist (1865–1945), born in the province of Izu. After studying anatomy in Germany, he returned to Japan, where he taught dissection. His research centered on comparing the Japanese "race" with European "races." Among his most notable works are *Nihon sekki-jidai zugai* (Crania from the Stone Age in Japan), showing that Japanese of that period were not Eskimos; *Nihonjin kinhakaku no tōkei* (Statistics on the Muscles of the Japanese); and *Nihonjin dōmyaku keitō* (Studies on the Anatomy of the Japanese).

Adachi Chōshun. Gynecologist (Mugai, 1775–1836), adopted son of Adachi Baian, who taught him the principles of Chinese medicine. He also studied European medicine with Yoshida Nagayoshi in 1831, and published *Ihō kenki,* his translation of a medical treatise by Austrian physician A. von Störk.

Adachi-hime. "Adachi's daughter." A character in Tokyo popular legend who may have lived in the tenth century. She married a warrior and is said to have been so bullied by her mother-in-law that she committed suicide by throwing herself into the Arakawa river along with her five servants. The young woman's father, despairing, made a pilgrimage to the temple of Gongen in the province of Kii and sculpted six statues of Amida Buddha, which he gave to six different temples. He sculpted another in a seventh temple, Shōō-ji, dedicated to Amida. The statues were to watch over his daughter's soul.

Adachi Kagemori. Noble warrior (d. 1248) from the province of Sagami. His daughter married Hōjō Tokiuji and bore two boys, Hōjō Tsunetoki and Hōjō Tokiyori. In 1218, the shogun Sanetomo appointed him vice-governor of the province of Dewa. In 1247, he formed an alliance with his grandson Hōjō Tokiyori to battle the rival Miura clan. Charged with the defense of the castle of Akita, he was appointed governor of the castle of Akita (Akitajō no Suke). Toward the end of his life, he became a Buddhist monk at Kōya-san under the name Gakuchi (Kakuchi, Kōya-nyūdō).

Adachi Kan. Physician (Kikkei, Yokudō, 1842–1917), student of Fukuzawa Yukichi and Ogata Kōan. After the Meiji Restoration (1868), he was appointed director of the military medical school. He wrote several medical works: *Geka gakuron, Bōfuteki chisōhō,* and *Kennyo tōketsu.*

Adachi Kenzō. Politician (1864 or 1868–1948), born near Kumamoto. In his first career as a journalist in China and Korea (where he founded two Japanese newspapers, *Chōsen Jihō* and *Kanjō Shimpō*), he was implicated in the assassination of Queen Min in 1895, but was acquitted. He returned to Japan and was elected in 1902 as a member of the Rikken Dōshikai (Constitutional Association of Friends). Reelected 14 times, he was minister of communications from 1925 to 1927 and minister of the interior in 1929 and 1931. After resigning from Rikken, he was leader of Kokumin Dōmei (Nationalist League), an ultranationalist party, from 1932 to 1939. He was a member of Konoe Fumimaro's second cabinet in 1940, after which he retired from public life.

Adachi Mineichirō. International jurist and diplomat (1869–1934), born in Yamagata. He accompanied the Japanese delegation to the Portsmouth conference, where the treaty ending the war with Russia was signed in 1905. As an ambassador, he was posted to Mexico (1913–16), Belgium (1917 and 1921–27), and France (1927–30). He represented Japan at the League of Nations starting in 1919. He was appointed a member of the Japan Academy (Nihon Gakushi-in) in 1925, and was also a member of the Academy of Belgium. In 1930, he was elected president of the International Court of Justice at the Hague, a position he held until his death.

Adachi Morinaga. Noble warrior (1135–1200) who sided with Minamoto no Yoritomo and helped him gain power in Kamakura. When Yoritomo died, in 1192, Adachi Morinaga was part of Minamoto no Yoriie's *bakufu* (military government). Later he became a Buddhist monk under the name Rensai.

Adachi-ryū. School of ikebana flower arrangement founded in 1912 by Adachi Chōka. She created a style that rejected all abstraction and emphasized the natural aspect of the elements used in flower arrangements.

Adachi Yasumori. Military governor (?–1285) of Akita castle and the province of Mutsu. His daughter married Hōjō Tokimune and was the mother of Hōjō Sadatoki. In 1282, he left his responsibilities to his son and became a Buddhist monk under the name Kakushin. However, he and his entire family were killed by Hōjō Sadatoki in a plot by a rival, Taira no Yoritsuna. *See* TAIRA NO YORITSUNA.

Adachi Yoshikage. Noble warrior (d. 1255), governor of the castle of Akita (Akitajō no Suke) and member of Hyōjō-shū of the Kamakara shogunate. He became a Buddhist monk under the name Ganchi.

Adams, Williams. English navigator (1564–1620), born in Gillingham, Kent. He was the captain of the Dutch ship *Liefde* that was shipwrecked on the coast of the province of Bungo, Japan, in April 1600. Taken prisoner with his crew, he gained his freedom thanks to his knowledge of ships. Shogun Tokugawa Ieyasu, who needed marine technicians, hired him to build an oceangoing fleet. He lived in Edo, married a Japanese woman (Magome Bikuni, d. 1634), and remained in the shogun's service until his death on May 16, 1620, in Hirado, where he was buried. He was highly regarded by Ieyasu, who gave him a property on the Miura Peninsula and a number of servants. Adams served as an intermediary between the shogunate and Dutch and English merchants at the port of Hirado. On behalf of the shogunate, he traveled to Okinawa, Cochin-China, and Siam to set up trading links. There is a ceremony in his honor each year in Hemi, near the monuments over the tombs of his wife and two sons. A memorial was built in Ito (near Shizuoka) in memory of his passage, and a monument to him was erected in his birthplace in England. A number of his letters inviting his compatriots to trade with Japan have been preserved. The novel *Shogun* (1976) by James Clavell gives a fictionalized account of his life. In Japan, he is better known as Miura Anjin, or simply Anjin (the pilot).

Adana. Nickname given to a person, or that a person gives himself or herself, to commemorate an event or simply to avoid using his or her *gō* or *azana*. *See* AZANA, GŌ, NAMES.

Adoption. Adoption has been a common practice in Japan throughout its history. According to Confucian philosophy, people who did not have an heir were allowed to adopt the children of other families of equal social status. The adopted children always took the name of their adoptive father and were considered full members of their adoptive family. It was also very common for a man with no son to succeed him to adopt his daughter's husband; this *yōshi* then had the right to his father's inheritance. In ancient times, this practice was current mainly among the aristocracy, adoption of another noble's child often increasing the prosperity of the adoptive family. At the beginning of the Meiji era (late nineteenth century), since a young man who was an only son could not be drafted into the army, it became customary for a family with two sons or more to allow one to be adopted by a family with no male heir. Today, this adoption custom is effected simply by making a declaration to the authorities. Even a foreigner who marries a Japanese woman can be adopted by his father-in-law as a son if his wife has no brothers. Throughout Japan's history, adoptions have been so common that it has always been difficult for historians and genealogists to trace natural filiations. This explains the large number of people who have a son with a different family name.

There are several types of adoption, depending on the status of the people involved. Some authors count at least ten different types: to keep a family from extinction, to avoid conscription (formerly), to perpetuate ancestral rites, to regulate the size of some families, to confirm the marriage of a daughter, etc.

Aeba Kōson. Writer and theater critic (Aeba Yosaburō, Takenoya Shujin, 1855–1922), born in Edo. He began his career as a journalist, then specialized in studying the popular literature of the Edo period. Later, influenced by Tsubouchi Shōyō, he studied Western literature and published translations and adaptations of American and European novels. While working at *Yomiuri Shimbun* and *Asahi Shimbun,* he wrote critiques of Kabuki theater and literature. Among his major works are *Tōse shōnin katagi* (1886), *Hasuha musume* (A Capricious Girl, 1888), *Horidashimono* (Used Goods, 1889), *Kachidoki* (Cry of Victory, 1892), *Muratake* (20 vols., collection of essays and stories, 1889–91), and *Takenoya gekihyōshū* (collection of theater criticism).

Aekuni-jinja. Shinto shrine founded in the ninth century in Ichinomiya (Miwa prefecture, formerly Iga province), in honor of the Aekuni no Kami (Ohiko no Mikoto), who died there. During the Kamakura period (1185–1333), it was renamed Nangū Daibosatsu. Destroyed by fire in the sixteenth century, it was rebuilt by the Tōdō family in the following century. In 1871, it was classified a *kuhei-chūsa*. Every year on December 5, a major festival is held there.

Agano-yaki. Type of pottery produced mainly in northern Kyushu in the early seventeenth century, created by the Korean potter Chöngye *(Jap.:* Sonkai, Agano Kizō) in the service of the Hosokawa family. Used primarily for bowls and accessories for the tea ceremony, it has a thick, cream-colored or white glaze with drips of brown iron oxide. In the eighteenth century, the Agano kilns also began to produce raku pottery with a blue-gray copper-oxide glaze. In the nineteenth century, the pieces became more colorful but were more crudely made.

Agari-tachi. *Tachi*-type sword, once carried by the nobles of the five first ranks *(see* I) of the imperial court during official ceremonies.

Agariya. Prison in the Kodemma-chō district of Edo, reserved for middle-rank warriors *(gokenin),* vassals of the small daimyo, monks, and physicians.
• The same word, pronounced AGEYA, designated a house where courtesans received customers.

Agata. Until 645 (Taika Reform), this word designated the fields owned by the court, the emperor's personal properties, and properties governed by a Kuni no Miyatsuko (then called Agata no Miyatsuko). The vice-governors of such properties held the title Agata-nushi.

Agata-miko. In the Shinto religion, a priestess *(miko)* with the gift of divination who was charged with transmitting to the gods the wishes and prayers of the faithful. Some cut their dependence on the shrines and became seers in their own right, to the profit of their customers. To invoke the *kami,* they often plucked the string of a small bow *(azusa-yumi),* and so they were sometimes called *azusa-miko.* The less formal names for them were Ichi or Ichiko. *See* AZUSA-MIKO, MIKO.

Agatamon. Literary school that flourished in Edo in the eighteenth century, bringing together the disciples of Kamo no Mabuchi. There were three important women writers in this school: Shindō Tsuku-bako (dates unknown), Udono Yonoko (1729–88), and Yuya Shizuko (1733–52). Collectively, they were called the Agatamon Sansaijo (the three women disciples of Agatamon).

Agata no Inukai no Michiyo. Lady of the court (d. 733) serving emperors Temmu and Shōmu. In 715,

Empress Gemmei gave her the name Tachibana. In her second marriage, she wed Fujiwara no Fuhito and had a daughter who married Emperor Shōmu and took the name Empress Kōmyō. One of her poems was included in the *Man'yōshū.* She had a magnificent portable altar *(zushi)* built. Called Nenjibutsu-zushi, it is preserved in the temple of Hōryū-ji. In 721, she became a Buddhist nun, and her husband also joined the religion. She is also known as Tachibana no Michiyo.

Agawa Hiroyuki. Writer, born in 1920 in Hiroshima). Heavily influenced by the works of Shiga Naoya, he wrote novels recounting his experiences as a marine officer in the Second World War. In 1979, he received the Japan Academy Prize (Nihon Gakushi-in-shō). Among his works are *Haru no shiro* (Spring Castle, 1952) and *Yamamoto Isoroku* (1980), a biography of the admiral who planned the Japanese attack on Pearl Harbor on December 7, 1941.

Agechi-rei. "Order to Requisition Land." Edict issued in 1843 by Mizuno Tadakuni in an attempt to regain the land belonging to the Edo shogunate, which had been dispersed. The properties within a perimeter of ten leagues *(ri)* around Edo and within five leagues around Osaka were to be returned to shogunal authority, the land thus recovered to be paid for with other property or with a certain quantity of rice. This measure met with such strong opposition by certain daimyo and *hatamoto* that it was retracted several days after it was issued, and Mizuno Tadakuni was obliged to resign his position.

Agemai. "Rice donation." In 1722, to solve his financial deficit, the shogun Tokugawa Yoshimune ordered all the daimyo to make a voluntary contribution, either in rice or in the equivalent amount of money, of 100 *koku* of rice for each 10,000 *koku* of their annual income. In exchange, they were no longer obliged to live in Edo for one year out of two, but only for six months. However, because this led to a relaxation in surveillance of the daimyo by the shogunate, it was revoked in 1731. *See* SANKIN-KŌTAI.

Ages. Ritual impurity being a serious concern, even in modern Japan, certain ages have been subject to taboos, and ceremonies are usually designed to ward off bad luck rather than to celebrate. The birth of a child, preferably male, is so desired by women that they often pray to a "child-giver" goddess (Koyasu). Childbirth itself is placed under the protection of a *kami* or a Buddhist deity, usually Jizō, to ensure that everything goes well. In previous times, and even today in the countryside, a small figurine of a dog or a monkey, associated with easy labor, was placed on the bedside table of the woman giving birth, and appeals were made to Ubugami, the "*kami* of births," who, according to tradition, arrived on horseback. It is perhaps because birth is closely associated with ritual impurity that birthdays are generally not celebrated; in fact, children are said to be one year older on each New Year's day, since human years cannot be divided. Thus, a child born on December 31, for example, would automatically be in his second year as of the next day. At one time, ages were divided into groups of 20 years: from birth to 20 years was youth; from 20 to 40 was middle age; from 40 to 60, old age. A person was then said to be reborn and start a new life cycle when he or she turned 61. A small family ceremony was (and is) conducted at that time—the only true "birthday" celebration. One exception, however, is made for the emperor, whose birthday is solemnly celebrated every year. In ancient Japan, however, some birthdays were celebrated: those at 40, 50, 60, 70, and over 70 years of age. Today, some birthdays, considered lucky, are celebrated in private: the 66th, 77th, and 88th birthdays, in which the doubled number is considered synonymous with happiness, 77 being *kiju* ("pleasure and long life") and 88 signifying "rice and long life." The 70th year (once called *koki,* "ancient and rare") is also honored. Some ages, though, are considered bad luck, such as 42 for men and 49 for women, because of a homophony between these numbers and terms for disaster and death.

Today, the age of legal majority is 20. In ancient times, it was around the age of 14 for boys, at the time of the ceremony of "giving the man's hat," the *gempuku* (or *gembuku*). For members in direct lineage of the imperial family, majority is set at 18. A married minor, however, is considered an adult and enjoys all the rights of majority.

Agetsuchi-mon. In the Kamakura period (1185–1333), entrance gates to samurai *(bushi)* houses of a style called *bushi-zukuri,* in which the roof was covered with wooden planks and a thick layer of earth, to keep possible assailants from setting them afire by shooting flaming arrows. A gate of this type can be seen in the temple of Hōryū-ji near Nara.

Ago Wan. Bay of Ago on the Shima Peninsula in Mie prefecture where, in 1883, Mikimoto Kōkichi began cultivating pearls using a method he developed.

Agriculture. Japan's agriculture is limited by the paucity of arable land, representing less than 14% of the country's area—a proportion that is shrinking daily with the continuing encroachment of cities and transportation systems. In addition, barely 4% of the land is pasture, which means that cattle breeding is not encouraged. Agriculture is practiced mainly in the plains and, where land conditions permit, in terraces; irrigated rice production is the dominant feature of the Japanese agricultural landscape. The average area cultivated per family or farm is about one hectare, resulting in a huge number (a total of just under 6 million) of very small operations and a divided landscape, since more than 2 million families cultivate half a hectare or less and 2 million others have only one hectare. Out of about 6 million hectares cultivated, 5.8 million are located in Honshu, Shikoku, and Kyushu. Hokkaido has only about 250,000 arable hectares (although this number is tending to increase as land is gained from cultivation in low-altitude forests). The small size of family operations means that farmers cannot in general live off just their production; more than two-thirds conduct supplementary activities, such as crafts, trades, or fishing, or work for a salary in factories or elsewhere.

Rice *(kome)* is the main crop; other cereals include barley, rye, oats, and wheat. Cultivation is so intensive that the harvest yield per area cultivated is the highest in Asia: Japan produces an average of more than 57 quintals of rice per hectare (world average: 31 quintals), and rice paddies account for 45% of cultivated land. This high average is obtained thanks to the use of select grains, modern chemical fertilizers, and proper irrigation, as well as the skill and hard work of the farmers. The amount of rice produced can feed 15 people per hectare cultivated (at a rate of 2,000 calories per day per person), whereas the same amount of wheat would feed only 9. But sales of rice and other cereals (wheat represents only 5% of land cultivated) do not provide enough income for a large "modern" family. Mechanization has helped to reduce greatly the farming population, from about 16 million in 1950 to about 9 million currently, representing only about 7.2% of the working population. In years of lower production, such as 1992 and 1993, when the summer was cold, Japan was obliged to import rice because its reserves (which normally should have been around a million tons) were at the insufficient level of only 300,000 to 400,000 tons. In general, agriculture is underproductive and the overall agricultural balance in Japan (including forestry and fishery) runs at a very high deficit. Most agricultural operations survive only due to government grants,

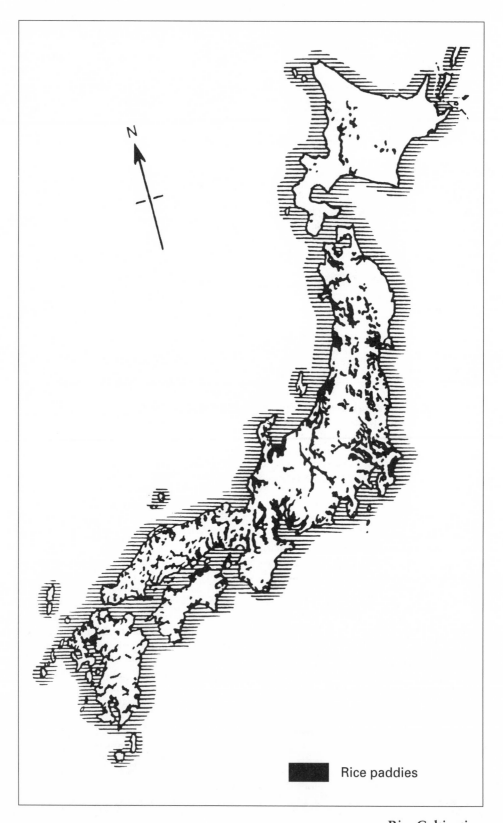

Rice paddies

Rice Cultivation

despite the double harvests reaped in southern Kantō (rice, then wheat and oats) and triple harvests in the southwest (rice, tobacco, and vegetables).

Aside from cereals, most farmers grow vegetables; in the south, there are tea and tobacco plantations; in the north, orchards (*nashi* pears). In Kyushu, a variety of oranges *(mikan)* are produced. In the north, trees producing other fruit, such as cherries, apricots, and peaches, are grown, and grapes thrive on the fertile volcanic slopes of central Honshu. On about 100,000 hectares of high-altitude land, blackberry bushes supply food for silkworms.

Cattle farming has never been intensive, due to lack of pastureland. Most stock is raised in northern Honshu and Hokkaido. Although more than half of all farms have a few animals (poultry, pigs, sometimes cattle), most animals are raised in Tohoku and eastern Hokkaido, where the best pastures are found. The government has strongly encouraged cattle farming (about 4.9 million head), mainly for dairy products. There are relatively few sheep (28,000), raised only for wool. Usually, pigs (which do not require pasture and are easy to feed) are raised in family operations (just over 11 million head). There are few horses (24,000) because of lack of pasture.

Japan can be divided into ten agricultural zones by region and main crop: 1) eastern Hokkaido (oats and cattle); 2) western Hokkaido and northeast Tōhoku (potatoes, peas, cattle, horses); 3) Tōhoku and the western part of the coast of the Sea of Japan (one harvest of rice per year, vegetables, fruits); 4) northern Chūbū, on the Sea of Japan (winter harvests of oats and wheat, rice); 5) the central mountainous part of Honshu (blackberries, tea, grapes); 6) Kantō and northern Kantō (barley and sweet potatoes, rice, wheat, vegetables); 7) central Honshu and the coast of the Inland Sea (vegetables, fruits and tea, rice); 8) Chūbū and the northwest coast of Shikoku, northeast Kyushu (fruits, industrial crops, vegetables, rice); 9) southwest Kyushu (summer rice and winter cereals, tobacco, fruits, rice); 10) southeast Kyushu and Shikoku, southern Osaka (sweet potatoes, rice, fruits).

Crops on the other southern islands are poor, consisting mainly of tropical fruits (pineapples, bananas) and sugar cane.

See CLIMATE, FISHING, GEOGRAPHY, GŌSHI, HANDEN, JŌRI, PEACHES, RŌNIN, RYŌMIN, SHINDEN, TONDEN-HEI.

Agui. Buddhist temple of the Tendai sect, located on Mt. Hiei, where the Buddhist Law was preached in the form of sermons called *shōdō*. It was the seat of many preachers, among them Chōken (ca. 1125–1205) and his son Shōgaku (?–1235), who created a sort of preachers' school known as Agui-ryū.

Ai. Indigo, from the indigo plant *(Indigofera tinctoria),* the leaves of which are used to make a blue fabric dye. There are a number of blue colors drawn from this plant (or from similar plants, such as *Isatis* and *Nerium*): pale blue *(asagi),* sky blue *(hanada),* dark blue *(kon),* and indigo *(ai).* This plant, which originated in southern China or India, seems to have been cultivated very early in Japan; the Shōso-in, an imperial storehouse in Nara, has some fabrics from the eighth century dyed with indigo. Indigo was also used during the Edo period to make blue inks for certain types of ukiyo-e prints of the *aizuri* technique. *See* AIZURI, AOYA.

• Concept expressing love, carnal or emotional. The word *ai* is, however, rarely used in daily life, and has been developed mainly in literature. In Buddhism, it is often synonymous with suffering.

→ *See* NOH.

Aichi. Name given to two warplanes used during the Second World War:

—**Aichi D.3–A.1.** American code name "Vals." Bomber used during the attack on Pearl Harbor (December 7, 1941). *Speed:* 387 km/h. *Range:* 920 km. *Weapons:* two 7.7 machine guns and one 400 kg bomb. The model D.3–A.2 was built in 1942.

—**Aichi E.16–A.1 (Zuiun).** American code name "Paul." Marine hydroplane bomber, built starting in 1942 (253 units built). *Speed:* 400 km/h. *Range:* 2,500 km. *Crew:* two. *Weapons:* two 20 mm cannons, one 12.7 machine gun, one 225 kg bomb.

Aichi-ken. Prefecture in the Chūbu region of Honshu, on the 35th parallel. Main city, Nagoya. Once composed of the provinces of Mikawa and Owari. *Area:* 5,114 km². *Pop.* 6.5 million. It is one of the main industrial centers of Japan (textiles, automobiles, steel mills, chemical products, lumber, ceramics). It is mountainous to the east (Mikawa range), and in the west is the Nōbi plain, irrigated by the Kiso and Yahagi rivers. *Main cities:* Okazaki, Toyota, Ichinomiya, Toyohashi.

Aichi Kiichi. Politician (1907–73) who held several ministerial positions. He played an important role after the Second World War, asking the Americans to return Okinawa from occupation. Fukuda Takeo succeeded him as minister of finance in December 1973.

Aida Yasuaki. Mathematician (1747–1817), author of many scientific works: *Sampō tenseihō shinan* (Treatise on Higher Mathematics, 1810), *Jū-jozan kajutsu* (Solutions to Advanced Equations with an Abacus), and *Taisūhyō kigen* (Studies of Logarithms). *See* WASAN.

Aiden-zukuri. Architectural style used in Shinto shrines, with two or several interior rooms for the veneration of several gods. This type of building can be seen in the Harima-sōsha at Himeji and in the Yamada-jinja at Shiga.

Aikawa. Town on the island of Sado, Niigata prefecture. It is an old mining city dating from 1601, when gold was discovered there. The mines were later abandoned, but every July a colorful festival celebrates its former activity. *Pop.:* 13,000.

Aikawa Yoshisuke. Financier (Ayukawa Gisuke, 1880–1967), founder of the Nissan zaibatsu before the Second World War. Born in Yamaguchi prefecture, he studied in the United States. In 1910, he founded the Tobata steelworks in Kyushu, which later became Nissan Motors. During the occupation of Manchuria in 1931–45, he was one of the promoters of industrialization of this region and had the Nissan plants transported to Mukden in 1937. After the Second World War, he was obliged to resign as president of the group, and he began a career in politics, being elected to the Chamber of Councillors in 1953.

Aikidō. "Path of Harmony with Universal Energy" (*ai:* union, harmony; *ki:* breath of life, energy; *dō:* path). A martial art *(budō)* created as a sport by Ueshiba Morihei (1883–1969) in Tokyo in 1931. For this art of self-defense he used ancient Chinese and Japanese techniques *(jū-jutsu)* comprising more than 700 movements and holds, most of them based on flexible body movements called *taisabaki*. The philosophy of *aikidō*, as conceived by Ueshiba, is a sort of art of living excluding violence, hand-to-hand combat, and competitive fighting. The skill of the *aikidō-ka* (*aikidō* practitioner) is, if attacked, to turn the strength of the adversary back against him without using any weapons. The mind of the *aikidō-ka* must be filled with harmony and peace. According to Ueshiba, only those who have fully realized within themselves an intuitive perception of the harmony existing among all things in the world, and who are thus imbued with a dispassionate love for all beings, can succeed to a higher state *(aikidō),* placing them beyond fear, weakness, laziness, and

pride, and thus making them truly "free." Beyond physical education, this martial art is a philosophy of life based on knowledge of oneself, one's body, and one's mind. All *aikidō* movements are thus designed to teach those who practice them to free themselves from psychic and muscular blockages so that they can live in full harmony with the world around them.

• **Aikidō-gi.** Clothing worn by those practicing *aikidō* in the *dōjō* (training room), consisting of *hakama* (traditional Japanese pants) and a jacket, white or black depending on the level.

• **Aikidō-ka.** A person who practices *aikidō*.

Aikoku Fujinkai. "Women's Patriotic Association." founded by Okumura Ioko (1845–1907) in 1901, when she returned from visiting Japanese soldiers on the front in northern China. She received support for this project from the military and from Konoe Atsumaru. Among members of the association were many women belonging to the aristocracy and the imperial family. It was also developed in Korea, Taiwan, and Manchuria. It had almost 4 million members assisting families of soldiers at the front and, in the interwar period, performing works of social welfare (orphanages, nurseries, etc.). In 1942, the association was absorbed by Dai Nihon Fujinkai.

• **Aikoku Kōtō.** "Public Party of Patriots." First political association, founded in 1874 by Itagaki Taisuke and other members of Parliament, Gotō Shōjirō, Etō Shimpei, and Soejima Taneomi. This party was opposed to the government's policies and wanted intervention in Korea. It also demanded adherence to French principles about the "natural rights of man" and the right to free thought. In 1874, it was absorbed into Aikoku-sha, which later became the Jiyūtō (Liberal party). *See* AIKOKU-SHA, JIYŪTŌ.

• **Aikoku-sha.** "Society of Patriots." Patriotic association founded in 1875 in Osaka, associating the Risshi-sha (Self-Help Society), created by Itagaki Taisuke in the province of Tosa, with various other movements for liberty and personal rights. It had very few members, all of them extremists, who demanded a national constitution. The society was dissolved one month after its creation when Ōkubo Toshimichi promised, on behalf of the government, to create a Constitution. Because it was slow in coming, Itagaki started his movement up again in

1878, gaining a great number of members (almost 100,000, from 27 different societies). In 1880, he named it Kokkai Kisei Dōmei (League for Establishing a National Assembly), which became the Liberal party (Jiyūtō) in October 1881. *See* AIKOKU-KŌTŌ, JIYŪTŌ.

Ai Kongō. "Diamond of Love." In Japanese Esoteric Buddhism, and mainly in the Shingon sect, this bodhisattva *(bosatsu)* is represented almost exclusively on mandalas, colored blue and holding a banner decorated with a head of Makara *(Jap.:* Makatsudō). Also called Kongō Ai. *See* AIZAN MYŌ-Ō.

Aikuchi. Short, single-edged dagger used by the samurai and nobles of the Kamakura and Muromachi periods as a complement to their swords. *See* HAMADASHI, KATANA.

• **Aikuchi-goshirae.** Type of sword handle without a guard *(tsuba),* typical of *aikuchi* and *tantō. See* TANTŌ.

Aikyōjuku. "Academy for the Love of One's Community." Nationalist society of farmers, founded in 1931 by Gondō Nariaki and Tachibana Kōzaburō (1893–1974) near Mito (Ibaraki prefecture) in the form of an educational institution for training the farmers in modern methods. The few students in this "school" were involved (along with Tachibana) in the incident of May 15, 1932 (Goichigo Jiken), an attempted coup d'état led by navy officers, and the institution was dissolved. It reopened a few months later, closing finally in 1933.

Ai Mitsu. Western-style painter (Ishimura Nichirō, 1907–46) born in Mibu, Hiroshima prefecture. At the beginning of his artistic career, he used the name Aikawa Mitsurō. His work was influenced by the Expressionists and Fauves of the Paris School. After a trip to China in 1935, he returned to Oriental painting, imitating somewhat the style of the painters of the Song period and adding Surrealist elements. He was a founder of Bijutsu Bunka Kyōkai in 1939 and, with other painters, started an artists' association against militarism, Shinjin Gakai (Society of New Painters). He died of dysentery in Shanghai.

Ainu. "Man" in the language of the aboriginals of Hokkaido. Word used to designate the populations of fishers and hunters of Hokkaido, the Kuril Islands, and Sakhalin, who probably arrived during a time when Asia was very active; the Ainu were related to the Siberian, Tungusic, Altaic, and Uralic peoples, although some of their physical features might be attributed to Caucasian ancestry. The Ainu originally peopled most of Honshu but were pushed north to the island of Hokkaido by the Japanese. They were of medium stature (160–165 cm) with a relatively heavy skeleton, flat face, deep-set chestnut-colored eyes under prominent orbits, white skin, and heavy body hair. Because of intermarriage with the Japanese, there are practically no racially pure Ainu left, and their language is also in danger of disappearing. Fortunately, it was studied at the beginning of the twentieth century by John Batchelor (1854–1944) and Kindaichi Kyōsuke (1882–1971). The Ainu language, limited phonetically, resembles Japanese in syntax, but there are notable differences between the two languages. Ainu has no written literature but a great oral tradition, consisting mainly of epic poems *(yukar).* There are at least three local dialects of Ainu. Ainu music, though influenced by Japanese music, uses mainly chants to accompany the *yukar* recitations and some simple instruments: drum, zither, and guimbarde. The men dance in a circle, stamping their feet *(tapkar).* The bear cult survives in the few remaining Ainu villages on Hokkaido. They worship spirits, or "forces of nature" *(kamuy),* which they symbolize by wood carvings placed in the northeast corner of their dwellings. Their dwellings are simple, with peaked thatched roofs. The Ainu are sometimes called Kai or Kehito (shaggy men). In Japanese history, they have been called Emishi, Ezo, or Mishibase (shaggy people), although it is not known if these terms are used only for the Ainu.

Ai Ō. Painter and printer (Ijima, Takao), born 1931 in Ibaraki prefecture. He experimented graphically with Demokorato, a group of avant-garde artists, then moved to the United States in 1958. He is known mainly for his brilliantly colorful silkscreens, which garnered him a number of awards, notably in Venice, Vancouver, and Tokyo.

Aioi. City in Hyogo prefecture, on the coast of the Inland Sea (Setonaikai), which, during the Edo period, became a post town *(shuku-eki)* on the San'yōdō road. Shipyards were established there in 1907. Every year on May 28, a race of traditional ships, called Peiron, is held.

Airaku-zō. The Buddha adorned with jewels and a crown, symbolizing the worldly aspects of divinity; used mainly in Esoteric Buddhism. This iconography originated in Southeast Asia, where it was a common representation of the Buddha.

Aiseki. Painter (early nineteenth century) born in Kishū. He was a student of Kaiseki, a master of the Nanga landscape school. He became a Buddhist monk under the name Shinzui.

Aizawa Saburō. Ultranationalist lieutenant-colonel (1889–1936) in the Kōdō-ha faction, which assassinated General Nagata Tetsuzan in 1935. His trial, known as Aizawa Jiken (the Aizawa Incident), provoked great political turmoil throughout Japan. He was executed in 1936. *See* NAGATA TETSUZAN, NINIROKU JIKEN.

Aizawa Tadahiro. Archeologist, born 1926 in Tokyo. He was the first to discover stone tools dating from the paleolithic age in Japan, at his excavations near the city of Kiryū, Gumma prefecture, in 1946. This discovery was followed by others, notably on the site of Iwaijuku, which provided confirmation that the Japanese islands were populated at least 30,000 years ago. *See* ARCHEOLOGY, IWAJUKU.

Aizawa Yasushi. Politician (Aizawa Seishisei: *gō:* Keisai; *azana:* Hakumin, 1782–1863), born in the province of Hitachi (Ibaraki prefecture). He was a member of the Mito school, where he was a student of Confucian philosopher Fujita Yūkoku. He played an important role in the reorganization of the Mito government (then run by Tokugawa Nariaki) and was a fervent promoter of the *sonnō jōi* movement. He wrote a number of political essays—*Tekii-hen, Kyūmon ihan, Kagaku jigen*—but is best known for his anti-Western work titled *Shinron* (New Thesis), which was based on Chinese Confucian teachings from the Zhu Xi (*Jap.:* Shushi) school and ended in a kind of mystical nationalism.

Aizen Myō-ō. Esoteric Buddhist deity, corresponding to the Sanskrit Rāgarāja, symbolizing carnal love. The Japanese Buddhist version of Eros, he is portrayed holding a bent bow and drawing an arrow made of flowers. His body is red, the color of passion. He has three faces and six arms. His main head has a mouth adorned with hooks and his hair stands on end, like that of all the Myō-ō (*Skt:* Vidyārāja). He is worshiped on the 26th of each month by dyers, who consider him their patron. Young people seeking love worship him in particular on New Year's day. *See* AI KONGŌ.

Aizu. Agricultural region in the western part of Fukushima prefecture, northern Honshu, famous for its pottery (Aizu-Hongō-*yaki*) and lacquered objects.

• **Aizu-Hongō-yaki.** Type of pottery produced in the region around the town of Hongō, in Fukushima prefecture, near Aizu-Wakamatsu. Production in this region began in 1645, when the daimyo of Aizu summoned a potter named Mizuno Genzaemon from the Mino pottery shops to make bowls for the tea ceremony. This pottery was made of a sort of brown sandstone, decorated around the edges with a white or black shiny glaze, or sometimes a white glaze with a gray-green or blue sheen. At the beginning of the nineteenth century, kilns were developed for blue porcelain with a clear glaze. They were partly destroyed in 1868 during the civil war (*see* BOSHIN SENSŌ) but were reopened at the end of the century. Their production is both industrial and artisanal.

• *Aizu nōsho.* Title of one of the oldest works on agriculture, written by Sase Yojiemon (1630–1711), a wealthy Aizu farmer, and completed by his adopted son Sase Rin'emon. What distinguishes it from other books of the period dealing with the same subject is that it refers to personal experience and not to the tradition inherited from China.

Aizuri. Technique of making ukiyo-e prints in the *nishiki-e* style, using mainly a blue color from the indigo plant (*see* AI), sometimes with red highlights. It was used mainly in the late eighteenth century by the painter Eishi and, starting in 1842, by Eisen.

• **Aizu-Wakamatsu.** Main city of the Aizu region, Fukushima prefecture, founded around a castle built in 1592. The city was partially destroyed during the Boshin Civil War (1868), but the ruins of its castle are still standing. The town is famous for lacquerware, textiles, and *sake. Pop.:* 120,000.
→ *See* BYAKKO-TAI.

Aizu Yaichi. Historian, poet, and calligrapher (Shūsō Dōjin, 1881–1956), born in Niigata. He wrote collections of *tanka* poems, imitating ancient styles. His best-known work is the collection *Nankyō shinshō* (1924), but he also wrote other works, such as *Rokumeishū* (1940), *Shūsho Dōjin no shō* (The Book of Shūshō Dōjin), and *Aizu yaichi zenkashū,* for which he won the *Yomiuri* Prize in 1951.

Ajari. Buddhist title (*Skt: āchārya,* "master") sometimes given to eminent monks of the Risshū, Shingon, and Tendai sects, and sometimes to nobles (*isshin-ajari*). It was conferred for the first time on the monk Kyōen Hōshi in 1034. Also written *azari.* *See* SŌ-KAN.

Aji-kan. In Japanese Esoteric Buddhism, a method of concentration and meditation based on contemplation of the Sanskrit Siddham script (*Jap.:* Shittan) letter *A,* symbolizing the eternal nature of the Self. The goal of this meditation is for the meditator to identify with Mahāvairochana (*Jap.:* Dainichi Nyorai) through chanting the sound represented by the letter. *See* A, GACHIRIN-KAN, SHITTAN.

Ajima Naonobu. Mathematician (1738–1796), the first in Japan to calculate integrals and differentials using Neper's logarithms. He also worked on geometrical calculation of circles and triangles. *See* WASAN.

Ajinomoto (Aji-no-moto). Food company that makes monosodium glutamate (MSG), an amino acid discovered in 1907 by Ikeda Kikunae and used as a seasoning to bring out the taste of foods. It began to be produced industrially in 1909 and was immediately successful in Japan; by 1917 it was popular in the United States and various other countries. However, after the Second World War, some researchers advised against its use, since monosodium glutamate could cause cerebral problems. The product nevertheless continues to be produced and sold, and Ajinomoto also makes a number of other food products (oils, coffee, soft drinks, etc.). Its head office is in Tokyo.

Ajiro Hironori. Shinto priest (*gō:* Ajiro Yutai, Gondayū, 1784–1856) and poet, born in Ise. He founded a traditionalist school and wrote many commentaries on ancient texts, notably on the *Kojiki,* the *Man'yōshū,* and the *Rikkokushi,* classifying the facts contained in them according to their analogies.

Akabane Kōsaku Bunkyoku. Government factory established in Tokyo's Akabane district around 1871. Its engineers imported their technology from Europe and produced boilers and various machinery for the public and private sectors. In 1883, it was placed under management of the navy. It contributed greatly to development of industrial techniques and training of engineers.

Akabashi Moritoki. Statesman (active 1326–33) of the Hōjō family. He was the last of the Kamakura regents (*shikken*), having succeeded Hōjō Takatoki when the latter became a Buddhist monk. Defeated by Ashikaga Takauji (who had married his sister), he committed suicide by *seppuku* when Kamakura was taken and set afire in 1333.

Akabori Shirō. Biochemist (1900–92), born in Shizuoka, known mainly for his research on the synthesis of amino acids. After studying in Japan, the United States, and Germany, he directed a number of research institutes in Japan. He was awarded the Order of Culture (Bunka-shō) in 1965.

Akaboshi. Type of Kagura dance performed to accompany the Shinto gods when they departed after an invocation. This dance generally ends the Kagura rites.

Akae. Decoration on the glaze of some pottery, using a Chinese technique adopted in Japan by the potter Sakaida Kakiemon in the mid-seventeenth century. It used mainly three colors (red, green, and yellow), to which Japanese ceramists added blue, purple, black, and gold. Also called *kakiemon, iro-e, uwa-e (Chin.: sancai, wucai).*
→ *See* HASHIMOTO CHIKANOBU.

Aka-ezo fūsetsu-kō. "Report on the Ezo Countries." Two-volume work presented to the Edo shogunate in 1783 by the physician-explorer Kudō Heisuke, in which he recounted the Russian advance on Kamchatka and the island of Sakhalin north of Hokkaido, then called Ezo. He called for trade negotiations to be opened with the Russians in order to forestall their potential aggression against Japan. He also stressed the need to develop Hokkaido, with a view to increasing the nation's resources. The Russians were often called Aza-Ezo, or "red-headed Ezo."

Aka-Fudō. Buddhist painting on silk portraying Achalanātha (*Jap.:* Fudō Myō-ō) sitting on a rock holding a sword in his hand. His body is colored red (whence his name). He is accompanied by two acolytes, Kongara Dōji and Seitaka Dōji. This painting, which probably dates from the fourteenth century, is by an unknown artist and is now in the Myō-ō-in on Kōyasan. *See* AOI-FUDŌ.

Akahata. "Red Flag." Newspaper of the Japanese Communist party, created in 1928 and called *Sekki* before the party was recognized by the authorities, it took the name *Akahata* in 1947. It was banned in 1935 but reappeared in 1945, only to be banned again from 1950 to 1952 by General MacArthur during the Korean War. This daily currently has a circulation of about 3.5 million. *See* SCAP.

• **Akahata Jiken.** "Red Flag Incident." Socialist riots that took place on June 22, 1908, in Tokyo, when socialists gathered to demand that the government free one of their members, Yamaguchi Gizō (1882–1920), from prison. Some, led by Ōsugi Sakae and Arahata Kanson, left the meeting room brandishing red flags to challenge the forces of order and were savagely attacked by the police. Their leaders, among them Ōsugi, Arahata, Sakai Toshihiko, and Yamakawa Hitoshi, were arrested, sentenced to two and a half years in prison, and fined. This incident marked the beginning of the fight of the imperial government (Katsura Tarō's cabinets) against the socialist movement.

Akahon. "Red books." Name given to a series of popular works with red covers published starting in 1662 and addressed mainly to children. They contained legends, ghost stories, and abridged versions of Kabuki theater pieces. They were popular until the end of the Edo period. *See* KUSAZŌSHI.

Akaishi. Volcano (3,120 m) in the Japanese Alps in Shizuoka prefecture (central Honshu), the summit of which abounds in the red quartzite that gave it its name, which means "red stone." This mountain is part of a north–south chain (Akaishi Sammyaku) about 120 km long between the Fuji and Tenryū rivers, in the prefectures of Shizuoka, Yamanashi, and Nagano.

Akai Tori. "The Red Bird." Literary magazine for youth, published 1908–36 (with an interruption 1929–31), the aim of which was to raise the intellectual level of young people. Many well-known writers published in it, including Mori Ōgai, Shimazaki Tōson, Akutagawa Ryūnosuke, and Nogami Yaeko. Its print run was 30,000 copies.

Akaji Yūsai. Lacquer artist (Sotoji, 1906–84) born in Kanazawa. He studied under Shimpo Kōjirō, then under Watanabe Kisaburō in Tokyo. He specialized in an ancient lacquer style called *magewazukur* that allowed for lacquering round-shaped objects. He was declared a Living National Treasure in 1974.

Akama-jingū. Shinto shrine in the city of Shimonoseki, dedicated to the memory of the child-emperor Antoku, who drowned during the naval battle of Dannoura in 1185, along with a number of warriors of the Taira clan. He was interred in a Buddhist temple in Amagasaki (now Shimonoseki), which Emperor Go-Toba renamed Amida-ji. This temple was converted into a Shinto shrine in 1875 and its name was changed to Akama-jingū. Every April 23–25, a festival, Senteisai, is held there in memory of Antoku. This shrine contains the *Nagato-bon,* a 20-volume manuscript of *Heike monogatari,* dating from the thirteenth century. *See* ANTOKU TENNŌ.

Akamatsu. Family of warriors of the Muromachi period (1333–1568) founded by Akamatsu Norimura, who joined with Ashikaga Takauji in 1336 to fight the Kamakura shogunate and was made *shugo-daimyō* of the province of Harima (Hyōgo). They lost their properties in 1521, when they were defeated by their rivals, the warriors of the Uragami family.

• **Akamatsu Mitsusuke.** Warrior (1381–1441), son of Akamutsu Yoshinori. With the help of his son Nariyasu, he assassinated the shogun Ashikaga Yoshinori. He was then attacked by warriors of the Yamana and Hosokawa families, who directed the shogunal forces. Defeated, he was forced to commit suicide (*see* KAKITSU NO HEN). He had become a Buddhist monk under the name Shōgu.

• **Akamatsu Nariyasu.** *See* AKAMATSU MITSUSUKE.

• **Akamatsu Norimura.** Warrior (1277–1350) in the service of Emperor Go-Daigo, assisting him in his fight against the Kamakura shogunate and assisting Ashikaga Takauji against the Hōjō regent (*shikken*) in 1333. Ashikaga Takauji made him a minister in his government. He became a Zen monk with the name Enshin.

• **Akamatsu Norisuke.** Governor (1311–71) of the provinces of Harima, Bizen, and Mimasaka, he fought alongside his father, Akamatsu Norimura, against the Hōjō regent in 1333. He became a Buddhist monk (Tendai sect) under the name Jiten.

• **Akamatsu Yoshinori.** Warrior and minister (1358–1427) under Ashikaga Yoshimitsu, and father of Akamatsu Mitsusuke. His very small stature earned him the nickname Sanshaku Nyūdo ("the three-foot-high monk"). He became a Buddhist monk under the name Shōshō.

Akamatsu Katsumaro. Politician (1894–1955), born in the province of Yamaguchi. A journalist by profession, he joined the Communist party in 1922, then, with other socialists, founded the Shakai Minshūtō (Socialist People's party) in 1923. He was named secretary-general of the party in 1930. In 1932, he organized a new party, Nihon Kokka Shakaitō (Socialist Party of the State of Japan) and in 1933 he was among the founders of the Kokumin Kyōkai (Nationalist Association). He was elected to the Diet in 1937. He then became a militarist and was sent on a mission to China. During the Second World War, he supported the government's war policy, but he was forced to withdraw from politics after Japan's defeat. *See* SHAKAI MINSHŪTŌ.

Akamatsu Noriyoshi. Samurai (1841–1920) in the final years of the Tokugawa shogunate. After studying in Holland in 1862 with Nishi Amane and other engineering students, he became vice-admiral of the imperial fleet. The founder of navy engineering in Japan, in 1876, he designed the first Japanese warship, the *Iwaki*. He ended his career as port-admiral of Sasebo and Yokosuka.

Akamatsu Sōshū. Confucian historian (1721–1801), author of many history books and a history of the 47 *rōnin*. *See* AKŌ-GISHI.

Akame Shijūhattaki. "The Forty-Eight Falls of Akame." Series of scenic waterfalls near the city of Nabari in Mie prefecture (Honshu). Despite the name, there are more than 50 waterfalls. It is an important tourist center.

Aka-mon. "Red gate." Ancient gateway to the Maeda family residence in Edo, in the seventeenth century. It was so named because the family painted it red to celebrate the marriage of the daughter of the shogun Tokugawa Ienari to Maeda Nariyasu. The gateway is now part of the University of Tokyo, and its name is often used to designate that institution. It has been classified a National Treasure.

Akan. Buddhist monk (1136–1207) who built a temple called Ama-no-Zan Kongō-ji (or Nyonin Kōya) in Kawachi, near Osaka, in 1178. The emperor and princes Go-Shirakawa, Morinaga, and Go-Murakami took refuge there at the end of the twelfth century during the disturbances that led to the creation of the Kamakura military government *(bakufu)*.

Akanishi kakita. Short story (30 pages) written by Shiga Naoya (1883–1971) in 1917 describing the adventures of a samurai called Akanishi of the Date clan. It inspired directors such as Yamanaka Sadao, who made a film of it in 1938, from a script by Itami Mansaka.

Akan Kokuritsu Kōen. Akan National Park is located in eastern Hokkaido, in a volcanic region with many crater lakes, among them Kutcharo (the largest), Machū (whose waters are transparent to a depth of 35 m), and Akankō, famous for a variety of globular algae *(Aegagropila, Jap.: marimo)* with a diameter from 3 to 15 cm, which rise to the surface only during the day. This last lake, at an altitude of 419 m, has an area of 12.7 km^2 and a depth of 36 m. It is surrounded by peaks, including Meakan-dake (1,500 m) and Oakan-dake (1,370 m) whose slopes are covered with pine forests. *See* NATIONAL PARKS.

Akasaka. District of Tokyo famous during the Edo period for its makers of *tsuba* (sword guards), such as Akasaka Tadamasa. A Buddhist temple dedicated to Avalokiteshvara *(Jap.: Kannon Bosatsu)* and a Shinto shrine (Hie-jinja) are located there; both were destroyed during an air raid on Tokyo in 1945 and reconstructed after the war.

• **Akasaka Rikyū.** Imperial palace built in the Akasaka district of Tokyo about 1872, to serve as a residence for Emperor Meiji from 1873 to 1888. It was rebuilt from 1898 to 1909 by architect Katayama Otokuma (1854–1917) with marble imported from Italy, and was decorated with nineteenth-century French and Japanese paintings. It served as a detached palace for the heir to the throne. Restored in 1970, it was home to the National Library and the ministry of justice, then was transformed into a residence for foreign diplomats.

Akasaka-jō. Name of two ancient castles, one built in 1331 by Kusunoki Masahige at Minami-Kawachi (near Osaka), the other the following year on Mt. Kiri (at 300 m) near the first, which had been besieged by the Hōjō army. The first was then called Shimo Akasaka-jō, the second Kami Akasaka-jō.

Akashi. City in western Honshu, in Hyōgo prefecture (previously the province of Harima), where a castle was built in 1617 by Ogasawara Tadazane to

control communications between Honshu and the island of Awagi, at the entrance to the Inland Sea (Setonaikai). It then became an important stop on the San'yōdō road. Its site was eulogized by poets of the *Man'yōshū* in the eighth century. In 1943, fossilized bones were found there, perhaps belonging to a man of the paleolithic era, who was named *Nipponanthropus akashiensis. Pop.*: 255,000.
→ *See* MATSUDAIRA.

• **Akashi Kaikyō.** Strait between the city of Akashi, on Honshu, and the island of Awaji, commanding the entrance to the Inland Sea, where strong currents make navigation difficult. Depth: 135 m.

Akashi Kakuichi. Famous fourteenth-century *biwa* player, related to the Ashikaga family. As a *biwa-hōshi*, a traveling bard, he helped to popularize the *Heike monogatari. See* BIWA, BIWA-HŌSHI.

Akashi Morishige. General (?–618) who fought alongside Konishi at the Battle of Sekigahara in 1600 and who opposed Tokugawa Ieyasu in Osaka in 1615. He converted to Christianity and took the name Akashi Kamon.

Akashi Motojirō. Military man (1864–1919) born in Fukuoka. He fought at Port Arthur and Taiwan and rose to the rank of general. He went to Sweden and gathered information for the government on the status of the Russian fleet in 1904. After suppressing several insurrections in Korea, he was named governor of Taiwan in 1918.

Akashi Shiganosuke. Famous sumo wrestler of the early Edo period between 1624 and 1643. The imperial court conferred the title of Kaizan on him. Also called Shikanosuke.

Akatsuka Jitoku. Decorative artist (Akatsuka Heizaemon, 1871–1936) famous for his lacquerware using the *maki-e* technique, as well as some oil paintings. His work was exhibited in Paris in 1929. He was a member of the Teikoku Geijutsu-in (Imperial Art Academy).

Akazome Emon. Poet (ca. 957–1041), lady-in-waiting to the wife of Fujiwara no Michinaga. She married Ōe no Masahira (952–1012) and, at the end of her life, became a Buddhist nun. She wrote mainly *waka* poems, 600 of which were published in the collection *Akazome emon-shū.* Various imperial anthologies, such as *Shūi wakashū,* include 92. She has also been credited with composition of part of *Eiga monogatari.* She wrote a travel diary, *Owari*

kikō, and is one of the Sanjūrokkasen (Thirty-Six Poetic Geniuses) of the Heian period.

Akebono. Sumo champion (Chadwick Rowan, American), born 1970 in Hawai'i. He won the title of 64th *yokozuna* in 1993; even though he is not Japanese, he was recognized as having the quality of *hinkaku* (dignity inherent to the sumo profession).

Akechi Mitsuharu. Warrior (Akechi Hidemitsu, ca. 1537–82), cousin of Akechi Mitsuhide. Having tried in vain to dissuade him, he agreed to help his cousin in a plot to assassinate Oda Nobunaga. When they were defeated, he killed all the members of his family, as well as the wife and children of his cousin, who had taken refuge in the Sakamoto castle, then committed suicide by *seppuku.*

Akechi Mitsuhide. Warrior (1526–82) born in the province of Mino. A cultured man, he was a great lover of the tea ceremony (*chanoyu*) and a poet. He served Oda Nobunaga under the name Koretō and became one of his generals. He received the Sakamoto castle for his services and was appointed governor of the province of Hyūga. He then conquered, for Oda Nobunaga, the province of Tamba (north of Kyoto). In 1580, he was put in charge of establishing the survey of Yamato (Nara prefecture); in 1581, that of the province of Tango (north of Kyoto). On June 21, 1582, for an unknown reason, he attempted to assassinate Oda Nobunaga at the Honnō-ji temple, where Nobunaga lived when he came to Kyoto; he involved his cousin, Akechi Mitsuharu, in this attack. On the verge of defeat, Oda Nobunaga killed his son, Nobutada, and committed suicide. Akechi Mitsuhide then took the title of commander in chief of the army, but he was attacked 11 days later by Toyotomi Hideyoshi at Yamazaki. He fled but was mercilessly pursued and killed two days later. His popular nickname was Jūsan-kobū ("the thirteen-day shogun"). One of his daughters married Hosokawa Tadaoki; she converted to Christianity and became famous as Gracia.

Akeji. Painter and calligrapher, born in 1935 in Kyoto. He traveled in Europe and had exhibitions in Tokyo (1970) and Paris (1973). Best known for his color calligraphy using vegetable dyes, he also wrote several books on calligraphy.

Akera Kankō. Poet (Yamazaki Kagemoto, Yamazaki Kagetsura; *gō*: Kankō, Junnandō, Shurakukan, 1740–1800), author of collections of *kyōka* including *Kokun bakashū, Kyōka daitai,* and *Kawabata yanagi.*

Akiba-jinja. Shinto shrine located on Mt. Akiha in Shizuoka prefecture. Founded in the eighth century, it was dedicated to Kagutsuchi, a fire spirit. It houses a splendid collection of ancient swords *(katana).* Every December 15–16 it is the site of a fire festival (Hi Matsuri) at which thousands of faithful gather. This shrine is also known by the popular name Sanjakubō.

Akihabara. Tokyo district known for its intense commercial activity focused on Japanese electrical and electronic goods. Its name is taken from that of the Akiba Shrine, founded in 1870 as a branch of Akiba-jinja. *See* AKIBA-JINJA, TOKYO.

Akihito. The 125th emperor of Japan (Prince Tsugu no Miya), born in Tokyo on December 23, 1933, eldest son of Hirohito, the Shōwa emperor, and Empress Nagako. He ascended to the throne upon the death of his father on January 7, 1989. In April 1959, he married a commoner, Shōda Michiko (b. October 20, 1934), with whom he had two sons, Naruhito (Hiro no Miya), born February 23, 1960, married to Owada Masako (b. December 9, 1963), and Fumihito (Akishino, Aya no Miya), born November 30, 1965, husband of Kawashima Kiko (b. September 11, 1966), and a daughter, Sayako (Nori no Miya), born April 18, 1969. Emperor Akihito has a brother, Prince Hitachi (Masahito), a biologist, married to Tsugaru Hanako in 1964, and three sisters: Taka no Miya, married to Takatsukasa Toshimichi; Yori no Miya, married to Ikeda Takamasa; and Suga no Miya, married to Shimazu Hisanaga. His fourth sister, Princess Teru no Miya, married to Higashikuni Morihiro, is deceased. He has a paternal aunt, Princess Chichibu, wife of Prince Chichibu (Yasuhito, deceased), and two paternal uncles, Takamatsu (Nobuhito, deceased), and Mikasa (Takahito), all three younger brothers of Emperor Hirohito. All of the emperor's other relatives lost their titles after the Second World War. When he ascended to the imperial throne, Emperor Akihito took the reign name of Heisei ("establishing peace"). The official coronation ceremony took place on November 12, 1990, followed by the Daijōsai ceremony on December 22. Akihito is the current emperor of Japan.
→ *See* SAKURAMACHI TENNŌ, SUTOKU TENNŌ.

• **Akihito Shinnō.** Imperial prince (1846–1903), eighth son of Fushimi no Miya Kuniie Shinnō. In 1858, he became a Buddhist monk, but he returned to lay life in 1867 and was named a general, then a marshal, in 1902. He represented the Emperor Meiji at the coronation of Queen Victoria.

Akimoto Matsuyo. Playwright, born 1911 in Kanagawa. Her first play produced was *Keijin,* in 1947, in which she dealt with the misfortunes of the lower classes. Among her major works are *Hitachibō kaison* (The Priest of Hitachi, 1964) and *Kasabuta shikibu kō* (1969).

Akimoto Nagatomo. Warrior (1546–1628) serving the Hōjō family, and later Tokugawa Ieyasu.

• **Akimoto Takatomo.** Warrior, grandson (1649–1714) of Akimoto Nagatomo. He was a daimyo of Tatebayashi in the province of Kōzuke, then, in 1704, of Kawagoe in Musashi. He was named a *rōjū* (senior councillor) in 1699.

Aki no Kuni. "Autumn Country." Ancient poetic name for the province of Hiroshima, in southwest Honshu.

Aki no Miya. "Autumn Palace." Poetic name given in ancient Japan to the empress and the palace in which she lived.

Akinoyo-no-naga monogatari. "Long Story of Autumn Nights." Novel by an unknown author, written about 1375–78, telling of the amorous adventures of Keikai (or Sensai), a Buddhist monk from Hiei-zan, with the young page *(chigo)* Umewaka, one of Minimato Arihito's sons, in the court of the Retired Emperor Go-Toba—adventures that led to a violent quarrel between the monks of Mt. Hiei and those of the Mii-dera temple in Ōtsu, ending with the death of Umekawa and Keikai's sincere repentance.

Akirame. "Renunciation." Feeling of self-confidence and control over one's behavior, part of the warriors' code of conduct inspired by the Confucian moral code. The sense of perseverance through misfortune that it implies also reflects the fatalism inherent to certain Buddhist beliefs, which see everything as transitory and thus to be endured with patience. It is in part because of *akirame* that, throughout their history, the Japanese have accepted their given place in society without overt recriminations and have borne the reverses that life dealt them. Emperor Hirohito spoke with *akirame* when, after the defeat of Japan in 1945, he declared that he must "accept the unacceptable and bear the unbearable."

Akishino-dera. Buddhist temple located at Sadaiji (Nara). It was founded in 780 by the monk Zenshu (723–97). Set afire many times during civil wars, it was reconstructed during the Kamakura period (1185–1333); the Kōdō and the Hondō were rebuilt in the primitive style in the late twelfth century. It houses a number of famous Buddhist statues, such as those of Gigei-ten and Kudatsu Bosatsu, the wooden bodies of which had to be refashioned in the late thirteenth century, their dry-lacquer heads having been preserved. This temple, affiliated with the Jōdo sect—although it was founded by a monk from the Hossō sect—was assigned to the Shingon sect in 834.

Akita. Main city in Akita prefecture (Akita-ken, *area*: 11,609 km²; *pop*.: 1.3 million), on the right bank of the Omono River. In the seventeenth century, it was the site of a castle belonging to the Satake family. It is now an industrial (petroleum, chemicals, lumber, etc.) and university city. *Pop*.: 300,000. Its main tourist attraction is its lantern festival (Kantō Matsuri), which takes place every August.

• **Akita-ha.** Painting school active in Akita in the mid-eighteenth century, under the patronage of daimyo Satake Shozan (1748–85) and his minister, Odano Kaotake (1749–80). The painters of this school adapted certain Western painting techniques to the traditional formats. When he visited Akita in 1773, Hiraga Gennai (1728–80) brought the laws of European perspective, which he had learned from the Dutch living in Nagasaki. The best-known painters of the school, among them Shozan, Naotake, and Satake Yoshimi (1749–1800), were remarkable for their precise observation of nature.

• **Akita inu.** Breed of Japanese dogs, famous for their bravery, bred for defense and fighting. *See* DOGS, ODATE.

• **Akita-jō.** Ancient post fortified against the Ainu (Ezo), established in 733 on the site of the modern city of Akita. This fort was abandoned in the ninth century and reconstructed farther north. All that is left of it are the ruins of a palisade and the foundations of a temple. Its governors had the title Akita-jō no Suke.

• **Akita-jō no Suke no Ran.** A civil war that broke out in 1285 between the Hōjō and Adachi families over the Akita region. The Adachi family was defeated and lost their privileges. Also called Shimotsuki Sōdō, Kōan Gassen.

• **Akita Risshikai.** Society of about 3,000 farmers and ex-samurai who planned an attack on government buildings for June 16, 1881. The plot was discovered and the head of the society, Shibata Asagorō, was arrested.

• **Akita Yuden.** Oil fields in the western part of Akita prefecture, producing about 20% (about 50,000 barrels) of Japan's total production. Main sites: Yabase, Shirakawa, offshore wells.

Akitsu. Port in Hiroshima prefecture on the Inland Sea (Setonaikai), known especially for its *sake* breweries and for its mussel and pearl-oyster cultivation. Some shipyards. *Pop*.: 15,000.

• **Akitsu-kunitama.** *See* ŌKUNI-NUSHI.

• **Akitsu-shima.** "Land of Dragonflies." Poetic name once used to designate Japan, notably in the *Kojiki* and the *Man'yōshū*. In the latter anthology, the emperor is called Akitsu-mikami ("the lord who gives rice in abundance"), the word *aki* also meaning "rice."

Akiyama Saneyuki. Architect and naval engineer (1868–1918), born in Matsuyama. He was sent to the United States to complete his education from 1897 to 1899, then became an instructor at the naval college in 1902. He was part of Admiral Tōgō Heihachirō's general staff during the Battle of Tsushima in May 1905. Promoted to rear admiral, he served as an adviser to the ministry of the navy at the beginning of the First World War. He was also known as Akiyama Masayuki.

Akiyama Teisuke. Politician and journalist (1868–1950), born in Kurashiki. In 1893, he founded a political journal, *Niroku Shimpō*, which ceased publication the following year but started up again in 1900. Elected to the Diet, he was obliged to resign because of his attacks on the policies of the Katsura cabinet. He nevertheless continued to exert a major influence on public opinion.

Akiyama Terukazu. Archeologist and art historian (b. 1918), author of many reference books on Japanese archeology and art.

Akiyama Yō. Modern-style ceramist, born 1953 in Shimonoseki. He received the *Yomiuri* Prize in 1987 and various other prizes at international exhibitions, notably in Faenza, Italy, in 1989.

Akiyoshidō. One of the largest natural caves in the world, located on the Akiyoshidai limestone plain, in the western part of Yamaguchi prefecture (Honshu). It is about 10 km long, of which about 1.5 km are open to the public, and is famous for its stalactites and stalagmites, waterfalls, and pools.

Akiyoshi Toshiko. Jazz pianist and composer, born 1929 in Dalian, Manchuria. She studied music at Berklee College in Boston from 1956 to 1959, married an American jazz musician, Lew Tabackin, and settled in California.

Akizuki no Ran. Revolt led by a group of ex-samurai in Fukuoka prefecture on October 27, 1876. Many warriors from the Akizuki estate, led by Iso Jun (ca. 1827–76) and Miyazaki Shanosuke (1835–76), attempted to involve other ex-samurai in their rebellion against conscription and the ban on carrying swords, also demanding that a military expedition be sent to Korea. Pursued by the regular army, the 400 rebels fled to the mountains. Their leaders committed suicide or were taken prisoner and beheaded. *See* SAGA NO RAN, SEINAN NO EKI.

Akkadō. Series of natural caves near Iwaizumi in Iwate prefecture (northern Honshu), with a total length of 7.6 km, the longest being 2.3 km, in which there are primitive marine animals of the genus *Nerillidae*.

Akogi. Title of a Noh play: an old fisherman, feeling guilty for killing fish, laments his shortcomings but, incapable of surviving in another way, starts to fish again and drowns in the sea.

• **Akogi-ura.** Coast of Mie prefecture, near the city of Tsu, on Ise Bay, reputed to be holy because of its proximity to Ise Shrine and its beauty. It was once forbidden to fish or hunt there.

Akō-gishi. "History of the Braves of Ako," the famous 47 *rōnin* (masterless samurai) who were the heroes of an incident in Edo in 1701–03, recounted in *Goban taiheiki,* a one-act drama by Chikamatsu Monzaemon performed in Osaka in 1706. In 1701, as he did each year, Emperor Higashiyama sent ambassadors from Kyoto, where he lived, to extend his greetings to shogun Tokugawa Tsunayoshi in Edo. To provide the imperial envoys with a dignified welcome, the shogun put two daimyo in his court in charge of organizing the ceremonies. One of them, Asano Naganori, the daimyo of the small estate of Akō in western Honshu, was inexperienced and unaware of the subtleties of the etiquette required in this particular case. He had to ask for advice from the chief of protocol, a cantankerous, corrupt old man named Kira Yoshinaka, of whose conduct Asano, a rigidly moral Confucian, disapproved. Kira felt that the gifts chosen by Asano were not consequential enough and, jealous of the young daimyo's wealth, tersely refused to help, which put Asano in an embarrassing situation. He repeatedly asked the old man for advice, but each time he was insulted and turned away; finally, in a fit of anger, he wounded Kira with his sword. Unsheathing a weapon in the shogunal palace was a serious breach of etiquette; when the shogun was informed, he demanded that Asano suffer exemplary punishment, and so he was condemned to ritual suicide by *seppuku*. According to custom, his possessions and property were confiscated by the shogun, who gave them to a daimyo of a different family. The 300 samurai of Akō found themselves, from one day to the next, without a master or employment, and they thus became *rōnin*. Most of them dispersed, but one, Ōishi Kuranosuke, feeling that Kira was responsible for what had happened, resolved to avenge his master. He called together 46 other samurai, told them his plan, and asked them to wait patiently for the moment of vengeance in such a way as to avoid the attention of Kira, who was likely to be on his guard. Finally, after preparing for two years in utter secrecy, the 47 conspirators met in Edo on December 14, 1702, and attacked Kira's residence under cover of night. When they got inside, they found Kira and beheaded him. They placed his head on the tomb of their master, then turned themselves in to the shogunal authorities. Although the people of Edo acclaimed them as heroes, the shogun condemned them all to the same fate that Asano Naganori had suffered. The 47 faithful samurai returned to the tomb of their master in the garden of the Sengaku-ji temple in Edo and committed ritual suicide on February 4, 1703. Only Terasaka Kichiemon escaped the fate of his comrades, having been charged by them to go to Akō and inform their confrères that vengeance had been carried out. When he returned to Edo and turned himself in to the authorities, the shogun pardoned him. But another Akō samurai, regretting that he had not participated in the attack on Kira's residence, proceeded to Asano's tomb and committed *seppuku*. The samurai who was pardoned died of old age and was buried beside his companions. Even today, the

47 *rōnin* are remembered: every year on December 14, pilgrims place flowers on the tombs of the brave samurai of Akō. This heroic tale aroused the popular imagination, and the people of Edo made the 47 *rōnin* into symbols of loyalty, honor, and courage, immortalizing them in plays and novels. *See* CHŪSHINGURA, KIRA YOSHINAKA, ŌISHI YOSHO.

List of the 47 *rōnin* of Akō according to the traditional order by attack group:

—Kataoka Gengoemon, Okuda Magodayū, Tomimori Sukeemon, Kakebayashi Yūshichi, Yada Gorōzaemon, Okajima Yasoemon, Katsuta Shinzaemon, Yoshida Sawaemon, Onodera Sachiemon.

—Hayamizu Tōzaemon, Otaka Gengo, Kanzaki Yogorō, Chikamatsu Kanroku, Yato Emonshichi, Hazama Jūjirō.

—Ōishi Kuranosuke, Hara Sōemon, Mase Hisadayū.

—Horibe Yahei, Muramatsu Kihei, Okamo Kinemon, Kaiga Yazaemon, Yokokawa Kampei.

—Horibe Yasubei, Isogoi Jūrōzaemon, Sugino Tōheiji, Ōishi Sezaemon, Akagaki Genzō, Kurahashi Densuke, Sugaya Hannojō, Muramatsu Sandayū, Mimura Jirōzaemon, Terasaka Kichiemon.

—Ōishi Chikara, Shioda Matanojō, Nakamura Kansuke, Okuda Sadaemon, Mase Mogokurō, Semba Saburobei, Ashino Kazusuke, Hazama Shinroku, Kimura Okaemon, Fuwa Kazuemon, Maehara Isuke.

—Yoshida Chūzaemon, Onodera ?, Hazama Kihei.

Akusō. "Rogue monks." Name given to Buddhist monks of the late Heian period who took an active part in the political struggles facing the Fujiwara clan, and later the warrior clans of the Taira and Minamoto at the end of the twelfth century. *See* HEISŌ, SŌHEI.

Akutagawa Hiroshi. Actor (1920–81), son of Akutagawa Ryūnosuke and Tsukamoto Fumiko. Director of the Bungakuza, he organized various theater companies and was one of the creators of the New Theater (Shingeki).

Akutagawa Ryūnosuke. Writer, poet, and essayist (1892–1927), born in Tokyo, son of Niihara Toshizō and adopted by his maternal uncle, Akutagawa Michiaki. He earned a degree in English literature from the University of Tokyo and was profoundly influenced by Mori Ōgai and Natsume Sōseki. After teaching for a short time in the naval college, he decided to devote himself completely to writing. He prided himself on being a poet more than a prose writer and used very pure language, emphasizing in his stories the strange, fantastic, and marvelous with sometimes caustic humor. He was often inspired by old Japanese legends, remodeling them to make completely modern texts that were also a reflection on the individual's inability to cope with modern society. His works are some of the richest in the pantheon of modern Japanese literature, in which he occupies a choice spot. Physically frail and sensitive, he committed suicide at age 35, for fear of going mad, as his mother had soon after his birth. He left almost 100 works, among the best known of which are *Rashōmon* (1915); *Akuma no tabako* (The Devil's Tobacco, 1916), which describes Satan from the Christian tradition; *Hana* (The Nose, 1916), the story of a monk with an extraordinarily huge nose; *Imogayu* (Sweet-Potato Broth, 1916); *Hankechi* (The Handkerchief, 1916); *Chūtō* (The Pirates, 1917); *Kesa to morito* (1918); *Hōkyonin no shi* (The Martyr, 1918); *Jigoku-hen* (Incident in Hell, 1918); *Kumo no ito* (Spiderweb, 1918); *Mikan* (Oranges, 1919); *Nankin no Kirisuto* (The Christ of Nanjing, 1920); *Yasukichi no techō kara* (From Yasukichi's Notebook, 1923); *Shūzanzu* (Painting of a Mountain in Autumn, 1921); *Yabu no naka* (In a Thicket, 1922); *Umi no hotori* (Beach, 1925); *Genkaku sambō* (1927); *Haguruma* (The Gears, 1927); *Anchū mondō* (Dialogue in a Park, 1927); *Kappa* (1927); and *Ahō no isshō* (Life of an Idiot, 1927). A literary prize bearing his name (Akutugawa-shō) was created in 1935 by the Bunka Shunjū-sha and is awarded twice a year to young literary writers.

Akutō. "Bandit gangs." Term applied during the Kamakura (1185–1333) and Nambokuchō (1333–92) periods to bands of malcontents comprised of bandits, peasants, and sometimes land stewards *(jitō)* and farmer-managers *(myōshu)* who tried unsuccessfully to take advantage of the disturbances to take over the estates *(shōen)* by force. They were enlisted in 1274 and 1281 to defend the country against attempted invasions by the Mongols. Many of them, having managed to seize land, became minor local lords *(kokujin)* during the Muromachi (1333–1568) period. *See* ASHIGARU.

Alcock, Rutherford. First British consul (1809–1907) in Japan, appointed in 1858. He arrived in Edo in 1859 and soon was promoted to ambassador. When he returned to Great Britain in 1862, he published an account of his experiences in Japan,

The Capital of the Tycoon (1863). When he went back to Japan, he advised the Europeans and Americans to bomb the Chōshū coastal batteries in reprisal for Western ships having been attacked in their passage through the Strait of Shimonoseki. Recalled to London in 1864, he was appointed ambassador to China the following year.

All Nippon Airways (ANA). Japanese airline (Zen Nippon Kūyu), at first mainly devoted to domestic traffic. In 1958, it merged with Far Eastern Airlines, and in 1971 it began to offer flights outside of Japan, first on East Asian routes, then to Europe, starting in 1988, thus competing with Japan Airlines (JAL).

Almeida, Luis de. Portuguese missionary and surgeon (1525–83). Having gone to Japan to trade, he entered the Company of Jesus in 1553 in Yamaguchi. He then founded a hospital in Funai (province of Bungo), where he taught European surgery methods. During the same time he evangelized in Kyushu. He died in Amakusa after 30 years of activity in Japan.

Ama. Term that once designated those involved in fishing and navigation. Before the Taika Reform (645), the *ama* were slaves, some of whom served the court. Later, other groups of *ama* specialized in deep-sea diving for shells, mainly abalone *(awabi),* and seaweed *(nori).* Divers of the Shima Peninsula (Mie prefecture) are mentioned in the *Man'yōshū.* The term *ama,* which originally included both male and female divers, is now used mainly for women who dive for pearl oysters and various shells.

• The name *ama* (written with different *kanji*) also designates women who leave lay life to become Buddhist nuns. The *Nihon shoki* recorded the names of the first *ama,* who entered the convent in 584, following the example of the nun Zenshin. Thereafter, their numbers increased considerably, and many girls from ruined noble families became *ama* (*Skt:* bikshunī, amba). Also called *bikuni, ni, nisō.* The convents were called *ama-dera.*

• Name of a Bugaku dance in the Rin'yūgaku style, performed with two dancers wearing rectangular masks *(zōmen)* made of cardboard covered with geometric-patterned silk.

• *Ama.* Noh play: a sea dragon covets three jewels belonging to a minister and manages to steal one. The minister, who goes in search of the jewel, meets an *ama* fisherwoman and falls in love with her child. When he grows up, the child becomes a minister. His mother recovers the jewel from the sea, but she drowns.

Ama-cha. Herbal tea made with chrysanthemum *(Hydrangea)* leaves for the Buddhist ceremony venerating a statue of the child Buddha (Tanjō-Butsu) performed each April 8. The monks bathe the statue in *ama-cha* during the ceremony, which is called Kambutsu-e. According to popular belief, *ama-cha* has special properties. Mixed with ink, for example, it has the power to improve children's calligraphy. In Okinawa, *ama-cha* is called *chikuzaki.*

Amadai Kannon. In Japanese Buddhism, one of 33 forms (*see* SANJŪSAN ŌGESHIN) of Kannon Bosatsu (*Skt:* Avalokiteshvara), the worship of whom was introduced from China in the ninth century. Represented sitting in the "royal ease" position on a rock or a white lion, he has three eyes and four arms and is playing the *hōkugo* (a type of small *koto*) or a sort of Chinese lute the neck of which is decorated with a phoenix head. His top right hand holds a *hakukichijō* (white pheasant) and his top left hand holds a *makatsugyo* (mythical sea animal resembling an Indian *makara*).

Amado. "Rain door." Sliding wooden shutters that protect the shoji windows from bad weather; used to close up traditional houses at night.

Amae. Japanese concept that describes how an individual expresses his or her desire (conscious or not) to depend on the goodwill of others. According to psychiatrist Doi Takeo (b. 1920), it is one of the linguistic elements that reflects the culture of society in a given period. The concept of *amae* is notable mainly in the child-mother relationship, but also between a woman and her husband, employees and bosses, and students and teachers. It implies a sort of accepted dependency, as well as a certain feeling of well-being and leniency on the part of the dominant individual. *Amae* is often expressed in words or turns of phrase that imply acceptance of such dependency. It is the concept that often links *giri* (social obligations) with *ninjō* (human feelings), which govern most relationships between Japanese.

Amagasaki. City in Hyōgo prefecture (Honshu) on Osaka Bay, linked to Kyoto by a river. It was an important port in the eighth century, and is now a major industrial center (metallurgy, chemistry, electricity, ceramics, machine tools, etc.). *Pop.:* 550,000. Close by is the Yayoi site (300 BC–AD 300) of Tono.

Amagi. Town in Fukuoka prefecture (Kyushu) famous for its dyed fabrics called *shibori*. It was an important transit point on the Bungo-kaidō road. Now it is a major agricultural market with some industry (lumber, pneumatics, fertilizers). *Pop.:* 45,000.

Amagoi. Shinto rain festival. During these festivals, the peasants made entreaties to Ryūjin (the dragon god) and Ryū-ō (king of the dragons), who were thought to be emanations of the *kami* of rain and clouds. The invocations recited during the ceremony were often accompanied by dances (Amagoi Odori), including lion dances *(shishi-mai)*, phoenix dances *(hōo-mai)*, and dragon dances *(ryū-mai)*. When the rains arrived, the peasants danced an *orei-odori* (or Hōnen Odori) to thank the gods. Many shrines are dedicated to the rain gods, and some, such as the Togakushi Shrine in Shinano, are visited mainly during dry periods: water drawn there is reverently deposited on the *kamidana* (household altar) in every home. Fire is also associated with prayers for rain; torches lit in the mountain shrines, called *hiburi,* are taken to fields and ponds with the goal of irritating the rain *kami*. In the Kyoto region, the farmers also pray to Jizō Bosatsu (*Skt:* Kshitigarbha) in the hope that he will intercede with the other Buddhist gods to make clouds cover the sky. Statues of this bodhisattva are taken and thrown in the water. In some other localities, the Shinto priest is thrown in a nearby lake or river. At one time, wrestling contests between women were organized (notably at Akita) or plays were performed in which the actors wore special masks (at Ōita, Kyushu). The beliefs and customs concerning these dances vary according to the province and region.

Amainukai no Okamaro. Poet who lived in the time of Emperor Shōmu (<701–756>).

Amako. Clan of the Chūgoku region, which became powerful at the end of the Muromachi period (1333–1574) during the Ōnin War (1467), thanks to the efforts of Amako Tsunehisa, who, in 1486, conquered the province of Izumo and the island of Oki. However, he ran up against the Ōuchi family, which controlled the San'yōdō region. After the death of Haruhisa, Tsunehisa's grandson, in 1566, the influence of the Amako clan began to decline and his castle at Tomito fell into the hands of the Mōri clan. Later, Amako Katsuhisa tried to bring the glory of the past back to his clan by going to Oda Nobunaga, but, besieged in 1578 in the Kōzuki castle (province of Harima), he committed suicide and the Amako clan faded from history.

• **Amako Haruhisa.** Warrior (1514–ca. 1562), grandson of Amako Tsunehisa and lord of the province of Izumo.

• **Amako Katsuhisa.** Warrior (1533–78), son of Amako Tsunehisa.

• **Amako Tsunehisa.** Warrior (1458–1541), a founder of the Amako clan.

• **Amako Yoshihisa.** Warrior (?–1610). He fought the Mōri clan. Conquered and abandoned by his vassals, he became a Buddhist monk under the name Yūrin in 1566.

Amakudari. "Descent from Heaven." Expression designating the reinsertion of retired bureaucrats into a private firm. This practice developed especially after the Second World War in the banking, transportation, and heavy-industry sectors, enabling private enterprise to have closer contacts with the ministries whose bureaucrats they had just hired. *See* TEINENSEI.

Amakuni. Famous sword maker in the seventh century, who is said to have forged the sword *(ken)* of the statue of Fudō Myō-ō of Narita, as well as one for Emperor Mommu. He created new blades, slightly curved but with a double-bladed point. His swords thus marked the transition from the *ken (tsurugi),* straight with a double blade, of ancient times, to the *tachi,* or single-bladed curved swords that developed thereafter, starting in the eighth century. The Shōsō-in of Nara housed 54 *tachi*-type swords.

Amakusa. Archipelago in the Bay of Yatsushiro, south of Nagasaki (Kumamoto prefecture, Kyushu), the main islands of which are joined by five bridges built in 1966 and totaling a length of 18 km. The archipelago comprises more than 100 mountainous islands and islets, with poor soil, inhabited mainly by fishers. There are some charcoal mines and stone quarries. The two largest islands, Shimoshima and Kamishima, as well as 65 others, are part of the Unzen-Amakusa National Park. *Total area*: 877 km². *Pop.:* 260,000.

• The town of Amakusa, on Shimoshima, is a fishing port around which slate is extracted for porcelain. In the seventeenth century, many Christians fleeing persecution took refuge there. *Pop.:* 7,000.

• **Amakusa Korejiyo.** Christian theology college founded about 1580 in Funai, then transferred to Yamaguchi in 1586, then to Arie and Amakusa in 1598, and finally to Nagasaki. It had a print shop with a movable-type press imported from Europe on which the first Christian works (*kirishitan-ban*) were printed.

Amakusa no Ran. *See* SHIMABARA NO RAN.

• **Amakusa Shirō.** Chief Christian (1612–38) of the Shimabara Revolt, killed during the assault on the castle of Hara by the shogunal troops. Also sometimes called Amakusa Tokisada, his real name was Masuda Tokisada.

Amami. Archipelago located about 400 km southwest of Kyushu, between Kyushu and the Ryukyu Islands. Its main islands are Oshima, Kikaishima, Tokunoshima, Okinoerabujima, and Yoronjima. In 1609, the Amami Islands came under the control of the Shimazu family, and they were included in Kagoshima prefecture at the end of the Meiji era. They were occupied by American troops from 1946 to 1953. The main crops are sugar cane, bananas, and pineapples. *Area:* 1,237 km². *Pop.:* 200,000. These islands are sometimes called Satsunan.

• **Amami-Ōshima.** This is the largest of the Amami Islands. Surrounded by coral reefs, it is mountainous and produces pineapples and bananas. This island is home to one of the few venomous snake species native to Japan, the *habu.* History reports that the court of Yamato, in 683, received envoys from this island. Saigō Takamori was exiled there. The island is famous for its silks, called Ōshima *tsumugi* (museum in Kagoshima), and it has an air force and naval base. *Area:* 710 km². *Pop.:* 86,000.

• **Amamiko.** Female creative divinity in Okinawa and Amami.

Amamimoto-amiko. Feudal relations existing between the owners of boats and nets and the fishers who use them.

Amano-gawa. "River of Heaven." Term for the Milky Way and, by extension, the Tanabata Festival, or the "meeting of stars."

Ama no Hashidate. One of Japan's "three famous landscapes" (Nihon Sankei): a sand spit bordered with pines located in the western part of the Bay of Wakasa on the Sea of Japan, in the northwest part

of Kyoto prefecture, portrayed in a painting by Sesshū in 1502. This beach was associated with the legend of the creation of the Japanese islands by Izanagi and Izanami, the two progenitor deities.

Ama no iwa. According to the legend of the origins of Japan told in the *Kojiki,* the name given to the cave where the sun goddess Amaterasu-Ōmikami took refuge when she was offended by the scandalous behavior of her half-brother Susanoo.

Amanojaku. A demon in Japanese Buddhist folklore who interfered with the propagation of the Law and opposed human desires. He was said to have the power to take the form of those he wanted to harm; for instance, he substituted himself for Uriko-hime at her wedding. In the *Kojiki,* this demon, called Amanosagume, incited the *kami* Amewaka-hiko to kill a white pheasant sent by Heaven to Izumo. In Buddhist iconography, he is shown trampled underfoot by one of the Shi-tennō.
• In popular language, what a person who acts against the wishes of others is called.
→ *See* URIKO-HIME.

Ama no mokuzu. Collection of ancient customs concerning Buddhist monastic life, in three volumes, written by the monk Senshū in 1694.

Amano Sadakage. Historian (*gō:* Hakkaō, 1616–1723), famous for his great erudition and his essays, such as *Shiojiri* in 100 volumes (the original was said to have comprised 1,000 volumes).

Amano Shōgetsu. Netsuke sculptor (b. 1889) who worked mainly in ivory.

• **Amano Shōfu.** Netsuke sculptor (*gō:* Shōzan), born 1917, son of Amano Shōgetsu.

Amano Tameyuki. Writer and economist (1859–1938). During the Meiji era, he introduced European economic theories to Japan and wrote many works on the subject, including *Keizai genron* (1886) and *Keizai kōyō.*

Amano Teiyū. Politician and philosopher (1874–1980) born in Kanagawa. He studied philosophy at Heidelberg (1923–24) and was influenced by Kant's work. Upon his return to Japan, he wrote, notably, *Dōri no kankaku* (The Meaning of the Law, 1937), which was censored by the government, and *San hihan.* Minister of education from 1950 to 1952, he tried to democratize the Japanese system. He then founded Dokkyō University.

Amano Tōkage. Warrior (1136–1208), son of Fujiwara Kagemitsu. He entered the service of Minamoto Yoritomo and fought the Taira forces at the Battle of Ishibashiyama in 1180. Defeated, he accompanied Yoritomo into exile in the province of Awa, then continued the struggle against the Taira with Minamoto Noriyori, Yoritomo's brother. In 1203, upon the order of Hōjō Tokimasa, he executed the leader of shogun Yoriie's supporters, Hiki Yoshikazu.

• **Amano Yasukage.** Warrior (1537–1613), descendant of Amano Tōkage. He entered the service of Tokugawa Ieyasu and repressed the Ikkō-ikki uprising. He took part in numerous battles, including that of Sekigahara (1600). Ieyasu gave him a fief of 10,000 *koku* and the Kōkokuuji castle in the province of Suruga. He was, however, sent to a Buddhist temple after he admitted responsibility for a murder committed by one of his samurai in 1611, and died there.

Amaribe. At the beginning of the formation of Japanese royalty, mainly in the states of Yamato and Izumo, a group of more than 50 households that was authorized to form a village *(be, ko)*, which was either incorporated into another village or obliged to found its own.

Ama Shogun. *See* HŌJŌ MASAKO.

Amaterasu-Ōmikami. "Great Goddess Who Lights Up the Sky." The main Shinto *kami*, symbolizing the sun and light. According to the *Kojiki,* she was born out of Izanagi's left eye and governed the "High Plain of Heaven" (Takamagahara). According to the *Nihon shoki,* she was born from the union of Izanagi and Izanami. She opposed her brother (or half-brother) Susanoo, the lord of Izumo. Her grandson, Ninigi no Mikoto, descended to Earth and became the first ruler of Japan. According to the *Kojiki,* it was her great-great-grandson, Jimmu Tennō, who became the first emperor circa 660 BC. Her main sanctuary is the Naikū (inner shrine) at Ise; she is the chief imperial *kami* and the personal divinity of the emperors. She is sometimes known by other names, such as Ō-hirume no Muchi, Shimmei, Daijingū, and Tenshōkō-daijin.

Legend has it that Amaterasu-Ōmikami took refuge in a cave to dissociate herself from the violent and irrational behavior of her brother, Susanoo no Mikoto. With the sun goddess shut away, the world was deprived of light. All the heavenly *kami* *(amatsu-kami)* gathered at the entrance to the cave to discuss the best way to get Amaterasu to come out. With everyone's approval, a goddess called Ame no Uzume began to dance on an overturned cask, holding a bamboo stalk, stamping her feet, and singing. As she danced, she began to undress, making the other gods and goddesses shriek with laughter. From the depths of her cave Amaterasu could hear the commotion. Curious, she moved aside the boulder *(ama no iwa)* with which she had blocked the entrance so she could see what was going on. At that moment, one *kami* handed her a mirror, in which she imagined she was seeing another sun goddess, while another very strong *kami* kept her from closing the cave again and drew her outside. All the gods rejoiced as the sun illuminated the world once more. This legend, told in the *Kojiki* and the *Nihon shoki,* was standardized by the publication (in 712 and 720) of these two works. Later, Buddhist monks of the Shingon and Kegon sects, in their attempt at syncretism, assimilated Amaterasu into the Great Sun Buddha Vairochana *(Jap.:* Dainichi Nyorai). Amaterasu gave her grandson Ninigi no Mikoto the imperial regalia—the mirror that had reflected her face, the jewels *(magatama)* that had decorated the tree under which Uzume had danced, and the sword belonging to her brother Susanoo—and they were passed down from generation to generation within the imperial family.

Amatsu-Kominato. Small town in Chiba prefecture, on the Bōsō Peninsula, north of Tokyo, famous mainly for Nichiren's stay there. A temple of the sect founded by Nichiren, Tanjō-ji, commemorates the visit. Nichiren retired to a nearby mountain, Kiyosumiyama, to meditate and study. *Pop.:* 10,000.

Amatsu-tsumi. At one time, categories of offenses *(tsumi)* against the heavenly *kami.* All of the offenses related to agriculture: destroying the rice-paddy breakwaters, filling in the irrigation ditches, not respecting the rules about the opening and closing of the sluices for the irrigation ditches, polluting the rice paddies, burning an animal alive, etc. *See* TSUMI.

Amatsu-yashiro. Name given to the Shinto shrines in which the heavenly *kami (amatsu-kami)* are worshiped. The terrestrial *kami* are worshiped in shrines called *kuni-yashiro. See* JINJA, YASHIRO.

Amazawa Taijirō. Contemporary poet (b. 1936).

Ame no Futotama no Mikoto. Heavenly *kami* (*Amatsu-kami*) who accompanied Ninigi no Mikoto when he descended to Earth. He is considered to be the ancestor of the priestly family who served as Shinto ritualists at the Yamato court (Imbe). *See* AMATERASU, NINIGI NO MIKOTO.

Ame no Hiboko. According to the *fudoki* and the *Nihon shoki,* a Korean prince who came to Japan during the reign of Emperor Suinin (third century?), bringing with him various valuable objects, particularly swords and lances. According to the *Kojiki,* Ame no Hiboko was the ancestor of Empress Jingū Kōgō; he was deified and is still worshiped in a shrine in Izushi (Hyōgo prefecture).

Ame no Kaguyama. Small hill in Nara prefecture, some distance from the Asuka River, which with two nearby hills form what are called the Yamato Sanzan (three mountains of Yamato). Legend has it that with the earth of this hill, Emperor Jimmu made the weapons with which he conquered the country. This hill has often been cited by poets, notably in the *Man'yōshū.*

Ame no Koyane. Heavenly *kami* (*amatsu-kami*) who accompanied Ninigi no Mikoto to Earth. Charged with the Shinto ritual, he is considered the ancestor of the Nakatome family and is worshiped at the Kasuga Shrine in Nara.

Ame no Minakanushi no Mikito. Heavenly *kami* who held himself immobile in the center of the sky; he was superior to Amaterasu-Ōmikami and the ancestor of all the gods. He is worshiped in the Ame no Minakanushi Shrine at Kagoshima (Kyushu).

Ame no Murakumo no Tsurugi. Magical sword found by Susanoo in the tail of an eight-headed dragon (Yamatano Orochi), which he fought in order to save a young woman, Kushi Inada-hime, from the Izumo region. Susanoo then married her. He offered the magical sword to his sister, Amaterasu, who then gave it to Ninigi no Mikoto. The sword became one of the three sacred treasures (*sanshu no jingi*) symbolic of the emperor's power, with the jewels (*magatama*) and the sacred mirror. It was carried to the depths of the sea by the child-emperor Antoku at Dannoura in 1185. Once recovered, it is said to have been placed in the Atsuta Shrine in Nagoya. Apparently, it disappeared when Nagoya was bombed in 1945. It is also known as

Kusanagi no Tsurugi ("grass-reaping sword"), for Susanoo used it to cut the high grass that the peasants had set afire (*Kojiki* I, 2). *See* ASHINA-ZUCHI, KUSHI INADA-HIME.

Amenomori Hōshū. Neo-Confucian historian and philosopher (Toshinaga; *azana*: Hakuyō; *gō*: Keishōdō, Hōshū, Kissō, 1668–1755), born in Ōmi. He became the disciple of Kinoshita Jun'an in Edo, then entered the service of the daimyo of Tsushima. Literate in both Chinese and Korean, he was charged with diplomatic relations with Korea. Because of his concept of society and the emperor's place in it—a concept arising from the Confucian philosophy of Zhu Xi (*Jap.*: Shushi)—he was opposed to shogunal advisor Harai Hakuseki's views on the attitude to take toward Korea. He wrote many literary works, including *Kissō yawa* (Kisō's Resolutions), *Hōshū kuju* (Literary Compositions), *Taware-gusa,* and *waka* poems. He is considered one of the Bokumon Jittetsu.

Ame no Ōshiki no Mikoto. Heavenly *kami* who, descending to Eearth with Ninigi no Mikoto, served as his bodyguard, according to the *Ki-ki.* He was the ancestor of the Ōtomo family.

Ame no Shihomimi no Mikoto. Heavenly *kami,* son of Amaterasu and father of Ninigi no Mikoto. It was said that he was born of the breath of Susanoo, who, as he was chewing on the sacred jewels, lectured his sister not to attempt to seize the High Plain of Heaven (Takamagarahara). *See* AMATERASU.

Ame no Taneko no Mikoto. Heavenly *kami* (*amatsu-kami*) who became Jimmu Tennō's minister. He was said to be the ancestor and patron of Japanese jurists and Shinto priests, and one of the ancestors of the Nakatomi family.

Ame no Tomi no Mikoto. *Kami* who built a palace for Emperor Jimmu during his reign and introduced the cultivation of hemp and blackberries to Awa province. He is worshiped in the Awa Shrine in Chiba.

Ame no Uzume no Mikoto. Female *kami* who, in the legend recorded in the *Kojiki,* danced before the cave where Amaterasu had taken refuge, chanting obscenities and undressing to entertain the other gods. She married Sarutahiko and gave birth to the Sarume no Kimi clan. Descending to Earth with Ninigi no Mikoto, she induced the fish of the sea to swear fidelity to her. Her dance in front of the cave was said to be the origin of the Kagura sacred dances. *See* AMATERASU.

Amida. Japanese name for Amitābha, supreme Buddha of the Western Paradise (Sukhāvatī, *Jap.*: Gokuraku), also called the Pure Land (Jōdo), where he is said to receive the souls of the faithful after death. The Amida cult, based on study of the *Sukhāvatī-vyūha sūtra* (*Jap.*: *Dai-muryōju-kyō*), was introduced from China and Korea, and spread through Japan in about the ninth century. The aristocracy was the first to build temples in Amida's honor (Amida-dō) using a particular type of architecture, in the middle of which sat a statue of Amida. He became better known thanks to the preaching of Kūya Shōnin, while remaining one of the main divinities of the Shingon and Tendaī sects. Monks of Amida sects such as Hōnen and Shinran accentuated piety and pure devotion to this Buddha, the very evocation of whose name (*nembutsu:* "Namu Amida Butsu") enabled them to save the faithful from hell. Devotion to Amida inspired many paintings (such as *Raigō-zu*, portraying Amida's descent to gather in the souls of the faithful) and sculptures mainly up to the end of the Kamakura period, and a great many temples were dedicated to him throughout the country. He is also called Amirita, Amidabaya, and Mida. *Chin.*: Amituo-fo. *See* RAIGŌ.

• **Amida Hijiri.** Name given to Kūya Shōnin (Kōshō) in the tenth century, then applied to wandering monks who preached devotion to Amida and chanted his name, carrying as an insignia a stick decorated with a deer antler. *See* NEMBUTSU.

• **Amida-in.** Mudra specific to Amida. There are nine mudras associated with Amida's "greeting" to paradise. *Skt:* Dhyāna-mudrā. Also called Amida Jō-in.

• **Amida kuji.** A type of lottery popular in the Muromachi period, in which the amount that each participant had to pay was recorded on a piece of paper folded into a fan shape resembling Amida's halo.

• **Amida-kyō.** Sects of devotees to Amida. The five main sects are Ji-shū, Jōdo-shū, Jōdo Shin-shū, Shinshū, and Yūzū Nembutsu. *See these names.*

• *Amida-kyō.* Title of one of the three major sutras (*kyō*) forming the basis of teachings of the Jōdo sect. In Sanskrit, *Sukhāvatī-vyūha.*

• *Amida no munewari.* A late-seventeenth-century Noh play in which the narrator *(jōruri)* describes a miracle in which the Amida Buddha offers himself as a victim to save someone.

• **Amida-sanzon.** Buddhist triad often portrayed in paintings and sculptures: Amida is flanked by two bodhisattvas, Kannon Bosatsu and Dai Seishi Bosatsu.

• **Amida Shinkō.** Devotion to Amida. Amidism. → *See* BUDDHISM.

Ami-ha. Painting school that began in the fifteenth century and revived the technique of *sumi-e* (ink painting) popular at the beginning of the Muromachi period. Before the Ōnin War (1467–77), artists benefited from two forms of sponsorship from the Ashikaga shoguns: either they lived in Zen monasteries, which were cultural and artistic centers at that time, or they were directly attached to the shogun, for whom they became a *dōbōshu* (attendant). The *dōbōshu* were painters, masters of the tea ceremony *(chanoyu)* or flower arrangement *(ikebana)*, playwrights, or curators of the shogun's works of art. Imbued with Chinese culture and fervent devotees of Amida Buddha, they included in their names the suffix "-ami" (for Amida). The "Ami" artists lived in the Muromachi period (e.g., Zen'ami, garden designer), but the name "Ami school" describes mainly three generations of painters: Nō-ami (1397–1471), Gei-ami (1431–85), and Sō-ami (ca. 1455–1525), son of Gei-ami. A few painters adopted some characteristics of the ancient Yamato-e style and used looser strokes in their compositons, making them freer than before. Although this painting school did not survive beyond the end of the sixteenth century, it influenced subsequent generations in the Edo period, notably painters such as Sōtatsu and the Rimpa school. *See* AN'AMI YŌ, SHUNSEN BŌEKI.

Amino Kiku. Contemporary author (1900–78) of novels and short stories, such as *Ichigo ichie* (Once in a Lifetime, 1967). She was a follower of Shiga Naoya.

Amma. Ancient Chinese massage technique, imported to Japan in the late seventh century, combining body massage with chiropractic and a form of acupuncture. The Japanese massage method was said to have been invented around 1320 by Akashi Kan'ichi, but it was only in the seventeenth century that it spread throughout Japanese society, where it was very popular and gave rise to numerous "schools." The current method of *amma* derives from that created during the Edo period by the Fujibayashi Ryōhaku school. Most *amma* (the word also designates those who practice this type of massage) were, and are to this day, blind. *See* SHIATSU, TSUNA.

Amō Eiji. Senior bureaucrat (1887–1968) in the ministry of foreign affairs. On April 17, 1934, he declared in a press conference that Japan would maintain close relations with China and Manchuria but would not allow interference from other countries. The European nations and the United States reacted so strongly to this announcement that Japan denounced his statement in order to stay on good terms with the West.

Ampa-sama. Shinto goddess worshiped mainly by fishers on the Pacific coast, her largest shrine is at Aba in the province of Hitachi (Ibaraki prefecture). During festivals in her honor, fishermen pile their nets on the beach and place a small shrine dedicated to her at the top. At one time, this rite corresponded to the fishermen's protest against the long hours imposed on them by their bosses. By doing this, they stopped working, and they started again only when the shrine was removed from the pile of nets and oars. The exact origin of this custom is unknown.

Anami Korechika. Statesman (1887–1945), general, and minister of war (April 1945) in Suzuki Kantarō's cabinet. He was a firm proponent of all-out war against the United States in the cabinet meeting of August 14, 1945, held to discuss the terms of the Declaration of Potsdam *(see this word)*. The emperor decided to surrender, and Anami Korechika committed suicide the following night, putting an end to an attempted coup d'état fomented by young officers counting on his support. He was then replaced as minister of war by Shinomura Sadamu.

An'ami Yō (Fu). School of Buddhist sculpture, characterized by calm, sensitive works, specializing in images of Amida. This style is similar to that created by Kaikei (late twelfth century). Also called An'ami Dabutsu. *See* KAIKEI, AMI-HA.

• **Anani-kyō.** Buddhist sect founded in 1949 by Nakano Yonosuke (b. 1887).

Anchi. Engraver (early eighteenth century) of the Kaigetsudō school.

Anchin. Name of a Buddhist monk, founder of the Dōjō-ji temple in the province of Kii, circa 928.

• **Anchin-hō.** Secret Buddhist ceremony within *mikkyō* (Esoteric Buddhism) during which the monks pray to Fudō Myō-ō, Monju Bosatsu, or Yōe Kannon for peace in the country or the society. The mandala (Anchin-*mandara*) related to the god invoked is then suspended from the main beam of the palace or house where the ceremony takes place. Generally, the image of Fudō Myō-ō (with two or four arms) is portrayed. This ceremony was introduced from China by the monk Jikaku and is said to have been performed for the first time in the imperial palace in 860.

• **Anchin-mandara.** *See* ANCHIN-HŌ.

Anderson, William Edwin. English physician (1842–1900) invited to teach at Japan's Naval Hospital in 1873. He collected art and wrote on the history of Japanese art, including *The Pictorial Art of Japan* (1886) and "A History of Japanese Art" in *Transactions of the Asiatic Society of Japan* (1879).

Ando. Ancient system of recognition by the lord of a vassal's rights regarding a piece of land or an estate; one of the key ties of allegiance. This system, which appeared during the Heian period, was reinforced during the Kamakura period, when the vassals became *honryō ando,* or inheritors. The *ando* certificate was called *ando-jō*. This certificate had to be produced if property was sold.

• **Ando-bugyō.** Justice officer in the shogunal administration of the Kamakura period, charged with questions of property (*see* ANDO) and inheritances. *See* BUGYŌ.

Ando Hirotarō. Agricultural technician (1871–1958) born in Hyōgo prefecture. Director of the experimental agricultural institute of the Ministry of Agriculture from 1920 to 1941 and professor at the University of Tokyo, he made great advances in Japanese agricultural methods and wrote a major work on agricultural technology (1951). He received the Order of Culture (Bunka-shō) in 1956.

Ando Ichirō. Poet and literary critic (1907–72) who used free verse in a Western style. He went to Europe in 1954.

Andō Jishō. Printer (1666–1745) and publisher who, using his house, Hachimonji-ya, as an imprint, published a great number of *ukiyo-zōshi* novels by authors such as Saikaku Ihara, Ejimaya Kiseki, and Ueda Akinara.

Andō Kō. Musician (1878–1963), sister of Kōda Rohan. She studied violin in Europe with Joseph Joachim (1831–1907), director of the Berlin Conservatory. Considered the best violinist in Japan, she was appointed a member of the Nihon Geijutsu-in.

Andon. Type of portable lantern with a wood-and-paper shade over an oil lamp, which appeared around the thirteenth century. During the Edo period, *andon* had various shapes—mounted on feet, hanging, or portable—and were often decorated with the name or *mon* (family crest) of their owner. These lanterns were made mainly in Gifu.

Andō Nakatarō. Painter (1861–1913), born and worked in Tokyo, who adopted a westernized style and who specialized in portraiture. A student of Takahashi Yuichi, he directed the painting school called Tenkaigakusha and founded an association of painters, the Hakubakai.

Andō Nobumasa. Politician (1820–71). First daimyo of Iwaki (Fukushima prefecture), he was appointed *rōjū* (senior councillor) to the Tokugawa shogunate in 1860, replacing Ii Naosuke, who had just been assassinated. An excellent administrator, he reorganized Japan's monetary system and tried to absorb the inflation resulting from foreign trade. He attempted to arrange the marriage of Princess Kazu, sister of Emperor Kōmei, to the shogun Tokugawa Iemochi, thus incurring the wrath of those who supported the separation of these two courts, who tried to assassinate him. Having failed to reinforce the shogunate as he had wished, he was obliged to resign in 1862. Faithful to his opinions during the Boshin Civil War, he was pardoned by Emperor Meiji when he acceded to power.

Andō Seian. Philosopher and writer (*azana:* Romoku; *gō:* Seian, Chisai, 1622–1701), disciple of Shunsui. He wrote numerous works on Confucian ethics, including *Seian ishū, Seian shoka, Shogaku shimpō, Shogaku ruihen,* and *Shinsō shāgo.*

Andō Shōeki. Writer and physician (ca. 1701– ca. 1750), born in Akita. He is best known for having written a 100-volume work (of which only 15 installments have survived), *Shizen shin'eidō* (abridged in 5 volumes as *Tōdō shinden*) in which

he expresses a utopian view of an egalitarian, agriculturally based society, revealing his resolute opposition to shogunal policies. He thus presaged modern ideas, although he had only limited knowledge of European philosophies of his time.

Andō Tadao. Architect, born 1941 in Osaka, where, in 1976, he built the Azuma House, which brought him immediate fame. Among his most remarkable works are the Japan pavilion at the Seville World's Fair in 1992, the Church of Light in Osaka (1989), and the Water Temple in Hyogo. He received the Alvar Aalto Prize in 1985, the gold medal of architecture awarded by France in 1991, and the Carlsberg architecture prize in 1992.

Andō Tameakira. Historian of Japanese literature (*gō:* Nenzan; 1656–1716), born in the province of Tamba. He entered the service of Tokugawa Mitsukuni at Mito. Author of seven studies on the work of Murasaki Shikibu *(The Tale of Genji)* entitled *Shiji shichiron,* writings on the poems of the *Man'yōshū,* and a collection of essays entitled *Nenzan kibun,* he was also one of the contributors to *Dai Nihon shi* (History of Greater Japan).

Andō Teru. Sculptor (1892–1945), creator of the statue of the dog Hachikō (facing the Shibuya train station in Tokyo) and that of Saigō Takamori at Ueno, Tokyo.

Andō Tōya. Confucian writer (1683–1719), disciple of Ogyū Sorai.

Ando Yasunori (Kaigetsudō). Painter (Okazawa Ando, Okazaki Genshichi; *azana:* Kaigetsudō; *gō:* Kan'unshi), active circa 1700–14, creator of ukiyo-e prints. He founded the Kaigetsudō school, which specialized in images of beautiful women *(bijin).* He is sometimes confused with Ankei. His students continued the Kaigetsudō-ryū.

Anegakōji Kintomo. Noble (1839–63) of the imperial court, of the Fujiwara family, and a firm proponent of the restoration of the emperor and of the *sonnō jōi* doctrine. The imperial envoy to Edo, he was assassinated by political adversaries as he left the shogunal palace.

Anegawa no Tatakai. "Battle of Anegawa." This decisive battle took place on July 30, 1570, in the northern part of the province of Ōmi, between Oda Nobunaga's troops, allied with Tokugawa Ieyasu's, and the troops of two daimyo, Asai Nagamasa of

Ōmi and Asakura Kagetake of Echizen. Assisted by Toyotomi Hideyoshi (then known as Kinoshita Tōkichirō), Nobunaga and Ieyasu crushed their adversaries and advanced freely toward Kyoto. This battle confirmed Oda Nobunaga's preeminence and paved his way to military dictatorship.

An'ei. Era of Emperor Go-Momozono: Nov. 1772–Mar. 1781. *See* NENGŌ.
→ *See* SUIBOKUSAI.

Anekawa Shinshirō. Kabuki actor (1685–1749) in Tokyo, specializing in the roles of *wakashū, onnagata,* and *tachiyaku. See* KABUKI.

Anesaki Masaharu. Writer (*gō:* Chōfū; 1873–1949) and religious philosopher, born in Kyoto. He studied in England, Germany, and India, and was editor of several literary and philosophy journals. His works spread knowledge of Christianity in Japan, and his speeches on Buddhism in foreign countries were seen as authoritative. In 1923, he was appointed a member of the Japan Academy (Nihon Gakushi-in); in 1939, he was appointed to the House of Peers (Kizoku-in). Influenced by his friend, Takayama Chōgyū, he converted to Nichiren Buddhism in 1916. He translated Schopenhauer's *Die Welt als Wille und Vorstellung (Ishi to genshiki to shite no sekai)* in 1910–11, and his studies on "fundamental" Buddhism *(Kompon bukkyō)* are still important.

Angura. Form of modern "underground" (whence its name) or avant-garde theater, inspired by Brecht, Beckett, and Ionesco and dealing mainly with contemporary social themes. Its best representatives are Fukuda Yoshiyuki (b. 1931), Shimizu Kunio (b. 1936), Betsuyaku Minoru (b. 1937), and especially writers Terayama Shūji (1936–83), Kara Jūrō (b. 1940), Satō Makoto (b. 1943), and Tsuka Kōhei (b. 1948).

Angya. Name given to certain Zen monks who wandered the country seeking a master to lead them to satori (enlightenment).

Ani-kōzan. Silver mine in Akita prefecture in operation since the late sixteenth century. In 1672, veins of copper ore were discovered there. Extracted by the daimyo of Akita, the copper was shipped to Nagasaki. In 1875, the government purchased the mine and turned over its management to European engineers, then resold it in 1885. It was temporarily abandoned, but operations started up again in 1933.

Anji. Before the seventeenth century in the Ryukyu Islands, title given to local lords who reigned over a *magiri* (group of tribes) and who had small forts. Their wives had the title Onajo, and their sons that of Wakaaji. After the seventeenth century, they were called Aji.

Anjirō. Name given to the first Japanese man to embrace Christianity, perhaps based on the name "Angelo." His real name may have been Yajirō (ca. 1512/1513–1551). Accused of murder, he took refuge on board a Portuguese ship that took him to Malacca, where Francis Xavier converted him. He returned to Japan with a missionary and lived with him for some time. Because of anti-Christian persecution, however, he fled to China, where he became a pirate. He died in China.

Anjō-ji. Buddhist temple of the Shingon sect, founded at Heian-kyō (Kyoto) by the monk Eun in 848. It contains magnificent works of art, including statues of Go-chi Nyorai.

• **Anjō-ji Sōzu.** *See* EUN.

Ankan Tennō. Posthumous name of the twenty-seventh emperor of Japan (Prince Magari no Oine Hirokuni Take Kahani, 466<534–35>), eldest son of and successor to Emperor Keitai. Senka Tennō succeeded him.

Ankei. Maker of ukiyo-e prints (Okazaki Genshichi; *gō:* Kaigetsudō Ando, early eighteenth century). He is often confused with Ando, another painter.

Ankoku-ji. Generic name given to all Buddhist temples built in Japan's 66 provinces under the reign of the Ashikaga shogun at the suggestion of Musō Kokushi (starting in 1339). The pagodas of these temples were called Ankoku-ji Rishō-tō.

Ankoku-ji Ekei. Daimyo (d. 1600) of Kanagawa (province of Aki) and a Buddhist monk. A friend of Mōri Terumoto, he served as a mediator between Oda Nobunaga and Ashikaga Yoshiaki, on one side, and Hideyoshi and Mōri Terumoto, on the other. He followed Hideyoshi's troops to Korea in 1592, was named abbot of Tōfuku-ji in Kyoto, and received a fief of 60,000 *koku* in the province of Iyo (Ehime prefecture). He fought Tokugawa Ieyasu at

Sekigahara in 1600, was taken prisoner, and was beheaded in Kyoto.

Ankoku-ron. "Treaties for Pacification of the State." Famous work written by Nichiren in 1260 in which the monk strongly criticizes the Kamakura shogunate and predicts an imminent attack by the Mongols, which resulted in his being exiled by Hōjō Tokyori to Ito, in the province of Izu.

• **Ankokuron-ji.** Buddhist temple of the Nichiren sect in Kamakura, founded in 1274. It was destroyed when Kamakura was taken in 1333. The current buildings date from 1751–53.

Ankō Tennō. Twentieth emperor of Japan (Prince Anaho, 401<454–56>), son of and successor to Emperor Inkyō. He assassinated his older brother, Kinashi no Karu no Ōji(-Miko) and his uncle Okusaka, but was in turn assassinated by Mayuwa (Mayowa) no Ō(-Okimi), the latter's son. Yūryaku Tennō succeeded him.

Anna. Era during the reign of Emperor Reizei: Aug. 968–Mar. 970. Also called Anwa. *See* NENGŌ.

• **Anna no Hen.** Conspiracy that took place when Emperor Reizei abdicated, in the second year of the Anna era (969). It enabled the Fujiwara family to depose the minister Minamoto no Takaakira (914–82), second son of Emperor Daigo, who was an obstacle to Fujiwara political ambitions. Following the plot, Takaakira was banished to Kyushu and replaced by Morotada (920–69), Saneyori's brother. Prince Morihira then ascended to the throne and took the name En'yū, and Fujiwara no Saneyori became *kampaku* (regent). The Fujiwara clan thus became dominant at court.

Annaka. Town in the southwest of Gumma prefecture, on the Usui River, ancient transit point on the Nakasendō road. Small zinc industries. *Pop.:* 50,000.

Annei Tennō. Third emperor of Japan (Prince Shikitsu-hiko Tamatemi, traditionally 567<548–511>BC, but probably lived in the first century AD), son of and successor to Suisei Tennō. Itoku succeeded him. *See* TENNŌ.

Annen. Buddhist monk (Godaijin Sentoku, Godaiin Ajari, 841–ca. 889 or 897) of the Tendai sect. Disciple of Ennin and Henjō, he spent his life studying Tendai *mikkyō* (the sect's esoteric doctrines) and wrote several treatises on *kenkyō* and *mikkyō*.

Anoku Kannon. One of the 33 forms (*see* SANJŪSAN ŌGESHIN) of Kannon Bosatsu (*Skt.:* Avalokiteshvara). As a protector against the dangers of the sea (monsters and drowning), she is represented sitting on a rock facing the sea, holding either a roll of sutras or a "magical pearl" *(hōshu).*

Anoo (Anō). Village near Nara, in the Yoshino district, that became famous for having been the refuge of emperors from the Southern Court during the Nambokuchō period (fourteenth century). It provided asylum for, among others, emperors Go-Daigo (in 1336), Go-Murakami (in 1348), and Go-Kameyama (in 1373). Its name is sometimes written Anō. *See* YOSHINO.

Anotsu. Old port in the province of Ise (Mie prefecture), now called Tsu. It was the main naval base for the Taira clan starting in the eleventh century. During the Muromachi period (1333–1568), it played a major role in trade with China; with Hakata and Bō no Tsu, it was one of the three largest ports in Japan. Although its port facilities were destroyed by an earthquake in 1468, it continued throughout the Edo period to serve as a stop for pilgrims traveling to Ise. *See* TSU.

Anraru. Buddhist monk (?–1206) of the Jōdo sect, born in Kyoto. Involved in political struggles, frequent at the time in the capital, he was beheaded.
• Netsuke sculptor (early nineteenth century). → *See* JŪREN.

• **Anraku-ji.** *See* DAZAIFU TEMMANGŪ.

• **Anraku-ji Tōba.** Octagonal, four-story, wooden Buddhist pagoda built in the thirteenth century in Nagano on the site of a temple founded in the eighth century, the pagoda of which was destroyed in a fire. The style of its construction combines the *kara-yō* and *wa-yō* methods.

Anrakuan Sakuden. Buddhist monk (1554–1642) of the Jōdo sect, master of the tea ceremony *(chanoyu)* and flower arrangement *(ikebana)*, and a poet. His collection of more than 100 anecdotes and stories, *Seisuishō* (To Laugh to Awaken), prefigured works of the same type in the Edo period called *hanashi-bon*. In 1594, he was appointed abbot of Shōbō-ji in Sakai; in 1596, abbot of Jōon-ji; and in 1613, abbot of Seigan-ji in Kyoto. He also wrote a work on camellias, *Hyakuchin-shū* (Collection of 100 Camellias).

Anrakuju-in. Buddhist temple of the Shingon sect (Chisan branch) established in Fushimi (Kyoto) by transforming Emperor Toba's (1103–58) former palace. The temple contains the emperor's tomb and a statue of Amida with a *manji* (swastika) on his chest.

Ansei. Era during the reign of Emperor Komei: Nov. 1854–Mar. 1860. *See* NENGŌ.

• **Ansei no Kari Jōyaku.** Provisional trade treaties signed in 1858 between Ii Naosuke, for the shogunate, and various Western countries (United States, Russia, Great Britain, France, and Holland), in which Japan agreed to open a certain number of ports—Kanagawa, Hyōgo, Niigata, Hakodate, Osaka, and Edo—to trade, receive diplomats, set customs laws, and recognize the right of exterritoriality. Ii Naosuke signed the treaties without warning the emperor of the measures he had taken. This caused irritation among supporters of the imperial restoration, who were against any dealings with the West, and he was assassinated. The *bakufu* then reneged on the agreement, but the foreign powers sent nine warships to the Bay of Hyōgo to enforce the treaties. With the threat of war, the imperial court finally gave its assent.

Ansei no Taigoku. "Ansei Purge." The Ansei no Kari Jōyaku resulted in the shogunate organizing a major purge, lasting from 1858 to 1860, to get rid of opponents to its policies. The first to be purged was Ii Naosuke, because of the imperial court's reaction to the treaties with the Western countries, and the purge ended only with his death. *See* SAKURADA-MONGAI JIKEN.

Antei. Era during the reign of Emperor Go-Horikawa: Dec. 1227–Mar. 1229. *See* NENGŌ.

Antoku Tennō. Eighty-first emperor of Japan (Prince Kotohito, 1178<1181–83>1185), son of and successor to Takakura Tennō and Kenreimon'in Tokuko (daughter of Taira no Kiyomori). When Minamoto Yoshinaka's forces entered Kyoto, the suporters of the Taira clan fled, taking with them the young emperor, then seven years old. They wandered aimlessly, going to Fukuhara (province of Settsu), Dazaifu (Kyushu), and Yashima (province of Sanuki). During the great naval battle of Dannoura in the third month of 1185, the young emperor drowned with his grandmother, Nii no Ama, who, according to Taira lore, threw herself into the sea with the child in her arms. The sacred sword sank to the depths with them. His tomb is in Shimonoseki. Go-Toba had already succeeded him the previous year (1184). Other relics of this child-emperor are preserved at Itsukushima Shrine, the Taira family shrine. *See* AKAMA-JINGŪ.

Anzai Fuyue. Poet (Anzai Masaru, 1898–1965), born in Nara. He lived in Manchuria, where he published his first collection, *Gunkan mari* (Battleship Mari, 1929). He was considered an avant-garde author in the 1930s, mainly because of his prose poems. Toward the end of his life, he devoted himself to film criticism. His poetry was anthologized in 1966 in *Anzai Fuyue zenshishū.*

Ao-byōshi. "Blue books." Series of books with blue covers, published in Edo from 1803 to 1814 by the Hyōjōsho, containing excerpts of court judgments.
• Book written in 1840 by Ono Hiroki giving general advice to the military and bureaucrats of the Tokugawa shogunate. It was censored by the authorities because it contained information that could be used by the shogunate's enemies.
• Title sometimes given to the version of *Genji monogatari (The Tale of Genji)* attributed to Fujiwara no Taika.

Aochi Rinsō. Scholar (Aochi Ei; *gō:* Hōko; *azana:* Shien, ca. 1775–ca. 1833), student of Sugita Gempaku and Baba Sajūrō. The son of a Matsuyama physician, he went to Edo to study "Dutch science" *(rangaku).* He entered the Astronomy Bureau in 1822, where he translated a number of Dutch scientific works and wrote the first Japanese treatise on physics, *Kikai kanran,* in 1827. He then served the Mito feudal lords, for whom he continued his physics experiments and produced more translations.

Aōdō Denzen. Painter (Nagata Zenkichi, 1748–1822), born in the province of Iwashiro (Fukushima prefecture). After studying European painting under Gessen and Kōhan, he specialized in copperplate engraving, a technique he learned from a Dutchman. In 1794, Matsudaira Sadanobu took him into his service and had him work with Bunchō. It was Sadanobu who gave him the name Aōdō, which means "Hall of Asia and Europe." He illustrated many books and greeting cards.

Aohon. "Green books." Series of books with pale-green paper covers, written for young people in the *kusazōshi* genre. Most of them were published in Edo between 1745 and 1774. The name was also given to a few works in the *kibyōshi* and *gōkan* genres. *See* KUSAZŌSHI.

Aoi. Plant *(Asarum caulescens)* whose leaves and flowers are often used as a model for designing *mon* (family crests), following the practice of Kamo-jinja priests in Kyoto, who often used them as insignia. During the Edo period, the Tokugawa family (some members of which were devotees of the Kamo-jinja *kami*) used it as their family crest; families not related to the Tokugawa were forbidden to do so.

Aoi bunko. Collection of books and documents of the Tokugawa shogunate, kept in the Shizuoka prefectural library. It contains a large number of works in Dutch, English, German, French, and Chinese from the private collections of the shoguns and various scholars, as well as official correspondence between the shogunate and the Dutch.

Aoi Fudō. Buddhist painting portraying Aoi Fudō Myō-ō (Skt: Achalanātha) with a dark-blue body, sitting on a rock, accompanied by two child-acolytes *(dōji)*. This famous painting, attributed to Genchō (late tenth century), is kept in the Shōren-in temple, Kyoto. Also Ao Fudō. *See* AKA-FUDŌ, FUDŌ MYŌ-Ō.

Aoi Matsuri. Kyoto festival that takes place every May 15, with Shinto and Buddhist origins dating back to the seventh century. A large procession of men and women dressed in Heian-period (794–1185) costumes goes to the old imperial palace, then proceeds with great pomp first to Shimogamo Shrine, then to Kamigamo Shrine, where ceremonies are conducted. The streets of Kyoto are beautifully decorated for the passage of the procession, and the festival attracts great numbers of spectators. It is one of Kyoto's three major festivals, along with Gion Matsuri and Jidai Matsuri.

Aoi no ue. Noh play, based on an episode from the *Genji monogatari (The Tale of Genji):* Lady Rokujō's jealousy causes Lady Aoi no Ue to fall ill. A sorceress and a demon cure the one of her jealousy and the other of her illness.

Aoki Hiroshi. Contemporary sculptor (b. 1933) in the constructivist style.

Aoki Kazuo. Politician, minister of "Greater Asia" (Dai-Tōa) from 1942 to 1944. Shigemitsu Mamoru succeeded him in this position.

Aoki Kon'yō. Confucian scholar (Aoki Atsubumi; *azana:* Bunzō, 1698–1769), born in Edo. In 1719–20, he entered the service of Tokugawa Yoshimune, who appointed him superintendent of the official archives in 1739. In 1735, he recommended that the shogun cultivate sweet potatoes, which he felt would mitigate chronic famine. He wrote a work on the cultivation of this tuber *(Ipomea aedulis)*, *Banshōkō*, in the same year, which earned him the nickname "Professor Sweet Potato" (Kansho-sensei). In 1740, at Yoshimune's request, he began to study Western—especially Dutch—agriculture. He then published several books on foreign subjects, including *Oranda kaheikō* (Notes on Dutch Currency, 1745) and *Oranda moji ryakkō* (Notes on the Dutch Language, 1746). In 1767, he managed the shogunal bookstore (Momijiya no Bunko).

Aoki Mokubei. Painter and ceramist (Kiya Sahei; Kiya Yasohachi; *gō:* Kukurin, Rōbei, Kokikan, Teiunrō, Hyakurokusanjin; *azana:* Serai, 1767–1833), born in Kyoto. He was a student of Okuda Eisen (1753–1811) and specialized in the reproduction of classic Chinese styles. He built two kilns, one in Kasugayama (Kanazawa) and the other in Awata (Kyoto), where he produced remarkable porcelain pieces for the tea ceremony. Toward the end of his life, he became less active in ceramics and took up painting in the Bunjinga style, featuring mainly tall, narrow of landscapes in ocher, red, and indigo inks. He also wrote *kanshi* poems (in Chinese, written in *kambun*).

Aokin-fun. Mixture of gold and silver powders used to decorate lacquerware beginning in the late Heian period.

Aoki Okikatsu. Confucian historian (1762–1812). He studied Dutch and wrote various books, including *Mondō jissaku* (1804) and *Waran kidan*.

Aoki Shigeru. Western-style painter (1882–1911), born in Kurume (Shizuoka). In Tokyo, he was a student of Kuroda Seiki (1866–1924) and Fujishima Takeji (1867–1943). His style was similar to that of the European romantics and, mainly in his seascapes, impressionism. He died of tuberculosis and was buried on Mt. Keshikeshi near Kurume, where a student raised a monument to his memory in 1948.

Aoki Shummei. Painter (Sōemon; *gō:* Shukuya, Suntō, Hachigaku, Yoshukuya, died 1802) of the Nanga school. He was a student of Ike no Taiga in Kyoto and was the adopted son of Kan Tenju (Dainen).

Aoki Shūzō. Politician and diplomat (1844–1914), originally from the province of Nagato. In 1868, he went to Germany to study law and political science. Appointed minister of foreign affairs in 1889, he resigned in 1891 after the Ōtsu Incident (Ōtsu Jiken). He was ambassador to Germany (1874, 1880, 1892), Great Britain (1894), and the United States (1899–1909) and an adviser to Emperor Meiji (1889–1905). He was also charged with studying a review of the Unequal Treaties (*see* JŌYAKU KAISEI).

Aoki Toku. Painter (*azana:* Shidō; *gō:* Shishin, Renzan, Gantoku, 1805–59), who studied under his father-in-law, Ganku. He also painted in the style of the Shijō school.

Aomori. Main city in Aomori prefecture, in the extreme north of Honshu, on the bay of the same name, which became an active port in 1624. The Seikan Tunnel connects this city to Hokkaido. Every August 1–7, the Nebuta Festival takes place in Aomori. It is also known for its museum dedicated to the artist Munakata Shikō and its major prefectural archeological museum, Aomori Kenritsu Kyōdokan, opened in 1973. *Pop.:* 300,000.

• **Aomori-ken.** Prefecture in northern Honshu, bordered by the Strait of Tsugaru and the Pacific Ocean. This region is irrigated by the Iwaki and Oirase rivers (the latter flowing from Lake Towada). This prefecture was first named Hirosaki. Agriculture, animal husbandry, forestry, and fishing are the main resources. Most of the territory is mountainous, except the Tsugaru Plain to the east, edging the Sea of Japan, and the eastern plain on the Pacific Ocean. A long peninsula extends to the north, forming the Bay of Mutsu, and on its tip is the Osorezan volcano (879 m), traditional site of shamanic cults. *Area:* 9,614 km²; *pop:* 1,525,000. *Main cities:* Aomori, Hirosaki, Towada, Goshogawara, Mutsu.

Aomugi. "Green Wheat." This novel by Niwa Fumio, published in 1953, is a sort of autobiography and critique of postwar Japanese society *(apure),* and also deals with the place of religion in the modern world.

Aonodōmon. Tunnel in the north of Ōita prefecture (northern Kyushu) that, according to legend, was dug by the monk Zenkai in the middle of the Edo period. He is said to have worked alone for 30 years to complete it. The tunnel is 187 m long and about 3.6 m wide, and crosses the gorges (called Yabakei) of the Yamakuni River at a picturesque site featuring fantastically shaped boulders.

Aono Heinai. Craftsman (late sixteenth century), nephew and student of Sen no Rikyū, famous for his beautiful bamboo vases.

Aono Sō. Contemporary writer who received the Akutagawa Prize in 1979 for his novels *Gusha no yoru* (Night of the Crazy Man) and *Yama-ai no kemuri* (Smoke in the Ravine), the latter written in collaboration with Shigekane Yoshiko.

Aono Suekichi. Writer and literary critic (1890–1961), born near Niigata. A political journalist affiliated with the Communist party, he later became a critic at *Bungei Sensen,* a proletarian magazine. He wrote a study on the works of Lenin (1923). At the end of the Second World War, he was elected president of the Association of Japanese Writers (Nihon Bungeika Kyōkai), and was able to revive the PEN club of Japan.

Aoshima. "Green Island" is about 1 km south of the city of Miyazaki (southeastern Kyushu) and is linked to the mainland at low tide. Despite its small size (0.04 km²), it is remarkable for its boulders and profuse subtropical flora.

Aoshima Gukio. Director of a number of important films, notably *Kane* (The Bell, 1968).

Aoshima Yukio. Politician and writer (b. 1940), elected to the Upper House of the Diet in 1968. He received the Naoki Prize in 1981 for his autobiographical novel *Ningen banji seio ga hinoe uma.*

Aoto Fujitsuna. Warrior and philosopher (thirteenth century) serving the regent *(shikken)* Hōjō Tokiyori. The *Taiheiki* tells how he rendered justice both fairly and firmly, but this personage may be legendary. Also called Aoto Saburō.

• *Aoto Fujitsuna moriyōan.* "The Judgments of Aoto Fujitsuna." Novel by Bakin, published in 1811, which contributed to the legitimacy of the legend of Aoto Fujitsuna.

Aoto Tsunayoshi. Warrior (ca. 1800?) in the service of a small-scale daimyo of Echigo, who, through studying the life cycle of salmon, was the first to farm them.

Aoya. Professional dyers' group that used indigo *(ai),* active from the medieval period to the beginning of the Edo period. They were often considered *hinin* (outcasts). *See* AI, BURAKUMIN, HININ.

Aoya Gen'emon. Potter and ceramist (1791–1863), born in Komatsu (Ishikawa prefecture). He worked in the Kutani style and was a student of Honda Sadakichi. In 1822, he built a kiln in Kaga and used the *gō* Tōkō to sign his works. His two main disciples were Matsuya Kikusaburō and Shōzō. His porcelain works were decorated before baking with a white slip covered with layers of colored glazes. He made many utilitarian objects, various types of boxes, clepsydras (water clocks), and fountainheads.

Aoyagi Tanenobu. Historian (Aoyagi Katsuji; *gō:* Ryūen, 1766–1825), born in the province of Chikuzen. Student of Motoori Norinaga, he worked in collaboration with Inō Tadataka. His best-known works are *Gokan kin'in kō, Sakimori nikki,* and *Chikuzen soku fudoki shūi.*

Aoyama Gakuin. Private colleges founded in Aoyama (Tokyo) by an American Methodist minister, Robert S. Maclay, and a group of young Christians in 1874. The colleges were renamed Tokyo Eiwa Gakkō in 1883 and took their current name, Aoyama Gakuin, only in 1894. They acquired the status of university in 1948. Aoyama Gakuin is known for its high quality of teaching in English, and it has research institutes in economics, science, and management. The student population is about 13,000.

Aoyama Nobumitsu. Historian (Aoyama Enkō; *gō:* Bansui, Shummu, ca. 1805 or 1807–70) of the Mito school. He was the son of Aoyama Nobuyuki, whose example he followed. His main work is *Kokushi kiji hommatsu.*

• **Aoyama Nobuyuki.** Confucian historian (Aoyama Ryōsuke; *azana:* Shisei; *gō:* Sessai, Unryū, 1776–1843), of the Mito school. He was the first president of the Kōdōkan and took part, with Tokugawa Mitsukuni, in the compilation of the *Dai Nihon shi* (History of Greater Japan), of which he assumed the editorship soon after. Among his own works are *Kōchō shiryaku* (Abridged History of the Emperors, 12 vols. written in *kambun*) and *Bun'en idan* (Biographical and Diverse Notes). He was Aoyama Nobomitsu's father.

Aoyama San'u. Calligrapher (1913–93) who established a modern style based on the Chinese Lishu and Zhuanshu styles. In 1966, he received the Japan Art Academy (Nihon Geijutsu-in) Prize; later, the Order of Culture (Bunka-shō).

Aoyama Tanemichi. Physician (1859–1917) for the imperial family. He studied in Germany and was appointed chancellor of Tokyo Medical College (Tōkyō Ika Daigaku). His activities greatly improved the teaching of medicine in Japan.

Arafutsukun. Ainu dance executed by two groups facing each other during certain ritual festivals, notably that of the bear sacrifice. This dance lasts several hours and stops only when one of the dancers drops from fatigue. *See* AINU.

Aragoto. A style of Kabuki performed in Edo from the early eighteenth century. The creators and best-known actors of this style of Kabuki were Ichikawa Danjūrō I and Ichikawa Danjūrō II. Some actors in the plays were disguised. These popular plays glorified heroism and gallantry, in contrast to *wagoto,* which expressed gentle, noble sentiments, and *jitsugoto,* featuring events in daily life. *See* KABUKI.

Aragyō. Ascetic practices of monks who followed the precepts of Shugendō, consisting of walking to exhaustion in the mountains, sleeping in the woods, frequent fasting, and diving into the freezing waters of raging rivers, in order to toughen the spirit and the body.

Arahata Kanson. Journalist and socialist politician (1887–1981), born in Yokohama. He was baptized in 1903 and became involved in socialist action in 1904, joining the movement against the Russo-Japanese War. He contributed to various proletarian publications, such as *Heinin Shimbun,* and wrote articles (such as those on the Ashio copper mines) that caused a sensation. In 1908, he was arrested with his wife, Kanno Suga, after the Akahata Incident (*see* AKAHATA JIKEN) and sentenced to two years in prison. He was arrested again in 1918 for having broken press laws. In 1922, he was a founder of the Communist party, which then sent him to Beijing and Moscow. In 1937, he was arrested once again for his writings, and spent the Second World War under house arrest, writing and producing translations. After the war, he took an active part in the union movements and helped to reorganize the Socialist party, for which he was elected to the Diet in 1946 and 1947. However, because of discord and electoral failures, he ended his political involvement in 1951. His autobiography, *Kanson jiden,* published in 1945 and revised in 1975, was his most important work. *See* KŌTOKU SHŪSUI, SAKAI TOSHIHIKO.

Arahitogami. "Living God." Title for the emperor of Japan until 1945. *See* IKIGAMI.

Arai Hakuseki. Historian and Confucian philosopher (Arai Kimiyoshi, Arai Kageyu; *azana:* Zaichū; *gō:* Shiyo, 1657–1725), born in the province of Kazusa (Chiba prefecture) into a minor samurai family. His father having been dismissed in 1677 after a dispute with other samurai, he became a *rōnin* and studied Confucianism, the ideals of which, based on the merits of man, remained with him throughout his life. In 1682, he entered the service of Hotta Masatoshi's family; in 1694, he tutored Tokugawa Tsunatoyo, who was to become the shogun Tokugawa Ienobu (1709–12), and he remained in the service of the Tokugawa shoguns Ienobu and Ietsugu as an adviser. He attempted to reform the shogunate according to Confucian ideas by investing it with more power and authority, giving the shogun the title of king in his diplomatic correspondence with the Koreans. Although his influence was very strong, his only reforms to survive concerned currency and the reorganization of the judiciary system. But more than a statesman, he was an accomplished scholar who wrote many historical works, including *Hankampu* (History of the Daimyo, 1701), *Oritaku shiba no ki* (Told Round a Brushwood Fire, ca. 1716), *Seiyō kibun* (Notes on Europe, after 1708), *Tokushi yoron* (Views on Japanese History, 1712), *Tōga* (Dictionary of Japanese Words), and *Sairan igen.* He is included in the list of Bokumon Jittetsu.

Arai Kampō. Painter (Arai Kanjūrō, 1878–1945), specializing in historic scenes and Buddhist religious painting.

Arai Ōsui. Head of a Christian community (1846–1922), born near Sendai. After studying Confucianism at Shōheikō, the Tokugawa academy in Edo, he joined the shogunal forces during the Boshin Civil War and enlisted in the navy led by Enomoto Takeaki, based in Hakodate. During the siege of this town by the imperial troops, he converted to Orthodox Christianity. In 1871, he entered the Brothers of New Life Christian community and went to the United States, first to New York, then California. He became head of the community in 1892. He decided to return to Japan in 1899 to preach his faith, publishing pamphlets called *Goroku* (Talks). He gained few converts, however. Having refused to marry or find employment, he died in poverty. After his death, his pamphlets were published in five volumes *(Ōsui koroku)* by one of his disciples.

Arai Ryōichirō. Businessman (1855–1939) of peasant origins who made his fortune in the silk trade and became a high-level intermediary between the United States and Japan. He started a family in San Francisco in 1876 and lived in the United States.

Arakatsu Bunsabe. Atomic physicist who worked with Nishina Yoshio and Sagane Ryōkichi in 1937.

Arakawa. River 177 km long, with its source in the Kantō mountains and its mouth in Tokyo Bay. A dam on its upper course created Lake Chichibu. Its lower course is called the Sumida River. Its hydrographic basin has an area of 3,130 km². *See* SUMIDAGAWA.

Arakawa Shūsaku. Western-style painter, born 1936 in Aichi prefecture. He became a conceptual artist and created a group called Neo-Dada about 1960. In 1961, he settled in the United States, where he painted groups of symbols on white backgrounds that he called "diagrams."

Arakawa Toyozō. Potter and ceramist (1894–1985), born in Gifu prefecture. He demonstrated that Shino-type pottery had been produced in the sixteenth century in the Mino région and not in Seto, as had been believed. He first studied painting, then became a ceramist under Miyanaga Tōzan (1868–1941). Becoming a professional in his own right in 1930, he conducted research on production from the Oribe and Shino kilns, which led him to discover a large kiln of Shino pottery in Mutabora, near Gifu. He then built a similar kiln on the ruins of the old one and produced beautiful objects in the purest Shino style. The government declared him a Living National Treasure in 1955. *See* SHINO-YAKI.

Araki-bune. "Araki ships." Large ships used by the Araki family of Nagasaki for foreign trade under shogunal licence. They featured a flag bearing the letters V.O.C. on the back, indicating that they belonged to the Vereenighde Oost (Indische) Companie (Dutch East India Company), which guaranteed them some protection from piracy. *See* SHUINSEN-BOEKI.

Arakida. Family of priests who inherited the Naikū (inner shrine) of Ise, competing with the Watari, who were in charge of the outer shrines (Gekū) of Ise. *See* ISE.

• **Arakida Hisaoi.** Priest of Ise Shrine (Arakida Hisaoyu; *gō:* Itsukien, 1746–1804), disciple of Kamo no Mabuchi. He wrote literary works and a commentary on the *Man'yōshū,* the *Norito,* and the *fudoki.*

• **Arakida Moritake.** Poet (Senku, Tobiume Senku, 1473–1549) and priest at Ise, author of many *renga* and *haikai* poems *(Haikai no renga),* gathered in a collection, *Haikai no renga dokugin senku* (also called *Tobiume senku* and *Moritake senku).*

Arakida Reijo. Woman of letters (Arakida Takako, 1732–1806), daughter of a priest at Ise, Arakida Moritō. She wrote historical novels and travel journals in an elegant style, such as *Ike no mokuzu,* a history of Japan from 1333 to 1603, and *Tsuki no yukue* (Where Is the Moon Going?), a story that takes places in the years 1168–85.

• **Arakida Takako.** *See* ARAKIDA REIJO.

Araki Jippo. Painter (1872–1944) in the Japanese style (Nihonga), who had an exhibit in Paris in 1900. He wrote an essay comparing Western and Eastern paintings entitled *Tōyōgaron.*

Araki Kampo. Painter (1831–1915), born in Tokyo. A student of Arakai Kankai, of the Bunchō school, he worked for the daimyo of Tosa in 1856, studied Western painting, then returned to traditional painting. His paintings of birds (peacocks) and of flowers are still highly regarded. He founded the Dokuga Kai, an artists' association, and taught at the Tokyo School of Fine Arts (Tōkyō Bijutsu Gakkō). He had an exhibit in Paris in 1900.

Araki Kodō. School of Kinko-*ryū shakuhachi* (vertical bamboo flute) players. The best musicians of this school were:
—Araki Kodō I (Araki Hanzaburō, 1823–1908), founder of the school. He transformed Komusō into a performance art, with accompaniment for the *shakuhachi* by shamisen and *shō,* and he composed music for these instruments. *See* FUE.
—Araki Kodō II (Araki Shinnosuke, 1879–1935).
—Araki Kodō III (Araki Shū, 1902–43).

Araki Mataemon. Warrior (1599–1638), born in the province of Iga. He studied the art of the sword under Yagyū Jūbei (1607–50). He helped the younger brother of his wife, Watanabe Kazuma, take revenge on his enemy Kawai Matagorō, and the story of this vengeance was the subject of many plays (along with the story of the 47 *rōnin* and the Soga brothers). He then became a master of weapons known throughout the country and the founder of a Kenjutsu school, Araki-*ryū* (*see* KENDŌ), using wooden swords *(shinai).* He was buried in the Genchū-ji temple, Tottori.

Araki Murashige. Warrior (d. 1586), born in the province of Settsu. He served, in turn, the Ikeda, the Miyoshi, and Oda Nobunaga. When he turned against the latter, he was defeated and went over to the Mōri. As a Buddhist monk, he became a disciple of Sen no Rikyū, who taught him the art of tea ceremony *(chanoyu),* of which he became one of the greatest masters.

Araki no miya. Building where the body of a deceased lay in state before his interment in a tumulus *(kofun)* so that offerings of food, chants, and dances could be made to him. This custom was abandoned in 646, when the practice of cremation became prevalent with Buddhism. *See* KOFUN, SENGONKO KOFUN.

Araki Ryōjun. Young man in the group that went to Rome at the beginning of the twelfth century. He was ordained a priest. Upon his return to Japan, he quarreled with the foreign missionaries, renounced Christianity, and helped the Nagasaki authorities persecute the Christians. Returning to Christian faith in 1637, he was persecuted in his turn and put to death. He had been baptized with the name Thomas Ryōjun.

Araki Sadao. Ultranationalist politician and general (1877–1966). After participating in the Russo-Japanese War of 1904–05, he obtained a diploma from the Army College in 1907. During the First World War, he was a military attaché in St. Petersburg. In 1930, he created a fascist group, Kōdōgikai, and hatched a plot with young officers who wanted him to become prime minister. Although the plot failed, he was named minister of the armed forces in 1932 by Inukai Tsuyoshi and Saitō Makoto. General Nagata, seen as more conservative, succeeded him in this position in 1934. Araki Sadao hoped that a new war would take place between Japan and the USSR, a view supported by the Kōdōha extremist faction. Following the failure of an attempted coup d'état by the faction in February 1936 (*see* NINIROKU JIKEN), which he had tacitly approved, he had to retire. Nevertheless, he was appointed minister of education in Konoe Fumimaro's cabinet, a position in which he was a proponent of military education at all levels. Declared a war criminal in 1945, he was sentenced to life in prison but was freed in 1955 and pardoned.

Araki Sōtarō. Trader, arms dealer, and navigator (?–1636), who, armed with a shogunate licence (*shuinjō*, "red seal"), conducted trade with Southeast Asia, notably Annam and Siam. After six voyages in these regions, he returned to Nagasaki, his home port, in 1619. He apparently married a daughter of King Nguyēn of Hué, capital of Annam. His ships bore the name *Araki-bune*.

Araki Takako. Ceramist, born 1921 in Nishinomiya (Hyōgo prefecture). Many of her works won awards in Japan and in various foreign cities, notably Paris (Mitsukoshi space) in 1994.

Araki Yojibei. Kabuki actor (1637–1700) and theater manager (*zamoto*) in Osaka. He played only male roles.

Ara Masahito. Literary critic (1913–79) born in Fukushima prefecture. A specialist in English literature, he was the founder of the literary journal *Kindai Bungaku* in 1946, in collaboration with Odagiri Hideo and Hirano Ken. He was the the first author to apply Freudian theories in literary criticism, notably in his critiques of Natsumi Sōseki's novels. He also translated works by Nathaniel Hawthorne and Emily Brontë and wrote essays on James Joyce and T. S. Eliot.

Arami meizukushi. Treatise on swords of the *shin* type (*shin-tō*), written by Hakuryūshi (Kanda Katsuhisa) in 1712, in which he describes swords (*katana*) made after 1596. This work became a standard reference on the subject.

Aramitama. According to Shinto belief, the *aramitama* is the active, violent, and destructive aspect of a *kami*, in contrast to the *nigimitama*, which is tranquil, passive, and in harmony with nature. At one time, when an unlucky event occurred people conducted ceremonies to appease the *aramitama* of the local *kami*, which was thought to have provoked the event. The afflicted family then entered a period of mourning and made offerings to the *kami* in the shrine dedicated to its *aramitama*. The *aramitama* and *nigimitama* of a *kami* had, and sometimes still have, separate shrines. Thus, for example, the *aramitama* of Ōmikami is worshiped in the Hirota Shrine in the province of Settsu (now Osaka and Hyōgo prefectures). *See* KAMI, MITAMA.

Arao. Mining town in Kumamoto prefecture (Kyushu) that developed during the Meiji era (1868–1912) when the Miike coal mines were in operation. The mines were closed after the Second World War and the town's inhabitants went to work in the sister city of Ōmuta, where chemical industries had been established. Arao also produces citrus fruits and *nori* seaweed. *Pop.*: 65,000.

Araragi. Journal devoted to *tanka* poetry, created in 1908 by Itō Sachio. It succeeded another journal, *Ashibi*, which folded in the same year. *Araragi* published young poets wishing to return to the old traditions, as well as essays on Western poets. It had a great influence on young people and still publishes "realist" poets writing in the *Man'yōshū* style.

• **Araragi-ha.** School of poetry for the development of *tanka*; it still has a number of devotees who publish in the journal *Araragi*.

Arashi Kanjūrō. Kabuki and film actor (1903–80), born in Kyoto. After starting his career in the theater, he began acting in silent films in 1927. He appeared in more than 100 films; before the Second World War, he was one of the most famous actors in Japanese cinema.

Arashi San'emon. Family of Kabuki actors active in Osaka from the seventeenth to the nineteenth century. The most famous were:
—Arashi San'emon I. Actor and *zamoto* (1635–90): *yatsushi* roles (*wagoto*, young lovers).
—Arashi San'emon II. Actor and *zamoto* (1661–1701).
—Arashi San'emon III. Actor and *zamoto* (1697–1754): *tachiyaku* and *oyajigata* roles.

• **Arashi Sanjūrō.** Actor (?–1750) in Osaka: *wakashū* and *tachiyaku* roles.

Arashiyama. Hilly area on the western outskirts of Kyoto, famous for its cherry trees and maples. The emperors and court nobles took excursions to this scenic spot. The Oi and Hozu rivers cut through Arashiyama, and a number of temples have been built there, including Seiryō-ji (known for its statue of Shaka Nyorai), Tenryū-ji (Zen monastery established in 1339 with a Zen garden by Musō Kokushi), Nison-in (founded in 850, reconstructed in the sixteenth century), and Hōrin-ji (founded in 713). The highest point is 375 m high. Sometimes called Ranzan.

• *Arashiyama.* Title of a Noh play: an imperial envoy goes to Arashiyama to contemplate the maples. There, he meets two *kami* disguised as old men.

Arashiyama Hoan. Physician (1632–93) who studied with Dutch physicians in Nagasaki. He wrote two works on Western medicine: *Bankoku chihō ruijū* and *Kōmōgeka sōden.*

Aratawake no Mikoto. Great-grandson of Emperor Suinin (early AD? *See* TENNŌ), who, according to the *Kojiki,* conquered the Korean Silla kingdom for Empress Jingū Kōgō. Tradition has it that he brought back the Korean scholar Wani, but this is doubtful.

Araya shiki. Buddhist concept of the state of awareness in which the spirit, finding itself beyond the notions of existence and nonexistence, can perceive the very source of the universe. It corresponds to the eighth level of consciousness, the highest level described in works on Zen and Esoteric Buddhism *(mikkyō)* in Japan.

Archeology. The islands of Japan were probably first inhabited at a time (30,000 BC?) when the archipelago was still linked to the continent by land bridges; however, there are few paleolithic sites. The stone tools uncovered at these sites have been dated to the late paleolithic or mesolithic period by comparing them with tools of the same type found at non-Japanese sites. In Iwajuku, near Tokyo, archeologists have discovered three levels of cut stones, the top level containing mainly mesolithic-type microliths. In level I at both Iwajuku and Takei, stone tools have been identified as contemporary with the Pajitanian (early paleolithic) industries of Java, but there has been no conclusive proof. In the Iwajuku II and Takei II levels, flint blades correspond to blades from Alaska and the Love Basin in eastern Siberia that date from the late paleolithic

age. They cannot be dated with certainty, however, because archeological evidence in Japan is unreliable due to the thin layers at sites and the history of earthquakes. Some sites in southern Okinawa, such as the one at Minatogawa, contain human fossils from circa 18,000 BC between layers of datable volcanic cinders. Pottery appeared very early, apparently with pebble culture (in Kansai), and microliths (in Kyushu, Kantō, and northern and western Honshu). Flat-bottomed pottery with corkscrew decorations has been found at the Fukui site in Kyushu, which date from 7500 BC according to carbon-14 dating, or 11,000 BC on the basis of comparative sequences. This "proto-Jōmon" pottery preceded (or was at least contemporary with) the oldest Jōmon pottery (decorated with impressions of cords), and includes vases with flat, pointed, or slightly rounded bottoms and decorated with marks made with fingernails or with a roller, and with impressions of cords and shells. Flat-bottomed pots from the beginning of the Jōmon period itself are more numerous; they are similarly decorated and, in the West, use relief ornamentation. This pottery is associated with microliths and polished axes, mainly at sites in northern Honshu, on the island of Rebun, near Muroran and Hakodate in southern Hokkaido, at Moraiso in Kanto, at Kitashirakawa (Honshu), and at Senokan (Kyushu). Thereafter, pottery became more diversified, in the West taking on elaborate, heavy decorative shapes. Rectangular-sectioned polished-stone axes have also been discovered (of a type probably from Yunnan, China), in addition to cut stones, stone arrowheads with tangs, and bone fishing harpoons and fishhooks.

In the following period, pottery seems to have taken three different directions, depending on the region. Vases were decorated with a "running water" motif and basketmaking and lacquer were introduced, as were harpoon points with multiple barbs. The most remarkable sites are at Ubayama, Harunouchi, and Kamegaoka near Aomori, in northern Honshu. Innumerable Jōmon pottery sites have been discovered all over Japan, mainly in the *kaizuka,* or "shell mounds" left by fishers and hunters at the mouths of rivers and on the coast. The Jōmon period, sometimes called "belated mesolithic" because agriculture was almost unknown (except the temporary cultivation of taro and yams), was suddenly followed (but not replaced) circa 300 BC by a new culture, the neolithic, with knowledge of the use of iron. Named after the Yayoi site near Tokyo, this neolithic culture first appeared in northern Kyushu and spread throughout the islands, arriving in northern Honshu around AD 100, while many island populations (especially in the extreme north) continued to live according to the Jōmon culture until at least the tenth century. In parallel to the Yayoi culture, in which rice was grown and iron tools used, came bronze, which was used only, it seems, for purposes of worship. The first evidence of woven fabrics dates from this period, and burials took on a different character, with bodies placed in a sepulcre or large urn *(kamekan),* following traditions imported from Korea and China. Pottery, at first made of mud and by hand, in the Jōmon tradition, gave way to pottery made on a wheel and smoothed. Shapes were almost entirely functional. The largest sites of this period, during which villages were organized into independent communities under the authority of a shaman (male or female), were the villages of Toro, Karako (near Nara), and Yamaki (near Shizuoka), where excavations have revealed the foundations of houses and the remains of organized fields. Near the coasts, boat construction developed, enabling the inhabitants to consume fewer shellfish and more fish, so the *kaizuka* were fewer and smaller. Some houses were elevated on pilings. A number of objects made in China were found (notably bronze mirrors; *see* KAGAMI), as were Japanese imitations of such objects.

The Yayoi culture, which probably lasted to the mid-third century, marks the true beginning of "proto-historic" Japan. Thereafter, it was transformed, politically at least, by the arrival from Korea of groups of horsemen clad in iron armor. These newcomers did not change the habits of the peasants or introduce new techniques; they simply organized them into small kingdoms *(kuni)* whose chiefs *(miyatsuko)* had huge tumuli of stone and earth *(kofun)* built to shelter their burials, similar to the Altaic *kurgan.* They introduced riding horses, particular shamanic beliefs that were superimposed over those of the Jōmon and Yayoi populations, probably linguistic elements that were adopted into the indigenous languages, some painted ornamentation (on the inside walls of tombs), and armaments that enabled them to establish political superiority. They were concentrated in the regions of most intense political activity: Yamato, Kinai, and Kanto. Excavations of some of the tombs and study of the *haniwa* (terracotta figures) buried there have provided insights into how these newcomers lived (*see* KIBA MINZOKU).

Starting in the late sixth century, Japan entered its historic period, and the era of large religious structures began with the introduction of Buddhism from Korea. The capital moved often during the Asuka period (ca. 538 or 552–ca. 645), but only within the region now called Nara. The true historic period, however, did not start until 710 with the establishment of a fixed capital city at Heijō-kyō (Nara). *See* AIZAWA TADAHIRO, AKIYAMA TERUKAZU, HAMADA KŌSAKU, HARADA YOSHITO, HASEBE KOTONDO, HOSHINO, KAIZUKA, KOFUN, TATARA, TATEANA.

Archery. The typically Japanese asymmetrical bow, used both for war and for hunting, is called the *yumi.* The arrows are called *ya,* and the art of archery is called Kyūdō. *See* AWA KENZO, AZUSA-MIKO, HACHIRŌ TAMETOMO, HAMAYA, HEKI MASATSUGU, HIRASE MITSUO, HORO, HOSHINO KANZAEMON, INU OI-MONO, MAKIWARA, MEIGEN, SAIGYŌ, SHADŌ, SHUNGYŪSAI, TOMO, WASA DAIHACHIRŌ, YABU-SAME.

Architecture. Japanese traditional architecture used wood exclusively. The Japanese had known carpentry techniques since prehistoric times, and high-quality wood was plentiful on the Japanese islands. The Koreans introduced Buddhist architectural styles at the end of the sixth century, along with the use of tile and metal roofs. It was only in the sixteenth century that stonework was used for castle foundations, and plaster to cover exterior structures. Stone and brick, which had always been used in Korea and China, appeared in Japan only at the beginning of the Meiji era, which marked the advent of modern architecture using materials such as cement, asphalt, and glass.

Japanese architecture differs from other Asian architecture in that it integrates with nature and is concerned with the notion of space (*see* MA), always linking the interior elements of a residence, shrine, or temple to the surrounding environment through the use of broad intercolumniations *(ken)* or bays and wraparound verandas. Another basic characteristic is the use of pilings to create a space for air circulation between the ground and the wooden structure, a practical design in a country that is humid and rainy. These pilings are not of ancient Japanese origin; the principle seems to have been introduced in the first millennium BC by populations from Micronesia and southern China. Architectural design has always favored horizontal lines; even today, rooflines still emphasize this aesthetic principle.

In traditional Japanese construction, the columns *(hashira)* that support the roof are of primary importance. There are few exterior and interior walls, and they do not fill the space between the columns except when needed; walls are made up of mobile pieces—sliding doors, shoji, and fusuma— sometimes pierced with square windows *(renji-madō)* or arched windows *(katō-madō)*. The roof is the most remarkable element in Japanese architecture: low and heavy, it is constructed of superimposed trusses of decreasing size; the eaves are supported by stacks of horizontal brackets *(hijiki)* held in place by cubical "dice" *(to)* in a variety of combinations, either requiring support from rafters or secured by interlocking pieces of wood *(taiheizuka, kaerumata)*. The roof joists are covered first with wooden planks, then with tiles, thatch, or bark shingles.

Pillars, columns, and beams are standardized according to the local size of the *ken* (about 1.9 m): the wood is cut in fixed lengths, generally a multiple of 3 *shaku* (about 91.2 cm), and the number of columns always determines the interior space available, calculated in squared *ken*—that is, in double tatami mats, the exterior surfaces having been calculated on the same basis in *tsubo* (equivalent to two *tatami,* or about 3.35 m²). It follows that all dimensions of the parts of a house are calculated in *ken* or tatami. The structures generally are not painted and the wood is left untreated, which enables it to better withstand changes in temperature and humidity. Large-diameter columns may be split so that the wood can expand without deforming, and the joints, which are often complex and do not involve nails, screws, or glue, are made so that they have free play (up to a certain point). Because of this, the joint pieces can slide over each other without compromising the structure; thus, the earthquakes that are so common in Japan are less likely to destroy these buildings, which can follow the movement of the ground by shifting slightly.

Another characteristic of traditional architecture is its lack of permanence. Knowing that everything comes to an end, both materials and the architectural ensemble, just as human life does, the Japanese have never sought to create permanent, monumental buildings. This is perhaps the most admirable feature of Japanese architectural production: even the most imposing structures relate to both nature and to the human dimension.

There are two types of traditional architecture in Japan, Shinto and Buddhist, in addition to the domestic architectural styles called *shinden, shoin,* and *sukiya,* as well as more specialized designs such as castle design *(jō, shiro; see* CASTLES). Prehistoric architecture consisted of simple cabins partially sunken into the earth (see TATARA). But true Japanese architecture started in the Yayoi period, with houses on low pilings and building types (such as the granaries of the time) that prefigured Shinto architecture, characterized by pillars set deeply into the earth, single or double roofs with a straight slope, partitions of intercolumniations formed by stacked wood (a little like the Russian izba) or by juxtaposed wooden planks. A derivative style, used for granaries (see KURA), called *azekura-zukuri,* is well preserved in Shōsō-in in Nara, for example. This Shinto style is found in a number of shrines, including those at Ise and Izumo. However, influenced by Buddhism and by new construction and roofing methods, it underwent numerous transformations over the centuries (see JINJA). Roofs were thatched or covered with cypress shingles and showed certain features portrayed on the *haniwa* representing houses (see CHIGI, HANIWA, KATSU-OGI). The single roofs did not have brackets to support the eaves, which generally were not very deep. The pilings were sometimes quite high, requiring stairs to access the level of the rooms, and supported the structure and the wraparound veranda. The entranceway was through doors either on the side or the gable end, and the fixed walls did not permit a full view of the environment. The doors were often full folding doors with pivoting hinges. Some shrines were surrounded by multiple palisades or simple fences, others by walls *(suiji)*. The approach was marked by simple gates called torii.

Buddhist styles of architecture, imported from Korea and China by the various sects that arrived from the continent, were more directly influenced by Chinese construction methods. Pillars supporting the roof were not set into the ground but rested on a stone terrace, sometimes with a stone base *(sōban),* carved or not. The roofs were hipped or hipped and gabled. A few octagonal or square structures had roofs with a number of slopes or pyramidal in shape. Buddhist buildings were usually grouped together in monasteries and included, within a corniced wall pierced with monumental gates, a main room *(kondō, hondō)* and one or two square-shaped pagodas with three-, five-, or seven-storied roofs supported by a series of sometimes very elaborate bracketing. Some pagodas, such as that of Yakushi-ji in Nara, had "intermediary roofs" called *mokoshi.* The interiors of Buddhist temples were adapted to the necessities of worship: the main statue *(honzon)* was either at the back of the main room or at the center so that one could walk around it, as was the case in Amida temples. Temple building underwent architectural modifications depending on whether the site was on flat ground or in the mountains; the latter were obliged to conform to the terrain. Many additional buildings were built: refectories, monks' quarters, pavilions for various ceremonies. Each temple also had a garden. Roofs were usually covered with tiles *(kawara),* although some had cypress shingles (such as the one at Murō-ji, for example). Temple architecture was modified in the eighth century, when the Chinese monk Ganjin introduced standardized components for carpentry and *sashi-hijiki,* or crossbeams. It was thus customary to distinguish in Buddhist construction three major "modes": *wa-yō, kara-yō,* and *tenjiku-yō,* which were sometimes mixed. Each sect, however, had its own style (for example, the Amida sects of Jodō and Jodō-Shinshū did not have pagodas, while Zen sects often had structures isolated from the main compound). Temples diversified and grew larger, and were surrounded with many walls requiring the erection of gates *(mon),* sometimes one or two stories high, known as *chūmon* and *sanmon.*

Domestic architecture derived from ancient architecture (on pilings) such as that in China. Starting in the seventh and eighth centuries, it was codified and called *shinden:* it involved essentially the body of a building *(taiya)* located at the back of a large enclosed garden, in front of which was a pond with three islets linked by bridges. Two pavilions *(tsuridono)* overhung the banks of the pond, linked to the main structure by roofed galleries on pilings. The floor was of wood, and people sat on straw-stuffed cushions *(zabuton).* The "walls" were composed of removable horizontal wooden folding doors *(shitomidō).* There were no windows, as the doors took their place.

In the medieval period, the interior underwent modifications, being divided into a number of rooms separated by fusuma, with the main structure growing larger as a result. The main room now contained the *tokonoma,* and after the fifteenth century, the floor was completely covered with tatami mats. There were not yet true doors, since people could enter between the open columns *(ken).* This was the palatial style, called *shoin-zukuri,* which was adapted for castles. The donjon had several stories made entirely of wood and roofed in tiles, but its "walls"—in general a light wood or bamboo lattice *(shinkabe)*—were covered with a thick layer of plaster. The lord did not live in the donjon *(tenshu)* except during wartime; his main home was a *shoin*-style palace at the foot of the imposing structure of the *tenshu,* within the inside wall of the castle. To repel an attacking enemy, the castle was surrounded with multiple walls, cul-de-sacs, drawbridges, and moats *(see* CASTLES).

Sukiya, or "teahouses," began to be built in the late fifteenth century with the development of the tea ceremony *(chanoyu):* they contrasted with domestic architecture in their "rural" simplicity *(see* CHANOYU, SUKIYA-ZUKURI).

Modern architecture dates from the Meiji era, with the arrival of foreign architects who introduced late-nineteenth-century Western styles and intensive use of brick and cement. The first "modern" Japanese architects attempted to imitate Western structures using traditional construction methods; in 1868, Shimizu Kisuke designed the Tsukiji Hotel in Tokyo in this way. Most of the first Western architects in Japan were British, the best known being Josiah Conder. They taught at the Industrial College, and their teachings were rapidly put into practice by the Japanese. Among the first famous Japanese architects were Itō Chūta and Sekino Tei, whose designs were executed between 1888 and 1900. However, traditional construction continued to be practiced, and it was only after the catastrophic earthquake of 1923 *(see* EARTHQUAKES), which the Imperial Hotel designed by Frank Lloyd Wright resisted well, that the new methods of mixing stone, brick, and concrete for public buildings, banks, and head offices of large companies began to be used in the Marunouchi district of Tokyo. However, domestic architecture is still wood frame, with lightweight walls made of chipboard and tile-covered roofs, while apartment buildings *(apātō)* and summer homes are often built in a Western style. After the Second World War, the reconstruction of Tokyo brought renewed interest in modern techniques, notably for prestressed concrete and interlocking designs using frets of welded reinforced concrete, reputed to be earthquake-proof. From then on, most large buildings were built according to strict standards including such safety measures. After the 1964 Olympics and designs introduced by modern architects *(see* TANGE KENZŌ), the emphasis shifted toward solutions with a more Japanese and original aesthetic, creating a new architectural style that was both futuristic and traditional. However, Japan's climate requires that these modern structures have highly effective insulation and expensive air-conditioning systems, so many modern architects are looking to new solutions, in which residences are designed on the principle of natural air exchange, such as the "breathing house" promoted by the firm National Jutaku, which uses the principle of natural ventilation.

→ *See* AGAETSUCHI-MON, AIDEN-ZUKURI, ASHIHARA YOSHINOBU, BUKE-ZUKURI, BUTSUDEN, CHASHITSU, CHIAGI-DANA DERA, DŌ, GOJU NOTŌ, IRIMOYA, ISOZAKI ARATA, JI, JINJA, KARA-HAFU, KARA-MON, MAEKAWA KUNIO, MAKI FUMIHIKO, MASSHA, MINKA, MITESAKI, MIYA, NAGARE masayuki, niwa nagahide, saeki no imaemishi, sakakura junzō, SANJUNO TŌ, SATŌ TAKEO, SEKINO TADASHI, SHIBI, SHIMMEI, SHIRAI SEIICHI, SHŌJI, SMEDLEY, SŌRIN, TAHŌ-TŌ, TANIGUCHI YOSHIRŌ, TATSUNO KINGO, TAUT, TENJŌ TŌ, YAMASAKI MINORU, YOSHIDA ISOYA, YOSHIMURA JUNZŌ.

Arechi. "Wasteland." Literary journal created just before the Second World War by students at Waseda University in Tokyo, edited by Ayukawa Nobuo and Morikawa Yoshinobu (1918–42), named after the T. S. Eliot poem *The Waste Land*. After the war, the journal expanded and published works by many young poets who were trying to reconstruct their devastated world. As an annual, it changed its name to *Arechi Shishū* in 1951. It was published until 1958.

Ariake Kai. "Sea of Ariake." Bay on the west coast of Kyushu, with exceptionally strong tides (6 m). This boggy inland sea is fed by the Chikugo and Yabe rivers. *Nori* seaweed is grown there.

• **Ariake Wan.** "Bay of Ariake." Former name of Shibushi Bay on the south coast of Kyushu.

Aridōshi. Title of a Noh play: a *kami* is angered by the poet Ki no Tsurayuki, who has dared to ride his horse through the shrine precincts. The poet appeases the god by composing a poem.

Ariga Nagao. Lawyer (1860–1921) specializing in international law, student of Lorenz von Stein in Germany. He was a legal adviser during the Sino-Japanese War (1894–95) and the Russo-Japanese War (1904–05). He translated a number of works by European authors and by American sociologist Ernest Fenellosa.

Arihisa. Painter (Kose Arihisa, fourteenth century), who was a member of the *e-dokoro* of the Tōji temple in Kyoto. He painted mainly Buddhist subjects. *See* KOSE-RYŪ.

Arima. Small town on the Shimabara Peninsula (Kyushu) where a castle (Hara-jō) was built. In it, 20,000 Christians commanded by Masuda (Amakusa) Shirō (1612–38) and Itakura Shigemasa resisted attacks by shogunal troops for six months in 1637. Almost all of them died. *See* SHIMABARA.

• **Arima Harunobu.** Christian daimyo (1567–1612) of the Hizen region (Kyushu), son of Arima Yoshisada (1521–77), who professed to favor the Christians in order to encourage trade with the Portuguese. Harunobu embraced Christianity in 1579, taking the name Jean Protose (or Protasio), in order to acquire weapons from the Portuguese to fight the daimyo of Saga, Ryūzōji Takanobu (1529–84), whom he defeated in 1584 thanks to an alliance with the Shimazu clan. He then served Hideyoshi and campaigned in Korea in 1592 and 1597 with Konishi Yukinaga, another Christian daimyo. At the Battle of Sekigahara in 1600, he turned against Konishi Yukinaga and fought for Tokugawa Ieyasu. He conducted sea trade with Macao, but following quarrels between Japanese and Portuguese sailors and the death of a number of men in his crew, he attacked the Portuguese ship *Madre de Dios,* commanded by Andrea Pessoa, in the port of Nagasaki in 1609. There followed a series of intrigues that led to Harunobu's being sent into exile and committing suicide. Although his conversion had originally been due to practical interests, he ended up a true convert. In 1582, he sent a number of young Japanese (led by Ōtomo Sōrin and Ōmura Sumitada) to Rome to study the Christian religion. His son, Arima Naozumi, renounced Christianity and was made daimyo of Arima, then, in 1614, of Nobeoka in the province of Hyūga (Miyazaki prefecture).

• **Arima Naozumi.** Samurai (1586–1641), son of Arima Harunobu, who became a Christian with the first name Miguel. When he married an adopted daughter of Tokugawa Ieyasu, he renounced his faith and persecuted Christians (ca. 1612–15). *See* ARIMA HARUNOBU.

• **Arima Seminariyo.** Christian school founded in 1580 by Jesuits at Arima (Kyushu) in the fief of Arima Harunobu. Four of the young Christians who had been sent to Rome studied there. Due to the persecution ordered by Hideyoshi, this school was obliged to change locations a number of times. It was reestablished in Arima in 1609 and found a permanent home in Nagasaki in 1612. Also called Arie Seminariyo.

• **Arima Sukemasa.** *See* BUSHIDŌ-SŌSHO.

Arima Ineko. Film actress (Nakanishi Seiko), born 1932 in Osaka. She was a member of the Takarazuka theater company and appeared in her first film in 1951, in a film by Hani Susumu. She has worked with a number of directors, including Ichikawa Kon and Ozu Yasujirō.

Arima no Miko. Imperial prince (640–58), son of Emperor Kōtoku. He opposed Empress Saimei and her son, Naka no Ōe, and was sentenced to death by strangulation; Naka no Ōe then became Emperor Tenji. Two of Arima no Miko's poems, composed just before his execution, were included in the *Man'yōshū.*

Arima Shinshichi. Samurai (1825–62) of the Satsuma (Kyushu) domain who supported the emperor against the shogunate in 1860 and conspired with other enemies of Ii Naosuke to assassinate him. Two years later, he organized another plot and raised an army to assassinate Tokugawa shogunate officials, but died in a skirmish with his enemies.

Arima Toyouji. Warrior and general (1559–1642) under Hideyoshi. He married one of Tokugawa Ieyasu's daughters and, after the Battle of Sekigahara (1600), was made daimyo of Fukuchiyama (province of Tamba). After the siege of Osaka, he was appointed daimyo of Kurume with a revenue of 220,000 *koku.*

Arimatsu-shibori. Cotton cloth, typical of the village of Arimatsu in Aichi prefecture, production of which probably started during the Keichō era (1596–1615) to be sold to travelers passing through the town, at the time a post town *(shuku-eki)* on the Tōkaidō road. This dark tie-dyed fabric is still produced today.

Arima Yorichika. Novelist (1918–80), author of a number of popular detective and science-fiction novels, including *Hōkai* (The Collapse, 1937), *Shūshin Miketsushū* (Detention for Life, 1954), and *Yonman-nin no Mokugekisha* (Forty Thousand Witnesses, 1959). He was one of Arima Yoriyasu's sons.

Arima Yoriyasu. Politician (1884–1957), born in Fukuoka prefecture. He created a Farmers' Union (Nihon Nōmin Kumiai) and was elected to the House of Representatives for the Rikken Seiyūkai (Friends of Constitutional Government party) in 1924. As a member of the Arima family, he was elected to the House of Peers as a count in 1929. He became minister of agriculture and industry in 1937 (in Konoe Fumimaro's cabinet). Tried as a war criminal after the Second World War, he was acquitted. He was the father of novelist Arima Yorichika.

Arima Yoriyuki. Mathematician (1714–83), author of a number of scientific treatises. In *Shūki*

sampō, he revealed the theories of *wasan* (higher mathematics).

Arisaka Hideo. Linguist (1908–52), born in Kure (Hiroshima prefecture), who conducted important studies on the phonology of the ancient Japanese language and helped develop the structuralist theory of language and phonology. His main work is *Kokugo on'in shi no kenkyū* (Studies on the History of Japanese Phonology, 1944 and 1947).

Arisaka Shōzō. Engineer, born 1868 in Tokyo, who studied in France and became an expert in naval weaponry. He created the automatic gun that bears his name, used during the Second World War by Japanese troops:
—**Type 38** (1936): *Caliber:* 6.5 mm. *Weight* (with bayonette): 4 kg. *Length:* 1.32 m. *Magazine:* 5 bullets. *Range:* 2,400 m. *Initial speed:* 730 m/sec.

Arisawa Hiromi. Economics scholar (1896–1988), born in Kōchi prefecture. He studied in Tokyo, then Berlin. His Marxist ideas led to his dismissal from the University of Tokyo in 1938. After the war, he became an adviser to Yoshida Shigeru and developed recovery plans mainly for two major sectors, coal and iron and steel, contributing to the resurgence of the Japanese economy.

Arishima Ikuma. Writer (Arishima Mibuma, 1882–1974) and painter, brother of Arishima Takeo and Satomi Ton. He studied Italian and entered the Rome School of Fine Arts in 1905, after studying with the painter Fujishima Takeji. He moved to Paris in 1907. On his return to Japan in 1910, he took part in the artistic-literary Shirakaba movement, writing a series of articles on Cézanne. He was appointed to the Imperial Academy (Teikoku Gakushi-in) in 1935 and named Person of Exceptional Merit in 1964. His style was influenced by late impressionism. He translated Émile Bernard's *Souvenirs de Cézanne* in 1920. See ISSUI-KAI, SATOMI TON.

Arishima Takeo. Writer (Arishima Takerō, Yukimasa, 1878–1923), born in Tokyo to a samurai family. He studied English in Yokohama and went to the Peers' School (Gakushūin). With his brothers Arishima Ikuma and Satomi Ton, he was a member of the Shirakaba movement, and considered himself a disciple of Walt Whitman. During a trip to Europe and the United States in 1907, he spent time with progressive thinkers. Upon his return, he began to write novels imbued with Christian idealism, having become a follower of a Calvinist sect. He distributed his entire fortune to poor peasants and then committed suicide with his mistress, a reporter at *Fujin Kōron,* a women's magazine. His voluminous body of work is infused with sometimes puritanical Christian yet somewhat progressive ideas. Among his main writings are *Aru onna* (A Certain Woman, 1917), the heroine of which is a mistress who succumbs to passion; *Sengen* (Statement, 1915); *Jikkenshitsu* (The Laboratory, 1917); *Kain no matsuei* (Descendants of Cain, 1918); *Umareizuru nayami* (The Agony of Being Born, 1918); *Seiza* (Constellations, 1922); *Oshiminaku ai wa ubau* (A Bold Love, 1920); *Shi* (Death); and *Hangyakusha* (Revolt).

Arisugawa no Miya. One of the four families of Hinnō (Shishinnō branch), founded in 1625 by Prince Yoshihito, son of Emperor Go-Yōzei, who took this name in 1672. However, at the end of the Meiji era, one of his descendants reverted to the original family name of Takamatsu. *See* KAN'IN NO MIYA.

• **Arisugawa no Miya Taruhito.** Imperial prince (1835–95), brother of Arisugawa no Miya Takehito. He played an important role during the 1868 Restoration by leading imperial troops against the Edo castle. Appointed minister of war in 1870, he repressed the Satsuma rebellion in 1877. Head marshal in 1878, he was promoted to commander of the armed forces in 1889. He died of illness in Hiroshima.

Arisugawa no Miya Takehito. Brother (1862–1913) of Arisugawa no Miya Taruhito, and an admiral.

Arita. Town in Saga prefecture (Kyushu), famous for its kilns and ceramics. *Pop.:* 15,000.

• **Arita-yaki.** "Porcelain of Arita." Often called Imari, for the name of the port from which they were exported, these ceramics are divided into two groups, Kakiemon and Nabeshima, named for the families of potters on whose properties the kilns were built. A Korean potter who came to Japan at the beginning of the seventeenth century, Ri Sampei, discovered clay suitable for modeling and baking on Izumiyama. He built kilns there and began to produce Korean-style ceramics in blue-and-white underglaze. Sakaida Kakiemon further developed this style after 1640 and produced porcelain decorated in a variety of colors, which was largely exported to Europe by Dutch traders in Nagasaki. In the late eighteenth century, however, mass production resulted in a decline in quality. The kilns were destroyed in a fire in 1818 and reconstructed at the beginning of the Meiji era; their tradition has continued to the present day. Arita porcelain is often decorated in red-brown, blue-green, yellow, blue, and gold, in typically Japanese designs (textile designs) and geometric shapes. *See* CERAMICS, IMAIZUMI IMAEMON, KAKIEMON, NABESHIMA-YAKI.

Arita Hachirō. Politician and diplomat (1884–1965) born on the island of Sado. After being appointed vice-prime minister in 1932, then minister of foreign affairs in 1936 (Hirota Kōki's cabinet), he served as ambassador to Germany, Austria, Belgium (1934–36), and China (1936). He was elected as an independent deputy to the Diet in 1952 and was an unsuccessful candidate for governor of Tokyo in 1955 and 1959.

Ariwara. Family of courtiers at the beginning of the Heian period (794–1185), descendants of one of Emperor Heizei's sons.

• **Ariwara no Moritaka.** Poet (ninth–tenth century), son of Ariwara no Munehari.

• **Ariwara no Munehari.** Poet (?–898), son of Ariwara no Narihara.

• **Ariwara no Narihara.** Imperial prince and poet (825–80), brother of Ariwara no Yukihira and father of Ariwara no Munehari. He composed numerous *waka* poems, 87 of which were included in the imperial anthologies *Kokinshū, Gosenshū, Shūishū,* and *Shin kokinshū.* He is sometimes credited (though not definitively) with the *Ise monogatari.* His tumultuous life, full of amorous adventures that occasionally led to his exile, gave rise to many legends. He was included in the lists of Rokkasen (Six Poetic Geniuses) and Sanjūrokkasen (Thirty-Six Poetic Geniuses). He was also a painter.

• **Ariwara no Yukihira.** Brother of Ariwara no Narihira and poet (818–93). His poems were included in the same anthologies as were his brother's. He founded a school, the Shōgaku-in, to educate the children of the Ariwara family.

Ariyasu Hidenoshin. Catholic missionary (1855–1939) who wrote major studies on Buddhism, including *Shin bukkyō no kaibō* (Analysis of True Buddhism).

Ariyoshi Sawako. Writer (1931–84), born in Wakayama. After studying English literature, in 1956 she began to publish novels that were instantly successful: *Jiuta,* which described the life of artists; *Kinokawa* (The Ki River, 1959), the story of a family in the Kii region; *Hanaoka seishū no tsuma* (The Doctor's Wife, 1966), the story of an eighteenth-century anesthesiologist; *Kōkotsu no hito* (People of Enchantment, 1972), on the problems the elderly face in modern society; and *Fukugō osen* (Compound Pollution, 1975), on pollution in Japan. She traveled in the United States and China and was interested in Nestorianism. Very devout, she contributed her royalties to assistance for the poor and aged, who came to be referred to by the name of her novel *Kōkotsu no hito.* Many of her novels were adapted for the screen.

Armed forces. The current Japanese army, called Jieitai, or Self-Defense Forces (SDF), consists of the armed forces *(jieikan)* and civil personnel *(bunkan).* It was created in 1945 as the National Police Reserve, not to number more than 75,000 men strong; its name was changed to the National Safety Forces in 1952, and to Boeichō, or Defense Agency, in 1954. The current SDF includes three corps, land-based (Rikujō Jieitai), maritime (Kaijō Jieitai), and air-based (Kōkū Jieitai), which recruit their members from among young volunteers aged 18 to 25 years. There are about 3,000 women in the SDF; total military personnel comprises about 180,000 in the infantry, 45,000 in the navy, about 45,000 in the air force (490 aircraft), and about 28,000 civilian staff. These figures vary according to the year and the recruitment opportunities. In addition, reserve personnel number about 40,000. The land-based armed forces comprise 13 divisions in five military regions, while the naval forces (160 ships), whose headquarters are in Yokosuka, are assigned to five maritime districts. There are three regions of air defense. Officers are recruited through the National Defense Academy (Bōei Daigakkō) and, for higher grades, by the National Institute for Defense Studies (Bōei Kenshūsho). Career soldiers retire at 50, 53, or 55 years of age, depending on their rank and the force they are in.

The SDF was established in contravention of article 9 of the 1947 constitution, which prohibits Japan from having any military forces. However, article 51 of the United Nations Charter, which recognizes that every independent country has the right to defend its territory, supported the creation of the SDF. Many groups in Japan feel that any military force, even for self-defense, is unconstitutional.

Nevertheless, since 1993, the SDF has assisted the UN in its humanitarian missions in foreign countries as an auxiliary force to the "Blue Helmets."

The national defense forces have modern equipment but no nuclear weapons. The United States would like Japan to take on a military role in the Pacific, but the Japanese, citing article 9, do not want to maintain a larger army.

Armor (gusoku, yoroi). The oldest armor dates back to the *kofun* era (third–seventh century). Archers on horseback (*see* KIBAMINZOKU-RON) were probably the first to wear armor, according to some *haniwa* and body armor *(dō)* remnants found in the tumuli. This armor consisted of plates of iron riveted together. The Shōso-in storehouse in Nara has preserved some armor from the eighth century of a slightly different type. During the twelfth century, when the warrior class was supplanting the aristocracy, armor covering not only the torso but the entire body *(ō-yoroi)* appeared, concurrently with breast protectors *(haramaki)* made of plates of leather laced up the back, reserved for ordinary warriors. The *ō-yoroi* then underwent some improvements, with the addition of articulated parts protecting the thighs and shoulders *(sode)* and leg guards *(suneate),* and an iron helmet *(kabuto),* sometimes with a mask *(hōate).* In the fifteenth century, the armor of wealthy samurai was decorated and the helmets had neck and throat protectors made of iron sheets, jointed and joined by colored cotton or silk laces. Horsemen also wore fabric sacks *(hōrō)* on their backs to stop arrows from behind, and sometimes carried a staff with a banner. With the advent of firearms (*see* TEPPŌ), armor no longer offered protection and became mainly decorative, a sort of insignia of high rank. *See* GUSOKU, KABUTO, KATCHŪ, KEIKŌ, MUSHA ROKUGU, TANKŌ, YOROI.

Art. *See* ARCHEOLOGY, ARCHITECTURE, CALLIGRAPHY, CERAMICS, CINEMA, DANCE, LACQUER, MUSIC, PAINTING, SCULPTURE, THEATER, UKIYO-E *(prints).*

Aruga Kizaemon. Sociologist (1897–1979), born in Nagano prefecture. He conducted important studies on kinship links within the social structures of various classes of the Japanese population through the ages. He attributed the lack of public social assistance in Japan to the strong familial system that governs Japanese social organization.

Asa. Name given to some varieties of hemp and, in general, all fibrous plants except cotton. From ancient times, the Japanese wove fabrics using *asa*, hemp *(taima)*, wisteria *(fuji)*, blackberry bark *(kōzo)*, and other fibers. In *Gishi wajin den (Chin.: Wei zhi)*, it is noted that *asa* fabrics were a Japanese specialty. Linen, however, seems to have been imported from the West; it was called *Seiyō asa, Seiyō* meaning "West."

Asabashō. Encyclopedia of Taimitsu (Esoteric Buddhism—*mikkyō*—according to the Tendai sect), illustrated, comprising more than 230 volumes. It is part of the *Bukkyō zenshō* (vols. 35–41). Also called *Ashō*.

Asada Gōryū. Astronomer (Ayabe Yasuaki; *gō:* Shōan, 1734–99), born in what is now Ōita prefecture, son of a Confucian physician, Ayabe Keisai (1676–1750). He studied Western mathematics and astronomy using Chinese texts, and made improvements to astronomical instruments used in Japan and new calculations for the calendar. He also published a book on human anatomy, *Shōchō kyūshoku hō*. His two disciples, Takahashi Sakuzaemon (Yoshitoki) and Hazama Shigetomi, continued his work.

Asada Sōhaku. Physician (*gō:* Ritsuen, 1815–94), born near Nagano. He studied in Kyoto, practiced in Edo using Chinese methods *(kampō),* and became the physician to the shogun's family. After 1868, he was named physician of the court. Among the texts he wrote, at least three are important: *Kōkoku meiiden* (Biographies of Japanese Herbalists and Physicians, 1851), *Sentetsu iwa,* and *Miyakuhō shigen.*

Asagao. Annual plant (*Pharbitis nil* or *Ipomea nil*), a variety of convolvulus known as morning glory, for its flowers which open early in the morning and have become symbolic of this time of day. Often used as decorative motifs, *asagao* are especially popular in Japan because of their short duration, as well as their bright colors. The seeds are used in medicine for their purifying and laxative properties.

• **Asagao-ichi.** Annual fair in early July in the Iriya district of Tokyo, near the Kishibojin temple, dedicated to the sale of *asagao* flowers.

Asagirishima Nosuke. Gardener at the Fushimi castle (Kyoto) in the late sixteenth century, said to be the creator of the garden at the Nishi Hongan-ji temple in Kyoto.

Asahara Tameyori. Warrior (d. 1290) of the province of Kai, related to the Minamoto family (Kai-Genji), notorious for his strength and his skill as an archer. He became a brigand and terrorized the Kyoto region. In 1290, assisted by his son, Mitsuyori, he forced his way into the imperial palace to assassinate Emperor Fushimi, who saved himself by fleeing, disguised as a woman. Surrounded by the palace guards, Asahara Tameyori committed suicide. Retired Emperor Kameyama (*see* INSEI), accused of having fomented this assassination attempt, was forced to become a Buddhist monk, but he was exonerated by the Kamakura *bakufu.*

Asahi-dake. Mountain (2,250 m) in the center of Hokkaido whose summit is the highest point on the island. Also called Ishikari-dake.

Asahifuji. Sumo wrestler (Seiya Suginomori), born 1960 in Aomori prefecture. From a family of fishers, he was ordained sixty-third Yokozuna (*see* SUMŌTORI) in July 1990.

Asahigawa. River 150 km long, running through Okayama prefecture (Honshu) to the Inland Sea (Setonaikai). The gorges of its upper valley are tourist attractions.

Asahi Gyokuzan. Sculptor of ivory (Tomisaburō, 1843–1923) born in Edo. He had a number of exhibitions starting in 1885, notably in Teiten, and he taught at the Tokyo School of Fine Arts. *See* GYOKUZAN.

Asahi Hōsō. Asahi Broadcasting Corporation (ABC). Radio and television station based in Osaka, part of the *Asahi Shimbun* organization since 1981.

Asahi no Kata. Half-sister (Suruga Gozen, Asahihime, 1543–90) of Toyotomi Hideyoshi. She married Tokugawa Ieyasu in 1886, after her first husband, Saji Hyūga no Kami, committed suicide.

Asahikawa. City in Hokkaido, located at the foot of Mt. Asahi, on the Ishikari River. Its industries are lumber and paper mills and *sake* breweries. It is the coldest city in Japan (–40°C in winter). *Pop.:* 350,000.

Asahi maru. Name of the first Western ship constructed in Japan, at Ishikawajima, on the orders of Tokugawa Nariaki in 1856.

Asahi no Miya. Former name of the Tenshō-daijin Shrine at Ise (Honshu).

Asahina Saburō. Late-thirteenth-century warrior whose exploits were popularized in literature and theater. It is not certain, however, that he actually existed.

Asahina Sanchi. Mountain range in the center of Yamagata prefecture (northern Honshu), part of the Japanese Alps; its highest peak is Oasahi-dake (1,870 m). Part of Bandai-Asahi National Park. Winter-sports resort.

Asahina Yasuhiko. Pharmacologist (1881–1975) whose research on Chinese traditional medicine *(kampō)* and plants helped to advance pharmacology in Japan. He received the Order of Culture (Bunka-shō) in 1943.

Asahisei. *See* GYOKUZAN.

Asahi Shimbun. One of the three largest Japanese newspapers, founded in 1879 in Osaka with the name *Ōsaka Asahi Shimbun.* It began to publish an edition in Tokyo in 1888, called *Tōkyō Asahi Shimbun.* It was notable for its progressive opinions, which led to its being banned several times, and for its cultural orientation. It also publishes editions in Osaka, Sapporo, Nagoya, and Kita-Kyushu, and has a print run of about 13 million (9 daily editions, 7 million copies for the morning edition, 3.5 million for the evening edition, and about 2.5 million for regional editions) and a network of 3,500 journalists, including more than 50 correspondents in 27 foreign bureaus. It also publishes a daily newspaper in English, the *Asahi Evening News;* nine weeklies, including *Shūkan Asahi,* founded in 1922; the weekly magazine *Aera,* created in 1988 (print run of 300,000); and four monthly magazines and various books. It is said to be influenced by the Sōka Gakkai.

Asahi Terebi. Television broadcasting company based in Tokyo. Created in 1959 as Nippon Educational Television, it took its current name in 1977. It is financed by the *Asahi Shimbun.*

Asahi-yaki. Type of pottery produced in Uji, near Kyoto, since the beginning of the seventeenth century. The Asahi kilns produce mainly bowls for the tea ceremony with a heavy, sandy clay that shows pinkish stains (called "pink speckles") through a transparent greenish or bluish glaze. These kilns were probably originally built by potters from Korea.

Asai Chū. Western-style painter *(gō:* Mokugo, Mokugyo, 1856–1907), born in Edo, best known for his lyrically tinted watercolors. A student of Kunisawa Shinkurō (1847–77) and Antonio Fontanesi (1818–82) in Tokyo, he founded the Meiji Artistic Society (Meiji Bijutsu-kai) in 1889 with other artists working in the same style. Heavily influenced by the impressionists, he also executed oil paintings of very dark landscapes, quite rare for the time. His main disciples were Ishii Hakutei (1882–1958), Umehara Ryūzaburō (1888–1981), and Yasui Sōtarō (1888–1955).

Asai Kan'emon. Western-style painter, born 1905 at Wakayama. In China during the Second World War, he executed realistic paintings with the war as subject matter, in contrast to his primary style, which resembled cubism. He established Shinju-kai, a sort of painting salon, and made portraits his specialty.

Asai Nagamasa. Warrior (Azai Nagamasa, 1545–73), daimyo of the Odani castle in the northern part of the province of Ōmi. Asai married a sister of Oda Nobunaga, Oichi (Odani no Kata), in 1568, but he turned against Nobunaga in 1570. After a war that lasted more than three years, he was defeated and committed suicide. Toyotomi Hideyoshi (then known as Kinoshita Tōkishirō) seized his properties, thus becoming a daimyo. The Asai family, which had been in the service of the Kyōgoku family of Ōmi since the mid-fourteenth century, died with him.

Asaino Sōzui. Gynecologist (d. ca. 1532) who was one of the pioneers of Japanese medicine according to Chinese methods *(kampō).* He translated *Yishu daquan,* a Chinese medical treatise by Xiong Jun, as *Isho taizen* (1528).

Asai Ryōi. Writer (1612–91), born in Edo. A *rōnin* (masterless samurai), he became a Buddhist monk at Honjō-ji in Kyoto and wrote a large number of novels in the *kana-zōshi* genre. His writings dealt with extremely diverse subjects: poetry, the art of war, Buddhism, tourist guides, legends inspired by Chinese folklore, fantasy stories, and so on. His best-known works are *Tōkaidō meishō-ki* (Traveler's Guide to the Tōkaidō, 1658), *Edo meishō-ki* (Guide to Edo, 1662), *Otogibōko* (1666) and *Inuhariko* (1692), both collections of Chinese and

Korean legends, *Kanninki* (Patient Notes, 1655), *Kōkō monogatari* (1666), *Honchō onna kagami* (Mirror of Women in Japan), and especially *Ukiyo monogatari* (Stories of the Floating World, 1660), which prefigured the stories and novels of Ihara Saikaku.

Asaka Gonsai. Confucian writer (Shigenobu; Yūsuke; *azana*: Asaka Shijun, 1791–1860), born in the province of Mutsu (northern Honshu) into a family of Shinto priests. A student of Satō Issai and Hayashi Jussai, he founded a private school in Edo in 1814, in which he taught Confucianism according to the Zhu Xi (*Jap.*: Shushi) school. He then filled various important positions in the shogunate's educational institutions. He wrote several books, including *Bunryaku yōgai kiryaku* (Notes on Europe), *Gonsai kanwa* (Precepts of Gonsai), and *Rongo kantanroku* (Notes on the *Analects*).

Asaka Tampaku. Confucian scholar (*azana*: Kakubei; *gō*: Rōho Jōzan, Rōgyu Koji, 1656–1737) of the Mito school, which followed the teachings of Zhu Xi (*Jap.*: Shushi). Born in the province of Hitachi, he studied under Shu Shunsui and contributed to the large edition of the *Dai Nihon shi* (History of Greater Japan). He also defined the essential principles of the neo-Confucian Mito school, which were "loyalty to one's superiors and respect for one's own condition." He also wrote other works, including *Resso seiseki* and *Kotei shōhitsu*.

Asakawa Kan'ichi. Historian (1873–1948) born in Fukushima. He studied at Yale University, where he then taught history and medieval civilization of Japan and Europe from 1910 to 1942. He wrote a number of studies in English on the subject, notably *Documents on the Iriki Family,* published in 1929 and 1953.

Asakawa Zen'an. Neo-Confucian writer (Kanae; *azana*: Gotei; *gō*: Zen'an, 1781–1849), disciple of Yamamoto Hokuzan. He specialized in the study of Chinese literary texts: the *Analects* (*Jap.*: Rongo; *Chin.*: Lunyu), *Kansetsu hakki*, and *Daigaku gempon yakugi*.

Asakura. Family of warriors and daimyo of the Muromachi period (1333–1568), who supported the Ashikaga shogun against Nitta Yoshisada in 1338. At first vassals of the Shiba, then governors of the province of Echizen, the Asakura replaced the Shiba when Asakura Toshikage, taking advantage of dissent within the Shiba clan, seized all of Echizen, thus becoming daimyo of the province. The family died out in 1573 with the suicide of Asakura Yoshikage.

• **Asakura Hirokage.** Warrior (1255–1352) who helped the Ashikaga in their struggle against Nitta Yoshisada in 1338 and became lord of the Kuromaru castle in the province of Echizen (Fukui prefecture) as a vassal of the Shiba family.

• **Asakura Kageaki.** Warrior (d. 1574). *See* ASAKURA YOSHIKAGE.

• **Asakura Masakage.** Warrior (1314–72), son of Hirokage. He expanded his properties in the province of Echizen, thus establishing his family's power.

• **Asakura Norikage.** Warrior (1474–1552). He fought the Ikkō sect and was killed in battle.

• **Asakura Toshikage.** Warrior (Takakage, 1428–81) in the service of the Muromachi shogunate. Having seized Echizen, then ruled by the Shiba family, he became a *shugo-daimyō* ("protector daimyo") in 1471. He is best known for his family code in 17 articles, *Asakura Toshikage jūshichikajō*.

• **Asakura Yoshikage.** Warrior (1533–73), grandson of Asakura Toshikage and daimyo of Echizen. In 1571, he defeated the Ikkō sect and forced them to make peace. Having quarreled with Oda Nobunaga, and with his fief of Ichijōtani destroyed due to the treason of one of his relatives, Asakura Kageaki, he committed suicide and his family line was extinguished.

Asakura Fumio. Sculptor (1883–1964), born in Ōita. A member of the Nihon Geijutsu-in (Japan Art Academy, University of Tokyo), his style was realism. He received the Order of Culture (Bunka-shō) in 1948.

• **Asakura Setsu.** Painter (b. 1922), daughter of Asakura Fumio, and theater set designer.

Asakusa. District of Tokyo, on the west bank of the Sumida River, which developed during the Edo period around the Sensō-ji temple (Asakusa Kannon-ji). It was one of the pleasure spots of the capital and is now devoted to entertainment and trade. Every year there are festivals there: in May, the Sanja Matsuri at Asakusa Kannon-ji; in July, the Hōzuki at the Sensō-ji; in November, the Tori no Ichi fair; and in December, the Hagoita Ichi fair.

- **Asakusa Hongan-ji.** Buddhist temple in the Tokyo district of Asakusa, branch of Kyoto's Higashi Hongan-ji, founded in 1657. Destroyed during the Second World War, it was later reconstructed in the original style.

- **Asakusa Kannon-ji.** Buddhist temple of the Tendai sect, founded in 1645 in the Tokyo district of Asakusa. Also called Kinryū-zan Sensō-ji. Damaged by the 1923 earthquake and in 1945 by the bombing of Tokyo, it was reconstructed after the war. It contains a small golden statue, 5.5 cm high, of the bodhisattva Kannon (*Skt.:* Avalokiteshvara). A long alley *(naka-mise)* lined with shops links the main gate (statues of Raijin and Fujin and a huge paper lantern) to the temple entrance. The temple has a number of annexes and a small Shinto shrine.

- **Asakusa-ningyō.** Type of doll created at Asakusa by the craftsman Fukushima Chikayori (1837–82) and very much in style as a decorative object or souvenir.

Asama Onsen. Hot spring in Matsumoto (Nagano prefecture), whose waters reach about 50°C. It has been in operation since the beginning of the seventeenth century.

Asama-yama. Active volcano (*alt.:* 2,542 m) in Gumma prefecture (Honshu). Mt. Asama erupted 66 times between 685 and 1900, and more than 2,000 times between 1900 and 1960. The most violent eruptions took place between 1783 and 1947. The town of Karuizawa is on its southern slope, which is least exposed to lava flows. The volcano is part of Jōshin'etsu Kōgen National Park.

Asami Keisai. Neo-Confucian scholar (Yasumawsa, Jūjirō; *gō:* Bōnanrō, 1652–1712), born in the province of Ōmi (Shiga prefecture). A physician by profession, he became a disciple of Yamazaki Ansai in Kyoto. He studied the history of Shintoism and became an ardent defender of the Akō-gishi (the 47 *rōnin*). His major works, *Seiken igen* and *Shiki satsuroku,* profoundly influenced the anti-shogunal forces at the end of the Edo period.

Asamushi Onsen. Hot spring in the town of Aomori in northern Honshu. Its slightly salty water contains gypsum, with temperatures varying from 30°C to about 70°C.

Asano Baidō. Scholar and painter (1816–80), disciple of Kurimoto Suihō. He was also a poet.

Asa no Katori. Poet and historian (774–843) who helped to compile the *Nihon kōki* with Fujiwara no Fuyutsugu and Fujiwara no Otsugu.

Asano Nagaakira. Samurai (1586–1632), son of Asano Nagamasa and brother of Asano Yoshinaga. He entered the service of Tokugawa Ieyasu and succeeded his brother as daimyo of Kii with an income of 24,000 *koku.* He participated in the siege of Osaka castle (Fuyu no Jin) and repressed peasant revolts, then succeeded Fukushima Masanori as daimyo of Aki with an income of 426,000 *koku.* He married one of Tokugawa Ieyasu's daughters.

- **Asano Nagamasa.** Samurai and general (Nagayoshi, Yazaemon, 1547–1611) of the province of Owari. Adopted by Asano Nagakatsu in the province of Mino, he served Oda Nobunaga, then Toyotomi Hideyoshi, and married the younger sister of Kōdai Fujin, Toyotomi's wife. Appointed inspector of the armies in Korea (Kangun), he received the fief of Kai, with an income of 215,000 *koku,* in 1593. His sons Yoshinaga and Nagaakira fought with him on Tokugawa Ieyasu's side in the Battle of Sekigahara (1600).

- **Asano Yoshinaga.** Samurai (1576–1613), son of Asano Nagasmasa and brother of Asano Nagaakira. He entered the service of Toyotomi Hideyoshi and helped Katō Kiyomasa to drive Chinese troops from Korea in 1597. As a reward, he and his father obtained the domain of Kai (Yamanashi prefecture). He fought alongside his father and Tokugawa Ieyasu in the Battle of Sekigahara (1600) and received a fief in the province of Kii (Wakayama prefecture) worth 376,000 *koku.*

Asano Nagakoto. Daimyo of Hiroshima (Shigekoto, 1842–1937), adopted by Asano Nagamichi, head of the main branch of the family. He advised shogun Tokugawa Yoshinobu to return power to the emperor but was opposed to a military settlement. In 1869, he inherited the title of daimyo of Asano, and was elected a member of the Kizoku-in (House of Peers) in 1880. In 1882, he was appointed ambassador to Italy. He was the last daimyo in Japan.

Asano Naganori. Samurai (1665–1701), daimyo of Akō (a small fief between Okayama and Himeji), one of the heroes of the Akō-gishi (the 47 *rōnin*). Sometimes called Asano Takumi no Kami.

Asano Sōichirō. Businessman (1848–1930), son of a physician in the province of Etchū. In 1898, he purchased from the government a company that he transformed into a cement works. Then he diversified, buying up various other firms and building a zaibatsu of 87 companies. Although his industrial empire was dismantled after 1945, his family continues to manage many companies that once belonged to his zaibatsu..

Asanuma Inejirō. Politician (1898–1960), born in Miyakejima. He joined the Communist party as a student and was sentenced to five months in prison for having waged a violent campaign supporting strikers at the Ashio Mines. He joined the Nihon Shakai Taishūtō (Japan Socialist Masses party) in 1936 and was elected to the House of Representatives, where he remained for 20 years. After the Second World War, he was elected secretary-general and then president of Nihon Shakaitō (Japan Socialist party). He was assassinated by a young right-wing extremist, an event witnessed live by thousands of television viewers.

Asao Tamajūrō. Name used by at least four Kabuki actors in Osaka and Kyoto. The first (1735–1804) was the best known.

Asari Keita. Theater producer, born 1923 in Tokyo. He became manager of the group Shiki in 1953 and was most interested in producing modern French plays. He then produced American musicals in Japan and *Madama Butterfly* at Milan's La Scala in 1985.

Asa Taishi. Japanese name of a son of a Paekche (Kudara) king, who, tradition has it, brought gifts to the court of Yamato in 597. The portrait of Shōtoku Taishi and his two sons (or nephews) is sometimes attributed to him.

Asayama Bontō-an. Poet of *renga* linked verse (Shuradayū Morotsuna, 1349–1417), student of Nijo Yoshimoto, in the service of shogun Ashikaga Yoshimitsu. He became a Buddhist monk and wrote a number of treatises on *renga* poetry, including *Bontō anshu hentō-shō* (Responses from Master Bontō on Questions Concerning *Renga,* 1417), *Renga awase jūgoban,* and *Chōtan-shō.*

Asayama Nichijō. Buddhist monk (d. 1577) of the Nichiren sect; birthplace uncertain, perhaps Izumo. Emperor Go-Nara is said to have given him his name. In 1568, he became the architecture adviser to Oda Nobunaga; he proved to be violently op-posed to Christianity and the activities of the Jesuit Luis Frois, and Oda Nobunaga banished him. His greatest achievement was rebuilding the imperial palace in Kyoto.

Ashiba Toshio. Painter (b. 1931) who moved to Paris in 1961 and has produced mainly lithographs.

Ashibetsu. Mining town in central Hokkaido, which developed around the former Ishikara charcoal mines. *Pop.:* 35,000.

• **Ashibetsu-dake.** Mountain (1,727 m) in central Hokkaido, in the Yūbari mountains. Winter-sports resort.

Ashida Enosuke. Educator (1873–1951), born in Hyōgo prefecture, who tried to introduce new teaching methods to motivate students, leaving them free to choose their examination subjects, in contrast to traditional education.

Ashida Hitoshi. Politician (1887–1959), born in Kyoto. He worked first at the department of foreign affairs, then joined the Rikken Seiyūkai (Friends of the Constitutional Government party) and was elected to the Diet starting in 1932 ten times. A devoted antimilitarist, he founded the Nihon Minshutō (Japan Democratic party) and was editor of the *Japan Times* from 1933 to 1940. In 1945, as minister of health, he formed the Nihon Jiyūtō (Japan Liberal party) with Hatoyama Ichirō. He was appointed minister of foreign affairs in 1947 (cabinet of Katayama Tetsu). In 1948, he became prime minister, a position he held for only six months; during his term he denied government bureaucrats the right to strike. He was obliged to resign because of his involvement in a bribery scandal, but his influence within the party remained great.

Ashide. "Reed writing." Calligraphy style created during the Heian period (794–1185), in which hiragana was written in imitation of reeds (hence the name *ashide*), rivers, trees, etc. These cursive, fluid characters were in style mainly after the tenth century. Around the twelfth century, they were combined, and sometimes merged, with drawings. *Ashide* sometimes designates collections of drawings or poems and Buddhist sutras *(kyō)* calligraphed in this style. Kanji are sometimes written in this way.

Ashigaru. Low-ranking foot soldiers *(zōhyō)* used during the Kamakura period, whose numbers multiplied during the Ōnin War (1467–77), when undisciplined armed bands of peasants *(nobushi)* and bandits *(akutō)* ravaged the region and the city of Kyoto. Hired by rival daimyo who were fighting each other at the time, the *ashigaru* were lightly armed (daggers, pikes, bows and arrows). In the sixteenth century, the daimyo taught them to use firearms (harquebuses), and Oda Nobunaga was the first to use large groups of *teppō-ashigaru* (harquebus foot soldiers). Thus armed, the *ashigaru* became a formidable force against the mounted samurai, who had only swords and bows and arrows. Oda Nobunaga owed his first great victory in Nagashino in 1575 to this light infantry (they had about 3,000 harquebuses at the time). However, though effective, the *ashigaru* were undisciplined and responsible for many massacres and much destruction and pillaging. It is sometimes said that Toyotomi Hideyoshi was the son of an *ashigaru*.

Ashiginu. A type of silk fabric woven on a thick warp (fine silk was called *katori*) produced starting in the seventh century and used to pay taxes or as gifts to the court. These fabrics were made in all provinces. Also called *futoginu*.

Ashihara no Nakatsu Kuni. "Country of Reeds." Ancient name for Japan, which, in mythology, was located between the Takamagahara (High Plain of Heaven) and Yomi no Kuni (land of dreams, death, and night). *See* TAKAMAGAHARA.

Ashihara Yoshinobu. Architect, born 1918 in Tokyo. After 1945, he studied in the United States with Marcel Breuer, then returned to Japan in 1954. He designed the Chūōkōron Building in Tokyo in 1956, then the Nikkō Hotel (1959) and the Sony Tower at Ginza (1966).

Ashikaga. City in Tochigi prefecture (Honshu), ancient seat of the Ashikaga family and important Buddhist center from the eleventh to the fourteenth century (Banna-ji temple, 1196). It was a post town *(shuku-eki)* on the Tōsandō road in the Nara period. In the Heian period, Fujiwara no Shigeyuki created an estate *(shōen)* there, which became that of the Ashikaga family. This city is famous for its textiles: since the eighth century, silks called *meisen* have been manufactured there. The ruins of the Ashikaga Gakkō, a Confucian school dating from 1394, are located here. It is now an industrial center (chemical products, machinery). *Pop.*: 170,000.
• Family of warriors founded by Yoshiyasu (1126–57), a grandson of Minamoto Yoshiie, ancestor of the Seiwa-Genji imperial family (descendants of Emperor Seiwa) in the twelfth century. His

name is that of the estate where his father, Yoshikuni, was born. This family of daimyo produced 15 shoguns, who ruled Japan from 1336 to 1573, and hundreds of brave warriors. List of Ashikaga shoguns:
1) Ashikaga Takauji (1305<1338–58>)
2) Ashikaga Yoshiakira (1330<1358–67>1368)
3) Ashikaga Yoshimitsu (1358<1367–95>1408)
4) Ashikaga Yoshimochi (1386<1395–1423>1428)
5) Ashikaga Yoshikazu (1407<1423–25>)
6) Ashikaga Yoshinori (1394<1428–41>)
7) Ashikaga Yoshikatsu (1433<1442–43>)
8) Ashikaga Yoshimasa (1435<1449–74>1490)
9) Ashikaga Yoshihisa (1465<1474–89>)
10) Ashikaga Yoshitane (1465<1490–93 and 1508–21>1522)
11) Ashikaga Yoshizumi (1478<1493–1508>1513)
12) Ashikaga Yoshiharu (1510<1521–45>1550)
13) Ashikaga Yoshiteru (1535<1545–65>)
14) Ashikaga Yoshihide (1538<1564–68>)
15) Ashikaga Yoshiaki (1537<1568–73>1597)
Their shogunate is known as the Muromachi period, for the district of Kyoto where the shogun's residence and general headquarters were located. They succeeded the Kanto Administrator (Kantō *kanryō*) of the Kamakura *bakufu*, after the latter's fall. This period is also known as the Ashikaga period. The Ashikaga family had many difficulties, with its members often fighting for supremacy and struggles for succession resulting in endless wars. Their shogunate was a dark period politically, with the country plunged into civil war. However, under these cultured shoguns, Japan developed new artistic forms (such as Noh theater) and breathed new life into trade, both domestic and foreign. The events of this period are complex, with coalitions constantly forming and breaking down, and treason (in the Western sense of the term) a common currency.

The Ashikaga period was one of incessant warfare. First was the war between the Northern and Southern Courts (1336–92), then the Ōnin War (1467–77), and finally a long period of wars between the clans, called Sengoku-jidai, or the Warring States period, which lasted some hundred years, until the rise to power of Oda Nobunaga, who unified Japan in 1573. A number of provinces had seceded and were refusing to pay taxes to the shogunate, so the financial situation of the Ashikaga *bakufu* was shaky; that of the imperial court was hardly better. Therefore, neither the emperor nor the shogun could afford armies sufficiently powerful to overwhelm those of the provincial governors. Once the two courts were reunited, the provincial lords fought for supremacy, and the city of Kyoto became a battlefield. Shogun succeeded shogun, most of them forced to abdicate or assassinated, and confusion reigned throughout the country, the *shugo-daimyō* ("protector-daimyo") becoming absolute masters of the lands they controlled, confiscating public and private property by force. It was the era of the *gekokujō* ("those of low extraction replacing the nobles"), in which Japan was divided into more than 20 rival "principalities."

The members of the Ashikaga family who played a role at this time are listed below in chronological order of succession (but dates of birth are not mentioned), and thereafter are described in alphabetical order:

—Yoshiyasu (d. 1157)
—Yoshikane (1147–99)
—Takauji (1305–58), shogun
—Tadayoshi (1306–52)
—Tadafuyu (1327–1400)
—Yoshiakira (1330–68), shogun
—Motouji (1340–67)
—Yoshimitsu (1358–1408), shogun
—Mitsukane (1376–1409)
—Yoshimochi (1386–1428), shogun
—Yoshinori (1394–1441), shogun
—Mochiuji (1398–1439)
—Yoshikazu (1407–25), shogun
—Yoshikatsu (1433–43), shogun
—Shigeuji (1434–97)
—Yoshimasa (1435–90), shogun
—Masatomo (1435–91)
—Yoshimi (1439–91)
—Chachamaru (d. 1491)
—Yoshihisa (1465–89), shogun
—Yoshitane (1465–1522), shogun
—Yoshizumi (1478–1513), shogun
—Yoshiharu (1510–50), shogun
—Yoshiteru (1535–65), shogun
—Yoshiaki (1537–97), shogun
—Yoshihide (1538–68), shogun

See MUROMACHI.

• *Ashikaga-bon*. Books printed with movable type by the Buddhist monk San'yō, who worked in the Ashikaga Gakkō in the seventeenth century.

• **Ashikaga Chachamaru**. Warrior (d. 1491), son of Ashikaga Masatomo. Jealous of the son of his father's second wife, he killed his father and the second wife, as well as a number of people in that household. Then, attacked by Hōjō Sōun (Hōjō Nagauji), he committed suicide.

• **Ashikaga Gakkō**. School founded by Ashikaga Yoshikane (1147–99) in Ashikaga and revived by Ashikaga Motouji and Nagao Kagehisa in 1394. The Buddhist monk Kaigen became its principal in 1439. This institution was famous for its teaching of Chinese studies and military strategy. Tokugawa Ieyasu donated a movable-type press to the school so that it could publish various scholarly books, collectively called *Ashikaga-bon*. It was closed in 1871.

• **Ashikaga Masatomo**. Warrior (1435–91), third son of Ashikaga Yoshinori, father of Ashikaga Yoshizumi and Ashikaga Chachamaru. In 1457, when he was a Buddhist monk in the Kōgon-in temple in Kyoto, he was appointed Kanto Administrator (Kantō *kanryō*) by Ashikaga Yoshimasa, but he could not take up his position because the warriors of Ashikaga Yoshiuji, the deposed Kanto Administrator, refused him access to the city. He therefore lived in Horiguchi, a small city in the province of Izu (whence his surname of Horiguchi-kubō), constantly making war against Ashikaga Shigeuji, who had settled in Koga in the province of Shimōsa (whence his title Koga-kubō). He was killed by his son, Ashikaga Chachamaru.

• **Ashikaga Mitsukane**. Warrior (1376–1409), son of Ashikaga Ujimitsu and father of Ashikaga Mochiuji and Ashikaga Mochinaka. He was the third Kanto Administrator.

• **Ashikaga Mochiuji**. Warrior (1398–1439), son of Ashikaga Mitsukane. He was appointed fourth Kantō Administrator, but he plotted against shogun Ashikaga Yoshinori and was obliged to commit suicide, along with his uncle Ashikaga Mitsusada. His sons were killed, except for Ashikaga Shigeuji. *See* EIKYŌ NO RAN.

• **Ashikaga Motouji**. Warrior (1340–67), fourth son of Ashikaga Takauji, he became the first Kanto Administrator in 1349. He was forced from Kamakura in 1352 by Nitta Yoshioki. When Nitta was killed by his vassals in 1358, Ashikaga Motouji pacified the Kantō region and repressed a local insurrection.

• **Ashikaga Saburō**. *See* ASHIKAGA YOSHIYASU.

• **Ashikaga Shigeuji**. Warrior (1434–97), fourth son of Ashikaga Mochiuji. Having escaped the massacre of his family (*see* ASHIKAGA MOCHIUJI), he was raised by one of his vassals in Kyoto. In 1449, he was welcomed into the Kantō region as Kantō Administrator; in 1454, he avenged his father by killing Uesugi Noritada, his steward. He then took refuge in Koga (province of Shimōsa) to defend himself against the troops sent by the *bakufu* to punish him. However, peace was made and Ashikaga Shigeuji became Koga-kubō, a title his descendants held until 1583.

• **Ashikaga Tadafuyu.** Eldest son (ca. 1327–1400) of Ashikaga Takauji by one of his concubines, he was adopted by his uncle, Ashikaga Tadayoshi. He was appointed governor of Nagano in 1349. When Ashikaga Tadayoshi died, he took the side of the Southern Court (Nanchō) against Ashikaga Takauji, whom he forced from Kyoto in 1352. However, he lost the province of Bingo in 1363 and finally made peace with the third shogun, Ashikaga Yoshimitsu.

• **Ashikaga Tadayoshi.** Brother (1306–52) of Ashikaga Takauji, with whom he was alternately friend and foe. Appointed governor of the province of Sagami, he went to Kamakura to protect Imperial Prince Shigenaga. He assassinated Prince Morinaga, who was being held prisoner, helped his brother against Ashikaga Tokiyuki, and entered Edo with Ashikaga Tadauji, founding the shogunate of Muromachi with him. Forced out of the city by his brother, he withdrew to Kyushu with his son, Ashikaga Tadafuyu. Expelled from that city, he supported Emperor Go-Murakami, defeated his brother, and killed Kō no Moronao. Upon his return to Kamakura, he apparently died of poisoning.

• **Ashikaga Takauji.** General (1305–58) in the service of Hōjō Takatoki. He supported Emperor Go-Daigo against the Kamakura shogunate, thus leading to the fall of the Kamakura *bakufu* in 1333. Then he turned against the imperial troops and his former allies Nitta Yoshisada, Kusunoki, Kitabatake, and Kikuchi, defeated them, and entered Kyoto as a conqueror. Appointed shogun by Emperor Kōmyō, son of Emperor Fushimi, whom he had helped ascend the throne by forcing Emperor Go-Daigo to take refuge in Yoshino, he established his own *bakufu* at Muromachi. There followed a long war between the supporters of the Northern Court (Hokuchō) and supporters of Ashikaga Takauji, a period called Nambokuchō (Northern and Southern Courts). However, he quarreled with his brother, Ashikaga Tadayoshi, and his adopted son,

Ashikaga Tadafuyu, whom he forced out of Kyoto. Takauji was a devout Buddhist, an excellent *waka* poet, a good painter, and a well-known *shō* musician. When he died, his son, Ashikaga Yoshiakira, became the second shogun of Muromachi.

• **Ashikaga Ujimitsu.** Warrior (1359–98), son of Ashikaga Motouji, succeeding him as Kanto Administrator in 1367. In 1378, he tried to unseat shogun Ashikaga Yoshimitsu, but was dissuaded from this attempt and pardoned. In 1392, he extended his authority to the provinces of Mutsu and Dewa in the extreme north of Honshu. He was the father of Ashikaga Mitsukane, Ashikaga Mitsutada, Ashikaga Mitsutaka, Ashikaga Mitsusada, and Ashikaga Mitsuhide.

• **Ashikaga Yoshiaki.** Fifteenth and last Ashikaga shogun (1537<1568–73>1597), third son of Ashikaga Yoshiharu (twelfth shogun). He became a Buddhist monk at Nara under the name Kakukei (or Gakkei). Oda Nobunaga appointed him shogun to succeed Ashikaga Yoshihide. But Yoshiaki, who feared Nobunaga's power, secretly allied himself with the Mōri, Asakura, and Takeda families and with the monks of Hongan-ji of Kyoto. When the plot failed, Oda Nobunaga forced him out of Kyoto in 1573, and the Muromachi *bakufu* collapsed. Later, he placed himself under the protection of Toyotomi Hideyoshi, who brought him to Osaka, where he returned to religious life with the name Shōzan.

• **Ashikaga Yoshiakira.** Second shogun of Muromachi (1330<1358–67>1368), son of Ashikaga Takauji. He served as a hostage at Kamakura when his father was sent to fight Emperor Go-Daigo (1333), but fled and joined Nitta Yoshisada to attack the Hōjō. After the fall of the Kamakura *bakufu*, he controlled the Kantō region until 1343, then went to Kyoto to help his father fight the supporters of the Nanchō (the Southern court). When Kyoto was taken by the armies of Emperor Go-Murakami, in 1351, he was able to recover it soon after. He succeeded to the shogunate when his father died, but in 1367, he abdicated in favor of his son, Ashikaga Yoshimitsu.

• **Ashikaga Yoshiharu.** Twelfth shogun of Muromachi (1510<1521–45>1550), succeeding his father, Ashikaga Yoshizumi. Forced to flee Kyoto because of the civil wars in 1528 and 1539, he returned in 1532 and 1542. He finally abdicated in 1545 in favor of his son, Ashikaga Yoshiteru.

• **Ashikaga Yoshihide.** Fourteenth shogun of Muromachi (1538<1564–68>), grandson of Ashikaga Yoshizumi and successor to Ashikaga Toshiteru. Attacked by Oda Nobunaga, he fled to the province of Settsu and may have been assassinated by Matsunaga Hisahide. Ashikaga Yoshiaki succeeded him.

Ashikaga Yoshihisa. Ninth shogun of Muromachi (1465<1474–89>), son of and successor to Ashikaga Yoshimasa. However, Yoshimasa's brother, Ashikaga Yoshimi, a Buddhist monk who had been designated by his older brother to succeed him, rebelled. Ashikaga Yoshihisa's mother, Hino Tomiko, fought him with the support of Yamana Mochitoyo, a powerful daimyo, and managed to name her son Ashikaga Yoshihisa as shogun in 1473, in the middle of a civil war. This was one of the causes of the Ōnin War. Ashikaga Yoshihisa was a good *waka* poet. Ashikaga Yoshitane succeeded him.

Ashikaga Yoshikane. Warrior (1147–99), Minamoto no Yoritomo's brother-in-law. He married one of Hōjō Tokimasa's daughters. He became a Buddhist monk under the name Gishō.

• **Ashikaga Yoshikatsu.** Seventh shogun of Muromachi (1433<1442–43>), son of and successor to Ashikaga Yoshinori. His adviser was Hatakeyama Mochikuni. He died of dysentery one year after he became shogun, and his brother Ashikaga Yoshimasa succeeded him.

• **Ashikaga Yoshikazu.** Fifth shogun of Muromachi (1407<1423–25>), son of and successor to Ashikaga Yoshimochi (who ruled from 1423 to 1428). Ashikaga Yoshinori succeeded him.

Ashikaga Yoshimasa. Eighth shogun of Muromachi (1435<1449–74>1490), brother of and successor to Ashikaga Yoshikatsu. He adopted his younger brother Ashikaga Yoshimi in 1464, but his wife, Hino Tomiko, bore him a son, Ashikaga Yoshihisa, and so his succession provoked quarrels between his two sons, which led to the Ōnin War (*see* ŌNIN NO RAN). He constructed the Silver Pavilion (Ginkaku-ji) at Higashiyama in Kyoto and, ignoring the civil war that was ravaging the country, was mainly preoccupied with Noh, organizing tea ceremonies, collecting Chinese ceramics, and promoting arts and letters, which resulted in his rule being named Higashiyama-bunka (Higashiyama culture). He abdicated in 1474 in favor of his son Ashikaga Yoshihisa, and retired to his villa in Higashiyama to devote himself to the arts. He was nicknamed Higashiyama-dono and Higashiyama shogun.

• **Ashikaga Yoshimi.** Son (1439–91) of Ashikaga Yoshinori and younger brother of Ashikaga Yoshimasa. A Buddhist monk under the name Gijin, he was adopted by his brother, who, not having a male heir, named him his successor. But Ashikaga Yoshimasa's wife, Hino Tomiko, bore him a son, Ashikaga Yoshihisa, late in life, and a conflict ensued that degenerated into civil war (*see* ŌNIN NO RAN). Ashikaga Yoshimi fled, soon returning under the protection of general Yamana Mochitoyo. Finally, in 1489, he made peace with Ashikaga Yoshimasa and returned to religious life in the Tsūgen-ji temple in Sanjō (Kyoto).

• **Ashikaga Yoshimitsu.** Third shogun of Muromachi (1358<1367–95>1408), son of and successor to Ashikaga Yoshiakira. Aided by the administrator Hosokawa Yoriyuki, he repressed revolts by *shugo-daimyō* in the provinces, notably those of Toki Yoriyasu in 1379, Yamana Ukimikiyo in 1391, and Ōuchi Yoshihira in 1399, and ended the Nambokuchō war (between the Southern and Northern Courts) in 1392. In 1394, Emperor Go-Komatsu gave him the title of Dajō-daijin. In 1401, he sent an ambassador to the Ming court in China. He had already abdicated, in 1395, in favor of his son, Ashikaga Yoshimochi, to devote himself to religious life. He had a luxurious villa, the Golden Pavilion (Kinkaju-ji), built at Kitayama in Kyoto in 1397. Retiring there as a Buddhist monk with the name Tenzan Dōgi, he continued until his death to concern himself with the country's affairs as adviser to his son. He was called Kitayama-dono.

• **Ashikaga Yoshimochi.** Fourth shogun of Muromachi (1386<1395–1423>1428), son of and successor to Ashikaga Yoshimitsu. He ended trade missions with China and, in 1418, had his brother Ashikaga Yoshitsugu assassinated. In 1423, he abdicated in favor of his son, Ashikaga Yoshikazu, but when Yoshikazu died, he took power again in 1425. His brother, Ashikaga Yoshinori, succeeded him.

• **Ashikaga Yoshinori.** Sixth shogun of Muromachi (1394<1428–41>), son of Ashikaga Yoshimitsu, brother of and successor to Ashikaga Yoshimochi. In 1439, he forced Ashikaga Mochiuji to commit suicide for having attempted independent rule in the Kantō region. This provoked the anger of Yoshinori's generals, and one of them, Akamatsu Mitsusuke, assassinated him. His son, Ashikaga Yoshikatsu, succeeded him.

• **Ashikaga Yoshitane.** Tenth shogun of Muro-machi (1465<1490–93 and 1508–21>1522), son of Ashikaga Yoshimi, adopted by Ashikaga Yoshimasa. He succeeded Ashikaga Yoshihisa but was beaten in battle by Hatakeyama Yoshitoyo and Hosokawa Masamoto and forced to flee to Kyoto. Ashikaga Yoshizumi was named shogun in his place in 1493. In 1508, however, Ashikaga Yoshitane managed, in his turn, to force out Ashikaga Yoshizumi and regained power. He was forced to flee once more in 1521 and took refuge on the island of Shikoku, where he died. He was called Shima-kobū. Ashikaga Yoshiharu succeeded him.

• **Ashikaga Yoshiteru.** Thirteenth shogun of Muromachi (1535<1546–65>), eldest son of and successor to Ashikaga Yoshiharu. He spent his time between Kyoto, torn by civil war, and Ōmi, where he took refuge. Attacked in 1549 by Hosokawa Harumoto, he was forced to flee once again and returned to Kyoto only in 1553. After the death of his ally, Miyoshi Nagayoshi, he was attacked in his Kyoto palace and killed by one of his vassals, Matsunaga Hisahide. Ashikaga Yoshihide succeeded him.

• **Ashikaga Yoshiyasu.** Grandson (d. 1157) of Minamoto no Yoshiie and brother of Nitta Yoshishige. He served emperors Toba and Go-Shirakawa, whom he supported during the war of the Hōgen era (*see* HŌGEN NO RAN) in 1156, and was appointed governor of the province of Mutsu. He was the founder of the Ashikaga family. Also called Ashikaga Saburō.

• **Ashikaga Yoshizumi.** Eleventh shogun of Muromachi (1478<1493–1508>1513), son of Ashikaga Masatomo. Beaten by Ashikaga Yoshitane, he fled to Ōmi in 1508.

Ashikari. Noh play: overwhelmed by his poverty, a man leaves his wife and becomes a wanderer. His wife goes to the capital, earns some money, and buys him new clothes.
→ *See* TANIZAKI JUN'ICHIRŌ.

Ashina. Family of powerful daimyo from the province of Aizu from about 1400 to 1589, when Date Masamune dispossessed them of their land.

Ashinaga. Mythical character in popular legends, supposed to have had very long legs, and often associated with his partner Tenaga, "Long Arms."

Ashinazuchi. In Shinto legends about Susanoo, notably in the *Kojiki,* Ashinazuchi was the father of Kushi Inada Hime (or Kushinada Hime), a young woman of the Izumo region who was to be sacrificed to an eight-headed monster, Yamata no Orochi, who haunted the region. She was saved from death by Susanoo, who killed the dragon and then married her. Her mother named her Tenazuchi. As for Ashinazuchi, he was said to be the son of Oyamazumi no Kami of Izumo. *See* KUSHI INADA HIME, INADA HIME.

Ashio. Mining town in Tochigi prefecture (central Honshu) at the foot of Mt. Akagi (2,010 m), located near silver and copper-ore mines that were in operation since the early sixteenth century. The mines were closed in 1973, when the ore ran out. *Pop.:* 6,000.

• **Ashio Dōzan Kōdoku Jiken.** "Ashio Copper Mines Incident." In 1877, operation of the copper mines at Ashio resulted in massive pollution of the Tone and Watarase rivers, which irrigated a large part of the northern Kantō plain, resulting in an agricultural disaster. The peasants of the region protested violently, and the affair was brought before the Diet. Pollution-control measures were introduced but not applied strictly enough, and the village of Yanaka, too severely damaged, had to be razed.

• **Ashio Dōzan sōgi.** "Ashio Copper miners' strikes." In 1907, more than 600 employees of the Furukawa Company, which operated the copper mines, led by union bosses such as Nagaoka Tsuruzō (1864–1914) and Minami Sukematsu (1873–1964), struck to demand better working conditions and higher wages. When the negotiations did not produce results, the miners got past the guard towers and set a number of buildings ablaze. The government then sent in the army, and 82 miners were arrested and sentenced to prison terms. This strike, the first under the Meiji government, led other workers throughout the country to demand improvements in their working conditions. It created a great stir in the press and among the population in general.

Ashiyuki. Painter of ukiyo-e prints (active ca. 1820), belonging to the Osaka school. *See* OSAKA SCHOOL.

Ashizuka Chūemon. Christian warrior (1578–1638), one of the leaders of the Shimabara revolt (1637–38), killed in battle.

Ashuku. Japanese transcription of the Sanskrit name for the Buddha Akshobhya, who ruled the Eastern Paradise according to Mahayana Buddhism. Also called Ashuku Butsu, Ashuku Nyorai, Hōtō Nyorai.

Ashura. Japanese transcription of *asura,* the "anti-gods" of Indian religious folklore, who fought the *deva,* or gods, of the Hindu and Buddhist pantheon. The most famous portrayal of one of the Ashura kings, Ashura-Ō, in dry lacquer, dating from 734, is in Kōfuku-ji in Nara. He symbolizes hunger, anger, and quarrels.

Aso. Town in the north of Kumamoto prefecture (Kyushu), on the Kurokawa river. Uchinomaki *onsen* (hot spring) is located there.

• **Aso-jinja.** Shinto shrine in the district of Aso (Kumamoto prefecture) dedicated to Takeiwatatsu no Mikoto and other *kami.* It is said to have been founded about two thousand years ago by the ancestors of the Aso clan. In 1017, a decree ordered the emperor to make an offering there at least once during his reign. Toyotomi Hideyoshi confiscated its properties in 1587. Its rice-planting festival, Mitaue Matsuri, takes place every July 28.

• **Aso Kokuritsu Kōen.** Aso National Park in south-central Kyushu, located around the Aso volcano. It also includes an extinguished volcano, Kujū (Kūjusan, 1,788 m), and Mt. Yufu (1,584 m). The park, with an area of 730 km², has numerous hot springs.

• **Aso-san.** Active volcano in southern Kyushu, Kumamoto prefecture, whose crater (caldera) is one of the largest in the world, with a circumference of 80 km. It is composed of five cones, called Takadake, Nakadake, Nekodake, Kishimadake, and Eboshidake, after their location or shape. The ash from this volcano fertilizes almost all of southern Kyushu and the neighboring islands for a radius of more than 100 km. Many of its frequent eruptions are dangerous: in 1979, it caused hundreds of deaths. There were 111 eruptions recorded between 796 and 1958. This volcano's highest spot is Takadake, with an altitude of 1,592 m. It is part of Aso National Park.

• **Aso-uji.** Powerful family of the province of Higo, descended, according to tradition, from the grandson of Emperor Jimmu, named Miyatsuko no Kuni of Aso. The lords of this family took sides with the Southern Court (Nanchō, *see* NAMBOKUCHŌ) against Ashikaga Takauji in the fourteenth century. Their descendants are traditionally charged with performing rites and ceremonies at the ancestral shrine of Aso, Aso-jinja.

Asō Hisashi. Socialist politician (1891–1940), born in Ōita. He was one of the leaders of the social conflict that set the miners of Ashio against their bosses in 1906–07 (*see* ASHIO DŌZAN SŌGI). He founded a number of political parties for peasants and workers. One of the founders of the Shakai Taishūtō (Socialist Masses party) in 1932, he was appointed its secretary-general. Elected to the House of Representatives in 1936 and 1937, he changed directions and allied himself with the militarist parties, at the side of the prime minister, Konoe Fumimaro. He wrote two books on politics: *Dakuryū ni oyogu* (Swimming in Troubled Waters) and *Reimei* (Dawn).

Asō Isoji. Writer and scholar (1896–1979), specializing in literature of the Edo period. Among his best-known works are *Chūgoku bungaku* (Chinese Literature), *Warai no kenkyū* (Study of Humor), *Hai shumi no hattatsu* (Evolution of the Haiku), and *Bashō monogatari* (Bashō's Novel).

Asomi (Ason). Starting in the seventh century, court title indicating a rank immediately below that of Mahito, according to the reform of eight classes of Kabane made by Emperor Temmu in 685. This title was later conferrred on all heads of powerful families and members of the imperial family to the fourth rank. Ministers had the right to add this title to their name. *See* I, HASSEI, KAN'I JŪNIKAI NO SEI, KŌBETSU, TACHIBANA, YAKUSA NO KABANE.

Asō Saburō. Western-style painter, born 1913 in Tokyo. He visited Europe in 1938; in 1943, he created the Shinjin Gakai (Society of New Painters) with Matsumoto Shunsuke, Ai Mitsu, and other artists.
• Figurative-style painter (1888–1963).

Aston, William George. English diplomat (1841–1911) and Japanese specialist born in Ulster. Sent to Japan in 1864, he was consul and secretary of the British delegation in Tokyo. He became known for his many translations of Japanese works, notably the *Nihon shoki* (1896), and for his authorship of *History of Japanese Literature* (1899).

Asuka. Village in the northern part of Nara prefecture, where a number of imperial palaces and Buddhist temples were established from the sixth to the eighth century, of which only ruins and tumuli *(kofun)* remain. "Asuka" means, in Ainu, "flying birds" or "morning fragrance." The first emperor to establish himself there was Inkyō Tennō (<412–53>). Then, from Empress Suiko (<593–628>) to Emperor Gemmei, all emperors (except Kōtoku Tennō and Tenchi Tennō) lived there. A number of Koreans also settled there. It was in Asuka that Buddhism gained its first foothold in Japan, and so it was the site of numerous temples. Because of this, it was the political and cultural center of the country for almost two centuries, until the capital was transferred to Heijō-kyō (Nara) in 710. Each palace was abandoned when its emperor died, and the ruins and foundations of many of them, such as that of the legendary Jimmu, Kashihara, Kyomihara, and Fujiwara-kyō, can still be seen. Asuka-dera is still standing, as are tomb chambers under *kofun,* the most famous of which (and the most recently excavated) is Takamatsuzuka. The culture of the Asuka period (which dates from the late sixth century to 710) was characterized by the introduction of Buddhism, the arrival of Korean immigrants (Aya family), and the early assimilation of Chinese culture. This influence was notable particularly in Buddhist sculpture and temple architecture, such as Hōryū-ji. One can also discern influences from Iran and Central Asia in the fabrics and decorations.
→ *See* TOYO-UKE KŌDAI-JINGŪ.

• **Asukabe.** *See* KŌMYŌ KŌGŌ.

• **Asuka-dera.** Buddhist temple built in Asuka between 588 and 596 by Soga no Umako. It houses the Asuka-daibutsu, a bronze statue of Shaka Nyorai (Shakyamuni) in a sitting position, perhaps by Korean sculptor and bronze artist Kuratsukuri no Tori, who would have made it in 606. This statue, 2.908 m high *(jōruku* size), has, unfortunately, been restored a great deal. In the Heian period, the temple was renamed Moto Gangō-ji, while another temple, transferred to Nara, kept the name Asuka-dera (or Gangō-ji). Its pagoda was destroyed by lightning in 1196. All of its buildings have disappeared, but excavations have revealed the original plan, which is similar to that of a Korean temple in Pyongyang of the same period. Asuka-dera was also known as Hōkō-ji and Angoin. *See* GANGŌ-JI.

• **Asukagawa.** River 23 km long, irrigating the Nara plain and emptying into the Yamato River. It flows through the former site of Asuka.

• *Asukagawa.* Noh play: a child who has lost his mother goes in search of her and finally finds her busy planting rice.

• **Asuka-jidai.** Historical period of Asuka, from 538 to 710. Sometimes called Suikochō-jidai (period of the Suiko court).

• *Asuka no kiyomihara ritsuryō.* Law code *(Temmu ritsuryō)* in 32 volumes, which were gathered by Emperor Temmu in 689 and published by Emperor Jitō in 697. These laws were replaced in 702 by the Taihō Code *(Taihō ritsuryō).* See JITŌ TENNŌ, KIYOMIHARA RITSURYŌ, TAIHŌ RITSURYŌ.

Asuka. Type of airplane (STOL) developed in Japan in 1985. *Length and wingspan:* 30 m; *weight:* 39,000 kg; 4 turbofan engines on the wings. It can take off and land in less than 600 m. *See* CIVIL AVIATION.

Asukabe Hime. Wife of Emperor Shōmu. *See* AGATA NO INUKAI NO MICHIYO.

Asukabe Tsunenori. Painter of the imperial court (tenth century). He painted the walls of Emperor Murakami's palace in 963 and 964. He also illustrated the *Genji monogatari* scroll calligraphed by Ono no Michikaze.

Asukai. Influential family *(shi, uji),* founded by Asukai Masatsune in the late twelfth century. Its members were known as *waka* poets, calligraphers, and *kemari* football players. Among the best known were Asukai Masaki (1611–79), poet; Asukai Masachika (1417–90), poet and calligrapher; Asukai Masatsune (1599–1615), famous *kemari* player; and Asukai Masamochi (1842–1906), *kemari* player and poet.

• **Asukai Masayasu.** Poet (fifteenth century), son of Asukai Masayo.

• **Asukai Masayo.** Poet and calligrapher (1390–1452). He compiled the last imperial anthology, *Shin zoku kokin waka-shū,* from 1434 to 1439. He also wrote *Fuji kikō* (Travels to Mt. Fuji).

Asukata Ichio. Politician (1915–90), born in Yokohama. In 1945, he participated in the revival of the

Socialist party of Japan and was elected to the House of Representatives in 1953; he became mayor of Yokohama in 1963. He was appointed president of the Socialist party in 1977, and reelected to the House of Representatives in 1979.

Atago Gongen. Shinto *kami,* considered a syncretic form *(gongen)* of the bodhisattva Kshitigarbha *(Jap.:* Jizō Bosatsu). Associated closely with Homusubi (or Kagutsuchi, the *kami* of fire). Also called Atago Jizō. He is worshiped at Atago Shrine.

• **Atago-jinja.** Shinto shrine on Mt. Atago, near Kyoto, whose main shrine is devoted to Izanami no Mikoto, Wakamusubi no Mikoto, and Atago Gongen. This shrine was said to have protected the imperial capital against fire. The shrine festival is on September 28. It has many branches throughout Japan.

• **Atago-yama.** Small mountain northwest of Kyoto, where Atago Shrine is located at 924 m.

Ataka. The Ataka Pass (Ataka no Seki) in Ishikawa prefecture was the site of a major battle between the Minamoto and Taira clans in 1183, and the events that took place there became the subject of a Noh play of the same name, as well as a Kabuki play *(Kanjinchō).* According to some writers, this pass, which bordered the seacoast, is now under water. *See* KOMATSU.
→ *See* JŌMON.

Atake-bune. Warships used in the late sixteenth and early seventeenth centuries by the armies of Hōjo Ujinao and Oda Nobunaga. These 55-meter-long ships, built in the ports of Ise and Shima provinces, had a wooden tower covered in copper plates whose walls were pierced with holes through which archers or harquebusiers could shoot. They were propelled by 20 to 25 oarsmen. The shogunate of Edo had one of these ships built, the *Atake Maru,* in 1635, inspired by the Korean admiral Yi Sun-sin's (1545–98) "tortoise boats" *(Kor.:* Gö-bug-sön).

Atami. Tourist town on the coast of Shizuoka prefecture, on the Izu Peninsula, in the Bay of Sagami, known since the eighth century for its chlorinated saltwater hot springs. Located only 70 km from Tokyo, it is a popular destination for city dwellers. Plum blossom festival in January; in the fall, festival in honor of writer Ozaki Kōyō, one of whose novels takes place in Atami. Small local museum, open since 1957. *Pop.:* 50,000.

Atemi. In martial arts, blow directed at a person's private parts with the goal of neutralizing him or her temporarily or even causing death. These blows are made with the side of the hand, the ends of the fingers, the fist, the elbow, the knee, the heel, and so on. The technique for using the *atemi* is called *atemi-waza.*

Atobe Yoshiaki. Shinto priest *(gō:* Kōkai, 1659–1729), disciple of Yasui Shinkai and Ogimachi Kimmichi, who encouraged the propagation of Suika Shinto. To this end, he wrote two works: *Shintō seishi no setsu* (Essay on Life and Death in Shinto) and *Shimoyo gakudan* (Dialogue on a Chilly Night).

Atomi Kakei. Woman of letters (Atomi Tokino, 1840–1926), born in Hyōgo prefecture. A painter and poet, she devoted herself to the education of women. In 1875, she founded a college in Kanda (Tokyo) called Atomi Jogakkō (Atomi School for Girls) and was its principal until 1919. It is now a secondary school.

Atsuakira Shinnō. Imperial prince (994–1051), son of Emperor Sanjō. Initially heir to the throne, he was replaced in 1018 by Atsuyoshi Shinnō, who became Emperor Go-Suzaku. *See* FUJIWARA NO ENSHI, KOICHIJŌ NO IN.

Atsugi. City in Kanagawa prefecture, post town *(shuku-eki)* on the Sagami River during the Edo period. It is now an important rail junction. In September 1945, the American occupation troops landed there. *Pop.:* 150,000.

Atsuita. Heavy brocade fabric imported from China, later produced in Kyoto *(nishiki).* This name was also applied to a short-sleeved kimono decorated with various embroidered or painted motifs, used as an undergarment by Noh actors. Also called *atsuita-ori. See* KOSODE.

Atsumi Hantō. Atsumi Peninsula, on the coast of Aichi prefecture (Honshu), south of Astumi Bay. It is famous for its rock formations and its greenhouse vegetable cultivation.

Atsumi Kiyoshi. Actor (Tadokoro Yasuo), born 1928 in Tokyo. He played mainly comic roles in movies and on television; the role of Tora-san made him famous. *See* HANI SUSUMU.

Atsumori. Title of a Noh play: Atsumori, a warrior of the Heike (Taira) clan, is killed at the Battle of Ichi no Tani by a warrior of the Genji (Minamoto) clan named Kumagai, who takes his flute and sends it back to his enemy's family.

Atsuta-jingū. Shinto shrine in Nagoya, said to have housed Susanoo's sword, called Kusanagi no Tsurugi. It was constructed in the *shimmei* style before the eighth century. Destroyed during bombing of the city in 1945, an exact replica was constructed in 1955, dedicated to the *kami* Atsuta Myōjin, but the sword was never recovered. It is one of the holiest shrines in Japan, after those at Ise and Izumo, since Emperor Meiji sent a personal envoy there in 1868, when he ascended to the throne: only the shrine at Ise had been blessed by this honor until then. Its annual festival takes place on June 5.

Atsuzane Shinnō. Eighth son (893–967) of Emperor Uda Tennō, ancestor of the Uda-Genji family. He became a Buddhist monk under the name Kakushin in 950. His name is still known because of his talent for playing the *biwa* and the *wagon* (a type of *koto*). *See* SEMIMARU.

Aum Shinri-kyō. "New Religion of Aum." Japanese millenarian sect falsely claiming to be Buddhist, led by a guru called Asahara Shōko, who recruited his followers in Japan and, since 1992, in Russia, where, according to some estimates, there are more than 30,000 members. This sect, which sequesters and brainwashes its followers, launched criminal activities with the goal of ending the civilized world. In April 1995, sect members set off cannisters of sarin gas in the Tokyo subway, killing 12 people and poisoning more than 5,000; a few weeks later, they did the same thing in Yokohama (though with fewer casualties). Members of this criminal sect were quickly arrested.

A-un. In Japanese Esoteric Buddhism, these two sounds symbolize the beginning and the end of all dharmas (phenomena): "A" *(alpha)* is produced when one opens one's mouth, and "un" *(omega)* when one closes one's mouth. The human and animal guardians at the entrances to Buddhist temples and Shinto shrines are always shown one with its mouth open, the other with its mouth closed, to portray this idea. *See* A, NI-Ō.

Aviation, airplanes. *See* AICHI, CIVIL AVIATION, ASUKA, FUJI JŪKŌGYŌ, HIROKOSHI JIRŌ, ITOKAWA HIDEO, JAL, KAMIKAZE, KANETAKA KAORU, KAWANISHI, KAWASAKI, KYUSHU, MITSUBISHI, NAKAJIMA, YOKOSUKA, YS-11.

Awabi. Name given to gastropods of the *Haliotis* genus (abalone), of which more than ten varieties are commonly found on the coasts of Japan. Their flesh is very popular in Japanese cuisine, particularly the Tokobushi *(Haliotis aquatilis).* They are now farmed. The Japanese have consumed abalone since prehistoric times, as evidenced by the innumerable shell mounds *(kaizuka)* on the coasts. Since the earliest poetry *(Man'yōshū),* their unique iridescent shells have been likened to unrequited love. The dried flesh is used to accompany gifts for the gods at the end of a fast. These *noshi* are now most often symbolized by a drawing made on the envelope of the gift.

• **Awabimusubi.** *See* MIZUHIKI.

Awaji. Island at the entrance to the Inland Sea (Setonaikai), forming Osaka Bay. Legend has it that it was the first created by Izanagi and Izanami, the primordial *kami.* It is separated from the island of Shikoku by the Strait of Naruto. Vaguely triangular in shape, its highest point, Mt. Yuzuraha, is only 609 m. Awaji has semitropical agriculture and pig husbandry; pottery and dolls of a specific type (Awaji-*ningyō*) are made there. It is now part of Hyōgo prefecture. The island was heavily affected by the Kōbe earthquake (Jan. 16–17, 1995), with 52 deaths. *Main town:* Sumoto. *Area:* 593 km². *Pop.:* 180,000.

• **Awaji no Haitei.** Name given to Emperor Junnin (753–765) after he was dethroned by Empress Shōtoku.

• **Awaji no Kimi.** Name given to Prince Sawara, exiled to Awaji for having killed Fujiwara no Tanetsugu, favorite of Emperor Kammu. He died on his way to exile, in 785.

• **Awa-jōruri.** A type of puppet theater performed in the province of Awa and on the island of Awaji (whence it draws its name).

Awa-jinja. Shinto shrine in Tateyama (Chiba prefecture), dedicated to Ame no Futotama no Mikoto, said to be the ancestor of the Imbe family of Shinto ritualists, cited in the *Kojiki* in relation to the legend of Amaterasu. This *kami* is said to have accompanied Ninigi no Mikoto when he "descended" to the islands of Japan. Every year on August 10, the shrine has a festival devoted to him. The shrine was founded before the eighth century. *See* AME NO TOMI NO MIKOTO.

Awa Kenzō. Grand master (1880–1939) of *kyūdō* (Japanese archery), who taught his art to German philosopher Eugen Herrigel from 1923 to 1929. His most famous disciple was Anzawa Heijirō (1887–1970).

Awa no Kuni. The name of one of the 15 provinces that the Tōkaidō road once crossed, now in Chiba prefecture.
• Also the name of one of the six provinces that the Nankaidō road crossed, now in Tokushima prefecture.

Awano Seiho. Haiku poet (1899–1992), born near Nara, member of the Hototogisu group. He published a number of poetry collections—*Manryō* (1931), *Teihon seho kushū* (1947), *Kōshien* (1972), *Ryojin o harau* (Brushing Off the Dust of Travel), *Anata konata* (Here and There), and *Haiku no kokoro* (Spirit of the Haiku)—and founded the literary magazine *Katsuragi*.

Awa Odori. Popular dance, variant of the peasants' Bon Odori (Hōnen Odori) traditionally performed in Tokushima prefecture (formerly Awa province) on August 12–15 of each year. This dance is said to have been created about 1600, when the daimyo of the city distributed large amounts of *sake* to the people to inaugurate his new castle; drunk, they began to dance.

Awasaka Tsumao. Writer (b. 1933) of a series of stories, *Kage kikyō* (Shadow of the Bellflower), which received the Akutagawa Prize in 1990.

Awaseguchi kamesō. Burial method practiced in the Yayoi period (ca. 300 BC–AD 300), consisting of enclosing the body in two large urns *(kamekan)* placed mouth to mouth. This type of burial has been found from northern Kyushu to the Osaka region. With the body were placed a number of ritual objects, shell rings and bronze weapons, bronze mirrors, and iron utensils, most imported from the continent. *See* ARCHEOLOGY, KAMEKAN.

Awata (or Awataguchi). Town east of Kyoto, where, starting in 1624, kilns were built by a potter from Seto called Katō or Nomomura Ninsei. The porcelain made in these kilns was called Awata-*yaki*, Kinkozan, Kyō-*yaki*, or Kiyomizu-*yaki*, the last in the style of the family of Kiyomizu Rokubei. Nineteenth-century ceramists Okuda Eisen, Aoki Mokubei, Ninnami, Dōhachi, Kenza, and others imitated the Awata style. Production was mainly for export. *See* AOKI MOKUBEI.

Awataguchi Yoshimitsu. Blacksmith and sword maker (Awataguchi Tōshirō, ca. 1227–ca. 1291), established in the Awata district of Kyoto. A descendant of Awataguchi Kuniyori and a student of Awataguchi Kuniyoshi, he excelled in the manufacture of very short swords *(katana;* shorter than a *shaku,* or 30 cm), treasured by samurai for their fine workmanship and beauty. *See* KATANA, SŌSHŪMONO.

Awata no Mahito. Noble (d. 719) of the Nara court, ambassador *(kentōshi)* from Yamato to the Tang court in 702. The empress of China, Wu Zetian, gave him the title "Chief valet of the imperial house" in 703. He returned to Japan in 704 and was appointed *chūnagon* (counselor) and governor of Dazaifu. In 700, he collaborated with Prince Ōsakabe and Fujiwara no Fuhito to write the law code of the Taihō era, the *Taihō ritsuryō*. His Chinese name was Sutian Zhenren.

Awazu. Site of the current town of Ōtsu, on the shore of Lake Biwa, where a number of battles between the Minamoto and Taira took place in 1184, and where Minamoto no Yoshinaka was killed by Minamoto no Yoritomo's troops. In the Gichū-ji temple, built early in 1553 in memory of the revolt, is the tomb of the poet Bashō (d. 1694 in Osaka). Also called Awazugahara.

Awazu Kiyoshi. Graphic artist, born 1929 in Tokyo, and illustrator (theater and movie posters). In 1962, he won the Prix de Paris for his movie posters and a silver medal at the Milan Triennale. He received the silver medal at the Poster Biennale of Warsaw in 1969 and the grand prize for book illustration at Leipzig in 1974.

Aya. In the Nara period, class of artisans who worked as saddlemakers, brocade weavers, and writers in the Kai, Tamba, Mino, Harima, and Hizen regions. Most of them were descendants of Korean immigrants, and they formed a distinct class called *ayabe* (or *ayabito, ayauji,* or *Yamato no aya no atae*).
• Silk brocade fabric used in Japan, consisting of threads woven on the diagonal, a technique im-

ported from Korea or China by *ayahatori* in the sixth and seventh centuries. Also called *ayaginu*.

• **Ayahatori.** Women who went to Japan from China and Korea before 645 and whose skills as weavers were highly appreciated at the court and in the shrines and temples. They introduced weaving techniques to Japan. Also called *kurahatori*.

Aya no tsuzumi. Title of Noh play: an elderly gardener falls in love with a lady of the palace, who asks him to make music with a drum of stretched silk. Unable to do so, in despair the old man drowns himself. A variation, called *Koi no Omoni*, replaces the drum with a heavy stone that the old man must carry around the garden a hundred times.

Ayatsuri-shibai. Puppet theater developed in Kyoto and Osaka in the early seventeenth century from the ancient art of puppeteers *(kugutsu)*, with the advent of the first *jōruri*, or recited dramas with shamisen accompaniment. *Ayatsuri-shibai* is the predecessor of the Bunraku puppet theater, which began in Osaka in 1734. European puppet theater is also called *ayatsuri-shibai*. Also called *ayatsuri-ningyō, ningyō-jōruri* (doll drama). *See* BUNRAKU, JŌRURI.

Ayu. "Sweetfish." Small freshwater fish *(Plecoglossus altivelis)* in the Salmoniformes order, about 15 to 20 cm long, much loved by the Japanese. *Ayu* are caught using trained cormorants, at night by the glow of torches, especially in Gifu, and they are also farmed. This fish, considered a good omen, is cited as such in the *Kojiki*, the *Nihon shoki*, and the *Man'yōshū*, in the eighth century. The fishing season for *ayu* begins about June 1. The image of this small fish adorns the Banzai flag, flown when an emperor is crowned.
→ *See* ISHIKAWA CHIYOMATSU.

Ayui-shō. Grammar treatise written in 1773 by Fujitana Shigeaya and published in 1778. It was the first grammar of the Japanese language.

Ayukawa Nobuo. Poet (Uemura Ryūichi, 1920–86), born in Tokyo. He was a member of the Arechi literary group. Among his most important works are *Ayukawa Nobuo shishū* (1955), *Shinda otoko* (The Dead Man, 1947), and *Gendaishi to wa nani ka* (1949), a book of critiques of modern Japanese poetry.

Azana. Name adopted by certain scholars and artists; their real name is reserved for use by their family and close friends. A person could use a number of *azana* over the course of his or her life, according to an ancient Chinese custom. *Chin.: zi. See* ADANA, GŌ, NAMES.

Azechi. Title of an inspector of the provincial government, created by Empress Gencho in 719, abolished a bit later, then reinstituted from 1868 to 1871. Also called *ansatsushi. See* JUNSATSUSHI.

Azechi Umetarō. Engraver, born 1912 in Ehime prefecture. A student of Un'ichi Hiratsuka, his subject matter was drawn from mountains and their inhabitants. He also wrote some books on Japan's mountain populations and the art of rock climbing. He had exhibitions in São Paulo, Lugano, Zurich, and other foreign cities.

Azekura-zukuri. Type of wooden construction specific to certain ancient buildings—storehouses, granaries, etc.—probably dating from the early centuries AD, built on short, massive pilings anchored deeply in the ground. The walls are made of stacks of beams, triangular in cross-section, set angle on angle. When the weather is dry, the wood contracts and allows air flow. When the air is humid, the wood swells and the structure is sealed. In this way, a constant humidity level is maintained in the building, allowing for excellent preservation of cereals and other goods stored in it. The best example of this architecture to be seen today is the Shōsō-in within the precincts of Tōdai-ji temple in Nara, which dates from the eighth century and has preserved intact to the present day the treasures that were stored there. Also called *seirōgumi. See* SHŌSŌ-IN.

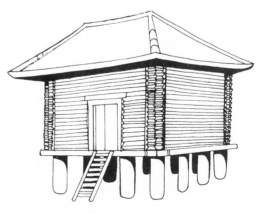

Azekura-zukuri granary

Azuchi. Small village near Lake Biwa, in the former province of Ōmi, where Oda Nobunaga had a castle designed by Niwa Nagahide in 1576. It was decorated by the best artists of the time and is considered the prototype of classic Japanese castles. Its donjon *(tenshu)* had seven stories, and the interior screens were painted by Kanō Eitoku. Each level had decorations of different styles and subjects. Destroyed by Akechi Mitsuhide in 1582, only its ruins remain. Today's town of Azuchi (Shiga prefecture) also contains the ruins of the Kannon-ji castle, which was the seat of the Sasaki family, and the Kuwanomi-dera temple, where, tradition has it, the first blackberry bushes brought from China by Fujiwara no Kamatari's son, then a monk under the name Jōe, were planted.

• **Azuchi-momoyama.** This name is given to the "dictators' period," from 1582 to 1600 (or from 1574 to 1615, depending on the writer), after the names of the castles of Nobunaga (in Azuchi) and Hideyoshi (in Momoyama, near Kyoto). *See* HISTORY, MOMOYAMA.

• **Azuchi shūron.** Great religious debate that took place in 1579 in the Azuchi castle, in the presence of Oda Nobunaga, between the monks of the Nichiren and Jōdo sects, following disturbances due to the intransigence of the Nichiren supporters. The debate turned against the Nichiren followers, and three of their most virulent preachers, among them Fuden Nichimon, were executed. The monks of the Nichiren temples, fearing more widespread persecution, admitted that they had overstepped themselves and promised to be less intolerant. They were nevertheless forced to pay a considerable fine to Oda Nobunaga's treasury.

Azukari-dokoro. Administrative office of the *shōen* (estates) which, in the late Heian period, was charged with collecting land taxes for the emperor and the aristocracy. This office was replaced by the *jitō* during the Kamakura period. *See* JITŌ.

• **Azukari-mōsu.** *See* KAMPAKU.

Azuki. Type of red beans *(Phaseolus angularis),* probably introduced from China before the fifth century and cultivated in Japan since that time. In Japanese cooking today, they may be simply boiled and served with rice *(sekihan),* or used to make sweets *(yōkan),* conserves *(ama-nattō),* soups, and so on. *Azuki* beans are cultivated mainly in

Hokkaido and constitute an important part of the Japanese diet. *See* COOKING, SEKIHAN.

Azuma. Former name for the eastern part of Japan. *See* AZUMA NO KUNI, BANDŌ.

• **Azuma-asobi.** Ancient chants and dances of the eastern islands of Japan, accompanied by musical instruments. During the Heian period, they were performed mainly during Buddhist or Shinto religious ceremonies and did not become truly popular until the Muromachi period, when they lost their religious character. These dances were revived after 1813 and are still performed in the Shinto shrines of Iwashimizu, Kamo, and Kasuga in Kyoto, as well as at the imperial court. Also called Azuma-*mai.*

• **Azuma-goto.** Another name for the *wagon,* a type of koto in style before the thirteen-string *sō* and the seven-string *kin* zithers were imported from China during the Asuka and Nara periods. The body of this type of koto is made of paulownia or Japanese cypress and is five to six *shaku* and three *sun* (1.5–1.9 m) in length. Its six strings are strummed with artificial fingernails made of water-buffalo horn. Also called Yamato-goto, Kami-goto, Mutsunoo, Tobinoo-goto. *See* KOTO.

• *Azuma-kagami.* "Mirror of the East." Historical chronicle about the period of the Kamakura *bakufu,* from 1180 to 1266, written in *kambun,* an ancient form of Chinese, by unknown authors, probably scribes of the shogunate. It has 52 chapters (or books). It is missing a number of events (which, perhaps, were never written about). About a dozen editions of this work are known; it is essential for knowledge of this period, with the Kanazawa Bunko and Kikkawa (found in 1911) being the most important.

• *Azuma-mondō.* Treatise on *renga* linked verse, composed by Sōgi Iio around 1470. Also titled *Sumidagawa.*

• **Azuma no Kuni.** Former name of all of the territory east of the Ashigara-dake pass (province of Sagami), which, before the sixth century, was a separate country populated by the Ainu, distinct from Yamato, which conquered and assimilated it in the sixth century.

• *Azuma-uta.* Poems of the *Man'yōshū* written by poets from eastern Japan and containing various dialectal expressions from the late seventh and early eighth centuries. There are about 230 of them.

• **Azuma-san.** Active volcanoes in Yamagata prefecture, culminating in Mt. Nishi Azuma (2,024 m). They last erupted in 1900.

Azuma Ryōtarō. Politican and physician (1893–1983), born in Osaka. He studied in London; upon his return to Japan, he specialized in sports physiology and became a professor of medicine at the University of Tokyo. He was president of a number or sports associations and, in 1953, became president of Ibaraki University. He was on the 1950 and 1964 Olympic committees, and was governor of Tokyo from 1959 to 1967.

Azuma Tsuneyori. Poet (Tō Tsuneyori, 1401–94), son of Tō Masayuki, also a poet. Having succeeded his father as daimyo of Shimotsuke, he lost his territories in the province of Mino during the Ōnin War and took refuge in the east (whence his chosen name, Azuma). He then went to Kyoto and devoted himself to poetry. His collections are titled *Tō yashū*

kikigaki, Tō yashū shōsoku, and *Tō yashū kashū.* The poet Iio Sōgi was his disciple.

Azumi no Hirafu. Imperial bureaucrat who, in the sixth century, was in charge of official relations between Korea and the court of Japan. Allied with Paekche (Kudara), he fought against the Silla (Shiragi) kingdom in 663 in the Battle of Hakusukinoe in Korea.

• **Azumi no Muraji.** Title given to bureaucrats charged with the imperial table in the seventh century. This charge was hereditary and reserved for the Azuchi family, which had controlled the fishers of Yamato.

Azusa. Catalpa tree *(Catalpa syringifolia)* with ornamental foliage that was used, with bamboo, to decorate archery bows.

Azusa-miko. Priestess in popular Shintoism who was a shamaness and soothsayer (*see* BOKUSEN); she invoked the gods by strumming the string of an archery bow called *azusa-yumi* or by various other methods. *See* AGATO-MIKO.

B. In Japanese, this consonant exists only in conjunction with a vowel: *ba, bi, bu, be, bo.* It is a "nigorization" (modification) of the corresponding sounds *ha, hi, hu, he, ho* of the hiragana and katakana syllabaries. *See* NIGORI.

Baba Keiji. Economist and administration theorist (1897–1961), born in Osaka. He studied the economic principles of Germany and the United States and attempted to apply some of them to Japan after the Second World War. His writings on the subject stimulated modernization of corporate management and encouraged Japan's economic recovery.

Baba Kochō. Writer (Baba Katsuya, 1869–1940), born in Kōchi. Baba Tatsui's younger brother, he joined the Bungaku Kai literary group. His novels were not very successful, so he became a translator of French writers, such as Alphonse Daudet, and of Russian writers, such as Tolstoy and Gorky.

Baba Sajūro. Interpreter (1787–1822) from Dutch for the Tokugawa shogunate and meteorologist. He wrote various works on this science, including *Kanji kōrei, Seiyō doryōkō,* and *Seisetsu zakki.*

Baba Tatsui. Political scientist and essayist (1850–88), son of a minor daimyo from Tosa (Kōchi prefecture) and older brother of Baba Kochō. He studied English, law, and political science in London and wrote editorials for *The Examiner* in which he demanded a review of the Unequal Treaties (*see* JŌYAKU KAISEI). He returned to Japan in 1878 and was a founder of the Jiyūtō (Liberal party) in 1881. He was sentenced to one year in prison in 1885 for his activism in favor of increased liberties; on his release, he went into exile in the United States. He died in Philadelphia. His most important work was written in English: *The Political Condition of Japan, Showing the Despotism and Incompetency of the Cabinet and the Aims of the Popular Parties* (1888).

Baba Tsunego. Journalist and politician (1875–1956). He worked at the *Japan Times* starting in 1900, as well as at various other newspapers, and was editor of the *Yomiuri Shimbun* in 1945.

Bachi. Large triangular plectrum made of wood or ivory, used to play the *biwa* and shamisen. *See* SHAMISEN.

Bachiru. Technique of engraving on ivory dyed blue, green, or red, made with a pointed tool of the same name. Practiced in China during the Tang dynasty, it was introduced to Japan during the Nara period.

Bahan-sen. Japanese pirate ships that sailed the coasts of Korea and China from the thirteenth to the sixteenth century. The name derives from Hachiman (god of war), whose name was written on their flags. These ships were also used, mainly in the sixteenth century, to transport contraband. After the Chinese executed the captain of the Ōchoku fleet, the ships gradually disappeared. *See* WAKŌ.

Baichō. "Annex" funerary tumuli built beside the large burial mounds *(kofun),* designed to bury votive objects and other items to accompany the dead interred in the main tomb. These subsidiary tumuli were sometimes built, according to the *Nihon shoki,* for people who died at the same time as the lord or for relatives of the lord, but this is not certain. Also called Baizuka. *See* KOFUN.

Baii. Trafficking in court ranks that took place in the Nara period to procure revenue for the state, running counter to the legal institutions for the sale of these titles, called *shokurō.* This practice continued after 800, when it was banned by the Dajōkan; it again became common during the Heian period and was even more widespread during the Kamakura period; the attribution of ranks and titles often having been a reward, the impoverished aristocracy resorted to their sale in order to sustain their lifestyle. However, the practice disappeared almost completely in the mid-fourteenth century, since court titles no longer had value under the Ashikaga shogunate. *See* I.

Baikun Jiken. Scandal that broke in 1929, when it became public that the head of the awards department, Amaoka Naoyoshi (or Naoka), had sold recommendations to individuals wanting to receive decorations. He was sentenced in 1933. Also called Kunshō Jiken.

Baiōken Nagaharu. Painter (Hasegawa Nagaharu; *gō:* Baiōken, Shōsuiken, Harunobu, Mitsunobu, active ca. 1710–55) of the Kaigetsudō school. His main output was ukiyo-e prints used for book illustration.

Baishin. Vassals of vassals, in the Japanese feudal system. During the Tokugawa period (1600–1868), the daimyo themselves, being direct vassals *(jikisan)* of the shogun, could have a number of vassals in their service. *See* JIKISAN.

Baishōron. "Discourse on Plum Trees and Pines." Fourteenth-century war chronicle *(gunkimono).* The writer is unknown, but was likely someone close to Ashikaga Takauji between 1352 and 1387; the text is quoted in the *Taiheiki,* especially in book 18. This short text deals essentially with the history of the Kamakura shogunate and is a valuable historical document because of its precision. No longer available in its entirety, the *Baishōron* was partially preserved in the Edo-period *Gunsho ruijū,* which treated it as a classic.

Ba-i sōshi emaki. An *emakimono* (illustrated handscroll) dealing with veterinary medicine, written and illustrated in the thirteenth century. Also called *Uma-i no sōshi.*

Baiu. "Rain of the plums." The rainy season, usually coinciding with the month of June. The extreme humidity is due to atmospheric depressions from the mainland moving eastward after passing over the Yellow Sea. It is the time when plums ripen and rice is planted. Also called *tsuyu.*

Baiyūken Katsunobu. Painter (early eighteenth century) of the Kaigetsudō school.

Bakan. Former name of the city of Shimonoseki.
   • Also, name given to Ma Han, a southern province on the Korean peninsula. *See* KUDARA.

Bakemono. General term for phantoms and ghosts. They play an important role in Noh and Kabuki, as well as in literature of the Edo period. They are also popular in children's literature. Phantom objects are also designated by this word (*see* BUMBUKU CHAGAMA). Also called *obake.*

Baku. Mythical animal of Chinese origin, vaguely resembling a tapir, supposed to be able to swallow anything, even mountains. It also swallows children's nightmares.

Bakufu. "Government under the tent." A word originally designating the quarters of a military commander during a war campaign. In the Kamakura period, it came to mean the seat of the shogunal military government; later, all forms of military government. There were three *bakufu* in Japan's history: Kamakura, Muromachi, and Edo. Also called *buke seiji* (warrior government). However, the Edo *bakufu* is now more commonly called *bakuhan taisei* (regime of the *bakufu* and the *han,* or clans).

• **Bakumatsu.** "End of the *bakufu.*" Term used to describe the period of instability in the Tokugawa shogunate between 1850 and 1868.

Bakurō. "Horse trader." Name given to horse and cattle traders of Kyushu, Chūgoku, and Tōhoku, whose profession was inherited.

• **Bakurō-gashira.** During the Edo period, title given to the shogunal bureaucrats charged with recruiting labor for public works. This duty was traditionally the aegis of the Yamamoto family.

Bälz, Erwin von. German physician (1849–1913) who lived in Japan from 1876 to 1905 and married a Japanese woman. A physiology professor at the

University of Tokyo, he also taught Western methods of obstetrics and gynecology and conducted research on parasitic worms. Interested in ethnicity, he established that the Japanese "race" had emerged from a mixture of Mongolian and Malaysian peoples. His journal, *Das Leben eines deutschen Arztes im erwachenden Japan* (1931), included notes on life in Japan during the Meiji era.

Bambayashi Mitsuhira. Writer (1813–64) and Buddhist monk of the Shinshū sect. When he returned to lay life, he aligned himself with the emperor during the *bakumatsu* disturbances and participated in the beginning of an insurrection against the shogunate in 1863. He was taken prisoner and beheaded in Kyoto. He is best known for his studies on the classics of Japanese literature. Also known as Tomobayashi Mitsuhira.

Bambetsu. Name given to foreigners, particularly Koreans, who settled in the country starting in the ninth century. *See also* KIKAJIN.

Bamboo. Plants of the family Gramineae *(Phyllostachys),* of which there are more than 400 species on the islands of Japan. Japanese bamboo forms horizontal rhizomes in which the roots are intertwined; villagers often take refuge in bamboo thickets during earthquakes. They can grow extremely quickly (30–40 cm in one night), and the largest can reach 20 m in height. There are two main categories of bamboo in Japan: *take* (the larger types), whose shoots *(takenoko)* are edible, and *sasa,* which do not grow over 2 m and form a dense carpet of vegetation. While *sasa* is not much appreciated except for its leaves, which are used in packaging, *take* is highly valued for its edible shoots and its woody stalks, which have many practical uses. The different varieties are used in various crafts. The *madake* has large leaves; the *kikkōchiku* is mainly ornamental; the *mōsōchiku* is used to make *shakuhachi* flutes; the *hoteichiku,* and so on. The *Bambusa* genus comprises most of the *sasa* bamboo, which has many varieties: *chimakizasa, azumazasa, kumazasa,* and so on. The stalks of a medium-sized bamboo, *yadake (Pseudosasa japonica),* were once used to make arrows. While *sasa* bamboo rarely flowers (and always in a group in a single region), *take* bamboo flowers only once every sixty years or so and dies afterward.

Ban. Ornamental banners used in Buddhist temples. They are generally composed of a triangular head *(bandō),* a vertical rectangular body *(ban-*

shin), and arms *(banshu)* and legs *(bansoku)* represented by ribbons. Some banners are round or oval and are made not of cloth but of leather or metal, cut out and gilded. Also called *hata. See also* BANZAI, KEMAN.

Ban Dainagon ekotoba. An *emakimono* attributed to Tokiwa Mitsunaga (late twelfth century). This illuminated handscroll portrays events that took place on March 10, 866, at one of the gates to the Kyoto imperial palace. On that day, Tomo no Yoshio, or Ban Dainagon, one of the grand counselors, set fire to the Ōtemmon gate, then circulated a rumor that his rival, Minamoto no Makoto, minister of the left, was responsible for the fire. The plot failed, and he was exiled to the province of Izu *(see* TOMO NO YOSHIO). *Ban Dainagon ekotoba* is more than 20 m long and about 31.5 cm high, with continuous illustration, colored in the traditional technique of *tsukuri-e.* The figures are portrayed in a realistic manner, with fluid lines in the free-style drawing typical of the Tosa family, to which Tokiwa Mitsunaga belonged. This *emakimono* is sometimes called *Tomo no Dainagon ekotoba.*

Bandaisan. Volcano (height: 1,819 m) in northern Fukushima prefecture. When it erupted in July 1888, the lava flows blocked the Nagase river system, resulting in the formation of a number of lakes. It currently has four distinct cones. This volcano is part of Bandai-Asahi National Park.

Bandō. Former name of the eight provinces located west of Osaka: Sagami, Musashi, Awa, Kazusa, Hitachi, Shimōsa, Shimotsuke, and Kōzuke, which were traditionally fiefs belonging to the Taira clan. *See also* AZUMA.

Bandō Hikosaburō. Family of Kabuki actors: B. H. I (1693–1751), the founder; II (1741–68); III (1754–1828); IV (1800–73); V (1832–77); VI (1886–1938); VII (b. 1916). This family changed its family name to Uzaemon during the twentieth century. *See* IEMOTO.

• **Bandō Mitsugorō.** Family of Kabuki actors: B. M. I (1745–82), the founder; II (dates unknown); III (1775–1831), son of I, famous for his *wagoto* roles and founder of Kabuki Bandōryū, the Kabuki classical dance and theater school; IV (1802–63); V (dates unknown); VI (dates unknown); VII (1872–1961); VIII (Yososuke, 1906–75), declared a Living National Treasure in 1973. He wrote a number of works on Kabuki.

• **Bandōryū.** *See* BANDŌ mitsugoro iii.

• **Bando Tamasaburō.** Kabuki actor (b. 1950) specializing in female roles *(onnagata)* and film actor.

• **Bando Tsumasaburō.** Film actor (Tamura Denkichi, 1901–53), also known as Bantsuma, born in Tokyo. He launched his own company in 1925; in 1926, he moved to Kyoto. Famous in silent films, this actor-producer faded from view during the era of the talkies, although he later appeared in a few films, notably, in Inagaki Hiroshi's *Muhō matsu no isshō* (The Life of Matsu the Untamed) in 1943.

Bangen. Master of the tea ceremony (*gō*: Kian, 1566–1653) of the Senke school. In 1600, he went to the Ryukyu Islands and became master of the tea ceremony in the king's court. He served as the intermediary between this court and the Edo *bakufu* during the 1669 invasion of the islands by the Shimazu warriors from the province of Satsuma.

Bankata. In the Edo period, a term used for the shogunate's military units, particularly the guards *(gokenin, hatamoto)* who took turns executing military obligations (service at the imperial palace, guarding the coasts, surveillance of the shogun's residences, defense of the castles, etc.). During the Meiji Restoration of 1868, the *bankata* formed the basis of the national army.

Bankei Eitaku. Buddhist monk (Bankei Yōtaku, 1622–93), born in Abashi. He belonged to the Rinzai sect of Zen. After studying under Umpo in the Zuiō-ji temple in Akō, he went to Nagasaki, where he served under the Chinese Chan (Zen) monk Daozhe Chaoyuan (*Jap.*: Dōja Chōgen). He is said to have had 50,000 disciples. He founded a number of temples and preached a simple doctrine favoring the eternal character of the spirit of Buddha *(fushōzen)* and rejecting the use of koan, which he felt were useless. Posthumously, he was given the name Bucchi-kōsai Zenji.

Banki. Fifth and last phase of the prehistoric period of Japan, corresponding to the late Jōmon. This word is also used to characterize the last period of an era or an art form. *See* JŌMON-JIDAI.

Ban Kōkei. Poet and scholar (Ban Sukeyoshi, Shōemon; *gō*: Kandenshi, Kandenro; *monk's name:* Kōkei, 1733–1806), born in Ōmi and lived in Kyoto. A scholar of Japanese literature, he wrote a number of historical and literary commentaries (such as *Kokka wakumon*), a history of style *(Kunitsubumi yoyo no ato),* a collection of essays (*Kanden kōhitsu,* ca. 1805), and a collection of biographies of famous people of his time *(Kenseikijinden)*. His poems, mainly in the *waka* genre, are collected in *Kanden eisō.*

Banko-yaki. Decorated pottery produced in Yokkaichi (Mie prefecture), beginning in the late eighteenth century by Nunami Rōzan (1718–77), and then at Ise and Edo; mainly bowls and accessories for the tea ceremony, *sake* bottles, platters, and so on, as well as Chinese Ming-style ewers. These ceramics had a pale-yellow milky glaze with red, green, and blue decoration. About 1830, Mori Yūsetsu (1808–82), another potter, rebuilt the kilns at Kuwana and Yokkaichi, which remained active through the Meiji era.

Banna-ji. Buddhist temple of the Shingi-Shingon sect, founded in 1196 in the town of Ashikaga by a monk named Banna, who installed there a statue of Dainichi Nyorai (*Skt.:* Mahāvairochana) sculpted by Unkei. The family of the Ashikaga shogun, who had property nearby, made it their temple of preference. Destroyed by fire in 1590, it was rebuilt in the seventeenth century in the style of the Kamakura period.

Ban Nobutomo. Confucian historian (Kotohi, 1773–1846), born in Wakasa. At first a simple warrior *(bushi),* in 1821, after a long illness, he fell in love with literary and historical studies and began to write works to refute the dogmatic theses of Hirata Atsutane about the superiority of the Japanese race, preferring a positivist approach to historical science. He wrote commentaries on the classics and more than 300 scholarly works, among them *Shiseiki nempyō* (Chronology of History Books), *Hikobai* (Essays), and *Jinja shikō* (Reflections on the Shinto Shrines). His theories on history were taken up and developed at the beginning of the Meiji era.

Banks. Before 1868 and the advent of the Meiji era, there were few banking institutions, each major clan issuing its own coins and the state controlling only the gold and silver currencies. Wealthy merchants often became bankers (or, rather, silver lenders), and the large temples often acted as sponsors for commercial enterprises. It was only in 1871 that Japanese currency was unified, based on the yen, which had parity with the Mexican silver dollar.

National and private banks were founded (such as the Mitsui Bank, founded in 1876). The Bank of Japan was created only in 1881, to respond to the needs of international trade. In 1897, Japan adopted the gold standard. The banks then became increasingly important as credit institutions and financing agencies: thus, large banks were created as part of the industrial and financial conglomerates *(zaibatsu),* such as Sumitomo, Mitsui, and Mitsubishi.

At the beginning of the twentieth century, although Japan's trade balance remained at a slight deficit, the banks rarely solicited foreign investors. After the Second World War, the yen was greatly devalued and it became easier to export from Japan. The banks then made loans to companies at low interest rates, making it easier for them to expand. Starting about 1975, capital investments caused a rise in the stock markets, and around 1980 the Tokyo Stock Exchange became one of the world's most important financial centers. After 1990, the fall in stock values and the rise in real-estate prices caused many bank failures. Despite the imposition of a value-added tax (1990) to ease the government deficit, the economy suffered and public debt grew.

The Japanese banking system, overall, is similar to banking in most countries, with the common financial instruments (deposits, bonds, portfolios, credit cards, etc.). Many banks have established subsidiaries in foreign cities. *See* CURRENCY, DAIICHI GINKŌ, ECONOMY, FUJI GINKŌ, GINZA, HOKKAIDŌ, TAKUSHOKI GINKŌ, JAPAN (STATISTICS), KŌNOIKE, MATSUKATA MASAYOSHI, MITSUBISHI, MITSUI, NIHON GINKŌ, RYŌGAISHŌ, SAITAMA GINKŌ, SANWA GINKŌ, SUMITOMO, TOKAI GINKŌ, TRADE, YASUDA, YEN.

Banri Shūkyū. Buddhist monk and poet (Shittō Banri; *gō:* Baian, 1428–after 1503), born in Ōmi. He belonged to the Rinzai sect of Zen and led a wandering life before settling permanently in the province of Mino, abandoning the monastic robes to marry. Literate in both Chinese and Japanese, he wrote commentaries *(Tenshihaku, Chōchūkō, Gyōfū-shū)* on Chinese poets and several interpretations of Buddhist texts. He also wrote a collection of Chinese poems, *Baika mujinzo,* named after his hermitage.

Banryūkyō. Bronze mirrors, Chinese (imported) and Japanese (from the first to the fifth century), generally with an alloy molding *(hakudō)* decorated with a motif called "tiger and dragon" on the back. They are divided into two main styles, those with one-headed dragons and those with four-headed dragons. These mirrors were found mainly in the *kofun* tumuli. Also called *ryūkokyō. See* KAGAMI, KYŌ.

Bansai Shichiyū. Collective name given in Japanese history to seven famous sixteenth-century warriors: Miyoshi Chōkei, Ōuchi Yoshitaka, Amako Haruhisa, Shimazu Yoshihisa, Mōri Motonari, Ōtomo Sōrin, and Chōsokabe Motochika.

Bansha. "Society of Barbarian Studies." Created circa 1830 by a group of scholars studying Western science and culture (among them Watanabe Kazan, Takano Chōei, and Ozeki San'ei), this society promoted Western Learning and criticized the National Seclusion policy. The shogunate brought them to trial (known as Bansha no Goku, "Imprisonment of the Bansha members") on charges of insurrection, which, in 1839, resulted in the sentencing of the most influential members: Kazan was placed under house arrest, while Chōei was sentenced to life in prison. This trial considerably slowed the growth in Western studies. *See* TORII YŌZŌ.

Banshō. During the Nara period, name for carpenters *(daiku)* specializing in construction of temples and shrines for the court, nobles with estates *(shōen),* monasteries, and the shogunate. These carpenters were also peasants who never left their villages unless they were asked to go somewhere.

Bansho Shirabe Dokoro. School created in Edo in 1856 to study and translate foreign books and teach Western sciences *(yōgaku).* It adopted the principles of the school created in 1811, Bansho-wage Goyō (Government Office for Translation of Barbarian Books). It was established in the Akasaka district in 1855 as the Yōgakusho, then in the Kudan district, and renamed the Bansho Shirabesho in 1862. This school later became the faculty of arts and sciences of the University of Tokyo.

Bantō. Head of a work unit in medieval villages belonging to an estate *(shōen)* collectively responsible for paying taxes. This position disappeared in the sixteenth century, but the word remained in the Edo period to designate clerks in trade companies.
→ *See* YAMAGATA BANTŌ.

Banzai. "Ten thousand years." Derived from the Chinese *wansui,* the cry or toast made as a sign of victory or congratulations. It implies "Long live the Emperor," equivalent to "Long live the King!"

• A banner of this name, bearing the image of a fish *(ayu)*, is raised in honor of the emperor during the coronation ceremony. *See* AYU.

• **Banzai Jiken.** Anti-Japanese uprising that began on March 1, 1919, in Seoul and spread rapidly throughout the Korean provinces. It was brutally suppressed by Japanese troops, who made more than 20,000 arrests. This repression provoked the creation in Shanghai of an anti-Japanese "provisional government in exile," which survived until 1934. Also called San'ichi Jiken, San'ichi Undō (March 1 Movement).

Banzuin Chōbei (Chōbe). Warrior (ca. 1622–51) born in Karatsu, famous for his skill as a fencer and his adherence to Bushido. He settled in the Asakusa district of Edo, where he established an employment bureau for masterless samurai *(rōnin)*. He was assassinated by Mizuno Jūrozaemon. His life and death were the subject of legend and inspired novels and Kabuki plays. *See* MACHI-YAKKO.

Baren. Ink pad made with bark or bamboo leaves, used by printers of ukiyo-e to ink the engraved woodblocks *(hangi)* before printing. *See* BOKASHI-ZURI, UKIYO-E.

Baseball. This American game was imported to Japan along with Western ideas of sports and competition. The first baseball games took place at Waseda University in Tokyo circa 1890. In 1905, the first national team, composed of students, was formed to play the Stanford University team in the United States. Although they lost, the Waseda students returned to Japan with standard baseball uniforms. The game was taken up again after the Second World War and quickly became extremely popular, especially among young people. The most famous player was Ō Sadaharu. Games and tournaments generally begin in spring and are widely televised. Along with sumo, baseball is the most popular sport in Japan.

Bashaku. Laborers who by the late Kamakura period (1185–1333) controlled the transportation of goods from the countryside to the cities; they used packhorses, breaking the custom that horses did not bear loads. The *bashaku* played an important role in popular uprisings during the Muromachi period by spreading news and ideas. During the Edo shogunate, the *bashaku* formed guilds, which, in addition to providing transportation of goods, supplied the relay points on major routes with horses. *See* BAKURŌ, MAGO.

Bashō. Poet (Matsuo Manefusa, Matsuo Chūzaemon; *gō*: Bashō, Mumei-an, Fura, Hyōchuan, Tōsei, 1644–94) and Zen monk, born in the province of Iga into a samurai family. In 1666, he left his clan, for unknown reasons, and went to Kyoto, where he studied haiku and *waka* poetry under Kitamura Kigin (1624–1705) and the Chinese classics under Itō Tan'an. Moving to Edo in 1672, he devoted himself to painting and composing haiku, the poetry form in which he excelled, mixing the sense of rhythm inherent to Chinese poetry with Japanese realism. Because his hermitage had a banana tree *(bashō)*, he chose Bashō as a pen name. Many disciples came to study with him. A Zen monk with no particular affiliation, in 1684 Bashō began to wander, returning from each of his travels with a "journal": *Nozaraki kikō* (1685), *Kashima kikō* (1687), *Sarashina kikō* (1688), *Oku no hosomichi* (Narrow Road to the Deep North, 1689), *Genjuan-ki* (1690), *Saga nikki* (1691), *Oi no kobumi*, and others. First influenced by the Kofu and Danrin schools, he later created his own style and published a number of collections of haiku, including *Minashiguri* (1683), *Fuyu no hi* (Winter Light, 1684), *Haru no hi* (Spring Light, 1686), *Arano* (1689), *Hisago* (1691), and *Sumidawara* (1694). In these poems, rhythmic notations of 17 syllables each, he evoked or suggested an ambience, a state of mind, the beauty inherent in things and beings, sentiments based on the feeling of *sabi* (simplicity), *shiori* (suggestion), *hosomi* (love of small things), and *karumi* (sense of humor). His style is called *shōfu*. Bashō died in Osaka in the house of the poetess Sono Jo. His disciples were called Bashō Juttetsu.

• *Bashō haikai shichibushū.* Collective name for seven collections of haiku written by Bashō and some of his disciples: *Fuyu no hi, Haru no hi, Arano, Hisago, Sarumino, Sumidawara,* and *Zuko sarumino* (published in 1698). *See* BASHŌ, HAIKU.

• *Bashō Juttetsu* (or Jittetsu). "Ten Great Disciples of Bashō." Includes some of the most famous haiku poets: Enomoto (Takarai) Kikaku (1661–1707), Hattori Ransetsu (1654–1707), Mukai Kyorai (1651–1704), Kagami Shikō (1665–1731), Naitō Jōsō (1662–1704), Sugiyama Sampū (1647–1732), Shida Yaha (1663–1740), Ōchi Etsujin (1656–1730), Tachibana Hokushi (1665–1718), Morikawa Kyoroku (1656–1715), and Bonchō (d. 1714).

Bashōfu. Type of Okinawa fabric, made with the fibers of a type of banana tree similar to the plantain.

Basshi. Small copper cymbals used during certain Buddhist ceremonies to punctuate the reading of sutras *(kyō).* Also called *nyōhashi.*
• In archeology, ritual tooth extraction, which seems to have been practiced during the Jōmon period, as evidenced by certain adult skeletons of the time.

Bassui Tokushō. Zen Buddhist monk (Battai Tokushō, 1327–87) of the Rinzai sect, born in the province of Sagami. His teachings, which he collected in a small book called *Wadei Bassui-shū* (1386), attracted a large number of disciples. He wrote other religious commentaries in Japanese (in contrast to the Zen tradition of writing in Chinese), including *Enzan kana hōgo* and *Bassui oshō goroku,* which were popular during the Edo period.

Basū Sennin. Japanese name of the Indian Buddhist sage Vasubandhu, considered one of the Nijūhachi Bushū. He is portrayed as an old man holding a scroll of his writings. There are few images of him; the best known, dating from the thirteenth century, is in the Sanjūsangendo in Kyoto.

Batchelor, John. Anglican missionary (1854–1944), born in London. He learned Chinese in Hong Kong, then went to Japan, where he spent most of his life. In 1877, he founded a school in Hakodate and began to study the Ainu language and customs. It is thanks to his efforts that studies on the Ainu were undertaken, for several Japanese scholars followed in his footsteps. His *Ainu–English–Japanese Dictionary* (1899) remains a remarkable source for this language. In 1940, the war forced him to leave Japan and return to England.

Bateren. Japanese pronunciation of the Portuguese *padre,* the word used starting in the sixteenth century for Christian missionaries, including priests Francis Xavier, Luis Frois, and Alessandro Valignano.

Batō. Type of Bugaku dance in the Rin'yūgaku style. *See* BUGAKU.

Batō Kannon. "Horse-Head Kannon." Japanese form of Hayagrīva, the Buddhist aspect of an avatar of the Hindu god Vishnu and the horse-savior Balāha, an incarnation of Avalokiteshvara. Also one of the "kings of wisdom" (Vidyārāja; *Jap.:* Myō-ō), an aspect of the Buddha Amida, in which he is represented with two horse heads in his hair, one white and one blue. Also called Batō Myō-ō, Mezu, Kichijō Komagata.

• **Batō-in.** Form of mudra specific to Batō Kannon and Batō Myō-ō.

Batsu (Hatsu). Modern word used as a suffix, designating a particular clique or faction composed of people with affinities that may be geographical, related to social or political status, or involving family ties. In combination, *hatsu* becomes *-batsu.* Thus, groups of students from the same university are called *gakubatsu;* groups formed of family alliances, *keibatsu* (or *mombatsu*); military cliques, *gumbatsu;* groups formed by members of former domains *(han), hambatsu;* and conglomerates created by groups of financiers, *zaibatsu. Kyōdobatsu* are influence groups comprising persons from the same region who control one or several industrial or business sectors.

Battles, naval (major).
—Battle of Hakusukinoe: 663.
—Battle of Dannoura: Apr. 25, 1185.
—Naval battle of Cheju (Korea): 1593.
—Battle of the Yellow Sea: Sept. 17, 1894. *See* KŌKAI KAISEN.
—Battle of Tsushima: 1905. *See* TSUSHIMA.
From 1941 to 1945:
—Japanese attack on Pearl Harbor: Dec. 7, 1941.
—Japanese attack on the Philippines: Dec. 8, 1941.
—Battle of the South China Sea: Dec. 10, 1941.
—Battle of Singapore: Feb. 15, 1942.
—Japanese landing at Java: Mar. 1, 1942.
—Japanese attack on the Ceylon fleet: Apr. 1942.
—Battle of the Coral Sea: May 6–8, 1942.
—Fall of Corregidor, Philippines, May 6, 1942.
—Battle of Midway: June 4–6, 1942.
—American landing at Guadalcanal: Aug. 7, 1942.
—Battles of the Aleutians: May 11, 1943–July 1943.
—Battle of the Philippine Sea: June 19–20, 1944.
—Battle of Saipan: June 15–July 9, 1944.
—Battle of Guam: July 21–Aug. 10, 1944.
—Battle of the Gulf of Leyte: Oct. 20–25, 1944.

—American landing at Luzon: Jan. 9, 1945.
—Battle of Iwo Jima: Feb. 19–Mar. 17, 1945.
—Battle of Okinawa: Apr. 1–July 2, 1945.
→ *See* KAIGUN.

Battleships. *See* katō yoshiaki, kurofune, musashi, mutsu, nagato, shokaku, submarines, yamato.

Be. Before the seventh century, occupational groupings associated with the Yamato court or lineage groups *(uji).* The *bumin* (people in a *be*) had to remit part of their production or supply a certain amount of labor to the *uji* to which they were subject. The *bumin* generally added the suffix *-be* to the name of their craft or occupation to create a family name. Some Shinto priests were thus called *kamibe* (the origin of the name of the city of Kobe). At first there were many such names: *yamabe,* or forestry worker; *tomobe,* or general worker; *hajibe,* or potter; *imube,* or Shinto ritualist; *nishigoribe,* or silk weaver; *kinunuibe,* or tailor; *kuratsukuribe,* or saddlemaker; *umakaibe,* or horse and cattle breeder; and so on. Also called *tomo* (companion). *See* HATA, HATTORI.

Beato, Felice. Italian photographer, born circa 1825 in Venice, who settled in Yokohama in 1863 at Charles Wirgman's invitation. His photographs provide a remarkable visual record of Japanese society in the process of change in the late Edo period. In 1868, he published two books of photographs on Japan, *Native Types* and *Views of Japan,* the proofs of which were hand-colored by Wirgman. By 1869, Beato was working for himself; in 1877, he began to trade in Japanese objets d'art. *See* RATENITZ, WIRGMAN.

Bedwell, Frederick Le Breton. English naval officer who accompanied Lord Elgin's mission to Japan in 1858 and went to Tsushima in 1859, then to Nagasaki in 1861, before returning to England. He left a great number of drawings and paintings of Japanese landscapes and flora and fauna.

Beisen. Painter and book illustrator (Kubota Hiroshi, 1852–1906). He went blind in 1900. His *Beisen gadan* (Dialogue on Painting), published in 1902, is still considered a classic.

Bekkei. Special performances of Noh plays in spring and fall. Name also given to these performances when they take place in tribute to an individual person and are performed by amateur troupes.

Bekkō. Stomach shell from a tortoise *(kame)* carapace, once used to tell the future according to an ancient Chinese method. A branding iron was applied to the shell and the answers to questions were read in the cracks produced by the heat. Hexagonal patterns inspired by these tortoiseshells are also called *bekkō.* Also called *taimai,* from the name given to a type of turtle commonly found in the waters off the Ryukyu Islands. *See* KAME.

• **Bekkō-zaiku.** Objects made of tortoiseshell. This material was used in ancient times to decorate objects (found in the Shōsō-in storehouse in Nara), but tortoiseshell objects became popular only during the Edo period, when women began to use combs and pins in their hair. Tortoiseshell is also used to make small boxes and various pieces of jewelry.

Bellecourt, Duchesne de. French diplomat, first general consul, then Napoleon III's ambassador to Japan, appointed in 1859. In 1864, he was replaced by another diplomat, Léon Roches. When he returned to France, in 1868, he wrote a detailed report on China and Japan.

Ben. Former title given to state advisers. First called *benkan,* they were divided into three double classes: *sadaiben* and *udaiben* (from the left, *sa,* and from the right, *u*); *sachūben* and *uchūben,* and *sashōben* and *ushōben,* corresponding to the upper, middle, and lower classes of advisers from the left and the right. They were under the dependency of a *gonkan,* or "controller." Collectively, they were called the *shichiben* (the seven *ben*) or, when an eighth person sometimes joined them, the *hachiben* (the eight *ben*).
→ *See* BEN NO NAISHI.

Benchūbenron. Japanese text from the Hossō sect, translation of the Sanskrit text *Madhyāntavibhanga* (Distinction Between the Middle and the Ends), a didactic treatise in Sanskrit attributed to the Indian Buddhist philosopher Asanga (Maitreyanātha).

Benedict, Ruth Fulton. American cultural anthropologist (1887–1948). A graduate of Columbia University, she worked in the War Information Bureau in Washington during the Second World War. Although she never went to Japan, she relied on Japanese-American sources to write her major work, *The Chrysanthemum and the Sword* (1946), designed to help American authorities in Japan to understand the country so that it could be transformed into a democratic state. This work was very popular and translated into Japanese as *Kiku to katana* in 1949. Now a bit dated, it was the first general study on Japanese behavior, motivations, and traditional social organization.

Ben'en. Buddhist monk (*azana:* Enni, 1202–80) of the Tendai and Rinzai Zen sects, founder of the Tōfuku-ji temple in Kyoto in 1243. Also known as Bennen and Shōikku-shi.

Bengyoku. Buddhist monk (Keia, 1818–80), poet, and historian, famous for the music he wrote for koto.

Benibana. Plant *(Carthamus tinctorius)* used for fabric dyes and cosmetics. From the ninth century, it was used to make *beniguchi* (lipstick and rouge); starting in the seventeenth century, it was used in the manufacture of printing inks for ukiyo-e prints of the *benizuri-e* and *beni-e* types.

• **Beni-e.** Type of ukiyo-e, printed in black with some color applied by brush, the deep pink *(benibana)* replacing the red lead pigment *(tan)* of earlier prints. These prints sometimes featured colors printed over saffron yellow with coppery stains.

• **Beni-girai.** Type of ukiyo-e in greenish gray and green tones (without any red), popular circa 1790–1800. Some, with a mainly purple hue, are called *murasaki-e*.

• **Beniguchi.** *See* BENIBANA.

• **Benizuri-e.** Type of early ukiyo-e produced between 1744 and 1765, printed with black outlines and three or four flat colors (red, indigo, yellow, and green).

Benkan. Former title of state advisers. *See* BEN.
• Former name of the Korean kingdom of Pyon Han (*Jap.:* Daikara or Benshin). In the fourth century, threatened by one of its neighbors, the Silla (*Jap.:* Shiragi), this small kingdom appealed to the Yamato state, which made it a protectorate, Kaya (Mimana), governed by an agency called Nihon-fu. However, the Japanese lost control of this state, which was conquered by the Silla in 562–63. *See* KAYA, MIMANA.

Benkei. Semi-legendary character (*childhood name:* Oniwaka-maru; *gō:* Musashi-bō, perhaps died 1189). According to the *Azuma kagami* and

the *Gigeiki,* he was an extraordinarily powerful warrior-monk. However, he was defeated by the young Minamoto no Yoshitsune and became his loyal retainer, following him in his flight from Minamoto no Yoritomo after the Taira-Minamoto War (1180–85) and committing suicide with him. Benkei's real and imagined exploits are the subject of all ballads dealing with the war between the Minamoto and the Taira, and are recounted in the *gunkimono* (war chronicles), such as the *Heike monogatari,* the *Gempei seisuiki,* the *Gigeiki,* and the *Benkei monogatari.* His legend has also been used in Noh and Kabuki (for example, *Kanjinchō*). He is one of the most colorful characters in Japanese legend. *See* JŪROKU MUSASHI, MINAMOTO NO YOSHITSUNE.

Benkei ga ana. "Benkei's hole." Burial mound *(kofun)* in Kumamoto prefecture (Kyushu), whose walls are decorated, notably, with a "ship of the dead" powered by oarsmen and steered by a horse (animal undertaker) through the heavens. In the Mezurashizuka tomb in Fukuoka prefecture, the ship is piloted by a bird. This *kofun* probably dates from the sixth century.

• ***Ben no Naishi nikki.*** "Journal of the Lady of the Ben Court." Text recounting the events that took place in the court of Kyoto from 1246 to 1251, attributed to Ben no Naishi. It is written in an elegant, classical style, and is accompanied by poems.

Benshi. Narrators of silent films, in the style of Rakugo artists, before the advent of the "talkies." *See* RAKUGOKA.

Bento. Boxed meals prepared in advance and sold to travelers in train stations. Their composition varies by region and town. A general term for travel provisions. Also called *kashi*.

Benyowsky, Moritz August Aldar, Count. Hungarian adventurer (1741–86). After years of wandering, he was exiled by the czar to Kamchatka, but he managed to flee in 1771. His memoirs, published in London in 1790, were translated into a number of languages. When he fled Kamchatka, he put into port at Amami Ōshima, where he warned the Dutch in Deshima (Nagasaki) about the danger that the Russian advance presented to the Far East. His letters were sent to the shogunate, where they caused some alarm, and certain scholars, such as Hayashi Shihei, favored measures to fend off any attack on

Japanese territory by the Russians. *Japanese name:* Han Bengorō.

Benzaiten. Buddhist goddess of the arts, love, music, and eloquence, corresponding to the Hindu goddess Sarasvati, who was claimed in Japan both by Buddhism and by Shinto. According to tradition, she was the sister of Lord Emma (*Skt.:* Yamarāja), the ruler of Hell. She is considered mainly a goddess of good luck. She is probably the Buddhist version of Ugajin, a Shinto water spirit often represented by a large white snake, since the popular effigies of her are often accompanied by such a snake. She is also, in Japanese Buddhism, one of Senju Kannon's Nijūhachi Bishū (Thousand-Armed Kannon's Twenty-Eight Bishū). In Shinto, she takes on various shapes but is always portrayed playing a *biwa* lute. She is also considered to be one of the Seven Gods of Good Fortune (Shichifukujin). She has several names in the Shinto tradition, including Kayane-hime, Bentensama, and Biditing (in Okinawa). In Buddhism, she is also called Dai Benzaiten, Benten, and Myōonten. She had 15 acolytes (*dōji*). This multifaceted goddess is worshiped mainly by artists, musicians, and merchants, who pray to her for wealth and luck. The shrines or temples dedicated to her are often on small islands. The most famous are those at Chikubujima (on Lake Biwa), Enoshima (near Kamakura), Itsukushima, Kinka-zan in northern Honshu, and Bentenjima on Lake Hamana (Shizuoka prefecture). *See* SHICHIFUKUJIN.

Beppu. *Onsen* (hot spring) town in Ōita prefecture (Kyushu) on the bay of the same name. Since ancient times, people have gone there for its waters (more than 3,000 hot springs), spas, and mud and sand baths. Known for bamboo crafts. *Pop.:* 140,000.

• **Beppu Wan.** Beppu Bay is the port at the entrance to the Strait of Bungo. Major sardine fishery and shrimp farming.

Berry, John Cutting. American missionary and physician (1847–1936). He arrived in Kobe in 1872 and headed a hospital in Okayama in 1879, then was named director of the Dōshisha University hospital in Kyoto in 1885, where he founded the first nursing school in Japan. Through his influence with the Japanese government, he helped bring about significant improvements in prison living conditions.

Bertin, Louis-Émile. French engineer (1840–1924). Invited to Japan as a special adviser, he stayed from 1886 to 1890 to supervise the construction of battleships, design port facilities, and train naval engineers.

Besshi Dōzan sōgi. Series of workers' strikes that began in June 1907, at the Besshi Copper Mine in Ehime prefecture, which had been operated since 1691 by the Sumitomo family. The strikers, along with miners in Ashio, were demanding higher wages and better working conditions. The army was sent in to break the strike. Other strikes took place in the same location in 1925–26, organized by the Sōdōmei (Japan Federation of Labor). These mines are still operated by Sumitomo; the ore is taken to the port of Niihama and refined on Shisakajima, an island in the Inland Sea.

Bessho Nagaharu. Lord (1558–80) of Miki castle in the province of Harima, who, besieged for two years by Hideyoshi and forced to surrender because of lack of provisions, asked for mercy for his men and committed suicide.

Besson-zakki. Collection of drawings of Buddhist gods in 57 volumes, made by Jōkin Shinkaku circa 1180–82. They were included in the encyclopedia on Buddhism, the *Taishō shinshū Daizō-kyō.* Also called *Gokikkan-shō.*

Betsuden. In Zen Buddhist doctrine, means of transmitting teachings "from mind to mind," from master to disciple without using words or a text.

Betsugen Enshi. Buddhist monk (1294–1364) of the Sōtō Zen sect, born in the province of Echizen (Fukui prefecture). He went to China in 1320 to study Chinese poetry and returned to Japan in 1329 with Sesson Yūbai. He wrote two anthologies of poems in Chinese, *Nan'yūshū* and *Tōkushū.*

Betsugi Shōzaemon. A *rōnin* (masterless samurai) who conspired against the *bakufu* in 1652, plotting to assassinate the *rōjū* (council of elders) during a ceremony in the Zōjō-ji temple in Edo. The plot was discovered; Betsugi Shōzaemon committed suicide in the temple and his accomplices were apprehended and crucified.

Betsu-in. Buddhist temple that is an annex (or a branch) of a main temple *(honji)* or a sect. Also called Matsu-ji.

Bettō. Title of a religious administrator in charge of a temple or a priest in a Shinto shrine, also given to the chief of protocol in the court of a retired emperor, or to the intendant of a family belonging to one of the five branches of the Fujiwara clan. Previously, the title given to a senior bureaucrat who moved to another government department. Also called *zasu, kengyō. See* JIMU.

• During the Kamakura period, title given to the heads of departments called the Samurai-dokoro and Mandokoro.

• **Bettō-ji.** *See* JINGŪ-JI.

Bigelow, William Sturgis. American physician (1850–1926). A brilliant medical student, he later abandoned medicine; in 1882, he accompanied Edward S. Morse and Ernest F. Fenellosa to Japan, where he became an art collector. He traveled a great deal, studied Buddhism, and provided financial assistance to Okakura Kakuzō to found the Japan Fine Arts Academy (Nihon Bijutsu-in). When he returned to the United States, he donated to the Boston Museum of Fine Arts more than 40,000 Japanese paintings and objets d'art. A convert to Buddhism, he died by self-immolation, with the request that his ashes be buried in the Hōmyō-in temple near Mii-dera, on the banks of Lake Biwa, with those of Fenellosa.

Bigot, Georges. French caricaturist (1860–1927), born in Paris, who went to Japan in 1883 and taught painting at the military academy. He provided illustrations for various newspapers and started a magazine for humorous drawings, *Tobae,* which appeared from 1887 to 1890. After working as a war correspondent during the 1894–95 Sino-Japanese War, he returned to France in 1899.

Bijutsu Gakkō. Fine arts school of Japan, founded in 1876 by Itō Hirobumi, and later renamed Kōbu Bijutsu Gakkō. Three Italian artists were invited to teach art there: Fontanesi, the painter; Ragusa, the sculptor; and Capelletti, the architect.

Bikuchi Kannon. Buddhist goddess, corresponding to the Sanskrit Bhrikuti, a Tantric aspect of Shō Kannon Bosatsu (Avalokiteshvara) depicted "knitting her brows." In some Japanese esoteric sects, she bears the secret name Joshō Kongō Bosatsu. She is rarely portrayed in Japan. *See* TARASON KANNON BOSATSU.

Bikuni. "Buddhist nun." Japanese adaptation of the Sanskrit *bhikshuni.* In the Edo period, this term was also used for prostitutes who disguised themselves as nuns. *See* AMA.

• **Bikuni-gosho.** Name given to Buddhist convents directed by imperial princesses or daughters of leading noble families.

Bimbōgami. In popular belief, Bimbōgami is a *kami* of poverty, who brings bad luck if one does not worship him in the appropriate manner. Generally portrayed as an emaciated character holding a battered fan *(shibu-uchiwa)* in his hand, he is mentioned for the first time in literature of the Edo period; his appearance coincided with the appearance of poor urban populations. Even today, people with constant bad luck are called *bimbōgami.*

• *Bimbō monogatari.* "History of Poverty." Socioeconomic novel written in 1917 by Kawakami Hajime (1879–1946). He then wrote *Daini bimbō monogatari,* published in 1930, in which he showed the need for socialist policies and gave a summary of the history of socialism in Russia.

Bingata. Fabric- or paper-dyeing technique using bright colors, generally applied in a stenciled pattern. Used to decorate kimonos and *byōbu* screens, and sometimes for book illustrations, it was also adopted in Okinawa (in Naha) to make certain fabrics: pounce bags, made with rice pulp, were used to transfer the design.

Bingo. Former province, now Hiroshima prefecture (Honshu).

Binzuru Sonja. Japanese arhat *(Jap.: rakan),* who, according to one Buddhist tradition, was run out of his religious community *(Skt.: sangha)* by the Buddha for having transgressed the vow of chastity. According to another tradition, he was, on the contrary, congratulated by the Buddha for having defeated heretics in argument. He was a physician. His effigy is often found at temple gates, and the faithful offer him red and white clothing so that he will protect them from illness. Effigies are also found in refectories of Zen temples, sitting on a chair against the western wall. He corresponds to Pindola Bharadvāja. Also called Binzuru Baradaja, Bindora.

Birōdo. Velvet fabric introduced to Japan by the Portuguese and manufactured locally starting in

1650. It takes its name from the Portuguese word *veludo,* which means "velvet."

Biruma no tategoto. This novel by Takeyama Michio, translated as *The Harp of Burma,* recounts the odyssey of Japanese soldiers in the jungles of Burma at the end of the Second World War. Written in 1956, it was adapted for the screen in the same year by Ichikawa Kon.

Bisai. Town in the north of Aichi prefecture (central Honshu) on the Kiso River, post town *(shuku-eki)* on the Minokaidō road in the Edo period. This town, known starting in the seventeenth century for its cotton production, was converted to industrial wool production circa 1900. *Pop.:* 55,000.

Bishamonten. One of the four Buddhist gods *(Skt.:* Vaishravana) of the horizons *(see* SHI-TENNŌ). This defender of Buddhist Law, who presides over the north, is represented by an armored warrior holding a pagoda in his hand. He was considered one of the Seven Gods of Good Fortune (Shichifukujin) in the seventeenth century. In popular Shinto, he is also considered one of the Three Gods of War (Sansenjin). Also called Tamonten.

Bishū. Former collective name of three provinces—Bizen, Bitchū, and Bungo—in the Kibi region. It was also the former name of the province of Owari.

Bitasen. Copper coins, sometimes containing more than 50% lead, struck by the provincial daimyo beginning in the sixteenth century and widely circulated. They were then exchanged for other currencies of better alloy in some provinces, according to variable rates. In 1570, in the Kanto region, the rate was four *bitasen* for one *eirakusen* (imported Chinese coin); this rate was imposed throughout Japan starting in 1604. Also called *akusen, yakusen, waresuri, okake, emyō, uchihirame, kyōsen, kinsen.*
• Iron or brass coins struck by the Tokugawa shogunate in the eighteenth century and known as Kan'ei-*tsūhō* (currency of the Kan'ei era).
→ *See* CURRENCY.

Bitatsu Tennō (Bidatsu Tennō). Thirtieth emperor of Japan (Osadan Nunakura Futotamashiki, 538<572–85>), son of and successor to Emperor Kimmei. He married Empress Suikō. He was an uncle of Prince Shōtoku. Yōmei Tennō succeeded him upon his death.

Bitchū. Former province, now Okayama prefecture.

• **Bitchū-in.** *See* UNKEI.

Bitō Nishū. Neo-Confucian philosopher (Bitō Jishū, Bitō Ryōsuke, Nishū, Yakuzan, 1745–1813), born in the province of Iyo (Ehime prefecture). At first a disciple of an ancient form of Confucianism *(kogaku),* he turned to the theories of the Zhu Xi *(Jap.:* Shushi) school favored by Rai Shunsui (1746–1816) and Nakai Chikuzan (1730–1804). He was appointed professor at Shōheikō, the shogunal academy for Confucian studies, in Edo in 1790, and was one of the three Kansai no Sansuke (or Sanhakase) with Koa Seiri and Shibano Ritsuzan. He wrote a number of commentaries on Confucian philosophy, including *Seigako shishō* (Manual of True Instruction). *See* HAKASE.

Biwa. Type of Chinese lute *(Chin.: pipa)* introduced to Japan during the Nara period, with a pear-shaped body and a short neck. There are a number of four- and five-stringed varieties. Very much in style for court music in the Nara period and in the Ryukyu Islands—there are magnificent examples in the Shōsō-in in Nara—the *biwa* was practically abandoned in the early Heian period but was brought back to prominence by the monks of the Tendai sect in the ninth century and in several provinces in the twelfth century. It was played mainly by blind monks *(mōsō).* At court, this instrument was generally used to accompany Bugaku plays. Starting in the fourteenth century, it was played by blind itinerant performers *(biwa-hōshi)* who sang heroic ballads of the war chronicles *(gunki-monogatari),* especially the *Heike monogatari.* A new type of music using the five-string *biwa* (Heike *biwa)* developed, and the *biwa* became popular within the samurai class during the Muromachi and Momoyama periods, especially in the Shimazu clan in Kyushu. There were various types of *biwa* used in Japan: the four-string *shigen-biwa* ("simple *biwa*"), the *gogen-biwa (Chin.: wuxian),* the *bugaku-biwa* (or *gaku-biwa)* with four strings and three frets, the *genkan (genkin-biwa)* with four strings and nine frets *(Chin.: yuanxian),* and the five-fret Heike *biwa.* The four-string, four-fret Satsuma *biwa,* 90 cm long, was most popular in Kyushu, while the 70-cm Chikuzen *biwa,* with four or five strings and five frets, was in style in northern Kyushu. The *ku* (four strings and nine frets), the *shigen* (similar to the *genkin),* and other types are still used. The *biwa* is played with a large triangular wood or ivory plectrum called a *bachi*.

• **Biwa-hōshi.** Bards, Buddhist monks mainly from the Tendai sect, many of them blind, who wandered the country singing or reciting ancient legends. They first appeared during the Heian period, but their numbers grew during the Kamakura period, and even more during the Muromachi period, when they specialized in reciting war chronicles *(gunki-monogatari)* such as the *Heike monogatari.* They belonged to two "schools," Yasaka and Ichikata, and were ranked according to their skill, the highest receiving the title *kengyō.* Some *biwa-hōshi* sang Buddhist texts, notably the *Jishin-gyō,* going from house to house to "purify the hearth." During the Edo period, some of them sang *jōruri,* accompanying themselves with a shamisen instead of a *biwa.*

• **Biwa-ko.** Large lake in central Honshu, so named because its shape is reminiscent of a *biwa.* Located in Shiga prefecture north of Kyoto, it is quite deep at the north end (50 m) and less deep at the south end (16 m), about 64 km long, and has an area of 674 m². Of volcanic origin, it was probably formed about 2,000 years ago. It is the source of the Yodo River, which flows into Osaka Bay. Its waters are used for irrigation and to supply potable water to Kyoto, Osaka, Nara, and neighboring towns. It is fairly rich in fish (trout, carp, *ayu*), and pearl oysters are cultivated. It has a few small islands, including Chikubushima, which is famous for its shrine dedicated to the *kami* of the waters and to Benzaiten. The largest lake in Japan, it is also known as Ōmi no Ko (Ōmi Lake) and Ōmi no Umi (Ōmi Sea).
• Shrub *(Eriobotrys japonica)* whose fruit, which ripen in early summer, are very popular. The plant was probably imported from China in the eighth century. The fruit is used to make an alcoholic beverage; its leaves, to make a tea *(biwa-yu)* said to have medicinal properties. In spite of this, people generally avoid planting it in their gardens, since it is thought to bring bad luck and illness.

• **Biwa-ko Sōsui.** Large canal linking the town of Ōtsu, on Lake Biwa, and Kyoto, and joining the Uji River at Fushimi. Begun in 1885, it was completed in 1890 and extended in 1912, for a total length of 20 km.

• *Biwa monogatari. See* FUNA YUGO.

• **Biwa no Daijin.** *See* FUJIWARA NO NAKAHIRA.

Bizen. Former province, now Okayama prefecture, and town (*Pop.:* 33,000) in the southeast part of this province, located on the Inland Sea (Setonaikai), known for its production of fireproof bricks and pottery. *See also* HIZEN.

• **Bizen-mono.** Generic name for goldsmiths and blacksmiths working in Bizen from the tenth to the nineteenth century. There were four "schools" *(ryū):* Bizen (tenth to thirteenth century); Ichimonji (thirteenth and fourteenth century); Yoshii (fourteenth to sixteenth century); and Osafune (from the village of the same name, thirteenth to nineteenth century).

• **Bizen-yaki.** Type of pottery produced in the former province of Bizen in the Kamakura period. These ceramics, fired at high temperature in the *anagama* and *noborigama* kilns, were unglazed and golden to dark brown in color. At first intended for daily use (pots, dishes, mortars, *sake* bottles, etc.), they became highly valued in the Muromachi period (*chawan* tea bowls). A number of families (Kimura, Mori, Ōai, Tongū, Kaneshige, and Terami) shared the kilns, forming three guilds in the service of the daimyo of the Ikeda family in Bizen. During the Meiji era (1868–1912), these kilns produced mainly tiles and bricks. Almost 200 potters have worked in Bizen in modern times, among the most important of whom are Fujiwara Kei (1899–1967) and Kaneshige Tōyō (1896–1967). Bizen pottery made for rituals or funeral ceremonies is called Imbe-*yaki* (for the village of Imbe, where a small museum, the Bizen Tōgei Kaikan, displays the most beautiful pieces produced at Bizen).

Blakiston, Thomas Wright. English ornithologist (1832–91) who moved to Hakodate (Hokkaido) in 1861 and devoted himself to describing the birds of Japan. He discovered that the Strait of Tsugaru formed a sort of border between Central Asian and Northern Asian fauna. This imaginary line is now called "the Blakiston line."

Blomhoff, Jan Cock. Dutch officer (1779–1853), supervisor of the Nagasaki trading post starting in 1809, and entrusted by the Edo shogunate with teaching English to Japanese interpreters. In 1817, he became the director *(kapitan)* of the Dejima (Deshima) trading post, succeeding Hendrik Doeff. He returned to Holland in 1824, having visited the shogun in Edo twice, in 1818 and 1822.

Bō. Ancient measure, equivalent to an area 528 m x 528 m. During the Nara and Heian periods, the *bō* was used as an administrative division for towns. It was generally divided into sixteen *tsubo* or *chō* (which were 117 m²), separated by streets 12 m wide. Each *chō* was in turn divided into 36 residential lots. One *chō* was worth four *ho.* Later, this name was also used to designate the districts where Buddhist monks lived, then monastic buildings, and finally the monks themselves. The term *bōzu* (monk belonging to a *bō*) acquired a somewhat pejorative meaning. It is behind the English word "bonze," meaning Buddhist monk but also suggesting an old fogey.

Bodai. "Enlightenment." Japanese transcription of the Sanskrit *bodhi,* awakening to the supreme consciousness of the Buddhist Law, attained by Buddha and leading to Nirvana, the goal of every devout Buddhist. Also called "the Path" *(dō)* and *kaku.*

• **Bodai-ji.** Buddhist ancestral temple.

• **Bodaiju.** Japanese name given to the sacred tree (pipal, *Ficus religiosa*) under which, at Bodh Gaya, the Buddha is said to have attained enlightenment.

• *Bodaishin-ron.* Esoteric Buddhist treatise of the Tendai sect, adaptation of the Sanskrit text *Bodhi-hridaya shāstra,* specifying that the only way to achieve enlightenment is to awaken in oneself the "consciousness of Buddha" by concentrating one's mind on a single point.

• **Bodai-Daruma.** Japanese name for Bodhidharma (fifth–sixth century), an Indian Buddhist monk said to have gone to Canton, China, in 470 (or 520?), bringing with him the begging bowl that belonged to the Buddha. A follower of the Indian Buddhist sect of *dhyāna* (meditation), he went to Luoyang to preach there, but then went into isolation to meditate. Legend has it that he remained in a sitting position for nine years, turned toward a wall, and lost the use of his legs. He is said to be the founder of the Chan sect (which was to become Zen in Japan) and martial arts. In fact, nothing is known about him. He is worshiped in Japan as Daruma, a legless man with protruding eyes and thick eyebrows. A popular practice is to buy, at the beginning of each year, an effigy of Daruma (made of papier-mâché or wood) and draw in one of his blank eyes while making a wish. If this wish is granted, one draws in the second eye, and at the end of the year the effigy is burned. Daruma is honored (Daruma-ki) on the fifth day of the fifth month (now May 5). The character of Daruma has inspired many painters, effigies of him have been made into dolls and rocking toys, and he is sometimes joined by a similar doll in female form, Hime-Daruma. He is always dressed in red.

Bo-in. Signature consisting of making a thumbprint on a document. Rural dwellers and illiterate people used this type of "seal" to identify various documents. The first mention found of such a signature dates from 1126.

Bōjutsu. Type of fencing practiced with a long stick *(bō)* held in both hands, very similar to the style of combat using a staff popular in medieval Europe. Warrior monks of the sixteenth century used sticks clad with iron *(kanabō).* The shogunal police force in the Edo period also adopted *bōjutsu* for defense against *rōnin* and brigands, using a type of stick called *keibō.*

Bokashi-zuri. Method of making ukiyo-e prints by rubbing the engraved wood with a colored pad *(baran)* over its entire surface *(fuki-bokashi)* or applying color at random *(atenashi-bokashi),* in graduated bands *(ichimonji-bokashi),* or by passing a sort of duster made of horsehair diagonally across it *(ita-bokashi).* Slightly damp paper is then placed on the block and pressed onto it. *See* BAREN, UKIYO-E.

Boki-ekotoba. *Emakimono* describing the life of Kakunyo, a Buddhist monk (1270–1351) at Hongan-ji in Kyoto. It was illustrated by Fujiwara no Takaaki and Fujiwara no Takamasa in the style of the Tosa school, and calligraphed by Jushin, Kakunyo's son. This *emakimono,* which comprises ten handscrolls, is dated 1351.

Boku Eikō. Japanese name of a Korean statesman (Pak Yŏng-hyo, 1861–1939) who supported Japan's policy of annexing Korea. In 1884, after a failed coup d'état, he took refuge in Japan. He returned to his native country in 1894, and after Japan's victory over China in 1895, he was named minister of the interior but was soon forced to resign. Considered a traitor by Koreans, he remained in Japan and was even appointed to the House of Peers (Kizoku-in) in 1932.

Bokumon Jittetsu (Juttetsu). Collective name given to the ten most famous disciples of Confucian philosopher Kinoshita Jun'an (1621–98): Arai Hakuseki (1657–1725), Muro Kyūsō (1658–1734),

Amenomori Hōshū (1668–1755), Gion Nankai (ca. 1677–1751), Sakakibara Kōshū (1658–1706), Nambu Nanzan, Matsuura Kashō, Miyake Kanran (1674–1718), Hattori Kansai, and Mukai Sōshū.

Bokusai. Zen Buddhist monk (Shōtō; *azana:* Motsurin, ?–1492), disciple of Ikkyū Ōshō and abbot of the Shūon-an monastery of Daitoku-ji in Kyoto. He painted using the Muromachi *suiboku* technique and is said to have been a student of Dasoku. It is possible that he is the same painter as the one known as Bokkei, who also lived in the fifteenth century.
• Netsuke sculptor (mid-eighteenth century) in Kyoto and Edo.
→ *See* DONKYŌ, IKKYŪ OSHŌ, KŌIN, TSUNENOBU.

Bokuseki. Name given to calligraphy in *sumi-e* (China ink) made by Zen Buddhist monks. Those by Eisai, Shunjō, Enni, Musō Kokushi, and Ikkyū are considered among the best.

Bokusen. *See* DIVINATION.

Bokusen. Painter (Maki Nobumitsu, Sukeemon; *go:* Hokusen, Hokutei, Gekkōtei, Hyakusai, Tokōrō, 1775–1824), born in Nagoya. A student of Utamaro and Hokusai, he produced many ukiyo-e prints and experimented with copperplate engraving. Also known as Maki Bokusen.

Bokushi. Zen Buddhist monk and painter (Shūsei; *azana:* Isan, ca. 1394–ca. 1469), belonging to the Muromachi *suiboku* school.

Bokutō. In the Edo period, wooden swords carried by physicians. This word was later used for the writing kits and small medicine boxes *(inrō)* that they usually wore on their belts. Also called *bokken. See* SHINAI.

Bombori. Type of small round or oval-shaped portable lantern *(andon),* sometimes mounted on a pedestal, in use during the Edo period.
• Name given to a half-open folding fan *(ōgi).* *See* ŌGI.

Bonchō. Poet (Tatsuju, Nozawa Bonchō, Miyake Bonchō, Miyagi Bonchō, Koshino Bonchō; *gō:* Kasei, Akei, ?–1714). A disciple of Bashō, he wrote many haiku and collaborated with him in 1691 to write *Sarumino,* the collection of poems that contains 41 of his compositions. After that time, imprisoned for a criminal act, Bonchō stopped writing. When he was freed, he settled in Osaka and died in misery. Some critics feel that his technique and descriptions of nature were superior to Bashō's. He has been classified among the Bashō Juttetsu (Ten Great Disciples of Bashō). His wife, Tome *(gō:* Ukō), was also an accomplished haiku poet.

Bonge. During the Kamakura period (1185–1333), general name given to those who were neither nobles *(kuge)* nor warriors *(bushi).*

Bonji. Brahmanic or Sanskrit letters *(Skt.:* Bīja, Siddham; *Jap.:* Shittan) sometimes engraved on Buddhist statues or swords. Certain letters represented the creative sound of a god and were often reproduced on the pedestal, halo, or body of a painted likeness of the deity.

Bon Odori. Popular dances of religious origin, generally performed from the 13th to the 15th day of the seventh month (either mid-July or mid-August) during the Urabon Festival. The musicians are placed high on a platform, and the villagers dance around them. At first, the dances were performed to console the souls of the deceased; they originated from an amalgam of Shinto religious dances performed at Ise (Ise Odori) and popular Buddhist dances (Nembutsu Odori) created by the monks Kūya (903–72) and Ippen (1239–89) to chant the name of Amida (Namu Amida Butsu, or *nembutsu).* In the Edo period, the dances *(odori)* lost all religious significance and came to be considered simply a form of popular diversion. They vary in style and music by region. In the Ryukyu Islands, they are called *shichigatsueisa* (dances of the seventh month).

Bō no Tsu. Former name of the port of Satsuma, now a small fishing village on the southwest coast of Kagoshima prefecture. During the Muromachi period (1336–1574) it was a very active port, with maritime traffic to China and the Ryukyu Islands. It was one of the "three great ports" *(sanshin)* with Nanotsu (Hakata) and Anotsu (Tsu). Development of the port of Nagasaki in the early seventeenth century led to its decline.

Bonsai. "Tray planting." This word refers to both a particular technique of growing potted trees or plants and the specimens themselves. The art of bonsai aims to produce miniature trees and shrubs. Placed in shallow earth, the plants grow slowly, and their growth is further slowed by pruning, binding the branches and roots, and repeated transplanting.

Bonsai is inspired by the fact that under certain climatic conditions and in poor soil, some trees that do not obtain enough nutritive substances develop slowly and grow very little. The technique appeared in China more than 1,000 years ago and was introduced to Japan during the Kamakura period (1185–1333) by Zen Buddhist monks. Over the centuries, many schools *(ryū)* have developed for different shapes—straight, leaning, cascading, waterfall, etc. The types are: *hako-niwa, bonkei,* and *saikei. Bonseki* are miniature landscapes produced on a tray, without vegetation but with sand, stones, and sometimes water, small houses, and miniature figures. Those with a little lake are called *suiseki.* The main bonsai schools created in the Edo period were named after their founders: Hosokawa, Chikuan, Hino, Sekishū. The aesthetic and the philosophical combine in this cultivation of nature, which must be asymmetrical: the center is reserved for the encounter of Heaven and Earth, of gods and humans. The art of the bonsai gardeners (or *bonsaidō*) was exported to the United States in the 1870s and to Europe after the Second World War.

Bonshō. Buddhist temple bells, which have no clapper. They are also called *tsurigane* and *tsurikane.* They are rung with a mallet or a hanging beam that hits the *tsukiza,* a specific spot on the wall of the bell reinforced for this purpose. These bells, which can be very large, are made of bronze. They are decorated in a traditional manner and have a handle (generally decorated with dragons, called *ryūzu),* a crown *(kasagata),* vertical and horizontal relief bands *(tatsuki),* a boss ornamenting the top of the wall *(chi),* and a lower border *(koma no tsume).* The flat surfaces bordered by the bands are called *ike no ma* (higher part) and *kusa no ma* (lower part). Sometimes there are texts, either engraved or cast in relief. These bells are often called simply *kane.* Very small bells, with a clapper, are called *fūrin.* Shinto shrines have small bells *(suzu,* also called *shō).*

Bonshun. Shinto priest and writer (1553–1632), son of Yoshida Kanesuke. He taught Shinto principles, according to the Yoshida school, to the shogun Tokugawa Ieyasu. His journal, *Bonshun nikki,* covers the years 1583 to 1632.

Bonten. Japanization of the Hindu god Brahmā, one of the Shichifukujin (Seven Gods of Good Fortune) of the Edo period and of the Jūni-ten (Twelve Gods) dating back to the Heian period. In Japan, he is generally portrayed holding a flower or a fan.

Some sculptures of him, in earthen clay on a core of wood or in dry lacquer, were made during the Nara period. Also called Baramonten.

Bosatsu. Japanization of the Sanskrit term bodhisattva. In Mahayana Buddhism, the bodhisattvas are exceptional beings who have achieved enlightenment but renounce Nirvana to help others who are struggling on the road to perfection. There are a great number of bodhisattvas. In Japan, multifaceted Kannon (*Skt.:* Avalokiteshvara), Jizō (*Skt.:* Kshitigarbha), Monju (*Skt.:* Mañjushrī), and Miroku (*Skt.:* Maitreya) are worshiped. The title of Bosatsu has sometimes been given to eminent religious leaders. Finally, in Shinto-Buddhist syncretism, certain Shinto gods, such as Hachiman, also bear the title Bosatsu.

Boshin Sensō. "Boshin Civil War." A civil war that lasted one year (1868–69) and resulted in the fall of the Tokugawa shogunate and the restoration of imperial power. The pro-imperial forces, led by the Satsuma and Chōshū clans, decided to take power by force and seized the Kyoto imperial palace on January 3, 1868, proclaiming the restoration of the emperor. Shogun Yoshinobu Tokugawa withdrew, but some of his vassals refused to surrender and were defeated in Toba and Fushimi. The victorious armies advanced to Edo through Tōkaido, Tōsandō, and Hokuridō. There was no battle for

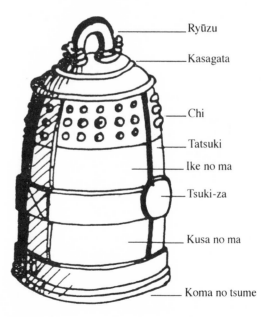

Ryūzu

Kasagata

Chi

Tatsuki

Ike no ma

Tsuki-za

Kusa no ma

Koma no tsume

Bonshō

Edo; the castle fell without a fight. Isolated groups continued the struggle, notably at Ueno (*see* SHŌGI-TAI), where they were decimated by artillery. Yoshinobu was then placed under house arrest in Mito. The *bakufu* war fleet, commanded by Enomoto Takeaki, refused to surrender and sailed north from Kanagawa. In northern Honshu, daimyo brought together under the authority of the Aizu clan surrendered (*see* BYAKKO-TAI) in October 1868. The last battle took place in Hakodate (*see* GORYŌKAKU NO TATAKAI), where Admiral Enomoto Takeaki finally surrendered on June 27, 1869, putting an end to the hostilities. Supporters of the shogunal regime in Edo were expelled from government and replaced by men from the Chōshū, Satsuma, and Tosa clans (the Satchūto). The imperial troops had borrowed heavily from merchants in Kyoto, Osaka, and Edo, which led to serious financial difficulties for the Meiji government. Also called Boshin no Eki.

Bōshu. In the traditional calendar of Chinese origin, 15-day period starting about June 5 marking the beginning of the sowing period. *See* NIJŪSHI-SETSU.

Bōsō Hantō. Mountainous peninsula (highest peak: Atagomaya, 408 m) on the coast of Chiba prefecture, north of Tokyo. With a total area of 2,600 km², it has a number of beautiful beaches on its south shore that are popular in summer. This peninsula, on the north side of the Bay of Tokyo, is a major industrial site and part of the Keiyō industrial complex.

Botchan. A novel by Natsume Sōseki, published in 1906 in the magazine *Hototogisu,* in which the qualities of Edokko ("children of Edo") are exalted. It was very popular and brought success to Sōseki. This novel was adapted for the screen by Kimura Kinka in 1927.

Bousquet, Georges. French lawyer (born ca. 1845), called in as a consultant by the Meiji government in 1872 to translate and comment on the Napoleonic Code, in collaboration with Gustave Émile Boissonnade de Fontarabie (1829–1910). He taught law at Meihōryō (law school of the Ministry of Justice) and helped write the Japanese civil code. Upon his return to France in 1876, he published a book of memoirs, *Le Japon de nos jours et les échelles de l'Extrême-Orient* (Today's Japan and the Scales of the Far East, 1877).

Boy Scouts. This youth organization, created by Lord Baden Powell, began to operate in Japan in 1915, although its existence was made official only in 1922. Because it had taken on a paramilitary nature, it was disbanded in 1945. It was reorganized soon after, and in 1971 an International Jamboree was held in Japan. Currently there are about 3,000 scout troops in Japan.

Brandt, Max August Scipio von. German diplomat (1835–1920) who was the first Prussian consul general to Japan in 1862. He left Japan in 1875 to become consul to China. He was the founder and first president of the Deutsche Gesellschaft für Natur-und Völkerkunde Ostasiens, an association for East Asian studies and culture. He wrote a book of observations on Japan, *Dreiunddreissig Jahre in Ost-Asien* (Thirty-three Years in East Asia, 1901).

Brangwin, Frank. British painter and engraver (1867–1956). He taught engraving to the potter Bernard Leach in 1908. Although he probably never went to Japan, many Japanese artists were among his students at Bruge, including Takeuchi Tsurunosuke, Kurihara Chūji, Matsukata Kōjirō, and Urushibara Mokuchū.

Bridgestone Tire Company. The largest firm manufacturing tires and other rubber products with Japanese capital and technology, founded in Kurume (Fukuoka prefecture) by Ishibashi Shōjirō in 1931. It exports more than 33% of its production throughout the world and recently formed a partnership with other European and American companies (notably Goodyear).

Brinkley, Frank. English journalist (1841–1912), born in Ireland. He went to Japan in 1867 as a military adviser, then taught mathematics at the National Engineering College (Kōbu Daigaku). He was owner and editor of the *Japan Mail,* an English-language newspaper, and a correspondent for the *Times* of London. His articles, favorable to Japan and resolutely hostile to the Unequal Treaties (*see* JŌYAKU), influenced British public opinion to accept the treaty of alliance signed in 1902 between Britain and Japan. Brinkley married the daughter of a former samurai and was as interested in Japanese culture as Japanese politics. He translated Noh plays and wrote a detailed study, *Japan: Its History, Arts, and Literature* (1901), and a landmark Japanese–English dictionary.

Brother Industries. Japanese company specializing in the design and construction of sewing machines, musical instruments, and more recently, typewriters, computer printers, and electronic equipment. It was created in 1934 but took its current name only in 1962. It exports more than 42% of its production throughout the world. Its head office is in Nagoya.

Brown, Samuel Robbins. American missionary (1810–80), the first foreign minister authorized to enter Japan since the seventeenth century. He preached and taught in Kanazawa, then Yokohama. He was one of the founders and the first president of the Asiatic Society of Japan and published an essay on Japanese vocabulary (*Colloquial Japanese,* 1863).

Brück, Karl Anton. German copperplate engraver (1839–80), employed by the Japanese Mint to design bank notes from 1874 to 1880, at the same time as the Italian engraver Eduardo Chiossone. He taught his craft to many Japanese after he left the Mint, in 1977. He died in Japan.

Brunet. French officer (1838–?) invited to Japan in 1867 with other officers to serve as army instructors. When the Meiji emperor canceled the contract linking his government to members of the French military missions, Brunet deserted and joined the shogunal forces, sailing on one of Enomoto Takeaki's ships. He helped to reinforce the defenses of Goryōkaku, the fort at Hakodate. When Enomoto's surrender was imminent, in 1869, he found a place on a French ship bound for Yokohama. He then returned to France, destitute, but was rehabilitated during the 1870 war and ended his career as a division general.

Brunton, Richard Henry. Scottish engineer (1841–1901) who, between 1868 and 1875, helped to improve Japan's ports and built 34 lighthouses along the coasts, thus continuing the work begun by François Verny, a French engineer. He also drew a detailed map of the Inland Sea (Setonaikai).

Brussels, Conference of. International conference (Nov. 3–15, 1937) held after the China Incident (*see* NISSHIN SENSŌ) of July 1937, following which Japan had refused to let China bring the affair before the League of Nations. Japan was accused of violating the Nine-Power Treaty (Great Britain, United States, France, Italy, Belgium, Netherlands, Portugal, China, and Japan) signed at the Washington Conference in 1922 and was summoned to resolve the conflict, but refused to attend the conference.

Bu. Former Japanese currency worth six *shu.* Four *bu* were worth one *ryō;* eight *bu,* one *dairyō. See* ICHI-BU-GIN.
• Measure of length equivalent to about 3 mm.
• Prior to the seventh century, an area unit equal to about 1 *koma-shaku* (0.35 m) squared (or 0.12225 m²). From the Kamakura to the Edo period, it was about 6 *shaku²* (or 1 *ken²,* or 1 *tsubo*). In 1596, it measured 6 *shaku* and 3 *sun²* (1 *ken²*). *See* SHAKU.

Buddhism. Japanese Buddhism grew out of the tradition of Mahayana Buddhism. However, it is quite different from forms of Buddhism that developed in other parts of Asia, both in its philosophical concepts and in its portrayal of the gods and "forces" worshiped by its various sects and "schools." In Japan, faced with a people and a folklore different from those of India, its country of origin, Buddhism took on very specific forms and retained elements that have long since disappeared from other regions where Buddhism had been established. It has become what one might call the "conservatory" of Buddhism's ancient forms.

About AD 538 (some say 552), the king of Paekche (Kudara) in Korea sent a letter to the ruler of Yamato in which he expounded the excellence of Buddhist principles and at the same time asked for assistance against his neighbor, the kingdom of Silla (Shiragi). With this letter, which was presented by a delegation of scholars and monks, were a number of sutras, a bronze image of the Buddha, perhaps others in wood, banners, and ritual objects. Thus, Buddhism made its entrance, officially at least, into the Yamato empire. (In fact, it is very likely that fragments of the doctrine had appeared well before this time, having come with Korean or even Chinese refugees, but without official support, the new religion did not spread.) Some local clans, imitating the court, converted to the new faith, which they associated with progress and power; they began to use the knowledge and talent of the monks, artists, and artisans who moved in large numbers from Korea after the Japanese were forced to abandon their hold on the peninsula in 562–63. But other clans were fiercely opposed to the adoption of Buddhism as a state religion, and sides soon formed, plunging the country, already unstabilized by struggles for influence between clans, into even greater confusion. The opponents of Buddhism were led by the Nakatomi clan, which included the priests of Japan's ancestral religion (which was soon afterward given the name Shinto to differentiate it from the imported religion, or Bukkyō), who officiated at the court. The others were led by the Soga clan and the prime minister, Soga no Iname, and were supporters of "Chinese-style" reforms, ready to adopt everything that came from China or Korea. There were a number of battles, culminating, in 587, with the defeat of the clans supporting Shinto. The battles were more over politics than religion. The entire court then converted to Buddhism, as did a certain number of noble families. The general population, however, remained largely unaware of the new religion. Prince Shōtoku (Shōtoku Taishi), a son of Emperor Yōmei who had become the regent to Empress Suiko, then issued an imperial edict calling for the promotion of Buddhism and rallied the clans that were still hesitant. He reviewed relations with China and the Korean kingdoms and encouraged exchanges between these countries and Japan. In the Seventeen-Article Constitution (Jūshichijō no Kempō), said to have been promulgated in 604 but probably written by his ministers soon after his death in 622, Prince Shōtoku urged his followers to live according to the Law of Buddha: "Worship wholeheartedly the three treasures: the Buddha, the Dharma [the Buddhist Law], and the Sangha [the monastic community], since they contain the ideal life and the wisdom of the nation."

As rulers made reforms in the spirit of the new religion, more and more people became interested in Buddhism, and many became monks. Starting in 607, Prince Shōtoku sent a number of missions to China to bring back knowledge of art and astronomy, architecture and administration, and literary and religious works. Kenzuishi and Kentoshi (ambassador to the Sui and, later, the Tang court) brought back a number of Buddhist texts, and introduced Taoist beliefs and Confucian principles. Shōtoku himself wrote three important commentaries on the sutras *(Jap.: kyō)*, which he felt would supply the people with an ethical foundation. He also had a number of temples built by Korean architects, including Shitennō-ji in Osaka, Hōryū-ji in Nara, and Chūgū-ji, to mention only the best known. When he died, according to the *Nihon shoki* (written in 720), there were 46 temples, 816 monks, and 569 nuns in Japan.

Promulgation, beginning in 645, of the Taika Reform, based on a Chinese model, owed much to Buddhism. Emperor Tenji (<662–71>) ordered the construction of temples in all provinces in order to spread Buddhist teachings. At this time, there were not yet true sects. Buddhism consisted in large part of worshiping relics *(shari)* and was not held to be different from Shinto in practice. It was appreciated for its magical and protective powers, mainly in the prevention and cure of diseases. Buddha Yakushi Nyorai (*Skt.:* Bhaishajyaguru), god of medicine, was thus especially popular. In the court, sutras were read to make rain fall, and Buddhist practices became mixed with Shinto ones. In the monasteries, monks familiarized themselves with the Buddhist documents and texts that they were translating and began to form opinions on the philosophies that they wanted to adopt. "National" Buddhism, as Buddhist doctrine in Japan at the time was called, would therefore soon become, like Chinese Buddhism, a religion of sects.

The transfer of the capital city from Asuka to Heijō-kyō (Nara) in 710 led to a proliferation of monasteries in Nara and its environs. Prince Shōtoku had studied the *Sanron (Skt.: Madhyāmika)* and *Jōjitsuron (Skt.: Satyasiddhishāstra)* doctrines under the leadership of Korean masters Eji, Esō, and Kanroku. In 653, the monk Dōshō of Gangō-ji brought back from China, where he had studied under Xuan Zang (*Jap.:* Genjō), doctrines of the Hossō sect (*Skt.:* Madhyāyāna) and transmitted them to the monk Gyōki (670–749). Five years later, two Japanese monks, Chitsū and Chitatsu, went to China and brought back a translation of the Sanskrit text *Abhidharmakoshashāstra.* In spite of the danger, more and more monks made the trip to China or Korea and returned loaded down with texts and holy images. In 749, after a smallpox epidemic decimated the country, against which invocations to the *kami* were ineffective, a colossal bronze statue (*see* DAIBUTSU) of the Buddha Vairochana (*Jap.:* Dainichi Nyorai) was installed at Tōdai-ji in Nara. Shinto was not, however, completely abandoned; in the court, imperial ceremonies were still led by priests, and a sort of Shinto-Buddhist syncretism began to develop. In the early eighth century, various trends appeared among the Buddhist clergy of Nara that were quickly concretized in the formation of the Nanto-rokushū (Six Sects of Nara), the doctrine of each based on a different text:

—The **Kusha** school embraced both the material and the spiritual and was based on the texts of the *Kusharon,* written in the fifth century by the Indian monk Vasubandhu (*Jap.:* Seshin).

—The **Jōjitsu** school was based on the Sanskrit treatise *Satyasiddhishāstra,* written in the early third century by the Indian monk Harivarman (*Jap.:* Karikatsuba).

—The **Hossō** sect was an intermediate step between the Hinayana and Mahayana traditions, favoring the "average vehicle," or Madhyāyāna. It was based on the teachings of the Sanskrit text *Yogāchāryabhūmishāstra (Jap.: Yugashijiron)*, written in the fifth century by Asanga (*Jap.:* Muchaku) and translated into Chinese by Xuan Zang.

—The **Sanron** school followed the principles of the "middle path" (*Skt.:* Madhyāmika), favored in the mid-second century by Nāgārjuna (*Jap.:* Ryūju), and was based on four main Sanskrit texts: the *Madhyāmikashāstra (Jap.: Chūron)* by Nāgārjuna, *Dvādasadvarashāstra (Jap.: Jūnimonron),* the *Shatashāstra (Jap.: Hyakuron),* and the *Prajñāpāramitāshāstra (Jap.: Daichidoron),* which had been introduced in 625 by the Korean monk Ekan.

—The **Ritsu** sect drew on both the Hinayana and the Mahayana traditions, emphasizing monastic discipline (*vinaya, Jap.: ritsu*). The doctrine was developed in China, using the Sanskrit text *Dharmaguptavinaya (Jap.: Shibunritsu),* written by the Chinese monk Dao Xuan (*Jap.:* Dōsen, 702–60) and introduced to Japan by Ganjin in 754.

—Finally, the **Kegon** sect, or "sect of flowery argument," founded in China and based on the Sanskrit texts *Avatamshakasūtra (Jap.: Kengon-kyō)* and *Dashabhūmivibhāshashāstra (Jap.: Jūjibibasharon).* It is said to have been introduced to Japan by Dōsen in 736.

The philosophical doctrines of these sects or "schools" were very difficult and probably understood only by the scholarly monks and a few aristocrats: the common folk felt that such speculations were beyond them. Some Buddhist notions, however, went beyond the narrow framework of the monasteries and the court to reach the population, such as retribution for acts according to the law of causation, a certain sense of impermanence in all things, and an increasingly strong belief in the saving powers of Buddhist divinities, the Tathāgata (*Jap.:* Nyorai) and bodhisattvas (*Jap.: bosatsu),* for these principles brought hope for survival in the hereafter that Shinto was unable to provide: Buddhism thus complemented Shinto.

When the capital was moved to Heian-kyō (Kyoto) in 894, Emperor Kammu, probably wanting to free himself from the overly cumbersome guardianship of the monks of the Six Sects of Nara (Nanto-rokushū), took measures to limit the proliferation of temples, monasteries, and monks. To renew Buddhism and infuse it with new concepts likely to counterbalance those of the Nara sects, he sent to China some relatively dissident monks, asking them to bring back the new esoteric doctrines. In 805, Saichō returned from Mt. Tiantai (*Jap.:* Tendai) in China and founded a monastery on Mt. Hiei, northeast of Heian-kyō, where he taught the principles of the Tendai sect. Another monk, Kūkai, who returned a year later, brought back doctrinal elements of another related Chinese sect, Shenyan (from "true word," *Jap.:* Shingon) and established himself some ten years later on Mt. Kōya, south of Nara. Buddhism of the Nara schools, though not totally abandoned, was nonetheless obliged to yield to the two new sects, which favored a partial syncretism with Shinto rituals and beliefs. The Shinto-Buddhist syncretism of the Tendai sect was called Ichijitsu Shintō, or "Shinto of the Only Truth," while that of the Shingon sect became Ryōbu Shinto, or "Shinto of Both Parts of the Universe." Both identified Buddhist divinities with Shinto *kami,* considered temporary incarnations (*gongen*) of them. However, the doctrines of these two new sects were even more obscure for most commoners, even literate ones, and reaction was not long in coming. Amidism returned Buddhism to simple doctrines practicable by all and bringing hope of salvation even to the most deprived. Named after the Buddha Amida (*Skt.:* Amitābha), it was created by Tendai monks such as Genshin (942–1017), then popularized by others, such as Kūya Shōnin. Buddhism of the Heian period was split among these three trends, the first two accentuating asceticism, the last offering access to Amida's paradise, or Pure Land. The belief in Mappō, or the "final period of the Buddhist Law"—which, according to certain sutras, was to mark the beginning of a new Buddhist cycle in 1052, and which predicted calamities and disturbances in that year—led many to devote themselves to the Amida cult, the only one offering to save them and guarantee them a life of bliss in the Pure Land (Jōdo). This belief in Amida had been introduced from China in 847 by Eun and developed slowly thanks to the writings of Genshin, Ryōnin (1073–1132), and especially Hōnen (1133–1212). Although the sect (Jōdo-shū) was not at first recognized as being independent from the Tendai sect, it was soon perceptibly separate, popularizing and spreading Buddhism thanks to the extreme clarity of its doctrine. Simple adoration of the Buddha Amida and the constant repetition of his name in the form of an invocation ("Namu Amida Butsu," abridged to *nembutsu*) were enough to ensure entry after death into the Western Paradise (Gokuraku Jōdo, *Skt.:* Sukhāvatī), where one could perfect oneself and finally reach the state of Buddha, for according to Nāgārjuna, "In the great ocean of the Law of Buddha, the only way to enter is faith."

With the decadence of the Fujiwara regime and the disturbances that followed in the mid-twelfth century, the "degeneration of the Buddhist Law" was manifested more dramatically. New sects appeared, imported from China or created in Japan, more or less in opposition to each other; some were considered aristocratic, such as Zen (*Chin.: Chan*), which was favored by high-ranking warriors, while others, such as Jōdo Shin-shū and Nichiren-shū, appealed mainly to the peasants and low-ranking warriors.

Jōdo Shin-shū, or "new Pure Land sect," was created by a disciple of Hōnen, Shinran, who, when his master died, provoked a schism within the Jōdo sect by publishing his teachings, *Kyōgyō-shinshō* (Doctrine, Practice, Faith, and Realization), in 1224. Thirty years after Shinran died, one of his disciples summarized this teaching in a small book called *Tannishō* (Opus on Deplorable Heterodoxies), a text that was to constitute the basis of teaching of the Jōdo Shin sect. Having faith in the original wish of Amida (which was to save all beings no matter what they had done) and reciting the *nembutsu* with sincerity were enough to ensure a happy rebirth in Amida's paradise. The faithful had to depend utterly on grace, or the "strength of the Other" *(tariki),* a belief that added mysticism to the simple piety of the Jōdo sect. The monks of this new sect were encouraged to have families in order to erase the traditional division between the clergy and the lay world. Although it was vigorously attacked by the other sects, the Jōdo Shin sect won over large numbers of people and soon began to offer military resistance to those in power, Oda Nobunaga and Toyotomi Hideyoshi (*see* IKKŌ-IKKI).

Zen doctrines were imported by Chinese Chan monks, first by Eisai in 1191, who established the Rinzai (*Chin.: Linzi*) branch in Japan, then by Dōgen, who founded the Sōtō (*Chin.: Caodong*) branch in 1227. Another branch, Obaku-shū, was established at the Mampuku-ji temple circa 1650. Zen advocated a particular type of transmission of teachings not based on any text; it rejected the worship of images, asking followers simply to recognize the nature of human thought to realize their buddha-nature. Its methods for achieving liberation, based more on experience than on study, involved the search for thought freed of all diversity *(zazen);* it recognized only the historical Buddha. Zen was successful almost immediately, especially among high-ranking warriors and intellectuals.

Nichiren-shū, named for its founder, Nichiren (1222–82), a Jōdo and Tendai monk, rejected the teachings of the other sects and founded its doctrine entirely on the *Lotus Sutra (Skt.: Saddharma-pundarīka-sūtra; Jap.: Hoke-kyō),* the title of which alone could be invoked to attain salvation. Its doc-

trines were to be intimately linked to Japan's political development. The Nichiren sect was very popular but was bitterly opposed by the authorities.

By the sixteenth century, the transformation of Buddhism in Japan was by and large complete. The existing sects—Jōdo, Jōdo Shin, Nichiren, Zen, Shingon, and Tendai—along with the minor sects and the innumerable "subsects" that were and still are being created, continued to evolve, but without any truly innovative spirit. However, the teachings of the Buddhist sects had by this time deeply penetrated all layers of Japanese society, becoming mixed (with the exception of Zen and Jōdo Shin) with popular and Shinto beliefs. With the advent of new social classes during the Tokugawa period, and with Chinese influence, some Buddhist divinities were shaded with a different personality, and cults unknown up to then appeared, some in the Chinese tradition, others emerging from local folklore (such as gods of happiness or good luck). Japanese Buddhism tended to become popularized and absorb a great variety of beliefs, which enabled it, in a certain sense, to survive its forced intellectual stagnation during the Edo period, when neo-Confucian philosophies and the Zen ethic were in almost exclusive favor. Buddhism was more and more confined to social roles (population registries, charitable works), and its temples organized in strict hierarchies. Nevertheless, a few major personalities dominated the religious scene, especially Zen monks such as Hakuin, Takuan, Suzuki Shōsan, and Ingen.

The restoration of imperial power in 1868 and the official separation of Shinto and Buddhism that followed forced Buddhism to turn in upon itself, distancing itself from popular worship—a phenomenon that no doubt encouraged the development of new independent sects, more or less syncretic, grouped under the name *shinkō shūkyō,* or New Religions. Among them, the most important are Tenri-kyō, or "Religion of the Divine Wisdom," Konkyō-kyō, or "Religion of the Golden Light," and P. L. Kyōdan. A modern semi-religious organization inspired by Nichiren Buddhism, Sōka Gakkai, "Society for the Study of Creative Values," has enjoyed spectacular growth. These modern sects and religions spend considerable effort proselytizing, both in Japan and abroad, while the "orthodox" sects (as much as there is a Buddhist orthodoxy) are currently experiencing a resurgence in popularity, the Japanese having retained a taste for worship of most of the Buddhist divinities.

Budō. "Way of Combat." Starting in the twentieth century, the name given to pacific martial arts in general, including physical and spiritual disciplines. All *budō*, now assimilated into sports, have a system of grades *(dan)*. The main Japanese *budō* are aikido, judo, karate, and kendo. The *budō* are contrasted to the *bugei*, which are martial-arts techniques using weapons. *See* MARTIAL ARTS.

• **Budōka.** one who practices a *budō* martial art.

• **Budōkan.** Martial-arts hall built in Tokyo in 1962 to replace the Kōdōkan. It is the Mecca of martial arts in Japan. *See* KŌDŌKAN.

• **Budōkukai.** Paramilitary school created in 1895 to prepare young people for the military: it taught the martial arts and weapons handling. It was shut down in 1945.

• *Budō shoshin-shū.* "Introduction to the Way of the Warriors." Instructional book by Daidōji Yūzan (1639–1730), in 44 chapters, in which a father gives advice to his son on neo-Confucian ethics, morality according to Bushido, and the correct attitude to take toward death. It also contained precepts on education, filial piety, and moral dignity. *See* BUSHIDO.

Bugaku. Traditional court dances with accompanying music, introduced to Japan in the Asuka period (before 645) from other parts of Asia: Tōgaku from the Chinese Tang empire, Tanjikugaku from India, Rin'yūgaku from Champā on the Annam coast, Bokkaigaku from southern Manchuria, and Komagaku and Sankagaku from Korea. The dances and music were performed at the imperial court and in Buddhist monasteries during the Nara period (710–794). During the Heian period, they were reserved for the imperial court, and became a sort of "national" entertainment. Chinese music (Tōgaku) was called "music of the left," while Korean music (Komagaku and Sankagaku) was called "music of the right." The dances were hieratic and slow, comprising two groups of dancers, one on the left and one on the right. They were accompanied by straight double-reed pipes *(hichiriki)* or transverse flutes *(ryuteki* or *ōteki)*, bamboo mouth organs *(shō)*, 13-string koto, drums, and gongs. Swords were used in some of the dances (Bu no Mai) and not in others (Bun no Mai). Masks were often used, especially to evoke mythical characters. Bugaku supplanted Gigaku, and the music alone was called Gagaku. Although these dances have not been performed for a very long time, certain aspects of them

are still used (notably from Tōgaku) during ceremonies at Shinto shrines during festivals. *See* AMA.

• **Bugaku-biwa.** *See* BIWA.

• **Bugaku-men.** Masks used in Kyoto Bugaku. They were smaller than those used in Gigaku.

Bugenchō. Registers of vassals, regularly drawn up by daimyo and the shogun and providing lists of landholders and revenue in *koku* of rice. The registers were started in the sixteenth century and continued under the Tokugawa shogunate; called *bukan,* they also included the location of the land and information on families and villages under shogunal authority. Hashimoto Hiroshi, a nineteenth-century historian, compiled a number of *bukan* in his *Daibukan* (13 volumes), a work republished in 1935–36 that is an important source of information on shogunal administration and the organization of fiefs during the Edo period.

Bugyō. During the Heian period, officials charged with the execution of a single decree or imperial order; their function ended when the task was accomplished. During the Edo period, they acted as commissioners or civil governors and were chosen from among the *fudai-daimyō.* This title was also given to property administrators from the Kamakura to the Edo period. Starting in 1863, *bugu-bugyō* were in charge of military weapons. This title replaced *gusoku-bugyō,* created in 1641 for *bakufu* bureaucrats in charge of equipment for the shogunal troops. The *kanjō-bugyō* had judiciary and financial control of estates belonging personally to the shogun; the *jisha-bugyō* supervised religious affairs, notably temples and shrines. The *machi-bugyō* were civil governors of the large cities under shogunal authority, such as Edo, Osaka, Nara, Nagasaki, and Nikkō, among others. There were many other types of *bugyō,* each with a specific task.

Būji. General name given to Buddhist monks in the Ryukyu Islands. Starting around 1600, these monks were ostracized somewhat by the population because of their links with death (they essentially took care of funerals and the future of the soul after death), which, in the Shinto way of thinking, made them impure. They thus constituted a particular caste.

Buke. General term for samurai and other warriors, often also placed in the category of *bushi*, and constituting the "warrior houses." *See* BUSHI.

• **Buke-bunka.** "*Buke* culture." Term designating all forms of culture created within the warrior class during the Kamakura period (1185–1333) and preserved by this class, as opposed to the aristocratic culture *(kuge-bunka)* of the imperial court. It tended to be typically Japanese in contrast to the Chinese Sui and Tang cultures that had prevailed up to then. This culture was close to that of the *kuge* during the Muromachi period and constituted what has come to be called Higashiyama *bunka* (Higashiyama culture), adding to the slightly rough culture of the *buke* the more refined culture of the Chinese Song and Yuan periods.

• *Buke-giri monogatari.* Popular novel *(ukiyo-zōshi)* from the Edo period, published by Ihara Saikaku in 1688, comprising 27 warrior stories contrasting the morality of the *buke (giri)* to that of the *chōnin* (townspeople).

• **Buke-hō.** Customary law (up to the thirteenth century) of the warrior class *(buke, bushi),* as opposed to that of the imperial aristocracy, the *kuge-hō.* *Buke-hō* was first codified in 1232 in the statutes of *Jōei shikimoku,* later complemented and augmented by the *Shikimoku tsuika.* Issuing from the military codes, it became the general code ruling Japanese society starting in the Muromachi period, *kuge-hō* remaining in force only at the imperial court in Kyoto and *ji-in-hō* being the law applied only within Buddhist monastic communities. Specific parallel laws, called *hampō,* existed on certain daimyo estates *(han),* based on local customs.

• *Buke-jiki.* Encyclopedia in 58 volumes written by Yamaga Sokō in 1673 for use by samurai in the *buke* class, providing articles and information on their history, how they should behave under various circumstances, rituals to follow, the etiquette appropriate for their status, military arts, and so on. This work helped to legitimize shogunal power.

• *Buke-keihō.* Criminal code concerning the warrior class *(buke),* in use from 1190 to 1600.

• **Buke-kojitsu.** Regulations governing the customs of the *buke* class, as opposed to those of the aristocrats, the *kuge-kojitsu.* These protocols were developed and recorded by "schools" such as those associated with the Ogasawara, Ise, and Imagawa families in the Edo period. These schools followed principles dating back to the Muromachi period and codified for the shogunate by Arai Hakuseki and Ise Sadatake, among others.

• *Bukemono.* Collection of war chronicles *(gunki-mono)* published by Ihara Saikaku from 1687 to 1688.

• *Buke myōmoku-shō.* Compilation of historical data of the Edo period as compared to preceding eras. Begun by Hanawa Hokiichi (1746–1841), continued by Nakayama Nobuna (1787–1836), it was finished after 1836 by other historians. It comprises 381 articles divided into 16 sections covering topics as varied as government administration, ceremonies, events, buildings, clothing, the arts, armor and weapons, archery, palanquins and horses, strategy, and many others.

• **Buke-seiji.** "Warrior government." Term analogous to *bakufu,* designating the types of government that ruled Japan from the Kamakura period to 1868.

• *Buke-shohatto.* Short work on the laws concerning the *buke (samurai* and *daimyō)* comprising 13 articles, issued in 1615 by Tokugawa Hidetada. The guidelines explain the fundamental laws of the Edo *bakufu.* These texts, which had been sketched out by Konchi-in Sūden, were then completed, notably in 1635 (six articles) and 1663 (two articles). A new text, influenced by Confucian morality, was published by Arai Hakuseki in 1710, but the 1683 text *(Tenna buke-shohatto)* remained in force until 1868.

Bukki. "Period of mourning" during which, following the death of a relative or an emperor, certain bans were observed that varied according to the relationship and the importance of the deceased. Laws *(bukki-ryō)* were written a number of times to regulate the duration and the customs observed. The first were decreed in 700–03 and called for a "grand mourning period" *(jūfuku)* of one year when a father or mother died. The common people could not conform to this requirement because it required them to abandon all activities. During the Edo period, new rules were established by Confucian philosophers Hayashi Hōkō and Kinoshita Jun'an, among others, that were to be applied to the entire population with the exception of the imperial aristocracy of Kyoto, setting the duration of the grand mourning period at 50 days. During the Meiji era, these prescriptions fell into disuse and the observation of mourning was left to individual families, although bureaucrats were still required to follow the old rules. Currently there are no set rules, the duration and modalities of mourning being left to individuals. Also called *kichū*. See FUNERALS.

Bukkigun emaki. Fifteenth-century *emakimono* (illustrated handscroll) telling the story of a bodhisattva of the Jōdo sect who assembled an army to battle demons and enable souls to escape from Hell.

Bukkō-ji. Buddhist temple of the Jōdo Shin sect, founded in Kyoto circa 1320 as Kōshō-ji by the monk Ryōgen, a disciple of Shinran. The site was changed in 1329, as was its name. Its buildings, destroyed in civil wars, were reconstructed during the Meiji era.

• **Bukkō-ji ha.** Branch of the Jōdo Shin sect established in Kyoto circa 1320 by Ryōgen, who, traditionally, was the seventh head of the Bukkō-ji temple after Shinran, Shimbutsu, Genkai, Ryōka, and Ryōen. This branch currently numbers about 200,000. Also called Shinshū Bukkō-ji ha.

• **Bukkō Zenji.** See SOGEN MUGAKU.

Bukkyō. "Buddhism." Also called *butsudō* (Path of Buddha) or *buppō* (Law of Buddha). The religion took this name only in the sixth century, thus distinguishing itself from the original Shinto beliefs. See BUDDHISM.

Bumbuku chagama. "The Enchanted Teapot." A popular tale in which a poor man, having saved the life of a *tanuki* badger *(Viverrinus),* watches as it transforms itself into a teapot, which he then sells to a temple. But when the teapot is polished, it is transformed back into a *tanuki* and returns to the poor man's house. It then metamorphoses into a young woman, who is sold into prostitution, then into a horse, sold to a wealthy man—each sale making the peasant a little wealthier. This legend, the Japanese version of "Aladdin's Lamp," has regional variants. See BAKEMONO, TANUKI.

Bummei (Bunmei). Era of Emperor Go-Tsuchimikado: Apr. 1469–July 1486. See NENGŌ.
• Painter (Oku Sadaaki; *azana:* Hakki, Junzō; *gō:* Seika, Rikuchinsai, ?–1813) of the Maruyama school and a student of Maruyama Ōkyo. He lived in Kyoto. Also called Oku Bummei.

• *Bummei ittō-ki.* "On the Unity of Knowledge and Culture." A work dealing with political ethics (1478) in which the philosopher Ichijō Kanera (1402–81) outlined in six points the duties of a prince.

• *Bummei-ron no gairyaku.* "Elements of a Theory of Civilization." An encyclopedia containing all that its author, Fukuzawa Yukichi, knew about Western civilizations. Ten chapters long, it was published in 1875, and often reprinted.

Bumpō. Era of Emperor Hanazono: Feb. 1317–Apr. 1319. See NENGŌ.
• Painter and netsuke sculptor (Kawamura Ki; *azana:* Shunsei, Goyū; *gō:* Shuyōkan, Bumpō, Hakurūdō, early nineteenth century), student of Ganku in Kyoto. Also called Kawamura Bumpō.

Bun. Term indicating the social status of an individual within Japanese society, which can vary with sex, age, and relationships between individuals. See OYABUN-KOBUN.
• Term indicating minutes or a unit of something, pronounced -*fun* in compound words.

Bun'an. Era of Emperor Go-Hanazono: Feb. 1444–July 1448. See NENGŌ.

Bunchi-shugi. Originally, Chinese political concept according to which society can improve, following the laws of nature, only if people receive appropriate education and conform strictly to ritual. This concept was adopted by the ruling classes of the Edo period, who were concerned with rallying support around the shogunate. It was based on the neo-Confucian principles then in style, as promoted by Arai Hakuseki and Hayashi Hōko. The concept had the force of law from Tokugawa Ietsuna's shogunate to Tokugawa Tsunayoshi's—that is, from the late seventeenth century to the early eighteenth century, a period called *bunchi-seiji.* The shogun Tokugawa Yoshimune, following plots against the shogunate, then decided to return to an authoritarian style of government.
→ *See* SUIAN.

Bunchō. Painter (Mori Bunchō, Ippitsusai Bunchō; Kishi Uemon; *gō:* Sōyōan, Hajintai, 1725–94) of ukiyo-e prints, influenced by Harunobu's style. In collaboration with Shunshō, he illustrated a three-volume work called *Butai Ōgi* in 1770.
• Painter (Tani Bunchō, Tani Masayasu; *azana:* Bunchō, Gungorō; *gō:* Shazanro, Gagakusai, Shōsō, Muni, Ichijo, Bun'ami, 1763–1840), in Edo, specializing in landscapes. A student of Bunrei and Kangan, he belonged to the Nanga (Bunjinga) lite-

rati school, a style that he introduced to Edo. Aside from book illustrations (such as those for *Shūko jsshu*), he wrote a number of works on painting techniques, including *Honshō gasan, Meizan gafu,* and *Bunchō gadan.*

Bunchū. Era of Emperor Go-Kameyama: Oct. 1372–May 1375. *See* NENGŌ.

Bundō Shunkai. Calligrapher (Keichū; *gō*: Shunkai, Kaiō, 1878–1970) and Buddhist monk, Sōjō (bishop) of the Tendai sect. He was a student of Nishikawa Shundō. His style was flexible yet firm.

Bun'ei. Era of Emperor Kameyama: Feb. 1264–Apr. 1275. *See* NENGŌ.

• **Bun'ei no Eki.** Name given to the Mongols' first attempt to invade the Japanese islands in 1274. Also called Genkō no Eki. A number of Chinese embassies had demanded that Japan submit to a tributary relationship preceding the invasion, but had been ignored. Kublai Khan, China's first Mongol emperor, dispatched a fleet of ships carrying 15,000 Mongols and 8,000 Koreans under the command of Hindu, Hong Chaqui, and Liu Fuheng. After conquering the islands of Tsushima and Iki, they reached the Bay of Hakata on the north coast of Kyushu, where they engaged Japanese troops in a fierce battle. When evening fell, the Mongols returned to their ships to rest. A typhoon appeared (it was October), dispersing the enemy ships. The survivors returned to Korea. This providential wind was then called Kamikaze ("divine wind").

Bungaku. "Literature." Scholars generally recognize six major periods in the history of Japanese literature: Jōko (Yamato period), Chūko (Heian period), Chūsei (Kamakura and Muromachi periods), Kinsei (Edo period), Kindai (Meiji era), and Gendai (contemporary period). *See* LITERATURE.

• *Bungaku-kai.* "Literary World." A literary periodical published in Tokyo from 1893 to 1898, promoting modern trends, romanticism, and idealism. Among those who worked on it were Shimazaki Tōson, Kitamura Tōkoku, Baba Kochō, and Ueda Bin.

• **Bungaku-za.** One of the largest contemporary theater companies in Japan, founded circa 1937 by writer-actors, including Kishida Kunio and Sugimura Haruko.

Bungei-bunka. Cultural and literary periodical, published from 1935 to 1944. It favored romanticism and eulogized Japanese classicism. Mishima Yukio and a number of other well-known writers worked on the periodical and were members of the Aoi Tori (Bluebird) group. *See also* NIHON ROMANHA.

• *Bungei-jidai. See* SHIN KANKAKU-HA, YOKOMITSU RIICHI.

• *Bungei-kurabu.* "Literary Club." A literary periodical, published from 1895 to 1933, to which a number of well-known authors contributed, including Izumi Kyōka, Kosugi Tengai, Kawakami Bizan, and Edogawa Rampo. At first a purely literary magazine, it was transformed into a popular magazine about 1907. It was unable to compete, however, and eventually ceased publication.

• **Bungei Kyōkai.** "Literary and Artistic Association," formed in 1906 by Tsubouchi Shōyō and Shimamuru Hōgetsu to encourage the spread of culture (literature, arts, theater). In reality, it was dedicated almost solely to theater. In 1911, it became a theater group, helping to popularize Western theater (Ibsen and Shakespeare) and New Theater (Shingeki). This group was dissolved in 1913; despite its short life, it had a great influence on innovative directors and on the actor's craft.

• *Bungei Sensen.* "Literary Battlefront." A leftist literary journal created in 1924, which gave birth to the communist-leaning Senki movement (NAPF) and the socialist-leaning periodical *Bunsen* (new name for *Bunge Sensen,* adopted in 1931). *See* AONO SUEKICHI.

Bungei Shunjū. "Literary and Artistic Annals of Spring and Fall." A literary periodical founded by Kikuchi Kan in 1923, designed to counter proletarian trends in the arts and literature. It was revamped in 1926 to a general-interest magazine; in 1935, it created the Akutagawa Prize to reward young talent. It is still the largest literary periodical in Japan. *See* KIKUCHI KAN.

Bungo. Former province in northeastern Kyushu, now Ōita prefecture.

• *Bungo-fudoki.* One of the four *fudoki* (reports on the geography and traditions of the provinces submitted to the central government) that has survived to the present, albeit incomplete. It deals with the province of Bungo, and was created either be-tween 732 and 749 or in the tenth century. Also called *Bungo no kuni fudoki.*

• **Bungo Kaikyō.** Strait 37 to 40 km wide, separat-ing the islands of Kyushu and Shikoku, and linking the Inland Sea (Setonaikai) to the Pacific Ocean. Also called Hoyō Kaikyō. *See* SETONAIKAI.

Bun'ichi. Painter (Tani Bun'ichi; *gō:* Chisai, 1787–1818) of the Nanga school, Bunchō's student and son-in-law. He was the son of an Edo physician. His style was very similar to Maruyama Ōkyo's.

Bunji. Era during the reign of Emperor Go-Toba: Aug. 1185–Apr. 1190. *See* NENGŌ.

Bunjin. "Literati," a Japanese term equivalent to the Chinese *wenren,* designating those who devoted themselves to studying literature and the arts.

• **Bunjinga.** "Literati painting" *(Chin.: wenren-hua),* an artistic genre formed by scholars who painted according to their own tastes and tempera-ments, without belonging to any school in particu-lar, and who sought to express in their work, aside from their own personalities, a certain poetic sense. This movement, also called the Nanga school (Southern painting)—because the style was brought to Nagasaki by Chinese painters circa 1700—spread rapidly throughout Japan thanks to the in-fluence of literati such as Gion Nankai (1677–1751) and Hattori Nankaku (1683–1759). This style is exemplified by the works of Yosa Buson (1716–83) and Ike no Taiga (1723–76), who broke away from the Chinese tradition to create a typically Japanese painting style. Among the most famous painters of the Nanga school are Uragami Gyokudō, Bunchō, Aoki Mokubei, Tanomura Chikuden, and Rai Sanyō, as well as the Meiji painter Tomioka Tessai (1836–1924).

Bunka. Era during the reign of Emperor Ninkō: Jan. 1804–Apr. 1817. *See* NENGŌ.
• This word also designates Japanese culture in the broadest sense.

• **Bunka-Bunsei jidai.** "Era of the Bunka [1804–18] and Bunsei [1818–29] reigns." During this era, under the shogun Tokugawa Ienari, Japan experi-enced serious currency inflation, social distur-bances, peasant revolts, and foreign threats. In spite of this, it was the last era of the shogunate with some political stability, economic prosperity, and flourishing of the *chōnin* (urban bourgeois) culture.

• **Bunka-kunshō (Bunka-shō).** "Order of Cul-ture." A decoration instituted in 1937 to reward those who have made significant contributions to the arts and sciences. The winners are chosen by the Cabinet from a list proposed by the minister of edu-cation. It can be awarded posthumously. This deco-ration is generally accompanied by an annual sti-pend. The winner may wear a mauve ribbon.

• *Bunka-shūrei-shū.* Three-volume collection of classical Chinese poetry *(kanshi),* compiled by Fujiwara no Fuyutsugu on the order of Emperor Saga in 818. It comprised 148 poems (only 143 of which have survived), written by emperors Saga and Junna, by Fujiwara no Fuyutsugu, and by 27 other authors whose names had been Sinicized (written with only three kanji).

Bunki. Era of Emperor Go-Kashiwabara: Feb. 1501–Feb. 1503. *See* NENGŌ.
→ *See* FUYŌ II.

Bunkōdō. Playwright (Matsuda Wakichi, ca. 1684–ca. 1741), author of Jōruri texts and four Ka-buki plays. He wrote other Kabuki plays in collabo-ration with various authors.

Bunkoku-hō. Legal codes decreed during the Sengoku (Warring States) period of the fifteenth and sixteenth centuries by provincial daimyo to counter the influence of the *bakufu* and of other daimyo. They consisted principally of the expansion of dai-myo family law to the general population of the do-main. The collection is composed essentially of the *ryōkoku-hō* and the *hampō,* or "laws of the *han.*" Most fell into disuse when the Tokugawa regime came into power in 1603. *See* IMAGAWA.

Bunkyō-hifu ron. "Hidden Mirror of Letters." A didactic work on esotericism in Chinese literature, written in 819 by the Buddhist monk Kūkai, to ex-plain to the nobility of his time the significance of Chinese literature and poetry. This work is impor-tant because it includes various Chinese texts, the originals of which are now lost.

Bunkyū. Era of Emperor Kōmei: Feb. 1861– Feb. 1863. *See* NENGŌ.

• **Bunkyū-heihō.** Small copper coin worth four *mon,* issued from 1863 to 1867. It was the last coin struck by the Tokugawa shogunate. *Weight:* 3.75 g; *diameter:* 27 mm. This coin did not replace the Kan'ei-*tsūhō,* issued starting in 1624, and circulated concurrently with it until 1868.

Bun'ō. Era of Emperor Kameyama: Apr. 1260– Feb. 1261. *See* NENGŌ.

Bunraku. Puppet theater created at the Bunraku-za Theater in Osaka in 1872 by a troupe handling *ayatsuri-shibai* puppets *(ayatsuri-ningyō)* while reciting *jōruri (ningyō-jōruri)* to the musical accompaniment of the shamisen. The puppets are approximately one-half to two-thirds life size; they are manipulated by one to three operators wearing black robes and hoods; only the principal operator does not wear a hood. The heads *(kashira)* of some puppets have movable jaws and eyelids. The main puppet characters were Musume (young woman), Fukeoyama (married woman), Chari (clown), Bunshichi (warrior), and Danshichi (braggart), but their heads could be used for a number of roles. The *ayatsuri-shibai* originated probably in the early seventeenth century, in Kyoto, and spread to Osaka and Edo, where traveling troupes performed the adventures of a certain Kimpira and his acolytes. The *ayatsuri-shibai* suffered in competition with the Kabuki theater. At the end of the eighteenth century, a *jōruri* singer, Uemura Kunrakuken, from Awaji, settled in Osaka and presented a new show using *ayatsuri-ningyō,* without great success. His son, however, followed in his footsteps, performing puppet shows in various places. His descendants created the Bunraku-za Theater in Osaka, giving the current form its name. The building was damaged by fire a number of times, and was last reconstructed in 1956. It is currently the only theater reserved exclusively for this type of performance, which draws most of its plays from the repertoire of Chikamatsu Monzaemon. *See* AYATSURI-SHIBAI.

Bunrei. "Emanation" of the *kami* of a major Shinto shrine *(honsha)* given to a secondary shrine *(massha).* Also called Kanjō.

Bunreki. Era of Emperor Shijō: Nov. 1234–Sept. 1235. Also sometimes written Bunryaku. *See* NENGŌ.

Bunrin. Painter (Shiokawa Bunrin; Zusho; *azana:* Shion; *gō:* Unshō, Kachikusai, 1808–77) of the Murayama (Shijō) school, student of Okamoto Toyohiko's in Kyoto. Deeply influenced by Goshun's work, he painted mainly landscapes.

Bunroku. Era of Emperor Go-Yōzei: Dec. 1592– Oct. 1595. *See* NENGŌ.

• **Bunroku Keichō no Eki.** Name given by Toyotomi Hideyoshi to the Korean invasion campaigns of 1592–93 and 1597–98, which ended when Hideyoshi's death was announced and Japanese troops were forced to retreat before the Chinese armies and the Korean resistance. Also called Chōsen Seibatsu.

• **Bunroku no Kenchi.** An agrarian reform launched from 1589 to 1595 by Hideyoshi, involving a general census of the population and the establishment of a national survey.

• **Bunroku-tsūhō.** Silver coins issued by Hideyoshi in 1592 to pay his troops. They had a diameter of 23.5 mm and weighed one *momme* (about 3.75 g). Copper coins called Bunroku-*tsūhō* were issued at the same time, but no examples have been preserved.

Bunsei. Era of Emperor Ninkō: Apr. 1818–Dec. 1829. *See* NENGŌ.

• **Bunsei Uchiharai-rei.** "Order for Repelling Foreign Ships" prescribed by the Edo *bakufu* in the eighth year of the Bunsei era (1825). According to this edict, coastal defense ships were to kill (or take prisoner) all foreigners attempting to set foot on the islands, and to oppose by all means necessary ships that wanted to put into the ports. In 1842, however, the shogunate reestablished the 1806 order allowing foreign ships to refuel and take on water without interference.

Bunsei. Painter (fifteenth century) known only by the seal placed on his works; he may have been a Korean painter who settled in Japan. He painted in the style of the Muromachi *suiboku* (ink painting) school, mainly landscapes of lakes and portraits of eminent Buddhist monks. A number of his paintings are known, among them several dated 1452 and 1457 (Yamato Bunkakan). He may have been a Zen monk of the Daitoku-ji temple in Kyoto.

Bunsen. Socialist-leaning literary periodical founded in 1931 and the literary movement born of the *Bungei Sensen. See* BUNGEI SENSEN.
→ *See* TOSHINOBU.

Bunsen-ō. Japanese transcription of the Chinese name Wenxuan Wang, one of the posthumous titles conferred upon Confucius during the Tang dynasty. Also called Kōshi.

Bunshō. Era of Emperor Go-Tsuchimikado: Feb. 1466–Mar. 1467. *See* NENGŌ.

• *Bunsho-zōshi.* Story for girls, one of the *otogi-zōshi* (medieval tales), most of which were published in collections in the sixteenth century. Also called *Shioyaki bunta monogatari, Funshō sōshi.* This story tells of a temple servant who, thanks to his honesty and hard work, becomes an imperial court minister. It was customary to give the *Bunsho-zōshi* to girls at New Year's to encourage virtuous behavior.

Bunshōjo. Female netsuke sculptor (Shimizu Bunshō, Seiyōdō Bunshōjo, 1764–1838) in Shimane prefecture.

Bunten. Abbreviation of "Ministry of Education Fine Arts Exhibition" (Mombushō Bijutsu Tenrankai), held in Tokyo starting in 1907 by the Ministry of National Education. In 1919, its name was changed to Teiten (abbreviation of Teikoku Bijutsu-in Tenrankai, "Imperial Exhibition of the School of Fine Arts") and came under the aegis of the Imperial Fine Arts Academy (Teikoku Bijutsu-in). *See* TEITEN.

Bunwa. Era of Emperor Go-Kōgon, who belonged to the "Northern Court" (Hokochū): Sept. 1352–Mar. 1355. *See* NENGŌ.

Bun'ya. Type of puppet show specific to the island of Sado, where it was created at the end of the Edo period by a popular singer, Bun'ya Okamoto. The show uses a single puppet, a narrator who recites a poem, and a shamisen player. *See* AYATSURI-SHIBAI, BUNRAKU.

Bun'ya no Watamaro. Military commander (763–821) who succeeded Sakanoue no Tamaramaro in northeastern Honshu and received the order to contain and push back the Ainu.

Bun'ya no Yasuhide. Poet whose works are collected in the *Kokin waka-shū.*

Bunzō. Sculptor of Noh masks (active during the Muromachi period), who specialized in male masks. Also called Fukuhara Bunzō.
→ *See* AOKI KON'YŌ, GOSHUN, KI'EN.

Bunzuke. In the early Edo period, a category of peasants who were sharecroppers. The landowners were required to pay taxes on revenues from the *bunzuke.*

Buraku Kaihō Undō. Popular social movements that arose periodically during the Meiji era, seeking equal status for *burakumin* and freedom to travel outside the districts to which they had been restricted.

Burakumin. "People of the villages *(buraku),*" also called *semmin, hinin* (nonhumans), *eta,* and sometimes even *yotsunin* ("those who walk on four legs"), a segment of the population that has been discriminated against since ancient times, although nothing distinguishes them racially from other Japanese. Their exact social origins are unknown, but their ancestors probably practiced trades "polluted" (in Shinto terms) by death or by animal slaughter, such as gravedigger, butcher, and leather workers. Even in the Nara period, those who did not take part in the imperial corvées were called *hinin,* as were vagabonds and beggars. Actors and other entertainers were sometimes included in this category. It was mainly during the Edo period that discrimination was strongest, with society separated into rigid classes—warriors, peasants, artisans, merchants, *eta,* and *hinin (shi-nō-kō-shō-eta-hinin).* The *eta-hinin* (two distinct endogamous groups with different occupations) were then obliged to live in separate village neighborhoods (whence the name *burakumin,* which was coined in the nineteenth century). The Meiji government theoretically abolished these distinctions and tried to integrate the *shinheimin* ("new common people"), but instead discrimination worsened, leading to the social movements known as Buraku Kaihō Undō. Many societies have been established to fight this discrimination, but they have not been very successful. Even today, the majority of Japanese do not associate with the *burakumin,* and even fewer want to do business with them. In 1974, there were estimated to be more than 3 million *burakumin,* some of whom have prospered in their new industrial or business trades. In fact, it is impossible for a stranger to distinguish a *burakumin* from an ordinary Japanese. The latter, however, claim to be able to tell them by their manners, education, and language. Before accepting a marriage proposal, the parents of a young woman (or young man) routinely investigate whether the intended is a *burakumin.* This situation continues to pose serious ethical and social problems for the government. *See* ETA, HININ.

Buretsu Tennō. Twenty-fifth emperor of Japan (Prince Ohatsuse-waka-sasagi, 489<499–506>), who, according to the *Nihon shoki,* succeeded his father, Emperor Ninken, but was so cruel that the people revolted and assassinated him. This is not, however, absolutely certain. His son, Keitai, succeeded him.

Busei. Painter (Kita Busei; *azana:* Shishin; *gō:* Kaan, Goseidō, Kakuō, 1776–1856) of the Nanga school. He was one of Bunchō's students in Edo. → *See* BUSON.

Bushi. "Man of arms." Since 721, this term was used for professional warriors, coming into general use in the late eleventh century and replacing the terms *mono-no-fu, tsuwamono, musha,* and *saburai,* which later became the word samurai. Starting in the Kamakura period, the *bushi* were part of the "warriors' house," or *buke,* an early designation of the shogun's entourage. Later, the term *buke* became synonymous with "*bushi* class" and encompassed all warriors. Leagues of warriors, or *bushidan,* especially in the provinces, gave rise to the great warrior clans, and thereafter the only true *bushi* were those in the *bushidan,* while others were called *tsuwamono.* During the Edo period, the *bushi* were classified according to a strict hierarchy, dominated by the shogun, within which each *bushi* occupied a place determined by his status (*daimyō, hatamoto, gokenin, hanhi,* etc.) and that of the lord he served. This hierarchy was abolished in 1869, and the former *bushi* became part of the new *shizoku* class. Finally, in 1947, all social distinctions were abolished and members of the *shizoku* class became simple citizens. *See* BUKE.

• **Bushidan.** Leagues of warriors that, from the late Heian to the end of the Muromachi period, gave rise to the warrior clans. The *bushidan* could be subordinate to each other, and a large *bushidan* could have smaller *bushidan* as a vassal.

Bushido. "Way of the Warriors." The ethical code governing the behavior of the warrior *(bushi),* based on the loyalty *(chū)* a retainer offered his lord in exchange for a fief or an allowance. By the Tokugawa period, the warrior owed his superior absolute allegiance. In addition, he was expected to exemplify such moral characteristics as courage, self-sacrifice, filial piety, generosity, courtesy, chiv-

alry, frugality, and selflessness. Bushido grew out of the unwritten code of *kyūba no michi* ("path of the bow and the horse"), tacitly observed since the Kamakura period, and developed during the Edo period under the influence of Zen and later, Confucianism. Only in the seventeenth century, when Yamaga Sōkō's theories were published, was the word "Bushido" used to replace the expressions *mono-no-fu no michi* and *tsuwamono no michi* to designate the *bushi* state of mind. The warrior ethic, according to which the warrior scorned death and acquired glory by dying for his lord, was codified in the *Hagakure,* written by a samurai from the province of Saga in the early eighteenth century. All *bushi* were expected to follow the Bushido code of honor, whose precepts continued to influence Japanese mentality until 1945. After the war, Bushido was no longer observed except by martial-arts practitioners, and attempts to revive it—by writer Mishima Yukio, for example—have met with little success.

• **Bushidō-sōsho.** Collection of literary works, codes of conduct, and poems about Bushido, written from the Muromachi period to the Meiji era and collected in three volumes by Inoue Tetsujirō and Arima Sukemasa in 1905.

• **Bushi-zukuri.** Architectural style adapted to the needs of the samurai class. Their residences *(yashiki)* were fortified and organized to include stables and lodgings for warriors. They also had a "meditation garden," located behind the main residence, and a separate kitchen. The entrance was protected by a large gate, the *agetsuchi-mon,* and the entire residence was surrounded by wooden walls or a palisade.

Buson. Painter (Taniguchi In, Taniguchi Chōkō; *gō:* Yosa Buson, Chōko, Shunsei, Sha-Shunsei, Yahantai, Busei, Sanka, Tōse-Saichō; Gasendō, Shimei, Shain, Hajin, Hekiundō, Hakuundō, Sha-Chōkō; *azana:* Shinshō, 1716–84), born in Settsu. He painted in the style of the Nanga literati school (Bunjinga). A haiku poet, he traveled throughout Japan, living in Edo and northern Honshu (following the footsteps of Bashō), and finally settled in Kyoto. He then took the name of his hermitage, Yahantai (Midnight Hermitage), in 1770, and sometimes signed his paintings Shunsei (Spring Star). He composed about 3,000 haiku, following Bashō's style; among his poetry collections, the best known is the first, *Hokuju Rōsen o itamu* (Elegy to Hokuju Rōsen, 1745). A talented poet and popular painter, Buson remains one of the great figures of the literati *(bunjin)* of his time.

Busshi. Buddhist artists who, mainly during the Nara period (645–710), painted or sculpted images for temples. The painters were called, more specifically, *e-busshi,* while the sculptors in wood were called *ki-busshi.* They were organized in categories and grades according to the task they performed or their degree of mastery: *sō-busshi* (master), *dai-busshi* (major), *gon-busshi* (assistant), *tō-busshi* (supervisor), and *shō-busshi* (apprentice). These designations remained in use until the Heian period. *See* BUSSHO.
• **Busshi-ryū.** School of Buddhist sculpture created in the eleventh century by Kōshō and Jōchō sculptors. Its best-known members were Kakujō, Kōjo, Kōkei, Raijo, Kōen, and especially, during the Kamakura period, Tankei and Unkei.

Bussho. In the Nara and Heian periods, workshops for *busshi* belonging to the imperial court, temples, and nobility. These workshops, which brought together masters and disciples, were directed by a *zōbutsusho,* in charge of making sure that works produced or repaired by sculptors conformed to the texts. Among the most important *bussho* in the capital of Heian-kyō were the Shichijō-*bussho,* founded by Kakujo; the Sanjō-*bussho,* founded by his disciple, Chōsei; the Shichijō-Ōmiya-*bussho,* created by another of Kakujo's sons, Injo; and the Rokujō-Menokōji-*bussho,* founded by Inchō, all named after their sites near the main bridges of the city. Unkei, Tankei, and Kaikei, the most important sculptors of the Kamakura period, were part of the Shichijō-ōmiya-*bussho.* The *bussho* workshops disappeared completely during the Edo period.

Busshō-zenji. Zen Buddhist monk (ca. 1222–97) from Kyoto, who was said to have taught the principles of the Fuke sect to Kakushin. Also known as Hakuun-egyō.

Bussoku-seki. "Stone footprints of the Buddha," a stone engraved with the image of one or both of Buddha's feet (*Skt.:* Buddhapāda) and bearing the sacred marks (*Skt.:* Lakshana) of the Sage. The oldest one is in the Yakushi-ji temple and dates from 753. These stones are highly revered by the faithful, following an ancient custom that originated in India and that was transmitted to Japan via China.

• **Bussoku-seki no uta.** Poem engraved on a stone bearing the imprint of Buddha's feet, found in the Yakushi-ji temple in Nara. It is a stele 1.88 m high and 0.47 m wide, on which are engraved 21 poems glorifying the *bussoku-seki,* written in *man'yōgana* characters. The poems each have six lines of 5, 7, 5, 7, 7, 7 syllables (corresponding to a *tanka* poem, plus one line of seven syllables). According to the inscription, this stele was carved on the order of a certain Bunya Mahito Chino in 753. Also called *Bussoku-seki katai* (or *kahi*). *See* WAKA.

Butchō. Groups of three, five, eight, or nine deities of Japanese Esoteric Buddhism that are grouped around the image of Dainichi Nyorai (*Skt.:* Mahāvairochana) in certain *mandara* (*Skt.:* mandala). In general, these are Byakusangai (*Skt.:* Sitātapatra), Shō (*Skt.:* Jaya), Saishō (*Skt.:* Vijaya), Kōju (*Skt.:* Tejorashī), Shajo or Zeizui (*Skt.:* Vikīrna), Kōshō or Daitenrin (*Skt.:* Mahosh-nīsha), Gokko (*Skt.:* Abhyudgata), Muhennon (*Skt.:* Anantasvaraghosha), and Kō (*Skt.:* Unnata).
• Zen Buddhist monk (1634–1715) and poet, who may have been Bashō's master.

Butō. Avant-garde dance form created in the late 1950s by dancer Hijikata Tatsumi (1928–86), who was inspired by gestures and body positions from the folk tradition. The most famous dancers in this style are Ono Kazuo (b. 1906), Teshigawara Saburō, Ikeda Carlotta, Tanaka Min, Hijikata Tatsumi (1928–1986), and Ashikawa Yōko. The Dai Rakudakan troupe (founded in 1972 by Maro Akaji (b. 1943) and the Sankai Juku troupe (founded by Amagatsu Ushio in 1975), whose dancers shave their heads and paint their bodies white (*Sholiba,* Tokyo, 1978), have gained an international audience through their performances at festivals (Brussels, 1989; *Yuragi,* in Théâtre de la Ville, 1993). *See also* BUYŌ.

Butoku. "Value of arms," a term used in many works glorifying the feats of warriors.

• ***Butoku hennen shūsei.*** "Annual Account of the Value of Arms." Anthology of warrior stories on the life and times of Tokugawa Ieyasu, compiled in 93 volumes by Kimura Takaatsu in 1741.

• **Butokukai.** "Society of Military Virtues." Created in 1895 to preserve the Bushido ethic, this society tried to foster martial fervor in the Japanese army.

• ***Butoku taisei-ki.*** "Account of the Great Work Accomplished by the Value of Arms." Anthology of warrior stories dealing with the life and work of Tokugawa Ieyasu, compiled on the order of Tokugawa Tsunayoshi by Hayashi Hōkō, Kinoshita Jun'an, and Hitomi Tomomoto in 1686, using exhaustive documentation provided by the daimyo, *hatamoto,* and other persons whose ancestors had been in the service of Ieyasu. This compilation preceded the longer anthology, *Butoku hennen shūsei,* by Kimura Takaatsu (1680–1742).

Butsu. Japanese term designating the Buddha himself and, by extension, all types of Buddhist deities. Also Butsumyō and, more generally, Hotoke; Buchi in Okinawa.

• **Butsudan.** A Buddhist altar containing a statue of Buddha and the ancestral tablets, found in every Buddhist home. On this altar (which is more or less elaborately decorated depending on the family's wealth or piety), it is customary to offer up the first fruits of the harvest, the monthly pay, or a donation that varies according to what one has received. Rice, water, and flowers are offered daily. In general, the *butsudan* comprises a small cabinet with a folding door *(zushi),* placed quite high as a sign of worship, in the main room or any other room, even the kitchen. The presence of a *butsudan* also means that the family is registered at a nearby temple. Called *buchidan* in Okinawa. *See also* KAMIDANA.

• **Butsuden.** Main room of a temple containing a statue of Buddha. Also called *butsudō.*

• **Butsudō.** "Way of the Buddha," term equivalent to *bukkyō,* "Buddhism." *See* BUTSUDEN.

• **Butsuji no mai.** Buddhist ritual dances intended to chase away evil spirits and demons *(oni)* and worship the gods. More recently, they were transformed into popular dances, such as the Bon Odori. Also called Ennen.

• **Butsumo.** Japanese identification of Buddha's mother, Māyā, and the aunt of the Wise Man, Mahāprajnāpatī.

• **Butsuzō.** Statue of the Buddha or of a Buddhist deity.

Butsurui shōkō. Compilation of Japanese dialectal expressions, sorted by subject (universe, moral principles, flora, fauna, instruments, clothing, and language),written by Koshigaya Gozan (1717–87),

haiku poet and master of Takizawa Bakin, and published in Edo in 1775.

Buyaku. System of corvée labor instituted in the seventh century as part of the *ritsuryō* system. At first called *yōeki,* this labor system called for each male commoner to devote several days a year to work of public service. It was only in the late Heian period that the word *buyaku* was used; it covered a number of other obligations as well, among them military service *(gun'yaku).* The *buyaku* represented a heavy burden for the peasantry; it was lightened somewhat by Oda Nobunaga and Toyotomi Hideyoshi and was then transformed, during the Edo period, into a tax payable in money or in rice. Nevertheless, the villagers still had to maintain the transit points *(sukegō)* along the main post roads, as well as the bridges on these routes. *See* KUJI, YŌEKI.

Buyō. Generally, grouped under this term are all Japanese "classical" dance forms—Dengaku, Kowaka-mai, Noh, Kyōgen, and others, but mainly the Kabuki dances and those derived from Kabuki, including some modern styles. There are two major *buyō* styles: the Kabuki-*buyō* of Kabuki theater, and the Ji-uta-mai performed in Kyoto. These dances are performed to the accompaniment of *naga-uta* singers and instruments such as the shamisen and the *hayashi* ensemble of flutes and drums used in Noh performances. The Onoe school, founded by Onoe Kikugorō VI (1885–1949), is currently attempting to revive *buyō* and introduce it to the West by organizing tours abroad. *See* ONOE.

Buzen. Former Japanese province, now included in the prefectures of Fukuoka and Ōita (Kyushu). Also, city on the Suō Sea near Kita-Kyushu.

Byakkō Kosei Kai. Popular Shinto religious sect, founded by Goi Masahisa after 1945. Also called Byakkō Shintō Kai.

Byakko-tai. "White Tiger Troupe," brigade of several hundred young samurai of the Aizu clan who, in March 1868, took the side of the *bakufu* against the imperial troops during the Boshin Civil War. They were completely crushed during the Battle of Tonokuchihara on October 8, 1868, after which the 20 survivors committed ritual suicide. They remained famous for their courage and their determination not to survive defeat. *See* BOSHIN SENSŌ, IMORIYAMA, SHŌGI-TAI.

Byakudan. White sandalwood *(Santalum album)* that has a very fine grain and was generally reserved for sculptures of the Buddha. Red sandalwood *(Pterocarpus santalinus* or *indicus),* with a coarser grain but a penetrating perfume, was also used for sculpture.

Byakue Kannon. One of the 33 forms (Sanjūsan Ōgeshin) of Kannon Bosatsu *(Skt.:* Avalokiteshvara), corresponding, perhaps, to the Indian Esoteric Buddhist god Pāṇḍaravāsinī. The "White-Robed Kannon" is generally portrayed sitting in *renge-za (Skt.: padmāsana),* the lotus position, on a lotus blossom, holding in her right hand a scroll from the *Prajñāpāramitā* sutra, or a "jewel" *(hōshū, Skt.: mani)* against her chest, her left hand resting on the pedestal and holding a string or a rosary. Sometimes a veil partly covers her face (Ryūzu Kannon). She is also portrayed sitting on a rock or standing on two lotus blossoms beside the sea. This may be the original form of Nyoirin Kannon.

Byakugō-ji. "Temple of the *Urnā*" *(byakugō,* tuft of hair in the middle of Buddha's forehead), founded in Nara in the eighth century. Its Hondō and Tahōtō date from the Kamakura period (1185–1333).

Byakurō. "White alloy" of lead and pewter, used in goldsmithing and to decorate Buddhist religious objects. It was also used as inlay in certain lacquer works.

Byō. Monument erected to commemorate a deceased person, and ceremonies performed in his or her honor. This monument generally resembles a group of Buddhist or Shinto buildings (temple or shrine).

Byōbu. Screens composed of several leaves (2, 3, 4, 6, or 8), jointed and decorated with paintings or calligraphy. In general (though not as a rule), they measure from 130 to 180 cm in height and, depending on their size, are called *honken, tachigaku,* or *kazeyoke. Furosaki-byōbu* are small screens 40 to 50 cm in height, in two leaves, used for the tea ceremony *(chanoyu).* The *namban-byōbu* ("screens of the southern Barbarians") were made in Nagasaki and the surrounding region in the sixteenth and seventeenth centuries and usually show scenes with foreigners (Portuguese and Dutch) and Western ships. They are sometimes also called *Nagasaki-byōbu* or *Koku-sen-byōbu. See* NAMBAN.

Byōdō-in. Buddhist temple of the Jōdo sect founded in the eleventh century in Uji, south of Kyoto. At first a villa belonging to Minamoto no Tōru (822–95), then to Fujiwara no Michinaga (866–1028), it was transformed into a temple by Fujiwara no Yorimichi, who dedicated it to Amida in 1052–53. Its main hall (Amida-dō) was also called Hōōdō (Phoenix Hall) because on the crest of its roof were two bronze phoenix covered in gold leaf. The Hōōdō contains a large wooden statue of Amida, covered in gold leaf, sculpted by Jōchō (a National Treasure), and 52 small wooden images of the bodhisattvas who accompanied Amida during his "descent" *(raigō)* to welcome the souls of the faithful. The statue of Amida, 2.78 m high, was created using the *yosegi-zukuri* technique, an assemblage of various pieces of wood. On his lotus pedestal and golden halo, both also sculpted by Jōchō, are 12 images representing the "emanations" of Amida, as well as one of Dainichi Nyorai. Many buildings originally surrounded the Hōōdō, which was restored during the Meiji era. The others, like the Kannondō (Kannon Hall) were destroyed by fire several times (including the statue of Dainichi Nyorai, in 1336) and reconstructed. The lake in front of the Hōōdō was larger at first and shaped like the Sanskrit letter (Siddham; *Jap.:* Shittan) "A" (for Amida). This temple, the first of the Tendai sect (Jimon branch), was dependent on Amida of the Jōdo sect in the fourteenth century, while continuing to belong to Tendai. It is no longer used for worship but has been transformed into a museum.

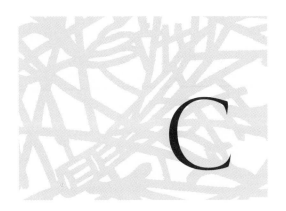

C

C. This consonant does not exist in Japanese. It is replaced by the syllables *ka, ki, ku, ke, ko,* or by *sa, shi, su, se, so.* The sound *ch* is replaced, in the katakana and hiragana syllabaries, by combinations: *cha (chi + ya), chu (chi + yu), cho (chi + yo);* the sound *che* does not exist. Finally, the sound *chi* is a form of *ta* on the table of 51 sounds (in which *ti* is replaced by *chi* and *tu* by *tsu,* since the syllables *ti* and *tu* do not exist). *See* GOJŪ-ON-ZU, HIRAGANA, KANA, KATAKANA.

Cabral, Francisco. Portuguese Jesuit (1529–1609), who served as Superior in Japan from 1570 to 1581. He had entered the Society of Jesus in India in 1550. His strict views clashed with the more liberal Alessandro Valignano, the official visitor to the missions in Asia, and he returned to India. He died in Goa. The Japanese had several names for him, among them Ōmura Sumitada, Ōtomo Yoshimune, and Ichijō Kanesada (in 1575).

Cachon, Mermet de. French Catholic priest (1828–70), member of the Foreign Missions. Arriving in Okinawa in 1855, he served as an interpreter for the first French embassy to Japan and then went to Hakodate, where he worked as a missionary and teacher for several years. He left Japan in 1863, but returned the following year to act as interpreter for ambassador Léon Roches; he also founded a school for teaching French in Yokohama. He accompanied the Japanese delegation, led by Tokugawa Yoshinobu's brother, Tokugawa Akitake, to the Paris World's Fair, and published a French–English–Japanese dictionary. The Japanese called him Kashun.

Cairo Declaration. Called Kairo Sengen or Kairo Kaigi, the Cairo Conference of November 22–25, 1943, brought together Franklin D. Roosevelt, Winston Churchill, and Chiang Kai-shek in an attempt to resolve the conflict with Japan. The statement that they issued confirmed their resolution to go to war with Japan, confiscate its colonies, and restore independence to Korea and Taiwan. This statement served as the basis for the Yalta Conference and the Potsdam Declaration regarding the fate of Japan.

Calendar.

Years. In 1873, Japan adopted the Gregorian calendar, while retaining the traditional calendar based on imperial eras *(nengō).* The method of counting years starting from the ascent to power of the mythical emperor Jimmu in 660 BC, which had never been widely used, was abandoned. However, rural dwellers used a different calendar, of Chinese origin, dividing the year into 24 "seasons" of about 15 days *(see* NIJŪSHI-SETSU), which determined dates for agricultural work. Another method of counting years, also of Chinese origin, was used concurrently with the calendar based on imperial eras. This method *(genka),* a sexagenary cycle, was divided into 12 "branches" *(shi),* corresponding to the 12 animal signs *(see* JŪNISHI), and five "stems" or "trunks" *(kan:* wood, fire, earth, metal, and water), considered major (positive, older brother: *-noe)* or minor (negative, younger brother: *-noto)* according to an alternating progression; thus, a composite sign returned once every 60 years. The first year of each cycle is always Rat-Wood-Positive, and the last is Boar-Water-Negative. There is thus the following sequence of years beginning each cycle (the system was adopted in 604):

604	904	1204	1504	1804
664	964	1264	1564	1864

724	1024	1324	1624	1924
784	1084	1384	1684	1984
844	1144	1444	1744	2044

Even years are positive in the order of the elements (Wood, Fire, Earth, Metal, and Water), while odd years are negative in the same order. The shortcoming of this system is that it does not provide the number in the cycle for these designations.

Imperial eras *(nengō)*, of varying lengths, were adopted in 645. A year was then designated by the name of its era followed by the chronological designation of the year by number; for example, "Shōwa 60" corresponds to 1985, the sixtieth year of the reign of Emperor Shōwa (Hirohito). Since 1868, there has been only one era per reign, beginning on January 1 of the year of that emperor's ascent to the throne. The word *kigen* (or *kōki*) is used to distinguish the date of the era from the date on the Gregorian calendar. See NENGŌ.

Hours. Traditionally, the Japanese hour *(koku)* corresponded to two Western hours, and the day was thus divided into twelve hours according to the following progression:

NIGHT *(gozen)*:

11 pm–1 am: hour of the Rat, Ne, Nezumi (9 bells, Kokonotsu).

1 am–3 am: hour of the Ox, Ushi (8 bells, Yatsu).

3 am–5 am: hour of the Tiger, Tora (7 bells, Nanatsu).

5 am–7 am: hour of the Hare, U, Usagi (6 bells, Mutsu).

7 am–9 am: hour of the Dragon, Tatsu (5 bells, Itsutsu).

9 am–11 am: hour of the Snake, Mi (4 bells, Yotsu).

DAY *(gogo)*:

11 am–1 pm: hour of the Horse, Uma (9 bells, Kokonotsu).

1 pm–3 pm: hour of the Sheep, Hitsuji (8 bells, Yatsu).

3 pm–5 pm: hour of the Monkey, Saru (7 bells, Nanatsu).

5 pm–7 pm: hour of the Rooster, Tori (6 bells, Mutsu).

7 pm–9 pm: hour of the Dog, Inu (5 bells, Itsutsu).

9 pm–11 pm: hour of the Boar, I, Inoshishi (4 bells, Yotsu).

The duration of these hours varied slightly according to the season and the time of day: for example, during the winter solstice, the duration of a *koku* was 1 hour 48 minutes during the day and 2 hours 12 minutes during the night; at the summer solstice, the *koku* was 2 hours 36 minutes during the day and 1 hour 21 minutes during the night.

There is a nine-hour difference between Japanese time and Greenwich Mean Time (or Universal Coordinated Time).

Months *(gatsu)* are designated by numbers: Ichigatsu (January, also called Shōgatsu), Nigatsu (February), Sangatsu (March), Shigatsu (April), Gogatsu (May), Rokugatsu (June), Shichigatsu (July), Hachigatsu (August), Kyūgatsu (September), Jūgatsu (October), Jūichigatsu (November), and Jūnigatsu (December). But in poetry and sometimes in common language, months are designated by typically Japanese expressions: Mutsuki, Kisaragi, Yayoi, Uzuki, Satsuki, Minazuki, Fuzuki, Hazuki, Nagatsuki, Kannazuki, Shimotsuki, and Shiwasu. The year is normally divided into four three-month seasons.

Days of the week *(shūkan)* are also designated, according to the Western custom, by names linked to the stars and to the five elements of Sino-Japanese cosmogony: Getsuyōbi ("moon day," Monday), Kayōbi ("fire day," Tuesday), Suiyōbi ("water day," Wednesday), Mokuyōbi ("wood day," Thursday), Kinyōbi ("metal day," Friday), Doyōbi ("earth day," Saturday), and Nichiyōbi ("sun day," Sunday).

The first calendars *(reki)* used to calculate time in Japan were introduced from China: Genka-*reki* (692), Gihō-*reki* (697), Taien-*reki* (764), Goki-*reki* (858), and Semmyō-*reki* (862), followed by those compiled in Japan: Jōkyō-*reki* (1685) by Shibukawa Shunkai, Hōreki Kōjutsu Gen-*reki* (1755) by Abe Yasukuni, Kansei-*reki* (1798) by Takahashi Yoshitoki, and Tempō-*reki* (1844) by Shibukawa Kagesuke. The last calendar was abandoned for the Western-style solar calendar by decree on December 9, 1872. The new calendar began on January 1, 1873, which corresponded to the 3rd day of the 12th month of Meiji 5. Nevertheless, both the traditional calendar *(nengō)* and the Western calendar are often used at the same time.

→ *See also* KICHIJITSU.

Calligraphy. The art of calligraphy appeared in Japan at the same time as the introduction of Sino-Japanese ideographs or "characters" *(kanji)* in the sixth century and has been kept alive, primarily based on Chinese models, to the present day. At first, scholars imitated the great calligraphers of the Sui and Tang dynasties, such as Wang Xijin (307–65), and many Japanese became expert calligraphers, including Saichō, Kūkai, and Emperor Saga. Starting in the tenth century, Japanese calligraphers began to develop styles unique to Japan though still

Sexagenary Cycle

Branch \ Stem	Kō WOOD + Kinoe	Otsu WOOD − Kinoto	Hei FIRE + Hinoe	Tei FIRE − Hinoto	Bo EARTH + Tsuchinoe	Ki EARTH − Tsuchinoto	Kō METAL + Kanoe	Shin METAL − Kanoto	Jin WATER + Mizunoe	Ki WATER − Mizunoto
RAT *Shi* Ne	1		13		25		37		49	
OX *Chū* Ushi		2		14		26		38		50
TIGER *In* Tora	51		3		15		27		39	
HARE *Bō* U		52		4		16		28		40
DRAGON *Shin* Tatsu	41		53		5		17		29	
SNAKE *Shi* Mi		42		54		6		18		30
HORSE *Go* Uma	31		43		55		7		19	
SHEEP *Bi* Hitsuji		32		44		56		8		20
MONKEY *Shin* Saru	21		33		45		57		9	
ROOSTER *Yū* Tori		22		34		46		58		10
DOG *Jutsu* Inu	11		23		35		47		59	
BOAR *Gai* I		12		24		36		48		60

Italics: Sino-Japanese pronunciation.

true to Wang's basic principles. Ono no Tōfū (894–966), Fujiwara no Sari (944–998), and Fujiwara no Yukinari (972–1028) were the most famous calligraphers of their time, known as the Sampitsu ("three brushes"). Their style is called Joōdai-yō. A new style developed based not on kanji but on the kana syllabaries, which were unique to Japan. In the Kamakura and Muromachi periods, Chinese calligraphy introduced by Zen monks followed the original canons.

After 1880, a new, modern style appeared in Japan, introduced by the Chinese calligrapher Yang Shoujing (1839–1915) and spread by Kusakabe Meikaku (1838–1922) and Iwaya Ichiroku (1834–1905), among others. It replaced the Ming Chinese style introduced by the Zen monk Yinyuan (1592–1673) and his disciples, called *kara-jō* (Chinese style), which had been favored throughout the Edo period. However, the ancient art continued to be practiced. Calligraphy is still popular, and competitions are organized in the schools at the beginning of each year. A person with good calligraphy is considered "culturally educated," while someone whose calligraphy is poor is seen as being uncultured.

Standard writing of Chinese characters, *kaisho,* is distinguished from cursive writing, *sōsho* ("grass writing," which gave rise to certain types of signatures, called *sōmyō* or *kaō*).
→ *See* AKEJI, ANDŌ SEIKŪ, ASHIDE, BOKU-SEKI, KANJI, KAŌ, NISHIKAWA SEIAN, ONO NO MICHIKAZE, SAMPITSU, SHOTAI.

Calpis ("karupisu"). Fermented drink based on *Lactobacillus acidophilus,* invented in 1919 by Mishima Kaiun and manufactured since 1948 by Karupisu Shokuhin Kōgyō. Refreshing and energizing, this drink is very popular in Japan and is exported, notably to the United States, as "Calpico."

Canon. Manufacturing firm founded by Mitarai Takeshi as Kannon, the name adopted by the Research Laboratories in Precision Optics in 1933, and specializing, since 1937, in the production of cameras, optical equipment, photocopiers, and computers. Canon's engineers introduced the ten-figure calculator (1964), the plain-paper photocopier (1968), the camera with integrated microchip (1976), and other innovations. The firm exports about 75% of its production under the Canon brand name.

Cappeletti, Giovanni Vicenzo. Italian architect (d. 1887) invited to Japan in 1876 to teach at the Bijutsu Gakkō, a newly created fine arts school. He designed many buildings between 1876 and 1885, among them the Yūshūkan weapons museum (at Yasukuni Shrine, Tokyo) in 1881. He then moved to San Francisco, where he lived for the rest of his life.

Capron, Horace. American agronomist (1804–85), born in Massachusetts. Invited to Japan in 1871 as a development consultant for the Hokkaido Colonization Office, he prepared plans for the agricultural development of the island and helped to found the Nōgakkō (Sapporo agronomy school). He returned to the United States in 1875.

Caron, François. French sailor (1600–73). Arriving in Japan with a Dutch trade mission in 1620, he learned Japanese and became an interpreter. In 1639, he was appointed manager of the Hirado trading post and became known for his diplomatic handling of disputes between the Dutch and the shogunal government. He left Japan in 1644 to become governor of Taiwan; in 1647, he was named director of the Dutch East India Company in Batavia. He perished on the way to Lisbon when the French East India Company ship he was commanding foundered.

Cary, Otis. American Congregational missionary (1851–1932), professor at Dōshisha Theological Seminary and long-time resident of Japan. He wrote *Japan and Its Regeneration* (1899) and *A History of Christianity in Japan* (1909).

Casio Computer Co. Western name of the company Kashio Keisanki, known mainly for its watches, calculators, and other high-technology electronic products. Founded in 1957, it currently exports more than 60% of its production under the brand name Casio.

Castles. What is most striking about Japanese castles, aside from their architecture, is that most of them were built between about 1550 and 1650, a period of 100 years. Before the mid-sixteenth century, there were only fortified houses *(yashiki)* and, in ancient times, small forts. After the mid-seventeenth century, castles were mainly palaces, though they retained the architectural form of fortified castles. The creation of Japanese castles is thus essentially linked to the social conditions that prevailed in the country during this relatively brief period in its history. During the Sengoku (Warring States) period, Japan was divided into a great number of estates whose heads, daimyo or others, were constantly at war to expand their territories and become favored vassals of the emperor, himself the puppet of the powerful men of the time, shoguns or others, many of whom were barely more powerful than the other lords in the provinces. To protect roads, mountain passes, and ports, each lord established fortresses on ridges, rocky spurs, or plains; these served no purpose except in times of war. Weapons and various provisions were stored in them, and their means of defense was adapted to the terrain. There were also a good number of monasteries or temples surrounded by thick walls and ditches, in the courtyards of which watchtowers were erected to survey the surrounding land. Small mountain forts *(sanjō)* had wooden walls covered with earth and sometimes faced with stones. Their massive gates were protected by lines of shields *(tate),* which was often an effective defense because armies fought on foot or horseback and had limited weapons—arrows, lances, and swords. In the late fifteenth century, these fortresses were modified so that families and members of religious sects could live within them permanently. The circumference of the walls expanded to hold a larger number of people and, eventually, armies. The residence of the daimyo, army leader, or sect leader was then enlarged, sometimes reaching seven stories in height, and served as the ultimate refuge and lookout point. The walls were doubled, then tripled, for better protection. The Inuyama castle, probably built around 1450; Edo castle, built by Ota Dōkan in 1457; the Yamashina fort near Kyoto, built in 1477 by the Ikkō sect of the Hongan-ji temple; and the fortified monastery at Ishiyama (Osaka), built in 1496 by

the same sect, each covered a very large area. These were the first attempts at true fortified castles; in the next century, castle architecture would undergo a radical transformation.

Two events in the mid-sixteenth century caused an upheaval in strategies and political conditions: in 1543, the first firearms were introduced into Japan by Portuguese traders; then, the major warlords—Oda Nobunaga, Toyotomi Hideyoshi, and Tokugawa Ieyasu—rose to power and made desperate efforts to unify Japan under their rule. But unification was not to occur without fierce battles between the various provincial and clan leaders. They followed Oda Nobunaga's example—who built the first true castle, Azuchi castle, in 1575 at Lake Biwa—and erected castles at strategic points on both mountains and plains *(hira-jō)* in their territories, in order to control troop movements and trade routes better. Azuchi castle served as a model for castles throughout Japan: it had a seven-story donjon *(tenshu),* and the interior was sumptuously decorated. Katō Kiyomasa (1562–1611) helped to build most of the castles of the period; his services were used by Oda Nobunaga, Toyotomi Hideyoshi, and Tokugawa Ieyasu. In 1583, Hideyoshi had a huge castle built in Osaka on the ruins of the Hongan-ji fortified monastery; to make it impenetrable, he had it constructed on enormous foundations of large boulders, fitted without cement, which were brought from the nearby island of Awaji. In 1594, he had another castle built in Fushimi, near Kyoto, in the Azuchi style. Although they stood up to enemy assaults, the Azuchi and Fushimi castles were vulnerable to fire because their superstructures were made of wood, then plastered to make them stronger and more solid. Each lord had one or more castles built; by the mid-seventeenth century, when peace was reestablished, there were several hundred of these complexes, which no longer served any use—from a military point of view, at any rate. Some were immense: the exterior wall of the Odawara castle was some 10 km long and defended by 20 towers *(yagura)*; in 1572, it was reinforced with 51 small forts. The castle in Himeji was expanded about 1600, on Ikeda Terumasa's orders; that in Nagoya was built in 1622 by Ieyasu, assisted by 22 daimyo of the western provinces; that in Kyoto (Nijō-jō), in 1603 by Ieyasu to serve as his residence. Many daimyo followed this example, erecting structures to serve as both a residence, a symbol of power and wealth, and, if necessary, a fortified place: at Wakayama (1585), Okayama (1573), Fukuyama (1619), Hiroshima (1589–93), Hikone (1604), Matsumoto (1594), Kumamoto (1601), Matsuyama (early seventeenth century),

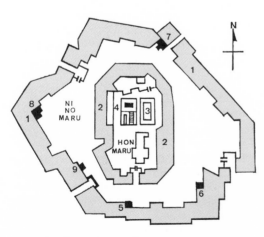

Plan of fortified castle in Osaka. 1. Exterior moats.
2. Interior moats. 3. Water reservoir. 4. Donjon.
5–9. Wall towers

and at Ōita, Kōchi, Sendai, Hirosaki, Takamatsu, Matsue, and Ōgaki, among other locations. These castles nevertheless proved to be vulnerable once the first cannons were introduced.

To establish his authority more firmly and discourage any warlike ambitions among the daimyo, Tokugawa Ieyasu forbade his vassals to build new castles or to make major repairs to those they owned, and had some castles demolished; most of the castles were then transformed into residential palaces. Successive courts added pleasure pavilions and other structures less austere than donjons. Gardens were laid out and the samurai carried out their drills within the disused walls. Nobles, courtiers, monks, and senior bureaucrats took up residence. In the space between the second and third walls, commoners lived, craftsmen worked and took refuge if they were threatened, and traveling merchants conducted business. Bureaucrats and samurai lived closer to the donjon, between the first and second walls *(ni-no-maru)*. The influx of people settling between the outside walls led to overflow conditions; gradually, towns *(jōka-machi)* developed around the castles as they had around monasteries *(monzen-machi)*. Some castle towns benefited from specific exemptions and grew considerably in the seventeenth century; the more powerful the daimyo living in the castle, the more bureaucrats he had, and the wealthier the town around the castle. Osaka and Edo, among others, owed their phenomenal expansion to the fact that their castles belonged to the shogun. Unfortunately, many castles were destroyed over the centuries, either by fire or in the civil war at the beginning of the Meiji era. Of those that remained standing, many were destroyed by the bombing during the Second World War. Some have been reconstructed according to the original plans, but in reinforced concrete. Since 1950, the government has undertaken to reconstruct the most beautiful castles that Japanese military genius created, thus preserving evidence of a dramatic period in the country's history. Some castles, such as the one in Osaka, have been converted into museums, and these "modern old castles" are attracting more tourists, both Japanese and foreign, every year.

Cats. Cats *(neko)* were introduced to Japan from Korea probably around the seventh century. Very rare at first, they were pets of court aristocrats, but they quickly multiplied and were abundant by the end of the Heian period (twelfth century). In the Heian court, cats had the privilege of the fifth rank of nobility and were thus among the emperor's familiars. They were called O-Koma-san ("Mister from Korea"). As in Europe, they were considered akin to witches in some regions, but they were not mistreated. It was also believed that *tanuki* or fox-witches *(kitsune)* could transform themselves into cats in order to enter houses more easily and to make fools of people. Many ghost stories involving cats *(bakeneko)* say that when they get old they can talk like humans. Traditionally, certain islands, called Neko-jima, are reserved for cats and no dogs are allowed to set foot on them. In the Edo period, cats, especially the short-tailed variety, were prized by artists and by geisha, who were sometimes also called *neko* (cat). Male calico cats *(mike-neko)*, which are rare, are considered good-luck charms. Black cats are supposed to cure certain illnesses. *Maneki-neko* ("cats that beckon") are sculpted and painted with one of their forepaws lifted as if to beckon someone, and this image is placed in many a shop window in the hope that it will attract customers and good luck. The Gotoku-ji temple became famous for having sheltered a cat that, it was said, invited passersby to enter. *See* HIDARI JINGORŌ, MANEKI-NEKO, MIKE, O-KOMA-SAN.

Ceramics. Pottery and ceramics techniques have been known in Japan since prehistory, beginning in the Jōmon period, and production continued without interruption in the Yayoi period. The potter's wheel *(rokuro)* may have been introduced as early as the Yayoi; however, ancient techniques continued to be used, such as coil-built *(himo-zukuri)*, ring-built *(tatara-zukuri)*, simple modeling *(tebineri)*, or molding on baskets *(kago-zukuri)*. The use of molds *(kata-zukuri)* appeared relatively late, with the need for mass production. The potter's wheel *(terokuro)* was set in motion by alternating pulls on a cord or with a stick; it was only at the end of the sixteenth century that Korean potters introduced the foot-driven wheel *(kerokuro)* to Japan. The early earthenware glazes were fortuitous, produced by ashes during firing. The first intentional glazes were lead-based celadon *(seiji)*, based on Chinese and Korean models, and appeared quite late. A type of white celadon, produced in the thirteenth and fourteenth centuries, is called *sei hakuji.*

Ceramic wares are called *yakimono* or more generally *setomono,* from the name of one of the most famous production sites. The different wares are most commonly named after the place of production: Seto-yaki, Oribe-yaki, and so on. It should be noted that the clay in Japan is different from that in China, where porcelain appeared very early.

Archeological excavations have changed the approach to studying ceramics as research has been conducted on mesolithic Jōmon and Yayoi sites and *kofun* burial mounds, as well as the sites of six kilns from the medieval period.

The first pottery (Jōmon, 11000 BC–ca. 300 BC) was very likely fired in pits. Each region had a local culture, but it was in Tōhoku that Jōmon pottery exhibited the most diversity. The most ancient pots have pointed bases; they were coil-built and fired at low temperature. On Kyushu, some pottery was incised with herringbone patterns, while in Tōhoku and Hokkaido designs were made by pressing cords into the clay. In Tōhoku, at the end of the Jōmon period, the Kamegaoka style revealed a new degree of creativity: vases, jugs, and small bowls have curvilinear designs and cord impressions that often create two decorative zones. The Jōmon clay was coarse and blackish. Large urns were used for burials, usually of children, in both the Kanto and Nagano regions in the third millennium BC. Figurines of human and animal shape *(dogū),* no doubt used for religious purposes, have been found from the early Jōmon period. Most of these figurines represent human females, often with a heart-shaped or triangular face, which evolved into a rounder form with "snow-goggle" eyes, especially in central and northern Japan.

The Yayoi period (ca. 300 BC–ca. AD 300) saw a change in forms and decoration. There is evidence that some of the pottery was made on a wheel, simply shaped with smooth surfaces. There were several basic types: pots for steaming, bowls, and dishes with feet. No kiln sites have been discovered yet, and it is likely that Yayoi pottery was fired in pits or in the open air under piles of straw and wood, which would seem to confirm that the black stains scattered on the bowls indicate where the wood touched the clay. Some examples of pottery decorated with drawings of animals, fish, people, and boats have been found, notably on the Itazuke site. Also appearing on Kyushu were new forms of burial in pairs of large urns joined at the neck (*see* KAMEKAN).

There were many advances during the *kofun* period (fourth–seventh century). New pottery techniques were introduced from Korea, resulting in *sue* stoneware, and Japanese reddish earthenware continued to be produced by the *hajibe* guild, makers of *haji* pottery. In the fifth century AD, the guild *(be)* of potters making *haniwa* began to compete with potters from the Korean Silla (Shiragi) dynasty, who had introduced *sue no utsuwa* pottery fired at high temperature in kilns built into hillsides. These potters created a new guild, *suetsukuribe,* which produced mainly vessels for religious use (*see* SUE-KI). The oldest *sue* kilns were discovered in 1961 south of Osaka, in Sakai, Izumi, Sayama, and Kishiwada.

These *anagama* kilns reached a temperature of at least 1200°C; the mainland models were quickly improved on and called *jagama* (also *teppōgama, hebigama*), based on their degree of sophistication and the arrangement of their combustion chambers. According to the *Nihon shoki,* the *sue* kilns were used by Korean potters in the service of Japanese clans. There are 500 of these kilns dating back to between the fifth and tenth centuries that have been discovered, but it is estimated that there were more than 2,000.

The Nara period (710–94) featured enameled ceramics imported from Tang-dynasty China (in China, called *sancai,* "three colors"), and ceramics made in Japan, enameled in one or two colors, imitating them. Examples have been found at the site of the ancient capital of Heijō-kyō, but the kilns that produced them have not yet been discovered.

In the Heian period, *sue* ceramics spread through the provinces, where they were produced on site or developed in the Yayoi pottery-production centers, notably Bizen, Tamba (Kyōto), and Seto (Owari), the last apparently having been the official supplier to the court in the ninth century. The manufacture of enameled tiles with a greenish tint, or with an ash slip fired at low temperature, the technique for which had been introduced from Korea or southern China (Yue kilns) at the end of the sixth century, continued unchanged, and pottery for daily use was still made according to the old methods. At Sanage near Nagoya (where the center for production of *sue-yaki* seems to have moved), however, white-clay pottery called *shirashi* was made. The nobles of the Heian period imported their ceramics from southern China, while local kilns were used only for utilitarian pieces; many potters reverted to earlier production methods, except in the centers of Bizen, Shigaraki, Iga, and Seto.

In the Kamakura and Muromachi periods, a number of trends arose: the Seto potters began to improve their Sanage-style ceramics, producing stoneware enameled in green and yellow, then in black and brown, influenced by Chinese wares of the Song and Ming dynasties. There was a search for new forms and an increase in incised decorations and applied glazes: urns with four handles, vases with lobed lips, and *meiping (Jap.: heishi)* flower vases (for plum branches). Their decoration was simple, consisting of impressions or engraved patterns with floral, plant, or fish motifs, sometimes obtained with molds, a technique that had long been in use for embossing tiles. Glazes were made either with wood ash or, in the fourteenth and fifteenth centuries, with iron oxide, which gave them a brownish tint. Particular shapes were developed for the tea ceremony: *temmoku* bowls, *cha-ire* (teapots), and so on, influenced by production in southern China.

In the twelfth century, the six "traditional" kilns included kilns for utilitarian production: *tsubo,* urns with narrow mouths and low shoulders; *kame,* jars with wide mouths and squat bodies; and *suribachi,* mortar bowls for grating foods. These three vessels reflected the transformation in nutrition resulting from the practices of Zen monks; they were used to store cereals, ferment foods, and grate roots. Added to this was regional production of cylindrical covered jars in which were placed bronze boxes designed to hold Buddhist sutras, which were buried in hillsides (*see* MAPPŌ). Recently, kilns were uncovered in Kaga (Ishikawa prefecture) and Suzu (Ishikawa prefecture), where blackish stoneware with floral decorations or printed or incised stamps were found, and Atsumi. Near the Hajibe traditional kilns were those of the *sue-ki* tradition (notably in Bizen, Shiragashi, Tamba, Suzu, and Kameyama), and stoneware in the *jiki* tradition: glazed ceramics from Seto, Sanage, Atami, Tokoname, Echizen, and other locations.

After 1404, when trade with China officially reopened, great quantities of Chinese ceramics were imported to be used by the Ashikaga shoguns and the great warriors for the tea ceremony (*chanoyu*) and to decorate palace interiors. Japanese potters began to produce special pieces for the tea ceremony, notably raku earthenware, which contrasted with the luxurious Chinese ceramics and corresponded better to the simple, refined taste (*wabi* and *sabi*) cultivated by Ashikaga Yoshimasa. New kilns, notably of the *ōgama* type, which allowed for more even firing and better-quality glazes, were built at the end of the sixteenth century to satisfy growing demand. There were many types of ceramics:

—Raku-*yaki,* comprising mainly tea bowls (*chawan*) made in the style created by Raku Chōjirō (1516–92), was continued by his son Jōkei and grandson Kichibei (Nonko, Donyu, 1599–1656), then imitated at many locations, notably Wakiyama. Tea bowls, incense holders, and urns, fired at low temperature, were enameled in red, white, or black. On some *chawan* were wave decorations (*maku-gusuri*) formed on the clay itself, which was often dark brown or blackish. The Ami family made remarkable pieces in this style. The pieces from the main kilns were called *hon-gama,* while those from auxiliary kilns were called *waki-gama.*

—The Shino kilns in Seto produced ceramics with a yellow enamel that was transparent (*guinomite*) or opaque *(ayamete),* sometimes decorated with stylized pressed or engraved designs, or with a blackish enamel *(hikidashiguro).* Some had a simple design made with a paintbrush (*e*-Shino) under a white glaze, while others had red (*beni*-Shino) or gray (*nezumi*-Shino) glazes. In the same region, the Oribe kilns produced dishes and bowls decorated with a paintbrush on one side only with simple motifs or bands, the rest of the surface being covered, for the first time, with a thick blue-green enamel (*e*-Oribe). Other pieces had a black or green glaze with stylized or geometrical designs in iron oxide.

—Bizen, Tamba, and Tokoname pottery, using clay with a high proportion of iron oxide (giving the clay a red tint), were generally fired and enameled at the same time, at a high temperature. Their geometrical shapes, often polygonal (at Tamba) required the use of molds to make bottles, pots, and various containers.

—In Iga and Shigaraki, the Tōdō family kilns produced sculptural works marked with black spots produced by an excess of carbon.

—In Kyushu, the potters brought to Japan by Toyotomi Hideyoshi when he returned from Korea produced Karatsu ware, sometimes simply decorated with a milky glaze over boldly applied brushstrokes in black iron underglaze on a gray background, the glaze scored in imitation of Korean pottery from the Yi period, such as the *Pun-ch'ŏng.* A number of potters followed this style, each adding variants, such as those at Nabeshima, Takatori, Hagi, and Satsuma in Kyushu, and Akahata, Zeze, Asahi, Shidoro, and Kosobe in Honshu.

At the beginning of the Edo period, when various types of ceramics developed in the preceding Muromachi and Azuchi-Momoyama periods were widespread, true porcelain, with its techniques of underglaze (*shita-etsuke*) or overglaze (*uwa-etsuke*) appeared, thanks to the discovery of kaolin by Ri Sampei, a Korean-born potter living in Kyushu, in 1616. The *noborigama,* a very elaborate type of kiln imported by Koreans, which could attain very high temperatures (1300–1400°C), was used. The first porcelain, white with cobalt decoration, was produced in the Tengudani kiln. Hon'ami Kōetsu and Sakaida Kakiemon built porcelain kilns in Kyushu, and other potters adopted the style in Kaga and Kutani. The Kakiemon method spread rapidly and was widely used. There were two main types: decorated on glaze in red, blue, and green on a white background (*nishikide*), with cobalt (*somenishikide*) or gold (*kinrande*), or underglaze; and designs painted in iron oxide in brown tones (*tetsu-e*), on cobalt in blue and white (*sometsuke*), and on copper in pink or red (*yūrikō*). The designs were inspired by the *suiboku* (ink painting) style of the time. Porcelain from the Kyushu kilns was exported in great quantities from the ports of Imari and Arita to Holland in particular, where such chinaware was highly appreciated and led to the development of Delft pottery. The Kutani potters imitated the techniques of their fellow potters in Kyushu, using Chinese or Japanese decorative motifs. When cobalt from China was no longer available, the ceramists turned to lower-quality Japanese cobalt. The first painted red decorations appeared around 1643, under the direction of Tōjima Tokuzaemon, with designs that were made in various colors by Sakaida Kakiemon. The Nabeshima kilns produced fewer pieces than did those at Arita, and these were reserved for the use of the local clan from 1675 to 1867. At the end of the seventeenth century, most kilns were producing porcelain, and the most famous painters were commissioned to decorate it. Each potter created his own style, recognizable in the shape and colors of the enamels he used. By the end of the period, production had grown considerably, often with a sacrifice in quality. The greatest ceramists of the time included Shonsui Gorōdayu, who made Chinese-style and blue-and-white pottery; (Nonomura) Ninsei (1595–1666); (Ogata) Kenzan (1663–1743), who opened a kiln in Kyoto where he fired pieces decorated with figurative motifs and calligraphy, some with designs by his brother, Ogata Kōrin; the Dōhachi family (1783–1858); and Hozen (1795–1855), who imitated Ming ceramics and made gold decorations on a red background.

In the Meiji era, it seems that the art of ceramics was somewhat neglected: a number of kilns closed and production consisted of pieces without great artistic merit, although there was a limited revival, encouraged by Yanagi Sōetsu and Hamada Shōji and inspired by Korean pottery. In the twentieth century, an English potter, Bernard Leach, studied Japanese pottery techniques and spread knowledge of them around the world. His books and studies stimulated new interest in Japanese folk art *(mingei)* and ceramics, and a number of traditional kilns were reopened. Today's Japanese potters, drawing on modern research, produce original works that are generally of very high quality.

Among the most common forms in Japanese ceramics are tea bowls *(chawan)*, bowls *(wan)*, sake cups *(choku* and *sakazuki)*, sake bottles *(tokkuri)*, large bowls *(domburi, hachi)*, incense holders *(kōrō)*, flower vases *(hana-ike, ueki-bachi)*, teapots *(chabin, kibisho, kinsu, dobin)*, large urns *(tsubo)*, jars for storing tea *(cha-ire, cha-tsubo)*, platters

(sara), and stacking boxes for food *(jubako)*. Modern potters have invented many other forms, most of them with a purely decorative purpose.

Main production sites: Agano, Arita, Atsumi, Banko, Bizen, Echizen, Hagi, Hirashimizu, Iga, Kaga, Kannei, Kameyama, Kanai, Karatsu, Koishiwara, Kosai, Kutani, Kyoto, Mashiko, Nakatsu-kawa, Onta, Sanage, Sasagami, Satsuma, Seto, Shigaraki, Shinanoura, Sōma, Sue, Suemura, Suzu, Takatori, Takōda, Tamba, Tōkita, Tokoname, Tsuboya, Tsutumi. *See* these entries and the towns mentioned in the text.

Cerqueira, Luis de. Portuguese Catholic priest (1552–1614), who became a bishop in 1593. He went to Japan in 1598 to succeed Bishop Pedro Martins (1542–98), the first bishop of Japan, and died in Nagasaki on the eve of the decree expelling foreign missionaries. He was thus the second and last Catholic bishop in Japan during the early period of Christianity.

Cespedes, Gregorio de. Portuguese Jesuit (1552–1611), who went to the Japanese province of Harima in 1578. He became a close friend of Konishi Yukinaga and accompanied him to Korea during Hideyoshi's invasion of that country. When he returned to Japan with the Japanese troops, he took refuge in Kokura, in the province of Buzen, where he died.

Cha. *See* TEA.

• **Cha no ma.** In a traditional Japanese house, this is the "tearoom," where visitors are usually received and served tea, and where family members gather to drink tea (or coffee), entertain themselves, and eat supper. In modern houses and apartments, the floor of this room is usually covered with tatami and has a *tokonoma* (raised alcove). *See* CHANOYU.

Chaguchagu Umakko. Horse festival, usually held on June 15 at the Komagata shrine in the city of Mizusawa, Iwate prefecture. The *kami* of horses is celebrated there because the region once specialized in horse breeding. During the festival, votive plaques *(ema)* are offered in the shrine and young men and women dance disguised as horses, decorated with small bells *(suzu)* that make a "chaguchagu" sound, the onomatopoeia that gave the festival its name. *See* MORIOKA.

Chakudasei. In ancient Japan, law obliging the *kebishi* (imperial police) to personally check the prisoners' chains during a particular ceremony twice a year, in May and December. This custom, inaugurated in the ninth century, became ritual at the end of the thirteenth century. Also called *chakuda no matsurigoto.*

Chamberlain, Basil Hall. Expert on Japan (1850–1935), born in Portsmouth, England. He went to Japan in 1873 to teach English at the Naval Academy, then taught linguistics at the University of Tokyo. A highly cultured man and a polyglot, he became very knowledgeable about the Japanese language and classical literature. He wrote many books, including translations of ancient poems and texts that are extremely useful to students of Japan. They include *The Classical Poetry of the Japanese* (1770), *Kojiki or Records of Ancient Matters* (1883), *A Handbook of Colloquial Japanese* (1888), *Things Japanese* (1890), and *A Practical Guide to the Study of Japanese Writing* (1905). Chamberlain amassed a major library of Chinese and Japanese texts, called Odō Bunko after his Japanese name, Odō. In 1911, he moved to Geneva, where he continued to study and write in spite of his declining health.

Chameshi. Dish of rice mixed with tea, said to have been invented in Nara by Buddhist monks during the Genroku era (1688–1703). Today, the tea is usually replaced by soy sauce (*shoyu*) and sweet *sake* (*mirin*), with the addition of azuki beans, meat, or fish. Many restaurants specialize in *chameshi.* In Osaka and Kyoto, a variety called *chagayu* is a gourmet delight.

Chanoine, Charles Sulpice Jules. French military adviser (1835–1915) posted to Japan in 1867 with a mission of 15 officers, after a brilliant career in China, to train and organize the shogunal troops. He returned to France at the beginning of 1869, after the Meiji Restoration, and was appointed a division general, then minister of war.

Chanoyu. Literally, "tea water," an expression designating the tea ceremony, also called *sadō* or *chadō,* "Way of Tea." Near the end of the Kamakura period, *chaya* (teahouses) opened near the temples, spreading the use of tea among the population; this beverage had previously been reserved almost exclusively for Zen monks and aristocrats. The faithful often gathered in *chaya;* in these meetings, first called *cha-yoriai* and later, during the Muromachi period, *tōcha* or *incha-shōbu,* participants tried to guess the provenances of the types of

tea that were being served. The *Taiheiki* provides splendid descriptions of this type of meeting. Other meetings, reserved for commoners, were more popular, however; they were often called *unkyaku-chakai,* "meeting of tea that leaves in a cloud," because of the tendency of green-tea froth to evaporate. In *cha-yoriai,* warriors often surrounded themselves with extravagant luxuries. The trend soon turned to moderation and, thanks to Nōami and the shogun Ashikaga Yoshimasa, the art of drinking tea was refined to become a ritual of aesthetics. In the fifteenth century, Murata Shukō devised new rules; these were refined by Takeno Jōō (1502–55) and his disciple Sen no Rikyū (1522–91), who recognized that the notion of *wabi,* or simplicity and restraint, should be observed. Toyotomi Hideyoshi organized huge tea meetings with thousands of people from all walks of life; the ceremony was soon monopolized by the *bushi* class, following recommendations by Furuta Oribe (1544–1615), and was transformed into the *daimyō-cha.* Following Furuta's teachings and those of his successors, Kobori Enshū (1579–1674) and Katagiri Sekishū, the tea ceremony became more spiritual and took the more appropriate name of *sadō.* Many tea-ceremony schools were founded based on rules formulated by past great masters: Katagari Sekishū's Fumai-ryū, Sen no Rikyū's Senke-ryū, his grandson Sōtan's Omote-Senke-ryū, and Sōtan's brothers' Ura-Senke and Mushanokōji-Senke, among others. At the end of the Edo period, the tea ceremony was once again transformed under the increasing influence of the *chōnin* (townspeople), and "classic" styles became formal and fixed. Other schools were founded, among them Oribe-ryū, Sekishū-ryū, and Enshū-ryū; because of the esotericism of their teachings, interest in the tea ceremony faded among the general population, and it fell into disuse during the Meiji era. After the Second World War, the tea ceremony was revived, and many foreigners came to Japan to learn about the art of *chanoyu* in one or another of the schools then active. The tea used for *chanoyu* is powdered green tea (*matcha*) that is mixed in the tea bowl, the best "vintage" being the first harvest of the year from Uji (Uji-*cha*).

The ceremony itself comprises various steps. First, the guests wait in the interior garden, having washed with water from the *chōzu-bachi* and rested for a few moments on the stone or wooden bench, called *koshikake machiai,* set out for this purpose. The host (*chasen* or *chajin*) fills the basin, washes, and invites the guests to do the same. Then the host enters the *chashitsu* to prepare; the others soon follow, crouching as a sign of humility as they pass through the *nijiriguchi* (low door). The host then bows to the *tokonoma* (raised alcove), on which a *kakemono* (hanging scroll) and a vase of flowers (*see* IKEBANA) have been placed, then takes his or her place near the square hearth while the guests sit facing the *tokonoma*. The host then serves a light meal *(kaiseki)* that has been prepared in an adjoining room *(mizuya)*, accompanied by *sake* and vegetables in brine *(kōnomono)*. Once this meal has been eaten, the host lights the charcoal fire, using special tools, and sets the water to boil for the tea: this is the first part of the ceremony, called *sumidemae*. The second part consists of offering sweets. Once the sweets have been eaten with bamboo chopsticks, the guests leave the *chashitsu* and go to the garden to rest and wash their mouths and hands again. This part, called *omogashi*, is followed by a "second entry" *(goiri)*; the guests take their places again while the tea master prepares the *matcha* (also called *koicha*) for each of them. Then the tea is presented *(koicha-demae)*. The host pours hot water on the powdered tea, mixes it with a small ladle *(hishaku)*, and whisks it to a froth with a bamboo whisk *(chashaku)*, then offers the bowl *(chawan)* of frothy tea. Each guest in turn is expected to lift the bowl to eye level, turning it to admire it from all sides, and finally taking a small mouthful of tea— the *itadakikata*. Then the bowl is passed to the next person, who does the same, wiping the rim of the bowl before taking a sip. Once everyone has taken a sip and praised the beauty of the bowl and the excellence of the tea, the various utensils that were used to prepare it are examined in the *dōgu no haiken*. The guests can then relax for a moment and even smoke. They are offered little candies *(higashi)*. Then the tea master, having been thanked with a bow, serves a light tea *(usucha)* while the participants continue to examine the other utensils. The host and guests then go out to the garden. The host bows deeply to the guests, who return the courtesy, and the ceremony is over. It is customary for the guests to return the next day to thank the host. *See* CHASHITSU, CHAWAN, CHAYA, KAISEKI.

Chashitsu. "Tearoom." A small room or hut of a particular architectural design, used only for the tea ceremony *(chanoyu)*. The first *chashitsu* was built by the shogun Ashikaga Yoshimasa in his Higashiyama villa in Kyoto. It was a small room of only four-and-a-half tatami. Sen no Rikyū (1521–91) wanted this room separated from the residence and had an extra pavilion, imitating a "grass-thatched hut" *(chashitsu)*, built in a specially designed garden. Made with simple (though sometimes expensive) materials, it was very small (two to five *tatami* in area) and the entrance was a low door (about 60 × 60 cm), the *nijiriguchi*. The interior was plain, decorated with flowers and a *kakemono* hanging scroll. A hearth *(ro)* was used to boil the water for tea, and a main pillar *(naka-bashira)*, generally wood with beautiful bark, supported the roof. Beside the main room *(chaji)* was a small room for storing utensils. This arrangement is still the basis of all *chashitsu*. The garden *(roji)* is divided into two parts separated by a rustic gate called *chūmon* (central gate). The entrance path is made of large stones so that guests do not get their feet wet. In the "interior" garden *(uji-roji)* is a stone basin, the *chōzubachi*, from which guests draw water using a long-handled bamboo ladle to cleanse their mouths and hands before they enter the *chashitsu*. The garden must be well maintained but give the appearance of being completely natural. When guests pass through the *chūmon*, they are expected to shed all worldly thought and immerse themselves in contemplation. The *chashitsu* is also called *chaseki*. *See* CHANOYU.

Chawan. "Tea bowl." The bowls used in the tea ceremony, in conformity with Sen no Rikyū's (1522–91) wishes, must appear rustic and simple. These modest-looking bowls are sometimes the work of master potters and passed down through the generations as family heirlooms. They are generally Raku-*yaki*, a type of blackish earthenware created by the Korean potter Chōjirō in the late sixteenth century on the orders of Sen no Rikyū. However, other types of pottery may be used for the tea ceremony, such as Hagi or Karatsu ware; Ido-*chawan* is currently the most popular. *See* CERAMICS, CHANOYU, RAKU, TEA.

Chawan-mushi. Clear bonito broth with beaten eggs, steam-cooked in covered bowls. Each region has a *chawan-mushi* specialty, made by adding *kamaboko* (fish-paste cake), mushrooms, *ginnan* (gingko fruit), bamboo shoots *(takenoko)*, and other ingredients.

Chaya. "Teahouse." A stall on the roadside or at the entrance to religious or public establishments, serving ordinary tea and some pastries, while giving travelers a chance to rest. Also called *chamise* ("tea shops"), *chaya* became very popular as soon as they sprang up, probably in the late Kamakura period (1185–1333), and they became widespread during the Edo period. As well as tea and cakes, many offered other, less innocent, diversions. The *chaya* tradition has been preserved; throughout Japan there are tea shops where tea and cakes, coffee, other beverages, and sometimes light meals are served. *See* CHASHITSU, TEA.

Chaya Shirōjirō. Family of wealthy Kyoto merchants, outfitters of trade ships *(shuin-sen),* and fabric merchants. The first merchant was probably Shirojirō Kiyonobu (1545–96), a masterless samurai *(rōnin)* adopted by the Chaya family. Tokugawa Ieyasu appointed him his fabric supplier. His sons, Shirojirō Kiyotada (1584–1603), Shirojirō Kiyotsugu, Shirojirō Michizumi, and Shirojirō Nobumune, helped develop the business by monopolizing the trade in raw silk and supplying many consumer goods to the *bakufu.* Starting in 1612, they obtained special licenses *(shuin)* to outfit the ships trading with Annam *(chaya-sen).* Their descendants, Nagayoshi and Koshirō Munekiyo, also served the Taokugawa shoguns and established trading branches of the Chaya house in the provinces of Owari and Kii.

Chaya Sōri. Weaver (active between about 1624 and 1644) of the Chaya fabric-trading family, who invented the indigo-based dyeing process *(see* AI) called Chaya-*zome,* used mainly for decorating *katabira* (summer kimonos). Also called Chaya Munemasa.

• **Chaya-tsuji.** General name given to weavers and dyers of the Edo period, suppliers to the imperial court and the Edo *bakufu.* Almost all of them belonged to the Chaya family.

• **Chaya-zome.** Indigo dyeing process in blue or brown tones, invented by Chaya Sōri around 1630. *See* KATABIRA.

Chazuke. Dish consisting of rice with tea added, and sometimes shredded salmon or other finely sliced fish. It is generally served at the end of the meal, especially in winter. *See* CHAMESHI.

Cherry tree. The *sakura* tree *(Prunus),* with its delicate pink flowers symbolizing the impermanence of all things, according to Buddhism, was closely associated with the samurai, for whom life was "as ephemeral as cherry blossoms." These flowers also became one of the symbols of Japan. In spring, the few days that the blossoms last is called *hanami* or *sakurami* ("cherry-blossom viewing"), when Japanese like to meet under the flowering trees to relax, eat, drink, and sing. There are more than 300 varieties of cherry trees *(sakura no ki)* in Japan, divided into *yamazakura* (mountain cherry trees) and *satozakura* (village cherry trees, more than 200 varieties). *See* HANAMI, SAKURA.

Chian Iji-hō. Peace Preservation Law of 1925, forbidding any attack on state security or individual property, and outlawing any organization having these goals, directed mainly against communists. In 1928, the law was modified to stipulate the death penalty or a life sentence of forced labor for those who broke it. It was the logical follow-up to another law, Chian Keisatsu-hō, promulgated in 1900, that aimed to control all political organizations, reinforcing the ban on freedom of expression and association, and thus giving full power to the police. Both laws were abolished in 1945.

Chiba. Main city of Chiba prefecture, on Tokyo Bay. During the Edo period, it was a castle town and transit point. Its very active port is one of the busiest in Japan. Not far from Chiba is an archeological site from the Jōmon period, the Kasori-*kaizuka.* Chiba University (Chiba Daigaku), founded in 1874 as a medical college and promoted to university status in 1949, has more than 10,000 students. *Pop.:* 800,000.
   • Family of powerful daimyo of the province of Shimōsa, descendants of Taira no Yoshibumi, who remained active until 1590. *See* CHIBA TSUNETANE.

• **Chiba-ken.** Chiba prefecture, on Tokyo Bay, includes what was once the provinces of Shimōsa, Kasuza, and Awa. It is a highly industrialized region. Narita international airport is located in Chiba. On the Pacific coast are excellent beaches which are extremely popular with Tokyo residents.

Chiba Ayano. Artisan dyer (1890–1980) from Miyagi prefecture, specializing in indigo *(see* AI). She received the title of Living National Treasure in 1955 for having preserved and taught traditional dyeing techniques.

Chiba Tsunetane. Warrior (1118–1201), son of Chiba Tsuneshige and leader of the Chiba clan of Shimōsa. In 1156, during the Hōnen uprising, he sided with Emperor Go-Shirakawa; in 1180, he supported Minamoto no Yoritomo, becoming a general famous for his military exploits. Having pacified the Kyoto region in 1187, he accompanied Yoritomo in his expedition north in 1189, then entered Kyoto with him in 1190.

Chichibu. Town in Saitama prefecture (Honshu), famous for its production of cement, manufactured from Bukōzan limestone since 1923, and for its silk. Mulberry bushes are grown on the Chichibu Plain (Chichibu Bonchi). *Pop.:* 65,000.

• **Chichibu Jiken.** Peasant revolt in the Chichibu region in November 1884. The peasants had been impoverished due to finance minister Matsukata Masayoshi's deflationary policies, and they intended to attack public buildings in order to destroy documents relating to their debts. Regiments sent from Tokyo managed to quell the revolt. More than 3,000 peasants were arrested and sentenced to prison terms, and their leaders received death sentences.

• **Chichibu no Miya Yasuhito.** Imperial prince (1902–53), younger brother of Emperor Shōwa, and a general. After the Second World War, he directed a number of sports associations. Also called Yasuhito Shinnō. *See* AKIHITO, HIROHITO.

• **Chichibu Matsuri.** Annual festival in Chichibu, with processions accompanied by a type of musical group, Chichibu-*daiko,* composed of one large and three small drums, a flute, and cymbals.

Chichijima. Main island of the Ogasawara archipelago, populated in 1830 by European and Hawaiian sailors, then by families of Japanese fishers. The island has a good port at Futami. Occupied in 1945 by the United States, it was returned to Japan in 1968. *Area:* 24.5 km². Also called Peel Island. *See* OGASAWARA GUNTŌ.

Chidaijōkanji. Official position created in the Nara period for a deputy to the *dajō-daijin* (grand minister of state) to control bureaucrats. This position, reserved for members of the imperial family, became honorary at the beginning of the tenth century, then disappeared.

Chi Den. Painter (*gō:* Tan'an, active ca. 1500) of the *suiboku* (ink painting) school of Muromachi, a student of Sōami. He was a Zen monk in Kyoto.

Chifijing. Title given to Shinto head priestesses on the Ryukyu Islands before the eighteenth century.

Chifuren. Abridged title of Zenkoku Chiiki Fujin Dantai Renraku Kyōgi-kai (National Federation of Regional Women's Organizations), an association founded in 1952 by Yamataka Shigeri to promote women's rights. It was active mainly in the economic sector. *See* YAMATAKA SHIGERI.

Chigai-dana. In domestic furniture, set of *tokowaki* ornamental shelves adjoining the *tokonoma* alcove and arranged in steps, often above a built-in cabinet. *See* TOKONOMA.

Chigai-hōken. "Law of extraterritoriality," imposed in Japan by the first foreign consuls in 1858, giving them the right to judge their own nationals, thus putting them beyond Japanese law. This law, imposed with the Unequal Treaties (Jōyaku), was abolished when these treaties were reviewed, in 1899.

Chigasaki. City in Kanagawa prefecture, residential and industrial suburb of the Tokyo-Yokohama metropolitan area. *Pop.:* 180,000.

Chigetsu-ni. *Haikai* poet (d. after 1706), wife of a merchant named Kawai, of Owari province. She became one of Bashō's disciples, as did her son, Kawai Otokuni. Around 1687, after her husband died, she became a Buddhist nun *(bikuni).*

Chigi. In Shinto architecture, ornamental roof beams that cross at each end of the ridge, extending into a V in the *shimmei* style. The *chigi* may have symbolized the stag antlers that shamans placed on the roofs of their huts to indicate their inviolable and sacred nature. The ends of the *chigi* are cut horizontally in the case of a shrine dedicated to a female *kami,* and vertically in the case of one dedicated to a male *kami.* In the *taisha* style (for instance, at Izumo), probably an older style, the *chigi* are separate from the gables and form an X at each end of the ridge. Sometimes called *higi.*
→ *See* TENDAI-SHŪ.

Chigo. "Little boy." At first, because of their presumed innocence and purity, *chigo* were supposed to represent *kami* during Shinto festivals. Later, the name was used for domestic servants of aristocratic families or temples. Later still, *chigo* replaced women who could not attend certain ceremonies *(ennen).* The term was then extended to include effeminate young men, partners of monks or nobles with "depraved morals." *See* DŌJI.

• *Chigo kannon engi.* "Legend of Chigo Kannon," a fourteenth-century Buddhist *emakimono* handscroll preserved in the Murakami collection (Hyōgo prefecture).

- *Chigo-monogatari.* Popular tale, one of the *otogi-zōshi,* dating from the Muromachi period, telling the story of a young page *(chigo)* in a Buddhist monastery. Also called *Ashibiki-e.*

Chigusa Tadaaki. General (d. 1336) of noble ancestry who assisted Emperor Go-Daigo. He went into exile with the emperor in 1331, escaped to Oki Island with him, and helped Ashikaga Takauji capture Rokuhara, the seat of the Kamakura *bakufu* in Kyoto. But he later opposed Takauji and died fighting against him in Sakamoto (Ōmi).

Chigyō. Feudal system of proprietorship, which developed during the Heian and Kamakura periods after the breakdown of the *ritsuryō* system. Combined with *shiki* (possession of land), the *chigyō* represented the actual exercise of those rights in terms of administration and taxation; the combination was called *shiki-chigyō.* The *shiki* fell into disuse in the thirteenth and fourteenth centuries, and only the *chigyō* remained in force. *See* JITŌ.

- **Chigyōkoku.** Province or estate whose proprietorship was conceded to an individual or a monastery. In the Kamakura period, most *chigyō-koku* became hereditary, but they disappeared during the civil wars of the fifteenth century.

Chihaya. Name given in 1937 to an armored vehicle (type 97) used by the Japanese troops in China and Burma during the Second World War. *Weight:* 15 tons; *length:* 5.5 m; *armor:* 25 mm; *crew:* 4; *speed:* 40 kmh; *range:* 190 km; *weapons:* one 57 mm cannon and two 7.7 mm machine guns.

Chihaya-jō. Fortress built by Kusunoki Masashige in 1332 on Mt. Kongō, at a height of 1,112 m, in Kawachi province. Conquered in 1390 by one of the generals of the Ashikaga *bakufu,* it was abandoned.

Chiji. Title of prefectural governors created by the Meiji government in 1868. They were called Kenrei (except in Kyoto, Osaka, and Tokyo) from 1871 to 1886, when the title Chiji was once again used. Since 1947, they have been elected by universal suffrage. *See* KENREI.

Chijimi. General name for cotton crepe fabrics, production of which started in Akashi in the seventeenth century. Crepe de chine (in silk) is called *chirimen.*

Chijin-godai. The Shinto "five generations of terrestrial *kami*" who succeeded the "seven generations of heavenly *kami*" (Tenjin-shichidai), and from whom the emperors of Japan are said to have descended. They themselves were the descendants of Izanagi and Izanami, the progenitors of the Japanese islands. According to the traditional mythological chronology, the five generations were:
   1) Amaterasu, Tsukiyomi, Susanoo;
   2) Amaterasu's sons (Mayasa-Akatsu-Kachi-Hayashi-Amano-Hoshohi-Mimi, Amano-Hoi, Amatsu-Hikon, Ikutsu-Hikone, Kumano-Kusubi);
   3) Amatsu-Hitaka-Hikoho no Ninigi (son of Masay-Akatsu) and his son Hosuseri;
   4) The youngest brother of the latter, Amatsu-Hitaka-Hiko-Hohodemi, and his brother, Hono-Akeri (Hoderi);
   5) The son of Hiko-Hohodemi, Amatsu-Hitaka-Hiko-Nagizatake-Ugaya-Fukisezu, and his sons Hiko-Itsuze, Inahi, Mike-Irino, and finally Kamu-Yamato-Iwarebiko (Jimmu Tennō, the first emperor).

Chjin no ai. "A Fool's Love." Novel by Tanizaki Jun'ichirō (1886–1965), published serially in Osaka in 1924–25. It is the story of a serious man who falls in love with a "modern" woman, marries her, and becomes her love slave, taking pleasure in being humiliated by her. This novel of social mores, dealing with problems of couples and those posed by a woman-child, was very successful and republished many times.

Chijiwa Seizaemon. Young devotee of Christianity (Chijiwa Miguel, born ca. 1550, date of death unknown) who was one of the four Japanese Christians sent to Rome in 1582 by Arima Harunobu and Ōmura Sumitada, the Kyushu daimyo. Chijiwa became a novice Jesuit in 1591, but seems to have renounced his faith a little later. It is not known what became of him.

Chijun. Buddhist painter (twelfth century) at the court of Retired Emperor Toba, who worked at temples founded by the emperor and his wife, Bifukumon-in. Chijun received the title Hōin in 1154. None of his works has survived to the present. It seems that he worked in Yamato-e style, as did his colleagues Fujiwara Takayoshi and Raishun.

Chikako. Poet (Jūsan'mi Chikako, Shinshi, thirteenth–fourteenth centuries), daughter of Minamoto no Morochika. Famous in her time, she took part in many literary competitions, notably in 1289 and 1303. The *Shin gosenshū* anthology includes 54 of her poems, and the *Gyokuyōshū* has 30. She became one of the concubines of Emperor Go-Daigo and was the mother of Morinaga Shinnō. She was also called Mimbu-kyō San'mi. *See* KAZU NO MIYA.

Chikakusan-minshū-kyō. Shinto subsect of Mitake-kosha, founded in 1929 by Nebashi Umetarō (1901–42).

Chikamasa. Sculptor of ivory netsuke (Shōminsai, early nineteenth century).

Chikamatsu Hanji. Playwright (1725–83), born in Osaka, who wrote for the puppet theater *(ayatsuri-shibai)*. Son of a Confucian scholar, Hozumi Ikan, he became a student of Takeda Izumo II and took the name Chikamatsu in tribute to Chikamatsu Monzaemon. He wrote some 50 plays for the Takemoto-za in Osaka (which later became the Bunraku-za) and specialized in adapting Noh plays, in collaboration with other authors. Among his best-known plays are *Ōshū adachiga hara* (1762), *Honchō nijūshikō* (1766), *Awa no naruto* (1768), and *Igagoe dōchū sugoroku* (1783). After he died, the puppet theater was overshadowed by the Kabuki theater and did not reemerge until the end of the nineteenth century, with the advent of Bunraku.

Chikamatsu Monazaemon. Playwright (Sugimori Nobumori; Heima; *gō:* Heiandō, Fui Sanjin, Sōrinshi, 1653–1724), born in Kyoto into a samurai family. He became a Buddhist monk at the Gonshō-ji monastery in Ōmi, where he completed his classical education. In 1676, he began to write *jōruri* for the puppet theater *(ayatsuri-shibai)*, for the more famous *jōruri* singers and Kabuki actors, such as Sakata Tōjūru, with whom he worked on *Fujitsubo no onryō* (The Evil Spirit of Lady Fujitsubo), written between 1675 and 1685, and other famous plays: *Shusse kagekiyo* (1686), *Keisei hotoke no hara* (1699), *Keisei mibu-dainembutsu* (1702). In 1686, he worked with Gidayū (d. 1714) and Masadayū (1691–1744), and his style was updated under the influence of these co-authors. He worked first for the Miyako Mandayū-za theater in Kyoto, then, starting in 1703, for the Takemoto-za in Osaka, which was directed by Gidayū, his style turning to realism. There are two phases in his production: the *jidaimono,* or stories of real, more or less contemporary events, and the *sewamono,* depicting mainly the sentiments of the *chōnin* (townspeople). Among Chikamatsu Monzaemon's masterpieces (which have been compared, justly, to

Shakespeare's plays), are *Sonezaki shinjū* (The Love Suicides at Sonezaki, 1703), *Yuki-onna gomai hagoita* (1705), *Kokusen'ya kassen* (The Battles of Koxinga, 1715), *Kokusen'ya konishi kassen* (The New Battles of Koxinga, 1717), *Shinjū Ten no Amijima* (ca. 1720), *Onna-goroshi abura no jigoku* (ca. 1721), *Kanhasshu tsunagi uma* (The Horse Relay of Kantō, 1724), and *Karabune hamashi ima no Kokusen'ya* (Story of a Chinese Boat, the Real Koxinga, 1727). Most Kabuki and Bunraku theaters still have Chikamatsu Monzaemon's plays in their repertoire, either in their complete versions, or as rewritten by Chikamatsu Hanji or other writers.

Chikamatsu Shūkō. Writer (Tokuda Hiroshi, 1876–1944), born in Okayama, in the naturalist school. His most successful novels are *Wakaretaru tsuma ni okuru tegami* (Letter to the Woman Who Left Me, 1910), *Giwaku* (1913), *Kurokami* (Black Hair, 1922), and *Ko no ai no tami ni* (1924); his novels tended to have many autobiographical elements.

Chikamori. In Kanazawa, Ishikawa prefecture, site of a typical Hokuriku prehistoric settlement dating from the Late and Final Jōmon periods (ca. 2000 BC–ca. 300 BC).

Chikara-ishi. Large rocks, usually rounded, placed in the courtyards of Buddhist temples and Shinto shrines. The faithful tried to lift them to demonstrate their strength and devotion and predict the future *(see* BOKUSEN). These rocks have many legends attached to them. Other, smaller stones, which in popular beliefs have protective powers, are sometimes placed in *tokonoma* alcoves or beside the beds of sleeping children to make them strong. Also called *hakara-ishi* and, in Okinawa, *bijuru.*

Chika-shiki yokoana. Burial method used in ancient times, consisting of a vertical shaft leading to a short horizontal gallery ending in a funerary chamber. The few tombs of this type discovered to date are located in northern Kyushu and in the Kanto region. Based on the funerary goods placed in them, they have been dated to the fifth or sixth century AD. *See* YOKOANA.

Chikayuki. Netsuke sculptor (Fukushima Chikayuki; *azana:* Kagon, Suginoya, 1837–82) in Edo and a maker of dolls called Asakusa-*ningyō*. He also sculpted some Noh masks and painted *kakemono* hanging scrolls in a highly decorative style.

Chiken-in. Mudra *(Jap.: in-zō)* of the "fist of wisdom" or the "six elements," specific to Dainichi Nyorai in his Kongō posture. The right hand is closed in a fist over the upright index finger of the left hand. Sometimes called Kakushō-in, Daichi-in, Dainichi-Ken-in. *See* DAINICHI.

Chikō. Buddhist monk (dates unknown, Nara period), famous for his erudition with regard to Buddhist texts. Like his master, Chizō, he belonged to the Sanron sect. He is said to have studied the texts for 30 years and come to the conclusion that the Buddha's teaching could be summarized in a single sutra, the *Hannyaharamita-shingyō (Skt.: Prajñāpāramitā-hridaya-sūtra),* on which he wrote a commentary, the *Hannya-shingyō jutsugi.* He also wrote other exegetic works. He is considered a precursor to the Pure Land (Jōdo) doctrines of Amidism.

Chikubashō. "Bamboo Stilt Anthology." A work of moral instruction for the samurai, written in 1383 by Shiba Toshimasa (1350–1410), a deputy shogun in the Ashikaga government.

Chikubu-jima (Chikubu-shima). Small island in north-central Lake Biwa (Biwa-ko), considered sacred since ancient times. On it is a Shinto shrine, the Tsukubasuma-jinja, dedicated to Benten and Asai-hime no Mikoto. In 1603, Hideyori, Hideyoshi's son, sent one of his ships from Fushimi castle (decorated with paintings by Kanō Eitoku) to have it dedicated to the cult of Asai-hime. Beside the Tsukubasuma-jinja is a Buddhist temple, the Hōgon-ji, which was likely founded by the monk Gyōgi in the eighth century. It is one of the Sanjūsan-sho (Thirty-Three Temples of the Western Pilgrimage) to Kannon. Close by is a shrine dedicated to Benzaiten, one of the three most visited Benten-dō in Japan, with those at Itsukushima and Enoshima. The island is only 0.14 km² in area and is known as one of the Eight Views of Lake Biwa (Biwa Hakkei). *See* BENZAITEN.

• *Chikubushima.* Title of a Noh play: a courtier visits the famous island on Lake Biwa in order to worship Benten.

Chikuden. Painter (Tanomura Kōken, Tanomura Ken; *azana:* Kun'i, Kōzō; *gō:* Kyūjō-senshi, Chikuden, Ransui-kyōkaku, Kōtō-shijin, Kachi-kuyūsō-shujin, Setsu-getsu-shōdo, Hosetsuro, 1777–1835), born in Takeda. He painted mainly flowers, landscapes, and generic scenes in the Nanga style, and worked with many other painters, including San'yō, Shōchiku, Mokube, and Unge. In 1801, he was a student of Tani Bunchō in Edo. Also a Confucian writer, he wrote a number of works on painting, including *Sanchūjin-jōzetsu* and *Chikuden-sō shiyū garoku.* He adopted the painter Tanomura Chokunyū. Sometimes called Tanomura Chikuden.

Chikudō. Painter (Kishi Shōroku; *azana:* Shiwa, Hachirō; *gō:* Chikudō), born in Kyoto, and a student of Kishi Renzan. He painted mainly animals. Also called Chikutō.

Chikugo. Former province in northern Kyushu, now Fukuoka prefecture.
• Town in southern Fukuoka prefecture, which produces, along with the nearby town of Kurume, fabrics dyed using the ikat method, called *kurume-gasuri. Pop.:* 45,000.

• **Chikugogawa.** River in Kyushu, 123 km long, crossing Ōita, Fukuoka, and Kumamoto prefectures. Its source is on the slopes of the Aso volcano. It is called Mikumigawa on its upper course, and it flows into the Bay of Ariake, having drained a basin measuring 2,860 km².

Chikuha. Painter (Odake Somekichi; *gō:* Chikuha, 1878–1936), born in Tokyo and a student of Gyokushō.

Chikuhō. City in northern Kyushu, in Fukuoka prefecture, and major coal-mining center, exporting through the ports of Fukuoka and Wakamatsu and by rail to Kita-Kyushu. Nearby is the largest coal bed in Japan, about 800 km² in area. However, most shafts stopped operating in the 1950s.

Chikukei. Painter (Nakabayashi Narishige; *azana:* Shōfu, Kingo; *gō:* Chikukei, 1816–67), son and student of Chikutō in Kyoto. He painted in the Nanga style.
→ *See* KI-EN.

Chikuma Shobō. Publishing house founded in 1940 by Furuta Akira and Usui Yoshimi, which became known for its encyclopedias on modern literature. After many financial difficulties, it closed in 1978, but resumed its activities soon after.

Chikuō. Painter (Katsuta Teikan, Katsuta Sadanori; *azana:* Shisoku, Yokei, Inosuke, Okinojō; *gō:* Tōhin, Shichikuan, Shūyūsai, Chikuō, mid-seventeenth century) of the Kanō school, student of Kyūhaku. He was the official painter of the shogun Tokugawa Iemitsu.

Chikurin-in. Buddhist temple in Yoshino; the garden was designed by Sen no Rikyū at the end of the sixteenth century.

• **Chikurin-ji.** Buddhist temple in Kōchi prefecture (Shikoku), founded in the eighth century, with a garden designed by Musō Kokushi. It has a Hondō (main hall) dating to the late sixteenth century, and an Edo-period Shoin.

Chikusai. Sculptor of wood netsuke (eighteenth century).
• Netsuke sculptor (late nineteenth century), working in Osaka.

Chikusai monogatari. Novel describing the famous sites in Japan, attributed to Karasumaru Mitsuhiro (1579–1638), in the *kana-zōshi* genre. It may, however, have been the work of Isoda Michiharu.

Chikuseki. Painter (Nagamachi Ki; *azana*: Kin'ō, Tokubei; *gō*: Kinken, Chikuseki, 1757–1806) of the Nanga school. A student of Ryōtai, he painted mainly landscapes.

Chikushō. "Animal world," one of the "six paths" (*rokudō, Skt.: gati*) to reincarnation according to certain Buddhist theories. It has become a common insult and swearword. *See* ROKUDŌ.

Chikutō. Painter (Nakabayashi Seishō; *azana*: Hakumei; *gō*: Taigen-an, Tōzanichi, Chūtan, Chikutō or Chikudō, 1776–1853). He was born in Nagoya and lived in Kyoto, where he was a student of Yamada Unsho and Kamiya Ten'yū, of the Nanga school. He wrote a number of works on the art of painting, including *Gadō kongō gine, Chikutō-gakō* (Texts on Painting), *Chikutō-garon* (Theories of Painting), *Chikutō sanjin jimbutsu* (Book of Drawings of Chinese Character Types, 1852), and *Bunga-yūeki*. He was Chikukei's father and teacher.

Chikuzen. Former province in northern Kyushu, now part of Fukuoka prefecture.

• **Chikuzen-biwa.** *See* BIWA.

• **Chikuzen no Kami.** *See* TOYOTOMI HIDEYOSHI.

Chimbata. Custom of lending a loom to peasants so that they could weave fabric at home. Home-based weavers were paid by the manufacturer, who took all of their production. This custom is still in effect for certain luxury fabrics. Also called *debata*.

Chinchō. Painter (Hakawa Chinchō, Manaka Chinchō; *azana*: Chūshin, Ōta Bengorō; *gō*: Sandō, Chinchō, d. 1754), born in Edo. A student of Kiyonobu, he produced mainly ukiyo-e prints.

Chinda Sutemi. Diplomat (1856–1929), consul in Shanghai (1895), then ambassador to Berlin (1908–11), Washington (1911–16), and London (1916–20). He was appointed Grand Chancellor of the Empire in 1927.

Chindon-ya. Almost extinct profession consisting of street performance to advertise for a show or a store. The *chindon-ya* was generally a man dressed in bright colors who played several instruments at once. In the Meiji era, this profession replaced that of *tōzai-ya* in the Edo period, in which men simply beat a drum or banged clappers to attract a crowd, whom they then harangued, crying, *"Tōzai! Tōzai!"* (From East to West, [Listen]!)

Chinjufu. Military district for "pacification and defense" of Japan, created during the Nara period in northern Honshu to fight the Ainu (Ezo) tribes. It was directed by a *sei-i-tai-shōgun* ("general against the barbarians"). At first located in Tagajō (Miyagi prefecture), it was moved farther north to Azawajō in 801, after Sakanoue no Tamuramaro's victories. Once Honshu was conquered, the clans of the north occupied the base, which was abandoned at the beginning of the fourteenth century.
• During the Meiji era, the Yokosuka Sasebo and Maizuru naval bases were called Chinjufu.

Chin Jūkan. Ceramist (1835–1906) from Kagoshima who built the first porcelain kiln in Naeshirogawa in 1857. He specialized in ceramics for export to the West and in the traditional decoration called *kinrande* ("with gold streaks"), also made mainly for export.

Chinju no kami. Guardian *kami* of a specific place or territory. Each province, region, and village had its own *chinju*, as did large cities such as Kyoto and, in former times, castles and their dependencies. *See* UBUSUNAGAMI, UJIGAMI.

Chinkai. Buddhist monk (1091–1152) of the Jōdo and Sanron sects, and a painter who was well known in his time. He was the son of painter Fujiwara no Motomitsu. His main subjects were religious, but no example of his work has survived, except through copies. He lived at the Tōdai-ji, in Nara, then the Zenri-ji, in Yamashiro. He wrote an exegetic text, *Ketsujō-ōjōshū* (Collection of Texts on the Certainty of Rebirth in Paradise) on devotion to Amida Buddha.

Chinkin. Method of decorating lacquered objects using inlaid gold wire. This Chinese technique goes back to the Song dynasty and was introduced to Japan during the Muromachi period. *Chin.: qiangjin.*

Chin-koro. Small dogs of mixed breed, in fashion during the Edo period and the Meiji era. Geisha were particularly fond of them, and ukiyo-e printmakers often portrayed geisha with their dogs or as a design decorating their kimonos. Japan exported these lapdogs to Europe during the Meiji era and offered a pair to Queen Victoria. They are now imported because the breed is almost extinct in Japan. *See* DOGS.

Chinnen. Painter (Ōnishi Chinnen; *azana:* Taiju, Yukinosuke; *gō:* Unkadō, Son'an, Kaō, 1792–1851) of the Nanga school. A samurai serving the Edo shogunate, he became a student of Bunchō.

Chinsetsu yumiharizuki. "The Chinsetsu Crescent Moon." A major *yomihon* novel in 30 volumes, written by Takizawa Bakin from 1807 to 1811 and illustrated with prints by Hokusai. It is a fantasy based on the feats of Minamoto no Tametomo, whose prowess with the bow and arrow was legendary, and on his exile in the Ryukyu Islands via Izu and Ōshima. This work, filled with warrior and Buddhist morals, is one of the weightiest by this productive author, along with *Nansō Satomi hakkenden* (Satomi and the Eight Dogs [Samurai]).

Chin Shunshin. Writer (b. 1924) of Chinese origin, naturalized Japanese, author of popular historical and mystery novels.

Chinsō. Portraits of great masters of Buddhist doctrine or of abbots of Zen monasteries, often used by monks to engage their minds during periods of meditation. A Zen master generally gave his portrait to those among his disciples whom he deemed to have absorbed his teachings, as a sort of diploma. This type of painting, of Chinese origin, was introduced to Japan in the Kamakura period and became so fashionable that certain well-known warriors (and some women) had themselves portrayed dressed as Zen monks (or nuns). Some sculptors made *chinsō* of monks standing, but Zen portraits usually showed the great master sitting on a highbacked chair, his legs folded under him and his hands in meditation posture *(zazen).* Also called *chinzō.*

Chintō-shōgun. Title of "general against the barbarians" given to eighth-century military leaders who fought in northern Honshu against the Ainu (Ezo) tribes. This title, as well as the similar ones of *sei-i-tai-shōgun, chinteki-shōgun,* and *chinju-shōgun,* were conferred upon generals by the emperor only in wartime. Later, it became a lifelong title and was replaced by *sei-i-tai-shōgun,* abridged to *shōgun. See* CHINJUFU.

Chin Wakei. Chinese bronze sculptor (Chen Heqing, twelfth–thirteenth century), said to have restored the large statue of Buddha at the Tōdai-ji in Nara, damaged by fire in 1180, at the request of Chōgen in 1182. He was assisted in this task by many other Chinese bronzesmiths, including his brother, Chen Foshou, and Japanese artisans. An architect, he helped to rebuild the great chamber (Butsuden) at Tōdai-ji and built a ship for the shogun Minamoto no Sanetomo in Kamakura.

Chinzan. Painter (Tsubaki Hitsu; *azana:* Tokuho, Chūta; *gō:* Takukadō, Kyūan, Shikyūan, Hekiinsambō, 1801–54) of the Nanga school. He was also a samurai famous for his sword-fighting technique, and an excellent musician.

Chinzei-fu. Military government in Kyushu established by the Kamakura shogunate in 1186, charged with pursuing and eliminating the last Taira supporters and led by a *chinzei-bugyō* (see BUGYŌ). The first *chinzei-bugyō* was Amano Tōkage. About 1193, Mutō Sukeyori succeeded him in this position, which then became hereditary. The *chinzei-fu* was established in Dazaifu. By the late thirteenth century, the title of *chinzei-bugyō* referred to an assistant of the *chinzei-tandai* or *tandai* (or *kanrei*), charged with control of Kyushu for the Kamakura shogunate.

• **Chinzei-keigoban.** Samurai officers charged with defending Kyushu against the Mongols at the end of the eighth century.

Chion-in. Buddhist temple and monastery in Kyoto, of the Jōdo sect, founded in 1211 by the monk Hōnen (Genkū) on the site of the hermitage that he had established at the foot of Higashiyama after leaving Mt. Hiei. Most of the buildings in this complex were rebuilt between 1619 and 1639, and the temple precincts were expanded. It contains many National Treasures, sutra scrolls, and statues. Its bell—6 m high, 2 m in diameter, and weighing more than 70 tons—was cast in 1633. The Chion-in is currently the head temple of the Jōdo sect.

Chiossone, Edoardo. Italian engraver (1832–98), born in Genoa, invited to Japan in 1875 to engrave bank notes and postage stamps. He also taught engraving to Japanese artists. After his retirement in 1891, he moved to Kamakura, where he assembled a large collection of Japanese art, now in a Genoa museum bearing his name. *See* BRÜCK.

Chiran. Village in Kagoshima prefecture (Kyushu) that has some good examples of samurai houses of the Sata family, a minor branch of the Shimazu clan, active during the Edo period. Some of the houses have magnificent gardens. A training base for kamikaze pilots was located there toward the end of the Second World War. *Pop.:* 15,000.
• Name of a Buddhist monk of Korean origin, of the Hossō sect, active around 703.

Chirimaki. Method of decoration on lacquer consisting of spreading gold or silver powder on the fresh lacquer and polishing it after it dries *(heijin)*. *See* LACQUER, MAKI-E.

Chirimen. Crepe fabric made with untwisted warp threads and twisted weft threads, then boiled in soda and soap. This technique was introduced to Japan in the seventeenth century by a Chinese weaver who set up shop in Sakai. *See* CHIJIMI, TANGO.

Chisahaku-in. Buddhist temple of the Shingon sect, founded in Kyoto at the foot of Higashiyama in 1598, on the ruins of the Negoro-ji temple. It was famous for its monk-soldiers *(sōhei);* on the orders of Oda Nobunaga, who felt that they threatened peace in the capital, they were subjugated by Hideyoshi in 1585. The monastery was rebuilt by the monk Gen'yū in 1601. It then became a major center of Buddhist studies, with room for about 3,000 disciples. After a short eclipse, it became prosperous again and now controls about 3,000 monasteries of the Chizan branch. Partly destroyed

by fire in 1947, it was rebuilt soon afterward. It contains valuable murals and fusuma paintings by Hasegawa Tōhaku and his students.

Chishiki. In Japanese Buddhism, this word means "knowledge" and connotes specifically all offerings made to a monk or a temple and, by extension, the benefactor himself. At first, however, *chishiki* designated a person who took care of a monk during his retreat, when he was occupied with studying or reading the sutras.

• **Chishiki-ji.** Buddhist temples and monasteries built thanks to donations from followers, mainly in the seventh and eighth centuries.

Chishima. "Thousand Islands." Japanese name for the Kuril archipelago, also called Chishima Rettō, comprising 32 islands. They were occupied by Russian settlers in 1738, who often attacked Japanese and Ainu settlers. The Russo-Japanese Treaty of February 7, 1855, delimited the zones of influence on the islands, with a border set between Etorofu and Uruppu. In May 1875, another treaty (called Chishima-Karafutō Kōkan Jōyaku) ratified the transfer of the island of Sakhalin to Russia in exchange for Japanese sovereignty over the Chishima Islands. The peace treaty of San Francisco, signed in 1951, returned the Chishima islands to the USSR. However, since the border was not really drawn, Japan continues to claim the islands of Kunashiri and Etorofu as part of Hokkaido. *See* KURIL ISLANDS.

• **Chishima-kan Jiken.** Diplomatic incident in November 1892, when the *Chishima,* a new Japanese torpedo gunboat, was hit by the *Ravenna,* an English ship of the Peninsular and Oriental Navigation Co., and sank. In 1895, the Japanese government's demand for compensation was reduced by the Yokohama Court of Justice to about a tenth of what had been claimed. This heightened Japanese demands for a review of the Unequal Treaties. *See* JŌYAKU.

• **Chishima Kazantai.** Volcanic arc formed by the Kuril Islands, extending almost 1,400 km, from central Hokkaido to Kamchatka and comprising a great number of active volcanoes and crater lakes.

Chishū Ryū. Film actor (1905–93), born in Kumamoto prefecture, son of a Buddhist monk. He began his career in 1925 with Shōchiku, then had his first big role in 1936, in a film directed by Ozu Yasujirō. He acted in Ozu's major films: *Late Spring* (1949),

Early Summer (1951), *Tokyo Story* (1953), and *An Autumn Afternoon* (1962). He also appeared in Kurosawa Akira's *Dreams*.

Chisso. Industrial and chemical complex whose fertilizer plant in Minamata caused severe pollution of the sea around 1955. Between 1973 and 1981, the company was finally forced to compensate victims of diseases caused by the pollution. *See* MINAMATA.

Chita. Town in Aichi prefecture, on the coast of the peninsula of the same name, famous for its cotton fabrics. *Pop.:* 65,000.

• **Chita Hantō.** Chita Peninsula, separating the Bay of Ise from the Bay of Mikawa, south of Nagoya. *Area:* 355 km^2.

Chitatsu. Buddhist monk (seventh century) of the Kusha sect, who went to China with Chitsū, returned with him, and helped to preach the doctrine of the Hossō sect about 660. Also called Chidatsu. *See* CHITSŪ.

Chitose. Suburb of Sapporo on the island of Hokkaido, created in 1869 for salmon fisheries. Sapporo's international airport is located in Chitose. *Pop.:* 70,000.

Chitsū. Buddhist monk (seventh century) of the Kusha sect who went to China in 658 with Chitatsu to study the precepts of the Hossō sect under Xuan Zang (*Jap.:* Genzō). When he returned to Japan around 660, he founded a monastery, Kannon-ji, in Yamato, where he preached the doctrine. He was named *sōjō* (head abbot) of the sect in 673. *See* CHITATSU, HOSSŌ-SHO.

Chiyo. Poet (Fukumasuya Chiyo; *gō:* Soen, Sōfū, 1703–75), born in Kanazawa to a family of poor artisans. She was married at age 19 to Fukuda Yahachi and traveled through Japan with him. Her husband and son died in 1727, and she became a Buddhist nun *(bikuni)* in 1729. Her poems, written in a popular style, were well liked and often recited. Also known as Kaga no Chiyojo. *Otoko nara / Hitoya nete min / Hana no yama* (If I were a man / I would sleep on the mountain / Under the blossoms).

Chiyoda. Tokyo city ward centered on the imperial palace. During the Edo period, most of its inhabitants were samurai.

• **Chiyoda-jō.** Name sometimes given to Edo castle, which is located in Chiyoda ward (Chiyoda-ku).

• **Chiyoda Kakō Kensetsu.** Petrochemical industrial complex founded in 1948 by engineers from Mitsubishi. Since 1960, Chiyoda has established branches and set up plants in many countries, including the United States, Saudi Arabia, Iran, and Singapore.

Chiyogami. Sheets of paper decorated with brightly colored woodblock print motifs used for gift wrapping and for making dolls and other items. These sheets of paper were produced starting in the late eighteenth century by ukiyo-e artists. *See* PAPER, WASHI.

Chiyonofuji. Famous sumo wrestler (Akimoto Mitsugu), born 1955 in Hokkaido. In the Kokonoe stable *(heya),* he fought his first matches in 1970 and became an Ōzeki in 1981, then a Yokozuna at Nagoya in the same year. He is 1.83 m tall and normally weighs between 118 and 125 kg. Although he is light compared to other *sumotori,* he is very quick. He has won more than 20 tournaments, including one in Paris in 1986. Experts consider him the greatest *sumotori* of all time. He is the fifty-eighth Yokozuna. *See* SUMO, SUMOTORI.

Chō. Former unit of length (108.06 m) divisible into 60 *ken.* Also an area (9,800 m^2) divisible into 10 *tan;* 36 *chō* equaled 1 *ri,* or about 3,909 m.
• A group of buildings between two streets 1 *chō* apart. The area of a *chō* is called *chōme.*
• Formerly, taxes payable in kind (other than in rice). The Taika Reform (645) made a distinction between the *denchō* and the *komaichō,* the latter being a rice tax. Corvées were also called *chō,* and only men had to take part in them. Bureaucrats charged with collecting these taxes in each province were called *chōchōshi.*
• From the Nara period to the fourteenth century, official orders sent to a subordinate.

Chobo. In Kabuki, *gidayū-* or *jōruri-*style music played by musicians sitting in the "music box" *(geza)* during certain performances.

Chō-Bō fudoki. Administrative report and geographical guide to the provinces of Suō and Nagao, compiled between 1842 and 1846. Also called *Bō-Chō fūdō chūshin'an.*

Chōbuku soga. Title of a Noh play: the Buddhist god Fudō Myō-ō (*Skt.*: Achalanātha) appears to ensure that the two Soga brothers' revenge is carried out. *See* SOGA SUKENARI.

Chōchin. Paper lanterns made, probably first in Gifu, in the seventeenth century. Translucent rice paper is glued onto a light bamboo frame that is either circular or square in shape. There were many types, depending on the region in which they were made: Gifu-*jōchin,* Yumihara-*chōchin,* Odawara-*chōchin,* Bura-*jōchin,* Takahari-*jōchin,* and others. They are now used as lampshades.

Chōchō. Decorative butterfly motif often used in Japanese art.

• **Chōchō-mage.** *See* MAGE.

• *Chōchō-san.* Japanese title for Puccini's *Madama Butterfly.*

Chōdai. Slightly raised platform (about 40 to 90 cm) in a reception hall, with an area of about two tatami. Before the seventeenth century, the lord sat on the *chōdai* to receive guests. Surrounded by drapes, it was sometimes used at night as a bed. During the Edo period, the *chōdai* was generally lower and used mainly as the shogun's or emperor's official seat. *See also* TATAMI, ZABUTON.
• During the Nara and Heian periods, bureaucrats fulfilling subordinate tasks and ensuring the safety of members of the imperial family. Also called *chōnai.*

Chōfu. Tokyo suburb, about 20 km from downtown, former transfer point on the Kōshū-Kaidō road in the Edo period. Airfield and botanical garden. *Pop.*: 180,000.
• Suburb of Shimonoseki (Yamaguchi prefecture), former capital of the province of Nagato. A castle was built there by the Mōri family.

Chōga. Painter and Buddhist monk (thirteenth century) in the Takuma school. In 1253, he decorated the Amida hall at Hōsho-ji in Kyoto and was promoted to the rank of Hōgen. Also known as Hōin Chōga.

Chōgaku-ji. Buddhist temple in Yanagimoto (Nara prefecture) founded in 824. Its buildings were reconstructed many times: the *gochidō* during the Kamakura period (1185–1333), the *rōmon* during

the Muromachi period, and the *hondō* in modern times.

Chōgen. Era during the reign of Emperor Go-Ichijō: July 1028–Apr. 1037. *See* NENGŌ.
• Buddhist monk (Urabe Shigesada, Shunjō, Chōgen, 1120–1206) at the Daigo-ji monastery, then of the Jōdo sect, as a disciple of Genkū. He traveled to China three times to visit the famous monasteries and study Chinese architectural techniques. When he returned in 1181, he directed the rebuilding of the Tōdai-ji in Nara, which had been destroyed by fire during the war between the Minamoto and Taira families, and traveled the country raising the funds needed for the reconstruction. He repaired the Great Buddha (Daibutsu), assisted by the Chinese bronze sculptor Chin Wakei, then rebuilt the large Daibutsuden structure. His statue, made soon after his death, is still in an annex of the Tōdai-ji that bears his name, the Shunjōdō. He wrote a treatise on Amidism, *Namu Amidabutsu sazen-shū,* in which he described the buildings he had constructed throughout Japan, the ports he had created, the ponds he had designed, and the roads he had repaired, as well as the temples and monasteries whose construction he had directed. He is also responsible for the great Nandaimon gate at Tōdai-ji in Nara. *See* CHIN WAKEI.

Chōgi. Blacksmith (fourteenth century) of the province of Bizen, in the Osafune school, famous mainly for his *tantō* and *tachi* sword blades, which featured a particular *nie.* He had many disciples, among them Kanenaga and Nagamori, but none were able to reach his level of accomplishment or style, which is considered unique.

Chōgin. Small silver coin issued by Tokugawa Ieyasu, weighing about 43 *momme* (161.2 g). A similar coin, called *mameitagin* (or *tōbangin*), was struck by slightly crushing a silver ball. *Chōgin* were reissued frequently during the Genroku era (1688–1703) but were often of inferior quality. Their units of weight were the *momme* (3.75 g) and the *kan* (worth 1,000 *momme*). *Chōgin* were issued a total of 11 times, each issue bearing the name of the era during which it was struck. The earliest ones bore on one face the effigy of the god of happiness (*see* SHICHI-FUKUJIN) Daikoku, a reference to Daikoku Jōze, the head of the coin-making workshop (*ginza*). *See* CURRENCY , SANKA.

Chōgosonshi-ji. Buddhist temple on the Shigisan hill, about 4 km north of Ōji (Osaka), also called

Shigisan-ji, and dedicated to Bishamon-ten. Its buildings date from the seventeenth century.

Chōhei-rei. Conscription law promulgated in 1873 by Yamagata Aritomo, making military service obligatory for all men, following the recommendations of Ōmura Masujirō, assassinated in 1869, and modeled on European and American practices. The law could be circumvented by making a proxy payment. This irritated the peasants and some samurai, who revolted under the leadership of Saigō Takamori. The law was amended and conscription became obligatory for all men who had reached the age of 20.

Chōhō. Era during the reign of Emperor Ichijō: Jan. 999–July 1004. *See* NENGŌ.

• **Chōhō-ji.** Buddhist temple founded about 1000 (Chōhō era) at Kami (Wakayama prefecture). Several old buildings survive: the *tahō-tō* (pagoda) and the *hondō* from 1311, the Amida-dō and the Chinjudō from 1300, and the *rōmon* from 1388.

Chō Isamu. Officer (1894–1945), who was a member of the Sakura Kai, a secret society, in 1930. He took part in an abortive coup (*see* JŪGATSU JIKEN) with Hashimoto Kingorō in 1931.

Chōji. Era during the reign of Emperor Horikawa: Feb. 1194–Apr. 1106. *See* NENGŌ.

Chōjirō. Ceramist (Tanaka Chōjirō, Raku I, 1516–92), son of a Korean potter named Ameya who specialized in the manufacture of tiles. His production came to the attention of Sen no Rikyū, who ordered bowls for the tea ceremony (*chanoya*). He thus inaugurated the raku style, rustic ceramics with a black or brown lead glaze, sometimes reddish or white, still sought after today.

Chōjō. Buddhist monk (1244–1323) of the Tendai sect, son of a governor of Izumo, from the Fujiwara family.

Chōjū-giga. Abbreviation of *Chōjū jimbutsu giga* (Scrolls of Frolicking Animals and Humans), an *emakimono* in four scrolls, drawn in ink with no text, about 31 cm high and 1 m long, kept at Kōzan-ji, a Kyoto temple. These scrolls of humorous drawings are traditionally attributed to Tōba Sōjō (Kakuyū, 1053–1140), although recent studies indicate that they are the work of a number of artists. A virulent satire of late Heian society, the scrolls fea-

ture situations in which animals exhibit human characteristics and behavior. In fact, the first two scrolls (scrolls A and B) may be from the end of the twelfth century, while the two others may date to the Kamakura period. There may have been a fifth scroll, of which only fragments have survived. Scroll C is dated 1253. These *emakimono*, the only ones of their kind in Japan, are the finest examples of the pictorial *hakubyō* (monochrome wash) technique. Some fragments (perhaps from the fifth scroll) are scattered in various private collections.

Chōka. Poetic ballads composed of an undetermined number of verses; lines of 5 and 7 syllables alternate, ending with a line of 7 syllables. Many *chōka* (the longest known is 148 verses) finish with a 31-syllable *tanka* called *hanka* or *kaeshiuta*. This type of poem was in style from the seventh to the twelfth century. The *Man'yōshū* contains 265 *chōka,* which are also called *naga-uta. See* NAGA-UTA, TANKA, WAKA.

Chōkai. "Neighborhood associations" (succeeding the *burakukai* in villages), groups of urban residents that are semi-officially charged with managing and coordinating their neighborhoods. They were very active after the 1923 earthquake in Tokyo. During the Second World War, they had official status and were charged with safety, regulations about defense and rationing, and other duties. *Chōkai* are especially concerned with the welfare of children, teenagers, women, and the elderly, and they are particularly vigilant in preventing crime, working closely with the police. Their main activity is to organize festivals on the local level. Also called *chōnaikai, jichikai. See* CHŌ.

Chōkai-san. Active volcano (2,230 m) located on the border of Akita and Yamagata prefectures, in northern Honshu. It last erupted in 1974.

• **Chōkai Kazantai.** Volcanic zone extending from southern Hokkaido to Niigata prefecture, including several volcanoes, the highest of which is Chōkai-san.

Chōkai Seiji. Western-style painter (Masao, 1902–72), born in Kanagawa. He traveled in Europe and Algeria in 1930, and in China in 1939. He specialized in landscapes and was an important collector of Japanese art.

Chōkaku Hōshinnō. Buddhist monk (1219–89), son of Rokujō no Miya (Masanari Shinnō, son of

Emperor Go-Toba), named abbot *(zasu)* of the Tendai sect in 1265.

Chōkan. Era during the reign of Emperor Nijō: Mar. 1163–June 1165. *See* NENGŌ.
→ *See* KUNAICHŌ.

Chōkei Tennō. The ninety-eighth emperor of Japan (Prince Yutanari, 1343<1368–83>1394), son of and successor to Emperor Go-Murakami. He abdicated in favor of his brother, Go-Kameyama. A member of the Southern Court (Nanchō), he was forced to move often to evade the Ashikaga troops and the emperors of the Northern Court (Hokuchō). He wrote a literary work on the *Genji monogatari,* called *Sengenshō.*

Chōki. Painter (Eishōsa Chōki; *gō:* Shikō, active from 1780 to the early nineteenth century). A student of Sekien, he produced ukiyo-e prints highly influenced by Utamaro.
• Painter (Miyagawa Chōki, active from 1715 to ca. 1750), student of Chōshun. He made ukiyo-e prints portraying beautiful women *(bijin).*

Chōkin. The art of sculpting and engraving metal, and the objects produced. Techniques are *takaniku* (high relief), *shishiai* (or *hanniku,* demi-relief), and *usuniku* (bas relief).
• Official visit made by the emperor to his predecessor at the beginning of the year of his coronation and after the heir to the throne's *gempuku* ceremony. This visit became customary after 810.

Chokkomon. Decorative drawings believed to have magical properties, painted or engraved on objects and sarcophagi during the Kofun period (fifth–seventh century). They adorned bracelets, bronze mirrors, sword guards, and sometimes the walls of funerary chambers. They were generally made of two lines crossing in an X, delimiting triangular zones crossed by curved lines that overlap irregularly. It is not known what they represented, but they probably bore some relationship to deer scapula or tortoiseshells used for divination. Some *haniwa* figurines are also decorated with *chokkomon.* Mirrors thus decorated are called *chokkomon-kyō. See* HANIWA, IDERA KOFUN, SENZOKU KOFUN.

Chokuan. Painter (Tanomura Chi; *azana:* Shōko; *gō:* Chokunyu, Ryū-ō, 1814–1907) of the Nanga school, specializing in landscapes, and a professor at the Tokyo School of Fine Arts (Tokyo Bijutsu Gakkō).

Chokugan-ji. Category of Buddhist temples "of the imperial wish," founded by an emperor in thanks when his prayers were answered. Among these temples are Tōdai-ji in Nara, and Tō-ji, Enryaku-ji, Daikaku-ji, and Ninna-ji in Kyoto. These temples enjoyed the highest status, but this distinction disappeared in 1871. Also called *gogan-ji.*

Chokusai. Netsuke sculptor (Miyagi Chokusai, b. 1877), student of Murata Naomitsu in Osaka.

Chokusen waka-shū. "Collection of *Waka* Poems." Name of all of the imperial *waka* anthologies (a total of 21) ordered by an emperor and compiled between 913 and 1439. Also called *Nijūichi daishū* (Twenty-One Great Collections). They are:
1) *Kokin waka-shū* (or *Kokin-shū*), collected on the order of Emperor Daigo, ca. 913–14.
2) *Gosen waka-shū* (or *Gosen-shū*), Emperor Murakami, ca. 951.
3) *Shūi waka-shū* (or *Shūi-shū*), Emperor Kazan, 1007.
4) *Go shūi waka-shū* (or *Go shūi-shu*), Emperor Shirakawa, 1086.
5) *Kin'yō waka-shū* (or *Kin'yō-shū*), Emperor Shirakawa, 1126–27.

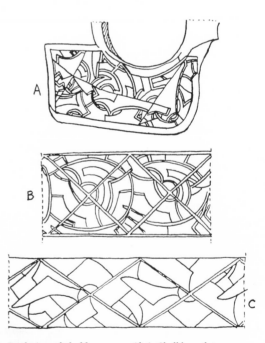

Evolution of *chokkomon* motif. A. Shell bracelet, Shikinzan tomb, Osaka, 4th century. B. Sarcophagus in the Sekijinyama tomb in Fukuoka, 5th century. C. Sarcophagus in the Nikenjaya tomb in Fukuoka, 6th century

6) *Shika waka-shū* (or *Shika-shū*), Emperor Sutoko, 1151.

7) *Senzai waka-shū* (or *Senzai-shū*), Emperor Go-Shirakawa, 1187.

8) *Shin kokin waka-shū* (or *Shin kokin-shū*), Emperor Go-Toba, 1205.

9) *Shin chokusen waka-shū*, Emperor Go-Horikawa, ca. 1234.

10) *Zoku gosen waka-shū* (or *Zoku gosen-shū*), Emperor Go-Saga, ca. 1251.

11) *Zoku kokin waka-shū* (or *Zoku kokin-shū*), Emperor Go-Saga, ca. 1265.

12) *Zoku shūi waka-shū* (or *Zoku shūi-shū*), Emperor Kameyama, 1278.

13) *Shin gosen waka-shū* (or *Shin gosen-shū*), Emperor Go-Uda, 1303.

14) *Gyokuyō waka-shū* (or *Gyokuyō-shū*), Emperor Fushimi, 1312.

15) *Zoku senzai waka-shū* (or *Zoku senzai-shū*), Emperor Go-Uda, 1320.

16) *Zoku go-shūi waka-shū* (or *Zoku go-shūi-shū*), Emperor Go-Daigo, 1325.

17) *Fūga waka-shū* (or *Fūga-shū*), Emperor Hanazono, 1346.

18) *Shin senzai waka-shū* (or *Shin senzai-shū*), Emperor Kōgon, 1359.

19) *Shin shūi waka-shū* (or *Shin shūi-shū*), Emperor Go-Kōgon, 1364.

20) *Shin go-shūi waka-shū* (or *Shin go-shūi-shū*), Emperor Go-En'yū, 1383.

21) *Shin zoku kokin waka-shū* (or *Shin zoku kokin-shū*), Emperor Go-Hanazono, 1439.

Each anthology comprises 20 volumes. The poems were selected by a committee working in a special office in the imperial palace, the Waka-dokoro. *See* WAKA.

Chokutō. Type of straight iron sword with a double blade and semicircular point, found in *kofun* burial mounds. Generally about 1 m long, they are divided into seven categories according to the shape of the pommel: ring (the oldest ones), cone, round, square, fern frond, antler, and closed fist. These swords were still in use in the Nara period. Also called *ken, tachi. See* KATANA, KEN, TSURUGI.

Chōkyō. Era during the reign of Emperor Go-Tsuchimikado: July 1486–Aug. 1488. *See* NENGŌ.

Chōkyōsai Eiri. A ukiyo-e artist (Hosoda Eiri, fl. late 18th century) who specialized in portraits of contemporary beauties *(bijinga)*. He was influenced by the style of Kitagawa Utamaro and may be the same person as Rekisentei Eiri or Shikyūsai Eiri.

Chōkyu. Era during the reign of Emperor Go-Shujaku: Nov. 1040–Nov. 1044. *See* NENGŌ.

Chokyū-ji. Buddhist temple founded in Ikoma (Nara prefecture) in 730 and reconstructed in 1279. The Hondō (1279) was the work of Koma no Sōgen.

Chōmoku. "Bird's eye." Name commonly given, starting in the Muromachi period, to copper coins *(zeni)* with a hole in the center, in imitation of Chinese coins. *See* CURRENCY .

Chōnen. Buddhist monk (938–1016) from a branch of the Fujiwara family. He entered Tōdai-ji, where he studied the doctrines of the Sanron sect. From 982 to 987 (or 991), he traveled in China; he brought back sutras *(Jap.: kyō)*, Buddhist statues (including the one at Seiryō-ji, according to tradition), and religious paintings made for him by Emperor Taizong of the Tang dynasty, who also gave him the Chinese title Fazi Dazhi *(Jap.: Hōsai Daishi*, "Great Master of the Law"). He is also known by the title Kōji Daishi.

Chōnen-taihō. Small copper coin issued from 848 to 859, in imitation of Chinese coins with a square hole in the center. It had a diameter of 2 cm and weighed 1.43 g. *See* CHŌMOKU, KŌCHU-JŪNISEN, CURRENCY.

Chōnin. Social class formed in the sixteenth century in castle towns *(jōka-machi),* which were populated mainly by merchants and artisans supplying lords and warriors. Later, other people—peasants, servants, and workers—came to the towns to serve the first inhabitants. Because peasants and warriors could not conduct trade for fear of losing their standing, the bourgeois in the towns quickly grew wealthy, often at the former's expense. During the Edo period, the *chōnin* (people of the *chō*) were placed lower on the social scale than *bushi*, peasants *(nō)*, and specialized artisans *(kō)*. These merchants *(shō)* became more and more numerous, and the label *chōnin* came to mean all townspeople who were not nobles, warriors, or peasants. Those who supplied rice were called *fudadashi* in Edo and *kakeya* in Osaka. Some became fabulously wealthy, to the point that they lent money to daimyo who were short of cash, while others founded major trading companies. Their wealth enabled them to develop within their class a popular bourgeois culture, which came to be called *chōnin-bunka*, including Kabuki, literary genres such as *chōnin-mono* and *ukiyo-zōshi, haikai* poems, and specific art forms such as ukiyo-e prints.

• **Chōnindō.** "Way of the *Chōnin*" (as opposed to Bushido, the warriors' code). Unwritten code that required *chōnin*, merchants, and others to devote themselves to the pursuit of profit while remaining scrupulously honest, and to cultivate the virtues of thrift and frugality.

• ***Chōnin kōken roku.*** Instructions left by the wealthy *chōnin* Mitsui Takafusa (1684–1748) to his descendants on ways to increase their inheritance, emphasizing *Chōnindō.* He advised them to act with dignity with regard to the samurai and not to lend money to daimyo, who might never pay it back. It is a key document on the life and ethics of *chōnin* during the Edo period.

• ***Chōnin-mono.*** Popular stories describing the lives of *chōnin,* written in the late seventeenth century. *See* LITERATURE, UKIYO-ZŌSHI.

Chon-mage (Chommage). Hairstyle for men, in fashion until the beginning of the Meiji era. The top of the forehead was shaved and the hair twisted and secured on top of the head. This was the standard hairstyle for samurai and is still used by certain *sumotori* (*sumo* wrestlers). *See* HAIRSTYLES, MAGE, SUMŌTORI.

Chōraku-ji. Buddhist temple in Kyoto, branch of the Jōdo sect, founded by Ryūkan Risshi, a disciple of Hōnen, at the beginning of the thirteenth century. It had previously (eighth–ninth century) belonged to the Tendai sect, and later one of the branches of the Ji sect. Its Hondō was reconstructed in 1893.

Chōreki. Era during the reign of Emperor Go-Shujaku: Apr. 1037–Nov. 1040. Also Chōryaku. *See* NENGŌ.

Chōri. Textile company based in Osaka that includes an industrial conglomerate (machinery, chemical products, etc.). It was founded in 1861 and works in cooperation with other large companies, such as Asahi and Teijin. It exports about 25% of its production through its foreign branches.

Chōroku. Era during the reign of Emperor Go-Hanazono: Sept. 1457–Dec. 1459. *See* NENGŌ.

Chōrō-Kyōkai. Presbyterian church of Japan, founded in 1859 by American pastors James Hep-

burn (1815–1911) and Samuel Robbins Brown (1810–80). They established the first church in 1872 in Yokohama (Yokohama Kirisuto Kyōkai). Also called Chōrōha.

Chō Ryō. Title of a Noh play: Chinese general Chō Ryō (Zhang Liang) visits a martial arts master, but is rejected a number of times and forced to do battle with a dragon to recover the sandal lost by the master. Finally, the master gives the general the coveted teachings. From a Chinese legend adapted by Kojirō Nobumitsu (1351–1416).

Chōsa. Type of ceramics produced by Korean potters who settled in the province of Ōsumi in the late seventeenth century, under the direction of a certain Hōshū. These ceramics feature a finely textured reddish or gray clay and a colored glaze. Also called *jōsa.*

Chōsai. Buddhist monk (Kakamyō-Shōnin, ca. 1184–1266), founder of the Kuhon-ji branch of the Jōdo sect. He wrote a number of exegetic works on Amidism, including *Nembutsu hongangi* and *Shogyō hongangi.*

Chō Sakurin Bakusatsu Jiken. The assassination of Zhang Zuolin (*Jap.*: Chō Sakurin), a Chinese general (1873–1928), as he fled from the Chinese Nationalists, on a train to Mukden (Shenyang). As he neared the city, he was seriously injured by a bomb and died a few days later. This assassination had been plotted by a Japanese officer, Colonel Kōmoto Daisaku, to compromise the Chinese Nationalist government, which was opposed to Japanese occupation of Manchuria. But the plot backfired because Zhang Zuolin's son, Zhang Xueliang, made a provisional alliance with Chiang Kai-shek's troops.

Chōsan. "Flight," describing the action of peasants on estates who, oppressed by taxes and compulsory labor, abandoned their land. These "flights" began in the Nara period and became more widespread during ensuing periods. Estate owners forbade *chōsan* and decreed severe punishment for those accused of it, but this had little effect on peasants, who fled to neighboring estates or to the cities throughout the Edo period. *See* RŌNIN.

Chōsei. Sculptor and Buddhist monk (1010–91), disciple of Jōchō and founder of Sanjō-*bussho* (*see* BUSSHO) and of the En school. He received the titles of Hokkyō in 1065, Hōgen in 1070, and Hōin in 1077. To him are attributed the statues of Nikkō

Bosatsu, Gakkō Bosatsu, and the Jūni Shinshō (in 1064) at Kōryū-ji in Kyoto.

Chōsei-kyō. Small Shinto subsect of the Shinri-kyō, founded in 1921 by Okabayashi Masakami (b. 1889). It drew only about 3,000 followers.

Chōsen. Japanese pronunciation of Josön (or Chosön), the Korean name for Korea. Throughout Japanese history, Korea has been known by various names, including Sankan, Kudara, Koma, Shiragi, and Kōrai (before 1392). The Japanese currently (since 1948) call South Korea Kankoku (*Kor.:* Hangug), while North Korea is still called Chōsen.

• *Chōsen-jihō. See* ADACHI KENZO.

• **Chōsen-karatsu.** *See* KARATSU-YAKI.

• **Chōsen ninjin.** Japanese name for ginseng (*Panax ginseng, Kor.:* In-sam) imported from Korea or China.

• **Chōsen Seibatsu.** *See* BUNROKU KEICHŌ NO EKI.

• **Chōsen Sensō.** Korean War (1950–53).

• **Chōsen Sōtokufu.** General Japanese government of Korea, from 1910 to 1945. *See* KANKOKU.

Chōshi. Major fishing port at the mouth of the Tone River, in Chiba prefecture, east of Tokyo. *Pop.:* 90,000.

Chōshitsu. Sculpted-lacquer objects with several coats of colored lacquer. There are three types (in black, *tsuikoku;* in red, *tsuishu;* in yellow, *tsuiō*) corresponding to similar Chinese techniques *(ti hong).* Other related techniques are called *kinshi, kyūrenshi, keishō,* and *guri. See* KANSHITSU, LACQUERS.

Chōshō. Era during the reign of Emperor Sutoku: Aug. 1132–Nov. 1135. *See* NENGŌ.

Chōshū. Former name of the provinces of Nagato and Suō, now in Yamaguchi prefecture (southern Honshu). Sometimes called Anato.

• **Chōshū-han.** Warrior clan of the Mōri family, founded in the sixteenth century by Mōri Motonari, who conquered a large part of the Chōshū and Kyushu regions. After the Battle of Sekigahara in 1600, the territory of Chōshū was reduced to the provinces of Nagato and Suō, and its daimyo had a revenue of only 369,000 *koku.* This clan comprised four fiefs, Chōfu, Tokuyama, Kiyosue, and Iwakuni, belonging to collateral branches of the Mōri family. Because the Mōri capital was in Hagi, the clan was also called Hagi-*han* and sometimes Mōri-*han.* After a difficult period punctuated by peasant revolts, the Mōri daimyo system became relatively powerful thanks to reforms imposed by Murata Seifū. At the end of the Edo shogunate *(bakumatsu),* the Chōshū clan took the emperor's side against the Edo *bakufu,* which sent two punitive forces (called Chōshū *sei-batsu*) against him: in 1864 (which ended without bloodshed, with the daimyo making apologies), and in 1865–66, resulting in a victory by the Chōshū. On the eve of the Meiji Restoration, the Chōshū clan, allied with the warriors of Satsuma and Tosa among others, played a very important role in supporting the imperial cause. Although clans and the daimyo system disappeared in 1871, when the territory was reorganized, the Chōshū clan continued to play a major political role in the government throughout the Meiji era, thanks to their cohesiveness (Chōshū-*batsu,* Chōshū clique).
→ *See* HOASHI KYŌU, SESSAI.

Chōshū-ki. "Notes of the Long Autumn." A 70-volume journal left by Minamoto no Morotoki (1077–1136), concerning the period from 1087 to 1136. Only 13 volumes, covering the years 1111–34, have survived. The work reveals the underside of court politics, describing both ceremonies and the disturbances provoked by armed monks and brigands. It is essential reading for an understanding of the Insei (Retired Emperors) regime and the events that pushed the Taira and Minamoto families into confrontation.

Chō Shūkoku. Chinese painter (Zhang Qiugu, Kun, late eighteenth century–early nineteenth century) born in Zhejiang, who went to Nagasaki in 1792. He introduced the Chinese Wenren (*Jap.:* Bunjin) painting style, Bunjinga (also called Nanga school). His style greatly influenced that of Tani Bunchō, and other Japanese painters joined his school. He also used the names Chō Shin (*Chin.:* Zhang Xin) and Shōkoku (*Chin.:* Qiugu) to sign his works, though some critics think that these were signatures of two different individuals.

Chōshun. Painter (Miyagawa Chōshun; Kiheiji, Chōzaemon, 1682–1752), born in Ōwari and died in Edo. He painted beautiful women *(bijin)* in the ukiyo-e style on *kakemono* hanging scrolls; he illustrated a scroll on theater sets titled *Engeki-zukan.* His art was similar to Moronobu's, but he made no prints. He had many disciples, among them Chōki, Isshō, Shunsui, and Nagafusa.

Chōsokabe. Major warrior family of the province of Tosa (Shikoku) that became famous during the Sengoku (Warring States) period in the sixteenth century and managed to conquer most of the island. However, they were defeated by Hideyoshi and lost their provinces, except for Tosa. Defeated again by Tokugawa Ieyasu, they were forced to abandon Tosa; in 1615, they sided with Hideyoshi's son and were annihilated during the siege of Osaka castle.

• **Chōsokabe Morichika.** Son of Chōsokabe Motochika. Defeated by Tokugawa Ieyasu during the Battle of Sekigahara in 1600, he lost the province of Tosa. When the Osaka castle was taken in 1615, he was taken prisoner and executed.

• **Chōsokabe Motochika.** Warrior (1539–99), son of Chōsokabe Kunichika (1502–60), lord of one of the fiefs of the province of Tosa. He became master of the province in 1575 and seized the entire island of Shikoku (provinces of Tosa, Awa, Sanuki, and Iyo) in 1585. He was defeated by Hideyoshi's generals, Hashiba Hidenaga and Hachisuka Masakatsu, retaining only the province of Tosa. He then took part in two campaigns in Korea with Hideyoshi, but he died when he returned to Fushimi, near Kyoto. He had had a survey of his province made in 1587 and is best known for the collection of estate laws *(bunkoku-hō)* that he had established in his province, the Chōsokabe Okitegaki (also called Chōsokabe Motochika Hyakkajō), an amalgam of laws inspired by the Kahō and the Ryōkoku-hō.

Chōtoku. Era during the reign of Emperor Ichijō: Feb. 995–Jan. 999. *See* NENGŌ.

Chōwa. Era during the reign of Emperor Sanjō: Dec. 1012–Apr. 1017. *See* NENGŌ.

Chōya-gunsai. "Collection of Texts of the Court and the Country." Prose and verse texts written in Sinicized Japanese, going back to the last decades of the Heian period, compiled in 1116 by Miyoshi Tameyasu (1049–1139). Tameyasu continued to add texts to the collection until his death.

Chōya-kyūbun hōkō. History of the Tokugawa shogunate, comprising 1,093 volumes, written by

Hayashi Kō (Jussai, 1768–1841) and his collaborators between 1819 and 1841.

Chōyōdō Anchi. Painter (early eighteenth century) of the Kaigetsudō school.

Chōyō no Sekku. Chrysanthemum festival, also called Kiku no Sekku (*Chin.:* Chongyang), held annually on the ninth day of the ninth month. This festival, originally Chinese, took place in the court during the Heian period and among warriors in the Kamakura period. It became popular during the Edo period but is now almost forgotten, having been replaced by the chrysanthemum fair that takes place in early November. During Chōyō no Sekku, which was the signal for everyone to change from summer clothes to warmer winter kimono, chrysanthemum wine *(kiku no sake)* and rice cooked with chestnuts *(kurimeshi)* were consumed. Many customs were associated with this festival, which symbolized the desire for youthfulness and longevity.

Chōyū. Buddhist monk (thirteenth century) of the Gokoku-ji temple in Kyoto, famous for his talent as a *shakuhachi* player. He was Kakushin's master.
• Sculptor and Buddhist monk (d. 1428) who worked in the Nōman-ji temple in Kawasaki (for which he made a statue of Kokuzō Bosatsu) and at Kokun-ji in Kamakura from 1401 to 1424 (statues of the twelve general-guardians [Jūni Shinshō] and Gakkō and Nikkō Bosatsu, among others). He received the titles of Hokkyō and Hōgen. His style was strongly influenced by Chinese art of the Song dynasty.

Chōzu-bachi. Basins of various shapes and sizes designed to hold water for ablutions. Generally made of stone or bronze, they are placed in gardens near houses or at entrances to teahouses *(chaseki),* temples, and shrines. Their water is drawn using a long-handled wooden ladle and used to rinse the mouth. *See* CHANOYU.

Christianity. The Christian doctrine was introduced to Japan by Francis Xavier in Kagoshima in 1549. It was welcomed by the Japanese, and the first Jesuit missionaries received permission from local authorities to preach freely and establish some churches, clinics, and schools. In 1570, the port of Nagasaki was opened to them, enabling the daimyo of Kyushu to trade with Portuguese ships. However, Francis Xavier failed in his missionary hopes at Kyoto, and Gaspard Vilela (d. 1570) received permission to spread the faith from Ashikaga

Yoshiteru. A number of Kyoto nobles converted, following the example of the daimyo of the Nagasaki region. Merchants supported the new religion, allowing it to be preached at Sakai, and in 1569 Oda Nobunaga lent his support to the foreign priests. Toyotomi Hideyoshi also favored the spread of Christianity at first, but, given the threat posed by the Spanish at Manila and the Portuguese at Macao, he proscribed it and ordered the persecution of Christians, notably in Nagasaki (*see* MARTYRS). The Christian daimyo of Kyushu (Ōmura, Ōtomo, and Arima) nevertheless sent a mission of four young converts to Rome in 1582. They returned to Japan in 1590, at a time when Christians were starting to be persecuted; like most other converts, they recanted or went into hiding *(kakure-kirishitan)*. Tokugawa Ieyasu seemed favorable to Christianity before the Battle of Sekigahara (1600), but, warned by Dutch Protestants that the Catholic nations wanted to seize Japan, he prohibited the foreign religion and reinforced his edicts of proscription in 1613. After the Shimabara uprising, caused only partly by persecuted Christians from Kyushu, the Tokugawa decided to close Japan in 1639; converts and foreign priests were threatened with death by the Shumon Aratame (Kaiyaku), an agency charged with repressing Christianity, established in 1640. The customary law of *fumi-e* (recanting) was established in all regions suspected of sheltering Christians, notably Nagasaki.

It was only after the Meiji Restoration in 1868 and the arrival, in relatively large numbers, of American missionaries that Protestantism was established. The missionaries, both men and women, began to found schools. Following the example of the wife of James Hepburn in this activity were new converts such as Niijima Jo, who, upon his return from a trip to the United States, founded Dōshisha University. In Hokkaido, pastor William Smith Clark was named director of the Sapporo Agricultural College in 1876, and his disciples founded other Christian-influenced educational institutions in many parts of the country. As books were imported and translated, Christianity's influence over education and literature grew. Although a number of Japanese philosophers and writers attempted to prove that Christianity contradicted traditional and Confucian teachings and was "irrational," Christianity won over many converts until the Imperial Rescript on Education was published in 1890. Although the Constitution allowed for free thought and worship, Christianity was not at all encouraged by the authorities, who preferred to emphasize Shinto, Buddhism, and Confucianism. The rise of nationalism after the Russo-Japanese War contributed greatly to the rejection of non-Japanese religions, and new syncretic religions, mixing Christian dogmas with Buddhist, Shinto, and Confucian doctrines, emerged. Christianity continued to expand, slowly, with the assistance of socialists such as Abe Isoo and Kōtoku Shūsui, who saw in it a means of propagating the notion of equality. The Salvation Army, established in Japan in 1895, took part in active proselytizing devoted to "social action."

In the 1930s, a number of Protestant movements were forced to unite in the Japanese Association of Christians (Nippon Kirisuto Kyōdan), while Catholic organizations formed the Japanese Association of Catholic Christians (Nippon Tenshū-kyō Kyōdan). Proselytization by converts was so effective that hundreds of churches and temples were opened and major educational institutions were founded under their aegis, including Dōshisha University, Aoyama Gakuin, Tsuda College, Kansei Gakuin, Meiji Gakuin, and the International Christian University of Tokyo. The establishment of the YWCA and YMCA drew a number of young people. Among the Catholic institutions that were created were Sophia (Jōchi) University and Seishin (Sacred Heart) University. The Episcopal Church (Nippon Seikō-kai), which was devoted exclusively to social works, opened clinics and hospitals, such as St. Luke International Hospital. The other significant Christian denominations in Japan are the Russian Orthodox Church (Nikolai Cathedral in Tokyo) and the Lutheran Church of Japan (Nihon Fukuin Rutero Kyōkai). Although it is a minority religion, involving about 1.4% of the population, or 1.5 million people, Christianity and its followers remain very active.

Chrysanthemum (kiku). Flowering plant *(Chrysanthemum morifolium)* with composite flowers, cultivated in Japan since ancient times (perhaps imported from China in the fifth century) for its medicinal properties. There are a number of varieties, most of which bloom in autumn. The flower, considered the most noble, was taken as an emblem by the imperial family. Every year since the Edo period, exhibitions of chrysanthemums are held all over Japan on the ninth day of the ninth month (the month of chrysanthemums, *kiku-zuki, naga-zuki*) during a festival called Kikka no En, Kiku no Sekku, or Chōyo no Sekku.

Chūai Tennō. Fourteenth emperor (Prince Tarashi Nakatsu-hiko, traditionally 149<192–200>?), husband of Jingū Kōgō. He was the son of Yamato Takero no Mikoto, nephew of and successor to Emperor Seimu. According to the *Kojiki* and the *Nihon shoki,* he probably died in Kyushu, while preparing to conquer the state of Silla (Shiragi) in Korea. Modern historians, however, believe that he did not really exist but was introduced into the imperial genealogy later (eighth century). Emperor Ōjin would have succeeded him.

Chuangzao She. Chinese expression meaning "Creation," name of a political and literary society founded by Chinese students in Japan in 1921 that published various periodicals in Chinese, such as *Chuangzao, Hongshui,* and *Wenhu Pipan.* This society was banned by the government in 1929, following the conflicts between China and Japan.

Chūan Shinkō. Zen Buddhist painter (Shinkō; *gō:* Kōseidō, Kyūkasanjin, Isoku-dōjin, mid-fifteenth century) of the Kenchō-ji temple in Kamakura, known for its *suiboku* images with thick lines and a generally dark tone. He is said to have been Shōkei's master. He sometimes signed with the name Kōseidō.

Chūbu. Central part of the island of Honshu, comprising nine prefectures *(ken):* Niigata, Nagano, Yamanashi, Aichi, Shizuoka, Gifu, Toyama, Ishikawa, and Fukui. It is a mountainous region dominated by the Japanese Alps, many volcanoes (including Mt. Fuji), and the longest rivers in Japan: Shinanogawa, Tenryūgawa, and Kisogawa. Its plains (Nōbi, Nagano, Matsumoto, Takayame, and Niigata) produce rice, tea, and citrus fruits. Fishing ports dot the coasts. The region has three large industrial centers: Chūkyō, around Nagoya, Tōkai (Shimizu, Hamamatsu), and Hokuriku (northern part). Chūbu contains a number of national parks and is popular with tourists. *See* NATIONAL PARKS.

• **Chūbu Nippon Shimbun.** See CHŪNICHI SHIMBUN.

Chūchō-jijitsu. "Verified Facts of the Middle Empire." Historical work written by Yamaga Sokō in 1669, in which the author minimizes the importance of China's influence on Japan and claims that Shinto teachings are not inferior to Chinese Confucianism. The title he gave his work inferred that the true "Middle Empire" was not China but Japan. This work, updated during the Second World War, served as a basis for nationalistic ideas. Also called *Chūchō-jitsuroku.*

Chūgai Shimbun. The oldest of Japan's modern newspapers, founded in February 1868 by Yanagawa Shunsan, a journalist and scholar of Western Learning. It stopped publication in June of that year because of government restrictions imposed on the press. It started up again in March 1869 but folded permanently in February 1870, when its founder died.

Chūgakkō. "Middle school," or secondary school. Children enter when they finish *shōgakkō* (elementary school) and take three years of classes before entering *kotogakkō,* or high school, then *daigaku,* or university. The *chūgakkō* have been co-ed institutions since the educational reform after the Second World War. *See* EDUCATION.

Chūgan Engetsu. Zen monk (1300–75) of the Rinzai sect, born in Kamakura. Having become religious at the age of eight, he studied Esoteric Buddhism (Tendai and Shingon) in Kyoto but finally returned to Zen. His highly reflective poems made him one of the most eminent poets of the Gozan (the five Zen monasteries in which Chinese literature was studied in detail). He traveled in China from 1325 to 1332; when he returned, he wrote the *Nihonsho,* which was banned by the emperor because its author had argued that the imperial lineage was descended from the Chinese Duke of Chou (Zhou). His poems were collected in the *Tōkai Ichiō-shū.*

Chūgen. Since the Kamakura period (1185–1333), a term encompassing all low-ranking retainers in *bushi* families. Later, it also designated the same category of persons in the service of nobles *(kuge)* or important monks. The Edo shogunal government employed a large number (between 540 and 560) of *chūgen* divided into a hierarchy according to the tasks they were assigned. After the Meiji Restoration (1868), they were assimilated into the ordinary citizenry *(heimin).*

• *Chūgen* are also ritual gifts given in mid-July. This tradition is derived from an ancient Chinese custom (Shangyuan), an annual Taoist rite. In Japan, the celebration takes on a Buddhist flavor and is sometimes associated with the "festival of souls" (Urabon). Especially during the Kamakura period, the custom was to offer small gifts (generally noodles or cakes) to be placed on the family altar *(butsudan).* The tradition is still faithfully observed and gives rise to a burst of retail activity July 1–15. *See also* GIFTS, O-CHŪGEN.

Chūgoku. Japanese pronunciation of the Chinese word Zhongguo, "Middle Kingdom," designating China.

• The southernmost part of the island of Honshu, including Hiroshima, Okayama, Tottori, Shimane, and Yamaguchi prefectures. The region is dominated by the Chūgoku mountain range, which runs east-west, creating a watershed that separates the northern (San'in) and southern (San'yō) regions of western Honshu. This range, with an average altitude of 1,000 m (1,339 m at Kammuriyama), is composed of granite with some lodes of ferriferous sand, which have been mined since the beginning of the modern era.

• **Chūgoku hanayome.** Chinese women (and, by extension, women from the countries of Southeast Asia, mainly Thailand and the Philippines), who, attracted by Japan's prosperity, came to marry Japanese men in rural areas. Marriage agencies in both Shanghai and Japan were created to profit from this situation.

• **Chūgoku Kokumin-tō.** Japanese name for the Chinese Nationalist party, founded by Sun Yat-sen (Sun Wun; *Jap.*: Son Bun) in 1912; later led by Chiang Kai-shek (Jiang Jieshi; *Jap.*: Shō Kaiseki) in China until 1949, and in Taiwan thereafter.

• **Chūgoku Kyōsan-tō.** Japanese name for the Chinese Communist party, founded in 1921 and led after 1927 by Mao Zedong (*Jap.*: Mō Takutō). Mao established the Red Army (Hongjun; *Jap.*: Kōgun), which battled the Japanese on Chinese soil during the Sino-Japanese War of 1937–45 (Nitchū Sensō), and against the Nationalist army of Chiang Kai-shek (Jiang Jieshi) until 1949.

Chūgū. Title given to the empress of Japan and her palace during the Heian period starting in the ninth century, replacing the title Kōgō. However, the latter title continued to be used to designate the dowager empress. Then, the two titles became interchangeable. The title Kōtaigō was used for the wife of an ex-emperor and that of Tai-Kōtaigō for the dowager empress. *See* KŌTAI-FUJIN.

• **Chūgū-ji.** Buddhist temple of the Shingon Risshū sect in Nara, near Hōryū-ji, founded by nuns of the Hossō sect in the seventh century, using the former palace of Prince Shōtoku (Shōtoku Taishi) constructed (according to tradition) in 595. The current buildings date from 1605. The temple has two National Treasures: a famous statue of Miroku

Bosatsu dating from the Asuka period (645–710), and fragments of two large embroideries of the Tenjukoku Mandala from the same period. This convent-temple is also called Ikaruga-dera, Ikaruga-gosho, and Chūgūni-ji.

Chū-i. Military grade equivalent to lieutenant.

Chū-in. In Japanese Buddhism, name of the intermediate period between death and rebirth (*Skt.*: Antarabhāva; *Chin.*: Zhongyin; *Tib.*: Bar-do), a 49-day period during which the family of the deceased must make offerings to ensure that the person's soul will rest. This period finishes with a large funeral service.

Chūjō. Military grade corresponding to lieutenant-general, before 1868. Also called *chūshō.*

Chūjō-hime. Buddhist nun (753–81) at the Taima-dera in Nara, and daughter of Fujiwara no Toyonari. According to legend, she wove the images of the paradise of the Pure Land (Jōdo) and of Kannon Bosatsu, with the help of this goddess. The tapestry, called Taima-*mandara,* is in the Taima-dera monastery. Her life has been the subject of many legends, Noh plays (*Hibari-yami, Taema*), Kabuki plays (*Chūjō-hime hachisu no mandara, Chūjō-hime kyō-hiina, Chūjō-hime hibari-yama,* and others), and various stories. One legend has it that she was an incarnation of Shō Kannon Bosatsu (*Skt.*: Avalokiteshvara).

Chūjō Seiichirō. *See* MIYAMOTO YURIKO.

Chūkaku-ha. Group of anti-imperialist extremists formed in 1990, who want to abolish the sovereignty of the emperor and who claim that imperial ceremonies will relaunch Japan into territorial expansionism. This group, which has about 5,000 members, is very active and violent; it has bombed imperial residences and Shinto shrines with missiles. Many smaller groups of the same kind are also active.

Chūkan-shōsetsu. "Middlebrow novels," genre of literature that was quite successful after the Second World War. Brought to prominence by Hayashi Fusao and writers such as Inoue Yasushi, Ishizaka Yōjirō, and others, it was considered a "high-class" popularization of literature. *See also* FŪZOKU-SHŌSETSU, SHIMBUN-SHŌSETSU, SHI-SHŌSETSU, SHŌSETSU.

Chūki. Third period of the Jōmon culture (middle Jōmon). This term is also used to describe all intermediate periods, historical or factual. *See* JŌMON-JIDAI.

Chūkin. Technique of casting metal, either solid or hollow, such that it contains a central core of clay or other material that disappears during the casting.

Chūkō-doki. Type of earthenware vase or container with a pouring spout, similar to a teapot, which appeared toward the end of the Jōmon period. Pieces of this type were found in large numbers in Jōmon sites.

Chūko no Sanjūrokkasen (Sanjū-roku Kasen). List of the 36 most famous poets in the eighth and ninth centuries, established by Fujiwara no Motoshi. They are: Izumi Shikibu, Sagama, Eikei-hōshi, Akazome-emon, No-in-hōshi, Ise no Ōsuke, Sone no Yoshitada, Dōmyō-ajari, Fujiwara no Sanekata, Fujiwara no Michinobu, Taira no Sadabumi, Kiyowara no Fukayabu, Ōe no Yoshitoki, Minamoto no Michinari, Fujiwara no Michiasa, Sōki-hōshi, Ariwara no Motokata, Ōe no Chisato, Fujiwara no Kintō, Onakatomi Sukechika, Fujiwara no Takatō, Uma no Naishi, Fujiwara no Yoshitaka, Murasaki Shikibu, the mother of Fujiwara no Michitsuna, Fujiwara no Nagayoshi, Fujiwara no Sadayari, Jōto-mon'in no Chūjō, Kane-ō, Ariwara no Munehari, Fumiya Yasuhide, Fujiwara no Tadafusa, Sugawara no Sukemasa, Ōe no Masahira, Ambō-hōshi, and Sei Shōnagon. *See* ROKKASEN.

Chūkyō. Industrial zone of Nagoya and region, stretching along the coast of the Inland Sea (Setonaikai) from Toyohashi to Gifu and Mie. It is home to many chemical and textile industries, ceramics and automobile (Toyota) plants, and petrochemical (Yokkaichi) and metallurgical (Nagoya) complexes.
→ *See* ŌSHIN.

Chūkyō Tennō. Twenty-fourth emperor (Prince Kanenari, 1218<1221>1242). Son of and successor to Emperor Juntoku, he ruled for only 70 days in the Kujō district of Kyoto, and was nicknamed Kujō-haitei. Having sided with Emperor Go-Toba against the Hōjō family of Kamakura, he was defeated and sent into exile, and was succeeded by Go-Horikawa. Emperor Chūkyō's posthumous title was conferred upon him only in 1870.

Chūma. Transportation system for agricultural supplies using packhorses dating back to the early Edo period in the mountains of the province of Shinano (Nagano prefecture), where waterways were not usable due to the difficult terrain. This system was legalized in 1673 by the shogunate, which began to regulate it in 1764. *See also* BASHAKU, HORSES, MAGO.

Chūnagon. Starting in the seventh century, title given to counselors of the second rank in the imperial court, who came after the *dainagon* and were superior to the *shōnagon.* Eliminated in 701, the position was reestablished in 705 and involved three title-holders. In 756, the number of *chūnagon* was raised to four, in 1015 to eight, and later up to ten. *See* NAGON.

• **Chūnagon-hōshi.** *See* RENNYO.

Chūnichi Shimbun. Daily newspaper published in Nagoya. In 1942, two local newspapers, *Shin Aichi* and *Nagoya Shimbun,* merged to become *Chūbu Nippon Shimbun,* which took its current name in 1965. The publishing company also puts out two other dailies, *Tōkyō Shimbun* and *Hokuriku Shimbun,* with a total print run of about 2 million copies.

Chūō. Section *(ku)* of Tokyo, retail and banking center comprising the districts of Nihonbashi, Ginza, Kabutochō, and Tsukiji (large wholesale market). Its population has been dropping since rents were raised in 1955, and there are now about 80,000 residents. Most buildings are used for corporate offices.

• **Chūō Daigaku.** Private university in the city of Hachiōji, west of Tokyo, descended from Igirisu Hōritsu Gakkō (School of English Law), founded in 1885. It changed its name to Tōkyō Hōgakuin Daigaku in 1903, taking its current name two years later. It has a number of faculties, but it is best known for its law school. Its annual student population is about 25,000.

Chūō Kōron. "Central Review." A monthly magazine founded in Kyoto in August 1887 as the organ of the Jōdo Shin sect, under the title *Hanseikai Zasshi* (Magazine of the Self-Examination Society). It was moved to Tokyo in 1892 and took its current title in 1899, abandoning all religious tendencies for literary criticism. In 1916, its editor-in-chief, Shimanaka Yūsaku, created a similar magazine for women, *Fujin Kōron*. The parent magazine was liberal in its outlook and was attacked by the government in the 1940s and suppressed in July 1944. It began publishing again in 1946 and was once again very successful. It is published by Chūō Kōron Sha, which, since 1929, has also published books aimed at the general public. In 1946 it created a science magazine, *Shizen* (Nature); in 1969, a literary magazine, *Umi* (The Sea).

Chūritsu Rōren. Abbreviation of Chūritsu Rōdō Kumiai Renraku Kaigi (Federation of Independent Unions), an association of 13 unions founded in 1956 and not affiliated with any political party. It now has about 1.5 million members.

Chūsa. Military grade in the Meiji era, corresponding to lieutenant-colonel in the infantry.

Chūsei. Historians' name for the Japanese "medieval" period, covering the Kamakura (1185–1333) and Muromachi-Momoyama (1333–1567) periods, or up to 1603, depending on the writer.

Chūseikai. "Upright party." Political party created in 1913 by a small group of parliamentarians, among them Ōzaki Yukio and Hayami Seiji (1868–1926), in opposition to the oligarchs *(genrō)* and the Seiyūkai party. By 1916, most of its members had joined the Kenseikai (Constitutional Association party) and the Chūseikai was dissolved.

Chūshi. Second-level Shinto festivals *(matsuri)* that, ritually, must be preceded by three days of purification ceremonies. The festivals are called Toshigoi, Tsukinami, Niiname, and Kamo no Matsuri.

Chūshingura. "The Treasury of Loyal Retainers," a Kabuki play in 12 acts by Takeda Izumo, Namiki Senryū, and Miyoshi Shōraku, performed at the Takemoto-za in Osaka in 1748. This tragedy recounts the story of the 47 *rōnin* of Akō (*see* AKŌ-GISHI). It was adapted for the stage many times and "novelized" by Tamenaga Shunsui (1789–ca. 1843). Also called *Kanadehon chūshingura*.

Chūson-ji. Head temple of the Tendai sect in the Tōhoku region, in Haraizumi (Iwate prefecture). Tradition attributes the founding of the temple to Ennin, 794–864. Fujiwara no Kiyohira (1056–1128) rebuilt the temple, wishing to provide solace to the souls of warriors killed during the civil wars of 1051–62 and 1083–87. Expanded by Fujiwara

no Motohira and his sons and grandsons, it comprised numerous buildings and many hundreds of monastic lodgings. Fire destroyed most of the structures in 1337; they were partly reconstructed by Date Masamune in the seventeenth century. Of the old buildings, only the Konjiki-dō and the Kyōrō (sutra repository) remain; the latter is mounted on an octagonal platform and its roof was destroyed in 1337. The Konjiki-do is a magnificent building, entirely clad in black lacquer inlaid with mother-of-pearl and decorated with paintings. It houses sculptures of Amida, Kannon, Jizō, and the Two Gods (Niten). Complete mummies of Fujiwara Kiyohira, Fujiwara Motohira, and Fujiwara Hidehara have been found there, along with the mummified head of Fujiwara Yasuhira (who had been beheaded). The Kyōrō contains magnificent artifacts, such as a large statue of Monju Bosatsu and many sutra boxes in decorated lacquer, as well as a complete edition of the Chinese Tripitaka from the Song dynasty. A small modern museum has been constructed beside it to house some sculptures, one of which is a rare statue of Ichiji-kinrin, an aspect of Dainichi Nyorai.

Chūyū-ki. Journal kept for about 52 years by Fujiwara no Munetada (1062–1141) and covering the period from 1087 to 1138. This work contains detailed documentation of the political, economic, social, and religious affairs of the time. The original has been lost, but over 100 volumes have survived.

Chūzan-ō. King of Chūzan, title given to the ruler of the kingdom of the Ryukyu Islands from the fourteenth century to 1879, when they were incorporated into Okinawa prefecture. Previously, three kingdoms had existed in the islands: Hokuzan (north), Chūzan (central), and Nanzan (south). They were united in 1422 by King Shō Hashi (1372–1439) of Chūzan. The Ryukyu Islands were then called Chūzan (or Chūsan).

Chūzenji-ko. Lake near the town of Nikkō (Tochigi prefecture), south of Mt. Nantai, whose waters form the famous Kegon waterfall. This volcanic lake, at an altitude of 1,270 m, has a depth of 163 m and an area of 11 km². Many temples and shrines have been built on its shores. It is in Nikkō National Park. *See* NIKKŌ.

Chūzō-katsuji. Metal movable-type characters imported by Christian missionaries at the beginning of the seventeenth century. Movable type was soon abandoned in favor of xylography, because it was difficult to procure the equipment. The technique was developed in Japan only at the end of the Edo period, when an American printer, W. Gamble, was invited to Nagasaki by Motoki Shōzō, an interpreter with the shogunate. Motoki founded a typography school in Nagasaki in 1869, then printed the first newspaper using lead movable type, *Yokohama Mainichi Shimbun,* in Yokohama in 1870. In 1872, a student of Motoki Shōzō, Hirano Tomiji, created a foundry of characters and a print shop called Tsukiji Kappanjo, for the name of the district in which it was located.

Citizen. Anglicized name of Shichizun Tokei Company, the second largest clockmaker in Japan, after Hattori (Seiko). Founded in the 1930s, it formed a partnership with the American company Bulova in 1960 and established branches throughout the world. It also makes computer parts and printers. Its head office is in Tokyo.

Civil aviation. Although the Japanese aeronautics industry dates back to 1911, it evolved very little until the Second World War, when Japanese industries redoubled their efforts to produce fast, high-performance airplanes. After 1945, the industry was partly converted to automobiles, but small numbers of tourist and business airplanes continue to be produced. Most of these aircraft, which have gained an international reputation, are sports planes, such as the single-engine Fuji FA-200 ("Aerosubaru"), and business planes such as the turboprop MU-2 (6–9-person aircraft with two engines per wing and fuel tanks at the ends of the wings), and the medium-range YS-11 turboprop transport plane (*see* YS-11), both of which can land on short runways. For coastal surveillance, Japan also developed an excellent four-engine hydroplane, the PX-S, equipped with a wave-control system. The Japanese industry is currently experimenting with other types of aircraft, particularly medium-range transport jets, and a few firms are even interested in ultra-light (ULM) and vertical-takeoff-and-landing (VTOL) aircraft. *See also* AIRPLANES, AVIATION.

Clark, Edward Warren. American Episcopalian minister (1849–1907), who was the first foreign teacher in Shizuoka, in 1871. He also taught chemistry at Kaisei Gakkō in Tokyo from 1873 to 1875. When he returned to the United States, he wrote several books on Japan, notably *Life and Adventures in Japan* (1878) and *Katz Awa, the Bismarck of Japan* (1904).

Clark, William Smith. American businessman and educator (1826–86) who was hired by the Meiji government in 1876 to establish Sapporo Agricultural College. During the year he spent in Hokkaido, he championed agricultural development on the island with modern growing methods and machinery.

Claudel, Paul Louis Charles. French diplomat and writer (1868–1955). As ambassador to Tokyo from December 1921 to February 1927, he tried to strengthen the ties between France and Japan, creating the Maison Franco-Japonaise (Nichi-futsukan). His writings on Japan were collected in *L'Oiseau noir dans le soleil levant* (Black Bird in the Rising Sun, 1928).

Climate. The islands of Japan are distributed over 16 degrees of latitude, located near the Siberian coast, and affected by ocean currents, both warm (Kuro-shio) and cold (Oya-shio); add to this the presence of mountain ranges, distinctive regional characteristics, and the proximity of the Pacific Ocean, and it is easy to see why the country has strongly differentiated climates. Although Japan is within the temperate zone of the northern hemisphere, its climates range from subtropical in the Ryukyu Islands to boreal in Hokkaido. In winter, Siberian winds blow against the mountain ranges, making the "back" side *(omote)* of the islands cold and often very snowy, while in Tokyo a cold but dry wind, the *karakaze* (Chinese wind), dominates. The Kansai region, although temperate, is very humid. Summers are generally hot or humid, especially in the rainy season *(baiu* or *tsuyu)*. Seasonal averages are as follows:

In January: Sapporo, −6.3°C; Tokyo, 4.4°C; Kagoshima: 6.9°C.

In July: Sapporo, 22.0°C; Tokyo, 26.3°C; Kagoshima: 27.7°C.

Annual precipitation: Sapporo, 1,104 mm; Tokyo, 1,023 mm; Kagoshima, 1,875 mm. The rainiest regions are the Pacific coast of the island of Shikoku (up to 2,600 mm) from May to September and along the Sea of Japan (average of 1,700 mm from July to February). Temperatures and precipitation vary widely according to local conditions. In spite of these considerable differences, Japan has four relatively well-defined seasons, of varying duration depending on the latitude. Spring and autumn are very warm throughout the country, while summers can be unbearably hot and humid and winters quite rigorous, especially in northern Honshu and Hokkaido.

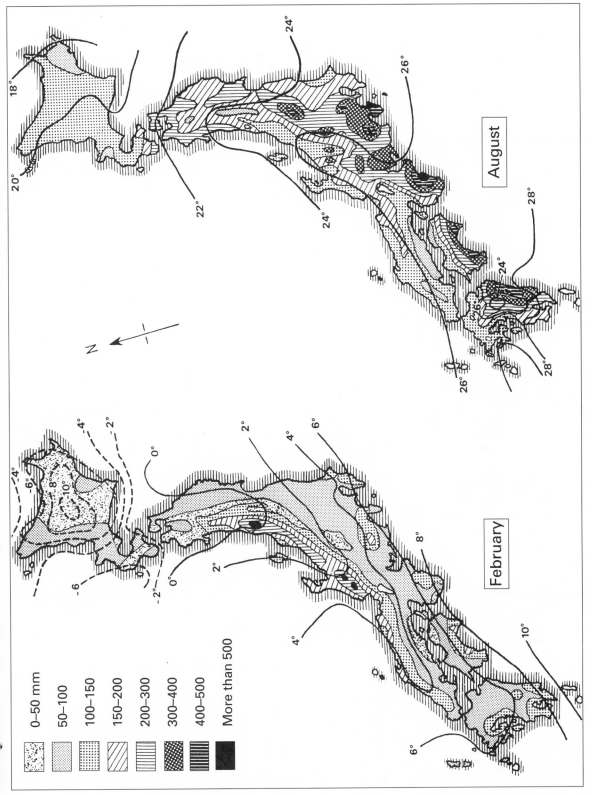

August

February

0–50 mm	
50–100	
100–150	
150–200	
200–300	
300–400	
400–500	
More than 500	

Temperature and Precipitation

Fierce typhoons (*see* TAIFŪ) from the Philippines hit the southeast coasts of the islands in September and October, but they can travel as far north as the Kanto region. *See* GEOGRAPHY.

Clocks. Mechanical clocks were introduced to Japan by Jesuit missionaries in the sixteenth century, but were not manufactured in Japan until about 1598, and then in very small numbers and more as objects of curiosity than of utility. The Japanese models *(tokei)* were German-type clocks with a small bell on top. The single hand was fixed and the face turned; holes pierced into the face activated the bell. The hours were indicated according to traditional Japanese timekeeping, either by the character of the respective animal or by numbers going from 9 to 4, sometimes both (*see* CALENDAR). The mechanism was activated by weights. Some faceless clocks had a hand attached to the cords of the weights and gave the time by pointing to a graduated scale. In 1612, Sebastian Vizcaino gave a clock made by Philip II's clockmaker as a gift to Tokugawa Ieyasu; this clock, kept in the Tōshōgū in Nikkō, is still in working order. In the late Edo period, some artisans produced clocks on this model. But it was not until the beginning of the Meiji era that European clocks and watches were imitated (some, being used to substitute for an *inrō*, were held on the belt by a netsuke). They came into common use in 1900, when they began to be manufactured in Japan in large numbers.

Sundials, which were in common use in China, were never popular in Japan. Some miniature Chinese-style ones were used as netsuke. To know the time, the Japanese relied on Buddhist temples, where the hours were marked by the tolling of a bell (from 9 strokes to 4 strokes). Time was also measured with primitive water clocks.

Clothing. The most common Japanese garment is the kimono, worn by both men and women, in contrast to Western clothing *(yōfuku)* and uniforms *(seifuku)*. At one time, clothing varied widely according to social class. Peasants wore simple shirts tied at the waist made of hemp or bark fabric, while the nobles wore court dress. In the fifth century, the clothing of the imperial court, copied from China and Korea, consisted of a shirt worn over wide pants that narrowed below the knee. This outfit is accurately portrayed in *haniwa*. In the Nara period, richer textiles, at first imported from China but soon made in Japan, included linen and hemp fabric, sometimes silk, always richly embroidered or dyed.

During the Heian period, court garments *(hō)* became diversified and typically Japanese. Because it was generally colder than it is today, warm clothing was required: women wore many layers, such as *jūni-hitoe,* and men wore various combinations, such as *sokutai* (ceremonial clothing), *nōshi,* or *kariginu* (hunting clothes). With the advent of the warrior class in the late twelfth century, clothing tended to become simpler. The short-sleeved kimono *(kosode)* became standard for women of all classes, and soon lower-class men were also wearing them.

At the end of the Muromachi period, styles introduced by the Spanish and Dutch began to appear, such as coats *(kapa, kappa),* baggy pants, and oversized jackets *(jimbaori)*. During the Edo period, clothes diversified with the advent of a new class, the merchants of the towns *(chōnin),* and advances in weaving techniques and fabric dyeing. The women's kimono had long sleeves *(furisode)* and men wore *kamishimo* and *hakama-haori*. These clothes were almost always accompanied by appropriate hairstyles (*see* HAIRSTYLES) and various types of shoes (*see* SHOES). Buddhist monks and Shinto priests wear special clothing *(kesa, juttoku)*.

Former court clothing for men: See HITATARE, HŌ, KATAGINU, SASHINUKI, SEKITAI, SHITA-GASANE, SOKUTAI.

Former court clothing for women: See HITOE, ITSUTSU-GINU, JŪNI-HITOE, KARA-GINU, KINU-YATSUGI, UCHI-KAKE.

Garments for priests and monks: See KESA, KOROMO.

Clothing of the Edo period: See FUNDOSHI, FURISODE, HAKAMA, HAORI, KIMONO, KOSODE, MINO, OBI, TASUKI, YUKATA.

See also ACCESSORIES, FABRICS, HAIRSTYLES, SHOES.

Clove, The. Name of the first British trade ship, commanded by John Saris, which sailed into the port of Hirado on June 12, 1613. Saris opened a trading post there. Before leaving in December of that year, he handed management of the trading post over to Richard Cocks (1560–1624), who held the position until December 1623. Accused of professional misconduct and recalled by the Dutch East India Company, Cocks died on the way home.

Cocks. Cockfighting *(tōkei, toriawase)* was introduced from China in the early eighth century and became a popular form of entertainment during the Kamakura period, when cockfights were traditionally held in March. During the Edo period, they grew in scale and were called *shamo*. Cockfighting was officially banned in 1873, but continued in many provinces.

• Long-necked cocks. *See* ONAGADORI.

Coelho, Gaspar. Portuguese Jesuit missionary (d. 1590), who arrived in Japan in 1572 and devoted himself to evangelizing in Kyushu. Accompanied by Father Luis Frois and Brother Lourenço, he visited Hideyoshi in Osaka in 1586. A protégé of the Arima family, Coelho died in Kazusa.

Coignet, François. French mining engineer (1835–1902), born in Saint-Étienne. He had worked in Algeria, Spain, Madagascar, and the United States, then was invited by the Satsuma clan in 1867 to improve mining operations in Japan. The Meiji government put him in charge of the Ikuno silver mines. When his mission ended, in 1878, he returned to France.

Coijet, Frederik. Swedish trader (ca. 1620–ca. 1678), named director of the Dutch trading post in Nagasaki in 1647 (1647–48 and 1652–53). He was then named governor of Formosa, which he had to abandon to the Chinese in 1662.

Conder, Josiah. British architect (1852–1920), invited to Japan in 1877 to teach architecture. He trained most of the major Japanese architects of the Meiji era and designed the Tokyo Imperial Museum in Ueno (1882), the Rokumeikan (1883), the University of Tokyo's faculty of law and arts building (1884), the Nikolai Cathedral (1891), and many public and private buildings. He worked in Japan until his death.

Confucianism (Jukyō). Political and ethical teachings attributed to the Chinese scholar Confucius (*Jap.*: Kōshi), probably transmitted to Japan via Korea in the sixth century, according to the *Nihon shoki.* This philosophy strongly influenced the thinking of Prince Shōtoku and contributed to the Taika Reform (645). Confucian studies underwent a revival during the Kamakura period under the influence of Zen monks, and many exegetic works were written on the Five Classics (*Gokyō, Chin.*: Wu Jing) and the Four Books (*Chin.: Daxue, Zhongyong, Lunyu,* and *Mengzi*). About 1200, the Neo-Confucian doctrines of Zhu Xi (*Jap.*: Shushi) were introduced to Japan by the Zen monks Shunjō (1166–1227) and Ben'en (1202–80) and by Chinese monks such as Rankei Dōryū and Taikyū Shōnen. This new philosophy was adopted by the emperors. During the Muromachi period, Neo-Confucianism developed quietly within the great Zen monasteries, then was disseminated through the provinces after the Ōnin War. Neo-Confucian thought supported the Tokugawa desire for political hegemony and was adopted by its shogun; thanks to learned scholars such as Fujiwara Seika (1561–1619) and Hayashi Razan (1583–1657), it was put on the curriculum of all official schools. Private schools *(juku)* were founded in the provinces to teach Confucian philosophy to the samurai and commoners. Other trends then developed, such as Wang Yangmei's (*Jap.*: Ō-Yōmei) Neo-Confucianism, known as the Yōmei school, which specialized in the study of Chinese and Japanese classics. In 1790, however, the shogunate banned all Neo-Confucian teachings other than the Zhu Xi school, thus instituting a sort of "state Confucianism." This philosophy strongly influenced the thinking of the bureaucrats and intellectuals of the Edo period. However, it lost some of its impact during the Meiji era, although imperial edicts and rescripts (such as that on education promulgated in 1890) were still under its influence. It underlay all political and intellectual activities until the end of the Second World War, since it gave a raison d'être for nationalism and justified the political thinking of the leaders. Also called Judō.

Constitutions. Japan has had three constitutions. The first, the Seventeen-Article Constitution (Jūshichijō no Kempō), was formulated by Shōtoku Taishi not long before his death in 622. The second, the Meiji Constitution or the Constitution of the Empire of Japan (Meiji Kempō, Dai Nihon Teikoku Kempō), was promulgated by Emperor Meiji on February 11, 1889, putting a definitive end to the shogunal regime and adopting certain Western principles of parliamentary government. Emperor Meiji was assisted in this project by a number of politicians, including Itagaki Taisuke, Iwakura Tomomi, Yamagata Aritomo, Itō Hirobumi, and Ōkuma Shigenobu. In its first article, it affirmed the preeminence of the emperor, considered the supreme leader of the empire, and established a constitutional government. The third constitution, the Constitution of Japan (Nihonkoku Kempō), approved on November 3, 1946, took effect on May 3, 1947 and was practically imposed by the Allied Occupation (S.C.A.P., 1945–52) after the defeat of Japan. It made the emperor the figurehead of the Japanese nation and set up a democratic government. Its most famous and controversial section is Article 9, which forbids Japan from maintaining armed forces (except for self-defense, with a small number of troops) and from armed participation in any war whatsoever. This constitution was supported by a security treaty signed between Japan and the United States. Still in force, it is, however, the object of bitter discussions and demands for its revision—in vain to date. *See* JUSHICHIJŌ NO KEMPŌ, SETAISHO.

Cuisine. Although Japanese cuisine is extremely varied, it is based on three main ingredients: rice *(gohan),* noodles (soba, udon, and others), and fish *(sakana).* It generally uses very little fat. Traditional cuisine includes seaweed, especially *nori* and *kombu;* soy-based products (soy sauce, tofu, miso); and various seasonings, such as *wasabi* (green horseradish), rice vinegar *(su),* red pepper *(tōgarashi),* seven-spice mixture *(shichimi), shiso* (*Perilla frutescens)* leaves, and a sort of clover called *mitsuba.* Japanese mustard *(nerigarashi)* is mild and slightly sweet. In addition, there are various sauces somewhat similar to Worcestershire sauce; various types of ground pepper *(koshō, sanshō);* and, of course, salt and MSG *(ajinomoto).* Japanese cuisine also uses sweet *sake (mirin)* in moderation. Accompanying all meals are a wide variety of pickles *(tsukemono, kōnomono,* etc.).

Rice is always cooked in water. Japanese rice is generally short-grained and slightly sticky, and it accompanies all dishes. There are a great many rice-based dishes; it is often served with curry (called *karē-raisu),* which was first introduced to Japan in the nineteenth century. When green tea, sliced fish, or fish broth is added to the rice bowl, it is called *chazuke,* a popular dish in winter. The most common dish is *domburi,* rice served in a deep bowl, topped with, for example, tempura (or breaded and fried fish, chicken, or pork). A variety of *domburi,* called *katsudon,* consists of a bowl of rice with breaded fried pork, thinly sliced white onions, and a beaten egg. There are an infinite number of rice-based dishes, according to individual taste, including rice balls *(onigiri)* and sushi. Pounded-rice cakes *(mochi)* are eaten as is, in soups, or grilled.

A wide variety of vegetables are rarely served raw; usually, they are boiled. Salads are of Western origin. Bamboo shoots *(takenoko),* boiled, fried, or in brine, are very popular, as are fern fronds, fresh soybeans *(edamame),* broad beans *(soramame),* azuki beans, eggplant *(nasu),* spinach *(hōrenso),* leeks *(negi),* chrysanthemum leaves *(shungiku),* and squash *(kabocha).* Chinese cabbage *(hakusai), daikon* (a type of large white radish), and mushrooms *(matsutake, shiitake,* and others) are also frequently used in cooking. Bitter vegetables, such as *fuki,* are eaten mainly in spring, boiled or fried. In winter, *chirinabe,* a sort of stew of vegetables and fish, or *shabu-shabu,* thinly sliced beef served with vegetables and dried mushrooms, cooked in water, is served. All sorts of other vegetables are found in the markets, including potatoes, taro, sweet potatoes, carrots, turnips *(kabu),* tomatoes, cucumbers, zucchini, and onions.

There are few varieties of meats. Beef, generally imported, is very expensive, and is usually served thinly sliced in sukiyaki or *shabu-shabu.* Kobe beef, a prized gourmet dish, is cooked in front of restaurant customers on a steel griddle. The other most popular meats are pork and chicken. Rabbit, game birds, mutton, and goat are consumed infrequently. Meat is served in croquettes, fried, or grilled on skewers. Eggs are eaten raw in sauce with certain meat dishes such as sukiyaki, or served as omelets. Boiled quail eggs are often added to dishes.

Fish is consumed in great quantity raw, boiled, fried, dried, in brine, and using other cooking methods. The most popular fish are *tai* (sea bream), considered a good omen and usually served on holidays; *katsuo* (bonito); *sake* (salmon); *same* (shark); *toro* and *maguro* (tuna); *hirame* (flounder); and *unagi* (eel); many other species are also eaten. Fish roe is also popular, along with sea urchin *(uni)* and various crustaceans—clams, winkles, shrimp *(ebi),* crab *(kani),* oysters, abalone *(awabi),* octopus *(tako),* and squid *(ika),* generally grilled with soy sauce. *Kamaboko* is a very popular fish-paste cake, while *surimi* is noodles made with fresh fish.

Noodles, of Chinese origin, consist of varieties of *soba* (buckwheat), served cold or hot, depending on the season, *udon* (wheat), and *ramen* (Chinese noodles). Some varieties, called *shirataki,* are made with a root vegetable called *konnyaku.* Chinese dumplings are also popular, *gyōza* (fried) or *shūmai* (steamed), served with a sauce of pepper, soy sauce, vinegar, and mustard.

There are few desserts, and they are generally not served at the end of the meal. Most Japanese sweets *(wagashi)* consist of a sort of steamed bread with *yōkan* (sweet bean paste) or stuffed pancakes. Each region has a specialty; though they often taste similar, these cakes go by a wide variety of names. Sometimes, *ammitsu* (or *mitsumame),* a sort of salad of sweet azuki beans, fruits, and agar-agar jelly *(kanten)* is served. There are many kinds of fruit, similar to those grown in Europe; the most popular, however, are *mikan* (mandarin orange), *nashi* (Japanese pear), apples, strawberries, peaches, and sweet chestnuts. Japanese candies are generally low in sugar. Those who wish to follow Western styles serve American-style pastries or cakes, often a sort of Genoa cake filled with jam, and ices. Yogurt is also sometimes considered a dessert.

The main beverages are tea (*cha, kōcha, ocha, sencha, bancha,* etc.); coffee *(kōhī);* Calpis, a milk-based drink; and various alcoholic beverages, including *sake,* wines, beers, and liquors (Japanese or imported). Only children drink milk. There are also soups, the most popular being miso-based *miso-shiru,* which sometimes take the place of a beverage. Alcoholic beverages are drunk more frequently in bars *(nomiya)* than at home or in a restaurant, and coffee is usually served in a café *(kissaten).*

Each region has its culinary specialties, and each family, its favorite recipes. Thus, one can taste thousands of dishes with different flavors when one travels through Japan, something impossible to do at Japanese restaurants in other countries. *See also* ITADAKIMASU, MEALS, PICKLES.

Currency. Currency appeared in Japan only in 708, trade having previously been conducted exclusively through barter. In that year (Wadō era), the Yamato court established a currency bureau on the Chinese model, issued silver and copper coins called Wadō-*keihin,* and produced twelve series of coins collectively called Kōchoō-*jūnisen,* struck near the Suō and Nagato mines. These coins were taken out of circulation in 987 and replaced in the twelfth century by imported Chinese coins *(eirakusen)* of excellent quality. Local lords also struck coins, but some of these, made of a poor-quality alloy, were banned. Toyotomi Hideyoshi struck gold coins *(ōban-kin),* then small gold coins *(koban-kin)* in 1585, which were widely circulated. In 1601, Tokugawa Ieyasu wanted to unify the monetary system. In the Edo period, the following coins were in use: *ōban,* in gold, worth 10 *ryō; koban,* in gold, worth 1 *ryō; chōgin* and *mama-itagin; ichibu-gin,* in silver; and *tsūhō,* in copper (various types). However, parities differed by region: in Edo, the gold standard was used, while in Osaka the silver standard was favored. Paper bills *(hansatsu)* issued by certain daimyo competed with these coins. It was not until 1871 that the currency was finally unified and minting regularized thanks to machines imported from England and the creation of a currency bureau *(zōhei-ryō).* The silver standard was adopted in 1878, but was dropped for the gold standard in 1897. *See* BITASEN, BU, BUNKYŪ-HEIHŌ, BUNROKU-TSŪHŌ, CHŌ-MOKU, CHŌNEN-TAIHŌ, ICHIBU-GIN, JINGŌ-KAIHŌ, JŌWA-SHŌHŌ, JUSENSHI, KAIKI, KAN'EI-TSŪHŌ, KASEN, KEICHŌ-TSŪHŌ, KENGEN-TAIHŌ, KENJI-KIN, KOBAN, KŌBU-TSŪSHŌ, KŌCHŌ-JŪNISEN, KYŌHŌ-KINGIN, ŌBAN, RYŌ, SHŌRYŌ, SHU, TEMPŌ-TSŪHŌ, TENSHŌ-TSŪHŌ, WADŌ-KAIHŌ.

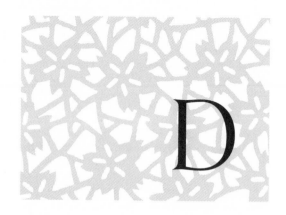

D. The sound *d (da, di, du, de, do)* is a "nigori-zation" of the sound *t (ta, chi, tsu, te, to);* the sounds *di* and *du* do not exist and are replaced by the syllables *ji* and *zu. See* KANA, NIGORI.

Dai. This syllable, generally meaning "big" or "important," is used in a great number of words, names, and titles.

• On the last day of the Urabon (Bon) Festival, bonfires form the ideograph "dai" on the slopes of certain mountains in Japan. The best known of these *daimonji* ("large characters") occurs every August 16 on a mountainside in eastern Kyoto. It is 77 m wide and more than 100 m long, and can best be seen from the Sanjō bridge. Also known as Daimonji Okuribi, and Daimonji Yaki, it commemorates the story of a fire at the Jōdo-ji temple, when the Buddha of the altar took refuge on Mt. Nyoigatake (Daimonji-yama, 466 m) and emitted a very bright light. At the same time, on other hills around Kyoto, bonfires are lit representing the "dai" ideograph on a smaller scale, the word *myōhō* (Buddhist Law), and designs such as that of a torii gate.

Dai-Ajia Kyōkai. "Society for Greater Asia." An ultra-imperialist party created in 1936 by Prime Minister Hirota Kōki (Hirota Hirotake, 1878–1948) to promote Japan's dominance in Asia.

Daian-ji. Buddhist temple in Nara, founded in 639 and reconstructed several times in different locations. One of the oldest Buddhist temples in Japan, it is a Sanron (Three Treatises) school center. First established by the Kudara River and called Kudara-daiji, the temple had a nine-story pagoda. It was reconstructed in 677 in Takechi and called Takechi-

daiji, then Daikan-daiji. Finally, it was moved to the new capital, Heijō-kyō (Nara), in 718, where it was renamed Daian-ji, probably about 729, and was one of the seven great temples of Nara. Fires and typhoons destroyed it completely over the centuries. Excavations have revealed that its plan was based on the Ximing temple in Chang'an, China. A modern hall houses nine *hinoki* cypress statues of Kannon Bosatsu (*Skt.:* Avalokiteshvara) and the Shi-tennō (*Skt.:* Chatur-mahrārāja), the Four Heavenly Kings, from the ancient temple.

Daibutsu. "Great Buddha," large bronze statues of Buddha, generally in a sitting position, higher than the traditional height of one *jōroku* (about 4.9 m), which would have been the height of the Buddha standing, according to certain legends. Several Daibutsu exist in Japan, all of them famous.

• The oldest, in poor condition, is that in the Asuka-dera, by Korean bronze sculptor Kuratsu-kuribe no Tori, and dates from 606.

• The Daibutsu of Tōdai-ji, in Nara, portrays Birushana (*Skt.:* Vairochana). It was cast in bronze from 749 to 752 by Kuninaka no Muraji Kimimaro, Takechi Makuni, Kakimoto Otama, and others, using the Igarakuri technique. It is 18 m high (including the pedestal) and weighs 450,000 kg. The bronze lotus seat has 56 petals, engraved with texts from the Sanskrit *Padmalokadhātu.* The halo was sculpted in wood and covered in gold leaf in the seventeenth century. This immense statue was damaged by fire a number of times, notably in 1180 and 1567 during civil wars, and the Daibutsu-den (the building that houses it) was destroyed. But it was repaired each time, once by Chōgen. There is almost nothing left of the original statue but the lotus petals at the base. Beside it sit late-seventeenth-century gold-leafed wooden statues of Nyoirin Kannon, Kokūzō Bosatsu, and other bodhisattvas. *See* TŌDAI-JI.

• The Daibutsu of Kamakura, cast in 1252 for the Kōtoku-in temple and representing Amida Buddha in meditation, is 11.5 m high and weighs 100,000 kg. It is said to have been the work of a certain Ono Goroēmon. The temple in which this statue sat was destroyed by a tsunami in 1495 and never reconstructed; the Daibutsu was left in the open. People can enter this Daibutsu through the back and climb inside to the head.

• Other Daibutsu were built in Japan, but they have since disappeared, including one at Hōkō-ji in Kyoto that was 18 m high and sculpted in 1587 on Hideyoshi's orders. Destroyed in 1596 by an earthquake, it was replaced in 1612 by a bronze Daibutsu (height: 19 m) that was destroyed by another earthquake in 1622.

• A Daibutsu was erected in Ueno (Tokyo) in modern times; it measures only 7 m in height.

• **Daibutsu-den.** Name given to the large wooden building housing the Daibutsu at Tōdai-ji in Nara. *See* TŌDAI-JI.

• *Daibutsu-kuyō.* Title of a Noh play: the Taira (Heike) warrior Kagekiyo disguises himself as a Buddhist monk and tries to attack Minamoto no Yoritomo during a ceremony. His plot is discovered, and he is forced to flee.

• **Daibutsu Nyorai.** *See* DAINICHI.

Daibutsu Sadafusa. Governor of Kyoto (1175–1240) for the Kamakura *bakufu*, and a poet. *See* HŌJŌ TOKIFUSA.

Daicel Chemical Company. Anglicized name of Daiseru Kagaku Kōgyō, one of the largest manufacturers of synthetic products (cellulose, Fuji film, etc.). It was founded in 1919 as a subsidiary of Mitsui. Its head office is split between Tokyo and Osaka, and it has branches in New York and Düsseldorf. It exports about 15% of its production.

Dai-dairi. The grounds of the inner imperial palace at Heian-kyō (Kyoto), built by Emperor Kammu in 794. The central part of the palace, where the emperor lived, was called Dairi, Kinri, or Kinchū. The palace itself was also called Ō-uchi, "the Great House," and was originally surrounded by walls. *See* GOSHO.

Daidan. Small table, generally placed before a small Buddhist statue, on which ritual implements *(daidan-gu)* are placed.

Dai-dembō-in. Buddhist temple in Wakayama, of the Shingi Shingon sect (separated from Kōya-san), founded by the monk Kakuban in 1130 and built around 1286–88. Destroyed by fire in 1585, it was reconstructed in 1623. Its pagoda *(tahō-tō)* dates from 1515. Also called Negoro-ji, Negoro-dera.

Daidō. Era during the reign of Emperor Junna: May 806–Sept. 810. *See* NENGŌ.

Daidōji Yūzan. Military strategist (Daidōji Shigesuke, 1639–1730), born in Yamashiro, raised in Edo by Hōjō Ujinaga (1609–70). He taught at various estates *(han)* and wrote a number of works on martial arts, notably the *Budō shoshin-shū* (Introduction to the Way of the Warrior), published after his death. His other, less-well-known works, such as *Ochiboshū* (Collection of Leaves) and *Iwabuchi yawa* (Night Stories of Iwabuchi), are accounts of the life of Tokugawa Ieyasu.

• **Daidōji Shigetoki.** *See* ISE TARŌ.

Daidō Tokoshukō. Steel company. Founded in 1916, it manufactures specialty steel; over 50% of its production goes to the automobile industry, especially Nissan. Head office in Nagoya.

Daie. Title of a Noh play: a Tengu steals an image of Buddha and brings it to a Buddhist monk to thank him for his kindness, but he is punished for his thievery.

Daiei. Film company, previously Dai Nippon Eiga, founded in 1942. It produced a number of films directed by Kurosawa Akira and Kinugasa Teinosuke. Daiei went bankrupt in 1971, but was reopened and continues to produce films.

• Major store chain founded in 1949 by Nakauchi Isao in Osaka and Kobe. It controls a large number of supermarkets throughout the country and is involved in many sectors, including clothing, pharmaceutical products, restaurants, and foodstuffs. It has partnerships with other major foreign stores, such as Printemps in Paris, Marks and Spencer in London, and J. C. Penney in the United States. Daiei is currently the top distribution chain in Japan.

Daie-kai. Modern Buddhist sect, founded in 1951.

Dai-ei (Tai-ei). Era during the reign of Emperor Go-Nara: Aug. 1521–Aug. 1527. *See* NENGŌ.

Daigaku. Literally, "great learning," *daigaku* means "university." It is the Japanese transcription of the Chinese work *Daxue,* the first of the Four Books, the Confucian classics. *See* UNIVERSITIES.

• Daigaku Bessho. *See* KANGAKU-IN.

• Daigaku-nankō. *See* KAISEI-SHO.

• Daigaku-rei. "Law on universities," promulgated in 1918, liberalizing education and recognizing private universities.

• Daigaku-ryō. Former imperial university of Kyoto, founded in the seventh century, where future administrators were trained according to Confucian philosophy. It was reorganized in 701, then expanded during the Heian period. It used Chinese Confucian texts such as the *Lunyu* (Analects) and the *Xiaojing* (Book of Filial Piety). The subjects taught were Confucian principles *(myōkyō),* mathematics *(san),* history *(kite, monjō),* and law *(myōhō)*—that is, the "four great sciences" *(daigaku-ryō no shidō).*

• Daigaku-shōsha. *See* KAISEKI.

• Daigaku Zenji. *See* RANKEI DŌRYŪ.

Daigenkai. Major Japanese dictionary, compiled from 1932 to 1937 by Otsuki Fumihiko. Comprising four volumes and listing about 100,000 words, it is an improved version of a similar work, *Genkai,* published in 1889–91. The *Daigenkai* stresses etymology, but some of the word roots it gives are contested by experts.

Daigen no Hō. Ceremony of the Buddhist Shingon sect. Starting in 840, it was performed at the beginning of each year at the Jibushō (Ministry of Civil Affairs) to pray for peace in the country. Also called Daigensui-hō.

Daigensui. Former title of the emperor, meaning "chief marshal."

• Daigensui Myō-ō. Japanese name of a *yaksha* of Indian Buddhist mythology (*Skt.*: Atavaka), general of the heavenly cohorts, who was accused of eating human flesh. He was a Vidyārāja (*Jap.*: Myō-ō), or "Wisdom King," and an acolyte of Vaishrāvana (*Jap.*: Bishamonten). Also called Atabaku, Kōyajin.

Daigo-genji. Branch of the Minamoto (Genji) family claiming direct descent from Emperor Daigo. *See* MINAMOTO.

Daigo-ji. Head temple of the Daigo branch of the Shingon sect, founded by Shōbō in 874. This religious complex, constructed midway up a hill in Fushimi, Kyoto, is typical of architecture of the ninth and tenth centuries. Beginning with Emperor Daigo, the imperial family maintained a close relationship with the temple. Emperor Daigo built a Shakadō (Buddha hall) in 926 and awarded the temple the imperial rank of Chokugan-ji. In 952, Empress Onshi had a five-story pagoda *(goju-no-tō)* built, which has been preserved and which houses valuable art of the time, notably paintings of mandalas and Shingon patriarchs. Destroyed (except for the pagoda) during the 1467 Ōnin War, the temple was rebuilt by Hideyoshi in the late sixteenth century. The 37-meter pagoda is the oldest five-story pagoda in Japan and is a National Treasure. Other buildings date from various eras: Sambō-in (1606), Yakushi-dō (1124), Godai-dō (1606), Haiden and Kiyotaki (fifteenth century), Kondō (Fujiwara style, 1600), Seiryū-gongen Shrine (1434), Kaisan-dō and Nyoirin-dō (1608). Certain structures are Shinto, others are associated with Shugendō, the sect of the mountain ascetics *(yamabushi);* the Sambō-in is the head temple of the Tōzan branch of the Shugendō sect. Daigo-ji houses many paintings and sculptures classified as National Treasures. It has about 850 annex temples throughout Japan.

Daigokuden. Great Hall of State, main building of the imperial palace in ancient Japan, where meetings of the state council were held and enthronement ceremonies took place. Each imperial palace had a Daigokuden, especially during the Asuka period. In the ninth century, these halls were replaced by Shishinden. In 1177, the former Daigokuden of Heian-kyō was destroyed by fire and was not rebuilt. Heian-jingū in Kyoto, built in 1895, represents this former imperial hall on a slightly reduced scale, but the original site is unknown.

Daigo Tennō. Sixtieth emperor of Japan (Prince Atsuhito, 885<898–930>), son and successor of Uda Tennō. Emperor Daigo's reign was characterized by a revival of arts and letters, especially during the Engi era (901–923). He had Ki no Tsurayuki and other poets compile a poetry anthology, *Kokin waka-shū*, in 905. In 902, he tried to stem the proliferation of *shōen* (private estates); he improved the government's finances by reforming the *ritsuryō* system.

Daigyaku Jiken. "Incident of High Treason." After the dissolution of the Socialist party in 1907 and the Akahata Incident, union groups in Aichi prefecture, along with Kōtoku Shūsui (1871–1911), conspired to assassinate Emperor Meiji. The plot was discovered in 1910 and the conspirators were arrested. The government accused Kōtoku Shūsui of being the leader of the conspiracy (which he was not) and sentenced him and several other people to death. This "incident" was the first act of a violently anti-socialist government.

Daihatsu Kōgyō. Automobile manufacturer (passenger cars and trucks) founded in 1907; since 1967, part of the Toyota group. It now specializes in the production of electric vehicles and exports to most countries in the world. Head office in Ikeda (Osaka).

Dai-hizen-kyō. Religious sect founded in 1949 by Orimo Nami (b. 1893).

Daihon'ei. Imperial General Headquarters during wartime. Under direct command of the emperor, it involved the top officers of all of the armed forces. Cabinet ministers did not take part in its deliberations. There have been three Daihon'ei: during the Sino-Japanese War (1894–95), during the Russo-Japanese War (1904–05), and during the Second World War.

Dai-hyakka jiten. "Great Japanese Encyclopedia" in 28 volumes, published from 1931 to 1935 and in 1939.

Dai-ichi Chūō Kisen Kaisha. Marine shipping company (freight and tankers) founded in 1960 and an affiliate of Mitsui Lines. Since 1970, it has operated in conjunction with marine shipping companies in Hong Kong and New York. Head office in Tokyo.

• **Dai-ichi Ginkō.** "First National Bank." A banking and commercial establishment founded in 1873 by Shibusawa Eiichi (1840–1931), in conjunction with the Mitsui and Ono merchant houses. It was active in the development of business and industry in Korea starting in 1878. In 1971, it was absorbed into the Dai-ichi Kangyō Ginkō.

• **Dai-ichi Kangyō Ginkō.** Major commercial bank, founded in 1971 by the merger of Dai-ichi Ginkō and Nippon Kangyō Ginkō (founded in 1897). It is now the largest bank in Japan. Head office in Tokyo.

• **Dai-ichi Seimei Hoken Sōgo Kaisha.** Life insurance company, founded in 1902 and active not only in Japan but in Brazil, the United States, and other countries. It was the first of its type in Japan.

Daiitoku Myō-ō. Buddhist goddess (*Skt.:* Yamāntaka), the "wrathful" emanation of Amida Buddha, who is said to have conquered Yama (death). She is a Tantric form of Monju Bosatsu (*Skt.:* Mañjushrī), who fights spiritual maladies and sin. This goddess, rarely portrayed, has six heads and six legs. She is sometimes considered a form of the Hindu god Shiva. Also called, depending on the form, Go-Emma-son, Emmatoku-kainu-ō, Rokumen-son, Rokuson Myō-ō.

Daiji. Era during the reign of Emperor Sutoku: Jan. 1126–Jan. 1131. *See* NENGŌ.

Daijin. Starting in 645, title of state ministers. They were divided into the minister of the left (*sadaijin*), the minister of the right (*udaijin*), and below them, the minister of domestic affairs (*naidaijin*). After 702, they were directed by a *dajō daijin*, or grand minister of state. Starting in 1885, the Grand Council of State comprised 10 *daijin. See* DAINAGON, NAGON.

• **Daijin zenji.** Title of "religious minister," given to Dōkyō by Empress Shōtoku in 764. The following year, she gave him the title *dajō daijin zenji. See* DŌKYŌ.

Daijizai-ten. Minor Buddhist deity (*Skt.:* Maheshvara), Japanese Buddhist form of Shiva. Also called Makeishura-ten.

Daijō-bukkyō. Japanese name for northern Buddhist schools, still called Mahyana, or "Great Vehicle" (for progress on the path to salvation).

• **Daijō-e.** Ritual conducted by a new emperor at the beginning of autumn following his enthronement to honor the ancestors. This is the third and final ceremony of the first year of a new reign, after the Senso (proclamation) and the Sokuirei, or formal enthronement at the Shishinden in the Imperial Palace. This ceremony was abandoned in 1947 after publication of new laws concerning the imperial family. It was reinstituted on November 22, 1990, after the coronation of Emperor Akihito. Also called Daijō-sai, Ōmube, Ōname, Ōni-e.

• *Daijō-in jisha zōji ki.* "Records on Miscellaneous Matters About the Monastery and the Shrine, Written at Daijō-in." Texts compiled by three monks from the Daijō-in in Nara and attached to Kōfuku-ji: Jinson (1430–1508), Seikaku (d. 1494), Kyōjin (d. 1526), and a few others, concerning the events that took place between 1450 and 1527.

• *Daijō-ji.* Buddhist temple founded in Kasumi (Hyōgo prefecture) in the eighth century and renovated in the eighteenth century. It was the residence of the painter Maruyama Ōkyo and his sons, who decorated it.

• *Daijōryūryōgakyō.* Japanese text of the Lankāvatāra-sūtra.

• *Daijōshōgonron.* Important Buddhist text of the Hossō sect, translation of the Sanskrit text *Mahāyānasūtrālamkāra.*

Daikaku. Buddhist monk (*posthumous name:* Myōjitsu, 1297–1364) who belonged to the Shingon and Nichiren sects. He may have been a son of the regent (*kampaku*) Konoe Tsunetada.

Daikaku-ji. Head temple of the Daikaku-ji branch of the Shingon sect, built in Kyoto in 876 on the site of the detached palace (823) of Emperor Saga, and dedicated to the five Myō-ō (Go-dai Myō-ō), the Wisdom Kings (*Skt.:* Vidyārāja). During the period of the Northern and Southern Courts (Nambo-kuchō), Emperor Go-Kameyama lived there and it was called Daikakuji-jō. Later it came under the patronage of the Ashikaga shogun, who embellished it. The temple's fusuma (sliding partitions) were decorated with paintings of flowers by Kanō Sanraku, Kanō Tan'yū, and other painters of the Kanō school. The Kyakuden and Shinden are examples of the *shoin-zukuri* style of the Azuchi-Momoyama period (1568–1600). The Hondō (main hall) houses a statue of Kongō Yasha (*Skt.:* Vajrayaksha), one of the Go-dai Myō-ō, sculpted by Myōen in 1176.

• *Daikaku-to.* "Imperial line of Daikaku-ji," emperors and princes descended from Emperor Kameyama (1249–1305). The Jimyō-in line is descended from Emperor Go-Fukakusa, and was named for the temple where he retired in 1259. The Kamakura shogunate decided that emperors would be chosen alternately from these two lines, but Emperor Go-Daigo of the Daitoku-ji line opposed this arrangement, which led to a civil war and the Kemmu Restoration. Ashikaga Takauji captured Kyoto, and Go-Daigo was forced to flee to Yoshino, where he established his own court. The period of the Northern and Southern Courts (Nambokuchō) that followed lasted until 1392.

Daikan. "Intendants," or local administrators of a fief (*gundai*) belonging to a *buke* (called *mokudai* when the fief was the property of a *kuge*) during the Kamakura period. In the mid-Muromachi period, a *daikan* was an intendant replacing a *shugo* (military governor) or a *jitō* (land steward). In the late sixteenth century, the title was applied to tax collectors. During the Edo period, *daikan* and *gundai* were administrators of shogunal estates. *See* JITŌ-DAI, MOKUDAI.

Dai kanwa jiten. Chinese and Japanese kanji dictionary, compiled by Morohashi Tetsuji and published in 12 volumes and an index from 1955 to 1960. It is the largest dictionary of its type, with about 50,000 entries and more than 520,000 compound words. An abridged edition was published in 1968. *See* MOROHASHI TETSUJI.

Daiken Kōgyō. Manufacturer of construction materials, founded in 1945 in Osaka. It exports much of its production to Asia, the Middle East, Europe, and the United States.

Daikokuten. Shinto form of a fierce manifestation of Kannon (*Skt.:* Mahākāla), protector of the Buddhist Law, guardian of monasteries, and associated with the *kami* Okuni-nushi no Mikoto. He is portrayed sitting or standing on a shield; when Daikokuten is portrayed with three heads (those of Bishamonten and Benzaiten or Marishiten), he is called Sanmen Daikoku. In his popular form, he is considered a kitchen god (Kōjin-sama). Starting in the early seventeenth century, he was incorporated into the Seven Gods of Good Fortune (Shichi-fukujin). He is portrayed as a fat, smiling man, sitting or standing on sacks of rice and holding a large bag containing wisdom and patience on his shoulder. He also sometimes carries a sort of wooden mallet (*uchide no kozuchi*). His followers use similar mallets, which they shake in the hope of obtaining wealth. In Shikoku and northern Kyushu, Daikokuten is considered a *Ta no kami* (*kami* of the fields), and prayers for good harvests are addressed to him. His main shrine is in Osaka, where there is a large festival in his honor every year.

• The wives of certain Buddhist monks are sometimes called Daikoku-san.

• **Daikokuya Kōdayū.** Sailor (1751–1828), born in the province of Ise, who was shipwrecked on the Siberian coast in 1787 and lived in Irkutsk, then St. Petersburg, where he was received by Catherine II. He returned to Japan in 1792 with the Russian envoy Adam Laxman, but was sentenced to house arrest for life for having broken the shogunate's laws forbidding travel abroad. The interrogation that he underwent on his stay in Russia was published in 1794 in a report titled *Hokusa bunryaku.*

Daikon. Type of large radish *(Raphanus sativus),* weighing up to 15 kg, used widely in Japanese cuisine. It is consumed raw, finely grated, or in brine *(takuan pickle).* It is also used as an ingredient in sauces and various seasonings.

Daikuhara Gintarō. Agricultural engineer and chemist (1868–1934). He invented a method (which bears his name) of measuring acidity in soil. He was the president of the University of Kyushu, then of Dōshisha University. His major work was *Dojōgaku kōgi,* published in 1920.

Daikyō Sekiyu. Oil company founded in 1939 by the merger of a number of oil producers in Nagano prefecture. It has been operating offshore wells in Abu Dhabi since 1968.

Daimaru. Department store chain based in Kansai. Daimaru includes supermarkets and restaurants, owned by a company founded in 1727 in Kyoto as a clothing store. It has many establishments in Japan and, since 1960, has opened branches in Hong Kong, Thailand, France (Paris), Singapore, and other countries. Head office in Osaka. *See also* MATSU-ZAKAYA.

Daimoku. In the Nichiren sect, recitation of the prayer "Namu Myōhō renge-kyō," the invocation of the *Lotus Sutra (Skt.: Saddharmapundarīkā-sūtra).*

Daimon. Upper garment *(hitatare)* worn by samurai from the Kamakura period to the Edo period. It bears five family crests *(mon),* embroidered or dyed, in the middle of the back, on the chest, and on the sleeves. The pants *(hakama)* also bear two *mon.*

During the Muromachi period, the *daimon* was a ceremonial garment for mid-ranking warriors. During the Edo period it became the official costume of the samurai of the fifth rank *(see* I). It is still a traditional formal-dress garment for men.

Daimon Shirō. Kabuki dancer (b. 1944) who has performed in many foreign countries.

Daimyō. "Great name." A title given to lords governing large territories and commanding a large number of vassals *(kenin)* starting in the Muromachi period, although the term was used in the eleventh century to designate major landowners, civil or military. At first used only for military men, in the Edo period it was applied to all owners of estates whose annual revenue was equal to or above 10,000 *koku* of rice *(see* KOKU). Those who had a lower income were called *shōmyō* (lit., "small names"). The *daimyō* were divided into several categories: *fudai-daimyō,* hereditary vassals; *tozama-daimyō* ("outside" *daimyō),* allies of the *bakufu;* and *shimpan-daimyō,* kinsmen of the Tokugawa family. Before the Muromachi period, however, the title *myōden* was more frequently used to designate owners of large estates, who were divided into *kokushu* (governing several provinces), *ryōshu* (governing a relatively small territory), and *jōshu* (governors of castles).

The *daimyō* conducted incessant wars with the aim of expanding their territories. In the fifteenth century, taking advantage of disturbances rocking the country, many military governors *(shugo)* appropriated land and became *shugo-daimyō,* building castles to defend themselves against the expansionist plans of their neighbors. They were pacified and their territories controlled only after the Battle of Sekigahara in 1600. At the end of the eighteenth century, there were 23 *shimpan-daimyō,* 45 *fudai-daimyō,* and 98 *tozama-daimyō* in Japan, and their total annual income was equivalent to about 19 million *koku,* while the territories directly under the shogun's control brought in only 6.8 million *koku (see* KAZOKU).

Although the *daimyō* had a certain amount of autonomy, they were subject to particular rules, the Laws for Military Households, codified in the *Buke-shohatto.* Among other obligations, they had to maintain a residence in Edo, remain there one year out of two (or six months per year), and leave their families and vassals in Edo as hostages *(see* SANKIN-KŌTAI). Starting in 1639, they no longer had permission to build castles or seaworthy ships, and they had to ensure that Christianity was banned in their territories. During the Meiji Restoration in 1868, certain *daimyō* were appointed governor of their provinces (then called *han*), but in 1871 all *han* were abolished and Japan was divided into prefectures *(ken)*. The former *daimyō* were then given pensions and forced to live in Tokyo.

• **Daimyō gyōretsu.** The procession that accompanied the *daimyō* on their annual or biannual journey to Edo to attend the shogun, as required by *sankin kōtai* ("alternate attendance"). The shogunate set rules for the number of vassals and size of the retinue according to the importance of the *daimyō*. These rules were not taken very seriously, and the *daimyō* were accompanied in their travels by a great number of people, sometimes thousands. The *daimyō* were gradually impoverished by this practice—a development that the *bakufu* encouraged. Many *daimyō* were forced to borrow from wealthy merchants, who ended up managing the finances of their estates. These loans to the *daimyō* (*daimyōgashi*) considerably enriched the merchant class, enabling it to expand. In addition, businesses, inns, and teahouses *(chaya)* sprang up along the post roads used by the *daimyō* to travel to and from Edo, stimulating the country's general economy. *See* KAZOKU.

Dainagon. Title given in 702 to government counselors. They had previously been called Oimonomōsu-tsukasa. *See* NAGON, DAIJIN.

• **Dainaiki.** Title given before 702 to the first secretary of the Ministry of Central Imperial Affairs (Nakatsukasashō).

Dainen. Painter (Nakagawa Tenju; Chōshirō; *gō:* Suishinsai, Kantenju; *azana:* Dainen, d. 1795) of the Nanga school, and a famous calligrapher. He illustrated books, including *Taigadō gafu* and *Ifukyū gafu.*

Daini. Title of the vice-governor of Dazaifu in northern Kyushu. *See also* GON NO SOTSO, TANGEN.

• *Daini bimbō monogatari.* See BIMBŌ MONOGATARI.

• **Daini no San'mi (Sammi).** Title of a famous early-eleventh-century poet, the daughter of Murasaki Shikibu. She was probably Fujiwara Kenshi (Satoku), wife of Fujiwara Kanetaka, with whom she had a daughter. She was married a second time, to Takashina Nariaki. She is sometimes credited with writing *Sagoromo monogatari.* Her poems are collected in the *Daini no San'mi-shū.* *See* SAGOROMO MONOGATARI, MURASAKI SHIKUBU.

Dainichi. "Great Sun." Dainichi Nyorai is the Japanese form of the Buddhist deity Vairochana or Mahāvairochana, who represents the highest expression of the godhead in Esoteric Buddhism. In the Tendai and Shingon sects, he is the central figure of the pantheon and the mandalas. He is the supreme Buddha of Light, the ultimate reality without beginning or end, manifest in two realms: the Diamond Realm (Kongō-kai, *Skt.:* Vajradhātu), which reveals his wisdom, and the Womb Realm (Taizō-kai, *Skt.:* Garbhadhātu), which represents his all-embracing enlightenment. The main mudras of Dainichi are the *chiken-in* in the Kongō-kai and the *hokaijō-in* in the Taizō-kai. He is also called Roshana Butsu, Birushana Butsu, Daibutsu Nyorai. *See* RYŌKAI MANDARA.

• **Dainichi Dairitsu-genri.** *See* ICHIGEN NO MIYA.

• **Dainichi Henjō.** Name given to Dainichi Nyorai at the Enryaku-ji temple on Mt. Hiei in the northeastern outskirts of Kyoto.

• **Dainichi ken-in.** Mudra (hand gesture) of the "sword of knowledge," specific to certain images of Dainichi Nyorai. Also called *mushofushi-in, ritō-in.* *See* CHIKEN-IN.

• *Dainichi-kyō.* Basic text of the Tendai and Shingon sects, Japanese translation of the Sanskrit *Mahāvairochana-sūtra (Bhisambodhi-sūtra).*

Dai-Nihon. "Great Japan," expression used in names relating to the history of Japan. Also Dai-Nippon.

• *Dai-Nihon chimei jisho.* Geographical dictionary of the Japanese archipelago in 11 volumes, written by Yoshida Tōgo, published from 1900 to 1907 and listing more than 40,000 place names, with their origins and descriptions. This work, compiled from archival documents, has never been equaled and remains an incomparable research tool.

• **Dai-Nihon Daidōkyō.** Subsect of Tenrikyō, founded in 1911 by Kanamori Umeko (1843–1924).

• *Dai-Nihon enkai jissoku zenzu.* Atlas of Japan written by Inō Tadataka, based on surveys he conducted on the coasts from 1800 to 1816. When the author died, work on this atlas was continued by Takahashi Kageyasu until 1821. It comprises more than 225 large-scale (1:36,000), mid-scale (1:216,000), and small-scale (1:432,000) maps. This collection of maps was the model for all those drawn thereafter in the nineteenth century; it is kept in the Tokyo National Museum and the Inō Tadataka Memorial in Sawara, Chiba prefecture.

• **Dai-Nihon Fujin-kai.** Women's association founded in 1942 to mobilize women in the war effort and assist soldiers on the front. It absorbed the Aikoku Fujin-kai and the Dai-Nippon Kokubo Fujin-kai.

• *Dai-Nihon kokugo jiten.* Four-volume dictionary of the Japanese language compiled by Ueda Kazutoshi, published from 1915 to 1919. It contains almost 200,000 articles, so accurate that this dictionary served as the basis for all those that followed.

• *Dai-Nihon komonjo.* "Archives of Great Japan." Chronologically ordered collection of documents on the history of Japan, published since 1901 by the University of Tokyo. There are now more than 150 volumes.

• **Dai-Nihon Rōdō Sōdōmei Yuai-kai.** *See* NIHON RŌDŌ SŌDŌMEI.

• **Dai-Nihon Sangyō Hōkoku-kai (SAMPO).** "Industrial Patriotic Association," an organization created in 1938 to replace labor unions, placing industry under direct state control. Dissolved in 1945.

• *Dai-Nihon shi.* "History of Great Japan," commissioned in 1657 by Tokugawa Mitsukuni (1622–1700), daimyo of Mito, and finished in 1906; 397 volumes. Written in classical Chinese *(kambun),* its original purpose was to affirm the legitimacy of the imperial throne and portray Japanese history according to the Neo-Confucian Zhu Xi *(Jap.:* Shushi) school. It begins with the ascent of Emperor Jimmu and ends with the reign of Emperor Go-Komatsu in 1412. Many scholars were contributors, among them Asaka Tampaku, Kuriyama Sempō, Miyake Kanran, Hanawa Hokiichi, and Kurita Hiroshi.

• *Dai-Nihon shiryō.* Collection of historical documents from 887, after the *Rikkoku-shi* (Six National Histories) were written, this is the follow-up to the historical work *Shiryō* (attributed to Hanawa Hokiichi). Published by the University of Tokyo starting in 1901, it covers Japanese history to 1868 and comprises more than 300 volumes. A huge 17-volume index was published from 1923 to 1963. The project is ongoing.

• **Dai-Nihon Teikoku.** Official name of the Empire of Japan until 1945. Also called Dai-Nippon Teikoku. Now replaced by Nihonkoku (or Nipponkoku).

• **Dai-Nihon Teikoku Kempō.** First imperial constitution, promulgated on February 11, 1889, and in effect as of November 29, 1890. This constitution was replaced in May 1947 by the current constitution, the Nihonkoku Kempō. *See* CONSTITUTIONS.

Dai-Nippon. "Great Japan," expression sometimes used instead of Dai-Nihon, but written with the same ideographs.

• **Dai-Nippon Inki Kagaku Kōgyō.** Dainippon Ink & Chemicals is a manufacturer of chemical products, inks, resins, plastics, and biochemical and petrochemical products. In 1962, it merged with Reichhold Chemicals of the United States and expanded into other countries through the acquisition of firms. It currently has some 30 international subsidiaries.

• **Dai-Nippon Insatsu (DNP).** Printing company founded in 1876 as Shūeisha; it took its current name in 1935. DNP prints books, papers, catalogues, and other products for Japanese and foreign companies, and manufactures precision components for the electronics industry. It has branches in many foreign cities, including Hong Kong, Singapore, Jakarta, San Francisco, New York, Sydney, Düsseldorf, and London. Head office in Tokyo.

• **Dai-Nippon Kokubo Fujin-kai.** "Women's Association for National Defense." Patriotic organization created in 1932 to assist soldiers on the Manchurian front, help families of war dead, and care for the wounded. In 1942, it merged with the Aikoku Fujin-kai to form Dai-Nihon Fujin-kai.

• **Dai-Nippon (Nihon) Kokusui-kai.** "National Essence Society." A right-wing political organization founded in 1919 by Tokonami Takejirō, then the home minister in the Hara cabinet, to counter socialism and sustain the cult of the emperor. This society, which sometimes resorted to violence, was dissolved in 1945.

• **Dai-Nippon Rengo Senendan.** Federation of Youth Groups of Japan, an association created in 1925 to promote patriotism; starting in 1931, it recruited young people for paramilitary organizations. In 1941, the federation became the nucleus of another organization, Dai-Nippon Seishōnendan, with even more militaristic goals. Both societies were dissolved in 1945.

• **Dai-Nippon Seinentō.** *See* HASHIMOTO KINGORŌ.

• **Dai-Nippon Sekiseikai.** *See* HASHIMOTO KINGORŌ.

Daiō Kokushi. Zen monk (1235–1308), born in the province of Suruga. He went to China in 1259. The abbot of Sōfuku-ji in Nagasaki for 30 years, he was a personal adviser to Hōjō Sadatoki. Also called Namban Shōmin. *See also* Ō-TŌ-KAN.

Dairi. In the Japanese legal system, the capacity of a person to act as an agent or proxy.
  • Inner palace, reserved for the emperor and, by extension, a name for the emperor himself. Also called Kinchū, Kinri. *See* DAI-DAIRI.

• **Dairi-bina.** Figurines portraying the emperor and empress in court robes, used in the exhibition of dolls mounted during the Doll Festival (Hina Matsuri), which takes place on March 3. *See* HINA MATSURI.

• *Dairi-shiki.* History book compiled by Yoshimine Yasuyo and others in 821.

Dai-Seishi Bosatsu. Japanese name of Mahāsthāmaprāpta, a bodhisattva *(Jap.: bosatsu)* symbolizing Amida's strength and wisdom. Dai-Seishi Bosatsu may also be a deification of the Buddha's disciple Mahāmaudgalyāyana, in which case he is portrayed as a monk with a shaved head. In the images called *raigō-zu,* he often accompanies Amida in his "descent" *(raigō),* in the company of Shō Kannon Bosatsu. Also called Seishi Bosatsu.

Daisen. Double-coned volcano (height: 1,711 m) in western Tottori prefecture (Honshu). Sometimes called Hōki no Fuji-san, Ōyama.

• **Daisen-ji.** Buddhist temple located on Mt. Daisen, near the city of Akasaki in Tottori prefecture. Founded in 817 as a center of the Tendai sect, it prospered until the Edo period, but few of its original buildings have survived. *See* NICHIREN SHŌSHŪ.

Daisen-in. "Monastery of the Great Hermit," a Zen temple founded by Kogaku Sōkō (1465–1548) in 1509 as a branch of Daitoku-ji in Kyoto. In this small temple are excellent fusuma decorated with paintings by Sō-ami, Kanō Motonobu, and Kanō Yukinobu. Its Zen garden is famous for its arrangement of sand and stones, symbolizing the sea and a ship.

Daisetsu. "Great Snow." The period of the year *(see* NIJŪSHI-SETSU) from about December 20 to January 5.

Daisetsu-zan. Group of volcanic mountains in central Hokkaido. More than 10 are over 2,000 m, including the island's highest peak, Asahidake (2,290 m). The range is in Daisetsu-zan National Park. Also called Taisetsu-zan.

Daishi. "Grand Master." Title given to the most deserving of Buddhist monks. *Standard form:* Taishi. *Chin.:* Dashi. *See* SŌ-KAN.
  • Nickname for Kūkai (Kōbō-daishi). Also O-Daishi-sama.

• **Daishi-dō.** *See* MIEI-DŌ.

• **Daishi-ko.** Major Shinto ceremonies for which purifications lasting up to several months are necessary. *See* DAIJŌ-E.

Daishikyō. Japanese title for a Christian archbishop.

Daisho. "Great Heat." The agricultural season *(see* NIJŪSHI-SETSU) from July 23 to August 8.

Daishō. Set of two swords (*katana* and *wakizashi*), one long and the other short, carried by samurai and high-ranking people from the Muromachi period to 1876, when carrying swords was banned except for military officers. *See* KATANA.

Daishō Kangi-ten. *See* KANGI-TEN.

Daishō Kongō. *See* FUGEN BOSATSU.

Daishō Myō-ō. *See* GUNDARI MYŌ-Ō.

Daishōwa Seishi. Manufacturer of paper and paper products, founded in Shizuoka prefecture in 1938. Daishōwa has subsidiaries in Canada, the United States, Australia, and Malaysia, where it operates forests. Head office in Fuji (Shizuoka prefecture).

Dai-sōjō. The highest title conferred on a Buddhist monk. *See* SŌ-KAN.

• **Dai-sōzu.** *See* SŌ-KAN.

Daitōa. "Greater East Asia." Political expansionism that arose in Japan after the Tanaka Report (1927) and that was behind Japan's decision to go to war with China and later to enter the Second World War.

• **Daitōa Kyōeiken.** "Greater East Asia Co-Prosperity Sphere." A euphemism for an alliance between Asian countries proposed by Japanese militarists in 1942 to justify their occupation of those countries. According to this concept, under Japanese leadership, the countries involved could create an economic and military sphere independent from the rest of the world. Top military commanders, led by Tōjō Hideki and minister of foreign affairs Shigemitsu Aoi, attempted to gain acceptance for the idea by publishing a communiqué (Daitōa Kyōdō Sengen) signed by authorities under Japanese control in China, Manchukuo, and the Philippines, and by representatives of India, Burma, and Thailand. A sort of cabinet was then formed by Aoki Kazuo (1942–44), Shigemitsu Mamoru (1944–45), and Tōgō Shigenori (1945) to implement the policy.

Daito-hijiki. In traditional architecture, eaves in which the top beam is supported by a horizontal bracket *(hijiki)* sitting on a large cubical die *(daito)* on top of a pillar. *See* TO.

Daitoku. "Great Virtue," title given to certain Buddhist monks.

• **Daitoku-ji.** Rinzai Zen temple founded by Myōchō (Sōhō Myōchō, Daitō-kokushi) in Kyoto in 1315 and dedicated in 1326. Most of its buildings were destroyed in a fire in 1453. They were rebuilt but ravaged again during the Ōnin War (1467–77). Reconstructed thanks to donations by merchants of Sakai, the temple was honored by Hideyoshi, who had Oda Nobunaga buried there.

In 1876, the temple became independent, although still part of the Rinzai sect. Of some 60 temples annexed to this large monastery, only some 20 are still standing; the most famous are Daisen-in (founded in 1509), Ryūgen-in (founded in 1502), Jukō-in (founded in 1566), and Kohō-an (founded in 1612). Daitoku-ji has many interesting buildings, the oldest of which date from its reconstruction in 1479. Among them are the Chokushi-mon (imperial gate, from 1640), the Kara-mon (a gate from the Jurakudai palace in Fushimi, late sixteenth century), the San-mon (designed by Sen no Rikyū in 1589), the residence of the monk Ikkyū (called Shinju-an, late fifteenth century), the garden attributed to Sō-ami, the Hondō (1665), the baths (1622), the library (1636), the Shōrō (1609), the Shindō (1636), the Hattō (1636), the Hondō of Ryōkō-in (1606), and the Hōjō by Kobori Enshū (1636). These buildings house many works of art and paintings by Mokkei (*Chin.*: Mu Qi) and Kanō Tan'yū, among others, from the fourteenth, fifteenth, and sixteenth centuries. *See* NAMBOKUCHŌ.

Daitsū-ji. Buddhist temple of the Jōdo Shin sect, founded in Nagahama, near Maibara (Shiga prefecture, Honshū), by the monk Sennyo (1581–1636). Momoyama-style buildings.

Daiwa Bōseki. Textile mill founded in 1941 in Osaka, using techniques from Czechoslovakia. It operates joint ventures with companies based in Brazil and Indonesia.

Daiwa Ginkō. Large bank founded in Osaka in 1918, with subsidiaries in many countries and correspondents in almost 700 foreign banks.

Daiwa Hausu Kōgyō. Daiwa House Industry specializes in the construction of prefabricated steel houses. Founded in 1955 in Osaka. It builds housing developments not only in Japan, but also in the United States, Brazil, and the Philippines. Also called Daiwa House.

Daiwa-jō. *See* GANJIN.

Daiwa Shōken. Daiwa Securities was founded in Tokyo in 1902 and incorporated as an international securities firm in 1943. It currently has some fifteen branches in foreign countries.

Daiyū-in. Shinto shrine built in Nikkō from 1651 to 1653 in memory of the shogun Tokugawa Iemitsu. It was designed by Kihara Yoshihira and

Heinouchi Masanobu, who imitated the Chinese Ming style of decoration. Also called Daiyū-byō.

Dai-za. Base of a statue, Buddhist or other. It has various names depending on its shape: *shumi-za* (stepped square, in imitation of Mt. Meru, Shumi), *renge-za* (lotus flower), *in-za* (rock), and others.

Daizan. Painter (Hirose Seifū; Shūzō, Undayū, Shogasai, Haku-unka, Rokumusai; *azana*: Bokuho; *gō*: Daizan, 1752–1813) of the Nanga school. A student of Gogaku, he painted mainly landscapes.

Daizōkyō. Compilation of sacred Buddhist writings, translated from the Chinese, comprising the words attributed to the Buddha Shakyamuni (*Jap.*: Shaka) and the texts left by his disciples and the faithful. The first edition of the collection (*Skt.*: Tripitaka) was made in China in 518 and titled *Dazang jing;* the first Japanese edition was published in 1630 under the direction of Tenkai (1536–1643) and Tetsugen (1630–82). The most recent and reliable edition, *Taishō shinshū Daizōkyō,* was published between 1923 and 1934 (title abridged to *Taishō Daizōkyō*). Also called *Issai-kyō (Chin.: Yiqie jing)* and *Zō-kyō (Chin.: Zang jing). See* TETSUGEN DŌKO.

• *Daizō ichiran.* Collection of Buddhist texts published in 1614 and printed with movable type.

Dajō daijin. The grand minister of state and chief of the emperor's Grand Council, created in 671. *See* DAIJIN, DAJŌKAN, FUJIWARA NO FUHITO.

• **Dajō-hōō.** *See* DAJŌ-KO, HŌ-Ō, MORISADA SHINNŌ.

• **Dajōkan.** Grand Council of State. Supreme council of the emperor, government agency created in 702 by the *ritsuryō* and Taihō codes. It was composed of three *daijin* (ministers), four *dainagon* (grand counselors), and three *shōnagon* (lesser counselors), directed by the *dajō-daijin* (grand minister of state). The *daijin* and *nagon* were assisted by Sabenkan (controllers of the left), Ubenkan (controllers of the right), and *geki* (secretaries). The Sabenkan controlled the ministries of central imperial affairs (Nakatsukasashō), ceremonial (Shiki-bushō), civil affairs (Jibushō), and the people (Mimbushō). The Ubenkan controlled the ministries of the imperial household (Kunaishō), finance (Okurashō), military affairs (Hyōbushō), and punishments (Gyōbushō). The Dajōkan was under the direct supervision of the emperor, who also directed

the ministry of the Shinto cult (Jingikan). This system was copied from that in force in the Chinese Tang court. To apply the decrees issued by the various ministries, other positions were created, such as that of administrator (called *chidajōkanji* in 703, *chūnagon* in 705, *naishin* in 721, and *sangi* in 729). During the Heian period, the Dajōkan was gradually supplanted by the agency of archives (Karōdo-dokoro) and the regency of the Fujiwara in 857, when the Dajōkan was consigned to a symbolic role. It was revived at the beginning of the Meiji era, from 1875 to 1885, and later abolished.

Dajōkan-satsu. The first national currency of the Meiji era, issued by the Dajōkan in July, 1868. These bank notes were easily counterfeited and rapidly lost their value, as they were not convertible into coins. New bank notes were issued in 1872, and the old ones disappeared completely from circulation in 1879. Also called *kinsatsu. See* YURI KIMIMASA.

Dajō-kō. Title given to an emperor after his abdication. Also called Jōkō, Dajō Tennō. When retired emperors decided to enter religious life, they were called Dajō-Hōō, or Hō-ō. *See also* GO-TOBA TENNŌ, HŌ-Ō, MASAHITO SHINNŌ.

Dajō-nyūdō. Title given to Taira no Kiyomori in 1168, when he took the monk's name Jōkai.

Dajō Tennō. *See* JITŌ tennō, masahito shinnō.

Dammari. In Kabuki theater, scene in which the heroes fight shadows. It is a pantomime, generally short, accompanied by music.

Dammono (Danmono). Form of musical composition for the koto, the invention of which is attributed to Yatsuhashi Kenkō in the eighteenth century.

Dampū. Title of a Noh play: story of revenge on the island of Sado in the Kamakura period.

Dan. Type of weaving in parallel bands; also, a dyeing technique for fabrics. Ordinary cotton fabrics imported from China were called *dantan.*
• In most of the martial arts, ranks attesting to the level of technique. There are most commonly 10 ranks. For beginners, lower levels *(kyū)* have been created; colored belts have been assigned to these *kyū:* white, yellow, orange, green, blue, and maroon, up to black on reaching the first *dan.* The highest *dan* is distinguished by a red-and-white belt.

• Certain other arts and techniques also use *dan* to indicate the degree of mastery attained by those who practice them.

Dances. Japanese dances are of ancient origin and draw on both popular and religious traditions. The oldest ones known were transmitted by the Kagura tradition, which mimes episodes of Shinto mythology. But probably just as old are dances related to food-producing activities such as planting rice, sowing, and fishing, including rain dances. These dances, with the suffix -*mai*, -*asobi*, or -*odori*, are extremely numerous and often specific to a village or region: Emburi, Bon Odori, Ta-asobi, Ta-ue Odori, Hōnen Odori, Awa Odori, Nembutsu Odori, Amagoi Odori, Shishi-mai, and so on. As a group, they are called *furyū*. Those related to Shinto shrines are collectively called Jinji-mai, while Buddhist dances are called Butsuji-no-mai. Ainu dances are called Tapkar or Upopo, Rimuse, Arafutsukun, or Nyenapukashi. The traditional dances of the Ryukyu Islands are classified into popular dances (various *odori* depending on the people—older women, youths, elders, or groups—that perform them), court dances *(kansen-odori)*, and theater dances *(kumi-odori)*, but each island has its own dances.

Buddhist temples often organized dance performances, Ennen Odori, for popular entertainment; some still do in rural areas. Dengaku were pastoral dances, as were Sarugaku, which were incorporated into the Noh theater.

The oldest of the "classical" dances are the Bugaku. Noh and Kabuki theater also created specific dances, for which various schools transmitted their family traditions *(see* IEMOTO). A new genre developed in the sixteenth century, mainly in Kyoto: *maiko* and geisha dances, called Kamogawa Odori and Miyako Odori; in Tokyo, Azuma Odori, Midori-kai, and Sanwa-kai; and so on, according to their district of origin. Of course, each large city— Osaka, Nagoya, and so on—had its own geisha dances.

Western-style dancing swept Japan from the middle of the Meiji era, but in modern times the only invaders are the latest American dance fads. As in Europe, ballet in Japan is strictly a spectator art. However, after the Second World War, many schools of modern dance were established, inspired by Martha Graham's techniques; they are attended mainly by young women who see it as a sort of exercise or sport. Some Japanese dancers have been noted for their choreography of original dances (Buyō, Butō) both in Japan and abroad. *See* these entries and ODORI, SAMBASŌ, SANJA MATSURI, SAOTOME, SARUKAWA, SHIRABYŌSHI, SHISHI-MAI, SHISHI ODORI, SHOSA.

Dan Ikuma. Musician (b. 1924) and composer, orchestra conductor, composer of the famous *Symphony No. 1 in A* (1950). He also composed Western-style operas, such as *Yūzuru* (The Crane, 1952), which was performed throughout the world, and *Chanchiki,* performed in Brussels in 1989. Grandson of Dan Takuma.

Danjōdai. High court of justice, replaced in 839 by the Keibiishi.

Danjūrō. School of classical *(see* IEMOTO) and Kabuki dance. This name was adopted by many families of Kabuki actors, such as Ichikawa Danjūrō *(see this entry)* and Ichikawa Ebizō.

Danka. "Donor house," term used to designate families of parishioners who have chosen a temple or shrine for all family ceremonies in their name, in return for a contribution toward the monks' sustenance or maintenance of the buildings. This practice was institutionalized by the Tokugawa shogunate, which forced families to register at the Buddhist temple or Shinto shrine near their home. *Skt.: dānapati. See* DANNA-DERA.

Dan Kazuo. Writer (1912–76), born in Yamanashi prefecture, disciple of Satō Haruo and Dazai Osamu. Among his main works are *Ritsuko sono ai* (Ritsuko's Love), *Ritsuko sono shi* (Ritsuko's Death, 1950), *Shinsetsu Ishikawa goemon* (winner of Naoki Prize in 1950), *Yūhi to kenjū* (1955), and *Kataku no hito* (1975).

Danna-dera. Buddhist temple to which a family makes donations in exchange for religious services. *See* DANKA.

Dannoura (Dan no Ura). The coast immediately east of Shimonoseki (Yamaguchi prefecture, Honshu), theater of a major naval battle (Dannoura Tatakai) on April 25, 1185, during which the Minamoto forces sank the Taira's ships. Minamoto no Yoshitsune had fewer ships, but he took advantage of the strong tidal currents in the Shimonoseki pass to drive Admiral Taira no Tomomori's ships against the rocks. It was during this battle that the child-emperor Antoku and the Taira admiral perished. This battle ended the 25-year hegemony of the Taira clan and began that of the Minamoto clan, which established its *bakufu* in Kamakura with the consent of the emperor in 1192.

Danrin. Empress (Tachibana no Kachiko, 786–850), daughter of Tachibana no Kiyomoto (757–89), wife of Emperor Saga (<810–23>), and mother of Emperor Nimmyō. A devout Buddhist, she founded many temples and sent the monk Egaku to China to invite the monk Yikong (*Jap.*: Gikū) to Japan to teach Chan (*Jap.*: Zen) at the Danrin-ji temple, which she had built west of Heian-kyō. With her brother, Tachibana Ujikimi, she also founded a school, Gakkan-in, to educate the children of the Tachibana family. She had the title Kōgō.

Danrin-fū. School of *haikai,* founded by Nishiyama Sōin (1605–82) in reaction to the style of Matsunaga Teitoku's *haikai,* judged to be too intellectual. In 1673, Ihara Saikaku, who was in this "avant-garde" school, and a group of poets in Osaka composed a 10,000-verse work called *Ikudama manku,* and in 1675, Tashiro Shōi and his disciples in Edo composed the *Danrin toppyaku-in,* a series of ten pieces of 100 verses, prefiguring the Bashō style. *See* HAIKAI, NISHIYAMA SŌIN.

Dansen. Special tax levied during the Muromachi period at the time of the investiture of an emperor and other important events. The bureaucrats charged with collecting this tax were called *dansen-bugyō. See* BUGYŌ.

Dan Takuma. Businessman (1858–1932), born in Fukuoka prefecture. He accompanied Iwakura's mission to the United States in 1871 and stayed there to study at M.I.T. When he returned to Japan, he became involved in mining operations and was appointed director of Mitsui. Considered too "westernized" by nationalist extremists, he was assassinated by Hishinuma Gorō in 1932. Grandfather of composer Dan Ikuma.

Danzan-jinja. Shinto shrine dedicated to the memory of Fujiwara no Kamatari in 701, located in Sakurai, Tōnomine (Nara prefecture). It was converted into a Buddhist temple of the Tendai sect until the Meiji era, when it reverted to a Shinto shrine (1870). Its most unusual building is a 13-story pagoda with false roofs covered with cypress boughs, dating from 1532; there are also a Rōmon and a Raiden (1668), a fifteenth-century Gonden, and a Honden from 1850. The other buildings are modern. The wooded, mountainous site is remarkable.

Danzō. Buddhist statues carved in sandalwood *(byakudan),* left unpainted so that the wood's aroma is released. *See* BYAKUDAN.

Daruma. *See* BODAI-DARUMA.

Dashi. Large processional float pulled by the faithful during a festival and decorated with a profusion of paintings, sculptures, and multicolored ribbons. Depending on the region and the shrine, the floats are called *yama* (mountain), *hoko* (e.g., Gion Matsuri in Kyoto), or *danjiri. See* MIKOSHI.

Dasoku. Painter (Soga Sōyo; *gō*: Jasoku, Dasoku, active between 1452 and 1483) of the Muromachi *suiboku* (ink painting) tradition. Born in the province of Echizen, he lived in Kyoto.

Dasokuken (Dasokugen). *See* SAN-SETSU.

Dasokuren. *See* SHŌHAKU.

Date. Town in southwest Hokkaido, on the Bay of Uchiura, founded by the Date family in 1870. Zenkō-ji temple located here. Fishing, agriculture, forestry industry. *Pop.*: 35,000.

Date Chichiro. Scholar (1802–77) of the Wakayama clan who, in 1868, fiercely defended the emperor's cause in his writings.

Date clan. Family of warriors founded by Isa Tomomune, who helped Minamoto no Yoritomo defeat his brother Yoshitsune in 1189. The clan then received the district of Date in the province of Mutsu (northern Honshu). During the Namboku-chō period, the Date clan fought for the Southern Court, then sided with the Ashikaga clan. By the 1500s, they were among the Sengoku (Warring States) daimyo. Having fought on Tokugawa Ieyasu's side at Sekigahara in 1600, they retained their lands and were classified among the *tozama daimyō,* with an annual revenue of 620,000 *koku.* The Date *sōdo,* a succession struggle, divided the family from 1660 to 1670, but they continued to play an important role until the end of the Edo period. Their familial and provincial code, *Jinkaishū,* promulgated by Date Tanemune (1488–1565) in 1536, remains a model of its genre.

• **Date Masamune.** Daimyo of the Date clan in the province of Mutsu (1567–1635), son of Date Teramune (d. 1584), lord of the Yonezawa castle. Having lost an eye to disease, he was nicknamed

Dokuganryū ("one-eyed dragon"). He expanded his family's landholdings at the expense of his neighbors and defeated the rival Aizu clan in 1589, but he was forced to surrender the Aizu castle to Toyotomi Hideyoshi the following year. He was at Toyotomi Hideyoshi's side during the invasions of Korea in 1592 and 1597, and he sided with Tokugawa Ieyasu at the Battle of Sekigahara in 1600, thus securing his lands with a revenue of 620,000 *koku*. He built the Sendai castle, conducted a census of his lands and vassals, created a salt-refining industry, and established other manufacturing, such as a silk industry. He also expanded horse breeding and the operation of gold and silver mines. Having permitted Christian missionaries to preach on his land and build a church in 1611, he considered entering into relations with the Pope and the king of Spain. To this end, he sent a mission led by Father Sotelo and Hasekura Tsunenaga to Mexico and Rome in 1613. Hasekura met Pope Paul V and Philip III, the king of Spain, and obtained permission to build a cathedral. But in the meantime the shogunate had banned Christianity, so Date Masamune had to ban Christians from his territory. A patron of arts and letters, Masamune was himself an excellent *waka* poet. He had also studied the arts of Noh theater, the incense ceremony, and calligraphy.

• *Date Masamune koi no higanoko.* See YAGURA NO OSHICHI.

• **Date Munekatsu.** Daimyo (1621–79) who was said to have plotted to have Date Tsunamune exiled and his underage son, Tsunamura, designated daimyo in order to take power more easily. After attempting to poison the young man, Munekatsu was banished by the shogunate to the province of Tosa.

• **Date sōdō.** Family quarrel that divided the Date clan for a decade, from 1660 to 1670, after the shogunate interfered in the succession of Date Tsunamune to daimyo by installing his son, Date Tsunamura. Power thus remained in the hands of Date Munekatsu, who had plotted to have Tsunamune exiled so that he could seize power. When Munekatsu was deposed by the shogunate for misbehavior, Tsunamura regained the title of daimyo.

• **Date Tanemune.** Daimyo of Mutsu (1488–1565), author of the Date provincial code, the *Jinkaishū,* in 1536. *See* DATE CLAN.

• **Date Tsunamune.** Daimyo of Mutsu (1640–1711), arrested by the shogunate because of disturbances in Sendai that had probably been fomented by Date Munekatsu.

• **Date Tsunamura.** Son (1659–1719) of Date Tsunamune and his successor in the Mutsu daimyo system. He improved the administration of his lands, returning them to the prosperity that had been weakened by the 1660–70 family quarrel (Date *sōdō*), and developed the arts, carrying on Date Masamune's policies.

Date Yasuke (V). Weaver and dyer (1844–92) born in Kyoto, fifth-generation artisan of Date Yasuke. His father, Date Yasuke (IV), attended the Vienna World Exhibition in 1873 and introduced Western weaving methods to Japan, leading to great advances, notably in the art of brocades *(nishiki).*

Dazai Osamu. Writer (Tsushima Shūji, 1909–48), born into a wealthy family in northern Honshu. After a lonely childhood and a suicide attempt in 1929, he enrolled in the French department at Tokyo University but did not graduate. Unhappy in love, he attempted double suicide by drowning; she died, but he survived. He then began to write, taking the pen name Dazai Osamu in 1933. When he was refused a job at a newspaper, he tried to kill himself a third time, this time by hanging. After this, he overdosed on drugs and entered a treatment program. Because the woman he was living with took a lover, he attempted double suicide yet again—yet again unsuccessfully. In 1939, he married a schoolteacher and continued to write throughout the Second World War, which he spent in Tokyo. His house was destroyed during the bombing, so he took refuge in Aomori. His novels began to achieve some success. Suffering from tuberculosis, he led a dissolute life and became more and more attached to writing. In June 1948, he committed suicide with his mistress; both died after throwing themselves into a river. His novels, most of them autobiographical and written in the first person, deal with problems of youth—*Shayō* (The Setting Sun, 1946) and *Ningen shikkaku* (No Longer Human, 1948)—but he also wrote novels and stories that were more distanced from his own life—*Shin Hamuretto* (The New Hamlet, 1941)—and children's stories—*Otogi-zōshi* (1945). Other works include "Gyakkō" (Regression, 1935), "Dōke no hana" (The Clown's Flowers, 1933), "Gyofukuki" (The Story of a Suicide, 1933), and "Bion no tsuma" (Villon's Wife, 1947). His other stories were collected in *Bannen* (Declining Years, 1936) and *Dazai Osamu zenshū* (published 1955–56). Dazai Osamu had two legitimate daughters, Tsushima Sonoko and Tsushima Yūko; the latter followed in her father's footsteps and became a writer. *See* TSUSHIMA YŪKO.

Dazai Shundai. Neo-Confucian scholar (1680–1747), born in the province of Shinano (Nagano prefecture). Entering the service of the daimyo of Izushi near Hyōgo, he studied under Nakano Iken. Later, having left the Izushi estate, he became a disciple of Ogyū Sorai. He then entered the service of the daimyo of Ōimi (Shimōsa) but soon decided to teach. His favorite subject was economics, and he published a number of works on the subject, the best known of which were *Keizairoku* (Discussions of Economics, 1729) and *Keizairokushū-i* (Discussions of Economics, part two). He wrote more than 50 works. Also called Dazai Shuntai.

Dazaifu. Town in Fukuoka prefecture (Kyushu) where government headquarters were established in the seventh century; officials had been posted there as early as the third century to oversee trade between Kyushu and the mainland. A fort was built in 664 to prevent Korean incursions after the battle of Hakusukinoe (662) resulted in the defeat of a Japanese fleet. During the eighth and ninth centuries, the town was known as the "distant capital." Later, governors of Dazaifu tended to live in Kyoto, and it became a site of exile. During the Kamakura period, Dazaifu and the castle, now the property of the Shōni family, played a major role in the defense of Kyushu against attempted Korean-Mongolian invasions (in 1274 and 1281). Thereafter, the town lost importance. A small museum is devoted to Sugawara no Michizane, who died in exile in 903.

• **Dazaifu Temmangū.** Shinto shrine built in Dazaifu in 919 in memory of Sugawara no Michizane, who died there in 903 and whose grave is located at the Anraku-ji temple. The shrine was rebuilt a number of times, notably in 1591 and 1914, and the current building dates from 1951. The annual festival is held on September 25; the Usokae ceremony is conducted on January 7, during which followers exchange bird-shaped talismans *(uso)* and circle a large tree in the hope of attracting good luck. On this day, a curious exorcism ceremony called Onisube also takes place. Also called Dazaifu-jinja.

Debayashi. In the Kabuki theater, the onstage orchestra that plays *nagauta, tokiwagu,* or *kiyomoto*

pieces with shamisen accompaniment. *See* GEZA-GAKU.

Deguchi Nao. Prophet (1837–1918), born in the province of Tamba, near Kyoto, wife of a carpenter named Shikata Toyosuke (Deguchi Seigorō, d. 1887) and mother of eight children. In 1892, Deguchi Nao began to have visions of a *kami* named Ushitora Konjin, who apparently dictated messages to her. Although she had little schooling, she wrote down these "revelations." These texts, called *Ofudesaki,* were to become the credo of a new religion called Ōmoto-kyō, created with the assistance of Ueda Kisaburō (Deguchi Onisaburō), who went through the same mystical experiences as Deguchi Nao and married her daughter Sumi (Ōmoto, 1883–1952). *See* DEGUCHI ONISABURŌ, ŌMOTO-KYŌ.

Deguchi Onisaburō. Peasant (Ueda Kisaburō, 1871–1948). He became a Shinto preacher, entering into a trance state to evoke the *kami.* He met Deguchi Nao in 1898, formed an alliance with her, and married her daughter, Sumi (Ōmoto, 1883–1952). Using Deguchi Nao's *Ofudesaki,* he created a new religion, Ōmoto-kyō, drawing on Shinto and on the Buddhist belief in Miroku (*Skt.:* Maitreya), the Buddha of the Future. Ōmoto-kyō was a threat to state Shinto and was suppressed in 1921. Onisaburō then began to write on his beliefs and published the 81-volume *Reikai monogatari* (1921–35), in which he described his spiritual journey. Persecuted, he took refuge in Mongolia, where he organized an army, proclaimed himself "Savior of the World," and founded Jinrui Aizen Kai (Association of Universal Love) in 1925. He also created other organizations and wanted to send missionaries throughout the world, but the state police arrested him in 1935. In prison, he wrote 600,000 religiously inspired poems. Freed at the end of the Second World War, he took up his missionary activities again, advocating use of Esperanto. He was also a potter, painter, and calligrapher. Omote-kyō still has many followers. *See* ŌMOTO-KYŌ, YŌWAN.

Degumi. In traditional architecture, eaves composed of a *demitsu-to* and a *hijiki* (horizontal bracket), with one or several *to* (dice) placed above the *demitsu-to* to support the *gangyō* beam. *See* TO, TO-KYŌ.

Dekasegi. "Work far from home," expression applied to workers whose jobs force them to work at distant locations for long periods. During these

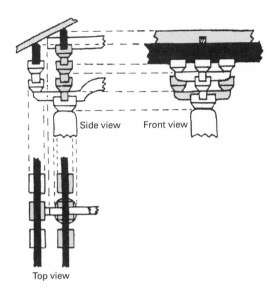

Type of *wa-yō* roof bracket: *degumi*

times, they live alone and send money to their families, returning home only for short vacations.

De Long, Charles E. American envoy to the kingdom of Hawai'i, sent to Japan by American president Ulysses S. Grant in 1869 to protest to its government the anti-Christian measures taken by the Tokugawa shogunate. In the name of the United States, he recognized the legitimacy of Japan's sovereignty over the Ryukyu Islands. In 1871, he negotiated a trade agreement between Hawai'i and Japan.

Deme. Family of sculptors of Noh masks and netsuke: Deme Jōman (early seventeenth century), Deme Eiman (d. 1705), Deme Taiman (early eighteenth century), Deme Uman (mid-eighteenth century), Deme Saman (eighteenth century).

• Deme Mitsuteru. Sculptor of Noh masks (ca. 1521–after 1581). One of the Jissaku, or "ten great sculptors of masks," he lived and worked in the province of Echizen (Fukui prefecture). He may have been the founder of the Deme family line, and he was also known as Jirōzaemon no Jō. He was followed by Deme Genkyū Mitsunaga in Kyoto.

Demitsu-to. In traditional architecture, eaves composed of a *hira-mitsu-to* with an extra *hijiki* (bracket) and a *to* (die) placed in the center of the overhang. *See* TO.

Dempōdō. "Sermon hall" of a Buddhist temple, a building generally reserved for instruction of the monks.

Denden-mono. Type of Kabuki play adapted for puppet theater (Bunraku). Also called *maruhon-mono.*

Denden-taiko (Dendon-daiko). Type of tambourine with a long handle and small bells attached. This children's toy was derived from a Chinese instrument, the *furitsuzumi,* used in Bugaku music.

Dengaku. General term designating popular dances and shows performed in the countryside to draw the favor of the *kami* and thereby ensure abundant rice harvests. The dances were accompanied by flutes, drums, and *sasara* (wooden clappers). Along with the Sarugaku, they were considered the ancestors of Noh dance, and were very popular during the Kamakura period. Provincial troupes perpetuated Dengaku performances, always in relation to work in the fields, especially the rice paddies. There were several types depending on the type of work being celebrated: Tamai Odori (plowing), of very ancient origin; Ta-asobi (care for the young rice shoots); Ta-ue Odori (planting the rice), and so on. These dances are often accompanied by licentious songs. *See* DANCES, TA-UE ODORI, TA-UE ZŌSHI.

Den Hideo. Politician, born 1925 in Tokyo. A journalist by trade, he joined the Socialist party in 1970 and was elected to the House of Councillors the following year. In 1977, however, he left the Socialist party to found another party, the Shakai Minshu Rengō (United Social Democratic party); he was elected secretary-general.

Denison, Henry Willard. American political consultant (1846–1914), born in Vermont. He went to Yokohama to assist the consul and was hired in 1880 by the minister of foreign affairs, Inoue Kaoru, as a consultant. He remained with the Japanese government until his death, playing an essential role in relations between Japan and Western countries, notably Russia and England. He represented the Japanese government at the International Court of Justice in The Hague and was decorated with the Order of the Rising Sun by the emperor.

Denka. Abbreviation for Denki Kagaku Kōgyō, a large conglomerate of chemical (plastics, fertilizers) and cement industries, founded in 1915. After the Second World War, it joined with Akzo Zout Chemicals of the Netherlands and created a subsidiary in the United States, Denka and Denak (the Japanese-Dutch company), which exports about 10% of its production. Head office in Tokyo.

Denki. Painter (Yasuda; *gō:* Tōgaku, Denki, 1784–1827) of the Yōga and Nanga schools, student of Aōdō Denzan. He painted mainly in the Western style.

Denki Rōren. Contraction of Zen Nihon Denki Kiki Rōdō Kumiai Rengōkai. National Federation of Workers' Unions in the Electrical Industries, created in 1953. This federation created another union federation, Chūritsu Rōren (Federation of Independent Unions) and founded the Japanese committee of the International Federation of Metallurgical Workers in 1964. It has more than 500,000 members.

Denkō-ji. Buddhist temple in Nara, founded, according to tradition, by the monk Shitaku, a disciple of Ganjin, about 775. It was called Jitsuen-ji at first and belonged to the Ritsu sect. The Hondō dates from 1585 and contains some good examples of Buddhist statuary from the Kamakura and Muromachi periods.

Denshū-dō. Clan school *(hangaku)* created in Hagi (Yamaguchi prefecture) in 1718 for the study of Western sciences *(rangaku)*. The philosophical works of Wang Yangming *(Jap.:* Ōyomei), translated by Miwa Shissai (1669–1744), were taught there. Also called Hyōchū Denshū-roku.

Dera. Allophonic form of the Japanese word *tera* (temple), set in words composed by "nigorization" of the initial *"t."* It is the equivalent of the Sanskrit *vihāra,* or Buddhist monastery. Also pronounced *-ji* (same character).

De Rijke, Johannes. Dutch engineer (b. 1842), invited to Japan by the Japanese government in 1873 to construct dams and regularize the flow of rivers, notably the Yodo and the Kiso rivers in the Osaka region. He also built the Tokyo sewer network. In 1901, he left Japan to work on regulating the flow of the Yangtze River in China.

Deshima (Dejima). Fan-shaped artificial island, created in the lee of Nagasaki from 1634 to 1636 with funds supplied by a group of 25 wealthy merchants, to lodge Portuguese merchants from other ports in Kyushu. In 1638–39, after the Shimabara

Christian uprising in 1637, the Edo shogunate decided to forbid the docking of Portuguese ships, and the Portuguese of Deshima and their families were forced to leave and settle in Macao. The Dutch of the port of Hirado were then transferred to Deshima, which in 1641 became the only trade port open to foreigners. There were 65 buildings on the island, housing not only the corporate offices of Dutch trading companies, but also their lodgings and housing for their families and for Japanese employees, notably interpreters. The Dutch were not allowed to leave Deshima except for official visits. Linked to the main island by a single bridge, the Deshima-bashi, the island also had gardens and pastures for cattle, sheep, and pigs. It was through Deshima that Dutch books entered Japan, enabling the Japanese to acquire some rudiments of Western sciences *(rangaku).* The Dutch East India Company had to pay an annual sum of 55 *kan* (about 206 kg) of silver to the city of Nagasaki as rent for the island. During the Meiji era, Deshima was attached to the main island, since it no longer served its original purpose. In 1957, however, it was restored to its original state as a historical monument.

• *Deshima rankan nikki.* Japanese name for the *Japan Dagregister in't Comptoir Nagasaki,* book of notes by Dutch directors of Deshima from 1631 to 1860, preserved in the archives at The Hague.

Deshimaru Taisen. Japanese Zen missionary (1915–82) who became a monk in 1965, went to Paris in 1967, and founded a temple there. He attracted many people through his "out of the ordinary" teaching. He created 110 Zen study centers in Europe and the Zen International Center of Cultural Exchanges in France. He also wrote many books on Zen.

Detchō-toji. "Butterfly binding," method of bookbinding used in the Heian period. Individual pages were printed on one side, folded, and bound so that the blank face was to the outside. Once the pages were compiled, they were glued together. Also called *kochōsō.*

Detsushi. Custom of unknown origin (perhaps from Southeast Asia) of blackening the teeth, practiced since at least the beginning of the Heian period. A mixture of iron powder dissolved in tea or vinegar and a medicinal powder were used. This custom was first observed among men of the aristocracy, but women of all classes soon followed. In the Edo period, it indicated that a woman had reached maturity (13 years of age); later, it indicated the status of a married woman. This custom was abandoned toward the end of the nineteenth century. Also called *kanetsuke*. *See* HAGUROME.

Dewa. Group of mountain ranges in Aomori, Akita, and Yamagata prefectures in northern Honshu, famous for pine and cedar forests, mines (gold, silver, copper), and Shinto shrines, the Dewa Sanzan-jinja.

• **Dewa no Kami.** *See* YANAGISAWA YOSHIYASU.

• **Dewa Sanzan-jinja.** Name for group of three Shinto shrines—Gassan, Ideha (or Dewa), and Yudonosan-jinja—located on three peaks with the same names. These shrines, founded in the seventh century, are visited mainly by monks of the Shugendō (sect of the mountain ascetics, the *yamabushi*). The Gassan-jinja is dedicated to the *kami* of the moon, Tsukiyomi no Mikoto. The Dewa-jinja, on Mt. Haguro, is devoted to a local *kami*, Ideha. The Yudonosan-jinja is dedicated to the cult of the *kami* of the mountain, Ō-yama-tsumi, represented by a boulder and a hot spring. In Honji-suijaku Shinto-Buddhist syncretism, these three shrines were called Haguro Sansho Gongen. A smaller shrine with easier access was constructed at the foot of Mt. Haguro; every July 15, there is a festival there that attracts thousands of the faithful and the curious. *See* HONJI-SUIJAKU, GONGEN.

Dialects. The Japanese language has a fairly large number of dialects *(hōgen)* corresponding roughly to the major regional divisions. The most important dialects are those of the Ryukyu Islands, Kagoshima (Kyushu), and the western (Kansai) and eastern (Kanto) regions of Honshū, the latter being considered the national language *(kokugo)*. The dialects differ in pronunciation of certain syllables or in their use of particular verbal forms. There are also dialectal forms associated with particular social groups: men use expressions that are different from those used by women *(see* NYŌBŌ-KOTOBA), and some words or expressions are taboo on certain occasions (similar to the theater tradition of never saying "good luck"). The imperial court used an ancient dialect *(kyūteigo)*. The army also uses particular expressions, as do the yakuza and several guilds. But the Japanese language is tending to become unified, mainly because of movies and television and the use of many "Japanized" English words.

Dickson, Walter George. English physician (1821–94) and painter, born in Edinburgh. He went to Japan in 1860–61 and published his drawings in *Japan, Being a Sketch of the History, Government and Officers of the Empire* (1869). He returned to Japan in 1883–84, then published *Gleanings from Japan* (1889) when he returned home.

Dictionaries. There are a great number of dictionaries in Japan, in at least three categories: *kanwa-jiten,* "dictionaries of Sino-Japanese characters *(kanji)*"; *kokugo-jiten,* "dictionaries of the Japanese language," very numerous especially during the Muromachi period, using both kanji and kana syllabaries; and *semmon-jiten,* which are thematic (sports, art, biography, literature, etc.). Bilingual dictionaries are included in this last category. Among the most complete dictionaries published in Japan are the *Dai kanwa jiten* (published 1955–60), with more than 50,000 kanji, and the *Nihon kokugo daijiten,* published in 1976. *See also* GAGEN SHŪRAN, IROHA, IROHA JIRUI-SHŌ, JIKYŌSHŪ, NIHON DAIJISHO.

Divers, Edward. English chemist (1837–1912) who was invited to Japan in 1873 to teach chemistry at the College of Engineers (Kōgakuryō) in Tokyo, then, starting in 1886, at the College of Sciences (Rika Daigaku), where he trained the top Japanese chemists. When he left Japan, in 1899, he was decorated with the Order of the Rising Sun.

Divination. In Japan, countless methods of divination *(bokusen, uranai)* have been used for religious purposes or to predict the future. As in China, deer scapula were heated *(futomani)* or brands were applied to the stomach shell of a tortoise carapace *(kiboku)* and the cracks thus produced were examined. These types of divination were conducted mostly in the imperial court, and a special bureau, the Jingikan, regulated the practices. The soothsayers belonged to the Urabe clan, which later became the Yoshida family. In both Japan and China, a divination method drawn from the *Yijin* (Book of Changes; *Jap.: Ekikyō*) is still used *(see* OMMYŌDŌ). There are an infinite number of ways to predict the future, among them observing water reflections *(mizu-ura)* or how the grass bends in the wind *(kusa-ura)*, examining the entrails of birds *(tori-ura)*, attributing a particular significance to words heard by chance on the street in the evening *(yūke-ura)*, playing "heads or tails" with coins *(zeni-ura)*, lifting a large stone *(ishi-ura)*, consulting the *kami* *(toshi-ura)* or an *azusa-miko* (woman shaman), purchasing a printed horoscope, and random draws *(mikuji)*. The Japanese are still fond of divination and are always looking for ways to predict the future. *See* AZUSA-MIKO, FUTOMANI, KOKKURI, OMIKUJI, TSUJI-URA, URABE, URANAI.

Divorce. Divorce *(rikon)* was once customary and was generally accomplished when the husband sent his wife a letter of repudiation *(mikudarihan)*. Women could not demand a divorce, so they often took refuge in a particular type of Buddhist temple (Kakekomi-dera), where they were considered legally divorced after two or three years of service. Only since 1947 has equality of the sexes been applied to marital separation. Many forms of divorce exist, from mutual agreement and joint declaration before the concerned authorities following a family breakup, to a legal decision (for infidelity, abandonment, absence for more than three years, incurable illness or madness, mistreatment). However, the court does not recognize the right of a guilty spouse to ask for a divorce. Custody of the children, if there are any, is decided by mutual agreement, but it is generally the mother (or a guardian) who is granted custody. The divorce rate has always been relatively high in Japan, with peaks at the beginning of the Meiji era and after the Second World War. It is estimated that one couple in six divorces after living together for an average of eight years. *See* ENKIRI-DERA, MARRIAGE, MAKUDARIHAN.

Dō. "The Path," the approach or discipline attained after intensive spiritual training, necessary to reach a goal in a particular art or technique. It is the equivalent of the Chinese Dao (Tao). This word is found in most disciplines: *jūdō, kendō, kadō, sadō, chadō,* and so on. In Buddhist philosophy, it sometimes conveys the Sanskrit term *bodhi,* which means supreme knowledge or enlightenment.
• Name given to a room in a Buddhist temple or monastery: *hondō, kondō, kōdō,* and so on. It may also designate a hall devoted to one of the primary deities: Fudō-dō, Aizen-dō, Kannon-dō. It corresponds to the former "-den" of the Shinto shrines.
• Object in bronze or alloy: *seido* (copper and brass), *sentoku* (copper, tin, and zinc), *sawari* (or *shirome*: copper, tin, lead, and arsenic), *shinchū* (brass), *hakudō* (bronze with a high proportion of tin or nickel), and so on. *See* MUSHA ROKUGU, YOROI.

Dō-ami. Famous Dengaku dancer (d. 1413), originally from the province of Ōmi (Shiga prefecture), whose talent was greatly admired by Ze-ami.

Dōan. Name of three painters:
• **Dōan (I).** Painter (Yamada Junsei; *azana:* Tarōzaemon; *gō:* Dōan, d. 1751) of the Muromachi-period *suiboku* school, specializing in flowers, birds, and faces. A high-ranking samurai, he was the lord of the castle of Yamada in the province of Yamashiro, near Kyoto.
• **Dōan (II).** Painter (sixteenth century) of the Muromachi-period *suiboku* school, perhaps a son of Dōan I. He was a samurai.
• **Dōan (III).** Painter (late sixteenth century) of the Muromachi-period *suiboku* school. He was a samurai, perhaps a descendant of Dōan I.

Dō-bachi. Copper cymbals. Also, a type of gong in copper alloy *(shibuichi),* in the form of a bowl, which is placed on a cushion. It is used in Buddhist worship to punctuate the recitation of the sutra *(Jap.: kyō).* Sometimes, *dō-bachi* are recast in silver or gold to give them a richer sound. Also called *dōhachi, dōra, basshi, nyōhachi, dōbyōshi* (in bronze). *See* INKIN.

Doban. Archeological objects, generally in terracotta, dating from the last phase of the Jōmon period. They are generally simplified forms of *dogū,* sometimes oval or rectangular, sometimes pierced and decorated with engravings on the sides. The masks thus produced are called Domen. Their usage and significance is not known; they may have been talismans or identification plaques. *See* DOGŪ.

Dobashi Jun. Painter, born in Tokyo in 1915. He has lived in France since 1953 and is known for his abstract compositions.

Dobei. In military architecture, clay wall protecting the base of the donjon *(tenshu)* of a castle *(jō, shiro).*

Dōbō-gashira. Title of the chief servant at the shogunal palace in the Edo period. This person was generally a Buddhist monk. The position was eliminated in 1866. Also called Bō-ami.

• **Dōbō-shū.** Buddhist monks who served as domestics in the court of the Muromachi *bakufu,* in Kyoto.

Dōboshu. Title of artistic consultant to the court of the Ashikaga shogun, charged with decorations, ceremonies, and selection of painters and other artists. *See* AMI-HA.

Dōcohū-sugoroku. Game using dice and a checker-board representing the 53 stages on the Tōkaidō road, somewhat similar to the American game "snakes and ladders," invented at the end of the Edo period and very popular. *See also* SUGOROKU.

Doeff, Hendrik. Dutch trader (1777–1835), director of the Dutch Factory on Deshima from 1803 to 1817, and its secretary starting in 1809. He visited the shogun in Edo three times. He defended Deshima against the attempt by Sir Thomas S. Raffles' fleet to annex it in 1811 and had a Dutch–Japanese dictionary compiled, the *Dōyaku Haruma* (or *Nagasaki Haruma*), which was published in 1833, the same year as were his memoirs (*Herinneringen uit Japan*).

Dōfuku. Everyday long robe worn by nobles or warriors who have become Buddhist monks and during religious ceremonies in the Muromachi period. It was the standard garment of Buddhist monks, and was adopted by nobles in the Heian period.

Dōgen. Buddhist monk (Buddō Zenji, Dōgen Kigen, Kigen Dōgen, 1200–53), founder of the Sōtō Zen sect in Japan. Born in Kyoto, he was the son of an influential courtier in the imperial court, Koga Michichika (1149–1202). His mother was one of Fujiwara no Motofusa's daughters. Orphaned, he entered religious life in 1213 at the Enryaku-ji monastery on Mt. Hiei, where he studied Tendai Esoteric Buddhism, later becoming the monk Kōin's (1145–1216) disciple at the monastery of Onjō-ji in Ōmi. In 1217, he entered the Kennin-ji monastery to learn about Rinzai Zen teachings under the direction of Myōzen (1184–1225), Eisai's disciple. The temple was destroyed in 1221. Dōgen went to China in 1223 and studied the Chan Caodong (Sōtō Zen) teachings under the master Zhangweng Rujing (1163–1228). In 1227, he received a certificate in the mastery of the doctrine of Chan Caodong directly from Zhangweng.

Dōgen returned to Japan, where he advocated Sōtō Zen practices at Kennin-ji, putting the principles in writing in *Fukan zazengi* (Universal Promotion of Zazen Principles, 1227). Rebuffed by the monks of the Tendai and Rinzai Zen sects, he moved to the An'yō-in temple in Fukakusa (Kyoto), where he wrote "Bendōwa" (Discourse on the Practice of the Way) in 1231. It was the first essay in what would be an immense 95-volume work, the *Shōbō-genzō* (1231–35), in which he posited that authentic personal experience is preferable to strict observance of doctrine. He took Koun Ejō (1198–1280) as a disciple in 1234 and expanded the Kannon Dōri-in monastery, where he was living, renaming it Kōshō Hōrin-ji; this was the first Sōtō Zen monastery in Japan.

Dōgen continued to write *Shōbō-genzō*. However, after he submitted to the court a memorial titled *Gokoku shōbōgi* (Significance of the True Dharma for the Protection of the Nation) about 1243, he was driven from the Kōsho Hōrin-ji. He took refuge in the province of Echizen and continued writing. In 1244, he founded the Daibatsu-ji monastery (which was renamed Eihei-ji in 1246), on Mt. Kichijō near Katsuyama, 17 km east of Fukui. There, he wrote a number of works on his doctrine, *Bendōhō* (Rules for Practicing the Path, 1245), *Chiji-shingi* (Rules for Monks, 1246), *Shuryō-shingi* (Rules for the Monastic Library, 1249), and others. He then taught the principles of Sōtō Zen to the shogunal regent (*shikken*) Hōjō Tokiyori in Kamakura and received a purple robe from the emperor. He died in Kyoto, just after finishing *Shōbō-genzō*. The posthumous name of Shōhyō Daishi was conferred upon him in 1800. He was the first patriarch of Sōtō Zen in Japan, and was succeeded by the monks Ekan and Gikai.

Dōgō. Landowners of humble origin under Hideyoshi and during the Tokugawa shogunate. They paid a minimal tax of 50 *koku* of rice. To work their land, they rented the services of poor peasants (*hikan* or *nago*) of the *kokujin* class.

Dōgo Onsen. Alkaline hot spring (42–50°C) in the town of Matsuyama (Ehime prefecture, Shikoku), one of the oldest in Japan, mentioned in the *Man'yōshū* (eighth century). *See* ONSEN.

Dogs. Small-sized dogs (*inu, ken*) were probably introduced from the mainland during the Jōmon period, around 5000 BC; their skeletons are sometimes found among burials of the Late Jōmon period. Other breeds arrived in Japan during the Yayoi period, and many of them were domesticated. In the Muromachi period, many dogs, generally called *tōken* and *kara-inu*, were introduced from Asia and Europe. They mixed with the local canine population, resulting in breeds such as the Tosa and the Akita. There is some evidence that dogs were eaten for medicinal purposes. However, the Japanese have always been fond of dogs; they have been used as guard dogs and for hunting. In the Kamakura period, they were entered in mass dogfights and obedience exercises (*inu oi-mono*). In some provinces, such as Kōchi (Tosa) and Akita, gambling on dogfights was popular but it is now illegal. These massive dogs were mixtures of typically Japanese dogs with European breeds. A breed of small dogs resembling the Pekinese, called *chin-koro* (or *chi-inu*) was very popular among bourgeois women, especially geisha, from the beginning of the Edo period. These companion dogs were exported to the United States after 1853, and to Europe, where they were officially recognized by the British in 1895 as "Japanese spaniels." At the beginning of the twentieth century, small terriers, white with black spots, were imported from Europe; bred in Japan, they were called *shika-bone*. Very popular before the Second World War, they are now rare. Dogs cannot roam freely in Japan and are always on leashes. *See* ANDŌ TERU, CHINKORO, HACHIKŌ, INU HARIKO, INU OI-MONO, SHŌRUI AWAREMI NO REI, TOKUGAWA TSŪNAYOSHI.

• Viverrine dogs; *see* TANUKI.

Dogū. Terra-cotta figurines portraying human beings, usually female, and sometimes animals, dating from the Middle Jōmon (Chūki) and Late Jōmon periods, often with protruding "snow goggle" eyes. These figurines, many of them decorated with complex geometrical designs, are portrayed in frontal view, with spread legs and relatively short arms. Their significance is not known, but it is likely that they played a role in ancient Japanese religious practices. *See also* DOBAN.

Dohi Keizō. Physician (1866–1931), born in the province of Echizen (Fukui prefecture). After studying in Europe, he taught at the University of Tokyo, contributing to the development of medical science in Japan. Among his works are *Hifukagaku* (Dermatology, 1910) and *Sekai baidoku-shi* (World History of Venereal Diseases, 1921).

Dōho. Lacquer artist (Igarashi Dōho, mid-sixteenth century–early seventeenth century) in the service of Maeda Toshitsune. In Kanazawa, he invented the technique called Kaga *maki-e* (Kaga style). His adoptive son, Kisaburō (Dōho II), followed in his artistic footsteps.

Dohyō. "Sacred circle." The ring where sumo matches take place. It is a platform about 5.7 m square, raised by 0.6 m, with a circular zone of hard-packed clay 4.55 m in diameter, delimited by partially buried straw bales. Above is a roof in the Shinto style called *shimmei-zukuri,* from the corners of which hang giant tassles in colors symboliz-

ing the seasons. Matches between sumo wrestlers *(sumotori)* and various ceremonies take place within the circular clay area.

• **Dohyō-iri.** Ceremony conducted before each sumo match, during which a *sumotori* asks the *kami* to help him obtain victory. *See* SUMŌ.

Doi. Warriors' residences *(yashiki)* in the Kamakura and Muromachi periods. This type of fortified house was surrounded by an earthen wall and a moat. It was often built on a site that was easy to defend and from which it was easy to survey the surrounding area. Also called *hori no uchi.*

Doi Bansui. Poet (Tsuchii Rinkichi, Tuschii Bansui, 1871–1952) and expert in English literature, born in Sendai. A professor at Tōhoku University, he translated a number of English, Latin, and Greek works. Among his most popular works is the poem "Kōjō no tsuki" (The Moon Above the Castle in Ruins), which was set to music by Taki Rentarō. Doi Bansui is also known for his translation of Homer's *Iliad* and his poetry collections *Tenchi ujō* (1899), *Banshō,* and *Bansui shishū.*

Doihara Kenji. General (1883–1948). He served in China in 1913 and from 1922 to 1929, and was involved mainly in espionage. After the Japanese military occupation of Manchuria, he was appointed mayor of Mukden in 1932 and, in this capacity, helped the former emperor Puyi escape from China. During the Second World War, he served as an army commander; in 1945 he was appointed the inspector general of military education. Convicted as a class-A war criminal by the Allies, he was executed on December 23, 1948. *See* WAR CRIMES.

Do-ikki. Leagues of peasants who revolted against the excesses of the *bushi* class and the merchants in the Ashikaga period. Organized in independent units, they fought for a reduction in their debts to wealthy moneylenders. The government attempted to defuse these uprisings by ordering imperial "edicts of pardon" *(tokusei),* but without much success. The first took place in 1428 in the province of Ōmi and spread rapidly to Yamashiro, Yamato, Kii, and Kawachi. In 1485, the peasants of Yamashiro rose up again. In the Edo period, these peasant uprisings were called *hyakushō-ikki.* Also known as *tokusei-ikki, tsuchi-ikki. See also* DOSŌ.

Doi Takako. Politician and judge, born in 1928 in Hyōgo. In 1969, she was elected to the House of

Representatives as a member of the Socialist party, of which she became president in September 1986. She resigned in June 1991, when she was defeated in an election; Tanabe Makoto succeeded her. In August 1993, when Hosokawa Morihiro was named prime minister, she was appointed Speaker of the Lower House.

Doi Tatsuo. Catholic priest (1892–1970), sixth archbishop of Tokyo and first Japanese cardinal, born in Sendai. He studied in Rome and was ordained a priest in 1921, then archbishop of Tokyo in 1939. Pope John XXIII made him a cardinal in 1960.

Doi Toshikatsu. Daimyo (1573–1644), son of Mizuno Nobutomo, but perhaps in fact one of Tokugawa Ieyasu's illegitimate sons, adopted by Doi Toshimasa. He became one of Tokugawa Hidetada's most influential advisers. After Hidetada's death in 1632, his influence diminished, although he was appointed great elder (tairō) in 1638. He received the daimyo estate of Koga (province of Shimōsa) with a revenue of 160,000 *koku*.

Doi Tsunehara. Writer (active ca. 1250) to whom composition of the *Genpei seisuiki* is sometimes attributed.

Dōji. In ancient Japan, young boys serving as domestics for, or disciples of, a Buddhist monk. Originally this was a title given to Buddhist deities. During the Heian period, *dōji* became armed guardians of the monasteries. They lived near the monasteries and performed all of the domestic tasks.
• Young boys, acolytes of a Buddhist deity (Skt.: *kumāra*). See FUDŌ MYŌ-Ō.

Dōjima kome ichiba. "Dōjima rice market," large market in Osaka, established in 1697, where the city's most important rice merchants and money-changers (ryōgaeshō) and their warehouses were located. This trading center conducted most transactions concerning rice until 1868, when it was reorganized. In 1939, it was absorbed into the Government Rice Agency (Nihon Beikoku Kabushiki Kaisha).

Dōjin-sha. Private school founded in Kioshikawa (Tokyo) in 1873 by Nakamura Keiu and Nakamura Masanao, to teach English. It was closed when Nakamura Keiu died in 1891.

Dōjō. Literally, the "hall of the Way." The training hall for martial arts (budō) where competitions also take place. The *dōjō* was once the room in Buddhist monasteries reserved for meditation. See JI.

• *Dōjō-ji.* Buddhist temple in Wakayama, founded in 701. Its Rōmon dates from about 1480, its three-story pagoda (sanjunotō) from 1762, and its Hondō from the late sixteenth century. It houses the manuscript of the *Dōjō-ji engi emaki.*

• *Dōjō-ji.* Title of a Noh play: a young woman falls in love with a Buddhist monk who flees from her and takes refuge in the Dōjō-ji temple. She then changes herself into a large snake and hides in the temple bell, which she breaks. But she is in her turn destroyed by the monks' prayers.

• *Dōjō-ji engi emaki.* "Story of Dōjō-ji." An *emakimono* attributed to Tosa Hirochika (ca. 1459–92) that tells, in images and text, the story of the foundation of the temple and the life of the monk Anchin. It is kept at Dōjō-ji.

Dojōsukui. Comical dance, characteristic of the town of Yasugi (Shimane prefecture), miming the movements made by fishers and iron prospectors. It is one of the town's major attractions during festivals and is accompanied by popular songs.

Dōkegata. In Kabuki theater, role of the comic dancer. This type of role fell into disuse at the beginning of the nineteenth century, but the word is still used to designate a clown. The role is now called Sammaime.

Dōken. Bronze sword dating from the Yayoi (300 BC–AD 300) and introduced from the mainland at that time (perhaps first or second century). They were found buried in large quantities with halberds (dōka) and lances (dōhoko) of the same origin, sometimes beside *dōtaku,* mainly in northern Kyushu and in the districts along the coast of the Inland Sea (Setonaikai). These weapons probably had ritual significance. See DŌTAKU.

Doki. Unglazed pottery, fired at low temperatures (less than 700°C), characteristic of the ceramic production of the Jōmon and Yayoi periods and of *haji* pottery.

Dōkō Toshio. Businessman and engineer (1896–1988), born in Okayama. During the Korean War, he supplied the United States armed forces with weapons, reorganizing for this purpose the Ishikawajima-Harima steelworks complex of which he became president in 1960. He then restructured Toshiba, using rigorous management to make it profitable. He was elected president of the powerful Federation of Economic Organizations (Keidanren) and opposed reform of the anti-trust laws.

Dokuritsu Bijutsu Kyōkai. Independent art society created in 1930 to succeed the "1930 Nen Kyōdai" founded in 1926, bringing together artists working in the Western style. It organized exhibitions and various artistic events until 1944, then was reorganized in 1947. It has an exhibition in Tokyo every November.

Dokushi yoron. "View of Japanese History," a three-volume historical and philosophical work published by Arai Hakuseki in 1712; it covers Japanese history from the country's beginnings to Hideyoshi. Also called *Tokushi Yoron.*

Dōkyō. Buddhist monk (d. 772) of the Hossō sect. In 761, he cured Empress Kōken and thus gained great influence with her. When she returned to the throne under the name Shōtoku, she appointed him *dajō daijin zenji,* against the advice of her ministers, giving him authority over civic and religious affairs; in 766, she conferred upon him the title of Hō-ō, making him virtually the heir to the throne. But Dōkyō's plot to seize the throne when the empress died was uncovered by Wake no Kiyomaro, and he was placed under house arrest near Osaka. When Empress Shōtoku died, in 770, he was banished to the province of Shimotsuke (Tochigi prefecture) by Emperor Kōnin. The ministers then decided that there would never again be an empress on the imperial throne. Thereafter, the emperors left Nara, where the Buddhist monks were too influential, and settled in Nagoka, then in Heian-kyō (Kyoto), where there were fewer Buddhist temples and their influence was weaker.
• Name given to the Chinese Taoist doctrines, such as Ommyōdo, and sometimes the Shugendō, before the fifth century.

Dolls. The oldest dolls *(ningyō)* date from the prehistoric Jōmon period. It seems that they were originally considered magical objects that could protect against illness and bad luck. *Katashiro* or *hitogata* ("human form") were used as substitutes to keep children from getting ill, and the custom quickly became to offer dolls *(anesama-ningyō,* made of

colored paper) to members of the imperial family so that the dolls would take illnesses upon themselves *(see* HINA-MATSURI). Doll-scarecrows *(kusahitogama)* were erected in fields to repel insects. After being used, these dolls (some of which represented dogs, *inu-hariko)* were burned or thrown into the river. The dolls probably gave rise to puppet shows *(ayatsuri-shiba).* Very early, children were given dolls made of wood with jointed limbs. During the Edo period, doll-making became an art unto itself; some dolls were decorative, while others were used in Shinto or family ceremonies. Types of dolls became more numerous, varying according to the region where they were made: *gosho-ningyō* ("palace dolls") from Kyoto quickly became famous. Other types of dolls appeared, not just for the Hina Matsuri, but also for the boys' festival (Tango no Sekku) and other occasions. Wealthy merchants liked to collect dolls representing Noh and Kabuki characters; *ishō-ningyō* and *kimekome-ningyō,* were designed to display their elaborate costumes. The Saga-*ningyō* represented mainly Buddhist subjects—divinities or monks—while the Nara-*ningyō* represented Shinto subjects or Noh characters. There were mechanical dolls *(karakuri-ningyō);* others were splendidly dressed in costumes of the time *(fuji-ningyō).* The art of *kokeshi*—simple and colorful human forms—developed in northern Honshu. European-style ornamental dolls greatly influenced the making of modern Japanese dolls, but the traditional types are still made by talented artisans, some of whom are honored with the title of Living National Treasure (Ningen Kokuhō). *See* ASAKUSA-NINGYŌ, FUJI-NINGYŌ, FUKUOKA, FUKUSUKE, FUSHIMI-NINGYŌ, GYŪKA, HAKATA-NINGYŌ, KAGOSHIMA JUZŌ, KOKESHI, NINGYŌ, UKIYO-NINGYŌ.

Dōmei. Abbreviation of Zen Nihon Rōdō Sōdōmei (Japanese Confederation of Labor), major labor federation (second in size only to the Sōhyō), created in 1964 by the merger of unions that had left Sōhyō and others opposed to the views of the Sōdōmei. Strongly anti-communist, it is closely associated with the Democratic Socialist party (Minshu Shakaitō). It has almost 2.5 million members.

Dōmei Tsūshinsha. Press agency, the only one authorized to function during the Second World War. Created in 1936, it was secretly hired by the government to produce propaganda. It was dissolved in 1945 and replaced by the Kyōdō News Service and Jiji Press.

Dominicans. The first Dominican brother arrived in Japan in 1602 and preached in Kyushu. Like other Catholic priests, the Dominicans were persecuted; 32 were martyred, the last in 1637. *See* JESUITS, CHRISTIANITY.

Domon Ken. Well-known photographer (1909–90), born in Sakata, Yamagata prefecture, where a museum bearing his name was opened in 1983 to preserve and exhibit more than 70,000 of his photographs.

Dōmoto Hisao. Painter, born in 1928 in Kyoto, who won the Nitten grand prize in 1951 and 1953. He studied at the École des Beaux-Arts in Paris in 1955. His primary influence was Sengai Gibon, a nineteenth-century Zen religious painter who tried to reduce all forms to a circle, symbolizing eternity. Dōmoto Hisao was one of the first Japanese painters to use acrylic paints. He exhibited internationally.

Dōmoto Inshō. Painter (Dōmoto Sannosuke, 1891–1975), born in Kyoto, who worked in the traditional style (Nihonga) and the modern Western style. He had regular exhibits in the Teiten, received the Imperial Academy of Fine Arts (Teikoku Bijutsu-in) Prize in 1925, and thereafter worked for the imperial household. He was decorated with the Order of Culture (Bunka-shō) in 1961. He designed the Dōmoto Art Museum in Kyoto to house his works. He also created wall paintings for Buddhist temples, notably for Shitennō-ji in Osaka.

Donchō. Korean painter (Tam-jing) and Buddhist monk of the Koguryō kingdom, who is said to have arrived in Japan in 610 and, according to the *Nihon shoki*, introduced paper-making techniques and the art of painting using ink wash. He is also credited with setting up the first water mill in Japan. According to legend, he worked on the interior decoration of the *kondō* at the Hōryū-ji temple in Nara.

Dōnin. Artisan (Hirata Dōnin, Hikoshirō; *azana:* Dōnin, 1598–1646), founder of the Hikoshirō family, which specialized in the manufacture of cloisonné objects.

Donker Curtius, Jan Henrik. Dutch diplomat (1813–79), last manager of the Dutch trading post at Nagasaki (Deshima) starting in 1852. In 1856, he concluded the Dutch-Japanese Treaty of Amity, then a trade treaty in 1858. In the meantime, he established a naval college in Nagasaki. When he returned to Holland, he helped create a chair of Japanese studies at the University of Leiden thanks to his knowledge of the Japanese language and the books he had brought back.

Donkyō. Painter (Ōhara Yoku; *azana:* Unkei, Sakingo; *gō:* Bokusai, Donkyō, d. 1810) of landscapes in the style of the Chinese painter Zhang Ruitu (ca. 1600–64).

Donsu. Damask fabric imported from China by Chinese weavers who settled in Sakai in the late sixteenth century. They transmitted their techniques to Japanese weavers of the Nishiki district in Kyoto (Nishijin), who produced brocades (damask) with Japanese motifs for obi sashes and slightly lighter fabrics for blankets. *See* MEIBUTSU-GIRE.

Dōnyū. Ceramist (Nonkō, 1599–1656), one of the most important members of the Raku family. His pieces were admired by Hon-ami Kōetsu, who considered him the best potter of his time. He invented new glazes, such as *ki-hage* (yellow) and incised black glazes, and he used white clay for the first time to produce red raku. The names of all of his descendants end with "-nyū." *See* RAKU.

Dōra. Gongs used in Buddhist ceremonies. They were probably imported from China in the Ashikaga period. *See* DŌ-BACHI, INKIN.

Dorei. In ancient Japan, a type of slave. *See also* NUHI, SEMMIN.

Doro-e. Pictures painted with colorings obtained from powdered calcified shells and vegetable or mineral pigments (*doro-enogu*) mixed with water. Easy to produce, these pigments were used during the Edo period to paint votive plaques (*e-ma*) or posters. These opaque colors were sometimes used by artists of the Yōga (Western-style painting) school who could not procure oil paints and wanted to imitate their effect.

Dōsei. Buddhist monk, head of the Daigo-ji monastery in Kyoto in the late thirteenth century. He was one of Emperor Kameyama's (<1260–74>) sons.
• Religious name taken by Hatakeyama Kunikiyo (d. 1364), a minister under the Kantō-kanryō (Kanto Administrator) Ashikaga Motouji.

Dōsen. Chinese Buddhist monk (Dao Xuan, 702–60) from Henan province who is said to have introduced the Zen (*Chin.:* Chan), Ritsu (*Chin.:* Lü), and Kegon (*Chin.:* Huayan) schools of thought to Japan in 736. He had arrived in the islands accompanied by a monk from India called Bodhisena, and a Tibetan monk from Champa called Fo-che. Dōsen lived in the Daian-ji temple in Nara, then in the Tōdai-ji monastery, where he taught these doctrines. He was the master of Gyōhō, who transmitted his teachings to Saichō, and Kūkai was his disciple in 743. He also participated in the inauguration ceremony for the Daibutsu of the Tōdai-ji in 749. *See* KEGON-SHŪ.

• Sculptor of netsuke (nineteenth century) and mosaicist.

Dōshaku-ga. Portraits of Buddhist, Taoist, and Confucian subjects. Also, Zen paintings portraying the life of the great masters of all sects, used for teaching.

Dōshin. Low-ranking samurai who, during the Edo period, served as shogunal constables in towns. They were armed with a *jitte* (a weapon used to deflect a sword blade) or a *manriki-gusari* instead of a sword, so that they could better fend off blows and take criminals prisoner. Their leader bore the title *yoriki* and carried a lance as a mark of office.

• Painter (early eighteenth century) of the Kaigetsu school.
→ *See* ZEN-SHŪ.

Dōshisha Daigaku. Private university founded in Kyoto in 1875 by Niijima Jō and Jerome Davis, a Congregational missionary. This university, which now has about 30,000 students, has faculties of letters, theology, law, economics, business, and engineering. It also has a women's college, a junior college, and various other lower schools associated with it, including a kindergarten. It was the first Japanese university to admit women.

Dōsho. Buddhist monk (629–700) of the Hossō sect, born in Kawachi near Osaka. In 653, he went to China, where he became a disciple of Xuang Zang (*Jap.:* Genzō) and of his student Kui Ji (*Jap.:* Kiki). When he returned to Japan (ca. 660–61), he taught the principles of the Hossō at the Asuka-dera and was Gyōki's master. He introduced the Buddhist custom of cremation and was the first Japanese to be cremated. He also had bridges and irrigation systems constructed.

• A monk of the Jōdo Shin sect who founded the Chōseiji-ha branch in the fourteenth century.

• Sculptor of netsuke (Kagei Dōshō, 1828–84) in Osaka.

Dōshū. Second-class Buddhist monks generally descended from former temple slaves *(nuhi),* who served as domestics in the monasteries. During the Heian period (794–1185), they formed armed groups *(sōhei)* to defend the temples and impose the monasteries' policies on the emperor. Also called *geshū, gyōnin, dōsō.*

• Painter (early eighteenth century) of the Kaigetsudō school.

Dosō. Bookmakers who operated mainly in Kyoto in the late Kamakura period and the Muromachi period. These usurers became wealthy enough to finance sea voyages and thus became shipowners. The high interest rates they demanded caused the peasants to revolt against them *(do-ikki)* and against the *sake* distillers *(sakaya),* who fixed their prices. The Muromachi shogunate nevertheless protected them because it drew a substantial part of its revenues from the taxes they paid. In the sixteenth century, the *dosō* spread into certain provinces and the daimyo were forced to promulgate laws to control their activities. They were called *dosō* after the underground warehouses *(dosō, kura)* in which they stored their merchandise. Also called *tokura.*

Dōsojin. Shinto gods of the roads, protectors of villages and travelers, said to banish evil spirits, demons *(oni),* and illness. These *Sae no kami (kami* of the roads) were represented by roughly sculpted stone markers of monkeys or couples, or by posts erected on roadsides or at the edges of fields or villages, often in phallic shapes. Associated with fertility cults, they were sometimes considered matchmaking gods. They were honored on January 14 or 15, when the New Year's decorations *(dondo)* are burned. Children searched for *mochi* (pounded-rice cakes) for the *Dōsojin.* Also called *Dōrokujin, Kunado no kami, Sae (Sai) no kami.* In Okinawa, they were called *Ishigantū. See* ISHIGAMA.

Dōtaku. Bronze ceremonial bells, from 0.2 to 1.2 m in height. They are decorated with story panels (village or hunt scenes), horizontal bands, flowing-water patterns, or rows of spirals. Dating from the Yayoi period, *dōtaku* are often found in groups, buried in a hillside along with imported weapons *(dōken).* A raised band on the sides forms a sort of handle on the top, more or less ornamented. The walls of the *dōtaku* are very thin; they could not have been used as musical instruments. Certain details of their construction suggest that they were a substitute for *kami* of the fields *(Ta no kami)* or of the mountains *(Yama no kami),* who "descended" from the mountains at village festivals, where they

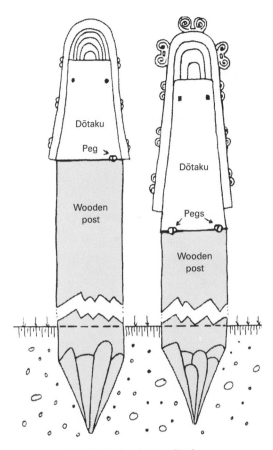

Reconstructed method of anchoring *dōtaku*

were placed on top of poles. They probably had some link with the fertility cults.

The Japanese *dōtaku* developed far beyond the Chinese and Korean prototypes. They have been found in northern Kyushu, southern Honshu, and Shikoku, but most come from the Kinai region (Kyoto-Nara-Osaka).

Dōto. Buddhist monk (seventh century) of the Genkō-ji temple, who built the Uji bridge in 646. On it he left an inscription in the Chinese Six Dynasties style, which is the oldest stone inscription in Japan.

Dōtoku Kagaku. "Moral science," syncretic Shinto sect based on morality, founded in 1928 by Hiroike Chikurō (b. 1893).

Dōwa chōnen. Collection of children's stories compiled by Kurosawa Okinamaro (1795–1859). Most of the ancient Japanese legends are found in this work, presented in a poetic form.

Dōza. Bureau to control copper refining and trading. First set up in Osaka as a subsidiary to the silver bureau *(ginza)* in 1738, it became independent in 1766, once copper became an important export item through the Deshima trading post in Nagasaki. Its role was to purchase the copper from the provincial mines, refine it, and ship to Nagasaki whatever was not used by Japanese artisans.

Dragons. Dragons *(ryū)*, mythical animals of Chinese origin, were generally considered benevolent, being symbols of rain that fertilized the fields. They were frequently portrayed by painters and sculptors, and always in relation with water. There are an infinite number of dragons: of the sea, the clouds, the ponds, the rivers, the rain, and so on, each with a particular legend. *See* RYŪ.

Dresser, Christopher. English connoisseur and designer (1834–1904). He visited Japan in 1876, via San Francisco, accompanying Prince Henry of Lichtenstein, Prince Alfred Montenuova, and two Japanese curators, Sekisawa Akiko and General Saigō Yorimichi. He returned with various objects for the imperial museum and collected numerous Japanese objets d'art and works of art for the Kensington Museum. He advised the Japanese government on which objects to export. During his stay in Japan, in 1876–77, he met the most famous Japanese painters and was received by Emperor Meiji on January 20, 1877. When he returned to England, he published *Japan, Its Architecture, Art and Art Manufactures* (1882).

Drums. There are many types of drums *(taiko)*: ō-*daiko*, a large temple drum of Chinese origin, decorated with a *mitsu-tomoe* motif; *ko-daiko*, a similar type but smaller, used for processions; *tsuri-daiko* (or *taiko*), a hanging gong; *kero*, a small gong-drum hung from the neck and used during processions, of Chinese origin; *da-daiko*, a large drum similar to the ō-*daiko*; *ni-daiko*, identical but carried by two men; *happu*, identical to the *ni-daiko* but half-filled with rice powder to deaden the sound; *kakko*, a small drum used in Bugaku orchestras; *daibyōshi* (or ō-*kakko*), used in Buddhist temples to mark the hours; *uta-daiko*, decorated with red cords and used in theater orchestras (also called *shime-daiko*, *geza-daiko*); *tsuzumi*, small double-faced hourglass drum, of various sizes; *uchiwa-daiko*, single-skinned tambourine with a short handle; *yagura-daiko*, large drum with skin nailed onto the body, not held by cords, specific to Shinto festivals, also called *tsuri-daiko; ninai-daiko,* drum attached to the end of a long pole, used in processions. Various other types, collectively called *gakudaiko,* were once used in orchestras that performed court music. Some village groups specialize in playing the large *ō-daiko* drum and have gained an international audience for their displays of rhythm and virtuosity.

Du Bousquet, Albert Charles. French military officer (1837–82), born in Belgium. He and other officers arrived in Japan in 1867, at the invitation of the shogunate, to reorganize the army along modern lines. After the Meiji Restoration, he remained in Tokyo as an interpreter for the French legation. At the same time, he served as a military adviser for various Japanese ministries. He was appointed French consul in 1880 and died in Tokyo.

Dumoulin, Louis. French painter (1860–1924), landscape artist. He went to Japan in 1887 and produced a great number of paintings, which he exhibited in Paris in December 1889.

Dury, Léon. Naval officer (d. 1891), France's vice-consul to Nagasaki from 1862 to 1870. He taught French in a number of cities, including Nagasaki, Kyoto, and Tokyo. When he returned to France, he was appointed Japan's honorary consul to Marseille.

Dyeing. The Japanese are past masters of the art of dyeing fabrics and have used most of the known techniques over their history. Each region had (and still has) its specialty, including stenciling *(komon-zome);* wax-resist methods similar to Indonesian batik *(rōkechi),* known since the Nara period (also called *sarasa, inkafu);* ink-block printing *(surizoe);* block-resist *(kyōkechi);* tie-dyeing *(kōkechi, yuhata, tsujigahama);* using rice paste *(yūzen)* for multicolored dyeing, or monochrome (generally with indigo, *ai*), called *chaya-zome,* and so on. *See* BINGATA, CHAYA-ZOME, CLOTHING, FABRICS, TSUJIGAHANA, YŪZEN-ZOME.

E. Fourth vowel of the Japanese syllabic alphabets *(kana),* always pronounced "ay" as in "say." It is combined with consonants to form the sounds *kay, say, tay, nay, hay, may, ray, way,* and the weakened ("nigorized") sounds *gay, zay, day, bay,* and *pay.*

• The Sino-Japanese character *e* generally means "image," and often follows (as does, sometimes, the character *gu,* "painting"), the name of the painter on a canvas or a print. It is sometimes replaced by the character *hitsu* ("painted by") or *sau.*

Ean. Buddhist monk (1225–77) of the Tendai sect. He switched to Rinzai Zen in 1257.

Earthquakes. Because the islands of Japan are located on a major fault line at the eastern edge of the Asian fault, under which the Pacific plate is sinking, they are subject to intense volcanic activity. There are also numerous earthquakes (more than 5,000 a year), some of which are catastrophic; most, however (an average of two or three per month), are not detectable except by high-precision instruments. The area most frequently affected by earthquakes is along the Pacific coast and on the continental slopes to about 1,000 to 3,000 m in depth. The epicenters are usually located along rivers, notably the Shinano and the Yado, and in the Nōbi, Tochigi, and Kanto plains. Many earthquakes are accompanied by landslides that cause major damage. When high-amplitude earthquakes take place on the ocean floor, they result in tidal waves *(tsunami),* which hit the coasts and reach gigantic proportions in the bays, destroying everything in their path. *See* map accompanying GEOGRAPHY.
→ *See* TANAKADATE AIKITSU, TSUNAMI, VOLCANOES.

East, Alfred. English art lover (1849–1913) sent to Japan in 1880 by the Fine Arts Society. During his visit, he was made an honorary member of the Meiji Fine Arts Society. A good painter, he illustrated Pigott's book *The Garden of Japan* (1882) and published *Landscape Painting in Oil Colour* (1906) and *Brush and Pencil Notes in Landscapes* (1914).

E-awase. Game popular among nobles in the twelfth and thirteenth centuries. Players were divided into two teams; each took a turn showing a painting or an *emakimono,* which the others had to identify and critique.

Ebashi Setsurō. Pharmacology professor (b. 1922) at the University of Tokyo, known for his applied research on muscular dystrophy. He received the Order of Culture (Bunka-shō) in 1975.

Ebi. Generic name for all crustaceans—shrimps, lobsters, prawns, and so on. The characters in *ebi* also mean "the old man of the sea," so the word is a symbol of long life. Preserved *ebi* used as door ornaments during New Year's celebrations are reputed to have the power to cure certain illnesses and to protect against bad luck.

• **Ebi-joro.** Formerly, small dolls made with eyes of an *ise-ebi,* a type of prawn with very large eyes, and very popular among children and young women in the Edo period.

• **Ebi-kōryō.** *See* KARA-YŌ, KŌRYŌ.

Ebihara Kinosuke. Figurative painter (b. 1904).

Ebina Danjō. Protestant minister (1856–1937) and educator, born in Fukuoka prefecture. He was active mainly in Kōbe, Kumamoto, and Gumma pre-

Major Earthquakes since 1847

Date	Location (Richter scale)	No. dead
1847, May 8	Nagano prefecture	12,000
1854, Dec. 23	Tōkai and Nankai	1,000
1854, Dec. 24	Shikoku and Kyushu coasts	3,000
1855, Nov. 11	Tokyo	7,000
1891, Oct. 28	Aichi and Gifu prefectures [Nōbi]	7,237
1896, June 15 (tsunami)	Tōhoku [Pacific coast]	27,122
1923, Sept. 1	Kantō (7.9–8.2)	142,807
1927, Mar. 7	Kitra Tango (7.3)	3,295
1933, Mar. 3	Tōhoku [Sanriku] (8.1)	3,064
1944, Dec. 7 (tsunami)	Wakayama prefecture	1,223
1945, Aug. 6	Tōkai (6.8)	2,300
1946, Dec. 21 (tsunami)	Nankaidō (8.0)	1,464
1948, June 28	Fukui prefecture (7.2)	3,895
1952, Mar. 4 (tsunami)	Southeast Hokkaido (8.2)	33
1960, May 24 (tsunami from Chile)	Northeast coast	991
1964	Niigata (7.5)	26
1968	Tokachioki (7.9)	52
1978	Izu (7.0)	25
1983	Miyagi (7.4)	28
1993, July 12	Okushiri, Hokkaido (7.8)	230
1995, Jan. 16–17	Kansai, Kobe (7.2)	5,250

fectures and was rector of Dōshisha University in Kyoto from 1920 to 1928.

Ebira. Title of a Noh play: the ghost of a warrior recounts how he adopted a flowering plum branch as an emblem before going off to the battle in which he died.

Ebisu. Term once applied to all non-Japanese peoples, then more specifically to the populations of the northern and eastern parts of the Japanese archipelago. Also called Ara-Ebisu, Tsugaru-Ebisu. *See also* EZO.

• Popular god, perhaps a *kami* or an ancient hero, who was considered a god of happiness and included among the Seven Gods of Good Fortune (Shichifukujin) in the seventeenth century. His origin is not clear. Some posit that he was likely the third son of Izanagi and Izanami, others that he was descended from Okuninushi no Mikoto and was in fact the *kami* Kotoshironushi; he would thus have been the ancestor of the Japanese people. He is the protector of work, health, and prosperity, very highly venerated by fishers and traders. He is portrayed dressed in a simple kimono and *hakama*, holding a fishing rod in one hand and a sea bream *(tai)* in the other. He is also considered a household god; in this context, his effigy often sits in kitchens alongside Daikoku-ten. He is reputed to be hard of hearing, which is why his followers make a loud noise before praying to him. His main shrine is the Nishinomiya-jinja in Hyōgo, where vendors of dolls in his image, the Ebisumawashi, used to gather. Ebisu is feted in October or January, depending on the locality. Also called Hiruko.

• **Ebisu-kō.** Shinto festival in honor of Ebisu, created in the sixteenth century, which takes place on January 10 (October 20 in Osaka) and is now a major commercial holiday.

Eboshi. Chinese-inspired headgear worn by nobles and warriors in the seventh century. It is a sort of hat made of gauze, horsehair, or lacquered paper in various shapes. A variation, similar to a creased bonnet, called *nae-eboshi,* was worn by commoners. Starting in the twelfth century, warriors wore a triangular-shaped *ji-eboshi.* The *eboshi* was worn only after a man had reached maturity and after the *gempuku. See also* HAIR STYLES, KAMMURI.

• **Eboshi-na.** Name given to a young man by his *eboshi-oya* (sponsor) during the "giving of the man's hat" *(gempuku)* ceremony. Also *kammei. See* GEMPUKU.

• **Eboshi-oya.** Sponsor of a young man, charged with giving him the *eboshi* hat and conferring on him his man's name *(eboshi-na)* during the *gempuku* ceremony. Also called *hikiire, kammuri-oya, kakan.*

E-busshi. Painters and sculptors who specialized in religious art, belonging to an official bureau of painting or sculpture *(e-dokoro)*. This term was not used, however, for Zen religious painters. *E-busshi* were active mainly in the Heian, Kamakura, and Muromachi periods. Lay painters were called *e-shi. See* BUSSHI.

Echigo. Former province in Honshu, now Niigata prefecture.

• **Echigo-chijimi.** *See* OJIYA.

• **Echigo-jishi.** *See* KAKUBEI-JISHI.

• **Echigo Sammyaku.** Mountain range in Niigata, Yamagata, Gumma, and Fukushima prefectures; highest peak, Dainaichi-dake (2,128 m).

• **Ehigo-ya.** Chain of stores founded in 1673 in Edo by Mitsui Takatoshi (Mitsui Hachirōemon, 1622–94). Its name was changed to Mitsui in 1896 and it gave rise to the company Mitsukoshi in 1904.

Echizen. Former province on the island of Honshu, now Fukui prefecture.

• **Echizen Deme.** *See* IZEKI CHIKANOBU.

• **Echizen Hokkyō.** *See* KAIKEI.

• **Echizen no Kami.** *See* MIZUNO TADAKUNI, ŌOKA TADASUKE.

• **Echizen'ya Chojirō.** *See* TAMENAGA SHUNSUI (I), MASAKAZU (II).

• **Echizen-yaki.** Type of ceramics produced in the late Heian period in the province of Echizen (Fukui prefecture), consisting mainly of pottery for domestic use. The pieces were rough in appearance and dark brown in color and were sometimes embellished with shoulders and green or light-brown borders, though they did not have a glaze. Their shapes were often asymmetrical and they sometimes had simple decorations made by pressing or with a "comb." In the Edo period, these ceramics were glazed and fired in a *noborigama* kiln. Their popularity declined in the Meiji era, but they seem currently to be regaining favor, thanks to efforts by director and potter Teshigahara Hiroshi and ceramist Hatakeyama Zekan, who have set up kilns in the village of Miyazaki.

Economy. Japan's economy is entirely based (except for agriculture, fishing, and forestry) on the import of raw materials needed for its industries and their transformation into manufactured products. It is even more fragile because Japan's soil is poor in useful ores: mines employ barely 1% of the active population, while industry employs almost 35%. One major feature of the Japanese economy is the large size of the services sector (tertiary sector), which represents more than 55% of economic activities and about 56% of GNP (the industrial sector represents 40%; agriculture, 3%).

The main mining resources are charcoal (usually of mediocre quality), average annual production of which is about 17 million tons (reserves of about 8 billion tons). Japan is the ninth-largest world producer of silver, with an annual average of 350 tons. The other mines are of low or very low yield: iron (340,000 tons), zinc (225,000 tons), copper (35,000 tons), talc, barite, lead, chrome, gold (3,000 kg).

Electricity production is at about 650 billion kwh, of which 130 billion are from nuclear power and 95 billion from hydroelectric power; the rest is supplied by coal-, oil-, and natural-gas–powered plants (production of natural gas is about 2 billion m^3 per year).

Industrial production is very important (steelworks, shipyards, automobile plants, etc.), and 90% is for export: to the United States (38%), South Korea and Germany (5%), China (4.7%), and the countries of the ex-USSR (1.5%). The main exports are automobiles and motorcycles, precision and electronic equipment, and computer components. Essential imports (raw materials, food products, etc.) come from the United States (23%), Indonesia (oil, 5.8%), Australia (5.5%), China (4.5%), South Korea (4.2%), Saudi Arabia (oil, 4.1%), Canada (4%), Malaysia (3%), and the countries of the ex-USSR (1.6%). Japan's foreign-trade balance is usually positive, especially because the government applies a non-tariff protective system.

Although the spectacular rise in value of the yen vis-à-vis the dollar in recent years has considerably hampered exports, it has allowed for massive in-

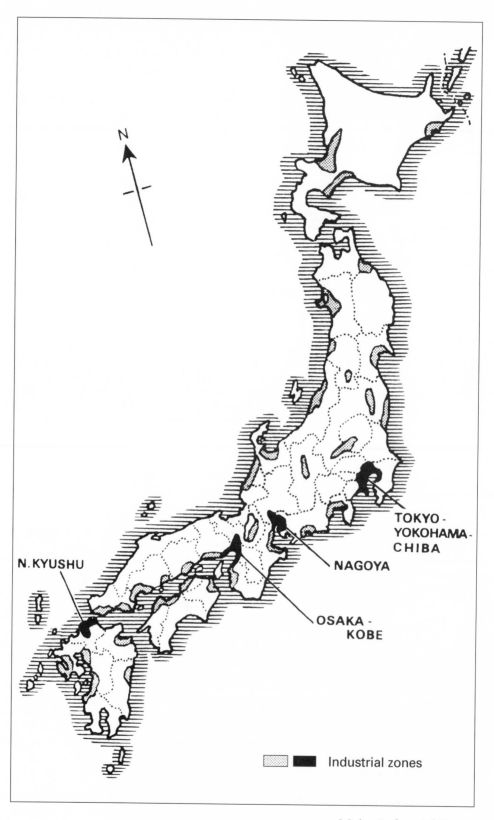

N

TOKYO-
YOKOHAMA-
CHIBA

NAGOYA

N.KYUSHU

OSAKA-
KOBE

Industrial zones

Major Industrial Zones

vestments in foreign countries (creation of subsidiary plants, acquisition of real estate and firms). The selling points of Japanese industry are quality and service. Its complex system enables it to remain strongly competitive with foreign products. The country has been forced to reduce its productivity in recent years. Although Japan is partly responsible for the world economic imbalance because its balance of trade is too high, the country's leaders claim that this is necessary to safeguard the existence of thousands of companies and thus the essential economy of the country, as well as its citizens' standard of living (GNP per inhabitant fourth out of 225 countries in the world, with annual income per family of about 5.5 million yen and savings at about 11%). GDP has been stagnant since the mid-1990s, and the unemployment rate in recent years has approached 5 percent. Revenues from tourism are over $80 million. *See* AGRICULTURE, FISHING.

Eda Saburō. Politician (1907–77), born in Okayama. Imprisoned a number of times for having participated in left-wing peasant movements in the 1930s, he went into voluntary exile in China, where he continued to be politically active. When he returned to Japan, in 1946, he helped reorganize the Socialist party and was elected to the House of Representatives in 1950. In 1960, as the party's secretary-general, he tried to free it from its Marxist-Leninist leanings; in 1977, he created a new party, Shakai Shimin Rengō (Socialist Citizens' League). Father of Eda Satsuki.

Eda Satsuki. Politician (b. 1941), son of Eda Saburō. Elected to the House of Representatives in 1977, he succeeded his father as leader of Shakai Shimin Rengō. But in July 1977, he decided to dissolve this association and replace it with another, Shakai Minshu Rengō (United Social Democratic party), by forming an alliance with the progressive members of the Diet.

E-den. In Shinto shrines and Buddhist temples, hall reserved for exhibition of religious images, votive or not. *See also* EMA, EMA-SHŌ.

Edo. "Entrance to the Bay," former name for Tokyo, used from 1180 to 1868. It was originally a fishers' village; in 1457, a minor lord, Ōta Dōkan, built a castle there for the Uesugi family. Edo was chosen by Tokugawa Ieyasu as the main center for his Kanto estates in 1590. A town *(jōka-machi)* then developed around the castle that Ieyasu had re-

constructed. In the early seventeenth century, Ieyasu decided to develop the capital of his *bakufu* in Edo and ordered his vassals to reside there, so lords' houses, palaces, temples, and shrines were erected. When the *sankin-kōtai* system was established, growing numbers of merchants and artisans followed the influx of wealthy daimyo and their retinues from the provinces and settled in Edo permanently, creating the *chōnin* (town dwellers), a new class distinct from the samurai and peasants. The population rose very rapidly and divided into various districts, spreading in all directions and swallowing up surrounding villages. In the eighteenth century, Edo's population was over 1 million and its area was about 60 km^2. The *chōnin* quickly became more numerous than the samurai, and the city continued to attract people from all parts of Japan. However, most construction was in wood, so enormous fires (the "blossoms of Edo") frequently ravaged the city. Houses began to be constructed of plaster and faced with tile to reduce the risk. A corps of firefighters was formed, and each group of houses had a tower for watchmen. Most samurai and lords lived inside the moats that surrounded the castle while the *chōnin* populated peripheral districts, mainly those near the bay and the shores of the Sumida-gawa. Pleasure districts were created, such as the famous Yoshiwara. But space soon ran out and land was reclaimed from the shallow waters of the bay to create new districts *(chō)*. The largest city in Japan, Edo had a profound influence on the national society, and the Edo culture spread into the provinces. In addition to being the seat of the shogunate, it was also a major trading center from which main roads ran in all directions. All distances were counted starting from Nihombashi (the bridge of Japan) located in the center of the city. A museum (Edo-Tokyo Museum) retracing the city's history opened in 1993 in the Sumida district. *See* TOKYO.

• **Edo-gawa.** Canal dug in 1641 to link the Rone River to the Kanto plain. It is 53 km long and supplies Tokyo with potable water.

• *Edo Haruma. See* HARUMA-WAGE.

• **Edo-jidai.** Artistic and historical period corresponding to the Tokugawa shogunate (1603–1868). Also called Kinsei (pre-modern) and Tokugawa-jidai.

• **Edo-jō.** "Castle of Edo." Built from 1603 to 1651 to be the seat of the Tokugawa shogunate, it was the nucleus of the city that developed around it. Its "outside" moat, fed (as were the other moats around it) by the waters of the Sumida River and the Bay of Edo, had a total length of about 16 km. The "inside" moat, which surrounded the castle itself, was 6.4 km long. Other moats defended the castle on the sea and the land sides. The Edo-jō, reconstructed on the foundations of a castle built by Ōta Dōkan in 1457, was occupied by the Hōjō family from 1525 to 1590, when it was passed on to Tokugawa Ieyasu. He and his successors had it completely reconstructed and expanded. It was destroyed by fire several times, notably during a terrible fire in 1657. Within its succession of walls lived warriors and servants, daimyo and bureaucrats. In the center of this immense complex was the shogunal residence, heavily defended by deep moats and enormous ramparts guarded by bastions. Most of the residences in the castle were destroyed by fires. Some were reconstructed, while others were abandoned. At the beginning of the Meiji era, in 1868, the castle was no longer in use as a fortress; all that remained of it were the inside moat, the walls made of enormous rocks with no cement, and a few palaces and guard towers. The buildings built for the emperor and his family were bombed during the Second World War. They were rebuilt in 1970 on a modernized traditional plan. The castle, however, remains the center of the city of Tokyo and constitutes an oasis of greenery in the Chiyoda district. *See* CASTLES.

• **Edo-kanō.** School of painting, branch of the Kanō school, established in Edo. It comprised five distinct "studios," called Kanō-ha. *See* KANŌ-HA.

• **Edo-ma.** *See* TATAMI.

• **Edo-machi bugyō.** Bureaucrats of the Edo *bakufu* responsible for maintaining order in the shogunal capital. Generally, two *hatamoto* fulfilled these duties, alternating month by month. They had under their command about 120 *dōshin* and *yoriki*. They also supervised construction, prisons, and firefighting brigades *(hikeshi)*.

• **Edo sampu.** Visits made annually by the head of the Dutch trading post at Deshima to the Edo shogun to receive confirmation of his trading and residential rights.

Edogawa Rampo. Writer (Hirai Tarō, 1894–1965), born in Mie, who lived mainly in Nagoya after studying at Waseda University in Tokyo. He took the pseudonym Rampo in tribute to Edgar Allan Poe, whose writing he admired. After working at several professions, including as a journalist, he began to write mystery novels and tragedies, modeling his writing on that of Poe and Arthur Conan Doyle. In 1922, he published two novellas, *Ichimai no kippu* (A Ticket) and *Nisen dōka* (Two Copper Coins) in the magazine *Shin Seinen*. They were very successful, so he began to write detective novels that were a little strange and sometimes even morbid, among them *Shinri shiken* (Psychological Examination, 1925), *Akai heya* (The Red Room, 1925), *Yaneura no sanōsha* (The Roofwalker, 1925), *Ningen isu* (Human Flesh, 1926), *Issumbōshi* (The Dwarf, 1927), *Kagami jigoku* (Hell of Mirrors, 1926), *Panorama-tō kitan* (The Strange History of the Panorama Islands, 1927), *Injū* (The Sinister Monster, 1928), *Kumo-otoko* (Spider Man, 1929–30), *Mōjū* (The Monster, 1928), *Kuro tokage* (Black Lizard, 1934), and *Kaijin nijūmensō* (The Monster with a Hundred Faces, 1936). He studied Western detective literature and published critiques of and essays on this literary genre, *Gen'ei-jō* (The Castle of Chimera, 1951) and *Tantei shōsetsu yonjū-nen* (Forty Years of Detective Literature, 1961). In 1954, he created a literature prize that bears his name, and in 1957 he became editor of the mystery magazine *Hōseki* (Gems). Many of his works were adapted for the screen.

E-dokoro. Official bureaus of painting, generally attached to the imperial court, the shogunate, or sometimes a large Buddhist temple or Shinto shrine. These agencies, created at the beginning of the Heian period, lasted until 1868. The most famous *e-dokoro* was the imperial one (Kyūtei E-dokoro) founded in the ninth century. From the *e-dokoro* came most of the major painting styles, including Yamato-e, and the Tosa and Kanō schools. The leader of the *e-dokoro* had the title E-dokoro Azukari.

Education. Since promulgation of the law *(gakusei)* of 1872, the Japanese educational system has been under the aegis of the Ministry of Education, which adopted the American and European systems. It underwent various reforms; in 1947, the militarist system adopted in 1917 and updated in 1937 was replaced by a single corpus defining the conditions of education, which became obligatory for all children up to the age of 15. In 1952, this system came under the aegis of a Central Council of Education (Chūō Kyōiku Shingi-kai) within the Ministry of Education. It consists of a normal system and a system for those with disabilities. The normal system involves optional preschool (1–3 years of age), then six years of primary school *(shōgakkō)* and three years of middle school *(chūgakkō),* both obligatory. Students can then opt for courses in a technical college or continue their regular studies for three or four years in a high school *(kōtōgakkō)* full time, part time, or by correspondence. They can then enter university if they pass an entrance exam.

The system for those with disabilities comprises six years of elementary education plus three years of secondary education, both obligatory, which can then be supplemented by three years of high-school education.

Japan has 231 public and 883 private universities, 4,183 public and 1,318 private secondary schools, 59 public and 3 private technical secondary schools, 10,674 public and 626 private colleges, 24,560 public and 170 private primary schools, 6,269 public and 8,737 private preschools, and many specialized schools, both public and private [source: *Asahi Shimbunsha*].

The Ministry of Education sets educational programs and controls textbooks. Primary and middle schools, being obligatory, are supported by the state and municipalities.

At the end of secondary school, more than 40% of students enter university, public (15%) or private (85%). Scholarships are rare, families are forced to make great sacrifices to ensure that their children receive a higher education. *See* ABE SHIGETAKA, ABE YOSHIHIGE, AMANO TEIYŪ, AOYAMA GAKUIN, ASHIDA ENOSUKE, ATOMI KAKEI, CHŪGAKKŌ, DAIGAKU, DEGREES, GAKKŌ, GŌGAKU, JUKU, KYŌIKU CHOKUGO, ŌSHEDASARE-SHO, SHIJUKU, SHŌGAKU-IN, SHŌHAN GAKKŌ, SHUGEISHUCHI-IN, SŌSHIN-IN, TERAKOYA, YAGAKU, YOBIKO.

"Eejanaika." "Why not?" Phrase sung by people in a sort of mass hysteria that swept Japan in 1867; they danced in the streets, dressed extravagantly, and acted in a manner diametrically opposed to the usual behavior required by the shogunate. A rumor had circulated in the Osaka region that amulets from the Ise shrine had fallen from Heaven onto the town of Nagoya; the population thought that this was heralding a new era of freedom, so men, women, and children threw aside their reserve and cried out "Eejanaika!" The mania quickly spread to Yokohama and Edo, causing quite a stir and creating disorder. This "liberation of the instincts" was interpreted as a chain reaction to the oppression of the *bakufu* and was triggered by the hope that a

new imperial era and a general liberalization of attitudes would take place.

E-fu. Bureau of the imperial guards, a sort of ministry created by the Taihō Reform of 701, on the model of a similar Chinese organization. It was charged with protection of the imperial family and policing within the palace walls. It was divided into sections: Emon-fu (general quarters of the guards), Sa-eji-fu (guards of the left), U-eji-fu (guards of the right), Sa-hyoe-fu (military quarters of the left), Chū-e-fu (of the center), Konoe-fu (or Jutoe-fu) and Gai-e-fu (until 722). The guards belonged to two classes: the Eji, from the provincial militias, and the Hyōe, from noble families. These responsibilities were replaced by those of the Kebiishi around 810.

• **E-fu no tachi.** *See* KENUKI-GATA NO TACHI.

E-fumi. Starting in 1628, following the prohibition on Christianity, annual ceremony in Nagasaki during which all who were suspected of following the Christian faith had to walk on an image *(fumi-e)* of the Virgin Mary, the Infant Jesus, or Christ to prove to the authorities that they were not Christians. *See* FUMI-E.

Egawa Tarōzaemon. Samurai and industrialist (Egawa Hidetatsu, Tan'an, 1801–55), born in Nirayama (province of Izu, Shizuoka prefecture). He went to Nagasaki in 1835 to study Western technologies, which he then taught in Edo. In 1842, he built the country's first reverberation blast furnace, in Nirayama, in order to cast cannons. In 1853, he was charged by the shogunate with reinforcing the defenses in the Bay of Edo when Commodore Perry's ships arrived, and he was assisted in this task by Western experts invited by the shogunate.

Egen. Zen Buddhist monk (Musō Daishi, Kanzan, 1277–1360), founder of the Myōshin-ji temple (Rinzai sect) in Kyoto in 1350.

Egōshū. "Town councillors," a body of wealthy urban merchants *(chōnin),* established to govern semi-autonomous towns during the Muromachi period (1333–1568). They administered local markets and paid taxes to the landowners. However, many *egōshū* managed to free themselves from the lords' grasp and establish local governments, as happened at Sakai.

Egoyomi. Illustrated calendars (often featuring ukiyo-e prints) made during the Edo period for illiterate people. Harunobu painted a number of prints for these tear-off calendars about 1765.

Eguchi. Title of a Noh play: the ghost of a courtesan from Eguchi appears to an itinerant Buddhist monk, revealing that she is really the Bodhisattva Fugen Bosatsu (*Skt.*: Samanthabhadra).

Eguchi Shin'ichi. Poet (1914–79), founder of the philanthropic Salt of the Earth movement in 1956. His hopes dashed, he committed suicide.

Ehime. Prefecture *(ken)* of the island of Shikoku, bordering the Inland Sea (Setonaikai). *Chief city:* Matsuyama. *Main towns:* Iyo, Hōjō, Tōyo, Saijō, Niihama, Imabari (all on the coast), and Ōzu. The mountainous nature of the region and its relatively warm climate allow for intensive citrus farming. Fishing is plentiful on the coasts. *Area:* 5,664 km². *Pop.:* 1.6 million.

E-hon wabigito. Book on art written by Nishikawa Sukenobu (1671–1751) in which the author expounds on the need for Japanese artists to discover their country's true spirit and stop imitating Chinese painters.

Eichō. Era during the reign of Emperor Horikawa: Dec. 1096–Nov. 1097. *See* NENGŌ.
• Zen Buddhist monk (d. 1247), Eisai's disciple. He preached Zen in eastern Japan and founded the Chōraku-ji temple in Kōzuke.
• Zen Buddhist monk (Tōyō Eichō, 1428–1504) of the Rinzai sect. He was appointed *jūji* of the Daitoku-ji in 1481 and founded the Shōrin-ji temple at Mino, where he died.

Eidaka. Tax payable in rice up to the mid-fifteenth century, and in cash with currency called Eiraku-tsūhō (Eiraku-sen), issued starting in 1412. *See* ERIAKU-TSŪHŌ.

Eien. Era during the reign of Emperor Ichijō: Apr. 987–Aug. 989. *See* NENGŌ.
• Buddhist monk (1048–1125) of the Hossō sect, from the Fujiwara family. He was a disciple of Raishin at the Kōfuku-ji temple in Nara and was appointed *sōzu* of the Kiyomizu-dera temple in Kyoto in 1113.

Eifuku-ji. Buddhist temple of the Shingon sect established in Osaka on the site of a temple built by Shōmu Tennō to commemorate the spot where Shōtoku Taishi was buried. Reconstructed in the twelfth century, it was destroyed by fire in 1574 and rebuilt on Hideyoshi's orders. It houses two statues portraying Shōtoku Taishi.

• **Eifuku Mon'in.** Empress (1271–1342), wife of Emperor Fushimi in 1288. Daughter of the noble Saionji Sanekane, she took the name Eifuku Mon'in when the emperor abdicated in 1298. She is best known as a *waka* poet in the *kyōgoku* style. Imperial anthologies, the *Gyokuyō wakashū* and the *Fūgashū,* contain about 150 of her poems. Also called Yōfuku Mon'in.

Eiga monogatari. "Story of Splendor." A novel attributed to Akazome Emon or to Fujiwara no Tamenari. The end of the work may have been written by Dewa no Ben. The first part was probably written between 1028 and 1034; the second part, between 1092 and 1107. It contained historical stories based on the life and exploits of Fujiwara no Michinaga and his family and was a sequel to the *Rikkokushi.* The manuscript comprises 40 scrolls *(makimono)* with poetic titles, which contain stories and notes *(nikki)* taken by noblewomen of the court. Twenty-eight scrolls are devoted to the government of Fujiwara no Michinaga. Written completely in hiragana characters, this work is of high literary quality and has sometimes been compared to the *Genji monogatari (The Tale of Genji).* Included are excerpts from the *Murasaki Shikibu nikki* and the *Ōjōyōshū.*

Eigen-ji. Zen Buddhist temple of the Rinzai sect, founded in Ōmi (Shiga prefecture) by Genkō in 1361. It was set on fire by Oda Nobunaga's troops about 1574 and rebuilt by Isshi Bunshu (1608–ca. 1646).

Eihei-ji. Zen Buddhist temple of the Sōtō sect founded by Dōgen near Katsuyama (17 km from Fukui) in 1243. It is still one of the sect's main temples, the other being the Sōji-ji in Tsurumi, near Yokohama. It was first called Daibutsu-ji but was renamed in 1246. The temple was partly destroyed by fire in 1473 and again in 1879, but many of its buildings have been rebuilt. It is at the head of more than 1,400 *matsu-ji* (attached temples) throughout Japan.

Eihō. Era during the reign of Emperor Shirakawa: Feb. 1081–Apr. 1084. *See* NENGŌ.

Eihō-ji. Zen Buddhist temple of the Rinzai sect, founded in Gifu on the orders of Ashikaga Takauji by Musō Kokushi in 1314. Its *kaisandō* (founder's hall) dates from 1352.

Eiji. Era during the reign of emperors Sutoku and Konoe: July 1141–Apr. 1142. *See* NENGŌ.

Eikai. Painter (Satake Aisetsu; Eishi; *gō:* Eikai, 1802–74). A student of Tani Bunchō, he painted mainly landscapes.

Eikan. Era during the reign of Emperor Enyū: Apr. 983–Apr. 985. *See* NENGŌ.
• Buddhist monk responsible for rebuilding the Eikan-ji temple in 983; the temple had been founded in 855 by Shinsho, a monk of the Jōdo sect.
• Buddhist monk (Yōkan, 1053–1132) of the Jōdo sect. He studied the doctrines of the Sanron and became a monk in the Zenrin-ji temple. He was then named *bettō* of the Tōdai-ji in Nara. He wrote a number of religious works, including the *Ōjōjūin* (10 vols.), the *Ojōkōshiki,* and the *Amidakyō yōki. See* ŌJŌJŪIN.

• **Eikan-dō.** *See* ZENRIN-JI.

Eika taigai. Poetry critique written in Chinese by Fujiwara no Taika (1162–1241).

Eikosaku. Rural leases given by some daimyo in the Edo period to encourage farmers to cultivate new crops. Farmers obtained a long-term contract and could pass on their rights, which remained inalienable even if the daimyo changed. When the land had been cultivated for more than 20 years, the contract could be considered permanent. Farmers then paid their taxes directly to the shogunal government. This system disappeared during the Meiji era. Also called *eitai-azukari, eitai-saku, seshū-kosaku.*

Eikyō. Era during the reign of Emperor Go-Hanazono: Sept. 1429–Feb. 1441. *See* NENGŌ.

• **Eikyō no Ran.** Revolt led by the Kanto Administrator (Kantō-kanryō) Ashikaga no Mochiuji against the Muromachi *bakufu* in 1438. Defeated the following year, Mochiuji committed suicide.

Eikyū. Era during the reign of Emperor Toba: July 1113–Apr. 1118. *See* NENGŌ.
• Painter (Matsuoka Teruo; *gō:* Eikyū, 1881–1938) in modern Japanese style.

Eiman. Era during the reign of Emperor Nijō: June 1165–Aug. 1166. *See* NENGŌ.

Einin. Era during the reign of Emperor Fushimi: Aug. 1293–Apr. 1299. *See* NENGŌ.

Einin Shinnō. Son (1356–1416) of Sukō Tennō of the Northern Court (Hokuchō). He became a Buddhist monk in 1398 under the name Tsūchi.

Einō. Painter (Kanō Yoshinobu; *azana:* Hakuju; Nuinosuike; *gō:* Ichiyōsai, Baigaku, Sojunken, Sansei, Kyo-ō, Einō, 1631/34–1697/1700), student of his father, Sansetsu, of the Kanō school. He wrote *Honchō gashi,* a history of Japanese painting, in 1693.

Eiraku Hozen. Ceramist (1795–1854), eleventh master of the Eiraku family of Kyoto. Adopted by the Nishimura family, he took the name Nishamura Zengorō XI. With his son, Wazen, he imitated Chinese ceramics of the Ming era and created an ornamental style of gold on a red background. He built a kiln at Midera, near Otsu, and produced ceramics called Konan-*yaki* (which he signed Konan Hozen) for one year, then moved to another kiln whose production was called Nagarayama-*yaki.* The Eirakyu family's production as a whole is called Eiraku-*yaki.* He also sculpted dolls and netsuke.

• **Eiraku Kōichi.** Contemporary ceramist and Nihonga painter, born in 1944 in Kyoto, seventeenth in the family line and son of Eiraku Jingorō, also a ceramist. He is a member of the International Ceramics Academy, and his works, most of them abstract, have been widely exhibited in foreign countries, including Cologne in 1991 and Paris in 1994.

• **Eiraku Wazen.** Ceramist (1821–96), son of Eiraku Hozen.

• **Eiraku-yaki.** *see* EIRAKU HOZEN.

Eiraku-tsūhō. Copper coins imported from China, issued in China during the Yongle (*Jap.:* Eiraku) era by shogun Ashikaga Yoshimitsu and widely used in Japan, notably in the Kanto region. These coins, which were used instead of rice to pay taxes (*see* EIDAKA), were banned by Tokugawa Ieyasu in 1609, but continued to be used unofficially until the mid-seventeenth century. Also called Eiraku-sen, Eisen. *Chin.:* Yongle Tongbao. *See also* BITASEN, ERIZENI, KŌBU TSŪHŌ.

Eiri. *See* CHŌKYŌSAI EIRI.

Eiroku. Era during the reign of Emperor Ogimachi: Feb. 1558–Apr. 1569. *See* NENGŌ.

Eiroku-ji. *See* NAMBAN-JI.

Eiryaku. Era during the reign of Emperor Nijō: Jan. 1160–Sept. 1161. *See* NENGŌ.

Eisai. Buddhist monk (Myōan Eisai, Yōsai, 1141–1215) of the Tendai sect, at the Enryaku-ji monastery on Mt. Hiei, which he entered at the age of 13. He went to China for five months in 1168 to visit the monasteries of Mt. Tiantai and gather texts. In 1187, he returned to the mainland intending to go to India, but the Chinese Song authorities refused him the necessary travel documents. He therefore remained in China for four years, studying the doctrines of the Chan sect of Linzi (Zen sect of Rinzai) under the direction of Xu'an Huaichang, whose confirmed disciple he became. When he returned to Japan, he tried to teach this doctrine but was rebuffed by the monks of the Enryaku-ji and the court. He went to Kamakura in 1199, where he was welcomed by Hōjō Masako and his son, Shogun Minamoto no Yoriie. In 1202, Yoriie asked him to start a new monastery in Kyoto, the Kennin-ji. The Kennin-ji was devoted to Zen, Tendai, and Shingon, reflecting Eisai's eclecticism. He wrote *Shukke taikō* (Essences of Monastic Life, 1192), *Kōzen gokokuron* (Zen as a Means of National Defense, 1198), the *Nihon buppō chūkō gammon* (Plea in Favor of Renewed Buddhism in Japan, 1204), and *Kissa yōjō-ki* (Tea as a Means of Cultivating Life, 1211). In addition, he cultivated tea plants to spread the use of tea among Buddhist monks. He received the title Dai-sōjō and the posthumous name Senkō Kokushi. *Chinese names:* Linzi, Huang Long.

Eisai Co. Pharmaceuticals firm, founded in 1941, with branches in a great many Asian and European countries, notably France and Switzerland. Head office in Tokyo.

Eisen. *Gō* of many painters.

• **Eisen.** Painter (Kanō Koshin; Shōzaburō; *gō:* Eisen, 1696–1731) of the Kobiki-chō branch of the Kanō school, son of Shūshin.

• **Eisen.** Painter (Kanō Sukenobu; *gō:* Eisen, Hakugyokusai, 1730–90) of the Kanō school, stu-

dent of Genshin. He was the fifth painter of the Kobiki-chō branch of the Kanō.

• **Eisen.** Painter (Ikeda Yoshinobu; *azana:* Konsei, Zenshirō, Teisuke; *gō:* Eisen, Keisai, Ippitsuan, Kokushunro, Hokugō, Mumeiō, Kakō, 1790–1848), of ukiyo-e prints, student of Eizan. He made erotic images, portraits of beautiful women *(bijin)*, and landscapes. He also wrote several books on art.

• **Eisen.** *See* MOTONOBU, EIRAKU-TSŪHŌ.

Eishi. Painter (Hosoda Jibukyō Tokitomi; *gō:* Hosoi Eishi, 1756–1829) of ukiyo-e prints and paintings in the Kanō style, serving shogun Tokugawa Ieharu. He painted mainly women's faces in a very elegant style, along with allegorical compositions. His main disciples were Eishō, Eiri, Eishin, and Eisui. Also called Chōbunsai Eishi.

Eishō. Painter (Chōkosai Eishō; *gō:* Shōeidō, active ca. 1794–97) of ukiyo-e prints, student of Eishi.
→ *See* O-KACHI NO KATA, EISHŌ-JI.
• Era during the reign of Emperor Go-Reizei: Apr. 1046–Jan. 1053. Also called Eijō. *See* NENGŌ.
• Era during the reign of Emperor Go-Kashiwabara: Feb. 1504–Aug. 1520. Also called Eijō. *See* NENGŌ.

Eishō-in. *See* O-KACHI NO KATA.

• **Eishō-ji.** Buddhist temple founded at Kamakura in 1636 to lodge nuns, constructed on the site of the former palace of Ōta Dōkan by the nun Eishō-in (O-kachi no Kata), a concubine of Tokugawa Ieyasu.

Eishō-ki. Journal kept by Fujiwara no Tametaka (1070–1130), covering the years 1105 to 1129.

Eishun. Painter (fifteenth century) of the Yamato-e school. He painted at least part of the *Yūzū-nembutsu-engi* scroll in 1414. The scroll is now in the Seiryō-ji temple in Kyoto.

Eiso. Era during the reign of Emperor Ichijō: Aug. 989–Nov. 990. *See* NENGŌ.

Eisō. King of the Ryukyu Islands in the thirteenth century, succeeding Yoshimoto. He was a member of the Tenson family. *Chin.:* Yingzu.

Eison. Buddhist monk (1201–90) of the Saidai-ji in Nara, belonging to the Ritsu sect, raised in the

Daigo-ji temple in Kyoto, where he studied the principles of the Hossō, Shingon, and Sanron schools. In 1236, he entered the Tōdai-ji temple in Nara where he continued his religious studies under Kakujō (1194–1249). In 1238, he began to reconstruct the Saidai-ji temple in Nara. He went to Kamakura in 1262 upon the invitation of Hōjō Tokiyori and established a great number of shrines where fishing and hunting were forbidden. With his disciple, Ninshō, he built bridges and roads and established an asylum for people with leprosy in Nara. Then he spread the teachings of the Shingon Ritsu sect, devoting himself to easing the miseries of the poor and outcast. He is said to have been in China from 1235 to 1238. In 1281, Emperor Go-Uda asked him to organize prayer sessions to ensure victory over the Mongols, who were trying to invade the islands. Eison wrote an autobiography, the *Kanjin gakushō-ki,* and many religious works, including the *Kōmyō shingon wasan,* the *Shingon anjin wasan,* and the *Bommō koshaku monjū.* Posthumous name: Kōshō Bosatsu. Also called Eizon.

Eitaku. Painter (Kobayashi Tokusen; Hidejirō; *gō:* Sensai, Eitaku, 1843–90) of the Kanō school. He painted mainly historical subjects in a realist style.

Eiten. "Honors," system of awards and honorific distinctions including decorations and court ranks, created in 1881. In 1937, decorations *(shō)* for notables who had distinguished themselves in the arts, music, culture, theatre, and the sciences were added. In 1947, however, court ranks were abolished, and only distinctions and decorations (with no attribution of privileges) awarding people of merit remained. *See* KUNSHŌ.

Eitoku. Era during the reign of Emperor Go-Komatsu: Feb. 1381–Feb. 1383. *See* NENGŌ.
• Painter (Kanō Kuninobu; Genshirō; *gō:* Eitoku, 1543–90) of the Kanō school, student of his father, Shōei. Considered the best painter of his time, he worked for Oda Nobunaga and Toyotomi Hideyoshi and decorated the fusuma in the Azuchi castle and the Jurakudai palace with flowers in the Shōheki-ga style. He also painted birds and flowers for the Daitoku-ji temple in Kyoto.
• Painter (Kanō Tsunenobu; *gō:* Seisetsu-sai, Eitoku, 1814–91), in the Kanō style, son of Kanō Isen'in. He painted faces and landscapes.

Eiwa. Era during the reign of Emperor Go-En'yū of the Northern Court (Hokuchō): Feb. 1375–Mar. 1378. *See* NENGŌ.

Eizan. Painter (Kikukawa Toshinobu, Omiya Toshinobu; Mangorō; *gō:* Chōkusai, Chōkyūsai, Eisan, Eizan, 1787–1867) of ukiyo-e prints, student of Hokusai. He formed a partnership with Toyokuni and painted mainly portraits of beautiful women *(bijin)* and of Kabuki actors, between 1810 and 1860. He was Eisen's master.

Eizan-ji. Buddhist temple near Nara, founded as a family temple of the Fujiwara in 718 and belonging to the Shingon sect. It has an eighth-century *kondō* (with a stone lantern dating from 1234); an octagonal structure, dating from 7674, adorned with twelfth-century paintings; and a seven-story pagoda from the late eighth century, on each floor of which is a Sanskrit monogram. The *shōro* has a bronze bell *(dōshyō)* 1.5 m high and 0.9 m in diameter, cast in 917 and bearing calligraphy attributed to Ono no Michikaze. Also called Eisan-ji.

Eji. Guards of the imperial palace, chosen from the provincial militias, and belonging to the Eji-fu corps. *See* E-FU.

Ejima. Noblewoman (1681–1741) of the shogunal household. She caused a scandal in 1714 because of her liaison with a Kabuki actor, Ikushima Shingorō (1671–1743), who entered the palace living quarters *(ōoku)* disguised as a woman. When the lovers were discovered, Ejima was exiled to the province of Shinano (Nagano prefecture) and Ikushima to the island of Miyakejima. To encourage those living in the *ōoku* to be more vigilant, shogun Tokugawa Ietsuna punished more than 1,000 individuals. This incident became the subject of novellas and Kabuki plays.

Ejimaya Kiseki. Writer (Ejima Kiseki, Shigetomo, Ichirōemon, 1666–1735), author of books in the *ukiyo-zōshi* genre, published by Andō Jishō. He began by writing *jōruri* plays for Matsumoto Jidayū, then wrote on the theater—*Yakusha kuchijamisen* (The Vocal Shamisen of the Actor, 1699)—and *ukiyo-zōshi* novels—*Keisei irojamisen* (The Vocal Shamisen of the Courtesan, 1701), *Keisei kintanki* (The Forbidden Character of the Courtesan, 1711). He then left his publisher and created his own publishing house, printing *katagi-mono,* or "character sketches," such as *Seken musuko katagi* (Behavior of Young Girls of Good Society), but later returned to Jishō and published a number of books jointly with him. His books are easy to read and often aimed at a working-class audience, but they describe accurately the customs of his times, which he sometimes caricatures fiercely.

Eki. Korean Buddhist monk who went to Japan in the seventh century; master of the Hossō doctrine, he taught Gyōki.

• Japanese name for the divination principles set out in the Chinese book *Yijing* (Jap.: *Eki-kyō*). Japanese studies on the *Yijing* are called Kigaku. *See* BOKUSEN, URANAI.

• "Station," name once used to designate the transit points *(ekiba)* where government couriers could obtain fresh horses (also called *ekisei*). This term now designates train and bus stations. Prepared meals, or *bentō*, distributed in the train stations are called *ekiben* (short for *eki-bentō*).

Ekibyōgami. *See* YAKUBYŌGAMI.

Eki-den. *See* FUYUSO-DEN.

Ekijin. *See* KOTOYŌKA, yakubyōgami.

Ekin. Painter (early nineteenth century), originally from Shikoku, notable for his surrealistic ukiyo-e prints.

Elgin, James Bruce, Eighth Duke of. English politician (1811–63), governor general of Canada (1846–54), appointed Great Britain's plentipotentiary minister to Japan in 1858. In 1862, he became the first viceroy of India.

Eliot, Charles Norton Edgcumbe. English diplomat and scholar (1862–1931), ambassador to Japan from 1919 to 1922. Returning to Japan in 1929, he devoted himself to studying Japanese religion. Among his most important works are *Letters from the Far-East* (1907), *Hinduism and Buddhism* (1921), and *Japanese Buddhism* (1935).

Élisséeff, Serge. French scholar (1889–1975), born in St. Petersburg. He studied with Serge Oldenburg, the famous Russian expert on the East, then went to Berlin, where he studied Japanese and Chinese, and to Japan, where he was a student at the University of Tokyo. Returning to Russia in 1914, he received his doctorate at the University of St. Petersburg in 1916. He left the Soviet Union in 1920 and went to Paris, where he taught at the Sorbonne and conducted research at the Guimet Museum. Invited to the United States by Harvard University, Élisséeff became director of the Harvard–Yenching Institute in 1934 and founded the *Harvard Journal of Asiatic*

Studies in 1936. With Edwin O. Reischauer, he wrote *Elementary Japanese for College Students* (1944), which became a standard work. He returned to Paris in 1957 and continued to teach there until his death. His sons Vadim and Nikita are also recognized experts on Eastern studies.

Ema. Literally, "images of horses." Votive tablets used in Shinto worship. They originally portrayed horses and were substitutes for the real animals, which were (and still are) kept in major shrines. These horses (generally white) are considered intermediaries that carry human beings' messages to the gods. This symbolism was probably introduced to Japan when the Altaic and Korean "horsemen-archers" arrived in about the third century AD, bringing certain beliefs that were integrated with those of the Yayoi and Jōmon peoples. In the early Nara period, the custom was introduced of replacing real horses, which were difficult to obtain, with images of horses, sculpted or painted, as offerings to the shrines in tribute to the *kami*. In northern Honshu (and probably also in other parts of the islands, although no example has survived), straw effigies *(wara-uma)* were also offered. Usually, however, an *ema* consisted of a small wooden board symbolizing the facade of a shrine, on which was drawn or painted the image of a horse. These boards became very popular and were later decorated with objects such as a part of the body or some other symbol (eyes for healing of an ocular affliction, a student's cap for success in an examination or to thank the *kami* for success, etc.). The popularization of *ema* seems to have started in the Muromachi period, and there were even *ema* on Buddhist themes (for example, a sword representing Fudō Myō-ō). Some *ema* were actual paintings and depicted complex sub-

Ema

jects or events; others symbolized a happy voyage (for example, the image of a boat); still others had a characteristic object glued to the votive board. Major Shinto shrines, which received many *ema* (some of them painted by famous artists), stored them in structures specially built for this purpose called *ema-sho* or *ema-dō*. *Ema* varied in size from postcard-sized to painting-sized; the latter were called *ō-ema* (large ema). They could be simple, portraying a single image, or elaborate, with an explanatory text or a poem, the donor's name, the artist's signature, and the date of the offering. The custom is still alive, and many temples and shrines provide the faithful with *ema* (generally images of the animal of the current year in the cycle) for a small sum of money during festivals or on New Year's Day. These *ema* are considered talismans. Some are made in naive style, while others are true works of art. Also called (but more rarely) *e-uma, emma.*

• **Ema-sho.** Special building in Shinto shrines for storage of *ema* offered by followers. Also called *ema-dō.*

Emakimono (E-makimono). Paintings illustrating literary or religious texts executed on long strips of paper rolled up around a stick, which were unrolled to be read from right to left. These illuminated scrolls, which measured up to 20 m in length and from 25 to 52 cm in height, appeared in Japan very early, in the Nara period, in imitation of Chinese scrolls. The oldest surviving *emakimono* is probably *Kako genzai inga-kyō* (Illustrated Sutra on Past and Present Causes and Effects), also called *E-inga-kyō*, dating from the eighth century and copied from a Chinese original of the Sui dynasty (589–618). The style became popular during the Heian period, especially within monasteries and among the aristocracy. Novels and famous stories (such as the *Genji monogatari*); stories of the founding of temples (such as the *Shigisan engi*); and Buddhist (*Jigoku-zōshi,* twelfth century), humorous (*Chōjū-giga,* late twelfth century), and historical *(Heiji monogatari)* themes were illustrated, as were some landscapes. In these illuminated scrolls (*emaki* or *emakimono*), painted scenes alternated with texts or were mixed in with texts or stories. Although most *emakimono* date from the thirteenth and fourteenth centuries, they were being produced until the nineteenth century. Scrolls with few or no illustrations are called *makimono.* They may comprise numerous scrolls, sometimes up to 60. *Chin.:* Juanzhou.

Ema Tsutomu. Historian (1885–1979) who was a pioneer in historical research about Japanese traditions and customs. His works have been collected in *Ema Tsotomu chosaku-shū.*

Embree, John Fee. American ethnologist (1908–50), born in New Haven, who specialized in studying Japanese society. Among his most notable works are *Suye Mura: A Japanese Village* (1939), *Some Social Functions of Religion in Rural Japan* (Chicago), and *The Distribution of Blood Groups in Ryukyus* (AJPA, Philadelphia). He also studied Thai society.

Embu. "Sword dance," performed at the beginning of every Bugaku performance.

Embu-kan. Clan school *(hankō)* founded in Kagoshima in 1773 to teach medicine.

• **Embu-kō.** Clan school *(hankō)* founded in Yonezawa in 1897 to teach medicine.

Embun. Era during the reign of Emperor Go-Kōgon of the dynasty of the North (Hokuchō): Mar. 1356–Mar. 1360. *See* NENGŌ.

Emma-ten. In the Buddhist pantheon, the Japanization of the Sanskrit name of the god of Hell and the first mortal man, Yama. Japanese images of him, inspired by Chinese ones, portray him as a king and a judge of Hell, assisted by a sort of "secretary," Chitragupta (*Jap.:* Gushō-jin, Taizan-ō, Taizan-fukun), who takes note of human facts; sometimes a female assistant *(kaguhana);* and eight other "kings" of Hell charged with judging humans after they die and having them reborn in one of the "ten destinies" *(gati; Jap.: rokudō).* Chin.: Yanluo Wang. Also called Emma-ō, Enra-ō, Emma Dai-ō.

Emmei. "He Who Prolongs Life." Nickname for Jizō Bosatsu and for one of the 33 forms (Sanjūsan Ōgeshin) of Kannon Bosatsu as "the prolonger of life," portrayed as appearing from behind a rock. This name is also applied to Fugen Bosatsu. Also called Emmyō. *See* ENNEN.

Emon-fu. Guards of the gates to the imperial palace, part of the *e-fu,* a sort of police force instituted in 643 by Empress Kōgyoku. *See* E-FU.

Emosaku. Painter (Yamada Emosaku; *gō:* Nobukata, early eighteenth century), one of the first artists to imitate Western styles, which he learned from a European missionary in Nagasaki. Having converted to Christianity, he was taken prisoner during the Shimabara revolt and sent to Edo. He painted mainly Christian-inspired subjects.

Empa (En-pa). Group of sculptors of Buddhist images, disciples of Jōchō and Chōsei of the Sanjō *(bussho)* school in Kyoto, active mainly during the Heian and Kamakura periods. Sculptors often added the suffix *-en* to their names. Myōen (d. 1199) was one of the last sculptors of this school. *See also* BUSSHO, IM-PA, KEI-HA.

Emperors. The emperors of Japan, designated by the title Tennō since the sixth or seventh century, truly ruled until the Heian period, but starting in the eleventh century, real government was in the hands of the regents *(kampaku)* of the Fujiwara family. With establishment of the Kamakura *bakufu* in 1185, power passed into the hands of the shogun and, apart from a few interruptions (the Kemmu Restoration), remained with the Kamakura, then the Muromachi, shogun. From 1574 to 1603, Japan was dominated by three "military dictators," Oda Nobunaga, Toyotomi Hideyoshi, and Tokugawa Ieyasu. When the latter was appointed shogun by the emperor in 1603, power passed into the hands of the Tokugawa shogunal line. It was not until 1868 that Emperor Mutsuhito (Meiji Tennō) took power of the government once again. But the emperors who succeeded him did not have his authority and became puppets of the military. On January 1, 1946, Emperor Hirohito (Shōwa Tennō), bowing to pressure from the American occupying force, officially declared that he was not really of divine ancestry, as his predecessors had always proclaimed, claiming to be descended from the *kami* Amaterasu-Ōmikami and the first (mythical) emperor, Jimmu Tennō. Thereafter, the emperor played the role of figurehead and adviser. In principle, until 1945, the "imperial system" (Tennōsei) consisted of an absolute monarchy by divine right, in which emperors succeeded each other in direct lineage (although there have been exceptions). In fact, it is not absolutely certain that all belonged to the same family. The emperor was the spiritual leader of the nation and the supreme Shinto priest. In 1945, this system was replaced by the "system of the imperial symbol" (Shōchō Tennōsei), according to which the emperor remains the symbol of the nation as both the Shinto leader and a constitutional monarch. His status is clearly indicated in the eight articles of the first chapter of the 1947 Constitution, which does not recognize his title as head of state but considers him simply a symbol. He enjoys all of the prerogatives available to Japanese nationals, and in addition, the reigning emperor cannot be taken to court. His "household" can neither accept nor offer gifts without the approval of the Diet (Kokka Gijidō). All imperial properties belong to the state. The emperor is, however, the guarantor of the country's integrity and unity, and he plays a representative role in all national events. *See* MIYATSUKO, TENNŌ (list of emperors).

Empo. Era during the reign of Emperor Higashiyama: Sept. 1673–Sept. 1680. *See* NENGō.

Empon. "One-yen books," published in Tokyo in the 1920s to encourage Japanese people to read more. These books of literature were sometimes more than 500 pages long and sold for one yen, which made them widely affordable. Many publishers launched similar series of books, which were very successful, but they quickly saturated the market. They stopped being published at the beginning of the 1930s.

Emura Sensei. Physician and poet (Emura Munetomo, 1565–1664) who preached temperance. His moralizing maxims and poems were collected by his friend Itō Tan'an in *Rōjin-zatsuwa*.

Enamels (shippō). Literally, "seven jewels." The oldest enameled metals found in Japan date from the Asuka period and were found in Kengoshi's *kofun*. They were enamels representing floral motifs, cast simply in a metal form. They no doubt came from Korea, where the technique seems to have already been in use. A mirror of the Shōsō-in treasure also has an enameled back, but it is in cloisonné style with gold and silver wires. Champlevé enamels decorating the gates of the Byōdō-in temple in Uji date from about 1053. It was not until the end of the fifteenth century, however, that enamels of Chinese provenance were found in Japan on vases. Sō-ami imitated them for his decorations of the Ginkaku-ji. For the shogun, a few objects (bowls, various stands) were enameled. The cloisonné technique dominated; starting with the Edo period, it was widely used in architectural decoration and to ornament objects such as writing implements, sword ornaments, and *tsuba*. By about 1634, enameled objects were no longer being imported from China, and Japanese artisans made them for the Nagoya castle and the Tōshōgū shrine in Nikkō. The most famous enameler was Hirata Dōnin (Hikoshirō, 1591–1646). One of his emulators, Kachō, enameled the fusuma handles *(hikite)* of the Katsura garden pavilions in Kyoto. Japanese enameling reached its peak in the late seventeenth and early eighteenth centuries, and descriptions of the time mention most of the Hirata family, including Hirata Narikado (1684–1757), as enamel artists. The decorations imitated the style of the Kanō painting school. In the mid-nineteenth century, the cloisonné method was revived by Kaji Tsunekichi (1803–83), who updated the techniques by studying European methods, but it was really the German artist Gottfried Wagener (or Wagner) who brought Japanese enamels back to high esteem about 1875. Most production from the workshops of Kyoto, Nagoya, and Tokyo was exported. Some netsuke were enameled. In 1880, Namikawa Sōsuke (1847–1910) inaugurated a new technique in Tokyo in which colors were not separated by "cloisons" *(musen shippō),* allowing for subtle color gradations, while other artists, such as Namikawa Yasuyuki (1845–1927), continued the traditional cloisonnée method in Kyoto. Today, some artists still practice the craft of enameling, using mainly the technique without cloisons, to decorate modern objects.

E-nashi-ji. "Pear-skinned" lacquered ornaments in which gold or silver beads of various sizes are sometimes used as a background for *maki-e* lacquers. Also called *nashi-ji.*

Enchi Fumiko. Writer (Ueda Fumi, Enchi Fumi, 1905–86), born in Tokyo, daughter of the scholar Ueda Mannen. In 1930, she married Enchi Yoshimatsu and began to write plays, such as *Banchun sōya* (A Rowdy Night in Late Spring), and novellas; she began writing novels after the Second World War. She twice received the prize for women writers, in 1954 for *Himoji tsukihi* (Days of Famine) and in 1965 for *Namimiko monogatari* (The Tale of Namimiko). She also won the Noma Prize for her novel *Onnazaka* (The Waiting Years, 1949–57) in 1978. She wrote more than 30 novels, 300 novellas, and 20 plays, and translated the *Genji monogatari* into modern Japanese in 1972–73. Most of her works deal with female psychology and sexuality. She was elected a member of the Arts Academy and was an important figure in contemporary Japanese literature.

Enchin. Buddhist monk (Onjin, ca. 814–91) of the Tendai sect, a descendant of Emperor Kaikō, born in the province of Sanuki (Kagawa prefecture). He entered religious life at the Enryaku-ji monastery on

Mt. Hiei, and traveled in China from 853 to 858. When he returned, he founded the Onjō-ji (Miidera) temple in Ōmi (Shiga prefecture) and spread Esoteric Buddhist beliefs based on the *Mahāvairochana-sūtra (Jap.: Dainichi-kyō),* creating the Ji-mon branch of the Tendai. He received from the court the titles of Hōkyo, Hōgan, and Ōshō. He wrote two treatises on the *Dainichi-kyō,* plus *Dengyō-daishi ryakuden* (a biography of Dengyō Daishi), *Sannōin Zaitoki,* and *Hokkeshūronki. Posthumous name:* Chishō Daishi. *See* TENDAI-SHŪ.

Enchō. Era during the reign of Emperor Daigo: Apr. 923–Apr. 931. *See* NENGŌ.
• Buddhist monk of the Tendai sect, disciple of Saichō. *Posthumous name:* Jakkō Daishi.
→ *See* SAN'TŪTEI ENCHŌ.

Enden. "Saltworks." The first seaside saltworks were created during the Nara period (710–94), and until recently they were the only source of salt available in Japan. There were various methods of extracting salt, among them boiling seawater *(sudaki)* to complete evaporation, sprinkling seaweed with water and burning it, letting seawater evaporate in slate reservoirs *(agehama),* and mixing seawater with sand.

Endō Shūsaku. Writer, born in 1923 in Tokyo. He spent his childhood in Dalian in Manchuria; when he returned to Kobe in 1934, he had himself baptized Catholic at his mother's request. He entered Keio University in Tokyo and studied French literature; in 1950, he went to Lyon, France, where he fell in love with Catholic literature. When he returned to Japan in 1953, he began a career as a novelist. One of his first novels, *Shiroi hito* (The White Man), won the Akutagawa Prize in 1955. All his work thereafter was dedicated to the spiritual conflict between his Catholicism and Japanese beliefs. He published *Kiiroi hito* (The Yellow Man, 1955), *Umi to dokuyaku* (The Sea and Poison, 1958), *Obakasan* (An Admirable Idiot, 1959), *Watashi ga suteta onna* (The Woman I Left, 1964), *Ryūgaku* (Studies Abroad, 1965), *Chinmoku* (Silence, 1966), *Iesu no shōgai* (The Life of Jesus, 1973), *Shikai no hotori* (Beside the Dead Sea, 1973), *Memamu-gawa no Nihon-jin* (The Japanese Man on the Shores of the River Menam, 1973), *Dokkoisho* (Oof!), *Kuchibue wo fukutoki* (Whistling to Myself), *Samurai* (1980), and *Fukai-kawa* (Deep River, 1993). Most of his novels have been translated into both

English and French, and a number have been made into movies.

En'en. Buddhist monk (tenth–eleventh century), creator of the garden at Fujiwara no Yorimichi's villa and well-known designer of rock gardens.

Energy. Japan has few coal mines (and the coal is of poor quality), so it must import vast quantities. It supplements this energy with oil (which it also imports), hydroelectric power (dams), and, more recently, nuclear plants, which have enabled it to become energy self-sufficient. In spite of this, it depends on imports for other sources of energy, both for industry and for domestic consumption (planes, automobiles, etc.). *See* JAPAN *(statistics)*.
→ *See* HARA, KI.

Engaku. Japanese transcription of the Sanskrit *pratyeka-buddha,* the eighth Buddhist rank, which is just below that of a fully awakened buddha. A character who comes to Earth only between two successive buddhas, an *engaku* is a "self-existent" buddha who has attained enlightenment on his own and only for himself. *Chin.*: Yuanjue.

• **Engaku-ji.** Zen temple founded in 1282 in Kamakura by Hōjō Tokimune to be the seat of the Rinzai sect, directed by the Chinese master Wuxue Zuyuan (*Jap.*: Mugaku Sogen), who had been invited to Japan in 1280. In 1386, it was named the second temple of the Gozan (five great Zen monasteries) of Kamakura. It was destroyed several times by war and fire—in 1400, in 1563—and by the 1923 earthquake, and each time it was rebuilt. It has a *shariden* (reliquary) in the Kara-yō style dating from 1285, and a bell dating from 1301. Also called Enkaku-ji.

Engen. Era during the reign of Emperor Go-Daigo: Feb. 1336–Apr. 1340. *See* NENGŌ.

Engetsu. Zen Buddhist monk (Chūgan, 1300–75), born in Kamakura. He lived in China from 1325 to 1332 and studied the Chan doctrines. He was a talented Chinese-language poet. His poems, collected in the *Tōkai ichiō-shū,* are among the most remarkable of those produced by the *gozan-bungaku* (culture of the five great Zen monasteries) of the Kamakura and Muromachi periods.

Engi. Era during the reign of Emperor Daigo: July 901–Apr. 923. *See* NENGŌ.

• *Engi kyaku-shiki.* Ten-volume collection of laws plus two supplements written between 690 and 907 by Tachibana no Kiyozume, Fujiwara no Hisatada, and several other scholars. *See* RITSURYŌ KYAKU-SHIKI.

• *Engi-shiki.* "Procedures of the Engi Era." Collection of 50 legal texts on all Shinto ceremonies and many other customs, compiled by Fujiwara no Tokihira (until 909) and his brother Fujiwara no Tadahira (until 927), which contained a number of *norito.* It is one of the Shinto sacred writings, with the *Kojiki* and the *Nihon shoki,* and one of the most important documents concerning customs, practices, foods, medicines, and other aspects of the Nara and Heian periods. *See* MASTUDAIRA NARITAKE.

• **Engi tenryaku no chi.** "Reigns of the Engi and Tenryaku eras," expression referring to the reigns of emperors Daigo and Murakami, considered by many historians a sort of "golden age" in the political and cultural sectors.

• **Engi-tsūhō.** *See* KŌCHŌ-JŪNISEN.

Engi. In Buddhism, the thesis that everything exists only thanks to the interaction of causes and conditions. Comprehending this is, in the Buddha's own words, attaining the very essence of awakening *(Skt.: bodhi).* It is the equivalent of the Sanskrit *pratītya-samutpāda* (lit., "conditioned/interdependent arising").
• Book or *emakimono* telling about the origin of a fact or an event, or about the foundation of a temple or shrine.

Engyō. Buddhist monk (799–852) of the Shingon sect, born in Kyoto. He went to China in 838–39; when he returned to Japan, he translated Chinese Buddhist texts.

En'i. Painter (thirteenth century) of the Yamato-e school. He painted, or helped to paint, the *Ippen Shōnin Eden Emakimono* in 1299.

Enichi. Buddhist monk (680–748) who lived in China for 15 years and brought back to Japan the Chinese medical techniques in use in the Sui and Tang dynasties.
• Japanese name of a Chinese Chan Buddhist monk (Huili, 1272–1340), invited to Japan by the Kamakura *bakufu* in 1309. He taught Zen in the temples of Kamakura, then went to Kyoto upon the

invitation of Emperor Go-Daigo. He died in Kamakura.

Enjaku. Buddhist monk (*gō:* Kōraku-ji, fourteenth century) and painter of religious subjects for the Jōdo Shin sect. He made portraits of some of the sect's patriarchs in 1351. He may have been the same painter as Enshun, who used the same *gō,* which shows that he belonged to the Kōraku-ji temple in Shiozaki (Naganoken); Enjaku, however, seems to have worked in Kyoto.

Enjitsu. Buddhist monk (thirteenth century) of the Shingon sect, who was named *bettō* of the Kōfuku-ji temple in Nara.

Enjō. Buddhist monk (1236–82) of the Shingon sect, seventh son of Emperor Go-Saga Tennō. He received the title Hōshinnō.

• **Enjō-ji.** Buddhist temple located about 14 km north of Nara, belonging to the Shingon sect, founded in the eighth century. It has a *rōmon* from 1466/68, a *kasugadō* from the thirteenth century renovated in 1464, and a magnificent statue of Dainichi Nyorai sculpted by Unkei. Also called Enshō-ji.

Enju Kunimura. Sword blacksmith (fourteenth century), founder of a school bearing his name. He was the son of Enju Hiromura of Yamashiro. His brothers, Enju Kuniyoshi and Enju Kunitoki, were also blacksmiths whose sword blades became well known. Enju's and his brothers' disciples belonged to his school, including Kuniyasu, Kuninobu, and Kunisuke, all of whom worked in the Kikuchi district of the province of Higo in the late Kamakura and early Muromachi periods.

Enkai. Traditional ceremonial meal taking place in a room on a floor covered with tatami, especially at the New Year *(shinnenkai)* and the end of the year *(bōnenkai,* "forgetting the past year"). But *enkai* may also be served to celebrate other events.

Enkan. Buddhist monk (Jii Oshō, 1281–1356) of the Tendai sect who practiced the *nembutsu* ("Namu Amida Butsu"). He took the side of Emperor Go-Daigo Tennō and was exiled to the province of Mutsu in 1333. Rehabilitated, he returned to Kyoto, where he died.

Enkei. Era during the reign of Emperor Hanazono: Oct. 1308–Apr. 1311. *See* NENGŌ.
→ *See* KYŌSHO.

Enkiri-dera. "Temple of Divorce," popular name for the Tōkei-ji temple in Kamakura, built in the thirteenth century by Mino no Tsubone, an aunt of Minamoto Yoritomo. In 1284, Kakuzan-zenni, the wife of Hōjō Tokimune, made it a refuge for mistreated or unhappily married women. Emperor Go-Uda gave it the equivalent of the freedom of a city and provided it with official guards; it was then sometimes called Matsugaoka. Every woman who entered was sheltered from the pursuits of a too-possessive husband; after spending three years as a nun, she was automatically divorced. Later, this period was reduced to two years. The temple was reserved for Buddhist nuns until 1868. It houses, among other valuable cult objects, a wooden statue portraying Suigetsu Kannon that dates from the fourteenth century. *See* DIVORCE.

Enkō Kannon. One of the 33 forms (Sanjūsan Ōgeshin) of Kannon Bosatsu (*Skt.:* Avalokiteshvara), portrayed in Japan sitting on a rainbow or surrounded by rays of light.

Enkū. Traveling Buddhist monk and sculptor (ca. 1632–95), born in the province of Mino (Gifu prefecture), Yamabushi of the Tendai sect. In his youth he expressed the wish to sculpt 120,000 Buddhist images in wood, since his father was a carpenter. He sculpted a great number with an ax (of which more than 7,000 survive) for peasants and the faithful of the Tendai sect to whom he preached. His crude pieces, sometimes left roughhewn so that each cut of the ax *(nata)* can be seen, were very quickly executed in various types of wood and show an original talent that was not appreciated until after the Second World War. They are found mainly in the temples in the prefectures of Aichi, Gifu, Saitama, and Tochigi. He also made a self-portrait that is housed in the Shimmei-ji temple in Seki. He was buried in the Miroku-ji temple in Seki (Gifu prefecture).

Enkyō. Era during the reign of Emperor Sakuramachi: Feb. 1744–July 1747. *See* NENGŌ.
→ *See* KAGAMI.

Enkyō-ji. Buddhist temple of the Tendai sect, founded in 988 near the city of Himeji. It is one of the Thirty-Three Temples of the Western Pilgrimage (*see* SANJŪSAN-SHO). Although it was destroyed several times by fire (in the fourteenth century, in 1898, in 1921), a pagoda from 1184, a fourteenth-century *daikōdō* and *shōro,* and a sixteenth-century *kongōdō* have survived.

Enkyoku. "Banquet songs." Songs and sung poems composed from the thirteenth to the fifteenth century for the pleasure parties of warriors, monks, and nobles. The songs were collected in a number of anthologies: *Enkyoku-shū* (before 1296), *Enkyoku-shō, Shinkyoku-shō,* and others. The Buddhist monk Myōkū (thirteenth century) was one of the main composers of these songs, which were inspired by history, legends, and classical literature and were often accompanied by a straight flute *(shakuhachi).* Also called *engyoku, sōga, eikyoku.*

Enkyū. Era during the reign of Emperor Go-Sanjō: Apr. 1069–Aug. 1074. *See* NENGŌ.

Ennen. "Long life." A group of plays, songs, and dances performed in public at the great Buddhist monasteries to mark the end of the long ceremonies of reading sutras *(Jap.: kyō).* Started in the Heian period, these shows expanded greatly during the Muromachi period. Parts of them were probably at the origin of Noh theater, notably the *kaiko* (invocation), *tōben* (sometimes humorous dialogue), *furyū* (play in costumes with props), and *renji* (type of chanted poem). These shows seem to have been inspired by Bugaku, Dengaku, and Sarugaku, and some Kagura. At the beginning, there were no fixed rules or specialized artists; the monks themselves were the performers. This type of entertainment was very popular until the end of the Muromachi period, but was tailored to the aristocracy during the Edo period and performed only during major warriors' visits to major temples. *See* EMMEI, FURYŪ, ITOYORI, MŌTSU-JI.

Ennichi. "Day of omens." A set day each month dedicated to worship of a particular Buddhist god. Worshipers who attend a ceremony performed on these days are ensured of acquiring righteousness. This custom originated in China. Even today, during holidays, temples are invaded by crowds who come to enjoy the outdoor shows and, incidentally, to pray at the temple.

Ennin. Buddhist monk (Mibu, 784–864) of the Tendai sect at the Enryaku-ji of Mt. Hiei, who went to China with a delegation in 837 and lived there for seven years. He was in Chang'an from 840 to 845 and visited most Buddhist sacred sites in China, meeting famous religious masters. When he returned to Japan, he wrote, in Chinese, a work on his experiences, the *Nittō guhō junrai koki,* in four scrolls *(makimono).* He then established the practice of *nembutsu* ("Namu Amida Butsu"), which he

had learned on Mt. Wutai in China, thus complementing the esoteric teachings of Saichō. He was appointed leader of the Enryaku-ji when he was 61. *Posthumous name:* Jikaku Daishi.

En no Gyōja. Buddhist monk and semi-legendary sorcerer (En no Ozuno, late seventh century), hermit on Mt. Katsuragi (Nara prefecture), who practiced a peculiar esoteric cult with shamanic aspects (Sangaku Shinkō). He is said to have been exiled to the island of Oshima in 699 due to a false accusation launched against him by a man jealous of his magical powers. Many legends formed over his claimed powers, and he is considered the founding father of the Shugendō and the orders of Yamabushi. Also called En no Shōkaku, Shimpen Dai Bosatsu (Great Miraculous Bodhisattva).

Ennō-ji. Buddhist temple in Kamakura, founded in 1250. It houses a famous fourteenth-century statue of Emma-ō. Also known as Arai-Emmadō.

Ennosuke. Family of Kabuki actors. Ennosuke III (b. 1940) updated the traditional style of the Kabuki performance, transforming it into a sort of opera mixing European characters and Japanese tradition.

En'ō. Era during the reign of Emperor Shijō: Feb. 1239–July 1240. *See* NENGŌ.

Enoki Misako. Pharmacist (b. 1946) and feminist militant. In 1976, she launched Josei Fukko, a sort of religion aiming for a "female renewal," and founded Chupiren, a women's emancipation movement. When she was defeated in the elections, she retired from political life.

Enomoto Ken'ichi. Actor and singer (Enoken, 1904–70), born in Tokyo. He founded a theater company, the Enoken Troupe, in 1931, and played in a great number of movie musicals directed by his partner, Yamamoto Kajirō, while directing European plays by Brecht *(Fourpenny Opera),* Jules Romain *(Knock),* Molière *(The Misanthrope),* and Molnar *(Liliom).* He also appeared in the first Japanese television series, *Mito Kōmon.* After the Second World War, he was a promoter of jazz and new music such as boogie-woogie and mambo.

Enomoto Kikaku. *See* KIKAKU.

Enomoto Seifujo. Buddhist nun (1732–1814) and famous haiku poet.

Enomoto Takeaki. Admiral and statesman (Enomoto Buyō, 1836–1908) born in Edo, serving the Edo shogunate, then the Meiji. From 1860 to 1866, he went to the Netherlands to study maritime technology, having studied Western sciences *(rangaku)* in Nagasaki in 1853. During the Boshin Civil War, in 1868, he escaped from Edo and rejoined Hakodate with his squadron; in January 1869, he proclaimed the "Independent Republic of Ezo." But, pressed by imperial troops, he was forced to surrender on June 27 of that year. He was sentenced to three years in prison, then granted amnesty in 1872 and appointed secretary-general for the settlement of Hokkaido. In 1874, now a vice-admiral, he was sent to Russia as a plenipotentiary minister to try to resolve the problem of the island of Sakhalin *(Jap.: Karafutō)*. He signed the Treaty of St. Petersburg (1875), in which Japan ceded Sakhalin to Russia in exchange for the Kuril Islands *(Jap.: Chishima Rettō)*. After serving as minister of the navy in 1880 and ambassador to China in 1882, he assumed a number of ministerial portfolios: education, communications, foreign affairs, agriculture, and commerce. He was raised to the peerage and appointed a member of the emperor's Privy Council in 1890. In 1897, in protest against the incidents in the Ashio mines *(see* ASHIO DŌZAN KŌDOKU JIKEN), he resigned from the government and retired from public affairs.

Enoshima. Small island *(area:* 0.2 km²) in the Bay of Sagami, 7 km southwest of Kamakura, facing the village of Katase, linked by a causeway and two bridges. Dedicated to Benten (Benzaiten) since the medieval period, it is famous for its small shrine dedicated to her and for its large natural cave in which, according to legend, she slew a one-eyed dragon. In 1182, Minamoto no Toritomo had a statue of Benten erected there and prayed to her to help him pacify the northern regions. The island also has a Buddhist temple, the Shōjōkō-ji, founded in 1325 and recently renovated. This small, mountainous isle is a favorite tourist site for residents of Tokyo and Kamakura. Its botanical garden, created in 1874 by Samuel Cockling, a British merchant, was renovated in 1949 and planted with tropical vegetation.

• *Enoshima.* Title of a Noh play.

Enryaku. Era during the reign of Emperor Kammu: Aug. 782–May 806. *See* NENGŌ.

• **Enryaku-ji.** Buddhist temple and monastery on Mt. Hiei northeast of Kyoto, founded by Saichō in 788 to protect the imperial palace from the evil influences that, according to tradition, came from the northeast. The temple was originally called Hieisan-ji and Ichijō Shikan'in, and took its final name only via an edict by Emperor Saga Tennō in 823. It rapidly became the center of Esoteric Buddhism in Japan and the seat of the Tendai sect established by Saichō when he returned from China in 805, and it developed considerably under the patronage of emperors. It maintained an army of monks *(sōhei)* who sometimes "descended upon" Kyoto to impose the will of the monastery leaders on the court. Because this complex occupied an important strategic position commanding the entrance to Kyoto from the provinces of Ōmi and Echizen and its monks had forged an alliance with powerful provincial leaders, Oda Nobunaga attacked it in 1571, slew 3,000 armed monks, and set the buildings on fire. The buildings were reconstructed under Toyotomi Hideyoshi and Tokugawa Ieyasu, but the monastery never regained its previous power. The current buildings are divided into three groups according to their location: Tōtō (of the west), Saitō (of the east), and Yokawa. The Tōtō is the oldest: the *sōrintō,* dating from 820, was renovated in the sixteenth century; the *kompon-chūdō* (a National Treasure) was built in 1642; the *daikōdō* was destroyed by fire in 1956 and rebuilt in 1961. Among the other interesting structures are the *kaidan'in,* the Amida-dō, the Jōdo-in, the Hokke-dō, and the Jōgyō-dō, all from the seventeenth century and containing numerous works of art.

Enryo. "Reserve," behavior that society expects from all well-raised Japanese, consistent with keeping a reserved and almost humble attitude under all circumstances, never acting aggressive, and speaking and acting with discretion, especially in the presence of acquaintances (with the exceptions of close friends and foreigners). *See* AMAE.

Ensei. Buddhist monk (d. 1134) of the Tendai sect and famous sculptor of Buddhist images. He received the titles Hokkyō and Hōin.

Enshin. Buddhist monk (eleventh century) and painter. None of his original work has survived, but his talent is known thanks to a copy of one of his paintings portraying Fudō Myō-ō, kept in the Daigo-ji temple in Kyoto. He may be the same painter as Enjin, another monk-painter of the same period.

→ *See* AKAMATSU NORIMURA, HŌGAI.

Entairyaku. Abbreviated title of the work *Nakazono Taishōkoku ryakki* (Journal of Great Minister Nakazono). Nakazono was the religious name of the author Tōin Kinkata (1291–1360), who was a minister and *dajō-daijin* in the Northern and Southern Courts (Nambokuchō) a number of times. The work originally comprised 120 scrolls, of which only one, dated 1311, has survived to the present day. *See* FUJIWARA NO KINKATA.

Entaku. Painter (Katō Moriyuki, 1643–1730) of the Kanō school, student of Kanō Tan'yu.

Entō. "Distant island." A sentence of exile to a distant island or province pronounced against major civil or religious notables fallen into disgrace or sentenced because of their illegal actions. Exiles who fled were sentenced to death. During the Edo period, defrocked monks, gamblers, assassins, and rapists were also exiled. The main islands of exile were Izu, Oki, and southern Kyushu. During the Heian period, people were exiled to the northern provinces and Kyushu (Dazaifu, among other towns). This custom disappeared during the Meiji era.

Entoku. Era during the reign of Emperor Go-Tsuchimikado: Aug. 1489–July 1492. *See* NENGŌ.

Entsuba Katsuzō. Sculptor (Katsuji), born in 1905 in the prefecture of Hiroshima. He was Sawa Weikō's student in Kyoto and had several exhibitions in Teiten. He was appointed a professor of sculpture at the Tama University of Fine Arts (Tama Bijutsu Daigaku) in 1947 and received the Nihon Geijutsu-in (Japan Art Academy) Prize in 1966. His wooden sculptures are usually of Buddhist inspiration, but he tends to plan the shapes so as to create a visual aesthetic that sometimes recalls that of the ancient Egyptians. In 1978, he sculpted the Ni-ō (two guardian deities) for the gate of the Hommon-jin temple in the Ikegami district of Tokyo.

En'ya Takasada. Warrior and statesman (d. 1341) who supported Emperor Go-Daigo, then shogun Ashikaga Takauji. He was apparently assassinated upon the orders of Kō no Moronao.

En'yū Tennō. Sixty-fourth emperor (Prince Morihira, 959<970–84>991), son of Murakami Tennō and successor to Reizei Tennō. He abdicated in favor of Kazan Tennō.

Enza. System of collective responsibility according to which the family of a criminal was sentenced at the same time as the criminal and faced the same punishment. It was applied, in case of rebellion or treason, starting with the promulgation of the Taihō Code in 701. During the Muromachi period, it was extended to most criminals. During the Edo period, however, it was applied to commoners only for very serious cases (murder of a family member or of a superior); among samurai, it was invoked for a great number of offenses. This practice, of Chinese origin, was abolished in 1882.

• Round, flat cushion of woven straw, placed on wood floors in houses and used as a seat. Use of the *enza* slowly disappeared, starting in the fifteenth century, as the use of tatami spread. *See* TATAMI, ZABUTON.

Enzan. Small town in the prefecture of Yamanashi (central Honshu) and former transit point on the Ōme-kaidō route. In the Erin-ji temple in this location are the tombs of Takida Shingen and Yanagisawa Yoshiyasu. Hot-spring resort. *Pop.* 27,000.
→ *See* GEN'YŪ.

• **Enzan-ryū.** Painting school founded by Maruyama Ōkyo and part of the Maryama-ryū.

Eras, Japanese. *See* NENGŌ.

Eri. Buddhist monk (852–935) of the Shingon sect, named *bettō* in 915 and *risshi* in 931. An architect and sculptor, he was involved in the erection of many buildings of worship and made repairs to the sculpture of the Shi-tennō of the Tōdai-ji in Nara in 907. He supervised construction of the pagoda of the Tō-ji in Kyoto in 920. He also painted many portraits of patriarchs of the Shingon sect. He was a student of Shōbō (832–909), another sculptor-monk of the Tō-ji monastery.

Erizeni. "Selection of coins." Of the great quantity of coins imported to Japan from China, many deteriorated due to fire or wear, so the custom was established to "select coins"—to evaluate them according to their condition and separate out the ones that were too damaged. This practice was detrimental to the circulation of coins, so it was forbidden a number of times, notably by the Muromachi government, but without obvious effect. It disappeared only at the beginning of the Edo period, when the Tokugawa established standardized currency for the entire country. *See* BITASEN, EIRAKU-TSŪHŌ, TSŪHŌ.

Eroticism. Neither the Japanese nor the Chinese subscribe to the same sexual taboos as do Westerners, so they have always considered erotic art a natural part of life and never made a mystery of the art of making love, called Shunga in poetry. Erotic books, prints (ukiyo-e), and paintings deal freely with these subjects, and "pleasure houses" have supplied an inexhaustible source of subject matter for both writers and artists. Although at one time the Edo shogunate tried to restrain what the Confucianist puritans considered an excess of licentiousness, the Japanese taste for eroticism (not for pornography) was always very strong. Even today, many *manga* (cartoons) deal with more or less erotic subject matter. Movies also use situations that Westerners might consider obscene but that do not shock the Japanese at all. *See* MANGA, PROSTITUTION, SHUNGA, UKIYO-E, YOSHIWARA.

Esaki Reona, Leonard (Leo). Physicist born in 1925 in Osaka. After studying at Tokyo University, he was hired as an engineer at Tokyo Tsūshin Kōgyō (later known as Sony) in 1956 and continued his research on electrical currents. In 1958, he invented the tunnel diode, known as the Esaki diode (transistor). In 1960, he went to IBM in the United States. He won the Nobel Prize for physics in 1973, and the Japanese government awarded him the Order of Culture (Bunka-shō) in 1974.

Eshin-ni. Buddhist nun (1182–ca. 1268), wife of Shinran. Her letters *(Eshin-ni shōsoku)* to her daughter, Kakushin-ni, provide information on Shinran's life. *See* SHINRAN SHŌNIN.

Eshin Sōzu. *See* GESHIN.

Eshi no sōshi. Colored *emakimono* on paper (790 × 30 cm) dating from the fourteenth century, describing the life and adventures of an impoverished painter. Imperial collection. Also called *Eshi-zōshi.*

Esperanto. This "universal language" began to be used in Japan about 1891, thanks to the efforts of biologist Oka Asakirō, and an Institute of Esperanto was founded in 1906. There are currently an estimated 10,000 Esperanto speakers in Japan.

Eta. "Impure." Low social class considered, since the thirteenth century at least, among the outcasts (although superior to the *hinin*), perhaps of foreign origin (China, Korea, and other countries); its members did work considered impure by Shinto and Buddhism. They were forced to be endogamous; by custom, they were not admitted into other families. Equality with other working classes was guaranteed to them in 1871 (when there were about 280,000 of them), and they were placed among the *heimin* and *shin-heimin.* The Meiji government used them in the lower ranks of the police. Some became wealthy, although they never gained respect from the other classes. *See* BURAKUMIN, HININ, SEMMIN.

Eta Funayama kofun. Tumulus *(kofun)* in Kumamoto prefecture, discovered and excavated in 1873. It contained many objects from the fifth century, including a sword blade engraved with the name of a sovereign, perhaps that of Yūryaku (Waka Takeru), although the characters are almost illegible. Bronze mirrors, earrings, and a golden crown were also uncovered in the stone sarcophagus, as were parts of horse harnesses and *sue*-type pottery.

Etajima. Small island situated at the entry to the Bay of Hiroshima, facing the port of Kure. Former headquarters of the Japanese Naval Academy, it was heavily bombarded at the end of the Second World War. *Pop.:* 18,000.

Etchū. Former province, now part of Toyama prefecture.

• **Etchū no Kami.** *See* MATSUDAIRA SADANOBU.

Ethnology. Most Japanese belong to the Mongoloid group, with skin color varying from ivory to brown; black or very dark brown hair, limp or straight; and eyes that are black at birth and sometimes very dark brown in adulthood. The upper eyelids have an epicanthic fold that is more or less pronounced. The average skull is mesocephalic with an index of about 80.2 mm. Cranial capacity varies from about 1,500 cc among men to more than 1,130 among women. At birth, 99% of babies have a blue birthmark (the "Mongolian blue spot") on the lower back, which is very pronounced at two years of age but gradually disappears by the age of 9–10 years. Average height varies quite widely depending on geographic origin, but is about 162 cm for men and 152 cm for women for people over 40 years of age. Since the end of the Second World War, children have benefited from better nutrition and have tended to grow taller than their parents, and student-aged individuals today may reach a height of more than 170 cm for men (with the exception of sumotori) and 160 cm for women.

During the Jōmon prehistoric period, various peoples arrived in Japan to fish and hunt, probably from Siberia and mainland Asia, but some people may also have come from Melanesia, as evidenced in certain "Malaysian" features among populations in southern Kyushu. They probably imported the practice of building houses on pilings and perhaps cultivation of taro. Shortly before the first century AD, it seems that there was a new influx of people from southern China, who imported rice cultivation. Then, in the third century, the arrival of other peoples from Korea and eastern Siberia considerably modified the physical characteristics of the Japanese. Similarly, in northern Honshu, there was much intermarriage between Japanese (themselves already a mix) and Ainu people. The Japanese people in its entirety is thus the result of a mixture of various peoples. However it is possible to distinguish at least three main ethnic types: "Malaysian" (small stature, dark skin) in southern Kyushu; Chinese (wide face, light skin, nose slightly flattened), mainly among rural populations; and "Altaic" (long face, nose sometimes aquiline and fine, pale skin) mostly among "aristocrats" and former samurai. There are many variations in these types, however, due to intermarriage.

Eto. Term used to describe the formulas defining the years according to the sixty-year cycle, *e* meaning "positive, older brother" and corresponding to yang, while *to* designates the years that are "negative, younger brother" and corresponding to yin. *See* CALENDAR, JIKKAN-JŪNISHI, JŪNI SHI, OMMYŌDŌ.

Etō Jun. Literary critic (Egashira Atsuo), born 1933 in Tokyo, and professor at the Tokyo Institute of Technology. He published many critical works on the writing of Natsume Sōseki and on literature in general, including *Natsume Sōseki-ron* (1955), *Sakka wa Kōdō Suru* (1959), *Kobayashi Hideo* (1962), and *Ichizoku Saikai* (1967–72). He lived in the United States for some time. In most of his writing, he shows little enthusiasm for post–Second World War Japanese intellectuals.

Etō Shimpei. Politician (1834–74) and low-ranked samurai of the Saga estate (Saga prefecture). He took part in the Boshin Civil War in 1868 and was named to a subordinate position in the Meiji government. He became minister of justice in 1872, then a councillor *(sangi)* in the Dajōkan. He sup-

ported Saigō Takamori's proposal to invade Korea, and was denounced by Iwakura Tomomi and Okubo Toshimichi, so he resigned in 1873 and returned to Saga, where he brought together discontent samurai in the Aikoku Kōtō (Public Party of Patriots). His views were not accepted by the government, so he and another rebel, Shima Yoshitaka (1822–74), rallied 3,000 samurai and instigated a revolt, attacking banks and government buildings in Saga. Defeated by the police, they fled by boat to Kōchi but were captured, convicted of rebellion, and executed.

Eulenburg, Friedrich Albert. Prussian diplomat (1815–81) who went to Japan in 1860 to sign a friendship and trade treaty with the Edo shogunate. When he returned to Germany, he published an interesting book on his experiences, *Ostasien 1860–1862* (East Asia, 1860–62).

Eun. Buddhist monk (798 or 800–869 or 871) of the Shingon sect, born in Kyoto. He was in China from 842 to 847 and brought back Amidist doctrines of the Jōdo sect. In 848, he founded the Anjō-ji temple in Kyoto and received the title Anjō-ji Sōzu.

Ezaki Glico. Manufacturer and distributor of all sorts of candies and sweets, founded by Ezaki Riichi in 1922. It has branches in Thailand and the United States (Glico Co.). Head office in Osaka.

Ezo. Name used until the end of the nineteenth century to designate the island of Hokkaido and its inhabitants, the Ainu. In the medieval period, it also designated all inhabitants of northwest Honshu, east of the Shinano River. The Ainu (or Ezo) were gradually pushed back to the island of Hokkaido. Some scholars dispute the theory that the Ezo were the ancestors of today's Ainu. Also called Ebisu, Emishi, Yezo. The region was called Ezo-chi and took the name Hokkaido only in 1869 (also called Watari-shima). *See* ABE NO HIRAFU, AINU, HOKKAIDO.

• **Ezo-kanryō.** Governor (or inspector) living in Tsugaru on the strait of the same name, whose function was to oversee Ezo (Ainu, Emishi) populations in northern Nonghu. This position was created in the Kamakura period to replace those of Chinjufu-shōgun and Akita-jo no Suke. It disappeared in 1333.

F. The syllable *hu* does not exist in Japanese, so it is replaced by the syllable *fu* in the kana syllabic series *ha, hi, fu, he, ho*. It is sometimes weakened (*see* NIGORI) to give the syllables *bu* and *pu*, especially in compound words. However, in some previous Japanese transcription systems, not the Hepburn system used here, the romanized syllable *hu* represents the sound *fu*. *See* GOJŪ-ON-ZU.

Fabian. Europeanized name of a Japanese Jesuit (Unguio Fabian, Fucan Fabian, Fukansai Habian, ca. 1565–after 1620), born in Kyoto. A novice in a Zen monastery, he converted to Christianity about 1583 and entered the Society of Jesus in 1586. He learned Latin and transcribed the *Heike monogatari* into Roman letters in 1592. He also translated *Aesop's Fables*. His book *Myōtei mondō* (Myōtei's Dialogues), written in 1605, was harshly criticized by Hayashi Razan. It seems that Fabian left the order in 1608. In 1618, he took part in the persecution of Christians at Nagasaki; two years later, he published a diatribe against Christianity, *Ha daiusu* (Deus Destroyed), which later served as a basis for refutation of that religion.

Fabric. The generic name *orimono* applies to all fabrics, while individual fabrics are named according to how they are woven, the fibers used, where they are made, and the type of dye applied to them. The oldest fabrics *(nuno, shizuri)* were woven from hemp *(asa)*, mulberry-bark fibers *(kōzō)*, and other local plants. Weaving was either simple *(atsuita)* or on the diagonal *(aya)*. Silk from China was used very early. Cotton appeared later, as did wool *(kamo*, part goat hair, part cotton). Certain specific fabrics, such as velvet *(birido, birōdo)*, were imitated in Japan in the seventeenth century. Sheep's-wool fabrics were adopted only in the late nineteenth century.

Silks included simple fabrics *(kaiki* or *gunnaori)*, brocades (such as *nishiki, kambata, ginran, kinran)*, satins *(donsu*, Ezo-*nishiki, rinzu, shusu*, etc.), gauzes *(kōhaku, ra, ro, sha)*, crepes *(chirimen)*, pongees *(tsumugi)*, taffetas *(kōhaku)*, and others *(seigō*, Isezaki-*meisen*, and others).

Cotton fabrics appeared in the mid-sixteenth century. In the category *momen* were a variety of fabrics, such as Satsume-*gasuri* (or Iyo-*gasuri)*, *tsumugi-momen, kurume-gasuri*, and others.
→ *See* BASHŌFU, CLOTHING, DYES, SŌ-HITTA.

Falconry. Hunting with falcons *(takagari)* seems to have been introduced to Japan from China about the fourth century, since images of falconers appear on certain *haniwa* (clay figures) and the *Kojiki* mentions such hunts. During the Heian period, the art of falconry was reserved for emperors and great nobles, but during the Kamakura period it became popular among the samurai, who created two schools of falconry, the Saion-ji and the Jimyō-in. During the Edo period, falconry was in great favor with the shogunate, and a special position, *takajō*, or "master falconer," was created in the government. Tokugawa Ieyasu was a passionate devotee of falconry. *See* KUDARA SAKE NO KIMI.

Family. The Japanese family is composed essentially of a husband, a wife, and their children. Theoretically, the husband is the head of the family, but his role has been so diminished that one could say he is a guest in his own home. His role is restricted to working to support his family, while his wife takes care of the children and everything concerning the household. Up to the Heian period, the woman usually lived with her parents, and her husband visited her there. During the Kamakura period, the husband was often a warrior, so the woman had the important task of taking care of the house *(yashiki)* during her husband's long absences. In peasant society, however, husband, wife, children, and often grandparents lived and worked together. Family arrangements were similar in merchant *(chōnin)* society in the Edo period. Thus, there were at least two types of husband-wife relations in Japan; in one, the wife was often the servant of her mother-in-law, and this sometimes led to marriage breakdown. There were different types of marital relationships depending on the social class: wives in samurai families had to respect etiquette very strictly, whereas those in working-class families had much more freedom and either worked for themselves or helped their husbands.

Currently, increasing numbers of couples are formed by affection and mutual interests, in the Western fashion, even though passion is still not considered important to marital happiness. In fact, romantic marriages are discouraged. Within Japanese families, even modern ones, emotional relationships run generationally, from grandparents to mother to children, while husband-wife relations are more practical. The husband's work is rarely discussed; in fact, husband and wife usually lead separate lives. In contrast, family feeling toward parents is very strong, reflecting the Confucian virtue of filial piety. *See* MARRIAGE.

Fane, Walter. English cavalry officer (1828–85) who served in the Punjab, India, and in China, and was sent to Japan in 1861, where he produced many drawings and sketches.

Fans. Fans, probably used in Japan since ancient times and certainly since the introduction of Buddhism, came to typify Japanese civilization, at least for Westerners. Their use is widespread in all classes of society, from the *shibu-uchiwa* used to stoke the embers in the kitchen (symbolic of the *kami* of poverty, Bimbō-gami), to the metal *gumpai-uchiwa* used by military leaders to direct their troops. Fans are used daily by Shinto priests, Buddhist monks, Noh actors, musicians, sumo referees, and every other social group. There are two types of fans: *uchiwa,* which do not fold, and *ōgi,* the folding fans. The oldest *uchiwa* were made of wood and sometimes had painted decorations. Later, they were made of lacquered leather; more recently, of paper stretched over fine blades of bamboo that came together at the base to form the handle. They were of various shapes, including round, oval, and square, and were often decorated by painters and calligraphers, especially during the Heian period.

Ōgi, used at first by men only, were originally made of small boards of wood tied together *(hiōgi)*. They then became lighter and were made of paper or fabric glued onto fine blades of wood or ivory. Some fans were so beautiful that they were unglued and used to decorate screens *(byōbu)*. *Ōgi* also inspired artists, who made paintings imitating their shape. And, like *uchiwa,* they were decorated with calligraphy of poems and Buddhist sutras. Fans were used by aristocrats to play games such as *tosenkyō* and *ōgi-nagashi*. Starting in the Edo period, they were often used for advertising. Even today, some restaurants and shops offer fans, either *uchiwa* or *ōgi,* marked with their name and address. Temples make a specialty of selling fan-shaped charms *(mamori)*; the Tōshōdai-ji in Nara, for example, sells *hōsen* engraved with Sanskrit characters. In 1701, the style of decorated fans had became so elaborate, with some worth a small fortune, that the shogunate promulgated an edict to forbid the manufacture and use of fans that were considered too luxurious. *See* GUMPAI-UCHIWA, GUNSEN, ŌGI, SHIBŪ-UCHIWA, UCHIWA.

Faulds, Henry. Scottish physician and missionary (1843–1930) who established a hospital in Tokyo in 1874 and a school for the blind, the Kummō-in, in 1880. When he examined the ancient pottery discovered by Edward S. Morse, he devised the theory that the fingerprints on them were different for each individual and thus could be used to identify these individuals; this, combined with the work of W. J. Herschell, led to the first use of fingerprints by the London police force, in 1901.

Fauna. Because of the extreme diversity in climate and altitude within the Japanese islands, the country's fauna is extremely varied. There are, however, two distinct regions, separated by the Watase line, which runs between the islands of Yaku and Tanegashima and the Amami Islands, forming an "eastern" zone to the southeast and a "paleo-arctic" zone comprising the rest of the islands. The latter zone is subdivided into the Manchurian and Siberian zones, separated by the Blackiston line, which runs along the Strait of Tsugaru. These zones, however, are theoretical, since animals do not respect them. Found mainly on Kyushu, Honshu, and Shikoku are the following mammals: *Macaca fuscata fuscata* (a type of monkey), *Vulpes vulpes japonica* (fox), *Nyctereutes procyonoides viver-*

rinus (raccoon dog, *tanuki*), *Ursus tibetanus japonicus* (bear), *Martes melampus meoamoys* (marten), *Pentalagus furnessi* (black hare), *Diplothrix legata* (long-haired rat), *Cervus nippon nippon* (Japanese deer), *Capricornis crispus* (antelope), and *Sus leucomystax* (boar). The main mammals on Hokkaido are *Ursus arctos yesoensis* (brown bear), *Martes zibellinobrachyura* (black marten), and *Mustela ermania Kanei* (Hokkaido skunk).

There are few snakes in Japan, except for a type of viper *(Agkistrodon blomhoffii)* and a few *Elaphe clomacophora*. The only truly dangerous snake is *Trimeresurus flavoridis (habu),* which is found in the southern islands, most frequently on Tokunoshima.

There are a great many kinds of birds, among which the most common are *Lalcitta lidthi* (emerald jay), *Phasianus versicolor* (pheasant), *Syrmaticus soemerringi scintillans* (golden pheasant), and on Hokkaido, *Tetrastes bonasia vicinitas* (Hokkaido pheasant); among the birds of prey are *Bibo blakistoni* (owl) and *Spilornis cheela perplexus* (Ryukyu serpent eagle), and others. *See also* CATS, DOGS, HORSES, TANUKI.

Fenellosa, Ernest Francisco. American sociologist (1853–1908) born in Massachusetts, who studied painting at the Boston Museum of Fine Arts in 1877. Invited to Japan by Edward S. Morse, he arrived in Tokyo in 1878 to teach philosophy at Tokyo University. He left his professorship in 1886 to devote himself to the evaluation of Japanese art and helped to found Tokyo Bijutsu Gakkō (Tokyo School of Fine Arts). After a study trip to Europe and the United States on behalf of the Japanese government, he directed the Eastern Studies department at the Boston Museum of Fine Arts, then returned to Japan in 1897. In 1900, he returned to the United States to teach at Columbia University. He was a pioneer in the study of Japanese art, and his many books offered Westerners a better understanding and appreciation of Japanese art: *The Masters of Ukiyoe* (1896), *Epochs of Chinese and Japanese Art* (1912), *Certain Noble Plays of Japan* (1916), and others, most of which were published after his death. *Japanese name:* Fenōrosa.

Ferreira, Cristoforo. Portuguese Jesuit who went to Japan in 1610 as the head of his order, succeeding Father de Couros. Arrested in 1633 in Nagasaki and tortured, he became an apostate and was then used as an interpreter for the daimyo of Nagasaki. According to some sources, he invented the *fumi-e.*

At the end of his life, however, he returned to Christianity and died a martyr about 1653.

Fesca, Max. German agricultural engineer (1846–1917), invited by the Japanese government to teach modern agricultural methods in 1882. He was instrumental in the development of scientific agriculture and cattle breeding. When he returned to Berlin, he became a professor at the Agricultural College.

Festivals. Japan draws its festival traditions from rural folklore and local beliefs. Customs and festivals are intimately linked to change, often emphasizing the transitory nature of things (the Buddhist notion of impermanence), and are more traditions than strict observances. Tied above all to the passage of time, they follow the 24 "seasons" *(jūnishisetsu)* and the equinoxes *(setsubun,* change of season), influencing clothing, food, and ritual. Festivals reflect the two sides of life—the extraordinary *(hare),* which determines the festival days *(harebi),* and daily life *(ke)*—without making any clear distinctions between them. Festivals are related to annual events *(nenchū-gyōji)* or to religious practice *(matsuri),* and often belong to both categories. Some festivals may or may not be linked to the types just mentioned, such as trade fairs *(ichi),* which generally take place on fixed dates, and the recently created "national festivals," which are also called *matsuri* but which are more often related to the *nenchū-gyōji* and have no religious associations. The current trend is to refer to every festival as a *matsuri.* In rural areas, the *matsuri* were a way of affirming the community's cohesiveness and were based on activities related to agriculture and worship of the Shinto *kami.* Buddhism simply added festivals to the ones that already existed. Groups of young people or associations of parishioners *(ujiko)* were charged with organizing them. Depending on the historical period and the location, festivals might also include some customs from other beliefs, such as the Way of Yin and Yang (*see* OMMYŌDŌ), Taoism, or Confucianism. They are thus extremely numerous. Most festivals are local, whereas others are shared to a greater or lesser extent by all Japanese, but they all give rise to celebrations, songs, dances, parades, and processions in period costume.

• **January.** This is Shōgatsu, the "auspicious month"; the entrances of houses are decorated with pine branches *(kadomatsu).* Meals include *mochi,* which symbolizes prosperity for the coming year. On New Year's Eve, people visit shrines or temples *(hatsu-mōde)*. On New Year's Day (a holiday), children play traditional games such as *hana-garuta* cards and *hanetsuki* (shuttlecock and battledore). In some villages, young people perform the lion dance *(shishi-mai)*. Traditionally, small gifts are offered to children *(otoshidama)*, who make good-luck calligraphy *(kakizome)*. Shinto shrines present Kagura shows and distribute charms to visitors:

—5th, the sacred cords *(shimenawa)* linking the two rocks of Futami ga Ura are replaced.

—6th, the great parade of firefighters *(dezome-shiki)* in Tokyo. Also, the beginning of the training season for various arts and sports, accompanied by customs such as ice baths *(kan-mairi)*.

—7th, the "day of humanity" *(jinjitsu):* a special soup, with seven types of herbs *(nanakusa),* is eaten.

—10th, in Osaka, the great festival of Ebisu called Tōka Ebisu: parades, processions of geisha.

—12th, Buddhist ceremony of making cutouts of carp in the Hō-on-ji temple in Kyoto.

—15th, start of the first sumo tournaments in Tokyo. At the imperial palace, appropriate poems are read. In Nara, herbs are burned on Wakayama. Throughout Japan, Coming of Age Day (Seijin no Hi) during which young people who have turned 20 are honored.

—16th, Akita's Hakata Matsuri. Beginning of annual vacation for all apprentices.

—17th, festival of Bonten, one of the Seven Gods of Good Fortune (Shichifukujin).

—21st, birthday of Kōbō Daishi, celebrated in many Buddhist temples *(hatsu-daishi)*.

—26th, annual festival of Tenrikyō, near Nara.

• **February**

—3rd and 4th, Setsubun, festival of the change of seasons *(o-harai)* throughout Japan. In Nara, *mandō-e,* "festival of lanterns," at Kasuga Shrine.

—4th, first "day of the horse," *matsuri* of shrines dedicated to Inari *(hatsu-uma)*. In Tokyo, pilgrimage to the tombs of the "47 *rōnin*" (*see* AKŌ-GISHI) at Sengaku-ji temple.

—5th and 6th, ice festival at Sapporo.

—8th, festival of needles *(hari-kuyō)*.

—10th, tumultuous rejoicing in many Shinto shrines.

—Until 1945, the 11th was a national festival: the anniversary of the (mythical) founding of the empire of Japan and of the proclamation of the Constitution of 1889. Called Kenkoku Kinen no Hi.

—12th, *omizutori* purification ceremony at Tōdai-ji in Nara (*see also* March 12).

—25th, ceremonies in memory of Sugawara no Michizane in all shrines dedicated to Tenjin. In Tōhoku, the Kamakura Festival.

• **March**

—3rd, Girls' Festival (Hina Matsuri or Joshi no Sekku). Dolls of the imperial court are exhibited.

—12th, the new *omizutori* ceremony at the Nigatsudo, Tōdai-ji.

—13th, Kasuga Matsuri in Nara: major processions, Kagura dances.

—15th, anniversary of the death of the Buddha. Beginning of sumo tournaments in Osaka.

—17th to 24th, vernal equinox: visits to tombs and ceremonies in memory of the deceased. Rice cakes (*mochi* and *ohagi*) are placed on the *butsudan* (Buddhist altar).

• **April**

—1st, beginning of "blossom viewing" season *(hanami)* for cherry trees *(sakura)*. Folk dances in Kyoto, Nara, Osaka.

—2nd and 3rd, designation of the Fukura parishoners *(ujiko)* at the Hachiman-gū Shrine.

—4th, beginning of the shell-gathering season on the beaches *(shiohigari)*.

—8th, birthday of Buddha. *See* TANJŌ-BUTSU.

—10th, start of "Women's Week," commemorating women's gaining the right to vote on April 10, 1945.

—11th, anniversary of the death of Shōtoku Taishi.

—13th, major festival in Kamakura in tribute to all local *kami*. Sannō Matsuri at the Hie Taisha shrine in Tokyo.

—13th to 15th, commemoration of the death of Hōnen at Zōjō-ji in Tokyo. Yayoi Matsuri in Nikkō. Sannō Matsuri of Takayama in Gifu (decorated carts). Festival of the *kami* on the island of Sado.

—21st to 25th, *matsuri* at Yasukuni Shrine in Tokyo to commemorate the war dead.

—21st to 30th, Kyōgen performances at Mibu temple in Kyoto.

• **May**

—1st, Labor Day.

—1st to 5th, major kite festival in Hamamatsu.

—2nd, Shōmu-sai festival, in memory of Emperor Shōmu.

—2nd and 3rd, village festival of the 88th day *(hachijūhachiya)* after Risshun, celebrating the beginning of sowing.

—3rd, national holiday, commemorates the day the Constitution of Japan became effective in 1947.

—5th, Children's Day (Kodomo no Hi, Tango no Sekku): paper or cloth carp streamers *(koinobori)* are flown to celebrate male children in the household.

—10th, beginning of Bird Protection Week.

—11th, beginning of fishing for *ayu* with cormorants at night, with torches, in Gifu.

—Second Sunday, Mother's Day.

—13th to 15th, festival of the Kanda district in Tokyo: parade of portable shrines *(mikoshi)*.

—14th, festival celebrating the opening of the port of Yokohama. Festival of godly vestments (Kami no Sai) at Ise Shrine. First summer sumo tournaments in Tokyo.

—15th, Aoi Matsuri of the two Kamo shrines in Kyoto: historically inspired carts and processions.

—16th to 18th, various festivals at the Asakusa Shrine in Tokyo. Festival at the Tōshōgū in Nikko with processions.

—17th, celebration in Shimoda of the arrival of Perry's "black boats" *(kurofune)*. Sanja Matsuri at the Asakusa Shrine in Tokyo: geisha dances.

—Third Sunday, Shūyū-sai (boat festival) at Saga, near Kyoto.

—19th, festival of Tōshōdai-ji in Nara.

—20th, commemoration of the birth of Shinran in all temples of the Jōdo Shin sect.

—24th to 26th, in Tsuruoka, festival of the founding of the Temmangū Shrine.

—28th, festival in all temples worshiping Fudō Myō-ō, such as Meguro in Tokyo.

• **June**

—1st and 2nd, performances of Noh plays starting at the Heian Shrine in Kyoto.

—5th and 6th, Agata Matsuri in Uji.

—6th, Ebara Matsuri in Tokyo, the fishers' festival.

—12th, beginning of the rainy season *(bai-u, tsuyu)*.

—14th, Shinto festival of transplanting the rice seedlings.

—15th, annual festival at Hie Shrine in Tokyo: lasts three days. Many Buddhist temples celebrate the birthday of Kōbō Daishi. In Nagasaki, there is a boat race called Peiron.

—15th to 17th, various festivals in honor of the imperial family (Tsukinami-sai) at Ise.

—20th, solemn cutting of the bamboo at the Kurama Shrine in Kyoto.

—21st, annual festival at Atsuta Shrine in Nagoya.

—21st and 22nd, summer solstice *(geshi)*.

—30th, great day of purification *(o-harai)* in all Shinto shrines.

• **July**

—1st, start of the season for climbing Mt. Fuji.

—1st to 15th, festival at Kushida Shrine in Kyoto.

—4th, great festival of the town of Nobeoka (Miyagi prefecture).

—7th, Tanabata Festival (the 5th in Akita).

—10th, great festival of the "46,000 days" at Sensō-ji temple in Asakusa (Tokyo).

—10th to 13th, "horse-taming" festival in Fukushima prefecture (Sōma Noma-oi Matsuri): horse races.

—13th to 15th, festival of souls (Urabon-e, Bon), Bon Odori dances.

—14th, festival of fans *(ōgi)* in Kumano: torchlit processions to the Nachi Waterfall.

—13th to 15th, festival at Yasukuni Shrine in Tokyo (Mitama Matsuri): Noh plays, fireworks.

—15th, beginning of summer vacation and the training season at the Kōdōkan in Tokyo. Music festival at Itsukushima Shrine in Miyajima. Annual festival of Osaka. Start of summer sumo tournaments in Nagoya.

—Third Saturday, fireworks in Tokyo.

—16th to 24th, Gion Festival, Yasaka Shrine in Kyoto: processions, parades in period costumes, floats.

—18th, festival of Mt. Ontake, near Nagoya.

—24th and 25th, in Osaka, festival at Temmangū in honor of Sugawara no Michizane: boat processions.

—The "day of beef," when smoked eels are eaten.

—31st, many festivals. The Kenka Matsuri in Ōita (Kyushu): *mikoshi* fights. Lantern festival on Lake Ashi near Hakone. Festival of Mt. Atago near Yonezawa and torchlit processions on all mountains in the country.

• **August**

—1st to 16th, period of O-Bon.

—6th, in Akita, Tanabata Matsuri and Kantō Matsuri (lantern festival). Festival of the Sumiyoshi Shrine in Tokyo. Festival of Peace in Hiroshima. Sacred dances *(waraku)* in Nikko. Tanabata in Sendai.

—8th, end of the rainy season; houses are aired out. Carnival in Kamakura (to the 16th): election of "Miss Carnival."

—10th to 17th, in Aomori and Hirosaki, Nebuta Matsuri (processions of elaborate floats).

—15th, festival of lanterns at Asakasa Kannon-ji in Tokyo and "moon viewing" *(tsukimi)*. Festival of lanterns at the Kasuga Shrine in Nara.

—21st to 25th, peasant dances (Awa Odori) in Takashima (Shikoku). Annual festival of the port of Niigata.

—26th, fire festival at the Sengen Shrine at the foot of Mt. Fuji.

—31st, closing of the mountain trails.

• **September**

—1st, commemoration of the 1923 earthquake.

—2nd to 17th, festival of Osaka: bullfights at the Bankyō Shrine.

—11th to 13th, festival of the temples of the Nichiren sect.

—11th, ginger fair (Shōga Matsuri) at Daijin-gū in Tokyo.

—14th and 15th, festivals of the shrines dedicated to Tenjin, especially in Kamakura.

—15th, Respect for the Aged Day (Keirō no Hi); major sumo tournaments in Tokyo.

—17th to 24th, archery (kyūdō) and other martial-arts demonstrations at Hachiman-gū in Kamakura.

—20th to 23rd, fall equinox. Visits to tombs, chrysanthemum exhibitions.

—23rd and 24th, festival of the sea on all coasts and lakeshores.

• October

—Start of the wedding season (except for the 10th, when the kami are absent, having all gone to Izumo; see KAMI-ARIZUKI). Festival of chrysanthemum dolls (kiku-ningyō) in Osaka (until the 17th).

—4th, festival of Kitano Tenjin of Kyoto, in memory of Sugawara no Michizane.

—5th to 28th, in Kyoto, traditional dance (Kamogawa Odori) performances.

—7th, 8th, and 9th, at Suwa Shrine in Nagasaki, dragon floats.

—9th to 11th, in Kotohira (Hikoku), annual Kompira Festival (also takes place in Tokyo).

—12th, in temples of the Nichiren sect, Nichiren's birthday, the Oeshiki is commemorated. Bullfights (ushi matsuri) at Uzumasa Shrine in Kyoto.

—14th and 15th, festival of Himeji castle.

—15th, opening of the hunting season. In Nara, the antlers of the sacred deer at Kasuga Shrine are trimmed.

—17th, festival of the Tōshōgū in Nikkō: processions in historical costumes.

—19th, in Tokyo, various fairs, including the Ebisu Fair.

—18th to 21st, fall festival at Yasukuni Shrine in Tokyo: parades in historical costumes.

—21st and 22nd, festival of Kobe.

—22nd, Kyoto's famous Jidai Matsuri. Festival of fire (Kurama no Hi) in Kyoto.

—26th, festival at Tenri Shrine near Nara.

• November

—1st, culture is celebrated and the treasures of the Shōsō-in in Nara are "aired out."

—1st to 7th, festival at Meiji-jingū in Tokyo to celebrate the birthday of Emperor Meiji.

—The 3rd is a national holiday: Culture Day (Bunka no Hi) is celebrated throughout Japan with many cultural events.

—The "day of the cock" is a fair (tori no ichi) in Tokyo: the custom on this day is to buy rakes (kumade) to "rake up happiness." Also on the 3rd, in Nara, at the Kasuga Shrine, Gagaku preformances. At Hakone, procession of daimyo of the Edo period.

—15th, the Shichigosan, celebration for girls seven years old, boys five years old, and all three-year-olds. In Fukuoka (Kyushu), the fall sumo tournaments begin.

—23rd, national Labor Thanksgiving Day (Kinrō Kansha no Hi). In the Jōdo Shinshū temples, commemoration of the death of Shinran.

• December. This is the month of year-end gifts and last-minute purchases. It is customary to pay all one's debts (or, if this is impossible, to leave for a distant destination!).

—5th, procession of floats to Suiten-gū in Tokyo, commemorating the battle of Dannoura.

—15th, festival of white horses at Hachiman-gū in Ogano-machi.

—16th, 17th, and 18th, Kasuga-Wakamiya Shrine festival in Nara (On Matsuri), which takes place at night: the shrine kami is carried off to the mountain and brought back the following day by two young children symbolizing the pure hearts of the samurai, along with a "messenger of the sun," always a member of the Fujiwara family.

—23rd, it is customary to take a bath scented with citronella or bitter orange (yuzu) to cleanse oneself. It is the winter solstice (tōji).

—25th, Christmas for Christians, and a commercial holiday for all.

—31st, the last day of the year (ōmisoka). At midnight, the Buddhist temples ring their bells 108 times (joya no kane) to dispel the evils of the past year. People stay away from their homes so as not to drive away the kami of the New Year, and visit temples or shrines. In Kyoto, the Gion Okera Matsuri takes place: the sacred fire at Yasaka Shrine is fetched to light the first fires of the year. In Akita, the namahage takes place, during which demons dressed in straw coats (mino) frighten the children into being good. Everyone waits for sunrise (hatsu-mōde) before going home.

These are just some of the holidays from among the hundreds that take place from one end of the year to the other in temples, shrines, and rural areas, and within families. Times when gifts are exchanged, during the winter season (seibo) and again in mid-July (chūgen), are also considered a sort of holiday. Each historical period has had its customs and traditions—especially culinary ones. There's a festival every day somewhere in Japan. *See* GIFTS.

Film. The first public film screenings (then called *katsudō-shashin*) were held in Osaka in 1897, using an apparatus similar to that used by the Lumière brothers. The first Japanese movie, made in 1899, was of a Kabuki play, *Momijigari,* and featured the famous actors Danjūrō IX and Kikugorō V. Reporters with cameras covered the theater of operations in China during the Boxer Rebellion in 1900, but it was only in 1912, with Nikkatsu, that the first Japanese movie-production company was founded. The technique was still imperfect, and the public generally preferred silent films imported from the United States.

Little by little, directors became bolder, employing actresses and using subtitles. One of the first films of this type was *Sei no kagayaki* (The Glow of Life), produced in 1919. Although it was not very successful, this film encouraged other filmmakers to improve their technique; in 1920, Shōchiku was founded in Tokyo to produce commercial films. After the 1923 earthquake in Tokyo, most film studios moved to Kyoto.

The public, although increasingly drawn to Western films, began to watch Japanese productions made by the many small companies. Techniques improved and the acting began to diverge from that of theater performance. While most imported films were fictional, the new Japanese cinema produced more realistic films, then, bowing to public demand, pure entertainment . Shōchiku produced the first talkie, *Madamu to nyobo* (The Neighbor's Wife and Mine), in 1931; it was directed by Goshō Heinosuke.

Until 1937, the Japanese movie industry expanded quickly and produced high-quality films. Most were adaptations of Japanese literary works, little known in the West. Japanese cinema was considered marginal on the international scene—an object of curiosity rather than a full member of the international movie industry. During the Second World War, Japanese studios produced propaganda films, with production strictly controlled by the government; by 1941, American and English films had disappeared from Japanese screens. In spite of the limitations imposed on them, Japanese filmmakers attempted to produce good work. Unfortunately, most prewar Japanese films have been lost.

Japanese cinema flourished after the war; in 1946, American films were once again allowed into the country. Technicians and actors trained abroad and returned with the latest techniques, determined to produce competitive work. The controls were lifted; a few movies promoted democractic ideals, but soon the film industry returned to fiction. The social difficulties of 1948 and 1949 caused the studios to unite in a sort of federation, comprising Tōhō, Shōchiku, Tōei, Daiei, and Nikkatsu, aimed at surviving the invasion of foreign films.

In 1951, Kurosawa Akira's *Rashōmon* won the grand prize at the Venice Film Festival, and exports of Japanese films picked up quickly. Also in 1951, the first major Japanese color film, *Karumen kokyō ni kaeru* (Carmen Comes Home), was produced. In 1953, Ozu Yasujirō made the remarkable *Tōkyo monogatari* (Tokyo Story), and Mizoguchi Kenji made *Saikaku ichidai onna* (The Life of Oharu). Now confident of their technical mastery, teams of technicians and directors produced films at a great rate. For example, Kinugasa Teinosuke made *Jigoku-mon* (Gate of Hell, 1953); Kurosawa made *Ikiru* (1953), *Shichinin no samurai* (Seven Samurai, 1954), *Yōjimbo* (1961), and *Akahige* (Red Beard, 1965); Ichikawa Kon made *Biruma no tategoto* (Harp of Burma, 1956); Shindō Kaneto made *Genbaku no ko* (Children of the Atom Bomb, 1952); and Kobayashi Masaki made *Seppuku* (Hara Kiri, 1962).

Currently, Japan is among the top countries in the world in terms of number of films produced, but they are of extremely variable quality: many "exportable" films are remarkable, such as Shindō Kaneto's *Hadaku no shima* (Naked Island, 1961), Teshigahara Hiroshi's *Suna no onna* (Woman in the Dunes, 1963), Ōshima Nagisa's *Ai no korīda* (In the Realm of the Senses, 1976), Kurosawa's *Kagemusha* (1980) and *Ran* (1985), and Imamura Shōhei's *Narayama-bushi kō* (Ballad of Narayama, 1983). Masterpieces such as these are rare, however, in comparison to the "domestic" films, which are generally hurried through production by mediocre directors.

The Japanese public prefers American and Western films on the one hand, and films dealing with specifically Japanese themes on the other. Japanese superproductions, very successful abroad, are shunned by Japanese audiences. In contrast, Japanese cartoons have been very successful in the West, notably in the television market. The three largest film studios are currently Tōhō, Matsutake, and Tōei; Nikkatsu went bankrupt in 1993. *See* ARIMA INEKO, ATSUMI KIYOSHI, FUJIMOTO SANEZUMI, GENDAI-GEKI, GOSHO HEINOSUKE, KUROSAWA AKIRA, MAKINO MASAHIRO, MAKINO SHŌZO, MATSUYAMA ZENZŌ, MIKUNI RENTARŌ, MIYAGAWA

KAZUO, MIZOGUCHIKENJI, MORIIWAO, MURATA MINORU, OZU YASUJIRŌ, and the names cited in the entry.

Fishing. Traditionally, fishing is the second-largest food industry in Japan, after agriculture. More than 2.2 million families and several thousand firms of various sizes are involved in this sector. Because of its insular nature, Japan has developed its coasts considerably, and because warm currrents (Kuroshio) and cold currents (Oyashio) meet at various points off its coasts, these waters are excellent for fish production. In 1986, 12,667,000 tons of fish were harvested, including 4,125,000 tons of sardines. In 1993, however, production declined slightly (to about 11 million tons). Inshore fishing (up to 20 nautical miles from shore) supplies the greatest quantity of seafood products. All types of fishing are practiced, including seining, trawling, fixed nets, and dragnets. Sardines, mackerel, tuna, and bonito are the most heavily fished species. Offshore fishing is conducted with trawlers, which catch mackerel, shark, whitefish, squid, tuna, sea bream, herring, eels, and other species. Salmon is fished mainly in the North Pacific. Crabs and spider crabs are abundant in the Sea of Okhotsk. Whaling is conducted with modern whaling ships accompanied by factory ships, mainly in the Arctic and Antarctic oceans (*see* WHALES). Most of the catch is consumed fresh, but a considerable proportion is canned for export (mainly tuna), used to make fish cakes *(kamaboko, surimi,)* or dried. The Japanese eat relatively little meat; they rely on fish for their protein, making it an essential component of their diet.

Seaweed *(nori, kombu,* and others), shrimp, carp, trout, *ayu* ("sweetfish"), and oysters (other than pearl oysters; *see* PEARLS) and various mollusks are farmed in the sea and in freshwater basins. *See* AYU, AOTŌ TSUNAYOSHI.

Flora. Japan's flora is in the holarctic category but comprises a large variety of plants and trees, thanks to the diversity of micro-climates and altitudes. There are four general botanical zones in Japan: southern, south-central, north-central, and northern:

—*Southern zone* (southern Kyushu and Shikoku, southern part of the Kii peninsula): broad-leafed evergreen trees, such as *kusunoki* (camphor tree; *Cinnamomum camphora)* and *tachibana (Citrus tachibana),* and tropical trees such as *sotetsu (Cycas revoluta)* and *birō (Livingstona sanglobosa),* whose seeds are carried along the coasts by warm sea currents (Kuroshio).

—*South-central zone* (northern Kyushu and Shikoku, coastal southern Honshu, and mountainous areas of Shikoku, Kyushu, and Kanto): temperate forests with broad-leafed evergreen trees, such as *kashiwa (Quercus dentata), shii (Shii sieboldi), sakaki (Cleyera japonica),* and *tsubaki (Camellia japonica). Kuromatsu* (Japanese black pine; *Pinus thunbergii)* are found near the coasts. But these zones have been largely deforested and at various times trees not native to the regions have been planted, such as *sugi (Cryptomeria japonica), hinoki (Chamaecyparis obtusa), kunugi (Quercus quercus),* and *konara (Quercus serrata).* Granite soils abound in *akamatsu* (Japanese red pine; *Pinus densiflora).*

—*North-central zone* (Chūbū; northeast and northern Honshu, southern Hokkaido): broad-leafed deciduous trees, such as *ōnara (Quercus crispula)* and *buna* (beech; *Fagus crenata),* and conifers—*hinoki* (cypress; *Chamaecyparis obtusa), hiba (Aesculus turbinata);* in certain regions, notably Aomori and Iwata prefectures, *harunire (Ulmus Davidiana, var. japonica)* and *sawakurumi (Pterocarya rhoifolia).*

—*North-central and northern zones* (mountains of northern Honshu and Hokkaido): mainly conifers such as the *shirabe (Abies Veitchii)* and *todomatsu (Abies Mariesii),* with broad-leafed trees typical of these regions, such as *kamba (Betula)* and *miya-nanakamado* (mountain ash; *Sorbus pseudogracilis). See also* BONSAI, GARDENS.

Flowers. Flowers have always inspired the Japanese, and poets and artists have celebrated them in their works. Flowers are symbols of beauty, all the more sought after when their blooms are short-lived. They symbolize the seasons and times of day, and they are arranged artistically to decorate houses and *tokonoma* alcoves. The most common are hollyhock, arum, morning glory *(asagao),* chrysanthemum *(kiku),* cherry blossoms *(sakura),* plum blossoms *(ume),* and peonies, but all flowers are appreciated. *See* these entries and BONSAI, FLORA, IKEBANA.

Flutes. Most flutes (vertical or transverse) are made of bamboo. A few are made of ivory, porcelain, or metal. Among the various types of flutes, the most common are:

—*yokobue,* general name for transverse flutes.

—*kichiriki,* shepherd's flute, vertical or transverse, with seven holes. Also called *ryūteki.*

—*Yamatobue,* concert flute with six holes and interior lacquered in red; length: 1 *shaku* 5 *sun.*

—*hichiriki,* reed flute with seven holes on the top and two on the bottom, about 18 cm long.

—*hitayokiri,* very long flute, in two parts.

—*shakuhachi,* vertical bamboo flute; length: 1 *shaku* and 8 *sun* (whence its name), with four holes on the top and one on the bottom. The mouthpiece is beveled and the sound is formed by pinching the lips. It is the classic instrument of traditional orchestras.

—Other types of flutes are called *seiteki, chi,* and *dōshō.*

—*shō no fue* is a type of Pan flute with 10, 12, 16, 22, 23, or 24 pipes.

—*shō* (or *shiyo*) are mouth organs with 17 pipes, similar to the Chinese *sheng.*

Folk art. *See* MINGEI.

Fontanesi, Antonio. Italian landscape painter (1818–82) in the French Barbizon style. In 1876, the Japanese government invited him, Giovanni Cappelletti, and Vincenzo Ragusa to teach Western painting and art techniques at the Kōbu Bijutsu Gakkō (Technical Fine Arts School) in Tokyo. He stayed for two years, but was forced to return to Turin in 1878 because of serious illness.

Franciscans. The Franciscans were among the first missionaries to arrive in Japan, in 1582. Of the 60 who preached there until 1632, 29 were martyred.

Frank, Junko. Painter, born in 1930 in Wakayama prefecture, wife of French Japanologist Bernard Frank. After graduating from the Tokyo Geijutsu Daigaku (Tokyo University of Fine Arts and Music) in 1955, she went to France. In 1964 she received the silver medal of Paris; in 1967, the gold medal of Athens. Her work has been exhibited in France and Japan. Since 1961, she has been a member of the Salon d'automne in Paris.

Frois, Luis. Portuguese Jesuit (1532–97), born in Lisbon. He arrived in Japan in 1563 and remained there until his death, except for two years spent in Macao. He met most of Japan's great lords, with whom he had many interviews, and wrote many reports on his missionary activities, collected in *Historia de Japam* (1594). His essays on Japanese customs and Toyotomi Hideyoshi's Korean campaign are important documents on the late sixteenth century.

Fubako. "Brush box," a writing kit with a drawer for paper, ink, and brushes, generally presented in a covered lacquer box and often decorated by a well-known artist.

Fubito. Before 644, court bureaucrats charged with writing the history of a province and collecting the documents belonging to the imperial archives and the major families. They were divided into a number of categories: *kuni-fubito* (imperial), *funa-fubito* (provincial), *tsu-fubito* (city), and so on; the suffix is a contraction of *fumi no obito.* In 644, when most archives were destroyed in the civil war between the Soga and Nakatomi families, the *funa-fubito* Esaka was able to preserve a few chronicles from destruction, and they were used as sources for the *Kojiki* and the *Nihon shoki.* Also called *fumi no nemaro.*

Fuchi (-buchi). "Support," extra allocation of rice given by a lord to his samurai, beyond the normal usufruct of their lands, in compensation for their services. In the Edo period, the *fuchi* constituted the basis of remuneration of ordinary samurai, who normally received their salary in rice *(kurumai).* This allocation was generally 5 *gō* (0.005 *koku,* or about 0.9 liter) per *fuchi* per day, which amounted to an annual allocation of about two *koku* (360 liters) per person *(ichinin-buchi).* Some high-ranking samurai, however, received larger quantities— *gonin-buchi* (*fuchi* for five people) or *jūnin-fuchi* (*fuchi* for ten people). These extra payments were then called *kafuchi.* Also called *fuchimai,* "rice support."

Fuchū. Satellite city of Tokyo, located on the north shore of the Tama River, which was the capital of Musashi province (Saitama prefecture and Tokyo) in the seventh century. It became an important transit point during the Edo period. Famous for its racetrack. *Pop.:* 200,000.

• Town in Hiroshima prefecture, on the Ashida River, former provincial capital. *Pop.:* 50,000.

• Former name of the cities of Shizuoka (also called Sumpu, Funai), Kōfu, Ishioka (Ibaraki prefecture), and Izu no Hara. *See* MATSUDAIRA.

Fudai. "Successive generations," vassals or servants whose position was hereditary, starting in the Muromachi period.
→ *See* NAGO.

• **Fudai-daimyō.** In the Edo period, hereditary vassals to the Tokugawa shogun; they had sided with

Tokugawa Ieyasu at the Battle of Sekigahara in 1600. There were 176 of them, and they generally had revenues of 10,000 *koku* or less. *See* DAIMYO, SHIMPAN-DAIMYŌ, TOZAMA-DAIMYŌ.

Fudaishi-ten. Chinese Buddhist monk (Fu Dashi, Shanhui Dashi, Fuxi, 497–569) considered an incarnation of Miroku (*Skt.:* Maitreya), deified in Japan as a fat, smiling Buddha (Warai-hotoke) and considered to be the guardian of libraries at Buddhist monasteries. He is sometimes portrayed accompanied by his two sons, Fujō and Fuken, who assist him in his tasks. Also called Fu Taishi, Fukyū, Sōrin Taishi, Tōyo Taishi.

Fudasashi. In the Edo period, rice dealers and financiers for samurai and *hatamoto* (bannermen) were paid in rice, which they exchanged for silver through the *fudasashi*. In 1724, the *fudasashi* created a monopolistic trade association *(kabuna-kama)* under the supervision (starting in 1777) of the Edo *machi-bugyō* (Edo city commissioners). The *fudasashi* also lent money, charging interest (12% to 15%), and became extremely wealthy. The government tried a number of times to regulate their trade, which was more or less illegal—notably in 1789 (Kienrei moratorium during the Kansei Reforms) and in the Tempō Reforms (1841–43)—but without great success. During the Meiji Restoration (1868), the *fudasashi* were eliminated, and thereafter all salaries were paid in cash, not rice. Also called *kurayado*.

Fūdo. Typically Japanese ecological concept that includes both all of the geographical aspects of a specific site and the ways of life of inhabitants of that site. It was perfectly expressed by Watsuji Tetsurō (1889–1960) in his essay *Fūdo* (1935) and other works, and by other philosophers, including Sabata Toyoyuki, Tsukuba Hisaharu, and Fukunaga Takehiko. *See* FUKUNAGA TAKEHIKO.

Fudoki. Official reports on the provinces, including notes on their history, geography, and customs, written in the early eighth century on the orders of Empress Gemmei (713). Only five *fudoki* have been preserved, some in their entirety and others not: those of the provinces of Bunto (Ōita prefecture), circa 740; Harima (Hyōgo prefecture), circa 715; Hitachi (Ibaraki prefecture), circa 715; Hizen (Saga prefecture), circa 740; and Izumo (Shimane prefecture), in 773, the only one to have been preserved in its original form. Some of the *fudoki* formed the basis of the *Nihon shoki*. There are also numerous fragments of other *fudoki* (there were about 60).

Some of them were completely modified and rewritten and republished, including the *Shimpen Musashi fudoki kō,* in 1828, and the *Kii zoku fudoki,* in 1839.

• Today, all reports on customs and life in regions of Japan are called *fudoki*.

Fudō Myō-ō. Japanese Buddhist form of Achalanātha, an esoteric divinity considered a "terrible emanation" *(funnu)* of Dainichi Nyorai (*Skt.:* Mahāvairochana). He is a Vidyarāja (Myō-ō) or "King of Magical Science" charged with fighting evil forces that are contrary to Buddhist Law and with protecting the faithful. He is portrayed standing or sitting, holding a sword (sometimes flaming) and a noose (to catch the evil or "tie together" the faithful). In general, he looks like a Myō-ō, but he is sometimes portrayed with the features of a young man, Fudōshisha (*Skt.:* Achalacheta). He has eight acolytes (*dōji*), two of whom are often portrayed with him, Seitaka-dōji (*Skt.:* Chetaka) and Kongara-dōji (*Skt.:* Kimkara). Fudō Myō-ō's sword is often portrayed alone as a symbol of his divinity. The most famous images of Fudō Myō-ō are called Aka Fudō (Red Fudō) and Aoi Fudō (Blue Fudō). He is very popular in Japan. *See* MYŌ-Ō.

• *Fudō Myō-ō.* Title of a Kabuki play, counted among the *Kabuki jūhachi-ban* but rarely performed.

• **Fudō-in.** Hand gesture *(Skt.: mudrā)* characteristic of Fudō Myō-ō, corresponding to the Sanskrit Tarjanī-mudrā, somewhat resembling the "devil's horns" (index and little fingers pointed). Also called *funnu-in.*

Fūgai. Zen Buddhist monk (1779–1847) of the Kōjaku-in temple in Mikawa and painter of the Nanga school.

• **Fūgai Ekun.** Zen Buddhist monk (1568–1654) of the Sōtō sect and painter. Born in Kōzuke (Gumma prefecture), he served in various temples but spent most of his life alone in caves meditating, whence his nickname Ana Fūgai. His paintings, most of which he made late in life, portrayed mainly Daruma or Hotei, but he also made some landscapes in ink in the Zen style. He is said to have asked to be shut into a cave on the day of his death.

Fugaku hyakkei. "One Hundred Views of Mt. Fuji." A series of ukiyo-e prints of Mt. Fuji made by Hokusai in 1834 and 1835.

- *Fugaku sanjūrokkei.* "Thirty-six Views of Mt. Fuji." A series of ukiyo-e prints portraying Mt. Fuji made by Hokusai from 1818 to 1829. In fact, he made 46.

Fūga waka-shū. "Elegant Collection of *Waka.*" The seventeenth imperial anthology of *waka* poems, compiled by Retired Emperor Hanazono in 1346. It includes 2,201 poems on 20 scrolls. Abridged as *Fūga-shū. See* CHOKUSEN WAKA-SHŪ.

Fugen Bosatsu. "Bodhisattva of Longevity," Japanization of the Buddhist deity of ecstatic contemplation, Sāmanthabhadra ("All Goodness"), an emanation of Dainichi Nyorai (*Skt.:* Mahāvairochana), representing the supreme intelligence of Buddhist Law. This divinity is often portrayed in images of Amida's *raigō* ("descent to welcome the souls of the faithful"), accompanied by Shō Kannon Bosatsu. Fugen Bosatsu is the main divinity of the Hokke Sammai, sometimes confused with (or identified as) Daishō Kongō. Also called Chakrapāni in Sanskrit. *Chin.:* Puxian, Xinli.

- Fugen-dōjin. *See* KŌKAN.

- Fugen Emmei Bosatsu. "Fugen, Prolonger of Life." Buddhist deity, a Tantric (esoteric) emanation of Fugen Bosatsu, corresponding to the Sanskrit Vajrāmoghasamayasattva. He is portrayed on one or several elephants, with four or sixteen arms.

Fugo. From the seventh to the twelfth century, groups of villages, families, houses, or slaves assigned to members of the imperial family, senior bureaucrats, or Buddhist temples, according to their rank or merit. *See* JIKIFU.

Fugu. General name for fish in the *Tetraodontides* family, commonly called sunfish, whose flesh is highly regarded by the Japanese, even though their ovaries and liver contain a potent poison. If *fugu* is improperly prepared, consuming it can be fatal; it has therefore been banned from time to time. Today, "*fugu* restaurants," under strict supervision, serve this fish almost without danger, though there is always a bit of doubt that supplies an extra thrill to those who like to eat it. *Fugu* skin (the variety called *Fugu rubripes, Jap.: torafugu*) is used to make lanterns.

Fu hakase. Musical-notation system used after 1050, replacing the old system called *ko-hakase,* derived from the *meyasu* system. It consists of small marks made to the right of characters of a text to be

sung, the precise orientation of which specifies the intonation. Also called *hakase.*

Fuhi Kannon. One of the 33 forms (Sanjūsan Ōgeshin) of Kannon Bosatsu (*Skt.:* Avalokiteshvara), representing universal compassion. This deity is portrayed with hands hidden in sleeves.

Fuji. City in Shizuoka prefecture (central Honshu) at the bottom of the southern slope of Mt. Fuji (*see* FUJI-SAN) facing the Bay of Suruga, created by the merger of the cities of Yoshiwara and Takaoka in 1966. Sea port. *Pop.:* 210,000.

- Fuji Gohō. Shinto sect founded in 1946 by Itō Gensaku.

- Fuji Hazumune. *See* HAZUMUNE.

- Fuji-hime. *See* SENGEN MYŌJIN, fuji-san.

- Fuji Hon-kyō. Shinto sect founded in 1948 by Tsubai Kunitarō (1889–1965).

- Fuji-kō. An association of worshipers of Mt. Fuji, established about 1630 by Hasegawa Takematsu, a Shinto priest. He died in one of the caves of the sacred volcano in 1646 and was thereafter known as Kakugyō. Thousands of pilgrims belonging to this religious group still climb the rocky slopes of the volcano each year, wearing white and singing hymns. *See* KŌ, FUJI-SAN.

- Fuji-kyō. Shinto sect of worshipers of Mt. Fuji, founded in 1948 by Hasegawa Teruhiro (1904–62).

- *Fuji musume.* "The Daughter of Mt. Fuji," a Kabuki play adapted from a Noh play of the same name by Katsui Gempachi in 1826. *See* FUJI-NINGYŌ, SAKURA-NINGYŌ.

- Fuji-san. "Mt. Fuji" (in the West erroneously called Fujiyama), a volcano in Yamanashi prefecture forming a perfect cone, and the highest peak in Japan (3,776 m). Its summit crater has a diameter of about 500 m and is about 250 m deep. Although it seems to be a single volcano, it is in fact accompanied by three subsidiary volcanoes called Komitake, Ko-Fuji, and Shin-Fuji. Shin-Fuji is the most active, its cinders and lava having covered the two other volcanoes. A small crater (conello) called Hōei was formed on the slopes of Fuji-san during the last eruption of Shin-Fuji in 1707. The first recorded eruption of this volcano took place in 864. The name Fuji is said to have come from an Ainu place name and to be associated with a fire god. Since the seventh century at least, Fuji-san has been worshiped by the Japanese as much for the great danger it represents as for its beauty, and its worship was mentioned as far back as the *Man'yōshū*. It has been given a great number of poetic names, including Chiri-yama, Fukukaze-ana-yama, Hatachi-yama, Fuji no Yama, Hagoromo-yama, Higashi-yama, Mikami-yama, Mie-yama, Midashi-yama, Nii-yama, Otome-yama, Narusawa no Takama, Sennin-yama, Taketori-yama, Tokiwa-yama, and Tokishiranu-yama. The Shinto gods Fuji-hime (Sengen Myōjin) and Sakuya-hime are said to live on its summit and slopes. Because Fuji-san is considered sacred, women did not have permission to climb it until 1872. Each summer from July to the end of September, great numbers of mountain climbers and tourists scale its slopes, at night if possible, stopping at one or another of the eight "waystations" set up for them. If they time their ascent properly, climbers can admire the sunrise over the Pacific Ocean and the long processions of Shinto devotees of the Fuji-kō and various sects that worship the volcano. The beauty of Fuji-san has been extolled throughout time by poets and reproduced in numerous paintings and prints (*see* FUGAKU HYAKKEI, FUGAKU SANJŪROKKEI), and it is still a favorite subject of photographers.

• **Fuji-san Goko.** "Fuji Five Lakes," a group of five lakes on the northern slopes of Mt. Fuji: Lake Yamanaka, Lake Kawaguchi, Lake Sai, Lake Shōji, and Lake Motosu, formed by lava obstructions in the valleys of the Misaka Mountains. Resorts and other tourist attractions are located on their shores, which provide beautiful views of the volcano's cone.

• **Fuji-san Hongū.** *See* SENGEN-JINJA.

• **Fuji-Yoshida.** Town in Yamanashi prefecture, at the foot of Mt. Fuji, that developed around Fuji Sengen Shrine (festival: August 26–27). It is the point of departure for pilgrims who want to climb Mt. Fuji. *Pop.:* 55,000.

Fuji. Wisteria *(Wisteria floribunda),* climbing leguminous plant with showy purplish flowers. There are many varieties: cultivated *(kushakufuji, shirobanafuji,* with white flowers; *akabonofu,* with pink flowers), which climbs in a clockwise direction, and wild *(yamafuji, Wisteria brachybotrys),* which climbs counterclockwise. Wisteria flowers in April. *See* FLORA.

• **Fuji-ningyō.** Dolls of geisha holding a branch of wisteria, made during the Meiji era. Also called *fuji-musume.*

Fuji-daiko. Title of a Noh play: the drummer Fuji is killed by another musician, Asama, who is jealous that his colleague was invited to play in the capital. Fuji's widow becomes a Buddhist nun and plays drums in his memory.

Fuji Denki. Fuji Electric Company is a leading manufacturer of heavy electrical equipment, created in 1923 with technology borrowed from Siemens. It produces hydroelectric and thermal turbines, atomic reactors, and so on. It exports about 22% of its production.

Fujieda. City in Shizuoka prefecture (central Honshu) that developed as a fortified town *(jōka-machi)* around the Tanaka castle during the Edo period and was a major post town. It is famous for its agricultural market, its tea, and its mushrooms *(shiitake).* Chemical and pharmaceutical industries. *Pop.:* 105,000.

Fujieda Shizuo. Physician and writer (Katsumi Jirō, 1907–93), born at Shizuoka. Some of his books, almost all of which are autobiographical, are erotic. Among his writings are *Michi* (1947), *Iperitto-gan* (1949), *Inu no chi* (1956), *Kyōto Tsuda Sanzō* (1961), and *Kūki atama* (1967).

Fujigawa no Tatakai. "Battle of Fujigawa" (November 1180), in which Minamoto no Yoritomo was victorious over the troops of the rival Taira clan. According to the *Azuma no kagami,* when Minamoto's soldiers disturbed a flock of wild geese, the troops of the Taira clan thought that it was a surprise attack and fled in disorder, thus providing Yoritomo with a victory (without a fight) and free rein to seize the eastern provinces. The name of this battle has come to mean a victory without a fight.

Fuji Ginkō. Major bank founded in 1864 by Yasuda Zenjirō and expanded in 1923 by a merger with 11 other banks. Currently the largest bank in Japan, Fuji Bank took its current name in 1948, after the dissolution of the Yasuda banks. It has international branches in London, New York, Hong Kong, Bangkok, Jakarta, Luxembourg, Toronto, and Switzerland, and more than 200 branches in Japan.

Fujihira Shin. Ceramist, born in 1922 in Kyoto. His work has been in numerous exhibitions, and he received the Order of Culture in 1985. In 1944, he had an exhibition at the Mitsukoshi space in Paris.

Fujiidera. Town near Osaka, former capital of Kawachi province and site of many *kofun* burial mounds and notable Buddhist temples, such as the Fujiidera and the Dōmyōji. *Pop.*: 65,000.

Fujii Heigo. Politician (1906–80), born in Gifu. First a journalist at *Asahi Shimbun,* he became a businessman and was named vice-president of Nippon Steel Corporation in 1962. He was elected to the House of Councillors in 1974.

Fujii Kenjirō. Physician and cytologist (1866–1952), born in Ishikawa prefecture. After studying in Europe, he became a professor at Tokyo University in 1911. His studies led him to found an international journal, *Cytologia,* in 1929. He received the Order of Culture in 1950.

Fujii Nitatsu. Buddhist monk of the Nichiren sect, born in 1885 in Kumamoto. He actively promoted realization of the ideal of Nichiren, the Risshō Ankoku, a national government based on the teachings of the *Lotus Sutra.* He then went to Manchuria to preach and establish temples, and to China, Burma, and India, where he met Mahatma Gandhi. After the Second World War, he changed his ideas, became a fervent promoter of peace, and led a number of anti-nuclear demonstrations, notably against American military bases. The sect he founded, Nihonzan Myōhō-ji, has few members in Japan.

Fujii Shigeo. Writer (1917–1979). At first a journalist with *Asahi Shimbun,* he began a career as a novelist, winning the Naoki Prize in 1965 for his novel *Niji* (Rainbow). Among his other books are *Kajin* (Beauty), *Owari naki chikonka* (Endless Requiem), and *Seika* (Gentle Melody).

Fujii Takanao. Writer (1764–1840), disciple of Motoori Norinaga, author of *Mitsu no shirube* (Introduction to Morals, Poetry, and Literature) and *Matsunoya bunchū* (Literary Essays), among others.

Fujii Teikan. Scholar and historian (Fujii Sadamoto, Tō Teikan, 1732–97) who specialized in historical accounts of the city of Edo, among them *Kōko shōroku* (1795), *Kōko ni hiroku* (1797), and *Shūkozu.*

Fujii Umon. Scholar (Fujii Naoakira, Yamato no Kami, 1720–67). He was beheaded for having written a book hostile to the shogun Tokugawa Ienari.

Fuji Jūkōgyō. Fuji Heavy Industries Ltd. is comprised of automobile, bus, and plane factories. The cars are known outside Japan by the brand name Subaru. Its predecessor was the Airplane Research Institute, founded in 1917 by Nakajima Chikuhei. The company is affiliated with Nissan Motors. Head office in Tokyo.

Fuji Junko. Actress (Shundō Junko), born in 1945 in Wakayama, daughter of producer Shundō Hiroshige. She played in a large number of gangster *(yakuza)* films, notably in series such as *Onna toseinin* (The Yakuza Women), where she handled a sword like a samurai. In 1972, she married the Kabuki actor Onoe Kikugorō VII, took the name Terashima Junko, and retired from acting.

Fujikawa Buzaemon. Kabuki actor (1618–1729) in Edo, Osaka, and Kyoto.

Fujikawa Yū. Medical historian (1865–1940), born in Aki province (Hiroshima prefecture). He studied in Germany; when he returned to Japan, he published a study of the history of the development of Japanese medicine, *Nihon igaku shi* (1904), translated into English as *Japanese Medicine.*

Fujikawa Yūzō. Sculptor (1883–1935). He studied in France from 1908 to 1916 and was an assistant to Auguste Rodin starting in 1910. He was elected a member of the Imperial Academy of Arts in 1935.

Fuji Kōsan. Oil company specializing in the manufacture and sale of oil and petroleum products, founded in 1949. Head office in Tokyo.

Fujikura Densen. Cable and electric wire manufacturer, founded in 1885. Its special cables (SZ), invented in 1965, helped it conquer an international market. Exports mainly to Brazil, Nigeria, Singapore, and Malaysia. Head office in Tokyo.

Fujima. Classical dance school founded between 1624 and 1643 (*see* IEMOTO).

- **Fujima Hideo.** *See* FUJIMA KANJŪRŌ.

- **Fujima Kan'emon.** *See* FUJIMA KANJŪRŌ.

- **Fujima Kanjūrō (VI).** Classical dancer (Onoe Umeo, Fujima Hideo) born in 1900 in Tokyo, sixth-generation descendant of the Fujima family, whose name he took in 1927. Designated a Living National Treasure in 1960, he received the grand prize of the Academy of the Arts and was decorated with the Order of Culture in 1982. His successor at the head of the Fujima dance school was Fujima Kan'emon VII.

Fujimori Seikichi. Writer and playwright (1892–1977), born in Nagano prefecture to a family of merchants. He studied German literature at Tokyo University, then was drawn to progressive movements and wrote very successful novels—*Nami* (1914, republished in 1920 as *Wakaki hi no nayamai*), *Haritsuke Mozaemon* (1926), *Gisei* (1926), *Nani ga kanojo o sō saseta ka* (1927)—and plays. Because of political pressure in the 1930s, he was forced to change his way of writing and confine himself to biographies and novels with no political overtones. He joined the Communist party after the Second World War and took up his previous activities. Among his major works are a biography of Watanabe Kazan (1935) and the autobiographical *Kanashi ai* (1955). *See* SENKI.

Fujimoto Sanezumi. Movie producer (1911–79) and director of Tōhō. Among his films are *Aoi sammyaku* (The Blue Mountains), *Meshi* (Boiled Rice), *Santō jūyaku* (The Third-class Agent), and *Kobayakawa ke no ki* (The Fall of the Kobayakawa Clan).

Fujimoto Tesseki. Painter (Shinkin; *azana:* Chūkō; *gō:* Tekkanshi, Kibidanshi, Tetsumon, Shinnosuke, 1816–63), born in Bizen province (Okayama prefecture) into the Katayama family and adopted by the Fujimoto family of the Ikeda clan. He painted in the Hokuga style at first, then in the Nanga style. He was also a samurai and a well-known calligrapher.

Fujimoto Yoshimichi. Ceramist (1919–92), famous for his multicolored porcelains with flower and bird designs. Former president of the Tokyo University of Fine Arts and Music (Tokyo Geijutsu Daigaku), he was declared a Living National Treasure in 1986.

Fujin. Before 850, title given to secondary wives of emperors. They were also called Kisaki and Mime-ōtoji. *See* KŌTAI-FUJIN.

- *Fujin Kōron.* Magazine for women founded in 1916 by Chūō Kōronsha. It immediately won over a large readership because it defended women's rights and demanded equality with men in Japanese society. The magazine dealt openly with subjects considered taboo, such as love and the mother's position in the family. In 1927 its editor-in-chief, Takanobu Kyōsui, further developed its editorial material by publishing autobiographical accounts of women and texts of famous writers. After the Second World War, *Fujin Kōron* expanded its readership by popularizing democratic ideals, becoming the top women's magazine in the country. *See* ARISHIMA TAKEO.

- *Fujin no Tomo.* "Woman's Friend." First women's magazine in Japan, founded in 1903 by Hani Motoko (1873–1957) and her husband, Hani Yoshikazu. First called *Katei no Tomo* (Friend of the Home), it changed names in 1908. *Fujin no Tomo* defended the rights of women and democratic views. In 1930, it gave rise to a national feminist organization, Tomo no Kai, to defend ideas promulgated in the magazine. *Fujin no Tomo* is still very popular today.

Fūjin. God of wind in the Shinto pantheon, corresponding to the Buddhist Fūten. He is one of the 28 acolytes (Nijūhachi Bushū) of Senju Kannon Bosatsu (Thousand-Armed Avalokiteshvara). He is portrayed, especially at the gates to Shinto shrines, with a green body, carrying a big bag full of wind, and looking at Raijin, the Shinto god of thunder. This pair of gods fulfils the same role of guardian as do the Ni-ō at the entrance to Buddhist temples. *Chin.:* Feilian.

Fujino Chūjirō. Businessman (b. 1902) elected president of Mitsubishi in 1974. During the Second World War, he lived in China, where he directed the company's Chinese branch.

Fujinoki (Fuji no Ki). Sixth-century round *kofun* burial mound found in the town of Ikaruga (Nara prefecture). It has a diameter of 40 m and a height of 8 m. Excavated in 1985, it revealed a wealth of funerary objects, including more than 3,000 fragments of horse harnesses in bronze and iron and a metal saddle decorated with elephant, tiger, dragon, phoenix, tortoise, and beehive motifs, showing a clear affinity with the cultures of Central Asia and Korea. It is not known whose tomb and house-shaped stone sarcophagus this was, but it was likely built for a member of the imperial family.

Fujioka. City in Gumma prefecture (central Honshu), former post town during the Edo period, and an active silkworm-breeding center. Many *kofun* burial mounds and pottery kilns, used in the Yayoi period to fire *haniwa,* have been found there. *Pop.:* 55,000.

Fujioka Tōho. Writer (Fujioka Sakutarō, 1870–1910), born in Kanazawa, and professor at Tokyo University. His books were profoundly influenced by the historical philosophy of Hippolyte Taine. He wrote a history of the arts of the Edo period *(Kinsei kaiga-shi)* in 1903, and *Koku bungaku zenshi* (Complete History of the Nation's Literature) in 1905, works that are still considered authoritative.

Fujisawa. City in Kanagawa (central Honshu), former post town on the Tōkaidō road during the Edo period, built up around the Yugyō-ji temple (Ji-shū sect) about 1325. Various industries, tourism (Bay of Sagami, island of Enoshima). *Pop.:* 300,000.

Fujisawa Takeo. Writer (b. 1904) with a proletarian bent, author of many working-class novels, such as *Shinsetsu,* which was adapted for the screen in 1942.

Fujisawa Yakuhin Kōgyō. Powerful pharmaceutical manufacturer founded in 1894; since the end of the Second World War, it has specialized in production of antibiotics. Head office in Osaka.

Fuji Shashin Fuirumu. Fuji Photo Film Company is a manufacturer of film for photography and cinematography, for both professionals and amateurs, founded in 1934. It also produces magnetic media (tapes and diskettes). In 1962, it formed a partnership with Rank Xerox to found Fuji Xerox Co. It has branches in New York, Honolulu, Canada, São Paulo, London, Düsseldorf, and Paris, and many offices in other countries. It controls about 70% of the domestic market for film. Head office in Minami Ashigara (Kanagawa prefecture).

Fujishima Takeji. Painter (1867–1943) in the Western style, born in Kagoshima prefecture. He studied Japanese-style painting in Tokyo in 1884, then began to paint in the Western style in the 1890s. A member of the Hakubakai (White Horse Society), he traveled in France and Italy and studied with Raphael Collin (1850–1917) and Carolus Duran (1838–1917) from 1905 to 1910. When he returned to Japan, he was appointed a professor at the Tokyo School of Fine Arts (Tokyo Bijutsu Gakkō), where

he taught for 30 years. His works are characterized by very bright colors and broad strokes. He was decorated with the Order of Culture in 1937.

Fuji Siyu. Manufacturer of comestible oils (soy, coconut, palm), founded in 1950 and part of the Itō (Itōh) group. Head office in Osaka.

Fujita Bijutsukan. Fujita Art Museum, in Osaka, founded in 1954 to exhibit Chinese and Japanese works of art (paintings, sculptures, ceramics, etc.) collected by Fujita Denzaburō (1841–1912) and his sons.

Fujita Bunzō. Sculptor (1861–1934). He studied in Italy under Vincenzo Raguza. When he returned to Japan, he was appointed a professor at the Tokyo Bijutsu Gakkō (Tokyo School of Fine Arts).

Fujita Denzaburō. Businessman (1841–1912) of the Chōshū clan. A *sake* manufacturer, he went to Osaka during the Meiji Restoration (1868) and made enormous profits dealing with the imperial military authorities. With his brothers and other partners, he used his political connections to found a number of trading and mining companies (Dōwa). An art connoisseur, he collected many Japanese and Chinese works of art throughout his life, which constituted the founding collection of the Osaka museum that bears his name (Fujita Bijutsukan).

Fujita Kōgyō. Major public-works company founded in 1937. It works mainly with Near Eastern countries. Head office in Tokyo.

Fujita Koheiji. Kabuki actor (died ca. 1700), creator of the genre called *jitsugoto* in Kyoto and Osaka.

• **Fujita Magojūrō.** Kabuki actor (seventeenth century).

Fujitani Mitsue. Poet and scholarly historian (1768–1823), born in Kyoto. His studies of ancient literature led him to theorize that the ancient texts were based, for the most part, on the concept of *kotodama* (the belief in the sacred power of words). Among his major books are *Kojiki tomoshibi,* a study of the *Kojiki* published in 1808; *Man'yōshu tomoshibi,* a study of the *Man'yōshū* (1822); and *Makoto ben* (ca. 1804–06). His poems, mainly *waka,* were collected by his disciples in the *Fujitani Mitsue ushi no ie no shū.* Son of Fujitani Nariakira.

• **Fujitana Nariakira.** Man of letters and grammarian (Minagawa Shigeaki, 1738–79), brother of Sinologist Minigawa Kien (1734–1807), adopted by the Fujitani family of the Yanagawa estate (Fukuoka prefecture). He sorted Japanese words into categories and collected them in two types of lexicons, the *Kazashishō* (1767) and the *Ayuishō* (1773, published in 1778). He is generally considered the true founder of Japanese grammar. Father of Fujitani Mitsue.

• **Fujitani Shigeaki.** *See* FUJITANI NARIAKIRA.

Fujita Sadasuke. Mathematician (1734–1807), author of *Seiyō sampō* (Essence of Mathematics), in 1781. *See* WASAN.

Fujita Tōko. Confucian scholar (Takeki, Hinkei, Takejirō, Toranosuke, 1806–55) of the Mito school, son of Fujita Yūkoku and professor in Shōkokan starting in 1827. In 1840, he was appointed Grand Chamberlain to Tokugawa Nariaki, and suffered the same fate of house arrest. During this period of seclusion, he wrote *Kōdōkan ki jutsugi,* which was to become the basic text of the Mito school. When Nariaki was granted amnesty in 1849, Fujita Tōko resumed his role as his adviser.

Fujita Toyohachi. Sinologist (1869–1928). He traveled to China in 1897 and became a friend of Luo Zhenyu (1866–1940), a famous scholar who had been the tutor of Emperor Puyi in Tianjin from 1925 to 1929 and studied the manuscripts of Dunhuang (*Jap.:* Tonkō). He returned to Japan with him and taught Chinese history at Tokyo University.

Fujita Tsuguharu. Painter (Fujita Tsuguji, Léonard Fujita, 1886–1968), born in Tokyo. He obtained a diploma from Tokyo University of Fine Arts in 1910; in 1912, he went to Paris, where he formed friendships with the Montparnasse painters—Soutine, Picasso, Modigliani, and others—and became a member of the "Paris school." He then became known for his drawings of women and of cats, which made him popular with the Parisian public. He returned to Japan during the Second World War and painted battle scenes for the army. Returning to France permanently in 1949, after a year in the United States, he became a naturalized French citizen in 1955; in 1957, he was decorated with the Legion of Honor. He converted to Catholicism in 1966 and took the name Léonard. He then devoted himself to painting religious subjects; he decorated the chapel of Notre-Dame de la Paix in Reims. He signed his work Fujita or Foujita.

Fujita Yūkoku. Confucian scholar (1774–1826) of the Mito school, a member of the Shōkōkan group that wrote *Dai Nihon shi.* He was particularly interested in rural and agricultural conditions; in 1799, he published *Kannō wakumon,* in which he analyzed the pitiful conditions in the villages at the time. He was appointed chief of the Shōkōkan in 1807. Father of Fujita Tōko.

Fuji Terebijon. Fuji Telecasting, the flagship television station based in Tokyo, was founded in 1959 as part of the Fuji Sankei group, a conservative media conglomerate that publishes the daily *Sankei Shimbun.* The network (FNN) has 27 stations.

Fujito. Title of a Noh play, based on a wartime episode between the Minamoto and Taira clans in 1184, attributed to Zeami (1363–1443).

Fujitsū. Manufacturer of electronic equipment and computers, exporting the brands Facom and Fetex (the latter for telecommunications equipment). The firm, founded in 1935, was originally the telephone department of Fuji Denki Seizō. The unique aspect of Fujitsū is that it uses an entirely Japanese technology. It has many foreign branches, notably in the United States, Brazil, Spain, Germany, Ireland, South Korea, and Australia, and exports more than 17% of its production. Head office in Tokyo.

Fujitsubo. Apartments reserved for women in the *seiryōden* of the imperial palace in Kyoto. Also called *higyōsha, ōoku. See* KOKIDEN.

• **Fujitsubo-ue no Mitsubone.** *See* KOKIDEN.

Fujiwara. Capital of the Yamato clan from 694 to 710, on the site of today's village of Kashihara (Nara prefecture), where Empress Jitō and emperors Mommu and Gemmei ruled. It was Empress Jitō, daughter of Emperor Temmu (who reigned at Asuka), who established the new capital. The site of Fujiwara-kyō was excavated in 1934, and it was possible to reconstruct some plans of the palaces, which had been faced with tiles. The town had an area of 3,210 m × 2,140 m and was laid out on a Chinese plan. More than 2,000 wooden tablets *(mokkan)* inscribed with Chinese characters have been discovered. The town was likely destroyed by fire in 711, but Nara (Heijō-kyō) had already been chosen as the new capital, so Fujiwara-kyō was not rebuilt. The town had been the fief of the Nakatomi family, whose duty at court was to ensure that Shinto, the indigenous faith of Japan, was strictly observed and to lead ceremonies having to do with worship of Amaterasu and Ninigi no Mikoto, the divine ancestors of the imperial family. Also called Fujiwara-kyō, Fujiwara no Miya.

• Powerful family of nobles and landowners of the Nakatomi clan who took over the Yamato court in the seventh century, from among whose leaders came the Shinto ritualists. In their political and religious opposition to the Soga family, they eliminated the most influential members of that family in 645 (*see* SOGA), thus reinforcing their influence at court. In 699, Emperor Tenji permitted Nakatomi no Kamatari to take the family name Fujiwara as compensation for services rendered. The first Fujiwara was thus Nakatomi no Kamatari's son, Fujiwara no Fuhito; one of his daughters married Emperor Mommu and another married Emperor Shōmu; the custom was thus started for emperors to marry Fujiwara women. Thanks to these family ties, the Fujiwara family soon became all-powerful in the court and supplied Japan with its greatest statesmen and poets until the twelfth century.

• **Fujiwara bunka.** The culture of the Fujiwara era, the aristocratic Japanese society that prevailed from the mid-ninth century to the late twelfth century, the latter date corresponding to the end of the Heian period, when emperors resided in Heian-kyō (Kyoto). In 894, official contact with China ceased, but cultural influences from the continent were assimilated and a brilliant native Japanese culture was developed under the aegis of the Fujiwara family. The Esoteric Buddhist sects, such as Shingon and Tendai, fell into decline, while pietistic sects, such as Jōdo, gained in popularity. New styles of painting and sculpture emerged, as did innovative architectural arrangements of temples and residences *(shinden-zukuri)*. The development of the kana syllabaries enabled literature to be popularized to a certain extent. Culture was no longer confined to Kyoto but spread to the provinces within newly established monasteries and local governments, reaching even remote regions thanks to itinerant Buddhist monks. Japan no longer imitated China but developed a typical indigenous culture. The brilliant Fujiwara period ended with the ascent to power of the warrior class *(bushi)* and the creation of Minsmoto no Yoritomo's *bakufu* in Kamakura in 1192.

• **Fujiwara no Akihira.** Poet (989–1066) whose works, written in Chinese, were inspired by Confucianism; he held the position of Monjō Hakase

in the court. About 1060, he compiled *Honchō monzui,* an anthology of 427 poems written in Chinese by Japanese authors (14 scrolls) and the *Meigō ōrai,* a collection of models for letter writing. Another work, *Shin sarugōki,* describes life in Kyoto in his times. His two sons, Atsumoto and Atsumitsu, were also renowned poets.

• **Fujiwara no Akiko.** Daughter (988–1074) of Fujiwara no Michinaga, Emperor Ichijō's wife (in 999), and mother of emperors Go-Ichijō and Go-Suzaku. She became a Buddhist nun in 1026 and took the name Jōtō Mon'in. She was the protector of the women writers Murasaki Shikibu, Izumi Shikibu, and Akazone Emon. Also called Fujiwara no Shōshi.

• **Fujiwara no Akimitsu.** Son (Akuryō-safu, 944–1021) of Fujiwara no Kanemichi and minister of the left *(sadaifu)*. His daughter, Enshi, married Crown Prince Ko-Ichijō no In (Atsuakira).

• **Fujiwara no Akirakeiko.** Daughter (829–900) of Fujiwara no Yoshifusa and wife of Emperor Montoku. She was the mother of Emperor Seiwa. Also called Fujiwara no Akiko.

• **Fujiwara no Akisue.** Poet (1054–1122), founder of a classical-poetry *(waka)* school. He occupied the official positions of *shuri-taiyū* and Rokujō *shuri-taiyū*. Father of Akisuke.

• **Fujiwara no Akisuke.** *Waka* poet (1090–1155), son of Fujiwara no Akisue. He compiled the imperial anthology *Shika waka-shū* between 1144 and 1151 (*see* CHOKUSEN WAKA-SHŪ) on the orders of Retired Emperor Sutoku. Of his own poems, 145 were preserved in *Akisuke shū,* and others (about 80) are in imperial anthologies. Also called Rokujō Akisuke because he was a member of the Rokujō poetry school founded by his father.

• **Fujiwara no Akitada.** Minister of the right *(udaijin;* 898–965), son of Fujiwara no Tokihira. Also known as Tomukōji Udaijin.

• **Fujiwara no Arihira.** Minister (891–970), appointed *udaijin,* then *sadaijin*. Grandson of Fujiwara no Yamakage. Known as Awada no Sadaijin.

• **Fujiwara no Ariie.** Poet (1155–1216).

• **Fujiwara no Atsumitsu.** Poet (1062–1144), son of Fujiwara no Akihira. He wrote mainly Confucian-inspired poems in Chinese. He held the position of Monjō Hakase.

• **Fujiwara no Atsutada.** Statesman and poet (906–43), son of Fujiwara no Tokihira. Also called Hon'in Chūnagon.

Fujiwara no Atsumoto. *See* FUJIWARA NO AKIHIRA.

• **Fujiwara no Enshi.** Daughter of Fujiwara no Akimitsu (944–1021) and wife of Crown Prince Atsuakira Shinnō (later Koichijō no In). When he took a second wife, Enshi returned to her family; she died (of heartbreak, it was said) soon after.

• **Fujiwara no Fuhito (Fubito).** Statesman (659–720), son of Nakatomi no Kamatari. Emperor Tenji conferred the family name Fujiwara upon him in 699. Appointed *udaijin,* he remained in this position through the reigns of Jitō Tennō, Gemmei Tennō, and Genshō Tennō. He helped to write the Taihō Code (701; *Taihō ritsuryō*) and had his daughters married to emperors Mommu and Shōmu. His four sons—Muchimaro (680–737), Fusasaki (681–737), Umakai (694–737), and Maro (695–737)—each founded a different branch of the Fujiwara family (Nanke, Hokke, Shikike, and Kyōke). Four of Fujiwara no Fuhoti's poems are included in the anthology *Kaifūsō.* He received the posthumous title *dajō daijin. See* AGATA NO INUKAI NO MICHIYO.

• **Fujiwara no Fujifusa.** Courtier (1295–ca. 1380) to Emperor Go-Daigo, son of Fujiwara no Nobufusa. He went into exile with Emperor Go-Daigo after the latter's attempted coup d'état against the Kamakura *bakufu* (Genkō Jiken, 1331), but he was taken prisoner and exiled to Hitachi province (Ibaraki prefecture). He returned to Heian-kyō during the Kammu Restoration of 1333, but his aspirations went unfulfilled and he became a Buddhist monk in 1335, abandoning public life.

• **Fujiwara no Fusasaki.** Son (681–737) of Fujiwara no Fuhito and founder of the Hokke branch of the Fujiwara family. Died of smallpox.

• **Fujiwara no Fuyutsugu.** Son (775–826) of Fujiwara no Uchimaro, of the Hokke branch of the Fujiwara family, appointed *sadaijin* in 825, having been the leader of the Kurōdo-dokoro (an informal imperial secretariat). A poet, he helped compile the *Bunka shūrei shū,* a collection of poems in Chinese, in 818, then a collection of jurisprudence, in 820.

He founded the Kangaku-in school in 821 for the education of his family. One of his daughters married Emperor Nimmyō. Also known as Kan'in no Sadaijin.

• **Fujiwara no Gōshin.** *See* GŌSHIN.

• **Fujiwara no Hamanari.** Great-grandson (711–90) of Nakatomi (Fujiwara) no Kamatari and minister (Dazai no Sōtsu) in 781. He wrote *Tensho,* a chronological history of Japan.

• **Fujiwara no Hidehira.** Lord (1096–1187) of Mutsu province (northern Honshu), of the Ōshu Fujiwara family, appointed Chinjufu-shōgun ("general against the Ainu"). He took in Minamoto no Yoshitsune when he fled to Mutsu in 1185. His mummified body was found under the main altar of the Konjiki-dō at Chūson-ji in Hirazumi, along with those of his father, Motohira, and his grandfather, Kiyohira (1056–1128), and the head of his son, Yasuhira, killed in battle against Minamoto no Yoritomo in 1189.

• **Fujiwara no Hidesato.** Military bureaucrat (tenth century) serving Emperor Suzaku; in 940, he formed an alliance with Taira no Sadamori and defeated the rebellious Taira no Masakado. He was then appointed Chinjufu-shōgun and governor of Shimotsuke. The Ōshū Fujiwara, Shimokōbe, Oyama, and Yūki families, among others, were descended from him. He was famous for his courage, and his life was the subject of many legends.

• **Fujiwara no Hirotsugu.** Leader of the Shikike branch of the Fujiwara family, and oldest son (715–40) of Fujiwara no Umakai. Appointed to a minor position in Dazaifu (northern Kyushu) in 738, he raised an army of 10,000 men and led a rebellion two years later. The imperial armies defeated him near the Itabitsu River, and he was captured and beheaded. His death marked the end of the Shikike branch and the rise in influence of the Nanke (Southern) branch. Some of his poems are included in the *Man'yoshū.*

• **Fujiwara no Ienaga.** Poet (1192–1264) who helped to compile the imperial anthology *Zoku kokin waka-shū* (1265).

• **Fujiwara no Ietaka.** Son (1158–1237) of Fujiwara no Mitsutaka and a poet, student of Fujiwara no Shunzei. He was the master of Emperor Go-Toba and worked with Fujiwara no Sadaie to compile the anthology *Shin waka-shū* (1205), which contains 43 of his poems. His personal collection, the *Minishū,* includes about 3,200 poems. He is considered the greatest poet of his time after Fujiwara no Teika. Also called Mibu-ni-i, Karyū.

• **Fujiwara no Iezane.** Statesman (1180–1283) who was a *sesshō* (regent to a minor) and then a *dajō daijin* (grand minister). He was the son of Fujiwara no Motonichi and the ancestor of the Konoe and Takatsukasa families.

• **Fujiwara no Ishi.** Daughter (999–1036) of Fujiwara no Michinaga; she married Emperor Go-Ichijō.

• **Fujiwara no Izuko.** Daughter (1351–1406) of Fujiwara no Kintada. She married Emperor Go-En'yū and was the mother of Emperor Go-Komatsu. In 1386, she became a Buddhist nun under the name Tsuyō Mon'in.

• **Fujiwara no Kadonomaro.** Son (late eighth–early ninth century) of Fujiwara no Oguromaro (733–794), a grandson of Fujiwara no Fusasaki. He was sent as ambassador to China in 804, and the Buddhist monk Kūkai accompanied him.

• **Fujiwara (Nakatomi) no Kamatari.** Landowner (614–69) and leader of the Shinto ritualists (Jingi no Haku), although the indigenous faith had been supplanted by Buddhism at court. The Soga family (Buddhist) had become too powerful, and Prince Naka no Ōe, son of Emperor Jomei, assisted by Nakatomi no Kamatari, led a coup d'état in 645 during which Soga no Iruka was killed and Soga no Emishi committed suicide. Empress Kōgyoku was forced to abdicate in favor of her younger brother Karu, who ascended to the throne under the name Kōtoku. Kamatari was appointed inner minister (*naidaijin* in 669). He then launched a program of reforms aimed at reinforcing imperial authority (Taika Reform, 645), modeled on Chinese institutions of the Tang dynasty. Before he died, Emperor Tenji (ex-Prince Naka no Ōe) conferred upon him the right to change his family name to Fujiwara. His nephew, Nakatomi no Omimaro (d. 711), became the head of the national shrines of Ise, keeping the Nakatomi family name.

Fujiwara no Kanehira. Statesman (1228–94), *dajō daijin* (grand minister), then *kampaku* (regent). Also called Takatsukasa no Kanehira.

• **Fujiwara no Kaneie.** Statesman (929–90), younger brother of Fujiwara no Kanemichi and son of Fujiwara no Morosuke.He held the positions of *sesshō* (987), *dajō daijin,* and *kampaku* (990). His daughter, Senshi, married Emperor En'yū, and he himself married a noblewoman, the author of *Kagerō nikki* (*see* FUJIWARA NO MOTOYASU). In 986, he forced Emperor Kazan to abdicate in favor of his own grandson, Ichijō. He was the father of Michitaka (953–95), Michikane (961–95), and Michinaga (966–1028). Also called Hōkō-in Daijin, Higashi-sanjō-dono.

• Fujiwara no Kaneko. *See* SANUKI TENJI.

• **Fujiwara no Kanemichi.** Statesman (925–77), son of Fujiwara no Morosuke (908–60). He became *sesshō* in 972, *kampaku* and *dajō daijin* in 974. To foil his rival, Fujiwara no Kaneie, he had his cousin, Fujiwara no Yoritada (924–89), appointed regent (*kampaku*) when he died. Also called Horikawa-dono. *Posthumous name:* Tōtōmi-kō.

Fujiwara no Kamatari, founder of the Fujiwara family in the 7th century (drawing by Kikuchi Yōsai)

• **Fujiwara no Kanesue.** Statesman (fourteenth century), appointed *udaijin* (minister of the right) in 1322–23. Also called Kikutai Udaijin.

• **Fujiwara no Kanesuke.** *Waka* poet (877–933) and mid-level bureaucrat (*chūnagon* in 930). About 55 of his poems were included in various imperial anthologies. His personal collection, *Kanesukeshū*, contains 125. He was included in the Sanjūrokkasen (Thirty-six Poetic Geniuses).

• **Fujiwara no Kanezane.** Statesman (1149–1207), son of Fujiwara no Tadamichi. He was appointed *sesshō* in 1185, then *kampaku* in 1190 under Emperor Go-Toba. He was the founder of the Kujō family, one of the five Fujiwara families (*see* GO-SEKKE) that supplied regents (*kampaku*) to the emperors. He wrote a diary, the *Gyokuyō*, covering the years 1164–1201. Also called Kujō no Kanezane, Tsuki no Wa no Kampaku.

• **Fujiwara no Kimiko.** Daughter (994–1027) of Fujiwara no Michinaga and wife of Sanjō Tennō.

• **Fujiwara no Kinkata.** Statesman (Tōin Kinkata, 1291–1360) who held the position of grand minister (*dajō daijin*). He wrote the *Shūkaisho*, a sort of encyclopedia (1320–41), and a diary called *Entairyaku*.

• **Fujiwara no Kinsue.** Statesman (956–1029), son of Fujiwara no Morosuke. He was appointed grand minister (*dajō daijin*) in 1021. *Posthumous name:* Kaikō.

• **Fujiwara no Kintō.** Statesman (966–1041) and poet, son of Fujiwara no Yoritada. His reputation as a poet in Japanese and Chinese and as a musician were such that he was cited in the works of Murasaki Shikibu and Sei Shōnagon and in many of the works of his time, including *Eiga monogatari*, *Konjaku monogatari*, and *Ōkagami*. More than 100 of his poems were included in imperial anthologies (*see* CHOKUSEN WAKA-SHŪ). He wrote a number of treatises on poetry, including *Waka kuhon* (The Nine Levels of Excellence of *Waka*), in which he classified poems in his order of preference, and *Shinsen zuinō*, as well as a personal anthology, the *Kintōshū*, containing 385 of his poems. Among his other poetry books, the best known are the *Wakan rōeishū* (Collection of Japanese and Chinese Songs, ca. 1013), comprising 217 Japanese and 587 Chinese poems. He also compiled a number of poetry anthologies, such as the *Nyioihōshū* (Collection of

Buddhist Treasures), containing 775 poems, and the *Shūi waka-shū*, an expansion in 20 scrolls of a previous poetry anthology called the *Shūishō*. He also established the Sanjūrokkasen (Thirty-Six Poetic Geniuses). His calligraphy was considered exemplary. Also called Shijō Dainagon.

• **Fujiwara no Kintsugu.** Statesman (1175–1227), *udaijin* in 1211, then *sadaijin* in 1221. Also called Nonomiya Sadaijin.

• **Fujiwara no Kintsune.** Statesman (d. 1244) and poet. He became a Buddhist monk.

• **Fujiwara no Kinyoshi.** *See* FUJIWARA NO MASUKO.

• **Fujiwara no Kiyohira.** Lord (1056–1128) of Mutsu province (northern Honshu) of the Ōshū Fujiwara family. He was the founder of the Chūsonji temple in Hiraizumi, where his mummified body was found. *See* FUJIWARA NO HIDEHIRA, CHŪSONJI.

• **Fujiwara no Kiyokawa.** Statesman (ca. 706–ca. 779), son of Fujiwara no Fusasaki. He was sent as an ambassador to China in 750; in 752, he was received by Emperor Xuanzong (*Jap.*: Genso) of the Tang dynasty. He attempted to return to Japan twice: the first time his ship was wrecked on the Annam coast; the second time, his plans were frustrated by the An Lushan Rebellion. He then settled in China, took a Chinese name, and held a position in the imperial court, as did Abe no Nakamaro.

• **Fujiwara no Kiyosuke.** *Waka* poet (1104–1177), son of Fujiwara no Akisuke. Some hundred of his poems were included in imperial anthologies (*see* CHOKUSEN WAKA-SHŪ). He also wrote treatises on poetry: *Ōgishō* (Notes on Basic Principles, ca. 1140), *Fukuro-zōshi* (Ordinary Book, ca. 1157), *Waka shogaku shō* (Notes on Japanese Poetry for Beginners), and *Waka ichiji shō* (Notes on Poetic Diction).

• **Fujiwara no Korechika.** Statesman (973–1010), son of Fujiwara no Michitaka. Accused of having shot an arrow at Emperor Kazan, he was exiled to Dazaifu in 996 but was granted amnesty the following year. He was the brother of Fujiwara no Teishi, a wife of Emperor Ichijō. Also called Gidō Sanchi, Sotsu no Naidaijin.

• **Fujiwara no Korekata.** Statesman (b. 1125). After taking part in the Heiji no Ran insurrection, he was sent into exile by Retired Emperor Go-Shirakawa, who had sided with the Taira clan. Also called Awada no Bettō.

• **Fujiwara no Koremichi.** Statesman (1093–1165), son of Fujiwara no Munemichi. He held the position of *naidaijin*, then of *sadaijin* (1157), during the reign of Emperor Sutoku, then that of *dajō daijin* in 1060. He wrote a critique of Emperor Nijō's policies in a book called *Taikai hishō*.

• **Fujiwara no Koretada.** Statesman (924–72), son of Fujiwara no Morosuke. He was appointed *udaijin* in 970, *sesshō* in 971, then *dajō daijin*. Also called Ichijō Sesshō, Mikawa-kō.

• **Fujiwara no Kōzei.** *See* FUJIWARA NO YUKINARI.

• **Fujiwara no Kurajimaro.** Statesman (734–75), who held the positions of *hyōbu-kyō* and *sangi* (councillor), but who was opposed to Fujiwara no Nakamaro.

Fujiwara no Kusuko. Daughter of Fujiwara no Tanetsugu (d. 810) and concubine of Emperor Heijō. She took part in a plot to restore Emperor Heijō to the throne (he had abdicated in favor of his brother, Saga) and reestablish the capital at Heijō-kyō (Nara). She poisoned herself when the plot was discovered. Also called Fujiwara no Kuzushi.

• **Fujiwara no Maro.** Son (695–737) of Fujiwara no Fuhito. He founded the Kyōke branch of the Fujiwara family. He and his brothers died in the smallpox epidemic that swept Japan in 737.

• **Fujiwara no Masako.** Daughter (1121–81) of Fujiwara no Tadamichi, who married Emperor Sutoku. She became a Buddhist nun in 1150 under the name Kōka Mon'in. Also called Fujiwara no Seishi.

• **Fujiwara no Masatsune.** Poet (1170–1221), founder of the Asukai family and famous in his time as a *kemari* player. He helped compile both the *Sengohyaku ban uta awase,* a collection of 1,500 "linked *waka*" poems, in 1201, and the imperial anthology (*see* CHOKUSEN WAKA-SHŪ) *Shin kokin waka-shū*.

• **Fujiwara no Masuko.** Daughter (1140–1201) of Fujiwara no Kin'yoshi, adopted by Fujiwara no Yorinaga. She married Emperor Konoe, then Emperor Nijō. Also known as Ōiko, Tashi, Tadako.

• **Fujiwara no Michichika.** Writer (1149–1200 or 1202) and statesman in the governments of seven successive emperors. He is sometimes credited with writing *Ima kagami*. Also known as Minamoto no Michichika.

• **Fujiwara no Michie.** *See* KUJŌ NO MICHIE.

• **Fujiwara no Michikane.** Statesman (961–95), son of Fujiwara no Kaneie. He was appointed *udaijin* in 994, then *kampaku* in 995. Since he held the latter position for only seven days, he was nicknamed Nanoka no Kampaku ("seven-day regent").

• **Fujiwara no Michinaga.** Statesman (966–1028), son of Fujiwara no Kaneie. He held a number of ministerial posts and was appointed *sesshō* in 1016. His three daughters, Akiko (Shōshi), Kenshi, and Ishi, married emperors Ichijō, Sanjō, and Go-Ichijō, so he became all-powerful at court and was appointed *dajō daijin* in 1018. Although he was never officially appointed *kampaku,* he had all the power associated with the position because he controlled the entire state apparatus. To reinforce his power, he formed an alliance with the Seiwa Genji branch of the powerful Minamoto warrior family and had his son, Fujiwara no Yorimichi, appointed to the position of regent *(kampaku)* and his other sons to various ministerial positions. In 1019, with his health in decline, he became a Buddhist monk, built Hōjō-ji temple, and retired from public life, while continuing to direct the policies of his son, Yorimichi. His other son, Norimichi, was also a regent *(kampaku)*. Michinaga was also known under the name of his residence, Midō, as Midō Kampaku, so he called his diary *Midō kampaku ki*. It is said that he was the model for Genji in Murasaki Shikibu's *Genji monogatari (The Tale of Genji)*. He received the posthumous name Hojō no Kampaku.

• **Fujiwara no Michinori.** Poet (1106–60) and Buddhist monk under the name Shinzei, son of Fujiwara no Sanekane. His wife was Emperor Go-Shirakawa's nurse, and he therefore had great influence at court. He was killed in battle with Minamoto no Yoritomo during the Heiji War. He compiled a history of Japan, *Honchō seiki*.

• **Fujiwara no Michitaka.** Statesman (953–95), son of Fujiwara no Kaneie. He was appointed *sesshō* in 990, then *kampaku* in 993 under Emperor

Ichijō, who married his daughter Teishi (Sadako). Also called Nijō Kampaku.

• **Fujiwara no Michitoshi.** *Waka* poet (1047–99), compiler of the imperial anthology (*see* CHOKUSEN WAKA-SHŪ) *Go shūi waka-shū* in 1086, on the orders of Emperor Shirakawa. Five of his own poems appear in it, while others are included in anthologies such as the *Zoku kokin waka-shū* (1265).

• **Fujiwara no Mitsunaga.** Painter (d. 1187) of the Kasuga school, who illustrated the *Nenjū gyōji emaki* handscroll. Also called Tokiwa Mitsunaga.

• **Fujiwara no Momokawa.** Statesman (732–79), son of Fujiwara no Umakai and minister under emperors Kōken, Shōtoku, and Kōnin. He had Prince Yamabe Shinnō named emperor (Emperor Kammu) in 773.

• **Fujiwara no Moroie.** *See* FUJIWARA NO MOTOFUSA.

• **Fujiwara no Moromichi.** Statesman (1062–99), son of Fujiwara no Morozane. He was appointed *kampaku* in 1094. He signed his memoir, *Go-Nijō kampaku ki,* with his nickname, *Go-Nijō Kampaku.*

• **Fujiwara no Moromitsu.** Statesman (d. 1117). Implicated in a plot concocted against the Taira family by Fujiwara no Narichika, he was executed, along with his two sons.

• **Fujiwara no Moronaga.** Statesman (1138–92), son of Fujiwara no Yorinaga. He was sent into exile after the Hōgen insurrection (Hōgen no Ran) in 1156; granted amnesty, he was appointed *dajō daijin* in 1177. Also called Myō-on'in Daijin.

• **Fujiwara no Morosuke.** Statesman (908–60), son of Fujiwara no Tadahira. Appointed *udaijin* in 947. He wrote a manual on official ceremonies, the *Kujō nenjū gyōji*. Also known as Kujō-dono and Hōjō Udaijin.

• **Fujiwara no Morozane.** Statesman (1042–1101), son of Fujiwara no Yorimichi. He held the positions of *kampaku* in 1075, *sesshō* in 1087, and *dajō daijin* under emperors Go-Reizei, Shirakawa, and Horikawa. His daughter, Kenshi, married Shirakawa Tennō. He wrote his memoirs *(Kyōgoku kampaku-ki)* and some poems. Also called Go-Uji Nyūdō, Kyōgoku Kampaku.

• **Fujiwara no Motofusa.** Statesman (1144–1230), son of Fujiwara no Tadamichi. He was appointed *sesshō* in 1166, *dajō daijin,* then *kampaku* in 1171. Taira no Kiyomori sent him into exile in Dazaifu (Kyushu) with the title Dazai no Gon no Sotsu, and his son, Moroie, was appointed *kampaku* in 1183 and 1184. Also called Matsudono, Bodai-in no Kampaku.

• **Fujiwara no Motohira.** *See* ōshū, fujiwara no kiyohira, fujiwara no hidehira, chūson-ji.

• **Fujiwara no Motoie.** Poet (thirteenth century), co-author, with Fujiwara no Mitsutoshi, of the imperial anthology (*see* CHOKUSEN WAKA-SHŪ) *Zoku kokin waka-shū* (1265).

• **Fujiwara no Motomichi.** Statesman (1160–1233), son of Fujiwara no Motozane. He was appointed *kampaku* in 1179, *sesshō* under Emperor Antoku in 1180, *sesshō* under Emperor Go-Toba in 1183, *kampaku* once again in 1196, and *sesshō* under Emperor Tsuchimikado from 1198 to 1202. After that, he became a Buddhist monk. Also called Fugenji-dono.

• **Fujiwara no Motomitsu.** Painter (eleventh century) said to have founded the Yamato-ryū school of traditional painting.

• **Fujiwara no Mototoshi.** *Waka* poet (ca. 1056–ca. 1138 or 1142), great-grandson of Fujiwara no Michinaga. He became a Buddhist monk in 1138. Some hundred of his poems are in imperial anthologies (*see* CHOKUSEN WAKA-SHŪ). He was the master of Fujiwara no Toshinari (Shunzei) and helped to compile the anthology *Shinsen rōeishū* (ca. 1110), a collection of Japanese and Chinese songs in verse.

• **Fujiwara no Mototsune.** Statesman (836–91), son of Fujiwara no Nagayoshi. He held the positions of *udaijin* in 872, *sesshō* in 876, and *dajō daijin* in 880. He deposed Emperor Yōzei and had Prince Tokiyasu enthroned as Emperor Kōkō. In 888, however, Mototsune deposed Kōkō to put Prince Uda on the throne. In 884, he was the first to receive the title *kampaku*. His two daughters, Onshi (I) and Onshi (II), married emperors Uda and Daigo. In collaboration with other authors, he wrote the *Montoku jitsuroku*. Also known as Horikawa Daijin.

• **Fujiwara no Motoyasu.** Scholar (tenth century), father of the woman of letters thought to have written the *Kagerō nikki* (translated into English as *The Gossamer Years*). This poet and author, whose real name is unkown, married Fujiwara no Kaneie, with whom she had a son, Michitsuna, in 954. She kept up a poetic correspondence with her husband.

• **Fujiwara no Motozane.** Statesman (1143–66), son of Fujiwara no Tadamichi. He was appointed *kampaku* in 1159 and *sesshō* under Emperor Rokujō in 1165. Also called Umezu-dono.

• **Fujiwara no Muchimaro.** Statesman (680–737), son of Fujiwara no Fuhito. He was appointed *udaijin* in 734, then *sadaijin* in 737. He founded the Nanke (Southern) branch of the Fujiwara family. He died in the smallpox epidemic of 737.

• **Fujiwara no Munehiro.** Court painter of the Kyūtei E-dokoro, the Imperial Court Office of Painting (active mid-twelfth century). In 1135, he made a plan of Emperor Tona's secondary palace south of Kyoto; in 1184, he painted screens for the Daijōsai ceremony. He supposedly also worked for the Eikyū-ji in Yamato province.

• **Fujiwara no Munetada.** Statesman (1062–1141) and poet. He served as *udaijin* under emperors Shirakawa, Horikawa, Toba, and Sutoku. His diary, the *Chūyu ki,* recounts 52 years of political life. Also called Nakamikado no Udaijin.

• **Fujiwara no Nagako.** *See* SANUKI TENJI.

• **Fujiwara no Nagataka.** *See* NAGATAKA.

• **Fujiwara no Nagate.** Statesman (714–71), son of Fujiwara no Fusasaki. He was *sadaijin* under emperors Shōmu, Kōken, Junnin, Shōtoku, and Kōnin. Also called Nagaoka Daijin.

• **Fujiwara no Nakahira.** Statesman (875–945), son of Fujiwara no Mototsune and brother of Tokihira. He was *sadaijin* under emperors Daigo and Suzaku. Also called Biwa no Daijin.

• **Fujiwara no Nakamoro.** Statesman (706–64), son of Fujiwara no Muchimaro. He was opposed to the undertakings of the monk Dōkyō but was defeated by his cousins, who took the monk's side and killed him and his two sons. Also called Emi no Oshikatsu.

• **Fujiwara no Nakanari.** Court noble (774–810), son of Fujiwara no Tanetsugu. He plotted (with his sister, Kusuko) against Emperor Saga and was beheaded.

• **Fujiwara no Narichika.** Statesman (1138–78), son of Fujiwara no Ienari. He was exiled and put to death by the Taira clan for having plotted against them. His son, Naritsune, was also exiled; he died in 1202.

• **Fujiwara no Naritsune.** *See* FUJIWARA NO NARICHIKA.

• **Fujiwara no Nobuyori.** Statesman (1133–59), son of Fujiwara no Tadataka. Having sided with the Minamoto clan during the Heiji no Ran insurrection in 1159, he was killed by the Taira clan.

• **Fujiwara no Nobuzane.** *Waka* poet and painter (ca. 1177–ca. 1265), son of Fujiwara no Takanobu. Specializing in portraits *(nise-e),* he worked for retired emperors Go-Toba and Go-Horikawa and for members of the Kujō family. No examples of his work have survived except, possibly, a portrait of Retired Emperor Go-Toba made in 1221, now the property of the Minase Shrine in Mishima (Osaka). He is credited, but with no certainty, with other portraits and a number of *emakimono* handscrolls, including *Zuijin teiki emaki, Murasaki Shikibu nikki emaki, Kitano Tenjin engi emaki,* and *Sanjūrokkasen emaki.* He is said to have signed some of his works with the *gō* Jakusai. He is better known under the single name Nobuzane. Father of Fujiwata no Tametsugu.

• **Fujiwara no Norikane.** Minister and poet (d. 1165).

• **Fujiwara no Norimichi.** Statesman (997–1075), son of Fujiwara no Michinaga. He became *kampaku* in 1068 and *dajō daijin* in 1070. His daughter, Kanshi, married Emperor Go-Reizei, and his younger daughter married Emperor Go-Suzaku. Also called O-Nijō-dono.

• **Fujiwara no Norinaga.** Poet and calligrapher (1109–77), son of Fujiwara no Tadanori. He wrote a commentary on the imperial anthology *Kokin waka-shū* in 1177.

• **Fujiwara no Oguromaro.** Commander of the imperial army (733–94), grandson of Fujiwara no Fusasaki, who went to war against the Ebisu clan in 780 and received the titles Ise no Kami and Mutsu no Kami. At court, his title was *dainagon.*

• **Fujiwara no Ōiko.** *See* FUJIWARA NO MASUKO.

• **Fujiwara no Onshi.** Name of two daughters of Fujiwara no Mototsune. The first (872–907) was the wife of Emperor Uda; the second (885–954), the wife of Emperor Daigo, was the mother of emperors Suzaku and Murakami.

• **Fujiwara no Otomuro.** Daughter (760–90) of Fujiwara no Yoshitsugu and wife of Emperor Kammu, with whom she had two sons who became emperors Heijō and Saga.

• **Fujiwara no Otsugu.** Son (773–843) of Fujiwara no Momokawa. He became *udaijin* in 825 and *sadaijin* in 832 under emperors Saga, Junna, and Nimmyō. He compiled the 40-volume *Nihon kōki*.

• **Fujiwara no Renshi.** Adoptive daughter (1301–59) of Fujiwara no Kintaka. She married Emperor Go-Daigo and was the mother of Emperor Go-Murakami. She became a Buddhist nun in 1351 under the name Shin Taiken Mon'in.

• **Fujiwara no Ryūsen.** *See* SHŪKI.

• **Fujiwara no Sadaie.** Poet and imperial bureaucrat (1162–1241), son of Fujiwara no Toshinari. He used the name Teika (the "Chinese" reading of Sadaie) to sign his works. A difficult personality, he was exiled in 1185 for hitting a superior. His career never advanced greatly, although he was rehabilitated in 1186; he obtained the title *gon chūnagon* (provisional middle counselor) only in 1232. He then became a Buddhist monk under the name Myōjō, while continuing to write poetry. His first collection, *Shūi gusō* (Foolish Verses of the Court Chamberlain) was published in 1216, followed by *Shūi gusō ingai* (Supplement to *Shūi gusō*). In 1232, Emperor Go-Horikawa asked him to compile the imperial anthologies *Shin chokusen waka-shū* and *Shin kokin waka-shū*. His diary, *Meigetsuki* (Diary of the Full Moon) and his *Meigetsushō* (Monthly Notes), written about 1219, provide important documentation of the times and of Sadaie's contemporaries during the period from 1180 to 1235. He is credited with having chosen poems for the collection *Hyakunin isshū*. His *Nishidaishū* (Collection of Two Times Four Eras), compiled about 1215, contains a selection of 873 classical poems by various authors. He was also responsible for collections such as *Kindai shūka* (Superior Poems of Our Time, ca. 1209) and *Eiga taigai* (Poetic Composition, ca. 1222). About 4,600 of his poems have survived to

the present day in various collections and imperial anthologies (*see* CHOKUSEN WAKA-SHŪ). Some of his poems, however, remain unpublished, having been jealously guarded by his descendants in the Reizei, Nijō, and Kyōgoku families. *See also* FUJIWARA NO TOSHINORI.

• **Fujiwara no Sadako.** Daughter (976–1000) of Fujiwara no Michitaka, who married Emperor Ichijō and was the patron of Sei Shōnagon. Also called Fujiwara no Teishi.

• **Fujiwara no Sadayori.** Statesman (995–1045), son of Fujiwara no Kintō. He was a minister and a poet well known in his time.

• **Fujiwara no Sanesuke.** Statesman (957–1046), son of Fujiwara no Tadatoshi. He was appointed *udaijin* in 1021. Author of a diary, *Shōyuki*. Also called Go-Ono no Miya.

• **Fujiwara no Saneuji.** Statesman (1194–1269), appointed *dajō daijin* in 1246. He became a Buddhist monk in 1260 under the name Jikku. Also called Tokiwa-nyūdō.

• **Fujiwara no Saneyori.** Statesman (900–970), son of Fujiwara no Tadahira. He became *kampaku* in 968 and *sesshō* under Emperor En'yū in 970. Also called Onomiya-dono.

• **Fujiwara no Satoko.** *See* DAINI NO SAN'MI.

• **Fujiwara no Seishi.** *See* FUJIWARA NO MASAKO.

• **Fujiwara no Senshi.** Daughter (967–1006) of Fujiwara no Kaneie. She married Emperor En'yū and was the mother of Emperor Ichijō. In 991, she became a Buddhist nun under the name Higashi Sanjō-in.

• **Fujiwara no Shimeko.** Daughter (1131–76) of Fujiwara no Tadamichi. She was a concubine of Emperor Konoe.

• **Fujiwara no Shōko.** Daughter (1101–45) of Fujiwara no Kinzane and wife of Emperor Toba. She was the mother of emperors Sutoku and Go-Shirakawa. Also called Fujiwara no Tamako.
• Daughter (1121–81) of Fujiwara no Tadamichi.

• **Fujiwara no Shōshi.** *See* FUJIWARA NO AKIKO, JŌTŌ MON'IN.

• **Fujiwara no Shunzei.** *See* FUJIWARA NO TOSHINARI.

• **Fujiwara no Sonohito.** *See* FUJIWARA NO SON'ONDO.

• **Fujiwara no Son'ondo.** Minister (756–818). He helped write *Shinsen shōjiroku,* a directory of noble families classified as Kōbetsu, Shimbetsu, and Shoban. Also called Yamashima Daijin, Fujiwara no Sonohito.

• **Fujiwara no Sukemasa.** Calligrapher (944–98), son of Fujiwara no Atsutoshi, one of the Sanseki, three great calligraphers of the tenth century. Also known under the single name Sukemasa.

• **Fujiwara no Suketaka.** Poet (twelfth century), author of *Renchūshō,* a small encyclopedia used by women of the aristocracy, circa 1170.

• **Fujiwara no Sumitomo.** Son of Fujiwara no Yoshinori (d. 941) who formed a secret alliance with Taira no Masakado in 940 and led a rebellion in the region of the Inland Sea (Setonaikai). He and Masakado were killed in 941 by General Fujiwara no Tadabumi.

• **Fujiwara no Tadabumi.** Son (873–947) of Fujiwara no Tsuneyoshi and general of the imperial troops. In 941, he received the title *sei-i-tai-shōgun* and the mission of putting down the revolt led by Fujiwara no Sumitono and Taira no Masakado. He was assisted at sea by Ono no Yoshifuru (884–968), who defeated Sumitomo's pirates, forcing Sumitomo to take refuge in Kyushu. Tadabumi tracked him down in Iyo and killed him. Also called Uji no Mibu-kyō.

• **Fujiwara no Tadahira.** Statesman and writer (880–949), son of Fujiwara no Mototsune and brother of Tokihira. He became *sesshō* in 931, *dajō daijin* in 936, and *kampaku* in 941. He finished writing *Engishiki* and published it in 927. His diary is titled *Teishinkō-ki.* Also called Ko-Ichijō Dajō Daijin.

• **Fujiwara no Tadako.** *See* FUJIWARA NO MASUKO.

• **Fujiwara no Tadamichi.** Statesman (1097–1164), son of Fujiwara no Tadazane. He was appointed *kampaku* in 1121, *sesshō* under Emperor Sutoku in 1123, and *dajō daijin* in 1129. His daughter Masako married Emperor Sutoku. He had five sons—Motozane, Motofusa, Kanezane, Kanefusa, and Jien (who became a Buddhist monk)—and another daughter, Seishi. He also adopted two other girls, Ikushi and Teishi, who married emperors. His memoirs were titled *Hōshō-ji kampaku-ki.* Also called Hōshō-ji kampaku.

• **Fujiwara no Tadanobu.** Statesman and poet (967–1035), son of Fujiwara no Tamemitsu.

• **Fujiwara no Tadazane.** Statesman (1078–1162), son of Fujiwara no Moromichi. He was *sesshō* (1108) then *kampaku* (1113) under Emperor Toba. Also called Fuke-dono.

• **Fujiwara no Takachika.** Painter (twelfth century) in the Yamato-e style.

• **Fujiwara no Takaie.** Imperial breaucrat (974–1044), son of Fujiwara no Michinaga and governor of Dazaifu (Kyushu). He fought the pirates based on the islands of Iki and Tsushima.

• **Fujiwara no Takamitsu.** Writer (d. 944), uncle of Fujiwara no Michinaga, who may have been the author of *Takamitsu nikki,* a diary about the years 961 and 962 (sometimes called *Tō no mine shōshō monogatari,* perhaps apocryphal). He became a Buddhist monk in 961 on Mt. Tō no Mine.

• **Fujiwara no Takanobu.** *See* TAKANOBU.

• **Fujiwara no Takasuke.** Painter (mid-fourteenth century), student of his father, Fujiwara no Nagataka.

• **Fujiwara no Takayoshi.** Painter (mid-twelfth century) in the Yamato-e school, maker of religious images and *emakimono (Takayoshi Genji)* hand-scrolls.

• **Fujiwara no Takekuni.** *See* FUSŌ-KYŌ.

• **Fujiwara no Tamako.** *See* FUJIWARA NO SHŌKO.

• **Fujiwara no Tameaki.** Statesman (d. 1364) and poet, minister under emperors Go-Daigo, Sukō, and Go-Kōgon. He was one of the compilers of the anthology *Shin shūi-shū,* from 1362 to 1364. Also known as Nijō Tameakira.

• **Fujiwara no Tameie.** Poet (1198–1275), son of Fujiwara no Sadaie. He was known mainly as a *kemari* player at the court of Emperor Juntoku. In

1234, continuing the family tradition, he began to write *waka* poetry. The retired emperor Go-Saga asked him to compile the tenth imperial anthology (*see* CHOKUSEN WAKA-SHŪ), *Shoka gosen-shū,* which he finished in 1251. He then compiled *Shoku kokin-shū,* in 1265. He married Abutsu-in (his second marriage) and had two sons. The older one, Tamesuke (1263–1328), contested his father's inheritance with the son from Tameie's first marriage, Tameuji (1222–86). Abutsu-in decided to go to Kamakura to fight for her son's rights. Tamenori (1227–79), Tameie and Abutsu-in's second son, also contested his father's inheritance. The dispute gave rise to three rival families of poets, Nijō, Kyōgoku, and Reizei. Fujiwara no Tameie held minor positions in the court: *gon dainagon* in 1241, and *mimbukyō* in 1250. In 1256, he retired from public life and became a Buddhist monk under the name Mimbukyō-nyūdō. He wrote more than 2,000 poems, 475 of which are included in various imperial anthologies.

• **Fujiwara no Tamekane.** Poet (1254–1332) who compiled the anthology *Gyokuyō-shū* in 1312. Also called Kyōgoku.

• **Fujiwara no Tamenari.** Historian (eleventh century) to whom is sometimes attributed the writing of the *Eiga monogatari,* the *Ō-kagami,* and the *Kachi-zusami,* but without certainty.

• **Fujiwara no Tamenobu.** Painter (Hōshōji Tamenobu, 1261–1304) in the Yamato-e style. He painted *emakimono* handscrolls and portraits of nobles. He became a Buddhist monk under the name Jakuyū. Also called simply Tamenobu.

• **Fujiwara no Tamesada.** *See* NIJŌ TAMESADA.

• **Fujiwara no Tametaka.** Statesman and writer (1070–1130), author of *Eishōki,* a diary dealing with the years 1105 to 1129.

• **Fujiwara no Tametsugu.** Painter (d. 1266) and poet, son of Fujiwara no Nobuzane. Also called simply Tametsugu.

• **Fujiwara no Tameuji.** Poet (1222–86), founder of the Nijō school of poetry. He was appointed *sangi,* then *dainagon,* and *gon dainagon* in 1285. He compiled various family anthologies, as well as an anthology called *Zoku shūi-shū,* ordered by Retired Emperor Kaneyama in 1276 and completed in 1278. His poems are in a number of imperial

anthologies (*see* CHOKUSEN WAKA-SHŪ). He was a son of Abutsu-in, with whom he contested for his father's inheritance against his half-brother Tamesuke.

• **Fujiwara no Tameyo.** *See* NIJŌ TAMEYO.

• **Fujiwara no Tanetsugu.** Courtier (737–85), favorite of Emperor Kammu. Prince Sawara assassinated him. He was posthumously appointed *dajō daijin.*

• **Fujiwara no Tashi.** *See* FUJIWARA NO MASUKO.

• **Fujiwara no Teika.** *See* FUJIWARA NO SADAIE.

• **Fujiwara no Teishi.** *See* FUJIWARA NO SADAKO.

• **Fujiwara no Tokihira.** Statesman (871–909), minister under Emperor Daigo. In 900 he accused Sugawara no Michizane of plotting against the emperor, which led to his exile. He wrote the *Sandai jitsuroku* and began to write the *Engi shiki,* which was completed by his brother Tadahira. Nicknamed Hon'in Daijin.

• **Fujiwara no Tokiko.** Daughter (d. 1185) of Fujiwara no Tokinobu and wife of Taira no Kiyomori.

• **Fujiwara no Tokinobu.** Noble (1102–49) officially adopted by the Taira clan; he took the name Taira no Tokinobu.

• **Fujiwara no Tokuko.** Daughter (1117–60) of Fujiwara no Nagazane and wife of Retired Emperor Toba. The emperor forced his son, Sutoku, to abdicate in favor of one of Tokuko's sons, Konoe. When Konoe died under mysterious circumstances in 1155, she opposed the throne returning to Sutoku's son, Shigehito. The dynastic crisis that ensued enabled another son of Toba's to take power under the name Go-Shirakawa, and this was one of the causes of the Hōgen era insurrection (*see* HŌGEN NO RAN). Tokuko became a Buddhist nun under the name Bifuku Mon'in. Also called Fujiwara no Tokushi.

• **Fujiwara no Tokushi.** *See* FUJIWARA NO TOKUKO.

• **Fujiwara no Toshinari.** Poet (1114–1204), father of Fujiwara no Sadaie. Having held a number of minor positions in the court, he became a Buddhist monk under the name Shakua in 1177. As a *waka* poet, however, he was better known as Fujiwara no Shunzei, or simply Shunzei. His poems, inspired by Chinese ideals from the late Tang dynasty, are mainly descriptive. His collection *Chōshū eisō* (Poems from the Palace of Long Autumns) contains 745 *waka* and 2 *chōka*. His other poems (numbering more than 430) are included in various imperial anthologies (*see* CHOKUSEN WAKA-SHŪ). In 1188, he compiled *Senzai waka-shū*, and, with the assistance of his son, compared various recensions of *Kokin-shū*. He also described his poetic concepts in a short book called *Korai fūtei shō* (Notes on Poetic Style Through the Ages) in 1197 and 1201. Also called Gojō San-i.

• **Fujiwara no Toshinari no Musume.** Granddaughter (ca. 1171–1254) of Fujiwara no Toshinari (her name is not known) and *waka* poet. The daughter of Toshinori's daughter Hachijō-in no Sanjō, she was adopted by her grandfather. About 1190, she married Minamoto no Michitomo, with whom she had a son and a daughter. She was quickly separated from her husband, and in 1202 became a concubine to Retired Emperor Go-Toba. She became a Buddhist nun in 1213. About 724 of her poems are in imperial anthologies (*see* CHOKUSEN WAKA-SHŪ). Also known by the nicknames Saga no Zenni ("nun of Saga") and Koshibe no Zenni ("nun of Koshibe"), for the names of the residences where she lived.

• **Fujiwara no Toshiyuki.** Poet (d. 707), some of whose poems were included in the *Kokin-shū*.

• **Fujiwara no Toyonari.** Statesman (704–65), son of Fujiwara no Muchimaro. He was a minister under emperors Genshō and Shōmu. Also called Naniwa no Daijin.

• **Fujiwara no Tsuginawa.** Statesman (727–96) and warrior, son of Fujiwara no Toyonari. Given the title *sei-i-tai-shōgun*, he was sent to northern Honshu to do battle with the Ebisu, then was appointed *udaijin* in 790. Also called Monozomo no Udaijin.

• **Fujiwara no Tsuneko.** Wife (d. 986) of Emperor Kazan.
→ *See* NAKATSUKASA NAISHI NIKKI.

• **Fujiwara no Tsunetaka.** Painter (late twelfth century) in the Yamato-e style, grandson of Fujiwara no Takayoshi. He founded the Tosa-ryū school of painting. He held the title Gon no Kami. Also called simply Tsunetaka or Tosa Tsunetaka.

• **Fujiwara no Tsunetugu.** Diplomat (ninth century) sent as ambassador to the Chinese court in 838. The Buddhist monk Ennin accompanied him. He was the last Japanese ambassador to China in the Heian period.

• **Fujiwara no Uchimaro.** Statesman (756–812), member of the Hokke branch. He was a minister at Nagaoka and called Nagaoka Daijin.

• **Fujiwara no Umakai.** Chief of protocol (694–737) at court with the title *shikibu-kyō*. He was the son of Fujiwara no Fuhito and founder of the Shikike branch of the family. He and all his brothers died of smallpox.

• **Fujiwara no Uona.** Statesman (721–83) who was a minister during the reigns of emperors Shōmu, Kōken, Junnin, Kōnin, and Kammu. He is considered the ancestor of the Ōshu Fujiwara and Date families of Mutsu (northern Honshu).

• **Fujiwara no Yasuhira.** Son (1155–89) of Fujiwara no Hidehira. He betrayed his father, who had given refuge to Minamoto no Yoshitsune, attacking Yoshitsune and forcing him and all his warriors to commit suicide during the Battle of Koromogawa. Minamoto no Yoritomo attempted to punish the traitor, but he fled to Hokkaido, where he was assassinated by one of his own warriors, Kawata Jirō, in 1189. His mummified head has been preserved in the Chūson-ji temple in Hiraizumi. *See* FUJIWARA NO HIDEHIRA.

• **Fujiwara no Yasuko.** Wife (1292–1357) of Emperor Go-Fushimi and mother of emperors Kōgon and Kōmyō. She became a Buddhist nun under the name Kōgi Mon'in.
• Second wife of Emperor Toba (twelfth century) and mother of Emperor Go-Shirakawa. She may have been a daughter of Fujiwara no Tadazane. Also called Koyo.

• **Fujiwara no Yasumasa.** Poet and musician (958–1036), famous in his time.

• **Fujiwara no Yorimichi.** Statesman (990–1074), Fujiwara no Michinaga's oldest son. He was *sesshō* and then *kampaku* under emperors Go-Ichijō, Go-Suzaku, and Go-Reizei, to whom he was related through the women of the Fujiwara family. In 1068, however, he was forced to accept the ascension to the throne of Emperor Go-Sanjō, who was not related to the Fujiwara family. Yorimichi then passed the position of regent *(kampaku)* to his younger brother Norimichi, retired to Uji, and converted his villa into a temple, the Byōdō-in, where he became a Buddhist monk in 1052. His daughters married emperors Go-Suzaku and Go-Reizei. Also called Uji-dono.

• **Fujiwara no Yorinaga.** Statesman (1120–1156), son of Fujiwara no Tadazane. He made a compromise with his allies in the Minamoto clan during the Hōgen insurrection (*see* HŌGEN NO RAN) and was killed in battle. He wrote a diary called *Daiki.* Also called Uji no Sadaijin, Akusafu.

• **Fujiwara no Yoritada.** Statesman (924–89), *udaijin* in 971, then *sesshō, kampaku,* and *dajō daijin* in 978. *Posthumous name:* Suruga-kō. Also called Sanjō-daijin.

• **Fujiwara no Yoritsugu.** Statesman (1239–56), son of Fujiwara no Yoritsune. He was appointed shogun of the Kamakura *bakufu* in 1244, succeeding his father, but was replaced in 1252 by Prince Munetaka.

• **Fujiwara no Yoritsune.** Son (1218–66) of Fujiwara no Michiie, appointed shogun of the Kamakura *bakufu* in 1226. In 1244, he abdicated in favor of his son Yoritsugu.

• **Fujiwara no Yoshifusa.** Noble (804–72), son of Fujiwara no Fuyutsugu. In 814, he married one of Emperor Saga's daughters and had a daughter, Akiko. He was appointed *dajō daijin* in 857. His sister, Junshi, married Emperor Nimmyō, with whom she had a son (Emperor Montoku); Yoshifusa had his daughter marry his nephew. When they had a son who was to become Emperor Seiwa, Yoshifusa appointed himself regent (*sesshō*) since Seiwa was a minor, thus starting the custom of having *sesshō* for emperors who were minors. Also called Somedono no Daijin, Shirakawa-dono.

• **Fujiwara no Yoshikado.** Statesman (eighth–ninth century), son of Fujiwara no Fuyutsugu. He held the title of *dajō daijin* and is considered the ancestor of the Uesugi, Ii, and Nichiren families. However, he adopted the family name Kanjuji, which he passed on to his descendants.

• **Fujiwara no Yoshiko.** Daughter (1225–92) of Fujiwara no Saneuji, who married Emperor Go-Saga and was the mother of emperors Go-Fukakusa and Kameyama.

• **Fujiwara no Yoshimizu.** *See* JIEN.

• **Fujiwara no Yoshino.** Historian (786–846), one of the compilers of the *Nihon kōki.*

• **Fujiwara no Yoshisuke.** Statesman (813–67), son of Fujiwara no Fuyutsugu. He was appointed *udaijin* in 857. He helped to write the *Shoku Nihon kōkoi.*

• **Fujiwara no Yoshitsugu.** Statesman (716–77), son of Fujiwara no Hirotsugu. Appointed *naidaijin* in 764, he opposed Fujiwara no Nakamaro and was sent into exile.

• **Fujiwara no Yoshitsune.** Statesman and poet (1169–1206), son of Kujō (Fujiwara) Kanezane. Through his marriage to a daughter of Fujiwara no Yoshiyasu, he became an ally of the Minamoto clan in 1190. He was *sesshō* under Emperor Tsuchimikado in 1202. However, he was better known as a poet than as a statesman. He wrote the preface to *Shin kōkin-shū* in 1205, in which 79 of his *waka* poems were included. His personal collection, *Akishino gessei shū* (Collection of Autumn Bamboo Grass and Moonlit Radiance), written circa 1204, contains more than 1,600 poems. More than 300 others were included in various imperial anthologies (*see* CHOKUSEN WAKA-SHŪ). Also called Go-Kyōgoku.

• **Fujiwara no Yukihiro.** *See* FUJIWARA NO YUKIMITSU.

• **Fujiwara no Yukiie.** Poet (1223–75), co-author, with Fujiwara no Mitsutoshi, Fujiwara no Motoie, and Fujiwara no Taneie, of the imperial anthology *Zoku kōkin-shū* (*see* CHOKUSEN WAKA-SHŪ) in 1265.

• **Fujiwara no Yukimitsu.** Painter (active between 1360 and 1371) in the Yamato-e style and leader of the Kyūtei E-dokoro, the Imperial Court Office of Painting. He founded the Tosa school. He specialized in painting Buddhist subjects and illustrating religious books, such as the *Jizō Reiken-ki.* His son, Yukihiro, continued his work. Also called Tosa Yukimitsu.

• **Fujiwara no Yukinaga.** Painter (1202–after 1221) in the Yamato-e style, perhaps the illustrator of the *Heike monogatari.*

• **Fujiwara no Yukinari.** Aristocrat (972–1027) and famous calligrapher in the style called Jīdaiyō, which gave rise to Sesonji-ryū calligraphy. He was considered one of the Sanseki ("Three Great Brushes"), with Ono no Tōfū and Fujiwara no Sukemasa, and was the master of Emperor Fushimi. His diary, *Gonki,* is an important source for information on political events at the Heian-period court. Also called Gon-seki, Fujiwara no Kōzei.

Fujiwara Kei. Potter and ceramist (1899–1983), born in Okayama. His pottery was in the Bizen style, which he modernized somewhat (*see* BIZEN-YAKI). He was declared a Living National Treasure in 1970.

Fujiwara Tsunenobu. Ceramist, born in 1939 at Matsubara (Osaka). His works were shown in the exhibition of ceramic art at the Mitsukoshi space in Paris in 1994.

• **Fujiwara Yu.** Ceramist, born in 1932 in Bizen (Oyakama prefecture). Declared a Living National Treasure in 1980. He has had frequent exhibitions abroad, notably at the Mitsukoshi gallery in Paris in 1994.

Fujiwara Seika. Philosopher (1561–1619), born in Harima, member of the Reizei branch of the Fujiwara family, and classical *waka* poet. He became a Zen monk, then abandoned Buddhism to devote himself to studying the neo-Confucianism of the Zhu Xi (*Jap.:* Shushi) school. Refusing all official positions, he became a hermit dedicated to studying and writing. He founded the Teisha school under the patronage of Tokugawa Ieyasu. Among his books are *Chiyomoyo-gusa* and *Shisho-gokyō wakun* (Explanation of the Four Books and the Five Classics of Chinese Confucianism). His most famous disciples were Hayashi Razan and Matsunaga Sekigo.

Fujiwara Tamezane. Historian (seventeenth century), author of *Reigi ruiten* (1710), written under the patronage of Tokugawa no Mitsukuni.

Fujiwara Uemon. Lacquer artist (nineteenth century) from Takamatsu. He was Zōkoku's master.

Fuji Xerox. Company founded in 1962 by Fuji Shashin and Rank Xerox of Great Britain to manufacture and distribute photocopiers, electric typewriters, and computers. It currently holds 90% of the Japanese market for photocopiers.

Fujiya. Large candy company, founded in 1938 by the Fuji family. Fujiya owns a large number of stores and restaurants in Japan, and has partnerships with Rowntree Macintosh and Hershey Foods Corporation abroad. Head office in Tokyo.

Fujiya Kōji. Painter (Fujiya Kazuo, 1899–1979) famous for his lyrical treatment of Japanese manners and customs of the Meiji and Taishō eras.

Fujiyama Aiichirō. Politician (1897–1985), born in Tokyo, son of Fujiyama Raita. The president of a major sugar company, he became chairman of the Chamber of Commerce and Industry in 1941. Although he distanced himself from politics after the Second World War, he was appointed minister of foreign affairs in Kishi Nobusuke's 1957 cabinet; in 1958, he was elected to the House of Councillors as a member of the LDP. Defeated in the 1964 election, he was replaced by Ikeda Hayato, then by Satō Eisaku at the head of the LDP. He retired from politics in 1975, after helping to restore diplomatic relations with China.

Fujiyama Raita. Businessman (1863–1938), born in Saga. He was employed by Mitsui, where he built a plant to manufacture Oji paper. He also founded the Tokyo Municipal Tramway Company (Tokyo Shigai Dentetsu) and a number of other companies, as well as the Teikoku (Imperial) Theater. He was chairman of the Chamber of Commerce and Industry. Father of Fujiyama Aiichirō.

Fuju Fuse. Literally, "Give nothing, receive nothing." A branch of the Nichiren sect that was founded in 1595 by the monk Nichi-ō, who was exiled by Tokugawa Ieyasu in 1608 along with another leader of Fuju Fuse, Nikkyō (1560–1620). Fuju Fuse was known mainly for its strictness; it often opposed the views of other Buddhists and government authorities. It was banned from 1614 to 1876, but its followers continued to practice clandestinely during this period; some were exiled or executed for disobeying the shogunate's orders. This sect (divided into two groups) currently has about 30,000 followers, mainly in Okayama and Chiba prefectures.

• **Fuju-Fuse Kōmon.** Branch of the Fuju-Fuse sect, founded by the monk Nikkō in Bizen in 1680.

Fukada Seishitsu. Geographer (seventeenth century) who drew Japan's first map of the world; he made the first Japanese globe in 1630.

Fukada Yasukazu. Philosopher (1878–1928), master of aesthetics.

Fukae Roshū. Painter (Shōroku, 1699–1757), born in Kyoto. He was probably a student of Ogata Kōrin and worked in the same style, decorating mainly fusuma (sliding partitions). *See* KŌRIN.

Fukae no Ura. Former name of Nagasaki. Also called Nigitatsu, Tama no Ura.

• **Fukae Hōjin.** *See* HONZŌ-WAMYŌ.

Fukagawa. Town in Hokkaido on the Ishikari Plain, founded in 1895 by the Tondenhei (colonist militia). It is irrigated by the Taishō Canal, which was dug from the Ishikari River in 1916. *Pop.:* 35,000.
• Tokyo district in which there is an annual festival during which young people try to balance on tree trunks *(kakunori)* floating in the canals. This sport, invented in Osaka in 1747, became popular in Edo and is now a major attraction in Fukagawa on certain festival days.

Fukami Jūsuke. Weaver (1885–1974), born in Kyoto, specializing in fabrics called *karakuni* (a Chinese technique). He worked mainly for Shinto shrines, as his family had for centuries, faithfully preserving his ancestral traditions. He was declared a Living National Treasure in 1956.

Fukami Sueharu. Ceramist in the modern style, born in 1947 in Kyoto. He has had many exhibitions both in Japan and abroad, notably in Chā teauroux (1985), Faenza (1986 and 1991), the United States (1988), Lausanne (1987), Mons, Belgium (1989), and Paris (Mitsukoshi Gallery, 1994).

Fukao Sumako. Writer and poet (1893–1974), born in Dairo-ji, author of a number of books of modern poetry. She lived in France and translated Colette's books.

Fukasaku Kinji. Film director (b. 1930), working mainly for Tōei since 1953. He specialized in gangster films, such as *Jingi naki tatakai* (Lawless Battle), a series made in the 1970s. Among his best-known films is *Gunki hatameku moto ni* (Under the Flag of the Rising Sun), produced in 1972, an anti-militarist tragedy set in New Guinea.

Fukazawa Shichirō. Writer and musician (1914–87), born in Yamanashi prefecture. His successful first novel, *Narayama-bushi kō* (Ballad of Narayama), based on the ancient legend of Obasute, earned him the *Chūō Koron* Prize in 1956. This novel was adapted for the screen in 1958 by Kinoshita Keisuke, and in 1983 by Imamura Shōhei. Among Fukazawa's other books (some of which caused a scandal because they attacked the imperial family, such as *Fūryū mutan* in 1960) are *Tōhoku no zummu-tachi* (The Trembling House, 1957), *Fuefukigawa* (1958), and *Shomin retsuden* (Working-Class Biographies, 1969). Several of his other novels were adapted for the screen. *See* NARAYAMA BUSHI-KŌ.

Fuke. Branch of Zen Buddhism composed of pilgrims (among them the Komusō) and itinerant monks, founded by the Chinese monk Fuke-zenji in the thirteenth century. It was banned in 1868 because its members had been used as spies by political parties. Also called Fuke-shū.

• **Fuke-dono.** *See* FUJIWARA NO TADAZANE.

• **Fuke-shū.** *See* BUSSHŌ-ZENJI, FUKE.

• **Fuke-zenji.** *See* FUKE, KOMUSŌ.

Fuki-age-hama. Part of the coast on the Satsuma Peninsula (Kagoshima prefecture, Kyushu), famous for its dunes and pines and protected as a prefectural natural park. It is about 40 km long and as wide as 3 km.

Fuki-dera. Buddhist temple of the Tendai sect in the town of Bungo Takada (Ōita prefecture, Kyushu), founded, according to tradition, by the monk Nimmon in 718. Its twelfth-century Amidadō (the oldest wooden structure in Kyushu) houses a beautiful statue of a seated Amida. Its main building (Ōdō) was restored in 1912 and 1965. Also called Fuki-ji.

Fukin. System allowing the general population to pay cash to lords and daimyo instead of taking part in the obligatory corvée. This system, called *fumai* (or *bumai*) when the payment was in rice, was in force mainly during the Edo period. There was, however, no official price, since the daimyo themselves set the amount. Also called *fugin* (or *bugin*).

Fukinuki-yatai. "Houses with blown-off roofs," an artistic convention used in paintings in the Yamato-e style, in which houses, seen from above, were drawn without a roof so that the interior could be seen.

Fukisumi. Type of decorative ink painting *(sumi-e)* with large splashes of color.

Fukki. Time off (one or several days) given to a bureaucrat or employee so that he or she can fulfill obligations with regard to a family event such as a birth, wedding, or death.

Fukko. "Old way," term used to designate a type of renewal, or a return to traditions.

• **Fukko-ha.** Neo-Confucian philosophical school founded by Itō Jinsai, Ogyū Sorai, Itō Tōgai, and other scholars in the seventeenth century. It was opposed to the teachings of the Teishu school. *See* TOKUGAWA-JIDAI NO KEIGAKU-HA, ITŌ JINSAI.

Fukko Shintō. "Restoration Shinto," a seventeenth-century philosophical and religious movement whose aim was to return Shinto to its original purity; according to its followers, it had been contaminated by Buddhism, Taoism, and Confucianism. Motoori Norinaga and Hirata Atsusane were the most ardent promoters of Fukko Shintō, which, in concert with the Kokugaku (National Learning), urged that the Japanese literary and artistic heritage be studied to rediscover the "true" spirit of ancient Japan. The movement's followers were violently opposed to Buddhism and Confucianism; during the Meiji Restoration of 1868, they were in favor of separating Shinto and Buddhism and felt that the emperor should worship Amaterasu. *See* HIRATA ATSUSANE.

• **Fukko Yamato-e.** Seventeenth- and eighteenth-century painting school based in Kyoto. It advocated a return to the classic Yamato-e painting style, according to the views of Tanaka Totsugen *(see* TOTSUGEN) and Reizei Tamechika, through studying *emakimono* handscrolls of the twelfth and thirteenth centuries. *See* YAMATO-E.

Fuko (Fugo). Starting in 645, form of salary paid to various government bureaucrats, with the amount varying according to rank *(ifu; see* I), position held *(shikifu, jikifu),* or services rendered *(kōfu).* This salary came, in whole or in part, from taxes in rice collected from households or villages. *Fuko* were eliminated in the late Heian period, when private estates *(shōen)* were formed. *See* JIKIFU.

Fūko. Modern painter (Matsumoto Takatada, 1840–1923), student of Eikai and Yōsaio. He painted mainly historical subjects.

Fukoku kyōhei. "Enrich the country and strengthen the military," a slogan used during the Meiji era to bring Japan up to Western standards by developing industry and trade and boosting its military potential. This policy became controversial in 1882, when politicians and writers claimed that there was a contradiction between the terms *fukoku* and *kyōhei,* in that the one could be accomplished only at the expense of the other. Despite this, the government continued with its military program, notably after the almost total retreat of Japanese troops from Korea in 1884. Various political parties, including the Liberal party (Jiyūtō), which had been anti-government, then proclaimed the necessity of *kyōhei* and of undertaking military action in China and Korea, which would, according to them, enrich the country *(fukoku).*

Fukuba Bisei. Kokugaku (National Learning) scholar and philosopher (Fukuba Yoshishizu, 1831–1907), born in Shimane prefecture. He was a disciple of Okuni Takamasa and Hirata Kanetane (1799–1880). A member of the Meiji government in the Jingikan (Office of Shinto Worship), he advocated a renaissance of Shinto *(see* FUKKO SHINTO). He then held a position in the Genrō-in (Chamber of Elders) and the House of Peers.

• **Fukuba Hayato.** Adoptive son (1856–1921) of Fukuba Bisei. He studied agronomic engineering in France and Germany; when he returned to Japan, he developed varieties of chrysanthemums and strawberry plants.

Fukubiki. "Good-luck draws," lotteries and random draws conducted in Japan at least since the eighth century and held usually at New Year's. Today, *fukibuki* are conducted by retailers in midsummer and at the end of the year.

Fukuchi Ōchi. Journalist and playwright (Fukuchi Gen'ichirō, 1841–1906), author of Kabuki plays. Born in Nagasaki, he studied Dutch, then went to Edo to learn English. Toward the end of the Tokugawa shogunate, he visited Europe twice; in 1868, he founded an illustrated newspaper, *Kōku Shimbun.* From 1874 to 1888, he was publisher of *Tōkyō Nichinichi Shimbun* (later *Mainichi Shimbun*). He became a politician (elected to the House of Councillors in 1904) while continuing his literary career, working with the actor Danjurō IX on Kabuki plays. He also wrote satirical and historical novels.

Fukuchiyama. Town in Kyoto prefecture, established at the confluence of the Hiji and Yura rivers, founded by Akechi Mitsuhide around his castle. Industrial center (machinery and textiles). *Pop.:* 65,000.

Fukuda Gyōkai. Buddhist monk (1806–88) of the Jōdō sect, abbot of the Zōjō-ji temple in Tokyo and of the Chion-in in Kyoto. He was known mainly for his defense of Buddhism in the face of rising anti-Buddhism among the followers of Fukko Shinto, and for his promotion of "purified" Buddhism.

Fukuda Heihachirō. Painter (1892–1974), born in Ōita (Kyushu), member of the Rikuchō-kai artists' group and professor at the Kyoto Shiritsu Kaiga Semmon Gakkō (now Kyoto City University of Arts). He was decorated with the Order of Culture in 1961. His paintings, in an independent style based on close observation of nature, evolved from intense realism to semi-abstract and depicted almost exclusively flowers, bamboo, birds, fish, and inanimate objects.

Fukuda Hideko. Feminist (Kageyama Hideko, 1865–1927), born in Okayama prefecture into a family of small-scale samurai. With her mother, Umeko, she founded a school for the girls in her village in 1883; the school was closed by prefectural decree the following year. She went to Kyoto and became involved in a political movement for human rights in Korea, and in 1885 she was sentenced to four years in prison along with Ōi Kentarō, with whom she had a son in 1890. After separating from Ōi Kentarō, she married Fukuda Yūsadu in 1892 and with him became involved in socialist and pacifist movements, notably against the Russo-Japanese War, while editing the women's magazine *Sekai Fujin*. She wrote two autobiographical books, *Warawa no hanshōgai* (Half of My Life, 1904) and *Warawa no omoide* (My Memories, 1905), as well as a number of articles promoting women's rights. *See* SEKAI FUJIN.

Fukuda Shigeo. Graphic designer, poster designer, and book illustrator, born in 1932 in Tokyo. His work has been featured in Japan and abroad, notably in Brno, Czechoslovakia, in 1970, Sofia in 1975, Warsaw, and Montreal. He received the award of the Ministry of Education (Geijutsu Senshō Shinjin-shō) in 1975.

Fukuda Takeo. Politician, born in 1905 in Gumma prefecture. After a career as a bureaucrat in the Ministry of Finance, he was appointed head of the budget department in 1947 but was involved in a scandal (Shōwa Denkō) and resigned the following year. Elected to the House of Councillors in 1952, he was minister of agriculture, finance, and foreign affairs in various cabinets. He was elected chairman of the Liberal Democratic party (LDP, Jiyū Minshutō) and prime minister in 1976, but was replaced in both positions, in November 1978, by Ōhira Masayoshi.

Fukuda Tokuzō. Economist (1874–1930), born in Tokyo. He studied in Germany and taught at Keiō University in 1901. His writings were collected in the *Fukuda Tokuzō keizaigaku zenshū,* published in Tokyo in 1925–27.

Fukuda Toyoshirō. Painter (Toyoshiro, 1904–70), born in Akita. A student of Tsuchida Bakusen, then of Kawabata Ryūshi, he was one of the founders of the Seiryūsha artists' group in 1929 and exhibited with them every year until 1939. Before the Second World War, his style was representative of the Nihonga style (modern Japanese painting). After the war, he painted in a modern style, portraying several subjects on a single canvas.

Fukuda Tsuneari. Playwright and literary critic, born in 1912 in Tokyo. At first a teacher, after the Second World War he became a highly acerbic critic of modern Japanese literature, protesting the simplification of Japanese writing. He translated Shakespeare into Japanese and wrote several major works: *Kitī taifū* (Typhoon Kitty, 1950), *Ryū o nadeta otoko* (The Man Who Patted the Dragon, 1952), and *Akechi Mitsuhide* (1957), a historical novel.

Fukuden-kai. Modern religious sect founded by Tada Seita (Tada Kōshi, 1862–1936) in 1900.

Fukue. Island in the Gotō archipelago off Nagasaki and main town, former castle town of the Gotō family. Ruins of a nineteenth-century castle. Agriculture and fishing. *Area:* 327 km². *Pop.:* 35,000. Also called Fukuejima.

Fukuhara. Port near Kobe (Hyōgo prefecture). In 1180, it was made the temporary capital of Japan by Taira no Kiyomori in order to keep the entire imperial family under his control. The court lived in the residence that he had had built in 1157. This transfer of the court angered most nobles and followers of the Taira clan; Minamoto no Yoritomo forced Taira no Kiyomori and the court to return to Kyoto after only five months in Fukuhara-kyō. Also called Fukuwara.

Fukuhara Gogaku. Painter of the Nanga school (Genso; *azana:* Taisho, Shijun; *gō:* Gogaku, Gyokuhō, Daisuke, 1730–99), born in Bizen province (Hiroshima prefecture). He was Ike no Taiga's disciple and specialized in the portrayal of famous people; he painted with heavy brushstrokes in a rough, austere style.

Fukuhara Tetsurō. Contemporary dancer and director, born in 1948 in Shizuoka. A specialist in Būto, he imbued this form of dance with a new dimension and produced a number of shows abroad, notably in Paris (1992), Berlin, Canada, and the United States.

Fukui. Main town of Fukui prefecture, in central Honshu, founded in 1575 as a castle town *(jōka-machi)* around Shibata Katsuie's castle. The town, destroyed by bombing in 1945, then by an earthquake in 1948, was completely rebuilt. Industries: chemicals, machine tools, textiles (silk and synthetics), paper. In the tenth century, it produced silk called *habutai.* It is a port on the Sea of Japan.

• **Fukui-ken.** Fukui prefecture, located on the Sea of Japan, north of Lake Biwa, in Chūbu (Honshu), former provinces of Echizen and Wakasa. One of its largest Buddhist temples is Eihei-ji. *Other major towns:* Sabae, Takefu, Tsuruga. *Area:* 4,188 km^2. *Pop.:* 800,000.

Fukui Cave. Archeological site in Fukui (Yoshii-chō) in Nagasaki prefecture, excavated in 1960. It has 15 levels of which at least seven contain proof of human habitation, thus comprising the most complete sequence of prehistoric cultures in the transition from the paleolithic to the Jōmon period. The lowest level (15) contains stone tools (dating from 32,000 years ago) from the paleolithic era. Level 3 (12,700±500 years) contains simple pottery, and level 2 (12,400±350 years) contains pottery decorated with marks made by fingernails and polished-stone tools. Level 1 has pottery decorated with rolling tools. The most recent levels are from the Yayoi period.

Fukui Ken'ichi. Chemist (1918–98), born in Nara, professor at Tokyo University. He received the Nobel Prize in 1981, with Ronald Hoffmann (United States), for having successfully applied quantum theories to chemical reactions. Between 1950 and 1970, Fukui developed an approximation method for simplifying calculations. He was decorated with the Order of Culture (Bunka-shō) in 1981.

Fukūkensaku Kannon. Buddhist god, a particular form of Avalokiteshvara (*Jap.:* Shō Kannon Bosatsu) who "traps souls" and who corresponds to the Sanskrit Amoghavajra. The most famous portrayal of him, executed in dry lacquer, is found in the Sangatsudō of Tōdai-ji temple in Nara, dating from the Tempyō period (710–94). Also called Fukūkenjaku Kannon.

Fukumoto Kazuo. Marxist philosopher (1894–1983), leading communist theoretician, born in Tottori prefecture. He studied in Europe and the United States. When he returned to Japan in 1924, he joined the Communist party and published a series of articles in the party paper, the *Marukusu Shugi.* In 1926, he was appointed head of the party's political department, but had to resign the following year because of criticism from the Comintern. He was arrested in 1928 and sentenced to 10 years of forced labor; he remained in prison for 14 years because of the war. He returned to political life in 1950, but was ejected from the Communist party in 1958 for insubordination. He wrote many articles on politics and economic history.

Fukunaga Takehiko. Writer and poet (1918–79), born in Fukuoka. She wrote many detective novels (under the pen name Kada Retarō) and science fiction novels (under the pen name Funada Gaku). She also translated some of Jean-Paul Sartre's work and wrote a critique of Paul Gauguin (*Gōgyan no sekai*) for which she received the *Mainichi Shimbun* Prize in 1961. Among her best-known books are *Fūdo* (Environment, 1957), *Bōkyaku no kawa* (River of Oblivion, 1964), *Shi no shima* (Island of Death), and *Kusa no hana* (Weed Flowers).

Fuku-nusubi. "Stealing luck," custom according to which people try to steal small effigies of Daruma or Daikoku from shop displays to bring themselves good luck during the year-end fair (Toshi no Ichi, in Asakusa, Tokyo). In other parts of Japan, during certain festivals, attempts are made to steal dolls (*fushimi-ningyō,* in Kyoto) or statuettes portraying *kami.* This is extremely difficult since merchants are particularly vigilant during these festivals. The custom comes from Manchuria or Mongolia.

Fukuoka. City in northern Kyushu and main city of Fukuoka prefecture, located on the Bay of Hakata. Formerly called Na no Tsu. It was a major port (Hakata) in the medieval period and the landing site of the Mongolian fleet in 1274 and 1281. A castle was built there in 1601. It is an industrial center, long known for its silks (Hakata-*ori*) and doll-making (Hakata-*ningyō*). Itazuke international airport is 10 km away. The city was destroyed by bombing during the Second World War and reconstructed. Various industries (machinery, textiles, shoes, paper). A festival called Hakata Dontaku is held every May 3–4. *Pop.:* 1.1 million.

• **Fukuoka-ken.** Fukuoka prefecture, in northern Kyushu. A mountainous region dominated by the Tsukushi range. The ancient kingdom of Yamatai mentioned in Chinese chronicles *(Weizhi)* was probably located there. The ancient city of Dazaifu was about 15 km south of the city of Fukuoka. Some coal mines at Miike and Kasuya. *Main cities:* Fukuoka, Kita Kyushu, Iizuka, Kasuga, Kurume, Onojō, Nōgata, Omuta. *Area:* 4,946 km². *Pop.:* 4.6 million.

Fukuoka Takachika. Statesman (1835–1919), born in Tosa province (Kōchi prefecture). He persuaded the shogun Tokugawa Yoshinobu to surrender power to Emperor Mutsuhito (Meiji). He then served the emperor and helped in the writing of the constitution. He was appointed minister of education and a councillor in 1891.

Fukurokuju. One of the Seven Gods of Good Fortune (Shichifukujin), of Chinese origin. He is also the god of the Southern Star, wisdom, virility, fertility, and longevity. He is portrayed as a little old bearded man with a head three times as big as his body (and often in a phallic shape). He is sometimes confused with Jurōjin. *Chin.:* Fuushou; *Kor.:* Susöng no In.

Fukuro-sōshi. Book on the *waka* style of poetry, written by Fujiwara no Kiyosuke in 1159.

Fukuro-toji. Common bookbinding method: the pages, printed on one side, are folded and sewn together along one edge. A similar method, but using only two threads to bind the pages, is called Yamato-toji.

Fukuryū-maru no. 5. Japanese fishing boat that was contaminated, along with its crew, by radiation from the American atom-bomb test at Bikini atoll on March 1, 1954. The crew was seriously affected by the radiation, and public opinion galvanized against such tests, with demonstrations held throughout Japan.

Fukusa. In the tea ceremony *(chanoyu),* a sort of brocade fabric used to cover lacquered objects and other objects when they are not in use. These fabrics are also used to present gifts. *See* FURISHIKI.

Fukushi Kōjirō. Poet (1889–1946) in the modern style, born in Aomori. He was the first to publish free verse written in everyday language, in *Taiyō no ko* (Children of the Sun, 1914). He also wrote in the dialect of the Aomori region.

Fukushima. Main city of Fukushima prefecture (northern Honshu) on the Abukama River, former castle town *(jōka-machi)* and post town on the Ōshu-kaidō road in the fifteenth century. Food industries, textiles, fruit orchards. *Pop.:* 270,000.

• **Fukushima Chikayuki.** *See* CHIKAYUKI.

• **Fukushima Jiken.** Popular uprising, the first of several that took place between 1882 and 1884 supporting the people's rights movement and protesting the appointment of Mishima Michitsune as governor of Fukushima; he wanted to impose local taxes and build new roads by having all men and women between the ages of 15 and 60 work on them for one day each month. A number of representatives from the Liberal party (Jiyūtō) were arrested as more than 1,000 peasants demonstrated. Mishima had 2,000 people arrested, and seven of them, including Kōno, the leader of the insurgents, were sentenced to seven years in prison.

• **Fukushima-ken.** Fukushima prefecture (northern Honshu), on the Pacific coast. Mountainous (Abukama, Ōu, Echigo ranges), irrigated by the Akuma, Nippashi, and Tadami rivers. Site of Bandai-Asahi National Park (Lake Inawashiro). Produces mainly fruit. *Main cities:* Fukushima, Aizu-Wakamatsu, Iwaki, Kōriyama, Sukagawa, Shirakawa, Sōma, Haramichi. *Area:* 13,782 km². *Pop.:* 2.1 million.

• **Fukushima Nei.** *See* RYŪHŌ.

Fukushima Kazuo. Composer, born 1930 in Tokyo. Encouraged by Stravinsky, he had his compositions performed at the international festival in Karuizawa in 1958 and in Los Angeles the following year. His pieces, mostly in twelve-tone mode, feature the flute, and many are inspired by the Noh theater and Buddhism.

Fukushima no Masanori. Daimyo (1561–1624), friend of Tokugawa Ieyasu and Hideyoshi. He had the castle at Nagoya rebuilt in 1610. His son, Fukushima no Masayuki, married one of Tokugawa Ieyasu's adoptive daughters. He received an estate of 113,000 *koku* in Iyo; in 1595, he was made daimyo of Kiyosu in Owari with a revenue of 240,000 *koku*. After he fought at Tokugawa Ieyasu's side at the Battle of Sekigahara (1600), his property was expanded and his revenue was raised to 498,000 *koku*. When he settled in Hiroshima, he was sympathetic to the Christians; for this, his properties were confiscated and his revenue reduced to 45,000 *koku*.

Fukushima Yasumasa. General (1852–1919) who commanded the Japanese troops in China fighting against the Boxer Rebellion in 1900. He proved to be a great proponent of fair play and did not allow his soldiers to pillage the Summer Palace. He also commanded an army during the Russo-Japanese War (1904–05). He had previously been famous for his solo 14-month trip (1892–93) on horseback from Berlin to Vladivostok through Siberia and then back to Germany, where he had been appointed military attaché.

Fukusuke. "Lucky man," doll portraying a small, fat man dressed in the old style, sitting and holding a fan, said to represent a late-eighteenth-century wealthy Kyoto merchant, Daimonjiya. Those who want good luck in business place this doll (or a picture of it) in their homes to bring them luck.

Fuku-warai. Child's game resembling "Pin the Tail on the Donkey," using an effigy of Otafuku instead of the donkey. A blindfolded child has to place the nose, eyes, eyebrows, and mouth on its face.

Fukuyama. City and seaport in Hiroshima prefecture. Industries: cotton, rubber. Castle (Fukuyama no jō) constructed by order of Tokugawa Ieyasu in 1619. The donjon *(tenshu)* was later constructed using material from Fushimi castle after it was torn down in 1623. *Pop.:* 350,000. *See* MATSUMAE.

Fukuzawa Ichirō. Western-style painter (1898–1992), born in Tomioka (Gumma prefecture). He traveled in Europe from 1924 to 1931, and adopted a surrealistic style, which he introduced to Japan.

After the Second World War, he went to Central America and began to paint in a primitive style, using very bright colors. He was decorated with the Order of Culture (Bunka-shō).

Fukuzawa Yukichi. Writer and philosopher (1835–1901), born in Ōita (Kyushu), died in Tokyo. As a journalist, he founded *Jiji Shimpō* news service and Keiō University in Tokyo. He studied the art of casting cannons in Nagasaki and "Dutch science" *(rangaku)* in Osaka under Ogata Kōan, and was a member of the first Japanese mission to the United States in 1860. Two years later, he went to Europe, where he became an avid student of various aspects of Western culture. When he returned to Japan, his observations were published in a hugely successful three-volume work, *Seiyō jijō* (Living Conditions in the West, 1866, 1868, 1870). He then devoted himself to making the West better known in Japan by teaching at Keiō University and writing books and articles. He defined the concept of *jitsugaku* (acquisition of practical knowledge), which became the slogan of an entire generation at the beginning of the Meiji era, and he became known as the "father of Japanese modernism." His writing had a profound influence on Japanese thinking of his time, and his modern ideas were enthusiastically received by young people. Among his most noted works are *Gakumon no susume* (Encouragement to Study, 1872–76), *Bummeiron no gairyaku* (Elements of a Theory of Civilization, 1875), *Tsūzoku minkenron* (On the Rights of the People, 1878), *Onna daigaku hyōron* and *Shin onna daigaku,* two books on education for women (1898), various essays *(Fukuō hyakuwa, Fukuō hyakuyowa),* and an autobiography, *Fukuō jiden* (1898). His two sons, Fukuzawa Ichitarō (1863–1938) and Fukuzawa Sutejirō (1865–1926), carried on his work.

Fumi-e. Plaque or bas-relief portraying Christ, the Virgin, or a Christian saint, used in the ceremony called *e-fumi,* in which Japanese suspected of sympathy for Christianity had to prove to the authorities that they did not belong to a Christian congregation by walking on the *fumi-e.* This practice began in Nagasaki in 1626 or 1629, following a ban on Christian worship decreed by the Edo shogunate in 1613, and was continued until 1858 in northern Kyushu. A few Christians had crosses made on which they placed a Buddha instead of Christ; they could then walk on the crucifix without remorse. *See* E-FUMI (also called E-bumi), FERREIRA, SHŪMON ARATAME.

Fumi-zuki. "Month of culture," name of the seventh month of the lunar-solar year (July–August). *See* NIJŪSHI-SETSU.

Funabashi. Title of a Noh play: a man and a woman tell a Buddhist monk the story of two lovers who arranged to meet on a bridge and then drowned together. They reveal themselves to be the spirits of the two lovers and ask the monk to recite prayers to put their souls at rest.

Funa-benkei. "Benkei on the Ship." A classic tragedy by Kanze Shojirō and the subject of a number of Noh plays *(Honganmono)* and of a Kabuki play by Mokuami. *See* BENKEI, TAIRA NO TOMOMORI.

• **Funa-Fubito.** *See* FUBITO.

Funadama. "Spirit of the Ship," a working-class divinity of fishers and sailors. An "image-support," or *shintai* (hair barrette, doll, or other object), is affixed to the central mast of a ship during a secret ceremony before the ship leaves on a voyage. Funadama is considered female. Sailors who consider a woman on board their ship to be bad luck do not place a *shintai* at the foot of the mast, even though they worship Funadama.

Funahashi Seiichi. Writer and playwright (1904–76) born in Tokyo. His first novel, *Daibingu* (Dive, 1934), was much admired in literary circles, especially among writers who belonged to the Shinkankaku school, as he did. He then wrote *Bokuseki* (1938) and *Shikkaiya Kōkichi* (1945), and the erotic novels *Yuki fujin ezu* (1950) and *Geisha Konatsu* (1952). Among his other works are *Aru onna no enkei* (1963), which won the *Mainichi Shimbun* Prize, and *Sukina onna no munekazari* (1967), which earned the Noma Prize. He was elected a member of the Academy of Arts in 1966. Also written Funabashi Seiichi.

Funa-hijiki. In traditional architecture, a type of overhang in which the upper beam *(gangyō)* is supported by a boat-shaped bracket *(hijiki)*. This form is typical of the Asuka period (552–645). *Chin.:* Zhoumu. *See* TO-KYŌ.

Funai. Former name of Shizuoka (also called Fuchū and Sumpu) and of Ōita (Kyushu), founded by the Ōtomo family. During the rule of its daimyo, Ōtomo Sōrin (1530–87), Ōita was the refuge for persecuted Christians. *See* KOKUFU, SUMPU.

Funakoshi Gichin. Master of martial arts (1869–1957), born in Okinawa. About 1921, he created the modern techniques of karate. His major book on this sport is the *Karate-dō kyōhan*. His son, Funakoshi Yoshitaka (d. 1953), succeeded him at the head of his main dojo in Tokyo, the Shotōkan.

Funakoshi Yasutake. Sculptor, born 1912 in Iwate prefecture, who carved marble busts of women. He converted to Catholicism in 1950, and thereafter his works were greatly influenced by his faith. His monument to the 36 martyrs of Nagasaki (1958–62) won the Takamura Kōtarō Prize and, later, the Nakahara Teijirō Prize. He was made a Knight of St. Gregory by the Pope in 1964. The recipient of many other awards, he was a professor at Tokyo University of Fine Arts from 1967 to 1980.

Funayama. Large funerary tumulus *(kofun)* in Kumamoto prefecture (Kyushu) dating from the fifth century, containing objects inscribed with Chinese characters.

Funayama Kaoru. Writer (1914–81).

Funa yujo. A Kabuki play performed through dance, created by Kawabata Yasunari in Osaka in 1956. Also called *Biwa monogatari*.

Fundoshi. "Loincloth," long strip of cotton used by men as underwear or a loincloth, traditional since ancient times (portrayed in fifth- and sixth-century *haniwa*) and still worn in rural areas and at festivals. At first woven of linen, they were made of cotton or silk in the Edo period. There are different types of various lengths and widths. *Sumotori* (sumo wrestlers) wear silk *fundoshi* called *mawashi* (or *shimekomi*). Also called *shita-obi* (underbelt).

Funerals. The funerary mode *(otsuya)* most widely used in Japan is cremation according to Buddhist rites. Shinto does not deal with funerals because contact with death is considered unclean. It is the duty of the closest relative to moisten the lips of the dying person. The dead body is washed in warm water, then dressed in white clothing *(kyōkatabira)*. Increasingly, however, these final tasks are performed by a mortuary, where the rites of washing the body *(yukan)*, the wake, the religious service, and the cremation take place. A monk is charged with writing the posthumous name *(kaimyō)* of the deceased on a tablet *(ihai)* that is placed on the altar before a photograph of the deceased. During the wake *(tsuya)*, the body is laid out with the head to the north and then covered with a white cloth. To the side, on a small table, are placed offerings of white rice, salt, and water, and incense sticks are kept burning while a Buddhist monk chants the sutras. By custom, guests at the wake bring white envelopes containing "incense money" *(kōden)* and flowers. The next day, the body is placed in a coffin made of white cypress and cremated. After this ceremony, close relatives gather some bones with chopsticks and put them in an urn *(kotsutsubo)*, which they place on a table at home beside a photograph of the deceased, an incense holder, and the funerary tablet. The urn is interred 49 days *(kichū)* after the cremation. During these seven weeks, the family refrains from celebrations. Theoretically, a religious service must be conducted every seven days during the period of mourning, and on the first, third, seventh, thirteenth, seventeenth, and thirty-third anniversaries of the death. Shinto funerals (which do in fact exist) are conducted in more or less the same way, except that the body is buried and not cremated. A Shinto priest performs purification ceremonies *(oharai)* before an altar decorated with *shimenawa* cords and *sakaki* branches. A spirit name *(mikoto)* is then added to the *kaimyō* on the tablet, and traditional music is played while the participants offer *sakaki* branches adorned with folded strips of white paper *(tamagushi)*.

The death is announced on a sheet of white paper with a black border affixed to the door of the deceased's home throughout the mourning period. Once the ceremonies have ended, the relatives of the deceased send a small gift "in return for incense" *(kōdengaeshi)* to thank those who took part in the wake.

Funerals are a very lucrative business for Buddhist temples and morticians, whose services are usually very expensive. The rites are generally observed, but they are often shortened, either to save money or to accommodate specific circumstances. The mourning period *(kichū)* may last only one or two weeks instead of the seven required by tradition; the rites are rarely performed in a spirit of devoutness but usually out of a sense of duty and custom. Their length and opulence generally depend on the social status of the deceased. Most emperors are buried in the Shinto mode, though many in the past were fervent Buddhists and were cremated. Since there is little open land in Japan, 90% of funerals end in cremation. Today, especially in large cities, funerals are often conducted with great ceremony, accompanied by performances, music, and video projections. Companies that provide these funerals vie for ingenuity and creativity, and the traditional simple contemplation is no longer considered adequate. *See* KŌDEN, TAISŌ.

Fun'ya no Watamaro. General (765–823). Having taken part in Fujiwara no Kusuko's revolt, he was imprisoned in 810, then granted amnesty and sent as *sei-i-tai-shōgun* to battle the Ezo in northern Honshu in 812. He held the position of *chūnagon* in 818.

Fun'ya no Yasuhide. Ninth-century poet, one of the Rokkasen (Six Poetic Geniuses). Many of his poems have been preserved, including five in the *Kokin-shū*. He was a friend of the poetess Ono no Komachi.

Funyū. The right of lords of private estates *(shōen)* to keep the tax agents of provincial governors *(kokushi)* from entering their property. This right, affirmed in the tenth century, along with those that exempted certain lay and religious estates from taxes *(fuyu)*, led to the increasing independence of the *shōen* from the central government.

Fūren-ko. Lake in eastern Hokkaido, near the town of Nemuro, famous for the swans that migrate from Siberia and live there from October to March. *Area:* 52 km^2. *Average depth:* 11 m.

Fūren Shōnyūdō. A pair of caves discovered in 1926 near Notsu, in Ōita prefecture (northern Kyushu), 420 m and 428 m deep, containing large quantities of splendid stalactites and stalagmites.

Furigana. Kana characters (hiragana or katakana) written in lower case at the right of Sino-Japanese characters (kanji) that are unusual or difficult to read, to make them easier to pronounce.

Fūrin. Small bronze or porcelain bell to the clapper of which is attached a long strip of paper *(tanzaku)*, bearing a poem or prayer, which flutters in the wind. The clear sound of these bells is said to freshen the air and ward off insects. They are usually hung in tree branches or along the eaves, mainly in summertime. *See* BONSHŌ, SHŌ.

Furisode. Long-sleeved, very ornate kimono worn by young women, children, *maiko* (apprentice geisha), and geisha on festival days.

• **Furisode Kaji.** "Fire of the Long Sleeves," name given to the major fire of January 18–19, 1657, which ravaged Edo and its castle, killing more than

100,000 people. It was so named because a man who was burning a *furisode* once worn by his deceased daughters lost control of the fire, which was fanned by the wind and burned the temple, then spread to the entire city. Also called Furisode no Taika, Meireki no Taika.

• **Furisode no Taika.** *See* FURISODE-KAJI.

Furitsuzumi. Child's toy consisting of a double-sided drum with a handle. When it is turned, a short cord with a small weight on the end hits each skin in turn, producing a drum-roll sound. This toy, of Chinese origin, is a replica of an ancient musical instrument used in religious ceremonies. In the Kyoto region, it is called *fureifuri taiko. Skt.: damarū. See* DENDEN-TAIKO.

Furnishings. The traditional Japanese house has few pieces of furniture. Cupboards are replaced by deep alcoves in the walls, and by three-door chests called *tansu,* used mainly to store kimono. Open shelving units *(kodansu)* are also used, and bedrooms sometimes have small dressing tables with mirrors. Aside from a low table, sometimes a *kotatsu,* and cushions, these are the only traditional furnishings. There are no beds; instead, thin futon mattresses are used; these are folded and stored in alcove cupboards during the day. More and more, however, Western-style furniture—sideboards, sofas, armchairs, chairs, and so on—is being used in Japanese houses, even traditional ones. Kitchens are now completely equipped with Western-style appliances, and very often floors are covered with carpeting. However, one room is sometimes reserved for greeting, covered with tatami and containing a *tokonoma.* Ancillary rooms such as bathrooms and entranceways also have modern furnishings. The traditional hibachi or *irori* may still be used for heating in rural houses, but most houses and apartments have natural-gas, electricity, or kerosene heaters. And, of course, every room has at least one television set.

Fu-rōnin. "Wandering peasants," farmers who avoided paying high imperial taxes by fleeing to serve lords of private estates *(shōen).* The large numbers of *fu-rōnin* pushed the *ritsuryō* administrative system into obsolescence at the end of the Nara period. *See also* RŌNIN.

Furoshiki. Square pieces of cotton or silk used by most Japanese women and men to wrap things and transport them more easily. At the beginning of the Edo period, *furoshiki* were used to wrap items used for bathing *(furo). Furoshiki* measure about 75 cm to 1 m per side. They are always highly appreciated gifts. See FUKUSA.

Furugaki Tetsurō. Diplomat and journalist (1900–87), born in Kagoshima. He studied in France and worked for the League of Nations in Geneva and as a correspondent for *Asahi Shimbun.* He became president of NHK (Nippon Hōsō Kyōkai, the Japan Broadcasting Corporation) in 1949, then was ambassador to France from 1956 to 1961.

Furuhashi Hironoshin. Athlete, born in 1928 in Shizuoka. In 1947, he set a world record in swimming, 4:38.04 minutes for the 400-meter freestyle, and the Japanese freestyle records for 400, 800 and 1,500 meters. In 1949, he set a world record, 18:19 minutes, for 1,500 meters. He is director of the Fédération internationale de natation amateur (FINA, International Amateur Swimming Federation) and a member of Japan's Olympic Committee.

Furuhata Tanemoto. Pathologist (1891–1975), born in Mie. He discovered blood type Q in 1934 and received the Order of Culture in 1956.

Furuhito Ōji. Imperial prince (seventh century), son of Emperor Jōmei, who became a Buddhist monk in 644 under the name Yoshino Taishi. After an attempted rebellion, he was condemned to death. His daughter married Emperor Tenji. Also called Furuhito Oine Shinnō.

• **Furuhito Oine Shinnō.** *See* FURUHITO ŌJI.

Furuichi Kimitake. Administrator, engineer, and researcher (1854–1934), born in Tokyo. Sent to France in 1875 to be educated in sciences, he obtained an "arts and manufacturing" engineering degree from the École Centrale in 1879 and a degree in mathematics from the Sorbonne in 1880. When he returned to Japan, in 1882, he entered the Ministry of Home Affairs and was put in charge of river-flow control. In 1888, he accompanied Minister of the Interior Yamagata Aritomo to Europe, then founded an engineering school in Tokyo. In 1905, he was named president of the Keifu Railway Company in Seoul. In 1917, he became president of the Civil Engineering Society; in 1920, he took charge of the Tokyo subway system. He directed the Institut Franco-Japonais (Nichi-futsu Kan) starting in 1932.

Furui Yoshikichi. Writer, born in 1937 in Tokyo. His novel *Yōko* won the Akutagawa Prize in 1970, and *Kushi no hi* (Fiery Comb, 1974) was very successful. His works describe daily life and reveal the secret motivations of individuals.

Furukawa. Town in Miyagi prefecture (northern Honshu), an important post town during the Edo period. *Pop.:* 60,000.
• Former zaibatsu founded by Furukawa Ichibei (1832–1903), a Kyoto entrepreneur who purchased the Ashio Copper Mines from the government in 1877. He then opened other copper mines in Japan, producing about 50% of the country's demands for this metal. After he died, the zaibatsu expanded, taking the name Furukawa Kōgyō Kaisha in 1905. By 1945, it was so diversified that it controlled 84 companies. In the 1970s, the companies, which had become independent, reunited to form a powerful industrial and financial group. One member company, Furukawa Denki Kōgyō (electrical equipment and nonferrous metals), in its turn controlled many other companies, including Fuji Electric, Nippon Light Metal, and Yokohama Rubber Co., and opened branches in a number of foreign countries (Brazil, Indonesia, Thailand, Saudi Arabia, and others). Head office in Tokyo.

• **Furukawa Ichibei.** *See* FURUKAWA.

Furukawa Ikurō. *See* FURUKAWA ROPPA.

Furukawa Roppa. Writer and actor (Furukawa Ikurō, 1903–61), born in Tokyo, known for the theater company he founded specializing in comedies and satires, Warai no Ōkoku (Great Company of Laughter), in 1933. In 1935, he founded another troupe (Roppa Troupe); he played many roles on stage and in various films produced by Tōhō, while continuing to work as a radio critic and journalist.

Furukawa Tomiko. *See* TANIZAKI JUN'ICHIRŌ.

Furusawa Shigeru. Politician (Furusawa Uruo, 1847–1911), born in Tosa (Kōchi prefecture). He studied in England after 1868 and worked with Itagaki Taisuke to establish an elected People's Assembly, which gave rise to the People's Movement for Freedom and Rights. He also helped to found the Risshisha and Aikokusha parties, as well as newspapers influenced by the Liberal party (Jiyūtō), such as *Ōsaka Nippō Shimbun* and *Jiyū Shimbun*. He was appointed governor of several prefectures (Nara, Yamaguchi, and Ishikawa) and elected to the House of Lords in 1904.

• **Furusawa Uruo.** *See* FURUSAWA SHIGERU.

Furu Tanuki. "Old *tanuki*," popular nickname for Tokugawa Ieyasu, of whom it was said that he was as cunning as an old *tanuki* (raccoon dog). *See* TANUKI.

Furuta Oribenoshō Shigenari. Warrior, potter, and master *(chajin)* of the tea ceremony, born in Mino province (Furuta Shigenari, 1544–1615). As a warrior, he served Oda Nobunaga, who gave him the title Oribe (an estate near Kyoto) no Kami with a revenue of 35,000 *koku*. He fought at Tokugawa Ieyasu's side at the Battle of Sekigahara (1600), but betrayed him during the siege of the Osaka castle and was forced to commit suicide. He was a student of Sen no Rikyū and became the leading tea master after Rikyū's death, creating the Oribe style. As a potter, he created a unique style called Oribe or Mino ware. He also designed the garden *(hira-niwa)* of Nanshū-ji temple in Sakai and invented stone lanterns *(ishidōrō)* for *chaseki* gardens, which are known as Oribe-*dōrō*.

Furuyama Komao. Writer, born in 1920 in Korea. After serving in Indochina during the Second World War, he was imprisoned by the French in 1946 as a war criminal. He returned to Japan in 1947 and worked at various newspapers, then began to write in 1969. His most famous book, *Pureō 8 no yoake*, describing the life of Japanese soldiers in a Saigon prison, received the Akutagawa Prize in 1970.

Furuyama Moromasa. Painter of ukiyo-e prints (Shinshichirō; *gō:* Bunshi, Getsugetsudō, ca. 1712–72), student of Hishikawa Moronobu. He painted mainly beautiful women *(bijin)* and adopted a Western-style perspective in his landscapes and genre scenes. Having also taken the name Hishikawa Masanori, he was the last artist in the Hishikawa family line.

• **Furuyama Moroshige.** *See* MOROSHIGE.

Furyū. Ancient traditional performances (part of the Ennen) involving sumptuous sets, music, dances, and chants. These performances take place at major festivals such as the Gion Matsuri in Kyoto, during the dances of the Urabon festival (Bon Odori), and at many working-class festivals. *See* JINJI-MAI, ENNEN.

Fūryū. Term used to describe a person with a refined aesthetic or artistic sense. This concept of simple beauty was behind many arts, such as Noh and the tea ceremony. The term encompasses all refinement, of any kind, in all areas, literary and artistic. A person with exquisitely good taste is also said to be *fūryū*.

Furyū monji. "Not holding to the letter," Zen Buddhist concept according to which candidates for enlightenment (satori) must avoid taking things literally but attempt to understand the spirit of things and to "realize" this spirit via experimentation or meditation.

Fūryū shidōkenden. "The Gallant Story of Shidōken." A novel in the *kokkei-bon* genre published in 1763 by Fūrai Sanjin (Hiraga Gennai), a sort of philosophical tale criticizing the customs of the Edo townspeople.

Fusa no Kuni. Traditional name of the former provinces of Shimōsa and Kazusa.

Fuse. Satellite city of Osaka, with a number of industries (ceramics, rubber, plastics, metallurgy). *Pop.*: 260,000.

Fuse Akiko. Contemporary writer and sociologist, author of books dealing with the Japanese family: *Gendai no kazoku* (The Contemporary Family, 1982), *Ararashii kazuko no sōzō* (Creation of a New Family, 1984).

Fusen Jōyaku. Japanese name for the Kellogg-Briand anti-aggression pact, signed in 1928 by 25 nations on the initiative of French Foreign Minister Aristide Briand and American Secretary of State Frank B. Kellogg.

Fusen Kakutoku Dōmei. "Women's Suffrage League," founded in 1924 to promote equality of the sexes through universal suffrage. It published a magazine called *Fusen* and also fought to lower food prices. It was dissolved in 1940. *See* ICHIKAWA FUSAE.

Fuseya Soteki. Scholar (Manchō Gonnoshin, Kimpan, 1747–1811), born in Kawachi. He studied "Dutch science" *(rangaku)*, mainly medicine. In 1803, he published *Oranda iwa* (History of Dutch Medicine), in which he described his own experiments on the formation of urine in the kidneys.

Fushimi. Site near Kyoto, on the Momoyama hill, where Toyotomi Hideyoshi had a castle built in 1593, in which he lived until his death in 1598. Tokugawa Ieyasu lived there until the fall of the Osaka castle in 1615. The castle was razed in 1623, and its treasures and furnishings were dispersed by Tokugawa Iemitsu. The town of Fushimi, now quite modest in size *(pop.:* 50,000), contains imperial tombs and a new castle, reconstructed according to the original plans.

• **Fushimi Inari Taisha.** Large Shinto shrine in Fushimi (Kyoto) dedicated to Uka no Mitama, a *kami* of agriculture, and several other *kami* presiding over activities of daily life. First built in 711 on the Inariyama hill in southwestern Kyoto, it was moved to its current site in 816 upon the request of the monk Kūkai. This very popular shrine is said to have more than 40,000 secondary shrines *(matsuji)* throughout Japan. The main shrine dates back to 1499. It is distinctive for its rows of red-painted torii gates (gifts from the faithful), which are crowded together to make covered alleys, and for its effigies of foxes *(kitsune)*, considered to be guardians of the crops. Its annual festival takes place on April 9.

• **Fushimi-ningyō.** Type of terra-cotta dolls made in Fushimi, intended for the Fushimi Inari Shrine, which were sold at shrine entrances throughout Japan in the Edo period. They portray characters that symbolize the person who is offering them, and they serve as substitutes in the case of disease or danger.

• **Fushimi Tōjūrō.** *See* SAKATA TŌJŪRŌ II.

Fushimi Sadanaru. Imperial prince (1858–1923), uncle of Emperor Taishō. An officer and a diplomat, he represented Emperor Meiji in the United States in 1904.

Fushimi Tennō. Ninety-second emperor of Japan (Prince Hirohito, 1265<1288–98>1317), second son of Emperor Go-Fukukusa and successor to Emperor Go-Uda. Having abdicated in favor of his son, Go Fushimi, he continued to rule as a retired emperor *(insei)* with the title Jimyō-in Hō-ō (his descendants were therefore called Jimyō-in Tō). He was an excellent *waka* poet and a good kana calligrapher, having had Ono no Tōfu and Fujiwara no Yukinari as masters. A few excerpts from his personal diary, the *Fushimi-in gyōki,* have survived, including entries concerning the years 1287–90, 1292–93, 1309, and 1311.

• **Fushimi no Miya.** *See* KAN'IN NO MIYA, KAMMON GYOKI.

Fushin-bugyō. Bureaucratic position created in 1652 to oversee the state of the walls and fortifications of the castle and city of Edo.

Fusō-koku. Former poetic name of Japan, based on the Chinese Fusang (a mythical country). Also called Fusō no Kuni.

• **Fusō no Kuni.** *See* FUSŌ-KOKU.

• **Fusō-kyō.** Shinto sect founded by Fujiwara no Takekuni (1541–ca. 1646?) and reorganized by Shishino Nakaba in 1873 to honor the Zōka no Sanjin. It is one of the 13 sects of Kyōha Shintō, which comprises more than 400,000 followers *(ujiko)*. It was divided into 12 branches *(ha)* in 1945: Fusō, Ishizuchi, Jitsugetsu, Kiso Mitake, Makotono Michi, P. L. Kyōdan, Seisei, Shinsei, Shintō Teruō, Shiogama, Sōgō Gimin, and Tenchi. These sects and subsects venerate the spirits of the mountains, particularly that of Mt. Fuji.

• *Fusō-ryakuki.* Japanese history book covering the period from 898 to 1198, written by Kōen, a Buddhist monk of the Tendai sect.

• *Fusō-shū yōshū.* Thirty-volume history, compiled by Tokugawa Mitsukuni and other historians of the Mito school.

Fusube-kawa. Leather colored by smoking with rice straw or pine needles, used to make armor in the medieval period *(see* YOROI*)*.

Fusuma. Window, door, or sliding partition connecting several rooms in a house or separating a single room into two or more parts. A fusuma is made of a wooden frame on which paper or fabric is stretched, thus forming an ideal support for decorative paintings. In the past, the greatest painters decorated fusuma for castles and aristocratic residences. Modern fusuma have glass panes in aluminum or plastic frames or sliding partitions; they are an indispensable part of Japanese houses. The immobile section between the ceiling and the fusuma, sometimes decorated with perforations, is called the *ramma. See also* SHŌJI.

Futabatei Shimei. Writer (Hasegawa Tatsunosuke, 1864–1909), born in Tokyo. He initiated the modern Japanese novel with *Ukigumo* (Drifting Clouds, 1887–89), which reflected his studies of characters in Russian novels and the emotional life of anti-heroes. He also translated many works of Russian literature into Japanese, including novels by Dosteovsky, Turgenev, Gogol, Tolstoy, Chekhov, and Gorky. Among his own novels are *Aibiki* (Lovers, 1888), *Meguriai* (Chance Encounter, 1889), *Chasengami* (Ladies' Hairdos, 1906), *Sono omokage* (An Adopted Husband, 1906), and *Heibon* (Mediocrity, 1907). His writings were collected in *Futabatei Shimei zenshū,* published in 1953–54. He died of illness on a ship bringing him back from Russia, where he had been sent as a correspondent for *Asahi Shimbun.*

Futago-zuka. "Twin hills," name sometimes given to *kofun* funerary mounds in a keyhole shape *(zempōkōen-fun)* to distinguish them from square- and round-shaped *kofun. See* KOFUN.

Futahaguro Koji. Sumo wrestler *(sumotori)* who attained the high rank of Yokozuna in 1986. Born in Hie prefecture, he weighs 151 kg and is 1.99 m tall. He directs the Tatsunami stable *(heya). See* CHIYONOFUJI SUMŌ.

Futai-ji. Buddhist temple founded in 847 in Nara. It houses a *nanmon* (southern gate) from 1317, a fourteenth-century *hondō,* and a one-story *tahō-tō* (originally a two-story pagoda) from the Kamakura period, restored in 1930.

Futaki Kenzō. Physician (1873–1966), born in Akita. Educated in Germany, he became director of the Komagome Hospital in Tokyo in 1919. He studied contagious diseases and is credited with discovering two dysentery bacilli (*Shigella flexneri* A and B) in 1903, and the *Streptobacillus moniloformis* bacillus in 1915. He was decorated with the Order of Culture (Bunka-shō) in 1955.

Futami ga Ura. Part of the coast facing Ise, famous for the linked rocks (*meoto-iwa,* "married rocks") not far from the rocky beach, believed to represent the progenitor *kami* of Japan, Izanagi and Izanami. The rocks are joined by a long cord *(shimenawa),* and a small torii gate has been erected on the larger rock. The cord is replaced every January 5 during a Shinto ceremony.

Futarasan-jingū. Group of three Shinto shrines in Nikkō, dedicated to Ōnamuchi no Mikoto, Tagorihime, and their son Ajisuki, founded in the tenth century. The current buildings date from the seventeenth century and are located in the town of Nikkō, on the shore of Lake Chūzenji and at the top of Mt. Futara. They were apparently built on the site of an older shrine venerated by the disciples of Shugendō. Also called Futarayama Shrine.

Futarayama-jinja. Shinto shrine of the town of Utsunomiya (Tochigi prefecture), dedicated to the spirit *(kami)* of the son of the legendary Emperor Suijin. Also called Utsunomiya Daimyōjin. Festival on October 21.

• **Futara-yama.** Former name of the city of Nikkō.

Futari shizuka. "The Two Shizuka," title of a Noh play: the spirit of Shizuka Gozen (Minamoto no Yoshitsune's teacher) takes possession of the spirit of another woman, then appears before her, dancing.

Futa-tesaki. In traditional architecture, type of eaves formed by a double *degumi*. *See* TO-KYŌ, WA-YŌ.

Futomani. Ancient method of divination, of Chinese origin, in which the future is predicted by reading the cracks produced by a red-hot brand applied to the scapula of a male deer, onto which certain lines have been drawn. This method seems to have been practiced before the introduction (from China) of divination using tortoiseshells *(kame-ura, kime)*. The *futomani* still takes place every year in the Shinto shrine at Mitake, near Tokyo, on January 3. Also called *shika-ura. See* BOKUSEN, URANAI.

Futon. Thin mattress (and padded cover) that is spread out on tatami mats at night to be used as a bed. In the morning, the futon is folded and stored in a wall cupboard, closed by a fusuma.

Futo no Yasumari no Ason. Bureaucrat *(ason)* who was commanded by Empress Gemmei to write out Hieda no Are's memories of the origins of Japan in 712. This text comprised the first history of Japan, the *Kojiki.* Futo no Yasumaro probably also helped write the *Nihon shoki* in 720. He was also known as Ō no Yasunaro. In 1979, his tomb was discovered in Konoe (Tawara-chō, Nara prefecture). It contains a wooden sarcophagus measuring 0.85 × 0.40 × 0.42 m and a copper plaque engraved with 41 Chinese characters.

Futsunushi no Kami. Shinto *kami* who, according to the *Kojiki,* descended to Earth to prepare it for the arrival of Ninigi no Mikoto. Also called Mikafutsu no Kami and Iwainushi no Kami.

Futtsu. Small town and industrial center in Chiba prefecture (central Honshu). It is known mainly for Takagoyama hill, on which colonies of Rhesus monkeys live, and a modern statue of Shō Kannon Bosatsu, 56 m high.

Fuwa Tetsuzō. Politician (Ueda Kenjirō, b. 1930), communist since 1947. Elected to the Diet as a member of the Communist party in 1969, he became the party's secretary-general the following year. In 1982, he took over the presidency from

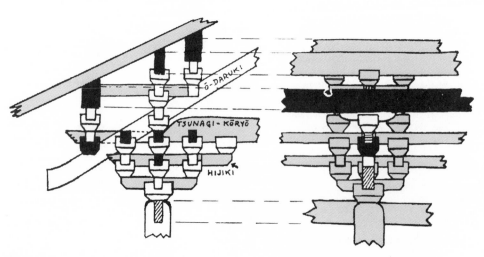

Type of *wa-yō* roof bracket: *futa-tesaki*

Miyamoto Kenji; his older brother was his assistant.

Fuyō. Painter (Oshima Mōhyū; *azana:* Juhi; Ikki, Kondō Itsuki; *gō:* Chūgakugashi, Hyōgaku-sanjin, Kantankyo, Kō Fuyō, 1722–84). He painted mainly landscapes in the Chinese style (he was a Confucian) and engraved seals.
 • Painter (Suzuki Yō; *azana:* Bunki; Shimbe; *gō:* Rōren, 1749–1816) of the Nanga school, student of Tani Bunchō. He was also a writer and poet.

Fuyuso-den. According to the *ritsuryō* administrative code (Nara period), properties and estates exempted from tax *(fuyu)*. These exemptions concerned imperial estates *(kanden);* estates belonging to shrines *(shinden),* Buddhist monasteries *(jiden),* government officers *(kugaiden),* and overseers of post towns *(ekiden);* and the properties of slaves serving government bureaucrats. During the Heian period, exemptions proliferated to the point that the government was losing all power over the various *shōen* (estates), whose owners had the right to forbid bureaucrats to collect taxes. *See* FUNYŪ.

Fūzoku-ga. Genre painting style that appeared in the late sixteenth century and evolved throughout the seventeenth century, portraying, sometimes humorously, scenes of daily life. The experts divide this type of painting into three eras, according to when it was produced: Keichō *fūzoka-ga,* attributed mainly to painters of the Kanō family, Kan'ei *fūzoka-ga,* and Kambun *fūzoka-ga.* The style was almost completely abandoned at the beginning of the eighteenth century, when it was replaced by ukiyo-e prints, which were popular among *chōnin* (townspeople) and less expensive.

 • **Fūzoku-shōsetsu.** Novels describing the customs and living conditions of the common people, written for them and therefore considered to have little literary value. Among the authors who wrote this type of novel in the nineteenth century were Kanagaki Rōbun, Ozaki Kōyō, and Kikuchi Kan. These working-class novels were also quite popular during the 1920s and 1930s, when they were composed by authors such as Kawabata Yasunari, Yokomitsu Riichi, and Kawaguchi Matsutarō. Some of these novels and their authors have been reassessed since the Second World War and their value recognized.

 • **Fūzoku-uta.** Popular songs in style at the imperial court during the Nara and Heian periods. In Kyoto, they were called *saibara.* Only 26 of these ballads have been preserved. *See* SAIBARA.

G. This consonant, which can be pronounced only when paired with the vowels *a, i, u, e,* and *o (ga, gi, gu, ge, go),* is a weakening (*see* NIGORI) of the sounds (*see* GOJŪ-ON-ZU) *ka, ki, ku, ke, ko.* The syllables *ga, gi, ge, gu,* and *go* are always pronounced with a hard *g,* as in "guest." They are partnered with the syllables *ya, yu, ye,* and *yo* to give the composites *gya, gyu, gye,* and *gyo.*

Ga. The Sino-Japanese character *(kanji)* representing the sound *ga,* meaning "painted by," is often found after the name of an artist on his or her work, notably on ukiyo-e prints. Also called *hitsu. See also* E, GIHITSU, ZU.
• When placed after a name, *ga* can also indicate a style of painting—for example, Bunjinga.

• **Ga-in.** "Imperial Academy of Painting," charged with setting the official rules for the arts, especially painting. *See* E-DOKORO, INTAI-GA.

Gachirin-kan. Meditation method based on contemplation of the moon used in some Buddhist sects. The meditator sits in the lotus position *(renge-in,* Skt.: *padmāsana)* in front of a *kakemono* or a painting portraying the letter A inscribed on a blossoming lotus flower or a moon. The meditator then chants the vowel "A" and tries to identify with the moon. This method is supposed to produce awakening to *bodhi* (enlightenment) through realization of the sound of the letter. *See* A, AJI-KAN.

Gachō. Albums of paintings made on separate sheets of paper *(shikishi).* These albums, in use for a very long time in China, became known in Japan only in the Edo period. Also called *gajō.*

Gagaku. "Elegant, refined music," imported from Korea and China in the ninth century and played in the imperial court to accompany Bugaku dances. When this music is played alone, it is called *kangen.* A sort of synthesis of ancient Asian aristocratic music and sacred (shamanic) Japanese music, the Gagaku tradition has been preserved more or less intact in the imperial court, in some temples (such as the Shitennō-ji in Osaka), and in the major Shinto shrines. *Kangen* is the oldest known orchestral form, with a repertoire comprising some 100 compositions and 56 dances. There are several types of Gagaku, among them the Komagaku, apparently from Korea; the Tōgaku, from China's Tang (*Jap.:* Tō) dynasty; and the Saibara, featuring very old Japanese popular songs. In addition, the Kagura (once called Mikagura in the court) involves dances and music associated with Shinto ritual. The instrumental ensemble used in the Gagaku *kangen* includes large drums *(taiko)* and small metal gongs *(shōko).* Depending on the form of Gagaku, additional instruments may include a two-sided drum *(san no tsuzumi)* or a small drum called *kakko;* sometimes, wooden clappers *(shakubyōshi)* punctuate the singers' performance. Two types of stringed instruments were used in the *kangen:* the koto (at the time called *gaku-sō,* with 13 strings) and the *biwa.* Shinto music, in contrast, uses the six-stringed *wagon,* a sort of koto. Rōei (compositions based on Chinese lyrics) and Saibara also use wind instruments such as flutes *(kagurabue, komabue,* or *ryūteki)* and 17-pipe mouth organs *(shō)* of Chinese origin. Komagaku use three musical modes inspired by Chinese music: Koma Ichikotsuchō, Koma Sōjō, and Koma Hyōjō; the first two are more common. Tōgaku is more complex: its 28 modes have been reduced to six—Ichikotsuchō, Hyōjō, Sōjō, Ōshi-kichō, Bashikichō, and Taishikichō—in addition to Rōei and Saibara. The compositions in these repertoires are divided into three parts of different lengths: *shōkyoku, chūkyoku,* and *taikyoku.* Every concert ends with a melody called *chōkeishi. Kor.:* Āg; *Viet.:* Nha Nhac. *See also* BUGAKU.

• **Gagaku-kyoku.** "Bureau of Painting," established in 1816; part of the Bansho-shirabe-dokoro. It was directed first by Kawakami Tōgai, then by Takahashi Yuichi.

• **Gagaku-ryō.** Gagaku-music school established in the ninth and tenth centuries. In 951, it was replaced by the Gaku-dokoro, where the main subject of study was Chinese music.

• **Gagakusai.** *See* BUNCHŌ (Tani Bunchō).

Gagen shuran. Major Japanese dictionary compiled by Ishikawa Masamochi (Gabō, 1753–1830) and published in 21 volumes starting in 1826. Work on this dictionary, which had not been completed, was continued by Nakajima Hirotari (1792–1864), and it was republished in 1887. The entries are arranged according to the *Iroha* traditional order.

Gahō. Modern-style painter (Hashimoto Masa-kuni; *go:* Shōen, Gahō, 1835–1908). He studied the style of the Kanō school with Kanō Shōsen-in (of the Kobikichō school) and studied with Fenollosa, who taught him the principles of Western painting. He also worked with Okakura Tenshin.
→ *See* HAYASHI RAZAN.

Gaikō. "Open space style," Western genre painting style executed in Japan for the first time by Seiki (early twentieth century). *See also* MA, SEIKI.

Gaikoku-bugyō. From *gaikoku,* "foreign country"; an administrative title created in 1858 for diplomats responsible for relations between the shogunate and foreigners. Their chief had the title *gaikoku-sōbugyō.* After 1862, they were assisted by other diplomats, the *gaikoku-bugyō-nami.* These positions fell into disuse in 1867, when the *rōjū* took over foreign affairs, and were dropped completely in 1869.

• **Gaikoku-hōjin.** Foreign juridical persons, states, administrative provinces, and trading companies recognized in Japan by the civil code (Article 36) and the commercial code.

• **Gaikokujin gakkō.** "Schools for foreigners" who do not enter the official education system. These schools are intended for foreign children, although some Japanese students are authorized to take courses in them. Japanese schools that teach foreign languages at various levels are also called *gaikokujin gakkō.*

• **Gaikokusen Uchiharai Rei.** "Order to Expel Foreign Ships." Edict issued in 1825 by the Edo shogunate to reinforce the policy of isolation inaugurated in 1639 and keep foreign ships from landing their crews on Japanese coasts. Although they had permission to take on provisions at certain ports (such as Nagasaki), the shogunate enforced this ban following various incidents between these ships and the Japanese authorities. In 1842, the shogunate once again allowed foreign ships to take on provisions in Japanese ports by issuing the Shinsui Kyōyo Rei (Order for the Provision of Firewood and Water).

• **Gaimushō.** "Ministry of Foreign Affairs," created in 1885. *See* MINISTRIES.

Gaki. Japanese equivalent of the Sanskrit *preta,* disembodied spirits condemned by their karma to perpetual wandering and hunger without hope of reincarnation; they haunt cemeteries and cremation sites. *Gaki* are also the spirits of the dead who did not have the benefit of burial or funeral services. *Chin.:* Gui, Egui, Guhun; *Mongol.:* Birit; *Tib.:* Yid-btags. *See* ROKUDŌ.

• **Gaki-zōshi.** Twelfth-century *emakimono* describing the six destinies of transmigration (*see* ROKUDŌ) according to Buddhist concepts.

Gakkan-in. School founded in the early ninth century by Empress Tachibana Kachiko and her brother, Tachibana Ujikimi, to educate the children of the Tachibana family. It was integrated with the Imperial Academy (Daigaku-ryō) in 960.

Gakken Co. (Gakushū Kenkyū-sha). A large publishing house founded by Furuoka Hideto in 1946; it publishes many scholarly works and more than 27 educational magazines. Head office in Tokyo.

Gakkō Bosatsu. Buddhist divinity symbolizing the lunar aspect (*Skt.:* Chandraprabha). He is one of the acolytes of Bhaishajyaguru (*Jap.:* Yakushi Nyorai), with Nikkō Bosatsu (*Skt.:* Sūryaprabha).

His role is to watch over living beings during the night.

Gakō. During the Edo period, name generally given to painters who engraved the plates for their ukiyo-e prints themselves.

- **Gakō-shi.** Official bureau charged with painting until 808, when it was replaced by the *e-dokoro.*

Gaku. Small wooden board inscribed with sacred or magical formulas *(darani)* hung on the walls of Buddhist temples for purposes of meditation.
- Term meaning "arts," "music," "culture."

Gakuan-ji. Buddhist temple founded, according to tradition, by Shōtoki Taishi (ca. 600) not far from the Hōryu-ji (Nara prefecture) and restored during the Kamakura period by the monk Ryōkan. This temple, at first dedicated to Yakushi Nyorai, is currently dedicated to Kokūzō Bosatsu. It houses two magnificent sculptures, in dry lacquer and wood, of Kokuzō and Monju Bosatsu, dating from the Nara and Heian periods, respectively.

Gakubatsu. *See* BATSU.

Gakuchi. *See* ADACHI KAGEMORI.

Gaku-daiko. *See* TAIKO.

Gakudō. *See* OZAKI TUKIO.

Gakudō-dōjyō. "Association for Self-Awakening," founded by a contemporary Zen philosopher, Hisa-matsu Shin'ichi, professor at Hanazono University and author of many books on Zen.

Gaku-dokoro. Japanese-music school. It replaced the Gagaku-ryō, which taught only Chinese music, in 951. *See* GAGAKU-RYŌ.

Gakufu. Old "stenographic" music-notation system.

Gakumon-jo. Name taken in 1797 by the Kōbunin, a school founded in Edo by Tokugawa Ieyasu and Tokugawa Iemitsu, and directed by the Hayashi family. *See also* SHŌHEI-KŌ.

- **Gakumonjo-ban.** Bureaucrat in the Kamakura *bakufu,* charged with horses, archery, and old warrior uniforms; a position of Chinese origin created in 1253. A bureau of the same name was created in

the Edo period for bureaucrats charged with Gakumon-jo schools, in 1798. *See* YUMI-YA-YARI BUGYŌ.

- *Gakumon no susume.* "Encouragement to Study the Sciences." A series of short books intended for the general public, published from 1872 to 1876 by Fukuzawa Yukichi. These books (a total of 17) were so popular that more than a million copies were sold. Starting from the philosophical assertion that "Heaven created no one superior or inferior to another," they contributed greatly to spreading the notions of freedom of thought and social equality.

Gakunin. Formerly, bureaucrat charged with court music. Title given to court musicians.

Gaku-ō. *See* MATSUDAIRA SADANOBU.

Gakuō Zōkyū. Painter (active between 1482 and 1514) and Zen monk at the Shōkoku-ji temple in Kyoto. He was a student of Shūbun, following the style of the Muromachi *suiboku* school. He painted mainly landscapes in the Chinese style of Xia Gui (active ca. 1195–1224). Although little is known about his life, enough of his works have survived that the development if his artistic career and his style can be traced.

Gakurazuka. *See* TORII.

Gakushū-in. School founded in Kyoto by Emperor Nikkō under the name Gakushūjo to educate the children of the nobility. The school was established in Tokyo in 1877 with the support of the House of Lords and became an imperial institution in 1884. It was transformed into a private university in 1947 and now comprises, among other faculties, a well-known institute of Eastern studies. It has about 7,000 students.

- **Gakushū-kan.** School *(shohan-gakkō)* founded in Wakayama in 1713 to teach Dutch.

Gaku-sō. Type of 13-string koto, used mainly in Gagaku orchestras. *See* GEI-AMI, KOTO.

Gambaru. "To persist," a term that had a negative value before the 1930s but gradually acquired a positive meaning, characterizing a passion for work and a sense of group responsibility.

Gamō. Family of Christian daimyo of northern Honshu, the most famous of whom were Gamō Katahide (1534–84) and Gamō Ujisato (1556–95). *See* GAMŌ UJISATO.

• **Gamō Kumpei.** Scholar (Fukuda Hidezane, 1768–1813) and historian, born in Utsunomiya (Tochigi prefecture), belonging to the Mito school. In a memorandum (*Sanryōshi*, 1808) addressed to the Edo *bakufu,* he deplored the state of neglect of the imperial tombs and revealed himself to be an early proponent of pro-imperial ideas, in opposition to the Edo shogunate.

• **Gamō Ujisato.** Daimyo (Gamō Masuhide, baptized Leao, 1556–95) of the Hino castle in Ōmi province (Shiga prefecture), Gamō Katahide's son. He assisted Oda Nobunaga and married his daughter. Then he entered the service of Toyotomi Hideyoshi in 1582 and received an estate in the Aizu Wakamatsu region with a revenue of 120,000 *koku*. In 1591, after he helped Hideyoshi conquer northern Honshu, the size of his estates was doubled and his revenue rose to almost 920,000 *koku,* making him one of the most powerful daimyo in Japan. After studying Zen and the arts of tea and poetry, he was converted to Christianity by Takayama Ukon in 1585, but quickly returned to his old faith after Hideyoshi edicted his anti-Christian laws, in 1587. He then changed his family name to Wakamatsu.

Gandate. Prayers accompanied by offerings, addressed to a Buddhist temple or a Shinto shrine by an individual, a village, or a family, to obtain a specific favor. Some pilgrimages are considered forms of *gandate*. Many customs are attached to these ritual offerings, varying by region or by site of worship. Also called *gankake*.

Gan'ei (or Gen'ei). Era of Emperor Toba: Apr. 1119–Apr. 1120. *See* NENGŌ.

Gangō-ji. Buddhist temple of the Kegon-shū sect, founded in Asuke (Nara prefecture) by Soga no Umako in 588 under the name Hōkō-ji, and now better known as Asuka-dera. *See* ASUKA-DERA.

Gangyō. Era of Emperor Yōzei: Apr. 877–Feb. 885. *See* NENGŌ.
• In traditional architecture, a horizontal beam, round in section, supporting the edges of a roof. Called *degeta* when it is square in section.

Ganjin. Chinese Buddhist monk (Jianzhen, 688–763) born in Yangzhou. Having been Daoan's (Taoan) disciple, he preached at Luoyang and Chang'an. The Japanese government decided to recall its ambassadors from China under the Tang (*Jap.:* Tō) dynasty in 732, and sent the monks Yōei and Fushō to ask Ganjin to go to Japan to teach. Ganjin accepted in 742; between 743 and 748, he tried five times to make the trip but was stopped each time by weather or pirates. He succeeded on his sixth attempt, arrived in Kyushu in 753, and went to Nara in 754, accompanied by a large group of disciples and artisans. By this time, however, he was almost totally blind. In Nara, he founded the Ritsu-shū sect (*Skt.:* Vināya) at the Tōdai-ji, establishing a strict monastic discipline and ordination rites *(kaidan; Skt.: sīmā)* for monks. He then created a number of charitable foundations and a garden of medicinal plants. He introduced to Japan the Chinese method of standardizing architectural elements so that the number of components in structures was reduced through prefabrication. In 759, he founded the Tōshōdai-ji temple, which became the center of teaching of the Ritsu-shū. He received the titles Taishin-Oshō, Daiwa-jō, Tōdai-Oshō, Kakai-daishi, and Ganjin Wajō. *Chinese titles:* Tang Da Heshang, Guo Hai Dashi. A sculpture portraying him sitting in meditation, in colored dry lacquer, 80 cm high, dating from 763, is housed in the Miei-dō of the Tōshōdai-ji (Nara prefecture).

• **Ganjin-wajō.** *See* GANJIN.

Ganjitsu no Sechi-e. Official ceremony that takes place every New Year's Day at the Imperial Palace. *See* GO SECHI-E, SECHI-E.

Gankō. "Incense ceremony," during which aesthetes meet to appreciate and guess the origin of various types of incense. It seems that this practice came into being in the fifteenth century. Also called Kōdō, Kō-awase. *See* GENJI-KŌ.

• **Gankō-ji ha.** *See* SANRON-SHŪ.

Ganku. Painter (Saeki Masaaki, Kishi Kū, Koma; *azana:* Funzen; *gō:* Kayō, Dōkōkan, Kakandō, Kotōkan, Tenkaikutsu, Ganku, 1756–1838), born in Kanazawa. He was governor of Echizen province. Having studied painting of the Kanō school and the works of Chinese painter Nampin, he created his own style, called Ganku-ryū or Kishi-ryū. He was famous mainly for his paintings of tigers. His son, Gantai, his son-in-law, Ganryō (1797–

1852), and his adoptive son, Renzan (1804–59), were his disciples.

Gantai. Painter (Saeki Tai; *azana:* Kunchin; Chikusen no Suke; *gō:* Takudō, Dōkokan, Gantai, 1782–1865), student of his father, Ganku. He painted mainly flowers and birds in his father's style. *See* GANKU.

Garabō. Method of spinning cotton using hydraulic pressure; invented in 1876 by the Buddhist monk Gaun Tatsumune (1842–1900), this procedure enabled production to be intensified. Spinning equipment was installed in ships furnished with paddles that kept the machinery working. About 1900, this process was replaced by more modern ones, but it continued to be used in the Mikawa (Aichi prefecture) region.

Garan. Term sometimes used to designate Buddhist temples, abridgment of *sōgaran,* which is a Japanization of the Sanskrit *samghārāma,* "retreat for monks." Also called *shichidō-garan. See* DERA, JI.

• **Garan'in.** Garden *(niwa)* in a Buddhist monastery.

Gardens. The oldest description of a Japanese garden is in the *Man'yōshū:* Prince Kusakabe, a son of Emperor Temmu's, admires "a piece of land with a pond edged with rocks and an island in the middle, surrounded by azalea bushes." But it was only during the Heian period, in the early ninth century, that gardens began to emerge as an art form. It seems that the first gardens were designed, following Chinese models, by Buddhist monks for their monasteries. In the same period, court nobles liked to place their residences in settings resembling landscaped gardens, with hills and artificial ponds. In the *shinden* housing style, the garden and pond were obligatory. This was, in fact, a natural development from the gardens that had been adorning residences for a long time: Empress Suiko (<592–628>) had her palace located in the middle of a sort of garden, and the minister Soga no Umako was said to have had a splendid garden near his home.

During the Heian period, garden plans were codified to provide space both for receptions and for contemplation of nature, and the plan of the residence was integrated with that of the garden. The main building had to face south; beyond an area of sand or gravel was an irregularly shaped pond, fed by a small stream *(yarimizu)* running from northwest to southeast, an orientation, according to the theories of Chinese geomancy, that would draw good influences. The pond had to have two or three islets of different sizes and shapes, linked to each other and to the shore by wooden or stone bridges. One or two small pavilions on pilings overlooked it, allowing for fishing or contemplation of the reflection of the moon on the water. These pavilions were linked to the main building by covered galleries called *tai no ya.* Artificial hills were made and planted with trees, and rocks of various shapes were placed around the pond and on the hills. There was no well-defined style; the owner's wishes were followed, although the rules propounded by the Ommyōdō about the influences of Yin and Yang were respected. Monastery gardens followed the same principle, although they seemed to obey a stricter set of rules. None of these gardens has survived; we know them from depictions in *emakimono.* According to the beliefs of the time, the arrangement of stones could not be haphazard, for such arrangements could bring good or bad luck. All symmetry was banished. In cases where running water was not available, it was symbolized by an arrangement of stones in the form of a dragon *(ryū),* the mythical animal that is the most powerful symbol of water.

Monastery gardens were almost always separated from the purely religious complex, though remaining closely linked to it. They were generally bordered on one side by a veranda from which the monks could contemplate them, since, unlike laical gardens, they were not meant to be walked in but to be enjoyed with the eyes only. Toward the end of the Heian period, and under the influence of the new Amida Buddhist sects, the style of gardens changed quite a bit. The *shinden* style of nobles' residences tended to become a sort of visualization of the Pure Land of Amida, and the lake became an essential component, symbolizing the river that separates life on Earth from the hereafter, where the Pure Land lies. Islands and bridges now symbolized the difficulties of passing from the world of earthly pleasures into that of eternal faith. These gardens might be extremely elaborate *(shin)* or relatively simple *(sō),* and flat or hilly, depending on the lay of the land. In general, monastery gardens were flat *(hiraniwa)* and arrangements of stones played an important role. Gardens with hills *(tsukiyama-sansui),* requiring a large area, were favored by nobles with sumptuous residences. In addition to the pond (which was sometimes made in the shape of the *shin* character *kokoro,* meaning "heart" or "spirit"), such gardens featured a waterfall *(taki),* paths skirting hills and rocks, and various ornaments such as fences of woven bamboo, jetties, and stone basins.

On the paths, strollers could enjoy different points of view, with the eye always drawn toward the main tree or the most remarkable rock (generally situated above the waterfall).

In the fourteenth century, Zen monks brought in a new style, epitomized by Musō Kokushi (1276–1351). He designed a number of gardens in which arrangements of sand and stones were more prevalent than vegetation. If they were to be used for contemplation, they had no paths, such as the Ryōan-ji's garden in Kyoto; if they were to be for contemplation of nature, they were arranged in such a way that no human touch could be discerned: they had to both symbolize and represent nature. Very often, a garden of sand and stones *(kare-sansui)* was flanked by a nearby "natural" garden in which running water was very important. With the appearance of large residences in *shoin* style in the sixteenth century, tea gardens *(sukiya-niwa)* came into fashion. These had to appear natural, but, according to the standard set by Sen no Rikyū, they had to be furnished with sliding gates, barriers and fences, basins for ablutions, flagstones, and resting pavilions in rustic style. *Sukiya-niwa* were small in size and had twisting paths. They were made not to be admired but to convey visitors to the teahouse at the back of the garden in an ambience of serenity, calm, and peace. In this sense, the Japanese garden provided a contrast with the great disorder of the cities and the chaos of the coasts and mountains, and it reduced the formidable and excessive to human proportions. Nature, which can be quite hostile, is at peace and under unseen discipline in the garden; it is a gentle friend, complementary and accommodating to human beings. The garden, small as it may be, is the part of dreaming, brought to life, that each Japanese carries within his or her heart.

Aristocrats also designed gardens, some of them immense, such as the park at the Katsura villa in Kyoto, and landscape artists were employed to create them for monasteries (Zen or other), for tea ceremonies, or for the pleasure of re-creating an ideal landscape. Emperor Go-Mizunoo designed the garden of the Shugaku-in. Buddhist monks such as Musō Kokushi, Sō Ami, and Kanō Tan'yū; clan chiefs such as Kobori Enshū; masters of the tea ceremony such as Sen no Rikyū; and famous painters, including Sesshū, Hon-ami Kōetsu, Ishikawa Kōzan, Kanō Motonobu, and Matsudaira Yorishige—all helped to create many gardens, most of them for major daimyo and shogun. Unfortunately, many gardens were left untended or destroyed by civil war, and it was only during the Meiji era that attempts were made to re-create

them. In modern times, architects and sculptors, inspired by old creations and basing their concept on Zen gardens, are designing gardens in which new materials are integrated to make symbolic "landscapes." The Japanese try to create gardens wherever possible, and they jealously tend their bits of land, often just a few square meters, around their homes. If they have no access to land, people create miniature landscapes with bonsai. *See* BONSAI, HONDA SEIROKU, KATSURA-RIKYŪ, KENROKU-EN, KŌRAKU-EN, RIKUGI-EN, RITSURIN-KŌEN, RYŌAN-JI, SHUGAKU-IN.

Gassan. Volcano (1,980 m) in Yamagata prefecture, northeast Honshu, part of the Dewa Sanzan and a Shigendō cult center of long standing (shrine at the summit). Winter resort.

• **Gassan-jinja.** *See* DEWA SANZAN-JINJA.

Gasshō. Hand gesture (mudra; *Jap.: in-zō*) of a Buddhist divinity indicating that divinity's action and powers (sometimes reputed to be magical). Hands joined in prayer.

• **Gasshō-in.** Mudra corresponding to the *añjali-mudrā (Skt.),* or mudra of greeting and veneration. Hands joined in prayer.

• **Gasshō Kannon.** One of the 33 forms of Kannon Bosatsu *(Skt.:* Avalokiteshvara) represented with the hands joined in *gasshō-in. See* SANJŪSAN ŌGESHIN.

Ge. "Outside." Also called *gai.*

• **Gejō.** *See* KŌZAMA.

• **Gejō Masao.** *See* KEIKOKU.

• **Gekan.** Title given to bureaucrats living outside of the capital, Kyoto, before the Edo period.

• **Gekū (Gegū).** In Ise, "outside" Shinto shrine dedicated originally to the *kami* of the crops Kunitokotachi no Mikoto and now to Ukemochi no Kami (Toyo-uke-hime no Mikoto).

Gebaku ken-in. Mudra *(Jap.: in-zō)* similar to the *gasshō-in,* but with the fingertips crossed facing outward, typical of certain Buddhist divinities, notably the Myō-ō *(Skt.:* Vidyarāja). A variant, with the fingertips crossed facing inward, is called *naibaku-in. Chin:* Waifuquan Yin.

Gedatsu234

Gedatsu. Religious sense of detachment from the material world.

Gedatsu-kai. Modern Shinto sect, created in 1929 by Okano Seiken (1881–1948).

Gegyō. Fishtail-shaped ornament made of wood or metal, concealing the end of the roof ridge beam under the gable. The oldest example of a *gegyō* is on the Kondō of the Hōryū-ji (ca. 607) near Nara. The motif was probably regarded as protection against fires. *See* KEGYŌ.

Gei-ami. Painter (Shingei; *gō:* Gakusō, Gei-ami, 1431–85) of the Muromachi *suiboku* school. He was the disciple of his father, Nō-ami, and, like him, a master *(chajin)* of the tea ceremony *(chanoyu)*. He also wrote highly popular *renga* (linked) poems.

Geisha. "Artist," woman specially trained from childhood in dancing, singing, and music, whose role is to entertain wealthy and influential men. *Geisha* generally have a protector, male or female

Geisha, by Utamaro

(danna), who assumes the cost of their education and living expenses. In Edo about 1660, *geisha* were considered models of good taste and elegance, highly appreciated by upper-class men, and many were confidants of and advisors to men in power. Originally, there were male *geisha (hōkan, taiko-mochi, otoko-geisha),* who were in charge of entertainment at parties. But this role was very quickly assumed by women, who were called *onna-geisha,* then simply *geisha.*

Apprentice *geisha (shikomi)* must join a "house" *(okiya)* for training. They are obliged to perform domestic services until they are fully accepted and become *maiko* (in Kyoto) or *oshaku* or *hangyoku* (in Edo). After passing an examination at the end of their apprenticeship and undergoing the *mizu-age* (deflowering) ceremony, they become full-fledged *geisha,* sometimes called *ippon* ("stick" of incense), since their worth was once evaluated by the number of incense sticks burned during their performance (no fewer than four sticks, representing about one hour). This remuneration was called *hanadai, senkōdai,* or *gyokudai.*

About 1700, the profession of *geisha* was combined (more or less) with that of prostitute, and geisha were forced to live (and *okiya* to be located) in "reserved districts" *(yūkaku, yūri),* such as Yoshiwara in Edo, Shimabara in Kyoto, Shimmachi in Osaka, Maruyama in Nagasaki, Kanayama in Sado, Chimori in Sakai, Kitsuji in Nara, and Shumokuchō in Fushimi. The first "licensed district" reserved for prostitutes and not for true *geisha* was probably created in the Rokujō district of Kyoto by Hideyoshi in 1589. There were, however, *geisha* who did not live in these areas or belong to an *okiya;* they worked alone in different districts called *okabasho,* such as Gion in Kyoto, and Fukagawa, Yanagibashi, and Akasaka in Edo, and formed groups to maintain the traditional culture and arts outside of the reserved districts. Many well-known *geisha* practiced their art in these districts. Ordinary courtesans (known generally as *jorō*) had their own "reserved quarters" *(yūri)* in each city. They were divided into two classes: the professionals, or *age-jorō,* highly educated in all arts and comparable to true geisha, and *mise-jorō,* or ordinary prostitutes. The geisha and *age-jorō* were also divided into classes depending on their talents in the arts, their general level of cultural knowledge, their elegance, and the way they attracted or retained their "clients." The highest rank was *taiyū,* followed by *tenjin* (or *kōshi*), *kakoi* (or *hikifune-jorō*), and the lowest rank, *sancha;* there were also four ranks among the *mise-jorō.* Books describing how the various *yūri* were organized and giving the names and classes of *geisha* and *jorō* included the *Shikidō okagami,* published in Edo circa 1678, and the *Shokoku irozato annai,* published in 1688. Today, small books still come out with similar information, along with photographs and (sometimes) biographies of true *geisha,* so that prospective clients can make a selection and find out where to go to procure their services.

It was once common (and even considered elegant) for a man in the public eye to "keep" a high-ranking *geisha,* an extremely expensive proposition. Even today, it is not unusual for a politician or financier to take on a geisha as part of his "standing." Each political party has its favorite *geisha* and district for meeting them, for what are called *machiai-seiji* (meeting-house policies). When a large company wants to hold a banquet for guests, it spends large sums for one or several *geisha.* Foreigners rarely appreciate this type of entertainment, since one must have perfect knowledge of all aspects of Japanese culture (and comprehension of their true value) to understand the attraction of the *geisha.* There are now relatively few *geisha;* there are fewer than 15,000 throughout Japan, of all classes, and they are in competition with bar "hostesses," who, less cultured and less expensive, are more likely to satisfy the tastes of a certain clientele. *Kor.:* Ki-saeng; *Okinawa:* Jūri. *See also* ONSEN, YOSHIWARA.

Geiyo Shotō. Group of small islands in the Inland Sea (Setonaikai) between Hiroshima and Shikoku; the main ones are Ōmishima, Innoshima, Mukai-shima, and Ikuchishima. A series of bridges connects them to each other and to Shikoku and Honshu. The main crop is citrus fruits; there are also shipyards on the islands.

Geji. Summer solstice period, lasting about 15 days starting on June 21. *Chin.:* Xiazhi. *See* NIJŪSHI-SETSU.

Gejin mikkyō. Important text of the Buddhist Hosshō-shū sect, translation of the Sanskrit *Sandinirmochāsana-sūtra.*

Gekkei. First- and second-rank nobles (*see* I). Also called Kandechime.
→ *See* GOSHUN.

• **Gekkei-unkaku.** Third-rank nobles (San-I). *See* I.

Gekkō. *See* OGATA GEKKŌ, NAKAJIMA J. I-N.

Gekokujō. "The lower commanding the upper," an expression designating a period at the end of the Ashikaga shogunate, when, due to civil war, many people of lower rank occupied ranks once held by warriors of noble lineage or nobles, and vassals became lords. This process, started in the thirteenth century when the warrior clans came to power, intensified and spread in the fifteenth and sixteenth centuries. The term was used again in the 1930s to describe military insubordination in Japan in which young officers contested the decisions made by their elders. *See* SENGOKU JIDAI.

Currently, the term designates the replacement of heads of enterprises by subordinates.

Gembō. Buddhist monk (d. 746) at the Kōfuku-ji temple and bureaucrat in the Nara court. He went to China with the mission led by Kibi no Makibi in 717 and studied the doctrines of the Hosshō-shū sect (*Chin.:* Faxian Zong). When he returned to Japan in 735, he brought with him some 5,000 Buddhist texts and cult objects (statues, paintings, and accessories). Emperor Shōmu appointed him Sōjō. However, he was opposed to Fujiwara no Nakamaro and was sent to Dazaifu in 745 to supervise construction of a temple. He died there the following year.

Gembu. Decorative motif symbolic of the direction north, consisting of a turtle and a snake intertwined, painted on the interior walls of some *kofun.* This Chinese-inspired motif is also found in tombs in northern Korea. *Chin.:* Xuanwu; *Kor.:* Hyön-mu.

Gembudō. Basaltic cave in Toyōka (Hyōgo prefecture), on the west bank of the Maruyama-gawa river. It is flanked by two similar but smaller caves called Seiryūdō and Suzakudō.

Gembun. Era of Emperor Sakuramachi: Apr. 1736–Feb. 1740. *See* NENGŌ.

Gembun-itchi. "Unification of written and spoken languages" that took place at the beginning of the Meiji era in an effort to make great literary works accessible to more people. In his novel *Ukigumo,* published from 1887 to 1889, Futabatei Shimei attempted to define the principles of a standardized language. Even today, however, literary language and spoken language are noticeably different.

Gemmei Tennō. Forty-third sovereign (Empress Abe no Hime-miko, O-Yamata-neko Amatsu-mihiro Toyokuninaru, 662<708–14>722), daughter of Tenji Tennō and successor to Mommu Tennō. She established her capital at Heijō-kyō (Nara) in 710, issued the first Japanese coins (Wadō-kaichin), and had the *Kojiki* and the *Fudoki* written. She abdicated in favor of her daughter, Genshō, in 714. Some of her poems were included in the *Man'yōshū*.

Gempei. Name compounded with those of two enemy families, the Minamoto (Genji) and the Taira (Heike) to describe the period, Gempei no Sōran, during which they confronted each other (1150–85).

• *Gempei jōsuiki.* See GEMPEI SEISUIKI.

• *Gempei nunobiki no taki.* Five-act Kabuki play in the *jidai-mono* genre, on an episode in the war between the Taira and Minamoto clans, written by Namiki Senryū in 1749.

• *Gempei seisuiki.* "Rise and Fall of the Minamoto and the Taira." An epic historical novel (*gunki-monogatari*) in 48 scrolls, attributed to Buddhist monk Genne or to Doi Tsunehira, but probably written by several authors. This famous war chronicle draws its subject matter from various other texts, such as *Kurakawa* and *Matsui*. It involves a mixture of Japanese and Sino-Japanese words, which makes it difficult reading at times. It describes the events that took place between 1160 and 1185 and the war between the Minamoto and the Taira clans, ending with the fall of the latter. This work had a great influence on later war literature and plays. Its date of creation is unknown (perhaps the fourteenth century); because it complements the *Heike monogatari,* it was also attributed to Hamuro Tokinaga, but with no certainty. Also called *Gempei jōsuiki.*

Gempuku (Gembuku). Ceremony of passage to adulthood, taking place when the boy is between the ages of 10 and 16 depending on the region, period, and family. In samurai families, the boy received a hat (*eboshi*) and an adult name (*eboshi-na*) during the ceremony. In the aristocracy, it was called *kanrei,* and the child received the *kammuri* hat. Among the common people, the young man received a *fundoshi* (loincloth) and the ceremony was called *heko-iwai.* Today, *gempuku* has its echoes in the celebration of attaining majority (20 years of age) during the national festival called Seijin no Hi (Day of Majority), which takes place each January 15 for young people of this age. During the ceremony for girls, they had their eyebrows shaved and

their teeth painted black, and received a kimono as a gift. This ceremony was called *mogi,* "putting on a dress." See EBOSHI, EBOSHI-OYA.

• *Gempuku-soga.* Title of a Noh play: Jūrō Soga conducts the *gempuku* rites for his younger brother, Gorō, before they leave on a campaign to take their vengeance on Minamoto no Yoritomo. The governor of their province gives them a sword.

Genchō. Painter (late tenth century) and Buddhist monk at the Ganjō-ji in Nara, to whom is attributed the painting called "Aoi-Fudō."

Genchū. Era of Emperor Go-Komatsu: Apr. 1384–Oct. 1392. See NENGŌ.

Gendai-geki. "Modern" films produced starting in 1912 by the Nikkatsu studio, as opposed to the films produced in Kyoto called *jidai-geki.*

Gen'e. Buddhist monk (1279–1350) and scholar of Confucian science. He was said to belong to the Tendai-shū sect and then to have turned to Zen. He supported Emperor Go-Daigo, whose tutor he was; after the fall of the Kamakura *bakufu,* he was hired by Ashikaga Takauji to write the *Kemmu Shikimoku,* in collaboration with the monks Ze-en, Shin-e, and others. He also wrote a correspondence manual called *Teikin-ōrai.* He is sometimes credited, though without certainty, with authorship of the *Taheiki.* See TEIKIN-ŌRAI.

Gen'ei. Era of Emperor Toba: Apr. 1119–Apr. 1120. See NENGŌ.

Gengō. Calendar system according to which the years are counted starting from the enthroning of an emperor. Also called Nengō. See NENGŌ.

Genji. Era of Emperor Kōmei: Feb. 1864–Apr. 1865. See NENGŌ.

• In the *Genji monogatari,* prince who plays the role of hero. His name became synonymous with the charm and elegance of a Don Juan–type character.

• Sino-Japanese pronunciation of the name of the Minamoto family. The family was divided into four branches, named after the emperors from whom they claimed to be descended: Seiwa-Genji, Uda-Genji, Murakami-Genji, and Daigo-Genji, collectively called Genji no Shisei.

→ See KANGETSU.

• **Genji no Choja.** One of the titles given to Tokugawa Ieyasu.

• **Genji no Heihō.** Group of war techniques, from the building of forts to strategy to individual combat, belonging, through inheritance, to the Minamoto family. These techniques were assembled by Prince Teijun, the sixth son of Emperor Seiwa. They were complemented by the warriors of the Takeda family, and were then called Takedo-heihō. It was based on some of these techniques that the martial arts called Daitō Aikidō or Daitō-ryū Aikijujitsi, which gave rise to today's aikido, were created in the seventeenth century.

• **Genji-ko.** Game once played by the aristocracy, consisting of guessing from their scents five different packages of incense and indicating the choice using special characters called Genji-mon during *kōdō* (incense) meetings. Also called *gankō.*

• *Genji kuyō.* Title of a Noh play: a woman asks a Buddhist monk to perform a service in memory of Prince Genji, so that his soul will rest. She then reveals herself to be the ghost of Lady Murasaki Shikibu, the author of the *Genji monogatari.* The monk, however, thinks she is an incarnation of Shō Kannon Bosatsu.

• **Genji-mon.** Series of 54 special characters used by Murasaki Shikibu to number the chapters of her work *Genji monogatari.* These characters were sometimes used for different purposes, as in the game Genji-ko, and as decorative elements. Their exact origin is not known.

• *Genji-monogatari.* "The Tale of Genji," a 54-chapter novel written in hiragana (*see* KANA) by Lady Murasaki Shikibu and probably finished between 1015 and 1020, making it one of the oldest novels in the world. It recounts the gallant adventures of Genji, a prince in the Heian court in the late tenth century, and of his "son," Kaoru. It is written in very pure classic language, expounding the Japanese concept of *mono no aware* (the fragility of things) and other ideas with Buddhist connotations. This work had a huge influence on subsequent literature. It is not known, however, whether Murasaki Shikibi was the sole author, nor whether this long work was completed. The action takes place at the court of Heian-kyō and spans three quarters of a century. The novel can be divided onto two main parts: the first 41 chapters, devoted to the life of Prince Genji, and the last 13 chapters, concerning mainly Kaoru, the self-styled son of the prince (in reality the grandson of one of his friends). There are a large number of characters (between 50 and 60), the most important being Genji, Kaoru, and Kaoru's friend Niou, and a number of women, including Fujitsubo and Murasaki. The original text is not known, for all that has survived are fragments and copies dating from the thirteenth to the sixteenth century. It is possible that the order of chapters was different; chapter four, for example, must have been written after chapter five. The 54 chapters are numbered using special characters called Genji-mon. The *Genji monogatari* has been imitated many times and has been the subject of numerous illustrated *emaki,* as well as exegeses and critical works, such as those by Keichū (1640–1701), Kitamura Kigin (1624–1705), Kamo Mabuchi (1697–1769), and Motoori Norinaga (1730–1801), to mention just a few. It was translated into English by Arthur Waley, and rewritten in modern Japanese by Tanizaki Jun'ichirō.

• *Genji monogatari emaki.* Twelfth-century *emakimono* illustrating the 54 chapters of the *Genji monogatari,* using the *tsukuri-e* technique. There

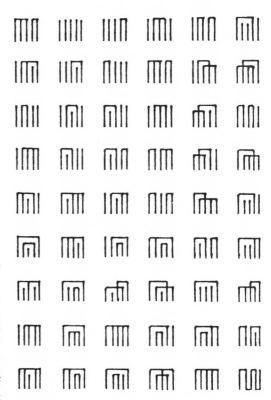

Genji-mon

are 19 paintings and 20 pages of text handwritten in kana in the four scrolls housed in the National Museum of Tokyo and the Gotō Art Museum in Tokyo. There are several other fragments in other collections. The complete set would have been about 10 scrolls. Each painting measures 21 to 22 cm in height and 39 to 48 cm in width. The technique used involved both *hikime-kagibana* and *fukinuki-yatai*. The colors are thick and brilliant, applied to paper made with *Wikstroemia sikokiana (Jap.: gampi)* fibres. These paintings have traditionally been attributed to Fujiwara no Takachika and Fujiwara no Takayoshi, and the calligraphy to Fujiwara no Korefusa, Fujiwara no Masatsune, Fujiwara no Takachika, and Jakuren. None of these attributions is certain. It can be said, however, that the paintings date from 1110–20.

Genji Keita. Writer (Tanaka Tomio, 1912–85), born in Toyama. He began his literary career with *Tabako musume* (The Tobacco Girl, 1947) and *Santō-jūyaku* (A Third-class Bureaucrat, 1951–52), while continuing to work in the office of a trading company. His book *Eigoya-san* (The English Interpreter, 1951) won the Naoki Prize. Among his other works, *Taifū-san* (Mr. Typhoon) was very successful. His novels described the lives of the urban middle class and office workers very vividly and humorously.

Genjō. Japanese name of the seventh-century Buddhist monk and traveler Zuanzang.
→ *See* KŌZAMA.

• *Genjō.* Title of a Noh play: a lute *(biwa)* player who wants to go to China to meet a master of his art plays for a couple of old men. In turn, they play a lute called *genjō* so marvelously that the musician abandons his notion of going to China. The old men then reveal themselves to him as the spirits of Emperor Murakami and his companion Nashitsubo. Mirakami Tennō then summons a dragon, asks him to bring a famous old lute, and gives it to the musician.

Genka-reki. The first Japanese calendar, imported from Korea by the Buddhist monk Kanroku Sōzu and used from 604 to 680. *See* CALENDARS, YAKOSHISO TAMAFURU.

Genkei. Era of Emperor Yōzei: Apr. 877–Feb. 885. Also Gangyo. *See* NENGŌ.

• Painter (Araki Shūhō, late eighteenth century) of the Yōga school in Nagasaki and Shūseki's student. He was an interpreter from Dutch.
• Sculptor (Shōun Genkei, 1684–1710), known for having vowed to sculpt a series of the *gohyaku-rakan* (Five Hundred Arhats). Of these sculptures, which were clearly influenced by the Chinese Ming dynasty, the Rakan-ji of Meguro (Tokyo) still houses about 300.
→ *See* GESSHŌ.

Genki. Era of Emperor Ōgimachi: Apr. 1570–July 1572. *See* NENGŌ.
• Painter (Kita Genki, active ca. 1671) of the Yōga school in Nagasaki. He painted mainly portraits of monks.
• Painter (Komai Ki-Minamoto, Yukino-suke; *azana:* Shi-on; *gō:* Genki, 1747–97), student of Maruyama Ōkyo. He painted Chinese women, flowers, and animals. Also called Kōnosuke.

Genkō. Era of Emperor Go-Daigo: Aug. 1331–Jan. 1334. Also Genkyō. *See* NENGŌ.
• General term for two attempts to invade the islands of Japan by Korean and Mongolian fleets in 1274 and 1281. Individually, the first is called Bun'ei no Eki and the second Kōan no Eki, from the names of the eras *(nengō)* during which they took place.
• Buddhist monk (1290–1367) of the Rinzai branch of the Zen-shū. He went to China during the Song dynasty, in 1320, and lived there for six years as a disciple of the monk Zhongfeng. When he returned to Ōmi, in 1326, he founded the Eigen-hi temple at the request of Lord Sasaki. He was appointed abbot of the Seiun-ji in Kai in 1359, and became Yakuō Tokken's disciple. He left a collection of thoughts, *Eigen Jakushitsi wajō goroku.* He was also an excellent classical poet. Also called Jakushitsu Genkō, Ennō Zenji, and Shōtō Kokushi.

• **Genkōbori.** Dry-stone wall about 2 m high, built along the beaches on the north side of Kyushu from 1274 to 1281 to defend the island against Mongolian invasions. All warriors on Kyushu had to contribute to its construction by supplying materials or workers.

• **Genkō no Ran.** A civil war of the Genkō era (1331–33) that led to the fall of the Kamakura *bakufu.* Emperor Go-Daigo decided to take back power and attacked the Hōjō family's *shikken* in Kamakura, but after various mishaps he was taken prisoner and sent into exile on the island of Oki.

His son Morinaga continued the struggle with the help of a large contingent of warriors, including Kusunoki Masashige. Go-Daigo managed to escape from Oki in 1333, and the general of the Hōjō family, Ashikaga Takauji, betrayed the *bakufu* and seized Kyoto in Emperor Go-Daigo's name, hoping to be named shogun. General Nitta Yoshisada then marched on Kamakura and set it afire, thus ending the regime of the Hōjō family *shikken* in Kamakura and, as a result, toppling the *bakufu*. Go-Daigo returned to Kyoto and inaugurated what has been called the Kemmu Restoration (1333–36). Also called Genkō no Hen.

• *Genkō shakusho.* The oldest account of Buddhism in Japan, finished during the Genkō era, whence its title. It was written by the Zen monk Kokan Shiren (1278–1346), one of the founders of the *gozan-bunka* belonging to the Tōfuku-ji temple in Nara. Written entirely in Chinese, it contains biographies of monks (more than 400), public records, and essays in which Kokan states that Japan is a land predestined to Buddhism, after the religion's failure in India and persecution of its practitioners in China, and that the *kami* of the Shinto had welcomed it happily.

Genkyū. Era of Emperor Tsuchimikado: Feb. 1203–Apr. 1206. *See* NENGŌ.

Genna. Era of Emperor Go-Mizunoo: July 1615–Feb. 1623. *See* NENGŌ.

• *Genna kokaisho.* Book on maritime navigation written by Kida Kōun in 1618.

Genne. Buddhist monk (1269–1350) who is sometimes credited with writing the *Gempei Seisuiki* and a version of the *Heike monogatari*.

Gennin. Era of Emperor Go-Horikawa: Nov. 1224–Apr. 1225. *See* NENGŌ.

Gen'o. Era of Emperor Go-Daigo: Apr. 1319–Feb. 1321. *See* NENGŌ.

Genrō. "Elder founders," group of nine (twelve in 1912) statesmen, advisers to the emperor during the Meiji period, who had the power to recommend the appointment of certain people to ministerial positions. The *genrō* were natural successors to the *rōjū* of the Edo period. They generally came from samurai families, with the exception of Saionji Kimmochi, the last *genrō*, who was from the aristocracy,

and most were from Satsuma and Chōshū provinces. They had the title *genkun*. About 1920, by which time their number and power had diminished considerably, the position of *genrō* was abolished.

• **Genrō-in.** "Hall of Elders," a sort of privy council to Emperor Meiji, prefiguring the future Senate, created in 1875 to prepare the new Constitution. It was dissolved when the Constitution was promulgated in 1890.

Genroku. Era of Emperor Higashiyama: Sept. 1688–Mar. 1703. *See* NENGŌ.
→ *See* MASANOBU.

• **Genroku-bunka.** "Culture of the Genroku era," corresponding approximately to the "reign" of the fifth shogun of Edo, Tokugawa Tsunayoshi (1680–1709). It was a very active period in all cultural areas. In literature, there were Ihara Saikau's popular works; in *jōruri* puppet theater, Chikamatsu Monzaemon's famous dramas. In poetry, haiku became popular thanks to Matsuo Bashō. Painting saw the blossoming of the Kanō and Tosa schools, and the decorative arts were epitomized by the works of Kōrin. Ukiyo-e prints evolved, gaining the status of art. This period saw the rise to financial prominence of the new *chōnin* class (urban dwellers), whose tastes differed profoundly from those of both warriors and aristocrats. Scholars such as Yamazaki Ansai, Kumazawa Banzan, and Itō Jinsai were developing Sinology, and Japanese literature *(kokugaku)* was being studied by Kitamira Kigin, Kada no Azumamaro, and Keichū. In the ruling classes, Noh theater was regaining popularity, while Kabuki was favored by the *chōnin*.

• **Genroku-jidai.** Period in Japanese history extending over about 30 years in the late seventeenth and early eighteenth centuries, during which Japan had no internal conflict and the government was able to devote itself to reorganizing the economy. The urban merchant class, the *chōnin*, became wealthy and influential in most areas, giving rise to the "culture of the Genroku era" *(Genroku-bunka)*, which was so rich and sumptuous that it sometimes approached decadence. It was the great epoch of geisha and the artists who celebrated them. The period of economic prosperity at the beginning of the 1970s, before the Nikuson Shokku (Nixon shock) of 1971, is sometimes called Shōwa Genroku.

Genryaku. Era of Emperor Go-Toba: Apr. 1184–Aug. 1185. Also called Genreki. *See* NENGŌ.

Gensen. Japanese dictionary, published, under the editorship of Haga Yaichi (1867–1927), until 1929. It has almost 300,000 encyclopedic articles.

Gensen. Buddhist monk (?–1055), who was *zasu* of the Tendai-shū.

Genshin. Buddhist monk (Urabe Genshin, Ima Kashō, Eshin Sōzu, 942–1017) of the Tendai-shū, born near Nara. He was Ryōgen's (912–985) disciple. His study of the *Lotus Sutra (Jap.: Hokke-kyō)* led him to a belief in the saving omnipotence of Amida Buddha, and he expounded his views in *Ōjōyōshū* (Essence of Rebirth on the Pure Land) in 985 and in *Ichijō-yōketsu.* He founded the Shin-in branch of the Tendai-shū and is considered the sixth patriarch of the Jōdo Shin-shū sect. As a painter, he made mainly images of the *raigō* of Amida and works of religious inspiration.
→ *See* SEKIHO.

Genshi-sai. Imperial Shinto festival held on the third day after the New Year, during which the emperor makes offerings to the spirits of his ancestors. *See* SECHI-E.

Genshō. Painter (Kankambō, 1146–ca. 1208 or 1223) and Buddhist monk of the Shingon-shū on Mt. Kōya (Kōya-san). He painted only Buddhist images.
→ *See* SHŪSEKI, UNZAN.

• **Genshōsai.** *See* ISEN.

• **Genshō Tennō.** Forty-fourth ruler (Empress Hitaka Yamato-neko Takamizu Kiyotarashi-hime, 681<715–23>748), daughter of and successor to Gemmei Tennō. She abdicated in favor of her nephew, Shōmu. She commissioned the *Nihon shoki,* written in 720.

Gensui. Military rank equivalent to that of general during the Edo period, and to that of marshal during the Meiji era. *Chin.:* Yuanshuai.

Gentai. Painter (Watanabe Ei; Matazō; *azana:* Enki; *gō:* Shōdai, Rinroku, Sōdō, 1749–1822) of the Nanga school, Binchō's student. He became a Buddhist monk and took the name Gentai.

Gentan. Painter (Shimada Gentan; Kiin, Kampo; *gō:* Gentan, 1778–1840) of the Maruyama school. He was likely a younger brother of Bunchō's and formed a partnership with Torei.

Gentoku. Era of Emperor Go-Horikawa: Aug. 1329–Apr. 1331. *See* NENGŌ.

Gen'ya. Painter (Kanō Gen'ya, mid-sixteenth century) of the Kanō school, Motonobu's and Shōei's student and Eitoku's master. He also signed his works Ken'ya.

Gen'yōsha. "Society of the Black Ocean." Ultranationalist terrorist group founded by Tōyama Mitsuru and Hiroka Kōtarō in 1881 in Fukuoka, demanding Japan's expansion into Asia and respect for traditional values. It replaced another political movement, Kōyōsha, founded in 1877 to demand the creation of a parliament. Its members supported their demands with violent acts; for example, in 1899 they threw a bomb at Ōkuma Shigenobu. In Korea, they undertook subversive actions, in liaison with the general headquarters of the armed forces, to force Japan to go to war. In Manchuria, they supported troops of bandits waging a guerrilla war, then were active in the process of annexation of Korea in 1910 and helped various revolutionary groups in China and Manchuria by assassinating their opponents. This society gave rise to other activist associations, including Kokuryūkai in 1901. It continued to have a very great influence on cultural and political milieus before the Second World War, favoring expansionist policies and worship of the emperor. After the war, the society was dissolved and one of its directors, Hirota Kōki, was sentenced to death for war crimes.

Gen'yū. Painter (Araki Gen'yū; Tamenoshin; *azana:* Shichō; *gō:* Enzan, Gen'yū, 1733–99). He studied oil-painting technique with a Dutch painter in Nagasaki.

Genzai-mono. "News items," a type of Noh play featuring common people of a period, as opposed to *onryo-mono,* portraying ghosts, and *oni-mono,* featuring demons.

Geography. The Japanese archipelago comprises almost 3,400 islands with a total area of about 372,000 km². Only four islands are large: Hokkaido in the north (about 77,000 km² in area), Honshu in the center (the largest island, about 228,000 km²), Kyushu to the southwest (about 36,000 km²), and Shikoku, to the southeast (the smallest of the four, about 18,000 km²). The topography is mountainous, and the country has a very long coastline (28,000 km). The surrounding bodies of water are the Sea of Japan (Nihonkai) to the west, the Sea of

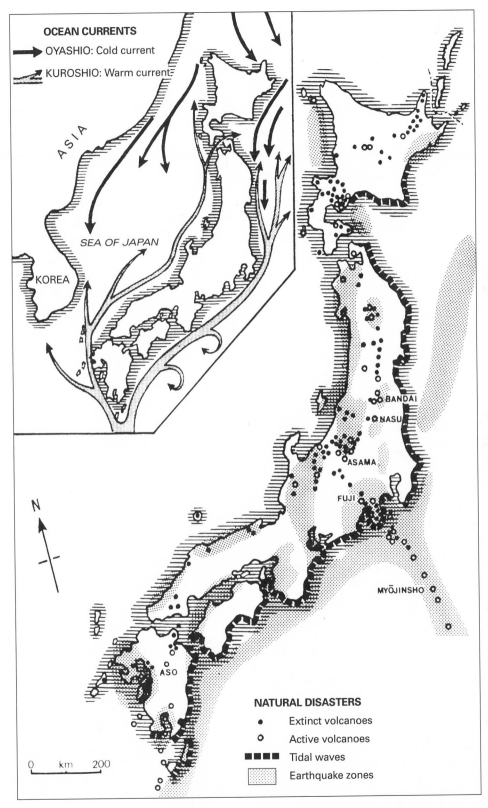

OYASHIO: Cold current

KUROSHIO: Warm current

ASIA

SEA OF JAPAN

KOREA

BANDAI

NASU

ASAMA

FUJI

N

MYŌJINSHO

ASO

NATURAL DISASTERS

•   Extinct volcanoes

○   Active volcanoes

■■■■   Tidal waves

Earthquake zones

0   km   200

Natural Disasters and Ocean Currents

Okhotsk to the north, the Pacific Ocean (Taiheiyō) to the east and south, the Sea of China to the southwest, and the Inland Sea (Setonaikai) between them. Japan has reminders of its active geological past (*see* GEOLOGY) in its volcanoes (*see* VOLCANOES); successive upthrusts have caused the appearance of archean, primary, secondary, and triassic areas (cretaceous on Shikoku and Hokkaido); and the sea has made limestone deposits. Plains and plateaus are formed of thin layers of tertiary limestone, alluvium, and quaternary coral deposits. Because of the perturbed orogeny and small size of the islands, rivers are many but short and become seasonal torrents whose erosive action is particularly strong. The rivers link the mountains, via the coastal plains, directly to the sea, and this powerful contrast has contributed largely to the modeling of both the landscape of Japan and the soul of the Japanese people.

The islands of Japan form a continuous chain in an arc from northeast to southwest between 30° and 46° north latitude and 128° and 146° east longitude, over approximately 2,200 km. They are extended to the south by the Ryukyu archipelago, which forms a sort of bridge between Kyushu and Taiwan, and to the north by two island groups that culminate in Sakhalin to the west and the Kamchatka Peninsula to the east, forming the Kuril archipelago. They are located at the same latitude as the city of Portland, Oregon (at the northern tip of Hokkaido), and Savannah, Georgia (at the southern tip of Kyushu). Tokyo is about at the latitude of Nashville, Tennessee. This elongated, chaotic configuration, featuring overlapping mountain ranges intercut with deep lateral valleys (*see* MOUNTAINS), explains why the Yamato rulers made slow progress in their conquest of the islands. They extended their territory from the shores of the Inland Sea toward central Kyushu to the south and toward central Honshu to the north in the seventh century, and reigned over all the islands in the twelfth century (except for Hokkaido, which was not completely occupied until the late eighteenth century). At the beginning of the eighteenth century, intrepid explorers such as Mamiya Rinzō and Mogami Tokunai pushed farther north toward the Kuril Islands (Chishima Rettō) and Sakhalin (Karafutō). To the south, the Ryukyu Islands were annexed by the Satsuma clan only in 1609.

The very jagged coasts of the Japanese islands, featuring peninsulas edged with abrupt cliffs, form excellent ports. Off the coasts are two major ocean currents, one from the north, the cold and relatively weak Oyashio, and the other from the equator, the powerful and warm Kuroshio. These currents collide and mix in the Sea of Japan and in the Pacific east of Honshu, creating zones that are alternately warm and cold—an environment very favorable to the reproduction of sea life. It was no doubt the existence of the warm current from the Philippines sweeping by the coast of the Ryukyu Islands that enabled peoples from the south to land on Kyushu in the prehistoric period. The islands of Japan, which are in fact the peaks of an enormous underwater mountain range, are bordered on the Pacific littoral by a sea trench 10,374 m long (Namposhōtō), extended southward by the Mariana Trench, 8,649 m deep off Iwo Jima and the Shichitō-Marianas and reaching a depth of 11,034 m south of Guam. The Sea of Japan is formed of underwater plateaus reaching a depth of 3,600 m in places, while the Inland Sea, divided into a number of basins (*see* SETONAIKAI) is relatively shallow but has violent currents.

One major feature of the Japanese landscape, due to its mountainous nature, is how the land is divided up: 67% of the total area consists of mountain forests, and only about 16% is arable land on the plains. These plains are small and densely populated; most are at the mouths of the major rivers, which flow into deep bays around which major urban agglomerations have developed. The rivers, not very long (few over 200 m), all have their sources in the mountains that constitute the "spine" of the islands. They flow either toward the Sea of Japan or toward the Pacific Ocean, draining the land and eroding it greatly, or else serving as an outlet for the many lakes, such as Lake Biwa. Many of the lakes sprinkled through the country are crater lakes, while others are lagoonal.

Geographic regions:
I. Northeast
  Hokkaido
  Tōhoku:
    a) Pacific coast
    b) coast of the Sea of Japan
II. Center
  Kantō (Tokyo region)
  Tōkai (coast of eastern Pacific)
  Hokuriku (coast of eastern Sea of Japan)
  Tōsan (mountainous region)
III. Southwest
  Kinki (former "central provinces")
  Chūgoku:
    a) San'in (coast of Sea of Japan)
    b) San'yō (north coast of Inland Sea)
  Shikoku:
    a) Northwest
    b) Southeast

REBUN
RISHIRI
Wakkanai

HOKKAIDO

Abashiri

Asahikawa

Sapporo

Hakodate

CHISHIMA
(KURIL)
ISLANDS

HOKKAIDO

AOMORI
Aomori

AKITA
Akita

Morioka

IWATE

TŌHOKU

REGION

YAMAGATA
Yamagata

MIYAGI

Sendai

Fukushima

SADO

FUKUSHIMA

Niigata

NIIGATA

TOCHIGI

Utsunomiya

Mito

NOTO PENINSULA

GUMMA

IBARAKI

Maebashi

SAITAMA

ISHIKAWA
TOYAMA

Toyama

Nagano

NAGANO

Urawa

KANTO

CHIBA

Kanazawa

GIFU

Kofu

Tokyo

Chiba

TOKYO

FUKUI
Fukui

Gifu

YAMANASHI

Yokohama

KANAGAWA

SEA

OF

JAPAN

HONSHU

OSAKA

Gifu

Nagoya
AICHI

Shizuoka

TOTTORI

KYOTO

SHIGA

Matsue

Tottori

Kyoto

Otsu

Tsu

SHIZUOKA

CHŪBU

CHŪGOKU

OKAYAMA

HYŌGO

Kobe

Nara

MIE

SHIMANE

Okayama

Osaka

NARA

KINKI

HIROSHIMA

Wakayama

YAMAGUCHI

Hiroshima

Takamatsu

Tokushima

WAKAYAMA

TSUSHIMA

Yamaguchi

Matsuyama

TOKUSHIMA

Kōchi

FUKUOKA

EHIME

KŌCHI

KAGAWA

SAGA

Fukuoka

SHIKOKU

GOTŌSHIMA

Saga

Ōita

ŌITA

PACIFIC

Kumamoto

OCEAN

Nagasaki

KUMAMOTO

MIYAZAKI

NAGASAKI

Kagoshima

Miyazaki

KYUSHU

KAGOSHIMA

RYUKYU ISLANDS

OKINAWA

Naha

0   km   200

RYUKYU ISLANDS

Prefectures and Major Cities

IV. South

Izu-Ogasawara island group
Amaami-Ryukyu island group

→ *See* AGRICULTURE, BIWA, CLIMATES, GEOLOGY, MOUNTAINS, PROVINCES AND PREFECTURES, VOLCANOES; names of islands: CHISHIMA, HOKKAIDO, HONSHU, KYUSHU, RYUKYU, SADO, SHIKOKU; names of seas; names of regions: CHŪBU, KANSAI, KANTŌ, KINAI, KINKI, OMOTE-NIHON, TŌHOKU; names of prefectures; names of rivers. *See also* FUKADA SEISHITSU, MAMIYA RINZŌ, MASTUURA TAKESHIRŌ, MOGAMI TOKUNAI, NAGAKUBO SEKISUI, OKAMOTO KANSUKE, SHIGA SHIGETAKA, TAKAHASHI KAGEYASU, YOSHIDA TŌGO.

Geology. The islands of Japan constitute the easternmost edge of the Asian continent and are in direct contact with the massive underwater Pacific plate, which is slowly subducting under the Eurasian plate; this means that the islands are often subjected to earthquakes and intensive volcanic activity (*see* VOLCANOES). The islands form a pair of arcs: the Kuril Islands, northern Honshu, and Izu-Ogasawara, then the southwestern arc of Honshu and the Ryukyu Islands. A major fault, the Fossa Magna, now buried under Neocene sediments and quaternary lava, crosses Honshu from Niigata prefecture to Nagano prefecture and from Yamanashi to Shizuoka. The fault is edged by belts of rock unique to each region; the oldest types, paleozoic and mesozoic, are most visible in the southwest, whereas in the northeast, where volcanic activity is most intense, neocene rock dominates. While the thickness of the Earth's crust varies from 7 to 10 km in the Pacific Ocean, it reaches a depth of 36 km in the Chūbu Mountains.

The islands of Japan were formed from a series of orogenic movements that have been going on since the Silurian period and that are continuing today. There are traces of pre-Cambrian metamorphism in the Hida Mountains (gneiss) and the Mino district (conglomerate gravel). The eastern part of Shikoku is composed of Ordovician granite. The oldest strata are from the Middle Silurian period, and fossils indicate that most of Japan was then underwater. In the Carboniferous period, the geosynclines, already filled with various sediments and ejecta from underwater volcanoes, began to move. It was probably during the Triassic period that the first foldings took place and the major faults were formed; these movements continued until the end of the Cretaceous period, as emergent metamorphic land was produced by intense orogenic activity. Terrestrial volcanoes appeared, the ejecta from which

gradually filled the hollows in the faults. The islands of Japan had emerged almost completely during the Paleocene period, but at the end of the Neocene period, the ocean began to invade the lowest-lying land. By the end of the Cretaceous period, the northeastern part of Honshu had risen once more, becoming the center of major volcanic activity. There were new foldings and new ocean encroachments on the lowest zones, where, in the Quaternary period, sediments were deposited that became the coastal plains. The physiognomy of the islands of Japan thus dates from this era. *See* LYMAN, MILNE, NAUMANN, OGAWA TAKUJI.

Geppō. Buddhist monk (Shinryō; *gō:* Kikukan, Geppa, 1760–1839) and painter, born in Kyoto. He was a student of Ikeno Taiga, of whom he made a portrait. He also wrote a number of books to make the work of his master known, including the album *Taigadō Gafu* (1804).

Gesaku-bungaku. General name for popular novels published between 1770 and the end of the nineteenth century, such as *sharebon, kibyōshi, ninjōbon, kokkeibon,* and *yomihon.* Hiraga Gennai is generally considered to have initiated the genre.

Gessen. Painter (Tan-ke Genzui; *azana:* Gyokusei; *gō:* Jakushū-shujin, 1721–1809); student of Sekkan and Ōkyo. He became a Buddhist monk at the Jōdo-shū monastery of the Jakushō-ji in Yamada (Ise) after living at the Zōjō-ji in Edo. He painted mainly landscapes and portraits in a darkly realistic style that earned him the nickname Kojiki Gessen ("Gessen the beggar"). He decorated many fusuma in the Myōhō-in in Kyoto.

• Sculptor of netsuke (early nineteenth century).
→ *See* SHABAKU.

• **Gessen Zenji.** Zen Buddhist monk (late eighteenth century), master of Sengai, who lived in Hakata (Kyushu).

Gesshō. Painter (Chō Yukisada; Shinzō, Kaisuke; *azana:* Genkei; *gō:* Suikadō, Gesshō, 1772–1832) in Ōmi. He painted mainly flowers and birds.

• Buddhist monk (1813–58), born in Osaka. Abbot of the Kiyomizu-dera temple in Kyoto, he resigned from his position to enter the service of the imperial cause in 1854, allying himself with Saigō Takamori and Umeda Umpin. He was pursued by shogunal troops and took refuge in Kagoshima, but drowned in the bay.

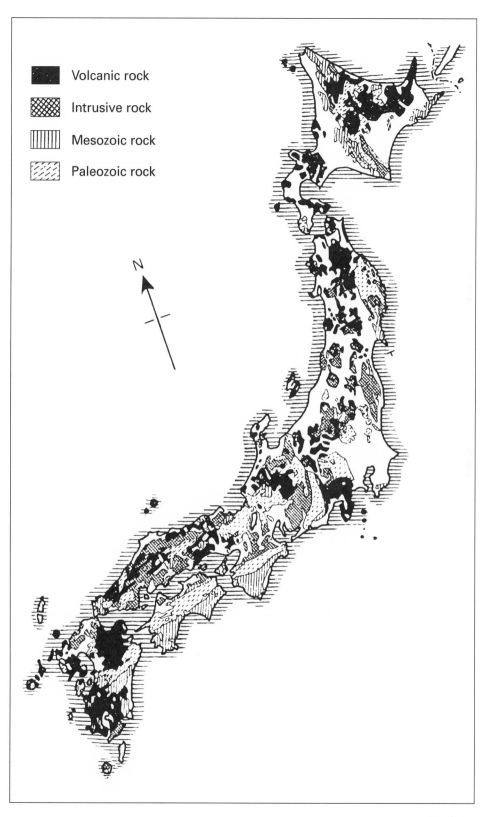

Volcanic rock

Intrusive rock

Mesozoic rock

Paleozoic rock

N

Geology

Geta. Shoes made of soles attached to clogs made of paulownia wood *(kiri)* by pegs of various heights *(ha)* and held on the feet by thongs running between the big toe and the other toes, used for outdoor work. This type of sandal, known from the Yayoi period (some were found on the Toro site), were at first called *ashida,* then *bokuri* during the Muromachi period, and finally *geta* during the Edo period. Among the types of *geta* are *takageta,* with very long pegs *(ha); tageta,* used by peasants to work in the rice paddies; *ama-geta,* worn in the rain; and *komageta* (or *pokkuri*), made of a single piece of wood. *See* SHOES, ZŌRI.

Getobōru. Japanization of the English term "gateball," a game similar to croquet involving two teams of five people, which has recently become popular in Japan. It is played mainly by elderly people, and there are annual national tournaments.

Geza-gaku. Type of music used in Kabuki. There are two types: *dagatari* to accompany *jōruri* and *gidayū,* and *debayashi* to accompany *naga-uta.*

• **Geza-daiko.** *See* TAIKO.

Gidayū. Type of *jōruri* narrative song, composed by Takemoto Gidayū (I) for his puppet theater, the Takemoto-za in Osaka, founded in 1684. These dramatic songs are accompanied by *dagatari* music (*see* GEZA-GAKU), generally played on the shamisen. Also called *gidayū-busi.*

Gidō Shūshin. Zen Buddhist monk (1325–88) of the Rinzai-shū sect, born in Tosa province (Kōchi prefecture). He was Musō Soseki's disciple and succeeded him in 1351. He worked at the Engaku-ji temple in Kamakura, then was invited to the Nanzen-ji in Kyoto in 1380. As a Confucian scholar, he was shogun Ashikaga Yoshimitsu's teacher. A famous Chinese-language poet, he was one of the leading lights of the *gozan-bunka,* and his poems were collected in an anthology called *Kūge-shū.* He also wrote notes, *Kūge nichiyō kufū-shū (Kūge nikku-shū),* which are an excellent source of information on the history of the period in which he lived.

Gien. Buddhist monk (d. 728) of the Hossō-shū sect, master of Gyōki (668–749).
• Buddhist monk (1557–1626) of the Shingon-shū sect.

Gifts. Following an ancient tradition, the Japanese like to exchange gifts at different events or times of year. In general, it is customary for visitors to offer their host a small gift, generally of food. When people move, they give a small gift (package of noodles, box of matches) to their neighbors. Gifts are always wrapped in white paper with a cord knotted in a particular way *(noshi)* and presented ceremoniously. The custom is never to offer in return a gift of greater value than the one received (except on Valentine's Day), so as to not oblige the first giver to offer a more expensive gift. It is also considered impolite to open a gift in the presence of the person who has given it. When a gift is composed of several small items, there must always be an odd number, or else more than ten. One should never give four objects, because the word meaning "four" *(shi)* is a homophone for the word meaning "death," nor three pieces *(mikire)* of food, for this means, again via a homophone, "to cut the body," which is a bad omen.
→ *See also* HIKIDEMONO, MIYAGE, NOSHI, O-CHŪGEN, OTOSHIDAMA.

Gifu. Chief city of Gifu prefecture, located on the Nōbi plain of Nagara-gawa river, founded as a castle town *(jōka-machi)* by the Toki family in the fifteenth century. Originally called Inokuchi, its name was changed by Oda Nobunaga in 1564. A way-station on the Nakasendō road, the town prospered during the Edo period and was known for its parasols, paper lanterns, and fans. It was destroyed by an earthquake in 1891 and rebuilt; its castle was reconstructed in 1956. Its institute of ethnology is famous and it is home to textile and machine-tool industries. Its most important tourist attraction is fishing with cormorants *(ukai)* on the Nagara-gawa. The Buddhist Shōhō-ji temple (founded in 1683) houses a statute of Buddha in wicker and lacquered paper. *Pop.:* 420,000.

• **Gifu-ken.** Prefecture in a mountainous region of central Honshu where some peaks (the Japanese Alps) reach an altitude of 3,000 m. To the south is the Nōbi plain, where the city of Gifu is located. The region is irrigated by the Kiso-gawa, Nagara-gawa, and Ibi-gawa rivers. *Main cities:* (south) Ōgaki, Tajimi, Kakamigahara, Toki; (north) Takayama. This prefecture was created in 1876 by amalgamation of the former provinces of Hida and Mino. *Area:* 10,596 km^2. *Pop.:* 2 million.

Gigaku. Ancient pantomime dance using masks (Gigaku-men), probably introduced from Korea

Gigaku

during the Nara period around 612. Gigaku danced dramas have a religious nature, and most are "farces" somewhat analogous to medieval Passion plays. Our knowledge of them is gleaned from masks, a short musical treatise written in the thirteenth century by Koma Chikazane, and a twelfth-century illustrated scroll *(emakimono)*, *Shinzei kogaku-zu* (Shinzei's Illustrations of Ancient Music), devoted to the Nara period. The music accompanying Gigaku dances was played by an instrumental ensemble including flutes, *tsuzumi* drums, and cymbals. The *shishi-mai,* or "lion dance," still performed during certain religious ceremonies, could be a surviving remnant of Gigaku dances. The museum at the Shōsō-in in Nara has a few costumes. *Kor.:* Sandaenoli. *See* BUGAKU.

• **Gigaku-men.** Colored wooden masks used by Gigaku dancers. They completely covered the head and often had comical expressions. Some of them had a movable lower jaw. Most portrayed Indian divinities such as Baramon (Brahmā), Karura

(Garuda), and Kongō Rikishi (Vajradhara). The museum at the Shōsō-in in Nara has 223 of them, all made of camphor-tree wood and brightly colored.

Gigei-ten. Buddhist divinity of the arts and the dance, corresponding, perhaps, to the Hindu divinity Devi, who was venerated in some Japanese temples from the ninth to the twelfth century and then abandoned. The only vestige of Gigei-ten is a ninth-century statue in dry lacquer, housed in the Akishino-dera (Nara prefecture). This statue was partially burned during a fire, so a new body was sculpted by Unkei in the twelfth century; only the head remained intact and is from the original statue.

Gihitsu. "From the brush of," characters often found on paintings following the name of the artist. Sometimes abridged to *hitsu. See* E, GA, SAN, ZU.

Gikan. Term designating all career bureaucrats who have received specific training, usually technical.

Gikeiki. "Chronicle of Yoshitsune," war novel *(gunki-monogatari)* wirtten by an unknown author in the early fifteenth century. It recounts the legendary lives and exploits of historic figures Minamoto no Yoshitsune and Shizuka Gozen, and fleshes out the Benkei legend. Also called *Gigeiki.*

Giko monogatari. "Stories according to the old ways," stories and novellas dating from the Kamakura period, imitating somewhat the style of authors from the Heian period and heavily influenced by the *Genji monogatari.* This literary genre continued to be used during the Muromachi period, but it had lost its vigor. During the Edo period, it was definitively supplanted by the *otogi-zōshi.* The first stories had been written by aristocrats for a literate readership; the most important ones were the *Sumiyoshi monogatari* and *Koke no koromo* (The Dress of Foam).

Gikū. Japanese name of a Chinese Buddhist monk (Yi Gong) said to have gone to Japan in 815 to preach Chan (Zen) doctrines. He soon returned to China.

Gikyō Daimyōjin. Divinity worshiped by the Ainu of Hokkaido, perhaps a divinization of Minamoto no Yoshitsune. Also Gikei Daimyōjin. *See* AINU, KAMUI.

Gilda. American code name for the "Little Boy" atom bomb that was dropped on Hiroshima on August 6, 1945, and completely destroyed the city, causing more than 180,000 deaths. *See* HIROSHIMA.

Ginji. Type of painting executed on leaves of silver, mainly to illustrate poems.

Ginkaku-ji. "Silver Pavilion," a pleasure villa built by Ashikaga Yoshimasa in his Higashiyama residence in Kyoto in 1473, and converted to a Zen Buddhist temple under the name Jishō-ji when the shogun died, in 1490. The Silver Pavilion is a two-story structure with a square plan, built to imitate the Kinaku-ji (Rokuon-ji), but with less sumptuous furnishings, and thus more in harmony with the surrounding countryside. On the first floor is a statue of Shō Kannon Bosatsu sitting in an artificial grotto. All wooden structures are covered with lacquer. To the side is the *tōgudō*, Ashikaga Yoshimasa's private chapel, rectangular in plan, with an *irimoya* roof. It is rustic-looking yet elegant. The Zen-style sand garden dates from the seventeenth century and was recently altered. Originally, the Ginkaku-ji comprised 12 buildings, but all except the Silver Pavilion and the *tōgudō* were destroyed in a fire about 1550. In the garden stands a *chashitsu* (teahouse) that may have been designed by Yoshimasa; it may be the oldest in Japan.

Ginza. "Seat of silver," the old mint district established during the Edo period south of the castle. It is now the most modern and commercial part of Tokyo. Most mints had previously been located in Sumpu (Shizuoka), Fushimi, Kyoto, Nagasaki, and Osaka, but in the Edo period the silver (Ginza) and gold (Kinza) mints were concentrated in Kyoto and Edo. The first plant for making gold coins *(koban, ichibu-kin)* was established in 1594 by Gotō Mitsutsugu on the order of Tokugawa Ieyasu, succeeding the one established by Gotō Yūjō in Kyoto for the Muromachi shogunate. Other plants operated on the island of Sado (near the gold mines) until about 1720, and in Kyoto until about 1800. In 1612, Tokugawa Ieyasu transferred the Ginza (silver mint) from Sumpu to Edo, then established another one at Nagasaki. The Kinza and Ginza were directed by descendants of Gotō Yūjō, who therefore had the right to ride a horse and carry a sword. Mints for copper coins *(zeniza)* were established in Edo in 1636 and in Sakamoto. In 1745, production of copper and iron coins was transferred to the Ginza and Kinza. In the Tokyo district that is now called Ginza (where the casting and striking work-shops for shogunal coins were located until about 1800) are the city's main banks and department stores. The Ginza is both a large central intersection and a commercial artery with shops selling luxury items (something like New York's Fifth Avenue). The street itself (which runs from the Ginza intersection to the Nihonbashi bridge, now destroyed) is quite narrow. *See* GOTŌ.

Giō-ji. Buddhist monastery in Kyoto. Formerly the *ōjō-in*, belonging to the Daikaku-ji branch of the Shingon-shū, it was rebuilt in 1895 and renamed in memory of Giō, a courtesan and erstwhile friend of Tairo no Kiyomori. When she fell out of favor, she became a Buddhist nun in the monastery, devoting herself to the adoration of Amida when she was only 21 years old (according to the *Heike monogatari*). Two wooden statues dating from the fourteenth century, representing Giō and her sister, are housed in the temple.

Gion. Kyoto district established around the Shinto Yasaka-jinja shrine (also called Gion no Yashiro), where annual dance and music festivals take place, famous for its geisha and *maiko*. In mid-July, there is a major *matsuri* related to the Yasaka-jinja to honor Gozu Tennō, a Shinto divinity who is the guardian of the Jetavana garden (in India; *Jap.:* Gion-shōja) and who ensures the health of his disciples. This festival started in 869, after a terrible epidemic. When 66 spears were erected in the imperial garden, each one representing a province, the emperor dedicated these symbols *(shintai)* to Gozu Tennō and donated them to the Yasaka shrine, along with those of the *kami* Susanoo and a one-eyed agrarian divinity *(Ta no kami)*. During the festival, devotees push floats *(yamaboko)* representing the ancient spears *(hoko)* through the city. These huge wheeled floats carry musicians playing Gion-bayashi music. Smaller floats are carried. They are all decorated with works of art, prized tapestries, and portraits of historical or mythical characters. The most magnificent parade takes place on July 17. This festival has given rise to imitations in other towns, notably Hakata (Gion Yamagasa), Gifu (Takayama Matsuri), and Edo (Sannō Matsuri).

• *Gion sairei shinkōki.* Five-act Kabuki play in the *jidai-mono* genre, produced by Asada Itchō in 1757.

• **Gion Tenjin.** Syncretic divinity *(kami)*, protector of the Gion shrine in Kyoto, sometimes considered an emanation of Yakushi Nyorai, the Buddha of

Medicine. Sometimes confused with Guzu Tennō. *See* YASAKA-JINJA.

Gion Nankai. Painter, calligrapher, and poet (Gion Yu; Yoichirō; *azana:* Hakugyoku; *gō:* Tekkandōjin, Shōun, Gi-Nankai, Nankai, 1677–1751). A Confucian scholar, he was one of Kinoshita Jun'an's ten disciples (Bokumon Jittetsu). He painted mainly landscapes and bamboo in the Nanga (Bujinga) style, somewhat imitating the style of the Chinese painter Tang Yin (1470–1523). His poems were written in Chinese.

Gion Yu. *See* GION NANKAI.

Girard, Prudence. French Catholic priest (1820–67) of the Foreign Mission in Paris, sent to Japan in 1859 as superior of the Japan mission. He had a church built in Yokohama in 1861. He went back to France, then returned to Japan, where he lived until his death.

Giri. Imperial duties or social obligations that a man must fulfill in order to hold an honorable place in Japanese society, on certain occasions and at certain times, toward society in general, then his superiors, his family, and, finally, himself. He is obliged to uphold his honor ("save face") if his reputation is tarnished, or if he has to compensate for a professional error or return a favor, and to observe all social conventions (never show his feelings, show respect, etc.). Warriors were expected to follow extremely strict *giri* that included sacrificing their lives for their lord, who fed and protected them, in order to return his *on* (favor given). From birth, Japanese people are subject to numerous *giri:* toward the nation and the emperor, their parents, nanny, teachers, and all debtors. When they enter employment, they must obey *giri* more directly related to their occupation, especially toward superiors. And soldiers must obey *giri* relating to their leaders, the emperor, and the nation. *Giri* are considered "burdens" by most Japanese. *See also* AMAE, NINJŌ, ON.

Gisei. "Sacrifice," consisting of an offering of rice, plants, *sake,* or fabric that is made to a Shinto or Buddhist divinity. After the ceremony, *gisei* are shared among followers during a common banquet called *naorai. See* SAKE.

Gishi. "Brave," a term for faithful vassals, very courageous men with unshakable morals, and heroes. It is traditionally used to describe the 47 *rōnin. See* AKŌ-GISHI.

Gishin. Buddhist monk (780–833) who studied under Saichō at Hiei-zan and helped him found a hermitage on Mt. Hiei. He served as Saichō's interpreter when they went to China in 805. When Saichō died, Gishin was appointed the first abbot of the Enryaku-ji temple. *Posthumous name:* Shūzen Daishi.

Gisō. Granaries set up by the Nara and Heian governments to prevent famines, and re-established during the Edo period. Also called Tensō.

Gitō. Painter (Shibata Gitō; *azana:* Ichū; *gō:* Kinchō, Kinkai, Kitarō, 1780–1819) of the Shijo school, Gekkei's student.

Glassware ("biidoro," "gyaman"). The art of glassmaking is not Japanese. Excavations of *kofun* have uncovered glass beads, and the treasures of the Shōsō-in include some glass cups and other objects, all of which were imported from the mainland, probably Persia, via the silk routes. During the Ashikaga period, some glassware came from China. It was not until the Edo period that glassware was made in Japan and the use of glass spread, though very slowly.

The first glassware was produced in Nagasaki about 1676; the words for glassware were adapted from the Portuguese word *vidro* and the Dutch word *gyaman* ("diamond"). Other glass factories were established in Osaka, Kyoto, and Edo. Use of industrial glass, especially for windows, using Western techniques, became common in the Meiji era. At the beginning of the twentieth century, glass began to be used in the arts, thanks to glassmakers such as Iwata Tōichi (1893–1980) and Kagami Kōzō (1896–1985).

Glover, Thomas Blake. Scottish merchant (1838–1911) who founded a trading company bearing his name in Nagasaki in 1859 to export gold and silver and to import ships and weapons for the Chōshū and Satsuma estates. In 1865, he imported the first locomotive, and he then established shipyards and operated mines. The Meiji government awarded him the Order of the Rising Sun in 1908.

Go. Chinese game (*Chin.:* Weiqi) probably imported to Japan by Kibi no Makibi in 735. It is played by two people on a thick wooden board marked with a grid of 19 × 19 lines, forming 361 intersections. Nine of the intersections are marked with a dot or a star *(hoshi)* for handicap stones during official games. Each player has a set number of pieces called *ishi* (stones)—181 for the person playing black, 180 for the person playing white—and takes a turn placing a stone on an intersection on the board. The objective of the game is to place stones on the grid in such a way as to gain as much territory as possible without being surrounded by the opponent's stones and, at the same time, to capture as many of the opponent's stones as possible. Although the basic rules are simple and easy to learn, the game itself is extremely difficult to play. The first *go* schools *(go-in)* were founded by Tokugawa Ieyasu in 1612 and directed by Hon'imbō, Hayashi, Inoue, and Yasui, each of whom initiated a style of play. Today's *go* associations are called *kiin*. There are several million *go* players in Japan, but only several hundred professionals. Players are ranked according to their talent in amateur *(kyū)* and professional *(dan)* levels in multiples of six and nine, respectively. This game, which has become popular in the West, is now featured in major international competitions. There are four basic rules:

1) Each player in turn must place stones on a free intersection. Black plays first.

2) When a group of stones (or one stone) is completely surrounded by the opponent's stones, it is captured and the stones are removed from the grid. If the surrounded group has two "eyes" *(nimoku)*, it cannot be captured.

3) Each captured stone and intersection counts for one point.

4) If placing a stone would entail capture, and the placement of a stone in the same spot by the opponent would cause a deadlock (which could be repeated endlessly), called a *kō,* then a stone cannot be placed in that spot by either player. Each impasse (intersection at which stones cannot be placed by either player), or *seki,* must be left empty until the end of the game. The game is finished when all of one player's stones are placed or all of the opponent's have been captured or are about to be; the points are then counted.

The board is called *goban;* the stones, *go-ishi* or simply *ishi;* the bowls containing the stones, *goke.* The game of *go* itself is sometimes called Igo. *Kor.: paduk, patuk.*

Go. Character meaning "behind" and used as a prefix to certain emperors' names or written names. *Chin.:* Hou, Qian.

• Honorific prefix placed before the name of a person or an object, equivalent to the prefix "O-" and corresponding to the formal form of "you" (similar to "vous" in French). *See* O.

• Character meaning "five." *Chin.: wu.*

→ *See* RENJU.

Gō. Unit of volume used mainly to measure liquids and grains, equivalent to 0.18 liter or 10 *seki. See* KOKI.

• Pseudonym taken by artists, writers, and poets, sometimes a nickname that has been given to them or that they have chosen. A person may use several different *gō* over a lifetime. *Chin.:* Hao. *See also* AZANA, NAMES.

• Administrative unit (village or borough) in use from the Nara to the Muromachi period. In 715, this unit was added to the older units of the *ritsuryō* system: *gun* (district), *kuni* (or *koku,* province), and *ri* (village). The old *ri* were then renamed *gō,* corresponding to hamlets. This distinction was abolished during the general land census ordered by Toyotomi Hideyoshi in the 1580s. *See* GŌRI-SEI, KOKUGUN-SE, RITSURYŌ SEIDO.

Gobō. Town in Wakayama prefecture (central Honshu) at the mouth of the Hidaka River. It developed around a temple *(monzen-machi)* that was a subsidiary of the Nishi Hongan-ji in Kyoto. In Gobō is the Dōjō-ji Buddhist temple, featured in a number of Noh and Kabuki plays. *Pop.:* 30,000.

Go-bō no keiji. "Five Public Notes," published by the Meiji government in 1868, exhorting the observance of Confucian virtues; condemning homicide in all of its forms, robbery, and tax evasion; banning Christianity and unrecognized sects; discouraging xenophobic behavior; and forbidding travel outside of Japan. These prescriptions, which were quite similar to those of the Edo shogunate, were a dead letter.

Go-bugyō. The "five administrators" *(see* BUGYŌ) named by Toyotomi Hideyoshi for the city of Kyoto in 1585.

Go-bushō. See SHINTŌ GOBUSHŌ.

Go-chi Nyorai. The "Five Buddhas of Wisdom" in Esoteric Buddhism:

—in the west: **Amida Nyorai** (*Skt.:* Amitābha)

—in the east: **Ashuku Nyorai** (*Skt.:* Akshobhya)

—in the center (zenith): **Dainichi Nyorai** (*Skt.:* Mahāvairochana)

—in the north: **Fukūjōju Nyorai** (*Skt.:* Amoghasiddhi)

—in the south: **Hōshō Nyorai** (*Skt.:* Ratnasambhava)

Yakushi Nyorai (*Skt.:* Bhaishajyaguru) sometimes replaces Ashuku Nyorai, and Tahō Nyorai (*Skt.:* Prabhūtaratna) sometimes replaces Amida Nyorai.

Depending on the mandala *(Jap.: mandara)* to which they refer, the Buddhas of Wisdom took different names. There are the following correspondences for the mandalas of the *Taizō-kai* and *Kongō-kai:*

Taizō-kai Mandara	Kongō-kai Mandara
Muryōko (Amida) Nyorai	Muryōju Nyorai
Ashuku Nyorai	Hōtō Nyorai
Dainichi Nyorai	Dainichi Nyorai
Fukūjōju Nyorai	Tenkuraion Nyorai
Hōshō Nyorai	Kaifuke-ō Nyorai

The Five Buddhas of Wisdom represented the five attitudes, functions, and attributes of Shaka Nyorai, the Buddha Shākyamuni. They personalized his five epithets and set the five great "moments" of his career. They were also the equivalents of the Dhyāni-buddhas of the Tibetan sects, the five Manushi-buddhas (the four human buddhas of today's *kalpa* plus the Buddha of the Future, Maitreya), corresponding to the "five elements" of Indian philosophy and the five spatial directions.

Go-Daigo Tennō. Ninety-sixth emperor (Prince Takaharu, 1287<1319–39>), second son of Go-Uda Tennō and successor to Hanazono Tennō. He belonged to the Daitoku-ji family line (which supplied emperors in alternation with the Jimyō-in line; *see* GO-FUKAKUSA). In an attempt to take back the power held by the *shikken* of the Hōjō family in Kamakura, he plotted a coup d'état, but the plot was uncovered in 1324. He tried to attack Kamakura again, but his army was beaten by Hōjō Takaoki in 1331. He then formed an alliance with several powerful warriors, including Kusunoki Masashige, and managed to persuade the general of the Hōjō family, Ashikaga Takauji, to come over to his side. Takauji easily defeated the Kamakura *bakufu,* and Go-Daigo returned to Kyoto and restored the imperial power in the Kemmu Restoration, in 1333. However, Takauji felt that he had been poorly compensated, so he revolted and drove Go-Daigo from Kyoto in 1335. The emperor took refuge in the Yoshino, where he established his Southern Court (Nanchō), while Takauji had another emperor, Kōmyō, of the Northern Court (Hokuchō), enthroned at Kyoto. The result was a civil war between the two courts (Nambokuchō) that lasted until 1392. In 1339, Go-Daigo abdicated in favor of his son, Go-Murakami, the day before he died.

Go-dai-riki Bosatsu. Group of five quick-tempered divinities (Bosatsu; *Skt.:* Bodhisattva) in the Esoteric Buddhist pantheon, transformative bodies of the five great Myō-ō (*Skt.:* Vidyārāja). They are, according to the *Ninnō-kyō:*
—to the east: **Kongō-shu Bosatsu** (or Kongō-ku Bosatsu)
—to the south: **Kongō-ō Bosatsu** (or Ryū-ō-ku Bosatsu)
—to the west: **Kongō-ri Bosatsu** (or Muijuriki-ku Bosatsu)
—to the north: **Kongō-yasha Bosatsu** (or Raiden-ku Bosatsu)
—in the center: **Kongō-hara Bosatsu** (or Muryōriki-ku Bosatsu)
Collectively, they are also called Go-dai-riki-son.

Go-dai tei-ō monogatari. "Story of the Five Imperial Reigns." History book by an unknown author, probably written in the late Kamakura period, describing the reigns of emperors Go-Horikawa, Shijō, Go-Saga, Go-Fukakusa, and Kameyama. It ends in 1272 with the death of Retired Emperor Go-Saga. Abridged title: *Go-dai-ō ki.*

Godai Tomoatsu. Samurai (1835–85) from Satsuma. After studying seamanship in Nagasaki and Shanghai from 1857 to 1859, he went to Europe with other samurai of his clan for a study trip. When he returned, he persuaded the daimyo of Satsuma to arm himself in the European style and purchase Western weapons. In the first Meiji government, he strove to make relations between Japan and foreign countries more flexible; in 1869, he became involved with industrial and trading businesses in order to develop Japan's economy. He then created the Osaka Chamber of Commerce in 1880 and a business school in Osaka, which later became Osaka University.

Gōda Kiyoshi. Painter (1862–1938). He studied copper engraving in France, then introduced the technique to Japan.

Go-En'yu Tennō. Fifth emperor of the Hokuchō, or Northern Court (Prince Ohito, 1359<1372–82>1393), succeeding Go-Kōgon Tennō. In 1391, he abdicated in favor of his son, Go-Komatsu.

Gofu. Protective amulet or charm sold by Shinto shrines and Buddhist temples to members of their congregations. It is usually a rectangular plaque made of paper, cardboard, or a thin slice of wood bearing the name of the temple or shrine, that of its divinity, stamps, sometimes magical formulas *(darani),* and a divine image. It is the custom to place *gofu* on the family altar (*kamidana* or *butsudana*) or to put them in a small brocade sack and carry them on one's person. Some *gofu* are even swallowed as medicine or were stuck to the walls of houses to keep bad luck away. Taxi and bus drivers and many other people hang them inside their cars. Also called O-fuda, O-mamori. *See* MANEKI-NEKO.

Go-Fukakusa Tennō. Eighty-ninth emperor (Prince Hisahito, 1243<1247–59>1304), son of and successor to Go-Saga Tennō. Go-Saga Tennō, though retired (*see* IN-SEI), continued to rule the country in the name of his underage son, and then forced him to abdicate in favor of his younger brother, Kameyama, in 1260. Go-Fukakusa then appealed to the Kamakura *bakufu* to recover his throne; in 1275, he enabled his own son, Fushime, to succeed Go-Uda Tennō. From this era dated the custom of alternating the reigns of emperors descended from Go-Fukakusa (the Jimyō-in line) and those descended from Kameyama (the Daikaku-ji line). The *Towazu-gatari*, written in 1307 by Lady Nijō, gives a detailed description of this unsettled period and of Go-Fukakusa's reign.

Gofun. Whitewash obtained by burning shells; used by painters as a base layer, as white paint (mixed with a binder), or in mixtures with other colors.

Go-Fushimi Tennō. Ninety-third emperor (Prince Tanehito, 1288<1299–1301>1366), son of and successor to Fushimi Tennō. He was forced to abdicate in favor of Go-Nijō in 1301.

Go-gaku. Term for the five sacred mountains of Japan: Hiei-zan, Kongōhō, Nyoi, Atago, and Takachito.
→ *See* FUKUHARA GOGAKU, SEIKI.

Gōgaku. "Village schools," created by the Edo *bakufu* and incorporated into the national education system in 1872. These schools (also called *gogakkō, gōgaku-sho,* and *gōkō*) were divided into two groups: those for educating vassals (and thus analogous to *hankō,* estate schools), and those for commoners (analogous to *terakoya*). Reading, writing, and mathematics were the main subjects taught in the *gōgaku*. *See* TERAKOYA.

Gogaku Shōnin. Painter (Hirano Bunkei; *gō:* Kochiku, 1809–93) and Zen Buddhist monk, famous for his paintings of landscapes.

Gogyō Setsu. Japanese theory of the "five elements" (*Chin.:* Wuxing) adopted from Taoism, ac-

cording to which living beings were constituted of five "elements" (earth, fire, metal, air, and ether). From the respective proportions of these elements in an individual's makeup, according to the principles of Ommyōdō, it was possible to predict his or her future.

Go-Hanazono Tennō. Hundred and second emperor (Prince Hikohito, 1419<1429–64>1471), son of Prince Fushimi no Miya Sadafusa, adopted by Retired Emperor Go-Konatsu, and successor to Shōkō Tennō. He abdicated in favor of his son, Go-Tsuchimikado, in 1465, and devoted himself to poetry and study. *See* GO-SUKŌ-IN.

Gohei. Shinto symbols made of strips of white paper folded into zigzags, either affixed to a pillar or another support or hung on a *shimenawa,* indicating the sacred nature of a location and the presence of a *kami. Gohei* are substitutes for offerings of fabrics made in former times. They are sometimes made of metal; more rarely, they are colored. When they are attached to a long handle and waved back and forth to cleanse the air, they are called *nusa.* The way the *gohei* is folded differs from shrine to shrine and indicates which *kami* it symbolizes. Also called *nigite, mitegura, shide.*

Go-Hōjō. Warrior family (not related to the Hōjō *shikken* of Kamakura) that controlled the town and castle of Odawara (Kanagawa prefecture) as Sengoku-daimyo during the Muromachi and Momoyama periods (sixteenth century). This family, founded by Hōjō Sōun (1432–1519), was finally wiped out by Toyotomi Hideyoshi in 1591. Its story is told in the *Hōjō godai-ki,* a military chronicle composed from notes (*Keichō kembunshū,* "Collection of Things Seen and Heard During the Keishō Era") made by a Hōjō vassal warrior, Miura Jōshin (1565–1644). The last of the Go-Hōjō was Hōjō Ujinao, who was defeated by Toyotomi Hideyoshi in 1591. Collectively, they were known as Hōjō Godai (the five generations of Hōjō) or Odawara Hōjō. The Go-Hōjō were: Hōjō Sūn (Nagauji), Hōjō Ujitsuna, Hōjō Ujiyasu, Hōjō Ujimasa, Hōjō Ujinao, and Hōjō Ujinori (*see* HŌJŌ GODAI). Also known as "later Hōjō." *See also* HŌJŌ SŌUN, HŌJŌ, ODAWARA.

Go-Horikawa Tennō. The eighty-sixth emperor (Prince Toyohito, 1212<1222–32>1234), successor to Chūkyō Tennō. He abdicated in favor of his son, Shijō.

Go-Ichijō Tennō. Sixty-eighth emperor (Prince Atsuhira, 1008<1017–1036>), son of Ichijō Tennō and Jōtō Mon'in (daughter of Fujiwara no Michinaga) and successor to Sanjō Tennō. He married another of Michinaga's daughters, Ishi, his maternal aunt. Go-Suzaku succeeded him.

Goju-no-tō. "Pagoda with five stories" of roofs, typical of buildings in Buddhist temples. Pagodas with three roof stories were called *sanju-no-tō;* those with seven stories, *shichiju-no-tō. See* TŌ.

Gojū-on-zu. "Diagram of the 50 sounds," represented by the "letters" of the *kana* syllabaries (*hiragana* and *katakana*), actually numbering 51 (including the nasal *n*), but representing 48 syllabic sounds. They are traditionally arranged in ten rows of five sounds corresponding to the vowels, an order said to have come from that defining the distribution of syllables in the Indian Sanskrit alphabet (Siddham; *Jap.*: Shittan). This order was sometimes used as a numbering system (as well as the *Iroha*) for series of objects or words (as in a dictionary). It is the equivalent of our alphabet. The *gojū-on* is as follows:

a	ka	sa	ta	na	ha	ma	ya	ra	wa	n
i	ki	shi	chi	ni	hi	mi	(i)	ri	(i)	
u	ku	su	tsu	nu	fu	mu	yu	ru	(u)	
e	ke	se	te	ne	he	me	(e)	re	(e)	
o	ko	so	to	no	ho	mo	yo	ro	(o)	

The order of reading is vertical. *See* KANA.

Go-kaden. Collective name for the five schools of sword blacksmiths (ancient swords, *kōtō*): Yamashiro, Yamato, Bizen, Sōshū, and Mino.

Go-kaidō. "Five great roads," general name for the major arteries linking the Nihonbashi, in Edo, to Shirakawa (Ōshū-kaidō); to Nikkō via Kurihashi (Nikkō-kaidō); to Kyoto and Osaka via Usui, Shimosuwa, Kiso Fukushima, and Kusatsu (Nakasendō); to Kyoto and Osaka via the coast, Kamakura, Hakone, Arai, and Kusatsu (Tōkaidō); and to Shimosuwa via Kobotoke and Kōfu (Kōshū-kaidō). The Nakasendō was sometimes called Kiso-kaidō; the Nikkō- kaidō was sometimes called Reihei-shi-kaidō. Less important roads were called *waki-kaidō*. Along the Go-kaidō were toll booths (*sekisho*) and waystations, or *shuku-eki* (53 on the Tōkaidō, 7 on the Nakasendō, and 17 on the Nikkō-kaidō and Ōshū-kaidō, which shared the same route part of the way). The longest road was the Tōkaidō. The Go-kaidō began to be developed in the Kamakura period, and the daimyo whose properties they crossed had to contribute to their upkeep and to that of the waystations. The waystations grew into towns, which were responsible for supplying horses, maintaining bridges, and running the inns that were constantly expanding. In 1659, the routes, used frequently for the annual processions of daimyo because of the Sankin-kōtai, came under the tighter control of a special bureaucrat, the Dōchū-bugyō. It was the establishment and control of these routes that contributed the most to unification of the provinces under the aegis of the Tokugawa shogunate. *See* KAIDŌ, TŌ KAIDO, WAKI-KAIDŌ.

Go-kajō no Goseimon. "The Five Articles of the Imperial Vow," published by Emperor Meiji when he came to power in 1868:

1) An assembly will be created, and discussion there will be free.

2) Superiors and subordinates must work with unity of spirit, and the economy and the treasury will be strengthened.

3) Both civil and military officials and commoners must be able to realize their aspirations in such a way that the spirit of the populace is not compromised.

4) The wrongful practices of the past must be abandoned and international conventions must be followed.

5) Knowledge will be sought throughout the world and the fundaments of imperial authority will be reinforced.

This "vow," which was to inaugurate the modern period of Japan and bring the country out of the feudal system, was reiterated on January 1, 1946, by Emperor Hirohito (Shōwa Tennō) to encourage the Japanese people to enter a new era. The Go-kajō no Goseimon had been written upon the order of Emperor Meiji by two advisers, Yuri Kimimasa and Fukuoka Takachika, and revised by Kido Takayoshi.

Go-Kameyama Tennō. The ninety-ninth emperor (Prince Norinari, ca. 1347<1383–92>1424), son of Go-Murakami Tennō and successor to Chōkei Tennō. He was the last emperor of the Southern Court (Nanchō); in 1392, on the request of shogun Ashikaga Yoshimitsu, he allowed the Northern and Southern Courts (Nambokuchō) to be reunified and agreed that emperors would be chosen alternately from the two courts. Go-Kameyama then ceded the throne to Go-Komatsu of the Northern Court (Hokuchō). After the death of Ashikaga Yoshi-

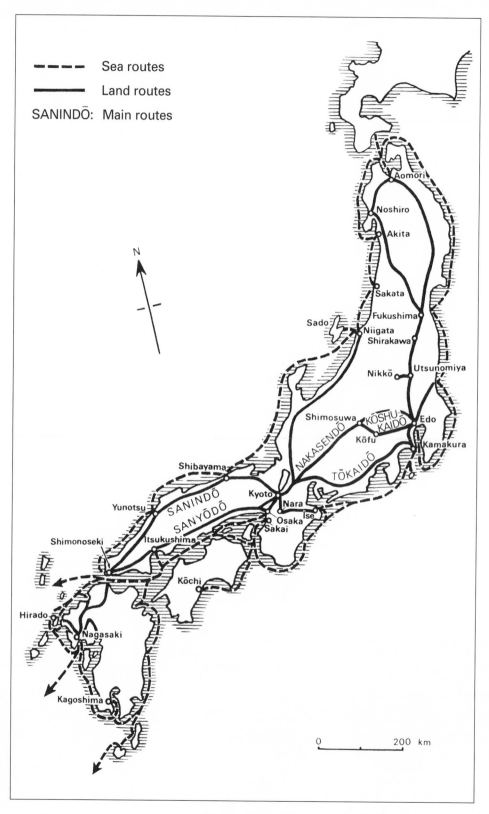

Land and Sea Routes in the Early 17th Century

mitsu, Go-Kameyama tried to re-create a Southern Court, but he changed his mind and returned to Kyoto the following year (1411).

Gōkan. "Bound-together volumes," works published in bound loose-leaf in the early nineteenth century, later replaced by the Kibyōshi. One of the first in this genre was *Ikazuchi Tarō gōaku monogatari* (1806) by Shiketei Samba. These books were usually illustrated with ukiyo-e prints and dealt with more or less factual history, extraordinary adventures, or events relating to Kabuki. Among the main authors were Ryūtei Tanehiko, Santō Kyōden, Jippensha Ikku, and Takizawa Bakin. This type of work disappeared when newspapers, with daily serials, began to be published in the late nineteenth century. *See* KIBYŌSHI.

Gokase-gawa. River 103 km long in northern Miyazaki prefecture (Kyushu) flowing into the sea near Nobeoka. It is said that the first terrestrial *kami*, ancestors of the Tennō of the historical period, descended from "Heaven" (Taka no Hara) to the mountains bordering its gorges.

Go-Kaishiwabara Tennō. Hundred and fourth emperor (Prince Katsuhito, 1464<1501–26>), son of and successor to Go-Tsuchimikado. Go-Nara Tennō succeeded him.

Gokenin. Direct vassals of a shogun. In the Kamakura period, term for some 2,000 samurai families who became hereditary vassals of Minamoto no Yoritomo and received land *(ando)* or became *jitō* or *shugo*. The *gokenin* served as the shogun's personal guard and constituted the basis of his army. In the Muromachi period, the *gokenin* were divided into two classes, those under direct control of the shogun, the *hōkōshū*, and those under a shugo, the *jitō-gokenin*. During the Edo period, the *gokenin* were the shogun's lowest-ranked direct vassals, below the *hatamoto,* and did not have the privilege of being received by the shogun. Their income varied widely but rarely exceeded 200 *koku,* which meant that many of them were impoverished and became merchants or artisans. *See* FUDAI-DAIMYŌ, HATAMOTO, JITŌ, KENIN, SHUGO.

Gōke-shidai. Encyclopedia of imperial ceremonies compiled in 1111 by Oe (Gōke) no Masafusa, on the order of *kampuku* Fujiwara no Moromichi. Nineteen chapters (out of the original 21) have been preserved; they are valuable for their information on court rites and customs in the early twelfth century.

Goki-shichidō. "Five provinces and seven circuits," general term for administrative units under the *ritsuryō* system (late seventh century). The five provinces (called *go-kinai* after 1760) were Yamashiro, Yamato, Settsu, Kawachi, and Izumi. The seven "circuits" (routes, *dō*) were the Tōkaidō, Tōsandō, Hokuridō, San'indō, Sany'ōdō, Nankaidō, and Saikaidō, roads running through the five provinces. *See* GO-KAIDŌ.

Gokō. Emperors' official visits within Japan. Also called *gyōkō, miyuki.*

Gokō-gomin. "Five for the lord, five for the people," an expression used during the Edo period, indicating that 50% of the harvest was to be paid to the lord and 50% remained the peasant's property. In practice, the share paid in tax rarely exceeded 50% and varied from estate to estate.

Go-Kōgon Tennō. Fourth emperor of the court of the North, "Hokuchō" (Prince Iyahito, 1338<1353–71>1374), son of Kōgon Tennō and successor to Sūkō Tennō. He abdicated in favor of his brother, Go-En'yū, in 1371.

Gōkoku. Tokyo painter (Kinugasa Shinkō; *azana:* Shinkei; *gō:* Tenchū-sanjin, Gōkoku, 1850–97) specializing in landscapes.

Gokoku-ji. Buddhist temple founded in Tokyo in 1681 by the monk Ryōken on the order of shogun Tokugawa Tsunayoshi and his mother, Keishō (1627–1705), and dedicated to Nyoirin Kannon Bosatsu. In it are the tombs of many Confucian scholars from the Edo period and members of the imperial family since 1873. This temple belongs to the Shingon-shū sect.

Go-Komatsu Tennō. Hundredth emperor (Prince Motohito, 1377<1392–1412>1433), oldest son of and successor to Go-En'yu Tennō in the Northern Court (Hokuchō). Emperor Go-Kameyama having agreed to end the war between the two courts (Nambokuchō) in 1392, Go-Komatsu became the only legitimate emperor, reigning in Kyoto. He had been emperor of the Northern Court from 1382 and was thus the last of this line. He abdicated in favor of his son, Shōkō Tennō, in 1412 and became a Buddhist monk in 1431.

Go-Kōmyō Tennō. Hundred and tenth emperor (Prince Tsugohito, 1633<1644–54>), son of Go-Minoo Tennō and successor to his sister, Myōshō Tennō. Go-Saiin succeeded him.

Gokuraku. Japanese equivalent of the Sanskrit Sukhāvatī, Amida Buddha's Western "Happy Land" or "Pure Land." Also called Gokuraku Jōdo, Gokuraku-sekai. *See* AMIDA.

• **Gokuraku Go-dō.** *See* TENJIN-SAMA.

• **Gokuraku-in.** Buddhist temple in Nara, founded in the eighth century by a monk called Chikō, who desired rebirth in Amida's "paradise." Hondō dating from 1265 containing a statue of Amida Nyorai in a sitting position, 1.6 m high, from the late Heian period. Zendō from the early Kamakura period (late twelfth century), five-story miniature pagoda (Goju no Tō), a model (0.53 m high) of the one at the Gangō-ji destroyed in 1859.

• **Gokuraku-ji.** Buddhist temple of the Jōdo-shū sect, founded in Kamakura in 1259. Restored and rebuilt a number of times. *See* JŌMYŌ-JI.

• **Gokuraku Jōdo.** *See* GOKURAKU, JŌDO-SHŪ.

Go-kyō. "Five Books," or Confucian classics *(Chin.: Wujing): Ekikyō (Chin.: Yijing), Shokyō (Chin.: Shujing), Shikyō (Chin.: Shijing), Raiki (Chin.: Liji),* and *Shunjū (Chin.: Chunqiu),* the main texts studied by Confucians and neo-Confucians in Japan, China, and Korea.

• **Go-kyō hakase.** "Doctor of Confucian classics," title given to the scholars who introduced the doctrines of Confucianism to Japan, including Tan Yōji (in 516), Kankō Ammō (in 516), and Ō Ryūki (in 554).

Golf. This sport was imported to Japan by an English merchant, Arthur H. Groom, who set up the first golf course in Kobe in 1903. Golf is currently enormously popular with the Japanese public; there are more than 1,000 golf courses in Japan, and more than 40 million Japanese play on them at least once a week. Most cities (and the roofs of many large buildings) have golf training centers, supplied with all the latest automatic devices and surrounded by immense green nets, that are always very busy. This sport is one of the most expensive in Japan (along with horseback riding); most of the time, large companies pay the high fees (entrance and an-

nual) for their employees. Japan has about 1,000 high-level professional golfers. *See* SPORTS.

Golovnin, Vassili Mikhailovich. Russian navy officer (1776–1831). After serving in the Russian navy, then in the English navy under Nelson's command, he captained the Russian frigate *Diana* on a worldwide voyage of exploration that took him to the Far East. In July 1811, he was taken prisoner by the Japanese in the Kuril Islands and held in captivity for three years. His memoirs on this period *(Memoirs of Captivity in Japan During the Years 1811, 1812, and 1813)* are a great source of information on the islands. Golovnin was interrogated extensively by the shogunal authorities on the countries of Europe and on Western science, and his responses enabled them to form a more informed opinion of the state of the world as a whole. A bay in the Bering Sea, in a strait between the Kuril Islands, and a mountain on the island of Noyaya Zemlia in the Arctic Ocean are named for him.

Goma. Plant *(Sesamum)* whose seeds supply an oil widely used in Japanese cuisine and are sometimes sprinkled on pastries and bowls of rice.
• Offering of incense to the divinities, made in a special room called *gomadō.*
• Former word for "horse" in northern Japan. *Normal form:* Koma. Horses were once given as offerings to the Shinto *kami. See* E-MA, MIHARU-GOMA.

• **Goma-zuri.** Technique for making ukiyo-e prints using sesame oil *(goma)* to make the colors transparent. It was used by Kiyonaga, Utamaro, Eishi, and other famous painters.

Gomi Yasusuke. Writer (1921–80), born in Osaka, author of popular novels in which the hero is often an experienced swordsman *(kengō)* or a spy *(ninja).* He received the 28th Akutagawa Prize in 1953 for his novel *Sōshin* (The Lost God, 1952). Among his other successful novels are *Futari no Musashi* (Two from the Musashi, 1956–57) and *Yagyū Ren'yasai* (1955).

Go-Mizunoo Tennō. Hundred and eighth emperor (Prince Kotohito, 1596<1611–29>1680), third son of Go-Yōzei Tennō, whom he succeeded. In 1624, he married Tokugawa Kazuko (Okiko, Tōfuku Mon'in), shogun Tokugawa Hidetada's daughter. In 1629, he abdicated in favor of his daughter Meishō (then five years old), who became the first empress since the eighth century. After he retired to the splendid villa he had built in Kyoto, the Shugaku-in, he spent the rest of his life writing *waka* poems (under the *gō* Go-Mizuno-in), which he collected in an anthology titled *Osō-shū* (A Gulls' Nest) and setting down his literary notes. Also called Go-Minoo Tennō.

Go-Momozono Tennō. Hundred and eighteenth emperor (Prince Hidehito, 1758<1771–79>), nephew of and successor to Go-Sakuramachi Tennō. Kōkaku Tennō succeeded him.

Gomon. Painter (Miura Korezumi; Sōsu-ke; *azana:* Sōryō; *gō:* Shūsei, Karyō, Gomon, 1809–60) of the Nanga school, a student of Kakushū in Nagasaki.

Go-Murakami Tennō. Ninety-seventh emperor (Prince Norinaga, 1328<1339–68>), son of and successor to Go-Daigo Tennō. Chōkei Tennō succeeded him.

Gōmyō. Buddhist monk (d. 834) of the Hossō-shū sect. Legend has it that Amida Buddha came in person to take him to his Pure Land paradise (Gokuraku Jōdo).

Gon. Character meaning "assistant" or "vice-"; used as a prefix to indicate a function below the one designated.

• **Gon no ben.** Vice-*chūben* (or vice-*shōben*) to the imperial court, corresponding to an undersecretary. Also called *gon no chūben, gon no shoben. See* BEN.

• **Gon-busshi.** *See* BUSSHI.

• **Gon-dainagon.** Vice-grand chancellor to the imperial court. *See* DAINAGON, NAGON.

• **Gon no Kami.** Title of provincial vice-governor *(kami).* This title was also conferred upon *dainagon* and *chūnagon* after their time in office.

• **Gon-negi.** *See* KANNUSHI.

• **Gon no sotsu.** Title of governors of Dazaifu (Kyushu). *See* DAINI.

• **Gon no suke.** *See* SUKE.

• **Gon-risshi, Gon-shō sōzu, Gon sōjō.** *See* SŌ-KAN.

• **Gon-seki.** *See* FUJIWARA NO YUKINARI.

Gonaisho. Personal letters by a shogun, either dictated or written in his own hand, signed with a monogram *(kaō)* or bearing (during the Edo period) his personal seal *(inchō).* These letters were sometimes used as requests or commands.

Go-Nara Tennō. Hundred and fifth emperor (Prince Tomohito, 1497<1527–57>), son of and successor to Go-Kashiwabara Tennō. Ogimachi Tennō succeeded him.

Gondō Nariaki. Writer (Gondō Seikyō, 1868–1937), born in Fukuoka. He was an ardent promoter of the Japanese expansionist movement and joined Kokuryūkai to publish his periodical journal *Tōa Geppō* (East Asia Monthly News). In 1920, he founded the Jichi Gakkai (Independent School) in Tokyo to spread his ideas that Japan should adopt a policy of self-sufficient village communities under direct authority of the emperor, without bureaucratic or capitalist interference, a doctrine whose basic principles he expounded in *Kōmin jichi hongi* (1920) and *Jichi mimpan* (Guide for the People's Self-Government, 1927). *See* AIKYŌ JUKU.

Gongen. According to the theories of the Ryōbu-shintō of the Shingon-shū, *kami* considered to be temporary incarnations of the Buddhist Nyorai (Tathāgatas) or Bosatsu (bodhisattvas). *See* HONJI-SUIJAKU, JINJA, RYŌBU SHINTŌ.

• **Gongen-sama.** Name given to Tokugawa Ieyasu by the people after his death, abridged from his posthumous title Tōshō Dai-gongen.

Gongenyama. Prehistoric site near Tokyo in the northern Kanto plain, where lithic Acheulean tools, especially bifaces and tools made with chipping, have been unearthed. Dating uncertain.

Go-Nijō Tennō. Ninety-fourth emperor (Prince Kuniharu, 1285<1302–08>), son of Go-Uda Tennō and successor to Fushimi Tennō. Hanazono Tennō succeeded him.

Go-nin gumi. "Group of five people," a social unit collectively responsible for all of its members (from their behavior to payment of their taxes), re-created in the early seventeenth century by the Tokugawa shogunate to control the populace more effectively. This system, based on one existing in China during the Tang dynasty, was introduced to Japan soon after 645 and called *goho*. Few people followed it until the late sixteenth century, when villagers and city-dwellers organized into groups of ten house-holds (called *jū-nin gumi*) to self-administer their assets and those of their communities more efficiently. Similarly, military units were organized into groups of five or ten soldiers. Thus, *go-nin gumi* and *jū-nin gumi* were composed not of five individuals, but of five (or ten) households. The daimyo organized their estates on the same model and established precise rules *(Tegata, Go-hatto Gaki, Go-uke Gaki)* to guide the members of these groups, whether it was for communal work, village defense, maintenance of roads and bridges, repression of banditry, or payment of taxes. Each group was led by an elected leader or an appointee called *gonin (jūnin) gumi gashira*. The system was abolished in 1868.

Gon-ki. Journal kept by Fujiwara no Yukinari (Fujiwara no Kōzei, 972–1027), covering the years 991–1011 in 50 chapters. It is important for knowledge of that period's history. Also titled *Tukinari kyō-ki.*

Gōnō. Wealthy farmers who were influential during the Edo period and the Meiji era. They played an important role in local administrations and popular uprisings. As they were opposed to feudalism and defended the interests of "wardens," they were somewhat instrumental in helping peasant society evolve. These wealthy landowners disappeared or were absorbed by the local bourgeoisie during the land-tax reform of 1873–81. *See* GŌSHI.

Gonse, Louis. French historian and art critic (1846–1921). He was among the first to provide a synthetic description of Japanese art, and he compared some aspects of it to French Gothic art. Gonse never went to Japan but drew upon the assistance of a Japanese merchant and collector, Hayashi Tademasa (?–Tokyo, 1906). His major work, *L'Art japonais* (Japanese Art, 1883), was reprinted a number of times.

Go-on. *Wu* pronunciation of certain Sino-Japanese characters *(kangi)*, part of the *on* (Chinese pronunciations). Each character can be pronounced two or three (sometimes more) different ways according to the time and place it was adopted. More specifically, the *go-on* are *on* pronunciations of characters introduced from Hina to Japan before the seventh century. After this time, new pronunciations called *kan-on* were introduced, corresponding to those in use in the Tang court; these were made official in 793. The *go-on* thus represented old pronuncia-

tions, some of which have survived to the present day. *See* KUN, ON.

Goraikō. Custom that has it that pilgrims (Fuji-kō) who climb Mt. Fuji (Fuji-san) start their ascent at night in order to be able to worship the rising sun from the summit of the mountain.

Go-Reizei Tennō. Seventieth emperor (Prince Chikahito, 1025 < 1046–68 >), son of and successor to Go-Suzaku Tennō. Go-Sanjō Tennō succeeded him.

Gorin-tō. "Pagoda of five circles," representing the five "elements." It is a composite vertical structure, formed by a cube (representing earth), a sphere (water), a pyramid (fire), a crescent or half-moon (air), and a flame or pointed ball (ether). *Gorin-tō* were introduced to Japan around the ninth century and were adopted by Buddhism as a symbol of the universe. Some are made of wood and adorn the tops of posts placed around cemeteries. Sometimes, each component is inscribed with a Sanskrit character. Also called *tōba. See* SHARI-TŌ.

• *Gorin no sho.* "Treatise of the Five Circles," a famous work on the martial arts and sword techniques *(ken-jutsu)* attributed to Miyamoto no Musashi and probably written about 1643. It is divided into five scrolls (whence its title) titled Earth, Water, Fire, Wind, and Sky. This work is considered a classic by martial-arts practitioners.

Gōri-sei. A *ritsuryō* administrative system that divided the country into villages *(gō)* and hamlets *(ri)*.

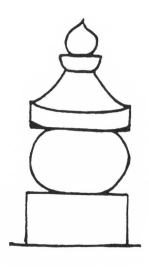

Gorin-tō

The Taika Reform (645) added to these units those of province *(kuni)* and district *(gun)*, with each new village *(ri)* comprising 50 households. This system was abandoned in 740 to return to the old system *(kuni, gun,* and *gō). See* GŌ, GUN, KUNI, RI.

Goroku. Written versions of the teachings of Zen masters, in spite of the doctrine of Furyū Monji ("Do not depend on words or letters"). The *goroku* written by disciples fell into several categories: the *kōroku* gave detailed descriptions of the teachings of a single master; the *goyō* dealt specifically with the master's spoken words; and the *tsūshū* dealt with teachings by various masters. By extension, the word *goroku* has come to designate any written text expounding a religious doctrine, Zen or other.

Gorō Masamune. *See* MASAMUNE.

Goryōkaku. Fortress built in 1855 in Hakodate (Hokkaido) by Takeda Hisaburō, on a model inspired by Vauban, to protect the Tsugaru Strait against possible invasion by the Russian fleet. *See* BRUNET, HAKODATE.

• **Goryōkaku no Tatakai.** "Battle of Goryōkaku," which took place June 20–27, 1869, in Hakodate between the pro-shogunal troops of Enomoto Takeaki, comprising eight ships and about 2,000 men, and those of the emperor. When Kuroda Kiyotaka's army arrived to provide reinforcement, the imperial troops attacked the fort. After a week of fighting, they captured it and forced Enomoto to surrender. This battle spelled the definitive end of the Edo shogunate. *See* BOSHIN SENSŌ.

Go-Saga Tennō. Eighty-eighth emperor (Prince Kunihito, 1220<1243–46>1272), son of Tsuchimikado Tennō and successor to Shijō Tennō. A Buddhist monk before his accession to the throne, he abandoned the robe to keep Prince Tadanari, a son of Retired Emperor Juntoko Tennō who was supported by the court, from being enthroned, and set a precedent by asking for assistance from the Kamakura *bakufu*. He abdicated after ruling for only four years but continued to govern in the name of his sons Go-Fukakusa and Kameyama, forcing Go-Fukakusa to abdicate in favor of his younger brother, Kameyama, in 1260. This was the origin of the alternation of reigns of the Jimyō-in and Daikaku-ji "family lines." Go-Saga was also a great *waka* poet. He compiled the *Soku kokin-shū.*

Go-Sanjō Tennō. Seventy-first emperor (Prince Takahito, 1034<1069–72>1073), son of Go-

Suzaku Tennō and Princess Teishi (Yōmei Mon'in). He succeeded his half-brother Go-Reizei Tennō. Because he was not related to the Fujiwara family, he held the reins of power on his own. After consolidating the imperial authority, he abdicated in favor of his son, Shirakawa, thus enabling two of his other sons (with a concubine belonging to the Minamoto family) to reign in their turn. He died several months after abdicating.

Gosan-ke. "The Three Successional Families" composed of the daimyo of Mito, Owari, and Kii, related to the Tokugawa, from which the shogun of Edo were chosen. These three major families of daimyo, whose ancestors went back to three sons of Tokugawa Ieyasu—Yoshinao (Owari), Yorinobu (Kii), and Yorifusa (Mito)—were extremely important in the political affairs of the shogunate because they were more powerful than all others, with revenues totaling around 1.62 million *koku. See also* GOSAN-KYŌ.

Gosan-kyō. "The Three Houses of Lords," collateral to the Tokugawa family, based on descendants of sons of the Tokugawa family by secondary wives. The Tayasu family was descended from Munetake, a son of Tokugawa Yoshimune; the Hitotsubashi family, from a son of Munetada, another of Tokugawa Yoshimune's sons; and the Shimizu family from Shigeyoshi, a son of Tokugawa Ieshige. These families each received an allocation of 100,000 *koku* but had no estates. *See* GOSAN-KE.

Gosannen no Eki. "Later Three Years' War" (1083–87), conducted in Mutsu province (northern Honshu) by Minamoto no Yoshiie to defeat the Abe clan and the Kiyohara family. *See* ZENKUNEN NO EKI.

• *Gosannen kassen emaki. Emakimono* relating some of the mishaps of the Gosannen no Eki, painted in the fourteenth century.

Gose. Town in Nara prefecture, former castle town *(jōka-machi)* in the Edo period, known for its Yamato-gasuri fabrics *(ikat)* and citrus fruits. The area around it has a number of *kofun. Pop.:* 40,000.

Go-sechi-e. Collective name for five imperial festivals: Ganjitsu no Seichi-e, Hakuba no Sechi-e, Haraka no Sō, Tango no Sekku, and Tōka-Ebisu. *See these names.*

• **Go-sechi no mai.** Bugaku dances (after 742) performed in court ceremonies by women, similar to those performed in the Yang dynasty court in China. During the Heian period, the dances were performed twice each year, during the Daijō-sai and Niname-sai festivals, by noblewomen. They were revived during the coronation ceremonies for emperors Taishō, in 1915, and Shōwa, in 1928. Previously, they had been performed only once a year, on the "Day of the Bull" in the eleventh month during the major *sechi-e.*

Goseda Iwakichi. Western-style painter (Genjirō, Denjirō, Kinjirō; *gō:* Hōryū, 1827–92), Higuchi Tangetsu's student.

• **Goseda Denjirō, Genjirō, Kinjirō.** *See* GOSEDA IWAKICHI.

• **Goseda Yōryū.** *See* YAMAMOTO HŌSUI.

• **Goseda Yoshimatsu.** Western-style painter (1855 –1915), student of Fontanesi and Charles Wirgman. He lived in France for some time, and studied with J. L. Bonnat. He was named Emperor Meiji's official painter.

Goseibai-shikimoku. Historically important legal code, promulgated by the Kamakura shogunate to be applied to its vassals, in 1232 (Jōei era, whence its other name, *Jōei-shikimoku).* Composed of 51 articles written by Miyoshi Yoshitsura, it was the first real Japanese legal code, and it was in force until 1868. From time to time, supplements *(tsuika)* were added to adapt it to societal changes, but it remained fundamentally unchanged. It was, in essence, a compendium of cases of jurisprudence concerning mainly civil suits, such as disputes over property rights.

Go-sekke. Collective name for the five main branches of the Fujiwara family—Ichijō, Konoe, Kujō, Nijō, and Takatsukasa—from which empresses and senior state bureaucrats were chosen during the Heian and early Kamakura periods. All were descended from Fujiwara no Michinaga and Fujiwara no Tadamichi. They took the names of the residences these families occupied in Kyoto.

Go-sekku. Collective name for the five major popular festivals *(matsuri):* Jinjitsu, Jōmi, Tango, Tanabata, and Chōyō. *See these names.*

Gosen. Town in Niigata prefecture (central Honshu), famous for its silk fabrics since the nineteenth century. It has the largest knitwear plants in Japan. *Pop.:* 40,000.

Gosen waka-shū. "Later Collection of Japanese Poems." Official anthology (*see* CHOKUSEN WAKA-SHŪ), compiled on Emperor Murakami's order in 951 by five bureaucrats of the House of Lords (Nashitsubo no Gonin): Ōnakatomi no Yoshinobu, Minamoto no Shitagau, Kiyohara no Motosuke, Sakanoue no Mochike, and Ki no Tokibumi. It comprises 20 books and 1,426 poems by 219 poets, among them Ki no Tsurayuki, Oshikōchi no Mitsune, and Fujiwara no Kanesuke, as well as poems that "answer" each other in a sort of poetic dialogue. Many poems in this anthology are preceded by prose notes about the circumstances under which they were written. Abridged title: *Gosen-shū.*

Gōshi. "Samurai peasants," term that applied originally to samurai who had to supply their war-related equipment out of the revenues from their own land when needed. During the Edo period, the term designated low-ranked samurai residing outside of the castle towns *(jōka-machi)* and living off the produce of their land while fulfilling a military or administrative function attached to their small estates. Starting in the Kamakura period, this type of land distribution was practiced mainly in the newly conquered territories of northern Honshu and on Shikoku and Kyushu. In 1872, these "semi-samurai" were classed among the *shizoku* and became "gentlemen farmers" *(inaka no shinshi)* who played an increasingly important role in domestic policy in the Meiji era. *See also* GŌNŌ, JI-SAMURAI.

Go-shichi-nichi no Mishiho. Major annual ceremony conducted from the third to the fifth day of the first month in the Tō-ji temple in Kyoto belonging to the Shingon-shū. It is said to have been created in 834 by Kōbō Daishi to ensure the empire's peace and prosperity.

Gōshin. Painter in the Yamato-e style (Fujiwara no Gōshin, late fifteenth century), son of a courtesan and a Buddhist monk. One of his few surviving works is a portrait of Hanazono Tennō, housed in the Chōfuku-ji (Kannon-dō) temple in Mie prefecture.

Goshintai. "Divine body," a sacred Shinto object considered to be a sort of receptacle for a *kami.* The *goshintai* (or *shintai, mitama no mikata, mitama-shiro, mishōtai)* can be a natural object, such as a rock or a tree, or a manufactured object (sword, mirror, *magatama* jewel, sculpture, painting, etc.). The *kami* invoked are said to "descend" into the *goshintai*. When it is a manufactured object, it is generally closed in a strongbox and kept in the shrine. Under the influence of Buddhism, sculptures or images representing a *kami* (or a Buddhist divinity) came to be considered *shintai*. *See* SHINTAI.

Go-Shirakawa Tennō. Seventy-seventh emperor (Prince Masahito, 1127<1155–58>1192), son of Toba Tennō and Empress Fujiwara Yasuko. He succeeded his brother, Konoe Tennō, but was opposed to Retired Emperor Sutoku, which led to the disturbances of the Hōgen era (*see* HŌGEN NO RAN) in 1156. He abdicated in favor of his son, Nijō (Morohito), in 1158, but continued to govern in retirement. He attempted to free himself from the guardianship of the Taira and skillfully exploited the warrior factions, the Taira and Minamoto, even managing to create conflict between Minamoto no Yoritomo and his half-brother, Minamoto Yoshitsune. A devious and unscrupulous politician, he was also a devout Buddhist and a very famous musician.

Goshkevich, Iossip Antonovich. Russian diplomat (d. 1875), born in Minsk. About 1839–40, he went to China, via Xinjiang and Tibet, with an Orthodox religious mission; settling in Beijing, he learned Chinese. From 1852 to 1855, he served as an interpreter to members of the Putiatine mission and learned Japanese. With the assistance of Tachibana Kōsai (who took the Russian name V. I. Yamatov), he compiled a Japanese–Russian dictionary that was published in 1857. He was named Russia's consul to Japan in 1858. When he returned to Russia, he wrote a book on the origins of the Japanese language, *O Korniakh Iaponskogo Iazika*, which was published in 1899, years after his death.

Gosho. Imperial palace in Kyoto, built by Kammu Tennō in 794. It was destroyed several times by war and fire, and some of its largest buildings were reconstructed according to the original plans in 1856. One part of the palace, called Sento-gosho, was designed by Koboro Enshū and built for retired emperors in 1627 on Go-Mizunoo Tennō's order. Another palace, Nyo-in, was added for Princess Tōfuku Mon'in about 1650. This palace was destroyed in fires in 1660 and again in 1673, and was rebuilt on a different plan. Destroyed once again by fire in 1684, it was reconstructed and expanded. In 1747, the Sento and Nyo-in gardens were joined together and their ponds linked by a canal. The site was then expanded northward to include a rice paddy for imperial ceremonies, only part of which has survived. *See* HEIAN-JINGŪ.

• **Gosho-bugyō.** Title given in 1204 to the intendant of the shogunal palace in Kamakura.

• **Gosho-dokoro.** Former name of the library in the imperial palace in Kyoto.

• **Gosho-guruma.** *See* GYŪSHA.

Go-sho. Collective name for the five greatest warriors of the medieval period: Taira Kiyomori, Minamoto no Yoritomo, Ashikaga Takauji, Oda Nobunaga, and Toyotomi Hideyoshi.

• **Go-sho Hachiman.** Collective name for the five great Shinto shrines dedicated to the *kami* of war, Hachiman (in Yawata): Owako no Miya (in Chikuzen), Chiguri no Miya (in Hizen), Fujisaki no Miya (in Higo), Nitta no Miya (in Satsuma), and Shō Hachiman no Miya (in Ōsumi).

Gosho Heinosuke. Director (1902–81), born in Tokyo. He was Shimazu's assistant and directed the first Japanese "talking" film, *Madamu to nyōbo* (Madame and the Neighbors) in 1931. His most famous silent film is *Not a Cloud in the Sky* (1925). He directed more than 150 feature-length films, all based on events of daily life, noted in numerous rapid touches. Among his most successful films are *Ōsaka no yado* (The Osaka Inn, 1954), *Entotsu no mieru basho* (Where One Sees Chimneys, 1953), and *Takekurabe* (Adolescence, 1955).

Gōshōji-ha. Branch of the Jōdo Shin-shū sect, founded in Echizen by the monk Shōsen in the fourteenth century. It currently has about 140,000 followers.

Go-shu-in. "Red seal," shogunal permission given to certain entities by special waiver:

• **Go-shuin bune.** Ships authorized, starting in 1593, to trade with China and the countries of Southeast Asia despite the ban against Japanese traveling outside of the country. The *go-shuin* had been promulgated by Hideyoshi to fight smuggling and piracy (*see* WAKŌ) and to ensure the safety of merchant ships. Ships that had a *go-shuin-jō* could make only a certain number of trips per year according to this mandate. Between 1593 and 1635, about 350 *go-shuin-jō* were granted, some of them to Chinese (43) and foreign (38) merchants. The ships exported mainly copper, iron, silver, sulfur, and objects such as swords and armor, and imported raw silk, spices, and medicinal plants. After 1604, the number of *go-shuin-jō* was reduced to about 15 per year; after 1615, there were only 8. They stopped being given about 1635 and Japan had to deal with foreign ships, mostly Dutch, for its foreign trade. Also called *go-shu-in sen.*

• **Go-shu-in chi.** Title of ownership given by the Tokugawa shogun for land or estates belonging to Buddhist temples, Shinto shrines, or daimyo, proving their unalienability.

Go shūi-shū. "Later *Shūi-shū,*" an official poetry anthology (*see* CHOKUSEN WAKA-SHŪ), compiled in 1086 by Fujiwara no Michitoshi. It comprises 1,208 poems in 20 scrolls. Also titled *Go shūi waka-shū.*

Goshun. Painter (Matsumura Toyoaki; Bunzō, Kaemon; *azana:* Hakubō; *gō:* Yūho, Katen, Sompaku, Sonjūhaku, Sonseki, Shōutei, Hyaku-shōdō, Gekkei, Goshun, 1752–1811), born in Kyoto and belonging to the Nanga and Shijō schools. He was first a student of Ōnishi Suigetsu and Bosun, then, in 1783, of Maruyama Ōkyo. With his brother, Keibun, he founded the Shijō school. Among his students were his brother, Matsumura Keibun, and Okamoto Toyohiko (1773–1845). Goshun was also a good *haikai* poet and a talented calligrapher.

Gōso. Protest or demand made by groups of malcontents. *Gōso* were organized mainly during the Heian period by monk-soldiers (*sōhei*) of the Enryaku-ji temples of Mt. Hiei and the Kōfuku-ji. Under the slightest pretext, they would make their way in a procession to the imperial palace (*gosho*) in Kyoto, carrying sacred images or palinquins, in an attempt to intimidate the emperor. They sometimes succeeded; at one point, Emperor Shirakawa complained that he "couldn't play dice without the monk-soldiers getting involved." During the Kamakura and Muromachi periods, the *gōso* were mainly peasants who were asking for help dealing with the extortion of *shōen* owners or demanding repayment of debts (*tokusei*).

Gōson. Semi-autonomous villages that developed within estates starting in the fourteenth century in Kinai, mainly around the capital, Kyoto, and Nara. During the gradual disintegration of the *myōden* system, some *myōshu* (landowners in the villages, or *gō*) organized so that they could better defend themselves against the authority of the *shōen* by taking charge of tax collection *(nengu)* and various peasant activities, and controlling local shrines. By freeing themselves from the old system, they gained partial autonomy for the villages under their control. During the Muromachi period, some became vassals of the major lords (*see* GEKOKUJŌ), mainly during the disturbances of the Sengoku-jidai period, and held the title *otona* or *toshiyori*. The division of society into distinct classes led to the gradual dissolution of this system, and as the *otona* became simple vassals, the *gōson* disappeared.

Gosu-aka-e. "Porcelain from Swatow [now Shantou]," a Chinese city producing *sencha* ceramics in the late Ming dynasty (early seventeenth century) enameled in cobalt blue *(gosu)* and red *(aka-e)*. It was imitated in Japan mainly by Okuda Eisen, in Kyoto, in the early eighteenth century.

Go-Sukō-in. Imperial prince (Sadafusa, 1372–1456), grandson of Sukō Tennō and son of Yoshihito Shinnō. His son, Hikohito, became Emperor Go-Hanazono.

Go-Suzaku Tennō. Sixty-ninth emperor (Prince Atsuyoshi, 1009<1037–45>), son of Ichijō Tennō and successor to his brother, Go-Ichijō Tennō. Go-Reizei succeeded him. His name is sometimes spelled Go-Shujaku.

Go-tairō. Collective name for five members of the state council created by Toyotomi Hideyoshi to act as regents while his son, Hideyori, was underage. The number of *tairō* was reduced to three in 1603, then to two, and finally to one. They were Ukita Hideie, Useugi Kagekatsu, Mōri Terumoto, Maeda Toshiie, and Tokugawa Ieyasu. *See* TAIRŌ.

Gotemba. Town in Shizuoka prefecture, at the foot of Mt. Fuji (Fuji-san), former waystation on the Tōkaidō road during the Edo period, near the Hakone "barrier" (*sekisho*). It is the point of departure for pilgrims and tourists intending to climb Mt. Fuji. Small botanical garden. *Pop.:* 70,000.

Gotō. Family of silver and iron jewelers, founded in Kyoto by Gotō Yūjō, a famous artisan. His successors were also noted for their talent as makers of precious objects, especially sword guards (*tsuba*):
  Gotō Sōjō (Takemitsu, 1461–1538)
  Gotō Jōshin (Yoshihisa, 1505–62)

Gotō Kōjō (Mitsuie, 1529–1620)
Gotō Tokujō (Mitsutsugu, 1550–1631)
Gotō Eijō (Masamitsu, 1577–1617)
Gotō Kenjō (Masatsugu, 1586–1663)
Gotō Sokujō (Misuhige, 1600–68)
Gotō Teijō (Mitsumasa, 1604–73)
Gotō Renjō (Mitsutomo, 1627–89)
Gotō Tsujō (Mitsunaga, 1663–1721)
Gotō Jūjō (Mitsutada, 1695–1742)
Gotō Enjō (Mistutaka, 1721–84)
Gotō Keijō (Mitsumori, 1751–1804)
Gotō Shinjō (Mitsuyoshi, 1783–1834)
Gotō Hojō (Mitsuaki, 1816–56)

Perhaps the best-known was Gotō Ichijō (Eijirō, Mitsuyuki; *gō:* Muan, Hakuō, Ichii, 1791–1876), although he may not have been directly in the Gotō family line.

Gotō akio. Writer (b. 1932), author of novels published serially in periodicals. His novels dealt mainly with people's reactions in a contemporary urban environment: *Shiteki seikatsu* (Private Life, 1968), *Warai jigoku* (Hell that Smiles, 1969).

Go-Toba Tennō. Eighty-second emperor (Prince Takahira, 1179<1184–98>1239), son of Takakura Tennō and successor to his brother, Antoku Tennō. He abdicated at age 18, but continued to govern during the reigns of his sons Tsuchimikado and Juntoku, and during the reign of the latter's son, Chūkyō. He decided to fight the Kamakura shogun to return full authority to the imperial family and began military preparations when Minamoto no Yoritomo died, in 1199. In 1221, he forced his son Juntoku to abdicate in favor of his grandson Chūkyō, then launched an attack against the Kyoto-kanrei. But reinforcements from Kamakura forced him to pull back; Chūkyō Tennō was deposed after a reign of only 70 days and replaced by Go-Horikawa, who was more favorably disposed toward Hōjō Tokyori, the *shikken* of Kamakura. The three ex-emperors were forced into exile, Go-Toba to the island of Oki, Tsuchimikado to Shikoku, and Juntoku to the island of Sado. A multitalented man, Go-Toba exerted an immense influence on the arts and technology of his country; he was interested in all aspects of culture, from cockfights to singing contests, archery, sword making, horseback riding, pilgrimages, *kemari* games (on which he wrote a short treatise, *Ommari no ki,* Chronicle of the Ball Game), and music (*Ombiwa-awase,* Biwa Contest). He was, above all, an excellent *waka* poet. He created a "poetry bureau" (Waka-dokoro) in his Nijō palace in 1201 and had a

new anthology, the *Shin kokin-shū,* compiled; it was completed in 1205. He also organized major poetry contests, such as the famous Sengohyakuban Uta-awase (1,500 poetic songs) in 1201–02. During his exile, he wrote a treatise on poetry, *Go-Toba no in gokuden* (Secret Teachings of ex-Emperor Go-Toba). Thirty-four of his own poems were included in the *Shin kokin-shū* and more than 200 others in various collections, such as the *Tsukuba-shū* (1356). He is also known as Kentoku and Dajō Tennō. When he became a Buddhist monk in 1221, he took the name Ryōzen.

Gotō Bijutsu-kan. Private museum in Tokyo, created to house Gotō Keita's collections. On display are beautiful collections of ceramics, paintings, and Chinese and Japanese objects. It houses a copy of the *Genji monogatari emaki* and other *emakimono.* A teahouse in its garden is open to visitors, and there is an adjoining library of Chinese and Japanese books (Dai Tōkyū). *See* MUSEUMS.

Gotō Chūgai. Writer (Gotō Toranosuke, 1866–1938), who wrote mainly novellas—*Funikudan* (1899)—and essays—*Hi shizen shugi* (1908). He published a major literary magazine, *Shinshōsetsu* (New Novel), to which writers of the Ken'yūsha (Friends of the Ink Slab) literary circle contributed.

Gotō Fumio. Politician (1884–1980), born in Ōita. A supporter of Japan's growing militarism, he held important positions in a number of government ministries in Japan and Taiwan and was admitted to the House of Peers in 1930. He was minister of agriculture in Saitō Makoto's cabinet, minister of the interior in Okada Keisuke's cabinet (June 1934–Mar. 1936), and minister of state in Tōjō Kideki's cabinet. In 1953, he was elected to the Chamber of Councillors.

Gotō Keiji. Architect (1883–1919). He designed many buildings, notably the Toyotama prison in 1915. His designs, in humanist style, bore no resemblance to the official architecture of the Meiji era.

Gotō Keita. Businessman (1882–1959) born in Nagano, founder of the Tōkyū stores in Tokyo. He headed a number of private railroad companies, and he founded chains of stores and a film company during the Second World War. When he returned to public life after the war, he created many schools and colleges (Gotō Ikueikai) and founded the Gotō

Bijutsu-kan museum to house his own art collection. Father of Gotō Noboru.

Gotō Konzan. Physician (Gotō Saichirō, 1659–1733), born in Edo, disciple of Nagoya Gen'i of the Koiho "experimental school" based on Chinese Confucian medicine, a theory according to which all diseases come from a "stagnation" of vital cosmic breath, the *ki* (*Chin.*: Qi). He favored acupuncture and *moxa,* among other treatments.

Gotō Midori. Prodigal violinist (b. 1972) who soloed with Leonard Bernstein's orchestra in the United States at age 14. After beginning her education in Osaka, she studied in Aspen, Colorado, in 1981, then at New York's Juilliard School of Music.

Gotō Miyoko. Classical *(waka)* poet (1899–1978). She was the teacher of heir to the throne Princess Michiko, daughter of Emperor Hirohito (Shōwa Tennō).

Gotō Mototsugu. Samurai (Gotō Matabei, d. 1615) who supported Toyotomi Hideyori against Tokugawa Ieyasu and died during Ieyasu's siege of the Osaka castle. His son, Gotō Ujifusa (1570–1615) was also killed at that time.

Gotō Noboru. Businessman (1916–89), born in Tokyo, oldest son of Gotō Keita. He became president of Tōkyū Corporation in 1954; in 1984, he was elected the fourteenth president of the Japanese Chamber of Commerce and Industry.

Gotō-reitō. Group of islands in the eastern China Sea, west of Nagasaki. It comprises five main islands, Nakadōrishima, Wakamatsujima, Narushima, Hisakajima, and Fukuejima, and some 100 small islands, 34 of which are inhabited. The five main islands are linked by modern bridges. Sweet potatoes are cultivated in terraced fields, but the main activity is fishing. The islands once served as bases for pirates and were refuges for Christians during times of persecution. *Total area:* 632 km². *Pop.:* 150,000.

Gotō Ryūnosuke. Politician (1889–1984). A classmate (*see* BATSU) of Konoe Fumimaro's at the University of Kyoto, he supported Konoe's career, helping him become prime minister by organizing various political associations (Nihon Seinenkan, Seinenkan, Sōnendan). In 1933, he created the Shōwa Kenkyūkai, a politics and economics study group; in 1940, he and Konoe established the Shin Taisei Undō (Movement for a New Order), but he was soon forced to resign because his political enemies denounced him as a communist. In 1945, he returned to politics by creating the Shōwa Dōjinkai (Fraternity of the Shōwa Era) to stimulate public debate on important issues concerning the reconstruction of Japan.

Gotō Shimpei. Politician and physician (1857–1929), son of a low-ranking samurai in Sendai. He studied medicine and was a military physician during Saigō Takamori's rebellion (1877). He was then appointed president of the Nagoya School of Medicine. In 1890, he went to Germany to continue his studies; in 1895, he was appointed director of the Military Quarantine. Three years later he became the civil governor of Taiwan, then he was elected to the House of Peers in 1903. In 1906, he was appointed president of the Manchurian Railroad; in 1908, minister of communications and director of railroads in Katsura Tarō's cabinet; he held the same positions in Katsura's second cabinet (1912). He was minister of state in 1916, then minister of foreign affairs in Terauchi Masatake's cabinet, supporting of the latter's expansionist policy. He became mayor of Tokyo in 1920 and was active in reconstruction of the capital after the earthquake of September 1923, and in the creation of many civil organizations.

Gotō Shōjirō. Samurai and politician (1838–97), born in Tosa. He took an active part in the Sonnō Jōi movement for restoration of imperial power and demanded that shogun Tokugawa Yoshinobu step down in favor of the emperor. After 1868, he held important positions in the Meiji government and was governor of Osaka prefecture. But after taking Itagaki Taisuke's side over Korea, he resigned from his position of councillor (*sangi*) in 1873 and founded the Aikoku Kōtō (Public Party of Patriots). Then, in 1881, he helped Itagaki form the Jiyūtō (Liberal party). The following year, he went to Europe to study political institutions; when he returned, he became a firm proponent of review of the Unequal Treaties (*see* JŌYAKU KAISEI). He was then minister of communications in the cabinets of Kuroda Kiyotaka, Yamagata Aritomo, and Matsukata Masayoshi, and minister of agriculture in Itō Hirobumi's cabinet.

Gotō Shōzaburō. Kyoto goldsmith (Gotō Mitsutsugu, 1571–1625), Gotō Tokujō's (*see* GOTŌ) disciple. He made gold coins under Tokugawa Ieyasu, then was named head of the Ginza Mint in

Edo, and helped Ieyasu standardize coins. His descendants adopted the name Shōzaburō and were directors of the Ginza until 1869.

Gotō Shuichi. Archeologist (1888–1960), born in Shizuoka prefecture. After working at the Tokyo National Museum, he traveled in Europe and the United States in 1927 to study museology. When he returned, he became a professor at Meiji University. He directed excavations at the Yayoi site in Toro and studied the circle of stones in Ōyu, as well as *kofun*. Among his books are *Nihon kōkogaku* (Archeology of Japan, 1927) and *Nihon rekishi kōkogaku* (Historical Archeology of Japan, 1937).

Gōtsu. Town in Shimane prefecture (Honshu) at the mouth of the Gō-gawa river, on the Sea of Japan. It produces ceramics known for their solidity, mainly tiles. Its annual Tōro Nagashi festival, which takes place in August, is famous.

Go-Tsuchimikado Tennō. Hundred and third emperor (Prince Fusahito, 1442<1465–1500>), son of and successor to Go-Hanazono Tennō. It was during his reign that the war of the Ōnin era (*see* ŌNIN NO RAN) took place. Go-Kashiwabara succeeded him.

Go-Uda Tennō. Ninety-first emperor (Prince Yohito, 1267<1275–87>1324), son of and successor to Kameyama Tennō. He belonged to the Daikaku-ji family line; his successors, Fushimi and Go-Fushimi, to the rival Jimyō-in line (*see* GO-FUKAKUSA). He abdicated in favor of his cousin, Fushimi; after his wife, Yūgi Mon'in, died in 1307, he became a Buddhist monk and devoted himself to the study of esoterism.

Go-un. Painter (Nishimura Genjirō; *gō:* Go-un, 1877–1938), student of Takeuchi Seihō in Kyoto. He painted mainly landscapes, flowers, and birds.

Goyō beya. Collective term for the great council of the Tokugawa shogun, composed of *tairō, rōjū,* and *waka-doshiyori.*

Goyō-shōnin. Merchants and financiers responsible for supplying the Edo shogun and the major daimyo. They also acted as "ministers of finance" for the latter, who regarded financial matters as beneath them, and many grew wealthy (often at the expense of the shogun and daimyo) by reselling the rice that had been allotted to them in payment (*kuramai*). However, precisely because they were wealthy, the *goyō-shōnin* were sometimes obliged to lend money (*goyō-kin*) to the shogunate when major expenditures had to be made. Such loans bore a very high interest rate—though they were not always paid back, since many daimyo opted to declare bankruptcy. The largest loan ever forced upon the *goyō-shōnin* was made by the shogunate during its second punitive expedition against the *chōshū* in 1866: 7 million *ryō* (the cash equivalent to 7 million *koku* of rice).

Go-Yōzei Tennō. Hundred and seventh emperor (Prince Katahito, 1571<1587–1611>1617), son of Prince Masahito Shinnō and grandson of and successor to Ōgimachi Tennō. He abdicated in favor of his son, Kotohito (Go-Mizunoo Tennō).

Go-yū. "The five braves," a collective name for the five greatest warriors of the sixteenth century: Mōri Motonari, Hōjō Ujiyasu, Uesugi Terutora, Takeda Harunobu, and Oda Nobunaga.

Gozan. "The five mountains" (Zen temples), a group of Zen temples officially recognized and supported by the Kamakura and Muromachi shogunates. The term refers to five Zen temples in Kamakura (Kenchō-ji, Engaku-ji, Jōmyō-ji, Jōchi-ji, and Jukufu-ji) and five in Kyoto (Nanzen-ji, Tenryū-ji, Manju-ji, Tōfuku-ji, and Kennin-ji). In fact, the *gozan* comprised more than 300 Zen temples (including their branches), most of which belonged to the Rinzai-shū branch. Their abbots and monks were appointed by the shogunal authorities. The monks in these temples studied mainly Chinese literature and poetry from the Song period (at the time, there was a similar organization of "official monasteries" in China) and disseminated them through the warrior class, thanks to the influence of the *jissatsu* (main temples of Kamakura and Kyoto) and the *shozan* (provincial monasteries). The *gozan* were financially dependent on the shoguns and answered only to them and to their warrior-patrons, who donated land and exempted them from taxes. The monks of the *gozan* invited to Japan a number of Chinese scholars, Chan monks and laymen, and artists. They thus brought Chinese culture to Japan and helped create a specific culture, called *gozan-bunka,* that dominated Japanese culture in the fourteenth and fifteenth centuries. However, the influence of the *gozan* waned when the monasteries began to lend money, which led to their being violently attacked by some borrowers, and they lost much of their land during the disturbances of the Warring States period (Sengoku-jidai, 1467–1568).

• **Gozan-bunka.** *See* GOZAN.

Gōzanze Myō-ō. Esoteric Buddhist divinity, corresponding to the Indian divinity Trailokyavijayarāja, a Myō-ō (King of Wisdom, Vidyārāja), associated with the east and considered an "angry emanation" of Ashuku Nyorai (*Skt.:* Ashobhya), conqueror of the "three poisons" (avarice, ignorance, and anger) and of the three worlds of passion. He is signified by a mudra (hand gesture) called Gōzanze-in (or Niwa-in, Shisetsu-in). He is also known by the names Bazara-un Kongō, Shōzanze, Somba Myō-ō, and Funnugatsu Enson.

Goze. Blind women who sang and played the shamisen. In the sixteenth century, they formed groups in order to survive and traveled throughout Japan. They were generally protected by the authorities and performed mainly in villages. Many of them were reputed to be witches, and they were asked to heal illnesses or protect against drought or too much rain. Their repertoire ranged from popular songs to long Buddhist hymns or Shinto incantations. They were the female counterpart of the *biwa-hōshi*. There are still a few *goze* today, mainly in Niigata prefecture. *See* BIWA-HŌSHI, ZA-TO.

Gozen. Title of respect once given to some high-ranking women, mainly during the Kamakura period.

Gozen kaigi. "Imperial conferences" convoked by the emperor under extraordinary circumstances, such as a declaration of war, the signature of a treaty of alliance, or, as was the case in 1945, making the decision to surrender. The emperor attended this conference but generally left his advisers and ministers to make the decision. He did, however, have the power (rarely used) to make his word stand.

Gozu Tennō. Shinto-Buddhist divinity, sometimes identified with an agrarian *kami* (in Kumamoto, he was a rice *kami* said to be one-eyed) and venerated mainly in the Yasaka-jinja in Kyoto, where he is called Gion, which is possibly a contraction of Gozu-dana (Lord Gozu). He is associated with Susanoo and some phallic cults. Portrayed (in Kyoto) as a bull's head, he is possibly also symbolic of beef eaters. *Chin.:* Niutou; *Skt.:* Goshirsha. *See* GION, SUSANOO.

Grew, Joseph Clark. American diplomat (1880–1965), born in Boston. He was ambassador to Denmark, Switzerland, and Turkey before being posted to Tokyo in 1932. In spite of his constant efforts to restore peace in Asia, he was not able to keep the Japanese from attacking Pearl Harbor in November 1941. He was then recalled to the United States, while Japanese diplomats were recalled to Japan.

Griffis, William Elliot. American Protestant pastor and educator (1843–1928), born in Philadelphia. In 1870, he was invited to teach in Fukui, then in Tokyo. He wrote 18 books on Japan, and when he returned to the United States in 1874, he gave many speeches. His most important book, *The Mikado's Empire,* was published in 1876. He was twice decorated with the Order of the Rising Sun.

Guandong ("Kantōgun"). Japanese army formed in 1906 to guard the territories in southern Manchuria and the south Manchurian railroad linking Port Arthur to Changchun. In 1919, the army was divided into military and civil administrations. The Guandong army became more and more independent from the civil government of Manchuria in the 1920s. Its officers, most of them extremists, plotted to assassinate Zhang Zuolin (*see* CHO SHURIN) in 1928; in 1931, they provoked various incidents that led the Japanese government to occupy all of Manchuria. In 1932, they helped set up the puppet government of Manchukuo, which became the base for Japanese military operations in northern China in 1937. In 1939, the Guandong army lost 18,000 soldiers in a series of battles against the Soviet army at Nomonham, on the Mongolian border. In 1941, its personnel comprised 700,000 men, but it had only a defensive role. In 1943, some members of its staff were transferred to the Pacific battlefields. The Guandong army that remained in Manchuria was attacked by the Soviets in August 1945, and suffered a crushing defeat, with almost 80,000 soldiers killed and more than 500,000 taken prisoner. The latter were repatriated to Japan between 1947 and 1950; their general, Yamada Otozō (1881–1965), in 1956.

Guérineau, Abel Jean-Louis. French military officer (1841–1929), painter, and architect who studied with Lenormand and Dubois in Paris. He went to Japan in 1874 upon invitation of the Ministry of War and worked there until 1880, teaching drafting to Japanese officers at the Numazu School and designing a variety of buildings. When he returned to France, in 1881, he exhibited his paintings at the Salon.

Guimet, Émile. French industrialist (1836–1918), born in Lyon, and lover of Eastern art. He traveled extensively in Asia and in East Asia, notably Japan, where he was sent in 1876 by the Ministry of Public Education to study religions. He brought back collections of art and archeological finds and created a museum bearing his name in Lyon in 1879. The museum was transferred to Paris in 1884, and was attached to the Musées Nationaux in 1945. He wrote two books on Japan, *Promenades japonaises I* (Japanese Walks I, 1878) and *Promenades japonaises II, Tokyo–Nikko* (Japanese Walks II, Tokyo–Nikko, 1880). In Japan, he traveled in the company of the painter Félix Régamey.

Guji. Chief priest of one or several Shinto shrines. *See* KANNUSHI.

Gukanshō. "Notes on Bizarre Ideas," a history of Japan written in 1219 by the Buddhist monk Jien (1155–1225) according to the views of the Tendai-shū sect and the idea that events are submitted to the will of contradictory divinities and "principles" *(dōri). See* JIEN.

Gukei. Painter (Sumiyoshi Hirozumi; Naiki; *gō:* Gukei, 1631–1705) and Buddhist monk. He studied with his father, Jokei, and created a style of his own for *emakimono* illustration, thus founding the Sumiyoshi school. He received the title of Hōgen and was a painter *(oku-eshi)* of the Edo shogunate.

Gukei Yūe. Zen Buddhist monk (Gen'an, fourteenth century) and painter, Tesshū Tokusai's disciple, head of the Manju-ji temple in Kyoto. In his images of divinities, he somewhat imitated Chinese styles, notably those of Yan Hui and Muqi. He also painted landscapes in ink imitating the style of the Chinese painter Yujian.

Gukyoku Reisai. Zen Buddhist monk and painter (1370–1452) who lived at the Kenchō-ji in Kamakura and the Tōfuku-ji in Kyoto, where he was Minchō's student.

Gumma-ken. Gumma prefecture in central Honshu, northwest of the Kantō. Most of the towns in this prefecture, which is mountainous except in the southeast, are on the Kanto plain. It was part of the former Kōzuke province, which was shared among a number of daimyo during the fifteenth and sixteenth centuries. The Tonegawa River crosses it. *Main city:* Maebashi. *Major cities:* Annaka, Fujioka, Kiryū, Ōta, Tatebayashi, Numata (in the north). *Area:* 6,356 km^2. *Pop.:* 2 million. This province has many archeological sites dating from the Jōmon to the Yayoi period; one of the most remarkable is in Iwa-juku.

• **Gumma Jiken.** Series of peasant riots that took place in the southern part of Gumma prefecture in May 1884, provoked by Matsutaka Masayoshi's deflationist policy. Because they were not able to demonstrate at the emperor's inauguration of a new train station—the ceremony had been postponed to avoid problems—more than 3,000 peasants attacked the house of a usurer and a police station. They were arrested, and their leaders were sentenced to prison in 1887.

Gumpai-uchiwa. Nonfolding fan *(uchiwa)* made of metal, leather, or wood, decorated with a sun on one side and a moon on the other. It was used during battles by commanders to indicate to their troops what movements to make or to transmit orders. It is still used by sumo referees. Also called *gumbai-uchiwa, gunsen. See* UCHIWA.

Gun. "War." This word indicates everything related to war and warriors. *See* GUNKI-MONOGATARI, GUNDAN.
   • Former administrative division corresponding to a district, governed by a *gunji* chosen from among the influential families in the region, who was subordinate to the *kokushi,* or lords of the *koku (kuni,* provinces) during the *ritsuryō* period (late seventh–late tenth century). The word *gun* is still used to mean "district."

• *Gunchūjō.* Reports made by samurai after a battle describing their exploits. The reports had to be verified by the superiors of the samurai, who put their monogram *(kaō)* on them, and they were then used to accord land, promotions, or honors.

• **Gundai.** Intendant of a region or administrator of a town, under the shogun's orders. In the Edo period, *gundai* were generally put in charge of shogunal lands *(tenryō)* whose revenue exceeded 100,000 *koku.* At the end of the Edo shogunate, there were four *gundai,* those of Kantō, Mino, Hida, and Saigoku. The daimyo also appointed *gundai* to administer the largest districts in their estates.

• **Gundan.** "Army corps." Provincial military troops before the ninth century. They were abolished by Emperor Kammu, with the exception of those defending northern Honshu and Kyushu.

• "War stories," accounts of battles and feats of war popular during the Edo period. They consisted mainly of more or less legendary biographies of famous warriors that had little to do with historical veracity. Many of these stories (which were inspired by the *Taiheiki*) were adapted for Kabuki theater. In the nineteenth century, stories drawn from Chinese epics and recent events such as the Opium War (1842) and the Taiping Rebellion (1850–84) were added. *See* GUNKI-MONOGATARI.

Gundari Myō-ō. Esoteric Buddhist divinity corresponding to the Indian divinity Kundalī, the "dispenser of Amrita" (*Jap.:* Kanro), an "angry manifestation" of Hōshō Nyorai (*Skt.:* Ratnasambhava) in the south, and sometimes also of Kokūzō Bosatsu (*Skt.:* Ākashagarbha) or Shō Kannon Bosatsu (*Skt.:* Avalokiteshvara). Also called Daishō Myō-ō, Kanro Gundari, Kirikiri Myō-ō, Nampō Gundari Yasha. *See* MYŌ-Ō.

• **Gundari-in (Gundari Ken-in).** Mudra *(Jap.: in)* specific to Gundari Myō-ō. Also called *tsurugi-in* (of the sword) and *myō-ō-in.*

Gunji Shigetada. Navy officer (Kōda Shigetada, 1860–1924), born in Edo. In 1892, disappointed that Japan seemed to have abandoned colonization of the Kuril Islands (Chishima Rettō), he resigned and founded a society; the following year, he and 60 volunteers left in five ships to colonize the island of Shimushiru. In 1904, he sent his troops on an assault of Kamchatka but was taken prisoner by the Russians. In 1914, he tried to settle in Siberia, but he was forced to return to Japan because of poor health in 1920. He was Kōda Rohan's older brother.

Gunka. "Military songs." These old marching songs had gradually been forgotten, but they were revived during the Russo-Japanese war (1904–05); during the Second World War, each soldier received a booklet containing the words to about 100 patriotic and war songs that he was supposed to learn by heart. Some songs were from the late nineteenth and early twentieth centuries, such as *Kitare ya kitare* (1893), *Gunkan kōshinkyoku* (Armored Advance, 1900), and *Sen'yū* (Death of the Brave Soldiers, 1905).

Gunkan. Title of general inspectors of the shogun's armies. Starting in 1829, the title of *gunkan-bugyō* was given to the minister of the navy in the Edo shogunate.

Gunki-monogatari. "War stories," a literary genre that developed late in the Kamakura period and that was very much in fashion during the Muromachi period. *Gunki-monogatari* told mainly about events that took place in the late twelfth century leading to the rise of Minamoto no Yoritomo. The main works in this "heroic" genre were the *Hōgen monogatari,* the *Heiji monogatari,* the *Gempei seisuiki,* and the *Taiheiki.* Many feats were later drawn from these epics and adapted for Noh and Kabuki theater. More recently, booklets by Chikamatsu Monzaemon and the *Chūshingura* were also considered *gunki-monogatari.* Sometimes shortened to *gunki-mono. See* GUNDAN.

Gunsen. War fan, similar to a *hi-ōgi,* whose blades were made of iron, sometimes used as a weapon. Its decoration and use were similar to those on *gumpai-uchiwa. See* FANS, ŌGI, UCHIWA.

Gunsho ichiran. Historical bibliography compiled by Osaki Masayoshi in 1802. This six-volume work gives short summaries of almost 1,700 history books.

• *Gunsho ruijū.* "Repertory of Classics," large bibliography of old history books, classic works, and documents, compiled by Hanwa Hokiichi from 1779 to 1819. It comprises 1,270 documents divided into 530 sections. It was supplemented in 1822 by *Zoku gunsho ruijū* (2,103 documents in 1,150 sections). Hanawa was assisted in this huge task by several scholars, among them Yashiro Hirokata and Nakayama Nobuna (1787–1836). The immense work was printed with 17,244 engraved wooden plates, with the financial assistance of the shogunate and the Kōnoike family. It was reprinted recently.

Gun'yaku. Military work parties imposed by warrior chiefs on their vassals in the Kamakura period. During the Edo period, the shogunate set precise rules for the nature and amount of services to be provided: a samurai with a revenue of 200 *koku,* for example, had to supply five men with their equipment; a daimyo worth 100,000 *koku* was obliged to provide, equipped, 1,500 men, 170 horsemen, 350 harquebusiers, 150 lancers, and 60 archers. The *gun'yaku* system was abandoned in 1867. *See* BUYAKU.

Gunze. Large thread, cotton, and silk manufacturer founded in 1896 in Kyoto. After the Second World War, it produced synthetic fibers and became one of the largest Japanese companies in this sector, with subsidiaries in Brazil, Korea, and Hong Kong, and dealers in the United States and Germany. Head office in Osaka.

Gusai. Zen Buddhist monk and poet (ca. 1280–ca. 1375), author of many *renga* ("linked *waka*") poems. In 1357, he compiled *Tsukuba-shū,* the first *renga* anthology, with the assistance of Nijō Yoshimoto, and he wrote a number of treatises on codification of *renga.* He included 136 of his own *renga* in *Tsukuba-shū.*

Gushōjin. Minor Buddhist divinity, "secretary" to the King of Hell, Emma-ten (*Skt.:* Yamarāja), corresponding to his Indian equivalent, Chitragupta.

Gusoku. Ornaments (flowers, vases, incense burners) on a Buddhist altar. Also called *mitsu-gusoku.*
• Type of light armor created in the late Muromachi period to be worn by foot soldiers *(ashigaru).* There were several types, which were more or less regulation-issue. Sometimes called *tōsei-gusoku. See also* KATCHŪ, YOROI-HITSU.

• **Gusoku-bugyō.** Starting in 1604, title of officers charged with the equipment for shogunal troops. They took the title *bugu-bugyō* after 1863. *See* BUGYŌ.

Gutai Bijutsu Kyōkai. "Art Society of the Gutai [concrete body]." An avant-garde art movement started in 1954 in the Kansai by the painter Yoshihara Jirō (?–1972) and his disciples to "create something that has never before existed." This association, praised in Europe by painters Michel Tapié and Georges Mathieu, was dissolved when its founder died.

Gyaku-enkin. Type of reversed perspective used by some painters, in which distant objects are shown as larger than closer objects.

Gyo. Fish-shaped wooden gong, used in some Buddhist temples to sound the hours.
→ *See* ROSETSU.

Gyō. Artistic style midway between the *sō* and *shin* styles.

Gyōbu-nashiji. Type of lacquered object with gold or silver inlay forming a sort of mosaic. *See* NASHIJI.

Gyōchi-sha. "Society of Heaven and Earth." A secret political organization promoting terrorism, created about 1920 by Ōkawa Shūmei, a disciple of Kita Ikki.

Gyōda. Town in northern Saitama prefecture (central Honshu) that developed around the Oshi castle in the late fifteenth century. Textile industry (mainly manufacture of *tabi). Pop.:* 75,000.

Gyōdō-men. Masks used by Buddhist monks during the *neri-kuyō* rituals, representing the faces of Buddhist divinities as they are traditionally portrayed.

Gyōgen. Buddhist monk (1097–1155) of the Tendai-shū, one of Fujiwara no Morozane's sons. He was appointed *zasu* of the Enryaku-ji, then *dai-sōjō.*
• Buddhist monk and painter (thirteenth century) of the Ichijō-ji temple. Starting in 1286, he made paintings for the Kasuga Shinto shrine in Nara. He received the title Hokkyō, then Hōgen.

Gyōkai. Sculptor (early thirteenth century), student of Kaikei, maker of Buddhist sculptures, including a Shaka Nyorai (at the Daihōn-ji) and the halo on the large statue of Jūichimen Kannon in the Hase-dera in 1220.

Gyōkei. Buddhist monk (1101–65), seventeenth son of Emperor Shirakawa. Also called Koma-sōjō, Sakurai-sōjō.

Gyōki (Gyōgi). Buddhist monk (688–749) of the Hossō-shū sect, born in Izumi province. He lived at the Yakushi-ji temple in Nara, then traveled throughout Japan with his disciples, building temples and creating charitable institutions. As an architect, he helped to build the great Tōdai-ji temple, which earned him the title and rank of Dai Bosatsu and Dai-sōjō (great bishop, or primate) awarded by Emperor Shōmu Tennō. A student of Eki, Gien, and Tokkō, he was one of the first to expound the doctrines of the Ryōbu-shintō (*see* GONGEN). He is said to have imported from Korea an improved potter's wheel *(rokuro).* He also sculpted Buddhist images.

Gyokudō. Painter (Uragami Gyokudō, Uragami Hitsu, Heiemon; *azana:* Kumpo; *gō:* Kinshi Gyokudō, 1745–1821) of the Nanga school, born in Bizen province. He was a major Chinese-language poet and composed many *saibara* for the koto. In 1794, after his wife died, he began to lead an itinerant life with his two sons, Shunkin and Shūkin, playing the koto and painting landscapes. Toward the end of his life, he lived in Kyoto with Shunkin and continued to paint landscapes in China ink on small pieces of paper. Also called Ki no Gyokudō. *See* KAWAI GYOKUDŌ, SHUNIN.

• **Gyokudō Bijutsu-kan.** Art museum in Ōme, a Tokyo suburb, devoted to works by the painter Kawai Gyokudō (1873–1957). It was built by Yoshida Isoya in 1961. *See* KAWAI GYOKUDŌ.

Gyokuembō. Zen Buddhist monk (d. 1661) who was probably the designer of the garden at the Chion-in in 1648. He was probably also a student of Kobori Enshū, and of his brother Kobori Masaharu, with whom he designed the garden for the Fumon-ji temple in Osaka prefecture.

Gyokuen. Zen Buddhist monk, scholar, and painter (Bompō, Gyokukei; *gō:* Shōrin, Gyokuen, 1348–ca. 1420), of the Muromachi *suiboku* school. He was abbot of the Kennin-ji and Nanzen-in temples in Kyoto. He painted mainly orchids, somewhat imitating the style of Tesshū Tokusai. He was also a poet, musician, and calligrapher.
→ *See* SESSAI.

Gyokugan. Technique of inlaying painted-glass or crystal eyes of statues in wood or lacquer from the back to make Buddhist images more lifelike. Pioneered by Unkei in the mid-twelfth century, it was part of the effort made by both painters and sculptors to attain greater realism.

Gyoku-hai. Rosary with wooden or ivory beads, hung from the belt *(hira-o)* of *sokutai* costumes. *See* JUZU.

Gyokuran. Painter (Ikeno Machi; *gō:* Kattankyo, Gyokuran, 1728–84) of the Nanga school, Ikeno Taiga's wife and student.

Gyokusan. Painter (Okada Shōyū; *azana:* Shitoku, 1737–1812) of ukiyo-e prints in Osaka. He specialized in illustrating books *(Taikōki)* and received the title Hokkyō.

Gyokusen. Kyoto painter (Mochizuki Shigemori; Tōbe; *gō:* Gyokusen, 1692–1755). His style shows the influence of Motonobu and Tosa Mitsushige.

• Painter (Mochizuki Shigemine; Shunzō; *azana:* Shuitsu; *gō:* Gyokkei, Gyokusen II, 1834–1913) who worked in Kyoto.
• Sculptor of netsuke (Isshu, born 1924).
→ *See* HOSOI KŌTAKU, MOTONOBU, NAO-TAKE (GYOKUSEN III), SEISEN-IN.

• **Gyokusen-ji.** Buddhist temple in Shimoda, where the first American consul, Townsend Harris, lived in 1856.

Gyokushō. Tokyo painter (Kawabata Takinosuke, Kawabata Gyokushō; *gō:* Keitei, 1842–1913). He studied Western painting with Charles Wirgman, then the Bunjinga (Nanga) style, and later worked in the style of the Maruyama-Shijō school, in the Nihonga genre. He had exhibits in Paris (1900) and St. Louis (1904) and taught at the Tokyo School of Fine Arts (Tokyo Bijutsu Gakkō) from 1890 to 1912. In 1909, he founded his own painting school and worked mainly for the imperial household. His best-known disciples are Yūki Somei (1875–1957) and Hirafuku Hyakusui.
→ *See* SHŌGI.

Gyokushū. Painter (Kuwayama Shisan; Sanai; *azana:* Meifu; *gō:* Kakuseki-en, Chōudo, Kasetsudō, Gyokushū, 1743–99) of the Nanga school, friend of Ikeno Taiga. He wrote two books on art theory, *Gyokushū-gashū* and *Kaiji-higen.*
→ *See* KAWAI GYOKUDŌ.

Gyokuyō. "Leaves of Jade," Kujō Kanezane's diary, in 66 chapters. It describes, in elegant Chinese prose, the events of the period from 1164 to 1200. Also titled *Gyokukai. See* FUJIWARA NO KANEZANE.

• *Gyokuyō waka-shū.* "Collection of *Waka* of the Leaves of Jade," the fourteenth official poetry anthology (*see* CHOKUSEN WAKA-SHŪ), compiled from 1312 to 1314 by Kyōgoku Tamekane on Emperor Fushimi's order. It is 20 volumes long and contains 2,796 poems. Title abridged to *Gyokuyō-shū.*

Gyokuzan. Family of nineteenth-century sculptors of netsuke:
—**Gyokuzan** (Isshinsai Gyokuzan).
—**Gyokuzan** (Asahi Gyokuzan, Asahisei, 1843–1923), sculptor of ivory. He was a professor at the Tokyo School of Fine Arts (Tokyo Bijutsu Gakkō).

Gyōnen. Buddhist monk (1240–1321) of the Kegon-shū sect, born in Iyo province (Ehime prefecture), who lived at the Tōdai-ji temple in Nara. He is said to have written more than 120 works on all aspects of Buddhism. His *Hasshū kōyō,* dated 1268, is an excellent introduction to Buddhist philosophy.

Gyoran Kannon Bosatsu. One of the 33 forms of Kannon Bosatsu (*Skt.:* Avalokiteshvara), portrayed as a woman holding a basket of fish. Sometimes portrayed standing or sitting on a carp *(koy),* as in a famous drawing in Hokusai's *Manga,* she is considered the protector of fishers and beings of the sea. Legend has it that she appeared in China, in Jiangxi province, in 818. *See* SANJŪSAN ŌGESHIN.

Gyōsai. Painter (Kawanabe Nobuyuki; Tōyū; *go:* Kyōsai, Gyōsai, 1831–89), born in Shimōsa province (Ibaraki prefecture) to a samurai family. He was Utagawa Kuniyoshi's student and then studied the painters of the Kanō family. He made ukiyo-e prints using a very personal technique, sometimes influenced by Hokusai. His caricatures displeased the Meiji government and landed him in jail for several months in 1869. He sent his works to the Vienna Exhibition in 1873 and to the Paris Exhibition in 1878. A very prolific artist, he was greatly popular and had many students, among them the English architect Josiah Conder. Also called Shōjō Kyōsai.
→ *See* HANKŌ (FUKUDA).

Gyōsei Shidō. "Administrative guide," extra-legal procedure through which government agencies control and regulate Japanese trade activities without recourse to the laws in force.

Gyōson Sōjō. Buddhist monk (ca. 1056–1135). Son of Sangi Minamoto no Motohira, he was appointed *zasu* of the Tendai-shū sect. He was a famous *waka* poet.

Gyotai. In the Nara and Heian periods, wooden box or shelf measuring about 8 × 3 cm, carried by courtiers and bureaucrats in the imperial court to indicate their rank. This custom was copied from that prevailing in the Tang court in China. *See* SHAKU.

Gyōyō. Metal ornaments on horses' harnesses, in the shape of a ginkgo *(itchō)* leaf, mainly in the Nara and Heian periods.

Gyūka. Nineteenth-century family of doll makers in Uji. The first (Kambayashi Gyūka, Rakushiken, 1801–70) also sculpted netsuke. His son (Gyūka II, Rakushiken Kyūsen) worked with him.

Gyūsha. Two-wheeled chariot pulled by an ox, used as a means of transport for the nobility in the Heian period. Although horses were used for riding, they were never used for pulling, a function reserved for oxen. The wheels of *gyūsha* were very large, often as tall as a man, with very wide rims and spokes. On the platform was a light wicker or wooden structure enclosed with curtains. Some *gyūsha* were sumptuously decorated, often to match the clothing of the owners. In the Kamakura period, use of *gyūsha* declined in favor of palanquins *(kago),* and they were used only to transport merchandise. Also called *gissha, hosho-guruma, kara-guruma.*

H

H. The consonant *h,* used only in conjunction with vowels to give the five primary sounds *ha, hi, fu, he, ho,* is always aspirated (except, obviously, in *fu*). When these syllables are weakened by a nigori sign ("or °), they become *ba, bi, bu, be bo* and *pa, pi, pu, pe, po*. Associated with the sounds *ya, yu,* and *yo,* they make the sounds *bya, byu, byo* and *pya, pyu, pyo*. It should be recalled that the sound *hu* is almost always pronounced *fu.*

Habaki. Piece of copper or brass used to keep a sword blade *(see* KATANA) in its guard *(tsuba)* and scabbard. It is sometimes reinforced with an extra piece, the *seppa. See* KYAHAN.

Haboku. Type of painting in China ink *(sumi-e)* in which the artist makes darker and lighter patches with a brush to obtain various tones of gray. This technique was imported from China in the fourteenth century and was used mainly by Zen painters and artists of the Muromachi *suiboku* school. The best-known artists using the *haboku* technique were Sesshū Tōyō, Kaihō Yūshō, and Kanō Tan'yū. *Chin.:* Pomo.

Habomai. Group of small islands linking the Kuril Islands (Chishima Rettō) to Hokkaido. The largest are Suishō *(Rus.:* Tanfiljeva; 20 km²), Yuri *(Rus.:* Juri; 10 km²), Shibotsu *(Rus.:* Zeleny; 45 km²), Taraku *(Rus.:* Polonskogo; 20 km²), Akiyuri (5 km²), and Shikotan (255 km²). Shikotan belongs to Russia; although the others have been occupied by the Russians since the end of the Second World War, they are still claimed by Japan. They are populated entirely by fishers.

Hachi bushū. In Japanese Buddhism, the "eight classes" of lower Buddhist divinities, protectors of the Law of Buddha and of the world, that do not have separate cults devoted to them: the dragons (Ryū, *Skt.:* Nāga), the titans (Yasha, *Skt.:* Yaksha), the heavenly musicians (Kandabba, *Skt.:* Gandharva), and the Kinnara (*Skt.:* Kimnara), the Karura (*Skt.:* Garuda), the Magoraka (*Skt.:* Mahorāga), and the ordinary gods (Ten, *Skt.:* Deva). Although these heavenly beings were sometimes represented (mainly during the Nara and Heian periods), only the dragons (Ryū) are the object of popular cults, and the ordinary gods (Ten) of some veneration.

Hachi dai-shū. General title for eight *(hachi)* official anthologies of *waka* poems published between 905 and 1205. *See* CHOKUSEN WAKA-SHŪ.

• *Hachi dai-shū shūitsu*. Anthology of 80 *waka* poems compiled in 1234 by Fujiwara no Teika.

Hachi-gyaku. "Eight crimes," according to the Taihō (701) and Yōrō (applied in 757) codes, liable for the death penalty, forced labor, or banishment depending on the social status of the criminal. The first three were all punishable by death for the accused and his family: (1) rebellion against the emperor, (2) desecration of holy sites, and (3) treason against the government. The other crimes were punished less severely: (4) murder of a member of one's own family, (5) murder of one's wife or members of her family, (6) theft or damage of imperial or religious property, (7) notorious ingratitude toward one's parents, and (8) murder of a superior or a teacher. These crimes could never be pardoned.

Hachihon. Branch of the Buddhist sect of the Hokke-shū founded by the monk Nichi-ryū in

Ikegami in 1240. His name was changed to Hommon Hokke-shū in 1898. *See* NICHIREN-SHŪ.

Hachijō-shima. Island in the Izu Shichitō archipelago, located south of Oshima, about 200 km southeast of the Izu Peninsula, and four volcanic islets (two dormant craters, 854 and 701 m in altitude), administered by Tokyo prefecture. During the Edo period, criminals were exiled to these islands, which are now populated by fishers and farmers. A high-quality natural yellow silk *(kihachijō)* is produced there. On holidays, bullfights are organized there. Also called Hachijō-jima.

Hachijō Toshihito. Imperial prince (1579–1629), younger brother of Emperor Go-Yōzei. He had the Katsura villa built in Kyoto. His son, Hachijō Noritada, expanded the building and the garden. *See* KATSURA RIKYŌ.

Hachi-kazuki. Book in the *otogi-zōshi* series recounting the famous story of a young woman with a bowl haircut who married a prince and who was thus the Japanese equivalent of Cinderella.

Hachikō. Famous statue of a dog by Andō Teru (1892–1945), located in front of the Shibuya railroad station in Tokyo, near a fountain. The dog came to this spot every evening at the same time to greet its master when he came home from work, and continued to come to the same place at the same time after its owner died. The city made the statue to honor the dog's loyalty. It is a favorite meeting place for Tokyo residents.

Hachimaki. Small towel *(tenugui)* or strip of canvas often worn tied around the head by men during certain festivals or religious ceremonies. The *hachimaki* (once called *makkō*) is also worn by manual laborers to keep perspiration from running down their foreheads. It is popular belief that the *hachimaki* makes its wearer stronger, and in the past many soldiers wore a *hachimaki* decorated with the emblem of the Rising Sun or other propitiatory calligraphy to show their determination in battle. On their birthdays (Tango no Sekku), boys also wear a sort of crown of iris leaves (which, because they are shaped like sword blades, are supposed to confer bravery) to symbolize a *hachimaki*. Women who are ill or in labor also sometimes wear a *hachimaki* to soak up perspiration. This very old custom is illustrated in *haniwa* (fifth–seventh century).

Hachiman Dai-myōjin. Popular *kami* of war and well-being (also called Yamata, of the "eight banners") and titular divinity of the Minamoto family. Starting in the Heian period, he was identified with the spirit of the semi-legendary Emperor Ōjin. The origins of this *kami* are mysterious; he may have come from the Usa region (northern Kyushu), where it is known that he was worshiped in the eighth century *(Shoku Nihongi)*. He was, in part, claimed by Buddhism after an oracle said that he would protect construction of the great Tōdai-ji temple in Nara. He was then called Hachiman Dai-bosatsu and Sōgyo Hachiman-shin. In 859, the Buddhist monk Gyōkyō had a shrine, the Iwashimizu Hachiman-gū, built for him in Kyoto. Thereafter, worship of Hachiman spread rapidly throughout Japan, and there are now almost 25,000 shrines dedicated to him. The most popular is the Tsurugaoka Hachiman-gū in Kamakura, founded in 1191 by Minamoto no Yoritomo to celebrate the foundation of the Kamakura *bakufu.* Two other characters are often associated with Ōjin Tennō: his wife, Hime Ōkami, and his mother, Ōkinaga-Ōtarashi-hime no Mikoto, all three being venerated under the generic name Hachiman Daimyōjin. *See* HAKOZAKI HACHIMAN-GŪ, ŪJIN TENNŌ, TORII, TSURUGAOKA HACHIMAN-GŪ.

• **Hachiman-jinja.** Shinto shrine founded near the Buddhist Yakushi-ji temple (Nara) in the late ninth century and restored in the fifteenth century (Wakamiya-shaden) and in 1603.

• *Hachiman matsuri yomiya no nigiai.* Kabuki play produced at the Saruzawa-sa theater in Edo by the actor Kumasaburō in 1860. "Sensational Event at the Hachiman Festival on a Night with a Full Moon" is the story of a young geisha, Minokichi, killed by a rejected lover, Jinnosuke.

Hachimonjiya-bon. Type of *ukiyo-zōshi* books containing popular novels, published in Kyoto by the publisher Hachimonjiya Jishō in the early eighteenth century, then by other publishers. Many of these novels, written by Ejima Kiseki among others, were adaptations of *jōruri* or Kabuki plays. Although their literary quality was mediocre, they had a great influence on subsequent literature, notably *yomi-hon.*

• **Hachimonjiya Jishō.** Writer and publisher (1666–1745) of *ukiyo-zōshi* novels, using the *gō* Jishō. His first publications were *jōruri* texts, followed by critical works on Kabuki theater *(Yakusha hyōbanki)*. He often signed the works of Ejima Kiseki, his main author, with his own publisher's name.

Hachinohe. City in Aomori prefecture (northern Honshu) and major fishing port on the Pacific Ocean, which developed around the Nambu castle during the Edo period. Main industries: fishing, chemicals, and paper. There is a major festival (Emburi Matsuri) February 17–20 to ensure good harvests; the city's great festival takes place around the Shinra Shinto shrine August 20–23. *Pop.*: 225,000.

Hachi no ki. Title of a Noh play: an old couple cut three sacred trees in their garden to make a fire so that they can provide a better reception for Hōjō Tokiyori. When he comes to power, the *shikken* thanks the couple by giving them gifts.

Hachiōji. District located about 40 km from central Tokyo; in the Edo period, it was an important waystation *(shuku-eki)* on the Koshū-kaidō road. It now has a military base and is the location of chemical and textile industries, as well as several university faculties. *Pop.*: 400,000.

Hachirōgata. Shallow (depth 4.7 m) lake in northwestern Akita prefecture, once the second largest in Japan after Lake Biwa. Most of it was drained from 1957 to 1966 to recover arable land. It originally had an area of 220 km² but is now only 48 km² in area and has a circumference of 78 km. Also called Koto-no-umi.

Hachirō Tametomo. Famous twelfth-century archer, hero of *Yumiharizuri,* a novel by Kyokutei Bakin. Also called Minamoto no Tametomo.

Hadaka no shima. "The Naked Island," a black-and-white film by director Shindō Kaneto, a huge success in the West and winner of the first prize at the 1961 Moscow Film Festival. It is about the hard, labor-filled life of a family of poor peasants on a small island in the Inland Sea with no source of fresh water. The stars were Tonoyama Taiji and Otowa Nobuko. This feature film is notable for having almost no dialogue.

Hagakure. "In the Shadow of the Leaves," abridged title of *Hagakure kikigaki* (Notes Heard in the Shadow of the Leaves), a didactic work for samurai containing about 1,300 stories and essays. It was compiled in 1716 by Yamamoto Tsunetomo (1659–1719), a samurai from Hizen province who became a monk after the death of his lord, Nabeshima Mitsushige (1632–1700). He is said to have dictated it to another samurai, Tashiro Tsuramoto (1687–1748). The first definition of the

notion of Bushido (the Way of the Warrior) as a path of dying in the service of one's lord is found in this work. It has become a classic for all martial-arts practitioners and was the subject of *Hagakure nyumon* (1968), a novel by author-actor Mishima Yukio.

Haga Yaichi. Professor (1856–1927) of Japanese literature at Tokyo University. He applied the German school's methods of philology to study of the classics in *Kokubungaku shi jikkō* (History of Classic Japanese Literature, 1899), *Meiji bunten* (Grammar of Modern Japanese, 1904), and *Kokuminsei jūron* (1907). *See* GENSEN.

Hagi. Port in Yamaguchi prefecture (Honshu) on the Sea of Japan, seat of the Mōri family daimyo system during the Edo period. In Hagi are the imposing ruins of the family's castle, many samurai houses, and the house in which Yoshida Shōin established his school, the Shōka Sonjuku. Hagi is known mainly for its ceramics (Hagi-*yaki*). Metallurgic industries and fishing. *Pop.*: 55,000. *See* CHŌSHŪ.

• **Hagi no Ran.** Rebellion by the samurai of Hagi, led by Maebara Issei, which took place in October 1876, when the Meiji government revoked their privileges. The imperial garrison of Hiroshima quickly quelled the rebellion, and Maebara and his accomplices were sentenced to death.

• **Hagi-yaki.** Ceramics fired at high temperature produced in Hagi and Fukuwa (town in Nagato), made by potters who went to Japan from Korea following the invasion of their country by Hideyoshi around 1598, and whose kilns were built by Rikei (Kōrazaemon). The kilns became known for their tea bowls *(chawan)* in a hard, dark clay covered with a light yellow or bluish glaze *(hakeme* type) or clay inlays *(mishima* type). These bowls may also be celadon, whitish, red, or brown, with splashes under a slip. The oldest of these kilns, with 14 firing chambers, was discovered about 1975. In the Edo period, the potters of the Saka and Miwa families, serving the Mōri family, directed production and took the names Kōrazaemon and Kyūsetsu. Other *noborigama*-type kilns were set up in Fukuwa. The tradition is alive today, and the kilns fire pottery at temperatures of 1200–1300°C. Three ceramics museums, the Kumaya Bijutsu-kan, the Ishii Chawan Bijutsu-kan, and the Hagi-yaki Tōgei Kaikan, display the best pieces produced in the region since the late sixteenth century. *See* MIWA KYŪWA.

Hagi. Plant *(Lespedeza bicolor)* in the legume family. It grows wild in Japan, producing pretty clusters of purple flowers in the fall. It was famous in antiquity as a symbol of autumn and was celebrated in many poems and anthologies (notably the *Man'yōshū*). There are many varieties.

Hagiwara (Hagihara) Hiromichi. Nationalist writer (1813–63) and scholar in traditional studies *(kokubunka)*, author of major studies on the *Genji monogatari*, the *Genji monogatari hyōshaku*, and the *Hongaku-teikō*.

Hagiwara (Hagihara) Kyōjiro. Anarchist poet (1899–1938), born in Gumma. With Tsuboi Shigeji and Okamoto Jun, he founded the poetry periodical *Aka to Kuro* (Red and Black). His main poetry collections are *Shikei senkoku* (Death Sentence, 1925) and *Dampen* (Fragments, 1931).

Hagiwara (Hagihara) Sakutarō. Symbolist poet (1886–1942), born in Gumma prefecture. He wrote a great number of *tanka* (modern *waka*) and free-verse poems and was quickly acclaimed as the best poet of his generation, in both classical and spoken language. He and a friend, poet Muroo Saisei, published a small poetry periodical, *Takujō Funsui* (Tabletop) in 1915, and another the following year, *Kanjō* (Feelings). Profoundly influenced by Edgar Allan Poe and Charles Baudelaire, Hagiwara Sakutarō had many collections published, including *Tsuki-in hoeru* (Baying at the Moon, 1917), *Atarashi yokujō* (A New Desire, 1922), *Ao neko* (The Blue Cat, 1923), *Kyomō no seigi* (Illusory Justice, 1929), *Shijin no shimei* (The Poet's Mission, 1937), *Hyōtō* (Island of Ice, 1934), *Muraka no teikō* (Resisting Nothingness, 1937), and *Shukumei* (Destiny: Prose Poems, 1939). These books had a very important influence on contemporary Japanese poetry. He also published a number of critical essays on poetry, including *Shi no genri* (Poetic Principles, 1925), *Ren'ai meika-shū* (The Best Love Poems, 1931), *Nihon-e no kaiki* (Return to Japanese Sources, 1938). After leading an itinerant and somewhat reckless life, Hagiwara Sakutarō died of pneumonia.

Hagiwara (Hagihara) Yūsuke. Astronomer and mathematician (1897–1979), born in Osaka. He was particularly interested in the mechanics of heavenly bodies. A professor at Tokyo University from 1946 to 1957, he was appointed director of the Tokyo astronomical observatory in 1954 and received the Order of Culture (Bunka-shō) the same year. Among his publications are *Temmongaku* (As-

tronomy, 1956), and *Celestial Mechanics* (1970, 1972). An asteroid between Mars and Jupiter has been named after him.

Hagoita. Small wooden racket used to play *hanetsuki*, or "shuttlecock game." It is decorated on the back with propitiatory symbols and sometimes the image of a geisha or Kabuki actor, which may be painted on silk and glued on. The custom seems to go back to the fifteenth century, when young noblewomen played in the imperial court. The players batted a shuttlecock *(hane)* adorned with feathers, trying to keep it in the air as long as possible. Points were awarded according to the number of times the *hane* fell to the ground. Although *hanetsuki* is rarely played today, custom has it that young women play at the beginning of the year and during some major festivals. At the end of each year, *hagoita* fairs *(hagoita ichi)* are held throughout Japan, and *hagoita* are purchased more as decorations or talismans than for use in playing *hanetsuki*. In Tokyo, this fair generally starts on December 15 at the Fudo shrine in Fukagawa and at the Asakusa-jinja. The game of *hanetsuki* is sometimes called *oibane*. See ASAKUSA.

Hagoromo. "The Dress of Feathers," an old story that inspired a famous Noh play: a heavenly divinity, descending to a beach to bathe, leaves her dress of feathers on the sand. A fisherman sees the young beauty and, desiring her, hides her dress. The divinity has no choice but to become the fisherman's wife. After bearing children with him, she begs her husband to return her dress of feathers. When he does so, she regains her divine nature; before she returns to her heavenly home, she dances for the fisherman to thank him.
→ *See* FUJI-SAN.

Hagurome. Paste for blackening the teeth, made mainly of iron oxide and gallnuts *(fushi)*, used until the Meiji period by women and men of the upper classes. See DETSUSHI.

Haguro-san. Hill 436 m high in Yamagata prefecture (northern Honshu), one of the three peaks of the Dewa-sanzan, along with the Gassan and the Yudono-san. Famous for the Shinto shrine on its summit, visited by Shu-gendō followers, and for its hundred-year-old cedars. *See* DEWASANZAN-JINJA.

Hai. "Forbidden," "banned." *See* hai-butsu, hai-chō, haihan chiken.
• "Okay," equivalent to "yes."

• **Haishitsu.** Tax exemption offered, in the code of the Taihō period, to people with disabilities or injuries.

• **Hai-tashi.** Term for imperial princes (Shinnō, Taishi) deprived of their titles because of their crimes.

• **Hai-tei.** Title for a deposed emperor or empress.

• **Haitōrei.** Decree issued in 1876, forbidding former samurai from carrying swords. Soldiers and police officers, however, were allowed to carry them, and they could be carried during certain ceremonies.

Haibun. Literary genre consisting of short prose essays, sprinkled with haiku, on light, even humorous subjects, addressed to the common people; quite popular during the Edo period. The first *haibun* collection was *Takagura* (An Attic of Treasures) by Yamaoka Genrin (1631–72); the master of the genre was Matsuō Bashō. The first *haibun* anthology, the *Fūzuoku monzen,* compiled by Morikawa Kyōroku, was published in 1706. Yosa Buson, Yokoi Yayū, and, in the nineteenth century, Kawakami Bizan were among the best *haibun* authors; two of the best examples are Yoshida Kenkō's *Tsurezure gusa* and Sei Shōnagon's *Makura no sōshi.*

Haibutsu kishaku. "Against the Buddha and against Shaka [Shakyamuni]," a religious reform movement in the very early Meiji period (from 1868 to 1871) that aimed to place Shinto shrines completely beyond the grasp of Buddhism and to promote Shinto as the state religion. This movement led to the destruction of some Buddhist temples, notably in Kyushu, but never took on the scope of a true persecutory movement. It ended up with the effective separation of state Shinto and Buddhism and the reorganization of both religions.

Haichō. Period of mourning observed in the former imperial court, lasting three days, when a high-ranking bureaucrat died. *See* FUNERALS.

Haiden. In a Shinto shrine, name for a room for worship before the Honden (Holy of Holies) and rooms used for offerings.

Haihan chiken. "Destruction of the *han* and establishment of the prefectures." This imperial order in 1871 abolished provincial estates and clans *(han)* and replaced them with new administrative divisions (prefectures) called *ken,* a consequence of the decree called Hanseki-hōkan (Donation of all lands and inhabitants to the emperor).

Haikai (Haiku). "Amusing pleasantry," a type of very short free-verse poem with 17 syllables (three lines of 5, 7, and 5 syllables), constituting the first part *(hokku)* of a classic *waka* or *renga* poem. Short poems of this type were first called *haikai-hokku,* which was later abridged to *haikai* or *haiku.* Some poets, however, extended them with two lines of 7 syllables each, to form series called *haikai no renga.* These "linked poems" came to be called *haikai,* while the first part of the *hokku* (5, 7, and 5 syllables), considered an isolated poem, was called *haiku.* But it was a subtle distinction, and the terms *haiku* and *haikai* are generally applied to all three-line poems with 17 syllables. These poems are descriptive, as are some *waka:* they have to suggest an idea, a fact, or a fleeting impression, and to encourage the reader or listener to reflect on the profound significance of the words that compose the poem. A very typical *haiku* is one by the poet Kaga no Chiyo-jo (*see* CHIYO): "Yu no Hana o / Maroū Tsutsumu ya / Oboro Tsuki" (Evening flowers / so delicately caressed: / the moon veils herself).

At first considered a form of entertainment, the genre began to be counted as "serious" poetry only in the early seventeenth century, although *haijin* (*haikai* poets) made liberal use of words and expressions generally banished from classic *waka* poetry. One of the first poets to popularize the genre was Matsunaga Teitoku (1571–1653), who used many *haigon* (words categorized as "nonclassical") in his compositions. But his approach was still considered too formal, and other poets, such as Nishiyama Sōin (1605–82), created a new *haiku* school, Danrin. It is said that Ihara Saikaku, on a wager, wrote 23,500 *haiku* in 24 hours in Osaka. But the poet who endowed the genre with nobility was Matsuo Bashō. He was followed by a galaxy of other poets, chief among them Uejima Onitsura, Konishi Raizan, and Yamaguchi Sodō. The Bashō Juttetsu (Ten Great Disciples of Bashō) also helped to elevate the writing of *haikai* to an art. Many artists then began to illustrate these poems with images called *haiga.* Various movements arose to reform *haikai* and return the genre to the purity of Bashō's style, as exemplified by Yosa Buson, Iwama Otsuni (1756–1823), and Kobayashi Issa. In 1892, Masaoka Shiki established a new school of "modern *haikai*" according to which the feelings suggested had to be drawn from daily life. Naturalist, symbolist, proletarian, and romantic poets tried to produce *haiku* in their respective styles, with varying degrees of success; many published their works or findings in the magazine *Hototogisu* or, more recently, in *Nihon.* Among the thousands of modernists who excelled at the genre were Kawahigashi Hekigotō, Osuga Otsuji, Ogiwara Seisensui, Taneda Santōka Ozaki Hōsai, Nakamura Kusatao, and Yamamoto Kenkichi. In the twentieth century, the *haiku* genre became known beyond Japan, and many foreign poets, writing mainly in English and French, tried their hand at writing *haiku* (also called "epigrams"), which thus exerted some influence on Western poetry.

• **Haikai no renga.** Poetry genre midway between *renga* and *haikai (haiku)* characterized by plays on words and a freer style than the *renga.* Yamazaki Sōkan and Arakida Moritake were the best poets of this genre. *See* HAIKAI.

Haikara. Japanese expression imitating the English expression "high collar," meaning, especially in the 1920s and 1930s, elegant and stylish.

Haiku. *See* HAIKAI.

Haimyō. Pen name or nickname adopted by many haiku poets *(haijin)* and by some actors, replacing the habitual *gō. See* NAMES.

Hairstyles. In the Asuka period, the hairstyles of the nobility, imitating those in the Chinese court, followed standards of shape and color that corresponded to the rank of those who wore them *(see* I*).* The ceremonial hairstyle, or *kammuri,* generally used gauze or black-lacquered horsehair, while the nobles usually wore *eboshi* in various shapes depending on whether the wearer was a low-ranking noble, a warrior, or a peasant. Warriors wore caps *(kabuto)* or, in some cases, iron, wooden, or lacquered-leather hats *(jingasa).* Women's hairstyles also varied according to their status and the period. *See* CHON-MAGE, EBOSHI, HACHIMAKI, ICHIMEGASA, KAMMURI, KAN'I JŪNIKAI NO SEI, KASA, MAGE, ZANGIRI-MONO, and words cited. *See also* ACCESSORIES, CLOTHING, FABRICS, SHOES.

Hai-yū. "Cinder glaze," an ordinary technique for glazing ceramics, produced naturally by mixing cinders with the pottery clay.

Haji. "Shame." This term was used by the American ethnologist Ruth Benedict to characterize an important aspect of Japanese culture, in which "relative" moral values exist only when they are seen as lacking in an individual by the society of which he or she is a part. The notion of "sin" does not exist, and transgressions causing shame are brought about only through societal sanction. In Japanese society, individuals who are thus sanctioned have a certain freedom of action. By extension, Japanese people would have a tendency to give freer rein to their instincts and feelings in a foreign country than at home, which would tend to explain certain "wild" behaviors by some Japanese in foreign countries during wartime. However, this definition of *haji* is not accepted by all ethnologists and sociologists.

Hajibe. Families or clans of potters (some from Korea) who, from about the fourth to the seventh century, produced unvarnished pottery, evolved from Yayoi pottery, mainly for the Yamato court; they probably also made *haniwa.* It is not known exactly how these potters' *be* (occupational groupings) were organized. Also called *hanibe, haijishi, hanishi. See* BE, HANIWA.

Haji-ki. Crude pottery, generally constructed in coils of clay and smoothed on the outside and the inside, produced by *hajibe,* mainly during the period of *kofun* (great burial places). This red-brown pottery, fired at low temperature, gradually became distinct from Yayoi pottery, with fewer decorations and more standardized shapes. A typical piece is a potbellied jar with a flared neck and round bottom. Some pottery, fired in reduced heat, was blackish; these pieces were commonly called *kokushokudoki* and gave rise to black textured tiles and bowls *(gaki).* The *haji-ki* tradition was maintained for quite a long period in some parts of Japan and influenced the northern culture called *satsumon.* Archeologists have classified successive phases of *haji-ki* pottery, named for the sites in Kanto where they have been discovered in quantity: Goryō (fourth century), Izumi, Yakuradai, Onitaka, Mama, Ochiai, and Kobuku (ninth century). Because of the standardized shapes of most *haji-ki* pots, however, it remains difficult to place them in precise sequences.

Hajin. Haiku poet (Hayano Hajin, Yahantei, 1677–1742), Yosa Buson's master. *See* BUSON.

Haji Seiji. Writer (Akamatsu Shizuta, 1893–1977), born in Okayama. At first a literary and theater critic in Osaka, he became known for his popular novels, such as *Suna-e shibari* (The Curse of the

Sand Painting, 1927), *Abare noshi* (1951), and *Fūsetsu no hito* (1958), written in a polished style.

Hajō. Buddhist monk (720–814) who became famous for having pinched the nose of one of his disciples to provoke his enlightenment *(satori).*

Hakama. Wide pants traditionally worn by both men and women, then only by men in the seventeenth century. In the Meiji period, female students and professors wore *hakama,* and today *miko* (female servants in Shinto shrines) and martial-arts practitioners wear them. Men still wear them with the traditional suit during official and religious ceremonies, but they are worn less and less. *Hakama* are slit on the sides and have five pleats in the front and one large pleat in back. They are held up by a belt *(koshi-ita)* tied over the lower back and are worn with a light kimono tucked in. They are usually dark in color, although those worn by *miko* are usually red. In the martial arts, their color sometimes indicates the grade *(dan)* of the person wearing them.

Hakase. "Professor," "doctor"; a title given to an official position in the government under the *ritsuryō* system, with responsibility for teaching in *kokugaku* schools and ministries. The term is often used to designate people with doctoral degrees. Also called *hakushi.*
• Musical-notation systems used by Buddhist monks for their chants. Each sect created its own system *(meyasu* for the Tendai-shū, *kari-bakase* or *kakui* for the Shingon-shū, and so on), and many *hakase* schools were created to attempt to impose a particular system, the most famous being the O-hara. *See* FU-HAKASE, MEYASU-HAKASE.

Hakata. Bay in northern Kyushu facing the city of Fukuoka, which was constructed over part of the ancient town of Hakata. Hakata was very important in the fifteenth and sixteenth centuries thanks to its trade with China. The town of Hakata and the new city of Fukuoka were united in 1889. Korean and Mongolian troops attempted to land in Hakata Bay in 1274 and 1281; during this period, the samurai of Kyushu built a defensive wall on the shore of the bay. *See* FUKUOKA.

• **Hakata Dontaku.** Major festival of Hakata May 3–5, during which floats *(dashi)* adorned with dolls (Hakata-ningyō) representing the Seven Gods of Good Fortune (Shichifukujin) are rolled through the streets. *See* FUKUOKA.

• *Hakata kojorō nami-makura.* "The Pillow of Waves of Hakata's Daughter," drama for *jōruri* theater by Chikamatsu Monzaemon.

• **Hakata-ningyō.** Decorated terra-cotta dolls produced in Hakata. Often very elaborately made, they portray actors, pretty women, or historical characters. More decorative objects than toys, they are often dressed in luxurious clothing. *See* FUKUOKA.

• **Hakata-ori.** Silk and cotton fabrics produced at Hakata since at least the fifteenth century and decorated with flowers and birds in golden and silver thread mixed with colored cotton thread. Also called Kara-ori, Wata-nishiki.

Hakeme. Type of porcelain with a painted decoration, somewhat analogous to the Korean Punchŏng ceramics, with a gray-green translucid glaze. Some pieces made of gray clay are covered with a white glaze. Others bear various decorations (usually floral) carved or painted with iron oxide. Still others, somewhat similar to celadon ceramics, have a greenish slip. Also called *mishima. See* HAGI-YAKI.

Hakkō-ichiu. "Eight directions, a single roof," an expression attributed to the mythical emperor Jimmu, according to the *Nihon shoki,* signifying that he wanted to unite all tribes in a single kingdom. It was used again, in a different sense, by the Japanese government from 1940 to 1945, and by expansionists who wanted Japan to rule all of East Asia. A stele was erected in 1940 in Miyazaki (Kyushu) bearing the expression to commemorate the twenty-six-hundredth anniversary of the founding of Japan by Jimmu Tennō. This stele is now called Heiwa no Tō (Tower of Peace).

Hakodate. Port in southern Hokkaido on the Strait of Tsugaru, founded in 1741 and opened to foreign traffic through the 1854 Kanagawa Treaty. The city and its fortress (Goryōkaku) were the site of the last battle of the Boshin Civil War in June 1869 *(see* GORYŌKAKU). Damaged in 1934 by a fire and intensively bombed in the Second World War, Hakodate has once again become a fishing port and developed a number of industries, including shipbuilding and machine-tool manufacturing. *Pop.:* 325,000.

• **Hakodate-bugyō.** Bureaucrats who succeeded the Ezo-bugyō, established in 1799 by the Edo shogunate; in the early nineteenth century, they were responsible for the defense of Hokkaido and surveillance of Russian ships navigating in the Sea of Japan.

• **Hakodate Docks.** Shipbuilding yards established in Hakodate by Shibusawa Eiichi and Okura Kihachirō in 1896, specializing in construction of medium-tonnage ships, salvage, and repairs. Head office in Tokyo.

Hakone. Small town in southern Kanagawa prefecture, on Lake Ashinoko, at the foot of Mt. Fuji. On November 3 (Bunka no Hi), the town hosts a great costumed procession re-creating the processions of daimyo going to or returning from Edo. Hakone is a tourist center; the region has a dormant volcano, 1,348 m altitude, featuring six peaks and a 91 km² crater with a lake. The town has several museums: the Hakone Bijutsu-kan (previously Kyūsei Hakone Bijutsu-kan), opened in 1952, features the ceramics collections amassed by Okada Mokichi; the Chōkoku no Mori Bijutsu-kan, an open-air museum created in 1969, displays Japanese and Western paintings and sculptures in a park. *Pop.:* 25,000.

• **Hakone Gongen-jinja.** Shinto shrine founded in Hakone in 757 (according to tradition) and dedicated to the *kami* Ninigi no Mikoto, Hiko Hohodemi no Mikoto, and Konohana Sakuyahime.

• **Hakone no seki.** Barrier 32 km long erected on the Tōkaidō road in 1618 on the difficult-to-access pass going from Mishima to Odawara (Hakone Tōge). Controls there were very strict, for the shogunal authorities wanted to ensure that no weapons were brought to Edo and that the families of daimyo restricted by Sankin-kōtai could not flee Edo. This barrier, of which some vestiges survive, was abolished in 1869.

• **Hakone yōsui.** Irrigation canal built in 1670 with its source in Lake Shinoko, in Kanagawa prefecture, crossing Shizuoka prefecture. Its water, which flows through a tunnel under Mt. Hakone-yama, irrigates more than 1,000 hectares of arable land.

Hako-niwa. Miniature landscapes created in flat boxes or ceramic platters, adorned with small figurines representing houses, bridges, and people. Of Chinese origin, they were popular during the Edo period and gave rise to the art of bonsai. *See* BON-SAI.

Hakozaki Hachiman-gū. Shinto shrine in Fukuoka (Kyushu), dedicated to the semi-mythical Emperor Ōjin and Empress Jingū Kōgō, and to Hachiman Dai-myōjin. Founded in the sixteenth century (in the tenth century according to tradition), it has a two-story-high door dating from 1595 and a small museum displaying artifacts from the invading Mongolian armies of 1274 and 1281. Annual festival September 15.

Haku. Former noble title equivalent to the Western title of count. Abolished in 1945.
• Prefix (or suffix) meaning "white."

• **Hakubakai.** "Society of the White Horse," an association of Western-style painters and sculptors founded by Kuroda Seiki and other artists in 1896 in opposition to the Meiji Bijutsukai, which sponsored "official art." Hakubakai included some famous artists, such as Andō Nakatarō (1861–1913), Kuroda Kiyoteru (1866–1924), and Kume Keiichirō (1866–1934), and was influenced by French impressionism. Dissolved in 1911.

• **Hakuba no Sechi-e.** "Imperial Ceremony of the White Horse," which once took place on the seventh day of the first month of the year and during which 21 white horses were led in a procession. Also called Ao-uma-no Sechi-e. *See* GO-SECHI-E.

• **Hakubyō-ga.** "Black-and-white painting," portraits in China ink *(sumi, sumi-e)* made in Japan starting in the late Heian period, using dry brush strokes with no wash. By extension, all drawings made with pure China ink.

• **Hakudō.** "White bronze," alloy containing 70–75% copper and 25–30% tin, once used to cast Buddhist statues. *See* DŌ.

• **Hakuro.** Period of the "white dew" in the ancient agrarian culture, starting September 1 and lasting about 15 days. *Chin.:* Bailu. *See* NIJŪSHI-SETSU.

• **Haku-zōsu.** "White monk." In popular stories, an old fox *(kitsune)* who sometimes took the form of a Buddhist monk to trick people.

Hakubunkan. One of the largest publishers in Japan, founded by Ohashi Sahei and his son, Ohashi Shintarō (1863–1944), in Tokyo in 1887. It published a great number of magazines of all types and inexpensive educational books such as the 200-

volume encyclopedia *Teikoku hyakka zenshu* and the *Teikoku bunko,* a compendium of excerpts of the best Japanese literature. The company was dissolved in 1947 and reorganized under the name Hakuban Shinsha. It spun off a major advertising agency, Hakuhōdō, the second largest in Japan, after Dentsū.

Hakuchi. Era of Emperor Kōtoku: Feb. 650–Dec. 654. *See* NENGŌ.

Hakuchi. "The Idiot," novel by Sakaguchi Ango (1906–55), published in 1946, describing the sad fate of victims of the Second World War.

Hakuhō. Historical and artistic period extending from the late seventh century to the early eighth century, named for the unofficial era *(nengō)* of Emperor Temmu, 673–686, when historians say it began. This period saw the continuation of the culture of the Asuka period and greater penetration of the Chinese Tang culture and of Gupta art from India, transmitted via China and Central Asia. It was followed by the Tempyō period, during which Chinese Buddhist culture flourished in Japan.

Hakuin Ekaku. *See* HAKUIN ZENJI.

Hakuin Zenji. Zen Buddhist monk (Hakuin Ekaku, 1686–1769) of the Rinzai-shū sect, famous painter and calligrapher, born in Hara (Shizuoka prefecture). He lived at the Shōin-ji temple in the village of Suruga, then wandered from temple to temple, preyed upon by doubt, until he suddenly attained enlightenment. He returned to his home temple in 1716 and gained a large number of disciples, to whom he posed difficult metaphysical questions called *kōan (Chin.: gong'an).* He wrote a large number of religious works expounding his views on Zen in the Rinzai (*Chin.:* Linji) tradition, including *Keisō dokuzui* (Stamens and Pistils Poisoned Like Thorns), *Hōgoroku* (Notes on Conversations about the Law), *Yasen kanna* (Evening Conversation on a Boat), and a treatise on epistolary correspondence, *Orate-gama* (The Teakettle, 1749). He began to paint when he was about 60 years old; he followed the principles of the Nanga school and used mainly the sumi-e technique to portray subjects likely to provoke enlightenment. Among his best-known painting disciples were Suiō Eiboku (1716–89) and Tōrei Enki (1721–92). *Posthumous names:* Shinki Dokumyō, Shōshū Kokushi.

Hakuji. Type of porcelain covered with a transparent white glaze, sometimes spotted with blue, yellow, or green due to air impurities in the kilns.

Hakuko-ji. Buddhist temple in Sakaide (Shikoku) founded in the Kamakura period. Stone pagodas of the thirteenth and fourteenth centuries, with 13 stories of false roofs.

Hakurai. "Having come from abroad," a term used since the Nara period to designate (with a sense of admiration) all imported products and techniques. The term is also used to describe all "high-quality" objects from the West during the early Meiji era, such as watches, razors, and pens. Also Hakuraihin.

Hakurakuten. Japanese name for the great Chinese poet Bai Juyi (772–846).

• *Hakurakuten.* Title of a Noh play: the Chinese poet Bai Juyi, on his way to Japan, is forced to return to China because of a storm created by the *kami* Sumiyoshi Myōjin.

Hakuryū. Painter (Sugawara Motomichi, 1833–98) of the Nanga school, whose subject was landscapes. He lived in Tokyo.
  • Sculptor of netsuke (Miyasaka Hakuryū, mid-nineteenth century) in Kyoto.

Haku-san. Old volcano located between Gifu and Ishikawa prefectures, reaching an altitude of 2,702 m in Gozemmine. Two other volcanic peaks, Onanjimine and Kengamine, have altitudes of 2,685 and 2,656 m, respectively. Haku-san, one of the three sacred mountains of Japan, along with Fuji-san and Tateyama, has a crater lake (Senjagaike) formed after its last eruption, in 1554. Its slopes can be climbed only in summer because they are snow-covered all winter. Haku-san is within a volcanic zone that bears its name (Hakusan Kazantai).

• **Hakusan-ro.** Incense holder shaped like a mountain (Haku-san), of Chinese origin, used by the Buddhist clergy for ceremonies. This type of cult object was introduced to Japan in the Nara period.

• **Hakusan-yajin.** *See* KAZUNOBU.

Hakusukinoe no Tatakai. Famous naval battle *(tatakai)* that took place in 662 (or 663) at the mouth of the Paegchon-gang River (Paeg-gang,

Güm-gang), Korea, between Korean and Chinese forces and the Japanese fleet sent by Emperor Tenji to rescue the Paekche government. The Japanese fleet, commanded by Admiral Abe no Hirafu, were defeated. Following this, Silla (Shiragi, Sin-ra) conquered Paekche, and Japan had to abandon all hope of holding on to the Mimana and its possessions on the Korean Peninsula. The Japanese, aware of China's superiority, then resolved to create a government imitating that of the Tang, which resulted in the Taihō Reform (701) complementing the Taika Reform (645). *See* TAKAYASU-JŌ, TENJI TENNŌ.

Hakuunsai. Sculptor of netsuke (Ichijō Hakuunsai, early nineteenth century) in Edo. His son Ichijō Kitarō succeeded him, also using the *gō* Hakuuansai.

Hakyō. Painter (Kakizaki Hirotoshi; *mei:* Shōgen; *azana:* Seyū; *gō:* Kyōu, Hakyō, 1764–1826) of the Maruyama school, Maruyama Ōkyo's student.

Hama-chō. Branch of the Edo-Kanō painting school, established in an Edo district called Hama. *See* KANŌ-HA.

Hamada. Town in Shimane prefecture, on the Sea of Japan, developed around a castle in the Edo period. It is one of the largest ports in western Japan, specializing in shipping wood and industries related to fishing. Ruins of the Hamada-jō castle (seventeenth century). *Pop.:* 50,000.

Hamada Hikozō. First Japanese (1837–97) to become a United States citizen. The son of a captain from Harima province, he was shipwrecked in 1850, and his disabled ship drifted for 52 days before he and his crew were rescued by the American ship the *Oakland,* which took them to San Francisco in February 1851. He converted to Catholicism in 1854, taking the name Joseph Heco, and became a U.S. citizen in 1858. He tried to return to Japan a number of times; when he finally obtained permission, he met Townsend Harris in Shanghai and accompanied him to Yokohama in June 1859. He opened a business in Yokohama and then returned to the United States, where he had an interview with President Abraham Lincoln in March 1862. When he went back to Yokohama, he founded a newspaper, *Kaigai Shimbun* (Overseas News), which was published 1864–65. He was appointed minister of finance in the first Meiji government and wrote two books, one in Japanese,

Hyōryū-ki (Journal of a Shipwrecked Man, 1863), and the other in English, *The Narrative of a Japanese* (1895). In Japan, he was known by the nickname Amerika Hikozō.

Hamada Hirosuke. Writer (1893–1973), born in Yamagata. He was interested mainly in English literature and wrote many books for young people, including *Taishō no dōzō* (The Bronze General, 1914), *Mukudori no yume* (Dreams of a Bird, 1921), *Naita aka oni* (The Red Demon Who Cried, 1934), and a collection of stories, *Hirosuke dōwa dokuhon* (5 vols., 1925–30).

Hamada Kōsaku. Archeologist (Hamata Seiryō, 1881–1938), born in Osaka. He studied in Tokyo and Kyoto and in England, was the first archeology professor at the University of Kyoto in 1917, and was appointed president of the university in 1937. He introduced modern research methods to Japan and led digs in Japan, Korea, and China. Among his scientific publications were *Shina komeiki deishō zusetsu* (Results of Excavations in China, 1927), *Tenshō Ken'o shisetsu-ki* (Study of Christian Missions of 1582, 1931), *Tsūron kōkugaku* (Lectures on Archeology, 1922), and *Kōkogaku nyūmon* (1930).

Hamada Kunimatsu. Politician (1868–1939), leader of the Rikken Seiyūkai (Friends of Constitutional Government party). He was firmly opposed to the rise of Japanese nationalism.

Hamada Shimei. Engraver (b. 1917) and painter. He specialized in copper engravings of caricatured grotesques and battle scenes. In 1956, he received the Lugano Biennial's international award; in 1960, the Contemporary Art of Japan Exhibition prize.

Hamada Shōji. Contemporary ceramist (1894–1978), born in Kawasaki. He accompanied Bernard Leach to England and helped him set up his kilns in St. Ives, Cornwall, then returned to Japan in 1924 and settled in Mashiko (Tochigi prefecture), where an active pottery center already existed. He traveled to Okinawa, Korea, and China, collecting folk-art *(mingei)* objects and developing his techniques. He used mainly Mashiko clay and created surprising effects with just a few salt and cinder glazes. He was designated a Living National Treasure in 1955 and received the Order of Culture (Bunka-shō) in 1968.

Hamada Yahyōe. Captain (ca. 1620–30) of a Shūin-sen ship sent to Taiwan by merchant Suetsugu Heizō in 1626. Kept from landing and trading by Dutch colonists, he returned to Japan, then went back to Taiwan accompanied by armed troops and obtained satisfaction through force. The Edo shogunate conducted reprisals against the Dutch in Japan. Good relations were not restored until a Dutch delegation apologized to shogun Tokugawa Iemitsu in 1737. *See* SUETSUGU HEIZŌ.

Hamaguchi Osachi. Politician (Hamaguchi Yūkō, 1870–1931), born in Kōchi prefecture. Elected to the House of Representatives in 1915 for the Kenseikai (Constitutional Association) party, he was minister of finance in both of Katō Takaaki's cabinets (1924 and 1925), then minister of the interior in Wakatsuki Reijirō's cabinet in 1926. He was elected president of the newly formed Rikken Minseitō (Constitutional Democratic party) in 1927 and became prime minister in 1929, replacing Tanaka Giichi following the incidents in Manchuria (assassination of Zhang Zuolin). He strengthened the national economy and signed the treaty issuing from the naval conferences in London in 1930. As a result, he was accused of betraying Japan's military interests, and he was shot by a young extremist in the Tokyo railroad station in November 1930. He died of his wounds in August of the following year.

Hamaguchi Yōzō. Painter and engraver, born 1909 in Wakayama prefecture. He studied sculpture, then went to France in 1930, where his work was exhibited in the Salon d'automne, the Salon des Indépendants, and the Salon des Tuileries. He returned to Japan in 1939; after the Second World War, he devoted himself to engraving. He settled in France permanently in 1953; his pieces were in various international exhibitions and won a number of prizes.

Hamaguri Gomon Jiken. Incident that took place in August 1864. Troops of the Chōshū clan wanted to return to Kyoto to present their regrets to the emperor about the battle that had taken place in June of that year, during which a number of Chōshū samurai had been killed by shogunal troops when they tried to enter Kyoto by force. The emperor refused to receive the Chōshū envoys sent by Maki Izumi and Kusaka Genzui, and they tried to force their way into the imperial palace through the *kimmon* (or *gomon*); a clash followed during which troops from Satsuma, Aizu, and Kuwama repelled the attackers. But during the battle of August 20, a fire was started in the city and 30,000 houses were destroyed. Maki Izumi and Kusaka Genzui committed suicide and the shogunate, on the emperor's order,

sent a punitive force to deal with the Chōshū. Also called Kimmon Jiken. *See* IKEDAYA JIKEN.

Hamakita. Town in Shizuoka prefecture (central Honshu), agricultural center, automobile and textile industries. A prehistoric site was uncovered there with several *Homo sapiens* skeletons the age of which has not yet been determined. Remains of an ancient checkpoint *(sekisho)* in the nearby town of Arai. *Pop.:* 75,000.

Hamamatsu. City in Shizuoka prefecture (central Honshu) on the Tenryū-gawa river, former castle town *(jōka-machi)* and waystation *(shuku-eki)* on the Tōkaidō road during the Edo period. The town has many industries (Yamaha musical instruments, Nippon Gakko Co., motorcycles, cotton fabrics). Nearby are the site of the battle of Mikatahara (1572), the Iba archeological site, and the Kanzan-ji Buddhist temple. Crater lake (Hamana-ko), previously called Tō Tsu no Umi, connected to the sea. Eel fishing and algae farming. May 3–5, major kite competition.

• *Hamamatsu chūnagon monogatari.* "The Story of the Adviser to the Hamamatsu Circle," six-volume novel written in the eleventh century in imitation of the *Genji monogatari,* but based on the adventures of an adviser *(chūnagon)* to the court in Japan and China. It may have been the work of the author of the *Sarashina nikki,* the daughter of Sugawara no Takasue, about 1053. This work was never finished, and the first volume has been lost.

Hamano Shozui. Blacksmith and goldsmith (Masayuki, 1695–1769), famous maker of sword guards *(tsuba),* Nara Toshinaga's student. He founded a school in Hamano to teach his art. Also called Hamano Seizui.

Hamao Arata. Educational administrator (1849–1925), born in Edo. He studied in Japan and the United States, then worked at the Ministry of Education starting in 1880. As president of Tokyo University from 1893 to 1897, then minister of education in 1897, and once again president of Tokyo University from 1905 to 1912, he considerably improved educational methods. He was finally appointed chairman of the emperor's Privy Council.

Hama-rikyū Kōen. "Hama Detached Palace Garden." Municipal park in Chūō-ku (Tokyo), former residence of the Mastudaira family of Kōshū prov-

ince and of the Tokugawa shogun. *Area: 25 hectares.*

Hamaya. Arrow-shaped talismans, sold at the beginning of the year in many Shinto shrines to followers on their first visit of the year *(hatsumōde)*
and reputed to have the power to chase away evil
spirits. As followers leave the shrine, they place
hamaya between the backs of their necks and their
collars. At one time, bows were also sold for this
purpose *(hamayumi)*; children trained with them,
they were used in archery competitions, and they
augured the yield of the year's harvest. *Hamaya,*
adorned with white feathers and with a *kabura*
("turnip-shaped" whistle) in their heads, are still
placed on rooftops of newly built houses to ward
off bad luck.

Hamidashi. Short (30 cm), single-bladed dagger,
somewhat similar to an *aikuchi,* but simpler in
shape and with only a single ring as a guard *(tsuba).*
It was used mainly by women in the warrior clans to
protect themselves from assault or to cut the carotid
artery to commit suicide. *See* KATANA.

Hamon. Line running the length of the edge of the
blade of a *katana* or *tachi* sword, produced by the
clay protection of the edge during the process of
soaking the blade. Each blacksmith has his own
method for applying the clay, so *hamon* differ sub-
stantially from artisan to artisan. A more or less
straight line is called *sugu-ha,* while a wavy line is
called *midareba.* It is one of the ways of recognizing
(and appraising) a blade. *See* KATANA.

Hamuro Tokinaga. Noble of the Kyoto court (thirteenth century) with the title *dainagon,* to whom
has been attributed (without certainty) the writing
of a number of literary works, such as the *Heike,
Hōgen,* and *Heiji monogatari* and the *Gempei
seisuiki.*

Han. Estate belonging to a warrior (after the
twelfth century) or to a daimyo (Edo period). From
1868 to 1871, daimyo owning *han* received the title
Han Chiji. The *han* disappeared in 1871, when the
Meiji government absorbed them and divided them
into prefectures *(ken).*
• Seal (in wood, stone, or ivory) generally used
by most Japanese as a signature on official papers.
Also called *hanko, incan. Chin.: yin.*

• **Han.** Current name for China and Chinese
people.

• **Han-yu.** Name for the Chinese monosyllabic
language.

Hana. "The Nose." A fantasy novel by Akutagawa
Ryūnosuke, written in 1916, in which the author
tells the story of a Buddhist monk with a gigantic
nose who tries to get rid of his grotesque appendage
by any means possible. Akutagawa took the story
from an old tale in the *Konjaku monogatari* and the
Uji shui monogatari.
• Pronounced with the accent on the second syllable, this word also means flower.

Hanabusa Itchō. Painter (Taga Shinkō, Taka
Chōko, Hanabusa Nobuka; *azana:* Kunju; *mei:*
Sukenoshin; *gō:* Hanabusa Itchō, Chōko, Sasui-ō,
Kyūsōdō, Ippō-kanjin, Waō, Rin-shōan, Rin-toan,
Gyōun, Kansetsu, Kan'un, Sesshō, Undō, Hokusō-
ō, Kanō Shinkō, Kyō-undō, 1652–1724), born in
Kyoto and the son of a physician. He studied with
Kanō Yasunobu, then created the Hanabusa school
in Edo, which was distinctive for its independence
of style, more poetic and less formalistic than the
Kanō school, and typical of the "bourgeois" spirit
of the Genroku period. Hanabusa was exiled to the
island of Miyakejima in 1698 for an unknown reason, and was granted amnesty only in 1709. He
took the name Hanabusa Itchō upon his return to
Edo in 1710. As a haiku poet, he studied with
Matsuo Bashō and proved to be an excellent calligrapher. The subject matter of most of his paintings
was the daily life of city residents. Also known as
Hishikawa Waō.

Hanada Kiyoteru. Writer (1909–74) and literary
critic, born in Fukuoka. In 1939, he founded an
antimilitarist magazine, *Bunka Soshiki;* after the
Second World War, he contributed to the magazine
Kindai Bungaku. He became known for his collection of antifascist essays, *Fukkōki no seishin*
(1946), which spread the notion of Marxist dialectics among the common people. His writings were
collected in *Hanada kiyotera chosaku-shū* (1963–
66).

Hana-garuta. Very popular card game (also called
hana-awase, hanafuda) played with 48 cards divided into 12 series of 4 cards, corresponding to the
months of the year. The cards represent flowers and
are worth points—20, 10, 5, or 1—depending on
the images depicted on them. The flowers are pine
(January), plum blossom (February), cherry blossom (March), wisteria (April), iris (May), poppy
(June), *hagi,* or Japanese bush clover (July), grass

(August), chrysanthemum (September), maple (October), rain and leaves (November), and paulownia (December). The rules differ greatly depending on the categories of players. In each series, the card that is worth the most points has the image of a bird, an animal, or the sun. The cards are small (about 6 × 4 cm) and have a black back. In the working class, people play for money. The game, it seems, was created during the Heian period and called *kachō-awase*. It became known by its current name in the late sixteenth century, when the Dutch imported European cards to Japan, but it did not become really popular until the early nineteenth century. *See* KARUTA.

Hana-gatami. Title of a Noh play: a weeping woman seeks her lover in vain and dances before the emperor (who had been her lover, but she doesn't recognize him) to express her sadness. She then gives him a bouquet of flowers as a gift.

Hana-hijiki. In traditional Japanese architecture, *hijiki* decorated with sculptures and moldings, especially in the Kara-yō mode of construction. *See* HIJIKI, TO-KYŌ.

Hanai Takuzō. Jurist (Tachihara Takuzō, 1868–1931), adopted by the Hanai family in 1888. President of the Tokyo bar in 1909, he wrote many law books and helped revise the criminal code (1907) and the laws ruling courts-martial (1921). As a lawyer, he became known for his involvement with the great criminal trials of his time. He was elected to the House of Representatives many times (1898–1903, 1904–20), to the House of Peers in 1922, and was an active participant in movements favoring universal suffrage.

Hana Matsuri. "Flower Festival," the name of several festivals, notably the *kambutsu-e* (Buddha's birthday, April 7) in various Shinto shrines in April and the festival of Kita Shitara (Aichi prefecture) at the end of the year; during these festivals, flowers are offered to the divinities.

Hanami. "Flower viewings," popular festivities during the first blossoming of the plum trees *(ume)* and cherry trees *(sakura),* celebrated on traditional dates in spring depending on the region. It is a time for people to rejoice and have pleasant picnics under flowering boughs. An aristocratic pastime since at least the Heian period, the *hamani* became popular during the Edo period and is now followed meticulously. Every day, announcements of where the cherry trees are blossoming are made on radio and television. Some sites have become famous for their flowers, and crowds gather to enjoy themselves by dancing, eating, singing, and drinking copious amounts of *sake.* Among the most popular sites are Ueno Park in Tokyo, the Arashiyama hill in Kyoto, the park and castle in Osaka, and Yoshinoyama Park in Nara.

Hanamichi. "Path of flowers," a raised passage crossing the hall in Kabuki theaters, allowing actors to go from their boxes to the stage so that the audience can see them up close. *See* HASHI-GAKARI.

Hanaoka Seishu. Physician (Hanaoka Shin, Hanaoka Zuiken, Umpei, Hakugyō, 1760–1835), born in Kii province (Wakayama prefecture), known for having performed, after 20 years of experimentation, the first operation under general anesthetic (with *datura*), for breast cancer, in 1805. The operation was a success, and he performed many others on people with malignant tumors, gangrene, and other serious conditions. He had many students eager to operate according to what was thereafter called the "Hanaoka method." *See* ARIYOSHI SAWAKO.

Hanasaka jijii. "The Old Man Who Makes the Trees Blossom," a popular legend telling the story of an old man who finds gold, assisted by a miraculous dog. One of his neighbors is jealous and kills the dog. The old man buries the dog under a tree that he later cuts down to make himself a mortar. Each time he piles rice in the mortar, the rice is transformed into pieces of gold. The evil neighbor borrows the marvelous mortar but cannot get anything from it; out of spite, he burns it. The old man then throws the ashes of the mortar onto dead trees, which miraculously begin to grow leaves and flower once again.

Hanasanjin. Writer (Hosakawa Namijirō; *gō:* Tōri Sanjin, Hanasanjin, 1790–1858), Santō Kyōden's disciple. He wrote many working-class novels in the *ninjōbon* genre. However, his writing quickly went out of style and he ended life as a seller of cheap books. Among his best works are *Satokagami* (Mirror of a Blossoming Village, 1822) and *Kuruwa zōdan* (Tales of the Pleasure Districts, 1825).

Hana-shizume no Matsuri. Old Shinto festival celebrated at the end of spring to honor the *kami* Omiwa and Sai, considered protectors against epidemics.

Hanawa Hokiichi (Hoki no Ichi). Low-ranking samurai (1746–1821). Although he went blind at 5 years of age, he went to Edo when he was 13 to learn acupuncture. He then met Kamo no Mabuchi, fell in love with Chinese and Japanese classical literature, and memorized many texts. With the help of the shogunate, he founded a school, Wagaku Kōdanshu, for the study of literature. He published many books (in collaboration with Yashiro Hirokata), such as the monumental 500-volume *Gunsho ruijū* (1779–1819), followed by the *Zoku gunsho ruijū*. After writing two books devoted to families of the nobility, the *Kaki* and *Buke myōmoku-shō*, he began to publish historical texts; this project was finished by other scholars in the twentieth century and called *Dai Nihon shiryō*. He became a Buddhist monk. *See* INAYAMA YUKINORI.

Hanayagi Shōtarō. Dancer and Kabuki actor (Aoyama Shōtarō, 1894–1965), specializing in female roles *(onnagata)*. He was a founder of the New Theater (Shingeki-za) in 1921 and updated the Shimpa theater, creating a school of dance (*see* IEMOTO) bearing his name. In 1939, he began what became a very successful career acting in films, and he wrote a few novels (*Kimono*, 1941). He received many awards and prizes and was designated a Living National Treasure in 1960.

Hanazono Tennō. Ninety-fifth emperor (Prince Tomohito, 1297<1308–18>1348), son of Fushimi Tennō and successor to Go-Nijō Tennō. He belonged to the Jimyō-in family line and was a follower of Zen Buddhism. He abdicated in favor of his cousin, Go-Daigo. A talented poet, he compiled the anthology *Fuga-shū* in 1346.

• *Hanazono Tennō shinki.* Emperor Hanazono's diary covering the years 1310–32, valuable for what it reveals about the rivalries between the Daikaku-ji and Jimyō-ji imperial family lines and the disturbances in the late Kamakura period.

Handen. System of land distribution *(handen shūju)* instituted by the Taika Reform (645), which attributed a lot of arable land, the size of which varied according to the size of the family, for six years. According to this system, one twentieth of the harvest had to be returned to the government as tax. The state inherited the lands at the end of six years and could redistribute them as it saw fit. These lands, called *handen shojo-hō*, were administered by a bureaucrat with the title *handen-taifu*, then *handen-shi*. The system was copied from one in use

in China during the Tang dynasty, called *juntian*. This system was difficult to enforce, however, and began to deteriorate because of population growth and a lack of land to allocate to peasants toward the end of the eighth century. Peasants began to leave government land to settle in virgin regions, or to enter the service of major noble landowners and monasteries that had huge *shōen* (*see* FU-RŌNIN). The *handen* system continued to function in certain parts of the country, but tended not to take hold when newly cleared land became the hereditary property of the pioneers, starting in 743 (*see* KONDEN). It disappeared completely during the ninth century.

Han Dōsei. Japanese name for a Chinese Buddhist monk (Fan Daosheng, seventeenth century) who went to Japan; he painted Buddhist images and directed the sculptors of wooden statues of the Rakan (*Skt.*: Arhat) in the Mampuku-ji temple in Kyoto around 1667.

Haneda. "Fields of Wings." Name of the first international airport in Tokyo, built on Tokyo Bay 12 km from the center of the city. When, in 1978, it became congested because of increases in traffic, it was replaced by the Narita International Airport, located about 100 km north of the capital. The Haneda airport is now used only for domestic flights. It is linked to Tokyo by an elevated monorail.

Haneda Tōru. Historian (1882–1955), born in Kyoto. President of the Imperial University of Tokyo from 1938 to 1945. He was known for his research on Ural-Altaic and Iranian languages and on the history of the Manchu, Mongolian, and Uighur peoples. He compiled a Manchurian–Japanese dictionary and wrote major works on Uighur populations.

Han'ei sembai. Trade monopolies set up by *han*, or daimyo estates, in the late Edo period, about 1760, involving mainly products such as salt, silk, paper, and iron ore. Starting in 1840, some estates *(han)* established monopolies on production of steel for weapons (high-temperature furnaces and shipyards, notably). These monopolies disappeared with the Meiji Restoration of 1868, when the government purchased the main estate-owned industries.

Haneji Tomohide. Statesman (Shō Shōgen, seventeenth century) from Okinawa. He was prime minister of the Ryukyu Islands from 1666 to 1696. He wrote a book on the Ryukyu Islands, *Chūzan seikan,* published in 1650. Also called Hameji Chōsū.

Hangaku. "*Han* schools," founded in the eighteenth century in the daimyo estates to educate young samurai. There were about 50 *hangaku,* almost one per province. The largest were the Zōshikan in Satsuma (1774), the Meirinkan in Owari, and the Kōdōkan in Mito (founded by Tokugawa Nariaki in the early nineteenth century). Also called *hankō, han-gakkō.*

Hangi. Wooden block (generally of cherry wood) used as a plate for engraving ukiyo-e prints. When very fine details had to be engraved, blocks of hardwood *(buis)* were set into these planks.

Hani Gorō. Historian (1901–83) and writer of Marxist persuasion. He received part of his education in Heidelberg, Germany, and wrote several books of Marxist-influenced history on the development of capitalism in Japan in the pre-Meiji and Meiji eras. Imprisoned during the Second World War because of his opinions, he was elected to the Chamber of Advisers in 1947. He was one of the founders of the National Library of the Diet. Father of director Hani Sumusu.

Hani Motoko. Journalist (Matsuoka Moto, 1873–1957), born in Hachinohe (Aomori prefecture). Converted to Christianity about 1890, she founded a school for women, the Jiyū Gakuen, then became the first woman reporter in Japan, working for the *Hōchi Shimbun* in 1897. She married a journalist, Hani Yoshikazu (1880–1955) in 1901, and they founded a women's newspaper, the *Katei no Tomo,* renamed *Katei Jogaku Kōgi,* then *Fujin no Tomo.* They then published children's magazines, including *Kodomo no Tomo* (Children's Friend) and *Shin Shōjo* (Modern Girls). They also continued to run the Jiyū Gakuen, which enrolled both young women and young men, and to teach in a liberal style in spite of orders issued by the minister of education during the Second World War. The school now has more than 1,000 students and 100 teachers.

Hani Setsuko. Author (1903–87).

Hani Susumu. Movie director (b. 1928), son of Hani Gorō and grandson of Hani Motoko, from whom he took courses in her school, Jiyū Gakuen. After careers as a reporter and a photographer, he directed a documentary, *Seikatsu no mizu* (Water of Life, 1952), for the company Iwanami. He then continued to make movies using new techniques, such as *Kyōshitsu no kodomotachi* (Children in School, 1955) and *E o kaku kodomotachi* (Children Drawing, 1956), inaugurating the "new wave" of Japanese cinema. He received a national first prize for his film *Furyō shōnen* (Bad Boys) in 1961, then produced "feminist" films such as *Mitasareta seikatsu* (A Very Full Life, 1962) and *Kanojo to kare* (This and That, 1963), in which his wife, actress Hidari Sachiko, played the lead role. Next came *Buwana Toshi no uta* (The Song of Bwana Toshi, 1965), shot in Africa with only one Japanese actor, Atsumi Kiyoshi. Hani Susumu then started his own production company and directed *Andesu no hanayome* (A Wife in the Andes, 1966), shot in Peru. In 1968, he shot *Hatsukoi jigokuhen* (The Hell of a First Love). He then returned to documentaries and went to Africa to shoot *Afurika monogatari* (African Story, 1980). In the meantime, he produced many other documentary and educational films, using mainly amateur actors and ordinary people, to the almost total exclusion of professional actors.

Haniwa. "Terra-cotta tubes," a term used to describe unvarnished terra-cotta figurines (made of rolls of clay coiled using a technique called *wasumi*) adorning clay tubes set in the ground in large numbers around major burial sites *(kofun)* and some holy sites. *Haniwa* were probably made by Hajibe potters between the fifth and seventh centuries. It has not been determined whether they were intended as religious symbols, images of courtesans to accompany the deceased, or simply reinforcements for the sides of the tombs. *Haniwa* are found outside of *kofun,* arranged in a number of fairly tight ranks. The earliest ones were simply terra-cotta tubes, but later ones were more ornate: figurines of men, women, sorcerers, arrow quivers, animals (monkeys, bears, horses, cocks, etc.), boats, houses, and so on; they are therefore an extraordinary source of details on customs, dress, armor, houses, and many other aspects of this epoch not provided in written sources. In the fourth and fifth centuries, most *haniwa* were made in Kinai; they became more numerous in Kanto, with the appearance of *kofun* with interior chambers and access corridors, in the fifth and sixth centuries. According to the *Nihon shoki, haniwa* were also placed on tombs to represent the unfortunate individuals who, according to Chinese custom, had to be interred with the deceased. But this hypothesis has no foundation in fact, both because no evidence of human sacrifice has been found in Japan and because the oldest *haniwa* do not represent human beings or objects. Their origin is more likely an evolution from the large hourglass-shaped jars common in the Yayoi period, and they were certainly used in connection with funerary ceremonies during this period. *Haniwa* may also derive from the Chinese habit of placing stone effigies of animals and warriors on and around tombs of well-known people. But none of these theories has been proven. Some later *haniwa* are decorated with painted red triangles and have traces of red paint on the faces. All the figurines are hollow, as are the eyes and mouths of the people and animals, giving them an intensely "alive" look. In their extreme simplicity, they are remarkable works of art, manifesting the stunning gifts of observation and stylization of their makers. All *haniwa* were modeled in the coil-built technique joined by clay plates, then fired at a low temperature in oxygen-reduction kilns. Some details were appliquéd or incised on the surface. Some *haniwa* have been discovered with traces of red, blue, and white pigments that emphasize designs, certain of which (such as the *chokkomon*) are enigmatic. In northern Kyushu, effigies of animals *(sekiba)* and human beings *(seki-jin)* carved in the lava of Mt. Aso were also sometimes placed on *kofun* dating from the fifth and sixth centuries.

Haniyasu-hiko. Male *kami* (Shinto divinity) of the earth. His female counterpart is called Haniyasu-hime.

Haniya Yutaka. Writer (Hannya Yutaka; 1910–97), born in Taiwan. He became a member of the Communist party in 1927, was imprisoned in 1932–33 for his opinions, then abandoned all political activity to devote himself to literature. He helped found the magazine *Kindai Bungaku,* where he first published the beginning of his major novel, *Shirei* (Dead Souls), from 1946 to 1949. In his later novels, he expressed anti-Stalinist views and preached a sort of existentialism that had a great influence on young intellectuals from the 1950s to the 1970s. He returned to work on *Shirei,* publishing five chapters in book form in 1976 and a final chapter in 1981; this novel won the Japan Literary Prize in 1976. Among his other books are *Genshi no naka no seiji* (Policy of Illusion, 1960) and *Yami no naka no kuroi uma* (A Black Horse at Night, 1970).

Hankampu (Hankanfu). "Genealogy of the Protectors of the Shogunate," history of the daimyo of Japan, written by Arai Hakuseki in 1701 on the order of Tokugawa Ienobu, at the time daimyo of the

han (estate) of Kōfu. This 13-volume study relates the history of the 337 daimyo with more than 10,000 *koku* in revenue between 1600 and 1680. A supplement, *Hankampu (Hankanfu) zokuhen,* was added in 1806 by Okada Kansen (1740–1816) and several other scholars. In general, this work is historically accurate.

Hanka-shiyui. Posture characteristic of some statues of Buddha, Miroku, and Nyoririn Kannon from the fifth to the eighth century in both Korea and Japan, in which divinities are portrayed sitting with the right ankle resting on the left knee, the fingers of the right hand lightly touching the right cheek, in the "thinker's" position. Also called *hanka-i, Miroku-in, shiyui.*

Hanko. Painter (Kajita Jōjirō, 1870–1917) of the Shijō school. He painted mainly portraits.
• Personal seal currently used in place of a signature. *See* HAN.

Hankō. Painter (Okada Shuku; *mei:* Uzaemon; *azana:* Shi-u; *gō:* Kanzan, Dokushōrō, Hankō, 1782–1846) of the Nanga school. He studied with his father, Beisan-jin, and he painted mainly landscapes.
• Painter (Fukuda Kitsu; *mei:* Kyōzaburō; *azana:* Kitsu-jin; *gō:* Gyōsai, Gyōmusei, Hankō, 1804–64), of the Nanga school and Kazan's disciple.
→ *See* HANGAKU, OKADA BEISAN-JIN, OKADA HANKŌ.

Hankyū Dentetsu. Private railroad 141 km long linking Kyoto to Kobe and Osaka, built in 1906 by Kobayashi Ichizō. In 1913, the company financed the famous music-hall group Takarazuka.

• **Hankyū Hyakkaten.** Chain of department stores belonging to the Hanyū Corporation (Hankyū Dentetsu), founded in Osaka in 1929, with branches in Tokyo, Kobe, Osaka, Los Angeles, Paris, London, and Milan.

Hankyū-ji. Buddhist temple located near Himeji, founded in the late sixth century and now part of the Hōryō-ji as a detached temple. Also called Ikaruga-dera.

Hannya. Mask used in some Noh plays, portraying a horned demon with a red face and large bulging eyes, characterizing jealousy. This very popular mask has become a decorative element.

• **Hannya Bosatsu.** Japanese divinity corresponding to the Indian Buddhist divinity Prajñāpāramitā, symbolizing the "perfection of divine wisdom." Also called Haramitsu, Dai Hannya.

• **Hannya-ji.** Buddhist temple in Nara, founded in 654 and restored in 902 and 1195, destroyed in 1490, and reconstructed in the late sixteenth century. Stone pagoda with 13 stories of false roofs, 15 m high, one of the most beautiful in Japan, dating from the Kamakura period. *Rōmon* in the *wa-yō* style dating from 1293–99.

• *Hannya-kyō.* Japanese title for the Sanskrit Buddhist text *Prajñāpāramitā-shāstra,* dealing with the perfection of qualities of the Buddhist, sometimes attributed to Nāgarjuna (*Jap.:* Ryūju, Ryūmyō, Ryūshō).

• **Hannya Yutaka.** *See* HANIYA YUTAKA.

Hansatsu. Paper currency issued by the *han* (daimyo estates) and by some vassals of the shogunate during the Edo period. They were generally of value only in the region where they were issued, although theoretically they could be converted into the currency of the shogunate. The first *hansatsu* were issued by the Fukui estate in 1661, and the other daimyo quickly followed. Because they were issued in very large quantities, however, they were rapidly devalued. All *hansatsu* were finally converted into national legal currency between 1871 and 1879.

Hansharo. Dutch-designed "high furnaces" (reverberation furnaces) introduced to Japan in 1842 and used in Satsuma in 1850 for production of steel to cast cannons. The Edo shogunate built the first *hansharo* in Nirayama (Ise province) under the direction of Egawa Tarōzaemon in 1855–57.

Hanshin. Industrial zone on the coast of the Inland Sea (Setonaikai) from Kobe to Osaka and including both cities, second in size only to the Keihin industrial zone around Tokyo. A great number of plants and corporations are located in Hanshin (steel mills, factories for automobiles and mechanical and electrical equipment, chemicals and textile plants, agri-food plants, etc.) Also called Keihanshin.

Hanshō Tennō. Eighteenth emperor (Prince Mizuhawake, ca. 342 < ca. 406–411 >, according to the traditional dates), son of Nintoku Tennō and successor to his brother, Richū. It is said that he assassi-

nated his other brother, Naka no Oji, who had fomented a rebellion. Inkyō Tennō succeeded him.

Hanwa Kōgyō. Major cargo-transport company founded in 1947, transporting and exporting all sorts of industrial and domestic products. Head office in Osaka.

Haori. Jacket with wide sleeves, made of a thick fabric, worn over kimono or work clothes by many laborers, artisans, peasants, and workers. *Haori* were once decorated on the back and the inside with the insignia *(mon)* of the head of the family. They still often bear the logo of the company for which the respective laborer works. Also called *happi.*

Hara. Japanese landscape between 300 and 1,500 m in altitude where mainly brambles and *sasa* (dwarf bamboo) grow.
• Geographical term meaning "plain."
• The physical center of a person, supposedly found two fingers' widths under the navel, where all strength or energy captured by the breath and the *ki* originates. It is also the body's center of gravity. Buddhists call it *tanden (Chin.: dantian).* The *hara* is also, in Japanese thought, the seat of a person's character, emotions, and secret thoughts. Many expressions use the word *hara* to define a person's character and the quality of relations that person has with others. A "black *hara*" *(hara ga kuroi)* designates a vile, evil person, an "open *hara*" *(hara o waru)* designates a frank person, and so on. A current expression, especially in business circles, is *haragei* (art of the *hara*), which describes a tacit agreement between two people, obviating the need to communicate verbally. A person who "feels the *hara*" of another person is sympathetic (or hostile) to that person, and if one feels one's own *hara* "stiffening," one is becoming angry.

• **Harakiri.** "Cutting the stomach." According to the theory of the *hara,* this is "cutting one's stomach open," a ritual mode of suicide among the samurai corresponding to separating one's ego from the cosmic energy. The word *harakiri* is rarely used by the Japanese, who consider it vulgar and prefer the nobler word *seppuku* (*see* SEPPUKU).
→ *See* HARA ZAICHŪ.

Harada Magoshichirō. Late-sixteenth-century trader and navigator who went to the Philippines many times with Harada Kiemon, his Nagasaki sponsor. In 1592, Toyotomi Hideyoshi sent him to Manila to ask the Spanish viceroy to form an alliance with

Japan. This mission failed, and Harada left the following year for Taiwan, where he made the same proposal (in vain) to the Dutch authorities of the island.

Harada Naojirō. Western-style painter (1863–99), born in Edo. He studied with Takahashi Yuichi, then went to Munich, where he studied with the realist painter Gabriel Max. When he returned to Japan, he founded his own school in Tokyo, the Shōbi-kan, where many artists, among them Wada Eisaku, learned oil-painting techniques.

Harada Yasuko. Writer (Sasaki Yasuko), born 1928 in Tokyo. She spent her childhood in Hokkaido, and most of her novels are set there. In 1954, she received the first prize for literature from *Shinchō* (a "new wave" literary magazine) for her novel *Sabita no kyoku* (Sabita's Memoirs, 1953). Her novel *Banka* (Elegy, 1955–56) was a bestseller and received the prize for literature by a woman. Among her other novels are *Yameru oka* (The Sick Hill, 1957), *Itazura* (The Joke, 1960), *Satsujin-sha* (The Assassin, 1961), and *Bōkyō* (Nostalgia, 1961).

Harada Yoshito. Historian and archeologist (1885–1974), born in Tokyo. He became known for his excavations of *kofun* in Saitobaru, then he went to the United States and Europe from 1921 to 1923 to further his education. With Hamada Kōsaku, he founded the Society for Archeological Study of the Far East in 1925, and he led excavations in China and Korea, notably on the site of the Chinese commander's residence in Luolang. His book *Tōa kobunka kenkyū* (Studies on the Culture of Eastern Asia, 1940) is still authoritative.

Hara Hiromu. Graphic artist and lithographer, born 1903 in Nagano. His art was influenced by the German Bauhaus school and by Russian constructivism. He painted the walls of the Japanese pavilions at the Paris World Fair in 1937 and the New York World Fair in 1939, illustrated books, and produced many posters; he also taught at Musashino Bijutsu Daigaku (Musashi Art University) in Tokyo.

Harai (or Harae). Shinto purification ceremony, generally performed with ablutions *(misogi)* and rites of repentance, in which followers "cleanse" themselves of actions contrary to Shinto ethics (i.e., anything "soiling," *kegare*). Some of these very ancient rites, performed during public ceremonies, are called *ō-harai*. Followers must purify themselves every time they feel soiled by something (a death or a degrading act) or by any crime *(tsumi)*, such as sacrilege. The *harai* has given rise to many Shinto rites and festivals *(matsuri)* during which priests *(kannushi)* purify those attending by shaking a large paper *gohei (haraigushi)* over their heads, or exorcise demons (evil thoughts) by throwing red peas *(azuki)*, as during the *setsubun* or the year-end festival *(ōmisoka)*. The *ō-harai* is also performed in the court during *sechi-e*. Indeed, a Shinto follower would not go to pray in the shrine without first being purified, in one way or another, usually by ablutions. *See also* KEGARE, Ō-HARAI, SETSUBUN.

Haraka no Sō. Imperial ceremony conducted on the first day of the year and part of the *go-sechi-e*, during which a trout *(haraka, masu)* is solemnly offered to the emperor.

Hara Kei. Statesman (Hara Takashi, Hara Satoshi, 1856–1921) born in Morioka (Iwate prefecture) into a samurai family. He converted to Catholicism about 1875 and was baptized David, studied English and French, then entered a school of administration. After working as a reporter for three years, he founded a newspaper, the *Daitō Nippō*, in Osaka in 1882, but folded it when he entered the Department of Foreign Affairs on the recommendation of Inoue Kaoru. He was then appointed attaché to the embassy in Tainjin, China, and first secretary to the embassy in Paris. In 1896, he was appointed ambassador to Korea, but soon resigned to become editor-in-chief of the *Ōsaka Mainichi Shimbun*. He became secretary-general of the Rikken Seiyūkai (Friends of Constitutional Government party) in 1900 and was leader of the party from 1914 until his death, succeeding Saionji Kimmochi in that position. In 1918, he was elected prime minister and governed with the assistance of the zaibatsu, mainly the Mitsui zaibatsu. The military often opposed his investment choices in his economic reconstruction policy. Accused of careerism, he gradually lost the public's confidence but nevertheless strengthened his party's influence in the country. He was assassinated on November 4, 1921, in the Tokyo train station, by a young right-wing extremist, Nakaoka Konichi. His ten-volume memoir, *Hara Takashi nikki,* was published in 1951.

Hara Kumatarō. Painter (*gō:* Bushō, ca. 1861–1907) in Western style. He moved to London in 1904, where he painted mainly portraits.

Haramaki. Armor consisting of pieces of leather laced together with colored cords. Foot soldiers *(ashigaru)* who wore this armor complemented their equipment with a flat hat made of lacquered boiled leather called a *jingasa. See* KATCHŪ, YOROI.

Hara, Martinho. Japanese convert (ca. 1570–1629). After studying at the Arima Seminary, he was sent to Rome with four other boys in 1582 by the Christian daimyo of Kyushu. He returned to Japan in 1590, entered the Company of Jesus in 1591, and was ordained a priest in 1608. In 1614, during the persecutions ordered by Tokugawa Ieyasu, he fled to Macao, where he taught Japanese at a Jesuit college until his death.

Hara Ryō. Writer (b. 1947), who received the 1990 Naoki Prize for his detective novel *Watakushi ga koroshita shōjo* (The Girl I Killed).

Hara Setsuko. Movie actress (Aida Masae) born 1920 in Yokohama. She was director Ozu Yasujirō's favorite actress and appeared in *Banshun* (Late Spring, 1949), *Bakushū* (Early Summer, 1951), *Tōkyō monogatari* (1953), and *Akibiyori* (Late Autumn, 1960). She also made several films with other directors, including Itami Mansaku. She retired in 1963, at the height of her career.

Hara Tamiki. Writer and poet (1905–51), born in Hiroshima. His poems reflect a sensitive yet pessimistic soul. He was irradiated in Hiroshima on August 6, 1945. He then wrote a series of novellas, which were collected in a book, *Natsu no hana* (Summer Flowers, 1947), that made him famous. Believing his illness incurable, he committed suicide in 1951.

Hara Zaichū. Painter (*mei:* Chien; *azana:* Shijū; *gō:* Gayū, 1750–1837), born in Kyoto, where he studied with Maruyama Ōkyo and Ishida Yūtei. He combined their styles with the Chinese Ming style to create a new style, which he called Hara, in which nature is precisely portrayed. He painted many fusuma, notably in the Ninna-ji temple in Kyoto.

Hare, Harebi. "Bright days," name for festivals and days off. *See* MATSURI.

Hari-bako. "Needle boxes," traditional sewing boxes that were part of a young woman's dowry, sometimes very elaborate and ornate. They were generally made of lacquered wood, with many small drawers. They are now prized by collectors.

• **Hari-kuyō.** "Service in memory of needles," family ceremony once observed by all women on December 8 (or February 8, depending on the region): they collected their worn or broken sewing needles, stuck them into a piece of tofu or *konnyaku,* and buried them while praying that their sewing talents would improve and their fingers would suffer fewer pricks; they thus hoped to appease the "spirits of needles."

Harima. Former province, now part of Hyōgo prefecture (Honshu). *See* SETONAIKAI.

• *Harima-fudoki.* One of the four *fudoki* found concerning the province of Harima. *See* FUDOKI.

• **Harima Nada.** Part of the Inland Sea (Setonaikai) in the south of the former Harima province, between Shikoku Island and the islands of Awaji and Shōdōshima, measuring about 60 × 40 km. It is shallow (about 40 m in depth) and was once highly stocked with fish, but is now polluted due to factories on its shores. It has a liberal sprinkling of picturesque islets and is part of the National Park of the Inland Sea (Setonaikai). *See* NATIONAL PARKS.

• **Harima Ninsei.** *See* NINSEI.

Harris, Merriman Colbert. American Methodist missionary (1846–1921), born in Ohio. He was consul to Hakodate and evangelized in Hokkaido. Then, after a stay in San Francisco, he was made a bishop in Japan and Korea from 1904 to 1916. He wrote three books on Christianity in Japan. His wife, Flora Best (1850–1909), was the first translator of Ki no Tsurayuki's *Tosa nikki.*

Harris, Townsend. American merchant (1804–78) and first American consul to Japan. After a mission in Siam, he went to Japan in 1856 to sign a trade treaty, but he was confined to the Buddhist Gyokusen-ji temple in Shimoda for 14 months. He finally was able to present his credentials to the shogun in Edo, and they signed the first American–Japanese treaty on July 28, 1858, opening six Japanese ports—Nagasaki, Kanagawa, Hyōgo, Shimoda, Niigata, and Hakodate—to trade with the United States. The treaty also provided for an exchange of consuls between the two countries, established the right for American citizens to live in these ports, and defined the principle of extraterritoriality. Although this treaty was not ratified by the emperor, Japan signed others several weeks later with the Netherlands, Russia, Great Britain, and France. It was replaced by another treaty only in 1894 (which did not take effect until five years later). These treaties provoked waves of protest throughout Japan and led to violence against foreigners and the assassination of Ii Naosuke. Harris, in poor health, resigned from his post in 1862 and returned to the United States. When he had resided in Shimoda, the shogunate had assigned him a Japanese servant, Okichi, and people invented a tragic love story between them that seems to have had no basis in reality, but that is still exploited for tourist purposes in Shimoda today. Harris left a journal on his years in Japan, describing the conversations he had with shogunal authorities and the events that resulted from the signing of the treaty.

Haru-ichiban. "First of the spring," name for the strong southwest winds that augur the end of winter and the beginning of spring. This is the time when the plum trees and camellias flower. These winds (along with those from Siberia) are created by an atmospheric depression over the Sea of Japan. They are accompanied by a sudden rise in temperature that provokes avalanches, especially in northern Honshu. *See* CLIMATE.

Haruki Nammei. Painter (Unosuke; *mei:* Shūki, Ryū; *azana:* Keiichi, Shishū; *gō:* Kōungyosha, Donzanrō, Nammei, 1795–1878), Haruki Nanko's son and student and Tani Bunchō's student. He adroitly mixed the Bunjinga of the North (Hokuga) and the South (Nanga), sometimes adding European elements. He painted mainly flowers and landscapes, as did his son, Haruki Nanka. His favorite disciple was Tazaki Sōun.

Haruma-wage. "Translation of Halma." The first Dutch–Japanese dictionary published in Japan (based on the Dutch–French dictionary by François Halma, published in 1708), compiled by Inamura Sampaku and several other *rangaku* ("Dutch science") scholars. Published in 1796 in Edo, the *Haruma-wage* comprises 80,000 entries and 27 volumes. One of Inamura's students, Fujibayashi Fuzan (1781–1836), published an abridged version in 1810 called *Yakuken* (Keys for Translation). Commonly called *Edo Haruma.*

Harunobu. Painter (Suzuki Harunobu, Hozumi Jihei, Hozumi Harunobu; *mei:* Jihei; *gō:* Chōeiken,

ca. 1725–70) of ukiyo-e prints, born in Kyoto or Edo. In Edo, he studied with Nishamura Shigenaga (ca. 1697–1756). His first paintings, in *hosoban* format, showed the influence of Okumura Masanobu, Ishikawa Moronobu, and the Chinese painter Qu Ying. In 1765, he was chosen by the wealthy *chōnin* to make illustrated calendars (*egoyomi),* which he designed in a larger format (*chūban)* and for which he invented a new technique of printing in several colors called *nishiki-e* (brocade of images). He also produced some 100 color images on separate pages and illustrated some 20 books in black and white, among them *Ehon kokinran* (Book Illustrated with Gold Brocade, 1763), *Ehon hanakazura* (1764), *Ehon sazareishi* (1766), *Ehon kotowazagusa* (1767), *Ehon nishiki no tamoto* (1767), *Ehon haru no yuji* (1767), *Ehon haru no tomo* (1768), *Ehon seira awase* (Book of Contrasts, 5 vols.), *Zashiki hakkei* (On Domestic Life, 8 vols.), *Yoshiwara bijin awase* (Yoshiwara's Beautiful Women, 5 vols., color, 1770), and *Kyokun iroha no uta* (1775). He also made a large number of erotic images (*shunga).* Among his many students were Koryūsai, Harushige, and Tanaka Masanobu; after his death, his works were imitated by several artists, notably Shiba Kōkan. *See* UKIYO-E.

→ *See* ARIMA HARUNOBU, BAIŌKEN NAGAHARU, TAKEDA HARUNOBU.

Haruyama Yukio. Poet and literary critic, born 1902 in Nagoya. He was particularly interested in the French surrealist poets, whose work he introduced to Japan through a quarterly magazine, *Shi to Shiron* (Poetic Theory), which he founded with several other poets in 1929. Among his poetry collections, the best known are *Tsukinoteru-machi* (The Rising Moon, 1925), *Shanikusai* (The Festival of Mid-fast, 1925), and *Shokubutsu no dammen* (Falling Leaves, 1930).

Hase. City in Nara prefecture, former waystation on the Ise road (Ise-kaidō), and favorite stopover for the nobility during the Heian period. It is famous for its blossoming cherry trees. Also called Hatsuse.

• **Hase-dera.** Buddhist temple located in Hase (Hatsuse), in the Buzan branch of the Shingon-shū sect, which was probably founded under the name Chōkoku-ji by the monk Dōmyō about 686. In 756, Gyōgi (Gyōki) blessed a large statue of the Eleven-headed Kannon (Jūichimen Kannon Bosatsu) carved in the trunk of a camphor tree (part of which is now housed in the Kannon-ji temple in Kamakura). This statue was remade in 1536, and the Kannondō was reconstructed in 1650. The Hasedera is one of the 33 temples in the Western circuit (Sanjūsangen-sho) of pilgrimages in honor of Kannon Bosatsu. Its other buildings date from the seventeenth and eighteenth centuries, except for the Fudōdō, which is from the thirteenth century. It houses many art objects, including the Taima Mandara.

• **Hase Kannon-ji.** Buddhist temple in Kamakura housing a large statue of Jūichimen Kannon Bosatsu, 10 m in height, in camphor wood. It is attributed to the monk-sculptor Tokudō Shōnin, who would have sculpted it about 721 in half of a tree trunk (the other half having been used to sculpt the statue at the Hase-dera).

Hasebe Kotondo. Archeologist and anthropologist (1882–1969), born in Tokyo. After studying medicine at Tokyo University and in Munich, he devoted himself to the study of skeletons found in the *kaizuka* and came to the conclusion that modern Japanese were the direct descendants of the Jōmon people and not the Ainu. He also studied the "Peking Man" skeletons found at Zhoukoudian, China.

Hasebe Kunishige. Sword maker (fourteenth century) in Kyoto, of the Hasebe school. His style was distinct from that of the Rai school, which was dominant during the Kamakura period. His descendants, Kuninobu, Munenobu, and Kunihira, perpetuated his style.

Hasegawa Fujihiro. Bureaucrat (1567–1617) of the Edo *bakufu* whose sister was one of Tokugawa Ieyasu's favorite concubines. He entered the shogun's service in 1602 and succeeded his older brother, Hasegawa Shigeyoshi, as governor *(bugyō)* of Nagasaki. When the Portuguese ship *Madre de Dios,* commanded by Andrea Pessoa, tried to force its way into the port in 1609, he attacked it, and Pessoa blew up his own ship. Hasegawa Fujihiro was then appointed governor of Sakai in 1615, and his nephew, Hasegawa Fujimasa, succeeded him in Nagasaki.

• **Hasegawa Fujimasa.** *See* HASEGAWA FUJIHIRO.

Hasegawa-ha. Painting school created by Hasegawa Tōhaku (1539–1610), a painter of the Muromachi *suiboku* school, specializing in the Chinese academic style *(kanga).* The painters in this school, of whom there were not a great number, lived in Kyoto and had been students of the masters of the Kanō school. Most of them were members of the Tōhaku family: his sons Kyūzō (1568–93), Sōtaku and Sakon (both active around 1650), and Sōya (d. 1667). They painted mainly fusuma. Their most remarkable work was decoration of the Chishaku-in in Kyoto (1592). The school disappeared in the late seventeenth century, though a few painters, such as Hasegawa Yōshin (d. 1726), perpetuated the Tōhaku style and kept the family name Hasegawa.

• **Hasegawa Tōhaku.** Painter (Okumura Tōhaku, 1539–1610), student of Kanō Eitoku in Kyoto. Considering himself the stylistic successor to Sesshū Tōyō, he painted mainly monkeys and pine trees in the Chinese style on fusuma. He also made color decorations for the temples of Kyoto, portraying subjects such as rocks, trees, and characters from Chinese legends. However, a number of works attributed to him were probably painted by his son (*see* HASEGAWA-HA) or by Kanō Sanraku.

Hasegawa Kazuo. Actor, born 1908 in Kyoto. He was very popular before the Second World War, playing the lead in the film *Yukinojō henge* (Yukinojō's Disguise, 1935). After the war, he was noted for his performance in Mizoguchi Kenji's film *Jigoku-mon* (The Doors of Hell, 1953). Soon after, he turned to directing, and his film *Berusayu no bara* (The Rose of Versailles) was very successful.

Hasegawa Kiyoshi. Painter and engraver (1891–1980), born in Yokohama, student of Kuroda Seiki, Okada Saburōsuke, and Fujishima Takeji. He visited the United States in 1918, then went to Paris the following year, where he settled and made a number of engravings in the "black style." He exhibited at the Salon d'automne in Paris and was decorated with the Legion of Honor in 1935. A recognized painter of the "Paris school style," he received the Order of Merit in 1966 and the city of Paris's Vermeil Medal in 1967.
→ *See* TAIWAN.

Hasegawa Nyozekan. Writer and journalist (Hasegawa Manjirō, 1875–1969), born in Tokyo. He contributed to a number of newspapers, including the *Osaka Asahi Shimbun,* where he was noted for his social commentaries. In all of his many writings (articles, novels, plays), he fought the rise of militarism and promoted democratic ideals. In 1948, he received the Order of Culture (Bunka-shō). His works, many of them written in popular language and some of them full of slang, were collected in the eight-volume *Hasegawa Nyozekan sen-shū* (1969–70).

Hasegawa Roka. Painter (Hasegawa Ryūzō, 1897–1967), born in Kanagawa. He studied in France from 1921 to 1927. After the Second World War, he decorated many public buildings in Japan with mosaics and frescoes. In 1955, he painted a fresco at the Civitavecchia in Italy commemorating Japanese Christian martyrs. He also created decorations for the Tokyo stadium. Invited to Italy by Pope Paul VI, he died en route.

Hasegawa Saburō. Western-style painter (1906–57), born in Chōfu (Yamaguchi prefecture). He studied Sesshū art, then traveled in the United States and France from 1929 to 1932 and exhibited at the Salon d'automne in Paris. He was influenced by Mondrian and Kandinsky, and when he returned to Japan he and Murai Masanari created an Art Nouveau group. A pioneer of abstract art in Japan, he wrote many books on this style of painting, including *Abusutoraku āto* (Abstract Art, 1937), *Atarashii-e miro tebiki* (Guide for Understanding the New Painting, 1948), *Mojiriani* (Modigliani, 1949), and *Modan-āto* (Modern Art, 1951). He died in San Francisco just after being appointed a professor at the California College of Art.

Hasegawa Senshi. Buddhist monk (1689–1733) and playwright, who collaborated with Takeda Izumo.

Hasegawa Shin. Writer (Hasegawa Shinjirō, 1884–1963) born in Yokohama. He became known for his novels and plays about the working class, in which the main characters were gamblers, samurai, gangsters, and outlaws. His best-known play, *Mabuta no haha* (Mother of My Dreams, 1930), features a legendary character, a sort of Robin Hood, called Bamba no Chūtarō, who goes in search of his mother. Hasegawa thus inaugurated a new literary genre, *matatabi-mono*, describing the life of outcasts. Another of his plays in this genre, *Ippon-gatana dohyōiri* (The Gangster Appears with a Sword, 1931) was also very famous, as was his novel *Araki Mataemon* (1937), a story of vengeance. He also wrote historical works, such as *Nihon horyo-shi* (History of Prisoners of War in Japan, 1950). When he died, a prize for popular literature was created in his name.

Hasegawa Shirō. Writer and poet (1909–87) born in Hakodate. He translated a number of authors into Japanese, including Franz Kafka, Bertolt Brecht, and Samuel Beckett. He was taken prisoner by the Russian army in Siberia and held for five years at the end of the Second World War. His account of his experiences, *Shiberiya monogatari,* published in 1951, earned him a place among the great postwar writers. Hayashi Fubō's brother.

Hasegawa Tenkai. Scholar and writer (Hasegawa Seiya, 1876–1940), born in Niigata, translator of many Western naturalist works, which he introduced to Japan through articles and literary critiques.

Hasegawa Toshiyuki. Painter (1891–1940) and *tanka* poet, born in Yamashina. He went to Tokyo in 1921, began to paint in Western style, and had several exhibitions that won him public acclaim. Very poor and living in the city's shabbier districts, he painted mainly homeless people. He died in poverty, for his works did not sell during his lifetime. Aside from his paintings, he left a collection of poems, *Mokui-shū* (Bouquet of Wood and Reeds), written in 1919.

Hasegawa Yoshimishi. Officer (Hasegawa Kōdō, 1850–1924), appointed commander-in-chief of the Japanese troops in Korea in 1905 and raised to the peerage in 1907 by Emperor Meiji.

Hasekura Tsunenaga. Samurai (Hasekura Rokuemon, 1571–1622) in the service of Date Masamune, daimyo of northern Honshu, who sent him to Mexico, Madrid, and Rome in search of trading partners. In October 1613, Hasekura set sail for Acapulco on a galleon, the *Date Maru* (renamed *San Juan Battista*), built in 45 days with the help of Spanish sailors and commanded by Mukai Shōgen, admiral of the shogunal fleet. He was accompanied by 180 people, including the Franciscan Luis Sotelo. He met the viceroy of Mexico in 1614; King Philip III of Spain in Madrid in 1615, where he was baptized Felipe Francisco on February 16; and Pope Paul V in October 1615. After visiting Italy, where he obtained Roman citizenship, he spent two years in the Philippines, then retraced his route to Japan in 1620. In the meantime, the Spanish had closed their ports and the Tokugawa clan had proscribed Christianity, so Hasekura's mission had no tangible effect. He was allowed by special permission to continue practicing his faith, but his son, Hasekura Tsuneyori, also a convert, was condemned to death in 1640 by Date Tadamune for having refused to recant. The Sendai Museum has a very good portrait of Hasekura Tsunenaga, in oil paint, executed about 1615 or 1616 in Rome or Madrid. Mention of Hasekura's trip was expunged by shogunal order, and it was not noted in the official histories of the Edo period. In 1873, Prince Iwakura Tomomi discovered documents and letters referring to Hasekura's voyage in the archives of the Serene Republic in Venice, although the report of Iwakura's mission makes no mention of this. However, on the initiative of Emperor Meiji, the account of Hasekura's mission was made public after more than 250 years of silence, and was published in the twelfth volume of *Dai Nihon shiryō* in 1909.

Hashiba. Name taken by Toyotomi Hideyoshi in 1575; he assumed the name Toyotomi only in 1585. *See* KINOSHITA, TOYOTOMI HIDEYOSHI.

• **Hashiba Hidekatsu.** Fourth son (1567–1593) of Oda Nobunaga, adopted by Hideyoshi. He died in Korea while directing an army sent by Hideyoshi.

• **Hashiba Hidenaga.** Hideyoshi's half-brother (1540–91). Appointed *gon-dainagon* in 1587. *See* TŌDŌ TAKATORA.

• **Hashiba Hidetoshi.** Son (1577–94) of Hideyoshi's older sister.

Hashi-benkei. Noh play telling how Ushiwaka (the young Minamoto no Yoshitsune), disguised as a girl and armed only with a fan, defeated the monk-soldier Benkei in hand-to-hand combat on a bridge, turning him into a faithful companion.

Hashi-gakari. Passage leading from backstage to the stage of a Noh theatre, located stage left, via which actors enter and on which they sometimes start to play or dance. *See also* HANAMICHI, NOH.

Hashiguchi Goyō. Painter and engraver (1880–1921), born in Kagoshima. A student of Hashimoto Gahō, he studied Western painting techniques and "new" Japanese painting (Nihonga). After 1911, he abandoned oil painting to devote himself to ukiyo-e prints in an attempt to update the style. He also made many illustrations for books and literary magazines.

Hashikawa Bunzō. Historian (1922–83), an expert on the history of modern Japanese political thought and a critic of the romantic school. Professor at Meiji University in Tokyo until his death.

Hashima. Small island located west of Nagasaki (Kyushu), where coal mines were opened in 1890. Drilling assays made by Mitsubishi reached a depth of 1,000 m below sea level. The mines were closed in 1974, and the island, which had up to 5,000 inhabitants, is now deserted. *Area:* 0.1 km².
• Town in Gumma prefecture (central Honshu), known for its wool crafts. *Pop.:* 60,000.

Hashimoto Chikanobu. Painter (Yōshō Chikanobu, Chikanobu, 1838–1912) of ukiyo-e prints. He studied with Utagawa Kuniyoshi and Kunisada I (Toyokuni III), and made triptychs on views of famous Tokyo sites and the Sino-Japanese War. His prints portraying foreigners are accurate and very well documented. He frequently used the aniline color red *(aka-e),* introduced to Japan shortly before and used mainly by artists of the Yokohama school (Yokohama-e) starting in 1865.

Hashimoto Eikichi. Writer (Shiraishi Kamekichi), born 1898 in Fukuoka. He practiced several trades and was a miner. In 1946, he began to write proletarian-style novels, influenced by Yokomitsu Riichi. His first book, *Fujisanchō* (The Top of Mt. Fuji, 1946 and 1948), was very successful. Following this, he wrote historical novels and studies such as *Tempyō, Keizu, Chūgi,* and *Tōhō no shizoku* (Races of the East).

Hashimoto Fumihiko. Musician (1904–50), composer of many songs and instrumental pieces.

Hashimoto Heihachi. Sculptor (1897–1935), born in Mie. Using a variation of the Enkū style, he drew his inspiration from Japanese folklore to create works of great originality.

Hashimoto Kansetsu. Painter (1883–1945), born in Kobe, the painter Hashimoto Kaikan's son. In 1903, he studied academic painting (Bunjin-ga) with Takeuchi Seihō, then mixed this style with that of the Maruyama-Shijō school and Western impressionism to create Shin Bungaku-ga, or "new academic painting." Although he was particularly interested in Chinese painting, he went on a study trip to Europe in 1921; thereafter, he spent part of each year in China. He was elected a member of the Teikoku Bijutsu-in (Imperial Academy of Art) in 1935. His house in Kyoto, the Hakusa Sonsō, was turned into a museum featuring his works. He also wrote essays, collected in the *Kansetsu zuihitsu*. He sometimes signed his work Kan'ichi.

Hashimoto Kingorō. Officer (1890–1957), born in Okayama. A firm proponent of Japanese expansionism, he organized the officers at general headquarters into secret societies, Sakura-kai and Kinki-kai, which attempted to overthrow the government on February 26, 1936. Transferred to the reserves, he founded a fascist party called Dai Nippon Seinen-tō (Great Japan Youth party). Sent to China during the Sino-Japanese War in 1937, he shot at the English ship the *Lady Bird*, which earned him a discharge. He was, however, elected to the Diet in 1944 for another party he had founded, the Dai Nippon Sekiseikai (Great Japan Loyalty Society). Condemned to prison for life as a war criminal by the Allies in 1948, he was freed in 1955. *See* CHŌ ISAMU.

Hashimoto Meiji. Painter, born 1904 in Hamada (Shimane prefecture), Matsuoka Eikyū's student. His style was related to Nihonga, or Japanese painting, and he won a number of prizes at Shin Bunten exhibitions, especially in 1937 and 1938. In 1940, he was involved in the group project to copy frescoes from the Kondō of the Hōryū-ji, which later enabled them to be reconstructed after the disastrous fire of 1949.

Hashimoto Ryūtarō. Politician, born in 1938, minister of labor and president of the Liberal Democratic party (LDP, Jiyū Minshutō). He succeeded Murayama Tomiichi as prime minister and served from January 1996 to August 1998.

Hashimoto Sachiko. Philanthropist, noted for her work with the International Red Cross. She received the Henri Dunant Medal in 1972.

Hashimoto Sadahide. Painter (1807–ca. 1878) of ukiyo-e prints, student of Kunisada I's (Toyokuni III), who made prints for the Paris World Fair in 1867. In addition to making portraits of actors and beautiful women *(bijin)*, he drew landscapes and illustrated fans and albums. His landscapes were often polytychs (three, six, or nine sheets stuck together or superimposed). Toward the end of his life, he also made several copper engravings. He worked in Yokohama and belonged to the Yokohama-e school.

Hashimoto Sanai. Physician (1834–59), born in Echizen (Fukui prefecture). He studied Western medicine with Ogata Kōan in Osaka; in 1854, when he became the head of his family, he studied languages and Chinese and Western science, then went to Edo to assist with the reform of the shogunate, upon the request of Tokugawa Yoshinaga. He was sent to Kyoto in 1858 to appoint Hitotsubashi Yoshinobu shogun, but following various incidents during the Ansei era (1859), Hitotsubashi and his followers were placed under house arrest and Hashimoto Sanai was sentenced to death and beheaded.

Hashimoto Shinkichi. Grammarian (1882–1945), born in Fukui, linguistics professor at Tokyo University starting in 1927. His studies on the phonology of old Japanese and the grammatical structure of modern Japanese were the basis of the standardized language taught in the schools today.

Hashimoto Shinobu. Writer, born 1918 in Hyōgo, author of successful screenplays for movies such as *Rashōmon* (1950), *Shichinin no samurai* (The Seven Samurai, 1954), and other films by Kurosawa Akira. He wrote many teleplays, and also wrote screenplays for directors Kobayashi Masaaki, Yamamoto Satsuo, Okamoto Kihachi, and Moritani Shirō.

Hashimoto Sōkichi. Geographer (1763–1836), creator of a two-hemisphere world map in 1796. He also was known for reproducing Benjamin Franklin's experiments with lightning conductors.

Hashira-kake. Narrow painting (often an ukiyo-e print) designed to be attached to an interior column of a house (*hashira,* or column). This form was probably invented by Okumura Masanobu (1684–1784). *Size:* approx. 67 × 12 cm. Also called *hose-e, hashira-e. See* UKIYO-E.

Hashira-mai. Dances performed by two actors during a Bugaku performance.

Hashiri-shū. Foot soldiers serving as the shogun's guard during the Kamakura period. Also called *kachi-hashiri-shū.*

Hashitomi. Noh play taken from an episode in the *Genji monogatari*: Prince Genji woos the young Yūgao, but she is killed by the jealous Lady Rokujō. The ghost of Yūgao then reveals herself to a Buddhist monk and asks him to pray for her soul to rest.

Hashiura Yasuo. Painter (1890–1979), one of the leaders of the "proletarian art" movement in the early Shōwa era (1926–89). He was also interested in Japanese folklore and worked with Yanagita Kunio.

Hassaku. In ancient Japan, ritual exchange of gifts between masters and servants on the first day of the eighth month. Also called Ta no Mi. *See* GIFTS.

Hassei. Collective name for eight titles of nobility *(kabane)* created by Emperor Temmu in 685: Mabito (Mando), Asomi (Ason), Sukune, Imiki, Michi no Shi, Ōmi, Muraji, and Inagi.

Hassendō. *See* HYAKUSEN, SAKAKI HYAKUSEN.

• **Hasshōdō.** The "Noble Eightfold Path" of the doctrines of early Buddhism.

• **Hasshū.** Collective name for the eight major sects of Buddhism in Japan: Sanron-shū, Hossō-shū, Kegon-shū, Ritsu-shū, Jōjitsu-shū, Tendai-shū, Jodō-shū, and Shingon-shū. The first six are sometimes called the Nanto-rokushū or Nara-shū (Six Sects of Nara).

• **Hassō.** In Buddhism, the "eight moments" of the career of Buddha Shakyamuni (*Jap.*: Shaka): birth, leaving the family, seeking the truth, descending from the mountain, awakening, preaching, establishment of the monastic community, and Parinirvāna (death, *Jap.*: Nehan).

Hata. Korean immigrants *(kika-jin)*, who went from Paeg-che to Japan in the fourth and fifth centuries, bringing the arts of sericulture and silk weaving. They planted many mulberry bushes for this purpose. They may also have introduced certain metallurgical and agricultural techniques. In the late fifth century, they obtained the right to the status *(kabane)* of Miyatsuko; in the seventh century, to that of Imiki. They established many Buddhist temples in the Nara and Kyoto regions, such as the Kōryū-ji, as well as Shinto shrines (Fushimi Inari, Matsunoo Taisha) and helped to found the new city of Heian-kyō. It is not known whether the origin of the name Hata is Chinese or Korean. Yūryaku Tennō gave them the family name Uzumasa in 471. The most famous members of the family were Hata no Kawakatsu, friend of Shōtoku Taishi, and Hata Sake no Kimi, grandfather of Yuzuki no Kimi. *See also* HATTORI.

• **Hata.** "Banner," a word that forms part of many words and names. *See* BAN, HATAMOTO, YAWATA.

• **Hata-bugyō.** Bureaucrat of the Edo *bakufu*, charged with banners and pennants.

Hata Chishin. *See* HATA CHITEI.

Hata Chitei. Painter (Hata Chishin, Chitei, Chishin, eleventh century). He painted the "Life of Shōtoku Taishi," comprising five silk panels, for the Hōryū-ji temple in 1069. This painting was restored in 1339, 1380, 1678, and 1878. It is now in the Tokyo National Museum. Hata Chitei also painted a wooden statue of Shōtoku Taishi sculpted by Enkei. Nothing is known about his life. He may have been a monk at the Hōryū-ji.

Hatakeyama. Famous warrior family in Musashi province (Kanto) in the Kamakura period, descended from a branch of the Taira family, according to tradition. Powerful during the Kamakura and Muromachi periods, the Hatakeyama lost their estates following the Ōnin War and disappeared from the political scene in 1574. Their descendants served Toyotomi Hideyoshi and Tokugawa Ieyasu. During the Edo period, they held the hereditary position of master of ceremonies *(kōke)*.

• **Hatakeyama Kinenkan.** Tokyo museum that was founded by Hatakeyama Issei in 1964. It contains paintings, ceramics, sculptures, gold pieces, Japanese lacquers, and Korean ceramics, along with Chinese bronzes and paintings.

• **Hatakeyama Kunikiyo.** *See* DŌSEI.

• **Hatakeyama Masanaga.** Warrior (d. 1493), adoptive son of Hatakeyama Mochikuni (1397–1455), who took part in the Ōnin War.

• **Hatakeyama Mitsue.** Statesman (Dōsui, d. 1433), appointed *kanryō* in 1410.

• **Hatakeyama Mochikuni.** *See* ASHIKAGA YOSHIKATSU, HATAKEYAMA MASANAGA, TOKUHON.

Hatakeyama Motokuni. Warrior, the first Hatakeyama to serve the Ashikaga shogun with the title of *kanrei*, in 1398. *See* TOKUGEN.

• **Hatakeyama Shigetada.** Warrior (1164–1205). He fought against Minamoto no Yoritomo, then took his side in the naval battle of Dan no Ura in

1185. When his son was killed by Hōjō Tokimasa, he protested, and he and his entire family were killed. His heroic actions became the stuff of legend, and in literature he is known for his bravery and strength.

• **Hatakeyama Yoshimune.** Statesman (d. 1480), appointed *kanryō* of Kyoto in 1473.

• **Hatakeyama Yoshinori.** Warrior (d. 1493), son of Hatakeyama Mochikuni. He took part in the Ōnin War.

Hatamoto. "Men of the banners" (*see* HATA). At first, this word meant a shogun's military camp. It later came to mean the men guarding the camp, a position to which the Tokugawa shogun appointed low-ranking vassals who had fought at Tokugawa Ieyasu's side in the Battle of Sekigahara in 1600 and their descendants. The *hatamoto* thus became direct vassals of the shogun, receiving an annual rice allocation of between 100 and 10,000 *koku,* a higher rank than the *gokenin,* who received under 100 *koku.* The *hatamoto* fulfilled various functions, military and civil, within the *bakufu,* in Edo or in the provinces. They were divided into three classes: Kōdaiyoriai, Yoriai, and Kofushin. All had the right to a direct audience with the shogun. There were about 5,000 *hatamoto* in the middle of the Edo period, and they were always firm supporters of the *bakufu* and valued for their abilities in the positions they filled. These positions were passed on to their direct heirs, or, if they were found to be inept, to their younger brothers or adoptive sons. By the eighteenth century, however, the *hatamoto* began to be impoverished, and many were obliged to sell their *kokudaka* to wealthy merchants for cash and to spend relatively large amounts to sustain their rank. A great number of them, deeply in debt and unwilling to perform manual labor or to become involved in business, became teachers of martial art or even bandits. During the Meiji Restoration of 1868, many *hatamoto* received a sort of salary from the government; nevertheless, their situation deteriorated and they chose—or were forced—to melt into the general population and earn a living as tradesmen or by their wits.

• **Hatamoto shohatto.** See HAYASHI RAZAN.

• **Hatamoto-yakko.** In the early seventeenth century, many young *hatamoto* were forced into idleness thanks to the peace established by the Tokugawa. Because they could not prove their valor, they acted outrageously and obnoxiously both with other *hatamoto* and with the general public, sometimes provoking disturbances by becoming violent with the *machi-yakko,* their counterparts among the *chōnin.* The shogunate reacted promptly by arresting some of these unruly characters, which cooled the ardor of the others. But Kabuki theater and literature seized on them as *kabukimono* or stock characters whom they invariably portrayed as quarrelsome, unstable, antisocial people. *See* MACHI-YAKKO.

Hatanaka Kenji. Officer who led an extremist coup d'état as Japan was about to surrender in August 1945, in an attempt to get the emperor to reverse his decision and continue the war. He and a few other officers assassinated General Mori Takeshi, who commanded the imperial guard corps, but his plot was discovered and he and his accomplices committed suicide.

Hatano Isoko. Writer (1905–78), author of the famous book *Hiroshima no ko* (Child of Hiroshima, 1950).

Hatano Seiichi. Writer and philosopher (1877–1950). After studying Greek writers and Spinoza's philosophy, he turned to the Bible and conceived his own philosophy of religion, which he expounded in *Toki to eien* (Time and Eternity, 1943). He taught at Kyoto University and was president of Tamagawa University.

Hata Sahachirō. Bacteriologist (1873–1938), born in Shimane prefecture. He conducted research on venereal diseases, notably syphilis, with Paul Ehrlich in Frankfurt, Germany, with whom he discovered the treatment Salvarsan for curing syphilis. When he returned to Japan, he was one of the founders of the Kitazato Institute and became a professor at Keiō University.

Hata Shunroku. Officer (1899–1962), general, then minister of war in 1939. He was commander-in-chief of the Japanese army in China in 1941.

Hata Toyokichi. Writer and translator (1892–1956), born in Tokyo. He translated works by Goethe (*The Sorrows of Young Werther*) and Erich-Marie Remarque (*All Quiet on the Western Front*); then, under the pseudonym Maruki Sado (a wordplay on "Marquis de Sade"), he wrote erotic novels and stories. At the Tōhō Company, he produced musical films.

Hata Tsutomu. Contemporary politician, succeeding prime minister Hosokawa Morihiro when he retired in April 1994 but serving only two months in office.

Hatogaya. Town in Saitama prefecture (central Honshu), waystation on the Nikkō-kaidō route in the Edo period. *Pop.:* 60,000.

Hatoyama Haruko. Educator (Hatoyama Taga, 1861–1938), born in Matsumoto (Nagano prefecture), wife of Hatoyama Kazuo and mother of Hatoyama Hideo and Hatoyama Ichirō. She helped create Kyōritsu University for Women, of which she was president in 1922, and the Aikoku Fujin-kai association. Her memoirs, *Waga jijoden,* were published in 1930.

Hatoyama Hideo. Politician (1884–1946), son of Hatoyama Kazuo and Hatoyama Haruko. In 1911, after studying at the University of Tokyo, he went to France and Germany. He was appointed a professor at the University of Tokyo in 1916. Having studied law, he exerted great influence on Japanese jurisprudence via his brother, Hatoyama Ichirō. He published a number of books on German legislation and on his ideas about its interpretation in Japan.

Hatoyama Ichirō. Politician (1883–1959), brother of Hatoyama Kazuo and Hatoyama Hideo, born in Tokyo. He was elected to the House of Representatives in 1915, then became secretary-general of the Rikken Seiyūkai (Friends of Constitutional Government party). He was director of Tanaka Giichi's cabinet from 1927 to 1929, then minister of education from 1931 to 1934, in the cabinets of Inukai Tsuyoshi and Saitō Makoto. In 1946, he reorganized the Liberal party (Nihon Jiyūtō), but he was rejected by the Occupation authorities and ceded leadership of the party to Yoshida Shigeru. Rehabilitated in 1951, he formed a new party, the Nihon Minshutō (Japan Democratic party) and was prime minister from December 1954 to December 1956, succeeding Yoshida Shigeru. He signed accords with the USSR and China to end the state of war with these countries and got Japan accepted into the United Nations in December 1956. In 1956, he was forced to resign and to retire from political life due to poor health, leaving his position to Ishibashi Tanzan.

Hatoyama Kazuo. Politician and jurist (1856–1911), born in Tokyo. Hatoyama Haruko's husband and father of Hatoyama Hideo and Hato-

yama Ichirō. He studied law at Cambridge and Yale; when he returned to Japan, he worked to revise the Unequal Treaties (*see* JŌYAKU KAISEI). In 1892, he was elected to the House of Representatives for the Rikken Kaishintō (Constitutional Reform party), then was appointed president of Waseda University.

Hatsu-uma. "First day of the Horse," in February, according to Japanese and Chinese computations (*see* JIKKAN-JŪNISHI), devoted to worship of the *kami* of harvests, Inari Daimyōjin. This Shinto festival is observed mainly at the Fushimi Inari Jinja in Kyoto, but also in other parts of Japan, where the *kami* of silkworms (eastern Japan) or the *kami* of draft animals (horses or cows) is honored.

Hatta Shūzō. Anarchist theoretician (1868–1934), born in Tsu. He became a pastor for the Presbyterian Church and tended his flock until 1924. He then abandoned his ministry, went to Tokyo, and became known for his articles favoring a decentralized economy based on free village communities. He was an active member of the Federation of Libertarian Unions (Zenkoku Rōdō Kumiai Jiyū Rengōkai, abridged to Zenkoku Jiren). His writings were collected in *Hatta Shūzō zenshu* (1983).

Hattō. In Zen monasteries, room reserved for sermons and study of the sutras *(kyō)*. Also called *kōdō*.

Hatto-gaki. Group of texts of ancient laws compiled by Tokugawa Yoshimune in 1725 to constitute a code of laws useful to the shogunate.

Hattori. In ancient Japan (Asuka and Nara periods), corporation *(be)* of silkworm breeders and silk weavers of Korean origin. Hattori became the family name of many families. *See* HATA.

Hattori Kintarō. Industrialist (1860–1934), born in Edo, and founder of the clock companies K. Hattori and Seikōsha, in 1881 and 1892. The latter makes Seiko watches and other precision instruments.

Hattori Nankaku. Confucian painter and poet (Fuku Nankaku, Nankaku, 1683–1759), born in Kyoto. He studied the Chinese classics under Ogyū Sorai, then opened his own school in 1716. His paintings, imitating the Chinese Qing-dynasty style, are Bunjinga, or "scholarly painting" (Nanga school).

Hattori Ransetsu. Haiku poet (Hattori Harusuke, 1654–1707), born in Edo. Matsuo Bashō's disciple (and one of the Bashō Juttetsu), he was a faithful follower of his master's tradition and founded his own school, called Setsumon, renamed Ransetsu-ryū by his disciples Sakurai Rito and Ōshima Ryōta. His poems were published in two collections, *Sono fukuro* (1690) and *Ramsetsu bunshū* (1774). He also wrote the poetry books *Aru toki-shū, Sono hamayū* (with Ishiuchi Chōsō), and *Gempōshū.*

Hattori Ryōichi. Composer (1908–93) of many popular songs with a jazz flavor, such as *Aoi sammyaku* (Blue Mountains), *Tokyo bugiugi* (Tokyo Boogie-Woogie), and *Wakare no burūsu* (Good-bye Blues).

Hattori Shirō. Linguist, born 1908 in Mie prefecture, and professor at the University of Tokyo. He is known mainly for his research on Altaic and non-Altaic languages of Asia, about which he wrote extensively. *Nihongo no keitō* (Genealogy of the Japanese Language), published in 1959, is essential reading for an understanding of the development of Japanese.

Hattori Tohō. Haiku poet (Hattori Dohō, Hattori Yasuhide, 1657–1730), born in Iga province (Mie prefecture), known mainly for his book *Sanzōshi,* on the teachings of his master, Matsuo Bashō, published in 1702. He collected his own poems and those of other haiku poets from Iga province in an anthology called *Minomushian-shū,* compiled between 1688 and 1729.

Hattori Unokichi. Sinologist (1867–1939), born in Fukushima. After studying at the University of Tokyo in 1890, he taught mainly in Korea and China.

Hayaishi Osamu. Biochemist, born 1920 in Kyoto. He discovered oxygenase while conducting research in the United States, and he received the Order of Culture (Bunka-shō) in 1972.

Hayakawa Sesshū. Movie actor (Hayakawa Sessue, Hayakawa Kintarō, 1886–1973), born in Chiba. He went to the United States and studied in Chicago. While acting in amateur theater companies, he was "discovered" by a director, Thomas Ince, who gave him a role in *Typhoon* (1914). After this, he was in great demand in Hollywood and was in more than 40 movies, the best known being *Yoshiwara* by Max Ophüls (1937) and *The Bridge Over the River Kwai* by David Lean (1957). He was

not well known in Japan, where he appeared in a few movies. He returned to his native country in 1949; becoming a Zen Buddhist monk late in life, he wrote a book on Zen, *Zen Showed Me the Way to Peace* (1960). He married actress Aoki Tsuru.

Hayakumo-za. Kabuki theater, built in Kyoto for the actor and *zamato* Hayakumo Chōkichi in 1669.

Hayama Yoshiki. Writer (1894–1945), born in Fukuoka prefecture. After an education cut short for lack of funds, he worked in various trades: sailor, laborer, bureaucrat. He became a journalist at the *Nagoya Shimbun* in 1920 and joined union movements, which earned him several stays in prison and an itinerant life. He began to write in the "proletarian" style, first stories, then novels. His story *Imbaifu* (The Prostitute), published in the magazine *Bungei Sensen* (Literary Front) in 1925, got him noticed in literary circles. He wrote many other stories on life in factories and on ships, then a long novel, *Umi ni ikuru hitobito* (Those Who Earn a Living from the Sea), published in 1926, which truly established him as an author. His narrative style was influenced by Russian writers, such as Dostoyevsky and especially Gorky. His works were collected in the six-volume *Hayama Yoshiki zenshū* (1975–76).

Hayami Gyoshū. Painter (Hayama Eiichi, Makita Eiichi, 1894–1935), born in Tokyo. Imamura Shikō's student, he took the name Hayami only in 1914. He traveled in Europe, Egypt, and Korea in 1930, and created a new "Japanese painting" style (Nihonga), interpreting the classical styles; then, after studying Chinese painters of the Song and Yuan periods, he devoted himself to realism. At the end of his life, he produced more symbolic and decorative works. He sometimes signed with the *gō* Kako.

Hayanari. *See* TACHIBANA HAYANARI.

Hayashi. Musical or vocal accompaniment for a singing, dancing, or theatrical performance. It can consist simply of clapping hands, snapping fingers, beating a drum, playing cymbals, or singing. In the case of Noh theater, a *hayashi* ensemble is composed of a flute and two or three drums *(taiko, tsuzumi)*. In Kabuki theater, the ensemble also includes a shamisen. *See* DEBAYASHI, GEZA-GAKU, HISAKUNI, NOH.

• **Hayashi-kata.** Orchestra accompanying Noh plays, composed of flutes and drums, whose role is to punctuate the recitation of the Yōkyoku and the actors' gestures.

Hayashi-bugyō. Bureaucrat in the Edo period responsible for surveillance and maintenance of shogunal forests. The position was created in 1685.

Hayashi Fubō. Writer (Hasegawa Umitarō; *gō:* Tani Jōji, Maki Itsuma, 1900–35), born on the island of Sado, Hasegawa Shirō's brother. After living in the United States for six years, he wrote stories about his life in that country (under the name Tani Jōji), then detective novels (under the name Maki Itsuma), and finally historical novels (under the name Hayashi Fubō) such as *Shimpan Ōoka seidan* (1928). He wrote so many novels that he was nicknamed "the literary monster." Among his best-known books are *Tekisasu mushuku* (Homeless in Texas, 1928) and *Chijō no seiza* (The Earth Constellation, 1934).

Hayashi Fumiko. Writer (1903–51) born in Yamaguchi prefecture. An illegitimate child, she spent her childhood traveling with her mother, an itinerant peddler. When she arrived in Tokyo, she worked at various trades and occupations and spent time in more or less anarchistic circles of poets. She began to write poems, then novels, which she published in various magazines; *Hōrōki* (1928), which describes the wanderings of her childhood, was an immediate success. It was followed by *Fūkin to sakana no machi* (A Town Full of Fish and Music, 1931), *Nakamushi kozō* (The Little Crybaby, 1935), *Inazuma* (Lightning, 1936), *Bangiku* (Last Chrysanthemums, 1948), *Shitamachi* (The Lower Town, 1949), and *Ukigumo* (Floating Clouds, 1950). She traveled in Japan, Europe, China, Manchuria, and Southeast Asia, from which she drew some of the material for her stories. Many of her books were adapted for the screen, notably *Hōrōki*, by Kimura Sotoji (1935), Hisamatsu Seiji (1954), and Naruse Mikio (1962), and *Nakimushi kozō*, by Toyoda Shirō (1938). Naruse Mikio was the most prolific adapter of her novels.

Hayashi Fusao. Writer and literary critic (Gotō Toshio, Shirai Akira, 1903–75), born in Ōita. His Marxist activities within student movements earned him two prison terms in the 1930s. He later changed his thinking and became an ultranationalist. After the Second World War, he wrote novels with no political slant, among them *Musuko no seishun* (1950), then returned to his polemics. His best-known novel is *Seinen* (Youth, 1932).

Hayashi Gahō. Confucian philosopher and historian (Hayashi Shunzai, 1618–80), Hayashi Razan's son, born in Kyoto. He went to Edo to teach Confucianism to shogun Tokugawa Iemitsu and, with his father, wrote a genealogy of warrior families, *Kan'ei shoka keizu-den,* and a history of Japan, *Honchō tsugan.* He succeeded his father as adviser to the shogun. Among his important writings were *Kokushi jitsuroki, Nihon Ōdai ichiran,* and *Kan'ei keizu* (1643). Hayashi Hōkō's father.

Hayashi Hiromori. Musician and composer (1821–86) who set Japan's national anthem to music. *See* KIMI-GA YO.

Hayashi Hōkō. Confucian scholar (1644–1732), Hayashi Gahō's son. He was the tutor of shogun Tokugawa Tsunayoshi and in 1691 became the first director of the official shogunate school (the Shōhei-kō), a position that remained hereditary in the Hayashi family from then on. On his suggestion, the shogun admitted Confucian scholars into the samurai class.

Hayashi Jikkō. Painter (1777–1813), in the Nanga style, who lived in Mito. Although he never studied painting, he produced very personal works, highly thought of by Tani Bunchō. He died in poverty.

Hayashi Jussai. Confucian historian and philosopher (Hayashi Kō, 1768–1841), Hayashi Jo's adoptive son, chosen by Mastudaira Sadanobu to be head of the Hayashi family when Hayashi Nobutaka died in 1793 (*see* SHŌHEI-KŌ). He reorganized the study cycles of Zhu Xi (*Jap.:* Shushi) philosophy, which he made the official doctrine of the shogunate. With other historians in his school, he compiled *Tokugawa jikki,* a history of the Tokugawa clan, and wrote *Chōya kyūbun bōkō.*

Hayashi Matsuhichi. Blacksmith (1613–99), maker of swords and sword guards *(tsuba),* serving the Hosokawa family of Higo province. Also called Hayashi Matashichi.

Hayashi Rashi. Writer (eighteenth century), author of a collection of popular stories, inspired by the Chinese *Jinqu qiguan,* titled *Gekka seidan* (Simple Conversations under the Moon), in 1790.

Hayashi Razan. Neo-Confucian scholar (Hayashi Nobukatsu, Hayashi Dōshun, 1583–1657), born in Kyoto, Hayashi Nobutoki's son and adopted by his uncle, Hayashi Yoshikatsu. After spending two years (1595–97) in the Zen Kennin-ji monastery, he plunged into study of Zhu Xi (*Jap.*: Shushi) philosophy. He then became Fujiwara Seika's student. In 1607, shogun Tokugawa Ieyasu forced him to become a Zen monk under the name Dōshun, and he worked for the shogunate as a secretary. Opposed to Buddhism, he founded a Shinto-Confucian sect that he named Ritō-shinchi Shintō. With two of his sons, Hayashi Gahō and Hayashi Morikatsu (Dokkō-sai, b. 1624), he compiled the *Honchō tsugan* (which his other son, Hayashi Jo, finished). In 1635, he collaborated with his younger brother, Hayashi Nobozumi (1585–1683), to write the second version of the *Buke-shohatto* and *Hatamoto-shohatto* (Laws Concerning the *Hatamoto*). As a promoter of Zhu Xi philosophy, he proved to be a fierce adversary of Christianity and Buddhism (even though he was a Zen monk) and of Wang Yang-ming's (*Jap.*: Ō-Yōmei) neo-Confucian philosophy, claiming that Shinto and the Confucianism that he himself favored were in essence identical.

Hayashi Senjuro. Officer and politician (1876–1943), born in Ishikawa prefecture. He commanded troops in Korea; in 1931, he sent reinforcements to the Chinese Army of the Guandong (Kantō-gun) without government authorization, but once he took control of Manchuria, he was praised. In 1932, he was promoted to general. He was minister of war in Saitō Makoto's cabinet in 1934 (succeeding Araki Sadao) and in Okada Keisuke's cabinet in 1935. He discharged from the army 5,000 officers whom he felt were fascists, provoking serious incidents (Feb. 26, 1936) that forced him to resign. Appointed prime minister (Feb.–June 1937) succeeding Hirota Kōki, he was not able to form a majority government and was replaced by Prince Konoe Fumimaro, then minister of war. *See* NINIROKU-JIKEN, TŌSEIHA.

Hayashi Shihei. Scholar and politician (Hayashi Tomonao, Rokumusai, 1738–93), born in Edo. Having taken the emperor's side against the shogunate, he was sent into exile in Sendai, where he spent the rest of his life. In 1785, he wrote an illustrated geographical treatise on the "three nations"—Korea, Hokkaido, and the Ryukyu Islands—titled *Sangoku tsūran zusetsu*. In a treatise on naval defense, *Kaikoku heidan,* published in 1791, he urged the shogunate to reinforce coastal defenses in anticipation of Russian landings and to retrain the samurai, who had become soft due to the long period of peace. He was exiled for expressing this opinion.

Hayashi Shōji. Architect, born 1928 in Tokyo. He designed many modern, functional buildings, among them Palaceside in Tokyo (1966), the Tōyō Shimpō Building (1961), and the IBM Building (1971).

Hayashi Tadasu. Diplomat (1850–1913), born in Shimōsa province (Chiba prefecture). He studied in Great Britain in 1866, then accompanied the Iwakura mission to Europe and the United States in 1870. Soon after, he was appointed governor of Hyōgo and Kanazawa, then vice-minister of foreign affairs, after working in the Ministry of Public Works. He was ambassador to China (1895–97), Russia (1897–99), and Great Britain (1899) and a delegate to the peace conference in The Hague in 1899. He signed a trade treaty between China and Japan (1896) and an alliance with England (1902 and 1905). As minister of foreign affairs from 1906 to 1908, he concluded a series of agreements with France (1907) and Russia. He served as minister of communications in Saionji's second cabinet in 1911–12.

Hayashi Takeshi. Western-style painter (Takeomi, 1896–1975), born in Tokyo. His first paintings, influenced by Matisse and Derain, earned him many awards in exhibitions in Japan, a chair at Tokyo Geijutsu Daigaku (Tokyo University of Fine Arts and Music) and the Order of Culture (Bunka-shō) in 1967. In his mature paintings, he used a very spare, "cerebral" cubist style.

Hayashi Yuzō. Politician (1842–1921), born in Tosa (Kōchi prefecture). He joined the Risshi-sha (Self-Help Society) formed by Itagaki in Kōchi and helped to found the Aikoku Kōtō party. He was imprisoned in 1877 for supplying weapons to Sutsuma; freed during the general amnesty, he was again imprisoned briefly in 1878 for anti-government activities. He then helped Itagaki reorganize the Aikoku Kōtō, which had been dissolved, and was elected to the Diet. He was minister of communications in Okuma Shigenobu's cabinet and minister of commerce and of agriculture in Itō Hirobumi's fourth cabinet. He retired from politics in 1908.

Hayato. An indigenous people inhabiting southern Kyushu at the beginning of the Japanese historical period, who resisted "pacification" attempts by the Yamato court until at least the early eighth century. General Otomo no Tabito finally subdued them. They were then integrated into society and became warriors responsible for guarding the imperial palace. One of their customs was to bay like dogs to frighten demons and enemies. They were recruited from their tribes by a special bureau established in the seventh century, the Hayato no Tsukasa, under the direction of the Emon-fu. After 808, they were recruited by the Hyōbu-shō and a Hayato no Kami was installed as their leader. The descendants of the Hayato (the name remained as a family name) have a special dance (Hayato-mai) celebrating, according to legend, their ancestors' surrender to Jimmu Tennō's grandfather. *See also* KUMASO.

• **Hayato-zuka.** Rectangular *kofun* in Hayato, Kagoshima prefecture (southern Kyushu), measuring about 15 m per side and 3 m in height; date of construction uncertain. Tradition has it that the conquerors of the Yamato had a stele and sculptures portraying the Shi Tennō constructed on top of it in order to keep the spirits of the Hayato and Kumaso from harming the state. These monuments date from the medieval period.

Hazama-gumi. Company that builds dams and executes other public works, founded in 1889. In 1908, it was one of the builders of the Seoul–Pusan railroad in Korea. Its foreign contracts comprise about 20% of its business volume. Head office in Tokyo.

Hazama Inosuke. Painter (b. 1895). He went to France and studied with Matisse. When he returned to Japan, he created a school of modern painting called Issui-kai and wrote several books on French painters Matisse and Courbet.

Ha-zuki. "Season of falling leaves," corresponding to the eighth month of the year in the Nijūshi-setsu calendar. Also called Tsukimi-zuki (month for contemplating the moon).

Hazumune. Engraver of ukiyo-e woodprints (Fuji Hazumune, late seventeenth century). He worked for many artists, among them Utamaro.

Hearn, Lafcadio. American writer (1850–1904), born on the island of Lefkas, Greece, to an Irish officer and a Greek mother. He was educated in Ireland, England, and France before emigrating to the United States in 1869. Although handicapped by partial blindness, he earned his living by translating French novels into English and working as a reporter. He went to Japan in 1889, upon the invitation of Basil Hall Chamberlain, who helped him

find a job as an English teacher in Matsue (Shimane prefecture). Two years later, he married Koizumi Setsuko, the daughter of a local low-ranking samurai. The following year, he became a professor at a government college in Kumamoto and wrote his first book on Japan, *Glimpses of an Unfamiliar Japan* (1894). Passionately devoted to his adoptive country, he applied for Japanese citizenship (which he received in 1894, was adopted by his wife's family, and took the name Koizumi Yakumo. Again with Chamberlain's help, he obtained a position as professor of English literature at University of Tokyo and continued to write: *Exotics and Retrospective* (1898), *In Ghostly Japan* (1899), *Shadowings* (1900), *Japanese Miscellany* (1901), *Kaidan* (1904), and *Japan: An Attempt at Interpretation* (1904). The last was his most famous work, published soon after his death on September 26, 1904. His tomb is in the Zōshigaya Cemetery in Ikebukuro (Tokyo). His wife wrote a memoir, *Reminiscences of Lafcadio Hearn* (1918).

Hebi to hato. "The Snake and the Pigeon," a satirical novel (1952) by Niwa Fumio, bitterly criticizing the new religious fads that sprang up after the Second World War and denouncing the way certain "priests" of these new religions strained the credulity of their followers.

Heguri. Lady of the imperial court of Heijō-kyō (Nara) in the eighth century and a poet famous in her time.

Heian-jidai. "Era of peace and tranquillity," name given by historians to the historical and artistic period that succeeded the Nara period (Nara-jidai), lasting from 794, when the court was established at Heian-kyō (Kyoto), to 1185, the beginning of the Kamakura period. In art, it is usually divided into three periods: Kōnin (or Jōgan, 794–868 or 877), Fujiwara (868 or 877–1086), and late Fujiwara (1087–1185). It was the great period of "classic" aristocratic culture in Japan.

• **Heian-jingū.** Shinto shrine in Kyoto built in 1895 to celebrate the 1,100th anniversary of the city's foundation, dedicated to the spirits of emperors Kammu and Kōmei. The main room, with red-painted pillars and a large gate, reproduces (on a reduced scale) the buildings of the old imperial palace *(gosho)*. The shrine is surrounded by a magnificent garden. A festival in memory of Emperor Kammu, the founder, is celebrated on April 3, and one in memory of Emperor Kōmei is celebrated on Janu-

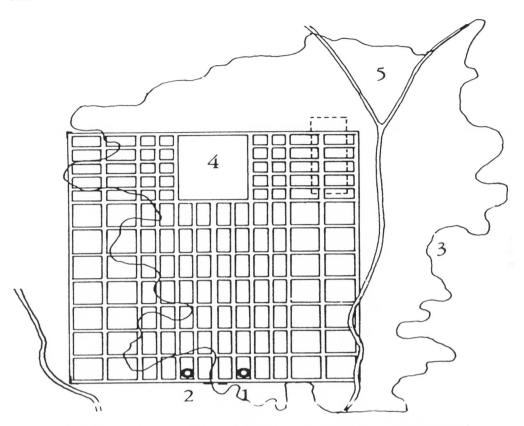

Plan of Heian-kyō (Kyoto) in 794. 1. Tō-ji, "eastern" Buddhist temple. 2. Sai-ji, "western" Buddhist temple. 3. The city today. 4. Imperial palace. 5. Kamo River

ary 30. On October 22, the costumed processions of the Jidai Matsuri leave from this splendid shrine. Damaged by fire in January 1976, it was quickly rebuilt.

• **Heian-kyō.** "Capital of Peace and Tranquillity," the name given to the city of Kyoto by Temmu Tennō when he inaugurated the new city in 794, after abandoning Nagaoka, which remained the imperial capital of Japan until 1868. Heian-kyō was planned on the checkerboard model of the Chinese capital, Chang'an, and built between the Kamo-gawa and Katsura-gawa rivers, on a plain bordered to the northeast by Mt. Hiei, to the west by the Higashiyama hill, and to the northwest by the Arashiyama hills. With the financial support of the Fujiwara and Hata families, who financed construction of the new capital, Emperor Kammu both freed the court from the grip of the six sects of Nara (*see* BUDDHISM) and reinforced the *ritsuryō* system. Huge works were executed to change the course of

the Kamo-gawa so that it would "frame" the capital, and canals were dug parallel to the major north–south avenues. Early plans called for the city to be 5.2 km north to south and 4.5 km east to west. Only two temples were to guard the southern entrances to the city, the Tō-ji and the Sai-ji. The palace *(daidairi, gosho)* was situated in the north part of the city and divided into two equal parts, east (Sa-kyō) and west (U-kyō), by a 84-meter-wide avenue, the Suzaku Oji. Each part of the city had a market. Transversal (east–west) avenues were named after the bridges over the canal that crossed the city north to south: Ichijō, Nijō, Sanjō, Shijō, Gojō, Rokujō, Shichijō, Hachijō, Kujō. Each part of the city was, in turn, divided into four large blocks by north–south streets. Other streets, less regularly laid out, crossed each block, dividing them into *chō* about 1,450 m², which in turn were divided into 32 lots of 16.6 × 8.3 m, called *henushi*. The residences of nobles and senior bureaucrats were in the north part of the city, on either side of the imperial palace.

In fact, however, the city very rapidly overflowed these theoretical limits; because the U-kyo district was unsanitary, the city developed mainly toward the Kamo River, in the Sa-kyo district to the east. Heian-kyo was victim to many fires, pillages, and wars, and was almost totally destroyed a number of times. The imperial palace caught fire 16 times between 960 and 1228, and finally was not restored. The city was more than half destroyed during the Ōnin War (1467–77), and it was not until Oda Nobunaga and Toyotomi Hideyoshi came to power that its streets were laid out again and the city and the *daidairi* were partially restored. In the eighteenth century, the palace buildings were moved to the center of the city, and some of its rooms were restored in the nineteenth century. Kyoto (which means "capital"), already the name of the city of Heijō-kyō (Nara), was not applied to Heian-kyo until the late eleventh century. It has remained the name of the previous imperial capital to the present day. Also called Miyako. *See* KYOTO.

Heibonsha. Publisher of dictionaries, encyclopedias, and scientific and philosophical books, founded in 1914 by Shimonaka Yasaburō in Tokyo. Since 1946, it has also published art books and literature magazines.

Heichū monogatari. Collection of 39 poetic tales containing 152 *waka* poems by an unknown author, probably written between 959 and 965, telling the story of a certain Heichū, perhaps Taira no Sadabumi (ca. 871–923). In this *uta-monogatari* (story in songs), the hero, Heichū, is contrasted to Prince Genji, and his amorous adventures almost invariably end in fiasco. The character was mocked and presented as a comic character in later novels such as the *Genji monogatari* and the *Konjaku monogatari,* which no doubt was not the author's intention.

Heida. In Noh theater, the mask representing a young man. *See* NŌMEN.

Heiden. In Shinto shrines, a room reserved for offerings made to the *kami* by followers.

Heiji. Era of Emperor Nijō: Apr. 1159–Jan. 1160. *See* NENGŌ.
• One of the names for the Taira family. Also Heike, Heishi.

• *Heiji monogatari.* "Story of the War of the Heiji Era," a war story *(gunki monogatari)* telling an em-

bellished version of the war between the Minamoto and Taira clans in the mid-twelfth century that resulted in the fall of the Fujiwara and the rise of the Kanto warrior clans. This text, sometimes attributed to Hamuro Tokinaga, was rewritten a number of times and was sung as a continuation of the *Hōgen monogatari.* Written in 36 chapters, the *Heiji monogatari* supplied countless themes to theater and literature in subsequent eras. *See also* GEMPEI SEISUIKI, HEIKE MONOGATARI, HEIKYOKU, HŌGEN MONOGATARI.

• *Heiji monogatari ekotoba.* *Emakimono* in color on paper, in five scrolls, dating from the thirteenth century, relating and illustrating some of the most notable episodes in the war between the Minamoto and Taira clans told in the *Heiji monogatari.* It is sometimes attributed, but without certainty, to Sumiyoshi Keion, a thirteenth-century painter. Also called *Heiji monogatari emaki.*

• **Heiji no Ran.** "Heiji War," a battle in January 1160 between Minamoto no Yoshitomo and Taira no Kiyomori. Yoshitomo took power, with the assistance of Fujiwara no Nobuyori (1133–60), and imprisoned emperors Go-Shirakawa and Nijō, but Taira no Kiyomori attacked him. Yoshitomo and Nobuyori were killed trying to flee, leaving the Taira victorious. The *Heiji monogatari* tells the story of this confrontation. *See* HŌGEN NO RAN.

Heijō. "Palace of Tranquillity," name for the imperial palace in Heijō-kyō (Nara).
• Japanese name for the Korean city Pyongyang.

• **Heijō-kyō.** Imperial capital of Japan from 710 to 784, on a site near the current city of Nara, built to replace the old capital city of Fujiwara-kyō, located about 18 km farther south. The site was irrigated by two small rivers, the Saho and the Akishino. Construction of the city took two years (707–09), and it was inaugurated by Empress Gemmei. The city followed the checkerboard plan of the Chinese Tang capital, Chang'an, but included an "outside" district to the east, the Ge-kyo, and two districts to the east and west called Sa-kyo and U-kyo (to the left and to the right), respectively. Measuring around 4.8 × 4.3 km, it was divided by evenly spaced streets into square blocks *(jō)* 550 m per side and had two large markets. (Its general plan was followed when Heian-kyō was built in 794, and the names of the streets were identical in both cities.) In the U-kyo section were three large Buddhist temples, the Saidai-ji, the Tōshōdai-ji, and the Yakushi-ji (from north to south). In the Sa-kyō was the Daian-ji; in the Ge-kyō were the Kōfuku-ji and the Gangō-ji. The Tō-ji was a bit farther east, outside the theoretical perimeter of the city. Heijō-kyō probably had a population of about 200,000 by the mid-eighth century. Excavations of the site have uncovered a large number of remains, including more than 20,000 inscribed tablets *(mokkan)* dating from between 709 and 782. In 784, the court left the city for Nagaoka, farther north, where it remained for ten years before moving on to Heian-kyō. The major temples remained, but the population moved farther east; today's city of Nara occupies the site of Ge-kyō. In the Nara period, emperors moved their palaces a number of times, establishing them at Kuni no Miya, Naniwa, and Shigaraki, but they returned each time to Heijō-kyō. Also called Taira no Miyako. *See* HEIAN-KYŌ, NAGAOKA, NARA.

• **Heijō Tennō.** Fifty-first emperor (Prince Ate, 744<806–09>824), son of and successor to Kammu Tennō. He abdicated in favor of his brother, Saga, but soon plotted against him with the help of his wife, Kusuriko. Defeated by the army of Sakanoue no Tamuramaro, he became a Buddhist monk. Also called Nara Tennō.

Heike. "Hei family," one of the names of the Taira family. Also Heiji. *See* TAIRA.

• *Heike monogatari.* "Account of the Heike," in 12 volumes, classical version of the *Gempei seisuiki,* written between 1202 and 1221 and attributed to Hamuro Tokinaga, Yukinaga, or Minamoto no Mitsuyuki. However, the sung version *(Heikyoku),* written by Akashi Kakuichi in 1371, is the one now accepted as definitive, since this "war story" *(gunki-monogatari)* was rewritten 100 times up to then. The original was written in Chinese *(kambun)* and incorporated various accounts and songs from different sources. The story relates the fortunes of the Taira clan after the Hōgen no Ran (1156) and the Heiji no Ran (1160), when they established supremacy over the rival Minamoto (Genji) clan. The main characters are Taira no Kiyomori in the first part and the Minamoto (Yoshinaka, Yoritomo, and Yoshitsune) in the second and third parts. The story ends in 1185, with the definitive victory of Minamoto no Yoritomo and the ultimate defeat of the Taira clan at the naval battle of Dan no Ura. This great epic abounds in battles and heroic feats and is imbued with Buddhist morals and piety, especially with the sense of impermanence of all things, sentiments that were probably added by the Buddhist singers *(biwa-hōshi)* who performed these stories. The *Heike monogatari* was adapted countless times for Noh theater and has been an inexhaustible source of inspiration for novelists and poets.

Heikyoku. Sung adaptation of episodes of the *Heike monogatari,* performed, according to Yoshida Kenkō, by Yukinaga, a courtier and monk of the Tendai-shū on Mt. Hiei, and a blind singer, Shōbutsu, about 1220. These songs, meant to be accompanied by a *biwa,* incorporated musical elements taken from Buddhist chants and court music. Schools of sung recitation of the *Heike monogatari (Heikyoku)* were founded by two of Shōbutsu's disciples, Ichikata-ryū and Yasaka-ryū, and others soon followed. The current repertoire of the *Heikyoku* comprises about 200 pieces categorized by genre.

Heimin. Commoners *(see also* ETA). At the beginning of the Meiji era (1868), Japanese society was divided into three classes: *heimin* (commoners), *kazoku* (former nobles and daimyo), and *shizoku* (former samurai). The *heimin* were authorized to use family names in 1870. *See* HYAKUSHŌ, KAZOKU.

• **Heiminsha.** "Society of Commoners," a socialist organization opposed to war against Russia, founded in 1908 by Kōtoku Shūsui and Sakai Toshihito in association with Christian socialists, including Ishikawa Sanshirō and Kinoshita Naoe. It published a weekly magazine, *Heimin Shimbun,* in 1903, which became a daily in 1907. This organ was replaced by another weekly, *Chokugen,* which was banned several months after it was launched. The society was dissolved in 1906 and its newspapers stopped publishing. The *Heimin Shimbun* was then taken over by the socialists, but was again banned in April 1907.

• **Heimin Shugi.** *See* TOKUTOMI SOHŌ.

Heimon. "Closed door." In the Edo period, punishment for samurai for minor offenses, in which they were not allowed to leave their house for a given period, generally between 50 and 100 days, or to receive visitors. The door was symbolically nailed shut. A similar punishment was meted out to monks. Commoners were sentenced to a similar punishment of confinement, called *tojime* or *hissoku,* but they were allowed to go out at night. *See* SHIOKI.

Heine, Peter Bernhard Wilhelm. German painter (1827–85), born and died in Dresden. He wanted to go to Japan, so he hired on to an American ship in order to sail with Commodore Perry in 1852 and 1854. He was the first Western painter to paint views of the coasts of Japan and Edo, which he published in *Graphic Scenes in the Japan Expedition,* in 1856, and in various magazines and newspapers. He returned to Japan in 1860, was named consul to Paris, then retired to Dresden in 1871, where he lived out his days finishing his travel sketches. A statue of him was erected facing the Staatliches Museum für Völkerkunde in Munich, where some of his works are on display. He illustrated *The Narrative of the Expedition to the China Seas and Japan* by Sir Francis Hawks, who had also accompanied Commodore Perry.

Heinouchi Osumi. Architect (1584–1645) from a famous family of builders; studied with his father, Heinouchi Yoshimasa (designer of Toyotomi Hideyoshi's mausoleum in Kyoto in 1598). Osumi worked for the Tokugawa shogunate, building various mausoleums, notably Nikkō's in 1634–36. He was responsible for construction of the inside shrine of the Tōshōgū and the Jōgyōdō of the Buddhist temple of the Rinno-ji in Nikkō. His descendants were all architects and builders.

Heisei. "Peace and Accomplishment." Name of the era chosen by Emperor Akihito when he ascended to the throne in 1989, succeeding his father, Hirohito (Shōwa Tennō); the era began in February 1989.

Heishi. Vase for a plum-tree branch, similar to the Chinese *mei-ping* and the Korean *mae-pyŏng,* with a wide shoulder and a very narrow mouth. This shape, which appeared in China under the Song dynasty, was imitated in Japan starting in the late Kamakura period. *See* CERAMICS.

Heisō. Warrior-monks responsible for defending the Buddhist temples; they often provoked disturbances. Also called Sōhei. *See* AKUSŌ.

Heki Masatsugu. Famous sixteenth-century samurai and archer who founded an archery school (Kyū-jutsu) named after him, Heki-ryū. He became a Buddhist monk on Mt. Kōya.

Hepburn, James Curtis. American missionary and physician (1815–1911) who lived in Japan from 1859 to 1892. From 1874 to 1888, with the help of other missionaries, he translated the Bible into Japanese and produced an English–Japanese dictionary for which he invented a system for romanizing sounds in the Japanese language. The Hepburn system is still the universally accepted standard for all translations from Japanese to English and French. *See also* CHŌRŌ-KYOKAI.

Heusken, Henry Hendrick, C. J. Secretary (1832–61) of the first American consul, Townsend Harris. He accompanied Harris to Japan in 1856. Dutch by birth, he spoke English, French, and Dutch fluently. In January 1861, he was assassinated by anti-foreigner elements of the Satsuma estate, and the shogunate was forced to pay an indemnity of 10,000 Mexican dollars to his family.

Heuvers, Herman. German Jesuit missionary (1891–1977) and Japanese-language poet. He was president of Sophia University in Tokyo and wrote Noh plays and a Kabuki play called *Hosokawa Gracia.*

Hibachi. Portable round or rectangular brazier, known in Japan since at least the Nara period. At first used only by nobles and important persons to heat their homes, their use spread in the mid-seventeenth century with the proliferation of *chōnin* houses, while peasants used *irori. Hibachi,* once called *hioke* and *hibitsu,* were made of porcelain or metal clad in wood. They were dangerous and caused many fires. Some houses use traditional *hibachi* even today, especially in the countryside. The charcoal used to fuel them is handled with large metal tongs called *hibashi. See* IRORI.

Hibakusha. Word coined in December 1945 to describe survivors, irradiated or not, of the atom-bomb attacks *(hibaku)* on Hiroshima and Nagasaki. The *hibakusha* formed associations to defend their rights and to fight against use of the atom bomb.

Hibari-yama. Title of a Noh play: upon the insistence of his second wife, a minister orders one of his servants to take his daughter, Chūjō, to Mt. Hibari and kill her. Instead of carrying out this barbaric order, the servant hides the girl. The nurse hears of this and sells flowers to provide concrete help. When the minister shows remorse over the death of his daughter, the nurse reveals the truth and asks him to take her back.
→ *See* TAEMA.

Hibino Gohō. Calligrapher (Hibino Makoto), born 1901 in Gifu. Ono Hyakuren's student, famous for his unique kana writings drawn from writing models of the Heian period.

Hibiya Kōen. Large park in central Tokyo near the imperial palace, created in 1903 on the estate of a former daimyo's residence. *Area:* 16 hectares. It is also the name of the surrounding neighborhood and a nearby subway station. In September 1905, it was the site of a huge riot (Hibiya Yakiuchi Jiken) as city residents protested the Portsmouth Treaty, which ended the Russo-Japanese War of 1904–05. They felt that the treaty was humiliating for Japan, and they appealed to the emperor himself. The government was forced to decree martial law after more than 350 public buildings, churches, and private homes had been set ablaze and looted by the rioters.

Hiburi-shima. Small island in the Suwa Sea, east of Shikoku, where Fujiwara no Sumitomo (killed in 941) built a fort and amassed a fleet to lead his men against the Heian government, thus supporting Tairo no Masakado's revolt. It was used as a place of exile during the Edo period. *Area:* 5 km².

Hibutsu. "Hidden Buddha": in Japanese Esoteric Buddhism *(mikkyō),* name for all divinities considered "secret" or "hidden," such as Kangi Ten.

Hichiriki. Sort of oboe made of bamboo. It is quite short (about 18 cm), lacquered in red or brown inside and out, with seven holes on the upper side and two on the lower side. The reed is made of two reed blades attached with a string. This Japanese version of the Central Asian *bili* is used mainly in Tōgaku and Komagaku Gagaku music. *See* FLUTES.

Hida. Former province, now part of Gifu prefecture (central Honshu).
• Mountain range running north–south, 130 km long, in northern Honshu, called the Japanese Alps. The range crosses Niigata, Toyama, Nagano, and Gifu prefectures. A number of its peaks are over 3,000 m in altitude.

• **Hida Kami-ji.** Former name of the region composed of the former provinces of Hitachi, Iwaki, and Rikuzen.

• **Hida Minzoku Mura.** Former village near Takayama (Gifu prefecture), transformed into an outdoor folklore museum featuring different housing styles in the region. Some private residences have also been converted into museums of local arts and crafts.

Hidai Tenrai. Calligrapher (Shōshi, 1872–1939), born in Nagano. Though he studied with Kusakabe Meikaku, he developed a very different style, creating a school of modern calligraphy (Shogaku-in) in Tokyo. His wife, Hidai Shōkin, herself an excellent kana calligrapher, also taught calligraphy.

Hidaka Sammyaku. Mountain range 130 km long in southern Hokkaido, north–south orientation. Its highest peak is Poroshirodake (2,052 m), and many other peaks are between 1,500 and 2,000 m in altitude.

Hida Keiko. Artist and calligrapher (b. 1913), creator of an art form called Kusa-e, consisting of pieces of paper cut out and pasted together to form "paintings."

Hidari Jingorō. Carpenter and sculptor in wood (Itami Toshikatsu, ca. 1584–1634), in the service of the Muromachi shogunate in Kyoto. He was left-handed (whence his surname Hidari). He worked at the Nishi Hongan-ji and the Chion-in in Kyoto (for which he built *uguisu-bari,* "singing floors") and at the Hōkō-ji (belltower). He then went to Edo and was sponsored by the Tokugawa clan to make sculptures at the Tōshō-gū in Nikkō (such as the *nemuri-neko,* or "sleeping cat"). The Hidari family has continued sculpting in wood to the present day.

Hidari Sachiko. Actress and movie director, born 1930 in Toyama. At first a music and gymnastics teacher, she was discovered in 1952 by Gosho Heinosuke, who featured her in a number of his films. She received the acting award at the Cork Film Festival in 1957 for her role in the film *Kamisaka Shirō no hanzai* (Kamisaka Shirō's Crime), directed by Hisamatsu Seiji. She then worked under director Imamura Shōhei (*Nippon konchū-ki,* "Story of the Insect-Woman of Japan," 1963). She married director Hani Susumu and acted in several other films for him, including *Kanojo to kare* (She and He, 1963), which earned her the best actress award at the Berlin festival in 1964. She then went to Paris, where she shot several short films in 1977 and launched her directing career with a feature called *Tōi ippon no michi* (The Long and Distant Road), which received an honorable mention from the Museum of Modern Art in New York and was presented at the Berlin festival in 1978. *See* TASAKA TOMOTAKA.

Hiden'in. Hostels for poor people and orphans set up at the same time as the *seiyaku-in* (dispensaries) by Shōtoku Taishi in the early seventh century, imitating similar institutions founded by Buddhist monks in China. The Kōfuku-ji temple in Nara housed such an institution in 723. These refuges also existed in the capital and in other regions under the direction of Buddhist temples until at least the tenth century, and some, such as those at the Sennyū-ji in Kyoto, operated until the fifteenth century. The Edo shogunate took over these charitable institutions and established others in a number of provinces. Also called *hiden-dokoro*.

Hideyori. Painter (Kanō Hideyori, d. 1557) of the Kanō school in Kyoto, Motonobu's son. He painted the "View of the Maples in Takao," a famous work now at the Tokyo National Museum.
→ *See* TOYOTOMI HIDEYORI.

Hideyoshi. *See* TOYOTOMI HIDEYOSHI.

Hieda no Are. Courtier or courtesan *(toneri)* serving Emperor Temmu (late seventh century). This person is said to have recited the ancient imperial legends and genealogies from memory to Ō no Yasumaro, who set them in writing to create the *Kojiki* (711–12), upon the request of Empress Gemmei. It is said that Hieda no Are was 65 years old at the time. It is not known whether this person was a man or a woman. Also written Ieda no Are.

Hiei-zan. Mountain (Mt. Hiei), altitude 848 m, located northeast of Kyoto, from the top of which there are extensive views of Lake Biwa and the city. On a north–south axis, it forms the border between Kyoto and Shiga prefectures. The Buddhist Enryaku-ji monastery was established on its eastern slopes in 788; there is also a Shinto shrine there, Hie-taisha, devoted to the mountain's *kami*, Ō-Yamakui, protector of the town of Kyoto and of the Enryaku-ji temple. *See* HIE-TAISHA, ENRYAKU-JI.

Hie-jinja. Shinto shrine in Tokyo, dedicated to Ō-Yamakui (Sannō Gongen), who is the *kami* of Mt. Hiei (Hiei-zan), and three other *kami*. It was transported from Kawagoe to Ōta Dōkan's castle in 1457, then, more recently, to the Chiyoda district of Tokyo. This *kami* was considered the guardian of the city of Edo. Every second year on June 10–16, a major festival, the Sannō Matsuri, takes place there,

alternating with the festival at the shrine in Kanda. Before 1870, this shrine was known as Sannō Gongen-jinja. *See* AKASAKA, SANNŌ-SAMA-JINJA.

Hie-taisha. Name of two Shinto shrines located on the eastern slope of Mt. Hiei (Hiei-zan) close to Kyoto. The one to the east is dedicated to Ō-Yamakui, *kami* of the mountain, and the one in the west is dedicated to Onamuchi no Mikoto, protector of the imperial court (*see* MIYA MYŌJIN). After 800, the shrines were viewed as protectors of the Buddhist Enryaku-ji monastery, and their *kami* as Gongen (Sannō Gongen). The main shrine of the Shinto Sannō Ichijitsu, the Hie-taisha was at the head of about 3,800 secondary shrines throughout Japan, one of the largest being the Hie-jinja in Tokyo. Its two main buildings were completely reconstructed by Toyotomi Hideyoshi in the *hiyoshi-zukuri* (or *shōtai-zukuri*) style. In partnership with the Enryaku-ji temple, it had a powerful army of monk-soldiers *(sōhei)* who did not hesitate to transport the *mikoshi* of the *kami* to the capital to intimidate the court. Legend has it that in 1156, Taira Kiyomori shot an arrow at the *mikoshi* to show his soldiers that the *kami* could not block the road and had no power to kill whoever molested the priests, as they claimed. Also called Hiyoshi-taisha.

Higaki. Title of a Noh play: an old woman, carrying water to a Buddhist temple, reveals herself to be the ghost of a famous dancer.

Higaki kaisen. Coastal cargo ships with a capacity of 200–300 *koku*. They transported various consumer goods, mainly wood and rice, from port to port starting in the fourteenth century. They were particularly active between Sakai and Edo in the seventeenth century, transporting rice, silk, cotton, and soy sauce to the shogunal capital. Ships transporting *sake* were called *taru kaisen*. *See* KAISEN.

Higan. Word meaning, literally, "the other side," used for the dates of two Buddhist festivals common to all sects, celebrated on the spring and autumn equinoxes. In fact, the word *higan* is an old Chinese pronunciation of the Sanskrit word *pāramitā*, indicating the attainment of supreme wisdom upon enlightenment. These Buddhist rites are intended to assist the spirits of those who have "passed to the other side." Followers of Amida pray turned toward the setting sun, in the west, where the "Pure Land" (Jōdo, *Skt.*: Sukhāvati) is supposedly found. Sutras *(Jap.: kyō)* are read in temples, and families pay visits to cemeteries. The word *higan* has become, in popular language, a synonym for "equinox." Also called *higan-e*.

Higashi. "Orient," "east," as opposed to *nichi*, "west." Many towns constituting districts located to the east of large cities had this name. Also *tō*, *azuma*.
→ *See* CHANOYU, HIGASHIYAMA.

• **Higashi Hongan-ji.** Buddhist temple in Kyoto, belonging to the Ōtani branch of the Jōdo Shin-shū sect, founded by Kyōnyo Kōju in 1603 following a dispute over succession that ended with the sect splitting into two rival branches. The Nishi Hongan-ji was founded by Junnyo, who claimed to be the twelfth *hossu* of the sect, succeeding their father, Kennyo Kōsa. Kyōnyo then created the Ōtani sect and moved to the Higashi Hongan-ji in 1603. When his sect was recognized by Tokugawa Ieyasu, in 1619, both temples had the same status. The buildings of the Higashi Hongan-ji were completely reconstructed between 1562 and 1670, but were destroyed by fire in 1788, 1823, 1858, and 1864. The grand hall dedicated to the founder was then rebuilt between 1880 and 1895 in huge proportions: 76 × 56 m and a height of 38 m. The rooftree beam was so heavy that no wire could hold it up, and the women of Kyoto donated their hair to braid a strong enough cable. The temple has a beautiful garden, designed by Kobori Enshū (sixteenth century). The sect of the Higashi Hongan-ji has about 6 million followers and many subsidiary temples. *See* HONGAN-JI, NISHI HONGAN-JI.

• **Higashi Nijō-in.** *See* FUJIWARA NO KIMIKO.

• **Higashi Ōtani.** Buddhist temple in Kyoto, built in 1671 in memory of the abbots of the Higashi Hongan-ji.

• **Higashi Sanjō.** *See* MINAMOTO NO TOKIWA, FUJI-WARA NO SENSHI.

• **Higashi Sanjō-dono.** *See* FUJIWARA NO KANEIE.

• **Higashikuni Naruhiko.** Imperial prince (1887–1990), one of Kuni no Miya Asahiko's (1824–91) sons, who married one of the Emperor Meiji's daughters. He received the name Higashikuni in 1906. A general during the Second World War, he was appointed prime minister in August 1945, just after Japan's surrender, and signed the official act of surrender on September 2, 1945; he resigned in October and withdrew from political life. Shidehara

Kijūrō succeeded him as government leader. In 1947, he renounced his rights as imperial prince and became an ordinary citizen.

• **Higashikuni Teru.** *See* HIROHITO.

Higashiyama. "Mountain of the east," hills bordering the Kyoto basin on the east, at the foot of which many Buddhist temples and Shinto shrines were established. This name (Higashiyama-dono) was given to shogun Ashikaga Yoshimasa when he had his residence, the Jishō-ji (Ginkaku-ji, "Silver Pavilion"), built on these hills.
→ *See* FUJI-SAN.

• **Higashiyama bunka.** "Higashiyama culture," aristocratic culture that developed under the aegis of shogun Ashikaga Yoshimasa, melding cultures from the Heian period and warrior cultures with Zen precepts. Yoshimasa retired at age 39 in favor of his brother Yoshimi and devoted the rest of his life to building an artistic culture, sponsoring esthetes, painters, poets, lacquer artists, literature and painting in general, the tea ceremony, Noh theater, flower arranging, and gardening. This culture was characterized by the concepts of *yūgen* and *wabi*, which gave the tone to all artistic endeavor. *See* YŪGEN, WABI.

• **Higashiyama Jō-en.** Large crematorium of the Jōdo Shin-shū sect, located on the Higashiyama hill in Kyoto, with a capacity of more than 20,000 urns. Buddhists of all sects (and even Christians) have reserved places there. The largest crematorium in the world, it is managed by the Ōtani family.

• *Higashiyama-orai*. Collection of letters written by a Kyoto Buddhist monk to his disciples in the twelfth century, setting out numerous details about the images of Buddhist divinities and the "paradises" attributed to them.

Higashiyama Chieko. Theater actress (1891–1980) in the Shingeki style. She studied acting in Moscow and also worked in film and television. She was declared a Cultural Person of Merit in 1966.

Higashiyama Kaii. Painter (Higashiyama Shinkichi), born 1908 in Yokohama. After studying with Yūki Somei, he continued his education in Germany from 1933 to 1935. His works were exhibited in Scandinavia in 1963, and he was appointed an academician and received the Order of Culture (Bunka-shō) in 1969. He decorated the fusuma in the imperial palace and the Tōshōdai-ji temple.

Higashiyama Tennō. One hundred and thirteenth emperor (Prince Asahito, 1675<1687–1709>), son of and successor to Reigen Tennō. Nakamikado succeeded him.

Higa Shunchō. Historian (1883–1977), born in Okinawa (Ryukyu), author of a history of Okinawa, *Okinawa no rikishi* (1959).

Hige-daimoku. Long, narrow board inscribed vertically with the invocation of the Lotus Sutra ("Namu Myōhō Renge-kyō") generally placed on the family altar *(butsudan)* of Buddhists who follow the teachings of Nichiren.

Higeki Kigeki. "Tragedy and Comedy." Quarterly theater magazine founded in 1928 by Kishida Kunio and his team, who published many Western works and those of modern Japanese playwrights. Publication stopped in 1929; when it started again in 1947, it was published monthly until 1964. It began a third time in 1966, and is now a very influential magazine in performance circles, with contributions from many well-known authors.

Higo. Name of a former province, now part of Kumamoto prefecture (southern Kyushu).

• **Higo-ha.** School of sword makers in Higo province.

• **Higo-nyūdō.** *See* TAIRA NO SADAYOSHI.

Higuchi Ichiyō. Well-known novelist and poet (Higuchi Natsuko, 1872–96), born in Tokyo. She published many stories in newspapers, mainly in *Bungaku-kai,* and led a somewhat itinerant life with her mother and sister. In 1894, she began to write novels: *Otsugomori* (The Last Day of the Year, 1894), *Takekurabe* (Rivalries, 1895), *Nigori-e* (Murky Bay, 1895), and *Jūsan'ya* (The Thirteenth Night, 1895) were published in serial form in various newspapers and magazines. She died of tuberculosis shortly after finishing a diary, *Wakaremichi* (Separate Paths) on her life from 1887 to 1896. Her style, very popular in her time, although it somewhat imitated that of Ihara Saikaku, was imbued with sadness yet not without humor. She also wrote more than 3,800 *tanka* poems and was among the top women poets of her time. *Nigori-e* was adapted

for the screen by Imai Tadashi in 1953; *Takekurabe,* by Gosho Heinosuke in 1955.

Hijikata Tatsumi. *Butō* dancer (1928–86), born in Akita. He started the trend to modern erotic dances, notably in his show called *Jōmon-shō* (Homage to Prehistory), which caused a scandal in the United States when one of his dancers killed himself by accident on stage in Seattle in 1985. Hijikata Tatsumi then stopped dancing but continued to direct the Sankai Juku troupe and taught choreography in Tokyo until his death.

Hijikata Tōrei. Painter (*mei:* Hirokuni, Hirosuke; *azana:* Shichoku; *gō:* Kosuiken, Gakoken, 1735–1807), born in Inaba province (Tottori prefecture), where he entered the service of daimyo Ikeda Narikuni. He painted mainly fusuma, and his images of carp are particularly well known. He sometimes signed with the family name Gōto, as he had been adopted by that family. He probably studied under Maruyama Ōkyo in Kyoto.

Hijiki. In traditional architecture, part of the console (wooden overhang supporting the roof), consisting of a relatively short strut supporting either the joists (*gangyō, degeta*) or the dies *(to).* *Hijiki* can be superimposed through the *to* or can simply cross at a right angle. The lowest *hijiki* rests directly on top of the pillar, in the *funa-hijiki* (Asuka style), or on a *dai-to* placed on the support pillar or on a *to* placed on another *hijiki. Chin.: huagong, queti. See* TO-KYŌ.

Hijiri. Name for highly esteemed Buddhist monks who led an ascetic or itinerant life. Before Buddhism was introduced to Japan, the word meant "emperor." In the eleventh and twelfth centuries, the main task of the *hijiri* was to collect funds for the construction or reconstruction of temples. As wanderers, they helped spread Buddhism among the people by distributing *fuda,* talismans inscribed with prayers or images of Buddhist divinities. They told stories and legends about their respective temples and sects in order to attract potential followers to Buddhism. *See* KŌYA-SAN, SHUGENDŌ.

• *Hijiri-yukaku.* Novel in Sharebon style by an unknown author, published in Osaka in 1757, telling about the lives of the *hijiri.*

Hi kangen. Chinese painter (Fei Hanyuan; *mei:* Ran; *azana:* Kangen, eighteenth century) who went to Nagasaki in 1734 and taught many Japanese painters the Chinese style of landscapes and faces then in style (Nanga).

Hikari. "Light," name of the ultra-rapid train *(shinkansen)* linking Tokyo to Osaka and Kyoto at a maximum speed of 210 km/h, inaugurated in 1964. In 1972, it was extended to Okayama; in 1975, to Hakata. *See* SHINKANSEN.

Hikawa-jinja. Shinto shrine in Ōmiya (Saitama prefecture) dedicated to Susanoo no Mikoto, which has a large number of branches around Tokyo (59 shrines) and in Saitama prefecture (162 shrines). These shrines are very old, but it is not known exactly when they were founded. They were regarded as very important (Myōjin Taisha) in the tenth century.

• **Hikawa-kyō.** Subsect of the Tenri-kyō founded in 1949 by Taida Toku.

Hikeshi. In the Edo period, brigades organized to fight the many fires that periodically ravaged the cities. The best-known fire-fighting brigades were those established by the shogun in Edo *(jōbikeshi)* and by the daimyo in their provinces *(daimyō-hikeshi)*. In Edo, each brigade, commanded by a *hatamoto*, comprised 36 paid samurai. The *chōnin* also organized their own brigades *(machi-hikeshi)*, but in 1629, the shogunate required that each daimyo supply Edo with a contingent of 30 men for every 10,000 *koku* of revenue. The *hikeshi* were assisted by observers *(hinoban)* perched in towers erected on the roofs of houses and at strategic points. In 1718, the *chōnin* established *machi-hikeshi* in Edo to safeguard their assets. In 1723, there were 48 of these brigades *(kumi)*, which were assisted by volunteers if disaster struck, but which did not have the right to intervene in the districts reserved for the *jōbikeshi*.

Hikidemono. Gifts given to guests after a celebratory meal (wedding, birthday, or other), generally consisting of small packages of food or various household items (e.g., vase, dish, spoon) bearing the guest's name. These gifts may be expensive, as at banquets organized by major industrial or retail firms, or symbolic (cake, *tsukemon,* etc.), for more modest celebrations. *See* GIFTS.

Hiki-mawashi. In the Edo period, the public display of criminals before their execution. The condemned person was taken through the city to the site of his execution on horseback, escorted by *hinin* carrying placards on which were written the reason for the sentence.

Hiki-me kagi-hana. "Wide-open eyes, hooked nose," an expression describing the stereotypical way that Yamato-e artists painted faces, with the eyes indicated by slightly curved lines and the nose by an angular hooked line.

Hikite. Small wooden or metal slot for the fingers placed on the edge of a fusuma (sliding partition) to slide it open or closed.

Hikitsuke. Court of justice established during the Kamakura period and the Muromachi shogunate to help the Hyōjōshū (Council of State) rule on cases submitted to it. This court was directed by a chairman *(tōnin)*, assisted by three to eight "secretaries" or fellow adjudicators *(hikitsukeshū)*. It was instituted in 1249 by Hōjō Tokiyori, the fifth *shikken* of Kamakura. *See* MONCHŪJO.

Hiki Yoshikazu. Warrior (d. 1203) and general, from Musashi province (Kanto), adopted son of Minamoto no Yoritomo's nurse. Because his daughter married Yoritomo's son, Minamoto no Yoriie, Yoshikazu had great influence over the shogunate. But when Yoriie died, in 1203, the regent *(shikken)*, Hōjō Tokimasa, had Hiki Yoshikazu and Yoriie's son assassinated.

Hiko. "Son of the Sun." Name formerly given to princes and often to Shinto *kami* who were ancestors of the imperial family. *See also* HIME.

• **Hiko Hohodemi no Mikoto.** Third son of Ninigi no Mikoto and Konohana Sakuya-hime. According to the *Kojiki,* he was Jimmu Tennō's grandfather. *See* HIKO-NAGISATAKE.

• **Hiko Isuseri Hiko no Mikoto.** *See* KIBITSU-HIKO.

• **Hiko Itsuse no Mikoto.** Jimmu Tennō's older brother, killed in battle against Nagasune-hiko.

• **Hiko Nagisatake Ugayafu-kiaezu no Mikoto.** Son of Hiko Hohodemi no Mikoto and Toyotama-hime. He was said to have had four sons, among them Jimmu Tennō.

• **Hikosan.** "Mountain of the Sons of the Sun," located between Ōita and Fukuoka prefectures in northern Kyushu, famous in ancient times as the center of worship for Shugendō followers. The

Hikosan-jinja, built on its peak, was probably founded by En no Gyōja in the late seventh century. Hikosan has an altitude of 1,200 m.

Hikone. City in Shiga prefecture (central Honshu), on the east shore of Lake Biwa. It houses the castle of the Ii family and many samurai houses from the Edo period. It was the site of the castle of Sawayama, the fiefdom of daimyo Ishida Mastunari; the castle was destroyed in 1600. *Pop.: 90,000.*

Hikyaku. "Flying feet," messengers on foot or horseback who delivered official orders and decrees, starting in the Kamakura period. They were capable of traveling from Kamakura to Kyoto (483 km) in just four days, thanks to relays set up along the major routes. In the Edo period, *hikyaku* serving the post office could get from Edo to Kyoto in about 68 hours via the Tōkaidō road. Daimyo and, later, large-scale merchants also established *hikyaku* systems, mainly to travel from Osaka to Edo once a week; this could ordinarily be done in six days by the fastest *hikyaku,* nicknamed *aihikyaku,* who could cover almost 100 km per day on foot and horseback. *Machi-hikyaku* (city messengers) were gradually replaced, after 1860, by more modern couriers and telegraphy, then by mail service.

Himachi. "Waiting for the sun," family and neighborhood meetings that once took place for communal enjoyment and meals, organized mainly by pilgrimage associations *(kō).* Some of the meetings were for women only. They were held, according to the Jikkan-jūnishi calendar, on predetermined days in the first, fifth, and ninth lunar months. Similar meetings called *tsukimachi,* "waiting for the moon," also took place.

Hime. "Daughter of the Sun." Title given in ancient times to imperial princesses and to female Shinto *kami* who were ancestors of the imperial family, corresponding to Hiko for princes. Also Hime-miko. Starting in 645, they bore the title Naishinnō or Nyo-ō. *See* HIMIKO.
• Shinto *kami* venerated in the Hirano-jinja shrine in Kyoto.

• **Himeji.** Literally, "Temple of the Daughter of the Sun," or "Temple of the Princess." A city in Hyōgo prefecture, on the Ichikawa river. The castle around which this former castle town *(jōka-machi)* developed is sometimes called Shirasagi ("of the egret") because of its elegance. The city itself is an impor-

tant industrial center *(pop.:* 450,000), specializing in production of textiles and petroleum and metallurgical products. The castle (Himeji-jō) was built by Akamatsu Sadanori in the fourteenth century, then completely reconstructed in 1608 by Ikeda Terumasa, who added 20 small manors *(yagura).* This huge castle is at the top of a hill about 45 m in altitude, overlooking the Harima plain and the city. Three rows of fortifications surround the donjon *(tenshu),* which has five stories on the outside and seven stories on the inside. Completely renovated after the Second World War, its walls are now painted white. It is the largest castle in Japan after the one in Osaka. Also called Hakuro-jō ("of the white heron") and Rojō.

Himetani-yaki. Red-glazed ceramics produced in the Bingo (Hiroshima prefecture) kilns during the Kambun era (1661–72).

Himeyuri-butai. "Star Lily Corps," a battalion of nurses from Okinawa organized on March 23, 1945, to fight the American invasion of the island. Many of the nurses committed suicide when Japan's surrender was announced, or were killed during battles for possession of the island. A novel by Ishino Keiichirō, *Himeyuri no tō* (1950), perpetuates the memory of these heroic young women, and a monument dedicated to them has been erected in Itoman (Okinawa).

Himiko. "Daughter of the Sun," name of a shamaness-queen *(miyatsuko)* of the kingdom of Yamatai (probably located in northern Kyushu), whose name may be identified with that of Hime-miko or Hi-miko. She is evoked in the Chinese annals of the Wei dynasty, the *Weizhi (Jap.: Gishi)* and is said to have sent a tribute to the emperor of China about 238. According to the *Kojiki* (712) and the *Nihon shoki* (720), she governed through the intervention of her brother and never appeared in public. Her role would thus have been, in all probability, more spiritual than temporal, the latter function having devolved to her young brother. She was the master of *kidō,* or the "art of subjugating demons." The *Weizhi* relates her sudden death and indicates that an immense tumulus was erected on her tomb, for more than 100 people accompanied her to her death (this is contradicted by the facts). It is possible that she was killed by other tribal chiefs, with her retinue, when her army was defeated in the battle against the state of Kona (or Kunu). The Wei emperor, Ming, sent her gifts, including a golden seal bearing the words "To the Wa sovereign, friend of the Wei," fabrics, and bronze mirrors, which were brought by Chinese envoys. One of her nieces, Iyō, is said to have succeeded her. In fact, the queen of Wa has not yet been identified; it is possible that she is the same person as Jingū Kōgō. Also called Pimiko. *See* HIME.

Himi Kōdō. Lacquer artist (Himi Yosaji, 1906–75), born in Ishikawa. He revived certain old techniques and made great use of marquetry *(moku-zōgan)* and inlays of metal wires *(kingisen-zōgan)*. Named a Living National Treasure in 1970.

Hina Matsuri. Annual festival for girls, celebrated on the third day of the third month (now March 3) and always an occasion for family festivities. On this date, courtesans usually offered the imperial family (particularly the princesses) dolls that were to serve as a magical substitute to preserve them from illness and bad luck. During the Edo period, it became the custom to offer such dolls to all little girls of all classes. Then, dolls were made to represent not only little girls but members of the imperial court, including the emperor and empress *(dairi-bina)* and their court *(hina ningyō)*, courtesans, and musicians. These dolls, often very expensively made, are placed on stepped shelves covered with red fabric, and girls invite their friends to admire them, then serve cake and tea. During the Hina Matsuri, all girls dress in the traditional costume of long-sleeved kimono *(furisode)*, receive gifts from their parents and friends, and go to pray at the shrine nearest their home, accompanied by their parents. Also called Jōmi, Jōshi.

Hinamishi. Imperial prince (seventh century), son of Temmu Tennō and father of Mommu Tennō. A highly regarded poet, his works were included in the *Man'yōshū.*

Hinatsu Kōnosuke. Scholar and poet (Higuchi Kunito, 1890–1971), born in Nagano. An expert in English literature, he translated works by Edgar Allan Poe, Oscar Wilde, and others, and wrote collections of "gothic" romantic poems *(Tenshin no shō,* 1917). His major work was the *Meiji Taishō shi shi* (History of Poetry of the Meiji and Taishō Eras), published in 1929, which earned him the *Yomiuri* Prize in 1950.

Hinawajū. Name for the first harquebuses, introduced to Japan by sailors from a Portuguese shipwreck in Tanegashima, in 1543. They were 1.3 m long and had a caliber of 22 mm. Their effective range was barely 60 m. Although they were relatively ineffective and heavy, these and related firearms continued to be used in Japan until the mid-nineteenth century. Also called Tanegashima, Teppō.

Hine Taizan. Nanga-style painter (Chōjirō; *mei:* Sei, Seichō, Chō; *azana:* Seigen, Shōnen; *gō:* Taizan, Bōkai, Kinrinshi, 1813–69), born near Osaka into a peasant family. He followed first the Tosa style, then that of the Bunjinga (Nanga) school of Kyoto.

Hinin. "Non-humans," term for the lowest Japanese social class, similar to the *eta* (*see* BURAKUMIN). In the Edo period, they did not have the right to practice any profession and were reduced to begging. They fulfilled the tasks that other Japanese rejected as repugnant, such as grave digging, occasionally leather tanning, and escorting those condemned to death. They were forced to live communally, they were not allowed to wear hats, and their robes could be no longer than knee-length. The women did not have the right to shave their eyebrows or tint their teeth black. There were two classes of *hinin:* those born of *hinin* parents and those who had lost their class status for one reason or another. Only the latter could, under certain circumstances, hope to be reintegrated into normal Japanese society. This class, along with the *eta* and *burakumin,* was abolished in 1871, when its members numbered about 23,500. The working class sometimes called them, derisively, *yotsunin* ("men with four paws"). *See* ETA, ŌE TAKU.

Hino. Site in the Uji region (Kyoto) whose name was used by a major family of courtesans and lords descended from Fujiwara no Uchimaro, who had founded a Buddhist temple, the Hōkai-ji, there in 822. One of Uchimaro's descendants, Fujiwara no Sukenari (990–1070), became a monk in this temple in 1051 and took the family name Hino.
• Small town near Tokyo. *See* HINO JIDŌSHA KŌGYŌ.

• **Hino Nariko.** Daughter (1352–1405) of Hino Tokumitsu (1328–67) and shogun Ashikaga Yoshimitsu's wife.

• **Hino Tomiko.** Sister (1440–96) of Hino Katsumitsu (1429–76) who married shogun Ashikaga Yoshimasa in 1455. Yoshimasa, who didn't have any sons, had named his younger brother Yoshimi as his successor. But Tomiko bore a son, Yoshihisa, late in life and claimed the title of shogun for him.

She allied herself with Yamana Sōzen to have her rights recognized, which provoked a ten-year civil war, the Ōnin War (1467–77). After the shogun retired to his Higashiyama villa, Tomiko, a canny businesswoman, amassed an enormous fortune by engaging in speculation on rice prices and usury.

Hino Ashihei. Writer (Tamai Katsunori, 1907–60), born in Fukuoka. His novella *Funnyō tan* (Medical Tales, 1937) earned him the Akutagawa Prize. He was a soldier in China and wrote about his experiences in his trilogy on the Sino-Japanese War, *Mugi to heitai* (Barley and Soldiers, 1938), *Tsuchi to heitai* (Land and Soldiers, 1938), and *Hana to heitai* (Flowers and Soldiers, 1939). He also published *Hana to ryū* (Flowers and Dragons, 1953) and an autobiographical novel, *Kakumei zengo* (Before and After the Revolution). He committed suicide.

Hino Jidōsha Kōgyō. Maker of Hino automobiles, specializing in diesel engines, created in 1910 and affiliated with Toyota since 1966. It produces mainly buses, luxury coaches, trucks, and diesel engines using a technology called HMMS (Hino Micro Mixing System) for the domestic market and for export. Head office in Hino (Tokyo).

Hinoki. "Fire tree," very common type of cypress *(Chamaecyparis obtusa)* whose wood is used in construction, carpentry, and sculpture. It can grow as tall as 30–40 m. Its name comes from the fact that it was once common to produce fire by rubbing two *hinoki* twigs together. The bark is used to make shingles *(hiwadabuki),* and the leaves yield an oil used in perfumes. There are many varieties, some of them called *hiba.* The *hinoki* grows mainly in Honshu, Shikoku, and Hokkaido.

Hi no Kuni. Former name of the region comprising Higo and Hizen provinces.

Hi no Moto. "Origin of the Sun," transcription of the Chinese Riben *(Jap.:* Nihon), designating Japan. Many religious sects have taken this name, among them Hinomoto-kyō, subsect of the Mitake Kosha founded in 1946 by Ishida Sakakimi (b. 1894); Hinomoto-kyōdan, founded in 1946 by Yamamoto Haruyuki (b. 1909); and Hinomoto Shinsei-kyō, subsect of the Tenri-kyō founded in 1950 by Okamoto Tsue (b. 1898).

• **Hi no Maru.** "Sun Circle," name of Japan's national flag, which was probably created during the Kamakura period and used by many warriors, including Useugi Kenshin, Takeda Shingen, and Toyotomi Hideyoshi. The flag was first flown on a Japanese ship, the *Kanrin Maru,* when it sailed for the United States in 1860. It was made official in 1870 by the Meiji government. Also called Kokki.

Hi no Michi no Shiri. Former name of Higo province.

Hi oki. Ancient system of computing time based on the lunar phases. It was replaced in 602 by the Chinese calendar *(yuanjia)* and used officially during the Taika Reform (645).

Hirabayashi Hatsunosuke. Writer and literary critic (1892–1931). He was one of the founders of the proletarian magazine *Tamemaku Hito* (The Sower) in 1921, and then became the most ardent defender of this type of literature, writing a literary critique based on dialectical materialism, *Musan kaikyū no bunka,* in 1923. He died in Paris during a study trip.

Hirabayashi Taiko. Writer (1905–1972), born in Nagano prefecture. She had an impoverished youth and wrote about this in a number of novels describing the difficulties encountered by the most disinherited classes. Expelled from Tokyo by the government, which accused her of Marxist activities, she went to Manchuria. When she returned to Tokyo in 1924, she joined up with anarchist and communist groups and began to write first novellas, then novels. In 1927, she married Kobori Jinji (1901–59), one of the editors of the magazine *Bungei Sensen* (Literary Front), where she published her stories, among them *Hitori yoku* (I Walk Alone, 1946), *Kō iu onna* (A Woman Like Her, 1946), *Watakushi wa ikuru* (I Live, 1947), *Kishimojin* (The Goddess of Children, 1946), *Kiyoko-zō* (Portrait of Kiyoko, 1948), *Kuro no jidai* (Dark Age, 1950), *Chitei no uta* (Subterranean Song, 1948), *Hito no inochi* (Life of a Man, 1950), and *Aijō ryokō* (Amorous Voyages, 1953). While writing fiction, she often traveled abroad. She also wrote several biographies of women, including *Hayashi Fumiko* (1969) and *Miyamoto Yuriko* (1972). An annual prize for a literary work by a woman was created in her name.

Hirado. Port on the northwest coast of Kyushu in Nagasaki prefecture, which was a fiefdom of the Matsuura family. The town was very active in the sixteenth century, and ships from China, Portugal, and Holland dropped anchor in the port. Hirado began to decline in 1641, when the Dutch living

there were transferred to the islet of Dejima in
Nagasaki. Vestiges from its period of prosperity include the ruins of the Matsuda castle (Hirado-jō)
and the Orandabashi, or "Dutch bridge." The town
occupied an entire island (Hiradoshima) attached
to the mainland by a bridge. It was called Firando
by the Portuguese, who were the first to land there
in 1549. The town was destroyed by fire in 1906
and reconstructed on a modern plan. François
Caron, the first Frenchman to arrive in Japan, lived
there, and Will Adams died there. *Pop.*: 30,000.

Hirado Renkichi. Modern poet (1893–1922), born
in Osaka. His style was futuristic, and he was not
much appreciated during his lifetime, but his works
were collected by some of his friends and published
in 1931 as *Hirado Renkichi shishū*.

Hirafuku Hyakusui. Painter (Hyakusui, Teizō,
1877–1933), born in Akita, painter Hirafuku
Suian's son and Kawabata Gokushō's student. He
painted in the "Japanese" style (Nihonga) and studied at the Tokyo School of Fine Arts (Teikoku
Bijutsu-in) while drawing illustrations for newspapers. Like a number of his colleagues, he was
opposed to the idealist romantic style of Okakura
Kokuzō. He went to Italy in 1930 and had his
works exhibited there. When he returned to Japan
in 1932, he was elected a member of the Imperial
Academy, then taught at the Tokyo School of Fine
Arts and had works exhibited in Bunten. He experimented with Rimpa style while continuing to paint
in the traditional Bujinga style. He also wrote poems that were collected in a volume called
Kanchiku (Chinese Bamboo).

Hiraga Gennai. Academic botanist and writer
(Shiroishi Gennai, Hiraga Kokurin, Kunitomo,
Fūrai Sanji, Kyukei, 1728–79), born in Sanuki
province (Kagawa prefecture) to a family of low-
ranking samurai. He first studied medicinal herbs in
Osaka with Toda Kyokuzan (1696–1769), then
went to Edo about 1757, where he studied with
Tamura Ransui (Tamura Gen'yū, 1718–76). He
wrote the *Butsurui hinshitsu* (Classification of Various Materials) in 1763; in the same year, he published two satirical novels, *Nenashi-gusa* (Grass
without Roots) and *Fūryū Shidōken den* (Brave
Story of Shidōken), which formed the roots of
kokkeibon literature. He also performed various
experiments, such as weaving asbestos (1765), calculating temperatures, and prospecting for ores,
and tried (without success) to have an old copper
mine opened in Akita in 1773. He learned Euro-

pean weaving methods, ceramics and painting
techniques, and conducted experiments with static
electricity. He tried to open another mine, this one
to exploit iron; angry that his fellow citizens were
offering no support, he killed one of his disciples
with a sword blow in a moment of madness. He was
sentenced to prison, where he died. Hiraga Gennai
used many pseudonyms, among them Fūrai Sanjin
(Wind Straddler), Kyūkei (Valley of Doves), and
Tenjiku Rōnin (Traveler from Elsewhere), with
which he signed his humorous and satirical works,
Fukuuchi Kigai (Demons Outside, Good Luck Inside), for his *jōruri* plays (such as *Shinrei Yaguchi no
watashi,* "Miracle When Yaguchi Passed," 1770),
Kinrazu Hinyaku (Happy to Be Poor and Have
Nothing to Eat), and Hinka Zeninai (Poor House,
No Money).

Hiraga Motoyoshi. Poet (1800–65) and samurai
of the Okayama estate (Okayama prefecture), author of *waka* poems modeled after those in the
Man'yōshū, but on war and patriotic themes.

Hiragana. Japanese syllabic writing, derived from
Chinese *caoshu* writing, invented in the early ninth
century to note sounds and grammatical inflections
of the Japanese language. Its creation has been attributed to Kūkai. Aristocratic women of the Heian
period used this writing, as most of them did not
have access to Chinese letters, to set down poems,
personal diaries, travel journals, and novels that are
now considered classics of Japanese literature. This
"alphabet," at the time called Onna-de (woman's
hand), comprised 51 letters (*see* GOJŪON-ZU), now
reduced to 46. It is still used to note grammatical
flexional endings and words in the Yamato language that do not have a phonetic transcription into
Sino-Japanese characters *(kanji),* concurrently with
kanji and the katakana syllabary. *See also* GOJŪON-
U, KANA, NIGORI.

Hiraga Renkichi. Forester born 1902 in Tokyo. He
immigrated to Brazil in 1931 and conducted important research on agriculture in tropical countries.
His wife, Hiraga Kiyoko, was nicknamed "the Angel of the Amazon" because of her tireless efforts on
behalf of the poorest populations of the Para region.

Hiraga Romomasa. Warrior (twelfth–thirteenth
century) of the Minamoto family, who married one
of Hōjō Tokimasa's daughters. He was appointed
shugo of Ise province in 1204; implicated in a plot

to replace shogun Sanetomo, he was defeated and killed in battle in Kyoto.

Hiraga Yuzuru. Naval engineer (1878–1943) born in Hiroshima. After serving as an officer in the Russo-Japanese War (1904–05), he went to Great Britain to study naval architecture. When he returned to Japan, he directed construction of many warships (notably the *Yamato*) and became known worldwide for his original techniques. He retired from active navy service in 1931 and was appointed a professor at the University of Tokyo, where he was president from 1938 until his death.

Hiragushi Denchū. Sculptor (Takutarō, 1872–1979), born in Okayama. At first a doll maker, he went to Tokyo, where he studied with Takamura Kōun. He had works in many exhibitions and founded the Nihon Chōkoku-kai (Association of Sculptors of Japan) in 1907 with Yonehara Unkai (1869–1925) and Yamazaki Chōun (1867–1954). He was elected to the Imperial Academy (Teikoku Geijutsu-in) in 1937, then taught at the Tokyo University of Fine Arts and Music (Tokyo Geijutsu Daigaku). He received the Order of Culture (Bunka-shō) in 1962.

Hiraide. Archeological site in Shiojiri (Nagano prefecture) discovered in 1947. Excavations have unearthed layers from the mid-Jōmon period (Chūki, ca. 4000–3000 BC) to the *kofun* (megalithic tomb) period. There are the remains of 17 half-buried round and oval houses from the Chūki period, and 49 half-buried rectangular houses from the *kofun* period, as well as various stone tools; Jōmon, *sue*, and *haji* pottery; and other remains. One of the prehistoric huts *(tatara, tataena)* has been reconstructed on the site.

Hirai Ikkan. Chinese lacquer artist (*gō:* Chōsetsusai, Kongō Sanjin, Chōchōshi, 1578–1657), who became a Japanese citizen and imported the technique of placing lacquered paper on a wooden core; this technique, *ikkanbari,* was named after him. A Zen Buddhist monk, he was also a painter and calligrapher. His descendants made lacquered utensils for the tea ceremony of the Senke school.

Hiraiwa Chikayoshi. Samurai (1542–1611), tutor of Tokugawa Ieyasu's sons.

Hiraizumi. Town in Iwate prefecture, on the Kitakami-gawa river, once a small fort built to defend against the Ainu. After 1094, the siege of the Fuji- wara no Kiyohira family (Ōshū family) took place there. Thanks to gold mines in the region, the Ōshū Fujiwara were able to construct the Chūson-ji monastic complex. Because Minamoto no Yoshitsune took refuge with the Ōshū Fujiwara family, it was attacked and wiped out by Minamoto no Yoritomo in 1189. *See* CHŪSON-JI.

Hiramatsu Kashin. Garden designer (1614–81) employed by Retired Emperor Go-Mizunoo. He designed a number of tea gardens *(sukiya)* and helped create the gardens of the Shūgaku-in in Kyoto. He also worked for the Konoe family.

Hira-mitsuto. In traditional architecture, type of wooden overhang in which three *to* (dados) are placed on the *daito-hijiki. See* HIJIKI, TO-KYŌ.

Hirano Ken. Literary critic and writer (Hirano Akira, 1907–78), born in Kyoto. A supporter of the proletariat, he contributed to the magazine *Kindai Bungaku* after 1946 and discovered a number of modern writers. He was best known for his biography of Shimazaki Tōson (1947) and a history of literature during the Shōwa era *(Shōwa bungaku-shi).*

Hirano Kuniomi. Politician and warrior (1828–64) from the Fukuoka estate, active in the struggle against the Edo shogunate and against allowing foreigners into Japan. He was arrested during Shimazu Hisamitsu's attempted coup d'état in 1863. Released soon after, he was involved in another coup attempt on September 30, 1863, when he tried to organize a peasant revolt in the Hyōgo region. He was defeated, taken prisoner, and executed. Two collections of his poems survive: *Hirano Kuniomi kashū* and *Reigo shōkō,* the latter containing poems written in prison as he awaited execution.

Hirano Yoshitarō. Writer (1897–1980), born in Tokyo. He studied at Tokyo University, then in Germany from 1927 to 1930. A communist, he was arrested and then released. He was a member of the Kōzaha group and published, with Noro Eitarō and Yamada Moritarō, the *Nihon shugi hattasu-shi kōza* (Discourse on the History of the Development of Japanese Capitalism, 1932–33). After the Second World War (during which he served in China and Southeast Asia), he was elected honorary chairman of the Nihon Heiwa I-inkai (Committee for Peace) and published his articles in *Nihon shihon shugi shakai no kikō* (Structure of Capitalist Society in Japan).

Hiranuma Kiichirō. Politician and jurist (1867–1952), born in Okayama prefecture. As minister of justice (1991–12), then adviser to the emperor (1926), he took a stand against corruption in political parties and the penetration of Western ideologies into Japan, and he had policing stepped up to check the inflow of foreign ideas. He was prime minister from January 1939 to January 1940, succeeding Konoe Fumimaro, and was replaced by General Abe Nobuyuki. A minister in Konoe Fumimaro's second cabinet, he resigned when Konoe lost power in October 1941. After the war, he was accused of war crimes and sentenced to life in prison.

Hiranuma Ryōzō. Politician and athlete (1879–1959), member of the House of Peers in 1932 and mayor of Yokohama in 1951. He led the Japanese delegation to the Olympic Games in Berlin in 1936, and founded the National Sports Festival. He received the Order of Culture (Bunka-shō) in 1955.

Hira-o. Type of belt that went with the *sokutai* costume, from which the *tachi* sword was hung.
→ *See* KUMIHIMO.

• **Hirao shita-gatane.** *See* SOKUTAI.

Hiraoka Kishio. Composer and pianist (1907–51), studied with Vincent d'Indy in France.

Hirase Mitsuō. Famous eighteenth-century archer, author of a book on Japanese archery *(kyūdō),* the *Shahō shinsho* (1796), modeled on the *Shexue zhengzong (Jap.: Shagaku seisō),* the major work on Chinese archery by Gao Yingshu (1610). Hirase's book was illustrated by Shungyōsai.

Hirase Sakugorō. Botanist (1856–1925), born in Fukui prefecture. After studying with Ikeno Seiichirō in Tokyo, he conducted research on gymnosperm plants and discovered the reproductive method of *Ginkgo biloba (Jap.:* Itchō) in 1896.

Hirashimizu-yaki. Very diverse types of pottery and porcelain made in the kilns at Hirashimizu (Yamagata prefecture) starting in 1800, using clay from nearby Mt. Chitose. The potters imitated the production from the Arita and Kutani kilns but were never able to match their technique. Starting in 1847, the Hirashimizu kilns began to produce porcelain while continuing to make stoneware for kitchen use. There are now five kilns in Hirashimizu, belonging to five families of potters: the Niwa, Abe, Bun'emon, Tentaku, and Shichiemon.

Hirata Atsutane. Philosopher (Owada Masayoshi; *gō:* Ibukinoya, 1776–1843), born in Akita. He studied Shinto and ancient Japanese history and became a champion of the movement to restore Shinto (Fukko Shintō) by expunging its Buddhist and Confucian influences. After studying Confucianism in Edo, he became interested in Zhuangzi's philosophy and in Taoism. He then became a passionate disciple of Motoori Norinaga's theories, but he claimed that the Japanese were superior to all other peoples and, although he studied Western science, he treated foreigners as unworthy of interest. He published his ideas in *Kamoshō* (1803), in which he criticized Buddhism, and in *Kodō taii* (1811), *Koshichō* (1811), *Tama no mihashira* (1812), *Tamadasuki* (1824), *Koshiden* (1825), and more than 100 books and lampoons. Having openly taken the emperor's side against the shogunate, the latter forbade him to write in 1841 and placed him under house arrest for the rest of his life.

Hirata Gōyō. Sculptor and doll maker (Hirata Tsuneo, 1903–81), born in Tokyo. His art was very highly regarded; he was invited to contribute to the Imperial Academy's annual exhibition in 1936 and was designated a Living National Treasure in 1955.

Hirata Guntō. Japanese name for the Paracel (Pratley) Islands. *Chin.:* Nansha.

Hirata Tokuboku. Writer (Hirata Kiichirō, 1873–1943), born in Tokyo. He joined the editorial team of the *Bungaku-kai* and translated many works by Keats, Dante, Dickens, and Lamb. He also translated some Noh plays into English.

Hirata Tōsuke. Politician (1849–1925), born in Yamagata prefecture. In 1871, he accompanied the Iwakura mission to Europe and the United States, then studied law in Germany. Appointed to the House of Peers in 1890, he was minister of the interior in Katsura Tarō's first and second cabinets (1901–05 and 1908–11). He was appointed Guardian of the Seals in 1922.

Hiratsuka Raichō. Writer (Hiratsuka Haruka, 1886–1971). She was interested in Western culture and in Zen, of which she was a fervent devotee throughout her life. Her affair with writer Morita Sōhei caused a scandal. In 1911, she founded the Bluestocking Society (Seitōsha) in an effort to defend women's rights and freedom of personal development in Japan. In her magazine *Seitō* (Bluestocking), she published a famous manifesto, *Genshi* *josei wa taiyō de atta* (In the Beginning, the Sun Was a Woman). She then married painter Okumura Hiroshi (1891–1964) while continuing her fight for women's emancipation, creating the Shin Fujin Kyōkai (Association of New Women). She also published articles in the *Fujin Sensen* (Feminine Front). After the Second World War, she returned to her cause.

Hiratsuka Tsunejirō. Politician (1881–1974), born in Hokkaido. In 1907, he set up a fishing company to operate in the Sea of Okhotsk and introduced new fishing methods. He was elected to the House of Representatives, appointed minister of transport in Yoshida Shigeru's first cabinet after the Second World War, and later became president of the Association of Fisheries of Japan (Dai Nippon Suisankai).

Hiratsuka Un'ichi. Contemporary painter (1895–1991), born in Matsue, who studied with Ishii Hakutei (1882–1958) and Umehara Ryūzaburō. He devoted himself to modern printmaking and was appointed professor of woodcuts and printing at Tokyo Geijutsu Daigakue (Tokyo University of Fine Arts and Music) in 1935. In 1927, he had written a book on printing techniques, *Hanga no gihō*. He lived in the United States for several years, and his works are better known there than in Japan. *See* MUNAKATA SHIKŌ.

Hirayama Ikuo. Contemporary painter, born 1930 in Hiroshima, and irradiated in the bombing of that city. He has devoted himself to research on peace. President of Tokyo Geijutsu Daigaku (Tokyo University of Fine Arts and Music), he is a goodwill ambassador for UNESCO and has created a fund for preservation of the monuments of Angkor.

Hirochika. Painter (Tosa Hirochika, active ca. 1459–92) in Tosa style, belonging to the imperial *e-dokoro*. He is credited with the *emakimono Dōjō-ji engi* (Sakai Collection).

Hirohito. Hundred and twenty-fourth emperor (Prince Michi no Miya, 1901<1926–89>), son of Taishō Tennō, whom he officially succeeded in 1926, inaugurating the Shōwa era. He was appointed regent in 1921, because his father was ill and unable to fulfill his duties. After visiting Great Britain, he married Princess Nagako (b. 1903), daughter of Prince Kuni no Miya Kumihiko, in 1924. They had two sons, Akihito (b. 1933) and Hitachi (who married Tsugaru Hanako in 1964),

and four daughters, Michiko (b. 1934) Higashikuni Teru, Toshimichi Takatsukasa, Takamusa Ikeda (Princess Yori), and Hisanaga Shimazu (Princess Suga). Among Hirohito's close relatives were his two brothers, Takamatsu and Mikasa; Princess Chichibu was the widow of the emperor's younger brother, Prince Chichibu. The other members of the imperial family lost their royal titles after the Second World War.

Emperor Hirohito did not exercise direct power. A moderate liberal, he could not express his opinions publicly and was obliged to endorse the Diet's decisions. In spite of this, he was sometimes able to impose his will, as he did during the attempted coup d'état of February 26, 1936. He was forced by his generals to sign the declaration of war against the United States, Great Britain, and the Netherlands in November 1941, and agreed to sign the Potsdam Declaration after Japan's defeat in 1945. The 1946 Constitution designated him simply a symbol of the state, stripping away all political power; this allowed him to devote himself to his favorite subject, marine biology, on which he wrote a number of scientific articles. The first Japanese emperor to travel abroad, he visited Europe and Paris in September–October 1971, and the United States in 1975. He died in January 1989. His son, Akihito, succeeded him on the throne soon after, with an official coronation. Emperor Hirohito is now referred to only by the name of his era, Shōwa Tennō. *See* AKIHITO.

Hirokoshi Jirō. Aeronautics engineer (1903–82), designer of the famous Zero war plane used by the Japanese in the Second World War. He also designed planes code-named Reiden and Reppu. *See* MITSU-BISHI (Airplanes).

Hiromasa. Painter (Itaya Hiromasa; *gō:* Hiroyoshi, Keishū, Hiromasa, 1729–97) of the Yamato-e school. He was the official painter of the Edo shogunate.
→ *See* MINAMOTO NO HIROMASA.

Hironaka Heisuke. Mathematician, born 1931 in Yamaguchi prefecture. In 1970, he received the Fields Prize in the United States for his research into algebraic functions, and he was awarded the Order of Culture (Bunka-shō) in 1975. He taught at Harvard University and the University of Kyoto.

Hiro no Miya Maruhito. Imperial prince (born 1960), oldest son of Emperor Akihito and crown prince since 1990.

Hirosaki. City in Aomori prefecture (northern Honshu), former castle town *(jōka-machi)*. Irrigated by the Iwaki-gawa river, it is known as a major center for production of apples *(nashi)*, rice, *sake,* and lacquered objects called Tsugaru-nuri. Ruins of the castle built by daimyo Tsugaru in 1601 (three-story donjon and ramparts). Saishō-in, seventeenth-century Buddhist temple with five-story pagoda *(gojunotō)*. *Pop.:* 180,000.

Hirose-jinja. Shinto shrine near Nara, dedicated to Waka-Ukanome no Mikoto, the female *kami* of grains, founded before 676 and famous for its charms that protected the harvests. Annual festival on April 4.

Hirose Taizan. Painter (Seifū; *azana:* Bokuho; *gō:* Shogasai, Hakuunka, Rokumusai, Shūzō, Undayū, Taizan, 1751–1813), born in Okayama prefecture, and bureaucrat serving the Tsuyama daimyo. He studied painting with Fukuhara Gogaku in Osaka and poetry with Hosoi Hansai, becoming very well known for his many landscapes in the Nanga style. Also called Taizan.

Hirose Tansō. Confucian scholar (1782–1856) in Bungo province (Ōita prefecture), founder of a very popular school teaching Chinese and Japanese literature and Confucian doctrines. His writings have been collected in a three-volume work, *Tansō zenshū,* published 1925–27.

Hiroshige. Painter (Andō Hiroshige; *mei:* Jūemon, Tokutarō; *gō:* Ichiyūsai, Ichiryūsai, Ryūsai, Tōkaido-utashige, Utagawa Hiroshige, Hiroshige, 1797–1858), born in Edo to the Tanaka samurai family, and adopted by the Andō family. He studied with Utagawa Toyokuni and Utagawa Toyohiro, taking the name Hiroshige in 1811, while his masters allowed him to take the artist's name Utagawa. His first ukiyo-e prints were not great works; he hit his stride as an artist only after 1818, with images of flowers and birds that were very popular. After 1830, the publisher Kawaguchi Shōzō ordered a series of ten views of Edo, which were printed with few colors: blue, pink, touches of brown and green. Now able to earn a living with his prints, Hiroshige passed on to his son his trade of firefighter *(hikeshi)* and devoted himself to art. He traveled from Edo to Kyoto and back, and was inspired to paint *Tōkaidō gojūsan-tsugi* (The Fifty-Three Stages of the Tōkaidō), which were published in part by publisher Takeuchi Hoeidō. Hiroshige then produced other series on the same subject, which were known

by the names of their publishers, Reisho Marusei and Gyōsho. He also produced "Eight Views of Ōmi" and a number of series of "Ten Views of Kyoto." In 1835, he began a series of 70 landscapes of the Kiso Kaidō (of which he completed only 46 views). Ten years later, he illustrated a number of literary and comical works *(kyōka)*. About 1850, he adopted a new printing format for his landscapes that was vertical instead of horizontal, and produced "Views of Sixty-nine Famous Sites" and *Maisho Edo hyakkei* (One Hundred Views of Edo—in reality, 118), as well as the famous *Fuji sanjurokkei* (Thirty-six Views of Mt. Fuji), published after his death. He died in 1858 in a cholera epidemic and was buried in the Zen temple (Sōtōshu) of the Tōgaku-ji in Asakusa (Edo). Over his lifetime, he completed over 10,000 works (not including book illustrations). He had few disciples, though two of his adoptive sons and a third artist adopted the name Hiroshige. However, his best-known artistic successors were Kobayashi Kiyochika and Yoshida Hiroshi in the Meiji period.

• **Hiroshige II.** Painter (Suzuki Chimpei; *mei:* Shigenobu, 1826–69). He married Tatsu, Hiroshige I's daughter, and took the name Ichiryūsai Hiroshige II; when the marriage ended, about 1865, he took the name Risshō. Although his ukiyo-e prints were exhibited in Paris in 1867, he had little success in Japan and was forced to paint lanterns to earn a living.

• **Hiroshige III.** Painter (Utagawa, Andō Hiroshige; *gō:* Shigemasa, 1841–94), Hiroshige I's student. He also married Tatsu, his master's daughter, after she split up with Hiroshige II. About 1869, he took the *gō* Hiroshige III. He portrayed mainly trains, ships, and buildings located in Edo and Yokohama (Yokohama-e style).

• **Hiroshige IV.** Painter (Kikuchi Kiichirō, Risshō II, dates unknown) who took the name Hiroshige IV in 1911. He drew prints in the same style as the other Hiroshige.

Hiroshima. Chief city of Hiroshima prefecture (western Honshu), located on the southwest coast of the Inland Sea (Setonaikai) in the plain of the Ōta-gawa river delta. The town developed around the castle of the Asano family, built in the late sixteenth century. A major port, completely rebuilt in 1889, Hiroshima was the seat of the general quarters of the imperial forces during the Sino-Japanese War (1894–95) and an important military center during the Second World War, linked with the port and naval base at Kure. Its university has more than 5,000 students. Hiroshima has the sad distinction of having been the first city destroyed by an atom bomb. On August 6, 1945, at 8:15:17 A.M., an American B–29 bomber, the *Enola Gay*, dropped an atom bomb called Little Boy ("Gilda"), with explosive power equivalent to 12,500 tons of TNT, over the city. It exploded 600 m above the city, instantly killing 80,000 people and destroying 90% of the city. Many survivors died of radiation sickness in the months and years that followed, bringing the number of victims to more than 200,000. Since then, the city has been completely reconstructed, including, in 1958, the castle (Koi no Jō, or Ri Jō, "castle of the carp"), originally built from 1589 to 1593 by Mōri Motonari. In the center of the city, however, a building in ruins (the former office of industrial promotion), known as the "Domb of the Bomb," bears witness to the city's martyrs. Beside it is a "Memorial to Peace" designed by architect Tange Kenzō, and other commemorative monuments, where a solemn ceremony in memory of the victims takes place every August 6. Surviving the bomb were the Shukkei-en, a 40,000 m² garden built for the Asano family in 1620, and some old houses in the suburbs. *Pop.:* 900,000. *See* PIKA.

• **Hiroshima-ken.** Hiroshima prefecture, comprising the Hiroshima plain, the six-armed delta of the Ōta-gawa river, and the foothills of the Chūgoku mountains. Hiroshima prefecture includes the former Bingo and Aki provinces. In the eleventh and twelfth centuries, it was a major fief of the Taira family. With the large chief city of Hiroshima, it is now a very industrialized region: shipyards, automobile and petrochemical industries, machinery manufacturing, and various food industries. Its main cities, aside from Hiroshima, are Fukuyama, Onomichi, and Kure. *Area:* 8,455 km². *Pop.:* 2.75 million.

• **Hiroshima Wan.** Bay at the bottom of which is the city of Hiroshima. It is very deep and a number of ports have been created on it, the main ones being Hiroshima, Ōtake, Kure, and Iwakuni. There are many small islands on the bay, the largest of which are Nomishima, Nijima, Kurashijima, Kamakarishima, Oshima, Suwajishima, and Nakashima.

Hirota-jinja. Shinto shrine in Nishinomiya (Hyōgo prefecture, Honshu), dedicated to the *aramitama* of Amaterasu-Ōmikami, which, according to the

Nihon shoki, was built by Empress Jingū Kōgō. The *kami* it houses were also protectors of *waka* poets. Festival on March 16.

Hirotaka. Painter (Kose Hirotaka, active ca. 1000) in the imperial court, in Yamato-e style. His works have been lost.

Hirota Kōki. Diplomat and politician (Hirota Hirotake, 1878–1948), born in Fukuoka. After holding various consular positions in China, Great Britain, the United States, and the Netherlands, he was appointed ambassador to Holland (1927–30) and the USSR (1930–32). He then became the minister of foreign affairs in the cabinets of Saitō Makoto (1933–34) and Okada Keisuke (1934–36). He succeeded Okada as prime minister in March 1936, and intensified Japan's war effort, proposing the creation of a China-Manchuria-Japan bloc. He signed an anti-Comintern pact with Germany and Italy, but was forced to resign following clashes between government members and his minister of war, Terauchi Hisaichi. Hayashi Senjūrō succeeded him. Hirota was then minister of foreign affairs in Konoe Fumimaro's cabinet (1937–39). During the Second World War, he tried but failed to negotiate a separate peace with the USSR. Convicted as a war criminal by the Allies, he was executed on December 23, 1948.

Hirotsu Kazuo. Writer (1891–1968), born in Tokyo. At first a literary critic, he was part of the proletarian literature movement in the 1930s, but distanced himself from it in 1941. After the Second World War, he wrote a couple of works in defense of the Matsukawa saboteurs: *Izumi e no michi* (The Road to Izumi, 1953) and *Matsukawa seiban* (The Matsukawa Judgment, 1958). He then wrote an autobiographical novel, *Nengetsu no ashioto* (The Steps of Time, 1961–63), which earned him the Noma Prize in 1963. Son of writer Hirotsu Ryūrō.

Hirotsu Ryūrō. Writer (Hirotsu Naoto, 1861–1928), born in Nagasaki prefecture. At first a ministerial employee, he joined the Ken'yūsha literary group and began to write "tragic" novels in 1895, including *Imado shinjū* (Suicide at Imado, 1986). He created a new genre with a sensational, dramatic flair and exaggerated romanticism, featuring highly colorful characters who were disinherited, mute, blind, lame, or otherwise disabled, but purehearted, all of whom come to a sad end. Hirotsu Kazuo's father.

Hiroyuki. Painter (Sumiyoshi Hiroyuki; *mei:* Naki; *gō:* Keikin'en, 1755–1811), Itaya Hiromasa's son and Sumiyoshi Hiromori's student. He was one of the official painters of the Edo shogunate.

Hiru no Omashi no Tsurugi. Celebrated sword that was one of the Sanshū no Jingi (Three Imperial Treasures) of the reign of Toba Tennō. This sword was supposedly lost during the naval battle of Dan no Ura in 1185, when it went overboard and sank with young Emperor Antoku. It was never found, although one legend has it that it is not at the bottom of the ocean but was taken and hidden in the Atsuita-jinja in Nagoya. But since this shrine was destroyed by bombing in 1945, the sword is now considered definitely lost.

Hisaakira Shinnō. Seventh son (1276–1328) of Emperor Go-Fukakusa. He was appointed shogun of Kamakura in 1289 to replace Koreyasu Shinnō. When he was deposed, in 1308, his son, Morikuni Shinnō, was appointed shogun.

Hisaita Eijirō. Playwright (1898–1976), born in Miyagi prefecture. His plays, inspired by the proletarian movement, described mainly the working-man's condition, as in *Hokutō no kaze* (Northeast Wind, 1937). After the Second World War, he wrote movie scripts for well-known directors such as Kurosawa Akira and Kinoshita Keisuke.

Hisakuni. Family of sword makers (twelfth century) of the Awataguchi school in Kyoto, founded by Kuniyori and continued by his six grandsons, Kunitomo, Kuniyasu, Kunikiyo, Arikuni, Hisakuni, and Kunitsuna, in the late twelfth century. Descendants of a branch of the Fujiwara family, they received the family name Hayashi. The best known was Hisakuni Tōjirō, who worked for Retired Emperor Go-Toba. He made mainly remarkably high-quality *tachi* swords and *tantō*.

Hisamatsu Sen'ichi. Writer and literature professor (1894–1976). He wrote many literary studies, notably on the work of Murasaki Shikibu.

Hisamatsu Shin'ichi. Philosopher (1889–1980), born in Gifu. A disciple of Nishida Kitarō, he was appointed a professor at the University of Kyoto. A fervent devotee of Zen philosophy, he attempted in his writings to compare Western and Eastern cultures from the religious point of view. He created a philosophical-religious association, Gyakudō-dojyō, also called FAS, "to awaken the formless

Self, to consider humanity as a whole, and to create a supra-historical history." His best-known books are *Tōyōteki mu* (Eastern Emptiness, 1939) and *Zen to bijutsu* (Zen and the Fine Arts, 1946).

Hisao Jūran. Writer (Abe Masao, 1902–57), born in Hokkaido. He went to France to study theater; when he returned to Japan, he began to write novels in different genres—detective, historical, and so on—in a polished style. His story *Suzuki mondo* (Suzuki's Interviews) earned him the Naoki Prize in 1951, and *Boshizō* (The Mother, 1954) won the *New York Herald-Tribune* Award.

Hishida Shunsō. Painter (Hishida Mioji, 1874–1911), born in Iida (Nagano prefecture). A child prodigy, he began to paint in the Kanō style at 10 years of age and entered Tokyo Bijutsu Gakkō (Tokyo School of Fine Arts) in 1890, where he studied with Hashimoto Gabō. In 1903, he followed Okakura Tenshin and Yokoyama Taikan to India, Europe, and the United States, where his paintings were exhibited. When he returned to Japan in 1905, he had an exhibit at Bunten. In his paintings (Buddhist images and landscapes), he used more color than lines. In later life, he turned more to the Rimpa style, while still favoring color over contour.

Hishikawa-ryū. School of painters of ukiyo-e prints founded by Moronobu (1618–94). Among the most important artists of this school *(ryū),* aside from Moronobu, were Hishikawa Morofusa, Hishikawa Moroshige, Hishikawa Morotane, and Hishikawa Waō (Furuyama Moromasa, Furuyama Moroshige, Furuyama Morotane). Almost all of them specialized in portrayals of beautiful women *(bijin)* and illustration of erotic books. *See* MORONOBU.

• **Hishikawa Masanori.** *See* FURUYAMA MOROMASA.

• **Hishikawa Morofusa.** Painter (Kichizaemon, Kichibe, active ca. 1700) of ukiyo-e prints, and oldest son of Hishikawa Moronobu (*see* MORONOBU). He portrayed mainly beautiful women *(bijin)* and illustrated erotic books.

• **Hishikawa Moronobu.** *See* MORONOBU.

• **Hishikawa Morotane.** Painter (Furuyama Morotane, active 1715–40) of ukiyo-e prints and *bijin* portraits.

• **Hishikawa Morotsugu.** Painter (active 1720–30) of ukiyo-e prints and *bijin* portraits.

• **Hishikawa Waō.** Painter (*gō*: Kuwabara, Moroshige, Fūyōken, Waō, active ca. 1700) of ukiyo-e prints. Some art historians feel that he was the same person as Hanabusa Itchō.

Hishū. Former name of the region comprising Hida, Hizen, and Higo provinces.

History. The historic period of Japan begins in the mid-sixth century, after a long prehistoric period (*see* JŌMON) and a proto-historical period that is generally divided into two distinct phases, the Yayoi and *kofun* periods (*see* KOFUN, YAYOI). In fact, information about the period before 712 comes essentially from two historical chronicles, the *Kojiki* (712) and the *Nihon shoki* (720), and from passages excerpted from ancient Chinese chronicles, notably the *Weizhi*. The traditional chronology setting the foundation of the Japanese empire with Emperor Jimmu in 660 BC has no historical basis, and it is likely that the first "emperors" (*see* KUNI, MIYATSUKO) are mythical. Thus, it is generally agreed that Japan's "historical" period began about 538, the probable year of the introduction of Buddhism to the islands. At the time, Japan had ongoing political and cultural ties with the Korean Peninsula and had previously been linked to China through trade and alliances. Japan evidently possessed a territory in southern Korea, Mimana, and exchanges of all sorts were taking place between the two countries. The ensuing Asuka period (645–710) was named for the village in which one of the capitals of the emperors of Yamato (the Nara region) was established. During this period, sovereigns moved around quite a bit, either on a whim or to satisfy a set of beliefs (called Shinto, to distinguish them from the newly imported Buddhism). The clans influential in the court became divided, with one faction led by the Mononobe, who favored Shinto, and the other by the Soga, who wanted Korean Buddhism and culture to become firmly entrenched. After many bloody conflicts, the Mononobe were defeated and the Soga triumphed. Empress Suiko (593–628) sent envoys directly to the Chinese Sui court, and her nephew, Prince Shōtoku Taishi (d. 622), a fervent Buddhist, had Buddhist temples built and promulgated a "Seventeen-Article Constitution" (Jūshichijō no Kempō) that set jurisprudence and that was emulated in later centuries. A flood of Buddhist texts then arrived from China, along with concepts of government and new philosophical and political ideas. From Korea came artists, architects, and artisans who created a true Japanese civilization in a purely indigenous context. As a result, when Shōtoku Taishi died, there was a movement to install a centralized government on the Chinese Tang model. The head of the Nakatomi clan rebelled against the ministers of the Soga family in 645 and promulgated a new code of laws inspired by the Chinese one, the Taika Code. Peasants and cultivated land were placed under the court's control and a new system of tax collection and justice, the *ritsuryō*, was implemented. In 663, the Japanese army was defeated (*see* HAKUSUKINOE) in Korea by the Chinese, allied with the kingdoms of the peninsula, and was forced to abandon its Korean territories. Many Koreans then settled in Japan, populating provinces such as Izumo, and bringing their own shamanic beliefs and their talent for imitating the arts and techniques of the Chinese Tang. In 672, Emperor Temmu drove out the clans opposed to the regime and, to reinforce the *ritsuryō*, promulgated a new, more precise and complete code of laws, the Taihō Code, which was completed only in 710. In 708, the Yamato court struck the first Japanese currency (*wadō-kaihō*) in copper, on the model of Chinese coins. As the state became more organized, the need for a stable capital was felt and the emperors decided to construct the city of Heijō-kyō (Nara) on the model of Chang'an, the Chinese Tang capital.

The Nara Period (710–94). Although Buddhism made enormous inroads, winning over most clans, the common people remained completely unaware of the religion and of the speculations of the monks in the capital's six major monasteries. When the Taihō Code was promulgated, land was redistributed and a military system created. Citizens' rights and duties were laid out and taxes set. In 712, Empress Gemmei had the *Kojiki* written to record the imperial genealogy and prove the divine origin of her family line, while organizing the beliefs of the common people according to a mythology involving various legends. Eight years later, the *Kojiki* was rewritten, with the same interpretation, in the *Nihon shoki*. Peasants on imperial lands were too heavily taxed, so they left to work for large monasteries or heads of clans. This considerably weakened imperial power, to the profit of monasteries and large-scale landowners, who paid almost no taxes and were able to use the new labor pool to expand their estates (which later became *shōen*, feudal estates). To spread Buddhism and solidify its hold on the provinces, Emperor Shōmu ordered in 741 that temples and pagodas be built in all provinces

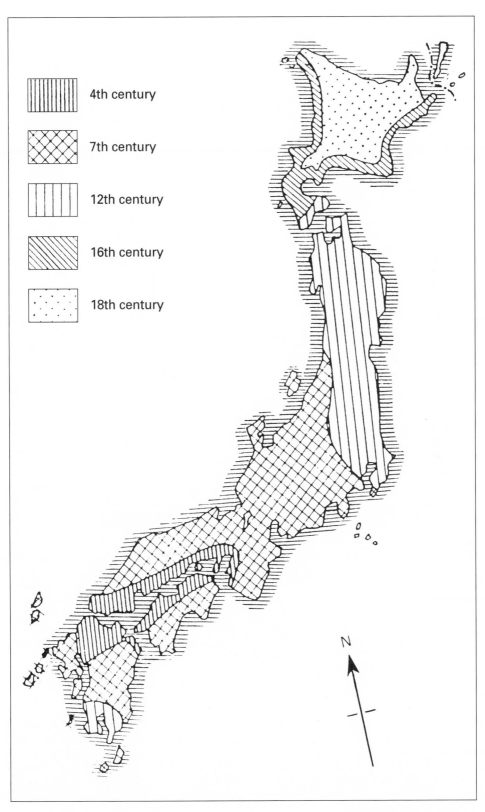

	4th century
	7th century
	12th century
	16th century
	18th century

N

Historical Development

(*kokubun-ji*); the cost of construction was also intended to weaken the major lords. Following a terrible smallpox epidemic (737), Emperor Shōmu ordered that a huge bronze statue of the Buddha be erected in the Tōdai-ji temple in Heijō-kyō; it was unveiled only in 749. But this enterprise bankrupted the state. Relations with the Chinese Tang continued, and in 754 the monk Ganjin arrived in Japan, accompanied by 24 students and technicians. In 756, Dowager Empress Kōmyō (or Kōmei) founded the oldest museum in the world, the Shōsō-in, in memory of Emperor Shōmu; it houses invaluable objects of the time, bearing witness to the intense trading activity that was taking place between China and Japan. The first poetry anthologies (written in Chinese, such as the *Kaifūsō*) were compiled, and the first major imperial anthology, the *Man'yō-shū,* was published about 759, containing some 4,500 compositions by a wide variety of poets. A few years later, in 764, an ambitious Buddhist monk, Dōkyō, Empress Shōtoku's protégé, had himself appointed prime minister, and his actions threatened the very existence of the imperial power. When the empress died, a palace revolt drove Dōkyō out, and in 781 the ministers decided never to allow a woman, who could too easily be swayed by Buddhism, on the throne again. Three years later, to free himself from the grasp of the monks of the six sects of Nara (*see* BUDDHISM), Emperor Kammu decided to move his capital, and he settled a little farther east, in Nagaoka. But the site was not very propitious, so he left it ten years later and had another capital built at Heian-kyō on the same plan as the Tang capital, Chang'an (today Xi'an) on the site of today's Kyoto. He transferred only a few temples to the new capital and located them in the south of the city. Nobles and artisans then left Heijō-kyō to move to Heian-kyō, which remained the capital of Japan until 1868. It was officially inaugurated in 794.

The Heian Period (794–1185). Once the empire was stable and power centralized, the war against the aboriginal Ebisu and Ainu tribes in northern Honshu was rekindled. In 803, General Sakanoue no Tamuramaro pushed them back to the extreme north of Honshu and to Hokkaido. This opened up new territories that were settled by thousands of peasants, who were promised complete exemption from taxes in return for defending their land against Ainu incursions. Thus, units of peasant-warriors began to form, living in relative autonomy and increasingly tending to shrug off the administrative grasp of the capital. Two rather dissident Buddhist monks, Saichō and Kūkai, were sent to China to

search for new doctrines. When they returned, they started two large sects similar to those in Tang-dynasty China, the Tendai and the Shingon, and inaugurated new forms of Buddhist art that evolved in Japan under the direction of Chinese masters. Buddhism became more widespread, although the common people did not rush to embrace it, even when Kūkai began to found schools for them. He is credited with the "invention" of kana characters, which were designed so that people could obtain an education without necessarily having to learn Chinese. The monks of the Tendai and the Shingon then tried to win over the common people by creating Shinto-Buddhist syncretic forms mixed with Confucian doctrines and Tao practices, thus setting the foundations upon which the Japanese people gradually liberated themselves from the Chinese cultural invasion. In 838, judging that China had nothing more to contribute and that Japan could take care of itself, the court stopped sending official envoys to the mainland, although trade and religious relations continued to link the two countries. A powerful noble family, the Fujiwara, soon took power in the court through a series of alliances with the imperial family; it appointed its choice of regents (*see* KAMPAKU, SESSHŌ), who increasingly governed in the emperor's name. Their greatest adversary, Sugawara no Michizane, was sent into exile on Kyushu, where he died in 903. The Fujiwara peacefully eliminated all their opponents and expanded their wealth and power by acquiring huge *shōen*, which they exempted from taxes. To protect their assets and perform policing duties, they hired troops of peasant-warriors from northern Honshu. Japan was thus divided into a large number of estates belonging either directly to the Fujiwara or to their lieges. Although the *ritsuryō* system was no longer in effect, peace reigned; under the aegis of the Fujiwara, an aristocratic culture developed that embodied the classic era of medieval Japan, in which women played a large role. This peaceful time did have its disturbances, notably a revolt by the head of a warrior clan of the Taira family, who proclaimed himself emperor in 940. The Fujiwara sent another warrior clan from the east, the Minamoto, to do battle with him. After the revolt was put down, the power of the warrior clans quickly became more entrenched. The imperial armies could not compete with them, and even the Fujiwara were often forced to negotiate with their leaders and give them access to the court. The two largest warrior clans of the east, the Taira and the Minamoto, became more organized and formed quasi-states within the state, though they did not dare to act outside the law and always recognized the authority of the emperor, if not that of the Fujiwara. In the court, the aristocratic culture continued to develop, while Buddhism began to spread among the common people thanks to a new form of pietist Buddhism, simple devotion to Amida Buddha. Literature and the arts evolved rapidly: many tales and "accounts" *(monogatari)* were written, mainly by women, and poetry proliferated. Many imperial *(see* CHOKUSEN WAKA-SHŪ*)* and private anthologies were published, as were the first major novels, such as Lady Murasaki Shikibu's *Genji monogatari.* The entire court was involved with noble arts, music, subtle games involving incense, and devotions. New types of Buddhist temples appeared to accommodate the faith in Amida. The architecture of Shinto shrines changed somewhat, influenced by designs favored by Buddhism. In rural areas, the peasants toiled ceaselessly for the lords of the *shōen,* and they formed military forces in the east. This social dichotomy was too deep to continue, and a series of disturbances soon caused a transformation in Japanese society.

In 1068, Emperor Go-Sanjō Tennō managed to free himself temporarily from the grasp of the Fujiwara and tried to institute reforms. To bring these changes to fruition, he abdicated in favor of his son and created a government "in retirement" *(see* INSEI*)*, which enabled him more room to maneuver to fight the influence of the Fujiwara. He inaugurated an era of parallel governments (which comprised up to five emperors—one as a figurehead and the others actually governing, though not always in concert). This state of affairs caused the fall of the Fujiwara; the family had become so large that there was dissent in the ranks, from which the leaders of the large warrior clans, eager to supplant them, skillfully profited. By the end of the eleventh century, almost half of government positions once occupied by the Fujiwara had been taken over by the Minamoto. To protect their territorial possessions, the large Buddhist monasteries entered the fray in their turn, forming associations with armed troops to resist the incursions of various groups. The court had to count on alliances (quickly formed and broken) to maintain a semblance of authority. However, the Minamoto clan was gaining more and more influence, and, thanks to the success of its armies in the service of the emperor (warrior-monks, bandits, and rebels of all sorts), it managed to supplant the Fujiwara in the court definitively. But another clan, the Taira, with strong maritime resources (they controlled the coast of the Inland Sea and traded with the mainland) also took over of-

ficial positions for the emperor. At this point, a merciless struggle for influence began between the two rival clans. In 1159–60, the head of the Taira clan, Kiyomori, was dispossessed by the Minamoto, who deposed the young emperor. This incident was the spark in the powder keg, and Kyoto was the site of a bloody battle between Taira (Heike) supporters and Minamoto (Genji) supporters. Kiyomori emerged victorious and was appointed chancellor of the empire. He decimated the vanquished, incurring the hatred of the population, and the capital was ravaged by fire. Partisans of the Minamoto were in constant revolt against the Taira, while misery ruled in the countryside and groups of bandits wreaked havoc even in the capital. In 1182, famine ravaged the region controlled by the Taira. The fiefdom of the Minamoto was Kanto, a region less severely affected; led by the young Minamoto no Yoritomo and his half-brother, Yoshitsune, the Minamoto regained their edge and annihilated the Taira family at Ichi no Tani and their fleet at Dan no Ura in 1185. The young Emperor Antoku, held hostage by the Taira, drowned during the final naval battle. Yoshitsune, who had plotted against the court, was forced to take refuge with the Fujiwara in the north; when the Fujiwara were attacked by Yoritomo, they betrayed Yoshitsune, who was forced to commit suicide. Minamoto no Yoritomo thus controlled all of northern and eastern Honshu and established his *bakufu* (military government) in Kamakura in 1192; the emperor, who had lost all but his moral authority, named him shogun. Yoritomo thus instituted a military and quasi-feudal regime, aiming to reunify the country and return it to prosperity by providing a just and strong government based on military power. He ended the period of "retired emperors" and reigned as master over the fate of Japan.

The Kamakura Period (1185 or 1192–1333). By 1181, Yoritomo had extended his territory by confiscating the lands of rebels "in the name of the emperor" and set up administrative offices for his *bakufu,* including the Samurai-dokoro, Kumonjo, and Monchūjo. He gave the peasants some freedom by allowing them, under certain conditions, to own the land they were cultivating, and he had intendants *(shugo)* appointed in each vassal state to represent him. In 1192, he appointed a senior representative *(tandai)* in Kyoto so that he could keep better track of the court. In 1186, he appointed a regent, Fujiwara Kanezane, and reinstated the policy of marriages between members of the Fujiwara family and imperial princesses. With Kanezane's help, he eliminated his last political enemies, and, in his new

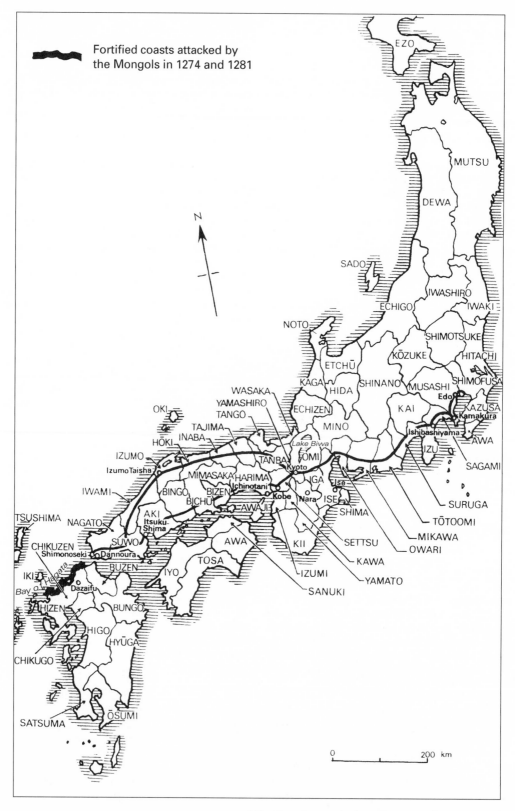

Fortified coasts attacked by
the Mongols in 1274 and 1281

EZO

MUTSU

DEWA

N

SADO

IWASHIRO

ECHIGO

IWAKI

NOTO

SHIMOTSUKE

KŌZUKE

HITACHI

ETCHŪ

SHIMOFUSA

KAGA

HIDA

SHINANO

MUSASHI

WASAKA

YAMASHIRO

TANGO

ECHIZEN

MINO

KAI

Edo

KAZUSA

Kamakura

OKI

TAJIMA

Lake Biwa

Ishibashiyama

AWA

INABA

ŌMI

IZU

HŌKI

TANBA

Kyoto

SAGAMI

IZUMO

IzumoTaisha

MIMASAKA

HARIMA

IGA

Ise

SURUGA

IWAMI

BINGO

BIZEN

Ichinotani

Kobe

Nara

ISE

TŌTOOMI

BICHŪ

AWAJI

SHIMA

MIKAWA

TSUSHIMA

AKI

Itsuku-
Shima

KII

SETTSU

OWARI

NAGATO

AWA

KAWA

CHIKUZEN

SUWO

Dannoura

Shimonoseki

IZUMI

YAMATO

IKI

BUZEN

TOSA

IYO

SANUKI

Bay

Hakata

Dazaifu

HIZEN

BUNGO

HIGO

HYŪGA

CHIKUGO

SATSUMA

ŌSUMI

0   200 km

The Provinces during the Kamakura Period

capacity as shogun, punished all rebels "in the name of the emperor." He died in 1199 due to injuries sustained from a fall from a horse, and his father-in-law, Hōjō Tokimasa, became the regent *(shikken)* of the shogunate. Yoriie, Yoritomo's oldest son, proved incapable of governing and was forced to abdicate his responsibilities in favor of his brother, Sanetomo; Yoriie was assassinated in 1203. Following a series of family quarrels, notably between Masako, Yoritomo's widow, and Makiko, *shikken* Hōjō Tokimasa's wife, Tokimasa was forced to resign and transfer his powers to his son, Hōjō Yoshitoki. Sanetomo was assassinated in his turn in 1219; Emperor Go-Toba tried to retake his power and declared a rebel *bakufu* in 1221, but his troops were defeated by the shogunate's forces at Uji and he was sent into exile. In 1232, he promulgated a new legal code, the *Jōei-shikimoku;* in 51 articles, it defined the duties of nobles, vassals, and peasants. It was revised and expanded in 1243 and 1286. This code replaced the *ritsuryō* code, which had long since lapsed, and was observed (on the whole) until 1868. Peace was not total, however; from time to time, vassals rose up, but they were defeated each time and lost their territories to the *bakufu.* Starting in 1247, shogun were chosen from among members of the imperial family so that no emperor could claim that they were rebels and treat them as such. These shogun were always underage, and true control remained in the hands of the *shikken* of the Hōjō family. At this time, the uncouth society of the Kamakura warriors began to become less boisterous and more refined in contact with the Kyoto court. At the same time, the Mongolians began to threaten Japan. After envoys from Kublai Khan were repelled or killed, the emperor of China, allied with the Koreans, launched two violent attacks on the Kyushu coast, in 1274 and 1281. The entire *bakufu* army was mobilized and the court was plunged into panic. Both attacks failed (*see* KAMIKAZE) and Kublai Khan died, so the Mongolians did not make further attempts. Japan was saved, but the *bakufu,* depleted by the defense effort, was unable to reward its vassals, who were not considered "patriotic" and who had fought only for profit; it could neither give them land nor compensate them for their expenses. Some vassals were thus forced to sell all or part of their land to merchants, monks, or artisans who were not part of the *bushi* class, which was in contravention of the laws in the *Jōei-shikimoku.* The *bakufu,* alarmed, forbade the sale of land; this further impoverished the warriors, who were no longer loyal to the shogun and the *shikken.* Merchants and artisans, however, grew very wealthy,

having profited from the general mobilization against the Mongolians, and they began to form a new class. Given this state of affairs, Emperor Go-Daigo refused to abdicate, as the Kamakura court was demanding. He was defeated and exiled. He managed to flee; he called together troops of malcontents, notably those of a dissident Minamoto, Ashikaga Takauji, and provoked a massive uprising of clan leaders; in 1333, they attacked the city of Kamakura and set it ablaze.

The Muromachi Period (1333–1574/1582). Go-Daigo then restored imperial power in the Kemmu Restoration. In 1336, Ashikaga Takauji, who was now the most powerful lord in Japan, turned against the imperial troops and established his own *bakufu* in the Muromachi district of Kyoto, naming emperors of his choice and exercising power in their name. He was appointed shogun. But the legitimate emperor's supporters revolted, and the Southern Court (Nanchō) took refuge in the Yoshino hills, while the Northern Court (based in Kyoto, named Hokuchō) remained under the control of the Ashikaga. War festered between the two courts (Nambokuchō)—that is, mainly between the Muromachi shogunate and the emperors of the Southern Court—and continued until 1392. The capital was captured, recaptured, and set afire several times, and provincial lords, taking sides depending on their immediate interests, waged bloody battles that destroyed villages and ruined the countryside. Despite this civil war, the Muromachi *bakufu* acted as lawmaker. Ashikaga Yoriyuki reformed the bureaucracy and administratively divided the country into three large regions, each governed by a *kanrei* (or *kanryō*) under the authority of a shogun. After subduing a revolt by the allied forces of the lords of Sakai and a group of pirates in 1401, the shogunate reopened official relations with the Ming-dynasty court of China, and the two countries cooperated in an attempt to stamp out piracy (*see* WAKŌ). Trade with the mainland flourished and the shogun inaugurated a new cultural era largely influenced by Chinese culture, although the domestic situation continued to deteriorate. While the shogun had luxurious villas built and generously sponsored new forms of art (*see* NOH), famine took hold in rural areas and the shogunate was forced a number of times to forgive the debts *(tokusei-rei)* of the peasants, who had formed "defense lines" in several provinces. In 1457, while shogun Yoshimasa was living an ostentatious life, famines and epidemics were decimating the countryside. Local lords hindered free trade by setting up toll barriers on their borders, causing prices to rise. Resorting to extreme

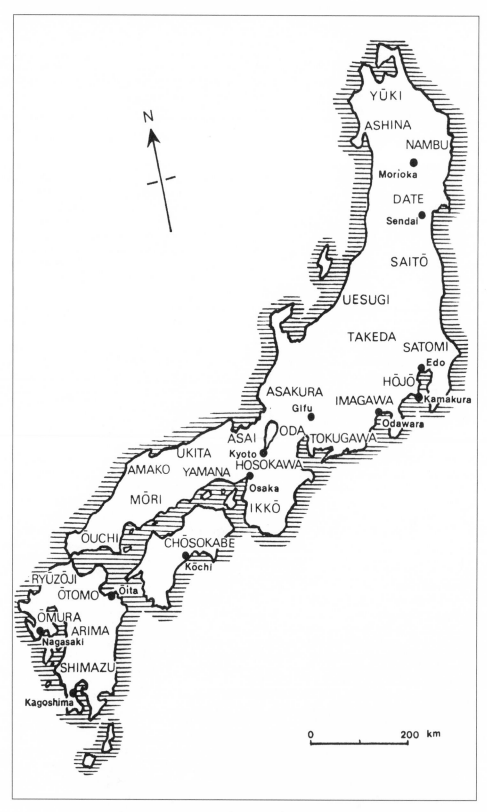

Approximate Distribution of Major Lords in the 16th Century

measures, the peasants signed up en masse for the lords' armies as foot soldiers *(ashigaru)* and became brigands as the lords used them in their attempts to gain hegemony. In 1467, a quarrel over succession flared up within the Ashikaga family. Supporters of the two pretenders to the shogunate confronted each other, even in Kyoto itself, in interminable battles that resulted in the almost total destruction of the city and its temples. This was the Ōnin War, which lasted ten years, continuing in the provinces well after the original antagonists had died. In 1485, tired of the soldiers' pillaging and other misdeeds, the peasants revolted and organized a sort of government in Uji, near Kyoto, that momentarily restored peace in the central provinces. Four years later, when the shogun Yoshihisa was assassinated, the warlords *(daimyō)* began doing battle again. There followed a long troubled and anarchic period of civil wars (Sengoku), during which lords confronted each other, sometimes for no reason other than to fight. This period lasted almost a century, until 1576. During this "Japanese Hundred Years' War," the imperial court—powerless and uninterested in the fate of the country, concerned only with surviving in its devastated capital, and prey to bandits of all sorts—was forced to place itself under the "protection" of whoever held power at the time. Japan was divided up among some 30 daimyo and more than 100 low-ranking lords who were constantly at war, obeying no law or rule of "chivalry"—samurai in name only. Each warlord followed his own interest or temperament, and the country fell into total anarchy. During this period, two events occurred that would have a great impact: in 1543, the arrival of the first harquebuses in Tanegashima; in 1549, the arrival in Kagoshima (Kyushu) of a Jesuit priest, Francis Xavier, as Portuguese, Spanish, and Dutch merchant ships were entering Japanese waters. Religious activity had not been slowed by the state of war that had devastated the country, and Buddhism was becoming increasingly popular, especially since the monks of the Amidist sects had formed defense leagues and taken up military opposition to those in power. Moreover, the Shinran, Nichiren, and Zen movements (begun during the Kamakura period) were spreading, and the population, more and more aware of its own strength and value, followed them. Monks and aristocrats took refuge in the arts and literature, which evolved considerably. Artisans, very sought after, honed their talents, while merchants became wealthy supplying war matériel to the shogun's court or trading with China, Korea, and even the Europeans who had come by sea.

In 1568, a low-ranking lord of humble origins, Oda Nobunaga, came to prominence through the luck of battle and his judicious use of troops armed with harquebuses. He defeated powerful rivals, captured Kyoto, and had himself appointed shogun. In a few years, he had reorganized the central provinces and gained the loyalty of large numbers of vassals, becoming the master of the country. In 1576, he had a magnificent castle built in Azuchi, on the shores of Lake Biwa, which became the prototype for all castles later built by lords. His rise to power was accomplished with brutality: in 1571, he had 3,000 rebellious monks from Mt. Hiei executed by sword. In 1573, he attacked shogun Yoshiaki, sent him fleeing, and was forced to do battle with the Buddhist Ikkō-ikki sect ensconced in the Ishiyama fortress in Osaka, which finally surrendered only in 1580. With his two generals, Toyotomi Hideyoshi and Tokugawa Ieyasu, he defeated all his enemies and finally installed some measure of peace throughout Japan. In 1582, under attack from a traitorous general, he committed suicide. Toyotomi Hideyoshi pursued the traitor, Akechi Mitsuhide, who had dared to proclaim himself shogun, and defeated him in battle 13 days later. Toyotomi Hideyoshi then officially succeeded Oda Nobunaga.

The Period of Dictators (1582–1616). Although Hideyoshi had Oda Nobunaga's young son named shogun in title, he retained power and continued the campaign to defeat recalcitrant vassals, notably those in Kyushu, in order to unify the country under his aegis. Granting his vassal Tokugawa Ieyasu the fiefdom of Kanto, he moved to Osaka and required his vassals to build him a huge fortified castle. He forced his other vassals to demolish their own fortresses, redistributed the land among his followers, and undertook a general survey of fields and harvests. To reinforce security, he ordered that all weapons be confiscated from the peasants *(katanagari)*, established the system of collective responsibility (adopted from China; *see* GO-NIN GUMI) in their communities, and set the tax rate at 40–50% of the harvest evaluated in *koku* (180 liters) of rice. The lords *(daimyō)* were then categorized according to the revenue of their provinces: Tokugawa Ieyasu, the most powerful, received 2.5 million *koku* per year. Hideyoshi struck his own currency and encouraged the development of mining operations. Now the wealthiest man in the country, he subsidized the extremely impoverished imperial court and became a generous patron of the arts. The emperor then named him *dajō-daijin* (prime minister), since he was unable to appoint him shogun because of his obscure family line. Although he was powerful, Hideyoshi still had to defeat a few recalcitrant daimyo, such as the Mōri and those in Kyushu. In 1586, he launched a major campaign, vanquishing them rapidly; he then attacked the castle in Odawara, the last bastion of the Hōjō clan, which he captured and had razed. In 1588, to reinforce his hold on the country, he forbade anyone who was not a warrior by birth or career to carry weapons. In 1592, he reached the peak of his own career by unifying Japan. He then named his nephew, Hidetsugu, his successor, and, with the (implicit) goal of getting rid of his too numerous and troublesome warriors, sent them off to conquer Korea. The operation was quite successful at first, so he set his sights on China. The Chinese, infuriated, formed an alliance with the Koreans and helped defend the peninsula. From a military walkover the invasion of Korea turned into a true war, and Japanese samurai suffered a number of reverses. Hidetsugu revealed himself to be a tyrant, and his uncle, to promote the son, Hideyori, whom his wife had just borne, ordered Hidetsugu to commit suicide. In Korea, the Japanese were pushed back on all sides and Hideyoshi's navy was crushed by that of Korean admiral Yi Sun-sin in 1596, even though Hideyoshi had sent an army of 100,000 men as reinforcements to his general, Konishi Yukinaga. When Hideyoshi died, in 1598, Konishi negotiated with the Chinese, and the Japanese troops, demoralized, returned to Japan, abandoning their dream of conquest. Tokugawa Ieyasu appointed himself "protector" of young Toyotomi Hideyori, but the generals who had returned from Korea, wanting to take power in their turn, divided into two opposing camps, supporting either Hideyori or Ieyasu. The conflict could not be resolved by political means, so confrontation was inevitable. Two hundred thousand men took part in the Battle of Sekigahara on October 20, 1600, which was to decide the fate of Japan. Tokugawa Ieyasu came out the winner. He had Konishi and the other leaders who had opposed him executed, and thus became the absolute master of Japan. In 1603, the emperor appointed him shogun. He then settled in Edo (today Tokyo), had a castle built, and began a remarkable career as a legislator, dividing the daimyo into three separate classes—*fudai, hatamoto,* and *tozama*—and society into four classes—samurai, peasants, artisans, and merchants. He surrounded himself with talented people—philosophers such as Hayashi Razan, foreign navigators such as William Adams, and well-informed merchants—and forced "outside" daimyo *(tozama)* to spend part of the year in Edo and leave their families there as hostages (*see* SANKIN-KŌTAI).

The role of emperor was reduced to an honorary one. However, many malcontents joined Hideyori, who had taken refuge in Osaka to prepare for an attempt to oppose Ieyasu's hegemony. In two campaigns (winter of 1614 and summer of 1615), Ieyasu captured the Osaka castle; Hideyori and his entire family were killed and the castle was destroyed. Injured during the latter siege, Tokugawa Ieyasu died the following year, leaving the responsibility of shogun to his son Hidetada (enthroned in 1605). Ieyasu's legacy was considerable: he had restored Japan's unity and installed a peace that was to last more than two and a half centuries. But he was fiercely opposed to Christianity, which he felt (justly, at the time), caused agitation and disturbances and was the harbinger of a foreign invasion.

The Edo Period (1616–1868). The role of the shogun in Edo had been set out by the founder of the *bakufu.* Hidetada set himself the task of strengthening the rules made by Toyotomi Hideyoshi and his father, and took severe measures against foreigners. In 1616, he forbade Europeans to settle in Japan and closed all ports (except Hirado and Nagasaki) in order to transfer to the *bakufu* the trade monopolies with European countries that some daimyo had retained. Then, out of fear of possible military action by the Spanish stationed in Manila or the Portuguese in Macao, he began to persecute Christian missionaries. His successor, Iemitsu, barred the Portuguese from access to Japan and forbade Japanese to trade with Manila. The English, in their turn, closed their trading post at Hirado. In 1637, the Christians of Kyushu, supported by hungry peasants and a few samurai defying the ban, revolted in Shimabara. The *bakufu* mercilessly repressed the rebellion and closed the country to foreigners in 1639. Only the Chinese and the Dutch (who were not given to religious proselytizing) had permission to live on the islet of Dejima at Nagasaki. Japan thus was in contact only with China, Korea, and the Ryukyu Islands, and secondarily with the Dutch.

Major roads (*see* GO-KAIDŌ) were built to facilitate trade, and the toll barriers were eliminated. Circulation of people and goods was overseen by fortified castles at strategic points. A few ships, armed with shogunal authorization (*see* SHUIN-SEN), received permission to trade with the countries of Southeast Asia three or four times a year, bringing back essential raw materials, silk, cotton, tin, and sugar. Trade prospered once again, and the new class of urban merchants, the *chōnin,* began to compete with the warrior class, which had become idle and had therefore turned into consumers. From

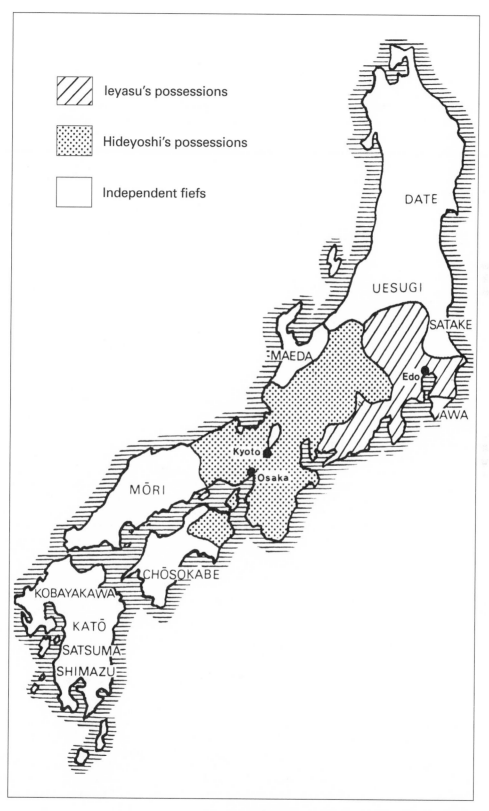

Japan at the Time of Hideyoshi's Death (1598)

time to time, there were revolts, such as the one in 1651 after the death of Tokugawa Iemitsu, but they were all harshly dealt with. Many samurai thus found themselves without a lord, and a number of these *rōnin* became brigands. They began to pose serious problems for the government, which didn't know what to do about them. In 1657, a gigantic fire ravaged Edo, causing more than 100,000 deaths. The capital was soon reconstructed on a new plan, which made merchants and entrepreneurs even wealthier. Shogun Tsunayoshi devalued the currency and was known mainly for his eccentricities and his inordinate love of dogs. Elsewhere, many daimyo, falling into debt because of the double life they were forced to sustain in Edo and in their provinces, began to depend on the merchants who lent them money. As trade flourished, the capital became a place of luxury and the *chōnin* encouraged the development of a new type of visual art, ukiyo-e prints. In parallel to warrior society and the static culture of the samurai, an evolutionary popular culture developed that raised Kabuki to a noble art. However, the spirit of the samurai had not died, as the famous incident of the Akō-gishi (or the 47 *rōnin*, 1701–03) shows. In 1709, the Confucian adviser to the shogunate, Arai Hakuseki, set the "rule of warrior houses" *(Buke-shohatto),* reformed the laws, stabilized the currency, and denounced the opulence displayed by some samurai. The *bakufu* was forced to revise its social policy because of the ever-growing influence of the *chōnin.* In the countryside, however, the peasantry still lived in misery, despite some agrarian reforms and the setting of rice prices by shogun Yoshimune. Pressured by taxes and prey to periodic famines, the peasants were in a state of continual revolt. Each time, the repression was merciless. In 1787, Matsudaira Sadanobu, an adviser to the shogun Ienari, tried to redress the situation: he fired corrupt bureaucrats, reduced public expenditures, stabilized finances, and tried to stem the flow of rural dwellers to the towns that were springing up at every crossroads, at the foot of castles, and around large temples and shrines. But these measures were not very effective. Matsudaira resigned, and Tokugawa Ienari took power in 1792, but he was an ineffectual leader. In the same year, Russian ships landed in Hokkaido; starting in 1797, European ships became more and more numerous off the Japanese coasts, which could not help but make the shogunate and the emperor nervous. In 1804, Russian admiral Rezanov dropped anchor in the port of Nagasaki, but the shogunate refused to open talks. Then, in 1804, an English ship threatened to bomb Nagasaki if it was not permitted to take on supplies. In 1825, the shogun ordered that any foreign ship caught trying to land in Japan be destroyed and its crew be executed. Indebted samurai and hungry peasants were still revolting, especially in rural areas. In 1844, the Dutch government, via Dejima, asked Japan to cease its isolationist policy. The shogunate seemed to soften its stand when it received an English warship in Nagasaki and two American warships off Edo (1845–46). Finally, in 1853, Commodore Perry's American fleet dropped anchor in the Bay of Uraga and demanded that the ports be opened. The *bakufu,* intimidated by the power of the American ships, agreed in 1854 to open two ports, Shimoda and Hakodate, and to receive a consul, Townsend Harris—without, however, submitting the matter to the emperor. Japan signed similar agreements with England, Russia, and Holland. In spite of passions that were tearing the country apart, the American consul was finally received by the shogun Iesada in 1857. After the shogunate signed trade and friendship treaties with the United States and France, part of the country rose up "against the barbarians," targeting the shogunate and advocating a return to imperial authority. When Ii Naosuke, the most listened-to adviser to the *bakufu,* was assassinated, the shogun was forced to consult with the emperor for the first time in two and a half centuries. After several displays of force by the allied ships, which bombed the port of Kagoshima and the city of Shimonoseki, the proponents of restoration of the emperor revolted and fought the *bakufu's* troops in 1864. Shogun Iemochi tried to reestablish order, then offered his resignation to the emperor. A provisional government was set up, excluding the Tokugawa. Finally, in 1868, after the Boshin Civil War, the emperor's supporters won on all fronts. The young emperor, Mutsuhito, then moved to Edo, where he made his new capital, Tokyo, and inaugurated the era of "enlightened government" (Meiji).

The Meiji Era (1868–1912). The clans, long victimized by the Tokugawa, raised their voices once more and asked to have their feudal rights recognized by the emperor. But he refused; having decided to modernize Japan, he brought the rebels to their senses and installed a series of reforms that were to cause lasting changes to Japanese society. He divided the country administratively into departments *(ken)* without taking the old feudal divisions into account, organized the population in new classes, denied samurai the right to bear swords, allowed peasants to own land, reestablished the freedom to buy and sell land, reorganized domestic and foreign trade, reformed the basis for taxes, created universities and schools, and updated the government system. Some samurai, unhappy that conscription had taken away their reason for being, rallied around Saigō Takamori and Etō Shimpei and revolted in Satsuma. The rebellion was finally quashed in 1877. The constitution promised by the emperor was eagerly awaited by the political parties that had started to form and that were demanding the extension of civil rights to all citizens and equality before the law. Japanese returning from study trips in the West brought back new ideas, expounded in the works of Fukuzawa Yukichi, among others. But it was only in 1885 that the emperor established a Western-style parliamentary cabinet, which was chaired by Ito Hirobumi. The constitution was finally promulgated by the emperor on February 11, 1889; it created two legislative chambers, the House of Peers and the House of Representatives. The latter assembly was reorganized in 1900 and 1902.

The industrialization of Japan proceeded in giant steps, laws were rewritten, the army was reorganized with the assistance of French and German military experts, the navy was rebuilt on modern principles, mining operations were intensified, and plants were purchased by the government and brought to the public sector. A railroad line from Yokohama to Tokyo was inaugurated in 1872, and others, built by private firms, rapidly followed. Roads were improved and a postal service instituted. In short, all of Japan was modernizing and westernizing at a frantic pace. Living conditions improved and the birth rate made a spectacular leap upward. In 1894, following a dispute over Korea, Japanese troops landed in China. The Chinese, poorly equipped and commanded, were beaten on land and at sea. The Japanese captured Taiwan. China was forced to admit defeat in the Treaty of Shimonoseki, signed on April 17, 1895. But the Western powers denied Japan one of its claims: Korea, cut off from Chinese influence, became a bone of contention between czarist Russia and Japan. Having assisted the allies in China in the Boxer Rebellion of 1900, Japan concluded a military alliance with England, directed against Russian aggression in Manchuria and Korea. Because Nicholas II had reinforced his troops in Manchuria, Japan attacked and blocked the Russian navy in Port Arthur, then landed troops in Chemulpo (In-ch'ŏn), Korea, and the Liaodong Peninsula in China in 1904. Japanese pressure on Port Arthur was so great that General Stœssel, its commandant, was forced to surrender while in Manchuria. Japanese troops were accumulating victories and captured Muken. In March

1905, the Russian Baltic fleet was caught and annihilated in a trap set by Admiral Tōgō in the Tsushima strait. Russia, defeated, signed the Portsmouth Treaty on September 5, 1905, which gave Japan the southern part of Sakhalin (Karafutō) and most of Korea and the Liaodong Peninsula. In return, Russians and Japanese agreed to leave Manchuria within 18 months. Itō Hirobumi, appointed president of Korea, began to colonize the country. In Japan, conservative and liberal parties alternated in power, while membership in progressive and socialist parties grew considerably. Militarists and liberals, the latter led by Saionji, continued to oppose each other. The military powers won out, and Saionji was forced to resign. On July 30, 1912, Emperor Mutsushito, thereafter called Meiji Tennō, died.

The Taihō Era (1912–26). Meiji Tennō's son, Yoshihito, succeeded him, but had neither his father's authority nor his abilities. After a liberal attempt, the emperor reappointed Katsura Tarō prime minister, but Tarō soon opposed the military and naval forces. The parliamentary seesaw continued, without bringing political stability. In 1913, following incidents in China, the Japanese sent forces to police that country; in 1914, Japan sided with the Allies, which enabled it to seize German possessions in China and gain a free rein on the continent. In 1915, it sent an ultimatum of "21 demands" to Yuan Shikai, who was forced to accept them, and the Japanese military triumphed. But when China entered the war on the Allies' side, in 1917, Japan found itself in a difficult position. In addition, the new Bolshevik government refused to recognize the accords signed with the czar. The Japanese invaded Siberia at the request of the Allies and did battle with the "Reds." When the Treaty of Versailles was signed in 1918, Japan had a position that was strong but difficult to maintain, since it and China were on the same side. It did obtain all German islands in the Pacific Ocean north of the equator, but had to agree to liberate the Liaodong Peninsula. In Korea, the death of the emperor in 1919 led to many nationalist disturbances, which Japanese troops bloodily put down. But the liberals had returned to power in Japan, and the triumphalist militarism seemed muffled. The war had upset the Japanese economy, and although Japan sought new trade outlets in Asia, Africa, and the United States, it met with reluctance everywhere. In 1921, an ill Emperor Yoshihito named his son, Hirohito, regent. On September 1, 1923, a catastrophic earthquake destroyed Tokyo and Yokohama, and Hirohito decreed martial law. An anti-Korean and anti-communist wave swept the country, causing thousands of deaths. Despite this, the progressives won the following election, although militarists and ultranationalists claimed power. Yoshihito (Taishō Tennō) died in 1926 and Hirohito succeeded him, naming his era Shōwa, or "Radiant Peace."

The Shōwa Era (1926–89): (1) The Rise of Fascism (1926–37). After a brief interval with a liberal government, the ultranationalists returned to power, supported to a great extent by the military. The Tanaka Memorandum of 1927 clearly laid out Japan's expansionist aims. In China, the dictator of Manchuria, Zhang Zuolin, held talks with the Japanese military while trying to maintain his independence from Chiang Kai-shek's (Jiang Jieshi) nationalists. But an assassination attempt against Zhang Zuolin provoked the resignation of the Japanese minister (1928). At the conference on global disarmament in 1930, the Japanese delegate was not able to win other delegates over to his country's views; soon after, the prime minister was assassinated. Minister Wakatsuki, a progressive, succeeded him, but the American financial crisis had profound repercussions on the shaky Japanese economy, setting off an acute social crisis. In spite of the emperor's disapproval, the Japanese military invaded Manchuria and, over the protests of the League of Nations, attacked China under false pretenses and bombed Shanghai. Japan withdrew from China under threat from the United States but created a puppet state, Manchukuo, in Manchuria, and installed the dethroned king of China, Puyi, as monarch. In Japan, Wakatsuki resigned because of plots against the government, but the military, which wanted to keep its grip on China, inaugurated a policy of assassinations in order to free itself from its adversaries. The assassination of Inukai (May 15, 1932) marked the end of parliamentarism in Japan. From then on, the military ran the country, launching it into a series of wars of conquest directed against China, imitating the rising German national socialism. On August 25, 1932, Manchuria was made a protectorate; in 1934, Puyi was officially named emperor of Manchukuo, with the Chinese ruling name of Kangde. Japan withdrew from the League of Nations, denounced the Washington and London accords on disarmament, and again invaded northern China (1934). In China, Chiang Kai-shek, with his personal policy of anti-communism, let the Japanese invade his country. In Tokyo, a wave of assassination attempts perpetrated by militarists was the prelude to a coup d'état, which, although it failed, did nothing to discourage the ultranationalists who supported military action in China with the tacit

approval of Chiang Kai-shek. Only Chinese communists and rural dwellers opposed the advance of the invader's troops. The Japanese provoked incident after incident in order to justify their intervention; at the beginning of 1937, a mobilized Japanese army landed in China in force.

(2) The Second World War (1937–45). In Nanjing, the Japanese installed a Chinese "cooperation" government led by Wang Jingwei, which enabled Japan rapidly to occupy the entire coast. Chiang Kai-shek and his senior staff withdrew to Chongqing, and he occupied himself exclusively with the struggle against Mao Zedong's communists, not concerning himself with the Japanese but encouraged by the Axis powers, especially Hitler's Germany. While the United States unreservedly backed Chiang Kai-shek's Guomindang, the English signed an accord with Japan recognizing its "special rights." For their part, the Japanese hesitated to join Germany for fear of the reactions of the United States, Russia, and Great Britain. There was a constant turnover in government ministers. In 1939, with the German-Soviet pact and the beginning of hostilities in Europe, Japan asked the Allies to withdraw their troops from China, but Japanese opinion was divided between those who wanted an alliance with the USSR, with Germany, and with Great Britain. In 1940, with France occupied by the Germans, the Japanese sent an ultimatum to General Catroux, commander of the troops in Indochina, then signed an accord with Great Britain to "close" the Burma route and deprive Chiang Kai-shek of all supplies. Prime Minister Konoe demanded free passage for his troops to Indochina; the Japanese military was actively supporting Thailand in its territorial claims on Cambodia, and called upon the Dutch government of Indonesia to deliver 3 million tons of oil. On September 27, 1940, the Japanese government joined the Axis and signed a tripartite treaty with it. Only England was still opposing Germany and Japan. On April 13, 1941, Japan signed a nonaggression pact with the Soviet Union; in response, the United States seized all Japanese property in its territory on July 25. Konoe wanted a policy of prudence, but General Tōjō was pushing for war; he replaced Konoe at the head of the government on October 16, and war was now inevitable. On December 7, 1941, without prior warning, the Japanese combined air-force and navy fleet bombed the American fleet based at Pearl Harbor, Hawai'i, destroying it almost completely. The United States was now forced to enter the war. The Japanese military, momentarily free to act, won battle after battle in its march south toward the Indonesian oil fields: Guam was occupied on December 10, 1941; the English navy was destroyed at Singapore on December 22; Wake fell the same day, Hong Kong on the 25th; Manila was taken on January 2, 1942. Singapore surrendered on February 15, 1942, and Indonesia was conquered in March. By May, all of Southeast Asia was in Japanese hands. But the Americans now took advantage of the fact that the extent of Japanese victories was causing problems with supplying the troops and forcing Japan to disperse its forces. On September 12, 1942, the Americans recaptured Guadalcanal, and in the course of 1943 the military picture was completely reversed. One by one, the Allies retook the Pacific islands, forcing the Japanese army, already harassed by local resistance movements, to withdraw. Despite often suicidal acts of heroism, the Japanese could not keep the American forces, with their superior weaponry, from pushing toward Japan. On June 15, 1944, they landed at Saipan. The fall of that island on July 7 caused General Tōjō to resign; he was replaced by an ultranationalist, Koiso Kuniaki, who, in spite of appeals for caution by experts (Japan had almost no raw materials or oil left), vowed to fight to the death. The Philippines were reconquered (the Battle of Leyte). The Japanese then invented suicide planes (*see* KAMIKAZE) and inflicted severe losses on the American army, but they could not keep it from landing on Okinawa on April 1, 1945. The incessant bombing of Tokyo and major industrial centers weakened the war effort, and the government grew concerned: Koiso resigned and the emperor asked the Soviets to open negotiations. But the Soviets, who had defeated Nazi Germany, were considering the possibility of attacking Japan in order to share in the spoils of war. Admiral Suzuki Kantarō, a moderate who had succeeded Koiso, tried to reopen talks, but the "Potsdam Treaties" remained without effect. President Truman then decided to use the atomic bomb to force Japan to surrender, in a bid to save many Allied lives. On August 6, 1945, the first atomic bomb was dropped on Hiroshima; three days later, another one was dropped on Nagasaki. On August 8, the USSR officially declared war on Japan. Emperor Hirohito agreed to an unconditional surrender, asking the Japanese people, in a historic speech, to "tolerate the intolerable and accept the unacceptable." On September 2, 1945, Japan's act of surrender was signed in Tokyo on the American warship *Missouri*, in the presence of General MacArthur.

(3) **The *Apure* (Postwar) Period (1945–93).** The emperor and General MacArthur worked together on reconstruction of Japan and its reorganization on a democratic basis. All of the country's industries had been destroyed, the problem of feeding the population was immense, and it no longer had its colonies to count on. General MacArthur organized his own "*bakufu*," creating an occupation agency called S.C.A.P., and an international court was convened to hear the cases of and set sentences for those responsible for the war (*see* WAR CRIMES). A new constitution took effect on May 3, 1947. The emperor renounced the fiction of his divine origins. The Diet was reorganized, the civil code modified, the education system reformed on American models, and S.C.A.P. relaunched agriculture and industry. Many American economic missions helped the country gradually get back on its feet. The way was not entirely smooth, however: after 1948, a year of strikes and riots, the government turned toward the right. Yoshida Shigeru, appointed prime minister with the cooperation of the American occupiers, tried to instill a new sense of courage and national pride in the population. On September 8, 1950, a peace was finally signed in San Francisco, and Japan was once again a free nation. It was at this point that the Korean War broke out. The American war effort was supported by Japan, which saw an unexpected opportunity to help its industries recover; it also benefited from American "military tourism." But General MacArthur proved too aggressive in his war effort, wanting to push ahead to China, and he was replaced by General Ridgway, who made Japan an "ally" of the United States. Thanks to its spectacular industrial recovery, Japan became the supplier of the American war machine. But once the Korean War was over, the situation remained difficult in Japan. Yoshida, faced with growing opposition, was forced to resign. Kishi Nobusuke tried to abrogate Article 9 of the Constitution, which forbade Japan to possess an offensive army, but he withdrew this notion under popular pressure and resigned in his turn. His successors were generally interested in transforming Japan's industrial power into an engine of economic development, under the leadership of Satō Eisaku. Japan's economy made a spectacular recovery, and the country held an Olympic Games in 1964, for which part of the Tokyo urban landscape was remodeled. The Liberal Democratic party (LDP, Jiyū Minshutō) was in power, and the prime ministers came from its ranks. Okinawa was returned to Japan in 1972, and relations with the People's Republic of China were normalized. Japan's extraordinary economic progress was somewhat damped by the "Nixon Shock" (*see* NIKUSON SHOKKU) in 1973, and Japan was forced to fight the threat of inflation. However, the Japa-

nese people, with their energy and sense of responsibility, overcame the crisis, and Japan's top-priority objective became to conquer, peacefully, the business world by producing high-tech, high-quality products. The United States was Japan's biggest customer, but Japanese products were also sold throughout Asia and Europe. For better penetration of European markets, Japanese firms set up joint ventures and foreign subsidiaries. Although competition in the business world was fierce, the Japanese gained firm footholds all over the world. The yen rose in value and became a currency of reference, although always in association with the American dollar. In 1989, Emperor Hirohito died, after the longest reign in the history of Japan; thereafter, he was referred to only by the name of his era, Shōwa Tennō. His son, Akihito, became emperor, inaugurating a new era (*see* NENGŌ) called Heisei ("Peace and Accomplishment").

Historical and Artistic Periods. In Japan, historical periods generally coincide with the country's major historical events. Japan has had a "linear" history in the sense that there were no major territorial modifications during the course of its historical development, so artistic currents varied only as a function of influences received, generally from Korea and China until the beginning of the nineteenth century, from the United States and Europe since. Japan's genius is in "Japanizing" these influences after a certain "absorption" period. It has also created its own forms of art and has preserved them carefully as part of an intangible heritage.

Because historical and artistic periods are referred to throughout this book, they are summarized below. (Note: double dates are due to varying opinions by historians.)

• *Prehistoric period* (Jōmon): From the tenth millennium BC to about 300 BC in Kyushu, with remnants persisting into the first millennium AD in northern Honshu. *See* JŌMON.

• *Protohistorical periods:*

(1) **Yayoi** (from ca. 300 BC to ca. AD 300), mainly in Honshu. *See* YAYOI.

(2) of the *kofun,* or megalithic tombs, from the late third century to the seventh century. *See* KIBA MINZOKU-RON, KOFUN.

• *"Historical" periods:*

—**Asuka** (from ca. 538 to 710)

—**Nara** (from 710 to 784 or 794)

—**Heian** (from 784/794 to 1185 or 1192): **Kōnin** and **Jōgan** (794–894), **Fujiwara** (894–1185 or 1192)

—**Kamakura** (from 1185/1192 to 1333)

—**Ashikaga** (or **Muromachi,** 1333–1574):

Nambokuchō (1336–92), **Ōnin** War (1467–77), **Sengoku** (Warring States, 1467–1567)

—**Dictators** (or **Azuchi-Momoyama,** from 1567 or 1574 to 1603 or 1615): **Oda Nobunaga, Toyotomi Hideyoshi, Tokugawa Ieyasu**

—**Edo** shogunate (or **Tokugawa** shogunate, 1603–1868)

—**Meiji** (1868–1912)

—**Modern** (1868–1990): **Taishō** (1912–26), **Shōwa** (1926–89), **Heisei** (1989–).

→ *See* ARCHEOLOGY, EMPERORS, JAPAN (STATISTICS), MIDWAY, MINISTERS, NAVAL BATTLES, POLITICAL PARTIES, PRIME MINISTERS, S.C.A.P., SINO-JAPANESE (WARS), UNITED NATIONS, WAR CRIMES, CHRONOLOGY.

Hita. Town in northern Ōita prefecture (northern Kyushu) on the Chikugogawa river, castle town (*jōka-machi*) in the Edo period, often called the "Kyoto of Kyushu," located in the center of a plateau with an altitude of about 700 m. Wood, lacquer, and pottery (*onta-yaki*) crafts. Remains of a *kofun* decorated with paintings. *Pop.:* 70,000.

Hitachi. City in Ibaraki prefecture (central Honshu) 130 km north of Tokyo, on the Pacific coast. Waystation on the Nikkō-Kaidō road during the Edo period. It developed around the Hitachi Copper Mines. Completely destroyed by bombing during the Second World War, it was reconstructed and is currently one of the most prosperous industrial cities in the country (copper, electrical cables, concrete, etc.). Its port, opened in 1960, is very busy. *Pop.:* 210,000.

• *Hitachi fudoki.* One of the rare *fudoki* (official reports) still in existence, concerning the former province of Hitachi (now Ibaraki prefecture).

• *Hitachi Ota.* Town in northern Ibaraki prefecture, former castle town (*jōka-machi*) of the Satake family and part of the Mito estate. Agricultural products, tobacco, paper (*washi*). *Pop.:* 37,000.

Hitachi Industries. A number of major industrial firms grouped together under the name Hitachi since the end of the Second World War, with their head office in Tokyo. The largest are Hitachi Densen, a cable and electrical-instruments maker founded in 1956 and exporting to many countries; Hitachi Kasei Kōgyō, founded in 1962, specializing in synthetic products (plastics, resins, etc.) and insulation, exporting throughout the world; Hitachi Kinzoku, founded in 1956 and specializing in production of specialized steels, exporting at least 25% of its production; Hitachi Seisakusho, founded in 1910 by Oadira Namuhei, producing heavy and light electrical equipment, specializing in locomotives, generators and transformers, radios, televisions, and household appliances, and, since 1959, computers and integrated circuits, exporting 30% of its production; Hitachi Kaden Hambai, which sells and distributes Hitachi products abroad, established in 1955; Hitachi Puranto Kensuetsu, founded in 1929, specializing in design and construction of factories and other buildings, which has worked in more than 45 countries; and Hitachi Zōzen, a ship- and factory-building company, previously Osaka Iron Works, which has become one of the three largest shipbuilding companies in the world (about 5% of annual world tonnage) with Ishakawajima Harima. Head office in Osaka.

Hitai tenri. Calligrapher (1872–1939), a founder of "modern" Japanese calligraphy.

Hitatare. Sort of shirt worn by nobles and samurai in the Kamakura period, tucked into *hakama* (pants).

Hitobashira. "Human pillar," human sacrifice once made to protect the spirit of a newly constructed building. Such sacrifices are mentioned in the *Nihon shoki* (720), but it is not certain that they were actually made in Japan, although they were in China. In many Asian and European countries, an ancient custom had it that a victim (preferably human) was buried under the threshold of a house under construction: this was why it is the custom never to set foot on the threshold when one enters a house, and why a man entering his home for the first time with his new wife must carry her so that her feet do not touch the threshold.

Hitodama. The spirit that leaves the human body after death. Some people say that they have seen this spirit in the form of a bluish ball of fire, which announced the death. Jack-o-lanterns in cemeteries are often taken for *hitodama.*

Hitoe. Type of undergarment kimono (longer for women than for men) worn by nobles in the Heian period. Women sometimes wore several colored *hitoe* in layers. *See* JŪNI-HITOE.

Hitogaeshi. "People going home," governmental incitement decreed in 1790 and 1843 to encourage peasants who had crowded into the cities to return to the countryside. It took the form of paying moving costs. In 1843, the shogunate ordered peasants to leave the cities, which were ravaged by the famines of 1833 and 1836, forbade them to come to Edo, and limited the amount of time peasants who had come to work for urban dwellers could stay.

Hitojichi. Holding of hostages by a lord or daimyo to ensure the loyalty of a vassal. This practice, current in the sixteenth century (Tokugawa Ieyasu took hostages for twelve years) was legalized by the Edo shogunate when the Sankin-kōtai was decreed. However, it was also practiced quite frequently among the common people when creditors took relatives or daughters of their debtors as hostages to ensure recovery of their loans. The custom was abolished in 1868. *See* SHICHI.

Hitorigoto. Two-volume collection of *haikai* poems and bits of prose by Kamijima Onitsura, published in 1716.

Hitotsubashi. Branch of the Tokugawa family, created by shogun Tokugawa Yoshimune in 1714 for his son, Tokugawa Munetada (1721–64). *See* SANKYŌ, TOKUGAWA.

• **Hitotsubashi Daigaku.** National university in Kunitachi (Tokyo), founded in 1875 by Mori Arinori as a school for business law. After having various names, it finally took its current name in 1949. It has a number of faculties of economic and business law and social sciences. It has about 3,000 students.

• **Hitotsubashi Keiki.** *See* TOKUGAWA YOSHINOBU.

Hitotsume kozō. Traditional character, a sort of demon *(oni)* or ghost *(bakemono)* with one eye in the middle of its forehead. This cyclops is often associated with a young Buddhist monk *(kozō),* or, in Shinto, with a *Ta no kami* (or *Yama no kami*). It is sometimes portrayed holding a grill with charcoal in its hand. People protect themselves from its spells by placing an upside-down basket on top of a pole in front of the house, especially on *kotoyōka* days (eighth day of the second and twelfth lunar months). *See* YAMA NO KAMI, KOTOYŌKA.

Hitoyogiri. Type of flute analogous to the *shakuhachi,* but shorter and with only five holes. It comprises only one bamboo knot, while *shakuhachi* may comprise several. This instrument stopped being used in the late eighteenth century. *See* FLUTES, SHAKUHACHI.

Hiuchi-bukuro. Box for cinders and embers used by smokers during the Edo period. A variant, called *hiuchi-bako,* had a mechanism that activated a lighter.

• **Hiuchi-dake (or Hiuchigadake).** Conical volcano in Fukushima prefecture (northern Honshu), 2,346 m in altitude, located in Nikkō National Park.

Hiyaka-me. Ancient unit of mass, weighing about 375.6 kg.

• **Hiyakkin.** Ancient unit of mass, weighing about 60 kg.

Hiyōe Kannon. One of the 33 forms (*see* SANJŪSAN ŌGESHIN) of Kannon Bosatsu (*Skt.:* Avalokiteshvara), corresponding to the Indian Buddhist divinity Parnashavarī (or Palāsambarī). In the Taizō-kai mandala, it is portrayed with two arms holding a *hōshu (Skt.: mani)* and a lotus flower. It is also sometimes portrayed with four arms, a small hatchet *(ono),* and a string. It is colored white. Also called Hae Kannon, Yōe Kannon Bosatsu.

Hizakurige. "Voyage on One Leg." A 56-volume travel book by Jippensha Ikku, published between 1802 and 1809. It is a picaresque, comic work *(kokkeibon),* parts of which are sometimes attributed to Santōan Kyōden. Its complete title is *Tōkaidōchū hizakurige.*

Hizen. Former province, now split between Nagasaki and Saga prefectures. Also sometimes written Bizen. *See* BIZEN.

Ho. Former measure of area comprising four *chō.* Four *ho* comprise a *bō.*

Hō. Long over-dress, with wide sleeves, part of the *sokutai* costume. Also called *hōeki-hō.*

Hō-an. Era of Emperor Toba: Apr. 1120–Apr. 1124. *See* NENGŌ.

Hoashi Banri. Confucian scholar (1778–1852), physician, and astronomer, born in Bungo province. He taught himself Dutch in order to have access to "Dutch science" *(rangaku),* and tried to combine Confucianism and Buddhism with science in his

work. His book *Kyūritsu* (Mastery of Truth, 1836) was concerned mainly with astronomy and physics. He also wrote treatises on Western medicine *(Igaku keimo)* and on economic policy *(Tōsempu ron,* Treaty by an Eastern Recluse). Also called simply Banri.

Hoashi Kyōu. Painter (Hoashi En; *mei:* Kumatarō, Yōhei; *azana:* Chidai; *gō:* Chōshū, Hannō, Kyōu, 1810–84), born in Bungo province (Ōita prefecture). He studied Nanga style with Tanomura Chikuden, then with Uragami Shunkin, and poetry with Rai San'yō, among others. He painted mainly in imitation of Chikuden in pure Nanga style.

Hōate. Mask made of iron or lacquered leather, which, in the samurai's complete armor, covered all or the upper part of the face. In some cases, the nose of the mask was detachable so that the warrior could blow his nose. The *hōate,* intended to protect the face from injury, was very realistic and often designed to evoke fear. A heavy mustache decorated the upper lip. The teeth were sometimes visible and gilded with gold or silver. Two hooks above the cheeks enabled the war mask to be attached to the helmet *(kabuto). See* KABUTO, MEMPŌ, MUSHA ROKUGU, SŌMEN, YOROI.

Hōchi Shimbun. Daily sports newspaper, very popular in Japan, with a circulation of about 850,000 (Tokyo and Osaka editions combined), founded in Tokyo in 1872 as *Yūbin Hōchi Shimbun.* It took its current name in 1894.

Hōdō. In a Buddhist temple or monastery, the "treasure room" in which relics, rare statues of divinities, and precious objects used in worship are kept.

• *Hōdō-kyō.* Japanese title of a major Buddhist Sanskrit text, the *Vaipulya-sūtra,* comprising three doctrinal texts of the Mahayana, the *Prajñā-pāramitā-sūtra,* the *Ratnakūta-sūtra,* and the *Buddhāvatamshaka-sūtra.* Sometimes, the *Mahāparinirvāna-sūtra,* the *Mahāsamnipāta-sūtra,* and the *Saddharmapundarīka-sūtra* are added.

Hōe-bugyō. In the Kamakura period, bureaucrat charged with official ceremonies in temples and shrines. *See* BUGYŌ.

Hōei. Era of Emperor Higashiyama: Mar. 1704– Apr. 1711. *See* NENGŌ.

Hōen. Era of Emperor Sutoku: Sept. 1135–July 1141. *See* NENGŌ.
• Painter (Nishiyama Seishō; *azana:* Shitatsu, 1804–67), of the Shijō school, Keibun's student in Osaka.

Hōgai. Painter (Kanō Enshin; *mei:* Enshin, 1828–88), studied with Kanō Shōsen'in and Kanō Masanobu in Edo.

Hōgaku. All music played on typically Japanese instruments, with or without vocal accompaniment.

Hōgen. Era of Emperor Go-Shirakawa: Apr. 1156–Apr. 1159. *See* NENGŌ.
• "Eye of the Law," Buddhist title conferred on important monks and sometimes on artists. *See* SŌ-KAN.

• **Hōgen monogatari.** Major war tale *(gunki monogatari)* relating the war of the Hōgen era and, like the *Heiji monogatari,* meant to be sung by *biwa-hōshi.* It was also written in the early fourteenth century, but has at least 38 different recensions. A number of later writers took the characters and episodes of this epic poem as models.

• **Hōgen no Ran.** Hōgen Civil War (1156–1159), in which the Taira clan, the Minamoto clan, and the Fujiwara family fought for predominance. After the death of Toba Tennō in 1156, the emperor who succeeded him, Go-Shirakawa, was supported by regent *(kampaku)* Fujiwara no Tadamichi, while Retired Emperor Sutoku was assisted by Tadamichi's younger brother, Yorinaga, and by Minamoto no Tameyoshi. The latter's son, Minamoto no Yoshitomo, formed an alliance with Taira no Kiyomori to support the titular emperor. Having attempted to retake power by force, Sutoku was attacked and defeated by Taira no Kiyomori. Fujiwara no Yorinaga was killed, Minamoto no Tameyoshi was executed, and Retired Emperor Sutoku was sent into exile. Go-Shirakawa thus retained power, but the Minamoto and Taira families made further attempts to grab power in their turns, which gave rise to another civil war in the Heiji era. Thus ended the Fujiwara rule and began a period of violence that would end with the installation of a warrior regime, the Kamakura *bakufu,* in 1185.

• **Hōgen Tadayoshi.** *See* TADAYOSHI.

Hōgu. Ritual objects used in Buddhist ceremonies, particularly by monks in "esoteric" sects *(mikkyō)* such as the Tendai-shū and the Shingon-shū.

Hōgyō. In traditional architecture, a type of roof with four, six, or eight slopes, whose apex is often a *rōban* (as at the Yume-dono of the Hōryū-ji complex). These types of roofs were used mainly for pavilions or Buddhist structures with a square, hexagonal, or octagonal plan.

Hōhei. Painter (Satake Seii; *gō:* Kibun-shujin, 1750–1807) of the Nanga school (Bujinga), Taiga's student. He painted mainly landscapes.

Ho-in. "Seal of the Law," the highest Buddhist title, above those of Hōgen and Hokkyō. It was conferred first upon artist-monks, then upon lay artists. *See* SŌ-KAN.

Hōitsu. Painter (Sakai Hōitsu, Sakai Tadanao; *azana:* Kishin; *gō:* Ōson, Keikyo-dōjin, Nison'an, Uka-an, 1761–1828), born in Edo to a wealthy samurai family. After experimenting with a wide variety of styles, he settled on the Rimpa. He became a Buddhist monk under the name Hōitsu at the Nishi Hongan-ji temple in Kyoto in 1797; in 1809, he returned to Edo, where he founded a painting school called Uka-an (Hermitage of the Rain of Flowers), faithfully emulating the style of Ogata Kōrin. A great observer of nature, he excelled in paintings of flowers and plants, but was never able to equal his master. He wrote two books in honor of Ogata Kōrin, *Kōrin hyaku-zu* (One Hundred Paintings by Kōrin) and *Ogata-ryū ryaku impu* (Seals of Ogata Kōrin's school), and one devoted to Kōrin's brother, Kenzan, *Kenzan oboku* (Kenzan's Washes).

Hōji. Era of Emperor Go-Fukakasa: Feb. 1247–Mar. 1249. *See* NENGŌ.

• **Hōji Kassen.** Battle that took place in 1247, during which the Hōjō regents *(shikken)* confirmed their authority by defeating the army of the Miura family, which was vying for their position. Hōjō Tokiyori, assisted by his relative Adachi Kagemori, attacked the Miura family and forced 500 of them to commit suicide, thus remaining alone in power under the increasingly theoretical authority of the shogun of the Minamoto family.

Hōjō. Name of two major warrior families. One supplied the *shikken* of Kamakura; the other, not related, controlled the Kanto from Odawara up to the sixteenth century (*see* GO-HŌJŌ).

The Hōjō (associated with the Kamakura) belonged to a minor branch of the Taira family and took their family name from the small town of Hōjō, which they controlled, in the Izu region. They became vassals of Minamoto no Yoritomo (who had married Hōjō Tokimasa's daughter, Hōjō Masako), and their talents soon caught the eye of the Minamoto shogun; they took responsibility for the office of regent *(shikken),* which became a hereditary position starting with Hōjō Tokimasa. The Hōjō regents were:

—Hōjō Tokimasa (1138<1199–1205>1215)
—Hōjō Yoshitoki (1163<1205–24>)
—Hōjō Yasutoki (1183<1224–42>)
—Hōjō Tsunetoki (1224<1242–46>)
—Hōjō Tokiyori (1226<1246–56>1263)
—Hōjō Tokimune (1251<1256–84>)
—Hōjō Sadatoki (1270<1284–1301>1311)
—Hōjō Morotoki (?<1301–11>)
—Hōjō Takatoki (1303<1311–33>)

Together, these nine Hōjō *shikken* are known as Hōjō Kudai.

→ *See* GO-HŌJŌ, HŌJŌ GODAI, ODAWARA.

Hōjō Masako. Oldest daughter (Taira no Masako, 1157–1225) of Hōjō Tokimasa, who married Minamoto no Yoritomo in 1177. She was the mother of two shoguns, Minamoto no Yoriie and Minamoto no Sanetomo. When Yoritomo died, in 1199, she became a Buddhist nun (and was then called Ama Shōgun) and fulfilled her duty to find a replacement for her dead husband. With the assistance of her father, she deposed the notoriously incompetent Yoriie and installed Sanetomo at the head of the shogunate. But Hōjō Tokimasa and his second wife (Omaki no Kata) had plotted to have their brother-in-law, Hiraga Tomomasa, take Sanetomo's place, so Masako and Hōjō Yoshitoki exiled their father and took control of the *bakufu.* In 1219, she chose the young noble Kujō Yoritsune (1218–56) from Kyoto to succeed Sanetomo, who was without a male heir. She nevertheless continued to exercise a strong influence on the shogunate until her death.

• Hōjō Masamura. Brother (1205–73) of Hōjō Shigetoki and assistant to *shikken* Hōjō Tokimune and to Hyōjō-shū. He tried to reconcile the Kyoto court and the Kamakura *bakufu* after the incident of the Jōkyū era in 1221 (*see* JŌKYŪ NO HEN).

• Hōjō Morotoki. Eighth *shikken* (?<1301–11>) of Kamakura, son-in-law of and successor to Hōjō

Sadatoki. However, Sadatoki continued to govern in Morotoki's place when Sadatoki became a Buddhist monk in 1301. Hōjō Takatoki succeeded him as *shikken.*

• Hōjō Nagatoki. Son (1230–64) of Hōjō Shigetoki. In 1256, he assisted the *shikken* Hōjō Tokimune with the title of Samurai-dokoro Bettō.

• Hōjō Sadatoki. Seventh *shikken* (1270<1284–1301>1311) of the Kamakura *bakufu,* son of and successor to Hōjō Tokimune. He became a Buddhist monk in 1301 with the name Sōen, but kept power while his son-in-law, Hōjō Morotoki, was appointed *shikken.*

• Hōjō Sanetoki. Scholar (active ca. 1270), grandson of Hōjō Yoshitoki. He was the founder of the Kamazawa-bunko Library (*see* KAMAZAWA-BUNKO).

• Hōjō Shigetoki. Brother (1198–1261) of Hōjō Yasutoki and Hōjō Tomoyoki. He assisted *shikken* Hōjō Tokiyori with his responsibilities.

• Hōjō Takatoki. Ninth and last *shikken* (1303<1311–33>) of the Kamakura *bakufu,* son of Hōjō Sadatoki and successor to Hōjō Morotoki. Although he became regent at the age of eight, power was held by his maternal grandmother, Adachi Tokiaki, and his minister, Nagasaki Takasuke (d. 1333). Takatoki fell ill in 1326, as the shogunate was under attack on all sides by the imperial armies, and he resigned and became a Buddhist monk. He and his entire family committed suicide on May 23, 1333, when Nitta Yoshisada's troops, allied with those of Ashikaga Takauji, captured and set fire to the city of Kamakura. The family line of the Hōjō *shikken* died with him. *See* AKABASHI MORITOKI.

• Hōjō Tokifusa. Brother (1175–1240) of Hōjō Yoshitoki. He was appointed governor of Kyoto (Kyoto-kanrei) in 1221. He became a Buddhist monk in the Tō-ji temple in Nara and was known as Daibutsu.

• Hōjō Tokimasa. First regent *(shikken)* of the Kamakura *bakufu* (1138<1199–1205>1215), upon the death of Minamoto no Yoritomo, after having been governor of Kyoto (Kyoto-kanrei) since 1185. His daughter, Hōjō Masako, had married the future shogun, Yoritomo, in 1177. With his daughter's help, Tokimasa took power from shogun Minamoto no Yoriie and created a regency, to which he appointed himself in 1203. He then had Yoriie assassinated and installed Minamoto no Sanetomo as shogun, keeping power for himself. After he plotted with his second wife, Omaki no Kata, to eliminate Sanetomo and replace him with his son-in-law, Hiraga Tomomasa, Masako and his son, Hōjō Yoshitoki, forced him to retire and go into exile in Izu province, where he became a Buddhist monk. Hōjō Yoshitoki then took over as *shikken.*

• **Hōjō Tokimune.** Sixth regent *(shikken)* of the Kamakura *bakufu* (1251<1256–84>), son of and successor to Hōjō Tokiyori. It was during his "reign" that the two attempted invasions by the Mongolians on the northern coast took place, in 1274 and 1281. He then organized Japan's defenses in a more effective way. A fervent devotee of Zen doctrine, he invited Chinese monks, such as Wuxue *(Jap.:* Mugaku), to Japan and had the Engaku-ji temple built at Kamakura. Hōjō Sadatoki succeeded him as shikken.

• **Hōjō Tokiuji.** One of Hōjō Yasutoki's sons (1203–30), appointed governor of Kyoto (Kyoto-kanrei) in 1224.

• **Hōjō Tokiyori.** Fifth *shikken* (1226<1246–56>1263) of the Kamakura *bakufu,* son of Hōjō Tokiuji and brother of Hōjō Tsunetoki, whom he succeeded. He successfully did battle with the "phantom shogun" Kujō Yoritsune and defeated the rival Miura family *(see* HŌJI KASSEN). He took the Buddhist robe in 1256 under the name Dōsō and left power to Hōjō Nagatoki to govern as *shikken* in the name of his son, Hōjō Tokimune, who was to succeed him at his death.

• **Hōjō Tokiyuki.** Son (d. 1333) of Hōjō Takatoki, who formed an alliance with his father's and Emperor Go-Daigo's enemies against the Kamakura *bakufu.* He was defeated and beheaded on Ashikaga Takauji's order.

• **Hōjō Tomotoki.** Brother (1193–1245) of Hōjō Yasutoki, appointed Hyōjō-shū Bettō.

• **Hōjō Tsunetoki.** Fourth *shikken* (1224<1242–46>) of the Kamakura *bakufu,* son of Hōjō Tokiuji and successor to Hōjō Tasutoki. He abdicated in favor of his brother, Hōjō Tokiyori, in 1246.

• **Hōjō Yasutoki.** Third *shikken* (1183<1224–42>) of the Kamakura *bakufu,* son of and successor to Hōjō Yoshitoki. He defeated the imperial

forces during the Jōkyū no Hen (1221), established his residence at Rokuhara (Kyoto), and held the position of *tandai* (deputy of the shogunate) until his father died. He created a State Council (Hyōjōshū) in 1226 and proclaimed the first code of shogunal law, the *Goseibai-shikimoku (Jōei-shikimoku),* in 1232, thus setting a basis for the legitimacy of the Kamakura shogunate. His most loyal adviser was the Zen Buddhist monk Myōe (Kōben).

• **Hōjō Yoshitoki.** Second *shikken* (1163<1205–24>) of the Kamakura *bakufu,* son of and successor to Hōjō Tokimasa and brother of Hōjō Masako. With Masako's help, he ousted his father and took over his position. After Minamoto no Sanetomo was assassinated in 1219, he assumed total power. The emperor's supporters tried to take back the reins of government in 1221 *(see* JŌKYŪ), but he defeated the troops of retired emperor Go-Toba and solidified the shogunate's hold over the entire country.

Hōjō Dansui. Writer (1663–1711) and haiku poet. Ihara Saikaku's disciple, he wrote many novels in the *ukiyo-zōshi* genre, such as *Chūya Yōjin-ki* (Account of Unfailing Vigilance, 1707).

Hōjōgawa. Title of a Noh play: two men carry fish, intending to release them in the Hōjō River.

Hōjō Godai (Odawara Hōjō). Warrior family that controlled Odawara in the fifteenth and sixteenth centuries *(see* GO-HŌJŌ). Its main members were:

• **Hōjō Sōun.** Warrior (Ise Shinkurō, Shinkurō Nagauji, 1432–1519), born in Ise province. A vassal of Imagawa Yoshitada (1442–76), *shugo* of Suruga, he received the Kōkoku-ji castle as compensation. This enabled him to seize Izu province in 1491 and the Odawara castle in 1495, where he and his descendants settled permanently, controlling all of Kanto. He became a Buddhist monk under the name Sōun and wrote a 21-chapter code of family law.

• **Hōjō Ujimasa.** Eldest son (1538–90) of Hōjō Ujiyasu. He became a Buddhist monk under the name Ryūsai. Attacked by Toyotomi Hideyoshi, he committed suicide. His son, Hōjō Ujinao, succeeded him.

• **Hōjō Ujinao.** Warrior (1562–91), son of and successor to Hōjō Ujimasa in Odawara. He married one of Tokugawa Ieyasu's daughters but, attacked by Toyotomi Hideyoshi and his father-in-law and defeated, he was sent into exile on Mt. Kōya, where he became a Buddhist monk. The Odawara castle was then dismantled. He was the last of the Hōjō of Odawara.

• **Hōjō Ujinori.** Son (d. 1600) of Hōjō Ujiyasu; he, like Hōjō Ujinao, was sent into exile on Mt. Kōya. However, Tokugawa Ieyasu later gave him the Sayama fiefdom.

• **Hōjō Ujitsuna.** Warrior (1487–1541), son of Hōjō Sōun (Nagauji). He conquered Kanto for his father and built a huge castle in Odawara, which became the residence of all of his descendants.

• **Hōjō Ujiyasu.** Warrior (1515–70), son of and successor in Odawara to Hōjō Ujitsuna. He completed the conquest of Kanto and defeated Uesugi Kenshin, who tried to steal his possessions.

Hōjō Hideji. Playwright (Ino Hideji, 1902–77) of the Shimpa theater school. He also wrote many popular and commercially successful plays for the New National Theater (Shinkokugeki). His best-known work is *Oshō* (The Master of Failure, 1947).

Hōjō Hiroshi. Buddhist monk (1923–81) who became the fourth president of Sōka Gakkai, succeeding Ikeda Daisaku, who devoted himself to foreign relations, in 1979. Hiroshi had a degree from the Naval Academy. When he died, Akiya Einosuke (b. 1930) succeeded him as fifth president of the religious society.

Hōjōki. "Memories of My Square Hut," small book of philosophical thoughts written by Kamo Chōmei (1154–1216) in a delicate style. This collection of essays is full of sensitive reflections, imbued with resignation and the Buddhist sentiment of the impermanence of all things. It was written about 1212.

Hōjō Tamio. Writer (1914–37), born in Seoul, Korea. He caught Hansen's disease (leprosy) at the age of 20 and wrote an account of his experiences in hospitals, *Maki rōjin* (Old Man Maki, 1935), a novella admired by Kawabata Yasunari, who encouraged him to write. He produced only novellas, including *Inochi no shoya* (The First Day of Life, 1936) and *Raiin jutai* (Pregnant in a Leper Colony, 1936).

Hōju. Family of sword makers whose members were active from the thirteenth to the fifteenth century in Mutsu province (northern Honshu) in Hiraizumi. Their products seemed less polished than those of the Kyoto and Bizen schools, but they nevertheless produced high-quality blades.

Hōka. Popular shows including dances and acrobatics with an accompaniment of bamboo sticks hit against each other, performed by itinerant performers in the streets, and common in the Muromachi and Edo periods. It is now the name for traditional dances in the Aichi region, in which the dancers carry enormous fans on their backs and play flutes and drums.

Hōkaibō. Title of a Kabuki play written in 1783: an evil Buddhist monk tries to seduce a young woman and kills a princess, whose ghost haunts him forever.

Hōkai-ji. Buddhist temple belonging to the Shingon-shū sect, situated in Fushimi (Kyoto). Founded in the ninth century, it was at first a Tendai-shū temple but came to be affiliated with the Shingon-shū during the Edo period. Its Amidadō dates from 1051 and houses a beautiful sculpture of Amida Buddha by Jōchō. The Yakushidō (1456) also houses a sculpture of Yakushi Nyorai dating from the late twelfth century.

Hōka-ji. Buddhist temple in Kamakura, founded in the late twelfth century. It houses beautiful sculptures dating from the Kamakura period.

Hōkan-ji. Five-story pagoda in Kyoto, also called Yasaka no Tō, dating from the early Muromachi period (fourteenth century). It is about 38 m high. Its roofs are covered with tiles and it is topped with a bronze *sōrin*. The temple to which it belonged was destroyed, so it is now in a park.

Hōkan-shō. Decoration of "the Order of the Crown," created in 1888 and reserved for deserving women. It has eight classes. Yellow-and-red ribbon.

Hōka-zō. Title of a Noh play: two brothers seeking revenge for an offense disguise themselves as Buddhist monks and kill their enemy.

Hoke-kyō. Japanese title of a Sanskrit Buddhist sutra, the *Saddharmapundarīka-sūtra* (Lotus of the True Law), part of the Tripitaka, in 27 chapters (prose and verse) explaining the Mahayanist conceptions of the Buddha and the bodhisattva *(Jap.: bosatsu)* and relating the sermons made by the Buddha Shakyamuni on Vulture's Peak in Rājagriha, India. Probably composed in the third century AD, this treatise was translated into Chinese by Dharmarākṣha in 286, then by Kumārajīva in 406, and by Jñānagupta and Dharmagupta in 589–601. The oldest illustrated edition, dating from 868, was found in Dunhuang, China: *Fahua jing, Miaofalianhua jing*; Mongolian: *Chagan lingqua*. Also called, in Japanese, *Hokke-kyō, Myōhō renge-kyō*. It is the most important sutra of the Nichiren sects. It is also the basic text of the Tendai-shū, and the text on which the Zen monk Dōgen based his work. The modern sects of Sōka Gakkai, Risshō Kōseikai, and Reiyūkai venerate him by reciting the name of his title, "Namu Myōhō renge-kyō" ("In the name of the *Lotus Sutra*").

• **Hōke-kyō-ji.** Buddhist temple in Shimōsa-Nakayama, founded in 1260 to be one of the four main centers of Nichiren's teachings. It contains sculptures attributed to Nichiren and his disciples.

Hōken. Term used by historians to describe the "pre-feudal" system of government of the Kamakura *bakufu*.

Hōki. Era of Emperor Kōnin: Oct. 770–Jan. 781. *See* NENGŌ.
• Name of a former province, now part of Tottori prefecture.
→ *See* WAKE NO HIROMUCHI.

• **Hōki no Kami Masayoshi.** *See* MASAYOSHI.

Hokkaido. The northernmost of the four largest islands in the Japanese archipelago, and the second largest in area after Honshu, from which it is separated by the Tsugaru Strait. *Total area:* 83,513 km². *Pop.:* 5.6 million. Hokkaido is administratively divided into 14 districts: Soya (far north), Rumoi (northwest coast), Abashiri (northeast coast), Nemuro (northeast cape), Kushiro (central southwest), Tokachi (central south), Hidaka (south cape), Hiburi (south coast), Oshima (eastern part of the southwest peninsula) Hiyama (western part of the southwest peninsula), Shiribeshi (southwest coast), Ishikari (west-southwest coast), Sorachi (central west), Kamigawa (central east), and the island of Junashiri in the Kuril Islands (Chishima Rettō). In the past called Ezo, Watari-shima, Yeddo, and Yezo, it has been called Hokkaido since only 1869. It is very mountainous and has a major central massif

from which the Teshio, Kitami, Ishikari, Hidaka, and Yubari ranges originate; they are extended by plateaus and bordered by coastal plains (Teshio, Tokachi, Ishikari). The climate, especially on the west coast, is harsh and swept by winds from Siberia, resulting in alpine and subarctic vegetation. Nevertheless, rice is cultivated and cattle breeding is intensive. Forestry is a major industry, providing raw materials for prosperous pulp and paper industries. The island was extensively settled and exploited only in the late nineteenth century, with assistance from American agricultural engineers. It is now a special prefecture *(dō)* of which the *chief city* is Sapporo. *Other important cities:* Hakodate, Asahikawa, Abashiri, Otaru, Mororan, Kushiro, Nemuro, Wakkanai, Tomakomai, Iwamizawa, Kitami, Obihiro. *See* AINU.

• **Hokkaido Daigaku.** National university of Sapporo, founded in 1876 as an agricultural college and becoming independent in 1918. It has many faculties, including medicine, literature, law, economics, and science, and accommodates about 10,000 students.

• **Hokkaido Minami-jinja.** Shinto sect belonging to Jinja Shinto, specific to Hokkaido, with about 60,000 followers.

• *Hokkaido Shimbun.* Hokkaido's major daily newspaper, founded in 1942 from the amalgamation of 11 local newspapers. Head office in Sapporo. *Circulation:* approximately 1 million.

• **Hokkaido Takushoku Ginkō.** Major Sapporo bank, founded in 1900, with about 150 branches throughout Japan and many branches in foreign cities, including New York, Los Angeles, Seattle, London, Brussels, and Hong Kong. It is mainly a business and commercial bank.

Hokkei. Painter (Totoya Hokkei, Iwakubo Tatsuyuki; *mei:* Hatsugorō, Ki-emon, Kinuemon; *gō:* Hokkei, Kosai, Kikō, Aoi-gaoka, 1780–1850) of ukiyo-e prints. A fish merchant by trade, he studied with Kanō Masanobu and Hokusai. He produced mainly *surimono* and illustrations for *kyōka* books.

Hokke-ji. Buddhist temple and monastery, located north of Hōryū-ji (Nara prefecture), founded as a women's institution in 638, at the time called Himuro-gosho. Originally Fujiwara no Fuhito's villa, it was converted into a monastery by Empress Kōmyō in 747. Renovated in the mid-thirteenth century, it was affiliated with the Shingon Ritsu-shū sect. It was rebuilt by Toyotomi Hideyori in 1601. Three-story pagoda *(sanju no tō)*, dating from 686, restored in 1263. Sammon and Hondō rebuilt in 1601. This temple houses a statue of Jūichimen Kannon dating from the ninth century, a National Treasure.

• **Hokke-kyō.** *See* HOKE-KYŌ.

• **Hokke matsuzai-ji.** *See* KOKUBUNJI.

• **Hokke-shū.** *See* TENDAI-SHŪ.

Hokke sammai. A sort of ecstatic contemplation practiced by some Buddhists in order to attain enlightenment; its main divinity is Fugen Myō-ō.

• **Hokke Sammai-dō.** In some Buddhist temples, room reserved for meditations on the *Hokke-kyō*.

Hokkyō. "Bridge of the Law," Buddhist title conferred on certain deserving monks and artists. *See also* HŌGEN, HŌ-IN, SŌ-KAN.

• **Hokkyō Hōzan.** *See* HŌZAN.

• **Hokkyō Sessai.** *See* SESSAI.

Hoko. Trident-shaped halberd, used in certain Esoteric Buddhist ceremonies *(mikkyō)* and as an emblem of some divinities. *Skt.:* Kunta.

Hōkō Guntō. Japanese name for the Pescadores Islands, located about 70 km east of the south coast of Taiwan. *Chin.:* P'enghu Ch'üntao. Also called Hōko-tō, Hōko-rettō.

Hōkō-ji. Buddhist temple of the Zen Rinzai-shū sect founded in Okuyama, near Kakegawa, by Mumon, one of Emperor Go-Daigo's sons, in the late fourteenth century. Also called Okuyama Han-sōbō.
→ *See* ASUKA-DERA, GANGŌ-JI.

Hōkoku-jinja. Shinto shrine built in Kyoto in 1599 and dedicated to the memory of Toyotomi Hideyoshi. It was rebuilt between 1868 and 1878. Its Karamon gate, dating from the late sixteenth century, was brought from the Fushimi castle.

Hokora. In a Shinto shrine, small wooden annex shrine dedicated to the worship of a *kami* considered inferior to that venerated in the main shrine.

Hokuba. Painter (Hoshino Mitsutaka; *mei:* Arisada Gorōhachi; *gō:* Teisai, Shunshuntei, Shunshunsai, Shūen, Hokuba, 1771–1844) of ukiyo-e prints. He was one of Hokusai's students and painted mainly *surimono* and illustrations for *kyōka* books.

Hokuchō. "Northern Court," term for the emperors (not officially recognized, but nevertheless included in the general list) who reigned in Kyoto from 1336 to 1392, when the Ashikaga *bakufu* was established (early Muromachi period), and who were opposed to the "legitimate" emperors of the Southern Court (Nanchō) during the Nambokuchō (Northern and Southern Courts) period. The emperors were: Kōgon Tennō (1313<1331–33> 1364); Kōmyō Tennō (1322<1336–48>1380); Sōkyō Tennō (1334<1349–52>1398); Go-Kōgon Tennō (1338<1353–71>1374); Go-En'yū Tennō (1359<1372–82>1393); Go-Komatsu Tennō (1377<1383–1412>1433). In 1392, Go-Komatsu Tennō became the only emperor of Japan, number 100 on the official list. *See* TENNŌ.

Hōkuei. Painter (1820–70) of ukiyo-e prints, belonging to the Osaka school. Also called Hōkushū. *See* OSAKA SCHOOL.

Hokujū. Painter (Kazumasa, Shōsai, Shōtei, active between 1802 and 1834) of ukiyo-e prints, Hokusai's student. He adapted European-style landscape painting to the ukiyo-e technique, creating an "avant-garde" art form.

Hokumen no bushi. Warriors from noble families who were in the service of retired emperors (*see* INSEI) in the twelfth century. This official position was created in 1087 by Emperor Shirakawa after his abdication. The warriors served to protect and, if necessary, as an army in the case of disturbances or power struggles. It is not known how many there were; probably, the number varied according to circumstances. Also known as In no Hokumen.

Hokurei. General term for all of the Buddhist temples built on Mt. Hiei, northeast of Kyoto.

Hokuriku. Former name of the northern region of Honshu, which was divided into seven provinces and is now made up of four prefectures, Niigata, Toyama, Ishikawa, and Fukui. It is now called Tōhoku.

• **Hokurikudō.** During the Edo period, major road linking Edo to northern Honshu via the Ōshu-kaidō, going from Maibara to Niigata via Tsuruga and Fukui.

• **Hokuriku Shimbun.** See CHŪNICHI SHIMBUN.

Hokusai. Painter (Nakajima, or Kusamura Tetsu-jirō, Tamekazu; *mei:* Tokitarō, Tetsuzō; *gō:* Katsu-shika Hokusai, Katsukawa Shunrō, Shunrō, Sōshunrō, Gunbatei Gyobutsu, Gamatei, Sōrei [Sōri], Gakyōjin, Shinsai, Kintaisha, Tamekazu, Raito, Raishin, Manji-ō, Manji-rōjin, Kakō, Iitsu, Hokusai, etc., 1760–1849), born in Edo to un-known parents. He was adopted by the Nakajima family of Ise when he was only three years old. As an apprentice woodcut printer at 13 years of age, he began to learn drawing. At 18, he entered the work-shop of Katsukawa Sunshō, a highly popular ukiyo-e print artist. He began with a series of portraits of actors, which he signed Katsukawa Shunrō, then he illustrated a number of books. Noticed by publisher Tsutaya Jūzaburō, he did a few color prints. He then changed his name to Kusamura and did com-mercial pieces and calendars, experimenting with various styles, sometimes signing his illustrations and *surimono* Sōri. These images were successful and began to be imitated by other artists in the Rimpa school. In 1796 (or 1798), he gave the name Sōri to one of his students and took the name Hokusai ("Northern Studio") in homage to the Buddhist divinity Myōken, representing the North Star. From then on he signed his works Hokusai, al-though he sometimes used other pseudonyms, such as Tatsumata, Raishin, and Raito, all of which evoked the seven stars of Ursa Minor; Tokitarō, for his commercial works; Kakō (or Sorobeku) for book illustrations; Fusenkyo, in 1799 only; and Gakyōjin Hokusai ("Hokusai the crazy painter") starting in 1800. As his popularity grew, he kept drawing and painting, sometimes performing pub-lic demonstrations of his talent by painting large panels for Zen Buddhist and other temples. When his art was criticized, he changed his name to Taito. He became friends with the painter Bokusen (1775–1824) and began to produce *Hokusai manga* (Ho-kusai's Drawings), published in Nagoya from 1814 to 1834. At age 60 he took the name Iitsu (Another Year) because he was beginning a new astrological 60-year cycle. About 1831, he produced his famous series *Fugaku sanjūrokkei* (Thirty-Six Views of Mt. Fuji); in 1834, when he was 74, he produced the se-ries *Fugaku hyakkei* (One Hundred Views of Mt. Fuji). He then left Edo to live on the Miura Penin-

sula, working on another series that was to crown his career, *Hyakunin isshu uba ga etoki* (Illustra-tions for the Poems of One Hundred Authors). In 1836, he returned to Edo, then ravaged by famine; three years later, his house burned down, with most of the documents that he had accumulated for the series, which was never finished. He produced few prints and drawings after 1840 and died in 1849. He was buried in the Seikyō-ji temple in Asakusa (Edo) and mourned by many students, who, in trib-ute to their master, included the name Hoku in their signatures. Among his best-known disciples were Katsushika Taito II (active 1820–50), Shinsai, Hokkei, Hokujū, Hokuba, and Issai.

Hokusō-ga. "Northern painting style," type of painting emulating the Chinese style of the North-ern Song dynasty (Bei Song; *Jap.:* Hokusō); one of the Bunjinga. Also called Hokuga. *See also* NANGA.

• **Hokusō-ō.** See HANABUSA ITCHŌ.

Hombyaku-shō. "Basic peasant class," a common term during the Edo period for peasants and farm-ers who owed allegiance to the *mizunomi-byaku-shō,* or landowners paying taxes *(nengu)* to the governors of shogunal estates. The *hombyaku-shō* were practically independent and, aside from their agricultural activities, did crafts work (raising silk-worms, weaving, growing cotton, etc.). They theo-retically could neither sell nor purchase land, al-though at the end of the Edo period some of them managed to become wealthy at the expense of their fellow peasants, who were reduced to working as agricultural laborers for them.

Homma Hisao. Historian (1897–1981) of Japa-nese literature, specializing in the Meiji era. He wrote a five-volume treatise on the subject, *Meiji bunkaku-shi* (History of the Literature of the Meiji Era).

Homma Masaharu. Officer (ca. 1888–1946). Mili-tary attaché in London in 1930, then commander of Japanese forces in Tianjin, China, in 1939. He led the force that invaded the Philippines (14th Army) in 1942 and captured the fort on Corregidor. Ar-rested after the Second World War and charged with mistreating prisoners of war (although probably not guilty of the atrocities committed), he was exe-cuted by firing squad.

Hommon-ji. Buddhist temple of the Nichiren sect, built in 1317 in Otaku (Tokyo), on the very site where the prophet died, by his disciple Nichirō (1243–1320). The temple was destroyed by a fire in 1710 and rebuilt by shogun Tokugawa Yoshimune in the early seventeenth century. It was again destroyed by bombs during the Second World War, and rebuilt; only its five-story pagoda (goju no tō) dating from 1608 was spared. In this temple, one of the four most important dates of the Nichiren-shū sect, the anniversary of Nichiren's death (1282), is commemorated every October 12–13 in a ceremony called Oeshiki.

Hompa-shiki. "Vestments in waves," a technique used mainly by sculptors of Buddhist images in the Heian period to portray the vestments of the divinities.

Hōmu. Title for a Buddhist monk responsible for the administration of a temple or a monastic community.

Homusubi. In Shinto legends, as told in the Kojiki, a fire kami who burned the genitals of his mother, Izanami, when he was born, causing her death. Also called Atago, Hi no Kagutsuchi.

Hon. "Origin," "root," "main thing." This word is used to compose a great many words and expressions, such as Nihon ("origin of the sun"), designating Japan. The character that symbolizes hon is pronounced moto in old Japanese.
  • Rank of imperial princes. Also Shinnō.
  • Numeral adjective, used for long, narrow objects.

Hon-ami. Family of artists, artisans, and aesthetes related to the Ami family and illustrious from the twelfth to the seventeenth century. Its most famous members were Zeami, Noami, Hon-ami Myōhon, Hon-ami Koetsu, Hon-ami Kōho, and Hon-ami Kōtoku. Most were devotees of the Nichiren-shū sect.

• *Hon-ami Gyōjō-ki.* "Memoirs of Hon-ami Gyōjō," a work attributed to painter Hon-ami Kōho (Hon-ami Gyōjō) on the life of his grandfather, Hon-ami Kōetsu.

• **Hon-ami Kōetsu.** Potter, calligrapher, lacquerer, and engraver (Hon-ami Jirosaburō; gō: Taikyoan, Jitokusai, Kūchūan, Tokukyūsai, Kōetsu, 1558–1637). Son of a polisher of sword blades, he studied with Kanō Eitoku and Yūshō, then began to paint in a decorative style resembling Tawaraya Sōtatsu's,

to whom he was related by marriage. He also studied the tea ceremony (chanoyu) with Furuta Oribe, and calligraphy, an art for which he was so highly regarded that he was considered one of the Sampitsu (Three Brushes) of the Kan'ei era. His lacquer works reveal his absolute mastery of the maki-e technique. As a sculptor, he produced Noh masks. A man of many talents, he designed gardens and made ceramic bowls for the tea ceremony.

• **Hon-ami Kōho.** Painter (Hon-ami Gyōjō; gō: Kūchūsai, Kōho, 1601–82); studied with his grandfather, Hon-ami Kōetsu, and his father, Hon-ami Kōsa. He was also a potter and master (chajin) of the tea ceremony. Author of Hon-ami Gyōjō-ki. He received the title Hōgen.

• **Hon-ami Kōtoku.** Maker of sword blades (1554–1620), related to Hon-ami Kōetsu.

• **Hon-ami Myōhon.** Sword maker (1252–1355), ancestor of the Hon-ami family.

Hon-bashira. In traditional architecture, main pillar (hashira) of a structure. Central column of a Buddhist pagoda, generally reinforced by four or six auxiliary columns called shiten-bashira.

Hon-bugyō. In the Kamakura period, main assessor in a court of law, charged specifically with examining indictments.

Honchō. "Japanese things," title of many paintings and albums of painting, poetry anthologies, catalogues, and chronicles about Japan.

• *Honchō gasan.* "Collection of Japanese Paintings," by Bunchō (1764–1840).

• *Honchō gashi.* "Biographies of Japanese Painters," attributed to Einō (1634–1700).

• *Honchō hennenroku.* "Chronological History of Japan," in 40 volumes, covering from the country's origins to 897, written by Hayashi Razan and published in 1645. The work was finished by Razan's son, Hayashi Jo, in 1670. See HONCHŌ TSUGAN.

• *Honchō monzui.* Anthology of waka poems and prose written in classical Chinese, compiled by Fujiwara no Akihira around 1060, imitating the Chinese anthology Wenxuan (Jap.: Monzen). It comprises 427 pieces by 70 Japanese authors from Saga Tennō's reign to Go-Ichijō Tennō's.

• *Honchō nijūshi-fukō.* "The Twenty-Four Examples of Filial Piety," a famous collection of Confucian tales based on the Chinese text *Ershisi Xiao,* written by Ihara Saikaku in 1686.

• *Honchō nijūshikō.* Kabuki play in five acts, in the *jidai-mono* genre, by Chikamatsu Monzaemon and Miyoshi Shōtaku.
• Bunraku play written in 1766: a princess uses the magical powers of a fox *(kitsune)* to win over the man she loves.

• *Honchō seiki.* "Chronicle of Imperial Reigns," official history *(seishi)* of Japan compiled by Fujiwara no Michinori on the order of Retired Emperor Toba. It was never completed and covers only the years 935 to 1135. Also called *Shikanki, Gekinikki.*

• *Honchō shojaku mokuroku.* Book catalogue, the oldest of its type known, produced between 1278 and 1292. Titles are catalogued in 20 categories and 493 entries. Also called *Ninnaji shojaku mokuroku, Omuro shojaku mokuroku.*

• *Honchō suibodai zenden.* "Illumination in a State of Rapture," novel by Santō Kyōden, written in 1806 as a supplement to his *Mukashi-gatari inazuma-byōshi.*

• *Honchō-tsugan.* "Complete Mirror of Japan,"a major history of Japan from its origins to 1611, produced by a group of historians under the direction of Hayashi Jo as a complement to Hayashi Razan's *Honchō hennenroku,* and published in 1671. This work bears some resemblance to the Chinese *Zizhi tongjian.*

Honda Giken Kōgyō (Honda Motor Company). Manufacturer of cars, motorcycles, and industrial motors founded in 1946 by Honda Sōichirō. Specializing in production of motorcycles, it is currently the world's top producer of these vehicles, exporting to most countries. Honda started to produce automobiles in 1963; they are now made in Japan or assembled in some 30 countries. It also makes motor coaches for Japan and the United States, as well as tractors. Head office in Tokyo.

Honda Ichirō. Movie director (Honda Hinmoshirō), born 1911 in Tokyo. He directed mainly fantasy and science-fiction movies.

Honda Kinkichirō. Western-style painter (*gō:* Keizan, 1850–1921), specializing in landscapes.

Honda Kōtarō. Physicist (1870–1954) and engineer, born in Aichi prefecture. After studying at the University of Tokyo and in Germany, he conducted research into special steels and created a laboratory for studying metals and alloys. He invented alloys with powerful magnetic properties in 1917. Appointed president of the University of Tōhoku in 1931, he received the Order of Culture (Bunka-shō) in 1937.

Honda Masanobu. Warrior (1539–1617), confidant of Tokugawa Ieyasu's and master falconer. He was appointed governor of the island of Sado, then Ieyasu's representative in the Kantō. He is sometimes credited with authorship of the *Honsaroku.*

Honda Seiroku. Botanist (1866–1952) born in Saitama prefecture, who studied forest exploitation. An excellent landscape designer, he helped create many national parks in Japan and designed the gardens of the Meiji Shrine in Tokyo.

Honda Shūgo. Literary critic born 1908 in Aichi, belonging to the "proletarian" literature movement. After the Second World War, he joined the editorial team of *Kindai Bungaku* (from 1946 to 1964) and wrote a major work of literary criticism, *Tenkō bungaku-ron* (Literature of Ideological Conversion) in 1957, in which he demonstrated the need to free literature from the influence of political ideologies. Among his other books are *Shirakaba-ha no bungaku* (Literature of the Shirakaba Group) and *Monogatari sengo bungaku-shi* (History of Modern Literature of Japan, 1953–63), which earned him the *Mainichi Shimbun* Literary Prize in 1965.

Honda Tadakatsu. Warrior (1548–1610), companion of Tokugawa Ieyasu, who named him daimyo of Ōtaki and of Kuwana. He took part in the Battle of Sekigahara (1600) with Ieyasu.

Honda Teikichi. Ceramist (1764–1819), born in Shimabara (Kyushu). He studied with Aoki Mokubei, with whom he collaborated.

Honda Toshiaki. Mathematician and navigator (1744–1821), born in Echigo province. He opened a school of mathematics and astronomy in Edo and studied these sciences in Western works. He explored the coasts of Japan, especially Hokkaido, in 1801. His research showed that Japan could not escape the economic impasse in which it was mired unless it adopted European economic management models. In his book *Keisei hisaku* (Secret Plan for Governing the Country), written in 1798, he recommended rational colonization of Hokkaido; in *Saiiki monogatari* (Tales of the West), published the same year, he proposed moving the capital of Japan from Edo to Kamchatka and abolishing the shogunal policy of national isolation in favor of participation in expanding international trade.

Honden. Main room in a Shinto shrine, in which the *mitama-shiro* of a *kami* is said to live. Also called Honsha.

Hondō. "Main island," former name of Honshu.
• Main room in a Buddhist temple, in which the *honzon* (main image) of a divinity is found. When the divinity is the Buddha Shakyamuni (*Jap.*: Shaka) himself, it is called Shakadō.

Honen. Buddhist monk (Genku, Hōnenbō, Hōnen Shōnin, 1133–1212), born in Mimasaka province (Okayama prefecture). At age 15, he entered the Tendai monastery of the Enryaku-ji on Mt. Hiei; in 1150, he withdrew to the Kurotani (one of the Hieizan hermitages) to meditate. Convinced that the road to salvation lay in pure devotion to Amida, he began to preach the practice of *nembutsu* in Kyoto in 1175, and he founded the Jōdo-shū sect, for which he laid out the basic tenets in *Senchaku hongan nembutsu-shū* (Choosing *Nembutsu* from Amida's Original Vow). The Tendai monks denounced him to the public authorities, and he was exiled to Shikoku and shorn of his capacity as a Buddhist monk; in addition, four of his companions were executed for "disturbing the public order." Granted amnesty in 1211, he returned to Kyoto, where he died the following year at the Chion-in monastery. He received the posthumous name Enkō Daishi. In preaching that recitation of the *nembutsu* alone would procure a "good death" *(ōjōyō)* and a pleasant rebirth in the "Pure Land" (Jōdo) of Amida Buddha, Hōnen followed the precepts given in China by the monks Daochuo (*Jap.*: Dōshaku, 562–645) and Shandao (*Jap.*: Zendō, 613–81). He claimed that in the Mappō era the practice of meditation was too difficult an approach for most people, who required a very simple devotional practice such as reciting the *nembutsu,* and he emphasized the eighteenth of Amida's 48 vows, made when he was still only the bodhisattva *(Jap.: bosatsu)* Hōzō

Bosatsu (*Skt.*: Dharma-ākara), in which he promised that he would save all of those who invoked his name even once. *See* JŌDO-SHŪ, MAPPŌ, NEMBUTSU.

• **Hōnen Odori.** Popular dances of the Shinto rites performed by villagers at New Year's and in the autumn to thank the *kami* for providing rain or an abundant harvest; it replaced the Amagoi Odori. Hōnen's name was given to these dances because he had invented a sort of analogous popular roundelay for the sung recitation of the *nembutsu,* intended to glorify not the *kami* but Amida Buddha. These dances are still performed in villages but have somewhat lost their religious and sacred character.

• *Hōnen shōnin e-den.* *Emakimono* describing Hōnen's life and sermons in 40 scrolls (234 texts and 230 images). It was written and painted between 1307 and 1317 by an unknown painter on the order of Emperor Go-Fushimi. Many artists probably collaborated on this gigantic work, the longest of its type. It is generally thought that at least eight painters and calligraphers worked on it; although certain names have been proposed, attribution has not been confirmed. The brightly colored images, seen from a three-quarters view from above, are very realistic, often humorous, and give an accurate picture of the life of monks and common people, as well as tools, boats, clothing, houses, and various occupations, providing an invaluable reference for historians. The scrolls are housed in the Chion-in in Kyoto.

Hongaku. In Mahayana Buddhism, this term, of Chinese origin, describes the internal enlightenment inherent to individuals and thus easily attainable by them, while its antonym, *shigaku,* describes an enlightenment attainable only by successive degrees. Mahayana theory was strongly refuted by Hōnen but was taken up by many followers of Zen sects. *Chin.*: Benjue.

Hongan-ji. Main temple of the Jōdo Shin-shū Buddhist sect, founded by Shinran in 1224 and built in Kyoto in 1591. The original Hongan-ji temple was a small chapel dedicated to Shinran and built by his daughter, Kakushin-ni (1124–ca. 1283), in the Ōtani district of Kyoto. When Shinran was reburied in this small temple, it was renamed Ōtani-byōdō (Ōtani Mausoleum). It was promoted to the rank of main temple in 1321 by Shinran's grandson, Kakunyo Sōsho (1270–1351), and renamed Hongan-ji (Temple of the Original Vow). Despite opposition by other members of the Amida sect, especially in the provinces of northern Honshu, the temple won followers and slowly expanded under the leadership of "abbots" *(hossu)* Zennyo Shungen (1333–89), Shakunyo Jigei (1350–93), Gyōnyo Genkō (1376–1440), and Zonnyo Enken (1396–1457), who were the fourth, fifth, sixth, and seventh patriarchs; the first three had been Shinran, Nyoshin, and Kakunyo. The eighth patriarch, Rennyo Kenju (1415–99), made the Hongan-ji the main temple of the sect after the Ōtani Hongan-ji was destroyed by the monk-soldiers of Mt. Hiei. Rennyo organized his followers into a military league (*see* IKKŌ IKKI) in order to defend himself against followers of other sects. Their struggle continued under the aegis of the ninth patriarch, Jitsunyo Kōken (1458–1525), who supported Hosokawa Masamoto's cause when a large fortified temple was built in Kyoto between 1479 and 1483. The tenth patriarch, Shōnyo Kōkyō (1516–54), consolidated the sect's strength with the addition of other temples from the Jōdo Shin-shū and established the Ishiyama Hongan-ji in Osaka, which became the center of the sect. His son, Kennyo Kōsa (1543–92), was officially appointed eleventh abbot in 1560, when the Hongan-ji was recognized by the emperor. The abbots of the Hongan-ji thereafter had a status equivalent to that of daimyo, court noble, or head of a monastery. Because the power of the Ishiyama Hongan-ji obstructed his "national" aims, Oda Nobunaga attacked the Ikkō Ikki. After ten years of conflict, Kennyo surrendered his Ishiyama Hongan-ji fortress in Osaka, but his son, Kyōnyo Kōju (1558–1614), refused to make peace and started the struggle again. Kennyo then disavowed Kyōnyo and appointed his other son, Junnyo Kōshō (1577–1631), *hossu;* this caused the Hongan-ji to split into two rival branches, with both Kennyo's sons claiming the title of twelfth *hossu.* Kyōnyo remained leader of the Higashi Hongan-ji, while Junnyo became the head of the Nishi Hongan-ji. In the meantime, the Ishiyama Hongan-ji in Osaka was destroyed by Oda Nobunaga on the very day of its surrender, and Toyotomi Hideyoshi begun construction of a large castle on its ruins. *See* IKKŌ IKKI, ISHIYAMA HONGAN-JI, JŌDO SHIN-SHŪ, MONTO, RENNYO, SHINRAN.

Hongawara-buki. In traditional architecture, type of facing in which the tiles *(kawara)* are in rows alternating round and flat tiles.

Hongō Shin. Sculptor, born 1905 in Sapporo. In 1928, he became Takamura Kōtarō's student. He produced several monumental works; as a refugee in Nara during the Second World War, he copied ancient works. Among his public sculptures is the "Mother and Child in the Storm" grouping in the Park of Peace in Hiroshima.

Hongū. In Nikkō, the main Shinto shrine of the Tōshōgū. It has a 5-meter-high stone torii in front and seventeenth-century buildings.

Hon'i. System of honorific ranks for imperial princes *(shinnō)* and princesses. There were four—Ippon, Nihon, Sambon, and Shihon (first, second, third, and fourth)—following the principles of the *Yōrōryō,* a code of laws promulgated at the beginning of the Nara period.

Hon'imbō. Title of grand master in the game of *go (igo),* taken from the name of a monastic residence of the Jakkō-ji, a Zen Buddhist temple in Kyoto, where a monk named Nikkai (1558–1623) taught Oda Nobunaga, Toyotomi Hideyoshi, and Tokugawa Ieyasu how to play the game. Thereafter, all uncontested masters of the game took the title, which was hereditary until 1939, when the National Go Association (Nihon Ki-in) decided that it would henceforth be awarded only to the winner of a national championship. *See* GO.

Hon-ji. Main temple of a Buddhist sect. Also called *honzan.* These temples had under their authority subsidiary temples called *matsu-ji* (or *betsu-in*), and they and the Hon-ji were linked via temples called Honji-fure-gashira. *See* JI-SHŪ.

Honjin. During the Edo period, inns established in waystation villages *(shuku-eki)* on the major routes, reserved for traveling daimyo and other officials. They were created by shogun Ashikaga Yoshiakira in 1363, but probably not made official until the establishment of the Sankin-kōtai at the beginning of the Tokugawa shogunate. They were closed down in 1870.

Honji-suijaku. Japanese syncretic religious doctrine according to which Shinto *kami* were considered by Buddhist sects to be emanations or incarnations *(gongen)* of Buddhist divinities *(hotoke).* It became customary in Buddhist temples to place shrines dedicated to *kami* of the soil in the walls of the monasteries to protect them. Buddhas thus "incarnated" in *kami* were called Honji-butsu. Thus, Dainichi Nyorai *(Skt.:* Mahāvairochana Buddha) was the *honji-butsu* of the sun *kami* Amaterasu-Ōmikami, and Yakushi Nyorai *(Skt.:* Bhaishajyaguru) was the *honji-butsu* of the *kami* Ōkuni-nushi no Mikoto. This doctrine, popularized in the ninth and tenth centuries, was observed until the separation of Buddhism and Shinto at the beginning of the Meiji era in 1868. *See* RYŌBU SHINTŌ.

Honjō. Japanese name of the *Jātaka* (tales of the former lives of the Buddha). Also *Honshōji.*

• **Honjō-ji.** Buddhist temple of the Hokke-shū, founded in 1320 in Echigo province by Nichi-i, a monk of the Nichiren-shū, to be the headquarters of the sect. *See* HONSEI-JI.

Honjō Mutsuo. Writer (1905–39), born in Hokkaido, member of the "progressive" literature movement of the 1920s. He wrote children's stories and novels in which he denounced social injustices. His best-known work is *Ishikarigawa* (The Ishikari River, 1938–39), in which the action takes place in Hokkaido at the beginning of the Meiji era.

Honjō Shigeru. Military officer (1876–1945) born in Hyogo to a peasant family. He took courses at the Military Academy until 1897. After holding several positions, including military adviser to Zhang Zuolin in Manchuria from 1920 to 1924, he was commander-in-chief of the Guandong army (the Japanese army in Manchuria) from August 1931 to July 1932. He was promoted to chief aide-de-camp to the emperor in April 1933. His son-in-law was implicated in the attempted coup d'état of February 26, 1936, so he tendered his resignation. At the end of the Second World War, to avoid being arrested by the Allies, he committed suicide by *seppuku.* The notebooks he left dealing with the conquest of Manchuria by the Japanese army and Emperor Shōwa Tennō's (Hirohito) behavior at the time have historical value.

Honkadori. Poetry technique consisting of taking one or two verses of an old poem and including them in a new *waka* poem. Many "classical" poets used the technique to remind readers of an old fact or to imbue their poems with a sense of purely poetic reminiscence. The verses borrowed were slightly modified so that they fit in with the rest of the poem.

Honke. "Main house," title for nobles and for owners of estates (*shō, shōen*) operated by *ryōke.* The *honke* controlled other families, called *bunke,* which owed them allegiance.

Honke-baeri. "Return to origins," name for the ceremony marking a person's sixtieth birthday and the beginning for that person of a new 60-year "cycle," following the traditional calendar. On this occasion, relatives and friends congratulate the person, make a banquet, and dress him or her in a red vest symbolic of new birth. The ceremony generally marks retirement for the person who has reached the age of 60.

Honken. Popular game played by two people, who must show a certain number of fingers at the same time while calling out the total number of fingers held out by both players. The person with the correct number wins. It is somewhat similar to the American game of "evens and odds." *See* JAN PREFECTURE-PON.

Honkoku-ji. Buddhist temple of the Nichiren-shū sect in Kyoto, transported from Kamakura in 1345 and reconstructed in the seventeenth century.

Hon-michi (Hommichi). Subsect of the Nichiren-shū (about 300,000 followers), divided into two branches, Hon-mon Butsu-ryū and Nichiren Shugi Butsuryū-kyō.

• **Hon-mon Hokke-shū.** Also called Hommon Hoke-shū. *See* HACHIHON, NICHIREN-SHŪ, NICHIRYŪ.
→ *See* HOMMON-JI.

• **Hon-myō Hoke-shū.** Buddhist sect of the Hokeshū, founded in 1898 in the Honryū-ji near Tokyo. Also called Hommyō Hoke-shū. *See* HACHIHON, HONRYŪ-JI, NICHIREN-SHŪ.

Honnō-ji. Buddhist temple of the Nichiren-shū sect in Kyoto, in which Oda Nobunaga, besieged by his general Akechi Mitsuhide, committed suicide with his son Nobutada (b. 1557) on June 21, 1582, by setting fire to the temple. Eleven days after this attack, called Honnō-ji no Hen, Akechi Mitsuhide was killed by Toyotomi Hideyoshi at the battle of Yamazaki.

Honryū-ji. Branch of the Nichiren-shū Buddhist sect, founded by the monk Nisshin at Hanazono (Kyoto) in 1485. It took the name Hon-myō (Hommyō) Hoke-shū in 1898.

Honsaroku. "Notes on the Government." A political work probably dictated (or inspired) by Tokugawa Ieyasu to his faithful companion Honda

Masanobu (1538–1616) to teach young Tokugawa Hidetada. This work, which contains the most intimate thoughts of the founder of the Tokugawa, which was also known as *Tenka kokkano yōroku* (Treatise on the Government of the Kingdom) and *Chiyō shichijō* (The Seven Essential Principles of Government). It has also been attributed, but without certainty, to Fujiwara Seika (1561–1619).

Honsei-ji. Branch of the Nichiren-shū sect founded at the Honjō-ji temple in Echigo province by the monk Nichi-in in 1320. Its name was changed to Hoke (Hokke)-shū in 1898.

Honsha. Main room of a Shinto shrine, containing the sacred mirror or *shintai (mitama-shiro).* The *honsha* authorities could issue *bunrei* (a sort of delegation) from their *kami* to subsidiary shrines *(massha).* Also called *honden.*
• "Main office" of an industrial or financial conglomerate *(zaibatsu).* Equivalent to head office.

Honshū. "Main region," name of the largest island of Japan, once called Hondō, where most of the population, arable land, and industries are concentrated. It is very mountainous and has few coastal plains, the largest being Kanto (where Tokyo is located). This large island is long, with its convex side curved toward the southeast. Its "belly" is along the north side of the Inland Sea (Setonaikai) and features an almost uninterrupted line, more than 1,000 km long, of cities and agglomerations from Tokyo to Shimonoseki, home to more than 50% of the population. The "back" of the island, facing the Sea of Japan, has a harsher climate and is relatively sparsely populated. The main regions of Honshū are, from north to south, Tōhoku, Hokuriku, Tōsan, Tōkai, Kantō, Kinki, and Chūgoku. Of Japan's 64 prefectures *(ken)*, 34 are on Honshū, as are the country's main cities, Tokyo, Osaka, and Kyoto. *Total area* (including small dependent islands): 230,897 km². *Pop.:* 95 million.

Honshū Seishi. Major producer of paper, cardboard, and various packing materials, working in partnership with various foreign companies, notably in Canada, and exploiting forests in Canada, New Guinea, and Taiwan. Head office in Tokyo.

Honshū-shikoku. Series of 17 huge bridges linking Honshu to Shikoku via small islands in the Inland Sea (Setonaikai), connecting Kobe to Naruto (two bridges via Awaji), Kojima to Sakaide (six bridges with supports on five islets), and Onomichi (Hiro-shima prefecture) to Imabari (Ehime prefecture) by nine bridges with supports on eight islets. Construction on these bridges started in 1959 and ended in 1990.

Honto-mononari. Annual tax paid by peasants during the Edo period. Based on average income from the land and the economic resources of villages, it was paid in rice and sometimes in cash. Villages' common land, forests, pastures, and swamps were not assessed. The tax could amount to 40–50% of peasants' overall income. It was replaced in 1868 by a system based on the market value of the land. Also called *hommen, mononari, marika, shomu, torika.*

Honzon. Main image of a divinity in a Buddhist temple. *See* HONDŌ.

Honzō-wamyō. "Japanese Names for Living Things," an 18-volume natural-sciences dictionary, written around 918 by Fukane Sukehito (or Fukae Hōjin), describing 1,025 types of plants, animals, and minerals. Other similar works were called *Honzō;* the best known are the *Honzō kōmoku,* a translation of the Chinese work *Bencao gangmu* (Classification of Herbs) by Li Shizhen, published in China in 1578, attributed to Hayashi Dōshun in 1590; and the *Honzō kōmoku keimō,* a work of the same type on the same subject, published by Ono Ranzan (1729–1810).

Hō-ō. Abridgment of Dajō Hō-ō, title for retired emperors who became Buddhist monks, starting with the abdication of Emperor Uda in 899. Retired Emperor Reigen was the last to bear this title, in 1686. Also called Dajō-kō, In, Jōkō. *See* HŌ-SHINNŌ, INSEI.
• "Phoenix" (*Chin.:* Fenghuang). *See* HYŌDŌ-IN.

• **Hō-ō-mai.** *See* AMAGOI.

• **Hō-ō-zan.** Mountain in Aichi prefecture on which there are Hōrai-ji, an old Buddhist monastery of the Shingon-shū founded at the beginning of the eighth century, and many mountain-climbing and winter-sports resorts. *Altitude:* 2,841 m.

Hō-on-ji. Buddhist temple located in Iwanogawa (Wakayama prefecture, Honshu), founded in the eighth century and reconstructed in 1457 for the Jōdo-shū sect. Its *hondō,* dating from 1457, houses a wooden statue of Amida from the Heian period, attributed, according to tradition, to Eshin (942–

1017), and one of Jūichimen Kannon, 107 cm in height, also from the Heian period.

Hora(-gai). Conch used in Buddhist ceremonies and as an attribute of certain divinities. Originally Indian, this instrument came to Japan via Korea during the Nara period. It was also used to signal troop movements during the Edo period. Yamabushi still sometimes use them.

Hōrai-ji. Buddhist temple in Aichi prefecture, on Mt. Aichi (*alt.:* 684 m), belonging to the Shingonshū, founded in the eighth century near Nagashino.

• **Hōrai-tō (or Hōrai-zan).** Mythical mountain located, according to Chinese tradition, in eastern China, and supposedly the abode of the gods, who kept their elixir of immortality there. The three summits of this mountain have inspired many artists. *Chin.:* Fenglai Dao. *See* JOFUKU.

Hōreki. Era of Emperor Momozono: Oct. 1751–June 1763. *See* NENGŌ.

• **Hōreki Jiken.** During the Hōreki era, an incident provoked in the Kyoto court by Takenouchi Shikibu and other nobles who were opposed to the shogunate. They taught the emperor the principles of Confucianism and, it is said, the martial arts. This was seen in a very poor light by the shogunal authorities, who sent Takenouchi and a number of his colleagues into exile in 1758.

• **Hōreki Kōjutsu Genreki.** *See* ABE YASUKUNI.

Hori Bakusui. Poet (Ikeya Chōzaemon, Shirakuan, Choan, 1718–1783), from Kanazawa. He studied "Dutch science" *(rangaku)* in Nagasaki. He lived in Kyoto, then Edo, and was a friend of Taniguchi Buson. He then settled in the Niigata region and wrote haiku poems, emulating Matsuo Bashō's style. When he returned to the Osaka region, he wrote a work on poetics, the *Shōmon ichiya kuju,* then an anthology of haiku, the *Shin minashiguri* (1777), in homage to Bashō.

Horie Ken'ichi. Navigator, born 1938 in Osaka. In 1962, he was the first Japanese to make a solo crossing of the Pacific Ocean, from Osaka to San Francisco. He accomplished this feat in 94 days without stopping, in a yacht he made himself, the 5.8 m *Mermaid I.* He also sailed around the world solo in another small yacht, the *Mermaid II,* from August 1973 to May 1974 (275 days), setting a world rec-

ord. He crossed the Pacific Ocean again, in just 40 days, in 1975.

Horiguchi Daigaku. Poet (1903–81) who introduced French surrealism to Japanese poetry and translated 66 modern French poets, including Jean Cocteau, Guillaume Apollinaire, and Paul Morand. He also wrote poetry collections, among them *Gekkō to piero* (1919) and *Ningen no uta* (Song of Humanity, 1947).

Horiguchi Sutemi. Architect, born 1895 in Gifu. Influenced by the Viennese school and German expressionism, he also studied Japanese traditional architecture and *sukiya (chashitsu).* He designed a number of buildings in these styles and wrote studies on Sen no Rikyū and the Katsura Rikyū garden in Kyoto.

Hori Hidemasa. Warrior (1533–90), born in Gifu, who helped Oda Nobunaga in his war against the Ikkō Ikki, then served Toyotomi Hideyoshi in Japan and Korea. He was killed during the siege of the Odawara castle.

Horikawa. Kyoto district where one of Emperor Horikawa's residences was located.

• **Horikawa-daijin.** *See* FUJIWARA NO MOTOTSUNE.

• **Horikawa-dono.** *See* FUJIWARA NO KANEMICHI.

• **Horikawa Gakkō.** School *(shohan gakkō)* founded by Itō Jinsai in the Horikawa district of Kyoto. *See* ITŌ JINSAI.

• **Horikawa Go-zō.** Collective name for Itō Jinsai's five sons, all of whom were eminent scholars and lived in Horikawa: Genzō, Jūzō, Shōzō, Heizō, and Saizō.

• *Horikawa-in nikki. See* SANUKI NO SUKE NO NIKKI.

• **Horikawa-safu.** *See* MINAMOTO NO TOSHIFUSA.

• **Horikawa Tennō.** Seventy-third emperor (Prince Taruhito, 1078<1087–1107>), son of and successor to Shirakawa Tennō. Toba succeeded him.

Horikoshi Nisōji. Playwright (1721–ca. 1781), author of a number of *tokiwazu* danced dramas for Kabuki theater.

Horimono. Engravings made on the blade of a sword *(katana)*. Also, name for the longitudinal groove made in the blade to lighten it. Also called *hi*. See KATANA, TATTOOS.

Hōrin-ji. Buddhist temple located north of the Hōryū-ji (Nara prefecture), founded in 622. It had a famous three-story pagoda *(sanju no tō)* dating from the seventh century, which was destroyed by fire in 1944. Kondō dating from 1737 with an old paved floor and a wooden statue of Yakushi Nyorai 106 cm high, dating from the Asuka period. It also houses beautiful statues of Shō Kannon, Jizō Bosatsu, Kichijō Ten, Bishamon Ten, and Kokuzō Bosatsu from the Asuka, Nara, and Heian periods. The *kōdō* houses a beautiful statue of Jūichimen Kannon in colored wood 3.6 m high, from the Heian period; other splendid works of ancient art are exhibited in a museum built beside the temple.
• Buddhist temple located on the Arashiyama hill in Kyoto, founded in 713.

Hori Ryūjo. Doll maker (Yamada Matsue, 1897– 1984). She created a particular style of *kimekomi-ningyō* (dolls sculpted in wood and clothed in glued brocades) that earned her, in 1955, the honor of being the first woman named a Living National Treasure.

Hori Shinji. Sculptor, born 1890 in Tokyo. His works, in realist style, earned him many distinctions at national exhibitions, among them the Nihon Geijutsu-in (Japan Art Academy) Prize in 1960.

Hori Tatsuo. Writer (1904–53) of the Shin Kangaku-ha group. He translated works by French poets and wrote poetry and prose. He was a friend of Akutogawa Ryūnosuke and published his works after his death. Among his own books are *Seika-zoku* (The Holy Family, 1930), *Utsukushi mura* (The Beautiful Village), *Kaze tachinu* (The Wind is Rising, 1938), and *Naoko* (1941).

Horiuchi Masakazu. Sculptor, born 1911 in Kyoto, noted for his "abstract" sculptures. Since 1954, he has used metal to create monumental works. He has received many prizes, including, in 1969, the prize in the First International Exhibition of Contemporary Sculpture in Hakone.

Horo. Sort of large canvas or silk sack supported on a bamboo frame, carried on the back of a warrior on horseback and designed, when inflated by wind, to protect him from arrows aimed at his back.

This piece of equipment, said to have been invented by Hatakeyama Masanaga about 1470, was probably of Chinese origin.

Hōroku. Large earthenware bowl with a cover, a typical traditional implement in Japanese kitchens, used to prepare a variety of foods. It was used to roast sesame seeds, to cook rice and vegetables, and to boil fish, mushrooms, and various vegetables with salt.

Horoscope. In Japan, there are various occasions for speculating on someone's future: when a baby arrives, when a young couple gets married, when a business is starting up, when a trip is planned, and many others. At these times, people may consult seers, very popular figures in Japanese society, who seek answers from the future in a variety of ways (*see* BOKUSEN), but they usually refer to horoscopes established according to their year of birth and the years of the "animals of the cycle" (*see* JIKKAN-JŪNISHI). These horoscopes are standardized but are followed with interest by many Japanese. They are often used for marriages.
—*Years of the Rat* (Ne): 1900, 1912, 1924, 1936, 1948, 1960, 1972, 1984 1996. People born in these years should marry a person born in the year of the Dragon, the Monkey, or the Bull (or, if necessary, the Rat, the Tiger, the Snake, the Dog, or the Boar), but must avoid a person born in the year of the Horse.
—*Years of the Bull* (Ushi): 1901, 1913, 1925, 1937, 1949, 1961, 1973, 1985. Those born in these years would make an excellent marriage with a person born in the year of the Snake, the Cock, or the Rat, but should avoid anyone born in the year of the Sheep, the Horse, or the Dog.
—*Years of the Tiger* (Tora): 1902, 1914, 1926, 1938, 1950, 1962, 1974, 1986. People born in these years would make a good marriage with someone born in the year of the Horse, the Dragon, or the Dog, and sometimes the Tiger, but must avoid a person born in the year of the Snake or the Monkey.
—*Years of the Rabbit* (U): 1903, 1915, 1927, 1939, 1951, 1963, 1975, 1987. People born in these years should marry a person born in the year of the Sheep, the Dog, or the Boar, but should avoid someone born in the year of the Rat or the Cock.
—*Years of the Dragon* (Tatsu): 1904, 1916, 1928, 1940, 1952, 1964, 1976, 1988. People born in these years will be happiest married to someone born in the year of the Rat, the Snake, the Monkey, or the Cock (or, if necessary, the Boar), but should

avoid anyone born in the year of the Bull, the Dog, the Rabbit, or the Dragon.

—*Years of the Snake* (**Mi**): 1905, 1917, 1929, 1941, 1953, 1965, 1977, 1989. Persons born in these years should marry someone born in the year of the Bull or the Cock, but avoid a person born in the year of the Tiger and the Boar.

—*Years of the Horse* (**Uma**): 1894, 1906, 1918, 1930, 1942, 1954, 1966, 1978, 1990. People born in these years would make a good marriage with someone born in the year of the Tiger, the Dog, or the Sheep, but a bad marriage with someone born in the year of the Rat.

—*Years of the Sheep:* (**Hitsu**): 1895, 1907, 1919, 1931, 1943, 1955, 1967, 1979, 1991. People born in these years should seek a marriage with someone born in the year of the Rabbit, the Horse, or the Boar, but avoid anyone born in the year of the Rat, the Bull, or the Dog.

—*Years of the Monkey* (**Saru**): 1896, 1908, 1920, 1932, 1944, 1956, 1968, 1980, 1992. People born in these years would make a good union with someone born in the year of the Dragon or the Rat, but should avoid a person born in the year of the Snake, the Boar, or the Tiger.

—*Years of the Cock* (**Tori**): 1897, 1909, 1921, 1933, 1945, 1957, 1969, 1981, 1993. People born in these years should marry someone born in the year of the Bull, the Snake, or the Dragon, but should mistrust someone born in the year of the Rat, the Cock, the Dog, and especially the Rabbit.

—*Years of the Dog* (**Inu**): 1898, 1910, 1922, 1934, 1946, 1958, 1970, 1982, 1994. People born in these years would be best matched with someone born in the year of the Horse, the Tiger, or the Rabbit, but should not marry someone born in the year of the Dragon or the Sheep.

—*Years of the Boar* (or *Pig,* **I**, **Inoshishi**): 1899, 1911, 1923, 1935, 1947, 1959, 1971, 1983, 1995. People born under this sign will form a good union with almost all others, except those born in the year of the Snake, the Monkey, or another Boar.

Many attempts have been made to link Japanese horoscopes to Western ones, based on the month of birth, but no real correspondences have been uncovered. Like Western horoscopes, the "signs" in the Japanese horoscope vary according to the time of birth (the hours also bear the names of animals in the cycle) and a series of parameters known only to seers, associated with predictions taken from study of the Chinese *Yijing* (Book of Changes), interpreted through the use of sticks called *zeichiku* and *sangi,* representing full and broken lines that in combination can produce 64 different hexagrams.

See BOKUSEN, JIKKAN JŪNISHI, KIBOKU, KOKKURI, OMIKUJI, URANAI.

Horses. Horses *(uma)* probably came to Japan from continental Asia around the fifth millennium BC. Remains of two types have been found: a pony similar to those found in the Ryukyu Islands, and a horse (not over 150 cm at the withers); the latter became widespread and were bred extensively until the nineteenth century. These horses, which probably were not used for riding, resembled the *tokara-uma* of the Ryukyu Islands and the *misaki-uma* and *kiso-uma* of the Meiji era, and were descended from Przevalsky horses, and perhaps from Tarpans. It was likely that horses were used in war and for transportation starting in the fourth century. The annals of the *Kojiki* and the *Nihon shoki* mention them. In the Meiji era, a large number of stallions from the West, mainly Arabians and Anglo-Normans, were imported to improve the breed. Since prehistoric times, white horses, said to carry the wishes of the faithful to Heaven, have been considered sacred by shamans. Even today, some large Shinto shrines keep white horses *(shimme),* considered holy, in their stables. By the medieval period, horses had become an essential part of samurai equipment, and each samurai kept one or several horses within the walls of his *yashiki.* Starting in the fourth century, pieces of harnesses (found, notably, in *kofun*), were increasingly elaborately decorated, indicating the care that warriors took of their steeds. The Chinese-type wooden saddle *(karakura)* was adopted in the Nara period. In the Heian period, Japanese saddles *(Yamatogura),* stirrups *(abumi),* and bits *(bagu)* were sometimes works of art, made of leather and metal often lacquered and inlaid with mother-of-pearl. The most famous horses in Japan were those bred in Nambu province (Iwate prefecture). They were rarely used in racing, except on rare occasions such as during festivals, notably in the Kamo shrines in Kyoto, when they were known as *Kurabe uma.* Westerners from Yokohama introduced racing about 1861, and a Frenchman, Descharmes, taught French equitation about 1872. An equestrian association was founded in Tokyo in 1889. Equitation *(bajutsu)* has always been held in high regard in Japan, and at the beginning of the Meiji era there were almost twenty riding schools *(ryū),* including those belonging to the Ogasawara, Ōtsubu, Hachijō, Araki, Sasaki, and Ueda families. Japan has been a member of the Fédération équestre internationale (FEI, International Equestrian Federation) since 1921, and sent riders to the Olympic Games for the first time in

1928 (Amsterdam); in 1932, a Japanese rider, Nichi Takeichi, won a gold medal at the Los Angeles Games. Having modernized its teams and equestrian infrastructure after the Second World War, Japan now has some good international-level riders. However, it is an extremely expensive sport, accessible only to people of considerable means. The custom in Japan is for horses' stalls to face the outside of the stable. *See* CHAGUCHAGU UMAKKO, CHŪMA, GOMA, HARAMACHI, HATSU-UMA, HŌSHU, KAMO NO KURABE-UMA, KIBAMINZOKU-RON, MIHARU-GOMA, YABUSAME.

Hōryū-ji. The oldest Buddhist temple still standing in Japan, located in Ikaruga (Nara prefecture), and the oldest wooden structure in the world. Founded by Prince Shōtoku Taishi in 607 near his palace, Ikaruga no Miya, in gratitude to Buddha for the cure of his father, Yomei Tennō, the temple was transformed into a monastery for the Hossō-shū sect. Most of the oldest structures were destroyed about 670 and reconstructed soon after on a larger scale, emulating the Korean-influenced Shitennō-ji in Osaka. The original axial plan was slightly changed, however, and the two-story *kondō* was placed near the five-story pagoda in the center of an enclosure with a rectangular arcade. These elements represented the traditional Chinese mode of construction. The buildings survived through the centuries, in spite of wars, but in 1949 the *kondō* was destroyed by a fire caused by an electrical short-circuit, and its magnificent interior murals were seriously damaged. Thanks to the existence of plans and drawings, it was reconstructed and the original paintings were restored; according to some sources, the paintings dated from 690 and 711 (or 750, according to other sources), and were typical of Chinese and Central Asian Buddhist art of the period. The five-story pagoda, 32.5 m in height, has on the ground floor many earthenware statues dating from 607. The current buildings comprise two distinct groups: the western part (Sai-in) and the eastern part (Tō-in). The *kondō* and pagoda are in the Sai-in. They were completed in 711 with the installation of two Ni-ō (guardian kings) statues and earthenware statuettes portraying scenes from Buddha's life in the *chūmon* (middle gate). In the *kondō* are a triad representing the Buddha Shakyamuni and two bodhisattvas sculpted by Kuratsukuribe no Tori in 623, a statue of Yakushi Nyorai (probably an early *honzon*) dating from 607, and a statue of Amida Buddha sculpted in 1232 by Kōshō. All these statues are in bronze. In the four corners of the ceiling (which symbolizes Mt. Meru, axis of the world according to Indian and Buddhist cosmogony) are images of the Shi-tennō (*Skt.*: Chaturmahārāja, Four Heavenly Kings), guardians of the world, which were probably made about 650 by sculptor Yamaguchi no Atai Oguchi. The other buildings (Tō-in) were linked to each other by covered walkways in the tenth century: the *kōdō* (991), *shōrō* (reconstructed ca. 900), *kairō* (seventh–eighth century), *kyōzō* (seventh century), *daikō-dō* (brought from the Fumio-ji in Yamashiro in 991), and others. Additional buildings, most of them in the Tō-in, are from later dates: the *saien-dō* (an octagonal room from the seventh century, reconstructed in 1250), the *shindō* (reconstructed in 1284), the *nandaimon* (large southern gate added in 1439), the *Kami no dō* (from 1311), the *sankyō-in* and *nishi-muro* (from 1231), the *shōryō-in* (from 1284), the *Jizō-dō* (reconstructed in 1372), the *yumedono* (an octagonal room dating from 739 but reconstructed in 1231), the *chūgū-in* (fifteenth century), and others. Around these buildings, to the east and west, are monastic districts (*higashi-muro* and *nishi-muro*). All contain remarkable works of art from the seventh to the fifteenth century. In 1941, a museum was built beside the group of buildings to display statues and objects belonging to the Hōryū-ji, notably the image of the Kadura Kannon and Lady Tachibana's Tamamushi no zushi. The buildings and works of art constitute a unique grouping, showing the Chinese and Korean influences of the seventh and eighth centuries and how they were absorbed and "Japanized" by artists.

• *Hōryū-ji engi shizai-cho.* General inventory of buildings and treasures of the Hōryū-ji dating from 747. It does not mention the murals in the *kondō* of the temple, which indicates that they were probably painted a little after this date, but Japanese historians do not agree on precisely when.

Hōsa Bunko. Library of Chinese and Japanese works collected by members of the Owari branch of the Tokugawa family, including works gathered by Tokugawa Ieyasu in Sumpu, and added to the library in 1616. Now located in Nagoya, the library is an important source for research on Chinese and Japanese history, especially information on the Tokugawa family.

Hōsai. *See* KAMEDA HŌSAI.

Hōsei Daigaku. Private university in Chiyoda-ku (Tokyo), founded in 1880 as Tokyo Hōgaku-sha (Tokyo Law School). It was given its current name

Pagoda of the Hōryū-ji

in 1903. It has faculties of law, sciences, arts, administration, and engineering, as well as several specialized institutes, and more than 20,000 students.

Hōseidō Kisanji. Writer (Hirasawa Tsunetomi; *gō:* Hirasawa Heikaku, Tegara no Okamochi, Kisanjin, Hōseido Kisanji, 1735–1813), author of satirical works in the *kibyōshi* genre, which earned him censure from the shogunate: *Bumbu futamichi mangoku-dōshi* (The Double Path for Those Who Follow the Literary and Martial Arts, 1788), *Omukaeshi bumbu no futamichi* (1789). He then stopped writing stories to devote himself to *kyōka*.

Hōshaku-ji. Buddhist temple founded in the eighth century north of Kyoto, belonging to the Shingon-shū sect. Dedicated to Jūichimen Kannon Bosatsu, it has a three-story pagoda *(sanju-no-tō)* from the late sixteenth century.

Hōshi. "Propagator of the Law," title once conferred upon itinerant Buddhist monks. *Chin.:* Fashi. *See* HŌGEN, HOKKYŌ, SŌ-KAN.
→ *See* GO.

Hoshikawa Seiji. Writer (b. 1927), who received the Naoki Prize in 1990 for his novel *Koden-shō* (The Life of Koden).

Hoshina Masayuki. Daimyo (Matsudaira Masayuki, 1611–72), son of Tokugawa Hidetada, adopted by the Hoshina family of the Takatō estate (Nagano prefecture). In 1643, he was appointed daimyo of Aizu (Fukushima prefecture), with a revenue of 230,000 *koku*. A capable administrator, he was Tokugawa Ietsuna's tutor. He was a Confucian (Zhu Xi school; *Jap.:* Shushi) and was noted for his sense of justice and for the public works he undertook—canals and bridges—to improve traffic circulation in Edo.

Hō-shinnō. Title for imperial princes who became Buddhist monks. *See* SHINNŌ.

Hoshino. Site of the town of Tochigi (Tochigi prefecture), which has been under excavation since 1965 by archeologist Serizawa Chōsuke. Thousands of paleolithic stone tools have been uncovered, some of which are 40,000 years old according to carbon dating, showing that the islands of Japan were occupied by human beings extremely early.

Hoshino Kanzaemon. Famous samurai archer, Nagaya Rokuzaemon's student. During the annual contest at the Sanjūsangen-dō (*see* RENGE-Ō-IN) in Kyoto in May 1669, he shot 12,042 arrows, of which about 8,000 reached the target, over 60 m away, in 18 hours of shooting. Exhausted, he then dropped out of the competition, which was to have lasted 24 hours. *See* WASA DAIHACHIRŌ.

Hoshi Shin'ichi. Science-fiction writer, born 1926 in Tokyo, who introduced the genre to Japan in 1957 with his novella *Sekisutora*. He also wrote some books in different genres, including a biography of his grandfather, *Koganei Yoshihiko* (1974). Most of his books have been widely translated into English, German, Swedish, and other languages.

Hoshi Tōru. Politician (1850–1901), born in Edo. He studied law in England from 1874 to 1877, then entered the Ministry of Justice, joining the Jiyūtō (Liberal party) in 1881. He was elected to the House of Representatives in 1892, and appointed ambassador to the United States in 1896; he then helped Itō Hirobumi form the Rikken Seiyūkai (Friends of Constitutional Government party) and was appointed minister of communications in Itō's fourth cabinet in 1900. Involved in a financial scandal, he was forced to resign two months later, and was then appointed head of the Tokyo Municipal Council. He was assassinated by a young weapons master, Iba Sōtarō (1851–1903), who thought he was a corrupt politician.

Hōshō-ryū. Famous family school of Noh writers and actors, descended from Kan'ami (Kanze-ryū), whose foundation is traditionally attributed to Ren-ami (d. 1468), one of Kanze Zeami's brothers. Among the most famous actors (*shite* roles) in this school were Hōzan (d. 1595), Katsuyoshi (d. 1630), Shigefusa (d. 1665), Shigetomo (d. 1685), Tomoharu (d. 1728), Nobuhide (d. 1730), Tomokiyo (d. 1772), Tomomichi (d. 1775), Tomokatsu (d. 1791), Hidekatsu (d. 1811), and Tomoyuki (d. 1863). In the early Meiji era, Hōshō Kuro (1837–1917) tried to revive this school, which was still producing a few talented actors, including Noguchi Kanesuke (1879–1953) and Kondō Kenzō (b. 1890).

Hōshō Sadayoshi. Sword maker (active in early fourteenth century) in Takaichi, Yamato province, who made heavy *tachi, ken,* and *tantō* swords, known for their solidity. The members of his family—Sadatsugu, Sadakiyo, and Sadaoki—followed his style through the first half of the fourteenth century.

Hōshu. "Precious stone," a sort of magical bead or jewel said to give its possessor what he or she desires or wishes for. As the story goes, the *hōshu* was jealously guarded by dragons at the bottom of the sea. It is one of the emblems of certain Buddhist divinities, such as Nyoirin Kannon and Jizō Bosatsu, and is sometimes portrayed with a halo of flames. In popular art, it sometimes appears on the back of a horse *(miharu-goma),* especially in northern Japan, as well as in some decorative elements on roofs of temples, such as *roban* (notably on the Yumedono of the Hōryū-ji). *Skt.:* Chintāmani (Mani). Also called *hōshu no tama.*

• **Hōshu-in.** Mudra *(Jap.: in-zō)* or hand gesture of certain Buddhist divinities holding a *hōshu;* often seen in statues of Jizō Bosatsu. Also called Jizō-in.

Hoso-ban. Format for ukiyo-e prints, generally about 22 × 15 cm. *See* UKIYO-E.

Hosoda Eiri. *See* EIRI.

• **Hosoda Eishi.** *See* EISHI.

• **Hosoda Eishō.** *See* EISHŌ.

Hosoe Eikō. Photographer, born 1933 in Yamagata, who has traveled abroad extensively, been in major international exhibitions, and lectured on art photography. He also collaborated on several movies shot during the Tokyo Olympic Games in 1964.

Hōsōge. Floral decorative element resembling a poppy, derived from Indian art; frequently used to ornament objects in both China and Japan during the Nara and Heian periods.

Hosoi Heishū. Confucian scholar (1728–1801), born in Owari. He opened a school in Edo and was invited by daimyo Uesugi Harunori to teach on his estates, but he returned to Owari in 1780, where he became principal of the province's schools.

Hosoi Kōtaku. Confucian physician (Hosoi Kōkin, Gyokusen, Kishōdō; *mei:* Chistin; *gō:* Kōtaku, 1658–1735) and famous calligrapher in Chinese style, born in Kyoto. He wrote a short treatise on calligraphy, the *Shibi jiyō,* in 1724, to show how to decompose the character "eternity" into eight brush strokes, the basis of calligraphy. He also en-

graved seals according to a technique imported to Japan by the Chinese Zen Buddhist monk Ōbaku Dokuryū.

Hosoi Nitatsu. Buddhist monk (1902–79) of the Nichiren-shū sect. He played a major role in resolving the doctrinal dispute between the clergy of the Nichiren Shōshū and the sect's large lay organization, the Sōka Gakkai.

Hosokawa. Family of noble warriors and daimyo descended from the Seiwa-Genji (Minamoto clan), who played an important role during the Muromachi period on the island of Shikoku and in central Honshu. In the mid-seventeenth century, they were among the most important daimyo of the *tozama,* ruling Higo province (Kumamoto prefecture) with a revenue of 540,000 *koku.*

• **Hosokawa Akiuji.** Lord of Mikawa province (Aichi prefecture), died 1352, who helped Ashikaga Takauji to found his Muromachi shogunate. He was then made *shugo* of seven provinces on Shikoku and in central Honshu.

• **Hosokawa Fujitaka.** Warrior (1534–1610), poet, and historian, who helped Oda Nobunaga and Toyotomi Hideyoshi consolidate their positions. At the end of his life, he became a Buddhist monk under the names Genshi Hō-in and Yūsai. He was an accomplished *waka* poet.

• **Hosokawa Gracia.** Wife (Hosokawa Tama, 1563–1600) of Hosokawa Tadaoki, and Akechi Mitsuhide's third daughter. When Akechi Mitsuhide rose against Oda Nobunaga in 1582, Hosokawa Tadaoki refused to support him and Hosokawa Tama was forced to flee to the mountains. Toyotomi Hideyoshi brought her back to Osaka two years later. In 1587, she converted to Christianity and took the name Gracia. In 1600, about to be taken hostage by the Tokugawa Ieyasu's enemy, Ishida Mitsunari, she was killed by Hosokawa Tadaoki's vassals, upon his order. *See* HEUVERS.

• **Hosokawa Harumoto.** Warrior (1519–63), son of Hosokawa Sunitomo. Named *kanryō* in 1546.

• **Hosokawa Katsumoto.** Son (1430–73) of Hosokawa Mochiyuki and military governor *(shugo)* of Settsu, Tamba, Tosa, and Sanuki provinces. He was *kanrei* three times, in 1445–49, 1452–64, and 1468–73. One of the most powerful warriors of his time, he opposed Yamana Sōzen during the successional dispute that began the Ōnin War (1467–77), during the course of which their armies devastated Kyoto. He had the Zen Ryōan-ji temple built in Kyoto.

• **Hosokawa Kiyouji.** Warrior who was killed by his cousin, Hosokawa Yoriyuki, in 1362.

• **Hosokawa Masamoto.** Son (1466–1507) of Hosokawa Matsumoto, appointed *kanrei* in 1494. He was assassinated by his rival, Kōsai Motochika.

• **Hosokawa Mochiyuki.** Warrior (1400–42), military governor *(shugo)* of Settsu, Tamba, Tosa, and Sanuki provinces. He passed on his responsibilities to his son, Hosokawa Katsumoto.

• **Hosokawa Shigekata.** Warrior (1718–85) and scholar, founder, in 1752, of the Jishukan school for the education of young samurai in Kumamoto.

• **Hosokawa Sumitomo.** Adoptive son (1496–1520) of Hosokawa Masamoto. He fought and killed Kōsai Motochika, his father's assassin, and Kōsai's ally, Hosokawa Sumiyuki, in 1507.

• **Hosokawa Sumiyuki.** Warrior (d. 1507), who helped Kōsai Motochika assassinate Hosokowa Masamoto. He was killed by Hosokawa Sumitomo.

• **Hosokawa Tadaoki.** Daimyo (Hosokawa Sansai, 1563–1646), son of Hosokawa Fujitaka. He was a faithful ally of Oda Nobunaga's, then of Toyotomi Hideyoshi's, and his wife, Hosokawa Tama (Gracia), was related to Akechi Mitsuhide. He succeeded his father as daimyo of Tango province (Kyoto), assisted Toyotomi Hideyoshi in his campaigns (Komaki Nagakute in 1584, Kyushu in 1587, Odawara in 1590, Korea in 1592), and fought at Tokugawa Ieyasu's side in Sekigahara in 1600. He then received Bungo and Bizen provinces as a fiefdom, with a revenue of 399,000 *koku*. In 1621, he passed his estates on to his son, Hosokawa Tadatoshi, and retired. An eminent warrior, Tadaoki was also a poet, painter, and expert in etiquette and the tea ceremony *(chanoyu)*.

• **Hosokawa Tadatoshi.** Daimyo (1586–1641), son of Hosokawa Tadaoki and successor to his father in his provinces. He also received a fiefdom in Higo province (Kumamoto prefecture), which raised his revenue to 540,000 *koku,* making him one of the most powerful *tozama-daimyō* in the country.

• **Hosokawa Takakuni.** Warrior (d. 1531), adoptive son of Hosokawa Masamoto. He rebelled against Masamoto, then against Ashikaga Yoshitane, whom he forced to flee in 1521.

• **Hosokawa Tama.** *See* HOSOKAWA GRACIA.

• **Hosokawa Yoriharu.** Warrior (1299–1352) who assisted Ashikaga Takauji in his fight against the Kamakura *bakufu* in 1333.

• **Hosokawa Yoriyuki.** Warrior (1329–92), son of Hosokawa Yoriharu. A minister for shogun Ashikaga Yoshiakira, he fought the warriors of the Yamana clan, defeating them in battle in 1361, and killed his cousin, Hosokawa Kiyouji, the following year.

• **Hosokawa Yūsai.** *See* HOSOKAWA FUJITAKA.

Hosokawa Morihiro. Politician, born 1938 in Kumamoto prefecture, eighteenth-generation descendant of Hosokawa Mochiyuki and grandson of Konoe Fumimaro. A dissident in the Liberal Democratic party (LDP, Jiyū Minshutō), he became the head of the Party of New Japan (Shinseitō) and was elected prime minister on August 5, 1993. He replaced Miyazawa Kiichi, who resigned after elections that saw the fall from power of the LDP (which had been in power for 38 years), and he obtained 262 votes against 244 for the LDP candidate, Kōno Yōhei. Involved in a political and financial scandal, Hosokawa Morihiro tendered his resignation on April 25, 1994, but his cabinet remained in place. Hata Tsutomu succeeded him as prime minister.

Hossō-shū. Buddhist sect founded in 653 by the monk Dōshō when he returned from China, where he had studied with Xuanzang, and updated about 712 by the Japanese monk Gembō. It is based on the teachings of *Joyui shiki-ron (Skt.: Vijñapti-matratasiddhi-shāstra),* according to which only thought is real; everything else is just illusion or dreams. The Hōryū-ji, Yakushi-ji, and Kōfuku-ji monasteries near Nara were built by monks of this sect, which now has very few followers. The Hossō-shū was one of the Six Sects of Nara (Nanto-rokushū).

Hossu. Title for superiors of the Higashi Hongan-ji and the Jodō Shin-shū sect.

Hosuseri no Mikoto. In the Shinto mythology described in the *Kojiki,* he was the oldest son of Ninigi no Mikoto and Konohana Sakuya-hime, the first celestial *kami (amatsu-kami)* who descended to Earth. He succeeded his father as sovereign but was forced to pass power to his brother, Hiko Hohodemi no Mikoto. Also called Honoseri no Mikoto.

Hotei. Japanized form of the Buddha of the Future, Maitreya, or perhaps a divinized form of the Chinese hermit Budai Heshang (d. 917), considered an incarnation of Maitreya *(Jap.:* Miroku Bosatsu). He is venerated particularly as one of the Seven Gods of Good Fortune (Shichifukujin) and, in some Zen monasteries, as the Mampuku-ji. He is portrayed as a plump, smiling man, raising both arms to the sky and sitting on a large bag reputedly full of treasures. His image was called "poussah" (meaning "pot-bellied man") in Europe, through corruption of the Chinese word *pu-sa,* meaning "bodhisattva."

Hotoke (-botoke). General popular name for all Buddhist divinities or those likened to buddhas. At first, this word designated the spirit of dead relatives. It is pronounced *-botoke* in composite words (such as *kake-botoke).* In Okinawa, a *futuke* (perhaps the origin or a corruption of the word *hotoke)* designates a male ancestral spirit.

• **Hotoke Gozen.** *See* TOKIWA GOZEN.

• **Hotoke Zenkō.** *See* SUZUKI ZENKŌ.

Hōtoku. Era of Emperor Go-Hanazono: July 1449–July 1452. *See* NENGŌ.
• Shinto sect founded by a peasant named Nimomiya Sontoku (1787–1856).
→ *See* SHUMMEI.

Hototogisu. "Cuckoo." A literary and poetry magazine dedicated to haiku, created in 1897 by Yanagihara Kyokudō (1867–1957) and Masaoka Shiki in Matsuyama (Ehime prefecture, Shikoku). Its offices were moved to Tokyo the following year by Takahama Kyoshi. The magazine expanded its editorial content and in 1906 became a stylish literary magazine, publishing works by many well-known authors, including Natsume Sōseki. It continued to publish modern haiku and was instrumental in launching a poetic and literary movement that bore its name.

• *Hototogisu.* "The Cuckoo." A novel by Tokutomi Kenjirō (Roka) published in 1898–99, which marked an important turning point in avant-garde literature of the time.

• *Hototogisu kojō no rakugetsu.* Kabuki play in three acts in the *jidai-mon* genre, written about 1907.

Hotta Masamori. Samurai (1606–51) serving shogun Tokugawa Iemitsu; he committed suicide when Iemitsu died so that he would not survive him. His name remained famous as a paragon of fidelity. He had been a senior councillor *(rōjū).* Father of Hotta Masatoshi.

• **Hotta Masatoshi.** Samurai (1634–1684), son of Hotta Masamori, adopted by Kasuga no Tsubone, Tokugawa Iemitsu's nurse, when his father died. He was appointed personal secretary to Tokugawa Ietsuna, then junior councillor *(wakadoshiyori)* in 1670 and senior councillor *(rōjū)* in 1679. Shogun Tokugawa Tsunayoshi, whom he had supported, gave him estates worth some 130,000 *koku.* He was assassinated for no apparent reason by one of his cousins, Inaba Masayasu (1640–84), who was condemned to death the same year. *See* INABA MASAYASU.

• **Hotta Masayoshi.** Daimyo (1810–64) of Sakura (Chiba prefecture). He succeeded Abe Masehiro as *rōjū* in 1855, and the shogunate gave him responsibility for concluding the Kanagawa Treaty with the United States and receiving Consul Townsend Harris. But when he went to Kyoto, he was not able to obtain Emperor Komei's approval. Ii Naosuke replaced him in 1858.

• **Hotta Zuishō.** *See* ZUISHŌ.

Hotta Yoshiie. Writer, born 1918 in Toyama. He lived in Shanghai during the Second World War and related his experiences in books that were very popular after the war, *Sokoku sōshitsu* (Loss of Homeland, 1950) and *Hiroba no kodoku* (Alone in the Marketplace, 1951), which won the twenty-sixth Akutagawa Prize. Most of his novels deal with political and conflictual relationships in the modern world—*Jikan* (Time, 1953)—and with the course of history—*Uminari no soko kara* (Under the Ocean's Roaring, 1960–63), which dealt with the events during the Shimabara Uprising. He also wrote a collection of essays, *Ransei no bungaku-sha,* in 1958. His works were translated into Russian, Estonian, and Bulgarian.

House, Edward Howard. American journalist (1836–1901), born in Boston. He went to Japan in 1871 as a correspondent for a number of newspapers. He taught at Kaisei Gakkō University and was noted for his pro-Japanese articles in favor of revising the Unequal Treaties and the principle of extraterritoriality. He accompanied the Japanese army when it conquered Taiwan in 1874; when he returned to Tokyo, he founded an English-language daily, the *Tokyo Times,* which he published until 1880, when he left Japan. Having become an invalid following a heart attack, he was offered a pension for life by the Japanese government, which awarded him the Order of the Sacred Treasure (Zuihō-shō) in recognition of services rendered. House then returned to Japan and, as a music critic, devoted himself to bringing Western music to that country.

Housing. Although stone is abundant in Japan, it is not very useful for making durable structures and has been used mainly for foundations of buildings and terraces. The ground shifts frequently due to earthquakes and run-off, so stone structures would be at a disadvantage. In addition, the sense of impermanence of all things, which is inherent to the Japanese soul, once inspired builders to use only wood precisely because no building is built for eternity. In fact, the use of wood and a construction system involving trusses and roof supports provided relative flexibility, enabling buildings to resist tremors better. The only drawback of wooden structures was their great susceptibility to fire, which meant that most old buildings were destroyed in one period or another, so that it is practically a miracle that some of them have survived to the present day.

There are three very distinct types of Japanese housing: rural houses *(minka),* lords' residences *(see* ARCHITECTURE, SHINDEN, SHOIN-ZUKURI), and modern cement housing units. Rural houses, made of wood covered with thatching, have always been built on the same principle: the rooms are organized around the fireplace *(irori)* and closed off from each other by sliding partitions *(fusuma, shōji).* The foundations rest on very short pilings that are either buried or sitting on stone bases *(soban).* The roofs, generally steeply sloping, are made of thick layers of reeds or thatching, with an opening left for smoke to escape. Roof styles vary slightly from region to region, but the general appearance of rural houses

has not changed much over time, deriving for the most part from houses portrayed on seventh-century *haniwa.* During the Meiji era, the style of houses changed slightly. Most, still built in wood, now had a second floor (rarely more) and were covered in colored plastic tiles, which were lighter and more waterproof than traditional tiles. Almost all rural houses follow these principles, which makes them inexpensive to build and easy to replace. The walls are made of plaster or an agglomerate of paper, straw, and plaster, and windows now have glass panes. There are no more fireplaces since electricity or gas stoves are used for heating. Only a few rural houses still use a small brazier *(hibachi).* All utility hookups are flexible to avoid ruptures during earthquakes.

During the Edo period, large cities began to feature multi-dwelling buildings constructed with plaster walls and tile roofs so that they would not catch fire so easily. During the Meiji era, Western influence was seen in urban housing: harder concrete, brick, stone, and cement began to be used in construction. Very quickly, concrete became the preferred construction material and Western standards were followed, with precautions (welded steel hoops surrounding structures like a net) taken to keep buildings from collapsing during earthquakes. In cities, buildings that generally respected safety standards went up, containing low-priced rental units *(apātō)* for rural in-migrants and workers. These buildings usually had four or five stories. Inside, the rooms were not arranged in the traditional way; instead, almost all gave onto outdoor or indoor corridors. The measure used for these modern structures was not the traditional *ken* (intercolumnation, usually 1.82 m) but the meter and its divisions, except for the room with tatami, which was always the same size (one *ken* by one-half *ken).* Large buildings are generally used for businesses or offices, for Japanese do not like living in skyscrapers (although the style is now beginning to catch on).

In every dwelling, traditional or not, there is usually a room with a floor covered in tatami, containing a *tokonoma* and at least one objet d'art (vase of flowers, *kakemono),* used as a reception area *(zashiki).* The walls are actually large cupboards used to store mattresses *(futon)* and clothing. Rooms that are for public use always have a floor slightly higher than that in the entranceway *(genkan),* where shoes and outerwear are left. Floors are often made of wood (sometimes carpeted, in luxurious Western-style residences), and tables, chairs, and sofas are used increasingly, except in rooms covered with tatami, where the tradition is to sit cross-legged at small folding tables or, in some cases, around a depression in the floor over which there are a table with a heating element (*kotatsu*) and covers to keep the legs warm in the winter. However, air flow in modern rooms cannot match the natural air movement in traditional wooden houses, so air conditioning is often used. Nowadays, most wooden houses have been replaced by modern standardized housing; wood is rarely used as a construction material, except in the case of individual houses commissioned by those enamored of tradition. *See* AMADO, ARCHITECTURE, BYŌBU, FURNISHINGS, FUSUMA, HIBACHI, IRORI, KAWARA, KEN, MINKA, ROOFS, SHŌJI, TATAMI, TOKONOMA, ZABUTON.

Hōzan. Ceramist (early nineteenth century), ninth director of the Awata ceramic manufacture and master of the modern ceramist Aoki Mokube.
• Sculptor (Takahashi Hōzan, Hokkyō Hōzan, mid-nineteenth century) of Buddhist images.
• Sculptor of netsuke (Tanaka Hōzan, mid-nineteenth century).
→ *See* HŌSHŌ-RYŪ.

Hōzan-ji. Buddhist temple in Nabata, Ikoma (Nara prefecture), belonging to the Shugendō sect, and dedicated to Fudō Myō-ō (*Skt.:* Achalanātha). Founded, according to tradition, by En no Gyōja, it was reconstructed in 1678 by the monk Tankai (1629–1716), who sculpted the small statue of Fudō (0.17 m high) in 1701. Also called Ikoma Shōten-ji.

• **Hōzan Tankai.** *See* HŌZAN-JI, TANKAI.

Hōzō-in Inei. Buddhist monk (1521–1607), guardian of the Nara temples, founder of a school for sword (*katana*) combat called Hōzō-ryū. All his successors were Buddhist monks: Hōzō Inshun (1589–1648), Hōzō Insei (1624–89), Hōzō Infū (1682–1731), Hōzō Inken (1746–1808), and others. The school was updated at the end of the nineteenth century, notably by Takeda Sōkaku Minamoto no Masayoshi (1858–1943), who used bamboo swords (*shinai*) for training.

Hōzuki. Very popular rattle made by little girls with the fruit of a plant (*Physalis alkekengi*) of the solanaceous family, which gave rise, during the Edo period, to a major fair (called *hōzuki-ichi*) in the Asakusa district every July 10. The monks of the Asakusa Kannon temple say that a prayer made to Kannon Bosatsu on this date is equivalent to 46,000 prayers recited on other days.

Hozumi. Family of jurists, in the Meiji and Taishō eras, who took part in writing the civil codes of Japan and were experts in constitutional law. They wrote many books on the subject that are still authoritative. The most famous were Hozumi Nobushige (1856–1926); his son, Hozumi Shigetō (1883–1951); and his brother, Hozumi Yatsuka (1860–1912).

• **Hozumi Harunobu, Hozumi Jihei.** *See* HARUNOBU.

Hozumi no Miko. *See* HOZUMI SHINNŌ.

Hozumi Shinnō. Imperial prince (d. 715), fifth son of Temmu Tennō. He was minister (*dajōkanji*) for Mommu Tennō and Gemmei Tennō. Four of his poems (*tanka*), included in the *Man'yōshū*, describe his tragic love affair with his half-sister Princess Tajima. He also had a relationship with Otomo no Sakanoue no Iratsume. Also called Hozumi no Miko.

Humbert-Droz, Aimé. Swiss clockmaker (1819–1900) who, as president of the Clockmakers' Union, was sent on a mission to Japan in 1863. When he returned, in 1864, he wrote a book about his voyage, *Japan Illustrated,* with many photographs by Felice Beato, Charles Wirgman, and Alfred Roussin, which was published in 1868. Appointed rector of the Neuchâtel Academy in 1866.

Humor. Westerners claim that the Japanese have no sense of humor. In fact, their sense of humor is very different from that in the West. During the Edo period, laughter was considered insulting by the samurai class; it was good manners never to do more than crack a smile and, especially, never to attempt to tell a joke. In the merchant class and among the common people, in contrast, drinking, singing, and jokes (often indecent or derisive) were much enjoyed. The arts of vaudeville and joketelling developed in large merchant cities such as Osaka, where wandering storytellers (*rakugo*) sent people into paroxysms of laughter. These entertainers were soon on stage performing monologues (*rakugo*) or dialogues (*manzai*) on politics, the news, and society. In the Ashikaga period, comic interludes (*kyōgen*) between Noh plays were designed to make the audience laugh and to relieve the tension caused by the dramas. This art was transferred to the screen, and there are still some performers on television whose particular humor can be truly appreciated only by a Japanese audience. *Manga* were also often imbued with humor, founded on the critical observation of customs or on caricature. The Japanese people are generally good-humored, and only in the samurai class was the behavior code so strict as to exclude laughing. Some daimyo were not above calling on humorists *(otogishū)* or clowns to entertain their guests. *See* MANZAI, RAKUGO, YOSE.

Hyakuman. Number equivalent to 100 *man* or one million.

• *Hyakuman.* Title of a Noh play: a woman who lost her son after her husband died finds the son during a religious service and takes him home, after telling her story to a monk at the temple.

Hyakunin isshu. "Simple Poems by One Hundred Poets." A poetry anthology compiled by Fujiwara Teika (Fujiwara no Sadaie) and revised by his son, Fujiwara no Tameie. These poems decorated the walls of their villa on Mt. Ogura (whence the anthology's other name, *Ogura hyakunin isshu,* or *Ogura sansō shikishi waka,* "One Hundred Poems on Cards in the Ogura Retreat") between 1229 and 1241. They were arranged in chronological order, going from Tenji Tennō to Juntoku Tennō, and were transcribed by Renshō in the thirteenth century. Most literate Japanese know them by heart. On New Year's Day, young people play a game *(uta-garuta)* consisting of guessing part of a poem from this anthology by listening to the first part of the *waka* and choosing the corresponding card bearing the second part. This collection inspired others of the same type, such as the *Buke hyakunin isshu* (Simple Poems by One Hundred Samurai), from the late Edo period, and the more modern *Aikoku hya-kunin isshu* (Simple Poems by One Hundred Patriots), dating from 1942.

Hyakurenshō. Historical work written in Chinese by an unknown author in the late thirteenth century, covering the years 968 to 1259. Only 14 of the 17 volumes of this important chronicle, dealing with the earlier years, have been found.

Hyakusen. Painter (Sakasi Shin'en; *gō*: Hōshū, Hassendō, Hyakusen, 1698–1753) of the Nanga school, and haiku poet.

Hyakushō (-byakushō). "Hundred names," a general term designating the social status of the peasants who worked freely on imperial estates, or *shōen,* and who enjoyed certain rights. A number of them became landowners in the Muromachi period and became vassals of the daimyo. In the Edo period, the term *hyakushō* became simply synony-mous with "peasant" *(nō),* as opposed to the other classes—samurai *(buke),* nobles *(kuge),* and townspeople *(chōnin).* There were several categories of *hyakushō*: those who were registered as landowners *(hom-byakushō),* those who were subordinate to them *(hikan-byakushō,* more commonly called *nago),* and those who owned no land *(mizunomi-byakushō).*

• **Hyakushō ikki.** Peasant uprisings. During the Edo period, taxes became increasingly onerous, provoking many revolts. There were more than 2,500 throughout the country during the Edo period, and they were particularly numerous and violent in 1780, 1830, and 1860, during periods of famine. At first simple acts of resistance, these movements were later marked by desertion of the land to avoid taxes. Discontent was sometimes channeled by village leaders into armed struggle. More than 200 villages took part in the Sakura Revolt in the 1640s. In the eighteenth century, the peasants were better organized and stood up not only to the authorities but also to unscrupulous traders. In the Meiji era, the motives became political. Marxist historians of the 1930s saw in the *hyakushō ikki* a manifestation of class struggle, while non-Marxists saw opposition to feudal injustice. *See also* HEIMIN.

• **Hyakushō-uke.** System for collecting taxes from peasants *(hyakushō, myōshu,* and *ji-samurai),* which, starting in the fourteenth century, instituted a sort of joint responsibility for payment under the aegis of the village leader. A similar system, called *egōshū,* was implemented later for urban dwellers. *See* GO-NIN GUMI, HYŌRŌMAI.

Hyakutake Kenkō. Painter (1842–87) and diplomat. He studied in France and Italy with Richardson, Bonnard, and Maccari, whose style he faithfully followed.

Hyōbusho. After 702, a sort of ministry of war, replacing the Hyōseikan created in 683. Also sometimes called Tsuwamono no Tsukasa.

Hyōgo prefecture. Prefecture in the Kinki region, located on the coast of the Inland Sea (Setonaikai) east of Kyoto, abutting the city on the coast of the Sea of Japan (Nihonkai). It is divided by the Chū-goku mountain range; the northern part is humid and cool, and the southern part is more temperate and drier. As the only passage between the south-eastern part of Honshu and the Osaka-Kyoto re-

The One Hundred Poets

1. Tenji Tennō
2. Jitō Tennō
3. Kakinomoto no Hitomaro
4. Yamabe no Akahito
5. Sarumaru Dayū
6. Otomo Yakamochi
7. Abe no Nakamaro
8. Kisen Hōshi
9. Ono no Komachi
10. Semimaru
11. Ono Takamura
12. Dōjō Henjō
13. Yōzei-in
14. Kawara no Sadaijin
15. Kōkō Tennō
16. Ariwara no Yukihira
17. Ariwara no Narihira
18. Fujiwara no Toshiyuki
19. Ise
20. Motoyoshi Shinō
21. Sosei no Hōshi
22. Bun'ya no Yasuhide
23. Ōe no Chisato
24. Kanke
25. Sanjō no Udaijin
26. Teishinkō
27. Fujiwara no Kansuke
28. Minamoto no Muneyuki
29. Ōshikōchi no Mitsune
30. Mibu no Tadamine
31. Sakanoue no Korenori
32. Harumichi no Tsuraki
33. Ki no Tomonori
34. Fujiwara no Ōkikaze
35. Ki no Tsurayuki
36. Kiyohara no Fukayabu
37. Bun'ya no Asayasu
38. Ukon
39. Sangi Hitoshi
40. Taira no Kiyomori
41. Mibu no Tadami
42. Kiyohara no Motosuke
43. Fujiwara no Atsutada
44. Fujiwara no Asatada
45. Kentokukō
46. Sone no Yoshitada
47. Ekei Hōshi
48. Minamoto no Shigeyuki
49. Ōnakatomi no Yoshinobu
50. Fujiwara no Yoshitaka
51. Fujiwara no Sanetaka
52. Fujiwara no Michinobu
53. Udaishō Michitsuna no Haha
54. Kidōsanchi no Haha
55. Fujiwara Kintō
56. Izumi Shikibu
57. Murasaki Shikibu
58. Daini no Sammi
59. Akazome Emon
60. Koshikibu no Naishi
61. Ise no Ōsuke
62. Sei Shōnagon
63. Sakyō no Daibu Michimasa
64. Fujiwara no Sadayori
65. Sagami
66. Saki no Dai-Sōjō Gyōson
67. Suhō no Naiji
68. Sanjō-in
69. Nō-in Hōshi
70. Ryōsen Hōshi
71. Dainagon Tsunenobu
72. Yūshi Naishinnō Kekii
73. Saki no Chūnagon Masafusa
74. Minamoto no Toshiyori
75. Fujiwara no Mototoshi
76. Hōshōji no Nyūdō
77. Sutoku-in
78. Minamoto no Kanemasa
79. Sakyo no Daibu Akisuke
80. Taikenmon'in Horikawa
81. Gotoku Daiji no Saidaijin
82. Dō-in Hōshi
83. Kōtaigō Gū no Daibu Toshinari
84. Fujiwara no Kiyosuke
85. Shun'e Hōshi
86. Saigyō Hōshi
87. Jakuren Hōshi
88. Kōkamon'in no Bettō
89. Shikishi Naishinnō
90. Imbumon'in no Tayū
91. Gokyōgoku Sesshō
92. Nijō-in no Sanuki
93. Kamakura no Udaijin
95. Dai Sōjō Ji'en
96. Nyūdō Saki no Dajō Daijin
97. Fujiwara no Sadaie (Taika)
98. Junii Ietaka
99. Go-Toba-in
100. Juntoku-in

gion, this prefecture was the site of many historic battles, including those between the Taira and the Minamoto in the twelfth century. It includes the island of Awaji, which separates, in the Inland Sea, the Harima Sea and Osaka Bay. *Chief city:* Kobe. *Main cities:* Nishinomiya, Himeji, Amagasaki, Akō, Ono; in the north, Toyooka and Kasumi. *Area:* 8,363 km². *Pop.:* 5.5 million. Former names: Muko no Minato, Wada no Tomaari.

• **Hyōgo-gusari.** Type of sword *(katana, tachi)* hung from the belt *(obi)* by a chain. Also called *ikamono-zukuri.*

Hyōjō-bugyō. Title of the chair of the board of the Kamakura *bakufu,* starting in 1249. *See* BUGYŌ.

• **Hyōjōsho.** During the Edo period, after 1636, the ministry that brought together the *jisha-bugyō, machi-bugyō,* and *kanjō-bugyō.* Its bureaucrats were called *hyōjōsho-jusha,* then, after 1693, *hyōjosho-meyasu-yomi.*

• **Hyōjoshū.** The highest authority of the Mandokoro of the Kamakura *bakufu* and the Muromachi shogunate, analogous to a state council, established in 1226 by Hōjō Yasutoki. During the Kamakura period, it comprised 11 members under the authority of the *shikken,* and decisions were made by the majority. The organization was abolished in the early sixteenth century.

Hyōmin Usaburō. "Usaburō Lost at Sea." Novel by Ibuse Masuji, published in 1956, describing a sea voyage made in 1839 and the first contacts between Japanese and foreigners.

Hyōmon. Technique of inlaying metals (gold, silver, pewter, bronze) on lacquer, imported from China *(Chin.: pingtuo)* during the Nara period. This technique was called *kanagai* during the Heian period. Also sometimes called *heidatsu.*

Hyōrōmai. Tax payable in rice levied during the Kamakura and Muromachi periods to support the war efforts. Minamoto no Yoritomo instituted the tax, which affected public and private estates and amounted to about 2% of the produce of the lands. During the Muromachi period, however, the tax grew, sometimes reaching 50% of the revenue of the *shōen.*

Hyōshigi. Sort of wooden castanets used by some orchestras accompanying Kagura dances.

Hyōtan. Dried gourds used in rural areas as bottles or jars to hold liquids. Small gourds (colocynths) used to contain *sake* or tea could be hung from the belt. Small wooden cups were attached to them to make drinking easier. Cut in half lengthwise, *hyōtan* were used as spoons or ladles. Also called *hisago.*

Hyottoko. Noh mask, perhaps an old mask used in Kagura, portraying a peasant with a stubbled face and protruding lips, with a comical appearance, Otafuku's companion. The *hyottoko* is also used in certain Kyōgen plays.

Hyūga. Former province, now included in Miyazaki prefecture.

I. Second vowel of the kana syllabic alphabet *(a, i, u, e, o)*.

• Court ranks in imperial Japan, introduced from China in 702 and in use until 1868, when they were changed. They originally comprised nine ranks, and the number grew to twelve a little later. Each rank was divided into two classes, superior *(shō)* and subordinate *(ju)*. The ranks from fifth to twelfth were also divided into subcategories, major *(jō)* and minor *(ge)*. The five top ranks were conferred by the emperor himself; the sixth and seventh were subject to approval by the emperor. The other ranks *(hanju)* were conferred by ministers. Each rank corresponded to an official position, with the highest being *dajō daijin* (grand minister of state). List of court ranks in the *ritsuryō* system:

First rank: **Shō-ichi-i**, superior (posthumous); **Ju-ichi-i**, subordinate (duke)

Second rank: **Shō-ni-i**, superior (marquis); **Ju-ni-i**, subordinate (count)

Third rank: **Shō-san-i**, superior (viscount); **Ju-san-i**, subordinate

Fourth rank: **Shō-shi-i-jō**, superior major (baron); **Shō-shi-i-ge**, superior minor; **Ju-shi-i-jō**, subordinate major; **Ju-shi-i-ge**, subordinate minor

Fifth rank: **Shō-go-i-jō**, superior major; **Shō-go-i-ge**, superior minor; **Ju-go-i-jō**, subordinate major; **Ju-go-i-ge**, subordinate minor

Sixth rank: **Shō-roku-i-jō**, superior major; **Shō-roku-i-ge**, superior minor; **Ju-roku-i-jō**, subordinate major; **Ju-roku-i-ge**, subordinate minor

Seventh rank: **Shō-shichi-i-jō**, superior major; **Shō-shichi-i-ge**, superior minor; **Ju-shichi-i-jō**, subordinate major; **Ju-shichi-i-ge**, subordinate minor

Eighth rank: **Shō-hachi-i-jō**, superior major; **Shō-hachi-i-ge**, superior minor; **Ju-hachi-i-jō**, subordinate major; **Ju-hachi-i-ge**, subordinate minor

Ninth rank: **Dai-so-i-jō**, superior major; **Dai-so-i-ge**, superior minor

Tenth rank: **Shō-so-i-jō**, superior major; **Shō-so-i-ge**, superior minor

Starting in 1868, the superior first rank was conferred only posthumously. The titles of duke, marquis, count, viscount, and baron were substituted for the former four top court ranks. This set of ranks was also called Ikai (I-kai). *See also* IHŌ, KABANE, KAN'I JŪNIKAI, YAKUSA NO KABANE.

→ *See* INOSHISHI.

Iai. Art of drawing the sword and striking the adversary in a single movement. This technique, part of samurai training at the Kenjutsu, was said to have originated with Hayashizaki Jinnosuke Shigenobu (b. 1542) in 1560, who founded a school *(ryū)* that bore his name. After being refined by the master of arms Eishin (Hasegawa Chikara no Suke Hidenobu, early eighteenth century) of the Musō Shinden-ryū school, it was called Hasegawa Eishin-ryū. *See* IAI-DŌ.

• **Iai-dō.** Martial-arts technique based on *iai*, comprising 24 basic movements *(kata)* for drawing the sword *(katana)* from its scabbard *(saya)* and 50 movements for cutting, practiced for training with the sword or for kendo.

Iba. Archeological site in Hamamatsu (Shizuoka prefecture), with remains from the Yayoi period (half-buried houses) and the *kofun* period. This site seems to have been an important center during the Nara period, and it is surrounded by a 13-meter-wide moat. More than 100 inscribed wooden tablets *(mokkan)* have been found there. Part of the ancient site is preserved in a park. *See* HAMMAMATSU, MOKKAN, TATARA, TATEANA.

Ibaragi Noriko. Writer and poet (b. 1926); she wrote stories and collections of modern poems.

Ibaraki. City in Osaka prefecture, located about 16 km north of Osaka, castle town *(jōka-machi)* from the late sixteenth century. A number of *kofun* are located in the surrounding area (notably in Shikinzan), as are houses from the Edo period (Kōriyama Honjin). A satellite city of Osaka, Ibaraki has some electrical-equipment plants. *Pop.:* 250,000.

• **Ibaraki-ken.** Prefecture in central Honshu, north of Tokyo and Chiba prefecture, with the Kanto plain on its northern border. Formerly Hitachi province. Main economic activities are agriculture, with a few industries, and fishing on the Pacific coast. The large lakes, Kasumigaura and Kitaura, and the Fukuroda waterfall are major tourist sites. The *chief city,* Mito, was a major center of historical and philosophical studies during the Edo period. The new town of Tsukuba contains a number of research institutes. *Main cities:* Mito, Tsuchiura, Hitachi, Koga. *Area:* 6,090 km². *Pop.:* 2.6 million.

Ibuka Masuru. Industrialist, born 1908 in Tochigi prefecture; founder, with Morita Akio, of Tokyo Tsūshin Kōgyo in 1946, renamed Sony in 1950. The company began by producing transistors in 1954 and exported part of its production to the United States, which enabled a large part of its budget to be devoted to research. Ibuka Masuru was appointed director general of the electronics manufacturer Sony in 1950 and was its president from 1971 to 1976.

Ibuse Masuji. Writer (1898–1993), born in Kamo (Hiroshima prefecture). After studying at Waseda University in Tokyo, he began to study French literature. He abandoned his studies in 1922 to devote himself to writing. He wrote mainly novellas, including *Yuhei* (1923), better known as *Sanshōuo* (The Salamander, 1929), *Koi* (The Carp, 1924), *Shigoto beya* (The Workroom, 1931), *Shūkin ryokō* (The Business Trip, 1935), *Tajinko mura* (The Village of Tajinko, 1939), and *Tange Shitei* (The House in Shitei, 1940). In a personal mode, he described the activities of his contemporaries using humor and symbolism. He also wrote historical novellas: *Sazamani gunki* (Chronicle of the Wavelets, 1938), *Kaikonmura no Yosaku* (The Yosaku Settler, 1955). His first true novel, *Kuroi ame* (Black Rain,

1965), inspired by the tragedy of Hiroshima, earned him international fame and the Noma Prize, the highest literary distinction in Japan. Among his other novels are *Ōshima no zonnensho* (Ōshima's Memoirs, 1950), *Ekinoe ryōkan* (The Train-Station Hotel, 1956), *Chimpindō shujin* (The Antique Dealer, 1959), and many stories, including *Kashima ari* (Room to Rent, 1948), *Honjitsu kyūshin* (No Consultations Today, 1949), and *Yōhai taishō* (Lieutenant Reverence, 1950). His body of work, written in an almost haiku-like poetic style, is more suggestive than descriptive. With acuity and often humor, in plain, polished language, he depicts the life of ordinary people with no moralistic pretensions. Many of his stories have been adapted for the screen in Japan, including *Tajinko mura, Honjitsu kyūshin, Ekimae ryōkan, Kashima ari,* and *Chimpindō shujin.*

Ichi. A term used mainly to designate markets and fairs. Before the seventh century, these events took place at crossroads of the main roads, under certain trees, as their ancient names testify: Tsubaki no Ichi (Camellia Market), Atokuwa no Ichi (Plum-Tree Market), and so on. When large cities such as Heijō-kyō (Nara) and Heian-kyō (Kyoto) were founded, two large permanent markets were set up in the eastern and western sectors, operating on an alternating schedule. Other markets took place at more or less regular intervals. As towns and villages developed, new markets were set up on private estates *(shōen),* giving rise to agglomerations of merchants, artisans, and innkeepers linked to each other via itinerant traders. These markets, some of which specialized in a particular foodstuffs, grew constantly in size. Market towns *(ichiba-machi)* developed concurrently with castle towns *(jōka-machi)* and monastery towns *(monzen-machi);* they enabled the economy to grow and the roads and communications systems to cover a large part of the country by the Edo period. The *ichi* began to fade in importance during the Meiji era in competition with wholesale trade, but some have survived to the present day because of their specialization and the fact that they are held on fixed dates during certain festivals.
• Term denoting any specific unit.

Ichiba Tsūshō. Writer (1739–1812) of *kusazōshi* works and author of many genre novels and novellas.

Ichiboku-zukuri. "Style of a single block of wood," an art technique consisting of carving an image (generally Buddhist) in a single piece of wood, with only the protruding parts (hands, arms) sculpted separately and added afterward. *See* YOSEGI-ZUKURI.

Ichibu. Title sometimes given to the Shijō, or bureaucrat working for a provincial governor.

Ichi-bu gin. Rectangular silver coin worth one *bu,* or one quarter of a *ryō,* issued during the Edo period starting in 1837 (Tempō 8). It weighed 8.66 g and was of almost pure (99%) silver. In 1859, it was devalued and reduced to 89% silver; in 1868, it was devalued again, with its silver content reduced to 81% and its weight to about 8.63 g. Exchange rates for the *ryō* were very favorable, so starting in 1860, foreign traders dealt the *ichi-bu gin* in such a way that a great quantity of gold left Japan (the coins were resold for double their value in Shanghai), impoverishing the country.

Ichibu-ichigen. In the traditional Japanese calendar, a period equivalent to 21 or 22 *gen,* starting with a Kanoto no Tori year and finishing with a Kanoe no Saru year. Its length is thus either 1,320 or 1,260 normal years. *See* CALENDAR.

Ichien. Buddhist monk (Ōnakatomi Masamune, 803–67) of the Shingon-shū, who was one of Emperor Saga Tennō's pages *(chigo)* about 820.

Ichiga. Painter (Oki Tei; *azana:* Shikei; *gō:* Sesai, 1830–55) of the Kano school. He was a member of the Tottori clan.

Ichigen no Miya. Modern Buddhist sect founded in 1950 by Motoki Isamu (b. 1906). Also called Dainichi Dairitsu-genri.

Ichigon hōdan. "Words of the Law." A collection of short religious works of the Buddhist Jōdo (Pure Land) sects, written by unknown authors between 1280 and 1330. They contain short maxims on principles that followers should observe, such as recitation of the *nembutsu,* the transitory nature of life, and so on, constituting a sort of memento to be used by Amidist believers.

Ichihara. Poet (eighth century) and architect, Prince Aki's son. He probably directed construction of the Tōdai-ji in Nara in 763.

Ichihara Tayojo. Haiku poet (1772–1865).

Ichijitsu Shintō. "Shinto of a Single Truth," a syncretic Shinto-Buddhist Tendai-shū sect. A famous work, *Ichijitsu shintō-ki,* by the monk Jihon (1795–1869) of the Tendai-shū, gives the history of the development of this type of syncretism, according to which the *kami* Ō-Yamakui, protector of Mt. Hiei, represented the highest teaching of the Tendai school. This 31-chapter work also contains an examination of many Shinto myths and biographies of the monks of the Enryaku-ji and the Hie shrines. Also called Sannō Ichijitsu Shintō.

Ichijō. Ancient noble family (one of the Go-sekke), descended from Fujiwara no Michie.

• **Ichijō Fuyuyoshi.** Statesman (Ichijō Fuyura, 1464–1514) who became a *kampaku.* He is sometimes attributed with authorship of the *Masu-kagami.*

• **Ichijō Kanera.** Philosopher (Ichijō Kaneyoshi, Go-shō-on-ji Kampaku, 1402–81) and poet. He was *dajō-daijin,* then *kampaku* in 1447. His Tokyo house was destroyed during the Ōnin War, so he resigned and took refuge in Nara in 1470, where he became a Buddhist monk in 1473. He returned to Kyoto in 1477 and was appointed tutor of the young shogun Ashikaga Yoshihisa. A great scholar of poetry, literature, and Chinese and Japanese history, and an expert in ritual and religion, he wrote many books on various subjects: *Kuji kongen* (Origin of the Court Ritual, ca. 1422), *Gōshidai-shō* (Notes on the Writings of Ōe Masafusa), *Nenchū gyōji taigai* (Annual Rites and Observances), *Kachō yojō* (Atmosphere of Flowers and Birds, 1472), *Gengo hiketsu* (Hidden Wisdom of the *Genji monogatari,* 1477), *Sayo no nezame* (Thoughts of the Early Hours, ca. 1478), and *Bummei ittō-ki* (On the Unity of Knowledge and Culture, ca. 1478). He also wrote on Shinto—*Nihon shoki sanso* (Notes on the *Nihongi*); on Buddhism—*Kanshū nembutsu-ki* (Appeal for the Recitation of Amida's Name); on Confucianism—*Shisho dōjikun* (The Four Classics for Children). He wrote the preface for the *Shin zoku kokin waka-shū,* the last of the 21 imperial anthologies (*see* CHOKUSEN WAKA-SHŪ), in 1439, and a number of treatises on classical poetry: *Karin ryōzai-shū* (Wood from the Forest of Verses), *Kokin dōmōshō* (Glimpses of the Kokinshū, 1476), *Renju gappeki-shū* (Jewels of Linked Verses, ca. 1476). He also wrote an annotated genealogy of his family, the *Tōka zuihō* (Leaves from a Blossoming of Peach Trees), in which he described the etiquette and ceremonies of the court in his time. Ichijō Norifusa's father.

• **Ichijō Norifusa.** Ichijō Kanera's son (1423–80), appointed *kampaku* in 1458. He resigned in 1467 and took refuge in Nara with his father, then returned to his fiefdom in Tosa, where, with the help of the Chōsokabe family, he founded a provincial cultural center in Nakamura.

• **Ichijō Sanetsune.** Founder (1223–84) of the Ichijō family of the Go-sekke. He was *kampaku* for Emperor Go-Saga and *sesshō* for young Emperor Go-Fukukusa in 1246. In 1265, he was appointed *kampaku* for Emperor Kameyama.

• **Ichijō-sesshō.** *See* FUJIWARA NO KORETADA.

• **Ichijō Tennō.** Sixty-sixth emperor (Prince Kanehito, 980<987–1011>), En'yū Tennō's son and successor to Kazan Tennō. Sanjō succeeded him. His mother was Senshi (Higashi Sanjō-in, 961–1001), Fujiwara no Kaneie's daughter. He had two empresses *(chūgū)* of equal rank: Fujiwara no Teishi, one of Fujiwara no Michitaka's daughters, and Fujiwara no Shōshi (Jōtō Mon-in), one of Fujiwara no Michinaga's daughters.

• **Ichijō Tsunetsugu.** Statesman (1358–1418), Nijō Yoshimoto's son, adopted by the Ichijō family. He was appointed *kampaku* for Emperor Go-Komatsu in 1394. He was a famous scholar in his time.

Ichijōgatani. Site of the town of Kukui (Fukui prefecture), famous for the remains of its fortified town *(jōka-machi)* dating from the Sengoku (Warring States) period, which was destroyed after Asakura Yoshikage was defeated by Oda Nobunaga in 1573. Excavations at the site after 1970 uncovered the remains of samurai houses and objects of the time that give a picture of life in a *jōka-machi* in that period.

Ichijō-yōketsu. Buddhist treatise expounding the doctrines of the Tendai-shū, written by Genshin (942–1017).

Ichikawa Beian. Calligrapher (Ichikawa Sangai, Ichikawa Beian, Kōyō; *azana:* Kōyō; *gō:* Hyakkasai, Kin'usanjin, Rakusai, 1779–1858), Ichikawa Kansai's (1749–1820) eldest son, and a Confucian scholar. He followed the Chinese style of Mi Fu of the Song dynasty and studied with Chinese calligrapher Hu Zhaoxin. When his father died, he entered the service of the daimyo of Kanazawa, a position he held until 1850. His calligraphy was so highly regarded that he was said to have had more than 5,000 students. He published a few authoritative books on his art, including *Beika shoketsu* (Calligraphy in the Style of Mi Fu) and *Beian bokudan* (Dissertation on Ink by Beian). He was one of the Sampitsu (Three Brushes) of the Edo period. He is also known simply as Beian.

Ichikawa Danjūrō. Famous family of Kabuki actors from the Edo period to the present. Actor Ichikawa Ebizō (who performed in Osaka and Kyoto) took the name Ebizō in 1735 and gave the name Danjūrō to his son. His family name was Horikoshi and his *haimyō* was Hakuen. Since then, all Kabuki actors in this family (or claiming to be in the family) have used the name Danjūrō. Among the most famous are:

Danjūrō I (1660–1704), creator of the *aragoto* style. He wrote some Kabuki plays that he signed with the *haimyō* Mimasuya Hyōgo.

Danjūrō II (1688–1758), his son, adapted for Kabuki *jōruri* plays written for puppet theater.

Danjūrō III (eighteenth century).

Danjūrō IV (1711–78), actor in *aragoto* style playing *onnagata* roles.

Danjūrō V (1741–1806), his son, who played all types of roles.

Danjūrō VI (eighteenth–nineteenth century).

Danjūrō VII (1791–1859) compiled the Kabuki-jūhachiban (Eighteen Best Kabuki Plays), the repertoire performed by actors in his family.

Danjūrō VIII (eighteenth–nineteenth century).

Danjūrō IX (1838–1903), Danjūrō VII's son; updated Kabuki theater and imbued it with more realism.

Danjūrō X (nineteenth century).

Danjūrō XI (1909–65), Matsumoto Kōshirō VII's (1870–1949) son, another Kabuki actor; adapted, among other plays, episodes from the *Genji monogatari* to the stage, and performed them with actor Onoe Baikō VII (b. 1915).

Danjūrō XII (Horikoshi Natsuo), born in Tokyo, Danjūrō XI's son. He performed not only in Tokyo's Kabukiza but in various American cities, including New York, Los Angeles, and Washington. He took the name Danjūrō XII only in 1975.

Many actors in Ichikawa Danjūrō's family were extraordinarily popular, and some fans came to commit suicide at their funerals.

Ichikawa Fusae. Politician (1893–1981), born in Aichi prefecture, who was known for her activities in favor of political rights for women. In 1924, she founded the Fusen Kakutoku Dōmei (Women's Suffrage League); in 1945, the Nihon Fujin Yūkensha Dōmei (League of Women Voters), which was renamed League of Japanese Women in 1950. In 1953, she was elected to the Diet, and she was elected five times to the House of Councillors. She campaigned against prostitution (1957) and founded an institute for developing women's political awareness. Defeated in the 1971 election, she was reelected in 1980.

Ichikawa Jun. Contemporary movie director, maker of intimist films showing modern relationships among family members, such as *Pancakes* (1993).

Ichikawa Kansai. Poet (Kōkoshirō, 1749–1820) and Confucianist scholar, born in Kōzuke province. Director of the Confucianist bureaucrats' school Shōheizaka Gakumonjo in Edo from 1785 to 1790, he then entered the service of the Toyama estate. His two sons, Ichikawa Beian and Ichikawa Shōin, became famous, the first as a calligrapher, the second as a painter.

Ichikawa Kon. Movie director, born 1915 in Ise, known mainly for his anti-war documentaries. His best-known movies (some written in collaboration with his wife, Wada Natto) are *Pūsan* (Mr. Pū, a comedy, 1953), *Okuman chōja* (A Millionaire, 1954), *Biruma no tategoto* (Burma's Harp, 1956), *Enjō* (Fire, 1958, an adaptation of a short story by Mishima Yukio), *Kagi* (The Key, 1959, based on a novel by Tanizaki Jun'ichirō), *Bonchi* (The Sin, 1960), *Hakai* (The Outcast, 1961), *Seishun* (Youth, 1968), and *Matatabi* (The Vagabonds, 1973). He also made a film on the 1964 Tokyo Olympic Games (1965).

Ichikawa Masamochi. Writer (1753–1830), who is known mainly for his popular *kibyōshi* books.

Ichikawa Sadanji. Family of Kabuki actors:

Ichikawa Sadanji I (1842–1904), born in Osaka, considered one of the three greatest actors of the Meiji era.

Ichikawa Sadanji II (1880–1940), Ichikawa Sadanji I's eldest son. He traveled in Europe; when he returned, he created a troupe called Jiyū Gekijō (Free Theater) in collaboration with Osanai Kaoru, to perform adaptations of European plays (by Ibsen and Gorky) and modern Japanese plays (by Mori Ōgai, among others). He also wrote plays for the "new Kabuki" *(shin Kabuki)*.

Ichikawa Sadanji III (1898–1964), adopted by the family in 1952. He specialized in romantic leads *(nimaime)* and women *(onnagata)*.

Ichikawa Sadanji IV (b. 1940), Ichikawa Sadanji III's son, specializing in roles of traitors *(katakiyaku)* and heroes. He took the name Sadanji only in 1979.

Ichikawa Shōichi. Politician (1892–1945), born in Yamaguchi prefecture. At first a journalist, he joined the Communist party in 1923 and edited the party's newspaper, *Sekki* (whose name was later changed to *Akahata*). He represented Japan at the sixth congress of the Comintern in Moscow in 1928, but was arrested the following year and sentenced to life in prison. He died in prison shortly before the end of the Second World War.

Ichikawa Utaemon. Movie actor, born 1907 in Kagawa prefecture. At first a Kabuki actor, he started his screen career in silent films in 1925 and was a popular actor until 1960, after which he appeared only occasionally in films.

Ichiko. Priestess-shamanesses who were said to have the ability to communicate with the spirits of the dead. They used a human skull and a bow *(azusa-yumi)* whose cord they strummed to summon the spirits and enter a trance. They recited invocations, Buddhist or Shinto. Some *ichiko* were men who used the same procedures. *Ichiko* are mentioned very early in literature, notably in the *Makura no sōshi* and *Eiga monogatari*, among others. *See* AZUSA-MIKO, MIKO.

Ichimegasa. Hat worn since at least the Heian period in harsher climates. *Ichimegasa* had a wide brim and a very high crown *(koji)*. Women often added a veil to hide their faces and as protection against dust. This travel hat (which may owe its name to the fact that women used it in the markets) was generally woven of salvia *(Carex)* fibers.

Ichimokuren. One-eyed dragon venerated in Ise province. He was said to have married Benzi-ten (Benten-sama), who rendered him harmless. He is invoked mainly to bring rain. *See* RYŪ.

Ichimonji-ha. Blacksmiths' school in Bizen province, founded by artisans mainly from Fukuoka and working in the *chōji-midare* style. They engraved their names on the tangs of the swords they forged, preceded by the character *ichi* ("one"), whence the name of their school. The best artisans from this workshop at the beginning of the Kamakura period were Norimune, Yoshioka, and Katayama. *See also* BIZEN-MONO.

• **Ichimonji Sukezane.** *See* SUKEZANE.

Ichimura Sanjirō. Scholar (1864–1947) born in Ibaraki prefecture, and professor at the University of Tokyo starting in 1905. He is best known for his research on the history of East Asian cultures, published in *Tōyōshi tō* (Detailed History of Eastern Asia, 4 vols., 1939–50).

Ichimura-za. One of the three largest Kabuki theaters in Edo, founded in 1604 by Murayama Matsaburō as the Murayama-za. The actor Ichimura Uzaemon bought and renamed it. It was then directed by Ichimura Uzaemon's successors until 1932, when it was destroyed by fire. The best-known actor-directors of the theater were:

Ichimura Uzaemon VIII (1692–1762), *onnagata, tachiyaku* (hero), and traitor *(katakiyaku)* roles.

Ichimura Uzaemon IX (1725–85), mainly a dancer *(shosagoto)*.

Ichimura Uzaemon XII (1812–51), *wagoto* roles.

Ichimura Uzaemon XIII (1844–1903), also known as Onoe Kikugorō V.

Ichimura Uzaemon XIV, also called Bandō Kakitsu.

Ichimura Uzaemon XV (1874–1945), who took the name Ichimura Kakitsu VI in 1893.

Ichimura Uzaemon XVI (1905–52), who also used the name Ichimura Kakitsu VII: *onnagata* and *wagoto* roles.

Ichimura Uzaemon XVII (b. 1916), who used the name Bandō Hokosaburō VII until 1955.

Ichinengi. Doctrine of the Jōdo-shū according to which a single recitation of the *nembutsu* could bring the faithful to be reborn in the "Pure Land" of Amida Buddha. This doctrine, supported by Hōnen's disciple Kōsai (1163–1247), among others, went against that of the *tanen*, according to which it was necessary to recite the *nembutsu* every day of one's life in order to be reborn in the Western Paradise. However, Shinran's (1173–1262) disciples felt that the term *ichinengi* applied to arriving in the faith, whereas *tanen* applied to daily recitation of the *nembutsu* in gratitude to Amida.

Ichi no Hito. "First Among Men," a title sometimes given to *kampaku* and *sesshō*. Also called Ichi no Tokoro, "First Place."

• **Ichi no Kami.** A title sometimes given to *sadaijin* and *udaijin. See* DAIJIN.

• **Ichi no Tsukasa.** A title once given to governors of Kyoto.

Ichinomiya. City in Aichi prefecture (central Honshu) northwest of Nagoya, which developed around the Masumida shrine during the Edo period. It has many wool-spinning mills. *Pop.*: 250,000.

Ichi no Miya. Name given to the main Shinto shrine in a province.

• Name also once given to a crown prince.

Ichinomiya Nagatsune. Well-known engraver (1722–86) from Kyoto.

Ichi-no-Tani. Naval base of the Taira (Heike) clan on the north shore of the Inland Sea, not far from Shimonoseki, which was conquered in 1185 by the Minamoto (Genji) clan after a hard battle during which Minamoto no Yoshitsune distinguished himself.

• *Ichi-no-Tani futabagunki.* Kabuki play in five acts, in the *jidai-mono* genre, created in 1751 and based on an episode from the *Heike monogatari* relating the Battle of Ichi-no-Tani.

Ichinyo Kannon. One of the 33 forms (Sanjūsan Ōgeshin) of Kannon Bosatsu, portrayed sitting in "royal ease" (*Skt.*: Lalitāsana) on a cloud.

Ichiō. Painter (Kanō Jūnō, Jūgō; *mei:* Kyūzō; *gō:* Ichiō, 1550–1616) of the Kanō school, serving the Hōjō family in Odawara.

Ichirakutai. Painter (active between 1797 and 1800) of ukiyo-e prints, disciple of Eishi (Hosoda). He portrayed mainly courtesans *(bijin)* in Utamaro's style.

Ichiri-zuka. Tumuli placed on the sides of routes to mark each *ri* (3,927 m during Oda Nobunaga's time). They were made by raising the land by about 3 m and planting trees on the mound. Distances were counted starting from the Nihombashi in Edo.

Ichiyō Kannon. One of the 33 forms (Sanjūsan Ōgeshin) of Kannon Bosatsu (Avalokiteshvara), portrayed sitting or standing on a lotus leaf floating on the ocean.

Ichō. Deciduous tree *(Gingko biloba),* brought to Japan from central China, whose origins go back to the Mesozoic era. It can grow to a height of more than 30 m, and its foliage turns golden in the fall. Its leaves are shaped like an open fan. It blossoms in April. Pollen from the flowers of the male tree is transported by the wind to the flowers of the female tree, which are fecund in the fall. The *ichō* forms fruits called *ginnan* that are considered a delicacy by gourmets. This very decorative tree was imported to Europe in the eighteenth century. It was studied in Japan by botanist Hirase Sakugorō.

Ida-ten. Buddhist divinity of uncertain origin, perhaps a Japanese assimilation of Veda (*Chin.*: Weituo) created in China in the twelfth century and adopted in Japan as a protector of the monasteries. He is sometimes portrayed as a young boy mounted on a winged wheel (like Hermes). Venerated mainly in Zen communities, he presides over prayers and helps calm the senses.

Iden. In ancient Japan, rice paddies given to nobles (*see* I) of the first five ranks, and to princes (the latter's paddies were called *honden*). These rice paddies were not considered inheritable assets and were subjected to real-estate tax. Some of the *iden* were used to put together the first private estates (*shōen*). *See also* IFU, KŌDEN.

Ide Nobumichi. Painter, born 1912 in Kumamoto prefecture. He studied at Tokyo Bijutsu Gakkō (Tokyo School of Fine Arts) and painted in oil in Western style. After the Second World War, he was on the panel of judges for the Nitten exhibition and visited Europe in 1955 and 1956. In 1967, he received the Japan Art Academy (Nihon Geijutsu-in) Prize; he was elected a member of the Academy in 1969. In 1974, he was appointed general director of the Nitten.

Idera kofun. Funerary tumulus in Kumamoto prefecture, consisting of an open path leading to a vaulted lava chamber in Mt. Aso that was once divided into three compartments. The vault of the *kofun* was decorated with red-and-white paintings, and its walls were adorned with drawings portraying *chokkomon*, "ladders," and circles.

Idojiri iseki. Archeological site near Fujimi (Nagano prefecture) where a museum displays the finds made at many other sites at the foot of Mt. Yatsugatake from the Middle Jōmon (Chūki) period. *See also* TOGARISHI.

Ie. Term for a fireplace, a household, sometimes a family, comprising not just all members related by blood but "customers" and domestics as well. It is the social basis of every community.

• **Iemochi.** General term for all *chōnin* (bourgeois) families owning a house and land in a town, and thus required to pay a special tax on urban properties analogous to the *nengu* for rural properties. The *iemochi* were also forced to participate in some corvées and were responsible for organizing and running the neighborhoods (*machikata*) in which they lived. Called *ienushi* in Osaka.

• **Iemoto.** Term for a family line of artists who transmit styles and traditions through heredity. It is somewhat analogous to a "school," except that one could not belong to an *iemoto* unless one was a member of the family (natural or adopted). Each *iemoto* comprised a "grand master," called Iemoto, and his students or disciples. This master exerted total authority over the members of his school. When he felt that they were worthy, he gave them a sort of license (*menkyō*) allowing them to teach in their turn. The *iemoto* system, which went back to the seventeenth century, involved almost all artistic genres, including classical ones such as Noh and dance, the tea ceremony (*chanoyu*), the art of bonsai, and most traditional sports. But it applied neither to puppet theaters (*see* BUNRAKU) nor to Kabuki. The system endures today, mainly for Noh, Kyōgen, and ikebana, as well as for classical dances (*buyō*). Some Kabuki actors recently tried to revive the old *iemoto* system for their art. Also sometimes called Fujima.

• **Ie no Hikari.** "Light of the Hearth." A monthly magazine founded in 1925 to popularize the agricultural-development movement. Its circulation topped 1 million before the Second World War and is now around 1.25 million. Its content is quite varied and addressed both to women and to farmers.

• **Ie-no-ko to rōtō.** From the ninth to the twelfth century, warriors who were hired by noble families to protect them and who were the direct ancestors of the samurai of the Kamakura period. Also called *ie-no-ko rōjū, ie-no-ko shojū*, with a few minor differences as to their degree of dependence on their "boss." They were called *hikan* in the Muromachi period.

Iezusu-kai. "Society of Jesus." The Jesuits arrived in Kagoshima with Francis Xavier in 1549 and were very active until Christianity was banned by the Tokugawa shogun. *See* JESUITS.

Ifu. In the old administrative system, fees paid by some households to certain bureaucrats. In the tenth century, for example, the first five ranks of nobility had the right to the revenues from 800 to 200 households (in descending order); others, from 300 to 100 households, depending on their grade. Women of equal rank received half these amounts. This remuneration system was abolished in the late Heian period. *See* I, IDEN.

Ifukube Akira. Contemporary musician and composer, born 1914 in Kushiro. A student of Alexander Tcherepnin, he composed a great number of ballets, symphonies, and concertos inspired mainly by Ainu and northern Honshu folklore.

Ifukyū. Japanese name of a Chinese painter (Yi Fujiu, mid-seventeenth century) from Zhejiang, who arrived in Nagasaki as a merchant in 1720 and who often made trips to China on business. A lover of painting, he worked in the Southern Song style (Nanga). Ike no Taiga was probably influenced by his work. He sometimes signed his paintings with the Chinese name Xinye. *See* UNSHITSU.

Iga. Former province, now Mie prefecture. It was in this province that the secret tradition of the *ninja* was born. The Iga peasants, very independent by nature, revolted against Oda Nobunaga, who was able to defeat them in 1581 thanks to his artillery. To resist the attacks of the daimyo, the warrior-peasants' leaders, hiding in the mountains, developed the *ninja* techniques. Tokugawa Ieyasu used them as mercenaries, thus perpetuating, almost in spite of himself, the *ninja* warrior tradition (also called Iga-*mono*). *See* NINJA.

• **Iga-yaki.** Type of ceramics specific to the Iga region (and its "capital," Ueno), produced mainly starting in 1600 for the tea ceremony *(chanoyu),* under the aegis of Furuta Oribe. Iga-*yaki* pieces are made of a mixture of two types of clay mixed using fine gravel. They are fired numerous times at about 1500°C (a temperature attained after 30 hours) in a pinewood fire whose smoke provides a sort of natural glaze. Production in these kilns stopped in the late eighteenth century, but was started again in 1937 by the potter Kikuyama Taneo. *See* SHIGA-RAKI-YAKI.

Igai Keisho. Confucianist scholar (Gempaku; *gō:* Bunkei, Kibun, 1761–1845), born in Kyoto. He opened his own school *(juku)* in Kyoto, then taught in various estates, notably at Izushi, Toyooka, and Tzu. He studied mainly the Chinese classics.

Igakusho (Igakujo). School for Western medicine *(igaku)* founded in Edo in 1858 by Itō Gemboku and other physicians familiar with "Dutch science" *(rangaku),* to teach about and administer anti-smallpox vaccinations. This school diversified its medical education and became the Faculty of Medicine at the University of Tokyo. Another, older medical school, called Igaku-kan, had been founded in Edo in 1765 by Taki Genkō under the name Saijū-kan. *See* OGATA KŌAN.

Igarakuri. Technique for casting large bronze statues, imported from Korea or China in the eighth century. It consisted of using the lost-wax method to cast horizontal sections of the statue and then assembled the sections with a tenon-and-mortise system planned for in the casting. The large statue of the Daibutsu in the Tōdai-ji in Nara was made using this method in 749. Also called *iguri.*

Igarashi-ryū. School of lacquerers specializing in *maki-e,* created by Igarashi Shinsai and Kōami Dōchō during shogun Ashikaga Yoshimasa's rule.

I Gyōmatsu. Japanese name of a Chinese sculptor (Yi Xingmo, d. 1260) who came from China of the Song dynasty to Kamakura and helped reconstruct the Tōdai-ji in Nara. He sculpted stone lions *(kara-shishi)* and lanterns, as well as many other religious objects for the temple, introducing to Japan techniques of Chinese stone sculpting in the Song style.

Iha Fuyū. Ethnologist (1876–1947) who studied the peoples of Okinawa and their language. Born in Naha (Okinawa), he studied at the universities of Kyoto and Tokyo, then in Okinawa, and he converted to Christianity. He was also the founder and first director of the large Okinawa prefectural library (more than 5,000 books on Okinawa). In 1924, he left that position and settled in Tokyo, where he conducted further research on the poetry, literature, religion, and language of Okinawa. He published a number of books on these subjects, including a dictionary of spoken language in Okinawa. His works were published as *Iha Fuyū zen-shū* in 1974–76 (11 vols.). Also known as Iba Fuyū.

Ihai. Rectangular wooden plaques, plain or lacquered, on which are inscribed the names of a family's deceased members. The plaque is placed on the family altar *(kamidana* or *butsudan)* to symbolize the presence of those who are no longer alive. The posthumous name of the deceased *(hōmyō)* is generally added to the personal name. There are several types of *ihai*: the *no-ihai*, in unpainted wood, is placed at the bedside of the deceased by his or her heir; the *tera-ihai* is a more luxurious plaque placed at the Buddhist temple; the *ihai* kept by the family is the *uchi-ihai*. It seems that this custom was imported from China to Japan in the Kamakura period, brought perhaps by Chan (Zen) monks. It became widespread only during the Edo period, when everyone was required to register at a Buddhist temple. Warriors' families used a special plaque called *rei-hai*, designed to receive prayers addressed to the deceased so that his spirit would rest. The word *ihai* is derived from confusion with the word *iwai*, "celebration."

Iha kaizuka. Prehistoric site in Iha, in the town of Ishikawa, in Okinawa, consisting of a deposit of shells *(kaizuka, kjökken-mödding)* that contained objects contemporary with the Late Jōmon period (2000–1000 BC). This deposit, about 0.6 m thick, was excavated in 1920, and flat-bottomed pottery and stone and bone tools were uncovered.

Ihara Saikaku. *See* SAIKAKU IHARA.

Ihō. Court apparel indicating the ranks of nobles and courtiers of imperial Japan, in use after the promulgation of the Taihō Code in 701. These costumes were distinguished by color: blue and yellow for the emperor, yellow and scarlet for princes. The first and second ranks were designated by dark purple, the third rank by light purple, the fifth by red, the sixth by dark green, the seventh by light green, the eighth by dark blue. The ninth, tenth, eleventh, and twelfth ranks wore light blue. However, these rankings by color were subject to variations according to the emperor's whims. Also called I no Hō. *See* HŌ, I, SOKUTAI.

Iida. Town in Nagano prefecture, castle town *(jōka-machi)* in the Edo period, on the shores of the Tenryū-gawa river. Its plum trees and orchards were famous. *Pop.*: 80,000.

• **Iida Jiken.** Aborted coup d'état attempted by the Jiyū Minken Undō (Freedom and People's Rights Movement) and members of the Kōdō Kyōkai (Justice Society) and the Aikoku Seirisha (Patriotic Truth Society), led by Muramatsu Aizō. These societies had organized peasants to protest against the deflationary measures taken by Matsukata Masa-

yoshi in 1884 and help the rebels of the Chichibu Jiken. The rebels were hunted down; in December 1884, the leaders of the conspiracy were caught and imprisoned, and peace returned.

Iida Dasoku. Haiku poet (Iida Takeharu; *gō*: Sanro, 1885–1962), born in Yamanashi prefecture. He was Takahama Kyōshi's disciple and worked at the magazine *Hototogisu* in 1914. His haiku, most of which describe nature, were collected in *Sanroshū* (1932) and *Kodamashū* (1940). Also called Iida Dakotsu.

Iida Takesato. Confucianist scholar (1827–1900) and historian. He wrote a commentary on the *Nihon shoki* in 1900.

Iidaya Hachirōemon. Potter (1804–52), born in Kaga province (Ishikawa prefecture). He built the Miyamotoya kiln near Yamashiro, where he produced ceramics decorated with gold *(kinrande)* overglaze, modeled after Kutani ceramics. He emulated Chinese porcelain that was decorated with delicate designs in red and gold.

Iijima Kōichi. Modern-style poet (b. 1930).

Iimoriyama. Hill in the town of Aizu-Wakamatsu (Fukushima prefecture), famous for the monument erected there in memory of young members of the Byakkotai who were supporters of the Edo *bakufu* and committed suicide in 1868 during the Boshin Civil War. The tombs of 19 of them surround the monument.

Ii Naomasa. Warrior (1561–1602) from Tōyōmi province (Shizuoka prefecture). He entered the service of Tokugawa Ieyasu in 1575 and was made governor of the Minowa castle (Gumma prefecture), receiving an estate with a revenue of 120,000 *koku*. After the Battle of Sekigahara in 1600, he received a fief in Ōmi that raised his revenue to 180,000 *koku*.

Ii Naosuke. Statesman (Ii Kamon no Kami, 1815–60), daimyo of the Hikone estate (350,000 *koku*). Appointed *tairō* in 1858, he signed treaties with the United States (July 29, 1858), Great Britain (Aug. 26, 1858), and France (Oct. 9, 1858). He tried to reconcile the shogunate with the court, in order to keep the latter and other malcontents from forming an alliance against the shogunate, and took severe measures against samurai who supported eviction of foreigners. He was assassinated on March 24,

1860, by a *rōnin* of the Satsuma clan from Mito province (*see* SAKURADAMONGAI JIKEN). Andō Nobumasa succeeded him in his position, assisted by Kuze Hirochika, and continued his policy of appeasement.

Iinuma Yokusai. Botanist (1782–1865) and physician, born in Ise. He studied "Dutch science" *(rangaku)* in Edo under Udagawa Yōan and Ono Ranzan. He is credited with introducing Western botanical studies into *honzōgaku* (traditional pharmacology). In 1856, he wrote a 20-volume atlas of plants *(Sōmoku zusetsu)* in which he described 1,215 plants classified in Linnaeus's system.

Iitoyo Ao no Kōjo. Stateswoman (440–485), Ichinobe Oshiha no Ōji's daughter and Richū Tennō's grandmother. She governed Yamato when Seinei Tennō died in 484, because her two brothers, Oke and Ōke, had refused to take the throne. When she died, however, Oke ascended to the throne, taking the name Kensō Tennō. *Posthumous name:* Seitei Tennō.

Ii Yōhō. Actor (Ii Shinzaburō, 1871–1932), first on stage, then on screen. In 1891, he founded his own troupe, Isami Engeki, and presented a number of modern plays; with Kitamura Rokurō and Kawai Takeo, he then created a new theater school called Shimpa (New School). He also appeared in several silent films in 1928.

Iizasa Chōisai. Samurai (Iizasa Ienao, ca. 1387–ca. 1488?) who had the title Yamashiro no Kami. He created a school *(ryū)* for sword and lance fencing *(yari, sōjutsu)* in the Katori Jingū shrine (Chiba prefecture) to fulfill a vow made in his youth. He called it Tenshin Seiden Shindō-ryū (abridged to Katori Shindō-ryū), and it is now the oldest martial-arts school in Japan, outside of the Takeda family school. Iizasa Chōisai became the master-at-arms for shogun Ashikaga Yoshimasa, then retired from active life and became a Buddhist monk. His favorite weapon was the short sword, the *kodachi*.

Iizawa Tadasu. Playwright (1909–94), born in Wakayama prefecture. At first a journalist, he began his literary career in the 1930s and was noted for his humor in the Kyōgen tradition. He received the first Kishida Prize for comedy in 1950, then wrote very popular children's plays for radio and television.

Iizuka Kōji. Geographer (1906–70), born in Tokyo. He studied at the University of Tokyo, then at the Sorbonne in Paris (1932–34), and translated Vidal de la Blache's *Principes de la géographie humaine* in 1940. He wrote other books on geography, among them *Sekai to Nihon* (The World and Japan, 1955), and directed the Institute of Eastern Culture at the University of Tokyo.

Iizuka Tōyō. Lacquer artist (active between 1764 and 1772 in Edo). He made objects in *maki-e* and especially *inrō*. He signed with his *gō* Kanshōsai and Tōyō. His descendants are still using these *gō*. *See* TŌYŌ.

Ijime. Hazing rituals, often very cruel, for newcomers to Japanese schools and colleges.

Ijūin. Small town in northern Kagoshima prefecture (Kyushu), where "Satsuma" ceramics were made in 1598 by potters from Korea. This pottery is known for its beige color with decorations in red, greenish blue, and gold.
• Family of provincial leaders belonging to the Shimazu family in southern Kyushu in the thirteenth century. Their castle was in Ijūin; only a few ruins of this castle remain.

Ijūin Gorō. Admiral (b. 1852), a hero of the Sino-Japanese War (1895) and the Russo-Japanese War (1904–05).

Ikakeji. Lacquer decoration using gold and silver, invented during the Heian period. This type of decoration was called *kinji, kindame,* and *fundame* in the nineteenth century.

Ikan. Ancient court costume, similar to the *sokutai* but without a train *(kyo)* or belt *(sekitai, hira-o)*. The *hō* was attached with another sort of belt, and a fan *(ōgi* or *hiōgi)* replaced the usual *shaku*. The *hakama* (called *sashi-nuki* or *nubakama*) was wide and so long that it could be walked on. *See* IHŌ, SOKUTAI.

Ikari kazuki. Title of a Noh play: an old boatman and the spirit of Tomomori tell a wandering Buddhist monk about the deaths of the child-emperor Antoku and the warrior Tomomori, who drowned himself during the Dan no Ura by holding an anchor in his arms.

Ikaruga. Small town in Nara prefecture, site of the residence (Ikaruga no Miya) of Prince Shōtoku in the early seventh century. Near it are many old temples and monasteries, such as the Hōryū-ji, Chūgū-ji, Hōrin-ji, and Hokki-ji. *Pop.:* 25,000.

• **Ikaruga-dera.** *See* HANKYŪ-JI, HŌRYŪ-JI.

• **Ikaruga no Miya.** Prince Shōtoku's residence in Ikaruga, built in 601 (according to the *Nihon shoki*). The site was excavated in 1934. The palace was destroyed by Soga no Iruka in 643. In 739, the monk Gyōshin built part of the Hōryū-ji temple on the site of the palace, now the pavilion called Yume-dono.

Ikazuchi. Collective name for the eight *kami* of thunder in Shinto mythology: Ō-Ikazuchi, Ho-no-Ikazuchi, Kuro-Ikazuchi, Saku-Ikazuchi, Waki-Ika-zuchi, Tsuchi-Ikazuchi, Naru-Ikazuchi, and Fushi-Ikazuchi, each one symbolizing a different type of storm.

Ikebana. The art of arranging flowers to honor a divinity, or simply to decorate a room or *tokonoma*. This art, also called *ka-dō* (Way of Flowers), is probably of Buddhist origin (it has been traced back to the Indian custom of offering flowers to the gods). It developed in Japan during the Muromachi period; the custom of admiring flowers placed in a vase was older, but not codified. During the Muro-machi period, the arranging of flowers (like the ar-ranging of incense) became standardized as *tate-bana* (trained flowers), then *nage-ire* (strewn flowers), for arrangements for worship or for the tea ceremony (*chanoyu*). In the sixteenth century, the art of arranging flowers, now called *ikebana*, became more popular, and many tea masters codified into "schools" (*ryū*) the various ways of presenting flowers and branches in vases or on dishes. The oldest school, which gave rise to the Ikenobō style, was supposedly descended from an art brought from China by Ono no Imoko when he returned from a mission in 607. By the fifteenth cen-tury, a number of styles of floral arrangement were recognized. The most classical, Rikka, is said to have been codified in 1462 by Sengyō of the Ikenobō school. He presented flowers in a triangu-lar arrangement involving seven branches of twigs, the upper ends called *ryō* (summit) or *shin*; the ones to the right, *shi* (city); and those to the left, *soe* or *yō* (positive). The other branches also bore meaningful names, to the right, *in* (negative) or *mikoshi, gaku* (hill) or *uke;* to the left, *hikae* or *bi* (valley). This type of arrangement could also be defined accord-ing to the sky (top), the earth (bottom), and humans (middle). The height of the vase had to be one quar-ter the total height of the arrangement. In the eigh-teenth century, nine branches were permitted. A number of Rikka schools developed over the centu-ries, each adopting a variation of the original Rikka. In the late sixteenth century, another school, Nageire, also developed, designed mainly for ar-rangements for the tea ceremony (*chabana*), usually comprising just one flower. A new style, Shōka, was created in the late seventeenth century for the mer-chant class and *chōnin;* this simplified form of the original Rikka combined Rikka with Nageire and was sometimes known as Seika. Each school used its own terminology to note the sizes, placing, and shapes of the different branches in the *ikebana*. During the Edo period, a "scholarly" style (Bunjin-ike) also appeared that differed from traditional ar-rangements. All styles, however, obeyed the "trian-gle rule." In modern times, aesthetes created many other styles of flower arrangement, such as Mori-bana, invented by Ōhara Unshin (1861–1914), con-sisting of flowers or branches arranged in a dish, and "free style," which gave rise to various avant-garde styles, such as the Teshigahara and Sōgetsu schools. Japan now has more than 3,000 schools teaching the art of *ikebana,* and more than 20 mil-lion practitioners (most of them young women). *Ikebana* has been exported to most countries, where the Ikenobō (traditional), Sōgetsu, and Ōhara styles are most often taught. Each school is directed by an Iemoto; among the main ones are Adachi, Ikenobō, Kohara, Koryū, Ichiyoshiki, Ikenobō-Ryūsei, Ōhara Senkei, Seifuheika, Ryūsei, Saga, Seigetsu, Sekiso, Shubō, Sōgetsu, and Yama-tokadō.

Ikebe Sanzan. Journalist (Ikebe Kichitarō; *gō:* Tek-konron, 1864–1912), born in Kumamoto. Paris correspondent for the *Nihon* starting in 1892, he sent his newspaper a series of sensational articles called *Pari tsūshin* (News from Paris). When he re-turned to Japan, he edited the *Ōsaka Asahi Shim-bun,* then, in Tokyo, the *Tōkyō Asahi Shimbun* (later called the *Asahi Shimbun*), introducing serials by Futabatei Shimei and Natsume Sōseki, among others.

Ikeda. Town northeast of Osaka where, according to tradition, the craft of weaving was introduced by Chinese (or Korean) artisans in the fourth century. On Ikeda's outskirts is the Osaka International Air-port.

• Name of many clans of ancient Japan and of many daimyo of the Edo period, in Okayama in Bizen province, and in Tottori in Inaba province.

They were said to have originated with an Ikeda family that would have settled in Ikeda in the Kamakura period.

Ikeda Daisaku. Third religious leader (b. 1928) of the Sōka Gakkai, succeeding Tōda Jōsei in 1960. In 1975, he became president of Sōka Gakkai International; Hōjō Hiroshi succeeded him as president of Sōkka Gakkai in 1979. His constant activity to promote peace and disarmament gave him the opportunity to meet many heads of state. In 1983, he received the United Nations Peace Prize; in 1986, the Cup of Peace and Friendship. Many universities (in Moscow and Beijing, among others) granted him honorary degrees. He wrote many books on Buddhism from the point of view of the Nichiren sect and published his interviews with Japanese personalities such as Inoue Yasushi and with foreign notables such as Toynbee, Peccei, and Huyghes. Among his books (translated into a dozen languages) are *The Human Revolution, The Enigma of Life, Choose Life, Buddhism, The First Millennium, Buddhism: Living Philosophy,* and *Before It Is Too Late.*

Ikeda Eisen. *See* KEISAI EISEN.

Ikeda Gentarō. Lacquer artist (twelfth century) said to have created the Tsugarunuri style.

Ikeda Hayato. Statesman (1899–1965), born in Hiroshima. At first a bureaucrat in the Ministry of Finance (1925), he was elected a representative from Hiroshima in 1949. He was minister of finance in 1951–52 and 1956, and minister of trade in between. He tried to stem inflation and was active in preparing the San Francisco Peace Treaty. He was prime minister following the resignation of Kishi Nobusuke (July 1960–Nov. 1964), and one of the organizers of the 1964 Tokyo Olympic Games. He fell ill and retired, dying soon after. Sato Eisaku succeeded him. Ikeda Hayato is remembered as an honest man and an advocate of expanding Japan's industrial and trade bases.

Ikeda Kentarō. Writer (Ikeda Yutaka, 1929–79) specializing in Russian literature and translator of works by Dostoyevsky and Pushkin. He won the *Yomiuri* Prize in 1974 for his body of work.

Ikeda Kikunae. Chemical engineer (1864–1936) who "invented" Ajinomoto by extracting monosodium glutamate from *kombu* algae, and who did major research on osmotic pressure. He was ap-

pointed professor at the University of Tokyo in 1901 and professor emeritus in 1923. *See* AJINOMOTO.

Ikeda Kōun. Astronomer (Sumida Kōun, seventeenth century), author of a famous book on navigation, the *Genna kokaishō,* in 1618.

Ikeda Masuo. Painter and engraver, born 1934 in Mukden. His drypoint and roulette engravings earned him the Ministry of Education's prize in 1960, the National Museum of Modern Art's prize in 1964, and the grand prize of the Tokyo International Print Biennial in 1961, as well as prizes in Vienna and Venice (1966). As a writer, he received the Akutagawa Prize in 1977 for his collection of stories, *Eige-kai ni sasageru* (Offering to the Aegean Sea), which he adapted for the screen. His main residence is in New York.

Ikeda Mitsumasa. Daimyo (Ikeda Shintarō, 1609–82), of Okayama (Bizen province). He inherited an estate of 420,000 *koku* in Harima province, which he exchanged for estates in Ōki and Inaba worth 320,000 *koku.* He was appointed daimyo of Okayama in 1632, and his revenues stood at 315,000 *koku.* A skillful administrator, he centralized the services on his estates, but as a devoted Confucian he fought against Buddhism, having more than half the monasteries in his provinces closed and expelling most of the monks. He then forced his vassals to register in Shinto shrines. Yet he developed the educational system, creating the first estate school *(hankō),* called Hanabatake Kyōjō, which was replaced in 1666 by the Karigakkan, a college for samurai. In 1668, he made a plan to create 123 elementary schools for young peasants on his estates, but the project was abandoned by his successor, Ikeda Tsunamasa (1638–1714), because it was deemed too expensive. The existing schools were united in a single school, Shizutani-gakkō, in 1675, which operated throughout the Edo period. *See* KUMAZAWA BANZAN.

Ikeda Nagaoki. Senior bureaucrat (Ikeda Chōhatsu, Ikeda Naganobu, 1837–79) in the Edo *bakufu,* born in Edo. In 1863, he was appointed governor *(bugyō)* of Kyoto and was sent to France to negotiate the suppression of free trade in the port of Yokohama. He failed in this mission but signed the Paris Convention, which modified the 1858 treaty and gave compensation to France for the Shimonoseki incidents. He was reprimanded when he returned to Japan, but he defended his position of support for friendly relations with foreign countries by publishing a treatise on the subject, the *Kengi-sho*. He then lost his title of foreign-affairs commissioner; he was appointed commissioner of naval affairs in 1867, but soon resigned due to poor health and retired to Okayama.

Ikeda Seihin. Politician and businessman (Ikeda Shigeaki, 1867–1950), born in Yonazawa (Yamagata prefecture). After studying at Keiō University and Harvard University, he was hired by the Mitsui Bank and married the daughter of the director, Nakamigawa Hikojirō. He was director of the bank from 1909 to 1933. In 1937, he was appointed governor of the Bank of Japan; from 1937 to 1939, he was minister of trade and industry in Konoe Fumimaro's cabinet. In 1941, he became a member of the emperor's Privy Council; because of this, he was banned from all political activity in 1945.

Ikeda Suisen. Physician (Ikeda Zuisen, 1734–1816) who studied with Saimon-ge, a Chinese physician living in Japan.

Ikeda Taishin. Lacquer artist (*go:* Taishin, 1825–1903), painter, and sculptor of netsuke, born in Tokyo. He was employed by the imperial court, for which he made *maki-e. See* TAISHIN.

Ikeda Terumasa. Daimyo (1564–1613) of the Ōgaki castle (Gifu prefecture), then the Yoshida castle in Mikawa (Aichi prefecture), serving Oda Nobunaga and Toyotomi Hideyoshi. His estates had a revenue of 152,000 *koku*. As a reward for assisting Tokugawa Ieyasu in the Battle of Sekigahara in 1600, he received the Harima estate (Hyōgo prefecture), worth 520,000 *koku*, and had the castle at Himeji restored and expanded.

Ikedaya Jiken. Skirmish between samurai supporting the emperor and the Edo shogunate's police forces, the Shinsengumi, which took place near an inn called Ikedaya, near Kyoto, in July 1864. During the battle, a number of activists were killed and some 20 arrested, most from the Chōshū clan. This incited the clan to try to recapture Kyoto by force, and they fought the shogunal troops in a battle called Hamaguri Gomon Jiken. *See* KONDŌ ISAMI.

Ikeda Yōson. Painter (1896–1988) specializing in landscapes, born in Okayama prefecture. He studied Western oil-painting techniques with Matsubara Sangorō in 1912, but in 1919 began to paint in the "Japanese style" (Nihonga). He received a num-

ber of prizes awarded by the Nitten and Teiten, as well as the Japan Art Academy (Nihon Geijutsu-in) Prize in 1959, becoming a member of the Academy in 1976. He sometimes signed with the name Shōichi. He received the Order of Culture (Bunka-shō) in 1987.

Ikegai Shōtarō. Industrialist and inventor (1869–1934), born in Tokyo. In 1889, he founded a company to make machine tools, then invented a semi-diesel motor that bears his name, as well as a number of other industrial procedures that helped modernize Japanese industry.

Ikegami Hommon-ji. Buddhist temple of the Nichiren sect, located in Ikegami Honchō in Tokyo. It was built by Nichiren's disciple, Ikegami Munenaka, on the spot where Nichiren was said to have died in 1282. It was destroyed in the bombing of Tokyo during the Second World War, but the Oeshiki ceremony is still celebrated there every October 12, drawing many followers of the Nichiren sects.

Ikei Shūtoku. Buddhist monk and painter (sixteenth century), Sesshū's disciple. He also painted in the style of Chinese painter Yujian (thirteenth century).

Ikenie. Old custom of making offerings to divinities of live animals—ones either caught and then released within the walls of the shrine, or sacrificed—to obtain some favor from the *kami*, generally rain. It is also possible that, before Buddhism arrived in Japan, human beings (generally volunteers) were immolated, as the *Nihon shoki* seems to indicate.

Ikenishi Gonsui. *Haikai* poet (1650–1722), born in Nara. He lived in Tokyo and various regions of Japan before settling permanently in Kyoto in 1684. His elegant and spontaneous poems were collected in *Edo shimmichi* (New Streets of Edo, 1678) and *Miyakoburi* (Kyoto Melodies, 1690).

Ike no Gyokuran. Painter (Tokuyama Gyokuran, Ike no Machi, ca. 1728–84) in the Nanga style (Bujinga) and *waka* poet, born in Kyoto, where her grandmother, Kaji, and her mother, Yuri, were also well-known poets. She studied painting with Yanagisawa Kien and married painter and poet Ike no Taiga, whose style she emulated. She painted mainly fans, which she sometimes signed with the name Shōfū Yūka.

Ike no mokuzu. "Grass Floating on the Pond." A major novel on the history of Japan, written by Arakida Kei in 1771. This novel is in fact a complement to the *Masu kagami,* covering the period from 1333 to 1603. It has little historical value but is considered a literary monument.

Ike no Seiichirō. Botanist (1866–1943), born in Edo, who worked with Hirase Sakugorō on gymnosperm plants (*see* ICHŌ). He also did research on genetics and published his findings in *Zikken idengaku,* written in Japanese with European letters *(romaji).*

Ike no Taiga. Painter and calligrapher (Ike no Arina, Ike no Tsutomu; *mei:* Shūhei; *azana:* Taisei, Mumei; *gō:* Kashō, Kyūka-sanshō, Fokuchōsō, Gyokukai, Chikukyo, Sangakudōja, Taikadō, Taigadō, 1723–76), in Nanga style (Bunjinga), born in Kyoto. A precocious talent, when he was six years old he won a calligraphy prize at the Mampuku-ji (Zen Ōbaku sect) in Uji. About 1738, he studied with Yanagisawa Kien and Gion Nankai. His paintings were influenced by Sōtatsu, Sōrin, and both Zen and Western painters (via artists based in Nagasaki, among them a Chinese merchant and amateur painter, Yi Fujiu, *Jap.:* I Fukyū). He, in turn, taught his wife, Ike no Gyokuran. A prolific artist, he is said to have painted more than 2,000 paintings, most of them landscapes (though he painted several other subjects), on scrolls, screens, fans, and separate sheets of paper, using techniques ranging from *sumi-e* to richly colored compositions. In calligraphy, he ingeniously re-created ancient Chinese writing in an elegant, fluid style. He had a very large number of disciples.

Ikenouchi Tomojirō. Musician and composer, born 1906 in Tokyo. He went to Paris in 1928 and studied with Caussade until 1936. He composed a number of "suites" for orchestra, quartets, and Noh music. He also wrote a treatise on harmony.

Ike no Zenni. Wife (twelfth century) of Taira no Tadamori. When Minamoto no Yoshitomo was defeated in 1160, she asked her husband to spare the life of Minamoto no Yoritomo, then aged 13, and send him into exile. According to the *Azuma kagami,* when Yoritomo returned to power, he showed his gratitude by giving Ike no Zenni's son, Taira no Yorimori (1131–86), a number of estates captured from the Taira.

Ikeuchi Hiroshi. Sinologist (1878–1952), specializing in Manchu and Korean civilizations, and a professor at the University of Tokyo.

Ikezawa Natsuki. Contemporary writer, author of a long novel, *Mashiasu Giri no shikkyaku* (The Fall of Macias Giri, 1993), which received the Tanizaki Prize in 1993.

Iki. Former province, now part of Nagasaki prefecture (Kyushu).
• Sentiment among the bourgeoisie of Edo that spread to the *chōnin* in the nineteenth century. It appealed to a new aesthetic sense, imbued with sensuality, and to a sense of morals according to which one must enjoy one's luck but have contempt for money. This sentiment was somewhat analogous to *sui,* which prevailed among the merchant class in seventeenth-century Osaka.
• Former diploma attesting to a rank of nobility conferred on an individual or awarded by an ecclesiastic or other dignity.

Ikigai. "Reason for living," an expression often used in Japan to describe everything that enhances and gives value to life—a son, the lure of money, the desire for comfort, work, or fame.

Ikigami. "Living *kami.*" People revered during their lifetime as divinities, such as emperors and some Shinto religious leaders. Buddhists prefer to use the term *ikibotoke* to indicate a "living Buddha"—a monk who has attained great holiness in the course of his life. Before 1945, emperors were also called Akitsukami and Arahitogami, terms that have almost the same meaning as *ikigami.*

Iki-ningyō. Life-sized dolls made in Osaka in the seventeenth century realistically portraying certain characters, sometimes from Kabuki, arranged in historical scenes. Similar dolls made in Edo by Yasumoto Kamehachi (who also made *kiku-ningyō,* or "chrysanthemum dolls") were particularly popular during the Edo period. This word now designates mannequins in store windows.

Iki no Hakatoko. Envoy from Yamato (seventh century) to the Chinese imperial court. He went to Luoyang in 659 and was held in Chang'an until 661, then led several missions to Korea, in Paekche and Silla (Shiragi, Sinra). He helped to write the Taihō Code of 701–02 and left a diary of notes, *Iki no muraji Hakatoko no fumi,* several passages of which have survived through inclusion in the *Nihon shoki*.

Iki-nyūdō. *See* KASAI KIYOSHIGE.

Iki-shiki. Ancient ceremony of passage from one rank to another (*see* I), described in detail in *Engishiki* and *Chōya-gunasi*.

Iki-shima. Small island off Hirado (northern Kyushu) in the Sea of Genkai, some miles from the coast of Saga prefecture and part of Nagasaki prefecture. It was attacked a number of times by pirates and occupied by the Mongols in 1274 and 1281. In ancient times, it was an almost obligatory stopover for navigators between the islands of Japan and the mainland. Its volcanic soil is poor but intensively cultivated (beans, sweet potatoes, tobacco). Fishing and pearl-oyster cultivation are also common activities. Highest point: the Dakenotsuji volcano, altitude 213 m. *Area:* 134 km²; *pop.:* 50,000. *Main town:* Gōnoura.

Ikitsuki-shima. Small island northwest of the Hirado Peninsula (Kyushu), populated with Christians descended from those who revolted against the Tokugawa shogunate in 1638. Although reputed to be Buddhists for the most part, the inhabitants of the island still practice Christianity in secret *(kakure)* and are baptized with Portuguese or Spanish names. Ikitsuki-shima was linked to Hirado by a bridge in 1990.

Ikkanbari. Sculptures or objects made by applying successive layers of paper covered with lacquer to a wooden form, a technique somewhat similar to papier mâché. Also called *shitai. See* HIRAI IKKAN.

Ikkei. Painter (Shigeyoshi; *mei:* Naizen, 1599–1662) of the Kanō school, Kanō Masanobu's student, in the service of the Hōjō of Odawara. He wrote an autobiography, *Tansei jakuboku shū.*
  • Painter (Toyotomi Kiminobu; *mei:* Kuranosuke; *gō:* Ukita Ikkei, 1795–1859) of the Fukku Yamato-e school. He studied with Tosa Mitsuzane and Tanaka Totsugen. Having too openly supported restoration of the emperor, he was arrested in 1858 during the purge of the Ansei era, and he died soon after he was imprisoned. He was an excellent haiku poet and a talented calligrapher.

Ikkei Dōsan. *See* MANASE DŌSAN.

Ikki. "Single path," name used by a number of leagues of common interest. During the Nambokuchō period, the term was applied to groups of warriors organized for a battle; starting in the early fifteenth century, to insurrectional groups in general composed of revolting peasants or Buddhist monks. *See* IKKŌ-IKKI.
  → *See* FUYŌ.

Ikkō. Sculptor of netsuke (Hasegawa Ikkō, late eighteenth century).
  → *See* KANEKO KICHIZAEMON, SHINGON HASSO.

Ikkō-ikki. "League of the Single Idea." A political and religious group of followers of the Jōdo Shinshū attached to the Hongan-ji temple and also called Ikkō. Under the aegis of Rennyo, *hossu* ("abbot") of the Shin-shū, peasants from village communities in a number of provinces organized groups to oppose the local lords, most of the time using force. In the sixteenth century, the authority of the Hongan-ji was extended to most provinces in central Japan, and the military forces of the Ikkō, directed by *ji-samurai* (peasant-samurai), were in some instances able to defeat the lords who were oppressing them. In 1563, they launched a major offensive against Tokugawa Ieyasu (then known as Matsudaira), who was trying to impose taxes on them to support his war effort. It took Ieyasu six months to defeat them. They then established their headquarters in Ishiyama, near Osaka, in the Ishiyama temple, a strongly defended fortress. They continued their fight against Oda Nobunaga, who was seeking to unify the country, and he launched several campaigns against them between 1570 and 1580. In 1574, he defeated the peasants in Ise province; in 1575, those in Echizen; two years later, the Ikkō-ikki of Kii province; finally, he besieged and destroyed the Ishiyama Hongan-ji in Osaka in 1580. The revolts were called Ikkōto no Ran. *See* IKKŌ-SHŪ.

  • **Ikkō-shū.** Branch of the Jōdo Shin-shū sect founded by Shinran Shōnin in 1224, with headquarters established at the Higashi Hongan-ji in Kyoto. Also called Monto-shū. The peasants and warrior-monks of the Ikkō-ikki were also called Ikkō-shū.

Ikkōsai. Sculptor of netsuke (Saitō Ikkōsai, 1805–76) in Edo. His son, Ikkōsai II (1833–93) continued his work and studied with Hōjitsu.
  → *See* TŌUN.

Ikkyū. Painter (Okubo Kōko; *azana*: Toshio, early nineteenth century) and samurai of the Yōga school. He was one of Kōkan's students.
→ *See* SAKE.

Ikkyū Ōshō. Zen Buddhist monk (Sōjun; *gō*: Kyōunshi, Mukei, Kokukei, 1394–1481) of the Rinzai sect and painter in Kyoto. He was said to be the son of one of Go-Komatsu Tennō's concubines. A renowned poet and calligrapher, he actively participated in rebuilding the temple of the Daitoku-ji following its destruction during the Ōnin War (1467–77). An eccentric personality, he often shocked his contemporaries with his outrageous behavior. He made his home in Sakai but wandered the country propagating a Zen doctrine stripped of the affectations of the monks of the court. He wrote a large number of poems in classical Chinese, such as *Kyōun-shū* (Crazy Cloud Anthology); at least eight prose essays, most of them sermons; and some commentaries on the *Mahāprajñāpāramitāhridaya-sūtra* (Jap.: *Maka-hannya-haramita Shingyō-ge*). His calligraphy was very diversified, ranging from fluid lines to rough brush strokes. A portrait of him (in the Tokyo National Museum) was made by his disciple and friend Bokusai (Motsurin Shōtō, d. 1496). Also known as Ikkyū Sōjun.

• **Ikkyū Sōjun.** *See* IKKYŪ ŌSHŌ, JASOKU.

Ikoku nikki. "Register of Foreign Affairs." A political work about Japan's relations with foreign countries, written by the Zen monk Sūdai and his successor as abbot of the Nanzen-ji in Kyoto, Saigaku Genryō (d. 1657). It is valuable for its information on shogunal Japan's relations with Korea, the Philippines, and Siam in the seventeenth century.

• **Ikoku keigo ban'yaku.** Armed service imposed by the Kamakura *bakufu* on the warriors of northern Kyushu in order to defend the coast against a foreign invasion. It was maintained until the beginning of the Muromachi period.

• **Ikokusen Uchiharai Rei.** *See* GAIKOKUSEN UCHI-HARAI REI.

• *Ikoku torai goshuin cho.* Official list of arrivals and departures of ships with a "red seal" *(shuin-sen)* during the Edo period.

Ikoma. Town in Nara prefecture that developed during the Taishō era (1912–26) as a suburb of Osaka, at the foot of the Ikoma-yama mountains,

altitude 640 m. It is the site of the Buddhist temple of the Hōzan-ji and the tomb of the monk Gyōki in the Chikurin-ji. At the top of Ikoma-yama is the observatory of the University of Kyoto.

Ikuno. Silver mine in Hyōgo prefecture, discovered in 807 and intensively exploited until the sixteenth century by the local daimyo, then by Oda Nobunaga and Toyotomi Hideyoshi, and finally by the Tokugawa shogunate. The Meiji government brought in French engineers to improve extraction techniques. The mine was exhausted and closed in 1973.

• **Ikuno no Hen.** Riot that took place in November 1863 in the mining town of Ikuno, where more than 2,000 pro-imperial peasants and warriors of the Chōshū clan attacked the shogunal authorities, which took three days to disperse the rioters.

Ikusa no Kimi. Former title of general-in-chief, before that of *sei-i-tai-shōgun*.

Ikushima Shingorō. Famous Kabuki actor (active between 1679 and 1743) in Edo, specializing in *wakashu-gata* and *tachiyaku* roles.

Ikuta atsumori. Noh play: Atsumori's child (*see* ATSUMORI) meets his father's spirit in Ikuta.

Ikuta Chōkō. Writer and literary critic (Ikuta Kōji, 1882–1936), born in Tottori prefecture. He translated works by Nietzsche *(Thus Spake Zarathustra),* D'Annunzio *(The Triumph of Death),* and Dante *(Divine Comedy).*

• **Ikuta Kōji.** *See* IKUTA CHŌKŌ.

Ikuta-jinja. Shinto shrine in the town of Kōbe, founded, according to tradition, in the third century and dedicated in the fourteenth century to Kusunoki Masashige (d. 1335). Destroyed in 1945, it was recently rebuilt.

Ikuta-koto. *See* KOTO.

Ikutama-jinja. Shinto shrine in Osaka dedicated to the *kami* that protect Japan, Ikushima no Kami and Tarushima no Kami. At each change of emperor, special envoys were sent to announce the news to the *kami*. This ancient shrine (date of foundation unknown) holds a major festival, the Yasoshima Matsuri (Festival of the Eighty Islands), every September 9. Also called Ikukunitama-jinja.

Ikuta Seihei. *See* IKUTA SHUNGETSU.

Ikuta Shungetsu. Poet (Ikuta Seihei, 1892–1930), born in Tottori prefecture, whose poems were influenced first by Christianity, then by nihilism. He translated the poems of Heinrich Heine and wrote collections of verse—*Reikon no aki* (Autumn of the Soul, 1917), *Shōchō no ika* (The Symbol of the Cuttlefish, 1930)—and a major autobiographical account, *Aiyori tamashii* (Meeting of Minds, 1921–24).

Ikuta Yorozu. Scholar (1801–37) from Echigo province (Niigata prefecture), who opened a school in Kashiwazaki to educate young peasants. During a severe famine in July 1837, in despair over not obtaining aid from local bureaucrats, he gathered some peasants and attacked the bureaucrats. His rebellion was disastrous and he committed suicide.

Imado-yaki. Type of porcelain produced at Imari, Bizen province, in the sixteenth century. *See* ISE GORŌDAYŪ SHŌZUI.

Imagawa. Family of warriors and lords of the Muromachi period, related to the Ashikaga, taking their name from the Imagawa estate in Mikawa province (Aichi prefecture). Their estates were invaded by Takeda Shingen and captured by Tokugawa Ieyasu. The family's last members then served the Edo shogunate and passed down by heredity the position of master of ceremonies for the court *(kōke).* A provincial code, *Imagawa kana mokuroku,* was promulgated in 1526 by Imagawa Ujichika (ca. 1473–1526) when he was lord of the Suruga and Tōtōmi estates (Shizuoka prefecture). This code, one of the first of its type *(bunkokuhō),* was widely imitated by other families that established estates, notably the Takeda. Originally comprising 31 or 33 articles, it was complemented by Imagawa Yoshimoto, who added 21 more in 1553.

• **Imagawa Sadayo.** General (b. 1326), son of Imagawa Norikuni, in the service of Ashikaga Yoshiakira as leader of the Samurai-dokoro (Board of Retainers) and *shugo* of Yamashiro province. When the shogun died, Imagawa became a Buddhist monk with the name Ryōshun; nevertheless, he then put down the revolt in Kyushu, and he was appointed *tandai* of Kyushu and *shugo* of Aki province. For the Ashikaga, he established complete control over the lords of Kyushu and battled pirates *(wakō).* Late in his life, he was forced to retire after taking part in a plot against the shogun. How he died is not known. A talented poet, he wrote a number of *renga* and some literary works, such as *Imagawa-sōshi* and *Kyūshū kasen-ki,* as well as *Imagawa-jō,* a manual for students in *terakoya* schools. He is also credited with writing *Nan Taiheiki,* a critique of the *Taiheiki,* and a description of his family's traditions. Also called Imagawa Ryōshun.

• **Imagawa Ujizane.** Warrior (1538–1614) serving Tokugawa Ieyasu. He became a Buddhist monk with the name Sōkan.

• **Imagawa Yoshimoto.** Daimyo (1519–60) of Suruga and Tōtōmi, Imagawa Ujichika's (ca. 1473–1526) third son. When his older brother, Imagawa Ujiteru, died in 1536, he left the monastery where he was studying to contest his other brother's right to inherit the estate. Then, in an alliance with the Takeda family of Kai province (Yamanashi prefecture), he attacked the Hōjō of Odawara, but he clashed with Oda Nobunaga in Owari province (Aichi prefecture) and was killed in the Battle of Okehazama. In 1553, he had complemented the code of laws promulgated by his father in 1526.

Imai Masayuki. Ceramist, born 1930 in Takehara (Hiroshima prefecture). His work has earned a number of prizes, notably in Vallauris, France, in 1974, and Hiroshima prefecture's Culture Prize in 1991. He also had exhibitions in the United States (1985) and in Paris (1994).

Imai Sōkun. Merchant in Sakai (Imai Hiratsuna, Imai Kanehisa; *gō:* Sōkun, 1552–1627), Imai Sōkyū's son. He was employed by Toyotomi Hideyoshi and became one of his advisers. When Hideyoshi died, Imai Sōkun worked for Tokugawa Ieyasu, who gave him an estate worth 1,300 *koku* and appointed him grand master of the tea ceremony *(chanoyu).*

Imai Sōkyū. Merchant in Sakai (1520–93). He became a master of the tea ceremony *(chanoyu)* after studying under Takeno Jōō, whose daughter he married. Oda Nobunaga then took him into his service. He continued his business activities, however, specializing in producing firearms and ammunition. He then entered the service of Toyotomi Hideyoshi, for whom he became, with Sen no Rikyū and Tsuda Sōkyū, one of the three great masters of the *chanoyu.* He was Imai Sōkun's father.

Imai Tadashi. Movie director (1912–91), born in Tokyo. In 1950, he began to produce movies influenced by Italian neo-realism and Marxist ideology: *Dokkoi ikiteru* (We Are Alive, 1951), *Himeyuri no to* (The Tower of Lilies, 1953), *Nigori-e* (Troubled Waters, 1954), *Aisureba koso* (Because I Love You, 1955), *Mahiruno ankoku* (Shadows in Full Light, 1956), *Kome* (Rice, 1957), *Jun'ai monogatari* (Story of a Pure Love, 1957), *Ani imoto* (Brother and Sister, 1976), and others.

Imai Toshimitsu. Painter in informal modern style, born 1928 in Kyoto. He studied and worked in Paris starting in 1952 and was part of the Paris School. He had many exhibitions in Europe, the United States, and Japan.

Imaizumi Imaemon. Family of ceramists in Arita founded in Nabeshima during the Edo period. The members of the family specialize in painting on porcelain. The last of this family, Imaiumi Imaemon XIII, born 1926 in Aritamachi (Saga prefecture), is noted for his painted porcelain (*see* NABESHIMA) and was designated a Living National Treasure in 1989.

Ima-kagami. "Mirror of the Present." Historical work written in kana about 1170 by Nakayama Tadachika (1131–95) or Minamoto no Michichika (1149–1200); sometimes also attributed to Fujiwara no Tametsune. It has 10 parts, devoted, respectively, to emperors, the Fujiwara, the Genji, and various events between 1025 and 1170. It contains mainly anecdotes that have little historical value but that are of literary interest. The stories related by the author are supposed to be the memories of a very old woman. This work is sometimes called the *Ko-kagami* (Little Mirror) to distinguish it from another of the same genre, the *Ō-kagami* (Large Mirror), written a little earlier.

Imamura Akitsune. Physicist (1870–1948), famous for his studies of the mechanisms behind earthquakes and volcanoes.

Imamura Arao. Physician (1887–1967), born in Nara prefecture. He was noted for his studies on the anti-tuberculosis vaccine B.C.G. and his personal crusade to spread its use throughout Japan to stem tuberculosis epidemics. He was elected president of the University of Osaka and made a member of the Academy of Japan in 1951.

Imamura Chishō. Mathematician (Imamura Tomoaki, seventeenth century), author of an authoritative work for its time, *Jugairoku* (1639).

Imamura Eisei. Scholar (1671–1736) in Nagasaki, interpreter from Dutch. He served as interpreter for the Italian missionary Giovanni Battista Sidotti, and translated various Dutch works on botany, equitation, and veterinary science upon order of the shogunate.

Imamura Shikō. Painter (Imamura Jusaburō, 1880–1916), born in Yokohama. He studied in Tokyo under the direction of Matsumoto Fūko, Yasuda Yukihiro, and Okakura Kakuzō. He experimented with various styles and techniques, then traveled in China, Korea, and India in 1914. When he returned, his exhibitions drew the attention of art circles and critics because of the new aspects he was bringing to Japanese visual art in his skillful combining of Nanga style with European realism.

Imamura Shōhei. Movie director, born 1926 in Tokyo. After the Second World War, he studied Western history at Waseda University, then became interested in theater and turned to acting. He was an assistant of Ōzu Yasujirō before hiring on with Nikkatsu. His movies are notable for their spontaneity and his search for the unusual and strange in daily life: *The Insect-Woman* (1963), *Desire to Kill* (1964), *The Deep Desire of the Gods* (1968), *Ningen jōhatsu* (A Man Disappears, 1967), *Nippon sengo-shi: madamu omboro no seiktasu* (History of Japan After the War Told by a Bar Hostess, 1970), *Karayuki-san* (Karayuki the Prostitute, 1973), *Fukushū suru wa ware ni ari* (Vengeance Shall Be Mine, 1979), *Eejanaika* (1980), *Narayama bushi-ko* (The Ballad of Narayama), which won the gold medal at Cannes in 1983, and others. He also produced television documentaries, notably in Southeast Asia.

Imanishi Kinji. Biology professor (1902–92), born in Kyoto. A devoted ethnologist, he became famous for his research on segregation due to habitat, and for his scientific expeditions to Mongolia (1938–39) and the Himalayas (1952). He also studied the behavior of primates, particularly Japanese monkeys *(Macaca fuscata),* and wrote many works on his research. He received the Order of Culture (Bunka-shō) in 1979.

Imanishi Ryū. Historian (1875–1932), who studied ancient Korean history and Korea's relations with Japan. He wrote an important book, *Shiragi-shi kenkyū* (Studies on the History of Paekche).

Imari. Town in Saga prefecture (Kyushu) on the Bay of Imari, former export port for ceramics produced there and in Arita. Imari now produces ceramics called Okawachi-*yaki*. Pop.: 60,000.

• **Imari-yaki.** Ceramics of the type made in Arita, bearing a floral decoration (or imitations of brocade designs) in blue under a glaze, or in "iron red" and gold on a white background. The first porcelain produced in Imari (called *ko*-Imari) was exported to Europe by the Dutch East India Company starting in 1646 and inspired certain decorations on Delft and Meissen porcelain. *See* ARITA-YAKI.

Imayō. Popular songs with a very simple text, often funny or satirical in style, written in the eleventh and twelfth centuries and sung by dancers performing in streets and villages. These songs originated in the Buddhist *wasan*. They were replaced in the thirteenth and fourteenth centuries by songs called *saibara*. There are many texts of *imayō* songs in *Ryōjin hishō*, published in 1177. They were generally composed of four lines of seven and five syllables. *See* RŌ-EI, SAIBARA, WASAN.

Imbe. During the Yamato period (fourth–seventh century), a family or guild (*see* BE) in which the members were responsible, through heredity, for religious affairs (Shinto), in competition with the Nakatomi family. The Imbe family's influence diminished in the eighth century with the emergence of the Nakatomi-Fujiwara family. One of the best-known members of the Imbe family, Imbe Hironari, wrote a work called *Kogo shūi* (Seeds of Ancient Stories, 807) to show that his family had at least as many rights as the rival Nakatomi. Also called Imibe, Imube.
• Former guild of artisans specifically responsible for making and keeping objects of Shinto worship. It was directed by Imbe no Obito. Sometimes written Imube, Imube no Obito. *See* AME NO FUTO-TAMA, AWA-JINJA, BE.

• **Imbe-yaki.** *See* BIZEN-YAKI.

Imi. "Interdiction," a Chinese Taoist rite consisting of abstaining from an action that is contrary to certain natural laws or likely to enrage a divinity. There were once numerous *imi*, or taboos, such as the *ara-imi*, which required that one abstain, for a certain period *(mono-imi),* from eating meat, attending a burial, enjoying oneself, or making music.

There were also, especially during the Heian period, many bans of direction *(kata-imi)* to obey the prescriptions of the Ommyōdō (Theories of Yin and Yang, In and Yō). Under these bans, on certain days, one had to abstain from going in a particular direction, visiting people who were in a state of ritual impurity, and so on. Some trade guilds had taboo words *(imi-kotoba)* that were never uttered to avoid calamity. However, there were certain ways of bypassing these bans, by practices called *kata-tagae*.

• **Imi-kotoba.** *See* IMI.

• **Imi-kura.** In Shinto shrines, a special room for storage of cult instruments and objects.
→ *See* YUME.

Imoji. Term for artisans *(be)* specializing in metal casting. Large organizations, such as the large Buddhist monasteries, had *imoji* working for them but also used the services of itinerant artisans. The *imoji* formed guilds *(za)* that monopolized the manufacture and sale of weapons and agricultural tools to major lords. Some production centers were very prosperous during the Edo period, and their factories formed the basis for Japanese industrial development in the Meiji era.

Imoseyama onna teikin. "Female Education on Mt. Imo and Mt. Se." A *jōruri* play in five acts for puppets *(ayatsuri-ningyō)* of the Takemoto-za in Osaka. Written by Chikamatsu Hanji in 1771, it dealt with the rivalry between the Soga and Fujiwara clans in the seventh century. This play was adapted for Kabuki.

Im-pa (In-pa). Buddhist school of sculpture based in Kyoto, whose workshops were set up at Shichijō (founded by Injo) and Rokujō Madenokōji (founded by Inchō). The sculptors of this school followed the style inaugurated by Jōchō in the eleventh century and incorporated into their names the kanji character for "In," thus distinguishing themselves from the En school (*see* EMPA) founded by Inkaku and Inson in the twelfth century.

Impan. Sculptor in the early Kamakura period, member of the Impa workshop, perhaps Inson's disciple. He worked on the halo on the large Buddha of the Tōdai-ji in Nara, and received the title Hōin in 1215 in compensation for his work on the pagoda of the Hosshō-ji temple in Kyoto. He also sculpted the Jū-chimen Kannon at the Hōshaku-ji in Kyoto, which is the only surviving work in Impa style.

Impo. Painter (Miyazaki Ki; *azana:* Shijō; *mei:* Shijō; *gō:* Jōnoshin, 1717–74), a founder of the Bunjinga (Nanga) school. A Confucian scholar, he painted mainly bamboo.

In. Part of a Buddhist monastery. By extension, title of a nun retired to the respective monastery and added to her name (eleventh century).

• Retired emperor and, by extension, his palace. His court was then called In-no-Chō. Also called Hōō, Jōkō. *See* INSEI.

• Japanese pronunciation of the Chinese term *Yin*, the principle both opposed and complementary to *Yang* (*Jap.:* Yō). *See* OMMYŌDŌ.

• Ritual gesture of the hands, corresponding to the Sanskrit mudra in Buddhist terminology. This term also means "seal." Also called *in-zō.*

• Granaries built by the government in certain regions, notably on Kyushu.

→ *See* INGA.

Inaba. Former province, now part of Tottori prefecture.

• **Inaba Masanari.** *See* KASUGA NO TSUBONE.

Inaba Masayasu. Daimyo (1640–84) of Mino province, appointed *wakadoshiyori* in Edo in 1682. He directed irrigation projects in Settsu and Kawachi provinces and was given a fiefdom worth 12,000 *koku* as remuneration by Tokugawa Tsunayoshi. It is not known why he assassinated *tairō* Hotta Masatoshi in the shogun's palace in Edo; he was then killed on the spot by his fellow disciples (or, according to some sources, condemned to death the same year). *See* HOTTA MASATOSHI.

Inada-hime. Mythical princess who, in Shinto legends, was the daughter of the *kami* Ashinazuchi and Tenazuchi. About to be devoured by the dragon Yamato no Orochi, she was saved by Susanoo. He then married her and moved her to Izumo. She was Onamuji's (Ōkuni-nushi no Mikoto) mother. Also sometimes called Kushinada-hime, Kushi Inada-hime.

Inada Ryōkichi. Physician (Inada Ryūki-chi, 1874–1950), born in Aichi. After studying in Tokyo and Germany, he taught medicine. In 1915, in collaboration with Ido Yutaka, he discovered *Leptospira icterohaemorrhagiae,* responsible for Weil's disease. He received the Imperial Prize (Gakushi-in Onshi-shō) of the Japan Academy (Nihon Gakushi-in) in 1916 and the Order of Culture (Bunka-shō) in 1944.

Inadome Ichimu. Engineer (Inadome Naoie; *gō:* Sukenao, 1552–1611), firearms expert. He founded an artillery school bearing his name, Inadome-ryū. Working for Hosokawa Tadaoki, then Tokugawa Ieyasu, he led an adventurous life until he donned the monk's habit with the name Ichimu. Ieyasu appointed him artillery master of the Edo *bakufu.*

• **Inadome-naoie.** *See* INADOME ICHIMU.

Inagaki Hiroshi. Movie director (1905–80). He began his career with a silent film, *Tenka taiheiki* (Peace on Earth) in 1928. Among his other movies, the best known are *Muhōmatsu no isshō* (Life of Matsu the Bandit, 1943, remade in 1958), *Miyamoto musashi* (1954–56, three episodes), and *Chūshingura* (1962). Most of the movies he directed before the Second World War have been lost. *Tomishima matsugōro den,* made in 1939, won the Venice Festival's grand prize in 1958. He also received the Academy of Japan's prize for *Miyamoto musashi.*

Inagaki Taruho. Writer and poet (1900–77), born near Osaka. After a brief career as a painter, he turned to literature, publishing his first novel, *Issen ichibyō monogatari* (The Story of a Thousand and One Seconds) in 1923, which established him as an innovative modern writer. An alcoholic, he left Tokyo for Kansai; when he returned to the capital in 1936, he produced very little because of his poor health. However, he began to write again after the Second World War, publishing *Miroku* (Maitreya, 1946) and *Karera* (Them, 1946–47), in which he dealt with problems of homosexuality, then numerous essays, most of them on the same subject. In 1969, he received the literary prize from Shinchōsha Publishing House for *Shōnen'ai no bigaku* (Aesthetics of Pederasty). He continued his literary elegy to homosexuality with *Hikōki yarōtachi* (The Flying Boys, 1969), *Vuanira to Manira* (Vanilla and Manila, 1969), *Raito kyōdai ni hajimaru* (Encounter with the Wright Brothers, 1970), and *Kinshoku no anus* (The Purple Anus, 1972). His books were a mitigated success, praised by some and despised by others, but they left no one indifferent. He died in Kyoto.

Inagaki Toshijirō. Fabric designer (1902–63) born in Kyoto, specializing in stencil designs on painted fabrics dyed in *yūzen* technique, portraying Buddhist divinities and subjects inspired by the classics of Japanese literature. He was declared a Living National Treasure in 1962.

Inagi. Former title of a senior bureaucrat responsible for collecting taxes paid in cereals and rice.
→ *See* HASSEI, YAKUSA NO KABANE.

Inahe no Mikoto. In Shinto legends, brother of Jimmu Tennō who became king of Shiragi (Silla) in Korea. Perhaps the same person as Hyukkusa (*Kor.:* Hyög-gö-se, 57 BC–4 AD), founder of the Pak dynasty of the kingdom of Silla (Sin-ra).

Inamura Sampaku. Physician (1758–1811) and proponent of "Dutch science" *(rangaku),* born in Matsui. In 1796, he wrote, in collaboration with colleagues Ishii Tsuneemon and Yasuoka Genshin, a Dutch–Japanese dictionary known as *Harumawage* (or sometimes *Edo Haruma*), modeled after François Halma's (1653–1722) Dutch–French dictionary. This dictionary contained about 80,000 translated words. Only about 30 copies were printed.

Inari. Shinto *kami* of cereals, then of foundries and trade, as well as guardian of houses *(yashikigami).* Its traditional messenger was the fox *(kitsune),* which came to be confused with the *kami* itself. According to the *Kojiki* and the *Nihon shoki,* Inari was none other than the *kami* Uka no Mitama (Uganomitama, Toyouke-hime, Toyuke no Kami) of the Ise outside shrine *(gekū),* also called Ukemochi no Kami, Miketsu Kami. A great number of shrines were built in Japan in honor of Inari, whose cult, created by the immigrant Korean Hata family, went back to 711. "Inari" was likely a condensed form of the word *inanari,* meaning "growing rice." It was probably originally a *kami* of the fields *(Ta no kami)* and became a titular divinity *(ujigami)* of the Hata clan, which had settled in Fushimi, near Kyoto. Soon, Inari became so popular that Buddhism caught hold of it and the monk Kūkai made it a protective *kami* of the Tō-ji temple. It is perhaps the same as Dakini Ten, worship of which was popularized in the seventeenth century. It is portrayed as an old person (man or woman). However, the Shinto divinity came to be called Inari Myōjin to distinguish it from the syncretic *kami* (called *gongen*) Inari Ten.

• **Inari-jinja.** Shinto shrine built in Fushimi, a suburb of Kyoto, dedicated to worship of Inari. Founded in 711, according to tradition, it was rebuilt in the Momoyama style in 1499. It is notable for its effigies of foxes *(kitsune)* and its innumerable red-painted torii offered by the faithful, which are placed in lines to form covered walkways.

• **Inari-kyō.** Shinto subsect of the Shinto-Taikyō, founded in 1950 by Shigemasa Mizunobu (1867–1953). About 5,000 followers.

Inari-san. *See* JŌMYŌ-JI.

• **Inari-shinkyō.** Shinto sect founded in 1950 by Nakamura Yukikazu (b. 1907).

Inariyama kofun. Funerary tumulus located in Gyōda, Saitama prefecture, and located within a group of 10 *kofun* called Sakitama. It is of the "keyhole" type *(zempō-kōen)* and is 120 m long. In it were found, in 1968, an earthenware sarcophagus, bronze small bells and mirrors, various jewels, pieces of harnesses, iron armor, and an iron épée whose blade has 115 Chinese characters in gold inlay, which date the weapon to 471 or 531 and attribute its manufacture to Yūryaku Tennō (late fifth century). Fragments of *haniwa* were also uncovered. The front part of the *kofun* was destroyed in 1938. The location of this *kofun* shows that Yamato's influence extended far into eastern Honshu.

Ina Tadatsugu. Senior bureaucrat (1550–1610), born in Mikawa province (Aichi prefecture). He served Tokugawa Ieyasu, who appointed him Kantō *gundai* (intendant of the eight provinces of the Kantō) in 1590. Although he owned an estate worth more than 10,000 *koku,* he did not have the rank of daimyo. He improved agriculture in Kanto by developing irrigation and putting fallow land into production; he also conducted a land survey that enabled him to set taxes. His initiatives were imitated and his descendants retained the title of Kantō *gundai* until 1792.

Inatomi Ichinu. Engineer and artilleryman (Inatomi Sukenao, Inatomi Naoie, Iga no Kami, 1552–1611), born near Kyoto. He became a Buddhist monk with the name Ichimusai. He studied with his grandfather, Inatomi Naotoki, founder of the family line of casters of Inatomi cannons, serving Tokugawa Ieyasu. Inatomi Ichinu was ordered to guard Hosokawa Gracia; when she was killed on her husband's order, he fled, but he was later pardoned. His techniques were recorded in two works, *Ichiryū ippen no sho* and *Gokui.*

Inawashiro Kensai. Poet (1452–1510), born in Aizu. When he was very young, he wrote *renga* that were so highly regarded that he was appointed master of the poetry bureau of the Kitano shrine in Kyoto in 1489, succeeding Sōgi. He left a collection of *renga (Renga entoku shō)* dedicated to the daimyo Ouchi Masahiro, and three works on the theory of *renga, Shinkei sōzu teikin* (1488), *Renga honshiki*, and *Yōjinshō*.

Inayama Yokinori. Historian (eighteenth century), student of Hanawa Hokiichi (1746–1821). He discovered the 10 lost volumes of the *Nihon kōki.*

Incense. Although the Japanese use few fragrances in general, reserving them for Buddhist worship, they often enjoy incense (imported); mainly in the Heian period, gatherings were organized for the appreciation of various incenses. *See* GANKŌ, GENJI-KŌ, KASHA, KŌDŌ, KŌGŌ.

Industry. The industrial revolution in Japan dates from the mid-nineteenth century, with the Meiji Restoration and investments by the state. Strongly influenced by the needs of military expansionism, it was oriented mainly toward heavy industry (ship-building, weapons) and textiles (many small companies). This led to the formation of conglomerates *(zaibatsu)* combining industrial, commercial, and financial concerns.

Because of a crucial lack of fuel and mining resources, Japanese industry had to import almost all the raw materials it used. It was thus based almost exclusively on manufacture and export of processed products, since the domestic market was rapidly saturated.

After the Second World War, Japan had a spectacular recovery and became a preponderant force in the world. Heavy industries and chemical and textile industries (cottons, synthetic fabrics) developed most quickly, thanks to the immense combines established on the coasts and near mining centers (Kita-Kyushu). After the 1970s, the market for heavy-industry products (ships, "turnkey" plants, etc.) slowed, and large steel complexes were found to pollute too much, so Japanese industry turned increasingly toward advanced products (vehicles, computers, electronics, telecommunications, aerospace, biotechnology, new materials, etc.), areas in which its research and engineering capacities are excellent. *See* ECONOMY, JAPAN (STATISTICS), MINES, MITI.

Inga. "Cause and effect," a basic concept of Buddhist belief, explaining the mechanism of rewards *(Skt.: karma)* according to which a cause *(in)* engenders a direct effect *(ka)*. Birth, living, and death are effects of acts or thoughts in a past life, and the cycle of births and rebirths *(Skt.: Samsāra; Jap.: Rinne)* continues without end unless the believer, through purity of thought, "extinguishes" the results of the past and enters Nirvana (absence of desires that govern life). A famous illuminated scroll, *Kako-genzai inga-kyō*, dating from the eighth century, illustrates this theory.

• *Inga monogatari.* Buddhist moralistic novel, in the *kanazōshi* genre, written by Suzuki Shōzō (Shōsan, 1579–1655) about 1640.

Ingen Ryūki. Japanese name of a Chinese monk (Lin Longqi, Yinyuan Longqi, 1592–1673) of the Chan sect who went to Japan in 1654 and introduced the Ōbaku-shū sect to the Mampuku-ji temple, which he had built near Uji. He became famous for his sermons and received the title of Daikō Fushō Kokushi from the emperor. He also introduced the Ming-era style of calligraphy to Japan.

Ingo. Slang specific to certain social groups or organizations. There are many forms of spoken slang, generally based on abridged, inverted, or other forms of words. Japanese students, like students in other countries, use various sorts of slang, often in fads. Many slang words have passed into the regular language. *See also* DIALECTS, RYŪKŌGO.

Ingyō Tennō. Nineteenth emperor (Prince Ō-Asatuma Wakugo no Sukune, 374<412–53>, according to traditional dates), Nintoku Tennō's fourth son and Richū Tennō's and Hanzei (Hanshō) Tennō's brother; he succeeded the latter. His sons were Ankō Tennō and Yūryaku Tennō. It seems that Korea (or at least one part thereof) paid a duty to the Yamato during his reign, according to the *Nihon shoki.*

Injiuchi. Game once played by children, usually featured during the festival for boys (May 5), in which children divided into two groups threw stones at each other. Starting in the late Heian period, it was adopted by men in the *bushi* class (warriors), but because it was becoming more and more violent, it was banned by the Edo shogunate. It disappeared almost completely during the Meiji era. Also called Ishigassen, Inji.

Ink (sumi). China ink, considered one of the four treasures of the literate, is generally made in sticks, often artistically decorated. To use it, the calligrapher or artist rubs one end of the stick for a long time on an "ink stone" *(suzuri)* on which he has poured a few drops of water from a sort of cruet *(mizu-ire),* producing a more or less fluid ink that is more or less dark and permits washes in an infinite number of shades. *See* SUIBOKU, SUMI, SUMIZURI-E, SUZURI.

Inka. Diploma or certificate given by a Zen or Buddhist master to one of his disciples attesting to the fact that he has attained satori (full enlightenment) or ending the cycle of his spiritual training. Also called *inkajō.*

Inkaku. Sculptor of Buddhist images (twelfth century) in Kyoto, Injo's son, belonging to the Shichijō school. He emulated the style of Jōchō (d. 1057).

Inkin. Method of decorating fabrics imported from China around the thirteenth century, consisting of application of gold leaf with lacquer.
→ *See* DŌ-BACHI.

Inkyo. Custom according to which a person retired voluntarily from his activities to leave his professional, material, or cultural heritage to his heirs or successors. People who retired from public life were generally older or heads of families who wanted to withdraw from the world. Very often they retired to a Buddhist monastery or led a religious life while remaining with their families. *See also* INSEI.

Innai Ginzan. Silver mine in the Okachi district of Akita prefecture, discovered in 1607. It produced more than three tons of silver in the nineteenth century, reaching maximum productivity in the late nineteenth century; it is still in operation today.

Inoe no Naishinnō. Daughter (717–75) of Shōmu Tennō and the high priestess of the Ise shrines. She married Prince Shirakabe no Ōji (Kōnin Tennō) and became empress.

Inō Jakusui. Physician and chemist (Inō Nariyoshi; *gō*: Akinobu, Seisui, Jakusui, 1655–1715). He studied the traditional pharmacopoeia *(honzōgaku)* and the properties of two thousand plants cited in the Chinese *Bencao gangmu.* He recorded the results of his research in *Bussan mokuroku* (Catalogue of Products, 1692) and *Shokumotsu denshikan* (Origin of Foods). In 1709, upon Arai Hakuseki's request, he wrote an explanation of *Shijing,* the *Shikyō shōshiki,* and began to write *Shobutsu ruisan,* a treatise on medicinal herbs that was completed by his disciples in the eighteenth century.

Inokuma Gen'ichirō. Western-style painter, born 1902 in Takamatsu, Fujishima Takeji's student. He visited Henri Matisse in Nice when he went to France in 1938–39, and later he had works in major international exhibitions, notably at the Willard Gallery in New York, where he lived from 1966 to 1969.

Inomata Tsunao. Economist (1889–1942) born in Niigata prefecture. He studied in the United States from 1915 to 1921, then learned Marxist theory under Katayama Sen. In 1922, he helped found the Japanese Communist party and the magazine *Rōnō.* His books were among the most important prewar works in economics: *Kin'yu shihon ron* (Theory of Financial Capital, 1925), *Kin no keizaigaku* (Gold-Based Economy, 1932), and *Nōson mondai nyūmon* (Introduction to Agricultural Problems, 1937). Arrested many times by the authorities for his political opinions, he died in prison.

Inoshishi. General term for boars. Their flesh was once highly prized by samurai and peasants, who also called them *yama-kujira* ("whales of the mountains") because their fat was used for the same purposes as whale blubber. The popular custom has it that simply invoking their name causes snakes to flee. The boar replaces the twelfth animal, the pig, in East Asian zodiac signs. Abridged to I. *See* JŪNISHI.

Inō Tadataka. Geographer and historian (Inō Tadayoshi, Inō Chūkei, 1745–1818), born in Kazusa province (Chiba prefecture). After studying with astronomer Takahashi Yoshitoki, he researched European astronomical theories and mathematics, revised the calendar on the order of the shogunate, and made a detailed survey of Hokkaido in 1800. He traveled the length and breadth of Honshu and drew an accurate map of its coasts. To accomplish this enormous task, he invented a number of instruments for measuring terrestrial distances from the positions of the stars and set the zero meridian at Kyoto. His disciples completed his map *(Dai Nihon enkai jissoku zenzu)* and his observations *(Dai Nihon enkai jissokuroku)* in 1821. Some of his maps were copied by Franz von Siebold, who published them in Europe. A museum is devoted to him in Sawara, Chiba prefecture. *See also* AOYAGI TANENOBU.

Inoue. Traditional Noh dance school in Kyoto, founded by Inoue Harima no Jō (1632–85), a *jōruri* composer. *See* IEMOTO.
→ *See* KŌNIN TENNŌ.

• **Inoue Akira.** *See* INOUE NISSHŌ.

Inoue Enryō. Philosopher (1858–1919) born in Niigata, who created an institute (Tetsugakukan) of Buddhist philosophy in 1887, based on the teachings of the Jōdo Shinshū sect. In his teachings, he attempted to forge a synthesis between Eastern philosophers (Buddha, Confucius) and Western philosophers (Socrates and Kant, among others). He wrote many books expounding his own philosophy.

Inoue Hisashi. Writer and playwright (Uchiyama Hisashi), born 1934 in Yamagata prefecture. He wrote a number of plays, including the successful comedies *Omoteura gennai kaeru gassen* (1971) and *Chin'yaku seisho* (1973). His novel *Tegusari shinjū* (Double Suicide in Handcuffs, 1972) won the Naoki Prize in the year it was published. Among his other works are a novel, *Dōgen no bōken* (The Adventures of Dōgen), published in 1971.

Inoue Junnosuke. Politician and financier (1869–1932), governor of the Bank of Japan in 1919. He was minister of finance three times, in 1923 (Yamamoto Gonnohyoe's cabinet), and in 1929–30 (Hamaguchi Osachi's cabinet) and 1931 (Wakatsuki Reijirō's cabinet), when Japan underwent a severe economic crisis, due mainly to the international situation, known as "the Shōwa Depression." Inoue Junnosuke was denounced by the military during the Manchuria crisis for having tried to reduce military expenditures, and he was assassinated by Onuma Shō (b. 1911), a member of the ultranationalist terrorist organization Ketsumeidan. Takahashi Korekiyo succeeded him as minister of finance.

Inoue Kaoru. Statesman (1835–1915) and samurai of the Chōshū clan, born in Yamaguchi. A friend of Itō Hirobumi, he accompanied him to Great Britain in 1863, but returned to Japan the following year to negotiate a cease-fire between the Chōshū and Western nations whose ships had been attacked. A resolute supporter of restoration of the emperor, he played an important role in the formation of the alliance between the Chōshū and the Satsuma to fight against the Edo shogunate, and he purchased weapons for the cause in England. After the Meiji Restoration, Inoue was appointed a member of the Genrō, then held various ministerial positions: foreign affairs from 1881 to 1887, agriculture, commerce, and interior. He was sent to Korea as a plenipotentiary representative in 1896, but Korea rejected his reform proposals. He was then named a special adviser to the emperor, who ennobled him in 1885 and 1907.

Inoue Katsunosuke. Financier and statesman (1861–1929), Inoue Kaoru's nephew. He was ambassador to Berlin (1906–08), Chile (1910–13), and Great Britain (1913–16), then director of the Manchurian railroad.

Inoue Kiyonao. Senior bureaucrat (1809–67) in the Edo shogunate, born in Edo, appointed *bugyō* of the port of Shimoda, which had recently been opened to international traffic. He signed the first trade treaty with Townsend Harris in 1858, then was *bugyō* of foreign affairs and, in 1862, *kanjō-bugyō* (commissioner of finances).

Inoue Kowashi. Politician (*gō*: Goin, 1843–95), born in Kumamoto fief. He accompanied Etō Shimpei to Germany and France; in 1881, he and colleagues Iwakura Tomomoi and Itō Hirobumi were asked to write Japan's Constitution. He asked for assistance from German jurist Karl Friedrich Hermann Rœsler and wrote a number of books (*Daikō-ryō, Sairyō, Ikensho*) to justify the measures to be taken. He was appointed head of the Bureau of Legislation, then general secretary of the emperor's Privy Council. He helped write the regulations of the imperial house and the Imperial Rescript on Education (see KYŌIKU CHOKUGO), and was minister of education in Itō Hirobumi's second cabinet in 1883.

Inoue Michiyasu. *Waka* poet (Matsuoka Michiyasu; *gō*: Nantensō, 1866–1941) and physician, named Adviser to the Court (Kyūchū Komonkan) in 1920. His brother, Yanagita Kunio, published his books. He conducted poetic studies of the *Man'yōshū*, including *Man'yōshū shinkō* (New Treatise on the *Man'yōshū*), and on the *fudoki* (*Harima fudoki shinkō*), and wrote a major historical work, *Jōdai rekishi chiri shinkō* (New Views on the Geography and History of Antiquity).

Inoue Mitsuharu. Writer, born 1926 in Manchuria. A Marxist, he wrote in the magazine *Shin Nihon Bungaku,* founded in 1945, but was expelled from the Communist party in 1950 for having written a novel, *Kakarezaru isshō,* in which he criticized the party's bureaucracy. In 1956, he founded the magazine *Gendai Hihyō,* in which he published in serial form his novel *Kyokō no kuren* (published in 1960), on living conditions in Japan during the Second World War.

Inoue Nisshō. Activist (Inoue Akira, 1886–1967), born in Gumma prefecture. He served as a military spy in China and Manchuria. Becoming a fervent

Nichiren follower in 1921, he took the family name Nisshō and founded an agriculture school; after the incidents in Manchuria in 1931, he created a terrorist group, the Ketsumeidan (League of Blood), inspired by Tōyama Mitsuru and Ōkawa Shūmei, and directed plots to assassinate Inukai Tsuyoshi, Dan Takuma, and Inoue Junnosuke. He surrendered to the authorities and was sentenced to life in prison in 1934, but he was freed in 1940 during the general amnesty. After 1945, he once again took up his ultranationalist activities, but he no longer had a following.

Inoue Ryōkai. Admiral (Inoue Yōshika, 1845–1929) from 1911 to his death. In 1881, he was one of the first Japanese students to go to the United States. He was ennobled in 1907.

Inoue Ryōsai. Potter (17th century), founder of the Seto kilns near Kyoto and creator of a type of porcelain named after him, Ryōsai-*yaki*.

Inoue Tetsujirō. Writer and philosopher (1855–1944), born in Fukuoka. He went to Germany to finish his studies, then was a philosophy professor at the University of Tokyo. He introduced Germanic idealism into Japanese literature *(shintai-shi)* and attempted a synthesis of Confucian, Buddhist, and Western philosophies, though he was fiercely opposed to Christianity. A fervent nationalist, he recommended devotion to emperor and country. Among his very numerous books are *Nihon rinri ihen* (1901–03), *Nihon kogakuha no tetsugaku* (1931), *Nihon yōmei gakuha no tetsugaku* (1932), *Nihon sushi gakuha no tetsugaku* (1933), and *Bushidō shōsho*. His writings were collected in *Inoue hakase kōronshū* (1894–95) and *Sonken rombunshū* (1899–1901).

Inoue Tsuyoki. Politician (*gō:* Bokudō, 1855–1932). At first a journalist, he became a bureaucrat in the Institute of Statistics and helped found the Rikken Kaishintō (Constitutional Reform party) with Ōkuma Shigenobu in 1882, then left for Korea to cover events for a number of newspapers. He was appointed minister of education in Ōkuma's first cabinet, succeeding Ozaki Yukio, but he resigned. In 1910, he founded a political party called Rikken Kokumintō (Constitutional Nationalist party), which he dissolved in 1922 and replaced with a "Reform Club" (Kakushin Kurabu) that was merged with the Rikken Seiyūkai (Friends of Constitutional Government party) in 1925. In 1931, he was appointed prime minister, replacing Waka-

tsuki, but was assassinated a few months later by a group of navy officers.

Inoue Yasushi. Writer (1907–91), born in Asahikawa, Hokkaido. He studied in Tokyo, then at the University of Kyoto, earning a degree in art and history. After working as a journalist for the *Mainichi Shimbun* and as a soldier in China in 1937, he devoted himself to literature. In 1949, he won the Akutagawa Prize for his novel *Tōgyū* (Bullfight, 1947), published in the magazine *Bungakukai*. His fluid, recitative style gained him public recognition, and his works were adapted for the screen. With his lyrical voice and respect for facts, he excelled at historical novellas and novels. Among his best-known works are *Tsuya no kyaku* (Guest at the Funeral Vigil, 1949), *Kuroi ushio* (Black Tide, 1950), *Hyōeki* (The Ice Wall, 1950, Academy of Arts Prize), *Yoru no koe* (A Voice in the Night, 1952), *Iiki no hito* (The Man from Foreign Lands, 1953), *Tempyō no iraka* (The Tile Roof in Tempyō, 1957, prize of the Ministry of Education), *Asunarō monogatari* (The Story of Asunarō, 1958), *Sanada gunki* (The Move of the Sanada, 1958), *Tonkō* (Dunhuang, Roads of the Desert, 1959), *Rōran* (Loulan, 1959), *Aoki okami* (The Blue Wolf, 1960), *Fūtō* (The Storm, 1963), *Saiiki monogatari* (Voyage to Beyond Samarkand, 1971), *Go-Shirakawa In* (1972), *Waga haha no ki* (Story of My Mother, 1975), and *Oroshakoku suimutan* (Russian Tales by a Drunkard). Many of Inoue Yasushi's works were translated into Western languages. Most of his novels were adapted for the screen by Masumura Yasuzō, Mori Kazuo, Inagaki Hiroshi, and others. He received the forty-second Noma Prize for his novel *Kōshi* (Confucius) in 1989. In 1993, an annual literary and cultural prize was created in his name; the first recipient was Ozawa Seiji.

Inrō. Small box with several compartments, for holding a seal and vermilion paste or medications. *Inrō* began to be used in the seventeenth century; they were usually attached to the belt by a string ending in a netsuke. They were often very elaborate, made of wood and lacquered by specialized artisans, with the different compartments linked by a cord that was difficult to adjust. Only men wore them. Two families, the Kajikawa and the Koma, produced the most beautiful examples. *Inrō* were rarely signed, however. They were in widespread use in the eighteenth century but gradually fell out of favor during the Meiji era, when the Japanese adopted Western clothing. *See* NETSUKE, OJIME.

Insei. "Retired government," a government system instituted by emperors who had retired to monasteries *(in)* to counterbalance the influence of the Fujiwara regents and the rising *bushi* class. Emperor Shirakawa inaugurated the system in 1087, and it remained in force until the Kamakura *bakufu* came to power in 1192. The retired emperors governed on behalf of the titular emperors and had their own courts (In no Chō) and administrations. Because of the frequency of abdications in the twelfth century, there were sometimes several retired emperors ruling at the same time; the oldest took the title of Hon'in. Holding this title (and truly governing the country) were emperors Shirakawa (*In* from 1087 to 1129), Toba (*In* from 1129 to 1156), and Go-Shirakawa (*In* from 1158 to 1192). The retired government imitated somewhat the various "familial governments," such as those founded by the Fujiwara, the Taira, and the Minamoto. The retired emperors held the title In, Hōō, or Jōkō. Orders issued by the *Insei* were called Inzen or Hōsho. *See also* HŌ-Ō, IN, INKYO.

In-sempō. In traditional Japanese music, a musical mode using the notes re, mi flat, sol, la, si flat, and re. *See* MUSIC, RYŌ-SEMPŌ.

Inson. Buddhist sculptor and monk (1120–98), who worked in Kyoto monasteries and produced a number of Buddhist statues. A member of Shichijō's studio (the Im-pa school), he helped with restoration of many temples in Nara, notably the Tōdai-ji and the Kōfuku-ji, and received the high distinctions of Hokkyō (1154) and Hōin (1183). He was Inkaku's son (or student). Currently, there is no known work that can be attributed to him with certainty.

Intai-ga. "Academic" style of painting whose standards were defined by the Imperial Academy of Painting (Ga-in). It was popular between the fourteenth and sixteenth centuries.

Inten. Abridgment of Nihon Bijutsu-in Tenrankai (Annual Exhibition of the Japan Fine Arts Academy), which, since it was inaugurated in 1898, has annually displayed the works of Nihonga-style painters. From 1914 to 1920, a section devoted to Yōga (Western influenced) painting was added; until 1961, there was a section reserved for sculpture. The Inten, a product of the Tokyo Bijutsu Gakkō (Tokyo School of Fine Arts), was founded by some painters of the school, among them Okakura Tenshin, Hashimoto Gahō, Yokoyama Taikan,

Shimomura Kanzan, and Hishida Shunshō. Its selections have become so broad that it bears only a distant relationship to the goals of its founders, but it has preserved the spirit of the Japan Fine Arts Academy. Its exhibitions are still very popular. *See* BUNTEN, NITTEN.

Inugami no Mitasuki. First Japanese ambassador to the Chinese Sui court in 614 and the Tang court in 630. He returned to Japan, with Chinese envoy Gao Biaoren, at the same time as Buddhist monks Ryōun and Min were returning from Korea. *See* KENTŌSHI.

Inu hariko. Popular talisman representing a young dog, said to protect the birth and health of children, used mainly during the Edo period. It originated with another, quite similar talisman, Inubako (dog-box). It was also customary to write the kanji character for dog *(inu)* on the forehead of children to keep them from falling ill. Today it is a toy, sometimes displayed during the festival for little girls (Hina Matsuri).

Inukai Tsuyoshi. Statesman (Ki Inukai, 1855–1932), born in Okayama prefecture. At first a journalist, he helped to found the liberal Rikken Kaishintō (Constitutional Reform party) in 1882. He was elected to the House of Representatives in 1890 as a member of the Shimpotō and the Kenseitō, and was reelected 18 times. He was appointed minister of education (Ōkuma's cabinet) in 1898, and continued his opposition to the clans' influence in the government. In 1923, he was minister of communications (Yamamoto Gonnohyōe's second cabinet), and in 1924 he held the same position in Katō Takaaki's cabinet. He was then elected to the House of Representatives as a member of the Rikken Seiyūkai. Appointed prime minister in December 1931, succeeding Wakatsuki Reijirō, he tried to resolve the conflict with China (as a friend of Sun Yatsen) and appointed Araki Sadao minister of war. He was assassinated by extremist officers (Koga and Yamagishi) on May 15, 1932. Admiral Saitō Makoto succeeded him as prime minister, retaining Araki as minister of war. An indefatigable orator and honest administrator, Inukai Tsuyoshi ceaselessly fought for parliamentary democracy and good relations with China.

Inu-kubō. "Shogun of Dogs," a nickname for shogun Tokugawa Tsunayoshi because of his inordinate love for dogs, which sometimes approached fanaticism. *See* SHŌRUI AWAREMI NO REI, TOKUGAWA TSUNAYOSHI.

Inu-oi-mono. "Dog hunt," sport practiced by samurai starting in the Kamakura period and consisting of shooting buttoned arrows at dogs. Within a large, roped-off circular area was another circle about 15 m in diameter in which dogs were released. Samurai on horseback galloped outside the larger circle, shooting at the dogs and trying to knock them over. This sport disappeared, along with the samurai class, in 1868. The game originated in China, where a popular Taoist divinity called Zhang Xian personified the art of archery (through confusion with the term *zhanggong,* "archery"), as he was represented holding hands with a child and hunting the heavenly dog with a bow and arrow. *See also* KASAGAKE, YABUSAME.

Inu tsukuba-shū. Collection of *haikai* and *renga* poems compiled by Yamazaki Sōkan (1465–ca. 1553) in 1514, 1523, or 1539 under the title *Shinsen inu tsukuba-shū.* It was the second *haikai* anthology (the first was the *Chikuba kyōginshū* in 1499) and the larger of the two.

Inuyama. Town in Aichi prefecture (central Honshu) on the Kiso-gawa river, and satellite city of Nagoya. It has a castle, built in 1440 by the daimyo of Chiba, that is the oldest standing military structure in Japan, famous for its wooden donjon with a circular balcony, also called Hakutei no Jō. The town also has a "Meiji village," featuring houses from all parts of Japan during the Meiji era. *Pop.:* 65,000.

In-yō gogyō-setsu. "Theory of Yin, Yang, and the five elements," imported from China, where it was developed before the Han era in the *Liji* (Canon of Confucian Rites), between the sixth and eighth century, via Korea. This theory, combined with concepts of the *mikkyō* (Esoteric Buddhism) and Shinto, gave rise to the Ommyōdō (Way of Yin and Yang), which, starting in the middle of the Heian period, strongly influenced the beliefs and behaviors of the aristocracy and then of the general population. *See* OMMYŌDŌ.

Iori kamban. A type of theater poster that bears the names of Kabuki actors playing in the advertised play, hanging at the entrance to the theater.

Ippen Shōnin. Buddhist monk (Yugyō Shōnin, Ōichi Michihide, Chishin, 1239–89) of the Tendai sect, born in Iyo (Ehimi prefecture, Shikoku). After studying at the Enryaku-ji monastery on Mt. Hiei, he went to Dazaifu, in Kyushu, where he converted to Buddhism of the Pure Land (Jōdo) in 1251. He abandoned his religious status after his father died in 1263 and married. Returning to the Shitennō-ji in Osaka in 1274, he decided to become itinerant in order to spread faith in Amida and encourage the people to recite the *nembutsu.* He founded the Ji(-shū) sect in 1276, gaining many disciples who "danced the *nembutsu*" in the manner of Kūya Shōnin. However, his teachings aroused strong resistance from the monks of the Tendai. Ippen returned to Shikoku, then went to Awaji and Hyōgo. He is said to have died in ecstasy, asking that no funeral rites be held for him. *Posthumous name:* Enshō-daishi. Also called Yugyō Shōnin ("the holy traveler").

• *Ippen hijiri-e.* An *emakimono* dating from the late thirteenth century (ca. 1298), illustrating legends relating to Ippen's sermons and voyages, and attributed to En-i (Hōgan). This 12-scroll *emakimono* has calligraphy by Shōkai, one of Ippen's disciples. Also called *Ippen Shōnin eden.* The scrolls are housed in the Kangikō-ji temple in Kyoto and the Tokyo National Museum.

Ippitsusai Bunchō. *See* BUNCHŌ.

Diagram of the donjon of the Inuyama castle

Ippō. Painter (Mori Takayuki; *azana:* Shikō; *mei:* Bumpei, 1798–1871) of the Maruyuma school. He was Tetsuzan's son and student in Osaka.

Ippon. "One point." In judo and other martial arts, the point awarding a victory.
• Also, a term (written with different characters) that designates a long thing or object.
→ *See* GEISHA.

Ippōsai. Famous sculptor of netsuke (Ōuchi Ippōsai, Jitsumin, 1829–95), Hōjitsu's student in Edo.

Irako Seihaku. Physician and poet (Irako Teruzō, 1877–1946), born in Tottori. He became known mainly as a writer of *waka* poems in modern style. His collection *Kujaku-bune* (The Peacock Boat), published in 1906 and 1929, was very highly regarded.

• **Irako Teruzō.** *See* IRAKO SEIHAKU.

Iratsuko, Iratsume (Hiratsu-hime). In ancient Japan, titles for young noblemen and noblewomen.
→ *See* MIYAKO NO IRATSUME.

Iriai. Collective peasant exploitation of fallow land, forests, and the ocean in order to produce consumer goods such as fodder, wood, various fruits, mushrooms, building stones, medicinal plants, and so on. Custom generally set the modalities of operating these public estates. The *iriai* disappeared after the Second World War, when most noncultivated lands were purchased by private companies.

Irie Garyū. Mathematician (nineteenth–twentieth century). In 1891, he made considerable improvements to the *soroban* (abacus), reducing the number of beads on the bottom from five to four and on the top from two to one.

Irie Takako. Film actress (Tōbōjō Hideko; 1911–95), born in Tokyo. She worked under director Mizoguchi Kenji, then separated from him and made many movies with other directors. Relatively unknown despite her great beauty, she was nicknamed Neko ("the cat").

Irimoya. In traditional architecture, a type of roof comprising four long slopes and two gables—in fact, a normal roof with four hips *(yosemune)* topped with a saddleback roof *(kirizuma)*. The Kondō of the Hōryū-ji has one of the oldest examples of this type of roof.

Irino Yoshirō. Composer (1921–80). He received the first prize at the 1962 Salzburg Opera Festival for *Aya no tsuzumi* (Aya's Tambourine).

Iro-e. Metal inlay on objects in a different metal, obtained by casting. Also applied to certain ceramic decorations painted on a glaze. *See also* AKAE.

Iro-gonomi. Said of a person who has "great sensitivity" and "a great comprehension of human nature." The expression was used in this sense mainly in the Middle Ages; today, it is used to describe a person who enjoys sensual pleasures.

Iroha. Poem *(uta)* written with the 47 characters of the kana syllabary (leaving out the *n'*) by an unknown author, although tradition attributes it to the Buddhist monk Kūkai. It appeared in literary sources only in the eleventh century. Its syllables are often used to enumerate lists, as we might use letters of the alphabet, but its use is fading in favor of the *Gojūon-zu* (50 syllabic sounds). It goes as follows:

I-ro-ha-ni-ho-he-to-chi-ri-nu-ru
(W)o-wa-ka(ga)-yo-ta-re-so(zo)-tsu-ne
Na-ra-mu-u-(w)i-no-o-ku-ya-ma
Ke-fu-ko-e-te-a-sa-ki-yu-me
Mi-shi-(w)e-hi-mo-se-su(n').

This means, approximately:

The blossoms disperse and fall.
In our world, what lasts forever?
Rather, let us cross the distant mountains of illusion
and no longer dream vainly or give in to intoxication.

• *Iroha-awase. See* IROHA-GARUTA.

• *Iroha bunko.* Collection of biographies in 52 volumes based on the story of the 47 *rōnin* (*see* AKŌ-GISHI), written by Tamenaga Shunsui I (Echizenya Chōjirō, 1789?–1843?) and Shunsui II (Somezaki Nobufusa, 1823–86). The complete title of this work is *Seishi jitsuden iroha bunko.* It was never finished.

• **Iroha-garuta.** Card game based on the principle of the 47 syllables of the *Iroha,* plus a 48th card bearing the character *kyō* (capital). Two decks of cards are used: one bears known proverbs, the other, syllables of the *Iroha* written using the hiragana syllabary (*see* KANA). The game consists of

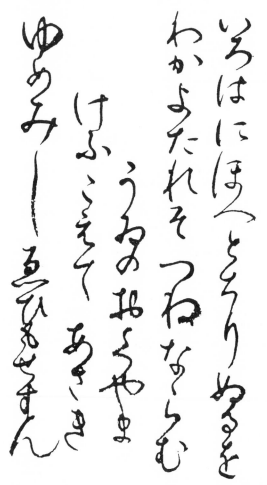

Iroha

taking the card corresponding to the proverb on a card in the second deck before the other players. The player who accumulates the most cards wins. This game, invented in Kyoto about 1850, is used mainly to familiarize children with proverbs and the *Iroha* "alphabet." Also called *Iroha-awase.* See KARUTA.

• **Iroha jirui-shō.** Japanese-language dictionary compiled in the late Heian period by Tachibana no Tadakane (late twelfth century), with divisions arranged according to the order of *Iroha* syllables, and giving the Chinese characters *(kanji)* corresponding to the words cited. Another 10-volume dictionary with the same title was produced during the Kamakura period to complement the first.

I-roku. Salary once paid in rice, hemp, silk, or other material, to bureaucrats of the fourth and fifth ranks. *See* I.

Irori. Open, fixed fireplace, generally square, located between the kitchen and the main room of a residence, mainly in rural houses, serving as a source of both heat and light. Family members gathered around the *irori* during long winter nights, each at his or her own reserved place. It was gradually replaced by portable braziers *(hibachi)* in the nineteenth century.

Irwin, Robert Walker. American diplomat (1844–1925). He went to Japan in 1866 as a negotiator and was hired by Mitsui. In 1884, he was the first consul general from Hawai'i to Japan; in this capacity, he organized Japanese immigration to Hawai'i. He became a Japanese citizen and received the Order of the Rising Sun and the Order of the Sacred Treasure.

Irwin, Sophia A. ("Bella Irwin"). Robert Walker Irwin's daughter (1884–1957), born in Tokyo. In 1917, she founded a school in Tokyo for nursery-school teachers, now known as the Irwin School. She became a Japanese citizen in 1942.

Isawa-jō. Small fort built by Sakanoue no Tamuramaro (758–811) to control Ainu populations on the site of today's town of Mizusawa (Iwate prefecture). It rapidly became an administrative center. Excavation of the site in 1954–55 revealed its enclosure wall, which was about 650 m per side. The fort and its administrative buildings disappeared after the eleventh century. Also called Izawa-jō.

Isawa Shūji. Musician and educator (1851–1917) who was sent to the United States to research new teaching methods. When he returned, he was appointed director of the Tokyo Normal School and reformed teaching of gymnastics and music in the schools. He founded the Tokyo Music School and, in 1890, started the Society for National Education (Kokka Kyōikusha). Sent to Taiwan in 1895, he attempted to assimilate indigenous peoples by using the new educational principles with them. He became a member of the House of Peers and was appointed director of the Superior Normal School in Tokyo. He also created a reading system for the visually impaired. His major work is the *Kyōgaku,* published in 1882. Also called Izawa Shūji.

Ise. Noblewoman (ca. 877–ca. 940) in the imperial court of Kyoto, Fujiwara no Tsugukage's daughter and Uda Tennō's favorite. She was a very talented poet, and some of her *waka* poems were included in the *Kokinshū* and the *Ise monogatari*. She was one of the Sanjūrokkasen (Thirty-Six Poetic Geniuses) of the tenth century.

• Former province, now part of Mie prefecture. The small city of Ise (where the most venerated Shinto shrines in Japan, the Ise Kōdai-jingū and the Ise Toyouke Daijingū, are located) was called Uji Yamada until 1956. *Pop.:* 105,000.

• *Ise daijingū sankeiki.* "Travel Diary of a Pilgrim to Ise," account of a trip made by Saka Jūbutsu in 1342.

• *Ise futadokoro dōdaijingū go-chinza denki.* Complement to the *Ise futadokoro kōdaijingū go-chinza shidaiki,* attributed to the latter's author and to the Shinto monk Asuka (ca. 507), but certainly an apocryphal text. It is considered one of the *Shintō gobushō.*

• *Ise futadokoro kōdaijingū go-chinza shidaiki.* "Memorandum on the August Consecrations Made to the Two Great Imperial Shrines of Ise." A text traditionally attributed to Abarawa no Mikoto (fifth century), but certainly apocryphal. It is one of the *Shintō gobushō.*

• Ise-kō. *See* ISE DAIJINGŪ, ISE SANGŪ, KŌ.

• **Ise Kōdaijingū (Kōtaijingū).** One of the two major shrines of Ise, called *naikū* (interior shrine), where the imperial *kami* Amaterasu-Ōmikami (Amaterashimasu Sumera Ōmikami) is venerated. It houses the sacred mirror *(yata no kagami).* This shrine, founded, according to tradition, in 478, has been rebuilt about every 20 years since the reign of Emperor Temmu (with a short interruption during the Muromachi period) in the same ancient style *(shimmei-zukuri),* using cypress wood from the nearby Kiso forest. The old shrine is demolished and cut into small pieces, which are sold as talismans. Two plots of land, situated side by side, are used alternately for the reconstructions. The last reconstruction *(sengūshiki)* took place in 1993. When the shrine is rebuilt, so is the Ujibashi bridge that provides access to it. Many pilgrims' associations (Ise-kō) organize trips to the two shrines of Ise, which are among the most venerated in Japan, at different times of the year.

• **Ise no Kuni.** Province in Ise (also called Seishū) on Tokaido, which was the fiefdom of the Ise Heichi branch of the Taira family in the late Heian period. It came under the control of the Ōuchi, then the Kitabatake and Toki families, before being recaptured by Oda Nobunaga.

• *Ise monogatari.* Collection of some 125 prose tales, with the addition of 209 poems, considered one of the first *monogatari* (with the *Taketori monogatari*). It is attributed to Ariwara no Narihira (825–80), although the oldest existing version dates from the era of Fujiwara no Sadaie (Taika, 1162–1241). It has been confirmed that this work dates from the tenth century, though the true author is not known. The poems it contains are by different authors, including the poet Ise, and each prose text explains a *waka* poem. This poetic work deals mainly with the harmonious relationships that should exist between men and women. Also called *Zaigo* (from the name of Prince Abo's fifth son, Narihira) *Chūjō monogatari, Zaigo-chūshō nikki, Zaigo-ga monogatari.*

• **Ise ondo.** Ancient Shinto religious dance performed by groups of girls during certain festivals *(matsuri)* at the Ise shrines, accompanied by music.

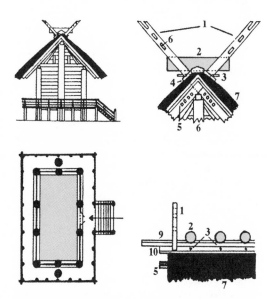

Plan of the major temple at Ise (Shimmei style). 1. *Chigi.* 2. *Katsuo-gi.* 3. *Himuki.* 4. *Afuri-ita.* 5. *Muchikake.* 6. Middle pillar. 7. Thatching. 8. *Kazu-kiri.* 9. *Iraka-ōi.* 10. *Afuri-ita*

• *Ise ondo koi no netaba*. Kabuki play in four acts, written by Chikamatsu Tokuzō in 1796: a samurai searching for a valuable sword is betrayed by the courtesan with whom he is in love, which gives rise to a massacre.

• Ise no Ōsuke. Poet (Ise no Taiyū, eleventh century), Ōnakatomi Sukechika's daughter, considered one of the Sanjūrokkasen (Thirty-Six Poetic Geniuses).

• Ise-sangū. Major pilgrimage to the two shrines of Ise, made at various times of the year by groups of pilgrims organized into associations called Ise-kō. These associations, created during the Muromachi period, proliferated during the Edo period, when almost every village had its own Ise-kō. Also called Ise-mairi, Ō-Ise-mairi, Sangū.

• *Ise shinmeisho uta-awase*. An *emakimono* created by sixteen painters and poets in 1295, describing eight famous sites in Ise, produced during an *uta-awase* meeting.

• Ise Shintō. Shinto philosophical school in Ise, founded by Watari Nobuyoshi (1615–91). *See* WATERAI-SHINTŌ.

• Ise Toyouke Daijingū. "Outer" shrine *(gekū)* in Ise dedicated to the *kami* of cereals Toyouke Ōmikami, located about 7 km from the "inner" shrine *(naikū)*; it has also been rebuilt every 20 years on the same model since the eighth century. It is said to have been transported to Ise from Tamba (near Kyoto) in 478. A number of festivals *(matsuri)* are celebrated there each year, notably on February 4 and 17, May 14, June 15 and 17, October 14, 15, and 17, November 23, and December 15 and 17. This shrine is small (11 × 7 × 6 m) and, like the *naikū*, is covered in thatching and surrounded by wooden palisades, within which a number of very simple buildings are designed to enclose cult objects. Outside the enclosure are pavilions dedicated to Kagura, Yamato-mai, Ninjō-mai, Bugaku, and other dances. *See* SENGŪSHIKI.

• Ise Wan. "Ise Bay," on the coast of Mie and Aichi prefectures, about 60 km long and 30 km wide, depth from 35 to 100 m. Its coasts are heavily industrialized, especially in the north around Nagoya, to the detriment of the fishing industry.

Ise Gorōdayū Shōzui. Ceramist (sixteenth century) who, in 1513, imported from southern China to

Imari (Hizen province) a type of kiln used to produce Imado-*yaki*, porcelain with blue decorations on a white background.

Iseki Nōki. Manufacturer of machine tools and agricultural implements, founded in 1936. It specializes in machines for transplanting rice and small tractors, which it exports to more than 50 countries. Head office in Tokyo.

Isen. Painter (Kanō Eishin; *gō*: Genshōsai, Isen, 1775–1828) of the Kanō school, Kanō Korenobu's son and student. He was the sixth Kobikichō painter in Edo.

Ise Sadachika. Ashikaga Yoshimasa's tutor (1417–73), appointed leader of the Mandokoro (general administration) of the *bakufu* in 1460. He wrote a short work on moral precepts, the *Ise Sadachika kyōkun*.

Ise Sadatake. Scholar (Ise Teijō; *gō*: Ansai, 1717–84) of the Edo shogunal bureau, titleholder to an estate worth 300 *koku* in Sagami province. He was a member of the shogun's personal guard from 1745 to 1784. He left a large number of notes valuable for what they reveal about customs and rites of the period during which he lived: *Ansai sōsho, Ansai zuihitsu, Teijō zakki*.

Isetan Co. Large store in Shinjuku, Tokyo, with branches in other districts and abroad. Founded in 1886 as Iseya Tanji, it is famous for its imported products and haute couture fabrics.

Ise Teijō. *See* ISE SADATAKE.

Ishibashi Masashi. Politician, born 1924 in Taibei (Taipei, Taiwan), elected to the House of Representatives in 1855 as a member of the Socialist party from Nagasaki prefecture. Elected secretary-general of the party in 1983, he resigned in 1986.

Ishibashi Ningetsu. Writer (Ishibashi Tomokichi, 1865–1926), born in Fukuoka prefecture. He specialized in literary criticism. His articles, published in *Kokumin no tomo*, were collected in *Ishibashi Ningetsu hyōron shū* (1939). Yamamoto Kenkichi's father.

Ishibashi Tanzan. Politician (1884–1973) born in Tokyo. At first a journalist, he edited the *Toyo Keizai Shimpō* starting in 1939. As minister of finance in 1946–47 (Yoshida Shigeru's cabinet), he was opposed to American influence on Japanese politics but was forced to resign due to American pressure. In 1954, he was appointed minister of international trade and industry in Hatoyama Ichirō's cabinet; in 1956 he was prime minister for only two months before falling seriously ill. He then attempted to improve relations between China and Japan.

Ishibashi Teikichi. *See* YAMAMOTO KENKICHI.

Ishibashi Tomokichi. *See* ISHIBASHI NINGETSU.

Ishibashi Wakun. Western-style painter (1876–1928). He lived mainly in London and Tokyo and was a member of the Imperial Academy.

Ishibutai. "Stone platform." Large funerary tumulus *(kofun)* dating from the seventh century and supposedly Soga no Umako's, located in the village of Asuka (Nara prefecture). On a large square platform about 54 m per side, enormous monoliths were heaped up to form a funerary chamber with a corridor leading to it. This tomb (which must once have been covered with earth that was swept away by the elements over time) was excavated in 1933 by Hamada Kōsaku. The chamber itself measures 7.7 × 3.5 m and is 4.8 m high; the two blocks making up its ceiling each weighs more than 70 tons. The corridor is 8.5 m long and 2.2 m wide. A ditch runs all the way around the platform.

Ishida Baigan. Philosopher and moralist (1685–1744), son of a peasant in Tamba province (near Kyoto). In 1729, he opened his own school in Kyoto, where he offered courses free of charge. His doctrines were simple and accessible to all, based on "inner knowledge" *(sekimon-shingaku)* and accepting all religions in Japan—but only their ethical aspects. Although he did not make new contributions, he had a large following. His best-known book is *Tohi mondō. See* SHINGAKU.

Ishida Eiichirō. Ethnologist (1903–68), born in Osaka. After studying at the University of Vienna, he was chair of the anthropology department at the University of Tokyo. In his studies, he tried to reconcile Marxist views with those of neo-evolutionism, using *Kulturkreislehre* comparative methods. His research on the myth of the *kappa (Kappa komahiki kō,* 1948) is of great interest. His other works were collected in eight volumes in 1970.

Ishida Hakyō. Haiku poet (Ishida Tetsuo, 1913–69) born in Ehime prefecture. His collection *Sha-*

kumyō (Desire to Live, 1950) made him one of the major poets of his generation.

Ishida Mitoku. *Kyōka* and haiku poet (1587–1669) born in Tokyo, Matsunaga Teitoku's disciple. His *kyōka* anthology *Gogin wakashū* (written from 1648 to 1651), parodying the *Kokin wakashū,* greatly influenced *kyōka* poetry.

Ishida Mitsunari. Warrior (1560–1600) from Ōmi province, serving Toyotomi Hideyoshi. He was chosen by Hideyoshi to be one of the five *bugyō* forming the administrative council for his government, then was given responsibility for the city of Sakai. He took part in almost all Hideyoshi's campaigns and was the administrator of Korean territories occupied by Japanese troops. In 1595, he obtained a fiefdom worth 190,000 *koku* and the Sawayama castle. When Hideyoshi died, Ishida Mitsunari allied himself with Tokugawa Ieyasu's adversaries and, with Mōri Terumoto, fought against Ieyasu at Sakigahara in 1600. Defeated and taken prisoner, he was executed in Kyoto. Christian missionaries gave him the name Gibounochio.

Ishida Yūtei. Painter (Tachibana Morinao, Ishida Morinao, 1721–86), born in Harima province. He worked as a painter for the Kyoto imperial palace and received the title of Hōgen. He was master to Maruyama Ōkyo and Tanaka Totsugen, to whom he taught the principles of the Kanō school (Tsuruzawa branch). *See* MARUYAMA ŌKYO.

Ishidōrō. Stone lanterns used both to light and to border walkways leading to a Shinto shrine or Buddhist temple. Some have now become simply decorative objects in gardens. They are made of a base *(jirin),* usually octagonal, with a stem *(sao)* topped by a capital *(chūdai)* supporting the actual body of the lantern *(hibukuro),* which is topped by a "hat" *(kasa)* finished with a five-part motif called *kūrin* or *gorintō (see* GŌRINTO, KŪRIN). There are various types of *ishodōrō,* the most popular of which are Oribe, Uzumasa, Rokujizō, and Kanshūki. *See* FURUTA ORIBENOSHŌ.

Ishigama. "Stone *kami,*" monoliths of various sizes. Commoners think that they are invested with a spirit *(kami)* and hence worship them. *Dōsojin* are one of the infinite varieties of sacred stones of Japan. Also called *shakuji, saguji. See* ŌYU.

Ishiguro Kazuo. Writer, born 1954 in Nagasaki. He went to London with his parents in 1959 and became a British subject. His first novels, *A Pale View of Hills* (1982) and *An Artist of the Floating World* (1986), written in English, received wide critical acclaim. He also produced television plays. In 1989, his novel *The Remains of the Day* won the Booker Prize.

Ishiguro Munemaro. Ceramist (1893–1968), born in Toyama prefecture. He made many tests of glazes on various pottery and finally managed to reproduce Temmoku ceramics, which earned him first prize at the Paris International Exposition in 1937. After the Second World War, he began experimenting again, and in 1955 he was designated a Living National Treasure.

Ishihara Jun. Physicist (1881–1947), born in Tokyo, who studied the theory of relativity and quantum theory. In 1911, he became chair of physics at the University of Tōhuko in Sendai; in 1919, he received the Imperial Academy's prize for his theoretical work. He was also a very talented poet and wrote *waka* poems of working-class inspiration. He was the editor of a number of scientific publications, among them *Kagaku* (Science), and helped to write the *Rikagaku jiten* (Dictionary of Physics and Chemistry). Also called Ishiwara Jun.

Ishihara Kanji. Army officer (1889–1949), born in Yamagata prefecture. He was sent to Germany to complete his studies, then was assigned to the headquarters of the Guandong (Kantō-gun) army in 1928. His speeches confirmed his aptitude as a theoretician. Collected in a book called *Sensō-shi taikan* (General View of the History of War), published in 1941 after he was transferred to the reserves, they give an accurate description of modern war and stress the importance of aviation. In 1931, he and Itadaki Seishirō were proponents of complete control of Manchuria; in 1935, he was assigned to the general headquarters of the armed forces. But his ideas on modern war were not accepted by the top military ranks, so he was transferred to the reserves. Also pronounced Ishiwara Kanji.

Ishihara Ken. Historian (1882–1976), born in Tokyo. He studied the history of Christianity and Christendom, and was president of the Women's University of Tokyo from 1940 to 1948, becoming a member of the Academy in 1953. Among his most important works are *Kirisuto-kyō shi* (History of Christendom, 1934), *Kirisuto-kyō shisō shi* (History of Christian Thought, 1949), and *Chūsei Kiri-*

suto-kyō kenkyū (Study of Medieval Christianity, 1952). Also called Ishiwara Ken.

Ishihara Shintarō. Writer and politician, born 1932 in Kobe. He published his first novel, *Hai-iro no kyōshitsu* (The Gray Class, 1954), when he was still a student, and soon followed it with a second, *Taiyo no kisetsu* (The Season of the Sun, 1955, Akutagawa Prize), in which he describes the behavior of youth of his time and their complete opposition to their elders' habits and customs. This novel, which caused a scandal for its freedom of expression, was soon followed by others in the same vein: *Shokei no heya* (The Torture Chamber, 1958), *Kiretsu* (The Fissure, 1958), *Chōsen* (The Challenge, 1959–60), *Okami ikiro buta wa shine* (Wolves, Live! Pigs, Burst!, 1960), and *Koi to shi* (Love and Death, 1964). In the political domain he founded the Seirankai (Blue Tempest) society in 1973 to expound his anti-communist and anti-imperialist opinions, thus becoming the leader of the right wing of the Jiyū Minshutō (Liberal Democratic party), and stopped writing. Most of his novels were adapted for the screen and were a mitigated success as movies. *See* TAIKŌ-ZOKU.

Ishii Hakutei. Painter (1882–1958) who attempted to modernize the ukiyo-e tradition, producing prints in a westernized style. *See* ASAI CHŪ, ISSUI-KAI.

Ishii Hida. Maker of puppets for the Osaka theater who may also have been a Kabuki actor about 1700. His real name may have been Yamamoto Hidanjō. He was also known as a doll maker.

Ishii Hida. *See* MARUOKA HIDEKO.

Ishii Kikujirō. Diplomat (1866–1945), born in Chiba. He was an attaché to the Paris legation (1890–96), consul to Korea (1896–1900), secretary to the Beijing legation (1900), then, after a period as an administrator, ambassador to France (1912–15), minister of foreign affairs (1915–16), special envoy (1917) and then ambassador to the United States (1918–19), and again ambassador to France (1920–27), during which time he was twice president (1923 and 1926) of the League of Nations. He retired in 1927.

Ishii Mitsujirō. Politician (1889–1981) and journalist. He edited the *Asahi Shimbun,* then was elected to the House of Representatives in 1946. In 1953, he was appointed minister of transportation, and he was minister of international trade and industry in Ikeda Hayato's cabinet. An influential member of the Jiyū Minshutō (Liberal Democratic party), he left the presidency of the party in 1960; Ikeda Hayato succeeded him.

Ishii Ryōsuke. Historian, born 1907 in Tokyo. He specialized in the history of judicial institutions and was a professor at the University of Tokyo. He wrote books on all aspects of Japanese law, including history of law—*Hōseishi Ronshū* (Collection of Essays on the History of Law, 1972 et seq.)—Japanese legislation in the Meiji era, and a history of political institutions in Japan (1980).

Ishii Tsuruzō. Painter and sculptor (1887–1973), born in Tokyo. He was greatly influenced both by Japanese sculpture of the Asuka era and by Auguste Rodin. From 1944 to 1959, he was a professor at the Tokyo National University of Fine Arts, and he was elected a member of the Academy. He also painted and produced woodcut prints for illustrations.

Ishikawa Chiyomatsu. Biologist (1861–1935), born in Edo and professor at the University of Tokyo. He studied in Germany and was known for his lectures and writings on theories of evolution. He also experimented with breeding fish, particularly *ayu.*

Ishikawa Gabō. *See* ISHIKAWA MASAMOCHI.

Ishikawa Goemon. Famous pirate (1596–1632) sentenced to being thrown alive into a cauldron of boiling oil. Before dying, he wrote a poem of farewell that has become famous.

Ishikawajima. Small island at the mouth of the Sumida-gawa river in Tokyo, now linked to land, where the shogunal government established major shipyards in 1853 at which the *Asahi Maru,* the first Western-style sailing ship, was built. These shipyards were expanded greatly; in 1960 they were merged with the Harima shipyards to form a heavy-industry complex called Ishikawajima-Harima.

Ishikawa Jōzan. Samurai (Ishikawa Shigeyuki, Ō; *gō:* Jōzan, Shisendō, 1583–1672) and Confucian scholar, from Mikawa province. At first a vassal of Tokugawa Ieyasu, he retired in 1636 to the Shisendō hermitage, near Kyoto, and devoted himself to poetry. He was influenced by his teacher Fujiwara no Seika and his friend Hayashi Razan, and

wrote many collections of poems, including *Shisensehi* and *Honchō senchū.*

Ishikawa Jun. Writer (1899–1987), expert in French literature, who translated Gide's and Molière's works and wrote many novels, among them *Fugen* (Akutagawa Prize, 1936), *The Falcon,* and *The Asters,* in which he revealed a fantastic imagination in an extremely pure language.

Ishikawa Masamochi. Poet (Yadoya no Meshimori; *gō:* Rokujuen, Gorōsai, Ishikawa Gabō, 1753–1830), painter Ishikawa Toyonobu's son. Although he studied painting in his youth, he later devoted himself to *kyōka* poetry, under the direction of Tsuburino Hikari and Ota Nampo. He wrote a great number of books of poems, including *Gagen shūran* and *Genchū yoteki,* as well as collections of archaistic poems *(Hokuri jūniji, Azuma namari, Miyako no teburi)* and *kibyōshi* and *yomihon* novels. He is better known as Ishikawa Gabō.

Ishikawa Sanshirō. Politician (1876–1956), Christian socialist, and political journalist. He objected to the opening of peace negotiations between Russia and Japan in 1904. Persecuted for his ideas, he moved to Europe in 1913 and lived there until 1922. When he returned to Japan, he left the socialist movement and advocated anarchy. He wrote *Nihon shakai shugi shi,* a history of Japanese socialism, translated works by Alphonse Daudet and Émile Zola, and wrote his autobiography, *Jijoden,* in 1956.

Ishikawa Takuboku. Poet and writer (Ishikawa Hajime, 1886–1912), son of a Zen monk from Iwate. He became known by publishing his *tanka* poems in the magazine *Myōjō;* his first collection, *Akogare* (Languor), was published in 1905, with a preface by Ueda Bin. While earning a living as a journalist, he continued to write poems, influenced by the naturalist school and socialist ideas: *Chōei* (1908), *Rōmaji nikki* (1909), *Ichiaku no suna* (A Handful of Sand, 1910), *Yobukoto-fue* (1912), *Kanashiki gangu* (My Sad Toys, 1912), and *Kikuchi-kun.* He also wrote in English and in *rōmaji.* A memorial to him was erected in Tamayama-mura, his birthplace, in 1986.

Ishikawa Tatsuzō. Writer (1905–85), born in Akita prefecture. After a short trip to Brazil, he wrote an account of his experiences, *Sōbō* (Immigrants, 1935–39), which won the Akutagawa Prize. After the Second World War, he wrote war stories, including *Ikite iru heitai* (The Living Soldier), *Kaze ni soyogu ashi* (1949–51), *Ningen no kabe* (The Human Wall, 1957–59), and *Kinkanshoku* (The Eclipse of the Gold Ring), placing him among the most important modern authors.

Ishikawa Tomonobu. Geographer (seventeenth–eighteenth century) who drew a map of the world (*Bankoku sokai-zu,* 1695) upon the request of the shogunate.

Ishikawa Toyonobu. Painter (Ishikawa Magosaburō, *mei:* Nukaya Shichibei; *gō:* Meijōdō Shūha, Nishimura Magosaburō Shigenobu, Tanjōdō, Shūha, 1711–85) of ukiyo-e prints, Nishimura Shigenobu's student in Edo. He produced prints in the style of the Torii school and painted, mainly in his own style, faces of beautiful women *(bijin)* on a background imitating wood texture, using *urushi-e* and *benizuri-e* techniques. Ishikawa Gabō's father (*see* ISHIKAWA MASAMOCHI).

Ishikoridome no Mikoto. According to a Shinto legend, the *kami* who made the sacred mirror, *yata no kagami,* and gave it to Amaterasu-Ōmikami when she left the cavern where she had been trapped; it was to become one of the three sacred treasures of the Japanese empire. He was the grandson of the *kami* Ame no Koyame no Mikoto.

Ishikura Chimata. Poet (1869–1942) born in Ehime prefecture, one of the founders (with Sasaki Nobutsuna) of the literary magazine *Kokoru no Hana.* He published a number of poetry collections in which he celebrated the sea: *Shionari* (The Sound of the Tide), *Kamome* (The Gulls), *Umi* (The Sea).

Ishikura Masayoshi. *See* MASAYOSHI.

Ishimoto Shizue. *See* KATŌ SHIZUE.

Ishimoto Umeko. Woman from Yokohama (1874–1921) who was born with paralyzed arms and legs, and who learned to write with her mouth. She was known as "the Helen Keller of Japan."

Ishimpō. Title of the oldest existing text on medicine in Japan, presented to Emperor En'yū in 982 by its author, Tamba no Yasuyori. This treatise is a compilation of Chinese works of the Sui and Tang eras. A revised version was published in Edo in 1860; a more recent edition, in China in 1955. This extremely precise work deals with acupuncture points, internal and external illnesses and their rem-

edies, gynecology, pediatrics, hygiene, and dietetics. It has 30 chapters. Chinese title: *Yixin fang.* Also called *Ishin-hō.*

Ishin Sūden. *See* KONCHI-IN SŪDEN.

Ishira Akira. Ceramist, born 1941 in Kamakura, who began to be noted for his very personal works in 1970. He had an exhibition in Paris in 1994.

Ishite-ji. Buddhist temple in Matsuyama (Shikoku), built in the Chinese style in the fourteenth century. Gate from the fourteenth century, *kondō* (1333), *gomadō* (1318), pagoda (mid-fourteenth century). *See* MATSUYAMA.

Ishiyama-dera. Buddhist temple in Ōtsu, on the shore of Lake Biwa, founded in 749 by the monk Rōben (689–773) in gratitude to Kongō Zaō and Kannon Bosatsu for the discovery of a lode of gold in Mutsu province that made it possible to gild the Daibutsu of the Tōdai-ji. The temple was very popular because the people believed that its *honzon* (main divinity) could accomplish miracles. It was transferred from the Tōdai-ji sect to the Shingonshū sect about 900. Murasaki Shikibu is said to have retired there to write the *Genji monogatari.* The temple was destroyed by fire in 1078 and reconstructed about 1096. Minamoto no Yoritomo added a pagoda *(tahō-tō)* that is now the oldest standing structure of its type in Japan. *Tōdaimon* from the twelfth–thirteenth centuries, *hondō* dating from 1096, *raidō* from 1602 (the temple having been partially reconstructed at the time).

• *Ishiyama-dera engi emaki.* An *emakimono* in seven scrolls relating the history and legends of the foundation of the Ishiyama-dera. It was created in the fourteenth century and painted in the style then in vogue, Yamato-e. The text of the three first scrolls is attributed to the monk Kōshū, with illustrations by Takashina Takakane. The fourth was probably written in 1497 by Sanjōnishi Sanetaka and illustrated by Tosa Mitsunobu. The fifth scroll featured text by Reizei Tameshige and images by Awataguchi Takamitsu. The sixth and seventh scrolls were written by Asukai Masaaki (1655), and the illustrations were made only in 1805 by Tani Bunchō.

• **Ishiyama Hongan-ji.** Temple of the Jōdo Shinshū sect built in 1496 by Rennyo in the area of today's Osaka. It was the headquarters of the Ikkō-ikki (*see* IKKŌ-IKKI). *See* HONGAN-JI.

Ishizaka Kimishige. Biologist, born 1925 in Tokyo. After studying in the United States, he isolated immunoglobulin E, a factor in certain cases of asthma and allergies, between 1960 and 1966. From 1974 to 1980, he was a professor at the University of Kyoto, and he received the Passano Prize, awarded to researchers in immunology in the United States. He also received the Order of Culture (Bunka-shō) in 1974. His wife worked with him for many years.

Ishizaka Taizō. Industrialist (1887–1975), born in Tokyo, who was one of the leaders of the economic boom in Japan after the Second World War. He was president of Toshiba, elected president of the Keidanren (Federation of Economic Organizations of Japan) in 1956, and president of the Osaka "Expo 70" World's Fair. He was also a potter and a talented calligrapher.

Ishizaka Yōjirō. Writer (1900–86), born in Aomori prefecture. His first novel, *Wakai Hito* (Young Man), published in serial form in the magazine *Mita Bungaku* from 1933 to 1937, established his reputation as a popular writer. His novels deal mainly with young people's problems, and many have been adapted for the screen. Among his best-known books are *Mugi Shinazu* (1936) and *Aoi Sammyaku* (1947).

Ishizuka Tatsumaro. Scholar and philosopher (1764–1823), born in Tōtōmi (Shizuoka prefecture), who specialized in literature of the Nara period. He discovered a very old form of kana writing *(man'yōgana)* derived from Chinese characters.

Ishō nihon-den. "Foreign Documents on Japan." A collection of 127 Chinese and Korean documents concerning Japan, collected by Matsuhita Kenrin (1637–1703) in 1688, and published in Osaka in 1693.

Ishū. Painter (Kikuta Hideyuki; *gō*: Shōu, Ishū, 1791–1852), Isen's student in Edo.

Islam. Islam has never had many followers in Japan, except for a few foreigners living temporarily in the country. Before 1945, there were only 400 Muslims, almost all of them foreigners. However, a small mosque was built in Tokyo in 1938. Since 1981, a great number of Iranians (called Bazarī in Japan), many of them illegal immigrants, have settled in Tokyo and other large Japanese cities, and this has begun to pose serious integration problems.

Isoda Kōichi. Literary critic (1931–87), born in Yokohama and specializing in English romantic poetry. In his works he makes note of a "traditional Japanese mentality" inherent to political ideology. Two of his essays, *Junkyō no bigaku* (1964) and *Seitō naki itan* (1969), were widely read. A professor at the Tokyo Institute of Technology, he also published many history books, including *Sengoshi no kūkan* (Postwar Developments, 1983) and *Rokumeikan no keifu* (The Heritage of the Rokumeikan, 1983), and biographies, such as *Nagai kafū* (1979).

Isoda Kōryūsai. Painter (Isoda Masakatsu; *gō*: Haruhiro, Kōryūsai, eighteenth century), Nishimura Shigenaga's student in Edo. He produced many *ukiyo-e* and *nishiki-e* prints in muted colors, on vaguely erotic subjects, as well as true *shunga* (erotic images). Toward the end of his life, he seems to have abandoned printmaking for painting; he received the title of Hokkyō in 1781. He was sometimes called Shōbei.

• **Isoda Masakatsu.** *See* ISODA KŌRYŪSAI.

Isoho monogatari. "Aesop's Fables," the first European book translated into *rōmaji*, by Portuguese missionaries in Nagasaki in 1593, titled *Esopo no Fabulas,* and republished constantly until the nineteenth century.

Isoi Joshin. Lacquer artist (1883–1964), born in Takamatsu (Shikoku), specializing in colored lacquer objects *(kinma)* and designated a Living National Treasure in 1956.

Isonokami-jingū. Shinto shrine located in Furu (Tenri, Nara prefecture), dedicated in the fourth century, according to tradition, to Futsu no Mitama no Tsurugi, a sacred sword. Its *haiden* dates from the Kamakura period and its *rōmon* from 1318. At first considered a *jinja,* it received the title *jingū* in 1883. Its *honden* was built only in 1913. This shrine, much venerated by the imperial family, has many ancient weapons in its collection of relics, including a seven-branched épée called Nanatsusaya no Tachi, bearing an inscription in inlaid gold on both sides of its blade, reading (with gaps): "The sixteenth day of the month . . . month of the Tahe era, this seven-branched épée was made with iron one hundred times beaten so that it will split enemies apart . . . it is the work of . . . until now there has never been a similar épée, the king of Paekche . . . had it made for the king of the Yamato, so that it will be transmitted to future centuries." This dates the épée to 369.

Isonokami Otomaro. Adviser to the state and poet, some of whose works appear in the *Man'yōshū.* He was exiled to Tosa in 739 and died in 750.

Isonokami no Yakatsugu. Senior bureaucrat (729–81) in the Nara court, *dainagon* in 780, and famous classical-Chinese poet, some of whose poems appeared in *Keikoku-shū* (827). He founded the first library in Japan, called Untei, in his residence; it was later transformed into a Buddhist temple. His friend, the poet Kaya no Toyotoshi (751–815), helped him gather works for the library.

Isozaki, Arata. Architect, born 1931 in Ōita prefecture, Kyushu. A student of Tange Kenzō, he designed a number of Futurist-style buildings, including the Ōita prefectural library (1966), the Fukuoka Mutual Bank (1971), the museum of modern art in Gumma prefecture (1974), and the municipal art museum in Kita Kyushu (1974). In 1985, he designed the Tsukuba municipal center; other Isozaki designs include the great stadium in Barcelona and the Los Angeles Museum of Contemporary Art.

Issai-kyō. Title of the complete collection of sacred writings of Buddhism, the Tripitaka. *Chin.: Yiqie jin. See* DAIZŌ-KYŌ.

• **Issai-shū.** Modern Buddhist sect founded in 1953 in Shimonoseki by Baba Bokushin (1889–1962).

Issan Ichinei. Japanese name of a Chinese Buddhist monk (Yishan Yining, 1244–1317), from Zhejiang, sent to Japan by Kublai Khan's successor to establish friendly relations with the Kamakura *bakufu.* Received by Hōjō Sadatoki, he was put in charge of the Zen Nanzen-ji temple in Kyoto. He had many disciples, among them Sesson Yūbai and Kokan Shiren. He is credited with starting the Chinese literary wave cultivated by the *gozan.* He also spread the Song dynasty's Chan (*Jap.*: Zen) among the Kamakura warrior class in Japan and among scholars such as Musō Soseki.

Isshi. Painter (*mei:* Kōzasu, early fifteenth century) of the Suiboko school in Muromachi. He may have been a Buddhist monk at the Nanzen-ji temple in Kyoto.

• Painter (Iwakura Fumimora, Iwakura Bunshu; *gō:* Tōkō, 1608–46) and calligrapher, portrait maker. He was a *chigo,* then a Zen monk in Kyoto. → *See* EIGEN-JI.

Isshō. *See* MARUYAMA ŌKYO.

Issui-kai. Group of painters with Western tendencies, issuing from the Naika-kai in 1936. Most of the founders of this group studied in Paris in the 1920s and 1930s, including Ishii Hakutei (1882–1958), Arishima Ikuma (1882–1974), Yamashita Shintarō (1881–1966) and Yasui Sōtarō (1888–1955). *See* HAZAMA INOSUKE.

Issumbōshi. "Inch-High Monk." A popular tale equivalent to "Tom Thumb," about a foundling only one inch high who, after extraordinary adventures, becomes a normal man and marries a wealthy heiress. This tale, published in the *otogi-zōshi* series, was very popular among the common people and is still the subject of cartoons today.

Isuzu Jidōsha. Japan automobile manufacturer founded in 1916, known for its industrial vehicles and diesel engines. It became affiliated with General Motors Corporation in 1971. It currently has the largest truck and bus plant in Japan. It exports about 55% of its production. Head office in Tokyo.

Itabi. Stone steles bearing votive inscriptions *(tōba)* placed on tombs. They were generally topped by a triangular capital, sometimes decorated with an engraving or sculpture of the Buddha and a few Sanskrit characters. They were in common use during the Kamakura and Muromachi periods and continued to be used until the seventeenth century, when they were gradually replaced by square steles.

Itadakimasu. Expression said at the beginning of a meal, somewhat equivalent to "Bon appetit!" It comes from the verb *itadaku,* meaning "to carry above the head." In ancient times, to thank the divinities, a simulation of offering them food was made by raising a platter over the head. Even today, to thank someone for a gift, recipients lift the gift with both hands to the height of their head or eyes. At the end of the meal, it is customary to express gratitude by saying *Gochisō-sama,* which is a way of excusing oneself for leaving the table; *gochisō* means, approximately, "Good meal, good food." *See* MEALS.

Itagaki Seishirō. General (1885–1948), born in Iwate prefecture. A graduate of the School of War in 1916, he was sent, with Ishihara Kanji, to the Guandong army in Manchuria. In 1937, he was appointed minister of war in Konoe Fumimaro's cabinet, then was leader of the expeditionary force in China (1939); he rose to the rank of general in 1941. In 1945, he was found to be a war criminal by the Allied court, and he was executed in 1948.

Itagaki Taisuke. Politician (1837–1919), born in Kōchi, firm supporter of the Jiyū Minken Undō (Freedom and People's Rights Movement). He supported the emperor during the Boshin Civil War and was appointed *sangi* in 1871, but, having been among the advisers supporting military intervention in Korea, he was forced to resign. He then founded a political society, the Aikoku Kōtō (Public Party of Patriots), and demanded that the government allow elected representation by the people. He also founded the Risshi-sha (Self-Help Society) in Kōchi, and soon after was a founder of the Aikoku-sha (Society of Patriots). In 1881, he founded the Jiyūtō (Liberal party), of which he became president. But because his supporters had caused some disturbances, after a stay abroad Itagaki dissolved the party; in 1889, he started a new Aikoku Kōtō which merged with the Rikken Jiyūtō (Constitutional Liberal party) to form a new party, of which he was president. He was appointed minister of the interior in 1896 (Itō Hirobumi's cabinet), a position he retained in Okuma Shigenobu's cabinet. In 1900, he and Itō Hirobumi founded another party, the Rikken Seiyūkai (Friends of Constitutional Government); he then retired from public life.

Itakeru no Kami. According to Shinto legends, one of Susanoo no Mikoto's sons who became a king in Korea. Also called Oyabiko no Kami.

Itakura Katsukiyo. Daimyo (1823–89) of Matsuyama, and adviser to the Tokugawa shogunate until 1868. He was an adviser to Tokugawa Yoshinobu and supported his reforms. He took the shogun's side against the emperor and was defeated, so he fled to Hakodate (Hokkaido), but was forced to surrender with Enomoto Takeaki in 1869. He was pardoned and freed in 1871.

Itakura Katsushige. Samurai (1545–1624), appointed Edo-*machi-bugyō* by Tokugawa Ieyasu in 1590. He fought at Ieyasu's side at the Battle of Sekigahara (1600) and was appointed Kyōto-*sho-shidai* in 1603. He passed the position on to his son,

Itakura Shigemune (1586–1656), and it remained a hereditary title in the Itakura family.

• **Itakura Shigemasa.** Itakura Katsushige's second son (1588–1638). He entered the service of Tokugawa Ieyasu and received a salary of 1,000 *koku*. After serving as an intermediary between Tokugawa Ieyasu and Toyotomi Hideyori in 1614, his income rose to 15,000 *koku*. He was killed when he attacked the Hara castle during the Shimabara Revolt in 1638.

• **Itakura Shigemune.** *See* ITAKURA KATSUSHIGE.

Itakura Keiichi. Biologist, born 1942 in Tokyo. He studied mainly in Canada and the United States and made a number of important discoveries, notably the synthesis of pancreatic hormone DNA.

Itami Mansaku. Movie director (Ikeuchi Yoshitoyo, 1900–46).

Itami Toshikatsu. *See* HIDARI JINGORŌ.

Itaya Hazan. Ceramist (Itaya Kashichi, 1872–1963), born in Ibaraki prefecture. He taught sculpture and ceramics at the Tokyo Industrial College, where he built his own kiln. His multicolored pieces earned him many awards and membership in the Imperial Academy of Fine Art. He worked mainly for the imperial court starting in 1934 and was decorated with the Order of Culture (Bunka-shō) in 1953.

• **Itaya Hiromasa.** *See* HIROMASA, HIROYUKI, ITAYA KEISHŪ.

• **Itaya Hiroyuki.** *See* ITAYA KEISHŪ.

• **Itaya Kashichi.** *See* ITAYA HAZAN.

Itaya Keishū. Painter (Itaya Hiromasa; *gō*: Keishū, 1729–97) who founded the school bearing his name, Itaya-ha, in the service of the shogunate. His style resembled that of the painters of the Sumiyoshi school. His son, Itaya Hiroyuki, became the fifth leader of the Sumiyoshi school, succeeding Sumiyoshi Hiromori.

Itazuke. Prehistoric site in Shizuoka prefecture, late Jōmon period, which contains a large number of objects from the period and many adults' and children's footprints that have been dated at 400 BC. *See* FUKUOKA, YAYOI.

Itchū-bushi. *Jōruri* school founded by Miyakodayū Itchū (1650–1724), which started a long family line of *jōruri* narrators.

Itō Daisuke. Movie director (1898–1981). His first effort was the silent film *Shuchū nikki* (1924). He then founded his own production company, Itō Eiga Kenkyūjo (Ito Center of Cinematographic Research), and directed a number of silent films. With the advent of sound, he directed "historical" films for the Nikkatsu studios. After the Second World War, he made some major feature films, including *Ōshō* (1948) and *Hangyaku-ji* (1961).

Itō Einosuke. Writer (1903–59), born in Akita, author of "proletarian" novels on the peasant class in Tōhoku. He then turned to popular literature, using a very direct style. His best-known work is *Keisatsu nikki* (The Diary of a Police Officer, 1952), a collection of stories on village life seen through the eyes of a local police officer.

Itō Gemboku. Physician (1800–71) who imported anti-smallpox vaccination methods to Japan. He studied with Franz von Siebold, then founded a school of Western medicine in Edo in 1826. Suspected of having passed maps of Japan to Siebold, he was imprisoned in 1828 but freed soon after. In 1858, he was appointed official physician to the shogunate. He translated an Austrian medical work from its Dutch translation, the *Iryō seishi*.

Itō Hirobumi. Statesman (Hayashi, Itō Shunsuke, 1841–1909), born to a peasant family on the estate of the Chōshū clan in Yamaguchi prefecture. Adopted by a samurai at the age of 14, he took the family name Itō. He went to Nagasaki to study European military methods, then accompanied Kido Takayoshi to Kyoto and Edo, where he joined rioters setting fire to the British legation. The head of the Chōshū clan made him a samurai in 1863. After the bombardment of Shimonoseki, he realized how powerful Western armaments were and became a proponent of opening up Japan.

After the Meiji Restoration, thanks to his friends in the Chōshū clan, he obtained the position of *san'yo* (junior adviser), then was appointed governor of Hyōgo prefecture. He then changed his personal name from Shunsuki to Hirobumi. He made the plans for construction of the railway from Yokohama to Tokyo (completed in 1872). In 1870, he was sent to the United States to study that country's monetary system; when he returned, in 1871, he was appointed president of the mint and vice-minis-

ter of public works. The following year, he was a member of the Iwakura mission to Europe and the United States. In 1873, he was appointed *sangi*, minister of public works, and chairman of the assembly of prefectural governors. After he helped subdue Saigō Takamori's revolt, he was appointed minister of the interior and, in opposition to Okuma Shigenobu, worked to establish a Prussiantype constitution, convinced that Japan should have a constitutional monarchy.

With the establishment of a modern cabinet system in 1885, Itō became chairman of the commission studying the creation of a constitution, which was completed in 1888. He then created a Privy Council (Sūmitsu-in) for the emperor, who proclaimed the Constitution on February 11, 1889. The Diet became bicameral, and Itō was leader of the upper chamber (the House of Peers), then prime minister in 1892, a position he held until 1896. At the end of the Sino–Japanese War of 1894–95, he represented Japan at the Shimonoseki conference. In 1898, he was appointed prime minister for the third time and dissolved the Diet because of opposition to his policy of reforming the Jiyūtō (Liberal) and Shimpotō (Progressive) parties, which soon merged to form the Kenseitō (Constitutional Party). In 1900, he organized the Rikken Seiyūkai (Friends of Constitutional Government party) and, with his supporters in government and the emperor's approval, had his tax-reform bill passed.

In 1901, exhausted, Itō stopped his political activities and went to Russia to try to establish friendly relations. In 1903, the emperor appointed him head of the Privy Council. After the Russo-Japanese War, Itō went to Korea; in 1905, he signed the Korean-Japanese agreement in which Russia recognized Japanese influence in Korea. He was appointed Resident General in Korea in 1906, a position he held until 1909. He then returned to Japan to direct the Privy Council. He was assassinated by a Korean nationalist, An Chung-gün, in Harbin during another inspection trip. Itō was also a poet who published his work under the pseudonym Shunho ("spring fields").

Itō Hyōdō. Contemporary ceramist, born 1951 in Yamagata prefecture. He put the Kaminohata-type kilns in Nagoya back in operation, and produced modern ceramics inspired by old works. He has a degree in French literature, and he has traveled in Asia, Africa, and Europe to further his knowledge. He is also a master of the tea ceremony *(chanoyu)*, a poet, and a calligrapher. He had a major exhibition in Paris in 1995.

Itō Jakuchū. Painter (Itō Shunkyo, Itō Jokin; *azana*: Keiwa; *gō*: Tobei-an, 1716–1800). He studied the styles of the Kano and Tosa schools and created a new style combining the characteristics of Chinese and Japanese painting. The son of a Kyoto grocer, he left the family trade to devote himself to painting in 1755. He loved plants and birds, painted them in detail, and kept an aviary filled with exotic birds in his garden. About 1758, he painted a series of 30 large *kakemono*, which he offered to the Shōkoku-ji temple in 1770. The temple gave them to the imperial family in 1889. Jakuchū then began to sculpt a series of the *gohyaku-rakan* (Five Hundred Arhats) for the Sekihō-ji temple in Tamba, trading his paintings (which he was signing Tobei-ō, "the old man of the bushel of rice") for food. The great fire in Kyoto in 1788 left him penniless and he became partially blind. He nevertheless continued his work until his death.

Itō Jinsai. Confucian writer and philosopher (Keisai, 1627–1705), born in Horikawa district near Kyoto to a family of traders. He studied the Zhu Xi (*Jap.:* Shushi) doctrines, from which he drew a personal philosophy that he expounded in *Taikyoku-ron* (Treatise on the Ultimate) and other works, such as *Seizen-ron* (On the Natural Goodness of the Human Being) and *Shingaku gen-ron* (Principles of Spiritual Study). He then abandoned the Zhu Xi teachings to study Wang Yangming (*Jap.:* Ōyōmei), creating a philosophical school that was sometimes known as Horikawa-gaku, but was better known as Kogi-gaku, a branch of the Kogaku-ha (School of Ancient Studies). Itō Jinsai considered Confucius's *Analects* the supreme book and the writings of Mencius (*Chin.:* Mengzi) simply an exegesis. He opened a school in Kyoto, which he called Kogidō (Hall of the Ancient Teachings) and refused to enter the service of a daimyo or the shogunate. His teachings, based mainly on the concept of *makoto* (sincerity of the heart), influenced a number of Confucian philosophers in the Edo period, not the least among them Ogyū Sorai. He founded a second school, Fukko-ha, and wrote other major works, including *Go mōjigi* (Commentary on the *Analects*, 1683). His son, Itō Tōgai (1670–1736), continued his work and also wrote a number of philosophy books.

Ito-jō. Excavations made in 1936 in Ito, near Maebaru (Fukuoka prefecture), revealed vestiges of a huge fortress constructed during the Nara period in anticipation of a Korean invasion. According to the *Shoku Nihongi*, it was built between 756 and 770 and was surrounded by walls more than 2 km long. It was probably Kimi no Makibi who proposed that it be built. But the Korean invasion never took place and the fortress was abandoned soon after it was completed. Remains of the walls, a gate, and an observation tower were uncovered. *See* ITOKOKU.

Itokawa Hideo. Aeronautical engineer, born 1912 in Tokyo. During the Second World War, he designed airplanes such as the Nakajima and Hanabusa. In 1951, he developed a design for rockets at the University of Tokyo (where he taught from 1948 to 1967).

Itō Keiichi. Writer, born 1917 in Mie prefecture. He was a soldier for many years in China and Manchuria during the Second World War, and drew on his experiences for his novels, which were not without lyricism: *Hotaru no kawa* (The Hotaru River, 1961), *Rakujitsu no senjō* (1965).

Itō Keisuke. Physician (1803–1901), born in Nagoya. He was Franz von Siebold's student in Nagasaki, and he specialized in the study of medicinal plants. Siebold gave him Carl Peter Thunberg's *Flora Japonica* as a gift, and he used it as a model for *Taisei honzō meisō* (1829), in which he named plants according to the Linnaean system of Latin names.

Itokoku. Former name of a vassal kingdom of the Yamatai, cited in the *Weizhi*, a history of the Chinese Wei dynasty written in the third century. It is presumed that the capital of this kingdom was near the town of Meibaru in Fukuoka prefecture (Kyushu). Itokoku (*see* ITO-JŌ) seems to have been a major cultural center during the Yayoi period (300 BC–AD 300).

Itoku Kannon. One of the 33 forms (Sanjūsan Ōgeshin) of Kannon Bosatsu (*Skt.:* Avalokiteshvara), portrayed sitting in "royal ease" and holding a lotus flower in his left hand.

Itoku Tennō. Fourth emperor (Ō-Yamato-hiko Suki-tomo no Mikoto, 553<510–477> BC, according to traditional dates), son of and successor to Annei Tennō. He probably actually lived in the early first century AD. Kōshō Tennō succeeded him.

Itō Mansho. Christian samurai (Itō Sukemasu, ca. 1570–1612), from Hyūga province (Miyazaki prefecture), leader of the mission sent to Europe in

1582 by the Christian daimyo of Kyushu. He was baptized with the name Mancio in 1580 in Arima. Received by the Pope in 1585, he returned to Japan in 1590 and was ordained a priest by the Company of Jesus in 1608.

Itō Miyoji. Politician (1857–1934), born in Nagasaki prefecture. He had a gift for foreign languages and was sent to Europe by Itō Hirobumi in 1882, then served as cabinet chief in Itō Hirobumi's government. He was minister of trade and agriculture in Itō's third cabinet in 1898, then a member of Emperor Meiji's Privy Council the following year, while he continued to publish the pro-government newspaper *Tōkyō Nichinichi Shimbun* (until 1904). He worked behind the scenes on the Privy Council and was very influential in political circles in the 1920s.

Itō Noe. Politician (1895–1923) of the Seitōsha group (Bluestocking Society) and publisher of its newspaper, *Seitō* (Bluestocking) in 1915–16. She married the writer Tsuji Jun (1884–1944), but left him soon after to live with the anarchist Osugi Sakae, with whom she founded the group of socialist women called Sekirankai in 1921. She and Osugi were killed two years later by the police during a riot following the Tokyo earthquake. She wrote a great number of articles on feminism and anarchism and published autobiographical novels such as *Zatsuon* (Noises, 1916) and *Tenki* (The Point of Return, 1918).

Itō Ren. Western-style painter, born 1898 in Nagoya. After studying at the Tokyo School of Fine Arts, he went to Paris in 1927, met members of the Fauvist group, and returned to Japan in 1930. He then had an exhibition that won the Nika Prize. In 1954, he was appointed a professor at the Tokyo National University of Fine Arts, which he left two years later due to compulsory retirement.

Itō Sachio. *Waka* poet (Itō Kōjirō, 1864–1913), born in Chiba prefecture. He became Masaoka Shiki's disciple, and he published the poetry magazine *Ashibi* from 1903 until his death. Also in 1903, he founded the magazine *Araragi*. He wrote several novels, the best known of which is *Nogiku no naka* (The Tomb in the Midst of the Asters, 1906). His poems were collected in *Sachio kashū* (1920).

Itō Sei. Writer and literary critic (Itō Hitoshi, 1905–69), born in Hokkaido. He began by publishing a book of poems, *Yukiakari no michi* (The Road

Lit by Snow), in 1926. Then, influenced by the proletarian movement and writers such as Marcel Proust and Virginia Woolf, he published some essays, including *Shin shinri shugi bungaku* (The New Psychological Literature, 1932) and a collection of stories called *Seibutsusai* (Festival of the Living, 1932). He then wrote novels marked by the psychological approach to his characters, such as *Yūki no machi* (The Phantom Town, 1937) and *Yūki no mura* (A Phantom Village, 1938), followed by *Tokunō Gorō no seikatsu to iken* (Life and Opinions of Tokunō Gorō, 1941), a story continued in *Narumi senkichi* (1946). He then returned to his career as a critic by publishing various essays on the new literature of novels written in the first person in *Shōsetsu no hōhō* (The Method of the Novel, 1948), *Shōsetsu no ninshiki* (Conscience of the Novel, 1955), *Geijutsu wa nan to tame ni aru ka* (Why Art?, 1957), and *Kyūdōsha to ninshikisha* (Searchers and Voyeurs, 1962). Meanwhile, he published *Nihon bundan shi* (History of Japanese Literary Circles, 1952–), which earned him the Kikuchi Kan Prize in 1963. Accused of immorality for his translation of D. H. Lawrence's *Lady Chatterley's Lover,* he wrote a series of articles defending freedom of expression, *Itō Sei no seikatsu no iken* (Life and Opinions of Itō Sei, 1951 and 1952). Among his other novels are *Hi no tori* (The Firebird, 1953), *Hanran* (Flood, 1958), *Hakkutsu* (Excavation, 1968), and *Hen'yō* (Change, 1968), for which he won the Shinchō Prize posthumously in 1970.

Itō Shinsui. Japanese-style painter (1898–1972), born in Tokyo. He produced color prints portraying beautiful women *(bijin)* starting in 1916, and was known for his series of landscapes titled *Ōmi hakkei* (Eight Views of Ōmi, 1917). His prints were produced by artisanal engravers and printers from his paintings.

Itō Shizuo. Symbolist poet (1906–53), born in Nagasaki prefecture: *Waga hito ni atauru aika* (Sad Poems for My Lady, 1935), *Natsubana* (Summer Flowers, 1940), *Haru ni isogi* (Waiting for Spring, 1943).

Itō Sukechika. Warrior (d. 1182), responsible for guarding the young Minamoto no Yoritomo when he was exiled to Izu by Taira no Kiyomori. Yoritomo seduced Itō's daughter, earning his profound hatred, and he went to battle against him in 1180. Captured and released, he committed suicide. Itō Sukechika is best known for the events that linked him to the vengeance of the Soga brothers. Because he had confiscated the estates of his nephew, Kudō Suketsune, in Izu, the latter had his son assassinated. To take revenge, Sukechika's grandsons, the Soga brothers, assassinated Kudō Suketsune in 1193. *See* SOGA MONOGATARI.

Itō Sukeyuki. Admiral (Itō Sukeyasu, Itō Sukenori, Itō Yukō, 1843–1914), born in Satsuma. He commanded the Japanese fleet that attacked China in 1894–95 and modernized the Japanese navy. He was ennobled in 1907.

Ito-wappu-nakama. Guild of raw-silk importers who distributed the fabric to artisans and set prices in the seventeenth and eighteenth centuries. The guild was created by the shogunate in 1604 to reinforce its control of trade in light of the Portuguese and, later, Dutch monopolies on imports from China. *See also* KABUNAKAMA.

Itoyori. Buddhist dance accompanied by singing and music, part of the Ennen, and generally performed by "pages" *(chigo).*

Itozono Wasaburō. Western-style painter, born 1911 in Ōita prefecture. He studied painting in Tokyo and was concerned mainly with creating and running art societies, while continuing to produce oil paintings of symbolic subjects based on daily life. His paintings earned many awards in various exhibitions.

Itsuki Hiroyuki. Writer, born 1932 in Fukuoka prefecture. He lived in Korea until the end of the Second World War, then studied Russian literature. His first novel, published in 1966, *Saraba Mosukuwa gurentai* (Farewell to Muscovite Misfits), began his literary career, and he won the Naoki Prize for his second novel, *Aozameta umao miyo* (Look at the Pale Horse, 1966). Among his other books are *Seishun no mon* (The Door to Youth, 1971), *Unicōn no tabi* (Voyages of a Unicorn, 1971), *Hitler no isan* (Hitler's Heritage, 1971), and *Sofia no aki* (Autumn in Sofia).

Itsuki no Miya. General title for imperial princesses who became grand priestesses in the Ise shrines. Also called Saigū-shinnō Saiō.

Itsukushima. Small island in Hiroshima Bay on which stands the Itsukushima-jinja shrine (or Aki no Miyajima, for the island's other name, Miyajima). It is one of the three most famous landscapes of Japan (Nihon Sankei). It has granitic soil and is covered with forests. *Area:* 30 km².

• **Itsukushima-jinja.** Shinto shrine built on the island of Itsukushima (Miyajima) at the foot of Mt. Misen (*alt.:* 590 m), in Hiroshima prefecture. According to tradition, it was founded in 593, but it is more likely that it was first built in 811. Taira no Kiyomori, who controlled that part of Japan, renovated it and had a huge torii erected in front of it, in the sea (it was rebuilt in 1875 and is 18 m high; it is painted red). Having become the tutelary shrine of the Taira, the Itsukushima-jinja was restored and expanded in 1167 and 1241 and was completely rebuilt in 1556. It is dedicated to Susanoo's three daughters and, since the Kamakura period, the syncretic divinity Benzai-ten (*Skt.:* Sarasvatī). This shrine has about 6,000 branches throughout Japan. It has a five-story pagoda built in 1587, an *araebisu-jinja* from 1591, and a Noh theater dating from about 1590. Its annual festival takes place on June 17. Also called Aki no Miyajima.

Itsunen. Japanese name of a Chinese painter (Yiran, 1601–68) of the Zen Ōbaku sect, who went to Japan in 1644. He persuaded the Chinese monk Ingen to join him in Nagasaki. Itsunen painted mainly Buddhist subjects in the late Ming style. *See* ŌBAKU-SHŪ, ZENGA.

Itsuō Bijutsukan. Museum in Ikeda, Osaka, displaying mainly paintings, calligraphy, and lacquered objects collected by Kobayashi Ichizō; opened in 1957 (expanded in 1973). Among the treasures on exhibit are *emakimono* from the Kamakura and Muromachi periods, Chinese porcelain, and many pieces of Japanese pottery. *See* MUSEUMS.

Itsutsu-ginu. Ceremonial garment reserved for noblewomen in the Heian and Kamakura periods, composed of many kimono worn one over another (between 5 and 20 during the Heian period, and 2 or 3 during the Kamakura period), and showing their colored hems at the neck and sleeves. Also called *go-i. See* JŪNI-HITOE.

• **Itsutsu-gusoku.** *See* MITSU-GUSOKU.

Itsu-un. Painter (Kinoshita Shōsai; *azana:* Kōsai; *mei:* Shiganosuke; *gō:* Butsubutsu-chi, Yoshikusanjin, Jorasanjin, Itsu-un, 1799–1866) of the Nanga school, Yūshi's and Kōhako's student. He painted almost exclusively landscapes and was a highly regarded poet.

Ittan. Samurai (Ittanfu, Kyōryūsai, d. 1877) in Nagoya and Gifu, known mainly as a sculptor of netsuke.

• **Ittanfu.** *See* ITTAN.

Ittō-en. Shinto-Buddhist syncretic sect founded by Nishida Tenkō (Tenkō-san, 1872–?) in Hokkaido in 1928. It promotes action and service and recognizes the universality of all religions. Also called Senko-sha.

Iwa-enogu. Mineral pigments that painters mixed with glue and used to color *emakimono* (mainly during the Kamakura and Muromachi periods).

Iwahashi Eien. Japanese-style (Nihonga) painter, born 1903 in Hokkaido. Yamanouchi Tamon's student in Tokyo, he founded the Shin Nihonga Kenkyū-kai (Society of Research on Nihonga Painting), which was dissolved in 1938. He then created another association of painters, and continued to have exhibitions regularly at the Inten. He received the grand prize from the Ministry of Education in 1959, was appointed a professor at the Tokyo School of Fine Arts in 1966, and retired in 1968.

Iwai. Ancient Japanese family that, according to the *Nihon shoki,* governed the Tsukushi region in the sixth century. Having refused to support the Mimana in their invasion of Korea in 527, the Iwai family was attacked by the Yamato armies commanded by Ōmi no Kenu and destroyed. A "keyhole" *kofun* 125 m long in the town of Yame (Fukuoka prefecture) is probably that of the head of the Iwai family. *See* IWATOYAMA KOFUN.
• Classical-dance school. *See* IEMOTO, IWAI HANSHIRŌ.
→ *See* IHAI.

Iwai Hanshirō. Family of Kabuki actors and dancers. Its most famous members were Iwai Hanshirō IV (1747–1800), known for his *onnagata* roles, and Iwai Hanshirō V (1776–1847). They created a dance school called Iwai.

• **Iwai Heijirō.** Famous Kabuki actor (*waka-onnagata* roles) in Kyoto and Edo about 1700.

Iwajuku. Archeological site in the village of Kasakake, Nitta (Gumma prefecture). In 1947, layers of silt were excavated and paleolithic stone tools (pre-

dating the Jōmon cultures) were found. Most of them were oval bifaces with traces of polishing and retouched edges (Iwajuku I). This culture probably dates from 20,000 BC. The site comprises four levels. In 1970 (Aizawa and Serizawa Chōsuke excavations), an earlier level (level 0) was discovered containing what seem to be tools dating to 40,000 years ago, but it is not known whether they were made by humans or were shaped by nature. *See* HISTORY, PREHISTORY.

Iwaki. Former province, now divided between Fukushima and Miyagi prefectures.
→ *See* AKAMATSU NORIYOSHI.

Iwakura. Town near Nagoya, in Aichi prefecture, where an important archeological site dating from the Yayoi period was discovered. Ruins of an ancient castle. *Pop.:* 45,000.

Iwakura Tomomi. Statesman (Horikawa Tomomi, 1825–83), born in Kyoto. Adopted by the Iwakura family, he became chamberlain under Emperor Kōmei in 1854. He participated actively in the movement to restore imperial power and was named minister of foreign affairs in 1868. He led a major information mission to Europe and the United States (Iwakara Mission, Iwakura Kengai Shisetsu) from 1871 to 1873, and was appointed to Emperor Meiji's Privy Council upon his return. Also called Iwakura Tomoyoshi.

• **Iwakura Kengai Shisetsu.** Major information mission sent to Europe and the United States by Emperor Meiji in 1871, led by Iwakura Tomomi. In addition to Iwakura, the mission comprised Okubo Toshimichi, Kido Takayoshi, Itō Hirobumi, Yamaguchi Naoyoshi (1842–94), Sasaki Takayuki (1830–1910), Tanaka Fujimaro, and Yamada Akiyoshi (1844–92), accompanied by secretaries, scholars, and students (including children aged 6 to 15 years), for a total of some 50 people, not counting servants. The mission left for Yokohama on December 23, 1871, crossed the Pacific Ocean, and arrived in San Francisco on January 15, 1872. The group arrived in Washington, D.C., on March 4, 1872, met with President Grant, toured Washington and Boston, and left the United States in August 1872. On August 17, 1872, the group landed at Liverpool and traveled to London for an audience with Queen Victoria on December 5. The mission then went to Paris, where its members met with President Thiers. Then came meetings with King Leopold II of Belgium (Feb. 18, 1873), King William III of Holland (Feb. 25), Emperor William I of Germany

(Mar. 11), Czar Alexander II in St. Petersburg (Apr. 3), King Christian IX of Denmark (Apr. 19), King Oskar II of Sweden (Apr. 25), King Victor-Emmanuel II of Italy (May 13), Emperor Franz-Joseph of Austria-Hungary (June 8), and King Cérésole of Switzerland (June 21, 1873). After a stop in Lyon, the mission went to Marseilles, leaving on July 20, 1873 for the return trip to Japan via Alexandria, Suez, Aden, Ceylon, Saigon, Taiwan, Shanghai, Nagasaki, and Kobe, reaching Yokohama on September 13, 1873. The information gathered by the members of the mission led the Meiji government to make reforms and to modernize so that Japan could catch up with the Western world in all sectors.

Iwami. Former province, now Shimane prefecture.

• **Iwami Ginzan.** Silver mine in Shimane prefecture, near the town of Oda, where major silver reserves were discovered in the early fourteenth century. Operations improved in the fifteenth and sixteenth centuries, thanks to new cupellation methods imported from Korea. The Mōri family controlled the mine at the time; the Tokugawa seized it in the early seventeenth century. The mine was exhausted and operation abandoned in 1923.

Iwami Masayoshi. *See* MASAYOSHI.

Iwamoto Konkan. Blacksmith and goldsmith (1744–1801) in Edo, Ryōkan I's student and Ryōkan II's adoptive son. He was famous for his sword guards *(tsuba).*

Iwamoto Mari. Virtuoso violinist (1926–79). She toured in Europe many times and in the United States in 1950. In 1967, she founded the Iwamoto Mari String Quartet in Japan.

Iwamura kofun. Large funerary tumulus in Kumamoto prefecture, featuring a drawing in the interior chamber portraying a huge épée (covering four flagstones trimmed with sandstone) and a decoration formed of concentric circles. Date uncertain, between the fourth and seventh centuries.

Iwanami Shoten. Major publishing house founded in 1913 in Tokyo (Kanda district) by Iwanami Shigeo (1881–1946). It published works by Natsume Sōseki, Kurata Hyakuzo, and Abe Jirō, and a philosophy periodical called *Shichō* in 1917, then *Shisō* in 1921. It also published a science magazine, *Kagaku,* starting in 1931, and the literary magazine *Bungaku* in 1933. It started a major series of literary works, the Iwanami Bunko (Iwanami Library)

in 1927. After the Second World War, it produced many translations of foreign books and published an opinion periodical, *Sekai,* starting in 1946.

Iwa no Hime. Empress (d. 347), who married Emperor Nintoku in 314. Poems that she exchanged with her husband inspired legends related in the *Kojiki* and *Nihon shoki.* Some of her poems were included in the *Man'yōshū.*

Iwano Hōmei. Writer and poet (Iwano Yoshie, 1873–1920), born on the island of Awaji to a samurai family. As a young man, he converted to Christianity, intending to become a missionary, but he abandoned this plan and turned to literature. He wrote several books of poetry, then became interested in poetics, publishing *Shintaishi no sahō* (Composition of Poems in the New Style, 1907) and *Shintaishi shi* (History of the New Poetic Style, 1907–08). He had previously written several Kabuki tragedies, including *Tama wa mayou getchū no yaiba* (Soul in Pain and the Lunar Sword, 1894, renamed *Katsura gorō*), but was not very successful in this genre. He published other critical works, including *Shimpiteki hanjū shugi* (The Principle of the Mystical Semi-Animal, 1906) and *Shin shizen shugi* (The New Naturalism, 1908), in which he advocated adoption of a style midway between naturalism and symbolism. He also founded a magazine to explain ancient Shinto, *Shin Nihon shugi* (The New Japanism), in 1916. He then began to write more or less autobiographical novels, including *Tandeki* (Decadence, 1909) and *Hōmei gobusaku* (The Five Lives of Iwano Hōmei, 1911), featuring a single hero in five episodes called *Hatten* (Development), *Dokuyaku o nomu onna* (The Women Who Drinks Poison), *Hōrō* (Wandering), *Dankyō* (The Destroyed Bridge), and *Tsukimono* (Possession). He also wrote many novellas, literary-criticism articles, and translations (notably of Plutarch).

Iwasaki Tsunemasa. Naturalist and draftsman (Iwasaki Kan'en, Genzo, 1786–1842) who studied pharmacological plants. He was one of Ono Ranzan's students and may have drawn a portrait of Franz von Siebold when he was in Edo. Iwasaki published *Honzō zufu,* a 92-volume work describing the plants of Japan, with magnificent illustrations.

Iwasaki Yatarō. Businessman (1835–85), born in Tosa to a samurai family. He directed the company Tosa Shōji in Nagasaki in 1867, reorganizing it as Tsukumo Co. and transferring it to Osaka, where it became Mitsubishi in 1873. Having obtained a monopoly on transporting troops to Taiwan in 1874, he then started a regular passenger line to Shanghai (which he bought from the American Pacific Steamship Company) and extended his company's activities to insurance, warehouses, and mining. The government created another shipping company, Kyōdō Un'yu Kaishi, and after Iwasaki Yatarō died, Mitsubishi merged with it to form Nihon Yūsen Kaisha (NYK). *See* MITSUBISHI.

Iwasa Matabei. Painter (Iwasa Katsumochi, Iwasa Shōi, Iwasa Matabe no Iō, Matabe no Iō; *gō:* Dōun, Un'ō, Unnō, Shōi, Kekishokyū, Ukiyo-Matabe, 1578–1650), son of a daimyo of Settsu Araki Murashige. He studied with Tosa Mitsunori in Sakai, then with Kanō Naizen. In 1637, he went to Edo to enter the service of Tokugawa Iemitsu. In addition to painting in the classic tradition of the Yamato-e, Matabei was one of the first ukiyo-e painters, working in Edo and Fukui. He painted mainly portraits, but also genre landscapes.

Iwase senzuka kofun-gun. Sixth- and seventh-century grouping of 500 to 600 tombs *(kofun)* in the hills near the Kinokawa river at Iwasi in Wakayama prefecture. Most of the *kofun* are round, though some are square or keyhole-shaped. Some of them were excavated between 1962 and 1965.

Iwashimizu Hachiman-gū. Shinto shrine (also called Otokoyama Hachiman-gū) in the Tsuzuki district of Kyoto and dedicated to Emperor Ōjin, Empress Jingū Kōgō, and *kami* Hime Ōkami, founded in 859 by a Buddhist monk named Gyōkō. It was venerated by the imperial family and by the Minamoto clan (whose guardian *kami* was Hachiman-Ōjin), which established a branch of the shrine, the Tsurugaoka Hachiman-gū, in Kamakura. Every September 15, a major festival, Iwashimizu Hōjōe, is held there. The buildings in this shrine date from 1651. *See* HACHIMAN DAI-MYŌJIN.

• **Iwashimizu Hōjōe.** *See* IWASHIMIZU HACHIMAN-GŪ.

• *Iwashimizu monogatari.* Thirteenth-century two-volume war novel *(gunki-monogatari)* by an anonymous author.

Iwashiro. Former province, now included in Fukushima prefecture.

Iwashita Shunsaku. Writer (1907–80) of many best-selling novels, including *Tomishima Matsu-*

gorō den (The Life of Tomishima Matsugorō, 1939), which was made into a movie, *Muhō matsu no isshō* (The Rickshaw Puller), directed by Imagaki Hiroshi, in 1943.

Iwashita Sōichi. Philosopher (1889–1940) and Catholic priest, born in Tokyo. He studied in Europe from 1919 to 1925 and was ordained a priest in Rome in 1925. Known for his research on medieval philosophy, he was director of the Fukusei leper colony in Shizuoka from 1930 to 1940. His philosophical works were collected in the nine-volume *Iwashita Sōichi zenshū,* published 1961–64.

Iwata Eikichi. Contemporary painter, born 1929 in Tokyo, a trompe-l'oeil realist in style. He has worked in Paris since 1957.

Iwata Masami. Painter, born 1893 in Niigata prefecture. He became Matsuoka Eikyū's student in Tokyo, working in the new Yamato-e style and painting mainly landscapes. He received many prizes following his exhibitions at various Teiten, Shin Bunten, and Nitten, and the Nihon Geijutsu-in (Japan Art Academy) Prize in 1961. He was elected a member of the Academy in 1977.

Iwate-ken. Prefecture in northern Honshu (Tōhoku) on the Pacific coast, the former Mutsu province. *Main city:* Morioka; *other major cities:* Miyako, Hanamaki, Ichinoseki, Hiraizumi. *Area:* 12,277 km²; *pop.:* 1.45 million. Its very jagged coastline has many very scenic spots and is part of Rikuchū National Park.

Iwato. Traditional musical scale. *See* MUSIC, RITSU, RYŌ.

Iwato Kannon. One of the 33 forms (Sanjūsan Ōgeshin) of Kannon Bosatsu (*Skt.:* Avalokiteshvara), perhaps a syncretic form of Amaterasu-Ōmikami, since she is often portrayed sitting at the entrance to a cave.

Iwatoyama kofun. Large funerary tumulus *(kofun)* in Chikugo-Fukushima (northern Kyushu) 125 m long and 14 m high; said to be the tomb of a member of the Iwai family, Tsukushi no Kimi, a low-level *miyatsuko* who rebelled against the Yamato court in 527 and committed suicide when he was defeated. This uniquely shaped *kofun* comprises a *bekku,* or platform on which the corpse was placed until the tomb was completed. On the *bekku* are a number of rough-hewn stone statues portraying men, bears, and a horse with a saddle and stirrups, probably dating from the seventh century. This *kofun* is cited in the Nara-period compilation *Chikugo no kuni fudoki.* Close by is another tumulus, the Noriba *kofun. See* IWAI, KOFUN.

Iwaya Ichiroku. Calligrapher (1834–1905), who studied with Chinese historian and calligrapher Yang Shoujing (1839–1914). Iwaya Sazanami's father.

Iwaya Sazanami. Writer and journalist (Iwaya Sueo, 1870–1933), born in Tokyo. He wrote mainly children's stories featuring talking animals: *Koganemaru* (1891). He also compiled a major 24-volume series of popular legends, *Nihon mukashibanashi* (Japanese Tales of Once Upon a Time, 1894–96). He taught Japanese at the University of Berlin starting in 1900. He was Iwaya Ichiroku's son.

• **Iwaya Sueo.** *See* IWAYA SAZANAMI.

Iyagarase no nenrei. "Years of Ingratitude." A novel by Niwa Fumio, published in 1947. In this sordid family tragedy, an old woman is mistreated by her family. It is an eloquent plea for the creation of retirement homes for elderly people.

Iyo. Former province, now part of Ehime prefecture (Shikoku). *See* SETONAIKAI.
→ *See* HIMIKO.

Iyo-gasuri. *See* SATSUMA-GASURI.

Iyo-nyūdō. *See* MINAMOTO NO YORIYOSHI.

Iyo Shinnō. One of Emperor Kammu's sons. He and his mother were accused of plotting to kill his brother, Emperor Heijō, and they poisoned themselves in 807.

Izanagi and Izanami no Mikoto. According to the *Kojiki,* a couple of primordial *kami* from whom came the islands of Japan and all other "earthly" *kami (kunitsu-kami).* Izanami was Izanagi's twin sister, in the seventh generation of heavenly spirits. They plunged a magical lance into the water and created an island called Onogorojima, to which they descended to procreate, giving birth to the Japanese islands, the first of which was Awaji, then to other *kami.* The *kami* of fire, Kagutsuchi no Kami, burned his mother's genitals as he was being born, and she died. A grieving Izanagi killed this mur-

derous *kami* and descended to the kingdom of darkness (Yomi no Kuni) to find his sister-wife. But when he saw her, he was horrified by the ravages of death; chased by 80 horrible females, he saved himself only by throwing his comb and a peach to them. He then blocked off the entrance to Hell (Yomotsu Hirasaka). To wash away the contact with death, he bathed *(misogi),* and from his eyes and all parts of his body thus purified, other *kami* were born: Amaterasu-Ōmikami *(kami* of the sun), Tsukumi no Mikoto *(kami* of the moon), and Susanoo no Mikoto. *See* CHIJIN GODAI, TENJIN SHICHIDAI.

Izawa-jō. Ancient fort built in 802 by Sakanoue no Tamuramaro in the town of Mizusawa (Iwate prefecture), at the confluence of the Kitami-gawa and Izawa-gawa rivers, to defend the region against the Ainu. Also called Isawa-jō.

Izayoi-nikki. "Journal of the Moon of the Sixteenth Night." An account of Abutsu-ni's trip from Kyoto to Kamakura to meet bureaucrats who might help her resolve the issue of her deceased husband's succession. This text, sprinkled with many poems, was written in 1277. The journal describes the Tōkaidō road, then Abutsu-ni's stay in Kamakura, and quotes long poems *(chōka)* of prayer to the *kami* of Tsurugaoka Hachiman-gū. On the whole, it is rather monotonous, but it reflects well the author's sensibilities. Also called *Izayoi no ki. See* ABUTSU-NI.

Izayoi-seishin. See SATOMOYŌ AZAMI NO IRONUI.

Izeki Chikanobu. Sculptor (sixteenth century) of Noh masks, founder of the Ōmi Izeki school of mask makers, one of the three most famous in Japan at the time; the other two were Echizen Deme and Ōno Deme. He was a disciple of Sankōbō (d. ca. 1532) and one of the Jissaku (Ten Famous Master Sculptors). His family line was extinguished with Kawachi Daijō Ieshige (d. 1645 in Edo).

Izu. Former province, now part of Shizuoka prefecture. It is a rocky peninsula with many hot springs (thus formerly named Yu-Izu, "hot spring"), a very jagged coast, and some small fishing ports. It is part of the Fuji-Hakone National Park. Its highest mountain is Amagi-san (1,406 m). Also called Izu Hantō.

• **Izu Kinzan.** Gold mines in Izu province, operated by the Tokugawa, mainly Toi, Yugashima, and Nawaji, starting in the late sixteenth century. The mines were flooded, so their production declined and they were gradually abandoned.

- **Izu Shotō.** Island group in the Pacific Ocean, extending to the southeast of the Izu peninsula, composed of the volcanic islets Ōshima, Toshima, Niijima, Kōzujima, Miyakejima, Mikurajima, Hachijōjima, Shikinejima, Udonejima, and others. They are under the administrative aegis of Tokyo. The highest point on the islands is the Miharayama (758 m) on Ōshima. The main town, Motomura, is also on Ōshima. The Miyakejima volcano was last active in 1952; the Ōshima volcano, in 1985. Discovered by De Vries in 1643, these islands were long called the De Vries Archipelago. Also called Izu-tō, Izu Shichi-tō.

Izumi Chikahira. Warrior, famous for his strength, who was killed in 1213 after rebelling against the Hōjō *shikken.*

Izumi Kyōka. Writer (Izuma Kyōtarō, 1873–1939), born in Kanazawa (Ishikawa prefecture). He studied in Tokyo with Oaki Kōyō, who encouraged him to write in the style of the Ken'yūsha school. He began his career at 20 and was almost immediately successful with his novels of ideas, *Giketsu kyōketsu* (Loyalty and Bravery, 1894), *Yakō junsa* (The Police Officer's Rounds, 1895), and *Gekashitsu* (The Operating Room, 1895). His style was refined and more poetic in *Teriha kyōgen* (1896) and *Kōya hijiri* (The Saint of Mt. Kōya, 1900). He then married a geisha and described the ephemeral world of the pleasure districts in *Yushima mōde* (Pilgrimage to Yushima, 1899), *Onna keizu* (Genealogies of Women, 1907), *Shirasagi* (The White Heron, 1909), and *Nihombashi* (1914). He also wrote symbolist novels such as *Uta andon* (The Oil Lamp, 1910). Not very popular in his time, Izumi Kyōka has been rediscovered and is now considered one of the most representative writers of his time. Films by directors Ichikawa Kon, Mizoguchi Kenzu, and Kinusaga Teinosuke, among others, drew on his novels.

Izumi-ryū. Theater school in Kyōgen, one of the three most famous, with the Okura and the Sagi, founded by Yamawaki Izumi no Kami Motoyoshi (d. 1659) in the Owari estate. Its style was followed mainly in Nagoya and Kyoto, while other schools seemed to be favored by the shogunate in Edo.

Izumi Seiichi. Ethnologist (1915–70), born in Tokyo. Influenced by the Malinovsky school, he conducted much research in Korea and on the island of Cheju, and he created the faculty of ethnology at the University of Tokyo. He then continued his research on pre-Columbian civilizations in Peru, excavating the Kotosh site.

Izumi Shikibu. Woman of letters (tenth–eleventh century) and lady in the company of Empress Fujiwara no Akiko (Jōtōmon'in, 988–1074). She was Ōe Koretoki's (Masemune) daughter and married to Tachibana Michisada, governor of Izumi. After her husband died, she married Fujiwara no Yasumasa. Her real name and dates of birth and death are not known. An excellent *waka* poet, she left a collection of 1,540 poems and her diary, *Izumi Shikibu nikki,* in which she speaks of herself in the third person. This diary, covering the years 1003 and 1004, is composed of love letters addressed to her by Prince Atsumichi, Tametaka's brother, who died in 1002. An important document on the life of a lady of the Heian court, it has sometimes been attributed to Fujiwara no Toshinari (1114–1204), though with no certainty. Her daughter, known as Ko-Shikibu (d. 1025), was also a talented poet.

Izumizaki kofun. Funerary tumulus *(kofun)* of the village of Kawasaki (Fukushima prefecture, Kyushu), dating from around 600. The interior walls of its chambers are decorated with paintings of a hunting scene, a group of four men and three women who seem to be dancing, a boat, and concentric circles.

Izumo. Former province, now included in Shimane prefecture, on the Sea of Japan. It was one of the eight provinces of San'indō. It was probably an old religious center (related to Korea) that rivaled the Yamato court for preeminence before the latter absorbed it. Its local legends are mixed with those of other provinces and constitute one of the main sources of the *Kojiki* and *Nihon shoki.*
- Town in Shimani prefecture, on the shore of the Sea of Japan and Lake Shinji; former merchant city in the fourteenth century and site of the Izumo Taisha Shrine. Textile industries. *Pop.:* 80,000.

- *Izumo fudoki.* One of the four surviving *fudoki* (dating from 733), relating legends of the province of Izumo.

- *Izumo ji-ha.* Branch of the Buddhist sect of the Jōdo Shin-shū established in Izumo. About 40,000 followers.

- **Izumo no Okuni.** *See* OKUNI.

- **Izumo no Oyashiro.** *See* IZUMO TAISHA.

- **Izumo Taisha.** Major Shinto shrine located near the town of Izumo and dedicated to the *kami* Ōkuninushi no Mikoto, Ame no Minakanushi no Kami, and Takamimusubi no Kami. A legend told in the *Kojiki* and *Nihon shiki* relates the mythical origin of this shrine: it was given to Ōkuninushi by Amaterasu-Ōmikami to reward him for having helped Ninigi no Mikoto by offering him this part of the country. Izumo Taisha's main shrine, built very long ago, seems to have been constructed on the plan for a royal palace. It was rebuilt in 1744 and 1874 in the same style. It is a wooden structure 24 m high (although it is said to have been 96 m high originally), supported on nine enormous wood pillars and a central pillar composed of nine pillars braced together. A 15-step staircase leads to its entrance, on the right side of the building. This shrine has been rebuilt 25 times since its foundation. Every October 11–17, a major festival takes place there (Kamiari Matsuri) to which all the *kami* of Japan are invited; this is why October is called Kamiarizuki ("without divinities"). During the month, large numbers of small wooden houses are built around the shrine for the *kami* to stay in. Since they are absent from the other shrines of Japan, people cannot marry in October. Another festival takes place at the Izumo Taisha on May 14. People have sometimes identified the *kami* of Izumo with the syncretic divinity Daikoku-ten (*Skt.:* Mahākalā). He is prayed to for marriages, to better one's luck, and for good harvests. This shrine is also known as Izumo no Oyashiro.

- **Izumo Taisha-kyō.** Shinto sect founded in Izumo in 1873 by Senge Sompuku (1845–1918), which drew 3.2 million followers. Also called Shintō Taisha-kyō.

Izumo Hirosada. Physician (eighth–ninth century). He and Abe no Manao were said to have written the oldest treatise on Japanese medicine, the 100-volume *Daidō-ruijūhō*, now lost.

Izuna Gongen. Shinto-Buddhist syncretic divinity of Mt. Izuna, often identified with Zaō Gongen. This "terrible aspect" of the divinity was "seen" for the first time by the monk Gyōki (668–749).

Izuruhara. Archeological site in Tochigi prefecture, discovered in 1961, revealing a series of 37 shaft tombs from the Yayoi period and 6 more from the *kofun* period. Also uncovered were more than 100 pieces of Yayoi pottery and 50 necklace beads.

Izutsu. "The Curb of the Well." The title of a Noh play by Zeami: a young woman tells a Buddhist monk the story of Arihara no Narihira and his love for Ki no Aritsune's daughter, then reveals that she is the spirit of the latter.

J. This consonant, used in conjunction with a vowel (*a, i, u,* or *o*) is a "nigorization" (*see* NIGORI) of the syllable *sa* to yield the syllables *ja, ji, ju,* and *jo.* When the syllable *ji* is obtained by writing the single kana character for *shi* (nigorized), the syllables *ja, ju,* and *jo* are obtained by combining the characters *ji + ya (ja), ji + yu (ju),* and *ji + yo (jo).* *See* GOJŪON-ZU, KANA.

Jagatara-bumi. Series of letters sent from Java by Japanese exiles (who could not return to Japan because of the political isolation of the shogunate in 1639) starting in 1655, when mail was once again let in. These letters, sent to families, are valuable records of the living conditions of Japanese and mixed-blood Dutch and Japanese in the seventeenth and eighteenth centuries.

Jakkō-in. Buddhist monastery in Kyoto, belonging to the Tendai sect, where Kenri Mon'in (1155–1213), a daughter of Taira no Kiyomori, lived. She married Emperor Takakura and was Antoku Tennō's mother. She is venerated there as the main divinity Jizō (*Skt.:* Kshitigarbha).

Jaku. In Zen Buddhism, the pure expression of serenity, which can be obtained only by a combination of *wa* (peace of heart), *kei* (respect for things), and *sei* (harmony with nature). *Skt.: shānta.*

Jakuchi Kizaemon. Painter (mid-eighteenth century) of landscapes in the Chinese style and goldsmith famous for his *tsuba.*

Jakugon. Buddhist monk (1702–71), born in Bitchū province (Okayama prefecture), famous Sanskrit scholar and renowned calligrapher.

Jakuren. Buddhist monk (Fujiwara no Sadanaga, ca. 1139–1202) and famous *waka* poet, one of the compilers of the *Shin kokin-shū* in 1201. He traveled throughout Japan composing poems and taking part in many poetry contests. His works, collected in the *Jakuren hōshi-shū,* are imbued with the aesthetic concepts of *yūgen* and *sabi.* One hundred seventeen of his *waka* were included in various anthologies, starting with the *Senzai waka-shū* (ca. 1188).

Jakusai. Painter (Rokkaku Jakusai, 1348–1424) of the Yamato-e school, member of the imperial *e-dokoro.* He painted part of the *Yūzu nembutsu-engi* in 1414. At the end of his life, he became a Buddhist monk. *See* FUJIWARA NO NOBUZANE, NOBUZANE.

Janes, Leroy Lansing. American officer (1838–1909) who was invited to Japan in 1871 to teach (in English) mathematics, history, and science at the Kumamoto Yōgakkō. A fervent Christian, he converted some of his students, among them Ebina Danjō and Ukita Kazutami. After the Kumamoto Yōgakkō closed in 1876, Janes taught for several months at the Ōsaka Eigakkō, returned to the United States, then went back to Japan in 1893, where he taught for two years at Kyoto's Third College before returning to California for good.

Jan-ken-pon. Children's game of Chinese origin, in which two players must simultaneously show a hand sign, either stone (fist), paper (open hand), or scissors (two spread fingers). Stone wins over scissors, scissors win over paper, and paper wins over stone by covering it. It is played for the best out of three rounds. The objects may change to, for instance, hunter, gun, and fox. This game is played in almost all countries of Asia and has spread to Europe and North America. Also called *misukumi*. *Chin.*: Jiandao Shidou Pu, Caiquan.

Japan. *Official name:* Nihon (sometimes pronounced Nippon). *Geographical location:* Island country in northeast Asia, extending north to south from 24° to 46° latitude, and essentially of volcanic nature.
→ *See* AGRICULTURE, ARCHEOLOGY, ARCHITECTURE, CALENDAR, CINEMA, CURRENCY, DANCE, EDUCATION, FAUNA, FISHING, FLORA, GEOGRAPHY, GEOLOGY, HISTORY, LITERATURE, MUSIC, PAINTING, POLITICAL PARTIES, PRIME MINISTERS, PROVINCES AND PREFECTURES, SCAP, SCULPTURE, SPORTS, THEATER, WEIGHTS AND MEASURES; CHRONOLOGY.

Japan Airlines (JAL, Nihon kōkū). Semi-nationalized airline founded in 1951 and reorganized in 1953. It operates on intercontinental routes from Tokyo (Narita Airport) and Osaka. It also owns an international hotel chain.

Japan Foundation (Kokusai Kōryū Kikin). Official institution attached to the foreign affairs ministry, responsible for spreading Japanese culture abroad through cultural exchanges of goods, people, publications, and a quarterly English-language newsletter *(The Japan Foundation Newsletter)*. It was founded in 1972 following reorganization of the Kokusai Bunka Shinkōkai (KBS, Japan Cultural Society), which had been created in 1934. The foundation has branches in Kyoto, Jakarta, Rome, and Cologne, with offices in Bangkok, London, Paris, Los Angeles, Washington, São Paulo, and Canberra. Its first president was writer Kon Hidemi.

Japan Herald. English-language weekly newspaper created in Yokohama by Albert W. Hansard in 1861. It became a daily in 1863 as the *Daily Japan Herald.* It ceased publication in 1914.

Japan Line, Ltd. Japanese shipping company created in 1964 by the merger of Nittō Shōsen and Daidō Kaiun. Starting in the 1960s, it specialized in construction of supertankers and owned the largest commercial fleet in the world. After the oil crisis of 1970, however, it was forced to lay off employees. Head office in Tokyo.

Japan Times. English-language newspaper, new name of the *Japan Commercial News*, published in Yokohama and bought up by Charles Rickerby in 1865. Along with the *Japan Times Overland Mail,* it was published weekly until about 1870.
• English-language pro-government daily founded by Japanese interests in Tokyo in 1897 with government assistance. It absorbed various other English-language newspapers, such as the *Japan Advertiser,* the *Japan Mail,* and the *Japan Chronicle.* Its name changed to the *Nippon Times* in 1943, then returned to *Japan Times* in 1956. It now comprises a weekly supplement, *Japan Times Weekly,* and a magazine, *Student Times,* and has a print run of more than 60,000.

Japan Travel Bureau (JTB, Nihon Kōtsū Kōsha). Major travel and tourism agency founded in 1912 in Tokyo. It has many foreign offices and agencies in every city in Japan. Besides organizing trips in Japan and selling bus, train, and plane tickets, it takes hotel reservations and publishes a series of illustrated books on various sites in Japan and on Japanese arts and crafts.

Jasoku. Painter (active ca. 1491), probably a Zen Buddhist monk of the Daitoku-ji temple in Kyoto, known for having produced paintings on fusuma for the Shinju-an, a subsidiary temple built in memory of the Zen monk Ikkyū Sōjun (1394–1491) about 1491. The fusuma, painted in China ink, are among the most typical of *suiboku* art of the Muromachi period. Nothing is known about the person who painted them.

Jesuits (Iezusukai, Society of Jesus). Catholic order founded in Paris in 1534 by Ignatius of Loyola. Francis Xavier, one of the founders of the order, arrived in Kagoshima in 1549, was well received by the daimyo of Kyushu, and began to preach. Foreign and converted Japanese Jesuits worked in Japan until Christianity was banned by the Tokugawa and a number of them were martyred. The Jesuits returned to Japan in the early twentieth century and founded Sophia University (Jōchi Daigaku) in Tokyo in 1913. It was the Jesuits who introduced the first Western-type printing press to Japan in 1590, through Alessandro Valignano. The press was set up first in Kazusa (Nagasaki prefecture), then in Amakusa (Kumamato prefecture), but was shipped back to Macao in 1614 because of persecutions. However, the Jesuits were allowed to print certain books, religious and laic, including a translation of *Aesop's Fables (Isoho monogatari)* and abridged versions of the *Heike monogatari* and the *Taiheiki;*

Japan: Statistics

Total length of coasts: 34,000 km. *See*
GEOGRAPHY, GEOLOGY.

Total population (in 1998): 126,398,000.
Projections call for a peak population of 136
million by the year 2013. *Urban population:*
77%; *rural population:* 23%. *Immigration:*
Approximately 1,354,000 (from North and
South Korea, 50%; Taiwan, Hong Kong, and
China, 16%; Brazil, 11.8%; Philippines,
6.3%; United States, 3.2%). *Average
population density:* 334 per km², but may
attain record numbers in large urban
agglomerations.

Monetary unit: the *yen* (¥), theoretically divided
into 100 sen. Monetary zone for the
American dollar.

Official religion: None. Most Japanese,
however, are Shinto or Buddhist. Significant
Christian minority (3.9%).

Official language: Japanese. Second most
frequently used language: English.

Capital: Tokyo, since 1868; previously Kyoto.

Government: Pluralist democracy.
Constitutional monarchy headed by an
emperor assisted by a National Diet
(parliament) composed of two legislative
chambers, the House of Peers (251 members
elected for six years, one-half eligible for
reelection every three years) and the House of
Representatives (512 members elected for
four years by direct universal suffrage). The
head of government is the prime minister,
who is responsible to the parliament and
belongs to the majority political party.
Constitution promulgated November 3,
1946, taking effect May 3, 1947. The
emperor's position is hereditary; he represents
the nation but has no power.

Society

Housing units: About 40,670,000, of which
7.3% date from before 1945; 23 million
(64%) are private property.

Number of families: About 40 million; average
size: 3.2 people.

Single people: about 8 million (7.2%).

People living in their place of birth: 24%.

Economically active population: 67.1 million
(63% of those aged 15 and over, and 40% of
women). More than 24% of the active
population works in the tertiary sector.
Agriculture and fishing employ only 7.7%
of workers; commerce, 22.5%; industry,

33.1%; construction and public works, about
10%.

Proportion of adults voting in national elections:
70% (in 1992).

Birth rate: 9.5/1,000; *death rate:* 7.4/1,000.

Fertility rate per woman: 1.4.

Living Standards

Average life expectancy: women: 82.8 years; men:
76.4 years.

Suicide rate: 19.5 per 100,000.

Average work time per capita: 44.3 hours per
week.

Average leisure time per capita: 5 hours 50
minutes per week.

Number of households with: a car, 80%; a
telephone, 100%; a color television, 99%; a
washing machine, 99%; a camera, 87%; a
microwave oven, 84%.

Average income per family per year: 6,849,800
yen (US$72,824).

GNP: Japan is the second richest country in the
world. *Per capita GNP* (more than US$40,000)
ranked it fourth among 225 nations.

Total average expenditures per family: food
(24.4%), transportation (10%), recreation
(9.1%), clothing (7.1%), various expenses and
housing (10%), medical care (2.5%).

Unemployment rate: 3.4% (tending to rise since
1993).

Unionization: about 25% of workers (71,880
unions).

Strike rate: about 0.1 day per 1,000 working days
per worker.

Criminality per 100,000 inhabitants: *homicide,*
about 1.4; *rape,* about 1.4; *robbery,* 1,130.

Immigration: The main group of immigrants are
Koreans (about 700,000). But there are also
many workers (about 100,000 illegal, it is
estimated) from the Philippines, Southeast Asia,
and the Near East.

Communications

Roads: 1,112,900 km (66% paved).

Railroads: 38,125 km; 341,136,000,000
passenger-kilometers/year.

Private automobiles: 29 million; *trucks:* 20
million; *buses:* 233,000.

Merchant marine, total tonnage: 48,450,000
tons.

Air traffic: 83,725,000,000 passenger-kilometers/
year; *cargo;* 4,180,000,000 tons/km. Number
of airports with regular flights: 65.

Passenger transportation: by automobile, 48%;

by bus, 11%; by rail, 37%; by plane, 4%; by boat, 0.6% (total % of people transported).

Number of radio stations (1993): 1,269; 413 of them commercial.

Number of television stations: 36,250; 18,900 of them commercial.

Number of daily newspapers: 122, with a total circulation of 72 million.

Number of new books published: about 37,000 per year, of which 7,000 are novels.

Number of magazines published: weekly, 105; monthly, 2,527.

Number of feature films produced: about 386 per year.

Health

Physicians: one for about every 546 persons; *dentists:* one for every 1,564 persons.

Hospital beds (public and private): one per 74 persons.

Calories absorbed daily (average): 2,900.

Education

Literacy: practically 100% of the adult population.

Number of schools: primary, 24,900; secondary, 16,800; higher, 125.

Number of teachers: primary, 445,000; secondary, 570,000; university and technical college, 142,000.

Commerce

Imports (1994): 29,007,000,000,000 yen (15.5% on food). *Main importing countries:* United States (22.4%), South Korea (6.3%), Australia (5.5%), China (5.3%), Indonesia (5.1%), Taiwan (4.7%), Canada (4.4%), Germany (4.3%).

Exports (1994): 43,928,000,000,000 yen (of which 17.8% motor vehicles). *Main destination countries:* United States (33.8%), Germany (6%), South Korea (5.8%), Taiwan (5.4%), Hong Kong (4.4%), United Kingdom (3.9%), China (3.6%).

Public debt (1988): US$1,240,700,000,000 (65% of GDP).

Balance of payments (1992): + $US119 billion.

Military expenditures: 1% of GDP.

Tourism (1988): Imports (mainly from the United States): US$2,893,000,000. Exports: US$18,682,000,000.

Approximate inflation rate: 1.7% per year (starting in 1992). It was 3.3% in 1991.

Growth rate (1993): about 2.3%.

Industry and Energy

Employment in industry: 33.1% of the active population.

Employment in mines: 1% of the active population.

Coal reserves: 8.58 billion tons. *Annual extraction:* about 8 million tons (and dropping).

Mine production (coal, lignite): 13,049,000 tons.

Silver production: 170,000 tons; *zinc production:* 133,000 tons.

Natural-gas production (1992): 2.17 billion m^3.

Employment in services: 58.7% of the active population.

Employment in agriculture: 7.2% of the active population.

Forestry (wood): about 30 million tons.

Electricity production: 698,970 billion kwh, including *nuclear:* 215 billion kwh; *hydroelectricity:* 90.3 billion kwh; *geothermic:* 1.7 billion kwh.

Consumption of petroleum products: 134,820,000 tons (including 60% gasoline, fuel oil, kerosene).

Share of energy sources: nuclear, 10.3%; oil, 55%; natural gas, 9.6%; coal, 19%; hydroelectricity, 5.3%.

Land use: forests, 66%; uncultivated land, 18.6%; cultivated land, 13%; pastureland, 1.7%.

[Figures from *Encyclopaedia Britannica* 1994–2001 and *Atlaseco 1994.*]

---

this collection of 30 works was known collectively as *Kirishitan-ban. See* ARIMA.

JETRO (Japan External Trade Organization, Nihon Bōeki Shinkōkai). Previously Japan Export Trade Research Association (JETRA), a para-gov-ernmental agency assisting with import of foreign products to Japan and export of Japanese products and techniques. It organizes expositions of foreign products in Japan (the World Trade Mart in Tokyo and others) and maintains bureaus in many foreign countries.

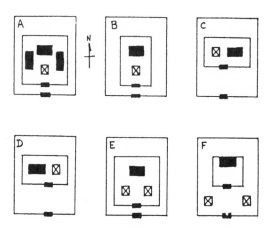

Six plans of monastery-temples, Asuka and Nara periods.
A. Asuka, ca. 560. B. Tennō-ji, ca. 600. C. Hōryu-ji,
ca. 610. D. Hokki-ji, ca. 650. E. Yakushi-ji, ca. 690.
F. Tōdai-ji, ca. 740

Ji. General term for a Buddhist temple. Also *tera*
(composite: *-dera*). Also sometimes called Shōja,
Dōjō, Garan. *See* HON-JI.
• Prefix meaning "by oneself" or "land" (a
"nigorization" of *chi*).

Jiaozhu (*Chin.*: Chiao-chow). Former Japanese
concession (Kōshūwan) on the southern coast of
Shandong province in China. At first a German possession, it was taken over by Japan in November
1914. It is an excellent port, located at the end of a
deep bay. Its main town is Qingdao. Japan refused
to cede this territory to China after 1918, but was
forced to do so after the Washington Conference of
1922, in return for compensation to defray the cost
of the improvements made.

Jibushō. In the *ritsuryō* era (eighth century), the
government department responsible for rules for
noble families above the fifth rank (*see* I), and for
foreigners, music, and imperial tombs. It was one of
the eight "ministries" created by the Taika Reform,
previously called Osamuru-tsukasa. A *jibu-kyō*,
subordinate bureaucrat, headed this department.

Jichirō. Abridgment of Zen Nihon Jichi Dantai
Rōdō Kumiai, a powerful union federation representing more than 1.5 million workers, organized in
1954. It is affiliated with the Sōhyō, the General
Council of Japanese Unions.

Jidai. Historical period or era.

• **Jidai-geki.** Historical films whose subjects were
taken from Japanese history before the Meiji period, and produced in Kyoto by Nikkatsu starting
in 1912. *See also* GENDAI GEKI.

• **Jidai-mono.** Kabuki plays dealing with historical
subjects before the Edo period. They are divided
into *odai-mono* and *oie-mono. See also* KABUKI,
KATSUREKI-MONO.

Ji-den. "Temple rice paddies." These lands, belonging to Buddhist monasteries, were neither redis-
tributable nor subject to land tax. However, lands
cleared by monks to make rice paddies after 743
were subject to land tax. *See* KŌDEN.

Jieitai. "Self-Defense Forces (SDF)." The armed
forces of Japan were dissolved by the occupying
forces on September 2, 1945, and the 1947 Constitution ratified this order: Chapter II, Article 9,
banned the country from ever having an offensive
army. In 1950, however, General MacArthur authorized Japan to form and maintain a "national reserve force" of 75,000 soldiers. The security treaty
attached to the Treaty of San Francisco, signed on
September 8, 1951, stipulated that Japan could possess an arsenal sufficient for self-defense. In 1952,
the "national reserve force" was expanded to
110,000 soldiers; in 1954, it became a "self-defense
army," composed of land-, sea-, and air-based
forces. It grew to comprise 250,000 soldiers, although the share of the national budget allocated to
these forces could not surpass 1%. In 1976, Japan
ratified the International Nonproliferation Treaty.
Article 9 of the Constitution is still the subject of
passionate debate, with a small portion of the population demanding that it be abrogated. *See* ARMED
FORCES.

Jien. Buddhist monk (Fujiwara no Yoshimizu, ca.
1155–1225), *kampaku* Fujiwara no Tadamichi's
son and Kujō Tadezane's brother. He became a
monk of the Tendai sect at 11 years of age, quickly
climbed the hierarchical ladder, and became Tendai-
zasu (superior) of the sect, then *daisōjō*. He studied
under the direction of the monk Myōun and became the chaplain of Retired Emperor Go-Toba.
He was also Jigen's (1219–55) master and admitted
Shinran into the Shōren-in monastery. A renowned
poet, he wrote an interesting chronicle on his times,
the *Gukanshō*, and a collection of *waka*, the *Shū-
gyoku-shū*. Some of his *waka* were included in anthologies, notably the *Senzai waka-shū* and the *Shin
kokin waka-shū*. He was one of the Shinrokkasen

(Six New Poetic Geniuses). Also sometimes called Yoshimizu Sōjō. *Posthumous name:* Jichin. *See* JIGEN.

Jigai. Type of suicide reserved for noblewomen and samurai. Women did not have the right to commit *seppuku*, so they bound their legs together in order to maintain a modest posture in death, then cut their carotid artery with a dagger. *See* SEPPUKU.

Jige. Lower social classes, generally peasants, as opposed to samurai. This term also designated all court bureaucrats below the third rank (*see* I); not having access to the Seiryōden, they had to live at the bottom of the stairs of this building. *See also* NAGO.

Jigei. Type of Kabuki with no music, performed very realistically, as opposed to plays in the *shosagoto* genre. Jigei were very much in style during the seventeenth century. Also called Ji-kyōgen.

Jigen. Buddhist monk (Eikū, 1219–55) of the Tendai-shū, member of the Fujiwara family and disciple of Jien and Ryōkai. He was *zasu* of the Tendaishū, succeeding Jien.

Jigoemon. Master lacquer craftsman (sixteenth century), creator of the Jōhana-*makie* style, a type of white lacquer.

Jigoku. Buddhist "Hell" that traditionally was made of eight main hells and sixteen subsidiary hells. *Skt.:* Naraka. *Chin.:* Diyu. *See also* ONI, ROKUDŌ.

• **Jigoku-dani sekkutsu-butsu.** *See* KASUGA YAMA SEKKUTSU-BUTSU.

• *Jigoku no hana.* "Infernal flowers." A collection of stories by Akutagawa Ryūnosuke (published in 1918) telling the tale of a painter who sees his daughter perish in a fire that destroys his house but who does nothing to help her because he is fascinated by the flames, which he wants to paint.

• *Jiguko-zōshi.* General term for the many *emakimono* that describe Buddhist hell. The best known have been attributed to Tosa Mitsunobu with texts by Jakuren. These *emakimono*, some of which are in the National Museum of Tokyo, are remarkable for the quality of their drawings, their colorful highlights, and their powerful evocation of the torment endured by the damned.

Jigon. Buddhist monk (b. ca. 1298) of the Tendaishū, who was appointed *zasu* of the sect in 1330.

Ji-in. Term sometimes used for some minor Buddhist temples. *See* JI.

• **Ji-in e-dokoro.** Painters' and sculptors' studios attached to minor temples or shrines (*ji-in*), active mainly during the Kamakura and Muromachi periods. The monks in these studios specialized in making *emakimono*.

• *Ji-in hatto.* Abridgment of *Shoshū ji-in hatto,* a group of 34 laws concerning Buddhist sects promulgated by the Edo shogunate between 1601 and 1616 and inspired by Konchin Sūden, one of Tokugawa Ieyasu's advisers. The government thus protected Buddhist sects so that they could continue to prosper, within certain limits.

• **Jo-in-hō.** *See* BUKE-HŌ.

Jijō. Era of Emperor Takakura: Aug. 1177–July 1181. Also called Jishō. *See* NENGŌ.

Jiki. Type of porcelain made in the Arita and Seto kilns in the seventeenth century.

Jikidō. In Buddhist temples, a room used as a refectory by the monks.

Jikifu. In ancient Japan, a remuneration system for bureaucrats. They received as salary a certain number of houses or royalties from houses, following a Chinese model. These allowances were different from those made as a consideration of rank (*see* IFU) or merit (*kōfu*). The persons concerned had the title *fushu* (master of allowance), and the households were called *fuko* (or *fugo*). However, these bureaucrats could not collect the royalties directly; payments were paid to the administration and ceded back to them. This archaic system disappeared after the tenth century.

Jikin. Buddhist monk (691–777) from Korea who had studied the doctrines of the Hossō and Kegon sects, and who was a confidant of Emperor Shōmu. He was appointed *bettō* of the Kōfuku-ji temple in Nara. Also perhaps called Jikun.

Jikisan. General term for warriors (*bushi*) who were direct vassals of the shogun during the Edo period, mainly relatives of the Tokugawa. However, only those with direct access to the shogun, thus the *hatamoto* and *gokenin,* had a right to the title *jikisan.* According to an estimate made in the early eighteenth century, the *jikisan* comprised 5,204 *hatamoto* and 17,309 *gokenin.* They were opposed to the *baishin,* or vassals, who did not have direct access to the shogun. The *jikisan* were forced to live in Edo.

Jikkan-jūnishi. "Ten trunks, twelve branches," a computation system of Chinese origin, in which a 60-year "Jupiterian cycle" was divided into 10 "heavenly trunks" *(kan),* each of which comprised twelve "terrestrial branches" *(shi).* The ten trunks were assimilated into the five elements—wood, fire, earth, metal, and water—to which were attributed a positive (Yang, Yō) or negative (Yin, In) value, while the twelve branches each bore the name of an animal of the Zodiac. This system applied not only to the years but to the hours of the day as well. The years were divided according to the order of the animals: Rat, Bull, Tiger, Rabbit, Dragon, Snake, Horse, Goat, Monkey, Bird, Dog, and Boar. The order of the elements, or "trunks," was: Wood, Fire, Earth, Metal, Water.

The directions were also assigned animals: Rat, the north; Rabbit, the east; Horse, the south; Bird, the west.

The hours *(koku)* were divided as follows: Rat: 11 P.M. to 1 A.M.; Bull: 1 A.M. to 3 A.M.; Tiger: 3 A.M. to 5 A.M.; Rabbit: 5 A.M. to 7 A.M.; Dragon: 7 A.M. to 9 A.M.; Snake, 9 A.M. to 11 A.M.; Horse: 11 A.M. to 1 P.M.; Goat: 1 P.M. to 3 P.M.; Monkey: 3 P.M. to 5 P.M.; Bird, 5 P.M. to 7 P.M.; Dog, 7 P.M. to 9 P.M.; Boar, 9 P.M. to 11 P.M.

However, the length of these "hours" was variable. At the winter solstice, for example, a *koku* was 1 hour and 48 minutes long during the daytime, and 2 hours and 12 minutes long at night, whereas at the summer solstice, it was 2 hours and 36 minutes long during the daytime and 1 hour and 21 minutes long at night.

This system was also called *kanshi* (trunk-branches) and *e-to* (older brother–younger brother), the latter used in the place of the Chinese terms Yang and Yin. Adoption of this calendar in Japan is attributed to Empress Suiko (554<593–628>) in 604.

Astrology has adopted these computations and attributes a particular personality to people according to the animal of their year of birth. *See* CALENDAR, HOROSCOPE, JŪNISHI.

Jikkin-shō. "Materials for Illustrating the Ten Moral Precepts." A work in three chapters and 280 anecdotes. It was written in 1252 by a samurai who became a Buddhist monk, perhaps named Nirō-zaemon, a representative of the Kamakura *bakufu* in Edo, although it is sometimes attributed to Tachibana no Narisue or Sugawara no Tamenaga. This small book, written specifically for the education of young samurai, was constantly republished and used up to the Meiji period. Also sometimes called *Jikkun-shō.*

Jikkō-kyō. One of the 13 sects of the Kyōha Shintō, founded by Hasegawa Kakugō (b. 1541) and updated by Shibata Janamori (1809–90). It was itself divided into a number of subsects: Jikkō (1945), Meiji-kyō (1946), Myōshō (1945), Shintō-komp'ira (1945), Shintō-kotohira-kyō (1946), and Onushi-kyō (or Yamato-kai, 1965). Its followers worship Mt. Fuji.

Jikō-in. A prayer room of the Zen sect, founded in 1633 by Katagiri Sekishu in Yamato-Kōriyama, south of Nara. It has a garden and a rustic-style tea pavilion *(chashitsu)* dating from the same period.

Jikuan. Japanese name of a Vietnamese Christian who went to Japan in 1644 with some Jesuit missionaries. Imprisoned in Edo, he died in 1700, aged 78.

Jikyō Kannon. One of the 33 forms (Sanjūsan Ōgeshin) of Kannon Bosatsu (*Skt.*: Avalokitshvara), portrayed as a woman holding a scroll of the sacred writings of Buddhism in her hand.

Jikyōshū. Dictionary of Japanese, written in 1245 and completed in 1416–17, probably compiled by Sugawara no Tamenaga (1158–1246). Words are classified according to the order of the 192 keys of Chinese characters *(kanji)* with their readings in *on* and *kun* written in katakana.

Jimmu Tennō. First emperor of Japan, according to tradition and the ancient chronicles, the *Kojiki* and *Nihon shoki.* He is said to have reigned from 660 to 585 BC, but these dates cannot be taken seriously because it is not certain that he actually existed. He was probably a composite of other characters, emperors Sujin and Keitai, whose legends are almost identical. The name Jimmu Tennō was given to the legendary Kamu Yamato Iware Hiko no Mikoto only in the eighth century. He was said to be the son of Hiko Nagisatake Ugaya Fukiaezu no Mikoto, a great-grandson of the sun *kami* Amaterasu-Ōmikami. His mother would have been Tamayori-hime, the daughter of the sea *kami*. Jimmu left his home in Hyūga (Kyushu, Miyazaki prefecture?) to conquer the Yamato. Crossing the sea and following the coastline, guided by a falcon, then fighting aboriginal tribes, he landed near the site of today's Osaka. Despite firm opposition by local populations, he managed to gain a foothold in the Nara basin and to have himself crowned emperor at the Kashihara palace. However, the *Kojiki* and *Nihon shoki* differ on many points of Jimmu's route. The ancient historians set the date at Kanoto-tori since it was, according to Chinese beliefs, symbolic of great change. In fact, both Sujin and Jimmu have been called Hatsu Kuni Shirasu Sumera no Mikoto ("first sovereign ruling the country"). Jimmu could thus be identified with Sujin Tennō, the tenth emperor, who, according to tradition, built the first shrine dedicated to Amaterasu-Ōmikami. He thus would have lived around the third century BC. His son, Susei, succeeded him.

• **Jimmu-kai.** Right-wing extremist party founded in 1932 by Okawa Shūmei (1886–1957) following developments in Manchuria. He demanded nationalization of Japanese interests in Manchuria and abolition of the zaibatsu. After he was arrested following a failed coup on May 15, 1932, the party faded from view, and it was dissolved in 1935.

Jimmyaku (Jin-myaku). In modern society, a network of personal relationships useful for promotions and career advancement.

Jimoku. During the Heian period, ceremonies for the appointment of court bureaucrats to a high position.

Jimon. Subsect of the Tendai-shū that separated from the Tendai of Mt. Hiei (called Sammon) established at the Mii-dera (Onjō-ji) in 993. Ennin's disciples set fire to the houses of Enchin's disciples and expelled them, so the monks belonging to Enchin's clan settled at the Onjō-ji founded by Enchin. The two rival clans often confronted each other thereafter, more for political than religious reasons. *See* SAMMON, TENDAI-SHŪ.

Jimotsu. Various objects or emblems held in the hands of Japanese Buddhist divinities to indicate their strengths and powers. *Approximate Sanskrit correspondence: lakshana.*

Jimpūren no Ran. Rebellion by former samurai of Kumamoto prefecture in 1876 to protest government measures depriving them of their privileges and banning them from carrying swords. It began on October 24 and was subdued the following day; a number of insurgents were killed, including their leader, Otaguro Tomoo (1836–76). It was one of many rebellions of a similar nature, inspiring, among others, those by Hagi and Akuzuki.

Jimu. One of the titles given to the religious leader of a Buddhist monastery. Also called *bettō, kengyō, zasu. See* SŌ-KAN.

Jimukan. Career administrative bureaucrat, as opposed to a "technician" bureaucrat *(gikan).*

Jimyō-in-tō. One of the two rival branches of the imperial family that fought over succession to the throne in the late Kamakura period. The other branch was called Daikoku-ji-tō. When Retired Emperor Go-Saga died in 1272, a conflict arose between his two sons; one settled in the Jimyō-in with his supporters, while the other and his supporters took refuge in the Daikoku-ji. The Kamakura shogunate decided to have emperors from each branch reign in alternation with each other. When the Kamakura *bakufu* fell, Ashikaga Takauji placed Kōmyō, from the Jimyō-ji family line, on the throne, while the rival branch started a dynasty in the south. There were then two imperial courts, the Northern Court (Hokuchō), in Kyoto, and the Southern Court (Namchō), in Yoshino. This situation lasted until 1392, when the emperors of the Southern Court gave up their rights after the war called Nambokuchō (Northern and Southern Courts), which had lasted 57 years. The Jimyō-ji family line continued to rule alone. *See* NAMBOKUCHŌ.

• **Jimyō-in Hōō.** Title taken by Emperor Fushimi after his abdication in 1298. *See* FUSHIMI TENNŌ.

• **Jimyō-ji San.** *See* UNEBI-YAMA.

Jinaichō. Urban areas that developed within the walls of certain Buddhist temples in the fifteenth and sixteenth centuries, notably those belonging to the Ikkō-shū. The modern city of Osaka, for instance, evolved from a *jinaichō* established in the Ishiyama Hongan-ji. Also called *jinai-machi. See also* ICHI, JŌKA-MACHI, MONZEN-MACHI.

Jindai. "Divine period," which, according to Shinto mythology, preceded the rise of Jimmu

Tennō. Also sometimes called *taiko, kamiyo. See* CHIJIN-GODAI, TENJIN-SHICHIDAI.

• **Jindai-ki.** "Narrative of the Divine Ages." A mythical story of protohistoric Japan published in 1599, based on the first two books of the *Nihon shoki*. This work was often annotated, notably in the *Nihon-shoki jindai gōkai* (1664) and the *Kamiyo no maki uzu no yamakage* by Motoori Norinaga (1730–1801). Also titled *Kamiyo no maki.*

• **Jindai-moji.** Written characters said to have existed before Chinese characters *(kanji)* were introduced to Japan; although their existence was posited by scholars such as Hirata Atsutane, it has been proved that they never existed.

Jindai-ji. Buddhist temple of the Tendai-shū in the town of Chōfu, near Tokyo. According to tradition, it was founded in 733 by the Hossō-shū sect, but was taken over by the Tendai in the ninth century. This temple, sponsored by the Minamoto family, became an important center of Esoteric Buddhism *(mikkyō)*. It houses a sculpture of Buddha Shakyamuni *(Jap.:* Shaka) from the late seventh century. Festival of the Daruma-ichi March 3–4.

Jingasa. Type of flat hat made of iron; wood, sometimes lacquered; or black-lacquered boiled leather, worn by soldiers and laborers in the Muromachi and Edo periods. *Jingasa* were worn by some laborers and rickshaw *(jinrikisha)* pullers in the early Meiji era. *See* KABUTO.

Jingi. Chinese philosophical concept issued by Mengzi (Mencius) integrating two Confucian philosophical virtues, fraternal love *(jin)* and sincere behavior *(gi)*. This concept, one of the codes of honor of many ancient and modern Japanese secret societies *(yakuza),* advocates fraternal assistance between all members of a given society.

Jingi-kan. Ministry of Shinto cults that replaced the department called *kami-tsukasa* in 645.

• **Jingi-kan no Hasshin.** Group of eight *kami* that were worshiped separately within the Jingi-kan: Kami-musubi, Takami-musubi, Tamatsune-musubi, Iku-musubi, Tara-musubi, Ō-miyama, Miketsu, and Kotoshiro-nushi.

• **Jingi-shō.** Name of the ministry of religious affairs responsible for administration of Shinto shrines, in 1868. It was replaced in 1872 by two other ministries, the Kunaishō, responsible for worship activities, and the Kyōbushō, responsible for the teaching of Shinto morals.

Jingo-ji. Major Buddhist temple of the Tō-ji sect of the Shingon-shū, established on Mt. Takao (Arashiyama) in Ukyō (Kyoto) in 824 and rebuilt in the twelfth century. It was said to have been built on the site of an older temple, the Takao-dera. Kūkai was its first leader; he was followed by his disciple Shinzei. The Jingo-ji was badly damaged during the Ōnin War and restored during the Edo period. It houses some beautiful works of art, including a bronze gong dating from 875 and portraits of Minamoto no Yoritomo and Taira no Shigemori that are attributed to Fujiwara no Takanobu. Also called Jingū-ji.

Jingo-jihen. Riots that took place in the Jingo year (1882) in Seoul, when Korean soldiers, unhappy with the idea that Queen Min planned to use Japanese officers to form the cadres of a new army, invaded the royal palace, assassinated the Japanese advisers, and attacked the Japanese legation. The regent father of the king, Dae Wŏn-gun, then seized power and supported the rebels. The Chinese sent troops, who arrested Dae Wŏn-gun, and Japan asked the Korean government for apologies and indemnities and demanded that the Treaty of Chemulpo *(Jap.:* Saimoppo), ratifying the presence of Chinese and Japanese armies in Seoul, be signed.

Jingō-kaihō. Japanese coin, issued from 765 to 796, one of the "12 Japanese coins" *(kōchō-jūnisen)*. This copper coin had a diameter of about 23 mm and a weight of between 3.4 and 4.5 grams.

Jingo-keiun. Era of Empress Shōtoku: Aug. 767–Oct. 770. *See* NENGŌ.

Jingū. Title for certain imperial Shinto shrines, including the Ise-jingū. Also called *gū, mia, yashiro. See* JINJA.

• **Jingū-ji.** Name for Buddhist temples that, starting in the eighth century, became associated with a Shinto shrine, following the theories of Ryōbu Shintō. These "mixed" temples were also called *shingan-ji, jingo-ji, jinku-ji, jingū-in, bettō-ji, miyadera.* They were abolished or separated by the law on separation of cults issued in 1868. *See also* HONJI-SUIJAKU, JINGO-JI.

• **Jingū-kōgō.** Empress (fourth century?) who was, according to the *Kojiki* and *Nihon shoki,* Emperor Chūai's wife and Ōjin Tennō's mother. She was in fact called Okinagatarashi-hime; Jingū-kōgō was her posthumous name. It is said that when her husband died, she took part in the conquest of Korea that defeated the three kingdoms of the peninsula, Silla (Shiragi), Koguryō, and Paegkche (Kudara). When she returned to Yamato, she gave birth to Ōjin, crushed a number of rebellions, and reigned as regent for her son Ōjin for 69 years. The events of her reign reported by the two ancient chronicles are mostly mythical, although they do attest to the relations that must have existed between the Korean Peninsula and Yamato in the fourth century. When Jingū-kōgō died, she was given the name Kashii Dai-myōjin. Certain authors liken her to Himiko in the Chinese chronicles *(Weizhi).* Also called Jingō-kōhō.

Jingū Bunko. Major library of works on the Shinto cults, comprising the ancient libraries of the Ise Shrines, located in the town of Ise (Mie prefecture). It comprises more than 250,000 volumes.

Jinin. People attached to a Shinto shrine and charged with nonspecific religious, domestic, or other tasks. Some *jinin,* responsible for guarding the shrines, later formed a sort of militia that assisted the warrior monks *(sōhei).* Others turned to trade or crafts and formed guilds *(za)* provided with certain privileges. During the Edo period, the *jinin* were replaced by simple "priests in charge of the shrines" called *shinshoku.* Also sometimes *jinnin.*

Jinja. General term for Shinto shrines. They are classified, depending on their importance, into *jingū* (or *gū*), *taisha* (or *ō-yashiro*), and simple *jinja* (or *miya, sha*). When the Shinto faith was in its infancy, no particular building was used to venerate the *kami,* who were said to reside in mountains and sacred spots. Then, temporary shrines were built in these locations to accommodate a particular ceremony and were destroyed afterward. Later, permanent shrines were established (although some, following the ancient custom according to which a new building was built for each major ceremony, were periodically rebuilt in the same form). It is felt that the oldest style of *jinja* architecture predates the introduction of Buddhism to Japan. This style is characterized by deeply anchored pillars, a raised floor, and a simple wooden structure covered in thatch. There are 11 styles of *jinja:*

1) The **taisha** style, typified by the Izumo Shrine, with the entrance on the gable side up a stairway.

2) The **shimmei** style, with entrance on one of the wide sides, as in the Ise Shrines.

3) The **otori** style, evolved from the *taisha* style, with the entrance in the center of the gable.

4) The **sumiyoshi** style, derived from the *otori* style, typified by the Sumiyoshi-jinja.

5) The **kasuga** style, with a roof in *kiri-zuma* and an awning above the gable entrance, as at the Kasuga-jinja.

6) The **nagare** style, with curved roof and entrance protected by an extension of the roof.

7) The **hachiman** style, formed by two rooms joined by the edges of their curved roofs.

8) The **hie** (or **hiyoshi**) **shōtai** style, with extended roof on the gables and the façade.

9) The **gion** style, comprising two rooms joined under a single roof.

10) The **gongen** style, an H-shaped structure comprising a small room joining the *honden* (main room) and the prayer room.

11) The **yatsumune,** rare, comprising multiple roofs, as at the Kitano-jinja.

Jinja architecture was influenced to a certain extent by Buddhist architecture starting in the Nara period (pillars on a stone base, tiled roofs, wood painted red, etc.). Most *jinja* are preceded by torii, or gates, usually between one and three, indicating the sacred nature of the site. Some later shrines also adopted a two-story gate structure *(rōmon)* inspired by Buddhist temples.

• **Jinja Honchō.** "Main Association of Shinto Shrines," created in 1946 and comprising the majority of shrines (about 80,000), with about 23,000 certified priests and more than 4,000 priestesses. *See also* SHIN SHŪKYŌ REMMEI.

• **Jinja-seido.** Early Shinto was not organized; during Emperor Temmu's reign it began to have an official structure, and the various *jinja* were subjected to regulation by the Jingi-kan, or minister of *kami.* In 1081, 22 governmental shrines *(kansha)* benefited from official offerings, while ordinary shrines survived only with assistance from followers. *See* JINGI-KAN.

• **Jinja Shintō.** Division of State Shinto (Kokutai Shintō) which, from 1871 to 1945, organized all sects of the Kyōha Shintō in associations named Hakuzan, Hokkaidō Minami-jinja, Inari-jinja, Jinja Honchō, Jinja Honkyō, Jinja Ubusuma, Kiso Mitake Honkyō, Shimmei Kyōdan, Shintō Dairei,

Soshin no Miyashiro Hankyō, and Tenshokyō Hombu. Each of these "associations" managed a certain number of shrines.

Jinji. Era of Emperor Shijō: July 1240–Feb. 1243. Also called Ninji. *See* NENGŌ.

Jinji-mai. Ritual Shinto dances, including Kagura, generally performed by *miko* during ceremonies and festivals, as they sang *jinji-uta*, or religious songs. Jinji-mai may be folkloric (Azuma-asobi, Yamato-mai), purely religious dances performed with a sword (Tsurugi no Mai, Tachi Odori), or have a magical meaning, such as the Shishi-mai ("lion dances") and *furyū-odori.*

Jinjitsu. Popular festival generally observed on the seventh day of the year according to the *inreki* calendar.

Jinkai-shū. Code of family laws *(bunkoku-hō)* of the Date clan in Mutsu province, compiled by Date Tanemune in 1536. Its 171 articles are strongly influenced by the Jōei Code (Jōei Shikimoku, 1232). Its title, "Dust and Cinders," indicates that it deals with a wide variety of subjects.

Jinki. Era of Emperor Shōmu: Feb. 724–Aug. 729. *See* NENGŌ.

Jinkōki. Mathematics book by Yoshida Mitsuyoshi, a wealthy Kyoto merchant, based on use of the abacus *(soroban).* It is a free interpretation of a similar Chinese work, the *Suanfa tongzong,* published in China in 1592, showing how to solve simple equations. It was the first Japanese book published in color, and was very popular.

Jinnō shōtō-ki. "Story of the Legitimate Succession of the Divine Emperors." A "historical" work by Kitabatake Chikafusa, written about 1339 for young Emperor Go-Murakami—or, rather, to encourage the Kanto warriors to take the side of the Southern Court (Nanchō). This book, divided into three parts (Sky, Earth, Men), was written from memory, which explains its inaccuracies. The author gives the filiation of all emperors from Jimmu Tennō and punctuates the text with moral and political considerations. *Jinnō shōtō-ki* was quite successful and was used as a basis for textbooks during the Meiji era.

Jinrikisha. Japanese name for the rickshaw, a two-wheeled vehicle pulled by a person, invented by Izumi Tōsuke, a Fukuoka samurai, about 1870. He formed a partnership with Takayama Kōsuke, Suzuki Tokujiro, and others to manufacture and sell *jinrikisha;* they immediately became very popular, replacing *kago* (palanquins) in the cities. Other companies then began to make them and rent them to the people who pulled them. By about 1876, there were more than 20,000 *jinrikisha* in Tokyo. The vehicle was then refined, provided with rubber tires and a hood, and Japan exported large numbers to China, Southeast Asia, India, and even South Africa. Also sometimes called *wansha, rikisha.*

Jinshin no Ran. "Riots of the Jinshin Year" (672). A dispute over succession that took place when Emperor Tenchi (Tenji) died. Having first designated his brother, Ōama, as his successor, Tenji changed his mind in favor of his son, Ōtomo. When he died, the nobles supported one or the other of the heirs, which led to civil war. Prince Ōtomo was defeated and committed suicide, and Ōama ascended to the throne, taking the name Temmu, in 673.

Jin'ya. Term used during the Kamakura period to designate an army's encampment. In the Edo period, it referred to the fortified residences of low-ranking daimyo who did not have a castle. Also called *jin'yashiki.*

• **Jin no za.** In ancient Japan, the place reserved for the emperor's guards within the walls of the imperial palace.

Jion-ō. Buddhist divinity of Hell (*see* JIGOKU); according to the Shingon-shū sect, the thirteenth sovereign of Hell, corresponding to Kokūzō Bosatsu. Families venerate him in the thirty-third year after the death of a family member. *See* JŪSAN BUTSU.

Jippensha Ikku. Writer (Shigeta Teiichi, Shigeta Sadakazu, 1765–1831), born in Suruga province (Shizuoka prefecture), son of a low-ranking bureaucrat. He went to Edo and entered the service of a warrior whom he followed to Osaka. In 1794, he returned to Edo and worked at the Tsutaya bookstore. He then began to write stories in *kibyōshi* style; in 1802, he published the first part of his humorous novel *Tōkaidō-chū hizakurige* (A Horse on Its Knees on the Tōkaidō), which he finished only in 1822. This multi-installment work in the *kokkeibon* genre was very successful, whereas his other books—comic verses *(kyōka), jōruri,* and *yomihon*—attracted fewer readers. He married three times, and his home was destroyed twice by fire. He often traveled to gather material for *Hizakurige* and led a fairly dissolute life. He asked that fireworks be lit over his body during his funeral to entertain his friends who attended.

Jiren Kannon. One of the 33 forms (Sanjūsan Ōgeshin) of Kannon Bosatsu (*Skt.:* Avalokiteshvara), portrayed holding a lotus blossom in both hands.

Jiryaku. Era of Emperor Go-Reizei: Aug. 1065–Apr. 1069. Also called Jireki. *See* NENGŌ.

Ji-samurai. During the Kamakura period, warrior assigned to a piece of land that he had to farm. The *ji-samurai* were in fact peasants who had to render armed service to the lord whom they served in case of war. They lived in fortified houses *(yashiki)* and had to have their own mount and armor. Also called *ji-zamurai.*

Jisha-bugyō. High-ranking bureaucrat (*see* BUGYŌ) charged with administering religious affairs starting in the Kamakura period. In 1635, four *jisha-bugyō* were appointed from among the *fudai-daimyō,* and they took turns in the position for one-month intervals. *See also* KANJŌ-BUGYŌ, MACHI-BUGYŌ.

Jishimban. Neighborhood surveillance system in cities (particularly Edo) organized by residents who took turns guarding against fires and maintaining order. The *jishimban* were abolished in 1868 and replaced by sapper-firefighters and police forces. *See also* JŌBIKESHI.

Jishō. Era of Emperor Takakura: Aug. 1177–July 1181. *See* NENGŌ.
• Buddhist monk (1291–1368) of the Tendai-shū.

Jishō-ji. *See* GINGAKU-JI.

Jishu. Buddhist monk responsible for the physical organization of a temple or monastery. *See* RISSHI.

Ji-shū. Buddhist sect, branch of the Jōdo-shū founded by Ippen Shōnin in 1275, dedicated to continuous recitation of the *nembutsu.* Its followers are called Jishū, Ikkō-shū, or Yugyō-shū. The center of the sect, established at the Muryōkō monastery in Sagami province, was transferred by the monk Donkai to the Yugyō-ji (also called Shōjōkō), also in Sagami province, in 1325. It was divided into 12 branches (called Honzan): Yūkō-ha, Ikkō-ji, Ōku-

tani-ha, Taima-ha, Shijō-ha, Rokujō-ha, Kaii-ha, Reizan-ha, Kōkua-ha, Ichiya-ha, Tendō-ha, and Mikagedō-ha, named according to the location of their temples, all recognizing the authority of the Chōraku-ji temple in Kyoto. It seems that these subsects have now been united in the Yugyō-ji. *See* AMIDA-KYŌ.

Jishūkan. Estate schools in the Edo period for the education of young samurai. The first was founded in Kumamoto in 1752 by Hosokawa Shigekata; others were soon set up in other *han* (estates): Sakurai-han (Kazusa), Ōtawara-han (Shimotsuke), Yoshida-han (Mikawa), Daishōji-han (Kaga), and Kojima-han (Suruga). The very liberal education dispensed in these schools was based on the Confucianism of the Shushi (*Chin.:* Zhu Xi) school. The schools operated until 1871, when the modern educational system was instituted.

Jishuku. "Voluntary self-restraint," self-discipline practiced by the Japanese that sometimes results in a reserved, humble attitude. It is part of the behavioral code that Japanese society expects everyone to observe under all circumstances.

Jishun. Buddhist monk (1295–1360) of the Jōdo Shin-shū, who was named *dainagon. See* NAGON.
→ *See* BOKI-EKOTOBA.

Jissaku. Collective name for ten sculptors of Noh masks considered the best of their time, including Tatsuemon (fourteenth century).

Jissatsu. Collective name for the ten Zen temples classified below the *gozan.* Starting in 1386, the *jissatsu* of Kyoto and the Kantō formed separate groups. These monasteries were sponsored by the *bakufu* and the daimyo.

Jite. Sort of lance *(yari)* with a cross-shaped spearhead sometimes used by foot soldiers *(zusa). See also* JITTE.

Jitō. In the late Heian period, land used to remunerate certain provincial bureaucrats or representatives of the *shōen* (intendants). Starting in the Kamakura period (or perhaps even a little before, in the mid-twelfth century), however, this term no longer referred to land but to estate intendants and tax collectors for the owners. The position of *jitō* became more or less hereditary starting in 1221. In the Muromachi period, "*jitō*" designated mainly a low-ranking local lord *(koku-jin);* in the Edo period, it was simply the title of a person with a certain share *(chigyō)* in a daimyo's fief.

• **Jitō-dai.** In the Kamakura period, a bureaucrat who lived on a *shōen,* substituting for the *jitō,* who lived in the court at Kyoto. Also called *gandai, daikan. See* DAIKAN, JITŌ-UKE.

• **Jitō-gokenin.** *See* GOKENIN.

• **Jitō-uke.** In the Kamakura period, a title for warriors who, in compensation for their services, were given a piece of land or the position of *jitō* on the estate on which they had been born, to replace the titular *jitō* living in the capital. Many *jitō-uke* (or sometimes *jitō-dai*), especially in Kanto, became independent low-ranking lords when they were able to free themselves from the grasp of the absent *jitō.*

Jitō Tennō. Forty-first sovereign (Empress Hironuhime, Uno no Sasara, 646<686–97>703), Tenji (Tenchi) Tennō's second daughter and wife of Prince Ōama, Tenji's younger brother, who became Emperor Temmu. When he died in 686, she ascended to the throne; she was officially crowned in 690. She abdicated in favor of her grandson, Karu (the future Emperor Mommu), and received the title Dajō Tennō. She promulgated the first Japanese legal code *(Asuka no kiyomihara risturyō).* A well-known *waka* poet, her works were included in the *Man'yōshū.* She was a fervent Buddhist and the first sovereign to ask to be cremated in the Buddhist manner.

Jitsue. Buddhist monk (785–847) belonging to the Shingon-shū, appointed councillor to emperors Saga and Seiwa. *Posthumous name:* Dōkō Daishi.

Jitsugen. Buddhist monk (fourteenth century) of the Hossō-shū, *kampaku* Konoe no Tsunetada's son.

Jitsugo-kyō. General term for an elementary textbook used in the schools from the late Heian period to the early Meiji era. This work by an unknown author, written in *kambun,* gave simple precepts of life and means of reasoning.

• **Jitsugoto.** Type of Kabuki play dealing with realities of daily life, as opposed to the *aragoto* and *wagoto* genres. Also called *tachiyaku.*

Jitsunyo. *See* KŌKEN.

Jitsuroku-mono. During the Edo period, name for popular documentary accounts that reported events of the time. Although these chronicles were banned by the shogunate in 1722, they continued to circulate in handwritten form until the late nineteenth century.

Jitsuzen. Buddhist monk (1141–1221) of the Tendai-shū, who was *zasu* of the sect in 1202–03.

Jitte. Weapon consisting of a long (about 45 cm) steel point with a sort of hook at its base that enabled its user to disarm the adversary by grabbing and twisting a sword blade. This weapon, of Chinese origin, was used mainly during the Edo period by police officers *(yoriki, dōshin). See also* JITE, SAI.

Ji-un. Buddhist monk (Onkō, 1718–1804) of the Shingon-shū who strove to spread Buddhism among the people. A Sanskrit scholar, he was also an excellent painter in the Sesshū style and a talented calligrapher (Chinese style). His works were published in *Jiun sonja zenshū,* but his major work, *Bongaku shinryō,* a study of Sanskrit grammar, remained in handwritten form. Also called Ji-un Sonja.

Ji-uta. Folksongs of the Osaka region, accompanied by the shamisen and sometimes danced *(ji-uta-mai).* The music used with these songs was called *kumi-uta;* in the late seventeenth century, some musicians added koto and *shakuhachi* flute to the *ji-uta.* They were probably the basis for Kabuki music.

• **Ji-utai.** *See* NOH.

• **Ji-uta-mai.** *See* BUYŌ.

Jiwari. Custom in certain villages consisting of dividing the land into equal parts, which were assigned to peasants for a set period so that the tax *(nengu)* could be more evenly distributed. This practice, which was unofficial but quite common, had different names from province to province, including *kadowari, gobanwari,* and *kujimochi.* It continued almost throughout the Edo period, with temporary revivals until as recently as the 1910s in Hokkaido.

Jiyū-gekijō. "Free Theater." The name for an association of actors under Ichikawa Sadanji II (1880–1940) and Osanai Kaoru (1881–1928). Their aim was to establish a purely artistic theater by performing Western plays (Ibsen, Gorky, etc.) in an updated style, not obeying the standards set by Kabuki. This style was performed mainly at the Yuraku-za in Tokyo from 1909 to 1919, when the Jiyū-gekijō folded. *See* OSANAI KAORU.

Jiyū Minken Undō. "Freedom and People's Rights Movement." A political party founded in 1874 by Itagaki Taisuke. It succeeded the Jiyū Minken-ron (People's Sovereignty Movement), founded around 1870. The party was renamed Jiyūtō in 1880.

• **Jiyū Minshutō.** "Liberal Democratic party (LDP)." Founded in November 1955 through the merger of the Jiyūtō (Liberal party) and the Nihon Minshutō (Japan Democratic party). Almost all prime ministers have come from this party (also called Jimintō) since 1955. *See* PRIME MINISTERS.

• **Jiyūtō.** "Liberal party." founded in 1880 by Itagaki Taisuke, based on the doctrines of philosophers Ueki Enori and Nakai Chōmin, to demand establishment of a constitution modeled after France's.

Jizai-kagi. Pot-hanger used to suspend a cauldron over an *irori* in traditional houses. The horizontal piece holding the pot-hanger (made of wood or iron) was often sculpted in the shape of a fish, a fan, an *uchide no kozuchi,* or another protective object. People believed that the home's *kami* resided in it.

Jizen. Buddhist monk (1231–76) of the Tendai-shū, who was successively *zasu* and *hōmu* of the sect. He was a disciple of Jigen.

Jizō Bosatsu. Japanese Buddhist form of the Bodhisattva Kshitigarbha, who was the object of widespread devotion in Japan during the Heian period. He is generally portrayed as a Buddhist monk with a shaven head, holding a pilgrim's stick *(Skt.: khakkara)* in his hand. Protector of travelers and children, he is said to save the faithful from hell. He is often confused (or combined) with Shinto *kami*. Because he is a guardian of roads, sculptures of him are often found on roadsides *(see* DŌSOJIN). Popular belief also sometimes accords him the faculty of "giving children" (in which role he is also known as Koyasu Jizō). Perhaps the most popular divinity in Japan, he is also portrayed holding a *hōshu (Skt.: chintāmani),* the "pearl that grants all wishes." He is often offered red-and-white bibs to thank him for protecting children. There are very many "aspects" of Jizō. *Chin.:* Dizang Pusa.

• **Jizō-in.** *See* HŌSHU-IN.

• **Jizō Shinkō.** "Devotion to Jizō Bosatsu," in order to obtain salvation, based on two sutras *(Jap.: kyō),* the *Jizō jūrin-kyō* and the *Jizō Bosatsu Hongan-kyō.* At first considered one of Amida's assistants, Jizō became assimilated to the Buddha and then, in popular belief, replaced him. In the early eleventh century, many popular ceremonies were created to spread worship of Jizō, who was prayed to for a long life (in which role he was also known as Emmei Jizō) and for the protection of children (in the Jizō-bon ceremony, on the 24th day of the 7th month), notably in the Kansai region.

Jō. Unit of length equivalent to 10 *shaku,* or about 3.03 m. Formerly called *tsue.*
   • Term for a fortified castle. Also called *shiro.* *See* CASTLES.

• **Jō-dai.** During the Edo period, a lord or bureaucrat responsible for defense and maintenance of a castle in the absence of a titular governor who was forced to reside in Edo by virtue of the *sankin-kōtai.* The title *jō-dai* was also given to certain lords responsible for guarding the castles belonging to the shogun.

Jō-an. Era of Emperor Takakura: Apr. 1171–July 1175. Also called Shō-an. *See* NENGŌ.
   → *See* KŌUN.

Jōban Tanden. Coal-bearing basin in Fukushima and Ibaraki prefectures, located along the Pacific coast. Although its coal is of poor quality, it was extensively used for industry and heating in the Tokyo region. Most of its shafts were closed in the early 1970s.

Jōbikeshi. Fire-watch system created in Edo about 1650, based on the organization of specialized brigades. They were called *daimyō-hikeshi* in the provincial lords' estates. *See also* HIKESHI, JISHIMBAN.

Jōchi. Lands exempted from tax because they belonged either to a Buddhist monastery or to a Shinto shrine, or sometimes to lords who had received them in compensation for services rendered. Also called *shuinshi* (land with a "red seal") and *yokechi.*
   • Buddhist monk (mid-twelfth century) on Mt. Kōya who was a painter. He produced the Buddhist paintings on the pillars of the Daidempō-in in 1147,

and of the "Zemmyō Ryū-ō" of the Kongōbu-ji on Mt. Kōya.

• **Jōchi Daigaku.** *See* JESUITS, SOPHIA UNIVERSITY.

• **Jōchi-ji.** Zen temple in Kamakura, founded by Hōjō Munemasa and Hōjō Morotoki in 1269. The Chinese Buddhist monk Gottan Funei (1197–1276) was its first abbot. This temple houses a statue of Jizō Bosatsu sculpted by Unkei.

Jōchō. Buddhist monk (d. 1057) and sculptor, Kōsho's son. He worked for Fujiwara no Michinaga and his son, Yorimichi. In 1022, he received the title *hokkyō* from the court; in 1048, that of *hōgen*. He established the principle of studios *(bussho)* and developed a joining technique for sculpture *(yosegi-zukuri)* that made it easier to produce Buddhist images. One of his most typical works is the large statue of Amida in the Hōō-dō of the Byōdō-in in Uji, sculpted in 1053. Jōchō is one of the Nara Horimono-ya. *See* SHICHIJŌ-BUSSHO.
• Sculptor (late twelfth century), Kōchō's son, who worked mainly at the Kōfuku-ji in Nara and received the title *hokkyō* in 1194. He also worked in Kamakura for Minamoto no Yoritomo.

Jōdaiyō. Calligraphic style in kana characters, particularly well represented by Ono no Tōfō, Fujiwara no Sari, and Fujiwara no Kōzei in the tenth century. It was very much in style in the late Heian period; in disuse for a long time, it is being rediscovered by modern calligraphers.

Jōdo. Abridgment of Saihō no Gokuraku no Jōdo (Western Paradise of the Pure Land, *Skt.:* Sukhavatī), a mythical region located to the west, where Amida Buddha is said to reside. *See* GOKURAKU, JŌDO SHIN-SHŪ, JŌDO-SHŪ.

• **Jōdo-goso.** *See* JODŌ-SHŪ.

• **Jōdo hensō.** Paintings of the Jōdo-shū illustrating Amida's "Pure Land" (Jōdo). Sometimes wrongly called Jōdo-mandara. *See* MANDALA.

• *Jōdo monrui jushō.* Buddhist text in which Shinran explains his doctrine of the Jōdo Shin-shū, written in 1252.

• **Jōdo Shin-shū.** "True Sect of the Pure Land." This Buddhist sect, founded by Shinran Shōnin in 1224, stressed unconditional devotion to Amida and taught that simply having faith in Amida and in

his "original vow" to save all creatures without exception was enough to be reborn in Amida's "Pure Land" (Jōdo). This sect, which now has almost 8 million followers, was also known as Ikkō-shū, Monto-shū, and Shin-shū. It is divided into ten main branches *(ha):*
  1) **Hongan-ji,** in Kyoto, founded in 1224.
  2) **Ōtani-ha,** in Kyoto, founded in 1602.
  3) **Takada-ha,** in Ise, founded in 1226.
  4) **Bukkō-ji-ha,** in Kyoto, founded in the fourteenth century.
  5) **Kibe-ha,** in Ōmi, founded in the thirteenth century *(see* SAMMON).
  6) **Senshō-ji-ha,** in Echizen, founded in 1280 by Jōdo (1253–1340).
  7) **Chōsei-ji-ha,** in Echizen, founded in the fourteenth century.
  8) **Jōshō-ji-ha,** in Echizen, founded in the fourteenth century by Jogaku.
  9) **Gōshō-ji-ha,** in Echizen, founded in the fourteenth century.
  10) **Izumi-ji-ha,** in Izumo.
There are other minor subsects and branches, such as the Joko-ji-ha, the Sammontō-ha, and the Yamamoto-ha. The seven masters of the sect were Shinran, Shimbutsu, Genkai, Ryōka, Seikai, Ryō-en, and Ryōgen. Its "abbots" have the title *hossu.*

• **Jōdo-shū.** "Sect of the Pure Land" (*see* JŌDO) devoted to Amida Buddha, imported from China (*Chin.:* Lianshe Zong, Jingtu Jiao, Jingxing She) by the monk Eun (798–869) in 847. This sect's goal was to popularize Buddhism, up to then reserved for the aristocracy, by reducing the rites of worship to a single act of faith in Amida. It was organized by Hōnen (Genkū, Enkō-daishi) in 1174. It was later divided into five main branches:
  1) **Chinzei** (Jōdo-shinzei), founded by Shōkō.
  2) **Seizan** (Jōdo-seizan), founded by Shōku. Divided into two subsects: Jōdo-seizan and Fudan Nembutsu (approx. 600,000 followers).
  3) **Chōraku-ji** (Jōdo-chōraku-ji), founded by Ryūkanrisshi.
  4) **Kuhon-ji** (Jōdo-kuhon-ji), founded by Chōsei.
  5) **Ichinengi** (Jōdo-ichinengi), founded by Gyōsei.
The Jōdo-shū (including its subsect, the Kurodani-jōdo) now has about 4.5 million followers. Its five "masters" (Jōdo-goso) are all Chinese:
  1) **Donran** (476–542). *Chin.:* Tanran.
  2) **Dōshaku** (562–645). *Chin.:* Daochuo.
  3) **Zendō** (613–81). *Chin.:* Chandao.
  4) **Ekan** (ca. 695). *Chin.:* Huigan.
  5) **Shōkō** (d. 805). *Chin.:* Shaokang.
→ *See also* AMIDA-KYŌ.

Jōe. Buddhist monk (643–ca. 714), Fujiwara no Kamatari's oldest son. He traveled to China in 653 with a mission and went to Chang'an, where he studied the doctrines of the Hossō sect. He returned to Japan via Korea and died the same year. *See* KENTŌSHI.

Jōei. Era of Emperor Go-Horikawa: Apr. 1232–Apr. 1233. Also called Tei-ei. *See* NENGŌ.

• *Jōei-shikimoku.* *See* GOSEIBAI-SHIKIMOKU.

Jōen. Buddhist monk and painter (Okamoto; *gō:* Gengenshi, 1628–73), Shōkadō's student in Kyoto.

Jōetsu. Town in Niigata prefecture, on the Sea of Japan (Nihonkai), created in 1971, by the merger of the towns of Takeda and Naoetsu, to become the political and cultural center of the region. During the Edo period, Naoetsu was an important way-station *(shuku-eki)* and a flourishing port, while Takeda was a castle town *(jōka-machi)* of the Uesugi family (remains of a fortress built by Uesugi Kenshin). Downhill skiing was introduced to Jōetsu in 1911 by an Austrian military instructor, Theodor von Lerch.

Jofuku. According to tradition, a physician who was sent (with another whose Japanese name was Zokuden) by Chinese emperor Qin Shihuangdi (*Jap.:* Shikō) to find the Islands of the Immortals (Hōraizan, *Chin.:* Fenglai Dao), traveling to Japan about 220 BC and bringing with him Confucius's (Kongzi) philosophical works. The Chinese names of the physicians (or Taoist monks) were Su She and Lu Ao. *See* HŌRAI-TŌ.

Jōga. Buddhist monk (active ca. 1295) at the Kōraku-ji temple of Shinano, and painter. He is said to have painted a "biography of Shinran."

Jogakkō. School for girls (Kōtō-jogakkō) founded in Tokyo in 1871, taken over by the government in 1899, with the goal of providing better education for girls so that they would become "good wives." Such schools were founded all over Japan, with different goals, but their number began to drop after 1947, when education generally became co-ed.

Jogaku Zasshi. "Magazine of Female Education." A Christian-inspired magazine, founded by Iwamoto Yoshiharu and several others, published in Tokyo from 1885 to 1904, and at first titled *Joaku Shinshi* (in 1884). It later published literary works

by women writers such as Kishida Toshiko (Shōen), Miyake Kaho, Wakamatsu Shizuko, and Kozai Shikin, and started the literary magazine *Bungaku-kai* in 1893.

Jōgan. Era of Emperor Seiwa: Apr. 859–Apr. 877. *See* NENGŌ.

• *Jōgan-ji.* Buddhist temple of the Shingon-shū, built in 872. In 874, it was raised to the rank of Jōgaku-ji, or private temple with official status. All that remains of it are some ruins south of Kyoto.

• *Jōgan Kyaku-shiki.* Legal code in 32 volumes, published in 868, comprising collections of laws and edicts issued since 811. *See* RITSURYŌ KYAKU-SHIKI.

Jōgen. Era of Emperor En'yu: July 976–Nov. 987. *See* NENGŌ.
• Era of Emperor Tsuchimikado: Oct. 1207–Mar. 1211. *See* NENGŌ.

Jogen. Painter (Araki Jogen; *mei:* Zenjūrō, 1765–1824) of the Yōga school, he was his father-in-law Gen'yū's student in Nagasaki. He produced mainly oil paintings in the European style.
→ *See* KŌYŌ.

Jōgyō. Buddhist monk (d. 865) in Nara, Kūkai's disciple. He traveled in China from 838 to 839.
• In temples dedicated to Amida, the room used for ritual circumambulation of the statue of Amida.

• *Jōgyō Bosatsu.* Bodhisattva (*Skt.:* Vishishtha) cited in the *Saddharmapundarīka-sūtra* (Sutra of the Lotus of the Good Law, *Jap.:* Hokke-kyō), with whom Nichiren identified himself.

Jōhei. Era of Emperor Shujaku: Apr. 931–May 938. *See* NENGŌ.

• *Jōhei Tengyō no Ran.* Name sometimes given to the rebellions led by Taira no Masakado (935) in Kanto and by Fujiwara no Sumitomo (939) on Kyushu. *See* FUJIWARA NO SUMITOMO, TAIRA NO MASAKADO.

Jōheisō. "Ordinary granaries," established in ancient Japan on a model imported from China, in which the government stored rice purchased in years of abundant harvests in order to control prices during times of scarcity. Emperor Junin was said to have introduced them to the provinces in

759. They were abolished during the Kamakura period, but after 1830 some daimyo reestablished them on their estates.

Johnston Report. Report written in 1948 by a 15-member commission, chaired by American congressman Percy H. Johnston, evaluating economic conditions in Japan. The report recommended that measures be taken to accelerate Japan's reconstruction and recovery of economic activities. Also called the Draper-Johnston Report.

Jōhō. Era of Emperor Shirakawa: Aug. 1074–Nov. 1077. *See* NENGŌ.

Jōi. Metal engraver (Nara Jōi, Sugiura Jōi, d. 1761), maker of *tsuba* and sculptor of netsuke in Edo.

Joji. Era of Emperor Go-Kōgon (Hokuchō dynasty): Sept. 1362–Feb. 1368. *See* NENGŌ.

Jōjin. Buddhist monk (1011–81) of the Tendai-shū, one of Fujiwara no Sukemasa's sons. He traveled in China in 1072 and wrote a travel journal, *Santendai godai sanki* (Pilgrimages to Mounts Tiantai and Wutai). He sent 527 scrolls of Buddhist texts to Japan in 1073 and donated statues of the *jūroku-rakan* (Sixteen Arhats) to the Dai-un-ji temple in 1074. Kept in China by Emperor Shenzong, who valued him highly, he died in Bianjing.

Jōjitsu-shū. Ancient Buddhist sect founded in Nara by the Korean monk Ekan in 625, based on the teachings of the *Jōjitsu-ron* (Skt.: *Satyasiddhishāstra*). It no longer exists. The original Sanskrit text, by Harivarman (ca. 250–350), has been lost, but it was translated into Chinese by Kumārajīva (344–413). This sect was one of the Six Sects of Nara (Nanto-rokushū) and was absorbed into the Sanron-shū sect.

Jojo-shi. "Lyrical Poems." A collection of poems published by a group of young poets in 1897 to display their concepts of lyrical poetry.

Jō-jutsu. Art of combat with a long stick (*jō*, made of wood or iron), practiced mainly by monk-soldiers during the medieval period. It is distinct from combat with a short stick, or *bo-jutsu. See also* JUTSU.

Jōkaku. Buddhist monk (early thirteenth century) and sculptor, Unkei's brother. He worked at the

Tōdai-ji with Kaikei, and they created the statues of the Ni-ō in the *chūmon.* He also helped to restore the Tōdai-ji.
• General term for fortresses and castles. Also *jō, shiro.*

Jōka-machi. Fortified towns that developed around castles (*jō*) in order to be under their protection. These towns were founded mainly from the sixteenth to the nineteenth century and grew rapidly. *See* ICHI, MACHI, MONZEN-MACHI.

Jokei. Buddhist monk (Sumiyoshi Hiromichi; *mei:* Naiki, 1599–1670) of the Sumiyoshi school in Edo. He was adopted by Tosa Mitsuyoshi, but left his master to work for the shogunate. He was Gukei's father.

Jōkei. Sculptor (born 1184) who worked at the Tōdai-ji in 1226 and received the titles *hokkyō* and *hōgen.* He was probably born in Higo province. He also worked at the Taima-dera and other monasteries. He sometimes signed his works with the title Daibusshi Nampōha (Master Sculptor of the Southern School).
→ *See* RAKU.

Jōkei. Buddhist monk (1155–1212) of the Hossō sect, Fujiwara no Michinori's grandson. His uncle, Kakuken, was his tutor at the Kōfuku-ji, but he retired to the Kasagi-dera in 1193 to escape corruption in the monastery. He wrote a commentary on the school of the Vijñānavādin, *Yuishiki dōgaku-shō,* and a text advocating devotion to Miroku Bosatsu, *Kōfuku-ji sōjō.*

Jōko. Traditional historical period extending from Jimmu Tennō to Kōgyoku Tenno (644).
→ *See* BUNGAKU.

Jōko. One of the titles for a retired emperor. *See* DAJŌ-KŌ, HŌ-Ō, IN, INSEI, KAKUTEI.
• Property title to a *shōen.* Also called *jōkō-shuin. See* JŌCHI.

Joko aishi. "Tragic History of Women Laborers," written by Hosoi Wakizō (1897–1925) in 1925, describing the miserable conditions in which some women laborers in the spinning mills worked in the years 1910–20.

Jo-kotoba. "Preface" comprising a sentence, long or short, placed at the beginning of a poem and having a metaphoric relationship with it. Generally used to introduce a *waka* poem. *See also* MAKURA-KOTOBA.

Jōkyō. Era of Emperor Reigen: Feb. 1684–Sept. 1688. Also called Teikyō. *See* NENGŌ.

• **Jōkyō Gekijō.** *See* KARA JŪRŌ.

• **Jōkyō-reki.** Lunar-solar calendar *(reki)* established by Shibukawa Shunkai and instituted in 1684. It replaced the Chinese calendar *(semmyō-reki),* which had been in force since 861, and was in use until 1753. Shibukawa calculated the length of the solar year at 365.2417 days. *See* ABE YASUKUNI, SHIBUKAWEA SHUNKAI, TEIKYŌ-REKI.

Jōkyoku. "High chamber" of the Deliberative Assembly established by Emperor Meiji in 1868, as opposed to the "Low Chamber," called the Kakyoku. It was composed of councillors chosen from among the imperial princes and high nobility and was responsible for laws, foreign relations, and recruitment of senior bureaucrats. The Low Chamber was composed of members elected by the estates and dealt with taxes, currency, and military affairs upon the orders of the High Chamber. The Jōkyoku became an administrative organ in 1869, and the Kakyoku became a Consultative Assembly (also called Shūgi-in, "house of representatives of the fiefs and prefectures").

Jōkyū. Era of Emperor Juntoku: Apr. 1219–Apr. 1222. Also called Shōkyū. *See* NENGŌ.

• *Jōkyū-bon.* Series of *emakimono* describing the life of Sugawara no Michizane, painted between 1194 and 1219. It was complemented by three other *emakimono* called *Kōan-bon,* in 1258. Also called *Kompon-engi.*

• **Jōkyū no Hen.** Revolt by Emperor Go-Toba, who tried in vain to take power back from the Kamakura *bakufu* in 1221. The death of Minamoto no Yoritomo in 1199 and the assassination of Minamoto no Sanetomo in 1219 led to disturbances among the vassals of the *bakufu,* and Retired Emperor Go-Toba amassed an army and attacked Hōjō Yoshitoki and Yoritomo's widow, Masako. Hōjō and Masako marched on Kyoto, deposed Emperor Chūkyō and replaced him with Go-Horikawa, and sent retired emperors Go-Toba and Juntoku into exile. The Kamakura *bakufu* then confiscated the estates of nobles who had helped Go-Toba and created a surveillance post for the Kyoto

court in the Rokuhara district. A representative of the *bakufu,* Rokuhara-tandai, was stationed there, thus reinforcing shogunal authority to the detriment to the Kyoto court. Also called Jōkyū no Ran.

Jomei Tennō. Thirty-fourth emperor (Okinaga Tarashi Hi Hiro Nuka no Mikoto, Prince Tamura, 593<629–41>), Bidatsu Tennō's grandson and Suiko's successor. Soga no Emishi helped him ascend to the throne, since Empress Suiko had died without an heir. He moved his palace to Asuka no Okamoto, then to Tanaka, and finally to Kudara. His wife was his niece Takara; she succeeded him when he died, under the reigning names Kōgyoku and Saimei. He was buried in the *kofun* in Ōshi-saka, in what is today the town of Sakurai (Nara prefecture).

Jōmi. Popular festival, also called Hina Matsuri, Jōshi, the "Festival of Girls" or "Festival of Dolls," held every March 3. *See* HINA MATSURI.

Jōmon-jidai. "Era of the Cord Decorations." Prehistoric period that began around the eleventh or tenth millennium BC and ended in the Tōhoku, around the tenth century AD. It is characterized by pottery with cord decorations, whence its name. Archeologists have divided it into six periods:

1) **Sōsōki** (or **Shigenki**), "the source," from about 11,000 to about 7000 BC. Perhaps microlithic.

2) **Sōki,** or early period, Neolithic, from about 7000 to about 5000 BC: sites at Senbagadani, Sōru-dai (Kyushu); Kamikuroiwa, Kōzanji, Yanagimata, Natsushima, Inaridai (Honshu).

3) **Zenki,** ancient period, from about 5000 to about 3300 BC: sites at Todoroki, Sobata (Kyushu); Kitashirakawa, Moroiso (Honshu).

4) **Chūki,** middle period, from about 3300 to about 2000 BC: sites at Ataka (Kyushu); Fukuda, Kasori (Honshu); Sannaimaru-yama (Aomori).

5) **Kōki,** low period, from about 2000 to about 1100 BC: sites at Mimanda, Ibusuki, Goryō (Kyushu); Fukuda III, Kasori, Angyō (Honshu).

6) **Banki,** late period, from about 1100 to about 100 BC: sites at Yūsu, Kurakawa (Kyushu); Kashiwara, Angyō III, Ubayama, Kamegaoka (Honshu). These dates are only very approximate indications and vary according to the sites and their levels. Some shell mounds *(kaizuka)* on coasts and riverbanks reveal populations of fishers, while remains found elsewhere show that there were also populations of hunters and gatherers. All the sites seem to have had inhabitants, at least in the middle periods, living in semi-buried round or square huts *(tateana-*

jukyō, tatara) with roofs of grass and foliage supported by a few wooden pillars. They were grouped into small hamlets of some dozen huts. In the low period, these hamlets became villages and houses were grouped around squares, cromlechs, or megalithic monuments. The deceased were buried in a squatting position, as their graves show. Study of skeletons has indicated that the custom of extracting teeth was common. In the low period, children were sometimes buried in jars. The presence of tools made of stone and bone (harpoons) does not prove that agriculture and fishing were practiced systematically. The Jōmon cultures were probably preceded by a microlithic culture (comparable to one called Sōsōki) characteristic of the Fukui, Nakatsuchi, Nakabayashi, Yasumiba, and Yadegawa sites, among others. The pottery (called Jōmon-*shikidoki*) was the most typical element of this prehistoric culture.

- **Jōmon-shikidoki.** Pottery from the Jōmon period, also called Neolithic, featuring decorations made with cords rolled on a stick and pressed into the surface. English archeologist E. S. Morse applied the term *jōmon* (cord mark) to this pottery. There were many variants depending on periods and regions. Those from the oldest periods seem to have had flat bottoms; later, pointed bottoms became widespread. In the middle period, decoration of the edges became more complicated and took fantastic shapes such as flame motifs. In the late Jōmon period, there were appliquéd decorations, sometimes of human figures or animals, as well as the appearance of a particular style of statuette, the *dogū*. *See* DOGŪ, HISTORY, YORI-ITO MONDOKI-BUNKA.

Jōmyō-ji. Buddhist monastery founded in 1005 in Kobata, near Heian-kyō, by Fujiwara no Michinaga, with the goal of acquiring merit and being reborn in the Pure Land (Jōdo) of Amida, and where he was buried. This monastery disappeared completely in the late Muromachi period.

- Zen Buddhist temple (Rinzai sect), also called Inari-san, founded in Kamakura in 1188 by Ashikaga Yoshikane for the Shingon-shū under the name Gokuraku-ji. His son, Yoshiuji, transferred it to the Rinzai sect in 1201. Ashikaga Sadauji was buried in this temple, so it was renamed Jōmyō-ji in 1331. Classified as one of the *gozan* of Kamakura, it comprised 33 subsidiary temples. Most of it was destroyed by fires in 1424 and 1429, but it still has a Yakushi-dō and a Tahō-tō from the late twelfth century. Its other buildings were reconstructed in 1756.

Jōnin. Buddhist monk (Enichibō, early thirteenth century) and painter, Kōben's disciple. He painted mainly Buddhist subjects and portraits (such as that of the monk Myōe in the Kōzan-ji). He may have been the author (or one of the authors) of the *Kegon-engi emaki.*

Jō-ō. Era of Emperor Go-Horikawa: Apr. 1222–Nov. 1224. *See* NENGŌ.

- Era of Emperor Go-Kōmyō: Sept. 1652–Apr. 1655. Also called Shōō. *See* NENGŌ.

Jo-ō. Zen Buddhist monk (1502–55) and poet, who worked with Sen no Rikyū. He combined the art of poetry with that of the tea ceremony *(chanoyu).*

- An emperor's third- and fourth-generation descendants (male branch).

Joosten van Lodensteijn, Jan. Dutch navigator (ca. 1560–1623) from Delft, officer on board the *Liefde,* which was wrecked on the coast of Kyushu in 1600. He lived with William Adams and was received with Adams by Tokugawa Ieyasu in Edo. Serving as an intermediary between the *bakufu* and the Dutch merchants of Hirado, he sent a number of ships with the "red seal" *(shuin-sen)* to Southeast Asia; he died in a shipwreck off the Paracel Islands. He was known in Japan as Yayōsu (or Yaesu). A district of Edo, Yaesugashi, was named after him. His son from his marriage to a Japanese woman in Edo continued to trade using his ships.

Jōri. During the Nara period, a type of land division and distribution in which arable land was divided into rectangular lots according to east-west *(jō)* and north-south *(ri)* axes. Each lot was 639 m (6 *chō*) per side and divided into 36 square parcels *(tsubo)* 106 m per side. The *tsubo* could in turn be divided into 10 bands *(tan)* with an area of about 1,130 m², in order to delimit rice paddies. Farms were grouped in no particular order in non-irrigated lands. Each *jōri* comprised a village composed of several *buraku* (hamlets) totaling about 30 to 50 houses. A new distribution of lands had to be made every six years according to the size of the families cultivating them. This type of land division left many traces on the countryside of the central provinces (especially Yamato), which were rapidly erased by the expansion of towns and road construction.

- Juridical term meaning, approximately, "that which is of the nature of things" or "that which emerges from the domain of reason," and which, theoretically, should designate a sort of standard of interpretation of laws.

Jorō. Professional courtesans. This term was applied, mainly in the Edo period, to all those who practiced this profession, from the highest rank *(tayū)* to the lowest *(mise-jorō)*. See GEISHA.

Joroku. "Sixteen feet," theoretical size of images of the Buddha portrayed standing (equivalent to about 4.85 m) or sitting (about 2.4 m).

Jōruri. Texts meant to be recited or chanted *(katari-mono);* with shamisen accompaniment or a puppet show, *jōruri* became a theater art in the late sixteenth century. The name comes from a popular fifteenth-century story, *Jōruri monogatari* (or *Jōruri jūnidan-sōshi)* telling of the love of the young Ushiwakamaru (Minamoto no Yoshitsune) for a young woman named Jōruri. At first sung by *biwa-hōshi, jōruri* were probably invented by Hamuro Tokinaga in the thirteenth century; in the late sixteenth century, Ono Tsū had the *Jōruri monogatari* set to music by Sawazumi Kengyō, a famous shamisen player. This type of sung recitation was later called *ko-jōruri* to distinguish it from the *shin-jōruri,* introduced by Chikamatsu Monzaemon in 1686, and is also called *gidayū (see* TAKEMOTO GIDAYŪ). The first *jōruri* performed in theaters accompanied *ayatsuri-shibai* shows, which became Bunraku in Osaka under the impetus of Uemura Bunrakuken I, who had founded his own puppet theater about 1800 to replace the Takemoto-za and Toyotake-za, which were declining in popularity. There are several "schools," or *bushi (fushi),* of *jōruri* recitation.

• *Jōruri jūnidan-sōshi.* "The Twelve Acts of Jōruri's Story." A mid-fifteenth-century play by an anonymous author (sometimes attributed to Ono Tsū) relating the gallant adventures of Ushiwakamaru and Jōruri. Also sometimes titled *Jōruri-hime monogatari, Jōruri monogatari.* See JŌRURI.

Jōruri-ji. Buddhist temple of the Shingon-ritsu sect, founded in Kyoto by the monk Gimyō Shōnin of the Taima-dera in 1047 to house a large statue of the Buddha Yakushi Nyorai, whose "paradise" was said to be of "pure beryl" *(jōruri).* This monastery was expanded considerably over the years, but was partly destroyed by a fire in 1343, leaving only the main hall (1157) and a three-story pagoda standing. In the hall are nine statues of Amida *(kuhon)* of *jōroku* size, sitting, in the Jōchō style (the only ex-

amples remaining from the period). The statue of Yakushi Nyorai is now housed in the pagoda. Also called Kutai-ji.

Jōryaku (or Jōreki). Era of Emperor Shirakawa: Nov. 1077–Feb. 1081. Also called Shōryaku. *See* NENGŌ.

Josetsu. Japanese name for a Chinese painter, naturalized in 1370, who founded a school of painting in Kyoto, introducing to Japan the landscape styles popular in China during the Song and Yuan dynasties. He used the *suiboko* technique (wash with colors), and his school was later known as Muromachi *suiboku.* Under the protection of shogun Ashikaga Yoshimochi, he participated in the decoration of many buildings and had many imitators, including Sesshū, Shūbun, and Kanō Masa Nobu. Also called Nyosetsu. *See* SUIBOKU.

Jōshi. Double suicide due to love. Mainly during the Edo period, some young people in love were not allowed to marry for family reasons, giving rise to the fad of double suicides. When these became too numerous, the shogunate forbade publication of works exalting *shinjū* (proof of fidelity) and use of the word in 1722. The penalty was death or outcast for any survivor *(see* HININ). Puppet and Kabuki theaters drew many plays from *jōshi.* See SHINJŪ.
→ *See* JUNKENSHI, JŌMI.

Joshi Eigaku Juku. School for girls founded by Tsuda Umeko in 1900 with an international vocation. It was transformed into a private university for women in 1948 and renamed Tsuda Juku Daigaku.

• **Joshi Shihan-gakkō.** Teacher-training college for women founded in Tokyo (Ochanomuzi district) in 1874. With a similar university, founded in Nara in 1908, it became the National University for Women (Ochanomizu Joshi Daigaku and Nara Joshi Daigaku).

Jōshū. Sculptor of netsuke (Shunchikudō, mid-nineteenth century).

Josō. Sculptor of netsuke (Miyazaki Josō, 1855–1910) in Tokyo.

Jōsui. Canals and trenches in cities carrying potable water to residents. Some were aqueducts, such as that of the Tamagawa river, which brought water into central Edo, and the Sen-gawa, built in the late seventeenth century. A water tax *(mizugin)* was imposed on all urban residents for construction and maintenance of the *jōsui* (not to be confused with the *gesui,* or sewers). Also called *yōsui.*

Jōtoku. Era of Emperor Horikawa: Nov. 1097–Aug. 1099. Also called Shōtoku. *See* NENGŌ.

Jotomba. In legends, name formed with the two characters *jō* and *uba,* symbols of longevity and happy marriage. Two characters with this name were also invented, who were supposed to have lived in the Takasago pine forest. Their life was the subject of many Noh plays, the best known being *Takasago.*

Jōtō Mon'in. Name of Fujiwara no Shōshi (Akiko, 988–1074) when she retired to a monastery in 1026. She was Fujiwara no Michinaga's daughter and became Emperor Ichijō's wife *(chūgū)* in 999. Her two sons became emperors Go-Ichijō and Go-Suzaku. Those in her service included Murasaki Shikibu, Izumi Shikibu, and perhaps Akazome Emon.

Jōwa. Era of Emperor Nimmyō: Jan. 834–July 848. *See* NENGŌ.
• Era of Emperor Kōmyō (Hokuchō dynasty): Oct. 1345–Feb. 1350. *See* NENGŌ.

• **Jōwa no Hen.** Disturbances that took place in Heian-kyō when Emperor Junna abdicated in 833 and his nephew Nimmyō ascended to the throne. Junna's son Tanesada was accused of conspiracy, and 60 people were sent into exile. Prince Michiyasu, one of Nimmyō's sons, was then declared crown prince; he became Emperor Montoku.

• **Jōwa-shōhō.** Name of one of the twelve types of coins *(kōchō-jūnisen)* issued in ancient Japan. These coins, struck from 835 to 847, had a diameter of 19 to 23 mm and a weight of 1.6 to 4.8 grams.

Jōyaku Kaisei. "Revision of the Unequal Treaties" *(fubyōdō-jōyaku)* signed by Japan between 1850 and 1860 with the United States, Holland, Russia, Great Britain, and France, limiting customs duties and establishing the principle of extraterritoriality. These treaties, whose terms were accepted by the Meiji government in 1868, drew the indignation of a population already prone to xenophobia. Starting in 1876, many senior bureaucrats demanded that the treaties be revised because they were keeping Japanese industry from developing due to strong competition from foreign products. After much bar-

gaining, led by Okuma Shigenobu, among others, Minister of Foreign Affairs Mutsu Munemitsu used diplomacy to reopen negotiations in 1892; in 1894, the Kimberly-Aoki agreement, abolishing the "Unequal Treaties" signed with England, was concluded. The other signatory nations followed Great Britain's example and committed themselves to rectifying the treaties in the five following years. Customs duties, however, returned to the Japanese only in 1911.

Jōyō-kanji. List of 1,945 Chinese characters *(kanji)* chosen by the Japanese government in 1981 for general use, replacing the list of 1,850 characters established in 1946 called Tōyo-kanji. A supplementary list of 166 characters was accepted only for transcription of proper nouns, which brought the total list of kanji to 2,111. The list includes 996 characters that should be learned by students during their first six years of school. *See* KANJI, TŌYO-KANJI.

Jōza. Former title of the director of general affairs for a monastery or Buddhist temple. *See* RISSHI.

• **Jōza no ma.** *See* SHOIN-ZUKURI.

Jozan. Painter (Watanabe Teiko; *azana:* Shukuho; *mei:* Gorō, 1817–37), Kazan's younger brother and also of the Nanga (Bunjinga) school.
→ *See* MIURA KŌHEIJI.

Jōzō. Buddhist monk (891–964) famous for his asceticism. His life was the subject of many popular legends.

Jūbako. Series of lacquered boxes, once used by nobles to send gifts. They were often valuable works of art.

Jū Dai Deshi. Group formed by the ten great disciples of Buddha, venerated as a group and sometimes portrayed surrounding the image of the Buddha Shaka Nyorai:
1) **Daikashō** *(Skt.:* Mahākāshyapa, Pippalayāna)
2) **Anaritsu** *(Skt.:* Aniruddha)
3) **Furuna** *(Skt.:* Pūrna, Maitreyāniputra)
4) **Kasenen** *(Skt.:* Kātyāyana, Nalada)
5) **Ubari** *(Skt.:* Upāli)
6) **Ragora** *(Skt.:* Rāhula)
7) **Sharihotsu** *(Skt.:* Shāriputra, Upatishya)
8) **Mokukenren** *(Skt.:* Maudgalyāyana)
9) **Ananda** *(Skt.:* Ānanda)
10) **Subodai** *(Skt.:* Subhūti)
The order of the disciples sometimes varies.

Judō. "Way of Suppleness." A nonviolent, non-offensive martial art and sport created in 1882 by Kanō Jigorō (1860–1938) based on the main techniques of *jū-jutsu* hand-to-hand combat practiced by the samurai. Its goal, according to its founder, is "to understand and rapidly demonstrate the living laws of motion." He codified a number of body, arm, and leg movements designed to unbalance *(kuzushi)* and immobilize the adversary without using any weapons. In the exercises *(randori)*, there is always "one who projects" *(tori)* and "one who submits" *(uke)*. *Judō* is practiced in a *dōjō*, a room with a floor covered with tatami. The grades comprise six "apprenticeships" *(kyū)* and ten masteries *(dan)*, indicated by belt colors. Since 1964 (when *judō* became an Olympic sport), championships have comprised seven weight categories.

• **Jūdōgi.** Garment worn by *judō* practitioners *(jūdōka)*.

Judō. Japanese name for Confucian philosophy. Also called Jukyō. *See* CONFUCIANISM.

Ju-ei. Era of Emperor Antoku: May 1182–Mar. 1185. *See* NENGŌ.

Jufuku-ji. Zen temple and monastery of the Rinzai sect, founded in 1200 in Kamakura by Hōjō Masako, Minamoto no Yoritomo's wife, for the monk Eisai. It was then directed by the monks Enni, Rankei Dōryū, and Gidō Shūshin. It was one of the *gozan* of Kamakura. The temple was destroyed by fire in 1247 and 1395. Two stone pagodas are said to be the tombs of Hōjō Masako and her son, Minamoto Sanetomo. All that remains is the *butsuden,* dating from 1200.

Jūgatsu Jiken. "October Incident." A plot discovered in October 1931, fomented by Lieutenant-Colonel Hashimoto Kingorō following the incidents in Manchuria and aimed at overthrowing the government of the Wakatsuki cabinet. Wakatsuki, forewarned, changed his military policy in Manchuria, and the conspirators were placed under house arrest.

Jugyoku. Sculptor of netsuke (Chōunsai, mid-nineteenth century).
• Sculptor of netsuke (Ueda Jugyoko, Ryūkōsai, late nineteenth century) in Tokyo.

Jūhachi Daitsū. "The Eighteen Commissioners," a group of wealthy merchants and samurai in Edo. During the An'ei and Temmei eras (1772–89), they provided a model for *chōnin* society and influenced art, theater, and literature through the principles of *iki* and *sui*. The number 18 was chosen for its symbolic value.

Jūji-ron. Text of the doctrine of the Hossō-shū, corresponding to the Sanskrit treatise *Dashabhūmika shāstra,* or "Treatise on the Ten Lands."

Jūjūshin-ron. Ten-volume treatise on Buddhist Shingon-shū philosophy, written about 830 by Kūkai, upon the order of Emperor Junna, to expound the sect's principles. This seminal work was later condensed as *Hizōhō-yaku* (Precious Key to the Sacred Treasure).

Jujutsu. "Magic," a group of techniques designed to master greater power practiced in most rituals in Shinto, Esoteric Buddhism, Ommyōdō, Shugendō, and divination. Most popular dances have a magical significance, as do major religious festivals *(matsuri)*. Also considered magical are charms *(omamori)* and various amulets, traditional foods, and so on. Certain magical acts have a harmful value, such as that of bewitching (*see* NINGYŌ), but most are designed to obtain some benefit, such as wealth or rain *(amagoi)*. Magic is thus an integral part of Japanese culture, underlying many everyday acts.

Jū-jutsu. "Technique of flexibility," combat using bare hands or weapons developed by the samurai of the Kamakura period from ancient fighting techniques called *kumi-uchi* or *yawara* (described, notably, in the *Konjaku monogatari*). Over the centuries, various schools *(ryū)* were created, each inventing new techniques that were part of the Kyūba no Michi (Path of the Bow and the Horse). They involved movements inspired by Chinese martial arts. *Jū-jutsu* developed as a martial art *(bujutsu)* only in the Edo period, and became a sport in the Meiji period. These deadly techniques, used mainly by bandits, were transformed into a "sport" by Kanō Jigorō, and his *judō,* along with *karate* and *aikidō,* officially replaced the offensive techniques of *jū-jutsu* in 1922. Also called, wrongly, *jiu-jitsu*.

Jukō. Buddhist monk (1422–1502), Ikkyū's disciple. He is considered to have "invented" the tea ceremony *(chanoyu)*. Also called Kyūshin Hōshi.

Juku. In the Edo period, private schools that taught Confucianism (Jukyō) to the samurai and to commoners who were protected by the shogunal government although they did not have official status.

Many *juku* also taught martial arts. In the Meiji era, *juku* became private schools teaching all sorts of subjects, but usually specializing in such subjects as English, piano, and *soroban* (abacus). Today, *juku* offer supplementary instruction to students preparing for entrance exams to universities; a sort of "cramming school," they are attended by more than 30% of public- and private-school students. Students in *juku* and *yobikō* (exam-preparation schools) take courses at night, after regular school hours, and during vacations. Although the cost of these extra courses is high, they are in great demand, and there are more than 100,000 *juku* in Japan, directed either by university students or retired teachers. *See* YOBIKŌ.

Jukyō. *See* CONFUCIANISM.

Jun-daijin. Title equivalent to vice-*daijin,* created by Fujiwara no Korechika in 1005. Also called Gidō-sanshi.

Jūni-hitoe. Ceremonial costume worn by women of the nobility and aristocracy during the Heian and Kamakura periods, consisting of a number of colored kimonos worn one over another. *Jūni-hitoe* consisted of wide red pants *(hakama),* worn under five kimonos—*hitoe, kasane-uchigi, uchiginu, uwagi,* and *karaginu*—with a matching train, *mo.* Depending on the style, as many as 12 *(jūni)* kimonos might be worn. This court costume was also called *karaginu no shōzoku, nyōbō shōzoku, shōzoku.*

Jūni Jinshō. "The Twelve Warriors," who, in Buddhist iconography, are supposed to have accompanied Yakushi Nyorai. They may have symbolized the 12 hours of the day. They are shown dressed in armor. These twelve warriors (rarely portrayed) are also the protectors of Buddhism and symbolize the twelve vows of Yakushi Nyorai. Their emblems and colors vary depending on the text. They have no independent existence and are venerated only when grouped with Yakushi Nyorai. The most representative groups of Jinshō are those at the Kōfuku-ji (Nara) and the Shin Yakushi-ji (Nara). They are:

1) **Kubira** (*Skt.:* Khumbīra)
2) **Basara, Bajira** (*Skt.:* Vajra)
3) **Mekira** (*Skt.:* Mikila, Mihira)
4) **Antera** (*Skt.:* Andira)
5) **Anira** (*Skt.:* Anila, Majila)
6) **Santera** (*Skt.:* Sandila)
7) **Indora** (*Skt.:* Indra)
8) **Haira** (*Skt.:* Pajira)
9) **Makora** (*Skt.:* Mahōrāga)
10) **Shindara** (*Skt.:* Sindūra, Kimnara)
11) **Shatora** (*Skt.:* Chatura)
12) **Bikara** (*Skt.:* Bikarāla)

This group is also sometimes called Jūni Taishō (Twelve Generals).

• **Jūnikō Gutsu.** "The Buddha of the Twelve Lights," one of the names of Amida Butsu in the esoteric doctrines of Buddhism.

Jūni Ritsu. In traditional Japanese music, the scale used mainly for Buddhist songs and prayers, corresponding to the twelve tones of the Chinese scale (Huangzhong):

1) **Ichikotsu** (Kōshō): **D.** *Chin.:* Huangzhong.
2) **Tangin** (Tairyo): **D sharp.** *Chin.:* Dalü.
3) **Hyōjō** (Taiso): **E.** *Chin.:* Taicou.
4) **Shōzetsu** (Kyōshō): **F.** *Chin.:* Jiazhong.
5) **Shimomu** (Kosen): **F sharp.** *Chin.:* Guxian.
6) **Sōjō** (Chūryo): **G.** *Chin.:* Zhonglü.
7) **Fushō** (Suihin): **G sharp.** *Chin.:* Ruibin.
8) **Oshiki** (Rinshō): **A.** *Chin.:* Linzhong.
9) **Rankei** (Isoku): **A sharp.** *Chin.:* Yizuo.
10) **Banshiki** (Nanryo): **B.** *Chin.:* Nanlü.
11) **Shinsen** (Bueki): **C.** *Chin.:* Wuyi.
12) **Kamimu** (Oshō): **C sharp.** *Chin.:* Yingzhong.

Jūnirui emaki. Group of three illustrated scrolls dating from the fifteenth century, author not confirmed. They tell about a poetry contest on the theme of the Jūnishi (Dōmoto Collection, Kyoto).

Jūnishi. The 12 animals of the 12-year cycle corresponding to the Chinese calendar *(Yuanjia)* called *genka-reki:*

1) **Ne, Nezumi** (Rat): . . . 1900, 1912, 1924, 1936, 1948, 1960, 1972, 1984, 1996 . . .
2) **Ushi** (Bull): . . . 1901, 1913, 1925, 1937, 1949, 1961, 1973, 1985, 1997 . . .
3) **Tora** (Tiger): . . . 1902, 1914, 1926, 1938, 1950, 1962, 1974, 1986, 1998 . . .
4) **U, Usagi** (Rabbit): . . . 1903, 1915, 1927, 1939, 1951, 1963, 1975, 1987, 1999 . . .
5) **Tatsu** (Dragon): . . . 1904, 1916, 1928, 1940, 1952, 1964, 1976, 1988, 2000 . . .
6) **Mi** (Snake): . . . 1905, 1917, 1929, 1941, 1953, 1965, 1977, 1989, 2001 . . .
7) **Uma** (Horse): . . . 1906, 1918, 1930, 1942, 1954, 1966, 1978, 1990, 2002 . . .
8) **Hitsuji** (Goat, Sheep): . . . 1907, 1919, 1931, 1943, 1955, 1967, 1979, 1991, 2003 . . .
9) **Saru** (Monkey): . . . 1896, 1908, 1920, 1932, 1944, 1956, 1968, 1980, 1992, 2004 . . .
10) **Tori** (Bird): . . . 1897, 1909, 1921, 1933, 1945, 1957, 1969, 1981, 1993, 2005 . . .

11) **Inu** (Dog): . . . 1898, 1910, 1922, 1934, 1946, 1958, 1970, 1982, 1994, 2006 . . .

12) **I, Inoshishi** (Boar, Pig): . . . 1899, 1911, 1923, 1935, 1947, 1959, 1971, 1983, 1995, 2007 . . .

These animals and their corresponding years are used mainly in astrology and were once also used to name the hours of the day and night. *See* CALENDAR, HOROSCOPE, JIKKAN-JŪNISHI.

Junkei. Sculptor (fourteenth century) who worked at the Kamidō of the Hōryū-ji (statue of Kōmo-kuten).

• Sculptor (early eighteenth century), maker of the statues of the Ni-ō in the *chūmon* of the Tōdai-ji in 1717. He worked with Kenkei on other statues in that temple, notably those of Nyoirin Kannon and Kokūzō Bosatsu.

Junkei Nagamitsu. *See* NAGAMITSU.

Junkenshi. In the Kamakura period (1185–1333), shogunal bureaucrats responsible for annual inspection of the provinces. They were called *jōshi* during the Muromachi period. In 1615, a new corps of *junkenshi* was instituted (also called *gojunken*), with 35 members. It operated until 1838. *See* JUN-SATSUSHI, NAIKENSHI.

Junna Tennō. Fifty-third emperor (Prince Otomo, 786<824–33>840), Kammu Tennō's third son and successor to his older brother, Saga Tennō. He abdicated in favor of Nimmyō, Saga Tennō's son, and retired to his "Western Residence," renamed Junna-in. An educated emperor, he was a major promoter of Chinese studies. *Posthumous name:* Yamato Neko Ame no Takayuzuru Iyatō no Sumera no Mikoto.

• **Junna-in.** Emperor Junna's residence in Tokyo, also called "Western Residence." It was transformed into a university for young nobles in 881, and was directed by a bureaucrat titled Junna-in Bettō. This title was later sometimes given to the Tokugawa shogun.

Junnin Tennō. Forty-seventh emperor (Prince Ōi, 733<759–64>765), successor to Empress Kōken. He was exiled to Awaji by the monk Dōkyō, who had been named prime minister (whence his nickname, Awaji-haitei). Empress Shōtoku succeeded him.

Junnyo. Buddhist monk (1577–1631), Kennyo's son. He was the twelfth abbot *(hossu)* of the Jōdo Shin-shū sect of the Hongan-ji in Kyoto.

Junrei. "Pilgrimages." The custom of making religious pilgrimages was established very early in Japan, but they became a regular event in the early Heian period. The monk Shinnyo (Prince Takaoka, 799–865) was the first, it seems, to attempt a pilgrimage to the holy Buddhist sites in India (he never reached that country but was shipwrecked on the coast of Malaysia). Devotion to Bodhisattva Kannon was at the origin of major Buddhist pilgrimage circuits to the 33 "Western Shrines" and the 33 "Eastern Shrines." Forty-eight-stage pilgrimages were also created on the path that Kūkai had taken on Shikoku, as were a number of other circuits organized by various Buddhist and Shinto sects (to the Ise Shrines, Ise-kō). These pilgrimages later became mainly an excuse for travel and recreation, and a number of Buddhists and Shinto followers today continue to make them without a religious goal. *See* SANJŪSAN-SHŌ.

Junsatsushi. Itinerant imperial bureaucrats responsible for inspecting provincial administrations from 694 to 826. This function was reestablished at the beginning of the Meiji era (1868), but the *junsatsushi* were quickly replaced by *azechi* in the Tōhoku provinces. They then operated irregularly, notably in 1882–83. *See* JUNKENSHI.

Junshi. "Suicide through fidelity," an ancient custom according to which the faithful servants of a sovereign committed suicide when their master died so that they would not outlive him and would accompany him to the Beyond. This custom, cited in the Chinese Wei chronicle *(Weizhi)* regarding the Yamato, was forbidden by decree in 646. Despite this, many samurai and servants killed themselves when their master or lord died. The last example of *junshi* occurred when General Nogi and his wife committed suicide when Emperor Meiji died in 1912. Throughout the Edo period, it was common practice for samurai close to a lord to commit *seppuku* when the lord died. *Junshi* was considered a *giri* (moral obligation). But many daimyo forbade it and, in 1683, the rules in the *Buke-shohatto* banned it again. The custom of double suicide, followed mainly at the beginning of the Edo period, called *jōshi (see* JŌSHI), was sometimes called *junshi* in order to give it the appearance of a noble act.

Juntoku Tennō. Eighty-fourth emperor (Prince Morihira, or Morinara, 1197<1221–21>1242), Go-Toba Tennō's third son and successor to his older brother, Tsuchimikado Tennō. To help his father, Retired Emperor Go-Toba, put up a better fight against the Kamakura *bakufu,* he abdicated in favor of Hūkyō, his three-year-old son. Defeated, he was sent into exile on Sado, where he died, leaving a diary and some writings on poetry and court protocol *(Kimpishō)*.

Jū-ō. The "Ten Kings" of Buddhist hell, venerated mainly by followers of the Shingon-shū sect. The Ten Kings—Byōdo-ō, Emma-ō, Gokan-ō, Gototenrin-ō, Hensei-ō, Shinkō-ō, Shokō-ō, Sōtei-ō, Taizan-ō, and Toshi-ō—are directed by Emma-ō *(Skt.:* Yamarāja). *See also* JŪSAN BUTSU.

Jurakudai. Fortified palace built in Kyoto by Toyotomi Hideyoshi in 1586 behind the imperial palace. This "pleasure villa" was used for only eight years; Hideyoshi had it destroyed after his nephew Hidetsugu committed suicide in 1595. It was huge and surrounded by a moat and a stone rampart. Its interior rooms were decorated sumptuously by the best artists of the time. Some parts of it were reused in other buildings, such as the Nishi Hongan-ji in Kyoto and the Daitoku-ji *(kara-mon* gate, among other things). Also called Jurakutei.

Jūren. Buddhist monk (eleventh–twelfth century) who was beheaded at the same time as his colleague Anraku, in 1206. He was one of Hōnen's disciples.

Jurōjin. One of the "Seven Gods of Good Fortune" (Shichifukujin), representing longevity; the Japanized form of the Chinese divinity Shouxing. Portrayed as an old man leaning on a long stick and often accompanied by a stork (or a crane), he is sometimes identified as the Chinese wise man Laozi *(Jap.:* Rōjin) and called Rōjinsei. The "book of knowledge" is often shown hooked on his stick. He is a heavenly divinity. His image is often reproduced alone (in the case of netsuke or good-luck statuettes) or with the other gods of happiness, posed in the "ship of treasures" *(takara-bune).* He is sometimes confused with Fukurokuju because of his high forehead. *See* SHICHIFUKUJIN.

Jūroku musashi. Popular game played on a checkerboard with 16 pieces (warriors) and a main piece called the *benkei* (after a famous twelfth-century monk-warrior). The goal is to push the *benkei* into a corner and keeping it from moving. The *benkei,* however, can "capture" the opposing player's pieces when they are in certain positions near it. This game, popular in the seventeenth century, is rarely played today.

Jūroku-rakan. *See* RAKAN.

Jūsan Butsu. Group of 13 Buddhist divinities venerated by followers of the Shingon sect during various periods following the death of a person in order to save that person's soul. These rituals are closely related to those of veneration of the Jū-ō (Ten Kings of Hell), whose names are in parentheses below:

1. **Fudō Myō-ō** (corresponding to Shinkō-ō), venerated during the first seven days after a death.
2. **Shaka Nyorai** (corresponding to Shokō-ō), during the second week.
3. **Monju Bosatsu** (corresponding to Sōtei-ō), during the third week.
4. **Fugen Bosatsu** (corresponding to Gokan-ō), during the fourth week.
5. **Jizō Bosatsu** (corresponding to Emma-ō), during the fifth week.
6. **Miroku Bosatsu** (corresponding to Hensei-ō), during the sixth week.
7. **Yakushi Nyorai** (corresponding to Taizan-ō), during the seventh week.
8. **Kannon Bosatsu** (corresponding to Byōdō-ō), on the hundredth day.
9. **Seishi Bosatsu** (corresponding to Toshi-ō), at the end of the first year.
10. **Mida Nyorai (Amida)** (corresponding to Gototenrin-ō), at the end of the third year.
11. **Ashuku Nyrorai,** at the end of the seventh year.
12. **Dainichi Nyorai,** at the end of the thirteenth year.
13. **Kokūzō Bosatsu** (corresponding to Jion-ō), at the end of the thirty-third year.

• **Jūsan Daishū.** "The Thirteen Anthologies of the Epoch," beginning with the *Shin chokusen wakashū* (1234) and ending with the *Shin zoku kokinshū* (1439). *See* CHOKUSEN WAKA-SHŪ.

Jusangō. "Privileges of the Three Empresses." The three *(sankō)*—the arch-dowager empress *(taikō-taigō),* the dowager empress *(kōtaigō),* and the reigning empress *(kōgō)*—had the privilege of appointing people of their choice to official positions at the beginning of each year.

Jūsan-mairi. "Festival of the Thirteenth Year." Children were considered to reach maturity at age 13, so a large festival was organized on this occasion, especially in the Kyoto and Osaka regions. It took place generally on the 13th day of the 13th month on the lunar calendar. Parents and children went to the temple or shrine to which they belonged and prayed for wisdom to be granted to them (this festival is thus sometimes called Chie-mairi).

Jusenshi. Title of the imperial bureaucrat in charge of issuing currency, starting in 694.

Jūshichijō no Kempō. "Seventeen-Article Constitution." The first "Constitution" of Japan, with 17 articles, written by Shōtoku Taishi and said to have been promulgated by him in 604, although it was probably promulgated after his death in 622. These articles truly gave birth to the Japanese nation and had a great influence on the Japanese way of acting and thinking:

1. *Respect above all Wa (peace, Japan). Your first duty is to avoid discord. There are people who do not love their parents and others who do not obey their masters. These people may cause dissent between themselves and their neighbors. If the highest class lives in harmony with the lowest class and if the low classes follow the best advice, all will go well and there will be few problems that cannot be resolved.*

2. *Venerate with all your heart the treasures that are the Buddha, the Dharma, and the Sangha, for in these are found the ideal life and the wisdom of the nation. There are not many truly evil men. Everyone can acquire a good education. But one cannot hope to straighten the tortuous paths of men without the help of these three treasures.*

3. *Listen with reverence to the Imperial Edicts. If the emperor can be likened to heaven, his subjects are the earth. With the heavens above and the earth below unified in the loyal accomplishment of their tasks in their respective positions, we will see the world managed in a perfect order and the harmonious turning of the four seasons. If the earth tries to replace the heavens, a catastrophe will occur. When the Lord speaks, his subjects must listen and obey. When he shows the way, they must follow it faithfully. If they disobey, it will be at their own risk.*

4. *All nobles, low and high, must observe the laws as being the root of all virtues. In governing the country, the first duty is to establish laws. If the upper class does not observe them, the low classes cannot be governed. If the low classes do not observe them, they will commit crimes. As long as the law is observed in relations between the upper and lower classes, perfect order will prevail and the stability of the state will be assured.*

5. *In hearing court cases that involve the ordinary people, the judges must curb their repose and detest their own interest. If there are a thousand cases to try each day, how many will there be to judge in a year? Thus, they must be diligent.*

6. *Our ancient wise men taught us to punish evil people and reward the virtuous. Do not conceal a person's kindness, nor his misdeeds if these are not repaired.*

7. *Each person has a duty to fulfill and must do so with faultless diligence. If wise and able people occupy high positions, unanimous voices of joyous approval will rise, but if evil employees occupy high positions, this will cause perpetual dissent and even upheavals. All of the state's affairs, large and small, will be conducted easily if the right people are in the right positions. This is the basis of a strong state and a prestigious, durable dynasty. The good leaders of ancient times used good men for high positions and did not reserve good positions for their favorites.*

8. *All nobles, high and low, must appear at their posts early in the morning and return home late at night. There are too many public affairs to be dealt with to have disposed with them at the end of each day.*

9. *Sincerity is the soul of good comportment. Be sincere every moment of your life. The success or failure of each task depends on your sincerity or lack of sincerity. When masters and servants are linked by feelings of sincerity, there is nothing they cannot accomplish. All work will fail if it is not thus performed.*

10. *Do not let yourself become angry. Forgive an angry eye. Avoid the resentment of those different from you. Each has his own mind and way of thinking. If you are right, I must be wrong. I am not always a saint and you are not always a sinner. We are both fallible mortals, and who is so wise as to judge which of us is good or bad? We are both alternately wise and foolish.*

11. *Distinguish between meritorious acts and misdeeds, and reward or punish them justly. In our times, merit is not necessarily rewarded and punishments are not always true punishments. Nobles, high and low, must receive the reward or punishment they deserve.*

12. *The governors and masters of the new territories must not impose taxes on their people. In this country there are not two sovereigns and the people do not have two masters to serve. There is only one lord in the person of the emperor. Governors and officers charged with administering local affairs are also among those under the emperor's rule.*

13. *All governors and officers must share their knowledge with regard to the duties of their responsibilities, since their absence, due to illness or travel, for any length of time could occasion difficulties in official work.*

14. *All bureaucrats, great and small, must take care not to be jealous of one another. If you are jeal-*

*ous of others, they will be jealous of you, and thus a
vicious circle will be perpetuated.*

15. *Public service to the sacrifice of one's own interest is the duty of a good noble. If a noble acts in
his own interest, he will provoke ill will among the
people. If there is such egotism on the one hand and
such ill will on the other, the result will be sacrifice
of the public welfare. The personal ambition of bureaucrats will keep law and order from reigning.
Thus, as is said in an article above, harmony is most
important; it cannot be overestimated.*

16. *The elders have taught us that it is wise to
choose the appropriate time for using the ordinary
people in public works. They may be profitably
used during the winter months, when they have free
time. From spring to fall, they are occupied in agriculture and sericulture and cannot be requisitioned.
Without agriculture, how would we all be fed, and
without blackberry cultivation, how would we be
clothed?*

17. *In important affairs, never act on your own
judgment alone, but deliberate with a number of
people. In affairs of little importance, you cannot
ask for the opinion of many people.*

This "Constitution" is also known as Kempō no
Jūshichijō. *See* CONSTITUTIONS.

Jushiki Wajin. When the Yi dynasty came to power
in Korea in 1392, neighborly relations were established between Japan and Korea. All Japanese who
had rendered services to Korea received honorific titles from the Korean government. The only obligation of the Jushiki Wajin was to present themselves
at the Korean court once a year, wearing the insignia that had been conferred on them.

Jūshin. Group of official advisers to the emperor,
who in effect made policy from the 1930s to the end
of the Second World War. The *jūshin* was composed
of former prime ministers and retired ministers.

Juso. Curse or magical spell cast on a person. In ancient times, it was considered a crime. Nevertheless,
the custom of sticking pins or nails into an earthen
or wooden effigy of the person whom one wants to
affect has always existed in Japan and is found today in various forms.

Jūshoku. Title for the head of the monks in a Buddhist temple. *See* SŌ-KAN.

• **Jūsō.** High-ranking monk in a Buddhist monastery. Also called hossu, ina, ino, jishu, jōza, jūshoku, risshi, sankō, sōjō, sōjō, sōzu, tsuina, zasu,
and other terms. See SŌ-KAN.

Jūtaku tōjin. In the Muromachi and Edo periods, a
term for Chinese who settled in Nagasaki and the
surrounding area, either for trade purposes or as
monks or artists.

Jutsu. "Art" or "technique" based on a traditional
school *(ryū)* and applied mainly to martial arts involving violence, as opposed to *dō*, a "way" or
"path," which is more spiritual. *See* JŪDŌ, JŪ-
JUTSU.

Juttoku. Black robe worn by some Buddhist
monks, and at one time by artists, poets, and old
men. It attaches at the right shoulder. Also called
jittoku.

Juzu. Rosary or string of beads used by Buddhist
monks to recite invocations to the Buddha or another divinity, or a group of prayers, notably the
nembutsu. This rosary is generally composed of 54
or 108 beads. In the case of 54-bead *juzu,* a "zero"
bead is inserted, at which the prayer sayer returns
down the beads in order to complete the 108 invocations. The beads are made of wood, hard seeds,
crystal, or any other convenient material. The most
popular are rosaries in pipal wood *(Ficus religiosa)*
or sandalwood *(Santalum album)*. Also called
nenju. Skt.: mālā.

K. The consonant K is always associated with one of the vowels—*a, i, u, e, o*—to form the syllabic sounds *ka, ki, ku, ke,* and *ko*. The syllable *ki*, associated with the sounds *ya, yu, yū, yo,* and *yō*, forms the complex syllables *kya, kyu, kyū, kyo,* and *kyō*. When it is "nigorized" (*see* NIGORI), it becomes a G. *See* KANA.

Kabane. Before 684, hereditary title of a bureaucrat or noble with an official responsibility in the court, indicating at the same time his rank as *uji no kami,* or head of a "family" *(uji)*. Later, "Kabane" became a family name conferred by the emperor. The titles *ōmi, muraji,* and *miyatsuko* were generally reserved for heads of *uji* actually at the court, while *kimi, atae,* and *obito* were titles for heads of *uji* living in the provinces. This system was reorganized in 684 and renamed *yakusa no kabane*. *See also* ASOMI, I.

Kabasan Jiken. "Incident on Mt. Kaba." One of the many popular uprisings that took place between 1880 and 1884 because of Prime Minister Matsukata Masayoshi's deflation policy. The goal of this uprising, instigated by left-wing members of the Jiyūtō (Liberal party), was to assassinate members of the government during an official ceremony inaugurating a building in Utsunomiya, near Mt. Kaba, in September 1884. The plot was discovered when a bomb made by the conspirators exploded prematurely. The police arrested several of them, while others fled to Mt. Kaba, proclaiming their desire to overthrow the "enemy of freedom" government. Besieged, they were forced into hiding and were captured soon after. Seven of them were sentenced to death by hanging, and the others to life in prison.

Kabayama Sukenori. Statesman and admiral (Hashiguchi, Kabayama Jiki, 1837–1922) from the Satsuma clan. He was appointed minister of the navy in 1889 in Yamagata Aritomo's cabinet and retained the position in Matsukata Masayoshi's cabinet (1891). After participating in the Sino-Japanese War of 1894–95, he was made an admiral and the governor-general of Taiwan. He was minister of the interior in Matsukata's second cabinet and minister of education in Yamagata's cabinet in 1898. Appointed marshal in 1893. *See* TAIWAN.

Kabegaki. Public posting for the general public's information of regulations and laws issued by the authorities, a custom started in 807 and continued during the Kamakura and Muromachi periods by provincial daimyo. Also sometimes called *hekisho.*

Kabuki. One of the major forms of Japanese theater, said to have been created by a dancer named Izumo Taisha, or Ōkuni, about 1603, when she gathered a troupe of dancers and singers to perform in the dry riverbed of the Kamo-gawa river in Kyoto. They were soon called "strange," "unusual" *(kabuki)*. This form of danced theater derived from sensual folkdances called Furyū-ō Odori and Nembu Odori, performed only by women. The actresses' performance was codified by Nagoya Sanzaburō, and "Kabuki" reached Edo in 1607. Because many of the actresses in this popular theater genre were also prostitutes, the shogunate banned women from going on stage in 1629. They were replaced by boys called *wakashu,* who, because they were generally under 15 years old, were the subject of numerous scandals and were also banned from the stage, in 1652. The shogunate ordered that Kabuki shows be based on the Noh theater's Kyōgen and be played by men *(yarō)*. Kabuki thus became a true professional theater form engaged in the arts of *ka* (singing), *bu* (dance), and *ki* (technique). The female roles *(onnagata)* were filled by men who specialized in playing women. Theaters were built in Edo, Osaka, and Kyoto for Kabuki performances, and changes were made to the stage with the invention of the *hanamichi* and the curtain, allowing actors to change costumes and sets to be changed every act. The plays performed became longer and were written especially for this new type of theater. Some famous actors, such as Ichikawa Danjūrō I, created new styles of plays, *aragoto,* featuring heroes.

During the Genroku era (late seventeenth century), Kabuki plays diversified; in addition to *aragoto* there were *jidai-mono* (historical plays), *sewa-mono* (more intimate plays), *shosagoto* (danced theater), and *jitsugoto* and *wagoto* (realistic plays), written by specialized authors such as Sakata Tōjūrō (*gō:* Mimasuya Hyōgo) and Chikamatsu Monzaemon (who also wrote for puppet theater, *ayatsuri,* then flourishing in Osaka). Plays from puppet theater were adapted for Kabuki; called *maruhon-mono,* they included *Kokusen'ya kasen* (The Battles of Koxinga, 1715), *Sugawara denju tenarai kagami* (The Secret of Sugawara's Calligraphy, 1746), *Yoshitsune sembon-zakura* (Yoshitsune's Thousand Cherry Trees, 1747), and *Kanadehon chūshingura* (The Faithful Vassals' Treasure, 1748). Namiki Shōzō and Namiki Gohei (1747–1808) were famous *shosagoto* actors, while Tsuruya Namboku IV (*Tōkaidō Yotsuya kaidan,* "The Ghosts of Yotsuya," 1825) shone in "realistic" plays *(kizewa-mono)*. Mokuami created the *shiranami-mono* genre featuring thieves and depraved people. He also tried to "modernize" Kabuki during the Meiji era by dressing actors in Western garb—the *zangiri-mono* (with short hair) genre—but *aragoto* remained the most popular genre. Many famous actors (Ichikawa Danjūrō, Onoe Kikugorō, Matsumoto Kōshirō, and Nakamura Kichiemon, among others) performed in plays written by Okamoto Kidō, Mayama Seika, Hasegawa Shin, and Kubota Mantarō, to mention only the best known of those who inaugurated a "new Kabuki" *(shin Kabuki)*.

After falling somewhat into disfavor in the early twentieth century, Kabuki became popular again after the Second World War, and performances are now given throughout the year in theaters designed specifically for this type of show. The plays are generally long, lasting up to four or five hours (including intermissions); very often, only the most popular scenes are performed. The actors' performance is strictly codified (*kata,* "forms") and often very stylized. The lead actors *(tachikayu)* often strike immobile poses called *mie* so that they can be admired, make a "dramatic exit" *(roppō)* via the *hanamichi,* or simulate a danced fight with characteristic poses, the *tate*. Their makeup is symbolic, with each color representing a character, and they often wear wigs. The costumes are always extremely elaborate, while the sets are generally simple and very suggestive. The stage itself is wide and has undergone various modifications since the beginnings of Kabuki. The *hanamichi,* created in 1670, was refined in 1740. Rising and descending devices were introduced in 1753 by Namiki Shozō, and a rotating stage brought a decisive change in direction in 1785. Stage music *(geza)* enlivens the stylized set; the songs *(naga-uta)* accompanying the dances vary according to the school. Very recently, actor-playwrights such as Ichikawa Ennosuke III have breathed new life into Kabuki by adding modern techniques inspired by Western theater.

• **Kabuki-jūhachiban.** "The Eighteen Best Kabuki Plays," a traditional list of works chosen by Ichikawa Danjūrō VII, most of them of the *aragoto* genre. Only ten are still performed today: *Narukami* (1684), *Shibaraku* (1697), *Fudō* (1697), *Zōbiki* (1701), *Sukeroku* (1713), *Yanone* (1720), *Kagekiyo* (1739), *Kenuki* (1742), *Kamahige* (1769), and *Kanjinchō* (1740). The others are *Fuwa* (1680), *Uwanari* (1699), *Uirō-uri* (1718), *Oshimodoshi* (1727), *Kan-u* (1737), *Nanatsu-men* (1740), *Gedatsu* (1760), and *Jayanagi* (1763). *See also* SHIN KABUKI-JŪHACHIBAN.

• **Kabuki-za.** Major Kabuki theater in Tokyo, built about 1660 and reconstructed using Western techniques in the Kobiki-chō district in 1889. Destroyed in the earthquake of September 1923, it was rebuilt in the style of the Momoyama era in 1924. Once again destroyed by bombing in 1945, it was reerected in the same style in 1951.

Kabukidō Enkyō. The artist's name used by Kabuki actor Nakamura Jūsuke (1749–1803), who made many ukiyo-e prints that were portraits of actors in the Sharaku style.

Kabuki-mon. Simple gate, somewhat similar to a torii, comprising two uprights joined by a crosspiece. At first reserved for the common people to pass through, it was used by samurai for the entrances to their *yashiki;* in the Edo period, it became the gate style adopted by the shogun and daimyo for their residences.

Kabu-nakama. Merchant guilds arising from merchants' associations called *nakama* (*uchi-nakama,* family groups; *kō,* compatriots; *kumiai,* professional groups) that received a monopoly in their respective trades from the Edo shogun, Some *nakama,* called *gomenkabu,* had a license to control prices and direct the trading operations of other *nakama.* Created in 1721 to replace the old guilds *(za),* they were dissolved in 1870 to make way for modern businesses. *See* FUDASASHI, TOIMARU.

Kaburagi Kiyokata. Painter (Kumeno Ken'ichi, Kaburagi Ken'ichi, 1878–1972) in the "Japanese style" (Nihonga), born in Tokyo. He painted prints in the ukiyo-e genre but in a modern style, and he illustrated many books. A member of the Academy in 1929, he received the Order of Culture (Bunka-shō) in 1954.

Kabura-ya. "Turnip-shaped arrow," with a bulging tip pierced in such a way that it made a shrill whistle when it was shot. These arrows were shot at the beginning of battles both to alert the enemy and to chase away evil spirits. They were also sold as charms in some Shinto shrines (the Meiji-jingū in Tokyo, for example) at the beginning of the year; carried on the back, they chased away the demons of the past year. *Chin.: mingdi. See also* KASAGAKE, YA.

Kabuto. "Helmet" worn by samurai. It was generally made of metal and decorated with horns *(kuwagata)* and "wings" *(fukigaeshi)* designed to deflect sword blows. The helmet itself was made of a "bowl" *(hachi),* sometimes signed by its maker inside the crown, a neck protector of jointed plates *(shikoro),* and a decorative piece on top *(mabesashi).* A hole *(tenen)* was made in the top of the "bowl" for air flow. Four "nails" were set on the sides of the helmet, symbolizing the four horizons. The visor *(maebashi)* was often decorated with a *mon* or *mabesashi.* The ornaments on top were called *maedate;* on the sides, *wakidate;* on the back, *ushirodate;* and on the tip, *kashiradate.* A mask *(men)* was attached covering either the entire face *(sōmen),* or just the cheeks and chin *(hōate),* or the cheeks, chin, and nose *(mempō).* The nose was sometimes protected by a removable piece. Parade helmets might be simple or complex in shape, some taking the shape of *eboshi,* others of animals. Their outside surface either was smooth or had protuber-

ances. Ordinary foot soldiers *(zusa)* wore a flat hat called a *jingasa. See* YOROI.

• **Kabutogane.** *See* KASHIRA.

Kabutsuchi no tachi. Type of straight épée, with a pommel ending in a fist-shaped bulge, found in many late-period (fifth–seventh century) *kofun.* Some were very long, up to 2.5 m. They probably had a ritual significance.

Kachikachi-yama. "Kachikachi Mountain." A famous tale in which a *tanuki* (badger or raccoon-dog, *Viverrinus*) teases an old couple so much that they threaten to boil it and eat it. But the *tanuki* kills the old woman, transforms itself to take her place, and gives the old man soup made with its victim's flesh. A rabbit sees this and decides to avenge the poor woman. It sets the *tanuki*'s fur on fire and drowns it. In some versions of this story, the main character is a fox *(kitsune)* or a monkey *(saru).*

Kachō-ga. "Painting of flowers and birds," a genre in which nature is depicted, as opposed to people *(jimbutsu-ga)* and landscapes *(sansui-ga).* It began in China toward the end of the Tang period and was developed during the Song dynasty. It was brought to Japan during the Kamakura period and became very popular during the Muromachi period because it was one of the favorite genres of painters of the Bujinga (Nanga) and Rimpa schools. Flowers and birds are still widely used as subjects by modern painters (Nihonga). *See* SANSUI-GA.

Kachōmai. During the Heian period, tax charged on rice grown on lands in public estates *(kokuga-ryō)* and *shōen,* in addition to regular tax *(nengu).* The *jitō* appointed by the Kamakura *bakufu* charged these taxes on lands they controlled, at five *shō* of rice per *tan* of rice paddy cultivated. This extra tax was sometimes called *komemai* or *nobemai* during the Edo period. *See* JITŌ, NENGU.

Kachō-yojō. "Atmosphere of Flowers and Birds." A 30-volume commentary on the *Genji monogatari,* written in 1472 by Ichijō Kanera, to complement and correct the previously published *Kakai-shō* by Yotsutsuji Yoshinari. This work is of prime importance for study of the *Genji monogatari.* Also titled *Kachō-yosei.*

Kada no Arimaro. Scholar and poet (1706–51) belonging to the school of "National Learning" (Kokugaku), born in Kyoto; Kada no Azumamaro's nephew and author of an excellent work on poetics, *Kokka hachiron* (1742).

• **Kada no Azumamaro.** Kokugaku (National Learning) scholar (1669–1736) and *waka* poet, born into a family of Shinto priests of the Fushimi Inari-jinja shrine in Kyoto. He was employed in Emperor Reigen's court, then went to Edo to work on the *bakufu's* historical archives. A fervent student of national history, he proposed that it replace Confucianism (Jukyō) as the state doctrine. He opened schools based on this premise, where he taught the ancient texts and the poetry of the *Man'yōshū*. His nephew and adoptive son, Kada no Arimaro, continued his work. His poems were collected in *Shun'yōshū* in 1798. Kamo Mabuchi was one of his disciples starting in 1733.

Kadensho. "Book of Transmission of Flowers," by Zeami Motokiyo, explaining Noh art. The oldest treatise on Japanese theater, it comprises seven books: the first deals with exercises according to age; the second, with mimicking; the third, with the origins of Noh; the fourth, with the presence of the actor on stage; the fifth, with the actor's life; the sixth, with the actor's art; the seventh, with oral tradition. It was probably completed in 1418. Its exact original title was *Fūshikaden* (Transmission of the Flower of Performance).

Kadokawa. Major publishing house (Kadokawa Shoten) founded in 1945 by Kadokawa Gen'yoshi (1917–75), specializing in classical literature. Gen'yoshi's son, Kadokawa Haruki, transformed the company into a publisher of pocket-books and a producer of television films and radio programs.

Kadota. Dry rice paddies located near a Buddhist monastery or a noble's residence, benefiting from special taxation. The warriors who cultivated them (called *ji-samurai*) or who had them cultivated ended up appropriating them and thus became landowners.

Kadoya Shichirobei. Shipowner and trader (1610–72), born in Ise, who established a Japanese colony on the coast of Annam, near today's Danang, in 1633, from which he sent local products to Japan. Unable to return to his country of birth due to the proscriptions of 1636, he married a local leader's daughter. After his death, his son continued to trade with Japan.

Kadozuke. Tradition in which, at certain times of year, groups of young people go from door to door dancing, singing, or performing a "lion dance" (Shishi-mai) to bring happiness to the inhabitants. In return, they receive a bit of money or rice. Once a religious rite, it is now just an entertaining custom.

Ka-ei. Era of Emperor Kōmei: Feb. 1848–Nov. 1854. *See* NENGŌ.

Kaei sandai-ki. "Journal of Three Generations of the Reign of Flowers," report on the Muromachi shogunate by an unknown author, covering the period from 1367 to 1425. Also titled *Muromachi-ki, Buke nikki.*

Kaempfer, Englebert. German physician and historian (1651–1716), born in northern Westphalia. Secretary to the Swedish embassy in Persia, he hired on with the Dutch East Indian Company and went to Batavia (Jakarta). He then sailed for Nagasaki, arriving in September 1690, and worked as a physician in Dejima. He accompanied the annual Dutch mission to the Edo court in 1691 and 1692 and wrote *History of Japan* (published 1727–28) on his stay in Japan. This inexhaustible mine of information on Japan during his times was translated into English (1727), French (1729), Dutch (1733), and German (1777). Kaempfer left Japan for Europe in 1692 and published his observations on the medicinal plants he studied in Asia in *Amoenitatum Exoticum*, in 1712. The original title of his book on Japan was *Geschichte und Beschreibung von Japan aus der Originalhand schriften des Verfassers.*

Kaerumata. "Frog-shaped" architectural element in traditional construction, separating and linking two horizontal beams. The simplest shape, called *ita-kaerumata*, generally supports a dado *(to)*. Chin.: *tuofeng* (camel back); a more frequently used shape is called *kentozuka* (bottle shape).

Kaezeni. During the Kamakura and Muromachi periods, notes of exchange used to pay taxes *(nengu)* from the *shōen* to the owners living in Kyoto. Payment was made using a sort of bank draft *(saifu)*, using merchants called *kaezen'ya* or *saifu-ya* as intermediaries. This form of transaction became more and more common; because currency was not in wide circulation, it facilitated exchanges between distant regions.

• **Kaezen'ya.** *See* SAIFU, KAEZENI.

Kafu. "Genealogies." Family and official records listing members of noble families and their places of birth. Such genealogies appeared in the *Kojiki* and *Nihon shoki*. Later, many genealogies were written; the *Honchō kōin shūnroku*, by Fujiwara no Michisue (ca. 1400), on the imperial family, has been updated to the present day. The Edo shogunate established genealogies of most of its vassals, daimyo, and *hatamoto;* rewritten a number of times, these culminated in a 1,530-chapter work, the *Kansei chōshu shokafu,* in 1812. Monks, artists, and peasants also established their own genealogies. Also called *kakei.*

Kaga. Former province, now included in Ishikawa prefecture. Long the fief of the Maeda family, Kaga-han once included the provinces of Kaga, Noto, and Etchū.
• Town in Ishikawa prefecture, on the Sea of Japan, former castle town *(jōka-machi)* in the Edo period, famous for its Kutani porcelain and silk fabrics *(habutae).* Fifth-century tombs at the Hōōzan and the Kitsune-yama. *Pop.:* 65,000.
• Style of lacquered objects. *See* DŌHO.

• **Kaga no Chiyojo.** *See* CHIYO.

• **Kaga-dainagon.** *See* MAEDA TOSHIIE.

Kagaku. "Art of Poetics," treatises on the composition of *waka,* or on the rules governing meetings of poets and poetry competitions and giving lists of preferred words and names to use in poetry. The first *kagaku* was the *Kakyō-hyōshiki,* by Fujiwara no Hamamari, which was simply an imitation of the Chinese genre. Then came the preface to the *Kokin waka-shū,* by Ki no Tsurayuki, written in kana, which was the first real critique of Japanese poetics. The genre then developed with the writings of Fujiwara no Kintō *(Shinsen-zuinō),* Fujiwara no Kiyosuke *(Ōgi-shō),* Kenshō *(Shūchū-shō),* belonging to the Rokujō-ke school, and more formalistic works by poets of the Nijō-ke school. It was continued in the Edo period by Kamo no Mabuchi (Agatai school), Kada no Arimaro, Motoori Norinaga, and Kagawa Kageki (Keien school).
• Schools created by artists or scholars and their disciples and students, who transmitted their knowledge or art by inheritance. With the establishment of universities and colleges in the Meiji era, this type of knowledge transmitted "from father to son" survived only in a few artists' and artisans' families. *See* IEMOTO.

• **Kagaku-ji.** *See* RINZAI-SHŪ.

• *Kagaku-shū.* Japanese-language dictionary compiled in 1444 by an anonymous monk from the Zen Kennin-ji temple in Kamakura. It is divided into 18 parts by subject (18 being a sacred number representing the alliance of Earth and Heaven), and the words are written in Chinese characters followed by a phonetic transcription *(furigana)* in katakana. Aimed mainly at the middle and lower classes, it includes many popular words and expressions. It was published only in 1617, but was republished and expanded in 1699 by Yamawaki Dōen under the title *Zōho kagaku-shū.*

Kagami. "Mirror" *(kyō).* Ancient Japanese mirrors, made of bronze, usually round (although some were octagonal, such as the famous *yata no kagami),* with a polished front; the back was decorated with molded or engraved reliefs, sometimes inlaid with gold or silver. On the center of the back is a pierced button so that a cord can be attached. The oldest examples found are from the Yayoi period (ca. 300 BC–AD 300) and were imported from China during that country's Warring States or Han period. Later, mirrors were cast in Japan on Chinese models, but were sometimes decorated with motifs specific to Japan, such as the *chokkomon.* In this category are the *kaokumon-kyō* (house decorations), *khishin-kyō* (with images of the four divinities), *kaijū-kyō* (with motifs of sea creatures), *shinjū-kyō* (with images of animals and divinities), and *sankaku-buchi shinjū-kyō,* which seem to have been imported from China but made for Japan. Mirrors from China continued to be imported (Tang period) and imitated *(wa-kyō).* Some mirrors are distinctive for their shape: *chōhōkei-kyō* (elongated form, tenth century), *e-kyō* (round with a handle, thirteenth century), *en-kyō* (round without a handle), *seihōkei-kyō* (square, eighth–thirteenth century), *rei-kyō* (round with bells around the outside), *kitsuneme-kyō* (eye-shaped, imported from China from the tenth to the thirteenth century, very rare), *tekkyō wa-kyō* (in bronze, made in Japan). These mirrors at first had a symbolic and ritual purpose (cult of Amaterasu), but they lost this aspect and became functional. They were used until the mid-nineteenth century. *Skt.: adarsha. See* KAIJŪ-BUDŌ-KYŌ.

"Magic mirrors": Certain mirrors were made in Japan with a polished surface that reveals various designs under indirect light or when fogged by being breathed on. The designs, which usually reproduce those on the back of the mirror, are probably due to a change (fibrous or crystalline) in the nature of the metal caused by pressure. These mirrors, called Oni-kagami, are relatively rare, but a very good example is on display at the British Museum in London. *Chin.:* Taoguang Jian.

Kagami-biraki. Annual martial-arts festival on June 7 and beginning the intensive training periods of the "great cold" *(kangeiko)*. On the first day, Shinto priests break a huge *kagami-mochi* with a wooden hammer and distribute pieces to all of the participants.

Kagami jishi. Kabuki play adapted from the Noh by Fukuchi Ochi in 1893.

Kagami Kenkichi. Businessman and executive (1868–1939), founder of the first Japanese insurance company. He was president of many firms, including the Nippon Yūsen and the Mitsubishi Bank.

Kagami Kōzō. Glass artist (b. 1896).

Kagami-mochi. Flattened ball of ground white rice, generally eaten on festival days. Often, another ball of ground rice, dyed red, is added. This rice is supposed to bring luck.

Kagami Shikō. Zen Buddhist monk and haiku poet (1665–1731), born in Mino province. He popularized Bashō's work throughout Japan after Bashō's death, and is known more as a haiku theoretician than for the quality of his poems. He was Kaga no Chiyojo's master and one of the Bashō Juttetsu.

Kaga Otohiko. Writer (Kogi Sadataka), born 1929 in Tokyo. A physician, he studied psychiatry in Paris from 1957 to 1960, then began to write novels. He gained notoriety for *Furandoru no fuyu* (1966), and he continued to write books with themes related to madness: *Bungaku to kyōki* (1971), *Kaerazaru natsu* (1974).

Kagariya-shugonin. Title for night watchmen in the town of Kyoto from 1238 to 1370; they served as personal guards to the shogun when he left his palace at night.

Kagawa Kageki. *Waka* poet (Okumura Juntoku; *gō:* Keien, Tōutei, Baigetsu-dō, 1768–1843), born in Tottori province. He studied with Ozawa Roan in Kyoto, then created a new poetry style that used simple words from daily language, and in which he emphasized *shirabe* (harmony of ideas and words).

He was one of the many disciples in the Keien-ha school, which had a major influence on modern poetry. Among his works are the *waka* collections *Niimanabi iken* (1811), *Keien isshi* (1828), *Kokinshū seigi sōron* (1823), and *Kagaku teiyō* (published posthumously in 1850). Also known under the name Kagawa Roeki. *See* KEIEN-HA.

Kagawa prefecture. Kagawa prefecture, in northeast Shikoku, bordering the Inland Sea (Setonaikai), formerly Sanuki province. It is mountainous (Sanuki range) and mainly agricultural. Fishing is conducted on the very jagged coasts, which form good ports (shipyards). *Chief city:* Takamatsu. *Main towns:* Zentsūji, Sakaide, Marugame, Kan'onji. *Area:* 1,879 km². *Pop.:* 1 million.

Kagawa Shūtoku. Physician (Kagawa Shūan, Ippondō, 1683–1775) who adopted certain aspects of Confucianism in his medical practice, following the *jui-ippon* doctrine according to which Jukyō (Confucianism) and medicine arose from the same principles.

Kagawa Toyohiko. Christian philosopher (1888–1960), born in Kobe, author of many religious essays and poems, who organized cooperatives and proposed social reforms. He traveled in the United States from 1914 to 1916, then became involved in the union movement, for which he was briefly imprisoned in 1921. A pacifist, he started an anti-war movement in 1928; attacked for his opinions in 1940, he took refuge in the United States in 1941. After the war, he returned to Japan and once again took up his activities supporting an international peace movement. Among his writings, the most interesting are *Himmin shinrino kenkyū*, a work on the psychology of poor people published in 1915, and *Shisen o koete* (After Death, 1920), an autobiographical novel. He also translated works by A. Schweitzer and G. Fox and wrote more than 150 books and articles on various subjects.

Kagei. Painter (Tatebayashi Rittoku, Shirai Sōken; *gō:* Tsurugaoka Itsumin, Kingyū-sanjin, Kiusai, eighteenth century) of the Kōrin school, Kenzan's student. He painted mainly flowers. He was also a physician.

Kagekiyo. Noh play attributed to Zeami (1363–1443) relating an episode in the life of warrior Taira no Kagekiyo, who was defeated by the Minamoto in 1184 and lived in exile on Kyushu.

• Kabuki play, one of the Kabuki-jūhachiban, rarely performed. It also relates the exploits of Taira no Kagekiyo, who was imprisoned by the Minamoto but refused to tell them where the treasure of the Taira was buried, in spite of threats, and who managed to escape with his wife and daughter.

Kagen. Era of Emperor Go-Nijō: Aug. 1303–Dec. 1306. *See* NENGŌ.
• Painter (Niwa Kagen; *azana:* Shōho; *mei:* Shinji; *gō:* Shūchindō, Fukuzensai, Sha-an, 1742–86) of the Nanga school (Bunjinga) in the Chinese Ming style.

Kagerō nikki. "Journal of a Dragonfly," written soon after 974 by a noblewoman whose name is not known but who was Fujiwara no Michitsuna's mother and Fujiwara no Tomoyasu's daughter. This three-volume journal, covering the years 954–974, tells of its author's life and her love for her husband, Fujiwara no Kaneie, who left her for his other wives and mistresses. It is one of the most important documents on life in the court and the condition of noblewomen in her times.

Kagi. "Key," one of the emblems *(jimotsu)* of some Buddhist divinities, symbolizing accession to Knowledge.
→ *See* TANIZAKI JUN'ICHIRŌ.

Kago. A sort of palanquin atop a long beam that was carried on the shoulders of two men, used widely as a means of transportation during the Muromachi period. *Kago* were closed in the front and back and had curtains on the sides. They generally held one person. The *kago* used by nobles and high-ranking people, highly decorated and made of lacquered and painted wood, were called *norimono*. In the middle of the Meiji era, they were replaced by *rikisha (jinrikisha)*.
• General term for reed or bamboo baskets or any other woven or interlaced material. Baskets are made in a wide variety of shapes (dating back to the Jōmon period) for different uses. Large ones used to store clothes are called *tsuzuka*; others, used to transport food, are called *warigo*.

Kagome kagome. Children's game: a group forms a circle around a participant who crouches in the middle. Those in the circle chant *"kagome, kagome,"* then stop suddenly. The player crouching in the middle must guess who is behind him or her.

Kagosaka-ō. One of Chūai Tennō's sons, who, according to the *Nihon shoki,* rebelled against Jingū Kōgō and was killed by Takeshiuchi no Sukune.

Kagoshima. City and port in Kagoshima prefecture, on Kagoshima Bay in southern Kyushu, former capital of the fiefdom of the Satsuma family, where the Shimazu family built a castle in 1602. Francis Xavier landed there in 1549. The city was bombed by the British fleet in 1863 (*see* SATUEI-SENSŌ), then was partly destroyed by fire in 1877 and by an eruption of the Sakurajima volcano in 1914. It is sometimes called "the Naples of Japan" because of its location at the end of a wide bay. It is the site of the ruins of the Shimazu family's Tsurumaru castle and of Nanshū shrine, dedicated to Saigō Takamori, in Shiroyama Park, where a commemorative festival is held in the cemetery reserved for those who fought in the 1877 Satsuma Rebellion every year on the 28th day of the 6th lunar month, according to the traditional calendar. *See* SATSUMA-YAKI.

• **Kagoshima Bōseki-kōjō.** First cotton spinning mill in Japan, established in Kagoshima in 1867 by Shimazu Tadayoshi, daimyo of Satsuma, who had the machines imported from Great Britain and recruited seven British engineers to set them up. It passed into the hands of private companies in 1871 and closed in 1898 due to strong competition.

• **Kagoshima prefecture.** Prefecture in southern Kyushu, volcanic in nature (Sakurajima, Kaimondake, and Kirishimayama volcanoes). This region was occupied very early (Jōmon period); in the proto-historic period, it was populated by tribes that the ancient chronicles called *kumaso* and *hayato*. The prefecture also includes the islands of Sakurajima, Ōsumi, Amami, Tokunoshima, Okinoerabujima, and Yoronjima, which are part of the Kirishima-Yaku National Park. Kagoshima Bay (also called Kinkō Wan) is one of the best ports in Japan. About 70 km long and 10 to 20 km wide, it contains the volcanic islet of Sakurajima, attached to the mainland by lava from the 1914 eruption; its highest point is Kitadake (1,117 m) and it opens into the Ōsumi Strait via a channel formed by the Satsuma and Ōsumi peninsulas. The prefecture's main activity is agriculture (semi-tropical fruits). In 1962, a major assembly plant and launch pad for satellites was established on the island of Uchinoura, at 31°3' latitude. This base, located on the flank of a mountain, is run by ISAS, the Japanese space agency. *See also* TANEGASHIMA, SATELLITES.

Chief city: Kagoshima. *Main cities:* Ibusuki, Kaseda, Kokubu, Kanoya, Izumi, Akune, Sendai, Okuchi, Naze. *Area:* 9,153 km². *Pop.:* 1.8 million. *See* NAMAMUGI-JIKEN, SATSUEI-SENSŌ.

Kagoshima Juzō. Poet and famous doll maker (1898–1982), born in Fukuoka, creator of *shiso* dolls, made by applying layers of paper to terracotta figures. He was designated a Living National Treasure in 1961 and received the Order of the Sacred Treasure (third class) in 1973. As a poet, he was a member of the Araragi group and wrote mainly *tanka*.

Kagu-hana. "The Nose that Smells Evil," a minor divinity of Buddhist hell *(jigoku),* said to be Emma-ō's "secretary"; his counterpart is Mirume, "The Eye that Sees Hidden Faults."

Kagura. Sacred Shinto dances whose origins go back to the early centuries AD; according to the *Kojiki,* they were created by Uzume no Mikoto when she danced in front of the cavern where Amaterasu-Ōmikami had taken refuge. This kind of sacred, danced performance gave rise to *saragaku* popular dances, performed with Chinese musical accompaniment *(sangaku).* There are many forms of Kagura (which means "temporary residence of the *kami,*" although the *kanji* characters used to write it mean, literally, "music of the gods"), generally grouped into two major categories: the *mikagura,* performed within the walls of major shrines or in the court, and the *sato-kagura* (or *minkan-kagura*), performed at minor shrines and in villages. The latter are subdivided into many categories, including *miko-kagura,* which are danced by *miko,* young female servants at the shrines; the *shishi-kagura,* dances mixed with Chinese "lion dances"; and various Kagura specific to major shrines such as those in Ise and Izumo. Kagura dances (some of which use masks) are generally performed in special theaters called *kagura-den.* They are often accompanied by songs called *kagura-uta.*

Kagura dances are performed for various reasons, either to invoke the *kami* and thank them for their kindness, or to ask them for good health and a long life during a ritual of Chinese origin called *chinkon.* Major Kagura performances are still given today on certain occasions, such as during the Daijōsai (Daijō-e) ceremony to celebrate the coronation of a new emperor, and by Yamabushi congregations. At the beginning of the Heian period, Kagura became an official rite of the imperial court; its songs, in *waka* form, were catalogued and codified (notably in the *Kokin waka-shū,* the *Shūi waka-shū,*

and the *Kagura-fu* by Fujiwara no Michinaga), and specific musical instruments were used, such as the *hichiriki,* the *wagon* (six-string *koto*), and the six-hole flute. The songs accompany the dancers (led by a *ninjō*) and the various scenes of the show: pantomimes of divine actions *(kamuwaza),* humans venerating the *kami (torimono),* and so on. There are a wide variety of *sato-kagura,* and in the medieval period there was some Buddhist influence in their performances, notably of the Nembutsu Odori. During the Edo period, some Kagura were influenced by Noh and even Kabuki. *See also* AKA-BOSHI, AME NO UZUME, GAGAKU, SAIBARA.

• **Kagura-zutome.** *See* TENRI-KYŌ.

Ka-hō. Groups of laws issued by noble families for their own use in the sixteenth and seventeenth centuries. Most of them were later included in codes promulgated in their estates by the daimyo *(ryō-koku-hō).*
• Era of Emperor Horikawa: Dec. 1094–Dec. 1096. *See* NENGŌ.

Kai. Former province on Honshu, in the current Yamanashi department. According to legends, it was to this region that Yamato Takeru no Mikoto came from the east. In the late Heian period, the lords of the Minamoto family, supporters of Minamoto no Yoritomo, settled there. This mountainous region, separated into two parts—western (Kuninaka) and eastern (Gunnai)—was always famous for its fabrics and its black horses *(kurokama).* After being a fiefdom of the Takeda, it came under the control of the Edo *bakufu,* and Tokugawa Ieyasu's descendants received estates there. It was named Kōfu prefecture in 1869, and renamed Yamanashi prefecture in 1871. Also called Kōshū.
→ *See* KAKI-HAN.
• Word meaning "sea," "shell."

Kai-awase. Old game using clamshells. To win, the two parts of the bivalves had to be matched by choosing them from separate piles. Toward the middle of the Heian period, the insides of the shells were painted and engraved with parts of *waka* poems that had to be matched. This game was the ancestor of card games such as *uta-garuta* and *utagai. See* KARUTA.

Kaibara Ekiken. Confucian writer and philosopher (Kaibara Atsunobu, Kaibara Ekken; *mei:* Sukesaburō, Jūsai, Kyūbei; *gō:* Shisei, Sonken, 1630–1714) from Fukuoka. A samurai, he became a *rōnin,* leading an itinerant life. He then settled in

Kyoto, where he received the patronage of daimyo Kuroda Mitsuyuki and became a disciple of Kinoshita Jun'an, Matsunaga Sekigo, and Yamazaki Ansai. After traveling throughout Japan and studying botany, he returned to Fukuoka, where he became a *bushi* serving the Kuroda and married Kaibara Tōken, also a scholar, writer, and calligrapher. He then began to write prolifically, publishing more than 100 works (some of which may in fact have been written by his wife), among which the best known are *Kuroda-kafu* (A Genealogy of the Kuroda Family), *Chikuzen no kuni zoku fudoki* (Sequel to the *Fudoki* of Chikuzen Province), and a number of Confucian philosophical works expounding views opposed to the then-accepted Zhu Xi (*Jap.*: Shushi) neo-Confucianism: *Shinshiroku* (Prudent Thoughts), *Daigiroku* (Thoughts of Great Doubt). He also wrote botany books—*Yamatao honzō* (Flora of Japan)—and works on other subjects, such as *Yōjō-kun* (Precepts of Hygiene), *Wazuko dōjikun* (Precepts for Children), and *Yamatozokkun* (Precepts of Customs for Children). Although he is often credited with writing *Onna daigaku* (School for Women), it seems that it was his wife who wrote it, according to a chapter in his *Wazoku dōjikun*.

Kaibo Seiryō (Kaihō Seiryō). Economist (Kaibo Kōkaku; *mei*: Gihei; *gō*: Banwa, Seiryō, 1755–1817), born in Tango province. A masterless samurai *(rōnin)*, he offered his services to various daimyo and taught the principles of Confucianism that he had learned by reading Ogyū Sorai's writings. He opened a school in Kyoto and wrote a number of books on economics, comparing relationships between individuals to types of trade operations. His teachings went against the principles of the samurai class and exalted the role of merchants in the country's economy. His best-known books are *Kaibo gihei-sho, Keiko-dan,* and *Masu-shōdan.*

Kaidaiki. Historical bibliography published in 1819, part of the *Koshi-chō* and *Koshi-seibun* by Hirata Atsutane. Also titled *Koshi-chō kaidaiki.*

Kaidan. "Ghost Stories." A book by Lafcadio Hearn based on old Japanese legends, a sort of adaptation of the *Ugetsu monogatari* by Ueda Akinari. Kobayashi Masaki made a movie of it in 1964. Formerly written Kwaidan.

• **Kaidan.** A sort of canopy used for ordination of Buddhist monks in monasteries. *See* NAMU MYŌ-HŌRENGE-KYŌ.

• **Kaidan-in.** Buddhist temple in Nara, part of the Tōdai-ji, founded in 754. Its current buildings date from 1731, but it houses beautiful statues in unfired clay dating from the eighth century, portraying the Four Heavenly Kings (Shi-tennō).

• **Kaidan-mono.** In Kabuki, plays featuring ghosts or spirits of the dead.

Kaidō. "Main routes." Starting in the Nara period, a number of major roads were built to facilitate trade between the capital and the provinces, notably the San'yō going to Daizaifu, the Tōkaidō and the Tōsandō going eastward, the San'indō, Hokurikudō, Nankaidō, Saikaidō, and others. In the Edo period, they were connected to Edo and five more roads, collectively called *gokaidō*, were added: the Tōkaidō (from Edo to Kyoto), the Nakasendō, the Kōshūkaidō, the Ōshū-kaido, and the Nikkō-kaido, which were under direct control of the shogunate. To these were added less important roads, the *waki-ōkan* and *waki-kaidō*. *See* GO-KAIDŌ, KŌSHŪ-KAIDŌ, TŌKAIDŌ.
→ *See* KATEN.

• *Kaidō-ki.* Travel journal telling of a trip from Kyoto to Kamakura during the Kamakura period. The unknown author, perhaps a Buddhist monk, described the events of the Jōkyū era (1221; *see* JŌKYŪ NO HEN) and the countryside he went through along the Tōkaidō. This trip is dated by its author as taking place in 1223. Written in classical Japanese sprinkled with Chinese expressions, it is mainly a philosophical reflection inspired by devotion to Amida Buddha. It has been attributed, but without certainty, to Kamo no Chōmei or Minamoto no Mitsuyuki.

Kaieki. Sanction used in medieval society and during the Edo period, consisting of stripping a samurai of his position and placing him among ordinary people *(shomin)*, causing him to lose all of his privileges and any land he possessed. This sanction could be applied by the shogunate against a daimyo or a simple samurai.

Kaifu Hana. Merchant and weaver (1831–1919), born in Tokushima. She invented a type of crêpe de Chine called *awashijira* and was the first to export her products to Korea, China, and Southeast Asia.

Kaifuke-ō Nyorai. Japanese name of the Esoteric Buddha Ratnasambhava, one of the five *jina* ("conquerors") of the horizons, corresponding to the South and to asceticism. In the Vajradhātu (Kongō-kai), he corresponds to Samkusumitarāja of the Garbhadhātu (Taizō-kai). Also called Hōshō Nyorai. He is portrayed accompanied by a pair of lions.

Kaifūsō. Collection of poems in Chinese compiled in 751 by Ōmi no Mifune or Isonokami no Yakatsugu (attribution is not certain). It is the oldest collection of its type to have survived to the present; it contains 120 poems by 64 authors from the late seventh century to early eighth century, some of whom also had works in the *Man'yōshu.*

Kaifū Toshiki. Politician, born 1931 in Nagoya. He studied law at Waseda University then joined the Jiyū Minshutō (Liberal Democrtic party, LDP). Elected to the Lower Chamber in 1960, he was minister of education in 1976 and 1985, then prime minister in 1989, replacing Uno Sōsuke. His mandate expired in November 1991, and Miyazawa Kiichi succeeded him. In December 1994, he formed an opposition party, the Party of the New Frontier of Japan, composed of nine conservative groups (most of them from the LDP), of which he was elected leader.

Kaigai Tokō Kinshi Rei. "Ban on Foreign Travel," an edict included in the general rules of national seclusion *(sakoku)* issued by the Tokugawa shogunate in 1635. It forbade Japanese ships, except those duly authorized by the shogunate *(shuin-sen),* from going to foreign countries and Japanese living abroad from returning to Japan; its goal was to keep missionaries out of the country.

Kaigen. The term for the period at a change of era *(nengō)* that occurred either due to the ascension of an emperor or when any event required the sovereign to change the name of an era.
• Buddhist monk (fifteenth century) famous for his vast scholarship, who was appointed leader of the Ashikaga-gakkō in 1439.
→ *See* KAKUTEI.

Kaigetsudō-ryū. School of painting and ukiyo-e printing founded in Edo about 1700–14 by Ando Yasunori (Okazawa, Okazaki Genshichi), a painter of beautiful women *(bijin).* His disciples, among them Dohan, Doshin, Doshu, Doshū, and Chōyōdō Anchi, took the pseudonym Kaigetsudō. After Ando's death, other painters who followed the canons of the school also took the name Kaigetsudō, including Tōsendō Rifū, Takizawa Shigenobu, Baiyūken Katsunobu, Baiōken Nagaharu, Takeda Harunobu, and others. Their works are character-ized by thick lines and bright colors and are quite stereotyped—in contrast to the prints of the Torii school. *See* ANDO YASUNORI.

Kaigun. "Navy." Because Japan is an archipelago, it seems to have had a powerful war fleet since antiquity. This naval force enabled Japan to conquer Mimana (southern Korea) in the third or fourth century, then Hideyoshi's troops to invade Korea in 1592. After the modernization of the Meiji era, the Japanese navy defeated the Chinese (1894–95) and Russian (1904–95) navies. During the Second World War, Japan had one of the most powerful fleets in the world. In the late Edo period, most navy officers were educated at the Nagasaki naval school (Kaigun Denshūjo) founded about 1850. Holland gave the shogunate a warship (in 1855), the *Soembing,* which was renamed the *Kankō Maru* and used as a training vessel. Other training centers were opened, notably in Edo (the Gunkan Kyōjusho, later called Gunkan Sōrenjo), succeeding the naval school in Nagasaki, which closed in 1859. The Edo naval school changed its name to Kaigun Heigakkō in 1876, then was transferred to Edajima, near Hiroshima, in the same year. It was closed in 1945. The minister of the navy is called the Kaigunshō. *See* BATTLES, NAVAL.

• **Kaigun Denshūjō.** *See* POMPE VAN MEERDERVOORT.

• **Kaigun-tō.** *See* KATANA.

Kaigyokusai Masatsugo. Famous sculptor of netsuke (Kaigyo, Masatsugo, 1813–92) who lived and worked in Osaka.

Kaihō-ha. Painting school created in Kyoto by Kaihō Yūshō (1533–1615), based on the principles of the Kanō school and the techniques of Chinese painters of the Song and Yuan periods, notably Liangkai (Liang Fengzai, d. 1225). Among the most important members of the school were Kaihō Yūshō, his son Kaihō Yūsetsu (1598–1677), his grandson Kaihō Yūchiku (1654–1728), Kaihō Yūsen (eighteenth century), Kaihō Yūtoku (1763–1847), and Kaihō Yūshō II (1818–69). Also called Kaihoku-ha.

• **Kaihō Yūshō.** Painter (Kaihō Shōeki; *gō:* Yūshō, Yūtoku, 1533–1615), born to a samurai family serving Asai Nagamasa, lord of Sataka in Ōmi. After Asai died in a battle against Oda Nobunaga, Kaihō left his samurai position and studied painting in Kyoto under the masters of the Kanō school, Kanō Eitoku and Kanō Motonobu. It seems that he then worked for Toyotomi Hideyoshi. His art was influenced by the masters of both the Kanō school and the Chinese schools (Liangkai in particular). Many of his works have survived: fusuma paintings in lively colors on a background of gold and large compositions in China ink, such as the fifty fusuma at the Kennin-ji temple, and the screens at the Myōshin-ji and Katano-jinja. Some of his works are in the Tokyo National Museum. *See* KAIHŌ-HA.

Kaijū-budō kyō. Polished-bronze mirrors imported from Tang-dynasty China (or imitations of them made in Japan). The back has a lion-shaped button in the center and decorations of sea animals *(kaijū)* and grapes *(budō)*. Although most of them are round, some are square. They have been found in large numbers in megalithic tombs *(kofun)*. *See* KAGAMI.

Kaika Tennō. Ninth emperor (Prince Waka-Ya-mato Nikohiko Ō-Hibi no Mikoto, traditionally 208<157–98> BC, but more likely early AD). He was Kōgen Tennō's third son and successor. Sujin Tennō succeeded him.

Kaikei. Sculptor (Echizen Hokkyō, Tamba Kōshi, An-Amida Butsu, An-ami, ca. 1183–ca. 1236) and Buddhist monk, disciple of the monk Chōgen (1121–1206). He learned sculpture under Kōkei and worked with his son, Unkei. His style (called An-ami) was distinctive for its elegance. He sculpted the images of Sōgyō Hachiman and Amida at the Tōdai-ji in Nara and, with Unkei, worked on the statues of the Ni-ō in the Nandaimon of the Tōdai-ji.
→ *See* AN-AMI YŌ.

Kaiki. Silk fabric produced in the Kai region between 1661 and 1672. Also called *gunnaori* and *gunnashima.*

Kaiki-shōhō. First gold coin struck in Japan in 760. It was worth 10 silver coins and 100 copper coins. It measured 2.4 cm in diameter and weighed about 13 g. It was in circulation for a very short time, and few examples have been found (about 30). *See* MANNEN-TSŪSHŌ, TAIHEI-GEMPŌ, WADŌ-KAIHŌ.

Kaikō. During the Kamakura and Muromachi periods, title held by ministers' secretaries. This title was also used by bureaucrats working in the Wakadokoro and Gosho-dokoro in the Heian period.

Kaikō Ken. Writer (Kaikō Takeshi) and journalist, born 1930 in Osaka. He married the poet Maki Yōko (Kotani Shōko, born 1923). In 1953, after a career as a journalist and publicist, he began to write stories, which were published in the magazines *Kindai Bungaku* and *Shin Nihon Bungaku,* and to translate works by Louis Aragon and Sherwood Anderson. His novel *Hadaka no ōsama* (The Naked King, 1957) won the Akutagawa Prize. His later works dealt mainly with problems of life: *Kagayakeru yami* (Under the Black Sun, 1968), recounting his experiences as a journalist during the Vietnam war, which won the *Mainichi Shimbun* Prize; *Nihon sammon Opera* (The Japanese Three-Penny Opera, 1959); *Robinson no matsuei* (Robinson's Descendants, 1960); *Aoi getsuyōbi* (Blue Monday, 1969); and *Natsu no yami* (Darkness in Summer, 1971). He also wrote books on fishing. His novels and stories were translated into many languages, and he is considered one of the best writers of the "postwar generation" *(apure).* A literary prize, the Kaikō Takeshi, was created in 1990 to reward a "positive work on observation of humanity."

Kaikoku-heidan. "Military Discussion of a Maritime Country." A 16-volume historical work published by Hayashi Shihei in 1791 exalting the authority of the emperor and describing principles of coastal defense and the art of war. It was banned by the shogunate in 1792; publication was allowed again in 1841, and it was republished 10 years later, when the foreign threat was weighing upon Japan.

Kaimaki. A sort of kimono-shaped, quilted cotton cover, once used for sleeping in winter. A larger, thicker variation was called *yagu.*

Kaimyō. Name of a temple given to Buddhist followers after their death and inscribed on their funerary tablet (*see* IHAI). Also called *hōmyō. See* NAMES.

Kainai San-kijin. Collective name for three writers who supported the emperor's cause against the Edo shogunate in the eighteenth century: Takayama Masayuki (1747–93), Hayashi Shihei (1738–93), and Gamō Kumpei (1768–1813).

Kainō Michitaka. Legal scholar (1908–75), born in Nagano prefecture. After the Second World War, he helped modernize Japan's judicial system and wrote two important works on the subject, *Iriai no kenkyū* (A History of Common Law, 1943) and

Hōritsu shakaigaku no shomondai (Various Problems in Social Jurisprudence, 1943), as well as many other authoritative works.

Kaionji Chōgorō. Writer (Suetomi Tōsaku, 1901–77), born in Kagoshima. He wrote great historical epics that were adapted for television and were very popular: *Tenshō onna gassen* (1936; Naoki Prize), *Taira no Masakado* (1954–57), *Saigō Takamori, ten to chi to* (1960–62). He received the Kikuchi Kan Prize in 1968 and the Academy of Arts Prize in 1976.

Kairitsu-shū. Buddhist sect of the Ritsu-shū (Risshū), created by the monk Ganjin in 754, whose doctrines were introduced to Japan by Zenshin-ni in 522. It was updated in the thirteenth century by the monk Ganjō-Risshi and underwent a certain renaissance after centuries of obscurity.

Kairō. In traditional architecture for Buddhist temples and nobles' residences *(shinden),* covered walkways linking various pavilions or rooms.

Kairyū. "Sea dragons," small submarines used at the end of the Second World War (in 1945) as suicide weapons *(kamikaze).* More than 200 units were built. *Tonnage:* 19 tons; *weapons:* 2,460 mm torpedo (or front load of 200 kg of TNT); *speed:* 17.5 knots surface, and 10 knots underwater. *See also* KAITEN, SUBMARINES.

Kairyū-ō-ji. Buddhist temple founded in Saidaiji (Nara prefecture) in 731. Its main hall *(kondō)* and library were renovated in the fourteenth century. Small five-story pagoda *(gojunotō)* about 3 m high, dating from the late Nara period. Eighth-century *saikondō* reconstructed in the thirteenth century in the original style. Thirteenth-century *kyōzō.*

Kaisandō. In a Buddhist temple or monastery, a room dedicated to the founder of the temple or of the sect to which it belongs. *See* MIEI-DŌ.

Kaisei-sho. Government college founded in Edo in 1863 to teach Western sciences. It was renamed Kaisei-gakkō in 1869, then Daigaku-Nankō and Daigaku-Tōkō. Finally, it became part of the imperial university (Tōkyō Daigaku) in 1877. *See also* BANSHO SHIRABE-DOKORO.

Kaiseki. Painter (Noro Ryū; *azana:* Ryū-nen, Daogoryū; *mei:* Kuichirō; *gō:* Waibai, Shiheki-dōjin, Daigaku-shōsha, Kaiseki, 1747–1828) of the Nanga school (Bunjinga), Taiga's student. He wrote a work on painting, *Shihekisai gawa.* He painted mainly landscapes.

• Ritual meal preceding the tea ceremony *(chanoyu)* composed of seasonal dishes prepared in a simple, elegant manner, according to Zen principles, and served on valuable ceramics. The term *kaiseki* comes from a word meaning "breast stone"; the Zen monks had a custom of keeping their stomachs warm by putting a heated stone *(yaku-seki)* against their chests inside their kimonos. This meal is served in a traditional order: *gohan* (rice cooked in water), *misoshiru* (light miso soup), *mukōzuke* (seafood), *wanmori* (boiled fish), *yakimono* (fried fish with vegetables), *azukebachi* (meat with salad), *hashiari* (light soup), *sake* (rice wine), *hassun* (fish and vegetables), *yōtukomono* (tea with vegetables in brine). *See* MEALS.

Kaisen. Painter (Oda Ei; *azana:* Kyokai; *mei:* Ryōhei; *gō:* Hyakukoku, Kaisen, 1785–1862), of the Nanga school (Bunjinga); studied with Goshun (of the Shijō school).

• Coastal ships and, more generally, especially in the Kamakura period, all commercial ships.

• *Kaisen-shikimoku.* Shipping law in 31 articles, the oldest code of Japanese maritime law, supposedly written in 1223, but neither the authors nor the precise date are certain. Based on the formulation of the text, some historians date it to a later period, the fifteenth or sixteenth century. About 10 articles have been added. This code was the basis of the more general code called *Kairo-shohatto* promulgated by Toyotomi Hideyoshi.

Kaishaku-nin. One who assists during the *seppuku* (suicide by cutting open the stomach) ritual. This person is charged with beheading, with one precise sword blow, the person who wants to die this way, at the very moment when he begins to make his incision. *See* HARA-KIRI, KUSUN-GOBU, SEPPUKU.

Kaishi. Sheets of paper, generally square, once carried by high-ranking people and samurai folded in their kimonos, used to write letters or poems. These pieces of paper, also called *tatōgami* and *hanagami,* were of different sizes and colors according to the rank and sex of those using them. In the court, etiquette had it that men carried white *kaishi,* while women wrote only on red paper. Such sheets of paper were also used during the tea ceremony; these were known as *kogikushi,* but were also called *kaishi. See* PAPER, WASHI.

Kaitai-shinsho. "New Treatise on Anatomy." A scientific work published by Maeno Ryōtaku and Sugita Gempaku in 1774, based on the *Tabulae anatomicae* written by Dutch physicians. It was revised by Ōtsuki Gentaku (1757–1827) and republished as *Jūtai-kaitai-shinso.*

Kaitakushi. Government bureau created at the beginning of the Meiji era to administer and develop Hokkaido. It was this agency that gave the island its current name; it had previously been called Ezochi (or Ezo). The Kaitakushi controlled not only Hokkaido but also the Kuril Islands after the Treaty of St. Petersburg (1875). It founded the Sapporo Agricultural College, facilitated immigration of former samurai (most of them belonging to the Satsuma clan) in order to develop agriculture, and invited a number of foreign experts (especially Americans) to assist. In 1882, following a financial scandal, the Kaitakushi was abolished and three prefectures were created: Hokodate, Sapporo, and Nemuro. In 1885, these prefectures merged to form Hokkaido prefecture.

Kaitei ritsurei. Criminal code, strongly influenced by principles of the French codes, that was added to the *Shinritsu kōryō* (1870) in 1873. It was replaced in 1882 by a new criminal code.

Kaiten. Small submarines used at the end of the Second World War as suicide weapons *(kamikaze).* They were launched from large ships or submarines. They were adapted to carry large Nagako torpedoes (93 mm, 610 mm types). *Length:* 15 m; *diameter:* 1 m; *range:* 23,000 m; *speed:* 30 knots; *crew:* one man; *explosive charge:* 1,500 kg. Between July 1944, and August 1945, 420 *kaiten* were built. *See also* KAIRYŪ, SUBMARINES.

Kaitokudō. Confucian school founded in Osaka by Nakai Shūan (1693–1758) in 1720 to educate the common people. This school, funded by wealthy merchants, was directed by Miyake Sekian, who taught Zhu Xi (*Jap.:* Shushi) philosophy and the rudiments of Wang Yangming (*Jap.:* Ō-Yōmei) philosophy. Nakai Shūan's son, Nakai Chikuzan (1730–1804), who succeeded his father as principal of the school, taught only Shushi neo-Confucian concepts. The school closed in 1869. Also called Kaitokushoin. *See* MIYAKE SEKIAN, NAKAI RIKEN.

Kai-tsūshō-kō. Two-volume work on foreign countries, written in 1695 by Dutch interpreter Nishikawa Joken (1648–1724). It was revised and expanded (to five volumes) in 1780. This "reflection on trade with China and other countries" dealt both with general geography and with trade.

Kaiyo Maru. Dutch steamship, purchased by the Edo shogunate in 1865. It sank during a storm off Esashi (Hokkaido) in 1868. *See* KAIGUN.

Kaizawa Tadashi. Ainu journalist (1913–92), born in Nibutani (Hokkaido), director of the Ainu Museum of Culture in Nibutani and leader of actions promoting the rights of the Ainu people. He published a journal, *Ainu-shi* (History of the Ainu), published by the Hokkaido Utari Society.

Kaizei Yakusho. "Tariff Convention." A trade agreement on customs rights made between the Edo shogunate and France, Great Britain, Holland, and the United States on June 25, 1866, according to which customs duty was lowered to 5% of the value of merchandise, payable in silver. It also gave foreigners the right to enter Japanese ports freely and establish warehouses in Japanese cities. This "unequal treaty" (*see* JŌYAKU) considerably weakened the country's financial resources. It was abrogated in 1894.

Kaizokushū. Groups of navy officers or armed sea merchants trading at sea, sometimes resorting to piracy. During the civil wars of the twelfth century between the Taira and the Minamoto, the *kaizokushū* were responsible for all sea transportation (warriors and horses, as well as consumer goods). They also took part in naval battles. During the Nambokuchō era (1336–92), they formed leagues and controlled all traffic on the Inland Sea (Setonaikai). Later, emboldened, they became pirates *(wakō),* following the example of their compatriots who had pillaged the coasts of southern Korea in 1226. *See* WAKŌ.

Kaizuka. Shell mounds *(kjökkenmödding)* left on coasts or riverbanks by prehistoric (Jōmon) populations, testifying to their fishing activities and consumption of shells. The *kaizuka,* also used as dumps (sometimes even as burial sites), contain great numbers of vestiges of ancient times: pottery, bones, tools, and so on. They are particularly numerous on the coasts of the Pacific Ocean and the Inland Sea. *Kaizuka* from the Yayoi or even more recent periods have also been found. *See* AWABI.

Kaizuka Shigeki. Sinologist (1904–87), born in Tokyo, disciple of Naitō Konan (1866–1934) and professor at the University of Kyoto since 1949. His major areas of study were ancient China and "oracular bones" *(Chin.: jiagu-wen)*. He received the Order of Culture (Bunka-shō) in 1984.

Kajii Motojirō. Writer (1901–32), born in Osaka. He entered the University of Tokyo in 1924, and he and some fellow students founded the magazine *Aozora* (Blue Sky) in 1925, in which he published his first stories, such as *Remon* (Lemon, 1925), which was later the title of a collection of 18 short stories (1931). He also published, in other literary magazines such as *Chūō Kōron,* stories influenced both by Baudelaire and by Marxism, such as *Nonki ka kanja* (The Neglected Patient), published a few months before his death. His stories show a great concern for realistic details and are imbued with a sort of moral despair that was common among young people of his time. He died from repeated bouts of tuberculosis.

Kajikawa Hikobei. Lacquer artist (seventeenth century), founder of a family of lacquer artisans in Edo whose members worked for the shogunate. His son, Kajikawa Kyūjirō (active 1660–80), also produced lacquer works and *inrō*. He passed his art on to his descendants.

Kaji-kitō. Term in Esoteric Buddhism *(mikkyō)* corresponding to the Sanskrit *adhishthāna,* describing relationships between the Buddhist divinities, living beings, and the Buddhist Law (Dharma). It is used to define the rites performed to obtain peace (for oneself and for the state), enlightenment, happiness, long life, and so on. To each of these goals corresponded a precise ritual *(hō): emmei-hō, keiai-hō, kōshō-hō, chōbuku-hō, sokusai-hō,* or *zōyaku-hō.* At first, they consisted of simple rituals of exorcism and magic, but they were later expanded, notably in the Shingon, Tendai, and Nichiren-shū sects.

Kaji Tameya. Painter (d. 1894) in Western style. He studied in the United States and Germany and produced mainly portraits in oil paints.

Kaji Tsunekichi. Enamel artist (1803–83) from Nagoya who was famous for his cloisonné enameling. In Nagoya, he founded a school of enamel decoration. *See* ENAMELS.

Kajiwara Kagetoki. Warrior (Kajiwara no Kagesue, ca. 1162–1200). Although he belonged to the Taira clan, he saved Minamoto no Yoritomo during the Battle of Ishibashiyama and became one of his most faithful vassals. He fought the Taira at Minamoto no Yoshitsune's side, but turned against him to humor Yoritomo. He was killed during a battle in Suruga by officers serving Minamoto no Yoriie. In warrior literature *(gunki-mono),* his name is synonymous with arrogance and treachery.

Kajiwara Shozen. Buddhist monk and physician (ca. 1265–ca. 1337), born in Sagami province (Kanagawa prefecture). He wrote a medical treatise, *Ton'ishō* (1303), in kana, and another, *Man'anhō* (Prescriptions for Happiness, 1315), in Chinese, summarizing medical science of his day. Also called Kajiwara Seizen.

Kajiyama kofun. Funerary tumulus in the Iwami district (Tottori prefecture) with a horizontal walkway decorated with murals portraying the sun, a sort of dragon, and a fish in red and yellow. This tomb, excavated in 1978, dates from the seventh century.

Kajiyama Toshiyuku. Writer (1929–75), born in Seoul, Korea. He wrote mainly detective and erotic novels in a journalistic style. Among his most representative works are *Kuro no shishōsha* (The Black Test Car, 1962) and *Akai daya* (Red Diamonds, 1963).

Kajō-shoku. Shinto ceremony performed on the 16th day of the 6th month to protect people from epidemics. It is rarely performed today.

Kakakiboku zempō kiso. Japanese title for a systematic 58-volume encyclopedia of plants, the oldest one in the world, of Chinese origin, which is said to have been compiled by a Chinese named Chen Jingchi in 1256 and printed with wood blocks. Only one copy has survived; it is in the archives of the imperial house in Tokyo.

Kakashi. "Scarecrows." In ancient times, human-shaped scarecrows were supposed to be *kami* of the fields *(Ta no kami)* charged with seeing to good harvests. Made of straw and dressed in clothes, they were supplied with a bow and arrows. These days, more modern methods are used.

Kake. General term for an object hung on the wall of a house or on a pillar.

• **Kakebotoke.** Wooden or metal plaque, engraved or painted, portraying a Shinto *kami* or Buddhist divinity *(hotoke),* used for syncretic worship *(Honji-suijaku)* mainly during the Heian and Kamakura periods. Also called *mishōtai. See* HOTOKE.

• **Kakego.** Toiletries case in the form of a box, designed to contain perfumes and makeup.

• **Kakemono.** "Hung object," usually a tall, narrow painting hung on a wall or in the *tokonoma,* generally mounted on paper or silk. Wooden rolls *(jiku)* attached to the top and bottom kept it stretched and flat. Paintings thus mounted could be of any type, including ukiyo-e prints. This type of mounting originated in China *(Chin.: biao-fa, guafu).* A pair of *kakemono* is called *sōfuku;* a triptych, *sampukutsui.* Also sometimes called *kakejiku. Kakemono-e* are a sort of ukiyo-e *(see* UKIYO-E*).* Specialized artisans called *hyōsōshi* usually attach the *kakemono* to the mounting, called *hyōsō,* which often has bands of silk brocade or embroidery called *kireji.* When the *kakemono* is not on display it is rolled around the bottom *jiku,* and the cord used to hang it is tied to the top *jiku* to keep it rolled. On the back of the *kakemono,* near the top *jiku,* are often the name of the author in colophon, sometimes that of the subject portrayed, and the name and seal of the collector. *See* KANSU-BON.

Kakei. Era of Emperor Go-Komatsu of the Northern Court (Hokuchō): Aug. 1387–Feb. 1389. *See* NENGŌ.
→ *See* KAFU, KEIBUN.

Kakei Katsuhiko. Shinto philosopher and jurist (1872–1961), born in Nagano prefecture. A graduate of the University of Tokyo, he went to Germany to continue his studies in legal history. When he returned, he taught at the University of Tokyo, while proving to be a firm supporter of Kokugaku (National Learning) based on the study of ancient chronicles such as the *Kojiki* and *Nihon shoki.* He published many books on Shinto, including *Koshintō taigi* (The Noble Path of Ancient Shinto, 1912), *Kokka no kenkyū* (Study on the State, 1913), and *Kami nagara no michi* (The Royal Way of the *Kami,* 1925).

Kakekomi-dera. Another name for refuge temples, or "divorce temples" (Enkiri-dera). Starting in the thirteenth century, such Buddhist temples accepted women fleeing abusive husbands and granted them a divorce after two years of service. During the Edo period, only the Tōjei-ji temple in Kamakura and the Mantoku-ji temple in Gumma continued with this custom. *See* DIVORCE, ENKIRI-DERA.

Kake-kotoba. "Pivotal words," used in poetry, mainly *waka,* that can have different meanings. They are generally homophones designed to add a certain ambiguity to the poems. This type of word began to replace the *makura-kotoba* around the ninth century. In prose, literary scholars sometimes used *kake-kotoba* to give underlying meaning to phrases that seem at first glance not to make sense. In poetry, they were frequently used in *renga,* or "linked *waka.*" *See* MAKURA-KOTOBA.

Kakeya Sōichi. Mathematician (1886–1947), born in Hiroshima prefecture. He became a professor at the University of Tokyo in 1935, and was appointed director of the Statistics Institute in 1944. He expressed the well-known Kakeya's theorem.

Kakiemon. Family of potters and ceramists in Hizen province (Saga and Nagasaki prefectures) founded about 1647 by Sakaida Kakiemon (1596–1666). He refined the method for obtaining a translucent white glaze that may have been transmitted to him by Tojima Tokuzaemon, who received it from Chinese potters. The ceramists in this family produced pieces with colorful clay decorated with gold, and pieces with a white glaze decorated with a sprinkling of little flowers (probably the inspiration for Meisen and Chantilly porcelain). Their decorations were asymmetrical on a white background; in Europe, they were called Korean-decorated ceramics. There are two types of Kakiemon pottery, *nishikite* and *some-nishikite,* sometimes called *nigoshide* and *nabeshima,* the latter currently perpetuated by the Imaemon family. The first polychrome Kakiemon were produced in 1643 with pigments imported from China: these pieces were also known as *ko*-Imari, since they were exported to China and Europe via the port of Imari. However, they were not yet very refined; it was Sakaida Kakiemon's fourth- and fifth-generation descendants who perfected them, using molds to make their pottery. Toward the end of the eighteenth century, the Kakiemon kilns fell into disuse; they were put back into service at the beginning of the twentieth century by Sakaida Kakiemon's twelfth- and thirteenth-generation descendants. Late-seventeenth-century Kakiemon porcelains were generally signed Kaki. Excavation of the Minamigawa kilns (near Arita) in 1975 showed that their production was widely imitated at other nearby kilns. Kakiemon XIV continues the tradition today, and his production has been declared an Intangible Cultural Asset. The largest European collections are currently those in Hampton Court near London, and in Suwienger in Dresden. *See* AKAE.

Kaki-han. Calligraphic signature in classic Chinese characters, which, after the tenth century, was generally replaced by a *kaō*. Also called *kai*.

Kakimoto Otama. Bronzesmith who worked from 749 to 752 on making the Daibutsu at the Tōdai-ji in Nara.

Kakinomoto no Hitomaro. Poet (active between 685 and 705 or 710) whose works were in the *Man'yōshū*. Lower-ranking noble in the court of emperors Jitō and Mommu, he lived in Heian-kyō but traveled around the country. Very little is known about his life, although, through his poems, it is known that he had at least two wives, who died before he did. Other poems appeared in the *Shin kokin-shū*, but their attribution is doubtful. He composed mainly *chōka* and *tanka* poems, which are still very highly regarded and earned him the title "Kami of Poetry." He was one of the five great poets of his time, the *Man'yō* no Go-taika.

Kakitsu. Era of Emperor Go-Hanazono: Feb. 1441–Feb. 1444. *See* NENGŌ.

• **Kakitsu no Hen.** Rebellion during which shogun Ashikaga Yoshinori was assassinated by Akamatsu Mitsusuke, in 1441, because Yoshinori had chosen one of his rivals, Akamatsu Sadaura, as leader of the Akamatsu clan. Mitsusuke organized a banquet during which he had the shogun assassinated. Yoshinori's death caused a rupture in the continuity of the shogunate; from then on, it was led by major warrior families such as the Yamana because Yoshinori's successors were too young or feeble-minded. The rivalry between the Hosokawa clans (allied with the Akamatsu) and the Yamana led to the Ōnin War. Mitsusuke, defeated in battle in Harima province, was forced to commit suicide. *See* ŌNIN NO RAN.

Kakitsubata. "Iris Flowers." Title of a Noh play: an itinerant monk meets a young noblewoman who invites him to spend the night in her home. She dresses him sumptuously and reveals herself to him as the spirit of the iris flower celebrated in a poem by Ariwara no Narihira.

• **Kakitsubata nanae no Someginu.** *See* TENA-RAIKO.

Kakō. Painter (Tsuji Unosuke; *gō:* Tsuji Kakō, 1877–1927) of the Shijō school, Bairei's student in Kyoto.
→ *See* EISEN (KEISAI), HOKUSAI, KEIZAN.

Kakogenzai inga-kyō emaki. An *emakimono* of the "Sutra of Cause and Effect," describing the former lives *(jātaka)* and earthly life of the Buddha Shakyamuni (*Jap.*: Shaka), drawn and handwritten in the seventh century. The painted images follow each other and a text runs underneath them, in the style of early comic strips. This *emakimono,* in a rather naive style and the oldest to survive to the present day, imitates a Chinese work. Only three fragments, kept at the Jōbonrendai-ji in the Hōon-in in Kyoto and at the Tokyo University of Fine Arts and Music (Tokyo Geijutsu Daigaku) have survived; they are of various lengths and a height of 26.5 cm. The text is written in Chinese characters from the Tang period. The illustrations are in the style of Six-Dynasties China and brightly colored. Another scroll on the same subject was painted by Keinin in 1254 (Nezu Museum, Tokyo). Also called *Inga-kyō, E-inga-kyō. See* INGA.

Kakoimai. "Rice in reserve," reserves of grain ordered by the Edo shogunate and many daimyo to moderate prices in times of famine and also to use as subsidies to the army in case of need. By 1840, these reserves amounted to 1.5 million *koku*. Also called *ogigome, tsumegome, kakoimomi.*

Kakuban. Buddhist monk (1095–1143) of the Shingon sect, founder of the Shingi Shingon-shū subsect. A descendant of Emperor Kammu, he was from a powerful family in Hizen province. He tried to forge a synthesis between the doctrines of the Shingon and those of the Pure Land (Jōdo). In 1134, he was appointed *zasu* of the Kongōbu-ji and the Daidempō-in on Mt. Kōya, but he resigned the following year to devote himself to meditation. Opposed to the monks of Mt. Kōya on points of doctrine, he left in 1140 and settled on Mt. Negoro, where he founded the Emmyō-ji temple (also called Negoro-ji). He wrote several works expounding his religious doctrines, among them *Gorin kyūji-hiyaku.* In 1690, he was given the *posthumous name* Kōkyō Daishi. Also sometimes called Kakuhan.

Kakubei-jishi. In the Edo period, folkdance performed by young people wearing lion masks and high *geta* shoes. It is sometimes called Echigo-jishi because it originated in Echigo province. This dance was accompanied by acrobatic leaps and drum music. It had some influence on Kabuki dances.

Kakuchō. Buddhist monk (952–ca. 1034) of the Tendai-shū, author of religious works *(Honchō kōsōden, Zuko honchō ōjōden).* He founded the Kawa no Ryū subsect in Taimitsu.

Kakuchū. Buddhist monk (ca. 1117–77), appointed *zasu* of the Tendai-shū.

Kakujin. Buddhist monk (1012–81), one of Fujiwara no Tadatsune's sons. He was *zasu* of the Tendai-shū from 1077 until his death.

Kakujo. Buddhist monk (d. 1077) and sculptor, Jōchō's son. His first son, Raijo, continued his work, but his second son, Injo (d. 1108), left his father's studio, located on the seventh street (Shichijō-bussho), to create another studio *(bussho)* on the third street (Sanjō-bussho) in Kyoto. *See* BUSSHO.

Kakumyō. Painter (Shinga; *mei:* Tayūbō; *gō:* Saibutsu, twelfth century) and Buddhist monk at the Kōraku-ji temple in Shinano province. He painted Buddhist subjects.

Kakun. Instructions written by the head of a family for the use of his family and descendants, mainly in samurai families. Study of these precepts is of great use for a better understanding of warriors' ethics and political thought. Most large families had such instructions—some moral, others practical—designed to ensure their prosperity and that of the family estate.

Kakunyo. Buddhist monk (1270–1351), third *hossu* of the Hongan-ji in Kyoto, Shinran's grandson via Kakue and Kakushin-ni. He wrote a genealogy of the Hongan-ji, the *Hongan-ji keizu,* various religious works (among them the *Hōōn kōshiki*), and an illustrated biography of Shinran (*Zenshin shōnin-e,* renamed *Hongan-ji shōnin Shinrandenne*). His life and activities were related in the *Boki ekotoba. See* HONGAN-JI.

Kakuon-ji. Buddhist temple in Kamakura, founded in 1218. It contains some works by the sculptor Unkei.

Kakure-kirishitan. "Clandestine Christians," a name for Christians during the period when Christianity was banned and Christians persecuted, from 1592 to 1868. *See* E-FUMI (FUMI-E), IKITSUKI-SHIMA, SHŪMON ARATAME.

Kakurezaiki Ryūichi. Contemporary ceramist, born 1950 in Fukue (Nagasaki prefecture), Isezaki Jun's student.

Kakure-zato. Character in popular legends with the power to abduct evil people and send them to hell.

Kakushi. Signature made with an imprint of the index finger—left for men, right for women—used during the Nara and Heian periods. This signature was replaced in the Kamakura period by a sort of paraph called *ryakyuō.* Also called *tenshi. See also* KAO.

Kakushin. Buddhist monk (1206–98) of the Rinzai-shū sect, and musician. He learned to play the *fuke-shū* from Busshō Zenji, but his master in the art of the flute was Chōyū. He went to China in 1249.
→ *See* ADACHI YASUMORI, ATSUZANE SHINNŌ.

• **Kakushin-ni.** Buddhist nun (1224–98), seventh daughter of Shinran and Eshin-ni. She founded temples (among them the Ōtani Hongan-ji in Kyoto in 1272) and was active in propagating the doctrines of the Jōdo Shin-shū. *See* ESHIN-NI, SHINRAN.

Kakushin Kurabu. "Reform Club," a small political party founded in 1922 by members of the Rikken Kokumintō (Constitutional Nationalist party) and the Kenseikai (Constitutional Association) to push for adoption of universal suffrage, a reduction in the military budget, and abrogation of the law allowing only generals and admirals to be ministers of war. Its main supporters were in the middle classes. In 1924, it joined the Rikken Seiyūkai (Friends of Constitutional Government party) and the Kenseikai (Consitutional Association party) in an attempt to "protect the constitutional government." After Inukai Tsuyoshi returned to the Seiyūkai in 1925, however, the Kakushin Kurabu was dissolved.

Kakushō Hōshinno. Buddhist monk (1129–69), Emperor Go-Toba's fifth son. He was appointed *isshin-ajari,* then *hōen,* and finally *kengyō* of the Tennō-ji temple in Kyoto in 1164.

Kakushū. Painter (Watanabe Shijitsu; *azana:* Gensei, 1778–1830) of the Nagasaki school; studied with his father, Shūsen.

• Painter (Sumiyoshi Hirotsugu, Sumiyoshi Hironatsu; *mei:* Kuranosuke, 1650–1731) of the Sumiyoshi school. He was Sumiyoshi Hiromichi's son.

Kakutei. Painter (Jōkō; *azana:* Kaigen; Etatsu; *gō:* Jubeiō, Gojian, Hakuyō-sanjin, Nansōō, Baisō, d. 1785) and Zen monk under the name Jōkō. He belonged to the Sumiyoshi school and was Yūhi's student. *See* KUMASHIRO YŪHI, YŪ HI.

Kakuyū. *See* CHŌJU GIGA, TOBA SŌJŌ.

Kakyō-hyōshiki. Title of the oldest known treatise on poetry, compiled in 772 by Fujiwara no Hamanari. Influenced by the Chinese, it was one of the "four poetic treatises" *(shika-shiki),* with the *Kisenshiki, Hikohime-shiki,* and *Iwamime-shiki.* Its title has not been definitively translated. Also titled *Kashiki, Hamanari-shiki.*

Kama. Kettle (or pot) made of molded cast iron, used to boil water for tea. Also called *chagama, chanoyu-gama.*

• Type of knife or sickle.

• **Kamado.** "Place for the pot," kitchen stoves, sometimes portable, but usually permanently placed and leaning against a wall in which a hole has been pierced to evacuate smoke. Symbolic of the house, in the sense of the "hearth," it is where the *kamada-gami,* the "stove *kami,*" guaranteeing the house's prosperity, is said to reside.

Kamada Ryūō. Scholar (1754–1821), born in Kii province, who studied the doctrines of the Shingaku (Teaching of the Heart) under the direction of Ishida Baigan. He attempted to amalgamate the theories of this school with the notions of "Dutch science" *(rangaku)* and Buddhism.

Kama-e. In Japanese Buddhism, excommunication or exclusion from a monastery, a sanction sometimes used during the Edo shogunate to make rebellious monks see reason.

Kamahige. "Shaving with a Sickle." Title of a Kabuki play, one of the Kabuki-jūhachiban, rarely performed today. The character called Kagekiyo (who figured in other plays, including *Kagekiyo*) takes refuge in the home of a blacksmith who recognizes him and, under the guise of shaving him, tries to kill him with a sickle. This does not work, however, because Kagekiyo is immortal.

Kamaishi. Town in Iwate prefecture, on the bay of the same name. Nearby are large deposits of iron ore, discovered in 1727, and the first European-type blast furnace *(hansharo)* was installed there in 1875. The blast furnace, run by a British engineer, did not work because the fuel used was coke instead of coal. Tests were conducted by Ōshima Takato, a military engineer of the Nambu clan, but efforts to produce steel came to fruition only twelve years later. The first Japanese steel cannons were then cast to replace the bronze cannons cast in Saga province. The port of Kamaishi can accommodate high-tonnage ships. *Pop.:* 70,000.

Kamakura. City in Kanagawa prefecture, on Sagami Bay, about 50 km south of Tokyo; its name, of Ainu origin, means "beyond the mountains," but the Sino-Japanese characters *(kanji)* used to write it mean, approximately, "granary of the sickles." Founded in the seventh or eighth century, it became important in 1192, when Minamoto no Yoritomo established his *bakufu* there, and it remained the military capital of Japan until 1333. The city, now mainly residential, has many Buddhist temples and Shinto shrines as well as two museums, one run by the prefecture and the other by the city, located within the walls of the Tsurigaoka Hachiman-jinja. Aside from this shrine, the most popular temples are the Engaku-ji (1282), the Tokei-ji (1284), the Jōchi-ji (1283), the Enno-ji (or Arai-Emmadō, 1250), the Kenchō-ji (1253), the Zaisen-ji (1327), the Jōmyō-ji (1188), the Hōkai-ji (twelfth century), the Eishō-ji (fifteenth century), the Hasedera, and the Kōtoku-in *(daibutsu* from 1252). *Pop.:* 180,000.

• Type of igloo built by children in the villages of Tōhoku (northern Honshu) during the winter in which they meet to venerate a *kami* in whose honor they drink sweet *sake.* Also called *bonzen.*

• **Kamakura bakufu kansei.** Name for the administration of the Kamakura *bakufu* (1192–1333). *See* KAMAKURA-JIDAI.

• **Kamakura bakufu shoshi.** In the Kamakura period, the main bureaucrats of the *bakufu:* the *jikken-shi, junken-shi, naiken-shi, kenchū-shi,* and *kenken-shi.*

• **Kamakura banshū.** Main bureaucrats of the Kamakura shogunal palace during the Kamakura period: the *gakumonjo-ban, kinju-ban, ō-ban, kōshi-ban, monkenzanketsu-ban, hisashi-ban,* and *hayahiru-ban.*

• **Kamakura-bori.** Objects made by applying red or green lacquer to a base of sculpted wood, imitating a Chinese technique. Also called *tsuishi, kōka rokuyō, negoro-nuri.*

• **Kamakura Daibutsu.** *See* DAIBUTSU.

• **Kamakura-dono.** "Lord of Kamakura," popular name for Minamoto no Yoritomo.

• **Kamakura Gongorō Kagemasa.** Warrior of the Minamoto clan (eleventh century), famous for having continued to fight in 1091 after losing an eye; he was only 16 years old at the time.

• **Kamakura gozan.** "The five mountains," the five great Zen monasteries of Kamakura: Kenchō-ji, Engaku-ji, Jufuku-ji, Jōchi-ji, and Jōmyō-ji. These monasteries, organized on a Chinese model, received official status in 1386, when preeminence was given by shogun Ashikaga Yoshimitsu to the *gozan* of Kyoto, established on the same model as those of Kamakura. *See* GOZAN.

• **Kamakura-jidai.** "Kamakura period," historical and cultural period from 1185 to 1333 corresponding to the government of the Kamakura *bakufu.* Sometimes, the Nambokuchō period (1333–92) is called "late Kamakura." This period was characterized by a military government *(bakufu)* created by Minamoto no Yoritomo, which had its headquarters in the city of Kamakura. It was directed by a shogun, assisted by a sort of regent or prime minister *(shikken)* from the Hōjō family. The shogun came from, in succession, the Minamoto, Fujiwara, and imperial families:
Minamoto family:
1) Yoritomo (1147<1192–99>)
2) Yoriie (1182<1202–03>1204)
3) Sanetomo (1192<1203–18>1219)
Fujiwara family:
1) Yoritsune (1218<1226–44>1266)
2) Yoritsugu (1239<1244–52>1256)
Imperial family:
1) Munetaka (1242<1252–66>1274)
2) Koreyasu (1264<1266–89>1326)
3) Hisa-akira (1274<1289–1308>1328)
4) Morikuni (1302<1308–33>)
5) Morinaga (1308<1333–34>1335)
6) Norinaga (1325<1334–38>)

This line of shoguns was replaced by the Ashikaga, which established its headquarters in Muromachi, near Kyoto. *See* SHIKKEN.

• **Kamakura no Noriyori.** Warrior of the Minamoto family (1156–93), Minamoto no Yoritomo's brother. He refused to fight his older brother, Minamoto no Yoshitsune; because of this, he was exiled, then assassinated on Yoritomo's order.

• *Kamakura ozōshi.* Military chronicle, probably written during the Muromachi period, describing the events that took place in the Kantō between 1379 and 1479. It is a sort of continuation of the *Taiheiki,* and is sometimes called *Taihei-kōki.*

• *Kamakura sandai-ki.* Kabuki play in 10 acts, in the *jidai-mono* genre, written by Chikamatsu Hanji in 1781.
• Puppet play *(ningyō-jōruri)* written in 1718 by Ki no Kaion.

Kamao kofun. Megalithic tomb *(kofun)* located on the flank of a hill near the Idoseri-gawa, north of the city of Kumamoto (Kyushu). It is square and preceded by a long corridor, and its interior is magnificently decorated with paintings in white, red, and blue of concentric circles, triangles, "stars," and "comets." It probably dates from the sixth century.

Kamasu. Very simple bags made of hemp or straw, once used by peasants and commoners to transport various merchandise. In modern times, they have been replaced by mass-produced bags. *See* FURO-SHIKI.

Kamata Itohei. Painter (1916–80), who received the grand prize at the International Art Festival in France in July 1975.

Kamban Batavia Shimbun. "Government Newspaper of Batavia," translation of a Dutch newspaper published in Batavia, Indonesia, in the early nineteenth century, which was the first modern newpaper in Japan.

Kambara Ariake. Poet (Kambara Hayao, 1876–1952) in the *shintaishi* (symbolist) trend, born in Tokyo. He also translated some Western poets, including Baudelaire and Verlaine. His poetry collections, *Kusawakaba* (1902) and *Dokugen aika* (1903), had a major influence on modern Japanese poetry.

Kambata. Type of silk brocade, similar to *nishiki.* Also called *kanhata.*

Kambayashi Akatsuki. Writer (Tokuhiro Iwaki, 1902–80), born in Kōchi. He wrote mainly autobiographical novels and stories: *Anjū no ie* (The House of Peaceful Life, 1938), *Sei Yohane Byōin Nite* (At St. John's Hospital, 1946), *Buronzu no kubi* (Bronze Head). He received several literary prizes.

Kambe. In ancient Japan, members of a community *(be)* attached to a Shinto shrine and responsible for maintaining its rice paddies. Later, this word was applied to peasants who owed the Shinto shrine in their village taxes or labor in corvées. The shrine's servants and *miko* were generally chosen from among the *kambe.* The word also signified the treasurer of a Shinto shrine. Also called *jinko, kamibe.*

Kambun. Literary compositions in classic Chinese by Chinese, Korean, or Japanese authors. These texts were read with a standardized pronunciation called *kundoku.* They had a profound influence on the Japanese language, which retained many of their features, such as the double negative. Purely Japanese literature is called *wabun,* while poems written in Chinese are called *kanshi. Chin.:* han-wen.
• Era of emperors Go-Saiin and Reigen: Apr. 1661–Sept. 1673. *See* NENGŌ.

• **Kambungaku.** Poetry or prose written in the traditional Chinese style. Also, Japanese literary works imitating the Chinese style, and the study of such texts. They are also called *kanshibun,* and are read with a mixture of *on* (Sino-Japanese) and *kun* (pure Japanese) pronunciations.

• **Kambun Kyōshō.** "Master of Kambun," name given to an unknown painter of ukiyo-e prints who was probably the creator, with Sugimura Jihei, of many works once attributed to Hishikawa Moronobu. He lived during the Kambun era (late seventeenth century) and painted mainly erotic images *(shunga).*

Kambutsu-e. Buddhist religious festival celebrating the birth of Gautama Buddha and consisting of bathing a statue representing him as a child (Tanjo-Butsu). It has taken place every April 8 since 840. The liquid used for the bath is a decoction *(ama-cha)* of chrysanthemum *(Hydrangea)* leaves, supposed to have curative properties and to endow schoolchildren with good handwriting. *Chin.:* Yufuhui. Also called Busshō-e. *See* AMA-CHA.

Kame. "Tortoise." Symbol of longevity and stability. A mythical tortoise, called *minogame,* lived 10,000 years, according to legend. It is portrayed with a long train or coat *(mino),* made of algae, attached to its carapace. *Chin.:* Gui.

Kameda Hōsai. Confucian philosopher (Bōsai, Hōsai, 1752–1826), poet, calligrapher, and painter in the Nanga (Bunjinga) style, born in Kōzuke (Gumma prefecture). He founded a school of Confucianism but was forced to close it, because only the teaching of Zhu Xi (*Jap.:* Shushi) was considered orthodox. He produced many calligraphic works for his painter friends, including Sakai Hōitsu and Tani Bunchō, and painted landscapes in delicate tones. Also called Kameda Chōko. *See* HŌSAI.

Kamegaoka-shikidoki. Pottery from the late Jōmon style found mainly on the Kamegaoka site in the Nishi-Tsugaru district of Aomori prefecture (northern Honshu). The objects are of various types, from fairly crude manufacture to relatively refined vases, pitchers, dishes with decorations (waves and spirals), incense holders with perforated sides, and other pieces. They were found in large quantities, along with lacquered woven-bamboo baskets. *See* JŌMON, KAMEKAN.

Kameido. Shinto shrine in a district of Tokyo, founded in 1662 and dedicated to Sugawara no Michizane.

• **Kameido Jiken.** Incident in the Kameido district of Tokyo on September 4, 1923, after the major earthquake. The police declared martial law, imprisoned many Koreans and Japanese who were members of socialist unions, and killed some 15 of them, including Ōsuge Sakae and his companion, Itō Noe.

Kamei Fumio. Movie director (1908–87). After studying in Moscow, he made mainly war movies in China and elsewhere, including *Senso to heiwa* (War and Peace, 1947).

Kamei Katsuichirō. Communist-leaning writer and literary critic (1907–66), born in Hakodate. Arrested in 1928 for his political views, he abandoned Marxism when he was released in 1930, a disavowal known as Tenkō. In 1932, he joined the proletarian-literature movement and helped found the progressive newspaper *Genjitsu* (Reality). He published a collection of literary essays, *Tenkeiki no bungaku* (Literature of a Period of Change, 1934), then created the Nihon Rōman-ha (Japanese Romantic school) with Yasuda Yojūrō, opposed to the proletarian current. He became an anti-communist and nationalist, publishing a series of works exalting the Japanese heritage, *Yamato koji fūbutsushi* (Pilgrimage to the Ancient Temples of the Yamato, 1943), *Shinran* (1944), *Shōtoku taishi* (1946), *Waga seishin no henreki* (The Pilgrimage of My Spirit, 1949), *Gendaijin no kenkyū* (Study of Modern Man, which won the *Yomiuri* Prize in 1951), and *Nihonjin no seishin shi kenkyū* (Study of the History of the Spirit of the Japanese People, Kikuchi Kan Prize in 1965). However, this last work, which was supposed to be 12 volumes long, was never completed; when Kamei Katsuichirō died, only the first four volumes had been written.

Kamei Shiichi. Painter (1843–1906), in Western style, from Tokyo.

Kamejo. Painter (?–1772) and metal engraver from Nagasaki. She produced many objects for the tea ceremony *(chanoyu)* that are still very much in demand today.

Kamekan. Large funerary urns, single- or double-sized, used by the peoples of northern Kyushu for burials in the Yayoi period (ca. 300 BC–ca. AD 300) and even in the late Jōmon period. These urns, found in cemeteries, were sometimes placed mouth to mouth *(awaseguchi)* in order to contain the body and the offerings (jewels, mirrors, etc.). Some were buried under stone dolmens *(shisekibo)*. *See also* KAMEGAOKA-SHIKI.

Kameoka. Town in Kyoto prefecture, former provincial capital in the Nara period. Akechi Mitsuhide had a castle built there in 1579. During the Edo period, it was a waystation on the San'in-dō road. Previously known as Kameyama. *Pop.:* 70,000.
→ *See* KIREI.

Kameyama. Town in Mie prefecture, on the Ise Peninsula, former castle town of Seki Munekazu (ca. mid-sixteenth century) and waystation *(shuku-eki)* on the Tōkaidō road during the Edo period. It was the headquarters of a fief worth 70,000 *koku*. *Pop.:* 35,000.
• Former name of the town of Kameoka.

• **Kameyama Tennō.** Ninetieth emperor (Prince Tsunehito, 1249<1260–74>1305), Saga Tennō's son and successor to his brother, Go-Fukakusa Tennō, who was forced to abdicate. Accused of complicity in the attempt to assassinate Emperor Fushimi, he was in his turn forced to abdicate, in favor of his son Go-Uda; he transformed his palace into a Buddhist monastery, the Nanzen-ji, in 1291, and took the religious name Kongōgen.

Kami. In Shinto, the original Japanese religion, the word *kami* designates all divine spirits, considered "superior" to the human condition. According to tradition, there are 88 million of them (this number signifies infinity). Shinto mythology distinguishes several types of *kami*: those who are "heavenly" *(amatsu-kami)*, such as Amaterasu-Ōmikami, and those who are "earthly" *(kunitsu-kami)*, such as Ōkuninushi no Mikoto. Exceptional human beings are also sometimes considered *kami*, being divinized after death, such as Sugawara no Michizane and Ōjin Tennō. By extension, the title *kami* is given to people who are considered exceptional for their talent or works. *Kami*, who are usually venerated (not adored) in shrines, may inhabit natural sites—rocks, mountains, rivers, and so on—and protect mountains *(Yama no kami)*, fields *(Ta no kami)*, or roads *(sae no kami)*. These "earthly" *kami* thus live in the world, whereas the "heavenly" *kami* are not occupied with the affairs of human beings and live on the High Plain of Heaven (Takamagahara). In general, *kami* at all levels are benevolent as long as they are regularly honored, although some can be vengeful spirits *(goryō)* who must be appeased *(tatari)* by propitiatory offerings and rituals. Each *kami* possesses an "active force" *(tama)* that is divided into a brutal aspect *(aramitama)* and a benevolent aspect *(nigimatama)*. Starting in the eighth century, with the appearance of the Esoteric Buddhist sects of Tendai and Shingon, there was a tendency to associate the Buddhist divinities *(hotoke)* with the *kami*; the latter were considered either "provisional incarnations" of Buddhist divinities *(gongen)*, or guardians of Buddhist Law *(see* GONGEN, HONJI-SUIJAKU, RYŌBU-SHINTŌ). Despite this, most *kami* still have a pronounced local character, which means that Shinto beliefs cannot be exported. *Chin.:* Shen. *See also* GOHEI, KAMUI, MITAMA, SHINTO.
• Starting in the seventh century, the title *kami* was given to all senior bureaucrats in provincial administrations, as an alternative reading of the titles *jikan, hangan,* and *shuten,* depending on their class.

• Also, the name for the northern part ("top") of a city or region. Kamigata, for example, is the region of Kyoto-Osaka, as opposed to that of Tokyo.

• With different (kanji) characters, this word means Japanese paper. It can also mean hair. *See* KAMIYUI.

• **Kami-ari-zuki.** The tenth month (October) of the lunar-solar year, so named because popular belief has it that on the tenth day of this month, all *kami* of Japan meet in the shrine in Izumo (Izumo-taisha). Because the *kami* are absent from the villages, marriages cannot be performed. Also called Kami-na-zuki, Kanna-zuki.

• **Kamibe.** *See* BE, KAMBE, KOBE.

• **Kamidana.** Household altar devoted to the family or regional *kami,* where custom has it that an offering of rice and water is made each day. It bears talismans (ofuda) received from the shrine, and workers place their paycheck there before using it. The altar is the equivalent of the Buddhist *butsu-dana.*

• **Kamigamo-jinja.** Shinto shrine in Kyoto dedicated to Wakeikazuchi no Kami, one of Tamayori-hime's sons, built around 678 in the Nagare style (*see* JINJA). It and the Shimogamo-jinja shrine form a pair called Kamo-jinja.

• **Kamigata.** Name for the Kyoto-Osaka region, as opposed to the Tokyo region. *See* KAMI.

• Classical-dance school in Osaka.

• **Kamikakushi.** "Hidden by the *kami,*" a term for people who disappeared from their homes and who were believed to have been kidnapped by the Tengū, or evil *kami.* Such people were usually runaway children, sleepwalkers, debtors, or those unhappy with their marriages who had in fact fled to another region and taken a different name to foil any search for them.

• **Kamikaze.** "Divine winds," providential typhoons which, in the autumns of 1274 and 1281, destroyed the Korean and Mongolian fleets on the north coast of Kyushu and thus saved Japan from imminent invasion. These winds were considered to be an intervention by the *kami.*

• **Kamikaze Tokubetsu Kogekitai.** "Kamikaze Special Intervention Corps," created by Admiral Onishi Takijirō in 1944 to make up for the lack of planes and fuel in the Japanese armed forces. The air force sent suicide pilots against American ships off the Philippines on October 25, 1944, each of their planes (Zero fighter planes) armed with a 250 kg bomb. The Japanese air force then used more than 2,000 of these suicide missions, with some craft specially constructed for the purpose and carrying a huge explosive charge and only enough fuel for the outward trip. Most of the pilots, hastily trained, were young men. It is estimated that over a period of about ten months (from October 1944 to August 1945), more than 2,000 pilots died this way, sinking 34 ships and seriously damaging 288 more. The navy, following this example, designed fleets of suicide submarines (*see* KAITEN), a type of human torpedo, hoping to sink a greater number of enemy ships. The pilots were called *kamikaze* (also called *jibaku,* "voluntary suicides"), as were their planes. Abridged to Tokkōtai.

• **Kami no Michibiki-kyō.** Shinto sect founded by Hosoya Shigematsu in 1950.

• **Kamimusubi no Kami.** One of the *kami* who created the universe, according to Shinto mythology. *See* JINGI-KAN NO HASSHIN.

• **Kaminari.** *Kami* of thunder, Shinto counterpart to the Buddhist divinity Raijin. He is portrayed at the entrance to shrines, colored red and hitting eight gongs placed in a halo around his head. He is associated with Fujin, the *kami* of wind.

• **Kami-tsukasa.** *See* JINGI-KAN.

• **Kamitsukenu.** Former name of Kōzuke province, now part of Gumma prefecture.

• **Kamiyui.** Hairdresser specializing in men's traditional hairstyles, especially those of samurai. In the eighteenth century, some *kamiyui* specialized in women's hairstyles (mage).

Kamichika Ichiko. Writer and politician (1888–1981), born in Nagasaki. At first a professor, then a reporter for the *Tōkyō Nichi-nichi Shimbun* (now the *Mainichi Shimbun*), she became famous for wounding her lover, the anarchist Ōsugi Sakae, who had left her to live with Itō Noe. Sentenced to two years in prison, she returned to journalism upon her release and published (with her husband, Suzuki Atsuchi, whom she had married in 1920) the magazine *Fujin Bungei.* After the Second World War, she was elected to the House of Representatives (from

1953 to 1969) for the Socialist party and began to campaign against prostitution and for women's rights. Her major work is *Kamichika Ichiko jiden: Waga ai waga tatakai* (Kamichika Ichiko's Autobiography: My Loves, My Battles, 1972).

Kamijima Onitsura. *Haikai* poet (1661–1738), author of *Hitorigoto* (1716), a two-volume collection of *haikai* and prose texts. *See* HITORIGOTO.

Kami no ku. "Top part"; in poetry, this is the name for the first three lines (of 5, 7, and 5 syllables) of a *waka* (5, 7, 5, 7, and 7 syllables): separated from the latter two lines, it became the haiku form in the seventeenth century. The two last lines (7 and 7 syllables) were then called *shimo no ku* (bottom part). *See* HAIKU, MANKU-AWASE, RENGA, WAKA.

Kaminohata. Type of ceramics kilns created in 1832 to produce pottery inspired by pottery from Imari. They were shut down about 1900, but were studied and rebuilt by the ceramist Itō Hyōdō in 1980 with white stone from the Yamagata region.

Kamishimo. Costume worn by warriors and, starting in the fifteenth century, by other people during certain ceremonies. It consists of a *kataginu* and a very long *hakama* (called *nagabakama*) made of the same fabric.

Kamitsukasa Shōken. Writer (Kamitsukasa Nobutaka, 1874–1947), born near Nara. He worked as a journalist for the *Yomiuri Shimbun*. Influenced by socialists Sakai Toshihiko and Kōtoku Shūsui, he wrote many essays and stories on the Osaka region, then on the condition of the poor classes. His most famous novel is *Hamo no kawa* (The Hamo River), published in 1933.

Kamiya Haruzane. Painter (nineteenth century) of the Kanō school in Owari. He is known for his paintings on screens and room dividers (*byōbu*), featuring mainly images of falcons.

Kamiyama Sōjin. Actor (Kamiyama Mitsugu, 1884–1954), born in Miyagi prefecture. He was a member of the Shingeki theater movement, then went to the United States, where he had a part in *The Thief of Baghdad* (1924), a film by Raoul Walsh starring Douglas Fairbanks. When he returned to Japan, he had a number of leading roles in movies directed by Shimazu Yasujirō and Shimizu Hiroshi. In spite of this, he was never very popular in Japan.

Kamiya Sōtan. Merchant and tea lover (1551–1635). His family had successfully operated the Iwami silver mines, and his father, Kamiya Jutei, and he outfitted merchant ships to trade with China and the Philippines, out of the port of Hakata. He also owned textile mills. His fortune was consolidated by his friendly relations with Toyotomi Hideyoshi, who ensured him of his cooperation during his expedition to Kyushu (1587) and his adventure in Korea (1592–97). He built a castle in Fukuoka for Kuroda Nagamasa and promoted industry and agriculture in the region. However, his fortune shrank during the Edo period because of competition from merchants close to the Tokugawa shogunate. A great tea connoisseur, he wrote an important work on the subject, *Kamiya sōtan nikki.*

Kammon gyoki. "Account of Things Seen and Heard," diary of imperial prince Fushimi no Miya Sadafusa (1372–1456), in 44 sections, covering the period from 1416 to 1448 (with a nine-year gap due to the loss of several volumes) and various subjects from politics to family events. This work is valuable for its author's knowledge of general conditions in the early Muromachi period.

Kammon Kaikyō. "Kammon Strait," another name for the Shimonoseki Strait, between Shimonoseki, in Honshu, and Kita-Kyushu (Fukuoka prefecture), forming a passage between the Inland Sea (Setonaikai) and the Sea of Japan. A tunnel under the strait was inaugurated in 1942 for the San'yō railroad, followed by a road tunnel in 1958, and one for the Shinkansen train in 1975. In 1973, a long bridge (about 800 m) was built over the strait. The strait is only about 10 to 20 m deep but has very violent currents.

Kammuri. Headdress worn in ancient Japan by nobles of the five highest ranks (*see* I). Made of black lacquered silk (or sometimes lacquered horsehair), it has one or two silk ribbons in the back, hanging or rolled on the vertical part of the hat (*koji*). This hat was attached to the wearer's hair, gathered in a bun, by wooden or metal pins (*kanzashi*). The headdress worn by the emperor was called *usubitai* (or *hanbitai*); that worn by the nobles, *atsubitai* (or *sukibitai*); that worn by nobles of the sixth to twelfth rank, *ōikake, ken-ei,* and *hoso-ei. See also* EBOSHI.

• **Kammmuri-oya.** *See* EBOSHI-OYA.

Kammu Tennō. Fiftieth emperor (Prince Yamabe Shinnō; *posthumous name:* Yamato-hiko Sumeragi-iyateru no Mikoto, 737<782–806>), born to a Korean mother of lower-class origins. He was raised to the dignity of crown prince thanks to the influence of his father-in-law, Fujiwara no Momokawa, and succeeded his father, Kōnin Tennō. Kammu Tennō established his capital in Yugi (Nara prefecture), then transferred it to Nagaoka (from 784 to 794) and finally to Heian-kyō, which he created wholesale in 794, the site of Nagaoka having been deemed inappropriate. He waged war against the indigenous peoples in northern Honshu, made important administrative reforms, sponsored the Buddhist monks Saichō and Kūkai, and gave posthumous names to past emperors. He was succeeded by Hijō Tennō. Also called Kashiwabara Tennō.

Kamo. Sheep's-wool fabrics, of recent manufacture (late nineteenth century). Before 1600, fabrics were sometimes made with goat hair mixed with cotton.

Kamo. Title of a Noh play: a Shinto priest discovers a platform near the bed of the Kamo River on which an arrow has been placed. A woman drawing water tells him its significance—it is the symbol of the *kami* of the shrine—then reveals herself to be the embodiment of a divinity. Also called *Yatategamo.*

Kamochi Masazumi. Scholar and poet (1791–1858) from Tosa province. A specialist in Kokugaku (National Learning), he spent 30 years writing an essay 124 volumes in length on the *Man'yōshū,* titled *Man'yōshū-kogi.*

Kamo no Chōmei. Buddhist monk, poet, and literary critic (ca. 1154 or 1156–1216), born in Kyoto. At about 30 years of age, he retired from the court and lived as a hermit on the bank of the Kamogawa, in Ōhara, northeast of Kyoto, leaving his retreat only occasionally to travel. He was appointed head of the poetry bureau by Retired Emperor Go-Toba around 1200, following presentation of a collection of 100 *waka,* the *Shōji ninen nido hyakushu* (Second Series of One Hundred Poems of the Shōji Era). In 1209, Kamo no Chōmei left his Ōhara hermitage and settled in Toyama on Mt. Hino, where he built a little hut in which he was to die. He proved to be a prolific writer, producing both poems and literary essays, such as the *Mumyōsho* (Untitled Notes, published after 1211) in 78 chapters on various subjects, notably aesthetics and poetic principles, in which he explains and advocates the

ideal of *yūgen* (*see* YŪGEN). He also wrote journals of his trips, *Iseki* (Account of a Voyage to Ise, ca. 1186), *Kaidōki* (Account of a Sea Voyage, ca. 1223), and *Tōkan kikō* (Voyage to the Western Gate, ca. 1242), an account of a trip he made to meet the poet Minamoto no Sanetomo in Kamakura. His best-known work is the *Hōjōki* (An Account of My Hut), written in 1212, a group of brief notes and reflections on the transitory nature of the world as the Buddhists conceived it. He also wrote a collection of Buddhist tales, *Hoshinshū* (Collection of Buddhist Thoughts, ca. 1214). He took Ren-in as his monk's name. Also known as Kamo no Nagaakira.

Kamo-gawa. River 35 km long with its source in the Tamba Mountains, crossing through Kyoto and flowing into the Katsura-gawa. Its course was slightly detoured by construction of Heian-kyō in 794 so that it could flow to the east of the imperial palace *(gosho).* It is often dry, and many bridges cross its bed in Kyoto. *See* KYOTO, HEIAN-KYŌ.

• **Kamo-gawa Odori.** *See* ODORI.

Kamogutsu. High, wide boots worn by officers *(uikin)* of the Imperial Guard and certain nobles who played *kemari,* during the Heian period. Also called *kamo-kutsu. See* SOKUTAI.

Kamo-jinja. Term for two large Shinto shrines in Kyoto, the Kamo Wakeikazuchi-jinja (Kamigamo-jinja) and the Kamo Mioya-jinja (Shimogamo-jinja), which were founded, according to tradition, in 678. Many festivals are held at the shrines every year, including the Aoi Matsuri, the Kamo no Kurabe-uma, and the Kamo no Matsuri. *See* KAMI-GAMO-JINJA, SHIMOGAMO-JINJA.

Kamo Kōsuke. Physicist, professor at the University of Kyoto, who invented a computer that can precisely predict volcanic eruptions. He predicted the eruption of Sakurajima on December 3, 1985.

Kamo no kurabe-uma. Horse race traditionally held on May 5 at the Kamogami-jinja Shinto shrine in Kyoto, with the goal of obtaining prosperity and good harvests from the *kami.* This race took place for the first time on the 5th day of the 5th month of 1093. During this ceremonial race, 20 riders dressed in the Heian style race two by two (one from the "left team," one from the "right team") on a course delimited by a cherry tree (start line, symbolizing spring) and a maple tree (finish line, symbolizing autumn). Victories are announced by priests with a drum roll for the left team or ringing bells for the right team. The camp with the greatest number of victories is declared the winner.

Kamo no Mabuchi. Scholar and *waka* poet (1697–1769), born near Hamamatsu, Shinto priest Ōkabe Masanobu's son. Kada Azumamaro's disciple in Kyoto from 1733 to 1736, he entered the service of Prince Tayasu Munetaki, shogun Tokugawa Yoshimune's son, and lived in Edo. A proponent of Kokugaku (National Learning), he advocated a return to the poetic style of the *Man'yōshū* and tried, in vain, to revive the *chōka* mode. He also wrote important studies on the *Man'yōshū*, such as *Man'yōkō* (between 1760 and 1768) and on other ancient works, such as *Kanjikō* (1757), *Genji monogatari shinshaku* (1758), and *Nimanabi* (1765). He also wrote a series of commentaries on Kokugaku, the *Bun'ikō* (1762), *Kaikō* (1764), *Kokuikō* (1765), *Shoikō* (1766), and *Goikō* (1769), in which he glorified the works of Japanese antiquity. His best-known disciple was Motoori Norinaga.

Kamo no Matsuri. Annual festival held in Kyoto on the day of the cock in the 4th month, in honor of *kami* venerated in the Kamo-jinja. In 889, another festival was created for the same reason, but taking place at the end of the 11th month, known as Kamo-rinji no Matsuri. *See* CHŪSHI.

• *Kamo no monogurui.* Title of a Noh play: a man returns to the capital after a three-month absence and finds that his wife, left alone, has gone mad.

Kamon. Title of noble families related to the Tokugawa shogun. Formerly called Kanimori and Kunaishō.
→ *See* KANIMORI NO TSUKASA.

Kampuku. Position of grand reporter, or regent, for an adult emperor, created in the Heian period by Emperor Kōkō, who gave the title to Fujiwara no Mototsune in 884, an appointment confirmed by Emperor Uda in 887. The Fujiwara family kept this position and the title relating to it. By the twelfth century, the position had become honorific and the Fujiwara no longer had the privilege of the title, which endured until 1867. The regent for an underage emperor was called *sesshō;* usually, the *sesshō*, by rights, became the *kampaku* when the emperor came of age. Before 884, this position had the title *azukari-mōsu. See also* SHIKKEN, SESSHŌ.

Kampeisha. "Government shrines," title given to certain Shinto shrines directly related to the Jingikan and honored by the imperial family, in contrast to the *kokuheisha,* simple provincial shrines receiving offerings only from the faithful and administrators. These titles, in use from the tenth century, were eliminated in 1945.

Kampō. Era of Emperor Sakuramachi: Feb. 1741–Feb. 1744. *See* NENGŌ.

Kampyō. Era of Emperor Uda: Apr. 889–Apr. 898. *See* NENGŌ.

• *Kampyō go-ikai.* Political will written by Emperor Uda for his son Daigo in 897. Also titled *Kampyō no Gyokuikai.*

• **Kampyō Hō-ō.** Title given to Emperor Uda after his abdication.

• **Kampyō-taihō.** *See* KŌCHŌ-JŪNISEN.

Kamui. Divinities or divinized ancestors of the Ainu. This may be the root (or a derivation) of the Japanese word *kami.* The *kamui* are symbolized in Ainu villages by rows of stakes bearing the skulls of ritually killed bears, located northeast of the settlements.

• **Kamuikotan.** Canyon in central Hokkaido, near the town of Askahigawa, formed by the waters of the Hishikari-gawa river. It is 10 km long and a remarkable site, once believed to be inhabited by gods *(kamui)* and thus sacred and inviolable. Site of Jōmon and Ainu houses.

Kamura Isota. Writer (1897–1933), born in Yamaguchi prefecture, author of autobiographical novels such as *Gōku* (1928) and *Tojō* (1932).

Kamu-ya-i-mimi no Mikoto. In Shinto mythology, Emperor Jimmu's second son. He was said to have killed his older brother, Tagishi-mimi no Mikoto, in order to seize power.

Kan. Former unit of mass, equivalent to about 1,000 *momme* (approximately 3.75 kg). Also called *ku'an. See* MŌ, MOMME.
• Japanese name for the Chinese Han dynasty, and prefix used to indicate Chinese origin: *kango* (Chinese language), *kan-on* (Chinese pronunciation), and so on.

• Japanese philosophical concept referring to a sort of intuition. It is a kind of sixth sense, of sudden realization with no premonition. It is cultivated in a number of Japanese arts, including Zen gestural painting and the martial arts.
→ *See* MARU.

Kana. Japanese phonetic written characters, created in the early ninth century (attributed to Kūkai, but without certainty), probably by Buddhist monks, and written with Chinese characters *(kanji)* used for their pronunciation *(karina,* as opposed to those used for their meaning, *mana).* As early as the seventh century, there existed a certain number of specific characters derived from the *kanji* and used only to denote their sound. These ancient characters, used notably in the *Man'yōshū,* were known as *man'yō-gana.* This type of writing was very complicated because it required knowledge of a great number of characters; it was transformed by simplifying the signs and retaining only a few *man'yō-gana* strokes for each sound. These gave rise to two sets of "provisional characters" *(karina,* whence *kana)* called *hiragana* and *katakana.*

The *hiragana,* corresponding to the 40 sounds (*see* GOJŪON-ZU) of the Japanese language, cursive in form and used to write poems, were first used by women, whence their name *onna-de* (woman's hand). This writing later gave rise to masterpieces of calligraphy and was used to note all sounds in the Japanese language that could not be transcribed with Chinese ideograms, including grammatical endings. *Katakana,* angular characters also drawn from the *Man'yō-gana,* appeared in the ninth century to facilitate reading of Chinese texts. Women thus had access to literature, which had theoretically been beyond their reach. At first, there were a great number of *kana,* but their number was reduced to 50 during the Muromachi period, and they are now used mainly for transcription of foreign words and on posters. The current form of *hiragana* and *katakana* was set in 1900; after the Second World War, several sounds pronounced similarly, such as *wi* and *we,* were eliminated and replaced by the sounds *i* and *e.* But simple sounds did not suffice to note all the sounds in Japanese, so very soon diacritical marks *(nigori)* were created to weaken or strengthen pronunciation of certain consonants: *ka* could become *ga; ho, po* or *bo; ta, da; ha, pa* or *ba;* and so on. There are two types of *nigori,* written to the upper right of the *kana,* in the form of a double accent (″) or a small circle (°), depending on their effect on the sound represented by the single *kana.* Certain complex sounds are written by combining two *kana,* the second being written smaller and combined in a single voice with the first, as in the "mixed" sounds *kya, sha,* and *ja,* made, respectively, by the combination of *ka + ya, shi + ya, shi (ji) + ya.* When these characters are written small beside *kanji* characters, in order to indicate pronunciation, they are called *furigana.*

Kana Nihongi. History of Japan which, according to the *Shoku Nihongi,* was written by Ki no Ason Kiyobito and Miyake no Ōmi Fujimaro in 714, now lost. Said to have been the first version of the *Nihongi,* it was in fact a transcription in kana characters (made between 720 and 878) of this work.

• **Kana-zōshi.** Series of books written in hiragana after 1596 for use by commoners, monks, and warriors, and dealing with romantic and educational themes, often illustrated with woodcut images. They were replaced by the *ukiyo-sōshi* in the late seventeenth century.

Kanabō. Sort of iron club, sometimes used by warriors in ancient times, and a favorite weapon of some monk-warriors *(heisō)* in the Heian and Kamakura periods. *See* BŌ-JUTSU.

Kanadehon chūshingura. See AKŌ-GISHI, CHŪSHIN-GURA.

Kanagaki Tobun. Writer and humorist (Nozaki Bunzō, 1829–94), born in Edo. He wrote many satirical novels in *kokkeibon* genre, somewhat influenced by Jippensha Ikku, including *Kokkei fuji mōde, Seiyō dōchū hizakurige* (On Foot Through the West, 1870–72), *Aguranabe* (The Eater of Beef, 1871), and *Kyūrizu-kai* (How to Use Cucumbers, 1972).

Kanagawa. Prefecture south of Tokyo on Tokyo and Sagami bays, formed of mountains to the west and a coastal plain to the east, created in 1876 by the former province of Sagami. It is irrigated by the Sagami-gawa and Tama-gawa rivers. *Chief city:* Yokohama; *other important cities:* Kamakura, Kawasaki, Fujisawa, Sagamihara, Hiratsuka. *Area:* 2,391 km². *Pop.:* 7 million.

Treaty of Kanagawa: Peace and friendship treaty signed on March 31, 1854, between the United States (represented by Commodore Perry) and the Tokugawa shogun, opening the ports of Shimoda and Hakodate to international trade, allowing ships to resupply in these ports, and establishing an American consulate at Shimoda. The shogunate was then forced to sign similar treaties with the British (1854), the Russians (1855), and the Dutch (1856).

Kanai Noboru. Economist (1865–1933), born in Shizuoka province. He went to Great Britain and Germany to study economics, and then taught the principles of German social economics at the University of Tokyo. He published at least two major books on the subject, *Shakai mondai* (Social Problems, 1892) and *Shakai keizaigaku* (Social Economics, 1902).

Kanai Sanshō. Famous Kabuki actor (1731–97), specializing in the dances of *jōruri* plays.

Kaname-ishi. Large rock within the walls of the Kashima-jingū shrine (Ibaraki prefecture), which, according to popular belief, was the head of a huge nail now underground, holding a giant Silurian fish that was accused of being the cause of earthquakes.

Kan'ami Kiyotsugu. Writer, poet, actor (Yūzaki Saburō, Kanze Kiyotsugu, 1333–84), and priest in the Kasuga-jinja Shinto shrine in Kyoto, serving Ashikaga no Yoshimochi. According to tradition, he was one of Kusunoki Masashige's sons. He wrote plays for Noh theater and triumphed as an actor in the play *Okina*, which was performed in 1374 for the shogun Ashikaga Yoshimitsu. He combined *sarugaku* dances with *kusemai* popular dances and created the first scenes for Noh theater, which his son Zeami took to its highest form of expression. He wrote many plays that were adapted by Zeami, such as *Okina, Eguchi, Sotoba komachi, Motomezuka,* and *Matsukaze. See* KANZE-RYŪ.

Kanamori Sōwa. Daimyo (seventeenth century) and master *(chajin)* of the tea ceremony *(chanoyu)*. He was a great collector of ceramic pieces made by Nonomura Ninsei.

Kanamori Tokujirō. Politician (1886–1959), born in Aichi. A senior bureaucrat in the Ministry of Finance, he was appointed director of the Bureau of Legislation in 1934, but, attacked by the right wing for having supported Minobe Tatsukichi's constitutional theories, he resigned in 1936. After the Second World War, he was a minister in Yoshida Shigeru's 1946 cabinet, and helped to write Japan's new Constitution. He retired in 1947 to direct the Diet National Library.

Kanawa. Title of a Noh play: a woman who was rejected by her husband and replaced by another goes to the shrine to ask for the help of its *kami.* She is told to wear an iron crown, paint her face red, and clothe herself in the same color to take her vengeance. Although a witch tries to protect her husband with charms, the abandoned woman manages to approach him and hits two dolls representing the new couple. But an army of divinities comes to the rescue of the husband and the vindictive woman leaves, saying that she will find a new opportunity to avenge herself.

Kanayama Hiko and Kanayama Hime. Pair of primordial *kami,* son *(hiko)* and sister *(hime)* of Izanagi and Izanami.

Kanazawa. City in Ishikawa prefecture (central Honshu), on the western coast, former capital of the Maeda clan in the seventeenth century. It developed in the fifteenth century around a temple of the Ikkō-shū sect, but the temple's supporters in the region were annihilated in 1580 by Sakuma Morimasa, who built a castle the same year. The town then came under the control of the Maeda. It is now an industrial city that retains its character as a feudal town (ruins of the Maeda castle). It has a prosperous crafts sector: *maki-e* lacquers, fabrics dyed using the Kaga-yūzen method, Kutani-style ceramics. *Pop.:* 420,000.

• **Kanazawa Bunko.** Library founded in the Kanazawa district of Yokohama by Hōjō Sanetoke in 1275 and transferred to Edo by Tokugawa Ieyasu in the early seventeenth century. It contains more than 20,000 works and 7,000 manuscripts, collected by Hōjō Sanetoki and his successors, as well as many works of art. At one point it was called Shōmyō-ji Bunko because the monks of the temple near the Shōmyō-ji were its curators after the fall of the Kamakura *bakufu* in 1333.

Kan Chazan. Poet and Confucian scholar (Kannami Hyakusuke; *gō:* Chazan, 1748–1827), from Bingo province. He opened a school in his village, then was hired by the daimyo of the Fukuyama fief to write a monograph on the estate, *Fukuyama shiryō.* He also wrote several philosophical essays and a poetry collection, *Kōyō-sekiyō-sonsha shi.*

Kanchō. Esoteric Buddhist rite of transmission of the doctrine of the Shingon-shū from master to disciple. *See also* TENDAI-SHŪ.

• **Kanchō-sensei.** *See* SŌ DOSHIN.

Kanchū-ki. Diary written by the courtier Kadeno-kōji Fujiwara no Kanenaka (1244–1308), a bureaucrat in the Archives Bureau (Kurōdokoro), relating the events of the period from 1268 to 1300, including the attempted invasions by the Mongols. This very detailed diary is a valuable source of information on this period. Also titled *Kananaka-kyō-ki, Kanenaka-ki, Kadenokōji chūnagon-ki.*

Kanda. Tokyo district (in Chiyoda-ku) and university center, where many bookstores and libraries are located. Also called "Tokyo's Latin Quarter."

• **Kanda-jinja.** Shinto shrine in the Kanda and Chiyoda-ku district of Tokyo, dedicated to the cult of Onamuchi no Mikoto and Sukunahikona no Mikoto, two *kami* responsible for maintaining peace in the territory. From the thirteenth to the sixteenth century, the spirit of the warrior Taira no Masakado was also venerated there, but he was replaced by Sukunahikona no Mikoto after the shrine dedicated to Taira no Masakado was destroyed by the 1923 earthquake. Every second year on May 15, there is a major festival, Kanda Matsuri, alternating with the Sannō Matsuri (at the Hie-jinja). On this occasion, carts are pulled in a procession, accompanied by musicians and dancers. This festival was formerly held on September 15. The shrine, also called Kanda Myōjin, was rebuilt in 1934.

• **Kanda-jōsui.** Aqueduct built in the late sixteenth century on Tokugawa Ieyasu's order to bring water from Lake Inokashira to Edo. It was about 17 km long, but comprised 23 km of various canals and 67 km of large pipes, which brought water to 3,660 reservoirs in Edo. The entire system was renovated in 1653, as was the Tamagawa-jōsui, enabling water to be brought to Edo from various places, some as far away as 86 km.

Kandachime (or Kandachibe). General term for nobles of the first three ranks (*see* I) before 645.
→ *See* GEKKEI.

Kandai-ji. Starting in 680, the title given to "official" Buddhist temples for which the state was responsible for construction and appointment of directors. During the Nara period, there were four: the Daian-ji, the Yakushi-ji, the Gangō-ji, and the Gufuku-ji; soon, the Tōdai-ji, the Kōfuku-ji, the Hōryū-ji, and the Saidai-ji were added. The number was raised to 10, then to 12, and finally to 15. These temples were organized differently from provincial temples *(kokubun-ji)* and private temples *(jōgaku-ji)*. Also called simply Dai-ji.

Kandaka. Method for determining the value of an estate during the Muromachi period, based on the *kan* (currency worth 1,000 copper *momme*) from the total of the taxes paid on the land, generally in produce (rice or other crops), converted into account currency. This system also permitted daimyo to calculate payments due from their vassals in horses, men, and weapons. *See* KOKU, KOKUDAKA.

Kanda Takahira. Scholar and bureaucrat (Kanda Kōhei, 1830–98), born in Gifu, professor at the Bansho Shirabesho, the shogunal school for "Dutch sciences" *(rangaku)*. He was appointed to the House of Peers in 1890. As an economist, he left one major work, the first of its type in Japan, *Keizai shōgaku* (Introduction to Economics, 1867), an adaptation of an English book by William Ellis.

Kaneakira Shinnō. Emperor Daigo's eleventh son (914–87), famous for his literary talent. He received the family name Minamoto in 920. Also called Miko-Sadaijin, Ogura Shinnō.

Kanebō. Firm that manufactures and sells textiles and cosmetics, founded in 1887. It has more than 100 subsidiaries in Japan and abroad. Head office in Osaka.

Kanehira. Title of a Noh play: a Buddhist monk on his way to Awazu falls asleep on the road and dreams of the battle during which Imai Kanehira and Kiso Yoshinaka died, in Awazu (Ōmi province) in 1184.

Kanehira. Famous sword maker (923–1000) from Bizen province.

Kan'ei. Era of Emperor Go-Minoo: Feb. 1624–Dec. 1644. *See* NENGŌ.

• **Kan'ei-ji.** Buddhist temple founded in Ueno (Tokyo) in 1625 by the monk Tenkai (ca. 1536–1643) for the Tendai-shū sect. Because it was built northeast of the shogunal palace, it was said to protect against evil influences. It was used as a cemetery for many members of the Tokugawa family, from among whom its abbots were chosen. Most of the temple's buildings were destroyed during the Boshin Civil War in 1868, and it was reconstructed in 1875 with parts of the Chōraku-ji temple of Gumma prefecture. Its five-story pagoda *(gojunotō)*, 35 m in height, dates from 1639. *See* UENO KŌEN.

• *Kan'ei shoka keizuden.* Historical work in 300 volumes, concerning the genealogies of the great families of Japan, written on Tokugawa Iemitsu's order by Hayashi Razan and his son, Hayashi Jo, from 1641 to 1643.

• *Kan'ei-tsūhō.* Coins worth one or four *mon,* issued starting in 1636 and in circulation until 1853. Their value was determined according to their diameter and their metal, brass or copper (or iron starting in 1739). *See* BITASEN.

Kaneko Kentarō. Politician (1853–1942), born to a samurai family in Fukuoka. He studied at Harvard University from 1872 to 1878. In 1880, he was appointed secretary of the Genrō-in; starting in 1884, he worked on writing the Constitution under Itō Hirobumi, whose private secretary he became. He was appointed secretary to the House of Peers in 1890; in 1898, he became minister of agriculture in Itō's cabinet. Two years later, he was minister of justice in Itō's fourth cabinet. He was sent to the United States in 1904–05 to speak with President Theodore Roosevelt on behalf of his government; when he returned, he was appointed a member of the emperor's Privy Council. He was ennobled three times: baron in 1900, viscount in 1907, and count in 1934.

Kaneko Kichizaemon. Author (Kaneko Ikkō, d. 1728) and actor in Kabuki and Bunraku plays, who worked with Chikamatsu Monzaeomon. His diary, dated 1698, was recently found.

Kaneko Kunen. Poet (1876–1951) of traditional *waka.* His main poetry collections are *Kataware-zuki* and *Shirasagi-shū.*

Kaneko Mitsuharu. Poet and writer (Oshika Yasu-makzu, 1895–1975), born in Tokyo, whose body of work can be defined as expressing absolute skepticism. Using his personal fortune, he published his first volume of poems, *Akatsuchi no ie* (The House of Red Earth) in 1919, then traveled in Europe. He published another collection, *Koganemushi* (The Golden Scarab) in 1923; one year later, he married a poet, Mori Michiyo (b. 1901). They took long trips abroad and he wrote other poetry books, such as *Same* (Sharks, 1937), and prose works, such as *Mare ran'in kikō* (Notes on Voyages in the Dutch Indies, 1940). During the Second World War, he

wrote pacifist poems that were published only starting in 1948, including *Ga* (Moths), *Rakkasan* (The Parachutist), *Oni no ko no uta* (The Song of a Son of the Demon, 1949). After the war, he wrote autobiographical novels—*Dokuro hai* (The Skull-Shaped Bowl, 1971), *Nemure pari* (Sleeping in Paris, 1973), *Nishi higashi* (East and West, 1974)—while continuing to write poetry—*Ningen no higeki* (The Human Tragedy, 1952), *Suisei* (The Strength of Water, 1956), *Il* (Him, 1965), *Wakaba no uta* (The Song of Wakaba, 1967–74). Among his other works are *Shijin* (The Poet, 1973), *Zetsubo no sei-shin shi* (Story of Desperate Souls, 1965), *Nippon-jin no higeki* (The Tragedy of the Japanese, 1967), and translations of French poets such as Rimbaud, Aragon, Baudelaire, and Verhaeren. In 1952, he received the *Yomiuri* Prize; in 1965, the Reikitei Prize for poetry.

Kaneko Rokuemon. Kabuki actor, active in Osaka and Kyoto about 1680, specializing in *tachiyaku* roles.

Kan'en. Era of Emperor Momozono: July 1748–Oct. 1751. *See* NENGŌ.
→ *See* IWASAKI TSUNEMASA, SESSAI.

Kanenaga Shinnō. The son of Emperor Go-Daigo (1329–83), he helped his father after the failure of the Kemmu Restoration. He managed to take control of Kyushu in 1361 for the Southern Court (Nanchō), but he was finally defeated by General Imagawa Sadayo in 1375. He retired to Chikugo province and was largely forgotten. Also called Kaneyoshi Shinnō.

Kaneshige Tōyō. Potter (Kaneshige Isamu, 1896–1967), from a family of potters in Bizen province (*see* BIZEN-YAKI), who inherited the family kilns in 1915 and revived the tradition. He created many ceramic sculptures and bowls for the tea ceremony. He was declared a Living National Treasure in 1956. After his death, his son, Kaneshige Michiaki (b. 1934 in Ibe-chō, Okayama prefecture) continued to work in the same style. The last of this family line of ceramists, Kaneshige Kōsuke, born 1943 in Bizen, is also a famous artist.

Kanetaka Kaoru. Writer, critic, and author of television plays. A sportswoman, she became famous in 1938 for circumnavigating the world from Tokyo to Tokyo in a plane in 81 hours. She was also the first Japanese woman to go to the South Pole and to parachute-jump. She wrote a number of books about her trips and experiences.

Kanga. "Chinese painting," style of painting popular mainly during the Muromachi period and also comprising Chinese paintings imported from China of the Song and Yuan dynasties (Hokuga style). Also called Kara-e.
Main artists working in this style:
—Josetsu, Shūbun's father.
—Shūbun, father of Oguri Sōtan (father of Sōkei and Kanō Masanobu), Shin-nō (Ami), Soga Dasoku, and Sesshū Tōyō.
—Sōkei, Sōritsu's father.
—Shin-no Ami, father of Shingei (father of Shinsō, who was the father of Tan'an Chiden and Shōkei).
—Soga Dasoku, father of Shōsen (father of Shōsō, father [?] of Chokuan, father of Nichokuan).
—Sesshū Tōyō, father of Tōetsu, Shūgetsu, Shūtoku (Tōgan), Sōen, Tōshun (Hasegawa, father of Tōhaku), and Sesson.

• **Kanga-kai.** "Association for Appreciation of Chinese Painting," founded by Okakura Kakuzō (1862–1913).

Kangaku. "Government schools," as opposed to private schools *(juku)*. In the Nara and Heian periods, name for universities *(daigaku)* in the capital and for schools (called *kokugaku*) established in the provinces *(koku)*. During the Edo period, this word applied to schools teaching the orthodox Confucian philosophy of Zhu Xi *(Jap.:* Shushi). Also called *kangakuryō*.
→ *See* SŌAMI.

• **Kangaku-in.** School founded in Heian-kyō in 821 by Fujiwara no Fuyutsugu to educate members of his family, with professors from the *kangakuryō* of the capital. This institution existed until the end of the Kamakura period. Also called *daigakubesshō*.
• Term for many schools founded by Buddhist monasteries, such as the Tōdai-ji, the Enryaku-ji, the Kōya-san, the Kōfuku-ji, the Onjō-ji, the Kan'ei-ji, the Hase-dera, and others.

• **Kangaku-sha.** Literary school of the seventeenth and eighteenth centuries, influenced by Chinese literature. Its followers wrote mainly works on politics, morals, and history.

Kangan. Painter (Kitayama Mōki, Ba Mōki; *azana:* Bunkei; *mei:* Gonnosuke, d. 1801), who was Bunchō's master. He painted landscapes and faces.

Kangeiko. Rigorous physical training conducted in the winter months, particularly during cold snaps in January. This practice, observed by Buddhist monks and Shinto priests since antiquity, is still in use by some traditional artists and practitioners of the martial arts; it sometimes involves pushing to the absolute limit of the body's resistance to cold and fatigue.

Kangen. Era of Emperor Go-Saga: Feb. 1243–Feb. 1247. *See* NENGŌ.
→ *See* GAGAKU, HI KANGEN.

Kangetsu. Painter (Shitomi Tokki; *azana:* Shion; *mei:* Genji; *gō:* Iyōsai, Kangetsu, 1747–97), from Osaka. He was also a good poet and a renowned calligrapher. He received the title of Hokkyō.

Kangin-shū. "Songs of Tranquillity," collection of 311 *ko-uta* songs compiled in 1518 by Sōchō (1448–1532), a *renga* poet. He collected popular songs of the Kamakura and Muromachi periods and songs drawn from Noh plays.

Kangi-ten. Secret divinity of syncretic Buddhism of the Shingon-shū and the Tendai-shū, representing the Hindu divinity Ganapati (Ganesha), Shiva's son, also symbolizing Āryāvalokiteshvara (*Jap.:* Shō Kannon Bosatsu). This double divinity (male and female) is usually portrayed in sexual union, signifying "joy without restriction" (*Skt.:* Nandikeshvara). It has many aspects and names in Tantric doctrines, and the common people endow it with great power. Because of its latent power, its images are shown only very rarely. It (or they) is portrayed as one (or two) human being(s) with an elephant's head, with two, four, six, eight, or twelve arms. Sometimes considered a sibling to Ida-ten and a protector of temples, it is venerated mainly by gamblers, geisha, actors, and people in the pleasure quarters. Its image, when it is displayed (rarely), is playfully desecrated. Also called Daishō Kangi-ten, Daishō-ten, Kangi Jizai-ten, Shōden-sama.

• *Kangi-ten reigen emaki.* Early-fourteenth-century *emakimono*, celebrating the miraculous effectiveness of the Kangi-ten and glorifying the role of the thirteenth *zasu* of the Tendai-shū, Son'i, in propagation of the cult of Kangi-ten.

Kangō. Signs of recognition given by the Chinese government to the Edo shogunate, which captains of Japanese ships had to present when they arrived in Chinese ports to prove that they were duly authorized traders and not pirates *(wakō)*. This regulation was applied by China in its trade with Japan from 1404 to about 1550. Trade with foreigners was prohibited in China, so merchandise was considered to be duty tax or gifts; this, obviously, often resulted in exchanges in which the Japanese came out ahead. This trade (called *kangō-bōeki*) was in the hands of two powerful clans, the Ōuchi (port of Hakata) and the Hosokawa (port of Sakai). But the constantly growing activity of *wakō* (Japanese pirates) and struggles between the two major clans, along with the arrival of Portuguese ships in Chinese waters, led to a decline in, then an almost complete stoppage of, trade between China and Japan. The trade was mainly in copper, sulfur, and weapons (swords), which were exchanged for Chinese currency, silk, and cotton. Trade with China did not start again until the Edo period, when ships carried a "red seal" *(shuin-sen)*.

Kan Hasshū. Generic term formerly designating the "eight provinces of the Kantō": Musashi, Sagami, Kazusa, Shimōsa, Awa, Kōzuke, Hitachi, and Shimotsuke.

Kan'i-hō. General name for medicine according to Chinese criteria, as opposed to Western medicine, called *ran'i-hō*.

Kan'i jūnikai no sei. "The twelve ranks of headdresses," first system of ranks in the court of Japan, based on the wearing of colored headdresses *(kan, kammuri)*, instituted in 604 by Shōtoku Taishi. The first six ranks (*see* I) were divided into two classes, high *(tai)* and low *(shō)*, named after the classic Confucian virtues:

1) **Toku** (moral excellence): purple
2) **Jin** (benevolence): green
3) **Rei** (splendor): red
4) **Shin** (fidelity): yellow
5) **Gi** (rectitude): white
6) **Chi** (wisdom): black

This system rewarded merit more than nobility. It was replaced in 647 by a system of 13 ranks, then abolished in 701 by the *ritsuryō* code and replaced by nine ranks divided into thirty classes.

Kanikō-sen. "The Crab-Fishing Boat." A novel by Kobayashi Takiji (1903–33) describing the difficult conditions and social problems of crab fishers in the Sea of Okhotsk. A movie, *The Boats of Hell,* directed by So Yamamura, was made from this novel in Europe in 1953.

Kanimoro no Tsukasa. Title of bureaucrats responsible for maintenance of and repairs to the imperial palace in Kyoto. It was replaced by the titles *kunai-shō* and *kamon* in the late Heian period. *See* KAMON.

Kan'in no Miya. One of the four hereditary palaces of the Edo period, founded by Prince Naohito (Hide no Miya), sixth son of Emperor Higashiyama. The others were called Fushimi no Miya, Arisugawa no Miya, and Kyōgoku no Miya.

Kanji. Era of Emperor Horikawa: Apr. 1087–Dec. 1094. *See* NENGŌ.

• Sino-Japanese characters used to transcribe Japanese. In Chinese, each character represents a word or idea (ideogram), while in Japanese these characters are often used to represent either an idea or a sound in the Japanese language. Unlike Chinese, Japanese sounds are not monosyllabic, so several characters were sometimes used to note Japanese sounds. *On* characters represent pronunciations, rather than meanings. To them were added Chinese characters chosen only for their meaning and pronounced according to their equivalent in Yamato language (original Japanese) and called *kun.* Thus, the same Sino-Japanese character could have several *on* pronunciations (*go-on,* before the sixth century; *kan-on,* in the Wu period; *tō-on,* in the Tang period) and other pronunciations in Yamato language. For example, the Sino-Japanese character for "on top" can have ten different pronunciations, two *on* and eight *kun—jō, ue, kami, uwa, a(-geru), kō, tate, nobu(-ru),* and so on—depending on whether the character is alone or in composition with another character or a verbal ending. In addition, several associated characters can have both an *on* and a *kun* pronunciation, such as the characters for "big" and "man," which can be read *"daijin"* or *"otona."* The combinations are infinite. As for verbs (which are represented in Chinese by a single character without verbal ending), in Japanese they are complemented by *hiragana* characters that are used to note grammatical endings. *Katakana* syllabic characters (*see* KANA) can also be used to note the sound of foreign words that have no equivalent in Japanese.

There are fewer Sino-Japanese characters (about 5,000) than Chinese characters (between 40,000 and 50,000). In 1981, a list was established for current use (*see* JŌYŌ-KANJI) of 1,945 characters (complementing another list of 1,850 characters established by the Ministry of Education in 1946, called *kyōiku-kanji*) to which some 166 characters are added for transcribing proper names. Because of all of this, it is sometimes difficult to read a Japanese text; readers might understand its meaning but have trouble discerning the exact pronunciation. In magazines and other publications, pronunciation of rare characters is generally indicated by their equivalent *(furigana)* in *hiragana* or *katakana* characters written beside the *kanji*. There are no precise rules about pronunciation of *kanji*, although in general any isolated character should be pronounced in Yamato *(kun)*, while any group of more than two characters should be pronounced in *on* (with many exceptions, of course). Thus, the characters for "mountain" *(san)* and "origin" *(hon)*, when together, must be pronounced not "Sambon" *(san + hon)* but "Yamamoto" *(yama+moto)*; and in the complex associating the characters forming the name Fuji with the character for "mountain," one must say Fuji-san and not Fuji-yama, because the latter character is considered isolated. In contrast, the characters for "now" *(ima)* and "day" *(hi)*, when associated, are pronounced, depending on context, as *kon-nichi* (*kon* and *nichi* being the *kun* pronunciations of *ima* and *hi*) or as the single syllable *kyō* (in *on*) to signify "today."

Writing of Sino-Japanese characters follows the rules of Chinese calligraphy, although, over the centuries, some Chinese characters have been abridged or simplified (characters called *zokuji*, "popular"). For printing, characters of various styles are used, modeled on those in use in China during the Song (960–1279), Ming (1279–1644), and Qing (1644–1912) periods. Handwriting uses at least four styles: *reisho* (bureaucratic), *kaisho* (standard), *gyōsho* (semi-cursive), and *sōsho* (cursive, also called "unripe," *Chin.*: *caoshu*, sometimes very difficult to read). For seals, the old Chinese characters, called *daiten* or *shōten*, with rounded strokes—derived from Chinese pictographic writing on divinatory bones, bronzes, or small bamboo plaques (called in Japanese, respectively, *kōkotsu-moji, kimbun,* and *kato-moji*)—are still sometimes used. Calligraphers use one or another of these styles, with a preference for semi-cursive or cursive characters. *See* CALLIGRAPHY.

Finally, Sino-Japanese characters are either simple, composed of several single characters ("keys," of which there are 214), or overlapping ones. In the latter case, each part of the composite character represents either a particular idea, or simply the sound according to which the entire character must be read, or a determinative (bird, animal, fish, grass, tree, fabric, element, various other categories) that defines the meaning of the ideogram.

Chinese characters were brought to Japan from Korea, probably in the fifth century, as inscriptions found on épés in the Inari-yama and Eda Fudayama *kofun* seem to indicate. The first scribes of the court were in fact Koreans called *fuhito*. However, tradition has it that it was the Korean Wani who introduced them in the fourth century, bringing to Japan examples of the "Interviews" *(Chin.: Lunyu; Jap.: Rongo)* with Confucius and the "Treatise of the Thousand Characters" *(Chin.: Qianzi-wen; Jap.: Senji-mon).*

Kanjinchō. Texts describing the raising of funds *(kanjin)* for construction or maintenance of religious buildings; subscription list.
• One-act Kabuki play (one of the Kabuki-jūhachiban), produced by Namiki Gohei III in 1840, adapted from the Noh play *Ataka.* This danced performance accompanied by songs *(naga-uta)* tells the story of the flight of Minamoto no Yoshitsune and the faithful monk Benkei to the north to escape the hatred of his half-brother, Minamoto no Yoritomo. When they reach the Ataka Pass, they cannot produce passports. Benkei claims that they are monks traveling to raise funds for the construction of a temple. The guard, Togashi, is not fooled by this stratagem, but he lets them pass. Another guard is suspicious, so Benkei hits Yoshitsune as if he were his servant, reassuring the guard. Once they are past the gate, Benkei asks Yoshitsune's pardon, but Yoshitsune congratulates him on his presence of mind. This play was very successful and is still one of the most popular plays in the Kabuki repertoire.

Kanjō. Buddhist monk (1206–86) of the Tendaishū, appointed Ajari in 1268.
→ *See* BUNREI.
• Japanese name for Seoul, Korea. Also Keijō.

• **Kanjō-in.** In Japanese Buddhist iconography, a mudra (hand gesture, *Jap.: in*) of consecration, corresponding to the Sanskrit *abhisheka.* It is used in the baptism of the statue of a divinity and in ritual ablutions.

• **Kanjō-jōyaku.** See SEOUL, TREATY OF.

Kanjō-bugyō. Superintendents of finances during the Edo period, recruited from among the *hatamoto* vassals. *See* BUGYŌ.

• **Kanjō-gimmiyaku.** Official inspectors of the Edo shogunate, established in 1682, whose main responsibility was to assist the *kanjō-bugyō*. They were recruited from among the *hatamoto*.

Kanjō Shimpō. See ADACHI KENZŌ.

Kanju-ji. Buddhist temple founded as a *honzan* of the Shingon-shū in the south part of Heian-kyō by Fujiwara no Sadakata in 900, on the order of Emperor Daigo's mother. It was renamed Jōgaku-ji in 905. Also sometimes called Kajū-ji. See FUJIWARA NO YOSHIKADO.

Kankai. Painter (Araki Shun; *azana:* Kyokō; *gō:* Hōseigajin, Tatsuan, Kankai, 1786–1860), Ezaki Kansai's student in Edo.

Kankai ibun. "Account of the Tour of Oceans," written in 1807 by Ōtsuki Gentaku (1757–1827), based on accounts given by Japanese sailors shipwrecked on the coast of Siberia and held in Russia. They were repatriated in 1804 by N. P. Rozanov's delegation after touring the world on a Russian ship.

Kankan. Painter (Hayashi Hama; *gō:* Suiran, Kankan, 1770–99), Bunchō's wife and student in Edo. She painted mainly landscapes, flowers, and birds.

Kanke bunsō. Collection of poems and prose pieces written by Sugawara no Michizane and his father and grandfather, presented to Emperor Daigo in 900, and considered a perfect example of poetry and literature of his time.

Kanki. Era of Emperor Go-Horikawa: Mar. 1229–Apr. 1232. See NENGŌ.
→ See AKERA KANKŌ.

Kankō. See KANRIN MARU.

Kankō-ji. Site of ancient tombs in Osaka prefecture (Kana-cho, Minami Kawachi-gun), where one of the few *kofun* that had not been pillaged was uncovered in 1991. The *kofun,* square in shape with an entrance corridor, dating from the mid-sixth century, contained weapons, armor made of gold decorated with "Iranian" motifs, and much crystal and silver jewelry. The grave, which contained two persons, may have belonged to the chief of the Ōtomo clan.

Kankoku. "Nation of the Han," name sometimes used in Japan for Korea. The Japanese Resident

General in Korea (starting in 1905) bore the title Kankoku Tōkanfu, renamed Chōsen Sōtokufu in 1910. See CHŌSEN.

• **Kankoku Heigō.** Treaty signed on August 22, 1910, under which Korea became a Japanese colony. The name Kankoku was replaced by Chōsen, and most Korean towns and regions were given Japanese names. This military occupation of the peninsula lasted until 1945. Also called Nikkan Heigō ni Kansuru Jōyaku.

Kankū. Buddhist monk (882–972) of the Shingon-shū who was raised to the ranks of *sōjō, jōmu,* and *dai-sōzu.* Also sometimes written Kangū.

Kan'na. Era of Emperor Kazan: Apr. 985–Apr. 987. See NENGŌ.

Kannagara. In Shinto belief, spirit of nature and creativity, expression of the desire of the *kami* to reach perfection in all things. Also called Kamunagara.

• **Kannagara-kyō.** Subsect of the Shintō-taikyō, founded by Mizuno Fusa (b. 1882) in 1907 in Nagoya. It had about 12,000 followers. Also called Kamunagara-kyō.

Kanname Matsuri. Shinto festival of offerings to the emperor or to the great Ise Shrine, held at the beginning of the year. It started in 721 when Emperor Genshō made a donation to the *naigū* and *gegū* shrines of Ise. This ceremony now takes place on the 16th day of the 9th month in the *naigū,* and on the 17th day of the 10th month (October) in the *gegū.* Also called Kanname-sai and Shinjō-sai.

Kannichi. Bad-luck days on the old calendar, on which people should not work in the fields or marry:
  —First month: day of the Dragon
  —Second month: day of the Bull
  —Third month: day of the Dog
  —Fourth month: day of the Sheep
  —Fifth month: day of the Hare
  —Sixth month: day of the Rat
  —Seventh month: day of the Cock
  —Eighth month: day of the Horse
  —Ninth month: day of the Tiger
  —Tenth month: day of the Boar
  —Eleventh month: day of the Monkey
  —Twelfth month: day of the Snake
→ *See also* KICHIJITSU.

Kannin. Era of Emperor Go-Ichijō: Apr. 1017–Feb. 1021. *See* NENGŌ.

Kannō. Era of Emperor Sūko (Northern Court [Hokuchō]): Feb. 1350–Sept. 1352. Also written Kan-ō. *See* NENGŌ.

• **Kanno no Jōran.** Civil war of the Kannō era, provoked by the antagonism between shogun Ashikaga Takauji and his brother, Ashikaga Tadayoshi. The latter, opposed to the influence of General Kō no Moronao, who sat on the shogunal council, revolted in the name of the Southern Court (Nanchō) in 1350. Kō no Moronao was killed in 1351 and the two brothers seemed to make peace, but war soon started up again and Takauji expelled his brother to Kamakura. They finally reconciled, and Tadayoshi's death in 1352 put a final end to the conflict.

Kanno Hachirō. Painter and calligrapher (b. 1944). He studied in France; Kanno Keiun's brother.

• **Kanno Keiun.** Painter and calligrapher (Kanno Ichirō, b. 1925), from Tochigi prefecture. Member of the Dobunkai and founder of the Ichigenkai school. Kanno Hachirō's brother.

Kannō-ji. Buddhist temple in Nishimo-miya, on Mt. Kabuto, belonging to the Shingon-shū, founded in the ninth century and renovated about 1190. Also called Jinju-ji.

Kannon Bosatsu. The most popular bodhisattva in Japan, corresponding to the Sanskrit Avalokiteshvara. It is the very expression of divine compassion, the main character in the *Lotus Sutra,* to whom a chapter called *Kannon-kyō* is devoted. At first a male divinity, it is often considered female in Japan (and in China) and is invoked by women who want to have children (Koyasu Kannon). It is the perfect bodhisattva, "He Who Looks Down [on the World]," the "Protector of the World," the "Brilliant." It is also called "He Who Slakes Thirst" and "He Who Listens to Prayers." Said to have been born from Amida's right eye, it is "the voice and the light of the world." To it are attributed a great number of aspects and shapes, and its images have been the object of great pilgrimages in Japan, including the 33 Western Pilgrimages (Sanjūsan-sho) and 33 Eastern Pilgrimages. It is the most frequently portrayed bodhisattva, in both sculpture and painting, and has been ever since Buddhism was introduced to Japan. Its emblems are the lotus flower and the water vase. Its images bear a small effigy of Amida in the headdress. Among the most venerated forms in Japan are Shō Kannon Bosatsu, Kongō-hō Bosatsu, Jū-ichimen Kannon, Senju Kannon, Nyoirin Kannon, Batō Kannon, Juntei Kannon, Fukūkensaku Kannon, and Bikuchi Kannon. Also called Kanjizai Bosatsu, Kanzeon Bosatsu, Kōzeon Bosatsu. *Chin.*: Guanyin; *Kor.*: Gwan-se-eum, Gwaneum Bo-sal; *Viet.*: Quan Am. *See* SANJŪSAN ŌGESHIN, SANJŪSAN-SHO.

Kanno Suga. Politician (1881–1911) and socialist journalist. She lived with the anarchist Arahata Kanson and was arrested with him in 1908 during

Kannon Bosatsu

the Akahata Incident. She then was involved with Kōtoku Shūsui and imprisoned with him for revolutionary activities. Implicated with Kōtoku Shūsui in the plot to assassinate the emperor, she was convicted, with Kōtoku and ten other people, and hanged in 1911. She wrote a journal during her last months in prison, *Shide no michikusa* (Grass on the Road to Death), which was published in 1950. *See* KŌTOKU SHŪSUI.

Kannushi. General term for priests in Shinto shrines. At first elected by the people, the *kannushi* often transmitted their responsibility from father to son, giving rise to families *(shake)* attached to certain major shrines, such as the Nakatomi, Imube, Kamo, Shirakawa, Aso, and Yoshida. There are several ranks in the hierarchy of *kannushi:* the *gūji* is the head priest, sometimes assisted by a *gongūji* (vice-head priest) and a *negi* (or titular second-rank priest), assisted by a *gonnegi.* Ordinary priests are called *shuten* (formerly *kafuri*); novices, *shusshi.* Also called *shinshoku, shinkan, kannagi.*

Kanō-ha. School of painting, created around the mid-tenth century by Kanō Masanobu and Kanō Motonobu, which mixed the styles of *suiboku* and the Tosa school. In the seventeenth century, this school was divided into several branches that took the names of the districts in Edo where their painters had their studios: Nakabashi, Kajibashi, Kobiki-chō, Surugadai, and Hama-chō. The painters of Edo (called Edo-Kanō) were called *oku-eshi* and *omote-eshi,* according to the location of their studios. The others were called *machi-eshi* and *machi-Kanō.* Another Kanō school was founded in Kaga. The Kanō artists, sponsored by various governments, formed family studios where particular formulas and styles were transmitted from father to son (or adopted son). They produced a great variety of paintings, from fusuma and screen decorations *(byōbu)* to illustrations of *emakimono, kakemono,* votive plaques *(ema),* and fans. They also worked in all genres, from Yamato-e to Suiboku-ga and Kanga (Chinese school of painting with ink). Their tradition continued during the Meiji era with the works of Kanō Hōgai and Hashimoto Gahō. Also called Kanō-ryū.

• **Kanō Chikanobu.** Painter (1660–1728), Kanō Tsunenobu's son, of the Kobiki-chō branch.

• **Kanō Dōeki.** Painter (d. 1841), Kanō Dōhaku's son, of the Surugadai branch.

• **Kanō Dōhaku.** Painter (d. 1851), of the Surugadai branch.

• **Kanō Dōshun.** Painter (d. 1724), Kanō Dōun's son, of the Surugadai branch. His grandson, who had the same name (1747–97), followed his tradition. Kanō Gensan's father.

• **Kanō Dōun.** Painter (1625–94), Kanō Tan'yū's adoptive son. He belonged to the Surugadai branch. Also called Kanō Tōun.

• **Kanō Eigaku.** Painter (1790–1867), Kanō Eishun's son, of the Kanō school in Kyoto.

• **Kanō Eihaku.** Painter (1687–1764), Kanō Eikei's son, of the Kanō school in Kyoto.

• **Kanō Eijō.** Painter (1731–87), Kanō Eiryō's son. Kanō school of Kyoto.

• **Kanō Eikei.** Painter (1662–1702), Kanō Einō's son. Kanō school of Kyoto.

• **Kanō Einō.** *See* EINŌ.

• **Kanō Eiryō.** Painter (1710?–70), Kano Eihaku's son. Kanō school of Kyoto.

• **Kanō Eisen.** *See* EISEN I, EISEN II.

• **Kanō Eishin.** *See* ISEN.

• **Kanō Eishun.** Painter (1763?–1830), Kanō Eijō's son. Kanō school of Kyoto.

• **Kanō Eitoku.** *See* EITOKU I, EITOKU II.

• **Kanō Enshin.** *See* HŌGAI.

• **Kanō Fukunobu.** *See* TŌSHUN.

• **Kanō Gensan.** Painter (1695–1751), Kanō Dōshun's son. Surugadai branch.

• **Kanō Gen'ya.** *See* GEN'YA.

• **Kanō Harunobu.** *See* TŌEKI.

• **Kanō Heishirō.** *See* SANSETSU.

• **Kanō Hideyori.** *See* HIDEYORI.

• **Kanō Hōgai.** *See* HŌGAI.

- **Kanō Ienobu.** *See* NAONOBU.

- **Kanō Jugō.** *See* ICHIŌ.

- **Kanō Kazunobu.** *See* KAZUNOBU.

- **Kanō Kōi.** *See* KŌI.

- **Kanō Korenobu.** Painter and sculptor (1753–1808). He worked at the Kagura-den of the Tō-shōgū Shrine in Nikkō.

- **Kanō Kōshin.** *See* EISEN.

- **Kanō Kōya.** *See* KŌYA (HAKUHŌ).

- **Kanō Kuninobu.** Painter (early nineteenth century), Kanō Yasunobu's son, of the Nakabashi branch. *See* YASUNOBU.
  → *See* EITOKU.

- **Kanō Kyūhaku.** *See* KYŪHAKU.

- **Kanō Masanobu.** *See* MASANOBU, SHŌSEN-IN.

- **Kanō Masunobu.** *See* TŌUN.

- **Kanō Minenobu.** *See* MINENOBU.

- **Kanō Mitsunobu.** *See* MITSUNOBU.

- **Kanō Mitsunori.** *See* MITSUNORI.

- **Kanō Morinobu.** *See* TAN'YŪ.

- **Kanō Moritaka.** *See* TAMBI.

- **Kanō Motohide.** *See* MOTOHIDE.

- **Kanō Motonobu.** *See* MOTONOBU.

- **Kanō Munenobu.** *See* MUNENOBU.

- **Kanō Naganobu.** *See* KYŪHAKU.

- **Kanō Naizen.** Painter (1570–161), famous for his paintings of genre scenes and screens, notably "Festivals of Toyokuni," made on the request of Toyotomi Hideyori to mark the seventh anniversary of the death of Hideyoshi (whose posthumous name was Toyokuni Daimyōjin).

- **Kanō Natsuō.** *See* NATSUŌ.

- **Kanō Norinobu.** Painter (1692–1731), Kanō Morinobu's son, of the Nakabashi branch.

- **Kanō Ryōji.** *See* SAMBOKU.

- **Kanō Sanraku.** *See* SANRAKU.

- **Kanō Sansetsu.** *See* SANSETSU.

- **Kanō Seisen.** *See* SEISEN-IN.

- **Kanō Shōei.** *See* SHŌEI.

- **Kanō Shōsen.** *See* SHŌSEN-IN.

- **Kanō Shō-un.** *See* SHŌ-UN.

- **Kanō Suenobu.** *See* SŌSHŪ.

- **Kanō Sukenobu.** *See* EISEN II.

- **Kanō Takanobu.** *See* TAKANOBU.

- **Kanō Tambaku.** Painter (1770–1842), Kanō Tanrin's son. Kajibashi branch.

- **Kanō Tan'en.** Painter (1795–1866), Kanō Tanshin's son. Kajibashi branch.

- **Kanō Tanjō.** Painter (d. 1756), Kanō Tansen's son. Kajibashi branch.

- **Kanō Tanrin.** Painter (d. 1777), Kanō Tanjo's son. Kajibashi branch.

- **Kanō Tansen.** Painter (d. 1728), Kanō Tanshin's son. Kajibashi branch.

- **Kanō Tansetsu.** Painter (nineteenth century), Kanō Tangen's son. Kajibashi branch.

- **Kanō Tanshin.** Painter (1653–1718), son of Kanō Tan'yū, of the Kajibashi branch. One of his descendants (same branch) of the same name (1785–1835) was Kanō Tansen's father.

- **Kanō Tan'yū.** *See* TAN'YŪ.

- **Kanō Terunobu.** Painter (1717–63), Kanō Norinobu's son. Nakabashi branch.

- **Kanō Tessai.** *See* TESSAI.

- **Kanō Tōun.** *See* KANŌ DŌUN, TŌUN.

• **Kanō Tsunenobu.** *See* TSUNENOBU.

• **Kanō Yasunobu.** *See* YASUNOBU.

• **Kanō Yoshin.** *See* SEISEN-IN.

• **Kanō Yoshinobu.** *See* EINŌ, TOSHUN, YOSHI-NOBU.

Kanō Jigorō. Master of martial arts (1860–1938), born in Mikatse, Hyōgo province (Kobe) to a family of senior bureaucrats. He practiced ju-jutsu in his youth and created his first *dōjō* in the Eishō-ji temple in Tokyo in 1882. He then designed a new, danger-free sport analogous to ju-jutsu. In 1893, he was appointed dean of the teacher-training college in Tokyo. He went to Europe and gave demonstrations of his sport, which he called judo, in Marseilles. He was then sent on several official missions to introduce the principles of judo to other countries, and he won a medal at the Olympics in Sweden in 1916. He then created a judo college, the Kōdōkan, in Japan. In 1938, he was Japan's delegate to the International Olympic Committee for the Cairo Games, and he died that year. *See* JUDŌ, MARTIAL ARTS.

Kanrei. Title of the representative of the Muromachi shogunate responsible for assisting the shogun in his transactions with the *shugo* (provincial military governors). This position was traditionally filled by the Shiba, Hosokawa, and Hatakeyama families, called the "three representatives" (*sankanrei; see* SANKAN). One of them was assigned to Kamakura and titled Kantō-kanrei. Also called *shitsuji, kanryō.*

Kanreki. First year of a 60-year cycle, or first year of a new era *(Genka-reki).* The word means "renewal," "new beginning." It is also applied to the banquet celebrating a person's 61st birthday. People thus honored are said to be entering a new life, and they must wear a red garment (symbol of life and happiness). In former times, people turning 60 also had to stop working and give their goods and titles to their oldest son. They then became *inkyō,* "retirees." *See* CALENDAR.

Kanrin. Painter (Okada Kanrin, Okada Ren; *azana:* Shihō, Sekihō; *gō:* Tei-in, Kanrin, 1780–1849), Bunchō's student in Edo.

Kanrin Maru. Japanese 300-ton steamship, 43 m long and 7.8 m wide, built in Holland, the first to fly the Japanese flag (Hi no Maru) abroad. Commanded by Admiral Kimura Yoshitake and Captain Katsu Kaishū, it crossed the Pacific Ocean to the United States in 1860, carrying the members of the delegation charged with ratifying the 1858 Harris Treaty. *See also* HI NO MARU, MAN'EN KEMBEI SHISETSU.

Kanro. In the old Japanese calendar, a 15-day period (of the "cold dew") beginning about September 20. *Chin.:* Hanlu. *See* NIJŪSHI-SETSU.
• Japanese name for the divine ambrosia, called *amrita* in Sanskrit, often mentioned in Buddhist treatises.

Kanroku. Japanese name for a Korean Buddhist monk (Gwan Rok, sixth–seventh century) who arrived in Japan in 602 bearing various scientific treatises. He settled in the Gangō-ji temple and taught calendar techniques to many nobles. Following an unfortunate affair of murder in which the Buddhist monks were implicated, the position of rector *(sōjō)* was created and given to Kanroku in 624.

Kansai. Region between Osaka, Kobe, and Kyoto, without well-defined borders (as opposed to the term Kinki). It means "west of the gate," as opposed to Kantō ("east of the gate"). This region also sometimes includes Shikoku and Chūgoku. The term also applies to the language spoken in the region. *See also* KINAI, KINKI.
• (Kansai style). *See* YAMAMOTO KANSAI.
• Painter (Ishakawa Ryūsuke; *azana:* Kōjō; *gō:* Nikyo-gaishi, Shinten-ō, Rōkōdō, Kansai, eighteenth century) of the Nanga school (Bunjinga), Shummei's student. He painted landscapes and bamboo.
• Painter (Mori Kōshoku; *mei:* Naotarō; *azana:* Shiyō; *gō:* Kansai, 1814–94), Mori Tetsuzan's student in Kyoto. He painted mainly landscapes.
• Lacquer artist (1767–1835), who made *inrō* and netsuke.

• **Kansai International Airport.** New international airport in Osaka, built on reclaimed land in Osaka Bay. Construction began in 1986 and the airport opened in September 1994. It required the flattening of three hills and the moving of some 185 million m³ of earth. Its runways are 3.5 km long, and it is open 24 hours a day. It complements the Itami Airport.

Kan Sazan. Confucian professor and educator (Kan Shinsui, 1748–1827), founder of a school in

Bingo province. He was Rai San'yo's master and wrote poems that had a great influence on Japanese poets writing in Chinese. He wrote a famous collection of poems, *Kōyō sekiyō sonsha shi* (1812–23), and a prose work, *Fude no susabi.*

Kansei. Era of Emperor Kōkaku: Jan. 1789–Feb. 1801. *See* NENGŌ.
→ *See* KŌRIN.

• *Kansei chōshū-shokafu.* Compilation of genealogies of daimyo and *hatamoto* families, ordered by the shogunate during the Kansei era. This list, which complemented the *Kan'ei shoka keifuden,* was assembled in 1793 by Hotta Settsu no Kami (Hotta Masaatsu, 1758–1832) and Yashiro Hirokata, with the help of 50 contributors. The completed work, comprising 1,535 handwritten volumes, was published from 1799 to 1812.

• **Kansei-reki.** Official calendar, revised and published by Takahashi Sakuzaemon in 1797.

• **Kansei no Sansuke.** "The Three Great Confucian Scholars of the Kansei Era," who wrote commentaries on Shushi (*Chin.*: Zhu Xi) philosophy: Koga Seiri, Bitō Nishū, and Shibano Ritsuzan.

Kanshi. Chinese poetry style written in *kambun,* as opposed to the typically Japanese *waka* style. *See* KAMBUN.

Kanshin-ji. Buddhist monastery of the Shingon-shū sect, located in the town of Kawachi-Nagano (near Osaka), founded by Jitsue, a disciple of Kūkai, and another disciple, Shinshō, about 827. It was completely rebuilt in the mid-fourteenth century in an original style mixing elements of the *kara-yō* and *tenjiku-yō* styles. One tradition has it that Kusunoki Masashige is buried there, and it contains Emperor Go-Murakami's mausoleum. It houses many artistic treasures, notably a statue of a sitting Nyoirin Kannon, in painted wood, 109 cm high, dating to between 824 and 848.

Kanshitsu. Technique of sculpting with dry lacquer (*urushi*) consisting of covering a form with bands of hemp fabric impregnated with lacquer, similar to the Chinese *jiachu* technique. During the Nara period, the technique was also known as *soku.* When the lacquered bands cover a core of clay, it is called *dakkatsu kanshitsu;* applied to a core of wood, the technique is called *mokushin kanshitsu.* The core of wood is sometimes replaced by a lattice of wood

called *kago-zukuri* (basket style). The fine details of the sculptures are then made using metal wire coated with liquid lacquer mixed with wood shavings (*kokuso*). Once dry, the lacquer is painted. *See* LACQUER, URUSHI.

• **Kanshitsu Genkitsu.** *See* SAN'YŌ.

• **Kanshitsukan.** Caskets made of *kanshitsu* lacquer, sometimes used during the *kofun* period. Also called *kyōchokan.*

Kanshō. Era of Emperor Go-Hanazono: Dec. 1460–Feb. 1466. *See* NENGŌ.

Kansu-bon. Texts or paintings mounted on a horizontal scroll (*makimono* or *emakimono*) made of silk or paper, which can be rolled on a cylinder (made of wood, metal or, sometimes, of ivory) called *jiku.* Its envelope is called *hyōshi.* Also called *kensu-bon. See also* KAKEMONO.

Kantan. Title of a Noh play: a young man seeking Truth goes to sleep on a magical pillow and then goes home, having acquired enlightenment.

Kantei. Painter (*mei:* Nara Hōgen, late fifteenth century) of the Muromachi *suiboku* school.

Kantei-ryū. Style of calligraphy invented in 1799 by Ozakiya Kanroku and used mainly in theater posters. *Banzuke,* or Kabuki posters, are written in this style.

Kantei Shōnin. Buddhist monk, founder of the Kurama-dera temple in 770.

Kantō. Part of the Tanabata Festival in the city of Akita, held August 5–7, during which young people carry long poles on their shoulders from which 24 or 48 paper lanterns (*kantō*) hang, which they try to keep in balance as they dance and sing.

Kantō. Region in eastern Honshu comprising Tokyo, Chiba, Kanagawa, Saitama, Gumma, Ibaraki, and Tochigi prefectures. The Kantō plain, the largest in Japan, has an area of 32,389 km^2 and a population of more than 35 million. Its coastal plain (Kantō-heya) on the Pacific Ocean has an area of about 15,000 km^2; Tokyo, Yokohama, Kawasaki, and other cities are located on the plain, and various types of crops are cultivated there. The mountainous part (Kantō-sanchi) to the west has a north–south range 130 km in length; its highest peaks are

Kimpusan (2,595 m) and Kokushigatake (2,592 m). The soil of this region comprises four thick layers of volcanic ash dating from 300,000 to 30,000 years ago, covered by a layer of humus, about 1 m deep, that formed over the last 10,000 years.

Kantō began to be developed only at the beginning of the Kamakura period (1185–1333). Its name, "east of the gate," indicates that it was considered distinct from the Kansai, from which it was separated by the Osaka (Ōtsu, Shiga prefecture) "gate" *(sekisho),* which was relocated to Hakone during the Edo period. It includes the major Keihin, Keiyō, and Kashima industrial zones *(see* KEIHIN, KEIYŌ, KASHIMA). A powerful earthquake was centered there in September 1923.

• **Kantō-gun.** *See* GUANDONG.

• **Kantō-kanrei.** Governor-general of Kantō during the Muromachi shogunate, located in Kamakura. Also called Kantō-kanryō. This position was held by members of the Uesugi family from 1363 to the late sixteenth century. *See* KANREI, KUBŌ.

Kan-tō. Political party founded in the early nineteenth century to support the Edo shogunate and promote liberalization of trade with foreign countries. It was opposed to the Sei-tō.
• Type of cotton fabric decorated with irregular lines imitating watered silk, made in Kanto.

Kantō Jidōsha Kōgyō. Automobile manufacturer, specializing in production of buses, founded in 1946 and affiliated with Toyota. It also produces small sailboats and motorboats. Head office in Yokosuka (Kanagawa prefecture).

Kantokoro. Estates conceded by the emperor to Shinto shrines for their subsistence. Also called *jinryō, kamutokoro, shinryō.*

Kantoku. Era of Emperor Go-Shujaku: Nov. 1044–Apr. 1046. *See* NENGŌ.
• Japanese title for Christian bishops.

Kantori-konkō-kyō. Subsect of the Shintō-taikyō, founded by Kantori Shige'emon (1823–89); about 10,000 followers.

Kan U. Japanese name for a famous Chinese general (Guan Yü, d. ca. 219), divinized as a protector of warriors in China. His military exploits were the subject of many works by Japanese painters inspired by Chinese techniques of painting with ink *(sumi-e)* during the Edo period.

Kanyō-dō. In Buddhist temples, rooms reserved for ablutions with holy water.

Kanyō-kyū. Title of a Noh play: a Chinese emperor, captured by two men from an enemy state, charms them with music played by his concubines, then kills them.

Kanzan. Painter (Shimomura Seizaburō, 1873–1930); studied with Kanō Hōgai and Hashimoto Gahō. Born in Wakayama prefecture to a family of Noh actors, he studied in England from 1903 to 1905, then helped reorganize the Japan Fine Arts Academy (Nihon Bijutsu-in). He was appointed an Artist for the Imperial Household (Teishitsu Gigei-in) in 1917. His works show influences of the Kanō and Rimpa schools and Western techniques.

Kanzan and Jittoku. Two legendary poets of the Tang era in China (Hanshan and Shide), who were said to have lived on Mt. Tiantai and whose life was often portrayed by Japanese painters using the *sumi-e* technique, since they symbolized the spirit of Zen. They are sometimes portrayed in the company of a monk who was their master, Bukan *(Chin.:* Fenggan), who traveled on the back of a tiger.

Kanzashi. Long pins (sometimes two-pronged) made of wood or finely wrought metal, used by nobles and warriors to keep their hats *(eboshi, kammuri)* on, and by women of the upper classes to keep their hairstyle in place. Some, made of steel, could also be used as a weapon. Formerly called *kazashi. See* KŌGAI, MAGE.

Kanze-ryū. Name of one of the five major schools of lead actors *(shite)* in Noh theater, founded by Kan'ami in the fourteenth century. The most famous actors and writers of this family school *(ryū)* were:
—Kanze Motokiyo. *See* ZE-AMI.
—Kanze Kiyotsugu. *See* KAN'AMI KIYOTSUGU.
—Kanze Motomasa (Jūrō, ca. 1394–1432), Zeami's son. He wrote several plays, including *Yoroboshi* and *Sumida-gawa.*
—Kanze Motoshige On-ami (1398–1467), Zeami's nephew.
—Kanze Masamori (d. 1501).
—Kanze (Kojirō) Nobumitsu (1435–1516), Onami's son. His most famous plays are *Funa Benkei,*

Dōjō-ji, Momijigari, and *Rashōmon.* Also known as Kanze Shōjirō.

　—Kanze (Yajirō) Nobutomo (1490–1541), On'ami's grandson.
　—Kanze Mototada (1509–83).
　—Kanze Kokuketsu (d. 1626).
　—Kanze Motoaki (1722–74).
　—Kanze Kiyotada (1837–88).
　—Kanze Yoshiyuki (1903–78).
　—Kanze Motomasa II (b. 1930), the twenty-fifth to bear the name.
Also called Kanze-tayū. *See* KOMPARU, NOH.

Kao. "Face," term used in many expressions, meaning approximately "reputation," "dignity." "Losing face" is said *memboku.* Also *men.*

Kaō. Era of Emperor Takakura: Apr. 1169–Apr. 1171. *See* NENGŌ.
　• Buddhist monk (fourteenth century) and painter of the Muromachi *suiboku* school.
　• Monograms derived from signatures and used by many important people to sign private or official acts at the beginning of the Heian period. During the Kamakura period, *kaō* were used to guarantee the authenticity of documents and were often placed beside the actual signature. Also called *kakihan.*
→ *See* CHINNEN.

Kaomise. Performances of Kabuki plays in Kyoto every December, during which all actors who will perform in the coming year are introduced and their names are posted on the facade of the Minamiza Theater.

Ka-ō Ninga. Painter (fourteenth century) whose name is not known, perhaps the Zen monk Kaō Sōnen (d. 1345) of the Kennin-ji temple in Kyoto. He painted in the Muromachi *suiboku* style.

　• **Kaō Sōnen.** *See* KA-Ō NINGA.

Kappa. Mythical character from Japanese folklore (particularly in Kyushu) and water genies, said to be the size of a three- or four-year-old child, with webbed feet and hands, a greenish body covered with scales, shaggy hair, and a skull in the form of a bowl containing water. If the water spills, the *kappa*'s powers disappear because this is its "life water." Depending on the region, *kappa* are seen as friendly or very cruel. They are held responsible for most drownings of children. But they can also show their gratitude to those who save their lives. In some regions, such as Tsugaru, they are thought to be water *kami* and are worshiped. Formerly called *mizuchi.*
→ *See* SUIJIN.

Kappo-zuri. Printing with stencils, sometimes used by ukiyo-e artists.

Kara. Former name for Korea, and for everything that came from China via the Korean Peninsula. This name was once also applied to everything from the Tang (*Jap.:* Tō) dynasty of China.

　• **Karabitsu.** Chests with feet, used to store clothes, once imported from China.

　• *Kara-bune emaki.* Name of two illustrated scrolls (*emakimono*) describing Chinese boats, dating from the seventeenth century.

　• *Kara-bune hanashi ima no kokusen'ya.* "Today's Koxinga, Story of a Chinese Boat," Kabuki play written by Chikamatsu Monzaemon in 1727 and the sequel to *Kokusen'ya kassen* and *Kokusen'ya go-nichi kassen,* by the same author.

　• **Kara-e.** General term for Japanese paintings of Chinese inspiration, as opposed to typically Japanese painting, or Yamato-e, of the Heian period. Works of the Tang period are called *kara-e,* while those from (or inspired by) the Song and Yuan periods are called, more specifically, *kanga-e.*

　• **Kara-ginu.** Short Chinese-style tunic, once worn by noblewomen over a *uwagi. See* JŪNI-HITOE.

　• **Kara-hafu.** Type of convex saddleback roof, imported from China in the sixteenth century and typical of Momoyama style. It is generally reserved for roofs over gates or entrances to buildings. However, there are rare examples of this type of roof dating back to the ninth and tenth centuries. Gates with a *kara-hafu* roof are called *kara-mon* (Chinese gates).

　• **Kara-kami.** *See* FUSUMA.

　• **Kara-kane.** Chinese metal alloy once used for objects (*dōgu*)—bells and statues—used in Buddhist worship. It is composed of 71–89% copper, 2–8% tin, and 5–15% lead.

　• **Kara-kasa.** Flexible parasols introduced from China in the late sixteenth century; previous parasols had been rigid. There are several types: *higasa* (parasol), *amagasa* (umbrella), *naga-e* (with a long handle). Also called *tsumaori-gasa, sashigasa,* *tegasa.* Western-style umbrellas are called *kōmori-gasa* (bat-shaped).

• **Kara-ko.** Type of doll portraying a boy dressed in Chinese style.

• **Karakuri-ningyō.** Type of mechanical puppet made in Nagoya.

• **Kara-kusa.** "Chinese grass," foliage decoration used in Japanese art, probably imported from central Asia in the seventh century.

• **Kara-minato.** "Chinese port," former name for the port of Bōnotsu, in Kyushu.

• **Kara-mon.** *See* KARA-HAFU.

• *Kara-monogatari.* "Chinese tales," anonymous work composed of 27 tales inspired by Chinese legends, and sprinkled with Japanese poems, written in the mid-Kamakura period.

• **Kara-mushi.** "Chinese grass," plant similar to hemp used in Japan to dye fabrics.

• **Kara-nishiki.** Type of brocade imported from Korea in the fifteenth century.

• **Kara-ori.** Type of fabric decorated with flowers and birds embroidered in silver, gold, and colored cotton thread, imported from Korea. Also called *Hakata-ori, watanishiki.*

• **Kara-shishi.** "Lion of China," one of the two mythical guardian animals often portrayed in sculpture at the entrance to Buddhist temples and Shinto shrines. It always has an open mouth, sometimes holding a ball. It symbolizes expressed power. Its opposite is the Koma-inu ("Dog of Korea"), with a closed mouth, symbolizing latent power. *See* A-UN, NI-Ō.

• **Kara-tachi.** Straight Chinese-style sword, generally richly decorated, carried by nobles and emperors in the Nara period. Some were imported from China.

• **Kara-yō.** "Chinese style" of architecture introduced to Japan by the Zen monk Eisai in Kamakura in the twelfth century and used mainly in construction of Zen buildings. Often combined with the *wa-yō* style, it has steeper roofs, more accentuated roof corners, more compactly shaped *to-kyō* (called *tsu-megumi*), fan-shaped joists, ends of *hijiki* shaped in quarter-circles, *kagami-tenjō* ceilings, and cylindrical pillars with bases in stone or wood. Some of the beams linking the pillars of the *mokoshi* to those of the main structure are curved and are called *ebi-koryō* (crab-shaped). The doors are of the *san-kara* (or *kara-dō*) type, the tops of the windows are curved, and the floors are usually paved with square stones laid in diagonals. *See* ARCHITECTURE, TENJI-KU-YŌ, WA-YŌ.

• **Karayuki-san.** "Women who go to China," a term for Japanese women who went to Korea, Manchuria, China, Southeast Asia, and even the United States to work as prostitutes at the time of the Russo-Japanese War (1904–05). It is estimated that there were more than 100,000 of them between 1868 and 1920; they were sold by their parents or went abroad more or less voluntarily, and sent money home to their families. After the Manchuria Incident (1931), many of the *karayuki-san* who had been in Korea were incorporated into the army, where they served as prostitutes *(ianfu)* for Japanese troops alongside growing numbers of Korean women. This custom disappeared after the Second World War.

• **Karazuri.** Technique of making ukiyo-e prints reproducing, in relief, the texture of wood blocks used for printing, with or without ink.

Karafuto. Japanese name for the island of Sakhalin, especially the southern part (south of 50°

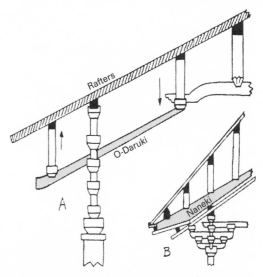

Roof-support systems. A. Cantilevered. B. Double joists (*kara-yō* style)

north latitude), which was occupied by Japan from 1905 (Treaty of Portsmouth) to 1946.

• **Karafuto-Chishima Kōkan Jōyaku.** "Treaty of St. Petersburg," signed between Japan and Russia in St. Petersburg on May 7, 1875, defining the border between Japanese and Russian possessions on Sakhalin and the Kuril Islands (Chishima Rettō). In the treaty, Japan abandoned its rights to Sakhalin in exchange for sovereignty over the Kuril Islands and fishing rights in the Sea of Okhotsk. The treaty was canceled at the end of the Russo-Japanese War in 1905.

Karagoromo Kisshū. Kyōka poet (Kojima Gen'nosuke, 1743–1802), born in Edo into a samurai family. With friends Ōta Nampo and Akera Kankō, he formed a group of humorist-poets. His works were collected in two anthologies, *Kyōka wakabashū* (1783) and *Suichikushū* (1802). Also called simply Kisshū.

Karai Senryū. Poet (Karai Hachiemon, 1718–90), born in Edo. He created a new poetic genre called *senryū*, derived from *haikai*. He collected a large number of poems of this genre by various authors that he included in a series of anthologies, published starting in 1765, under the titles *Haifū yamagidaru* and *Senryūhyō manku-awase*.

Kara Jūrō. Actor and playwright (Otsuru Yoshihide, b. 1941) who created a sort of strolling theater (Jōkyō Gekijō) that performed under a red tent; the goal was to make theater accessible to a very large public. With his wife (a Korean, Yi Yŏng-son, *Jap.:* Ri Reisen), he performed his own humorous plays, featuring many plays on words: *Giri ninjō iroha nihoheto-hen* (List of Obligations Contrary to Sentiments, 1967), *Aribaba* (Ali Baba, 1967), *Kyūketsu ki* (The Vampire Princess, 1971), *Nito monogatari* (Tale of Two Towns, 1972), *Bengaru no tora* (The Bengal Tiger, 1973), and others. He also made movies and wrote popular songs.

Karako iseki. Archeological site typical of the Yayoi period (300 BC–AD 300), located near the small town of Kashiwabara in Nara prefecture, excavated in 1936. It contained a large amount of pottery, classified into five types, that served as standards for pottery from other sites. Also discovered there were objects and agricultural tools made of wood, stone, and bone, as well as molds used to cast *dōtaku*. It comprised more than 100 pits from houses and silos. Study of the site revealed much about society in the Yayoi period.

Karaoke. "Empty orchestra," recordings of songs without the voices, used to accompany amateur singers. Starting in 1970, it became a fad in many public venues to encourage customers to sing using *karaoke* accompaniment. Many homes also have such tapes, which are used on festive occasions for entertainment, with people singing classical or pop tunes. The *karaoke* fad spread to the United States, and hit Europe in the 1990s.

Karasumaru Mitsuhiro. *Waka* poet and calligrapher (1579–1638), member of the Nijō school, who studied with his father-in-law, Hosokawa Yūsai. In his works—*Jiteiki* (ca. 1602) and *Kōyō wakashū* (published after his death, in 1669)—he combined the classicism of the Nijō school with the freedom of expression of Zen poets.

Karate. "Empty hands," a martial-arts *(budō)* fighting method based on old forms of self-defense called Okinawa-te and the Chinese art of *kempō*. *Karate* (at the time written with *kanji* characters meaning "Chinese hands") was developed in Okinawa in the fifteenth century to fight Japanese troops, who had disarmed the population, more effectively. The technique consists mainly of delivering violent blows *(atemi)* to the adversary's vital organs in order to neutralize him. Unlike *judō* and related sports, in *karate* there is never contact with the adversary. It is training for real combat that can be fatal if the blows are landed; as a sport, however, it is not dangerous and is used to help people conquer their fear of being assaulted. However, one form of *karate*, created in the United States and called "full contact," uses real blows, and the fighters wear protective gear. Other forms of *karate* use weapons such as the *nunchaku*, but this cannot be called an art of "empty hands." For individual training, cushions made of pressed straw *(makiwara)* or other materials are used to strengthen the hands and feet. One form of training consists of breaking wooden planks or bricks with the hands, feet, or head. It is very spectacular and an excellent preparation for street fighting.

The creator of *karate*, Funakoshi Gichin (1869–1957) codified the movements of this martial art by unifying the various styles of Okinawa-te. It then became a sport, divided into various schools, including Shōtōkan, Wadō-ryū, Sankukai, Gojū-ryū, and Shitō-ryū. National and international competitions take place throughout the world; competitors are divided into weight classes similar to those for *judō*. Competitions for women began in 1981. The adversaries (called *karateka*) wear a specific training costume called *keikogi* or *karategi*. There are about 15 million *karate* practitioners throughout the world.

• **Karateka.** Karate practitioner.

Karatsu. Town in Saga prefecture (Kyushu) on Karatsu Bay, and port once used for trade with Korea. During the Meiji era, it was a major port for shipping charcoal from the nearby mines. Ruins of a castle dating from 1602. *Pop.*: 80,000.
• Chinese calligraphy style, popular during the Edo period, imported by the Zen Buddhist (Ōbakushū) monk Ingen in the early seventeenth century, and contrasted with the typically Japanese *wa-yo* (Ō-ie-ryū) style. Followers of this style included Arai Hakuseki, Ogyū Sorei, and other well-known calligraphers.

• **Karatsu-yaki.** General term for pottery and ceramics produced in Hizen province (Saga prefecture) in some 100 high-temperature kilns starting in 1550. Although they were of very diverse styles, these ceramics can be classified into three main groups: *muji-karatsu* (simply varnished), *chōsen-karatsu* (Korean type, with an opaque dark-brown or black glaze), and *e-karatsu* (with decorations under a whitish translucent glaze). The oldest pieces (*ko-karatsu*) were produced mainly for the tea ceremony (*chanoyu*). The various pottery types from the Karatsu region are known by many names that describe the quality of the glaze, the color, or the decorations. Some kilns are still active, notably those of Nakazato Tarōemon XII (Muan, b. 1895) and his son, Nakazato Tarōemon XIII (b. 1923), who produce traditional-style ceramics.

Kare-sansui. "Dry landscape," garden style in Zen monasteries, developed during the Muromachi period and in use until the early Edo period, composed mainly of sand, gravel, and stones. The most famous are those at the Ryōan-ji and Daitoku-ji (Daisen-in) temples in Kyoto. Also called *kara-sansui, ko-senzui.*

Kari. Former unit of area, worth about one fifth of a *tan* or three *bu* (three *tsubo*), or about 11 m².

Kari-ginu. "Hunting costume," everyday coat for imperial bureaucrats and warriors until 1868. It had a round collar, long sleeves, and cuffs closed with cords. Also called *hōi, karigoromo.*

Karikura. Local lords' hunting preserves. Hunting was banned in the Edo period, and these lands were used for military exercises. Also called *takasuyama, kakurayama.*

Karimata. Former term for arrows with a fork-shaped head. There were many types. *See* YA.

Karō. During the Edo period, title held by the daimyo's most senior bureaucrats. They had the same functions as the *rōjū* in the shogunate. Also called *karei, toshiyori.*

Karoku. Era of Emperor Go-Horikawa: Apr. 1225–Dec. 1227. *See* NENGŌ.

Karōshi. "Killed by overwork," a modern concept designating people who fall seriously ill or even die following exhausting work forced on them by the company for which they work, usually meaning overtime totaling more than 20 hours per month.

Karuizawa. Town in Nagano prefecture, on the southern slope of the Asama volcano, a former waystation in the Edo period. It was developed, mainly in the late nineteenth century, as a health resort (it is located on a forested plateau about 1,000 m in altitude), and is now mainly residential during the warm season. A nearby lava field called Onioshidashi, the result of an eruption of Asama-yama in 1773, is a major tourist attraction. *Pop.*: 15,000.

Karu no Ōji. Emperor Ankō's older brother, assassinated by Ankō in 454. Also called Kinashikaru-ōji.
→ *See* MOMMU TENNŌ.

Karuta. Playing cards, derived from the Portuguese word *carta*. Card games were introduced to Japan by the Portuguese in the early sixteenth century, and they spread so rapidly that the Tokugawa shogunate banned card and betting games in the early seventeenth century. There are currently various sorts of cards; among the most popular are *hanafuda* (*hana-awase*), *uta-garata*, and *irohagaruta*. European-style card games are called *torampu*.

Karyaku. Era of Emperor Go-Daigo: Apr. 1326–Aug. 1329. Also called Kareki. *See* NENGŌ.

Karyōbin. Type of Bugaku dance of the Rinyūgaku genre, performed by four boys costumed as birds *(karyōbinga)* accompanied by Gagaku melodies.

• **Karyōbinga.** Legendary birds of Buddhist folklore, with melodious voices, corresponding to the Kalavinka of Indian legend.

Kasa. General term for hats worn by peasants, usually made of braided straw or bamboo. This term is also used for umbrellas and parasols *(see* KARA-KASA).

• **Kasagake.** "Hanging hat," a sport or military training exercise for mounted samurai in the Kamakura period, consisting of shooting arrows at a target (a hat hung between two posts) as they passed at full gallop. This target was generally at a distance of ten unstrung bows (about 23 m). It was sometimes made of a circular piece of wood covered with leather, about 50 cm in diameter; the archers used arrows with a buttoned, whistling head called *kaburaya*. Also called *kasakake. See also* INU-OI-MONO, YABUSAME.

• **Kasa Jizō.** "Jizō with a Bamboo Hat," a character in a folk tale. An old man and his wife make bamboo hats *(kasa)* to sell at the market and thus enable them to buy rice to celebrate the New Year. As they travel, they find statues of Jizō Bosatsu covered with snow beside the road, and they shelter them with some of their hats. When they return home, they find a large pile of rice cakes at their door.

• **Kasayaki.** Major festival that takes place every May 28 at the Jozen-ji temple near Odawara, to celebrate the vengeance of the Soga brothers, during which old hats and parasols donated by actors and innkeepers are burned. Children organize and perform sumo shows. *See* SOGA SUKENARI.

Kasa. Poet (eighth century), 29 of whose poems are included in the *Man'yōshū,* all dedicated to Otomo Yakamochi. She may have been related to Kasa no Kamamura, and her name may have been Kasa no Iratsume.

• **Kasa no Kanamura.** Poet (active ca. 715–33) of the Nara imperial court, 45 of whose poems (11 *chōka* and 34 *tanka*) are included in the *Man'yō-shū.* He also wrote elegies upon the death of imperial princes. Nothing is known about his life; he may have been related to the poet Kasa.

Kasagi. Granitic mountain *(alt.:* 289 m) near Kyoto, overlooking the valley of the Kizu-gawa river. On it is a famous Buddhist temple, the Kasagi-dera (date unknown), in which enormous blocks of granite are sculpted with bas-reliefs of Buddhist images, probably dating from the late Nara period (late eighth century). During the Heian period, it became an active center for the propagation of faith in Miroku *(Skt.:* Maitreya) related to beliefs in "the final period of the Good [Buddhist] Law" *(mappō).* Emperor Go-Daigo took refuge there in 1331 and was besieged by the troops of the Kamakura *bakufu,* who burned the buildings. Rebuilt in 1381, it was again destroyed by fire in 1398. Only a few chapels and a *shōrō* (belltower) remain.
→ *See* TORII.

Kasai. Town in Hyōgo prefecture, once famous for its tatami and cotton factories *(banshū-ori).* Famous temples, such as the Ichijō-ji (founded in the seventh century), and a group of Gohyaku-Rakan are located there. Pop.: 50,000.

Kasai Kiyoshige. Warrior (thirteenth century) of the Taira family, governor of Mutsu province (northern Honshu). He became a Buddhist monk with the name Iki-nyūdo in 1215.

Kasai Zenzō. Writer and journalist (1887–1928) with a personal and realistic style, who described poverty, illness, and loneliness in his novels, among them *Kanashiki chichi* (1912), *Akuma* (1912), *Kohan shuki* (Memories of the Lakeshore, 1924), *Kootsurete* (With a Child).

Kasama. Town in Ibaraki prefecture, castle town and waystation during the Edo period, then a shrine town (Inari-jinja) during the Meiji era. Major center of production of utilitarian ceramics since 1770. Also, a term for the barrels used for locally produced *sake.* Pop.: 35,000.

Kasamaro. Warrior (active ca. 700–after 723) and poet. He had the Kiso-kaidō route built in 724 and the Kanzeon-ji temple constructed in Kyushu in 723. He became a Buddhist monk in 721 with the name Manzei.

Kasane no enkon. "The Ghost of Kasane." Kasane was a seventeenth-century woman who was accused of having drowned her husband. Her story became the subject of legend and of Kabuki plays, and she was often portrayed in ukiyo-e prints.

Kasane no irome. During the Heian period, a series of robes *(kimono)* with hems of different colors according to the rules governing the ranks of those who wore them. *See* JŪNI-HITOE.

Kasei. "Holy poet," a title once given to the best poets, particularly those whose works appeared in the *Man'yōshū. See also* KASEN.
→ *See* BONCHŌ.

Kasen. "Immortal poets" of *waka* poems. There were various famous groups, such as the "Six Poetic Geniuses" (Rokkasen), the "Thirty-Six Poetic Geniuses" (Sanjūrokkasen), and others. *See* KASEI, ROKKASEN, SANJŪROKKASEN.
• Chinese coins about 3 cm in diameter, cast in bronze during the Wang Mang period (8–22 AD) and found in Japan in some sites from the Yayoi period; their presence enabled these sites to be dated.

• **Kasen-e.** "Paintings of the immortal poets," idealized portraits of the *kasen* poets, often imaginary, typical of Yamato-e artists of the Kamakura and Muromachi periods. These paintings were the subject of *emakimono, kakemono,* and albums. This genre also included illustrated cards based on the *Hyakunin-isshū. See* SANJŪROKKASEN.

Kasha. Sort of incense holder, round with three short feet, often used during ceremonies of Esoteric Buddhism *(mikkyō).*

Kashiage. During the Heian and Kamakura periods, usurers who lent to local lords at high interest rates. When the lords were not able to repay their loans, the *kashiage* accepted payment in rights to their debtors' estates. The Kamakura *bakufu* was forced to ban this practice in order to preserve the heritage of its vassals. The word fell into disuse in the fifteenth century and was replaced by *dosō* ("usury, usurer").

Kashihara. City in Nara prefecture, the site where, according to legend, Emperor Jimmu Tennō was enthroned as emperor, and where the ancient capital of Yamato, Fujiwara-kyō, was located. *Pop.:* 110,000. Also called Kashiwara.

• **Kashihara-jingū.** Shinto shrine in Kashihara, dedicated to the spirits of Emperor Jimmu Tennō and his wife, Himetatarai Suzu-hime no Mikoto. It was built in 1889 using the remains of the former imperial palace *(gosho)* of Kyoto and renovated in 1940 (2,600th anniversary of Jimmu Tennō's acces-

sion to the throne). Annual festival on February 11, called Kenkoku Kinembi, formerly Kigensetsu. Also called Kashiwara-jingū.

Kashii no Miya. Shinto shrine in Fukuoka (Kyushu), former imperial mausoleum transformed in the eleventh century and dedicated to the spirits of Empress Jingū Kōgō and Emperor Chūai. It was built in the Kashii-*zukuri* style during the Edo period. Annual festival on October 29. *See* JINGŪ-KŌGŌ.

Kashiko-dokoro. Site of the imperial palace where the sacred mirror *(yata no kagami),* one of the three symbols of imperial power, was kept, guarded by women who worked inside the palace, the *naishi-dokoro.* This building was destroyed by successive fires in 960, 1005, and 1040, and the mirror was damaged. When the emperor moved to Tokyo in 1869, a new *kashiko-dokoro* was built to house the relic.

Kashima-jingū. Shinto shrine in Kashimi, Ibaraki prefecture, dedicated to the *kami* Takemikazuchi, a local warrior divinity of ancient origin venerated by samurai. This *kami* later became one of the tutelary divinities of the Fujiwara clan, which installed it in the Kasuga-jinja beside the Futsunushi *kami.* On the grounds of this famous shrine live many sacred deer *(shika).* Annual festival on September 1. Every 12 years, on September 2, the shrine's priests go down the Tone-gawa river, escorting the *mikoshi* of the *kami* to the Katori shrine. An officiating priest, called Kashima no kotobure, gives oracles during New Year ceremonies. *See* KANAME-ISHI, KASUGA-TAISHA, KATORI-JINGŪ.

Kashira. Pommel of a sword or épée guard. Also called *kabutogane. See* KATANA, TSUKA.

• **Kashiradate.** *See* KABUTO.

• **Kashira-e.** *See* SAYA.

• **Kashira-nuki.** *See* MADO.

Kashiwabara. Town in Nara prefecture, site of the ancient capital of Yamato under the reigns of Temmu Tennō and Kammu Tennō. Nearby are the remains of the Yayoi village Karako. Also called Kashihabara.

• **Kashiwabara-jingū.** *See* UNEBI-YAMA.

• **Kashiwabara Tennō.** *See* KAMMU TENNŌ.

Kashiwabara Hyōzō. Writer (1933–72), born in Chiba prefecture. His novel *Tokuyama Michisuke no kikyō* (The Return of Tokuyama Michisuke, 1967) won the Akutagawa Prize. Most of his other books are autobiographical: *Nagai michi* (The Long Road, 1969), *Berurin hyōhaku* (Wandering in Berlin, 1972).

Kashiwade. Form of salutation used by Shinto followers to draw the attention of the *kami,* made by clapping the hands several times and sliding them lightly against each other while bowing and reciting the appropriate invocation.

• **Kashiwade no Ōmi-tsukasa.** Bureaucrat responsible for preparing the imperial family's meals. This position traditionally fell to the Ōtomo family.

Kashiwagi Gien. Protestant philosopher (Kashiwaki Yoshimaru, 1860–1938), born in Niigata prefecture, whose thought was influenced by Niijima Jō. A dedicated pacifist, he opposed the Russo-Japanese War in his monthly magazine *Jōmō Kyōkai Geppo* (published 1898–1936) and supported the strikers at the Ashio Mines in 1907.

Kashiwazaki. Title of a Noh play: the servant of a man who dies on his way to Kamakura takes a letter from the son informing him that he intends to become a Buddhist monk. His mother goes in search of the son and finally finds him in the Zenkō-ji temple.

Kashiyama. Industrial textile firm founded in 1947, using the brand name "Onward," specializing in uniforms. It also makes other sorts of clothing and has subsidiaries in Paris, Rome, and New York. Head office in Tokyo.

Kashō. Era of Emperor Nimmyō: June 848–Apr. 851. *See* NENGŌ.
• Era of Emperor Horikawa: Apr. 1106–Aug. 1108. *See* NENGŌ.
→ *See* OSHŌ.

Kasho. A pass allowing its bearer to go through the gates *(sekisho)* between the provinces without paying tolls. Called *tegata* during the Edo period.

• **Kasho-bune.** In the Edo period, trade ships with the official right to trade between Kyoto and Osaka on the Yodo-gawa river. Also called *kasho-sen.*

Kashū. Poetry anthologies compiled by poets not commissioned by the imperial authority (see CHOKUSEN WAKA-SHŪ). The *Man'yōshū* is in this category.

Kasō. Funerary custom of cremating the body, adopted by Buddhists and transmitted from China and Korea to Japan in the late seventh century. The first person in Japan to be cremated was the Buddhist monk Dōshō in 700, and Empress Jitō was cremated in 702, thus ending the custom of burying the deceased in large tombs *(kofun),* which had been practiced since the fourth century. In the Edo period, many shogun and daimyo preferred to be buried, and the practice of cremation was banned for the common people. A law passed in 1897 ordered cremation to be used, however, to keep disease from spreading. It is now practiced throughout Japan, except for a few locations. Only emperors, as the Shinto high priests, are buried. *See* FUNERALS, TAISŌ.
• According to Chinese laws of geomancy, arrangement of houses and buildings following precise rules on orientation, avoiding the *kimon,* or inauspicious direction (the northeast). *See* OMMYŌDŌ.

Kasori kaizuka. Prehistoric site in Kasori (Chiba prefecture), with two circular shell mounds *(kaizuka)* covering an area of about 400 × 200 m, from the middle and late Jōmon periods (ca. 3500–ca. 1000 BC). Excavations have uncovered vestiges of semi-buried cabins, tombs (bodies half-bent), stone and bone tools, and much pottery. A small museum has been established on the site.

Kasuga Ikkō. Politician, born 1910 in Gifu, elected to the House of Representatives in 1952 for the Socialist party. He left that party in 1960 to found the Democratic Socialist party (Minshu Shakaitō), of which he was president from 1971 to 1977.

Kasuga-taisha. Shinto shrine established on the small Kasuga hill in Nara in 768 to honor the tutelary divinities *(kami)* of the Fujiwara family. It is dedicated to the *kami* Takemikazuchi, Futsunishi, Ame no Koyama no Mikoto, and Ame's wife, Hime Ōkami. It is associated with the Kashima and Hiraoka-jinja shrines (in Osaka). This shrine succeeded one founded on a nearby hill, the Mikasayama. It was then rebuilt on its current site in the Kasuga-*zukuri* style. Its park is home to many deer, considered to be messengers of the *kami.* This shrine's annual festival is celebrated on March 13, and another festival (Ommatsuri) is held every December 17 in the attached Kasuga Wakamiya-jinja shrine. The main buildings, always well funded by the Fujiwara, were often rebuilt, although there are some remaining from the medieval period: *heiden* and *naoraiden* (859), *kura* (807), *kurumayadori, utsushidono, chakutō-den* (916), *wakamiya-jinja* (1135), *kagura-den, hosodono, onrō* (ca. 1178), *yuya* (rebuilt in 1415), south gate and west gallery (1179), *tōmon* (ca. 1190), *shōrō* (1279), *hettsui-dono* (1632), *itagura* (859, rebuilt in the seventeenth century), *sakedono* (859, rebuilt in 1388), *haisha* (1863), *honden* (rebuilt in the late eighteenth century), and others. More than 3,000 bronze and stone lanterns adorn the buildings and the park. They are lit twice a year, on the nights of Setsubun and Ōbon.

• *Kasuga-ban.* Texts of the Buddhist canon engraved in wood and published at the Kōfuku-ji temple in Nara in the late Heian and early Kamakura periods, then offered to the Kasuga-taishi shrine, where the *kami* were considered to be guardians and protectors of the monastery.

• **Kasuga-busshi.** General term for sculptors of Buddhist images attached to the Kasuga-taisha in Nara.

• *Kasuga gongen reigen-ki.* An *emakimono* in 20 scrolls, describing stories related to the founding of the Kasuga-taisha shrine. It comprises 94 texts and 93 illustrations made by Takashima Takekane around 1309. The definitive texts were by Takasukasa Mototada and his sons, assisted by the monks of the Kōfuku-ji, including Kakuen, Jishin, and Hanken. This *emakimono* is now in the imperial collection.

• **Kasuga-ryū.** Painting school founded by Fujiwara no Motomitsu in the late tenth century and part of the Yamato-e current. Among the most representative painters of this school are Fujiwara no Takayoshi, Fujiwara no Takachika, Fujiwara no Mitsunaga, Fujiwara no Takanobu, Fujiwara no Nobuzane, Shiba Keishun, Shiba Ringen, and Shiba Jiyū. *See* YAMATO-E.

• *Kasuga ryūjin.* Title of a Noh play: a man intends to go to China to study Buddhism, but a messenger from the *kami* of the Kasuga-taisha informs him that he can find these teachings in Japan. A dragon then descends from Heaven and the man decides not to make his trip.

• **Kasuga no Tsubone.** Nurse (1579–1643) to shogun Tokugawa Iemitsu. She was the daughter of Saitō Toshimitsu, a vassal of Akechi Mitsuhide, and the wife of Inaba Masanara, a vassal of the shogunate. She was named director of the women's quarters (*ōoku*) of the shogunal palace.

• **Kasuga-wakamiya.** Shinto shrine attached to the Kasuga-taisha, dedicated to the *kami* Ame no Oshikumo no Mikoto, one of Ame no Koyane no Mikoto's sons, built in the Kasuga-*zukuri* style and restored in 1863. Kagura-den dating from the twelfth century. *See* KASUGA-TAISHA.

• **Kasuga-yama.** Hill in the eastern part of Nara, covered with a forest whose trees, considered sacred, have never been felled. At its feet are the buildings of the Kasuga-taisha and the Kasuga-wakamiya. *Alt.:* 496 m. *See* KASUGA-YAMA SEKKUTSU-BUTSU.

• **Kasuga-yama sekkutsu-butsu.** Name of three groups of haut-relief Buddhist sculptures decorating the caves of Kasuga-yama hill: Takisada (1265), Kasuga-yama (1155–57), and Jigoku-dani (late Heian period).

Kasuga-zukuri shrine

• **Kasuga-zukuri.** Shinto architectural style inaugurated with the Kasuga-taisha in 768, consisting of a single room on pilings, surrounded by a balcony. One of the slopes of the roof is elongated to protect the entrance stairs, located on the long side. *See* JINJA.

Kasumi ga ura. Large lake in Ibaraki prefecture, second in size after Lake Biwa, located about 140 km north of Tokyo, on the Tone-gawa River. *Area: 178 km²; average depth: 7 m.*

Kasuri. Type of weaving and dying analogous to the Indonesian *ikat* technique. The fabrics are mainly in cotton and hemp dyed with indigo blue with designs in undyed white. *Kasuri* (which was used mainly to make peasants' clothing) was introduced to Japan in the fourteenth century from the Ryukyu Islands, and the fabrics were included in the annual tax paid by the sovereigns of the islands to the lords of Satsuma in the seventeenth century. The designs consist of broken lines surrounding images of fish, tortoises, arrows, wells, or stylized birds called *e-gasuri*. Kasuri are made mainly in Kurume and Niigata. Also called *asa-gasuri*.

Kata. "Forms." In martial arts, the arts, and other disciplines, stylized forms of theoretical movements used to teach perfect execution. There are six *kata* in judo and ten in karate. This term is also used for teaching and development of actors' movements in Noh and Kabuki theater.

Katabira. Light cotton kimono dyed using the *chayazone* process, worn mainly by women in summertime. Also, a type of short-sleeved kimono *(kosode)* in woven hemp.

Katada Tokurō. Western-style painter (1889–1934).

Katagami Noburu. Writer (*go*: Katagami Tengen, 1884–1928) and literary critic specializing in Russian literature.

Katagi. At first, this term designated an engraved wooden plank to be used for printing images, but it came to mean a person's mind and usual character in relationship to the social group to which he or she belongs. In the Edo period, it gave rise to *katagi-mono*, stories and novels describing the customs and habits of certain categories of people. Andō Jishō and Ejimaya Kiseki inaugurated and popularized this genre in the eighteenth century.

Kataginu. Sleeveless vest with broad shoulders, part of the *kami-shimo* costume, worn mainly by men from the fifteenth to the nineteenth century.

Katagiri Katsumoto. Warrior (1556–1615) who was one of Toyotomi Hideyoshi's "seven lances" *(shichi-hon'yari)* during the Battle of Shizugatake in 1583. He was appointed a daimyo in 1585 with a revenue of 10,000 *koku*. After Hideyoshi's death, Katagiri served Tokugawa Ieyasu, who gave him an estate worth 28,000 *koku* and appointed him tutor to the young Toyotomi Hideyori. But Tokugawa Ieyasu forced him to fight at his side at the two sieges of the Osaka castle (1614–15), which resulted in Hideyori's defeat. Ieyasu rewarded Katagiri by granting him a fief of 43,000 *koku,* but he died soon after. *See* KIODE HIDEMASA.

• **Katagiri Sekishū.** Buddhist monk (Katagiri Sadamasa, 1605–73) who founded the small Jikō-in hermitage near Nara in 1633. He was theoretically appointed governor of Iwami province in 1624. Master of the tea ceremony *(chajin)* for shogun Tokugawa Ietsuna, he wrote a treatise on the subject, *Sekishū sambyakkajō* (Sekishū's Three Hundred Articles) and had many disciples. He was also a painter.

Kata-imi. In the doctrines of Ommyōdō, a ritual ban on traveling in certain directions on certain days and at certain times, based on the concept of Yugyō-jin, because divinities were considered to be traveling during these periods. A way of circumventing these bans was called *kata-tagae. See* IMI, KATA-TAGAE, MONO-IMI.

Katakana. Series of syllabic characters derived from simplified Chinese characters, used mainly for phonetic notation of foreign words, for telegrams, and for posters. *See* FURIGANA, GOJŪON-ZU, HIRAGANA, KANA.
→ *See* KIBI NO MAKIBI.

Kataki-uchi. Family vendetta, based on a sentence from "Memoranda on the Rituals," a Confucian classic *(Chin.: Liji):* "No one can live under the same sky as the enemy of his father" (or his hierarchical superior). *Kataki-uchi* became a fairly common practice in Japan, as exemplified by the vendetta between the Soga brothers in 1193, and especially that of the 47 *rōnin* of Ako (Akō-gishi) in 1703. Vendettas of this type were declared illegal in 1873. However, they are still in force in some milieus, such as the yakuza.

• **Kataki-yaku.** In Kabuki theater, the villain. The actor wears makeup featuring contrasting colors. Also called *akunin-gata, nikugata,* and *jitsu-aku.*

Katakura-gumi. Industrial group (spinning mills) founded in 1895, which also had agricultural concerns in Hokkaido, Korea, and Taiwan. Between 1920 and 1945, it was one of the largest textile companies in Japan. It closed in 1945.

Katami-gawari. Type of kimono *(kosode)* made of two different fabrics, worn during the Heian period by certain nobles and sometimes by Noh actors.

Katana. "Sword" with a single sharp edge on the convex side of the blade, worn on the belt *(obi),* edge upward, by samurai starting in the Muromachi period. Along with the shorter sword called *wakizashi* (belt companion), it was part of the ensemble called *daishō,* distinguishing samurai from other people, such as physicians and certain artists, who had the right to carry a single sword.

The length of *katana* was not standardized. Generally, they were made to order by master blacksmiths who were also Shinto priests, using secret forging techniques transmitted from father to son. The parts of a *katana* are the handle *(tsuka),* composed of a pommel *(kashira),* a mounting *(tsukaito),* a sharkskin cover *(same),* a copper collar holding the blade *(fuchi),* a guard *(tsuba)* and a copper collar holding the *tsuba (seppa* and *habaki).* The blade itself, forged with a special steel called *tama-hagane,* has various parts: the point *(kissaki),* the tempered part *(bōshi),* the line dividing it and the thick part of the blade *(yokote),* the edge *(hasaki),* the straight or wavy line marking the tempering *(hamon),* the ridge of the blade *(shinogi),* the back *(mune),* and the grooves *(hi).* The tang of the blade *(nakago)* has holes to which a handle can be attached *(mekugi-ana),* file marks *(yasuri-me),* and an engraved inscription *(mei).*

Some blades also have engraved drawings or inscriptions called *horimono.* Accessories included a scabbard *(saya),* a small knife *(kozuka)* and pick *(kōgai),* bolts attaching the various parts to each other *(mekugi),* a protective ferrule on the scabbard *(kojiri),* a sort of ring or hook to keep the scabbard from sliding on the belt *(origane, sakatsuno),* a reinforcement ring at the top of the scabbard *(koiguchi, kuchi-gane),* and a decorated ring *(kurikata, kurigata)* to hold the safety cord *(sageo),* which was knotted in a special way. Some *katana* had two holes *(ude-nūki-ana),* one larger than the other, drilled into the handle through which a cord *(ude-*

nūki) could be passed to provide a more secure grip. When the *katana* was not in use, it was disassembled and the blade was placed, sharp edge up, on a special rack called *katana-kake,* or in a black-lacquered box often inlaid with mother-of-pearl, called *katana-zutsu.*

Blacksmiths belonging to various schools *(mono)* produced *katana,* which have been classified into various categories. The *ko-tō,* or "ancient swords," were made before 1596 and forged by *go-kaden* or their disciples; the *shin-tō,* forged between 1596 and 1804; and *shinshin-tō,* forged after 1804 for army officers, called *shinshin-tō* and *kyūshin-tō* from 1867 to 1937, and *shingun-tō* after 1937 *(kaigun-tō* for navy officers). From 1804 to 1867, *katana* were called *fukkō-tō* (of the "renewal"). The best blacksmiths of these "new swords" were Taikei Naotane and Minamoto Kiyomaro. *See also* DAISHŌ, TACHI, TSUBA, UCHIGATANA, WAKIZASHI.

• **Katana-gari.** "Pulling of Swords." An edict of suppression of weapons affecting everyone who did not belong to the *bushi* (warrior) class, ordered by Toyotomi Hideyoshi in 1588. Swords and other weapons were collected to be melted down and converted into agricultural tools or into nails and spikes to be used to hold together a large statue of the Buddha that was to be erected in Kyoto; it was never built.

Kataoka Chiezō. Actor (Ueki Masayoshi, 1903–83), born in Gumma prefecture. At first a Kabuki actor, he became a movie actor, appearing in many films directed by Makino Shōzō. In 1928, he founded his own production company, featuring directors Inagaki Hiroshi, Uchida Tomo, and Matsuda Teiji, and others.

Kataoka Kenkichi. Politician (1843–1903) born to a samurai family of the Tosa clan. He fought in the Boshin Civil War (1868) with Itagaki Taisuke then, after the Restoration, traveled to the United States and Europe (1871–72) to study the military. When he returned, he became a captain in the navy. He had created a paramilitary society, the Kainan Gisha, which supported the Risshi-sha (Self-Help Society), in 1874. The following year, he helped Itagaki to found the Aikoku-sha (Society of Patriots). He was also active in the creation of the Jiyūtō (Liberal party) in 1881. Arrested for demonstrating in favor of revision of the Unequal Treaties *(see* JŌYAKU*)* and freedom of expression, he was freed in 1889. He was elected to the House of Representatives in 1890, and constantly reelected until his death.

Kataoka Nizaemon. Kabuki actor (1656–1715) and famous shamisen musician. He was director *(zamoto)* of theaters in Osaka and Kyoto.

• Kabuki actor (1904–94) and author of a number of books on theater, including *Yakusha nana-jūnen* (Seventy Years of Theater, 1976). He was named a Living National Treasure (Ningen Kokuhō).

Kataoka Tamako. Painter, born 1905 in Sapporo (Hokkaido), who received the Order of Culture (Bunka-shō) in 1992. She painted many portraits in the modern Nihonga style and tried to update ukiyo-e art by using broad strokes and thick colors. She painted mainly screens *(byōbu)*.

Kataoka Teppei. Writer (1894–1944), born in Okayama. At first a journalist at the *Bungei Jidai,* the magazine of the *Shin-kankaku* ("New Sensibility") literary society, he then turned toward "proletarian" literature and joined the Communist party. Imprisoned for his ideas, he left the party upon his liberation in 1934 and began to write popular novels, such as *Tsuna no ue no shōjo* (1927) and *Aijō no mondai* (1931).

Katari-be. Ancient guild *(be)* of storytellers responsible for reciting sacred texts during court ceremonies. Hieda no Are, the reciter of the *Kojiki,* may have been a member of the Katari-be.

Katashiro. "Scapegoat," a piece of paper with an image on it that is buried as magical words are said, with the intention of causing problems for the person symbolized by the image. To avoid being affected by the spell, the targeted person has to rub his or her body with a similar image that has been purified by a *misogi.* This image is supposed to take all the evil onto itself *(waziwai);* it must then be thrown into a river or burned. This custom also takes place in Shinto shrines during exorcism rites *(kegare).* *Anesama-ningyō* paper dolls were also used to keep disease away from the person to whom they were offered: this is the origin of the Festival of Dolls (Hina Matsuri).

Katasuso. Type of kimono *(kosode)* with decorations only on the ends of the sleeves, the shoulders, and the hem.

Kata-tagae. According to Ommyōdō doctrines, taboos of direction obliging believers to change roads to go from one point to another in such a way as to avoid angering certain divinities (Yugyō-jin) and thus avoid the taboo *(kata-imi). See* IMI, KATA-IMI, YUGYŌ-JIN.

Katayama Kenzan. Confucian scholar (1730–82) from Kōzuke, belonging to the Setchū school (Setchū-ha).

Katayama Nampu. Painter (1887–1980) in Japanese style (Nihonga), Yokoyama Taikan's disciple, who painted mainly flowers and birds. He received the Order of Cultural Merit in 1968.

Katayama Sen. Politician (Yabuki Sugatarō, 1860–1933) and union leader. After studying in the United States (1884–94), he converted to Christianity. When he returned to Japan, he founded the first unionist newspaper, *Rōdō Sekai* (The World of Labor); it was bilingual (English and Japanese), and was published until 1904 (a total of 100 issues). He then joined with Kōtoku Shūsui and others in forming several socialistic groups and parties, and went again to the United States and to Europe (1903–05). His activities and socialist writings earned him the international nickname "Apostle of the Comintern." He returned to the United States in 1914 and settled in California. In 1921, he went to Moscow, where he was warmly received, and lived there until his death. He was buried in the wall of the Kremlin.

Katayama Tetsu. Politician (1887–1978) and socialist leader, born in Wakayama. Influenced by Abe Isoo, he converted to Christianity and helped Abe found the Shakai Minshutō (Socialist Democratic party), a party he later quit. After the Second World War, he helped found the Nihon Shakaitō (Japan Socialist party) and was elected prime minister (May 1947–Mar. 1948), succeeding Yoshida Shigeru. Ashida Hitoshi succeeded him. He retired from politics following his electoral defeat, and was actively involved in the restoration of diplomatic relations with China in 1972.

Katazome. Fabric-dying method, using a stencil *(katagami)* made from blackberry-bark *(kōzo)* paper treated with persimmon *(kaki)* juice. The stencil is applied to the fabric with glutinous rice, and the dye is applied by hand on the uncovered part; the motif is repeated many times.

Katchū. General term for warriors' armor, including the armor itself *(yoroi),* the helmet *(kabuto),* and the arm and leg protectors. Ancient armor was probably made of wood and leather (Yayoi period). In the *kofun* period (probably beginning in the fourth century), it was made of iron, with a simple corselet and a skirt *(keikō)* made of articulated plates. This type of armor was considerably improved in the eleventh century to accommodate mounted warriors: called "great armor" *(ō-yoroi),* it comprised a breastplate *(dō),* shoulder-pieces *(ōsode),* and a skirt *(kusazuri).* In the fourteenth century, lighter, shorter armor appeared *(dōmaru* and *haramaki).* In the fifteenth and sixteenth centuries, armor was reinforced (because of the use of firearms) and complemented with gloves *(kote),* greaves (or tibia protectors, *sune-ate),* a throat-piece *(nodowa),* tall boots *(haidate),* and sometimes a mask *(ho-ate, men).* Also called *gusoku. See* KABUTO, YOROI.

Katei. Era of Emperor Shijō: Sept. 1235–Nov. 1238. *See* NENGŌ.
• Painter (Taki Ken; *azana:* Shichoku, 1830–1901), Araki Kankai's and Ooka Umpō's student.
• Painter (Kodama Michihiro; *azana:* Shiki, 1841–1913), Chokunyū's student.
→ *See* SHISEKI.

• **Katei-dōjin.** *See* SHŌKA.

Katen. Painter (Mikuma Shikō; *mei:* Shukei; *azana:* Kaidō, 1730–94), from Nagasaki, Gekko's student.
→ *See* GOSHUN.

Katō Chikage. Writer (Ukerazono, 1735–1808), Katō Enao's son. Author of *Man'yōshū ryakukai, Ukeragahama,* and other works. Also called Tachibana Chikage.

• **Katō Enao.** Writer (Hagizono, 1692–1785) and poet, Kamo no Mabuchi's friend. He wrote mainly poems in the ancient style. Katō Chikage's father.

Katō Gen'ichi. Physician and physiologist (1890–1979) known for his neural research, author of *Seirigaku* (Physiology, 1925).

Katō Hajime. Ceramist (1900–68), born in Seto (Aichi prefecture). He became known for re-creating Chinese polychrome porcelain from the Ming period and producing ceramics in the Mino and Seto styles, excelling mainly in pieces in the Oribe style. He also made pieces emulating Song porcelain; he was made a Living National Treasure in 1961.

Katō Hiroyuki. Politician, scholar, and writer (1836–1916), specializing in the study of "Dutch science" *(rangaku)* in the Bansho Shirabesho of the *bakufu.* He studied German and encouraged adoption of new political structures. Appointed dean of Tokyo's imperial university in 1881 and a member of the House of Peers in 1890, he ended his career as director of the Imperial Academy (Teikoku Gakushi-in), a position he took in 1906. He wrote many political-science works, including *Shinsei taii, Kokutai shinron,* and *Jinken shinsetsu.*

Katō Kagemasa. Ceramist (thirteenth century) who accompanied the monk Dōgen to China in 1228 and brought porcelain techniques back to Seto. He was known as Tōshirō.
→ *See* SOBOKAI-YAKI.

Katō Kanji. Admiral (Katō Hiroharu, 1870–1939), born in Fukui prefecture. He attended the naval conference in Washington in 1921–22 that set the relative sizes of the navies of the United States, Great Britain, and Japan at 10, 10, and 6. He was named chief of all fleets in 1925 and opposed disarmament proposals at the London Conference. After retiring from active service in 1935, he actively advocated increasing Japan's military potential.

Katō Kiyomasa. Warrior (Katō Toranosuke, 1562–1611) who fought at Toyotomi Hideyoshi's side in the Battle of Shizugatake in 1583; he earned the title of one of the dictator's "seven lances" *(shichihon'yari)* and received a fief of 3,000 *koku* in Kumamoto. He commanded part of the Japanese army sent to Korea by Hideyoshi in 1592 and 1597, and proved so skilled that his soldiers nicknamed him Kishōkan ("the demon general"). After Hideyoshi's death, he sided with Tokugawa Ieyasu, fighting at his side at Sekigahara (1600), and received an estate of 520,000 *koku.* A follower of Nichiren, he took the religious name Seishō-kō a few years before he died.

Katō Kiyoyuki. Contemporary ceramist, born 1931 in Seto (Aichi prefecture). He has had exhibitions in Australia (1976) and France (1994) and won many prizes.

Katō Kyōtai. Haiku poet (1732–92), born to a samurai family in Nagoya. With Yosa Buson, he tried to restore haiku to the form created by Bashō;

in 1772, he published an anthology of his poems and those of some of his disciples, *Aki no hi,* then had the *Kyōrai-shō* printed in 1775. Most of his haiku were published in the *Kyōtai kushū* (1809). Also called Kyōtai.

Kato-madō. In traditional architecture, in *kara-yō* and composite styles, window with a scalloped upper contour and window bars arranged asymmetrically. *See also* RENJI-MADŌ.

Katō Michio. Playwright (1918–53), born in Fukuoka, who wrote plays inspired by those of Jean Giraudoux, as well as historical plays: *Nayotake* (1946), *Episōdo* (1948), *Omoide o uru otoko* (1951). He committed suicide.

Katori. Ancient fine silk fabric. *See* ASHIGINU.

Katori-jingū. Shinto shrine in Sawara (Chiba prefecture) that may have been founded in the eighth century, dedicated to the *kami* Futsunushi, a tutelary divinity *(ujigami)* of the Fujiwara. Futsunushi was a favorite *kami* of warriors (the name means "sword edge"). Annual festival April 14. Every twelve years there is a festival on April 12, related to the festival at the Kashima shrine.

Katori Nahiko. Scholar and poet (1723–82), Kamo no Mabuchi's disciple. He compiled a dictionary of words in the classical language, the *Kogentai* (1765), and a *waka* anthology, the *Nahiko kashū* (1777), in which his poems imitated somewhat those in the *Man'yōshū.* Also known as Nahiko. He was also famous for his paintings of carp and flowers.

Katō Shigeru. Sinologist and economist (1880–1946), author of major studies on the Chinese Tang, Song, and Qing dynasties: *Shin-keizai shi kōshō.*

Katō Shin'ya. Contemporary ceramist, born 1940 in Seto (Aichi prefecture), professor (1992) at the Aichi University of Arts.

Katō Shizue. Politician, born 1898 in Tokyo to a samurai family. In 1919, with her husband, Ishimoto Keikichi, she went to the United States, where she met the American feminist Margaret Sanger; when she returned, she led a major campaign promoting birth control. Her husband was killed in Manchuria, and in 1944 she married union leader Katō Kanjū (1892–1978). She was elected to the House of Representatives as a member of the Social-ist party in 1946, then to the Chamber of Councillors in 1950, and she constantly campaigned for women's rights and nature conservation. She wrote two autobiographical books, *Facing Two Ways* (1935, in English), and *Hitosuji no michi* (A Straight Road, 1936). She retired from public life in 1974.

Katō Shūichi. Writer and physician, born 1919 in Tokyo. He taught in the United States and Berlin, and at Sophia University in Tokyo. He then turned to literature, writing essays—*1946 Bungakuteki kōsatsu* (1947), *Zasshu bunka* (1956), *Shōshin dokugo* (1972)—and an anti-war novel, *Aru hareta hi ni* (1949). He is best known for *Nihon bungakushi josetsu* (History of Japanese Literature).

Katō Shūson. Haiku poet (Katō Takeo), born 1905 in Tokyo, founder of a poetry magazine, *Kanrai* (1940), and author of studies on Bashō.

Katō Takaaki (Takaakira). Statesman (Hattori Sōkichi, Katō Kōmei, 1860–1926), born in Nagoya. He studied law and English civilization, then hired on with Mitsubishi and went to Great Britain in 1883, where he studied the merchant marine. In 1884, he married Mitsubishi founder Iwasaki Yatarō's oldest daughter. He then worked for the government and was appointed ambassador to London (1894–98 and 1908–12). In 1914, he was minister of foreign affairs in Ōkuma's cabinet, succeeding Kiyoura, then prime minister from 1924 to 1926. Founder of the Kenseikai (Constitutional Association) party, he militated in favor of adoption of universal suffrage (1925). His minister of the interior, Wakatsuki Reijirō, succeeded him as prime minister when he died, in 1926.

Katō Takuo. Ceramist, born 1917 in Tajimi (Gifu prefecture), who was decorated many times and received prestigious prizes for his works, notably his glossy patinas and his blue and "three-color" enamels.

• **Katō Tamikichi.** Ceramist (1771–1824) from Seto, who rediscovered the techniques used by potters in Hizen in the sixteenth century.

• **Katō Tokurō.** Ceramist (1898–1985), born in Seto. He studied the old kilns of Mino, Seto, and Karatsu and rediscovered some of the techniques used by late-sixteenth-century potters to make bowls for the tea ceremony *(chanoyu).* He wrote a great number of articles and books on his art.

• **Katō Tomotarō.** Ceramist (1851–1916) who worked in Tokyo. In 1899, he produced color glazes fired at high temperatures.

Katō Tomosaburō. Politician (1861–1923) and navy officer, born near Hiroshima. He took part in the naval battle of Tsushima in May 1905, under admiral Tōgō Heihachirō, then was appointed commanding admiral of the Kure base. Appointed minister of the navy in Ōkuma Shigenobu's second cabinet, he retained this position until 1922, when he became prime minister, succeeding Takahashi. He reduced the size of the army and navy to respect the agreements concluded at the 1922 Washington Conference. When he died, Admiral Yamamoto Gompei succeeded him as prime minister.

Katō Umaki. Writer (1721–77), author of various historical works, such as the *Kojiki-kai* and the *Tosanikki-kai*. He was Ueda Akinara's master; Ueda finished his work on the *Ise monogatari*.

Katō Yoshiaki. Admiral (1563–1631) who commanded the Japanese fleet during the war against Korea under the command of Toyotomi Hideyoshi. His fleet was destroyed by Korean admiral Yi Sun-sin's "turtle ships." He returned to Japan and, after Hideyoshi's death, took Tokugawa Ieyasu's side in the Battle of Sekigahara (1600). He captured Gifu and received an estate of 200,000 *koku*, then, after restoring various castles, the fief of Aizu (400,000 *koku*). He was well known as an administrator.

Katsui Gempachi. Playwright (1778–1828) who adapted a number of Noh plays for Kabuki theater.

Katsu Kaishū. Politician (Katsu Rintarō, Katsu Yasuyoshi, Katsu Yoshikuni, Awa no Kami, Katsu Awa; *gō*: Kaishū, 1823–99), born in Edo to a Hatamoto family. He studied "Dutch science" *(rangaku)* and military arts (artillery and navigation) with Sakuma Shōzan. In 1850, he founded his own school and made guns and cannons for various fiefs. Sent to Nagasaki by the *bakufu*, he formed a modern navy and commanded the ship *Kanrin Maru*, which took Japanese delegates to San Francisco to sign a trade and friendship treaty in 1860. When he returned, he held various important positions in the shogunate, notably chief engineer of the navy at the Kobe school (1863). He tried to persuade shogun Yoshinobu to leave his position in order to avoid civil war, and later followed him into exile on Suruga. In 1869, he was appointed a foreign-affairs adviser; he became a member of the Genrō-in in

1875 and of the emperor's Privy Council in 1888. He wrote many historical works (*Katsu kaishū zenshū*, 23 vols., published 1970–82). Although he had physical disabilities, he was one of the best fencers of his time.

Katsukawa. Family and school of painters and makers of ukiyo-e prints in the eighteenth and nineteenth centuries. Among the best-known artists in this school:
—Katsukawa Shunchō (*see* SHUNCHŌ).
—Katsukawa Shun'ei (*see* SHUN'EI).
—Katsukawa Shunkō (*see* SHUNKŌ).
—Katsukawa Shunshō (*see* SHUNSHŌ).
—Katsukawa Shunshui (*see* SHUNSHUI).
—Katsukawa Shuntei (*see* SHUNTEI).
—Katsukawa Shunzan (*see* SHUNZAN).

Katsumata Chieko. Ceramist, born 1950 in Gotemba (Shizuoka prefecture). She went to study at the University of Applied and Decorative Arts in France under professors France Frank and Pierre Roulot in 1973.

Katsumoto Seiichirō. Writer and literary critic (1899–1967), born in Tokyo, member of the proletarian-literature movement. He lived in Germany from 1929 to 1933 and was invited to the Comintern Writers' Conference in Kharkov in 1930. He was a founder of the P.E.N. Club of Japan in 1936, but was ejected because of his political beliefs. He was appointed president of the UNESCO National Commission after the Second World War.

Katsunuma Seizō. Physician (1886–1963), born in Shizuoka. His research on geriatrics and on enzymes earned him an international reputation, as well as the prize of the Japan Academy (Nihon Gakushi-in) in 1926. He was appointed president of Nagoya University in 1949 and honored with the Order of Culture (Bunka-shō) in 1954.

Katsuogi. In the oldest examples of Shinto architectural styles, *shimmei* and *taishi*, wood logs attached horizontally to the ridges of roofs of shrines or nobles' houses to hold the thatched cover. The number varied according to the importance of the shrine (10 at Ise, 3 at Izumo), but might also have had another meaning that has been lost. *Katsuogi* were used as far back as the *kofun* period, for they have been portrayed on *haniwa* of houses (numbering five to seven); they are slightly curved upward, leading to the hypothesis that the first ones were not

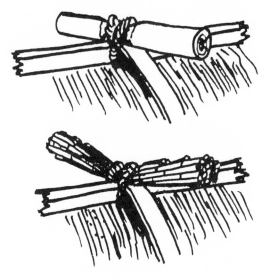

Katsuogi

logs but bunches of straw. They now have an exclusively decorative function.

Katsurabara Shinnō. Imperial prince (786–853), Emperor Kammu's son, considered to be the ancestor of the founder of the Taira (Heike) family.

Katsurada Fujio. Physician (1867–1946), born in Ishikawa prefecture. After studying at Utrecht University, he did interesting research on parasitology in Japan (on *Schistosomiasis japonica,* among others). He received the Japan Academy Prize (Nihon Gakushi-in-shō) for his work in 1918.

Katsurada Yoshie. Mathematician (1912–80), first Japanese woman to receive a doctorate in mathematics and to be a university professor (1967).

Katsura-gawa. River 31 km long, tributary of the Yodo-gawa near Kyoto. Its very swift upper course, running through the gorges of Arashiyama, is called Hozu-gawa, while its middle course is called Ōi-gawa. *See* KYOTO.

Katsuragawa Hochiku. Physician and surgeon (1661–1747) who learned his craft from Dutch physicians in Nagasaki. He was appointed official physician to the shogunate in 1696.
• Official translator (1767–1844) from Dutch for the Edo *bakufu.* His son, Katsuragawa Hoken (1797–1844), held the same position, as did his

brothers, Katsuragawa Hosan (1754–1808) and Katsuragawa Hoshū.

• **Katsuragawa Hoshū.** Physician (Katsuragawa Kuniakira, 1751–1809) and translator from Dutch for the shogunate; Katsuragawa Hosan's brother. Appointed the shogun's personal physician in 1777, he received the title Hōgen. In 1794, he was appointed a professor at the shogunal school of medicine. He helped to translate a Western treatise on anatomy, *Kaitai shinsho.*

Katsurame. Women from the village of Katsura, near Kyoto, who, in ancient times, were *miko* at the Shinto shrines of the capital and participated in its rituals, weddings, and other ceremonies. They wore white headbands, called *Katsura-zutsumi,* and still do during certain festivals, such as the Jidai Matsuri in Kyoto.

Katsura Rikyū. Separate imperial palace constructed starting in 1642 by Kobori Enshū (1579–1647) at the instigation of Prince Toshihito, an uncle of Emperor Go-Minoo's, and his son Toshitada, who had married one of daimyo Maeda Toshitsune's daughters. The existing garden was completely redesigned and the various buildings, typical of the *sukiya-zukuri* style, comprise a masterpiece of mid-seventeenth-century architecture. The palace and gardens were restored in 1982. The buildings, raised on high pilings, were decorated with paintings by artists of the Kanō school. The landscaped garden includes a large lake with an island in the middle.

Katsura Tarō. Politician and general (1847–1913), born in Hagi in the Chōshū estate, died in Tokyo. He fought for the restoration of Emperor Meiji in 1868 and was sent to Germany from 1870 to 1873 to study weaponry. Two years later, he was appointed military attaché to the Japanese embassy in Germany; he returned to Europe in 1884–85 to accompany a military mission led by Ōyama Iwao. Promoted to general, he served in China in 1894–95; in 1896, he was appointed governor-general of Taiwan. In 1898, he was minister of the army in Yamagata's and Ōyama's governments. Due to his effectiveness in this position, he was appointed prime minister in 1901, succeeding Itō Hirobumi; he held this position until 1906, when Saionji replaced him. He returned to power from 1908 to 1911. Saionji again succeeded him, but he formed a third government from 1912 to 1913. When he died, Admiral Yamamoto replaced him. It was under his government that Korea was annexed (1910).

Katsura Yukiko. Avant-garde painter (b. 1913).

Katsureki-mono. Kabuki plays, performed after 1868, whose themes were even more realistic than the *jidai-mono* plays.

Katsuhige. Painter (Iwasa Katsuhige; *mei:* Gembei; d. 1673). He studied with his father, Iwasa Matabei, and worked with him on decorating the Fukui castle in 1669.

Katsu Shintarō. Actor (Okumura Toshio), born 1931 in Tokyo. He became famous for his portrayal of the blind samurai Zatōichi in a series of movies starting in 1962. He started his own production company, Katsu, in 1967.

Katsu-yu. Japanese name for Thai ceramics (*see* TEMMOKU) from the Sukhōtai and Sawankhalōk kilns in the fifteenth and sixteenth centuries. These ceramics had a dark-brown glaze and some were decorated under a slip. They were imported to Japan and used in the tea ceremony *(chanoyu)*.

Kauffman, James Lee. American architect and jurist (1886–1968), from Pennsylvania. A professor of English at the Tokyo Law University from 1913 to 1919, he founded an architectural firm and designed the modern buildings in Tokyo's Marunouchi district. After the Second World War, he advised the S.C.A.P., advocating massive foreign investment for Japan's reconstruction. For this, he was decorated with the Order of the Rising Sun and the Order of the Sacred Treasure.

Kawabata Bōsha. Haiku poet (Kawabata Nobukazu, 1900–41), born in Tokyo. He worked on the literary magazine *Hototogisu* and was one of Takahama Kyoshi's assistants. His works were collected in *Kegon,* published in 1939.

Kawabata Ryūshi. Painter (Kawabata Shōtarō, 1885–1966), born in Wakayama prefecture. After studying Western-style painting (Yōga), he produced illustrations for various magazines, then traveled in the United States in 1913. When he returned, in 1914, he turned toward Japanese-style painting (Nihonga), and his works were exhibited a number of times at the Inten, the official exhibition of the Nihon Bijutsu-in (Japan Fine Arts Academy). In 1928, he created his own group, Seiryūsha,

which was dissolved upon his death in 1966. He was decorated with the Order of Culture (Bunka-shō) in 1959.

Kawabata Yasunari. Writer (1899–1972), born in Osaka to a family of physicians. Orphaned early (his father died in 1900 and his mother the year after), he was raised by his grandmother and older sister. He studied literature at the University of Tokyo at age 15, living alone under the guardianship of one of his cousins living in Tokyo. In 1921, he began to write, publishing *Jūrokusai no nikki* (Diary of a Sixteen-year-old Boy), in which he described the death of his grandfather, and founded a small literary magazine, *Shinshichō* (New Thought). He came to the notice of Kikuchi Kan, who allowed him to contribute to his magazine, *Bungei Shunjū*. He was then part of a literary group called Shinkankaku (neo-sensualist school), which studied Western literature.

Kawabata's first major novel, *Izu no odoriko* (The Dancer of Izu, published 1926), was an immediate success. In the same year, he helped write film scripts and worked at the magazine *Bungei Jidai* (Literary Era). He then wrote a large number of novels and stories, many of them unfinished, and in 1935 a first version of *Yuki-guni* (The Country of Snow), which was finished only in 1947, as well as an autobiography, *Bungakuteki jijiden* (Literary Autobiography, 1934). After the Second World War, he gained international renown through translations of his works. He published *Semba-zuru* (Clouds of White Birds, 1949), *Yama no oto* (The Mountain Rumbles, 1949–54), *Mizu-umi* (The Lake, 1954), *Nemureru bijo* (The Sleeping Beauties, 1960), *Koto* (The Old Capital, 1961), *Utsukushisa to kanashimi* (Sadness and Beauty, 1961), and *Meijin* (The Go Master, published in looseleaf in 1951–52). Among his other works are *Asakura kurenaidan* (unfinished, 1929–30), *Kinjū* (Animals, 1933), and a great number of stories.

Some critics have called Kawabata's writing "decadent" in the sense that it exhibits a sort of morbid fascination with beauty and sadness, purity and idealism: "Since Japan has been conquered," he wrote, "the only thing left for me is to return to the traditional spiritual sadness of the Japanese." His entire body of work consisted of suggesting, rather than describing, characters and situations in a classical, plain language. Profoundly affected by the transformation of Japan and the gradual disappearance of the traditional spirit, Kawabata Yasunari committed suicide on April 16, 1972, four years after receiving the Nobel Prize for literature. Most of his works have been adapted for movies in Japan by directors Kinugasa Teinosuke, Takami Sadae, Gosho Heinosuke, Naruse Mikio, Shima Kōji, Hisamatsu Seiji, Toyoda Shirō, Nakamura Noboru, Ichikawa Kon, and others. Almost all of them were translated into various languages.

Kawabe Torashirō. General (1890–1960). On the personal order of Emperor Hirohito, he went to Manila on August 10, 1945, to negotiate Japan's surrender with American general Sutherland, General MacArthur's assistant.

Kawabiraki. "Opening of the River," annual festival celebrating the beginning of summer, on the third Saturday of July. Until recently, it was accompanied by fireworks over the shores of the Sumidagawa in Tokyo. It also marks the beginning of the fishing season.

Kawachi. Former name of a province now included in Osaka prefecture.

• **Kawachi, Master of.** Painter (sixteenth century) whose name is not known, working in Osaka.

• **Kawachi Nagano.** Town in Osaka prefecture, industrial suburb (metallurgy, *sake* breweries). Kanshin-ji and Emmei-ji Buddhist temples, founded, according to tradition, by Kūkai. *Pop.*: 80,000.

Kawade Nunjirō. Peasant (1814–83), who, in 1859, founded a new religion called Konkō-kyō. Also known as Konkō Daijin. *See* KONKŌ-KYŌ.

Kawagoe. Former lord's estate in Musashi province (Saitama prefecture), fief of *fudai-daimyō* families in the Edo period. It was transformed into a department of the same name in 1871, renamed Kumagaya in 1873, then integrated into Saitama prefecture in 1876.
→ *See* MASTUDAIRA.

Kawaguchi Ekai. Buddhist monk and explorer (Ekai, 1866–1945) of the Zen Ōbaku-shū sect, born in Sakai. He traveled extensively in Tibet, Nepal, and India, searching for ancient Sanskrit texts, and met theThirteenth Dalai Lama, with whom he exchanged Buddhist manuscripts. He returned to Japan in 1916, bringing back many manuscripts and works of art. In 1935, he renounced the ecclesiastic state and wrote accounts of his travels—*Chibetto ryokōki* (Records of a Tibetan Journey, published in

English in London in 1909)—and a book on Tibetan grammar.

Kawaguchi Matsutarō. Writer and movie producer (1899–1985), born in Tokyo. He became known for writing popular novels and stories such as *Aizen Katsura* (1936–38). In 1947, he joined the Daiei film-production company, and in 1965 he was elected a member of the Japan Art Academy (Nihon Gakushi-in).

Kawahigashi Hekigotō. Haiku poet (Kawahigashi Heigorō, 1873–1937), born in Ehime prefecture, Masaoka Shiki's disciple and contributor to the magazine *Hototogisu*. He tried to reform the haiku form by freeing it from the traditional framework of lines of 5, 7, and 5 syllables. His works were collected in *Sanzenri* (1906) and *Hikigotō kushū* (1916).

Kawai Eijirō. Philosopher (1891–1944), born in Tokyo, specializing in political thought, which, he felt, was the only way to bring about reforms based on personal fulfillment. He became a bureaucrat in the Ministry of Agriculture and Trade, devoting himself to the well-being of laborers, then resigned to teach. He advocated the sharing of production goods among the workers, although his "socializing" ideal was far removed from the goals of socialists such as the communists. Arrested in 1938 for his opinions, he was forced to stop teaching.

Kawai Gyokudō. Painter (Kawai Yoshisaburō; *gō*: Gyokudō, Gyokushu, 1873–1957), born in Aichi; he studied with Kōno Bairen and Mochizuki Gyokusen (of the Shijō school in Kyoto), then with Hashimoto Gahō (Kanō school of Tokyo). He became a professor at the Tokyo School of Fine Arts and was elected a member of the Imperial Fine Arts Academy (Teikoku Bijutsu-in) in 1919. He received the Order of Culture (Bunka-shō) in 1940. His style represents a sort of compromise between the Kanō school of Edo and the Maruyama school. *See* GYOKUDŌ BIJUTSU-KAN.

Kawai Kanjirō. Ceramist (1890–1966), born in Shimane prefecture, who worked in Kyoto. A lover of folk art, he and Yanagi Muneyoshi founded the Nihon Mingei Kyōkai (Japanese Association for Folk Art) and published a magazine, *Kōgei*, in 1931. He then opened a museum of folk art in Tokyo in 1936. After the Second World War, he created his own ceramics style, inspired by ancient pottery of Japan and Korea (where he traveled frequently), making rustic-style pottery decorated with haut-relief and varnished in bright colors.

• **Kawai Seitoku.** Ceramist, born 1927 in Kunimi-chō (Ōita prefecture).

Kawaishi Mikinosuke. Master of martial arts (d. 1969), specialist in judo at the Kōdōkan. He went to France in 1935 and adapted Japanese judo, founding a club that merged with France's Jū-jutsu Club in 1938. He moved to France in 1949 to teach his own judo method.

Kawai Sora. Samurai and haiku poet (1649–1710), born in Shinano province (Nagano prefecture), Bashō's disciple. He accompanied Bashō on his travels and wrote a book of notes, *Oku no hoso-michi zuikō nikki,* that is important for the study of Bashō's life.

Kawai Suimei. Poet (Kawai Matahei, 1874–1965), born in Osaka. In a romantic and lyrical style, he wrote works in popular language and free verse: *Mugenkyū* (1901) and *Tōei* (1905). He was elected a member of the Nihon Geijutsu-in (Japan Art Academy) in 1937.

Kawai Tsugunosuke. Samurai (1827–68) of the Nagaoka estate (Niigata prefecture), who wanted the estate to remain neutral during the Boshin Civil War (1868). When the Nagaoka castle was occupied by imperial troops, he tried to retake it by force, but he was fatally wounded during the battle.

Kawaji Ryūko. Poet (Kawaji Makoto, 1888–1959), born in Tokyo, author of free verse in modern language that had a major influence on development of contemporary poetry: *Nami* (Waves, 1957), *Robō no hana* (1910), *Ayumu hito* (1922), and others.

Kawaji Toshiakira. Bureaucrat (1801–68) of the Edo shogunate, Inoue Kiyonao's brother, appointed *kanjō-bugyō* (commissioner of finances) in 1852, responsible for defense of the coasts. He began negotiations in Nagasaki with the Russian envoy Putiatine in 1853, and signed a friendship treaty with Russia in 1855. In 1860, he was responsible for foreign affairs as *gaikoku-bugyō.* He committed suicide when the Edo castle was captured by imperial troops.

Kawaji Toshiyoshi. Samurai (1834–79) of the Kagoshima estate. He fought with the imperial troops in the Boshin Civil War (1868), then was responsible for his province's armaments. Summoned to Tokyo in 1872 to direct the police force, he went to Europe to study police operations. Upon his return, he was appointed commissioner of the Tokyo police and reorganized the force. He also reorganized the sapper-firefighter force along the lines of France's force.

Kawakami Bizan. Writer and poet (Kawakami Akira, 1869–1908), born in Osaka. He joined the Ken'yūsha group in 1886, then contributed to the *Bungaku-kai* starting in 1893, and finally joined the Ryūdo-kai group around 1904. He wrote many *haibun* poems in an eloquent, flowery style, and travel journals such as *Futokoro-nikki* (1897), as well as romantic stories, such as *Ōsaka-zuki, Sho-kikan, Ura-omote,* and *Yamishio,* in which he criticized the business circles of his time. Then, influenced by Zola, he began once again to write works that combined romanticism and naturalism, including *Kannon-iwa* (1907) and *Harin* (1907).

Kawakami Hajime. Marxist economic theoretician (1879–1946), son of a samurai of the Chōshū clan, appointed instructor of economics in Kyoto. After studying law in Europe from 1913 to 1915, he published a Marxist-leaning economics magazine, *Shakai Mondai Kenkyū* (Studies on Social Problems), translated *Das Kapital* by Karl Marx (*Shihon-ron,* 1927–29), and wrote many essays, including *Keizaigaku taiko* (Economic Sketches, 1928). He then began to write novels and stories, publishing his autobiography, *Jijoden* (1947–48) and poems (1946). His major works are *Bimbō monogatari* (Novel About a Poor Man, 1917) and *Daini bimbō monogatari* (1930). Arrested in 1933 for his membership in the Communist party, he was sentenced to five years in prison but was freed in 1937.

Kawakami Jōtaro. Politician (1889–1965) with socialist leanings, elected to the House of Representatives in 1928 for the Nihon Rōnōtō (Japan Labor-Farmer party). After the Second World War, he helped revive the Socialist party, succeeding Asanuma Inejirō as president in 1960. He retired a few months before his death.

Kawakami Kan. Painter (*azana:* Shiritsu; *mei:* Mannojō; *gō:* Tōgai, 1827–81) in Western style (Yōga, oil painting), who worked in Tokyo.

Kawakami Otojirō. Actor (1864–1911), born in Hakata (Fukuoka prefecture). At first a Buddhist novitiate, he worked at various trades before becoming a political agitator for the Jiyū Minken Undō (Freedom and People's Rights Movement), which got him arrested several times. He then began to tell stories *(yose)* and composed songs that quickly became popular, such as *Oppekepei bushi,* in which he ridiculed the elites of his time. With some friends, he created a touring theater troupe in 1891, performing political plays that somewhat imitated Kabuki. He traveled in Europe in 1893 to study theater; on his return, he produced modern plays (such as *Igai,* "Surprise") and patriotic plays. His company then toured Europe and North America and, from 1903 to 1906, adapted Shakespeare's plays, performing with his wife, Sada Yakko, one of Itō Hirobumi's favorite geisha. Kawakami Otojirō was thus the first promoter of modern theater (Shimpa) in Japan.

Kawakami Sokun. Writer (b. 1923) of works dealing with sexual problems and detective novels based, according to him, on his own experiences.

Kawakami Tetsutarō. Writer and literary critic (1902–80), born in Nagasaki. He translated works by French symbolists such as Léon Chestov. Among his best-known works are *Shizen to junsui* (Nature and Purity, 1932), *Nihon no autosaida* (Outsiders in Japan, 1959), *Watakushi no shi to shinjitsu* (My Poetry and the Truth), and *Yoshida shōin.* He was elected a member of the Japan Art Academy (Nihon Gakushi-in) in 1962.

Kawakita Michisuke. Painter (1850–1905), Kawakami Kan's student. He studied in Paris.

Kawamori Yoshizō. Writer and literary critic, born 1902 in Sakai, specializing in studies of French literature and poetry of the fifteenth and sixteenth centuries. He was elected a member of the Japan Art Academy (Nihon Gakushi-in).

Kawamoto Kōmin. Scholar, physician, and physicist (Kawamoto Yukitami, 1810–71), who studied "Dutch sciences" *(rangaku)* and medicine in Edo. He taught physics and chemistry at the Bansho Shirabesho and was appointed counselor to Shimazu Nariakira, the daimyo of Satsuma. He wrote a number of works on chemistry and a 15-volume encyclopedia on the sciences, *Kikai kanran kōgi* (Observing the Waves of the Sea, 1851–56). He also experimented with photography.

Kawamura Jakushi. Painter (1630–1707) of the Nagasaki school.

Kawamura Kiyoo. Painter (1852–1934) in Western style (Yōga), Kawakami Kan's student. He studied in Venice and painted mainly portraits.

Kawamura Manshū. Painter (1880–1942) of the Kōrin school. His works were exhibited in Paris in 1929.

Kawamura Zuiken. Wealthy Edo merchant (1617–99), born in Ise, who made a fortune in the lumber business when Edo was reconstructed following the disastrous fire of the Meireki era in 1657. He also built irrigation canals in the Edo region and regulated the flow of the Yodo-gawa river near Osaka. In recognition of his work, the shogunate granted him the title of *hatamoto,* even though he was of common birth.

Kawanakajima no Tatakai. "Battles of Kawanakajima." A series of battles that took place in 1553, 1555, 1557, 1561, and 1564 between the daimyo Uesugi Kenchin and Takeda Shingen in Shinano province (Nagano prefecture). Although they were not very important militarily, they were celebrated in warrior novels of the Edo period, including the *Kōyō gunkan,* which related the exploits (more or less fictitious) of Kenshin and Shingen. A *byōbu-e* (painted screen) was recently discovered in the possession of a family in Wakayama prefecture portraying one of these battles, probably the work of an artist of the Kanō school from the early seventeenth century.

Kawanishi. Series of planes built and used during the Second World War:

—**Kawanishi H.6 K.** Hydroplane built in 1943 in Kawanishi (U.S. code name "Mavis"), of which 217 were operational. They were powered by four 1300 HP engines. *Maximum speed:* 384 km/h; *range:* 6,750 km; *crew:* 9; *weapons:* one 20 mm cannon, four 7.7 mm machine guns, bomb load of 1,600 kg. This model was replaced in 1943–44 by the **Kawanishi H.8 K2** (U.S. code name "Emily"), which had more weaponry, and the H.6 K was transformed into a troop-transport craft (18 soldiers).

—**Kawanishi N.1 K1.J, N.1 K2.J.** Fighter planes called Shiden-kai (U.S. code name "George"). During the Second World War, 5,428 K1s and 10,071 K2s were built. *Maximum speed:* 600 km/h; *range:* 3,400 km; *crew:* one; *weapons:* four 20 mm cannons and two 7.7 mm machine guns.

Kawanobe Itchō. Lacquer artist (1830–1910), specializing in *maki-e*.

Kawanoe. Town in Ehime prefecture (Shikoku), seat of the *bugyō* during the Edo period, a commercial town with activities related to the nearby Besshi Copper Mines, and relay point on the Tosa Kaidō route. Paper industry. *Pop.:* 40,000.

Kawara (-gawara). "Tiles." The system of cladding buildings with tiles was imported from Korea in the late sixth century, and the first structure cladded was that of the Asuka-dera (588–96) in Nara. There are different types of tiles depending on the use and their placement on roofs. Those that cover the slopes of roofs are called *abumi-gawara* (stirrup-shaped), *maru-gawara* (round), and *hira-gawara* (flat). Ridge tiles are called *noshi-gawara*. Tiles that ornament the edges of roofs, usually decorated with relief designs—arabesques, lotus flowers or chrysanthemums, kanji characters, or others—are called *renge-mon*, *karakusa-mon*, and so on. Those that ornament gables and bear the image of a dragon (or demon) are called *oni-gawara*.
→ *See* KOKURA.

Kawaraban. News sheets published starting in the early Edo period, for commercial and sometimes political purposes. *Kawaraban* (which took their name from *kawara*, the word for the use of tile as blocks for printing) first appeared in Kyoto in 1615 to inform the population that Tokugawa Ieyasu had captured the Osaka castle. These broadsheets were about 24 × 13 cm in size. They later proliferated and were more widely distributed. As they were read in public, they were called *yomiuri*. They were often illustrated with ukiyo-e prints.

• **Kawara-kyō.** Tile-shaped plates of terra-cotta about 30 cm per side, engraved with Buddhist texts, produced mainly in the eleventh and twelfth centuries. Also called Ga-kyō.

Kawara-dera. Site of a Buddhist temple in the village of Asuka (Nara prefecture) founded on the former site of Saimei Tennō's palace. Excavations made on the site of this seventh-century temple have shown that it was constructed on a unique plan, different from those of the Hōryū-ji and the Shitennō-ji, imitating a Chinese Tang-dynasty plan. This temple was not transferred to Heian-kyō in 794, so it went into decline and rapidly fell into ruins; all that remains is its stone foundation. Also sometimes called Yamada-dera and Gufuku-ji.

Kawaramono. The term for people who lived beside the rivers *(kawa)* in Kyoto in the medieval period, whose occupation consisted of dismembering animals and using the skins to make leather *(kawa)*. They also worked as laborers on construction sites and on embankments for gardens. These people of very low status were also executioners and scavengers, since victims of torture were generally placed on exhibit on riverbanks. They were later confused with the *eta,* and then were assimilated with the *hinin* in the Edo period. Kabuki actors were sometimes also called *kawaramono* because they were mistrusted by other social classes.

Kawara Sadaijin. *See* MINAMOTO NO TŌRU.

Kawarasaki Chōjūrō. Kabuki actor (1903–81) who helped to found the Shingeki (New Theater) in 1925 and started a group whose goal was to reform Kabuki about 1931.

Kawasaki. City in Kanagawa prefecture, near Tokyo, of which it is a suburb, beyond the Tama-gawa river. A waystation *(shuku-eki)* during the Edo period, it was transformed into an industrial city in 1927 (automobile and motorcycle manufacturing, petrochemical and chemical industries, cement works, etc.) because of its river port, and became the center of the Keihin industrial zone. Heigen-ji (Kawasaki Daishi) Buddhist temple. *Pop.:* 1.1 million.
• Series of war planes made and used during the Second World War:
—**Kawasaki 88.** Light observation plane designed in 1929 and transformed into a bomber. It was replaced by the K.1–32.
—**Kawasaki K.1–32.** Bomber produced in 1938 to replace the Kawasaki 88. *Payload:* 3,400 kg; *length:* 11.35 m; *wing span:* 14.75 m; *engines:* two 850 HP; *maximum speed:* 420 kmh; *maximum altitude:* 8,800 m; *crew:* two; *weapons:* two 7.7 mm machine guns and 4,500 kg of bombs.
—**Kawasaki K.1–45.** Keihei, Tōryū fighter plane (U.S. code name "Nick"), of which 1,700 were built during the Second World War. *Engines:* two 1080 HP; *maximum speed:* 550 km/h; *range:* 1,500 km; *weapons:* one 37 mm cannon and two 20 mm cannons. It was used mainly in 1945 to fight the American B–29 "Flying Fortress" bombers.
—**Kawasaki K.1–48 II.** Bomber built beginning in 1940 (U.S. code name "Lily"). *Total weight:* 6,750 kg; *length:* 12.55 m; *wing span:* 17.20 m; *engines:* two Nakajima Ha-115, 1130 HP each; *maximum altitude:* 10,000 m; *range:* 2,400 km; *crew:*

four; *weapons:* three 7.7 mm machine guns and 800 kg of bombs.

—Kawasaki K.1–61. Hien fighter plane (U.S. code name "Tony"), of which 2,800 were built in 1945. *Engine:* one 1500 HP; *maximum speed:* 560 km/h; *range:* 1,900 km; *weapons:* two 20 mm cannons and one 12.7 mm machine gun.

—Kawasaki K.1–102 B. Experimental fighter plane (U.S. code name "Randt"), built in 1943. *Maximum speed:* 585 km/h; *range:* 4,000 km; *crew:* two; *weapons:* one 57 mm cannon, two 20 mm cannons, and one 12.7 mm machine gun.

• **Kawasaki-byō.** Disease characterized by intense fever, usually affecting children under four years of age, and discovered in 1967 by Kawasaki Tomisaku. The cause is unknown; the only treatment is aspirin.

• **Kawasaki Daishi.** Buddhist temple in the town of Kawasaki, formerly called Heigen-ji, belonging to the Chizan branch of the Shingon-shū. It was likely founded in 1127 by a warrior who, according to tradition, had found a statue of Kōbō Daishi in the sea. The temple was destroyed by bombing in 1945 and rebuilt after the Second World War. Annual festivals on the 21st of January, March, May, and September.

• **Kawasaki Jūkōgyō.** Shipbuilder and maker of machinery, motor vehicles, and plants, founded in Tokyo in 1878 by Kawasaki Shōzō; it took its current name in 1939. It built large tanker ships and, in partnership with Kawasaki Car and Kawasaki Aircraft Co., became a large industrial conglomerate. It now has six branches abroad and is the third-largest zaibatsu in Japan, exporting more than 57% of its production. Its motorcycles are famous. Head office in Kobe.

• **Kawasaki Kisen Kaisha.** Shipping company (better known as K Lines), affiliated with Kawasaki Jūkōgyō and Kawasaki Seitetsu, founded in 1919 and owning about 60 high-tonnage ships. Head office in Tokyo.

• **Kawasaki Seitetsu.** Steelworks founded in Kobe in 1906, then established in Chiba in 1951, now producing about 12 million tons of steel per year, thanks to a new plant in Mizushima (Okayama prefecture). It exports about 45% of its production. Head office in Kobe.

Kawasaki Chōtarō. Writer (1901–85), born in Kanagawa prefecture. With some friends, he started an anarchist-leaning poetry magazine, *Aka to Kuro* (Red and Black) in 1923. He then wrote autobiographical novels, such as *Michikua* (Road Grass), and stories.

Kawasaki Hideji. Politician (1911–78), member of the Jiyū Minshutō (Liberal Democratic party). He directed the UNESCO national commission and was a member of the Olympic Committee.

Kawasaki Natsu. Christian politician, who founded a sort of cultural academy (Bunka Gaku-in) with Yosano Akiko, then contributed to the *Yomiuri Shimbun* from 1921 to 1934 as a women's rights advocate. During the Second World War, she was elected to the House of Peers (1947) and continued her activities on behalf of women's rights, peace, and social reforms as a member of various international organizations, including those dedicated to women's rights.

Kawasaki Shōzō. Famous art collector (1837–1912), businessman, and patron.

Kawase Hasui. Engraver (Bunjirō, 1883–1957) of ukiyo-e prints in modern style.

Kawashima Kōgyoku. Contemporary sculptor of netsuke. He signs his works with various pseudonyms, including Kōgyoku, Koichi, Koji, Masatoshi, Yuji, and Shuzan.

Kawatake Mokuami. Actor and writer (Kawatake Shinshichi, 1747–95), author of, among other plays, *Kanjinchō.*

• **Kawatake Mokuami II.** Actor and writer (Yoshimura Shinshichi, 1816–93), born in Edo. After studying with Tsuruya Namboku V, he was hired by the Ichimura-za troupe, then went to the Kawarazaki-za in 1841. He wrote more than 360 plays. Among the most frequently performed, and among the most typical of nineteenth-century Kabuki, were *Murai chōan benten kōzō* and *Shinobu no sōta.*

• **Kawatake Mokuami III.** Actor and writer (1842–1901) of Kabuki plays, Kawatake Mokuami II's disciple.

Kawazoe. Archeological site recently discovered on the banks of the Hirazuka-gawa in Amagi

(Fukuoka prefecture, Kyushu), containing the remains of a town from the Yayoi period, surrounded by six moats.

Kawazu. Type of Noh (and Kyōgen) mask portraying a frog.

Kawazura Bonji. Writer (1862–1929) and Shinto priest, author of many pamphlets that were very influential in the development and modern conceptions of this religion.

Kaya. Imperial prince (b. 1900), older brother of princes Higashikuni and Asaka. He was a lieutenant general in 1943.

• Name for a region in southern Korea attached to the Mimana, controlled by Yamato between the third and sixth centuries. It was conquered by the Silla (Sinra, Shiragi) kingdom in 532 and 562. *See* BENKAN.

• Tree in the *Myristica moschata* family, whose wood was once burned (reduced to dust and mixed with sulfur) to produce smoke *(kayara)* to repel insects. The word *kayari* is often synonymous with "summer" in poetry.

Kayama Matazō. Painter, born 1927 in Kyoto, the son of a weaver in the Nishijin district. He painted in a traditional decorative style inspired by nature.

Kayanu-hime. In Shinto mythology, a female *kami,* Izanagi and Izanami's daughter. Also called Nozuchi no Kami.

Kaya Seiji. Physicist, born 1898 in Kanagawa prefecture. He studied the properties of ferromagnetic crystals and was one of the founders of the Nihon Gakujutsu Kaigi (Scientific Council of Japan) after the Second World War. President of the University of Tokyo from 1957 to 1963, he was decorated with the Order of Culture (Bunka-shō) in 1964.

Kaya Shirao. Haiku poet (1738–91) who tried to return to the purity of Bashō's style in his work: *Kazarinashi* (Without Artifice, 1771). He had a great many disciples.

Kayō. Painter (Shirai Kagehiro; *azana:* Shijun; *gō:* Baisen, active ca. 1840), Ganku's student. He painted mainly animals and wrote a book on painting called *Gajō yōryaku.*

Kayoi-komachi. Title of a Noh play: the spirit of Ono no Komachi appears to a Buddhist monk and asks him to recite prayers for him, but the spirit of one of his rejected lovers, called Fukakusa no Shō-shō, then appears and asks that Ono no Komachi burn in hell forever.

Kazan. Painter (Yokoyama Ishhō, *azana:* Shunrō, 1784–1837), Ganku's student.

• Painter (Watanabe Kazan, Watanabe Sada-yasu; *mei:* Nobori; *azana:* Shi'an, Hakuto; *gō:* Gūkaidō, Zenrakudō, Sakuhi-koji, Kintonkyō, Zui'an-koji, Kazan, 1793–1841) and samurai who studied with Bunchō and Kaneko Kinryō. He introduced European oil-painting techniques for portraits, flowers, and birds to Japan. Imprisoned for his Western sympathies and unable to work, he committed suicide.

→ *See* VOLCANOES.

Kazan-in Morotaka. Warrior (1301–32) of the Southern Court (Nanchō). Taken prisoner by the Muromachi shogunal troops, he was sent into exile in Shimōsa province, where he died.

Kazan Rettō. Generic term for a group of three islands south of the Ogasawara islands: Iō-jima (Iwojima or Naka-iō), Minami-iō, and Kita-iō. Also sometimes called Iō Rettō. *See* OGASAWARA-GUNTŌ.

Kazan Tennō. Sixty-fifth emperor (Prince Morisada, 968<984–86>1008), Reizei Tennō's oldest son, and En-yū Tennō's nephew and successor. When his wife, Fujiwara Tsuneko, died, he was forced to abdicate by Fujiwara no Kaneie, and he was replaced on the throne by Kaneie's grandson, Ichijō. Kazan retired to the Kazan-ji monastery, where he became a Buddhist monk. An excellent poet, he is sometimes credited with compilation of the *Shūi-shū* anthology. His reign marked the beginning of the preeminence in the court of regents of the Fujiwara family.

Kazari-tachi. Large, elaborately decorated ceremonial sword worn by nobles of the court in the eighth century.

Kazoku. "Class of flowers," second level in the social classes established by Emperor Meiji in 1869: *kōzoku* (imperial family), *kazoku* (nobility), *shizoku* (warriors), and *heimin* (commoners). The *kazoku* replaced the old division of the nobility into *kugyō* and *daimyō.* Its members benefited from privileges and were automatically admitted to the House of Peers (Kizoku-in). They received new titles corresponding to European ones: Kōshaku (duke), Hōshaku (marquis), Hakushaku (count), Shishaku (viscount), and Danshaku (baron). In 1869, this class comprised 1,478 families; in 1905, only 781 families. All noble titles and the division of society into classes were abolished in 1947.

• **Kazoku Kaikan.** *See* ROKUMEIKAN.

• **Kazoku-kokka.** "Family-state," a term used in the Meiji era to designate the Japanese state as resembling a large family in which the emperor was the father and his subjects the children.

Kazunobu. Painter (Kanō Kazunobu; *mei:* Kumenosuke; *gō:* Chinshidō, Hakuchisō, Hakusen-yajin, Shōunsai-rishi, active ca. 1740) of the Kanō school who studied with his father, Shōun. He entered the service of the daimyo of Tsukushi.
→ *See* NAONOBU.

Kazu no Miya. Princess (Chikako, 1846–77), Emperor Kōmei's sister and shogun Tokugawa Iemochi's wife; this match was made (in 1862) by the advisers *(rōjū)* Andō Nobumasa and Kuze Hirochika, in order to forge closer ties between the shogunate and the imperial court. When her husband died, Kazu no Miya became a Buddhist nun in Edo with the name Seikan'in no Miya. She was an excellent calligrapher and highly regarded *waka* poet.

Kazuraki. Title of a Noh play: a mountain *kami* disguised as a woman gives refuge to three Yamabushi and tells them that she was sentenced to wander for having refused to build a bridge for En'no Gyōja. The prayers of the three monks free her from her punishment.

• **Kazura-mono.** In Noh theater, plays in which female characters appear to expound the concepts of *yūgen.*

• **Kazura-obi.** Long, narrow band of decorated fabric worn around the head by Noh actors performing female roles, going under the mask. Its decorations indicate the nature of the role: *iro-iri* (red decoration) for young women, *iro-nashi* (without red) for middle-aged women. Those with fish-scale *(uroku)* motifs indicate the lead role in the second part of some plays, such as *Dōjō-ji* and *Aio no ue.*

Kazusa. One of the "provinces of the Eastern Sea" (Tōkaidō), now included in Chiba prefecture. Formerly called Kamitsufusa.

Ke. All things of daily life, except for those concerning religious rites and ceremonies, which were grouped under the term *hare. See* HAREBI.
• Also "hair," "family."

Kebiishi. Imperial police force established in Heian-kyō by Emperor Saga in 839 to maintain order in the capital and prevent usurpation of the throne. It was directed by a bureaucrat with the rank of *bettō* who controlled officers of various ranks—*suke, jō,* and *sakan.* This police department (Kebiishi-chō) was replaced by the Samurai-dokoro during the Muromachi period. *See also* DANJŌDAI.

Kebori. Metal-engraving style using very fine cuts. Also called *senkoku. See* CHŌKIN.

Kebutsu. Manifestations of a buddha or a bodhisattva *(bosatsu),* portrayed in sculpture and painting by small images placed on the head of certain Buddhist divinities, such as Kannon Bosatsu, or on the halo *(kōhai)* placed behind their head.

Kebyō. In Esoteric Buddhist *(mikkyō)* ceremonies, a type of long-necked vase used to offer flowers to the divinities.

Keenan, Joseph Berry. American jurist (1888–1954), born in Rhode Island, appointed chief attorney in the court charged with judging the war crimes committed by the Japanese. He published a book (with B. F. Brown) on these trials, *Crimes Against International Law. See* WAR CRIMES.

Kegare. Purely Japanese (Shinto) concept of ritual purity and impurity, associated long ago with the notion of crime or sin *(tsumi).* Because blemishes or impurities could be transmitted from one person to another, it was necessary to undergo *misogi,* or purification by water. The most common *kegare* was contact with death, but others were destroying crops, incest, arson, and for women, menstrual periods. *See* HARAI, KATASHIRO, TATARI.

Kegon-shū. Buddhist sect of the *Flower Garland Sutra,* whose doctrine was based on the concept of the buddha-nature in all things. This sect was created in China by the monk Fazhun (557–640) under the name Huayan Jiao, and was introduced to Japan by the Chinese monk Daoxuan (*Jap.:* Dōsen) in 736. The Kegon-shū, which was one of the largest of the Six Sects of Nara (Nanto-rokushū), drew its doctrine from the texts of the *Dashabhūmi-vibhasha-shāstra* (Sutra Explaining the "Ten

Lands" of Buddha, *Jap.: Jūjiron, Jūjibibasha-ron*), in which Amida is mentioned for the first time. These texts are also used by the Hossō-shū sect. The Tōdai-ji temple in Nara is one of the main sites of this sect, which has 47 secondary temples. *See* BUD-DHISM.

• *Kegon engi emaki.* An *emakimono* describing the foundation of the Kegon-shū sect in Korea and the life of two monks of the sect who are called Gishō and Gengyō in Japanese. It comprises six scrolls, attributed to Ennichibō (thirteenth century). Also called *Kegon-shū-sōshi-eden.*

• *Kegon gojūgosho emaki.* An *emakimono* describing the life of the Buddhist monk Zenzai Dōji. It is a single scroll and probably dates from the tenth century.

• **Kegon-ji.** Buddhist temple belonging to the Tendai-shū sect, founded in Gifu in 798 and dedicated to Jūichimen Kannon. It is one of the Sanjū-san-sho (Thirty-Three Temples of the Western Pilgrimage).

Kegon no Taki. Famous waterfall in Tochigi prefecture, in Nikkō National Park. One of the highest waterfalls in Japan (97 m), it is on the Daiya-gawa river, whose source is in Lake Chūzenji.

Kegyō. Architectural ornamentation generally consisting of a decorated, more or less hexagonal plaque attached to the ends of the ridge beams of a roof to hide them and protect them from elements. Also called *gegyō.*

Kehi-jingū. Shinto shrine in Tsuruga (Fukui prefecture), dedicated to a *kami,* Izasawake, who, according to legend, was Emperor Ōjin's personal *kami.* In front of it is a large four-pillar torii, a very rare form, erected in 1645. Annual festival September 4.

Kei. Former unit of volume equivalent to 64 *kibi* (*Panicum miliaceum,* sorghum) seeds:
—10 *kei* were worth 1 *shō.*
—10 *shō* were worth 1 *sai.*
—10 *sai* were worth 1 *shaku* (1.8 cl).
—10 *shaku* were worth 1 *gō* (1.8 dl).
—10 *gō* were worth 1 *shō* (1.8 liters).
—10 *shō* were worth 1 *to* (18 liters).
—10 *to* were worth 1 *koku* (180 liters).
—4 *koku* were worth 1 *hyō* (720 liters).
• Mission mark or sign of recognition, pyramidal or triangular, of Chinese origin, once symboliz-ing the mission or responsibility of an envoy or a daimyo.
• Gong in a Buddhist temple or Shinto shrine, in thick metal, round, hexagonal or another shape, from 25 to 40 cm in diameter, used for certain ceremonies. Also called *hokyo.*

Kei'an. Era of Emperor Go-Kōmyō: Feb. 1648–Sept. 1652. *See* NENGŌ.

• *Kei'an Jiken.* "Incident of the Kei'an Era." An aborted coup d'état led by a handful of *rōnin* samurai against the shogunate in 1651, when shogun Tokugawa Iemitsu died and the young Tokugawa Ietsuna (then ten years old) came to power. This coup had been planned by a *rōnin* named Yui Shōsetsu, a master of martial arts, and his associate, Marubashi Chūya. The plot was discovered; Chūya was captured and executed, while Yui Shōsetsu committed suicide. Their unfortunate venture was the subject of many novels and Kabuki plays, such as *Kusunokiryū hanami no makubari,* by Kawatake Mokuami. One of the most famous novels describing this affair is the *Kei'an taiheiki.*

• *Kei'an no ofuregaki.* Confucian-inspired 32-article legal code concerning only peasants, promulgated in 1649 by Tokugawa Iemitsu. The code promoted the virtues of frugality and obedience among the peasant class, restricting their right to consume costly goods and encouraging them to save so that they could pay their taxes *(nengu)* more regularly.

Keian Genju. Zen Buddhist monk (1427–1508) of the Rinzai sect, born in Nagato province. He studied in the *gozan* of Kyoto and was sent to China in 1645 as a member of the mission led by Ten'yo Seikei, the abbot of the Kennin-ji monastery. When he returned, he preached the neo-Confucian doctrines of Zhu Xi (*Jap.:* Shushi) and the principles of Zen Buddhism.

Keibatsu. "Party, clique," composed of families linked by marriage that worked as a unit and that were influential in political and social circles. Also called *mombatsu. See* BATSU.

Keibun. Painter (Matsumara Keibun; *mei:* Kanama; *Azana:* Shisō; *gō:* Kakei, Keibun, 1779–1843) of the Shijō school who studied with his brother, Goshun, in Kyoto. He then associated himself with the Confucian scholar Koishi Genzui.

Keichitsu. In the old agricultural calendar, period of "awakening of the insects," lasting about 15 days and starting around March 5. *Chin.:* Jingzhe. *See* NIJŪSHI-SETSU.

Keichō. Era of emperors Go-Yōzei and Go-Minoo: Oct. 1596–July 1615. *See* NENGŌ.

• **Keichō-chokuhan.** Imperial publications of the Keichō era, produced on the order of Emperor Go-Yōzei with movable type, a printing technique imported from Korea following Toyotomi Hideyoshi's expeditions. Also called Keichō Shinkoku-bon.

• **Keichō no katsuji-ban.** First works printed with movable type made of wood, during the Keichō era.

• *Keichō kemmon-shū.* "Things Seen and Heard During the Keichō Era." A collection of anecdotes and tales by Miura Jōshin (1565–1644), a samurai of the Odawara fief, who became a merchant in Edo, then a Buddhist monk, and devoted his life to the description of mores, customs, and events of his times. Also titled *Kembun-shū.*

• **Keichō-tsuhō.** Copper and silver coins, issued during the Keichō era, perhaps in 1606. They had a diameter of 2.3 cm and weighed from 2.33 g (silver) to 4.13 g (copper). Only one side was engraved. Concurrently with these coins, gold coins, small and large, called Keichō *ōban-koban,* were issued in 1600–01; they were in circulation until 1695. The oval-shaped *ōban* (10 × 15 cm) weighed 165.375 g, while the *koban* (7 × 4 cm) weighed only 17.85 g. These coins helped unify the currency system and were accepted throughout the country. Banned in 1695, they were again authorized from 1714 to 1736. *See* CURRENCY, RYŌ.

Keichō. Registers established by bureaucrats during the Taika Reform (645), noting all information needed to set distribution of land to the peasants according to the *handen shūju* system and listing those who should be charged tax. These registers were updated every six years and transmitted directly to the State Grand Council (Dajōkan). They stopped being kept in the ninth century.

Keichū. Buddhist monk (Shimokawa Kūshin, Keichū, 1640–1701), born in Amagasaki, of the Shingon-shū sect, appointed *ajari* of the Kōya-san monastery. A scholar and poet, he wrote commentaries on the *Man'yōshū* (*Man'yō daishō,* between 1683 and 1690), the *Ise monogatari,* the *Genji monoga-*

tari, and other classics, and a study of kana (*Waji shōran-shō,* 1693).

→ *See* BUNDŌ SHUNKAI.

Keidanren. Abridgment of Keizei Dantai Rengōkai (Federation of Economic Organizations), a major union association founded in 1946 involving workers from more than 100 companies. It is one of the four largest unions, with the Nikkeiren, the Chamber of Commerce, and the Committee for Economic Development. Its influence in economic circles is so great that the government is forced to negotiate with it, as are other political parties, because it controls the country's major industries.

Keien-ha. Poetry school founded by Kagawa Kageki (Keien) in the nineteenth century on the principles laid down by Ozawa Roan, and seeking to reconcile rhythm with word meanings.

Keiga. Painter (Kawahara Keiga, Kawahara Toyosuke, Taguchi, ca. 1786–ca. 1860), born in Nagasaki. He studied with Ishizaki Yūshi (1786–1846), who gave him access to Dejima, where he met Franz von Siebold and viewed many Dutch paintings. He then painted portraits (including one of Hendrick Doeff) and illustrated Siebold's work in a style that tended to meld European art of the time with Yamato-e painting techniques. After the shogunate accused Siebold of smuggling maps of Japan out of the country in 1829, Keiga changed his name to Taguchi. He continued to paint portraits, decorate buildings, and draw plants. The works that he produced with Yūshi bore the seal Tanemi. His son, Taguchi Rokoku, continued his work.

Keigo. "Honorific or polite language," involving a degree of politeness in the formulation of sentences corresponding to the social situation or sex of the person saying them in relation to the person to whom they are addressed. There are more than 12 conversational "levels" in classical language, although there are fewer in everyday language. Depending on the case, one uses particular nouns and verbs, verbal endings (such as *degozaimasu* for *imasu*), and honorific prefixes (such as O, Go); speaks of oneself and one's family with "humble" words; and usually avoids personal pronouns, which are replaced by the title of the person to whom one is speaking if he or she is of a higher class. It is an extremely complex system, and one to which foreigners are generally not required to adhere as long as they express themselves politely. *See also* DIALECTS, KOKUGO.

Keigyoku. Blind man (1712–85) of humble origins, from Yamagata prefecture, often cited as an example for his devotion toward his parents.

Kei-ha. Group of sculptors of Buddhist images of the Kamakura period, belonging to the Shichijō studio in Nara. Most of the artists in this school included the character *kei* in their names (whence the name given to this school, or *bussho*): Kōkei, Unkei, Kaikei, Tankei, and so on. The Kei-ha survived the In and En schools and lasted until the Edo period, although works by artists from the latter period were not highly valued by their contemporaries.

Keihin Kōgyō Chitai. "Keihin Industrial Zone." Industrial zone including the Tokyo area, stretching from the coast to the cities of Kawasaki and Yokohama. This industrial megalopolis (steel mills, petrochemical plants, shipyards, thermal power plants, food industries, electrical equipment, automobile plants, etc.) supplies about half of Japan's industrial production. In Chiba prefecture, in the north, it extends beside the Keiyō Industrial Zone, and in Ibaraki prefecture it continues by the Kashima Industrial Zone. However, the industrial concentration is now so high that many industries have been forced in recent years to relocate to other regions due to a lack of fresh water.

Keijō. Former Japanese name for Seoul, Korea. Also sometimes called Kanyojō, Kanjō.

Keikō. Type of armor used by warriors in the *kofun* period (fourth–seventh century), longer than *tankō* armor and composed of plates of iron juxtaposed and interlaced. It was probably imported from Korea around the fifth century. Also called *kakeyoroi.* See KATCHŪ, YOROI.

Keikoku. Painter (Gejō Masao, 1842–1920) of the Nanga school (Bunjinga) in Tokyo, who produced landscapes.

Keikoku-bidan. "Beautiful Story of the Classical Countries." A historical novel set in ancient Greece during the time of Epaminondas and evoking the struggle for democracy, written by Yano Ryūkei (1850–1931), leader of the Shimpotō (Progressive party). It was published in two volumes: the first in 1883 and the second in 1884.

• *Keikoku-shū.* Historical work written in 827 by Yoshimine no Yasuyo and several contributors, in 20 volumes (6 of which have not survived), bringing together the works of Chinese and Japanese poets. Originally, it contained 1,033 poems by 178 poets who lived between 707 and 827 and wrote in Chinese in a wide variety of styles.

Keikō Tennō. Twelfth emperor (Prince Otarashi-hiko Oshiro-wake no Mikoto, traditionally 12<71–130>), who probably actually lived in the second or third century, succeeding his father, Suinin Tennō. He was said to have led an expedition in southern Kyushu against the Kumaso tribes, then another against the Ezo in northern Honshu with the help of his son, Yamato-takeru, who succeeded him with the reigning name Seimu.

Keimon'e. Buddhist monk (eighth century) and sculptor of Buddhist images. Also called Keishu-kun.

Keinen. Painter (Imao Eikan; *azana:* Shiyū; *gō:* Yōsosai, Keinen, 1845–1924), Suzuki Kyakunen's student.

Keinin. Painter (Sumiyoshi Keinin, thirteenth century). Assisted by his son, Shōjumaru, he painted a scroll titled *Kako-Genzai inga-kyō* in 1252. Sometimes pronounced (wrongly) Keion.

Keiō. Era of Emperor Kōmei: Apr. 1865–Sept. 1868. See NENGŌ.
→ *See* UNCHIKU.

• **Keiō Gijuku Daigaku.** Keiō University, a private institution founded by Fukuzawa Yukichi in Tokyo in 1858 to teach foreign languages. It was raised to the rank of a university in 1890 and has faculties of literature, law, business, medicine, economics, and engineering, as well as various schools, institutes, and laboratories. It now has more than 23,000 students.

Keiretsu. Groups of enterprises, generally linked by financial interests, some of which have replaced the old zaibatsu since the Second World War.

Keisai. Painter (Onishi In; *azana:* Shukumei; *gō:* Yūkei, Issa Enkaku, Shōchidōjin, Keisai, active ca. 1820) of the Nanga school, Bunchō's student in Edo.
→ *See* AIZAWA YASUSHI, MASAYOSHI.

• **Keisai Eisen.** Painter (Ikeda Yoshinobu, Keisai Shōsen, Chiyoda Saiichi, Ippitsuan Kakō, Mumeiō, Kaedegawa, Shiin, Insai, Insai Hakusui, Koku-shunrō, Hokutei, Hokkatei, 1790–1848), author of stories and poems that he signed with various names, using the *gō* Eisen starting only in 1816. He studied with Kanō Hakkeisai and was inspired by the works of Hokusai. He produced hundreds of ukiyo-e prints, most portraying beautiful women and erotic scenes. He also began a series of landscapes, *Kiso kaidō rokujūkutsugi* (The Sixty-Nine Stages of the Kiso Road, 1835), which was finished by Hiroshige. After 1830, Keisai stopped painting and devoted himself to writing: *Mumeiō zuihitsu* (Essays on a Nameless Man, 1833) and *Ukiyo-e ruikō,* a collection of anthologies of ukiyo-e painters that is very useful for learning about the lives of painters of his time.

Keisatsu Yobitai. "National Reserve Force," established with the consent of General MacArthur at the suggestion of Yoshida Shigeru on July 8, 1950, to replace the national army. Its staff was set at 75,000 soldiers. This armed force was reorganized in 1952 and became the "Self-Defense Forces" (SDF, or Jieitai) in 1954. It now has about 250,000 members. *See* ARMED FORCES, JIEITAI.

Keisei. In Kabuki theater, the role of a courtesan, played by an *onnagata* actor.

• *Keisei Kokusen'ya.* "Koxinga Among the Courtesans." A Kabuki play written in 1713 by Ki no Kaion (1663–1742). *See* KOKUSEN'YA.

Keisen. Painter (Tomita Shigegorō: *gō*: Keisanjin, 1879–1935), Tsuji Kakō's student.

Keison. Painter (*gō*: Kyūgetsusai, fifteenth–sixteenth century), of the *suiboku* school in Muromachi.

Keitai Tennō. Twenty-sixth emperor (Prince Ohodo no Mikoto, Hikofuto no Mikoto, 450<507–31>531), Buretsu's son and successor. According to the *Nihon shoki,* he was not related to the imperial family and was enthroned by the Mononobe family, which provoked strong opposition and caused disturbances in Yamato. Forced to abdicate in favor of his son (?) Ankan, he died soon after. However, his traditional dates given in the *Nihon shoki* are controversial.

Kei'un. Era of Emperor Mommu: May 704–Jan. 708. *See* NENGŌ.

Keiyō. Industrial zone east of Tokyo, around Kisarazu and Chiba, where most heavy industry (oil refineries, shipyards, thermal power plants, automobile plants, etc.) are concentrated along the coast. *See also* BŌSŌ HANTŌ, KEIHIN.

Keizan. Painter (Ōhara Keizan; *gō*: Kakō, d. 1723), of the Nagasaki school.
• Buddhist monk (Keizan Jōkin, 1268–1325) of the Sōtō Zen sect, from Fukui. He studied Zen under Gikai (1219–1309), Dōgen's disciple, and founded the Sōji-ji temple in 1321, which became one of the headquarters of the Sōtō sect, with the Eihei-ji. He wrote a set of monastic regulations called *Keizan ōshō shingi* and a collection of sermons, *Denkō-noku* (Collection of Transmission of the Light). He succeeded Gikai as patriarch of the Zen sect.
→ *See* HONDA KINKICHIRŌ.

• **Keizan Jōkin.** *See* SŌTŌ-SHŪ.

Keko. Sort of flat, shallow vase, in which Buddhist followers place flowers to offer them to the divinities. *See* IKEBANA.

Keman. Metal ornament (sometimes, but rarely, made of gold-leafed wood or fabric) symbolizing, in Buddhism, an offering of flowers. Generally, a *keman* in a screen is placed before a lamp. *Keman* are made in various shapes, most frequently a nonfolding fan *(uchiwa);* they are perforated and decorated with propitiatory motifs such as pine trees or cherry blossoms. The faithful sometimes offer them in homage to the Buddha.

Kemari. Traditional football game in which a number of people form a circle *(kakari)* about 3 m in diameter and try to keep a deerskin ball *(mari)* about 25 cm in diameter in the air. This game was very popular during the Nara, Heian, and Kamakura periods but then fell out of fashion, although some commoners and warriors still played. Both men and women participated, dressed in special garb with very wide pants *(hakama)* and boots. Today, *kemari* is played only in temples and during certain ceremonies with a historical character. *Chin.: zuzhu.* Also sometimes called *shūkiku.*

Kembyō. Small table screen, often highly ornate, once used for protection from the wind or to hide one's face.

Kemmu. Era of Emperor Kōgon of the Northern Court (Hokuchō): Jan. 1334–Aug. 1338. *See* NENGŌ.

• **Kemmu no Chūkō.** "Kemmu Restoration." An attempt made in 1333 by Emperor Go-Daigo to restore imperial authority when the Kamakura *bakufu* fell. He succeeded temporarily, but in 1336 Ashikaga Takauji reestablished the shogunate, establishing his headquarters in Muromachi, a Kyoto district, so that he could control the actions of the court and appoint the emperors. The end of this "restoration" led to the creation of two rival courts (Nambokuchō) that fought for power until 1392; the Northern Court (Hokuchō) was supported by the Muromachi shogunate.

• *Kemmu nenchū gyōji.* Book written about 1334 on the order of Emperor Go-Daigo and describing the ceremonies of the court. Written in Japanese, its purpose was to revive ancient etiquette.

• *Kemmu nenkan ki.* Chronicle of the Kemmu era compiled by an anonymous author about 1336, providing valuable information on laws, government, bureaucrats, and *shōen* during the time of Emperor Go-Daigo's "restoration" of imperial power.

• *Kemmu-shikimoku.* Legal code in 17 articles, promulgated by Ashikaga Takauji in 1336, attempting to regulate the behavior of the nobles. It was written by the Buddhist monks Gen'e, Ze-en, and Shin'e and their collaborators, who wanted to emulate Prince Shōtoku's Seventeen-Article Constitution of 604 (*see* JŪSHICHIJŌ NO KEMPŌ).

Kempeitai. Government police created in 1910 to control populations in occupied Korea; it was extremely active in all countries invaded by Japan, notably in Southeast Asia, until 1945.

Kempō. Japanese name for a Chinese sword-fighting art (*Chin.*: Quanfa) that was transformed into fist fighting *(ken'yu).* When it was imported to Okinawa, before 1600, it modified somewhat the original techniques of Okinawa-te, which led to the creation of karate and kendo.
• Era of Emperor Juntoku: Dec. 1213–Apr. 1219. *See* NENGŌ.
• "Constitution." *See* CONSTITUTION.

• **Kempō no Jūshichijō.** *See* JŪSHICHIJŌ NO KEMPŌ.

• **Kempō Kinenbi.** Annual commemoration of the promulgation of Japan's second Constitution, which took place on May 3, 1947.

• *Kempō satsuyō.* A work about the Constitution promulgated by Emperor Meiji in 1880, published in 1923 by Minobe Tatsukichi. Its interpretation of the role of the emperor was denounced by the militarist government of the 1930s, which banned publication of *Kempō satsuyō* in 1935.

Kempon Hokke-shū. Buddhist subsect of the Hokke-shū with its headquarters in the Myōman-ji temple in Kyoto.

Ken. "Fist," a term used in all games (from China) in which the players try to outguess each other by making figures with their hands or fingers, as in *jan-ken-pon. Kazu-ken* is a variant of this game in which one player must guess the number of fingers the other player shows. A very popular variation of *jan-ken-pon* is *kitsune-ken,* in which the traditional paper, stone, and scissors are replaced by the hunter (who kills the fox), the village chief (who beats the hunter), and the fox (who tricks the village chief). This game is also called *tōhachi-ken. See* JAN-KEN-PON.
• Unit of length used mainly in architecture to measure the space between two pillars. It is also the unit of length of tatami. It is equivalent to 6 *shaku* (1.818 m) in Nagoya, 6.3 *shaku* (1.9 m) in Kyoto, and 5.8 *shaku* (1.75 m) in Tokyo; 1 ken^2 is equal to 1 *tsubo* (about 3.3 m²). *Chin.: jian.*
• Straight épée with a double blade, used mainly in rituals and in portrayals of Buddhist divinities, in which it is the symbol of the divinities' fight against ignorance. Corresponds to the Sanskrit *khadga. See* JIMOTSU, TSURUGI.
• Prefectures (departments), administrative divisions established in 1868 and 1876 to replace the former provinces. There are currently 47 (including Okinawa).
• Alternative pronunciation *(on)* of the character meaning "dog" *(inu).*

Kencha-sai. Festival of the tea ceremony *(chanoyu)* that takes place every December 1 in the gardens of the Kumano-jinja Shinto shrine in Kyoto. On the same day, many people in Kyoto organize similar private ceremonies in honor of their invited guests.

Kenchi. "Measuring the land," a land census taken during certain periods to determine the size of the harvest and thus set taxes. This survey was sometimes used to produce land registers. *Kenchi* became generalized during Toyotomi Hideyoshi's time, when it was undertaken on a national scale (Taikō-kenchi) in 1582. During the Edo period, the *kenchi* underwent a number of reforms in order to reinforce the domination of the shogun and the daimyo over the peasant class so that they would be subjugated more completely. The results of surveys were recorded in registers called *kenchi-chō*, in which the names of the peasant-owners *(sakunin)* who had to pay tax *(nengo)* were listed. See KENCHŪ-SHI.

Kenchiku-girei. Set of magical and religious rites presiding over construction of a building, private house, or temple, to invoke the divinities and ask for their protection. These rites seem to have been of Chinese origin (they appeared during the Heian period). There were a great many at first, but there are now just two. The *jichinsai* is conducted to consecrate the soil where the structure is to be erected: the site is defined by planting bamboo branches at the four corners and linking them with a sacred cord *(shimenawa)*. The *muneage* (or *tatemae)* consists of attaching sacred folded papers *(gohei)* to the top of the completed frame and throwing down ground-rice cakes *(mochi)* to people who will benefit from the building, in order to draw the blessing of the *kami* to them and to the building. Sometimes, the master pillars *(hon-bashira)* of the house are covered with cooked rice *(shinchiku-iwai)*. Other ceremonies or rites may be performed in various regions.

Kenchō. Era of Emperor Go-Fukakusa: Mar. 1249–Oct. 1256. See NENGō.

• **Kenchō-ji.** Zen Buddhist temple in Kamakura, founded in 1249 by the Chinese monk Daigaku Zenji (Rankei Dōryū, *Chin.*: Lanqi Daolong, 1213–78) of the Rinzai sect, on the model of the Chinese Jingshan temple (Hangzhou province). Often destroyed by fires, notably in 1315, it was reconstructed, always in the original style, in the fifteenth, seventeenth, and twentieth centuries. This temple, sponsored by the family of the Hōjō *shikken*, was exempted from tax payments. It contains invaluable art objects from the Kamakura period. Its *butsuden* and *kara-mon* are in the Muromachi style.

• **Kenchōji-bune.** Merchant ships sent to China in 1325 by the Kamakura shogunate, profits from which were used to finance construction of the Kenchō-ji temple.

Kenchū-mikkan. Famous commentary on the *Kokin-shū*, written in 1212 by Fujiwara no Teika.

Kenchū-shi. Bureaucrats of the Kamakura *bakufu* charged by the *shugo* and *jitō* with producing a register *(kenchi)* of lands under their jurisdiction, giving rise to the creation of documents called *kenchi-chō*. Also called *nawa-uchi, sao-ire*. See KAMAKURA BAKUFU SHOSHI, KENCHI.

Kendan. During the Kamakura and Muromachi periods, policing and judicial functions devolved to the *jitō* and *shugo* of the estates. In Kyoto, this authority was given to the *kebiishi*, then, in the late fourteenth century, to the Samurai-dokoro. In the provinces, many lords of small holdings assumed the right of *kendan*, and sometimes banned *(funyū)* access to their *shōen* to the *shugo* responsible for capturing criminals.

Kendō. "Way of the Sword." Martial art of training to handle the sword *(ken)*, formerly called *ken-jutsu*, Ken no Michi, or *gekken*. This art, banned in 1876, was transformed into a combat sport by Sakakibara Kenkichi (1830–94) for the physical and mental training of young people, and the name *ken-jutsu* was replaced by the less warrior-like *kendō* in 1900. *Kendō* practitioners use swords with bamboo blades called *shinai* and protection over the face *(men)*, chest *(dō)*, stomach *(tare, tare-obi)*, and hands. The combatants wear *kendōgi* and wide *hakama*. They fight in an area measuring 9 × 11 m. The *shinai* are of different lengths and weights depending on the ages of the combatants. Perhaps the most popular combat sport in Japan, *kendō* requires energy, quick decision-making, and composure. Strictly codified, it has six grades *(kyū)* of students and ten ranks *(dan)* of masters. The International Kendo Federation was established in 1970, and *kendō* has become popular in the West.

Ken'ei. Era of Emperor Tsuchimikado: Apr. 1206–Oct. 1207. See NENGō.
• Era of Emperor Go-Nijō: Nov. 1302–Aug. 1303. Also called Kengen. See NENGō.
→ See KAMMURI.

Kengen. Era of Emperor Go-Nijō: Nov. 1302–Aug. 1303. See NENGō.

Kengen-taihō. Coins made of a copper alloy with a high proportion of lead, issued by the court in 958. They had a diameter of between 18 and 20 mm and weighed between 1.8 and 3 grams. They stopped being used in the late tenth century and were replaced by coins imported from Song-dynasty China. *See* KŌCHŌ-JŪNISEN.

Kengyō. Former title of the head of a Buddhist monastery. *See* SŌ-KAN.
→ *See* BETTŌ, BIWA HŌSHI, JIMU, KENKYŌ.

Kenin. "Man of the family," liege of a warrior or noble in ancient times and in the Kamakura period. In the Edo period, the name *gokenin* was given to all vassals of the shogunate. Also sometimes called *kerai* (in the case of vassals of a *daimyō*). *See* GOKENIN, SEMMIN.

Ken-in. Name for the *in-zō (Skt.: mudrā)*, or specific hand (or fist) positions symbolic of the powers of angry (against evil) Buddhist divinities such as the Myō-ō. *Skt.: Mushti-mudrā.*

Kenji. Era of Emperor Go-Uda: Apr. 1275–Feb. 1278. *See* NENGŌ.

Kenji-kin. Gold coin issued during the Edo period, in the Hōei era. Its circulation was interrupted from 1722 to 1730, and it stopped being used completely in 1736. It weighed 2.5 *momme,* or 8.4 grams. Also called Hōei-kin.

Kenjō. A samurai whose main responsibility was to carry and maintain the swords of the daimyo whom he served.

Kenkairon engi. Two-volume Buddhist philosophical work, written in 822 by the monk Saichō (767–822), complementing his earlier work, the three-volume *Kenkairon,* written in 820. This "Treatise to Bring Out the Facts of the Commandments" was intended to defend the new esoteric theories that he had brought back from China against the accusations made by the sects of Nara (*see* NANTO-ROKU-SHŪ) and to show that they alone could be said to belong to the Mahayana (Great Vehicle) branch of Buddhism.

Kenkō Hōshi. Buddhist name of the monk and writer Urabe Kaneyoshi (Yoshida Kaneyoshi, Urabe Kenkō, Yoshida Kenkō, 1283–1350), born in Iga to a family of Shinto priests. An officer in the Imperial Guard, he converted to Buddhism upon the death of Go-Uda Tennō in 1324 and retired to a hill near the Ninna-ji temple in Kyoto, then returned to his Kunimiyama hermitage in Iga in 1340. He wrote *Tsurezuregusa.*

Kenkui. Type of Noh theater mask portraying a fox *(kitsune)* disguised as a Buddhist monk.

Kenkyō. General term for all exoteric Buddhist sects, including Zen and Amida-kyō, as opposed to esoteric sects, or *mikkyō* (Shingon-shū, Tendai-shū, etc.). Also called *kengyō. See* MIKKYŌ.

Kenkyū. Era of Emperor Go-Toba: Apr. 1190–Apr. 1199. *See* NENGŌ.

Kennai-ki. Abridgment of *Kensei-in naifu-ki,* Madenokōji Tokifusa's (1394–1457) diary, of which some fragments have survived; very important for what it tells about the early Muromachi period. The diary covers the years 1414 to 1455 and is very detailed; its author was the rapporteur *(densō)* for the emperor.

Kennin. Era of Emperor Tsuchimikado: Feb. 1201–Feb. 1204. *See* NENGŌ.
• **Kennin-ji.** Zen temple and monastery in the Rinzai sect, founded in Kyoto by the monk Eisai (Yōsai) in 1202 on the order of shogun Minamoto no Yoriie, and built on the model of the Chinese Baizhang monastery. It was named one of the *gozan* of Kyoto in 1334. This temple gave instruction on Rinzai Zen to many monks, among them Dōgen and Muszō Soseki. It became a major center of Chinese literature in the Muromachi period. What remains of it are a *chūmon* from 1202 and a five-story pagoda (the Yasaka no Tō), 38 m high, built in 1440 and restored in 1618. The other buildings date from the eighteenth century. It currently controls about 70 subsidiary temples *(matsu-ji).*

Kennyo Shōnin. Buddhist monk (1543–92) of the Jōdo Shin-shū, eleventh leader *(hossu)* of the sect, who succeeded his father, Shōnyo, in 1555 at the head of the Hongan-ji in Osaka. He opposed Toyotomi Hideyoshi, who wanted to overthrow the Ishiyama-dera, which was occupied by the Ikkō-ikki, and who was at war with him from 1576 to 1580. He was then obligated to make peace with Hideyoshi, who gave him the site of the Nishi Hongan-ji in Kyoto in 1591. His sons Kōchō and Kōjū succeeded him at the head of the Jōdo Shin-shū sect, and Kōjū founded the Higashi Hongan-ji temple in Kyoto in 1602. Also called Kōsa. *See* HONGAN-JI, IKKŌ-IKKI.

Kenrei. Title of prefecture *(ken)* governors from 1871 to 1886; the title was then changed to *chiji.*

Kenrei mon'in ukyō no Daibu-shū. "The Poetic Memoirs of Lady Daibu." A collection of 359 poems written by a woman in the retinue of Empress Taira no Tokuko (1155–1213). Sprinkled with prose texts, it comprises a sort of autobiography in which the author describes her love affairs with the poet and painter Fujiwara no Takanobu and with a grandson of Taira no Kiyomori, Taira no Sukemori, as well as the war between the Taira and the Minamoto. This work, which may date from after 1233, does not have great literary or poetic qualities but is valuable for the events it recounts. *See* TAIRA NO TOKUKO.

Kenroku-en. Garden in the city of Kanazawa (Ishikawa prefecture) created, according to tradition, by Kobori Enshū in the seventeenth century, but completely remade in 1822 by daimyo Maeda Norinaga. One of the three most famous gardens in Japan, with the Kairaku-en and the Kōraku-en, it contains the "six desirable features" of a garden.

Kenryaku. Era of Emperor Juntoku: Mar. 1211–Dec. 1213. *See* NENGŌ.

• **Kenryaku gyoki.** See KIMPISHŌ.

Kensai. Painter (Hirai Shin; *mei:* Jiroku; *azana:* Kimpu; *gō:* Sankoku-shanshō, Kensai, 1802–56), who studied with Bunchō, Kazan, and Aigai.

Kenseitō. "Constitutional party," founded in 1898 by an alliance between the Jiyūto (Liberal party) and the Shimpotō (Progressive party). In 1899, it was divided to form the Kensei Hontō (1899), then, later, the Rikken Kokumintō (1910) and the Rikken Dōshikai (created by Katsura to counter Itō Hirobumi's Seiyūkai). The Rikken Dōshikai (Constitutional Association of Friends) took the name Kenseikai (Constitutional Association) in 1916 and Rikken Minseitō (Constitutional Democratic party) in 1927. The Kenseitō changed its name to Rikken Seiyūkai (Friends of Constitutional Government party) in 1900. *See* KENSEIKAI.

• **Kensei Hontō.** "True Constitutional party," created in 1898 by some members of the Kenseitō; Okuma Shigenobu became its president in 1900. In 1910, weakened by much internal dissension, it allied itself with other political groups to form the Rikken Kokumintō (Constitutional Nationalist party). *See* KENSEIKAI, KENSEITŌ.

• **Kenseikai.** "Constitutional Association," political party founded in 1916 by the merger of the Rikken Dōshikai (Constitutional Assocation of Friends), the Chūseikai (Upright party), and the Kōyū Kurabu (Kōyū club), thus gaining a majority of seats (197) in the House of Representatives. However, because its president, Katō Takaaki, had not been chosen by the *genro* to become president of the Council, it won fewer seats in ensuing elections. Once again allied with the Rikken Seiyūkai (Friends of Consitutional Government) in 1924, it regained its lost seats. Katō Takaaki was then able to form a coalition cabinet, which opened diplomatic relations with the USSR and reduced armaments in 1925. In 1927, the party united with the Seiyū Hontō (True Seiyū party) to form the Rikken Minseitō (Constitutional Democratic party). *See* KENSEITŌ, RIKKEN DŌSHIKAI.

Kenshin. Buddhist monk (1132–92), one of Myōun's disciples, who became *zasu* of the Tendaishū in 1190.

→ *See* USESUGI TERUTORA.

• **Kenshin Daishi.** *See* SHINRIN SHŌNIN.

Kenshō. Poet and Buddhist monk (ca. 1160–1207), Fujiwara no Akisuke's adoptive son. He wrote commentaries on the *Man'yōshū* and classical anthologies (see CHOKUSEN WAKA-SHŪ). Thirteen of his poems *(waka)* were included in the *Senzai waka-shū*.

• **Kenshō-in.** *See* YAMANOUCHI KAZUTOYO.

Kenshun. Buddhist monk (1299–1356) of the Shingon-shū sect, who sided with Ashikaga Takauji during the restoration of the Kemmu era. Appointed *zasu* of the Daigo-ji temple, then *choja* of the Tōdai-ji temple in Kyoto, he became the most important monk of his time. He accompanied Ashikaga Takauji on his expedition against Kyushu, earning the nickname Shōgun-monzeki ("monk-general").

• **Kenshun Mon'in.** *See* TAIRA NO SHIGEKO.

Kensō Tennō. Twenty-third emperor (Prince Ōke no Inasu-wake, 440<485–87>), who, according to the *Kojiki,* succeeded Seinei Tennō after the interim (484–85) of Iitoyo Ao no Kōjo. Emperor Ninken succeeded him.

Kentoku. Era of Emperor Go-Kōgon: July 1370–Apr. 1372. *See* NENGŌ.

Kentōshi. Title for Japanese delegations sent to the Tang court between 630 and 894. Such delegations comprised up to 500 people, among them monks and students, divided among four ships that sailed along the coast. The most famous members of the *kentōshi* were Awa no Mahito (702), Abe no Nakamaro, Kibi no Makibi, and Sugawara no Kiyokimi (804). The last delegation left in 838, and only Japanese merchants continued to have steady relations with China after this date. Japanese envoys to the Sui court in China (in 607 and 608) had the title *kenzuishi*: Ono no Imoko, Takamuko no Kuromaro, and Minabuchi no Shūan held this title.

Kentozuka. In traditional architecture, short pillars, square in section, separating (or uniting) two horizontal beams. They were sometimes topped by a *to* (dado). *See also* KAERUMATA.

Kenuki. "Tweezers." Kabuki play, one of the Kabuki-jūhachiban, revived in 1910 by the actor Sadanji II (d. 1940). This play, which had originally been called *Narukami fudō Kitayama-zakura,* tells the story of a princess forced to put off her wedding because her hair suddenly stands up on end and she cannot style it. The hero of the play discovers that magnetic iron *kanzashi* have been substituted for the princess's silver ones.

Kenuki-gata no tachi. Type of sword whose handle is perforated to make it lighter. Also called Efu no tachi.

Ken'yakurei. Sumptuary edicts issued by the Tokugawa shogunate from time to time to restrain expenditures by peasants, *chōnin,* and samurai. The most typical *ken'yakurei* were those of the Keian, Kyōhō, Kansei, and Tempō eras.

Ken'ya Miura. *See* MIURA KEN'YA.

Ken'yūsha. "Friends of the Ink Block," a student association, formed in 1885 by Ozaki Kōyō (1867–1903), which became a literary group of reference. It published a magazine, *Garakuta Bunko,* and gathered a number of talented writers, including Yamada Bimyō, Kawakami Bizan, Iwaya Sazanami, Hirotsu Ryōrō, and Kōda Rohan. In 1890, the association expanded with the inclusion of other famous writers, such as Izumi Kyōka, Tokuda Shūsei, Nagai Kafū, Tayama Katai, and others, all of whom contributed to the development of popular novels and novels of morals. The first literary society of its type, it was very influential until it was dissolved in 1903.

Kenzan. Painter and ceramist (Ogata Shinsei, Ogata Kenzan; *azana:* I-in; *gō:* Shōkosai, Shūseidō, Shisui, Reikai, Tōin, 1663–1743), Ogata Kōrin's brother. He may have been a descendant of Hon'ami Koetsu. Born in Edo, Kenzan first studied with his older brother to learn poetry (almost all his paintings included a poem he wrote out in calligraphy), then ceramics under Nonomura Ninsei. In 1699, he built a kiln in Narutaki, northwest of Kyoto, which he called Inuiyama (another reading of Inui is "Kenzan"). Kōrin decorated some of his ceramic production but, lacking sufficient financial means, in 1712 he was forced to close his kiln and open a pottery shop in Kyoto. Finally, supported by a wealthy Edo monk, he built another kiln in Iriya, near Edo, and produced ceramics in a unique style called Kenzan-*yaki.* He was also known as a master *(chajin)* of the tea ceremony *(chanoyu).*

Keppan. Ancient signature made by making a print with one's index finger using one's own blood, used around the fourteenth century by people of all classes to solemnize a contract or a commitment. Some people wrote such contracts with their blood *(kessho)* or with blood mixed with China ink. *See also* KAŌ.

Keren. In Kabuki theater, magical apparitions that are a part of some plays.

Keribori. Type of decorative engraving on metal comprising triangular points executed with the point of a tool. Also called *senkoku.*

Keshin. "Transformative incarnation" assumed by the Buddha and some bodhisattvas *(bosatsu)* in order to save people. *Keshin* are sometimes portrayed atop the heads of Buddhist images as small effigies or heads. *See* KEBUTSU.

Ketsujō. In ancient Japan and the Ryukyu Islands, cords knotted in a certain way, used as a sort of accounting method, similar to the *quipu* (or *quipos*) in ancient Peru.

Ketsu-meidan. "Fraternity of Blood," a secret ultranationalist society active between 1920 and 1930, some of whose members committed political assassinations, including those of Inoue Junnosuke, secretary of the Rikken Minseitō (Constitutional Democratic party) and Dan Takuma, director of the

Mitsui Bank, in 1932. The assassins, Konuma Tadashi and Hishinuma Gorō, supported in part by the peasant class, were freed in 1940. This association, to which some navy officers also belonged, was led by Inoue Nishhō. *See* INOUE JUNNOSUKE, INOUE NISSHO.

Ki. Ancient unit of length equivalent to one *sun* (about 3.3 m). *See also* SHAKU.

• Word that conveys an extremely broad concept associated with energy, spirit, intellect, and emotion, and often used as a psychological definition. It can define health (moral or physical), will (good or bad), nervous state (apathy or excitation), temperament (timidity or boldness), and so on. *Ki (Chin.: qi)* is thus a sort of force or energy that acts upon or through an individual in a variety of ways. It is somewhat equivalent to the Chinese Taoist "field of cinnabar" *(Chin.: dantian)* and the Indian *prāna,* which correspond, more or less, to the Western concept of the "soul." Essentially, it is the bit of cosmic energy that is inherent in all living beings, giving them their personality. One may have strong *ki (tsuyo-ki)* or weak *ki (yowa-ki).* An individual's *ki* may be remote from him or her (unconsciousness), "short" (a person who is quick to anger), "small" (a timid person), "long" (a patient person), and so on. The *ki* is located in the *hara* (abdomen). The instant liberation of *ki* during a sudden effort is accompanied by a sort of cry (exhalation) called *ki-ai,* somewhat analogous to the woodsman's "Hunh!" The notion of *ki* is at the basis of all martial arts because it expresses the coalescence and liberation of a person's energy.

• **Ki-ai.** In martial arts, a specific cry made at the psychological point of an attack or a violent effort, expressing the liberation of the energy accumulated or concentrated in the *hara* (abdomen) during preparation for the action. *See* KI.

Ki Baitei. Painter (Baitei Ki Jibin, Konan Kyūrō, Kyūrō Sanshō, Jibin, Bai Tei, 1734–1810), born in Ōtsu, Buson's disciple. Also a haiku poet, he was better known as a painter in the Bunjinga style. His main subjects were landscapes, flowers, and birds, but he also illustrated haiku *(haiga)* and painted beautiful women *(bijin),* humorous scenes *(kyōga),* and other subjects. Many of his paintings were reproduced in ukiyo-e prints collected in albums, such as *Kyūru gafu.* He was also known as Ōmi Buson because he lived in Ōmi.

Kibaminzoku-ron. Historical theory of "horse-riding peoples" proposed by Professor Egami in 1950, according to which Altaic "horsemen-archers," armed with iron épées and armor, conquered Japan more or less peacefully before the sixth century and imposed themselves as lords over the Yayoi agricultural population. They brought with them shamanic beliefs that would contribute to the creation of Shinto, myths, and a civilization that has been called the *kofun* period because of the megalithic tombs that they erected in great numbers to bury the members of their aristocracy. These Altaic peoples, who came in small groups from the Korean Peninsula, settled on Kyushu or in Yamato starting in the late third or early fourth century, thus transforming an agricultural society that was not very hierarchized into a highly structured society that gave rise to "historical" Japan. This theory is now universally accepted with a few minor modifications because it has been largely corroborated by excavation of *kofun. See* KOFUN.

Kibe-ha. Branch of the Jōdo Shin-shū, founded in Ōmi by the Buddhist monk Shōshun in the thirteenth century, currently with about 100,000 followers. Also called Kinshokuji-ha.

Kibi. Former region in southwest Japan corresponding to today's Okayama and Hiroshima prefectures, which was divided into three provinces in 701—Bizen, Bitchū, and Bingo—and into four provinces in 713 with the addition of Mimasa province, created by dividing Bizen. This maritime region very quickly opened relations with the Korean Peninsula, but in the sixth century it came under the control of Yamato. The heads of the region's clans were buried in gigantic *kofun* (megalithic tombs). Also called Kibi no Kuni.
→ *See* KEI.

• **Kibi no Makibi.** Literate noble of the Nara court (695–775), from Kibi no Kuni, who went to China in 717 as part of an envoy to the Tang court (*see* KENTŌSHI) with Abe no Nakamoro and the Buddhist monk Gembō. When he returned, in 734, he brought back many Chinese administrative texts, the art of embroidery, and the games of *biwa* and *go (igo).* Appointed a counselor, he opposed Fujiwara no Nakamaro, who sent him to a posting in Kyushu. He then went to China again in 752 as vice-ambassador. Recalled to the court in 764, he directed construction of the Tōdai-ji and was appointed *dainagon* (grand counselor). He withdrew from public affairs in 771 and devoted himself to the study of Confucian rites, which he adapted to the Japanese administration. He is sometimes credited with invention of the katakana syllabary.

• **Kibi no Michi no Naka.** Former name of Bitchū province.

• **Kibi no Saki.** Former name of Bizen province. Also Kibi no Michi no Kuchi.

• **Kibi Yakehiko no Mikoto.** In Shinto legend, Yamato-Takeru's companion in the wars against the Ebisu.

Kibitsu-hiko no Mikoto. Imperial prince (Hiko Isuseri-hiko no Mikoto, traditionally first century AD), son of Kōrei Tennō, who, according to the *Nihon shoki*, put down revolts in Kibi no Kuni and Izumo. He was divinized as a *kami*.

• **Kibitsu-jinja.** Shinto shrine in Kibitsu (Okayama prefecture) dedicated to the *kami* Kibitsu-hiko no Mikoto and built between 1390 and 1402.

Kiboku. Divinatory procedure using tortoise shells *(kame)* imported from China, where this art had been practiced since prehistoric times. Analogous to divination with deer scapula, it was performed by applying a red-hot brand to the underneath of a tortoise shell, which caused cracks that were then interpreted by seers. It was perhaps these cracks that were stylized in drawings called *chokkomon*, found on certain objects and sarcophagi in *kofun. See* DIVINATION.

Kibumi no Eshi. Group of Korean and Chinese painters who settled in Yamato in 604 and received various names according to where they lived. They worked mainly for the court and the Buddhist monasteries of Nara. In 701, they became attached to an official Bureau of Painting (Edakumi no Tsukasa) of the ministry of court affairs, the Nakatsukasa-shō.

Kibyōshi. "Yellow books." A series of inexpensive books with yellow covers, written in the *gesaku* and *kusazōshi* genres. *Kibyōshi* contained various types of literature, from children's stories to novels for adults, in a small format (about 18 × 13 cm), and included a large number of woodcut illustrations. Some were more specifically made for children (starting in 1720). *Kibyōshi* for adults appeared about 1775, and many dealt with satirical subjects, written by such authors as Santō Kyōden and Hōseidō Kisanji. More than 2,000 titles were published between 1775 and 1806. They were then replaced in popularity by the *gōkan* (bound-volume) genre, featuring longer works by authors such as Shikitei Samba. *See* KINKIN SENSEI EIGA NO YUME.

Kichi. Painter (fifteenth century?) of the Muromachi *suiboku* school, perhaps one of Sesshū's students.

Kichibei. Ceramist (Raku III, 1599–1658), who also signed his works Ronko and Don'yu.
→ *See* MORONOBU.

Kichijitsu. According to the ancient lunar calendar and a number of superstitions arising both from natural beliefs and from Taoism and Buddhism, the Japanese are convinced that there are lucky *(kichijitsu)* and unlucky days. It is important to begin something on a lucky day and to avoid days considered unlucky. Thus, in almanacs, days are always designated by one in a cycle of six names that characterize each day's potential:

1) **Sensho** (of the first victory): Lucky in the morning, unlucky in the afternoon.

2) **Tomo-biki** (which gains friends): Unlucky only around midday.

3) **Sembu** (first defeat): Unlucky in the morning, lucky in the afternoon.

4) **Butsu-metsu** (Buddha's ruin): Unlucky all day.

5) **Daian** (great peace): Lucky all day.

6) **Shakko** (red mouth): Bad luck all day except around midday.

For example, it is believed that if a funeral is held on a Tomo-biki, it will soon be followed by others (unless one places a substitute doll in the coffin of the deceased person). It is also strongly ill-advised to marry on a Butsu-metsu, and so on. *See* KANNICHI.

Kichijō. Buddhist divinity of Good Luck, Merit, and Beauty, perhaps corresponding to the Hindu divinity Lakshmī (Shrī). It is portrayed as a beautiful Chinese woman. It was not very popular and was rarely portrayed. Starting in the fifteenth century, it was supplanted by Benzai-ten. Also called Kudoku-ten, Kichijō-ten.

• **Kichijō-in.** Mudra specific to the preaching Buddha and to Kichijō-ten, the hand extended with the palm forward and the ring finger forming a circle with the thumb. Also called *chikichijō-in.*

• **Kichijō-komagata.** Syncretic Shinto-Buddhist aspect of Batō Kannon (*Skt.*: Hayagrīva) in the Kumano-ōji shrines.

• **Kichijō-za-zō.** Name sometimes given to the "lotus" sitting position *(Skt.: padmāsana)* of some Buddhist divinities.

Kichō. Curtain hanging from a wooden frame, once used to close off part of a room if a fusuma was not available.

Kida Minoru. Writer and ethnologist (Yamada Yoshihiko, 1895–1975), born in Kagoshima. He studied at the Université de Paris (1933–39) and was a reporter for Agence France Presse. In 1958, he translated Jean Henri Fabre's 10-volume *Souvenirs entomologiques*. His novel *Kichigai buraku shūyū kikō* won the *Mainichi Shimbun* Prize. He also translated French sociology and ethnology works.

Kido Kōichi. Politician (1889–1977), Kido Takayoshi's grandson, born in Tokyo. He was appointed minister of education in Konoe Fumimaro's cabinet in 1937, then minister of the interior in Hiranuma Kiichirō's cabinet in 1939. A member *(naidaijin)* of the emperor's Privy Council, he was among the "hawks" during the Second World War and had Tōjō Hideki appointed to replace Konoe Fumimaro in 1941. However, he advised the emperor to accept Japan's surrender in 1945. Considered a war criminal by the Allies, he was sentenced to life in prison in 1948, but was freed in 1955. His *Kido nikki* (Kido's Diary, 1966) remains an excellent source of information on Japanese politics between 1930 and 1945.

Kido Shirō. Movie producer (1894–1977), born in Tokyo, who became head of the Shōchiku movie studio in 1924 and hired famous directors, including Ozu Yasujirō and Kinoshita Keisuke. During the Second World War, he produced movies to encourage the war effort; after 1945, he returned to a lighter style. He was appointed president of Shōchiku Co. in 1954.

Kido Takayoshi. Politician (Kido Kōin, Kido Takamasa, Katsura Kogorō, 1833–77), head of the Chōshū clan, who played an important role in the restoration of the emperor in 1868, having sided with his former enemies from the Satsuma clan (Sat-Chō Dōmei), Saigō Takamori and Ōkubo Toshimichi, to overthrow the shogunate. He then worked to modernize Japan and helped write the "Oath in Five Articles" (Gokajō no Seimon) taken by the emperor on April 6, 1868. An ambassador to Europe and to the United States from 1871 to 1873, he was then appointed minister of public education and the interior, but resigned because of his opposition to Ōkubo's decision to send troops to Taiwan. He returned to government under the aegis of Itagaki Taisuke, then was appointed president of the Assembly of Prefects in 1876.

Ki'en. Painter (Yanagisawa Rikyō; *mei:* Gondayū, Ryūrikyō, *azana:* Kōbi; *gō:* Chikukei, Gyokukei, Ki'en, 1706–58), one of the founders of the Nanga school and the Bunjinga style.
• Painter (Minigawa Ken; *mei:* Bunzō; *azana:* Hakukyō; *gō:* Yūhisai, Kyōsai, Donkai, Ki'en, 1734–1807), Gyokusen's and Ōkyo's student in Kyoto. A Confucian scholar, he wrote a number of works on Confucianism. He painted mainly bamboo and orchids.

Kien-rei. Cancellation of the debts of vassals of the Edo shogunate, ordered at various times to save them from ruin, since they were often deeply indebted to the *fudasashi* who bought the rice that was their salary. The first of these moratoria took place in 1789 on the order of Matsudaira Sadanobu, and some debts were then converted into interest payable in annual installments. Another was decreed in 1843, and others were ordered by daimyo; this caused the ruin of the *fudasashi* but did not much ameliorate the situation of the *hatamoto* and other indebted vassals. *See* FUDASASHI, TOKUSEI.

Kigen. Chronological system of Japanese history setting the ascension of Jimmu Tennō (traditionally February 11, 660 BC) as the beginning of calculation of time. This date was probably established by Shōtoku Taishi, but was officially set in 1872 by Emperor Meiji, who created a commemorative festival celebrating the beginning of this era, the Kigensetsu, coinciding with publication of Japan's first Constitution on February 11 (first day of the new moon), 1889. It was observed mainly during the Meiji era. However, over the opposition of many parliamentarians, this commemoration, which had been abolished in 1948, was converted into a national holiday called Kenkoku Kinembi (Statutory Holiday of Foundation of the Nation) in 1966.

• **Kigensetsu.** *See* KASHIHARA JINGŪ.

Kiguchi Kohei. Soldier (1873–94), one of the heroes of the Sino-Japanese War of 1894–95, born in Okayama prefecture. Wounded, he used his gun as a crutch and continued to sound the bugle until he died.

Kigyoku. Painter (Kurokawa Yasusada; *mei:* Mangorō; *azana:* Shimo; *gō:* Shōrakan, Shōzan-shōshi, Kigyoku, d. 1756), one of Kanō Kyūshin's students.
• Sculptor (early nineteenth century) of Noh masks and netsuke.

Kihara Hitoshi. Biologist (1893–1986), known for his research on the origins of wheat and his important studies on chromosomes. He was decorated with the Order of Culture (Bunka-shō) in 1948.

Kihara Kōichi. Poet and playwright (Ōta Tadashi, 1922–79), author of many plays, including *Ichiban takai basho* (The Highest Place, 1957) and *Gyosha Paetōn* (Phaeton the Driver, 1965), a musical in verse.

Kihei-tai. Irregular military groups that sprang up in Chōshu in 1863 to fight against the Tokugawa shogunate. These elite units, raised by Takasugi Shinsaku, were formed of volunteers from all classes and commanded by officers appointed more on merit than on social standing, and perfectly trained. After defeating the Tokugawa regiments at Kokuraguchi in 1866, they entered Kyoto in 1868 to protect the imperial palace and took part in the major battles of the Boshin Civil War (1868). The units were dissolved in 1869, when a national army was created; the successful warriors were not, for the most part, from the samurai class, and this fact contributed greatly to formation of an army based on universal conscription, as advocated by Yamagata Aritomo, one of the commanding officers of the Kihei-tai. *See* MIURA GORŌ, TAKASUGI SHINSAKU.

Kihira Tadayoshi. Philosopher (Kihira Masami, 1874–1949), born in Mie prefecture, who propagated Hegel's ideas in Japan and wrote an important work on epistemology, *Ninshiki-ron* (1915). He also wrote *Gyō no tetsugaku* (Philosophy of Spiritual Discipline, 1923) and works on nationalist philosophy, such as *Nihon seishin* (The Spirit of Japan, 1930). Recently, more than 1,200 letters written and received by Kihira were discovered in his house in Mie prefecture, including correspondence with other philosophers such as Nishida Kitarō and Watsuji Tetsurō.

Kii. Former province, now part of Wakayama and Mie prefectures.
• Branch of the Tokugawa family, formed by the descendants of Tokugawa Yorinobu, Tokugawa Ieyasu's eighth son. *See* SAN-KE, TOKUGAWA.

• Fortress built about 663 to protect the city of Dazaifu (northern Kyushu) against potential invasion by the Koreans.

Kiichi hōgen sanryaku no maki. Kabuki play in five acts, in the *jidai-mono* genre, produced by Bunkodō and Hasegawa in 1731.

Kiitsu. Painter (Suzuki Motonaga; *mei:* Tamesaburō; *azana:* Shi'en; *gō:* Kaikai, Seisei, Kiitsu, 1796–1858) of the Kōrin school, Sakai Hōitsu's student. He was the first to use the purple ink called *murasaki-zome.*

Kijiya. Wood turners, living mainly in the mountains and villages of northern Honshu, where their families make *kokeshi* dolls. They claim to be descendants of Prince Koretaka (844–97), Emperor Montoku's oldest son, whom they credit with inventing the wood lathe *(rokuro).* They also make lacquered pieces. *See* KOKESHI.

Kijyoku. Type of decorated fabric once used for tablecloths. Also called *ochi-shiki.*

Kikajin. According to the *Nihon shoki* (720), groups of Korean immigrants from the Paekche kingdom who settled in Japan around 400 under the leadership of Yuzuki no Kimi. This name was also applied to their descendants. These immigrants held important positions in all spheres of lay and religious activity and were behind the formation of clans *(uji)* such as the Hata, the Aya, and the Sakanoue. Other Koreans, who arrived in Japan in the sixth and seventh centuries, and who introduced Buddhism and a number of arts and crafts, were also called *kikajin. See* HATA, YUZUKI NO KIMI.

Kikaku. *Haikai* poet (Enomoto Kikaku, Takarai Kikaku, 1661–1707), a disciple of Bashō, to whom he dedicated a collection called *Kare obana* and a short work describing his master's last days, *Bashō-ō shūen-ki* (1694). He created a *haikai* school in Edo that had more brilliance and spirit than Bashō's.

Kiki. Collective term for two major ancient histories of Japan, the *Kojiki* (712) and the *Nihon shoki* (720).

Kikka no En. National chrysanthemum festival on the ninth day of the ninth month, with public exhibitions of the best varieties grown by horticulturists. In Hakata, a small town between Kyoto and

Osaka, *kiku-ningyō,* dolls made with chrysanthemum flowers and dressed in ancient costumes, are put on display. Also called Kiku no Sekku, Chōyō no Sekku. *See* CHRYSANTHEMUM.

• **Kikka-shō.** "Order of the Chrysanthemum," decoration *(kunshō)* consisting of a purple-and-red ribbon, created in 1876 and reserved for sovereigns and princes to reward services rendered to the country. This order was eliminated several years after it was created, and reestablished in 1888. Also called Kikuka-shō. *See* KUNSHŌ.

Kikkawa Motoharu. General (1530–86), Mōri Motonari's son, adopted in 1547 by the Kikkawa family. He pacified Iwami and Izumo provinces and, in 1569, captured the Tachibana castle in Chikuzen province. He defeated Ōuchi Teruhiro's army and won a number of battles in Izumo and Inaba. In 1578, allied with Kobayakawa Takakage, he besieged the Kōzuki castle in Harima, causing its defender, Amako Katsuhisa, to commit suicide. Kikkawa then opposed Toyotomi Hideyoshi, but became his vassal after the assassination of Oda Nobunaga. He died during the expedition to Kyushu.

• **Kikkawa Hiroie.** General (1561–1625), Kikkawa Motoharu's son, who became the head of the Kikkawa house after his father and older brother died in Kyushu in 1586. A vassal of Mōri Terumoto, he received a fief of 140,000 *koku* in Izumo and other provinces, and had a castle built in Oda (Izumo). He took part in two expeditions to Korea led by Toyotomi Hideyoshi. During the Battle of Sekigahara (1600), he contacted Tokugawa Ieyasu in an effort to preserve some of the land of the Mōri, although they had sided with the losing side; he kept for himself an estate worth only 30,000 *koku* in Iwakuni. He retired in 1616 and compiled a collection of his edicts.

• **Kikkawa Hitoshi.** *See* REIKA.

• **Kikkawa Koretari.** *See* YOSHIKAWA KORETARI.

• **Kikkawa Reika.** *See* REIKA.

• **Kikkawa Saburō.** *See* REIKA.

Kikki. Fujiwara no Tsunefusa's (1143–1200) diary, also called *Kichidai-ki* (Notes of the Grand Counselor) and *Kikko-ki,* concerning the years 1166 to 1198 (with some interruptions). It provides very interesting information on the rivalry between the Taira and the Minamoto.

Kikkōman. The largest manufacturer of soy sauce in Japan. It also owns restaurant chains and plants making various food products. Founded in 1917 in Noda, Chiba prefecture, it has a number of foreign subsidiaries, notably in Wisconsin and Germany. It also distributes a number of Italian and English products and Coca-Cola. *See* SHŌYU.

Kikō bungaku. "Travel literature," a literary genre that began during the Heian period, comprising almost exclusively the accounts of more or less official people who were traveling. These journals, many of them in prose sprinkled with poems, were very popular until the Meiji period. There are about 70 dating from before the Edo period. The oldest seems to be *Tosa nikki* (935) by Ki no Tsurayuki; other famous ones are *Sarashina nikki* (1059), *Izayoi nikki,* and *Towazu monogatari.* Some *kikō* were included in longer novels, such as *gunki-monogatari* and warrior novels. During the Edo period, poets such as Bashō also wrote travel journals in poetry; in the Meiji era, Tayama Katei, among other writers, continued the tradition. *See also* HOKKEI, NIKKI.

Kikō-ji. Buddhist temple located near Nara (Ikoma-gun) that was said to be the imperial temple of Gemmei, Genshō, and Shōmu Tennō. It was apparently founded by the monk Gyōki in 721 for the Hosshō-shū sect. Almost completely destroyed (except for the *kondō*) in the late sixteenth century, it was reconstructed in the Momoyama style. The *kondō,* in the Nara style, contains a triad of Amida, in wood, 2.24 m high, in the Jōchō style (late twelfth century). Also called Sugawara-dera.

Kiku. *See* CHRYSANTHEMUM.

• **Kiku-ningyō.** *See* IKI-NINGYŌ, KIKKA NO EN.
→ *See* KIKKA-SHŌ.

Kikuchi Dairoku. Mathematician (1855–1917), born in Edo. He studied at the Bansho Shirabesho, then in England from 1866 to 1868 and 1870 to 1877. He was then appointed a professor at the University of Tokyo. His mathematics textbook (*Shotō kikagaku kyōkasho,* 1881) was the most used book in schools until 1945. He was president of the University of Tokyo (1898–1901), minister of education (1901–03), and subsequently director of the Physics and Chemistry Research Institute.

Kikuchi Kan. Author and playwright (Kikuchi Hiroshi, 1888–1948), born in Takamatsu (Kōchi prefecture). A disciple of Mori Ōgai, he and Mori, along with other writers, started the literary magazine *Bungei Shunjū* in 1923; he was friends with Akutagawa Ryūnosuke. He had studied at the University of Tokyo, then the University of Kyoto, where he specialized in English and Irish literature. He began to write for the student magazine in Kyoto, *Shinshi-chō*, and penned short plays such as *Chichi kaeru* (The Return of the Father, 1917), then turned to stories—*Mumei sakka no nikki* (Diary of an Unknown Writer, 1918), *Tadanao kyō gyōjō-ki* (On the Behavior of Lord Tadanao, 1918)—and novels—*Shinju fujin* (Madame Pearl, 1920). Among his other major works are *Okujō no kyōjin* (A Madman on the Roof, ca. 1916), *Onshū no kanatani, Gokuraku* (Paradise), *Reigan* (The Cold Look), *Gaki* (The Urchin), *Dōri* (Reason, 1919), and *Doku no hana* (The Flowers of Evil). He was nicknamed Bundan no Ogosho ("prince of the novel"). He created two important literary awards in 1935, the Akutagawa Ryūnosuke Prize and the Naoki Sanjūgo Prize, in memory of his two friends. Even today, these are two of the most prestigious literary prizes. In 1952, a major literary award was created in his name.

Kikuchi Keigetsu. Painter (1879–1955) in "Japanese style" (Nihonga).

Kikuchi Kōsai. Confucian scholar and writer (1618–82), who lived in Kyoto. Among his works are *Shichisho kōgi tsūkō* (7 vols.) and *Honchō rekidai Meijin-den* (14 vols.).

Kikuchi Seishi. Physicist (1920–74), born in Tokyo, who developed nuclear science in Japan. He directed construction of the two cyclotrons at the University of Osaka and received the Order of Culture (Bunka-shō) in 1951.

Kikuchi Takemitsu. General (?–1373), who, serving the Southern Court (Nanchō), battled the troops of the Ashikaga in Kyushu and captured Dazaifu in 1361. When he died, General Imagawa Ryōshun regained control of the island.

Kikuchi Yōsai. Painter (Kikuchi Takeyasu; *mei:* Kikuchi Yōsai, Kawahara Ryōhei; *gō:* Ryōhei, Yōsai, 1788–1878), of the Kanō, Bunchō, and Ōkyo schools. A student of Takada Enjō, he painted mainly historical subjects, for which he performed detailed historical and archeological research. In 1878, he produced a series of ten albums of woodcuts (in black and white) titled *Zenken ko-jitsu,* portraying more than 500 famous figures from Japanese history.

Kikumura Itaru. Writer, born 1925 in Kanagawa. A war correspondent for the *Yomiuri Shimbun* during the Second World War, he wrote a story, *Iōjima,* in 1957 that won the Akutagawa Prize. He wrote fiction and biographies.

Kikuta Kazuo. Actor and radio personality (1908–73), who wrote very popular comedies, such as *Hana saku minato* (The Port Where the Flowers Bloom, 1943), and radio serials, including *Kane no naru oka* (The Hills Where the Bells Ring, 1947–50), *Yama kara kita otoko* (The Man from the Mountains, 1945), and *Kimi no na wa* (What Is Your Name? 1952–54). He ran several studios for Tōhō and produced Broadway-style musical comedies, adapting *My Fair Lady* for Japanese theater.

Kikutake Kiyonori. Architect (b. 1928), one of the founders of the Metabolism group that planned coastal towns and designed some interesting buildings, such as the Tōkōen Hotel (1964) and the Kurume Civic Center (1969).

Kimbusen-ji. Buddhist temple established in Yoshino, near Nara. According to tradition, it was founded by En no Gyōja in the late seventh century for the Shugendō sect. During the Nambokuchō War, it was the headquarters of emperors of the Southern Court (Nanchō). The syncretic divinity Zaō Gongen is venerated there. In 1872, because the Shugendō sect had been abolished, the temple came under the obedience of the Tendai-shū, but it became independent again in 1945. Fifteenth-century *zaō-dō* and *ni-ō-mon*. Also called Kimpusen-ji, Zaō-dō.

Kimedashi. In ukiyo-e printing technique, inkless relief printing on the edges of the images and in some uncolored parts of the print, often used by Harunobu. Also, a term for a paper texture reproducing the veins of the printing woodblock through application of pressure. Also called *kimekomi, nikuzuri.*

Kimekomi-ningyō. Type of doll sculpted in light wood (usually paulownia, *kiri*), with brocade fabric glued on. The head and hands are often made of porcelain or painted terra-cotta, and the base is sculpted to represent feet. These dolls are difficult to make; about 10 to 20 cm high, they portray mainly characters from Noh and Kabuki theater. Con-

いよゝ広せたゝずも仮だ呂立じれ。
れも広心やゝひ呂小火れ。松の下に宿り

16th-century noble warrior, by Kikuchi Yōsai

sidered objets d'art, they are collected and offered as highly prized gifts. Specialized schools teach women and girls to make this type of doll. *See* NENGYŌ.

→ *See* KIMEDASHI.

Kimi. Former title for high-level bureaucrats that became a family name. In current usage, it is an in-formal mode of address between persons of the same age and social rank with a certain level of fa-miliarity. *See also* KABANE, KUNI, KUNI NO MIYA-TSUKO, OKIMI.

Kimigayo. Japan's national anthem, a 31-syllable *tanka* poem excerpted from the *Kokin-shū*, set to music by Hayashi Hiromori and harmonized by

Franz Eckert, the navy's orchestra conductor from 1879 to 1898. It was played for the first time at the imperial court in 1880. The lyrics are: *Kimi ga yo wa / Chi yo ni yachi yo ni / Sazare ishi no / Iwao to narite / Koke no musu made* (The reign of our lord / shall last eight thousand and one generations / until stones / become boulders / and are covered with moss).

Kimii-dera. Buddhist temple in Wakayama, one of the Shingon sect's Sanjūsan-sho (Guze Kannon branch). It was founded, according to tradition, in 770 by the Chinese Buddhist monk Weiguang (*Jap.*: Ikō), who placed statues of Senju Kannon and Jūichimen Kannon that he had sculpted on the site. This temple (also called Nagusazan Gokoku-in) was designated an imperial temple by Retired Emperor Go-Shirakawa. Located on a hill overlooking the city and the island of Awaji, it has many old structures: *hondō* (eighteenth century), *tahōtō* (1449), *rōmon* (1588, restored in 1789), *shōrō* (1588), *daishidō* (1753), *rokkaku-dō* (Edo period), *kaisandō* (ca. 1600), and others.

Kimitada. Painter (Kose Kimitada, active ca. 950) of the Yamato-e school, perhaps Kose Kanaoka's grandson.

Kimma. Objects made with thin strips of bamboo or braided horsehair and covered with several layers of different-colored lacquers that are then engraved to make colored designs. Few *kimma* were made in Japan; most were imported from Burma and Thailand.

Kimmei Tennō. Twenty-ninth emperor (Prince Ame-kuni Oshi Haruki Hironiha no Mikoto, traditionally 509<540–71>); according to the *Nihon shoki,* Emperor Keitai's third son and successor to his brother, Senka, after a long dispute over the throne between him and his two brothers, Ankan and Senka. It was likely under his reign that Buddhism was imported from Korea (in 538 or 552), when more than 5,000 Korean families (*see* KIKAJIN) settled in Japan. Bitatsu Tennō succeeded him.

Kimono. General term for the Japanese national costume for both men and women. It is a long robe, open in front, which is crossed left over right and held closed with a fabric belt *(obi)*. The *kimono* succeeded the short-sleeved *kosode* (worn as an undergarment in the Nara period, which became an overgarment in the sixteenth century), becoming

the standard garment. Until the seventeenth century, women held their *kimono* closed with a flexible fabric belt, but this was then replaced by a wide rigid belt with a knot on the back. However, courtesans continued to close their *kimono* with a flexible belt knotted in front.

All *kimono* are shaped the same way; only their decoration and fabric differentiate them. In general, men wear *kimono* in dark colors; ceremonial *kimono* are sometimes decorated with the family *mon*. They are worn over pants *(hakama)* and a loose-fitting vest *(haori)*. In summer, wool or silk *kimono* are replaced by *kimono* made of light cotton, printed (or dyed) in indigo on a white background, called *yukata*. In the winter, a loose-fitting jacket in thick fabric *(tanzen)* is worn over the *kimono* at home. Women's *kimono* are decorated, sometimes luxuriously, with motifs and colors corresponding to the seasons. The ceremonial *kimono* is black and bears the family's *mon*. Girls wear long-sleeved *kimono (furisode)* with long panels, brightly painted or embroidered with various motifs, with an *obi* usually knotted in the back. On stage, Noh and Kabuki actors wear shaped *kimono* in sumptuous fabrics. Wedding *kimono* are usually very long and have padding on the bottom to make them heavier.

The *kimono* is worn with *tabi* (socks with sepa-

Kimono motif

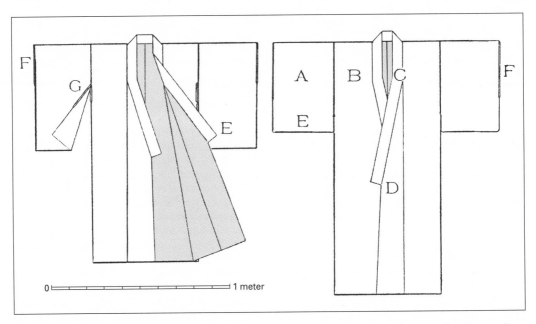

Kimono: *left*, woman's; *right*, man's. A. Sleeve. B. Front. C. Collar. D. Front extension. E. Sleeve part forming a pocket. F. Opening for hand. G. Opening for arm

rated toes) and clogs (*zōri* or *geta*). While *kimono* for men have short sleeves and closed armpits, those for women have slightly longer sleeves and are not sewn at the armpits. In general, a *kimono* should be about 20 cm longer than the height of the person wearing it. The excess fabric is folded at the waist and the *kimono* is kept at the correct length with crepe belts and *obi*. A *kimono* is usually made in eight rectangular pieces cut from a single piece of fabric about 11 × 0.36 m, regardless of the size of the person wearing it. It is assembled with straight seams. *Kimono* must be folded in a certain way to preserve their natural pleats, and they are stored in special chests *(tansu)*. Although *kimono* are often worn by both men and women at home and during festivals, Western clothing *(yōfuku)* has been adopted for working, and it is rare to see people, except for the elderly, wearing *kimono* except on special occasions. Luxurious *kimono* are sometimes worth a great deal of money; it is not unusual to have to rent them for major ceremonies and weddings. Many families pass down sumptuous ceremonial *kimono*. Also called, rarely, *wafuku*. See KOSODE, YUKATA.

Kimpishō. A three-volume work describing court ceremonies, compiled by Emperor Juntoku about 1213 or 1221, frequently imitated by later emper-

ors. Also called *Kinchūshō, Juntoku-in mishō, Kenryaku gyoki*. See JUNTOKU TENNŌ.

Kimura Heitarō. General (1888–1948) who fought in Burma in 1942. Accused of war crimes by the Allies in 1948, he was hanged. *See* WAR CRIMES.

Kimura Hisashi. Astronomer (1870–1943), born in Ishikawa, who discovered the Z term of latitude variations (variations in the terrestrial axis). He received the Order of Culture (Bunka-shō) in 1937.

Kimura Ki. Writer and literary historian (1894–1980), born in Okayama prefecture; his studies on the culture of the Meiji era earned him the Kikuchi Kan Prize in 1978. Editor of many magazines and publications, he wrote a historical novel, *Shimabara bishōnen-roku* (1927), and a major study on literary exchanges between Japan and the United States, *Nichibei bungaku kōryūshi no kenkyū* (1960).

Kimura Kinka. Silent-movie director, primarily known for his production of *Botchan,* after the novel by Natsume Sōseki, in 1927.

Kimura Motoo. Geneticist, born 1924 in Aichi prefecture. He rejected Darwin's theory of evolution, proposing instead a neutral theory based on discoveries made about DNA mutations. He received the Order of Culture (Bunka-shō) in 1976 for his body of work.

Kimura Shigenari. Warrior (ca. 1592–1615) in the service of Toyotomi Hideyori, who distinguished himself during the summer siege (Natsu no Jin, 1615) of the Osaka castle and who was killed in the battle against the troops of Tōdō Takatora and Ii Naotaka acting under the orders of Tokugawa Ieyasu.

Kimura Sōhachi. Painter (1893–1958) in Fauvist style who worked in Paris.

Kimura Susumu. Vice-admiral (d. 1942) who commanded the ship the *Nagara* of the tenth destroyer fleet in the Battle of Midway (Apr. 6, 1942), and who died in combat.

Kimura Takaatsu. Writer and historian (1680–1742), author of *Butoku hennen shūsei* (1741).

Kimura Yoshio. Contemporary ceramist, born 1946 in Imabari (Ehime prefecture). His works were exhibited in the United States, Eastern Europe, Faenza, Italy (1991), and Paris (1994).

Kimura Yoshitake. Vassal (Kimura Kaishū, 1830–1901) of the Edo shogunate, officer on board the *Kanrin Maru* (1860). He worked on modernizing the shogunate's navy at the same time as Katsu Kaishū, having the Edo government hire British naval engineers. During the Meiji Restoration of 1868, he abandoned all public activity and retired to write his memoirs.

Kin. Former unit of mass equivalent to 100, 120, 160, or 180 *momme,* depending on the region. Another unit of mass was equal to about 600 grams.
• Word meaning "metal" and used in many composite terms. It also often means "gold."
→ *See* SHICHIGEN-KIN.

Kinai. Former name for provinces around the capital (Nara and Heian-kyō). In 645, during the Taika Reform, it comprised Yamato, Yamashiro, Kawachi, and Settsu provinces. This region is still called Kinai, though its area now corresponds only vaguely to the provinces it once encompassed. Also sometimes called Go-kinai. *See also* KINKI, KANSAI.

Kinashi no Karu no Ōji. Imperial prince (d. 454), Ingyo Tennō's son. According to the *Nihon shoki,* when his father died, he was attacked by his brother Anaho (Ankō Tennō) and committed suicide. Also called Karu no Ōji.

Kin-bugyō. During the Edo period, after 1646, the title of bureaucrats in the Ministry of Finance. Also called *kane-bugyō. See also* BUGYŌ.

Kinchū-jōmoku. Seventeen-article legal code promulgated by Tokugawa Ieyasu in 1615, somewhat resembling Shōtoku Taishi's legal code (622; see JŪSHICHIJŌ NO KEMPŌ) and regulating the activities of emperors and nobles. Also called *Kinchū narabi-ni kuge shohatto, Kuge shohatto, Kinchūgata gojōmoku.* It remained in force until the end of the Edo shogunate.

Kindai Bungaku. "Modern Literature." A literary magazine that was published from 1946 to 1964 by a group of writers who wanted to establish a "new left-leaning literature," and that had a major influence on writers of the postwar generation *(apure).*

Kindaichi Kyōsuke. Ethnologist (1882–1971), born in Morioka. He studied the customs, legends, and language of the Ainu tribes, produced several dictionaries, and translated the *Yūkara,* a legend cycle, into Japanese in *Ainu jojishi yūkara no kenkyū* (1931). He also wrote a study on the origins of the Japanese language, *Kokugo-shi keitō-ron* (1938), and compiled a Japanese dictionary, *Meikai kokugo jiten* (1943). He was honored with the Imperial Prize (Gakushi-in Onshi-shō) and the Order of Culture (Bunka-shō). *See* AINU.

Kindei-gaki. Painting technique consisting of sprinkling gold dust into a mixture of glue, water, and ground pigment, used mainly during the Kamakura period for decoration.

Kimena Jumpō. Major cinema magazine, founded in the Taishō era (1912–26), which created a prestigious prize awarded to the best Japanese films.

Kinensai. Prayers for abundant harvests, made in the court before the spring planting, giving rise to ritual festivals *(matsuri)* and officialized in 675 as a state ritual. This ritual disappeared after the Ōnin War but was reestablished at the Shinto shrine in Ise in 1699, then at the imperial court in 1869. It is still practiced in most Shinto shrines.

Kineya Rokuzaemon. Great singer (1901–81) who wrote about 400 modern pieces for the *naga-uta* repertoire. He was declared a Living National Treasure in 1974.

Kingai. Fabric slippers, once worn by nobles in their palaces.

Kingin-e. Decoration on lacquer obtained by drawing on the lacquer with a mixture of silver powder, gold powder, and glue. This technique was specific to the artists of the Heian period. *See also* KINDEI-GAKI.

Kingo. A name once sometimes given to officers of the Imperial Guard *(emon-fu)*.
→ *See* CHIKUKEI, RYŌTAI.

Kingu. "King," a popular monthly magazine founded in 1925 by Noma Seiji and the publisher Kōdansha, which reached a circulation of more than 1 million in 1927. Renamed *Fuji* in 1943, it returned to the name *Kingu* in 1946; publication ceased in 1957.

Kingyo. "Goldfish" or carp *(koi)* in colors ranging from red to white, sometimes multicolored, bred as pond ornaments. There are said to be 97 types. Also called *nichiki-goi, higoi.*

Kinji. Lacquer decoration in which fresh lacquer was sprinkled with gold powder, used mainly after the Muromachi period. *See* KINDEI-GAKI, KINGIN-E.
→ *See* IKAKEJI.

Kinjō. A polite term designating the reigning emperor.

Kinju-ban. Title of bureaucrats of the Kamakura and Muromachi *bakufu* responsible for servants at the imperial court.

Kinkafu. Collection of 22 musical scores for the koto, dating from the Nara period to the mid-tenth century. They have musical notations and indications for voices, and are accompanied by notes on their composition. They are the oldest musical scores found to date.

Kinkai-shū. Collection of poems by Minamoto no Sanetomo (1192–1219), constituting a sort of exercise in style, which he sent to his master, Fujiwara no Teika. This collection was later expanded to 716 *waka* poems. Also known by the title *Kinkai waka-shū.*

Kinkaku-ji. "Temple of the Golden Pavilion," in Kyoto, within the walls of the Rokuon-ji temple, and former pleasure-palace of shogun Ashikaga Yoshimitsu, who had it built between 1397 and 1407, at the same time as various palaces and two pagodas with three and seven stories. This grouping was called Kitayama-dono. When Yoshimitsu died in 1408, it was converted into a temple and called Rokuon-ji; its first honorary abbot was Musō Kokushi (1275–1351). The Rokuon-ji was set on fire during the Ōnin War (1467–77), restored, then destroyed again in 1565; all that remained were the Kinkaku pavilion and the Fudō-dō. The Kinkaku was totally destroyed by arson in 1950; it was reconstructed according to the original plans in 1955. Standing beside a lake in a rustic garden, it is square in plan and has three levels representing the *shinden* (ground floor), *buke-zukuri* (second floor), and *shariden* (third floor) architectural styles. Each level houses statues of Amida Buddha, Shō Kannon Bosatsu, and various Buddhist divinities. Its exterior structures are completely covered in gold leaf, whence its name. It belongs to the Shōkoku-ji branch of the Zen Rinzai sect.

• *Kinkaku-ji.* Novel by Mishima Yukio, written in 1956, drawing its theme from the willful destruction of the Golden Pavilion by a young, mentally unbalanced monk.

Kinkei Gaku-in. "Association of the Golden Pheasant." An ultranationalist society founded by Yasuoka Masaatsu in 1926, that advocated the bowlderization of books used in schools in order to promote patriotism among students.

Kinki. Industrial region surrounding Osaka, Hyōgo, Kyoto, Shiga, Mie, Nara, and Wakayama, the second largest after the Keihin region, and formerly the political and cultural center of Japan. *See also* KANSAI, KINAI.

• *Kinki-kai.* "Society of the Imperial Flag." A group of ultranationalist officers in the 1930s who had some influence on Japan's political aggressiveness at the time. *See* HASHIMOTO KINGORŌ.

• **Kinki Kekko-kai.** "Banner of the Empire." A secret ultranationalist society in existence from 1920 to 1930.

Kinkin sensei eiga no yume. "Master Kinki's Dreams of Greatness," a realist novel in the *kibyōshi* genre. Published by Koikawa Harumachi in 1775, it revived the *kusazōshi* genre.

Kinko. Historical term generally designating Japan's medieval period, which lasted from 1185 to 1603. Also called Chūsei. *See also* KINSEI.

Kinkoku. Painter (Yokoi Myōdō, eighteenth century) of the Nanga school who was Buson's student at Ōtsu in Ōmi.
• Samurai and painter (Yamamoto Ken; *azana:* Shijō; *gō:* Chichisai, Kinkoku, 1811–73) of the Nanga school, Kazan's student. He painted landscapes.

Kinko-ryū. *Shakuhachi* music school founded by Kuroda Kinko between 1764 and 1772. *See* ARAKI KODŌ.

Kinkōzan. Type of porcelain made with dark clay, decorated in blue, yellow, white, and green. It was created in Awata, near Kyoto, by a ceramist called Kinkōzan in the late seventeenth century. *See* AWATA.

Kinkyō-rei. Edicts banning Christianity, promulgated in 1612 and 1614, in which Tokugawa Ieyasu forbade missionaries from preaching, gathered them in Nagasaki, and expelled them to Manila and Macao. He accused Christian priests of obeying the Pope before obeying his own laws, of quarreling among themselves, and of cornering trade and favoring Portugal and Spain, whose fleets, based in Manila and Macao, were a concern to him. Japanese Christians were then persecuted, notably in Nagasaki in 1622 and in Shimabara in 1637. The ban on Christianity, reinforced in 1640 by a bureau charged with the repression and seeking out of clandestine Christians, remained in force until 1873. *See* CHRISTIANITY, KAKURE-KIRISHITAN.

Kin-ma. Polychrome lacquers, with several colored and incised layers, produced mainly in the Takamatsu region; the technique was imported from Burma or Thailand in the late Edo period. Also called *kimma.*

Kinnara. A mythical being of Hindu folklore and Buddhism, corresponding to the Sanskrit *Kimnara,* with a man's body and a horse's head. As heavenly musicians and singers, companions of the Apsarās (*Jap.:* Tennin, Hiten), *kinnara* were often portrayed accompanying the *raigō* ("descent") of Amida and in scenes of Buddhist paradise.

Ki no Haseo. Scholar and poet (845–912), Sugawara no Michizane's disciple, who intended to go to China with him in 894, but the plan was aborted. Appointed *chūnagon* in 911, he was Emperor Uda's confidant and helped write the laws of the Engi era *(Engi-shiki).* As a Chinese-language poet, he was considered the equal of Bai Juyi (772–846), but his works have been lost, except for some fragments of his collection *Kika-shū* and some poems published in collections such as the *Honchō monzui* and *Fusō-shū.*

Ki no Kaion. Writer and playwright (Enami Kiemon, 1663–1742), born in Osaka, author of some fifty *jōruri* plays for the puppet theater *(ayatsuri-ningyō)* at the Toyotakeza, an Osaka theater founded in 1704. In his plays (*jidai-mono* genre), he somewhat emulated Chikamatsu Monzaemon's style, and some of his *jōruri* were later adapted for Kabuki, among them *Yaoya ō-shichi, Kamakura sandai-ki* (Chronicle of the Three Ages of Kamakura, 1718), *Osome Hisamatsu tamoto no chirachibori* (Story of Osome and Hisamatsu, 1711), *Keisei Kokusen'ya* (Koxinga and the Courtesans, 1713).

Ki no Kiyohito. Scholar and poet (d. 753) said to have compiled a history of Japan in 714, now lost. He was the master of literature at the court in 741.

Kinokuniya Bunzaemon. Merchant (Kibun, ca. 1669–1734) who traded in citrus fruit, salted salmon, and lumber, and who amassed a huge fortune thanks to the protection of the shogunate's intendant of finances, Ogiwara Shigehide, and counselor Yanagisawa Yoshiyasu. When these two senior bureaucrats retired, he lost his status of favored merchant and retired from business.

Ki no Ōiwa. Warrior (late fifth century) who tried to carve out a kingdom for himself in Korea about 487. He founded a capital, Taizanjō, and took the royal name Shinsei, but he was almost immediately defeated by the king of Kudara (Paekche).

Kinoshita. "Under the Tree," a family name adopted by Toyotomi Hideyoshi when he married Kinoshita Iesada's (1543–1608) sister. He changed his name to Hashiba in 1575. *See* TOYOTOMI HIDEYOSHI.

Kinoshita Jun'an. Neo-Confucian philosopher (Kinoshita Sadamasa; *mei:* Heinojō; *gō:* Kinri, Jun'an, 1621–98), born in Kyoto. He wrote history books and worked for Maeda Tsunanori. Tokugawa Tsunayoshi appointed him master of Confucianism for the *bakufu*. He had many disciples, among them Amenomori Hōshū, Arai Hakuseki, Sakakibara Kōshū, and Muro Kyūsō. A collection of his writings was published under the title *Kinri sensei bunshū*. His sons, Kinoshita Kyokan and Kinoshita Nyohitsu, continued his work. His ten most important disciples were called, collectively, Bokumon Jittetsu.

Kinoshita Junji. Contemporary playwright (b. 1914), author of many plays for the stage and radio. He studied Elizabethan theater under Nakano Yoshio, then created, with Yamamoto Yasue, a "theater of the Left" (Budō no kai) with populist leanings, drawing its subjects from folklore. He also translated some plays. In 1949, he received literary awards for his plays *Fūrō* (Wind and Waves, 1934) and *Yūzuru* (Cranes at Dusk, 1949). Among his other successful plays are *Tsuru nyōbō* (The Heron's Wife, 1943), *Yamanami* (Mountain Range, 1949), *Kurai hibana* (Dark Sparks, 1950), *Kaeru shōten* (A Frog's Leap, 1951), *Onnyoro seisuiki* (Onnyoro's Grandeur and Decadence, 1957), *Okinawa* (1961), *Ottō to yobareru Nihonjin* (A Japanese Called Otto, 1962), *Fuyu no jidai* (The Winter Season, 1964, the story of the spy Sorge), and *Shimpan* (The Judgment, 1970). He also wrote a novel, *Mugen kidō* (Road Without End, 1966).

Kinoshita Katsutoshi. Poet (Kinoshita Chōshōshi, 1569–1649), Kinoshita Iesada's son, Toyotomi Hideyoshi's father-in-law, and nephew of Hideyoshi's wife, Kita no Mandokoro. He accompanied Hideyoshi to Korea, then converted to Christianity in 1588, taking the first name Pierre. Although he did not take part in the Battle of Sekigahara (1600) and was therefore stripped of his small fief of the Ōbama castle in Wakasa (Fukui prefecture), he gave his daughter's hand in marriage to Tokugawa Ieyasu's fifth son, Nobuyoshi. He wrote many works, among them *Kyūshū no michi no ki* (The Road that Leads to Kyushu) and *Kyohaku-shū*. According to some critics, his poems influenced Bashō's.

Kinoshita Keisuke. Movie director (1912–98), born in Hamamatsu. He directed the first Japanese color film, *Karumen kokyō ni kaeru* (The Return of Carmen, 1951). Among his other films: *Osoneke no*

asa (The Osone Family's Morning, 1946, winner of the Kinema Jumpō Award), *Nihon no higeki* (A Japanese Tragedy, 1953), *Nijūshi no hitomi* (Twenty-Four Eyes, 1954, which also won the Kinema Jumpō Award), *Narayama bushi-kō* (The Ballad of Narayama, 1958, another winner of the Kinema Jumpō Award). He worked mainly for the Shōchiku production company, with his brother, Kinoshita Chūji, composing the music for his movies and his brother-in-law as his chief cameraman.

Kinoshita Mokutarō. Playwright, poet, and writer (Ōta Masao, 1885–1945), born in Shizuoka prefecture. He contributed to many poetry magazines, including *Subaru* and *Okujō Teien*. A physician by profession, he traveled in Manchuria and China in 1916 and became known in Japan and abroad for his dermatological research, for which he was decorated with the Legion of Honor in France. Among his literary works are *Shokugo no uta* (poems) and *Irumiya somemonoten* (a play). His complete works were published in 12 volumes in *Kinoshita Mokutarō zenshū* (1948–51).

Kinoshita Naoe. Writer and Christian socialist (Kinoshita Shōkō, 1869–1937), born in Matsumoto. At first a journalist, he was a famous anti-war orator, for he felt that war was incompatible with the Christian spirit. He was one of the founders of the Shakai Minshūtō (Socialist People's party), with Abe Isoo. His novels conveyed both his socialism and his pacifism: *Hi no hashira* (The Pillar of Fire, 1904), which was banned by the police in 1910, *Ryōjin no jihaku,* and others. He also fought for the workers at the Ashio Copper Mines (1900) and against the pollution caused by the mines; toward the end of his life, he tried to reconcile Buddhism and Christianity in a sort of silent meditation called Seiza.

Kinoshita Rigen. *Tanka* poet (Kinoshita Toshiharu, 1886–1925), born in Okayama prefecture; founder, with Shiga Naoya and Mushanokōji Saneatsu, of the literary magazine *Shirakaba* in 1910. Among his poetry collections, the best known are *Kōgyoku* (1919) and *Ichiro* (1924).

Kinoshita Takafumi. *Waka* poet (1789–1821), born in Bitchū province, Kagawa Kageki's disciple. His works were collected in *Sayasaya ikō*.

Kinoshita Toshimasa. Warrior (1603–61), founder of a school for combat with lances (Sō-jutsu) called Kinoshita-ryū and Awaji-ryū.

Kinoshita Yūji. Modernist poet (1914–65), author of many collections.

Ki no Tokibumi. Poet (tenth century), Ki no Tsurayuki's son, who compiled the *Gosen waka-shū* in 951. *See* NASHITSUBO NO GONIN.

Ki no Tomonori. *Waka* poet (tenth century) who began to compile the *Kokin-shū* in 905 on the order of Emperor Daigo, but who died before finishing his work. The *Kokin-shū* contains 46 of his poems, and others are included in various anthologies.

Ki no Tsurayuki. *Waka* poet (ca. 883–945), vice-governor of Kaga province (after 917), and governor of Tosa province in 930. He was then appointed director of the imperial library and head of palace repairs, with the subordinate fourth rank of nobility (*see* I). In 905, Emperor Daigo asked him to finish compiling the *Kokin-shū*, started by Ki no Tomonori. He also wrote a famous travel journal, *Tosa nikki*, after a trip he made from Tosa to Kyoto in 934–35, perhaps in memory of his daughter, who died in Tosa. About 500 poems attributed to him (including 100 in the *Kokin-shū*) are included in various anthologies and in a collection titled *Tsurayuki-shū*. Ki no Tokibumi's father.

Ki no Yoshimochi. Poet (?–919), Ki no Tsurayuki's adoptive son. He wrote a preface *(manajo)* in *mana* to the *Kokin-shū*.

Kinouchi Shōhan. Geologist, author of the first work on mineralogy in Japan, *Unkon-shi*, in 1771.

Kinran. Silk and gold-thread brocade, the weaving technique for which was introduced from China to Japan via the port of Sakai in the late sixteenth century; it was developed in the Nishijin district of Kyoto. When these brocades are woven with silver thread, they are called *ginran*. *Chin.*: Zhijin. *See* NISHIKI.

• **Kinrande.** "Gold brocade," name for Chinese ceramics from the Jiajing era (1522–66), profusely decorated with gold decorations on a background of red (sometimes blue) enamel; imitated in Japan, it gave rise to the Ko-Imari style.

Kinrei-zuka. *Kofun* (megalithic burial site) located near Kisarazu on the coast of Tokyo Bay and the Tōkaidō road, excavated in 1950. It contained three graves and iron armor, helmets, bronze épées,

and many objects showing a continental influence. It has been dated to around the fifth century.

Kinri. Name once sometimes used for the imperial palace and, by extension, for the emperor himself. *See* DAI-DAIRI, DAIRI.

→ *See* KINOSHITA JUN'AN.

• **Kinri-kugonin.** Persons or associations whose custom it was to provide the emperor with products for his dining table: rice, fish, vegetables, and sometimes everyday utensils. In the fourteenth century, the *kugonin* settled in Kyoto as merchants.

• **Kinri-zuki.** In the Edo period, inspector of the imperial palace. Also called Kinchū no Mamorishū.

Kinro Gyōja. Physician and Sinologist (Tsuga Teishō, eighteenth century), author of a collection of fantasy tales, inspired by Chinese folklore, titled *Hanabusa-zōshi*, published in *yomi-hon* in 1749.

Kinrō Kansha no Hi. Labor Day, celebrated on November 23. National statutory holiday. *See* NIINAMESAI.

Kinryō. Painter (Kaneko Inkei; *azana*: Kunshō; *gō*: Jitsu-u-tei, Kinryō, d. 1817) of the Nanga school, Bunchō's student.

Kinsei. "Modern era," historians' term for the period from 1568 to 1868. It immediately precedes the "contemporary period" (*kindai*, from 1868 to the present) and follows the medieval period (*chūsei*, *kinko*, from 1185 to about 1568). However, historians do not agree on the precise beginning and end of this period; the dates 1590, 1600, and 1615 have been proposed for its start, and the dates for 1853, 1854, and 1868, among others, for its end.

• *Kinsei kijin den.* "Tales About the Extraordinary People of Our Day." A collection of biographies of more than 100 famous people of the Edo period, published by Ban Kōkei (1733–1806) in 1790. A supplement was added in 1798, written by Ban Kōkei and Katen (Mikuma Shikō); Katen also illustrated it.

Kinshi Kunshō. "Order of the Golden Falcon," a decoration conferred by the emperor on military men to reward their acts of bravery, created on February 11, 1890. It had seven degrees. *See* KUNSHŌ.

Kintai-bashi. Wooden bridge on stone pilings, 250 m long, with five barrel arches *(taiko-bashi),* crossing the Nishiki-gawa river near Nishi-Iwakuni in southwest Honshu. It was built in 1673, destroyed by a typhoon in 1950, and reconstructed in 1953. It is a major tourist attraction, especially during the summer season of fishing with cormorants by torchlight. *See* MEGANE-BASHI.

Kintarō. "Golden boy," a child-hero of folk tales, thought to have been Sakata no Kintoki, a faithful samurai serving Minamoto no Yorimitsu. Legend describes him as the son of a mountain sorcerer (Yamamba) with Herculean strength. He is portrayed as a stout child brandishing an ax, the typical instrument of the *kami* of thunder in the Ashigara region. The character was featured in *jōruri* and Kabuki under the name Kaidōmaru. Pregnant women pray to the *kami* to give birth to a child as beautiful and strong as Kintarō, and venerate his image. *See* SAKATA NO KINTOKI.

Kinugasa Teinosuke. Movie director (Kinusaga Kukame, 1896–1982), born in Tokyo. His first career was as a Kabuki actor, playing *onnagata* roles in dozens of silent films. He then began to direct; after 1923, he directed more than 150 films, the best known of which are *Kurutta ippeiji* (A Page of Madness, 1926), *Jūjiro* (Crossroads, 1928), and *Jigokumon* (The Doors of Hell, 1953), which won the gold medal at the Cannes Film Festival in 1953 and the prize for Best Foreign Film in 1955.

Kinuta. Japanese name for Chinese ceramics (celadons) produced in the Longquan kilns during the Song dynasty and imported to Japan. *See* CERAMICS, SEIJI.

Kinuta. Title of a Noh play: a young woman complains about her husband's absence. A messenger arrives and announces that her husband will not be able to come to see her at the end of the year, as he had promised. The young woman then falls into melancholy and dies.

Kinutatsugi. Kimono for traveling, with a part that could be folded over the head, once worn by noblewomen with a very wide-brimmed hat, the *kinugasa.* Also called *kinutazuki.*

Kin'yō-shū. "Collection of Gold Leaves." The fifth imperial anthology *(see* CHOKUSEN WAKA-SHŪ), compiled by Minamoto no Toshiyori on the order of Retired Emperor Shirakawa between 1124 and 1127. Depending on the edition, it contains between 648 and 712 poems, arranged in ten books. There are 27 poems by Minamoto no Toshiyori; 37 by his father, Minamoto no Tsunenobu; 20 by Fujiwara no Akisue; 15 by Fujiwara no Tadamichi; 15 by Fujiwara no Nagazane; and others by *waka, tanka,* and *renga* poets. Also titled *Kin'yō waka-shū.*

Kiraba-e. Type of ukiyo-e prints printed on a micaceous background, used by Sharaku, among other artists, in 1794. *See also* KIRAZURI.

Kirare yosaburō. Kabuki play in the *kizewa-mono* genre, first produced by Jokō Segawa III about 1853. Also titled *Yowanasake Ukina no Yokoku-shi.*

Kira Yoshinaka. Samurai (1641–1703), master of ceremonies at the shogun's court with the title Kōzuke no Suke. He had a reputation for arrogance; when he refused to help Asano Naganori, Asano wounded him slightly in the shogunal palace. Asano was sentenced to commit suicide by *seppuku,* so his vassals decided to avenge him; on a winter night in 1703, they attacked Kira's house and killed him. *See* AKŌ-GISHI, ASANO NAGANORI, ŌISHI YOSHIO.

Kirazuri. Decorative paper for writing poems or painting, made with mica powder and a black or yellow background, used during the Heian period and by some ukiyo-e artists. *See also* KIRABA-E.

Kirei. Painter (Kameoka Kirei; *mei:* Kijūrō; *azana:* Shikyō; *gō:* Kirei, 1770–1835) of the Maruyama school, Maruyama Ōkyō's student. He painted mainly landscapes and flowers.

Kiribi. "Sacred fire," used during certain Shinto ceremonies, produced by the rubbing together of two pieces of wood, generally cypress *(hinoki),* or by striking a flint against iron. The sparks produced by the flint were once supposed to purify the person who received them, a custom still sometimes practiced to purify and protect a person leaving a house.

Kirikane. "Cut gold," leaves of gold cut into small squares, applied on fresh lacquer to decorate lacquer objects and statues. Sheets of paper *(shikishi)* were also decorated this way for the writing of poems *(kirihaku).* When *kirikane* were applied on colored lacquer or paper, it was called *kirikane-saishoku.* Also called *kirigane.*

Kiri no ki. Rapidly growing deciduous tree (paulownia) whose blossoms, stylized, were used as an emblem by empresses. It flowers in early summer. Its fine-grained, very light wood is used mainly to make chests of drawers *(tansu)*, boxes, musical instruments *(koto)*, and *geta;* its charcoal, to make powder for fireworks; its bark, to dye fabrics; and its leaves, in medicine. Formerly, a *kiri no ki* was planted when a girl was born; when she was of marriageable age, it was cut down to make *tansu* to hold her trousseau.

• *Kiri hitoha (hitoba)*. "Paulownia leaves." A Kabuki play in the *jidai-mono* genre, in eight acts, written by Tsubouchi Shōyō in 1895 and first produced in 1904.

Kirimai. Salary in rice once given by a daimyo or shogun to vassals in his service who did not have estates. Starting in the eighteenth century, *kirimai* were often paid in cash. Samurai receiving rice generally exchanged it for cash with the *fudasashi*, merchants specializing in this trade. Also called *kurumai*.

Kirin. Mythical animal resembling a winged unicorn, emblem of kindness and charity, borrowed from Chinese folklore *(Chin.: qilin)*.
• Japanese name for a former province of Manchuria, under Japanese occupation (Manchukuo from 1932 to 1945); it corresponded to the Chinese province of Jilin.

Kirinami Senju. Kabuki actor *(keisei* roles) active in Kyoto around 1700–10.

Kirino Toshiaki. Samurai (Nakamura Hanjirō, 1838–77), born in Satsuma province, serving daimyo Shimazu Hisamitsu in Kyoto. He fought on the emperor's behalf against the Edo shogunate and was appointed battalion leader in Kagoshima in 1869, then battalion leader of the Imperial Guard (Goshimpei) in Tokyo in 1871. Having sided with Saigō Takamori on the issue of Korea, he resigned from his position and opened a fencing school in Satsuma. He was killed in combat fighting at Saigō Takamori's side.

Kirishitan. General term for Christians. Also *kirisutan, kirisuto*. The Christian religion is called *kirishitan-shū* or *kirishitan-kyō*. *See* CHRISTIANITY.

• **Kirishitan-ban.** *See* JESUITS.

• *Kirishitan monogatari*. "Tales of the Christians." A book published anonymously in 1638 to denigrate Christians and show them and missionaries in a grotesque light. This work inspired others in the same vein, such as the *Kirishitan shūmon raichō jikki* (True Account of the Arrival of the Christian Religion in Our Empire) and the *Nambanji kōhai ki* (Grandeur and Decadence of the Church of the Southern Barbarians, ca. 1695).

Kirishitan Yashiki. "House of the Christians," name for a building in Edo (a former school) where people suspected of being Christians were held and interrogated starting in 1646. Giuseppe Chiara (Okamoto San'emon, d. 1685) and Giovanni Battista Sidotti (who died there in 1714) were incarcerated and tortured there. This prison was destroyed by a fire in 1725, and inquisitorial practices were abolished in 1792; the Kirishitan Yashiki, having no more purpose, was torn down.

Kirisute-gomen. "Permission to cut," given to all samurai during the Edo period. They thus had the right to kill anyone in the lower classes who showed a lack of respect or seriously offended them. However, the shogunate reserved the right to punish samurai who abused this right. Also called *bureiuchi*, "punishing disrespect."

Kiritake Monjūrō II. *Bunraku* puppeteer (1900–70), born in Osaka, Yoshida Bungorō III's disciple. He was declared a Living National Treasure in 1965.

Kirizuma. In traditional architecture, a saddleback roof with two panels and no gable, considered to be the oldest form (it is the roof form of the Ise and Izumo shrines). *See* IRIMOYA, ROOFS.

Kirokusho. "Registration Commission," a bureau created in 1069 by Emperor Go-Sanjō to counterbalance the growing influence of the Fujiwara family in the justice and administration systems. The institution was updated in 1111 by Retired Emperor Shirakawa, then in 1156 but for a different reason—to control more closely disputes that might arise between provincial governors and other lords. In 1187 Emperor Go-Shirakawa established another Kirokusho that served as a court of justice and a management council for the court. It was reestablished in 1333 during the Kemmu Restoration, but abolished in the late fourteenth century.

Kisaki. Former title for an emperor's second wife; now one of the empress's titles. Also, a term for the Buddhist semi-divinity Yamī, sister and wife of the King of Hell, Emma-ō (*Skt.:* Yamarāja).

Kisaragi. "Double garment," the former name of the second month of the lunar-solar year, corresponding to February or March.

Kiseru. Long pipe with a small bowl *(gankubi)* and metal mouthpiece *(suikochi)*, whose stem *(rao)* was usually made from bamboo imported from Laos. During the Edo period, it was used by both men and women, who kept their tobacco and deposited their ashes in a special box called *tobako-bon.*

Ki-seto. Ceramic objects produced in Mino province during the Momoyama period (1573–1603). These pieces were usually varnished in yellow, sometimes with green run-outs *(tampan). See* CERAMICS.

Kisetsugo. "Seasonal words," poetic terms evoking the seasons *(kisetsu),* used mainly by haiku poets. Also called *kigo.*

Kishida Ginkō. Journalist and pharmacist (Kishida Ginji, 1833–1905), born in Okayama prefecture. He helped James Curtis Hepburn compile his Japanese–English dictionary and published, with Hamada Hikozō, the first modern newspaper in Japan, the *Kaigai Shimbun.* He then became a reporter at the *Tokyo Nichinichi Shimbun (Mainichi Shimbun).* The first Japanese war correspondent, he covered the expedition to Taiwan in 1874. Kishida Ryūsei's father.

Kishida Kunio. Playwright (1890–1954) born in Tokyo. He went to Paris in 1921–22 and worked with Jacques Copeau; when he returned to Japan in 1929, he founded the Bungaku-za (Literary Theater) group and wrote many plays in dialogue form for it, among them *Kami fūsen* (Paper Ball, 1925), *Ochiba nikki* (Journal of Dead Leaves, 1927), and *Sawa shi no futari musume* (The Two Daughters of the Sawa Family, 1935).

Kishida Ryūsei. Painter (Ryūsai, 1891–1929), born in Tokyo, Kishida Ginkō's son. At first painting in the Western style (Yōga), he worked in the Hakuba-kai group with Kuroda Seiki and studied European art, especially the French Fauvists. He founded the Sō-dosha group in 1914, then distanced himself from Western influences and studied Chinese art,

painting in the Bunjinga style. After 1923, he moved his studio to Kyoto, then to Kamakura, and took part in exhibitions of the Shun'yō-kai group. Subsequently, he returned to the "Japanese style" (Nihonga) and to ukiyo-e.

Kishida Tohō. Writer (late eighteenth century), in *kibyōshi* genre: *Kusazōshi nendaiki* (Chronology of the *Kusazōshi,* 1783).

Kishida Toshiko. Politician and writer (Nakajima Toshiko; *gō:* Nakajima Shōen, 1863–1901), born in Kyoto. Although she was of modest origins, her talents in Chinese and Japanese literature earned her the honor of being chosen by Empress Shōken (1850–1914), Emperor Meiji's wife, to be a lady-in-waiting. She left this position in 1882 to travel the country making political speeches supporting the Jiyūtō (Liberal party). She then married Nakajima Nobuyuki, one of the party's leaders; while continuing her political activities, she wrote for the feminist magazine *Jogaku Zasshi.* Her memoirs, *Shōen nikki,* were published in 1903. *See* NAKAJIMA NOBUYUKI.

Kishi Keiko. Movie actress (b. 1932), who married French director Yves Ciampi (b. 1921). She made a number of films with him, including *Typhoon over Nagasaki* (1956). She was divorced in 1975 and continued her career in Japan and the United States.

Kishimojin. Female Buddhist divinity, "giver of children" *(koyasu),* a Japanized form of the Hindu divinity Hārītī. She is most frequently portrayed as a beautiful woman holding a pomegranate and a child. Considered a guardian of the *Lotus Sutra (Renge-kyō),* she is venerated by followers of the Nichiren sect. Also called Kariteimo, Koyasu Kannon. *See* KOYASU.

Kishimoto Kennin. Contemporary ceramist, born 1945 in Nagoya. He exhibited his works in Japan, Germany (1989), and Paris (1994).

Kishi Nobusuke. Politician (1896–1987), born in Yamaguchi prefecture, Satō Eisaku's brother. He entered the Department of Agriculture and Trade in 1920; his abilities were noticed, and he was made responsible for reorganizing the economy of Manchuria (Manchukuo) and northern China under Japanese occupation. As vice-minister of industry and trade in 1939–40, then minister of trade in 1941–42 in Tōjō Hideki's cabinet, he transformed Japanese industry to put it on a war footing. In

1946, he was convicted of war crimes by the Allies, but was freed in 1948 and quickly became the leader of the democratic movement. He was elected to the House of Representatives in 1953, and in 1955 he helped form the Jiyū Minshutō (Liberal Democratic party), of which he became the secretary-general. Appointed minister of foreign affairs in Ishibashi Tanzan's cabinet in 1957, he became prime minister, succeeding Ishibashi (Feb. 1957–July 1960). In this position, he ratified the security treaty with the United States in 1960 but was forced to resign because of public hostility, and Ikeda Hayato succeeded him. He remained leader of the LDP and a member of the House of Representatives.

Kishi Seiichi. Jurist (1867–1933), born in Shimane prefecture, president of the Japanese Amateur Sports Association and member of the International Olympic Committee. He had a sports arena built in Tokyo that bears his name.
  • Jurist (1908–1979) and judge at the Supreme Court who helped revise the criminal code in 1948.

Kiso. Title of a Noh play: before a battle, Yoshinaka sends a petition to Hachiman in a note attached to an arrow. The *kami* sends it back accompanied by pigeons to announce victory.

Kiso. *See* minamoto no yoshinaka.

Kiso, Forest of. *See* ISE.

Kiso-gawa. River 193 km long, crossing Nagano, Gifu, Aichi, and Mie prefectures and flowing into the Bay of Ise near Nagoya. It irrigates the Nōbe plain, where its course is diked to protect farmland.

Kiso Sammyaku. Mountain range that is part of the "Japanese Alps," crossing Nagano prefecture from north to south. Highest peak: Komagatake (2,956 m).

Kissaten. General term for cafés and Western-style nonalcoholic bars where consumers can drink tea, coffee, and other beverages while listening to music, often classical European. People meet to discuss and do business in *kissaten* because private homes are too cramped to allow for meetings.

Kissa yōjō-ki. "Notes on the Good Influence of Tea." The first work devoted to tea, written in two volumes by the Buddhist monk Eisai (1141–1215) in 1211–14 for Minamoto no Sanetomo. In this work, Eisai treats tea as a medication.

Kita. Term for the north. Also *hoku.*
  • Family of playwrights and composers of Noh and Sarugaku plays, founded by Kita Daifu (1586–1653). It was revived by Kita Roppeita (1874–1971) and his son, Kita Minoru (b. 1900), who set up a theater in the Meguro district of Tokyo in 1954. Also called Kita-ryū. *See* NOH.

  • **Kita Nagayo.** Contemporary Noh actor, sixteenth-generation descendant of Kita Daifu (Nanadayū), a famous flautist and Noh dancer in Sakai, to whom Tokugawa Ieyasu gave the nickname Roppeita (after the leather purse a Portuguese man had given him). Educated by his grandfather, he became an exemplar of his art; after the Second World War, he was one of the most popular Noh actors. He was declared a Living National Treasure in 1986.

Kitabatake Akiie. General (1318–38), Kitabatake Chikafusa's son, appointed governor of Mutsu province in 1333, then *chinjufu-shogun* for all of northeast Honshu in 1334. He opposed Ashikaga Takauji on behalf of the emperors of the Southern Court (Nanchō); after defeating the troops of the Ashikaga, he was killed in battle in Ishuzu (Izumi province).

  • **Kitabatake Chikafusa.** Statesman and historian (1293–1354), Kitabatake Akiie's father. Appointed *dainagon* by Emperor Go-Daigo, he was Prince Tokinaga's tutor; when Tokinaga died, he became a Buddhist monk with the name Sōgen. He helped his son pacify the northeast regions and fought the Ashikaga at his side. He wrote a major work justifying the legitimacy of the emperors of the Southern Court, *Jinnō shōtō-ki,* and another political work, *Shokugen-kō.*

Kitadake. Second highest mountain in Japan (after Mt. Fuji), located in Yamanashi prefecture in the northern section of the Akaishi Mountains (central Honshu). *Alt.:* 3,192 m.
→ *See* KAGOSHIMA PREFECTURE.

Kitade Fujio. Ceramist, born 1919 in Kaga (Ishikawa prefecture). His works (porcelain) received many awards both in Japan and abroad.

Kitagawa Fuyuhiko. Poet and movie critic (Taguro Tadahiko, 1900–90), born in Shiga prefecture. His poems were clearly influenced by French surrealism and dadaism, notably in his anti-war works, such as *Sensō* (1929). He founded a poetry magazine, *Shi to Shiron,* in 1928. His poems were collected in two books, *Iyarashii kami* (1936) and *Jikkenshitsu* (1941).

Kitagawa-ha. School of artists of ukiyo-e prints from the late Edo period, founded by Kitagawa Utamaro (*see* UTAMARO), which included artists such as Utamaro II, Tsukimaro, and Fujimaro. The Kitagawa-ha disappeared after Utamaro's death in 1806.

Kitahara Hakushū. Poet (Kitahara Ryūkichi, 1885–1942), born in Fukuoka, writer of *tanka* and modern symbolic poems, co-founder of the poetry group Pan no Kai. He published *Jashūmon* (Heretics, 1909), *Omoide* (Memories, 1911); then *tanka* collections, such as *Kiri no Hana* (Paulownia Blossoms, 1913), and religious poems *(wasan),* such as those in *Shinju-shō* (Selection of Pearls, 1914), *Hakkin no koma* (Peak of Platinum, 1914), and *Suiboku-shū* (Collection of Ink Drawings, 1923). He returned to *tanka* in *Suzume no tamago* (Sparrow Eggs, 1921). He published more than 200 books and edited several literary magazines and children's magazines with poems, set to music by Yamada Kōsaku, which are still very popular today.

Kitahara Takeo. Writer (1907–73), born in Kanagawa prefecture. He translated works by Jean Cocteau and Raymond Radiguet and wrote novels, a few of which, such as *Tsuma* (Wife, 1938), were very successful. His second wife was writer Uno Chiyo, and they published a women's fashion magazine. Most of his novels deal with women's problems.

Kita Ikki. Politician (Kita Terujirō, 1883–1937), born on Sado Island. A friend of Kōtoku Shūsui, he left for China after the 1912 Revolution and took part in the subsequent events, but was expelled by Yuan Shikai. He returned there in 1916 and wrote *Shina kakumei gaishi* (History of the Chinese Revolution), criticizing Japanese policy. In 1919, he helped Okawa Shūmei found the Yūzonsha, an ultranationalist party, and became the theoretician of Japanese fascism, advocating "Asian nationalism" in two of his books, *Kobutai ron oyobi junsei shakai shugi* (National Politics and Pure Socialism, 1906) and *Nihon kaizo hōan taikō* (Essay on a Plan to Reorganize Japan, 1923). Accused of complicity in the rebellion of February 26, 1936 (Niniroku Jiken), he was executed by firing squad.

Kita-in-ji. Buddhist temple in Kawagoe (Saitama prefecture) founded by Ennin for the Tendai sect in 830. His sculptures of the *gohyaku-rakan* (Five Hundred Arhats) are famous.

Kita-Kyūshū. Name of the conurbation connecting the industrial cities of Moji, Tobata, Yahata, Kokura, and Wakamatsu (Fukuoka prefecture, Kyushu), facing Shimonoseki. More than 30% of Japan's heavy industry (metallurgy, shipyards, coal fields), the largest metallurgical complex in the world (Yahata), the largest artificial port in Asia, and the longest suspension bridge in Asia (more than 2 km long) are located there. Two tunnels, one for cars and one for trains, link Moji to Shimonoseki (*see* KAMMON KAIKYŌ). Kita-Kyūshū covers about 480 km^2 (30 km of coastline) and has a population of almost 1.2 million.

Kita Morio. Writer and physician (Saitō Sōkichi), born 1927 in Tokyo, poet Saitō Mokichi's son. His novels *Yori to kiri no sumide* (Between Night and Mist) and *Yūrei* (Ghosts) won the Akutagawa Prize in 1960. His serial *Dokutoru Mambō* (Dr. Mambō), begun in 1960, was very successful, and his more or less autobiographical novel *Nireke no hitobito* won the *Mainichi Shimbun* Prize in 1964.

Kitamura Kigin. *Waka* and haiku poet (1624–1705) Bashō's master and Matsunaga Teitoku's disciple, born in Ōmi province. Appointed master of *waka* of the Edo shogunate, he wrote commentaries on the *Man'yōshū*, the *Genji monogatari,* and the *Makura no sōshi,* and several anthologies, such as the *Tsukuba-shū.*

Kitamura Rokurō. Stage and movie actor (1871–1961), born in Tokyo. He founded the theater group Seibidan in Osaka and performed in Shimpa plays in Tokyo starting in 1906. He was in only one movie, *Noroi no fue* (The Magic Flute, 1958). He was designated a Living National Treasure in 1955.

Kitamura Sayo. Peasant (1900–67) from Yamaguchi prefecture, who, after hearing heavenly voices, declared that she was Amaterasu-Ōmikami's daughter. In 1946, she founded a religion related to Shinto, the Tenshō Kōtai Jingū-kyō, whose followers express their faith by dancing and singing, whence their name, Odori-shūkyō. This religion now has about 40,000 followers.

Kitamura Tōkoku. Writer (1868–1894) and poet (blank verse and rhythmic prose) of romantic inspiration (*shintaishi* style), who founded the literary magazine *Bungaku-kai* in 1893 and who also published his works in the pacifist magazine *Heiwa*. He was influenced by Byron and by Christianity, and in his poems he attempted a sort of harmonious synthesis between Eastern thought and Western spirit; he inspired Shimazaki Tōson.

Kitano Tenjin. Posthumous name for Sugawara no Michizane, deified as a *kami* of literature.

• *Kitano tenjin engi.* An *emakimono* illustrating the foundation of Kitano Tenjin-jinja and the divine life of Sugawara no Michizane, dated 1219 and attributed to Fujiwara no Nobuzane (9 scrolls) and Fujiwara no Yukimitsu (2 scrolls). There are several versions.

• **Kitano Tenjin-jinja.** Shinto shrine built in Kyoto in 947 to honor the memory of Sugawara no Michizane. Toyotomi Hideyoshi had an immense tea ceremony held there in 1587, in which 1,000 people from all social classes participated. The current buildings date from 1607. Also called Kitano Temmangū. *See* TEMMANGŪ.

Kitanoumi. Sumo wrestler (Ogata Toshimitsu), born 1953 in Hokkaido, and the youngest *sumotori* to attain the title of Yokozuna (the 55th) in 1975, when he was only 21. *See* SUMO.

Kitaōji Rosanjin. Ceramist (Kitaōji Fusajirō, 1883–1959), born in Kyoto. He studied Kutani ceramics in Kanazawa from 1915 to 1917, then built a kiln in Kita Kamakura, producing porcelain in the Arita, Bizen, and Mino styles. His works were in a number of exhibitions abroad, including San Francisco in 1964 and New York in 1972.

Kitasato Shibasaburō. Bacteriologist (1853–1931), born in Kumamoto. He studied with R. Koch in Germany starting in 1885. In 1889, he isolated the agent responsible for tetanus and discovered an antibody that could counteract it. During an epidemic in Hong Kong in 1894, he discovered, concurrently with A. Yersin, the bacilla that causes the plague. In 1914, he founded a research institute that bore his name. He was elected a member of the Academy, appointed to the House of Peers, and ennobled in 1924. Also called Kitazato Shibasaburō.

Kitashirakawa Yoshihisa. Imperial prince (Rinnōji no Miya, 1845–95), leader of the Shinto shrines of Ueno (Tokyo) and Nikkō. He lived in Europe for seven years; when he returned, he commanded the Japanese army sent to Taiwan, where he died.

Kitayama bunka. "Kitayama culture," an expression designating the society of the era of shogun Ashikaga Yoshimitsu (1358–1408), centered at the Katayama palace in Kyoto. This period was typified politically by the merger between the Northern and Southern courts and the reestablishment of relations with Ming-dynasty China. The latter led to an influx of Chinese techniques, products, and philosophies that helped define the new Muromachi culture and that provoked intense cultural activity: development of Chinese *gozan* literature, painting with ink (*sumi-e* and *suiboku*), theater (Noh), the art of gardening, the tea ceremony, and ceramics. It was followed by another "shogunal culture," called Higashiyama.

• **Kitayama-dono.** *See* ASHIKAGA YOSHIMITSU, KINKAKU-JI.

• **Kitayama Jūhakken-dō.** Leper colony founded in Nara in the thirteenth century by the Buddhist monk Ninshō (1217–1303), in a building 37 m long with 18 bays (*ken,* intercolumnations), defining 18 rooms (whence its name). It was destroyed by fire in 1567 and rebuilt in the style of the Kamakura period.

Kitazono Katsue. Poet (Hashimoto Kenkichi, 1902–78), born in Mie prefecture. His style was avant-garde and surrealist; he founded a poetry magazine, *VOU,* in 1935 and translated poems by Éluard and Mallarmé.

Kites. Kites (*tako, ika*) were imported from China in the medieval period and were immediately adopted by the Japanese as a form of entertainment for children and adults alike. Although they were mentioned for the first time in a tenth-century work by Minamoto no Shitagō, they had certainly been known for centuries. Kites underwent considerable development during the Edo period, and were called *ikanobori* (paper falcons), an ancient term. They were sometimes used by armies to signal troop movements or to give orders to soldiers, especially in the eleventh and twelfth centuries. During the Tokugawa period, kites dotted the skies of Edo, if one believes ukiyo-e prints of the time. They had a wide variety of shapes and were ornamented with kanji characters, legendary figures, or dragons. Currently, it is traditional to fly kites on New Year's Day, during the girls' (Hina Matsuri) and boys'

(Tango no Sekku) festivals in March and April, and in certain provinces during the Bon (Urabon) festivals. Kite battles often take place at the beginning of May in Hamamatsu (Shizuoka prefecture). Some of these enormous kites, armed with cutting strings designed to sever those of the *tako* of the "enemy" village, require several dozen men to handle them, as for example in Shirone (Niitaga prefecture, early June) and Ōjūbana (Saitama prefecture, May 3–5). In March 1980, an *ōtako* (large *tako*) launched at Shirone measured 19 × 14 m—a record. Many collectors value *tako* for their shapes or decorations, and this has induced many regions and municipalities to produce kites of high artistic quality and a wide variety of shapes. The most famous, aside from those cited above, are made at Nagasaki, Aomori, Fukushima, Chiba, Fukuoka, and Aichi.

Kitoshi. Buddhist monks and Shinto priests specializing in healing, who made charms and amulets to ward off illness.

Kitsune. In popular and Shinto legend, a mythical fox that had the power to transform itself into a woman or a monk to cause problems for humans. It is an important character in Noh theater (mask) and Kabuki. *Kitsune* are also guardians of Shinto shrines dedicated to the *kami* of grains (Inari). For this reason, effigies of *kitsune* are placed at shrine gates. *Chin.: hulijing. See also* INARI, KENKUI, TANUKI.

• **Kitsune prefecture.** *See* JAN PREFECTURE-PON, KEN.

Kiuchi Sekitei. Archeologist (1724–1808), born in Ōmi province. Conducting research throughout Japan, he devised the theory that flint arrowheads were prehistoric weapons and developed a comparative theory in *Unkonshi* (Petrography), written from 1772 to 1801. Also called Kinouchi Sekitei.

Kiuchi Shinzō. Geographer (1910–93), born in Tokyo. A member of many international geographical organizations, he received several honorific distinctions (Berlin and United States). Among his works are *Toshi no chirigakuteki kenkyū* (Studies on the Geography of Cities, 1949), *Toshi chirigaku kenkyū* (Study of Urban Geography, 1951), *Chiiki gairon* (Introduction to Regional Studies, 1968), *Toshi chirigaku genri* (Principles of Urban Geography, 1979).

Kiyochika. Painter (Kobayashi Kiyochika, 1847–1915) of ukiyo-e prints in Tokyo. He studied Western painting with Charles Wirgman and, in prints he made starting in 1876, skillfully dealt with shadows and light, somewhat in the manner of La Tour. In 1888, he abandoned Western subjects to devote himself to historical triptychs, notably on episodes from the 1894–95 Sino-Japanese War. It was said that he was so attracted to light that in 1891 he let his own house burn in order to contemplate the flames.

Kiyohara no Motosuke. Poet (908–90), Sei Shōnagon's father and one of the Sanjūrokkasen (Thirty-Six Poetic Geniuses). He compiled (with the Nashitsubo no Gonin) the *Gosen waka-shū* in 951. Also called Kiyowara no Motosuke.

Kiyohara no Natsuno. Imperial prince (Shigeno, 782–837) and *udaijin,* one of the authors of the *Ryō no gige* in 833. Also called Narabi no Oka Daijin.

Kiyohara Tama. Painter (*gō:* Eleonora Ragusa, 1861–1939), born in Tokyo. She lived in Sicily and studied classical European styles with her husband, Vincenzo Ragusa, and S. Lo Forte. Also called Raguza Tama.

Kiyoharu. Painter (Kondō Kiyoharu; *mei:* Sukegorō, eighteenth century) of ukiyo-e prints, Kiyonobu's student. He illustrated books and wrote satirical pieces.

Kiyohiro. Painter (Torii Kiyohiro; *mei:* Shichinosuke, active ca. 1750–60, died ca. 1776), Kiyomitsu I's disciple. He produced prints in *benizuri-e* style.

Kiyokaze Yohei. Family of ceramists (late nineteenth century) in Kyoto. The best-known member is Kiyokaze Yohei III.

Kiyomasu. Painter (Torii Kiyomasu; *mei:* Shōjirō, 1706–63) of ukiyo-e prints, son (or brother) of Kiyonobu of the Torii school. He produced prints in *sumizuri-e* and *tan-e* styles.
• Another painter of the same name (active between 1697 and 1725), perhaps Torii Kiyonobu's brother, or another ukiyo-e artist working in Edo and not in Ōsaka, as his namesakes did.
• Painter (Kiyomasu II, active from 1720 to 1750) who produced portraits of actors in *urushi-e* and *benizuri-e* styles. Perhaps the same artist as the one above. *See* KIYOMITSU.

Kiyomihara ritsuryō. Legal code written on the order of Emperor Temmu in 689 and promulgated by

Jitō Tennō in 697. Also called *Asuka no kiyomihara ritsuryō.*

Kiyomitsu. Painter (Torii Kiyomitsu; *mei:* Kamejirō, 1735–85) of ukiyo-e prints. He produced theater posters and portraits of actors in *beni-e* and *nishiki-e* styles. He studied with his father, Kiyomasu, in Edo.
→ *See* OSAFUNE KAJI.

• **Kiyomitsu II.** Painter (Torii Kiyomitsu II; *mei:* Shōnosuke; *gō:* Kiyomine, Seriyū prefecture, 1787–1868) of ukiyo-e prints, Kiyonaga's student in Edo. His works were mainly of theater sets.

Kiyomizu-dera. Buddhist temple of the Hossō-shū and Shingon-shū sects, founded in Higashiyama (Kyoto) in 798 by Enchin for Sakanoue Tamuramaro, and dedicated to worship of Jūichimen Kannon (Kannon with Eleven Faces). It was set afire several times in the late Heian period (twelfth century), then in 1629, and was rebuilt on the order of Tokugawa Iemitsu in the Momoyama style in 1633. Located on a hill, it has a *hondō* supported by a structure of latticed wood formed of 139 pillars, a roof covered with cypress shingles, and a *kara-hafu*-type porch roof. It also has a small three-story pagoda and, at the bottom of the hill, a spring where pilgrims perform their ablutions. In the Edo period, a business district developed and inns sprang up all around this temple.

• Another Buddhist temple, also dedicated to Kannon Bosatsu, built in Yonago near Matsue. Eighteenth-century pagoda.

• *Kiyomizu-dera engi.* An *emakimono* relating the foundation of the Kiyomizu-dera in Kyoto, attributed to Tosa Mitsunobu (sixteenth century).

• **Kiyomizu-yaki.** Ceramics produced in Kyoto in the sixteenth century, revived in the seventeenth century by Nonomura Ninsei. The Kiyomizu kilns produced porcelain pieces (as did related kilns in Omuro, Awataguchi, and Mizoro) to be used in the tea ceremony *(chanoyu)*. Starting in the eighteenth century, these ceramics were decorated with Chinese motifs. Most of the artists who worked in this style belonged to the Rokubei family (Kiyomizu Rokubei). Its best-known members were Kiyomizu Rokubei IV, Kiyomizu Rokubei V (b. 1901), and Rokubei VI (1902–80), who received the Order of Cultural Merit in 1976.

Kiyomoto. Painter (Torii Kiyomoto, Miyamoto, 1645–1702) of ukiyo-e prints in Osaka. He produced mainly Kabuki theater scenes and posters.

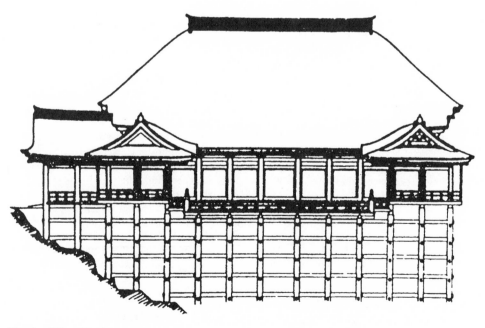

Temple of Kiyomizu-dera

Kiyomoto-bushi. Type of music for Kabuki theater, with shamisen and drums, created by Kiyomoto Enjudayū (1777–1825) and perpetuated by his son Kiyomoto Enjudayū II (1801–55) in Edo. The Kiyomoto-bushi repertoire originally comprised about 300 pieces, of which only about 40 are still played today. *See also* NAGA-UTA, TOKIWAZU-BUSHI.

Kiyonaga. Painter (Sekiguchi Shinsuke; *mei:* Shirakoya Ichibe I; *gō:* Torii Kiyonaga, 1752–1815) of ukiyo-e prints, student of and successor to Torii Kiyomitsu with the name Torii IV. He painted portraits of Kabuki actors and *bijin* (beautiful women).

Kiyonobu. Painter (Torii Kiyonobu; *mei:* Shōbe, 1664–1729) of ukiyo-e prints who studied with his father, Kiyomoto (Miyamoto). He was known for his portrayals of actors and Kabuki scenes in Edo, using *sumizuri-e, tan-e,* and *urushi-e* techniques. His art was influenced by the Kanō and Tosa schools and by Moronobu.

• **Kiyonobu II.** Painter (Torii Kiyonobu II, 1702–ca. 1752) of ukiyo-e prints, active from 1720 to 1750. He produced portraits of Kabuki actors in *urushi-e* and *benizuri-e* styles.

Kiyono Kenji. Physician and ethnologist (1885–1955), born in Okayama prefecture. After studying in Germany, he was a professor at the University of Kyoto from 1921 to 1938. He had excavated many *kaizuka* in 1919 and examined the skeletons they contained, coming to the conclusion that they belonged to a mixed Korean and Japanese race whose members were the forebears of today's Japanese people.

Kiyonori Kikutake. Contemporary architect, creator of the "new monumental metabolism" style (ca. 1960). He designed many plans for new cities in association with Tange Kenzō and Irozaki Arota.

Kiyooka Takayuki. Poet and writer, born 1922 in Dalian, China, and professor of French at Hōsei University. He published a collection of surrealist poems, *Kōtta honoo,* in 1959, and wrote novels, including *Akashiya no dairen,* which received the Akutagawa Prize in 1969; stories, including *Furūto to ōboe* (1971); and a poetry collection, *Nichijō* (1962).

Kiyoshige. Painter (Torii Kiyoshige; *gō:* Seichōken, ca. 1720–60) of ukiyo-e prints, Kiyonobu I's student. He produced portraits of Kabuki actors in *urushi-e* and *benizuri-e* styles.

Kiyotada. Painter (Torii Kiyotada, active 1725–45) of ukiyo-e and *eki-e* prints. He was Kiyonobu I's student in Edo. His two disciples took his name and were known as Kiyotada I and Kiyotada II.

Kiyotomo. Painter (Torii Kiyotomo, active 1720–40), Kiyonobu I's student.

Kiyotsune. Painter (Torii Kiyotsune; *mei:* Nakajima Daijirō; *gō:* Daijirō, active 1760–80), Kiyomitsu's student. He illustrated many books with ukiyo-e prints (*benizuri-e* and *nishiki-e*).

• *Kiyotsune.* Noh play, attributed to Zeami (1363–1443), about the suicide of warrior Taira no Kiyotsune after he was defeated by the Minamoto in 1184.

Kiyoura Keigo. Politician (1850–1942), born in Kumamoto. Thanks to his friendship with Yamagata Aritomo, he was minister of justice in Matsukata Masayoshi's second cabinet in 1896 and in Yamagata's cabinet (1898), then minister of the interior, trade, and agriculture in Katsura Tarō's cabinet (1901). Elected president of the emperor's Privy Council in 1922, he became prime minister in January 1924. But, strongly attacked by most parties, he was forced to resign six months later. Kato Kōmei succeeded him. Abandoning politics, he remained an adviser to Emperor Hirohito until the end of his life.

Kiyozawa Manshi. Buddhist monk (Tokunaga Manshi, 1863–1903) and philosopher. A professor of French history and Western philosophy, he left his official position because of uncertain health and, starting in 1894, took on the duty of reviving the Ōtani branch of the Jōdo Shin-shū. He was appointed dean of Shinshū University (which became Ōtani University in 1901), then founded a spiritualist movement (Seishin Shugi) in Tokyo. He wrote many religious books, among them *Shūkyō tetsugaku gaikotsu* (Plan of Religious Philosophy, 1892), *Tarikimon tetsugaku gaikotsu shikō* (Outline of *Tariki* Philosophy, 1892), *Zaishō zange roku* (Repentance During Illness, 1894), and *Waga shinnen* (My Faith, 1903). *See* TANNISHŌ.

Kiyū shōran. "Amusing Entertainment." A 12-volume collection of texts read and annotated by Kitamura Nobuyo (1784–1856), dealing with a wide variety of subjects, published in 1830. It comprises more than 4,000 articles, all annotated and referenced, making it an essential work for knowledge of customs and practices during the Edo period in the Edo, Osaka, and Kyoto regions.

Kiza-zō. Respectful position, kneeling on the heels, adopted by all Japanese during visits and ceremonies. Some portrayals of Buddhist divinities and praying figures also use this position. Also called *sonkyō-zō.*

Kizewa-mono. Type of Kabuki play describing habits, customs, and social conditions in Edo around 1800, typified by works by Tsuruya Namboku IV and Kawataka Shinshichi.

• **Kizewa-kyōgen.** *See* TSURUYA NAMBOKU.

Kizoku bunka. "Aristocratic culture," a term designating the aristocratic society of the Heian period.

• **Kizoku-in.** "House of Peers," one of the two chambers in the Diet after 1889, the other being the House of Representatives (Shūgi-in). Its members were aristocrats and members of the imperial family or high nobles *(kazoku),* appointed for life, and people whom the emperor wanted to honor, appointed for seven years. It had the same powers as the House of Representatives but had no say in the writing of the budget, which meant that a true parliamentary regime could not exist. It was dissolved in 1946. *See* KAZOKU.

• **Kizoku-sarugaku.** Pantomimes and danced dramas performed by nobles in the imperial court during the Heian period.

Ko. Administrative unit in the *ko-ku-gun* system, created by the *ritsuryō* laws in the mid-seventh century and corresponding to a hamlet of about 50–100 people. It was the basis for allocation of lands according to the *handen* system. In general, all members of a ko belonged to a single "extended" family, registered in a special register called *koseki,* and were led by a *koshu,* "family head."

Kō. Noble title corresponding to "duke" for civilians and "marquis" for military men (from 1870 to 1945).
• Religious associations responsible for organizing ceremonies and, especially, pilgrimages; raising funds for works, shrines, or temples; and, in the Heian and Kamakura periods, listening in groups to the reading of sacred texts. Many ancient Buddhist *kō,* such as the Amida-*kō,* are still in existence, as are many Shinto *kō,* such as the Ise-*kō* and Kumano-*kō,* responsible for the pilgrimages to Ise and Kumano, and the Fuji-*kō,* responsible for annual pilgrimages up Mt. Fuji. The members of a *kō* were required to help each other when the need arose.

Kō-ami. Family of lacquer artists whose members worked for the court of the Tokugawa shogun in the eighteenth and nineteenth centuries. *See* NAGASHIGE KŌ-AMI.

Kōan. "Questions and answers," a method used in the Zen Rinzai sect to evaluate a monk's state of spirituality and to develop his sense of philosophical reflection. When the master asked a particular disciple a *kōan,* the disciple had to supply a satisfactory answer, the range of which was limited to his degree of enlightenment. A *kōan* thus could not be considered to have a universal value; rather, it was designed by the Zen master so as to be apparently illogical, in order to force the disciple to make a personal effort of reflection and not give a conventional response. These sorts of paradoxes were at the core of Chan (Zen) in China in the Song period (960–1279) and were developed in Japan in the early thirteenth century. They were based on two important Chinese Chan works, the *Biyanlu* (*Jap.: Hekigan-roku,* "Account of the Blue Mountains") and the *Wumenguan* (*Jap.: Mumonkan,* "The Gate with No Entrance"). The *kōan* tradition was initiated in Japan by the Zen monk Hakuin. Although the *kōan* are specific to the Zen Rinzai branch, the Sōtō branch also uses them, but without according them so much importance. *Chin.: gong'an. See* ZEN.

Kōan. Era of Emperor Go-Uda: Feb. 1278–Apr. 1288. *See* NENGŌ.
• Era of Emperor Go-Kōgon of the Northern Court (Hokuchō): Mar. 1361–Sept. 1362. *See* NENGŌ.

Kōan no Eki. "Kōan War." The name sometimes given to the second Mongolian attempt to invade Japan in 1281, following the unsuccessful attempt of the Bun'ei era (1274). Two fleets sailed for Japan, one from Korea with 900 ships and 40,000 men, the other from China with 3,500 ships and almost 100,000 men. These fleets were to meet off the island of Iki and jointly attack the port of Hakata (Kyushu). But they were unable to meet and so attacked separately, the first at Hakata, the second at

Hirado, using the island of Takashima as a base. On August 23, 1281, a typhoon dispersed the ships of both fleets. Some of the Koreans and Mongolians who took refuge on Takashima were annihilated by samurai, while the rest of the invading fleet tried to return to the mainland.

• **Kōan Tennō.** Sixth emperor (O-Yamata Tarashi-hiko Kuni Oshihito no Mikoto, traditionally 427<392–291> BC), son of and successor to Kōshō Tennō; Kōrei Tennō was said to have succeeded him. He was probably a mythical character or someone who lived in the first century BC.

Koban. Gold coins issued starting in 1601, worth one *ryō*. They were oval-shaped and quite thin, measuring about 7.5 × 3.5 cm and weighing about 17.85 g, with a gold content of 84.30%. However, the weight and gold content varied over time; in the Gembun era, they weighed only 13.13 g and were 65.70% gold. The weight and purity continued to drop; by the end of the Edo period (Man'en *koban*), they weighed 3.30 g and had a gold content of 56.80%. *Koban* were recalled and reissued nine times, each bearing the name of an era: Keichō (1601–1738), Genroku (1695–1717), Hōei (1710–19), Shōtoku (1714–1860), Gembun (1736–1827), Bunsei (1819–42), Tempō (1837–74), Ansei (1859–74), Man'en (1860–1974). *See* CURRENCY, KEICHŌ-TSŪHŌ, ŌBAN, RYŌ.
→ *See* UKIYO-E.

Kōban. "Police station," police units responsible for patrolling the country to maintain order. These units (which could comprise anywhere from two officers to fifty or more) were generally set up at major crossroads in towns. *Kōban* were also called *chūzaisho* in the countryside and *hashutsujo* in urban areas.

Kobanashi. "Short stories." Stories of various lengths, generally humorous, published from the seventeenth to the nineteenth century, mainly in Edo. They dealt with all sorts of subjects, religious and lay; their sole purpose was entertainment, and they were very popular. They were called *karuku-chi-hon* in the Kyoto and Osaka regions, and *otoshibanashibon* in Edo, but all were included in the genre called *hanashibon, shōwa-hon,* or *kobanashibon*. In the late nineteenth century, under the influence of *rakugo* recited by professionals, *kobanashi* became longer and were called *nagabanashi,* "long stories." *See also* RAKUGO.

Kiobayakawa Hideaki. Daimyo (1582–1602), nephew of Toyotomi Hideyoshi's wife, Kita no Mandokoro, and Hideyoshi's adoptive son, lord of an estate in the Fukuoka region in 1598, following the death of his protector, Kobayakawa Takakage (1533–97). In the Battle of Sekigahara (1600) he betrayed his allies, enabling Tokugawa Ieyasu to seize victory. Ieyasu rewarded him by granting him an estate of 510,000 *koku* in Okayama, a fief left vacant by the death of its legitimate owner, Ukita Hideie, but Hideaki died soon after, leaving no heir.

Kobayakawa Takakage. Warrior (1533–97), Mōri Motonari's son. When he became head of the Kobayakawa clan upon the death of his father in 1545, he expanded his territories almost throughout Chūgoku. He opposed Oda Nobunaga and Toyotomi Hideyoshi but made a pact with the latter, who appointed him *tairō*. From then on, he fought on Hideyoshi's side and received an estate of 350,000 *koku* in Iyo and Chikuzen. He had a castle built in Najima (Chikuzen) and joined Hideyoshi's army that went to Korea. He then adopted one of Hideyoshi's adoptive sons, Hideaki, and gave him his name before retiring from active life. *See* KOBAYA-KAWA HIDEAKI.

Kobayashi Beika. Western jurist and writer (Joseph-Ernest de Becker, 1863–1929) who became a Japanese citizen in 1892; author of many works on jurisprudence.

Kobayashi Hideo. Writer and literary critic (1902–83), born in Tokyo. With his writings and studies on Dostoyevsky, Mozart, and modern Japanese writers, he helped establish independent literary criticism. He proved to be a fierce opponent of the "first-person" novel *(watakushi-shōsetsu)* that was then in style and founded the literary magazine *Bungaku-kai* along with Kawabata Yasunari, Takeda Rinarō, and several other writers. He received the Order of Culture (Bunka-shō) in 1967. His critical works were collected in the 13-volume *Kobayashi Hideo zenshū* (1978–79).

Kobayashi Issa. Haiku poet (Kobayashi Yatarō, Kobayashi Nobuyuki, 1763–1827), born in Shimano province (Nagano prefecture). He emulated Bashō both in life style—he became an itinerant monk—and in his poems. His haiku collections include *Kansei-kuchō* (1794), *Kansei kikō* (1795), *Chichi no shūen nikki* (Journal of My Father's Death, 1801), *Kyōwa kuchō* (1803), *Bunka kuchō* (1808), *Oraga haru* (The Years of My Life, 1819),

Shichiban nikki (1818), *Hachiban nikki* (1821), *Kuban nikki* (1824). Often called simply Issa.

Kobayashi Kokei. Painter (Kobayashi Shigeru, 1883–1957), born in Niigata. He was Kajita Hanko's (1870–1917) student in Tokyo and painted in the Yamato-e style, then in the style of the Rimpa school. He went to Europe in 1922 with Maeda Seison and made copies of ancient Chinese paintings (notably by Gu Kaizhi, ca. 345–ca. 411) for the British Museum. He was made a member of the Japanese Fine Arts Academy (Nihon Bijutsu-in) in 1912 and of the Imperial Academy (Teikoku Geijutsu-in) in 1937; became an Artist for the Imperial Household (Teishitsu Gigei-in) in 1944; and received the Order of Culture (Bunka-shō) in 1950.

Kobayashi Masaki. Movie director (1916–96), born in Ōtaru (Hokkaido). He was Kinoshita Keisuke's assistant. Taken prisoner in Okinawa at the end of the Second World War, he was freed in 1950. He drew on his experiences in the war and in captivity for films such as *Kabe atsuki heya* (The Room with Thick Walls, 1953), then continued his career with *Ningen no jōken* (The Human Condition, 1959–61, after a novel by Gomikawa Junpei); *Seppuku* (Hara-kiri, 1964), a three-part film lasting a total of 9 hours and 43 minutes, on the survival of a Japanese soldier during the war; *Kaidan* (1965, after stories by Lafcadio Hearn); and *Kaseki,* produced for television in 1973.

Kobayashi Takiji. Writer (1903–33), born in Akita, one of the most representative of the proletarian-literarature movement. At first a bank employee, he went to Tokyo in 1930 and joined the Communist party. Inspired by Dostoyevsky and Chekhov, he began to publish stories and translations of Henri Barbusse's works. He then created the magazine *Kurarute* (Clarity) with friends and became involved in the proletarian movement, publishing stories with political and social resonance: *Tenkeiki no hitobito* (Living in an Era of Transition, 1931), *Tōseikatsusha* (Living for the Party, 1932), and a novel that made him famous, *Kami-kōsen* (The Cannery Boat, 1929), which was adapted for the screen by Yamamura Sō in 1953 as *The Boats of Hell.* Among his other works, mostly stories, are *Higashi Kutchan kō* (Voyage to Eastern Kuchan, 1928), *Kōba saibō* (The Factory Cell, 1930), *Orugu* (The Organizer, 1931), *Yasuko* (1931), and *Numa-iri mura* (The Village of Numairi, 1932).

Kobe. Main city in Hyōgo prefecture and major port on Osaka Bay, located 32 km southwest of Osaka, to which it is linked by an industrial conurbation (metallurgy, heavy industry, shipyards and airplane plants, automobile plants petrochemicals, etc.), most of whose installations are on landfill. The second largest port in Japan, Kobe exports mainly textiles and automobiles, and has a long tradition of trade (with China) going back to the fifteenth century. It was designated an open port by the 1858 treaties (*see* ANSEI NO KAI JŌYAKU). Heavily bombed during the Second World War, it was reconstructed after 1945. It was once the town of Kamibe (*see* BE), where the Ikuta-jinja—a shrine whose foundation, according to tradition, goes back to the third century—is located. A very busy business center, its Motomachi and Sanchika districts are known throughout Japan for their activity. The city has a university and a museum (Hakutsuru Art Museum). Nearby, on Mt. Rokkō, overlooking the city, are hot springs. *Pop.:* 1.4 million. A 7-magnitude earthquake on the night of January 16–17, 1995, killed almost 4,800 and caused considerable damage to buildings in and around the city.

• **Kōbe Daigaku.** Kobe national university, founded in 1902 as a business school; it became a university in 1949. It has a large number of faculties and a student population of about 9,000.

Kōben. *See* MYŌE.

Kōbetsu. Category of titles of nobility and aristocratic families. These families, related to (or issuing from) the imperial family line, claimed that their ancestry went back to the time of Jimmu Tennō. In the early ninth century, according to the *Shinsen shōjiroku,* there were 335. Starting with the reign of Emperor Temmu, all their members received the title of Ason (or Asoni). There were two types of *kōbetsu* families: those truly of "divine descendancy" *(shembitsu),* and those of foreign origin *(shoban).* *See* SHIMBETSU.

Kobikichō. Branch of the Kanō school of painting, created in the district of this name in Edo. *See* KANŌ-HA, OKU-ESHI.

Ko-bizen. Nickname for sword makers belonging to a single family that worked in Bizen province from the tenth to the thirteenth century. The best known were Tomonari and Masatsune.

Kōbō Daishi. *See* KŪKAI.

Kobori Enshū. Master of the tea ceremony *(chanoyu),* warrior, calligrapher, gardener, and architect

(Kobori no Masakazu, 1579–1647) serving Toyotomi Hideyoshi, born in Ōmi province. He was master of the tea ceremony under the first three Tokugawa shoguns. He is also credited with construction of several teahouses (chashitsu) in Kyoto, notably those at the Nanzen-ji and Katsura Rikyū, and is said to have been associated with the erection of the Nijō-jō castle in Kyoto. Among his many activities, he sponsored the kilns of potters making pieces for the tea ceremony. Little is known about his personal life. His style of ceremony is known as Enshū-ryū.

Kōbun-in. School founded around 800 by Wake Hiroyo to educate the children in his family. It had a library of about 6,000 works. The school founded by Tokugawa Ieyasu in Edo in 1632 was given this name by Tokugawa Iemitsu.
→ *See* SHŌHEI-KŌ.

Kobunji-gaku. Confucianist school of "the old rhetoric" whose most famous theoretician was Ogyū Sorai. Its members opposed the schools of Wang Yangming (Yōmei-gaku), Zhu Xi (Shushi-gaku), and Itō Jinsai (Kogi-gaku), and advocated study of the ancient Confucian texts. Also called Ken'en-gaku.

Kōbun Tennō. Thirty-ninth emperor (Prince Otomo, Iga no Oji, 648<672>), Tenji Tennō's son and heir. At his ascension, the throne was contested by his uncle, O-Ama no Oji, who attacked and defeated him during the Jishin Jiken. Kōbun Tennō committed suicide after ruling for only eight months, and Prince O-Ama succeeded him with the name Temmu. The *posthumous name* Kōbun Tennō was given to him by Emperor Meiji in 1870. Two poems by this unfortunate sovereign are contained in the *Kaifūsō.*

Kobushin. In the Edo period, bureaucrats responsible for maintenance of and repairs to public buildings, starting in 1685. *Kobushin* were generally from the *hatamoto* or *gokenin,* and unable to perform military service; they received an annual salary of at least 3,000 *koku.* Also called *kobushin-bugyō.*

Kōbushō. Military school for young samurai, created in Edo in 1855. It was called Rikugunsho starting in 1866. This school, established in Tsukiji, was mainly for *hatamoto* and *gokenin.* It taught swimming, fencing, and artillery. A naval section was founded in 1857. Another center for military instruction was started in Osaka in 1865.

Kobutori jijii. Folk tale in which an old man with a large wart on his cheek meets a group of demons *(oni),* and sings and dances for them in such a pleasing manner that they remove his wart. Another old man, similarly afflicted, tries to imitate the first, but his performance is so awful that the demons make a second wart grow on his other cheek. This tale is in the *Uji shūi monogatari* (thirteenth century).

Kōbu-tsūhō. Chinese copper coins from the Ming dynasty, imported to Japan during the Muromachi period and in use until the beginning of the Edo period. In the late Muromachi period, these coins were struck in Japan and called *kajiki-sen.* They had five values, from 1 to 10 *mon,* according to their size. Also called *kōbu-sen.*

Kōchi. "Cochin-China." Ceramics typical of southern China that were imitated in Japan. They were decorated with relief motifs and were enameled in yellow, green, and aubergine.

Kōchi. Main city in Kōchi prefecture on Shikoku and an important port on the Kagami River and Urado Bay, founded as a castle town *(jōka-machi)* around Yamanouchi Kazutoyo's castle, built in 1603 and renovated in 1748, with five stories and an outside gallery. It is the site of Chikurin-ji temple, founded by Gyōki and adorned with a garden designed by Musō Kokushi *(hondō* from the Muromachi period), the Buddhist Sekkei-ji temple (founded in the twelfth century), and the Sōan-ji temple dedicated to worship of Fudō Myō-ō. The city has several small industrial concerns. *Pop.:* 300,000.

• **Kōchi prefecture.** Prefecture in southern Shikoku, former Tosa province, created in 1871, former fief of the Chōsokabe and Yamanouchi families. It is famous for its breeding operations, producing long-tailed cocks *(onagadori)* in the town of Gomen and fighting dogs (Tosa-inu). One of the hottest regions of Japan, it has two rice harvests per year, some lumber and paper industry, and fishing on the Pacific coast. *Main city:* Kōchi. *Other major cities:* Nakamura, Nankoku, Tosa. *Area:* 7,107 km². *Pop.:* 900,000.

Kōchiyama to naozamurai. Title of a seven-act Kabuki play, first produced in 1881 by Kawataka Mokuami: a corrupt daimyo tries to seduce a young woman with whom the hero is in love. Also titled *Kumo ni magon ueno no hatsuhana.*

Kōchō. Era of Emperor Kameyama: Feb. 1261–
Feb. 1262. *See* NENGŌ.
→ *See* KENNYŌ SHŌNIN.

• Kōchō-jūnisen. General term for 12 Japanese
imperial issues of copper coins, copies of Chinese
coins, during the Nara and Heian periods. The
coins had limited circulation in the region around
the capitals and among aristocrats, while commoners continued to use the barter system. These coins
were replaced in the late tenth century by other
coins imported from China. The 12 *kōchō-sen*
were:
1. **Wadō-kaihō** (708)
2. **Mannen-tsūho** (760)
3. **Jinkō-kaihō** (or Jingū-kaihō, 765)
4. **Ryūhei-eihō** (796)
5. **Fuju-shimpō** (818)
6. **Shōwa-shōhō** (or Jōwa-shōhō, 835)
7. **Chōnen-taihō** (848)
8. **Jōeki-shimpō** (859)
9. **Jōgan-eihō** (870)
10. **Kampyō-taihō** (890)
11. **Engi-tsūhō** (907)
12. **Kengen-taihō** (948)
→ *See* CURRENCY.

Kōda Aya. Novelist and essayist (1904–90), Kōda
Rohan's daughter, born in Tokyo. After her father
died, she began to write essays and articles about
him—*Shūen* (Last Moment, 1947), *Chichi sono shi*
(My Father, His Death, 1953), *Chichi konno koto*
(My Father, These Things, 1954)—and stories such
as *Kuroi suso* (The Black Kimono Hem, 1955), *Chi-
giregumo* (Wild Clouds, 1956), *Nagareru* (Hesi-
tation, which won the Nihon Geijutus-in Prize in
1957), *Fue* (The Flute, 1957), *Otōto* (My Younger
Brother, 1957), *Tō* (Combat, 1972). Her novels
Nagareru and *Otōto* were adapted to the screen by
Naruse Mikio (1956) and Ichikawa Kon (1960).

Kōdai-in. Toyotomi Hideyoshi's wife (1549–
1624). When her husband died in 1598, she became
a Buddhist nun. Also called Kita no Mandokoro.
Hideyoshi's nickname for her was Nene.

• Kōdai-ji. Buddhist temple in Kyoto, built by
Kōdai-in in memory of her husband in 1606.
Kaisan-dō and funerary chapel from 1606, Omote-
mon from the late sixteenth century, brought from
Fushimi's castle in 1606.

• Kōdai-jimaki-e. Lacquered objects *(maki-e)* from
the late sixteenth century, taking their name from

the Kōdai-ji collections. These objects are decorated
with flowers and plants distributed in discrete areas
on their surface, and made in *hira-maki-e*—that is,
by sprinkling gold and silver on black lacquer without further polishing.

• Kōdai-jingu. *See* ISE KŌDAI-JINGŪ.

Kodaira Kunihiko. Internationally renowned
mathematician (1915–97), born in Tokyo, who
taught at Princeton University and other major
American universities before holding the chair at
the University of Tokyo in 1967. He received many
foreign distinctions, as well as the Order of Culture
(Bunka-shō) in 1957.

Kodama Gentarō. General (1852–1906), born in
Suō province (Yamaguchi prefecture). He fought in
the imperial troops during the Boshin Civil War
(1868), and later reorganized the army along German principles. After fighting in the Sino-Japanese
War (1894–95), he was appointed governor-general
of Taiwan. Minister of war in 1900 in Itō Hirobumi's then Katsura Tarō's cabinet, he was also
minister of the interior and of education. He received marshal's stripes in 1904, during the Russo-
Japanese War, and commanded an army at Port Arthur. Appointed chief of staff in 1906.

Kodama Kagai. Poet (Kagai, 1874–1943), inventor
of a genre of socialist-inspired popular poetry about
1902: *Shakaishugi shishū, Kagai shishō,* etc.

Kodama Yoshio. Politician and businessman (1911
–84), born in Fukushima. He joined right-wing
parties in 1929 and tried to have the minister of
finance, Inoue Junnosuke, assassinated in 1931. He
was arrested and imprisoned, then tried to assassinate other politicians opposed to his views in
1932. When he left prison in 1937, he went to Manchuria and northern China on the pretext of an official mission; in 1941 he was made responsible for
organizing a trade network (called Kodama-kikan)
in Shanghai to procure war materiel for the army.
He published an extremist magazine, *Taigi,* in
1942. Taken prisoner by the Allies in 1945, he was
declared a war criminal and imprisoned. He was
freed in 1948, thanks to the huge fortune he had
amassed in China; he backed the Jiyū Minshutō
(Liberal Democratic party) and remained active behind the scenes. A secret agent for Lockheed (air-
plane-purchasing scandal involving the Japanese
government in 1976), he was arraigned and sent to
trial, but died before he was sentenced. He had writ-

ten a book on politics, *Akusei jusei ransei* (Bad Policy, Gunshots, and a Troubled World), in 1961.

Kōdan. Historical tales and legends, recited by professional storytellers, that were very popular (as were *rakugo*) in the late Edo period and in the Meiji era. They were previously called *kōshaku*. This art is still alive and is practiced by four different schools, but audiences are small. *See* RAKUGO, YOSE.

Kōdansha. Publishing house founded in Tokyo in 1909 by Noma Seiji (1878–1938) under the name Dai Nippon Yūben-kai (Oratory Society of Greater Japan), which published the magazine *Yūben*. It was renamed Kōdansha in 1911, when it published a more popular magazine called *Kōdan Kurabu*, followed by several others, which made Kōdansha the largest magazine publisher in Japan before the Second World War. Because the goal of these publications was to bring culture to a greater number of readers, there was talk of a "Kōdansha culture" (Kōdansha-bunka). After the Second World War, Kōdansha started up again, publishing various magazines, art books, and culturally oriented books, and rapidly became the largest publisher in Japan, with more than 1,500 titles published each year. Starting in 1963, Kōdansha also published books in English through a newly created company, Kōdansha International, Ltd.

Kōda Rohan. Writer (Kōda Shigeyuki, 1867–1947), born in Tokyo to a family of low-level samurai, brother of explorer Gunji Shigetada (1860–1924), musicians Kōda Nobu (1870–1946) and Andō Kōko (1878–1963), and scholar Kōda Shigetomo (1873–1954), and novelist Kōda Aya's father. He worked at various trades before beginning to write stories, then novels, somewhat influenced by classical Chinese culture and Buddhism and by his colleagues from the Ken'yūsha: *Fūryū butsu* (The Buddha of Love, 1889), *Gojunotō* (The Five-Story Pagoda, 1891), *Isanatori* (The Whaleboat, 1892), *Fūryū mijinzō* (The Warehouse of Life's Dust, 1893), *Sora utsunami* (Ten *Utsanami*, 1904), *Senshin-roku* (Purifying One's Heart, 1914), *Rangen* (Soothing Stories, 1901) *Ummei* (Destiny, 1919), *Chikutō* (Pieces of Bamboo, 1939), *Renkanki* (Chains, 1940), commentaries on Bashō's poems (1947), and a large number of historical stories: *Wankyū monogatari, Yoritomo, Taira no Masakado,* and others. He was elected a member of the Imperial Academy (Teikoku Geijutsu-in) in 1937.

Kōden. In ancient Japan, public rice paddies or fields generally given (either permanently or temporarily) to certain people as a reward for their services rendered to the court. These lands were different from *shiden* (private properties), but the distinction later faded. They were classified in four major categories: *shikiden* (for senior bureaucrats), *iden* (for nobles), *jiden* (for Buddhist temples), and *shinden* (for Shinto shrines). After 743, there was a clearer distinction between *kōden* and *shiden,* which were controlled either by the government or by private institutions.
→ *See* KOKURYŌ.
• Sum of money that funeral attendees pay to the family of the deceased to help defray costs. Wealthy families often return part of this sum to the donors *(kōden-gaeshi).* This custom replaces the former donation of rice and food by the community. *See* FUNERALS.

Kōdō. In Buddhist temples and monasteries, a room reserved for sermons or meetings of the monks. *See* HATTŌ.
• Art of appreciating the scent of incense and distinguishing its provenance. It was codified by Sanjōnishi Sanetaka (1455–1537), who created a school called Ōe-ryū. His disciple, Shino Munenobu, created another Kōdō school, called Shino-ryū.

Kōdō-ha. "'Imperial Way' faction." A military faction formed about 1932 by ultranationalist officers opposed to the Tōsei-ha and directed by generals Araki Sadao and Mazaki Jinzaburō. It advocated total devotion to the emperor and military reform based on opposition to the Soviet Union. One of its officers, Aizawa Saburō (1889–1936), assassinated a general of the Tōsei-ha, Nagata Tetsuzan, in 1936, and others provoked serious incidents, such as the one on February 26, 1936 that attempted to establish a military regime. This movement failed, and Araki Sadao was "retired"; the Tōsei-ha regained control of the army. *See* MAZAKI JINZABURŌ, NINIROKU JIKEN.

• **Kōdō-kai.** Ultranationalist secret society founded around 1933 by general Araki Sadao, who recruited his members from among army officers. *See* KŌDO-HA.

Kōdōkan. Sports arena devoted to teaching the martial arts, mainly judo and aikido, founded by Kanzo Jigorō in 1883 within the walls of the Eishō-ji Buddhist temple in Tokyo. A new building, called

Budōkan, was erected in Tokyo in 1962 to replace the Kōdōkan, which had fallen into disrepair.

• School *(shohan-gakkō)* founded in Mito in 1838 by Tokugawa Nariaki to develop historical and Confucian studies; many scholars met there, forming what has been dubbed the "Mito school."

Koeckebaecker, Nicolas. Dutch director of the Dejima trading post from 1633 to 1639. On request of the shogunate, he attacked the rebels of the Shimabara Peninsula, bombing them from his ship *De Ryp* in February 1638, then returned to Dejima after donating some cannons to the shogunal troops.

Kōei. Era of Emperor Kōmyō, of the dynasty of the North: Apr. 1342–Oct. 1345. *See* NENGŌ.

Kōen. Buddhist monk (b. 1207) and sculptor, Unkei's grandson. He sculpted the statue of Senju Kannon at the Sanjūsangandō in Kyoto.

• Buddhist monk (d. 1169) of the Tendai-shū at Mt. Hiei; author, after 1198, of the *Fusōryakuki,* a historical work on the period from 898 to 1198.
→ *See* KŌIN.

Kōfuku-ji. Buddhist temple of the Hossō-shū sect, founded in Yamashina in 669 by Kagami no Ōkimi (d. 683), Fujiwara no Kamatari's wife, under the name Yamashina-dera, and transported to Nara in 710. She had a large statue *(jōroku* size) of Shakyamuni Buddha installed there. The Kōfuku-ji became the family temple of the Fujiwara family, where the doctrines of the Hossō sect, brought to Japan in 735 by the monk Gembō (d. 746), were taught. This temple has many ancient buildings, among them a five-story pagoda 50 m high, built in 730 and reconstructed in the same style in 1426; three-story pagoda built in 1143 and reconstructed about 1250; *hokuen-dō* (octagonal) built in 721 and reconstructed in 1240; *nanendō* (octagonal), built in 813 (bronze lantern from the period) and reconstructed in 1789; *chū-kondō* (beautiful sculpture museum, Koku-hōkan) from 1819; *tō-kondō* built in 726 and reconstructed in 1425. Also called Nanto Hokurei.

Kofun. Large megalithic tombs of earthen tumuli, erected by members of the aristocracy between the late third century and the very early eighth century on Kyushu and Honshu, for which the corresponding period of Japanese history is named. Excavation of *kofun* is the only definite source of study for this period, which was divided into three stages:

Early kofun. Although some archeologists think that this type of tomb existed in Japan during the Yayoi period (ca. 300 BC–ca. AD 300), it was probably imported from Korea in the late third century by groups of Altaic "horsemen-archers" with iron armor who came from the mainland and took political control of Yamato (*see* KIBAMINZOKU-RON). The oldest *kofun* were found in the Kinai region, built on top of hills overlooking cultivated plains. A *kofun* was a sort of well that was faced with stones, at the bottom of which a wooden casket was placed. It was protected by boulders covered with a mound of earth on which were placed terra-cotta tubes *(haniwa).* Excavation of these *kofun* has uncovered mainly ceremonial objects, Chinese bronze mirrors, *magatama* necklaces, and various bracelets. In the late fourth century, this burial style spread to eastern Japan (Kanto) and to the west coast, and the *kofun* were made in various shapes: round, square, gourd-shaped. Sarcophagi were in stone or wood and enclosed in terra-cotta walls.

Middle period. This period began in the fifth century, with the appearance of megalithic tombs built on large terraces and surrounded with moats. These tumuli were often accompanied by small annex mounds *(baichō)* that contained large amounts of funerary property—mainly weapons, iron armor, and objects showing that Japan had close relations with the Korean kingdoms. There was also a new type of tomb, imported from Korea, with an entrance corridor *(yokoana-sekishitsu)* that allowed for multiple burials.

Late period. In the sixth and seventh centuries, the size of *kofun* shrank and their numbers grew, with local populations tending to bury their dead in *kofun* grouped in giant "cemeteries." Funerary property became more utilitarian and was placed not only in the funerary chamber itself but also in the access corridor. *Sue* and *haji* pottery has been found, as have objects that belonged to the deceased. These *kofun* show fairly wide regional differences: on Kyushu, they were made of lava and tuff and were decorated with lava sculptures; elsewhere, the interior was decorated with symbolic paintings and was surrounded by many rows of *haniwa* portraying objects, people, and animals.

There are at least four forms of *kofun:* round *(empun),* square *(hōfun),* "keyhole" *(zempō-kōen-fun),* and square preceded by a rectangle *(zempō-kōhō-fun).* The erection of such structures (some, such as the tomb said to belong to Nintoku Tennō, are immense), which was very expensive and required a huge amount of labor, was banned by Emperor Kōtoku, but construction of small *kofun* continued for some time before the custom of cremation became common. *Kofun* also exist on the Ryukyu Islands, where they are called *paka* (or *haka*). The main *kofun* are:

—*In Kinai:* Samita, Ishibutai, Takamatsukasa, Niiyama, Iwase, Chūson-ji, Nintoku, Mozu, Ōjin, Tsubai Otsukayama.

—*In Kantō:* Shiraishi Inariyama, Sakitama, Inariyama.

—*On the west coast:* Chūsen-ji.

—*On Kyushu:* Takehara, Ikisan Chōshizuka, Ōzuka, Yame, Takehara, Iwatoyama, Sekiji-yama, Saitobaru, Eta Funayama.

Excavation of "imperial" *kofun (misa-sagi)* was banned before the Second World War, so archeologists could open only those considered "common," and certain restrictions are still in effect for opening large *kofun*. The period during which these megalithic tombs were built is called *kofun-jidai,* and the corresponding civilization is called *kofun-bunka. See* ARAKI NO MIYA, HABIKINO, HAYATO-ZUKA, HIRAIDE.

Kōfu-saishō. "Daimyo of Kōfu," title for Tokugawa Tsunashige, brother of Tokugawa Ietsuna and Tokugawa Tsunayoshi.

Koga-biko. Biography of painters of the Edo period, published in 53 volumes by Kōtei (Asaoka Okisada, 1800–56).

Koga-kubō. Title for Ashikaga Shigeuji and his descendants after Shigeuji took refuge at Koga (Ibaraki prefecture). *See* ASHIKAGA SHIGEUJI, ASHIKAGA MASATOMO, KYŌTOKU NO RAN.

Kōgai. Small stiletto that generally accompanied the *kozuka* or *umabari* on the scabbard *(saya)* of a *katana* sword. It was used to repair armor and pick out horse's hooves. *Kōgai* could also be used as chopsticks for eating. Also, a decorative hairpin in metal, wood, tortoiseshell, or other material, very ornate, used by women to hold their bun in place. *See also* KANZASHI, KOZUKA.

Koga Issaku. Engineer (1899–1982), born in Saga prefecture, who invented the quartz-crystal resonator and the procedure for splitting quartz to obtain crystals with a stable resonance frequency. He taught at the University of Tokyo starting in 1944 and received the Order of Culture (Bunka-shō) in 1963.

Kogaku-ha. "School of Ancient Studies," an important current of Confucian thought in the Edo period criticizing Zhu Xi (*Jap.:* Shushi) theories and advocating a return to Confucius's original thought. The main masters of this school were Yamaga Sokō, Itō Jinsai, and Ogyū Sorai, who, though often opposed on details, were firm supporters of Confucian thought stripped of Taoist and Buddhist concepts.

• "Ancient studies," works dealing with the study of ancient Japanese literature. *See* KOKUGAKU.

Kōgaku Shinnō. Imperial prince (d. 865), Heijō Tennō's son. Implicated in a conspiracy, he became a Buddhist monk with the name Shinnyo and a disciple of Kūkai. He traveled in China in 862, then went from Canton to Malaysia, where he died. Also called Takaoka Shinnō, Shinnyo Shōnin.

Koga Masao. Composer (1904–78) of popular music, born in Fukuoka prefecture, who wrote very well-known songs such as *Kage o shitaite* (Dark Desire, 1924) and *Sake wa namida ka tameiki* (Is the Wine Tears or Sighs? 1930).

Kōga Mineichi. Admiral (ca. 1885–1944) who succeeded Yamamoto Isoroku as chief commander of Japan's naval and air forces in April 1943. He continued his predecessor's offensive tactics but perished in a plane accident while he was preparing to launch "Operation Z," a large-scale naval attack on Palaos. Admiral Toyoda Sōemu succeeded him.

Kogan. Sculptor and painter (Tobari, 1882–1927). After studying in the United States, he created an artists' association, the Nihon Sōsaku Hanga Kyōkai, in Japan.

Koga Seiri. Confucian scholar (1750–1817) and Chinese professor at the Shōheikō in Edo. A member of the Teishu-ha, he wrote a large number of books on this philosophy, including *Shisho shōyaku, Kinshiroku,* and *Susetsu.* He was one of the three Kansai no Sansuke (or San-hakase), with Bitō Nishū and Shibano Ritsuzan. *See* HAKASE.

Kōgen. Era of Emperor Go-Fukakusa: Oct. 1256–Mar. 1257. *See* NENGŌ.

Kōgen Tennō. Eighth emperor, according to the traditional genealogy (Prince O-Yamato Nekohito Kuni Kuru no Mikoto, 273<214–158> BC), Kōrei Tennō's son and successor. His son, Kaika, would have succeeded him.

Kogidō. Private school for commoners founded in 1662 in Kyoto by Itō Jinsai, teaching principles of Confucian philosophy based on the *Analects* and the *Doctrine of the Mean*. This school remained open to all until the early Meiji era. Also called for the name of the district in which it was located, Horikawa-gakkō.

Kōgō. Incense holder made of wood, ceramic, or lacquer, with a decorated cover.
• Title for a nonreigning empress, generally an emperor's wife who has given birth to the heir to the throne. This title, still in use, was sometimes conferred on the widow of a prince or on a princess whose son became emperor.
→ *See* ŌKISAKI.

Kogō. Title of a Noh play: the noblewoman Kogō no Tsubone, favorite of Emperor Takakura, leaves the capital because Taira no Kiyomori's daughter has become empress. But the emperor searches for her and finally finds her when he hears the sound of her *biwa*.

• **Kogō no Tsubone.** Lady of the Heian court, Fujiwara no Shigenori's daughter. One of Emperor Takakura's favorites, she was a famous *biwa* player. She became a Buddhist nun when she was 23 years old.

Kōgoishi. Earthen walls built on a foundation of stone to surround sacred sites, erected probably in the sixth or seventh century in northern Kyushu and coastal regions on the Inland Sea (Setonaikai). One of the largest was that around the summit of Mt. Kōra (near Fukuoka), which was 2.3 km long. Eight of these walls have been discovered in Fukuoka prefecture. Some may have been built in anticipation of an attack from Korea, though this has not been proven. Archeologist Tsuboi Shōgorō gave them this name, which means "stones of divine protection."

Kōgon Tennō. First emperor (Prince Kazuhito, 1313<1331–33>1364) of the dynasty of the North (Hokuchō), Go-Fushimi's son, placed on the throne in Kyoto after Go-Daigo was exiled. He belonged to the Jimyō-in family line but was forced to abdicate when Go-Daigo managed to oust the Kamakura shogunate and reestablish shogunal authority (Kemmu Restoration). Becoming a retired emperor, Kōgon continued to govern in fact until his death. He compiled a poetry anthology, *Fūga waka-shū*, in

1346. Kōmyō Tennō succeeded him on the Kyoto throne.

Kogo-shūi. "Collection of Ancient Stories." A one-volume historical work compiled in 807 by Imbe no Ironari to complement the *Nihongi*. It deals mainly with ancient legends and customs. Also called *Kogo-jūi*.

Kōgyo. Painter (Terazaki Hironari; *gō*: Sōzan, Tenrai Sanjin, Kōgyo, 1866–1919) of the Kanō school, who studied with Hirafuku Suian and Komuro Hidetoshi. He painted in the Japanese style (Nihonga) and, with Okakura Kokuzō, founded the Nihon Bijutsu-in (Japan Fine Arts Academy) in 1898. He visited China in 1910 with Yokoyama Taikan and brought back many paintings.

Kōgyoku Tennō. Thirty-fifth sovereign (empress, Princess Ametoyo Takara Ikashi Hitarashi Hime, 594<642–45>661), Shōtoku Taishi's granddaughter and Jomei Tennō's wife; she succeeded Jomei. She abdicated in favor of her brother Kōtoku, and took the name Sume-mi-oya no Mikoto. But she returned to the throne 10 years later with the ruling name Saimei (*see* SAIMEI).

Kōhai. In traditional architecture, the protruding part of a roof over the entrance to a Shinto shrine, designed to shelter priests and worshipers. Also called *gōhai*.
• Halo or aura placed behind the statue of a Buddhist divinity. It is called *zukōhai* when it is behind the head, and *kyōshinkōhai* when it is behind the body.

Kōhei. Era of Emperor Go-Reizei: Aug. 1058–Aug. 1065. *See* NENGŌ.

Kohitsu. Type of kana calligraphy, used from the eighth to the fifteenth century, mainly for decorative purposes, for example on *kakemono (kohitsu-gire)* exhibited during the tea ceremony *(chanoyu)*.
• Family of aesthetes and connoisseurs of the tea ceremony. Among its best-known members: Kohitsu Ryōsa (1582–1662), Kohitsu Ryūnin (1614–77), Kohitsu Ryūei (1617–78), Kohitsu Ryūyū (1648–87), Kohitsu Ryūchū (1656–1736), Kohitsu Ryūon (1664–1725), Kohitsu Ryūen (1704–74), Kohitsu Ryūi (1751–1834), Kohitsu Ryūhan (1790–1853), Kohitsu Ryūhaku (1836–1862).

Kōhō. Era of Emperor Murakami: July 964–Aug. 968. *See* NENGŌ.

Kōi. Noblewoman responsible for dressing the sovereigns, usually one of the emperor's secondary wives. This role disappeared in the late tenth century, when the Fujiwara became all-powerful and installed their daughters as empresses.

• In ancient Japan, officer commanding 200 men *(gundan)*.

• Painter (Kanō Kōi; *azana:* Chūri, d. 1636) of the Kanō school, Mitsunobu's student and master to Tan'yū, Naonobu, and Yasunobu.

Koibikyaku yamato orai. Three-act Kabuki play, of the *sewa-mono* genre, written by Chikamatsu Monzaemon in 1711.

Koichijō no In. One of the assumed names of Prince Atsuakira (994–1051), Sanjō Tennō and Fujiwara no Ishi's oldest son. Empress Fujiwara no Shōshi, Fujiwara no Michinaga's daughter and Go-Ichijō's wife, gave birth to a son (who became Emperor Go-Suzaku in 1036), so Atsuakira was forced to renounce his title as crown prince; he retired to the Koichijō-in palace, whose name he took.

Koide Hidemasa. Warrior (1540–1604), related to Toyotomi Hideyoshi. He and Katagiri no Katsumoto were tutors to the young Toyotomi Hideyori.

Koide Narashige. Painter (1887–1931) born in Osaka. He studied traditional Japanese painting (Nihonga) and Western painting (Yōga); in 1919, he had work exhibited at the Nika-kai, where he received awards. After a trip to France and Germany (1921–22), he became a member of the Nika-kai. His nudes were very popular. He wrote a book on landscape painting, *Medetaki fūkei.*

Koie Ryōji. Ceramist, born 1938 in Tokoname (Aichi prefecture), whose works, often called avant-garde, have been exhibited in the United States (1970), Canada and Mexico (1971), Switzerland (1983), the Pompidou Center in Paris (1986), Spain (1988), England (1991), and Paris (1994).

Ko-ihō. Medical school (I-hō, seventeenth–eighteenth century), based on traditional Chinese and Confucian practice.
→ *See* GOTŌ KONZAN.

Koikawa Harumachi. Writer and illustrator (1744–89), born to a samurai family in Suruga province (Shizuoka prefecture). He wrote the first known *kibyōshi* (small illustrated fiction books with a yellow cover), *Kinkin sensei eiga no yume*

(Master Kinkin's Dreams of Grandeur, 1778), and some 30 others, which were censored by the government. He then committed suicide. He also wrote some *kyōka* poems, which he published under the pseudonym Saka no Ue no Furachi, as well as novels in the *sharebon* genre, such as *Mudaiki* (1779). Under the name Shunchō, he produced many ukiyo-e prints, and he was Sekien's student in Edo. He used a number of different names, including Kurahashi Kaku, Kurahashi Juhei, Kakuju Sanjin, and Shunchōbō.

Ko-imari. Porcelain produced in Arita during the Genroku era (1688–1704) and exported through the port of Imari. *See* ARITA-YAKI.

Kōin. Painter (Nagayama Kōin; *azana:* Shiryō; *gō:* Kōen, Gorei, Bokusai, 1765–1849), Gekkei's student. He also wrote humorous *tanka* poems. He worked mainly in Osaka.
→ *See* KIDO TAKAYOSHI.

Koi-nobori. "Rising carp." Carp-shaped pennants placed on tall poles set in front of all houses during the boys' festival (Kodomo no Hi, Tango no Sekku) on May 5 of each year. Generally, hooked to these bamboo poles are cascades of ribbons or a colored banner *(fukinagashi)*, a black carp *(magoi)* representing the father of the family, a red carp *(higoi)* for the mother, and small black-and-white carp for each of the male children. The carp is supposed to swim upstream without ever getting tired, and is thus in this context a symbol of perseverance and tenacity.
→ *See* KINGYO.

Koishikawa-yaki. A type of pottery and ceramics produced in the village of Koishiwara (or Koishibara) in Fukuoka prefecture, which were said to have been created in the Sarama kilns in 1682, under the rule of daimyo Kuroda Mitsuyuki. Designed almost solely for domestic use, this pottery has a semi-transparent *(ame)* or transparent *(tōmei)* slip on a white background with touches of green, white, or yellow applied over the glaze *(uchikake, nagashigake)*. These kilns fell into disuse before the Second World War, but were reactivated around 1952–53 and automated. Their production resembles that of the Onta-*yaki* kilns.

Koishikawa Yōjōsho. Hospital founded in Edo in 1722 by the shogunate, at the request of Ōgawa Shōsen (1672–1760), and built in the Koishikawa Shokubutsuen botanical garden created in 1638.

Managed by 20 doctors, it could house from 40 to 170 ill people considered too poor to pay for ordinary medical help. It was incorporated into the shogunal medical school (Igaku-jo) in 1868, then became the hospital of the University of Tokyo.

Koiso Kuniaki. General and politician (1880–1950), born in Tochigi prefecture. After an eventful political career, he was minister of colonial affairs in Hiranuma Kiichirō's cabinet in 1939 and in Yonai Mitsumasa's cabinet in 1940, and then governor-general of Korea (Chōsen). He succeeded Tōjō Hideki as prime minister from July 1944 to April 1945, and lowered the minimum age of conscription to 17. Condemned as a war criminal in 1948, he was sentenced to life imprisonment and died in prison. Also called Koiso Kuniteru.

Koiso Ryōhei. Painter (1903–88), born in Hyōgo prefecture. He studied in France from 1928 to 1930 and had works in the Salon d'automne. A professor at the Tokyo University of Fine Arts and Music (Tokyo Geijutsu Daigaku) starting in 1950, he was elected a member of the Japan Art Academy (Nihon Geijutsu-in) in 1983 and received the Order of Culture (Bunka-shō) the following year. He painted mainly nudes and groups of women and also produced many magazine illustrations.

Koito Gentarō. Painter (1889–1978) in the Japanese style (Nihonga) and haiku poet, elected member of the Japan Art Academy (Nihon Geijutsu-in) in 1959.

Koizumi Chikashi. *Tanka* poet (1886–1927), born in Chiba prefecture, member of the Araragi poetry group. His collections of poems were called *Kawa no hotori* (1925) and *Okujō no tsuchi* (1928).

Koizumi Shinzō. Economist and essayist (1888–1966), born in Tokyo. He studied in Europe from 1912 to 1916, then was appointed president of Keiō University. After the Second World War, he was tutor to Crown Prince Akihito. Among his most representative works: *Marukuso shigo gojūnen* (Fifty Years After Marx, 1958), *Kyōsan shugi hihan no jōshiki* (Bases for a Critique of Communism, 1949).

• **Koizumi Yagumo.** *See* HEARN.

Kōji. Era of Emperor Konoe: Apr. 1142–Feb. 1144. *See* NENGŌ.
• Era of Emperor Go-Nara: Oct. 1555–Feb. 1558. *See* NENGŌ.

Kojidan. "Tales About the Past." A nine-chapter collection of historical anecdotes written in *kirokutai* (classical Japanized Chinese writing), compiled about 1212–15 by Minamoto no Akikane (1160–1215).

Kōji-kai. Group of painters of the early twentieth century who advocated adoption of a "new Japanese style" (Shin Nihonga); a prominent member was Nakamura Gakuryō.

Kojiki. "Account of Ancient Things." The oldest surviving chronicle of Japan, compiled in 712 by Ō no Yasumaro on the order of Empress Gemmei, with the assistance of memoirs by Hieda no Are (or Ieda no Are). This work, which deals with the origins of Japan and its attendant myths, as well as events in Yamato, is divided into three volumes. The first deals with the history of the *kami*, the second with history from Jimmu Tennō to Ōjin Tennō, the third with history up to the time of Empress Suiko Tennō in 628 (it was not finished). The texts are sprinkled with ritual poems *(norito)*. They were written in pure Yamato language but transcribed into Chinese characters, which makes reading and comprehension difficult. The *Kojiki* takes some of its material from the ancient *fudoki* and from genealogical lists produced on the order of Emperor Temmu, the *Teiki* and the *Kyūji* (now lost). There is no existing copy of the original text; the oldest known version is a copy made in 1371–72 and kept in the Shimpuku-ji temple in Nagoya. The *Kojiki* is cited in the *Man'yōshū* and the *Shōhei no shiki*, dating from 936. The most famous commentary on this ancient text is Motoori Norinaga's *Kojiki-den*. The *Kojiki* was rewritten and complemented by the *Nihon shoki* in 720. Also called *Furu koto-bumi*.

• *Kojiki-den.* "Commentary on the *Kojiki*." A 44-volume work written from 1789 to 1822 by Motoori Norinaga and several authors who were part of the *wagakusha*. It is the most representative work of the Kokugaku (National Learning).

Kojima Hōshi. Buddhist monk (d. 1374), probably a Yamabushi ascetic from Kojima (Bizen province), who is sometimes credited (but without certainty) with writing the *Taihei-ki*. He may be the same person as Kojima Takanori.

• **Kojima Takanori.** Scholar and samurai (fourteenth century) who took Emperor Go-Daigo's side against the Kamakura shogunate. He also fought in support of Emperor Go-Murakami in 1352, and he became a Buddhist monk with the name Shijun. Perhaps the same person as Kojima Hōshi. Also known as Bingo Saburō.

Kojima Iken. Samurai and jurist (1837–1908), born in Iyo province (Ehime prefecture), who took an active part in the battles of the Boshin Civil War (1868) and then entered the Ministry of Justice. He became president of the High Court in 1891, and was elected a member of the House of Peers in 1894, then of the House of Representatives in 1898.

Kojima Nobuo. Writer, born 1915 in Gifu prefecture, specialist in English literature. In 1954, his novel *Amerikan sukūru* (American School) won the Akutagawa Prize. He also received the Tanizaki Jun'ichirō Prize in 1965 for *Hōyō kazoku.* He wrote a three-volume series of biographies of modern Japanese authors, *Watakushi no sakka hyōden* (1972–73).

Kojima Torajirō. Painter (1881–1929) in the Western style, who studied with painter E. Aman-Jean in France.

• **Kojima Zenzaburō.** Painter (1893–1962) in the Western style.

Kōjindani. Archeological site from the Yayoi period, excavated in the town of Hikawa (Shimane prefecture) in 1984. A group of 358 bronze épées about 50 cm long, from the first two centuries AD, was uncovered. The following year, another group of objects was discovered: 6 *dōtaku* about 20 cm high, and 16 bronze lance points. This discovery shows that there was a close cultural relationship between northern Kyushu and the Yamato region at the time.

Kōjin-sama. *Kami* of the family hearth, of Chinese origin (*Chin.:* Shimei). *See* DAIKOKU-TEN, SAMBŌ KŌJIN.

Kojiri. Tip of the scabbard *(saya)* for a *katana* sword, generally made of metal and decorated. Also called *ishizuri. See* KATANA, SAYA.

Koji-ruien. Major historical encyclopedia, in a thousand installments, grouping a large number of documents, conceived in 1879 by Nishimura Shigeki, given to the Bureau of Shinto Shrines, and completed with government assistance in 1914. It was followed by the *Kojitsu-sōshu,* a collection of

historical texts specifically concerning manners and customs, published in Tokyo starting in 1904.

Ko-jōruri. *Jōruri* texts written in Edo, Osaka, and Kyoto between 1625 and 1685, dealing specifically with fantasy and magic, love stories, and various anecdotes; the most typical of the genre is *Jōruri jūnidan sōshi. See* JORURI.

Kōjū. Buddhist monk (seventeenth century) of the Jōdo Shin-shū, founder of the Ōtani-ha branch of the sect in 1602.
→ *See* KENNYO SHŌNIN.

Kōka. Era of Emperor Ninkō: Dec. 1844–Feb. 1848. *See* NENGŌ.

Kōkai Kaisen. Naval battle at the mouth of the Yalu (*Kor.:* Abnog) River on September 17, 1894, between the ships of the imperial fleet commanded by Admiral Itō Sukeyuki and a Chinese fleet under the orders of Admiral Ding Ruchang. The outcome of the confrontation, during which five Chinese ships were sunk or crippled, was to enable Japan to control the Yellow Sea. *See* BATTLES, NAVAL.

Kokaji. Title of a Noh play: a Kyoto blacksmith must make a sword for the emperor. Since he does not have an assistant, he solicits the help of the *kami* Inari, who agrees to come to his aid.

Kōkaku Tennō. Hundred and nineteenth emperor (Prince Kanehito, 1771<1780–1816>1840), Higashiyama Tennō's great-grandson and successor to Go-Momozono Tennō. He abdicated in favor of his son, Ninkō.

Kōka Mon'in. *See* FUJIWARA NO MASAKO.

Kokan. Buddhist monk and painter (Myōyo; *gō:* Kyoshū, 1653–1717) of the Kanō school, Eihō's student. He painted mainly Buddhist subjects.

Kōkan. Painter (Shiba Shun; *mei:* Andō Kichijirō, Katsusaburō, Magodayū; *azana:* Kungaku; *gō:* Fugen-dōjin, Rantei, Shumparō, Suzuki Harushige, 1738/1747–1818) of the Yōga school, who studied with Kanō Furunobu, Sō Shiseki, Suzuki Harunobu, and Hiraga Gennai. He produced copper engravings, ukiyo-e prints, and paintings in the Western style. He was the first artist in Japan to use acid for etchings.

Kokan Shiren. Zen Buddhist monk (1278–1346) of the Rinzai school, member of the Fujiwara family. He was the senior abbot of the Tōfuku-ji and Nanzen-ji temples in Kyoto. In 1342, he retired to the Kaizō-in of the Tōfuku-ji, where he wrote a number of Buddhist works, among them the *Genkō shakusho*, a major collection of biographies of Japanese monks, in *kambun* style, published in 1322. Also called Kaizō Oshō.

Kokata. In Noh theater, actor playing the role of a child under the direction of a *waki* or a *shite*. He does not wear a mask.

Kōkatō Jōyaku. "Treaty of Kanghwa," signed between Korea and Japan on February 27, 1876, giving the Japanese the right to free trade with the Korean Peninsula. It was imposed on Korea by force: the Japanese delegation was led by Kuroda Kiyotaka and Inoue Kaoru and accompanied by a war fleet. The treaty comprised 12 articles in which it was stipulated that Korea was an independent nation, that it was to exchange diplomatic delegations with Japan on a basis of equality, that Pusan and other ports were open to international trade, and that Japan could establish consulates in these ports. Though it was called "unequal," this treaty was the first step toward modernization of Korea.

Kokatsuji-ban. Works printed using wooden movable type, imitating Korean copper type. This technique was used to publish books from 1593 to 1647, but it was found to be too slow, and printers returned to engraved woodblocks.

Kokawa-dera. Buddhist temple built in 770 in Naga (Wakayama prefecture) by Otomo no Kujiko, of the Tendai-shū sect, and dedicated to Kannon Bosatsu. It is one of the Thirty-Three Temples of the Western Pilgrimage (Sanjūsan-sho) of Kannon. It expanded constantly over the years; destroyed by fire several times and rebuilt each time, it housed several hundred monks in the fifteenth century. Toyotomi Hideyoshi burned it down again in 1585, and it was rebuilt in the seventeenth century.

• *Kokawa-dera engi emaki.* An *emakimono* housed in the Kokawa-dera that recounts the origin of the statue of Senju Kannon venerated in the temple and describes the miracles it accomplished. A single scroll, it dates from the thirteenth century.

Kōke. Bureaucrats of the Edo shogunate responsible for official rituals and ceremonies. Only 26 families were allowed to hold these positions, among them the Kira, Hatakeyama, Kyōgoku, and Ōtomo. → *See* KUGE.

Kōkechi. Method of dyeing fabrics known as "tie-dyeing," in which certain parts of the fabric are knotted and the knots are dipped in dye. This technique was imported from China and Southeast Asia. In the eighth century, it was called *yuhata*.

Koke-dera. *See* SAIHŌ-JI.

Kōkei. Buddhist monk (twelfth century) and sculptor of Buddhist images, Unke's father and Kaikei's master, of the Kei-ha school. One of his major works is the statue of Fukukensaku Kannon of the Kōfuku-ji temple in Nara.
• Painter (Yoshimura Kōkei; *mei:* Yōzō; *azana:* Mui; *gō:* Ranryō, Ryūsen, Kōkei, 1769–1836) of the Maruyama school, Ōkyo's student in Kyoto.
→ *See* BAN KŌKEI, MAGE.

Kokei sanshō. "The Three Laughers of Tiger Ravine." A story of Chinese origin that has become a favorite subject of Japanese art and literature: the Buddhist monk Huiyuan had wished never to leave his monastery by the Hu River. One day, absorbed in a discussion with his two brothers, he crosses this limit without wanting to; when they realize this, the three companions laugh heartily at their adventure.

Kōken. Buddhist monk (1458–1525) of the Jōdo Shin-shū, ninth patriarch of the sect, starting in 1489. He compiled a collection of writings by his father, Rennyo, which became the basic text of the set. Also called Jitsunyo.
• Title for a member of the Tokugawa family appointed tutor to a young shogun.
• In a Noh play, a *shite*'s assistant responsible for adjusting his mask and costume and for handling props *(kodōgu)*. *See* KUROGO.
→ *See* MYŌTAKU.

Kōken Tennō. Forty-sixth sovereign (empress, Princess Abe Naishinnō, 718<749–58>770), Shōmu Tennō's daughter and successor. A pious Buddhist, she ordered a colossal statue of Vairochana Buddha (Daibutsu) to be erected in the Tōdai-ji in Nara. She abdicated in 758 in favor of Prince Toneri, who became Emperor Junnin, and became a nun with the name Takano Tennō. Following the actions of the monk Dōkyō, she deposed Junnin and ascended once again to the throne in

764 with the name Shōtoku (*see* SHŌTOKU), thus becoming the forty-eighth sovereign of Japan.

Kokeshi. Wooden dolls made on a lathe, decorated with floral motifs, traditionally made for at least 150 years by peasant families in the prefectures of northern Honshu during long winter evenings. They are generally cylindrical in shape, without arms or legs, some with a rotating head. There are at least 250 types, corresponding to as many families of seasonal artisans, classed into ten main categories according to their provenance: Kijiyama, Nambu, Narugo, Hijiori, Sakumani, Tsuchiyu, Tōgatta, Tsugaru, Yajirō, and Zaō. Dolls decorated with three rows of flowers are made by the oldest member of the family, and those with a single flower are made by apprentices. Their height varies from a few centimeters to more than 1 m; they are often signed and are highly prized by collectors. Their exact origin is not known, although some researchers believe that they are derived from the Shinto symbol of Susanoo, the *somin-shōrai*. They may also be sexual symbols or substitutes somewhat analogous to *anesama-ningyō*. Modern artisans make purely decorative shapes. *See* KIJIYA, OBOKO.

Kokiden. Part of the imperial palace generally reserved for the empress and her ladies-in-waiting.

Kokeshi dolls

The parts reserved for the women of the palace were called Koki-den no Ue no Mitsubone, Fujitsubo-ue no Mitsubone, or Ue no Mitsubone or Ōoku (in the shogunal palace).

Kokin waka-shū. "Collection of Ancient and Modern Poems." The first of 21 imperial anthologies (*see* CHOKUSEN WAKA-SHŪ), compiled starting in 905 on the order of Emperor Daigo by Ki no Tsurayuki, Ki no Tomonori, Mibu no Tadamine, and Oshikōchi no Mitsune. It contains 1,100 poems in 20 sections and was the first to classify the contents by theme: seasons, nature, love, travel, feelings, and so on. At first considered a continuation of the *Man'yōshū*, it was titled *Shoku Man'yōshū*. In it are poems by the Rokkasen (Six Poetic Geniuses) of the preceding century and works by the compilers and their contemporaries. The preface *(kanajo)*, written by Ki no Tsurayuki, is important from the point of view of literary criticism and for its defense of the *waka* style. Another preface *(manajo)* was written in Chinese by Ki no Yoshimochi. Abridged to *Kokin-shū*.

• *Kokin waka rokujō.* A six-volume anthology of *waka* poems, compiled about 950 as a continuation of the *Kokin waka-shū*.

• *Kokin waka-shū-chū.* Commentaries on the *Kokin waka-shū* written by Fujiwara no Norinaga (of the Rokujō school) in 1177 and by Kenshō about 1185–91.

Kokiroku. "Ancient Chronicles." The name for accounts, historical or not, by private individuals, written by members of the aristocracy or even emperors, starting in about the ninth century. These "ancient *kiroku,*" of which there are a great number, are essential for study of Japanese history. They are distinguished from the *Rikkokushi* (Six National Histories), or official chronicles.

Kokka. "National Flowers." The title of an art magazine founded in 1889 by Kuki Ryūichi (1852–1931), Okakura Kakuzō, and Takahashi Kenzō (1885–98). It was devoted to Asian, and especially Japanese, art, in reaction to what its founders considered to be an excessive infatuation with Western art in Japan. This magazine is still one of the most influential in the art world.

Kokkai Gijidō. "Building of the National Diet," designed by Austrian architects and erected on Kasumigaseki hill in Tokyo in 1936. It is a granite structure 66 m high, crowned by a square tower with a stepped pyramidal roof. It has 390 rooms, some decorated with marble tiles, and contains the Chamber of Councillors (250 seats) and the House of Representatives (467 seats), as well as visitors' galleries (seating: 1,692). Nearby is the Ozaki Memorial Hall, a monument dedicated to the memory of Ozaki Yukio, the "father of parliamentarism."

• **Kokkai Kisei Dōmei.** "League for Establishing a National Assembly," established in 1880.

Kokkaku-ki. General term for all archeological objects made with animal matter (bone, shell, horn, teeth, fins, etc.).

Kokka Shintō. *See* KOKUTAI SHINTŌ.

Kokkei-bon. "Funny books," a genre of picaresque, comic, and satirical novels, popular in Edo starting in 1738 and succeeded by the *sharebon* genre about 1790. These books were generally printed on *chūbon*-format (medium-size) pages. They were derived from *dangi-bon,* a genre of moralizing novels created in Osaka by Jōkambō Kōa, a physician, about 1752, with *Imayō heta dangi* (Bizarre Sermons of Now). The most important *kokkei-bon* authors were Hiraga Gennai, Jippensha Ikku, and Shikitei Samba.

Kokki. Annual imperial ceremony celebrated since 1868 in the Koreiden of the imperial palace to commemorate the anniversary of the death of the preceding emperor.
  • National flag of Japan, consisting of a red disk, representing the sun, on a white field. Also called Hi no Maru. Legend has it that the Buddhist monk Nichiren presented such a flag to the Kamakura shogun to fly over the troops that were to fight the Mongols. Takeda Shingen, Uesugi Kenshin, and Date Masamune also adopted it as a battlefield symbol; Toyotomi Hideyoshi flew it when he fought in Korea. In 1600, the Tokugawa shogunate placed the Hi no Maru on the mast of its ships. The flag was flown on the ship the *Kanrin Maru* in 1860, but it was made the national flag by the Meiji government only on January 27, 1870.

• *Kokki.* Title of a historical work written, according to tradition, by Shōtoku Taishi about 612, now lost. Also titled *Koku-ki.*

Kokkuri. Popular divination procedure, consisting of dropping sticks on a plank on which the numbers 1 to 10 and the 50 characters of the phonetic alphabet *(kana)* are inscribed. The operator is in a trance

and is blindfolded. An interpretation is given based on the position of the sticks. *See* BOKUSEN.

Kōkoku. Era of Emperor Go-Murakami: Apr. 1340–Dec. 1346. *See* NENGŌ.

Kokon chōmon-shū. "Collection of Ancient and Modern Tales" with a moral and didactic content, written for young people, compiled by Tachibana no Narisue and complemented by other authors starting in the early Kamakura period (1254). It contains more than 700 tales and legends, of Chinese and Japanese origin, classified into categories. This work was a valuable source for many writers, including Akutagawa Ryūnosuke. Also titled *Kokin chōmon-shū.*

Kokorozuke. General term for all gifts given to reward a service, analogous to a tip. Also called *shūgi. Kokorozuke* (generally cash) are always presented in an envelope decorated with a particular *mizuhiki* ("ribbons") and *noshi* ("frills") design.

Kōkō Tennō. Fifty-eighth emperor (Prince Tokuyasu, 830<885–87>), Nimmyō Tennō's son and Yōzei Tennō's successor. He created the position of *kampaku.* Uda succeeded him.

Koku. Unit of volume used to measure rice, equivalent to about 180 liters, the quantity needed to feed one person for a year. When this unit was used to measure products other than rice, it was equivalent to 10 cubic *shaku* (0.28 m³). One *koku* = 10 *to;* 1 *to* = 10 *shō;* 1 *shō* = 10 *gō.* These units were standardized by Toyotomi Hideyoshi; in the seventh century, they were worth about half the volume of the measures he adopted. The value of estates assigned to various lords and daimyo during the Edo period was measured in *koku.* The practice of paying the annual tax *(nengu)* in cash rather than rice, which became common during the Edo period, was called *kokudainō.* The annual yield value of land, measured in rice *koku,* was called *kokudaka;* it replaced the old method of determining an estate's revenue *(kandaka)* based on an estimation of the value in money of harvests, in use from the Kamakura period.
  • Former denomination of provinces. Also called *kuni. See* KOKUGUN.
  • "Hours." *See* CALENDAR.

• **Kokudainō, kokudaka.** *See* KOKU.

Kokubunji. Buddhist "provincial temples" whose construction in each province was ordered by Emperor Shōmu in 741. They had to be associated with a monastery for women called *kokubunni-ji* (or *hokke-matsuzai-ji*). In addition to the usual buildings, each temple (also called *shin-kōmyō shi-tennō gokoku-ji*) had to have a hall *(hondō)* and a pagoda. Starting in 752, provincial monasteries and temples for men were attached to the Tōdai-ji in Nara, while those for women were placed under the jurisdiction of the Hokke-ji. *See* SHINGON-SHŪ.

Kokufu. "Provincial capitals" established throughout Japan as chief towns of provinces starting in the late seventh century. They were laid out on a grid plan similar to that for Heijō-kyō (Nara) and Heian-kyō (Kyoto), and they had to contain a *kokubun-ji*. The *kokushi,* or provincial governor, lived there. Also called *fuchū, funai.*

Kokuga-kai. Association of painters founded in 1918. In 1926, a section devoted to painters in the Western style (Yōga) was added; this was the only part to survive after 1928. This association succeeded another of the same type, called Kokuga Sōsaku-kyōkai, created by Umehara Ryūzaburō.

Kokugaku. "National Learning" (or national education, ancient studies), a literary and historical movement for the study of classical Japanese literature, with the goal of promoting Japanese culture, as opposed to Chinese culture. Developed in the seventeenth century, this movement was exemplified by the works of Kada no Azumamaro (1669–1736), Kamo no Mabuchi (1697–1769), Motoori Norinaga (1730–1801), and Hirata Atsutane (1776–1843). In the modern era, Kokugaku also included works intended to glorify the origins of the Japanese nation and the role of the emperor *(kokutai)*. *See also* KOGAKU-HA, WAGAKUSHA.
• Schools established in the provinces *(koku)* by the *ritsuryō* system to educate the children of administrators *(gunji)* and governors *(kokushi)* and dispensing a Confucian-type curriculum. The best students were then admitted to the *daigaku* (major school) of the capital and could become bureaucrats. These schools disappeared in the late twelfth century.

• **Kokugaku-in.** Private university in Tokyo, founded in 1882, under the name Kōten Kōkyōjo, as a Kokugaku (National Learning) research institute. It took its current name in 1890 and obtained the status of university in 1906; a department for the education of Shinto priests was established in 1927. It is attended by about 10,000 students.

Kokugikan. Large sumo stadium, built in Tokyo in 1909 and reconstructed in the Kuramae district in 1954. Six tournaments take place there each year, in January, May, and September. Capacity: 12,000. *See* SUMO.

Kokugo. "National language," the everyday language spoken by the Japanese, as opposed to the more formal *nihongo,* "Japanese language." *Kokugo* includes popular and informal expressions. For example, a man may speak of his wife as *kanai* ("she who is inside the house") or *gusai* ("my stupid wife"), whereas in *nihongo* he would say *watakushi no tsuma. Nihongo* is rarely used except in formal discourse and highly literary texts; however, everyone understands it. The two terms are often confused. *See* INGO, KEIGO.

Kokugun. System of dividing the country into provinces *(koku, kuni)* and districts *(gun, kōri)*, created by the *ritsuryō* system and the Taihō Code (701). Japan comprised 58 *kuni* and 3 islands. In the ninth century, it was redivided into 66 provinces and 2 islands. This system remained in force until the Meiji era (1870), when it was replaced by the prefecture *(ken)* system.

Kokuhei-sha. Class of Shinto shrines financed by the state, created in 1871 and composed of 188 *daisha* (large shrines), a large number of *chūsha* (medium-sized shrines), and 2,207 *shosha* (small shrines). *See* JINJA.

Kokuhon-sha. "Society of the National Foundation." A nationalist association founded by Hiranuma Kiichirō in 1924 to oppose democracy and socialism, which he deemed to be contrary to the development of national values. In 1936, the Kokuhon-sha claimed to have about 80,000 members. Hiranuma dissolved the association after the events of February 26, 1936 (*see* NINIROKU JIKEN), for fear that it would be confused with extremist and fascist associations such as the Kokui-kai (Society for Defense of the National Prestige) founded in 1932, and other similar organizations.

Kokujin. "Provincials," a term used in the late Heian period (twelfth century) to designate warriors attached to a provincial lord or a public estate. In the fourteenth century, it designated small local lords, generally former *jitō* or newly wealthy peasants who had become independent. They formed leagues *(ikki)* during the Nambokuchō period to support the military actions of the *shugo*, but they were not attached to the *shugo,* and they disappeared in the early sixteenth century when the country was organized by powerful warlords who assimilated them.

Kokumin. Provincial governor. Also "spiritual master of the country," a title conferred upon eminent Buddhist monks.

• **Kokumin Dōmei.** "Nationalist League." A fascist party created in 1932 by Adachi Kenzō, Nakano Seigō, and 28 other elected representatives to demand government control of strategic industries and financial firms and creation of a Japan–Manchuria economic bloc. The party split into two factions in 1938, and Nakano Seigō then founded the Tōhōkai (Far East Society). The party was dissolved in 1940 and its members joined the Taisei Yokusankai (Imperial Rule Assistance Association).

• **Kokumin-gakkō.** "National people's schools," a system of compulsory schools run from 1941 to 1947 on the model of the German *Volksschule,* with the goal of inculcating young people with the ideal of loyalty toward emperor and nation.

• **Kokumin Kyōdōtō.** The "People's Cooperative party." Political party created in 1947 by the merger of the Kokumintō (People's party) and the Kyōdō Minshutō (Cooperative Democratic party). Miki Takeo was its secretary-general. A moderate party, it merged with the Minshutō (Democratic party) in 1950 to form the Kokumin Minshutō (People's Democratic party). It was reorganized in 1952 and became the Kaishintō (Reform party), which in its turn merged with the Jiyū Minshutō (Liberal Democratic party, or LDP).

• **Kokumin Kyōkai.** "Nationalist Association." A pro-government political group created in 1892 by Shinagawa Yakirō, Saigō Tsugumichi, and other politicians to counterbalance the action of opposing parties such as the Jiyūto (Liberal party) and the Rikken Kaishintō (Constitutional Reform party). Dissolved in 1899, it was reorganized under the name Taikokutō (Imperial party).

• Ultranationalist group founded in 1933 by Akamatsu Katsumaro. In 1937, with other extremist associations, it formed the Nihon Kakushintō (Japan Renovation party).

Kokumin no Tomo. "The Nation's Friend." Christian-leaning literary and scientific magazine published by the Min'yūsha (Society of Friends Democ-

racy), founded by Tokutomi Soho in 1887 to support the activities of the Jiyū Minken Undō (Freedom and People's Rights Movement). Among the contributors were Futabatei Shimei, Kunikida Roppo, Uchida Roan, and Yamada Bimyō. It had an English-language edition, *The Far East,* published from 1896 to 1898. *Kokumin no Tomo,* which had a great influence on democratic thought in its time, stopped publication in 1898, its founder having transformed its original universalist orientation to a nationalist one. He replaced it with a pro-government political newspaper that he had founded in 1890. *Kokumin Shimbun* was published until 1942, when it was merged with the *Miyako Shimbun* to form the *Tōkyō Shimbun.*

Kokura. Former lord's estate in Buzen province, belonging to the Mōri. After the Battle of Sekigahara in 1600, it was given to the Hosokawa, with a revenue of 399,000 *koku.* In 1632, the Edo *bakufu* gave it to the Ogasawara and its revenue was reduced to 150,000 *koku.* It changed names a number of times, becoming Kawara in 1866, then Toyotsu in 1869. In 1876, it was incorporated into Fukuoka prefecture.

Kokuren. "United Nations," abridgment of Kokusai-rengō.

• "League of Nations," abridgment of Kokusairenmei.

Kokuritsu kōen. *See* NATIONAL PARKS.

Kokuryō. Starting in the tenth century, estates controlled by provincial or shogunal authorities, as opposed to private estates, or *shōen.* To preserve their privileges, emperors delegated their powers over provincial estates and authorized governors *(kokushi)* to charge tax not on individuals but on rice paddies, which were registered under the name *(myō)* of the peasants cultivating them. In the Edo period, this system, also called *kōryō,* designated lands administered directly by the shogun. Also called *kōden, tenryō.*

Kokuryūkai. "Amur River Society" (literally, "Black Dragon Society"). A secret, ultranationalist political association founded by Uchida Ryōhei in 1901, succeeding the Gen'yōsha, whose goals were to promote a "Greater Asia" (Dai Tōa) led by Japan. Its members conducted intensive clandestine activities during the Russo-Japanese War (1904–05), the events in Korea (1910) and Manchuria (1931), and the war against China (1937), serving mainly as spies for the Japanese government. It was dissolved in 1946. *See also* GEN'YŌSHA, TŌYAMA MITSURU.

Kokusen'ya. Japanese name for Zheng Chenggong, commonly called Koxinga (1624–62). He was a Chinese general with a Japanese mother, born in Hirado, who fought the Qing for the Ming dynasty and established a kingdom in Taiwan, having expelled the Dutch. His story and the legends that were created around his name and exploits gave rise to many Kabuki plays, notably those written by Chikamatsu Monzaemon.

• *Kokusen'ya go-nichi kassen.* "The Continuing Battles of Koxinga." A play by Chikamatsu Monzaemon, a continuation of *Kokusen'ya kassen,* written in 1717.

• *Kokusen'ya kassen.* "The Battles of Koxinga." A historical drama in five acts by Chikamatsu Monzaemon, first produced at the Takemoto-za in Osaka in 1715.

Kokushi. "National master," a title conferred by the imperial court on Buddhist monks emeritus. *Chin.: guoshi.*
• Title of provincial governors *(kokufu)* appointed by the imperial government, starting in the Nara period. Also called *kokushu. See also* DAIMYO, KUNI NO MIYATSUKO.

• *Kokushi taikei.* Compilation of historical and juridical texts from the fourteenth century, published in Tokyo from 1897 to 1904 (32 volumes) and followed by a supplement, *Zoku kokushi taikei* (66 volumes, 1929–66).

Kokuso. Paste made by mixing hemp fiber, lacquer *(urushi),* and boiled rice (or sawdust), used by sculptors to finish lacquer statues and as a support for the lacquering of various objects. *See* KANSHITSU.
• "Provincial appeals": during the Edo period, petitions made by peasants to the shogunate to ask it to right wrongs perpetrated against them by merchant guilds that monopolized trade. Most appeals were made by small-scale local negotiators harmed by the activities of *kabu-nakama,* mainly in the early nineteenth century.

Kokutai. "National polity" or "national essence," a nationalist concept encompassing all archetypes referring to the sacred nature of Japanese culture and the divine authority of the emperor, and tending to symbolize the nation itself.
• Sports festivals, held at various places and times of year throughout Japan.

• **Kokutai Shintō.** Doctrine of State Shinto, put into practice in 1871 during the separation of Buddhist and Shinto cults, which lasted until 1945. It was a nonreligious organization, comprising the Kyōha Shintō and the Jinja Shintō, whose goal was to glorify the role of the emperor, the imperial *kami* Amaterasu, and the nation. Also called Kokka Shintō.

Ko-kutani. "Ancient Kutani," decorated porcelain produced in the kilns in Kutani (Ishikawa) and Arita from the mid-seventeenth to the mid-eighteenth century. They featured a white, slightly bluish clay and simple painted decorations. *See* ARITA-YAKI, CERAMICS, KUTANI-YAKI.

Kokuten. "Society of National Art." An association of painters who belonged to a school of national painting (Nihonga) created by Tsuchida Bakusen, Murakami Kagaku, Ono Chikuyō, and Sakakibara Shihō about 1910.

Koku-u. In the old agrarian calendar, period of "rain favorable to rice," beginning around April 20 and lasting 15 days. *Chin.:* Guyu. *See* NIJŪSHI-SETSU.

Kokūzō Bosatsu. The Bodhisattva "Receptacle of Emptiness" (and of Compassion and Wisdom), a guardian of the Buddhist Law, sometimes portrayed in the center of the lunar disk. This esoteric divinity, venerated mainly in the Shingon and Tendai sects, corresponds to the Sanskrit Ākāshagarbha.

Kokyū. A fretted stringed instrument, similar in shape to the shamisen but smaller, played with a horsehair bow. It generally has four strings. There are several varieties: the *keikin* (4 strings), the *kokin* (2 strings), the *teikin* (2 strings), and two types from Korea, the *kokun* (*Kor.:* Go-güm) and the *nisen.* The original *kokyū* was derived from the Portuguese *rebec* and imported from the Ryukyu Islands in the sixteenth century. It is rarely played today, although it was in style in Edo in the early eighteenth century.
→ *See* RYŪKŌKA.

Koma (-goma). Old word for "horse" in the northern provinces of Honshu.
→ *See* SHŌGI.

• Top, toy brought from Korea in the eighth century, at first used by nobles in the court. This toy (analogous to European tops) became popular in the seventeenth century and is still a favorite among children.

• Former name of the Korean kingdom of Kōrai (Shin-kan) from 37 BC to AD 668, when it was conquered by Shiragi (Ban-kan). Many objects from Korea bear this name.

• **Koma-inu.** "Dog of Korea," statue of a dog (or lion) gracing the entrance to Shinto shrines and facing a Kara-shishi ("Lion of China"). It has a closed mouth, corresponding to unexpressed power. Its role, like that of the Kara-shishi (with an open mouth) is to frighten evil spirits.

• **Koma-shaku.** Unit of length imported from Korea and used before the fifth century to measure fabrics. It was equivalent to about 35.5 cm. Also called *koma-jaku.*

Komachi. Type of mask *(nōmen)* in Noh theater, portraying a woman with an emaciated face.
→ *See* ONO NO KOMACHI.

Koma Chikazane. Musician (1177–1242), author of a musicology treatise describing Gigaku music and dance.

Komaki Nagakute no Tatakai. Prolonged engagement near the town of Komaki in 1584 between Toyotomi Hideyoshi and the combined forces of Tokugawa Ieyasu and Oda Nobukatsu (1558–1630), Oda Nobunaga's son. After several battles with no clear victor, Toyotomi Hideyoshi made peace with Oda Nobukatsu and Tokugawa Ieyasu, who became his allies. Hideyoshi adopted Ieyasu's son, Hideyasu, and continued his reunification of the country.

Koma Kyui. Famous lacquer artist (d. 1663) who worked for shogun Tokugawa Iemitsu in Edo. His son, Koma Kitoe (d. 1774), continued his work and founded the family line of lacquer artists called Koma-ryū (or Koma-ha).

Koma no Sōgen. Architect and Buddhist monk (thirteenth century) from Korea, founder of a number of temples, among them the Chōkyū-ji, in 1279.

Komatsu. City in Ishikawa prefecture, on the Sea of Japan, former castle town *(jōka-machi)* in the seventeenth century. It was famous for its Katuni-style ceramics and silk factories. Hot springs; Nata-

dera Buddhist temple, founded, according to tradition, in the eighth century; and site of an ancient toll gate, Akata no Seki. *Pop.:* 105,000.

Komatsubara Eitarō. Politician and journalist (1852–1919), born in Okayama prefecture. Appointed police chief in 1891, he became a member of the House of Peers in 1900, then was minister of education in Katsura Tarō's second cabinet in 1908. He was editor of the newspaper *Ōsaka Mainichi Shimbun,* which later became the *Mainichi Shimbun.*

Komatsu Sakyō. Writer (Komatsu Minoru), born 1931 in Osaka. He studied Italian literature, and started writing science-fiction novels in the early 1960s: *Nihon apatchi zoku* (1964), *Nihon chimbotsu* (Japan's Nightmare, 1973); the latter was successfully adapted into a horror movie.

Komatsu Tatewaki. Samurai (1835–70) of the Satsuma estate. He took part in the Boshin Civil War in 1868, served the Meiji government, and helped it achieve its reforms by facilitating an alliance between the Chōshu and Satsuma clans. He was minister of foreign affairs in 1870.

Kombu. Edible marine algae (kelp, *Laminaria*), cultivated in shallow water and commonly used in Japanese cuisine. *Chin.:* Haidai.

Kōmei Tennō. Hundred and twenty-first emperor (Prince Osahito, 1831 < 1846–67 >), Ninkō Tennō's successor. He agreed to sign the Treaty of Kanagawa in 1854, but approved of only half of the Harris Treaty in 1859. In 1863, he signed a decree ordering the expulsion of all foreigners, but he was forced to ratify the Harris Treaty and the treaties of the "Ansei era" in 1865. He died of smallpox in January 1867 and was succeeded by the young Mutsuhito, who was enthroned with the name Emperor Meiji.

Komeitō. "Clean Government party." Political and theocratic party linked to the Sōka Gakkai, founded in late 1964 by that organization, which supplied financial and electoral support. It had representatives in the Diet for the first time in 1967. It theoretically became independent in 1970, and its elected representatives demanded stabilization of government policy. In 1977, the Komeitō won 56 seats in the House of Representatives and 28 in the Chamber of Councillors, thus becoming the second-largest opposition party. The party publishes several newspapers, including the daily *Kōmei Shimbun* (circulation 800,000), the monthly *Kōmei Gurafu* (350,000 subscribers), and the political monthly *Kōmei.*

Kome-shōgun. "Shogun of Rice," a nickname for Tokugawa Yoshimune, who ordered that massive amounts of rice be distributed to the population during periods of famine.

Ko-mikkyō. A sort of ancient Buddhist esoterism, antedating the importation of the Shingon and Tendai sects (early ninth century), still poorly defined.

Komiya Toyotaka. Writer and literary critic (1884–1966), specializing in German literature, and Natsume Sōseki's disciple. A theater lover, he wrote mainly on Noh and Kabuki; he also penned two important essays on his master, *Natsume Sōseki* (1938) and *Sōseki no geijutsu* (1942).

Kommintō. "Indigents' party." A groups of peasants who, impoverished by Matsukata Masayoshi's deflationary measures, rebelled between 1883 and 1885 to demand that their debts be forgiven. These uprisings took place mainly in the Chūbu region. Also called Shakkintō (Debtors' party).

Kōmoku-ten. "He Who Sees All," a minor Buddhist divinity corresponding to the Sanskrit Virūpāksha ("With Strange Eyes"), one of the Shi-tennō (Four Heavenly Kings), generally portrayed as a warrior wearing armor and with an angry face. He is colored white and brandishes a sword. He presides over the West and autumn. Also called Birubakusha-ten.

Ko-mononari. Various taxes (not including the annual *nengu* tax) levied by the Edo shogunate and the daimyo of the Edo period on tea, forestry products, and other products. The taxes were spread among various classes, could be temporary or permanent, and were to be paid in rice. Those called *ukiyaku* were not registered because they were temporary or subject to changing rates. Also called *myōgakin, unjō,* and other names. All these taxes were abolished in 1873 with the reform of real-estate taxes.

Komonzome. Fabric-dyeing method, similar to stenciling, consisting of repeating small motifs.

Komparu. Traditional Noh theater school reserved for *shite* roles, which drew its name from Zeami's son-in-law, Komparu Ujinobu (also called Zenchiku), who gave it its definitive status in the Muromachi period. It was previously known as Takeda and Emman'i, and is still active under the name Komparu-ryū. Among the Noh actors and authors belonging to this school are:

—Komparu Ujinobu (1405–ca. 1470). He wrote several treatises, including *Kabu zuinō ki* (Essence of Song and Dance, 1456) and *Rokurin ichiro* (The Six Wheels and the Dew Drop, 1455), and Noh plays. *See* ZENCHIKU.

—Komparu Zempō (b. 1454).

—Komparu Toyouji (d. 1458).

—Komparu Zenkyoku (1549–1621).

—Komparu Yasuteru (d. 1628).

—Komparu Hiroshige (d. 1896), perhaps the best known.

—Komparu Nobutaka (b. 1920).

→ *See* NOH, ZENCHIKU.

Kompira. Shinto-Buddhist divinity (also called Kubira, Zōzugen Kompira Gongen) of wealth and happiness, venerated mainly on Shikoku, where he is considered the protector of sailors. He may be a divinization of the hero Kotohira or Emperor Sutoku; perhaps also the same divinity as Kuvera (Kubera).

• **Kompira-gū.** Shinto shrine built in Kotohira (Shikoku) in honor of Kompira and the *kami* Omononushi no Mikoto. It was rebuilt in 1878. *See* KOTOHIRA-GŪ.

• **Kompira-kyō.** Modern Shinto sect founded in 1947 by Yamaji Kazuomaro (b. 1918).

Komura Jutarō. Statesman and diplomat (1855–1911), born in southern Kyushu. After studying English in Nagasaki and law at Harvard (1875–78), he worked for the Ministry of Justice, then the Ministry of Foreign Affairs, and was secretary of the Beijing legation in 1893. During the Sino-Japanese War, he worked in Manchuria and Korea, where he signed a pact with Russia (the Komura-Veber Memorandum, 1896) that called for joint Russian and Japanese management of Korea. Komura was ambassador to Washington in 1898, then to Russia in 1900. Katsura Tarō appointed him minister of foreign affairs in his first cabinet in 1901. He was ambassador to Great Britain (1906–08), then again minister of foreign affairs (1908–11) in Katsura's second cabinet. He concluded several trade treaties with other countries and was ennobled in 1907 and 1911.

Komusō. Buddhist monks who were itinerant musicians, belonging to the Fuke-shūsect. Their name apparently came from a disciple of Fuke-zenji's named Komu, who, like Kichiku, Kakushin, and Chōyū, was a famous *shakuhachi* player. During the Edo period, the *komusō* were in the habit of concealing their faces behind a sort of basket *(fukaamigasa, tengai)*. They did not wear a monk's habit and were recruited mainly from the warrior class *(bushi)*. Many outlaws disguised themselves as *komusō* to escape the police, who, in turn, often sent spies, also disguised as *komusō*. The name *komusō* means "monk from nothing." They were also called *boroji* ("monks in rags"). *See* ARAKI KODŌ, FUKE.

Kōmyō-ji. Buddhist temple of the Jōdo-shū, built in 1253 near Kyoto. Also called Aoi Kōmyō-ji.

Kōmyō Kōgō. Empress (Princess Asukabe, Kōmyōshi, 701–60), Fujiwara no Fuhito's daughter and Emperor Shōmu's wife. A devout Buddhist, she had a number of temples and pagodas built, including the Kōfuku-ji, the Hokke-ji, and the Shin Yakushi-ji, and she helped erect the Tōdai-ji and founded many charitable institutions. In 749, her daughter Kōken acceded to the throne, and power passed in fact to her nephew, Fujiwara no Nakamaro. When her husband died, Kōmyō Kōgō donated his accumulated treasures to the Tōdai-ji; they were placed in the Shōsō-in, where they can still be viewed and admired. She then became a Buddhist nun under the name Mampuku. She was an excellent calligrapher whose works (notably *Gakki-ron*) are housed in the Shōsō-in in Nara.

Kōmyō Tennō. Second emperor (Prince Toyohito, 1322<1336–48>1380) in the court of the North (Hokuchō), Fushimi Tennō's ninth son, placed on the throne by Ashikaga Takauji. In 1348, he abdicated in favor of his nephew Sukō, the son of his older brother Kōgon Tennō, and became a Buddhist monk. He and Sukō were held prisoner from 1351 to 1357 by Emperor Go-Murakami of the Southern Court (Nanchō); he then returned to Kyoto, where he lived in various monasteries. He wrote a diary, of which some excerpts have been found that relate to the period between 1342 and 1345.

Konakamura Kiyonori. Historian (1821–95), author of two major works, *Yōshunro zakkō* and *Kokushigaku no shiori*.

Konchi-in Sūden. Buddhist monk (Isshiki Ishin, Ishin, 1569–1633) of the Zen Rinzai sect, who was ordered by Tokugawa Ieyasu to record the diplomatic actions of the shogunate, which he collected in the *Ikoku nikki* (Chronicle of Relations with Foreign Countries). He then directed the general administration of Buddhist temples and Shinto shrines, a task he shared with Itakura Katsushige. He inaugurated a temple in Sumpu, the Konchi-in, where he made his home, then another, also called Konchi-in, in Shiba (Edo) in 1618. Emperor Go-Mizunoo gave him the honorific title Enshō Honkō Kokushi in 1626. An *eminence grise* for Tokugawa Ieyasu, he was responsible for the banning of Christianity in 1614. His main work, the *Honkō kokushi nikki* (Memoirs for the Spiritual Master Honkō), is a valuable document for what it reveals about diplomatic relations of his time.

Kondei. Rural militia created in 792 to replace imperial troops after the conquest of northern Honshu, charged with cultivating the new lands and defending them against incursions of the Ezo. These "strongmen" also had to guard the public granaries and provincial government centers. The regulations of the Engi era set their total number at 3,964 men (between 20 and 200 per province), but the system began to fall into disuse in the tenth century.

Konden. Development of fallow land or creation of new rice paddies. A law promulgated during the Nara period allowed farmers and soldiers who had conquered (notably from the Ezo tribes) and cleared new lands to own them individually for a period of three generations (723), then in perpetuity (in 743). This law (called Konden Einen Shizai Hō or Konden Eisei Shizai Hō), which rendered those of the *ritsuryō* null and void, allowed large monasteries and nobles to accumulate land, leading to the establishment of private estates *(shōen)*. Also called *harita. See also* SHINDEN KAIHATSU.
→ *See* KONDŌ.

Kondō. "Golden room" in Buddhist temples, where the main image *(honzon)* of the divinity to which the temple is dedicated is found. Also called *hondō* ("main room"). It was the equivalent to the *konden* and *honden* of Shinto shrines.
  • Gold-plated copper or copper-based alloy, used for decoration. The Kondō Butsu Buddhist statues were made of bronze (alloy of copper, tin, and lead in various proportions). They were molded or cast using the lost-wax method, then plated with an amalgam of gold and mercury.

Kondō Heisaburō. Chemist (1877–1963), born in Shizuoka prefecture, who made important discoveries in alkaloids. He was a professor at the University of Tokyo and received the Order of Culture (Bunka-shō) in 1958.

Kondō Isami. Warrior (1834–68) of peasant origin, born in Musashi province, and famous swashbuckler (Kondo Shūsuke's student). He joined in the Shinsengumi, the special police serving the Edo shogunate, in Kyoto in 1863, and was named commandant of the force in 1864. The same year, he opposed the samurai of the Chōshū (*see* IKEDAYA JIKEN), then raised a sort of anti-imperial army in Edo, the Kōyō Chimbutai. He was captured by loyalist forces and executed in 1868.

Kondō Jūzō. Senior bureaucrat (Kondo Morishige; *gō*: Seisai, 1771–1829), sent by the Edo shogunate to explore the island of Ezo (Hokkaido). He was assisted by a merchant from the island, Takataya Kahei; when he returned to Edo, he submitted to the shogunate a report on Hokkaido and the Kuril Islands (Chishima), including a map. He helped to "Japanize" the Ainu of the Kuril Islands; in his memoirs *(Hen'yō bunkai zukō)*, he recommended that the *bakufu* defend the islands against a possible future claim by the Aka-Ezo (Russians).

Kondō Keitarō. Writer, born 1920 in Mie prefecture, author of popular novels and stories relating to the sea. Her novel *Amabune* (The Divers, 1956) received the Akutagawa Prize.

Kondō Nobutake. Vice-admiral (1886–1953) of the Japanese fleet that attacked Pearl Harbor on December 7, 1941.

Kongō. Japanese equivalent to the Sanskrit *vajra*. In Esoteric Buddhism, it is the symbol of emptiness *(Skt.: shūnya),* as indestructible as a diamond and analogous to lightning. It is also, in the same sects, a cult object formed of a short stick with points on the ends (which number 1, 3, 5, 7, or 9), symbolizing the strength and indestructibility of the spirit, almost always associated with a small bell *(kongōrei)* with a handle decorated with an identical *kongō.* Also called *kō.*

• **Kongōbu-ji.** Buddhist temple built on Mt. Kōya by Kūkai in 816, comprising a great number of buildings. A major center for teaching Shingon, it was destroyed and restored several times, the last time in 1869, when two of its temples, the Seigan-ji

and the Kōzan-ji, were united. This sacred plateau, at an altitude of about 1,000 m, was barred to women until 1872. Among its buildings, the Oku no In is Kūkai's mausoleum (Kōbō Daishi), and along the walkways leading to this holy of holies are more than 250,000 ancient tombs belonging to individuals, monks, and daimyo, in the midst of giant cryptomeres several hundred years old. One enters the religious complex by the *daimon* gate, then arrives at the *kondō* (or *gogandō,* imperial votive hall), rebuilt in 1934, passing in front of the Fudō-dō, the *daitō,* or grand *stūpa* (also reconstructed in 1934), the *miei-do* (bronze lantern dating from 1543), and other major buildings (*saitō, rokkaku-kyōzō,* etc.), before arriving, at the end of a long forest road, at the Oku no In. On exhibit in the Reihōkan are a great number of artistic treasures—sculptures, paintings, and valuable objects—dating from all periods. Nearby are houses for pilgrims and more than 110 annex temples. Also called Nanzan-ji. *See* KŌYA-SAN.

• **Kongō-kai.** In Esoteric Buddhism, "the world of the indestructible spirit" *(kongō),* the very essence of the divine. In Shingon-shū doctrine, it is the counterpart to the "transitory" world where the divinities manifest themselves (Taizō-kai), yet inseparable from it.

• **Kongō ken-in.** Mudra (symbolic and ritual hand gesture; *Jap: in*) of certain Buddhist divinities, used during esoteric *(mikkyō)* ceremonies: fists are held in front of the chest and the thumbs are clasped.

• **Kongōsen-ji.** Buddhist temple built in Yata (Ikoma-gun, Nara prefecture), dedicated to Jizō Bosatsu in 679. Current buildings dating from the Heian period. Also called Yata-dera, Yata no Jizō-san Ji.

• **Kongōsho-ji.** Buddhist temple founded in the ninth century in Asama (Mie prefecture, Honshu). *Hondō* (Mani-den) rebuilt in 1609.

Kongō-ryū. Name of one of the four or five major schools for actors *(shite)* in Noh theater, arising from the Sakado-za Sarugaku troupe serving the Hōryū-ji temple near Nara during the Kamakura period. This school was developed during the Muromachi period under the aegis of Saburō Masaaki (Kongō, 1449–1526), then was revived by his grandson, Shinroku Ujimasa (1507–76), who was also a playwright. The main members of this school were Shinroku Magojirō, Shinroku Ujimasa's son and a famous sculptor of Noh masks; Ukon Ujinari (1815–84); Sakado Ukiyō Ujiyasu (1872–1936); Sakado Kongō Iwao (1886–1951); and Sakado Kongō Iwao II (b. 1924).

Kon Hidemi. Writer (1903–84), born in Hokkaido, Kon Tōkō's younger brother. He studied French literature; after the Second World War, he began to write novels and stories, some based on his experiences during the war, such as *Sanchū hōrō* (1949) and *Tennō no bōshi,* which earned the Naoki Prize in 1950. He founded the Annual Arts Festival of Japan, and became president of the Japan Foundation in 1972.

Kōnin. Era of Emperor Saga: Sept. 810–Jan. 824. *See* NENGŌ.
→ *See* HEIAN-JIDAI, ZEN-SHŪ.

• **Kōnin-jōgan.** Period of the Kōnin and Jōgan eras, from 810 to 877 (emperors Saga and Seiwa), during which Buddhist doctrines of the Shingon and Tendai schools were imported from China, and the arts flourished. They were typified by sculptures made from single blocks of wood *(ichiboku-zukuri)* and the rendering of draped fabric in "waves" *(hompa-shiki).* Painting was epitomized by mandalas *(Jap.: mandara)* and images of Buddhist divinities. Shinto-Buddhist syncretism also appeared, with some portrayals of *kami* in human form. In religious architecture, the symmetrical temple plans of the Nara period gave way to arrangements more adapted to the nature of the terrain, such as the Murō-ji, the only example preserved from the time.

• **Kōnin kyaku-shiki.** Legal code in 50 volumes, promulgated in 820 and including all laws and edicts since 701. These new rules were complemented then put into effect in 840. *See* RITSURYŌ.

• **Kōnin shiki.** Official commentary on the *Nihongi,* written in 812, of which only a few fragments have been preserved in the *Shoku Nihongi.*

Kōnin Tennō. Forty-ninth emperor (Prince Shirakabe no Ōji, Yamato-neko Ame-mune Takatsuki no Mikoto, 709<770–81>), Tenji Tennō's grandson and Shōtoku Tennō's successor. He banished the monk Dōkyō, recalled the minister Wake no Kiyomaro from exile, and raised his wife, Inoue, to the rank of empress. His son Yamabe succeeded him, with the name Temmu (Kammu).

Konishi Raizan. Haiku poet (1634–1716), born in Osaka; Nishiyama Sōin's disciple. His poems are imbued with the sentiment of *makoto* and are closer to Bashō's than to the poems of the Danrin school. After his death, his works were anthologized in *Imamiyagusa,* published in 1734.

Konishiroku Shashin Kōgyō. Manufacturer of photographic products, cameras, and optical devices, founded in 1876 and reorganized in 1936. Since 1974, it has been the second largest producer of light-sensitive materials in Japan, after Fuji, and of automatic cameras under the brand name Konica. It exports about 53% of its production. Head office in Tokyo.

Konishi Yukinaga. Warrior (ca. 1556–1600), a Kyoto merchant's son and Toyotomi Hideyoshi's main lieutenant. A convert to Christianity, like his father, he took the name Dom Agostinho. He entered Hideyoshi's service in 1581 and commanded the military dictator's fleet. After helping Katō Kiyomasa pacify the Higo provinces, he and Katō transported Hideyoshi's troops to Korea in 1592 and 1597. When Hideyoshi died, Konishi allied himself with Ishida Mitsunari against Tokugawa Ieyasu. Conquered and taken prisoner at the Battle of Sekigahara in 1600, he was executed, and his estate in Uto (Amakusa Islands) was given to his rival, Katō Kiyomasa, who had supported Tokugawa Ieyasu.

Konjaku monogatari. "Tales of Times Now Past." A collection of about 1,000 short stories compiled by Minamoto no Takakuni (1004–77), who gathered tales and legends from China, India, and Japan related to him by travelers passing through. This work, in a rather rough, common, often even Rabelaisian language, was written for the religious and moral education of the common people according to Buddhist philosophy. It may not have been completed. Of the 31 sections that have survived to the present, 5 concern China (180 tales); 5, India (187 tales); and 21, Japan (736 tales). Volumes 8 and 18 and part of volume 21 are lost. These tales are extremely valuable for study of society in the Heian period, because they give precise descriptions of the life of commoners and not just aristocrats. The writer Akutagawa Ryūnosuke was inspired greatly by the works in the *Konjaku monogatari.* Also sometimes titled *Uji Dainagon monogatari.*

Konjichō. A sort of Garuda (mythical bird associated with Vishnu in Indian mythology), a guardian of Buddhism, portrayed as a man with a bird's head and playing the flute. It is very rarely portrayed in Japan (eighth-century dry-lacquer statue at the Kōfuku-in museum in Nara).

Konjin. Divinity of the points of the compass, belonging to the Taoist pantheon of Ommyōdō, both feared and venerated by followers of this doctrine when they travel. Also called Tenchi Kane no Kami. *See* KATA-IMI, KATA-TAGAE, KONKŌ-KYŌ, OMMYŌDŌ.

• **Konjin-nyo.** *See* ZAIKE.

Konjō. "Spirit of perseverance," a characteristic of sports and other kinds of undertakings, implying a sustained effort to the limit of the individual's capacities, beyond suffering, in order better to master the body and spirit.

Konketsuji. Term sometimes used for children of mixed race born in Japan, generally to Japanese and Chinese (or Korean) parents. It was also used, after the Second World War, for children resulting from the union of African Americans and Japanese women, of whom there were more than 100,000. After 1970, many *konketsuji* emigrated to the United States because they were subject to discrimination in Japan. Those who remained acquired Japanese citizenship and were more or less integrated. Children of mixed European and Japanese blood are more easily accepted into Japanese society than are those with a black parent.

Konkō-kyō. Modern syncretic Shinto-Buddhist religion founded in 1859 by a farmer from Okayama prefecture, Kawate Bunjirō (1814–83). He elevated the divinity Tenchi-kane no Kami (also called Konjin) to a Supreme Being, rejecting the Shinto rites. Kawate Bunjirō, who changed his name to Bunji Daimyōjin, then Konkō Daijin (Grand Divinity of the Golden Light), preached a life of harmony with nature and equality among all people (called *ujiko*), and rejected all superstition as contrary to divine principles. Although its beliefs were denounced repeatedly by the authorities and by other sects, such as the Shugendō, Konkō-kyō spread rapidly among the peasants and lower classes of the coastal regions around the Inland Sea (Setonaikai). In 1873 and 1874, Kawate Bunjirō wrote books intended to enlighten believers, *Tenchi kakitsuke* and *Konkō daijin oboe*. His followers grew in numbers in the Kyoto and Osaka regions, but he refused to have his religion integrated into State Shinto; it was later forced to affiliate with the Shinto Bureau (Kyōha-shintō) from 1871 to 1946. This sect now has about 500,000 followers. Its headquarters are at the Konkō-cho, in Okayama. *See also* KONJIN, KYŌHA SHINTŌ, SHINKO-SHŪKYŌ.

Konō Bairei. Painter (Konō Naotoyo; *azana:* Shijun; *gō:* Chōandō, Seiryūkan, Omu, Bairei, 1844–95), born in Kyoto. He was a member of the Maruyama-shijō school and was Shiokawa Bunrin's (1808–77) disciple. He founded the Kyoto-fu Gagakkō (Kyoto Prefectural School of Painting) in 1880, then started his own school the following year. Appointed an Artist for the Imperial Household (Teishitsu Gigei-in) in 1893, he had a great many students, among them Kawai Gyokudō and Uemura Shōen. He painted landscapes, flowers, and birds, often inspired by Chinese themes, in a fairly conventional style.

Konoe Atsumaro. Politician (1863–1904), born in Kyoto, Fumimaro Konoe's father. After studying at the University of Leipzig, he was appointed a prince—due to his noble origins (the Konoe were one of the *go-sekke*, "five families" issuing from the northern branch of the Fujiwara)—and entered the House of Peers in 1890; he became Speaker of the House in 1895. In 1889, he founded the Tōa Dōbunkai (Cultural Society of Eastern Asia), an association designed to forge closer links between Asian countries and Japan and to counterbalance European influences. In 1900, he founded the Kokumin Dōmeikai to resolve the problem posed by Manchuria; in 1901, he bought the *Nihon Shimbun-sha* newspaper. Vigorously opposed to Russian policy in Asia, he founded an anti-Russian association, Tairō Dōshikai, in 1903, in an effort to win over Japanese public opinion.

Konoe Fumimaro. Politician (Konoe Ayamaro, 1891–1945), born in Tokyo, Konoe Atsumaro's son, from whom he inherited the title of prince. He entered the House of Peers in 1916 and was part of the Japanese delegation to the peace conference in Paris in 1919; after visiting Europe and North America, he was Speaker of the House of Peers from 1933 to 1937. His impartiality in public affairs earned him the chair of the Council (June 1937–Jan. 1939), succeeding Hayashi Senjūro. Hiranuma Kiichirō replaced him, but he returned to power (July 1940–Oct. 1941), succeeding General Abe Nobuyuki. Tōjō Hideki succeeded him. During his ministry, he signed the "tripartite pact" with Germany and Italy (September 27, 1940) and founded the Taisei Yokusankai (Imperial Rule Assistance Association), a political movement advocating a "Sphere of Asian Co-Prosperity." He tried, in vain, to obtain an interview with American president Franklin D. Roosevelt, hoping to avoid a direct confrontation with the United States; he failed, and resigned on October 26, 1941. Although he had no official responsibility in the Japanese government during the Second World War, he used his influence during the negotiations over Japan's surrender in 1945. He was handed over to the war-crimes court and committed suicide on December 16, 1945. He wrote a book on his actions as prime minister, *Ushina wareshi seiji* (Prince Konoe's Memoirs), and some articles on historical subjects.

Konoe Fusatsugu. Architect (fourteenth century) in Go-Daigo Tennō's court, who drew up plans for the Muromachi shogunate's quarters in Kyoto about 1333–36.

Konoe Iehiro. Imperial prince (1667–1736) who married Emperor Reigen's daughter. He was appointed regent *(kampaku)* in 1709 and became a Buddhist monk in 1725 with the name Yorakuin. A master calligrapher and expert in the tea ceremony *(chanoyu)* and flower arranging *(kadō, ikebana),* he was also a major collector of objets d'art (now part of the Konoe collection of the Yōmei Bunko in Kyoto). He was also interested in the art of gardens, painting, and poetry, but he is best known as an expert calligrapher in the five styles of Chinese writing and kana.

• **Konoe Nobuhiro.** Imperial prince (1599–1649), Emperor Go-Yōzei's son. He was appointed *kampaku* (regent) in 1623.

• **Konoe Nobutada.** Calligrapher and statesman *(gō:* Sammyaku-in, Nobutada, 1565–1614), Konoe Sakihisa's son. He was appointed *sadaijin,* then *kampaku* in 1605. An excellent *waka* poet, he created a literary school (Konoe-ryū) in Kyoto, and he was also a painter. His calligraphic style was highly valued, and he was considered one of the Sampitsu (Three Brushes) of the Kan'ei era, with Hon-Ami Kōetsu and Shōkadō Shōjō. He painted a few works in the Zen tradition.

• **Konoe Sakihasa.** Statesman (Konoe Harutsugu, Konoe Sakitsugu, 1536–1612), born in Kyoto, Konoe Nobutada's father. He was appointed *kampaku* in 1554. In 1573, he wrote the *Saga-ki,* a work

on Saga province, and he became a Buddhist monk in 1582 with the name Ryūzan.

Konoe Tennō. Seventy-sixth emperor (Prince Narihito, 1139<1142–55>), Toba Tennō and Fujiwara Tokuko's son. He succeeded Sutoku Tennō, and Go-Shirakawa Tennō succeeded him upon his death.

Konoe Tsunetada. Statesman (1302–52) who was *sesshō* in the Southern Court (Nanchō). His son was Jitsugen, a Buddhist monk of the Hossō-shū.

Konohana no Sakuya-hime. Female Shinto divinity, daughter of Ōyamatsumi *(kami* of the mountains) and wife of Ninigi no Mikoto. She is considered the protective *kami* of Mt. Fuji and the spirit of the cherry blossoms. Also called Sengen, Asama. *See* SENGEN MYŌJIN.

Kōno Hironaka. Politician (1849–1923), born in Fukushima prefecture to a family of land-owning samurai. He took part in the Boshin Civil War (1868) with the imperial troops, then, influenced by Itagaki Taisuke, became one of the pioneers of the Jiyū Minken Undō (Freedom and People's Rights Movement) and advocated the creation of a parliament in 1880. After the announcement that a Constitution was to be written, Kōno Hironaka took an active part in founding the Liberty party (Jiyūtō), but, having been involved in the Fukushima "affair," he was arrested and sentenced to seven years in prison. Pardoned in 1890, he was elected to the House of Representatives and reelected constantly until 1920, having been appointed Speaker of the House in 1903. He founded many patriotic associations and the National Constitutional party, and was minister of agriculture and commerce in 1915 in Ōkuma's second cabinet. His advocacy of universal suffrage was constant and fervent.

Kōno Ichirō. Politician (1898–1965), born in Kanagawa prefecture. At first a journalist, he ran for the House of Representatives for the Rikken Seiyūkai (Friends of Constitutional Government party) and was elected in 1932. Although he was kept from being politically active by the Occupation authorities from 1946 to 1951, he was appointed minister of agriculture and forests by Hatoyama in 1954, then by Ikeda Hayato in 1961. His son, Kōno Yōhei, and his brother, Kōno Kenzō, continued his political activities.

• **Kōno Kenzō.** Politician (1901–83), Kōno Ichirō's brother, elected to the Chamber of Councillors in 1953 for the Jiyū Minshutō (Liberal Democratic party), after having been in the House of Representatives for many years. As Speaker of the Chamber of Councillors from 1971 to 1977, he resigned from the LDP in order to remain impartial.

• **Kōno Yōhei.** Politician (b. 1927). Member of the Jiyū Minshutō (Liberal Democratic party), he succeeded his father, Kōno Ichirō, in the House of Representatives in 1967 and was vice-minister of education in 1973.

Kōnoike. Large Osaka family of merchants founded in the village of Kōnoike by Yamanaka Shinroku (1570–1650), who set up a *sake* brewery there. He then moved to Osaka and supplied Edo with *sake,* which he transported by boat. Purchasing rice *(kuramai)* from samurai, daimyo, and *hatamoto,* he produced increasing quantities of *sake* and became extremely wealthy. His son, Kōnoike Zen'emon (1608–93), continued the *sake* business and set up money-lending bureaus; the interest he collected added to the family fortune. Kōnoike Zen'emon II (1643–96) followed in his footsteps, as did Kōnoike Zen'emon III, who diversified the family's activities from *sake*-making to insurance, money-lending, and banking. The family is still active in Osaka, although it suffered some financial setbacks in the early twentieth century.

Kōno Michiari. Warrior (late twelfth century) who was military governor of Iyo province. During the attempted invasion by the Mongols in 1281 (*see* KŌAN NO EKI), he performed with prowess and captured an enemy admiral. His exploits are described in the *Mōko shūrai ekotoba,* an *emakimono* commissioned by Takezaki Suenaga.

Kō no Moronao. Warrior (d. 1351), vassal of the Ashikaga, minister for and secretary to shogun Ashikaga Takauji. He defeated and killed the generals of the Southern Court (Nanchō), Kitabatake Akiie and Kusunoki Masayuki. But he himself was killed by Uesugi Yoshinori while doing battle with Ashikaga Takauji's younger brother, Ashikaga Tadayoshi. One of his brothers, Kō no Morofuyu, died with him; his other brother, Kō no Moroyasu, was assassinated the same year.

Kōno Togama. Politician (1844–95) from the Tosa estate (Kyushu), and Confucian scholar, Yasui Sokken's student in Edo. He served in the ranks of the anti-shogunal forces; after the Meiji Restoration, he was appointed Guard of the Seals, then, in 1881, minister of agriculture and trade, but he re-

signed almost immediately to form the Rikken Kaishintō (Constitutional Reform party) with Ōkuma Shigenobu. He was once again appointed minister of agriculture in 1892 in Matsukata Masayoshi's first cabinet; he was then, in succession, minister of justice, of the interior, and of education.

Konrad, Nikolai Iossifovich. Russian scholar (1891–1970), born in St. Petersburg, specializing in Japanese studies. He studied in Japan from 1912 to 1917, and obtained a number of academic distinctions in Leningrad and at the Institute of Asian Studies in Moscow (1941–49). He directed the compilation of a major Japanese–Russian dictionary and was decorated with the Order of the Rising Sun in 1969.

Konron-hassen. Sort of Gagaku dance performed by four people wearing bird-head masks, with musical accompaniment. Also called *tsuru-mai* (dance of the crane).

Konsei. Popular Shinto divinity, supposed to protect women in labor and considered a protector of marriage. It is represented as a stone phallus, mainly in northern Honshu and in the Kanto region. It is likely one of the forms of a *Sae no kami* or *Dōsojin.*

Kon Tōkō. Buddhist monk and writer (1898–1977), born in Kanagawa prefecture, Kon Hidemi's older brother. After a rather adventurous life, during which he was identified with the proletarian-literature movement, he became a Buddhist monk in 1930. He resumed his interrupted literary career in 1956, publishing *Ogin sama,* a novel that won the Naoki Prize. Appointed *hossō* of the Tendai-shū sect in 1966, he continued to write; in 1968 he was elected to the Chamber of Councillors. Among his other important works are *Shundei ni shō* (1957) and *Akumyō* (1961).

Kō-ō. Era of Emperor Go-Komatsu of the Northern Court (Hokuchō): Feb. 1389–Mar. 1390. *See* NENGŌ.

Kōotsunin. "Nameless person," formerly a person without rank, or someone deprived of privileges or status. *See* BONGE.

Kōraku-en. Landscaped garden at the Bunkyō-ku (Tokyo), featuring a lake with an island in the middle, created by Tokudaiji Sahei for Tokugawa Mitsukuni and Tokugawa Yorifusa in 1629. This garden, whose design was influenced by Chinese gardens, has magnificent rocks from all provinces of Japan. Its *taiko-bashi,* or barrel-arch bridge, is famous. *Area:* about 7 hectares. An amusement park and a stadium have been built nearby.

• Landscaped garden created in Okayama by one of Kobori Enshū's students, who designed it in 1700 for the daimyo Ikeda Tsunamasa. It comprises several lakes, a teahouse *(chashitsu),* and a stage for Noh theater. *Area:* about 13 hectares.

Korea. Korea often found itself closely linked to Japan, first during the third century, when the horsemen-archers arrived (*see* KIBAMINZOKU-RON), then before 663, when it seems the Japanese conquered a part of the Korean Peninsula (*see* JINGŪ, KŌGŌ, MIMANA). It was from Korea that Confucianism, Taoism, and Buddhism arrived in Japan. Then, when many Korean émigrés settled in Japan, Korea became a practically obligatory intermediary between Japan and China, since the ocean crossing between the two countries was relatively easy. In 1582, Korea became a bone of contention between Japan and China, when Toyotomi Hideyoshi attacked the peninsula. At the end of this invasion attempt, a number of Korean artisans, notably potters, moved to Japan. After conquering China in 1895, Japan once again set its sights for Korea, which was the object of rivalry among China, Russia, and the Empire of the Rising Sun. In 1905 and 1910, Japan managed to oust its adversaries and colonize the peninsula, imposing its laws and language by force. At the end of the Second World War, Korea regained its independence but was divided in two because of diverging political ideologies: North Korea with a Marxist ideology, and South Korea under American influence. War broke out in 1950, with the Americans and their allies on one side and Communist China on the other. Japan, not having an army (it had been eliminated by the 1947 Constitution), did not take part in the war, but it nevertheless benefited from it enormously, experiencing an economic boom resulting from being the supplier for the American army. At the end of the war (1953), relations between Korea and Japan remained tense, with the Koreans not forgiving the Japanese for the atrocities they committed during their occupation of the country. Diplomatic relations between the two countries, however, are now good, although often delicate, because of the relatively precarious situation of many Koreans who moved to Japan. *See* CHŌSEN.

• **Japanese Occupation of Korea:** The Korean Peninsula was occupied from 1910 to 1945 by Japanese forces, making it a colony; it was directed by 12 governors-general: Itō Hirobumi (1905–09); Sōji Arasuke (1909–10); Terauchi Masaki (1910–16); Hasegawa Yoshimichi (1916–19); Saitō Makoto (1919–27); Ugaki Issei (1927); Yamanashi Hanzō (1927–29); Saitō Minoru (1929–31); Ugaki Issei (1931–36); Minami Jirō (1936–42); Koiso Kuniaki (1942–44); Abe Nobuyuki (1944–45)

Kōrei Tennō. Seventh emperor (Prince O-Yamato-neko Hiko-futo-ni no Mikoto, traditionally 342 <290–15> BC), successor to Kōan Tennō. He very likely lived in the first century AD. Kōgen Tennō would have succeeded him.

Korenobu. Painter (Fujiwara no Korenobu, thirteenth century), Fujiwara no Nobuzane's grandson, of the Yamato-e school in Kyoto.

Koretaka Shinnō. Imperial prince and *waka* poet (844–97). He became a Buddhist monk. Also known by the name Ono no Miya.

Koreyasu Shinnō. Imperial prince (1264<1266–89>1326) and seventh shogun of Kamakura, succeeding Munetaka Shinnō. He was deposed and became a Buddhist monk. Hisaakira succeeded him.

Kōri Kannon. One of the 33 forms (*see* SANJŪSAN ŌGESHIN) of Kannon Bosatsu (*Skt.:* Avalokiteshvara), portrayed holding a seashell. Perhaps a divinity that protects fishers.

Kōrin. Painter (Ogata Kōrin, Ogata Koretomi; *mei:* Kariganeya Tōjūrō, Katsuroku; *gō:* Hōshuku, Jakumei, Dōsū, Kansei, Iryō, Seiseidō, Chōkōken, Kōrin, 1658–1716) of the Rimpa school, son of a Kyoto fabric merchant and related to Hon'ami Kōetsu through his grandfather. He first followed the style of the Kanō school with Yamamoto Soken (d. 1706) and began to paint on fabric, then he decorated the ceramics made by his brother, Ogata Kenzan. He also worked independently on painting screens, which he decorated with magnificent paintings on a gold background in an essentially decorative style. In 1704, he went to Edo and produced various paintings and portraits for the daimyo, but he returned to Kyoto in 1711 and continued to paint there, despite serious reversals in his fortunes. His style, influenced by Sōtatsu and Kōetsu, earned him many disciples—among them Watanabe Shikō, Tatebayashi Kagei, and Fukae Roshū (1699–1757)—who founded the Kōrin school (Kōrin-ha). Kōrin was also an excellent lacquer artist *(maki-e)* and a good calligrapher. He is said to have invented some accessories for the tea ceremony *(chanoyu).* He received the title Hokkyō.

• *Kōrin hyakuzu.* "Kōrin's Hundred Paintings." An art-criticism book by Hōitsu (1761–1828) devoted to Ogata Kōrin's work.

Koromo (-goromo). Type of robe worn by Buddhist monks over a white kimono. Also, sort of decorated coat once worn by noblewomen.

Koropokguru. Ainu word designating ancient peoples who lived on the islands of Japan; theoretically, these peoples preceded the Ainu. The word *koropokguru,* which means "spider people," may be equivalent to Kumaso, Kobito, and Tsuchigumo, used in the *Kojiki* and the *Nihon shoki* to designate aboriginal populations.

Koroshi-ba. In Kabuki theater, scenes portraying a massacre.

Kōryaku. Era of Emperor Go-En'yū, of the Northern Court (Hokuchō): Mar. 1379–Feb. 1381. *See* NENGŌ.

Kōryō. In traditional architecture, a type of decorated beam linking two pillars to provide reinforcement. A variant, called *ebi-kōryō,* is curved in a "crab shape." The *kōryō* were used mainly in *karayō*-type structures.
→ *See* KOKURYŌ, NOMURA MOTONI.

Kō Ryōsai. Physician (1799–1846) who was one of Franz von Siebold's students in Nagasaki.

Kōryū. Small submarines used at the end of the Second World War for suicide missions. About 100 of them were built in 1945. *Crew: 5. Weapons: 2* torpedoes. *See* KAIRYŪ, KAITEN, SUBMARINES.

Kōryū-ji. Buddhist temple belonging to the Shingon-shū sect, built in the Uzumasa district of Kyoto (whence its other name, Uzumasa-dera) in 622 to house a statue of the Buddha that Shōtoku Taishi had received from Korea in 603. It was first built on the right bank of the Kamiya-gawa river, then transferred to its current site in 1150 by Fujiwara no Nobuyori. It is the oldest Buddhist site in Kyoto. In it, followers worship images of Yakushi Nyorai and Miroku Bosatsu. Sermon hall *(kōdō)* dating from 1185, *keigū-in* from 1251, Amida-dō from the ninth century. The Reihōkan museum has art treasures from the sixth and seventh centuries. Also sometimes called Hachioka-dera.

Kōsa. *See* KENNYO SHŌNIN.

Kōsai. Buddhist monk (Jōkakubō Kōsai, 1163–1247), Hōnen's disciple, considered a heretic by the followers of the Jōdo-shū.
• Sculptor of netsuke (Yukawa Kōsai, active until ca. 1887).

Kōsaka Masanobu. Warrior (d. 1578). He was chosen by Takeda Shingen to perpetuate the Kōsaka family line of Shinano, which he had exterminated in 1561, and asked to guard a castle threatened by Takeda's enemy, Uesugi Kenshin. He began to write the *Kōyō gunkan,* which was completed by Obata Kagenori. *See* KŌYŌ GUNKAN.

Kōsaku. Ancient official ceremony during which the emperor was informed of the legal positions taken during the preceding months. Also called *kokusaku.*

Kosaku. Farmers who, from medieval times to 1940, paid an annual rent in various products to the owners of the lands they were developing. Also called *mizunomi byakusho* (water drinkers). *See also* JI-SAMURAI (JIZAMURAI).

Kōsatsu. Posters displayed on wood panels in cities to announce rules made by the local lord of the government, in use in the Muromachi and Edo periods. Also called *seisatsu.*

Kose Kanaoka. Painter (active between 850 and 890) of the Yamato-e school, founder of the Kose-ryū school in Kyoto. Although none of his works has survived, it is known that he painted portraits of famous Confucian scholars and works on Buddhist subjects. He was closely linked with Sugawara no Michizane. His son (?), Kose Aimi (Kose Ōmi, tenth century) perpetuated his style.

• **Kose-ryū.** The oldest school of painting in Japan. It was founded by Kose Kanaoka, who was inspired largely by models supplied by Chinese artists of the Tang dynasty (622–907). Among the painters of this school, the best known are Kose Aimi, Kose Kintada (ca. 950), Kose Kimitada, Kose Kimmochi (ca. 980), Kose Hirotaka (ca. 1000), Kose Arihisa, Kose Muneyoshi (ca. 1100), Kose Masumune (ca. 1115), Kose Nobushige (ca. 1060), Kose Tomomune (ca. 1155), Kose Sōshin (ca. 1180), Kose Nagamochi (ca. 1245), Kose Mitsuyasu (ca. 1290), Kose Ariie (ca. 1320), and Kose Ariyasu (ca. 1350).

Kōsen. Zen Buddhist monk (1816–92) from Settsu, Daisetsu's disciple at the Shōkaku-ji temple. He di-

rected the Engaku-ji temple (Rinzai sect) in Kamakura in 1875. Author of a major work on Zen philosophy, *Zenkai ichiran* (Waves on the Sea of Zen).
→ *See* SHŌNYO.

Kōsen-ga. "Image of light beams," name for ukiyo-e prints made in a chiaroscuro style. The main artist using this technique was Kobayashi Kiyochika (1847–1915).

Ko-seto. Type of ceramics produced in the Seto kilns during the Muromachi and Edo periods, imitating Chinese celadons. Their glaze ranged from light yellow-brown to dark brown. *See* SETO.

Kōsetsu. Painter (Sakamoto Chokudai; *mai:* Kōzen; *azana:* Ou; *gō:* Shōsōrinsho, Kōson, Kōsetsu, 1800–53) of orchids and other flowers. He was also a physician and botanist.
→ *See* TAIGAN.

Kōshi. In the early Meiji era (1868–1912), representatives of the estates of the daimyo in the Assembly. There had to be three for estates with a revenue of more than 400,000 *koku,* two for those with a revenue of between 100,000 and 400,000 *koku,* and just one for the others. The *kōshi* thus became members of the "Lower Chamber" (*kakyoku,* then *kōshi-taisakujō*). The term *kōshi* was quickly replaced by *kōmunin* (people charged with public affairs).
• In traditional architecture, window bars.
• Type of fabric in which the weft and warp form a checkerboard or latticework design, used mainly for obi (kimono belts) for costumes in Noh theater of the *atsu-ita* genre.
• Japanese name for Confucius.
→ *See* BUNSEN-Ō, GEISHA.

• **Kōshi-ban.** Functionary in the Kamakura *bakufu* charged with opening and closing the gates of the shogunal palace.

Koshi. Type of palanquin used by aristocrats for traveling, mainly during the Nara and Heian periods. Later, samurai and other individuals used *koshi,* but in the Edo period they were replaced by *kago. Koshi* are still sometimes used to transport *mikoshi,* or portable shrines, during festivals. Also called *ren.*
• Former name for the region comprising Echigo, Etchū, Noto, Kaga, and Echizen provinces, whose inhabitants, called Koshi-bito, were said to be of foreign origin (from Manchuria and Korea).

Koshigatana. Relatively short sword (about 30 cm long) mounted in the *aikuchi* style—that is, without *tsuba*—used after the Kamakura period. *See* TANTŌ.

Koshigaya Gozan. *Haikai* poet (eighteenth century). In 1775, he compiled *Butsurui shōko.*

Koshiki. Kitchen utensil, terra-cotta container with holes in the bottom used for steaming rice, known since the Yayoi period (around the first century AD) and sometimes still used in rural areas, called *mushiki.* It is somewhat similar to a couscous cooker.

Ko-shikibu no Naishi. Poet (late ninth century), Izumi Shikibu and Tachibana no Michisada's daughter, and Empress Jōtō Mon'in's lady-in-waiting.

Koshimaki. Short-sleeved, very long kimono (*kosode*), held at the waist by a soft-fabric obi and generally worn over a *katabira* by courtesans and geisha in the Edo period. The obi was knotted in front.

Kōshin. Japanese reading of two Chinese characters typifying, in the Jikkan-jūnishi system, the 57th year or day of a cycle of 60 respective periods, and called Kanoe Saru ("positive metal monkey"). According to ancient beliefs arising from Taoism, on the night of a *kōshin* day, three "souls" or "insects" (*sanshi*) leave a person's body and go to the Supreme Being, to whom they describe the faults that person committed, causing death as he or she sleeps. Therefore, on this night, those who believe in *kōshin* do not sleep (Kōshin-machi). This belief (*kōshin-kō*) was probably imported to Japan from Korea during the Heian period. *Kōshin* is also called Shōmen Kongō. *See* KŌSHIN-SHINKŌ.
→ *See* MONKAN, SAMBŌ KŌJIN, SHŌMEN KONGŌ.

• **Kōshin-shinkō.** Taoist-influenced syncretic cult, imported from China in the late ninth century (?), whose main divinity is Shōmen Kongō (also called Kōshin).

Koshira-e. All parts of a sword (*katana*) except for the blade, also called *tōsō* or *gaisō,* including the handle (*tsuka*), the sheath (*saya*), and the guard (*tsuba*). During the Muromachi period, some accessories were added to these parts: a small knife (*kozuka*), a stiletto (*kogai*), and handle ornaments called *menuki.*

Kōshitsu. Term often used for the imperial residence.

Kōshō. Era of Emperor Go-Hanazono: July 1455–Sept. 1457. *See* NENGŌ.

• Buddhist monk and sculptor (eleventh century), Jōchō's father.

→ *See* KŪYA SHŌNIN.

• **Kōsho-ji.** *See* BUKKŌ-JI.

• **Kōshōji-ha.** Secondary branch of the Jōdo Shin-shū sect, founded in Kyoto by Renkyo in the fourteenth century.

Kōshō. "Pages," during the Muromachi and Edo periods, that is, warriors who assisted a lord (daimyo) or the shogun. Those directly attached to the shogun had the title *nakaoku-koshō* (there were 50 of them) and *oku-koshō*. They were generally recruited by the *hatamoto*. The *koshō-shū* were a corps of 30 samurai charged with serving the shogun in his Edo palace. *See also* CHIGO.

Kōshoku-bon. "Love books," series of fiction books dealing mainly with love, slightly erotic, in favor among the merchant class *(chōnin)* and people frequenting the pleasure districts during the Edo period. The most representative were by Ihara Saikaku, Nishizawa Ippū, and Ejima Kiseki. Books called *ukiyo-zōshi* replaced them after 1716.

• **Kōshoku-mono.** "Tales of Gallantry." A series of erotic works and stories of chivalry published in the early Edo period. They were repeatedly censored by the shogunate, notably from 1721 to 1723. Ihara Saikaku wrote a few, but more audacious works, by writers such as Tōrindō Chōmaro (active between 1688 and 1711) and Hachimonjiya Jishō (d. 1745 in Kyoto), some of them frankly pornographic *(shumpon)*, typified the genre.

Kōshō Tennō. Fifth emperor (Prince Mimatsu-hiko Kae-shine no Mikoto, traditionally 506<475–393> BC), who would have succeeded Itoku Tennō and been succeeded by Kōan Tennō. This emperor, more or less mythical, could only have lived (if he existed) in the early years AD.

Kōshū-kaidō. In the Edo period, 139 km road linking Edo to Fuchū and meeting the Nakasendō road at Shimosuwa. It passed through the Kobotoke gate *(sekisho)* and the city of Kōfu, north of Mt. Fuji. It had between 33 and 47 waystations *(shukuba),* each of which could hold 25 men and horses. Also called Kōshū-dōchū. *See* GO-KAIDŌ, TŌ-KAIDŌ.

Kosode. Short-sleeved kimono, usually worn by married women. It is the current style of women's kimono. Children and teenaged girls wear *nagasode* ("long sleeves"). *See* KIMONO.

Kosode soga. Noh play: two brothers, Jūrō and Gorō Soga, receive their mother's forgiveness once they have achieved their vengeance.

Kosoku. In Japanese colleges and schools, a group of rigid and often useless rules that all students must absolutely follow under pain of sanctions. The rules vary from school to school and make school life a sort of "regimental prison." The vile and often vexatious *kosoku* are often denounced by students in mass protests, but to no avail. Their goal is to teach young people absolute conformity with the group to which they belong, under pain of *naishinsho,* a defamatory report on their conduct, which can have a detrimental effect on their further studies.

Koson. Painter (Ikeda Sanshin; *azana:* Shūji; *gō:* Gasenken, Kyūshō prefecture, Koson, 1801–66), Hōitsu's student in Edo. He also painted in Chinese style.

Kosugi Tengai. Writer (Kosugi Tamezō, 1865–1952), born in Akita prefecture. Greatly influenced by the French naturalist movement and by Émile Zola's works, he tried to emulate them, but he was unable to convey the most profound reaches of the human soul and restricted himself to appearances. His most important books are *Hatsusugata* (1900), *Hayara-uta,* and *Makaze koitaze.* He was elected a member of the Japan Art Academy (Nihon Geijutsu-in) in 1948.

Kōtai-fujin. Term for the mother of an emperor until 702; thereafter, Kōtaigō. Also Fujin, Nyōgo, Chūgū.

• **Kōtai-shi.** Title for the heir to the imperial throne. If it was one of the emperor's brothers, this title became Kōtai-tei. Also called Choni, Taishi, Haru no Miya, Hitsugi no Miya, Shōyō, Tōgu.

Kōtai-yoriai. During the Edo period, name for *hatamoto* samurai who had no official function and who received an average salary above 3,000 *koku* of rice. They were required to live in Edo, like the daimyo who were bound by the *sankin-kōtai.* However, some *hatamoto* with a lower income could have this title by derogation, such as those of the Sakakibara family.

Kotani Kimi. Reformer (1901–71), born in Miura (Kanagawa prefecture), who founded the Reiyūkai lay sect with her husband, Kotani Yasukichi, and her brother-in-law, Kubo Kakutarō (1892–1944). She cured the ill with prayer and advocated preservation of family traditions. When her brother-in-law died, she became the leader of the sect. *See* REIYŪKAI.

Kotatsu. Low table with a heating lamp and covered with thick fabric, used today in houses to warm the feet and legs of those sitting at it, especially during winter.

Kōtei. Title of a Noh play: Princess Yōhiki (*Chin.*: Yang Guifei) is ill, and Emperor Xuanzong, of the Tang dynasty, is visited by the spirit of Shōki (*Chin.*: Zhonghui), a bureaucrat whom he had promoted posthumously, who orders him to make a mirror and place it beside the princess's bed, so that her spirit will eventually attack and vanquish the demon responsible for her illness.

Kōtei. Painter (Asaoka Kōtei, Asaoka Okisada; *mei*:: Sanjirō; *gō*: Heishū, Sanraku, Kōtei, 1800–56) of the Kanō school, who studied with his father, Isen-in. He wrote major biographies of Japanese painters of the Edo period in the *Kogu-bikō*.
• One of the emperor's titles.

Kotenjō. In traditional architecture, type of ceiling (*tenjō*) made of a wood latticework, generally used for roof awnings and the edges of coffered ceilings.

Kotetsu Nagasone. *See* OKISATO.

Koto. Japanese zither, about 1.9 m long, made of paulownia (Kiri no ki) wood; today, it has 13 silk strings. The ancestor of this instrument, of Chinese and Korean origin, was the Yamato-goto (or *wagon*), used before the seventh century; it had only five strings and was 90 cm long. In the Nara period, a sixth string was added and another *koto*, similar to the one used now, was invented, called *gakusō*. *Koto* have movable frets that are used for tuning, since each string has its own bridge. The strings are strung at equal tension; it is the position of the bridges that gives each its pitch. The *koto* is played with artificial fingernails (*koto-tsume*) placed on three fingers of one hand, while the other hand presses on the strings to change the pitch. There are many varieties:
—**Azuma-goto.**
—**Han-koto,** of Chinese origin, small.

—**Ichigen kin,** of Chinese origin, with 12 strings.
—**Hitsu no koto,** with 12, 20, 23, 25, or even 50 strings.
—**Shō-hitsu no koto,** with 25 strings.
—**Chiku no koto,** with 13 strings.
—**Yamato-koto** *(wagon)*, the oldest, with 5 strings.
—**Ikuta-koto,** with 13 strings, currently the most frequently used in concerts. Also called Sō no koto. *Kor.*: go-gŭm.

Kotō. "Ancient swords," sword blades forged before 1596 by the *go-kaden* or their disciples, as opposed to the *shotō*, or "new swords," forged after that date.
→ *See* TOTSUGEN.

Kotobuki. Characters *(kanji)* used mainly in calligraphy and meaning "wishes for long life" and "words of congratulations." These propitiatory characters are found, often stylized, as decorations on objects, notably those made of porcelain and bronze.

Kotodama. Ancient belief according to which each Japanese word has a good or bad magical effect according to the use to which it is put and the moment when it is said. This belief may have given rise to the *norito*, ancient invocations to the *kami*.

Kotohira-gū. Shinto shrine (also called Kompira-gū or Kompira-san) in Kotohira (Shikoku, Kagawa prefecture) dedicated to the *kami* Omononushi no Kami and the spirit of Emperor Sutoku (who died in exile in Sanuki). This shrine, founded in the early eleventh century, was first dedicated to Kompira Daigongen, a Shinto-Buddhist syncretic divinity assimilated with the Indian divinity Kumbhīra, symbolic of the waters of the Ganges and considered in Japan to be a protector of sailors and fishers. Only when the cults were separated in 1868 was the Kompira-gū associated solely with Omononushi, a *kami* that, according to the *Kojiki*, "lit up the sea." It has a major festival every October 10. *See* KOMPIRA.

Kōtoku-in. Former Buddhist temple in Kamakura that housed a large statue of the Daibutsu cast in 1252. It was destroyed by a tidal wave in the fifteenth century and never rebuilt, leaving the Daibutsu in the open air. *See* DAIBUTSU, KAMAKURA.

Kōtoku Shūsui. Political agitator (Kōtoku Denjirō, 1871–1911) born in Nakamura, a village in Kōchi prefecture, to a family of small-scale merchants. He became interested in the Jiyū Minken Undō (Freedom and People's Rights Movement) and was so active that he was expelled from Tokyo, where he had gone to study, in 1887. He then went to Osaka and became Nakae Chōmin's student. In 1898, Kōtoku, Katayama Sen, and Murai Tomoyoshi (1861–1944) founded the Shakai Shugi Kenkyūkai (Society for the Study of Socialism). He wrote political works: *Nijisseiki no kaibutsu teikoku shugi* (Imperialism: The Specter of the Twentieth Century, 1901), then *Shakai shugi shinzui* (The Quintessence of Socialism, 1903). A pacifist, he argued against the Russo-Japanese War (1904–05) in the magazine he founded, *Heimin Shimbun,* and was sentenced to five months in prison in 1905. He then went to the United States; upon his return, he advocated "direct action" and general strikes to oppose government policy. Though he was disowned by the Socialist party, he continued his activities, inspiring young Japanese anarchists (including his wife, Kanno Suga), who plotted to assassinate Emperor Meiji. The plot was discovered, and Kōtoku Shūsui and 23 of his companions were arrested and sentenced to death on January 18, 1911. He was hanged six days later. *See also* ABE ISOO, HEIMIN-SHA.

Kōtoku Tennō. Thirty-sixth emperor (Prince Ame Yorozu Toyoshi no Mikoto, 597<645–54>), successor to his sister, Kōgyoku. He transferred his capital from Asuka to Naniwa and wrote the articles of the Taika Reform with the assistance of Prince Naka no Ōe (the future Emperor Tenji) and Fujiwara no Nakatomi (Kamatari no Nakatomi). He forbade construction of *kofun* because they were too expensive and strengthened the ties between Japan, Korea, and China. Late in Kōtoku Tennō's life, Prince Naka no Ōe moved the court back to Asuka, and Kōtoku Tennō, left in Naniwa, faded into obscurity.

Kotoshironushi no Kami. Shinto *kami,* Okuninushi no Mikoto's son and Tateminakata no Kami's brother. Chief of the Izumo region, he yielded to Ninigi no Mikoto. Also called Katsuragi Hitokotonushi, Yae-kotoshironushi. *See* JINGI-KAN NO HASSHIN.

Kotowaza. "Proverbs." This term also includes sayings and dictums, common phrases and adages, sometimes even insults and repartee. True proverbs from folk wisdom are quite similar to those in the West, though adapted to Japanese life; they deal with time, people's actions, and sometimes wordplay and repartee.

Kotoyōka. "Little eighth day," agricultural ceremonies held on the eighth day of the second and twelfth months of the year to ward off the demons of epidemics such as Ekijin. In the Kantō region, baskets are placed upside down on poles in fields in order to keep *hitotsume kōzō* (one-eyed demons) from disturbing the peace of the fields. This ceremony is also held during the festival of Setsubun. The rites vary from region to region.

Kōu. Title of a Noh play: A boatman reveals to his passengers that he is the spirit of General Kōu (*Chin.:* Xiang Yü, 232–02 BC), a general who rebelled after the death of Qin Shihuangdi and committed suicide when he was defeated; the boatman then reveals his true form.

Kōun. Painter (Kōtari Kōun; *mei:* Zen'emon; *gō:* Yūsan, Jōan, Kōun, active ca. 1670) of the Kanō school, Kanō Tan'yū's student.
→ *See* TAKAMURA KŌUN.

Kōunsai. Painter and samurai of the Mito clan (Takeda Seisei; *mei:* Iga no Kami; *gō:* Jo-un, 1803–65).

Ko-uta. "Short songs," a type of folk song composed of short poems, performed with shamisen accompaniment, invented in the sixteenth century. They were in style mainly in the Edo region, while similar songs, called *kamigata-uta,* were also popular in the Kyoto-Osaka region. Today's *ko-uta* are derived directly from other folk songs called *ha-uta,* favored by geisha in the late nineteenth century, and are sung by professionals, such as Tade Kōchō (1869–1958), Kasuga Toyo (1881–1962), Motoki Sui (1888–1979), and Gotō Ichimaru (b. 1906). The best-known collections of old *ko-uta* are *Kangin-shū* (311 *ko-uta* compiled in 1518 by Sōchō, 1448–1532) and the *Muromachi-jidai ko-uta-shū,* compiled in the early sixteenth century, perhaps by Sōan.

Kōwa. Era of Emperor Horikawa: Aug. 1099–Feb. 1104. *See* NENGŌ.
• Era of Emperor Go-Kameyama: Feb. 1381–Apr. 1384. *See* NENGŌ.

Kōwaka-mai. Danced dramas (also called *mai-mai*) created, according to tradition, by Kōwakamaru (Momonoi Kōwakamaru Naoaki, 1403–80), a dancer and poet who drew his themes from Sara-gaku theater and epics *(gunki-mono)* and who cre-ated dances to portray the feats of warriors. These dances were directly related to Noh theater and supplied it with dramatic elements. About 50 *kōwaka-mai* are known, of which 36 are part of the traditional repertoire, most of them dealing with episodes in wars between the Tairo and the Mina-moto in the late twelfth century. Kōwakamuru may have written these plays at the request of Retired Emperor Go-Komatsu. The texts were meant to be declaimed to the rhythm of a slow dance either by choruses or by three Noh actors *(tayū, waki,* and *tsure).* Most are inspired by the *Gikei-ki,* the *Soga monogatari,* and the *Heike monogatari.* Very popu-lar among the warrior class in the Muromachi pe-riod, *kōwaka-mai* had practically disappeared by the end of the seventeenth century, and their tradi-tion was maintained only by the Daigashira family in Fukuoka prefecture. The texts are called *mai no hon;* the dances, *kuse-mai* or *daigashira-mai.*

Kōya. Painter (Kanō Kōya; *mei:* Ri-emon, Gyōbu; *gō:* Hakuho, Kōya, ?–1672) of the Kanō school. He studied with his father, Kōi, and received the title of Hokkyō from the court.

Kōya-gire. Fragments of the oldest existing copies (in *kana)* of the *Kōkin-shū,* dating from the mid-eleventh century, and kept in the monasteries of Mt. Kōya *(see* KŌYA-SAN).

Koyama Shōtarō. Painter *(gō:* Senraku, 1857–1916) in Western style, student of Kawakami Tōgai and Fontanesi.

Koyama Yūshi. Playwright (1906–82) born in Hi-roshima prefecture, Kishida Kunio's student. Among his most successful plays are *Setonaikai no kodomo* (The Children of the Inland Sea, 1936) and *Nihon no yūrei* (The Ghosts of Japan, 1965).

Kōya monogurui. Title of a Noh play: a boy who has lost his father becomes a Buddhist monk on Mt. Kōya. A servant of his father finally finds him among the monks and takes him home.

Kōya-san. "Mt. Kōya," mountainous plateau *(alt.:* approx. 900 m) in the northern part of the Kii Pen-insula (Wakayama prefecture), surrounded by eight peaks with an altitude of over 1,000 m. It is covered with cedar, cypress, and pine forest, in the middle of which is the Kōya-san monastic complex.

• Group of Buddhist temples belonging to the Shingon-shū sect, founded in 816 by Kūkai (Kōbō Daishi) on Mt. Kōya, comprising more than 110 religious buildings, the main one of which is the Kongōbu-ji. The various monastic buildings in the grouping once housed up to 90,000 monks. Mt. Kōya was already a religious site before Kūkai ar-rived; Kūkai founded a single hermitage, and the main buildings were the work of the second abbot of the Shingon-shū, Shinnen (804–91). Ravaged by fire in 994, they were restored by Myōsan (1021–1106), and the Kōya-san became an important cen-ter for the *hijiri* of Amida under the direction of monks such as Kyōkai (1001–93), Chōgen (1121–1206), and Myōhen (1142–1224). It became cus-tomary for nobles and samurai to have their ashes buried near this sacred site. Although the monastic community was impeded by suppression by mili-tary dictators Oda Nobunaga and Toyotomi Hide-yoshi (who massacred some 1,000 *hijiri*) and suc-cessive fires (especially in 1521, 1888, and 1926), the temples there continued to prosper. At first, women did not have the right to enter; only in 1872 was this interdiction lifted. *See* KONGŌBU-JI.

• **Kōya-san Shingon.** Buddhist sect of the Shingon-shū, divided into six subsects, with a total of 4.5 million followers: Kōyasan Shingon, Gochi Kyō-dan, Kannon-shū (the largest, with more than 200,000 followers), Reiun-ji, Shūgen, and Suma-dera.

Koyasu. Particular class of syncretic Shinto-Bud-dhist divinities that is considered to be "givers of children" and that women invoke against sterility. Folklore has endowed certain Buddhist divinities with this aspect, including Jizō Bosatsu (once known as Koyasu Jizō) and Shō Kannon (Koyasu Kannon); the latter has an aspect of Juntei Kannon (Kishimojin or Kariteimo), representing a benevo-lent aspect of the demon of Indian Buddhist folk-lore, Hāritī. The Shinto *kami* presiding over easy childbirths was invoked under the name Koyasu-gami or Koyasu-sama.

Kōyō. Painter (Nakayama Kiyoshi; *mei:* Sei-emon; *azana:* Jogen; *gō:* Suiboku-sanjin, Gansei-dōjin, Shōseki-sai, Kōyō, 1717–80) of the Nanga school (Bunjinga), perhaps one of Hyakusen's students. An excellent calligrapher, he wrote a work on aesthet-ics, *Gadan keiroku.*

Kōyō gunkan. Twenty-volume military treatise at-tributed to Kōsaka Masanobu (?–1578) but probably dating from about 1625, describing the virtues required to be a perfect samurai and taking as examples generals Takeda Shingen and his son, Takeda Katsuyori, daimyo of Kai province, who, it was said, were never defeated in combat. It was in this work that the Bushido was first mentioned. According to the latest research, this work was probably written by a strategist called Obata Kagenori (1572–1663).

Ko-za. In Noh theater, the back part of the stage, where the musicians sit.

Kozai Shikin. Novelist and essayist (Shimizu Toyoko, 1868–1933), born in Okayama prefecture. At first she signed her works, many of which dealt with women's conditions in Japan, Shimizu Shiken. She adopted the name Kozai when she married a well-known chemist, Kozai Yoshinao (1864–1934), who became president of the University of Tokyo. Her most important novels were *Koware yubiwa* (The Broken Ring, 1891), *Kokoro no oni* (The Heart's Demon, 1897), and *Imin gakuen* (Immigrants' School, 1899).

Kōzama. Decorations on side panels of pedestals for Buddhist statues. Also called *gejō, genjō.*

Kōzan-ji. Buddhist temple in Kyoto, attached to the Shingon-shū sect (Omuro branch). Its date of foundation is not known, but it predates 870. This temple, at first called Toganoo-dera, was restored by the monk Myōe and renamed Kōzan-ji: doctrines of the Kegon and Shingon sects were studied there. It was expanded thanks to the patronage of Oda Nobunaga, Toyotomi Hideyoshi, and Tokugawa Ieyasu, and was rebuilt in 1636. It has the oldest known "tea garden," planted by Eisai (1141–1245). Among its treasures are most of the *Chōjū giga* scrolls. Aside from its *mie-dō,* which was built in the Kamakura period, its buildings date from 1636.

Kōzen gokoku-ron. "For the Promotion of Zen and Protection of the Nation." A religious text composed by Eisai in 1198 to explicate the doctrine of the Rinzai sect, which he had founded when he returned from China in 1191.

Kōzo. Paper with a fairly irregular texture, made with mulberry bark, used mainly for calligraphy and painting. Now, it is used as decorative paper. *See* PAPER, WASHI.

Kozuka. Small knife on the scabbard *(saya)* of a sword *(katana),* usually attached on the side opposite the stiletto *(kogai).* This small knife with no guard *(tsuba)* was used as a paper cutter, projectile, or to finish off an enemy. *See* KATANA, KŌGAI, KOSHIRA-E, UMABARI.

Kōzuke. Former province (previously called Kami-tsukenu), now Gumma prefecture.

• **Kōzuke sampi.** Name for three monuments in Gumma prefecture dating from the seventh and eighth centuries: a stele erected in Yamanoue in 681 or 741 by a Buddhist monk called Chōri on his mother's tomb, near a *kofun* with a corridor; in Tago, another stele commemorating the creation of the district in 711; and in Kanaizawa, a boulder erected in 726 following a vow made by nine Buddhist inhabitants of the area. The steles are engraved with Chinese characters transcribing Japanese words.

• **Kōzume Shinnō.** *See* MUNENAGA SHINNŌ.

Kōzume no Suke. Title of the chief of protocol at the Edo shogunal palace. *See* KIRA YOSHINAKA.

Kuatsu. In Japanese medicine, especially in martial-arts techniques, a method of reviving a person through pressure or blows applied to certain specific parts of the body and nerves (neural centers) or reflexogenic zones, usually corresponding to acupuncture points and meridians. It is a para-medical procedure, sometimes called "bare-hands acupuncture."

Kubō. Abridgment of "Kuge no Kata," title at first given to the emperor, shogun, and highest-ranked daimyo. In the Muromachi period, this title was given to delegates of the Ashikaga shogun in Kanto and in Kamakura. Also sometimes called *ōyake-kata. See* KANTŌ-KANREI.

Kubokawa Tsurujirō. Literary critic and essayist (1903–74). A member of the proletarian literature movement and the Communist party, he was imprisoned in 1932. After the Second World War, he once again took up his literary activities. Sata Ineko's first husband.

Kubo Ryōgo. Physicist, born 1920 in Tokyo, known for his work on magnetic resonance. He studied in Chicago, then at the University of Tokyo, and received the Order of Culture (Bunka-shō) in 1973.

Kubo Sakae. Writer (1901–58), born in Hokkaidō. He wrote plays and translated early-twentieth-century German playwrights such as Wedekind and Toller. He committed suicide in 1958. Among his plays are *Goryōkaku kessho* (1933), *Kazan baichi* (1937), and *Ringoen nikki;* he also wrote the novel *Noborigama* (1952).

Kubota. Japan's consul to Phnom Penh who declared Cambodia's independence on March 10, 1945, thus ending French rule over its protectorate. This act of independence was ratified two days later by royal proclamation.

Kubota Ichiku. Master dyer, born 1917 in Tokyo. In the 1950s, after many attempts, he was able to re-create the *tsujigahana* decoration style for kimonos. He had many exhibitions in Japan and abroad, notably at the Tokyo Palace in Paris in 1990.

Kubota Mantarō. Writer, playwright, and poet (1889–1963), born in Tokyo. He worked at the Tokyo Broadcasting Station radio station (NHK's predecessor) and wrote excellent haiku and collections of stories in a simple, pure language, such as *Asakusa* (1911), *Yuki* (Snow, 1913), *Uragare* (1917), *Shundei* (1928). His best-known plays are *Odera gakkō* (1927) and *Hanabie* (1938).

Kubota Utsubo. *Waka* poet (1877–1967) born in Nagano prefecture, author of new-style *(shintaishi)* poems and *chōka.* He published several poetry collections—*Mahiruno* (1905), *Tsuchi o nagamete* (1918), *Kyonen no yuki* (1967), *Chōsei-shū*—and a collection of stories, *Rohen* (1911).

Kubunden. Former system of proportional distribution of lands based on the Chinese *Koufentian* system (*see* RITSURYŌ) in effect under the Tang dynasty and inaugurated in Japan in the eighth century with the goal of establishing a basis for taxation. According to this system, each able-bodied man had the right to cultivate two *tan* (about 2400 m²) of arable land, and each adult woman had the right to about 1600 m². Servants and slaves could own only 800 m². These lands were allocated for a duration of six years and then redistributed. The system was abandoned in the tenth century.

Kuchi-zusami. "Ritornello." A small encyclopedia for children compiled by Minamoto no Tamenari (or Minamoto no Shitagō) in 970. It was rewritten about 1123 by Miyoshi no Tameyasu, who retitled it *Shōchū-reki* (Pocket Almanac). It had 19 sections.

Kudan. Character in tales and legends with three eyes on its forehead and three more in the back of its head, hooves, a lion's tail, and horns; it was said to be incapable of lying.

Kudara. Former name of Korea, or at least the part called Paekche (*see* PAEKCHE), comprising, before the seventh century, the tribal Hakusai and Benkan territories, which were conquered by Jingū Kōgō. Also called Bakan.
• Site of an ancient Buddhist temple, in the town of Hirakata near Osaka, where remains of buildings arranged in a way analogous to those of the Yakushi-ji, covering an area of about 4 hectares, were discovered in 1932 and 1965. This temple was probably built in the seventh century by Korean nobles who had emigrated from Paekche. Also called Kudara-dera.

• **Kudara Kannon.** Famous painted statue, more than 2 m high, carved from a single piece of camphor-tree wood, portraying Shō Kannon Bosatsu and dating from the Asuka era (early seventh century). It is housed in the Hōryū-ji.

• **Kudara Kawanari.** Warrior, painter, and poet (Aguri, 782–853) of Korean origin. He painted in the realist style of the Tang era; none of his works has survived.

• **Kudara Keifuku.** Governor (698–766) of Mutsu province, of Korean origin. He supplied some of the gold used in the gold leafing of the statue of the Daibutsu at the Tōdai-ji in Nara.

• **Kudara Sake no Kimi.** Grandson of a king of Kudara (Korea) who, according to tradition, introduced the art of falconry to Japan around 360.

Kudō Heisuke. Physician (1734–1800) from Kii province. He studied "Dutch sciences" *(rangaku)* and is known mainly for having written the *Aka-ezo fūsetsu kō,* a report on colonization of Hokkaido, in which he suggested measures to defend the island against Russian (Aka-ezo) incursions.

Kudō Tetsumi. Sculptor, born 1935 in Osaka. He studied at the University of Tokyo from 1954 to 1958, then went to France in 1962, where he worked in Arman's style, producing "accumulations in boxes": *Portrait of Ionesco, Your Portrait* (1970–71), and others.

Kuga Katsunan. Journalist (Nakada Minoru, 1857–1907), born in Tsugaru, founder of the newspaper *Tōkyō Dempō* (Tokyo Telegram) in 1888, after a brief career in the Ministry of Justice. In 1889, he founded another opinion journal, *Nihon* (Japan), in which he criticized the influence of provincial cliques *(hambatsu)* called Satchū-to-hi on government policy. He wrote a book on his ideas, *Kinji seiron kō* (Thoughts on Current Policy), in 1891, using the name Katsunan.

Kugatachi. A sort of ordeal inflicted on people suspected of a misdeed, in use before the eighth century and mentioned in the *Nihon shōki* (720). The accused had to grab a stone placed at the bottom of a pot full of boiling water without burning himself. A similar trial, called *yugishō,* was applied during the Muromachi period. Also known as *kukadachi, kukatachi, ukehiyu.*

Kuge. Term that originally designated the emperor's residence. It was later applied to all high-level bureaucrats and nobles, as opposed to *buke,* or warrior families. Formerly sometimes called *kōke* or *oyake. See* KUGYŌ.

• **Kuge-aku.** In Kabuki theater, the role of the conspirator.

• **Kuge-hō.** *See* BUKE-HŌ.

• **Kuge-kojitsu.** *See* BUKE-KOJITSU.

Kuge-shohatto. See KINCHŪ-JŌMOKU, BUKE SHO-HATTO.

Kugutsu. Troupes of itinerant actors and performers who entertained commoners with dance, song, and puppet shows. *Kugutsu* were made up of people, some of them foreigners, who had no well-defined social status. They formed during the Heian period, and the women members were sometimes prostitutes. Some of these troupes specialized in a particular genre, such as puppet theater *(ayatsuri-shibai),* and were known as *tekugutsu* or *kairaishi.* The plays they performed, called *kugutsu-mawashi,* were very popular in the fourteenth century; they complemented the *jōruri* repertoire in the following century, and shamisen accompaniment was added during the Edo period. The *kugutsu* used painted wooden or terra-cotta puppets and were the fore-runners of *ningyō-jōruri* and Bunraku. *See* AYA-TSURI-SHIBAI.

Kugyō. Former title for nobles of third rank and above (*see* I) and assimilated with the *kuge. See* KAZUKO, MINAMOTO NO SANETOMO, MINAMOTO NO YORIIE.

• Third son (1200–19) of shogun Minamoto no Yoriie of Kamakura. His grandmother, Hōjō Masako, had him enter the Buddhist orders and be named *bettō* of a temple attached to the Tsurugaoka Hachiman-gū in Kamakura. But Kugyō, who wanted to become shogun and believed that Minamoto no Sanetomo had plotted to kill Yoriie, slew the young Sanetomo with his sword within the very walls of the temple and was killed immediately by the warriors in the shogun's retinue.

Kugyō-zō. In Zen monasteries, a form of portrayal of the Buddha as an emaciated ascetic, common starting in the fourteenth century.

Kuhara Fusanosuke. Politician and industrialist (1869–1965), director of the Kuhara Mining Company (which became Nippon Sangyō, or Nissan, about 1930). He became extremely rich and powerful thanks to his copper mines, and he helped to fund development of Manchuria. He then turned to politics, joining the Rikken Seiyūkai (Friends of Constitutional Government party). Tanaka Giichi appointed him minister of communications in 1928. He favored military action on the mainland. After the Second World War, he was banned from having a political career by the Occupation authorities, but he worked on reopening negotiations with China after 1951.

Kui-awase. Popular belief according to which the association of certain foods could provoke illness or poisoning, such as eels and *umeboshi,* or eels and watermelon, or crab and *kaki* (persimmon). Also called *tabe-awase.*

Kuji. Taxation system established in the *shōen* and distinct from the *nengu,* applied from about the tenth to the fifteenth century. *Kuji* included work parties *(buyaku)* and barter (excluding rice), and was levied on independent landowners *(myōshu).*

Kujikata osadame-gaki. Legal code promulgated in 1742 by Tokugawa Yoshimune and written under the direction of Matsudaira Norimura (1686–1746). It was divided into two sections: civil and administrative laws (81 articles) and criminal laws

(103 articles). It was one of the reforms of the Kyōho era. *See* RENZA.

Kujiki. A history of Japan (also titled *Sendai kuji hongi*) traditionally attributed to Shōtoku Taishi and Sōga no Umako, who would have written it about 620. This work, published for the first time in 1644, is in fact apocryphal. However, it probably includes some fragments of the *Tsugibumi,* a sixth-century work destroyed around 644 and probably rewritten between 823 and 904.

Kujira-shaku. Former unit of length for fabrics, slightly longer than the traditional *kane-shaku.* Also called *kujira-zashi. See* SHAKU.

Kujō. One of the five families *(go-sekke)* of the northern branch of the Fujiwara, from among whom the regents *(sesshō* and *kampaku)* were chosen. Its members received the title of prince *(kō-shaku)* in 1868; a princess from the family married Taishō Tennō and was Shōwa Tennō's (Hirohito's) mother.

• **Kujō-dono.** *See* FUJIWARA NO MOROSUKE.

• **Kujō Haitei.** Name for Emperor Chukyō after he was dethroned by Hōjō Yoshitoki. *See* CHŪKYŌ TENNŌ.

• **Kujō no Kanezane.** *See* FUJIWARA NO KANEZANE.

• **Kujō Kintsune.** *See* SAIONJI KINTSUNE.

• **Kujō no Michie.** Statesman (Fujiwara no Michie, 1193–1252), Fujiwara no Yoshitsune's son. He became *susshō* in 1221, then *kampaku* in 1228. His son, Fujiwara no Yoritsune, was appointed shogun of the Kamakura *bakufu* in 1226, and had the Kofuku-ji temple built in Kyoto between 1236 and 1252.

• **Kujō no Norizane.** Statesman (Tōin Sesshō, 1210–35), appointed *kampaku* in 1231 and *sesshō* in 1233.

• **Kujō no Sukezane.** Statesman (1669–1729) who became *kampaku.* He was an excellent painter.

• **Kujō Takeko.** Poet (1887–1928).

• **Kujō Yoritsune.** *See* HŌJŌ MASAKO.

Kūkai. Buddhist monk (Kōbō Daishi, 774–835), born in Sanumi province (Shikoku). He entered the orders very young, and denounced Confucianism and Taoism in a pamphlet titled *Rōko shiki* (renamed *Sangō shiki*) in 798. In 804, he left for China with Fujiwara no Kadonomaro's delegation and went to Chang'an, the Tang capital, where he studied the Zhenyang doctrine under the direction of the monk Huiguo (*Jap.:* Keika) and became a master of esoterism in 806. When he returned to Japan, he established the Takaosan-ji temple (later known as Jingo-ji) in Kyoto and became the leader of thought among aristocratic society of the Heian period, to whom he preached a new Buddhist doctrine, the Shingon (lit., "True Speech"; *see* SHINGON-SHŪ). In 819, he received imperial authorization to build a hermitage on Mt. Kōya (*see* KŌYA-SAN, KONGOBU-JI). Emperor Saga offered him the directorship of the Tō-ji temple in Kyoto in 823. Kūkai spent most of his life, however, on Mt. Kōya, composing some 50 religious works on the dogmas of Shingon, which he felt was the only path to attainment of spiritual enlightenment during one's lifetime. He created a pilgrimage circuit of 88 temples on Shikoku and urged the creation of mandalas and works of art on the models of those that he had brought back from China. He is also credited (but without certainty) with invention of the kana syllabary. An eminent architect, painter, sculptor, and calligrapher, he compiled the oldest dictionary in Japan, *Tenrai banshō myōgi,* and founded a school (Shugei Shuchi-in in Kyoto) open to all without regard for class. He is generally considered the father of classic Japanese culture. He was posthumously given the title Kōbō Daishi in 911. Also called Daishi Ō-Daishi-sama.

Kūki-enkin. In Japanese painting, concept of the "aerial perspective" in which objects that are farther away are painted higher on the pictorial plane and in soft tones.

Kuki Shūzō. Philosopher (1888–1941), born in Tokyo. He went to Europe in 1922 and studied under Henri Bergson and Martin Heidegger; in 1929, he obtained a philosophy chair at the University of Kyoto. His most famous works, *Iki no kōzō* (The Structure of the Iki, 1930) and *Gūzensei no mondai* (The Problem of the Accidental, 1935), show an "aesthetic" approach to existentialism.

Kuki Yoshitaka. Admiral (1542–1600) from Shima province, serving the Kitabatake clan and then Oda Nobunaga. As commander of Nobunaga's fleet, he led the blockade of Ishiyama-dera that enabled the military dictator to conquer the Hongan-ji and the Ikkō-ikki. When Nobunaga died, Kuki Yoshitaka entered the service of Toyotomi Hideyoshi and commanded the invading fleets that Hideyoshi sent to Korea in 1592 and 1597; he was also involved in the expeditions to Kyushu and Shikoku. During the Battle of Sekigahara (1600), he chose to remain neutral, thus coming into conflict with his son, Kuki Moritaka, who had taken Tokugawa Ieyasu's side. After Ieyasu's victory, Yoshitaka committed suicide, even though Ieyasu had pardoned him.

Kumadori. Painting technique using two paintbrushes at a time, one depositing the color, the other making the gradations or shadings.
  • A sort of makeup used by Kabuki actors, designating a mask with a number of colors: red, blue, green, black, and gray.

Kumagai Naoyoshi. *Waka* poet (1782–1862), born in Suō province (Yamaguchi prefecture). Kagawa Kageki's student, he went to Osaka, where he taught poetry. His main work, the *Ryōjin kōshō* (1860), developed Kageki's theories on poetry.

Kumagai Naozane. Warrior (1141–1208), who fought at Minamoto no Yoritomo's side at the Battle of Ichinotani in 1184. He was then Hōnen's disciple and became a Buddhist monk with the name Renshō in 1192. His life, parts of which were featured in the *Heike monogatari,* was the subject of Noh plays *(Atsumori)* and Kabuki plays *(Ichinotani Futaba Gunki). See* KUMAGAYA.

Kumagai Taizō. Physician (1880–1962) born in Nagano prefecture, who was known for his research on tuberculosis. He was president of Tōhoku University, became a member of the Japan Academy (Nihon Gakushi-in) in 1943, and received the Order of Culture (Bunka-shō) in 1952.

Kumagaya. City in Saitama prefecture, on the Arakawa river, former waystation *(shuku-eki)* on the Nakasendō route in the Edo period. It has two famous fan *(uchiwa)* festivals: in the Yasaka Shinto shrine in July, and in Ebisu in November. Yūkoku-ji Buddhist temple founded, according to tradition, by Kumagai Naozane. *Pop.:* 150,000.

Kumai Kei. Movie director (b. 1930), who directed realist, documentary-style films for the Nikkatsu studios—*Shinobu kawa* (The Long Darkness, 1972) and *Sandakan hachiban shōkan: bōkyō* (San-

dakan no. 8, Bordello no. 8, 1974)—which won many awards. He also directed, in the latter film, actress Tanaka Kinuyo, hailed as the best actress of the year at the Berlin Festival. In 1989, he directed *The Death of a Tea Master,* in which Mifune Toshiro played Sen no Rikyū.

Kumamoto. Main city in Kumamoto prefecture, Kyushu. It began to develop in 1600 around the castle built by Katō Kiyomasa (destroyed by fire in 1877 and rebuilt). The city has textile and electrical industries and is a major transportation hub (railroad, airport). It contains the tombs of Hosokawa Gracia and Miyamoto Musashi and a major art museum, designed by Maekawa Kunio, that opened in 1976. *Pop.:* 500,000.

  • **Kumamoto prefecture.** Kumamoto prefecture in southern Kyushu, south of Nagasaki prefecture, bordering the Shimabara and Yatsuhiro seas, and including the Amakusa Islands. It is essentially agricultural and tourist-oriented (Mt. Aso National Park). *Main city:* Kumamoto; *major cities:* Yatsushiro, Tamana, Hitoyoshi, Uto, Hondo, Arao. *Area:* 7,400 km². *Pop.:* 1.8 million.

  • **Kumamoto Yōgakkō.** School created in 1871 in Kumamoto to teach Western sciences to young people from the samurai class. The professors were foreigners, and instruction was given in English. Christianity was also taught, but because this displeased the authorities, the school was closed in 1877.

Kumano Hayatama-taisha. Shinto shrine located in Shingū (Wakayama prefecture), dedicated to the *kami* Kumano Hatayama, Kumano Fusumi, and Ketsumiko. Reconstructed in 1894; small museum.

  • **Kumano Hongū-taisha.** Shinto shrine founded in the eighth century (?) and dedicated to the *kami* Ketsumiko (Susanoo no Mikoto).

  • *Kumano honji emaki.* Group of three illuminated scrolls describing the shrines of Kumano and discovered recently (1986) in the Itsuō museum in Osaka. The partially damaged scrolls, about 26.6 m long, comprise 15 series of colored illustrations.

  • **Kumano Nachi-taisha.** Shinto shrine founded in Nachi Katsura, dedicated to the *kami* Kumano Fusumi. Three shrines (Hayatama, Hongū, and Nachi), collectively called Kumano Sansha, were the seat of a major syncretic Shinto-Buddhist (Honji-suijaku) movement in which the *kami* of

Kumano were considered *gongen,* or manifestations of Amida Buddha. These shrines were also very popular among followers *(yamabushi)* of the Shūgendō and became destinations for numerous pilgrimages.

Kumasaka. Title of a Noh play: an itinerant Buddhist monk meets another monk who invites him home to pray for the soul of a deceased person. The monk discovers that his host's house is full of weapons. Suddenly, the house disappears and he finds himself sleeping under a tree. Then the monk who had issued the invitation comes and reveals that he is the spirit of Kumasaka, a bandit killed at this site by Minamoto no Yoshitsune.

Kumashiro Tatsumi. Movie producer (1927–95) born in Saga prefecture. He worked for the Shochiku studios, then for Nikkatsu. As a director, he was not very successful, so he produced television series. He then produced pornographic films for Nikkatsu, such as *Nureta kuchibiru* (Moist Lips), *Ichiji Sayume, nureta yokujo* (Sayumi the Striptease Artist, Moist Desire), *Kagi* (The Key, 1974), *Akasen tamanoi nukereremasu* (Street of Joy, 1974), *Bō no kanashimi* (The Sadness of a Stick). One of his greatest successes was *Yojōhan fusuma no urabari* (The Fusuma in the Four-and-a-Half-Tatami Room, 1973), which was hailed as a masterpiece by Japanese critics.

Kumashiro Yūhi. Painter (Kumashiro Hi; *azana:* Kitan; *gō:* Shūkō, Yūhi, 1713–72) of the Yōga school in Nagasaki, Shen Nampin's student. His works, directly copying nature, were brightly colored. His students included Mori Ransei (d. 1801) and Kakutei (d. 1785).

Kumaso. Ancient tribes in central and southern Kyushu, perhaps of Malaysian or Malayo-Polynesian origin, whom certain authors assimilate with the Hayato. They would have been defeated in the fourth century by Prince Yamato Takeru and conquered by Jingū Kōgō. *See* KOROPOKGURU.

Kumazawa Banzan. Confucian scholar (Kumazawa Ryōkai, Nojiri Jirōhachi, 1619–91), born in Kyoto and son of a *rōnin,* serving Ikeda Mitsumasa (1609–82), daimyo of Bizen province from 1634 to 1639. He studied Wang Yangming's *(Jap.:* Ō-Yōmei) Confucianism under Nakae Tōju (1608–48), then returned to the service of the Ikeda clan until 1656. He then left Kyoto and led an itinerant life while writing philosophy and economics works

—*Shūgi washo, Shūgi gaisho, Daigaku wakomon* (Questions About the Great Study of Confucius)— and commentaries on the Confucian classics and the *Genji monogatari.* His philosophy had some influence on the *kogaku* (ancient studies) in favor in the early eighteenth century. He was imprisoned in 1685 for criticizing the shogunal administration but was freed soon after and placed under house arrest in Koga, Shimōsa province, where he died.

Kume Keiichirō. Painter (1866–1934) who studied in France and Italy and who was Raphael Collin's student. When he returned to Japan, he founded the Hakuba-kai art society. *See* OKADA SABURŌSUKE.

Kume Kunitake. Writer and historian (1838–1931), born in Saga province. In 1871, he went to Europe and the United States with Iwakura Tomomi's delegation, for which he was the secretary. He wrote the report for the delegation, titled *Tokumei zenken taishi: Beiō kairan jikki* (1878), then contributed to various histories and encyclopedias. Because he had openly criticized Shinto, he was forced to resign from his professorship at the University of Kyoto. He then taught at Semmon Gakkō University (Waseda).

Kume Masao. Writer (1891–1952), born in Nagano prefecture. A successful playwright, he began to write novels, influenced by his friends Kikuchi Kan and Akutagawa Ryūnosuke: *Ten to chi to, hotarugusa* (1918), *Hasen* (1922), *Tsuki yori no shisha* (1933).

Kumi. "Neighborly relations," a very important concept in the villages, especially in the Edo period, according to which families formed groups to do farmwork and to provide mutual assistance and help. This concept remains alive today, underlying a number of typically Japanese behaviors. *Kumi* had various names, depending on the region: *kaito, keiyaku, tsubo,* and so on. During the Second World War, the *kumi* were reorganized and called *tonari-gumi* and *impohan.* In composite words, *-gumi. See also* GO-NIN GUMI.
→ *See* HIKESHI, MACHI-YAKKO.

• **Kumi-gashira.** "Group leader," a military function designating the officer commanding a group of either foot soldiers *(ashigaru)* or fusiliers *(teppō-gumi).* In the Edo period, the title also designated the officer commanding the shogunal palace guard. It was also given to representatives of groups *(kumi)* of five families *(gonin-gumi)* or ten families *(jūnin-*

gumi), who were responsible to the authorities for the behavior of the families they led. This term also designates any group leader in a plant, an association, or a guild.

• **Kumi-uchi.** *See* JŪ-JUTSU.

• **Kumi-uta.** *See* JI-UTA.

Kumihimo. Ribbons or bands of silk woven on the bias, used to make cords and laces for armor, banners, bandoliers, and so on, a technique known since at least the eighth century (some examples are in the Shōsō-in in Nara). In the Nara and Heian periods, *kumihimo* called *hirao,* 2 m long and about 9 cm wide, were worn by bureaucrats in the court, in various colors to indicate their rank.

Kumo-gata. "Cloud-shaped," a pictorial technique consisting of portraying fog or clouds to separate various scenes in a landscape and leave room for the imagination. This technique was used mainly on fusuma and screens *(byōbu),* as well as on *kakemono.* It is sort of a concretization of the concept of *ma* in art.

Kumoi Tatsuo. Politician (Kojima Moriyoshi, 1844–70) and samurai of the Yonezawa estate (Yamagata prefecture). After 1868, he became a bureaucrat in the Meiji government in Kyoto, but resigned to form a league of malcontents. Suspected of trying to assassinate senior bureaucrats and of plotting the restoration of the shogunate, he was arrested and executed.

Kumon. "Documents." At first, *kumon* were registers of taxes and other archives, but during the Heian and Kamakura periods, the term designated bureaucrats responsible for writing the official documents of the noble houses and monasteries.

• **Kumonjo.** Department of archives of the Kamakura *bakufu,* in operation from 1184 to 1191. It was absorbed into the Mandokoro in 1192. The first director of the Kumonjo was Ōe no Hiromoto.

Kumo-to. In traditional architecture, a *to* (dado) sculpted in the shape of a cloud, in Chinese style, typical of the Asuka period. *See* TO-KYŌ.

Kun. Japanese pronunciation (Yamato language) of Chinese characters *(kanji). See also* KANJI, ON.

• **Kundoku.** Chinese characters *(kanji)* used only for their meaning, but read in Japanese fashion *(kun).* Thus, for instance, the Chinese character for "mountain" would be pronounced "san" in *kan-on,* but "yama" in *kun.*

Kunaichō. "Imperial Household Agency," responsible for the staff around the emperor and his family, for ceremonies, and for everything to do with the imperial house *(kōshitsu).* In 1947, it replaced the old Kunaishō (Ministry of the Imperial House). Its director *(chōkan)* is appointed directly by the prime minister.

• **Kunaishō.** Department of the imperial government directed, after 645, by a minister charged with collecting taxes on imperial estates. It then became a particular ministry charged with everything concerning the imperial family. Replaced in 1947 by the Kunaichō. Also called Miya no Uchi no Tsukusa. *See* JINGI-SHŌ, KAMON, KANIMORI NO TSUKASA.

Kuni. From the third to the seventh century, "states" or "kingdoms," or groups of villages directed by a clan leader *(miyatsuko, kimi).* This term *(Chin.: guo)* was later applied to the provinces of Japan.
   • Town in Yamashiro province that was the temporary capital of Yamato from 765 to 770, during the reign of Empress Shōtoku.
→ *See* CHIKUDEN, KOKUGUN.

• **Kuni-bugyō.** A sort of military judge appointed at the head of each province by Minamoto no Yoritomo in 1184 to assist the *shugo.* Also called *zatsumu-bugyō.*

• **Kuni-gae.** In the Edo period, transfer of daimyo from one province to another in order to avoid abuses of power.

• **Kuni-ikki.** Popular uprisings that took place throughout the Muromachi period, led by provincial warriors *(kokujin)* and local landowners who wanted to oust the provincial *shugo* and take over. *See* IKKI.

• **Kuni-kyō.** Capital of Emperor Shōmu, built in 740 on the Izumi-gawa river by Tachibana no Moroe (684–757) and abandoned in 744. Also called Kuni no Miyako.

• **Kuni no Miyatsuko.** Local chiefs who governed small territories under the control of the Yamato court in the sixth and seventh centuries. They were also administrators *(agatanushi)*. They had the titles *ōmi, kimi,* and *atae.* Starting in 645 (Taika Reform), they were called Kuni no Mikotomochi, or *kokushi.* Later, the title Kuni no Miyatsuko was reserved for leaders of provincial Shinto shrines *(kuni),* also called Shin Kokuzō.

Kun-i. Ranks of nobility attributed not by birth but by merit. From 702 to 1875, there were 12 *kuni-i* ranks; later, this number was reduced to 8. *See* I.

Kunihiro. Sword maker (Horikawa Kunihiro, 1531–1614), founder of the Horikawa-ryū school and creator of the *shin-tō* sword style in Hyūga and Kyoto.

Kunikida Doppo. Writer and poet (Kunikida Tetsuo, 1871–1908), born in Chiba prefecture. He studied English literature at the Tokyo Semmon Gakkō (Waseda), then converted to Christianity. As a journalist at the *Kokumin Shimbun,* he was a war correspondent in China in 1894–95. After an unhappy marriage, he began to write in a naturalist and romantic style, influenced by Maupassant's works. His literary career is divided into three periods. In the first (1897–1901), he was romantic in spirit and wrote mainly stories, among them *Gen oji* (Uncle Gen, 1897), *Musashino* (1898), and *Kawagiri* (River Mist, 1898). In the second (1901–04), his works were more realistic, with *Gyūniku to bareisho* (Meat and Potatoes, 1901), *Ummei ronja* (The Fatalist, 1903), *Haru no tori* (Spring Birds, 1904). The third period was fully naturalistic: *Kyūshi* (Death of a Poor Man, 1907) and *Take no kido* (The Bamboo Gate, 1908). He also wrote poems in which he celebrated his love of nature. He died of tuberculosis in 1908.

Kunimaru. Painter (Utagawa Kunimaru; *mei:* Iseya Ihachi; *gō:* Ichi-ensai, Gosairō, Honchōan, Keiuntei, Saikarō, Kunimaru, 1794–1830) of ukiyo-e prints, Toyokuni's student. He painted mainly portraits of Kabuki actors in Edo, and he was an excellent *haikai* poet.

Kunimasa. Painter (Utagawa Kunimasa; *mei:* Jinsuke; *gō:* Ichijūsai, 1773–1810) of ukiyo-e prints, Toyokuni's student. He produced portraits of Kabuki actors in Edo.
→ *See* TOYOKUNI I.

Kuni Nagako. Empress Dowager (b. Mar. 6, 1903), Prince Kuni Kuniyoshi's daughter, who married Crown Prince Hirohito (Shōwa Tennō) in January 1924. She went to the Peers' School for young women and studied music and painting. She is also an excellent poet and calligrapher. Because she is from a family descended from the Shimazu, former daimyo of Satsuma, her marriage to Prince Hirohito caused some opposition among senior dignitaries from the Chōshū, such as Yamagata Aritomo. She had six children: Prince Hitachi, Prince Akihito (who became emperor in 1989), and four daughters. Also called Kuninomiya Nagako. *See* HIROHITO.

Kuninaka no Muraji Kimimaro. Sculptor (?–774) from Korea, who directed the casting of the statue of the Daibutsu in the Tōdai-ji in Nara from 749 to 752, and who was responsible for construction of the Tōdai-ji temple in 761. He apparently retired from public life in 767.

Kuninao. Painter (Utagawa Kuninao; *mei:* Taizō; *gō:* Ukiyo-an, Ichi-ensai, Dokushuisha, Enryūrō, Shashinsai, 1793–1854) of ukiyo-e prints, Toyokuni's student. He imitated Hokusai's technique.

Kuninori. Imperial prince (b. 1867), Prince Kuni Asahiko's (1824–91) second son. He became head of the Ise shrines, with the title Kayo no Miya, in 1890.

Kunisada. Painter (Tsunoda Kunisada; *mei:* Shōzō; *gō:* Utagawa Kunisada, Utagawa Toyokuni III, Ichiyūsai, Gotoei, Kōchirō, Kinraisha, Gepparō, Ichiyōsai, 1786–1864) of ukiyo-e prints, Toyokuni's student. His prints were influenced by the art of Itchō and Ikkei. He illustrated books and made portraits of beautiful women *(bijin)* and of Kabuki actors in Edo.
→ *See* SHINKAI.

Kunitomo. Famous sword maker (Awataguchi Kunitomo, 1146–1214) from Yamashiro. *See* AWATAGUCHI.
→ *See* HIRAGA GENNAI.

• **Kunitomo Teppō-kaji.** *See* KUNITOMO TŌBEI.

• **Kunitomo Tōbei.** Famous maker of firearms *(teppō,* harquebuses) and engineer (1778–1840) from a family of artisans and artillerymen in the village of Kunitomo, Ōmi province, working for the Edo shogunate. In 1819, he made a compressed-air pistol on a Dutch model, and he produced a reflector telescope in 1837. A talented inventor, he also created a pocket fountain-pen, a bronze cross-bow, and a water pump, and made observations of sunspots. Popularly known as Kunitomo Teppō-kaji.

• **Kunitsuna.** Sword maker (Awataguchi Tōro-kurō, 1163–1255) in Sagami. *See* AWATAGUCHI.

• **Kuniyasu.** Sword maker (Awataguchi Kuniyasu, active ca. 1200) in Yamashiro. *See* AWATAGUCHI.

Kuniyoshi. Painter (Igusa Kuniyoshi; *mei:* Mago-saburō, Tarōemon; *gō:* Utagawa Kuniyoshi, Ichi-yūsai, Chōōrō, 1797–1861) of ukiyo-e prints, Toyokuni's student. He painted portraits of Kabuki actors and samurai, landscapes influenced by West-ern engraving techniques, and fish. He also tried his hand at caricature and designed many tattoos.
→ *See* TOYOKUNI I.

Kuniyoshi Yasuo. Painter (1893–1953), born in Okayama. He lived in New York and Los Angeles, where he studied painting, and his works were ex-hibited at the Museum of Modern Art for the first time in 1929. His paintings, of natural subjects, show a great concern with detail. He lived most of his life in the United States and died in New York.

Kuno Yasushi. Physician (1882–1977) born in Aichi prefecture. A specialist in respiratory prob-lems, he taught at the University of Nagoya. His work earned him the prize of the Japan Academy (Nihon Gakushi-in) in 1941 and the Order of Cul-ture (Bunka-shō) in 1963.

Kunrei. Former system of romanization of Japa-nese, now replaced by the Hepburn system, which is used in this book.

Kunshō. Orders of "chivalry," the highest honor-ific distinctions conferred on people of eminent merit. There are seven orders:
   1) **Kikuka-shō,** of the Chrysanthemum
   2) **Tōka-shō,** of the Paulownia
   3) **Kyokujitsu-shō,** of the Rising Sun
   4) **Zuihō-shō,** of the Sacred Treasure
   5) **Hōkan-shō,** of the Crown
   6) **Kinshi-shō,** of the Golden Falcon
   7) **Bunka-shō** (or **Bunka-kunshō**), of Culture (since 1937)
→ *See* BAIKUN JIKEN, KINRYŌ.

Kuon-ji. *See* MINOBU-SAN.

Kura. Storehouses with thick earthen walls faced with tiles, used to hold a family's treasures and safe-guard them from thieves and fires.

• **Kura-bugyō.** Tax collector for the Kamakura shogunate. In the Edo period, the title of a bureau-crat responsible for distributing salaries and in-specting rice *(kuramai)* reserves in shogunal or urban warehouses *(kurayashiki)*. Also called *kuramoto.*

Kurahara Korehito. Writer (1902–91), born in To-kyo, specializing in Russian literature, which he studied in Russia. He was a member of the proletar-ian-literature movement, then joined the Commu-nist party, publishing Marxist magazines, which earned him long stretches in prison between 1930 and 1940. After the Second World War, he again be-came politically active within the Japanese Commu-nist party.

Kurahashi Yumiko. Novelist born 1935 in Kōchi prefecture. Her novels seem to have been influenced by those by Franz Kafka and other European au-thors: *Parutai* (The Party, 1960), *Kon'yaku* (The Engagement, 1961), *Kurai tabi* (Dark Journey, 1961), *Sumiyakisuto Q no bōken* (The Adventures of Sumiyakist Q, 1969), *Yume no ukihashi* (The Bridge of Dreams, 1971), *Hanhigeki* (Anti-Trag-edies, 1971).

Kurama-dera. Buddhist temple founded on the slopes of Mt. Kurama (*alt.:* 570 m), north of Kyoto, in 796 by the monk Kantei Shōnin; Minamoto no Yoshitsune was brought up there. This temple was reconstructed in 1872. Every January it celebrates a "festival of torches" *(hi-matsuri)* that draws large crowds.

• *Kurama tengu.* Title of a Noh play: the young Ushiwaka (Minamoto no Yoshitsune) meets some *tengu* on Mt. Kurama, near Tokyo, who teach him the arts of war.
→ *See* OSARAGI JIRŌ.

Kuramoto. *See* KURA-BUGYŌ.

Kurashiki. City in Okayama prefecture, large com-mercial center and river port in the Edo period. In-dustrial center: textiles, metallurgy (uranite mines), and petrochemicals. The district on the bank of the Kurashiki-gawa river is famous for its many houses belonging to samurai and wealthy merchants from the Edo period. Museums of art (Ohara Museum), archeology, and crafts. *Pop.:* 410,000.

Kurata Hakuyō. Painter (Kurata Shigeyoshi; *gō:* Hakuyō, 1881–1938) in the Western style, Asai Chū's student. He specialized in landscapes.

Kurata Hyakuzō. Writer and playwright (1891–1943), born in Hiroshima prefecture, Nishida Kitarō's disciple. He wrote mainly religious plays, such as *Shukke to sono deshi* (The Priest and His Disciples, 1916) and *Ai to ninshiki to no shuppatsu* (The Beginning of Love and Comprehension, 1922), heavily imbued with both Buddhism and Christianity.

Kuratsukuribe no Tori. Famous sculptor (early seventh century) of Chinese origin, son of sculptor Kuratsukuribe no Tasuna, who settled in Nara. He worked for the Yamato court and made a large statue of the Buddha Shakyamuni (*Jap.:* Shaka) for the Asuka-dera temple on the order of Shōtoku Taishi in 606. He also made the large Shaka triad at the Hōryū-ji temple, which he dedicated to the memory of Shōtoku Taishi and Empress Suiko in 623. His art was greatly influenced by the Northern Wei of China. *See* BE.

Kure. City in Hiroshima prefecture, located at the entrance to the bay; its excellent natural port served as a naval base until the end of the Second World War. It has a naval school, dockyards, shipyards, and museum of marine history. *Pop.:* 250,000. *See* HIROSHIMA.

Kure Ken. Physician (1883–1940) born in Kyoto, internationally known for his studies on the nervous and parasympathetic systems. He received the prize of the Japan Academy (Nihon Gakushi-in) in 1939.

Kuribayashi Tadamichi. Lieutenant-general and head of the Imperial Guard who defended Iō-jima (Iwo Jima) against American attacks in 1944–45. He committed suicide with the last defenders of the island on March 10, 1945.

Kurihama. Port on the coast of Kanagawa prefecture, near Yokosuka, where Commodore Perry landed in 1853. This event is celebrated every July 14 at the Kurofune Matsuri (Festival of Black Boats). *See* URAGA.

Kurikara-dani. Site of a battle that took place in 1183 between the Taira and Minamoto armies in the Tonamiyama mountains, at the Kurikara pass between Etchū and Kaga provinces. Minamoto no Yoshinaka drove before him herds of cattle with torches attached to their horns; this panicked the Taira ranks, providing Yoshinaka with an easy victory, even though the Taira had numerical superiority. The ruse enabled Yoshinaka to enter Kyoto unencumbered.

Kuriki Tatsusuke. Contemporary ceramist, born 1943 in Seto (Aichi prefecture). His porcelain pieces are very popular both in Japan and abroad (Mons Art Museum, Belgium, 1989).

Kuril Islands. Volcanic archipelago that belonged to Japan until 1945 (Chishima Rettō; *Rus.:* Kurilskiye Ostrova), separating the Sea of Okhotsk from the Pacific Ocean and linking the Kamchatka Peninsula to the eastern tip of Hokkaido. It is bordered to the east by an ocean trench 10,542 m deep. The islands were discovered by Martin de Vries in 1634 and conquered by Japan in 1875. The archipelago comprises 32 islands with a total area of 15,652 km². Its highest peak is on the island of Araito (*Rus.:* Alaid), *alt.:* 2,240 m. Humid climate, cold in winter. The islands' soil is not arable; there are several mines (sulfur, copper, iron, gold) that are not actively operated. The population of about 20,000 (Japanese, Russians, Ainu) are mostly fishers (salmon) and hunters. Only the southernmost islands have some agriculture. The largest islands are, from north to south, Shumushu (*Rus.:* Shumshu), Araito (*Rus.:* Alaid), Paramushiro (*Rus.:* Paramushir), Onnekotan (*Rus.:* Onekotan), Harimukotan, Shashikotan (*Rus.:* Shiashkotan), Matsuwa (*Rus.:* Matua), Rashowa (*Rus.:* Rauke, Raseva), Ketoi, Shinshiru or Shimushiri (*Rus.:* Simusir), Uruppu (*Rus.:* Urup), Etorofu (*Rus.:* Iturup), Kunashiri (*Rus.:* Kunashir), Shikotan, and the Habomai islands. *See also* CHISHIMA, OYASHIO.

Kurimoto Joun. Senior bureaucrat (Kurimoto Kon, Kurimoto Hōan, 1822–97) of the Edo shogunate, commissioner of the navy and of foreign affairs. He went to the Paris World's Fair in 1867 with shogun Tokugawa Yoshinobu's brother, Tokugawa Akitane. In 1872, he joined the editorial team of the *Yokohama Mainichi Shimbun,* and he was editor-in-chief of the *Yūbin Hōchi Shimbun* in 1873. He also used the *gō* Hōan.

Kūrin. In Buddhist architecture, the middle part of a *sōrin,* a mast bearing 9 to 11 bronze rings surmounting the roof. *Kūrin* (also called *kyūrin*) are reminiscent of the *chattra* surmounting *stūpa* in India. On certain Buddhist buildings, this name is given to a type of finial in the shape of a *gorin. See* GORIN, ISHIDŌRŌ, SŌRIN.

Kurino Shin'ichirō. Diplomat (1851–1937). He was ambassador to Washington (1894–96), Rome (1896), Paris (1897–1901), St. Petersburg (1901–04), and Paris again (1906–12).

Kurishima Sumiko. Stage and movie actress (b. 1902) who appeared in many films directed by her husband, Ikeda Yoshinobu, for the Shōchiku studios. She also directed the Mizuki school of traditional dance.

Kurisu Hiroomi. General (b. 1920), chairman of the board of the Self-Defense Forces (Jieitai) in 1977. He was forced to resign from this position in 1978 after criticizing civil control of the army.

Kurita Kan. Confucian philosopher and historian (Kurita Hiroshi, 1835–99) of the Mito school. He wrote historical works, including *Hyōchū kofudoki*, *Shiryō taikan* (a collection of 62 essays, 1868), *Shōen kō*, and other works.

Kuriyagawa Hakuson. Writer and literary critic (Kuriyagawa Tatsuo, 1880–1923), born in Kyoto. His best-known works are *Kindai bungaku jukkō* (Ten Aspects of Modern Literature, 1912) and *Kindai no ren'aikan* (Modern Views of Love, 1921).

Kuriyama Sempō. Confucian historian (Kuriyama Gen, 1671–1706) of the Mito school, Yamazaki Ansai's disciple. He was appointed head of the Shōkōkan in Edo, where he helped to compile a major history of Japan, *Dai Nihon shi*.

Kuri Yōji. Cartoon director (b. 1928), maker of more than 500 films noted for their strange, sometimes erotic, content. Among the best known are *Locus* (1963), *Samurai* (1965), *Sadono tamago* (The Eggs, 1966), *Kemeko* (1968), *Pop* (1970), *Imus* (1973), *Manga* (1977), and *Shometsu* (1978).

Kuroda Aki. Contemporary painter, living and working in France. He has had many exhibitions, starting in 1976; since 1984, he has been represented by the Maeght Gallery. He had an exhibition at the Grand Palais, Paris (1978), and his work has been shown in many galleries and museums in the West and in Japan. He also founded an art magazine, *Noise,* which received the Vasary Prize for best art magazine, and created sets for the Opéra de Paris and the Papal Palace in Avignon (1993).

Kuroda Kiyotaka. Politician (1840–1900), born in Kagoshima. In 1868, he was appointed assistant manager *(kaitakushi)* of the Hokkaido Colonization Bureau (Hokkaidō Kaitakuschi) and was one of the initiators of the St. Petersburg Treaty (1875), which gave Japan the Kuril Islands in exchange for the island of Sakhalin. He reorganized agriculture on Hokkaido by creating *tondenhei* (militias of peasant-soldiers). In 1877, he commanded the imperial troops in battle against the Satsuma. Appointed minister of agriculture in 1977 in Itō Hirobumi's first cabinet, he succeeded Itō as prime minister the following year; General Yamagata succeeded him in 1889. He was minister of communications in Itō Hirobumi's second cabinet in 1892, then chairman of the Privy Council in 1895.

Kuroda Kiyoteru. Painter (Kuroda Seiki; *gō*: Seiki, 1866–1924) from Satsuma. He studied in France and Italy and was Raphael Collin's student. He was the first artist in Japan to produce oil paintings of nude women. In 1910, he was appointed an Artist for the Imperial House (Teishitsu Gigei-in); in 1922, he was elected president of the Imperial Fine Arts Academy (Teikoku Bijutsu-in). He became a member of the House of Peers in 1920. *See* HAKUBAKAI.

Kuroda Mototaka. Warrior (1524–85) serving Oda Nobunaga. He became a Buddhist monk with the name Sōen. Kuroda Yoshitaka's father.

• **Kuroda Nagamasa.** Warrior and daimyo (1568–1623), Kuroda Yoshitaka's son. He succeeded his father in his Bizen estate and served Toyotomi Hideyoshi, notably in the Battle of Shizugatake (1583) and the invasion of Korea (1592–97). He then went over to Tokugawa Ieyasu's side and seconded him at the Battle of Sekigahara (1600), which earned him an estate worth 523,000 *koku* in Fukuoka. He converted to Christianity with the name Damien, but later abandoned Christianity. He also fought at Ieyasu's side at the siege of the Osaka castle (1615).

• **Kuroda Yoshitaka.** Warrior (Kuroda Josui, Kodera Kambyōe, 1546–1604), Kuroda Mototaka's son. He became a Christian, with the name Siméon Condera, in 1583. He fought on Kyushu at Tokugawa Ieyasu's side and was rewarded with a fief worth 120,000 *koku* in Bizen province. He retired in 1589 and gave his estate to his son, Kuroda Nagamasa.

Kurodani Kōmyō-ji. Buddhist temple belonging to the Jōdo-shū, founded about 1212 by Hōnen in Kyoto. It has a three-story pagoda *(sanju no tō)* dating from 1710 and a statue portraying Monju Bosatsu, attributed to Unkei. This temple is the headquarters of the Kurodani Jōdo subsect, with about 350,000 followers.

Kurōdo. In ancient Japan, archivists responsible for transcribing imperial decrees. Also called *kurando*.

• **Kurōdo-dokoro.** Bureau of Archivists, established by Emperor Saga in 810. The bureaucrats *(kurōdo)* in this bureau gradually acquired great political influence at the court and were behind the rise to power of the Fujiwara. Starting in 897, they were directed by a *bettō*. Retired emperors and the Fujiwara also established *kurōdo-dokoro* for their own purposes. *See* MANDOKORO.

Kurofune. "Black boats," a term for foreign sailing ships and steamships that appeared off the Japanese coast in the Edo period, starting in 1853, and particularly the warships in Commodore Perry's fleet, which had their hulls painted black.

• **Kurofune Matsuri.** Folk festival celebrated every April 10 to commemorate the arrival of Commodore Perry's ships at Shimoda in 1853. A similar festival, celebrated July 14, takes place in Kurihama. *See also* URAGA.

Kurogo. In a Kabuki play, the assistant who is on stage, wearing black clothing and a hood, to help the actors and move the props. He is in his turn assisted by a man who does not wear a mask, called a *kōken*. Also called *kurombo*.

Kurohon. "Black books." Popular works in the *kusazōshi* genre, most of them warrior stories, published in the eighteenth century. *See* KUSAZŌSHI.

Kuroi Senji. Writer (Osabe Shunjirō), born 1932 in Tokyo. A factory worker, he described people's alienation from machinery in his novels: *Mekanisumu no. 1* (Mechanism no. 1, 1958), *Jikan* (1969), and *Hashiru kazoku* (1971).

Kuroita Katsumi. Historian (1874–1946), born in Nagasaki prefecture. A bureaucrat in the Ministry of Education, he sponsored major historical publications and worked to protect monuments and an-

cient sites. He was also among the first to teach Esperanto in Japan.

Kuroiwa Jūgo. Writer, born 1924 in Osaka. His novel *Haitoku no mesu* (1960) won the Naoki Prize. Among his other works: *Hadaka no haitokusha* (1965), *Maboroshi-e no shissō* (1975), *Kuroi yuki* (Black Snow, 1978).

Kuroiwa Ruikō. Writer and journalist (Kuroiwa Shūroku, 1862–1920), born in Kōchi prefecture. He edited a number of literary publications, wrote successful novels, and translated Victor Hugo's *Les Misérables* (*Aa mujō*, 1902–03) and Alexandre Dumas's *The Count of Monte Cristo* (*Gankutsuō*, 1901–02).

Kurokawa Kishō. Architect, born 1934 in Aichi prefecture. A student of Tange Kenzō, he was part of the "metabolism" group and opened his own architecture practice in 1962. Among his most remarkable designs are various pavilions for the Osaka World Fair (1970) and the Sony skyscraper in Osaka (1976).

Kurokawa Oriaki. Architect, born 1934 in Nagoya. Among the many buildings he has designed are the Yamagata Cultural Center, the Goshikidai holiday resort (1967), the Nitto plant, and the Aichi Social Center (1967).

Kurokawa Toshio. Physician (1897–1988), born in Hokkaido, author of several books on the organs in the digestive system. He was decorated with the Order of Culture (Bunka-shō) in 1968.

Kuroki Tametomo. General (Kuroki Tamesada, 1844–1923), born in Satsuma, died in Tokyo. He commanded the Japanese troops in China (1895) and Korea (on the Yalu against the Russians in 1904–95). Appointed a member of the Senior War Council in 1904, he was ennobled with the title of count.

Kuromaku. Traders with great financial power who influenced government policy after the Second World War. Among the best known are Kodama Yoshio (implicated in the Lockheed scandal in 1976) and Sasakawa Ryōichi.

Kurosawa Akira. Movie director, born 1910 in Tokyo. He began his career with *Sugata Sanshirō* (1943), a film on judo, and went on to make *Tora no oo fumu otokotachi* (The Man Who Walked on the Tiger's Tail, 1945), based on the Kabuki play *Kanjinchō*; *Waga seishun ni kui nashi* (No Regrets for Our Youth, 1946); and *Yoidore tenshi* (The Drunken Angels, 1948), featuring actor Mifune Toshirō. His best-known films are *Norainu* (Mad Dog, 1949); *Rashōmon* (1950); *Ikiru* (Living, 1952); *Shichinin no samurai* (The Seven Samurai, 1954); *Kumonosujō* (The Hidden Fortress, 1957), an adaptation of *Macbeth*; *Yōjimbō* (The Bodyguard, 1961); *Tsubaki sanjūrō* (1962); *Tengoku to jigoku* (From Heaven to Hell, 1963); *Akohige* (Red Beard, 1965); *Tora, tora, tora* (which he wrote, directed by Richard Fleischer); *Dodesukaden* (1970); *Derusu uzāra* (1975); *Kagemusha* (The Shadow, 1980); *Ran* (Riot, 1986); *Yume* (Dreams, 1990); "Rhapsody in August" (presented at the Cannes Film Festival, 1991). These movies earned him an international reputation and the grand prize of the Venice Film Festival in 1951. Among his other movies are *Shizukanaru kettō* (The Quiet Duel, 1949), *Shūbun* (Scandal, 1950), *Hakuchi* (The Idiot, 1951), *Donzoko* (1957), *Warui yatsu hodo yoko nemuru* (The Evil Sleep Well, 1960). His movies have triumphed in many countries, although they are not always popular in Japan because they portray a historical reality that many modern Japanese prefer to forget.

Kurosawa Okinamaro. Writer (1795–1859), author of many children's stories, collected in *Dōwa chōhen*.

Kuroshima Denji. Writer (1898–1943). Sent to Siberia in 1919 and exempted from military service in 1921 because of illness, he began to write novels whose theme was the horror of war, such as *Sōri* (1927) and *Uzumakeru karasu no mure* (1928). A member of the proletarian-literature movement, he also wrote fiction on peasant life.

Kuroshio. "Black current," a warm current from the Philippines that flows by the east coast of Japan and the Kuril Islands. One of its branches flows through the Shimonoseki Strait and meets the cold current from the polar region in northern Japan (Oyashio), forming a region propitious to fish production. This current, with a temperature of 18°C to 27°C in summer, tempers Japan's climate. It is about 50–75 km wide, 500 m deep, and flows at a rate of about 5 knots. Sometimes written Kuroshivo.

Kuroyanagi Tetsuko. Television actress, born 1933 in Tokyo. She became famous when she wrote an autobiographical novel, *Madogiwa na totto-chan* (The Little Girl at the Window), which sold more than 6 million copies and was translated into a number of languages. She was Japan's ambassador to UNICEF in 1984 and created a foundation, Totto, to assist people with physical and hearing disabilities.

Kurozuka. Noh play: a Buddhist monk and his servants take shelter for the night with an old woman who is working at her spinning wheel. They soon discover that she is a cannibal ogress.

Kurozumi Munetada. Shinto priest (1780–1850), son of an Okayama priest. He had a dream linking him to the sun *kami* Amaterasu-Ōmikami, and in 1814 he founded a new Shinto sect, Kurozumi-kyō, which became one of the 13 official sects of Kyōha Shintō. It has about 250,000 followers, and its main shrine is in Okayama. Kurozumi Munetada wrote a group of letters and poems that comprise the sacred writings of the sect, the *Osadamegaki. Posthumous name:* Munetada Daimyōjin.

Kuruma zō. Title of a Noh play: a crafty, skillful *tengu* opposes a Buddhist monk, but must finally admit defeat.

Kurume-gasuri. Cotton fabric woven in the *kasuri* (ikat) technique, also called *arare-ori* and *shimofuri-ori*. It has been produced mainly in Kurume (Fukuoka prefecture, Kyushu) since 1800. It is often decorated with designs in indigo. *See* CHIKUGO, KASURI.

Kurusu Saburō. Diplomat (1886–1954), born in Kanagawa prefecture, ambassador to Germany in 1939, who signed the "tripartite pact" with Germany and Italy in 1940. A special envoy to Washington in 1941, he tried in vain, with ambassador Nomura Kichisaburō, to ease the growing tension between Japan and the United States. He returned to Japan in 1942 in an exchange of diplomats. He had married an American woman.

Kusado-sengen. Medieval village at the mouth of the Ashida-gawa river on the Inland Sea (Hiroshima prefecture), destroyed by a flood in 1673. The site, excavated superficially in 1928 and more intensively starting in 1961, shows that this village existed in the twelfth century. Many objects of daily life were uncovered, enabling study of village life at the time.

Kusaka Genzui. Samurai (1840–64) of the Chōshū clan, Yoshida Shōin's brother-in-law. In 1862, he left his estate to serve in the imperial troops; in 1863, with Takasugi Shinsaku, he set the British legation in Shinagawa on fire. Returning to Chōshū, he bombarded the European ships that were trying to force their way through the Shimonoseki Strait, then was involved in a number of actions against the Satsuma and Aizu armies. Wounded in battle, he committed suicide.

Kusama Naokata. Wealthy Osaka merchant (Kusama Isuke, 1753–1831) and famous numismatist, author of a major encyclopedia on Japanese currency from 1575 to 1800, *Sanka zui,* which took 30 years to complete and was published only in 1916. He also wrote other books devoted to utensils for the tea ceremony *(chanoyu)* and various essays on agrarian policy.

Kusano Shimpei. Poet (1903–88), born in Fukushima prefecture, whose works, influenced by the anarchist movement, were collected in *Teihon kaeru* (Things Seen by a Frog, 1948), which won the *Yomiuri* Prize. He also wrote two other poetry collections, *Daihyaku kaikyū* (1928) and *Fuji-san* (1943).

Kusaribane. Weapon used by certain schools of martial arts, derived from the sickle that Okinawa peasants used to defend themselves against samurai. It is a sickle with a long (2–3 m) iron chain ballasted with a lead or iron ball. The blade was used to cut horses' hocks; the chain, to disarm samurai. This weapon was also used by *ninja* and police forces in the Edo period. Its use is now taught in some martial-arts schools, such as Araki-ryū. A slightly different form, with a very short handle, is called *chigiriki.* Also called *kusarigama.*

Kusari-renga. "Linked *renga,*" type of poem in which long (17-syllable) and short (14-syllable) elements alternate. A variety of poets used this form, which appeared in the late Heian period. In the thirteenth century, it became the "normal" *renga* form.

Kusazōshi. Inexpensive illustrated books written mainly for women and children, later for all adults, published throughout the Edo period. These publications were known as *akahon, aohon, kurohon, gōkan,* and *kibyōshi,* depending on the color of their cover and their content. These works, whose name means "that which smells bad," owe their name to the poor quality of the ink used in printing

them, which had a tenacious odor. They were thin, composed of five double pages of about 19 x 13 cm, and had many illustrations, often woodblock prints *(ukiyo-e). See* AKAHON, AOHON, GŌKAN, KIBYŌSHI, KUROHON.

Kusazuri. In *yoroi* armor, the four-part chest plate covering the chest, the stomach, and the thighs.

Kuse-mai. Ancient dance of good augury *(see* KŌWAKA-MAI), with no musical accompaniment, performed by Shirabyōshi during Suraguku shows in the Kamakura period. This dance contributed to the creation of Noh theater. *See* KAN'AMI KIYOTSUGU.

Kusha-shū. Old Buddhist sect, based on the Sanskrit text *Abhidharmakosha (Jap.: Abidurama kusha-ron)* by the Indian philosopher Vasubandhu, introduced from China (where it had been called *Jushe)* by the monks Dōshō, Chitatsu, and Chitsū about 660. It was one of the "Six Sects of Nara" (Nanto-rokushū).

Kushibaru kaizuka. Site of a prehistoric *kaizuka* (shell mound) at Ie-son (Okinawa) whose layers date from the early Jōmon period to the late Yayoi period, showing that trade took place in these periods between the Ryukyu Islands and Kyushu.

Kushi Inada-hime. According to Shinto legend, a daughter of the chiefs of the Izumo region, Ashinazuchi and Tenazuchi; she married Susanoo after he was saved from a dragon. Also called Kushinadahime, Inada-hime. *See* SUSANOO.

Kushiro. Name for certain bracelets made of metal, bone, stone, or shells, typical of Yayoi sites and *kofun.* Some, in bronze, are decorated with small bells *(suzuri-kushiro).*

Kussō. Former burial method consisting of bending the limbs of the body, binding them in this position, and burying the body either sitting or lying on the back. *Kussō* was in common use during the Jōmon period and gradually abandoned during the Yayoi period.

Kusumi Morikage. Painter *(Mei:* Hambei; *gō:* Mugesai, Morikage, ca. 1620–ca. 1690) of the Kanō school, born in Kaga province. He studied with Kanō Tan'yū, who disapproved of his style, which he felt to be too personal. He went to Kanazawa, where he worked for the potters of the Kutani kilns. He painted all sorts of subjects—landscapes, flowers, Buddhist themes, etc.—in colored China ink *(suiboku-ga),* and excelled in decoration of fusuma and screens *(byōbu).*

Kusumoto Ine. Franz von Siebold's daughter (1827–1903) resulting from von Siebold's affair with a Japanese woman named Taki, born in Nagasaki. She studied with her father and was the first woman gynecologist to experiment with Western childbirth methods.

Kusun-gobu. "Nine inches and five *bu,*" a dagger of this length (about 25 cm) generally used by samurai to cut their stomach during *seppuku,* whence the name sometimes given to this action.

Kusunoki Masashige. Warrior (1294–1336) from Kawachi province, who fought under the orders of Emperor Go-Daigo during the restoration of the Kemmu era and who died in his service. An important character in the *Taiheiki,* he was honored for his courage and loyalty and is often presented as an example of the perfect samurai. All that is known of him is drawn from legends and feats recounted in the *Taiheiki.* His sons, Kusunoki Masatsura and Kusonoki Masanori, continued the fight against the Muromachi shogunate.

• **Kusunoki Masatora.** Warrior serving shogun Ashikaga Yoshiaka. He became a Buddhist monk with the name Shiki-bugyō Hō-in.

Kutani-yaki. Pottery from Kutani, porcelain used for daily needs and for the tea ceremony, produced from 1655 to 1704 (and again from 1807 to the present) in Kaga province (Ishikawa prefecture). The main general category is *ko*-Kutani, produced by potters from Arita (such as Gotō Saijirō, d. 1704), with a coarse-grained gray clay, covered with a whitish or bluish-white enamel with decorations under blue slip, or in three colors *(kōchi),* gold, red, and blue, inspired by Chinese production, in various styles. Real Kutani were produced from 1807 on and have a richer decoration, mainly in gold and red; the main master was Kutani Shōzō (1816–83). *See also* AOYA GEN'EMON, KO-KUTANI.

Kutsu. General term for shoes. *See* GETA, KAMO-GUTSU, KINGAI, SHOES, ZŌRI.

Kuwabara Jitsuzō. Sinologist (1870–1931). After studying in China from 1907 to 1909, he taught at the University of Kyoto, and he was the first Japa-

nese historian to apply Western methodology to the study of Chinese history. Kuwabara Takeo's father.

• **Kuwabara Takeo.** Writer and mountain climber (1904–88), Kuwabara Jitsuzō's son, expert on French literature. He translated books by Stendhal and Alain and wrote some literary criticism, notably on Nakae Chōmin's works.

Kuwada Yoshinari. Physician and cytologist (1882–1981), born in Osaka, noted for his research on chromosome structure. He was decorated with the Order of Culture (Bunka-shō) in 1962.

Kuwagata. Horn- or antler-shaped ornaments (sometimes a crescent moon or a sun) generally in bronze or gold-plated tin, placed on the front of helmets *(kabuto)* of high-ranking samurai.

Kuwaki Gen'yoku. Philosopher (1874–1946) born in Tokyo, influenced by neo-Kantian thought and realist criticism. He studied in Germany starting in 1907, then taught at the University of Tokyo from 1914 to 1935. Among his major works: *Tetsugaku gairon* (Outlines of Philosophy, 1900), *Kanto to gendai no tetsugaku* (Kant and Contemporary Philosophy, 1917).

Kūya Shōnin. Imperial prince (Kūya, Kōshō, 903–72) and itinerant monk of the Tendai-shū sect, one of the *hijiri* of the Kōya-san. He popularized belief in the saving power of Amida Buddha, preaching in villages and continuously chanting the *nembutsu.* He was given the nickname Ichi no Shōnin (or Ichi no Hijiri), "the saint of the markets." Ordained only in 948 on Mt. Hiei, with the monk's name Kōshō, he built many temples and bridges and opened new roads. In Kyoto, he founded the Roku-haramitsu-ji temple. He is generally portrayed as a monk with small images of Amida Buddha emanating from (or entering) his mouth (statue at the Rokuharamitsu-ji), dressed in a deerskin, leaning on a stick topped with antlers and hitting a gong suspended from his neck. He is also known by the name Kōya Shōnin.

Kuze Hirochika. Daimyo (1819–64) from a small estate in what is now Chiba prefecture, born in Edo. He became a councillor *(rōjū)* to the shogunate in 1852 but was relieved of his duties in 1858 for having openly criticized Ii Naosuke's domestic policy about the purges of the Ansei era. After the assassination of Ii Naosuke, Kuze Hirochika once again became a *rōjū* and, with Andō Nobumasa, worked to reinforce the structures of the shogunate. They arranged a marriage between Princess Kazu, Emperor Kōmei's sister, and shogun Tokugawa Iemochi. However, accused of collusion with foreign countries, he was once again relieved of his duties and placed under house arrest in 1863.

Kuzu. Prehistoric site in Tochigi prefecture, excavation of which uncovered remains of Neanderthal peoples.

Kuzu. Title of a Noh play: as he flees to Yoshino, Emperor Temmu meets an old couple, who hide him from his pursuers in a boat. The old people then become *kami.*

Kyahan. Leggings or greaves made of straw or foliage once used by peasants and workers to protect themselves from the cold, then called *habaki.* Starting in the Muromachi period, these greaves were usually made of cotton. They were held on by cords going around the leg. Depending on their shape and the region, they were also called Edo-*kyahan,* Otsu-*kyahan,* or *tsutsu-kyahan.*

Kyo. The tail or train of the robe called *sokutai,* up to several meters long (during the Heian period). It was attached and separated from the garment from underneath the *shitagasane.*

Kyō. Buddhist writings *(Skt.: sūtra).*
• Also, "mirrors." *See* KAGAMI.

Kyōbin. Buddhist monk (ninth century) who founded the Mangan-ji temple in Nikkō and became its first abbot, in 818.

Kyōbushō. Ministry of Religion, created in April 1872, to replace the Jingisho (Shinto Ministry), overseeing both Shinto shrines and Buddhist temples. It was abolished in 1877 when the Meiji government decided to liberalize its religious policy. Religious affairs were then controlled by the Ministry of the Interior (Naimushō). *See* JINGI-SHO.

Kyōden. *See* SANTŌ KYŌDEN.

Kyōdotō. Cooperativist political party founded in 1946 by parliamentarians elected by the peasantry. In 1951, it was merged into the Shakaitō.

Kyōdō Tsūshinsha. "Kyōdō Press Agency," a cooperative involving 63 newspapers and the national radio and television station NHK; it replaced the Dōmei Tsūshinsha in 1945. It is one of the most prestigious press agencies in the world, linked to almost all the major international agencies. It has some 30 foreign bureaus and a large number of correspondents.

Kyōgamine kofun. Group of 10 tombs *(kofun),* perhaps dating from the sixth century, carved out of the rock on the banks of the Kuma-gawa river, looking north, in Kumomoto prefecture. The interiors of the tombs are decorated with engravings and paintings portraying quivers, concentric circles, and a drawn épée.

Kyōgen. Comic theater, closely associated with Noh theater, performed between the acts of a Noh play by actors who are sometimes masked, to provide comic relief for the audience. Directly inspired by Sarugaku, Kyōgen is a sort of satirical comedy (or medieval farce) that was integrated into Noh performances in the Edo period. It never has musical accompaniment. It is sometimes called Ai-kyōgen. There are currently 250 Kyōgen and Ai-kyōgen plays. Of the two schools existing in the Edo period, the Okura-ryū and the Sagi-ryū, only the former has survived. The term Kyōgen has also sometimes been applied to Kabuki performances. Among the masks (Kyōgen-men) used in these plays, the most popular are those representing Otafuku (a chubby peasant woman) and Hyottoko (a simple but crafty peasant man).

Kyōgoku Tamekane. Senior bureaucrat (1254–1332) of the Kamakura *bakufu* and poet, Fujiwara no Tameie's grandson. He founded the Kyōgoku-ha poetry school, with a freer style than that favored by the rival Nijō-ha school. A faithful servant to Emperor Fushimi, he was sent into exile on the island of Sado in 1298, then to Tosa. His poems were included in a few official anthologies, including the *Zoku shūi-shū.*

Kyōgyōshinshō. "Teaching, Practice, Faith, Proof." An important text in six sections, written by Shinran to expound the principles of the Jōdo Shin-shū sect, between 1224 and 1247. It is the major text of the sect, kept in the Higashi Hongan-ji temple in Kyoto.

Kyōha Shintō. "Shinto of the Sects." A group of 13 Shinto sects officially recognized by the Meiji government in 1871, not belonging to State Shinto: Fuso-kyō, Jikkyō-kyō, Konkyō-kyō, Kurozumi-kyō, Misogi-kyō, Mitake-kyō, Shinri-kyō, Shinshū-kyō, Shusei-kyō, Tai-kyō (Shinto-honkyoku), Taisei-kyō, Taisha-kyō, Tenri-kyō. They are also collectively called Shūha Shintō. *See also* KOKUTAI SHINTŌ.

Kyōhō. Era of Emperor Nakamikado: July 1716– Apr. 1735. *See* NENGŌ.

• **Kyōhō-kingin.** Series of coins issued during the Kyōhō era; the main coins were a gold *ōban* and a *koban* that was 86.22% fine gold.

Kyōiku Chokugo. "Imperial Rescript on Education." An important decree written by Inoue Kowashi and Motoda Nagazane and issued on October 30, 1890, by Emperor Meiji. Founded on Confucian morals, the rescript advocated the virtues of loyalty, filial piety, fraternity, and devotion to serving the state. It was distributed in all schools with portraits of the imperial couple. This text, which exalted nationalism, was abolished in 1948.

• **Kyōiku Kihon-hō.** "Fundamental Law on Education," promulgated in 1947 by an education-reform commission, based on the advice of American delegations. This 11-article law defines the objectives of education: democratic ideals and the search for peace, respect for others, co-ed schools, and independence from politics and religion.

Kyōka. "Mad poems," 31-syllable poems, identical to *waka* but humorous and making great use of "pivot words" (*kakekotoba*) with several meanings. According to tradition, this style goes back to the *Man'yōshu* (eighth century), but it in fact developed during the Kamakura period. During the Edo period, *kyōka* were very fashionable and were written by many poets, among the best known of whom were Ōta Nampo, Ishikawa Gabō (1753–1830), and Shokusanjin. Sometimes called *kyōku*. *See also* ZAPPAI.

Kyōkaku. During the Edo period, outlaw bands claiming to right wrongs, à la "Robin Hood," generally from the *hatamoto* class. The shogunal authorities fought these bands (*hatamoto-yakko, daishō jingi-gumi, yoshiya-gumi, machi-yakko*), managing to defeat them only in the late seventeenth century. Individual outlaws (*yakuza* or *kyōkaku*), however, continued to subsist; they became journeymen workers or professional players. They are the direct ancestors of today's *yakuza*.

Kyōkechi. Old dyeing technique in which the fabric was folded in two or four and pressed between two planks of wood pierced with holes into which the dye was poured. A more recent procedure, similar in principle, is called *itajime-zome*.

Kyōko. In some Buddhist temples and monasteries, a particular room in which the sacred writings are kept. Also called *kyōzō, kyōrō*.

Kyō-kudari-bugyō. Senior bureaucrat in Kyoto, appointed by the Kamakura *bakufu* to render justice in the shogun's name. Also called Kyō-kudari-shippitsu.

Kyokujitsu-shō. "Chivalric order" (*see* KUNSHŌ) of the Rising Sun, created in 1875 to honor civil and military services rendered to the state. Red-and-blue sash.

Kyokuroku-za. High, wide chair with curved arms, on which senior Buddhist dignitaries, especially Zen ones, sat with their legs folded under them.

Kyokusui no en. Game in style in the imperial court in the eighth and ninth centuries, in which nobles, sitting in a boat floating on the current, had to catch floating cups filled with *sake* with their fans. This game usually took place on the third day of the third month.

Kyokutō Kokusai Gunji Saiban. "East Asian International Military Court" established by the Allies in January 1946, to hear the cases of eminent Japanese suspected of having committed war crimes. The trials of the 25 accused began on May 3, 1946, and lasted until November 12, 1948. All accused were found guilty, and seven of them (including General Tōjō) were sentenced to death; the others served terms of seven years to life. *See* WAR CRIMES.

Kyō Machiko. Movie actress (Yano Motoko), born 1924 in Osaka, who starred in films directed by Kurosawa Akira (*Rashōmon*), Mizoguchi Kenji (*Ugetsu monogatari*), Kinugasa Teinosuke (*Jigokumon*), Naruse Mikio, Ichikawa Kon, and Yoshimura Kōzaburō. She also appeared in some foreign films, such as *Teahouse of the August Moon*, directed by Daniel Mann (1956).

Kyōmasu. Carved-wood container used as a measure of volume, equivalent to about 1 *shō* (a bit more than 1.8 liters). Smaller units are still used to measure *sake*. Also called simply *masu*.

Kyō-mono. Group of sword-blade makers working in Kyoto and the surrounding area and making *ko-tō* swords. The best known were:
—*Heian period:* Sanjō Munechika, Yoshiie, Gojō Kananaga, Kuninaga.
—*Kamakura period:* Hisakuni, Norikuni, Kuniyoshi, Yoshimitsu, Sadatoshi.
—*Early Muromachi period* (fourteenth–fifteenth century): Sanjō Yoshinori, Heianjō Nagayoshi.
These blacksmiths belonged to various schools, including Awataguchi, Rai, Ayakōji, Hasebe, and Nobokuni.

Kyōō Gokoku-ji. Buddhist temple built about 823 in Kyoto for Kūkai, whose mission was to protect the south part of the city. It was destroyed several times by wars and fires and rebuilt each time, and most of its current buildings date from the early seventeenth century. Five-story pagoda *(goju-no-tō)* 61 m high in the style of the one built in 826. This temple houses invaluable sculpture masterpieces from the Heian and Kamakura periods. One of the buildings, called Tōji Hōmotsuden, was transformed into a museum in 1965. Better known as Tōji.

Kyorai. *Haikai* poet (1651–1704), Bashō's disciple and Bonchō's companion, whose works, notably *Kukai kyorai* and *Kyoraishō,* were collected in *Sarumino.*

Kyoroku. Painter (Morikawa Hyakuchū; *mei:* Gosuke; *azana:* Ukan; *gō:* Kikuabutsu, Ragetsudō, Josekishi, Rokurokusai, 1656–1715), Yasunobu's student. Better known as a *haikai* poet than as a painter, he was one of Bashō's ten disciples (Bashō Juttetsu).

Kyōroku. Era of Emperor Go-Nara: Aug. 1528– July 1532. *See* NENGŌ.

Kyōsai Shōfu. Painter (Kawanabe Kyōsai, Kyōsai Kawanabe, Kyōsai Shōjō, 1831–89), born in Kaga province. He studied with Kuniyoshi (Utagawa) and Kanō Tōhaku, and his work was influenced by Hokusai's art. He painted insects, birds, and fish, and made caricatures that got him arrested several times by the shogunal authorities. When they visited Japan in 1876, Émile Guimet and Félix Régamey met Kyōsai Shōfu, who was famous in Japan, and admired his ukiyo-e prints and his paintings in Kanō style. He signed his works Kanō Tōiku, and sometimes Shōjō Kyōsai. Also called Kawanabe Shūzaburō.

Kyōsantō. Japanese Communist party, which is generally neutral on foreign affairs and moderate on domestic policy, usually limiting itself to supporting the unions. Its daily, *Akahata* (Red Flag), is very widely read by all sectors of the population.

Kyōsei-gun. Japanese name for the Salvation Army.

Kyōshi. Poems, written entirely in Chinese characters, that were quite popular between 1770 and 1800. *Kyōshi* poets deliberately used "non-poetic" and sometimes humorous expressions. The poets who wrote in this genre were usually lower-ranking samurai and some literate *chōnin,* but the genre disappeared very quickly. One of the best-known poets who wrote in this style was Ōta Nampo. Most *kyōshi* poets also wrote *kyōka* poems. Those who used only Chinese characters to write prose *(kyōbun)* were in the same social categories. *See also* SENRYŪ.

Kyōsho. Painter (Tachihara Nin; *mei:* Jintarō; *azana:* Enkei; *gō:* Tōken, Gyokusōsha, Kōanshōshi, Kyōsho, 1785–1840) of the Nanga (Bunjinga) school, and Tani Bunchō's student. He was a samurai and Confucian philosopher, friends with Chinzan and Kazan.

Kyōsoku. Supports, generally in lacquered wood, placed on tatami to be used as armrests to make people who were sitting down more comfortable.

Kyōto. Main city in Kyōto prefecture, located at the bottom of a small plain in central Honshu at the foot of the Tamba mountains, with Mounts Hieizan and Atagoyama to the northeast and northwest. It was built between two rivers flowing southward from these mountains, the Kamo-gawa to the east and the Katsura-gawa to the west, which join the Yodo-gawa, flowing into Osaka Bay, to the south. This enclosed position gives it a humid climate that is hot in summer (33°C), with abundant summer rain, and very cold in winter.

The site of this historic city bears signs of human occupation from the Jōmon period; it was "settled" in the sixth century by a family from Korea, the Hata, who were involved in the silk trade. In 794, in an attempt to free himself from political pressure from the monks of the Six Sects of Nara (Nantorokushū), Emperor Kammu decided to make his capital there, after an unsuccessful attempt to establish it on the nearby site of Nagaoka in 784. However, even before Kammu's capital was constructed there, the site had been home to the Hata, Izumo, and Kamo families, who built Buddhist temples (Kōryū-ji, seventh century) and Shinto shrines (Kamo-jinja) there. At first called Yamashiro, the new "capital city" (Kyō-to) was then renamed Heian-kyō. Emperor Kammu had it built in a grid plan, inspired by Chang'an, the capital of the Tang dynasty of China, as the city of Heijō-kyō (Nara) had been built. At first it measured about 5 km from north to south and 4.5 km from east to west; because it was not surrounded by walls, it grew very rapidly, with the districts of Saga and Uzamasa to the west; Shirakawa, Keage, Gion, Higashiyama, and Yamashina to the east; and Fushimi and Momoyama to the south. In more modern times, it expanded southward toward Yamato onto the old site of Nagaoka, and to the northeast toward Mt. Hiei and Yase. During the Kamakura period, the Rokuhara district, on the left bank of the Kamo-gawa, became the political center of the capital; in the ensuing period, the Muromachi took over this role.

The city was theoretically divided into two large parts (left and right), separated by a wide north-south avenue ending, to the north, at the wall of the imperial palace (gosho). Each part was divided into rectangular blocks separated by streets and had markets. The transversal streets were named for their respective bridges over the Kamo-gawa—starting from the palace, Ichijō, Nijō, Sanjō, Shijō, and so on. Around these bridges grew new trade and religious districts that helped develop the city toward the east. Over the centuries, temples, shrines, monasteries, and gardens were built in the foothills around the city. South of the city, near the markets, merchants and artisans settled.

From the ninth to the twelfth century, Heian-kyō was the seat of a brilliant aristocratic society that was to become the classical civilization of Japan. During the Ōnin War (1467–77), however, the city and the buildings of the imperial palace were almost completely destroyed by fires. It was reborn from its ashes only during the dictatorship of Toyotomi Hideyoshi, who had it rebuilt in the late sixteenth century, creating new streets and districts. The city then grew quickly; by the beginning of the Edo period, it had about 600,000 inhabitants—nobles, warriors, merchants, and artisans. It became famous for its brocade fabrics (from the Nishijin district, northwest of the palace), pottery (kyō-yaki), artists' studios (bushi, most of them along the Kamo River), and temples and shrines, which drew a considerable number of followers and pilgrims. The city was modernized during the Meiji era, with development of scientific and educational institutions (the imperial university, Kyōto Teikoku Dai-

gaku, was founded in 1897). Electricity was installed, and artisans were able to develop their crafts. Museums and art institutes were founded, and tourism was developed. Kyōto was spared being bombed during the Second World War, thanks to the advice of Japanologists from many countries who were aware of the inestimable value of the city's cultural heritage. It therefore has important monuments from its illustrious past, some of them in the city itself and many more in its immediate environs.

The population of Kyōto declined when Emperor Meiji decided to transfer the capital to Tokyo ("city of the east") in 1868, giving rise to a major migration in which all bureaucrats and the court left Kyōto for Edo (Tokyo). It is now a provincial city, still very active, linked to Tokyo and Osaka by the Shinkansen rapid train and to Osaka and Kobe by a highway (Meishin), making it an important transportation hub. It has few industries, except in the Hanshin industrial district, which is served by railroad and road (the old Tōkaidō route). It now has 39 universities and colleges, 34 museums, and many hotels and conference centers, making it a top-notch academic and cultural center: according to recent estimates, it contains 202 National Treasures and 1,596 Cultural Treasures, considered the most valuable heritage of Japan. It has a number of festivals and matsuri, among the most noted of which are Gion, Jidai Matsuri, and Aoi Matsuri; Noh and Kabuki seasons; and various performances—sumo, traditional dance (Mibu Kyōgen, Miyako Odori, etc.). The art of the tea ceremony (chanoyu) developed there, as did the art of flower arranging (ikebana).

Life is less hurried in Kyōto than in Osaka and Tokyo. The city is surrounded with pleasant sites and green spaces, such as the Arashiyama hills to the west, the Higashiyama hills to the east, and Lake Biwa, which is about 5 km northwest of the city. It was also called Miyako (called Miaco by foreigners in the sixteenth century). A very large city, it now covers more than 610 km², including its suburbs, and has a population of around 1.4 million. See HEIAN-KYŌ.

Main monuments:

—In the city: Former imperial palace (Kyōto-gosho), Nijō-jō, Higashi Hongan-ji, Nishi Hongan-ji, Heian-jingū, Sanjusangendō, Yasaka-jinja, Chion-in, Kyōō Gakoku-ji (Tōji), Kiyomizu-dera, Nanzen-ji, Zenri-ji, Shōren-ji, Kennin-ji, Roku-haramitsu-ji, and more.

—To the south: The Senryū-ji, Fushimi Inari-jinja, Mampuku-ji, Daigo-ji, Sambō-in, Hōkai-ji, and farther south, near Uji, Byōdō-in.

—*To the north and northeast:* Kurodani Kōkyō-ji, Shinnyo-dō, Hōnen-in, Ginkaku-ji, Shisen-dō, Manshu-in, and farther in the same direction, toward Yase, the Sanzen-ji, the Jakkō-in, and the monasteries of Mt. Hiei.

—*To the northwest:* Shimo-gano and Kami-gamo shrines, Entsū-ji temple.

—*To the west:* Shōkoku-ji, Daitoku-ji, Jingo-ji, Kinkaku-ji, Kitano Tenjin, Hirano, Myōshin-ji, Ryōan-ji, Ninna-ji, Kōryū-ji, and farther west, temples of Arashiyama, Tenryū-ji, Nison-in, Hōrin-ji, Daikaku-ji, Koke-dera (Saihō-ji), Katsura (gardens), Kōzan-ji, and more.

• **Kyōto-fu.** Kyoto prefecture, located between Nara prefecture, to the south; Hyōgo and Osaka prefectures to the west; Fukui, Mie, and Shige prefectures to the east; and the Sea of Japan to the north. Oriented northwest-southeast, the prefecture is mountainous (Tamba Mountains near Kyoto, Tango Mountains farther north) and is irrigated by the Uji-gawa, Kamo-gawa, Katsura-gawa, Yodo-gawa, and, in the north, Yura-gawa rivers. It was formed in 1871 by the merger of the former Tamba, Yamashiro, and Tango provinces. Only the southern part is industrialized (Hanshin zone). *Chief city:* Kyoto. *Main cities:* Uji, Jōyō, Yawata, Kameoka in the south; Ayabe, Miyazu, Maizuru, Fukuchiyama in the north. *Area:* 4,620 km². *Pop.:* 2.6 million.

• **Kyōto machi-bugyō.** Prefect of Kyoto, title created in 1665 to replace the former governor. There were in fact two prefects, one for the east and one for the west, who alternated their duties every other month. This title was abolished in 1868.

• **Kyōto-shoshidai.** Governor of Kyoto, the representative of the military dictators Oda Nobunaga and Toyotomi Hideyoshi and the Edo shogun in the capital. His task was to protect the imperial family, ensure justice in the eight provinces under his jurisdiction, and keep watch on the daimyo in western Japan. This position was abolished in 1868.

• **Kyōto-shugoshoku.** Military governor of Kyoto, position created in 1862 to maintain order in the city and surrounding areas, as well as in Osaka. This position was abolished in 1868.

• **Kyōto Teikoku Daigaku.** Imperial University of Kyoto, founded in 1897. In 1949, it became the University of Kyoto (called, for short, Kyōdai) and it now has 9 faculties and 18 research institutes. Attendance is about 12,000 full-time students. This

university is the most sought-after in Japan, on an equal footing with the prestigious University of Tokyo (for short, Tōdai).

Kyōtoku. Era of Emperor Go-Hanazono: July 1452–July 1455. *See* NENGŌ.

Kyōtoku no Ran. Series of battles and skirmishes that took place starting in 1454 in the Kantō, following the assassination of Uesugi Noritada, the Kantō-kanrei, by Ashikaga Shigeuji (Ashikaga Mochiuji's son). The clans took sides, and wars broke out defending or attacking Shigeuji. One of the allies of the *bakufu,* Imagawa Noritada, captured and set fire to Kamakura, where Shigeuji was living. Shigeuji fled to Koga, whence the name Koga-kubō given to him and his descendants. The new *kubō* of Kanto, who could not live in Kamakura because the city had been destroyed, established his headquarters in Horikoshi in 1457 and was therefore called Horikoshi-kubō. The two *kubō* continued to do battle until 1482, when the Horikoshi-kubō (or Kamakura-kubō) made a provisional peace with the Koga-kubō.

Kyō-u. *See* HAKYŌ, HOASHI KYŌU.

Kyōwa. Era of Emperor Kōkaku: Feb. 1801–Feb. 1804. *See* NENGŌ.

Kyōzuka. Small tumuli in which Buddhists once had the custom of burying sacred writings to preserve them from destruction when *mappō* (the final period of the Good [Buddhist] Law) started; later, they conducted a service in tribute to the deceased in this way. The Buddhist writings *(kyō)* were enclosed in bronze or pottery boxes *(kyōzutsu)* and placed in stone vaults in pits, accompanied by various offerings. The same thing was done when Buddhists wanted to transmit the texts to the future world in which Miroku Bosatsu (the Bodhisattva Maitreya) is to return to Earth as the Buddha. This custom was followed mainly from the eleventh to the thirteenth century, but was still sometimes practiced during the Edo period. *See* MAPPŌ.

Kyū-an. Era of Emperor Konoe: July 1145–Jan. 1151. *See* NENGŌ.
→ *see* CHINZAN.

Kyūba no Michi. "Path of the Bow and the Horse." A group of unwritten rules to which warriors *(bushi)* and samurai were supposed to conform. They appeared around the tenth century and constituted a sort of physical and moral training for warriors, with the ideals of courage, disregard for death, and impassiveness. Like knights of the medieval period, *bushi* were bound to protect women. In the Edo period, this practical ideal became more philosophical and was called Bushido, "Way of the Warriors." *See* BUSHIDO.

Kyūbei. Famous metal engraver (Karamono Kyūbei, mid-eighteenth century) and sculptor of netsuke in metal from Sakai.

Kyūdō. "Way of the Bow." Traditional art of archery, created during the Edo period to replace *kyūjutsu,* the art of archery for war. It was the first of 18 warrior techniques *(kakutō-bugei)* that all warriors had to study. At first handled by foot soldiers, the bow was adopted, despite its length, by samurai on horseback, who invented specific techniques for its use. After the sixteenth century, firearms came into common use, the bow became marginal to warfare, and archery was converted into a training sport for warriors; from *bu-jutsu* (an "art of war"), it became a mental discipline, or *budō* ("warrior's path"). It is still practiced today as a mental and physical discipline in many clubs; practitioners seek not absolute precision or efficiency, but concentration and mastery of their bodies and minds. The emphasis is on the correctness of positions, which must bring harmony *(wa)*. A federation of *kyūdō* clubs (Zen Nihon Kyūdō Renmei) was founded in Tokyo in 1948 to regulate the sport. Archery as a sport is called *kyū-jutsu,* as distinguished from the spiritual form, which is called *shadō. Kyūdō* was codified in the *Shagakuseidō* and the *Shahō-shinshō,* two eighteenth-century works, adaptations of the Chinese *Shexue zhengzong. See* INU-OI-MONO, REISHA, SHADŌ, YABUSAME, YUMI.

Kyūhaku. Painter (Kanō Naganobu; *mei*: Genshichirō, 1577–1654) of the Kanō school, Kanzō Shōei's son and student (Kanō branch in Kaga). He worked in Tsuruga for the Tokugawa family. His son, Kyūhaku II (d. 1602), was a painter of the same school.

Kyūichi. *See* TAKEUCHI KYŪICHI.

Kyūji. Ancient collection of myths and legends, now lost, that was said to have been compiled at the Yamato court in the sixth century, and on which the compilers of the *Kojiki* and the *Nihon shoki* based their work. Also titled *Kuji. See also* KOJIKI, TEIKI.

Kyūjo. Painter (Ido Kōryō, Naomichi; *azana*: Chūgyo; *gō*: Tōkyūjo, Kōsenkoji, Kōro-en Tonkashitsu, Tonsai, 1744–1802) of the Nagasaki school, Sō Shiseki's student in Edo. He was a samurai.

Kyūju. Era of Emperor Konoe: Oct. 1154–Apr. 1156. *See* NENGŌ.

Kyūkakoku Jōyaku. "Treaty of the Nine Powers" (United States, Belgium, France, Italy, Great Britain, the Netherlands, Portugal, China, and Japan), signed at the conference of Washington in 1922 and entering into force in 1925, stipulating the independence of China, the integrity of its territory, and freedom of trade for all nations with it. This treaty, repudiated in fact by Tanaka Giichi in 1927, was rendered null and void by the annexation of Manchuria, considered a "special territory," by Japan in 1931, and the establishment of Manchukuo in 1932.

Kyūsai. Sculptor of netsuke (Hirai Kyūsai, Tetsugen, Tetsugendō, nineteenth century) in Osaka.

Kyūshitsu. Term designating all objects in undecorated lacquer, made with coats of primer *(shitaji)* and finishing glaze *(uwanuri, rō ironuri, rō irourushi, nuritate)*. These lacquers are usually black or red. *See* LACQUER, URUSHI.

Kyūshū. Third largest island in the Japanese archipelago, located to the extreme south. Mountainous and volcanic, it is surrounded by a large number of small islands. Once divided into nine provinces (whence its name), it now comprises seven prefectures: Fukuoka, Nagasaki, Ōita, Kumamoto, Miyazaki, Saga, and Kagoshima. The main islands around it are Amakusa, Satsunan, Gotō, Hirado, Iki, Satsuma, and Koshiki. Kyūshū is separated from Honshu by the Kammon Strait (also called Shimonoseki). A large mountain range divides the island into two parts, southeast and northwest, and its highest peak is Sobosan (1,757 m); a number of swift-flowing small rivers, the most important of which are the Mimikawa, Onoga-gawa, and Kumagawa, flow from the mountains into coastal plains. Kyūshū's volcanic topography (Mt. Aso) is sprinkled with hot springs. Six national parks preserve the untamed nature of the island: Unzen-Amakusa, Kirishima-Yaku, Saikai, Aso, Setonaikai, and Iriomote. The northern region, the first to be colonized by the Chinese and Koreans, is now the most industrialized (Kita-Kyūshū, Fukuoka). The extremely indented coastline has provided for excellent ports at the bottom of deep roads, such as Nagasaki and Kagoshima. The subtropical climate allows for cultivation of rice, tobacco, citrus fruit, pineapples, and sugar cane, and there is very active fishing on all coasts. There are some coal mines, but with very low yield. Main cities: Fukuoka, Nagasaki, Beppū, Kagoshima, Kumamoto, Ōita. *Total area:* 43,000 km². *Pop.:* approx. 15 million. *See* KITA-KYŪSHŪ.

• Name of several types of warplanes used in the Second World War:

—**Kyūshū J.7 W.1.** Experimental plane, only two of which were built in 1943, called Shinden. *Speed:* 750 kmh; *range:* 1,500 km; *weapons:* four 30 mm cannons, four 30 to 60 kg bombs; *crew:* 1 pilot.

—**Kyūshū Q.1 W.** Bomber seaplane, built in 1944 to attack submarines, called Tokai. *Weight:* 5,300 kg; *length:* 11.9 m; *motors:* two 160 HP Hitachi Tempu; *speed:* 320 km/h; *range:* 1,300 km; *weapons:* one 20 mm cannon, one 7.7 kmm machine gun, and 500 kg of bombs; *crew:* 3–4 men.

• **Kyūshū Daigaku.** National university, founded in Fukuoka in 1910. It comprises many faculties and research institutes. Attendance is about 10,000 students. Also called Kyūdai.

• **Kyūshū-mono.** Name of several sword-blade makers who worked on Kyushu and made mainly "*shin-tō*" blades (*see* KATANA) until the sixteenth century: Chōen, Yukihira, Miike Tenta, Naminohira, Samonji, Tadayoshi, Ishidō. *See also* BIZEN-MONO.

Kyūtei E-dokoro. Imperial Court Office of Painting, established in the late Heian period; its main artists were Tokiwa Mitsunaga, Takashima Takakane, and Tosa Mitsunobu.

Kyūzō. Painter (Hasegawa Kyūzō, 1568–93) of the Hasegawa school who studied with his father Tōhaku.

→ *See* ICHIŌ.

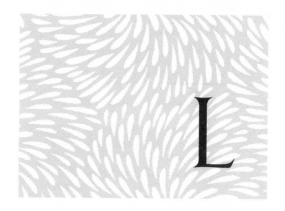

L. The sound represented by *l* does not exist in transcription of Japanese language; it is replaced by *r*. However, pronunciation of *r* is midway between *l* and *r*. Japanese people who are not familiar with the Hepburn transcription system (which is internationally known and is used in this book) often confuse the two letters.

Lacquers. Lacquer itself, or *urushi* (taken from the sap of a tree, *Rhus vernicifera*), and lacquered objects, or *shikki,* are often confused in Japan. The lacquering techniques used throughout Asia were brought to a degree of expertise in Japan seldom seen elsewhere. Japanese artisans, with their prodigious manual skill and patience, worked with renowned painters and decorators to create true masterpieces. In pre-Buddhist times, lacquer was used in Japan to make basketwork, ceramics, and terracotta pieces waterproof, and to decorate combs and bows. Lacquer objects have been found associated with Late Jōmon–period pottery (Torihama site, Fukui prefecture), and other objects decorated in this way have been found in *kofun*. The guild *(be)* of lacquerers was one of the first to be founded, and tradition has it that a certain Mimi no Sukune, who lived in the era of the mythical emperor Kōan, was the first chief of this *urushi-be*.

Objects and sculptures decorated with lacquer were very popular during the Asuka and Nara periods. The famous portable shrine *(zushi)* called Tamamushi is completely covered with black lacquer and Buddhist religious decorations in colored painted lacquer. The Shōsō-in treasury has many eighth-century objects—bowls, boxes, musical instruments—covered with lacquer and paint and inlaid with mother-of-pearl. Until the Heian period, decorative motifs in lacquer and the techniques for

applying it were inspired mainly by Chinese techniques. Leather, wood, hemp fabrics, and bamboo basketwork were the most commonly used supports, and the layers were decorated with inlays of mother-of-pearl or precious metal, and with paintings made with ground pigments in oil mixed with the liquid lacquer. Buddhist sculptures were made in colored lacquer, either on a core of solid wood *(mokushin kanshitsu)* or on a light frame covered with hemp fabric *(dakkanshitsu, dakkatsu kanshitsu)*.

Lacquer seemed so essential in the Nara period that the government, by order in the Taihō Code, encouraged the cultivation of *Rhus vernicifera (urushi no ki)*, whose sap was the raw material, and asked all peasant families to devote a parcel of land to growing the trees alongside mulberry bushes. Lacquer was so much in favor that it may be one of the reasons that ceramics developed relatively late in Japan. The *maki-e* technique, in which metallic powders (gold, silver, copper) were applied on still-wet lacquer, supplanted most ancient techniques during the Heian period. In the early Heian period, decorations on lacquer continued to be inspired by Chinese models (arabesques, *hosoge* and lotus blossoms, and fabulous birds—*hō-ō* phoenixes and *karyōbinga*), but in the late tenth century, they gradually became more typically Japanese, simpler and often diagrammatic; by the Fujiwara period, there was a truly indigenous style (images of wheels floating on waves, for example). Lacquer was used to decorate temple structures (as at the Chūson-ji in Hiraizumi) and to cover chests, saddles, tables, and most objects commonly used by the aristocracy and Buddhist monks. *Maki-e* and lacquers inlaid with mother-of-pearl and sprinkled with gold and silver powder or flakes were highly valued on the Korean and Chinese markets and were exported in great numbers. The best painters contributed their images and their sense of color and composition to ornamentation of lacquered objects, which became more and more naturalistic: birds on riverbanks, autumn foliage. Gold powder, used almost exclusively at the beginning in *maki-e* technique, was soon augmented by silver powder and by *aogin-fun,* or "pale gold," a mixture of gold and silver. These powders were densely or lightly sprinkled, and were sometimes accompanied by mother-of-pearl inlays.

In the Kamakura period, larger and more solid objects were decorated with more realistic images: toiletry chests are the most famous examples. Lacquer decoration followed trends in painting, especially the Yamato-e, and the use of metallic powders was complemented by that of small leaves of gold *(kirikane),* for more striking effects. Relief decorations *(taka maki-e)* began to appear, as did many motifs with a literary allusion in which kanji characters and syllabaries were mixed with decorations involving trees and rocks on makeup boxes, toiletry cases, and writing cases. During the period of the Ashikaga shoguns, the aristocracy favored lacquered objects imitating paintings in the monochrome style inspired by Chinese Song and Yuan painters such as Sō-ami and Nō-ami. Because of the shoguns' taste for imported Chinese products, artisans learned new techniques and forms from the Chinese Ming dynasty. The most notable are the lacquers called *Kamakura-bori* (lacquers on relief-sculpted wood) and *chinkin* (using gold inlays to highlight the images on the decorations).

In parallel to production for nobility and high-level warriors, lacquers for religious use were developed, attaining a high degree of finish, such as those of *Negoro,* which use applications of red lacquer on a base of black lacquer. During the Azuchi-Momoyama period (late sixteenth century), the trend was toward plainer decorations. The most typical lacquers were those made for Toyotomi Hideyoshi and the ornamentation of his mausoleum at the Kōdai-ji, where artists used only flower motifs and autumn foliage in gold *maki-e* on a plain black background. Tables, dishes, cabinets, and various cases and writing cases were decorated in the Kōdai-ji style. The arrival of the Portuguese gave rise to production of lacquers made for export to Europe—valises, cabinets, and objects for Christian worship, such as host boxes, altar pieces, and lecterns inlaid with mother-of-pearl, sharkskin, and Jesuit and Christian symbols. The attempt to annex Korea by Toyotomi Hideyoshi caused a revival of techniques, bringing back to Japan methods of inlaying mother-of-pearl that had been largely supplanted throughout the Muromachi period by the use of *maki-e.* Hon-Ami Kōetsu was one of the major artists to return to this procedure; he was also behind a decorative movement inspired by the classical art of the Yamato-e and seeking to illustrate the classical literature of the Heian period in a more modern style. The lacquers he made (or inspired) are known as "Kōetsu lacquers." Most of them are writing cases with a concave cover decorated with motifs arranged in an original way, using tin or lead cutouts of leaves mixed with mother-of-pearl inlays and *maki-e.* His movement, in which the painter Sōtatsu participated, was perpetuated by Ogata Kōrin and painters of the Rimpa school in the eighteenth century. Throughout the Edo period, there was a proliferation of forms, and lacquer was applied to all sorts of utilitarian objects, from the smallest (combs, *inrō*) to the largest (tables, vanities, toiletry kits, headrests, bottles, etc.). The fashion of lacquering *inrō* (pill or seal boxes), scabbards *(saya),* writing kits, and smoking kits *(tobako-bon)* supplied artisans with new supports that enabled them to diversify their talents and techniques. Outside of major centers, such as Kyoto and Edo, provincial schools developed in Iwate, Yamaguchi, Shikoku, Toyama, Nagasaki, Niigata, Wakayama, Akita, Tsugaru, and elsewhere, and their artisans equaled their co-workers in Edo in terms of innovation. Their products are still highly valued for their originality and the quality of their execution. After the Meiji Restoration (1868), lacquer decorators, influenced by Western art, updated their techniques. Inspired by informal art or returning to traditional motifs, they used new forms of supports and produced objects and furniture of high quality. Among the best-known "modern" artists were Shibata Zeshin (1807–91), Matsuda Gonroku (1896–1986), and Ban'ura Shōgo (1901–82); there were hundreds of others. There are a number of types of lacquered objects: aside from *maki-e,* there are sculpted lacquers *(chōshitsu),* gold-inlaid lacquers *(chinkin),* undecorated lacquers *(kyûshitsu),* and polychrome lacquers *(kin-ma, kimma). See* AKA-TSUKA JIYOKU, AOKIN-FUN, CHINKIN, CHŌSHITSU, GYŌBU NASHI-JI, KANSHITSU, KIN-MA, KYŪSHITSU, MAKI-E, MOKUSHIN KANSHITSU, NASHIJI, SHIKKI, SHUNKEI-NURI, TSUGARU-NURI, URUSHI.

Ladybird. Name of a British gunboat that accompanied several merchant ships on the Yangzi-jiang in China. On December 12, 1937, the Japanese army attacked it near the city of Wuhu, killing one sailor and wounding several others. The same day, other foreign ships were also attacked, notably the English gunboats the *Cricket,* the *Scarab,* and the *Bee,* and the American ship the *Panay.* The Japanese minister of foreign affairs, Hirota Kōki, was forced to make official apologies to avoid having this incident become an international crisis. After the Second World War, it was revealed that Japanese general Yanagawa Heisuke (1879–1945) had given the order to sink all foreign ships on the Yangzi-jiang that were trying to reach Nanjing. This incident was known as the Ladybird Incident.

Lafarge, John. American painter (1835–1910), related to Commodore Perry, who went to Japan in 1866 to study Japanese art, along with the historian Henry Adams. When he returned to Boston, he exhibited some works that he had painted in Japan, and he published *An Artist's Letter from Japan* in 1897.

Landor, Alfred Henry Savage. American painter (d. 1924), sculptor, and traveler, born in Florence, Italy. He lived in Japan from 1869 to 1891, executing numerous paintings and portraits. He published a book of memoirs, *Everywhere,* in 1924.

Language. It is difficult to classify the Japanese language, and ethnologists and linguists are still debating this issue. Some place Japanese in the Korean, Ainu, and Ryukyu group, while others put it in the Chinese group, with Tibetan, Burmese, Uralo-Altaic, Mōn-Khmer, Polynesian, and other languages. In reality, Japanese can be considered an isolated idiom that occupies a unique position in the distribution of world languages. Its fundamental structure has remained unchanged probably since prehistory, while its vocabulary has been greatly influenced by Chinese, Korean, and Ainu contributions. It is said that about 40% of the words in contemporary Japanese come from Chinese (although they have been somewhat altered over the centuries), written in Sino-Japanese characters *(kanji).* Conversely, Japanese has influenced Korean, Ainu, and the indigenous languages of the Ryukyu Islands. The original Japanese language, Yamato-kotoba, is polysyllabic, whereas words borrowed from Chinese are usually monosyllabic. The adoption of Chinese characters to express Japanese words led to a variety of pronunciations. Thus, the word that means "man" can be written with the Chinese character with the same meaning, which is pronounced *jin,* while in its Yamato pronunciation and kana transcription, it is pronounced *hito.* However, although the pure Yamato vocabulary is relatively limited, the number of words used in Japa-

nese is considerable: the *Dai Nippon kokugo jiten* lists more than 200,000, and Ueda's *Daijiten* lists almost 700,000. Formation of the Japanese language was not systematic and was influenced by various local usages. Of the eight vowels that Japanese phonetics used in the late eighth century, only five have been retained (*see* GOJŪ-ON-ZU). Consonants such as *p* were gradually abandoned in the early Edo period. In addition, words arrived in Japan at various times and from different regions of China, with the result that a single Sino-Japanese character, representing a single idea, can have several different pronunciations (*see* KUN, ON). Syntax is also specific, and the meaning of a sentence is generally determined by the participles (verbal or not) that end it. The verb generally comes at the end of a sentence (which means that to translate a sentence, one must start reading it from the end), and adjectives always precede the noun they qualify. A Japanese sentence is composed of ten main parts: noun, verb, adjective, verbal adjective, adverb, auxiliary verb, verb participle or not, copula, conjunction, and interjection. Enclitics, such as *ni, de, wa,* and *ga,* modify the meaning of words that precede them. Both the genitive and possessive cases are expressed by the participle *no.* The honorific participles *O* and *Go* often precede the name (or the object) that they distinguish.

There are no articles in Japanese, and nouns are not modified by gender. Nor are nouns modified by their number: singular and plural have the same form. In verb conjugation, the past, present, and future are expressed not by modification of the verb but by the respective auxiliary verb. Finally, great use is made of participles following the verb root (which does not change) according to whether it is given a negative *(-nai),* doubtful *(-kana),* conjectural *(-darō),* affirmative *(-yo),* continuative *(-te),* conclusive *(-kaku),* conditional *(-ba),* imperative *(-kake),* or exclamative *(-na)* value. Adjectives and auxiliary verbs are conjugated in different ways, and there are a great number of irregular verbs, auxiliaries, and adjectives. Finally, in common language there exist not only innumerable forms of politeness and apology, but complete phrases (sometimes with no real meaning) designed to soften a sentence that might seem too abrupt. These expressions are usually local. There are at least six levels of politeness (there were once up to twelve), and women use different nouns, verbs, and expressions from those used by men (*see* NYŌBŌ-KOTOBA). *See also* DIALECTS, INGO, KEIGO, KOKUGO, NIHONGO.

Lansing, Robert. Adviser (1864–1928) to American president Woodrow Wilson and Secretary of

State in 1915. On November 2, 1917, he signed an agreement with Japan, represented by Ishii Kiku-jirō, according to which both countries would favor an open-door policy toward China while respecting its independence and its territorial and administrative integrity. This agreement is known in Japan as the Ishii-Ranshingu Kyōtei. Lansing urged the American government to recognize Japan's "unique position" in Manchuria; at the Conference of Paris in 1919, he supported Japan, on the understanding that it would not become imperialistic. American policy was thus indecisive, notably with regard to Shandong: Lansing often opposed the views of the President, who was more pro-China.

La Pérouse, Jean-François de Galaup, Count of. French navigator (1741–88). During a trip around the world with the ships the *Boussole* and the *Astrolabe,* he reached Japan in 1786 and discovered the strait separating the islands of Sakhalin and Hokkaido, which was named for him (today called Sōya Kaikyō). He discovered Kamchatka, then sailed southward; he was killed by Samoan natives.

Laxman, Adam Erikovitch. Russian officer (1766–after 1796), son of Finnish naturalist Eric Laxman. In 1792–93, he directed an expedition to Japan, on the order of Czarina Catherine the Great, with the official goal of repatriating Japanese sailors who had been shipwrecked, but in reality to study the coasts of Japan and seek means of opening trade relations with the country. Laxman and his companions were cordially received in Nemuro (Hokkaido), set sail for Hakodate, then traveled to Matsumae over land. The Japanese refused to open negotiations, however, and Laxman was forced to return to Russia.

Lay, Horatio Nelson. British agent (1833–98) in China, charged by the Meiji government with securing a loan from London to fund the building of the first railway line (Yokohama–Tokyo). He was able to obtain a loan of £1 million in London in 1869, as well as the aid of British engineers. But Lay tried to speculate on this loan on the London Stock Exchange, and the Japanese government fired him and dealt with the agent of the British Oriental Bank Corporation. The railway was inaugurated in 1872.

Leach, Bernard. British potter (1887–1979) born in Hong Kong. He lived in Japan from 1909 to 1920 and became familiar with Japanese ceramic arts. He tried to export techniques to England, assisted by Hamada Shōji. They built a kiln in Cornwall, and Leach returned to Japan a number of times, notably in 1934–35. In 1916, Leach had reconstructed the Kenzan kilns in Japan. His work *A Potter's Book,* published in 1960, had a major influence on European ceramics. His other works include *Kenzan and His Tradition* (1966), *A Potter's Work* (1967), *Hamada, Potter* (1975), *The Potter's Challenge* (1977), *Beyond East and West* (1978).

Le Gendre, Charles William. American general (1830–99) who advised Japan's Ministry of Foreign Affairs from 1872 to 1875. Appointed consul to Xiamen, China, he led a punitive expedition against the Taiwan indigenous people who had massacred the crew of a shipwrecked American ship. He was then hired by Soejima Tanemoi, who also sent him on a punitive expedition against Taiwan because the Taiwanese had also massacred inhabitants of the Ryukyu Islands in 1871. Le Gendre advised the Japanese government and trained soldiers for the expedition. He was decorated with the Order of the Rising Sun (*see* KUNSHŌ) and remained in Japan until 1890, freelancing as an adviser to Ōkuma Shigenobu, then to the government of Korea. He died in Korea.

Lemaire, Maxemilien. Dutch director of the Hirado trading post. When he arrived in Japan in 1641, he asked in vain for an audience with shogun Iemitsu, who notified him of the order to leave Hirado for the island of Dejima at Nagasaki. Hirado was therefore abandoned.

Lerch, Theodor von. Austrian officer (1869–1945), military attaché to the Austrian embassy in 1910. In 1911, he introduced alpine skiing to the soldiers stationed in Niigata and Hokkaido; he returned to Austria in 1912. *See* JŌETSU.

Liefde. Dutch ship that ran aground in the Bay of Usuki (Bungo province, Ōita prefecture). Only 24 sailors out of the crew of 110 survived the storms, among them the captain, Jacob Quaeckernaeck, the second mate, Jan Joosten, and the English pilot, Will Adams. *See* ADAMS, JOOSTEN.

Lighthouses ("tōdai"). The first modern lighthouses in Japan were built in 1869. They were erected in the Tokyo region (Cape Kannonzaki) by the French architect François Léonce Verny. Other lighthouses were quickly built, notably at Nojimazaki (1869), Shinagawa (1870), and Jōgashima (Kanagawa prefecture, 1870). The English engineer Richard Henry Brunton continued Verny's work; starting in 1880, lighthouses were designed by Japanese architects. *See* VERNY.

Lindau, Rudolf. Swiss writer (1829–1909), a French citizen, who became a minister in Jules Ferry's cabinet. He was sent to Japan as a representative of Swiss trade interests. He visited Nagasaki and Hakodate, where he met Abbot Mermet of Cachon; the last ambassador of the Tokugawa to France, Kurimoto Kon; and the painter and photographer Charles Wirgman. In 1864, he was appointed Swiss consul general to Yokohama, a position he handed over to Kaspar Brennwald in 1866. He left Japan in 1869 and wrote several works on the country: *Un voyage autour du Japon* (A Trip Through Japan, 1864) and *Aus China und Japan, Reiseerinnerungen* (Travel Memoirs from China and Japan, 1896).

Linschooten, John Hugues van. Dutch navigator (sixteenth century) who reached Japan in 1584, thus encouraging his compatriots to supplant the Portuguese in Japanese waters.

Lions Club. The Lions Club of Japan was founded in Tokyo in 1952 and became a national association in 1958. It now has about 150,000 members.

Literacy. It is estimated that the literacy rate of the Japanese population (men and women) is currently higher than 99.9%, equal to the rate of school attendance. The literacy rate was about 45% for boys and only 15% for girls at the beginning of the Meiji era.

Literature. The beginnings of Japanese literature coincide with the foundation of the first major administrative capital, Heijō-kyō (Nara), and the establishment of a centralized government. Most of the first literary texts were official compilations with a specific political goal: the creation of a religious and political ideology affirming the preeminence of the most important clan, whose leader was the emperor. The oldest text is Shōtoku Taishi's "Seventeen-Article Constitution" (*see* JŪSHICHIJŌ no kempō), probably written in 622 or soon after. Other studies with a religious or supposed historical content were written in the seventh century but have since been lost. The oldest surviving text is the *Kojiki*, written in 712, complemented eight years later by the *Nihon shoki*; these works were written in Chinese because the Japanese language did not yet have a written form. From the same era are provincial chronicles, *fudoki*, few of which have survived to the present day; *norito*, invocations to the Shinto *kami*; and *semmyō*, or imperial rescripts. In the following century, the first of the major impe-

rial anthologies, the *Man'yōshū*, was compiled; this work marked the real inception of what is called poetic literature, a genre that constantly flourished thereafter. Another type of literature arose around the same time, written in Chinese, comprising mainly Buddhist and Confucian texts. The tradition of *waka* poetry anthologies gave rise to new genres, such as collections of tales *(uta-monogatari)*—including the *Ise monogatari*, *Yamato monogatari*, and *Taketori monogatari*—most of which were composed in the early tenth century. Poetry imitated the works in the *Man'yōshū*, but its forms were concretized in the major imperial anthologies (*see* CHOKUSEN WAKA-SHŪ), which were compiled at emperors' command, such as the *Kokin-shū*. Among the major poets of this period were Arihira Narihira, Ono no Komachi, and Sugawara no Michizane. Then a new and different style arose: descriptive poems, such as Ki no Tsurayuki's *Tosa nikki*. Literature was divided into three genres: poetry, tales *(monogatari)*, and poetic journals *(nikki)*. The two most important *monogatari* that have survived from this period (tenth century) are the *Utsubo monogatari* and *Ochikubo monogatari*, by unknown authors. The *nikki* genre is typified by works by women, who wrote in Japanese in kana characters, probably created in the early ninth century, while men continued to write in Chinese. Two *nikki* have been preserved, the *Takamitsu nikki*, attributed to Fujiwara no Takamitsu but probably apocryphal, and the *Kagerō nikki*, composed by a woman in the Fujiwara family. Around the year 1000, the Japanese aristocracy benefited from an extremely brilliant society, that of the Fujiwara regents. Poetry ruled at the court, written in both Chinese and Japanese, as evidenced in the collection *Wakan-rōei-shū*, compiled by Fujiwara no Kintō. But the *monogatari* genre soon gained its letters of nobility with the *Genji monogatari*, by Murasaki Shikibu, and the *Makura no sōshi*, by Sei Shōnagon. Although they are very different, these two masterful works by ladies of the court are typical of dominant attitudes in aristocratic circles in the capital, Heian-kyō, at the time; the more romantic *Genji monogatari* was the true genesis of the Japanese novel. Many *nikki* were written at the same time by Murasaki Shikibu, Izumi Shikibu, and other women; the *Sarashina nikki* depicts the life of a provincial governor's wife.

The high quality of the *Genji monogatari* led to many attempts at emulation. In the eleventh and twelfth centuries, the myth of the unassailable masterpiece was born, accompanied by a certain nostalgia, and literature began to be oriented in slightly different directions. But the *Genji* left a considerable heritage: the *Sagoromo monogatari, Hammatsu-chūnagon monogatari, Yowa no nezame, Tsutsumi-chūnagon monogatari, Heichū monogatari,* and *Torikaebaya monogatari* are works of varying degrees of value, containing elements of both novel and tale. In the late eleventh century, other genres appeared, including *setsuwa,* or collections of tales and legends. Some, of Buddhist inspiration, were written in Chinese, such as the *Nihon-ryūi-ki* and *Sambō-ekotoba,* but the genre was quickly distanced from religious tradition with the *Konjaku monogatari,* attributed to Minamoto no Takakuni, and the *Uji-shūi monogatari,* perhaps by the same author. Other collections of the same type followed in the twelfth and thirteenth centuries, such as the *Kokon-chomon-shū,* attributed to Tachibana no Narisue. In parallel, there were historical chronicles, the oldest example of which seems to be the *Eiga monogatari,* soon followed by *O kagami, Ima kagami,* and later by *Azuma kagami* and *Masu kagami.*

With the rise of warrior clans and the weakening of the imperial court, literature turned to warrior tales, such as the *Hōgen monogatari* and *Heiji monogatari,* which told of battles for preeminence between the warrior clans and the court in the late twelfth century. The most famous of these epics is the *Heike monogatari* (of which more than 70 variants exist), a sort of epic poem that was recited by itinerant monks called *biwa-hōshi,* who accompanied themselves on the *biwa.* This work greatly influenced subsequent literature, especially the *Taiheiki* (fourteenth century), *Gikei-ki,* and *Soga monogatari* (late fourteenth century).

At the court, poetry remained very popular and imperial poetry anthologies, such as the *Shinkokin-shū,* continued to be produced, complemented by poetry anthologies written by individual authors, among them the great *waka* masters Saigyō, Fujiwara no Sadaie, and Minamoto no Sanetomo. The *nikki* style was not lost, but it was difficult to innovate in this genre. "Travel notes" *(kikō),* in contrast, such as the *Izayoi nikki,* began to be very successful, as were "various notes" *(zuihitsu),* the major works of which were the *Hōjō-ki,* by Kamo no Chōmei, and *Tsurezure-gusa,* by Kenkō Hōshi.

Japanese Theater: Noh. In the time of the Ashikaga shoguns (Muromachi period), culture was oriented toward China, especially in the arts, but remained resolutely Japanese in the literary domain. A composite form of theater arose in which aesthetics played a large part; mixing completely different genres, its origins were in popular dance, Sarugaku,

and it referred to ancient forms of danced theater, such as the Bugaku and Gagaku, and to recitation of epic poems or tales. Most plays in this new theater form, called *sarugaku no nō,* were written by Zeami, Kan'ami, Motomasa, and Zenchiku, all from the same family. The scripts were long poems intercut with songs, a synthesis of such diverse genres as epic *(gunki-monogatari), monogatari,* poems, tales, and legends, all with a strong Buddhist or Shinto connotation. These plays were broken up by a type of farce, Kyōgen, similar to fables of the Western medieval period and resembling comedies of manners. These were not literary masterpieces, but their influence on the literature of subsequent centuries was great. This type of aristocratic theater was then codified and became a sort of solemn, formal entertainment.

Popular Literature. Itinerant storytellers and touring theater troupes helped decentralize culture, and romantic works began to replace the old *monogatari,* which were no longer the exclusive domain of aristocrats (who were still devoted to poetry), and which thus became available to people of more modest milieus. With the appearance of a new urban merchant class, the *chōnin,* in the sixteenth and early seventeenth centuries, public taste turned toward more accessible works, signaling the passing of the novel. In fashion were *otogi-zōshi,* romances incorporating love stories, hagiographies, more or less historically accurate legends and stories, fairytales, and animal stories. Some of these works, written in kana characters, incorporated tales translated from Chinese or even from Western languages, such as the *Isopo monogatari,* a transcription of Aesop's *Fables.* At the same time, a new form of theater was born with the appearance of the *Jōruri jūnidan-sōshi,* written about 1570—a form that was aptly dubbed *jōruri. Jōruri* texts were soon adapted for puppet theater, *ayatsuri-shibai,* especially in Osaka, and became very popular in the seventeenth century with plays by Chikamatsu Monzaemon, who has justly been called the "Shakespeare of Japan." Poetry was revived with *renga,* or "linked verses," which had been composed for a long time as a sort of parlor game but which now became a poetic genre in their own right: many were contained in the anthology *Tsukuba-shū,* dating from 1356. At the same time, a new poetic form called *haikai* (or *haiku*) arose; at first simple poetic entertainment, after Bashō it became a literary genre of its own that is still in use today.

In the early seventeenth century, after peace returned and the Tokugawa shogunate was established, attitudes and tastes changed. Although many "Sinologists," such as Hayashi Dōshun and Kaibara Ekiken, continued to advocate the study of Chinese letters and Confucianism, other scholars tried to revive purely Japanese traditions. The *kana-zōshi* genre was revived by Ihara Saikaku, who wrote many works (called *ukiyo-zōshi*) dealing with commonplace subjects, such as love *(kōshoku-mono)*, war *(buke-mono)*, and interactions among urban merchants *(chōnin-mono)*. Saikaku was followed by many authors, among them Andō Jishō and Ejimaya Kiseki. These novels (or stories of time passing) were extremely popular, as were *jōruri* plays, and they gave rise to a highly colorful theater genre, Kabuki. In poetry, the haiku genre gained increasing numbers of followers, most writers of the time tried their hand at the form, and many haiku collections were published.

In the mid-eighteenth century, a period of returning to sources began, under the impetus of philologists and historians such as Motoori Norinaga and Ueda Akinari. A new style of novel, the *yomi-hon*, mixed historical tales with fantasy, as in the *Hanabusa-zōshi*, by Kinryō Gyōja, and *Ugetsu monogatari* (Tales of the Rain and the Moon), by Ueda Akinari, published in 1775. After this, a wide variety of tales, stories, and histories were classified in the *kusa-zōzhi, share-bon,* and *kokkei-bon* genres, typified by works by Jippensha Ikku and Shikitei Samba. Other categories of books were popular with the public, such as sentimental *(gōkan)* and romantic *(ninjō-bon)* stories.

In Kabuki theater, a form that developed rapidly, styles followed the subject represented: historical plays, such as those written by Ki no Kaion and Takeda Izumo; plays on current topics, such as those inspired by Chikamatsu Monzemon's and Chikamatsu Hanji's works; and plays on fantastic subjects, such as *Yotsuya kaidan* by Tsuruya Namboku. Kabuki theater also drew upon many puppet-theater plays, which were gradually losing their audiences (except in Osaka, where, in the late eighteenth century, this genre was known by the name of its most famous theater, Bunraku) to Kabuki. One of the most famous writers of this period was Kawatake Mokuami (1816–93).

Poets were still intensely active. Haiku became very popular, with works emulating those of Bashō, Buson, and Issa; the genre was supplemented by humorous and satirical poems called *senryū*. Classical poetry, although still being written, notably by Ryōkan, fell to secondary importance, despite the appearance of a genre of *waka* that was quite humorous, called *kyōka*, which was more entertainment for poets than literature of high value.

Until the Meiji Restoration (1868), popular literature and poetry were fertile ground for writers, whose numbers swelled; they wrote in a wide variety of genres, with different degrees of success. Although some works were worthy of being called literature, most no longer have any but anecdotal interest. Some *ninjō-bon*, for example, were simply erotic stories. Their value is in illustrating the extreme diversity of genres, many of which were classified according to book cover. Some *share-bon* were frankly vulgar, as opposed to *yomi-hon*, which retained a certain decorum, while *kuza-sōshi* (covers colored yellow, black, red, blue, etc.) still had some literary pretensions. The most interesting, perhaps, were *kokkei-bon*, or "droll books," of which some titles showed a definite humorous quality in relatively chaste language—for example, the famous *Hizakurige,* by Jippensha Ikku, published in 1802, and Shikitai Samba's *Ukiyo-buro* and *Ukiyo-doko*. The *Genji monogatari* had its imitators, and still does today, notably Ryūtei Tanehiko, who wrote *Nise-murasaki inaka Genji* (The Genji Peasant), which takes place during the Ashikaga period.

Modern Literature. The Meiji era, which started in 1868, saw a phenomenal infatuation with Western studies and a proliferation of "schools." The rise of scientific literature, following the works by Fukuzawa Yukichi, led to a clear degradation in popular romantic literature, while the supporters of classical Chinese literature struggled desperately to preserve their status. Western-type novels began to appear, and Tsubouchi Shōyō published *Shōsetsu-shinzui* (Substantive Marrow of the Novel), in which he stated that writing novels is an art unto itself, though it must obey certain laws. He was followed by Ozaki Kōyō, who returned to national sources, though he was not unaware of the lessons of the West. Yamada Bimyo and Kōda Rohan were the most representative authors of this first "modern school." There were, of course, reactions, especially that of the Bungakukai (Literary World) group, into which Kitamura Tōkoku gathered such authors as Shimazaki Tōson, Higuchi Ichiyo, and two "old-fashioned romantics," Tokutomi Roka and Izumi Kyōka.

Like European literature, Japanese literature was divided into trends: the naturalists were well represented by Kunikida Doppo, Shimazaki Tōson, Tayama Katai, Iwano Hōmei, and Tokuda Shūsai; the symbolists were led by Mori Ogai and Natsume Sōseki. Other groups followed several influences at once. Some, publishing in the magazine *Shirakaba*, such as Mushano-kōji Saneatsu, Shiga Naoya, Arishima Takeo, and Akutagawa Ryūnosuke, were influenced by Tolstoy and Maeterlinck, as opposed to the prosaic views of Nagai Kafū and Masamune Hakuchō. Other writers belonged to no particular trend, such as Tanizaki Jun'ichirō, who was beginning to publish at the time. In 1920, many intellectuals began to subscribe to socialist theories; a group of "proletarian" writers united in a "federation," the NAPF: Kobayashi Takiji was one of its best representatives. However, the naturalist trend did not weaken, and Shimazaki Tōson continued to be very successful. In the meantime, theater was revived with the adaptation of foreign plays and the new Shingeki style, in which original plays were produced. After 1937, proletarian literature disappeared due to government censorship, and it was not until 1945 and the end of the Second World War that a new generation of writers stepped forward, such as Noma Hiroshi, Shiina Rinzō, Ōoka Shōhei, Umezaki Haruo, and Dazai Osamu, many of whom drew on their experiences in the war. There were a number of different literary currents, which was a good thing because the number of authors was increasing exponentially, some returning to the roots of the Japanese character, such as Kawabata Asunari; others attempting literary experiments, such as Mishima Yukio; some writing psychological novels, such as Abe Kōbō; still others devoted to current affairs or social conditions, such as Ōe Kenzaburō. The confrontation between the Japanese literary and poetic world and the West led to a total revolution in genres and a proliferation of new talent. Liberated from taboos and conventions, modern Japanese literature, often of very high quality in both poetry and theater and novels, is extremely fecund at present.

Living National Treasures (Ningen Kokuhō). Established in 1950 and awarded since 1955, a title given by the government to people recognized as "bearers of important intangible cultural assets" (Jūyō Mukei Bunkazai Hojisha). This high distinction, rarely granted, rewards efforts made in all traditional fields by a wide variety of artists and artisans. It is accompanied by an annual stipend.

Loew, Oscar. German agronomist (1844–1941), professor of biochemistry at the University of Tokyo from 1893 to 1907. He and Oscar Kellner initiated biochemical agricultural methods in Japan.

Loti, Pierre. Navy officer (Louis Marie Julien Viaud, 1850–1923). He visited Japan in 1885 and 1900–01 and wrote several novels dealing with Japanese customs, such as *Madame Chrysanthème* (Madam Chrysanthemum, 1887) and *Japoneries d'automne* (Japan's Autumn Art, 1889), which, in their naiveté and total contempt for Japanese civilization, unfortunately gave the French a completely false idea of the country. He also wrote other novels on the countries of the Near East, which, though very literary, were nevertheless superficial.

Lowell, Percival. American astronomer and writer (1855–1916), born in Boston. After traveling extensively in the Far East, he wrote several important works on Asian thought, such as *The Soul of the Far East* (1888) and *Occult Japan* (1895), in which he showed a real comprehension of Asian attitudes and Shinto rites.

Lyman, Benjamin Smith. American geologist (1835–1920), invited to Japan by the Meiji government to supervise Japanese coal mines and oil wells, in 1872. He introduced modern mining operations to Japan and drew the first geological map of Hokkaido, *Nihon Ezo chishitsu yōryaku no zu*, in 1876. He returned to the United States in 1881.

Lytton Commission. In December 1931, the League of Nations sent to Japan and Manchuria a five-person commission, led by Count Lytton, to determine the causes of the "Manchuria Incident" (September 18–19, 1931), which had led to the creation of the state of Manchukuo by the Guandong (Kantō-gun) army, paid for by the Japanese government. This commission concluded that Japan had been the aggressor in this affair, and the League of Nations adopted the Lytton Report, so the Japanese delegate quit the General Assembly and Japan withdrew from the League of Nations in March 1933.

M. This consonant is found in Japanese only in association with one of the five vowels, to give the sounds *ma, mi, mu, me,* and *mo.* It can also be combined with *yō* to form the composite syllable *myō* *(mi + yo + u).* In phonetic transcription, the sound *m* also replaces the final letter *n* of a syllable preceding the sounds *n* and *h (b, p),* as in, for example, *homma* for *hon'ma, shimbun* for *shin'bun. See* N.

Ma. Concept of space or emptiness between two things, used mainly in Japanese arts (painting, theater, music, martial arts) to describe a gap. In music, dance, and theater, there are several types of *ma:* total *(homma),* transitory *(hamma),* and very short *(hayama).* The concept of immobilization between two movements in Kabuki theater is called *mie.* In painting, *ma* is an empty space leaving room for the imagination. The concept is also used in garden design and literature. According to *ma,* everything is integrated with nature and is defined by its own space-time *(ma-ai). See* NAITŌ AKIRA.

• **Ma-ai.** According to the concept of *ma,* the space-time or distance-time that allows for a general evaluation of movements or situations against each other or in relation to their situation in space or time. In martial arts, it is the ideal distance between two combatants, and the one who "penetrates" the *ma-ai* of the adversary is able to defeat him or her. It is also any pause in a sequence of facts or ideas, intended to give more significance to those that follow.

Mabe Manabu. Painter, born 1924 in Kumamoto prefecture, who emigrated to Brazil in 1934 to operate a farm in São Paulo State. He quickly turned to painting and gained an international reputation for his exhibitions in Europe and America. His works bear a resemblance to the French "informal" style.

Mabiki. "Lightening the harvest," a term used, especially during the Edo period, to characterize infanticide or abortion, practiced among peasants during periods of famine. Also called *yomogi-tsugi ni yaru, yama-e asobi ni yaru* ("sending children to play on the mountain").

MacArthur, Douglas. American general (1880–1964), General Arthur MacArthur's (1845–1912) son, born in Arkansas. An observer for the United States during the Russo-Japanese War of 1904–05, he fought in the First World War and was wounded twice. After serving in the Philippines, he was chief of staff from 1930 to 1935, then was sent back to the Philippines, where, starting in 1937, he devoted himself to reorganizing the army. President Franklin D. Roosevelt appointed him commander-in-chief of the American forces in the Far East on July 28, 1941. In March 1942, he was forced to withdraw from the Philippines (Bataan) by the Japanese forces, and he established headquarters in Australia. In October 1944, he landed on Leyte and began to recapture the archipelago. He accepted the Japanese forces' surrender on September 2, 1945, on board the *Missouri,* then began the process of "democratizing" Japan, dismantling the zaibatsu and organizing a major anti-communist campaign *(see* S.C.A.P.). During the Korean War, which began on June 25, 1950, he opposed the views of the American government with regard to Chinese engagement, and President Harry Truman relieved him of duty. He spent the rest of his life in retirement, retaining his rank of five-star general.

MacDonald, Ranald. American adventurer (1824–94), born in Oregon, of Chinook mixed blood. A sailor on a whaling ship, he landed on the Japanese islands of Rishiri and Yagishiri in 1848. He was arrested by the shogunal authorities, sent to Nagasaki, and held as a prisoner for five months, during which time he taught English to several Dutch interpreters. When he was freed, in April 1849, he was repatriated by an American ship, along with other shipwrecked sailors. He then went to Australia and prospected for gold. When he returned to the United States, he wrote his memoirs, which were published posthumously.

Machi. "City," "town," or district of a large city.

• **Machi-bugyō.** City governor under the authority of the Edo shogunate, administering the affairs of the *chōnin*. There was one in each large city: Edo, Kyoto, Nara, Sakai, Nagasaki, Nikkō, Niigata, and others. *Machi-bugyō* was one of the three senior bureaucratic positions (with *jisha-bugyō* and *kanjō-bugyō*) collectively called *sambugyō*. See BUGYŌ.

• **Machi-kanō.** School of painting frequented by painters of the Kanō school living in Edo. They were self-employed, as opposed to working for the shogunate, and belonged to neither the *oku-eshi* nor the *omote-eshi*. Also called *machi-eshi* (urban painters).

• **Machi-shū.** Term for urban dwellers, mainly in Kyoto, Sakai, and other large cities, during the Muromachi and Momoyama periods. In the late sixteenth century, some *machi-shū* formed associations, *machi-gumi*, for self-defense and administrative needs. The *machi-shū* were called *chōnin* in the Edo period.

• **Machi-yakko.** During the Edo period, delinquent boys who organized in troops *(kumi)* in the large cities, controlling the labor market for commoners. They often violently attacked the *hatamoto-yakko,* who played the same role among the *hatamoto.* The Tokugawa shogunate sometimes used them as auxiliary police. One of their most famous members was Banzuiin Chōbei (1622–51). *See* BUGYŌ, YAKKO.

• **Machi-yakunin.** During the Edo period, civil bureaucrats of the *chōnin* class who represented associations of commoners. They served as deputies to the *machi-bugyō,* overseeing and assisting people and forming firefighting *(hikeshi)* and police units.

Machi Shunsō. Contemporary calligrapher, founder of the Nanihazu school of photography and author of books on calligraphy. She had several exhibitions in the United States and Europe, and she received the grand prize of the National Academy of Calligraphy of Japan in 1946.

Mado. "Windows." Windows in the traditional architectural styles *wa-yō* (panes with vertical window bars) and *kara-yō* (with curved frame and interlaced window bars). *Mado* are generally placed between two horizontal beams, called *uchinori-nageshi* or *kashira-nuki* on top and *koshi-nageshi* or *koshi-nuki* on the bottom. They are sometimes protected by full sliding wood shutters called *amado.*

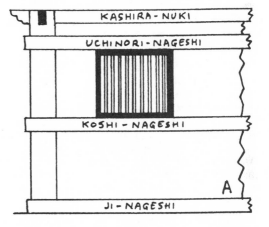

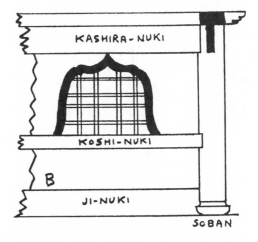

Mado windows. A. *Wa-yō.* B. *Kara-yō*

Madre de Deus. Portuguese ship, commanded by Andrea Pessoa, that sailed into Nagasaki in 1609. In 1608, following a riot involving Japanese sailors from a ship belonging to the Christian daimyo Amira Harunobu and one belonging to the Portuguese of Macao, the *Madre de Deus* was attacked by Arima's fleet on the orders of Tokugawa Ieyasu. Pessoa sank his ship, rather than surrendering it, on January 6, 1610. *See* ARIMA HARUNOBU, HASEGAWA FUJIHIRO.

Maebara Issei. Samurai (1834–76) of the Chōshū estate who held several important positions in the new Meiji government; he was minister of war in 1870, a position that he held for only a short time before falling ill. Unhappy that the government had eliminated the privileges of the samurai, he organized a group of rebel samurai in Hagi in October 1876; he was defeated, taken prisoner, and executed.

Maebashi. City in Gumma prefecture, about 100 km northwest of Tokyo, on the Tone-gawa river, former castle town *(jōka-machi)* and headquarters of the Matsudaira family, once called Umayabashi. It has silk mills and automobile and electrical industry, Futagoyama and Hachimanyama ancient tombs *(kofun)*. University founded in 1949. *Pop.:* 270,000.
→ *See* KABUTO.

Maeda Kanji. Painter (1896–1930) in Western style, who studied in France.

Maeda Kensetsu Kōgyō. Public-works and construction firm, founded in 1919, also active in Hong Kong and Southeast Asia. Head office in Tokyo.

Maedakō Hiroichirō. Writer (Maedakō Kōichirō, 1888–1957), born in Sendai. Taokutomi Roka's disciple, in 1907 he left for the United States, where he became familiar with the socialist ideas of Kaneko Kiichi (1876–1909) and his wife, Josephine Conder Kaneko. He began to write plays, then moved from Chicago to New York in 1915 and wrote novels and essays, while working for various newspapers (writing in English). When he returned to Japan, in 1920, he introduced the "proletarian" style of novel. He traveled in China in 1928–29, and translated novels by Upton Sinclair and Sinclair Lewis. Among his best-known works are *Daibōfūu jidai* (The Age of Tempests, 1924), *Jūnenkan* (Ten Years, 1930), *Ningen* (The Human Being, 1938),

Seishun no jigazō (Self-Portrait of a Young Man, 1958).

Maeda Magoemon. Samurai (1818–64) of the Chōshū clan. Having sided with the emperor against the Edo shogunate, he was taken prisoner during the expedition against the Chōshū and executed.

Maeda Masahiro. Ceramist, born 1948 near Kyoto. He had exhibitions in the Mitsukoshi space in Paris in 1994.

Maeda Munehisa. Buddhist monk (Maeda Gen'i, Mimbukyō Hō-in, Tokuzen'in Gen'i, 1539–1602) and statesman, adviser to Toyotomi Hideyoshi, appointed *soshidai* of Kyoto. He modified etiquette at the Jūrakudai and protected Christian missionaries.

Maedare. A sort of apron made of coarse canvas generally worn by laborers. Also called *maekake.*

Maeda Seison. Painter (Maeda Renzō, 1885–1977), born in Gifu prefecture. He studied the techniques of the Maruyama school in Tokyo, under Kajita Hanko (1870–1917). He then visited Europe in 1922 and 1923 and China in 1938, after being elected a member of the Imperial Fine Arts Academy (Teikoku Bijutsu-in). Appointed an Artist of the Imperial Household (Teishitsu Gigei-in) in 1944, and a professor at the Tokyo School of Fine Arts (Tokyo Bijutsu Gakkō), he was responsible for restoration of the frescos in the *kondō* of the Hōryū-ji, which had been damaged by fire in 1949, and received the Order of Culture (Bunka-shō) in 1955. From 1959 until his death, he gave painting lessons to Empress Nagako. He worked mainly in Nihonga style.

Maeda Tamon. Politician (1884–1962) born in Osaka, Japan's delegate to the International Labor Organization in 1923, then director of the Japanese Cultural Center in New York from 1938 to 1941. He was minister of education (1945–46) in Shidehara Kijūrō's cabinet and wrote the imperial proclamation in which the emperor renounced his divinity. He converted to Christianity and became a Quaker.

Maeda Toshiie. Samurai (ca. 1538–99) from Owari, who was a page *(koshō)* for Oda Nobunaga in 1551 in Nagoya. He fought in most of Nobunaga's campaigns and commanded his troop of harquebusiers *(teppō-ashigaru)* in the battle of Nagashino (1575). Nobunaga gave him a fief in Noto province, through which he acceded to the rank of daimyo. When Nobunaga died in 1582, Toshiie fought on Toyotomi Hideyoshi's side against his rival, Shibata Katsuie, and received other estates as a reward, including that of Kanazawa, worth about 1 million *koku*. One of his daughters, Maa (Kagadono, 1572–1605), became a concubine of Hideyoshi, and two others, Kiku (1578–84) and Gō (1574–1634), were adopted by Hideyoshi. In 1595, Maeda Toshiie was one of the five *tairō (go-tairō)* responsible for tutoring the young Toyotomi Hideyori. Also known under the title Kaga-dainagon. *See* SONKEIKAKU BUNKŌ.

Maeda Tsunanori. Daimyo (1643–1724) of the Kanazawa estate, Maeda Toshiie's and Maeda Toshitsune's (1593–1658) grandson. He converted the rents from the fiefs of his samurai into salaries, established a land survey of his estates, and reorganized the tax-collection system. He took in the Confucian scholar Kinoshita Jun'an and allowed him to gather a large collection of Japanese and Chinese works and documents, which formed the Sonkeikaku library. *See* KANAZAWA BUNKŌ.

Maeda Yūgure. Poet (Maeda Yōzō, 1883–1951) born in Kanagawa prefecture, author of *waka* collections in the naturalist style of Shimazaki Tōson and Tayama Katai: *Shūkaku* (1910), *Genseirin, Suigen chitai* (1932).

Maehara. Archeological site in the town of Koganei west of Tokyo, excavated in 1975. Hundreds of stone tools were found from seven pre-ceramic cultural levels, the oldest going back 22,000 to 23,000 years. It seems that the site was also occupied during a large part of the Jōmon period (tombs and piles of debris, ceramic shards, a stone phallus, and some arrowheads).

Maejima Hisoka. Politician (1835–1919), born in Echigo province, of peasant origins. After studying Chinese, literature, military and naval sciences, and English, he traveled extensively throughout Japan and became a low-level bureaucrat in the Edo shogunate. He then worked in the Meiji government's Ministry of People's Affairs (Mimbushō) in 1870, where he was noticed by Ōkuma Shigenobu and Itō Hirobumi. That same year, they provided him with the opportunity to create a national postal service, which was inaugurated in April 1871, with 65 post offices along the Tōkaidō road. Maejima also formed an international postal service and had Japan admitted to the Universal Postal Union in 1877. He founded the first major daily newspaper, the *Yūbin Hōchi Shimbun* (which became the *Yomiuri Shimbun* in 1942) and another newspaper, written entirely in kana, the *Mainichi Hiragana Shimbun.* He advocated the adoption of kana syllabaries to replace Chinese ideograms *(kanji).* From 1886 to 1890, he was the second president of the University of Waseda, which he had helped to found after resigning from his official position in 1881; after this, he directed private railroad companies. He was vice-minister of communications from 1888 to 1891, and elected to the House of Peers in 1904.

Maekawa Kunio. Painter and architect (1905–86), born in Niigata, student of Le Corbusier in Paris until 1935, and Tange Kenzō's teacher. He belonged to the avant-garde Kosaku Bunka Remma movement. In 1963, he received the Benjamin Perret Prize for his architectural projects in prestressed concrete. Among his most typical works are the International House of Tokyo (1955), the city hall in Fukushima (1958), the Harumi apartment buildings (1959), the Setagaya Community Center in Tokyo (1959), the Tokyo festival hall (1961), the Saitama prefectural museum (1971), the Kyoto Kaikan, the Tokyo Bunka Kaikan, the Tokyo Kaijō Building (1974), and the Japanese pavilions at the Brussels International Exposition.

Maeno Ryōtaku. Physician and scholar (1723–1803) in "Dutch sciences" *(rangaku),* born in Edo. A student of Aoki Kon'yō, he conducted anatomy experiments following directions in a Dutch work that he had translated with the assistance of Sugita Gempaku in 1774, *Kaitai shinsho* (New Book on Anatomy). A naturally curious man, he also studied astronomy, the natural sciences, and architecture. Among his other works, the best known is *Rangaku kotohajime* (Encounters with Western Science), published in 1744.

Mafune Yutaka. Playwright (1902–77), born in Fukushima prefecture. He studied English and Irish literature, then wrote short plays dealing with the life of peasants and urban dwellers, such as *Itachi* (The Weasel, 1934) and *Hadaka no machi* (The Naked City, 1936). After the Second World War, he wrote comedies and worked in radio. His complete works, *Mafune Yutaka zenshū,* was published in five volumes from 1948 to 1950.

Magatama. Prehistoric and proto-historic hook- or comma-shaped magical ornaments made of amber, stone, jade, and even glass, found in Late Jōmon and Yayoi sites and in *kofun*. These amulets, which comprised one of the Mi-kusa no Kandakara (Three Sacred Treasures) were perhaps at first a sort of "passport" to Heaven, used by shamans for their "voyages." Shamans' vestments and the harnesses of white horses were adorned with *magatama,* as were the crowns of Korean kings. They have been found in Altaic tombs in Pazyryk, Siberia, dating to the fifth century BC. *Magatama* (also called *mitama*) are still worn on necklaces by priestesses in Okinawa during Shinto ceremonies. A sandstone mold for casting *matagama* in glass (about 4 cm long) was found in Akaide (Fukuoka prefecture) in 1977. *See also* MITAMA, TAMA, YASAKANI NO MAGATAMA.

Mage. Hairstyles once worn by women and men according to their status or for specific events. There were more than 35 different *mage,* varying widely within and between eras, especially in the Edo period.

For men, the main *mage* were:

—*in the fifth and sixth centuries:* the *mizura,* with a curl on either side of the face.

—*from the seventh to ninth century:* the *kanka no ikkei,* with a high bun.

—*starting in the twelfth century:* the hairstyles of the *bushi* featured a shaved front of the scalp and hair gathered on top of the head in a bun, called *chasen-mage, chon-mage, honda-mage, ōsakayaki,* etc.

Among the many women's hairstyles were:

—*until the seventh century:* the *shimada-mage,* two loops of hair on the head, and the *kōkei,* with two raised loops.

—*in the Heian period:* the *suihatsu,* long straight hair, and the *tamamusubi,* flat style with hair rolled on the nape.

—*in the Muromachi period:* the *karawa-mage* and *hyōgo-mage,* more elaborate hair styles with a high braided bun held by a comb.

—*in the Edo period:* various types of buns, held by combs and pins *(kanzashi),* called *shimada-mage, katsuyama-mage, ichō-gaeshi,* etc. The most common form for married women was the *marumage;* for girls, the *ichō-gaeshi* (or *chocho-mage*); and for young women of marriageable age, the *shimada-mage.* For weddings, women styled their hair in *tsuno-kakushi* (hidden horns).

Modern hairstyles are called *seiyō-agemaki* (for women) and *zangiri* (for men). Although hairstyles were greatly influenced by Chinese styles at the beginning of the historical period, in the Edo period they took typically Japanese forms, distinguishing

men and women by age, status, and social class. Hairstyles for women of high society also followed fashion, while men's hairstyles changed less. Some people with "no rank" allowed their hair to grow long, while Buddhist monks shaved their heads. Rural dwellers had no particular hairstyles. In the 1920s and 1930s, the fashion for women was to have "Joan of Arc" haircuts, while boys had "bowl" cuts. Curling irons, imported from France, began to be used about 1920. Traditional hairstyles are now usually worn only as hairpieces during festivals and historical reconstructions, in Noh and Kabuki theater, and by *sumotori.* Hairstyles in general are known as *kamigata. See also* ACCESSORIES, CHON-MAGE, HAIRSTYLES, ZANGIRI.

Mago. Former name for packhorse-men. These people led the horse by the bridle and did not ride. Their numbers increased starting in the Kamakura period (they were then called *bashaku*), as transport needs grew. In the Edo period, *mago* were assigned to relays *(shukuba)* on the major roads. Organized in guilds, they monopolized land transport. *See also* BASHAKU, SHUKU-EKI.

Magojirō. Sculptor (Ukyō Hisatsugu; *mei:* Shintarō, 1538–64) of Noh masks, son of Kongō Shiroku Ujimasa, a famous maker of masks portraying girls.
→ *See* SHIGENAGA.

Magome Tōge. "Magome Pass," located in southwestern Nagano prefecture, on the Nakasendō road, very busy during the Edo period. A waystation *(shuku-eki)* was installed there. *Alt.:* 800 m.

Maigo-fuda. Formerly, a copper tag attached to a child's belts bearing his or her name and address, for easy identification if he or she got lost. The tags also often bore the animal symbol of the child's year of birth (*see* JIKKAN JŪNI-SHI). *Maigo-fuda* have now been replaced, for nursery- and pre-school children, by a pouch hung from their necks containing their vital information.

Maiko. In Kyoto, a term for apprentice geisha. *See* GEISHA.

Mainichi Hōsō. The first commercial radio station in Japan, established by the *Mainichi Shimbun* in 1950. In 1956, it merged with the Asahi Broadcasting Corporation to form the Osaka Terebi, which became the Mainichi Broadcasting System in 1958.

• *Mainichi Shimbun.* Daily newspaper, founded in 1876 in Osaka as *Osaka Nippo,* then called *Osaka Mainichi;* it took the name *Mainichi Shimbun* in 1911. It is one of the largest newspapers in Japan, with a daily circulation of almost 5 million. It also publishes an English-language edition, the *Mainichi Daily News,* and has major regional bureaus in Tokyo, Osaka, Nagoya, Kita-Kyushu, and Sapporo, as well as more than 20 foreign bureaus connected to major international press agencies such as Agence France-Presse, United Press International, and the Tass Agency.

Mājan. Japanese name for the Chinese game *mahjong,* introduced to Japan in the early twentieth century and extremely popular in the 1920s. The game lost popularity after 1932, but was taken up again after the Second World War, and there are currently millions of players in Japan, organized in more than 50,000 clubs. Many *mājan* schools were created, attended by both men and women. However, young people today seem less interested in *mājan* than in sports.

Majima Toshiyuki. Chemist (1874–1962), born in Kyoto. After studying in Great Britain, Switzerland, and Germany, he was a professor at the University of Tōhoku starting in 1911, and president of the University of Osaka from 1943 to 1946. His research on alkaloids and pigments is authoritative. He received the Order of Culture (Bunka-shō) in 1949.

Maki. Old measure of land corresponding to the area needed to sow 1 *shō* of seeds, and equivalent to about 0.1 or 0.2 *tan* (100 to 200 m²). *See* KOKU, SHŌ, TAN.
• Name for pastureland, considered essential for horse-breeding operations during the Edo period.

Maki-e. Type of decoration on lacquer using gold and silver powder spread on the surface while the lacquer is still moist. This technique, invented in the eighth century, was called *makkinru.* There are different types of *maki-e: togidashi* (polished after decoration), *hira maki-e* (decoration covered with transparent lacquer), *taka maki-e* (metallic powder on "sculpted" lacquer, a decorative technique that appeared during the Kamakura period), and *nashiji* (irregular sprinkling on different layers of translucent lacquer). These techniques were sometimes combined or used with *kirikane* or mother-of-pearl inlay *(raden). See* LACQUER, URUSHI.

Maki Fumihiko. Architect, born 1928 in Tokyo. After studying in the United States, he worked in Japan and the United States. Among his major works are the Toyota Memorial Auditorium (University of Nagoya, 1960), Risshō University in Kumagaya (1968), the Daikan'yama apartment building, the Katō Gakuen elementary school (1972), the Osaka sports center (1972), and the Okinawa aquarium (1975).

Makiginu. Title of a Noh play: a man, delivering silk to the emperor, stops at the Otonashi shrine to perform his devotions. Because of this, he should have been punished for arriving at the palace late, but the *kami* of Otonashi appears disguised as a shamaness who dances and asks that he be pardoned.

Makiguchi Jōzaburō. Religious leader (Makiguchi Tsunesaburō, 1871–1944), born near Niigata. At first a teacher in Hokkaido (he was a graduate of the Sapporo Teachers' College in 1893), he went to Tokyo in 1901 and wrote a number of books while continuing his career as a professor: *Jinsei chirigaku* (Geography of Human Life, 1901), *Kyōdoka kenkyū* (Studies in Folklore, 1912), *Sōka kyōigaku taikaei* (Pedagogical System Based on Creative Values, 1930). In 1928, he became a follower of Nichiren's doctrines, and in 1930 he created the Sōka Gakkai, a religious and political society advocating the virtues of education according to creative values. In 1943, he and some of his assistants were imprisoned for their opposition to the war, and he died in prison on November 18, 1944. *See* SŌKA GAKKAI.

Maki Izumi. Politician (Maki Yasuomi, 1813–64), born on the Kurume estate (Fukuoka prefecture) into a family of Shinto priests. Influenced by the Mito historical school, he tried to foment anti-shogunal ideas in the Kurume estate but was placed under house arrest. He escaped to Kagoshima but was taken prisoner during a battle between the shogunate's warriors and samurai faithful to the emperor. Freed in 1863, he was a professor at the Gakushū-in in Kyoto for a short time; he then joined the forces of the Chōshū trying to recapture Kyoto from the shogunal troops. The Chōshū army was forced to retreat on August 20, 1864, and Maki Izumi committed suicide two days later.

Makimono. Horizontal scroll bearing a text in calligraphy (novel or poetry) with no illustrations, as opposed to *emakimono,* or illustrated scroll. *Chin.:* Shoujuan. *See* KAKEMONO.

Makino Eiichi. Jurist (1878–1970), born in Takayama. He studied law at the University of Tokyo, then in Germany, Italy, and Great Britain. When he returned to Japan in 1913, he became a professor at the University of Tokyo, a position he held until his retirement in 1938. He was particularly interested in criminal law and legislation and wrote a large number of works aimed at reforming the Japanese criminal code, notably *Nihon keihō* (Japan's Penal Code, 1916) and *Keihō kenkyū* (Study of the Penal Code, 1919–1967). He received the Order of Culture (Bunka-shō) in 1950.

Makinohara. Site in Shizuoka prefecture where a *kofun* containing magnificent pieces of horses' harnesses in gold-plated bronze, decorated with Korean and Chinese designs, was excavated.

Makino Masahiro. Movie director (1908–93), son of Makino Shōzō. He directed 255 movies between 1926 and 1972, most of them for the Tōei company. Among his best-known movies are *Rōningai* (The Street of Masterless Samurai, 1928), the first in a long series on historical themes in which the hero is an outcast—*rōnin,* musician, vagabond, etc.; others in this genre were *Aoi me no ningyō* (The Blue-Eyed Doll) and *Nihon kyōkaku den* (Tales of Japanese Chivalry, 1964–71). He also collaborated with Itō Daisuke.

• **Makino Shōzō.** Movie director (1878–1929), born in Kyoto, Makino Masahiro's father. He was a pioneer of Japanese cinema, directing "Kabuki" films for the Nikkatsu company, such as *Honnō-ji gassen* (1908). He directed several hundred films over a little more than ten years with his main actor, Onoe Matsunosuke. He is considered the "father" of Japanese cinema.

Makino Nobuaki. Statesman (Makino Shinken, 1861–1949), born in Kagoshima, Ōkubo Toshimichi's son. He accompanied the Iwakura delegation in 1871 and stayed in the United States until 1874. In 1880, he was appointed ambassador to Italy; he was minister of education in Saionji Kimmochi's cabinet (1906–08) and of foreign affairs in Yamamoto Gonnohyōe's cabinet (1913–14). In 1919, he attended the Peace Conference in Versailles, then was minister of the imperial house starting in 1921. However, criticized by the militarists, he was forced to resign in 1935. Yoshida

Shigeru had married one of his daughters. His memoirs covering the years 1921–38 were published in 1990.

Makino Shin'ichi. Writer (1896–1936), born in Kanagawa prefecture, author of many novels in "personal" style *(watakushi-shōsetsu),* such as *Chichi o uru ko* (1924) and *Kinada mura* (1936). He fell ill and committed suicide.

Makino Tomitarō. Naturalist and botanist (1862–1957), born in Kōchi prefecture. His research on plants earned him the nickname "the Linnaeus of Japan." In *Nihon shokubutsu zukan* (Illustrated Herbarium of Japan, 1940), he described more than 1,000 new plants. He received the Order of Culture (Bunka-shō) posthumously.

Makino Torao. Painter (1890–1946) in Nihonga style. He had an exhibition in Paris in 1922.

Makiwara. A very hard cushion, stuffed with straw or another material, struck by karate practitioners in order to harden their hands and feet. *Makiwara* are sometimes made of a thick cord of straw or raffia wound around a wood post. In *kyūdō* (traditional archery), a *makiwara* is a target about 60 cm in diameter used for training, made of intertwined wisps of straw; archers stand about 2 m away from it. *See* KARATE, KYŪDŌ.

Makoto. A typically Japanese sentiment of "sincerity," an ethical and religious concept that, it is claimed, cannot be really understood except by the Japanese. It includes a sense of moral and physical "cleanliness" (the Shinto notion of *kiyoshi*), symbolized by the cherry blossoms and white snow, and is one of the cardinal virtues of Confucianism contained in the *chū-yō* (*Chin.:* Zhongyong, "Doctrine of the Middle"). The notion of *makoto* was interpreted by Itō Jinsai (and other non-orthodox Confucians) as a sincerity of mind and heart that alone could lead to harmonious relations among people and between people and nature. For Shinto followers, *makoto* (or the True Word) consists of being naturally in harmony with oneself and nature. It is thus the equivalent of the "pure heart" of Western philosophy. Artists and poets are supposed to define *makoto* in their compositions. All self-respecting Japanese must strive for *makoto. Chin.: ching.*
→ *See* ITŌ JINSAI.

• **Makoto no Michi Kyō.** Shinto sect founded in 1925 by Matsumoto Tsunetarō (1887–1944), based on respect for *makoto*. Also called Shin no Michi Kyō. *See* FUSŌ-KYŌ.

• Shinto sect founded in 1949 by Shinoya Nobuo (b. 1927).

Maku. Wide curtain dividing a room into several parts, or encircling a particular spot in a garden to preserve its intimacy. Also, near the battlefield, a curtain enclosing a space reserved for commanding officers.

• **Maku-shita.** *See* SUMO, SUMOTORI.

• **Maku-uchi.** *See* SUMOTORI.

Makura. "Pillow," generally small and made of a hard material—lacquered wood or porcelain. In former times, women used a *makura* under the nape of the neck to preserve their hairstyles while they slept. Some women used a hexagonal *makura,* called *hako-makura,* in which they stored hairpins and small items that might come in handy at night.

• *Makura-jidō.* Title of a Noh play: in ancient China, a man who has inadvertently stepped on the emperor's pillow is exiled to Mt. Rekken. An emperor's envoy finds him centuries later, now 700 years old. The man, called Jidō, tells the envoy that he had written two verses of a Buddhist text on chrysanthemum leaves embroidered on the pillow. Every morning, he has used the dew that covered them to make an elixir of longevity. Jidō then serves a cup of this elixir to the envoy.

• **Makura-kotoba.** "Pillow word," an epithet, sometimes in poetry, to change the meaning of certain words. In general, this epithet had five syllables in *waka* poems. The *Man'yōshū* contains many examples of this literary device, which was later replaced by a *kake-motoba,* or "pivot word," because the real meaning of the *makura-kotoba* was often lost.

• *Makura no sōshi.* "Pillow Book of Sei Shōnagon" (literally, "Night-Table Notes"). A book in 300 short chapters, a sort of personal notebook in the *zuihitsu* genre, written in a poetic style by Sei Shōnagon, lady-in-waiting to Empress Fujiwara Sadako (<997–1000>), describing the ways and customs of the Heian-kyō court.

Makura no sōshi emaki. Single-scroll *emakimono* illustrating the text of *Makura no sōshi,* handwritten by the Buddhist monk Gokōken-in. The illustra-

tions were produced by an unknown woman painter in fourteenth-century Yamato-e style.

Mamiya Rinzō. Explorer (1775–1844) born in Hitachi province (Ibaraki prefecture). After studying cartography with Inō Tadataka, he was sent by the shogunate to survey Hokkaido and the Kuril Islands, and then to reconnoiter the coasts of Sakhalin with another geographer, Matsuda Denjirō (b. 1769) in 1808. He discovered that Sakhalin is separated from the mainland by a strait, crossed it, and visited eastern Siberia in 1809, returning to Japan via China. He was then used as a spy by the shogunate. His reports, *Kita Ezo zusetsu* (Illustrated Notes on Northern Ezo) and *Tōdatsu kikō* (Voyages in Manchuria), contain valuable geographical and ethnographic information. When Franz von Siebold returned to Europe, he named the strait Rinzō; it is now called Nevel Skogo or Tatarskij Proliv (Tatar Strait) in Russian.

Mamori-gatana. Small wooden (bamboo) sword carried by boys in the samurai class and used in combat training. *See* KATANA.

Mampuku-ji. Zen Buddhist temple of the Ōbaku-shū sect, located in Uji (Kyoto-fu) and established by the Chinese monk Ingen (1592–1673), who built it in the Chinese Ming style from 1662 to 1669 on land conceded by shogun Tokugawa Ietsuna. It was directed exclusively by Chinese monks until 1740, when the Japanese monk Ryūtō Gentō (1663–1746) became its abbot. Chinese and Japanese monks then alternated at the head of the monastery until 1786, after which the Mampuku-ji was always directed by Japanese. The group of buildings includes a hall of the Buddha *(butsuden),* a hall of divine kings *(tennōden),* and a large aligned gate *(sammon).* The various buildings house beautiful statues of the Rakan, Hotei, and Ida-ten, sculpted by the Chinese Han Dōsei (Fan Daosheng); many art works and calligraphies by Mokuan (1611–84), Ingen, and Sokuhi (1616–71), Sampitsu (Three Brushes) of the Ōbaku sect; and paintings by Kanō Tan'yū, Ikeno Taiga, and other artists.

Mana. This term, meaning "true writing," designates Chinese characters *(kanji)* used in prose and poetry, as opposed to *kana,* or "borrowed writing." *See* KANA, KOKIN WAKA-SHŪ.

• **Manajo.** Preface or foreword to a book or poetry collection, written in *mana* characters.

Manabe Akifusa. Samurai (1667–1720), born in Musashi province, who became a page *(koshō)* for Tokugawa Ienobu in 1684. He was appointed grand chamberlain in 1709 and was an adviser to the shogun Tokugawa Ienobu and Tokugawa Ietsugu.

• **Manabe Akikatsu.** Senior councillor (1804–84) to the Edo shogunate, and daimyo of a small estate in what is now Fukui prefecture. He took the side of Ii Naosuke, who appointed him *rōjū* in 1858. But he lost the favor of his protector and was forced to retire from public affairs.

Manase. Family of scholars and poets in the sixteenth and seventeenth centuries.

• **Manase Dōsan.** Scholar and physician (Manase Shōkei, Ikkei Dōsan, 1506–94). He was a Zen Buddhist monk at the Shōkoku-ji temple in Kyoto, but abandoned the robe to study medicine. Physician to the imperial family and shogun Ashikaga Yoshiteru, he founded his own school, Keiteki-in, where he taught medicine to many disciples using the Chinese Li-Zhu method (of physicians Li Dongtan and Zhu Danqi, Song period). He became a Christian in 1684 with the name Melchior. His nephew and adoptive son Manase Gensaku (1551–1632) was also an excellent physician, as was his other son, Manase Genkan (Imaōji, ?–1626). They used the names Dōsan II and Dōsan III. The other members of the Manase family, Gen'en (1636–86), Shōchin (1644–1728), and Shōrin (?–1601), were all physicians, as were their descendants up to the nineteenth century.

Manchukuo. State of Manchuria, placed under Japanese control following occupation of the territory in September 1931 and the Manchuria Incident (Manshū Jihen), and called Manshūkoku. It theoretically became independent in March 1932, with its capital in Xinjing (Changchun, *Jap.:* Shinkyō), and the ex-emperor of China, Puyi, became head of state with the Chinese era name Kangde in March 1934. This state remained a Japanese protectorate until the Japanese were defeated in 1945, when it was returned to China. The state of Manchukuo was recognized by the Axis powers, Spain, Finland, Thailand, and the Vatican, among other nations. After 1932, many contingents of Japanese, both civil and military, settled in Manchukuo, which was occupied by the Guandong army, to develop agriculture and build roads. But the Japanese occupation of Manshūkoku was not without major dif-

ficulties, including increasing numbers of attacks on the Japanese immigrants by Russians and Chinese. Puyi abdicated on August 18, 1945; he was captured by the Russians and returned some years later to China, where he was "re-educated." *See* GUANDONG, MANSHŪ JIHEN.

Mandala ("mandara"). Diagrams symbolic of the divinities of Esoteric Buddhism and their "forces." Although *mandara* were introduced from China to Japan by Kūkai and Saichō in their esoteric conception, they were already known from the introduction of Buddhism in the sixth century. But it was mainly through study of the *Dainichi-kyō (Skt.: Mahāvairochana-sūtra)* of the Shingon sect that the art and veneration of *mandara* developed for teaching purposes and as a support for meditation. The two most famous *mandara,* inseparable from the Shingon, are the *taizō-kai* and the *kongō-kai.* In the Nara period, *mandara* of the sect of the Pure Land (Jōdo-shū), Amida-mandara, began to appear. But most sects, both exoteric and esoteric, have used *mandara* of one type or another, some of which are true masterpieces. There are also *mandara* belonging to syncretic Shinto-Buddhist sects, and some are dedicated to particular shrines, such as the Kasuga-mandara and the Hie-mandara. There are, in general, Buddhist *mandara (miya-mandara* or *honji-mandara)* and syncretic *mandara (suijaku-mandara).* It is sometimes difficult, however, to make the distinction, especially in the case of *honji-mandara.*

Mandokoro. Administrative bureau of the high-ranking nobles of the Heian period, composed of a Kurōdo (Secretariat) and a Kumonjo (Archives Bureau). During the Kamakura period, the Mandokoro was the most important administrative organ in the *bakufu;* Ōe no Hiromoto was its first director. But soon, under the *shikken* of the Hōjō family, it became responsible only for administering the finances of the *bakufu.* The Mandokoro was retained by the Muromachi shogunate. *See* KUMONJO.

Maneki-neko. "Calling cat," a popular figurine portraying a cat sitting and lifting its right paw, as if to beckon someone, often placed in shop windows to "call in" customers and bring good luck. Some *maneki-neko* have the left paw raised, for no apparent reason. Some Buddhist temples and Shinto shrines sell *maneki-neko* as protective amulets *(gofu),* and terra-cotta versions are used as children's piggy banks. *See* CATS.

Man'en. Era of Emperor Kōmei: Mar. 1860–Feb. 1861. *See* NENGŌ.

• **Man'en Kembei Shisetsu.** Name of the Japanese delegation sent to the United States by the shogunate in 1860 to ratify the trade and friendship treaty signed by consul Townsend Harris in 1858. This 81-person delegation was led by Shimmi Masaoka and Muragaki Norimasa, along with Ogura Tadamasa. The Man'en Kembei Shisetsu left Japan on the American ship the *Powhattan,* accompanied by the *Kanrin Maru,* commanded by Katsu Kaishū, and was greeted in Washington by President James Buchanan. The delegation left the United States two months later on the warship the *Niagara,* sailed around the Cape of Good Hope, and reached Japan in October, 1860.

Manga. "Sketches," a term for all humorous drawings and caricatures, and more recently for comic strips. The art of *manga* is very old in Japan: caricatures were found among the treasures of the Shōsō-in (eighth century). Some *emakimono,* such as the *Ban dainagon ekotoba,* could also be considered *manga,* along with the *Shigisan engi emaki, Gaki-zōshi,* and *Yamai no sōshi.* The tradition continued during the Edo period with ukiyo-e artists, and reached a peak with Hokusai's *Manga.* One of the most famous producers of *manga,* nicknamed "Japan's Walt Disney," was Tezuka Osamu (1926–89), who created the famous "Astroboy" (Tetsuwan Atomu), a Robin Hood–like robot, in 1951. Japanese of all ages love *manga* and comics, which represent about 40% of the annual output of all Japanese publishers.
• Title of a group of 15 books of sketches by Hokusai, *Hokusai Manga,* published from 1814 to 1878, containing thousands of serious and humorous drawings on all subjects.

Mangan-ji. Buddhist temple founded in Nikkō by the monk Kyōbin in 810, according to tradition; renamed Rinnō-ji by the Tendai-shū sect in 1654 and completely rebuilt at that time.

Mangetsu-ji. Buddhist temple in Usuki, near Fukuda (Kyushu), built between the ninth and twelfth century against a high rock cliff into which some 50 images of Buddhist divinities were carved.

Manji. Era of Emperor Go-Sai-in: July 1658–Apr. 1661. *See* NENGŌ.

Manjū. Era of Emperor Go-Ichijō: July 1024–July 1028. *See* NENGŌ.
• *See* MANJI.

Manjū. Title of a Noh play: a man, embittered because his son has learned nothing in school, orders his servant to kill him. But the faithful servant instead kills his own son, who has offered himself as a substitute. When the father regrets his order and finds his son, the servant grieves over the death of his own child.
→ *See* NETSUKE.

Manku-awase. Collection of *tanka* poems in which the first lines *(kami no ku)* were composed by Karai Senryū, and the last lines *(shimo no ku)* by the public, published in 1757. *See* HAIKAI.

Mannen-tsūhō. Copper coins issued in 760, worth one tenth of a silver *taihei-gempō. See* KŌCHŌ-JŪNISEN.

Manriki-gusari. Chain ballasted with lead or iron and used as a weapon by *dōshin,* sometimes in conjunction with a *jitte.* The weapon was said to have been invented by Masaki Toshimitsu, a famous sword expert from Edo. This chain "of the ten thousand powers," skillfully handled, could easily disarm a man armed with a sword. Also called *kusari.*

Mansai. Buddhist monk (1378–1435) of the Shingon-shū sect, son of Fujiwara no Morofuyu (Imakōji), abbot of the Daigo-ji temple in 1395. Ashikaga Yoshimitsu's adoptive son and confidant, he also served Yoshimitsu's two successors, Ashikaga Yoshimochi and Ashikaga Yoshinori. As an éminence grise, he conducted covert activities on behalf of the Muromachi shogunate. He left a book of notes on the years 1411–35, the *Mansai jugō nikki,* which is an invaluable source on the policies of the Ashikaga during this period. He received the title of *jugō,* reserved for empresses and imperial princes, in 1428. Also written Manzei.

Manshū Jihen. "Manchuria Incident." The term for the conquest of Manchuria (Manshūkoku) by the Japanese Guandong army from September 1931 to January 1933. It began with a night attack on September 18–19, 1931, on the Chinese garrison of the town of Mukden (Shenyang). Japan had long been battling China and the Soviet Union for control of this vast underpopulated and underexploited territory. After the fall of the Qing dynasty in Beijing in 1912, control of Manchuria fell to more or less independent Chinese warlords and, after 1920, to a Chinese marshal, Zhang Zuolin. The officers of the Guandong army had the marshal assassinated in 1928, and his son, Zhang Xueliang, succeeded him. Zhang agreed to recognize the Nationalist government of Jiang Jieshi (Chang Kai-shek). The Japanese, concerned with protecting their interests in southern Manchuria, decided to annex the territory. Ultranationalist Japanese officers—Itagaki Seishirō, Ishihara Kanji, Hanaya Tadashi, Chō Isamu, Inada, and some others—tried to take it by force, attacking Zhang Xueliang's army in Mukden, supposedly in reprisal for destruction of the trans-Manchurian railroad. They were acting for their own leader, but with the tacit approval of the militarist faction of the Japanese government. Despite the numerical superiority of the Chinese, the Guandong army was victorious, capturing Mukden and then attacking other cities, including Changchun, Jilin, and Daxing. The Guandong officers set up a puppet state, Manchukuo. The League of Nations appointed a commission of inquiry (*see* LYTTON), but remained neutral, which enabled Japan to tighten its grip on Manchuria. *See* MANCHUKUO, MUKEN.

• *Manshukoku Seifu Kōhō.* Official newssheet of Manchukuo (Manshūkoku), published from April 1, 1932, to July 26, 1945, by the Japanese occupying forces in Manchuria.

Man'yōshū. "Collection of Ten Thousand Pages." A major poetry anthology compiled by Otomo no Yakamochi around 760, containing the works of court poets and commoners—peasants and others. The 20-volume *Man'yōshū* comprises 4,516 poems (4,173 *tanka,* 260 *chōka,* 62 *sedoka,* and 21 *nagauta*) by 561 authors (among them 70 women). The longest *chōka* is 149 stanzas of 5 and 7 syllables and ends with a triplet of 5, 7, and 7 syllables. The poems in the *Man'yōshū* (like those in the *Kojiki*) were written in *man'yōgana,* Chinese characters used only for their phonetic value. It is quite difficult to decipher the poems, both because many used *makura-kotoba* ("pillow words") and because writing in *man'yōgana* can sometimes lead to confusion. Most of the poems are lyrical, while some are epic. The main themes are the joys and pains of love, the glory of the imperial house, and veneration of the *kami.* To the usual Chinese repertory were added flowers, the moon, nightingales, insects, and more. This huge anthology, considered a classic of Japanese literature, has been the subject of many commentaries. So many studies have been written on the *Man'yōshū* at various times—by Shimokōbe

Chōryū Keichū, Kada no Azumamaro, Katō Chikage, and other exegetes—that its adaptation into modern Japanese poses very few difficulties. It was translated in its entirety into English by J. L. Pierson and into Russian by A. Y. Gluskina, and a number of partial translations into other languages have been published.

• *Man'yo daishōki.* A major 54-volume commentary on the *Man'yōshū,* written by Keichū (1640–1701) around 1690.

• **Man'yō no Go-taika.** General term for the five most famous poets in the *Man'yōshū:* Kakinomoto no Hitomaro, Yamabe no Akihito, Yamanoe no Okura, Otomo no Yakamochi, and Otomo no Tabito.

• *Man'yōshū kogi.* A commentary on the *Man'yōshū* in 124 or 141 volumes, depending on the version, composed by Tachibana Chikage (1734–1808).

Manzai. Type of show in which two actors engage in a comic dialogue, traditionally performed, since the Nara period, on New Year's Day to bring luck to homes. Each region of Japan has its own style of *manzai,* notably Yamato, Owari, Iyo, Mikawa, and Akita. In the Edo period, *manzai* made its way onto the stage and was treated as a theater art in its own right. In the twentieth century, *manzai* have been accompanied by music and dances; they are now featured on a popular television show, and the actors are considered stars. *See* RAKUGO, TAUE ODORI, YOSE.

Mappō. "Final period of the Good [Buddhist] Law," which, according to the Buddhist interpretation of certain texts, notably the *Saddharma-pundarīka-sūtra (Jap.:* Hokke-kyō, Myōhōrenge-kyō), corresponded to the degeneration of Buddhism; it began in AD 1052. This belief in the advent of *mappō* gave rise to a sort of fear in Japanese Buddhist milieus (somewhat similar to "millennium fear" in Europe) that greatly contributed to the development of the Jōdo-shū sect and faith in Amida. *Chin.:* Houfa.

Marco Polo Bridge Incident. Skirmish between Chinese and Japanese troops that started on July 7, 1937, near the Marco Polo Bridge (*Jap.:* Rokōkyō) about 20 km south of Beijing. Shots were fired by both sides until July 11, when a cease-fire was forged between the Chinese general, Song Zheyuan, and the Japanese commander. But the Japanese government sent reinforcement troops and the Chinese government decided to recapture Beijing. A battle ensued at the end of which the Japanese, under the command of General Katsuki Kiyoshi, attacked and occupied Beijing and Tianjin; this set off the second Sino-Japanese war, which lasted until 1945.

Marebito. "Guests"; according to folk beliefs, divine beings from the other world who come to bring luck and wealth to the people. They may present themselves in various forms, such as aged couples, nobles, monks, or beggars. Also called *marōdo.*

Marriage. Today, Japanese marriages *(kekkon, kon'in)* tend to follow Western customs, and couples are formed according to affinity or love, especially in large cities. However, families generally make sure that couples belong to the same social class, and discreet inquiries are always made to ensure that the future husband and wife will be of more or less equal social status. Most Japanese families, for example, avoid a marriage into a family believed to be of the *burakumin* class.

Generally, marriages are arranged by families (although there are more and more exceptions) with the assistance of a carefully chosen matchmaker *(nakōdo).* The horoscope also plays a large role in determining whether or not the spouses will get along: for example, a person born in the year of the Rat should marry a person born in the year of the Dragon, the Monkey, or the Bull, but should avoid those born in the year of the Horse (*see* HOROSCOPES). A woman born in the year of the Horse (Hinoe-uma) is reputed to "kill her husband"—that is, to outlive him—and is avoided.

Weddings are generally held in autumn (except on October 10, said to be "without *kami,*" who have gone en masse to Izumo). Traditionally, the *nakōdo* arranges a meeting *(miai)* between the future spouses, after they have been chosen by the respective families, but this meeting does not oblige them to contract a marriage. If there is a negative outcome, the *nakōdo* (one or more) seeks another partner and arranges another *miai.* When the future spouses agree, a date is set for the marriage. The wedding is always an intimate family ceremony. People get married at home, usually in the groom's parents' house, at a Buddhist temple or Shinto shrine of their choice, or in a hall rented for the occasion. Nowadays, specialized stores or restaurants organize "made to measure" marriages in which everything is included in the price: clothing rental, meals, gifts, ceremony, transportation, photography, and sometimes honeymoon. Buildings are specially arranged to accommodate couples, relatives, and guests. Such weddings are quite expensive, and both sets of parents usually share the cost. But since the point is to make the ceremony unforgettable, every luxury (even extravagant ones) is permitted, for the décor, clothing, the traditional cake (Western style), and gifts alike.

Christians marry in a church or a temple; in this case, the ceremony is exactly the same as that for a Western marriage, with the bride *(yome)* wearing a white dress and a veil instead of the traditional kimono, and the groom *(muko)* in a tuxedo. However, almost 90% of weddings take place in a Shinto shrine, in a short ceremony during which the bride and groom simply exchange three cups of *sake* from which they must drink three times *(san-san-ku-do),* which definitively seals their union before the family and relatives, as well as before the *kami* or Buddha. The bride wears an extremely opulent kimono, embroidered with gold and silver threads (these are often worth a fortune, and are usually rented for the ceremony), and a traditional hairpiece partly concealed by a white headband *(tsunokakushi).* The groom may be simply dressed in dark clothes. During a Buddhist wedding in a temple, the rite is more or less the same, but the officiating monk makes a speech and gives the bride and groom rosaries, made of white beads for the man and red beads for the woman. Once the ceremony is over, relatives, guests, and newlyweds go to a restaurant for a banquet, during which *sake* and other alcoholic beverages are served, to celebrate the union of the two families. The *nakōdo* presents the newlyweds to the guests, and then the heads of the two families make speeches to give their best wishes. A large wedding cake generally ends the banquet. Then one of the hosts may sing a song or perform an excerpt from a Noh play, usually *Takasago.* Before the end of the meal, the newlyweds discreetly slip away. As they leave, guests receive small gifts, usually food, in return for their gifts (usually money) offered in a traditional envelope adorned with a *noshi* in gold or silver thread. According to custom, the groom's parents offer a dowry to the bride's parents (a relic of the custom of purchasing the woman), equivalent to about three months' salary. Part of this sum is always returned by the bride's parents, to signify that their daughter is not really worth so much. This money is usually given to the couple to help them get settled. The honeymoon, during which the bride wears a small round hat, is generally spent by the sea, in the mountains, at a spa, or, for wealthier couples, abroad, usually in Okinawa or Hawai'i.

Often, wedding styles are mixed, and a couple may get married at a Shinto shrine, a Buddhist temple, and at a church (or Protestant temple). In addition, sometimes couples who are not officially married are recognized as such by their families at a banquet. Although this is not a legal (or registered) ceremony, it has social value for the families concerned. In some cases, the groom is adopted by his bride's family (*see* ADOPTION) and takes that family's name. Rites also vary considerably depending on whether the wedding involves peasants, merchants, samurai, or *kuge* (nobles). In most cases, families consider the marriage of their children valid only when a first child is born, since the goal of Japanese marriage is, above all, to make a family.

In the Nara and Heian periods, marriages in aristocratic families were usually endogamous. The wife lived in her father's house and the husband visited her when he felt like it and led a very free life. Accounts from the Heian period are full of stories of abandoned wives waiting in vain for their husband to deign to visit them *(yobai)* or for their true love to slip in secretly at dusk and leave at dawn. In later periods, marriages within the warrior classes were usually subject to the constraints of military alliances, and women were often used as hostages. It was only in the Edo period that marriages were recorded in family registers. Until recently, villages had "houses for young people" *(wakamono yado)* where couples could meet freely before their marriage, which was recognized only when a child was born. In cities, however, love matches *(ren'ai kekkon)* were strongly discouraged, which sometimes led to lovers' committing suicide (*see* JUNSHI). However, all forms of unions took place (a custom that is now dying in Japan), leaving great sexual freedom to young people, although they did not seem to abuse it. Certain things are still left to tradition, and the good offices of a *nakōdo* are often required after the young people have freely chosen each other. Only one rule seems to be respected most of the time, that of equality of social status.

The average age at marriage is about 29–34 for men and 20–30 for women. Only 8% of women are still single after the age of 35. Although marriage between blood relations is illegal, marriage between distant cousins is not that uncommon, especially in rural areas. The minimum age for marriage is 18 years for men and 16 for women. Minors (under 20 years of age) must obtain their parents' consent; however, a married minor is considered an adult. A woman may not remarry within six months after divorce. Bigamy is forbidden by law. Couples may adopt the wife's or the husband's family name.

Marriages with foreigners are generally disapproved of and are poorly accepted by society. A foreigner married to a Japanese woman, even if he speaks Japanese and conforms to the customs, will have difficulty renting an apartment, for example, because Japanese fear that foreigners will upset their customary way of life. (This is a recent attitude that developed after about 1990, especially in the middle classes.) Children resulting from these unions, called *nisei,* have difficulty in school and at work. The problem is not as serious when the marriage is between a European and a Japanese, but it is much more so when the non-Japanese spouse is black or Korean.

→ *See* ADOPTION, DIVORCE, MIAI, MUKOI-RIKON, SAN-SAN-KU-DO, YOBAI, YOMEI-RIKON.

Martial arts. The Japanese martial arts *(bujutsu, budō, bugei)* were practiced by warriors *(buke, bushi, samurai)* since at least the Kamakura period. At first, they were classified under the general category "Path of the Bow and the Horse" (Kyūba no Michi); in the Edo period, they were absorbed into the warrior arts called Bushido. In the twentieth century, they gained an international following and inspired imitations and the development of related martial arts mainly in Korea, China, Vietnam, India, and Indonesia, giving rise in these countries to a resurgence of ancient, noncodified arts relating to defense and attack with or without weapons. In Japan, these martial arts, originally designed to develop the military education of warriors, were transformed into sports at the end of the nineteenth century; *bu-jutsu,* or "war techniques" became *budō,* or "the (spiritual) way of combat." In the Meiji era, the samurai lost their status of professional warriors, and some of them modified the warrior arts learned within the various *ryū,* or "schools," many of which were hereditary within *bushi* families, into corporal techniques designed to enable young people to fight and defend themselves effectively, while instilling in them an ethic directly descended from that of the Bushido. The *bugei,* or "martial arts," then underwent a rapid evolution that involved both physical training *(waza)* and moral discipline *(dō, michi),* which together constituted a sort of search for a noble spirit that combined the art of defense against an aggressor and the sentiments of fearlessness, self-control, strong character, and benevolence *(kokoro, shin).* Many people created specific martial arts, based on traditional warrior arts, to develop an ethic of behavior among those who practiced them; in teaching the art of self-defense, they invoked at the same time nonviolence and nonaggressiveness. Martial sports spread quickly and were gradually codified and regulated to make them safer for the people who practiced them. There were sports without weapons *(budō)*, such as *aikido, judō,* and *karate,* and the arts of defense with weapons, such as *kendō* (sword), *kyūdō* (bow and arrow), and *naginata* training. *Karate,* a group of techniques adapted from the methods used by the peasants of Okinawa to protect themselves against bandits and samurai, uses specific weapons: the *nunchaku, sai,* and *tonfa,* among others. *Jujutsu* was transformed into *judō,* which became a "path to flexibility" under the guidance of Kanō Jigorō, who established the first school for this kind of sport, Kōdōkan, in 1882 in Tokyo. Thereafter, great numbers of schools were created, using different names and teaching various techniques, though all were based on those of the ancient schools. In the West, especially the United States, some of these schools, claiming to teach Japanese martial arts, became, in contrast to true *budō,* schools for offensive, not just defensive, combat, with certain forms of *karate* and "full-contact" combat. Other schools stressed both the mystical and the acquisition of physical discipline rather than defensive techniques, such as those claiming (often erroneously) to teach the practices of Shugendō. Currently, there are hundreds of "schools" of "martial arts" (bearing some resemblance to sects) throughout the world, with tens of millions of practitioners. However, the true Japanese martial arts, based on tradition, remain *aikido, judō,* and *karate* on the one hand, and *kendō* and *kyūdō* on the other. *See* AIKIDŌ, BŌ-JUTSU, FUNAKOSHI GICHIN, GENJI NO HEIHŌ, IAI-DŌ, JUDŌ, KANŌ JIGORŌ, KARATE, KATA, KENDŌ, KYŪDŌ, MA-AI, UESHIBA MORIHEI, UKEMI.

Martyrs. A group of 6 Spanish Franciscans, 3 Spanish Jesuits, and 17 "tertiary" Franciscans were executed in Nagasaki on February 5, 1597 on the order of Toyotomi Hideyoshi, and are generally termed the "Japanese martyrs." These 26 martyrs were beatified in 1627 and canonized by Pop Pius IX in 1862. *See* CHRISTIANITY.

Maru. "Circle," a term for most Japanese merchant ships (and sometimes warships). Although its origin is uncertain, this word may come from *toimaru,* a name given to large trading companies in the Edo period. The ships used by these companies to transport merchandise (mainly rice, *sake,* and wood) had the name of the company painted on their hull, followed by the word *"toimaru,"* often abridged to *"maru."* However, many warships had their name followed by the word *kan,* a Japanese adaptation of the Chinese word *lan,* meaning "warship."

• Name for successive courts surrounding a castle *(jō, shiro)* or a palace: *ni no maru* (second court), *san no maru* (third court), and so on.

• Another way of writing the first name Maro.

• **Maru-gawara.** *See* KAWARA.

Marubashi Chūya. *Rōnin* samurai from Yamagata (Dewa province), supposedly a son of Chōsokabe Motochika. In 1651, to avenge his father (killed 30 years before), he and Yūi Shōsetsu plotted to assassinate shogun Tokugawa Ietsuna, blow up the arsenal with the assistance of its commandant, Kawara Jūrōbei, and attack the Edo castle. The plot was discovered and Marubashi was arrested and sentenced to death, along with 33 of his companions, on September 24, 1651. He was executed and Yūi Shōsetsu committed suicide. *See* KEI'AN JIKEN.

• *Marubashi chūya.* Title of an eight-act Kabuki play in *kizewa-mono* genre, written by Mokuami in 1870. Also titled *Keian Taiheiki.*

Marubeni Shōsha. Major financial and trading company involved in many industrial sectors and part of the Fuyō group, created in 1858 and reorganized in 1949. It has more than 50 subsidiaries in Japan and about 130 foreign offices. About 62% of its activities are related to exports. Head office in Tokyo.

Maru-mage. Women's hairstyle in fashion in Edo starting in the Genroku era (1688–1704) and adopted by married women in the aristocracy after 1870. *See* HAIR STYLES, MAGE.

Maruoka Hideko. Sociologist (Ishii Hide, 1903–90), born in Nagano prefecture. She was interested mainly in the condition of women in Japan in rural areas and published an important work on this subject, *Nihon nōson fujin mondai* (Women's Problems in the Villages of Japan, 1937). She lived in China during the Second World War, but returned to Japan afterward and continued her research, publishing *Aru sengo seishin* (Postwar Conscience), dealing with nuclear problems and living conditions in the new Japan, in 1969.

Murayama Kaoru. Poet (1899–1974) born in Ōita prefecture. He is best known as a "poet of the sea," because all his works deal with the ocean: *Ho,* *rampu, kamome* (Veils, Lamps, and Seagulls, 1932), *Tenshō naru tokoro* (When the Bells Toll, 1943), *Tsuresarareta umi* (The Kidnapped Sea, 1962), *Tsuki wataru* (The Moon Passes, 1972), *Ari no iru kao* (Face Covered with Ants, 1973). He was a member of the Shiki group in 1934.

Maruyama Kenji. Writer, born 1943 in Nagano prefecture. His novel *Natsu no nagare,* published in 1966, won the Akutagawa Prize. Among his other works are *Mahiru nari* (1968) and *Asahi no ataru ie* (1970); influenced by Hemingway, he deals mainly with the plight of young workers.

Maruyama Kyōkai. Shinto mountain sect founded in 1853 by Itō Rokurōbei (1829–94) as a subsidiary to the Fusō-kyo sect. It currently claims to have about 100,000 followers. *See* SHINTŌ HONKYOKU.

Maruyama Ōkyo. Painter (Maruyama Masataka, Maruyama Mondo; *mei:* Iwajirō; *azana:* Chūsen; *gō:* Sensai, Isshō, Ka-un, Untei, Senrei, Rakuyō-sanjin, Seishūkan, Ōkyo, 1733–95), born in Tamba province near Kyoto. He studied the Kanō style with Ishida Yūtei (1721–86), then was influenced by the painters of the Nagasaki school (Yōga). He took the name Ōkyo in 1766. He also studied the works of painters of the Tosa and Rimpa schools and those of Chinese painters, and he inaugurated a particular, very decorative style. His very numerous works range from simple paintings and lacquer decorations to large decorative compositions on walls, fusuma, and screens *(byōbu);* he was particularly skilled in the portrayal of flowers and trees—so much so that his paintings were often imitated and sometimes even counterfeited. He had a huge influence on many artists, who created the Maruyama-ha and Maruyama-Shijō schools based on his work. The latter was founded in Kyoto by one of his students, Matsumura Goshun (1752–1811), who, with his own disciples, used European principles of perspective and sketches from nature in his decorative paintings *(shasei-ga).* This school, in its turn, influenced the Fukku Yamato-e and Rimpa schools.

Maruya Saiichi. Writer (Nemura Saiichi), born 1925 in Yamagata prefecture. With critic Shinoda Hajime (b. 1927), he founded the literary magazine *Chitsujo* (published from 1952 to 1963), in which he published his first works, notably *Ehoba no kao o sakete.* In 1968, he won the Akutagawa Prize for his story *Toshi no nokori.* He also published *Tatta hitori no hanran* in 1972 and *Uragoe d'utae kimigayo* in 1982, as well as studies and critical es-

says such as *Go-Toba-in* (*Yomiuri* Prize in 1973) and *Chūshingura to wa nani ka* (1984).

Maruzen. Publisher and bookstore specializing in the import of foreign books. The bookstore was founded in Yokohama in 1869 under the name Maruya Shōsha. It was moved to Tokyo in 1893 and still has an international reputation in the publishing world.

Maruzen Sekiyū. Japanese oil company, founded in 1933. After the Second World War, it specialized in refining petroleum products, importing oil mainly from China, Indonesia, Mexico, and Abu Dhabi. Head office in Tokyo.

Masahide. Sculptor of netsuke (Kurokawa Masahide, mid-eighteenth century) who worked in Nagasaki and sculpted mainly coconut shells.
• Maker of sword blades (Kawabe Suishinshi, 1750–1825) in Edo.

Masahiro. Painter of ukiyo-e prints (Kitao Masahiro, late eighteenth century).

Masahito Shinnō. Imperial prince (1552–86), Ogimachi Tennō's son and Go-Yōzei's father. He received the posthumous names Dajō Tennō and Yōkō-in.
→ *See* GO-SHIRIKAWA TENNŌ.

Masakatsu. Sculptor of netsuke (Suzuki Masakatsu, 1840–99), Masanao's son.

Masakazu. Sculptor of netsuke (Sawaki Masakazu, Kihōdō, Kohōsai, 1839–91), born in Nagoya; he worked in Osaka.

• **Masakazu II.** Sculptor (Echizen'ya, Masanao II, 1848–1922), born in Uji-Yamada. Masanao's student.
→ *See* MASATOSHI.

Masakiyo. Sculptor of netsuke in wood (Sakai Masakiyo, nineteenth century) in Mie prefecture.
→ *See* MONDO NO SHŌ MASAKIYO.

Masamitsu. Sculptor of netsuke (Ejima Masamitsu, 1837–1909), active in Niigata.

Masamune. Maker of sword blades (Gorō Nyūdō Masamune, 1264–1343) from Sagami province. A number of his descendants bore the same name. Among the most famous members of his school were Masamune Jittetsu (or Jūtetsu, *see* MINO-MONO) and Masamune Yukimitsu, who worked in the Kunimitsu style, only three of whose blades have survived. Among his students, collectively called Jūtetsu, the best known were Rai Kunitsugu (1247–1327) of Yamashiro, Kinjū Kaneshige (1232–1322) of Mino, Keanemitsu (1280–1344) of Bizen, Shizu Kaneuji (1284–1344) of Mino, Gō Yoshihiro (1299–1325) of Etchū, Sayeki Norishige (1290–1366) of Etchū, Naotsune (1280–1348) of Iwami, Chōgi Nagayoshi (1288–1370) of Bizen, and Masamune Sadamune (1298–1349). *See* ICHIEN, RAI KUNITSUGU.

Masamune Hakuchō. Writer and literary critic (Masamune Tadao, 1879–1962) of the naturalist school, born in Okayama prefecture. He studied English and the Bible and converted to Protestantism. In 1896, he went to Tokyo, where he contributed to the *Yomiuri Shimbun* and began his literary career by writing stories: *Sekibaku* (Solitude, 1904), *Jin'ai* (Dust, 1907), *Doko-e* (Where? 1908), *Bikō* (Soft Light, 1910), *Doro Ningyō* (The Earthen Doll, 1911). He then turned to novels, with *Shisha seisha* (The Dead and the Living, 1916), and plays, with *Jinsei no kōfuku* (The Joys of Life, 1924). After the Second World War, he continued to write stories, novels, and plays until his death. His work, imbued with pessimism and skepticism, nevertheless has Christian resonances.

Masanao. Name of a number of sculptors of netsuke: Isshinsai (mid-seventeenth century), Suzuki Masanao (late eighteenth century) in Kyoto; Miyake Masanao (Masanao II, 1848–1922), Masanao III (b. 1890). *See* MASAKAZU II.

Masanobu. Painter (Kanō Masanobu; *mei:* Shirojirō; *gō:* Yūsei, 1434–1530), founder of the Kanō school, Kanō Kagenobu's son. He was a samurai serving the Ashikaga shogun. *See* KANŌ.
• Painter (Okumura Masanobu; *mei:* Genroku, Genhachi; *gō:* Tanchōsai, Bunkaku, Shimmyō, Baiō, Hōgetsudō, Gempachi-rō, Mangetsudō, 1686–1764). He owned a small printing business in Edo that published ukiyo-e prints. He also produced prints in the style of his master, Kiyonobu, and created the *uki-e* and *hashira-e* genres, which he printed for the first time in *benizuri-e* (two colors) and *urushi-e* (black lacquered inks). He painted court scenes, beautiful women *(bijin),* and Kabuki scenes. He was also a haiku poet.
→ *See* MINAMOTO NO MASUNOBU, SANTŌ KYŌDEN, SETTEI, SHŌSEN-IN, TŌUN.

Masaoka Shiki. Poet (Masaoka Tsunenori, 1867–1902), born in Matsuyama, died in Tokyo. A member of the Ototogisu group, he wrote many *tanka* and haiku (*Haigai-taigai,* 1897) and essays influenced by the works of Tsubouchi Shōyō and Futabatei Shimei: *Jojibun* (Reports), *Byōshō rokushaku* (The Six-Foot-Long Sickbed), *Tsuki no miyako* (The Capital of the Moon, 1892), *Bokuju itteki* (A Drop of Ink, 1901), *Gyōga manroku* (Notes of a Man at Rest, 1902), and others. His complete works were published in Tokyo from 1924 to 1926 as *Shiki zenshū.* Commonly known as Shiki.

Masashige. Famous maker of sword blades (Tegarayama Masashige, 1754–1824) from Mutsu province.

Masatami. Sculptor of netsuke (Moribe Masatami, 1854–1928) in Nagoya.
• Sculptor of netsuke (mid-nineteenth century) in Osaka.

Masatoshi. Sculptor of netsuke (Sawaki Masatoshi, 1835–84) in Nagoya, Masakazu's brother.
→ *See* KAWASHIMA KŌGYOKU.

Masatsune. Maker of sword blades (Ōshū Masatsune, 962–1023) in Bizen province. *See* BIZEN-MONO, KO-BIZEN.
→ *See* FUJIWARA NO MASATSUNE.

Masayoshi. Painter of ukiyo-e prints (Kitao Masayoshi, Akabane Masayoshi, Kuwagata Masayoshi; *mei:* Sanjirō; *azana:* Shikei; *gō:* Keisai, Tsugazane, ca. 1761/1764–1824). The son of a tatami manufacturer in Edo, he produced mainly caricatures and book illustrations (between 1780 and 1796) but also painted beautiful women *(bijin),* warriors, and landscapes.
• Name of many sculptors of netsuke, among them Ishikura Masayoshi and Gotō Masayoshi (1820–65) in Niigata.
• Sculptor on metal (Iwami Masayoshi, 1764–1837) of the Nara school.
• Maker of sword blades (Hōki no Kami Masayoshi, 1731–1819) from Satsuma.
• Maker of sword blades (Hosokawa Masayoshi, mid-nineteenth century) in Edo.

Masayuki. Physician (Katō Masayuki, mid-nineteenth century) in Tokyo, and amateur sculptor of netsuke.

• Sculptor of netsuke (Hōshunsai, early nineteenth century).

→ *See* HAMANOSHOZUI.

Mashiko-yaki. Pottery in a folk style made in the town of Mashiko (Tochigi prefecture), first used during the Edo period for mortars *(suribachi)* and kitchen utensils. Starting in 1853, some of the kilns began to produce ceramics in the Shimotsuke and Sōma styles. Hamada Shōji settled in Mashiko in 1919 and revived this declining industry.

Masks. Masks have always been used by people to transform themselves or assume the identity of another, for magical purposes, dances and ceremonies, or theatrical performances, generally of religious origin. Masks were used in Japan from prehistoric times, as evidenced by certain *dogū* from the Jōmon period. They were indispensable for shamanic dances of the lion and the deer, as well as for Shinto Kagura dances. Noh theater makes great use of them, although, among the actors, only the *shite* and sometimes the *shitezure* wear them; the ancient forms of danced theater, such as Bugaku, used a great number. Just as each gesture is symbolic of a thought, an emotion, a sentiment, each mask symbolizes a character. Noh actors consider their masks sacred, for through them they truly become the soul of their character. *See* NŌMEN.

Noh masks. Sculpted in wood and painted, they have traditionally been categorized according to the characters they represent. The main ones are:

1. *Female masks:*

a) Young:

—**Ko-Omote:** thick, high eyebrows, smiling face.

—**Maki Masu:** noblewoman.

—**Waka Onna:** smiling, high eyebrows.

b) Middle-aged:

—**Shakumi:** calm expression.

—**Fukai:** serious expression.

—**Daigan:** spiteful expression.

c) Elderly:

—**Uba:** calm and modest expression, somewhat wrinkled.

—**Rōjo:** very aged, very wrinkled.

d) Comical:

—**O-Kame** (Otafuku): chubby, smiling, peasant.

e) Evil:

—**Hannya:** horned, green skin, bulging eyes.

2. *Male masks:*

a) Aged *(jo):*

—**Ko-jo:** noble, bearded, not very wrinkled.

—**Sanko-jo:** humble, bearded, very wrinkled.

—**Chu-jo:** noble warrior, anxious eyebrows.

—**Mai-jo:** bald old man.

—**Hakujiki-jo:** white eyebrows and beard (used in the Noh play *Okina*).

—**Yorimasa:** aged warrior.

—**Heida:** warrior in the prime of life.

b) Young:

—**Kasshiki:** young assistant, bangs over the forehead.

—**Jidō:** child demi-god.

c) Comical:

—**Hyottoko** or **Shio-fuki:** twisted mouth, asymmetrical eyes.

3. *Ghosts.* These are often portrayed as blind men or women.

4. *Gods and demons:*

—**Shishi-guchi:** lion's head, open mouth.

—**O-Beshimi:** powerful monster, closed mouth.

—**O-Tobide:** divinity with prestige and power, open mouth, bulging eyes.

—**Tengu:** demons, sometimes winged, with a long neck and red face.

—**Kurihige:** chief of the dragons, with a black beard.

—**Nyodo:** demon with three eyes.

—**Oni:** various demons, horned, red face.

—**Shōjō:** sea genie with red hair.

—**Buaku:** demon with large mouth (used in Kyōgen).

5. *Animal masks:*

—**Kawazu:** frog.

—**Kitsune:** fox.

—**Saru:** monkey.

These masks all have fixed expressions. Only one mask used in the play *Okina* has a mobile lower jaw.

Dance masks. The oldest dance masks that have survived to the present day are those of the Gigaku, dating from the Nara period. The most typical characters are the king Gōto, the herald Chidō, and Kongō Rikishi; some of the other masks are called Ayakiri, Saruta, Genjoroku, Ranryū-ō. In Bugaku, the masks are lighter and cover only the face. They often have a mobile lower jaw.

Other types of masks. In folk dancing, there is a wide variety of masks according to region and type of dance or performance. Masks used in Kagura are often analogous to those used in Noh, but sometimes portray different characters, representing characters in Shinto mythology. Among the other common masks:

—**Kamado-sama:** symbolizes the spirit of the home. It is a roughly carved mask and represents a very ugly boy.

—**Otafuku** and **Hyottoko:** the same as those used in Noh and Kyōgen, and often considered lucky charms.

—**Mibu-kyōgen:** specific to performances that have been taking place once a year, from April 21 to May 10, at the Mii-dera temple in Kyoto since 1300, and originally used for the propagation of Buddhism.

—In some parts of the country, notably in the south, during prayers to bring rain *(amagoi),* the officiants wear masks representing a dragon (**Ryū-ō**) painted green.

This list is not exhaustive; there are many popular and other masks, and they are used in most religious ceremonies and popular festivals *(matsuri).*

→ *See* AMA, BUGAKU, GIGAKU, GYŌDŌ-MEN, HAN-NYA, HEIDA, HŌATE, HYOTTOKO, KAGURA, MEMPŌ, NOH, NŌMEN, OAKU-JŌ, O-BESHIMI, OKAME, OKINA, OTAFUKU, SŌMEN, USOBUKI, YASHAO, YORIMASA.

Mason, Luther Whiting. American musician (1818–96) who, on request of the Ministry of Education, introduced instruction in Western music in the schools. He founded the Tokyo Ongaku Gakkō (Tokyo Music School), which later became part of Tokyo University of Fine Arts and Music, and organized concerts. He also created a school for making Western musical instruments. The Japanese government decorated him with the Order of the Sacred Treasure (*see* KUNSHŌ) posthumously.

Massha. Term for a Shinto shrine attached to a more important one *(honsha),* which confers *bunrei* upon it. Also called *bunsha. See* BUNREI, JINJA.

Masuda Kimiyo. Contemporary painter, born in Kumamoto. She went to Paris in 1968 and took part in a number of solo and group exhibitions (Salon des artistes français, Salon d'automne, Salon nationale des beaux-arts, and others). She received the Deauville International Grand Prize in 1974. Her works, influenced by Marie Laurencin and Matisse, are imbued with great delicacy.

Masuda Nagamori. Warrior (1545–1615), adviser to Toyotomi Hideyoshi. Exiled to Mt. Kōya by Tokugawa Ieyasu for having taken Toyotomi Hideyori's side, he committed suicide.

Masujima Ran'en. Scholar (Masujima Konnojō, Masujima Mōkyō, 1768–1839) and botanist who wrote books on botany in Chinese.

Masu-kagami. Abridged title of *Masumi no kagami,* "Clear Mirror," a historical chronicle covering a period of about 154 years, from 1180 to 1333, and probably written between 1338 and 1376 by Nichijō Yoshimoto, although it is some-

times attributed to Ichijō Fuyuyoshi (1464–1514). This work, imitating the style of the *Genji monogatari,* is remarkable for its objectivity.

Masumoto Hakaru. Metallurgist (1895–1987), inventor of "invar" steel in 1929, KS magnetic steel (in collaboration with Honda Kōtarō) in 1934, and other alloys. He received the Order of Culture (Bunka-shō) in 1955.

Masumura Yasuzō. Movie director, born 1924 in Tokyo, assistant to Mizoguchi and Kon Ichikawa. He wrote a history of Japanese film.

Matagi. An ancient people still existing in the Tōhoku Mountains, living in huts and subsisting on hunting activities. They once supplied the daimyo with bear livers (used in some medicinal preparations) and fur. They have specific customs and speak a dialect called *yama-kotoba* (mountain speech). Formerly called Yamadachi.

Matara Shin (Matara-jin). Shinto *kami,* tutelary guardian of the Enryaku-ji Buddhist temple on Mount Hiei, near Kyoto, sometimes portrayed with three heads and six arms. It is probably an ancient syncretic Buddhist divinity.

Mathematics (sūgaku, wasan). The development of Japanese mathematics is divided into two distinct periods: that of Chinese influence, and that of modern mathematics (before the introduction of Western mathematics). Starting in the seventh century, Chinese principles, confined to simple operations, were used. Algebraic rules, laid out in the *Suanxue qimeng* by Zhu Shijie, were discovered by Japanese scholars in Korea; they arrived in Japan during Hideyoshi's time and were published in 1299. The properties of numbers began to be studied, using sticks *(sangi).* The introduction, in the early seventeenth century, of the Chinese abacus *(soroban)* facilitated arithmetic operations; later, a scholar in the court of the shogun, Seki Takakuzu (d. 1708), invented a notation system for calculations. It was not until the late eighteenth century that mathematics was accepted as a science; it had previously been considered a mind game without any real utility. However, many scholars who had learned about "Dutch science" *(rangaku)* were attracted to mathematics, studied the works of Newton, and attempted to apply his principles, with the help of Dutch instructors, to shipbuilding, astronomy, and surveying. In the Meiji era, Western mathematics spread more widely in Japan, and the authorities founded schools for the study and practice of mathematics. Japanese *wasan* mathematical procedures were then abandoned in favor of Western science, and universities opened faculties of mathematics, first in Tokyo in 1877, then in Kyoto and Sendai. *See* AIDA YASUAKI, AJIMA NAONOBU, OGARA KINNOSUKE, SANGI, SHŌDA KENJIRŌ, SOROBAN, TAKAGI TEIJI, TAKEBE KATAHIRO, WASAN, YOSHIDA MITSUYOSHI.

Matora. Painter (Ōishi Matora; *mei:* Koizumi Monkichi, Ōishi Komonta; *gō:* Tomonoya, Shōkoku, 1794–1833), born in Nagoya, Gesshō's student. He produced mainly book illustrations.

Matsubame-mono. Type of Kabuki show, in the *sewamono* genre, in which the emphasis is placed on danced action. It draws its themes from Noh and Kyōgen. *See* SHOSA.

Matsubara Saburō. Art critic (b. 1918) and professor at the University of Tokyo, known mainly for his scholarly studies of Chinese and Korean paintings.

Matsubase kofun. *Kofun* located in the city of Matsubashi (Kumamoto prefecture, Kyushu), whose funerary chamber is decorated with circles and triangles, once painted red, carved into the rock. The chamber is now in the open air, and rain has washed away the color.

Matsu-cha (Matcha). Type of powdered green tea used mainly in the tea ceremony. It has a taste that is initially bitter but that becomes sweet when held in the mouth. It is reputed to be very energizing, with a high vitamin C content. Also called *hiki-cha. See* CHANOYU, TEA.

Matsudaira. Families descended from the Tokugawa and consisting of collateral branches of that family:
—Echizen family, descended from Matsudaira (Yūki) Hideyasu (1574–1607), which in turn gave rise to the Itoigawa, Matsue (Hirose and Mori), Askashi, Tsuyama, and Kawagoe families.
—Matsudaira family of Takasu, from the Tokugawa of Owari.
—Matsudaira families of Saijō and Yada, from the Tokugawa of Kii.
—Matsudaira families of Takamatsu, Moriyama, Fuchū, and Shishido, from the Tokugawa of Mito.
—Matsudaira (Ochi) family of Hamada, from the Tokugawa of Kōfu.

→ *See* NABESHIMA, OKUDAIRA TADAAKI, SANKE, SANKYŌ, TOKUGAWA.

Matsudaira Hideyasu. Toyotomi Hideyoshi's adoptive son (1574–1607). He was also adopted by Yūki Harumoto, a daimyo in Shimōsa. Having fought at Tokugawa Ieyasu's side at the Battle of Sekigahara (1600), he received part of Echizen province as a fief.

Matsudaira Ietada. Warrior (Matsudaira Tonomo no Suke, 1555–1600), head of the Fūzoku branch of the Matsudaira family of Mikawa province (Aichi prefecture). Having fought on Tokugawa Ieyasu's side against Takeda Katsuyori, he received a fief worth 100,000 *koku* in Ōshi in Musashi (Saitama prefecture). He was transferred to Kashira (Shimōsa province) in 1592, then to Ōmigawa (Shimōsa) two years later. In 1599, he was commander of the Fushimi castle near Kyoto; he was killed at Sekigahara in the battle against Ishida Mitsunari.

Matsudaira Ietada. Daimyo (Jintarō, 1548–82), who died without an heir; his estates were annexed by one of Tokugawa Ieyasu's sons, Matsudaira Tadayoshi. Also called Kii no Kami.

Matsudaira Katamori. Daimyo (1835–93) of the Aizu estate, appointed military governor of Kyoto in 1862 to combat extremists and the emperor's supporters. He advocated closer cooperation between the shogunate and the court and created *shinsengumi,* or police militias. In 1863, he led the Satsuma and Aizu troops against the Chōshu extremists, whom he expelled from Kyoto in 1864 (*see* HAMAGURI GOMON). During the Boshin Civil War, he was attacked by the imperialists and surrendered only when his castle in Wakamatsu was captured. He was then stripped of all of his government positions.

Matsudaira Naritake. Scholar (1815–63) who revised and complemented the *Engi-shiki* in 1848.

Matsudaira Nobutsuna. Administrator (Izu no Kami, 1596–1662) and *rōjū* under the aegis of shoguns Tokugawa Iemitsu and Tokugawa Ietsuna. He took an active part in putting down the revolt of the Christians of Shimabara (1637–38) and in repression of the Keian uprisings (1651). He was later replaced by Sakai Tadakiyo. Also called Chie Izu no Kami ("Intelligent Izu no Kami").

Matsudaira Nobuyasu. One of Tokugawa Ieyasu's sons (1559–79). In 1573, he married Tokuhime, one of Oda Nobunaga's daughters.

Matsudaira Sadanobu. Daimyo (Tayasu Sadanobu, 1758–1829) in Shirakawa (Fukushima) and *rōjū* of the shogunate, born in Edo. He was one of Tayasu Munetake's sons and Tokugawa Yoshimune's grandson. Yoshimune had him adopted by Matsudaira Sadakuni, the daimyo of Shirakawa, in order to distance himself from him. But when Tokugawa Ienari came to power, Sadanobu once again became *rōjū*, as well as regent *(hosa)* for the shogun. He succeeded his adopted father as daimyo of Shirakawa in 1783. He fortified Japan's coasts, then retired from public affairs in 1812, becoming a Buddhist monk with the name Gaku-ō, and writing several works on Confucian ethics. Also called Etchū no Kami.

Matsudaira Tadanao. Tokugawa Ieyasu's grandson (1595–1650) and son of Yūki Hieyasu (1574–1607), daimyo of Echizen. He fought beside Ieyasu at the siege of Osaka (1615); after the shogun's death, however, he became tyrannical and undisciplined. He was therefore stripped of his estates in 1623 and exiled to Bungo province.

Matsudaira Tadayoshi. Tokugawa Ieyasu's fourth son (1580–1607). In 1592, he received an estate worth 120,000 *koku* in Ōshi, Saitama province, where he had major works executed to regulate the flow of the Tone-gawa river. He took part in the Battle of Sekigahara in 1600 and received a fief in Owari province worth 520,000 *koku*.

Matsudaira Tsuneo. Politician and diplomat (1877 –1949) who was ambassador to the United States from 1925 to 1928, and to Great Britain from 1929 to 1936. He was an adviser to Emperor Hirohito from 1936 to 1945 and was elected president of the Chamber of Councillors in 1947.

Matsudaira Yoritsune. Composer, born 1907 in Tokyo. A student of Nicholas Tcherepnin's, he wrote many pieces for piano and orchestra.

Matsudaira Yoshinaga. Daimyo (Tayasu Yoshinaga, Matsudaira Keiei; *gō*: Shungaku, 1828–90), adoptive son of Matsudaira Nariyoshi, daimyo of Echizen. He advocated the opening of Japan to foreign relations, but at the same time reinforced the country's coastal defenses. In 1862, he was appointed the shogun's prime minister; in this capac-

ity, he abolished the custom of alternating presence at the court *(sankin-kōtai)*. Having asked shogun Tokugawa Iemochi to resign from his position in favor of the emperor, he was forced to resign. After the Meiji Restoration, in 1868, he held a number of positions in government.

Matsue. Chief city of Shimane prefecture, port on the Sea of Japan at the mouth of the Ōhashi-gawa river, about 150 km northeast of Hiroshima, and part of the Nakaumi industrial complex. Castle (Shirayama-jō) built by the daimyo of Horio in 1611 (five-story *donjon*). Koizumi Yakumo museum dedicated to the memory of Lafcadio Hearn, who lived in Matsue. There are a number of *kofun* nearby, in Fodoki no Oka park. Eighteenth-century Buddhist temple and Lake Shinji-ko. *Pop.*: 135,000.
→ *See* MATSUDAIRA.

Matsue Shigeyori. Poet (1602–80) and merchant in Kyoto. He studied with Matsunaga Teitoku and was active in developing the haiku form. Author of the anthology *Enokoshū* (1633) and a treatise on haiku, the *Kefukigusa*, in 1638. He also compiled a poetry anthology featuring Bashō's first published poems, *Sayo no nakayama-shū*, in 1664.

Matsugaoka Bunko. "Matsugaoka Library," founded in Kamakura in 1946 by D. T. Suzuki to honor the memory of his Zen master, Shaku Shōen (1859–1919). Its collection contains more than 50,000 volumes on Zen from Japan, China, and Europe.

Matsuhime monogatari emaki. "Tale Illustrated by Matsuhime," describing the life of a noble who falls in love with the beautiful Matsuhime. It is a single scroll painted by an amateur in a naive style in 1526, conserved at the University of Tokyo.

Matsui Keishirō. Diplomat (1868–1946), ambassador to France (1914–20) and Great Britain (1925–28), and minister of foreign affairs in 1924.

Matsui Kōsei. Ceramist, born 1927 in Nagano prefecture. He won the prize of excellence awarded by the imperial family in 1973, and exhibited in Monz, Belgium, in 1989, and in Scandinavia and Paris (Mitsukoshi space) in 1994.

Matsui Sumako. Actress (Kobayashi Masako, 1886–1919), born to a samurai family in Nagano. Joining the Bungei Kyōkai theater company directed by Tsubouchi Shōyō in 1919, she performed in Western plays, notably Shakespeare, and was thus the first Western-style stage actress in Japan. She committed suicide after the death of Shimamura Hōgetsu, with whom she had founded another theater company, the Geijutsu-za, in 1913. *See* SHIMAMURA HŌGETSU.

Matsu-ji. Annex temple in a Buddhist grouping. Also called *betsu-in*. *See* BETSU-IN, HON-JI.

Matsukata Kōjirō. Industrialist (1865–1950) and naval engineer (Kawasaki shipyards), Matsukata Masayoshi's son. After studying in the United States, London, and Paris, he began in 1916 to collect art (including 34 paintings by Monet), creating what became the core of the current collection of the Tokyo Museum of Western Art. He also bought 8,000 ukiyo-e prints from the Vever Collection and organized the first major ukiyo-e exhibition in Tokyo in 1925.

Matsukata Masayoshi. Imperial prince (1835–1924) of the Satsuma clan, and statesman. He was prime minister in 1891–92, succeeding Yamagata. His cabinet included Vice-Admiral Enomoto as minister of foreign affairs and senior ministers Shinagawa, Soejima, and Kōno Togama. Itō Hirobumi succeeded him, but he was prime minister again in 1896–97. During his term as minister of finance, from 1881 to 1885, he instituted profound financial reforms that caused a monetary deflation and restored the value of the currency. In 1882, he founded the Bank of Japan, which stimulated industrial growth to the detriment of the peasantry. He was Privy Chancellor in 1917 and ennobled in 1922. Matsukata Kōjirō's father.

Matsukaze. Title of a Noh play: the spirits of Matsukaze and Murasame, two young women who were lovers of Prince Yukihira, appear as poor salt venders to a Buddhist monk whom they have taken in for the night, and they dance in his honor.

Matsukura Shigemasa. Daimyo (?–1630) of Iga and Yamato provinces, who fought in the Battle of Sekigahara (1600) at Tokugawa Ieyasu's side. He was rewarded with the concession to the former estate (worth 10,000 *koku*) of his suzerain, Tsutsui Sadatsugu (1562–1615), who had fallen into disgrace; he then received the Shimabara estate (Kyushu), worth 40,000 *koku,* in 1616. He fought to suppress Christianity. His son, Matsukura Katsuie, succeeded him, but he was held responsible

for the revolt of Christians in Shimabara and sentenced to death in 1638.

Matsumae Suehiro. First settler on Hokkaido in the sixteenth century, also known as Kakizaki no Suehiro. His son Matsumae Yoshihiro (1550–1618) continued his colonization work.

Matsumoto. City in Nagano prefecture, former provincial capital in the eighth century, and castle town during the Edo period. Castle (Fukashi-jō) built in 1504 by Shimadate, a vassal of the Ogasawara family. The Takeda occupied it from 1555 to 1582, when it returned to the Ogasawara. The Ishikawa family expanded it and added a five-story donjon *(tenshu)* in 1594. Folk-art museum. Many hot springs in the area. Site of Shinshū University. Small silk and electricity industries. *Pop.:* 195,000.

Matsumoto Jiichirō. *Burakumin* leader (1887–1966), one of the founders of the Buraku Kaihō Dōmei (League for the Liberation of the *Burakumin*), elected to the vice-presidency of the Chamber of Councillors in 1947. Having refused to defer to the emperor, he was forced to resign in 1948, but he was granted amnesty and reinstated in 1951.

Matsumoto Jōji. Statesman and jurist (1877–1954), born in Tokyo, professor of law at the University of Tokyo. In 1919, he was vice-president of the trans-Manchuria railroad; in 1923, director of the legislative cabinet; in 1934, appointed minister of finance by Saitō Makoto. A minister in Shidehara Kijūrō's cabinet in 1945, he was made responsible for writing a new constitution, but his proposal was rejected by the American Occupation authorities. He wrote many works on law and legislation and worked to revise Japan's commercial code.

Matsumoto Kōshirō. Family of Kabuki actors. The best-known members were Matsumoto Kōshirō IV (1737–1802) and Matsumoto Kōshirō V (1764–1838). Matsumoto Kōshirō VIII (Fujima Junjirō, 1910–82), Matsumoto Kōjirō VII's (1870–1949) son, debuted in 1926 and first took the stage name Ichikawa Somegorō in 1930, acceding to the family name only in 1949. He was designated a Living National Treasure in 1975 and received the Order of Culture (Bunka-shō) in 1981. He then passed the name Matsumoto Kōjirō on to his oldest son and retired with the name Matsumoto Hakuō.

Matsumoto Nazaemon. Kabuki actors (father and son) in the late seventeenth century. The father (?– ca. 1685) founded a theater in Osaka.

Matsumoto Ryōjun. Physician (1832–1907); with the help of Dutch physicians, he founded a school for Western medicine in Nagasaki in 1861. *See* SEITOKU-KAN.

Matsumoto Seichō. Writer (Matsumoto Kiyoharu, 1909–92), born in Fukuoka prefecture (Kyushu). A journalist at the *Asahi Shimbun* from 1937 to 1957, he began to write novels after the Second World War and received the Akutagawa Prize in 1952 for *Aru kokura nikki den.* He then wrote a number of detective novels that quickly became best-sellers— *Ten no sen* (Points and Lines, 1957–58), *Me no kabe* (1957), *Kuroi gashū* (1958), *Nihon no kuroi kiri* (Black Fog on Japan, 1960)—and the historical works *Kodaishi-gi* (1967) and *Shōwashi hakkutsu,* a 13-volume history of the Shōwa period (1926–90).

Matsumura Kenzō. Politician (1883–1971), born in Toyama prefecture. He was elected to the House of Representatives 13 times (from 1928 to 1969; out of office 1946–49) and was minister of education in Hagashikuni Naruhiko's cabinet (1945), then minister of agriculture in Hatoyama Ichirō's cabinet (1955).

Matsumushi. Title of a Noh play, sometimes attributed to Zeami, in which cricket *(matsumushi)* chirps bring back the memories of people who have died: at the Abeno market, a man recalls that once two friends were walking when one of them suddenly died. The narrator admits that he is the spirit of the deceased, and dances and sings to the chirping of crickets.

Matsunaga Hisahide. Warrior (1510–77) who was an important figure during the Sengoku era and who was responsible for the suicide of shogun Ashikaga Yoshiteru in 1565. Oda Nobunaga appointed him *shugo* of Yamato, but he rebelled and was forced to commit suicide.

Matsunaga Sekigo. Confucian scholar (Matsunaga Shōsan, 1592–1657), born in Kyoto, Matsunaga Teitoku's son and Fujiwara Seika's disciple. He opened his own school of Confucianism in 1648, where he taught more than 5,000 students.

• **Matsunaga Teitoku.** Poet (1571–1653), born in Kyoto. He studied *renga* and *waka* with Hosokawa Yūsai and Satomura Jōha, then founded his own *haikai* school, Teimon-ha. As Toyotomi Hideyoshi's secretary, he acquired an encyclopedic body of knowledge and worked to spread education to the widest number of people possible. *Gosan* (1651), a collection of his *haikai* poems, defined the rules for their composition according to the Teimon-ha. Matsunaga Sekigo's father. *See* TEIMON-HA.

Matsunaga Yasuzaemon. Businessman (1875–1971), born in Nagasaki, builder of railroad lines in Kyushu in 1909. He was elected president of the Association of Electrical Industries of Japan in 1924. When his businesses were nationalized in 1936, he retired from public affairs. In 1953, he was appointed director of the Japanese Center for Research on Electrical Energy. An important art collector, he founded a gallery (now called Matsunaga Kinenkan) in Odawara (Kanagawa prefecture) in 1959; it was moved to the Fukuoka Art Museum (Kyushu) in 1980. His collection included objects in lacquer, jade, and bronze, sculpture, *emakimono,* and many ancient Japanese and Chinese paintings.

Matsunoo-dera. Buddhist temple of the Shingon sect, founded around 717–23 in Yamada (Ikoma, Nara prefecture) and reconstructed twice, in the thirteenth century and from 1596 to 1614.

• **Matsunoo-jinja.** Shinto shrine in Arashiyama (Kyoto) dedicated to the *kami* Oyamakui no Mikoto.

Matsuoka Yōsuke. Politician and diplomat (1880–1946), born in Yamaguchi prefecture, died in Tokyo. He studied law in Oregon from 1893 to 1902, then began his diplomatic career in 1940 with postings in Shanghai, Dalian, Beijing, St. Petersburg, and Paris. He was Japan's delegate to the League of Nations in 1932–33, then director of the Southern Manchuria Railroad from 1935 to 1939. As minister of foreign affairs in Konoe Fumimaro's cabinet from June 22, 1940 to July 18, 1941, he signed the Tripartite Pact with Germany and Italy on September 27, 1940, then a pact of neutrality with the Soviet Union on April 13, 1941. When Konoe refused to attack Siberia as Germany wanted, Matsuoka resigned. Taken prisoner by the Soviets in Manchuria and indicted by the war-crimes court, he died before his court appearance.

Matsuo Taseko. Woman of letters (Kinnō Basan, 1811–94), born in Nagano prefecture, of the Hirata school. She wrote mainly collections of poems, including *Matsu no homara* and *Miyako no tsuto*.

Matsura Sayohime. Wife (sixth century) of the warrior Ōtomo Sadehiko. According to legend, she was turned to stone as she waited on top of a mountain for her husband to return from Korea, where he had gone to fight.

Matsuri. Religious and agrarian festivals associated with Shinto or folk Buddhism, held on set dates at temples and shrines. There are two main categories: *matsuri,* which are religious in nature, and *nenchō-gyōji* (seasonal rites), which are calendar-related (often also called *matsuri*). *Matsuri* may be local or national, and they relate to two "dimensions" of life: *hare* (all that is out of the ordinary and therefore a celebration, *harebi* meaning "propitiatory day"), and *ke* (lay family festivities); however, there is no clear distinction between the two. Other *matsuri* are simply commercial festivals, such as fairs and Christmas celebrations. The major national and "historic" festivals, which were created relatively recently and which are political in nature, are also sometimes called *matsuri*. In villages, *matsuri* are a way of affirming the cohesion of the community, based on agricultural activities with which Shinto *kami* are always associated. In cities, *matsuri* were sometimes organized to invoke *kami* and Buddhist divinities to counter epidemics. *See* FESTIVALS.

Matsushima. "Islands of Pines." A group of about 260 small islands in Matsuhima Bay, in Miyagi prefecture, in a sandy lagoon on the Pacific coast. It is one of the Nihon Sankei (Three Views of Japan), along with Amanohashidate and Istukushima. Several Buddhist temples were established in the lagoon, such as the Zuigan-ji (renovated in 1604), the Go-Daidō (built by Date Masamune in 1610), and the Kanrantei (seventeenth century). *See* NIHON SANKEI, SANKEI.

Matsushita Daisaburō. Grammarian (1878–1935), born in Shizuoka prefecture. He conducted fundamental studies on the Japanese language and its syntax, and wrote a number of works on these subjects.

Matsushita Kōnosuke. Industrialist and philanthropist (1895–1989), born in Osaka, founder of manufacturers and distributors of electrical and electronic equipment (Matsushita Denki Sangyō, Matsushita Denki Bōeki, Matsushita Denkō) mainly under the brand names National, Quasar, Panasonic, and Technics. In 1935, Matsushita Kōnosuke founded a company called Matsushita Denki Sangyō, from a small store opened in 1918. He reorganized his company in 1947, then affiliated with the Dutch company Phillips in 1952 and opened a large number of branches in Japan and abroad, exporting up to 42% of production through 32 trading companies established in 33 countries. A proponent of "Japanese-style" work organization, in 1946 he founded a movement called P.H.P. (Peace, Happiness, Prosperity) that promoted peace and prosperity through well-understood and well-organized work. He also created business schools and a labor organization and was a member of many philanthropic associations. The head offices of his companies are in Osaka. The subsidiaries are Matsushita Kotobuki Denshi Kōgyō, founded in 1969 to manufacture video equipment (head office in Takamatsu), and Matsushita Reiki Co. (founded in 1939), specializing in refrigeration equipment and air conditioners. Another major subsidiary is Matsushita Tsūshin Kōgyō, which makes telecommunications equipment and computers under the brand name Panasonic, exporting about 30% of its production; head office in Yokohama. In 1991, Matsushita purchased MCA and Universal Studios and began to specialize in high technology, including high-definition television (HDTV). In 1992, Matsushita began to expand to other countries; by 1994, it had 152 subsidiaries, including 68 in Asia, 43 in the Americas, and 41 in Europe and Africa. Its main markets are China (13 subsidiaries) and Malaysia (16 subsidiaries).

Matsutani Takesada. Contemporary painter, born 1937 in Osaka; has lived and worked in France since 1968. He has had many exhibitions in France (almost every year since 1968), Germany (1979), Belgium (1980), San Francisco (1982), Geneva (1985), Honolulu (1986), and Japan. In 1966, he received the grand prize of the Franco-Japanese Institute; he received other awards in Yugoslavia, England, and San Francisco.

Matsuura Shigenobu. Warrior (1549–1614) who became famous for his courage when he fought in Korea in Toyotomi Hideyoshi's army. When he returned, he became a Buddhist monk with the name Sōsei Hō-in.

Matsuura Takeshirō. Geographer (1818–88), born in Ise province, who led three exploratory expeditions to the island of Ezo and drew maps of the island in 1845. He renamed Ezo, calling it Hokkaido.

Matsuyama. Chief city of Ehima prefecture (Shikoku) and port on the northwest coast. It developed around the castle built in 1603 by Katō Yoshiakira, which was later occupied by the Matsudaira family. This castle, destroyed by fire in 1854, had three fortress walls and four gates. The city has several Buddhist temples, among them the Ishite-ji, founded in 1318, which has a *kondō* and a pagoda dating from 1333 and a *gomadō* from 1318. The industrial district (oil refineries, mechanical and textile plants) is also the seat of the University of Ehime, founded in 1949, and a number of literary associations. *Pop.:* 400,000.
• Name for a geomagnetic period, which ended 700,000 years ago, that involved an inversion of the terrestrial magnetic field.

Matsuyama kagami. Title of a Noh play: a young woman, devastated by the death of her mother, fiercely guards a mirror in which her mother's face appears every day. Her mother's spirit returns to visit and console her. Glancing at the mirror, the spirit sees that, thanks to her daughter's love, all her sins have been pardoned. She then enters Amida's Pure Land.

• *Matsuyama tengu.* Title of a Noh play: the spirits of an emperor and a *tengu* appear to the poet Saigyō.

Matsuyama Zenzō. Movie director and set designer (b. 1925) who worked for the Shochiku company starting in 1948 and was Kinoshita Keisuke's assistant. He worked on many movies, the most famous being *Ningen no jōken* (The Human Condition) in 1961. He married the actress Takamine Hideko.

Matsuzakaya. Large store founded in 1611 in Nagoya. It currently has nine branches, notably in Tokyo and Osaka, and is associated with Daimaru, a food distributor. This chain distributes a wide variety of products and has a partner in Hong Kong called Hang Long.

Matsuzaki Hakkei. Samurai and scholar (1682–1753), disciple of Itō Tōgai and Ogyū Sorai. He wrote many works on Confucianism.

Matsuzaki Tenjin engi. "Legend of the Shrine of Matsuzaki Tenjin," a six-scroll *emakimono* dating from the early fourteenth century and telling of the life of Sugawara no Michizane. It is kept in the Bōfu Temmangū in Yamaguchi prefecture.

Mawari-butai. In Kabuki theater, a revolving stage, apparently invented by Namiki Shōzō (1730–73) in Osaka. This stage enabled sets to be changed easily and the artists to change costumes out of sight of the audience. It helped to popularize Kabuki theater.

• **Mawari-dōrō.** Revolving magic lantern, moved by warm air from a flame, that projects silhouettes cut out from the paper on its outside surface. Originally from China, it was very popular during the Edo period.

Mawashi. Belt worn by *sumotori,* consisting of a long band of silk (11 × 0.6 m), usually black, folded six times and rolled around the wrestler's waist. It is very heavy (13–15 kg) and adorned with cords of silk that have been hardened with glue, *sagari,* whose role is purely decorative. *See* OBI, SUMO, SUMOTORI.

Mayama Seika. Writer and playwright (1878–1948), born in Sendai. He wrote naturalist-style novels, notably on peasant life, such as *Minami koizumi mura* (The Village of Minami Koizumi, 1907), and plays for the Shimpa. After 1924, he wrote many historical plays (more than 200), some of which are still being produced.

Mayet, Paul. German economist (1846–1920). Invited to Japan by the Meiji government in 1875, he taught in several universities and advised the government on matters such as insurance, postal savings bonds, and agriculture. In 1893, he returned to Germany, where he became director of the Statistics Bureau.

Mayoke. Charms and amulets designed to keep evil spirits and demons from entering houses or causing illness. They take a wide variety of forms: shells, pine cones, mushrooms, magical inscriptions, and so on. They are hung at the door to houses on New Year's Day *(kadomatsu),* or attached to clothing or worn by those seeking their protection. Amulets *(gofu)* sold by temples and shrines are also *mayoke.*

Mayuzumi Toshirō. Composer, born 1929 in Yokohama, who studied in Tokyo and Paris (where he was Tony Aubin's student). In 1953, he introduced electronic music and "concrete music" to Japan. He composed an opera, drawn from Mishima Yukio's novel *Kinkaku-ji,* which was performed at the Berlin Opera in 1976.

Mazaki Jinzaburō. General (1876–1956), born in Saga prefecture, inspector general of military education in 1934. With Araki Sadao, he commanded the Kōdōha, and because of this he was stripped of his position in 1935. After the Second World War, he was sentenced to two years in prison for war crimes.

Meals. In Japan, a meal *(meshi)* is more than a simple act of nourishment: it is a family ritual (except, of course, for meals eaten in restaurants), which it is important to observe down to the smallest detail in order to feel at peace with oneself and one's food, which is a part of nature. Thus, one does not eat just anything at random. Just as each season produces specific foodstuffs, so each meal requires the preparation and eating of certain dishes. Japanese dishes are generally prepared so that their arrangement is pleasing to the eye. Foods must taste as natural as possible. An ordinary meal is composed of three to five dishes as well as a bowl of plain rice, soup, and condiments, such as vegetables in brine *(tsukemono).* These dishes are served all at the same time, arranged on a lacquered-wood tray with no cloth on it, accompanied by a small paper napkin. The most typical dishes are:

—Cooked rice *(gohan),* served in a covered bowl.

—Clear soup *(suimono)* or miso soup *(misohiru)* in the morning.

—*Nimono* (vegetables, fish).

—*Yakimono* or *agemono* (grilled or fried vegetables, fish, or meat).

—*Sunomono* (vegetables, shellfish, or fish in a vinegar sauce) or *aemono* (vegetables mixed with another food) or *hitashimono* (boiled green vegetables with soy sauce).

—*Mushimono* (steamed vegetables, mushrooms, or seafood).

—*Sashimi* (slices of raw fish with soy sauce and grated horseradish, *wasabi*).

—*Sushi* (rice rolls with fish or shellfish and *nori* algae).

—*Kōnomono* or *tsukemono,* vegetables in brine. It is customary, before beginning the meal, to bow slightly and say *"itadakimasu"* (see ITADAKIMASU). Chopsticks are used for eating, and spoons are used for liquid foods. Japanese chopsticks *(hashi)* are shorter and pointier than Chinese ones. Soup is sipped from the bowl and accompanies other dishes because usually nothing is drunk with the meal, but only before or after (see SAKE). It is permitted to make noise while drinking soup or tea or eating noodles. Chopsticks must never be placed in the rice bowl, for this is how food is offered to the souls of the deceased, and food must never be passed between sets of chopsticks because this is a funerary rite. Chopsticks should not be used to stab a piece of food, and they must not be waved around while a person speaks, as this is considered impolite. Chopsticks must be placed on a chopstick rest before a dish is picked up with the hands. In principle, one should not start eating until the person who is serving the dishes has placed them all on the table and invited the guests to eat.

Traditionally, there are several types of meals: family, formal *(honzen),* and light *(kaiseki).* In *honzen* meals, the dishes are placed on three trays and a small separate table. There are also various ways of presenting dishes, depending on the seasons and the circumstances, and specific foods are served on certain days or in certain periods.

Restaurants serve both traditional Japanese meals and Western-style food; most have rooms set up for both styles of dining. There are many types of traditional restaurants specializing in one dish or another. The most popular are the *sushi-ya* (mainly sushi); *soba-ya* (buckwheat noodles); *sukiyaki-ya* (sukiyaki and *shabu-shabu*); *tempura-ya* (fried fish, shellfish, and vegetables, served at a counter); *tonkatsu-ya* (breaded fried pork cutlets and other fried foods); *ramen-ya* (Chinese noodles); *oden-ya* (fish cakes with noodles and other ingredients); *yakiniku-ya* (Korean-style marinated and grilled meats); *yakitori-ya* (grilled chicken brochettes). Recently, restaurant-inns *(robatayaki-ya)* have been set up in rural areas (and some cities) serving "family food," usually grilled on a wood fire. In large cities, there has been a great infatuation with American-style "fast food" and take-out establishments in recent years. This type of meal is found all over the world and is not at all traditional, but it is a sign of the times. *See* CUISINE, KAISEKI, MESHI.

Meckel, Klemens Wilhelm Jakob. German officer (1842–1906), born in Köln, invited by the Meiji government in 1885 to teach at the Military College and modernize military training. When he returned to Germany, in 1888, he was appointed head instructor of the general staff.

Medals. There are five types of honorific medals in Japan, conferred by the emperor upon ministerial recommendation: a red ribbon (for rescuers), green (rewarding virtue), blue (for philanthropists), yellow (rewarding industrial success), and purple (for social works). These medals were created in 1881. *See also* KUNSHŌ.

Medicine (i-hō). Japanese traditional medicine is almost entirely rooted in Chinese medicine *(kan'i-hō)*, which was superimposed on "folk medicines" used since prehistory, mixing magic and plant decoctions. The *Kojiki* and *Nihon shoki* recount that two *kami* taught medicine to the Japanese, but in fact medicine did not arrive on the islands until it was brought by Chinese and Korean practitioners in the sixth century. A medical code translated from the Chinese, *Itsuryō* (757), sheds some light on how physicians worked; in the late eighth century, Emperor Heizei had a major medical work written, the *Daidō-ruijūhō*, now lost. The oldest surviving medical work is the *Ishimpō*, dating from 982 and credited to Tamba no Yasuyori (912–82), a court physician who used a great many Chinese books, including the *Xianjinfang* and the *Zhubing yuanhu*, in writing his work. He deals with acupuncture, preparation of remedies, obstetrics, sexuality, and diet, among other subjects, as well as magical recipes and the Chinese theory of the interaction of Yin and Yang.

Buddhism somewhat encouraged the growth of medicine through the intercession of the great "Medicine Buddha" Bhaishajya-guru *(Jap.*: Yakushi Nyorai), and monks who returned from China and Korea brought techniques and remedies. This importation of medical methods and procedures continued until relatively recently; the first written mentions of Western medicine *(ran'i-hō)* were made by Manase Dōsan (1506–94), one of Toyotomi Hideyoshi's physicians, and Nagata Tokuhon (1513–1610). Schools were founded advocating various methods, but most were still inspired by Chinese concepts.

The first Jesuits to arrive in Japan, in the mid-sixteenth century, brought new Western therapeutic methods, but few of these were adopted by the Japanese. It was not until the eighteenth century that they began to be seriously considered, thanks to contacts established with the Dutch in Dejima at Nagasaki. The first dissections, using Western medical illustrations, were performed in 1754 by Yamawaki Tōyo (1705–62) and Sugita Genpaku (1733–1817), who translated a Dutch treatise, *Kaitaishinsho* (New Treatise on Anatomy). Dutch physicians such as Engelbert Kaempfer (1651–1716) and Philipp Franz von Siebold (1796–1866) also shared their knowledge with their Japanese colleagues. The first Western-style hospital was founded in Nagasaki in 1860 by the Dutch physician Pompe van

Meerdervoort (1829–1908). But it was only in the Meiji era that the Western system of medicine (mainly German) was officially adopted, relegating traditional Chinese medicine to a secondary role.

From then on, the progress of Japanese medicine followed that of Western medicine. After the Second World War, a great number of Japanese physicians studied in the United States and Europe, and medicine was taught at many national and private universities. Currently, the Japanese enjoy certain social benefits, and people over 60 receive free medical care. Therapy, surgery, and cosmetic procedures performed in state hospitals or in the large number of private clinics are now as advanced as Western techniques, and many Japanese researchers are receiving great distinction for their discoveries.

See entries for names cited and ACUPUNCTURE, BOKUTŌ, EMBU-KŌ, IGAKUSHO, JAPAN (STATISTICS), JOFUKU, KUATSU, MOGUSA, OGINO GINKO, OGINO KYŪSAKU, SEITOKU-KAN.

Megane-bashi. "Lunette bridge," a term for double-arched bridges. The most famous one is in Uragami (Kyushu), built in stone in 1634 by a Chinese Buddhist monk *(Jap.*: Jotei) and still used today. *See* KINTAI-BASHI, NAGASAKI.

Megijima. Small island in the eastern Inland Sea (Setonaikai), north of the city of Takamatsu (Shikoku), made famous by Momotarō's story in which it is called Onigashima ("island of ogres"). *Area:* 2.7 km².

Mei. Familiar name by which a person is often known. On tangs of sword blades, blacksmiths' signatures are also called *mei*. Unsigned blades are called *mumei* (without *mei*). *See* KATANA, NAMES.

Meibutsu. Utensils used in the tea ceremony *(chanoyu)*.

• **Meibutsu-gire.** High-quality silk imported from China from the fourteenth to the seventeenth century and particularly valued by noble warriors and those who performed the tea ceremony *(chanoyu)*. These silks were damask *(donsu)*, brocades *(nishiki)*, and other types of fabric. Some also came from Persia, India, and Southeast Asia via China.

Meigen. Custom according to which, when the emperor gets into his bath, a servant plucks the string of a bow in order to keep evil spirits away. This custom is still observed when a prince is born and in some rural areas.

Meigetsuki. Book of notes by the poet and courtier Fujiwara no Sadaie, written in Chinese *(kambun)* and covering the years 1180–1235. This historical work served as a basis for the *Azuma kagami* and is still a valuable source for study of the period's history. Also titled *Shōkōki.*

Meiji. Era name meaning "enlightened government," corresponding to the reign of Emperor Meiji (Mutsuhito): Sept. 1868–July 1912. *See* NENGŌ.

• **Meiji Daigaku.** "Meiji University," a private institution created in 1903 in Chiyoda-ku (Tokyo) to succeed the Meiji Hōritsu Gakkō (Meiji Law School), founded in 1881. Its largest faculties—law, business, economics, and engineering—are located in Chiyoda-ku, Suginami-ku, and the city of Kawasaki. Attendance is currently more than 25,000 students.

• **Meiji Gaku-in Daigaku.** "Meiji Private University," founded in Minato-ku (Tokyo) in 1886 by descendants of James Curtis Hepburn and Samuel Robbins Brown. This multidisciplinary school was raised to the rank of university in 1949. It has a number of faculties, and attendance is about 8,000 students.

• **Meiji-isshin.** "Meiji Restoration." A revolution in 1868 that defeated the Edo shogunate and brought Emperor Mutsuhito (Meiji) to power. The capital was moved from Kyoto to Edo, and the latter city was renamed Tokyo. *See* BOSHIN-SENSŌ.

• **Meiji-jidai.** "Meiji era," corresponding to Emperor Meiji's reign and characterized by modernization, adoption of a constitution (1889–90) and a parliament (created in 1885 by Itō Hirobumi), updating of the army and navy, victorious wars against China (1894–95) and Russia (1904–05), and territorial expansion (occupation of Manchuria, Korea, the Kuril Islands, and Taiwan), making Japan one of the great global powers. *See* MEIJI TENNŌ.

• **Meiji-jingū.** Shinto shrine built in a magnificent park in the Harajuku district of Tokyo, dedicated to the memory of Emperor Meiji in 1920. The park has trees donated by people from all parts of the country.

• **Meiji-kyō.** Shinto subsect of the Jikkō-kyō, founded in 1946 by Eno Tasuku (1876–1952). It has about 3,000 followers.

• **Meiji-kyōdan.** Shinto sect founded in 1950 by Ota Eizaburō.

• **Meiji Tennō.** Hundred and twenty-second emperor (Mutsuhito, 1852<1866–1912>), son of Kōmei Tennō and Nakayama Yoshiko, the daughter of grand counselor *(dainagon)* Nakayama Tadayasu (1809–88). Meiji acceded to the throne in 1866 under the regency *(sesshō)* of Nijō Nariyuki (1816–78). He married Ichijō Haruko (Shōken Kōtaigō, 1850–1914), who gave birth to Crown Prince Yoshihito in 1879. In 1868, Meiji's supporters overthrew the Tokugawa shogunal regime and brought him to power, following the short Boshin Civil War. He then concentrated all power in his own hands and transferred his capital to Edo, which he renamed Tokyo ("capital of the east"). Aided by advisers most of whom belonged to the major southern clans, especially the Chōshū and the *hambatsu (han* cliques), and by remarkable statesmen such as Itō Hirobumi, Saigō Takamori, Okubo Toshimichi, and Kido Takayoshi, the emperor undertook to modernize Japan, although he had to deal with various domestic difficulties (Saigō Takamori's revolt in 1877). He created a Western-style army and navy, ended the privileges of the samurai and former nobles, divided the country into departments *(ken),* had public education improved, instituted means of communication such as telegraphy and the railroad, improved the postal system, and more. However, he was forced to support two wars, against China in 1894–95 and against Russia (1904–05). His influence was huge in all sectors, which earned him the nickname "the father of modern Japan." A literate and traditionalist emperor and an excellent poet, he was clearly influenced by the Confucianism of one of his tutors, Motoda Nagazane. Although he did not like the Western life style, he realized that adoption of the techniques and knowledge of the West could help with his country's modernization, and he invited to Japan a number of experts in various areas: law, army, navy, education, sciences. He had a constitution written and adopted and created a parliament (the Diet). Finally, he expanded diplomatic relations with other countries, had the "Unequal Treaties" revised *(see* JŌYAKU), concluded an alliance with Great Britain, approved the annexation of Korea (1910), and encouraged the development of industry. He died on July 30, 1912, and was buried in the Fushimi mausoleum near Kyoto. His son Yoshihito succeeded him on the throne with the era name Taishō.

Meiji Nyōgyō. Large distributor of dairy and frozen products in Japan (using the Meiji brand name) and the United States (under the Borden brand name), where it has subsidiaries. It is a partner of Meiji Seika Kaisha, a distributor of food products, pharmaceuticals, sweets, and canned fruits. Both companies were established in 1917. Meiji Seika has branches in most countries of Southeast Asia, Korea, Brazil, and the United States. Meiji Seitō, a sugar refinery created in Taiwan in 1906, is affiliated with Mitsubishi Corporation.

Mei-ō. Era of Emperor Go-Tsuchimikado: July 1492–Feb. 1501. *See* NENGŌ.

Meipin. Vase for holding a plum-tree branch, with very wide shoulders, a narrow mouth, and a narrow base, of Chinese origin *(Chin.: mei-ping);* its shape probably appeared during the Song dynasty in China. *Kor.: mae-pyöng.*

Meireki. Era of Emperor Go-Saiin: Apr. 1655–July 1658. *See* NENGŌ.

• **Meireki no Taika.** A huge fire that swept Edo in March 1657, killing more than 100,000 people. It was supposedly caused when the kimono sleeves of a young woman caught on fire during an exorcism ceremony, whence its other name, Furisode no Taika. Edo was then reconstructed on an expanded plan, which emptied the state's coffers and led to a devaluation of the currency.

Meirin-dō. Confucian schools (Shohan-gakkō) founded in 1749 in Nagoya and in 1792 in Kanazawa. *See* MIWA SHISSAI.

• **Meirin-kan.** Confucian school (Shohan-gakkō) founded for the study of "Dutch sciences" *(rangaku)* in Hagi in 1718. *See* RANGAKU.

Meiroku-sha. "Society of the Year 6 [of the Meiji era]," founded in 1874 by Mori Arinori to promote civilization and modernism. It published a newspaper, *Meiroku-zasshi,* and organized many conferences aimed at spreading Western ideas among the population. It had only 33 members to start with—including Katō Hiroyuki, Kanda Takahira, Fukuzawa Yukichi, Nishimura Shigeki, Nishi Amane, and Tsuda Sen—who were very influential in all areas of thought and who had studied the principles of Confucianism and foreign languages—Dutch, English, French, Russian, German. However, these scholars soon became divided over whether or not to participate in governing the country. The society stopped publication of its paper in September 1875;

although its members continued to meet until 1900, the influence of the Meiroku-sha, very great at first, declined over time.

Meiryō Kōhan. "Illustrious Examples," a 40-volume collection of stories and anecdotes about famous men who lived under the first five Tokugawa shoguns, compiled by a samurai, Sanada Zōyo, from 1680 to 1700.

Meisei-kyo. Shinto sect founded in 1946 by Omori Mume (1881–1965). *See* SHINRI-KYŌ, SHIN SHŪ-KYŌ.

Meishi. "Visiting cards." These are indispensable in Japanese life; when people meet, they unfailingly exchange *meishi* bearing their name, home and work addresses, and telephone number. Japanese in constant contact with foreigners have their visiting cards printed with information in Japanese characters on one side and in roman letters on the other. Women use *meishi* that are usually smaller and have rounded corners. The custom of exchanging visiting cards was imported in the early nineteenth century, but became more widespread during the Meiji era. Today, it is considered de rigueur.

Meishō Tennō. Hundred and ninth sovereign (Princess Okiko, 1623<1630–43>1696), daughter of and successor to Go-Mizunoo (*see* TOKUGAWA KAZUKO). She abdicated in favor of her brother Tsuguhito, who took the emperor's name Go-Komyō. Also called Myōshō Tennō.

Meisho-zue. Illustrated guides for travelers published during the Edo period, to facilitate the movements of pilgrims and promote "tourism."

Meitoku. Era of Emperor Go-Komatsu (dynasty of the North): Mar. 1390–July 1394. *See* NENGŌ.

• **Meitoku no Ran.** Attempted coup d'état planned in 1391 by Yamana Ujikiyo (1344–91) and his nephew, Yamana Mitsuyuki (d. 1395), to overthrow shogun Ashikaga Yoshimitsu. Ujikiyo and Mitsuyuki, very powerful daimyo, attacked Kyoto, but were defeated by the shogunal troops. Ujikiyo was killed, and their estates were divided up among the victorious generals.

Meiwa. Era of Empress Go-Sakurama-chi: June 1764–Nov. 1772. *See* NENGŌ.

Mekki. Metal-plating technique. When it is gold plating, it is called *kin-kise, kin-mekki,* or *tokin.*

Mekugi-ana. Holes made in the tang of a sword blade (*see* KATANA, TACHI) for insertion of the fixtures (usually wooden pegs) for the handle (*tsuka*).

Mempō. Samurai mask (*men*) covering the warrior's chin, cheeks, and nose. It was made of leather or iron, lacquered, generally in black, and decorated with a mustache. Sometimes teeth were painted on in gold or silver. On some masks, the nose was detachable so that the warrior could blow his nose. These masks were meant not only to protect the warrior but to frighten the enemy. *See* HŌATE, KABUTO, SŌMEN.

Mendenhall, Thomas Corvin. American physicist (1841–1924), invited to Japan by the Meiji government in 1878 to teach physics, on the recommendation of Edward S. Morse. He set up the first physics lab at the University of Tokyo, founded the Seismology Society, and made meteorological observations. He returned to the United States in 1881 to direct the Polytechnic Institute in Worcester.

Menko. Children's game consisting of throwing a piece (generally square, in clay, lead, or cardboard) at another in order to flip it over. Sometimes the pieces are brightly decorated. Similar pieces are used to count the points scored.

Menpes, Mortimer. Australian painter and engraver (ca. 1860–1938), born in Port Adelaide. In 1887, he visited Japan and made a great many paintings and prints, which he exhibited in London the following year. While in Japan, he met the painter Kyōsai, who taught him the rudiments of ukiyo-e printing. He returned to Japan in 1896 during a trip to East Asia and had another exhibition. He published several works on his voyages and experiences, including *Japan, A Record in Color* (1901).

Menukiya Chōzaburō. Famous shamisen player (late sixteenth–early seventeenth century) and puppeteer in Kyoto, Osaka, and Edo. He also sang *jōruri* and, in collaboration with the puppeteer Hikita, created many *ningyō-jōruri* plays.

Merōfu Kannon. One of the 33 forms (*see* SAN-JŪSAN ŌGESHIN) of Kannon Bosatsu (*Skt.*: Avalokiteshvara), represented as a Chinese lady. She was a divinization of the virtuous wife of a holy man named Ma. In China, she is considered an incarna-

tion of Guanyin. This divinity is venerated mainly by fishers in Nagasaki.

Meshi. Literally, "boiled rice"; also called, more politely, *gohan*. Because rice is the main staple consumed, the term *meshi* has come to mean all meals.

Metezashi. Small stiletto dagger, used by medieval warriors to pierce the armor of their defeated enemies. Also called *yoroi-dōshi*.

Metropolitan ("Chikatetsu"). The first subway line was opened in Tokyo on December 30, 1927, to link the Asakusa and Ueno districts. Osaka opened a subway line in 1933, followed by Nagoya (1957), Kobe (1968), Sapporo (1971), Yokohama (1977), Kyoto (1981), Fukuoka (1981), and Sendai (1982). Every year, these systems add new lines to improve circulation. Most of them link up to railroad networks, and the price of tickets is calculated according to distance traveled.

Metsuke. In the Edo period, censors and police officers used by *wakadoshiyori* (young councillors) to oversee the *hatamoto* and *gokenin*. There were ten, chosen from among the *hatamoto*. The daimyo also had a *metsuke* system. Also called *yokome*. *See also* ŌMETSUKE.

Meyasu-bako. Boxes for suggestions and petitions, placed by shogun Tokugawa Yoshimune at the gate to his Edo castle in 1721 to gather criticisms and suggestions made by the people. The shogun personally read the messages that were left in the boxes. Also called *jikiso-bako*.

Meyasu-hakase. System of musical notation of religious songs from the Tendai-shū sect, based on *fu-hakase* (or *fushi-hakase*) notation, the invention of which is attributed to the monk Ryōnin (1073–1132).

Mezu. Folkloric demon, corresponding to the Buddhist demon Ashvamukha, portrayed with a horse's head and symbolizing the souls of those who mistreated horses. It is often associated, notably during the Gion Matsuri in Kyoto, with Gozu (*Skt.*: Goshirsha), a demon with a bull's head, said to symbolize the souls of those who mistreated cattle. *Chin.*: Mamian. *See* GION-TENJIN.

• **Mezu Kannon.** Japanese name for the Buddhist divinity Hayagrīva ("Horse's Neck"), a Buddhist form of Vishnu considered an incarnation of Kannon Bosatsu, and a slightly wrathful form of Amida in Esoteric Buddhism. Also called Batō Kannon, Dairiki Myō-ō, Kichijō Komagata.

Mezurashizuka. Partly destroyed *kofun* in Fukuoka prefecture (northern Kyushu) with engraved decorations on its interior walls portraying quivers, a frog, horns, and a boat with a raven on its prow. It probably dates from the sixth century. *See also* TORAZUKA.

Miai. "Meeting" between a prospective bride and groom organized by a *nakōdo* (official matchmaker) and the parents of the future spouses, generally followed by a meal in a restaurant. After this meal, the young man and woman are free to do what they like, because the *miai* is considered a sort of marriage without the ceremony. Marriages thus arranged are called *miai-kekkon,* whereas love marriages (not arranged by a *nakōdo*) are called *ren'ai-kekkon.* Also called *O-miai. See* MARRIAGE.

Mibuchi Tadahiko. Politician (1880–1950), born in Okayama prefecture. He became a judge in 1907, but resigned in 1925 to hire on with Mitsui. As minister of justice and chief justice of the Supreme Court in 1947, he strengthened the role of the court as guardian of the new Constitution. He wrote important works on the civil code and legal interpretation.

Mibu-dera. Buddhist temple of the Ritsu-shū sect, established in Kyoto in 991 by the monk Kaiken of the Mii-dera. The temple was completed in 1005 and raised to the rank of Chokugan-ji in 1077. Shukō (1223–1311), a monk of the Shingon-shū, moved there in 1299 and introduced the custom of chanting the *nembutsu.* Often destroyed and rebuilt, the temple's current buildings date from 1825; its *hondō,* destroyed by fire in 1862, was restored in 1967. It houses a famous statue of Jizō Bosatsu, sculpted by Jōchō about 1150. Every April 21–29, a very old masked pantomime, the *mibu-kyōgen,* is performed there; there are about 30 Buddhist plays in its repertoire.

Mibu no Tadamine. Poet (active in the tenth century) of the Heian court, one of the compilers of the first *waka* anthology, the *Kokin-shū,* and one of the Sanjūrokkasen (Thirty-Six Poetic Geniuses) of the period. Although he had only a minor position in the court, he was considered an eminent poet. He wrote an anthology of poems, *Tadamine-shū* (which contains 50 or 122 poems, depending on the

version) and a treatise on poetry, dated 945, *Tadamine juttei* (or *Wakatei jisshu,* "Ten Poetic Styles"), in which he gives a clear description of ten different styles of *waka;* this work became a sort of classic memento used by poets of later periods.

Michi. "Path," or "road," a term that can be used in the spiritual sense of "discipline" or "virtue" or in the more prosaic sense of "road." Also pronounced *-dō* in composite words (and *on* in reading). It is the equivalent of the Chinese Dao (Tao). *See* DŌ.

Michi-ae no Matsuri. Ancient Shinto ceremony meant to chase away evil spirits, celebrated each year on the fifteenth day of the sixth moon of the lunar-solar year.

Michikata-gakari. Senior bureaucrat in the Edo shogunate, responsible, starting in 1658, for public works and maintenance of roads and streets in Edo.

Michiko. Emperor Akihito's wife (Shōda Michiko, b. Oct. 10, 1934), daughter of industrialist and mill owner Shōda Eizaburō. She married Prince Akihito in 1959 and became empress when her husband was crowned, in 1990. She has three children: Naruhito (Prince Hiro no Miya), Fumihito (Prince Aya no Miya), and Sayako (Princess Nori no Miya). *See* AKIHITO, HIROHITO.

Michimori. Noh play: the spirits of Michimori and his wife (who drowned herself when she heard of her husband's death) appear to a Buddhist monk praying that the spirits of warriors of the Heike (Taira) killed in battle will rest in peace.

Michinaga Shinnō. Imperial prince (d. 1360), Prince Morinaga's son and Emperor Daigo's grandson. He fought the Ashikaga shogun and then sided with the Northern Court (Hokuchō).

Michi no Ōmi no Mikoto. Warrior of Shinto legend who, according to the *Kojiki,* helped Emperor Jimmu Tennō conquer Yamato by "opening the roads." Also called Hi no Ōmi.

Michi-yuki. Literary genre, typified by the *Taiheiki,* describing a voyage in a poetic manner, in which literary reminiscences accompany descriptions of places visited.
→ *See* NOH.

Midō Kampaku. One of Fujiwara no Michinaga's titles.

• *Midō Kampaku-ki.* Diary kept by Fujiwara no Michinaga (966–1028) covering the years 998 to 1021. Fourteen chapters of this work were written by Fujiwara no Michinaga, while the 12 following chapters were written by other nobles. This manuscript, extremely important for an understanding of the history of the period, is kept in the Yōmei Bunko in Kyoto. Also titled *Hōjō-ji Nyūdō Sadaijin-ki.*

Midori. *See* GOTŌ MIDORI.

Midorikawa kofun. Large *kofun* in Kumamoto prefecture, on the bank of the Midorikawa river. It has a large inner chamber made of large stones, one of which, almost 2 m wide, bears paintings of twelve boats.

Midway, Battle of. Decisive Second World War naval battle between the United States and Japan on June 4–6, 1942, off the Midway Islands, an archipelago (two islands and an atoll) in the Pacific Ocean about 1,300 miles northwest of Hawai'i, discovered in 1859 by Captain Brooks and annexed by the United States in 1867. The American fleet, commanded by Admiral Nimitz, defeated the Japanese *Kidō-butai* (mobile units) fleet, accompanied by four aircraft carriers, which had attacked the islands; the Japanese suffered the heavy loss of four aircraft carriers, a heavy cruiser, and many planes. The battle changed the course of the war, with the advantage turning to the American naval forces. The Japanese fleet was under the command of admirals Yamamoto, Nagumo, and Kondō. *See* BATTLES, NAVAL; KIMURA SUSUMU.

Mie. In Kabuki theater, mainly, when an actor "freezes" in a pose characteristic of his role, designed to highlight both the actor and the action. *See* MA.

Miei-dō. In a Buddhist temple or monastery, a building or room dedicated to the founder of the sect or temple, or to a master of the sect whose portrait is exhibited there. Also called *daishi-dō, kaisan-dō, shōryō-in, soshi-dō.*

Mie prefecture. Prefecture on Honshu, located east of the Kii Peninsula on the Inland Sea (Setonaikai). The southern part of the prefecture is mountainous, the northern part has plains (Ueno), and the coast comprises lowlands (Ise plain). It was constituted in 1876 by the merging of the former provinces of Ise, Shima, and Iga. Its most famous sites are the Ise shrines and the Yoshino Mountains. *Chief city:* Tsu. *Other important cities:* Ise, Matsusaka, Yokkaichi, Ueno, Suzuka, Kuwana, Kameyama, Hisai. *Area:* 5,774 km². *Pop.:* 1.7 million.

Mifune Kyūzō. Judo master (1883–1965) who joined the Kōdōkan in 1903. He attained the tenth *dan,* the highest grade, in 1945, and published his memoirs, *Jūdō kaikoroku,* in 1953.

Mifune Toshirō. Movie actor born 1920 in Qingdao (Manchuria). He began his career in 1948 with the director Kurosawa Akira (*Yoidore tenshi,* "Black Angels"), then received an Academy Award for his work in *Rashōmon* in 1951, the Venice International Award in 1952 for *La Vie d'Oharu* (Oharu's Life), the Silver Bear in the Berlin Festival in 1959 for *La Forteresse cachée* (The Hidden Fortress), the prize of the San Francisco festival in 1961 for *Animas Trujano,* the Golden Harvest in 1962 for *Sanjūrō,* the Grand Prize of Venice in 1967, and other awards. An internationally known actor, he acted in most of the films directed by Kurosawa. In 1960, however, he left Kurosawa to found his own film and television company. He is also known as an archer *(yabusame).*

Migita Toshihide. Painter (1862–1925) of ukiyo-e prints and in Western style; he studied with Tsukioka Yoshitsohi (1839–92) and Kunisawa Shimburō (1847–77), an artist trained in Great Britain. He illustrated many magazines and newspapers starting in 1877 and also painted Kabuki actors. His triptychs on the Sino-Japanese War (1894–95) and the Russo-Japanese War (1904–05) are excellent historical documents. He sometimes signed his works Oju Toshihide or simply Toshihide.

Miharu-goma. Straw or wood (sometimes paper) effigies of horses bearing on their back a *hōshu* (magical bead) or Buddhist emblem. They are supposed to transmit the wishes of the faithful to the *kami* and are thus analogous to Tibetan *rLung-ta* (horses of the wind). *See* HŌSHU.

Mii-dera. Major Buddhist temple of the Ji-mon branch of the Tendai-shū sect, founded in 744 in the town of Ōtsu (Shiga prefecture) by Prince Ōtomo no Yota and restored in 859 by the monk Enchin (814–91). It was a major center for teaching Tendai and Shugendō. Its monks often opposed those of the Enryaku-ji, and its buildings were set on fire and razed by the soldier-monks of Mt. Hiei several times between the late tenth and the fifteenth century, but were rebuilt each time. It is one of the Saikoku Sanjūsansho (Thirty-Three Temples) of the circuit of pilgrimages to Kannon Bosatsu. Because it was protected by the court, the Ashikaga shogun, and the Minamoto family, the temple contains magnificent artistic treasures (*hondō* from 1559) and a small Shinto shrine dedicated to Shiragi Myōjin, *kami* of poets and warriors.

• *Mii-dera.* Title of a Noh play: a woman searching for her son who had become a Buddhist monk arrives at the Mii-dera and asks to ring the temple's big bell. She then recognizes her son among the monks, and the two go home together.

Miike Tankō. Coal mines located on Ariake Bay, astride the border between Fukuoka and Kumamoto prefectures, discovered in the late fifteenth century. They were nationalized in 1873, and prisoners were used as miners. In 1899, the government sold them to Mitsui, which built new extraction facilities. In 1960, the miners began a strike (Miike-sōgi) that lasted 282 days, and in 1963 a firedamp explosion claimed 458 victims. The mines currently produce about 5 million tons of coal per year.

Mikado. "Noble Gate," former name for the imperial palace in Heian-kyō (Kyoto), symbolizing the emperor. *See also* TENNŌ.

• *The Mikado.* English comic opera by W. S. Gilbert and Arthur Sullivan (1885), set in Japan.

Mi-kagami. "Sacred mirror," name for the symbol of Amaterasu-Ōmikami, in the form of a mirror, generally placed in Shinto shrines and representing the sun, the soul, or the *kami* that is venerated there. Also called *yata no kagami. See* KAGAMI.

Mikami Akira. Linguist and mathematician (1903–71), born in Hiroshima prefecture, author of many works on the specifics of Japanese syntax.

Mikami Sanji. Historian (1865–1939), born in Harima province (Hyōgo prefecture), adviser to the imperial house and publisher of the major encyclopedia on historic sources of Japan, the *Dai Nihon shiryō.* He also wrote historical works mainly on the Edo period, such as *Edo jidai-shi* (1943–44).

Mikan. Variety of citrus fruit specific to Japan *(Citrus unshiu, Citrus deliciosa),* resembling an orange (whence its name "Satsuma orange"); highly regarded, they are exported to Canada and other countries. *Mikan* trees exported from Japan have been introduced to Florida and Alabama, the Black Sea coast, and Spain. Originally from China, *mikan* trees were planted on Kyushu about 400 years ago. They are now cultivated mainly on the southern tip of the archipelago.

Mikasa. Imperial prince (Mikasa no Miya Takahito, b. 1915), Taishō Tennō's fourth son and Shōwa Tennō's brother. He was an officer in China and served at the army's general quarters during the Second World War. After the war, he studied the history of the Near East; in 1954, he became director of the Society for Study of the Near East. *See* AKIHITO, HIROHITO.

• *Mikasa.* Flagship (14,900 tons; *speed:* 18 knots) commanded by Admiral Tōgō during the Battle of Tsushima on May 27, 1905.

Mikasa Jōemon. Kabuki actor (*tachiyaku* roles) active in Kyoto around 1700–06 and in Osaka from 1706 to 1715.

Mikata Shami. Buddhist monk (Yamada Mikata, late seventh century), tutor to imperial princes and poet writing in Chinese.

Mikawa. Former province, now part of Aichi prefecture.

• *Mikawa monogatari.* Three-volume work written in 1622 by Okubo Hikozaemon, a *hatamoto* from the Mikawa estate, dealing with the history of the Tokugawa shoguns and of his own family.

Mike. "Three hairs"; cats, usually female, with tricolor coats. Males with this coat, very rare, are considered good-luck charms in Japan, and are often ships' mascots. They have a very short tail. *See* CATS.

Miki Bukichi. Politician (1884–1956), born in Kagawa prefecture, elected to the House of Representatives for the Kenseikai (Constitutional Association party) in 1917 and to the Tokyo municipal council in 1922. After the Second World War, in 1946, he was once again elected to the House of Representatives, and he was appointed secretary-general of the Jiyū Minshutō (Liberal Democratic party) in 1953. The following year, he and Hato-yama Ichirō founded the Japan Democratic party (Nihon Minshutō).

Miki Kiyoshi. Philosopher (1897–1945), born in Hyōgo prefecture, a disciple while in Europe of Martin Heidegger and Heinrich Rickert. When he returned to Japan in 1928, he taught Marxist philosophy from a humanitarian viewpoint, but he was arrested for his opinions in 1930 and fired from his professor's position. He then earned a living as a journalist, but was arrested again in 1945 for having harbored a communist and died in prison.

Mikimoto Kōkichi. Oyster farmer (1858–1954), born in Mie prefecture. In 1883, he began to raise pearl oysters in Ago Bay, and developed the technique of culturing pearls between 1893 and 1897. Two years later, he opened a shop in Tokyo to sell natural and cultured pearls. By 1911, he had several stores abroad—in London, New York, Chicago, Los Angeles, San Francisco, and Beijing—and had gained an international reputation for his pearls. He had based his research on the work of the Chinese Ye Jinyan (twelfth century). The "farm" he created in Ago Bay is still the center for growing pearl oysters in Japan. *See* PEARLS.

Miki Rofū. Poet (Miki Masao, 1889–1964), born in Hyōgo prefecture, baptized as a Christian in 1922. He wrote many poetry collections and essays, including *Shinkō no akebono* (Dawn of Faith, 1922), *Kami to hito* (Gods and Men, 1926), and *Nihon Katorikku-kyō-shi* (History of Catholicism in Japan, 1929). The Vatican decorated him with the title of Knight of the Holy Sepulcher of Jerusalem in 1927.

Miki Takeo. Politician (1907–88), born in Tokushima. Elected to the House of Representatives and a minister in Katayama Tetsu's cabinet in 1947. He joined the Liberal Democratic party (LDP, Jiyū Minshutō) and was minister of trade and industry (1965–66) and of foreign affairs (1966–67) in Satō Eisaku's cabinet. He was elected president of the LDP and prime minister in 1974. Implicated in the Lockheed scandal, he resigned in 1976; Fukuda Takeo replaced him in December of that year.

Miki Tokuchika. Religious reformer (1900–83) born in Ehime prefecture, son of a Zen monk of the Ōbaku-shū sect, Miki Tokuharu (1871–1938), and founder of a religious sect called Tokumitsu-kyō. All the leaders of this organization were arrested,

and the followers dispersed. When Miki Tokuchika was freed in 1946, they reunited under the denomination of P. L. Kyōdan (Church of Perfect Liberty), advocating peace through tolerance and stating that "life is an art." *See* P. L. KYŌDAN.

Mikkabi. Town in Shizuoka prefecture where remains of human beings from the Paleolithic period ("Mikkabi man") were found. *Pop.:* 16,000.

Mikkyō. Doctrines of Esoteric Buddhism advocated by the Tendai-shū and Shingon-shō sects. Before these doctrines arrived in Japan, in the early thirteenth century, similar ideas were already circulating, known generally as *ko-mikkyō,* or "ancient esoterism," although their exact content is not known. The esoteric doctrines were named to distinguish them from exoteric doctrines *(kenkyō)* such as, for example, faith in Amida and Zen. There are several forms of esoterism, such as *taimitsu,* specific to Tendai-shū, and *tōmitsu,* specific to Shingon-shū. Shugendō also has its own form of esoterism, connected to Taimitsu. Also called *misshū.*

Miko. Before 702, *miko* was a title given to imperial princes. It was replaced by *shinnō* after this date.
• In Shinto beliefs, a shamaness, acting as a medium during certain rites *(matsuri),* who evoked the spirit of dead people and who acted as an intermediary between the *kami* and human beings when she was in a trance. Most frequently, however, the word *miko* designates a girl or young woman who serves in a shrine and assists the *kannushi;* she does not need to have any special skills except for knowing how to dance for the *kami* and in the *matsuri.* After the Taika Reform (seventh century), former *miko* were banished from ceremonies in the court, which had been converted to Buddhism, and had to officiate outside of the capital. On *haniwa* of the *kofun* period, some *miko* are portrayed wearing *magatama* necklaces. According to the *Kojiki,* they officiated in association with female assistants called *saniwa.* The ancient *miko* are still well represented in the beliefs of Okinawa, where they are called *nuru* (or *noro*) or *yuta.* The Ainu also had shamanesses called *tsusu.* Today, aside from *miko* officiating in shrines (who are recognized by their red *hakama* and white blouses), there are still shamanesses in rural areas predicting the future and evoking spirits, such as the *itako* in Aomori prefecture; most of them are blind. Some founders of modern Shinto sects, such as Nakayama Miki and

Deguchi Nao, were *miko* in a sense. They are sometimes called *kannagi. See* HIMIKO, OKUNI.

• **Miko-sadaijin.** *See* KANEAKIRA SHINNŌ.

Mikoshi. Portable Shinto shrine, a very ornate replica of a shrine, carried on the shoulders on two long wooden poles, which is why they are called palanquins. The custom of carrying a *mikoshi* during certain ceremonies and *matsuri* replaced that of carrying a *sakaki* branch and a sacred mirror in processions in the eighth century. *Mikoshi,* said to represent the "soul" *(mitama)* of the *kami,* were used to transport the *kami* from their original shrine to other places; in the late Heian period, the monks of Mt. Hiei used them to intimidate the imperial powers and make them accede to their demands. Today, *ujiko* (or "parishioners") usually transport the *mikoshi* of the shrine to which they belong during major religious processions and *matsuri.* They set them down in certain traditional places *(otabisho)* to rest before continuing the trip through the streets of the village or town. During some *matsuri, mikoshi* battles are staged: young men carrying *mikoshi* on their shoulders throw themselves violently at their adversaries or competitors to tip over their *mikoshi;* this is to augur good future harvests. Some *mikoshi* are mounted on chariots and pulled; the largest ones have room for dancers and musicians. They are the major attraction of all *matsuri.* Also called *shin'yo.*

• **Mikoshi-nyūdō.** A demon in folk legends, said to have a third eye on its forehead and a very long tongue.

Mikoto. Title formerly given to important people, notably chiefs of tribes or clans in ancient Japan. Later, the title was reserved for Shinto *kami* and for imperial princes after their death.

• **Mikotonori.** During the Nara period, imperial edict. Some of them were preserved in the *Shoku Nihongi.* Also called *semmyō. See* SHŌ.

Mikudarihan. "Three and a half lines"; a letter of divorce of this length, written by a man to his wife to inform her that he wanted to separate from her and giving her complete freedom to remarry. This form of divorce, in use during the Edo period among commoners, did not exist in samurai families, whose members had to apply to the shogunate to obtain approval for a divorce. *See* DIVORCE, ENKIRI-DERA, MARRIAGE.

Mikumari-jinja. Shinto shrine built in Yoshino (Nara prefecture) in 1604 in the style of the Momoyama era.

Mikuni Rentarō. Actor (Satō Masao) and movie director, born 1923 in Gumma prefecture, who performed in many films directed by Kinoshita Keisuke for the Shōchiku company. He received the Cannes Festival Award in 1987 for his first directing effort, *Shinran. See* SEPPUKU (HARA-KIRI).

Mi-kusa no Kandakara. Collective term for the "Three Sacred Treasures," emblems of imperial power, the mirror *(yata no kagami),* the sword (Ame no Murakumo no Tsurugi; later renamed Kusanagi no Tsurugi), and the jewels *(yasakani no magatama).* According to legend, Amaterasu-Ōmikami gave them to Ninigi no Mikoto when the latter descended to Earth. Also called *sanshu no jingi.*

Milne, John. English geologist (1850–1913), born in Liverpool, invited to Japan by the Meiji government in 1876 to teach geology and mineralogy. After the earthquake of February 22, 1880, he founded the Seismology Society and invented a seismograph that was used at many sites in the country. He received the Order of the Rising Sun *(see* KUNSHŌ) in 1895.

Mimai. Manifestation of sympathy, in words or through gifts, to an esteemed person before an important event or after a death or catastrophe. The *mimai* must be made during a visit or, if this is not possible, by letter or telephone. During a *mimai* visit, a gift, generally food, is offered. This custom of encouragement or condolence is one of the obligatory social rites *(on)* that must be scrupulously observed. *See* GIRI, ON.

Mimana. Japanese name for an ancient state on the southeast coast of the Korean Peninsula (Kaya), conquered, according to tradition, by Empress Jingū Kōgō. It remained under Japanese administration until 562, when the state of Sinra (Silla) or Shiragi annexed it. It may be, however, that Mamana conquered Yamatai. Also called Karaka (*Kor.:* Garag), Benshin (*Kor.:* Pyŏjin, Pyŏhan). *See* BENKAN, HAKUSUKINOE, KAYA, YAMATAI-KOKU.

Mimasaka. Former province, now part of Okayama prefecture.

Mimbu-shō. Ministry created in 646 and directed by a *mimbu-kyō,* whose main task was controlling agriculture. Among those who held this position was Fujiwara no Tameie.

Minabuchi no Shōan. Buddhist monk (Minamibuchi no Shōan, seventh century) of Chinese origin, who went to China in 608 to study Confucianism and remained there for 32 years. When he returned, he taught Confucianism to imperial princes and to Fujiwara no Kamatari. *See* KENTŌSHI.

Minakami Takitarō. Writer (Abe Shōzō, 1887–1940), born in Tokyo. He launched his literary career after studying in the United States and traveling in Europe. Most of his novels describe the life of office workers *(sarariman): Ōsaka no yado* (1925), *Kaigara tsuihō* (essays published from 1918 to 1939).

Minakami Tsutomu. Writer (b. 1919), son of a carpenter in Fukui prefecture. After being a novice in two Buddhist temples, he began a literary career while doing odd jobs to earn a living. His first novel, *Furaipan no uta* (The Song of the Stove, 1948), went almost unnoticed, and it was not until 1959 that he found success with a detective novel, *Kiri to kage* (Fog and Shadow), followed by *Umi no kiba* (Seaside Resort, 1960). He then published *Gan no tera* (The Temple of the Wild Geese, 1961), which won the Naoki Prize; *Gobanchō yūgirirō* (District Five, Manor of Mists, 1962); *Kiga kaikyō* (The Strait of Hunger, 1962); and others. A number of his novels were made into movies by Ishi Teruo, Imai Tadashi, and other directors.

Minakata Kumakusu. Ethnologist and biologist (1867–1941), born in Kii province. After studying for 15 years in Europe and the United States, notably at the British Museum, he specialized in Japanese folklore and wrote hundreds of articles and several important books on the subject, such as *Jūnishi-kō* (On the Twelve Hourly Signs, published from 1914 to 1924). His complete works, *Minikata Kumakusu zenshū,* were published in 12 volumes from 1971 to 1975 by Heibonsha.

Minamata. Small port on the Yatsushiro Sea, in Kumamoto prefecture (Kyushu). Its name was given to a terrible illness (called *itai-itai*) produced by the ingestion of seafood polluted with industrial discharge (mercury by-products) from a plant belonging to Nihon Chisso Hiryō, a chemical-products company, between 1960 and 1974. Hundreds of people fell seriously ill with neural disorders, and long trials took place; this tragedy alerted the public to the dangers of uncontrolled pollution.

Minami Hokke-ji. "Southern Hokke-ji," a Buddhist temple built in Tsubosaka, Takai-chi (Nara prefecture). It has a three-story pagoda *(sanju no tō)* dating from the fifteenth century.

Minami Jirō. General (1874–1955), born in Ōita prefecture, promoted in 1930. In 1931, he was minister of war in Wakatsuki Reijirō's second cabinet; in 1934, he was appointed commander-in-chief of the Guandong army in Manchuria and Japan's ambassador to Manchukuo. After the revolt of February 26, 1936 (*see* NINIROKU JIKEN), he was returned to the reserves, and from 1936 to 1942 he was governor-general of Korea. Convicted of war crimes after the Second World War, he was sentenced to life in prison.

Minami kikan. Japanese military organization operating in Burma during the Second World War, which, under the command of Colonel Suzuki Keiji (b. 1897, *Bur.:* Bo Mogyo), recruited young Burmese nationalists (including Aung San). Its mission was to destroy the road linking China to Burma (established from 1939 to 1941) in order to cut supplies to the troops allied with the Chinese government.

Minamoto. Major family of warriors and statesmen who dominated politics in Japan during the Heian and Kamakura periods, some of whose members remained influential until the Meiji era, also known by the name Genji. Settling in the Kanto region in the ninth century, the Minamoto became the uncontested lords of the region; starting in the midtwelfth century, they began to rival the Taira (Heike) family as the Fujiwara began to lose their influence in the court. They are traditionally divided into four "branches"—Seiwa-Genji, Murakami-Genji, Daigo-Genji, and Uda-Genji—according to the imperial ancestor they claimed. Emperor Saga created the family name Minamoto in 814, and gave it to 33 of his 50 children. Later, the branches of the Minamoto became more or less independent of the imperial power, either remaining in Heiankyō and serving the court or various administrations, or creating fiefdoms in the provinces. One of them, however, Minamoto no Sadami, was reintegrated into the imperial genealogy and became Emperor Uda in 887, thus creating a new branch of the Minamoto family. The Seiwa-Genji branch produced Minamoto no Yoritomo, the founder of the

Kamakura *bakufu,* in the late twelfth century. The Minamoto were known mainly for their wars against the Taira, struggles that were the subject of innumerable warrior tales *(gunji-monogatari)* and epic songs, poems, and plays. *See also* GENJI, TAIRA.

• **Minamoto no Akikane.** Writer (1160–1215), author of *Kojidan.*

• **Minamoto no Akira.** Imperial prince (814–52), Emperor Nimmyō's brother and Emperor Saga's son. He became a Buddhist monk with the name Sosa. Also known as Yogawa-Saishō-nyūdō.

• **Minamoto no Hideakira.** Imperial prince (?–940) and senior bureaucrat in the court, maternally descended from Sugawara no Michizane.

• **Minamoto no Hikaru.** Imperial prince (845–913), Emperor Nimmyō's son. Appointed *udaijin* to replace Sugawara no Michizane in 901. Also called Nishi-sanjō Udaijin.

• **Minamoto no Hiromasa.** Imperial prince (918–80), Emperor Daigo's grandson and famous *biwa* player, Semimaru's student. Also called Hakuga no Sammi.

• **Minamoto no Ienaga.** Noble (1170–1234) of the Heian court and poet, author of a journal, *Minamoto no Ienaga nikki,* covering the years 1196–1207.

• **Minamoto no Kanemasa.** Poet (?–1112).

• **Minamoto no Makoto.** Emperor Saga's seventh son (810–68), who received the family name Minamoto in 814, thus founding the Minamoto family. He was the brother of Emperor Nimmyō, Minamoto no Tokiwa (812–54), and Minamoto no Tōru (822–95). Also called Kitabe-daijin. *See* ŌTEMMON NO HEN, TOMO NO YOSHIO.

• **Minamoto no Masanobu.** Imperial prince (920–93) and *sadaijin,* of the Uda-Genji branch of the Minamoto. Also called Tsuchimikado no Masanobu.

• **Minamoto no Masazane.** Senior bureaucrat (1059–1127), appointed *dajō-daijin* in 1122. Author of a journal, *Kuga-shōkoku-ki.* Also called Kuga.

• **Minamoto no Michichika.** *See* FUJIWARA NO MICHICHIKA.

• **Minamoto no Mitsunaka.** Son (912–97) of Minamoto no Tsunemoto (Seiwa-Genji branch), brother of Minamoto no Mitsumasa, Minamoto no Mitsusue, and Minamoto no Mitsuyoshi. He was *chinjufu-shōgun.* Also called Tada Manjū.

• **Minamoto no Mitsuyuki.** Writer (1163–1244), supposedly one of the authors of the *Heike monogatari* (ca. 1203–ca. 1221).

• **Minamoto no Morofusa.** Imperial prince (ca. 1005–1077), who received the family name Minamoto (Murakami-Genji branch) in 1020. He was *udaijin* and received the title *dajō-daijin* posthumously. Also called Tsuchimikado no Morofusa. He was a renowned poet.

• **Minamoto no Morotoki.** Writer and poet (1077–1136), author of a journal, *Chōshū-ki* (Notes on a Long Autumn), covering the years 1087 to 1136.

• **Minamoto no Moroyori.** Writer and poet (1070–1139), also called Ono no Miya.

• **Minamoto no Motohira.** Senior bureaucrat (eleventh–twelfth century) who was *sangi* in the Heian court.

• **Minamoto no Noriyori.** *See* KAMAKURA NO NORIYORI.

• **Minamoto no Sadamu.** Imperial prince (815–63) and musician, also known by the title Shijō Dainagon.

• **Minamoto no Sadazumi.** Imperial prince (884–916), Emperor Yōzei's brother and Minamoto no Tsunemoto's father (Seiwa-Genji branch).

• **Minamoto no Sanetomo.** Third shogun (Semman, 1192<1203–19>) of the Kamakura *bakufu,* Minamoto no Yoritomo's son and Minamoto no Yoriie's brother; he succeeded Yoriie. In 1204, he married the daughter of an adviser to the Heian court, Fujiwara no Nobukiyo, and received the title *udaijin* (minister of the right) in 1218. The regent *(shikken)* Hōjō Tokimasa plotted to assassinate him and put one of his sons-in-law in his place; however, the plot was exposed by his own daughter, the shogun's mother, Hōjō no Masako, and his son, Hōjō

Yoshitoki, and he was exiled to Izu. But Sanetomo was assassinated anyway, by one of his nephews, the Shinto priest Kugyō, one of Minamoto no Yoriie's sons, who held him responsible for the death of his father. Minamoto no Sanetomo was a famous *waka* poet and *kemari* player. He emulated the poems in the *Man'yōshū* in his first works (which he submitted to Fujiwara no Teika in 1209), and Teika included his poems in the *Shin chokusen-shū* around 1234; they were also in other imperial anthologies. His own collection, *Kinkai waka-shū* (also titled *Kinkai-shū*), of which at least three versions exist, has 716 poems in the most complete version; Fujiwara no Teika himself transcribed 663 of them in 1213.

• **Minamoto no Senjumaru.** Third son (1201–14) of Minamoto no Yoriie, Minamoto no Kugyō's brother (see KUGYŌ), who became a Buddhist monk in 1213 with the name Eijitsu. He was killed in battle.

• **Minamoto no Semman.** *See* MINAMOTO NO SANETOMO.

• **Minamoto Settei.** *See* SETTEI.

• **Minamoto no Shitagō (Shitagau).** Poet (911–83), one of the five chosen by Emperor Murakami in 951 to compile the *Gosen waka-shū*, in which his poems were published. He was one of the Chūko no Sanjūrokkasen (Thirty-Six Poetic Geniuses). Between 931 and 937, he compiled a sort of dictionary of Chinese characters, *Wamyō ruiju-shō (Wamyō-shō)* and wrote a collection of poems, the *Minamoto no shitagau-shū*. He is also credited, but without certainty, with writing the *Ochikubo monogatari* and *Utsubo monogatari*. He became a Buddhist monk with the name Ambō-hōshi. *See* NASHITSUBO NO GONIN, CHOKUSEN WAKA-SHŪ.

• **Minamoto no Tadakatsu.** Noble (seventeenth century), protector of Hayashi Shunzai (1618–80).

• **Minamoto no Takaakira.** Imperial prince (914–83), Emperor Daigo's seventeenth son, who received the family name Minamoto (Daigo-Genji branch) in 920. He was appointed *udaijin* in 966 and *sadaijin* in 968. After taking part in a plot to dethrone Reizei Tennō, he was exiled. He wrote several poetry collections and an autobiography. Also called Nishi no Miya no Sadaijin.

• **Minamoto no Takakuni.** Poet and writer (1004–77) who is credited with writing the *Konjaku monogatari* and, sometimes, the *Uji monogatari*. Also called Uji no Dainagon. *See* TOBA SŌJŌ.

• **Minamoto no Tamenori.** Poet (?–1011), author of *Sambō-e* around 984.

• **Minamoto no Tametomo.** Warrior (1139–70) whose exploits were famous. He was one of Minamoto no Tadayoshi's sons. According to some legends, he was an ancestor of the kings of the Ryukyu Islands. He died in exile in Oshima. Also called Chinzei Hachirō Tametomo.

• **Minamoto no Tameyoshi.** Warrior (1096–1156), Minamoto no Yoshichika's son, of the Seiwa-Genji branch. He sided with Retired Emperor Sutoku to defeat his uncle, Minamoto no Toshitsuna, but was taken prisoner in 1156 (*see* HEIJI NO RAN) and executed on the order of Taira no Kiyomori. Also called Mutsu Shirō.

• **Minamoto no Tokiwa.** Imperial prince (812–54), ninth son of Emperor Saga. Appointed *udaijin* in 840 and *sadaijin* in 849. His poems are in the *Kokin-shū*, and he compiled the *Nihon kōki*. Also called Higashi-sanjo no Sadaijin, Tō-sanjō no Sadaijin.

• **Minamoto no Tōru.** Imperial prince (822–95), son of Emperor Saga and brother of Emperor Nimmyō, Minamoto no Makoto, and Minamoto no Tokiwa. He was *sadaijin* in 872. He built the first villa, which was to become the Byōdō-in in Uji. Also called Kawara Sadaijin.

• **Minamoto no Toshiaki.** Statesman (1044–1114), who was *bettō* in the court of Retired Emperor Shirakawa, then inspector general of Mutsu and Dewa provinces.

• **Minamoto no Toshifusa.** Imperial prince (1035–1121), Minamoto no Morofusa's son (Murakami-Genji branch), appointed *sadaijin* in 1083. He became a Buddhist monk with the name Jakushun, and wrote an autobiographical journal, *Suisa-ki*. Also called Horikawa Safu.

• **Minamoto no Toshikata.** Statesman and poet (960–1027), one of the Shinagon.

• **Minamoto no Toshiyori.** Poet (1055–1129), Minamoto no Tsunenobu's son, author of a poetry anthology, *Kin'yō-shū* (Collection of Autumn Leaves), around 1127. Also called Minamoto no Shunrai.

• **Minamoto no Tsunemoto.** Imperial prince (894–961), Prince Sadazumi's (884–916) son and Emperor Seiwa's grandson. He received the family name Minamoto (Seiwa-Genji branch) in 961, thus founding the family from which the Minamoto, Ashikaga, and Tokugawa shoguns were descended. Minamoto no Mitsunaka's father.

• **Minamoto no Tsunenobu.** Statesman (1016–97) and poet, one of the Shinagon.

• **Minamoto no Yoriie.** Second shogun (1182 <1202–03>1204) of the Kamakura *bakufu,* son of Minamoto no Yoritomo and Hōjō Masako. He plotted with his father-in-law, Hiki Yoshikazu, against his grandfather, Hōjō Tokimasa; the plot failed, Yoshikazu was killed, and Yoriie was exiled to a Buddhist temple in Izu. He was assassinated there the following year, on the order, it is said, of Hōjō Tokimasa. He had three sons, Ichiman (?–1203), Kugyō (1200–19), and Senju. His brother, Minamoto no Sanetomo, succeeded him as the third shogun of Kamakura.

• **Minamoto no Yorimasa.** Warrior (1104–80), famous for having killed a *nue* (cloudbird?) with a single arrow in 1153. He took the side of Retired Emperor Go-Shirakawa in 1156 and 1159 (*see* HŌGEN NO RAN, HEIJI NO RAN); defeated in Uji by Taira no Kiyomori, he was forced to commit suicide in the Byōdō-in temple. He had become a Buddhist monk with the name Gensan-in Nyūdō. His poems were collected in the anthology *Yorimasa kashū* and in the imperial anthologies *Shin kokin-shū* and *Senzai waka-shū.* Also called Gensammi Yorimasa.

• **Minamoto no Yoritomo.** Warrior and first shogun (1147<1192–99>) of the Kamakura *bakufu,* son of Minamoto no Yoshitomo and brother of Minamoto no Yoshihira (1141–60), Minamoto no Tomonaga (?–ca. 1160), Minamoto no Mareyoshi (?–1182), Minamoto no Noriyori (?–1193), Minamoto no Zenjo (Ano Zenjo, 1153–1203), Minamoto no Gien (?–1181), Minamoto no Yoshitsune (1159–89), and Minamoto no Yoshinaka. Having been saved by Taira no Kiyomori after his father was defeated, he was raised by Kiyomori's supporters, and when he was of fighting age he amassed an army. After a long war against the Taira (Heike), he

defeated them, with the help of his general and half-brother Minamoto no Yoshitsune, at the Battle of Ichi no Tani, then on sea at Dan no Ura in 1185. But, jealous of Yoshitsune's popularity, he attacked him, forcing him to flee to the north and eventually to commit suicide with his last followers in 1189. Yoritomo then established his military government *(bakufu)* in Kamakura, forcing the emperor to confer upon him the title of *sei-i-tai-shōgun* in 1192. He died in 1199 from injuries due to a fall from his horse. His father-in-law, Hōjō Tokimasa, then assumed the regency *(shikken)* on behalf of the young Minamoto no Yoriie, the second shogun, with the assistance of Yoritomo's widow, Hōjō Masako. Also called Kamakura-dono, Kamakura Udaisho.

• **Minamoto no Yoriyoshi.** Warrior (988–1075), son of Minamoto no Yorinobu (968–1048), who was the son of Minamoto no Mitsunaka. Yoriyoshi was governor of Mutsu and Sagami provinces and became a Buddhist monk with the name Iyo-nyūdō. *See* TSURUGAOKA HACHIMAN-GŪ.

• **Minamoto no Yoshichika.** Son (?–1108) of Minamoto no Yoshiie. Having rebelled several times, he was exiled, then defeated in battle and executed.

• **Minamoto no Yoshihira.** Warrior (1141–60), Minamoto no Yoritomo's older brother; he fought the Taira at Yoritomo's side and was killed in battle. Also called Kamakura Aku-genda.

• **Minamoto no Yoshiie.** Warrior (Hachiman Tarō, 1041–1108), Minamoto no Yoriyoshi's son, whose military exploits were the subject of many legends.

• **Minamoto no Yoshikuni.** Second son (ca. 1090–1155) of Minamoto no Yoshiie and brother of Minamoto no Yoshichika and Minamoto no Yoshikiyo (1094–1145). He retired to Ashikaga in 1150, and was the direct ancestor of the Ashikaga and Nitta families.

• **Minamoto no Yoshimitsu.** Warrior (1045–1127) of the Satake family, Minamoto no Yoshiie's brother. Also called Shinra Saburō.

• **Minamoto no Yoshinaka.** Warrior (1154–84), brother of Minamoto no Yoritomo and Minamoto no Yoshitsune, founder of the Kiso family. He fought the Taira and joined his uncle, Minamoto no Yukiie, in 1182. He took Retired Emperor Go-Shirakawa as a prisoner; Go-Shirakawa appointed him shogun, but he was attacked and killed by Minamoto no Noriyori and Minamoto no Yoshitsune. His mistress, Tomoe Gozen, was famous for her physical strength. Also called Kiso Yoshinaka.

• **Minamoto no Yoshitomo.** Warrior (1123–60), Minamoto no Tameyoshi's son. He fought on the side of the Taira in 1156, but revolted against them after his father was killed on the order of Taira no Kiyomori. Defeated, he fled, but was assassinated. His wife, Tokiwa Gozen, Minamoto no Yoshitsune's mother, then took refuge with Minamoto no Yoritomo.

• **Minamoto no Yoshitsuna.** Warrior (?–1134), Minamoto no Yoshiie's brother. When his son, Minamoto no Yoshiaki, was sentenced for committing a crime, he rebelled, but he was defeated by Minamoto no Tameyoshi and exiled on the island of Sado. Also called Kamo Jirō.

• **Minamoto no Yoshitsune.** Half-brother (1159–89) of Minamoto no Yoritomo and son of Minamoto no Yoshitomo and Tokiwa Gozen. Raised on Mt. Kurama by monks *(yamabushi)* under the name Ushiwaka, he was noted as a youth for his talents as a warrior. Accompanied by a brigand-monk named Benkei, he became a general under the command of Yoritomo, whom he helped defeat the Taira, notably in the 1185 battles of Ichi no Tani and Dan no Ura. He became the target of Yoritomo's jealousy and took refuge in Mutsu province, where, betrayed, he was forced to commit suicide with his supporters, his wife, and his children. The stories of his adventures, battles, life with his mistress, the beautiful Shizuka Gozan, and heroic death were the subject of many legends and stories (including the *Heike monogatari*), often portrayed on stage (Noh and Kabuki).

• **Minamoto no Yukiie.** Warrior (Minamoto no Yoshimori, Shingū Jūrō, d. 1186), Minamoto no Yoshitomo's brother. Having taken the side of Minamoto no Yoshitsune against Minamoto no Yoritomo, he was assassinated on the order of the latter.

Minase sangin hyaku-in. Collection of *renga* poems written by Sōgi, Sōchō, and Shōhaku, published in 1488.

Minatogawa. Archeological site on the south coast of Okinawa (Ryukyu) at which paleolithic-type lithic tools were uncovered in association with human skeletons *(Homo sapiens),* which, according to carbon-14 dating, date to about 18,000 BC.

Minato-gawa no Takakai. Battle on July 4, 1336, between the forces of Ashikaga Takauji and those of Nitta Yoshisada and Kusunoki Masashige in Settsu province (Hyōgo prefecture) near Kobe. Ashikaga Takauji had rebelled against Emperor Go-Daigo, who had retaken power during the Kemmu era; Takauji attacked and defeated the imperial forces led by Kusunoki Masashige, who committed suicide. Then, after defeating Nitta Yoshisada, Ashikaga Takauji entered Kyoto as a conqueror and established his *bakufu* in the Muromachi district, enthroning Emperor Kōmyō. War between the Northern (Kyoto) and Southern (Yoshino) Courts (Nambokuchō) thus became inevitable.

Minazuki. "Month without water," name for the sixth lunar month in the old lunar-solar calendar.

• **Minazuki-barai.** *See* NAGOSHI NO HARAI.

Minchō. Zen Buddhist monk (Kitsuzan, Kichizan Minchō; *mei:* Chōdensu; *gō:* Hasō-ai, Minchō, 1352–1431) from the island of Awaji, and a painter at the Kōfuku-ji temple in Kyoto. He followed the style of the Muromachi *suiboku* school, influenced

Minamoto no Yoshitsune

by the Chinese painters of Zhejiang. He produced many portraits and landscapes in ink, as well as Buddhist images, most of them now housed in the Tōfuku-ji and the Chion-in in Kyoto. Some of his paintings, notably the religious ones, were clearly influenced by the Chinese painter Yan Hui (thirteenth–fourteenth century).

Minenobu. Painter (Kanō Minenobu; *gō:* Zuisen, Kakuryūsai, 1662–1708), of the Kanō school in Hamachō (Edo). *See* KANŌ.

Mingei. "Folk art," a term coined by Yanagi Muneyoshi in 1926 to describe utilitarian objects made by artisans and folk-art objects, as opposed to *kōgei,* aristocratic or industrial-art objects, although many types of *kōgei* could be assimilated with *mingei.* The latter comprises innumerable objects in a wide variety of categories, including ceramics, wood sculptures, lacquers, furniture, basketwork, textiles, bamboo utensils, metal objects, dolls, folk statuettes of divinities, paper *(washi),* and dyed fabrics. Objects made by the Ainu are also considered *mingei.* Formerly, objects and figurines found in tombs were called *mingei,* after the Chinese *mingqi. See* MINGEI UNDŌ, MINGU.

• **Mingei tōki.** "Folk" ceramics, a term often used for utilitarian pottery.

• **Mingei Undō.** A movement for the appreciation and preservation of *mingei,* launched by Yanagi Muneyoshi in 1926. The potters Kawai Kanjirō (in Kyoto) and Hamada Shōji (in Tokyo) belonged to this modern school, which gave rise to another of the same type, the Sōdeisha, in 1948.

• **Mingu.** "Folk objects," sometimes also considered *mingei,* but not necessarily of an artistic nature, such as ordinary objects of worship, kitchen and general utensils, fishing and hunting implements, calendars, medicines, propitiatory decorations, and so on.

Mining, coal ("yama"). Coal, most of it of mediocre quality, has been actively mined since the Edo period, mostly by the firms Mitsui, Mitsubishi, Hokutan, and Sumitomo. The largest deposits are in Hokkaido and northern Kyushu. Producing more than 5.5 million tons in 1961, the coal mines provided work for more than 300,000 miners. But after a number of catastrophes (notably in Yubari, Hokkaido, in 1981) and a drop in domestic demand, Japanese coal became more expensive than imported coal, and most mines were forced to close down, including those in Kamisunagawa, Yubari, Mikasa, Ashibetsu, and Akibira (closed in 1994). Consumption of coal by Japanese industry reached 114 million tons in 1992, of which 7% came from the country's mines. According to union sources, coal is the only energy resource in which Japan could be self-sufficient.

Ministries. Names of current ministries:
—Foreign affairs: **Gaimu-shō,** 4,600 employees. Diplomatic relations with foreign countries.
—Agriculture, forestry, and fishing: **Nōrin Shuisan-shō.**
—International trade and industry (MITI): **Tsūsan-shō.** *See* MITI.
—Construction: **Kensetsu-shō,** 24,000 employees. Oversees regional development, urbanization, water drainage, river control, roads, and housing.
—Education: **Mombu-shō.**
—Finance: **Ōkura-shō,** 70,000 employees. Insurance, financial institutions.
—Interior: **Jichi-shō.**
—Justice: **Hōmu-shō.**
—Post and telecommunications: **Yūsei-shō,** 300,000 employees. Telephone, telegraph, radio broadcasting, telecommunications, television.
—Health and welfare: **Kōsei-shō.**
—Transport: **Un'yu-shō,** 38,000 employees. Directs transportation systems, the merchant marine, and civil aviation, tourism, the automobile industry, highways, and ports.
—Labor: **Rōdō-shō.**

Minka. Term for all rural and traditional architectural styles in towns and villages, except for palace, temple, and Western-influenced architecture. *Minka* styles include semi-buried huts *(tate-ana jūkyo)* from the prehistoric period; peasants' wooden houses with roofs of thatching *(kayabuki),* wood shingles *(ishioki),* or tiles *(kawarabuki),* and artisans' and retailers' shops in towns and granaries and warehouses *(dozō, kura). See* ARCHITECTURE.

Minkan. Forms of uncodified folk Shinto belief, comprising many superstitions, perhaps one of the oldest forms of Shinto.

• *Minkan Denshō.* "Oral Folklore," a scholarly journal on Japanese folklore and ethnology, founded in 1935 by Minka Denshō-kai. Publication ceased in 1952, but it was followed by others of the same type, such as the *Nihon Minzokugaku.*

• **Minkan Shintō.** *See* SHINTO.

• **Minkan-kagura.** *See* KAGURA.

Minkō. Sculptor of netsuke (Tanaka Minkō, 1835–1916) who worked in Ise.
• Sculptor of netsuke (late eighteenth century) who portrayed mainly insects and animals.

Minkoku. Sculptor (Genryōsai, late eighteenth century) in Edo.

Mino. Former province, now part of Gifu prefecture. Also sometimes called Minu, Nōshū.
• Straw jacket once worn by peasants and workers to protect them from the cold, rain, and snow.

• **Mino-yaki.** Type of ceramics produced in Mino province, developed in the late sixteenth century and used to make utensils and bowls for the tea ceremony. The tradition of Mino pottery goes back at least to the seventh century. Until 1868, Mino pottery was mistaken for that from the Seto kilns. In the late sixteenth century, *noborigama*-type kilns replaced the old *anagama* and *ōgama* types, allowing for diversification and thus for production of Oribe-type pieces. These kilns were rediscovered by Arakawa Toyozō in 1930 and reopened to produce Shino-type ceramics.

Minobe Ryōkichi. Politician and economist (1904–84), born in Tokyo, Minobe Tatsukichi's son. Because of his Marxist leanings, he was arrested in 1938 and fired from his professorship at Hōsei University. After the Second World War, he became a professor at the University of Tokyo. Elected governor of Tokyo in 1967 and reelected in 1971 and 1975, he became a member of the Chamber of Councillors in 1980.

• **Minobe Tatsukichi.** Jurist (1873–1948), born in Hyōgo, proponent of the nondivinity of the emperor. In 1935, he was forced to resign from the House of Peers, to which he had been appointed in 1932, and his books were banned. He helped write the 1945 Constitution. Among his best-known works are *Kempō satsuyō* (Outline of a Constitution, 1923) and *Nihon-koku kempō genron* (Principles of a Constitution for Japan, 1946). He was Minobe Ryōkichi's father.

Minobu-san. Main temple of the Buddhist Nichiren sect, established in 1281 by Hakii Sanenaga in Minami Koma, Yamanashi prefecture, near the small town of Minobu (*pop.*: 10,000), on the site of a small hermitage where Nichiren had taken refuge when he returned from exile on the island of Sado in 1274. This temple, called Kuon-ji, houses Nichiren's tomb. It was protected by the Takeda and Tokugawa families and was consecrated Chokugan-ji in 1706. Destroyed by a fire in 1875, it was rebuilt soon after.

Minogame. Mythical turtle *(kame)* that is said to have lived for 500 years (sometimes 10,000 years) and that is a symbol of longevity. It is portrayed as a sea tortoise whose shell is covered with a long train of algae. *See* KAME.

Minolta. Manufacturer of photographic equipment, optical products, and photocopiers, specializing in production of lenses, founded in 1937. In partnership with Wetszler's Leitz plants in Germany, it has subsidiaries in the United States, Europe, and Southeast Asia, and exports more than 80% of its production. Head office in Osaka.

Mino-mono. Blacksmiths' school for makers of sword blades, one of the *gokaden,* created by Shizu Saburō Kaneuji and Shizu Saburō Kinjū. In the Muromachi period, the two most famous representatives of this school were Kanesada and Kanemoto.

Minomura Rizaemon. Businessman (1821–77), born in Shinano (Nagano prefecture), founder of Mitsui. *See* MITSUI.

Minsei. Abridgment of Nihon Minshu Seinen Dōmei (Democratic Youth League of Japan) with communist leanings, created in 1923 as Nihon Kyōsan Seinen Dōmei and suppressed in 1933. It was reorganized in 1956 and gave rise to the Zengakuren movement.

• **Minseitō.** Liberal party created by the merger of the Kenseikai (Constitutional Association party) and the Seiyū Hontō (True Seiyū party). It succeeded the Rikken Kaishintō (Constitutional Reform party) in 1927, with Hamaguchi Yūkō as leader. It was dissolved in 1940. Also called Rikken Minseitō (Constitutional Democratic party). *See* RIKKEN DŌSHIKAI, RIKKEN MINSEITŌ.

Minshugaku. Songs of Chinese origin, in fashion mainly in the Nagasaki region in the eighteenth and nineteenth centuries. According to tradition, they were imported by a Chinese musician named Wei Hou in the sixteenth century. One of this artist's descendants, Wei Hao, performed the songs in Kyoto, where they were quite popular. But they disappeared almost completely in the late nineteenth century because of the war with China. Only a few musicians in Nagasaki continue the tradition today.

Minshuku. Private houses that may, upon occasion, provide room and board for travelers and tourists for a relatively modest sum. According to an official survey by the Japan Travel Bureau, there are currently about 28,000. Some are equipped to host foreigners.

Minshu Shakaitō. "Democratic Socialist party," founded in 1960. It is divided into three sections, Nichio, Ito, and Mizutami. Also sometimes called Minshatō.

• **Minshutō.** Social-democratic party created circa 1930, giving rise (in 1931–32) to the Nihon Kokka Shakaitō (Socialist Party of the State of Japan), led by the former secretary-general of the Minshutō, Akamatsu Katsumaro. *See* SHAKAI MINSHUTŌ, SHIMPOTŌ.

• Democratic party founded in March 1947 by Ashida Hitoshi. It united with the Socialist party and the Kokumin Kyōdōtō (People's Cooperative party) to form a coalition cabinet headed by Katayama Tetsu in May 1947. This party was dissolved in 1950; some of its members joined the Jiyū Minshutō (Liberal Democratic party, LDP), while others joined the Nihon Kaishintō (Japan Reform party), created in 1952.

Mintō. "Popular parties," such as the Rikken Kaishintō (Constitutional Reform party) and the Jiyūtō (Liberal party). They sat in opposition to the so-called *ritō,* or "bureaucrat's parties," such as the Kokumin Kyōkai (Nationalist Association).

Min'yō. General term for folk songs, also called *fōku-songu,* always enjoyed by Japanese of all classes, who enjoy singing together at family and professional meetings (or even in bars). Also the term used by young people for foreign songs, such as those by Bob Dylan, popularized mainly on television since 1977. *See* KARAOKE.

Min'yūsha. "Society of Friends of Democracy," a literary group created by Tokutomi Sohō (1863–1957), which published the *Kokumin Shimbun* starting in 1890.

Miroku Bosatsu. Japanese form of the Bodhisattva Maitreya, the Future Buddha, residing currently in Tushita Heaven *(Jap.:* Tosotsu). Miroku was one of the first bodhisattvas to be venerated in Japan; according to tradition, a stone statue of him was brought from the kingdom of Paekche in Korea in 584. In the seventh century, Miroku was honored in many Buddhist temples, such as the Chūgū-ji and the Kōryū-ji in Heian-kyō and the Hōryū-ji in Nara. His cult diminished in intensity in the tenth century as followers turned in growing numbers to Amida Butsu. However, he is still largely revered by followers, notably those of the "modern" sects such as the Omoto-kyō and the Reiyūkai. *Kor.:* Mi-rük; *Chin.:* Mi-luo Fo.

• **Miroku-in.** Mudra *(Jap.: in-zō),* or hand gesture, specific to Miroku Bosatsu, in a pensive pose *(shiyui-in),* the right hand lightly touching the cheek, the right leg crossed over the left knee.

Miruna no zashiki. "The Forbidden Room," a popular tale (also called *Uguisu no ichimon,* "The Nightingale's Coin"): a man taking shelter for the night in an isolated house on a mountain is asked to look after the house by its owner, a young, beautiful woman, but not to try to find out what is in a closed room. He promises and keeps his word. After a year, the owner returns; seeing that the forbidden room has not been opened, she rewards the traveler with a roll of fabric and a small coin *(mon)* that soon reveals itself to be an infinite treasure, as it constantly duplicates itself. One of his neighbors, having heard about this good luck, asks to stay in the house, and the same condition is imposed on him. But he is unable to resist his curiosity and opens the door, instantly releasing demons that overwhelm him with troubles.

Misasagi. Term for tombs (generally *kofun*) of the emperors and members of the imperial family, before 701. *See* KOFUN.

Mishihase. According to the *Nihon shoki* (720), an indigenous people who lived in northern Japan, perhaps an Ainu (Ezo) tribe, who were conquered by general Abe no Hirafu in 658. The name was probably taken from the Chinese word *sushen,* which was applied to the Tungusic populations on the banks of the Amur River (Heilongjiang). The term can also be read Shukushin. *See* AINU.

Mishima Tokushichi. Metallurgist and physicist (1893–1975) who invented an alloy called MK that was used to make Alnico V magnetic material, used mainly in loudspeakers. Mishima taught solid-state physics at the University of Tokyo from 1921 to 1953 and received the Order of Culture (Bunka-shō) in 1950.

Mishima Tsūyō. Prefectural governor (Mishima Michitsune, 1835–88) and senior bureaucrat in the Meiji government, born in the Satsuma estate (Kyushu). He was noted mainly for his iron fist during local incidents in Fukushima prefecture; in 1885, he was appointed superintendent of police in Tokyo, where he applied the laws extremely strictly.

Mishima Yukio. Writer (Hiraoka Kimitake, 1925–70). He studied law at the Gakushūin (Peers' School) in Tokyo and began to write very early, fascinated by the magic of words. He first wrote some *waka* poems, influenced by Tachibana Michizō, that were published in his school paper, and stories such as *Hanazakari no mori* (The Blossoming Forest, 1941), then he was deeply attracted to the works of Oscar Wilde. He took the *gō* Mishima Yukio. He became interested in psychoanalysis and fell in love with Western literature, which he tried to emulate in his early stories, describing, in a rather morbid style, the life of young people of the *apure* (postwar period).

In 1949, when he was 24, he published his first major novel, *Kamen no kakokuhaku* (Confessions of a Mask); largely autobiographical, it prefigured the essence of his entire literary oeuvre: a taste for beauty mixed with a morbid attachment to death, voyeurism associated with narcissism, a devotion to heroism, and a conviction that all people will come to a tragic end. Although his thought was very westernized, he was, paradoxically, fiercely attached to the traditions of his country, which he linked to military spirit (with which he was inculcated at the Peers' School in his youth, an experience that seems to have strongly affected him). A prolific writer, he produced novel after novel, essays, plays, and screenplays. He was of slight build and was constantly bodybuilding, partly to stay healthy, partly to "be beautiful," since he unreservedly admired men's bodies, revealing his penchant for homosexuality. He wrote *Ai no kawaki* (Thirst for Love, 1951), *Kinjiki* (Forbidden Pleasures, 1952), *Shiosai* (The Sound of Waves, 1954), *Kinkakuji* (1956), *Kindai nōgakushū* (Five Modern Noh Plays, 1956), *Utage no ato* (After the Banquet, 1960), *Gogo no eikō* (The Sailor Who Fell from Grace with the Sea, 1963), *Sado kōshaku fujin* (Madame de Sade, 1965), *Hōjō no umi* (The Sea of Fertility, 1970), and a tetralogy concerning four reincarnations of the same person, completed just before his death:

Haru no yuki (Spring Snow, 1965), *Homba* (Runaway Horses, 1967), *Akatsuki no tera* (The Temple of Dawn, 1969), and *Tennin gosui* (The Decay of the Angel, 1970).

Mishima Yukio published a great number of stories, including *Jumpaku no yoru* (The Pure White Night), *Nipponsei* (Made in Japan), *Nagasugita haru* (The Too-Long Spring), *Kujaku* (The Peacocks, 1965), *Manatsu no shi* (Death in Midsummer, 1952), *Bitoku no yoromeki* (Unsteady Virtue), *Ojōsan* (The Young Lady), *Ken* (The Sword), *Are no yori* (From the Depth of Solitude), *Kemono no tawamure* (Beastly Games), and adaptations of plays, including *Kurotokage* (The Black Lizard), *Kurobara no yakata* (The House of the Black Rose), *Rokumeikan* (The Festival Palace). He also acted in various films, and even tried directing, with *Seppuku,* a movie on traditional samurai suicide. He lived for a while with a famous tennis player, Shoda Michiko, and in 1957 he married the daughter of a traditional painter, Sugiyama Yōko, with whom he had two children. Some of his novels were failures, such as *Kyōko no ie* (The House in Kyoko, 1959); others raised controversy, such as *Kinjiki* (Forbidden Colors, 1951), on homosexuals in Tokyo. But his reputation was truly established with publication of *Ai no kawaki.*

In 1952, he went on a long trip around the world. In 1968, he formed the Tate no Kai (Shield Society), a sort of militia (numbering some 100 men) whose members dressed in uniforms he had designed; his goal was to preserve Japan's ancestral military values. This idea was disapproved of or viewed with derision by most Japanese. On November 25, 1970, he tried to harangue the Jieitai (Self-Defense Forces) but was shouted down and ultimately unsuccessful (he was wounded and sequestered from the officers). He committed suicide in a spectacular manner, with the help of his assistant, Morita, by performing *seppuku* in the headquarters of the Self-Defense Forces in Tokyo. This insane gesture, which was nevertheless in line with his thinking, drew the attention of foreigners to his work, which was then translated into many languages, although it was not very popular among the Japanese, who seemed to rediscover it via Western critiques. Almost all his novels and stories have been adapted for the screen, some by directors as prestigious as Ichikawa Kon and Fukusaku Kinji.

Mishōtai. Sacred Shinto image, consisting of a metal disk bearing the image of a divinity, sometimes Buddhist, at its center, and associated with syncretic beliefs that developed in the ninth century.

Mishōtai were often offered in tribute at the shrine by worshipers; their popularity was at its peak from the thirteenth to the sixteenth century. Also popularly called *kakebotoke, goshintai.*

Miso. Indispensable condiment in Japanese cuisine: a brown paste made from boiled and fermented soybeans, with salt, wheat, rice, and a ferment drawn from *Aspergillus* added. Miso was introduced from China in the eighth century. It is used to season vegetables, in *kombu* soup *(miso-shiro),* or as a light seasoning mixed with rice vinegar *(sumiso)* or lemon juice *(yuzumiso),* or kneaded with sesame seeds *(gomamiso).* Each housewife has her own *miso* recipe, but *miso* is now produced commercially by food manufacturers.

Misogi. Shinto ablution ritual for purification from all blemishes. It consists of showering or of washing the hands, feet, and mouth with pure water. In some cases, *misogi* is performed by complete immersion under a waterfall or in the sea. The origin of this ritual, according to the *Kojiki,* is the following: Izanagi no Mikoto, returning from Yomi no Kuni, where he had searched for his wife-sister Izanami, washed away his impurity (having been in contact with death) in the water of a river, giving birth to three great *kami*: Amaterasu, Susanoo, and Tsukiyomi no Mikoto (the moon). At the entrance to every shrine is a basin or fountain *(mitarashi, temizuya, chōzuya)* where worshipers can perform a cursory *misogi* before entering the inner sanctum. Also called *harai. Okinawa: amichujing. See* HARAI, KEGARE.

• **Misogi-kyō.** One of the 13 sects of Kyōha Shintō, founded to emulate the Tofukami-kyō by Inoue Masakane in 1872. It makes great use of purification *(misogi)* practices and breathing exercises intended to cleanse the mind. Formerly called Tōkami-kyō.

Misoka. Old term for the last day of the month. The last day of the year is *ō-misoka* (the great *misoka*).

Misora Hibari. Singer (Katō Kazue, 1937–89), born in Yokohama, where she was the queen of pop music in the years following the Second World War. Her hoarse voice and sentimental songs gained her a large following. Nicknamed "the Japanese Édith Piaf," she frequently performed on stage and screen.

Misu. Bamboo screen once used in the court to hide the emperor or other important people during interviews with people of modest means and during official ceremonies.

Mita Bungaku. Literary journal founded by Nagai Kafū in 1910 at Keiō University in Tokyo. It published works by important authors such as Mori Ōgai, Izumi Kyōka, Yosano Akiko, and Tanizaki Jun'ichirō. Publication was interrupted for several months in 1925 and from 1944 to 1946. *See* WASEDA BUNGAKU.

Mitake-kosha. Sect of the Kyōha Shintō, branch of the Mitake-kyō, founded by Shimoyama Ōsuke in 1873. It is divided into 15 subsects: Naobi-kyō (founded in 1893), Shinsen-kyō (1924), Chikakusan-minshū (1929), Hino-oshie (1931), Tenjō-kyō (1931), Mitake-kyō Shūsei-ha (1939), Tokashin-kyō (1940), Hinomoto-kyō (1946), Nichigetsu-kyō (1946), Mitama-kyō (1949), Mitakesan-soma Honkyō (1949), Shinsen-reidō-kyō (1950), Shintoku-kyō-dan (1950), Kyūseishū-kyō (1956), Tokumitsu-kyō *(see* P. L. KYŌDAN). *See* MITAKE-KYŌ.

• **Mitake-kyō.** Sect of the Kyōha Shintō, dedicated to veneration of Mount Ontake (south of Nara), founded by Aoki Kōkichi (b. 1909) in 1939. It is divided into six subsects—Mitake, Hino, Hinomoto, Naobi, Ontake-kyō-shūsei, and Shinrei-kai—and has about 1.7 million followers. *See* MITAKE-KOSHA.

• **Mitakesan-soma Honkyō.** Shinto subsect of the Mitake-kosha, founded by Yoneda Shūichi in 1949.

Mitama. In Shinto belief, the "spirit" (or "soul") of a *kami* or an individual. There are several kinds of *mitama: nigi-mitama,* of peaceful, amiable nature, representing the "essential" part of the *mitama; ara-mitama,* which is active and sometimes destructive, and represents the manifested part of the *mitama; saki-mitama,* the creative and "happy" part of the *mitama;* and *kushi-mitama,* which symbolizes the hidden part, the "wisdom," of an individual's spirit. *See* MAGATAMA.

• **Mitama-kyō.** Subsect of the Mitake-kosha, founded in Chiba by Nagata Fuku (b. 1891) in 1949.

• **Mitama-shiro.** "Spirit" or "substitute body" of a Shinto *kami,* object into which the *kami* is said to descend temporarily during ceremonies. The *mita-*

ma-shiro may be a single object—a mirror, a sword, or, in syncretic cult, a statuette of a Buddhist or other divinity. *See* GOSHINTAI, SHINTAI.

Mitamura Engyo. Historian (Mitamura Genryū, 1870–1952), born in Hachiōji (Tokyo), specializing in society during the Edo period. His works were published in *Mitamura Engyo zenshū* in 1975.

Mitarashi. Basin or fountain used by worshipers at a Shinto shrine to perform their ritual ablutions before entering the shrine. Also called Chōzuya, Temizuya. *See* MISOGI.

Mitesaki. In traditional architecture, a type of very elaborate corbelling, composed of a projected triple degumi supporting the master beam *(gangyō, degeta),* used mainly in *wa-yō* construction modes. In Zen temple architecture, the *mitesaki* is sometimes double. *See* TO-KYŌ.

Mitford, Algernon, Baron Redesdale. English diplomat and writer (1837–1915) attached to the British delegation to Edo and Tokyo from 1866 to 1870. He studied Japanese there with E. Satow; after he retired to London, he wrote several volumes of memoirs, some of which concern Japan, such as *Tales of Old Japan* (1871), *Bamboo Garden* (1896), and *Garter Mission to Japan* (1906), in which he tells of King Edward VII's nephew's visit to Emperor Meiji to decorate him with the Order of the Garter after the signature of the Anglo–Japanese alliance in 1902.

MITI (Tsūshō Sangyō Shō, abbrev. Tsūsanshō). "Ministry of International Trade and Industry." Official agency responsible for Japan's trade and industrial policy, to which firms wishing to trade or import products must apply. This powerful ministry directs the Agency for Natural Resources and Energy, the Patent and Trademark Bureau, the Agency for Small and Medium-Sized Enterprises, the Administration for International Trade, the Bureau of the Environment, the Industry Information Agencies, and others. It has more than 12,000 employees and controls basic industry (steelworks, iron, petrochemicals), technology, computers, textiles, and equipment. In June 1993, Sakamoto Yoshihiro (b. 1948), a senior administrator in the ministry, was appointed its director general.

Mito. Chief city of Ibaraki prefecture, on the Naka-gawa river, north of Tokyo, which developed around a fortress built during the Kamakura period. After the Battle of Sekigahara (1600), Tokugawa Ieyasu's eleventh son, Tokugawa Yorifusa, had a castle built there. The castle became a center of historical and Confucian studies called Mitogaku, then housed the Kōdōkan created by Tokugawa Nariaki in 1841. Mito is now a prosperous agricultural city. *Pop.:* 215,000.

The Mito region was the site of a major insurrection (known as Tengutō no Ran) in 1864, when a pro-imperial faction opposed the orders of the Edo shogunate and firmly supported expulsion of foreigners. Pro-imperial samurai, under the leadership of Fujita Koshirō (1842–65), one of Fujita Tōko's sons, and Takeda Kōunsai, met near Mt. Tsukuba and battled the troops of daimyo Tokugawa Yoshiatsu. The shogunate sent more than 12,000 soldiers to fight the insurgents (about 2,000 in number), and the fighting lasted three months. The rebels were defeated and severely punished, but the quarrel between supporters of restoration of the emperor and those who remained faithful to the shogunate did not die down within the community of Mito.

• **Mitogaku.** "Mito School," a Shinto-Confucian society established in Mito by Tokugawa Mitsukuni as a "center for historical research" in the late seventeenth century. Its goal was to compile a major history of Japan, *Dai Nihon-shi* (which was completed only in 1906). This historical society, whose

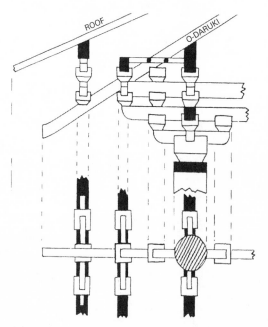

Type of *wa-yō* roof bracket: *mitesaki*

most influential members were Fujita Yūkoku, Aizawa Seishisai, and Fujita Tōko, favored nationalism and espoused principles of neo-Confucian Zhu Xi (*Jap.*: Shushi) philosophy, Wang Yangming (*Jap.*: Ō-Yōmei), and Kokugaku (National Learning). This view of history based on the cult of the emperor was expounded in many works and debated in an academy founded by Tokugawa Nariaki, the Kōdōkan, which attempted to find a solution to the problem posed by the decadence of the shogunate and the arrival of foreign ships in Japanese waters, and proposed political and military reforms. However, it leaned toward political conservatism and was increasingly opposed to the shogunal regime. The Mito School was very influential after the Meiji Restoration (1868) and continued to exert political pressure until the Second World War, supported by scholars who wanted to preserve the national heritage.

• **Mito-kaidō.** *See* WAKI-KAIDŌ.

• **Mito Lōmon.** *See* TOKUGAWA MITSUKUNI.

Mitori. In the Edo period, a bureaucrat responsible for collecting taxes on shogunal estates. Also called *kemitori, mitorikemi.*

Mitsuaki. Painter (Tosa Mitsuaki, late fourteenth century) of the Tosa school. He was daimyo of Echizen province, but lived and painted mainly in Kyoto.

Mitsuatsu. Painter (Tosa Mitsuatsu, 1734–64) of the Tosa school, Mitsuyoshi's son.

Mitsubishi. "Three Diamonds," an industrial and financial conglomerate *(zaibatsu)* founded in 1871 in Nagasaki by Iwasaki Yatarō (1834–85), a samurai from the Tosa clan, under the name Tsukumo. At first, it was a shipping and trading company with just 11 ships. During the expedition to Taiwan, the government provided Yatarō with 13 more ships for troop transport, and Tsukumo was renamed Mitsubishi Kisen Kaisha (Mitsubishi Shipping Company) in 1875. Later, Iwasaki Yatarō's brother, Iwasaki Yanosuke (1851–1908), expanded the fleet with government assistance; he founded another shipping company, Kyōdō Un'yu Kaisha, and obtained an almost complete monopoly on shipping in Japan. When Yatarō died, Yanosuke assumed control of the group and diversified its activities. His son, Iwasaki Koyata, succeeded him in 1916, taking over an ever-growing trading and industrial empire. The Iwasaki family directed Mitsubishi until 1945.

In 1940, it controlled 200 companies, including aircraft factories. The zaibatsu was broken up in 1945 and reconstituted in 1952 as Fuji Trading Co., but it later took back the name Mitsubishi. It currently controls a number of companies, including Mitsubishi Kasei Kōgyō (chemicals), Mitsubishi Shōji (international trading), Mitsubishi Denki (electrical appliances), Mitsubishi Jisho (real estate), Mitsubishi Gasu Chemical (chemicals, plastics, petroleum products, fertilizers, etc.), Mitsubishi Ginkō (banking), Mitsubishi Jūkōgyō (heavy industry, dockyards, various factories), Mitsubishi Kinzoku (nonferrous metals), Mitsubishi Jidōsha (automobiles), Mitsubishi Sekiyu (oil refineries), Mitsubishi Seishi (paper products), Mitsubishi Yuka (chemical products, ethylene), Mitsubishi Seikō (specialized steels), Mitsubishi Shintaku Ginkō (financial and banking institutions), Mitsubishi Sōkō (transport and warehousing).

The group currently has more than 350,000 employees and produces more than 10% of Japan's GNP. Its member companies have immense production complexes, both in Japan and abroad.

• The Mitsubishi aeronautics company actively participated in Japan's war effort by producing many types of fighter planes and bombers:

—**Mitsubishi A.6 M.2/M.3/M.5:** single-seat fighter plane (Zeke, U.S. code name "Zero"), Japan's most famous, produced in 1940. *Maximum speed:* 570 km/h; *range:* 1,800 km; *weapons:* two 20 mm cannons, two 7.7 mm machine guns. A version of this plane was called Zero-sen. *Engine for the A.6 M.3 (1940):* 925 HP; *engine for the A.6 M.5 (1942):* 1,130 HP. Three thousand of these planes were built by Mitsubishi and 6,200 by Nakajima. They were used in the attack on Pearl Harbor on December 7, 1941.

—**Mitsubishi A.7 M.2:** Fighter plane (Reppū, U.S. code name "Sam"), built starting in May, 1944. It could reach an altitude of 13,000 m. Only eight were built before the plants were destroyed by American bombing.

—**Mitsubishi B.2 M:** Bomber invented in 1927 and in operation in China from 1932 to 1937. *Total weight:* 3,557 kg; *length:* 9.1 m; *wing span:* 15.22 m; *engine:* one 600 HP Mitsubishi-Hispano-Suiza; *crew:* three; *speed:* 211 km/h; *maximum altitude:* 5,290 m; *range:* 1,760 km; *weapon:* one 789 kg torpedo.

—**Mitsubishi F.1 M.2:** Imperial Navy hydroplane (U.S. code name "Pete") with four wings, three floats, and one engine.

—**Mitsubishi G.3 M.2:** Bomber rolled out in 1935 (U.S. code name "Nell"). *Engines:* two 1,075 HP Mitsubishi Kensei; *weapons:* one 20 mm cannon and four 7.7 mm machine guns; *payload:* 850 kg of bombs; *maximum speed:* 350 km/h; *maximum altitude:* 10,000 m; *range:* 4,500 km; *length:* 13.5 m; *wing span:* 20 m.

—**Mitsubishi G.4 M:** Bomber produced in 1941 (U.S. code name "Betty"). *Range:* 4,800 km. It was equipped to carry the Oka bomb in 1944–45.

—**Mitsubishi J.2 M:** Fighter-interceptor (Raiden, U.S. code name "Jack") built starting in late 1943; 500 were built. *Engine:* one 1,850 HP; *maximum speed:* 600 km/h; *range:* 1,050 km; *weapons:* four 20 mm cannons.

—**Mitsubishi J.8 M.1** (or **K1–200**): Shusui jet interceptor, designed in 1945 but never built, based on plans for the German Messerschmidt Me 163 B "Komet."

—**Mitsubishi K.1 21:** Fighter-bomber (U.S. code name "Sally") produced starting in 1937 and replaced in 1942 by the Nakajima K.1 49 (U.S. code name "Helen"). *Weight:* 9,700 kg; *length:* 15.75 m; *wing span:* 22.10 m; *engines:* two 1,450 HP Mitsubishi Ha-101; *crew:* five; *speed:* 475 km/h; *range:* 2,100 km; *weapons:* five 7.7 mm machine guns and one 12.7 mm machine gun; *payload:* 1,000 kg of bombs.

—**Mitsubishi K.1 30:** Light bomber, produced before 1942. *Total weight:* 3,300 kg; *length:* 10.7 m; *wing span:* 14.3 m; *engine:* one 850 HP Nakajima; *speed:* 420 km/h; *crew:* two; *range:* 1,700 km; *maximum altitude:* 8,400 m; *weapons:* two 7.7 mm machine guns; *payload:* 300 kg of bombs.

—**Mitsubishi K.1 46 III:** Two-engine infantry-support plane (U.S. code name "Dinah"). *Speed:* 630 km/h; *range:* 5,000 km; *crew:* two. Only 611 of these planes were built during the Second World War, most of them in 1943.

—**Mitsubishi K.1 67:** Navy bomber (U.S. code name "Peggy") built in 1944. *Length:* 18.4 m; *wing span:* 22.15 m; *total weight:* 13,850 kg; *crew:* six; *engines:* two 1,900 HP Mitsubishi AH–104; *speed:* 540 km/h; *maximum altitude:* 9,000 m; *weapons:* one 20 mm cannon, two 7.7 mm machine guns, two 12.7 mm machine guns (in 1945).

—**Mitsubishi OB 01:** Bomber (U.S. code name "Betty"). *Maximum speed:* 445 km/h; *range:* 4,200 km; *weapons:* five 7.7 mm machine guns; *payload:* 800 kg of bombs.

—**Mitsubishi OB 97–1:** Bomber (U.S. code name "Sally"). *Maximum speed:* 400 km/h; *range:* 1,900 km; *weapons:* five 7.7 mm machine guns; *payload:* 1,000 kg of bombs.

Mitsubumi. Painter (Tosa Mitsubumi, 1812–79) of the Tosa school.

Mitsubuse. Unit of length equivalent to the width of three fingers.

Mitsuchi Chūzō. Politician (1871–1948), born in Kagawa prefecture. After studying in Europe, he taught in Japan, became a journalist, then campaigned for the Rikken Seiyūkai (Friends of Constitutional Government party). He was elected to the Diet in 1908 and reelected to the lower chamber 11 times. He was Takahashi's cabinet chief (1921–22), minister of finance in Tanaka Giichi's cabinet (1927–29), minister of communications in Inukai Tsuyoshi's cabinet (1931–32), and minister of railroads in Saitō Makoto's cabinet (1932–34). He became a member of the Privy Council in 1940; after the Second World War, he was minister of transport in Shidehara Kijūrō's cabinet.

Mitsudae. Pigment containing sesame oil and lead monoxide *(mitsudasō)* or litharge, used by painters in the Nara period, in emulation of Chinese painters of the Tang dynasty.

Mitsu-gusoku. The three ritual accessories (incense holder, candelabrum, and flower vase) used in Buddhist ceremonies mainly during the Kamakura period. Another group of five accessories, adding a second candelabrum and vase, is called *itsutsu-gusoku. See* GUSOKU.

Mitsui. Conglomerate of trading companies *(zaibatsu)* founded in 1673 in Kyoto by Mitsui Takatoshi. It monopolized the silk trade and the money-changing business in Edo (1683), Kyoto (1686), and Osaka (1691) with the approval of the Edo shogunate, which granted charters (Goyō Shōnin) to members of the Mitsui family. In the Meiji period, Mitsui (which had been divided into several branches) bought up factories from the government, diversifying its activities and extending its trade and industrial empire to the entire country by constantly investing in new firms—trading, banking, mining, and so on. By the end of the Second World War, Mitsui controlled 273 companies and was the largest zaibatsu in Japan. When the zaibatsu were dismantled, in 1945–46, the firms that had been part of the Mitsui group became independent. About 1950, they began to regroup in *keiretsu* (holding companies), the number of which rose into the dozens (up to 70), in a similar fashion to Mitsubishi and Sumitomo, with members of the Mitsui family controlling the most important ones. While Mitsubishi supported the Rikken Minseitō (Constitutional Democratic party), Mitsui helped finance the Rikken Seiyūkai (Friends of Constitutional Government party). Among the members of the Mitsui family who helped the firm grow and industrialize in the interwar period in Manchuria, Taiwan, and Korea, the best known are Mitsui Hachirōemon (Takatoshi, 1622–94), the founder; Mitsui Takayasu (1850–1922); Mitsui Hachirōemon II (1857–1948); and Mitsui Takamine (?–1933).

The Mitsui group comprises a large number of companies, including Mitsui Bussan (general trading, metals, machinery, chemical products, etc.), Mitsui Ginkō (banking), Mitsui Kensetsu (construction), Mitsui Kinzoku Kōgyō (nonferrous metals), Mitsui Kōzan (mines and construction materials), Mitsui Ōsaka Shōsen Sempaku (O.S.K. shipping companies), Mitsui Fudōsan (real estate), Mitsui Sekiyu Kagaku (petrochemicals), Mitsui Seitō (sugar refineries), Mitsui Tōatsu Kagaku (various chemical products, colorants), Mitsui Shintaku Ginkō (banking), Mitsui Sōtō (transport and warehousing), Mitsui Zōzen (heavy industry, plants, shipyards). The group established Mitsui Bunko, a library and museum located in Tokyo that is dedicated to the Mitsui family and its activities since the firm's foundation, and a research institute for social and economic history.

Mitsukiyo. Painter (Tosa Mitsukiyo, d. 1862) of the Tosa school, student of his father, Mitsuzane.

Mitsukoshi. The largest chain of stores in Japan, created in 1673 by Mitsui Takatoshi, who opened a shop called Echigo-ya in Nihombashi (Edo). The success of this store, which offered a wide variety of wares with prices displayed, was the cornerstone of the Mitsui family's fortune and zaibatsu. In 1908, Echigo-ya opened a large European-style three-story store in Tokyo and drew customers by organizing exhibitions. This store was renamed Mitsukoshi in 1928. After the Second World War and some financial difficulties, it regained popularity by emphasizing fashion and objets d'art. It opened a branch in Paris in 1971, then branches in Rome, Dusseldorf, and Singapore, which specialized in exhibitions of works by contemporary Japanese artists. The chain has some 15 ultramodern stores in Japan.

Mitsukuri. Major family of scholars.

• **Mitsukuri Gempachi.** Historian (1862–1919), Mitsukuri Gempo's grandson and Mitsukuri Shūsei's (1826–86) son, born in Edo. He studied Western history and zoology (in Germany from 1886 to 1890), then was a professor of Western history at the University of Tokyo. He wrote *Furansu dai kakumei-shi* (History of the French Revolution) in 1920, *Naporeon jidai-shi* (History of the Napoleonic Period) in 1923, and other works.

• **Mitsukuri Gempo.** Physician (1799–1863) and scholar in "Dutch sciences" *(rangaku),* son of a physician for the daimyo of Tsuyama. He was the official interpreter for the Astronomy Bureau (Temmonkata) in Edo, and took part in the discussions with the Russian envoy E. V. Putiatin and in the conclusion of the Kanagawa Treaty with the United States. He was a professor at the Bansho Shirabesho and translated technical works, some of which were used by the Satsuma clan to build the first Japanese steamship.

• **Mitsukuri Rinshō.** Jurist (1846–97), born in Edo, Mistukuri Gempo's grandson and his successor at the Bansho Shirabesho in 1864. He went to the Paris World's Fair in 1867 with the shogunal delegation. In collaboration with Gustave Émile Boissonnade, he wrote a plan for a civil and commercial code. He was vice-minister of justice in Kuroda Kiyotaka's cabinet (1888–89) and was raised to the peerage.

Mitsumine-jinja. Shinto shrine founded, according to tradition, in the second century by Yamato Takeru at the foot of the Mitsumine mountains *(alt.: 1,100 m)* in Saitama prefecture, and dedicated to the *kami* Izanagi and Izanami. It was very popular during the Kamakura period, when it became a center for the Shugendō cult and a meeting place for Yamabushi, and during the Edo period. Annual *matsuri* on April 8.

Mitsumochi. Painter (Tosa Mitsumochi, active ca. 1550), who studied with his father, Mitsunobu, and was Mitsumoto's master. He illustrated the *Kuwa-no-midera engi* in 1534.

Mitsumoto. Painter (Tosa Mitsumoto, 1530–69) of the Tosa school. He studied with his father, Mitsumochi, and was head of the Kyūtei E-dokoro (Imperial Court Office of Painting).

Mitsunaga. Painter (Tosa Mitsunaga, Tokiwa Mitsunaga, active ca. 1173) in the Heian court, of the Yamato-e school. He illustrated a number of *emakimono,* including *Ban dainagon ekotoba.*

Mitsunari. Painter (Tosa Mitsunari, 1646–1710) of the Tosa school.

Mitsunobu. Painter (Tosa Mitsunobu, ca. 1434–ca. 1525) of the Yamato-e school and head of the imperial *e-dokoro* (*see* KYŪTEI E-DOKORO). He illustrated a number of *emakimono,* including *Kiyomizu-dera engi* and *Kitano-tenjin engi.*
• Painter (Kanō Mitsunobu; *mei:* Ukyō-noshin, 1565–1608) of the Kano school; he studied with his father, Eitoku, in Kyoto.
→ *See* BAIŌKEN NAGAHARU.

Mitsunori. Painter (Tosa Mitsunori, 1583–1638) of the Tosa school, Mitsuyoshi's son and student and Mitsuoki's father. He became a Buddhist monk with the name Sōjin.
• Painter (Kanō Mitsunori; *mei:* Shurinosuke, early seventeenth century) of the Kanō school, who studied with his father, Sanraku.

Mitsuoki. Painter (Tosa Mitsuoki; *gō:* Jōshō, Sunkaken, 1617–91), born in Sakai, died in Kyoto. He studied with his father, Mitsunori, of the Tosa school, and was head of the imperial *e-dokoro* (*see* KYŪTEI E-DOKORO). He produced decorative compositions whose style represented a mixture of techniques of the Tosa and Kanō schools. He became a Buddhist monk with the name Jōshō and received the title Hōgen.
• Sculptor of netsuke (Ōtsuki Mitsuoki, Ryūsai, early nineteenth century) and goldsmith in Edo.

Mitsusada. Painter (Tosa Mitsusada, 1738–1806) of the Tosa school, Mitsuyoshi's son and student.

Mitsusuke. Painter (Tosa Mitsusuke, 1675–1710) of the Tosa school.

Mitsutada. Maker of sword blades (1194–1271) in Bizen. *See* BIZEN-MONO.

Mitsutani Kunishirō. Painter (1874–1936) in the Western style, born in Okayama prefecture. He studied painting at Koyama Shōtarō's (1857–1916) school in Tokyo, then went to Paris in 1900–01, where he worked in Jean-Paul Laurens's studio. He lived in Paris again from 1911 to 1914 and was strongly influenced by Matisse. He was elected a member of the Imperial Fine Arts Academy (Teikoku Bijutsu-in) in 1925.

Mitsutoki. Painter (Tosa Mitsutoki, 1765–1819) of the Tosa school.
→ *See* TAKAHASHI DŌHACHI.

Mitsu-tomoe (Mitsu-domoe). Symbolic decoration formed by a spiral made of three apostrophe-shaped branches within a circle, generally used on drum skins and the ends of round tiles. When the decoration comprises only two branches in the spiral, representing Yin and Yang intertwined (*Jap.:* In-yō), it is called *futatsu-tomoe.*

Mitsutoshi. Netsuke sculptor (Ōtani Mitsutoshi, mid-nineteenth century) in ivory, in Edo.

Mitsuyama. Noh play: the spirit of a woman tells a Buddhist monk the story of two women deceived by the man they loved, who committed suicide. The spirit of the second woman arrives and argues with the first about the dead man, but the monk manages to reconcile them.

Mitsuyoshi. Painter (Tosa Mitsuyoshi; *mei:* Gyō-bu; *gō:* Kyūkoku, 1539–1613) of the Tosa school, Mitsumochi's son and student. He was head of the imperial *e-dokoro* (*see* KYŪTEI E-DOKORO) in Kyoto and became a Buddhist monk in Sakai.
• Painter (Tosa Mitsuyoshi, 1700–71) of the Tosa school, Mitsusuke's son and student.

Mitsuzaki. Composer (mid-nineteenth century) of pieces for *koto, sangen,* and *shakuhachi.*

Mitsuzane. Painter (Tosa Mitsuzane, 1780–1852) of the Tosa school.

Miura Anjin. *See* ADAMS, WILLIAM.

Miura Baien. Philosopher and physician (1723–89) born in Bungo province (Ōita prefecture), whose thought, imbued with skepticism, somewhat resembled Hegel's dialectics. He studied all religious doctrines of Asia and learned Dutch, then opened a school in his province, drawing numerous disciples. His trilogy *Kango, Gengo,* and *Zeigo,* published in 1763, presents philosophical doctrines that were completely new for his time, and he tried to apply them concretely in a fourth volume, *Kagen,* published in 1773. He led a frugal life, helping his poorest students and making no class distinction between them and their professors.

Miura Chora. Haiku poet (1729)–80, born in Shima province (Mie prefecture), who was a member of the same poetry group as Yosa Buson and, like Yosa, showed a sense of *mono no aware* in his work.

Miura Gorō. Politician and officer (1846–1926) of the Kiheitai in the Chōshū estate. After the 1868 Restoration, he led the repression of the Hagi and Satsuma revolts; in 1884, he accompanied General Oyama Iwao to Europe to study armed-forces organizations, but he was sent to the reserves because of his insistence on following through with reforms. A minister in Korea, he was implicated in the assassination of Queen Min in 1895, but was absolved of any involvement. He was appointed to the Privy Council in 1910.

Miura Hiroyuki. Historian (Mirua Kaneyuki, 1871–1931), born in Shimane prefecture, expert in Japanese medieval history and professor at the University of Kyoto starting in 1909. He received the Imperial Academy Prize (Teikoku Gakushi-in shō) for his work on the history of legislation in Japan, *Hōseishi no kenkyū*, in 1919.

Miura Ken'ya. Ceramist (1821–89), born in Edo. He studied painting under Tani Bunchō, as well as *maki-e* lacquer techniques. Curious about Western sciences, he studied ship construction in Nagasaki with Dutch engineers and constructed the first modern ship for the daimyo of Sendai. He also conducted many other scientific experiments and was interested in geology, but he is best known for his ceramics in the Kenzan and Oribe style, which he produced in Edo. Also called simply Ken'ya, Ken'ya Miura.

Miura Kōheiji. Contemporary ceramist, born 1933 on the island of Sado; he made celadons in new colors, thus reviving this type of ceramics. He belonged to the Jozan family tradition. He had a number of exhibitions abroad, lectured at the Musée Guimet in Paris on celadons in 1990, and was represented in the exhibition of ceramic arts in Paris (Mitsukoshi space) in 1994.

Miura Shumon. Writer, born 1926 in Tokyo and literature professor at Nihon University. His early stories were based on Chinese legends; later, he wrote novels portraying the life of bureaucrats after the Second World War, such as *Meifu sansuizu* (1951) and *Hakoniwa* (1967). His wife, Sono Ayako, is also a talented author.

Miura Taneyoshi. Warrior (?–1221). He plotted against the Hōjō *shikken* and was killed by his brother, Miura Yoshimura.

• **Miura Yasumura.** Warrior (Suruga Jirō, 1194–1247), appointed Hyōjoshū in 1235. He and his

brother, Miura Mitsumura, were killed in battle against Adachi Kagemori.

• **Miura Yoshiaki.** Warrior (1092–1120).

• **Miura Yoshimura.** Warrior (?–1239), serving the Kamakura *bakufu*. He defended the Hōjō *shikken* against his brother, Miura Taneyoshi, whom he killed in battle in 1221.

• **Miura Yoshitsura.** Warrior (Sawara Jūrō) who fought the Taira at Ichi no Tani in 1185 on behalf of Minamoto no Yoritomo.

• **Miura Yoshizumi.** Warrior (Arajirō, 1127–1200), who assisted Minamoto no Yoritomo in his fight against the Taira.

Miura Tetsuo. Writer (Miura Tetsurō), born 1931 in Aomori prefecture. His works, mainly autobiographical, revealed his despair at having people close to him die and belonging to a family that he believed was under a curse. He won the Akutagawa Prize for his story *Shinobugawa*, in 1960. Among his other works, the most important is probably *Umi no michi* (The Roads of the Sea, 1969).

Miura Tokitada. Daimyo (1416–94) of Sagami province. He adopted Miura Yoshiatsu, but Yoshiatsu rebelled against him, killed him, and seized his estates.

• **Miura Yoshiatsu.** Warrior (?–1516), Miura Tokitada's adoptive son. He rebelled against Tokitada and killed him, seizing his property. But he was attacked by Hōjō Sōun and committed suicide. He had become a Buddhist monk with the name Dōsun.

Miwa. School of sculptors of netsuke that flourished in Edo in the mid-eighteenth century. One of its most famous members was Hiromori Miwa.
  • Shinto sacred mountain, in Nara prefecture, near the town of Sakurai, at the foot of which is the oldest known "keyhole" *kofun* (third–fourth century). Excavations revealed objects from the Yayoi period, mainly pottery shards and *haniwa*.

• *Miwa.* Noh play: a priest gives a pious woman a coat to protect her against the cold, but a little later, he finds the coat hanging on a tree. The *kami* of Miwa appears to him, tells him her story, and dances for him.

Miwa Kazuhiko. Ceramist, born 1951 in Hagi (Yamaguchi prefecture), whose works have been exhibited in Japan and in a group exhibition in Paris (Mitsukoshi space) in 1994.

• **Miwar Ryūsaku.** Sculptor and ceramist, born 1940 in Hagi (Yamaguchi prefecture), organizer of many art events and exhibitions. He was in a group exhibition in Paris (Mitsukoshi space) in 1994.

Miwa Kyūwa. Ceramist (Miwa Kunihiro, 1895–1981) from Hagi (Yamaguchi prefecture) in the tradition of the Hagi family. He took the name Kyūsetsu when his father died, in 1927. His brother, Miwa Setsuo (b. 1910) also used the gō Kyūsetsu. Kyūwa made mainly Korean-style bowls for the tea ceremony, with a thick, whitish glaze. Declared a Living National Treasure in 1970.

Miwa Myōjin. See ŌMIWA-JINJA.

Miwa Shissai. Confucian philosopher (1669–1744), Satō Naokata's and Yamazaki Ansai's disciple, and scholar in the tradition of Wang Yangming (*Jap.*: Ō-Yōmei). He founded his own school, the Meirindō, in Edo. He translated the works of Chinese philosopher Wang Yangming into Japanese under the title *Denshūroku,* and he tried to popularize Wang's teachings, which advocated unity of knowledge and action through meditation.

Miwata Masako. Scholar (Uda Masako, 1843–1927) of Chinese and Japanese literature, daughter of a teacher at a private school in Kyoto. In 1869, she married a politician, Miwata Mototsuna (Miwata Tsunaichirō, 1829–79); after he died, she founded a school in Tokyo, helping to organize the Women's University of Japan (then called Nihon Joshi Daigakkō). She published several works on girls' education.

Miya. Former name of the imperial palace. Also called *mi-araka, momoshiki, gosho.*
• Title for imperial princes and princesses. Also called Shinnō.
• Term often used for Shinto shrines. Also called *jinja, jingu, yashiro,* etc. See JINJA, JINGU, MIYAZA, YASHIRO.
→ *See* TORII.

Miyagawa Kazuo. Cameraman (1908–99), born in Kyoto. He became famous for his work in *Rashōmon,* a film by Kurosawa Akira (1950), which had an influence on a number of French cameramen. He also shot the 1964 Tokyo Olympics with a hand-held camera.

Miyagawa Kōzan. Ceramist (1842–1916) who established his kilns in Kyoto about 1900. Also called Miyakawa Kōzan.

Miyage. Custom has it that when Japanese come home from a trip, they offer small gifts—souvenirs from the place they visited—to loved ones; these are called *miyage.* When people leave on a long trip, their loved ones offer them gifts (called *sembetsu*). The *miyage* tradition requires them to bring home gifts of at least equal value to the *sembetsu* received upon their departure. A similar custom, called *temiyage,* has it that people visiting friends or relatives bring a small gift, usually pastry or fruit. *See* GIFTS.

Miyagi prefecture. Prefecture in northern Honshu, bordering the Pacific Ocean and irrigated by the Abukuma-gawa and Kitakami-gawa rivers. The territory of this prefecture was once part of Mutsu province. Its western border is formed by the Ōu mountains; between the mountains and the ocean is the Sendai plain, which is intensively cultivated (mainly rice). *Chief city:* Sendai. *Other major cities:* Natori, Kakuda, Tagajō, Ishinomaki, Kesennuma, Furikawa, Shiroishi, Izumi. *Area:* 7,290 km². *Pop.:* 2.1 million.

Miyagi Michio. Blind composer (1894–1956), born in Kobe. He began by writing works for koto (*Sōkyoku*) and *shakuhachi* that showed some Western influence. He also invented a 17-string koto, called *jūshichigen.* His most famous work, for Japanese and Western instruments, is *Haru no umi* (Spring Sea, 1929). His works for koto are in the style of the Ikuta school.

Miyagi Tamayo. Politician (Ueda Tamayo, 1892–1960), born in Yamaguchi prefecture. She studied social sciences in the United States from 1922 to 1924, then became a juvenile-court judge in Japan. In 1927, she married Miyagi Chōgorō (1878–1942), who became minister of justice in 1939. From 1947 to 1959, she was a member of the Chamber of Councillors (in the Ryokufūkai group). She fought against prostitution and campaigned for the prevention of juvenile delinquency.

Miyagi Yotoku. Painter (1903–45), born in Okinawa. He went to the United States to pursue his artistic studies and had an exhibit in Los Angeles in

1925. He became affiliated with the Communist party and returned to Japan as an agent of the Comintern in 1933, working under the orders of the spy Richard Sorge, as did his compatriot and friend Kitabayashi Tomo. Arrested with Sorge in 1941, he died of tuberculosis in prison. *See* SORGE.

Miyaichi Temmangū. Shinto shrine established in Mitagiri, near Yashiro (Hyōgo prefecture), dedicated to the memory of Sugawara no Michizane. Also called Hōfu Temmangū, Matsugasaki-jinja. A famous *emakimono* describing the foundation of this shrine, dating from the late Kamakura period, is called *Matsugasaki tenjin engi.*

Miyake. In ancient Japan, imperial rice paddies, and term for state granaries in which the harvest from these rice paddies was stored.

Miyake Issei. Fashion designer, born 1938, in Hiroshima prefecture, who created clothing lines for men and women that were very successful in Europe and the United States in the 1980s. He received the *Mainichi* Prize for his work in 1976 and was invited to participate in the Autumn Festival in Paris that year. His unconventional fashions have been featured in many exhibitions and fashion shows in Paris and New York and gained an international reputation.

Miyake Kaho. Writer (Tanabe Tatsuko, 1868–1943) and poet, born in Tokyo, Tanabe Taichi's daughter. Her early works, such as *Yabu no ugiusu* (The Garden Nightingale, 1888), dealt with Japan's modernization. She married the philosopher Miyake Setsurei in 1892 and published a number of articles in the magazine he edited, *Josei Nihonjin* (Japanese Women). Her poems were collected in *Hana no shumi* (To the Glory of Flowers), in 1909.

Miyake Kanran. Confucian philosopher (1674–1718), born in Kyoto, Asami Keisai's and Kinoshita Jun'an's disciple. He began to work for Tokugawa Mitsukuni, daimyo of Mito, in 1699, and helped to write the *Dai Nihon shi.* He was an adviser to the Edo shogunate and one of the Bokumon Jittetsu. Miyake Sekian's brother.

• **Miyake Kisai.** Confucian philosopher (1580–1649) of the Teishū-ha.

• **Miyake Sekian.** Confucian scholar (1665–1730), Miyake Kanran's brother. He was also a disciple of Asami Keisai in the Zhu Xi (*Jap.*: Shushi)

school. He opened a private school in Osaka and directed the Kaitoku-dō school, founded by his disciple, Nakai Shūan (1693–1758), to teach philosophy (mixture of Shushi and Ō-Yōmei doctrines) to the city's merchants.

Miyake Setsurei. Writer and journalist (Miyake Yūjirō, 1860–1945), born in Kanazawa. With friends, among them Shiga Shigetaka and Sugiura Shigetake, he created a political organization, Seikyōsha, in 1888 to provide political education to the people, and a magazine, *Nihonjin* (The Japanese). He tried to forge a synthesis between Eastern and Western philosophies in *Uchū* (The World), published in 1908, and wrote a six-volume chronicle of events of his time, *Dōjidai-shi.* In 1920, he and his wife, Miyake Kaho, founded the women's magazine *Josei Nihonjin.*

Miyake Shōsai. Confucian philosopher (1662–1741), born in Harima province, Yamazaki Ansai's and Asami Keisai's disciple. He opened a school in Kyoto. *See also* MIYAKE KANRAN, MIYAKE SEKIAN.

Miyake Yoshinobu. Athlete, born 1939 in Miyagi prefecture. He won a gold medal at the 1964 Olympics in Tokyo (weightlifting, featherweight class), another (same discipline) at the 1968 Olympics in Mexico City, and was world champion in 1969. He retired from competition after winning another gold medal at the 1972 Olympics.

Miyako. Name, especially in literature, for the imperial city of Kyoto. Sometimes written by Europeans as Miaco, Miako, Meaco. *See also* KYOTO, MIYA.

• **Miyako-fuji.** Literary name sometimes given to Mt. Hiei-zan.

• **Miyako Mandayū.** Famous *jōruri* singer (active ca. 1700 to 1710) and Kabuki actor in Kyoto.

• **Miyako Odori.** Dance performed by the *maiko* and geisha of Kyoto, created in 1872.

• *Miyako Shimbun.* First Japanese evening daily, founded as *Konnichi Shimbun* in 1884; its name was changed in 1888. It published a number of literary serials (such as *Daibosatsu tōge* by Nakazato Kaizan). In 1942, it merged with the *Kokumin Shimbun* to form the *Tokyo Shimbun.*

Miyako no Iratsume. Mommu Tennō's wife (?–754) and Shōmu Tennō's mother.

Miyako no Nishiki. Writer, born 1675 in Settsu, Nishizawa Ippū's disciple and author of novels in the *ukiyo-zōshi* genre. Among his works was *Genroku taiheiki* (1702).

Miyako no Yoshika. Poet and historian (834–79), one of the compilers of *Montoku jitsuroku* in 879. He was ambassador to the Korean kingdom of Pohai in 872. His poems, written in Chinese, are collected in *Toshi bunshū*.

Miya-mairi. Custom of presenting a newborn child at the shrine *(miya)* on the twentieth, thirtieth, fiftieth, and hundredth days after its birth, so that the baby will be recognized by the *kami (ujigami)* of its birthplace. This family ritual is still widely performed.

Miya Monzeki. Name for Buddhist temples directed by an imperial prince. There were once 13 of them. *See* MONZEKI.

Miyamoto Kenji. Politician, born 1908 in Yamaguchi prefecture. He joined the Communist party in 1931 and continued his writing career within the Puroretariya Sakka Dōmei (Union of Proletarian Writers), which he had begun in 1929 with a story, *Haiboku no bungaku* (The Literature of Defeat), dedicated to Akutagawa Ryūnosuke. Elected a member of the party's Central Committee in 1933 (secretly, for the Communist party had been banned), he was arrested and sentenced to life in prison, but was freed in 1945. He became the secretary-general of the Nihon Kyōsantō (Japan Communist party) in 1958, and was elected to the Chamber of Councillors in 1977. In 1932, he married the writer Miyamoto Yuriko.

Miyamoto Musashi. Painter and warrior (Niten, 1584–1645), born in Kansai. He became a *rōnin* after the Battle of Sekigahara (1600), in which his masters had fought Tokugawa Ieyasu, and became a master of arms, inventing a style of combat with two swords *(nitō-ryū)*. He claimed to have won 50 duels and was considered the best swordsman in Japan. His exploits inspired a number of legends. In 1637, he went to work for the Tokugawa, fighting for them against the Shimabara rebels, and in 1650, he became a martial-arts instructor for the daimyo of the Hosokawa family in Kumamoto. He wrote a work on martial arts in 1643 that has become a classic of the genre, the *Gorin no sho* (Book of the Five Circles). As a painter, he belonged to the Muromachi *suiboku* school; his main subjects were birds and Zen patriarchs, executed in brush strokes as incisive as sword strokes. His exploits were brought to the Kabuki stage by Tsuruya Namboku and featured in a major novel by Yoshikawa Eiji, published from 1935 to 1939. Miyamoto Musashi was also an excellent calligrapher. *See also* KATŌ KYIYOMASA, SASAKI KOJIRO.

Miyamoto Yuriko. Woman of letters (Chūjō Yuriko, 1899–1951), born in Tokyo, daughter of Chūjō Seiichirō (1868–1936), a well-known architect, and Chūjō Ashie, one of Nishimura Shigeki's daughters. She began to write stories when she was 12, then studied the works of Russian writers when she attended the women's college at Ochanomizu. Her first novel, *Mazushiki hitobito no mure* (A Herd of Poor People), was published in the magazine *Chūōkōron* in 1916, when she was only 17. She accompanied her father to New York in 1918 and married a linguist, Araki Shigeru. Her marriage was a disaster; soon after, she wrote an autobiographical novel, *Nobuko* (1924–26). In 1927 she went to the Soviet Union, where she stayed for three years. When she returned to Japan, she joined the NAPF and edited a magazine published by the association, *Hataraku Fujin* (Women at Work). She joined the Communist party in 1931 and met Miyamoto Kenji, whom she married in 1932. She was arrested several times for her Marxist ideas, but continued to write: *Futatsu no niwa* (The Two Gardens, 1947), *Dōhyō* (Road Signs, 1950). Her letters to her imprisoned husband were collected in *Jūninen no tegami* (Twelve Years of Letters) in 1952. Other letters exchanged with women writers were collected in *Fujin to bungaku* (Women and Literature, 1948). Among her other works are *Fūchiso* (1946) and *Banshū heiya* (Banshū Plain, 1947), which won the *Mainichi* Prize in 1947. Her stories were published in *Sangatsu no daiyon nichiyō* (The Fourth Sunday in March) in 1940.

Miyanaga Rikichi. Ceramist, born 1935 in Kyoto. His work was included in many exhibitions abroad, notably in the United States (1971), Germany (1976), Denver (1979), Spain (1986), Australia (1987), and Paris (Mitsukoshi space, 1994).

Miyashita Zenji. Contemporary ceramist, born 1939 in Kyoto. He took part in many group exhibitions abroad, including Australia (1977), Italy, (1982), and Paris (1994).

Mi-yasu-dokoro. Bedrooms in the imperial palace reserved for the emperor. In the ninth century, this term also applied to emperors' second wives, then to wives of imperial princes. *See* KŌTAI-SHI.

Miyatake Gaikotsu. Writer and journalist (Miyatake Tobone, 1867–1955), born in Sanuki province. He became known for writing very licentious novels, and he published more than 100 works on a wide variety of topics, including *Tobakushi* (History of Wagering Games) and *Meiji enzetsu-shi* (History of Orators of the Meiji Period).

Miyatsuko. Before 645, title for provincial governors and clan chiefs *(ujizoku)* governing a group of villages *(kuni)*. *See* HATA KABANE, KUNI.
• (King) of the state of Wa (in northern Kyushu?), according to Chinese chronicles, he sent a delegation to the Southern Song Court (Nanchō; *Chin.*: Liu Song) in 462. This king probably corresponds to Emperor Ankō on the traditional list of Japanese sovereigns.

Miyaza. Council of elders representing the heads of families attached to a single Shinto shrine. The council presided over the organization of festivals and local *matsuri*. In the Edo period, *miyaza* were gradually replaced by groups of "parishioners" called *ujiko*.

Miyazaki Giheita. Kabuki actor (active between 1690 and 1730) in Kyoto and Osaka.

Miyazaki Ichisada. Historian, born 1901 in Nagano prefecture, professor of Chinese history at the University of Kyoto and author of many history books, among them *Kakyō* (Examination System, 1946), *Kyūhin kanjin hō no kenkyū: kakyō zenshi* (Studies on Bureaucratic Advancement before the Examination System, 1956), *Rongo no shin kenkyō* (Study on Confucius's Analects, 1974), *Ajiashi ronkō* (Studies on the History of Asia, 1976).

Miyazaki-jingū. Shinto shrine in Miyazaki (Kyushu), dedicated to Jimmu Tennō and his parents, Ugayafukiaezu no Mikoto and Tamayori-hime no Mikoto. According to legend, it was founded during the rule of Emperor Kaiko. Annual festival on October 26.

• **Miyazaki prefecture.** Prefecture in southeast Kyushu, mountainous (Kyushu mountains), bordering on the Hyūga Sea (Pacific Ocean) on the east, which exposes it to catastrophic typhoons. Mainly agricultural, in spite of its poor soil, this prefecture has few industries. *Chief city:* Miyazaki. *Other major cities:* Miyanokojō, Hyūga, Nobeoka, Kobayashi, Saito. *Area:* 7,734 km². *Pop.:* 1,160,000.

Miyazaki Koshoshi. Poet (1864–1922) in the Shintai-shi style.

Miyazaki Tōten. Politician (Myazaki Torazō, 1871–1922), born in Kumamoto prefecture. A firm supporter of the political unity of Asia, he was an informant for China in 1899, then met Sun Yat-sen in Japan, with whom he became friends. Both tried, unsuccessfully, to convince the Japanese government to send help to the Filipino Aguinaldo, head of the independence movement in the Philippines. Returning to China with Sun Yat-sen, Miyazaki Tōten took part in the Huizhou Revolt; when he went back to Japan, he wrote an account of this adventure, *Sanjūsannen no yume* (A Thirty-Year Dream, 1902). He then helped Sun Yat-sen and Huang Xing create the Tongmen Hui. In 1912, he again went to China and took part in the revolution that overthrew the emperor and established a republic.

Miyazaki Yasusada. Agricultural engineer (1623–97), born in the Hiroshima region. He conducted many experiments, which he described in a book on agricultural techniques, *Nōgyō zensho* (Agricultural Encyclopedia, 1696).

Miyazawa Kenji. Writer and poet (1896–1933), born in Iwate prefecture. A pious Buddhist of the Nichiren sect, he devoted himself to relieving the peasants' misery. When he moved to Tokyo, he wrote a large number of tales and stories for children, as well as novels dealing with the peasants' problems: *Haru to shura* (Demons and Springtime, 1922), *Koiwa nōjō* (Koiwa's Farm), *Kaze no Matasaburō* (Matasaburō of the Wind), *Ginga tetsudō no yoru* (Night on the Train), *Chūmon no oi ryōriten* (A Good Restaurant, 1924), and others. The peasants sometimes called him Kenji Bosatsu ("the bodhisattva Kenji").

Miyazawa Kiichi. Politician (b. 1919), minister of finance, foreign affairs, and international trade and industry. In October 1991, he was elected president of the Jiyū Minshutō (Liberal Democratic party, LDP); in early November 1991, he became prime minister, succeeding Kaifū Toshiki. Defeated in the elections of July 1993, he was forced to resign in August of that year and was succeeded by Hosokawa Morihiro, head of a coalition of seven political parties most of which contained LDP dissidents.

Miyazono Senju IV. *Jōruri* singer (1900–85), only surviving performer of the Miyazono style that was popular in the middle of the Edo period. He was named a Living National Treasure.

Miyoshi Jūrō. Poet and playwright (1902–58) in the proletarian style (*see* NAPF). He wrote plays dealing with the lives of ordinary people: *Kikare no senta* (1934), *Bui* (1940), *Honoo no hito* (1951), *Suohito o shirazu,* and others.

Miyoshi Kiyoyuki. Scholar and statesman (847–918) in the Heian period. He was opposed to the views of Sugawara no Michizane and was in part responsible for Sugawara's withdrawal to Dazaifu in 901. He wrote a history of the reigns of emperors Seiwa, Yōzei, and Kōkō, and an essay on administrative techniques (914). He was also an excellent poet, writing in Chinese.

Miyoshi Manabu. Botanist (1861–1939) and ecologist *(seitaigaku),* author of many books on botany and nature-preservation techniques.

Miyoshi Sanninshū. "The Miyoshi Triumvirate." Family of daimyo, generals for Miyoshi Nagayoshi (Miyoshi Chōkei, 1522–64): Miyoshi Nagayuki, Miyoshi Masayasu, and Iwanari Tomomichi, who dominated the Kyoto region from their base in Sakai after 1564. Allied with the daimyo of Yamato province, Matsunaga Hisahide (1510–77), they attacked and killed shogun Ashikaga Yoshiteru in 1565, and installed Ashikaga Yoshihide in his place in 1568. However, they were attacked and defeated by Oda Nobunaga, who installed Ashikaga Yoshiaki. Having revolted and been defeated again, they took refuge in Osaka, where they had supporters at the Hongan-ji. Their hold on the region ended when Iwanari Tomomichi was killed in battle by Oda Nobunaga in 1573.

Miyoshi Shōraku. Playwright (1696–ca. 1772), perhaps a Buddhist monk, known for having written, with Takeda Izumo and Namiki Senryū, the famous Kabuki play *Chūshingura.*

Miyoshi Tameyasu. Poet (1049–1139), author of *Chōya gunsai* and *Shōchū-reki. See* CHŌYA GUNSAI.

Miyoshi Tatsuji. Poet (1900–64), born in Osaka. After studying at the Tokyo Military Academy

(1915–21), he devoted himself to poetry. At first a surrealist, he quickly returned to classicism, studying French authors such as Francis Jammes. In 1928, he and some poet friends founded the magazine *Shi to Shiron* (Poems and Poetics), and he translated works by Beaudelaire. His first collection of free verse, *Sokuryōsen* (The Oceangoing Ship), was published in 1930. He then wrote more books of poetry: *Nansō-shū* (South Window, 1932), *Kanka-shū* (Among the Flowers, 1934), *Sanka-shū* (Mountain Fruit), *Haru no misaki* (The Course of Spring, 1936), *Suna no toride* (The Sand Castle, 1946), *Tōkyō-zakki* (Notes on Tokyo, 1950), *Rakuda no kobu ni matagatte* (Between the Camel's Humps, 1952), *Robō no aki* (Autumn on the Side of the Road, 1958), *Sōjōki* (Writings on Grass, 1963). His style varied greatly, ranging through all aspects of modern poetry, but he preferred free verse in which imagery was very important. He is considered the greatest Japanese twentieth-century poet.

Miyoshi Yasunobu. Warrior (1140–1221), son of Minamoto no Yoritomo's nurse's sister. He supported Yoritomo's cause in 1184 and was appointed *monchūjō* and *jitō* in Bingo province, where he helped Oe no Hiromoto organize the Kamakura *bakufu.*

Miyoshi Yoshifusa. Daimyo of Owari province, who married one of Toyotomi Hideyoshi's sisters.

Miyoshi Yoshitsura. Bureaucrat in the Kamakura *bakufu;* he published the *Jōei-shikimoku* in 1232 on the order of Hōjō Yasutoki.

Mizoguchi Kenji. Movie director (1898–1956), born in Tokyo. At first a painter, he began to direct in 1922. He directed more than 85 films, including *Nihombashi* (1929), *Tōjin Okichi* (Okichi, the Foreigner's Mistress, 1930), *Taki no Shiraito* (The Water Magician, 1933), *Orizuru osen* (Osen's Downfall, 1934, or "The Paper Stork," after Izumi Kyōka's *Kamonanban baishoku*), *Oyuki the Virgin* (1935, adaptation of de Maupassant's *Ball of Fat*), *Gubijinso* (The Poppies, 1935, after a novel by Sōseki Natsume), *Naniwa erejii* (Osaka Elegy, 1936), *Gion no shimei* (Sisters of the Gion, 1936), *Sangiku monogatari* (The Story of the Last Chrysanthemum, 1939). During the Second World War, he was forced to produce nationalist-inspired films, such as *Genroku chūshingura* (The Loyal Forty-Seven Samurai of the Genroku Era, 1941), but he did not reach his full stride until after the war, with *Yoru no onnatachi* (Women of the Night, 1948),

Saikaku ichidai onna (The Life of Oharu, 1952, which won the Silver Lion directorial prize at the Venice Film Festival), *Ugetsu monogatari* (Tales of Rain and the Moon, 1953), *Chikamatsu monogatari* (The Crucified Lovers, 1954), *The Sacrilegious Hero* (1955), *Yōhiki* (Empress Yang Guifei, 1955), *Akasen chitai* (Street of Shame, 1956).

Mizuhara Shūōshi. Haiku poet (Mizuhara Yutaka, 1892–1981), born in Tokyo, Takahama Kyoshi's disciple and member of the Hototogisu group. He founded a poetry magazine with expressionist leanings, *Ashibi*, in 1928. He entered the Nihon Geijutsu-in (Japan Art Academy) in 1966. Among his books of poetry, the best known are *Katsushika* (1930) and *Shūen* (1935).

Mizuhiki. Cord traditionally wrapped around gifts offered as congratulations or in celebration of a particular event. It is generally made of a number of strings placed flat beside each other and glued in the middle. The ends are knotted in three different ways depending on the occasion: simple *(musubikiri),* in a bow *(kaishimusubi),* or double *(awabimusubi).* The first is used for weddings or deaths; the two others, for births, birthdays, or celebrations of success. In all cases, the colors of the cords are significant: gold and silver for weddings, red and white for other occasions, white and gray or yellow for condolence ceremonies. Usually, a *noshi,* a small piece of red-and-white folded paper—holding (in theory) a bit of dried tuna—is added. Nowadays, however, *mizuhiki* and *noshi* are usually printed directly on wrapping paper. *See* KOKOROZUKE, NOSHI.

Mizu-ire. Small vases, in a variety of shapes, used to hold water to moisten China-ink blocks *(suzuri)* to dilute the ink *(sumi)* for calligraphy or painting. These vases, often shaped like animals, are generally made of painted porcelain. Some of them are true works of art. *See* SUZURI-BAKO.

Mizu-kagami. "Mirror of Water." A historical work about the period from the accession of the mythical emperor Jimmu Tennō to the reign of Emperor Nimmyō (ca. 850), written by Nakayama no Tadachika (1131–95).

Mizuki. "Wall of Water," a defensive earthen wall reinforced with a ditch, built about 664 to protect the town of Dazaifu (northern Kyushu) from a possible invasion by the Koreans. It is almost 14 m high and about 1 km long (in two sections).

• Kabuki classical-dance school, founded circa 1700 by the actor and dancer Mizuki Tatsunosuke (1673–1745). *See* IEMOTO.
→ *See* KURISHIMA SUMIKO.

Mizuki Yōko. Screenwriter (Takagi Tomiko), born 1913 in Tokyo. She wrote screenplays for Yasumi Toshio, Kamei Fumio, Imai Tadashi, Naruse Mikio, and other directors, and adapted *Kaidan* (1964) from the novel by Lafcadio Hearn for Kobayashi Masaki. She also wrote scripts for television.

Mizunomi-byakushō. "Water-drinking peasants," name during the Edo period for the poorest landless peasants, whose diet was reduced to the very basics. A number of small-scale farmers, ruined by taxes and forced to sell their land to survive working for others, were also lumped under this sobriquet. *See* HOMBYAKUSHŌ, HYAKUSHŌ.

Mizuno Rentarō. Politician (1868–1949), born in Tokyo. He was minister of the interior in Terauchi Masatake's cabinet (1918), in Katō Tomosaburō's cabinet (1922), and under Kiyoura Keigo (1924). A member of the Rikken Seiyūkai (Friends of Constitutional Government party), he was once again a minister, this time of education, in Tanaka Giichi's cabinet (1927), but he resigned the following year. He retired from public affairs, and from the Rikken Seiyūkai, in 1935.

Mizuno Rochō. Painter (*gō:* Seisenkan, Hanrinsai Chōkōsai, Chōkyūsai, b. 1748), active from 1793 to 1830. He produced mainly book illustrations.

Mizuno Tadakuni. Daimyo (1794–1851) in Hamamatsu (Shizuoka prefecture), born in Edo, son of the daimyo of Karatsu (Saga prefecture, Kyushu), Mizuno Tadamitsu. A follower of Confucianism, he became *jisha-bugyō* and was assigned to Hamamatsu; he was appointed governor *(jōdai)* of the Osaka castle in 1825, then governor of Kyoto (1827), which earned him the title Echizen no Kami. Appointed *rōjū* by the shogunate during the Tempō era, in 1834, he tried to promote reforms to improve the disastrous conditions among the peasantry, but his plans were rejected and he resigned in 1843. Made responsible for the corruption of his subordinates, he was forced to give up his daimyo's position in 1846.

Mizuno Toshikata. Painter and engraver (1866–1908), born in Edo, Tsukioka Yoshitoshi's student, and Yama Ryūtō's student for painting on ceramics.

He made illustrations for newspapers in ukiyo-e prints, executed in *nishiki-e.* He signed many of his engravings, illustrating the Sino-Japanese and Russo-Japanese wars, Oju Toshikata and Toshikata.

Mizusawa. Town in Iwate prefecture, on the Kitakami-gawa river, former military fort founded by Sakanoue no Tamuramaro in 802. The Date family had a castle built there in the early Edo period. An astronomical observatory (Mizusawa Ido Kansokujo) was founded in 1899.

Mizusawa Ken'ichi. Writer (b. 1910), specializing in Japanese folklore.

Mizushima San'ichirō. Chemist (1899–1983) born in Tokyo, famous for his work on molecular structure and the "Raman effect" (1954). He received the Order of Culture (Bunka-shō) in 1961.

Mizutani Yaeko. Stage and screen actress (Matsuno Yaeko, 1905–79), born in Tokyo. She appeared in numerous films and received the Japan Art Academy (Nihon Geijutsu-in) Prize in 1956. She was designated a "Person of Cultural Merit" (Bunka Kōrō-sha) in 1971. Her daughter, Mizutani Yoshie, is also an actress. Yaeko used a pseudonym, Fukumen Reijō (Young Masked Girl) at least once (for the film *Kantsubaki,* "Winter Camellia," produced by Hatanaka Ryōha, in 1921). She was decorated with the medal of honor (red sash).

Mō. Ancient unit of mass equivalent to about 3.75 centigrams:
—10 *mō* = 1 *rin* = 3.75 decigrams
—10 *rin* = 1 *momme* = 3.75 grams
Chin.: Mao. *See* KIN, MOMME, RIN.

Mo. Sort of apron once worn by women of the aristocracy, tied with a double cord called *hiki-koshi.*

Mochizuki. Title of a Noh play: story of vengeance told by the spirits of the victim's wife and son.

Mochizuki Yūko. Movie actress (Suzuki Mieko, 1917–77), born in Tokyo. At first she was a dancer; she was discovered by the Shōchiku production house, which hired her to play in movies by Shibuya Minoru. She also worked under directors Kinoshita Keisuke, Naruse Mikio, and Yamamoto Satsuo, among others. She ran in the 1971 elections and was elected to the Chamber of Councillors thanks

to the vote of women, for whom she embodied the ideal Japanese woman.

Moga. Abridgment of the term *mōdan-gāru* ("modern girl"), describing modern young women in the 1920s and 1930s. Young men were called *mobo* (an abridgment of *mōdan-boy,* "modern boy").

Mogami Tokunai. Geographer (1755–1836), born in Dewa province (Yamagata prefecture). He explored Hokkaido and Sakhalin (Karafutō) and some of the Kuril Islands (Chishima Rettō) in 1785 and 1786, and then continued his explorations, emphasizing in his reports to the shogunate the need to defend the islands. He learned Ainu and Russian so that he could better study Hokkaido and Sakhalin, which he described in a book called *Ezo-zōshi.*

Mogusa. Japanese for *moxa,* small quantities of medicinal herbs placed on certain parts of the body and burned in order to provoke physiological reactions, procedure used in ancient times in China to complement acupuncture. Modern medicine sometimes replaces *mogusa* with electrical "points of fire" or vibrating apparatuses. *Chin.:* Jiu.

Mokkan. Roughly oblong wooden tablets used to write on in the seventh and eighth centuries. They were written on in ink on both sides. In 1961, a large number of *mokkan* was discovered during excavations on the site of the Heijō-kyō (Nara) imperial palace; in 1980, more than 36,000 were uncovered at some 40 other sites, mostly former capitals; in 1985, about 100 dating from the late seventh century were found in the former capital Asuka. *Mokkan* were used for various purposes, including recording taxes received and providing instructions to the people about certain edicts. It is thought that they were also used for the oldest Japanese chronicles, the *Kojiki* and *Nihon shoki. See* HEIJŌ-KYŌ.

Mokkei. Japanese name for a Chinese painter (Muqi, ca. 1215–ca. 1270), born in Sichuan province, who was a Chan monk living at the Liutong-si monastery near Hangzhou. A disciple of Wuzhun (d. 1249), he painted mainly animals (monkeys), flowers, and vegetation, in a plain, unembellished style that was often emulated in Japan, where most of his works in ink *(sumi-e)* are now kept.

Mokkotsu. Landscape-painting technique in which flowers and leaves are indicated simply by dots of ink or color without outlines. A modern technique derived from *mokkotsu* is called *mōrōtai.*

Mōko. Japanese term for Mongolians.

• *Mōko-shūrai ekotoba.* An *emakimono* in two scrolls describing the two attempts by the Mongolians to invade Japan in 1274 and 1281, and their defeat by samurai and storm *(kamikaze)*. These scrolls were painted about 1293 on order of a Kyushu samurai, Takezaki Suenaga, to commemorate his exploits in these wars. They are kept in the imperial collection in Tokyo.

Mokoshi. In traditional architecture, an extra roof surrounding the upper floor of a building; its joists are supported by extra pillars, generally linked to the main pillars by beams called *ebi-kōryō*. In some old structures, such as the pagoda of the Yakushi-ji, they are intermediary roofs. *See* KARA-YŌ.

Mokuan Rei'en. Buddhist monk and painter (Zeichi Rei'en, active from 1323 to ca. 1345), one of the first creators of *suiboku* in the Muromachi school, having studied this technique during a ten-year stay in China starting in 1326. His painting greatly resembles Mokkei's. While he was in China, the famous Chinese calligraphers Yue-jiang Zhengyin, Liao-an Qingyu, and Chushi Fanqi *(Jap.: Soseki Bonki)* made inscriptions on his paintings. He probably died in China just before he was to return to Japan.

Mokuan Shōtō. Zen Buddhist monk (Mu-an, 1611–84) who was abbot of the Mampuku-ji temple in Kyoto, succeeding in 1664 the Chinese monk Yin Yuan *(Jap.:* Ryūki, 1592–1673), founder of the Ōbaku-shū sect and the Mampuku-ji in 1659–61. *See* MAMPUKU-JI, ŌBAKU-SHŪ.

Mokudai. Title of a bureaucrat responsible for residing in a province to replace its governor *(kokushi)* who was residing at the Heian-kyō court. Also sometimes called *rusu-shoku, daikan. See* YŌNIN.

Mokuga. Technique of inlaying various materials (shells, mother-of-pearl, metal) in an object or a wooden sculpture.

Mokugyo. Wooden gong in the shape of a fish rolled upon itself or another round object, generally lacquered in red, used by Buddhist monks to punctuate their readings of sacred texts *(sūtra, kyō)*. *Chin.: muyü.*
→ *See* ASAI CHŪ.

Mokujiki. "Wood eater," term for an ascetic discipline practiced by some Buddhist monks consisting of eating only uncooked vegetables and fruit. Many monks who practiced *mokujiki* (of Chinese Taoist origin) used this word as a family name.

• **Mokujiki Myōman (Gogyō).** Buddhist monk (1718–1810) of the Shingon sect. A sculptor, he created more than a thousand Buddhist images that he gave to the temples he visited on his wanderings. His works are crude and lack detail but have a certain rustic charm.

• **Mokujiki Ōgo.** *See* ŌGO.

Mokukenren. Japanese name for one of the ten major disciples of Buddha, Mahāmaudgalyāna. Also called Mokuren. *See* JŪ DAI DESHI.

Mokushin kanshitsu. Sculpture technique of applying dry lacquer to a core of rough-hewn wood, which remains in place once the sculpture is finished. *See* KANSHITSU.

Momijigari. "Maple Hunt," a traditional autumn festival celebrated since the Heian period; it had become popular among commoners by the Edo period. It consists of making excursions to places known for the beautiful red foliage of the maples *(momiji)*, such as the Arashiyama hill near Kyoto. This custom is still followed by most Japanese and many tourists. *See also* HANAMI.

• *Momijigari.* Title of a Noh play: the warrior Koremochi is captivated by a woman's song and falls asleep. In his dream, a *kami* appears to him, tells him that the singer is in fact a demon, and gives him a sword. When he awakes, he kills the singer.
• Kabuki play, adapted from Noh theater in 1887 by Kawatake Mokuami.

Momme. Former unit of mass, equivalent to about 3.75 g, and a term often used for a small copper coin of this weight. *See* MŌ.

Mommu Tennō. Forty-second emperor (Prince Karu no Ōji, Ama no Mamunetoyo-ihoji, 683 <697–707>), son of Prince Kusakabe (Emperor Temmu's oldest son) and successor to his grandmother, Jitō. He married Fujiwara no Kyūshi, Fujiwara no Fuhito's daughter. He established his capital at Fujiwara in 691 and had the Taihō Code promulgated in 702. His mother, Gemmei Tennō, succeeded him in 707.

Momoshiki. One of the former names for the imperial palace in Kyoto. *See* DAIRI, MIYA.

Momotarō. "Peach Boy," a character in a very popular folk tale in which a child is born in a peach and found by a woman doing her laundry on the riverbank. Endowed with Herculean strength, he performs incredible feats. He forms a friendship with a cock, a dog, and a monkey, and they go to conquer the "island of ogres" (Onigashima) and chase away the demons. This tale was popularized during the Edo period by works in the *kusa-zōshi* genre and is still told to children in many forms. Also called simply Tarō. *See* MEGIJIMA, URIKOHIME.

Momoyama-jidai. "Momoyama era," a historical and artistic period from 1568 or 1573 to 1615, during which Japan was controlled by military dictators (Oda Nobunaga, Toyotomi Hideyoshi, and Tokugawa Ieyasu) who fought the feudal lords in order to unite Japan. The name is from a hill in Fushimi, near Tokyo, where Toyotomi Hideyoshi had a magnificent castle built. Some historians contend that this period ended in 1603, when Tokugawa Ieyasu established his *bakufu* in Edo. Also called Azuchi-Momoyama.

Momozono Tennō. Hundred and sixteenth emperor (Prince Tohito, 1741<1746–62>), successor to Sakuramachi Tennō. Empress Go-Sakuramachi succeeded him.

Mon. Family insignia used by samurai from the Kamakura period on, so that they could recognize each other more easily on the battlefield. Later, all families adopted their own *mon,* usually a stylized design (object, animal, plant, characters) within a circle (or sometimes another geometric figure). In the Edo period, daimyo had the right to have two different *mon,* while simple samurai had the right to only one. Commoners did not have *mon.* After 1868, use of these distinctive emblems spread among commoners, and towns and administrative and other bodies also adopted them. The imperial *mon,* called *kikumon,* is a golden chrysanthemum *(kiku)* with 15 petals. Today, ceremonial clothing for both men and women bears the family *mon* in five places: on the lapels, in the middle of the back, and on the sleeves.
• Copper coin issued by the Tokugawa during the Edo period (*see* SANKA) whose diameter was commonly used for measurements, especially for the body and for shoes. A coin worth several *mon* was commonly called *sen.* A thousand *mon* were

equivalent to a *kammon,* and four *kammon* to one gold *ryō.*

Mon. "The Door." A famous novel (1910) by Natsume Sōseki describing the psychology of a couple through their daily actions.

Monchūjo. High court of justice during the Kamakura and Muromachi periods, created in 1184 by Minamoto no Yoritomo, intended to arbitrate quarrels between vassals *(gokenin, kenin)* of the shogun. The Monchūjo was somewhat supplanted after 1249 by another judicial body called Hikitsuke, and it became responsible only for business transactions and litigation. In the late Muromachi period, most of its prerogatives were ceded to the Kyoto Mandokoro, and it was occupied with affairs concerning the archives.

Mondo. Bureaucrat in charge of water supply for the court and Shinto shrines. During the Edo period, this position fell to engineers responsible for irrigation works and river management.
• Sculptor (Tanaka Mondo, 1857–1917) of Buddhist images and netsuke in Osaka.

Mondō. In monasteries of Zen sects, dialogue, sometimes seemingly illogical, undertaken between a master and his disciple to bring the latter to enlightenment and a true understanding of the intimate nature of things and of Divinity. *See* KŌAN.
→ *See* NOH.

Mon

Mondo no Sho Masakiyo. Famous maker of sword blades (1670–1730) from Satsuma province.

Mongaku Shōnin. Buddhist monk (Endō Moritō, ca. 1120–ca. 1200) and warrior serving Jōsai Mon'in, one of Emperor Toba's daughters. He inadvertently killed Minamoto no Kesa (Kesa Gozen), one of Minamoto no Wataru's daughters, mistaking her for his lover. In remorse, he renounced the world and became a hermit at the Jingo-ji temple on Mt. Takao, near Kyoto. Having unsuccessfully requested funds from Emperor Go-Shirakawa to repair the temple, he was exiled to Izu province, where he became a friend of the young Minamoto no Yoritomo, who had been in exile since 1160. He took Yoritomo's side, but he was implicated in a plot hatched by Minamoto no Michichika and was further exiled to the island of Sado, then to Kyushu, where he died at the age of 80. His story has been the subject of many legends, Kabuki plays, and novels, such as Akutagawa Ryūnosuke's *Kesa to moritō,* which was adapted for the screen as *Jigokumon* (The Gates of Hell) in 1953. The tragic story of Mongaku and Kesa Gozen was told in the *Taiheiki.*

Monjō Hakase. During the Nara and Heian periods, title for scholars who studied Chinese society and literature.

Monju Bosatsu. Japanese name for Bodhisattva Mañjushrī, symbolizing youth, beauty, and intelligence, considered the founder of Tibet and Manchuria (whence his name). *Chin.:* Wenshu.

Monkan. Buddhist monk (Kōshin, 1287–1357), sixty-fourth head of the Daigo-ji temple in Kyoto. A famous warrior, he fought the Hōjō *shikken,* then Ashikaga Takauji. Defeated in battle by Takauji, he was exiled to Iwo Jima, in the Ryukyu Islands, then to Kai province, where he died.

Monnō. Buddhist monk and philologist (1700–63), born in Tamba province, author of important studies on the phonetics of Chinese characters *(kanji): Makō inkyō* (1744), *San'on seika* (1752), *Waji taikan-shō* (1754). He was also an astronomer.

Monogatari. "Tale," a term for many novels and romances, epic songs, and various accounts in the form of long texts. Prose literature written in Japan from about the ninth to the fifteenth century was called *monogatari-bungaku;* it was differentiated by its novelistic or narrative content from *waka-bungaku* (poetry), *zuihitsu-bungaku* (essays), and *nikki-bungaku* (travel accounts). There are several types of *monogatari: uta-monogatari* (stories drawn from poems), *tsukuri-monogatari* (aristocratic romances), *rekisihi-monogatari* (historical novels), *gunki-monogatari* (epic novels), and *setsuwa* (collections of various anecdotes).

Monogurui. In Noh theater, type of play in which a character goes mad following the loss of a loved one.

Mono-ha. Modern-art group of esoteric leanings, whose members explore relations between objects and nature. Among the most typical artists of this movement, which exhibited at the Anvers Biennial in 1989, were sculptors Yayoi Kusama (who worked with Andy Warhol in New York), Nobuo Sekine, and Tomio Miki (?–1979).

Mono-imi. "Things to avoid," taboos that arise from the theories of the Ommyōdō, and that can be gotten around by practicing *kata-tagae. See* IMI.

Monomane. "Imitation of things," concept used in Noh theater to portray objects and actions, in conjunction with the concept of *yūgen.*

Mono no aware. "Emotional sense of things," an expression used to describe a feeling that gives rise to an emotional impulse, frequently used in the arts and literature since the Heian period. This fleeting, diffuse feeling, which may be shared by several people at once, involves a certain melancholy or unexpressed regret, related to the Buddhist sentiment of the impermanence of all things *(mujō).* Admiring cherry blossoms *(hanami)* may be considered *mono no aware,* as may contemplation of the red leaves of maples *(momijigari);* observing falling leaves or snow, a misty day, or fine rain; or seeing a ship leaving or a loved one disappear around a bend in a road. *Mono no aware* was used skillfully in the *Genji monogatari,* by Murasaki Shikibu, and has been imitated many times thereafter; previously, poets had rarely alluded to it.

Mononobe. Before the sixth century, a title for guards of the imperial palace and certain warriors who founded a noble family, generally strongly opposed to the introduction of Buddhism to Japan, and as a consequence enemies of the Soga family. The best-known members of this powerful family line were Mononobe no Me, Mononobe no Okoshi, Mononobe no Arakabi (d. 535), and Mononobe no Moriya.

Mononobe no Moriya. Son (?–587) of the senior bureaucrat Mononobe no Okoshi, appointed *ōmuraji* by emperors Bidatsu and Yōmei. He strongly opposed the Soga family, which wanted to introduce Buddhism to the court; set fire to the first temples; and threw into the Naniwa canal the first images of Buddha imported from Korea. He and his entire family were killed by Soga no Umako.

Mono no fu. In both literature and art, a war-like sense of virility and strength. It is often used in conjunction with *mono no aware* and *mono no ke*.
• Before the eighth century, a term often used to designate warriors. *See* BUSHI, BUSHIDŌ.

Mono no ke. The way in which objects, beings, and wandering spirits that "possess" an individual and cause disease or death appear to a poet or painter. According to this concept, a person's spirit may momentarily separate itself from its physical being during a moment of intense emotion. When it is consumed with jealousy, anger, or vengeance, this spirit can take possession of another person. *See also* MUSHI.

Monsu. Title for imperial princes named abbots of Buddhist monasteries.

Montblanc, Charles, Comte des Cantons de. Belgian count (1832–93) who went to Japan in 1861–62 and offered his services to the shogunate but was turned down. He made friends with some students from Satsuma province in London and became an agent for Satsuma, arranging its participation in the Paris World's Fair of 1867. The following year, he accompanied Satsuma representatives to Kyoto and was appointed Japan's consul general to Paris for the first government of the Meiji era, a position he held until an ambassador was officially appointed in 1870.

Monto. Buddhist disciple. This title was used specifically by lay members of the Jōdo Shin-shū sect, also called Monto-shū.

Montoku Tennō. Fifty-fifth emperor (Prince Michiyasu, 827<851–58>), successor to Nimmyō Tennō. Emperor Seiwa succeeded him.

• *Montoku jitsuroku.* "History of the Reign of Montoku Tennō," the fifth of the *Rikkokushi* (Six National Histories), compiled in 10 volumes by Fujiwara no Mototsune, Sugawara no Koreyoshi,

Miyako Yoshika, Shimada Yoshiomi, and several other historians in 879.

Monzeki. Title for imperial princes (*shinnō*) who became Buddhist monks (*hō-shinnō*). By extension, the term for the temples to which they retired. Also, the title for some other Buddhist temples during the Muromachi period.

Monzen-machi. Towns that developed around Buddhist temples or Shinto shrines and along roads leading to them, at first lined with shops selling religious objects. Especially from the thirteenth to the sixteenth century, major pilgrimages required the establishment, near religious centers, of inns and all the conveniences needed by pilgrims, which were supplied by these towns. *See also* JŌKA-MACHI.

Moraes, Wenceslau de. Portuguese navy officer and writer (1854–1929). He arrived in Japan in 1889 and liked the country, so in 1898 he resigned from the navy and entered the diplomatic service so that he could live there. He was appointed vice-consul from Portugal to Osaka and married a Japanese woman, Fukumoto Yone. When she died in 1912, he retired, moved to Tokushima (Shikoku), and wrote his memoirs in Japanese, *Teihon Moraesu zenshū*, published in 1969.

Morgan, Yuki. Geisha (Katō Yuki, 1881–1963) from Kyoto. She married American financier J. P. Morgan's nephew, G. D. Morgan, in 1904, and moved to France with him. Her husband died in 1915, but she stayed in France until 1938, when she returned to Japan. She converted to Catholicism in 1953. Her life has been the subject of a number of novels and a musical in Japan.

Mōri. Family of daimyo who managed the estates in the western part of Honshu from the twelfth to the nineteenth century, and took part in many battles during the Muromachi period. In the Edo period, they were considered *tozamada-daimyō*. The best known are:
—Mōri Motonari (1497–1571). *See this name.*
—Mōri Terumoto (1553–1625). He was one of Toyotomi Hideyoshi's *go-tairō*.
—Mōri Takamasa (1556–1628).
—Mōri Hidekane (1566–1601).
—Mōri Hidemoto (1579–1650).
—Mōri Motokiyo (late sixteenth century).
—Mōri Katsunobu (d. 1601).
—Mōri Hidenari (1595–1651).
—Mōri Motonori (1839–96).

Mōri Terumoto, defeated in the Battle of Seki-gahara in 1600, saw his holdings reduced to Suō and Nagano provinces (Chōshū). The Mōri did, however, keep their castle in Hagi until 1863, when they moved to Yamaguchi. The last of the Mōri, Yoshichika, made his estate the center of the anti-shogunal movement in 1867 and 1868. *See* CHŌ-SHŪ-HAN.

Mori Arimasa. Writer and philosopher (1911–76), born in Tokyo, professor of Japanese language and literature at the Sorbonne and the Institute of Eastern Languages in Paris starting in 1950. He wrote a number of works in which he developed a sort of personal philosophy based on experience *(keiken)* and translated a number of Japanese books into French. He died in Paris. Among his works: *Pasu-karu no hōhō* (Pascal's Path, 1938), *Babiron no nagare no hatori nite* (On the Shores of the River of Babylon, 1957), *Jōmon no kawara nite* (On Gates in Walls, 1963), *Harukana Nōtoru-Damu* (In the Distance, Notre Dame, 1967), *Sabaku ni mukatte* (Toward the Desert, 1969), *Kigi wa hikari wo abite* (Trees Bathed in Light, 1973), *Paridaiyori* (Letters from Paris, 1974), *Shisaku no keiken wo megutte* (On Thought and Experience, 1976), *Tsuchi no utsuwa ni* (In an Earthen Vase, 1976), *Ikani ikuru ka* (How to Live? 1976), *Uchimura Kanzō* (1976). He was Mori Arinori's grandson.

Mori Arinori. Politician and diplomat (1847–89), born on the Satsuma estate. In 1873, after spending several years in the United States and serving as the first plenipotentiary envoy to Washington in 1871, he founded a study group on English society called the Group of Six. He was ambassador to Beijing from 1876 to 1877, then to London in 1879. As minister of education in 1886 in Itō Hirobumi's first cabinet, he made numerous educational reforms. He was, notably, the founder of the first business college, Shōhō Kōshūjo (now Hitotsubashi University), in 1875. During his term as minister of education (1886–89), he reorganized education in the schools, regimenting students as if they were in military service, and raised the University of Tokyo to the rank of imperial university. He was nicknamed the "father of modern education." He was assassinated on February 11, 1889 by a fanatical Shinto priest who blamed him for having removed the veil hiding the holy of holies in a shrine. He was Mori Arimasa's grandfather.

Mori Atsushi. Writer (1912–89), Yokomitsu Rii-chi's disciple. With Dasai Osamu and Dan Kazuo,

he started the literary magazine *Aoi Hana* (Blue Flower); he published his first novel, *Yoidore bune* (The Drunken Boat), in the *Mainichi Shimbun* in 1933. He led an itinerant life, sometimes working as a construction worker to earn a living. After abandoning literature for 40 years, he published *Gassan* (Mount Gassan) in 1973, which won the Akutagawa Prize; in 1967, he received the Noma Prize for his novel *Ware yuku mono no gotoshi* (I Am Like a Dying Man).

Mōri Genju. Painter and naturalist (Mōri Moto-hisa, Bai'en, Shashinsai, Shaseisai, 1815–81), specializing in portrayals of birds, insects, fish, and shells.

Mori Hanae. Fashion designer, born 1926 in Shimane prefecture. Her haute couture designs were presented in Paris and New York, where she opened boutiques. She also designed uniforms for China.

Morihasa. Title of a Noh play: in prison in Kamakura, Taira no Morihisa passes the time before his execution reading Buddhist sutras. He falls asleep, and in his dream he sees the executioner blinded by the light emanating from the sutra scrolls. When he awakes, Minamoto no Yoritomo pardons him, and the two drink *sake* and dance together.

Mori Iwao. Movie producer (1899–1979) for the Tōhō company starting in 1937. He produced many movies directed by Kurosawa Akira, Yamamoto Kajirō, and other directors.

Morikage Kyoroku. Haiku poet (Morikawa Kyoroku, 1656–1715) and Bashō's main disciple. A samurai from Ōmi province, he was also a painter (in the style of the Kanō school). He explicated Bashō's poems in a number of works, such as *Hentsuki,* a poetry anthology published in 1698; *Uda no hōshi,* a philosophical work on Bashō's poems; *Haikai mondō,* a debate on poetics with Mukai Kyorai. He also compiled the *Fūzoku monzen* (Honchō monzen, 1706), an anthology of prose written by Bashō's disciples.

Mori Kansai. Painter (1814–94), born in Hagi (Yamaguchi prefecture), son of a Chōshū warrior of the Mōri family. He was adopted by Mōri Tetsuzan (1775–1841), whose daughter he married. He worked in the tradition of the Maruyama-Shijō school and was appointed an Artist of the Imperial Household (Teishitsu Gigei-in) in 1890. He taught art at the prefectural school of painting in Kyoto

(Kyōto-fu Gagakkō) starting in 1880, then opened his own school. His main students were Yamamoto Shunkyo (1871–1933) and Nomura Bunkyo (1854–1911).

Morikuni Shinnō. Imperial prince (1301<1308–33>), appointed shogun of Kamakura, son of and successor to Hisaakira. Morinaga succeeded him.

Mori Masayuki. Actor (Arishima Ikumitsu, 1911–73), Arishima Takeo's son, born in Tokyo. He performed first at the Gekidan theater, where he was very popular. His screen debut was in *Haha no chizu* (The Mother's Map, 1942), directed by Shimazu Yasujirō; he then appeared in films directed by, among others, Kurosawa Akira (*Rashōmon,* 1950, *Hakuchi,* 1951), Naruse Mikio (*Ukigumo,* 1955), and Mizoguchi.

Morimoto Kaoru. Playwright (1912–46), born in Osaka. Many of his plays were produced at Kishida Kunio's Bungakuza theater, including *Hanabanashiki ichizoku* (1935), *Taikutsu na jikan* (1937), *Tomishima matsugorō den* (1942, adapted for the screen as *Muhōmatsu no isshō,* The Rickshaw Puller, in 1958), and *Onna no Isshō* (A Woman's Life, 1945). He also translated Western plays.

Mōri Motonari. Daimyo (1497–1571) from western Honshu. During the Sengoku period, he allied himself with the Amako and Ōuchi families in order to acquire large estates in Aki and Bingo provinces. In 1540, he turned against the Amako and defeated them, appropriating their lands. He then attacked the assassin of his ally Ōuchi Yoshitaka, defeating him in 1555 in Utsukushima, and occupied the lands of the Ōuchi. Finally, he attacked the Ōtomo family on Kyushu, thus becoming the master of a huge estate comprising Aki, Bingo, Suō, Nagato, Bitchū, Inaba, Hōki, Izumo, Oki, and Iwami provinces, which enabled him to oppose Oda Nobunaga. Two of his sons (Kobayakawa Takakage, 1533–97, and Kikkawa Motoharu, 1530–86) were adopted by other daimyo, which increased his power even more. He was also a talented poet. *See* MŌRI.

Morimoto Rokuji. Archeologist (1903–36). In 1929, he founded the Tokyo Archeological Society (Tōkyō Kōko Gakkai) and its journal, *Kōkogaku.* He went to France in 1931–32 and studied the agricultural techniques of the Yayoi and *kofun* periods.

Morinaga Seika. Large sugar manufacturer established in 1899 in Tokyo, known mainly for its candies and various products (jams, soft drinks), with a worldwide distribution network for its products. It is affiliated with the American Sunkist Company. Head office in Tokyo.

• **Morinaga Nyūgyō.** Dairy company founded by Morinaga Seika in 1921; it became independent in 1949. It produces mainly powdered milk, cheese, and yogurt. In 1955, improper inspection of the products used in making the powdered milk led to the death of more than 130 children and serious illness among more than 12,000 others. Lengthy trials followed, which ended only in 1973 with the indemnization of the victims and their families.

Morinaga Shinnō. Imperial prince (Moriyoshi, Daitō no Miya, Otō no Miya, 1308<1355>), Emperor Go-Daigo's oldest son. He became a Buddhist monk and was appointed head *(zasu)* of the Tendai sect on Mount Hiei in 1327, with the name Son'un. In 1331, he fought alongside his father against the Kamakura shogunate; in 1333, during the Kemmu Restoration, he was made shogun, replacing Morikuni. But Ashikaga Takauji defeated Go-Daigo, and Morinaga was imprisoned in Kamakura and killed by Ashikaga Tadayoshi, his guardian.

Morino Taimei. Ceramist, born 1934 in Kyoto, whose porcelain gained an international reputation. His works were in the exhibition in the Mitsukoshi space in Paris in 1994.

Mori Ōgai. Writer (Mori Rintarō, 1862–1922), born in Iwami province (Shimane prefecture) into a family of physicians serving the daimyo of Tsuwano. He studied medicine and Confucianism, as well as German and Dutch. He then took medical courses with German professors at the University of Tokyo after 1877. Later, he studied Chinese literature with Yoda Gakkai (1833–1909) and Satō Genchō (1818–97). A medical officer in the army, he was sent to Germany from 1884 to 1888, where he studied in Leipzig, Dresden, Munich, and Berlin. While continuing the research on nutrition that he had begun in Germany, he launched a literary career and founded a magazine for diffusion of modern literature, *Shigarami Sōshi* (Magazine of the Dam), resolutely anti-realist, in line with his feeling that literature belonged to the areas of the spirit and emotions serving an ideal. He wrote a number of stories, including *Maihime* (The Dancer, 1890), *Utakata no ki* (The Mirage, 1890), and *Fumizukai* (The Mailman, 1891), in which he denounced Wagner's work and supported Goethe's. He married

Akamatsu Toshiko, Vice-Admiral Akamatsu Nori-yoshi's (1841–1920) daughter, in 1889, but divorced the following year. Fifteen years later, he married Araki Shigeko and moved to Sendagi, a Tokyo suburb. In 1894, he was sent to Manchuria; the following year, to Taiwan. He was appointed head of the army's medical service in Kokura (Kyushu), then head surgeon of the armed forces in 1897, a position he held until he retired in 1916. Meanwhile, his literary career continued, with *Sokkyo shijin* (a translation of Hans Christian Andersen's *Improvisations*) and a journal about his stay in Germany, *Doitsu nikki* (1884–88). In 1909, Mori Ōgai began to devote himself fully to literature, publishing stories and novels: *Wita sekusuarisu* (Vita Sexualis, 1909), *Seinen* (The Young Man, 1910), *Asobi* (Games, 1910), *Gan* (The Wild Goose, 1911), *Kaijin* (Ruins, 1912 [unfinished]), *Ka no yoni* (As if . . . , 1912), *Chimmoku no tō* (The Towers of Silence, 1913), *Sakai jiken* (The Sakai Incident, 1914), *Sanshō dayū* (Intendant Sanshō, 1915), *Takase bune* (The Boat on the Takase, 1916), *Izawa ranken* (a biography of Shibue Chūsai, an early-nineteenth-century physician, 1916). He also wrote some plays: *Urashima, Nichiren, Ikutagawa, Purumūra* (1909), *Abe ichizoku* (1912), *Okitsu Yagoemon no isho* (Okitsu Yagoemon's Will, 1912). Some of his works were adapted for the screen, including *Abe ichizoku* (by Kumagai Hisatora in 1938), *Gan* (by Toyoda Shirō in 1953), *Ikehiro kazuo* (by Toyoda Shirō in 1966), *Sanshō dayū* (by Mizoguchi Kenji, 1954).

Morioka. City in Iwate prefecture, about 180 km north of Sendai, on the Kitakami-gawa river. Formerly a castle town *(jōka-machi)* in the Nambu estate, it has been known since the fourteenth century for its artisans who make iron kettles *(kama)*. Ruins of the castle dating from 1599. The Chagu-chagu Umakko, a festival of caparisoned horses, takes place there every June. Pop.: 230,000.

Mori Rammaru. Page *(koshō)* for Oda Nobunaga (Naritoshi, ca. 1565–82), son of Mori Yoshinari (1523–70) and brother of Mori Katsuzō (1558–84), both of whom were Oda Nobunaga's generals. As Nobunaga's secretary, he died with him, as did his two young brothers, Mori Bōmaru and Mori Rikimaru, when Akechi Mitsuhide attacked Nobunaga (*see* HONNŌ-JI JIKEN).

Morisada Shinnō. Imperial prince (1179–1223), Takakura Tennō's son. Also called Dajō-ō-ō, Ga-Takakura-In, Jimyō-in.

Morishige Hisaya. Actor, born 1913 in Osaka. He worked in various theaters and made his movie debut in 1950 in Namiki Kyōratō's *Koshinuke nitōryū* (The Chicken Swordsman) in a comic role. He then acted in many films and television series. Also a singer, he is most popular among people of his own generation, who appreciate his *morishige-bushi* style.

Morishita Yōko. Dancer, born 1948 in Hiroshima, who won a gold medal at the international competition in Varna, Bulgaria, in 1974, and became internationally known. She danced with Rudolf Nureyev in London in 1985 and received the Laurence Olivier Prize that year. She is only 1.5 m tall. Her husband, Shimizu Tetsutarō (b. 1948), is also a ballet dancer.

Mori Sosen. Painter (Mori Shushō, 1747–1821), born in Osaka. He became famous for his paintings of monkeys in the style of the Kanō school. Influenced by the painters of the Maruyama school, he also had a talent for painting various animals, including deer, although his other paintings (figures, landscapes) are less elaborate. He began a family line of artists that continued with his brothers Mori Yōshin (1730–1822) and Mori Shūhō (1738–1823) and ended with Mori Kansai (*see* MORI KANSAI).

Morita Akio. Businessman, born 1921 in Nagoya to a family of *sake* brewers. An electronics engineer, he founded, with Ibuka Masaru, the Tokyo Telecom Engineering Company in 1946, which became Sony Corporation in 1958. He became president of Sony in 1976. He registered Sony on the New York Stock Exchange, helping internationalize the firm. *See* SONY.

Morita Kan'ya. Family of Kabuki actors founded by Morita Kan'ya I (?–1679), actor and *zamoto* at the Morita-za, one of the three major Kabuki theaters in Edo. The most famous actors in this family are:
—Morita Kan'ya I (?–1679).
—Morita Kan'ya II (1676–1734).
—Morita Kan'ya III (?–1722).
—Morita Kan'ya IV (?–1743).
—Morita Kan'ya VI (1724–80), *tachiyaku* roles.
—Morita Kan'ya VIII (1759–1814), *onnagata* roles.
—Morita Kan'ya IX (1800–1863), *tachiyaku* roles.
—Morita Kan'ya XII (Furukawa Shinsui, 1846–97), who developed Kabuki to attract an international audience, and wrote a number of plays.

—Morita Kan'ya XIII (1885–1932), *wagoto* roles.
—Morita Kan'ya XIV (1907–75).

Morita ryōhō. Psychotherapy method developed by the physician Morita Masatake (Morita Shōma, 1874–1938), intended to treat a type of nervousness. Called *shinkeishitsu,* it was taught mainly at the Jikkei University of Medicine in Tokyo.

Morita Sōhei. Writer (Morita Yonematsu, 1881–1949), born in Gifu prefecture. A disciple of Natsume Sōseki, he became known for his novel *Baien* (Smoke), which appeared in serial form in the *Asahi Shimbun* in 1909. He tried to commit double suicide *(junshi)* with his mistress, Hiratsuka Raichō (Haruko), which caused a scandal, but he did not succeed, and later he became a professor at Hōsei University. He then devoted himself to translation of foreign novels, mostly Russian (Gogol, Dostoyevsky); after the Second World War, he joined the Community party. His best-known works are the novels *Rinne* (Reincarnation, 1925) and *Hosokawa Garashiya* (Life of Hosokawa Gracia, 1950), and a two-volume biography of Natsume Sōseki.

Morita Tsunetomo. Painter (1881–1933) in the Western style; he studied with Koyama Shōtarō and Nakamura Fusetsu.

Morita Yoshimitsu. Contemporary movie director, who made successful films such as *Kitchen* (1989), adapted from a novel by Yoshimoto Banana.

Mori Tōgaku. Ceramist, born 1937 in Bizen (Okayama prefecture). His works won a number of awards in Japan. He also exhibited in Paris (Mitsukoshi space) in 1994.

Morito Tatsuo. Politician and economist (1888–1984), assistant professor at the University of Tokyo. In 1920, he was fired after he published an article on Kropotkin's thought; he was also sued, as was Ōuichi Hyōe, the publisher of the periodical that had published the article, and was sentenced to three months in prison. This trial, which was in fact about freedom of thought and expression, marked the beginning of increasingly severe government control over thinkers suspected of sympathies with the Left. After the Second World War, as minister of education in the cabinets of Katayama Tetsu and Ashida Hitoshi, from May 1947 to October 1948, Morito Tatsuo undertook numerous educational reforms. He was then president of the University of Hiroshima and chairman of the Central Education Council.

Moriyama Takichirō. Interpreter from the Dutch (1820–71) in Nagasaki. He studied English with an expatriate American, Ranald MacDonald, and was Admiral Putianin's interpreter in Nagasaki in 1853, and Commodore Matthew Perry's in 1854. He accompanied Takenouchi Yasunori's shogunal mission to Europe in 1862, then retired in 1868 to open a school for interpreters in Tokyo.

Morohashi Tetsuji. Sinologist and lexicographer (1883–1982), born in Niigata prefecture. In addition to writing a number of works on Confucian philosophy during the Song dynasty, the Chinese classics, and the family system in China, he compiled one of the largest dictionaries in the world, the *Dai kanwa jiten* (Big Dictionary of Sino-Japanese Characters, 1955–60), with 15,416 pages and 50,294 entries. Although most of his notes were destroyed in a bombardment in February 1945, he managed to finish his major work (13 volumes). After his death, it was revised and supplemented by his students Komata Tadashi and Yoneyama Toratarō, who published the completed work in 1986 (with the Taishūkan Shoten publishing house in Tokyo), as well as his collected works, *Morohashi Tetsuji zenshū* (10 volumes).

Moroi Makoto. Musician and composer of twelve-tone music (b. 1930) who studied with his father, Moroi Saburō. He taught at the Tōhō Gakuen Daigaku (Tōhō Gakuen School of Music) in Tokyo.

• **Moroi Saburō.** Musician and composer, born 1903 in Tokyo. He studied music in Tokyo and Berlin (1932–34) and wrote a large number of symphonies and concerti. Moroi Makoto's father.

Moronobu. Painter (Hishikawa Moronobu; *mei:* Kichibei; *gō:* Yūchiku, ca. 1618–94) of ukiyo-e prints, born in Chiba prefecture, son of a brocade weaver, Hishikawa Kichizaemon. He produced the first *sumizuri-e* prints (in black) and illustrated many works using this genre, including *Buke hyakunin hisshu* (Simple Poems by One Hundred Warriors) in 1672. He became the most popular print maker in Edo, illustrating more than 150 novels and various books. His two sons, Morofusa and Moronaga, perpetuated his style. Among his best-known disciples are Torii Kiyonobu, Okumura Masanobu, and the painters of the Kaigetsudō school. He founded the Hishikawa school.

Moroshige. Painter (Furuyama Moroshige; *mei:* Tarobei, active ca. 1700) of ukiyo-e prints, Moronobu's student in Edo.

Morrison. American merchant ship that approached Japan in 1837 to return seven shipwrecked Japanese sailors. It was driven away by cannon shot in Uraga Bay, then in Kagoshima Bay, in conformity with the orders of the Edo shogunate not to allow any foreign ship in Japanese waters.

• **Morrison Bunko.** *See* TŌYŌ BUNKO.

Morse, Edward Sylvester. American biologist (1838–1925) who traveled to Japan several times from 1877 to 1883 and founded a marine-biology laboratory in Enoshima. He taught at the University of Tokyo and also conducted archeological research (notably at the *kaizuka* in Ōmori). A good artist, he made many sketches of Japan. He collected ceramics, amassing what became the Japanese ceramics collection at the Boston Museum of Fine Arts. He was decorated with the Order of the Rising Sun (Kyokujitsu-shō) in 1898 and with the Order of the Sacred Treasure (Zuihō-shō) in 1922.

Mosse, Albert. German jurist (1846–1925) who was Itō Hirobumi's professor when the latter traveled to Berlin and was invited to teach in Japan in 1886. He helped Inoue Kawashi define the broad lines of the 1899 Constitution. When he returned to Germany in 1890, he held senior administrative positions in Königsberg and Berlin.

Motoda Nagazane. Confucian scholar (Motoda Eifu, 1818–91) of the Kumamoto fief (Kyushu). He was appointed Emperor Meiji's tutor *(jidoku)* in 1871, and became a member of the emperor's Privy Council (Sūmitsu-in) in 1888. He was involved with educational reform and helped to write the Imperial Rescript on Education (Kyōiku Chokugo) promulgated in 1890. Among his works, *Yōgaku kōyō* (Essential Principles for Education of the Young, 1882) became a classic on education of the Meiji era.

Motohide. Painter (Kanō Motohide; *mei:* Jinnojō; *gō:* Shinsetsu, early sixteenth century) of the Kanō school, Munehide's son and student and one of Kanō Eitoku's younger brothers.

Motohira. Sword-blade maker (Oku Yamato no Kami, 1743–1827) from the Satsuma estate.

Motokawa Tatsuo. Contemporary biologist and writer, whose book *Zo no jikan, nezumi no jikan* (Elephant Time, Mouse Time, 1992), questioning the meaning of time, was very successful.

Motoki Shozaemon. Grammarian (1767–1822), author of the first Japanese–English dictionaries (published 1811 and 1814).

Motome-zuka. Title of a Noh play: a woman tells a Buddhist monk the story of a young woman who loved two suitors. Unable to choose between them, she drowned herself; the two suitors killed each other so that they would not survive her. Then the woman disappears into a nearby tomb. The monk prays for her soul's rest, and she reappears to thank him and describe to him the horrors of Hell.

Motonobu. Painter (Kanō Motonobu; *mei:* Shirojirō; *gō:* Eisen, Gyokusen, Ko-Hōgen, 1476–1559) of the Kanō school, Masanobu's son and student, who worked for the Ashikaga shogun. He received the title Hōgen.

Motoori Norinaga. Scholar and philosopher (Ozu Norinaga; *gō:* Suzunoya, 1730–1801), born in Matsuzaka (Ise prefecture). He received an excellent education in all the arts (including the tea ceremony, archery, and Chinese and Japanese classics), then decided to become a physician and went to Kyoto to study under a scholar, Hori Keizan (1688–1757), and physicians such as Hori Genkō (1686–1754) and Takekawa Kōjun (1725–80). He also studied poetry *(waka)* and published his first works on this subject, which led to an interest in the Japanese classics, phonology, and etymology. He then wrote a large number of works of literary criticism, notably on the *Man'yōshū,* the *Genji monogatari,* and the imperial anthologies (*see* CHOKUSEN WAKA-SHŪ). From his studies on early Shinto, he developed theories based on the study of ancient things *(kokugaku)* and tried to breathe new life into Shinto. Most of his works expounded the great value of Japan's classical literature and showed that it was at the origin of Japanese thought. He summarized his reflections in the monumental *Kojiki-den,* a remarkable 44-volume study on the *Kojiki.* At the same time, he continued to study and write, producing at least 90 books totaling about 260 volumes, including the voluminous *Tamakatsuma* (started in 1793), a collection of 1,000 articles and essays, and *Uiyamabumi* (ca. 1799), a literary guide for students. In 1798, he compiled an anthology of his own writings, *Suzunoya-shū,* containing about

2,500 of his own *waka*. He had a large number of students and disciples, among them his sons Motoori Haruniwa and Motoori Ohira, and his grandson, Motoori Uchitō (1792–1855). The latter finished publishing his grandfather's complete works, which were finally published in their entirety in Tokyo in 1926 as *Zōhō Motoori Norinaga zenshū*.

• **Motoori Haruniwa.** Philosopher and writer (1873–1828), born in Ise, Motoori Norinaga's son. After going blind at age 20, he became an acupuncturist and grammarian, publishing two important works on grammar, *Kotoba no yachimata* (1808) and *Kotoba no kayoji* (1828), in which he attempted a classification of verbs.

• **Motoori Ōhira.** Motoori Norinaga's adoptive son (1756–1833), who continued his father's work in support of Kokugaku (National Learning) and wrote several works, including *Kogakuyō* (1809) and *Kagurauta shinshaku* 1827).

Motoyakushi-ji. Remains of a Buddhist temple built by Emperor Temmu from 680 to 698 in Kidano, near Kashiwara (Nara prefecture). It remained standing until the eleventh century. Excavations made in 1937 revealed its plan, similar to that of the Yakushi-ji.

Mōtsu-ji. Remains of a Buddhist temple in Haraizumi (Iwate prefecture), founded by Ennin in 850 and reconstructed by the Fujiwara family (Kiyohira and his son, Motohira) starting in 1105. It was dedicated to Yakushi Nyorai. This temple, once huge, had more than 40 secondary temples. The new building was erected on the ancient site in 1899 and was excavated in 1972. There are plans to reconstruct it in its original state. Annual festival (14th–20th day of the first moon) famous for Ennen-type dances. Small museum on the site.

Mountains. Japan is an essentially mountainous country, with a succession of ranges most of which are in volcanic "zones" (*see* VOLCANOES). The main ranges are, from north to south:

On Hokkaido: Kitami, Hidaka, Teshio, Yūbari.

On Honshu: Ōu Sammyaku, Dewa, Echigo, Abukuma, Mikuni, Kantō, Akaishi, Kiso, Hida (the three latter comprising the core of the Japanese "Alps"), Suzuka, Kii, Tamba, Chūgoku.

On Shikoku (not one of the volcanic zones): Sanuki, Shikoku.

On Kyushu: Tsukushi, Kyushu.

The highest mountains are on Honshu:
—Fuji-san (3,776 m)
—Shirane or Kitadake (3,192 m)
—Hodake (3,190 m)
—Ontake (3,063 m)
—Hakuba (2,933 m)
—Asama (2,560 m)
On Hokkaido are the following mountains:
—Nantai (2,484 m)
—Daisetsu (2,290 m)
—Hojiri (2,052 m)
—Iwate (2,041 m)
On Kyushu, the highest mountains are under 2,000 m altitude:
—Ishizuchi (1,982 m)
—Miyanouradake (1,935 m)
—Ōmine (1,915 m)

Moyoro. Prehistoric site located in the dunes at the mouth of the Abashiri River, near the town of Abashiri, on the north coast of Hokkaido, where many remains from the Late Jōmon period to the twelfth century were uncovered. A number of semi-buried houses and tombs were reconstructed there. *Moyoro* is an Ainu word meaning "bay." Small museum on the site. *See* ABASHIRI.

Mozume Takami. Kokugaku (National Learning) scholar (1847–1928), born in Bungo province (Ōita prefecture), and professor at the University of Tokyo, author of dictionaries (*Kotoba no hayashi,* 1888; *Nihon daijirin,* 1894), and compiler of a 20-volume collection of Chinese and Japanese classical texts, *Kōbunko* (1918).

Mozuna Kikō. Contemporary architect who has designed many buildings in Japan, including the port complex on Hokkaido, the Ainu cultural museum, hotels, and private residences. He is known for the originality of his work, which he says is founded on a philosophy arising from Tantric Buddhism.

Mudōki-bunka. Term used in archeology to define an "a-ceramic" culture dating from the paleolithic era and preceding the Jōmon period. Main sites in Sōzudai (Ōita prefecture), Dewa (Miyazaki prefecture), and Hoshino (Tochigi prefecture). Also called Sendōki-bunka.

Mujō. "The impermanence of all things," a Buddhist concept according to which everything that comes into existence must necessarily, someday, die out and disappear. It was largely accepted as an underlying concept of most areas of Japanese thought. Literature made great use of it, as did the warrior philosophies. Also called *tsunenashi,* from its Japanese pronunciation.

• **Mujōkan.** A sense of the ephemeral, used mainly in literature.

Mujū Ichien. Buddhist monk (1226–1312), author of a famous Zen Buddhist treatise, *Shaseki-shū* (Collection of Sand and Stones, 1279–83), comprising 134 short stories with didactic content. Ichien belonged to the Zen Rinzai sect and was Enni's (1202–80) disciple; Enni was the founder of the Tōfuku-ji temple. Ichien reconstructed the Chōbo-ji temple in Nagoya, where he lived his entire life, and wrote other treatises on Buddhism and education, such as *Tsuma kagami* (Mirror for Women, 1300).

Mukade. Large venomous centipedes, common in Japan, considered symbols of evil in folk literature. Some villages in Saitama prefecture consider them messengers of the local *kami.* When peasants caught them, the custom was to put them in oil, which they felt gave it medicinal properties, and it was often used on burns and wounds to speed scarring.

Mukai Genshō. Astronomer, physician, and naturalist (1607–77) who wrote a book on edible animals and plants in Japan in 1671.

Mukai Kyorai. Haiku poet (Mukai Kanetoki, 1651–1704), one of Bashō's ten main disciples (Bashō Juttetsu); he met Bashō in Ise in 1686. He wrote works on poetics and the *Koraishō* (1704), which reports his conversations with Bashō on the aesthetics of haiku.

Mukan Fumon. Zen Buddhist monk (1211–91) who was in China of the Southern Song dynasty from 1251 to 1262. Upon his return, he founded the Nanzen-ji (Rinzai sect) temple in Kyoto. *Posthumous names:* Busshin Zenshi, Daimyō Kokushi.

Mukden. City in Manchuria (now called Shenyang), site of a major battle between Russian and Japanese forces on March 10, 1905. The Russians had 320,000 troops, while the Japanese had only 250,000. Although the Russians fiercely defended the city, the Japanese captured it, but they were not able to annihilate the Russian army as they had hoped. The anniversary of this battle was celebrated

in Japan every year until 1945. In Japan, the battle is called Hōten-kaisen.

Mukōgaoka kaizuka. Shell mound *(kaizuka)* in Yayoi-chō in the Mukōgaoka district of Tokyo, where, in 1884, archeologists Tsuboi Shōgorō and Arisaka Shōzō discovered pottery that seemed to belong to the Late Jōmon period, but that was recognized in 1923 to belong to a distinct period, the Yayoi, dating from about 300 BC to AD 300.

Mukoirikon. Ancient practice of matrilocal marriage, which seems to have been the custom in the Nara and Heian periods among all social classes. This custom disappeared almost completely in the Kamakura period, but is still practiced in some fishing communities.

Mukyōkai. "Without a Church," a Japanese Christian religious group created by Uchimura Kanzō about 1900 that rejected Western religious institutions. This "religion" is practiced by small Bible-study groups and asks its members to observe the virtues of work, honesty, and sense of duty. Other nonconformist Christian movements sprang up in imitation of the Mukyōkai, notably the Makuya (Tabernacle), founded by Teshima Ikurō (1910–73). They have about 100,000 followers.

Mumyō-zōshi. "Untitled Book." A work written in kana by an adoptive daughter of Fujiwara no Toshinari (or by another woman of the same period) about 1196–1202, constituting one of the first literary critiques of works of the Heian period. It is presented as a conversation between two characters discussing both famous works and others that had faded from view.

Munabetsusen. Tax levied on each building during the Kamakura and Muromachi periods. At first applied to construction of shrines and temples at certain times, it became permanent. It disappeared in the early seventeenth century with the establishment of more regular taxes, the *honto-mononari.* Also called *muneyaku, munabechisen.*

Munakata Shikō. Painter and wood-block printer (1903–75), born in Aomori; Hiratsuka Un'ichi's student. Some of his woodcuts were destroyed during the Second World War, when Tokyo was bombed, in May 1945. After the war, however, his talent was recognized, and he had exhibitions in Japan and other countries, receiving awards at the São Paulo Biennial (1955) and the Venice Biennial

(1956). He was decorated with the Order of Culture (Bunka-shō) in 1970.

Mune. Term for the flat part of the back of a sword blade. *See* KATANA.

• **Munechika.** Sword-blade maker (Sanjō Kokaji Munechika, 938–1014) in Kyoto.

Munenaga Shinnō. Imperial prince (Kōzuke Shinnō, Shinano no Miya, 1311–85), Go-Daigo Tennō's second son and half-brother to Morinaga Shinnō, whom he succeeded as head *(zasu)* of the Buddhist Tendai sect, where he was a monk with the name Sonshō. He tried to help his father during the Kemmu Restoration in 1333; forsaking his monk's robe in 1337, he took part in many battles against Ashikaga Takeuji. He finally retired to the Southern Court (Nanchō) in 1374 and devoted himself to poetry, compiling a major anthology, *Shin'yō wakashū* (Collection of New Pages, 1381).

Munen-bara. Type of ritual suicide practiced in the recent past by some Japanese for the purpose of being pardoned for a transgression, real or imaginary.

Munenobu. Painter (Kanō Munenobu; *mei:* Shirojirō; *gō:* Yūsei, Yūsetsu, 1514–62) of the Kanō school; studied with his father, Motonobu. He worked for the Ashikaga shogun.
→ *See* HASEBE KUNISHIGE.

Munetaka Shinnō. Imperial prince and shogun of Kamakura (1242<1252–66>1274), Emperor Go-Saga's second son. He was chosen by *shikken* (regent) Hōjō Tokiyori to become the sixth shogun and successor to Fujiwara no Yoritsugu. Implicated in a plot aimed at overthrowing the Hōjō in 1266, he was deposed and replaced by Koreyasu Shinnō. He took refuge in Kyoto, where he became a Buddhist monk with the name Gyōshō in 1272. A talented poet, he wrote several *waka* collections, notably *Keigyoku wakashū* (Collection of Precious Stones) and *Ryūyō wakashū* (Collection of Willow Leaves).

Mura. "Village," the smallest administrative unit; before the Taika Reform in 645, *mura* were probably counted as divisions of *agata*, or *kuni* districts. This basic unit was replaced by the *gō* in 710, then by the *ri,* comprising five households, in 715. However, the *mura* came into use again during the Heian period and has remained the basic social unit to the present day.

• **Murahachibu.** "Village outcasting," the practice of socially isolating a family when its members behaved reprehensibly—if, for example, they had cut wood in a communal estate without permission or denounced someone to the authorities. This ostracism, which lasted for a predetermined period, forbade the family from participating in rites, marriages and funerals, and festivals. In some cases, if the offense was almost unpardonable, the affected family was forced to move to another village. The practice was not officially recognized but had great value in the eyes of the villagers, who used it whenever one of their members behaved in such a way as to "disrupt the harmony among all people."

Muragaki Norimasa. Senior bureaucrat (1813–80) of the Tokugawa *bakufu,* born in Edo, who in 1854 was made responsible for managing the affairs of the shogunate and inspecting the coastal defenses of Ezo (Hokkaido). He was an intermediary with the Russian E. V. Putianin, then he was appointed *bugyō* in Hakodate and *gaikoku-bugyō* (*bugyō* for foreign affairs). He had Hokkaido's coastal defenses fortified; in 1860, he was vice-ambassador for the delegation sent by the shogunate to the United States to ratify the treaty signed with Townsend Harris. During the Meiji Restoration in 1868, he retired from public life.

Murai chōan. Title of a Kabuki play, in the *kizewamono* genre, written by Kawatake Mokuami in 1862. Also titled *Kanzen Chōaku Nozoki Karakuri.*

Murakami Genzō. Writer, born 1910 in Korea. He received the Naoki Prize in 1940 for his historical novel *Kazusa fudoki.* After the Second World War, he became quite well known for *Sasaki Kojirō* (1950), about the rivalry between the title character and the famous swashbuckler Miyamoto Musashi. He also wrote other works, including the biographical novels *Minamoto no Yoshitsune* (1955) and *Hiraga Gennai* (1957).

Murakami Haruki. Writer, born 1949 in Kobe. After studying at Waseda University, he began in 1981 to write novels that were immediately extremely successful, especially among young people (millions of copies of each title sold), as well as many stories and essays. He received the Gunzō Prize in 1980 for *Hear the Wind,* the Noma Prize in 1982 for *A Wild Sheep Chase,* and the Tanizaki Prize in 1985 for *The End of the World* and *Hard-boiled Wonderland.* Among his other successful books are *Norwegian Wood* (1989) and *Dance, Dance, Dance* (1988).

Murakami Kagaku. Painter (Murakami Shin'ichi, 1888–1939), born in Osaka, who worked in modern Japanese style (Nihonga) and had works shown in the various Bunten. He painted mountain landscapes and, toward the end of his life, Buddhist subjects.

Murakami Kijō. Poet (Murakami Shōtarō, Kijō, 1865–1930), born in Edo. He lost his hearing and was unable to pursue a military and administrative career, so he lived with his family in the town of Takasaki. He became friends with Masaoka Shiki and Takahama Kyoshi and began to write haiku poems that were so well liked that he was soon a member of the Hototogisu group. He described animals and insects with great precision. Among his works are the collections *Kijō kushū* (1917), *Teihon Kijō kushū* (1940), and *Kijō haiku hairon-shū* (1947); the latter two were published posthumously.

Murakami Namiroku. Writer (Murakami Makoto, 1865–1944), born in Sakai, author of popular historical novels that were very successful in the 1920s. His most famous novel is *Mikazuki,* describing the life of a swordsman and imbued with traditional values.

Murakami Naojirō. Historian (1868–1966), born in Ōita prefecture. After traveling in Europe and Taiwan, where he was a professor, he was named president of Jōshi (Sophia) University in Tokyo in 1945. His main field of study was the relations between the Dutch merchants of Nagasaki and the shogunate during the Edo period, and he translated reports made by Jesuit missionaries in the sixteenth century.

Murakami Ryū. Writer (b. 1954) in modern style, who received the Akutagawa Prize in 1976 for his novel *Kagirinaku tōmeini chikai bleu* (Almost Transparent Blue).

Murakami Tennō. Sixty-second emperor (Prince Nariakira, 926<947–67>), successor to his brother, Shujaku Tennō. His descendants received the family name Minamoto and were known by the generic name Murakami-Genji. Emperor Reizei succeeded him.

Muramasa. Famous maker of sword blades (active ca. 1500) in Ise province. The blades that he and his descendants forged had a reputation of being eager for blood and bringing bad luck, to the point that their use was banned in the Tokugawa court.

Muramatsu Shōfu. Writer (Muramatsu Giichi, 1889–1961), born in Shizuoka prefecture. He wrote popular historical novels and many biographical novels: *Shōden shimizu jirochō* (1928), *Honchō gajin-den* (1943), *Kinsei meishōbu monogatari* (1961).

Muramatsu Takeshi. Literary critic (1929–94), author of major works on the writers Mishima Yukio and André Malraux. His biography of Kidō Takayoshi, *Sameta homoo* (Awakened Flame) won the Kikuchi Kan Prize in 1962. Among his other works is *Shi no Nihon bungakushi* (History of Japanese Literature on Death), published in 1951.

Murano Shirō. Poet (1901–75), born in Tokyo, and influential literary critic in the early twentieth century. He wrote haiku in free verse, then turned toward more modern forms, while pursuing a business career. He also wrote critical works on modern poetry and was an editor of the poetry magazine *Mugen* (Infinity).

Murano Tōgo. Architect (1891–1984), born in Saga prefecture, Watanabe Setsu's student. He designed many buildings in ultramodern style, such as the Sogō store in Osaka (1936), the Nippon Life insurance company building in Hibiya (Tokyo, 1963), the Cathedral of Peace (1953), and the Lutheran Theology Seminary (1970).

Muraoka Hanako. Writer (Yasunaka Hana, 1893–1968), born in Yamanashi prefecture, specializing in writing and translating children's stories. As a radio personality, she was concerned with improving women's conditions; she was appointed vice-president of the National Commission for UNESCO. She also translated works by Pearl Buck and Emily Dickinson, and edited the Christian magazine *New Age.*

Murasaki Shikibu. Writer (Tō no Shikibu, active ca. 1000), who probably belonged to the Fujiwara family (Tō being the Chinese pronunciation of the word *fuji,* "wisteria," and the title Shikibu indicating that she was related to a minister of the Department of Rites, Shikibu-shō). Almost nothing is known about her life except that she was married to Fujiwara no Nobutaka and was a lady-in-waiting to Empress Fujiwara no Akiko (Jōtō-mon'in, 988–1074), Emperor Ichijō's second wife. She is credited with writing a large part of the first major Japanese novel, the *Genji monogatari,* as well as a work of her own, *Murasaki Shikibu nikki.* It is likely her daughter, known as Daini no Sammi, wrote the last chapters of the *Genji monogatari,* but this is not certain. Murasaki Shikibu also contributed to the poetry anthology *Murasaki Shikibu-shū.* It seems that she was not considered a great poet in her time, and only the *Genji monogatari* survived for posterity as a great Japanese literary work. Her supposed life has been the subject of a number of novels and a Noh play, *Genji kuyō,* in which she is portrayed as an incarnation of Kannon Bosatsu. Her work, often imitated, was somewhat forgotten over the centuries, but was rediscovered in the late nineteenth century and gained an international reputation through translations. Sometimes called Nihonki no Tsubone.

• *Murasaki Shikibu nikki emaki.* Thirteenth-century *emakimono* in several scrolls illustrated by Fujiwara no Yoshitsune using the *tsukuri-e* technique, and handwritten by Fujiwara no Nobuzane.

Murata. Officer who invented a gun named after him in 1873. The Murata was replaced in 1897 by an improved model, the Arisaka. *See* ARISAKA.

Murata Harumi. Poet (1746–1811), born in Edo, Kamo no Mabuchi's student. He wrote *waka* and scholarly studies on the *Kokin-shū,* and was a member of the group of followers of Kokugaku (National Learning). He rediscovered the lost manuscript of the *Shinsen jikyō,* the oldest known Chinese–Japanese dictionary, dating from the late ninth or tenth century.

Murata Minoru. Movie director (1894–1937). At first a director for the Shingeki theater, he joined the movie company Sōchiku Kinema in 1920 and worked with Osanai Kaoru on the film *Rojō no reikon* (Souls on the Road, 1921). He also adapted many Western stories to the screen, transforming them to conform to Japanese criteria, in a realist style.

Murata Ryō'a. Writer (1773–1843), author of *Rigen shūren* (Panorama of the Common Language), published in 1900.

Murata Seifū. Samurai (1783–1855), minister of the Chōshū estate in 1838. He managed to pay off the estate's enormous financial debt by taking severe measures, and he had low-ranking samurai admitted to the Meirikan estate academy. But merchants whose businesses were suffering due to his measures forced him to resign in 1845. He returned

to power in 1855 but died before he could complete his reforms.

Murata Seimin. Sculptor and engraver (1761–1837), maker of sculptures portraying mainly animals.

Murayama Heiemon. Family of Kabuki actors whose most important members were Murayama Matabe (ca. 1655–70), actor and *zamoto* in Kyoto, founder of the Maruyama-za theater and the Murayama Heiemon, and Murayama Kurōemon (Kozakura Sennosuke II, d. 1692).

Murayama Riu. Writer (1903–94) known mainly for her studies on the *Genji monogatari,* notably *Watashi no Genji monogatari* (My Tales of Genji, 1977).

Murayama Tomiichi. Politician, born 1924, son of a fisherman and former socialist union leader, elected prime minister succeeding Hata Tsutomo on June 28, 1994, following elections in which he won 261 votes, against 214 for Kaifu and 29 abstentions. He was the second socialist prime minister elected to the Diet since 1945. His coalition cabinet comprised thirteen members of the Jiyū Minshutō (Liberal Democratic party, LDP), five socialists, and two ministers belonging to the Sakigake, an organization that had supported the candidacies of Hata and Hosokawa. The new minister of the MITI, Hashimoto Ryūtaro, and the vice-premier, Konō Yōhei, were both LDP members. Murayama resigned on January 3, 1996, and Hashimoto Ryūtaro succeeded him.

Murayama Tomoyoshi. Playwright and theater producer (1901–77), born in Tokyo. He studied painting in Germany, then became one of the leaders of the proletarian-literature movement (theater section). After the Second World War, he directed the Artistic Troupe of Tokyo (Tokyō Geijutsu-za), which performed in China. He also wrote a number of plays, which were collected in *Murayama Tomoyoshi gikyokushū* in 1971.

Murdoch, James. British journalist and writer (1856–1921), born near Aberdeen, Scotland. After studying languages in Aberdeen, Oxford, and Paris, he went to Australia, then arrived in Japan in 1889 to teach in various government schools. In 1917, when he returned to Australia, he created a chair of Japanese studies at the University of Sydney. With the assistance of Yamagata Isoo (1869–1959), he wrote the first major Western history of Japan *(His-*

tory of Japan) from 1903 to 1917; it was published only in 1926.

Murei. Japanese name for a sovereign of the Ryukyu Islands, placed on the throne of Okinawa by the Chinese when his father, Satsudo, died in 1404. He was overthrown by Shōhashi, the *anji* (lord) of Sashiki, who proclaimed his own father, Shishō, king in 1405. *Chin.:* Wuling.

Murō–ji. Buddhist temple founded in 681 (or, according to some, in the late eighth century) on a beautiful forested, mountainous site in Nara prefecture, about 25 km southwest of the city of Nara. The buildings are on small terraces, set between cryptomeria and giant gingko trees. The Murō-ji is affiliated with the Buzan branch of the Shingon sect. The temple was apparently reconstructed by Kūkai in 824. Its five-story pagoda, 16.2 m high (the smallest in Japan), dating from the late eighth century, is extremely well preserved. *Kondō* from the ninth century, *mie-dō* from the Kamakura period, *hondō (kanchō-dō)* from the thirteenth century, *raidō* from 1672, Miroku-dō from the ninth century. The Murō-ji contains many art works and sculptures. Below the wide steps leading to the temple is an old barrel-arch bridge *(taiko-bashi)* over the river. Because it was open to women for ceremonies, the temple was commonly known as Nyonin Kōya (Mt. Kōya for Women). A stele placed at the entrance is a reminder that women have always been welcome.

Muro Kyūsō. Neo-Confucian philosopher (Muro Naokiyo, 1658–1734) born in Edo, where he was a disciple of Arai Hakuseki and Kinoshita Jun'an. In 1722, he was appointed private tutor to shogun Tokugawa Yoshimune, and strictly applied the Chinese philosophy of Zhu Xi *(Jap.:* Shushi), refusing to "Japanize" his teachings. He wrote a famous book in memory of the "47 *rōnin*" of Akō *(see* AKŌ-GISHI), titled *Akō gijin roku* (1703 and 1709), as well as several philosophical essays. He was one of the Bokumon Jittetsu. His son, Muro Fukken (Muro Kōkan, 1706–39), complemented his works.

Muromachi-jidai. "Muromachi period." An artistic and historical period (from 1333 or 1336 to 1568 or 1574) during which Japan was controlled from Kyoto by the shogun of the Ashikaga family. The name of this period comes from the site in Kyoto where the Ashikaga decided to establish their *bakufu,* in the Hana no gosho (or Muromachi-dono, Karasumaru-dono) of the Muromachi district. This period was marked by a renaissance of

Chinese style and the reopening of relations with China. It was a time of political turmoil—the war between the Northern and Southern Courts (Nambokuchō, 1336–92), the Ōnin War (1467–77), the Warring States (Sengoku, 1467–1568)—but also of innovation in the arts: the decline of sculpture in favor of Chinese-style ink painting *(suiboku),* the development of Zen, the creation of Noh theater, the flourishing of crafts and ceramics for the tea ceremony *(chanoyu),* and so on. This period ended when Oda Nobunaga expelled the last Ashikaga shogun, Ashikaga Yoshiaki, from Kyoto and inaugurated the period called Azuchi-Momoyama (1568–1600). *See* ASHIKAGA.

• *Muromachi-jidai ko-uta-shū.* Collection of *ko-uta* songs compiled in the late fifteenth or early sixteenth century, perhaps by the monk Sōan.

Muroo Saisei. Poet and writer (Obata Terumichi, 1889–1962), born in Ishikawa prefecture. He composed haiku and many collections of modern poetry, including *Ai no shishū* (Love Poems, 1918). In 1918, he and novelist Akutagawa Ryūnosuke began to collaborate on several major novels: *Yōnen jidai* (Years of My Youth, ca. 1919), *Sei ni mezameru koro* (My Awakening to Sexuality, 1919), *Aru shōjo no shi made* (The Death of a Certain Young Woman, 1919). His novel *Anzukko* (The Apricot Child, 1957) won the *Yomiuri* Prize in 1958; the following year, he received the *Mainichi* Prize for his critical essay *Waga aisuru shijin no denki* (Lives of Beloved Poets). He also won the Noma Prize in 1959 for *Kagerō no nikki ibun,* his study on *Kagerō nikki,* in which he gives a novelistic account of life in the court in the Heian period. In 1960, he created a literary prize bearing his name.

Murray, David. American educator (1830–1905) invited to Japan in 1873 by the Meiji government, at Mori Arinori's suggestion, to advise the Ministry of Education. It was at his instigation that the first university for women (Ochanomizu) was opened in Tokyo, as were playgrounds for children. He also established a system of university examinations based on those in use in the United States and Great Britain. He returned to the United States in 1879.

Musashi. Former province, replaced by Tōkyō-to, Saitama, and Kanagawa prefectures, encompassing most of Kantō. Also called Bushū. The region was populated in the seventh century by Korean émigrés (Kikajin), who developed it. During the Kamakura period, it was the fief of the Minamoto and Hōjō families, then of the Usegui during the Muromachi

Murō-ji pagoda near Nara

period. It became the political center of Japan in 1603, when Tokugawa Ieyasu established his *bakufu* there.

• *Musashi.* Battleship of the *Yamato* class, built from 1938 to 1942, and flagship starting in 1943. It was sunk by American planes at the Battle of Leyte on October 24, 1944. The 64,000-ton ship was 250 m long and armed with a main battery of nine 460 mm cannons.

• **Musashi-bō.** *See* BENKEI.

• *Musashi fudoki.* A work in 165 volumes describing the customs and ways, culture, and economy of Musashi province, compiled on the order of the Tokugawa shogunate and published in 1884 by the Meiji government as *Shimpen Musashi fudoki* (New Edition of the *Musashi fudoki*).

• **Musashi Miyamoto.** *See* MIYAMOTO MUSASHI.

• **Musashi Shichitō.** Bands of warriors *(bushidan)* active in Musashi in the tenth century, which supposedly gave rise to the great Minamoto and Hōjō warrior clans. Seven are known, the most famous of which were the Yokohama and the Kodama. The warrior chronicles *(gunki-mono) Gempei seisuki* and *Taiheiki* mention them.

Museums. Thanks to its long religious and artistic tradition, Japan has a great number of museums, either created as conservatories, as was the case for Buddhist temples, or established by the government. The oldest museum in the world is the Shōsō-in in Nara, dating from the eighth century. In more recent times, many collectors have founded private museums and the various levels of government have opened national, prefectural, and municipal museums. Religious museums are in temples and shrines. Some museums specialize in a specific area, such as paintings, ceramics, folk objects *(mingei),* archeology, or ethnography. National and prefectural museums often organize temporary exhibitions through loans from religious institutions or private foundations, and many large stores and galleries exhibit works also on loan from such organizations. Thus Japan is a country of museums; some 2,500 have been counted. Below is a list of just some of the major ones.

National museums

In Tokyo:

—National Museum (Ueno Park), founded in 1871; Asian and Japanese art.

—National Museum of Western Art (Ueno Park): Matsutaka's collections of Western art; paintings by Monet, Renoir, and others; sculptures by Rodin.

—National Museum of Modern Art (Kitanomaru Park, Chiyoda-ku): modern Japanese art.

—Tokyo-Edo Museum, founded in 1994: reconstruction of life in Tokyo during the Edo period.

In Kyoto:

—National Museum of Modern Art (Okazaki Park), founded in 1897.

In Nara:

—National Museum (50 Noboriojichō), founded in 1895: Buddhist art, archeology.

—Shōsō-in Museum in the Tōdai-ji.

In Osaka:

—National Museum of Art: various exhibitions.

—National Museum of Ethnology (Suita Park): objects from around the world.

In Kamakura:

—National Museum, created in 1928: art mainly from the Kamakura and Muromachi periods.

Prefectural museums

In Tokyo:

—Tokyo Metropolitan Teien Art Museum (5–21–9 Shiroganedai, Minato-ku): various exhibitions.

In Nara, Kyoto, and other cities:

—Prefectural Art Museum (Kyoto, 10–6 Noboriojichō): various collections.

—Kyoto Museum (Sanjo Takakura, Nagakyo-ku).

—Various museums in the prefectures of Aomori (1973), Arita (Saga-ke, Kyushu, 1980: ceramics), Fukui (Kenritsu Hakubutsukan, 1984), Fukuoka (1985), Fukushima (1984), Gifu (1982), Gumma (in Takasaki, 1974), Hokkaido (in Sapporo, 1983), Hyōgo (in Himeji, 1983), Ibaraki (in Mito, 1906), Ishikawa (in Kanazawa, 1983), Iwate (in Morioka), Kagawa (in Takamatsu, 1966), Kagoshima (1983), Kōchi, Kumamoto (1976), Mie (in Tsu, 1982), Miyagi (in Sendai, 1981, from Tōhoku to Tagajō), Nagasaki (1965), Nara (Archeological Institute in Kashihara, 1980), Niigata (1981), Ōita (in Usa, 1981), Okayama, Okinawa (in Naha), Saga, Saitama (in Omiya, 1971), Tochigi (in Utsunomiya, 1982), Toyama (1981), Wakayama, and others. Most display works from recent periods of Japan or by local artists or from local history, as well as Western works.

Municipal museums

There are many municipal museums, established relatively recently in large cities or in cities known to be cultural centers, including Arita (Kyushu Ceramics Museum, 1980), Izumi (Ōsaka-fu, Kobusō Memorial, 1982), Kagoshima (Museum of Western Art, 1985), Kita-Kyushu (1974), Kobe (Amagasaki

Cultural Center; Kobe City Museum, 24 Kyomachi, Chūō-ku; Municipal Museum, 1982; Science Museum, 1984), Kumamoto (1978), Kurayoshi (1972), Kushiro (1983), Kyoto (Municipal Art Museum in Okazaki, Sakyo-ku; Municipal Museum of History in Teramachi, Kamigyō-ku; Municipal Museum of Traditional Industries, Okazaki, Sakyo-ku), Nagano (1981) Nagoya (1977), Osaka (Municipal Museum, 1960; Municipal Museum of Fine Arts; Museum of Eastern Ceramics, 1982), Saitama (9–30–1 Tokiwa, Urawa), Sendai (1961, 1985), Shimonoseki (1983), Yokohama (Art Museum), and others.

Private and other museums

In Tokyo:

—Bridgestone Art Museum (Western art, 1–10–1 Kyobashi, Chūō-ku)

—Azabu Museum (Roppongi, 1987)

—Gotō Museum (Setagaya-ku)

—Suntory Museum of Art (Akasaka, Minato-ku)

—Okura Shūkokan (2–10–3 Toranomon)

—Shoto Art Museum (2–14–14, Shibuya-ku)

—Meguro Art Museum (2–4–36 Meguro-ku)

—Nezu Institute of Fine Arts (very beautiful garden, 6–5 Minami Aoyama, Minato-ku)

—Sōgetsu Art Museum (7–2–21 Akasaka, Minato-ku)

—Itabashi Art Museum (5–34–27 Akatsuka, Itabashi-ku)

In Osaka:

—Navio Art Museum (Navio Hankyū, Kita-ku)

—Kintetsu Museum of Art (Abeno)

—Itsuo Museum of Art (Tateichichō, Ikeda)

—Manno Art Museum (Shoho Building, Chūō-ku)

—Aquarium (Museum of the Sea)

In Kyoto:

—Kōryō Museum of Art (Kamikishichō, Shichi-ku, Kita-ku)

In Nara:

—Yamato Bunkakan (1–16–6 Gakuen Minami)

—Tenri University Museum (Furucho 1, Tenri)

In Kobe and Hyōgo:

—Tekisui Museum (13–3 Yamaashiyachō, Ashiya, Hyōgo)

—Tawara Museum (Tsukiwakachō 6–1, Ashiya, Hyōgo)

—Emba Museum of Fine Arts (12–1 Okuikechō, Ashiya, Hyōgo)

—Itami City Museum (Miyanomaechō, Itami, Hyōgo)

—Tatsuuma Archeological Museum (28 Matsushitachō, Nishinomiya, Hyōgo)

—Okanoyama Art Museum (345–1 Kamihiechō, Nishiwaki, Hyōgo)

Specialized museums

Many such museums are sprinkled throughout Japan, most of them dedicated to a particular art, artisanal or industrial. In Tokyo, there are the Museum of Calligraphy (1936), the Japan Calligraphy Museum (1873), and the Museum of Weapons (1967); the museums of arms and armor at the Kyoto-Arashiyama Art Museum and at the Nishimura Museum in Iwakuni (Yamaguchi-ken); the Hida Takayama Shunkei Institute in Takayama (Gifu-ken) and the Kaisendō Museum in Kaminoyama (Yamagata-ken), featuring lacquers; the Ninja Museum (Igaryū Ninja Yashiki in Ueno, Mie-ken).

The archeology museums, such as the Ainu Museum in Shiraoi (Hokkaido, 1984), are generally located on the sites of excavations, such as the ones in Toro, Moyoro, Saitobaru, Idojiri (in Sakai), Hachinoe (Aomori-ken, 1975), Togariishi (Nagano-ken), Shiojiri (Nagano-ken, 1954), Beppu (Oita-ken, university, 1978); there are also collections at the Tokyo and Nara national museums, among others.

The ethnography museums are also remarkable, and their collections often overlap with those of archeology museums. Most of these museums are dedicated to folklore, including those in Kurashiki, Tsuruoka (Chidō Museum, Yamagata-ken), Matsumoto (Nagano-ken), Osaka (in Suita), Takamatsu (Sanuki Folk Museum, Kagawa-ken), Toyama (1965), Tottori (Yoshida Shōya collections), the Hida village in Takayama (Gifu-ken), the village of Edo in Yuwaku-machi (Kanazawa-ken), Kurashiki (old town), Sankeien Park in Yokohama (1906).

Ceramics have been featured in many museums, aside from collections of the major organizations, such as those in Bizen (Okayama-ken, 1977), Arita (1954), Seto (Aichi-ken, 1878), the Hakone and Moa museums (in Hakone), and the Idemitsu Museum in Tokyo.

There are also museums devoted to the works of particular artists: to sculptor Asakura Fumio in Asakura; to Gyōkudō in Ome; to Yokoyama Taikan, Kawai, Kanjirō, and Kawabata Ryūshi, all in Tokyo; to Munakata Shikō in Aomori; to Tomioka Tesai in Takarazuka (Hyōgoken); to Enkū in the Senkō-ji temple near Takayama (Gifu-ken); to Ikeno Taiga in Kyoto; to Maruyama Okyo in Kushimoto (Wakayama-ken); and others.

Other types of museums

Most larger Buddhist temples and Shinto shrines have their own collections of Buddhist art, and they often lend pieces to major national museums and private galleries for temporary exhibitions. The Tō-ji and the Sanujusangendō in Kyoto are just two of these, but there are numerous private foundations, both religious and lay, that open their doors to the public from time to time. The major galleries in Tokyo, Kyoto, Osaka, and other cities also often have exhibitions of art from private collections.

Although admission fees to national, prefectural, and municipal museums are generally low, they may vary considerably from one to another. Photography rights are high, especially in Buddhist temples, when permission is given by the religious authorities. Private museums are open on different dates and at different times, and travelers should check ahead before visiting.

Art galleries

Among the major galleries (many of them located on upper floors or in large stores) in Tokyo are the Striped House (5–10–33 Roppongi, Minato-ku), the Center for Contemporary Sculpture (3–10–19 Ginza, Chūō-ku), Yoseidō Reflection Gallery (5–5–9 Ginza, Chūō-ku), Grafica Tokio (7–8–9 Ginza), the Interior Gallery (2–19–1, Shinjuku-ku), the Art Forum in the Seibu department store (Ikebukuro), the Marlborough Gallery (1–13–12 Moto Akasaka, Minato-ku), the Sogo Art Gallery in Yokohama, Kōgei Gallery (Seibu department store, Shibuya-ku), Kabutoya Gallery (8–8–7 Ginza, Chūō-ku). In Osaka: the Imax Gallery (7–1 Shimmachi, 1-Chōme, Nishi-ku), Fujikawa Gallery (1–7 Kawaramachi, Chūō-ku), Itsuō Museum (7–17 Tataeichi, Ikeda). In Kobe: Tsukashin Hall Gallery (8–1 Tsukaguchi Honmachi 4-chōme, Amagasaki, Hyōgo).

There is also the Museum of Modern Literature (Nihon Kindai Bungakukan), founded in 1967, in Komaba Park (Meguro-ku, Tokyo), which contains about 200,000 books and thousands of newspapers.

This list is nowhere near exhaustive, since new museums are opened every year by municipalities and private foundations.

Musha. Former name for warriors.

• **Musha-e.** A term for paintings and prints portraying warriors or war scenes.

• **Musha rokugu.** The six main parts of samurai armor: *sune-ate* (greaves), *hagi-te* (thigh guards), *dō* (corselet), *kote* (armbands), *kubi-yoroi* (neck protector), and *hō-ate* (or *kabuto*, helmet). See YOROI.

• **Musha shugyō.** In martial arts, the period of study during which some samurai traveled around the country to train and learn the secrets of their art in various schools. This custom took shape during the Edo period. The best-known itinerant samurai seeking perfection was Miyamoto Musashi.

Mushanokōji Saneatsu. Writer, playwright, and painter (Mushakōji Saneatsu, 1885–1976), born in Tokyo. He was from an aristocratic family (his father, Mushanokōji Saneyo, had accompanied the Iwakura delegation to Europe) and studied at the Peers' School (Gakushū-in). In 1907, he, Shiga Naoya, and some other poets formed a literary group called Jūyokka-kai, which became the nucleus of the Shirakaba (White Birch), publishing a handwritten journal called *Bōya* (Perspectives). A utopian, he created a village community, Atarashiki Mura. In 1927, he founded another literary magazine, *Daichōwa* (Great Harmony), with illustrations by himself and Hokusai, in which he published discussions on Western art. He had a number of exhibitions of his paintings starting in 1929. In 1936, he traveled in the United States and Europe to further his knowledge of painting. His books, somewhat naive, imbued with idealism, and influenced by Christianity, were not without their psychological aspects: *Omedetaki hito* (A Naive Man, 1910), *Aru otoko* (That Man, 1922), *Ningen banzai* (Up with Humanity, 1922), *Aiyoku* (Desire, 1926), *Ai to shi* (Love and Death, 1939), *Shinri Sensei* (1950), and others. He was decorated with the Order of Culture (Bunka-shō) in 1952.

• **Mushanokōji-Senke.** See CHANOYU.

Mushi. Literally, "worm, insect." This word was—and still is—used to define certain emotions inherent to a person's nature. The "worm" is said to live within individual people, causing them to act in aberrant ways, provoking anger, bad moods, depression, and so on, and it symbolizes an impulsive temperament. However, some Shinto detoxification methods can, in certain cases, "close all exits to the worm" *(mushifūji)* so that the possessed person can return to normal behavior. To keep the *mushi* from causing upset or re-emerging, magical formulas for exorcism are sometimes placed on the hands, soles of the feet, or forehead of the person at risk. *See also* MONO NO KE.

Mushin. "Without heart," a term sometimes used to define a lack of aesthetics or of depth in a work. Thus, comic poetry (which is popular, common) is called *mushin,* as opposed to "aristocratic" poetry, which is termed *ushin* ("with heart"). Among commoners (*kokoronashi* in Japanese), *mushin* usually designates a person who lacks judgment or feeling. In Buddhism, *mushin* means a person without worldly attachments, thus "enlightened," whereas in common language it often means one who begs. *See* USHIN.

Mushofushi-in. "Mudra of the Three Mysteries," or "Mudra of Ubiquity," used in some Esoteric Buddhist sects to make oneself invisible. It is formed with the two hands together, fingers intertwined, the index fingers straight and touching at the tips, and the middle fingers straight. Also called *ritō-in, tō-in, Dai-sotoba-in.* Chin.: Wusuo Buzhi-yin.

Music. The history of traditional Japanese music follows, more or less, the major historical periods:

Before the sixth century: early music of the peoples of Japan.

Asuka, Nara, and early Heian periods: music influenced by Korean and Chinese music.

Late Heian, Kamakura, Muromachi, and Edo periods: development of "national" music.

From 1868 to the present: music influenced by Western music.

None of the early music of Japan is known, although it seems to have been associated with dances (Kagura), as reported in mythological legends in the *Kojiki.* During the *kofun* period, it seems plausible that it had affinities with the shamanic music of western Siberia and the Korean Peninsula. Instruments were probably very simple, consisting mainly of drums, flutes, and zithers (some ancient types are portrayed on *haniwa; see* KOTO). Some folk-music traditions probably date from this proto-historical period, but it is difficult to trace them back except perhaps through *norito,* and it is not known how they were chanted or sung. From this ancient sung music came *mi-kagura,* which was court music, and *sato-kagura,* which was folkloric and used in Shinto ceremonies. Because this music did not have a notation form, it cannot be studied. Music can be traced directly from the time Buddhism was introduced to Japan from Korea; this music was religious and followed the Korean-Chinese canon, consisting mainly of Buddhist chants *(shōmyō)* and sutra recitations with the accompaniment of simple instruments. Japan had had "foreign" music, generally Chinese, from the early fifth century, but it was played only by foreign artists. The oldest Japanese musical form, Gigaku, was probably introduced in 612 from Paekche, Korea, by someone named Mimashi, who taught it to young nobles in the Yamato court with the approval of Prince Shōtoku Taishi. Later, other styles of music arrived in Japan from Sankan (Sam-han, Korea), Tang-dynasty China, Manchu-

ria, and perhaps from Southeast Asia via China. Music was performed only in the temples and the court; in 701, a Department of Music (Gagaku-ryō) was established in Heijō-kyō. In ensuing periods, as the influence from the mainland increased, Japanese court musicians and Buddhist monks assimilated imported musical styles and used them to compose original music—vocal compositions such as Saibara and Rōei, from which a court music called Gagaku was developed—while commoners developed *sarugaku,* evolved from *sangaku* imported from Korea during the Nara period, and songs called *imayō.* In the Kamakura and Muromachi periods (twelfth to sixteenth century), court music was not very popular among the warriors, who preferred more rustic folk music: *sarugaku, ennen,* and *dengaku* (or *heikyoku*), and *biwa-hōshi* songs, which were accompanied by the *biwa,* an instrument imported from China.

Truly Japanese music developed during the Edo period with the appearance of new instruments such as the shamisen (from China via the Ryukyu Islands in 1562) and the *shakuhachi* flute (also of Chinese origin). Shamisen provided accompaniment for folk songs, ballads *(ko-uta)* and *ningyō-jōruri,* while a distinct musical style, *sōkyoku,* developed in Kyushu using the Gagaku koto. Three *sōkyoku* "schools" were formed: Yatsuhashi, Yamada, and Ikuta. In the Kansai region, *ji-uta* were also accompanied by shamisen; in Edo, the *ji-uta* evolved into *naga-uta* through Kabuki theater. At the same time, also in the Kyoto region, several types of instrumental music were developed, such as *bungo-bushi,* which, in Edo, gave rise to other genres: *tokiwazu* (named after Tokiwazu Mojidayū in 1717)—which led to *tomimoto* and *kiyomoto* (named after its inventor, Kiyomoto Enjudayū in 1814)—and *fujimatsu* (created in 1745 by Satsuma Fujimatsu, and which led to the *tsuruga* and *sinnai* styles). In Osaka, *jōruri* were in their turn behind the development of *gidayū.*

In the Meiji era, Japanese musical styles were greatly influenced by Western music, and as the koto increased in popularity, many musicians wrote new pieces for this instrument. In addition, *naga-uta, tokiwazu,* and *kiyomoto* were transformed. But it was not until the 1920s that Western music was fully accepted and Japanese musicians began to use Western instruments such as the piano and violin. Traditional music evolved, especially for koto, while retaining some of its historical characteristics.

Thus, there were two major categories of music in Japan: *hōgaku,* or music played on typically Japanese (or imported Chinese) instruments, and

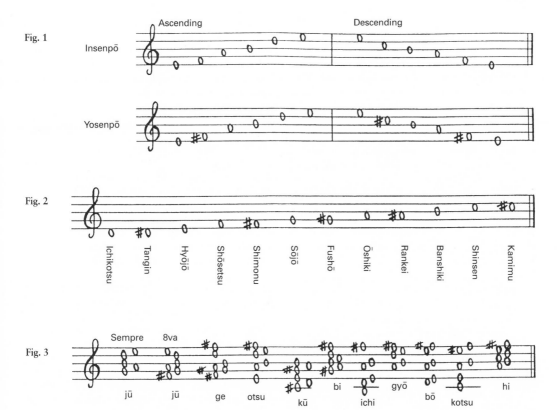

Fig. 1

Fig. 2

Fig. 3

yōgaku, which first arose in Nagasaki with religious instruments and songs brought by Christian missionaries in the second half of the sixteenth century.

Japanese music as a whole is monophonic, except for Gagaku instrumental ensembles. It seems that polyphony was never highly developed. Folk music, such as that for the koto and the shamisen, is based mainly on two pentatonal scales, *In-sempō* and *Yō-sempō* (figure 1), while Gagaku uses a heptatonal scale (figure 2). Noh music is based on a tetrachord scale (figure 3). However, modes use a twelve-tone system. Rhythms are generally free and not based on measures composed of beats. Melodies are juxtapositions of themes. Classical instruments have few different timbres (compared to those used in the West), so great emphasis is placed on differences in sonority among instruments in each category (percussion, plucked string instruments, wind instruments). Each instrument is tuned according to the type of music to be played. Purely instrumental music is found only in Gagaku, *koto* concerts, and *shakuhachi* solos. It seems that vocal music has always been preferred, although certain theater forms, such as Noh, have synthesized the forms.

Contemporary music is represented mainly by bands such as the Yellow Magic Orchestra (YMO), which performs techno-pop and uses many electronic instruments. Musical groups in other styles are also quite popular, such as Shang Shang Typhoon, The Boom from Okinawa, and B'z, whose performances are widely televised.

Instrumental music:
→ See BIWA, FLUTES, GAGAKU, HAKASE, IN-SEMPŌ, JŪNI RITSU, KOTO, MASON, MEYASU HAKASE, RITSU, RYŌ, RYŌ-SEMPŌ, RYUKYU-SEMPŌ, SASARA, SŌ-KYOKO (DAMMANO), SHAKUHACHI, SHAMISEN, SHI-CHIGEN-KIN, SHŌ, TAIKŌ, YŌKYOKU, YŌ-SEMPŌ.

Vocal music:
→ See GIDAYŪ, HEIKYOKU, JI-UTA, KIYOMOTO-BUSHI, KO-UTA, NAGA-UTA, RŌEI, SAIBARA, SŌ-KYOKU, TOKIWAZU-BUSHI.

Musicians:
→ See ANDŌ KŌ, ATSUZANE SHINNŌ, BIWA-HŌSHI, FUKUSHIMA KAZUO, GOTŌ MIDORI, GOZE, MA-

TSUDAIRA YORITSUNE, MAYAZUMI TOSHIRŌ, MENU-
KIYA CHŌZABURŌ, MITSU-ZAKI, MOROI MAKOTO,
MOROI SABURŌ, ŌTAGURO MOTOO, OWARI NO
HAMANUSHI, OZAWA SEIJI, SAWAZUMI KENGYŌ,
SEMIMARU, TAKEMITSU TORU, TAKI RENTARŌ, TŌGI
TETTEKI, TSURUTA KINSHI.
See also BUGAKU, KABUKI, NOH, WASAN.

Musō Soseki. Zen Buddhist monk (Chikaku,
1275–1351), one of the masters of thought of the
Kamakura *gozan*. He was born into a noble family
(he was a descendant of Emperor Uda) in Ise province, and studied esoterism of the Shingon-shū sect
at the Tōdai in Nara, where he was ordained in
1292. He then studied Zen at the Rinzai temple of
the Kenchō-ji in Kamakura under the direction of
the Chinese monk Yishan Yining (*Jap.*: Issan Ichinei, 1244–1317), and later at the Mampuku-ji with
Kōhō Kennichi (1241–1316). He then retired to
meditate; in 1325, at the request of Emperor Go-
Daigo, he agreed to become *zasu* (head abbot) of
the Nanzen-ji temple in Kyoto. One year later, however, he returned to Kamakura, then to the Nanzen-
ji in 1334. After Go-Daigo's downfall, he entered
the service of the Ashikaga. In 1939, he converted
the Saihō-ji temple, attached to the Jōdo-shū, into a
Zen monastery. He is credited with designing the
Zen gardens of the Kinkaku-ji and the Ginkaku-ji in
Kyoto, and especially with establishing the *gozan*
system. He founded the Zen-ō-ji temples in Ise in
1325, then the Tenryū-ji in 1342. He took the name
Soseki in 1289, and his *posthumous name* was
Musō Kokushi. It was thanks to his actions that the
Zen Rinzai sect was firmly established in Japan.

Mutai Risaku. Philosopher (1890–1974), born in
Nagano prefecture, Nishida Kitarō's disciple, and
Husserl's disciple in Germany in 1926. In his works,
he attempted to reconcile the methodological theories of phenomenology with Hegel's and Nishida
Kitarō's philosophies of history. He also attempted,
in *Daisan hyumanizumu to heiwa* (The Third Great
Humanism and Peace, 1951) to formulate a socialist humanism based on Marxism and existentialism.

Mutesaki. In traditional *tenjiku-yō* architectural
style, a type of overhang composed of six *degumi*
projecting to support the *gangyō*, with some *sashi-
hijiki* inserted on the main pillar. Good examples of
this relatively rare type of overhang are the *nandaimon* gate and the Daibutsu-den of the Tōdai-ji temple in Nara. *See* TO-KYŌ.

Mutō Akira. Officer (1892–1948), born in Kumamoto, head of operations at general quarters in
China in 1937. He was appointed commander-in-
chief of the Imperial Guard in 1942 and led the occupying forces in the Philippines in 1944. Found
guilty of war crimes in 1947 by the Allied war-
crimes court, he was executed in 1948.

Mutō Kiyoshi. Architect (1903–89), born in Ibaraki prefecture, and professor at the University of
Tokyo starting in 1927. He calculated the resistance
of structures to seismic disturbances and invented
ways for high-rise buildings to withstand strong
earthquakes. Among his designs were those for the
36-story, 147m-high tower in Kasumigaseki, built
in Tokyo in 1968, and the Sunshine building (60
stories, 240 m high) built in Tokyo in 1978. He received the Order of Culture (Bunka-shō) in 1983.

Mutsu. Former province in northern Honshu, now
included in Aomori and Iwate prefectures. Formerly called Michinoku, Ōshū, Rikushū, it was one
of the eight provinces of the Tōsandō (Eastern
Mountain Road) and was populated mainly by Ezo
tribes. Mutsu was conquered by Sakanoue no
Tamuramaro in 801, belonged to the Ōshū Fujiwara family (*see* HIRAIZUMI) during the Heian period, then passed into the hands of the Date family
in the Muromachi and Edo periods.

• *Mutsu.* Warship of the *Nagato* class, built in
Yokosuka in 1921. It weighed 43,000 tonnes, had a
maximum speed of 25 knots, and was armed with a
main battery of eight 400 mm cannons. It sank in
June 8, 1943, in Hiroshima Bay, following an explosion in its powder magazine.
• Name of the first nuclear-powered ship
launched in Japan in June 1969. This cargo ship,
150 m long and weighing 4,096 tonnes, had a maximum speed of 16 knots and was propelled by a
reactor that developed 36,000 kw. At first, it was
anchored in the port of Mutsu, but there were protests; tests in 1974 revealed a leak in the reactor. It
was repaired and based in Sasebo.

• **Mutsu Shiro.** *See* MINAMOTO NO TAMEYOSHI.

Mutsuki. "Month of good relations," former name
for the first month of the year.

Mutsu Munemitsu. Politician (1844–97), born in
the Wakayama estate. He joined the pro-imperial
movement in 1868 and obtained a ministerial position in the first government of the Meiji era; he was

governor of Kanagawa province in 1870 and became a member of the Genrō-in in 1875. He was sentenced to five years in prison for his part in the Satsuma Rebellion in 1878. Freed and rehabilitated in 1883, he returned to the government thanks to the efforts of his friend Itō Hirobumi, then went to Europe in 1884, where he continued his studies in London and Vienna. When he returned to Japan in 1886, he was appointed minister of foreign affairs (Gaimushō) and worked on revision of the "Unequal Treaties" (*see* JŌYAKU KAISEI). He was ambassador to the United States in 1888, and minister of agriculture in 1890 in Yamagata Aritomo's cabinet. Once again minister of foreign affairs in Itō Hirobumi's cabinet in 1892, he concluded the revisions to the Unequal Treaties, and he signed a trade treaty with Great Britain in 1894. During the Sino-Japanese War of 1894–95, he skillfully conducted Japanese diplomacy and represented Japan at the Shimonoseki Conference (1895). He resigned in 1896 for health reasons and died the following year, having completed the *Kenkenroku* (Report on Sufferance) describing his diplomatic activities during the Sino-Japanese War.

Myōchin. Family of sword-blade makers active from 1200 to 1850. Its members used the family name Masuda until 1155. Among the most famous blacksmiths of this family were Myōchin no Munesuke (twelfth century, in Kyoto) and his son, Myōchin no Munekiyo (in Kamakura), then Myōchin Nobuie (the seventeenth, 1485–1564), Myōchin Yoshimichi, Myōchin Takayoshi, and their successors until 1756. The first ten generations (Myōchin jūdai) did not sign their blades; their names began with *So.* The following six generations signed *Gi.* There were a total of 24 master blacksmiths in the direct family line, the last being Myōchin Kunimichi (1624–43) and Myōchin Munemasa (1688–1740).

Myōchō. *See* SHŪHŌ.

Myōden. Before the twelfth century, cultivated lands belonging not to the government but to the *myōju (daimyō, shōmyō)* who were farming them.

Myōe. Buddhist monk (1173–1232) of the Kegonshū sect, who lived at the Tōdai-ji monastery in Nara and at the Kōzan-ji monastery in Takao. A fertile thinker, he kept an esoteric, dream-based journal, *Yume no ki* (Dream Diary), that reported his visions for almost his entire life. His main disciples in esoterism were Ninshin (b. 1178), Kikai (1178–

1250), and Ryūben (active ca. 1214–39). When he was 24, he cut off part of his right ear as an offering to his chosen divinity, Butsugen-Butsumo, and during a meditation, he received "natural" ordination from the bodhisattva *(bosatsu)* Mañjushrī. He founded a studio for the artists of the Kōzan-ji. Also known as Kōben.

Myo'en. Buddhist monk (d. 1199) and sculptor of Buddhist images, Chū'en's son. He was principal of the Sanjō Bussho (En-pa) school and worked with Inson at the Daikaku-ji temple in Kyoto.

Myōgakin. During the Edo period, taxes levied on artisans, fishers, and traders who did not pay land tax. A special tax in this category was also levied on *kabunakama* (guilds). These taxes constituted an important source of revenue for the shogunate. *See* KO-MONONARI.

Myōha. Zen Buddhist monk (1311–88) of the Rinzai sect, founder of the Shōkoku-ji temple in Yamashiro, in 1383.

Myōhō. Buddhist temple of the Tendai-shū sect, founded in the sixteenth century on Mt. Hiei and transported to Kyoto in the seventeenth century. It has paintings from the sixteenth century. Its *ojo-in* dates from 1619. The *renge-ō-in* is part of this temple.

Myōho-in no Miya. *See* RYŌSHŌ HŌSHINNŌ.

Myōhon-ji. Buddhist temple of the Nichiren sect, founded in Kamakura in 1275.

Myōhōrenge-kyō. See HOKE-KYŌ.

Myōjō. "Bright Star." A literary magazine and intellectual movement launched in 1900 by Yosano Tekkan; it belonged to the Romantic-influenced Araragi group. The magazine ceased publication about 1910, but was published again from 1921 to 1927 and from 1947 to 1949. Its first series featured prestigious figures of the literary scene of the time, such as Yosano Akiko, Masaoka Shiki, Satō Haruo, and Mori Ōgai, and it had a major influence on the thinking of writers and poets of the late Meiji period. *See* SUBARU.

Myōju Shigeyoshi. Maker of sword blades (Umetada Shigeyoshi, 1558–1631) in Kyoto.

Myōki-an. Zen Buddhist temple (Rinzai sect) founded in Yamazaki, near Osaka, in the fifteenth century. Shōin (residence) dating from 1469–87 and tea pavilion *(chashitsu)* by Sen no Rikyū (1521–91).

Myōman-ji. Branch of the Buddhist Nichiren-shū sect, founded in 1381 in Kamakura by the monk Nisshū. Its name was changed to Kempon Hokke-shū in 1898.

• Buddhist temple belonging to the Nichiren-shū sect, founded in the thirteenth century in Kyoto by the monk Nichiju.

Myō-ō. Kings of magical science (*Skt.:* Vidyarāja) constituting the third class of Buddhist divinities, after the buddhas *(nyorai)* and bodhisattvas *(bosatsu)*. The kings were Fudō Myō-ō (*Skt.:* Achalanātha), Gōzanze Myō-ō (*Skt.:* Trailokyavijava), Gundari Myō-ō (*Skt.:* Kundali), Daiitoku Myō-ō (*Skt.:* Yamāntaka), Kongō Yasha Myō-ō (*Skt.:* Vajrayaksha), Kujaku Myō-ō (*Skt.:* Mayūrāsana), and Aizen Myō-ō (*Skt.:* Rāgarāja). The first five were considered major (Go-dai Myō-ō). They were said to save people through the power of their magical incantations (*daranī, Skt.:* mantra). Of these divinities, Fudō Myō-ō was the most popular.

Myōsen. Buddhist monk (789–868) of the Hossō-shu sect, who received, in succession, the titles *sōgō, risshi,* and finally *dai-sōzu* (in 864).

• Buddhist monk (1166–1242) of the Tendai-shū sect, son of *sangi* Fujiwara no Noriyori.

Myōshin-ji. Former palace of Emperor Hanazono in Kyoto, transformed into a Buddhist temple for the Zen Rinzai sect in 1337 by the monk Kanzan Egen (1277–1360) and his master, Daitō Kokushi. The Zen monk Nippō Sōshun (1368–1448) renovated the temple, but it was almost completely destroyed during the Ōnin War (1467–77). It was restored by Sekkō Sōjin (1408–86), the ninth abbot, supported by Emperor Go-Tsuchimikado. It comprises 57 secondary temples and 3,444 affiliated temples. It includes a *san-mon* (from 1599), *chokushi-mon* (1610), *kuri* (1654), *hōjō* (1654), library (1673), *shōrō* (1639), *hattō* (1657), *shindō* (1654), Butsuden (reconstructed in 1830), *kaisandō* gate (1409), *tenkyū* (1635), and other structures. These various buildings contain magnificent works of art, notably a bell (in the *chokushi-mon*) dating from 690–98, the oldest in Japan. Its Zen-style gardens are famous.

Myōtaku. Buddhist monk (Ryūshū Shūtaku; *gō:* Koken, 1308–38) and painter of the Muromachi *suiboku* school; he painted Buddhist subjects.

Myō-un. Buddhist monk (1115–83), Minamoto no Akimitsu's son, who was *zasu* of the Tendai-shū in 1167 and 1179. He was killed by Minamoto no Yoshinaka.

Mythology. Japanese mythologies flow from two very distinct sources, one indigenous to the territory and forming the basis of "national" beliefs, or Shinto, and the other from Buddhism, an imported religion. Shinto mythology is quite hazy because it was codified very late, with the writing of the *Kojiki* and the *Nihon shoki* in the early eighth century. Some provincial chronicles, the *fudoki,* also supply some information on ancient beliefs, and there are *norito,* ancient poetic invocations to the divinities of the soil, or *kami.* Although they have a common foundation, the traditions reported by these texts differ and were not synthesized and interpreted until relatively recently, notably by Motoori Norinaga (1730–1801) and other modern thinkers who wanted to add foreign elements to original Japanese thought, such as the Chinese notions of Yin and Yang and their interaction.

In fact, there is no truly indigenous Japanese mythology, but an odd assortment of ancient myths that owes much to shamanic concepts introduced from Korea by the "horsemen-archers" who arrived on the islands in the late third or early fourth century (*see* HISTORY). This mythology offers a particular view of the world that explains the creation of Japan and its gods and that justifies the imperial succession. It thus offers a rather blurred distinction between the divine and the historical, based on the main myth setting Amaterasu, the sun goddess, against her "brother" Susanoo, who probably represented the invasive element from Korea.

Over the centuries, the beliefs issuing from this duality were polarized in the cult centers of Ise and Izumo. The imperial family having chosen Amaterasu as its ancestor, worship of Susanoo was relegated to secondary importance. In fact, the works dealing with Shinto mythology are only a sort of ordering of local myths, in which the authors of the earliest texts made choices based on imperial orders. Thus, Japanese mythology can in no way be compared to Western mythologies. In reality, aside from the more or less coherent story of the unpleasantries between Amaterasu and Susanoo and the role that various *kami* played, there is no unanimity of opinion on the succession of the *kami.*

The *kami* themselves were arbitrarily and relatively recently divided into "heavenly" *(amatsu-kami)* and "earthly" *(kunitsu-kami),* especially because each region worships its own *kami* and every prominent person was elevated to the rank of *kami* after his or her death. Trying to establish a hierarchy among the *kami* is therefore impossible. There is a clear distinction between destructive fire and life-giving water, typical of agricultural populations, which was added to beliefs dating from Japanese prehistory (about which there is no information) to constitute a particular mythological ensemble that gave Japan its "soul." *See* names cited, BUDDHISM, CHIJIN-GODAI, KOJIKI, NIHON SHOKI, SHINTO, TENJIN SHICHI-DAI.

N. The consonant *n* is usually associated with the vowels *a, e, i, o,* and *u* to give the sounds *na, ne, ni, no, nu*. However, there is a letter in kana that represents the nasalized end of syllables, transcribed as *n* without a vowel attached, as in *shimbun*. As a general rule, this final vowel is transformed into an *m* when it is placed directly before a *b* or a *p*: *shin'bun* thus becomes *shimbun*.

Naba Kassho. Confucian philosopher (1595–1658) of the Teishu-ha school.

Nabeshima. Family of daimyo from Hizen province (Saga and Nagasaki prefectures, Kyushu). Some of its members assisted Tokugawa Ieyasu at the Battle of Sekigahara in 1600 and thus had their estates confirmed; these had been stolen from Ryūzōji Masaie (1566–1607) by Nabeshima Nasoshige (1538–1618) and had been raised in value to 357,000 *koku* by Toyotomi Hideyoshi. This family received the family name Matsudaira in 1648.

• **Nabeshima Kansō.** Daimyo (Nabeshima Naomasa, 1814–71) of Hizen, famous for reorganizing the finances of his estates and encouraging trade (porcelain, coal), which enabled him to build a large military force. After 1868, he was appointed head of the Hokkaido *kaitakushi*.

• **Nabeshima Katsushige.** Daimyo (1580–1657), Nabeshima Naoshige's son and successor to his estates in Hizen. He fought Tokugawa Ieyasu at the Battle of Sekigahara (1600) but soon after declared himself Ieyasu's vassal, thus preserving his own inheritance.

• **Nabeshima Naoshige.** Daimyo of Hizen (1538–1618), who succeeded Ryūzōji Masaie; he fought under Hideyoshi in 1592 and 1597. He brought potters back from Korea and settled them in his fief (*see* NABESHIMA-YAKI).

• **Nabeshima-yaki.** Nabeshima pottery, term for blue-and-white, celadon, and polychrome porcelain pieces made in Arita by potters brought from Korea by Nabeshima Naoshige. The kiln at Iwayagawachi produced porcelain painted in blue and white under a slip from 1628 to 1661; the kiln in Okawachi, perhaps the largest, was active from 1675 to 1871, producing very beautiful porcelain of the same type, but of better quality. Some pieces were decorated under a slip and fired a second time. The kilns produced decorated dishes with a sort of scalloped decoration, as well as *sake* flasks, various vases, and other table utensils. The main decorations, generally applied in blue under a slip, were complemented by designs in transparent colors (*iro-nabeshima*) in red, blue-green, or yellow under a slip, mainly plant motifs (flowers, fruits, leaves). Starting in the late seventeenth century, some pieces from Imari were imitated with a white reverse design. The best-known potters working in the Nabeshima kilns were those of the Soeda family, including Soeda Kizaemon (?–1654) and his descendants, most of whom used the name Soeda Imaemon (or simply Imeamon). The Nabeshima ceramics tradition was revived in the nineteenth century by Soeda Imaemon XII (1897–1975) and his son, Soeda Imaemon XIII (b. 1926), whose works were exhibited in Paris in 1994.

Nabeta. Group of 54 tombs carved into the rock near the town of Yamaga in Kumamoto prefecture (Kyushu); some of their walls are decorated with bas-reliefs portraying military equipment. Date uncertain.

Nabeyama Sadachika. Political writer (1902–79) and Marxist theoretician, one of the founders of the Japanese Communist party in 1922. He left the party in the 1930s.

Nachi no Taki. Major waterfall, 133 m high, on the upper part of the Nachi-gawa river (Wakayama prefecture). The most famous of the 48 waterfalls along the river's course, it is sacred to those who worship at the nearby Kumano Nachi shrines and Buddhist Seigantō-ji temple. This waterfall is in the Nachisan mountain range, with peaks from 750 to 1,000 m altitude. Annual festivals (Hi Matsuri) on January 1, January 7, and July 14.

Nagabakama. Type of long pants *(hakama),* once worn by men with the *kami-shimo* costume during religious ceremonies or at the court.

Naga-e no kasa. Large parasol with a very long handle, used to protect senior bureaucrats and nobles from sun and rain during processions or trips. *See* KARA-KASA.

Nagahara Kōtarō. Painter (gō: Shisui, 1864–1930) in Western style, Koyama Shōtarō's student.

Nagai Kafū. Writer (Nagai Sōkichi, 1879–1959), born in Tokyo to a family of samurai who had become senior bureaucrats. Sent to the United States and Europe to study, he worked in New York in 1903, then in Paris and Lyon as an employee for a Japanese bank. When he returned to Japan in 1908, he published accounts of his travels in two works, *Amerika monogatari* (Stories of America, 1908) and *Furansu monogatari* (Stories of France, 1909). Strongly influenced by Émile Zola's works, he became a naturalist and began a very fertile career, although two of his early works, *Furansu monogatari* and *Kanraku* (Pleasures, 1909), were banned by the government because of their criticism of Japanese society. He nevertheless became a professor of literature at Keiō Gijuku University, where he founded a literary magazine, *Mita Bungaku.* In 1910, to please his father, he married Saitō Yone, but he divorced soon after, following his father's death, and married the woman he loved, Uchida Yai, a former geisha, who left him some years later because of his infidelity. He left his professor's position in 1916 to devote himself to writing: *Udekurabe* (Geisha Rivalry, 1917), *Ame shōshō* (Quiet Rain, 1917), *Okamezasa* (Dwarf Bamboo, 1918). For the next 10 years he did not write much; then he began again in 1931: *Tsuyu no ato saki* (After the Rainy Season, 1931) and *Bokutō kidan* (Strange Tale from East of the River, 1937). Many of his books were banned by the censors and published only after the Second World War: early works of his youth, such as *Yume no onna* (The Dream Woman, 1903), *Sumidagawa* (Sumida River, 1909), *Jigoku no hana* (Flowers of Hell, 1902), *Yojōhan no shitabarai* (Behind the Fusuma in the Little Bedroom, 1915), and later works, such as *Towazu gatari* (Volunteered Remarks, 1946). He received the Order of Cultural Merit in 1952 and was elected to the Nihon Geijutsu-in (Japan Art Academy) in 1954. Some of his novels were adapted for the screen, including *Bokutō kidan* (by Toyoda Shirō in 1960) and *Ratai* (The Naked Body, by Narusawa Masashige in 1962). All of Nagai Kafū's books (commonly called *Kafū*) deal with the pleasures of the lower districts of Tokyo in the late Edo period and the Meiji period, and very precisely describe urban culture of those times in a colorful and sometimes lyrical style imbued with nostalgia.

Nagai Nagayoshi. Pharmacist (1845–1929) born in Awa province. Sent to Europe by the government, he went to school in Berlin. When he returned to Japan, he studied medicinal plants and isolated ephedrine from *Ephedra sinica.* He taught at the University of Tokyo and was president of the Pharmacology Society of Japan.

Nagai, Paul. Christian physician and writer (Nagai Takashi, 1908–56) who died of radiation sickness due to exposure at Hiroshima. He wrote novels in the form of tales: *The Bells of Nagasaki* (1947), *Here Are My Children* (1948), and others.

Nagai Ryūtarō. Politician (1881–1944), born in Saga to a samurai family. A convert to Christianity in 1898, he completed his studies at Oxford. He was appointed a professor at Waseda University in Tokyo, where he stayed until 1917, when he left teaching to devote himself to politics. His liberal ideas and oratorical talents made him famous as a "champion of the people." In 1920, he was elected to the Diet and became the leader of the Rikken Minseitō (Constitutional Democratic party). He was minister of colonies from 1932 to 1934 in Saitō Makoto's cabinet, minister of communications under Konoe Fumimaro, and minister of railroads under Abe Nobuyuki.

Nagai Tatsuo. Writer (1904–90), born in Tokyo. After holding various jobs, notably in Manchuria, and editing the literary magazine *Bungei Shunju,* he continued to write, mostly stories, including a collection called *Ikko sono ta,* which received the

Noma Prize and the Nihon Geijutsu-in (Japan Art Academy) Prize in 1965. Elected to the Academy in 1969, he was decorated with the Order of Culture (Bunka-shō) in 1981. He also received the Yokomitsu Riichi Prize in 1950.

Nagako. Empress Dowager. *See* KUNI NAGAKO, HIROHITO.

Nagakubo Sekisui. Geographer (1717–1801) of the Mito clan. He made the first map of Japan using the Western system of latitudes and longitudes, *Nihon yochi rotei zenzu* (1775–79). Also a Confucian scholar, he helped to write the *Dai Nihon-shi.*

Nagamitsu. Sword maker (Junkei Nagamitsu, 1222–97) in Osafune. *See* OSAFUNE-KAJI.

Nagamochi. Oblong coffer without feet, generally made of *kiri* (paulownia) wood, up to 2 m long, used until the very early twentieth century to hold clothes. It was part of a bride's trousseau: when a girl was born, it was customary to plant a *kiri no ki,* a tree that grows very rapidly and yields light, non-rotting wood. The tree was cut when she married, and used to make one or several *nagamochi* to hold her kimonos. *See also* KIRI NO KI, TANSU.

Nagano. Chief city of Nagano prefecture (Nagano prefecture), about 180 km north of Tokyo. During the Kamakura period, it developed around the Zenkō-ji temple as a *monzen-machi.* It was an important waystation *(shuku-eki)* on the Hokkoku-kaidō road in the Edo period. Site of 1998 Winter Olympic Games. Agriculture, printing firms, electricity, and textiles (silk). *Pop.:* 340,000.

• **Nagano prefecture.** Province in central Honshu, located between Niigata, Gumma, Saitama, Yamanashi, Aichi, and Toyama prefectures. Largely mountainous (Japanese Alps), it is irrigated by the Shinano-gawa, Kiso-gawa, Tenryū-gawa, and Himekawa rivers. It was formerly Nagano province, which was divided into a large number of estates during the Edo period. Agriculture (rice), cattle breeding. *Main cities:* Matsumoto, Ueda, Iida, Shiojiri, Okaya, Suwa, Chine, Ina, Komagane. *Chief city:* Nagano. *Area:* 13,585 km². *Pop.:* 2.1 million.

Nagano Osami. Admiral (1880–1947), born in Kōchi prefecture. He was the naval attaché to the United States embassy, then promoted to admiral in 1934. He represented Japan at the Naval Conference in London in 1935 and was minister of the navy in Hirota Kōki's cabinet in 1936. Promoted to commander of the combined fleets in 1937, then to commander of the general quarters of the imperial naval forces in 1941, he planned and organized the Japanese attack against Pearl Harbor on December 7, 1941. He was arrested in 1945 by the occupying forces and found guilty of war crimes, and he died of disease in prison two years later.

Nagaoka Hantarō. Physicist (1865–1950), born in Ōmura (Nagasaki prefecture), best known for his research on electromagnetics and his production of an atomic model (1903) that was confirmed by Rutherford. He was a professor at the University of Tokyo (1896), then president of Osaka University and the Japan Academy (Nihon Gakushi-in). Decorated with the Order of Culture (Bunka-shō) in 1937.

Nagaoka-kyō. City located between Osaka and Kyoto. The site was chosen in 784 to build the new capital, succeeding Heijō-kyo (Nara). But Emperor Kammu abandoned it in 794 and moved the capital to Heian-kyō, following fires and sudden deaths that had sullied the site. The city developed rapidly, but the foundations of the ancient capital and the Buddhist Kōmyō-ji temple, where Hōnen lived, have been preserved. *Pop.:* 75,000.

Nagare Masayuki. Contemporary sculptor and architect. A former suicide-plane pilot *(kamikaze)* who managed to evade death, he launched his career after 1945, creating a number of gardens and fountains. In 1963, he received Japan's Grand Prize for Architecture and was responsible for designing the Japanese pavilion at the New York World Fair. This colossal project required 600 tons of granite from Awaji, where he works. Among his other accomplishments are the sculptures in Ueno Park in Tokyo and the stunning garden in Ōita.

Nagare-zukuri. Type of architecture for Shinto shrines in which the roof slopes are asymmetrical, with the long part on the shrine side. *See* JINJA.

Nagasaki. Chief city of Nagasaki prefecture (Nagasaki prefecture) and major port since 1571, founded by daimyo Ōmura Sumitada at the request of the Portuguese. It was formerly called Fukae no Ura, Tama no Ura, and Nigitatsu. It was one of Japan's main ports for trade with China, Korea, Southeast Asia, and Western countries until the nineteenth century. After Japan's isolationist laws were enacted, a fan-shaped artificial island called

Dejima was built there from 1634 to 1636 to house foreign citizens, mainly Dutch. A bridge linked the island to the rest of the city. Located at the foot of a deep bay opening onto Gotō Sea and protected by the Nagasaki Peninsula *(hantō)*, the port could accommodate very large ships and had major shipyards (founded in 1855–61). The city was partially destroyed by the second atom bomb dropped by the United States on Japan, on August 9, 1945, at 11:02 A.M.: the US B-29 bomber *Bockscar* released a bomb called "Fat Boy" or "Big Guy," equivalent to 22,000 tons of TNT, which exploded at an altitude of 515 mm, instantly killing 26,000 people and injuring more than 40,000 more. The city was completely rebuilt after the war and is now a major cultural and industrial center: Mitsubishi shipyards, various factories. Urakami Catholic church, university, Sōfuku-ji temple (Ōbaku sect, built in 1629), Meganebashi (Chinese-style bridge dating from 1634), remains of the Dutch occupation at Dejima, Glover gardens and residences in the Victorian style (nineteenth century), various temples in the Chinese Ming style. Airport at Ōmura. Ōkunchi festival in October, Peiron race in June, kite competition in April. *Pop.:* 450,000.

• **Nagasaki-bugyō.** Senior bureaucrat in Edo and governor of Nagasaki, responsible for controlling trade with China and Holland via the island of Dejima. This position was created in 1603.

• **Nagasaki-ha.** Painting school founded in Nagasaki in the seventeenth century by painters, in contact with Chinese and European artists, who worked in a wide variety of styles, often influenced by the works of Chin Nampin (*Chin.:* Shen Nanpin), who taught the Zen arts and Chinese painting (*kanga* and *bunjinga*) in Nagasaki from 1731 to 1733. They also painted screens *(namban-byōbu)* with scenes portraying the "Southern Barbarians" and their ships. The Nagasaki school included official painters, called *kara-e mekiki,* who were responsible for making copies of important Chinese works; painters from the Chin Nampin school; many other independent painters, such as Kawahara Keiga; and woodcut engravers who made hand-colored prints as travel souvenirs. *See also* YŌGA.

• **Nagasaki prefecture.** Prefecture on Kyushu, on the extremely jagged coast of the Gotō Sea, composed of four mountainous peninsulas: Kita Matsuura, Nishi Sonogi, Nagasaki, and Shimabara to the south. It is bordered on the east by Saga prefecture.

It has excellent ports, including Hirado, Sasebo, and Nagasaki, and many islands, including Hirado-shima, Gotō, Iki-shima, and Tsushima, and intensive fishing, pearl-oyster and algae farming, cattle breeding (on Gotō and Hirado), coal mines, shipyards. There is also some farming, mainly of sweet potatoes. *Main cities:* Nagasaki (chief city), Sasebo, Ōmura, Isahaya, Matsuura, Hirado. *Area:* 4,102 km². *Pop.:* 1.6 million.

• **Nagasaki Nijūroku Shōnin.** "The Twenty-Six Saints of Nagasaki," name for the first Christian martyrs tortured in Nagasaki on February 5, 1597. *See* MARTYRS.

• **Nagasaki Zōsensho.** Major shipyards in Nagasaki, built by the Tokugawa shogunate from 1855 to 1861 with the assistance of Dutch engineers. The shipyards were taken over by the Meiji government in 1868 and sold to Iwasaki Yatarō in 1884 and to Mitsubishi in 1887.

Nagasawa Rosetsu. *See* ROSETSU.

Nagasawa Shogetsuma. Blacksmith who wrote a technical essay on the manufacturing and use of firearms, *Teppō-shu* (1612–16), which was a classic throughout the Edo period.

Nagaseko kofun. Group of megalithic tombs *(kofun)* in the villages of Ryūho and Amura, near Tankochi, Kumamoto prefecture (Kyushu), with beautiful interior paintings of mirrors, concentric circles, broken lines, and other patterns.

Nagase Yoshirō. Painter and sculptor (b. 1891), who studied in France from 1927 to 1934. In 1974, he had an exhibition in Paris of his very modern-style ukiyo-e prints.

Nagashige Kōami. Lacquer artist (1599–1651), famous for his objects decorated in *maki-e,* made for the Edo shogunate.

Nagashino Tatakai. Major battle on June 29, 1575. The armies of Oda Nobunaga and his ally, Tokugawa Ieyasu (about 40,000 soldiers), defeated the forces of Takeda Katsuyori, who had besieged the fortress in Nagashino (Hōrai-chō, in today's Aichi prefecture). Oda Nobunaga was then able to turn, unencumbered, to his fight with the Ikkō-ikki of Echizen province. It was in this battle that Oda Nobunaga used *teppō-ashigaru* (harquebusiers) for the first time; there were about 3,000 of them, and they easily defeated samurai on horseback. This battle was depicted in the film *Kagemusha* (1980), by Kurosawa Akira.

Nagasune-hiko. Mythical governor of Yamato. According to the *Kojiki,* he was defeated by Jimmu Tennō after a heroic struggle, then killed by his nephew, Umashimate no Mikoto.

Nagataka. Painter (Fujiwara no Nagataka, late thirteenth century) and Buddhist monk under the names Kaishin and Kaikan, who studied with his father, Ienobu, in Kyoto. He painted in the Yamato-e style.

Nagata Masaichi. Film producer (1906–85). He first worked at Nikkatsu, starting in 1925, then founded his own company, Daiichi Eiga-sha, in 1934. His directors included Mizoguchi Kenji *(Naniwa erejii, Gion no shimai)* and Kurosawa Akira *(Rashōmon, Shaka).*

Nagata Teiryū. *Kyōka* poet (Taiya Teiryū, Yuensai, 1654–1734) in Osaka, Ki no Kaion's younger brother. His poems, humorous and written in simple language, were collected in two anthologies, *Kyōka iezutu* (1729) and *Yuensai okimiyage* (1734).

Nagata Tetsuzan. Military officer and politician (1884–1935), born in Nagano prefecture. As a military attaché abroad after the First World War, his abilities as a strategist were noted, and he was promoted to major general in 1932, then to commander of the Military Affairs Bureau in 1934, succeeding General Araki Sadao as minister of war. He was assassinated by Aizawa Saburo (1889–1936), a lieutenant colonel of the Kōdō-ha faction.

Nagata Tokuhon. Physician (Kai no Tokuhon, ca. 1513–1610) serving the Takeda family in Kai province. He used the Chinese Han medical methods. Also called Tokuhon.

Nagato. Former province now in Yamaguchi prefecture.

• *Nagato.* Japanese warship, built in the Kure shipyards between 1917 and 1920. It weighed 43,000 tons, had a maximum speed of 25 knots, and was armed with eight 400 mm cannons. It took part in most of the major naval battles of the Second World War, notably those at Midway and the Gulf of Leyte. Damaged by an air raid on the port of Yokosuka in July 1945, it was used by the United States as a target for atom-bomb tests on the Bikini atoll after the Second World War.

• **Nagato Keigo-ban.** Corps of guards created in 1275 to protect the coasts of Nagato province against an eventual attack by the Mongols, and maintained until 1330. It was commanded by a Nagato-tandai (Chūgoku-tandai) from the Hōjō family.

Nagatsuka Takashi. Writer (1879–1915) and *waka* poet, born in Ibaraki prefecture, Masaoka Shiki's disciple. He was a member of the Araragi group; with Itō Sachio, he founded the poetry magazine *Ashibi* in 1903. His best-known work is a long novel on peasant customs, *Tsuchi* (The Earth, 1910).

Naga-uta. Poetic form, also called *chōka,* consisting of long descriptive poems composed of alternating verses of five and seven syllables and finishing with a triplet of five, seven, and seven syllables. These poems were meant to be sung with shamisen accompaniment during Kabuki plays or in concerts. This type of "long song" developed in Edo in the early eighteenth century from *ji-uta* and *yōkyoku.* Today, *naga-uta* are sung by choruses, accompanied by ensembles comprising several shamisen, a flute, and several drums. There are currently about 100 *naga-uta* pieces, most of them written by musicians such as Kineya Rokuzaemon IX (d. 1819) and his successors, Kineya Rokuzaemon X (1800–59) and Kineya Shōjirō III (1851–96). *See* CHŌKA.

Nagaya-mon. Monumental gate used exclusively for the residences of high-ranking nobles during the Edo period.

Nagaya no Ō. Politician (676 or 684?–729), Emperor Temmu's grandson and Prince Takechi's son. He was minister of the left *(sadaijin)* in 724. He plotted against Shōmu Tennō, and he and his entire family were forced to commit suicide. In 1988, more than 30,000 *mokkan* (engraved tablets) were found in the ruins of his residence. Nagaya no Ō was an excellent poet writing in Chinese.

Nagayo Sensai. Physician (1838–1920), born to a family of physicians in Hizen province (Nagasaki prefecture). He accompanied the Iwakura delegation to Europe and the United States (1871–73). When he returned, he founded Japan's modern medical system. He had a law passed making vaccination against smallpox mandatory and directed the Bureau of Health in the Ministry of the Interior. Nagayo Yoshirō's father.

Nagayo Yoshirō. Writer and playwright (1888–1961) born in Tokyo, Nagayo Sensai's son. He contributed to the Peers' School's (Gakushūin) literary magazine *Shirakaba.* Among his best-known works are the plays *Kōu to Ryūhō* (1917) and *Inadara no ko* (1920); the novel *Takezawa sensei to iu hito* (1925); an autobiographical work, *Waga kokoro no henreki* (1959); and a book on philosophy, *Seidō no Kirisuto* (The Bronze Christ, 1941).

Nagi kofun. Group of more than 40 tombs dug out of the rock near Ishinuki, Kumamoto prefecture, Kyushu, with an entrance decorated with concentric circles and interior chambers decorated with paintings of épées, triangles, and boats.

Naginami Futabashira. "The Two Pillars of Nami and Nagi," a term sometimes used for Izanagi and Izanami, the *kami* who created the islands of Japan and the other "terrestrial" *kami (kunitsu-kami).*

Naginata. A kind of halberd composed of a long curved blade and a long bamboo handle, used mainly by warrior-monks *(heisō)* in the Ashikaga period of medieval times, and by foot soldiers *(ashigaru)* and women in the Edo period. There were several types: *kozori* (with a long, very curved blade), *shira-e* (with a white-painted handle), *shobu-gata* (with a blade shaped like an iris leaf), *hirumaki* (with a ring), and others. A *naginata* halberd could be up to 2 m long; its blade, with a convex edge, was from 0.6 to 1 m long. *Naginata* were used mainly to cut the hocks of horses. Some warriors used a similar weapon, but with a shorter handle and longer blade, called *nagakami.* Some *naginata* had a steel point called *ishizuki* on the end of the handle, used to pierce armor. Peasants and *ninja* sometimes used a particular type of *naginata,* a double-edged sword with a short, thick blade, called *bisen-tō.* The art of *naginata,* still very popular among Japanese women, is practiced with a halberd with a bamboo blade. Today, there are still at least four schools *(ryū)* for using this weapon: Jikishin Kage-ryū, Todaha-ryū, Tendō-ryū, and Katori Shindō-ryū.

Nago. A term once used to designate landless peasants working for landowners *(hombyakushō, myōshu).* They had various designations depending on the region and the period: *myōshi, fudai, tsukurigo,* *hikan, jige,* and so on. *See also* MIZUNOMI BYAKUSHŌ.

Nagon. Former title for secretary of state, ranked below *udaijin* and *sadaijin.* There were three classes of *nagon: dainagon, chūnagon,* and *shōnagon* (large, medium, and small).

Nagoshi no harae (harai). Annual Shinto ritual of purification *(misogi, harai),* generally performed on the last day of the sixth month in the lunar calendar. On this occasion, worshipers pass through a ring made of interlaced reeds or undergo symbolic flagellation with a paper or straw doll to rid themselves of their blemishes. *See* KATASHIRO, MISOGI.

Nagoya. Chief city of Aichi prefecture (Honshu), on Ise Bay, at the bottom of the Nōbi Plain. It was formed in medieval times around several groups of *kofun,* and developed in the Muromachi period as a *monzen-machi* around the Atsuta-jinja shrine. The town was the seat of the Imagawa family in the sixteenth century and was conquered by Oda Nobunaga. The Owari family built a castle there (1609–14) for the Tokugawa. Heavily damaged by bombing during the Second World War, it was reconstructed on a modern plan, and its castle was rebuilt in 1959. Nagoya is the center of the Chūkyō industrial conurbation and has rapidly become the fourth largest city in Japan, after Tokyo, Yokohama, and Osaka, due mainly to its port. The city is built on alluvial soil that is sometimes below sea level, and it is protected from the ocean by dikes. It was opened to international trade in 1907. Its twin city is Los Angeles. It has an airport and ceramics, aeronautical, railroad, chemical, and other factories. Among its main monuments: the Atsuta-jinja shrine, the Shimpuku-ji Buddhist temple (Ōsu Kannon-ji) of the Shingon sect. Nanzan University (founded 1939), cultural centers, and prefectural arts and sciences museums. Festival of the Atsuta-jinji in May, and of the Tōshōgū shrine in April. *Pop.:* 2.1 million.

• **Nagoya Daigaku.** National university of Nagoya, founded in 1881 as the Aichi Medical College. It became an imperial university in 1939 and the University of Nagoya in 1949. It has faculties of literature, law, economics, medicine, sciences, and agriculture, and many science research institutes. Annual attendance: more than 7,000 students.

• **Nagoya-jōshi.** Nagoya's castle, built for Tokugawa Ieyasu between 1609 and 1614. It was destroyed in 1945 and rebuilt in concrete in 1959; its keep, 48 m high, is decorated with gold-leaf dolphins and now houses a history museum.

Nagoya Gen'i. Physician (Nagoya Tansuishi, 1628–96), born in Kyoto, founder of the traditional Chinese school of medicine in Japan, based on teachings from the Chinese treatise of the Han period, *Shang hanlun.* He inaugurated experimental methods in medicine.

Nagoya Sanzaemon. Masterless samurai, or *rōnin* (Nagoya Sanzaburō, ?–1603), who became an actor in itinerant troupes; with Ō-Kuni of Izumo, he founded the Kabuki theaters in Kyoto and Edo. *See* KABUKI.

Naha. Chief city of, and largest city on, Okinawa (Ryukyu Islands), located on the island's southwest coast. At first occupied by the Japanese troops of Shimazu Iehisa (Shimazu Tadatsune) in 1609, it became the seat of the local and prefectural administration in 1879. It was the theater of terrible fighting between Japanese and Americans in May and June 1945, and was totally destroyed. Reconstructed, it remained under American administration until 1972. Local crafts, *bingata* fabrics. International airport. Tombs of the ancient kings of the Ryukyu Islands. Also sometimes called Naba, Nawa. *Pop.:* 300,000.

Nahiko. *See* KATORI NAHIKO.

Nai. Prefix indicating everything "inside," as opposed to *gai (ge),* "outside."

• **Naibu-kan.** Imperial guard formed of six *e-fu.* *See* E-FU.

• **Naidaijin.** Minister assisting an udaijin or sadaijin. Also called naijin, naifu, uchi no otoko, uchi no ō-ōmi.

• **Naidōjō.** Formerly, Buddhist temple established within the palace and reserved for the imperial family.

• **Nai-en.** Lay festival *(sechi-e)* once held at the imperial palace on the 21st, 22nd, and 23rd days of the first month of the year and devoted to reading poems. This tradition is still alive today.

• **Naijudokoro.** Bureau directing young servants and bureaucrats under 16 years of age who served the *kampaku* in the Heian period. The *kampaku* sometimes bore the title Naijudokoro no Bettō.

• **Naikaku.** Since 1885, the Council of Ministers.

• **Nai-kanrei.** Title held by prime ministers of the Hōjō *shikken* in Kamakura from 1200 to 1333.

• **Naikenshi.** Bureaucrats of the Kamakura *bakufu* responsible for setting prices for harvests. Also called *junkenshi.*

• **Naiki.** Former title for the secretary of the state archives.
→ *See* GUKEI, HIROYUKI, JOKEI.

• **Naikū.** *See* ISE KODAIJINGŪ.

• **Naikubu.** Group of ten Buddhist monks responsible for explaining the Buddhist Law in the imperial palace during the Gosai-e (June 8–14). Also called *naigu.*

• **Naikyōbō.** Pavilion within the imperial palace reserved for the women of the imperial family, for instruction in music, dance, and singing. Created in 765.

• **Naimushō.** Ministry of the Interior. *See* MINISTRIES.

• **Nairai-shi.** Before 808, the bureau of the imperial palace responsible for etiquette, justice, and ceremonies; part of the Danjō-dai.

• **Nairan.** The shogunate's delegate to the imperial court of Kyoto. Also called *shoshidai.*

• **Naishi-dokoro.** Room in the imperial palace reserved for emblems. *See* KASHIKO-DOKORO.

• **Naishin.** Honorific title conferred by the emperor before the ninth century, notably on Nakatomi no Kamatari in 645 and on Fujiwara no Yoshitsugu in 770. Also called Uchitsu-omi.

• **Naishinnō.** Title for an emperor's legitimate daughters and granddaughters. *See* SHINNŌ.

• **Naishi no Tsukasa.** Empress's household, including only female domestics from the imperial palace. Also called *ōoku* (in the shogunal palace).

• **Naiyaku-shi.** Imperial bureau of medicine, annexed to the Tenyaku-ryō in 736. Also called Uchi no Kusuri no Tsukasa.

- **Nai-zenshi.** Former position of emperor's official food taster. Also called Uchi no Kashiwade no Tsukasa.

Naiben. Senior bureaucrat responsible for festivities *(sechi-e)* at the imperial court.

Naitō Akira. Professor of architecture, born 1932 in Tokyo, president of Aichi-Sangyō University in 1993, author of "Research on the Concept of *Ma: Interval*" (Academy Architecture Prize) and of *Katsura* (International Book Award).

Naitō Arō. Writer (1883–1977) specializing in French literature and the translator of several French classics, among them Saint-Exupéry's *The Little Prince*.

Naitō Jōsō. Haiku poet (Jōsō, 1662–1704) and samurai from Owari province, one of Bashō's ten disciples (Bashō Juttetsu). He became a Buddhist monk in 1688 and joined Bashō in 1689. His poems perfectly expressed the concept of *sabi* so dear to his master. When Bashō died, Naitō Jōsō wrote an essay on him, *Nekorobigusa* (1694) and a collection of essays called *Nembutsu sōshi* (1774). His poems, published in the anthology *Sarumino* (1691), are also in a collection, *Jōsō hokkushū* (1774).

Naitō Torajirō. Sinologist (Naitō Konan, 1866–1934), born in Akita. At first a journalist, he traveled frequently in China and became a professor of Chinese civilization at the University of Kyoto in 1909. He wrote many works on Sinology and was a famous expert on Chinese art. He also wrote poems in Chinese and was an excellent calligrapher. His complete works, *Naitō Konan zenshū,* were published from 1969 to 1976.

Naitō Yukiyasu. Daimyo (d. 1626) sent by Toyotomi Hideyoshi as an ambassador to the Beijing imperial court to demand the surrender of the emperor of China. His mission having failed, Naitō Yukiyasu returned to Japan and converted to Christianity in 1604, taking the first name Joan. Sent into exile in Manila in 1614, he remained there until his death.

Nakabayashi Chikutō. *See* CHIKUTŌ.

Nakadai Tatsuya. Stage and movie actor (Nakadai Motohisa, b. 1932) noted for his character roles. His first movie role was under director Kurosawa

Akira in *Shichinin no samurai* (The Seven Samurai, 1954); he then worked under directors Ichikawa Kon, Kobayashi Masaki, and others. He also appeared in one of Kurosawa's last films, *Kagemusha*.

Nakae Chōmin. Philosopher (Nakae Tokusuke, 1847–1901), born in Kōchi to a family of small-scale samurai. After studying Confucianism (Shushi and Ō-Yōmei schools) and learning Dutch and French in Nagasaki (he served as interpreter for French envoy Léon Roches), he was sent to France in 1871, where he studied literature and philosophy. When he returned, he taught at the Tokyo Foreign Language School and was appointed secretary of the Genrō-in; he left in 1877 to teach in his own school (founded 1874) and to study Zen Buddhism and the Chinese classics. In 1880, he and Saionji Kimmochi founded the newspaper *Tōyō Jiyū Shimbun* (Oriental Free Press), in which he wrote articles demanding the establishment of a parliamentary system of government. He then published his own magazine, *Seiri Sōdan* (Anecdotes of Statecraft), in which he published his translation of J. J. Rousseau's *Social Contract*. He was considered one of the spiritual leaders of the Jiyū Minken Undō (Freedom and People's Rights Movement) and was called "the Rousseau of the East." Elected to the Diet in 1890, he came under pressure and quickly resigned. He then made a living from odd jobs. In 1900 and 1901, although very ill, he wrote his two most important philosophical works, following on his *Rigaku kōgen* (Research on Philosophical Principles, 1886): *Ichinen yūhan* (A Year and a Half) and *Zoku ichinen yūhan* (A Year and a Half, Continued), expounding the principles of his materialist philosophy of "no God, no spirit." He also wrote a great number of articles tending to reconcile the idealism of the Tokugawa period with the modern scientific spirit, such as *Sansujin keirin mondō* (A Discourse by Three Drunkards on Government, 1887).

Nakae Tōju. Neo-Confucian philosopher (Gen, Mokken, 1608–48), born in Ōmi to a family of peasant samurai. He first studied Zhu Xi (*Jap.:* Shushi) philosophy, then became a follower of Wang Yangming (*Jap.:* Ō-Yōmei). He entered the service of the daimyo of Ōsu and taught Yōmei-gaku, writing more than 200 works on this philosophy; among the best known (which strongly influenced the thought of anti-shogunal proponents in the mid-nineteenth century) were *Okina mondō* (Dialogue with an Old Man), *Daigaku-mōchū, Daigaku-kai, Daigaku-kō, Kohon daigaku zenkai,* and *Kagami-gusa* (Mirror for Women).

Nakagami Kenji. Writer (1946–92), born in Waka-yama prefecture. He went to Tokyo, where he fell in love with jazz and theater. In 1973, while working at the Haneda Airport, he began to write stories, such as *Jūkyūsai no chizu* (The Nineteen-Year Plan, 1974), which were very successful. His first major novel, *Misaki* (The Cape, 1975) won the Akuta-gawa Prize; *Karekinada* (The Kareki Sea, 1977) won the *Mainichi* Prize. He then published continu-ally—*Hōsenka* (Balsam, 1980), *Sennen no yuraku* (The Joy of a Thousand Years, 1982), *Chi no hate, shijō no toki* (End of the Earth, Supreme Time, 1983), *Sanka* (Songs of Praise, 1990)—and traveled in the United States, Europe, Korea, and Southeast Asia. In 1986, he was invited to lecture at Columbia University. Many of his stories were adapted for the screen in Japan.

Nakagawa Gorōji. Interpreter (1768–1848) in the Kuril Islands, taken prisoner by the Russians and sent into captivity in Siberia in 1807, where he learned about vaccinations against smallpox. When he returned to Japan in 1812, following an ex-change of prisoners, he put his medical knowledge to the test, attempting to vaccinate people during the epidemics that decimated the country in 1824, 1835, and 1842.

Nakagawa Hachirō. Painter (1877–1922) in the Western style, Koyama Shōtarō's student. He stud-ied in the United States and Europe and painted mainly landscapes.

Nakagawa Ichirō. Politician (1925–83), born in Hokkaido. Elected to the Diet in 1963, he created a secret ultra-conservative group, the Seiran-kai (So-ciety of the Blue Storm), in 1973, to attempt to de-stabilize the party in power, the Jiyū Minshutō (Lib-eral Democratic party). Distraught at not being able to take over the presidency of that party, he commit-ted suicide.

Nakagawa Jun'an. Physician (1739–86), born in Fukui prefecture, who, with Hiraga Gennai, con-ducted many scientific experiments (he invented an asbestos fabric) and studied Western medical tech-niques. In collaboration with Maeno Ryōtaku and Sugita Gempaku, he translated a Dutch anatomy treatise called *Kaitai shinsho* (New Anatomy Book, 1774), which enabled Japanese medicine to make great advances.

Nakagawa Kazumasa. Painter (1894–1991) of the Nanga school, known for his bright colors and fluid lines. He was also a scholar of classic Chinese litera-ture; he was decorated with the Order of Culture (Bunka-shō) in 1975.

Nakagawa Yoichi. Writer and poet (1897–1994), born in Kagawa prefecture. He first published his *waka* poems in the literary magazine *Bungei Jidai,* then wrote stories and novels: *Ten no yūgao* (1938), *Shitsuraku no niwa* (1950), *Tambi no yoro* (1958).

Nakahama Manjirō. Fisherman (John Manjirō, John Mung, 1827–98). Shipwrecked, he was res-cued by an American whaling ship. His companions debarked in Hawai'i, but Nakahama Manjirō went to the United States, where he studied in Massachu-setts. He returned to Japan via Okinawa in 1851. He was employed as an interpreter by the shogunal authorities during Commodore Perry's visit and became an instructor of interpreting in Nagasaki. In 1859, he published the first English–Japanese phrase book, *Eibei taiwa shōkei.* He was sent to the United States as an interpreter for the delegation (1860) that was to ratify the treaty signed with Townsend Harris. When he returned, he taught English, as well as navigational and whaling tech-niques, in Tokyo. Also called Manjirō.

Nakahara Chūya. Poet (1907–37), born in Yama-guchi prefecture. At first a *waka* poet, he began to compose free verse, inspired by the dadaist poet Takahashi Shinkichi, then by the works of Verlaine and Rimbaud: *Yagi no uta* (1934), *Arishi hi no uta* (published 1938).

Nakai Riken. Neo-Confucian philosopher (1732–1817) from Osaka who, with his brother, Nakai Chikuzan (1730–1804), directed the Kaitoku-dō school. Their instruction was very liberal and did not faithfully follow Zhu Xi (*Jap.:* Shushi). Chiku-zan published several works on economics, includ-ing *Sōbō kigen* (Humble Words on Herbs and Thickets, ca. 1789). Both were sons of Nakai Shūan (1693–1758), also a neo-Confucian philosopher, founder of the Kaitoku-dō.

Nakajima. Marque of many fighter planes, most of which were used during the Second World War:
—**Nakajima B.5–N2:** Torpedo plane (U.S. code name "Kate") made in 1941. *Speed:* 380 km/h; *range:* 1,200 km; *weapons:* one 800 kg torpedo or three 250 kg bombs, one 7.7 machine gun.
—**Nakajima B.6–N:** Tenzan torpedo plane (U.S. code name "Jill") that replaced the B.5–N2 in 1944; 1,268 were built. One 1,850 HP engine; *maximum*

speed: 480 km/h; *range:* 2,500 km; *weapons:* two 7.7 mm machine guns (or one 13 mm machine gun), one 800 kg torpedo.

—**Nakajima C.6–N1:** Saiun navy fighter plane (U.S. code name "Myrt"); 498 built in 1944. *Maximum speed:* 620 km/h; *range:* 5,300 km; *crew:* three; *weapon:* one 7.7 mm machine gun.

—**Nakajima J.1–N:** Gekkō fighter and escort plane (U.S. code name "Irving"), 470 built. Two 1,130 HP engines; *maximum speed:* 505 km/h; *range:* 2,200 km; *crew:* two; *weapons:* two 20 mm cannons.

—**Nakajima Ki–43:** Hayabusa fighter plane (U.S. code name "Oscar"), 5,751 built. Single engine; *maximum speed:* 550 km/h; *range:* 1,200 km; *weapons:* two 12.7 mm machine guns. It was used in Burma in 1942.

—**Nakajima Ki–44:** Ōtsu Shoki single-engine fighter plane (U.S. code name "Tojo"), built starting in 1944.

—**Nakajima Ki–49:** Donryū bomber (U.S. code name "Helen") that replaced the Mitsubishi Ki–21 in 1942. *Weight with payload:* 11,400 kg; *length:* 24.5 m; *wing span:* 20 m; two Nakajima Ha–109 1,450 HP engines; *crew:* eight; *maximum speed:* 490 km/h; *range:* 2,900 km; *maximum altitude:* 9,000 m; *weapons:* one 20 mm cannon, five 12.7 mm machine guns; *payload:* 1,000 kg of bombs.

—**Nakajima Ki–84:** Hayate fighter plane (U.S. code name "Frank"), 3,500 built to support ground forces. *Maximum speed:* 630 km/h; *range:* 2,900 km; *crew:* one; *weapons:* two 20 mm cannons, two 12.7 mm machine guns; *payload:* two 225 kg bombs.

—**Nakajima Ki–115:** Tsurugi fighter plane, used as "kamikaze" plane. *Maximum speed:* 550 km/h; *range:* 2,400 km; *weapon:* one 500 kg bomb.

—**Nakajima Ki–201:** Karyū jet fighter plane (prototype in 1945). *Engines:* two NE–230 (or NE–130) turbo-jets, 1,000 kg thrust each; *length:* 12 m; *wing span:* 14 m; *maximum speed:* 1,000 km/h; *weapons:* two 210 mm cannons and two 30 mm cannons.

—**Nakajima P1–Yi:** Ginga navy bomber (U.S. code name "Frances"), 1,000 built in 1944, used as a "kamikaze" plane. *Maximum speed:* 560 km/h; *range:* 4,400 km; *crew:* three; *weapons:* two 20 mm cannons, one 12.7 mm machine gun; *payload:* 850 kg of bombs.

→ *See* NAKAJIMA CHIKUHEI.

Nakajima Atsushi. Writer (Nakajima Tōn, 1909–42), born in Tokyo. She taught at a girls' school in Yokohama and wrote tales in classic style: *Kotan* (1942), *Hikari to kaze to yumi* (Light, Wind, and Sand, 1942), *Deshi* (The Apprentice), *Sangetsuki* (The Moon on the Mountains), and others. She also wrote a history of R. L. Stevenson's life in Samoa, *Riryō* (The Chinese Doctor, published 1943).

Nakajima Chikuhei. Industrialist and politician (1884–1949), born in Gumma prefecture. In 1917, he founded the Nakajima Institute of Aeronautics Research, which became the Nakajima Aeronautics Company, building planes and engines for other planes, including some Mitsubishi (Zero). He was elected to the House of Representatives in 1930 for the Rikken Seiyūkai (Friends of Constitutional Government party), then was minister of railroads (1937–39) and of trade and industry (1945). His aeronautics company was dismantled after 1945, and some of its subsidiaries were bought up by the Fuji industrial complex.

Nakajima Hiroshi. Ceramist, born 1941 in Takeo (Saga prefecture). Named a Living National Treasure in 1990; exhibited at the Mitsukoshi space in Paris in 1994.

Nakajima Nobuyuki. Politician (1846–99), born in Tosa province, who took part in the anti-shogunal movement in the 1860s. Appointed governor of Kanagawa province in 1874, then a member of the Genrō-in, he joined the Jiyūtō (Liberal party) when it was founded in 1881, but was exiled for his political activities. In 1890, however, he was elected to the House of Representatives for the Rikken Jiyūto (Constitutional Liberal party); he left that party two years later, when he became ambassador to Italy and a member of the House of Peers. He was married to Kishida Toshiko.

Nakajima Yoshimichi. Contemporary writer and philosopher, expert in studies on time. He wrote a highly regarded book, *Jikan to jiyu* (Time and Freedom, 1992), in which he notes, among other things, that the notion of time is changing because of the collapse of the old objective reality of the world.

Naka Kansuke. Writer (1885–1965), born in Tokyo, Natsume Sōseki's student, author of essays and novels with a pessimistic bent: *Gin no saji* (The Silver Spoon, 1913), *Inu* (The Dog, 1922), *Rōkan* (Poetry Collection, 1935).

Nakamaru Seijūrō. Painter (*gō:* Kimpō, 1841–96) in Western and Japanese (Nihonga) styles, disciple of Taizan, Kawakami Tōgai, and Fontanesi.

Naka Michiyo. Historian (1851–1908), expert on Chinese civilization and pioneer of modern Sinology in Japan. He proved that the date 660 BC, traditionally accepted for Jimmu Tennō, could not be true, and translated *The Secret History of the Mongols* into Japanese.

Nakamikado Tennō. Hundred and fourteenth emperor (Prince Yasuhito, 1702<1710–35>1737), Higashiyama Tennō's fifth son and successor. He abdicated in favor of his son Sakuramachi.

Nakamura. Town in Kōchi prefecture (Shikoku) that developed in the fifteenth century with the arrival of Ichijō Norifusa (1423–80), who was fleeing the disturbances of the Ōnin era. Agriculture and fishing. *Pop.*: 37,000.
• Kabuki classical-dance school founded by Nakamura Denjirō (1673–1729), a famous Kabuki actor in Edo. *See* IEMOTO.
—**Nakamura Jōgorō:** Kabuki actor and dancer (1711–63) and playwright.
—**Nakamura Kanzaburō XVII:** Actor (Namino Seiji, Nakamura Yonekichi, Nakamura Moshio, b. 1909 in Tokyo), Nakamura Kichiemon's (1886–1954) younger brother. Designated a Living National Treasure in 1975 and decorated with the Order of Culture (Bunka-shō) in 1980.
—**Nakamura Kumetarō:** Kabuki actor and dancer (1724–77).
—**Nakamura Nakazō:** Kabuki actor and dancer (1736–90), creator of new folk dances. *See also* SHIGAYAMA MANSAKU.
—**Nakamura Shichisaburō:** Kabuki actor (Shōchō, 1662–1708) in Edo, then in Kyoto starting in 1697.
—**Nakamura Shirogorō:** Kabuki actor (*tachiyaku* roles, d. 1712) in Osaka around 1695, then in Kyoto.
—**Nakamura Tomijūrō:** Kabuki actor and dancer (*onnagata* roles, 1719–86) in Edo.
—**Nakamura Utaemon:** *See entry under this name.*
—**Nakamura Yahachi:** Kabuki actor (1703–77) in Edo.

Nakamura Fusetsu. Painter (Nakamura Sakutarō, 1866–1943), born in Tokyo, Koyama Shōtarō's (1857–1916) student. He lived in Paris, where he studied in J. P. Laurens's studio. When he returned to Japan in 1905, he painted historical subjects in a very academic style. He was a well-known calligrapher; in 1936, he founded the Shodō Hakubutsukan (Calligraphy Museum) in Tokyo.

Nakamura Gakuryō. Painter (Nakamura Tsunekichi, 1890–1969), born in Shizuoka prefecture. At first, he followed the style of the Tosa school and was a member of the Nihon Bijutsu-in (Japan Fine Arts Academy). He is best known for his copies of the frescos of the *kondō* in the Hōryū-ji in Nara and his frescos in the Shitennō-ji in Osaka, for which he received the Order of Culture (Bunka-shō) in 1962. His son, Nakamura Tani-o (b. 1921), is an art historian and critic who has written extensively.

Nakamura Hajime. Historian of Buddhism, born 1921 in Matsue. He wrote works on Indian philosophies and Buddhism that gained him an international reputation—*Tōyōjin no shii hōhō* (Ways of Thinking of Eastern Peoples, 1963), *Bukkyōgo daijiten* (Dictionary of Buddhist Terms)—and founded an academy for the study of East Asian thought, the Tōyō Gakuin.

Nakamura Keiu. Writer (Nakamura Masanao, 1832–91), born in Edo, founder of the Dōjin-sha in Tokyo and professor at the University of Tokyo. He converted to Christianity in 1874. Known mainly for his translation of Samuel Smiles's *Self Help (Saigoku risshi hen)* in 1871, which became the "bible" of the Meiji era.

Nakamura Kenkichi. *Waka* poet (1889–1934), born in Hiroshima prefecture, a contributor to the magazine *Araragi*. His works were collected in *Rinsenshū* (1916) and *Keiraishū* (1931).

Nakamura Kimpei. Contemporary sculptor and ceramist, born 1935 in Kanazawa (Ishikawa prefecture). He worked in the Sèvres national manufacture in France in 1985 and wrote several works on ceramics.

Nakamura Kusatao. Poet (Nakamura Seiichirō, 1901–83), born in China. He wrote mainly haiku in the style of the Hototogisu literary group, and founded his own poetry magazine, *Banryoku*, in 1946.

Nakamura Mitsuo. Writer (Koba Ichirō, 1911–88) and literary critic, born in Tokyo, who made a study trip to France in 1938–39. Influenced by French literature, he advocated a Japanese literature more centered on social criticism. His critical works on Futabatei Shimmei, Shiga Naoya, and Tanizaki Jun'ichirō were highly respected and earned several literary awards. Professor emeritus at Meiji University, he was president of the P.E.N. club of Japan.

Nakamura Shin'ichirō. Writer (1918–97), born in Tokyo. He gained some notoriety for publishing a series of five novels written in a rather Proustian style, beginning with *Shi no kage no moto ni* (1947) and ending with *Nagai tabi no owari* (1952). Among his other novels are *Kaiten mokuba* (1957) and *Kūchū teien* (1953). He also wrote many articles of literary criticism and an analytical biography of Rai San'yō.

Nakamura Teii. Painter (1900–82) in the Japanese style (Nihonga), born in Osaka, Hasegawa Sadanobu's student. Because of a congenital malformation, he had to paint holding his brush in both hands. After the Second World War, he inaugurated a new style of painting portraits of women in a very realistic style.

Nakamura Teruo. Soldier (*Chin.*: Li Guanhui, 1918–79), from an Ami tribe in Taiwan, who, as a Japanese soldier, fought in the jungle of the island of Morotai, Indonesia. Unaware that the Second World War had ended, he continued to fight for 30 years. He was found in 1974. Another Japanese soldier, Lieutenant Onoda Hiroo (b. 1922), underwent a similar ordeal; he was found, also in 1974, in the jungle on the island of Lubang, the Philippines.

Nakamura Utaemon. Family of Kabuki actors from the Kinai region. *See also* NAKAMURA.
—Nakamura Utameon I (1714–91), *jitsuaku* roles.
—Nakamura Utaemon III (1778–1838), actor and dancer, Nakamura Utaemon I's son, men's and *onnagata* roles.
—Nakamura Utaemon IV (Kaneru, 1798–1852), various roles.
—Nakamura Utaemon V (1865–1940), *onnagata* roles.
—Nakamura Utaemon VI (b. 1917), Nakamura Utaemon V's son, *onnagata* roles. Designated a Living National Treasure.

Nakano. Archeological site from the Jōmon period (ca. 6000 BC) near Hakodate (Hokkaido), discovered in 1995 and comprising some 50 foundations of semi-buried huts but few ceramic remains. It is the largest Jōmon agglomeration discovered to date. It seems to resemble the Sannaimaru-yama site near Aomori, on the northern tip of Honshu, which is 2,000 years more recent. *See* JŌMON.

Naka no Ōji. Imperial prince (fifth century), Emperor Richū's son. He was killed by his brother, Mizuha-wake (the future Hansō Tennō), on the premise that he had rebelled.

Nakano Ryōko. Contemporary movie actress who began her career in 1970. She is known for her television role in a series of historical adventures in 1971 (NHK network). She acted in numerous films, including *Kimi yo ikari no kawa wo watare* (You Must Cross the River of Anger) and *Ogin-sama* (Story of Lady Ogin) in 1976, as well as in plays. A participant in many symposiums on international exchanges, she founded a cultural-exchange center called WILL (World Inspiration for Liberty and Love) in 1994.

Nakano Seigō. Journalist and politician (1886–1943). Elected to the House of Representatives in 1920, he helped found the Kokumin Dōmei (Nationalist League) in 1932, then founded the Tōhōkai (Far East Society) in 1938. Imprisoned for his opposition to General Tōjō, he committed suicide by *seppuku.*

Nakano Shigeharu. Writer (1902–79), born in Fukui prefecture, part of the "proletarian" Shijikai group starting in 1925. He was also a member of the Nihon Puroretaria Geijutsu Remmei (League for the Proletarian Arts of Japan). He was elected a member of the Nippona Artista Proletaria Federacio (NAPF) in 1927. After marrying a Shingeki stage actress, Hara Masano, in 1930, he joined the Communist party, which was banned, and began to write critical works and poetry anthologies: *Kūsōkato shinario* (1939), *Tetsu no hanashi* (History of Iron), *Uta no wakare* (Farewell to Songs, 1939), *Go-shaku no sake* (Five Cups of Sake, 1947), *Muragimo* (The Soul, 1954), *Nashi no hana* (Pear-Tree Blossoms, 1958), *Kō, otsu, hei, tei* (A, B, C, D, 1965–69), and others. He left the Communist party in 1964. His opinions earned him several prison terms between 1932 and 1941. He received the *Yomiuri* Prize in 1960.

Nakanoshima Kin'ichi. Musician and composer (1904–84) of music for the koto, in the *sōkyoku* genre, son of a famous *shakuhachi* player and grandson of a koto musician of the Yamada school. He became a professor at the Tokyo music school, a position he held until his death. He was also an expert koto player and often gave concerts with his wife, Imai Keiko, the daughter of another musician of the Yamada school, Imai Keishō (1871–1947).

Nakano Takeko. Poet (1847–68), calligrapher, and warrior, born in Edo, expert in *naginata*. She became famous for taking part, with her mother and her sister, Nakano Yūko, in the battle of the Tsuruga castle in Izu, in which she died.

Nakano Yoshio. Writer and literary critic (1903–85), born in Ehime province. He translated a number of English-language works, including *The Merchant of Venice* and *Gulliver's Travels,* and wrote critical books on Elizabethan theater and a biography of Tokutomi Roka.

Nakasendō. Major road linking Edo to Kyoto via central Honshu, Ōmiya, Karuizawa, Fukushima, Ōta, and Sekigahara, and meeting the Tōkaidō at Kusatsu. Opened in 702, it was 542 km long; it had 69 waystations *(shukuba)* and two toll gates *(sekisho),* at Usui (Gumma prefecture) and Kiso Fukushima. Also known as Kiso-kaidō and Kisoji. It was one of the five main roads *(gokaidō)* in the Edo period. *See* GOKAIDŌ, TŌKAIDŌ.

Nakasone Yasuhiro. Politician, born 1918 in Gumma prefecture. After studying law at the University of Tokyo, he served in the navy during the Second World War. Thanks to Tanaka Kakuei, he entered politics in 1947, when he was elected to the House of Representatives for the Jiyū Minshutō (Liberal Democratic party), and he was reelected a number of times. He was minister of communications in Satō Eisaku's cabinet, held several other ministerial positions, then became prime minister in November 1982, as head of the LDP. He resigned in January 1987 and was replaced by Takeshita Noboru. *See* PRIME MINISTERS.

Nakatomi no Kamako. Minister (sixth century) under Emperor Kimmei, strongly opposed to the introduction of Buddhism into the court and to the Soga family. His son, Nakatomi no Katsumi, was killed by the Soga in 587.

• **Nakatomi no Kamatari.** *See* FUJIWARA NO KAMATARI.

• **Nakatomi no Kiyomaro.** Noble and Shinto priest (702–88), head of the Jingi-kan in Nara. The emperor conferred upon him the name Onakamoti no Kiyomaro.

• **Nakatomi no Yakamori.** Poet (active ca. 740) famous for his exchange of poems with his wife, Sanu Chigami. His poems are included in the *Man'yōshū.*

Nakatsukasa naishi no nikki. Journal, probably written by Fujiwara no Tsuneko, lady-in-waiting to Emperor Fushimi, in the late thirteenth century, dealing with the years 1280–92. The title *Nakatsukasa* indicates that she may have belonged to the government's bureau of central affairs (Nakatsukasa-shō). This text, sprinkled with some 150 *waka* poems that convey a profound sense of *mono no aware,* deals mainly with events in the court and with the festivals that took place there.

• **Nakatsukasa-shō.** The court's Department of Central Affairs, created in 649 to form a liaison between the emperor and the State Council (Dajō-kan), directed by a minister with the title Nakatsukasa-kyō. Starting in the eleventh century, an imperial prince always held this position.

Nakaura, Julian. Christian (ca. 1570–1633) sent to Rome in 1582 by the Christian daimyo of Kyushu after completing his studies at the Arima Seminary. When he returned to Japan in 1591, he became a Jesuit; he was ordained a priest in 1608 and martyred in 1633.

Nakayama Gishū. Writer (Nakayama Yoshihide, 1900–69), born in Fukushima prefecture. His first novel, *Atsumonozaki,* published in 1938, won the Akutagawa Prize. A war correspondent in the Pacific during the Second World War, he wrote novels dealing with this period, then historical novels; *Shōan,* on the life of warrior Akechi Mitsuhide, received the Noma Prize in 1963.

Nakayama Ichirō. Economist (1898–1980), born in Mie prefecture, who completed his studies in Germany. An adviser to several successive governments, he was one of the most influential figures in the economic development of Japan after 1950. He was decorated with the Order of the Rising Sun, First Class (*see* KUNSHŌ) in 1974. Author of a number of books on economics.

Nakayama Komin. Lacquer artist (Komin, 1808–70) and sculptor of netsuke in Edo.

Nakayama Miki. Peasant (Maekawa Miki, Ō-Miki, Miki, 1798–1887), born in a small village (now Tenri) in Yamato. After she was married at the age of 13, she became increasingly pious and mystical, losing herself in devotion to the *kami*. On December 9, 1838, when she was about 40, she received a "revelation" from a *kami* named Tenri Ō Mikoto and began to travel the region preaching an ideal of faith and justice, ridding herself of all her possessions by distributing them to the needy. About 1858, she began to heal by the laying on of hands and recitation of prayers. She wrote many religious texts on her beliefs, including *Mikagura uta* (Songs for Sacred Dances) and *Ofudesaki* (Born of the Divine Brush), which became sacred writings of the Tenri-kyō sect. Sect members called her Oyasama ("venerated parent"). *See* TENRI-KYŌ.

Nakayama Shimpei. Composer (1887–1952), born in Nagano prefecture. He wrote a great number of popular songs and melodies, which were performed by the greatest singers of his times and recorded on Victor records (JV–1024/5).

Nakayama Tadachika. Writer and historian (1132–95) who is sometimes credited with writing the *Mizu kagami* and *Ima kagami.*

Nakayama Ukichirō. Physicist (1900–62), born in Kaga, famous for his study on snow and low temperatures, *Fuyu no hana* (Winter Flowers, 1938).

Nakazato Kaizan. Writer (Nakazato Yanosuke, 1885–1944), born in Hamura, near Tokyo. After holding various jobs, in 1906 he joined the newspaper *Miyako*, where he published his first historical novel, *Kōya no gijin* (The Wise Man of Mt. Kōya, 1910), and, starting in 1913, a very long novel, *Daibosatsu tōge* (The Passing of the Bodhisattva), of which he completed 32 volumes before he died. The first two parts of this immense work were adapted for the screen, notably by directors Inagaki Hiroshi, Yamanaka Sadao, and Arai Ryōhei in 1935, then by Watanabe Kunio (1953), Uchida Tomu (1957–59), and Okamoto Kihachi (1966).

Nakazato Takashi. Ceramist, born 1937 in Karatsu (Saga prefecture). Lecturer in Ohio (1967). In 1971, he opened a kiln in Tanegashima. His works were exhibited at the Mitsukoshi space in Paris in 1994.

Nakazato Tsuneko. Writer (Nakazato Tsune, 1909–87), born in Kanazawa prefecture. She was the first woman to receive the Akutagawa Prize, in 1938, for a story called *Noriai basha*. After the Second World War, she wrote novels dealing with marriages with foreigners, including *Mariannu monogatari* (or *Bochi no haru*, 1946) and *Kusari* (1959). In 1973, she received the *Yomiuri* Prize for her novel *Utamakura;* she received the Nihon Geijutsu-

in (Japan Art Academy) Prize the following year. She was elected a member of the Academy in 1983.

Nakazawa Dōni. Philosopher (Nakazawa Yoshimichi, Dōni, 1725–1803) of the Sekimon school founded by Ishida Baigan. Born to a family of weavers in Kyoto, he was a devotee of Nichiren before he studied Confucianism. He opened a lecture hall that anyone could attend in Edo in 1779, to spread his teachings among commoners and warriors; encouraged by Matsudaira Sadanobu, he extended his activities to Kyoto and Osaka. His lectures were collected in *Dōni ō dōwa* (Discourse on the Path by Dōni). Also known as Dōni.

Nakazawa Rinsen. Social historian (Shiozawa Shigeo, 1878–1920) and electrical engineer. He wrote many works intended to educate the Japanese about Western societies, and books about works by European philosophers such as Bergson and Nietzsche.

Naki-fudō emaki. Thirteenth-century *emakimono* of "Fudō crying."

• **Naki-masu.** Noh mask portraying the face of a sad young woman. *See* MASKS, NŌ-MEN.

Nakōdo. People responsible for arranging marriages and serving as intermediaries between the families and the future husband and wife. They are charged with seeking the ideal partner for the son or daughter of the family that requests this service. *Nakōdo* play an extremely important social role; on the wedding day, they are the first to make a speech, in which they present to the families the young people who have decided to unite in marriage (*engumi, miai-kekkon,* or *ren'ai-kekkon*). *Nakōdo* (usually a couple) are generally chosen from among aged, respected people. *See* MARRIAGE.

Nakoku. According to the Chinese chronicle the *Weizhi,* a small sovereign state in northern Kyushu during the second and third centuries, ruling over about 30 small *miyatsuko*. It was the Wa no Nakoku of the *Hou hanshu,* perhaps identical to the town and region of Nanoagata or Nanotsu, mentioned as being located near Hakata in the *Nihon shoki.* Also called Na no Kuni. *See* SUKU.

Nakoso no seki. Fortified barrier erected in the eighth century (called Kikuta no seki) near the town of Iwaki (Fukushima prefecture) to contain the Ezo tribes. It was one of three large barriers built in the region in this period; the others were the Shirakawa no seki and the Nezu no seki. In poetry, it was called Uta-makura and evoked solitude and distance from the capital.

Namahage. Tradition according to which, on the eve of the day called *koshōgatsu* (15th day of the first month), foreigners living in the villages disguised themselves as gods or demons and visited houses to ask whether the children had been good. They were given *mochi* or a little money. The visitors were often played by young men of the village. This custom was observed mostly in the Akita region.

Namamugi Jiken. Incident on September 14, 1862, between some British travelers and samurai escorting Shimazu Hisamitsu, daimyo of Satsuma, in the village of Namamugi near Yokohama. The foreigners had not bowed as the daimyo passed, so several samurai, outraged, attacked them, killing a British merchant, Charles Richardson, and injuring two of his companions. The British government demanded an apology and an indemnity of 100,000 pounds sterling from the Edo shogunate, as well as punishment of the samurai. The shogunate agreed, but Satsuma refused to pay the indemnity of 25,000 pounds sterling demanded of it. In reprisal, the British bombed Kagoshima on August 15, 1863. *See* SATSUEI SENSŌ.

Namban. "Southern Barbarians," a term for most of the foreigners trading with Japan via the ports of Kyushu, especially Nagasaki, in the sixteenth century, as opposed to *kōmōjin*, or "red-skinned men" (Aka-Ezo), the term for the Russians, English, and Dutch who arrived in Japan in the early seventeenth century. *Namban* was also applied to most imported objects; to objects portraying foreigners, such as *namban-byōbu*, or "screens portraying the Southern Barbarians"; and to foreign customs. *Namban* art was represented mainly by copies of foreign paintings (notably Christian ones). These paintings were introduced to Japan in 1683 by the Italian Jesuit Giovanni Niccolo, who inaugurated Christian religious painting in the country. However, Japanese artists preferred to portray lay scenes in which the "barbarians" were shown as objects of curiosity. Most of these screens are not signed, and only one of the artists, Nobutaka, is known; he placed his seal on several of his works. Some artists of the Kano school worked in this style (also called the Nagasaki style), including Kanō Naizen (1570–1616) and Kanō Mitsunobu.

• **Namban-byōbu.** *See* NAMBAN.

• **Namban-ji.** Jesuit church built in Kyoto in 1576 and destroyed in 1588 on the order of Toyotomi Hideyoshi. All that remains of it is a bell engraved with the monogram IHS and the date 1577, now kept in the Myōshin-ji temple in Kyoto. Also called Eiroku-ji.

Nambokuchō. The imperial Northern Court (Hokuchō) and Southern Court (Nanchō), which conducted a civil war from 1336 to 1392. In the thirteenth century, the imperial family separated into two factions, the Jimyō-in (descendants of Emperor Go-Fukakusa) and the Daitoku-ji (descendants of Emperor Kameyama), and a compromise was forged according to which emperors from each faction would reign alternately. But when Ashikaga Takauji placed Emperor Kōgon (of the Jimyō-in) on the throne in Kyoto and had him followed by Kōmyō, another emperor of the same branch, the two branches separated, with the Daikaku-ji taking refuge in Yoshino, while emperors of the Jimyō-in reigned in Kyoto. The emperors of the Northern Court were not recognized in the legitimate succession of imperial power. The lords rallied behind one of the two courts (the Northern Court was supported by the Ashikaga shogun), and war broke out. The two courts reconciled only in 1392, when Emperor Go-Komatsu of the Northern Court was accepted as the legitimate sovereign by both factions, on condition that the alternation resume. But this did not happen, and the Southern Court was eliminated.

Nambō Sōkei. Master of the tea ceremony (*chanoyu*) who lived in the late sixteenth century and who was a disciple of Sen no Rikyū. He was probably a merchant in Sakai. His only work, *Nambōroku* (Nambō's Notes), in seven scrolls, completed in 1593, was published in 1686 and 1690 by Tachibana Jitsuzan. It is considered one of the main texts on *chanoyu*, with the *Yamanoue sōji-ki*. *See* SEN NO RIKYŪ, YAMANOUE SŌJI.

Nambu. Automatic pistol (model 14) in use in the army in 1926, the ammunition for which was also used in model 94, produced in 1934. This pistol, invented by Colonel Nambu Kijirō (1869–1949), replaced the old T26 (9 mm) dating from 1893. *Total weight:* 920 g; *length:* 228 mm; *magazine:* eight 8 mm bullets; *initial velocity:* 330 m/sec.; *range:* 50 m. Model 94 was slightly smaller than model 14 and had a seven-bullet magazine.

• **Nambu-Goma.** *See* CHAGU-CHAGU, UMAKKO.

Names ("Myō"). Proper names in Japan fall into four main categories: place names, family names, men's names, and women's names, to which are added special names, names of Buddhist monks, and honorifics.

—Place names: The origin of place names is not always certain, but they are usually derived from physical or historical specificities. The most common are taken from the name of a river *(kawa, -gawa)*, a plain *(hara)*, a mountain *(-san, yama, take, -gake)*, a valley *(tani, -dani)*, a bay *(kata, -gata)*, or an island *(shima, -jima)*, and may have a qualificative such as big *(ō)*, small *(ko, o)*, high *(taka)*, long *(naga)*, or a direction—north *(kita hoku)*, south *(nan, nam, minami)*, east *(higashi, tō)*, or west *(nishi, sai)*. Many place names come from ancient Ainu designations, such as those ending in *-betsu* and *-nai*. Others originated in administrative divisions: prefecture *(ken)*, village *(mura)*, town *(machi, chō)*, road *(dō, michi)*. Of course, the combinations are infinite.

—Family names: At first, there were no family names, but clan names *(uji, kabane)*, to which were often added words describing a function, such as *ason, asomi, imiki, omi, muraji, mahito,* and so on. In the Heian period, family names diversified and were created, generally by emperors, by adopting place names, such as *Fujiwara, Ichijō, Satō,* and so on. Commoners did not have family names but used their first names, sometimes adding a specification relating to their parentage, village, or occupation. In 1868, family names were made compulsory for all, both nobles and peasants. These names had to be different from first names and sobriquets.

—Men's names: People's true names were once rarely used, the belief being that the person who knew someone's name could influence that person's fate. Asking a young woman her personal name was equivalent to a marriage proposal, and if the young woman gave it, it was equivalent to accepting. Therefore, another name—sobriquet, name of function, title, and so on—was used instead, especially in relations with superiors. Personal names *(tsūshō* or *yobina)* were very diverse and could have to do with birth order, such as *Tarō* (big male), *Ichirō* (first male), *Jirō, Saburō, Katorō* (small male), and so on, or to the family or clan to which they belonged, such as *Gen* (for Genji), or *Hei* (for Heike), leading to names such as Gentarō and Heitarō. Childhood names *(yōmyō, dōmyō)* were also used, often ending in *-waka, -maro, -maru, -ō;* these were sometimes used throughout life. When men reached adulthood (around 13–14 years of age), they were given their true name *(jitsumyō, nanori)*, which was often covered by a sort of taboo *(imina)* but which were used to distinguish them officially, in the *gempuku* ceremony.

—Women's names: Before the ninth century, almost all noblewomen's names ended with *-me, -iratsume,* or *-toji.* Later, these names gained the suffix *-ko.* Other women's names (drawn from names of virtues or flowers, for example) ended with syllables such as *-e, -i,* or *-o.* Starting in the Meiji era, with names no longer regulated, many women adopted the suffix *-ko* (girl, princess) and the most popular names became Yōko (daughter of the sun), Sachiko (happy girl), Kazuko (girl of peace), Fumiko (literate girl), Shizuko (tranquil girl), Hisako (long-lived girl), and so on. The modern trend is to return to less "standard" names and drop the suffix *-ko,* for names such as Shizue and Harue.

—Other names: There are other categories of names used in preference to men's and women's personal names, such as *azana* (pseudonyms in two *kanji* characters), *gō* (artists' names, also called *gagō)*, names of Buddhist monks *(hōmyō)*, and posthumous names *(kaimyō, okurina)*. Geimyō, names given to artists, and *haimyō,* given to haiku poets, are in the *gō* category. *Mei,* or "familiar names," were used in place of personal names in certain circumstances. Some artists had several *gō* (Hokusai, for example, used 30). Many people were known only by their sobriquet *(adana, azana)*— such as Hidari Jingorō ("Jingorō the left-handed") —comprising either an adjective or the name of a place or a building, such as *yagō,* used by some Kabuki actors. Other names used in daily life (in the *tsūshō* category) were called *zokumyō, kemyō,* and so on.

—Emperors' names: These are not family names but princes' personal names, designated after their death by the name of their era followed by their posthumous title *(tennō)*. (Thus, Hirohito, after 1990, was known as Shōwa Tennō.) Some emperors, however, were given other posthumous names in the course of history.

—Polite names: In general, all people are addressed by following their family name with the suffix *-san* (very polite, *-sama)*. Married women have the title *okusan* ("she of the back room," once reserved for women) or *okusama*. Personal names (or sobriquets) of most children (boys and girls) are followed by the affectionate suffix *-chan*. According to Eastern custom, the family name always precedes the personal name—Tange Kenzō, for example, not Kenzō Tange. When a Japanese introduces himself,

he always gives his business card *(meishi)* as he says his name, since it is often difficult to read kanji characters (even though their number is limited by law; *see* KANJI): one character can have up to 10 different pronunciations, and one sound *(taka, moto, nobu,* etc.) can be represented by dozens of characters. *See* AZANA, DAIMYO, GŌ, HAIMYŌ, HYAKUSHŌ, MEI, YAGŌ, YOBINA, YŌMYŌ, ZOKUMYŌ.

Namie Kokan. Famous Kabuki actor *(onnagata* roles) active in Kyoto and Osaka between 1659 and 1694.

Namikawa Banri. Contemporary photographer, famous for his images of the Japanese heritage and for photographs he took on the Silk Road in China for television and UNESCO.

Namikawa Sōsuke. Enamel artisan (1847–1910).

• **Namikawa Yasuyuki.** Enamel artisan (1845–1927).

Namiki. Family of actors and Kabuki playwrights:
—Namiki Gohei I: Kabuki actor (1747–1808), Namiki Shōzō's student in Osaka and Edo, author of famous plays: *Kimon gosan no kiri* (The Thief of the Temple Gate, 1778), *Keisei kogane no sachihoko* (The Thief of Fish Scales, 1782), *Kanjin kammon tekuda no hajimari* (Murder of a Foreign Envoy, 1789), *Godairiki koi no fūjime* (1794), *Sumida no hara geisha-katagi* (1796), and others. He wrote more than 110 historical *(jidai-mono)* and current-events *(sewa-mono)* plays.
—Namiki Gohei II: Kabuki actor (Shinoda Kinji I, 1768–1819).
—Namiki Gohei III: Kabuki actor (1790–1855), author of *Kanjinchō* (The Subscription List, 1840).
—Namiki Senryū: Actor and playwright (Namiki Sōsuke, 1695–ca. 1751), author of more than 40 *jōruri* plays for the Takemoto-za in Osaka, to be used in puppet shows *(ningyō-jōruri)*. He worked with Takeda Izumo and Miyoshi Shōraku *(Chishingura,* 1748).
—Namiki Shōzō I: Kabuki actor and playwright (1730–73) in Kyoto and Osaka, author of some 100 plays *(jidai-mono)*. He invented the revolving stage *(mawari-butai)* and the *seri-age.*
—Namiki Shōzō II: Kabuki actor (d. 1807), author of a technical work on Kabuki, *Gezairoku,* in 1801.

Nammei. *See* HARUKI NAMMEI.

Nampin. Chinese painter (Chin Nampin; *azana:* Shen Quan, Hengzhai; *Chin.:* Shen Nanpin, active between 1725 and 1780). He went to Nagasaki in 1731 and taught there until 1733; his style profoundly influenced Itō Jakuchū and the artists of the Bunjinga (Nanga) school. He painted mainly animals, flowers, and birds.

Nampo Jōmyō. *See* DAIŌ KOKUSHI.

Namu Amida Butsu. "In the name of Amida Buddha," a magical and devotional formula recited by followers of the Jōdo-shū sect for the purpose of being reborn in Amida's paradise (Jōdo, "Pure Earth") after their death. Called *nembutsu,* it is also recited by devotees of the Jōdo Shin-shū. Also called Nammanda Butsu. *Okinawa: Nimbuchi; Chin.: Nianfo.*

• **Namu Myōhō renge-kyō.** "In the name of the *Lotus Sutra,"* a magical and devotional formula recited by followers of the Nichiren and Sōka Gakkai sects. It is one of the *sandai-hihō* of the Nichiren-shū sect, along with the cult object *(honzon,* often the written formula) and the *kaidan* (ordination platform). Recitation of this sutra title *(Jap.: kyō)* is supposed to bring happiness, health, and prosperity to followers and lead them to supreme bliss. This sacred formula is called *dainoku. See* HOKE-KYŌ.

Nanako. Type of decoration on metal made by incising the background with a pointed engraving tool to produce granular surfaces.

Nanakusa no kayu. Soup made with seven types of herbs. Custom (of Chinese origin) has it that it is eaten on the seventh day of the month in order to enjoy good health all year.

Nanatesaki. In traditional architecture, a type of overhang (in the *tenjiku-yō* mode) formed by seven projected *degumi* with a *shashi-hijiki* inserted. *See* MUTESAKI, TO-KYŌ.

Nando-yaku. During the Edo period, the bureau responsible for jewels and objects belonging to the shogun, directed by a *nando-gashira* with 60 assistants. Also called *nando-gata.*

Nanga. "Southern paintings," an alternate term for Bunjinga, or "literate painting," a style created in the seventeenth century and in use mainly during the ensuing two centuries, in which painters were freer in their interpretation and techniques. Landscapes, trees, and flowers were their favorite subjects. Painters of this school were also poets. Also called Nanshūga. *See also* BUNJINGA.

Nangaku. *See* WATANABE IWAO.

Nangaku-ha. "School of the Southern Teaching," a branch of the Zhu Xi (*Jap.*: Shushi) school of philosophy, founded in 1548 in Tosa by a Zen monk, Minamimura Baiken. It had some influence on the anti-shogunal school in that province.

Naniwa. Ancient port and capital founded about 683 by Emperor Temmu, now a district (Hōenzakachō) of Osaka. A number of sovereigns (Kōgyoku Tennō, Saimei Tennō, Kōtoku Tennō, Jitō Tennō, Mommu Tennō, Shōmu Tennō) had their pleasure palaces there in the seventh and eighth centuries; these were often destroyed by fires. Naniwa stopped being the capital when the sovereigns moved to Shigaraki no Miya and Heijō-kyō in 745. Also called Naniwa no Tsu, Naniwa-kyō.

• **Naniwa-bushi.** Ballads sung with shamisen accompaniment; this genre developed in the Osaka and Kyoto regions in the early Edo period. Often humorous, *naniwa-bushi* were very popular until the Second World War, but are now performed mainly in the countryside. Better known as *rō-kyoku*. *See* YOSE.

• **Naniwa no Horie.** Canal dug by Koreans in 323, according to tradition, to keep the town of Naniwa from being flooded by the sea. Legend has it that Emperor Kimmei had the Buddhist statues that had been sent to the Japanese court by the Korean king of Kudara thrown into this canal in 553.

• *Naniwa miyage.* Title of a work on Chikamatsu Monzaemon's *jōruri,* written by one of his contemporaries, Hozumi Ikan (1692–1769), a Confucian scholar (Chikamatsu Hanji's father), and published in 1738.

Nanjō Bun'yū. Buddhist monk (1849–1927) of the Ōtani branch of the Jōdo Shin-shū sect, born in Mino province (Gifu prefecture), who studied Buddhism and Sanskrit under Max Müller at Oxford starting in 1876. When he returned to Japan, he published many translations of Buddhist texts, taught at the University of Kyoto, and was president of Ōtani University (formerly Shinshū University). His best-known book is *Catalogue of Chinese*

Transcriptions of the Tripitaka (also known as the *Nanjō Catalogue*), published in 1883.

Nanjō Tokimitsu. Militarist governor (1259–1332) of the Ueno region of Suruga province (Shizuoka prefecture), who became a disciple of Nichiren. He donated a parcel of land in Ōishigahara to Nikkō Shōnin, who had directed the Minobu temple after Nichiren's death but had left it; Nikkō Shōnin constructed a small temple there called Daibo in 1290. It later became the Taiseki-ji temple, headquarters of the Nichiren sect. *See* TAISEKI-JI.

Nanki Bunko. "Nanki Library," containing more than 100,000 works gathered by various members of the Nanki branch of the Tokugawa, and belonging to the University of Tokyo. *See also* AOI BUNKO.

Nanko. Painter (Haruki Kon; *mei:* Mon'ya; *azana:* Shigyo; *gō:* Enka-chōsō, Yūsei-kitei, Dombokuō, 1759–1839) of the Nanga school, who studied with Sensei and Tani Bunchō. He painted mainly landscapes. Nammei's father.

Nansō Satomi hakkenden. "The Eight Dogs of Satomi." A 181-chapter historical novel by Takizawa Bakin, published from 1814 to 1842 in Edo, describing a rebellion that took place in 1441 as told by eight "dogs" (warriors) of the Satomi family. This *yomihon,* written in a simplified form of classical Japanese, features a moralizing plot. This novel has remained famous as a classic of the *yomihon* genre and *gesaku* literature.

Nanto-rokushū. "The Six Sects of Nara," Buddhist sects that had a great influence on politics in the Nara period: Kusha-shū, Jōjitsu-shū, Hossō-shū, Sanron-shū, Ritsu-shū, and Kegon-shū. *See* BUDDHISM.

• **Nanto Shichidai-ji.** "The Seven Great Buddhist Temples of the Nanto [Nara] Period": Tōdai-ji, Kōfuku-ji, Saidai-ji, Genkō-ji, Taian-ji, Yakushi-ji, and Hōryū-ji.

Nanushi. In the Edo period, mayor of a village or small town. *See also* SHŌYA.

Nanzan Daigaku. Private university founded in Nagoya in 1946, which became a national university in 1949. Many faculties; annual attendance, about 6,000 students.

Nanzen-ji. Major Zen Buddhist temple of the Rinzai branch, established in 1291 in Kyoto in the former villa of Retired Emperor Kameyama, who first called it Ryūzan Zenrin Zen-ji, then Zuiryūzan Nanzen-ji. The first abbot of this temple was Mukan Fumon (1212–91). The Nanzen-ji was raised to the rank of first *gozan* temple in Kyoto in 1334, and Musō Kokushi was its head abbot. In 1393, the warrior-monks of the Hiei-zan (Enryaku-ji) attacked the temple and set it ablaze. It was rebuilt by Ashikaga Yoshimochi but destroyed again in 1447 and 1467 (Ōnin War). Toyotomi Hideyoshi and the Tokugawa shogun had it reconstructed: the abbot's apartments were transported from the imperial palace and the demolished castle in Fushimi. It has a San-mon (Tenka Ryūmon) in Zen style rebuilt in 1628, *hōjō* from 1611, and *hondō* built in 1909. This temple houses beautiful paintings by Kanō Tan'yū (ceiling of the San-mon), and paintings by Kanō Motonobu, Kanō Sanraku, Kanō Mitsunobu, and Minchō. The *daihōjō* has a beautiful sand-and-stone garden, designed by Kobori Enshū, and the *nanzen-in,* a garden in the style of the Kamakura period.

Naohiko. Painter (Kumagawa Naohiko; *gō:* Tokuga, 1828–1913) in modern Japanese style (Nihonga).

Naokata. Painter (Shirai Naokata; *mei:* Chūhachirō; *azana:* Shisai; *gō:* Bunkyo, active ca. 1810) of the Maruyama school, Ōkyo's student. He painted mainly animals.

Naoki Sanjūgo. Writer (Uemira Sōichi, 1891–1934), born in Osaka. He changed pseudonyms almost every year to reflect his age, and adopted Sanjūgo ("thirty-five") only when he was 35 years old. He wrote many stories for the *Bungei shunjū* and a few historical novels, such as *Nangoku taiheiki* (1931) and *Kusunoki masashige* (1932). The prestigious Naoki Literary Prize was created in his honor by his friend Kikuchi Kan.

Naonobu. Painter (Kanō Naonobu, Kanō Kazunobu, Kanō Ienobu; *mei:* Shume; *gō:* Jitekisai, 1607–50) of the Kanō school, who studied with Kanō Kōi; his father, Kanō Takanobu; and his older brother, Kanō Tan'yū. He created the Kobikichō branch of the Kanō school in Edo and worked in the *e-dokoro* of the Tokugawa shogun. *See* KANŌ-HA.

Naorai. Shinto rite of communion between the *kami* and the faithful, performed generally at the end of a period of *imi* (abstinence, mourning, or purification) during a banquet at which *sake* and various foods were offered to the divinities. A *naorai* sometimes took place among the followers of a Buddhist divinity after "sacrifices" (ritual offerings) called *gisei* were made.

Naoshi. Robe *(kimono)* once worn at home by nobles in place of the official *hō.* Also sometimes called *nōshi.*

Naotake. *See* ODANO NAOTAKE.

Naotomo. Painter (Isshiki Naotomo; *gō:* Getsuan, Rosetsu, d. 1597) of the Muromachi *suiboku* school, influenced by Sesshū. He was a samurai.

NAPF. Abbreviation of Nippona Artista Proletaria Federacio, the Esperanto name of an association of writers with communist leanings ("proletarian" literature) created in 1924 by writers from the magazine *Bungei Sensen;* NAPF separated from *Bungei Sensen* around 1930. Also called *Senki* (The Flag). *See* BUNGEI SENSEN, SENKI.

Nara. Chief city of Nara prefecture (Honshu) about 20 km southeast of Kyoto, on the Yamato plateau, built in 710 as Heijō-kyō to be the capital of the state of Yamato. The city was laid out on a checkerboard plan, imitating that of Chang'an, the Chinese Tang capital, and measured about 4.8 by 4.3 km. It was in and around this city that the Buddhist "Six Sects of Nara" (Nanto-rokushū) developed; they had a major influence on emperors' policies until 784, when the capital was transferred to Nagaoka (then to Heian-kyō in 794). Heijō-kyō was then renamed Nanto and lost some of its importance. The city was decimated several times in civil wars and was set afire by the Taira clan in 1180. However, many monuments have survived, including the Tōdai-ji (749), the Kōfuku-ji (669), transferred to Nara in 710), the Kasuga-jinja (1135), the Shin Yakushi-ji (747), and the Shōsō-in Museum (749). There are many more in the surrounding area: Saidai-ji, Hōryū-hi, Akishino-dera, Hokke-ji, Hase-dera, Danzan-jinja, Morū-ji, Bunkakan Museum of Yamata, and others. The city of Nara has few industries; the main economic activities are tourism, sumi (China ink) crafts, and manufacturing of brushes, dolls, fans, and bamboo and lacquer objects. Pop.: 300,000.

• **Nara-jidai.** "Nara era," from 710 to 784 (or 794, according to some historians). This period saw the development of the *ritsuryō* system, the introduction from China of government systems, Buddhist sects, art forms ("Tempyō culture"), and the beginnings of Japanese literature, with the *Kojiki* and *Nihongi*.

• **Nara-ken.** Nara prefecture, surrounded by Kyoto, Mie, Osaka, and Wakayama prefectures; it has no direct access to the sea and is irrigated by the Yoshino-gawa, Yamato-gawa, and Totsukawa rivers. This mountainous prefecture has always had a base in agriculture and crafts. Its very numerous historic sites make it a favorite tourist region. *Main cities:* Kashihara, Ikoma, Tenri, Gose, Gojō, Takada, Sakurai. It also has the Yoshino-Kumano National Park. *Area:* 3,692 km². *Pop.:* 2,330,000.

• **Nara Horimono-ya.** Collective name for sculptors from the Kōshō, Jōchō, Unkei, and other family lines who worked in Nara.

• **Nara Joshi Daigaku.** Women's university in Nara, founded in 1908 as a teaching college, and raised to the rank of university in 1949. It has faculties of literature, science, and domestic economics. Attendance: about 1,600 students.

• **Nara Kokuritsu Hakubutsukan.** National museum of Nara, founded in 1899, devoted to Buddhist art and religion of the Nara region. It also displays Shinto cult objects and various collections. Tea house *(hassōan)* in Oribe style. *See* MUSEUMS.

• **Nara, Master of.** Unknown painter who probably lived in Nara in the late sixth century and was a Buddhist monk. Nothing is known about his life.

• **Nara Sansaku.** Collective term for the three best metal engravers who worked in Nara in the seventeenth and eighteenth centuries: Tsuchiya Yasuchika, Nara Toshinaga, and Sugiura Jōi.

Narayama-bushi kō. "The Songs of Oak Mountain." A novel by Fukazawa Shichirō on the legend of Obasute, published in 1956. A movie on this subject was made by Kinoshita Keisuke in 1958. *See* OBASUTE.

Naraya Mozaemon. Family of wood merchants who made their fortune in Edo during the Tokugawa shogunate; they contributed to the reconstruction of the Tōshōgū shrine in Nikkō after it was partially destroyed by the earthquake of 1683.

Narihasa. *See* DŌNIN.

Narinaga Shinnō. Imperial prince (1325–38), Go-Daigo Tennō's tenth son, who was appointed Kantō-kanryō in 1333, then shogun in Kamakura. He and his brother, Tsunenaga Shinnō, were killed in the disturbances following the fall of the Kamakura shogunate.

Narita. City in Chiba prefecture, about 66 km northeast of Tokyo, which developed as a *monzen-machi* around the Shinshō-ji Buddhist temple. It is home to the New Tokyo International Airport, which opened in 1978 to replace the overly congested Haneda Airport as Tokyo's chief international airport. The airport has runways 4,000 m long and covers an area of 550 hectares, soon to be expanded to 1,065 hectares. *See* CHIBA PREFECTURE, TOKYO.

Narita Tomomi. Politician (1912–79), born in Kagawa prefecture, elected to the House of Representatives in 1947 for the Nihon Shakaitō (Japan Socialist party). He was secretary-general of the party in 1962, and its president from 1968 to 1977.

Naruhito. Crown prince of Japan, born 1960, oldest son of Emperor Akihito. In 1993, he married Owada Masako, the daughter of a senior bureaucrat in the Ministry of Foreign Affairs, with degrees from Harvard and Oxford, born 1964. *See* AKIHITO.

Naru-ita. In the palaces and houses of samurai in the Edo period, a method of constructing veranda floors so that they creaked when they were walked on, providing a warning that someone was there. Also called *genzan no ita, uguisu-bari* (nightingale floor).

Narukami. "The *Kami* of Thunder." A one-act play, one of the Kabuki-jūhachiban, written by Ichikawa Danjūrō I (1660–1704), first performed in 1742, and re-created about 1911 by Sadanji II: to take revenge on the emperor, a Buddhist monk named Narukami imprisons the dragon of rain, thus provoking a severe drought. The emperor sends one of his daughters to the monk's retreat to seduce him. She succeeds, and when he falls asleep she frees the dragon, enabling the rain to fall again. → *See* KAMINARI.

Naruse Mikio. Movie director (1905–69). Starting in 1930, he produced a number of silent films imbued with melancholy, mostly on social behavior and women. He started to produce talking pictures in 1934, working for Tōhō. His first movie with sound, *Tsuma yo bara no yō ni* (Woman, Be Like a Rose, 1935), was successful, and he married the lead actress, Chiba Sachiko. After a fallow period, he directed *Meshi* (The Meal, 1951), *Inazuma* (Lightning, 1952), *Okasan* (The Mother, 1952), *Bangiku* (Late Chrysanthemum, 1954), *Ukigumo* (Wandering Clouds, 1955), his greatest success, and *Hōrōki* (Traveler's Notes, 1962), in which he directed his favorite actress, Takamine Hideko.

Narushima Ryōjō. Historian and writer (Narushima Chikuzan, 1803–1854), author of *Nochikagami (Kōkan),* a history of the Ashikaga shoguns, complementing the *Azuma-kagami.*

Narushima Ryūhoku. Journalist and writer (Narushima Korehiro, 1837–84), born in Edo, author of a series of anecdotes and books on life in Edo, such as *Ryūkyō shinshi* (1860). After the Meiji Restoration, he traveled in Europe; when he returned in 1873, he became editor-in-chief of the *Chōya Shimbun,* an anti-government newspaper. He published the second part of *Ryūkyō shinshi* in 1874, and the third part in 1876 (it was censored, and only the preface survived). In 1884, he published a journal on his trip to Europe, *Kōsei nichijō.*

Narutaki-juku. School established near Nagasaki by Franz von Siebold to teach medicine and Western sciences.
→ *See* JUKU.

Naruto Kaikyō. Strait between the island of Awaji and the city of Naruto on Shikoku. Because it is narrow (1,300 m), it has strong currents and undertows between the Kii Sea and the eastern part of the Inland Sea (Setonaikai). It is dangerous for shipping because the current can reach 18 km/h. A bridge linking Honshu to Shikoku crosses the strait.

Nashiji. Lacquer technique in which tiny grains of silver and gold are mixed with the lacquer in different layers, giving the appearance of pear skin *(nashi).* This type of lacquer was produced mainly in the fourteenth and fifteenth centuries. *See* E-NASHIJI, LACQUER, MAKI-E, URUSHI.

Nashimoto. Imperial prince (1874–?), made marshal in 1932 and chief priest of the Shinto shrines in Ise in 1937.

Nashitsubo. In the old imperial palace, apartments reserved for ladies-in-waiting.

• **Nashitsubo no Gonin.** Collective term given in 951 to five poets: Ōnakatomi no Yoshinobu, Kiyohara Motosuke, Minamoto no Shitagō, Ki no Tokibumi, and Sakanoue no Mochiki, who helped to compile the *Gosen waka-shū.*

• **Nashitsubo no Kasen.** Title for the court poetesses Murasaki Shikibu, Akazome Emon, Uma no Naishi, Ise Ōsuke, Sei Shōnagon, and Ko-Shikibu, among others.

Nasu no Yoichi. Famous archer (twelfth century) of the Minamoto (Genji) clan who, according to the *Heike monogatari,* was killed in the Battle of Kashima in 1184 by an arrow that hit him on the shore. The arrow had been fired by the Taira from the top of the mast of one of their ships.

Natabori. A type of wooden sculpture in which the wood is left undressed after rough hewing and sculpting; there is no polishing or painting, and the chisel marks are left visible. This style was predominant in the provinces during the Heian period.

National Parks (Kokuritsu kōen). Zones in Japan corresponding to specific historical, geographic, and natural sites and subject to laws concerning preservation of such sites and of nature. There are currently 27, among them:
—On Kyushu: Saikai, Unzen Amakusa, Kirishima-Yaku.
—On Shikoku: Ashizuri-Uawakai.
—On Honshu: Setonaikai, Daisen-Oki, Yoshino-Kumano, Fuji-Hakone-Izu, Jōshin'etsu Kōgen, Bandai-Asahi, Towada-Hachimantai.
—On Hokkaido: Shikotsu-Tōya, Rishiri-Rebun-Sarobetsu.
—On the Ryukyu Islands: Ogasawara, Okinawa.
There are also 51 "quasi-national" parks *(kokutei kōen),* including:
—On Kyushu: Aso.
—On Honshu: San'in Coast, Ise-Shima, Southern Alps, Hakusan, Chūbu-Sangaku, Chichibu-Tama, Nikkō, Rikuchū.
—On Hokkaido: Daisetsuzan, Akan, Shiretoko.
—On the Ryukyu Islands: Iriomote.

Natsume Sōseki. Writer (Natsume Kinnosuke, 1867–1916), born in Tokyo. He studied Chinese literature, then specialized in English literature. He taught English in a number of schools, then went to

England from 1900 to 1903 to further his studies. When he returned, he taught at the University of Tokyo (1903–05), then abandoned his professorship to become an editor at the *Asahi Shimbun* in 1907. In his works, he skillfully describes the shock of the meeting of two civilizations, Western and Japanese, with acuity and often humor. Collections of his lectures were published—*Bungaku-ron* (Treatise on Literature) and *Bungaku-hyōron* (Literary Criticism)—and then he wrote his first novel, *Wagahai wa neko de aru* (I Am a Cat, published 1905), a direct satire of society as seen through the eyes of a cat (the author himself). His second novel, *Gubi-jinsō* (The Poppy, 1907), involved love triangles, a theme he further developed in *Sorekara* (And After? 1909) and *Kokoro* (The Poor Hearts of Men, 1914). He then wrote an autobiographical novel, *Michikusa* (Grass by the Roadside, 1915), and began another major novel, *Meian* (Light and Shadow, 1916), which was never finished. Among his other important works are *Botchan* (A Good Boy, 1906), *Kusamakura* (The Grass Pillow, 1906), *Omoidasu koto nado* (Things I Remember, 1910), *Kōjin* (The Traveler, 1913); collections of stories, *Uzurakago* (The Basket of Shells, 1906), *Yōkyoshū* (1906), *Nowaki* (The Storm, 1907), *Sanshirō* (1908), *Kōfu* (The Miner, 1908), *Mon* (The Door, 1910); and individual stories and a few short plays, in an elegant style that gained him recognition as one of the major authors of the Meiji era. He was also an excellent haiku poet.

Natsuo. Painter (Kanō Natsuo; *mei:* Fushimi; *gō:* Jurō, 1828–98) and metal engraver *(chōkin)* for the imperial court. He created accessories for swords and sculpted netsuke. He was director of the Mint and of the National Arts School in Tokyo.

Natsushima. Site near Yokohama, former island now attached to the mainland, famous for its shell mound *(kaizuka)*. Excavation of the shell mound revealed many objects from the Jōmon era, dating from 7000 to 6000 BC. *See* JŌMON.

Naumann, Edmund. German geologist (1854–1927) who taught geology at the University of Tokyo from 1875 to 1885, and who conducted geological research in Japan. When he returned to Germany, he published the results of his studies in *Geologische Arbeiten in Japan* (1901). A fossil elephant found in Japan is named for him.

Nawabari. "String border," a term used to demarcate a sacred or other particular territory, from the ancient custom of bordering it with a string *(shimenawa)*. It later came to mean all "reserved" territory, and currently is used by yakuza to indicate their sphere of influence. *See also* NUSA, SHIMENAWA.

Nawa Nagatoshi. Warrior (?–1336) known for his fidelity to Emperor Kemmu, whom he helped to restore to power. He drove Ashikaga Takauji toward Kyushu in 1336, but was killed by Takauji when he returned a few months later. Nawa Nagatoshi remains a symbol of loyalty and fidelity. The story of his life was told in an eponymous play by Kōda Rohan in 1913, and a shrine was built in his honor in Tottori, his birthplace, about 1870.

Nayotake monogatari emaki. "Illustrated Tale of a Young Bamboo Plant." An *emakimono* from the early fourteenth century describing life in Emperor Go-Saga's court and the emperor's amorous adventures. One scroll.

Nebuta Matsuri. Major festival taking place during the Bon season in various Japanese towns, notably Aomori and Hirosaki, from August 1 to August 7. Large chariots bearing paintings portraying historical and legendary heroes, backlit at night, are pulled toward the town. Also called *nemurinagashi*.

Negi. Formerly, a Shinto priest responsible for making offerings to Amaterasu in the Ise *naikū*. *See* KANNUSHI.

Negishi-ha. Group of writers active during the Meiji era, living in the Negishi district of Tokyo. Among its members were Aeba Kōson, Morita Shiken, Kōda Rohan, and Suō Nansui.
• Group of haiku and *tanka* poets surrounding Masaoka Shiki and also living in the Negishi district of Tokyo.

Negoro-nuri. Type of lacquered objects produced starting in 1288 by Buddhist monks of the Negoro-ji temple (*see* DAI DEMBŌ-IN) in Wakayama prefecture, with irregular black stains due to wearing of the top layer of red lacquer. This type of lacquer was often imitated. *See also* KAMAKURA-BORI, LACQUER.

Nehan. Japanese translation of the Sanskrit word "Nirvana," designating the extinction of desires and the absence of rebirth according to Buddhist philosophy. A Buddhist ceremony commemorating the Buddha's ascendance to Parinirvāna, celebrated every year on the 25th day of the second month, is called *nehan-e*. A *nehan-zu* is a painting showing the Buddha's death; a *nehan-zō* is a statue of the same subject.

Nembutsu. Buddhist invocation meaning "in the name of the Buddha" (abridgment of "Namu Amida Butsu"), recited by followers of Amida (*Skt.:* Amitābha) in the Jōdo-shū and Jōdo Shin-shū sects, in the hope of being reborn in Amida's paradise (Gokuraku-jōdo). There are several types of *nembutsu: shōmyō-nembutsu* (simple invocation), *okunen-nembutsu* (meditative), *kannen-nembutsu* (purely contemplative). This invocation (imported from China) became known in Japan when Genshin's *Ōjōyōshū* was published, in 985. Other monks, such as Kūya Shōnin, spread its use among commoners, along with dances accompanying the recitation of the invocation, Nembutsu Odori. *See* AMIDA BUTSU, HŌNEN, NAMU.

Nene. Childhood name of Sugaihara Yasuko (O-yae, 1549–1624), Toyotomi Hideyoshi's wife. Also known as Nemoji and Kōdai-in. She did not bear a child, and Hideyoshi took a concubine, Yodogimi (Chacha), who gave him a son, Tsurumatsu.

Nenga. "Paintings of the year," generally used as decorations on New Year's Day.

Nengajō. "New Year's cards." Following an American custom, the Japanese have adopted the habit of sending large numbers of best-wishes cards on New Year's Day, to make sure their friends and acquaintances remember them fondly. Christmas cards are also sent. Firms and individuals of all classes and professions send these cards on December 25 and 28; they are collected by the post office and distributed en masse on January 1. *See also* MEISHI.

Nengō. Era names. Upon his or her ascendance to the throne, each sovereign decreed a new era, which was changed if circumstances demanded, or simply to mark a break in the continuity in his or her reign. Until 1868, most sovereigns had several era names. The first era name was inaugurated, in the Chinese style, in 645: it was the Taika era, or "era of great change." Starting in 1868, there was only one era per sovereign, and each emperor was named for his era *(nengō)* after his death. Thus, Emperor Mutsuhito was renamed Meiji Tennō in 1912; Emperor Yoshihito, Taishō Tennō in 1926; Emperor Hirohito, Shōwa Tennō in 1990. The era of the current sovereign, Akihito, is called Heisei. Also sometimes called Gengō. *Chin.* Nianhao; *Viet.:* Niēn-hiēu. *See* CALENDAR.

Nengu. Starting in the Heian period, annual tax paid to estate owners, and later to the daimyo. It was distinct from other taxes on grain *(so)* and manufactured fabrics *(chō, zōkuji)*, and from working parties *(yō, buyaku)*. Those who paid this tax were the *myōshū*, or farmers with certain rights *(shiki)* on the lands they worked. After Toyotomi Hideyoshi's agrarian reform *(nenchi,* 1582) the value of lands assessed for payment of the *nengu* was evaluated in *koku* (about 180 liters) of rice; peasants had to pay two-thirds of their harvest each year as *nengu,* plus a tax, called *kuchimai,* of about 2 *shō* (3.6 liters of grain) per *koku*. The annual tax was then called *honnengu*. There were also many other taxes, local and provincial, temporary and permanent, levied on the peasants. In the Edo period, the *jōmen* was instituted, based on the average of annual harvests calculated over several years and set for a determined period of between three and ten years. Each village was assessed, and the leaders were responsible for distributing tax payment among the *hyakushō* (peasants).

Nenji Butsu. In Japanese Buddhism, a protective divinity, buddha, or bodhisattva venerated by an individual, a family, or a group.

• **Nenji-butsu zushi.** Portable altar *(zushi)* belonging to Lady Tachibana (*see* AGATA NO INUKAI NO MICHIYO), made about 730 and cast in bronze. It contains statuettes (26 to 33 cm high) of Amida and his two assistants, Kannon and Seishi Bosatsu, sitting on lotus flowers supported by stems. The gates of the altar are in lacquered wood and painted with religious scenes ornamented with elytrons. Kept in the museum of the Hōryū-ji temple (Nara prefecture). Also called Tachibana no zushi, Den Tachibana Fujin Nenji-butsu.

Nenju. Rosary used by Buddhists and composed of beads numbering 54, 108, or other multiples of nine. *Skt.: mālā. See also* JUZU.

NenjūGyōji emaki. An *emakimono* attributed to Fujiwara no Mitsunaga (ca. 1180), portraying the annual rites and ceremonies in the imperial court. It comprised 60 scrolls, but by the seventeenth century only 16 scrolls remained; these were copied, on imperial order, by Sumiyoshi Jokei in 1626. Also titled *Nenjū Gioji no Sōshi*.

Nenkō-joretsu. Traditional system applied in the work environment since the First World War, according to which seniority counts more for promotions and salaries than do the abilities of employees.

This system is reinforced by lifetime job security and compulsory retirement at age 60. Advancement depends not only on seniority, but also on education level, sex, and type of job. Recently, this system has begun to weaken as companies pay more attention than previously to merit because of international competition. *See also* SEMPAI-KŌHAI.

Ne no Kuni. "Land of the Departed," or "Place of Death." In Shinto legends and the *Kojiki,* the realm where Izanagi went to search for his sister-wife Izanami after she died giving birth to the *kami* of fire. Also called Yomi no Kuni, Yomotsu-kuni. *Chin.:* Huangquan ("Yellow Springs").

Neri-age. Ceramics technique of adding clays of different colors to the usual clay. This very old technique of Chinese origin (Cizhou kilns) was used mainly to decorate sandstone pieces that were not enameled. It was revived in Japan in the 1960s by the modern ceramist Matsui Kōsei, superior of the Gesso-ji temple near Tokyo, who was designated a Living National Treasure in 1993.

Netsuke. Small object designed to attach to a belt *(obi)* the cord of an *inro* (medicine box), a smoking kit or writing kit, a tobacco pouch, or a purse. *Netsuke* were used (by both men and women) starting in the sixteenth century. These objects were made of a wide variety of materials: bone, ivory, wood, ceramics, metal. They had a sliding oval button *(ojime)* to hold shut the object worn on the belt. *Netsuke* had to be pleasant to the touch and have no sharp angles that could injure their wearer. Not considered works of art before the Meiji era, they were rediscovered by Europeans, who began to collect them. Many sculptors and artisans then began to make them for collectors, although they were no longer worn, since the Japanese had adopted Western clothing with pockets.

Netsuke were categorized either according to what they were made of or, more commonly, according to their shape. There were *katabori* (sculpted objects), *kagami-buta* (shaped like a small container with a cover), *manjū* (shaped like round, flat, or oval buttons), *ryūsa* (openwork), *sashi-netsuke* (oblong), and *ichiraku* (in a fine basketweave). Some *netsuke* were shaped like everyday objects, such as a small shovel (used as an ashtray) or *soroban. Katabori netsuke* are the most sought-after because they are magnificent miniature works of art, portraying masks (Noh or Gigaku), animals, legendary characters, plants, flowers, fruits, fish, shellfish, and more—the imagination of *netsuke*

sculptors (who were sometimes also painters or engravers) knew no bounds.

Most well-made *netsuke* were signed or had a seal carved into them. The signatures were sometimes sculpted in relief (rare). Up to the present, more than 3,000 artists have been catalogued, some of whom specialized in *netsuke,* while others were also goldsmiths, sculptors of Noh masks, ceramists, or *tsuba* makers. The signature is often followed by one or two kanji characters meaning "old man" *(ō, sō, rōjin),* "made by" *(saku),* "copied by" *(utsusu),* "made for" *(ōju, okō),* or a religious title, usually Hōgan or Hōkkyō. The characters *Ten ka ichi* ("first under Heaven") meant that the *netsuke* had been made by a famous sculptor of masks. Sometimes, the signature was engraved on a separate piece that was inlaid. Many books have been written about *netsuke* as collectors' objects, listing the names and signatures of their makers. The best-known sculptors of *netsuke* were Shūzan (late sixteenth century), Ryūkei (early eighteenth century), members of the Miwa school (mid-eighteenth century), Norikazu, Gambun, Ikkō (late eighteenth century), Norisane, Anrakusai, Masatsugu, Shibiyama (mid-nineteenth century).

Nevski, Nikolai Aleksandrovich. Russian philologist (1892–1945), born in Yaroslav. He learned Japanese in St. Petersburg and went to Japan, where he taught Russian, in 1915. He also did research on the Tangut peoples in Japan and China. He returned to the Soviet Union in 1929 and taught Japanese at the University of Leningrad and the Hermitage Museum. In 1937, he and his Japanese wife were arrested as spies and sent to a prison camp in Siberia, where he died in 1945. He was posthumously rehabilitated in 1957 and awarded the Lenin Prize for his work.

Nezami monogatari emaki. Single-scroll *emakimono* painted in *tsukuri-e* style, measuring about 508 × 26 cm, depicting the eleventh-century novel *Nezame monogatari* (or *Yoru no nezame*). The images, which evoke those of the *Genji monogatari emaki,* show buildings from a very high perspective *(fukinuki-yatai).* It is typical of *emakimono* of the late Heian period. Kept in the Yamato Bunkaken (Nara prefecture). *See* YŌHA NO NEZAME.

Nezu Bijutsukan. Art museum in Tokyo, housing collections assembled by Nezu Kaichirō, opened in 1940 and reorganized in a new building in 1955. It has sections on painting, calligraphy, ceramics, lacquer, and Chinese art. Exhibitions are usually accompanied by catalogues. *See* MUSEUMS.

Nengō

Many of the dates below are approximate and may vary by one year due to differences in calendars. See respective entries for more details.

Taika (645–50)
Hakuchi (650–55)
Saimei (655–62)
Tenji (or Tenchi, 662–72)
Kōbun (672–73)
Temmu (673–86)
Shuchō (686–87)
Jitō (687–97)
Mommu (697–701)
Taihō (701–04)
Keiun (704–08)
Wadō (708–15)
Reiki (715–17)
Yōrō (717–24)
Jinki (724–29)
Tempyō (729–48)
Tempyō-Kampō (749)
Tempyō-Shōhō (749)
Tempyō-Hōji (749–65)
Tempyō-Jingō (765–67)
Jingo-Keiun (767–70)
Hōki (770–81)
Ten-ō (781–82)
Enryaku (782–806)
Daidō (806–10)
Kōnin (810–24)
Tenchō (824–34)
Jōwa (Shōwa, 834–48)
Kashō (848–51)
Ninju (851–54)
Saikō (854–57)
Ten'an (857–59)
Jōgan (859–77)
Gangyō (877–85)
Ninna (885–89)
Kampyō (889–98)
Shōtai (898–901)
Engi (901–23)
Enchō (923–31)
Shōhei (Jōhei, 931–938)
Tengyō (938–47)
Tenryaku (947–57)
Tentoku (957–61)
Ōwa (961–64)
Kōhō (964–68)
Anna (968–70)

Tenroku (970–73)
Ten'en (973–76)
Jōgen (976–78)
Tengen (978–83)
Eikan (983–85)
Kan'na (Kanwa, 985–87)
Eien (987–89)
Eiso (989–90)
Shōryaku (Shōreki, 990–95)
Chōtoku (995–99)
Chōhō (999–1004)
Kankō (1004–12)
Chōwa (1012–17)
Kannin (1017–21)
Chi'an (Ji'an, 1021–24)
Manju (1024–28)
Chōgen (1028–37)
Chōryaku (Chōreki, 1037–40)
Chōkyū (1040–44)
Kantoku (1044–46)
Eishō (Eijō, 1046–53)
Tengi (1053–58)
Kōhei (1058–65)
Jiryaku (1065–69)
Enkyū (1069–74)
Shōryaku (Shōreki, 1077–81)
Eihō (1081–84)
Ōtoku (1084–87)
Kanji (1087–94)
Kahō (1094–96)
Eichō (1096–97)
Shōtoku (Jōtoku, 1097–99)
Kōwa (1099–1104)
Chōji (1104–06)
Kashō (Kajō, 1106–08)
Tennin (1108–10)
Ten'ei (1110–13)
Eikyū (1113–18)
Ge'ei (1119–20)
Hōan (1120–24)
Tenchi (Tenji, 1124–26)
Daiji (1126–31)
Tenshō (1131–32)
Chōshō (1132–35)
Hōen (1135–41)
Eiji (1141–42)
Kōji (1142–44)
Ten'yō (1144–45)
Kyūan (1145–51)
Nimpei (Nimbyō, 1151–54)
Kyūju (1154–56)
Hōgen (1156–59)
Heiji (1159–60)
Eiryaku (1160–61)

Ōhō (1161–63)
Chōkan (1163–65)
Eiman (1165–66)
Ninnan (1166–69)
Kaō (1169–71)
Jōan (1171–75)
Angen (1175–77)
Jishō (1177–81)
Yōwa (1181–82)
Juei (1182–84)
Genryaku (Genreki, 1184–85)
Bunji (1185–90)
Kenkyū (1190–99)
Shōji (1199–1201)
Kennin (1201–04)
Genkyū (1204–06)
Ken'ei (1206–07)
Jōgen (1207–11)
Kenryaku (Kenreki, 1211–13)
Kempō (1213–29)
Jōkyū (1219–22)
Jōō (1222–24)
Gennin (1224–25)
Karoku (1225–27)
Antei (1227–29)
Kanki (Kangi, 1229–32)
Jōei (1232–33)
Tempuku (1233–34)
Bunryaku (Bunreki, 1234–35)
Katei (1235–38)
Ryakunin (1238–39)
En-ō (1239–40)
Ninji (1240–43)
Kangen (1243–47)
Hōji (1247–49)
Kenchō (1249–56)
Kōgen (1256–57)
Shōka (1257–59)
Shōgen (1259–60)
Bun'ō (1260–61)
Kōchō (1261–64)
Bun'ei (1264–75)
Kenji (1275–78)
Kōan (1278–88)
Shō-ō (1288–93)
Einin (1293–99)
Shōan (1299–1302)
Kangen (Kengen, Ken'ei, 1302–03)
Kagen (1303–06)
Tokuji (1306–08)

• **Nezu Kaichirō.** Politician (1860–1940) and major art collector. The president of railroad companies, he used his immense fortune to collect valuable art works, which were placed in a museum named after him. He was elected to the House of Representatives in 1904, then to the House of Peers.

• **Nezu no seki.** *See* NAKOSO NO SEKI.

NHK (Nippon Hōsō Kyōkai). "Japanese Broadcasting Company." A public, noncommercial radio and television network founded in 1926 by the merger of a number of broadcasting companies. It began broadcasting television in 1953. It has two television networks and one FM and two AM radio networks. NHK also broadcasts a number of programs in foreign languages and has more than 20,000 employees.

Nibutani. Site in the Hidaka region on Hokkaido, sacred for the Ainu, where, according to legend, the god *(kamui)* Okikurumi appeared, bringing culture to the Ainu peoples. A dam project that would have flooded this region, where the Ainu traditionally celebrate the "return of the salmon," met with strong opposition from local residents.

Nichi-in. Buddhist monk (1264–1328). In 1297, he founded the Seiren-ji temple in Echigo to be the seat of the Hokke-shū; it was later called Honjō-ji.

Nichiin. Buddhist monk (?–1180) of the Tendai-shū sect, Minamoto no Yoritomo's confidant. He and Prince Mochihito were killed by the Taira at the same time.

Nichi no Oka kofun. Large keyhole-shaped *kofun* in Fukuoka prefecture (northern Kyushu), excavated in 1890. The walls of the inner chamber are decorated with concentric circles in red and with motifs of horns, triangles, boats, and quivers. Nearby is Tsuki no Oka's tomb, containing an enormous stone sarcophagus and fragments of *haniwa*.

Nichi-ō. Buddhist monk (1565–1630) of the Nichiren sect, founder of the Fuju Fuse branch in Bizen in 1595. As abbot of the Myōkaku-ji temple in Kyoto, he opposed Toyotomi Hideyoshi's plan to have an inter-sect service conducted in honor of his ancestors when the large image of the Buddha at the Hōkō-ji temple was completed. Nichi-ō and his disciples withdrew until the dictator died. In 1599, Ieyasu Tokugawa invited him to expound his doctrine of "give nothing, receive nothing" *(fuju fuse)*, but he criticized the supremacy of lay power and was sent into exile on the island of Tsushima, where he lived until 1612. His supporters were declared outlaws by the shogunate in 1691 and went underground until 1876. *See* FUJU FUSE.

Nichiren. Buddhist monk (Zennichi Maru, Renchō; *posthumous name:* Risshō Daishi, 1222–82), born in Kominato (Awa province) to a family of poor fishers. Sent as a novice to the Kiyomizu-dera temple of the Tendai-shū when he was 12, he was ordained when he was 16; he visited most of the temples in Kansai and studied at the Hiei-zan and Onjō-ji and on Mt. Kōya. But he then had doubts about the effectiveness of the Jōdo doctrines and made Kokūzo Bosatsu (*Skt.:* Ākāshagarbha) and the *Lotus Sutra (Hokke-kyō; Skt.: Saddharmapundarīka-sūtra)* his chosen divinities. In 1253, he began to preach his own doctrine, opposed to those of Jōdo and Zen, at the Kiyomizu-dera temple, but his teachings went against the beliefs of the local lord, and he was expelled from Awa province. Taking refuge in Kamakura, he continued to spread his faith in the exclusive salvational power of the *Hokke-kyō* and the Buddha Shakyamuni (*Jap.:* Shaka). He then advocated recitation of the invocation *(daimoku)* Namu Myōhō renge-kyō, supposed to procure salvation for the faithful, similar to the *nembutsu* of the Jōdo sects. In 1260, Nichiren codified his doctrine (which involved the idea of heresy, a concept then unknown in Buddhism) in *Risshō ankoku-ron* (Treatise on Pacification of the State Through Orthodoxy), attacking the Jōdo sects and accusing them of responsibility for the misfortunes besetting Japan. His work was considered subversive, and Hōjō Tokiyori, *shikken* of Kamakura, exiled him to Izu in 1261. When he returned to Kamakura two years later, and after two trips to Awa, he saw in the Mongolian claims (1268 delegation) the realization of the prophecies made in *Risshō ankoku-ron;* his denunciations of the Jōdo, Shingon, Tendai, and Risshu sects became so violent that the Kamakura authorities sentenced him to death.

Having narrowly escaped execution in September 1271, Nichiren was banished to the island of Sado, where he wrote *Kaimoku-shō* (Opening People's Eyes, 1272), in which he detailed his doctrine of intolerance of the other Buddhist sects and his faith in the effectiveness of recitation of the *daimoku*, identified his mission with that of two bodhisattvas of the *Lotus Sutra,* Jōfukyo (*Skt.:* Sadāparaibhūta) and Jōgyō (*Skt.:* Vishishtacharitra), and claimed that he wanted to revive faith in the Buddha at the onset of *mappō* ("the final period of the Good [Buddhist] Law," which, theoretically, had begun in 1052). He also advocated *shaku-buku*, a doctrine of intolerance aimed at instituting veneration of the *Lotus Sutra* as the only acceptable Buddhist doctrine, to which all Buddhists must be converted—by force if necessary. He began to attract disciples, and he wrote another treatise for them in 1273, *Kanjin honzon-shō* (The Object of Adoration in Contemplation), presenting the *daimoku* as *honzon* and claiming that only his doctrine could save the country from disintegration in the face of Mongolian attacks and the other sects' doctrines of tolerance. Finally freed from his exile in 1274, he returned to Kamakura, but he was not able to convince the Hōjō of the validity of his ideas, so he moved to Minobu in Kai province (Yamanashi prefecture), where, surrounded by his disciples, he spent his last years in the Kuon-ji temple. Among his other religious works are *Shuga kokka-ron* and *Sainan taiji* (1272). Nichiren fell ill in 1278 and visited hot springs a number of times. He died en route to Ikegami, near Tokyo, on November 21, 1282. He is also called Nichiren Daishōnin, Zenshōbō Renchō. The Sōka Gakkai lay sect claims to follow his teachings.

• **Nichiren-Kōmon.** Subsect of the Nichiren-shū, with about 5,000 followers.

• **Nichiren-shō.** Subsect of the Nichiren-shū, with about 150,000 followers.

• **Nichiren Shō-shū.** "True Nichiren sect." A branch of Nichiren-shū that developed mainly after 1950 with the Sōka Gakkai, based on the doctrines of the monk Nikkō, who preached at the Daisen-ji (at the foot of Mt. Fuji) in 1290. His followers venerated the *daigo-honzon,* a tall wooden board engraved with the invocation titled *Hokke-kyō, Namu Myōho renge-kyō.* Nichiren Shō-shū separated from Sōka Gakkai in 1989.

• **Nichiren-shū.** Pietist Buddhist sect, at first called Hokke-shū, founded by Nichiren in 1253 and based on the teachings (interpreted by Nichiren) of the *Lotus Sutra.* It was divided into nine branches—Itchi, Shōretsu, Honseiji, Myōman-ji, Honjō-ji, Hachi-mon, Honryū-ji, Fuju Fuse, Fuju-Fuse Kōmon—and nine subsects: Hokke, Hommon Butsu-ryū, Myō-Hokke, Nakayama-myō, Nichiren, Nichiren-Kōmon, Nichiren-shō, Shōwa Hon, and Zaike Nichiren Jōfukai. The Nichiren-shū is also divided into numerous more recent subsects. *See also* SŌKA GAKKAI.

• **Nichirō.** Buddhist monk (1243–1320), Nichiren's disciple and founder of the Itchi branch of the Nichiren-shū. *Posthumous names:* Daikoku-ajari, Daikoku Bosatsu.

• **Nichiryū.** Buddhist monk (1384–1464) of the Nichiren-shū, founder of the Hachi-mon branch in Ikegami (near Tokyo) in 1420.

• **Nichizō.** Buddhist monk (1269–1342), disciple of Nichirō in the Nichiren-shū sect. He received the posthumous title Bosatsu in 1369.

Nichirinji. Keyhole-shaped *kofun* near the town of Kurume (Fukuoka prefecture, northern Kyushu); its inner chamber is decorated with friezes of *chokko-mon* motifs.

Nichokuan. Painter (Soga Nichokuan; *mei:* Sahe, Sahei, mid-seventeenth century) who studied with his father, Chokuan, in Sakai. He specialized in painting birds.

Nichōsai. Painter (Matsuya Heisaburō, d. 1793) and bookseller in Osaka. His caricatures are famous.

Nidō-mon. Decorative beehive motif used mainly in architecture of the Asuka and Nara periods.

Nie. Crystalline structure (martensite) produced in steel during the tempering process, forming undulating lines. It is used to decorate the cutting edge of sword blades. When the tempering is invisible, it is called *nioi. See* KATANA.

Nigao-e. In painting, especially in ukiyo-e prints, a life-like portrait. *See also* NISE-E.

Nigihayahi no Mikoto. A *kami* of Shinto legend, descendant of Ninigi no Mikoto's older brother and Umashimate's father. He married Kashikiya Hime, Nahasune-hiko's sister. Also called Kushitama Nigihayabi no Mikoto.

Nigite. In Shinto, bands of white paper or hemp fabric generally hung from a string called *shimenawa,* symbolizing the presence of one or more *kami. See also* GOHEI, NUSA.

Nigori. Diacritical marks that alter the primary sounds in the Japanese language, placed to the upper right of *kana* characters (*katakana* and *hiragana*). There are two: the *dakuon* (represented by ") and the *handakuon* (represented by °).

The (") modifies sounds in the following way: *Ka* to *ga, sa* to *za, ta* to *da, ha* to *ba, ki* to *gi, shi* to *ji, chi* to *ji, hi* to *bi, ku* to *gu, su* to *zu, tsu* to *zu, hu* to *bu, ke* to *ge, se* to *ze, te* to *de, he* to *be, ko* to *go, so* to *zo, to* to *do, ho* to *bo.*

The (°) modifies only aspirated sounds: *ha* to *pa, hi* to *pi, hu* to *pu, he* to *pe,* and *ho* to *po.* Both types of *nigori* apply also to complex syllables. The (") modifies them as follows: *kya* to *gya, kyu* to *gyu, kyo* to *gyo, sha* to *ja, shu* to *ju, sho* to *jo, hya* to *bya, hyu* to *byu, hyo* to *byo;* (°) modifies them thus: *hya* to *pya, hyu* to *pyu,* and *hyo* to *pyo.*

A sound is said to be "nigorized" when it is altered by either diacritical mark. *See* GOJŪ-ON-ZU.

• **Nigori-zake.** *See* SAKE.

Nihon. Japanese pronunciation of the Chinese *Riben* ("origin of the sun"), designating the East, the name for the islands of Japan since 671. Also, in certain cases, pronounced "Nippon."
→ *See* JAPAN, NIPPON.

• **Nihon.** Newspaper created by Kuga Katsunan in 1889 to support the cause of "Japanism" (*Nihon-shugi*) and counterbalance Western influences. Some 20 issues of *Nihon* were considered anti-constitutional and were suppressed by the government. When its founder died, *Nihon* became the organ of the Rikken Seiyūkai (Friends of Constitutional Government party); it ceased publication in 1914.

• **Nihon Bijutsu-in.** "Japan Fine Arts Academy." Association of artists founded by Okakura Kakuzō in 1898, and composed mainly of painters in the Nihonga style.

• **Nihon Bijutsu Kyōkai.** Association of painters in the Japanese (Nihonga) style, founded in 1887 as a branch of the Ryūchi-kai (founded in 1878).

• **Nihon Bungaku Hōkoku-kai.** "Patriotic Association for a Japanese Literature," created in 1942 for propaganda purposes. It published a magazine, *Bungaku Hōkoku* (Literature in the Service of Patriotism), and contributors included such eminent men of letters as Yoshikawa Eiji and Kikuchi Kan. It ceased publication in 1945.

• *Nihon daijisho.* Japanese-language dictionary compiled by Yamada Bimyō in 1893. This 12-volume work was the first truly modern Japanese dictionary (along with Otsuki Fumihiko's *Genkai,* published in 1891).

• **Nihonga.** Modern Japanese style of painting, blending Western techniques with Japanese pictorial traditions, in contrast to purely Western-style painting, which is called Yōga. This style of painting originated in the early nineteenth century; it developed mainly during the Meiji era and was perpetuated by artists such as Okakura Kokuzō, Ernest Fenollosa, Kampo Hōgai, Hashimoto Gahō, and Yokoyama Taikan. The school was officially recognized in 1907 by the Ministry of Education, which organized the Bunten exhibitions featuring works by members of both the Nihonga and the Yōga schools.

• *Nihon gaishi.* "Unofficial History of Japan," in 12 volumes, published in Chinese in 1829 by Rai San'yō, covering Japanese history from the twelfth to the nineteenth century. Rai San'yō complemented this work with the 16-volume *Nihon seiki.*

• **Nihon Gakushi-in.** "Japan Academy," founded in 1879 and bringing together eminent scholars. It comprises 150 titular members: 70 representing the human and social sciences, and 80 representing the natural sciences. Academics are elected for life and receive an annual grant. The Academy gives out awards each year: the Imperial Prize (Gakushi-in Onshi-shō) and the Academy Prize (Gakushi-in-

shō). It also publishes reports in the *Gakushi-in kiyō.*

• **Nihon Geijutsu-in.** "Japan Art Academy," founded in 1947, composed of 120 members representing painting, sculpture, music, literature, dance, and theater. This academy gives out annual prizes. *See* BUNTEN.

• **Nihongi.** See NIHON SHOKI.

• **Nihon Ginkō.** "Bank of Japan," the country's central bank, authorized to issue Japanese currency. Founded in Tokyo in 1882, it controls fluctuations in and ensures stability of the currency. It was reorganized in 1942 and in 1949.

• **Nihon-ha.** School of haiku poetry founded by a disciple of Bashō, Shiki Masaoka (1867–1902).

• *Nihon Hyōron.* General-interest magazine founded in 1926 as *Keizai Ōrai.* It took its definitive name in 1935; during the Second World War, it was renamed *Keizai Hyōron,* but it returned to the name *Nihon Hyōron* in 1945. It was suppressed in 1956 because it printed opinions contrary to those of the Occupation Authorities. It was published again in that year, but ceased publication a few months later.

• *Nihonjin.* "The Japanese." A literary-criticism magazine founded in 1888 by Miyake Setsurei, Shiga Shigetaka, and the Seikyōsha group to counter excessive westernization of Japan; for this reason, it was banned several times. It then took other titles, such as *Ajia Nihon Oyobi Nihonjin* (Japan and the Japanese). It ceased publication in 1923.

• **Nihon Hōsō Kyōkai.** *See* NHK.

• **Nihon Jūni-kei.** "The Twelve Views of Japan." The twelve most beautiful landscapes in Japan: Tago no Ura, Matsushima, Hakosaki, Ama no Hashidate, Waka no Ura, Biwa-ko, Itsukushima, Kisakata, Asama-yama, Matsue, Akashi, and Kanazawa. *See* NIHON SANKEI.

• **Nihonkai.** "Sea of Japan," located between the Japanese islands and the coasts of Korea and Manchuria, probably resulting from a subsidence during the Quatenary Era. The sea is oriented NNE–SSW and extends from 43° to 53° north latitude, opening into the Sea of Okhotsk via Sakhalin Strait and La Perouse Strait (Sōya Kaikyō) and into the Pacific Ocean via Tsugaru Strait. It is connected to the

China Sea via Tsushima Strait to the south. Its waters are cold, but the less cold Oyashio and warm Kuroshio currents run through it, making it a very fertile breeding ground for fish. Its northern part, between Sakhalin and the Siberian coast, is often frozen over in winter. *Area:* 1,011,660 km²; *average depth:* 1,350 m; *deepest point:* 3,742 m.

• *Nihon Keizai Shimbun.* Major financial newspaper, founded in 1876 by Masuda Takahashi as the *Chūgai Bukka Shimpō;* it became the *Chūgai Shōgyō Shimpō* in 1889. At first published by Mitsui, it became independent and absorbed other financial and trade magazines, taking its current title in 1946. Its current circulation is about 2 million copies daily.

• *Nihon kiryaku.* "Short Report on Japan." A 34-chapter history of Japan, composed during the Heian period by an unknown author and covering the period from the mythical era to the reign of Emperor Go-Ichijō, based on the *Nihon shoki.* It is a supplement to the *Rikkokushi* (Six National Histories).

• *Nihon kōki.* "Continuation of the Annals of Japan." The third of the *Rikkokushi,* completed in 843, consisting of 40 volumes (only 10 of which have survived to the present) covering the period from 697 to 832. This work was the result of a collaborative effort by Fujiwara no Otsugu (773–843), Fujiwara no Yoshino (786–846), Fujiwara no Yoshifusa (804–72), Minamoto no Tokiwa (812–54), Asa no Katori (774–843), Yamada no Furutsugu, and several other historians. Part of the original text, which had been lost, was found in the eighteenth century by Inayama Yukinori.

• Nihon Koku Kempō. The current Constitution of Japan, promulgated in 1947 and replacing the Dai-Nihon Teikoku Kempō.

• Nihon Kōsaku Bunka Remmei. Modern architecture movement influenced by Walter Gropius and Le Corbusier, which publishes the magazine *Kōsaku Bunka.* Also known as Kōsaku Bunka Remmei.

• Nihon Kyōsantō. "Japan Communist party," founded in 1922 as a branch of the Comintern by a group of socialists whose members included Arahata Kanson, Sakai Toshihiko, Yamakawa Hitoshi, and Tokuda Kyūichi. Before the Second World War, it was often outlawed, but it managed to publish newspapers such as *Sekki* and *Akahata.* Starting in 1928, and especially after 1932, its members were persecuted for their activities. The Communist party was legalized in 1945, and has since played an important role in Japanese domestic politics, having broken away from the Chinese Communist movement and taken a nationalist position. It has remained a small party, however, with barely 400,000 members.

• Nihon Minshutō. "Japan Democratic party," politically conservative, founded in 1954 by Hatoyama Ichirō, Shigemitsu Mamoru, and Kishi Nobusuke to oppose Yoshida Shirgeu's Liberal party (Jiyūtō). In October 1955, it joined the Jiyūtō to form the Liberal Democratic party (Jiyū Minshutō).

• Nihon Musantō. "Japan Proletarian party," founded in 1937 by Katō Kanjū (1892–1978) and Suzuki Mosaburō to oppose a growing militarist influence, but it was not able to form a union with the Socialist Party of the Masses (Shakai Taishūtō). A few months after its foundation, the party was dissolved and its leaders arrested.

• *Nihon-ō dai ichi ran.* "Great Panorama of the Sovereigns of Japan," history book compiled in 1662 by Hayashi Shunzai on the orders of Minamoto no Tadakatsu.

• Nihon Rōdō Nōmintō. "Japan Labor-Farmer party," organized in 1926. It split into several other parties: the Shakai Minshūtō (Socialist People's party), the Nippon Rōdō-nō-tō, and the Rōdō Nōmintō (Labor-Farmer party).

• Nihon Rōdō Sōdōmei. "Japan Federation of Labor." A union federation founded in 1912 by Suzuki Bunji, a militant socialist union leader, as Yūaikai (Friendship Association). The federation took the name Dai Nihon Rōdō Sōdōmei Yūaikai in 1919, and its definitive name in 1921. It was the largest union organization in Japan during the Taishō and Shōwa eras, but was dismantled in 1940.

• Nihon Roman-ha. "Japanese Romantic school." A nationalist literary movement and the title of a magazine created in 1935 by Jimbō Kōtarō, Kamei Katsuichirō, Nakajima Eijirō, Nakatani Takao, Ogata Takashi, and Yasuda Yojūrō. Dazai Osamu joined the movement in 1938, after quitting the Aoi Tori (Bluebird) school. This magazine published the works of about 50 authors and had a major influence on literature before the Second World War. It ceased publication in 1938. In 1979, a new magazine of the same name was published to revive the Romantic movement.

• **Nihon Rōnōtō.** "Japan Labor-Farmer party," founded in 1926 by the moderate members of the Rōdō Nōmintō (Labor-Farmer party) to promote unification of the "proletarian" parties, excluding the communists. In 1928, it joined the Nihon Nōmintō (Japan Farmers' party) to form another party, the Nihon Taishūtō (Japan Masses party), which lasted only a few months. Also called Nichirōtō.

• *Nihon ryōiki.* "Chronicle of Natural and Supernatural Events in Japan." The oldest collection of Buddhist tales *(setsuwa)* in Japan, composed in Chinese in 822 by the Buddhist monk Kyōkai (or Keikai), who was inspired by the Chinese collection *Ming-baoji.* This work contains 116 tales describing the relations of cause and effect *(inga).* Complete title: *Nihon koku gempō zen'aku ryōiki.*

• **Nihon Sankei.** "The Three Views of Japan." Traditionally, the three most famous landscapes or sites in Japan: Itsukushima, Ama no Hashidate, and Matsushima. *See* NIHON JŪNI-KEI.

• **Nihon Seiki.** Japanese name for a Korean Buddhist monk who was said to have written a history of Japan about 622. This work apparently served as the basis for the *Nihon shoki.*

• **Nihon Shakai Shugi Dōmei.** "Japan Socialist League." A federation of socialist organizations founded in 1920 by Yamakawa Hitsohi, Sakai Toshihiko, and others. Because of a lack of agreement between its members, the league was dissolved in 1921, with the communists and anarchists splitting off from the socialists.

• **Nihon Shakaitō.** "Japan Socialist party," founded in 1906 by Sakai Toshihiko, Katayama Sen, Tazoe Tetsuji and Nishikawa Mitsujirō, and dissolved the following year. It was re-formed in November 1945, and has remained the largest opposition party since. It lost two-thirds of its seats in the Diet in the 1949 elections, but regained some in the late 1950s. In 1980, it had 107 seats in the Lower Chamber and only 47 in the Upper Chamber.

• **Nihon Shi-sei.** Collective name for the four largest families in ancient Japan: the Fujiwara, the Taira, the Minamoto, and the Tachibana.

• *Nihon shoki.* "Chronicle of Japan." An ancient official history of Japan, written in 720 by Prince Toneri (675–735), Futo no Yasumaro, and several other historians, to complement the *Kojiki.* This work takes from the *Kojiki* the description of the origins of Japan (with a few variations) up to 697. It often contains several versions of the same stories and legends, and was probably compiled from the *fudoki* and other works that have been lost. Its 30 volumes are divided as follows:
　—Vols. 1–2: Jindaiki, or history of the epoch of the *kami.*
　—Vols. 3–15: from Jimmu Tennō to the reign of Ninken Tennō.
　—Vols. 16–30: historical period from 498 to 697. The work also contains 132 poems, texts drawn from Chinese chronicles *(Weizhi)* and Korean chronicles, as well as a few Buddhist texts. No complete copies have survived, but partial copies do exist, the oldest seeming to date from the late Nara or early Heian period. Among the many commentaries that have been made on this work, the most important are the *Shaku Nihongi* (Kamakura period) and those written by Ichijō Kaneyoshi, Tanigawa Kotosuga, Kawamura Hidene (1723–92), Suzuki Shigetani, and Ban Nobutomo. Also titled *Nihongi. See* KOJIKI.

• **Nihon-shugi.** "Japanism," a nationalist ideology opposed to democracy and socialism and rejecting westernization. This ideology, which advocated traditional Japanese virtues, was launched in the 1880s by Inoue Tetsujirō, Takayama Chogyū, and other intellectuals who were worried that typically Japanese values would be replaced by Western ones. This movement did not outlive the nineteenth century, but was revived during the 1930s by ultranationalist parties.

• **Nihon-siki.** Former system of transliterating Japanese into Roman letters, now replaced by the Hepburn system.

• **Nihon University (Nihon Daigaku).** Private university founded in 1899 in Tokyo by Kaneko Kentarō, Yamagata Aritomo, and Yamada Akiyoshi (1844–92), which received university status in 1920. It has many faculties and scientific research institutes, as well as a number of associated colleges and schools. Annual attendance is more than 75,000 students.

Nihon Densuke. Actor and choreographer (active 1629–52) in Osaka. Father of actor Takejima Kozaemon (d. 1712).

Niigata. Chief city in Niigata prefecture, on the Sea of Japan, facing the island of Sado, and major port at the mouth of the Shinano-gawa river. Once the main port on the west coast of Honshu, it gradually silted up, and shipping traffic declined. It was opened to trade with the West in 1859, and still does business with the Russian ports of Nakhodka and Vladivostok. It exports locally produced oil. Fishing, chemical and petrochemical industries, textile plants. Major local festival (fireworks) in August. *Pop.:* 475,000.

• **Niigata-ken.** Niigata prefecture, on the Sea of Japan (Nihonkai), facing the island of Sado, with mountainous topography (Echigo range). Major rice producer, and important industrial centers. Old mines on Sado. *Main cities:* Niigata, Nagaoka, Tsubame, Mitsuke, Tochio, Toyosaka, Murakami, Sanjō, Ojiya, Jōetsu, Itoigawa, Kashiwazaki. *Area:* 12,577 km². *Pop.:* 2.5 million.

Niijima Jō. Protestant pastor and educator (Joseph Hardy Neesima, 1843–90), born in Edo to a samurai family. He studied Dutch at the shogunal naval school (Gunkan Sōrenjo) and learned the rudiments of Western science. Intrigued when he read a Chinese translation of *Genesis* and geography books on the United States, he stowed away in 1864 on the *Wild* Rover, an American ship anchored in Hakodate, and arrived in Boston in 1865. He continued his studies in Amherst, and in 1870 entered the Andover Seminary. Upon the request of Mori Arinori, he worked as an interpreter for the Iwakura mission to the United States, then returned to Japan. With funds gathered in the United States and Yamamoto Kakuma's support, he created a Christian school, Dōshisha, in Kyoto, where he taught from 1875 to 1890. He went to Europe and the United States in 1884, for further studies, and received a degree from Amherst College in 1889. He was buried in Nyakōji, east of Kyoto. Dōshisha received university status in 1921.

Niinamesai. Annual imperial ritual on November 23, during which the emperor makes an offering of new rice to the *kami* of Heaven and Earth (Tenjin Chigi). This ritual, also called Shinjōsai and Niiname Matsuri, has been faithfully conducted since ancient times, except from the beginning of the Ōnin War (1467–77) to 1739. In 1948, November 23 was chosen as the day for celebration of the national Labor Day festivities (Kinrō Kansha no Hi), during which peasant communities offer rice to their agrarian divinities.

Ni-i no Ama. Title for Tokiko (Taira no Kiyomori's wife) and Masako (Minamoto no Yoritomo's wife), who held the second rank (Ni-i, *see* NI) at the imperial court. *See* TAIRA NO MUNEMORI.

Niitaka-yama nobore. "Climb Mt. Niitaka," a phrase used by the general quarters of the Japanese navy and air force to confirm to Admiral Nagumo the plan to attack Pearl Harbor on December 1, 1941 (code: "Tora, tora, tora!"). Mt. Niitaka was the Japanese name for Mt. Morrison (*Chin.*: Yushan) in Taiwan.

Nijō. Branch of the Fujiwara family. *See* FUJIWARA.
• Imperial concubine (b. 1258) and woman of letters, author of a book of notes, the *Towazugatari,* in 1313. She lived in Emperor Go-Fukakusa's court, whence the name sometimes used for her, Go-Fukakusa-in no Nijō. Also known as Nijō no Tsubone.

• **Nijō jin'ya.** Former lord's residence in Kyoto, near the Nijō-jō castle, designed in the seventeenth century to receive guests passing through. Its unusual architecture includes hidden corridors, suspended ceilings, and various systems designed to prevent all intrusion ("nightingale floors," trap doors, and so on).

• **Nijō-jō.** Pleasure castle built in Kyoto by Tokugawa Ieyasu in 1603 and expanded by Tokugawa Iemitsu in 1624 with parts of the Fushimi castle, in the *shoin* style. Its interior decoration includes paintings by artists of the Kanō family, and it has a garden designed by Kobori Enshū. The palace itself is surrounded by moats. Karamisu imperial gate, Ni no Maru pavilions with "nightingale floors" (*uguisu-bari*). It was in this palace that Emperor Meiji's government first sat in 1868. Total area of the palace and its garden: 275,000 m².

• **Nijō no Michihira.** Statesman (1288–1335), *kampaku* in 1316 and 1327. He received the name Nochi no Kōmyōshō-in. Nijō Yoshimoto's father.

- **Nijō no Mochimoto.** Statesman (1390–1445) and *kampaku*. He received the title Nochi no Fuku-shō-in.

- **Nijō Takako.** Nonreigning empress (842–910), Emperor Seiwa's wife. She was an excellent poet.

- **Nijō Tameakira.** *See* FUJIWARA NO TAMEAKI.

- **Nijō Tamefuji.** Poet (?–1324) who helped compile the *Zoku go-shūi-shū,* completed in 1325, and the *Zoku shūi-shū* in 1278. Also called Fujiwara no Tamefuji.

- **Nijō Tamesada.** Poet (1293–1360) who helped compile the *Zoku go-shūi-shū* of 1325 and the *Shin senzai-shū* in 1359. Also called Fujiwara no Tamesada.

- **Nijō Tameshige.** Poet (?–1385), one of the compilers of the *Shin go-shūi-shū* in 1383.

- **Nijō Tameto.** Poet (?–1381), one of the compilers of the *Shin go-shūi-shū.*

- **Nijō Tameuji.** Poet (1222–86), one of the compilers of the *Zoku shūi-shū* in 1278. Nijō Tameyo's father.

- **Nijō Tameyo.** Poet (ca. 1250–1338), Fujiwara no Tameuji's son. He compiled the imperial anthology *Shin gosen-shū* (1303), then the *Zoku senzai-shū* (ca. 1320). Toward the end of his life, because of rivalries dividing the poets of the court, he retired to Mt. Kōya. He wrote two poetics treatises, *Waka teikin-shō* (Notes on Poetics for Beginners, 1326) and *Waka yōi jōjō,* which simply reiterated the ideas of his predecessors. Although he was influential in the court, he was a mediocre poet and made no innovations.

- **Nijō Tennō.** Seventy-eighth emperor (Prince Morihito, 1143<1159–65>), son of and successor to Shirakawa Tennō. Rokujō succeeded him.

- **Nijō Yoshimoto.** Statesman (1320–88) and *renga* poet, Nijō no Michihira's son. He served the emperors of the Northern Court (Hokuchō) in Kyoto and was *kampaku* four times. He is best known for his works on customs and ceremonies and his treatises on poetry, such as *Gumon kenchū* (Wise Responses to Pointless Questions, 1363, also attributed to Ton'a); *Kinrai fūtei-shō* (Notes on Poetic Styles of the Recent Past, 1387); *Renga*

shinshiki (New Rules Concerning *Renga*), also titled *Ōan shiki* (New Rules of the Ōan Era, 1372); *Renri hishō* (Secret Notes on *Renga,* ca. 1349); *Renga jūyō* (Ten Styles of *Renga,* 1379); *Tsukuba Mondō* (Questions and Answers on *Renga,* 1372). He received the name Nochi no Fukōon-in.

- **Nijō Yoshizane.** Statesman (1216–70), who was *sadaijin,* then *kampaku.* He received the name Fukōon-in.

Nijūgo Bosatsu. "The Twenty-Five Bodhisattvas," the most venerated in Japanese Esoteric Buddhism: Kannon, Seishi, Yaku-ō, Yakujō, Fugen, Bunshu, Shishikū, Darani, Kokuzō, Tokuzō, Hōzō, Sankai-e, Kongō, Konzō, Komyō-ō, Kagen-ō, Shuhō-ō, Nikkō-ō, Gakkō-ō, Sammai-ō, Seijison-ō, Daijizai-ō, Daiitoku-ō, Muhenshin, Hakugu-ō. These *bosatsu* are not all portrayed, and some are theoretical. Some of them are shown accompanying Amida in his *raigō* ("descent").

Nijūhachi Bushū. "The Twenty-Eight Acolytes of Senju Bosatsu," who personified, in Esoteric Buddhism, the 28 constellations: Misshaku-kongō Rikishi (*Skt.:* Vajrapāni), Naraenkengō-ō (*Skt.:* Nārāyana), Kompira-ō (*Skt.:* Kubera?), Manzensha-ō, Mawara-nyo, Hitsubakara-ō (or Bibakara-ō), Gobujō, Taishaku-ten (*Skt.:* Devendrachakra), Dai Benzai-ten (*Skt.:* Sarasvatī?), Tōhō-ten (or Jikoku Tennō?), Birokusha Tennō (or Zōchō Tennō, *Skt.:* Virūdhaka), Birubakusha Tennō (or Kōmoku Tennō, *Skt.:* Virūpaksha), Bishamon Tennō (*Skt.:* Vaishravana), Kujaku Tennō (or Konjiki Kujaku-ō, *Skt.:* Mahāmayūrī), Basu Sennin, Sanshi Tennō (or Jinja Tennō, *Skt.:* Samjñeya?), Nanda Ryū-ō, Sakara Ryū-ō, Ashura-ō (*Skt.:* Asurarāja), Kendatsuba-ō (*Skt.:* Gandharva), Karura-ō (*Skt.:* Garuda), Kinnara-ō (*Skt.:* Kimnara), Magoraka-ō (*Skt.:* Mahōrāga), Daibon Tennō (*Skt.:* Mahābrahmādeva), Kindai-ō, and Mansen-ō. These 28 *bushū* are not venerated individually, but only as a group. They are very rarely portrayed (notably at the Sanjūsangendō in Kyoto, in sculpture).

Nijūikkajō Yōkyū. "The Twenty-One Demands" made by the Japanese government to China in 1915, among them recognition of Japan's rights in Manchuria. At first rejected en masse by China, these "demands" (except for five) were finally accepted in May 1915, leaving Japan's hands free in Manchuria.

Nijūni-sha. "The Twenty-Two Shinto Shrines" that are the most venerated: Ise, Iwashimizu, Kamo, Matsuo, Hirano, Inari, Kasuga, Ohara-no, Iso no Kami, Yamato, Hirose, Atsuta, Sumiyoshi, Hiyoshi, Ume no Miya, Yoshida, Hirota, Gion, Kitano, Mibu, Kibune, and Miwa.

Nijūshi-kō. "The Twenty-Four Examples of Filial Piety." A series of biographies of men and women offered by Confucians as examples with which to educate the people and illustrate the virtues of filial piety *(oyako-kō).* These examples were borrowed from China, and most were improbable stories taken from folklore. *Chin.: Ershisi xiao.*

Nijūshi-setsu. "The twenty-four seasons," former divisions of the agricultural calendar, copied from the Chinese *Qijie,* each comprising about 15 days, starting at the beginning of spring, theoretically February 5: **Risshun** (beginning of spring, Feb. 5–19), **Usui** (rain, Feb. 20–Mar. 3), **Keichitsu** (awakening of insects, Mar. 3–20), **Shunbun** (vernal equinox, Mar. 3–Apr. 5), **Seimei** (clear and light, Apr. 5–20), **Koku-u** (rain of seeds, Apr. 20–May 5), **Rikka** (beginning of summer, May 5–20), **Shōman** (growth of seeds, May 20–June 5), **Bōshu** (formation of heads of grain, June 5–20), **Geji** (summer solstice, June 20–July 5), **Shōsho** (little heat, July 5–20), **Daisho** (great heat, July 20–Aug. 5), **Risshū** (beginning of autumn, Aug. 5–20), **Shosho** (end of the great heat, Aug. 20–Sept. 5), **Hakuro** (white dew, Sept. 5–20), **Shūbun** (autumn equinox, Sept. 20–Oct. 5), **Kanro** (cold dew, Oct. 5–20), **Sōkō** (first frost, Oct. 20–Nov. 5), **Rittō** (beginning of winter, Nov. 5–20), **Shōsetsu** (little snow, Nov. 20–Dec. 5), **Daisetsu** (great snow, Dec. 5–20), **Tōji** (winter solstice, Dec. 20–Jan. 5), **Shōkan** (small cold, Jan. 5–20), and **Sekki** (intense cold, Jan. 20–Feb. 5). These periods correspond to the sun's entry into Zodiac constellations, starting with Libra. They were used to determine agricultural activities; although they were officially abandoned, they are still used by peasants. (The above dates may vary by one or two days depending on the region.) Also called Nijūshi-ki, Ki, Setsu, Sekki.

Nikaidō. Major family related to the Fujiwara, founded in the late twelfth century in Kamakura by Fujiwara no Yukimasa, with the assistance of Minamoto no Yoritomo; it took the name of its residence, Nikaidō. Its descendants held numerous administrative positions in the Kamakura *bakufu;* Nikaidō Yukimori (1181–1253) helped write the *Jōei-shikimoku. See also* TON'A.

Nika-kai. Art society founded in 1914 by Western-style artists who were opposed to the Bunten government exhibitions. It is still active.

Nikka Jihen. Name given to Japan during the Sino-Japanese War of 1937–45. Also called Nichū Sensō. *See* NISSHIN SENSŌ.

Nikkan. Buddhist monk (1665–1726), founder of the Nichiren Shō-shū sect, which Sōka Gakkai currently claims to follow.
→ *See* TAISEKI-JI.

• **Nikkan Heigō.** *See* KANKOKU HEIGŌ.

Nikkatsu. Movie-production company, founded in 1912 as Nippon Katsudō Shashin. During the Second World War, it was absorbed by Daiei, but it became independent again after 1945. It is known for its films on youth starting in 1950, then its pornographic movies *(poruno-firumu),* produced starting in 1980 in its Tokyo studios. It went bankrupt in 1993, following rash investments.

Nikka Whisky Distilling Co. Large manufacturer and distributor of alcoholic beverages, notably whiskey; it also imports gin, vodka, and other types of liquor. Founded in 1934, it has distilleries in Hokkaido, Sendai, and Nishinomiya. It is the second largest liquor-production company in Japan, after Suntory. Head office in Tokyo.

Nikkei. Press group publishing mainly financial information and the newspapers *Nihon Keizai Shimbun* (daily, founded in 1876, circulation more than 2 million), *Nikkei Sangyō Shimbun* (daily, circulation 270,000), *Nikkei Ryutsu Shimbun* (tri-weekly, circulation 360,000), and the *Nikkei Weekly* (weekly, in English, circulation 36,500). The group employs more than 1,300 journalists and has 90 bureaus, including 32 overseas.

Nikkeiren. Federation of employers' associations in Japan, founded in 1948. Its members include the directors of 47 employers' organizations and more than 50 industrial groups. *See also* KEI-DANREN.

Nikki. "Notes" or "diary." A traditional literary genre, written mainly by women of the imperial court, sometimes by courtesans, either in Chinese or in kana, from the tenth to the thirteenth century. The first *nikki* was Ki no Tsurayuki's *Tosa-nikki,* written in 935. Among the most famous are *Kagerō-nikki, Izumi shikibu nikki, Murasaki shi-*

kibu nikki, Sarashina-nikki, Sanuki no Nikki, Sanuki no suke Nikki, Minamoto Ienaga Nikki, Izayoi-nikki, Nakatsukasa naishi no nikki, and *Towazu-gatari.* Continuing the tradition, other *nikki* were written in later periods, most of them personal diaries or confessions. Modern writers best known for their *nikki* include Natsume Sōseki, Kunikida Doppo, Nagai Kafū, and Higuchi Ichiyō. *See also* KIKŌ BUNGAKU.

Nikkō. Town in Tochigi prefecture, about 120 km north of Tokyo; according to legend, an ancient religious center going back to the eighth century. It was chosen by the Tokugawa shogun to be the site of the mausoleum dedicated to the memory of Tokugawa Ieyasu, the Tōshōgū. It is a base for tours to the cryptomere forests in the area, the Tōshōgū shrine, Lake Chūsen-ji, the Kegon waterfall, and sites in Nikkō National Park. Daiyū-in temple. *Pop.:* 25,000. A famous saying goes, "Never say *kekkō* [marvelous] until you've seen Nikkō." *See* TŌ-SHŌGŪ.
→*See* SHIN SHŪ-KYŌ.
• Buddhist monk (1246–1333), Nichiren's disciple and founder of the Kōmon branch (Hommon-shū) of the Nichiren-shū.
• Buddhist monk (1626–98), Nichi-ō's disciple and founder of the Fuju-Fuse Kōmon branch of the Nichiren-shū, in Bizen.

• **Nikkō Bosatsu.** Japanese name for Sūryaprabha, a bodhisattva, acolyte of Bhaishaijyaguru (*Jap.:* Yakushi Nyorai), symbolizing the light of the sun, thus watching over people during daylight hours. He is inextricably paired with Gakkō Bosatsu (*Skt.:* Chandraprabha), symbolizing the light of the moon and the night. Also called Nitten.

• **Nikkō-kaidō.** Former road 146 km long linking Edo to Nikkō, built by Tokugawa Ieyasu, who had it edged with cryptomeres. It went through Taka-zaki, Ashikaga, and Mibu. Also called O-nari Kaidō, Reihei-shi Kaidō. *See also* GO-KAIDŌ, TŌ-KAIDŌ.

Nikō Jiken. Incident that took place from February to May 1920, in the town of Nikolayev at the mouth of the Heilongjiang (Amur) river, in eastern Siberia, during which the Japanese garrison and settlers living in the town as a result of the 1918 intervention in Siberia were massacred by Bolshevik troops commanded by Yakov Triapitsin. The Soviet government, which had not ordered this action, had Triapitsin executed. In reprisal for the attacks, the Japanese occupied the north part of Sakhalin and refused (until 1925) to recognize the Soviet government.

Nikolai. Russian Orthodox archbishop (Ioan Dmitrievich Kasatkin, 1836–1912), born in St. Petersburg, sent to Japan in 1861 to be a monk at Hakodate, and raised to the dignity of patriarch in 1880. He had the Orthodox cathedral of Tokyo (called Nikoraidō) built in 1884.

Nikuson shokku. "Nixon Shock," an expression referring to two decisions made in 1971 by President Richard Nixon of the United States without consulting the Japanese government beforehand: détente with China, and devaluation of the dollar. These decisions deeply wounded Japanese pride and provoked an economic crisis, and they weighed heavily on subsequent relations between Japan and the United States.
→ *See* GENROKU-JIDAI.

Nimmyō Tennō. Fifty-fourth emperor (Prince Masaro, 810<834–50>), nephew of and successor to Junwa Tennō. He was a famous poet and musician. Montoku succeeded him. *Posthumous name:* Fukakusa Tennō.

Nimpyō. Era of Emperor Konoe: Jan. 1151–Oct. 1154. Sometimes called Nimpei. *See* NENGŌ.

Nin'an. Era of Emperor Rokujō: Aug. 1166–Apr. 1169. *See* NENGŌ.

Ningen kokuhō. The title "Living National Treasure," conferred by the government on living people whose talent and skill in the traditional arts are considered worthy of being preserved for future generations.

Ningyo. Sirens and other sea-dwelling beings with a human aspect, sometimes evoked in legends.

Ningyō. "Dolls." Very popular in Japan, where they are both toys and objets d'art. They fall into six categories:
—*In colored wood: kokeshi, gosho-ningyō,* Saga-*ningyō,* Nara-*ningyō.*
—*With fabric clothing: kimekomi-ningyō, ukiyo-ningyō,* Yamato-*ningyō* (dressed at home), *mitsu-ore-ningyō* (jointed), *sakura-ningyō.*
—*Dolls for children's festivals: hina-ningyō* (for the Hina Matsuri), dolls representing Momotarō, warriors, etc. (boys' festivals).

Anesama-ningyō dolls

—*Folk dolls in clay:* Fushimi-*ningyō,* Hakata-*ningyō.*
—*Porcelain and modern dolls:* sakura-*ningyō,* gosho-*ningyō,* Furansu-*ningyō,* and others.
—*"Magical" dolls (hitogata):* anesama-*ningyō,* Amagatsu, Hōko.

• **Ningyō-jōruri.** *See* AYATSURI-SHIBAI, BUNRAKU, MENUKIYA CHŌZABURŌ, PUPPETS.

Ninigi no Mikoto. In Shinto legends and the *Kojiki,* the grandson (Amatsu-hiko Hikoho no Ninigi) of Amaterasu-Ōmikami, sent by his grandfathers, Takamimusubi and Amaterasu, to Earth to reign over the islands of Japan. Amaterasu gave him the three symbols of his sovereignty *(sanshū no shiki):* the sword, the *magatama,* and the sacred mirror. Ninigi "descended" to Earth on Mt. Taka-

chihonomine (in southern Kyushu) and conquered the country. He married Konohana no Sakuya-hime and was the grandfather of the legendary first emperor of Japan, Jimmu Tennō.

Niniroku Jiken. Attempted coup d'état on February 27, 1936, by ultranationalists led by Nonaka Shirō, aiming to overthrow the government and assassinate a number of members of Parliament. Following the battle that ensued, Admiral Saito Makoto, General Watanabe Jōtarō, and Minister Takahashi Korekiyo were killed. Emperor Hirohito pronounced himself opposed to the rebels, who surrendered on February 29 and were tried by a military court. Seventeen of the accused were sentenced to death and executed, and 65 others were sentenced to prison terms. However, the attempted coup brought an ultranationalist, Hirota Kōki, to power as prime minister, and the emperor asked him to form a new cabinet.

Ninja. Category of men specially trained for espionage and assassinations. This category was created, according to legend, in the late Heian period in the mountains around Kyoto, where *ninja* were sometimes mistaken for Yamabushi. Most of these peasants came from Kōga and Iga provinces (east of Lake Biwa), where entire villages were devoted to these activities; starting in the fifteenth century, they were used mainly by daimyo to assassinate their enemies and penetrate their fortresses and castles. There were three classes of *ninja: jōnin,* who commanded actions; *chūnin,* who were responsible for preparation; and *genin,* who executed the plans. They were experts in all sorts of disguises and wore special black garments during their night missions. Experienced in all sorts of tricks and acrobatics, they used a wide variety of non-noble weapons—daggers, poisons, iron claws *(shukō),* spears *(shuriken, shaken),* incendiary and smoke bombs, and more—to achieve their ends. Ordinary peasants feared them, and when they captured *ninja,* they tortured them to find out their secrets. During the Edo period, most *ninja* became pirates and assassins for hire. In an attempt to eradicate them, Oda Nobunaga sent a force of 46,000 men against them in Iga in 1581, of whom, legend has it, 4,000 were killed. *Ninja,* now the stuff of legend, have been the subject of many films, novels, and cartoons *(manga),* and martial-arts practitioners have created *ninja* schools (though not for the purposes of assassination) to develop certain physical attributes among their followers, manufacturing a sort of magical mysticism around them; this has nothing in common with the real *ninja,* but it is good marketing! Their "art" is called *ninjutsu, nimpō,* or *shinobi,* and their followers are *ninjutsu-ka. Ninja* were sometimes called Iga-*mono. See* IGA, TOGA-KURE-RYŪ.

Ninji. Era of Emperor Shijō (also called Jinji): Aug. 1240–Jan. 1243. *See* NENGŌ.

Ninjō. "Sentiments." *See* AMAE.

• **Ninjō-bon.** "Books of sentiments," a type of literature derived from the *sharebon,* which developed after 1790, when the *sharebon* disappeared. These novels gave amusing descriptions of daily life of ordinary citizens *(chōnin)* in large cities, such as Edo and Osaka, and many reflected on the moral decadence of the *chōnin* in the late eighteenth century. Among the best-known authors in this genre were Santō Kyōden, Umebori Kokuga (1750–1821), and especially Tamenaga Shunsui.

Ninju. Era of Emperor Montoku: Apr. 851–Nov. 854. *See* NENGŌ.

Ninkan. Buddhist monk (1057–1123), founder of the Tachikawa branch of the Shingon-shū. He advocated Tantric sexual rites and the use of a "great seal" *(Skt.: mahāmudrā),* considered the very essence of the *Ryōkai mandara.* Although it was banned, this sect continued to exist secretly until at least the seventeenth century.

Ninken Tennō. Twenty-fourth emperor (Prince Ōke, traditionally 448<488–98>), successor to his brother, Kenso. Buretsu succeeded him. *See* ŌKE.

Ninkō Tennō. Hundred and twentieth emperor (Prince Ayahito, 1800<1817–46>), successor to Momozono Tennō. Kōmei succeeded him.

Ninna. Era of Emperor Kōkō: Feb. 885–Apr. 889. *See* NENGŌ.

• **Ninna-ji.** Buddhist temple of the Shingon-shū sect, built in Kyoto in 886 on the former Omuro-gosho imperial residence on the order of Emperor Kōkō, "for the protection of the country," and completed by his son, Uda Tennō (who was buried in its wall). This temple *(monzeki)* was traditionally directed by members of the imperial family who had taken religious status. It was burned down during the Ōnin War (1467–77) and restored by Tokugawa

Iemitsu in 1634. Pagoda *(goju no tō)* 35 m high, dating from 1637.

• **Ninnaji shokaku mokoroku.** See HONCHŌ SHO-JAKU MOKUROKU.

Ninomiya Chūhachi. Aeronautical engineer (1866–1936). In 1891, he built a model helicopter with an engine made of rubber.

Ninomiya Sontoku. Agrarian reformer and philosopher (Ninomiya Kinjirō, 1787–1856), born in Sagami province, who instigated new agricultural methods. He was involved in the draining of lakes to create new land for farming, as well as road construction and bridge repair. Because his methods, based on rational irrigation and use of fertilizer, had improved the harvests, he was asked by the shogunate to develop villages around Nikkō. He taught the peasants his Hōtoku doctrine, according to which Heaven dispenses its goodness, and when the Earth and its people recognize this, an era of peace and prosperity will come. He also created credit unions *(Hōtoku-sha)* to assist the peasants. His frugal life was considered a model of filial piety *(oyako-kō)* and was used as an example in all of Japan's elementary schools.

Ninsei. Painter and ceramist (Nonomura Ninsei, Nonomura Seiemon; *mei:* Seibe, Seibei, Seisuke, ca. 1595/98–1666), born in the village of Nonomura (Tamba province, near Kyoto), who studied with a Korean potter. From 1630 to 1640, he worked at a kiln he built in Omuro (Kyoto) and made pottery (Kyō-*yaki*) characterized by symmetrical shapes covered with a beige glaze with touches of gold and decorated with blue and green flowers. His first pieces were signed Harima Ninsei. He later produced pieces for the tea ceremony *(chanoyu)* in the style of the Seto and Shigaraki kilns.

Ninshō. Buddhist monk (1217–1303) of the Shingon-shū who, against the advice of his masters, devoted himself entirely to the service of others, with the goal of becoming a bodhisattva.

Nintoku Tennō. Sixteenth emperor (Prince Ō-Sasagi, ca. 290<313–99>), fourth son of and successor to Ōjin Tennō. His dates are to be treated with caution because they are traditional and open to being revised. According to the *Kojiki* and *Nihon shoki,* his reign was prosperous and he exempted the people from work parties for three years. He established his capital at Naniwa. He can probably be identified, thanks to Chinese chronicles, as a *miyatsuko* who reigned in the Naniwa region in the early fifth century.

He is credited with building a huge keyhole-shaped *kofun (zempō-kōen-fun)*, 486 m long, surrounded with a triple row of moats and covering an area of 32 hectares (*width:* 305 m; *height:* 30 m). This *kofun,* the largest grave in the world, is located in Mozuno-machi, near Sakai. It has not been excavated, but hundreds of *haniwa* have been found on its surface. Part of the central monticule collapsed in 1872, revealing armor and iron and bronze weapons, a glass vase from Persia, a stone sarcophagus, and other items.

Ni-ō. Pair of guardian deities of Buddhist temples, whose effigies are generally placed on either side of the main gate, representing latent power (closed mouth) and expressed power (open mouth) capable of chasing away evil spirits. They symbolize the beginning and end of all things, and correspond to the Chinese divinities of the same order called Jingang ("Latency") and Lishi ("Expression"), and to the Indian Dvārapāla Vajradhara (*Jap.:* Bazara-un) and Rākshasa (*Jap.:* Rasetsu-ten). They have a threatening stance and are dressed in robes or armor. They are also called Kongō (*Skt.:* Vajrapāni) and Misshaku, and in this case they correspond to the Buddhist divinities Rāga (*Jap.:* Aizen Myō-ō) and Achalanātha (*Jap.:* Fudō Myō-ō). Misshaku has an open mouth; Kongō, a closed mouth. *See* A.

Nippon. Alternate pronunciation of Nihon (Japan). The names of many industrial and commercial companies start with this word. *See* NIHON.

• **Nippon Bunka Hōsō.** Commercial radio station based in Tokyo, created in 1952 with funds from the Catholic St. Paul Society. In 1956, its Christian orientation was replaced by cultural programming.

• **Nippon Columbia Co.** Record-making company founded by an American, F. W. Horn, as Nipponophone Co., in 1910. It now produces not only music albums but tape recorders, television sets, and other electronic equipment, which it exports under the brand name Denon. It was taken over by Hitachi in 1969. Head office in Tokyo.

• **Nippon Denki.** Also called Nippon Electric Co. (NEC), a major manufacturer of telecommunications equipment and of computers and peripherals, founded in 1899, and now part of the Sumitomo group. Nippon Denki has subsidiaries throughout the world, notably in the United States (NEC America), and plants in 10 countries. It is one of the largest computer manufacturers in Japan. Head office in Tokyo.

• **Nippon Gakki.** Manufacturer of musical instruments (Yamaha brand, the largest in the world by volume, 70% of production), motorcycles, audiovisual equipment, and rare alloys; founded in 1897 by Yamaha Torakusu (an organ maker). It also produces world-famous competition archery bows. Head office in Hamamatsu (Shizuoka prefecture).

• **Nippon Hōsō.** Commercial radio station based in Tokyo, broadcasting throughout the Kanto plain, created in 1954. *See* NHK.

• **Nippon Kōgaku.** Maker of photographic equipment and precision instruments (Nikon brand), member of the Mitsubishi group, founded in 1917 by Iwasaki Koyata. It made the first Nikon camera in 1948. The firm now has subsidiaries in New York, Switzerland, the Netherlands, Germany, Canada, and the United Kingdom. It exports more than 50% of its production. Head office in Tokyo.

• **Nippon Sekiyu.** The first oil company in Japan, founded in 1888. It dug wells in the Niigata region in 1890, and began to refine crude oil in 1922. In 1941, it absorbed Kokura Sekiyu; in 1951, it amalgamated with Caltex. Nippon Sekiyu also has supertankers and major storage facilities, notably in Kagoshima. It conducts oil exploration in the China Sea (in partnership with Texaco and Standard Oil of California) and has interests in some 20 other oil companies. Head office in Tokyo.

• **Nippon Terebi Hōsōmō.** Commercial television channel based in Tokyo. It started broadcasting in 1952 as NTV (Nippon Television Network), in collaboration with the *Yomiuri Shimbun.*

• **Nippon Yūsen.** Japanese shipping line (NYK) founded by Iwasaki Yatarō as a department of Mitsubishi in 1870. It is affiliated with more than 70 other shipping companies. After a merger with the Shōwa Line in 1998, its operations included 545 vessels. Head office in Tokyo.

Nise-e. A type of realistic portraits painted mainly in the Kamakura period. Those that were faithful portrayals of their models were called *ni-gao.*

Nisei. "Two origins," name for a person born to a Japanese man or woman and a foreigner, and for Japanese people born in a foreign country and considered foreign citizens *(gaijin)*. Many Nisei, born in the United States, Europe, or Hawai'i, do not speak Japanese.

Nise monogatari. Collection of short humorous stories in the *kanazōshi* genre, published in Edo by an unknown author about 1620.

• *Nise murasaki inaka-genji.* "False Murasaki and the Peasant Genji." A novel of morals by Ryūtei Tenehiko, in 152 volumes and 40 parts, with illustrations by Utagawa Kunisada, published in 1835.

Nishi Amane. Writer and philosopher (1829–97), born in Shimane prefecture to a family of samurai physicians. In 1862, the shogunate sent him to Holland, where he learned about Western culture. When he returned in 1865, he became a fervent positivist, arguing that European civilization was superior to Asian society. He gave a series of lectures on this subject and was a firm supporter of the ideas propagated by the Meiroku-sha. Emulating Auguste Comte, he published a sort of encyclopedia of Western sciences, the *Hyakugaku renkan* (1870), and translated the works of J. Stuart Mill, E. Kant, J. Haven, and other Western writers. In *Hyakuichi shinron* (The New Theory of the 101), he tried to show that Confucianism was not adapted to modern life in Japan; in *Jinsei sampō setsu* (Theory of the Three Treasures of Humanity, 1875), he urged his compatriots to seek health, knowledge, and wealth through adoption of Western civilization. He helped write the edict on conscription *(chō-heirei)* in 1873 and the imperial rescript for soldiers and sailors *(gunjin-chokuyu)* of 1882.

Nishida Kitarō. Writer and philosopher (Nishida Ikutarō, 1870–1945), born in Ishikawa prefecture, whose philosophy, based on the concept of "pure experience" *(junsui-keiken)* as the only reality, became a school. In his later years, he tried to bring his concepts together with the philosophy of Zen *mu* (nothingness). A graduate of the University of Tokyo in 1894, he taught in various institutions, then at the University of Kyoto starting in 1910. His major works were *Zenno kenkyū* (An Inquiry into the Good, 1911), *Jikaku ni okeru chokkan to hansei* (Intuition and Reflections on Consciousness, 1917), *Ishiki no mondai* (Problems of Consciousness, 1920), *Geijutsu to dōtoku* (Art and Morality, 1923), *Hataraku mono kara miru mono-e* (From

Action to Vision, 1927), *Ippansha no jikakuteki taikei* (The System of Consciousness of the Universal, 1930), *Mu no jikakuteki gentei* (The Conscious Determination of Nothingness, 1932), *Tetsugaku no kompon mondai* (Fundamental Problems of Philosophy, 1934), and *Tetsugaku rombunshū* (Philosophical Essays, 1937–46). He was internationally known and was regarded as the greatest philosopher Japan ever produced, as the creator of what is now called the "Kyoto school of philosophy." One of his main disciples is Abe Masao.

Nishida Mitsugu. Politician (Nishida Mitsugi, Nishida Zei, 1901–37) and military officer who organized a secret group of young officers from the Military Academy to discuss political affairs in 1922. He resigned in 1925 for health reasons and became a disciple of ultranationalist theoretician Kita Ikki. In 1927, he attempted to found another secret society, the Tenkentō (Party of the Sacred Word), but his plans were uncovered by the police. He refused to take part in the plot that led to the assassination of Prime Minister Inukai Tsuyoshi in 1932, and was seriously wounded by one of the terrorists. However, he was the theoretician behind the rebellion of February 26, 1936 (*see* NINROKU JIKEN). Arrested with Kita Ikki, he was sentenced to death and executed by firing squad in 1937.

Nishida Tenkō. Politician and Shinto priest (1872–1968) who founded a syncretic sect, the Ittō-en (or Senko-sha), in 1928. He lived on Hokkaido and tried to develop agriculture there. Familiarly called Tenkō-san.

Nishihata Tadashi. Contemporary ceramist, born 1948 near Hyōgo. His works were exhibited at the Mitsukoshi space in Paris in 1994.

Nishi Hongan-ji. Buddhist temple belonging to the Jōdo Shin-shū sect, founded in 1591 in Kyoto by the eleventh abbot *(hossu),* Kennyo Kōsa (1543–92), on a lot conceded by Toyotomi Hideyoshi, and renovated with parts of the Jurakudai and the Fushimi castle in 1618. This temple replaced the Honkoku-ji, which had been transported to Kyoto from Kamakura in 1545. It has many structures dating from the Momoyama period, including two Noh theaters. *Hondo* (reconstructed in 1760), *seimon* (1645), *hiunkaku* (1587, once part of the Jurakudai), *daishidō* (1637), *seishō-kō* and *shōrō* (sixteenth century, bell dating from 1165?), *shoin* from the Fushimi castle (1594, transported in 1630), *kokeitei* garden (designed by Asagari Shimano-suke), and others. This temple is distinct from the Higashi Hongan-ji, located nearby, and it fell to Kyōnyo in 1603, when he contested the title of twelfth *hossu* with his brother Junnyo. Kyōnyo Kōju (1558–1614) then moved to the Higashi Hongan-ji, and Junnyo Kōshō (1577–1631) went to the Nishi Hongan-ji when their father, Kennyo Kōsa, died. The Nishi Hongan-ji is the main temple of the Hongan-ji sect, controlling more than 10,000 subsidiary temples and with about 7 million followers in Japan. *See* HIGASHI HONGAN-JI, HONGAN-JI.

Nishijin-ori. High-quality silk fabrics made in the workshops of the Nishijin district of Kyoto in the late eighth century. *See* NISHIKI.

Nishikawa. Classical Kabuki dance school founded in Nagoya and Edo by Nishikawa Senzō I (d. 1756). Nishikawa Senzō IV (1792–1845) is probably the most famous dancer of this school. The current head of the Tokyo branch is Nishikawa Senzō X. Nishikawa Koisaburō IV is the head of the Nagoya branch; he was a disciple of Nishikawa Senzō IV, Nishikawa Yoshijirō, who created the Hanayagi and Wakayagi dance schools. *See* IEMOTO.

Nishikawa Joken. Astronomer (Nishikawa Tadahide, 1648–1724), born near Nagasaki, serving the shogunate; author of works on "Dutch science" *(rangaku)* and a book of practical advice for merchants, *Chōnin-bukuro* (Merchants' Wallet, 1719). He also wrote the first book describing the world and Europe, *Ka-i tsūshōkō* (1695) and a "Treatise on the Customs of Forty-Eight Nations" (1714).

Nishikawa Kazumi. Government agent (b. 1918). In 1943, he penetrated the Chinese lines and traveled by foot throughout Inner Mongolia, Gansu, Xinjiang, and Tibet, crossing the Himalayas seven times. At the end of the Second World War, cut off from the Japanese army, he spent several years in Tibet, Nepal, and India, before finally being repatriated in 1950. He wrote a book on his travels, *Hikyō seiiki hachinen no senkō* (Eight Years as a Secret Agent in the Banned Lands of Central Asia, 1967), which was very successful.

Nishikawa Kōjirō. Politician (Nishikawa Mitsujirō, 1876–1940), born in Hyōgo prefecture, and a Christian socialist, Nitobe Inazō's disciple. He contributed to magazines founded by Katayama Sen; together, they founded the Socialist Democratic party (Shakai Minshutō). Sentenced to two years in prison in 1908, for having organized a demonstration in the streets of Tokyo, he abandoned all political activity.

Nishikawa Seian. Calligrapher (Nishikawa Yasushi), born 1902 in Tokyo. He studied calligraphy and Chinese literature in Beijing, and created his own style imitating Chinese calligraphers of the Six Dynasties period (222–589). Made a member of the Nihon Geijutsu-in (Japan Art Academy) in 1969; received the Order of Culture (Bunka-shō) in 1985.

Nishikawa Shōji. Physicist (1884–1952), born in Tokyo, and professor at the University of Tokyo from 1915 to his death. His work on x-ray defraction and the atomic structure of crystals earned him an international reputation and the Order of Culture (Bunka-shō) in 1952.

Nishikawa Sukenobu. Painter (Nishikawa Yūsuke; *mei:* Ukyō, Magoemon; *gō:* Jitokusai, Bunkadō, Sukenobu, 1671–1751) of ukiyo-e prints, student of Kanō Einō and Tosa Mitsusuke in Kyoto. He founded his own school, illustrated more than 50 works and texts for Kabuki, and produced many fashionable drawings and a few erotic books *(shunga).* He also wrote *Ehon wagibito,* a book in which he advised painters of his time to free themselves from Chinese styles and return to purely Japanese concepts. His son Suketada and the painters Suzuki Harunobu and Katsukawa Shinshō were his close disciples.

Nishiki. Multicolored silk brocades with gold and silver threads; the manufacturing techniques were imported from China in the seventh and eighth centuries and developed by the artisans of the Nishijin district of Kyoto. There are several types: *nuki-nishiki* (with several wefts), *tate-nishiki* (with several warps, invented in the seventh century), *kara-nishiki, tsuzure-nishiki,* and others. In the *keikin* type, the background and the designs are backed by a colored warp; in the *ikin* type, they are backed by a colored weft. *Chin.:* Huawenjin. *See* KARA-ORI, KINRAN, NISHIJIN-ORI.
→ *See* RICE.

• **Nishiki-e.** Printing technique for ukiyo-e prints using five to ten colors (and as many printing blocks) created by Suzuki Harunobu in 1765. Also called *Edo-e.*

• **Nishiki-goi.** Ornamental multicolored carp. *See* KINGYO.

- **Nishikite.** Type of porcelain in Kakiemon genre, with red, green, and blue decorations on a white background over glaze, somewhat imitating brocade. *See* KAKIEMON.

Nishimaru. Palace built west of the Edo castle in 1592 by Tokugawa Ieyasu to serve as his son's residence. No longer standing.

Nishimura Dōnin. Blacksmith (sixteenth century) famous for his iron kettles *(tetsubin)* for the tea ceremony. Also called Dōnin.

Nishimura Shigeki. Writer and philosopher (Nishimura Hakuō, 1828–1902), born in Chiba prefecture to a family of samurai serving Hotta Masayoshi. He studied "Dutch science" *(rangaku),* artillery, and Confucianism. He translated several Western works, including Laurent Hickok's *Moral Science,* and wrote a large number of works (more than 130), mainly on morals, the best known being *Nihon dōtokuron* (Treatise on Japanese Morals) and *Fujo kagami* (The Women's Mirror). In 1875, he succeeded Katō Hiroyuki as head of the emperor's reading bureau; in 1888, he was appointed director of Joshi Gakushū-in University. Two years later, he was admitted to the House of Peers and ennobled.

Nishina Yoshio. Physicist (1890–1951) born in Okayama prefecture. He studied in Great Britain and Germany, was Niels Bohr's student in Copenhagen from 1923 to 1928, and became famous for his work on atomic particles (Klein-Nishina formula) and cosmic rays. He was Nagaoka Hantarō's disciple, and his students were Yukawa Hideki, Tomonaga Shin'ichirō, and Sakata Shōichi. In 1937, he built the first cyclotron *(riken)* in the laboratory he had founded for atomic research, and he worked with Arakatsu Binsahe, Takeuchi, and Sagane Ryōkichi. He received the Order of Culture (Bunka-shō) in 1946.

Nishi Nippon Shimbun. Daily newspaper published in Fukuoka (Kyushu), founded in 1877 as *Tsukushi Shimbun;* its name was then changed to *Fukuoka Nichinichi Shimbun.* In 1942, it took over another Kyushu newspaper, the *Kyūshū Nippō.* Its current print run is around 600,000 copies.

Nishio Suehiro. Politician (1891–1981), born in Kagawa prefecture. A unionist, he joined the Yūaikai (Friendship Association) in 1919 and was elected president of the Sōdōmei in 1924, helping

form the Shakai Minshutō (Socialist Democratic party). He was elected to the Diet in 1928 and was an elected representative for 15 years. In 1945, after the Second World War, he organized the Socialist party with Katayama Tetsu. He was a member of several cabinets, notably under Ashida Hitoshi (1948). Opposed to collaboration with the communists, he founded the Democratic Socialist party (Minshu Shakaitō) in 1960 and was its president until 1967. He retired from public life in 1972.

Nishi-ōtani. Buddhist temple of the Jōdo Shin-shū sect (Ōtani-ha branch), founded in Kyoto in 1709.

Nishi Takeichi. Sportsman and military officer (1902–45), born in Tokyo. He won a gold medal in equitation (show jumping) on his mare Urania at the 1932 Olympic Games in Los Angeles. During the American attack on Iwo Jima, he committed suicide rather than surrender.

Nishiwaki Junzaburō. Poet (1894–1982) born in Tokyo. He tended toward surrealism, strongly influenced by Western writers such as Ezra Pound, T. S. Eliot, and French poets. He wrote his first poems in French and English, then returned to Japanese. Among his major collections are *Ambervalia* (1933), *Poems Barbarous* (1934), *Tabibito kaerazu* (The Traveler Who Does Not Return, 1947), and *Ushinawareta* (Lost Time, 1960). He also wrote studies on modern poetry, such as *Chogen jitsushugi-ron* (On Surrealist Poetry, 1929).

Nishiyama Sōin. Poet (1605–82), born in Higo province (Kumamoto prefecture, Kyushu), samurai serving daimyo Katō Masakata. He wrote mainly *renga* and *haikai* in the style of the Danrin school (Danrin-fū), which he helped to create. He became a *rōnin* in 1632, then a monk. In 1670, he started to write *haikai,* which earned him and his disciples much criticism from the other *haikai* poetry school, the Teimon-ha. His main poetry collections are *Saiō toppyaku-in* (Series of One Hundred Verses, between 1661 and 1670) and *Danrin toppyaku-in* (Series of One Hundred *Danrin* Verses, ca. 1675). *See* HAIKAI.

Nishiyama Suishō. Painter (Nishiyama Usaburō, 1879–1958), born in Kyoto. Takeuchi Seihō's student, he painted in the Nihonga style and showed his works in the Bunten starting in 1907, receiving numerous awards. He was elected to the Imperial Fine Arts Academy (Teikoku Bijutsu-in) in 1929, and had Dōmoto Sinshō as his student. He received the Order of Culture (Bunka-shō) in 1957.

Nishizawa Ippū. Writer and publisher (1665–1731) in Osaka, author of some 20 novels in *ukiyo-zōshi* genre and 10 puppet-theater plays. His history of puppet theater (*Imamukashi ayatsuri nendaiki,* 1727) is still a valuable source of information.

Nison-in. Buddhist temple (formerly Ogurayama Nison-in Ketai-ji) built in Arashiyama (Kyoto) between 834 and 837 by the monk Jikaku Daishi (Ennin). It houses the tombs (Santei-ryō) of emperors Tsuchimikado, Go-Saga, and Kameyama. It was in this temple that Fujiwara no Sadaie compiled the anthology *Hyakunin-isshū.* It has two very beautiful sculptures of Amida and Buddha Shakyamuni (*Jap.*: Shaka) and paintings by Kanō Eitoku.

Nissan Jidōsha. Manufacturer of Datsun and Nissan automobiles and engines, founded in 1933 by Aikawa Yoshisuke as Jidōsha Seizō. It also makes trucks and buses, and during the Second World War it produced military vehicles. In 1966, it took over its competitor, Prince. It exports more than 53% of its production abroad, where it has many subsidiaries and assembly plants. Nissan Jidōsha is affiliated with Nissan Dizeru Kōgyō (Nissan Diesel), which produces tractors (exported to Russia) and engines (in partnership with Chrysler), and Nissan Shatai, which assembles Nissan cars. Head offices in Tokyo (Nissan Jidōsha) and Hiratsuka (Nissan Shatai).

Nisshin. Expression meaning "Japan and China."
• Buddhist monk (1444–1528) who founded the Honryū-ji temple about 1520 to be the seat of the Hommyō Hokke-shū sect in Musashi.
→ *See* RŌEN.

• **Nisshin-kan.** School (*shohan-gakkō*) founded in Wakamatsu in 1788.

• **Nisshin Sensō.** Name for the Sino-Japanese War of 1894–95. The Sino-Japanese War of 1937–45 was called Nitchū Sensō or Nikka Jihen.

Nitesaki. In traditional architecture (*wa-yō* mode), a type of overhang with two stories of *degumi* with a cantilevered projection. *See* TO-KYŌ.

Nitobe Inazō. Protestant minister (1862–1933) and educator, born in Morioka. He learned English very young and studied modern agricultural tech-

niques. A friend of Uchimura Kanzō, he converted to Christianity and in 1884 left Japan to travel in the United States, Europe, China, and Southeast Asia for 18 years. He married a young Quaker from Philadelphia, Mary Elkington. With degrees from American and Japanese universities, he taught in Sapporo and at private schools. He moved to the West Coast of the United States in 1897, where he wrote *Bushidō: The Soul of Japan,* which was very successful and which popularized Bushido theories in the West. When he returned to Japan in 1900, he held various positions in the Ministry of Colonies; in 1918, he attended the Peace Conference in Versailles, then remained in Geneva as a delegate to the League of Nations. He died during a diplomatic mission to Canada. He wrote several works on agriculture, including *Nōgyō honron.*

Nitta. Warrior family founded by Minamoto no Yoshishige (1135–1202), Minamoto no Yoshiie's grandson, in Kōzuke province (Nitta estate). It became powerful during the Kamakura era and helped Emperor Go-Daigo destroy the Hōjō *shikken* in 1333. However, the Nitta remained faithful to the emperors of the Southern Court (Nanchō) after 1336, and were almost completely annihilated by the Ashikaga shoguns.

• **Nitta Yoshisada.** Warrior (1301–38), the most famous member of the Nitta family. Turning against the Hōjō, he took the side of Emperor Go-Daigo and captured Kamakura, then assisted Go-Daigo during the Kemmu Restoration (1333–36). He was appointed governor of Echigo province (Niigata prefecture) and vice-governor of Harima province (Hyōgo prefecture). He clashed with Ashikaga Takauji and attacked him at Takenoshita but was defeated, then turned against the shogunal forces at Hyōgo. He and his sons Nitta Yoshiaki, Nitta Yoshioki, and Nitta Yoshimune were killed by one of Takauji's allies, Shiba Takatsune (1305–67), in Echizen province.

Nitta Isamu. Chemist (1899–1984), born in Tokyo, famous for his work on the organic structure of certain compounds and his analysis of tetrodotoxin, a deadly poison found in *fugu* fish. He received the Order of Culture (Bunka-shō) in 1966.

Nitta Jirō. Writer and mountain-dweller (1913–80), who wrote many novels set on mountains, such as *Gōriki-den* (1951); *Kazan-gun* (Range of Volcanoes, 1957); *Jūsōrō* (Mountain Trail, 1958); *Hakkōdasan shi no hōkō* (Fatal Walk on Mount

Hakkōda, 1958), which was adapted for the screen by Kurosawa Akira in *Dreams (Yume);* and several historical novels, such as *Takeda shingen* (1969), for which he received the Yoshikawa Eiji Prize in 1974.

Nitten. Abbreviation of Nihon Bijutsu Tenrankai (Japan Art Exhibition), an annual official painting and sculpture exhibition organized, after 1945, by the Imperial Fine Arts Academy (Teikoku Bijutsu-in). *See* BUNTEN, TEITEN.
→ *See* NIKKŌ BOSATSU.

Nittō Hakke. Collective term for the eight major Buddhist monks (including Kūkai and Saichō) who went to Tang-dynasty China.

Niwa Fumio. Writer, born 1904 in Mie prefecture. He was a Buddhist monk until 1932, when he abandoned the robe to devote himself to literature, writing mainly *fūzoku-shōsetsu,* novels dealing with urban life; Buddhism played an important role in most of his works. He wrote more than 80 novels and many essays and stories; he received the *Chūō-koron* Prize (1942), the Noma Prize (1953), the *Mainichi* Prize (1960), the Kikuchi Kan Prize (1949), and was decorated with the Bunka Kunshō in 1977. He became a member of the Nihon Gei-jutsu-in (Japan Art Academy) in 1964 and was president of the Association of Writers of Japan from 1966 to 1972. Among his best-known works: *Ayu* (1932), *Iyagarase no nenrei* (Years of Ingratitude, 1947), *Hōkō* (Wanderings, 1944), *Aomugi* (Green Wheat, 1953), *Hebi to hato* (The Snake and the Pigeon, 1952), *Bodaiju* (The Buddha Tree, 1966), and *Shinran* (a biography, 1969). Many of his novels were translated into European languages.

Niwa Nagahide. Samurai (1535–85) serving Oda Nobunaga. As an architect, he designed the Azuchi castle (Azuchi-jō) in 1576.

Niwano Nikkyō (Nikkei). Monk (b. 1906), founder of the Risshō Kōseikai sect in 1938. At first a follower of the Reiyūkai (founded in 1924), he separated from it; he and one of his disciples, Naga-numa Myōkō (1889–1957), founded a new religion based on veneration of the *Lotus Sutra (Renge-kyō).* After the Second World War, he was active in the peace and ban-the-bomb movements.

Niwa Yasujirō. Electrical engineer (1893–1975), born in Mie prefecture. He worked in the Bell Laboratories in the United States starting in 1925; in

1936, he invented a system for transmission of images that is the basis for all current fax systems (NE type) used today. He received the Order of Culture (Bunka-shō) in 1959.

Nō. *See* NOH.

Nō-ami. Painter (Nakao Shinnō; *gō:* Ōsai, Shun-Ōsai, 1397–1471), attached to the house of the Ashikaga shogun, and a *renga* poet. An art lover, he amassed important collections of Chinese paintings and objets d'art for the shogun. He painted in the *suiboku* style of his time (Muromachi-jidai) and was also known for his knowledge in the arts of incense *(kō-awase)* and the tea ceremony *(chanoyu).* Shūbun's student, he painted mainly landscapes. He was one of the three Ami (San-ami), with Gei-ami and Sō-ami.

Nōbi. Large plain (approx. 1,800 km²) in Aichi and Gifu prefectures, in the Tōkai region, bordering Ise Bay on the Inland Sea (Setonaikai), formed by alluvia from the Kisogawa, Nagara-gawa, and Ibi-gawa rivers. Its coast is heavily industrialized. A major earthquake hit the plain on October 28, 1891, causing 7,237 casualties.

Nobi. See ŌOKA SHŌHEI.

Noborigama. Korean-style potter's kiln, hollowed out of a hill with a slope of about 30° and comprising multiple firing chambers (between 3 and 20), layered on top of each other, each with its own source of heat and opening for loading. It is in these types of kilns that celadon ceramics were made. They replaced the *anagama* kilns around 1600. *See also* ŌGAMA.

Nobukado. Painter (Takeda Nobukado; *mei:* No-butsuna; *gō:* Shōyōken, Kaiten, Nobukado, d. 1582), Takeda Nobutora's fourth son. He painted a portrait of his parents.

Nōbushi. "Peasant-warriors." From the fourteenth to the sixteenth century, bands of peasants, aided by samurai who had broken their ban *(rōnin),* made their living by assassinating and robbing isolated samurai or serving as spies for the daimyo. Some became famous for their exploits, such as Hachisuka Koroku (Hachisuka Masakatsu, 1526–86), who was employed by Toyotomi Hideyoshi, and Ishikawa Goemon. Their adventures were portrayed in Kabuki plays and in movies, notably *Kwaidan (Kaidan).* Also called *nōbuseri.*

Nobuzane. *See* FUJIWARA NO NOBUZANE.

Noda Kōgo. Writer (1893–1968), born in Hokkaido, known mainly for his movie dialogues and screenplays. He worked notably for Ozu Yasujirō and wrote many plays.

Nogami Yaeko. Novelist (Kotegawa Yae, 1885–1985), born in Ōita prefecture (Kyushu). After studying Chinese and Japanese literature, she moved to Tokyo and married Nogami Toyoichirō (1883–1950), a disciple of Natsume Sōseki. She began by writing stories for the magazines *Chūō-kōron* and *Shinchō,* and she also wrote children's stories. Her best-known novels include *Enishi* (Love Stories, 1907); *Kaijin maru* (The *Neptune,* 1922); *Ōishi yoshio,* a historical novel (1926); *Machiko* (1930); *Meiro* (Labyrinth, 1936–56); *Kitsune* (1946); and *Hideyoshi to rikyū* (1963); other works include *Mori* (an autobiography, 1972) and *Hana* (a collection of essays, 1977). She also translated works by a few English authors, including Jane Austen and Charles Lamb. She was decorated with the Order of Culture (Bunka-shō) in 1971.

Nogawa. Archeological site from the paleolithic era, on the terrace of the Nogawa river in the town of Chōfu near Tokyo. When it was excavated, in 1968–70, nine levels of human occupation were discovered extending over a period of 5,000 years, and many lithic tools were found.

Nogi Kiten. General (Nogi Maresuke, 1849–1912), born in Yamaguchi prefecture to a samurai family of the Chōshū. In 1877, during Saigō Takamori's revolt, Nogi Kiten's regiment lost its flag, an unacceptable disgrace. Despite this, Nogi had a brilliant career, becoming a general in 1885. During the Sino-Japanese War of 1894–95, he captured the Liaodong Peninsula and the city of Port Arthur (Lüda), which earned him the noble title of baron. He was also governor-general of Taiwan from 1896 to 1898. During the Russo-Japanese War of 1904–05, he commanded the Third Army during the assault on Port Arthur, losing 56,000 Japanese soldiers. The city was finally taken thanks only to the intervention of General Kodama Gentarō. Nogi Kiten's two sons died during the battle for Mukden. Made a count in 1907, he was appointed director of the Peers' School (Gakushū-in). He and his wife committed suicide on the eve of the burial of Emperor Meiji. This act aroused national pride and inspired many novelists to write on the themes of patriotism, fidelity, and *junshi* (ritual suicide), including Natsume Sōseki *(Kokoro)* and Mōri Ōgai *(Abe ichizoku).*

Noguchi Hideyo. Physician and bacteriologist (1876–1928), born in Fukushima prefecture. He worked at the University of Pennsylvania in 1899, and at the Rockefeller Institute from 1904 to his death. He became famous for his work on white treponoma, which causes syphilis; yellow fever; and poisonous snake venom. He received an imperial award in 1915; he died of yellow fever in Accra.

Noguchi Isamu. Japanese-American sculptor and architect (1904–88), born in Los Angeles. He received a grant from the Guggenheim Foundation in 1927 and studied in Paris with Constantin Brancusi. He then traveled in China, Japan, and Mexico. After the Second World War (he was interned in Arizona from 1941 to 1945), he produced many abstract sculptures and designed furniture and objects inspired by Japanese tradition. Among his most representative works are the Civic Center in Detroit, the Park of Peace in Hiroshima (1952), and the UNESCO garden in Paris (1958). He was poet Noguchi Yonejirō's son.

Noguchi Yonejirō. Poet (*gō:* Yone Noguchi, 1875–1947), born in Aichi prefecture. He went to the United States in 1894, worked for a Japanese newspaper in San Francisco, and married an American poet, Leonie Gilmour, with whom he had a son, Noguchi Isamu. He began writing haiku and poems in the style of E. A. Poe, then moved to London and wrote poems in English, collected in *Seen and Unseen, The Voice of the Valley* (1897), and *From the Eastern Sea.* When he returned to Japan, he was an English professor at Keiō University; he also wrote poems in Japanese, notably *Nijū kokusekisha no shi* (1921), and essays on the art of ukiyo-e prints.

Nōgyō zensho. First basic treatise on architecture, written in 1697 by Miyazaki Yasusada and republished in 1721 by Suyama Don'o (Suyama Totsuan, 1657–1732).

Noh. Abridgment of "Sarugaku no Nō," an aristocratic form of sung and danced performance developed from Kagura plays, *sarugaku,* and folk dances *(dengaku, mai)* by Kan-ami and his son Ze-ami in the fourteenth and fifteenth centuries, on the order of shogun Ashikaga Yoshimitsu. It uses specific masks based on *gigaku* masks. This theatrical genre involves two types of plays: those dealing with reality-based stories, and those in which supernatural beings intervene; both include a sort of syncretic Buddhism and Shinto beliefs. The texts, always very poetic and written in a language that is often difficult to understand, are either *yōkyoku* (recited) or *utai* (chanted), accompanied by drums and flutes supported by a spoken chorus.

Noh plays are performed on a raised stage called a *butai,* about 6 m per side, with a traditional Shinto roof supported by five pillars at the corners, linked to the dressing room (on the upstage left of the stage) by an open corridor *(hashi-gakari)* decorated with three potted pines. The back of the stage has a simple set composed of a curtain, generally portraying pine branches. The orchestra, located upstage, comprises four musicians *(hayashi),* who play a flute *(fue),* two drums (*ō-tsuzumi* and *ko-tsuzumi*), and a larger drum *(taiko).* The chorus *(jiutai)* is on the right. The backstage area *(kagami no ma)* is generally in a small separate building, linked to the stage by the *hashi-gakari.* Actors move onstage via a small, three-step staircase at the front. This arrangement dates only from the eighteenth century; older Noh performances took place on more or less symmetrically arranged stages. All around the stage, which is open on three sides, is a band of stones about 1 m wide. The audience is beyond this space.

The actors, always sumptuously costumed, are all men. The cast generally includes a *shite* (lead actor) and a *tsure* (assistant actor), who sometimes wear masks *(nōmen),* plus other, unmasked actors *(waki).* The *waki* vary in number depending on the play, but there are generally only one or two *(waki* and *kokata).* The plays themselves are often in two acts, the *mae* (first) and the *nochi* (ending), separated by a sort of interlude called *ai.* The texts on which the plays are based are usually short, in prose *(kotoba)* or verse *(utai),* and have few musical indications (except for drumbeats) and no directions. The *yōkyoku* are not at all high literature, for they serve only to illustrate the actors' gestures and dances, to confer a theatrical significance upon them. The aesthetic importance of the performance resides in the music (*jo,* introduction; *ha,* exposition; and *kyū,* finale) and in the actors' dancing.

Usually, the *waki* enters first, stopping on the *hashi-gakari* to sing a sort of introduction *(shidai)* to the play, accompanied by the chorus. He slowly proceeds to the pillar *(shite-hashira)* located at the exit from the corridor, declaiming *(nanori)* his names and the reason for his presence. Then he sings a recitative *(michiuki)* situating the locale and the era of the action that will follow, and sits down.

The *shite* (lead actor) enters to sing a first song *(issei),* followed by a recitative *(sashi)* and by songs *(sage-ute, age-uta)* in which he gives his name and his function in the play, as well as the place where the action takes place, supported by the chorus. The second part of the show consists of a sort of dialogue *(mondō)* between the *shite* and the *waki,* intended to specify (through question and answer) the reason for the action, with the responses repeated in song by the chorus *(shodō).* The *waki* then asks the *shite* who he really is, and the *shite* answers by dancing *(kuse),* with the chorus supplying the words. Then the *shite* exits by the *hashi-gakari,* while the *kyōgen* actors (comedians) come on stage to explain, in plain language, the subject of the play (the *ai-kyōgen*); they then retire in their turn while the *waki* intones a "waiting song" *(machi-utai).* The *shite* reappears, having changed his costume and mask, and dances another *kuse* describing the action (called *iguse* when he remains immobile during this time). He then dances rapidly *(waka),* withdraws to near the pillar and stamps on the ground to signify that the act is over, and leaves for the *kagami no ma* (backstage) very slowly, like a ghost disappearing.

A Noh performance usually consists of three to five "acts" (plays with different subjects), separated by comical interludes *(kyōgen)* designed to relieve tension in the audience. A performance can last several hours. Although this form of theater has evolved since it was created, it has little in common with Western theater (in contrast with Kabuki); it is, above all, intended to provide audiences with a pure aesthetic experience through the costumes, the dance, the music (in which silences, or "spaces," *ma,* are very important), and the very codified gestures of the actors. There are few or no props; sometimes a light bamboo gondola symbolizes a boat, a house, or a chariot. Each actor *(shite* or *waki)* has a folding fan *(chūkei),* which he uses only to indicate the beginning of a dance or a chorus and to convey, by its position or how far it is open, a particular object or sentiment. The *chūkei* is generally painted gold on one side, silver on the other, and bears drawings related to the subject of the play. The other actors and choristers have regular folding fans *(ōgi)* on which are drawn the *mon* (insignia) of the schools to which they belong.

There are currently five main Noh schools: Kanze, Hōshō, Kita, Kongō, and Komparu. There are also specialized schools for the secondary roles, including the Shimogakari, Hōshō, Takayasu, and Fukuō. The Tokyo University of Fine Arts and Music gives courses in Noh. The most popular school is

the Kanze, which claims about one million practitioners, most of them amateurs. Performances,
mainly in Kyoto, Nagoya, and Tokyo, are attended
for the most part by Noh fans and drama students,
but it is considered good form to go and "suffer
through" a Noh play at least once in one's life; Noh
is preserved only as a tradition that should be duti-
fully observed. Among the most frequently performed Noh plays today are *Okina* (the oldest), *Aoi
no ue, Ataka, Aya no tsuzumi, Hagoromo, Izutsu,
Kamo, Kantan, Kiyotsune, Matsukaze, Momijigari,
Saigyō-zakura, Shakkyō, Sumida-gawa, Takasago,
Tomoe, Yashima,* and *Yuya* (*see* these titles).

• **Nōmen.** Noh masks. These masks are slightly
smaller than, and partially cover, the face. Relatively flat, they are carved from wood and painted.
They symbolize seven traditional types of conven-
tional characters:
  —*Masks used for a single play,* such as *Kagekiyo,
Okina.*
  —*Women's masks:* Omote, Ko-Omote, Nari-
masu, Okame, Uba, and others.
  —*Men's masks:* Heida, Yorimasa, Okina, Shio-
fuki, Jō, Kasshiki, Maijo, and others.
  —*Animal masks:* Kitsune, Ko-Tengū, Kawazu
(frog), Kinkui (fox in the form of a monk), Saru
(monkey), Shōjō, and others.
  —*Demon masks:* O-Beshi-mi, Oni, Tengū, Hannya, and others.
  —*Masks representing ghosts and spirits.*
  —*Kyōgen masks, often grotesque,* such as Hyottoko, Otafuku, and Kobuaku.
The masks are often signed by the artists who
sculpted them, the most famous of whom lived in
the fourteenth and fifteenth centuries: Shakuzuru,
Koushi, Fukurai, Tatsuemon, Yasha. Other famous
sculptors worked in the seventeenth century, including Zekan, Kawachi, and Yūkan. The art of sculpting Noh and Kyōgen masks continues today,
though the quality varies. There are currently more
than 200 types of Noh and Kyōgen masks, of which
80 are commonly used. These masks are held in
great respect by the actors, who treat them almost
as cult objects. Some of them are true masterpieces.
See MASKS.

• **Nō-shōzoku.** Kimono or robes for Noh theater.
They may have wide *(hirosode)* or narrow *(kosode)*
sleeves, but are always made of luxurious fabrics,
painted or embroidered.

• **Nō-tori-mono.** Kabuki plays adapted from Noh
or Kyōgen.

→ *See* AKOGI, AMA, AMIDA NO MUNEWARI, AOI NO
UE, ARASHIYAMA, ARIDŌSHI, ASHIKARI, ATSUMORI,
AYA NO TSUZUMI, FUJITO, FUTARI SHIZUKA,
GEMPUKU SOGA, GENJI-KUYŌ, HACHINOKI, HAKU-
RAKUTEN, HASHI-BENKEI, HIBARI-YAMA, HIGAKI,
HŌJŌ-GAWA, HŌKA-ZŌ, HYAKUMAN, IKARI KAZUKI,
IKUTA ATSUMORI, IZUTSU, MAKI-GINU, MAKURA-
JIDŌ, MANJŪ, MATSUKAZE, MATSUMUSHI, MATSU-
YAMA KAGAMI, MATSUYAMA TENGU, MICHIMORI,
MII-DERA, MITSUYAMA, MIWA, MOCHIZUKI, MORI-
HISA, MOTOME-ZUKA, OCHIBA, OHARA GOKŌ, OMI-
NAESHI, OMU KOMACHI, OSHIO, SEIGAN-JI, SEKI-
DERA KOMACHI, SEKIHARA YOICHI, SHAKKYŌ,
SHIGEHIRA, SHITE, SHŌJŌ, SHŌKUN, SHUN'EI, SHUN-
KAN, SHURAMONO, SŌSHI-ARAI KOMACHI, SUMIDA-
GAWA, SUMIYOSHI MODE, TAKASAGO, TAKE NO YUKI,
TAMURA, TEIKA, TENKO, TŌBOKU, TŌEI, TOMOA-
KIRA, TOMOE GOZEN, TORI OI, TŌRU, TSUCHIGUMO,
TSUCHI-GURUMA, TSUNEMASA, UKIFUNE, UNRIN-IN,
UROKO-GATA, UTA-URA, WAKI, YORO-BOSHI, YO-
SHINO SHIZUKA, YOUCHI SOGA, YUYA, ZEGAI.

• Term often used to designate the peasant class.
See NŌBUSHI.

Nō-in Hōshi. *Waka* poet (Tachibana no Nagayasu,
998–ca. 1050) who became a Buddhist monk in
1013. He led an itinerant life around Kyoto, composing poems that he gathered into collections: *Nō-
in utamakaru* (Poetic Places Seen by Nō-in), *Gen-
genshū* (Depth on Depth, ca. 1046), *Nō-in hōshi-
shū* (Collection by the Monk Nō-in, before 1049).
The imperial anthology *Go shūi-shū* (1086) contains 31 of his poems. He was one of the Chūko no
Sanjūrokkasen (Thirty-Six Poetic Geniuses).

Noma Hiroshi. Writer (1915–91), born in Kobe.
His father was an electrician and leader of a lay
Buddhist association (Jōdo Shin-shū sect). He studied French literature at the University of Kyoto, and
in 1938 he worked in the Osaka mayor's office,
where he was responsible for the *burakumin.* Sent
to the Philippines front in 1942 and repatriated
due to ill health, he was interned in 1943 because of
his communist sympathies. He wrote poems in his
youth, but published novels after the Second World
War: *Kurai-e* (Dark Painting, 1946), *Kao no naka
no akai tsuki* (Full Red Moon, 1947), *Nikutai wa
nureta* (Clammy Flesh, 1947). He joined the Communist party and described the life of workers in
Shinkū chitai (Empty Zone, 1952); he then wrote a
social satire, *Saikoro no sora* (The Sky of Dice,
1959); *Waga tōwa soko ni tatsu* (an autobiography,
1960); *Seinin no wa* (The Circle of Youth, 1971), a
huge work begun in 1947 in which he described the

world of the *burakumin*. His later novels were influenced by Buddhism, notably biographical novels: *Tannishō* (1969), *Shinran* (1973). Among his other works: *Futatsu no nikutai* (Two Bodies of Flesh, 1946), *Hōkai kankaku* (A Sense of Disintegration, 1948), *Sayama saiban* (Sayama's Judgment, 1977). Some of his novels were adapted to the screen, notably *Shinkū chitai* by Yamamoto Satsuo in 1952.

Noma-oi. "Wild-horse hunt," a reenactment performed every year at the Ōta Shinto shrine in the town of Haramachi (Fukushima prefecture), in tribute to the *kami* that protect horses.

Noma Seiji. Writer (1878–1938), born in Gumma prefecture. In 1910, he published the literary magazine *Yūben* (Discourse); the next year, he founded his own publishing company, Kōdansha, to publish other magazines, such as *Kōdan Kurabu* (Kōdan Club), *Shōnen Kurabu* (1914), *Omoshiro Kurabu* (1916), *Gendai* (1920), *Fujin Kurabu* (1920), *Shōjo Kurabu* (1923), *Kingu* (1925), *Yōnen Kurabu* (1926). He changed the name of the publishing company to Dai Nippon Yūben Kai Kōdansha in 1925. He also wrote several books, including *Shisei no michi* (1930) and *Sakaeyuku-michi* (1932). *See* KŌDANSHA.

• **Noma Shōichi.** Publisher (1911–84), born in Shizuoka prefecture, who became fourth president of the Kōdansha Publishing Company in 1945. He rebuilt the company founded by Noma Seiji; changed its name to the original one, Kōdansha, from Dai Nippon Yūben Kai Kōdansha, in 1958; and concentrated on publishing educational works for the people. In 1963, he established Kōdansha International to publish books in English translated from Japanese and books about Japan, making Kōdansha one of the wealthiest publishing companies in Japan. He retired in 1981, leaving the presidency to his adoptive son, Noma Koremichi. *See* KŌDANSHA.

Nomi no Sukune. Head of the *hanibe* guild (third–fourth century?), renowned for his strength. According to legend, he defeated his adversary, Taema no Kuehaya, in a sumo match. He is credited with devising the rules for sumo and making the first *haniwa*.

Nomori. Title of a Noh play: a Buddhist monk learns that a pond has the same name as a mirror owned by a demon. The narrator reveals himself to be the demon, then appears carrying the mirror.

Nomura Heiji. Jurist (1903–79) and union leader, author of many works on labor and unions, among them *Nihon rōdōhō no keise katei to riron* (Japanese Laws on Labor: Genesis and Theories), *Rōdō kyōkaku* (Union Accords), *Rōdōhō nōto* (Notes on Labor Laws).

Nomura Kichisaburō. Politician and admiral (1877–1964), born in Wakayama prefecture. He was the naval attaché to the Japanese delegation to Washington during the First World War, promoted to admiral in 1933, and made director of the Peers' School (Gakushū-in) in 1937. As minister of foreign affairs in Abe Nobuyuki's cabinet (1939), he was sent to Washington as an extraordinary ambassador in 1941. After the Second World War, he was elected to the Chamber of Councillors.

Nomura Kodō. Writer and music critic (Nomura Osakazu, 1882–1963), born in Iwate prefecture, author of popular and detective novels featuring Detective Heiji and his associate Hachigorō (analogous to Sherlock Holmes and Dr. Watson) in plots that take place during the Edo period. His series called *Zenigata heiji torimono higae,* published from 1931 to 1958, earned him the Kikuchi Kan Prize in 1958.

Nomura Manzō. Principal (1899–1978) of the Izumi school for Kyōgen. His three sons, Nomura Mannojō, Nomura Manasaku, and Nomura Mannosuke, were famous Kyōgen actors.

Nomura Motoni. Poet (Nomura Moto; *gō*: Kōryō, 1806–67), born in Fukuoka prefecture (Kyushu) to a samurai family. She became a Buddhist nun when her husband died, in 1859, and wrote many *waka* imbued with patriotic sentiment: *Kōryōshū* (1863).

Nomura Naokuni. Politician (1885–1973); minister of the navy in 1944, succeeding Shimada Shigetarō. Yonai Mitsumasa replaced him.

Nomura Yasushi. Politician (1842–1909), born in Yamaguchi prefecture. He was minister of the interior in Itō Hirobumi's second cabinet (1892–96), then minister of communications in Matsukata Masayoshi's second cabinet (1896–98).

Nomura Yoshiteru. Contemporary painter in the Nihonga style, born 1945 in Osaka. After studying with Maeda Seison and Hirayama Ikuo, he specialized in restoration of old works. He traveled extensively in France, Greece, Spain, and Italy, where he had exhibitions of his works. His paintings, executed with ground-mineral pigments in somber blue tones, portray mainly monuments and urban sites. His first exhibition in France was in Paris in 1992–93.

Nonaka Kenzan. Confucian philosopher (1615–63), born in the Tosa estate, serving the daimyo of Tosa province. He belonged to the Teishu-ha branch of neo-Confucian studies. He tried to develop the estate for which he was responsible, but his often unfortunate attempts resulted in the estate being taken away from him.

Nonaka Shirō. Captain (1903–36) who directed the aborted coup d'état of February 26, 1936, during which the banker Takahashi Korekiyo, General Watanabe Jōtarō, Admiral Saitō Makoto, Admiral Suzuki, and several other government representatives were assassinated. As he was about to be arrested, he committed suicide. *See* NINIROKU-JIKEN.

Nonoguchi Ryūho. *Haikai* poet (1595–1669) of the early Edo period. A wealthy, literate merchant, he studied poetry with Matsunaga Teitoku, then left the Teimon-ha school to found his own school and publish his anthology, *Haikai hokkuchō* (1633). He wrote a number of prose pieces in the elliptical *haibun* style. An experienced literary critic, he showed how *haikai* were derived from *renga* and favored the linking of ideas rather than of words (*Kawabune tokumanzai,* 1653). He was also a talented painter.

Nonoguchi Takamasa. Samurai (1792–1871) and political writer. He was the first to dare to demand that the emperor return to the head of government, thus opposing the Tokugawa shogunate. Also known under the name Ō-Kuni Takamasa.

Nonomiya. Noh play, based on an episode described in the *Genji monogatari* involving Lady Rokujō's jealousy of Aoi no Ue.

Nonomura Ninsei. Ceramist (Nonomura Seiemon) active in the mid-seventeenth century. He was asked to create pottery kilns at the Ninnaji temple in Kyoto. His production varied widely but was essentially based on tea services: rustic vases and elegant bowls and teapots. He liked gold and silver decorations and was famous for his delicate colors and the sense of space in his designs, which featured moons and cherry blossoms.

Nopperabō. In ghost stories, a faceless demon, portrayed as a young woman who turns toward travelers who meet her revealing a completely blank, featureless face.

Noren. Split half-curtain hung at the entrance to stores and residences, decorated with the merchant's insignia or the family's *mon.* Such curtains are of ancient origin (probably dating back to the Heian period); their early function was to keep evil spirits from entering the establishment by "brushing" the heads of all who entered. Later, this function was lost and they were used simply as dust guards. *Noren* are generally made of dark-blue cotton or hemp fabric with white decorations. They can be of various lengths and split into two or more parts. They are sometimes used to separate parts of a room. *Noren* made of woven straw are used by low-class bars. When a *noren* is hung at the entrance to a shop, it means that it is open to the public; this custom originated in China.

Nori. Algae of the *Porphyra* genus, widely used in Japanese cuisine. Once harvested, it is finely chopped and laid out to dry on planks to form thin, paper-like sheets *(hoshinori).* It is used as a condiment with rice and pasta, and as an ingredient in sauces; it is heated to make it more crumbly. Once cultivated in abundance on the coasts of Japan, it is now often imported from Korea because Japanese waters are too polluted to allow large-scale production. *Nori* is an essential ingredient in Japanese cuisine, as it contains protein, vitamins A and B, and minerals.

Noriba kofun. Large keyhole-shaped *kofun* (*zempō-kōen-fun*) facing the Iwatoyama *kofun* on Kyushu. Its stone funerary chamber is decorated with painted red-and-white designs.

Noritake. Brand name of high-quality porcelain produced in Nagoya (Noritake district) by Nippon Tōki starting in 1904. The company also makes all sorts of ceramics for domestic, sanitary, and industrial (insulators, etc.) use. Noritake porcelain is exported to more than 110 countries. Head office in Nagoya.

Norito. Shinto ritual formulas composed of poems of invocation to the *kami.* According to the *Kojiki, norito* were created by the *kami* Amenokoyane no Mikoto, who recited them in front of the cave where Amaterasu-Ōmikami had hidden in order to convince her to emerge. *Norito* may be simple thanks to the *kami,* invocations recalling particular events, or prayers. They are written in Chinese characters; their unique aspect is that their grammatical endings are written not in kana but in Chinese characters *(kanji),* in smaller type, to signify that they should be read phonetically *(semmyō-gaki).* The 27 oldest *norito* appear in the *Engi-shiki* (927); they are also found in the *Man'yōshū* and the *Taiki bekki* (1142). Most *norito* were composed by Shinto priests. Their use was regulated in the early Meiji era.

→ *See* KOTODAMA, YOGOTO.

Noro Eitarō. Economist (1900–34) and Marxist theoretician for the Japanese Communist party, who wrote essays on capitalism (1927). He was arrested for his political activities and died in prison.

Noro Genjō. Botanist (1693–1761), born in Ise province, Inō Jakusai's student. Official physician to shogun Tokugawa Yoshimune, he was ordered to study Dutch and to translate a book on medical botanicals, *Cruydeboek,* published by Rembert Dodens in 1554. This work was published as *Oranda honzō age* (Dutch Herbarium Translated).

Noro Kuninobu. Writer (1938–80) who won the Akutagawa Prize in 1974 for his novel *Kusa no tsurugi* (The Sword That Cut Grass). He also wrote *Ara otoko no kokyō* (A Man's Homeland) and a historical novel, *Isahaya shōbu nikki.*

Nosaka Akiyuki. Writer, born 1930 in Kanagawa prefecture. After working at various more or less respectable trades, he became a publicist, then began to publish novels in the Osaka dialect, stunning for both their style and their violence: *Erogotoshitachi* (The Pornographers, 1963), *Tomuraishitachi* (The Gravediggers, 1966), *Amerika hijiki* (1967), *Hotaru no haka* (The Tomb of the Fireflies, 1968), *Honegami tōge hotokekazura* (The Vine of the Dead on the Necks of the Gods, 1969), and others; *Erogotoshitachi* was adapted for the screen by Imamura Shōhei; *Tomuraishitachi,* by Misumi Kenji. Nosaka Akiyuki's life was chaotic, and he tried his hand at all sorts of professions, including radio and television singer, boxer, rugby player, and even politician, running in the 1974 and 1984 legislative elections.

Nosaka Sanzō. Politician (1892–1993), born in Yamaguchi prefecture. He joined Suzuki Bunji's Yūaikai (Friendship Association) party, then left for Great Britain in 1919, where he became affiliated with the British Communist party. Expelled from Great Britain, he went to France, then to Germany and the Soviet Union. In 1922, when he returned to Japan, he joined the newly founded Communist party. He went to the Soviet Union again in 1931 as a representative of the Comintern, then to the United States several times. In 1940, he went to Yan'an, China, and worked with Mao Zedong to indoctrinate Japanese soldiers who had been taken prisoner. He returned to Japan in 1946 and was elected to the Diet on behalf of the revived Communist party. A member of the Chamber of Councillors from 1956 to 1977, he was president of the party's Central Committee from 1958 to 1982. However, he was stripped of his honorary presidency of the party in September 1992, for having denounced one of his companions in the Comintern during the Stalinist purges.

Nōshi. Everyday garb for nobles during the Heian period, which became a ceremonial costume during the Edo period. *See* HŌ, NAOSHI, SOKUTAI.

Noshi. Emblem on a gift, once composed of a long band of dried *awabi* (abalone) folded in a special way in a piece of white-and-red paper and tied with one or several gold or silver cords *(mizuhiki).* It was an essential part of gifts of food offered to a person for whom a period of mourning or ritual abstinence was ending, and had to be glued on the upper-right part of the wrapping. Today, the original significance of the *noshi-awabi* has been lost, but gifts are always accompanied by a paper *noshi,* often simply printed on the wrapping paper. Sometimes the *noshi* is even replaced by the word *"noshi"* written in *harigana* characters. There are several types of *noshi,* depending on the purpose of the gift: *naga-noshi,* used for gifts signifying a commitment of some sort (usually marriage); *kazarinoshi,* decorated with propitiatory symbols (pins, bamboo, plum trees); *warabinoshi; ryō-ori-noshi;* and others. *See* MIZUHIKI.

Noto. Former province, now included in Ishikawa prefecture, including the Noto Peninsula (Noto Hantō), which extends into the Sea of Japan. This mountainous peninsula is famous for its landscapes, beaches, and hot springs. Fishing, pearl-oyster cultivation, lacquer objects.

Nozawa Bonchō. *See* BONCHŌ.

Nozu Michitsura. General (1841–1908), born in Kagoshima. He was sent to the United States in

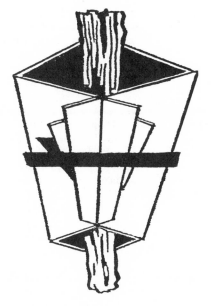

Noshi

1876, then to Europe in 1881 to study military techniques. He fought in China (1894–95), then in Mukden in 1905 under Nogi Kiten's orders.

Nue. Legendary mythical, composite-winged monster that is a harbinger of troubled times. According to the *Heike monogatari,* such a demon was killed by Minamoto no Yorimasa with a bow and arrow in 1153, when it landed on the roof of the imperial palace.

Nuhi. During the Asuka period (sixth century), "slaves," male *(nu)* and female *(hi),* a class of persons of low birth who were distinguished from free people *(ryōmin).* They were generally prisoners of war (Korean) or criminals condemned to be *semmin* (outcasts). According to the Taihō Code (701), *nuhi* (or *menoyakko)* were divided into five categories, depending on whether they were public slaves or belonged to individuals. They could marry only within their categories. Slavery was officially abolished in 907, and the *nuhi* became peasants or domestics. Also called *dorei. See* SEMMIN.

Nukata no Ōkimi. Poet (ca. 630–after 690), wife of Prince Ōama (Emperor Temmu), then of Prince Naka no Ōe (Emperor Tenji). A high-ranking Shinto priestess, she could not be empress. Only 12 of her poems (three *chōka* and nine *tanka)* are

known, because they were recorded in the *Man'yōshū.* She was probably a sister of Fujiwara no Kamatari's wife. Also called Nukuda-hime.

Nukina Kaioku. Confucian scholar (Nukina Kane, Nukina Sūō, Nukina Hō, Kaioku, 1778–1863), calligrapher, and painter in the Nanga (Bunjinga) style, born to a samurai family in Awa province. His calligraphic style followed the Chinese Tang style.

Numa Morikazu. Politician and journalist (1844–90), born in Edo. A member of the Genrō-in, he resigned in 1879 to have the right to speak freely and joined the Jiyū Minken Undō (Freedom and People's Rights Movement). He helped found the Jiyūtō (Liberal party) in 1881, but left this party to join the Rikken Kaishintō (Constitutional Reform party). He was president of the Tokyo Prefectural Assembly.

Numanami Rōzan. Ceramist (active 1736–46) at the Banto and Antō kilns in Kyoto, and in Kuwana (Ise province). He produced works in a wide variety of styles.

Nunchaku. Weapon consisting of two wooden handles joined by a chain or horsehair cord, inspired by the flail used by Okinawa peasants. The handles varied in length but were usually from 25 to 35 cm long. The art of using the *nunchaku,* adopted by karate practitioners, was popularized in the West by Bruce Lee films, and is part of the teachings of the martial arts in the *ko-budō.* Some *nunchaku,* of Chinese or Vietnamese origin, have three wooden parts. Also called *nunjaku, so-setsu-kon.*

Nuno. Former method of weaving plant fibers: *tae (shirotae)-nuno,* made with plum-tree bark *(kōzo),* and *asa-nuno,* made with hemp.

• **Nunome-zuri.** Method of printing ukiyo-e prints, using *nuno* fabric glued onto the woodblock *(hangi).*

Nuri-mono. General term for lacquered objects and utensils. Also called *urushi no mono. See* LACQUER, SHIKKI, URUSHI.

Nuru. In Okinawa, the head priestess of cults related to Shinto, often assisted by a second priestess called *nigami,* and generally residing in the shrine *(nundunchi).* Sometimes written *noro. See* MIKO, RYUKYU.

Nusa. In Shinto, a sacred hemp cord, symbol of the *kami. See also* GOHEI, SHIMENAWA.

Nyōbō. Title for noblewomen serving in the imperial or shogunal palace.

• **Nyōbō-kotoba.** Dialect developed by the women of the aristocracy during the Muromachi period in order to remain elegant while discussing trivial things among themselves. These special words and verbs, numbering about 1,000, were indispensable to all cultivated women during the Edo period. A certain number of words from *nyōbō-kotoba,* characterizing women's speech, still exist today.

Nyo-i. Curved stick made of wood, metal, or ivory, used to scratch the back, and representing the rank of the Buddhist monk who carries it. *Chin.:* Jui, Rui.

Nyo-in. Title for the mother of an emperor. When she is a widow and has become a Buddhist nun, she takes the title Mon-in.
→ *See* GOSHO.

• **Nyo . . . no Miya.** Title for the daughters of an emperor: Nyoni no Miya (second princess), Nyosan no Miya (third princess), Nyoshi no Miya (fourth princess), and so on.

• **Nyogo.** Title for an emperor's second wife, since 800.
→ *See* KŌTAIFUJIN.

• **Nyokōba.** Schools for young women created in the early Meiji era, notably in Kyoto in 1872, to teach girls and women sewing, some "feminine" arts, and English.

• **Nyonindō.** In some Buddhist temples, a room reserved for women.

• **Nyo-ō.** Title for women descended from an emperor, up to the fourth generation.

• **Nyotei.** Title sometimes given to empresses.

Nyoirin Kannon. Hypostasis of Kannon Bosatsu (*Skt.:* Avalokiteshvara) corresponding to the Bodhisattva Chintāmani-chakra, representing, in Buddhism, a form of bodhisattva said to grant the wishes of the faithful. *Chin.:* Ruyilin Guanyin. Also called Seiryū Gongen in Buddhist-Shinto syncretism.

• **Nyoirin-ji.** Buddhist temple founded in Yoshino (Nara prefecture) about 910. *Hondō* rebuilt in 1650; *tahōtō* restored in 1925.

Nyorai. Title for some major buddhas, corresponding to the Sanskrit *Tathāgata.* Among the buddhas with a right to this title are the Go-chi Nyorai (Five Buddhas of Wisdom), Buddha Shakyamuni, and Dainichi Nyorai, the Sun Buddha, central divinity of the esoteric pantheon. *Chin.:* Rulai; *Kor.:* Yo-rae.

• **Nyorai ken-in.** Mudra *(Jap.: in-zō)* specific to some Buddhist divinities in the esoteric pantheon, made with the two fists placed one on top of the other in front of the chest.

• **Nyorai Kōjin.** *See* SAMBŌ KŌJIN.

Nyū. Paleolithic site on a plateau 8 km east of Ōita. Excavation by amateur archeologists in 1982 revealed "arranged pebbles" similar to those of the early paleolithic era in Africa, India, and Southeast Asia, as well as picks, flakes, blades, points, and microliths. It is difficult to date them because of the geological activity of the region. It could be that these "tools" were not the result of human activity, but they do pose the question of when the Japanese islands were first inhabited by human beings.

Nyūdō. A lay Buddhist disciple, belonging to no particular monastery or temple. Also called *shami.*

• **Nyūdō Masamune.** *See* MASAMUNE.

• **Nyūdō Shinnō.** Title for imperial princes who became lay Buddhist disciples *(nyūdō).* Also called *hō-shinnō.*

O. Fifth vowel of the kana alphabet (*see* GOJŪ-ON ZU).

• Honorific particle placed before a name or title as a sign of importance or respect. This vowel is often placed before the name of an object belonging to another person in order to show that it belongs to the honored person. As a particle, it is equivalent to the formal "you" of French and other languages. It is not directly translatable, though the word "honorable" is often used. Also, in certain cases, replaced with *Go*.

→ *See* ISHIKAWA JŌZAN.

Ō. "Grand," a title once given to legitimate male descendants of an emperor up to the third or fourth generation. This long vowel also means "king" (*Chin.*: Wang). *See* JO-Ō.

• Also, court garment.

Oakujō. Type of Noh mask (*nōmen*) representing a bearded, smiling old man.

Ō-an. Era of emperors Go-Kōgon and Go-En'yū of the Northern Court (Hokuchō): Feb. 1368–Feb. 1375. *See* NENGŌ.

Ōba Kagechika. Warrior (d. 1180) from Sagami province who served Minamoto no Yoshitomo in 1156 (*see* HŌGEN NO RAN), then aligned himself with the Taira in 1180. Defeated that year, he surrendered and was decapitated by the Minamoto.

Obake. Human-like ghosts often described in legends and folk tales. A "nice" ghost, called Oba-Q, was recently created in a children's cartoon. Ghostly objects are called *bakemono*. *Okinawa*: Majimung.

Ōbaku-shū. Zen Buddhist sect imported to Japan by Chinese monks in the mid-seventeenth century—notably, by Yiran (*Jap.*: Itsunen) to Nagasaki in 1644. In 1659, the monks of this sect established their headquarters in Uji, thanks to the arrival in Japan of the monk Yinyuan (*Jap.*: Ingen, 1592–1673), 20 of his disciples, and 10 artisans who built the Mampuku-ji on the Ōbaku-san hill. The Ōbaku-shū advocated a certain syncretism with the doctrines of the Jōdo-shū, including adoption of recitation of the *nembutsu*. The Chinese monks also brought Ming architectural styles and, especially, calligraphy styles, exemplified in works by the Ōbaku Sampitsu (Ōbaku Three Brushes), Ingen and his disciples Mokuan (1611–84) and Sokuhi (1616–71). Currently, the Ōbaku sect is divided into two branches, the Ōbaku-shū (about 120,000 followers) and the Guze-shū (about 5,000 followers). *Chin.*: Huangmo.

Ōba Minako. Contemporary author (b. 1930). She has written many very successful works of fiction, including *Sambiki no kani* (Three Crabs), which won the Akutagawa Prize in 1968; *Naku tori no* (The Bird Cry), Noma Prize in 1986; and *Tsuda Umeko* (1993).

Ōban. Format of printing paper (about 38 × 25 cm) used for certain ukiyo-e prints.

• Guards of the Kamakura shogunal palace, generally recruited from the eastern provinces (Azuma), who served for only one year before being replaced.

• Starting in 1573, large, thin, more or less oval gold coins (10 to 15 cm long), weighing about 165 g, worth 10 *ryō*. They were ink-engraved and bore the seal of the Gotō family, directors of the Mint.

The first official *ōban* were issued in 1588 on the order of Toyotomi Hideyoshi, and Tokugawa Ieyasu made them the model of the national currency. At first, they were struck with 16-carat gold, but they gradually lost their gold content in subsequent reissues. *See* CURRENCY, KOBAN, RYŌ.

Obara Kuniyoshi. Educator (1887–1977). In 1929, he founded Tanagawa University, where he implemented his ideas on education, which involved practice concurrent with theory for full realization of the complete human being *(zenjin kyō-iku)*. He wrote many educational works.

Obasute. Custom observed (rarely) in some mountainous regions of Japan in times of famine, consisting of abandoning old people on the mountain, mainly on Obasute-yama (also called Ubasute-yama, Kamuriki-yama) in Nagano prefecture. This custom, of Chinese origin, has become legendary; it was the subject of a number of Noh plays (such as Zeami's *Obasute*) and is mentioned in the *Konjaku monogatari* (twelfth century). A modern novel called *Narayama bushi-kō*, by Fukazawa Shichirō (1956), recounts this legend, and it was adapted for the screen by Kinoshita Keisuke in 1958. *See* NARAYAMA BUSHI-KŌ.

Obata Kagenori. Confucian scholar (Dōgyū, 1572–1663), Matabei Masamori's third son, serving the Takeda family. He founded a school for studying the arts of war, the Kōshū-ryū Gungaku (also called Obata-ryū Gungaku), and he fought in the Battle of Sekigahara (1600), with Ii Naomasa, and at the siege of Osaka (1615), on behalf of Tokugawa Ieyasu. He completed Kōsaka Masanobu's *Kōyō gunkan*. *See* KŌYŌ GUNKAN.

Ō-beshi-mi. Type of Noh mask *(nōmen)* representing a demon.

Obi. "Belt." Large fabric belt used to keep the kimono closed. Before the eighth century, a flexible, narrow belt or a simple cord was used. With the adoption of the new kimono *(kosode)* during the Nara period, the belt became wider and was made of expensive fabrics; it was called *kantai* (for men) and *soe-obi* (for women). During the Heian period, *obi* for men were often made of leather decorated with precious stones (*see* SEKITAI), while women of the aristocracy did not wear an *obi* with the garment called *jūnohitoe*. In the Edo period, *obi* became quite elaborate, especially for women's kimono. Men wore various sorts of fabric *obi* called

shigoki-obi (in white cotton), *heko-obi*, or *kaku-obi*. Married women knotted the *obi* in front, whereas young women knotted it in the back; courtesans, however, tied their *obi* in front, and the tails sometimes fell to the floor. The manner of knotting the *obi*, the material of which it was made, and its width gave indications of the age and status of the woman wearing it. Today, *obi* are wide and rigid. They have a large knot in the back (sometimes separate from the *obi* itself) made of brocade, called *otaiko* for married women and *fukurasuzume* for young women. The knot is supported by a pad *(obi-makura)* and kept in place by a cord *(obijime)*. Other accessories often complement the *obi*, such as the *obi-dome*, a brooch on the *obijime*, and the *obiage*, a crepe belt holding the *obi-makura*. A rigid panel *(obiita)* is placed against the stomach under the *obi* to keep it from creasing. The *obi* is the ultimate adornment for the kimono. *See also* KAZURA-OBI, MAWASHI.

• **Obi iwai.** A custom according to which a pregnant woman wears a special *obi* called *iwata-obi* tied around her chest on the day of the dog (Inu no Hi), starting in the fifth month of pregnancy, in order to have an easy delivery.

Obito. In ancient Japan, before the seventh century, an honorific title for chiefs of guilds *(be)*. *See* KABANE.

Obitoke-dera. Buddhist temple in Imaichi (Nara prefecture), founded in the mid-ninth century. *Hondō* from the Kamakura period.

Oboko. Man-shaped rattle with an egg-shaped papier mâché head and a short handle made of light wood (sometimes with a whistle). This *mingei*, often considered a charm *(engi)*, was placed on a pregnant woman's bedside table so that she would give birth to a boy. It would later be given to the child. *Oboko* were probably first made in Miyagi prefecture (then under the Date clan) in the seventeenth century, and, according to certain authors, were the forerunners of *kokeshi*.

Ōbunsha (Ōbunsha Kakushiki Kaisha). Textbook publishing company founded in 1931 by Akao Yoshio. It publishes many reference books and magazines for students.

Obusuma saburō ekotoba. "Story of the Samurai Saburō." A late-thirteenth-century one-scroll *ema-kimono* describing the daily life of rural dwellers.

Ochanomizu Joshi Daigaku. University of Ocha-nomizu (Tokyo district), founded for young women in 1874; it obtained university status in 1949. Attendance: about 1,700 students.

O-cha no Tsubone. Wife (d. 1637) of Takeda Shinden, Toyotomi Hideyoshi's adoptive father in Imagawa. Having reached the first rank of nobility in the imperial court, she acted as the intermediary between Tokugawa Ieyasu and Toyotomi Hideyori during the first siege of Osaka *(fuyu no jin)* in January 1615.

Ochiai Eiji. Chemist (1898–1974), born in Chiba prefecture. He studied in Germany from 1930 to 1932 and became known for his many scientific articles on the properties of plants and on alkaloids. He received the Imperial Academy Prize (Teikoku Gakushi-in shō) in 1944 and the Order of Culture (Bunka-shō) in 1969.

Ochiai Naobumi. Poet and philologist (*gō:* Haginoya, 1861–1903), born in Miyagi prefecture. He formed the Asakasha poetry group and wrote mainly *tanka,* attempting to revive *waka* style. Among his works: *Shinsen katen* (New Code for Short Poems, 1891), *Nihon dai bunten* (Study of the Japanese Language, 1897), and a collection of poems, *Haginoya ikō* (published posthumously in 1904).

Ochiai Yoshihiku. Painter of ukiyo-e prints (1833–1904) who studied with Utakaga Kuniyoshi and Yoshitoshi. In 1854, he began to produce prints in *nishiki-e* on a wide variety of subjects—foreigners, women, Kabuki actors, military scenes, and others—for various newspapers and the theater magazine *Kabuku Shimpō.* His late portraits were inspired by photographs. He sometimes signed his works Igeisai Yoshiiku, Yoshihiku.

Ochiba. Title of a Noh play inspired by an episode from the *Genji monogatari:* the spirit of Princess Ochiba appears to a Buddhist monk and tells him about the love she felt for Prince Genji.

Ochi Etsujin. Haiku poet (1656–ca. 1739), one of Bashō's ten main disciples (Bashō Juttetsu). He accompanied Bashō on a trip from Kyoto to Nagoya and Edo in 1688. His poems were published in *Sarashina nikki, Arano,* and *Sarumino.* His own anthology is called *Shakubikan* (1717).

Ochikubo monogatari. "Tale of the Lower Room," written between 960 and 970 and often attributed (without certainty) to Minamoto no Shitagō (911–83). It tells of an unhappy young woman from a good family, persecuted by her stepmother, who forced her to live in a room below those of her sisters. She married secretly, thus managing to escape her family's grasp; her husband tried to avenge her but finally gave up at his wife's insistence. This tale is the equivalent of "Cinderella" and belongs to the *mamago-monogatari* genre (stories of stepmothers). It was in the realist style and four scrolls long.

Ōchō. Era of Emperor Hanazono: Apr. 1311–Feb. 1312. *See* NENGŌ.

• **Ōchō-jidai.** "Ōchō period," the name for the era when emperors governed alone, from the beginning until around 1185–92.

• **Ōchō-mono.** *See* ŌDAI-MONO.

O-chūgen. Time in the middle of the year (July 1–15) when custom has it that gifts, usually of food, are offered to friends and relatives. Also called *chūgen. See* GIFTS.

Odagiri Hideo. Literary critic and Marxist theoretician, born 1916 in Tokyo. In 1946, he helped to found the magazine *Kindai Bungaku,* which advanced the idea that Marxism was compatible with freedom of expression.

Odagiri Susumu. Literary critic (1924–92), author of works on literature of the Shōwa era. He was director of the Museum of Modern Japanese Literature.

Oda Hidenobu. Oda Nobunaga's grandson (Sambōshi, 1580–1605). He converted to Christianity and opposed Toyotomi Hideyoshi; he was forced to recant and became a Buddhist monk on Mt. Kōya in 1600.

Ōdai-mono. Type of Kabuki play, in the *jidai-mono* genre, whose subjects are based on the lives of nobles in Kyoto before the twelfth century. Also called *ōchō-mono.*

O-dai no Kata. Mizuno Tadamasa's daughter (1528–1602) and Tokugawa Ieyasu's mother. Repudiated by her first husband in 1545, she married

Hisamatsu Toshikatsu. *Posthumous name:* Denzū-in (or Dentsū-in).

Odaira Namihei. Industrialist (1874–1951), born in Tochigi province, founder of the manufacturer of electrical appliances Hitachi, of which he was president from 1929 to 1947.

Oda Makoto. Writer, born 1943 in Osaka prefecture. After studying in the United States, he published an account of his stay there, *Nandemo mite yarō* (1931) and a major novel on racial discrimination in America, *Amerika* (1962). During the Vietnam War, he was active in the anti-war movement.

Oda Nagamasu. Daimyo (Oda Uraku, Urakusai, 1547–1621), Oda Nobunaga's younger brother. He assisted Tokugawa Ieyasu at the Battle of Sekigahara in 1600 and received an estate worth 30,000 *koku*. After taking Toyotomi Hideyori's side at the Battle of Osaka in 1615, he abandoned public life. He became a Buddhist monk with the name Urakusai-joan and was a famous master *(chajin)* of the tea ceremony *(chanoyu)*, a disciple of Sen no Rikyū, and established his own school, called Uraku. The Yūrakuchō district of Tokyo was named for his hermitage. He apparently converted to Christianity in 1588.

Odani no Kata. Oda Nobunaga's younger sister (Oichi no Kata, 1548–83), famous for her beauty. When she was 15, she married the daimyo of Ōmi, Asai Nagamasa, who had revolted against Oda Nobunaga and was killed by him in 1573. Odani no Kata and her daughters were spared, but her two sons were put to death. After Oda Nobunaga was assassinated, she was forced to marry daimyo Shibata Katsuie, but one year later he was attacked and killed by Toyotomi Hideyoshi. She perished when her castle was set afire, but her three daughters (Yodogimi, Kyōgoku Maria, and Sūgen-in) were saved. Yodogimi became Toyotomi Hideyoshi's favorite, and Sūgen-in (1573–1626) married Tokugawa Hidetada.

Oda Nobukane. One of Oda Nobunaga's brothers (1543–1614), who became a Buddhist monk in 1594 with the name Rōtaisai. He was also a painter. *See* ODA NOBUNAGA.

Oda Nobunaga. Warrior (1534–82) and primary unifier of Japan. He was born of humble origins in Owari province, the son of Oda Nobuhide (1510–51), one of the warlords of the Sengoku (Warring States) period and lord of the Nagoya castle. When Nobuhide died, Oda Nobunaga succeeded him; assisted by his uncle, Oda Nobumitsu (killed in 1556), he began to expand his estate. He had his younger brother, Oda Nobuyuki, whom he suspected of plotting against him, assassinated, and drove the other members of the Oda family from Owari province. After defeating the superior forces of daimyo Imagawa Yoshimoto at the Battle of Okehazama in 1560, he concluded an alliance with Matsudaira Motoyasu (the future Tokugawa Ieyasu) in 1562. Continuing his series of conquests, he placed his son, Oda Nobutaka (1558–83) at the head of Ise province, and his brother Oda Nobukane (1543–1614) at the head of Mino province.

He took as his motto *"Tenka fubu"* ("Empire under the military") and installed shogun Ashikaga Yoshiaki in Kyoto, taking advantage of this to occupy Kyoto in 1568 on the pretext of protecting Emperor Ogimachi and the shogun. He then reduced the shogun's power and continued his "pacification": he invaded Echizen province, which was held by Asakura Yoshikage, in 1570, and battled Asai Nagamasa, whom he defeated only in 1573, although both Asakura and Asai were allied with the "abbot" *(hossu)* of the Hongan-ji in Osaka, Kennyo Kōsa. In 1574, he defeated the Ikkō-ikki leagues, immolating almost 20,000 monks and massacring those on Mt. Hiei, who were allied with Asai and Asakura. In 1572, shogun Ashikaga Yoshiaki had plotted with Takeda Shingen, the powerful daimyo of Kai, Shinano, Suruga, and Hida provinces, and he defeated Oda Nobunaga's and Tokugawa Ieyasu's troops at Mitagahara in Tōtomi on January 6, 1573, then seized the Noda castle in Mikawa. Ashikaga Yoshiaki then openly declared himself opposed to Oda Nobunaga, but Takeda Shingen had died, so Oda Nobunaga surrounded Kyoto and set fire to its suburbs, then drove Yoshiaki from the city, thus putting an end (de facto if not de jure) to the Muromachi shogunate. The Hongan-ji of Osaka rebelled again, assisted by Takeda Shingen's son, Takeda Katsuyori. But Katsuyori was defeated by Oda Nobunaga at the Battle of Nagashino and the *monto* (disciples of the Hongan-ji) were massacred.

Oda Nobunaga was now free to organize his conquests into a military dictatorship *(shokuhō)*: he confiscated the peasants' weapons *(katanagari)*, divided the population into military and peasant classes, and began to conduct a general land census *(kenchi)*. In 1576, he had a splendid castle built in Azuchi (Shiga prefecture), which he had decorated with paintings by Kanō Eitoku; it became his official residence in 1579.

Oda Nobunaga's "reign" did not, however, go uncontested: in 1576, a second coalition of daimyo formed to oppose his hegemony, led by exiled shogun Ashikaga Yoshiaki and the monks of the Hongan-ji. Mōri Terumoto, daimyo of Aki, and Uesugi Kenshin, of Echigo, also united against him. But their efforts were unsuccessful against the ripostes of his generals Akechi Mitsuhide, Hosokawa Yūsai, Tsutsui Junkei, and Oda Nobutada. Uesugi Kenshin died in 1578, and Oda Nobunaga took over some of his territories in order to oppose Mōri Terumasa more effectively. He finally defeated Takeda Katsuyori in 1582, and the imperial court proposed that he become shogun, elevating him to the third rank of nobility.

However, the war continued, both in Shikoku and in the provinces held by the Mōri. On June 21, 1582, Oda's general, Akechi Mitsuhide, suddenly turned against him and attacked him while he was resting in the Honnō-ji temple in Kyoto. Wounded, Oda Nobunaga took refuge with his oldest son, Oda Nobutaka, in the back of the flaming temple, and committed suicide by *seppuku*. The emperor gave him the posthumous name Sōgen-in. His general and ally, Toyotomi Hideyoshi, pursued and killed Akechi Mitsuhide, then succeeded Oda Nobunaga as leader of his troops and continued his efforts at pacification.

Odano Naotake. Painter (1749–80) and samurai in Akita. He first studied the style of the Kanō school, then learned about Western painting from Hiraga Gennai. He illustrated some works by Sugita Gempaku, notably the *Kaitai shinsho*. He painted a wide variety of subjects with a naturalist technique imitating Western style, and was one of the most influential painters of the "Akita school."

Oda Sakunosuke. Writer (1913–47), born near Osaka to a family of fish merchants. In spite of his modest means, he managed to go to teachers' college. In 1937, he went to Kyoto and began to write stories and novels. *Meoto zensai* (A Couple's Good Luck, 1940) was very successful. He then published a series of novels, *Nijūsai* (Twenty Years, 1941), *Seishun no gyakusetsu* (The Paradox of Youth, 1941), and *Wagamachi* (My City, 1942), in which he depicted the life of ordinary people in Osaka. After the Second World War, he wrote other novels, including *Sesō* (The Climate, 1946) and *Keiba* (The Horse Race, 1946). He died of tuberculosis. Most

of his works were made into movies by directors such as Toyoda Shirō and Gosho Heinosuke.

Oda Takeo. Writer (1901–79), author of many successful novels, including *Jōgai* (Outside of the Castle, 1936) and *Iku Tatsuo Den* (Life of Yū Dafu, 1975).

Odawara. City in Kanagawa prefecture, on Sagami Bay, which developed around a fortress built in the twelfth century and a castle belonging to the Ōkubo family during the Edo period. It was an important waystation *(shuku-eki)* on the Tōkaidō road. A huge castle built there by the Hōjō family (see GO-HŌJŌ) was razed to its foundations by Toyotomi Hideyoshi in 1590, during the "Odawara campaign" (Odawara-seibatsu), because Hōjō Ujimasa and his son Hōjō Ijinao refused to surrender. The fortress, believed to be impenetrable, fell after 100 days, ending the campaign of "pacification of the territory" started by Oda Nobunaga. Toyotomi Hideyoshi gave the Hōjō estate to his most powerful vassal, Tokugawa Ieyasu, who then became the uncontested master of Kanto. *Pop.*: 180,000.

• **Odawara Hōjō.** *See* GO-HŌJŌ, HŌJŌ.

Odori. General term for folk dances of ancient origins. Dances of this type executed by geisha and *maiko* are recent, however—created only in the late nineteenth century. The best known are the Miyako Odori, Kamogawa Odori (in Kyoto), Azuma Odori and Sanwa-mai (in the Tokyo region), Nagoya Odori, and Osaka Odori. Also called *mai*. Some *odori* are of religious origin, such as the Nembutsu Odori (*see* NEMBUTSU).

Odoshi. Technique of lacing the plates of samurai armor *(yoroi)* with cords of silk, cotton, or leather.

Ōei. Era of Emperor Go-Komatsu: July 1394–Apr. 1428. *See* NENGŌ.

• **Ōei no Gaikō.** Korean attack on the island of Tsushima in 1419 against pirates *(wakō)* who had settled there in order to reach the coasts of the Korean Peninsula more easily. More than 200 ships and 17,000 soldiers took part in this operation.

• **Ōei no Ran.** Revolt led by Ōuchi Yoshihiro (1356–1400), *shugo* of the western provinces, against the Muromachi shogunate. Allied with the Kantō-kanrei Ashikaga Mitsukane (1378–1409), he retrenched in Sakai but was killed after a two-month siege in 1399–1400. Also called Ōei Jiken.

Ōe Kenzaburo. Writer, born 1935 in Shikoku, Ehime prefecture. After studying French literature at university (thesis on Jean-Paul Sartre), he began to write and publish stories and novels in a very analytical style with a "commitment" to the Left, such as *Hiroshima nōto* (Notes from Hiroshima, 1965). He lived in Mexico, where he was a professor; after his son Hikari was born with mental disabilities, he devoted a large part of his writing to the subject of maladjusted childhood, as in *Sora no kabutsu agui* (Agui, the Monster of the Clouds, 1964) and *Kojinteki na taiken* (A Personal Affair, 1964). It was with *Man'en gan'en no futtobōru* (The Football Game of the First *Man'en* Year, 1967, Tanizaki Prize) that Ōe Kenzaburō reached the peak of his narrative talent. He received the Akutagawa Prize in 1958 for his novel *Shiiku* (Breeding). He then wrote many stories: *Warera no kyōki o iki nobiru michi o oshieyo* (Tell Us How to Survive Our Madness, 1969), *Kōzui wa waga tamashi ni oyobi* (Flood Reaching to My Soul, 1973), *Dōjidai gemu* (Contemporary Game, 1979), *Reintsuri o kiku onnatachi* (The Women Who Listen to the Rain-Tree, 1982), *Nan to mo shirenai mirai ni* (The Mad Iris and Other Stories from After the Atom Bomb, 1983), *Atarashi hito yo mezame yo* (Wake up, Young People of a New Age, 1983), *Kaba ni kamateru* (Bitten by a Hippopotamus, 1985), *Shizukana seikatsu* (A Peaceful Existence, 1990), and more. He received the 1989 Itō Sei Prize for *Jinsei no shinseki*. A number of his works were adapted for the screen by Ōshima Nagisa, Masumura Yasuzo, and Kurahara Koreyoshi, among others. He received the Nobel Prize for literature in 1994. In 1995, he declared that he no longer wanted to write novels and devoted himself to reflection on the meaning of life.

Ōendan. Custom, originating in the United States, of encouraging a sports or other team with cries such as "*Fure, Fure*" ("Hurrah, Hurrah!") or, more commonly, "*Banzai*," and waving sticks, pompoms, or flags.

Ōe no Asatsuna. Historian (886–957), Ōe no Otondo's grandson. Author of *Shin kokushi* (New History of Japan). Also known as Nochi no Kōsōkō.

• **Ōe no Chisato.** Poet (ninth century), Ōe no Otondo's son.

• **Ōe no Hiromoto.** Politician (1148–1225), head of the Kumonjō and the Mandokoro in Kamakura. Adviser to Minamoto no Yoritomo. He became a Buddhist monk in 1217.

• **Ōe no Koretoki.** Poet (888–963), author of an anthology of *rō-ei*, the *Senzai-kaku*.
• Poet (955–1010), Ōe no Koretoki's son.

• **Ōe no Masafusa.** Poet and politician (1041–1111), governor of Dazaifu. He was known for his knowledge of the Chinese classics. He wrote many works, among them *Gōke shidai* (Ceremonial Customs, 1111), and collections of strange tales in the Chinese style: *Gōdanshō* (Tales of Master Ōe, ca. 1107), *Kobi no ki* (Tales of Foxes, 1110), and others. One hundred twenty of his poems were included in various anthologies. His personal collection, *Gō no sōchi-shū*, comprises 518 *tanka* and various other poems.

• **Ōe no Masahira.** Poet (952–1012), Akazome Emon's husband.

• **Ōe no Otondo.** Politician and writer (811–877). Author of many works; he worked on the *Jōkan kyakushiki* in 871. Also called Kōsōkō.

Ōe Taku. Politician (1847–1921), born in Tosa province, who devoted himself to defending the rights of outcasts *(hinin)*. Appointed governor of Kanagawa prefecture, he was compromised in the Satsuma Rebellion in 1877 and sentenced to ten years in prison. He was freed in 1884 and continued his fight; in 1890, he was elected to the Diet as a member of the Jiyūtō (Liberal party). He was defeated in the elections of 1892, left politics, became a Buddhist monk, and once again took up his fight against discrimination against the *hinin (burakumin)*.

Ōeyama. Mountain in Kyoto prefecture, 833 m high, on which, legend has it, an ogre named Shuten-dōji lived; he was killed by Minamoto no Yorimitsu.

• *Ōeyama.* Title of a Noh play: the demon Shuten-dōji is killed by Raikō, who is able to find him thanks to a woman held captive on Mt. Ōeyama.

Ofuda. Religious images given or sold by Buddhist temples and Shinto shrines as charms or talismans. Most *ofuda* consist of bands of paper inscribed with the name of a temple or shrine and bearing its seal. Pilgrims like to collect *ofuda* in albums.

Ofudasaki. "On the Point of the Brush," a collection of 1,711 "revealed" texts, of Shinto character, written between 1859 and 1882 by Nakayama Miki. *See* TENRI-KYŌ.

Ōgaki. City in Gifu prefecture that was the general quarters of the armies of Ishida Mitsunari during the Battle of Sekigahara in 1600. Castle town of the Toda family and important waystation *(shuku-eki)* in the Edo period. Castle built in 1596 by the daimyo of Itō, with a unique four-story donjon. *Pop.:* 150,000.

Ōgama. Potters' kilns replacing the *anagama* type during the Muromachi period (sixteenth century) in the Seto and Mino regions. The *ōgama* kilns were built underground, with a vault supported by three or four central pillars. The entrance was on the side. An almost identical type, *jagama,* with a long combustion chamber, was used mainly in Tamba. *See* ANAGAMA, NOBORIGAMA.

Ogasawara. Family of warriors and daimyo related to the Minamoto family (Seiwa Genji branch), active from the Kamakura to the Edo period. Its members did battle with Toyotomi Hideyoshi and Tokugawa Ieyasu. They were divided into the Fukashi Ogasawara and Matsuo Ogasawara branches, which managed large estates in the Edo period in Harima and Buzen provinces (Kyushu). Ogasawara Sadamune (1294–1350) codified warrior etiquette, notably for certain martial sports such as *yabusame, inu-oi-mono,* and *kasagake,* in Ogasawara-ryū, which is still observed in some martial-arts circles.

• **Ogasawara Guntō.** Group of volcanic islands that owe their name to the fact that they were explored by Ogasawara Sadayori (d. 1625) in 1593, though they were discovered by Villalobos in 1543. This archipelago, about 900 km south of Tokyo, comprises three island groups called Bailey, Beechy, and Parry by the Americans, and four main islands: Chichijima, Hanajima, Mukojima, and Yomejima. Settled by Hawai'ians in 1830, they were annexed by Japan in 1876. American and English whaling ships established shipyards there in 1820 and 1830. Once sparsely populated, the islands were called *bunin* ("without men"), whence "Bonin," the name frequently used for them. Strategically placed, they were the theater of terrible battles during the Sec-

ond World War, notably on the small island of Iōjima in February 1945, and were under American control from 1945 to 1968. Near the islands is a deep underwater trench (10,374 m). *Total area:* about 106 km². *Population* (farmers): about 700. Also called Kazan Rettō, Ogasawara Shotō.

• **Ogasawara Ichian.** First governor of Nagasaki and controller of the island of Dejima in 1603.

• **Ogasawara Nagahide.** Samurai (fifteenth century) who, following Ogasawara Sadamune's (1294–1350) codification, wrote the Ogasawara-ryū etiquette for the Path of the Arrow and the Horse (Kyūba no Michi), in collaboration with Ise Mitsusada and Imagawa Ujiyori.

• **Ogasawara Nagatoki.** Samurai (1514–83), master-at-arms for shogun Ashikaga Yoshiteru.

• **Ogasawara-ryū.** *See* OGASAWARA, OGASAWARA NAGAHIDE.

Ogata Gekkō. Painter (1859–1920) of ukiyo-e prints and ceramics. Inspired by Hokusai, he drew a series of 100 views of Mt. Fuji in a very decorative style belonging more to Nihonga than to traditional ukiyo-e. His work was exhibited in various Bunten, and in Chicago (1893), Paris (1900), and London (1910). He signed his work simply Gekkō.

Ogata Kōan. Physician (1810–63), born in Bitchū province (Okayama prefecture), who studied "Dutch science" *(rangaku)* in Nagasaki and medicine in Osaka. In 1838, he opened a medical school *(tekijuku)* in Osaka that later became the University of Osaka. A student of the Dutch physician Niemann, he had many followers, among them Fukuzawa Yukichi. In Osaka, he popularized smallpox vaccination, which had been introduced to Nagasaki by the Dutch in the 1840s. He was appointed head of the shogunal institute of Western medicine (Igagakujo) in 1862, and was the shogun's personal physician.

• **Ogata Koreyoshi.** Physician (1843–1909), born in Osaka, Ogata Kōan's son. He went to Holland and studied in Utrecht. Starting in 1868, he was the physician of the imperial house and president of the army's school of medicine. He established two hospitals in Osaka, the Ogata and the Osaka Jike.

Ogata Shūhei. Ceramist (1788–1830), famous for his figurines and teapots.

Ogata Taketora. Politician (1888–1956), born in Yamagata prefecture, related to Ogata Kōan and Ogata Koreyoshi. He was a correspondent in London and Washington for the *Tōkyō Asahi Shimbun* from 1920 to 1922, then editor-in-chief of the *Asahi Shimbun* in 1934. Minister of information in Koiso Kuniaki's cabinet during the Second World War, he tried to negotiate a separate peace with Jiang Jieshi (Chang Kai-shek), then was a minister in Prince Higashikuni Naruhiko's cabinet in 1945. He was elected to the House of Representatives in 1952, and was vice–prime minister under Yoshida Shigeru from 1952 to 1954. Elected president of the Liberal party (Jiyūtō) in 1954, he joined the LDP (Jiyū Minshutō) in 1955. He wrote biographies of his friends Nakano Seigō and Yonai Mitsumasa.

Ogata Tomosaburō. Physician and researcher (1883–1973), Ogata Koreyoshi's son, famous for his research on bone growth, vitamin B1, and salivary glands. He received the Imperial Academy Prize (Teikoku Gakushi-in shō) in 1944 for his work. Decorated with the Order of Culture (Bunka-shō) in 1957.

Ogawa Akimichi. Writer (1737–1814), author of a book of famous essays, *Chirizuka-dan* (Words Without Value), describing life in Edo in his times. He was probably a physician.

Ogawa Heikichi. Politician (1870–1942), born in Nagano prefecture. He helped Konoe Atsumaro found the Tōa Dōbunkai (East Asia Common Culture Society), then joined the Rikken Seiyūkai (Friends of Constitutional Government party) in 1903, and was elected to the Diet ten times. Minister of justice in Katō Takaaki's first cabinet (1924–25), and of railroads in Tanaka Giichi's cabinet (1927–29). Implicated in a financial scandal, he was sentenced to two years in prison in 1936.

Ogawa Kunio. Writer (b. 1927). After studying at the University of Tokyo and in France, he published his first novel in 1937—*Aporon no shima* (The Island of Apollo), on the islands of the Mediterranean—but became widely known only after the Second World War, with *Kokoromi no kishi* (1970) and *Kare no kokyō* (1971), works written in an autobiographical style.

Ogawa Machiko. Contemporary ceramist, born 1946 in Sapporo (Hokkaido), known mainly for her works for the tea ceremony *(chanoyu).*

Ogawa Mimei. Writer (Ogawa Kensaku, 1882–1961), born in Niigata prefecture. His novels for adults were influenced by socialism and tended to promote anti-militarism. Starting in the late 1920s, however, he devoted himself to writing children's stories, and he was considered one of the greatest authors for young people: *Akai fune* (The Red Boats, 1910), *Rondon no neko* (The Cat of London, 1912), *Akai rōsoku to ningyo* (The Red Candle and the Siren, 1921), *Tsukiyo to megane* (Moonlight and Glasses, 1922), and others. He was elected a member of the Nihon Geijutsu-in (Japan Art Academy) in 1953.

Ogawa Takuji. Geologist and geographer (1870–1941), born in Wakayama prefecture. He conducted important geological research in Korea and China and taught at the University of Kyoto. Yukawa Hideki's and Kaizuka Shigeki's father.

Ogawa Usen. Painter (Ogawa Mokichi, 1868–1938), born in Tokyo to a family of poor samurai. He studied Bunjinga (Nanga) painting, then worked in the Nihonga style. He is best known for his many caricatures and drawings done for newspapers. He was elected a member of the Nihon Bijutsu-in (Japan Fine Arts Academy) in 1917. Also called Usen.

Ōgeshin. In Japanese Esoteric Buddhism, "transformation of the body" performed by a buddha or a bodhisattva in order to appear to the faithful. Also called *keshin*. *See* SANJŪSAN ŌGESHIN.

Ōgi. Folding fan. Several types exist in Japan: *hi-ōgi*, made with slats of wood (*hinoki* cypress) joined with silk strings and sometimes painted; *shojōsen* (or *sensu*), the current type of fan, divided into two types: with flat ribs (*kawa-hori*) and with very fine ribs (*suehiro, chūkei, chū-ukei, bombori*). A variety of these, called *kame-ōgi*, used by women, have 39 ribs. These fans, probably a Japanese invention, began to be used in the seventh century, concurrently with flat fans (*uchiwa*) imported from China via Korea. Paper and silk *ōgi* have bamboo, or sometimes ivory, ribs. Some large fans, such as *umaji-rushi*, were used by the Tokugawa as curtains, and were placed on top of large poles. In the tea ceremony (*chanoyu*), a decorated fan called *rikyū-ōgi* is used. *Mai-gōgi* are used in folk dances, while brightly decorated *chūkei* are used by Noh actors. Folding fans were imported from Japan to Portugal and Spain starting in the sixteenth century. *See* BOMBORI, FANS, GUMPAI-UCHIWA, GUNSEN, UCHIWA.

• **Ōgi-awase.** In the courts of ancient Japan, contests of poetry handwritten on fans.

• **Ōgi-daruki.** In traditional architecture, fan-shaped chevrons at the corners of roofs, mainly in the *kara-yō* and *tenjiku-yō* styles.

• **Ōgi-nagashi.** Aristocratic game played by nobles in the Heian period, in which they threw *ōgi* into the water of a river and composed poems about the sensations they felt upon throwing them.

• **Ōgi-otoshi.** Ancient aristocratic game consisting of throwing an open fan at a set target, such as a small object. Played mainly by women. Also called *tōsenkyō*.

Ogidō kaizuka. Prehistoric shell mound *(kaizuka)* site from the Jōmon period, located in the village of Nagakusuku, Okinawa (Ryukyu Islands), excavated in 1919. It contains many stone and bone tools and flat-bottomed pottery of the type found in the *kaizuka* in Iha.

Ōgimachi Tennō. Hundred and sixth emperor (Prince Katahito, 1517<1558–86>1593), son of and successor to Go-Nara Tennō. He abdicated in favor of his grandson, Go-Yōzei.

Ogin. Daughter of master of the tea ceremony Sen no Rikyū; she was said to have committed suicide with her father on the order of Toyotomi Hideyoshi. A movie about her life *(Ogin-sama)* was made in 1976 by director Kumai Kei, with the role of the heroine played by Nakano Ryōko.

Ogino Ginko. Physician (1851–1913), born in Saitama prefecture, the first Japanese woman authorized (in 1885) to practice Western medicine. She practiced in Tokyo, then on Hokkaido.

Ogino Kyūsaku. Gynecologist (1882–1975), born in Aichi prefecture. From his research on menstrual cycles, he invented a method of contraception in 1924; associated with the method devised by Austrian gynecologist Herman Knaus (1934), it was called the Ogino-Knaus method.

Ogino Samanojō. Famous Kabuki actor (Ogino Sawanojō, 1656–1704) in Osaka and Edo. He specialized in female *(onnagata)* roles.

Ogisu Takanori. Painter (1901–86) in the Western style, born in Aichi prefecture; Fujishima Takeji's student. In 1926, he went to Paris and had works in several Paris salons as well as a number of European galleries. The Paris Museum of Modern Art bought two of his canvases in 1936 and 1937. When he returned to Japan in 1940, he was sent to Indochina. After the Second World War, he returned to France (1948) and received the Legion of Honor. A retrospective of his works was organized at Bagatelle (Paris) in 1978.

Ogiwara Morie. Sculptor (*gō*: Rokuzan, 1879–1910), born in Nagano prefecture. He first studied oil painting; in 1901, he went to New York and Europe to study. In Paris, he was a student at Académie Julian; he became friends with Auguste Rodin and Antoine Bourdelle and began to devote himself to sculpture. When he returned to Japan in 1908, his works were exhibited in the various Bunten. A museum containing his most famous works, the Rokuzan-kan, was opened in Matsumoto (Nagano prefecture).

Ogiwara Seisensui. Modern haiku poet (Ogiwara Tōkichi, 1884–1976), born in Tokyo. In 1911, he founded the poetry magazine *Sōun*. His most important collections are *Waki-izuru mono* (1920) and *Chōryū* (1964). He was elected a member of the Japan Art Academy (Nihon Geijutsu-in) in 1965.

Ogiwara Shigehide. Politician (1658–1713), son of a private physician serving shogun Tokugawa Tsunayoshi. He was minister of finance from 1696 to 1712; in this position, attempting to stabilize the currency, he proceeded with a series of devaluations. He opposed Arai Hakuseki and was forced to resign in 1712.

Ōgo. Buddhist monk (Mokujiki Shōnin, 1537–1608) and *renga* poet, serving the Sasaki family in Ōmi. He was responsible for organizing Toyotomi Hideyoshi's funeral. He wrote a three-chapter treatise on versification of *renga*, the *Mugonshō* (1603).

Ōgosho. "Retired shogun," the title taken by Tokugawa Ieyasu in 1605, when he transferred his responsibilities to his son Tokugawa Hidetada and retired to Sumpu. This title was also taken by Tokugawa Ienari in 1837. It was sometimes used by the Ashikaga shoguns when they retired.

• **Ōgosho-jidai.** Period of Tokugawa Ienari's retirement, from 1837 to 1841. Also, a name given to the Bunka-Bunsei era (1804–30).

Oguma Hideo. Poet (1901–40) from Hokkaido. His violently anti-militarist works were directed mainly against the war with China. His most important work was a long epic poem, *Tobu sori*, published in 1935.

Ogura Kinnosuke. Mathematician (1885–1962), born in Yamagata prefecture, who took part in the major mathematics reform movement in the late nineteenth and early twentieth century. He wrote a number of scientific treatises that had an important impact on Japanese mathematics. *See* WASAN.

Ogura Masatsune. Businessman (1875–1961) born in Ishikawa prefecture. He joined the Sumitomo Company in 1899 and devoted himself to developing the firm, transforming it into a zaibatsu of which he became president in 1930. Appointed minister of finance in 1941.

Ogura no Ōji. Imperial prince (?–1443), Go-Kameyama Tennō's grandson. Shogun Ashikaga Yoshinori ousted him from the throne in 1428 and forced him to become a Buddhist monk.

Ogura Shimpei. Philologist (1882–1944), born in Sendai, an expert on Korean language and culture and the author of major scientific works on these subjects. He received the Imperial Academy Prize (Teikoku Gakushi-in shō) in 1935.

Ogurayama. Hill northwest of Kyoto, on the north bank of the Hozu-gawa river, where a number of important temples are located, including the Tenryū-ji, the Nison-in, and the Giō-ji. This hill, famous for its cherry blossoms in springtime and the red foliage of its maples in autumn, has often been cited in poems.

Ogura Yuki. Painter (Mizogami Yuki), born 1895 in Ōtsu. A professor of Japanese and Chinese literature, she began to paint in 1920 under Yasuda Yukihiko (1884–1978), and her works were exhibited regularly in the Bunten. She was elected a member of Japan Art Academy (Nihon Geijutsu-in) in 1926 and received the Order of Culture (Bunka-shō) in 1980.

Oguri Fūyō. Writer (Oguri Isoo, 1875–1926), born in Aichi prefecture. He was a member of the Ken'yūsha group and the disciple of Ozaki Kōyō, whose *Konjiki yasha* he finished when Ozaki died, in 1903. His own works are mainly realistic family dramas in the style of Émile Zola; *Seishun* (Youth, 1906) is his best-known work.

Oguri Hangan. Legendary character (perhaps Oguri Sōtan, ca. 1398–1468?) who became popular due to his incredible adventures with his wife, Teruta Hime. *See* OGURI SŌTAN.

Oguri Mushitarō. Writer (Oguri Eijirō, 1901–46), born in Tokyo. He wrote many detective and horror novels, as well as legends: *Kanzen hanzai* (1933), *Yūbijin* (1944), and others.

Oguri Sōtan. Painter and Zen monk (Oguri Sukeshige; *gō*: Sotan, Jiboku, 1413–81), famous in his time for his *suiboku* paintings and polychrome paintings of flowers and birds in the Chinese Muqi (*Jap.*: Mokkei) style. He was Shūbun's disciple and worked mainly for the Muromachi shogunate starting in 1463. None of his own works have survived, but a number of panels of calligraphy in his style were produced in 1490 by his son, Oguri Sōkei, for the Yōtoku-in, a temple attached to the Daitoku-ji in Kyoto. Perhaps the same person as Oguri Hangan.

Oguri Tadamasa. Senior bureaucrat (1827–68) in the Tokugawa shogunate, born in Edo. Sent to the United States with a delegation in 1860, he later held various important positions in the shogunal administration and was a *kanjō-bugyō* from 1865 to 1868. He founded the Yokosuka shipyards. However, he took the shogunate's side against the emperor and was fired from his position in 1868; he and his son were then arrested and executed. Also known as Oguri Kōzuke no Suke, as his ancestral estate was in Kōzuke province.

Ogyū Sorai. Confucian scholar (1666–1728), born in Edo to a family of physicians and samurai. His father was exiled to Kazusa in 1679, so he did not pursue regular studies until 1690, when his father was made personal physician to shogun Tokugawa Tsunayoshi and returned to Edo. Ogyū Sorai then abandoned medicine to devote himself to Confucian studies; in 1696 he entered the service of adviser Yanagisawa Yoshiyasu, a position he held until Yanagisawa died in 1709. In 1721, he became the personal adviser to shogun Tokugawa Yoshimune.

Ogyū Sorai composed more than 600 poems and wrote many letters that have been preserved. He was opposed to the doctrines of the Zhu Xi (*Jap.*: Shushi) school then in favor in Japan, and his scholarship took the philological viewpoint of classical and modern Chinese. His thought was very influential for the development of modern rationalism in Japan. He wrote many books on his ideas, including

Seidan and *Bendō,* as well as "instructions" for his disciples, among them Dazai Shuntai. Ogyū Sorai was also a famous archer. Also sometimes called Butsu Sorai.

Ohajiki. Children's game similar to marbles, played with stones, shells, coins, or pieces of glass or plastic shaped like coins. This game, introduced from China in the eighth century, was at the time called *tagi* and *ishihajiki* (thrown stones).

Ohara gokō. Title of a Noh play: Empress Kenrei, Antoku Tennō's mother, lives in the hut she has retired to. When a visitor arrives, she tells him about her past.

Ō-harai. "Great purification," a solemn Shinto ceremony that generally takes place in shrines on the last day of the sixth and twelfth months. *See* HARAI, MISOGI, SETSUBUN.

Oharame. Women from the villages around Kyoto who peddle their wares in the streets of Kyoto and who are responsible for maintaining the gardens of the imperial palace. They are known by their special costume: black gloves, and white apron and leggings.

Ohara Yūgaku. Agricultural technician (1797–1858), born in Nagoya, who devoted himself to improving farming conditions for the peasantry. In 1850, he opened the Kai-shinrō, a school for the education of peasants, in Shimōsa province. He was arrested for contravening the shogunal regulations but was released soon after. He committed suicide.

Oharuda. Former name of Owari province.

Ohashi Junzō. Samurai (Totsuan, 1816–62) and expert on Chinese literature. He was firmly opposed to the opening of Japan to foreigners; accused of plotting against the shogunate, he was condemned to death and executed.

Ohi Chōzaemon. Contemporary ceramist (Ohi Toshiro, b. 1927 in Kanazawa, Ishikawa prefecture), tenth-generation artist in a family of potters. A professor at Kanazawa University, he won many awards in Japan and took part in a group exhibition in Paris in 1994, with other well-known artists.

Ohira Masayoshi. Politician (1910–80), born in Kagawa prefecture. After working in the Ministry of Finance, he became Ikeda Hayato's secretary, then was elected to the House of Representatives in 1952 for the Jiyūtō (Liberal party). Minister of foreign affairs (1960–64) in the cabinets of Tanaka Kakuei and Miki Takeo, then minister of international trade and industry; president of the Jiyū Minshutō (Liberal Democratic party, 1964–72); once again minister of foreign affairs (1972–74); and secretary-general of the LDP (1977–78). He was elected prime minister on December 7, 1978, and reelected in 1979. When he died, Suzuki Zenkō succeeded him as prime minister. Nicknamed Otochan ("papa") by his followers.

Ōhiroma. Large hall in the part of the castle of Edo outside the wall *(hommaru),* where the most important *tozama-daimyo* gathered for their annual interview with the shogun. This room was also used to receive foreign visitors and senior bureaucrats. Its floor was completely covered with tatami and had a raised platform on which the shogun sat.

Ōhō. Era of Emperor Nijō: Sept. 1161–Mar. 1163. *See* NENGŌ.

Oi. Large wooden box, often lacquered, with doors and drawers, used by traveling Buddhist monks to hold sacred writings and personal effects. Also called *katabako.*
→ *See* JUNNIN TENNŌ.

Oibane. Game resembling badminton, played with decorated wooden rackets *(hagoita),* mainly by young women on New Year's Day. *See* HAGOITA.

Oie-mono. Type of Kabuki play *(jidai-mono* genre) whose plots generally deal with domestic scandals among the daimyo.

O-ie-ryū. Style of Chinese calligraphy created in Japan by imperial prince Son'en Hōshinnō (Seiren-in no Miya, 1298–1356), Emperor Fushimi's son. Also called Son'en-ryū.

Ōi Kentarō. Politician (1843–1922), born in Ōita (Kyushu). He joined the Jiyūtō (Liberal party) in 1882, but was arrested in 1885 for having taken part in a peasant revolt (Chichibu Jiken) and for plotting to establish reforms in the Korean government (Ōsaka Jiken). Freed in 1889, he campaigned for universal suffrage; in 1892, he formed his own party, the Tōyō Jiyūtō (Asian Liberal party), which was dissolved two months later. He then retired from politics.

Ōi-mōchi-gimi. Title for *sadaijin* and *udaijin* ministers before 645.

• **Ōi-mono-mōsu Tsukasa.** Title for ministers *(dainagon)* before 645.

Ōishi Yoshio. Samurai (Ōishi Kuranosuke, 1659–1703) of the Ako estate (Hyōgo prefecture), leader of the 47 *rōnin* who avenged the death of their master, Asano Nagaomori (*see* AKŌ-GISHI). He had studied martial arts with Yamaga Sokō and Confucianism under Itō Jinsai. He was also a talented amateur painter. In literature, he is sometimes given the name Ōboshi Yarunosuke.

Ōita. Chief city of Ōita prefecture (Kyushu), on Beppu Bay. In the sixteenth century, its daimyo, Ōtomo Sōrin, opened trade with the Portuguese. Castle built in 1597 by the Fukuhara family and occupied the same year by Matsudaira Ōgi. Only a few *yagura* and *ishiotoshi* remain. Many petrochemical and metallurgical plants; orange groves. *Pop.*: 360,000.

• **Ōita-ken.** Ōita prefecture, located in northern Kyushu and bordering the Inland Sea (Setonaikai). It is very mountainous (Kyushu mountains). Archeological research has shown that it was occupied as early as the Jōmon period. The prefecture was created in 1876 by the amalgamation of Toyo, Buzen, and Bungo provinces. *Main cities:* Nakatsu, Usa, Bungo Takada, Beppu, Usuki, Taketa, Saiki, Hita. *Area:* 6,331 km². *Pop.*: 1,250,000.

O-iwa. In popular legend, the ghost of a young woman murdered by her husband. Her story was told in *Yotsuya-kaidan*, a famous Kabuki play.

Ojigi. Form of salutation consisting of bowing to a person one greets or honors; it is performed standing or sitting. There are many rules for making this salutation, which is more or less pronounced depending on the status of the person saluting and the person being saluted. There are different rules for *ojigi* during the tea ceremony.

Ojime. Oval-shaped button pierced with a longitudinal hole, used to tighten the cord holding a netsuke to an *inrō* or other object worn on the belt *(obi)*. Some, made of wood, ivory, or ceramic, are, like netsuke, ornately decorated, and are sought after by collectors. *See* INRŌ, NETSUKE.

Ōjin Tennō. Fifteenth emperor (Prince Hondawake, Homatawaki no Mikoto, Otomo-wake, traditionally 210<270–310>? but probably late fourth to early fifth century). Chūai Tennō and Empress Jingū's fourth son. According to some historians, he was one of the "five kings of Wa" (mid-fifth century). He was venerated under the name Hachiman, first in Usa (Kyushu), then in other Shinto shrines, as a *kami* of war (Yawata, "Eight Banners"). His mother Jingū Kōgo was regent of the kingdom during his reign until her death. It was under Ōjin Tennō's reign that Korean immigrants such as Wani and Yuzuki no Kimi arrived in Japan. He created guilds *(be)* and sent Takenouchi no Sukune to conquer Kyushu. A huge *kofun* (415 × 240 m) located in Habikino, near Osaka, surrounded by two ditches and a talus, is considered to be his tomb. It is on a raised terrace and faces north. A large number of *haniwa* were found on the site, but the tomb itself has not been excavated. Nintoku succeeded him.

Ōjōjūin. "The Ten Conditions of Rebirth in Amida's Paradise." A Buddhist text on devotion to Amida, attributed to Eikan (1053–1132).

• *Ōjōyōshū.* "Treatise on Rebirth in the Western Paradise." A 10-chapter Buddhist text compiled in 985 by Genshin, a monk of the Tendai-shū. It is based on Chinese and Sanskrit texts such as the *Amitāyurdhyāna-sūtra*. This text became the basis for the teachings of the Jōdo-shū sect.

Ōju. Painter (Kinoshita Naoichi; *azana:* Kunrai; *gō:* Suiseki, 1777–1815); he studied with his father, Ōkyo, and was Ōshin's father.

Ōka. Flying bomb (Yokosuke MXY-7) used in late 1945 by kamikaze pilots against ships in the American fleet. It was carried under the fuselage of a G.4 M.2 "Betty" bomber and was propelled by three or five rockets. It weighed about 800 kg. *Number built:* 755. *Maximum speed:* 650–920 km/h; *range:* 32 km; *payload:* 1,200 kg trinitro-aminol; *total loaded weight:* approx. 2,400 kg; *crew:* one pilot; *wing span:* 4.92 m. Model 43 K1, the Kai, also made in 1945, had two seats and was used to train pilots of the Ōka. Only two were built, called Wakazakura (Young Cherry Blossoms). Also called Baka (Crazy).

Oka Asajirō. Biologist (1868–1944), born in Shizuoka prefecture, who became known for applying

Darwin's evolutionary theories to human societies with the goal of finding the perfect type of society.

Okabe Kinjirō. Engineer (1896–1984), born in Nagoya; author of theoretical works on microwaves and radar. He received the Order of Culture (Bunka-shō) in 1944.

O Kachi no Kata. One of Tokugawa Ieyasu's concubines (O Kachi no Tsubone, 1578–1642). She bore him two children; when he died, she became a Buddhist nun with the name Eishō-in. *See* EISHŌ-JI.

Okada Beisanjin. Painter (Okada Koku; *azana:* Shigen; *gō:* Beisanjin, Beiō, 1744–1820) and rice merchant in Osaka, born in Yokohama. He was an officer for a daimyo in Tsu. His paintings, highly regarded, belong to the Bunjinga (Nanga) school of Osaka and feature large landscapes, executed with broad brushstrokes, and portraits, often caricatured. His son, Okada Hankō (1782–1846), inherited the collection of his works.

• **Okada Hankō.** Painter (Okada Shuku; *azana:* Shiu; *gō:* Hankō, 1782–1846), Okada Beisanjin's son, born in Osaka. Like his father, he worked for the large Tōdō family of rice merchants. He also painted in the Bunjinga (Nanga) style but had a wide range of talents.

Okada Keisuke. Admiral and politician (1868–1952), born in Fukui prefecture. He was promoted to admiral in 1924 after serving in the Sino-Japanese (1894–95) and Russo-Japanese (1904–05) wars. He was minister of the navy in 1927 in Tanaka Giichi's cabinet and in Saitō Makoto's cabinet (1932–34), and became prime minister in July 1934. He resigned, with his entire cabinet, after the events of February 26, 1936 (*see* NINIROKU-JIKEN); his minister of foreign affairs, Hirota Kōki, succeeded him.

Okada Kenzō. Painter in the Western style, born 1905 in Yokohama. He studied in Paris starting in 1924, along with Fujita Tsuguharu, then exhibited at the Nika-kai when he returned to Japan in 1927. He moved to the United States in 1950 and won awards for various exhibitions he had there. In 1957, he was named one of the eight most important artists in the United States; he later had exhibitions in São Paulo, Venice, and Japan. In 1960, he won the Ford Foundation Prize; in 1967, the *Mainichi* Prize.

Okada Mokichi. Founder (1882–1955) of a new religion, Sekai Kyūsei-kyō; he claimed to be the Messiah who had come to deliver the world from misery and to restore peace. *See* SEKAI KYŪSEI-KYŌ.

Okada Saburōsuke. Painter (1869–1939) in the Western style (Yōga), born in Saga prefecture; he studied with Kuroda Seiki, Soyama Yukihiko (1859–92), and Kume Keiichirō (1866–1934) in Tokyo and was one of the founders of the Hakubakai group. He went to France in 1897 and studied with Raphael Collin until 1902. He was elected a member of the Imperial Academy in 1919, became artist of the court in 1934, and received the Order of Culture (Bunka-shō) in 1938. He painted mainly landscapes and portraits of women in a very decorative style. Okada Yachiyo's husband.

Okada Samanosuke. Kabuki actor (active 1680–1700) in Osaka, specializing in *onnagata* roles.

Okada Tamechika. Painter (Kanō Tamechika, Ryū Rikyō; *mei:* Saburō, Shin'ichi, Shinzō; *gō:* Matsudono, Sugawara, 1823–64) of the Fukko Yamato-e school, Kanō Eitai's third son. He painted Buddhist subjects and made many copies of old paintings and *emakimono*. A fervent supporter of the emperor, he was assassinated by a *rōnin*. Also called Tamechika and Reizei Tamechika.

Okada Yachiyo. Writer (nineteenth–twentieth century), Osanai Kaoru's sister. She began to write novels, stories, and plays in 1902. Her collection of stories, *Enogu bako* (The Color Box), earned her some success in 1912. She married the painter Okada Saburōsuke.

Oka-dera. Buddhist temple (formerly called Ryūgai-ji) located in Asuka (Nara prefecture), belonging to the Buzan branch of the Shingon-shū, founded in 663 by Emperor Tenji. Its first superior was the monk Gien (d. 728). Kūkai made it into a center for Esoteric Buddhism; the temple houses a splendid statue of Nyoirin Kannon, sculpted, it is believed, by Kūkai himself. It is one of the Thirty-Three Temples of the Western Pilgrimage (Saigoku Sanjūsan-sho). It was rebuilt in the seventeenth century in the style of the Nara period.

Ōkagami. "The Great Mirror." A history of Japan that is part of the *Rekishi monogatari* (written in Japanese), dealing mainly with the period from 850 to 1025 and the major families, such as the Fujiwara. This work contains many biographical essays and anecdotes written in a style approaching spoken language. It is relatively objective, and its lively narrative style was widely imitated by historians in following centuries. The name of its author is not known, but he probably lived in the eleventh or twelfth century. The work comprises eight volumes, divided into three sections.

Okakura Kakuzō. Philosopher and art critic (Okakura Tenshin; *gō:* Tenshin, 1862–1913), born in Yokohama. After studying English and art at the University of Tokyo, where his professors included Ernest F. Fenollosa (with whom he founded the Kangakai), he traveled in Europe and the United States in 1886 to study art. When he returned, he founded the first art school (Tōkyō Bijutsu Gakkō), now the Fine Arts and Music Department of the University of Tokyo; he was dean of the University of Tokyo from 1890 to 1898, after which he directed the museum of the imperial house. He also founded the first art magazine in Japan, *Kokka*. After visiting India and China, he returned to Europe and the United States in 1904, and he wrote a number of very successful works in English: *The Ideals of the East* (1903), *The Awakening of Japan* (1904), *The Book of Tea* (1906).

Okame. Type of Kyōgen mask often used as a decoration, representing a plump, smiling peasant woman, a sign of prosperity. This mask is often associated with the character of Hyottoko, a peasant with protruding lips twisted to the side, who appears in the Kyōgen *Usobuki*. These masks are often used in folk dances. Also called Otafuku. *See* MASKS, NŌ-MEN.

Okamoto. Site in the town of Kasuga (Fukuoka prefecture, Kyushu) where tombs typical of the Yayoi period, dating from the early years AD, have been discovered.
→ *See* JŌEN, YODOYA TATSUGORŌ.

Okamoto Kanoko. Writer (Onuki Kano, 1889–1939) and poet, born in Tokyo. She wrote *tanka* and free verse. Her first collection of *tanka, Karoki netani,* published in 1912, established her reputation. After an unhappy marriage to the designer Okamoto Ippei (1886–1984), she became very interested in Buddhism of the Jōdo Shin-shū and began to write novels on Buddhism. Following a four-year stay in Europe, she published *Boshi jojō* (1927), then, a few years later, *Tsuru wa yamiki* (1936). She wrote in a steady stream thereafter,

publishing stories and novels that drew varied reactions from critics.

Okamoto Kansuke. Geographer (1839–1904) born in Awa province. As a shogunal bureaucrat, he explored all of Sakhalin, recommending in his reports that Japan annex the island. He also organized groups of settlers to colonize the Kuril Islands.

Okamoto Kidō. Playwright (Okamoto Keiji, 1872–1939), born in Tokyo. He wrote more than 100 modern plays for Kabuki theater; among the best known are *Shuzenji monogatari* (1911) and *Toribeyama shinjū* (1915).

Okamoto Tarō. Painter, sculptor, and decorator (1912–96), born in Tokyo. He went to Paris in 1929 to study sociology under Marcel Mauss. As a painter, he refused to affiliate himself with any school and developed his own avant-garde style. He painted the famous "sun tower" at the Osaka World Fair (70 m high, 1970) and decorated many public buildings in Japan. He wrote several works on aesthetics, including *Bino juryoku* (Aesthetics and the Sacred, 1975).

Okamoto Toyohiko. Painter (*mei:* Shiba, Shume; *azana:* Shigen; *gō:* Kōson, Rikyō, Chōshinsai, Tangaku-sanjin, 1773–1845), born in Bitchū province. In Kyoto, he studied with Ryōzan and Goshun. Although he belonged to the Shijō school, his landscapes were influenced by the techniques of the Bunjinga painters.

Okando. First chamberlain for a daimyo, in the Edo period. It was the highest position to which a simple samurai could accede. This person was responsible for servants, gardeners, grooms, and all staff in the daimyo's house.

Okanishi Ichū. Poet (1639–1711), born in Inaba province, and theoretician of haiku of the Danrin school. He also wrote *renga* and Chinese classical verses.

Okano Keijirō. Politician (1865–1925), born in Kōzuke province, minister of justice in Katō Tomosaburo's cabinet in 1922, then minister of education, agriculture, and commerce under Yamamoto Gonnohyōe. He helped write commercial codes and wrote works on commercial jurisprudence.

Okano Sekiho. *See* SEKIHO.

Okashi. "Charmed," a term denoting, especially in the Heian period, a sense of ecstasy or amazement upon seeing a performance that is worthy of admiration or simply pleasant because of its beauty, according to the criteria of the time. Starting in the Kamakura period, it meant, more specifically, a sense of admiring amusement, the meaning it has kept to the present.

Oka Shigeki. Journalist (1878–1959), born in Kōchi prefecture. Fired from the newspaper at which he worked because of his socialist views, he went to the United States, where, following Kōtoku Shūsui's directives, he organized a group of socialist activists. During the Second World War, he enlisted in the British army in India. After the end of hostilities, he founded companies that printed Japanese works in San Francisco, Los Angeles, and other American cities.

Oka Shikanosuke. Painter (1899–1978) in modern Western style. He studied in France and was profoundly influenced by Seurat and Rousseau.

Okatomo. Sculptor of netsuke (Yamaguchi Okatomo, mid-eighteenth century) in Kyoto. His brother, Okatori, was also known for his netsuke.

Ōkawa Shūmei. Philosopher (1886–1957), born in Yamagata prefecture. He was interested in various world religions but was convinced that Japan needed to return to tradition. While working as a government bureaucrat (notably for the Manchurian railroad), he joined extreme-right-wing parties and founded other extremist organizations. He wrote a treatise in favor of the reforming of Japan, *Nihon oyobi nihonjin no michi* (Japan and the Path of the Japanese, 1926), which was very popular in nationalist circles. Arrested in 1932 for conspiracy, he was sentenced to five years in prison, but was granted amnesty in 1937 and again became active in Manchuria, publishing more works expounding his nationalist ideas. After the Second World War, he was arrested as a war criminal but was released, considered to be feeble-minded. He nevertheless continued to write, publishing an autobiography and a translation of the *Koran* titled *Anraku no mon* (The Gate to Tranquillity). *See* INOUE NISSHŌ.

Okayama. Chief city of Okayama prefecture, former castle-town *(jōka-machi)* and trade center. Garden (Kōrakuen) from the seventeenth century. Castle built by Ukida Naoie in 1573, with a six-story donjon *(tenshu),* called U-jō (Castle of Crows), re-built in 1966. Local fine-arts museum. A festival is held every February at the Saidai-ji temple (founded in 781), during which hundreds of young men dressed only in loincloths *(fundoshi)* race to grab two sacred sticks that are supposed to bring luck. *Pop.:* 550,000.

• **Okayama-ken.** Okayama prefecture, located on the Inland Sea (Setonaikai) between Hiroshima and Hyōgo prefectures. It is mountainous in the north (Chūgoku mountains) and has a large coastal plain irrigated by the Yoshii-gawa, Asahi-gawa, and Takahashi-gawa rivers. This prefecture was established in 1876 by an amalgamation of the former Bizen, Bitchū, and Mimasaka provinces. Fruit (grapes, peaches) and rice production. *Main cities:* Okayama, Kurashiki, Niimi, Tamano, Bizen, Tsuyama, Kasaoka. *Area:* 7,079 km². *Pop.:* 1.9 million.

Okazaki Katsuo. Politician (1897–1965), born in Tokyo. Vice-minister of foreign affairs in Yoshida Shigeru's and Ashida Hitoshi's cabinets (1947–48). Elected a member of the House of Representatives in 1949, then minister of foreign affairs in Yoshida Shigeru's fourth and fifth cabinets. Ambassador to the United States from 1961 to 1963.

Okazaki Kunisuke. Politician (1854–1936), born in Wakayama prefecture, Mutsu Minemitsu's cousin. He accompanied Mutsu to the United States in 1888. One of the leaders of the Jiyūtō (Liberal party) and the Rikken Seiyūkai (Friends of Constitutional Government), he was minister of agriculture and forests in Katō Takaaki's cabinet in 1925. He was elected to the House of Peers in 1928, then retired from politics.

Okehazama Tatakai. Battle won on June 12, 1560, by the young Oda Nobunaga over his rival, Imagawa Yoshimoto, near the town of Toyoake (Aichi prefecture); Imagawa was killed in the battle. Oda Nobunaga had only 3,000 soldiers, as opposed to his adversary's 25,000, but he took advantage of a storm to surround and annihilate the enemy. This victory opened the way for him to further conquests, and to dictatorship.

Ōke Shinnō. Imperial prince, older brother of Iitoyo-Ao no Kōjo and Oke Shinnō. He refused to take the throne, withdrawing in favor of his brother, Oke, who became Emperor Kensō in 485. However, he succeeded Oke with the ruling name Ninken.

Okhotsk. Open sea between Sakhalin and Hokkaido, connected to the Sea of Japan (Nihonkai) by the La Perouse Strait (Sōya Kaikyō). An arm of the Pacific Ocean, it has a great abundance of fish (mainly salmon). *Average depth:* 840 m. *Area:* approx. 1.6 million km². *Japanese:* Ohōkotsu-kai.

• Hunting and fishing culture that flourished from the eighth to the twelfth century on the coasts of Sakhalin, Hokkaido, and the Kuril Islands (Chishima), as the local extension of the Jōmon culture. However, it has more affinity with Siberian cultures than with Ainu culture (*see* SATSUMON), because it was characterized by pentagonal semi-buried huts with a central fireplace and niches for ceremonial objects (bones). Main site in Moyoro. Called Ohōtsuku Bunka.

Oki Guntō. Group of islands in the Sea of Japan (Nihonkai), close to the coast of Shimane prefecture, with two main islands, Dōzen and Dōgo, and about 180 small islands. Dōgo, the largest island, is also called Hahajima. The Dōzen group includes Nishinoshima, Nakanoshima, Chibaru, and a few other volcanic islands, among them Takeshima, which is still claimed by Korea. Most of the islands are mountainous and have a warm climate, thanks to the Tsushima current. They were once a site of exile; Emperor Go-Daigo was sent there by the Kamakura *bakufu*. Fishing, cattle and horse breeding. *Total area:* 348 km². *Pop.:* approx. 50,000. Also called Oki Shotō, Oki Rettō.

• **Oki** is also the name of a former province, now Shimane prefecture.

O-kiku. In folk legends, a ghost or spirit of wells (Ido no Bōkon).

Ōkimi. In the fifth and sixth centuries, the title for the emperor or king controlling a number of *kuni* (states of Yamato) and leader *(miyatsuko, kimi)* of all princes governing these states. The title "Tennō" was used for emperors starting only in the seventh century.

Okimono. Term for many art objects, generally small, made to be exhibited in the *tokonoma* or to be offered as gifts and placed on display shelves *(chigai-dana)* in *tokowaki*. Usually, they were sculpted in ivory by netsuke artists.

Ōkin. Painter (*azana:* Kōyu; *gō:* Tenryū-Dōjin, seventeenth–eighteenth century), known mainly for his paintings of grapes.

Okina. Noh mask *(nōmen)* representing an old man with white hair, typical of the Noh play of this name.

• *Okina.* Noh play performed during propitiatory events. It is composed of three dances, called Senzai, Okin, and Sambasō, in which the Okina mask is used.

Okinaka Shigeo. Physician (1902–92), born in Ishikawa prefecture. He wrote many studies on pathology of the brain and the sympathetic and parasympathetic nervous systems. Former director of the Toranomon Hospital in Tokyo, he received the Order of Culture (Bunka-shō) in 1970.

Okinawa. City on Okinawa (Ryukyu Islands), created in 1974 by the merger of the towns of Koza and Misato. It is the second largest city after Naha, the chief city of Okinawa prefecture. Former American military base. Botanical garden. *Pop.:* 95,000.

• **Okinawa-ken.** Okinawa prefecture (Ryukyu Islands), composed of about 50 islands extending south from Kyushu and separating, from north to south, the eastern China Sea from the Pacific Ocean. The largest island, Okinawa, is also the political and cultural center of the prefecture; its capital is Naha, on the southeast coast. Subtropical climate, with abundant rain. The islands are hit by typhoons, especially from the Philippines, in late September and early October. They were the theater of fierce fighting between Japanese and Americans in 1945, and remained under American control until 1972. Because of a lack of potable water, the islands developed slowly. Nevertheless, pineapples and sugar cane are cultivated, and are the most important export products. Okinawan society, made up of family clans (*monchū,* whose members have a common tomb), is distinct and more open than the rest of Japanese society. Although the average income of Okinawans is lower than that of Japanese on the four main islands, the favored life style is based on a sort of egalitarianism in which mutual aid is the dominant value. The main religion of Okinawans is directly related to ancestor worship (the main manifestation of which is the Seimei Festival, locally called Shimi) and worship of nature. Traditionally open to foreigners, Okinawan culture has a heterogeneous, welcoming aspect, and mixed marriages are more frequent there than in the rest of Japan. *Main cities:* Naha, Okinawa, Ginowan, Urasoe, Gushikawa, Ishikawa, Itoman. *Main islands:* Okinawa Iejima, Kerama, Kumejima, Miyakojima,

Sakishima, Yaeyama, Daitō Rettō. *Area:* 2,246 km². *Pop.:* 1.1 million. *See* RYUKYU ISLANDS.

• **Okinawa-te.** Former name for martial-arts techniques that were codified in karate; they were used by Okinawan peasants against the samurai of the Satsuma clan and pirates in the seventeenth century.

Oki no Shima. Island in the Strait of Korea, located between Tsushima and Fukuoka prefecture (Kyushu), former port of call for ships en route to or from Korea. It has basaltic soil and is forested. Its highly venerated Minikata Shrine is closed to women. Some dozen archeological sites containing offerings made by travelers between the fourth and ninth centuries were uncovered there, most of them placed in rocky shelters; these were generally from the *kofun* and Nara periods, with some sites going back to the Jōmon period. *Area:* 0.7 km². *Pop.:* 3,000. *See* OKI GUNTŌ.

Ōkisaki. Former title for an emperor's wife, replaced in 702 by Kōgō.

Okisato. Famous maker of sword blades (Nagasone Kotetsu Okisato, 1599–1678) in Edo. His blades are highly sought after by collectors.

Ōki Takatō. Politician (1832–99), born in northern Kyushu. Having helped with the restoration of the emperor, he was appointed governor of Tokyo in 1868 and minister of justice in 1873. He was president of the Genrō-in in 1885 and of the emperor's Privy Council in 1889.

Okita Saburō. Politician and economist (1914–93), adviser to a number of prime ministers and to the Jiyū Minshutō (Liberal Democratic party). In 1977, he left the LDP to join the New Liberal Club, formed in June 1976, and led by Kono Yōhei. He was instrumental in the effort to rebuild Japan after the Second World War.

Ōkōchi Denjirō. Theater and movie actor (Obe Masuo, 1898–1962), born in Fukuoka. He played mainly villains in movies by Kinugasa Teinosuke, Itō Daisuke, and other directors. He was very popular with the public.

Ōkōchi Masatoshi. Engineer (1878–1952), born in Tokyo. After studying in Germany and Austria from 1908 to 1911, he was a professor at the University of Tokyo. As director of the Institute of Physics and Chemistry Research (Rikagaku Ken-

kyūjo), which he had founded, he promoted applied science in industry and modernization of Japanese firms between 1921 and 1946. Among his many books are *Kōgyō keiei sōron* (General Theory of Industrial Management, 1936) and *Moteru kuni Nihon* (Japan, the Model Nation, 1939).

O-koma-san. "Master from Korea," a name given in deference to cats when they were imported from Korea around the tenth century; they were coveted by aristocrats in the imperial court. *See* CATS.

Ōkubi-e. Style of ukiyo-e prints featuring mainly portraits of actors, created by Sharaku in 1794 in Osaka and followed by a number of artists, including Utamaro.

Ōkubo Hikozaemon. Warrior (Ōkubo Tadataka, 1560–1639) who faithfully served the Tokugawa family and fought under Ieyasu. He is best known as the author of the *Mikawa monogatari*.

Ōkubo Nagayasu. Director of mines (1545–1613) serving the Takeda family and then Ōkubo Tadachika (1553–1628), daimyo of Sagami province. He directed the silver mines at Sagami starting in 1601, then those at Sado (1603) and Izu (1606), improving their production, which earned him an estate worth 30,000 *koku*. After his death, however, his fief was confiscated, and his sons, suspected of having misused public funds, were condemned to suicide.

Ōkubo Toshimichi. Politician (1830–78), born in Kagoshima to a family of samurai serving the Shimazu family. After the 1868 Restoration, his talents earned him a place in Emperor Meiji's Privy Council; he was minister of finance (1871), then ambassador to China, Europe, and the United States, and minister of domestic affairs in 1874. He opposed the Satsuma Rebellion led by Saigō Takamori and was assassinated on May 14, 1878, by a group of six samurai from Satsuma, who considered him a traitor to their clan.

Okuda. Family of daimyo descended from Minamoto no Yoshiuji (1189–1243) of the Seiwa Genji branch. Some of them took the family name Hori in the late sixteenth century and kept it until 1868. This large family was divided into several branches, whose members were ennobled during the Meiji era.

• **Okuda Naomasa.** Warrior (d. 1608) serving Hori Hidemasa and Toyotomi Hideyoshi in 1598. He changed his family name to Hori.

• **Okuda Naoyori.** Warrior (1577–1639) serving Tokugawa Ieyasu, famous for having captured the Nagoka castle in 1616 and the Murakami castle in 1618.

Okuda Eisen. Ceramist (Okuda Yōtoku, 1753–1811), born in Kyoto. A painter by training, he decorated ceramics in the styles of Nonomura Ninsei and Ogata Kenzan, introducing the art of painted porcelain to Kyoto. His students were Aoki Mokubei and Nin'ami Dōhachi. He produced Sencha ceramics in the Sometsuke and Gosuakae styles, decorated with flowers, birds, dragons, and Chinese motifs, under a thick transparent slip.

Okuda Gensō. Painter (Okuda Genzō) in Japanese (Nihonga) style, born 1912 in Hiroshima prefecture. Made a member of the Japan Art Academy (Nihon Geijutsu-in) in 1974, he received the Order of Culture (Bunka-shō) in 1984. He painted mainly landscapes.

Okudaira Tadaaki. Warrior (1583–1644) and Tokugawa Ieyasu's adoptive son. Ieyasu gave him the family name Matsudaira.

Oku-eshi. Term for the four branches of painters of the Kanō school who settled in Edo and worked for the shogunate—Nakabashi, Surugadai, Kajibashi, and Kobikichō, named for the districts where they were established. These painters were opposed to the *omote-eshi.* Also called *oku*-Kanō. *See* KANŌ-HA, MACHI-KANŌ.

Okugaki. "Colophon," inscription at the end of a book or scroll *(emaki)* giving the author's name, the place and date of production, and sometimes the sources of the work. Also sometimes added were the names and seals of the collectors or libraries *(bunko)* that owned the works. *Chin.: kuan, tan-kuan, shuangkuan.*

Okuhara Seiko. Painter (Ikeda Setsu; *gō:* Sekihō, 1837–1913) of the Nanga (Bunjinga) school, born in Koga (Ibaraki prefecture). A lover of Chinese culture, she was also a skilled writer of *waka* and haiku and a master of the tea ceremony *(chanoyu).*

Okujiri. Small island southwest of Hokkaido, with a population of about 4,600. It was almost completely destroyed in June 1993 by a tsunami resulting from an underwater earthquake that registered 7.8 on the Richter scale. More than 200 people were killed. The tsunami also ravaged several villages on the southwest coast of Hokkaido and the northwest coast of Tōhoku.

Ōkuma Kotomichi. *Waka* poet (1798–1868), born in Chikuzen province (Fukuoka prefecture), author of an essay on *waka, Hitorigochi* (1857) and a collection of *waka, Sōkeishū* (1863).

Ōkuma Shigenobu. Politician (1838–1922), born in Saga prefecture to a family of samurai serving the daimyo of Nagasaki, Nabeshima Kansō. He learned English and Dutch; in 1868, he left Nagasaki for Kyoto, where he actively supported the imperial cause. He was appointed trade attaché in Nagasaki, then *sangi* (state councillor) in Tokyo from 1873 to 1881, after accompanying the Iwakura delegation to Europe and the United States. He was then appointed secretary-general of the bureau of indigenous affairs in Taiwan. A member of the Kenseitō (Constitutional party), he founded the Rikken Kaishintō (Constitutional Reform party) in 1882 and the Shimpoto (Progressive party) in 1896; after holding various positions in the ministry of finance, he was appointed minister of foreign affairs (1896–97), then prime minister (1898), succeeding Itō Hirobumi, retaining the position of minister of foreign affairs (Waihan cabinet). Yamagata Aritomo succeeded him. He retired from politics after being wounded in an assassination attempt by Kurushima Tsuneki, a student inspired by the Kokuryū-kai (Amur River Society), but was prime minister again from 1914 to October 1916, succeeding Yamamoto Gonnohyōe, and signed an alliance pact with Russia in 1916. In 1882, he had founded Waseda University in Tokyo. When he died, he left a collection of documents he had amassed under the title *Ōkuma monjo,* valuable for information on history of the Meiji era.

Okumiya Takeyuki. Socialist agitator (Okumiya Kenshi, 1857–1911), born in Tosa province. A member of the Jiyūtō (Liberal party), he organized the Shakaitō (Rickshaw party), then was compromised in the Nagoya Incident. Arrested and sentenced to life in prison, he was freed in 1897. He went to Europe and the United States; when he returned, he joined Kōtoku Shūsui's socialists. Arrested again in 1910 as Kōtoku's accomplice, he was executed in 1911.

Oku Mumeo. Feminist (Wada Mumeo; 1895–1997), born in Fukui prefecture. She helped to found the Shin Fujin Kyōkai (New Woman's Association) in 1920 and was elected its president in 1922. She published a feminist magazine, *Shokugyō Fujin* (Women at Work), which became *Fujin Undō* (Feminist Movement). After the Second World War, she was elected to the Chamber of Councillors three times in succession.

Okumura Ioko. Politician (1845–1907), daughter of a Buddhist monk, born in Hizen province (Saga prefecture). She joined the pro-imperial movement and took part in Saigō Takamori's rebellion in 1877, acting as a courier. She lived in Korea but went to China during the Boxer Rebellion (1900) to help wounded Japanese soldiers. In 1901, she founded the Women's Patriotic Association (Aikoku Fujin), which later became a very large organization.

Okumura Togyū. Painter in Japanese (Nihonga) style (Gizō, 1889–1990), born in Tokyo. His works were exhibited in various Bunten and he was elected a member of the Japan Art Academy (Nihon Geijutsu-in) in 1947, receiving the Order of Culture (Bunka-shō) in 1962. He directed the Japan Fine Arts Academy (Nihon Bijutsu-in). His work was influenced by Cézanne and other Western artists. Also known as Okumura Dogyū, Okumura Yoshizō.

Okuni. Sacred dancer (*miko*, d. ca. 1640), said to be the creator of Kabuki theater. She was likely a servant at the Izumo Shrine, whence the name Izumo no Okuni. She created a company of women dancers and singers who performed at the Kitano Shrine and on the banks of the Kamo River in Kyoto around 1603. Not much is known about her life, except that she had a very public affair with a warrior named Nagoya Sanzaburō (?–1603). The form of danced theater she created, soon emulated by other troupes of women, was called Shibai. *See* KABUKI.

Ōkuni-nushi no Mikoto. Shinto *kami* who, according to the *Kojiki* and *Nihon shoki*, was a son (or a descendant) of Susanoo and governor of Izumo. At first a local divinity in Izumo, he was incorporated into the national Shinto pantheon at the time the *Kojiki* was compiled (712). He is presented as a beneficent *kami,* with a civilizing role. According to legend, he saved a hare from his brothers, and he learned from it that he was to marry the beautiful Yagami-hime. His brothers, out of jealousy, set him afire, but he was revived by his mother and the *kami* Kamimusubi. Still facing the hostility of his brothers, he was banished to Ki province and took refuge in Ne no Kuni (Hell), ruled over by Susanoo, whose daughter, Suseri-hime, he married. When he returned from Ne no Kuni with Susanoo's blessing, he expelled his brothers from Izumo, assisted by his son, Kotoshironushi no Kami. He thus brought peace to Izumo, which he then gave to Amaterasu-Ōmikami's envoys. In Izumo, he was considered the creator of the world, the *kami* of agriculture and of the "great country." In addition, he is worshiped as the divinity of war under the name Yachihoko no Kami ("*kami* of the 8,000 lances"). In syncretic Buddhism, he is sometimes identified with Daikoku-ten (*Skt.:* Mahākāla), one of the Seven Gods of Good Fortune (Shichifukujin). He is also called Akitsu-Kunitama, Ashihara Shikō-ō, Hie, Hiyoshi, Ōnamuji, Ōkunitama, Ōmononushi (in the Ōmiwa Shrine, Nara prefecture), Sannō, and other names.

Ōkura. In ancient times, a warehouse in the imperial palace (*see* KURA), reinforced with layers of plaster, in which the imperial treasures were kept. Also called Iwaigura, Uchikura.
• Zaibatsu founded in 1873 by Ōkura Kihachirō (1837–1928) as Ōkura-gumi Shōkai. From 1910 to 1945, it operated coal and iron mines in Korea. After the Second World War, the zaibatsu was dismantled and split into a number of associated companies operating mines in China and constructing public works. Head office in Tokyo.
→ *See* IZUMI-RYŪ.

Ōkurakyō. Buddhist monk and painter (thirteenth century) who painted a portrait of Nichiren now housed in the Myōhokken-ji temple in Shizuoka.

Ōkura-ryū. One of the three major Kyōgen schools *(ryū),* once part of the Komparu school of Noh, founded by Komparu Shirojirō in the sixteenth century. It still exists today. *See* IZUMI-RYŪ.

Ōkura-shō. Since 1885, the name of the Ministry of Finance. Also called Ōkura no Tsukasa. *See* MINISTRIES.

Okurina. Term for the posthumous name given to high-ranking people. In 784, Ōmi Mifune set the *okurina* of the previous emperors. *See* NAMES.

Ōkusaka no Miko. Imperial prince (d. 455), Emperor Inkyō's brother. He was assassinated by his nephew Ankō; his son, Mayuwa no Ō, assassinated Emperor Ankō the following year.

Oku Yasutaka. Military officer (1846–1930), born in Fukuoka. He fought in the Sino-Japanese (1894–95) and Russo-Japanese (1904–05) wars and was promoted to marshal. He was ambassador to India in 1898 and chief of general quarters from 1906 to 1912, and was ennobled (becoming a count) in 1911.

Old age. The age of retirement in Japan is 60 years, when the cycle of 5 times 12 years is completed, according to the principles of the Jikkan-jūnishi. When a person has reached this age, he or she is said to have entered old age—in other words, to have been reborn (*see* HONKE-GAERI, KANREKI). The life expectancy of people in Japan is rising every year, reaching 76 years for men and 83 years for women in 1995. This is causing serious problems both for society and for the old people themselves, who often have difficulty surviving after they retire. The problem is likely to grow because many companies are now retiring employees at 55 years of age.

There is no pension system in Japan analogous to those in Western countries, but custom has it that when people retire, the company that employed them pays them a large sum of money, which they are free to dispose of as they choose. Although a national festival honoring old people was instituted in 1963, retirees are still considered social outsiders because they are no longer producers but only consumers. This, however, involves only administrative, business, and industrial employees and managers. Retailers, members of the liberal professions, and peasants, who do not benefit from a global pension allowance, generally work until they die, or until illness keeps them from continuing to work. Workers who are "redundant" and in good health often seek another job, which means that the average real age at retirement is around 70 years. Those who have a family can generally count on their relatives to help provide them with a generally worry-free old age, but isolated people, if they did not make provisions in one way or another (insurance, savings, investments), often have a harder time.

The government provides social assistance for old people; since 1973, medical care has been free for those over 70, and 70% of the cost of such care is reimbursed for those between 65 and 70, with some municipalities paying the balance (law called Rōjin Fukushi Hō). People who return to work after retirement often find work in private firms, sports, charities, or educational institutions, or op-

erate small independent businesses (corner stores, cafés, second-hand shops). Recently, clubs for old people have sprung up to help retirees "recycle" themselves, or even to create jobs or firms. In fact, the protection traditionally offered by the family is often illusory because children may live far from their aged parents and young couples are not eager to have an extra mouth to feed; thus, the problem of housing, always very difficult, is acute for the aged. The best-off retirees are managers from government agencies, who usually receive a government pension. Others must make do, either with assistance from their families, by using their own means, or with help from associations. Poverty-stricken old people are sometimes helped by Buddhist temples or by Christian or other charitable institutions, but in general the Japanese hate living off charity, and few do. Those with the least means often simply cut back severely. *See also* AMAKUDARI, IN, INSEI, TEINENSEI.

Oliphant, Lawrence. British journalist and writer (1829–88), born in South Africa. He went to Japan in 1857 and became the embassy secretary in Tokyo in 1861. After being injured by a group of xenophobic samurai, he returned to England, then went to the United States. There, he and Thomas Harris founded the Society of the Fraternity of New Life, which he then exported to Palestine, and which he convinced six Japanese friends of the Satsuma clan to join.

Ombu. Traditional manner for a mother or an older sister to carry a young child on her back, in a wide belt strapped to her shoulders.

Ōmetsuke. In the Edo period, general inspectors of the *hatamoto* class, responsible for overseeing main roads and daimyo. In 1632, when they were created, they were called Sōmetsuke, to distinguish them from ordinary inspectors, or Metsuke.

Ōmi. Former province, now included in Shiga prefecture.
• Town in Yamato (also called Ōmi-Ōtsu), capital of Tenji Tennō and Kōbun Tennō from 667 to 673. It was on the shore of Lake Biwa (which is sometimes called Ōmi no Umi).
• Painter (Kose Ōmi, tenth century) of the Yamato-e school. Nothing is known about his life.
→ *See* HASSEI, YAKUSA NO KABANE.

• *Ōmi genji senjin yakata.* Nine-act play written for puppet theater *(ayatsuri-shibai)* by Chikamatsu

Hanji and Miyoshi Shōraku in 1769, and subsequently adapted for Kabuki theater.

• **Ōmi Hachiman.** Town in Shiga prefecture, on the eastern shore of Lake Biwa, where Toyotomi Hideyori built a castle in 1585. It contains ruins of the castle and old houses, Chōme-ji Buddhist temple, and Himuri Hachiman Shinto shrine dating from the twelfth century. *Pop.:* 60,000.

• **Ōmi Hakkei.** "The Eight Landscapes of Ōmi," often cited in poetry after 1500.

• **Ōmi no Mifune.** Imperial prince (Ōmi no Mabito, 722–85) who set the posthumous names *(okurina)* of emperors and who compiled the *Kaifusō.*

• **Ōmi-ryō.** Name sometimes used for the Taika Reform (645), which remained in force until the reform of the Taihō era in 701.

• *Ōmi-ryō.* First Japanese legal code, compiled on the Chinese model by Nakatomi no Kamatari and promulgated by Tenji Tennō about 668. It was 22 volumes long and finished only in 689. It is now lost. *See* RITSURYŌ entries.

Omikuji. Divination method used by temples and shrines, consisting of shaking a wooden rod marked with a number out of a bamboo tube. For a small donation, the monk or priest interprets this number, referring to the *Book of Changes (Chin.: Yijing).* Japanese often consult the *omikuji* before taking a trip or making a business decision, or before an important event. When the prediction written on the paper given back by the officiant is dire, it is averted by knotting the notice in the branches of a tree near the holy site.

Ominaeshi. Title of a Noh play: a Buddhist monk on his travels is about to pick a yellow *ominaeshi* flower *(Patrinia scabiosaefolia)* but is stopped by an old man who explains that there is a relationship between this flower and a couple whose tomb is nearby. The spirits of the deceased then appear, tell their story to the monk, and dance to express the torment they are suffering in Hell.
• In ancient literature, the *ominaeshi* was symbolic of autumn and of pretty women.

Ōmine-san. Mountain in southern Nara prefecture, once sacred for members of the Shugendō sect; climbing it was forbidden to women until 1960. *Alt.:* 1,719 m. Also called Sanjōgatake.

Ō-misoka. The last day of the year. Custom has it that, on midnight of this day, people leave their homes to visit temples and shrines so as not to anger the spirits who change the year. Noodles *(soba)* called *kake* ("debts") are eaten with a hot soup, symbolizing the fact that people have settled all of their debts. Buddhist temples toll their bells eight times to announce new life with the new year, which starts after midnight, to great celebration.

Ōmiwa-jinja. Shinto shrine in the town of Sakurai (Nara prefecture), dedicated to the *kami* Ōmononushi, Ōkuninushi no Mikoto's son. It is one of the oldest shrines in Japan; instead of a *honden,* it has the summit of Mt. Ōmiwa (Miwa-yama), which it is forbidden to climb. It is believed that the *kami* venerated there has the ability to cure diseases. The Ōmiwa-jinja was declared an imperial shrine about 910. *Haiden* rebuilt in 1644, Ōtodaneko-jinja Shoden dating from 1285, torii in "Miwa" style. Annual festival on April 9. Also called Miwa Myōjin. *See* HANA SHIZUME.

Ōmiya-kyō. Name of two subsects of the Shintō Taikyō, one founded in 1882; the other, founded in 1921 by Sako Kan (1878–1931), has about 10,000 followers.

Ō-mizutori. "Great Drawing of Water," a Buddhist rite observed every March at the Nigatsudō temple of the Tōdai-ji (Nara) to celebrate spring. The monks (having themselves undergone purification tests for a month) wave large torches over the heads of the faithful to purify them, then solemnly draw water from an adjacent well to offer it to Eleven-Headed Kannon Bosatsu (Jūichimen Kannon), the central divinity of the temple. Also called Ō-taimatsu ("Great Festival of Torches").

Ommitsu. General term for all spies used by the Tokugawa during the Edo period to keep tabs on the movements and actions of the daimyo. The daimyo, in turn, used spies to keep an eye on their vassals. The *ommitsu* were often *ninja.* Also called *kakushi-metsuke* (secret agents), *shinobi-metsuke* (agents in disguise). *See* METSUKE, NINJA, Ō-METSUKE.

Ommyōdō. "Way of Yin and Yang," a Taoist theory imported from China around the sixth or seventh century, based on interaction of the "five elements" *(Chin.:* Wuxing; *Jap.:* Gogyō) and Yin and Yang *(Jap.:* In, Yō) according to the *Book of Changes (Chin.: Yijing).* Ommyōdō dealt with the influences of the elements and of active and passive forces on individuals. In the seventh century, a Bureau of Ommyōdō (On'yō-ryō) was established, directed by theoreticians of the doctrine, the Ommyōhakase and Ommyōji. These theories, which gave rise to many Japanese beliefs about bans on directions (*see* IMI) and the determination of lucky and unlucky days, were expounded by Kamo no Tadayuki, his son Kamo no Yasunori (?–977), and Abe no Seimei (921–1005), among others. Also called On'yōdō, On'yō-gogyō. *See* GOGYŌ-SETSU, IN-YŌ, JIKKAN-JŪNISHI.

Omoide no ki. "The Tree of Memories." A novel by Tokutomi Kenjirō (1868–1927), partly autobiographical, describing the life of a young Japanese man of the Meiji era wishing to become educated in order to gain celebrity. Published in 1901, it was very popular.

Ōmori Fusakichi. Geologist (1868–1923), born in Fukui prefecture, pioneer of seismological research in Japan, and professor at the University of Tokyo.

Ōmori kaizuka. Shell mounds (*kaizuka, kjökkenmödding*) in the Ōta and Shinagawa districts of Tokyo, excavated by Edward S. Morse in 1877, which contained a great number of remains (kept at the University of Tokyo) from the Late and Final Jōmon periods. These shell mounds have now disappeared due to urbanization, and two monuments have been erected to indicate their former location.

Ōmori Shozō. Contemporary author (b. 1921)and philosopher. He wrote books on time, among them the very successful *Jikan to jiga* (Time and the Ego, which received the Tetsurō Watsuji in 1992) and *Jikan to sonzai* (Time and Existence, 1994).

Omori-sōshi. Collection of 1,554 ancient religious songs (*umui*) from Okinawa and the other Ryukyu Islands, written in archaic language; compiled from 1531 to 1623.

Omote-eshi. "Painters from outside," a term during the Edo period for painters of the Kanō school who lived in Edo but did not belong to the *oku-eshi.* They were divided into 15 families that were led by the branch in the Surugadai district. Also called *omote-*Kanō. *See* KANŌ-HA, MACHI-KANŌ.

Omote Nihon. Part of Honshu along the coasts of the Pacific Ocean and the Inland Sea (Setonaikai), very industrialized, considered the "belly" of Japan, as opposed to its "back" (Ura Nihon), comprising

the coast of Honshu along the Sea of Japan (Nihonkai), which is less developed.

Ōmoto-kyō. Internationalist religious sect founded in Ayabe by Deguchi Nao (1837–1918) and her son-in-law, Ueda Kitasaburō (Deguchi Onisaburō, 1871–1948). It still has several hundred thousand followers. *See* DEGUCHI NAO.

Omron Tateishi Denki. Manufacturer and distributor of electronic parts, founded in 1933 by Tateishi Kazuma, internationally known for its industrial and other types of robots. Branches in Chicago, Amsterdam, Hamburg, Singapore, and Hong Kong. It exports about 15% of its production under the brand name Omron. Head office in Kyoto.

Omu Komachi. Title of a Noh play: the poet Ono no Komachi receives a poem from the emperor; she returns it to him with only one word changed.

Ōmura. Town in Nagasaki prefecture (Kyushu), former castle-town (*jōka-machi*) of the Ōmura family, which had trade relations with Portugal in the sixteenth century. Site of Nagasaki Airport, about 20 km north of Nagasaki, built in 1975. *Pop.:* 70,000.

→ *See* SHIRAMOTO KOFUN.

Ōmura Masujirō. Military expert (1824–69) of the Chōshū clan, for the Tokugawa shogunate. He learned "Dutch science" (*rangaku*) and studied English with James C. Hepburn in Yokohama, but turned against the shogunate when it attacked the Chōshū in 1866 and, thanks to his techniques, defeated them on the battlefield. After the Meiji Restoration in 1868 (he defeated the Shogitai troops at Ueno), as vice-minister of military affairs, he reorganized the imperial army. His advocacy of conscription earned him the hate of the proponents of a professional army, who assassinated him in October 1869, in Kyoto. A bronze statue of him faces the Shōkonsha shrine in Tokyo.

Ōmura Sumitada. Daimyo of Hizen province (1533–87) who converted to Christianity (making him one of the first Christian daimyo on Kyushu) and took the name Bartholomew. The son of daimyo Arima Haruzumi (1483–1566), he was adopted by the Ōmura family, of which he became the head. He made important territorial concessions to the Portuguese Jesuits and opened the port of Nakae (Nagasaki) to them in 1571, but the Shimazu of Kagoshima attacked him and captured Nagasaki in 1587. A religious zealot, he had converted more than 60,000 of his citizens and destroyed Buddhist temples and Shinto shrines; Toyotomi Hideyoshi reacted by banning Christianity. Ōmura was one of the daimyo who had helped a mission of young converts to Europe in 1582. *See also* CABRAL.

On. Fundamental concept in Japanese ethics, consisting of favors that each person receives from society or from other persons, thus placing that person in an indebted situation and making him or her subject to mandatory obligations. These obligations can be considered passive in the case of *kō-on* (favors received from the emperor), *oya no on* (from relatives), *nushi no on* (from the lord), and *shi no on* (from teachers). The person from whom favors are procured is called *onjin*. Those who receive favors must perform various types of active obligations: *gimu* (permanent duty to the emperor, the state, and relatives), *giri* (mandatory duties engendered by the reception of favors or gifts), and duties toward oneself. Among Buddhists, another obligation is added: that toward humanity in general. From medieval times to the Edo period, *go-on* were duties owed to a lord by a person who had received land and benefits from him. Those who did not obey this rule were called *on-shirazu* and were automatically banned by society because they were considered to have committed a serious offense. *See* OYABUN KOBUN.
 • Chinese reading of a kanji character, opposed to its Yamato, or "Japanese," reading, which is called *kun*. There are, in general, three ways to pronounce kanji characters, called *ondoku*: in the manner of the Han Chinese *(kan'on)*, the Wei Chinese *(go-on)*, and the Tang Chinese *(tō-on)*. All nouns of foreign origin, such as Ainu words, transcribed with kanji characters must be read with the *on* pronunciation. According to the rules for reading Sino-Japanese characters *(kanji)*, *on* and *kun* readings must not be mixed in a significant text—although there are exceptions, of course. *See* KUN, YAMA.

 • **Ondoku.** *See* ON.

Onagadori. Breed of cock with a very long tail (sometimes more than 7 m) raised in Kōchi prefecture and used to ornament gardens. To let their tails develop fully, they are kept and fed on high perches. Their plumage is usually black and white or completely white.

Ōnakatomi. Ancient noble family, once charged with imperial rites. Also sometimes called Nakatomi.

 • **Ōnakatomi no Sukechika.** Senior bureaucrat and Shinto priest (954–1038), father of poet Ise no Ōsuke.

 • **Ōnakatomi no Yoshinobu.** Shinto priest of noble birth and poet (921–91), head of the priests in Ise. He wrote many *waka* poems and compiled the *Gosen waka-shū* in 951. His poems also appeared in anthologies, such as the *Shūi-shū* (997), and in his personal collection, *Yoshinobu-shū,* containing 485 poems. He is one of the Sanjūrokkasen (Thirty-Six Poetic Geniuses) and one of the Nashitsubo no Gonin (Compilers of the *Gosen waka-shū*).

Onchi Kōshirō. Printer and poet (1891–1955), and art lover. After studying oil painting and sculpture at the Tokyo Bijutsu Gakkō (now Tokyo University of Fine Arts and Music), he published the poetry magazines *Tsukehae* (Bright Moon) in 1913 and *Kanjō* (Emotion) in 1916, with several illustrator friends. He produced many illustrations drawn and printed in a very decorative modern style.

Ongyō-in. Buddhist mudra (hand position) of "dissimulation of shapes," specific to the divinity Marishi-ten. It is made with the right hand extended, palm down, and placed on the closed left fist held at chest level. This mudra *(Jap.: in-zō)* is supposed to have magical powers, rendering the person who makes it invisible. *Chin.:* Yinxing Yin.

Oni. General term for all folkloric demons with horns, large bulging eyes, and a red face. They are often portrayed on stage, during popular festivals as well as in Noh and Kabuki performances. Buddhists think that Hell is populated with wild and cruel *oni*. However, it may be that *oni* were former Shinto *kami;* they are not all cruel, and their nature is sometimes ambivalent. Some of them symbolize human passions, such as Hannya, who is represented in several Noh plays by an *oni* mask. Called *uni* in Okinawa.

Oni ga Shima. Former name of the island of Ao ga Shima. *See* MOMOTARŌ, TAKAMATSU.

 • **Onigawara.** Roof ornament made of tiles or metal in the form of a demon's head, generally put on roofs to keep evil spirits away. *Chin.: guilonhzi; Kor.: jab-sang. See* KAWARA.

 • **Oni-harai.** Public ceremony at the beginning of spring *(risshun, setsubun)* in which demons that haunt houses and public places are banished by throwing soybeans into the air and shouting "*Oni* *wa soto, fuku wa uchi"* ("Out with demons! In with happiness!") This ceremony provides an opportunity for great festivities, with well-known artists and political celebrities often taking part. Also called Mamemaki, Ō-harai. *Kor.:* An-taeg. *See also* HARAI.

• **Oni-kagami.** "Demon mirror," a mirror with special reflective properties. *See* KAGAMI.

Ōnin. Era of Emperor Go-Tsuchimikado: Mar. 1467–Apr. 1469. *See* NENGŌ.

• **Ōnin no Ran.** "The Onin War." A civil war that began in 1467, at the time of the succession of shogun Ashikaga Yoshimasa, in which two clans of daimyo, the Hosokawa and the Yamana, did battle. It lasted 11 years, until 1477, and caused the destruction of the city of Kyoto, which was the theater of battles between the families and their allies. It was the beginning of a series of civil wars and disturbances called Sengoku (Warring States), which lasted sporadically until 1568. Relations deteriorated between the Ashikaga shoguns and the *shugo-daimyō* of the provinces after the war of the Northern and Southern courts (Nambokuchō), when Ashikaga Yoshimasa persuaded his brother, Ashikaga Yoshimi, to abandon the robes of a Buddhist monk and succeed him. Yoshimasa's wife, Tomiko, had given birth to a male child, Yoshihisa, and claimed the title of shogun for him. Hosokawa Katsumoto took Yoshimi's side and thus found himself opposed to Yamana Sōzen (his father-in-law), who supported Tomiko and Yoshihisa. The war that broke out between the two sides ended in 1473 with the death of both adversaries and the official appointment of Yoshihisa, but their allies and descendants continued the struggle for dominance. They finally gave up in 1568, under pressure from Oda Nobunaga, but the country had been left in ruins.

Ōnishi Hajime. Philosopher (1864–1900), born in Okayama prefecture. A convert to Christianity, he postulated that religion should have precedence over the state and looked to socialism to protect freedom of thought. He expounded his ideas in various writings, collected in *Ōnishi hakase zenshū*.

Ōnishi Takijirō. Admiral (1891–1945) who assembled teams of kamikaze pilots in 1944; his goal was to ease the shortage of aviation fuel while maintaining an effective attack against the American fleet.

He committed suicide when Japan's surrender was announced. *See* KAMIKAZE.

Oniwa-yaki. In the Tokugawa period, a term for ceramics made exclusively for a daimyo within the walls of his castle or residence. The most famous of these ceramics were the Ofuke-*yaki* of the Tokugawa of Owari, the Kairakuen-*yaki* of the Tokugawa of Kii, the Kōrakuen-*yaki* of the Tokugawa of Mito, the Rakurakuen-*yaki* of the Ikeda, and the Ōsaki Oniwa-*yaki* of the Matsudaira of Izumo.

Onna. Generic term for women, as opposed to *otoko,* "man."

• **Onna-budō.** In Kabuki theater, the role of a warrior's wife. *See* ONNAGATA, ONNA PREFECTUREGEKI.

• *Onna daigaku.* "Great Science for Women." A 19-chapter manual of social behavior for women, attributed to Confucian philosopher Kaibara Ekiken, published in 1716. Kaibara's wife, Kaibara Tōken (1652–1713), may have been his co-author. This work had an enormous influence on the ideas that Japanese society formed about the role and place of women, but it was strongly criticized after 1868, notably by Fukuzawa Yukichi in *Shin onna daigaku* (1898).

• **Onna-de.** "Women's hand," a term once used for hiragana writing, which was reserved for women who did not have access to Chinese literature (Kambungaku).

• **Onna-e.** "Women's style," a term for Yamato-e paintings that illustrated the great novels written by women in the late Heian period.

• **Onnagata.** In Kabuki theater, women's roles, played by men after 1629, when women were banned from the stage. These roles have specific names depending on the character portrayed: *kashagata, keisei, onna-budō, oyama,* and others.

• *Onna goroshi abura jigoku.* "Murder of a Woman in an Inferno of Oil." A play by Chikamatsu Monzaemon portraying a contemporary event, performed in 1721.

• **Onna-kabuki.** Early form of Kabuki theater in which all actors were women. It was banned for reasons of morality in 1629. *See* ONNAGATA.

• **Onna prefecturegeki.** Type of Kabuki theater in which the warrior heroes are women (played by men). *See* ONNA-BUDŌ.

Ono Azusa. Economist and jurist (1852–86) who studied the banking systems in the United States and London from 1871 to 1874. He helped Ōkuma Shigenobu found the Rikken Kaishintō (Constitutional Reform party) and plan the Constitution of Japan.

Ōno Bamboku. Politician (1890–1964), born in Gifu prefecture. Elected to the House of Representatives for the Rikken Seiyūkai (Friends of Constitutional Government party) in 1930, after the Second World War he helped to found the Nihon Jiyūtō (Japan Liberal party), of which he became the secretary-general. He was minister of state in Yoshida's fifth cabinet in 1953, and vice-president of the LDP (Jiyū Minshūtō) until his death.

Ono Chikkyō. Painter (Ono Hidekichi, 1889–1979), born in Okayama prefecture. He specialized in landscapes in the Nihonga style and was influenced by Cézanne and the post-impressionists. With compatriots Bakusen, Shihō, Kagaku, and Nonagase Banka, he founded the Kokuga Sōsaku Kyōkai (National Association of Creative Painting). He was elected a member of the Japan Art Academy (Nihon Geijutsu-in) in 1947 and decorated with the Order of Cultural Merit in 1968.

Onoe. Family of Kabuki actors and dancers founded by Onoe Kikugorō I (1717–83) in Kyoto. His descendants performed mainly in Edo: Onoe Kikugorō III (1784–1849), adoptive son of Onoe Matsusuke I (1744–1815); Onoe Kikugorō IV (1808–60); Onoe Kikugorō V (1844–1903); Onoe Kikugorō VI (1885–1949); Onoe Kikugorō VII (b. 1942), and One Shōroku II (1914–89) are the best known. In 1988, Onoe Kikuya (Hamada Masako) founded a group called Masako, whose mandate is to spread the principles of the Onoe school to other countries. *See* FUJIMA, IEMOTO.

Onoe Matsunosuke. Actor (Nakamura Tsuruzō, 1875–1926) in Kabuki theater and movies, nicknamed Medaman no Matchan ("Matchan with rolling eyes") because of his mime work. He played in hundreds of silent films, and directed several. He became the director of Nikkatsu in 1923.

Onoe Saishū. *Waka* poet (Onoe Hachirō, 1876–1957), born in Okayama prefecture, disciple of Ochiai Naobumi. Considered a great scholar of *waka* in his time, he was elected to the Nihon Geijutsu-in (Japan Art Academy) in 1937; he was also a talented calligrapher. He wrote two poetry collections, *Nikki no hashi yori* (1913) and *Shiroki michi* (1914).

Ōno Gorōemon. Dancer and bronze sculptor (thirteenth century), maker of the great Daibatsu of Kamakura in 1252. *See* DAIBUTSU.

Ōno Harunaga. Warrior (?–1615) serving Toyotomi Hideyoshi and his son, Toyotomi Hideyori, who was a favorite of his mother, Yodogimi. Ōno Harunaga tried to assassinate Tokugawa Ieyasu in 1599. In 1615, he defended the Osaka castle, which was besieged by Tokugawa Ieyasu; he committed suicide with Hideyori and Yodogimi in June 1615, when the castle fell.

Onokoro-jima. According to legends related in the *Kojiki,* a mythical island to which the *kami* Izanagi and Izanami descended from the "Bridge of Heaven" when they united to form the islands of Japan.

Onomichi. City in Hiroshima prefecture, on the Inland Sea (Setonaikai), important commercial port in the twelfth century, and the site of the Jōdo-ji, Saikoku-ji, and Senkō-ji Buddhist temples, some founded in the seventh century. According to custom, large straw sandals *(waraji)* are given as offerings to the Ni-ō of the Saikoku-ji. *Pop.:* 110,000.

Ono no Imoko. Senior bureaucrat (seventh century) in the court of Empress Suiko; first ambassador *(kenzui-shi)* to China, sent by Prince Shōtoku Taishi in 607. He returned to China the following year with several other envoys, among them Takamuko no Kuromaro, Minabuchi no Shōan, and the Buddhist monk Sōmin, thus establishing fruitful diplomatic relations with the Sui Chinese that had a profound influence on the development of Japanese civilization. *See* KENTŌSHI.

Ono no Komachi. Poet (mid-ninth century), classified among the Six Poetic Geniuses (Rokkasen) of the period. According to tradition, she was the daughter of Ono no Yoshizane, a governor of Dewa province, in northern Honshu. She was a lady-in-waiting at the imperial court of Heian-kyō (Kyoto) from 850 to 869. Eighteen of her poems have been preserved in various anthologies. Nothing is known about her life but there are many legends about her, according to which she was very beautiful and had many lovers. She went mad when the love of her life, Fukakusa, died in a snowstorm as he was coming to visit her for the hundredth time, and she thereafter led a miserable existence. Her life and legends were the subject of many Noh plays *(Sotoba Komachi)* and a novel *(Tamatsukuri Komachi seisui sho)*. *See also* KAYOI KOMACHI, OMU KOMACHI, SEKIDERA KOMACHI.

• **Ono no Michikaze.** Calligrapher (894–966), one of the Sanseki (Three Pens) of the tenth century, with Fujiwara no Sari and Fujiwara no Yukinari. Also known by the names Yaseki Tōfū and Ono no Tōfū. He is sometimes considered the founder of Japanese calligraphy.

• **Ono no Minemori.** Poet writing in Chinese (770/778–830), author of a collection called *Ryōun shinshū* (or *Ryōun-shū*) in 814.

• **Ono no Takamura.** Poet (802–after 852), perhaps from Mutsu province (northern Honshu), and noble in the Heian-kyō court. He wrote various collections of poems and prose texts in Chinese, of which a small number have been preserved. He was shipwrecked during a mission to China in 834, and refused to re-embark because of illness. Relatively little is known about his life, but many legends have been attached to his name.

Ono Ranzan. Botanist and physician (1729–1810). His 48-volume work on plants used in medicine, *Honzō kōmoku keimō,* earned him the nickname "the Linnaeus of Japan."

Ono Seiichirō. Jurist (1891–1986), born in Morioka, an expert in criminal procedure and professor at the University of Tokyo, succeeding Makino Eiichi. After the Second World War, he helped rewrite the Japanese penal code.

Ōno Taiichi. Engineer (1912–90), inventor of a production method that he applied in Toyota's plants, enabling that company to become third largest in the world. He wrote many books on his methods, which gained worldwide recognition: *Toyota Production System, Workplace Management,* and others.

Ono Tōzaburō. Poet (1903–96), born in Osaka, an advocate of social realism and author of several collections of modern poems, including *Ōsaka* (1939),

Fūkeishi-sho (1943), and *Jūyū Fuji* (1956), and an essay on poetry, *Shiron* (1947).

Ono Tsū. Lady-in-waiting (1559–1616) for Oda Nobunaga, credited with writing the *Jōruri-hime monogatari* and *Jōruri jūnidan sōshi.* She was also a painter. *See* JŌRURI.

Ō no Yasumaro. *See* FUTO NO YASUMARO.

Ono Yōko. Musician, born 1933 in Tokyo to a family of bankers. In 1952, she took part in avantgarde art movements in New York. In 1956, she married Japanese composer Ichiyanagi Toshi (b. 1933); in 1963, she wed an American artist, Anthony Cox, with whom she had a daughter, Kyōko. In 1969, she married English musician John Lennon (of the Beatles), who was assassinated by a psychopath in 1980. She recorded a number of albums with her husband and was known mainly for her eccentricities.

Onsen. "Hot spring." Due to its volcanic topography, Japan has a great many hot springs—a total of 2,237, according to estimates made by the geology department in 1975—which have drawn visitors since antiquity, being famous for their curative properties. Some have hot sand and lakes of hot mud that are used for medicinal purposes. The largest *onsen* are surrounded by hotels, restaurants, and recreational areas; others are used as geothermic energy sources by industry. They are found throughout Japan, mainly in proximity to volcanoes. The most famous are in Beppo (Kyushu), Noboribetsu (Hokkaido), Kirishima (Kagoshima prefecture), Narugo (Miyagi prefecture), and Kusatsu (Gumma prefecture).
    • **Onsen-geisha** are prostitutes who frequent the hot springs and who aspire to be true geisha, although their clothes and makeup are very ordinary and they have little talent. *See* GEISHA.

Ontake. Volcano (*alt.:* 3,063 m) between Gifu and Nagano prefectures, composed of five peaks and surrounded by lakes, one of which, Ni no Ike, is the highest in Japan. The volcano erupted for the first time in 1979. Every year, many pilgrims dress in white to climb Ontake, a custom going back to the fifteenth century, because this mountain is the most sacred in Japan after Mt. Fuji. Also called Kisokomatake.
    • Many other mountains bear this name and are considered sacred. Also sometimes called Mitake or Ōtake.

Onta-yaki. Type of porcelain made in the village of Sarayama in Ōita prefecture (Kyushu) starting in 1720, and somewhat similar to Koishikawa ceramics. The pieces often have a yellow-and-green glaze produced without chemical products and are fired in wood-fueled *noborigama* kilns. Also called Onda-*yaki*. See KOISHIKAWA-YAKI.

Ōnuma Chinzan. Poet (1818–91) writing in Chinese in the style of the Song dynasty; Yanagawa Seigan's student. His best-known collection is *Chinzan shishō,* published from 1859 to 1867.

On'yō-ryō. "Bureau of Yin and Yang," a government agency created by the Taihō Code (701) to direct the activities of experts *(hakase)* in Ommyōdō, astrologers, geomancers, and other scholars of "Chinese science." It was directed by members of the Abe family starting in the tenth century and by their descendants from the Tsuchimikado family in the late twelfth century. See OMMYŌDŌ.

Ōoka Makoto. Poet, born 1931 in Shizuoka prefecture, and professor at Meiji University. He was known for his linked poems *(renga)* and was appointed professor at the Tokyo University of Fine Arts and Music in 1988. He was the eleventh president of the P.E.N. Club of Japan, succeeding Endō Shūsaku. Among his most notable works: *Tōji no kakei* (1969), *Ki no tsurayuki* (1971), and *Nihon shiika kikō* (Voyages Through the Poetry of Japan, 1978).

Ōoka meiyo seidan. "The Glorious Judgments of Ōoka." An eighteenth-century historical novel by an unknown author, a sort of collection of detective stories. See ŌOKA TADASUKE.

Ōoka Rei. Modern writer (b. 1959), who received the Akutagawa Prize in 1990 for his novel *Hyōsō sekatsu* (The Outside of Life, 1989).

Ōoka Shōhei. Writer (1909–88), born in Tokyo. He studied French literature at the University of Tokyo, began to write when he was 19, and translated Stendhal's work. Among his early writings are stories, critical essays (notably on the poet Nakahara Chūya), and poems. Mobilized in 1944, he was sent to the Philippines, where he was taken prisoner. He returned to Japan in 1945 and wrote *Furyo-ki* (Diary of a Prisoner of War, 1948), which won the Yokomitsu Prize in 1949. He continued to write war novels, including *Nōbi* (Fire on the Plain, 1951), *Reteno ame* (Rain over Leyte, 1948), *Ikite-*

iryu horyo (Living Prisoners, 1949), *Reite sen-ki* (Diary of the Battle of Leyte, 1967), as well as novels of morals, such as *Musashino fujin* (The Lady of Musashino, 1950), *Sanso* (Oxygen, 1955), and *Kaei* (The Shadow of the Flowers, 1959), and was regarded as one of the best writers of his generation. Many of his novels were adapted for the screen by Mizoguchi Kenji, Ichidawa Kon, Kawashina Yūzō, Nomura Yoshitarō, and other directors.

Ōoka Shunboku. Painter (Ōoka Aitō, 1680–1763), born in Osaka. He studied the paintings of the Kanō school and the Chinese masters and received the honorific title Hōgen. He wrote some works on painting, among them *Gahon tekagami* (1720) and *Gakō senran,* mainly about technique.

Ōoka Tadasuke. Civil governor (1677–1751), or Edo *machi-bugyō,* in the era of shogun Tokugawa Yoshimune, who noticed him when he was a judge in Ise. The justice of his rulings became proverbial, as did his integrity, and many legends and stories were written on the affairs he had knowledge of, the most famous of which is *Ōoka meiyo seidan.* His diary was published as *Ōoka Echizen no Kami Tadasuke nikki* from 1972 to 1975. Also very well known by his title, Echizen no Kami.

Ōoku. "Great interior," a district reserved for women within the walls of the shogunal palace in the Edo period. In this district, women of all ranks were submitted to a strict hierarchy, and each had one or several apartments.

Oppler, Alfred C. American jurist (1893–1982) of German descent, attached to General MacArthur's general quarters in Tokyo in 1946. With his extensive knowledge of national and international law, he helped MacArthur set up the judicial reforms that were deemed necessary to transform Japan after the Second World War. He retired in 1959 and wrote many books on law, among them *Contemporary Japan* (1952), *The Sukanawa Case* (1961), and *Legal Reforms in Japan during the Allied Occupation* (1977).

Ōrai-mono. Manuals or guides to writing letters, managing one's affairs, and providing assistance to travelers. Many of these works were textbooks, used in the Edo period in *terakoya* (village schools). They were written in the eleventh century; one of the oldest, the *Meigō ōrai,* dates from 1058.

Oranda. Japanese name for Holland; until the Meiji era, a specific term designating everything from the West. As a consequence, "Dutch science" was called *rangaku* (a contraction of *Oranda-gaku*).

• **Oranda-bashi.** *See* HIRADO.

• *Oranda fūsetsu-gaki.* Reports on international current events (especially from Europe) brought to Nagasaki (Dejima) by Dutch merchants, and translated for the shogunate by official interpreters living in Nagasaki called *Oranda-tsūji*. These interpreters *(tsūji),* directed by a head interpreter *(ō-tsūji),* numbered several dozen. They also translated science books brought by Dutch sailors, and some of them wrote Dutch–Japanese dictionaries for their own use.

Oribako. A type of round box made with a single thin piece of wood rolled on itself, not painted but often decorated, used in certain Shinto ceremonies.

Oribe-ryū. School for the tea ceremony *(chanoyu)* founded by Furuta no Shigenari (Furuta Oribe). Furuta also founded a special type of pottery for his school about 1600 in Mino province (Gifu prefecture), called Oribe-*yaki. See* MINO, FURUTA ORIBE.

Origami. The art of folding squares of white or colored paper to make objects or animals. At first a pastime for children, *origami* has become more and more complex, and some pieces are true masterpieces. *Origami* can be traced back to the Shinto *gohei* and *katashiro,* in which the *kami* are symbolized by folded pieces of paper. In more practical terms, the art of *origami* also involves how paper is folded around gifts and purchases, as well as the *noshi* that accompany these packages. There are many forms of *origami,* depending on the way the paper is folded, the color, the decoration, or the way several foldings are arranged. *Origami* is taught in elementary schools to develop manual dexterity and a sense of surfaces and volumes. There are many associations of *origami* aficionados, not only in Japan but in Europe and America.

Orihon. Bookbinding method in which sheets of paper are glued end to end and folded in accordion style before being sewn together. Each page is therefore double, with a single side printed. This is the "classic" Japanese binding.

Orikuchi Shinobu. Poet (Shaku Chōkū, 1887–1953), born in Osaka prefecture. He studied Japanese folk literature and folklore with Yanagita Kunio and wrote *tanka* poems during his travels throughout Japan researching ancient customs. His most important work is the three-volume *Kodai kenkyū* (Studies on Ancient Times, 1930). He also wrote several poetry collections—*Umi yama no aida* (Between Sea and Mountains, 1925), *Kodai kannai-shū* (Poems Inspired by Ancient Times, 1947)—and a novel, *Shisha no sho* (Writings of the Dead, 1939). Also written Origuchi Shinobu.

Orimpasu Kōgaku Kōgyō. Manufacturer of cameras, tape recorders, and precision optical instruments, founded in 1919. In 1959, this company made the first pocket camera under the brand name Olympus, and it has continued to make increasingly sophisticated cameras both for the domestic market and for export. It exports 70% of its production. Head office in Tokyo.

Orlik, Emil. Designer and poster artist (ca. 1870–1932) from central Europe. He went to Japan in 1900–01 and learned the techniques of ukiyo-e prints, which he then taught to Pissarro in Paris. He visited Japan again in 1911.

Ōryōshi. Ancient title for military leader and provincial governor, created in 878. This position disappeared during the Kamakura period, when it was replaced by that of *shugo*.

Osa. Term for the first interpreters *(tsūji)* from Chinese and Korean in the Yamato court in the sixth century. Most of them were Korean.

Ō Sadaharu. Athlete, born 1940 in Tokyo of Chinese parents from Taiwan. One of the greatest baseball players Japan has known, he set the world record for home runs in 1977, with 868. He retired in 1980. Also written Oh Sadaharu.

Osafune Kaji. Famous school for makers of sword blades in Bizen founded in the thirteenth century by Mitsutada. Its best-known members were Nagamitsu, Kagemitsu (Kamakura period); Kanemitsu, Tomomitsu, Motomitsu (Nambokuchō period); Morimitsu, Yasumitsu (of the Ōe Bizen school, Muromachi period); Katsumitsu, Sukemitsu, Kiyomitsu (of the Sue Bizen school, late Muromachi period).

Ōsaka. Chief city of Ōsaka prefecture (Ōsaka-fu), located at the bottom of Ōsaka Bay, on the Inland Sea (Setonaikai), commercial center of Japan and third largest city, after Tokyo and Yokohama. The axis of a large coastal industrial zone called Hanshin, it is served by rail *(shinkansen)* and by two international airports: Itami (14 km away) and Kansai, constructed on landfill in the sea and opened in September 1994. The port of Naniwa, founded in the third century, was expanded by Toyotomi Hideyoshi, who had an immense castle built there in 1583. Ōsaka is famous for its commercial activities (rice; textiles; manufactured products; electrical, mechanical, and automobile industries), retail trade (Semba district), and pleasure district (Dōtombori). A seaside city, Ōsaka has canals and branches of the Yodogawa river delta running through it, forming a series of islands. The largest is Naka no Shima (Middle Island), 3.5 km long, where the administrative center is located. The city was almost completely destroyed by bombing in 1945, but was quickly reconstructed on a modern plan. It hosted a world fair in 1970. Its very active port is third in the country in terms of tonnage transited. Open to visitors are the castle (Ōsaka-jō), the remains of the ancient Naniwa-kyō and the Shitennō-ji temple, the Bunraku theater, municipal art museums (*see* MUSEUMS), and a huge aquarium. University (faculties of medicine, dentistry, foreign languages, etc.) founded in 1931. *Pop.*: 2.7 million.

• **Ōsaka Daigaku.** Osaka University, founded in 1931 to replace a college (Tekijuku) founded in 1838 by Ogata Kōan. Faculties of literature, science, law, economics, medicine, dentistry, pharmacology, engineering, and a number of scientific institutes. Attendance: about 10,000 students.

• **Ōsaka-fu.** Osaka prefecture, created in 1887 in the Kinki region, on the wide Yodo-gawa river plain, ringed by mountains and facing Osaka Bay on the Inland Sea. It was populated in ancient times, and remains from the Jōmon, Yayoi, and *kofun* periods abound on its coasts and hills. Along the coast is the Hanshin Industrial Zone, linking the old port of Sakai to Kobe via the prefecture's chief city, Osaka. This region was rapidly reconstructed and developed after the Second World War. *Main rivers:* Yodo-gawa, Yamato-gawa. *Main cities:* Osaka, Sakai, Izumi Ōtsu, Toyonaka, Ikeda, Minoo, Ibaraki, Moriguchi. *Area:* 1,858 km². *Pop.*: 8.5 million.

• **Ōsaka Gaikokugo Daigaku.** Osaka University of Foreign Languages, mainly Asian, located in Minoo (Ōsaka-fu). It was founded in 1921 and became a university in 1948. Attendance: about 2,000 students.

• **Ōsaka-jō.** Castle in Osaka, built by Toyotomi Hideyoshi, starting in 1583, on the site of the Higashiyama Hongan-ji; it was finished in 1586. Huge rocks were brought from the island of Awaji for its construction. The castle and its outbuildings originally covered an area of 3.3 km by 2.4 km. It was magnificently decorated with paintings by the best artists of the time (from the Kanō family). Damaged during the siege of 1615, restored in 1620 by Tokugawa Ieyasu, and destroyed during the Second World War, it was reconstructed in cement (1947) and transformed into a museum.

• **Osaka school.** School of ukiyo-e print artists that developed in Osaka and environs in the mid-seventeenth century, specializing in images of Kabuki scenes and actors. Among the exemplary artists of this school were Ashiyuki (ca. 1820), Harusada (ca. 1822), Nishikawa Hirosada (ca. 1845), Konishi Hirosada (?–1863?), Nakai Yoshitaki (1841–99), Hōkuei, Nakamura Nagahide, Ryūsai Shigeharu, and especially Sharaku (active ca. 1794–95), the most famous of them. They used a rich palette of colors reminiscent of the tonalities in Yamato-e painting.

Osakabe Shinnō no Ōji. Imperial prince (Osakabe Otomaro, d. 705), who, with Fujiwara no Fuhito, compiled the Taihō Code (701–02; *see* TAIHŌ RITSURYŌ). One of his poems was included in the *Man'yōshū.*

Osako Mikio. Contemporary ceramist, born 1940 in Usa (Ōita prefecture), who received the Grand Prize of Honor at the International Biennial of Ceramics in Vallauris, France, in 1972. He has had many exhibitions in Japan, and in Paris in 1994.

Osanai Kaoru. Playwright and director (1881–1928), born in Hiroshima; he wrote many screenplays and translated modern European plays. In 1909, he and Ichikawa Sadanji (1880–1940) founded the Jiyū Geki-jō (Liberal Theater); in 1924, he founded the Tsukiji Shōgekijō (Little Theater of Tsukiji), which was dissolved after his death. Among his most notable works are the novel *Okawabata* (1911) and the plays *Daiichi no sekai* (1921) and *Musuko* (The Son, 1922). His works were republished in Tokyo under the title *Osanai Kaoru engekiron zen-shū* (1968).

Osano Kenji. Businessman (1917–86) who made a huge fortune selling spare parts for automobiles. A friend of Tanaka Kakuei, he was implicated in the Lockheed Scandal in 1981 and 1983. He owned hotel chains in Japan and Hawai'i and various companies worth a total of $6 billion.

Osaragi Jirō. Writer (Nijiri Kiyohiko, 1897–1973), born in Yokohama. After 1923, he devoted himself to literature, resigning from his job as a bureaucrat in the Ministry of Foreign Affairs. He published his first historical novel, *Hayabusa no Genji,* in 1924, then continued with *Karana tengu,* an extremely popular series of novels published from 1924 to 1959. He then wrote other series of novels in the same vein, such as *Teru hi kumoru hi* (Sunny Days, Cloudy Days, 1927) and *Akō rōshi* (1928). He also wrote novels of morals, including *Nadarae* (Avalanche, 1936) and *Kōri no kaidan* (Ice Staircase, 1940); novels based on various historical events, *Dorefusu-kjiken* (The Dreyfus Affair, 1930), *Būranje shōgun no higeki* (The Tragedy of General Boulanger, 1935); and a long historical novel, *Tennō no seiki* (The Century of Emperors), which he finished in 1973. Among his other works: *Ahensensō* (The Opium War, 1942), *Kikyō* (Homecoming, 1948). He also wrote several plays, including *Yō Kihi* (Yang Guifei, 1951), *Wakaki hi no Nobunaga* (Young Oda Nobunaga, 1952), and *Sekigahara zen'ya* (The Eve of the Battle of Sekigahara, 1958), which were adapted for Kabuki. An annual literary prize was created in his name in 1973.

Ōsawa, Jean-Georges. Physician and philosopher (Sakurazawa Nyoichi, 1893–1966). Imprisoned in 1944 for his "subversive" ideas, he went to the United States after the Second World War. He then moved to France, where he advocated "macrobiotic" medicine and a naturalist and pacifist philosophy, based in part on alternations of Yin and Yang (*see* OMMYŌDŌ); he published a number of works on the subject. Also written Ohsawa, Jean-Georges.

Ōseidasare-sho. "Proclamation on Encouragement of Education," an important text published in 1872 by the Meiji government to explain the terms and applications of the Imperial Rescript on Education (Kyōiku Chokugo). Also titled *Gakuji shōrei ni kansuru ōseidasare-sho. See* GAKUMON NO SUSUME.

Ōsei Fukko. "Restoration of the Imperial Government," the name for the coup d'état of January 3, 1868, the outcome of which was the abolition of the Tokugawa shogunate and the taking of all power by Emperor Meiji. The Meiji Restoration, as it is sometimes called, was the culmination of the Boshin Civil War, in which the imperial troops decisively defeated the shogunate's supporters. *See* BOSHIN SENSŌ.

Ō-setsu-ma. In contemporary Japanese homes, a room with Western-style furnishings for receiving visitors. It is usually located near the entrance and does not have tatami.

Oshi. In certain Buddhist and syncretic sects, such as Shugendō, the title for "masters of exorcism," who are supposed to have supernatural powers. In many shrines, as at Ise, low-ranked Shinto priests fulfilled this function (which was then called *onshi*). These "masters of powers," created in the twelfth century at the Kumano Shrine, lost their official status in 1871.

O-shichi. Title of a Bunraku play first produced in 1773: the title character is a young woman in love who sounds the alarm bell in her village so that, in the confusion and under cover of night, she can meet with her beloved.

Oshidashi-butsu. Religious image, generally Buddhist, embossed with fine copper leaf and gold leaf. The technique of embossing, which enabled many images to be made inexpensively, was imported from China in the seventh and eighth centuries. Also called *tsuiki-butsu.*

Oshigata mondoki bunka. Prehistoric culture in Kanto and the Chūbū region, dating from the Early Jōmon period. It is characterized by pottery with various pressed designs, perhaps borrowed from the peoples of the Yori-ito mondoki bunka.

Ōshikōchi no Mitsune. Poet (?–after 921) who, with a few others, compiled the first imperial anthology, the *Kokin-shū,* around 905. He was one of the Sanjūrokkasen (Thirty-Six Poetic Geniuses), with Ki no Tsurayuki and Mibu no Tadamine. Sixty of his poems were included in the *Kokin-shū,* and his personal collection, *Mitsune-shū,* contains between 140 and 384 poems, depending on the edition.

Oshikuma Ōji. Imperial prince (fourth–fifth century?), Emperor Chūai's son. He rebelled against Empress Jingū Kogō and was killed by Takeshiuchi no Sukune.

Ōshima. Volcanic island about 12 miles from the coast of the Izu Peninsula, part of the Iazu-tō; its volcano is Miharayama (*alt.* 758 m). The beauty of its landscape makes it very popular with tourists. *Area:* 91 km²; *pop.:* 15,000. Also called Izu Ōshima.
• Several other small islands also have this name (Kii Ōshima, Duō Ōshima).
• Japanese name for De Vries Island.

Ōshima Hiroshi. Politician and general (1886–1975), born in Gifu prefecture, an expert in German affairs. When he was a military attaché in Germany, he and von Ribbentrop wrote the "anti-Comintern pact." He was ambassador to Germany in 1938, and again after the signature of the 1940 "tripartite pact"; he remained in this position until the end of the Second World War. Sentenced to life in prison for war crimes in 1948, he was freed in 1955.

Ōshima Nagisa. Movie director, born 1932 in Kyoto. He started work for Shōchiku as an assistant in 1954, and began directing movies in 1959. Strongly influenced by Marxism and the French "New Wave," he drew most of his subjects from real events. In 1965, he founded his own production house, Sōzōsha, specializing in films on sex and violence: *Shōnen* (Boy, 1969), *Gishiki* (The Ceremony, 1971), both made with the help of a French producer, and *Ai no korīda* (The Empire of the Senses, 1976) are among his best-known movies. He received the award for best director at the Cannes Film Festival in 1978 for his series called *Ai no bōrei* (The Empire of Passion). He also worked in television. Among his movies distributed in Europe are *Yumbogi's Nikki* (1965), *The Treachery of Bizarre Songs* (1967), *Koshi-kei* (The Hanging, 1968), and *A Little Sister for the Summer* (1972).

Ōshima Ryōta. Haiku poet (1718–87) in Bashō's style. He had a large number of disciples. He published critical editions of Bashō's works, *Bashō kukai* (1757), and some collections of his poems, including *Haikai jūsanjō* (1767).

Ōshima Takatō. Engineer (1826–1901), born in Morioka; he built the first reverberation blast furnace *(hantarō)* in 1858 in Kamaishi and made the first Western-style gun in Mito. He participated actively in developing Japan's mines after 1868.

Ōshin. Painter (Maruyama Oshin; *azana:* Chūkyō; *gō:* Hyakuri, Hōko, Seishūkan, 1790–1838) of the Maruyama school; he studied with his father, Ōju, and was Ōzui's adoptive son.

Oshin. Famous television series from a script by Hashido Sugako, broadcast by NHK. Since 1981, it has gained a huge audience (more than a 50% share of mornings from 8:15 to 8:30 and at lunchtime). It is the story of a nonconformist 83-year-old woman who works hard to take care of her family, thus celebrating the traditional virtues of Japanese women.

Oshio. Noh play: an old man recites the poems of Ariwara no Narihira, evoking the spirit of the poet, who then appears and dances to thank him.

Ōshio Heihachiro. Neo-Confucian philosopher (Ōshio Chūsai, 1793–1837) of the Ō-Yōmei (*Chin.:* Wang Yangming) school, who led a rebellion in Osaka in 1837 (Tempō Jiken). A former police officer, he rose up against the Tokugawa shogunate, intending to force it to make reforms to help the poorest classes. The rebels set fire to the city, partly destroying it, and attacked the castle. When they were about to be captured by the shogunal troops, they committed suicide, on March 27, 1837. However, many peasants refused to believe that Ōshio Heihachirō was dead and continued to rebel sporadically.

Oshiroi. White paste made with plant extracts and sometimes lead oxide, used during the Edo period as face makeup. *See also* BENI-BANA.

Ōshita Tōjirō. Painter (1870–1911), most of whose works were landscapes in watercolor. He went to Europe in 1902.

Oshō. Title of "professor" given by Buddhist disciples to their masters and to heads of temples. Also called Kashō, Wajō. *Chin.: heshang.*

O-shōgatsu. Festival of the new year, lasting three days (formerly seven), during which Japanese drink a soft drink called *otoso (toso)* and eat *mochi* made from crushed rice. This word also designates the first month of the year, the "exemplary month," full of celebrations and festivals of all sorts.

Ōshū Fujiwara. Powerful warrior family that ruled Mutsu and Dewa provinces in the eleventh and twelfth centuries from their capital, Hiraizumi, which was founded by Fujiwara no Tsunekiyo, a descendant of the Hidesato branch of the Fujiwara of Heian-kyō, vassal of Abe no Yoritoki. His son, Fujiwara no Kiyohira (1056–1128), built a fort at Haraizumi. Fujiwara no Motohira (?–1157) succeeded him, followed by his grandson, Fujiwara no Hidehira (1096–1187). Hidehira took in Minamoto no Yoshitsune, thus incurring the wrath of Minamoto no Yoritomo, who invaded the estates of the Ōshū, captured and set fire to Hiraizumi, and destroyed the Ōshū Fujiwara family by Fujiwara no Yasuhira, killing the last offspring of this illustrious family. *See* HIRAIZUMI.

Ōshū-kaidō. Major road, 786 km long, linking Edo to Aomori through the waystation towns of Utsunomiya, Shirakawa, Fukushima, and Sendai, created during the Edo period. Also called Riku-u Kaidō, Ō-u Kaidō. *See* GO-KAIDŌ, TŌKAIDO.

Ōsō. Itinerant divinity (Yugyō-jin) of the Ommyōdō, whose movements must never be interfered with by human beings, giving rise to certain bans on direction *(imi)*. This divinity, of Chinese origin, is perhaps composed of two entities, Ōjin and Sōjin. *See* KATA-IMI, KATA-TAGAE.

O-some hisamatsu tamoto no shirashibori. "Story of Hisamatsu and O-Some." A three-act play written for puppet theater by Ki no Kaion in 1711. It was adapted for Kabuki by Chikamatsu Hanji with the title *O-some hisamatsu shimpan utazaimon.*

Osore-yama. Volcano (alt. 879 m) in Aomori prefecture, with a crater lake called Usori-yama on the shores of which a Buddhist temple, Entsū-ji, was founded in the ninth century by the monk Ennin. This volcano is one of the sacred sites of Japanese shamans *(itako),* who gather there, usually on July 20–24, and invoke the spirits of the dead. Also called Osorezan.

Ōsuga Otsuji. Haiku poet (Ōsuga Isao, Otsuji, 1881–1920), born in Fukushima prefecture, Kawahigashi Hekigotō's disciple. He wrote collections and essays on poetics: *Otsuji kushū* (1921), *Otsuji haironsū* (1921), and *Otsuji shokanshū* (1922).

Ōsugi Sakae. Politician (1885–1923) and anarchist, born in Kagawa prefecture. He was a profes-

sor of French in the army college (Rikugun Daigaku) after being fired from the cadets' school in Nagoya for insubordination. He became friends with Kōtoku Shūsui and Sakai Toshihiko, and took part in political actions that got him arrested and imprisoned in 1906. When he was freed in 1910, he studied Marxist theorists, then began to take part in various socialist activities, going to Shanghai in 1920 at the invitation of the Communist International. In 1922, he went to France, but he was arrested and sent back to Japan in 1923. After the riots that followed the major earthquake in Tokyo in September 1923, he was arrested by the police and beaten to death.

Ōsumi. First Japanese artificial satellite, launched on February 11, 1970. *Weight:* 22 kg. It was followed by the Tonsei satellite (65 kg) on February 16, 1971, then by the Shinsei satellite (31 kg) on September 29, 1971. *See* SATELLITES.

• **Ōsumi.** Name of a former province, now Kagoshima prefecture (Kyushu).

• **Ōsumi Guntō.** Group of islands south of Kyushu, extending from the Ōsumi Peninsula (Ōsumi Hantō), on which there is a satellite-launch base. The group includes the island of Tanegashima, the Yaku Islands, and many islets. *Area:* 1,030 km². *Pop.:* 60,000. Also known as the Van Diemen Islands.

Ōta Dōkan. Small-scale daimyo (Ōta Sukenaga, 1432–86), vassal of the Uesugi family, who served Minamoto no Yorimasa. As Kantō-kanrei, he built a castle in Edo in 1457, which was expanded by Tokugawa Ieyasu in 1590. He became a Buddhist monk with the name Dōkan and devoted himself to *waka* poetry. He was assassinated on the order of Sadamasa, the head of the Uesugi family, because of a false accusation of disloyalty. He was the true founder of Edo.

Otafuku. *See* HYOTTOKO, MASKS, NŌMEN, OKAME.

Ōtagaki Rengetsu. Poet (Tōdō, Nobu, 1791–1875), painter, ceramist, and calligrapher, born to a samurai family. After serving at the Kameoka castle (Kyōto-fu) as a lady-in-waiting and getting married, she became a Buddhist nun in 1823, adopting the name Rengetsu (Lotus Moon) at the Chion'in Zen temple. She then lived in various temples and composed *waka,* illustrating them with her own paintings. She was also known for her pottery for the tea ceremony and for other talents, notably in the martial arts. Her poems were collected in *Ama no karumo.*

Ōtaguro Motoo. Musicologist (1893–1979) who wrote a number of major works.

Ōta Hisa. Artist (Hanako, 1868–1945). She went to Paris in 1910 and became sculptor Auguste Rodin's friend and favorite model. She is better known by her personal name, Hanako.

Ōta Kinjō. Neo-Confucian philosopher (1765–1825). He wrote a number of philosophy books and founded a school of Confucianism.

Ōta Mizuho. *Tanka* poet (1876–1955), born in Nagano prefecture, author of a number of poetry collections, including *Tsuyu kusa* (1902), *Sanjō kojō* (1905), *Unchō, Fuyuma, Sagi, Raden, Ryūō,* and critical works on poetry.

Ōta Nampo. Poet (Ōta Tan; *gō:* Kyōkaen, Yomo no Akara, Shokusanjin, 1749–1823), born in Edo to a family of samurai and bureaucrats serving the Tokugawa shogunate. He wrote satirical verses *(kyōshi)* in Chinese and comical verses *(kyōka)* in *waka* form. He also wrote many popular novels in the *kokkeibon* and *sharebon* genres *(kusazōshi* series): *Kikujusō* (Eternal Chrysanthemums, 1781), *Okame hachimoku* (The Observer, 1782), *Neboke sensei bunchū* (Professor Neboke's Literature Collection, 1767), and others. Among his best-known *kyōka* collections are *Manzai kyōka-shū, Shokusan hyaku-shū* (1818), and a collection of essays, *Ichiwa ichigen,* published in 1820. He sometimes signed his "erotic" *sharebon* works with the pseudonym Yamanote no Bakabito ("the madman of Yamanote," a district of Edo).

Ōtani. Noble family descended from the Fujiwara and related to the imperial family, whose heads have traditionally been, since Shinran, the directors of the Hongan-ji branch (in Kyoto) of the Jōdo Shin-shū sect. A collateral branch, called Ōtani-ha, was founded by Kōju in 1602 at the Higashi Hongan-ji in Kyoto. *See* HONGAN-JI.

• **Ōtani Chōjun.** Buddhist monk (Ōtani Tsunemaro), born 1929 in Kyoto, high dignitary of the Jōdo Shin-shū sect. He received a doctorate from the University of Paris and wrote a number of works in French, among them *Pages de Shinran* (Shinran's Pages, 1969), *Les Problèmes de la foi et*

de la pratique chez Rennyo à travers ses lettres (Rennyo's Problems of Faith and Practice from his Letters, 1991). A history aficionado, he became very interested in the life of Joan of Arc and published a number of articles and books in Japanese on this subject.

• **Ōtani Daigaku.** Private Buddhist college founded in Kyoto as a seminary of the Hongan-ji temple in 1665 under the name Shinshū Daigaku. The college was elevated to university rank in 1949. Faculties of literature and Buddhist studies. Attendance: about 2,000 students.

• **Ōtani Kōzui.** Buddhist monk (1876–1948) of the Jōdo Shin-shū sect and twenty-second abbot *(hossu)* of the Higashi Hongan-ji in Kyoto with the name Kyōnyo, succeeding his father, Ōtani Kōson. He visited China, Europe, and India; in 1902, he went to Russia to explore Buddhist sites in Central Asia. He purchased manuscripts in Dunhuang *(Jap.:* Tonkō), amassing one of the most important collections on Buddhist Central Asia. He returned to Europe in 1909–10, then sent three expeditions to Central Asia to draw up maps. Involved in a financial scandal in 1914, he was forced to resign as *hossu* of the Jōdo Shin-shū.

Ōta Shogo. Contemporary playwright, internationally known for his silent plays, notably *Suna no eki* (The Sand Train Station) and *Element,* performed in 1993 and 1994, both dealing with the problem of time.

Ōta Zensai. Philologist (1759–1829), known mainly for writing *Rigen shūran* (Panorama of Common Language), a nine-volume dictionary, sometimes attributed to Murata Ryō-a (1773–1843). This work was published as a supplement to *Gagen shūran* in 1900.

Otedama. Game consisting of tossing small canvas sacks filled with beans, played mainly by little girls. The sacks, often made with luxurious fabrics, were made in the seventeenth century to replace the stones used in a similar game called *ishi-nago.* It is comparable to the game of knucklebones.

Ōtemmon no Hen. Incident that took place in Heian-kyō, during which the Ōtemmon gate was set afire, described in detail in *Ban Dainagon ekotoba.* Tomo no Yoshio (Ban, 809–68), a descendant of the Ōtomo family, accused his political rival, Minamoto no Makoto (810–68), of having set the fire, and his son Yoshio and members of their clan were sent into exile.

Ōte Takuji. Poet (1887–1934), born in Gumma prefecture, whose works were strongly influenced by French symbolism. His poems were published after his death: *Ai iro no hiki* (1936), *Hebi no hanayome* (1945), *Ōte takuji shishū* (1948).

Otogi-bōko. Title of a novel published by Asai Ryōi in 1666, one of the *kana-zōshi*. It is a collection of 68 fantastic tales, 21 of which were adapted from the Chinese novel *Jiangdeng xinhua* by Qu Zongji.

• **Otogishū.** In the Edo period, readers at the courts of the daimyo and the shogun responsible for entertaining them and receiving their confidences. *Otogishū* were often scholars. This term also designated pages *(koshō)* of the young nobles and sons of major daimyo.

• *Otogi-zōshi.* Collection of 23 tales "for the education of women and children," published in Osaka in 1720 and reprinted in 1891. A new selection of 20 tales was added in 1901. A total of more than 80 were published. This name also designates a genre of popular novels based on tales and legends, which emerged in the fifteenth century and developed fully in the late Edo period. Although the literary value of these tales is sometimes debated, they remain interesting for the legends they recount and for their description of details of daily life. Also called *Otogibanashi.*

Ō-tō-kan. Collective name for three Zen monks of the Rinzai sect, Dai-ō, Daitō Kokushi (Shuhō), and Kanzan (Egen), active in the fourteenth century.

Otoko-e. "Male image," a label sometimes used for Chinese-inspired monochrome paintings, as opposed to *onno-e* paintings, which were a sort of reaction against the Chinese style of painting. This style began with the *Chōjū giga* and the scroll called *Shigisan engi.*

Ōtoku. Era of Emperor Shirakawa: Feb. 1084–Apr. 1087. *See* NENGŌ.

Ōtomo. Powerful family or clan *(uji)* in the Yamato court, which, according to the *Kojiki,* was descended from the *kami* who accompanied Ninigi no Mikoto on his descent to earth. This *uji* supplied the warriors who enabled the Yamato clan to establish itself in the sixth and seventh centuries.

• **Ōtomo no Kanamura.** Warrior of the Ōmoto clan (active 495–540) who, according to the *Kojiki* and the *Nihon shoki,* played an important role in Emperor Buretsu's accession to the throne. Implicated in an unfortunate diplomatic affair with Korea (Paekche kingdom), he was removed from office and probably assassinated by his rivals.

• **Ōtomo no Koshibi.** Ambassador (695–777) from Yamato to the Chinese court in 752. *See* KENTŌSHI.

• **Ōtomo no Kui.** General under Soga no Umako who led two military expeditions to Korea, in 590 and 601. He was Ōtomo no Kanamura's son.

• **Ōtomo no Miyori.** Poet (?–774) whose works appeared in the *Man'yōshū.*

• **Ōtomo no Sadehiko.** General who led a military expedition to Mimana (Korea) in 562. *See* MATSURA SAYOHIME.

• **Ōtomo no Sakanoue no Iratsume.** Poet (active 728–46), leader of the Ōtomo clan, 84 of whose poems appeared in the *Man'yōshū* (77 *tanka,* 6 *chōka,* and 1 *sedōka*). She was one of the favorites of Prince Hozumi, Emperor Temmu's son, and married Fujiwara no Maro (695–737), then Ōtomo no Sukemaro. She lived in Nara and Dazaifu. She was Otomo no Tabio's half-sister.

• **Ōtomo no Tabito.** Poet (665–731) and statesman, governor-general of Dazaifu and grand councillor; Ōto no Yakamochi's father and Ōtomo no Sakanoue no Iratsume's half-brother. He was one of the *Man'yō* no Go-taika.

• **Ōtomo no Yakamochi.** Poet (737–85), Ōtomo no Tabito's son and one of the *Man'yō* no Go-taika. He was probably the compiler of the *Man'yōshū,* in which 481 of his poems appeared (434 *tanka,* 46 *chōka,* and 1 *sedōka*).

• **Ōtomo no Yoshimune.** *See* CABRAL, ŌTOMO NO YOSHISHIGE.

• **Ōtomo no Yoshishige.** Daimyo (1530–87) from Kagoshima, who welcomed Francis Xavier in 1578. Also called Ōtomo Sōrin, Sambisai Sōrin. He became a Buddhist monk with the name Sōrin in

1562, but converted to Christianity in 1578 with the name Francisco. He opposed Shimazu Yoshihisa (1533–1611), but his 60,000-soldier army was defeated in Mimigawa and he lost most of his territorial possessions. It was he who encouraged Toyotomi Hideyoshi to conquer Kyushu. The Jesuit chronicles call him the "King of Bungo." He sent delegations to Goa in 1551 and 1553, and probably helped to send young Japanese Christians to Rome in 1582 (although this cannot be proved). His son Ōtomo Yoshimune was also baptized, with the name Constantinho, but he turned against the Christians after Toyotomi Hideyoshi confirmed his estates. However, since he did not perform well during the invasion of Korea in 1593, Toyotomi Hideyoshi took away his land, putting an end to the powerful Ōtomo family. *See also* CABRAL.

Ōtomo Katsuhiro. Author (b. 1954) of comic books and contemporary science fiction (*Akira*, 1984) who is well known in the West. Some of his comic books have been made into cartoons, such as *Akira* (1990).

Otona. "Elders," a term for heads of villages in the Muromachi and Momoyama periods, landowners (*myōshu*), and heads of Shinto ritualist associations. Elected by the villagers, they were responsible for payment of taxes (*nengu*). In the Edo period, they were exempted from certain taxes and called *mura yakunin*. *See* GŌSON.

Ōtori Keisuke. Samurai (1832–191) serving the Tokugawa shogunate, born in Harima province. A military instructor using Western methods, which he had learned in Osaka with Ogata Kōan and Egawa Tarōzaemon, he defended the Edo castle during the Boshin Civil War (1868) and joined Enomoto Takeaki in Hakodate. He was sent to prison and then granted amnesty in 1872; later, he held various ministerial positions and was made ambassador to China (1889) and Korea (1893).

Otoshidama. New Year's gifts, once food distributed by temples and shrines to their followers, now simply toys or, more often, money, given to children by their parents, friends, or neighbors, to celebrate the New Year. *See* GIFTS.

Ōtoshi no kyaku. "The New Year's Eve Visitor." Popular tales in which an unexpected visitor shows up on the last day of December and is welcomed; during the night he changes into a treasure. These tales derive from an old belief that on New Year's Eve divine charitable beings visit houses to bring luck to worthy inhabitants.

Oto-tachibana Hime. In Shinto legend, Yamato-takeru no Mikoto's wife. She was thrown into Sagami Bay to appease a tempest in which her husband was at risk of dying.

Otowa. Family of Kabuki actors and dancers in Osaka, founded by Otowa Jirōsaburō (?–1732), who created a classical-dance school. *See* IEMOTO.

• **Otowa Nobuko.** Actor (Kaji Nobuko, Shindō Nobuko), born 1924 in Osaka. At first a dancer at the Takarazuka Kagekidan, she was discovered by director Shindō Kaneto, who gave her her first movie role in *Aisai monogatari* (Story of a Beloved Wife) in 1951. She then appeared in all of Shindō's movies, and was noted internationally in *The Naked Island* (*Hadaka no shima*, 1960), receiving the prize of the Moscow festival in 1978.

Ōtsu. Chief city of Shiga prefecture, on the south shore of Lake Biwa, former imperial residence in the seventh century and waystation (*shuku-eki*) on the Tōkaidō road in the Edo period. It includes the Ishiyama-dera temple (Bashō's tomb) and Enryaku-ji temple, remains of the castle (Zeze), and Hie Shinto Shrine, and is home to electrical and textile industries and a major rice market. *Pop.*: 220,000.
　　On May 11, 1891, there was an attempt to assassinate the Russian crown prince, Nicholas Alexander (the future Alexander II), who was on a tourist visit, by a police officer in his escort, Tsuda Sanzō (1854–91), who believed that the prince had come to Japan to plan for an invasion. Tsuda Sanzō was sentenced to life in prison and died soon after.

• **Ōtsu-e.** Folk images once sold in shops along the road leading to Ōtsu and at the Mii-dera temple during the Edo period. These Buddhist-inspired images, drawn in ink, then colored, were often naive in style. The Ōtsu-e of the nineteenth century, influenced by ukiyo-e prints, also portrayed beautiful women (*bijin*) and Kabuki actors. Although they are generally of mediocre quality, they are actively sought by collectors.

• **Ōtsu no Miya.** Imperial palace in use from 667 to 672, located in Ōtsu, whose remains were found recently. Established by Emperor Tenji, it was abandoned for Asuka when he died.

• **Ōtsu no Ōji.** Imperial prince (663–86), Emperor Temmu's son. He tried, in vain, to seize the throne when his father died and was condemned to death. He was an excellent poet. Also called Ōtsu no Shinnō.

Ōtsuka kofun. Large keyhole-shaped *kofun* on the bank of the Honami River (Fukuoka prefecture, Kyushu), excavated in 1934. It is 70 m long, built of granite, andesite, and sandstone, and its interior chamber is decorated with paintings of horses (in black and red) and riders, "horns," fans, ceremonies, triangles, quivers, and épées in yellow, black, red, and green. The vault is studded with yellow dots on a red background. It may date from about the fifth century.

Ōtsuki. Major family of scholars, whose most famous members were Ōtsuki Gentaku, Ōtsuki Banri (1787–1838), Ōtsuki Bankei (1801–78), Ōtsuki Fumihiko, and Ōtsuki Joden.

• **Ōtsuki Fumihiko.** Philologist (1847–1928), Sinologist, and lexicographer, pioneer in modern study of the Japanese language, author of dictionaries and grammar books.

• **Ōsuki Gentaku.** Scholar and physician (Ōtsuki Bansui, 1757–1827), astronomer, and geographer; Sugita Gempaku's student. He wrote in both Japanese and Dutch. *See* KAITAI-SHINSHO, RANGAKU-KAITEI.

• **Ōtsuki Joden.** Man of letters and lexicographer (Nyoden, 1845–1931), born in Sendai, son of Confucian scholar Ōtsuki Bankei and Ōtsuki Gentaku's grandson. He wrote a number of books on literature and helped compose the dictionary *Shinsen jisho* in 1872. He was a great connoisseur of Japanese traditional music.

O-tsuki-mi. Festival of the "sight of the full moon," generally in mid-September. Once, official ceremonies were conducted in honor of the moon, during which poets composed works to its glory. It is still customary for people to get together to admire the full moon and eat *o-dango*, rice-paste balls. This custom is said to have been started by Emperor Montoku in 851, but it became a popular celebration in the seventeenth century. *Chin.:* Zhongqiu.

Ott, Eugen. German general (1889–1976), appointed military attaché to Japan in 1934, then German ambassador in 1938. He was removed from office in 1942 because of his friendship with Richard Sorge. *See* SORGE.

Ōuchi. Major family of daimyo that controlled a large part of Chūgoku and the Suō region during the Muromachi period. It was of Korean origin. In the fourteenth century, Ōuchi Hiroyo (?–1380) entered the service of the Ashikaga shogun, but his son, Ōuchi Yoshihiro (1356–1400), rebelled (*see* ŌEI NO RAN). When he died, his brother Ōuchi Morimi (1377–1431) began to trade intensively with China; he regilded the family's coat of arms and became a patron of the arts. *See* ŌUCHI YOSHITAKA.

• **Ōuchi-ke kabegaki.** Code of family laws (*bunkoku-hō*) established by the heads of the Ōuchi family between 1459 and 1495, comprising some 50 articles concerning trade and administration of the Suō estate.

• **Ōuchi Yoshitaka.** Daimyo (1507–51) of Suō, Ōuchi Yoshioki's (1477–1529) son. He opposed the Ōtomi of Kyushu and the Amako of Izumo for control of trade with China and Korea. In an attempt to make his capital, Yamaguchi, as flourishing a city as Kyoto, he attracted a large number of artists, such as Sesshū Tōyō and Sōgi. He also welcomed Francis Xavier in 1550 and 1551, giving him permission to preach in his estates. The Jesuits called him "King of Yamaguchi." However, his vassal Sue Harukata (1521–55) revolted and forced him to commit suicide, which led to the disappearance of the Ōuchi family.

Ōura Kanetake. Politician (1850–1918) of the Satsuma estate (Kyushu). He supported the imperial cause during the Boshin Civil War (1868); after holding various positions in the Meiji government, he was appointed a provincial governor. Minister of the interior in Ōkuma Shigenobu's cabinet in 1915, he was implicated in various scandals and was forced to resign.

Ōura Okei. Businesswoman (1828–84), born in Nagasaki. Profiting from her close relations with foreigners, she launched a tea-exporting company and quickly made her fortune, part of which she used to provide financial support to patriots (such as Sakamoto Ryōma). She was so widely known that General Grant invited her on board his ship when he was in Japan in 1879.

Ōura Tenshudō. The oldest Catholic church in Japan, founded in 1865 in Nagasaki by Father B. T. Petitjean. *See* NAMBAN-JI.

Ōu Sammyaku. Major mountain range on Honshu, called the "Japanese Alps," stretching about 450 km from Aomori to Kantō. It includes several volcanoes more than 2,000 m high, including Iwate-san and Azuma-san. *See* MOUNTAINS.

Ōwa. Era of Emperor Murakami: Feb. 961–July 964. *See* NENGŌ.

Owari. Former province, one of the 15 provinces traversed by the Tōkaidō road. Created in 646, it is now included in Aichi prefecture. Also called Oharuda.
• Branch *(ke)* of the Tokugawa family, established by Tokugawa Yoshinao (1600–50), Tokugawa Ieyasu's ninth son, in Nagoya, Owari province. *See* SAN-KE.

• **Owari no Hamanushi.** Famous Bugaku musician (733–?), from Owari province.

Oyabun-kobun. Primordial relationship in Japanese society, established at the beginning of Japan's history, that forges an almost indissoluble link between parents and children, superiors and inferiors, at all levels of society. This concept implies duties that are owed (*see* ON) by *kobun (kokata)*—children, people under obligation, inferiors, and so on—toward *oyabun (oyakata)*—parents, teachers, superiors, and so on. *Kobun* owe absolute obedience and unfailing loyalty to their *oyabun,* who may also be directors of the company at which the *kobun* work. *Kobun* must show their allegiance to *oyabun* on a specific date each year by offering them small gifts or paying them a visit. These relations exist among almost all Japanese groups and are faithfully observed in yakuza societies. Also called *oyakata-kokata. See* GIRI, ON.

• **Oyaji-gata.** In Kabuki theater, the role of an old man. Also called *rōnin-yaku.*

• **Oyako-kō.** Confucian virtues of "filial piety." *Chin.: xiaojing.*

Oyama-e. In ukiyo-e prints, a courtesan's or geisha's face.

Ōyama Ikuo. Politician and writer (Fukumoto Ikuo, 1880–1955), born in Hyōgo prefecture. He studied sociology in Chicago and Munich from 1910 to 1914. When he returned to Japan, he was a professor at Waseda University. He resigned from this position in 1917 and began to write for newspapers, notably the *Ōsaka Asahi Shimbun.* An advocate of democratic ideals, he and Kawakami Hajime founded the political and literary magazine *Warera* in 1919. He was recalled to Waseda University in 1920. In 1926, he was elected president of the Labor-Farmer party (Rōdō Nōmintō, abridged to Rōnōtō) and was once more forced to resign from his professor's position. He was finally elected to the House of Representatives in 1930. Because of his opposition to the government's bellicose policy, he went into self-imposed exile in the United States with his wife in 1933; he returned to Japan only in 1947, once again taking up his position at Waseda. He was again elected to the Diet in 1950 and received the Stalin Peace Prize in 1951.

Ōyama Iwao. General (1842–1916), born in Kagoshima, Saigō Takamori's nephew. He studied the art of artillery and invented a modern gun, the *yasukehō,* then fought in the Boshin Civil War (1868) as a supporter of the imperial restoration. He continued to study military strategy in France; after he returned to Japan, he was appointed minister of war in 1880 and head of general quarters in 1882. In the Sino-Japanese War (1894–95), he captured Port Arthur and Mukden, receiving the title "Duke of Mukden." He then commanded the Manchurian army during the Russo-Japanese War (1904–05) and was raised to the dignity of Privy Councillor to Emperor Meiji in 1914. Ennobled several times, he was made a prince in 1907.

Ō-Yamato. Ancient name for Japan, meaning "Great Yamato" and used mainly in literature. Many emperors received this name posthumously, including Itoku Tennō (Ō-Yamato Hiko Sukitomo no Mikoto), Gemmei Tennō (Ō-Yamato Neko Amatsu Mihiro Toyokuni-naru), Jitō Tennō (Ō-Yamato Neko Ame no Hironu-hime no Mikoto), Kōrei Tennō (Ō-Yamato Neko Hiko Futo-ni no Mikoto), Kōgen Tennō (Ō-Yamato Neko Hiko Kuni-kuru), and Kōan Tennō (Ō-Yamato Tarashi-hiko-kuni-kuru no Mikoto).

• **Ō-Yamato Toyo Akitsu Shima.** "Fertile Island of Grand Yamato, Land of Dragonflies," an ancient poetic name for Honshu.

• **Ō-Yamato-tsumi.** Shinto *kami* of the mountains, son of Izanagi and Izanami.

Oyama Tokujirō. Modern *tanka* poet (1889–1963), born in Kanazawa. He helped edit a number of poetry magazines and began to publish collections of his verses in 1912: *Sasurai* was followed by 11 other anthologies. *Tofu no sugagomo* won the Academy of Arts prize.

Ō-ya-shima no Kuni. "Country of the Eight Great Islands," an ancient poetic name for Japan.

Oyashio. Cold ocean current descending from the North Pole and flowing alongside the Kuril Islands, the east coast of Hokkaido, and northern Honshu, where it meets the warm waters of the Kuroshio current, forming a mix of water very propitious for fish production. Also called Okhotsk current and Chishima-kairyū (Kuril Islands current).

Ōya Tōru. Philologist (1850–1928), born in Niigata prefecture, pioneer of research on the Japanese language and author of many important works on the subject. He received an Imperial Prize for his body of work.

Ōyu. Circles of stones arranged on the ground, dating from the Jōmon period. It was discovered in 1931 in the Ōyu district, near the town of Kazuno (Akita prefecture), and excavated in 1952. The two circles studied have diameters of 42 and 46 m and are made of concentric rows of stones. Between the two concentric rows of the 42 m circle is a sort of sundial with a type of menhir 0.85 m high at its center. They may have been tombs or cult sites; Jōmon stone tools and pottery were found on the site.

Ō-yumi. Type of Korean crossbow sometimes used in Japan in the seventh century. *See* YUMI.

Ozaki Hōsai. Haiku poet (1885–1926), born in Tottori prefecture. He traveled in Manchuria and worked in Korea, and he was employed as a lay Buddhist in several Japanese temples. His collection of poems, *Taikū* (1926), was published after his death, as were various essays that he wrote during his itinerant life.

Ozaki Kazuo. Writer (1899–1983), born in Mie prefecture, elected to the Japan Art Academy (Nihon Geijutsu-in) in 1964. He received the Noma Prize for his novel *Maboroshi no ki* in 1961. Among his other works: *Nonki megane* (1937, Akutagawa Prize), *Mushi no iroiro* (Various Types of Insects, 1948), *Mushi mo ki mo* (1965).

Ozaki Kōyō. Writer (Ozaki Tokutarō, Kōjō Sanjin, 1867–1903), born in Edo. He was a member of the Ken'yūsha literary group and became known for his long, passionate novels. At first a journalist at the *Yomiuri Shimbun,* he began his literary career after creating a magazine devoted to novels, *Garakuta Bunko* (Library of Mixtures); he later organized another literary circle to study haiku poems. His first novel was *Ninin bikuni irozange* (Amorous Confessions of Two Nuns, 1889); it was followed by *Kyara makura* (Pillow of Aloe, 1890), *Futari nyōbō* (Two Wives, 1891), *Sanninzuma* (Three Wives, 1892), *Tajō takon* (Full of Love, Full of Regret, 1896). *Konijiki-yasha* (The Golden Demon, 1902) was his last, and perhaps most accomplished, novel.

Ozaki Shirō. Writer (1898–1964), born in Aichi prefecture. At first a journalist, he started his literary career in the 1920s. His writings were felt to be too nationalistic, however, and after the Second World War he was banned from all public activity by the Occupation authorities. His most notable work was the seven-volume *Jinsei gekijō,* written between 1933 and 1960. Among his other works are *Kagaribi* (1941) and *Tennō kikan setsu* (1951).

Ozaki Yukio. Politician (Gakudō, 1859–1954), born to a samurai family in Sagami province. A protégé of Ōkuma Shigenobu, he was elected to the House of Representatives 25 times for the Rikken Kaishintō (Constitutional Reform party). He was mayor of Tokyo in 1893 and from 1903 to 1912, and minister of justice in Ōkuma's cabinet. A strong anti-militarist, he was nicknamed the "father of parliamentarism." He was imprisoned from 1941 to 1945 because of his political activities. A pavilion was erected in his memory near the Diet (Kokkai Gijidō) in Tokyo.

Ozawa Ichirō. Politician (b. 1942) from Iwate prefecture, son of a parliamentarian, Ozawa Saeki. A member of the House of Representatives in 1969, then secretary-general of the Jiyū Minshutō (Liberal Democratic party) in 1989, he left that party in 1992 to become the secretary-general of the Shinseitō (Party of New Japan), which was founded after the LDP was defeated in the election and which became part of the coalition government under Prime Minister Hosokawa. A political theoretician, Ozawa directed the formulation of a "Plan for the Restructuring of Japan," advocating decentralization and deregulation, in 1993. He was elected president of the newly formed New Frontier party.

Ozawa Jizaburō. Admiral (1886–1966) of the Japanese fleet defending the Mariana Islands in 1944 and commander-in-chief of the navy in 1945.

Ozawa Roan. Poet (1723–1801), born in Owari province, specializing in traditional waka. He wrote a collection of classic *waka, Rokujō eisō* (1811), and essays on poetics.

Ozawa Seiji. Contemporary musician, born 1935 in Shenyang, China, Saitō Hideo's (1920–74) student. A talented pianist, he studied conducting and won first prize in the 1959 international competition in Besançon, France. In 1972, he conducted the New Japan Philharmonic Orchestra and received the Japan Art Academy (Nihon Geijutsu-in) Prize. Appointed conductor of the Boston Symphony Orchestra in 1973, he has also conducted a number of orchestras in France and other European countries. He received the first Inoue Yasushi Prize in 1993.

Ozeki San'ei. Physician (1787–1839), born in Dewa province. A student of Franz von Siebold in Nagasaki, he practiced Western medicine in Sendai and Osaka. He committed suicide during the great purge of *rangaku* students (Bansha no Goku) ordered by the Tokugawa shogunate in 1839.

Ōzozō kofun. Simple-shaped *kofun,* in Kumamoto prefecture, whose inner chamber is decorated with paintings of quivers, concentric circles, épées, and "hanging mirrors."

Ōzui. Painter (Maruyama Ōzui; *mei:* Ukon; *azana:* Gihō; *gō:* Ishindō, 1766–1829) of the Maruyama school; he studied with his father, Maruyama Ōkyo.

Ōzuka. Large keyhole-shaped tomb *(kofun)* in Fukuoka prefecture (Kyushu), probably dating from the mid-sixth century; it was excavated in 1934. Its inner chamber is decorated with paintings of quivers, shields, épées, and triangles in red, green, black, and yellow. Bronze mirrors, gold ornaments, horse harnesses, and weapons were found there.

Ozu Yasujirō. Movie director (1903–63), born in Tokyo. He made at least 54 films, most dealing with social and family life in Japan, in an intimist style. He began his movie career in 1927, working in silent films, and continued without interruption until his death, producing some of the most remarkable movies in Japanese cinema. Among the most notable are *Chichi ariki* (He Was a Father, 1942), *Tōkyō monogatari* (Tokyo Story, 1953), *Banshun* (Late Spring, 1949), *Sōshun* (Beginning of Spring, 1956). No one else was able to show with such emotional intensity the life of ordinary Japanese people. Recently, one of his early films was discovered, *Tokkan kozō* (A Malicious Kid), dating from 1929, starring Aoki Tonio, which had been very successful at the time but had since been lost.

PQ

P. The sound *p* does not exist in Japanese except as a "nigorization" (*see* NIGORI) of the syllables *ha, hi, hu, he,* and *ho,* to give the sounds *pa, pi, pu, pe,* and *po.*

Pabst, Jean-Charles. Dutch diplomat (1873–1942), sent to Japan as a military attaché in 1910. Appointed a minister in 1923, he promoted the strengthening of friendship bonds between Holland and Japan. He died in Tokyo.

Pachinko. Game somewhat similar to pinball, but played on a vertical panel. The player launches balls, propelled by a small lever on a spring, that have to fall into boxes of various values but that are deflected by fixed steel bolts. Invented in Nagoya in 1948, this game quickly became a fad throughout Japan, and tens of millions of Japanese spend hours playing. Pachinko parlors offer players row upon row of these machines, and people set their eyes on the balls, forget their work and worries, and empty their minds as they play. Pachinko balls are purchased at a counter; when people have finished playing, they exchange their remaining balls (or those they have won) for merchandise, chocolate bars, cigarettes, or canned foods. Some players resell these products outside the parlor. The name "pachinko" comes from an onomatopoeia, "pachin," analogous to "clink." Some pachinko games are computer controlled.

Paekche (Paeg-che, *Jap.:* Kudara). One of the Three Kingdoms of early Korean history, along with Silla and Koguryō. Paekche (ca. 350–663), on the southwestern quarter of the Korean Peninsula, was responsible for introducing Buddhism and many other features of continental civilization to Japan.

Pages, Léon. French diplomat and writer (1814–86), born in Paris, attaché to the Chinese embassy from 1847 to 1851. A Japanophile, he wrote a great deal about the country and its history, particularly the beginnings of Christianity in Japan. He also wrote *Essai de grammaire japonaise* (Essay on Japanese Grammar, 1861) and *Dictionnaire japonais-français* (Japanese–French Dictionary, 1862–68).

Painting. The oldest Japanese paintings have been found in fairly large numbers on the walls of funerary chambers of *kofun,* and can thus be dated from about the fourth to the seventh century. Some show a close resemblance to those in similar tombs in Korea and Manchuria (notably in Tong-gou). Aside from purely Chinese motifs, these paintings portrayed allegories of the four horizons (Takamatsuzaka tomb) in fairly unsophisticated designs in three or four colors—red, blue, ocher, and white—portraying single objects: boats, horses, stars, "ceremonial fans" (?), "comets" (?), and, more rarely, human figures.

True painting in Japan began with the introduction, at the same time as Buddhism, of techniques and models from China and Central Asia. These involved mainly decorative elements, although the treasures of the Shōsō-in contain a few portraits that are colored drawings. The ancient chronicles recorded the names of some painters, including Hakuga (who came from Korea about 588); a few masters, including Kibun, Yamashiro, Suhata, Kawachi, and Nara; and artists such as Yamato no Aya no Maken, Aya no Nukakori, Koma no Kasei, and others whose works have not survived, except for the panels in a portable sanctuary, the Tamamushi-zushi, probably dating to before 645 and preserved at the Hōryū-ji. These paint-on-lacquer panels are in a clearly Central Asian style, with conventional decorative elements and characters executed in fluid lines. Painting in the following period, the Nara, has clearly Chinese characteristics; the Chinese Tang tradition is noted in portraits and sutra illustrations (such as *Kakogenzai inga-kyō,* dating from 735). These paintings were generally executed with China ink applied to hemp canvas with fine brushes and were sometimes adorned with feathers attached to the surface. The colors were pure and bright. Some dyed fabrics show Iranian and Byzantine influences, transmitted via China, in their designs. Painters belonged to "bureaus" *(e-dokoro)* sponsored by sovereigns or major monasteries.

Starting in the ninth century, religious paintings became prominent (mainly mandalas and portraits of divinities) with the introduction of new sects from China—the Tendai-shū and Shingon-shū in particular. Almost all these paintings were copies based on Chinese models and were executed as simple line drawings in China ink *(sumi-e),* sometimes brilliantly colored ("Aka-Fudō" of the Kōya-san). Portraits of sect patriarchs, also a genre imported from China, had none of the spontaneity of the originals and were generally graceless and frozen looking. When Amidist sects blossomed during the Fujiwara period, religious painting was concentrated on portrayals of Amida and his "Pure Land." Two major currents began to emerge: the Chinese style, Kara-e, and styles drawing inspiration from typically Japanese subjects, collectively called Yamato-e. The latter school was not confined to Buddhist subjects but was also used to decorate doors and mobile partitions in houses, fans, shells, and objects for daily and cult use. Subjects also included monthly work *(tsukinami-e),* the seasons *(shiki-e),* and famous places *(meisho-e),* or took their inspiration from scenes from literature *(monogatari-e)* for illustrating *emakimono* (illuminated scrolls). Drawings, executed with fluid lines, adopted a high perspective *(futai-nuki)* for interior scenes, without showing ceilings or roofs. People were portrayed in a stereotypical fashion, with extremely simplified faces (in *hikime-kagihana),* and the colors used were pure, sometimes bright. Paintings showed either a transition between the Kara-e and the Yamato-e, such as those of Kose no Takaoka's school (ninth century), or the new official style, such as the works of Kose Hirotaka (eleventh century). But few works from this period can be attributed to painters working in these two trends. Also appearing at this time were drawings with no or little color, arranged in tableaus that succeeded each other from right to left on very long scrolls, such as the *Shigisan engi*

emaki and a series of humorous drawings attributed to Toba Sōjō. A clear desire was evident to withdraw from Chinese models and create a typically Japanese art, in which realism and humor vied for attention.

In the thirteenth century, new currents arriving from Song-dynasty China updated the Yamato-e and Buddhist painting styles. Buddhist images, which had been static up to then, began to portray movement, and compositions became dynamic *(haya raigō-zu).* Paintings in *emakimono,* in contrast, remained quite isolated from Chinese influence, showing great vitality and an increased concern with realism. Scenes from life and realistic portraits *(nise-e)* became the rule. The lines used for faces were clean, supple, and sometimes weighted with color. These *emakimono*—recounting edifying stories, the founding of temples, miracles, war scenes, travel impressions, or enlightening tales— were now on paper, whereas Buddhist paintings were still executed on silk in the Chinese mode. Subjects varied, but points of view were always from on high and from a certain distance, so as to integrate elements of the environment such as houses, landscapes, and monasteries; these works were forerunners of the landscapes of the following period. There was a diversification of subjects and of ways of treating them, but it was still aristocratic painting, although a number of subjects were drawn from ordinary life. "Literary" *emakimono* continued in the pure Yamato-e tradition, with illustrated versions of great works, such as the *Genji monogatari,* being produced.

The Muromachi period (1333–ca. 1573) saw new styles form with a reemergence of Chinese influence due to the growing importance of Zen monks in society. Although some monks imitated Chinese style, others were more authentically Japanese and used the Chinese *suiboku* (China-ink wash) technique to create a new genre in which supple, flowing lines were used both to define contours and to suggest volume. Rather than simply portraying nature, painting began to seek its essence. Painters, most of them Zen monks, specialized in such subjects as bamboo, flowers, landscapes, portraits *(chinsō)* of great masters of the Buddhist doctrine, or themes designed to provoke a spiritual awakening in the viewer *(dōshaku-ga).* Because Zen had rejected the Buddhist scriptures, portrayals of Buddhist subjects became rarer, giving way to portraits of the great monks, and were made only by official painters within the *e-dokoro,* who still followed the Yamato-e style. Starting in the late fourteenth century, *suiboku* painters began to produce landscapes on horizontal and vertical scrolls (*kakemono* and *shijiku*) designed to be hung on a wall. They were often executed in black ink *(sumi-e)* and adorned with handwritten poems, with the poetry and the painting considered complementary. Most landscape painters followed the Chinese Song and Yuan styles of portraying a hermitage *(shozai-zu)*; Shūbun was one of the first to work in this genre, and, as director of the shogunal *e-dokoro,* he also painted landscapes with no religious connotation on screens. After traveling in China, Tōyō Sesshū (1420–1506) painted Chinese landscapes in the *haboku* (raised wash) technique of the Ming dynasty, with a truly Japanese spirit. He also painted flowers and birds in Japanese style, and his style was faithfully followed by many painters in ensuing generations. At almost the same time, Soga Dasoku created a more original style characterized by powerful brush strokes, which was followed by the painters of the Soga school. The painters of the Yamato-e continued to illustrate religious *emakimono* and produce portraits, but Tosa Mitsunobu (1434–1525) provided a unity of style. Another painter, Kanō Masanobu (1434–1530), using Chinese *kanga-e* techniques, inaugurated a more typically Japanese "warrior" style. His son, Motonobu, introduced color into the *suiboku-ga,* creating a style that grew in popularity during the Azuchi-Momoyama era in the late sixteenth century. After schools of religious painters were attacked by Oda Nobunaga and Toyotomi Hideyoshi, patronage of art fell to great warriors who wanted to decorate their castles and palaces as sumptuously as possible. The best-known artists of the time, most of them belonging to the Kanō family line, were freed from religious banalities and began to draw their inspiration from profane subjects, using more energetic brush strokes. For decoration of vast surfaces, they combined the decorative painting *(shōheki-ga)* of the Yamato-e with Chinese monochrome, using gold-leaf backgrounds *(kirikane):* it was the time of sweeping compositions in which the subjects had no superfluous details and were reduced to their essentials. In other schools, painters emulated the Muromachi *suiboku-ga,* such as Unkoku Tōgan, Hasegawa Tōhaku, Kaihō Yūshō, and Soga Chokuan; Tawaraya Sōtatsu drew on literary works to make very personal paintings. Elsewhere, painters of the Tosa school in Sakai and Osaka continued in the Yamato-e tradition of illustrating literary works and painting fans, but their style had grown stale and most painters of this declining school joined the Kanō school. Toward the end of the period and the beginning of the following one, a sort of genre

painting arose to satisfy the tastes of the new citizen class *(chōnin);* it soon evolved into wood-block prints *(ukiyo-e).* In Kyushu, European-style oil painting, called Yōga, appeared, portraying mainly foreign subjects from Portugal and Holland, in emulation of Western paintings brought by European merchants and missionaries. These paintings, most of them on large screens *(namban-byōbu),* were by unknown Japanese converts to Christianity.

Painting in the Edo period (1600–1868) was noted for its originality and truly Japanese character: it owed little to China. The Kanō school continued to be active in Kyoto and especially in Edo *(omote-eshi* and *machi-eshi),* creating various studios named after the districts in which they were established. Other styles developed in the Tosa school, the Kōrin school, the Shijō-Maruyama school, the Nanga school (also called Bunjinga), and *ukiyo-e* prints, a separate genre that is often placed among schools of painting.

—The **Tosa school,** composed of painters of the imperial *e-dokoro* in Kyoto (*see* KYŪTEI E-DO-KORO), continued to imitate Chinese styles, but some of its members, such as the Sumiyoshi, moved to Edo and adopted the *kanga-e* style, infusing it with a certain vigor. Toward the end of the period, the Yamato-e strongly reemerged, and this updated style, called Fukko Yamato-e, was briefly popular.

—The **Kōrin school,** inaugurated by Sōtatsu, arose with the extremely decorative works of Ogata Kōrin (1658–1716) in Edo. His disciples brought freshness and youth to Japanese painting by depicting nature in a style that was both realistic and decorative.

—The **Shijō-Maruyama school,** created by Maruyama Ōkyo (1733–95), was inspired by Chinese subjects but added a note of realism. The painters of this group worked mainly in Kyoto and added a certain poetic touch to their works.

—The **Nanga** and **Hokuga schools** (from southern and northern China) developed mainly among Confucianist men of letters *(bunjin,* whence the name *bunjin-ga)* and amateur painters. Their works, imitating those of Chinese painters but imbued with Zen spirit and more freedom of expression, were sometimes very original. They mistrusted the classic canons and tried to express their feelings freely, considering this more important than form. Yosa Buson and Ike no Taiga were among the pioneers of this genre, which had followers in Kyoto, Osaka, and Edo.

Ukiyo-e ("images of the Floating World"), the first works of which were painted and not printed, was more illustration than true painting, portraying the life of gallant women with greater realism, to please the *chōnin*. Hishikawa Moronobu (1618–94) began to produce prints using woodblocks portraying beautiful women *(bijin)* and Kabuki actors. These prints, little sought-after by Japanese connoisseurs, were "discovered" by Westerners in the late nineteenth century and reevaluated. Most of the first *ukiyo-e* were simply depictions of daily life; at first, the styles of printers and illustrators were similar. In the late eighteenth century, however, true artists distinguished themselves from the crowd of *ukiyo-e* printers. Suzuki Harunobu (1725–70) inaugurated a personal style and new coloring techniques *(nishiki-e)*, and soon *bijin* portraits began to emerge from the stereotypical mold of the early works to become truly personal creations; Shunshō, Bunchō, and Sharaku (active only 1794–75 in Osaka) did the same for portraits of actors. But it was Hokusai and Andō Hiroshige who raised the art of *ukiyo-e* to its peak with their series of landscapes and theater scenes. Other artists became famous for their skill in this genre, including Kuniyoshi and Utamaro. *See* UKIYO-E.

After 1868, *ukiyo-e* seemed to decline, even though many artists used prints for illustrations in newspapers and gazettes. Styles evolved, influenced by the European art of etching on copper and techniques of perspective. Some gained genuine fame in their genre, but overall, their style did not keep up with the times. Japanese painters tried to imitate European art; under the aegis of teachers such as Fenellosa, they created a new genre of painting called Nihonga ("Japanese painting"), in which the influence of the Kanō, Tosa, Kōrin, and Yamato-e schools was evident. Oil paints became the preferred medium. However, some, including Yokoyama Taikan, tried to update the *suiboka-ga* style; others, such as Shimomura Kanzan, tried to revive the Yamato-e style. Still others returned to ancient Chinese sources, among them Maeda Seizon, or continued the *sumi-e* tradition, including Hishida Shunshō. The era saw the emergence of a wide variety of styles belonging to no school in particular, and painters often turned from one to another without showing great creativity. Until the end of the Second World War, there was a sort of cultural stagnation, and painting simply followed literary currents. Some names emerged, such as Fujita Tsuguharu, Higashiyama Kaii, Hashimoto Meiji, and Kobayashi Kokei, but they were really only minor painters. Many became involved in research that led nowhere. After the Second World War, Japanese painters went abroad and integrated with the Paris and New York schools, completely breaking with Japanese tradition. All trends are represented in modern Japanese painting, which has not shaken off the influence of the Paris and New York schools. *See names cited.*

Paleolithic. *See* ARCHEOLOGY.

Pan no Kai. "Society of Pan," a literary and art group formed in 1908 by Kinoshita Mokutarō, Kitahara Hakushū, and Nagata Hideo (1882–1949), and named after the Greek god Pan. Tanizaki Jun'ichirō, Nagai Kafū, and Osanai Kaoru were members. This group, which followed Ueda Bin, favored symbolism in literature and impressionism in painting, and was influenced by French artists and writers. It had some impact on intellectuals of the late Meiji era, but its members went their separate ways in 1912, dissolving the group.

Paper. Traditional handmade Japanese paper *(washi)*, with its varied textures, is highly appreciated in other countries. In 610, the Korean Buddhist monk Doncho introduced paper-making and brush-making techniques to Japan, although it seems that a type of paper made from bark was known in Japan before this date. Paper was made by artisans, peasants, and families until the Muromachi period, when needs expanded greatly because of an exploding bureaucracy and the growing fashion of *shoji,* and paper-making became an industry. *Washi* paper is made mainly from a base of plum-tree bark *(kōzō, Broussonetia kajinoki)* of various sorts, including at least two types of *mitsumata (Edgeworthia papyrifera)* and *gampi (Lichnis coronata).* It was said that paper made from *gambi* was noble, paper made from *kōzō* was masculine, and paper made from *mitsumata* was feminine. Each region developed its own techniques; paper was at first reserved for very specific purposes: *sumi-e,* calligraphy, painting, writing, *shoji,* parasols, lanterns, fans, and so on. However, the habit quickly developed of carrying squares of paper to be used as handkerchiefs or napkins.

The wood is boiled so that the bark can be separated easily, then the bark is grated and carefully washed. It is boiled with potash from domestic fireplace cinders, then washed in running water to eliminate the potash. The softened bark is beaten and reduced to pulp. Once it is fine enough, the pulp is mixed with plant lime taken from the root of a plant called *tororo,* a variety of hibiscus, and rice water. Great importance is attached to the purity and temperature of the water used—the colder, the

Paper-making

better—and paper made in winter is most highly prized. After being shaped in vats on screens of silk or straw, depending on the texture desired, the sheets are pressed to squeeze out excess water and dried in the sun on tilted planks of wood. The beauty of the paper comes from the tangling of its fibers, the fineness of the fiber mixture, and additions made by the artisan: dried leaves or flowers, sometimes butterfly wings. Some paper, very thick and heavily sized, is called "Japan paper." Other paper, finer and with little size, is used for calligraphy. Artisans make colored paper by adding plant dyes to the pulp. Each family of artisans had its own procedures, and paper artisans are still very active, making mainly decorative paper. Today, paper is made industrially from various materials, including wood imported from Canada and Siberia. It is used for many purposes, but one of its greatest uses, aside from newspapers and books, is gift wrapping, an art in which the Japanese excel.

The various formats of paper used in Japan over the ages are:

—*Kaishi,* paper carried on the person, usually white, used for writing poems. About 30 × 39 cm.

—*Shikishi,* thick white paper, sometimes decorated. Two sizes: 19.5 × 16.9 cm and 18 × 15.9 cm.

—*Tanzaku,* about 5.10 × 36 cm, also for writing poems.

—*Semmen,* various sizes, for making fans or writing.

→ See CHIYOGAMI, KIRAZURI, ŌBAN, ORIGAMI, SAISEN, SHIKISHI, SHŌMEN-ZURI, SOMEGAMI, TOBI-GUMO, WASHI.

Parkes, Harry Smith. British ambassador (1828–85) to Japan from 1858 to 1883. In 1868, he was the first diplomat to recognize the Meiji government, which he supported and assisted by allowing British engineers and officers to train the Japanese navy. In 1883, he became ambassador to China, where he died.

Pasokon. A term adapted from the English "personal computer," designating personal computers introduced by IBM in 1979. Very inexpensive "family" computers, called Famikon, later became popular in Japan.

Pearl Harbor. Major port in Hawai'i, famous for having been the target of the surprise attack by the Japanese air force and navy on December 7, 1941, that began hostilities between Japan and the United States. The attack (called Shinjuwan Kōgeki in Japanese) was planned by Admiral Yamamoto Isoroku, and it sank four battleships, seriously damaged four more battleships and a dozen other ships, destroyed 188 airplanes on the ground, and killed about 3,700 American soldiers and sailors. The Japanese lost only 29 planes and 5 submarines. The attack, made without a preceding declaration of war, brought the United States into the Pacific War.

Pearls. The cultivation of pearl oysters, introduced by Mikimoto Kōkichi, has benefited from modern research and technology. The most-used oysters are *Pinctata mortensii* (Drunker); other species, such as *Pinctata maxima* (Jamson), *Pinctata margaritifera* (Dinne), *Pteria Penguin,* and *Hyriopsis schegelii* (var. *Martens*), may also be used. The old iron-wire racks have been replaced by ones made of synthetic fibers, and chemical products are used to accelerate formation of nacre. A national park and a research laboratory have been set up in Kashikojima, Mie prefecture. The pearls produced are inspected before being marketed or exported, mainly to the United States. The pearl industry annually produces between 17,000 and 20,000 kg of pearls of various qualities, about one-tenth of which are premium quality. *See* MIKIMOTO KŌKICHI.

Peiron. Race between Chinese-style rowboats (introduced from southern China) that takes place in Nagasaki in mid-June (formerly held during the Boys' Festival, or Tango no Sekku, on May 5). The boats are about 12 m long; their prows are adorned with a dragon (whence the name Peiron, from the Chinese *palong,* "dragon"), and they are crewed by 36 oarsmen. During the race, they are cheered on by gongs and drums. There are two categories of oarsmen, young and old. Also called Oshifune and Funaguro.

Perry, Matthew Calbraith. American navy officer (1794–1858) who, after a full career, was asked by American president Millard Fillmore to establish trade relations with Japan. In 1852, he set sail with a fleet of four ships (two steamships and two sailing ships); he put into port at Naha (Ryukyu Islands), then arrived in Edo Bay on July 8, 1853, and dropped anchor in front of Uraga. He delivered his credentials to the shogunal authorities and requested more humane treatment of shipwrecked sailors and the opening of ports to trade and resupply. He left for Hong Kong but returned for the Japanese response in February 1854, this time with nine ships. On March 31, 1854, he forced the shogunate to sign the Kanagawa Treaty, according to which the shogunate agreed to open the ports of Shimoda and Hakodate for resupplying ships and to accept an American consul in Shimoda. Perry then explored the coasts of Honshu and the Ryukyu Islands and returned to the United States. His black-painted ships greatly impressed the Japanese, who called them *kurofune* ("black ships"). Perry, nicknamed "Old Matt" and "the old bear" by his sailors, died without achieving the rank of admiral of the Mediterranean fleet that he had coveted.

Philippine Sea, Battle of (Mariana Oki Kaisen). "Battle of the Mariana Islands." This major naval battle took place between Japanese and American forces west of the Mariana Islands on June 19–20, 1944. The American objective was to capture the island of Saipan. The Japanese forces were commanded by Vice-Admiral Ozawa Jisaburō; the American fleet, by Admiral R. Ames Spruance. The Japanese base at Saipan was finally captured by American soldiers and served as a base for the bombing of Japan. *See* BATTLES, NAVAL.

Photography (shashin). Photography was imported to Japan in the early Meiji era by European photographers such as Felice Beato (ca. 1870) and was quickly taken up by professionals who captured the images of their time, often coloring the prints by hand. Portraits, studies of customs, landscapes, and war scenes were among the main subjects. The Japanese became infatuated with this art form, which enabled them to preserve the images that were important to them in their own way. Many schools of photography were formed, each with its own style. Photography really became popular after the Second World War, with the manufacture of Japanese cameras. These cameras, at first copies of German models, evolved rapidly and gradually took over the world market from the best American and German products, with Canon, Fuji, Minolta, Nikon, Pentax, and other brands benefiting from highly skilled labor and huge progress made in the areas of miniaturization, electronics, and optics. *See* BEATO, HOSOE EIKŌ, SAUNDERS, SAWADA KYŌICHI, SHIMIZU TŌKOKU.

Pia. Biweekly magazine published in Tokyo by Pia, Ltd., starting in 1972; current circulation, almost 500,000. The magazine gives information on shows, exhibitions, movies, concerts, libraries, celebrities, and so on, to help Tokyo inhabitants decide what to do for entertainment. An edition published in Osaka since 1985 and covering the Kansai region prints more than 100,000 copies.

Pickles (tsukemono). Vegetables or sea products dried and preserved in salt or vinegar and soy sauce, *miso,* and sometimes *sake.* There are a great number of different recipes for these pickles, and each family has its own. The Japanese are very fond of them, and always buy *tsukemono* typical of the places they visit, either to eat themselves or to give as gifts, for they are highly appreciated as presents. They are eaten with rice, tea, or *sake.* The most famous *tsukemono* are *ume-boshi,* plums soaked for a very long time in *sake* and salt. Another type of very popular *tsukemono, takuan,* consists of *daikon* (a sort of large, strong radish) soaked in salted rice alcohol. *See* CUISINE, TSUKEMONO.

Piggott, Francis Stewart. English military attaché (1883–1966) to the British embassy in Japan. After the Second World War, he became president of the Japan Society in London. In 1950, he wrote an account of his three stays in Japan, *The Broken Thread.*

Pika. "Flash of light," a word generally used to describe the atom bomb and its fatal flash.

Pilgrimages. In Japan, the custom of making pilgrimages *(junrei)* goes back to the Nara period, but it became truly popular in the Heian period, with the development of Buddhism and its spread into the lower classes. Buddhist pilgrimages are generally made in groups and consist of going to venerate, in order, the 33 western temples (Sanjūsan-sho), the 33 eastern temples, or the 88 temples of Shikoku (in Kotohira). Shinto pilgrimages, also undertaken in groups (*see* KŌ), visit specific sites such as the sanctuaries in Ise and Izumo, on Mounts Fuji and Ontake, and others. Some Buddhist pilgrims do not go on the "circuits" (which require much time) but visit a particular temple. The custom of making such pilgrimages (under religious pretext, but more often as a holiday) spread mainly in the Edo period and has remained de rigueur among many Japanese groups. *See* SANJŪSAN-SHO.

P. L. Kyōdan (Pī Eru Kyōdan). "Church of Perfect Liberty." Created in 1946 on the model of a religious organization called Tokumitsu-kyo, which was founded in 1912 by Kanada Tokumitsu (1863–1919) and renamed Hito no Michi Kyōdan (Organization of the Path of Man) in 1931 by Miki Tokuchika. Although it was of Shinto belief and followed the new order of the Meiji era, the society was dissolved by the authorities during the Second World War. Miki Tokuchika reorganized it in 1946 under its current name. It teaches that life is an art and that man has a divine nature that he must express through creativity. This organization, whose head office is in Osaka, has branches in many foreign countries and claims to have more than 2.5 million followers. Every August 1, it holds a large festival in Osaka, featuring fireworks.

Political parties. There have always been a great many political parties in Japan, especially between 1868 and 1945. Since the end of the Second World War, the main parties have been:
—The Communist party (**Nihon Kyōsantō**, founded 1945).
—The Socialist party (**Nihon Shakaitō**, founded 1945), which had various names and many factions before uniting under the name **Shakai Minshu Rengō** (United Social Democratic party) in March 1978.
—The Liberal party (**Nihon Jiyūtō**, founded 1945), which underwent many transformations and adopted various names over the years: **Minshu Jiyūtō** (1948), **Jiyūtō** (1950), **Nihon Jiyūtō** (1953), **Jiyū Minshutō** (1955), and others. The Jiyū Minshutō (Liberal Democratic party, or LDP) held power from 1955 to 1993, and all prime ministers came from its ranks, but it suffered a devastating electoral defeat in July 1993, after many of its members left to form "dissident parties," including the

Party of New Japan (**Shinseitō**), leaving it very weakened.
—The Progressive party (**Nihon Shimpotō**, founded 1945), sometimes associated with the Socialist party and giving rise to many groups: the **Minshu Jiyūtō** (1948), the **Jiyūtō** (1950), the **Nihon Jiyūtō** (1953), the **Nihon Minshutō** (1954), the **Jiyū Minshutō** (1955), the **Kokumin Minshutō** (1950), and others.
—The Cooperative party (**Nihon Kyōdōtō**, founded 1945), called **Kokumin Kyōdōtō** in 1947, which merged with the **Kokumin Minshutō** in 1950.
—The Clean Government party (**Kōmeitō**), founded in 1964. *See* SŌKA GAKKAI.
See also, for the period before the Second World War, AIKOKU KŌTŌ, JIYŪTŌ, KENSEITŌ, KOKUMIN DŌMEI, NIHON RŌDŌTŌ, RIKKEN KAISHINTŌ, RIKKEN MINSEITŌ, RIKKEN SEIYŪKAI, SEIYŪ HONTŌ, SHAKAI MINSHŪTŌ, SHAKAITŌ.

Pompe van Meerdervoort, Johannes Lydius Catherinus. Dutch navy officer and physician (1829–1908), invited by the Tokugawa shogunate in 1857 to teach medicine at the naval school (Kaigun Denshūjō) in Nagasaki, where he established the first Western-type hospital in Japan. One of his best-known students was Enomoto Takeaki. He returned to Holland in 1862, accompanied by two of his students, who finished their studies in Europe. From 1875 to 1877, he served as adviser to Enomoto Takeaki in St. Petersburg. He wrote a book about his stay in Japan, *Vijf jaren in Japan* (Five Years in Japan, 1863).

Port Arthur. Major Chinese port in the city of Dairen (Liaodong) where a number of major battles took place. The first occurred during the Sino-Japanese War (1894–95), when Port Arthur was taken by the Japanese, who suffered enormous losses, on November 21, 1894. It was conceded to Russia by tripartite intervention, which took away some of the gains Japan had made from the Treaty of Shimonoseki. During the Russo-Japanese War (1904–95), the third Japanese army, under the command of General Nogi Maresuke, took Port Arthur on January 2, 1905, after a seven-month siege that cost the lives of almost 60,000 soldiers. During the Second World War, Soviet troops captured Port Arthur on August 22, 1945, after a battle lasting only several hours. The Soviets occupied the city until 1955. Today called Lüda.

Portman, Anton L. C. American diplomat (late nineteenth century), who went to Japan with Commodore Perry as an interpreter from the Dutch. He returned to Japan in 1861 and was responsible for the American government's affairs there until 1866, when he returned to his position as secretary of the American delegation. He negotiated the establishment of a railroad connection between Edo and Yokohama with the shogunate; this line was finally built by the Meiji government in 1872, with English financial and technical assistance.

Portsmouth, Treaty of. Treaty signed on September 5, 1905, in Portsmouth, New Hampshire, between Japan and Russia, ending the Russo-Japanese War of 1904–05. Japan was represented by Komura Jitarō; Russia, by Sergei I. Witte. With this treaty, Japan obtained military and economic predominance in Korea, and Russia ceded its territories of Port Arthur and Dalian in Shandong, China, and its rights to the Manchuria railroad south of Changchun. This treaty was followed, in December 1905, by another signed between Japan and China in Beijing. However, Japan did not obtain everything it wanted from this treaty, notably an indemnity and cession of the island of Sakhalin. Both President Roosevelt, who had acted as mediator between Russia and Japan, and France had applied pressure so that Japan would not become too powerful in the Far East, and Japan had to be content with occupying the south part of Sakhalin (Karafutō).

Postage stamps. The first postage stamps issued in Japan, in 1871, were the "dragon series." They were square, unperforated, and featured a filet framework and dragons; their value in kanji characters was written at the center, from top to bottom. In 1872, this series was followed by another issue of the same stamps (with some variations in the border decoration), except that they were crudely perforated, and by new perforated stamps on Japanese paper, worth a half-*sen* and a *sen* (values written in kanji on the frame on the sides, and in roman letters on the frame on the top and bottom), called the "cherry-blossom series." The frames of these stamps were either square or oval or had fan-shaped corners, and bore the 16-petaled imperial chrysanthemum. The first illuminated series (images of a crane, a magpie, or a falcon), in a double circle containing the face value in Japanese and roman type, appeared in 1875 in the "bird" series. Also in that year, stamps were printed on imported paper with variable colors, bearing face values of 0.5, 1, 4, 10, 20, and 30 *sen*. The first stamps bearing a portrait (in an oval frame) were in the *kiku* (chrysanthemum) series and were issued from 1899 to 1908: the portrait (face values of 5 and 10 *yen*)

replaced the central imperial chrysanthemum. Japanese stamps overlaid with black kanji characters were used for Korea starting in 1900, for China from 1900 to 1926 (military stamps overlaid with two characters meaning "military letter"), and for the Ryukyu Islands (1948, 1949, and 1950, overlaid in 1952, then replaced by "regular" stamps in that year). From 1958 to 1961, ungummed temporary stamps were issued with face values in American cents.

The first airmail stamps, called "Ryukyu Islands," were issued in 1950 and portrayed a bird in flight. They were followed, in 1951–54, by other stamps showing the image of a celestial being *(tennin)* and bearing the words "Air Mail." Some were overlaid with new values in American denominations in 1959 and 1960.

The Japanese also issued special stamps for their occupation of Burma in 1942–43: square, perforated, and portraying a Burmese laborer in a rice paddy, with the inscription "Burma Post" in katakana and kanji characters. New stamps were issued in 1943 to celebrate Burma's "independence," but this time they did not bear Burmese characters, or they were Japanese stamps overlaid with Burmese characters.

In 1943–44, the Japanese post office issued stamps for Java, Malaysia, North Borneo, Sumatra, and the Philippines, bearing words in kanji and katakana. An unperforated stamp was also issued for the Philippines in 1945 to celebrate the first anniversary of this country's "independence."

The first stamps issued by Japan after the end of the Second World War appeared in 1946 to celebrate the 75th anniversary of the postal service.

Prehistory. *See* ARCHEOLOGY.

Press. In general, the Japanese are fervent readers of newspapers (90% read at least one newspaper per day). While almost all the dailies are delivered to subscribers' residences by a dense network of carriers (usually students), weeklies and monthlies are usually bought in bookstores. There are about 122 daily newspapers—though the number varies as titles cease publication, merge, or start up—divided among morning, evening, and regional editions, with a total circulation of 72 million. About 4 billion copies of periodicals are published per year. The growth of radio and television has had little impact on newspaper circulation, except for advertising, although it still accounts for almost 50% of revenues for the written press.

Most major dailies are parts of groups that also finance weeklies, monthlies, and radio and televi-

Prime Ministers

1. Itō Hirobumi, Dec. 22, 1885–Apr. 30, 1888
2. Kuroda Kiyotaka, Apr. 30, 1888–Dec. 25, 1889
3. Yamagata Aritomo, Dec. 24, 1889–May 6, 1891
4. Matsukata Masayoshi, May 6, 1891–Aug. 8, 1892
5. Itō Hirobumi (2), Aug. 8, 1892–Sept. 18, 1896
6. Matsukata Masayoshi (2), Sept. 18, 1896–Jan. 12, 1898
7. Itō Hirobumi (3), Jan. 12, 1898–June 30, 1898
8. Okuma Shigenobu, June 30, 1898–Nov. 8, 1898
9. Yamagata Aritomo (2), Nov. 8, 1898–Oct. 19, 1900
10. Itō Hirobumi (4), Oct. 19, 1900–June 2, 1901
11. Katsura Tarō, June 2, 1901–Jan. 7, 1906
12. Saionji Kimmochi, Jan. 7, 1906–July 14, 1908
13. Katsura Tarō (2), July 14, 1908–Aug. 30, 1911
14. Saionji Kimmochi (2), Aug. 30, 1911–Dec. 21, 1912
15. Katsura Tarō (3), Dec. 21, 1912–Feb. 20, 1913
16. Yamamoto Gonnohyōe, Feb. 20, 1913–Apr. 16, 1914
17. Okuma Shigenobu (2), Apr. 16, 1914–Oct. 9, 1916
18. Terauchi Masatake, Oct. 9, 1916–Sept. 29, 1918
19. Hara Takashi, Sept. 29, 1918–Nov. 13, 1921
20. Takahashi Korekiyo, Nov. 13, 1921–June 12, 1922
21. Katō Tomosaburō, June 12, 1922–Sept. 2, 1923
22. Yamamoto Gonnohyōe (2), Sept. 2, 1923–Jan. 7, 1924
23. Kiyoura Keigo, Jan. 7, 1924–June 11, 1924
24. Katō Takaaki, June 11, 1924–Aug. 2, 1925
25. Katō Takaaki (2), Aug. 2, 1925–Jan. 30, 1926
26. Wakatsuki Reijirō, Jan. 30, 1926–Apr. 20, 1927
27. Tanaka Giichi, Apr. 20, 1927–July 2, 1929
28. Hamaguchi Osashi, July 2, 1929–Apr. 14, 1931
29. Wakatsuki Reijirō (2), Apr. 14, 1931–Dec. 13, 1931

30. Inukai Tsuyoshi, Dec. 13, 1931–May 16, 1932
31. Saitō Makoto, May 16, 1932–July 8, 1934
32. Okada Keisuke, July 8, 1934–Mar. 9, 1936
33. Hirota Kōki, Mar. 9, 1936–Feb. 2, 1937
34. Hayashi Senjūrō, Feb. 2, 1937–June 4, 1937
35. Konoe Fumimaro, June 4, 1937–June 5, 1939
36. Hiranuma Kiichirō, June 5, 1939–Aug. 30, 1939
37. Abe Nobuyuki, Aug. 30, 1939–Jan. 16, 1940
38. Yonai Mitsumasa, Jan 16, 1940–July 22, 1940
39. Konoe Fumimaro (2), July 22, 1940–July 18, 1941
40. Konoe Fumimaro (3), July 18, 1941–Oct. 18, 1941
41. Tōjō Hideki, Oct. 18, 1941–July 22, 1944
42. Koiso Kuniaki, July 22, 1944–Apr. 7, 1945
43. Suzuki Kantarō, Apr. 8, 1945–Aug. 17, 1945
44. Higashikuni Naruhiko, Aug. 17, 1945–Oct. 9, 1945
45. Shidehara Kijūrō, Oct. 9, 1945–May 22, 1946
46. Yoshida Shigeru, May 22, 1946–May 24, 1947
47. Katayama Tetsu, May 24, 1947–Mar. 10, 1948
48. Ashida Hitoshi, Mar. 10, 1948–Oct. 15, 1948
49. Yoshida Shigeru (2), Oct. 15, 1948–Feb. 16, 1949
50. Yoshida Shigeru (3), Feb. 16, 1949–Oct. 30, 1952
51. Yoshida Shigeru (4), Oct. 30, 1952–May 21, 1953
52. Yoshida Shigeru (5), May 21, 1953–Dec. 10, 1954
53. Hatoyama Ichirō, Dec. 10, 1954–Mar. 19, 1955
54. Hatoyama Ichirō (2), Mar. 19, 1955–Nov. 22, 1955
55. Hatoyama Ichirō, (3), Nov. 22, 1955–Dec. 23, 1956
56. Ishibashi Tanzan, Dec. 23, 1956–Feb. 25, 1957
57. Kishi Nobusuke, Feb. 25, 1957–June 12, 1958
58. Kishi Nobusuke (2), June 12, 1958–July 19, 1960
59. Ikeda Hayato, July 19, 1960–Dec. 8, 1960
60. Ikeda Hayato (2), Dec. 8, 1960–Dec. 9, 1963
61. Ikeda Hayato (3), Dec. 9, 1963–Nov. 9, 1964
62. Satō Eisaku, Nov. 9, 1964–Feb. 17, 1967
63. Satō Eisaku (2), Feb. 17, 1967–Jan. 14, 1970
64. Satō Eisaku (3), Jan. 14, 1970–July 7, 1972

---

65. Tanaka Kakuei, July 7, 1972–Dec. 22, 1972
66. Tanaka Kakuei (2), Dec. 22, 1972–Dec. 9, 1974
67. Miki Takeo, Dec. 9, 1974–Dec. 24, 1976
68. Fukuda Takeo, Dec. 24, 1976–Dec. 7, 1978
69. Ōhira Masayoshi, Dec. 7, 1978–Nov. 9, 1979
70. Ōhira Masayoshi (2), Nov. 9, 1979–July 17, 1980
71. Suzuki Zenkō, July 17, 1980–Nov. 27, 1982
72. Nakasone Yasuhiro, Nov. 27, 1982–Nov. 6, 1987
73. Takeshita Noboru, Nov. 6, 1987–June 2, 1989

74. Unō Sōsuke, June 2, 1989–Aug. 9, 1989
75. Kaifū Toshiki, Aug. 9, 1989–Oct. 15, 1991
76. Miyazawa Kiichi, Nov. 5, 1991–Aug. 5, 1993
77. Hosokawa Morihiro, Aug. 5, 1993–Apr. 8, 1994
78. Hata Tsutomu, Apr. 15, 1994–June 23, 1994
79. Murayama Tomiichi, June 28, 1994–Jan. 3, 1996
80. Hashimoto Ryūtarō, Jan. 11, 1996–July 30, 1998
81. Obuchi Keizo, July 30, 1998–Apr. 5, 2000
82. Mori Yoshiro, Apr. 5, 2000–Apr. 26, 2001
83. Koizumi Junichiro, Apr. 26, 2001–

---

sion stations, as well as publishing houses, sports teams, theater companies, and orchestras. The largest of these financial groups associated with television networks are Asahi (TV Asahi), Yomiuri (Nippon Television Network), Fuji-Sankei (Fuji TV), Mainichi (Tokyo Broadcasting System), and Nikkei (Tokyo TV). They are assisted by national press agencies, such as the Kyōdō News Service and Jiji Press, which provide news from abroad; each newspaper has its own correspondents within Japan. The major "national" dailies, among them the *Yomiuri Shimbun,* the *Asahi Shimbun,* the *Mainichi Shimbun,* the *Sankei Shimbun,* and the *Nihon Keizai Shimbun,* alone account for almost half of total sales. They are published morning and evening in the major regions of Japan by a telematics system and are supplemented with local sections. There is also a regional press providing news that affects readers more directly. Many people subscribe to both types of publication.

Finally, there are many daily, weekly, and monthly sports newspapers (the largest being the *Nikkan Sports,* published by the Asahi group), newspapers aimed at young people and women, others devoted to *manga* (comics for young people and for adults), and professional journals with a more limited circulation. Economics newspapers, such as the *Nihon Keizai Shimbun,* the largest, are also widely read.

The dailies are usually well written and generally conservative and careful in their editorials, as they are controlled by "press clubs" that act as moderators, whereas some weeklies and monthlies put out by publishing houses feature stronger opinions, as they are often attached to large political or financial groups.

In addition to distribution within the country, the Japanese press publishes some titles (transmitted by satellite) for Japanese residing abroad, enabling them to keep up to date on happenings at home.
→ *See* ASAHI SHIMBUN, CHŪNICHI SHIMBUN, DŌMEI TSŪSHINSHA, FUJI TEREBIJON, KYŌDŌ TSŪSHINSHA, MAINICHI SHIMBUN, NIHON KEIZAI SHIMBUN, SANKEI SHIMBUN, SHIMBUN.

Prime ministers. *See* accompanying list.

Prints. *See* UKIYO-E.

Prostitution. Once quite common in Japan and confined to quasi-official pleasure districts, prostitution, in its various forms, has taken on alarming proportions since 1945. The sex industry, according to the latest official estimates, represents about 1% of the GNP. The main activities are X-rated movies and videos, prostitution in clubs and cabarets, bath houses and massage parlors, "meeting clubs" and Turkish baths, "love hotels," and "pink telephones" (Dial Q2). Annual revenues from prostitution activities (discreetly called "industries of desire") are estimated at about 4.6 billion yen (US$38 million). Given the great demand for women engendered by this flourishing industry, Japan is turning increasingly to foreigners, generally young women who come "under contract" from the Philippines or Thailand. In reality, they are imported by people who pay for their travel and force them to prostitute themselves to repay their "debt," which can be between 2 and 3 million yen. Recently, in large Japanese cities, a hue and cry has arisen over a particular form of prostitution involving schoolgirls who have agreed to pose for pornographic photographs or appear in pornographic movies. *See* GEISHA, YOSHIWARA.

Provinces and Prefectures

Provinces of the Kinai

Yamashiro (Kyoto and Nara)
Yamato (Nara)
Kawachi (Osaka)
Izumi (Osaka)
Settsu (Osaka, Hyōgo)

Tōsando circuit (northern and central Honshu):

Mutsu (Aomori, Iwate, Akita, Miyagi,
    Fukushima)
Dewa (Akita, Yamagata)
Shimotsuke (Tochigi)
Kōzuke (Gumma)
Shinano (Nagano)
Hida (Gifu)
Mino (Gifu)
Omi (Shiga)

Hokurikudō circuit (central coast of the
    Sea of Japan):

Sado (Niigata)
Echigo (Niigata)
Etchū (Toyama)
Noto (Ishikawa)
Kaga (Ishikawa)
Echizen (Fukui)
Wakasa (Fukui)

San'indō circuit (southern coast of the
    Sea of Japan):

Tango (Kyoto)
Tamba (Kyoto, Hyōgo)
Tajima (Hyōgo)
Inaba (Tottori)
Oki (Shimane)
Hōki (Tottori)
Izumo (Shimane)
Iwami (Shimane)

Tōkaidō circuit (Tokyo–Osaka region):

Hitachi (Ibaraki)
Shimōsa (Chiba, Ibaraki)

Kazusa (Chiba)
Awa (Chiba)
Musashi (Saitama, Tokyo, Kanagawa)
Kai (Yamanashi)
Sagami (Kanagawa)
Izu (Shizuoka)
Suruga (Shizuoka)
Tōtōmi (Shizuoka)
Mikawa (Aichi)
Owari (Aichi)
Ise (Mie)
Iga (Mie)

Nankaidō circuit (Shikoku and region):

Kii (Wakayama, Mie)
Awaji (Hyōgo)
Sanuki (Kagawa)
Awa (Tokushima)
Tosa (Kōchi)
Iyo (Ehime)

San'yōdō circuit (southern Honshu):

Harima (Hyōgo)
Bizen (Okayama)
Mimasaka (Okayama)
Bitchū (Okayama)
Bingo (Hiroshima)
Aki (Hiroshima)
Suō (Yamaguchi)
Nagato (Yamaguchi)

Saikaidō circuit (Kyushu):

Buzen (Ōita, Fukuoka)
Chikuzen (Fukuoka)
Iki (Nagasaki)
Tsushima (Nagasaki)
Hizen (Nagasaki, Saga)
Chikugo (Fukuoka)
Higo (Kumamoto)
Bungo (Ōita)
Hyūga (Miyazaki)
Satsuma (Kagoshima)
Osumi (Kagoshima)

Provinces and prefectures. Japan's former provinces were converted into prefectures (departments) by the Meiji government between 1870 and 1876. Japan was thus redivided and the traditional provinces were split up; the new prefectures (*ku, fu,* or *to*) were grouped, according to geographic position, into the "five provinces of the Kinai" and "seven circuits."

PS–1. Short-takeoff-and-landing sea plane, built after the Second World War for coastal surveillance missions and sea rescue operations. *See* CIVIL AVIATION.

Publishing. Publishing in Japan cannot be dissociated from the press in general because most major publishers are partners in newspapers or publish weeklies and monthlies themselves. Although there are some 4,300 publishing houses putting out books and magazines of all types and in all subject areas, as well as comics *(manga)*, audio books, compact disks, and so on, most are small, relatively specialized publishers. Most of the market falls to four major publishers: Kōdansha, Gakken, Shōgakkan, and Shūeisha, which together account for almost 40% of published titles.

One of the characteristics of Japanese books is their quality of presentation and binding. Another is the large number of paperbacks, which are very inexpensive despite their high quality. More than half of all works published are sold through a few large "national" distributors such as Tōhan (Tōkyō Shuppan Hambai) and Nippan (Nippon Shuppan Hambai), partly financed by the publishers.

The Japanese read a great deal. The most popular books are nonfiction—history, various essays, and eyewitness accounts—followed by novels and art books (which are of very high quality and affordable). Many novels are published first in serial form in daily or weekly newspapers. Print runs are often at least one million, and sales of more than 100,000 are frequent. Every year, about 37,000 new titles are published, including 7,000 novels. Sometimes, up to one-third of a print run goes unsold, a loss that is compensated for in part by diversification in "product." Publishers advertise their most recent publications in the newspapers and have inserts in the largest newspapers. In-depth articles are published on their works and their authors in these same newspapers. They also advertise on radio and television. *See* IWANAMI SHOTEN, KŌDANSHA, MARUZEN, PRESS.

Punishment (shioki). Punishments imposed on criminals during the Edo period fell into several categories defined in the *Hyakkajō:*

—*Capital punishment* (**seimeikei**): beheading *(zanzai)*, *seppuku* (for the samurai), sawing up the body *(nokogiri-biki)*, crucifixion *(haritsuke)*, pillory *(gokumon)*, burning at the stake (for commoners). Public exhibition of the head was called *sarashi-kubi.*

—*Corporal punishment* (**shintaikei**), imposed only on commoners: whipping *(tataki)*, tattooing *(irezumi).*

—*Imprisonment* (**jiyūkei**), including exile *(entō)* or confinement in a determined location *(tsuihō)*, various deprivations of liberty *(heimon,* for nobles and samurai), *jurō* and *teijō* (with chains) for ordinary people.

—*Loss of goods and property* (**zaisankei**).

—*Loss of social status* (**mibunkei**), reduction to status of *hinin* or *yakko* (for women), among others.

—*Loss of honor* (**eiyokei**)—that is, of official employment *(inkyo)*—or reprimand *(shikari).*

—*Fines* (**karyō**).

Before the seventeenth century, other forms of capital punishment were used, mainly against Christians and bandits, such as immersion in a cauldron of boiling water or oil *(hiaburi)*, piercing with a lance *(haritsuke)*, and quartering using cattle *(ushizaki)*. All of these were abolished by the new penal code promulgated in 1868. Also called *shizai.*

Puppets. *See* AWA-JŌRURI, AYATSURI-SHIBAI, BUNRAKU, BUN'YA, DOLLS, KUGUTSU.

Putiatin, Evfimii Vasilievich. Russian navy officer (1803–84), appointed vice-admiral and sent on a mission to establish relations with Japan in 1852–55. He arrived in Nagasaki on August 21, 1853, on board the *Pallada,* accompanied by four other ships. He concluded a treaty (Nichiro Washin Jōyaku), under which the Kuril Islands south of Iturup would belong to Japan, while those to the north went to Russia, and Sakhalin remained divided between the two nations. Putiatin's secretary, Ivan Aleksandrovich Goncharov, wrote a famous novel on Putiatin's negotiations, *Fregat Pallada.* At the end of his expedition (which now involved a single ship, the *Diana*), Putiatin was shipwrecked on the coast of Shimoda. With the help of Japanese carpenters, his sailors rebuilt the ship, with which they were able to set sail for Russia on May 8, 1855. Putiatin returned to Japan in 1858 to sign a friendship and trade treaty (August 19, 1858, treaty of the Ansei era). His daughter, Olga, became deaconess of the Russian Orthodox Church of Japan in the year her father died. *See* ANSEI NO KARI JŌYAKU, ANSEI NO TAIGAKU.

Qingdao (Chin.: Ts'ing-tao). Chinese port on the Shandong coast and industrial city built in the early twentieth century by the Germans and Japanese. The Germans had forced China to cede this territory for 99 years in 1898, but the Japanese captured it at the beginning of the First World War, along with other German possessions in Shandong. They kept it following the Treaty of Versailles (1919) but, faced with Chinese protests, restored it to China following the Washington Conference (1921–22). Japan again occupied Qingdao in 1937, during the Sino-Japanese War, but was forced to return it to China once again in 1945.

R

R. The consonant *r* (pronounced somewhere between *r* and *l*) is always associated in the syllabary (see GOJŪ-ON-ZU) with vowels to give the sounds *ra, ri, ru, re,* and *ro.* It is never isolated and thus cannot be pronounced aloud in combination with other consonants.

Ra. Type of fabric imported from Han-dynasty China, somewhat similar to fabrics found among pre-Inca peoples of South America. It became popular in Japan in the seventh century. Also called Ro, Sha, Usabata, Usumono.

Raden. Technique of inlaying pearls or mother-of-pearl in lacquer. Also called *aogai, kaizuri.* See MAKI-E.

Raguza, Vincenzo. Italian sculptor (1841–1928) from Palermo, who lived in Japan from 1876 to 1882 and imported the European method of casting bronze, the use of plaster-of-Paris, and the technique of modeling clay on a frame. He, Fontanesi, and architect Cappelletti taught Western art at the Kōbu Bijutsu Gakkō (Technical School of Fine Art). Raguza had a major influence on sculpture and ceramics in the Meiji era and had many students. He married the Japanese painter Kiyohara Tama (1861–1939), of whom he made a bust. Among his best-known works are bronze busts of Okubu Toshimichi and the Kabuki actor Ichikawa Danjūrō IX. *See* KIYOHARA TAMA.

Raidō. In Buddhist monasteries and temples, a room reserved for adoration and prayer.

Raigō. The "descent" of Amida Buddha to welcome the faithful when they die and take them to his Paradise of the Pure Land (Jōdo). In Jōdo-shū belief, Amida himself, accompanied by a cohort of bodhisattvas *(bosatsu)* and musicians, descends to Earth to welcome the souls of his followers at the time of their death. In the late Heian period, this concept was often portrayed in paintings called *raigō-zu,* showing Amida on clouds, accompanied by 20 to 25 bodhisattvas. *Raigō-zu* were more rarely portrayed in sculpture, but some magnificent examples can be found in the main hall of the Byōdō-in temple in Uji, dating from about 1050, and in the Jōruri-ji temple in Kyoto. In painting, Amida is most often shown accompanied only by his twelve "emanations" *(busshin),* by Kōbutsu (Buddha of Light), or by portrayals of the beings of the "six paths" *(rokudō; Skt.: gati).* Amida's different types of "welcomes" *(raigō-in)* to his paradise are described in the *Sukhāvatīvyūha (Jap.: Daimuryōju-kyō).* Some *raigō-zu* paintings, typical of the Kamakura period and Amidist sects (Jōdo-shū, Jōdo Shin-shū), are of the "dynamic" type *(hayaraigō),* in "rapid descent." First developed within the Tendai sect, to which *raigō-zu* were imported from China by the monk Ennin, *raigō* seem originally to have been mimed by costumed and masked monks during ceremonies called *mukaekō.* Later, some *raigō-zu* also included images of Miroku *(Skt.:* Maitreya), Shaka Butsu (the Buddha Shakyamuni), Jizō, and even Kannon Bosatsu (Avalokiteshvara) in one of her/his multiple forms. Also called *shōju raigō-zu, gōshō hensō, gōshō-mandara.*

• **Raigō-in.** A mudra *(Jap.: in-zō,* hand gesture) representing Amida welcoming an ordinary follower into his Paradise of the Pure Land. In Japan, these mudras are divided into nine classes, corresponding to the stage of evolution of the soul welcomed. These classes *(kubon)* are, from highest to lowest:

High class:

   Jōbon Jōshō: Jō-in (thumb on index finger)
   Jōbon Chūshō: Seppō-in (thumb on index finger)
   Jōbon Geshō: Raigō-in (thumb on index finger)

Middle class:

   Chūbon Jōshō: Jō-in (thumb on middle finger)
   Chūbon Chūshō: Seppō-in (thumb on middle finger)
   Chūbon Geshō: Raigō-in (thumb on middle finger)

Low class:

   Gebon Jōshō: Jō-in (thumb on ring finger)
   Gebon Chūshō: Seppō-in (thumb on ring finger)
   Gebon Geshō: Raigō-in (thumb on ring finger)

Raijin. The Japanese Buddhist god of thunder, a "Buddhization" of the Shinto *kami* Kaminari. His effigy is often placed at the main gate to Buddhist temples (and Shinto shrines), facing that of Fūjin (god of wind). His body is green, and he has a halo made of tambourines to chase away evil spirits. Sometimes called Raiden. *Chin.:* Lei Gong. *See also* FŪJIN.

Raijō. Buddhist monk (1044–1119) and sculptor of sacred images, Kakujō's son and Jōchō's grandson.

Raikan. Crowns worked in metal, similar to those found in Korea, uncovered in some large *kofun* dating from the fifth and sixth centuries. Also called Gyokukan.

Rai Kunitsugu. Blacksmith (1247–1327) in Kyoto, famous manufacturer of sword blades. *See also* MASAMUNE.

• **Rai Kuniyoshi.** Blacksmith (1240–ca. 1344?) in Kyoto, maker of sword blades. Also called Magotarō.

Rai San'yō. Poet (1781–1832), historian, and painter of the Nanga (Bunjinga) school; Rai Shunsui's son, born in Osaka. He studied with Furukawa Koshōken (1726–1807), Bitō Nishū, and Shibano Ritsuzan (1736–1807). Disowned by his father in 1804, he was forced to write to earn his living, so he became a historian. His works were clearly influenced by the thought of Arai Hakuseki. His main work was the *Nihon gaishi* (which took him 25 years to complete), a military history of Japan from the rise to power of the Taira to 1603; it was fin-

ished in 1827. He also wrote another historical work, *Nihon seiki.*

• **Rai Shunsui.** Historian (1746–1816), father of Rai San'yō; he belonged to the Teishū-ha school of Hiroshima, where he was principal of the academy of Confucianism in the Aki estate. He wrote many history books, among them *Fushin-shi, Shiyū-shi, Ittokuroku, Zaishin-kiji, Zaikō-kiji, Takehara bunchū, Shunsui-ikō.*

Rai Yu. Buddhist monk (1226–1304) of the Shingon-shū sect, who was director of education at Mt. Kōya in 1266 and founded the "new school" *(shingi-ha)* of the Shingon. Made a scapegoat for opposition to the traditional *kogi-ha* school, he retired from Kōya-san and made the *shingi-ha* an independent school.

Rakan. "Saints" *(Skt.:* Arhat). A term defining all Buddhists who, in ancient times, managed to free themselves completely from the ten links of karma. In the Buddhist hierarchy, they comprise the sixth rank of saintliness and are considered protectors and keepers of the Buddhist Law. According to tradition, there were 500 *(gohyaku-rakan),* but usually only 16 are portrayed *(jūroku-rakan),* although in China there are sometimes 18. They are not venerated individually and are usually represented in a group, as in the Rakan-ji temple in Ōita (Kyushu) and the Gohyaku-rakan-ji temple in Tokyo. Also called Arakan.

Rakkan. Signature or seal placed by an artist in an unused space in a painting or calligraphy. The *rakkan* sometimes bears the date on which the work was executed. This signature is sometimes represented by a *kaō.* It appeared on works more and more frequently starting in the twelfth century; before that, works were generally not signed. *See also* SAN.

Raku. Former name of Kyoto. Also called Rakuyō, Rakuchū, Saikyō.

• Family of potters from Kyoto, founded by Chōjirō (1516–92), on whom Toyotomi Hideyoshi conferred the family name Raku (I), a word that means "joy," in 1580. These potters produced ceramics called *raku-yaki,* covered with a lead glaze and fired at a low temperature (between 800° and 1,000°), used mainly for the tea ceremony *(chanoyu).* The translucent glaze was invented by Chōjirō and Sen no Rikyū, probably inspired by Korean production following Hideyoshi's invasions of Korea. *Raku-yaki* bowls were round, with a slightly narrower lip in a reddish color (ferruginous clay), or sometimes black or whitish. The glaze covers the clay only partly, and sometimes shows drips. In general, *raku-yaki* pottery is in simple shapes, with thick sides, often roughly textured. The pieces are fired in simple cylindrical kilns made of bricks covered with slate; the fireplace is placed at a right angle to the kiln itself. Chōjirō's son Jōkei and his grandson Nonkō (Donyū) also worked in this style for Hideyoshi. *Raku-yaki* not made by Chōjirō's descendants are called *wakigama*. Ceramics of this type are still being produced today. Among the most important artists following the tradition of the Raku family were Dōnyū (Nonkō, 1599–1656), Sonyū (1664–1716), Sōnyū (1685–1739), Chōnyū (1714–70), Tokunyū (1745–74), Ryōnyū (1756–1834), Tannyū (1795–1854), Keinyū (1817–1902), Kōnyū (1858–1932), and Seinyū (1885–1944). *See* AGANO-YAKI, CERAMICS, DŌNYŪ.

• **Raku Kichizaemon.** Contemporary ceramist, born 1949 in Kyoto, fifteenth generation. He took part in the Mitsukoshi exhibition in Paris in 1994.

• **Raku III.** *See* KICHIBEI.

• **Rakuza.** *See* RAKUICHI.

Rakugo. Short, humorous stories, often satirical, told by professional storytellers (*rakugoka*), often adopted by popular writers. Today, descendants of *rakugoka* families still perform in a few specialized theaters in large cities. The classic repertoire (quite reduced), is often transformed; performers improvise according to the news of the day, criticizing society and people in high places. In the era of silent movies, *rakugoka* called *benshi* were often employed to narrate the movie being shown. The most famous *rakugoka* was San'yūtei Enchō (1838–1900). *Rakugo* were also sometimes called *tsuji-banashi* (stories of the crossroads), *zashiki-banashi* (stories of the anterooms), *otoshi-banashi* (funny stories), and, in Osaka-Kyoto, *karukuchi-banashi* (stories by great talkers). Theaters used for *rakugo* are called *yose*; they were once very numerous (there were up to 392 in Edo at the end of the Tokugawa era), but very few remain.

Rakuichi. "Free markets" created by Oda Nobunaga in 1577, where *rakuza* (independent guilds, created in 1577) could freely sell their products.

Ramen. Seasoned wheat-flour noodles, eaten almost daily by most Japanese. They are sold in packaged individual servings; the noodles are boiled in water for a few minutes, then the packet of sauce and spices is added. Many small restaurants specialize in ramen, which is a strange word adapted from the Chinese *la-mian,* "stretched noodles."

Randori. In martial arts, combat training exercises, during which etiquette must be scrupulously observed and the movements (*kata,* "forms") executed precisely.

Rangaku. "Dutch science," a word derived from "Oranda-gaku," and signifying all educational studies using Western methods, which were imported to Japan in the Edo period. *See* ORANDA.

• *Rangaku kaitei.* "Introduction to Dutch Science," book written by Ōtsuki Gentaku in 1788, presenting the rudiments of Dutch.

• *Rangaku kotohajime.* "Beginning of Dutch Science," book written by Sugita Gempaku in 1815, describing work undertaken by *rangaku* scholars, notably himself and Ōtsuki Gentaku, in medicine and anatomy.

Rankei Dōryū. Buddhist monk of Chinese origin (Lanqi Daolong, 1213–78), born in Sichuan, China. He went to Kyushu in 1246 to spread the doctrines of Chan (*Jap.*: Zen), and was invited to Kamakura by Hōjō Tokiyori, where he founded the Kenchō-ji temple in 1253. He then lived at the Kennin-ji and the Zenkō-ji, having been banished a number of times because of his scandalous behavior. *Posthumous titles:* Daigaku Zenji, Daikaku Zenji.

Rashōmon. Famous film directed by Kurosawa Akira in 1950, from a story by Akutagawa Ryūnosuke and Hashimoto Shinobu, adapted by Kurosawa: it shows three versions, by each of the protagonists, of a rape and a murder. Mifune Toshirō, Kyō Machiko, Shimura Takashi, and Mori Masayuki were remarkable in the starring roles. The original, magnificent cinematography was by Miyagawa Kazuo. *Rashōmon* received the top prize at the Venice Film Festival in 1951. *See* CINEMA.

Ratenitz, Baron von Stillfried. Former Austrian officer. In 1877, he purchased Felice Beato and Charles Wirgman's photography business and started a portrait studio in Yokohama. He sold his business to Japanese photographer Kusakabe Kim-bei in 1887; between then and 1912, Kusakabe made many portraits, mainly of women and children. Von Ratenitz and another photographer, H. Andersen, published a photography book called *Views and Costumes of Japan* about 1880.

Raymond, Antonin. American architect (1888–1976) of Czech origin, who worked in Japan with Frank Lloyd Wright in 1919 and helped design the Imperial Hotel (Teikoku hōteru). Until 1937, he worked with Japanese architects, including Maekawa Kunio and Yoshimura Junzō, on many skyscrapers and concrete buildings. He returned to Japan in 1948 and designed skyscrapers, embassies, and other buildings in Tokyo.

Rebun-tō. Island in the northern Sea of Japan (Nihonkai), about 30 miles west of the port of Wakkanai (Hokkaido). With the island of Rishiri, it forms a nature park where flora and fauna are preserved. On a cliff on the island's west coast, immense basaltic columns "in the sun" dominate an archeological site from the Jōmon period. Highest peak, Rebun-dake (490 m). Fishing is the main economic activity. *Area:* 82 km². Also called Rebunjima. *See* RISHIRI-TŌ.

Red Army. *See* SEKIGUN-HA.

Red Cross (Nihon Sekijūjisha). Affiliated with the International Red Cross, the Japanese Red Cross was founded in 1877 as Hakuaisha by Sano Tsunetami. It joined the International Red Cross in 1887 and gained legal status in 1952. *See* HASHIMOTO SACHIKO, SANO TSUNETAMI.

Régamey, Félix. French painter (1844–1907), professor of drawing for the city of Paris. He accompanied Émile Guimet to Japan in 1876, then returned in 1899 to study teaching fine arts. He wrote and illustrated several interesting works on Japan: *Okoma* (1883), *Le Japon vu par un artiste* (Japan Through the Eyes of an Artist, 1890), *Le Japon pratique* (Japan in Practice, 1891), *Le Cahier rose de Madame Chrysanthème* (Madame Chrysanthemum's Pink Notebook, 1894), *Japon* (Japan, 1903), *Le Japon en images* (Japan in Images, 1904), and others. He also illustrated works of Émile Guimet, such as *Les Promenades japonaises* (Japanese Promenades).

Rei. Term for the rites (*Chin.:* Li) used mainly by Confucians who based themselves on the *Li ji (Jap.: Reiki)* to build their philosophy of observance of rites, conforming to tradition and emphasizing the importance of etiquette.

• *Reigi ruiten.* Historical work, a sort of repertory of ceremonies, rites, and imperial festivals, comprising 515 volumes and completed by Fujiwara no Tamezane in 1710. It was probably published by Mito Mitsukuni (Mito Kōmon). *See* TOKUGAWA MITSUKUNI.

Reietsu. Painter (seventeenth century) of the *suiboku* school in Muromachi.

Reigen Tennō. Hundred and twelfth emperor (Prince Satohito, 1654<1663–86>1732), Go-Mizunoo Tennō's son and successor to his brother, Sai-in. He abdicated in 1686, and Higashiyama Tennō succeeded him.

Reiheishi kaidō. *See* NIKKŌ-KAIDŌ.

Reika. Painter (Kikkawa Reika, Kikkawa Hitoshi; *mei:* Saburō, 1875–1929) of the New Yamato-e school in Tokyo. *See* FUKKO YAMATO-E.

Reiki. Era of Empress Genshō: Sept. 715–Nov. 717. *See* NENGŌ.

Reimeikai. "Society of the Dawn," a group formed in 1918 by a few liberal thinkers, including Yoshino Sakuzō and Fukuda Tokuzō, to propagate ideas of democracy among the people; it advocated universal suffrage and the lifting of restrictions on the right to strike and freedom of assembly. The group was dissolved in 1920 because its members had diverging opinions.

Reisai. Painter (active ca. 1435) of the *suiboku* school in Muromachi.

Reischauer, August Karl. American Presbyterian missionary (1879–1971). He lived in Japan from 1905 to 1941, and founded the Christian College for Young Women (Tōkyō Joshi Daigaku) in Tokyo in 1918, and a school for deaf-mutes, the Nihon Rōwa Gakkō, in 1920. He studied Buddhism (*Studies in Japanese Buddhism,* 1917) from the Christian point of view. His son, Robert, wrote a major work, *Early Japanese History, 40 BC–AD 1167.* Among A. K. Reischauer's other books was *Ōjōyōshū, Collected Essays on Birth into Paradise* (1930). Edwin O. Reischauer's father.

• **Reischauer, Edwin Oldfather.** American diplomat (1910–90), August Karl Reischauer's son, born in Tokyo. He studied with Serge Elisséeff at Harvard, then completed his education in Europe. A federal bureaucrat in the United States from 1941 to 1946, he became ambassador to Japan in 1961. He married Matsukata Masayoshi's granddaughter, Matsukata Haru, in 1956. When he returned to the United States in 1966, he taught at Harvard until he retired in 1981. He wrote many books on Japan: *Japan, Past and Present* (1946), *The United States and Japan* (1950), *Ennin's Diary: The Record of Pilgrimage in T'ang China* (1955), *East Asia: The Great Tradition* (1960), *East Asia: Modern Transformation* (1965), *Japan: The Story of a Nation* (1970), *The Japanese Today* (1988).

Reisha. Traditional, formal style of archery *(kyūdō)*, performed in a costume that leaves the left shoulder naked.

Reishi. Type of mushroom (*Ganoderma lucidum* Leys, ex. Fr. Karst) with hallucinogenic properties, called "divine mushroom of immortality," known since ancient times in China and Japan and used by shamans and Shinto priests. It grows normally in full light but is shaped like deer antlers when grown in complete darkness, which is why it was always associated with the concept of long life and venerated by Taoists and shamans. In Japan and China, it is a symbol of luck. Also called *kinoko, mannentake, waraitake.* Chin.: *lingzhi.*

Reisho. "Square" characters in Chinese *lishu* writing, used by some Japanese calligraphers. *See* CALLIGRAPHY, KANJI, SHOTAI.

Reishōjō. Japanese name for a Chinese heroine of filial piety, Lingchao, often portrayed in Zen-influenced painting as a young woman carrying a basket full of flowers. She symbolizes the virtues of Confucianism as well as the magical powers of Taoism and Zen thought.

Reiso Shintō. Syncretic Shinto-Buddhist sect (Shugen-ichijitsu Shintō) founded by Join, a monk of the Tendai-shū, in the early eighteenth century.

Reiyūkai. "Society of Friends of the Spirit." A modern religious sect issuing from Nichiren Buddhism, founded in 1915 by carpenters and cabinetmakers under leader Nishida Toshizō, and updated in 1925 by Kubo Kakutarō (1892–1944); his brother, Kotani Yasukichi (1895–1929); and Yasu-

kichi's wife, Kotani Kimi (1901–71). This largely lay movement advocates veneration of the *Lotus Sutra (Renge-kyō)* and of ancestors, as well as recitation of the title of the sutra, "Namu Myōhō renge-kyō." The sect developed during the Second World War; afterward, it was led by Kotani Kimi, who could not prevent schisms from forming within it. When Kotani Kimi died, his son, Kotani Tsugunari (b. 1936), tried to "Buddhize" the sect, building a headquarters in Tokyo in 1975. The sect claims to have almost 3 million followers throughout the world, as branches have been founded in a number of European countries and the United States. It recruits its followers mainly among housewives and low-level employees. Also called Reiyūkai-kyōdan.

Reizei Tamesuke. Poet (1263–1328) of classical *waka,* son of Fujiwara no Tameie (1198–1275), who founded the Reizei poetry school; he was opposed to the Nijō and Kyōgoku schools. About 65 of his poems were included in the anthology *Shoku gosen-shū* (1251), and his personal collection includes 319. His *Tamesuke kyōsen-shū* contains 994.

• The documents of the Reizei family, kept secret for 800 years by imperial order, were made public by Reizei Tametō (1914–86) in 1980. They included about 200,000 works and various texts, some categorized as National Treasures. They have not yet all been identified. A special library was created in Tokyo in 1981 to house them.

Reizei Tennō. Sixty-third emperor (Prince Norihira, 950<968–69>1011), son of and successor to Murakami Tennō. He abdicated in favor of his brother Morihira (En'yū Tennō) after ruling for only one year, and retired to the Reizei-in Buddhist monastery in Kyoto.

Rekishi monogatari. "Historical accounts," a literary genre somewhat imitating the style of the *Genji monogatari,* but based on facts. This genre succeeded the *Rikkokushi.* The *Eiga monogatari,* the *Ōkagami,* the *Imakagami,* the *Mizukagami,* and the *Masukagami* are in this genre.

Remmon-kyō. Shinto sect affiliated with the Taisei sect, founded in the nineteenth century by Shimamura Mitsu. It combines the theories of the Fuju Fuse (Nichiren-shū) and popular Confucianism. *See* TAISEI-KYŌ.

Rendai. Very simple wooden palanquin consisting of a platform on poles, carried on the shoulders of several men. *Rendai* were used to transport travelers across watercourses that crossed the Tōkaidō because the Edo shogunate had forbidden construction of bridges to protect itself against possible attacks. There were several types classified by size, called *hira-rendai* and *daikōran. See* KAGO, KOSHI.

Rendaku. Change in pronunciation of the first letter of a word, often to make it sound euphonious. Thus, first letters such as *h* and *f* may be changed to *b*, *t* to *d*, *s* and *ts* to *z*, *sh* and *ch* to *j*, and *k* to *g*. For example, Hito-hito becomes Hitobito, Hana-karuta becomes Hanagaruta, Iō-shima becomes Iōjima. *See* GOJŪON-ZU, NIGORI.

Renga. Poetic form created in the thirteenth century, consisting of *waka* "linked" to each other, in which ideas progressed logically. This type of "poetic entertainment" fell into disuse around the seventeenth century, when it was replaced by *haikai* and *haiku. Renga* could be quite long, from 100 to 1,000 stanzas of 5, 7, 5 lines and 7, 7 lines (*kami no ku* and *shimo no ku*). *See* WAKA.

Renga Kannon. One of the 33 forms of Kannon Bosatsu (*Skt.*: Avalokiteshvara), usually portrayed as a young woman sitting on a lotus flower. *See* SANJŪSAN ŌGESHIN.

Renge-ō-in. Buddhist temple of the Shingon-shū sect, founded in Kyoto in 1132 and rebuilt in 1251–56. It is a wooden structure 118.22 m long and 16 m wide, composed of 33 *ken* (bays between pillars), whence its popular name, Sanjūsan-gendō. It houses 1,001 statues of Jūichimen Kannon in gold-leafed wood, each about 1.2 m high, and, in the back gallery, 28 statues of Nijūhachi Bushū made by Unkei, Kōkei, and their students in the twelfth and thirteenth centuries. This large hall was part of the Myōhō-in temple. Archery contests took place on the temple's veranda every April and May: for 24 consecutive hours, the best archers in Japan competed to shoot the largest number of arrows at a target 60 to 118 m away. This contest, inaugurated in 1696, is still held every year. *See* HOSHINO KANZAEMON, WASA DAIHACHIRŌ.

Rengyō. Buddhist monk (*mei*: Rokurobei, active ca. 1298) and painter, author of the *emakimono Tōsei e-den*.

Renji-mado. In traditional architecture, a rectangular window with many vertical bars, vertical in section, typical of the *wa-yō* construction mode. *See also* KATO-MADO.

Renjō. Painter (Shimo Oka Renjō, 1823–1914), lithographer and photographer; Yokoyama Matsusaburō's master in Tokyo.

Renjō-ō. In Buddhist cosmogony, particularly that of the Shingon-shū sect, the eleventh "king of hell," corresponding to Ashuku Nyorai (*Skt.*: Akshobhya), venerated in the seventh year following a person's death. *See* JIGOKU.

Renju. Game analogous to *go*, played with black and white "stones" *(ishi)* on a checkerboard with 15 x 15 lines. The goal is to be the first to line up five stones at the intersections of the lines. Also called *gomoku narabe, kakugo, kyōgo.*

Renkyō. Buddhist monk (sixteenth century), founder of the Kōshōji-ha branch of the Jōdo Shin-shū in Kyoto.

Rennyo. Buddhist monk (Rennyo, Kenju, Rennyo Shōnin, 1415–99), eighth *hossu* of the Hongan-ji temple, headquarters of the Jōdo Shin-shū sect in Kyoto, succeeding his father, Zennyo, in 1457. The monk-soldiers of the Tendai monastery on Mt. Hiei attacked him in 1465, and he took refuge at the Mii-dera temple in Ōmi, then in Yoshizaki, on the Sea of Japan, in 1471. There, he wrote a great number of *Ofumi* (sermon-letters), thus helping disseminate Shinran's thought. In 1475, he rebuilt the Hongan-ji in Yamashina, near Kyoto, then passed his position on to Kōken in 1489. His descendants, all in the Ōtani family, are traditionally the *hossu* of the Hongan-ji sect in Kyoto. Rennyō is also known by the title Chūnagon-hōshi. *Posthumous name:* Etō-daishi. *See* HONGAN-JI.

Rensha. Small, two-wheeled enclosed cart, pulled by men. It was used during the Heian period by members of the imperial family and great nobles to move around inside the palace. *See* GYŪSHA.

Rensho. Title of a senior bureaucrat in the Kamakura *bakufu*, the *shikken's* assistant. This position was created in 1224 by Hōjō Tokifusa (1175–1240). He had to place his signature beside the *shikken's* for official acts. Also called *rempan. See* SHIKKEN.

Renza. A principle establishing joint responsibility by members of a given group *(kumi),* applied from the Heian period until 1868. *Renza* also applied both to an entire village and to groups of five people *(gonin-gumi)* or ten people *(jūnin-gumi).* If a crime was committed by one member of a *renza,* the entire group, considered a unit, was punished. This principle of collective responsibility was codified in the *Kujikata osadame-gaki* in the eighteenth century.

Rezanov, Nikolai Petrovich. Russian noble (1764–1807) sent by Czar Alexander I as Russia's representative in an around-the-world mission led by Ivan Fedorovich Krusenstern. Rezanov went with Krusenstern to Nagasaki on the merchant ship *Nadejda* in 1804, repatriating several shipwrecked Japanese and bearing gifts for the shogun. The Russian delegation waited for several months, but the shogunate refused to open negotiations and returned the gifts. Rezanov was forced to leave Japan; he went to the United States, and died as he was returning to Europe.

Rhodes, Alexandre de. French Jesuit priest (1591–1660) who settled in Japan. He learned Japanese syllabic writing and designed, with a team of linguists, the system of romanization (Qu'o'c-ngu') for Vietnamese that has been in official use since 1919. He died during a mission to Ispahan.

Ri. Former measure of length defined by the *ritsuryō* (late seventh century) as the equivalent of 16 *chō* (about 650 m). During the Heian period, a *ri* was a unit of length measuring 36 *chō* (3,927 m), a value it retained until 1868. In some regions, however, the *ri* measured 42 or 50 *chō* (4,582 or 5,454 m). The 36-*chō ri* remained in force throughout Japan until the metric system was adopted in 1951. Also called *kami-michi. See* SHIMO-MICHI.
• Unit of area equivalent to 6 *chō* according to the *ritsuryō* system, then to 36 *chō* (15.42 km²) starting in the Heian period. *See* TSUBO.
• According to the *ritsuryō* system, a term for the smallest administrative division, consisting of a hamlet of 50 households led by a *richō.* Several *ri* comprised a *gun,* and several *gun* made up a *kunin (koku),* or province. In 715, under the *gōri* system, *ri* were renamed *gō.* The *ri* was abandoned in 740.
• Legal principle *(Chin.: li)* that is the basis of the Confucian Zhu Xi *(Jap.:* Shushi) metaphysical system and seen as the source of all existence. In this philosophical system, *ri* is immanent, permanent, self-existent, formless, and motionless. The material world is the product of interaction between

ri and *ki (Chin.: qi).* However, other Confucian schools limited *ri* to its primary meaning: natural and social laws.

Rice. Japanese rice (*Oryza sativa,* var. *glutinosa*) has always been one of the country's main crops. Since its use was generalized among the common people during the Edo period, it has become a staple. There are a number of varieties, the most popular being Kōshihikari, from Niigata prefecture. Once cultivated for the wealthy and noble classes, this variety has now become common. Other types of rice, whose taste derives from the consistency of the grains and their ease of agglutinization, locally grown or imported from abroad, are called Nishiki. The quality of rice also depends on its age and on husking, drying, and storage techniques. If it is not consumed within a certain time after husking, the grains begin to oxidize and absorb water less well in the cooking process, and the taste deteriorates. It had been widely believed that rice growing began about 300 BC, coinciding with the beginning of the Yayoi culture, but a recent discovery (1992) made in Okayama prefecture, in Soja, indicates that rice was cultivated on Kyushu as early as the Late Jōmon period, about 1500 BC, about 1,000 years earlier.

Richū Tennō. Seventeenth emperor (Prince Ōeizao-wake, traditionally 336<400–05>), son of and successor to Nintoku Tennō. Hanshō Tennō succeeded him.

Ricoh (Rikō). Company that manufactures and distributes cameras, electronic instruments, and photocopiers, founded in 1936 as Riken Kanōshi to make sensitive surfaces. Its name was changed to Ricoh in 1963. It distributes products throughout the world, some of which are made in the United States, Korea, and Taiwan. Ricoh has many commercial branches abroad and exports about 35% of its production. Head office in Tokyo.

Riess, Ludwig. German historian (1861–1928), invited to teach Western history at the University of Tokyo by the Meiji government in 1887. He married a Japanese woman, Ōtsuka Fuku, and helped found the modern school of Japanese history and the magazine *Shigaku Zasshi* (Historical Journal) in 1889. After he returned to Germany in 1902, Riess published a book, *Allerlei aus Japan* (1908), a collection of his articles on Japan.

Rigen shūran. "Panorama of Popular Language," a Japanese dictionary published in 26 installments (nine volumes) in 1900 as a supplement to *Gagen shūran*. It is attributed to Ōta Zensai (1759–1829) or, with less certainty, to Murata Ryō-a (1773–1843). The revised edition, published in 1900, was called *Zōho rigen shūran*.

Ri Kaisei. Writer (Yi Hoe-sŏng) of Korean descent, born 1935 on Sakhalin; he moved to Japan in 1947. After studying Russian literature at Waseda University in Tokyo, he began to write stories and novels in Japanese. *Kinuta o utsu onna* (The Laundress) won the Akutagawa Prize in 1972. His other well-known works are *Warera seishun no tojō nite* (1973) and the six-volume *Mihatenu yume* (Endless Dreams), completed in 1979.

Rikka. Season in the old *nijūshi-setsu* calendar, corresponding to the beginning of summer, around May 5. *Chin.: lixia.*
→ *See* IKEBANA.

Rikkā Bijutsukan. "Riccar Museum," founded in Tokyo in 1972 to exhibit ukiyo-e prints. Its collection includes about 6,000 prints, and it organizes exhibitions of prints held in public and foreign collections. Its library dedicated to ukiyo-e is a valuable source for research into the art of Japanese printing. *See* MUSEUMS.

Rikken. "Constitutional," a name used by a number of political parties.

• **Rikken Dōshikai.** "Constitutional Association of Friends," a political party founded in 1913 by Katsura Tarō in order to weaken the Rikken Seiyūkai party, then in power. Katsura Tarō died in October 1913, and Katō Takaaki was elected the party's secretary-general. The Rikken Dōshikai formed a majority in the Diet after the 1915 election. In October 1916, it united with other parties to form the Kenseikai (Constitutional Association party). Also called simply Dōshikai. *See* KENSEITŌ.

• **Rikken Kaishintō.** "Constitutional Reform party," founded in 1882 by Ōkuma Shigenobu, with a moderate program advocating the establishment of a British-type parliamentary democracy. It won 46 seats in the House of Representatives in 1890. In 1896, it merged with other nationalist parties to form the Shimpotō (Progressive party). Also called Kaishintō.

• **Rikken Kokumintō.** "Constitutional Nationalist party," founded in 1910 by the merger of the Kensei Hontō (True Constitutional party) and other minority groups in the Diet. In 1922, it merged with the Kakushin Kurabu (Reform Club) and disappeared.

• **Rikken Minseitō.** "Constitutional Democratic party," founded in 1927 by the merger of the Kenseikai (Constitutional Association party) and the Seiyū Hontō (True Seiyū party), with Hamaguchi Osachi as leader. It won 216 of the 464 seats in the Diet in 1928, and Hamaguchi became prime minister in 1929. In 1930, he obtained an absolute majority with 273 seats. When he was assassinated by a terrorist, Shidehara Kijūrō became party leader, followed by Machida Chūji (1863–1946). Opposed to the rising militarism, the Rikken Minseitō had to bow to the inevitable, and it was finally dissolved in 1940, absorbed by the Taisei Yokusankai (Imperial Rule Assistance Association). Also called Minseitō (*see* MINSEITŌ).

• **Rikken Seiyūkai.** "Friends of Constitutional Government party," founded in 1900 by Itō Hirobumi to replace the Jiyūtō (Liberal party). In 1930, Saionji Kimmochi replaced Itō as its leader; Hara Takashi became leader in 1914. The party gained an absolute majority in the Diet in the 1920 election. Hara Takashi was assassinated in 1921, and Takahashi Korekiyo succeeded him as party leader and was elected prime minister. Tanaka Giichi succeeded Takahashi at the head of the party in 1925 and became prime minister in 1927. Then Inukai Tsuyoshi, elected party leader in 1929, became prime minister in 1931. After he was assassinated in 1932, Suzuki Kisaburō took over. But internal dissension weakened the party, and Suzuki announced its dissolution in 1940. Most of its members joined the Taisei Yokusankai (Imperial Rule Assistance Association). Also called Seiyūkai. *See* KENSEITŌ.

• **Rikken Teiseitō.** "Constitutional Imperial Rule party," founded in 1882 by Fukuchi Gen'ichirō and several other political journalists to boost government policy through columns in his newspaper, the *Tōkyō Nichi Nichi Shimbun*. It was dissolved in September 1883 because it did not have the government's support.

Rikkokushi. "The Six National Histories." A generic term for six historical works written in Chinese and compiled on the order of emperors, from the beginnings of Japan to 889:

1. *Nihongi (Nihon shoki)*
2. *Shoku Nihongi*
3. *Nihon kōki*
4. *Shoku Nihon-kōki*
5. *Montoku jitsuroku (Nihon Montoku Tennō jitsuroku)*
6. *Sandai jitsuroku (Nihon sandai jitsuroku)*

Rikkyō Daigaku. Private university founded in Tsukiji (Tokyo) in 1874 by the American Episcopal missionary Channing Moore Williams. It has five faculties—literature, economics, law, sociology, and sciences—with which numerous research institutes are associated. Attendance: about 12,000 students.

Rikuchū. Former province in northern Honshu, now included in Iwate and Akita prefectures.

Rikuentai. Military group (militia) organized in 1867 by Nakaoka Shintarō to support the pro-imperial faction opposing the Edo shogunate. It involved about 50 samurai operating in Kyoto. After Nakaoka Shintarō was assassinated, this commando unit continued its activities under Tanaka Mitsuaki. It was dismantled after the Restoration of 1868.

Rikugi-en. Municipal garden in Bunkyō-ku (Tokyo) created in the early seventeenth century by Yanagisawa Yoshiyasu, with a lake and hills. *Area:* approx. 10 hectares.

Rikugun Shikan Gakkō. "Army Academy," the main school of the imperial army, founded in 1868 in Kyoto, transferred to Tokyo, and then to Sagamihara (Kanagawa prefecture) in 1937. More than 50,000 officers were trained there. It was closed in 1945.

• **Rikugun-shō.** Ministry of the Army, created in 1872 by Yamagata Aritomo to replace the Hyōbu-shō (Ministry of Military Affairs). It was under the direct responsibility of the emperor. It was dissolved in December 1945. *See also* KŌBUSHŌ, MINISTRIES.

Rikuoku. Former name of Mutsu province, in northern Honshu.

• **Rikuzen.** Former province in northern Honshu, now constituting Miyagi and Iwate prefectures. Major fishing port (Rikuzen Takata) in Iwate prefecture. *Pop.:* 30,000.

Rimpa. School of painting founded about 1600 by Sōtatsu and Hon'ami Kōetsu and revived in the eighteenth and nineteenth centuries by Ogata Kōrin and Sakai Hōitsu. The paintings of this school, mainly decorative, had a great deal of gold and silver in association with bright colors, and subjects were drawn mainly from nature and the classics. The school was also known, mainly in the seventeenth and nineteenth centuries, as the Kōetsu school, Kōrin school, and Sōtatsu-Kōrin school. Okakura Kakuzō rediscovered it in 1905 and proposed that it serve as a model for modern Japanese painting (Nihonga).

Rimuse. Traditional group dance performed by the Ainu, also called Horippa.

Rin. Former unit of currency equivalent to about one thousandth of a yen. *See* YEN.
• Former unit of length, measuring 0.303 mm:
—10 rin = 1 *bu* = 0.00303 m
—10 bu = 1 *sun* = 0.0303 m
—12 *sun* = 1 *kane-shaku* = 0.30303 m
→ *See* SHAKU.
• Former unit of mass, equivalent to 10 *mō,* or 0.0375 gram.

Rinken. Painter (Shiba Rinken, sixteenth century) of Buddhist images, of the Kasuga school (Kasuga-ryū).

Rinkyō. Painter (Ishii Kisaburō; *gō:* Tempu, 1884–1930), of the Nanga (Bunjinga) school.

Rinne. Japanese transcription of the Sanskrit *samsāra,* "cycle of births and rebirths," which, according to Buddhist belief, causes all beings to be reborn after death and a time of "purification" in a sort of purgatory or hell (Jigoku), determined according to their karma *(Jap.: inga). See* INGA.

Rinnō-ji. Buddhist temple of the Tendai-shū sect, founded in Nikkō in 848. Its current buildings date from the seventeenth century. Large statue (9 m high) of Senju Kannon Bosatsu, Amida, and Batō Kannon, and other statues from the same period. Also called Mangan-ji.

• **Rinnō-ji no Miya.** *See* KITASHIRA-KAWA YOSHI-HISA.

• **Rinnō-zō.** Posture *(zō; Skt.: āsana)* of Buddhist statues corresponding to the Sanskrit *rājalīlāsana,* in which the divinity is portrayed sitting, one leg folded under itself and the other hanging vertical.

Rintō. In Buddhist temples, bronze lamp hung before the image of a divinity. *See also* KEMAN.

Rinzai-shū. Branch of Zen Buddhism by Eisai (Rinzen Zenshi) in 1191, following the beliefs of the Chan Linji (or Huanglong) sect, founded by the monk Linji (Yixuan, d. ca. 867) in China. The Linji sect belonged to the Southern school of Chan, which advocated "sudden enlightenment," as opposed to the "gradual enlightenment" advocated by the Northern school (followed in Japan by the Sōtō branch of Zen). The Rinzai-shū was revitalized in 1654 by the arrival of another Chinese Chan monk, Yinyuan Longji (*Jap.*: Ingen Ryūki, 1592–1673), of the Ōbaku-shū (*Chin.*: Huangbo) sect, then by the monk Hakuin (1686–1769), of the Myōshin-ji, and a few others who wanted to spread Zen teachings. This doctrine was introduced to the West by Suzuki Daisetsu. It makes great use of *kōan* to provoke *satori* (awakening of the spirit) among its followers. In Japan, the Rinzai has 15 subsidiary branches *(ha)* in the Kennin-ji, Tōfuku-ji, Kenchō-ji, Engaku-ji, Nanzen-ji, Eigen-ji, Daitoku-ji, Tenryū-ji, Myōshin-ji, Shōkoku-ji, Buttsu-ji, Hako-ji, Kagaku-ji, Kokutai-ji, and Ryōbō-zen-ji temples. It has about 2.5 million followers.

• **Rinzai-ji.** Zen Buddhist temple of the Rinzai sect founded in the early sixteenth century in Shizuoka. Decorated with paintings by Kanō Tan'yū (1602–74).

Rinzō. In Buddhist temples, a large rotating bookshelf, usually octagonal in shape, designed to house the sacred scriptures *(kyō)*.
→ *See* MAMIYA RINZŌ.

Ri Sampei. Korean potter (Yi Sam-pyŏng, Kanegai Sampei, Sambei, 1579–1655). He went to Japan in 1598, following Toyotomi Hideyoshi's invasion of Korea, and settled on Kyushu, where he built a number of pottery kilns in the Karatsu style. In 1616, he discovered a large vein of kaolin in Izumiyama, near Arita, which enabled him to make porcelain in a kiln that he built, with 18 other Korean potters, in Tengudani. He produced white-and-blue pieces in the Korean style of the Yi dynasty (1392–1910), and in the Chinese Ming and Qing styles, thus revolutionizing Japanese ceramics production.

Rishiri-tō. Island in the Sea of Japan (Nihonkai), located about 19 miles west of the port of Wakkanai (northern Hokkaido), south of the island of Rebun. It has a large volcano (Rishiri-zan), with an altitude of 1,719 m. Its port, Kutsugata, is an important fishing center. *Area*: 183 km². It is part of the Rishiri-Rebun-Sarobetsu National Park (Kokuritsu-kōen). *See* REBUN-TŌ.

Risshaku-ji. Buddhist temple of the Tendai-shū sect in Yamagata (Yamagata prefecture), affiliated with the Enryaku-ji temple on Mt. Hiei, founded by the monk Ennin in 860. It was rebuilt in 1543 by the monk Enkai. Ennin was buried in this temple, which houses important works of art from the Muromachi period and a statue of Yakushi Nyorai dating from the Heian period. Also called Yamadera.

Risshi. In the Buddhist hierarchy, the title of "master of discipline." Also called *jishu, jōza, jūsō, sankō, tsuina*. *See* SŌ-KAN.

Risshi-sha. "Self-Help Society," a political group founded in 1874 in Kōchi prefecture by Itagaki Daisuke to promote the Freedom and People's Rights Movement (Jiyū Minken Undō). It had originally been created to assist impoverished older samurai in Tosa province. In 1883, its name was changed to Kainan Jiyūto. *See also* AIKOKU-SHA.

Risshō ankoku-ron. "Treatise on Pacifying the State by Establishing Orthodoxy," an acerbic pamphlet written by Nichiren in 1258–60 against the Jōdo Shin-shū and Jōdo-shū. This pamphlet earned its author exile in Izu in 1261. Nichiren revised his text, making it even more virulent, in the 1270s.

Risshō Kōseikai. Buddhist organization for "friendly relations," inspired by Nichiren's doctrines, founded by Niwano Nikkyō (b. 1906) and Naganuma Myōkō (1889–1957) as Dai Nippon Risshō Kōseikai in 1938 in Tokyo. This lay organization is not affiliated with any sect, but is strictly hierarchical. One of the most powerful of its type in Japan, it has about 1 million followers, who meet in discussion groups *(hōza)*. It advocates peace and cooperation among all religions.

Risshū. In the old agricultural calendar *(nijūshisetsu)*, a 15-day period corresponding to the beginning of autumn, around August 7. *Chin.*: Liqiu.
→ *See* KAIRITSU-SHŪ, RITSU-SHŪ.

- **Rishhun.** In the old calendar, the period corresponding to the beginning of spring, around February 4 or 5. *Chin.*: Lichun. *See* NIJŪSHI-SETSU.

Ritsu. Musical scale of Chinese origin: D, E, G, B, B sharp, D. *Chin.*: *lü.* Also called Ritsu-sempō. *See* RYŌ.
  - Criminal code.
  - In Buddhism, code of monastic discipline. *Skt.*: *vinaya. See* RITSU-SHŪ.

- *Ritsuryō kyaku-shiki.* "*Ritsuryō* code." Collection of civil and criminal codes published between 800 and 1200: *ritsu* (criminal code), *ryō* (civil code), *kyaku* (decrees), *shiki* (festivals and ceremonies). It includes the codes called *Ōmi-ryō, Taihō ritsuryō, Kōnin kyaku-shiki, Jōgan kyaku-shiki,* and *Engi kyaku-shiki* (each named for the era in which it was promulgated); the last three comprise the *Sandai kyaku-shiki.*

- *Ritsuryō seido.* "*Ritsuryō* system." General legal code written in the late seventh and early eighth centuries, establishing the political and moral supremacy of the emperor and the great nobles, as well as written law. The *ryō* comprised about 900 articles dealing with functions and ranks, nobles and bureaucrats, religions and religious personnel, private houses, arable lands, taxes, the army, official costumes, state granaries, medicine, festivals, funerals, markets, criminal procedures, and more. The *ritsu,* divided into 12 chapters, dealt with the same subjects, but from the legal point of view (what was and was not permitted). Other codes were written at various intervals, adding specifics to the preceding ones. *See* RITSURYŌ KYAKU-SHIKI.

Ritsumeikan. Private university for law and politics founded by Saionji Kimmochi in Kinugasa (Kyoto) in 1900 as Kyōto Hōsei Gakkō. It now has several other faculties and a number of research institutes. Attendance: about 16,000 students.

Ritsuō. Painter, lacquerer, and sculptor of netsuke (Ogawa Haritsu, Ogawa Kan, Ukanshi Kan; *mei:* Heisuke, Kin'ya; *azana:* Shōkō; *gō:* Ritsuō, Haritsu, Bōkanshi, Muchūan, 1663–1747), born in Edo, Inchō's disciple. His lacquer works in *chōshitsu* and *maki-e* are called Haritsu-zaiku. He was also a haiku poet and Bashō's disciple.

Ritsuren-kōen. Large park and gardens in Takamatsu (Kagawa prefecture, Shikoku), including several lakes and hills, owned by the Matsudaira family in the eighteenth century, and opened to the public in 1875. *Area:* 78 hectares.

Ritsu-shū. Buddhist sect introduced from China by the Chinese monk Ganjin in 754; one of the Six Sects of Nara (Nanto-rokushū). Its doctrine draws on the teachings of the Hinayana but puts emphasis on monastic discipline *(ritsu; Skt.: vinaya).* This school of Buddhism declined in the middle of the Heian period, although it was revived during the Kamakura period thanks to the efforts of monks such as Shunjō (1166–1227), Kakujō (1194–1249), Ninshō (1217–1303), and Eizon (1201–90); Eizon founded a syncretic sect called Shingon-ritsu. Its main temple is the Tōshōdai-ji in Nara. It now has relatively few followers. *Chin.*: Nanshan Lü Zong. Also called Risshū. *See* KAIRITSU-SHŪ.

Rittō. In the old agricultural calendar, a 15-day period corresponding to the beginning of winter, around November 7. *Chin.*: Lidong. *See* NIJŪSHI-SETSU.

Rivers. The topography of Japan's islands does not allow for the formation of great rivers *(kawa, -gawa)* because of the steep slopes of the mountain ranges and the relatively short distances separating river sources from the sea. Abundant precipitation nevertheless creates a great number of small rivers and rapids whose rapid flow erodes their banks and forms major alluvial deposits at their mouths. Of more than 100 rivers, the major ones are the Shinano-gawa (about 367 km), on Honshu, which flows into the Sea of Japan near Niigata; the Ishikarai-gawa (approx. 430 km), in western Hokkaido; the Tone-gawa (322 km), in Kantō; and the Sumida-gawa (290 km) and Tama-gawa (140 km), which flow into the Bay of Tokyo. A number of rivers form lakes *(ko, ike),* some of which are large, and impressive waterfalls *(taki),* such as the one at Kegon (106 m) in Nikkō, and at Nachi (131 m). Most rivers are navigable only in their lower stretches through the plains; their upper stretches feature rapids snaking through picturesque gorges, such as the Hozū-gawa, the Kiso-gawa (175 km, also called the "Japanese Rhine") in central Honshu, and the Kuma-gawa (63 km) in Kumamoto prefecture on Kyushu. Rivers flowing through plains have been admired by poets through the ages, such as the Yodo-gawa (78 km), which irrigates the Kinai plain, and the Uji-gawa, whose source is in Lake Biwa and which meets the Yodo-gawa (also called the Katsura-gawa) near Kyoto.

Riyū. In the Ryukyu Islands, a noble who overthrew the Tenson dynasty in 1187. He was defeated and killed by Sundun (or Sondon), who proclaimed himself king under the Japanese name Shunten. *Chin.*: Liyong.

Ro. Small square fireplace, about 0.3 m per side, recessed in the floor to the same level as the tatami, used in tea ceremonies *(chanoyu)* held in *chashitsu*. *See* IRORI.
→ *See* RA.

Roads. *See* GO-KAIDŌ, NAKASENDŌ, TO-KAIDŌ.

Roban. In traditional architecture, a cubic block at the end of a *hōgyō*-type roof (with four or six slopes) supporting a bronze ornament, generally a *hōshu* or a *sōrin*.

Rōben. Buddhist monk (Ryōben, 689–773) of the Kegon-shū sect, born in Sagami province, who succeeded Korean monk Shinjō (Sim-pyöng) as leader of the sect. He was involved in construction of the Daibutsu-den of the Tōdai-ji in Nara and the casting of the great Daibutsu from 746 to 749. An adviser to Emperor Shōmu and a disciple of Dōsen, he was named head abbot of the Tōdai-ji. He was said to have introduced to Japan the text of the *Avatamshaka-sūtra (Jap.: Kegon-kyō)*. Also known by the name Ryōben. *See* KEGON-SHŪ.

Roches, Léon. French diplomat (1809–1901), born in Grenoble, sent as a plenipotentiary minister to Japan in 1864. He took part in the Western military expedition against the Chōshū clan and the bombing of Shimonoseki, then supported the modernization effort undertaken by the Edo shogunate. He allowed the export of silkworm cocoons to France to palliate the shortage of silkworms due to disease, and persuaded the shogunate to hire French military officers and engineers to construct arsenals and shipyards, such as the one at Yokosuka, begun in 1865. He also induced the French Société Générale de Banque to create a company for developing trade with Japan; when the company failed, he was forced to resign. From Paris, he continued to support the shogunate's cause in 1868. He then retired from public life.

Rōdō Nōmintō. "Labor-Farmer party," founded in 1926 by socialists, communists, and Oyama Ikuo to improve living conditions for the peasant class. In February 1928, in the first election with universal suffrage, it won only two seats. Declared illegal in April of that year because of its communist sympathies, the party was reorganized in 1929 as Rōdōsha Nōmintō (better known as Rōnōtō), but the communists had abandoned it, leaving it with no foundation. It returned to the political scene in 1948 under the impetus of Kuroda Hisao, Kimura Heihachirō (1901–75), and dissidents from the Socialist party, but it did not gain popular support and was dissolved in 1957; most of its members joined the Nihon Shakaitō (Japan Socialist party).

Rodrigues, João. Portuguese Jesuit (ca. 1561–1633), who arrived in Japan in 1577. He learned Japanese and was nicknamed Tçuz-zu (*tsūji*, interpreter). In 1591, he met Toyotomi Hideyoshi and became involved in business ventures with him, which he continued with Tokugawa Ieyasu. However, a plot against him in Nagasaki ended with his expulsion from Japan in 1610. He fled to China and died in Macao. He wrote two books on Japanese grammar, *Arte da Lingoa de Iapam* (1608) and *Arte Breve da Lingoa Iapoa* (1620).

Rō-ei. Folk songs, originally translated from Chinese. After the ninth century, this name was also given to Japanese songs accompanied by instruments. A number of *rō-ei* were included in anthologies (*Wakan rō-ei-shū, Senzai-kaku,* etc.) and novels of the Heian period. *See* IMAYŌ, SAIBARA, WAKAN.

Rōen. Painter (Hayashi Shin; *mei:* Shūzō; *azana:* Nisshin; *gō:* Shōrei, Rōen, nineteenth century) of the Nanga (Bunjinga) school; Gogaku's student in Osaka.

Roesler, Karl Friedrich Hermann. German lawyer (1834–94). In 1878, he was asked by the Meiji government to help write the Constitution (1889) and commercial code (published in 1899). He returned to Germany in 1893.

Rōgata chūzō. Lost-wax method of bronze casting, known in Japan since the sixth century; it was imported from Korea by Buddhist bronzesmiths. *See* IGARAKURI.

Rōjo. Type of Noh mask *(nōmen)* portraying a crafty young woman. *See* MASKS, NŌMEN.

Rōjū. During the Muromachi period, a direct vassal of the shogun. Starting in 1620, this title was given to the "elders" acting as advisers to the shogun. The "Council of Elders" was composed of four or five *fudai-daimyō* who alternated leadership.

They exercised a sort of dictatorship over the shogunate's bureaucrats, supervising foreign affairs, the shogun's house, the imperial house, the daimyo, religious establishments, and all citizens. They were usually chosen by the shogun from among the *wakadoshiyori*, or "young advisers." The *rōjū* of the shogunal estates were called *karō*. Also sometimes known as *toshiyori* or *rōchū*.

Rōka. Buddhist monk (1671–1703) and haiku poet.

Rōkeichi. Type of wax used in the batik method of dyeing fabrics. Also, the name for fabrics dyed with this technique starting in the eighth century. Also called Inkafu, Rōketsu-zōme, Sarasa, Shamuro-zōme.

Rokkaku. Family of *shugo* (military governors) descended from a branch of the Minamoto (Uda Genji) clan, founded by Sasaki Yasutsuna in Ōmi province in the thirteenth century; it took the name Rokkaku from that of its residence in Kyoto. Family members faithfully served the Ashikaga, but their fortunes declined after the war of the Ōnin era (1467–77). The Rokkaku resisted Oda Nobunaga, but they were defeated and their role dwindled to insignificance. *See* YOSHIHARU SHIKIMOKU.

- **Rokkaku Jakusai.** *See* JAKUSAI.

- **Rokkaku Shisui.** Lacquer master (1858–1950).

- **Rokkaku Yoshikata.** Samurai (1521–98) and Buddhist monk under the name Shōtei. He created a school of martial arts called Sasaki-ryū.

Rokkasen. The "Six Poetic Geniuses" cited in the *Kokin-shū*: Ariwara no Narihira, Ono no Komachi, Bun'ya no Yasuhide (Fun'ya no Yasuhide), Ōtomo no Kuronushi, and the Buddhist monks Henjō (816–90) and Kisen Hōshi. *See also* SANJŪROK-KASEN.

Rokkō-san. Hill 932 m high behind the port of Kobe; on it are many Buddhist temples (Tenjo-ji, dedicated to the Buddha's mother, Māyā; Tairyū-ji; etc.) and many recreational centers. Its peak is linked to the city of Kobe by a cable-car system and by roads.

Rokuchō-kai. Art group founded by a few painters in the early twentieth century, members included

Fukuda Heihachirō, Nakamura Gakuryō, and Yamaguchi Hōshun.

Rokudō. "The six paths" to reincarnation, or "the six modes of existence" *(Skt.: gati),* according to Buddhist cosmogony: Gati (ghosts), Chikushō (animals), Shura (asuras), Ningen (humans), Ten (gods), and Budda (buddhas). The images portraying them are called *rokudō-e. See also* JIGOKU.

Rokuhara. Taira no Kiyomori's palace, located in the Kyoto district of Rokuhara. In 1221, it became the residence of the two Kyoto-*tandai* (Rokuhara-*tandai*), who were chosen from members of the Hōjō family and governed jointly. This position was eliminated in 1333, when the Kamakura *bakufu* fell.

- **Rokuharamitsu-ji.** Buddhist temple founded in Higashiyama (Kyoto), as a branch (Chishaku-in) of the Shingon-shū sect, by the monk Kūya Shōnin in 963 to shelter a statue of Jūichimen Kannon that he had sculpted. It was originally called Saikō-ji. Its buildings were rebuilt in 1463 and in the sixteenth century. It contains many sculptures from the Kamakura period. This temple was one of the Thirty-Three Temples on the Western Pilgrimage dedicated to Kannon Bosatsu (*see* SANJŪSAN-SHO).

Rokuji Kannon Bosatsu. One of the 33 forms of Kannon Bosatsu (*see* SANJŪSAN ŌGESHIN), perhaps symbolizing the "six hours" of the day, portrayed holding a book.

Rokujō. In the *Genji monogatari*, a lady of the court in love with Prince Genji but spurned by him. *See* HASHITOMI.
- "Sixth bridge" of Kyoto.

- **Rokujō no Akisuke.** *See* FUJIWARA NO AKISUKE.

- **Rokujō Bussho.** *See* BUSSHO.

- **Rokujō-ke.** *See* KAGAKU.

- **Rokujō Tennō.** Seventy-ninth emperor (Prince Nobuhito, 1164<1166–68>1176), son of and successor to Nijō Tennō. He was dethroned by Takakura Tennō, who succeeded him.

Rokumeikan. "Pavilion of the Rutting Deer," a building constructed in 1883 in Hibiya (Tokyo) by architect Josiah Conder, in which Meiji high society met for sumptuous receptions and balls. It became the symbol of the westernization of Japan. The empress herself was seen there in a crinoline dress. It was renamed Kazoku Kaikan (House of Peers) in 1890. Destroyed in 1941.

• **Rokumeikan-jidai.** Period (1885–86) that saw the westernization of Japan adopted as a principle by Prime Minister Itō Hirobumi. It was symbolized by the building called the Rokumeikan.

Rokumeishū. "Where the Deer Rut," a collection of *waka* poems by Aizu Yaichi (1881–1956), published in 1940, a republication of the *Nankyō shinshō* and *Nankyō yoshō,* originally published from 1924 to 1934.

Rokuon-ji. Name given in 1408 to Ashikaga Yoshimitsu's villa in Kitayama, located near the Saion-ji temple (near Kyoto), where he had the Kinkaku-ji (Golden Pavilion) built.

Rokuon nichiroku. Journal covering the period from 1487 to 1651, kept by the Buddhist monks *(sōroku)* of the Roku-in, a temple attached to the Shōkoku-ji in Kyoto. It was written on the order of the Muromachi and Edo shogunates. These texts contain valuable information on organization of Zen temples and Kyoto society.

Rokuro. Potter's wheels that began to be used in the Yayoi period; examples have been found in Karako. They were turned by a rope wound around their axis, the ends of which were pulled alternately *(te-rokuro).* Wheels moved by the feet *(kerokuro, keri-rokuro)* and by water *(mizu-rokuro)* were introduced later, perhaps in the ninth century. *See* KIJIYA.

Rokuro-kubi. In legends and folk tales, the ghost of a woman with a disproportionately long neck who disturbs people's sleep.

Rokusai. Game similar to *sugoroku* (a type of backgammon), but played with a single die.

Rokusai-nichi. Days during which pious Buddhists fasted or were abstinent, generally the eighth, fourteenth, fifteenth, twenty-third, twenty-ninth, and thirtieth days of each month.

Rokusaku. Title for the group of six most famous sculptors of Noh masks. *See* ZŌ-AMI.

Romanization ("romaji"). The first system of romanizing syllables in the Japanese language was invented in Japan in the sixteenth century by European missionaries (among them Alexandre de Rhodes). Since then, a number of systems have been used. Aoki Kon'yō and Ōtsuki Gentaku created a romanization system based on Dutch pronunciation, rather than Portuguese. This system, *rōmajikwai,* was replaced about 1885 by a system invented by James Curtis Hepburn and the system called *kunrei,* developed by Tanakadate Aikitsu (1856–1952) in 1909, which was officially adopted by the government in 1937 and called *kokutei.* After the Second World War, this system was revised according to Hepburn's principles and called *hyōjun.* However, both systems continued to be used in Japan until the modified Hepburn system was officially adopted in the 1960s. It has been used in this book, although we have maintained the euphonic link that changes an *n* into an *m* in front of syllables starting with *b, m,* and *p. See* GOJŪ-ON-ZU, KUN, NIGORI, ON.

Rōmon. In Buddhist temples and Shinto shrines, a monumental two-story gate, faced with tiles.

Rōnin. "Men floating (with the wind)," a term originally used for peasants who had been dispossessed of their land and were working as traveling agricultural laborers. Later, the term was applied to warriors and samurai who no longer had a master or lord following a conquest or who had been dispossessed of their territory, and who therefore had to rent their services to those who needed them. They grew in numbers during the Ōnin War; some became highway bandits, others were forced to ply a trade to earn a living, and many became teachers of martial arts or guards in the corps of important personalities. Today, students who have failed to pass the entrance examination to the university of their choice and who are waiting to be accepted at another school are called *rōnin,* as are individuals who do not conform to the laws of Japanese society; the latter designation has a strongly pejorative implication. *See also* AKŌ-GISHI.

• **Rōninkai.** "Society of Masterless Samurai," a nationalist group created in 1908 by Tōyama Mitsuru, Miura Gorō, and other extremists. Its goals were imprecise, but it tended to promote the preeminence of Japan in Eastern Asia, advocating terrorism as a means of action.

Rōnō-ha. "Labor-Farmer faction," created by Marxist theoreticians opposed to the Japanese Communist party in the 1920s and 1930s. It published a newspaper called *Rōnō*. This political group disappeared in 1937 with the arrest and imprisonment of most of its members. After the Second World War, an attempt was made to revive it, with the assistance of the most left-wing faction of the Socialist party, and it published a magazine, *Zenshin.*

Roofs. Various types of traditional roofs, faced with tiles, were used for temples and palaces. The most widely used were *kirizuma* (a saddleback roof with two single slopes), *hōgyō* (with four or eight equal slopes, as at the Yume-dono of the Hōryū-ji in Nara), *yosemune* (also called *shishō*, with four slopes in a longitudinal plan), and *irimoya* (two slopes, gables and auxiliary slopes arranged around them, to which were sometimes added a sort of awning, *gohai*). The hips of these roofs were usually upturned, and their ridge beams were decorated with dolphins or stylized horse heads. The roofs of Shinto shrines followed normal styles (*see* JINJA). Ordinary houses were usually covered with thatching or cypress boughs. Some religious structures were also covered with boughs. In the Momoyama and Edo periods, some temples had roofs (notably those in *kara-hafu*) covered with copper plates. *See* ARCHITECTURE, HŌGYŌ, HONGAWARA-BUKI, IRIMOYA, KAKA-HAFU, KIRIZUMA, MINKA, MOKOSHI.

Roppō. In Kabuki theater, acrobatic dance movement performed by an actor entering or exiting the stage. Called *deha* in Osaka and *tanzen* in Tokyo.

Rosetsu. Painter (Nakasawa Gyo, Nagasawa Masakatsu; *mei:* Kazu-e; *azana:* Hyōkei; *gō:* Kataoka, Kanshū, Gyōsha, Rosetsu, 1755–99); he studied with Maruyama Ōkyo, who later repudiated him. He was a samurai in Yamashiro province (Kyoto). After leaving Ōkyo, he created his own style and exhibited his works, which featured (for the first time in Japan) mainly ordinary people, as well as animals and birds, often portrayed in a humorous manner.
→ *See* NAOTOMO.

Roshū. Painter (early seventeenth century), Sōsatsu's student.
• Painter (Nagasawa Rin; *azana:* Donkō; *gō:* Roshū, 1767–1847); he studied in Kyoto with his father-in-law and adoptive father, Rosetsu. He was a samurai in Yodo near Kyoto.

• Sculptor of netsuke (Seiryū-un, early nineteenth century) and lacquer artist in Edo.

Rosny, Léon Louis Lucien Prunol de. French Japanologist (1837–1916), who wrote many works on China, Japan, and Korea. He talked and wrote Japanese fluently, although he never went to Japan; after 1868, he often served as an interpreter for Japanese who traveled in Europe and was a correspondent for the Tokugawa shogun in the 1860s. He tried to live in Japanese style in Paris, where he was a teacher at the school of Eastern languages. He was also a founder of the Society of American and Far Eastern Ethnography (in 1858) and of the International Congress of Orientalists (in 1873).

Ruijū kokushi. "Classified National History." A work on the ancient history of Japan, compiled in 892 by Sugawara no Michizane, drawing information from the *Rikkokushi* (Six National Histories) and divided into categories in chronological order. This work comprised 200 volumes, of which only 61 have survived.

Ruijū myōgi shō. Dictionary of Sino-Japanese characters *(kanji)* compiled in the twelfth century by an unknown author, perhaps a Buddhist monk, in which each character is noted with its Japanese *(kun)* and Chinese *(on)* pronunciations. It is the oldest work of its type.

Ruson Sukezaemon. Merchant (Naya Sukezaemon, sixteenth century) from Sakai. He returned from a trip to the Philippines with large ceramic jars that were admired by Toyotomi Hideyoshi and sold for their weight in gold. These jars, used as containers for tea, had been used in the Philippines for burials, and in fact came from Song and Yuan China.

Ryakunin. Era of Emperor Shijō: Nov. 1238–Apr. 1239. *See* NENGŌ.

Ryaku-ō. Era of Emperor Kōmyō (Northern Court, Hokuchō): Aug. 1338–Apr. 1342. *See* NENGŌ.
→ *See* KAKUSHI.

Ryō. Unit of mass adopted from Chinese standards of the Tang dynasty for the *ritsuryō* codes, corresponding to about 16.08 g. It was divided into 24 *shu* (a *shu* was equivalent to 100 millet seeds), and 16 *ryō* equaled 1 *kin* (257.28 g). From the thirteenth to the sixteenth century, the *ryō* was a unit of

Roof styles. A. *Kirizuma*. B. *Hōgyō*. C. *Yosemune* or *shishū*. D. *Irimoya* (with stippled porch roof).
E. *Engaku-ji* type (13th century)

mass for precious metals, whose value varied between 4 and 5 *momme* (3.75 g) depending on the location. In the Edo period, the *ryō* became the standard gold coin of the shogunate, minted on thin, wide oval sheets and engraved with ink; it was known as the *koban,* and its weight was 4 *bu* or 16 *shu.* Another coin, called *ōban,* was worth 10 *ryō* at first, but it was devalued a number of times; by the late Edo period it was worth only 7 *ryō* and 2 *bu.* The *keichō-koban,* issued in 1601, weighed 15 g of gold at about 850 thousandths. They could be exchanged for 50 *momme* of silver or 1 *kan* (1,000 *momme*) of Chinese-type bronze coins *(zeni).* The *ryō* was renamed *yen* in 1871. Also called *shōryō.* *See* CURRENCY, MON.

• Sculptor of netsuke (Kawahara Ryō, mid-nineteenth century) in Edo.
• Name of a musical scale of Chinese origin. *See* RITSU, RYŌ-SEMPŌ.

• **Ryō-ori-noshi.** *See* NOSHI.

• **Ryō-un shinshū.** *See* RYŌUN-SHŪ.

Ryōan-ji. Buddhist temple of the Myōshin-ji branch of the Zen Rinzai-shū sect, built in Ukyō-ku (near Kyoto) by Hosokawa Katsumoto in 1450 for the monk Giten Genshō (1396–1465), fifth abbot of the Myōshin-ji. This temple, which had the sponsorship of Toyotomi Hideyoshi and Tokugawa

Ieyasu, was almost completely destroyed by fire in 1797. It is famous mainly for its sand-and-stones garden *(karesansui)*, designed by Sōami about 1455. The garden is 23 m long and 9 m wide, covered with sand that is raked every day to resemble ocean waves, and has 15 "islands," or stones, divided into five groups (5, 2, 3, 2, 3), arranged so that only 14 can be seen from any one viewpoint. It is surrounded by walls on three sides; the fourth side abuts the veranda of the main hall of the temple.

Ryōbu Shintō. "Dual Shinto," a syncretic Shinto-Buddhist school tending to assimilate the beliefs of the Shingon-shū sect with those of the shrines of Ise, in which Amaterasu is considered to be a manifestation of Dainichi Nyorai. This syncretic school probably arose shortly before the eleventh century, although its foundations are attributed to Gyōki or Kūkai. The Ryōbu Shintō was quickly divided into subschools according to the location where it was practiced. It involved secret or esoteric rituals, including that of consecration *(jingi-kanjō)*. It had almost disappeared by the nineteenth century, although some of its principles are still observed, such as the *kami* being considered temporary incarnations *(gongen)* of Buddhist divinities. *See also* HONJI-SUIJAKU, SHIMBTSU BUNRI.

Ryōchi. In the time of the Ashikaga shoguns, an estate provided to a noble *(ryōshu)*.

Ryōchū. Buddhist monk (1199–1287) from Kamakura; in 1240, he founded the Renge-ji (Kōmyō-in) temple belonging to the Jōdo-shū.
• Buddhist monk (?–1333) of the Fujiwara family. He was allied with Morinaga Shinnō and fought the Hōjō, but was killed when the Kamakura *bakufu* fell.

Ryōgae-shō. In the Edo period, merchants who specialized in money-changing and various financial operations, and who sometimes lent money to indebted daimyo. Some of them founded what became the large modern banks, such as Mitsui and Sumitomo.

Ryōgen. Buddhist monk (912–85) of the Tendai-shū, born in Ōmi. He was head of the sect *(ajari,* then *zasu)* from 966 to 985, and in this capacity had many buildings on Mt. Hiei rebuilt. He tried, in vain, to pacify the warrior-monks *(sōhei)* of the Enryaku-ji by edicting strict regulations. He received the title Hōmu in 971 and Dai-sōjō in 981,

and he was Genshin's master. The posthumous name Jie Daishi was conferred upon him in 987.
• Buddhist monk (d. 1336), founder of the Bukkō-ji branch of the Jōdo Shin-shū in Kyoto. *See* BUKKŌ-JI.

Ryōge no kan. Imperial edicts intended to complement the *ritsuryō* code of the Taihō era (701). This term also designated senior bureaucrats *(chūnagon, naidaijin,* etc.) after 702.

Ryōiki. *See* NIHON KOKU GEMPŌ ZENAKU RYŌIKI.

Ryōjin hishō. "Secret Selection of Dust." A 24-volume collection of folk songs and poems *(imayō* and *saibara)* from the late Heian period, compiled by Retired Emperor Go-Shirakawa about 1169. Only four volumes have survived.

Ryōkai. Buddhist monk (1185–1242), Fujiwara no Kanezane's eighth son and Kakujū's disciple. He was *zasu* of the Tendai-shū in 1229.

Ryōkai mandara. "Mandala of the Two Worlds," a group of two great mandalas *(Jap.: mandara)* of the Shingon-shū sect, the *Taizo-kai mandara (Skt.: Garbhadhātu)* of the manifest world, and the *Kongō-kai mandara (Skt.: Vajradhātu)* of the world of the spirit, used for meditation; their interpretation is founded on the esoteric teachings of the Shingon-shū. These two complementary mandalas are based on texts in the *Dainichi-kyō (Skt.: Mahāvairochana-sūtra)* and the *Kongōchō-gyō (Skt.: Vajrashekhara-sūtra)*, belonging to Indian, Chinese, and Tibetan canons. The *Taizō-kai mandara* comprises 12 sections portraying all the divinities of Buddhism arranged around the Chūtai Hachiyō-in (an eight-petaled lotus supporting Dainichi Nyorai and his emanations): in the north, Hōto Nyorai; in the east, Kaifuke-ō Nyorai; in the south, Muryōju Nyorai; in the west, Tenkuraion Nyorai; in the northeast, Fugen Bosatsu; in the southeast, Monju Bosatsu; in the southwest, Kanjizai Bosatsu; and in the northwest, Miroku Bosatsu. The *Kongō-kai mandara* is divided into nine equal squares portraying the attributes of the respective divinities in the *Taizō-kai mandara*. Although these two mandalas are complementary, they are not interdependent.

Ryōkan. Japanese-style inns. Usually set up in traditional houses with gardens, they offer travelers Japanese-style hospitality (tatami, futon, o-*furo,* etc.). Guests take off their shoes at the front door and give a "tip" *(hanadai)* to the hostess when they enter. Breakfast and dinner are usually included in the price.

Ryōkan Zenji. Zen Buddhist monk *(gō:* Taigu, 1758–1831) of the Sōtō-shū sect, famous calligrapher and *waka* poet, born in Echigo province. He wrote more than 400 poems in Chinese, and about 1,400 of his poems in Japanese—*waka, tanka, chōka,* and *haiku*—were included in various collections. About 150 of his poems imitate those in the *Man'yōshū.*

Ryōke. In the medieval period, a tenant farmer and operator of a *shō (shōen)* in the absence of its legal owner, usually a *honke* (noble) living in Heian-kyō. *See* RYŌSHU.

Ryōko. Calligrapher (Maki Ryōko; *mei:* Maki Tainin; *azana:* Chien; *gō:* Ryōko, 1777–1843) and founder of a calligraphy school bearing his name. He studied Chinese calligraphy styles of the Tang period, particularly those of Uyang Xun (557–641) and Li Beihai. He is considered one of the Sampitsu (Three Brushes) of the Edo period.
→ *See* SEMMIN.

Ryōkoku-hō. Legal codes promulgated by daimyo concerning their estates. Also called *bunkoku-hō, hampō (han-hō).*

Ryokuyū. Type of varnished ceramic with a green or greenish tint, obtained with copper and lead oxides, used for tiles and tiling in the Nara and Heian periods. Some jars were also varnished in this way. The name Ryokuyū comes from a town in Korea where this type of pottery was made.

Ryōmin. "Good people," a term for free people, bureaucrats or peasants, in the Nara period. The lower classes were called *semmin,* and marriages between people in these two classes were forbidden, although they sometimes took place (their children belonged to the *ryōmin* class). This distinction became completely obsolete about 900. Also called *kōmin* (little people).
• Sculptor of netsuke (Ono Ryōmin, mid-nineteenth century).

Ryōnin. Buddhist monk (1073–1132) of the Tendai-shū sect, born in Owari province, founder of the Yūzū Nembutsu in 1123. He invented a musical-notation system for Buddhist songs called Meyasu-hakase and created a school of music called Ohara-

ryū. He received the posthumous name Shō-ō Daishi. *See* MEYASU-HAKASE, YŪZŪ NEMBUTSU.

Ryō no gige. Ten-volume commentary on the Chinese legal code *(Myōhō)* written by Kiyowara no Natsuno about 833. The *Ryō no shūge,* compiled by Koremune Naomoto in 920 (30 volumes), complemented it. These two works constituted a supplement to the *Taihō ritsuryō,* written in 701.

Ryō-ō. Style of dance belonging to Bugaku, of the Rinyūgaku type.

Ryōsai-yaki. Type of porcelain created in Seto in the nineteenth century by the potter Inoue Ryōsai. He also built kilns in Edo in 1848 and in Yokohama in 1868. Also called Sumida-*yaki.*

Ryō-sempō. Japanese musical mode (D, E, F, B, B-sharp, D) divided into two types: Yō-sempō to express joy, and In-sempō to express delicacy.

Ryōsen. Painter (fourteenth–fifteenth century) of the Muromachi *suiboku* school; he made Buddhist images, mainly of Kannon Bosatsu. Sometimes also written Rōzen.
• Painter (late sixteenth century) of the Muromachi *suiboku* school.

• **Ryōsen-ji.** Buddhist temple in Shimoda, with a curious small museum on religious and folk eroticism.
• Buddhist temple founded in Ikoma (Nara prefecture) in 755. *Hondō* dating from 1283 and three-story pagoda *(sanju-no-tō)* from the thirteenth century.

Ryoshi. In ancient Japan, a commander of 100 soldiers.

Ryōshin. Buddhist monk (1024–96), *zasu* of the Tendai-shū from 1081 to his death.

Ryōshō. Buddhist monk (1622–93), *zasu* of the Tendai-shū.

• **Ryōshō Hōshinnō.** Buddhist (fourteenth century), ninth son of Emperor Go-Fushimi, *zasu* of the Tendai-shū about 1346. Also called Myōhō-in no Miya.

Ryōshu. Managers of *shōen* with effective control over their estates; they collected taxes, which were instituted in the tenth century, when the large familial and monastic estates were created. These owners, who previously had to pay taxes to the government (according to the rules of the *ritsuryō*), obtained exemptions and collected taxes for themselves. The central owners *(ryōke)* lived in the capital and left the administration and development of their lands to other, less powerful *ryōshu,* the *zaichi-ryōshu, shōkan,* or *shōke,* who lived on the land and paid a royalty to them. This system, which had weakened by the Kamakura period, disappeared completely in the sixteenth century and was replaced by the *bakuhan* system in the Edo period. *See* DAIMYŌ.

Ryōtai. *See* TAKEBE AYATARI.

Ryōtō Hantō. Japanese name for the Chinese Liaodong Peninsula. *See* PORT ARTHUR.

• **Ryōyō.** Japanese name for the city of Liaoyang, Manchuria.

Ryōun-shū. An anthology of poems in verses of seven syllables, written in Chinese and compiled by Ono no Minemori and Sugawara no Kiyokimi (770–842) on the order of Emperor Saga in 814. It includes 93 poems written by 33 authors between 782 and 814. Also called *Ryō-un shinshū.*

Ryū. "Dragons," divinities of water, rain, and clouds, associated with water cults. There are three categories of Japanese dragons: celestial (guardians of the divinities), of the clouds (guardians of rain), and terrestrial (guardians of rivers and ponds). There are a number of types: *kōryū* (with scales), *kyūryū* (with horns), *ōryū* (winged), *ichimokuren* (cyclops, rainmaker), and others. They also symbolize equinoxes: *nobori-ryū* (ascendant, in springtime), and *kudari-ryū* (descending, in autumn). A great many legends have a dragon as the central character. They are generally beneficent, and it is believed that they have the power to protect from fires, which is why their effigies are often found on the roofs of houses. Their body is never seen in its entirety, as it is partially hidden by clouds or water. While Chinese dragons generally have four or five claws, Japanese dragons have only three (or sometimes four). Dragon dances *(ryū-mai, see* AMAGOI), of Chinese origin, are often performed in villages to bring good luck or rain. *Skt.: nāga; Chin.: long; Tib.: drug, druk, brug; Kor.: ryong.*
• Term for a religious, art, or martial-arts school. *See* YAMAZAKI-RYŪ.

Ryūchi-kai. Association of partners and sculptors in the "Japanese style" (Nihonga), founded in 1878 by E. Fenellosa for the preservation of traditional arts. It gave rise to the Nihon Bijutsu Kyōkai, founded in 1887.

Ryū Chishū. Movie actor (1906–93), born in Kumamoto. He was one of director Ozu Yasujirō's favorite actors starting in 1935, and he appeared in many movies directed by Kinoshita Keisuke and Kurosawa Akira *(Akahige, Yume).*

Ryūei. Painter (Momota Morimitsu; *mei:* Buzaemon; *gō:* Yūkōsai Ryūei, 1647–98) of the Kanō school; Kanō Tan'yū's student in Edo.

Ryūen. Buddhist monk (?–1015) of the Ritsu-shū sect, eighth son of Kampaku Fujiwara no Michitaka. He was *risshi,* then *sōzu* in 994.
→ *See* AOYAGI TANENOBU.

Ryūho. Painter (Nonoguchi Chikashige, Hinaya Ryūhō; *gō:* Shōō Ryūhō, ca. 1595 or 1599–1669), Kanō Tan'yū's student in Edo, and haiku poet (Teitoku's disciple). He also sculpted dolls and netsuke.
• Painter (Fukushima Nei; *mei:* Shigeji-rō; *azana:* Shichoku; *gō:* Mokudō, Ryūhō, 1820–89) of the Nanga school (Bunjinga); Zeshin's student in Edo.

Ryūkaku. Buddhist monk (1088–1158), *sōjō* of the Hossō-shu.

Ryūkan. Buddhist monk (Muga, Kaikū, 1148–1227) of the Jōdo-shū, Hōnen's disciple and author of works on faith in Amida. He founded the Chōraku-ji of the Jōdo-shū.

Ryūko. Painter (Takaku Ryūko; *mei:* Onoshirō; *azana:* Jutsuji; *gō:* Ryūko, 1801–59) of the Fukko Yamato-e school, Aigai's adoptive son; studied with Kyoshi and Ikke. He painted mainly historical subjects.

Ryūkō. Buddhist monk (1649–1724) of the Chikaku-in temple, shogun Tokugawa Tsunayoshi's friend and adviser.

Ryūkōgo. Words and phrases typical of a period or a region, generally created (or adapted) by people to describe new situations and social or economic changes. Since the end of the Second World War, they have generally been foreign words, many of them from English. *See* INGO.

Ryūkōka. Folk songs influenced by European music, which came into fashion after the Meiji Restoration (1868), taken from European plays and movies, children's songs with Western tunes and Japanese words, war songs, various lyrics *(jojōka)*, and work songs *(rōdōka)*. Before the popularization of records and tapes, these songs were performed for the general public by street singers *(enkashi)*, accompanying themselves on a sort of violin *(kokyū)* or a shamisen. These songs are now inspired by recordings and television, and many famous singers (Misora Hibari, for example) perform them. *See also* IMAYŌ, KARAOKE.

Ryūkyū Islands (*Chin.:* Luchu.). Archipelago between Kyushu and Taiwan, extending more than 1,200 km from north to south. Its islands are divided into three groups: Amami to the north, Okinawa in the center, and Sakishima to the south. There are about 60 islands and several hundred islets, covering an area of about 3,300 km²; the total population is about 1.2 million. The main, and largest, island is Okinawa. The other major islands include Kume, Kerama, Tonaki, Aguni, Ie, Iheya, Izena, Yoron, and Okinoerabu; most of them are volcanic or coralline. These islands were the theater of terrible battles between American and Japanese troops in 1945. After the Second World War, they were placed under American administration, but were returned to Japan in 1953 and 1972.

According to legend, the kingdom of the Ryūkyū Islands was founded by the dynasty of the Tenson (*Chin.:* Tiansun) family *(shi)*, whose descendants are said to have reigned for 25 successive generations. The dynasty was defeated in 1187 by a noble called Riyū (*Chin.:* Li Yong); Riyū was in his turn defeated by Sonton (Sundin, *Chin.:* Suntian), who proclaimed himself king with the name Shunten-ō. Shunten's grandfather, Yi Ben (Yoshimoto), had abdicated in favor of a descendant of the Tenson, Ying Zu (Eizō). After the fourth generation, the country was split into two rival kingdoms, Samboku in the north and Sannan in the south. King Yucheng Wang (Gyokusei-ō) then changed his title to Zhongshan Wang (*Jap.:* Chūsan-ō), king of Chūsan. When he died in 1337, the *anji* of Urasoi, Satsudo (Chadu), was elected king of Chūsan. He opposed the kingdoms of Samboku and Sannan, and paid tax to the Ming Chinese starting in 1372. In 1404, the Chinese emperors placed imperial prince Wuling (*Jap.:* Murei) on the throne of Chūsan. He was overthrown the following year by the *anji* of Sashiki, Shang Bazhi (*Jap.:* Shōhashi), who put his father, Si Shao (*Jap.:* Shishō), on the throne; he managed to reunite the three kingdoms and declared his own era *(nengō)*, Shōhashi (1422–39). In 1469, when Shangde Wang (*Jap.:* Shōtoku-ō) died, a descendant of Shunten-ō, Shang Yuan (*Jap.:* Shōen), was elected king of Chūsan. His family line continued to rule until Shang Ning (*Jap.:* Shōrei), who was captured in 1609 by troops sent by the daimyo of Satsuma (Kyushu) and brought to Edo. Japan then annexed the Amami Islands and declared the Ryūkyū Islands a vassal state. The last king of the Ryūkyū Islands was taken prisoner by the Japanese in 1879, and thereafter the Ryūkyū Islands were an integral part of the Japanese empire.

The inhabitants of the Ryūkyū Islands practice a sort of primitive Shinto religion with priestess-shamanesses *(nuru, noro)* as officiants. The language of Okinawa and the other islands resembles Japanese, but with considerable variants from one island to another, especially in terms of pronunciation. The dialects of the Ryūkyū Islands also have typical words that are not found in Japanese. This is due to the fact that from prehistoric times, the islands of the north had close relations with Kyushu, while the southern islands were closer to Taiwan. Japanese seems to have been introduced to the islands around the second century AD; in the seventeenth century, the conquerors of the Shimazu family imposed their language on the inhabitants, while depriving them of all of their weapons (even simple knives) to prevent any rebellion. Okinawans defended themselves against the samurai by inventing bare-hands combat techniques (Okinawa-te) or using agricultural instruments that were later adapted for use in the Japanese karate and *ko-budō* techniques.

• **Ryūkyū Daigaku.** National university founded in Naha (Okinawa-ku) in 1950, which received official status in 1972. It includes a number of faculties (sciences, education, engineering, agriculture, etc.); attendance, about 4,500 students.

• **Ryūkyū kizoku mondai.** A dispute between China and Japan at the beginning of the Meiji period over possession of the Ryūkyū Islands, on the pretext that the ancient sovereigns of the islands had always paid an allegiance tax to China. The king of the Ryūkyū Islands had signed a treaty with Commodore Perry in 1854, and one with France in 1855. But after the Japanese expedition was launched against Taiwan in 1874, China tacitly recognized Japanese sovereignty over the islands by agreeing to pay Japan an indemnity for the massacre of 54 shipwrecked sailors from the islands by aboriginals on Taiwan. The islands were included in Okinawa prefecture in 1879, over China's protests. The Ryūkyū Islands became definitively Japanese after the Treaty of Shimonoseki (1895) was signed to end the war between China and Japan (1894–95).

• **Ryūkyū sempō.** Okinawan musical mode (D, F, G, B, C, D) used in traditional Japanese music.

• *Ryūkyū shintō-ki.* Book describing the Ryūkyū Islands and their inhabitants, written by a Japanese Buddhist monk, Taichū Shōnin, in 1648.

• **Ryūkyū tōki.** Type of pottery, for daily use, made on the Ryūkyū Islands according to techniques from China and Korea. Types include *arayachi* (in the south), *jōyachi* (with slip), and *tsuboya.*

Ryūmei. Buddhist monk (1020–ca. 1104) of the Tendai-shū, grandson of *kampaku* Fujiwara no Michitaka. Appointed *sōjō* in 1091, he was chaplain to the imperial court. Also called Ryūmyō.
• Name given to Indian monk Nāgārjuna. Also called Ryūmyō.

Ryūsai Shigeharu. Painter of ukiyo-e prints (1820–70) in Osaka.

Ryūtatsu-bushi. Folk songs from the early Edo period, originally written by the Buddhist monk Ryūtatsu, of the Nichiren sect, performed with accompaniment by tambourines and *shakuhachi*. *See* IMAYŌ, RYŪKŌKA.

Ryūtei Rijō. Writer (Ikeda Yaemon, d. 1841), born in Edo, perhaps Tamenaga Shunsui's brother. He wrote many popular novels in the *kokkeibon* genre, describing the light side of life of Edo residents. His most famous novels are *Hanagoyomi hasshōjin* and *Kokkei wagōjin,* which were finished by other authors after his death.

Ryūtei Tanehiko. Writer (Takaya Hikoshirō, 1783–1842), born in Edo to a samurai family, author of light novels *(gesaku)* and historical novels *(yomihon),* as well as essays on the literature of his time. He is best known for *Inaka Genji,* published from 1829 to 1842, a rustic parody of the *Genji monogatari* (complete title: *Nise-Murasaki inaka Genji,* A False Murasaki and a Mystical Genji), and *Ukiyo-gata rokumai byōbu* (Six Screens Around the World, 1821).

Ryūteki. Concert flute used in *gagaku* orchestras. Also called Ryōteki. *See* FLUTES.

Ryūzan Tokuken. Buddhist monk (1284–1359) famous for having traveled to Yuan-dynasty China arbout 1305.

Ryūzōji. Family of provincial lords and daimyo of western Kyushu, founded in 1186 by Fujiwara no Sueie, *jitō* in Hizen province. Its members took Ashikaga Takauji's side in 1336, but they were defeated in an attempt to conquer the territories of the Ōtomi and Shimazu families, and their estate was taken over by neighbors. The most famous members of this family were Ryūzōji Takanobu (1529–1584), who expanded his territories at the expense of the Shōni, and his son, Ryūzōji Masaie (1566–1607), who was killed in battle.

Ryūzū Kannon. One of the 33 forms (Sanjūsan Ōgeshin) of Kannon Bosatsu (*Skt.:* Avalokiteshvara), portrayed as a woman sitting on a dragon *(ryū)* or on the back of a sea turtle *(kame).* The veil on her head partly hides the small effigy *(kebutsu)* of Amida in her hair. In her hand she holds a blossoming lotus flower, or she holds her hands in the *dhyana-mudrā (Jap.: jō-in)* hidden under her dress. A large modern statue of this Bodhisattva, in cement, was recently erected at the foot of the Higashiyama hill in Kyoto.

S. This consonant is always associated with vowels to give *sa, si, su, se,* and *so.* The syllable *si* does not exist in Hepburn transcription (used in this book), although it does exist in the previous system of transcription; it is now replaced by the syllable *shi.* It is combined with the syllables *ya, yo, yō, yu,* and *yū* to give the complex syllables *sha, sho, shō, shu,* and *shū.*

Sabi. Aesthetic concept that developed during the Muromachi period, in which restraint and simplicity are more important than brilliant appearance. The interior nature of things is considered primarily, and less attention is paid to their exterior. In art, this concept was used mainly in the tea ceremony *(chanoyu),* and it is the basis for the visual simplicity of teahouses *(chashitsu)* and of the pottery *(chasen)* and implements used in the tea ceremony. In the twelfth century, the concept appeared in literature and poetry, proposing that descriptions be more allusive and suggestive than factual. One of the first poets to use *sabi* was Fujiwara no Toshinari (1114–1204), but Matsuo Bashō expressed it the best in his haiku, by emphasizing the beauty of natural things. *Sabi* also includes a feeling of solitude *(sabishi),* desolation *(susabi),* and serene resignation. *See also* YŪGEN.

Saburai. Old form of the word "samurai," derived from the verb *sabaru,* "to stay to the side." Guards in the corps of great nobles and vassals were called *saburai* in the ninth and tenth centuries. *See* SAMURAI-DOKORO.

• **Saburai-dokoro.** In the Kamakura period, the military department of the *bakufu. See* SAMURAI-DOKORO.

Sadaijin. In the ancient imperial government, "minister of the left" *(sa),* with a rank between *dajō-daijin* and *udaijin.* Also called Ichi no Kami, *safu. See* DAIJIN, ZUISHIN.

Sada Keiji. Movie actor (Nakai Hiroshi, 1926–64), born in Kyoto, who worked for the Shōchiku Company. After making his debut in 1937, in a movie by Kinoshita Keisuke, *Fushichō* (The Phoenix), he rapidly became a star. He also worked with directors Oba Hideo and Ozu Yasujirō. He died in an automobile accident.

Sado. Island in the Sea of Japan (Nihonkai) 35 km offshore from Niigata. It is mountainous: the highest peak in the Osado mountains, in the north, is Kimpoku-san (1,173 m), while the Kosado hills, in the south, reach a peak of 1,640 m. Between these ranges is the wide Kuninaka plain. Sado was an independent province until 1871, when it became part of Niigata prefecture. In the Kamakura period, it was a site of exile; Nichiren spent some time there, as did Emperor Juntoku, Fujiwara no Tamekane, and Zeami. Several gold mines opened near the village of Aikawa in 1601; they produced up to 100 tons of ore annually until the mid-eighteenth century, when production dropped to less than 1 ton. Now operated by Mitsubishi with modern mining techniques, the mines are again more productive. In the Edo period, Sado province was administered by a Sado-*bugyō;* the first was Ōkubo Nagayasu, appointed by Tokugawa Ieyasu. The island produces rice and is famous for its miso and its folk dances called *okesa. Main port:* Ryotsu *(pop.:* 60,000). *Other ports:* Ogi and Aikawa *(pop.:* 30,000) on the west coast. *Area:* 857 km². *Pop.:* 90,000. Also called Sadoshima, Sadogashima.

Sadoshima Chōgorō. Kabuki actor (Renchibō, 1700–57) and playwright, Sadoshima Dempachi's son.

• **Sadoshima Dempachi.** Kabuki actor and dancer (?–1712), Sadoshima Chōgorō's father.

Saeki no Imaemishi. Architect (719–90) who directed construction of the Tōdai-ji temple in Nara in 741 and drew up the plans for the new capital of Nagaoka in 784.

Saeki Yūzō. Painter (1898–1928) in the Western style. The son of a Buddhist monk in Osaka, he studied at the Tokyo Bijutsu Gakkō (Tokyo School of Fine Arts). He married another painter, Ikeda Yoneko, in 1921, then continued his education in France, where he worked with Vlaminck and Utrillo. When he returned to Japan in 1926, he formed an artists' society called 1930-nen Kyōkai (Society of the Year 1930). He went back to France in 1927, and died destitute in Paris in August 1928. His work, based mainly on urban landscapes, is somewhat reminiscent of Van Gogh's.

Saga. Chief city of Saga prefecture, on Ariake Bay on Kyushu, former estate of the Ryūzōji family during the Kamakura period. It developed in the seventeenth century around the castle belonging to the Nabeshima family. Industries: textiles, electrical, paper. *Pop.:* 175,000.

• **Saga prefecture.** Saga prefecture, in northwest Kyushu, between Fukuoka prefecture, to the north, and Nagasaki prefecture, to the south; formerly Hizen province. The region, which is moderately mountainous (Mt. Sefuri and Mt. Tsukushi) and surrounds Ariake Bay, has a subtropical climate. It is relatively wealthy; some areas are famous for their ceramics industries, including Karatsu, Arita, and Imari. Its very jagged coast is propitious for fishing. *Main cities:* Saga, Imari, Tasa, Kashima. *Area:* 2,418 km². *Pop.:* 900,000.

• **Saga no Ran.** Insurrection by discontent samurai in Saga in 1874, led by Etō Shimpei and Shima Yoshitake (1822–74), to induce the Meiji government to send a military expedition to Korea. Okubo Toshimichi sent troops to quell the rebellion, and Etō and Shima were captured and executed.

Sagane Ryōkichi. Physicist. Before the Second World War, he worked in the United States with E. O. Lawrence. In Japan, he and Nishina Yoshio

built an experimental cyclotron 180 cm in diameter at the Rikagkyu Kenkyūjo (Institute of Physical and Chemical Research, abbreviated Riken) in Wakō, which was destroyed by American aerial bombing in 1945.

Sagara Morio. Professor (1895–1989) of German literature at the University of Tokyo from 1947 to 1956. He wrote a number of books and a German–Japanese dictionary, and translated works from German *(Faust, Nibelungen)*. He was decorated with the Order of Culture (Bunka-shō) in 1895.

Sagara Sōzō. Samurai (1839–68) from Shimōsa, born in Edo. He studied "Dutch science" *(rangaku)* and supported the imperial cause, rebelling against the Tokugawa shogunate with several other samurai in Mito. When the rebellion was put down, he fled to Kyoto, where he met Saigō Takamori, then went to Edo to try to encourage other samurai to join his cause. Unable to do so, he returned to Kyoto and raised his own army to attack Edo. The imperial court declared him a rebel, and he was arrested and executed. In 1928, he was honored posthumously by Emperor Hirohito (Shōwa Tennō).

Saga Tennō. Fifty-second emperor (Prince Kaminu, 785<810–23>842). He created a police force called *kebiishi* and buttressed imperial power. He was a renowned poet and a great calligrapher, counted among the Sampitsu (Three Brushes) of the Kōnin era.

Sagi-mai. "Dance of the heron," a traditional folk dance *(minzoku-buyō)* typical of Kyoto and the Tsuwano region (near Hiroshima); today, it is performed throughout Japan. The dancers wear costumes representing herons and other animals.

Sagoromo monogatari. "Tale of Sagoromo," written between 1070 and 1090 by an author whose identity is not certain—perhaps Daini no San'mi (ca. 1080?), Murasaki Shikibu's daughter, or Seji, a lady in the court of Imperial Princess Baishi (1039–96). This four-volume work relates the amorous adventures of Sagoromo, a young noble whose advances are rebuffed by his adoptive sister, Genji no Miya. A pale imitation of the *Genji monogatari*, it was illustrated in an *emakimono* in the early fourteenth century.

Sahari. Alloy of copper and tin (a sort of bronze) used mainly to make *dora,* gongs with sustained resonance.

Sai. Steel trident once used by peasants and some warriors to fend off sword blows by samurai. The middle tine is longer than the other two. This weapon was probably created in the eighteenth century by peasants in Okinawa, and was used by police officers in the Edo period. It was also used as a thrusting weapon. It is sometimes used in karate training *(sai-jutsu)* to strengthen the wrists. A particular type of *sai,* with a single hook at the base of the largest tine, was called *jitte* (or *jutte).*
- Shinto *kami* considered to be a protector against diseases.
- In Chinese reading *(on),* the character meaning "west." Pronounced *nishi* in *kun.*

Sai-an. Painter (sixteenth century) of the Muromachi *suiboku* school. He may have been a Buddhist monk at the Shōkoku-ji temple in Kyoto.

Saibara. Type of ballad or folk song with musical accompaniment (reed flutes, *biwa,* and koto) popular in the Heian court. These songs, with lines alternating between 5 and 7 syllables and a refrain, usually relate love stories in a very direct style. *Saibara* were supplanted in the late Heian period by folk songs called *imayō.* They are still sung during Gagaku performances at the court. *See* IMAYŌ, RŌ-EI.

Saibun. Message sent to the *kami* by the faithful during certain Shinto ceremonies. Also called *saimon.*

Saichō. Buddhist monk (Mitsukube Hirono, 767–822), born in Ōmi province to a family of Chinese immigrants; he took the name Saichō at his ordination in 785. He then left Nara and built a hermitage on Mt. Hiei, northeast of Heian-kyō, to devote himself to meditation. He studied the texts of the Chinese Buddhist Tiantai sect, and his sermons earned him the protection of Emperor Kammu, who wanted to free himself from the very firm grasp of the monks of the Six Sects of Nara (Nantorokushū). In 802, Kammu ordered Saichō to go to China with an official delegation to the Tang court. Kūkai also went with this delegation but on another ship. Saichō left in 804 and arrived in Chang'an a few months later; he stayed in China for nine months and visited the monasteries of Mt. Tiantai. In 805, he learned the sects' esoteric rituals.

When he returned to Japan in 806, Saichō founded the Japanese Tiantai sect, the Tendai, on Mt. Hiei, with the approval of Emperor Kammu, who died several months later. When Kūkai returned from China with the teachings of the Shingon *(Chin.:* Zhen-yan), Saichō became his disciple, receiving major ordination *(kanjō)* from him. But he later became angry with Kūkai, who had taken away one of his favorite disciples in 816—a practice that was legal according to the rules in effect—as ordinations took place only in Nara. Saichō asked the court (in three written submissions known as *Sange gakushō shiki)* for permission to institute his own system of ordination on Mt. Hiei. There was strong opposition from the monks of Nara, and Saichō wrote his famous *Kenkairon* (Manifestation of Precepts, 820), but the response did not come until June (or July) 822, several days after his death. The Tendai-shū sect was thus officially founded. In 866, the court conferred upon Saichō the posthumous title of Dengyō Daishi (Great Master Teaching the Doctrine). Also known by the title Dengyō Hōshi. *See* GISHIN, HIEI-ZAN, TENDAI-SHŪ.

Saidai-ji. "Great Western Temple," built in Nara in 765, on the order of Empress Shōtoku, as the headquarters of the Ritsu-shū sect and an annex to the Tōdai-ji temple, the "Great Eastern Temple." The monk Eizon was its first abbot. This Buddhist temple and monastery published many religious works (called *Saidaiji-han)* until the Muromachi period. It houses many national art treasures (sculptures from the eighth to the twelfth century). Most of its buildings were rebuilt in the eighteenth century: *shakadō* (1752), *chiodō* (1771), *kondō* (ca. 1760), *shōdō* (1711). It is famous for its tea ceremonies *(ochamori),* which generally take place in April.
→ *See* OKAYAMA.

Saifu. Payment vouchers that came into use in the Kamakura and Muromachi periods to facilitate trade; sometimes used to pay the annual tax *(nengu).* Moneychangers called *saifuya* (or *kaezeniya)* were responsible for converting these vouchers to the standardized currency in the Edo period. *See* KAIZENI.

Saigen. Buddhist monk, *zasu* of the Tendai-shū in 1282.

Saigoku Sanjūsan-sho. *See* SANJŪSAN-SHO.

Saigō Takamori. Samurai (1827–77) of the Satsuma estate. After a strict military education, he went to Edo in 1854 to serve Shimazu Nariakira, daimyo of Satsuma, who was trying to promote an alliance between the shogunate and the imperial court to confront the danger represented by the arrival of Commodore Perry's ships. When Ii Naosuke took the Edo shogunate's side, however, Saigō Takamori was forced to return to Satsuma. Shimazu Nariakira had died, so Saigō tried to commit suicide by throwing himself into Kagoshima Bay, but he was saved by fishers and exiled on the island of Amami Ōshima, where he lived for three years. When he returned, he entered the service of Shimazu Hisamitsu, but they did not get along, so Saigō was again sent into exile, this time on the island of Tokunoshima. Granted amnesty by his daimyo in 1864, he went back to Satsuma to tend to the clan's business, with Ōkubo Toshimichi and Komatsu Tatewaki, as commander of the troops. In 1868, he took the emperor's side and defeated the shogunal forces at Toba and Fushimi, then marched on Edo. As the top general in the new Meiji government's army, he favored intervention in Korea in 1873, in opposition to Iwakura. He and several other senior bureaucrats quit, and he returned to Satsuma, where he founded a private military-training school for young samurai. The government wanted to dismantle the arsenal in Kagoshima, and Saigō's samurai began an open rebellion in 1877. After several months of fighting, Saigō's forces were defeated, and Saigō committed suicide on September 24, 1877. A bronze statue by sculptor Takamura Kōun was raised in his memory in Ueno (Tokyo) after he was posthumously rehabilitated by the emperor in 1891.

Saigō Tsugumichi. Politician and admiral (1843–1902), born in Satsuma, Saigō Takamori's brother. He and his brother fought against the Tokugawa shogunate in 1868 and led the punitive expedition sent to Taiwan in 1874. He refused, however, to help his brother in his rebellion in 1877 and remained faithful to the Meiji government. Several times minister of the navy (in 1885 and from 1892 to 1902), he reorganized Japan's navy and was a private adviser to the emperor. He was one of the founders of the Kokumin Kyōkai (Nationalist Association) in 1892. Also called Saigō Yorimichi.

Saigusa Hiroto. Philosopher (1892–1963), born in Hiroshima prefecture. After studying the works of nineteenth-century European philosophers, he formulated a materialist philosophy. He was arrested in 1935 on suspicion of belonging to the Communist party. After the Second World War, in 1946, he founded a private academy called Kamakura Academy; in 1952, he became president of Yokohama University. His philosophical writings, mainly concerning materialist theories, were published in 1973 in 12 volumes.

Saigusa no Matsuri. Ancient Shinto ceremony during which *sake* was solemnly presented to the *kami* of the Isagawa Shrine.

Saigyō. Buddhist monk (Satō Norikiyo, 1118–90) of the Shingon-shū sect, *waka* poet, and famous archer. He became a monk at age 23, first in the Tendai-shū, then in the Jōdo-shū. He traveled throughout Japan making pilgrimages and composing *waka* and *tanka* poems, which were included in the anthologies *Senzai-shū* (1183) and *Shin kokin-shū* (94 *tanka*, 1206). Most of his other poems (at least 1,571) were collected in *Sanka-shū* (Poems of the Mountain Hermitage), *Mimosugawa uta-awase* (Poetry Contest on the Mimosu River, 1187), and *Miyagawa uta-awase* (Poetry Competition on the Miya River, 1189). Recently, two more collections of his poems were found, *Kikigaki-shū* and *Kikigaki zan-shū*, which were supplements to *Sanka-shū*. Saigyō is considered one of the major poets of his time, and one of the first to have used the concept of *sabi* in his compositions. Matsuo Bashō greatly admired his poems. Also called Saigyō Hōshi.

• *Saigyō monogatari emaki.* Thirteenth-century illuminated scroll *(emakimono)* attributed to Tosa Tsunekata, describing and embellishing the life and travels of Saigyō. This single-scroll *emakimono* is part of the collection in Ohara (Okayama prefecture).

• **Saigyō Zakura.** In Noh plays, the spirit of the cherry trees, portrayed as an old man.

Saihai. Command baton once used on the battlefield by troop leaders, decorated with bands of white paper that floated in the wind. It was used to direct soldiers in maneuvers. *See also* GUMPAI-UCHIWA.

Saihō-ji. Zen Buddhist temple of the Tenryū-ji branch of the Rinzai sect, built in Ukyō-ku (Kyoto) by Gyōki in 731 and rebuilt by Musō Kokushi in 1339. It has a Chinese-style *shōnantai* teahouse (late sixteenth century) and a moss garden (whence its nickname *kokedera*) with more than 140 varieties of moss, also created by Musō Kokushi, in the middle of a beautiful stand of bamboo.

Saiiki monogatari. "Western Tales," a three-volume government treatise written by Honda Toshiaki in 1798, describing the laws and customs of Western countries and advocating the reopening of trade with other nations and the colonization of Hokkaido. Also titled *Seiki monogatari.*

Saijiki. Specific words used mainly in haiku to denote the seasons, collected in glossaries for the use of poets and published since the beginning of the Edo period.

Saijō-ji. Zen Buddhist temple of the Sōtō-shū sect, built in Odawara in the fifteenth century and dedicated to the worship of Kannon Bosatsu. It houses many statues portraying *tengu.*

Saijō Yaso. Poet (1892–1970) influenced by French and English symbolists, professor at Waseda University in Tokyo. He lived in France from 1924 to 1926 and became friends with Stéphane Mallarmé. Among his collections are *Sakin* (1919) and *Rōningyō* (1922).

Saikaku Ihara. Writer and *haikai* poet (Hirayama Tōgo; *gō:* Kakuei, 1642–93), born in Osaka. He studied traditional *haikai,* then *haikai* of the Danrin school. In 1673, he published, in the latter style, a collection of 10,000 *ku* titled *Ikutama manku;* two years later, he wrote 1,000 *ku* in a single day in memory of his wife, who had died at age 25. He then increased his production; it is said that he composed 23,500 *ku* in 24 hours, which earned him the nickname Niman-ō ("the lord of 20,000"). He then began to write tales and novels in *ukiyo-zōshi* style on the daily life, characters, and morals of his time, most of which were published by Andō Jishū of the Hachimonjiya publishing house. Ihara Saikaku's body of work is extraordinarily fecund, and is usually divided into three periods. In the first (1682–86), he wrote mainly gallant stories: *Kōshoku ichidai otoko* (Life of a Friend of Pleasure, 1682); *Shoen okagami* (The Great Mirror of Gallantry, 1684); a sequel to the first, *Kōshoku ichidai otoko* (Life of a Woman Friend of Pleasure, 1684); *Kōshoku godai onna* (Five Women in Love). He also wrote "provincial" stories, such as *Shokokubanashi,* and tales about straying from the duties of filial piety: *Honchō nijū fukō.* In the second period, he wrote warrior stories *(buke-mono),* such as *Budō denrai-ki, Nanshoku ōkagami* (Great Mirror of Pederasty), and *Buke giri monogatari,* a novel on warrior fidelity. In the third period (1688–93), he described the lives of *chōnin* in *Nippon eitaigura* (The Storehouse of Eternal Treasures, 1688) and *Seiken munesan'yō* (The Accounts, 1693). Some of his works were published after his death, including *Saikaku okimiyage* (Gift Left by Saikaku, 1693) and the epistolary *Yorozu no Fumi gōgo* (Many Letters to Throw Out, 1696). Saikaku Ihara's works were very successful during his lifetime; his style was widely imitated by many authors writing in the *ukiyo-zōshi* genre, but none matched his precise, imaginative, and very spontaneous style. Saikaku was later somewhat forgotten, but his works became popular again in the Meiji era, when they were "rediscovered" by Kōda Rohan, Ōzaki Kōyō, and Mori Ōgai, among others. His name is sometimes written Ibara Saikaku and Ihara Saikaku.

Saikei. The art of making miniaturized landscapes. *Bonkei* are *saikei* placed on dishes or in large, low-sided bowls. *See* BONSAI.

Saikō. Painter (Ema Tahoko; *azana:* Ryokugyoku; *gō:* Kizan, Shōmu, Saikō, 1787–1861) of the Nanga (Bunjinga) school; she studied with Rai San'yō. She painted mainly flowers.

Saikō-kai. Society of modern painters, founded about 1920 by Nakamura Gakuryō, Fukuda Heihachirō, Okumura Dogyū, Yamaguchi Hōshun, Tokuoka Shinsen, and Ono Chikuyō.

• **Saikō Nippon Bijutsu-in.** Association of painters in the "Japanese" style (Nihonga), founded in 1914 by Yokoyama Taikan and Shimomura Kanzan.

Saikyō. "Western Capital," the name given to Kyoto in 1868 to differentiate it from the new capital, Tokyo ("Eastern Capital"), formerly Edo; the name was rarely used.
→ *See* HEIAN-KYŌ, RAKU.

Saimei Tennō. Thirty-seventh sovereign (Empress Hitarashi Hime, 594<655–61>) in her second reign. She had previously occupied the throne from 642 to 645 as thirty-fifth sovereign under the name Kōgyoku. She was the wife of Emperor Jomei and the mother of emperors Tenji and Temmu. When she became empress again upon the death of Jomei Tennō, she gave the throne to her brother Kōtoku in 645, but she took control of the empire when he died in 654. She sent a number of military expeditions against the Ezo in northern Kyushu and dispatched troops to Korea to assist the kingdom of Paekche (Kudara), which had been attacked by Silla (*Jap.:* Shiragi, Sinra) and the Tang-dynasty Chinese. Her son Tenji succeeded her. *See* KŌGYOKU TENNŌ.

Saimyō-ji. Buddhist temple founded in Kyoto about 832 and rebuilt in 1699.

St. Petersburg, Treaty of. Treaty signed between Russia and Japan on May 7, 1875, under which Japan renounced its claim to Sakhalin in exchange for acquisition of the Kuril Islands and free use of Russian ports. This treaty annulled one signed in February 1855 and an accord signed in 1867.

Saionji Kimmochi. Statesman (Tokudaiji Kimmochi, 1849–1940), born in Kyoto to a noble family and adopted by the Saionji family, a branch of the Fujiwara family. Appointed *san'yo* (councillor) in 1867, he took part in the Boshin Civil War in 1868 on the side of the imperial troops in northern Honshu. From 1871 to 1880, he lived in Europe and France, where he studied law; upon his return in 1881, he founded the Meiji Hōritsu Gakkō (Meiji Law School), which later became Meiji University. He also helped found the anti-government *Tōyō Jiyū Shimbun* (Liberal Newspaper of the East) but had to resign from his official position. In 1882, he accompanied Itō Hirobumi to Europe; he was ambassador to Austria, then to Germany. A member of the emperor's Privy Council and vice-chairman of the House of Peers, he was minister of education in Itō's second and third cabinets (1892–96 and 1898). In 1898, he succeeded Itō Hirobumi at the head of the Privy Council, and in 1903 he was elected leader of the Rikken Seiyūkai (Friends of Constitutional Government party). He succeeded Katsura Tarō as prime minister from 1906 to 1908. Katsura Tarō then returned as prime minister; Saionji again succeeded him in 1911–12; and Katsura Tarō then returned once again to the head of the government. The last of the *tairō*, Saionji was made a prince by the emperor and continued to play an important role in domestic policy until his death. His brother, Tokudaiji Sanenori (1839–1919), had replaced him at the head of his family clan; his younger brother, Tokudaiji Takamaro (1864–1926), adopted by the Sumitomo family, took the name Sumitomo Kichizaemon (or Sumitomo Tomozumi) and headed the Sumitomo zaibatsu.

Saionji Kintsune. Noble (Kujō Kintsune, 1171–1244), born in Kyoto, of the Fujiwara family and allied with the Minamoto family; grandfather of Kujō Yoritsune, fourth shogun of Kamakura, and minister of state *(dajō-daijin)* in 1222. He had a temple built (1224) north of Kyoto, the Saion-ji, and took the name of the temple as his family name.

Saipan. Pacific island, one of the Mariana Islands, discovered by Magellan in 1521. It belonged to Spain, then to Germany, and finally to the United States after the U.S.–Philippines war of 1899. After 1918, it came under Japanese administration. There was terrible fighting there between American and Japanese forces in 1943 and 1944. In 1945, it became an American possession.

Sairai-ji. Buddhist temple of the Tendai-shū built in 1490 in Tushi (Mie prefecture) and rebuilt in the original style in 1605. Belongs to the Maeda foundation in Tokyo.

Saisei-ichi. Political-religious theory of "the unity of rites and government" that was dominant when State Shinto (Kokusai Shintō) was instituted in 1870.

Saisen. Type of paper imported from China, colored and sprinkled with mica flakes, used to write poems on in the twelfth century. *See* PAPER, WASHI.

Saishō-e. Buddhist ceremonies created in 693; starting in 830, official prayers for peace were said during the annual ceremonies. These grand ceremonies took place mainly in the Yakushi-ji (starting in 830) and Enshū-ji (starting in 1072) temples.

• **Saishō-in.** Buddhist temple in Hirosaki (northern Honshu) with a five-story pagoda *(goju-no-tō)* 12 m high, dating from 1668.

Saitama Ginko. "Saitama Bank," founded in 1943 in Saitama prefecture and in Tokyo. It has more than 175 branches throughout Japan and a number of others abroad, notably in Singapore, London, New York, Hong Kong, and Brussels. Head office in Urawa (Saitama prefecture).

• **Saitama prefecture.** Saitama prefecture, located north of Tokyo in the northern part of the Kanto plain, irrigated by the Arakawa and Tone-gawa rivers. Before 1876, it was part of Musashi province. It is an essentially agricultural prefecture, "Tokyo's granary," famous for its green tea. *Chief city:* Urawa; *main cities:* Sayama, Sakado, Chichibu, Kawagoe, Niiza, Toda, Asaka, Kawaguchi, Ōmiya, Kumagaya. *Area:* 3,799 km²; *pop.:* 5.5 million.

Saito-baru. Group of 329 megalithic tombs *(kofun)* dating from the fifth and sixth centuries, located near the town of Saito (Miyazaki prefecture). The *kofun* are of different shapes and sizes, from 30 m to 219 m long. Those that have been excavated contained weapons, horse harnesses, and armor, as well as *haniwa,* now on display in a local museum, the Tokyo National Museum, and the museum of the University of Tokyo.

Saitō Bishu. Sculptor of netsuke and *okimono* (Mishiu, Shōsai, Baisho, Baishodō, b. 1843). He sometimes signed his works in the name of his cousin and partner, Yasufusa.

Saitō Chikudō. Confucian scholar (1815–52), born in Sendai; Asaka Gonsai's student.

Saitō Dōsan. Warrior (Saitō Toshimasa, ca. 1494–1556) of unknown origins, small-scale vassal of the *shugo* of Mino province, Toki Yorinari (1502–82). At first a Buddhist monk, he became a warrior and assassinated Toki Jirō, Toki Yoshinari's son. He expelled Toki Yoshinari from the province, and Toki took refuge with Oda Nobuhide (1510–51), daimyo of Owari province. Saitō Dōsan married his daughter to Oda Nobuhide's son, the future Oda Nobunaga. But his own son, Saitō Yoshitatsu (ca. 1527–61), attacked him, and he was killed in battle soon after.

Saitō Gesshin. Writer (1804–78), born in Edo, expert in Chinese classical studies. He continued the journal started by his grandfather on the city of Edo, *Edo meisho-zue* (20 volumes), and compiled a history of folk songs, *Seikyoku ruisan,* and a description of the life of the common people, *Bukō nempyō.*

Saitō Hikomaro. Confucian scholar (1768–1854), Motoori Norinaga's disciple.

Saitō Hiroshi. Diplomat (1886–1939), born in Niigata, ambassador to Holland (1933) and the United States (1934–38), where he died. He wrote classical poetry in Chinese and translated works by English poets into Japanese.

Saitō Jirō. Officer (b. 1893) who was the head of the Japanese secret service in Southeast Asia. He reorganized the Thai army in 1934 and was active in Indochina in 1940 and 1941.

Saitō Koichi. Movie director, born 1929 in Tokyo. He worked with Imai Tadashi, Ichikawa Kon, and Imamura Shōhei, and began to write screenplays in 1962. He made his first film, *Sasayaki no Jo* (Whispering Jo) in 1967. He then directed films on popu-

lar singers and, starting in 1971, more personal movies focusing on problems of youth: *Yakusoku* (Meeting, 1972), *Tabi no omosa* (Solitary Journey, 1972), *Tsugaru jongara bushi* (The Ballad of Tsugaru, 1973), and others.

Saitō Makoto. Politician (1858–1936) and admiral, born in Iwate prefecture. He was vice-minister of the navy during the Russo-Japanese War of 1904–05, then minister of the navy from 1906 to 1914; having modernized the fleet, he was promoted to admiral in 1912. From 1919 to 1927, he was governor-general of Korea. After Inukai Tsuyoshi was assassinated, in 1932, he became prime minister, keeping General Araki as minister of war. He resigned in 1934 following a scandal, and was assassinated during the incidents of February 26, 1939 (*see* NINIROKU JIKEN), by extremist officers who felt that he was too moderate.

Saitō Mokichi. Psychiatrist and poet (Moriya Mokichi, Saitō Shigeyoshi, 1882–1953), born in Yamagata prefecture. As a poet, he was a disciple of Itō Sachio of the Araragi-ha school. He studied psychiatry in Vienna and Munich, where he lived from 1921 to 1924, after teaching in Nagasaki. He was better known for his collections of *tanka* poems than for his work as a psychiatrist. Among his most popular collections: *Shakko* (Red Light, 1913), *Aratama* (Jewel in the Rough, 1921), *Shiroki yama* (White Mountain, 1949), *Renzan* (1950). He also wrote several essays on folklore. His complete works comprise 56 volumes. He was writer Kita Morio's father.

Saitō Ryokū. Writer (Saitō Masaru; *gō:* Shōjiki Shōdayū, 1867–1904), born in Ise province. At first a literary critic, he became known when he began to publish humorous and satirical novels, such as *Abura jigoku* (Inferno of Oil, 1891). His critical essays were collected in *Shōsetsu hasshū* (1889).

Saitō Sanemori. Warrior (1111–83) who fought on the side of the Taira. According to the *Heike monogatari* and *Hōgen monogatari,* in his old age, he dyed his hair and beard so that he could continue to fight. He was killed in a battle against Minamoto no Yoshinaka.

Saitō Satoshi. Ceramist, born 1935 in Tokyo; he studied in Japan and Canada and settled in Quebec. He produces ceramics in shapes that are new but related to Japanese tradition; his work has been in exhibitions in Japan, Canada, and Paris. His wife,

Louise Doucet (b. 1938 in Montreal), is a painter whose works are known mainly in Canada.

Saitō Setsudō. Confucian scholar (Saitō Tekkan, 1797–1865), born in Edo, where he was Koga Seiri's (1750–1817) disciple. In 1844, he became director of the Yūzōkan, a school of Confucianism founded in the Tsu estate (Ise province), where he introduced study of "Dutch science" *(rangaku).*

Saitō Yori. Painter (1885–1959) of the Fauvist school in Paris.

• **Saitō Yoshishige.** Painter in Western avant-garde style, born 1904 in Tokyo. His works were exhibited in Japan and in foreign cities, including São Paulo and New York, and received numerous awards.

Sai-un Hōshinno. Buddhist monk (1104–62), son of Emperor Horikawa and *zasu* of the Tendai-shū.

Saji Keizō. Industrialist, born 1919 in Osaka, son of Torii Shinjirō, the founder of Suntory, a manufacturer of whiskey and beer. He founded the Suntory Art Museum and the Suntory Music Foundation in Tokyo.

Sakagami Hiroshi. Writer, born 1936 in Tokyo, author of many stories in autobiographical style, dealing with the urban middle class. He received the *Chūō Kōron* Prize in 1959.

Sakaguchi Ango. Writer (Sakaguchi Heigo, 1906–55), born in Niigata. After studying religion and French literature, he launched his literary career with an autobiographical novel, *Fubuki monogatari* (Tale of the Snowstorm, 1938), which was not very successful, and wrote screenplays. After the Second World War, he wrote many popular novels and essays. He gained public recognition with *Hakuchi* (The Idiot, 1946), then *Daraku-ron* (On Falling, 1946) and *Furenzoku satsujin jiken* (Murders out of Context, 1947). Among his other important stories are *Murasaki Dainagon* (1939), *Bungaku no furusato* (The True Homeland of Literature, 1942), and *Shinju* (The Pearl, 1942).

Sakaguchi Kin'ichiro. Bacteriologist (1897–1994) in Niigata. His research on ferments earned him the Japan Academy Prize (Nihon Gakushi-in-shō) in 1950 and the Order of Culture (Bunka-shō) in 1968.

Sakai. Port on the Inland Sea (Setonaikai) located south of Osaka at the mouth of the Yodo-gawa river. Populated as early as the Yayoi period, it was very active until the seventeenth century, when it was gradually supplanted by Osaka. The city was almost completely destroyed in 1399, following the rebellion of its lord, Ōuchi Yoshihiro (1356–1400), after the Ōei War; it then came under the direct control of the Muromachi shogunate. The merchants of Sakai became wealthy during the Ōnin War because it was the only port that was open and served as a departure point for missions to China. The city was administered by a council of merchants, the *egōshū.* Sakai is now a modern port and a major industrial center (chemical, automobile, mechanical, textile plants, etc.). In the immediate surroundings are many *kofun,* among them one built for Emperor Nintoku. *Pop.:* 850,000.

Sakaibe no Iwatsumi. Scholar (seventh century) who went to China and returned in 653 with a 44-volume dictionary, now lost.

Sakaibe no Ōkita. Ambassador to China from 701 to 718. Also called Sakaibe no Ōwake.

Sakaida Kakiemon. Potter and ceramist (1596–1666) from Arita (Hizen province, Saga prefecture). He made the first painted porcelain around 1650; this type of porcelain bears his name (Kakiemon). *See* AKAE, CERAMICS, KAKIEMON. The last ceramist by this name, born 1934 in Arita-machi (Aichi prefecture), exhibited his works in Japan and throughout Europe, including Moscow (1990), Germany (1991) and Paris (1994).

Sakai, Frankie. Actor (Sakai Masatoshi), born 1929 in Kagoshima prefecture. At first a jazz musician (whence his nickname Frankie), he made his movie debut in 1957 in a film by Kawashima Yūzō, *Bakumatsu taiyō den* (The Sunset of the Shogunate), then acted under Toyoda Shirō and other directors of comedies and science-fiction movies. He received a number of awards for his performances.

Sakai Tadakiyo. Statesman (1624–81), *rōjū* and *tairō* for shogun Tokugawa Ietsuna in 1662. He was very powerful (the *daimyō* of a huge estate in Kōzuke province) and was nicknamed *geba-shōgun* because he established his residence in Edo facing the spot where it was obligatory to dismount *(geba)* before entering the castle by the Ōtemmon gate. He resigned from his position when Tokugawa Tsunayoshi came to power, and Tsunayoshi replaced him with Hotta Masatoshi in 1680. Also called Taka-sago-shōgun.

Sakai Toshihiko. Politician (*gō:* Sakai Kosen, 1870–1933) and journalist. In 1910, he created a company for the diffusion of literary works, Bai-bun-sha, which rapidly became a sort of socialist political club opposed to the government. Ōsugi Sakae, Arahata Kanson, and Yamakawa Hitoshi were active members. The society was dissolved in 1918. Sakai was a founding member of the Japan Socialist party (Nihon Shakaitō) in 1906 and, with Yamakawa Hitoshi and Arahata Kanson, of the Japan Communist party (Nihon Kyōsantō) in 1922.

Saka Jūbutsu. Buddhist monk (fourteenth century) and personal physician to shogun Ashikaga Taka-uji. He wrote the *Ise daijingū sankeiki* in 1342.

Sakaki. Evergreen tree *(Cleyera ochnacea)* of the tea-tree family, growing in its wild state in the hottest regions of Japan, including Kyushu, Shikoku, and southern Honshu. It can reach 10 m in height. This tree, whose name means "tree of prosperity," has whitish five-petaled flowers and a round fruit with a large number of seeds. It seems that the *sakaki* was considered sacred in early Shinto, as it was said to be the permanent or temporary home of *kami.* Its branches are often used in rituals and offered in tribute *(tamagushi)* to the *kami.* According to the *Kojiki,* the *kami* hung jewels and mirrors in a *sasaki* tree to draw the goddess Amaterasu from the cavern where she had hidden.

Sakakibara Yasumasa. General (1548–1606) under Tokugawa Ieyasu. With Sakai Tadatsugu (1527–96), Ii Naomasa, and Honda Tadakatsu (1548–1610), he was one of the Tokugawa Shitennō (Four Heavenly Kings of the Tokugawa), known for their fidelity to the Tokugawa. He fought under Tokugawa Ieyasu in most of his battles and received an estate of 100,000 *koku* near Edo. After the Battle of Sekigahara (1600), he actively participated in redistribution of estates among the daimyo.

Sakaki Hyakusen. Painter (Sakaki Shin'en; *gō:* Hōshū, Hassendō, Hyakusen, 1697–1752) of the Nanga (Bunjinga) school and haiku poet, born in Nagoya. He imitated the Chinese painters of the Ming and Qing dynasties and painted mainly landscapes in their style.

Sakakiyama Koshirō. Famous Kabuki actor (1671–1747) in Kyoto and Osaka.

Sakakura Junzō. Architect (1901–69) who studied with Le Corbusier in Paris from 1929 to 1936. In Paris, he designed the Japanese Pavilion for the 1937 World Exposition; in Japan, the Kanagawa Museum (1951), the Shibuya railway and subway station (1954–56), the Shinjuku Station Square (1966–68), and the Ashiya Cultural Center (1969) in Tokyo; and the Osaka Youth Center (1967).

Sakamoto Hanjirō. Painter (1882–1969) in the Western style, born in Hiroshima prefecture, working in the French impressionist style. He lived in France from 1921 to 1924. He painted mainly animals, particularly cattle and horses. Decorated with the Order of Culture (Bunka-shō) in 1956.

Sakamoto Kōzen. Botanist (1800–53), born in Kii province; he also painted cherry blossoms in the style of the Kanō school.

Sakamoto Ryōma. Samurai (1836–67) of the Tosa estate (Kōchi prefecture). An expert in swordplay *(ken-jutsu),* he went to Edo in 1853 and soon joined the anti-foreign and pro-imperial movements. After the assassination of the minister of Tosa, Yoshida Tōyō, in 1862, he became a *rōnin* and entered the service of Katsu Kaishū, helping him organize a naval school in Hyōgo. He assembled a fleet of merchant ships to supply the Chōshū and constantly opposed the shogunate. He was assassinated, at the same time as Nakaoka Shintarō, by *rōnin* employed by the Tokugawa.

Sakamoto Tarō. Historian (1901–87) in Shizuoka prefecture, whose areas of expertise were the *ritsuryō* system and the ancient Japanese histories called the *Rikkokushi.* His books and studies earned him the Order of Culture (Bunka-shō) in 1982.

Sakanishi Shiho. Essayist and translator (1896–1976), born in Tokyo. She went to the United States in 1922, where she completed her studies in aesthetics and literature at the University of Michigan; she then worked at the Library of Congress from 1930 to 1942. After the Second World War, she was an adviser to the Japanese government. Her writings deal mainly with women's issues and international relations: *Chi no shio* (The Salt of the Earth, 1947), *Toki no ashioto* (The Steps of Time, 1970). When she wrote in English, she used the name Shio Sakanishi.

Sakanoue no Mokichi. Poet (tenth century) who helped to compile the *Gosen waka-shū,* with other poets who were part of the Nashitsubo no Gonin.

Sakanoue no Tamuramaro. General (758–811) belonging to a family of chief warriors serving the imperial court since the seventh century, Sakanoue no Karitamaro's (728–86) son. Emperor Kammu sent him to fight the Ezo tribes in northern Honshu in 791 and gave him the title *sei-i-tai-shōgun* (commander-in-chief against the barbarians) following his victories. Tamuramaro, perhaps a descendant of Achi no Ōmi, had started his military career as a lieutenant under Ōtomo no Otomaro. Just before his death, he was appointed *dainagon* and *hyō-bukyō* (minister of war). Tradition has it that he founded the Buddhist Kiyomizu-dera temple in Kyoto. His tomb is in Shōgun-zuka, east of Kyoto.

Sakashitamon Jiken. Assassination attempt made on February 13, 1862, against Andō Nobumasa, a *rōjū* of the Edo shogunate, by supporters of the emperor who suspected him of plotting to dethrone Emperor Kōmei. Andō had in fact arranged the marriage of Imperial Princess Kazu to shogun Tokugawa Iemochi. He was injured in the attempt, which took place near the Sakashita gate of the Edo palace; his six assailants were killed on the spot by his bodyguards.

Sakata Heiichi. Lacquer artist (nineteenth century) from Matsue. In 1888, he invented a decoration technique called *yagumo-nuri.*

Sakata no Kintoki. Samurai (?–1021) serving Minamoto no Yorimitsu, whose feats in his youth were celebrated in legends and attributed to a character bearing his name as a young man, Kintarō. *See* KINTARŌ.

Sakata Shōichi. Physicist (1911–70), born in Tokyo, internationally known for his theoretical work on atomic structure and his two-meson theory (1942). After the Second World War, he joined Yukawa Hideki and Tomonaga Shin'ichirō to campaign for peaceful uses of atomic energy.

Sakata Tōjūrō. Family of Kabuki actors in Kyoto and Osaka. Sakata Tōjūrō I (1647–1709) was the most famous of its members, playing *tachiyaku* roles. He also wrote plays for Kabuki, the most famous of which is *Yūgiri nagori no shōgatsu.*

• **Sakata Tōjūrō II.** Kabuki actor (1669–1724), Sakata Tōjūrō I's student in Kyoto and Osaka. Also called Fushimi Tōjūrō.

• **Sakata Tōjūrō III.** Kabuki actor (1701–74) in the family line of his two predecessors.

Sake. General term for all alcoholic beverages made with fermented rice (with boiled rice, *koji,* augmented with *Aspergillus oryzae*). Refined *sake* (which titrates at 17–20°) is normally called *seishu* or *nihonshu* (as opposed to foreign alcoholic beverages, called *yōshu*). A *sake* that is popular but less refined than *seishu* is *shōchū,* which may also be made with fermented millet (notably in Okinawa, where it is called *awamori*), potatoes, or barley added to fermented rice, and can titrate at up to 80°. There are several qualities of refined *sake: ikkyū* (first degree), *nikyū* (second degree), and *tokkyū* (special degree); the lowest quality is called *nigori-zake.*

Sake seems to have been made at the time that rice cultivation was introduced to Japan, around the third century BC; at first, it was used in religious ceremonies as an offering *(gisei)* to the *kami.* It was later distilled for nobles and the court. Around the twelfth century, it started to be distilled for use among the common people.

Sake is generally drunk before meals or to accompany certain dishes, such as crab *(kani),* sometimes cold but usually lukewarm. It is heated in a double-boiler in bottle-shaped containers called *tokkori,* and is drunk at a temperature of about 35°C from small cups *(sakozuki).* A sweet *sake (mirin)* is used in cooking to heighten the flavor of dishes. In ancient Japan, guilds of *sake* distillers were called *sakabe (see* BE), and merchants were also grouped in guilds *(sakaya).* Called *saki* in Okinawa.

Sakhalin. Large island in the Sea of Okhotsk, north of Hokkaido, from which it is separated by the La Perouse Strait *(Jap.:* Sōya Kaikyō), and east of Siberia, from which it is separated by the Tatar Strait *(Rus.:* Tatarskij Proliv) at 52° north latitude. The narrowest part of this channel (called Nevelskogo Proliv) is only a few kilometers wide and 4 m deep; it freezes in winter, allowing easy passage between the mainland and the island. Sakhalin stretches along a north-south axis between 46° and 55° north latitude. Its two parallel mountain ranges—culminating to the east with Mt. Nevelski (1,900 m)—frame the valley of the Poronaj River, which empties into the Sea of Okhotsk (Terpenija Gulf) via a marshy delta. The northern part of the island is flat and marshy in summer; the rest of the island is covered with forests. Its general climate is cold and foggy. There are some oil fields in the north and coal mines in the central region. Sakhalin was occupied by the Russians starting in 1857, and it was a site of exile for Russian political outlaws before the Russian revolution. The Portsmouth Treaty (1905) gave the part south of the 50th parallel to Japan, which named it Karafutō, but the entire island was returned to the Soviet Union in 1945. *Main cities:* Juzno-Sakhalinsk (on the southwest coast), Aleksandrovsk Sakhalinskij (on the northwest coast). *Area:* 76,000 km²; *length:* 948 km. *Pop.:* 700,000.

Sakimori. In the seventh and eighth centuries, a term for soldiers sent to Kyushu to defend the island against possible attack by the Koreans. They were commanded from Dazaifu by a Sakimori no Tsukasa (minister of *sakimori*). These peasant-soldiers had to see to their own needs and were exempt from taxes. The *sakimori* were dismissed in 795 and replaced by local militias and volunteers from other provinces. Many *sakimori,* far from home, wrote poems *(sakimori-uta),* 98 of which were included in the *Man'yōshū* (books 14 and 20).

Sakisaka Itsurō. Political scientist (1897–1985) and Marxist theoretician, born in Fukuoka prefecture (Kyushu). After living in Germany from 1922 to 1925, he taught at the University of Kyushu. He was forced to resign his position in 1928, however, because of his political views, and was imprisoned from 1937 to 1939 for the same reason. After the Second World War, he published a journal of opinion, *Zenshin,* and helped found a socialist association (1960), after retiring as a professor. He published the complete works of Karl Marx and Engels *(Marukusu Engerusu zanshū)* in 27 volumes in 1935, and translated Marx's *Das Kapital (Shihonron)* in 1956. He also wrote a biography of Marx *(Marukusu den)* in 1962, as well as various other political works.

Sakishima Shōtō. Archipelago comprising some 20 islands located between the Ryukyu Islands and northeast Taiwan. The three largest are Miyakojima (main city: Hirata), Ishigaki-jima, and Iriomote-jima. The islands are divided into two groups, the Miyako and the Yaeyama. Administratively, it is part of Okinawa prefecture. *Total area:* 811 km²; *pop.:* 100,000.

Sakoku-rei. "Isolationist policy," applied from 1639 to 1868, under which relations with European countries was forbidden on pain of death (with the exception of the Dutch on the islet of Dejima in Nagasaki) and relations with Asian countries were strictly controlled by the government. *See* DEJIMA.

Sakomizu Hisatsune. Politician (1920–77) from Kagoshima prefecture. In 1945, he wrote Japan's imperial document of surrender. He was banned from politics until 1952 by the Occupation forces (S.C.A.P.), but was then elected twice to the House of Representatives for the Liberal Democratic party (Jiyū Minshutō), appointed minister of communications in 1962, and elected a member of the Upper House of the Diet.

Sakon. Painter (Hasegawa Sakon, late seventeenth century) of the Hasegawa school, perhaps one of Tōhaku's sons. *See* HASEGAWA-HA.

Saku. Barriers built in northern Honshu on imperial order starting in the mid-seventh century, intended to contain the Ezo tribes. *Saku* consisted of forts surrounded by palisades with watchtowers, sometimes reinforced by earth ramparts and moats. In addition to being military posts, the forts were administrative centers. Also called *ki, jō. See* AKITA-JŌ, IZAWA-JŌ, SEKISHO, TAGA-JŌ.

Sakugen Shūryō. Buddhist monk (1501–79) of the Tenryū-ji, who was in China from 1538 to 1541 and from 1546 to 1550.

Sakuma Kanae. Psychologist (1888–1970), born in Chiba prefecture, who introduced Gestalt psychology to Japan and conducted important research on the phonetics of Japanese. Elected a member of the Japan Academy (Nihon Gakushi-in).

Sakuma Shōzan. Samurai (1811–64), physicist, and military engineer, born in the Matsushiro estate (Nagano prefecture). He studied "Dutch science *(rangaku)* with Egawa Tarōzaemon and other scholars of his time, then opened a school in 1850 to teach the principles of European artillery and crafts such as glass making. He married Katsu Junko, Katsu Kaishū's daughter, in 1853. In 1854, he tried to go to the United States with one of the ships in Commodore Perry's fleet, but was arrested and imprisoned. In his own defense, he wrote *Seikenroku,* in which he advocated the opening of Japanese ports to Western trade. In 1858, he made a Daniell-type battery and an electromagnet. However, some supporters of the shogunate hated him for his pro-European ideas, and they assassinated him. Also called Sakuma Zōzan. *See* SATŌ ISSAI.

Sakuma Tōgan. Painter (1658–1736) and writer from Sendai.

Sakunin. Peasant serving a *myōshu.*

Sakura. *See* CHERRY TREE.

• *Sakura-gawa.* Title of a Noh play: a boy sells himself to a child merchant to relieve his family's misery. His mother searches for him for three years, and during a party under the cherry trees *(sakurami),* she dances to express her sadness. A Buddhist monk arrives, bringing her son with him, and he allows the boy to rejoin her.

• **Sakura-kai.** "Society of Cherry Trees," an extreme-right-wing political group founded by military officers in 1930 and dissolved in 1931.

• **Sakura-ningyō.** "Cherry-tree dolls," made on the model of French dolls introduced to Japan in the late nineteenth century. There are two types: those dressed in French clothes *(Furansu-ningyō),* made during the Taishō era, and those dressed in kimono and posed as dancers *(fuji-ningyō).* These dolls, usually made by young women using a French technique, portray classic dances such as *Fuji-musume* and *Musume Dōjō-ji* (from the title of a Kabuki play written by Miyake Shūtarō).

Sakuraba Masaru. Contemporary painter, born 1940 in Yokohama. He went to Paris and studied at the École des beaux-arts in 1968; he is noted for his realistic trompe-l'oeil paintings.

Sakurada Ichirō. Chemist (1904–86) born near Kyoto, famous for his work on synthetic fibers. Professor at the University of Kyoto; he retired in 1967.

Sakurada Jisuke. Kabuki actor and playwright (1754–1806), author of such famous plays as *Gohiiki Kanjinshō* (Kanjincho the Favorite) and *Keisei azuma kagami,* danced performances, and *jōruri* texts. He wrote more than 120 Kabuki plays, most of them in *jidai-mon*o genre, and more than 100 danced performances *(shosagoto).* He started a family line of actors of the same name: Sakurada Jisuke II (1768–1829), Sakurada Jisuke III (1802–77), Sakurada Jisuke IV (dates uncertain, nineteenth–twentieth century).

Sakurada-mongai Jiken. Incident that resulted in the assassination of Ii Naosuke on March 24, 1860, in front of the Sakurada gate of the Edo castle by a conspiracy of 18 samurai of the Mito and Satsuma clans, who blamed him for having capitulated to foreign powers by signing the trade treaties of the Ansei era *(see* ANSEI NO KARI JŌYAKU, ANSEI NO TAIGAKU). Only two of Ii Naosuke's assailants survived the repression that followed.

• **Sakuradamon Jiken.** Attempted assassination of Emperor Hirohito that took place on January 8, 1932, as he was returning from a military review and entering his palace by the Sakurada gate. The grenade thrown by a Korean anarchist caused little damage and injured no one. The Korean was arrested, tried in camera, and executed.

Sakurajima. Volcano on an island in Kagoshima Bay (Kyushu), linked since 1914 to the Ōsumi Peninsula by an accumulation of cinders. It is 1,117 m high and still active, constantly spewing cinders. Most recent eruptions in 1779 and 1914. The island has an area of 77 km^2.

Sakuramachi Tennō. Hundred and fifteenth emperor (Prince Akihito, 1720<1736–46>1750), son of and successor to Nakamikado Tennō. He abdicated in favor of his son Momozono.

Sakuranoue. Group of tombs *(kofun)* hollowed out of rock, located near Yamagata (Kumamoto prefecture, Kyushu). Tomb no. 2 is decorated with a human figure and boats (?) in white on a red background.

Sakura Sōgorō. Leader (Kiuchi Sōgorō, Sakura Sōgo, seventeenth century) of a small village *(kōzu)* in the Sakura estate (Chiba prefecture) who personally presented a petition to shogun Tokugawa Ietsuna in which he denounced the tyranny of the local daimyo and demanded that taxes be lowered. Although his request was satisfied, he and his entire family were condemned to crucifixion, probably between 1645 and 1652, so that his act would not be repeated. Considered a hero, he was the subject of a Kabuki play called *Sakura gimin den.*

Sakurayama Shōzaemon. Kabuki actor (Sakurayama Rinnosuke, Ōzan, ca. 1664–1714) in Osaka.

Salvation Army. *See* KYŌSEI-GUN.

Sambasō. Kabuki dance, adapted from the Noh play called *Okina*.
• In Kabuki theater, character who raises the curtain.

Sambiki-zaru. "The three monkeys," a traditional image, of Chinese origin, of three monkeys, one with its hands over its eyes, one with its hands over its ears, and one with its hands over its mouth. They symbolize the old adage "See no evil, hear no evil, speak no evil," counseling discretion. This image, popularized in painting and sculpture, was introduced to Japan in the seventeenth century. A sculpture by Tōshōgū in Nikkō made it famous.

Sambō. In Buddhism and Shinto, a small wooden table, bare or lacquered, used to present offerings to the divinities.
• "Three treasures," a generic term for the three greatest writers of the eleventh century: Ōe Tadafusa, Fujiwara no Korefusa, and Fujiwara no Nagafusa.

• *Sambō-e.* "Painting of the Three Treasures," an ethics work written by Minamoto no Tamenori in 984. The scroll of illustrations accompanying it has been lost. Also titled *Tamenori no Ki*.

• *Sambō-ekotoba.* "Tale of the Three Brothers," a collection of tenth-century folk tales, written in Chinese.

• *Sambō-in.* Buddhist temple of the Shingon-shū, founded in Heian-kyō (Kyoto) in 1115 by Shō Kaku, abbot of the Daigo-ji. The current buildings and garden date from the late sixteenth century. Paintings from the same period.

• *Sambō Kōjin.* Syncretic folk divinity of the Honji-suijaku and the Tendai-shū sect, portrayed with several pairs of arms. He is the familiar divinity of kitchens and hearths, sometimes confused with minor aspects of Monju Bosatsu. This divinity assumes various forms and names, among them Kōjin, Kōshin, Nyorai Kōjin, Kojima Kōjin. He is sometimes symbolized by a scarf hung on the kitchen wall. Also sometimes pronounced Sampō Kōjin.

Samboku. Painter (Kanō Ryōji; *gō:* Fukyūshi, Samboku; seventeenth–eighteenth century) of the Kanō school, a disciple of Kanō Sanraku in Kyoto.
• Japanese name for a kingdom in the Ryukyu Islands, on northern Okinawa, rival of the Sannan kingdom (on southern Okinawa) in the fourteenth and fifteenth centuries. Shō Shashi united them to make the "central kingdom," Chūsan. *See* RYUKYU, SATSUDŌ.

Sambugyō. Generic term for the three most important senior bureaucrats of the Edo period: the Edo *machi-bugyō,* the *kanjō-bugyō,* and the *jisha-bugyō. See* BUGYŌ, MACHI-BUGYŌ.

Sambu honsho. The "three classic books" of Shinto: *Kojiki, Jujiki,* and *Nihongi. See also* KIKI.

Samisen. *See* SHAMISEN.

Sammai-dō. In Buddhist temples, the hall reserved for meditation.

Sammichi. Collective term for three *kampaku* (regents) who succeeded each other in the late tenth century: Fujiwara no Michitaka (993), Fujiwara no Michikane (995), and Fujiwara no Michinaga (995). They were brothers.

Sammon. Main branch of the Buddhist Tendai-shū sect, created by Saichō in 805 at the Enryaku-ji on Mt. Hiei.
→ *See* SAN-MON.

Sammon gosan no kiri. Kabuki play, in the *jidai-mono* genre, first produced in Osaka in 1778.

Sampitsu. "The Three Brushes," the name for the three best calligraphers of a given period or sect. For example: *in the early tenth century,* Hayanari, Kūkai, and Emperor Saga; *in the Kan'ei era,* Kōetsu, Nobutada, and Shōkadō Shōjō; *of the Ōbaku-shū sect,* Ingen, Mokuan, and Sokuhi. *See also* SANSEKI.
→ *See* ISHIKAWA BEIAN.

Samurai. Class of warriors *(bushi)* who were vassals of a military leader, a daimyo, or a shogun. This class appeared in the eastern provinces of Japan in the mid-tenth century, when the great warrior clans were being formed. The samurai were guards *(saburai)* serving the lords of the court, but in the twelfth century they became powerful enough to command attention in the court with the Taira clans and the Minamoto. Starting in the Kamakura period, they were organized by the *bakufu,* gained hereditary status, and were expected to follow an unwritten warrior code called Kyūba no Michi, or "Way of the Bow and the Horse," which was modified and institutionalized in the seventeenth century under the name Bushido, or "Way of the Warrior."

In the Edo period, samurai received a sort of pension from their direct leader (daimyo or shogun) to whom they had sworn unconditional fidelity until death. The most important samurai also received land in compensation for their services. In the Kamakura and Muromachi periods, "peasant-samurai" *(jizamurai, ji-samurai)* had their own estates but were obliged to assist their suzerains in case of war. During the disturbances that swept Japan in the fourteenth, fifteenth, and sixteenth centuries, many *jizamurai* became independent, and some conquered provinces and became daimyo in their own right *(see* GEKOKUJŌ). In the Edo period, they constituted a sort of military aristocracy, distinguishing themselves from simple soldiers by carrying two swords *(see* DAISHŌ, KATANA). Their emblem was the cherry blossom *(sakura)* because their lives were as fragile as those of the flowers, which lasted only several days.

After the Meiji Restoration, samurai were included in the *shizoku* class and considered ordinary subjects. In 1876, they were forbidden to carry swords, which caused several rebellions; a few years later, the establishment of conscription deprived them of the rest of their privileges. *See* AKŌ-GISHI, BUKE-SHOHATTO, BUSHIDŌ, IENOKO-RŌTŌ, KŌYŌ GUNKAN, SABURAI.

• **Samurai-dokoro.** "Board of Retainers." In the Kamakura period, a ministry charged with military affairs. Also called Saburai-dokoro, *"saburai"* being an old form of the word *"samurai,"* meaning "at the service of."

San. "Three." In front of a *b, p,* or *m,* this syllable is pronounced *"sam."* Japanese reading *(kun):* mi, mitsu.

• Sino-Japanese reading *(on)* of the ideogram meaning "mountain." Japanese reading *(kun):* yama.

• Inscription (poem or prose) on a painting in *suiboku,* generally a *kakemono. See* SUIBOKU.

• Honorific suffix, corresponding to Mr., Mrs., or Miss, placed after a family or personal name. Very polite form: Sama.

→ *See* DAIGAKU-RYŌ.

Sanada Nobushige. Warrior and strategist (Sanada Yukimura, 1576–1615), son of Sanada Masayuki (1545–1609), lord of the Ueda estate in Shinano province (Nagano prefecture). He served Toyotomi Hideyoshi in Japan and in Korea starting in 1587.

At the Battle of Sekigahara (1600), he initially took Tokugawa Ieyasu's side, but he left Ieyasu to second Ishida Mitsunari, while his brother, Sanada Nobuyuki (1566–1658) remained faithful to Ieyasu. Pardoned, Nobushige settled on Mt. Kōya, but he opposed Ieyasu again during the siege of the Osaka castle. He was killed in battle on the eve of the surrender of the castle.

Sanage. Site near Nagoya (Aichi prefecture) where ceramics kilns were built in the eighth century to produce *sue* pottery and imitations of Chinese celadons. These kilns were in use until the late twelfth century. Only recently (in 1954) was the exact location of the site, extending over an immense territory, rediscovered. More than 438 kilns from ancient times were uncovered, as were about 800 from the Kamakura and Muromachi periods; the latter were producing only unvarnished tea bowls because the master ceramists of Sanage had migrated to Seto, where they taught their skills to the potters of that region.

Sanchū. "The Three Great Models of Fidelity" (to the emperor): Taira no Shigenori, Fujiwara no Fujifusa, and Kusunoki Masashige.

San-daijin. Collective term for three famous writers: Motoori Norinaga, Kamo no Mabuchi, and Kada no Azumamaro. When Hirata Atsutane is added to this group, it is called Kokugaku Shidaika.

Sandai jitsuroku. "Story of the Three Reigns." A 50-volume history book, the sixth work of the *Rikkokushi,* compiled in 901 by Fujiwara no Tokihira, Sugawara no Michizane, Mimune no Masahira, and Ōkura no Yoshiyuki. It covers the period from 859 to 889 and the rules of emperors Seiwa, Yōzei, and Kōkō.

Sandai kyaku-shiki. Collective term for the three great collections of laws: *Kōnin kyaku-shiki, Jōgan kyaku-shiki,* and *Engi kyaku-shiki. See* RITSURYŌ KYAKU-SHIKI.

San daishū. Collective name for three famous poetry anthologies: *Kokin-shū* (913–14), *Gosen-shū* (951), and *Shūi-shū* (1007). *See* CHOKUSEN WAKA-SHŪ.

Sanda-yaki. Celadon-type ceramics produced in Sanda (Settsu province) starting in 1788 by a potter named Kanda Sōbei.

Sandō. "Three lines" drawn on the necks of Buddhist divinities portrayed in sculpture and painting, and characteristic of the images of the late Heian period. These three lines are part of the Chinese canon of beauty.
→ *See* CHINCHŌ.

Sane-hijiki. In traditional architecture, *hijiki* (strut) placed on the farthest outside (die) of an overhang, supporting the main beam (*degeta* or *gangyō*). *See* TO-KYŌ.

Sanetaka kō ki. Diary of the courtesan Sanjōnishi Sanetaka, describing events that took place from 1474 to 1536 under three emperors of the Muromachi period: Go-Hanazono, Go-Tsuchimikado, and Go-Kashiwabara. This 60-chapter work of memories and accounts is a valuable source of information on this turbulent epoch.

San Feripe gō Jiken. In December 1596, Toyotomi Hideyoshi seized a Spanish galleon, the *San Felipe,* which, en route from Manila to Acapulco, was shipwrecked and sank on the coast of Urado in Tosa province. He confiscated the cargo and began persecuting Spanish and Portuguese missionaries, whom he suspected of plotting with the Philippines and Macao.

San Francisco, Treaty of. Treaty signed between the Allied forces and Japan on September 8, 1951, in San Francisco, officially ending the war. On the Allied side, 48 nations countersigned the treaty ending the occupation of Japan. It was signed by Foster Dulles and Dean Acheson for the United States, and by Prime Minister Yoshida Shigeru for Japan. It was followed, on April 28, 1952, by another treaty in which Japan made peace with China. The Treaty of San Francisco allowed the United States to maintain military bases in Japan and to occupy Okinawa. Japan lost all the territories it had conquered after 1895—Taiwan, Korea, Karafutō (southern Sakhalin); agreed to prosecute war criminals; and renounced all claims to its former colonies. The treaty officially took effect after it was ratified by the U.S. Senate on April 28, 1952.

Sangi. Old method of calculating using short wooden sticks. The numbers 1 to 5 were represented by sticks placed beside each other. The same sticks, on top of another horizontal stick, represented the numbers 6 to 9. Groups of 10 were represented by horizontal sticks (10 to 50) and by combinations of horizontal and vertical sticks (60 to 90).

Hundreds were symbolized by dots, zero by a circle. Negative numbers were represented by an oblique bar on the last figure on the right (except for zero). In the seventeenth century, use of the *soroban* spread, and *sangi* were abandoned.
• Former title for the imperial counselor to the *dajōkan.* This position was eliminated in 1885, when the ministerial cabinet system was adopted.

San Giovanni, Achille. Italian painter (nineteenth century) who taught at the Technical School of Arts from 1880 to 1883, after having been officially invited to give courses in anatomy drawing at the University of Tokyo.

Sangoku-shi. Japanese title for the famous Chinese work *Sanguozh* (Chronicle of the Three Kingdoms), dating from the late third century and translated many times.

Sangyō gisho. Group of three famous commentaries on Buddhist texts written between 609 and 615 and attributed to Shōtoku Taishi: the *Hokke-kyō gisho (Skt.: Saddharmapundarīka-sūtra),* the *Yuima-kyō gisho (Skt.: Vimalakīrti-sūtra),* and the *Shoman-gyō gisho (Skt.: Shrīmālādevī-sūtra).*

Sangyō hokokukai. "Patriotic industrial associations," groups formed before and during the Second World War to rally workers in plants and factories who wanted to help increase production.

San gyokushū. Collective term for three poetry anthologies: Haku gyokushū, Heki gyokushū, and Settsu gyokushū.

San'in. Northern part of southern Honshu, on the Sea of Japan (Nihonkai), as opposed to San'yō, the southern part on the Interior Sea (Setonaikai). The San'in region includes Kyoto, Hyōgo, and Tottori prefectures.

Sanja Matsuri. "Festival of the Three [Shinto] Shrines" of Asakusa (Tokyo), which takes place every May at the Asakusa-jinja. During the festival, more than a hundred *mikoshi* (portable shrines) are carried in processions, and ancient dances of rice-paddy fertility rites (*binzasara no mai*) and dances by geisha (*teko-mai*) are performed.

• *Sanja matsuri.* Kabuki play, adapted from a Noh play by Segawa Jokō II in 1832.

The Thirty-Six Poetic Geniuses

1. Kakinomoto no Hitomaro (?–between 708 and 715)
2. Ki no Tusrayuki (ca. 883–945)
3. Ōshikōchi no Mitsune (active ca. 898–922)
4. Ise (ca. 877–ca. 940?), woman poet
5. Ōtomo no Yakamochi (717–85)
6. Yamabe no Akahito (active between 724 and 737)
7. Ariwara no Narihira (825–80)
8. Henjō (ca. 816–90)
9. Sosei (active 859–923)
10. Sarumarudayū (ninth century)
11. Ki no Tomonori (active between 850 and 904)
12. Fujiwara no Kanesuke (877–933)
13. Ono no Komachi (active between 834 and 857), woman poet
14. Fujiwara no Atsutada (906–43)
15. Fujiwara no Asatada (ca. 910–66)
16. Fujiwara no Takamitsu (d. 994)
17. Fujiwara no Toshiyuki (881–907)
18. Fujiwara no Kiyotada (?–958)
19. Fujiwara no Okikaze (early tenth century)
20. Fujiwara no Motoyoshi (tenth century)
21. Fujiwara no Nakabumi (908–78)
22. Minamoto no Kintada (889–948)
23. Minamoto no Shigeyuki (?–ca. 1000)
24. Minamoto no Muneyuki (?–ca. 939)
25. Minamoto no Nobuakira (909–70)
26. Minamoto no Shitagō (911–83)
27. Mibu no Tadamine (active from 898 to 920)
28. Mibu no Tadami (early tenth century)
29. Saigū no Nyōgo (929–85), Emperor Murakami's wife
30. Ōnakatomi no Yoritomo (?–958)
31. Kiyohara no Motosuke (ca. 908–90)
32. Sakanoue no Korenori (?–930)
33. Ōnakatomi no Yoshinobu (921–91)
34. Taira no Kanemori (?–980)
35. Nakatsukasa (ca. 920–80), woman poet
36. Ki no Tomonori (?–915), woman poet, sometimes replaced by woman poet Kodai no Kimi

Sanjō-bussho. Artists' studio of the En-pa (Empa) school, established on Third Avenue (Sanjō) in Kyoto by Chōsei (a disciple of Jōchō) and his son, Ensei (d. 1134). Its best-known members were:

—**Chōsei,** Ensei and Kenkei's father
—**Ensei,** Chōen and Ken'en's father
—**Chōen,** Enshin and Chōshun's father
—**Ken'en,** Gan'en, Chūen, and Enshun's father
—**Mei'en,** Chōen and Kan'en's father

Sanjō-daijin. *See* FUJIWARA NO YORITADA.

• **Sanjō Kokaji Munechika.** *See* MUNECHIKA.

• **Sanjō Tennō.** Sixty-seventh emperor (Prince Okisada, 976<1012–16>1017), Reizei Tennō's son and successor to his cousin, Ichijō Tennō. He went blind and abdicated in favor of his other cousin, Go-Ichijō.

Sanjōnishi Sanetaka. Poet (Fujiwara Sanetaka, 1455–1537), son of *naidaijin* Fujiwara Kin'yasu (?–1460) and also appointed *naidaijin*. His poems, mainly *renga,* were compiled in the *Setsu gyokushū* and *Chōsetsu-shū.* He wrote a Noh play, *Sagoromo,* and a number of treatises on poetics, as well as an important historical work, the *Sanetaka kō ki.*

Sanjō Sanetomi. Politician (1837–91) belonging to a branch of a Fujiwara family, personal adviser to Emperor Mutsuhito. Appointed *udaijin* in 1869, then *dajō-daijin* from 1871 to 1885. He led the government from 1889 to his death.

Sanjūniban shokunin uta-awasa emaki. "Poetic Competition in Thirty-Two Parts Held by the Members of Various Professions." A fifteenth-century *emakimono* describing merchants and artisans at work, each image accompanied by a *waka* poem.

Sanju-no-tō. "Pagoda with three stories" of roofs, generally Buddhist. A unique variant is found at the Shin Yakushi-ji, near Nara (*see* MOKOSHI). *See also* GOJU-NO-TŌ, TAHŌ-TŌ.

Sanjūrokkasen. "Thirty-Six Poetic Geniuses." A group of 36 famous poets who lived before the eleventh century, according to the list established by Fujiwara no Kintō. The order of this list of "immortal poets" may vary. These poets were often portrayed in paintings (called *kasen-e*), alone or in groups, starting in the twelfth–thirteenth century. Later, compilers chose other poets to constitute different groups of "36 poetic geniuses," represented in Sanjūrokkasen-*emaki*. The most famous one was by Fujiwara no Nobuzane (1177–1265), in which each portrait is accompanied by a handwritten

---

The Thirty-Three Forms of Kannon Bosatsu

1. Yōryū Kannon Bosatsu
2. Ryūzu Kannon Bosatsu
3. Jikyō Kannon Bosatsu
4. Enkō Kannon Bosatsu
5. Yūge Kannon Bosatsu
6. Byakue Kannon Bosatsu
7. Renga Kannon Bosatsu
8. Takimi Kannon Bosatsu
9. Seyaku Kannon Bosatsu
10. Gyoran Kannon Bosatsu
11. Toku-ō Kannon Bosatsu
12. Suigetsu Kannon Bosatsu
13. Ichiyō Kannon Bosatsu
14. Shōkyō (or Seitsu) Kannon Bosatsu
15. Itoku Kannon Bosatsu
16. Emmei (or Emmyō) Kannon Bosatsu
17. Shūhō Kannon Bosatsu
18. Iwato Kannon Bosatsu
19. Nōjyō (or Nōshō) Kannon Bosatsu
20. Anoku Kannon Bosatsu
21. Amadai Kannon Bosatsu
22. Hae (or Hyoe) Kannon Bosatsu
23. Ruri Kannon Bosatsu
24. Tarason Kannon Bosatsu
25. Kōri Kannon Bosatsu
26. Rokuji Kannon Bosatsu
27. Fuhi Kannon Bosatsu
28. Merōfu Kannon Bosatsu
29. Gasshō Kannon Bosatsu
30. Ichinyō Kannon Bosatsu
31. Funi Kannon Bosatsu
32. Jiren Kannon Bosatsu
33. Shasui Kannon Bosatsu

---

poem. Then Izumi Shikibu, Murasaki Shikibu, Sei Shōnagon, and others were added to the list. The Buddhist monk Eikai (1288–1347) also selected "36 Buddhist poets"; in the Kamakura period, there was also a list of "36 immortal women poets."

Sanjūsangendō. *See* RENGE-Ō-IN.

Sanjūsan Ōgeshin. "Thirty-Three Forms of Kannon Bosatsu" (*Skt:* Avalokiteshvara), which are emanations (or correspondences, incarnations, or "transformation bodies") of this bodhisattva of Chinese origin (*Chin.:* Guanyin Sanshi'er Xiang). These forms *(ōgeshin)* gave rise to a famous pilgrimage to the 33 temples of the provinces of the West (*see* SANJŪSAN-SHO). Neither the list nor the order is definitive, and there are many variations. There are also other groups of Kannon Bosatsu, such as the "100 Kannon of the Hōjō-ji," the "1,001 Kannon" of the Renge-ō-in (Sanjūsangendō), the "3,000 Kannon" of Shizuoka, and so on. These forms also have various names, such as the Nurete ("wet hand") Kannon of the Kiyomizu-dera temple in Kyoto.

• **Sanjūsan-sho.** "The Thirty-Three Temples of the Western Pilgrimage." A group of Buddhist temples dedicated to Shō Kannon Bosatsu (*see* SANJŪSAN ŌGESHIN). Also collectively called Saikoku Sanjū-san-sho.

Sanka. "Mountain grotto," a name given to itinerant aboriginal hunter-fisher groups living in the mountains. Their origin is not well known, and people often assimilate them with *hinin* and *semmin.* Also called *yamabito* (men of the mountains) and sometimes referred to as the "Japanese gypsies." They are mentioned in texts as far back as the eleventh century. *See also* ETA.

• Currency system of "three coins"—in gold *(ryō),* silver *(chōgin),* and copper *(mon)*—created by Tokugawa Ieyasu in the early seventeenth century.
→ *See* BUSON.

San-kaidan. Generic term for the three main temples of the Buddhist Tendai-shū sect: Tōdai-ji, Yakushi-ji (Shimotsuke no Kuni), and Kanzeon-ji.

Sankan. Collective term for three major noble families (Hosokawa, Shiba, and Hatakeyama) that inherited the highest administrative positions and whose authority sometimes surpassed that of the Ashikaga shoguns in the fourteenth and fifteenth centuries.

• Japanese name for the three Korean provinces conquered by Jingū Kōgō: Shinra (*Kor.:* Sinla, Silla), Kōrai (*Kor.:* Kōryö), and Hakusai, corresponding to the Korean kingdoms of Ma-han on the west coast, Pyŏn-han in the far south, and Chin-han in the east. *Chin.:* San Han.

San-ke. The "three families" of the Tokugawa, descended from Tokugawa Ieyasu's sons, from among which the shoguns of the Edo period not belonging to the direct line were chosen: Owari, Kii, and Mito. *See* SHIMPAN-DAIMYŌ.

The Thirty-Three Temples of the Western Pilgrimage

1. Nyorin-ji, in Nachi (Kii province)
2. Kakawa-dera, in Kokawa (Kii)
3. Fujii-dera, in Nakano (Kawachi)
4. Kongō-hō-ji, in the Kimii-dera (Kii)
5. Sefuku-ji, in Makino-o (Izumi)
6. Minami Hokke-ji, in Tsubosaka (Yamato)
7. Ryūkai-ji, in Okadera (Yamato)
8. Hase-dera, in Hase (Yamato)
9. Nan'en-dō, in Nara
10. Mimurodō-dera, in Uji
11. Kami no Daigo-dera, in Uji
12. Shōhō-ji, in Iwama (Ōmi)
13. Ishiyama-dera, in Ishiyama (Ōmi)
14. Onjō-ji (Mii-dera), in Ōtsu (Ōmi)
15. Shin Kumano-dera, in Kyoto
16. Kiyomizu-dera, in Kyoto
17. Rokuharamitsu-ji, in Kyoto
18. Rokkaku-dō, in Kyoto
19. Gyōkan-ji (or Kōtō-ji), in Kyoto
20. Yoshimine-dera, in Kyoto
21. Bodai-ji, in Anō (Tamba)
22. Sōzen-ji, in Settsu
23. Kachiō-dera, in Toyokawa (Settsu)
24. Nakayama-dera, in Kobe (Settsu)
25. Shin Kiyomizu-dera, in Kamogawa (Harima)
26. Hokke-ji, in Harima
27. Nyorin-dō, at Shosha-zan (Harima)
28. Seisō-ji, at the Nairai-yama (Tango)
29. Matsuno-o-dera, in Wakasa
30. Chikubu-ji, on the island of Chikubu-shima (Ōmi)
31. Chōmei-ji, on the island of Oku-shima (Ōmi)
32. Kannon-ji, in Ashi-ura (Ōmi)
33. Kegon-ji, in Tanigumi (Mino)

• **Sankyō.** Term for three branches of the Tokugawa family: Tayasu, Hitotsubashi, and Shimizu.

Sankei. The most famous "three landscapes" in Japan: Itsukushima, Matsushima, and Ama no Hashidate, often cited in literature. *See also* NIHON SANKEI.

• **Sankei-en.** Garden in Yokohama, created in 1906 by a wealthy merchant, Hara Tomitarō. As well as a number of ponds and flowering trees, it features old farms and a teahouse *(chashitsu)* built for shogun Tokugawa Iemitsu.

Sankei Shimbun. Daily newspaper founded by Maeda Hisakichi in Osaka in 1933 under the name *Nihon Kōgyō Shimbun.* It took its current name in 1958, after absorbing other newspapers and undergoing several name changes. This general-interest newspaper, with a moderate but anti-communist political stance, is part of the Fuji-Sankei group and has correspondents in many countries. Circulation is about 2 million. Head offices in Osaka and Tokyo. *See* FUJI TEREBIJON, PRESS.

Sankin-kōtai. "Alternating presence," a system inaugurated in 1635 by the Tokugawa shogunate to ensure the loyalty of the *tozama-daimyō.* According to the *sankin-kōtai,* the provincial daimyo were forced to maintain a residence *(yashiki)* in Edo, live there one year out of two (or several months a year), and leave their family living there permanently.

Tokugawa Iemitsu decreed this system obligatory so that he could control the daimyo better. Travel by the daimyo to and from Edo was regulated: their retinue could not be more than several hundred people, and their procession had to follow a set itinerary. This system was expensive for the daimyo, who had to pay for their *yashiki,* stays, and travels, draining their finances and thus strengthening the shogunate. The *sankin-kōtai* was temporarily suspended from 1722 to 1730 because of serious famines, but was not eliminated until 1862. The settling of the families of the daimyo in Edo and their constant traveling contributed to the creation of a national economy and the development of Edo and the waystations *(shukuba, shuku-eki)* on the major roads *(see* GO-KAIDŌ). It also provided the country with some unity and was a powerful tool for organizing the state during the Meiji Restoration of 1868.

Sankyōku. Music written for the *kokyū* (three-stringed violin), the koto, and the shamisen (or *shakuhachi*).

San-mon. In a Buddhist monastery, the main gate *(mon),* generally two stories with roofs covered with tiles, located on the main path to the shrine. Also called *sammon.*

Sannaimaru-yama. Jōmon prehistoric site on the hills north of Aomori, excavated in 1992, which revealed the vestiges of a sizable community of hunter-gatherers (perhaps 500 people) who built large warehouses on pilings (chestnut-tree trunks with a diameter of 0.8 m). This village dates back to about 3500 BC, when the climate was slightly warmer than it is now. A large quantity of pottery and bones of small animals were discovered there. The village was probably abandoned during a chilling of the climate about 1,500 years after its most prosperous period.

Sannan. "Southern" kingdom of the Ryukyu Islands, on Okinawa, rivaling the Samboku kingdom on the north part of the island, from the thirteenth to the fifteenth century. King Shō Hashi united them in the kingdom of Chūsan. *See* RYUKYU, SAMBOKU, SATSUDO.

Sannō. Popular name for the Shinto *kami* Ōkuninushi no Mikoto, also called Hie, Hiyoshi, Onamuji, Sannō Sama, Sannō Gongen.
→ *See* TORII.

• **Sannō Ichijitsu Shintō.** Syncretic Shinto-Buddhist sect created by the Tendai-shū sect in the ninth century. It developed in the thirteenth century and expanded greatly in the sixteenth century under the impetus of the monk Tenkai (1536–1643), but disappeared about 1868. *See* ICHIJITSU SHINTŌ.

• **Sannō Matsuri.** Grand festival of the Shinto Hie Shrine in Tokyo, celebrated in mid-June of odd-numbered years. This festival features processions of chariots and *mikoshi*. It originated in a similar *matsuri* at the Hie Shrine (Hiyoshi-taisha) in Ōtsu, which generally took place in April. Also called Hie Matsuri.

• **Sannō-sama-jinja.** Shinto shrine in Tokyo, dedicated to the *kami* Ōkuninushi no Mikoto, built by Tokugawa Ieyasu in 1615 with the assent of the Sannō Ichijitsu sect. Also called Hie-jinja.

San no tsuzumi. Small hourglass-shaped drum with two skins and a striking cord, used mainly in *gagaku* music.

Sanogawa Mangiku. Kabuki actor (1690–1747), active in Osaka.

Sano Manabu. Economist (1892–1953), born in Ōita. He joined the Communist party in 1922; following the persecution after the major earthquake of September 1923, he fled to the USSR. He returned to Japan in 1925 and became active in the party, but left again for the USSR in 1928. When he once again returned, he was arrested by the Japanese in Shanghai and sentenced to life in prison. In 1933, he renounced communism and was freed.

Sano no Chigami no Otome. Poet (early eighth century) and priestess at the Ise Shrine. After she secretly married Nakatomi no Yakamori, he was exiled to Echizen, about 738. Sixty-three poems exchanged between Chigami and Yakamori were included in the *Man'yōshū*, 23 of which were by Chigami. Also called Sanu Chigami, Sano no Otogami no Otome.

Sano Tsunehiko. Shinto priest (1834–1906), founder of the Shinri-kyō sect in the late nineteenth century.

Sano Tsunetami. Politician and navy officer (1822–1902), born in Saga province. After studying "Dutch science" *(rangaku),* he went to Europe in 1867 to complete his education in naval techniques, and in 1868 he helped organize the Japanese navy. In 1877, during the war against Satsuma, he created Hakuaisha, a humanitarian organization to assist the injured, which became the Japanese Red Cross in 1887. He also held several ministerial portfolios, including finance.

Sanraku. Painter (Kanō Sanraku, Kanō Mitsuyori, Kimura Mitsuyori; *mei:* Heizō, Suri; *gō:* Sanraku, 1559–1635), born in Kyoto, painter Kimura Nagamitsu's son and Kanō Eitoku's adoptive son. He worked for Toyotomi Hideyoshi and decorated many fusuma, creating the Kyō Kanō school. His son, Sansetsu, succeeded him at the head of his Kyoto studio.
→ *See* KŌTEI.

Sanron-shū. Buddhist sect of the "Three Treatises," whose philosophy, part of the Madhyāmika (*Jap.:* Chūron) school, was founded on three major texts of this religious current: the *Chūron (Skt.: Madhyamika-shāstra)* and *Jūnimonron (Skt.: Dvādashamukha-shāstra)* by Nāgārjuna (*Jap.:* Ryūju, Ryū-myō), and the *Hyakurion (Skt.: Shata-shāstra)* by Āryadeva. The sect was imported from China via Korea by the monk Ekan in 625 and was established in Nara. It was divided into two branches, the Gankō-ji-ha and the Taian-ji-ha (which no longer exists). The Sanron-shū still had followers until the beginning of the Edo period. *Chin.:* Sanlun Zong. Also called Ichi-dai Kyō-shū.

San-san-ku-do. "Three times three," the traditional marriage ceremony *(kekkon)* during which the newlyweds exchange three cups of *sake* that they must drink in three swallows in order to seal their union definitively. This ceremony may take place at the Buddhist temple, at the Shinto shrine, or during a banquet to which relatives and friends are invited. *See* MARRIAGE.

Sanseki. Collective term for the three greatest calligraphers of the tenth century: Ono no Michikaze (Yaseki), Fujiwara no Yukinari (Gonseki), and Fujiwara no Sari (Saseki). Some lists replace Ono no Michikaze with Kaneakira Shinnō. This term is also used for the three best calligraphers of a given period. *See also* KANEAKIRA, SAMPITSU.
→ *See* TACHIBANA HAYANARI.

Sansen-jin. Collective term for three Buddhist and Shinto warrior divinities, Marishi-ten, Bishamonten, and Daikoku-ten, sometimes portrayed with a single body, three heads, and six arms.

Sansetsu. Painter (Kanō Heishirō, Kanō Sansetsu; *mei:* Nui no Suke; *gō:* Dasoku-gen, Shōhaku-sanjin, Tōgenshi, Sansetsu, 1589–1651) of the Kyō Kanō school, who succeeded his father, Sanraku, at the head of his Kyoto studio.

Sanshō. Famous sculptor of netsuke (Wada Sanshō, Kokeisai, 1871–1936), in Osaka.

Sanshoku. "The Three Offices," established on January 3, 1868, to constitute the first government of the Meiji era: the Sōsai (presidential office), the Gijō (administrative office), and the San'yo (office of advisers). Several months later, seven departments were added, charged with the budget, domestic and external affairs, trade, and so on. Together they were called Sanshoku Shichika. All these offices were replaced on June 11, 1868, by the Dajōkan (Great State Council), which truly inaugurated the new Restoration regime. The first president of the Sanshoku was Arisugawa no Miya Taruhito, an imperial prince. Much earlier, in the eighth century, this term had designated the three offices of the minister of state *(dajō-daijin),* the ministers of the right and the left *(udaijin* and *sadaijin),* and the councillors *(sangi).*

Sansom, George Bailey. English diplomat and Japanologist (1883–1965), born in Kent and educated in France. As a consular employee, he was posted to Japan from 1939 to 1941. His research on Japanese society led to important books on the subject, including *An Historical Grammar of Japanese* (1928), *Japan: A Short Cultural History* (1931), *The Western World and Japan* (1951), *A History of Japan* (1958–63). He was knighted in 1935.

Sansui Denki. Manufacturer and distributor of audiovisual equipment (tape recorders, video recorders, television sets, etc.) under the brand name Sansui. Founded in 1960, it currently exports more than 60% of its production. Head office in Tokyo.

Sansui-ga. "Landscape painting," as distinct from *kachō-ga* (paintings of flowers and birds) and *jimbutsu-ga* (paintings of people and theater scenes).

Santō Kyōden. Writer and painter (Iwase Denzō, Iwase Sei, Haida Sei; *mei:* Denzō, Iwase Samuru; *azana:* Yūsei, Hakkei; *gō:* Kitao Masanobu, Masanobu, Rissai, Santōkyō, Santōan, Seiseisai, Santōkutsu, Kyōden, Migaru Orisuke, 1761–1816), born in Edo. He was Kitao Shigemasa's student and painted mainly ukiyo-e prints, specializing in portrayals of beautiful women *(bijin)* and courtesans of the Yoshiwara district (he married two of them, Okiku, then Yuri). He earned a living by running a tobacco store and organizing artists' and writers' meetings.

He began his literary career about 1775 publishing novels in *kibyōshi* genre *(Edo umare uwaki no kabayaki),* then, starting in 1785, works in *sharebon (Tsūgen sōmagaki)* and *yomihon* genres. He also wrote erotic novels with complex plots: *Gozonji no shōbai-mono* (The Famous, 1782), *Shingaku hayasome kusa* (Good and Bad Eggs, 1790), *Kataki-uchi ato no matsuri* (Vengeance and Celebration, 1788), and others. Three of his *sharebon* became very popular, but earned him three months in prison for immorality: *Shōgi kinuburui, Nishiki no ura,* and *Shikake bunko.*

Santō Kyōden also wrote a sort of biography of Confucius, *Tsūzoku daiseiden* (1790), and conducted studies on customs and mores of the Edo period: *Ukiyo-e ruikō tsuikō* (Classification of Ukiyo-e Prints, 1802), *Kottōshū* (Antique Collection, 1804), *Kinsei kisekikō* (Extraordinary Facts of the Present Day, 1815), *Mukashi-gatari inazuma byōshi* (or *Mukashi-banashi inazuma byoshi,* Light on Ancient Stories, 1806), *Honchō suibodai zenden,* and *Sakura hide abebo no sōshi* (1805). An active member of a number of literary circles, he also wrote *kyōka* poems. It is thought that he collaborated with Jippensha Ikku to write *Hizakurige.* His brother, Santō Kyōzan (ca. 1769–1858), also wrote *gesaku,* and his sister, Santō Yone (1771–88), wrote humorous poems *(kyōka)* and *kibyōshi* under the pseudonym Kurotobi Shikibu.

Sanuki. Former name of a province on Shikoku, now included in Kagawa prefecture.

• *Sanuki no suke no nikki.* "Sanuki Tenji's Diary," a work by a lady-in-waiting called Sanuki Tenji, written around 1107–08. Also titled *Sanuki Tenji nikki, Horikawa-in nikki.*

• *Sanuki Tenji.* Lady of the court (Fujiwara no Nagako, ca. 1079–early twelfth century), serving Emperor Horikawa, then Emperor Toba. Her diary *(Sanuki no suke no nikki)* gives an emotional account of her relationship with Emperor Horikawa and of life in the court between 1107 and 1109. She is still sometimes considered to be the same person as her sister, Fujiwara no Kaneko (1050–1133).

• *Sanuki tenui nikki.* See SANUKI NO SUKE NO NIKKI.

Sanwa Ginkō. Large commercial bank, founded in 1933 by the merger of several local banks. It is now one of the five largest financial institutions in Japan by volume of deposits, and has many foreign subsidiaries, including in San Francisco, London, and Southeast Asia. Head office in Osaka.

San'yō. Buddhist monk (Kanshitsu Genkitsu, 1548–1612), director of the school created by Tokugawa Ieyasu in Fushimi (Kyoto) in 1601 and professor at the Ashikaga-gakkō. He invented moving characters for book printing, a system he called Ashikaga-bon.
• Painter (Rai Jō; *mei:* Kyūtarō; *azana:* Shisei; *gō:* Sanjūroppō Gaishi, San'yō, 1780–1832) of the Nanga (Bunjinga) school, Rai Shunsui's son and student. He painted mainly landscapes *(sansui-ga).* Also a historian and calligrapher, he wrote many works, including *Nihon gaishi* (History of Japan). → *See* SAN'IN.

San'yō Denki. Manufacturer of electrical and electronic equipment, various instruments, household appliances, and computers, founded in 1947. It began to distribute radio receivers and rotary washing machines in 1953, and now has more than 28 plants in 19 countries. It exports 40% of its production and is the second largest manufacturer of household appliances in Japan, after Matsushita. Head office in Moriguchi, Ōsaka-fu. Also called Sanyo.

San'yūtei Enchō. Writer (Izubuchi Jirokichi; *gō:* Koenta, 1839–1900) and *rakugo* artist, of the San'yū school in Edo; he studied with San'yūtei Enshō II (1806–62). In addition to stories (which he dictated to a stenographer), he wrote a play, *Botan tōrō* (The Peony Lamp), based on a Chinese collection of ghost stories, *Jiandeng xinhua,* by Qu Zongji. Also known as Enchō.

Sanzen-in. Buddhist temple founded in the ninth century in Ōhara (Kyoto) by Saichō to house Buddhist images, including several of Yakushi Nyorai. In 1086, nine statues of Amida in gold-leafed wood were moved there. Starting in 1130, the temple was directed by an imperial prince, Saiun (1104–62), Emperor Horikawa's son. It was moved several times, and was built on the current site only about 1480. The main hall (Ōjō Gokuraku-in) probably dates from 985 and was built by the monk Genshin. The other buildings date from the sixteenth and seventeenth centuries.

Sanzō. "The Three Treasures" of Buddhism, composed of canonical texts: the Sutras *(Jap.: kyō),* the Vinaya (rules of monastic discipline; *Jap.: ritsu),* and the Abhidharma (didactic treatises; *Jap.: ron),* comprising a total of 1,662 volumes. *Chin.:* Sanzang; *Skt.:* Tripitaka.

Sanzon. "The Three Venerable Ones." Triads of Buddhist divinities comprising one *nyorai* and two *bosatsu,* or three *bosatsu,* or three *myō-ō,* or three *ten,* and so on. The oldest *sanzon,* portraying Shaka (Shakyamuni Buddha) accompanied by Monju Bosatsu and Fugen Bosatsu, made in bronze by Kuratsukuri no Tori in the early seventh century, is in the Hōryū-ji (Nara). *Sanzon* are also synonymous with the "Three Precious Jewels" of Buddhism: the Buddha, the Dharma (the Law), and the Sangha (monastic community). *Chin.: sanzun.*

Saotome. Term for women who were responsible for transplanting rice seedlings in the rice paddies. They were usually young women who came from other villages to help with this essential task. They performed their work with joy in order to please the *kami* of the fields *(Ta no kami);* in the evenings, the village danced rounds called Saotome Odori (Ta-ue Odori).

• **Saotome Odori.** See SAOTOME, TA-UE ODORI.

Sapporo. Chief city of Hokkaido prefecture and of the island of Hokkaido, located at the opening to the Ishikari plain in the southwest part of the island. The city was built from scratch in 1869 on a checkerboard plan. It became a prefecture in 1886. It hosted the Winter Olympic Games in 1972 (Teine ski resort) and is the home of Chitose International Airport. Its climate is relatively cool and humid. It expanded considerably after the Second World War, and it produces *sake* and Western-style liquors (whiskey, cognac) as well as Sapporo brand beer. It is also home to some textile, furniture, and machine-tool manufacturers. Every January, a major ice-sculpture festival draws large numbers of visitors. University of Hokkaido, founded 1918. Botanical gardens and zoo. *Pop.*: 1,450,000.

Sarakin. Credit institutions specializing in making loans to salaried workers (*see* SARARĪMAN) without requiring collateral, but at high interest rates; these institutions appeared officially in the early 1950s. Since 1983, the *sarakin* have been regulated by law, which governs the interest charged and bans the use of threats or violence (which are often used to recover debts when they are made by yakuza).

Sararīman. "Salary man," a term for all white-collar workers with a regular salary. Society expects them to conform strictly to custom and to be discreet. They must also show unfailing loyalty to the company that employs and pays them, and they are the most conservative social group in today's Japan.

Sarasa. Cotton calico fabrics, imported from India by the Portuguese and Dutch in the sixteenth and seventeenth centuries. Made in Japan in the late Edo period, they were called *wasarasa*. Each region had its own special type of cotton named after it. The designs on these fabrics were copied onto silk after 1945.

Sarashina-nikki. Diary written in the eleventh century by a lady of the Heian court, born about 1009, Sugawara no Takasue's daughter and the wife of Tachibana no Toshimichi (?–1058), governor of Shinano province. After her husband died, she became a Buddhist nun. Unlike the other *nikki* of the time, the *Sarashima-nikki* deals mainly with events in its author's personal life, her dreams, and her children. It is the diary of an ordinary woman, unconcerned with politics or the court, which had little to do with her life, but it is nevertheless full of sensitivity and written in a simple, elegant style.

• **Sarashina-kikō.** See BASHŌ.

Saris, John. English navigator (ca. 1580–1643) and trader from Java who arrived in Hirado in June 1613, bearing credentials from James I and hoping to open a trading post. Through William Adams, he obtained interviews with shogun Tokugawa Ieyasu and with Tokugawa Hidetada, who gave him permission to trade in Japan and to establish a trading post in Hirado in November 1613. Saris left Japan that December, leaving his assistant, Richard Cocks, in charge of the new trading post. The post was abandoned in 1623, as it did not prove profitable. Saris's memoirs were published by E. M. Satow in 1900. *See* CLOVE.

Saru (-zaru). "Monkey"; a type of Noh mask *(nōmen)* symbolizing a monkey. *See also* SAMBIKI-ZARU, TOYOTOMI HIDEYOSHI.

• **Saruda-hiko.** Shinto *kami,* the husband of Ame no Uzume no Mikoto, who was said to have preceded the *kami* Ninigi no Mikoto on Earth. A divinity of fertility and fecundity, often portrayed as a monkey, he is particularly venerated in the Hie shrines (Sannō). Also called Sadabiko, Otsuchi no Kami. *See also* SHŌMEN KONGŌ, TSUBAKI DAIJINGU.

• **Sarugaku.** Ancient peasant dance that originated, according to the *Kojiki,* in the dance that Ame no Uzume performed before the cave where Amaterasu-Ōmikami had hidden, which made all of the other *kami* burst into laughter. This "monkey music" was in its turn behind the creation of some Noh dances. The *sarugaku* came from China (*Chin.: sanyue*) and were apparently incorporated into Bugaku theater (*see* GAGAKU). Also called Sangaku until the tenth century.

• *Sarugaku-dangi.* Treatise on the art of Noh theater, written by Zeami in 1430.

• *Sarugaku shi-za.* Collective term for four fifteenth-century families that held a monopoly on the composition of Noh plays and the organization of Noh performances: the Kanze, Komparu, Hōshō, and Kongō. *See* KYŌGEN, NOH.

• *Sarukani kassen.* "War Between the Monkey and the Crab." A folk tale: a crab has planted *kaki* (persimmon) seeds, for which he had traded a handful of rice with a monkey; now he is waiting for the tree to bear fruit. But the monkey climbs the tree and eats the ripe *kaki,* then throws the unripe fruit at the crab, killing it. The crab's children decide to avenge their father, assisted by several other animals.

• **Sarukawa.** Former Noh classical dance school. *See* IEMOTO.

• **Sarumaru-dayū.** Pseudonym for a ninth-century poet, perhaps Prince Yamashiro no Ōe, one of the Sanjūrokkasen.

Sarumino. "The Monkey's Raincoat." An anthology of *haikai* and *haiku* poems by Bashō, Bonchō, and Kyorai, published in 1691; it defined the rules of *haiku* of Bashō's school.

Sasa. Variety of dwarf bamboo that spreads rapidly and forms prairies that destroy farmland, especially in northern Japan. *See* BAMBOO.

Sasagawa Ryōichi. Ultranationalist philanthropist (1899–1995) and aviator. During the Second World War, he created an independent force of 20 bombers to support Japan's war effort, and he went to Rome on board a bomber to meet Mussolini. A member of Parliament, he favored total war and expansion of the conflict. The Allied war-crimes court sentenced him to four years in prison in 1947. After he was freed, he raced motorboats, gambled, built a financial empire, and devoted a great part of his fortune to charitable and educational works.

Sasaki Kiyōshi. Ethnologist (Sasaki Kyōseki, 1886 –1933) who worked closely with Yanagita Kunio.

Sasaki Kojirō. Famous expert in martial arts, killed by Miyamoto Musashi in a swordfight on the beach of Ogura in 1612. Also called. Sasaki Ganryū. *See* MIYAMOTO MUSASHI.

Sasaki Kōzō. Politician (1900–85), elected to the House of Representatives in 1948 for the Socialist party, which he led from 1965 to 1967.

Sasaki Nobutsuna. Poet who wrote traditional *waka* (1872–1963), born in Mie prefecture. He wrote important studies on classical poetry, notably the *Man'yōshū*; he was elected to the Academy of Japan in 1917 and received the Order of Culture (Bunka-shō) in 1937. Among his *waka* collections were *Omoigusa* (1903) and *Shingetsu* (1912).

Sasaki Ryōsaku. Politician(1915–92), born in Hyōgo prefecture, elected to the Chamber of Coun-

cillors in 1947 and the House of Representatives in 1955. In 1960, he left the leadership of the Japan Socialist party (Nihon Shakaitō) to found the Democratic Socialist party (Minshu Shakaitō); he became leader of this party, succeeding Kasuga Ikkō, in 1977.

Sasaki Sōichi. Jurist (1878–1965), born in Tottori prefecture. He studied law in France and Germany from 1909 to 1912, then directed Ritsumeikan University. In 1945, he was appointed *naidaijin*. His writings concerning constitutional law earned him the Order of Culture (Bunka-shō) in 1952.

Sasaki Takatsuna. Warrior (?–1214), Minamoto no Tameyoshi's grandson. In 1180, he saved Minamoto no Yoritomo's life in the Battle of Ishibashiyama and was made governor *(shugo)* of Nagato province. In 1195, he became a Buddhist monk on Mt. Kōya. His military feats became the stuff of legend.

Sasaki Takauji. General (1306–73), born in Ōmi, who helped Ashikaga Takauji recapture power after the restoration of the Kemmu era in 1336. He was *shugo* of six provinces and directed the Mandokoro starting in 1354. He was known as an excellent *waka* and *renga* poet. Toward the end of his life, he became a Buddhist monk with the name Sasaki Dōyo.

Sasaki Takayuki. Politician (1830–1910) and samurai from Tosa province. He actively participated in the movement to restore imperial power in 1868 and went to Europe in 1871 with the Iwakura mission to study judicial systems there. He was tutor to the young crown prince, the future Taishō Tennō.

Sasaki Toyoju. Politician (Hoshi Toyoshi, 1853–1901), born near Sendai. She and Yamija Kajiko founded a temperance league and political-discussion clubs.

Sasame-goto. "Whispered Conversations." A treatise on the art of writing *renga* poems written by the monk Shinkei about 1461 or 1463. He attempted to apply the principles of Buddhist asceticism to the composition of poems and advocated the use of *sabi*.

Sasano-bori. Small sculptures, mainly of birds and animals, carved out of softwood with a long knife called *sarukiri*. These folk sculptures were made by peasants in the Sasano region of Yamagata prefecture starting in about the fourteenth century, to be used as *mayoke* (talismans). They were made in the winter, when farm work was finished for the year. In the Meiji era, the art was taken up by professional sculptors, who exhibited their work at the annual Sasano Kannon fair held each January. *See* MINGEI.

Sasara. Musical instrument, made of blades of bamboo that are hit against each other or a notched bamboo pole that is rubbed with a stick, used mainly in Dengaku music.

Sasebo. Port on Nagasaki Bay (Kyushu) about 40 km west of Nagasaki, created in 1886. It was transformed into a naval base by the Americans in 1945. Large construction and repair shipyards. *Pop.:* 260,000.

Sashi-hijiki. In traditional architecture (*tenjiku-yō* construction mode), the beam *(hijiki)* of an overhang crossing a support pillar *(hashira)*. The overhangs at the Nandaimon of the Tōdai-ji in Nara, dating from 1199, are of this type. *See* TO-KYŌ.

Sashimi. Fillets of raw fish served with soy sauce and *wasabi* (very strong horseradish paste), one of the main elements of Japanese cuisine. The art of making *sashimi* lies in the choice of fish ("tai" dorado, tuna, etc.) and the filleting of the pieces. They are served with daikon and seasoned with *chiso (Perilla frutescens)* leaves, or eaten with rice, algae *(nori),* and thin slices of fresh vegetables. *See* CUISINE, MEALS.

Sashimono. Small fabric banner with a *mon,* attached to a short pole and worn by samurai on the back of their armor *(yoroi)* to indicate their family or clan. This system became common after 1573. Also called *shirushi.*

Sashi no Kuni. Former name of Sagami province. Also called Sashi-kami.

Sashinuki. Very long, very wide pants *(hakama),* laced at the ankles and completely hiding the feet, worn by courtesans in the Kamakura period. Also called *nubakama. See* HAKAMA.

Sasshi-bon. Bookbinding technique in which the pages are sewn together, used since the ninth century.

Sata Ineko. Writer (Tajima Ine; 1904–98), born in Nagasaki. After making a living at various jobs, she married a student, Kobori Keizō, in 1924, but left him a few months later and returned to her parents' home. When she went to Tokyo, she met writers and began to publish stories in the magazine *Roba* (The Mule). She joined the movement for proletarian literature (*see* NAPF), and published *Karameru Kōjō kara* (In a Caramel Factory, 1928); in 1932, she joined the Communist party, even though it was banned. She was imprisoned for two months in 1935 for her political activities; when she was freed, she wrote an account of her experiences, *Kurenai* (Vermilion, 1936).

From 1940 to 1943, she visited Korea, China, and Southeast Asia with Hayashi Fumiko, and wrote *Suashi no musume* (The Barefoot Girl, 1940). After the Second World War, she was expelled from the new Communist party, allowed to join again in 1955, then permanently expelled in 1964; she took this opportunity to publish *Sozō* (Plastic Sculpture, 1966). Among her best-known novels are *Watashi no Tōkyō chizu* (My Map of Tokyo, 1948), *Kikai no naka no seishun* (Youth among Machines, 1954), *Hai iro no gogo* (A Dark Afternoon, 1959), *Onna no yado* (Women's Apartments, 1963), *Omoki nagare ni* (The Pressure of the Current, 1968), and *Juei* (The Shade of Trees, 1972). Her complete works were published in 18 volumes in 1979. *See* KUBOKAWA TSURIJIRŌ.

Satake Eikai. Painter (1802–74), Tani Bunchō's disciple.

Satake Shozan. Daimyo (Satake Yoshiatsu, 1748–85) of Akita and painter, born in Edo. After studying with Hiraga Gennai, he founded the Akita school of Western painting. He and Odano Naotake wrote three treatises to explain the techniques of European painting and the laws of perspective, using Dutch works as examples.

Satake Yoshinori. Daimyo (1395–1462) of Kanto, and a famous warrior, painter, and writer.

Sat-chō Dōmei. Secret military alliance concluded between the Satsuma and Chōshū clans in 1866 against the Tokugawa shogunate. After the Meiji Restoration (1868), the politicians of these two clans continued to impose their will on the new government by occupying key positions in it. *See* SAT-CHŌ-TO-HI.

• **Sat-chō-to-hi.** Generic term for the four great clans, Satsuma, Chōshū, Tosa, and Hizen, that played an essential role in the restoration of imperial power from 1862 to 1868 and then in the Meiji government. The alliance between the Satsuma and Chōshū was called Sat-chō Dōmei.

Satellites. Of all Asian countries, Japan has launched the most satellites. Following Japan's decision to participate in the International Year of Geophysics in 1957–58, there was much experimentation, punctuated with many failures:

1. On February 11, 1970, scientists successfully launched **Ōsumi** from the Tanegashima base. It was propelled by a Lamda L-45 rocket and made a complete revolution of the Earth in 114 minutes. It weighed 23.8 kg.

2. **Tansei** was launched on February 16, 1971, by an Mu 4S rocket into an orbit of 611/685 km. *Weight:* approx. 70 kg.

3. **Shinsei** was launched by a similar rocket on September 29, 1971, and placed in an orbit of 284/2,814 km. *Weight:* approx. 80 kg.

4. **Dempa** was put into an orbit of 250/2,800 km on August 19, 1972. *Revolution time:* 116 minutes.

5. **Tansei II,** launched on February 16, 1974, into an orbit of 293/3,329 km, inclined at 31°2'.

6. **Taiyō,** an 86 kg STRATS, launched on February 24, 1975, into an orbit of 250/3,408 km, inclined at 31°5', by an Mu 3c rocket. *See also* ŌSUMI.

7. **Ume,** an 86 kg ETS I, launched February 29, 1976, for scientific tests, into an orbit of 994/1,012 km inclined at 69° east.

8. **Tansei III,** 134 kg, launched February 19, 1977 into an orbit of 795/3,814 km, inclined at 67°7', by an Mu–3H rocket. *Revolution time:* 134 minutes.

9. **Kiku II,** a 254 kg ETS, launched on February 23, 1977, by a type N rocket into an orbit of 34,060/35,576 km, inclined at 0°5'. Geosynchronous.

10. **Himawari,** a GMS II launched on July 14, 1977, into an orbit inclined at 140° east. *Weight:* 350 kg. Delta Y rocket.

11. A CS, launched on November 17, 1977, into an orbit inclined at 135° east.

12. **Sakura,** launched on December 15, 1977, by a Delta rocket into an orbit of 35,560/36,157 km (geosynchronous), inclined at 0°. *Weight:* approx. 340 kg.

13. **Kyokkō,** an Exos A launched on February 4, 1978, with a solid-fuel Mu-3H rocket, into an orbit of 560/4,000 km, inclined at 60°, from the Uchinoura base, by the University of Tokyo.

14. An Exos B, launched September 16, 1978, into an orbit of 250/30,000 km inclined at 0°. *Weight:* 72 kg. *Revolution time:* 8 hours 45 minutes.

15. An ISS B, launched on February 2, 1978, by an Mu–3 rocket into an orbit of 978/35,661 km, inclined at 69°30', for ionospheric research.

16. **Yuri,** launched on April 7, 1978, on a geosynchronous orbit of 35,114/35,661 km for telecommunications, from Cape Kennedy. *Weight:* 350 kg.

17. **Ayame,** launched in February 1979, from Tanegashima by an N 1 rocket. Launch aborted.

18. **Ayame II,** communications satellite launched on June 2, 1979, into an orbit of 33,966/35,421 km, inclined at 0°4'. *Weight* 260 kg. *Revolution time:* 1,380 minutes.

19. **Hakuchō,** launched by an Mu–3c rocket on December 2, 1979, into an orbit of 538/568 km, inclined at 29°9'. *Weight:* 96 kg. *Revolution time:* 95 minutes. Research on soft x-rays.

20. **Yuri–2a,** communications satellite, launched on January 23, 1984.

21. **Yuri–2b,** communications satellite, launched on February 12, 1986.

22. **Suisei,** launched in August, 1985, to observe Halley's comet, by an M3–SII (solid fuel) rocket, from the Uchinoura base. *Weight:* 140 kg (including an ultraviolet camera). On March 8, 1986, it passed about 15,000 km from the comet.

Japan's space program involves a large number of satellites, with a number of launches in recent years; they are to be used mainly for oceanography research, surveillance, geodesy, telecommunications, television broadcasting, meteorology, navigation, and astronomy. *See* TANEGASHIMA.

Sato-dairi. During the Heian period, a "country palace." Annex imperial palaces where emperors and their courts took refuge during the fires that frequently ravaged the main palace *(gosho, dairi).* There were up to 30 different *sato-dairi* during different eras and events. During the Muromachi period, the Higashi no Tōin Tsuchimikado in Kyoto was the most often used; it is now the Kyōto-gosho.

Satō Eisaku. Politician (1901–75), born in Yamaguchi, Kishi Nobusuke's brother. He studied law at the University of Tokyo and was appointed director of railroads in 1945. In 1949, he was elected a representative for the Liberal Democratic party (Jiyū Minshutō) and held ministerial positions (post office, construction) in Yoshida Shigeru's cabinets from 1948 to 1955, then was minister of finance from 1958 to 1959 in Kishi Nobusuke's cabinet. As minister of trade in 1963–64, he organized the 1964 Olympic Games in Tokyo and renovated the capital's central district. In November 1964, he succeeded Ikeda Hayato as prime minister, and was reelected in 1971. He resigned in 1972 and was replaced by Tanaka Kakuei. He received the Nobel Peace Prize in 1974. *See* PRIME MINISTERS.

Satogo. In the sixteenth century, a common practice among aristocrats of sending their children to families in the countryside for their health. *Satogo* was also used when children were born of illegitimate unions. The children were then generally returned to their respective families, although this was not always the case.

Satō Gōsai. Confucian scholar (1650–1719), one of Yamazaki Ansai's most faithful disciples.

Satō Hachirō. Lyric poet (1903–73), born in Tokyo, son of writer Satō Kōroku, author of poetry collections and songs that became very popular on radio and television.

Satō Haruo. Poet and writer (1892–1964), born in Wakayama prefecture. He studied with Nagai Kafū at Waseda University in Tokyo and wrote *waka* and modern verses; in 1913, he turned to novels, becoming one of the most representative writers of his generation: *Den'en no yūutsu* (Rural Melancholy, 1919), *Tokai no yūutsu* (Urban Melancholy, 1922), *Kōseiki* (Chronicle of a Renaissance, 1929), *Kono mittsu no mono* (These Three Things, 1926), *Akiko mandara* (The Circle of Yosano Akiko, 1955; Yomiuri Prize). His lyrically inspired poems were published in the collections *Junjō shishū* (Poems of Innocence, 1921) and *Shajinshū* (Dust Wagon, 1929).
→ *See* TANIZAKI JUN'ICHIRŌ.

Satō Issai. Confucian scholar (1772–1859), born to a samurai family in the Iwamura estate (now in Gifu prefecture). After studying in Osaka, Kyoto, and Edo under various renowned masters, he became a professor at the Shōheikō and was an adviser to the shogun of Edo. He taught the official Shushi (*Chin.*: Zhu Xi) philosophy, sometimes tinged with Ō-Yōmei (*Chin.*: Wang Yangming). He was Watanabe Kazan and Sakuma Shōzan's master.

Satō Key. Painter (Sato Kei, 1906–78), born in Ōita (Kyushu), died in Paris. He studied Western painting in Tokyo, then in France from 1930 to 1935, and moved to Paris in 1952. His paintings were abstract compositions in flat colors in which the materials used were very important. His son, Satō Ado, born 1936 in Tokyo, was a photographer at first,

then created a new graphical style in painting, resembling his photographic research.

Satō Kōroku. Writer (1874–1949), born in Aomori prefecture. He wrote mainly works for young people and modern haiku similar to those by Masaoka Shiki. His son, Sato Haichirō, became a famous poet, and his daughter, Sato Aikō (b. 1923), is also a talented writer.

Satomi Ton. Writer (Yamanouchi Hideo, 1888–1983), born in Kanagawa prefecture, Arishima Takeo's younger brother. He joined the Shirakaba group and began to write novels that were both realistic and romantic: *Zenshin akushi* (Good Heart, Bad Heart, 1916), *Tajō busshin* (1923), *Taika* (The Great Fire), *Chichi-oya* (The Father), *Gokuraku tombo* (A Joyous Companion, 1961). He was decorated with the Order of Culture (Bunka-shō) in 1959. His other brother, Arishima Ikuma, was a famous painter.

Satomoyō azumi no ironui. Kabuki play in four acts, written in the *kizewa-mono* genre by Kawatake Mokuami in 1859. Also titled *Izayoi Seishin*.

Satomura Joha. *Renga* poet (Matsumura Shōha, Satomura Shōha, 1524 or 1527–1602), born in Nara, where he began his career as a Buddhist monk at the Kōfuku-ji temple. His works earned him a reputation as the greatest *renga* poet of his time: *Renga shihō-shō* (Treasures of Linked Verses, 1585). He also wrote *haikai*. Also called Satomura Shōha.

Satomura Kinzō. Writer (1902–45) of the Bungei Sensen movement; he wrote works on war.

Satō Naokata. Neo-Confucian scholar (1650–1719) born in Fukuyama (Hiroshima prefecture), Tamazaki Ansai's student in Kyoto. He was severely critical of the samurai of Ako who avenged their master (*see* AKO-GISHI).

Satō Naotake. Diplomat (1882–1971), born in Osaka. He was, in succession, consul to Russia, Manchuria, Switzerland, and France, then ambassador to Poland in 1923, delegate to the League of Nations in 1931–32, ambassador to France from 1933 to 1936, minister of foreign affairs in 1937–38, and ambassador to the Soviet Union from 1942 to 1945. He was elected to the Chamber of Councillors (1947), which he chaired from 1954 to 1958.

He retired from public affairs in 1965 and published his memoirs.

Satō Nobuhiro. Confucian philosopher (1769–1850), born in Dewa province. After studying "Dutch science" *(rangaku),* he specialized in agronomy. In his book *Fukkohō gaigen,* he advocated the unification of Japan and centralization of power under a single sovereign.

Satori. "Awakening," or enlightenment, according to the Zen doctrines. This "awakening" (to the awareness that a buddha experiences) may be sudden (according to the Sōtō sect) or gradual (according to the Rinzai sect). *Chin.: wu; Skt.: bodhi, moksha.*

Satō Satarō. *Waka* poet (1909–87) in Miyage prefecture, author of the collections *Hodō* (1940) and *Kichō* (1952; winner of the *Yomiuri* Literary Prize). He published the works of his master, Saitō Mokichi.

Satō Seiyū. Botanist and physician (Satō Chūryō; *gō:* Onkosai, 1762–1848), born in Kagoshima, and senior bureaucrat in the Mito estate. He wrote many works on plants.

Satō Seizō. Sculptor (Satō Gengen; *gō:* Chōzan, 1888–1963); he studied with Bourdelle in Paris and Yamazaki Chōun in Japan.

Satō Takeo. Architect (1899–1972), born in Nagoya. He specialized in acoustic structures and theaters, as well as large public buildings such as the Waseda Okuma auditorium (1927) and the city halls in Kōfu (1960), Okayama (1963), and Ōtsu (1967).

Satowaki Asajirō. Catholic archbishop (b. 1904) of Nagasaki, made cardinal in 1979, succeeding Doi Tatsuo and Taguchi Yoshigorō.

Satow, Ernest Mason. English diplomat and Japanologist (1843–1929). He was a member of the English diplomatic delegation to Japan from 1862 to 1882, then plenipotentiary minister to Japan from 1895 to 1900, and to China from 1900 to 1906. Thanks to his mastery of Chinese and Japanese, he was a valuable asset to the Japanese government in its relations with Western countries. After retiring from diplomatic service in 1907, he wrote articles on Japan, published in the *Transac-* *tions of the Asiatic Society of Japan,* and works on various subjects related to his activities in Japan.

Satsudo. King (<1337>) of the Ryukyu Islands, successor to Gyokusei-ō. *Anji* of Urasoi, he was made king of Chūsan. He then fought the rival Sannan and Samboku kingdoms and agreed to pay a (nominal) tax to China. His son Murei was made king by the Chinese in 1404. *Chin.:* Chadu. *See* MUREI, RYUKYU.

Satsuei Sensō. "War between Satsuma and England." In 1862, an English merchant, Charles Richardson, was killed by samurai from Satsuma; the British government demanded an indemnity from the shogunate and Satsuma as well as punishment of the murderers. Satsuma refused to pay the £25,000 demanded, and a squadron of seven British ships entered Kagoshima Bay to force the Satsuma clan to negotiate. The spokesmen did not come to agreement, and the result was partial destruction of the city. But a typhoon dispersed the British fleet, which took some losses. Finally, Satsuma agreed to pay and to punish the murderers. *See* KAGOSHIMA, NAMAMUGI JIKEN.

Satsuki. In the old Japanese agricultural calendar (*see* NIJŪSHI-SETSU), fifth month of the year (May–June), "propitious for sowing."

Satsuma. Former province on Kyushu, now Kagoshima prefecture. This province was governed by the Shimazu family in the twelfth century. In the seventeenth century, as the fief of a *tozama-daimyō,* it produced a revenue of 770,000 *koku.* It was one of the "11 provinces of the Saikai-dō" (circuit of the Western Sea), and the site of a major rebellion led by Saigō Takamori in 1877 (*see* SEINAN NO EKI). *See also* SAT-CHŌ-TO-HI, SAT-CHŌ DŌMEI.

• Ceramics kilns founded in the fifteenth century in Satsuma province, producing pottery with a black or whitish slip, sometimes pierced or decorated with gold, following a technique imported by Korean potters and called Satsuma-*yaki.* There were several varieties of this style, used mainly for the tea ceremony *(chanoyu).* The best-known Korean potters working at the kilns in Kagoshima were Kim Hai (*Jap.:* Kin Kai, Hoshiyama Chūji, 1570–1621) and Pak Pyŏng-hüi (*Jap.:* Boku Heii, Kiyoemon, 1560–1629). Other types of Satsuma ceramics, black or dark red, were produced in the Naeshirogawa kilns, built in 1604 and still active. The production of the other Satsuma kilns (Tateno,

Ryūmonji, Nishimochida, Hirasa, etc.) emulated Siamese pottery imported from Sawankhalōk in the seventeenth and eighteenth centuries. Each kiln had its specialty, and their production was exported in large quantities to the West during the Meiji period. *See* IJŪIN.

• **Satsuma-gasuri.** Type of cotton fabric made in Satsuma in 1820. Also called Iyo-gasuri.

• **Satsuma-imo.** *See* SWEET POTATO.

Satsumon bunka. Proto-historical culture on Hokkaido and northern Honshu, characterized by iron tools, which flourished between about the eighth and twelfth centuries, drawing its technology from the *kofun* period and directly succeeding the Jōmon period in these regions. It is typified by pottery with the outside smoothed with a blade of wood (whence the name *satsumon,* "scratched design"), iron implements, and square, semi-buried cabins *(yokoana, tatara)* with fireplace against the interior wall. *See* HAJI-KI.

Sa-u-daijin. Term for the two ministers (of the left, *sa,* and the right, *u*) in the old imperial government (Nara and Heian periods). They were controlled by the grand minister of state *(dajō daijin). See* DAIJIN.

Saumarez, James St. Vincent, de. English diplomat (1843–1937), assigned to Tokyo from 1875 to 1880. He imported to his home in Guernsey a number of Japanese plants, which he had tended by Japanese gardeners, as well as a small Shinto shrine and a Japanese house.

Saunders, Elisabeth. *See* SAWADA MIKI.

Saunders, William. English photographer who traveled to Japan in 1862 and worked in Shanghai from 1864 to 1888. Although he was in Japan for only a few months, he was the first photographer to take pictures of senior bureaucrats in the shogunal government.

Sawada Kyōichi. Photographer (1936–70) who received the Pulitzer Prize for his photographs taken in Vietnam during the war. He was killed in Cambodia while on assignment. He had been one of the official photographers for the 1964 Olympic Games in Tokyo. His collection comprises about 30,000 black-and-white and color photographs.

Sawada Miki. Philanthropist (1901–80), founder of an institution (Elisabeth Saunders Home) to help mixed-blood children born during the Second World War and the Allied occupation. She constantly traveled between the United States and Japan to raise funds for her foundation, and received the Prime Minister's Award in 1966 for her humanitarian activities. Bridgeport University in the United States awarded her an honorary doctorate in law in 1970.

Sawada Shōjirō. Actor and playwright (1892–1929), born in Ōtsu. He studied with Tsubouchi Shōyō and acted in many plays at the Shingeki Theater, then created the Shinkokugeki (New National Theater) company in 1917. He specialized in heroic roles and historical tragedies. More than 100,000 people attended his funeral.

Sawada Tōkō. Writer (1732–96) who wrote many novels in the *sharebon* genre, such as *Iso rokujō* (1757).

Sawamura Sōjūrō. Family of Kabuki actors and musicians in Kyoto and Edo, specializing in *onnagata* roles. The best-known members of this large family were Sawamura Sōjūrō I (1685–1756), Sawamura Sōjūrō II (1713–70), Sawamura Sōjūrō III (1753–1801), Sawamura Sōjūrō V (1802–53), Sawamura Sōjūrō VII (1875–1949), Sawamura Sōjūrō VIII (1908–75), and his son, Sawamura Sōjūrō IX (Sawamura Tosshō V, b. 1933).

Sawa Nobuyoshi. Noble (1836–73) of the imperial court, who played a very active role during the disturbances in the country that led to the restoration of imperial power in 1868. He was appointed minister of foreign affairs in 1869, then ambassador to Russia in the year of his death.

Sawano Chūan. Japanese name for a Portuguese pirate, Cristovão Ferreira (ca. 1580–ca. 1650), a renegade Christian who lived in Japan and translated Portuguese science books. He wrote *Namban geka hidensho* (Secrets of Western Medicine) about 1650.

Sawara Shinnō. Imperial prince (757–85), Emperor Kōnin's fifth son. Implicated in the murder of Fujiwara no Tanetsugu, he was exiled to the island of Awaji, where he starved himself to death.

Sawayanagi Masatarō. Educator (1865–1927), born in Nagano prefecture. He was vice-minister of education and rector of the University of Kyoto. In 1917, he founded experimental schools to promote a more modern educational system that was better adapted to the country's needs.

Sawazumi Kengyō. Musician (late fourteenth–early fifteenth century) who apparently introduced the shamisen to orchestras accompanying *jōruri*.

Saya. Scabbard for a sword (*katana* or other), generally made of red- or black-lacquered wood or covered with shark skin *(same)*. Its decoration, sometimes very elaborate in the case of swords belonging to important personages, is called *kanamono;* its chape, *kojiri* or *ishizuki;* the rings holding the cord on the scabbard, *kurikata;* the cord itself used to hang the *saya* from the belt, *ageo.* Also called *gaishō, kashira-e, tsukuri. See* KATANA, SHIRAZAYA, YARI.

S.C.A.P. "Supreme Commander for the Allied Powers," the name both for the head of the organization and for the organization itself, established in Tokyo in 1945 by the Allies after the defeat of Japan in 1945, and used mainly as an American administrative base controlling the occupation of Japan. The first head of S.C.A.P. was General Douglas MacArthur; he was followed by General Matthew B. Ridgway. S.C.A.P. then became part of a larger organization, the United States Far-East Command (US-FEC). It was dissolved in 1952.

Scott, Marion McCarrell. American educator (1843–1922). He went to Japan in 1871 and taught at the University of Tokyo (then the Daigaku Nankō), then at Tokyo Teachers' College. There, he introduced American educational methods with books imported from the United States, thus helping create the Japanese national educational system. He returned to the United States in 1881.

Sculpture. In Japan, the stone is of volcanic origin and difficult to carve; aside from some relatively crude ancient works on tombs on Kyushu and some Buddhist works, it was rarely used. Marble and other rare calcareous stone are not found at all. Wood, however, is abundant and was used both for architecture and for sculpture. Sculptures were carved out of solid wood (*ichimoku-zukuri*) or made from assembled parts (*yōsegi-zukuri*). In the Nara and early Heian periods, images were made of dry lacquer modeled on a core of solid wood (*mokushin-kanshitsu*) or a hollow frame (*dakkatsu-kanshitsu*). Clay is also abundant and was widely used, mixed with mica flakes and often covered with a coating after drying, or fired in a kiln. Bronze, known since the early years AD, was also widely used to make Buddhist statues. Bone, ivory, hard stone, and very fine-grained precious wood were used only for very small pieces, such as *netsuke.* Contemporary sculptors have turned to working with stone, mainly granite, because modern tools make carving it possible.

Subjects were mainly religious; since Shinto cults, in principle, did not use icons, Buddhism supplied most subjects, which were, in fact, often copied from Chinese works. Nonreligious sculpture was generally confined to portraits and masks for theater. Ornamental sculpture began to develop with the early styles of Buddhist architecture and cannot be separated from them. Sculptors, like painters, were first grouped together in guilds *(be),* and later in studios *(bussho)* under the patronage of the court or large monasteries. Most sculptors were also Buddhist monks, so their works were not signed, though literature has supplied us with the names of the most famous artists. Like artists of the medieval period in the West, Japanese sculptors were multitalented, also being painters, calligraphers, and poets, since the Japanese aesthetic made few distinctions between the fine arts. In general, development of sculpture in Japan followed that in the other arts. Conventionally, it is generally divided into periods corresponding to the major historical epochs.

The Prehistoric Period. Toward the end of the Jōmon period, in the first millennium BC, some pottery was decorated with string impressions, portraying human figures with short arms and legs and large heads with bulging eyes or goggles *(dogū)*. Masks (or objects evoking masks) called *domen* were also characteristic of this period, but it is not known whether these terra-cotta pieces were truly indigenous or were inspired by Siberian neolithic art.

The Pre-Buddhist Period. There are few vestiges of sculpture from the Yayoi period; pottery was mainly utilitarian, and it was only starting in the fourth century that a completely new type of sculpture, *haniwa,* was created, linked to large grave sites *(kofun)*. The earliest of these "terra-cotta tubes," found in great numbers arranged in lines around funerary tumuli, were not decorated, but as time passed their tops became ornamented with various representations: men, women, shamans, animals, boats, houses, and various objects. These *haniwa,* modeled according to the *wasumi* technique (mounds of coils of clay), often resemble modern sculpture. There were several types, depending on the region, but they all have the same characteristics: they are hollow, and openings are made in the clay to signify the eyes or mouths of the people or animals, or the entrances to houses. Although it is impossible to say whether this art is directly descended from that of the Jōmon peoples, *haniwa* represent the true beginning of sculpture in Japan: concern for realism, simplification, and "blending" of form with feeling are found throughout the centuries in Japanese sculpted and modeled works.

The Asuka Period (538 or 552–645). In the sixth century, Buddhist doctrines and religious images were introduced from Korea and Korean artists arrived in Japan. According to the ancient chronicles, one of the first Buddhist sculptors was Kuratsukuribe no Tasuna, who made a statue of the Buddha 5 m high. Since it is no longer in existence, its style cannot be determined, but it probably obeyed the canons of Korean Buddhist sculpture of the time. The creation of monasteries and the constantly growing demand for religious images to decorate temples led to a certain amount of imitation among artists. Almost all sculptors were immigrants from China or Korea who worked in a Chinese style close to that found in the Buddhist grottos in Yüngang and Longmen. The first Japanese sculptors were descendants or students of these artists. They were inspired mainly by mainland models of the Northern Wei or Southern Sui dynasty, somewhat modified by their transmittal through Korea. One of the most famous sculptors of this period was Kuratsukuribe no Tori (the son of Kuratsukuribe no Tasuna), who made a famous Buddhist triad in bronze, now in the Hōryū-ji monastery. Most of the sculptures of this time were cast in bronze and gold-leafed or carved in camphor-tree wood; the latter were coated and painted. Of course, they were Buddhist images or Gigaku masks. The faces are long, with wide-open eyes and a gently smiling mouth. The proportions are elongated, the shapes symmetrical, designed to be seen only from the front. Nimbuses or haloes, in the shape of a pippal leaf or a magical jewel *(hōs-shu)*, were widely used.

The Nara Period (645–794). The earliest part of this period, the Hakuhō era, was characterized by the importation and copying of new models. Sculptors were inspired by both Chinese art from the early Tang dynasty and Indian art from the Gupta period, transmitted via China; Korean art gradually gave way to Chinese art. Bodies were more realistic, faces fuller, than during the preceding period; however, a frontal view and symmetry were still the rule. Some pieces in repoussé copper from this period could easily be confused with Chinese works. But

over all, sculpture of the Hakuhō era presents an art in transition. Two works give a perfect demonstration of the trends under way: the bronze "Kannon" at the Tō-in-dō in Nara, and the very remarkable head, also in bronze, of the Buddha Yakushi at the Kōfuku-ji in Nara, the latter showing an effort at stylization heralding the "Japanization" of Chinese art. The second era of the Nara period, the Tempyō, saw the advent of a "national" Buddhism under which the government had colossal works in bronze, such as the Daibutsu at the Tōdai-ji in Nara, executed in a style that started to show some independence from its models. Chinese Tang-dynasty culture had been assimilated, and the works of the Tempyō era bore the imprint of a new national style. Though it was realistic in appearance (sense of movement, facial expressions, heavy drapings in *hompa-shiki*), sculpture nevertheless retained profoundly idealistic characteristics. Bronze was reserved for large statues and abandoned for other statues, in favor of the less cumbersome techniques of applying clay and lacquer to frames made of wood and rice straw. Some Buddhist subjects drew their supernatural appearance (three eyes, many arms) from Hindu religious images, but they were designed not from models but by following directions in the sacred texts. Lay subjects (portraits of Ganjin in the Tōshōdai-ji, of Gyōshin in the Hōryū-ji, Gigaku and Bugaku masks) skillfully drew on the new techniques and reflected the taste for realism. Some clay statuettes retained a clear influence from the Tang dynasty, while others, in dry lacquer, obeyed more typically Japanese criteria. This new art was still seeking its definitive expression, and although remarkable works were produced (Shūkongō-shin in the Hokke-dō of the Tōdai-ji, Hachi-Bushū of the Kōfuku-ji in Nara), in very different materials, a movement toward creative thought without Chinese influence was arising. Lay sculptures were ahead of their time and truly creative, while Buddhist artists still hesitated to distance themselves from mainland models.

The Heian Period (794–1185). During the Jōgan (also called Kōnin) era that marked the beginnings of society in the new capital of Heian-kyō, Chinese influence remained very strong in all areas, and exchanges with the mainland were frequent, but the "Japanizing" trend begun at the end of the preceding period became stronger. The importing of new Buddhist sects (the Tendai-shū and Shingon-shū) allowed religious art to develop along personal lines. Religious representations became more solemn and rather austere as artists distanced themselves from simple realism to adopt an "extra-human" style, thus losing some freedom of expression. Techniques using clay and lacquer were gradually abandoned for sculpture in wood; bronze, which had become very expensive, was rarely used. The Japanese technique of carving wood still seemed relatively primitive: the head and body of a statue were carved in a single block, and the limbs, sculpted separately, were added on. A fine coat of glaze or lacquer covered the hewn form, and modeling added the final touch. In general, the style was tending to become increasingly distanced from realism, with pieces becoming more massive and giving an impression of power. Faces were impersonal and devoid of life, with features obeying canons set by the scriptures. A number of styles coexisted: imitations of Tang-dynasty works in sandalwood (Kumon Kannon at the Hōryū-ji, Jūichimen Kannon at the Hokke-ji), a continuation of the Nara style (Yakushi Nyorai at the Jingō-ji), a transition between styles of the late Nara and Heian periods (Nyoirin Kannon of the Kanshin-ji), and local styles drawing on several trends at once. Shinto sculpture, which appeared for the first time with Shinto-Buddhist syncretism, executed by artists trained at the Buddhist school, retained realistic characteristics belonging to the late Nara period, as did portraits (of Rōben at the Tōdai-ji, for example). Only statues made of sandalwood (a precious wood imported from Southeast Asia) were not painted, to preserve the fragrance of the wood, except sometimes for hair, eyebrows, eyes, and a thin mustache.

During the last, sumptuous era of the Heian period, the Fujiwara, true Japanization of Chinese culture arose. The era of prosperity and the refined taste of the nobility of the times enabled Buddhist sculpture to attain maturity. The massiveness of forms gave way to more delicacy and elegance. The proportions of the body were well observed, shapes became harmonious, and a sense of balance was the artists' main aim. Wood was used almost exclusively, but in the new *yōsegi* technique, each statue was made by assembling many pieces sculpted separately, making great detail possible. The most famous sculptors of this period were Kōshō, his son Jochō ("Amida Nyorai" at the Byōdō-in in Uji, 1053), and their descendants and collaterals, who made up the family studios *(bussho)*. The "Fujiwara style" was defined by Jochō: a massive, correctly proportioned body, attractive face, and a sense of movement both fluid and majestic. It was, above all, art for the aristocracy. But toward the end of the period, the positions of the characters became more conformist and rigid, while there was a return to the realism of the Nara period: portraits ("Shōtoku

Taishi" by Enkei, 1069) showed a stylization that did not at all exclude an expressive realism subtler than that of the preceding period.

The Kamakura Period (1185–1333). The creation and increasing spread of doctrines of the new Buddhist sects—Jōdo-shū, Ji-shū, Jōdo Shin-shū, Nichiren-shū, Zen—and the revival of old ones, such as the Kegon-shū and Ritsu-shū, brought some resurgence of Chinese influence (mainly from the Song dynasty) and of the spirit of the Nara period. There was a certain democratization of art because the taste of the warrior classes was different from that of the aristocrats of Heian-kyō. Buddhist statues became overloaded with ornamentation, the expression in the faces became softer, and the addition of painted-glass eyes *(gyoku-gan)* gave them a more lifelike appearance. Two currents began to be defined: traditional, represented by the works of sculptors such as Mei-en and Inson, who continued the Heian styles and added a touch of realism; and a new style, typified by Kōkei, Unkei, Kaikei, and their school, characterized by total realism and very vigorous treatment. This school produced very remarkable works—the most Japanese, perhaps, of all sculpture in Japan. The colossal statues of the Ni-ō in the *nandaimon* of the Tōdai-ji, sculpted by Unkei and Kaikei in 1203, the "Maitreya" by Unkei at the Kōfuku-ji, the "Hachiman" by Kaikei at the Tōdai-ji, and the "Vimalakīrti" and "Kongō-riki-shi" by Jōkei at the Kōfuku-ji are good examples of the warrior and folk trends in this period. The portraits are remarkable for the accuracy of the expressions and the precision of detail and are, it seems, absolutely faithful to the model ("Shunjō" at the Tōdai-ji, "Uesugi Shigefusa" by Meigetsu-in), with attitudes truthfully rendered ("Basu Sennin" of the Myōhō-in by Tankei, 1254). Religious works were still influenced by those from China (Daibutsu of Kamakura, 1252) or retained some characteristics of the Fujiwara era ("Dainichi Nyorai" by Unkei, at the Enjō-ji in Nara). Statues of animals were rare, except for portrayals of the Koma-inu and Kara-shishi at the entrances to Shinto shrines, which precisely followed the Chinese Sui and Tang styles. At the end of the period, Noh masks began to be made, inaugurating a specific genre, while those of Gigaku and Bugaku followed the era's trend toward fantastic realism.

The Modern Periods (Sixteenth–Twentieth Century). After the Kamakura period, it seems that sculptors lost all inspiration. The Ashikaga shoguns preferred ceramics and paintings, which almost completely replaced sculpture. Sculptures became decorations, executed according to painters'

sketches, and were made by artisans without great imagination. Starting in the seventeenth century, temples and shrines were adorned with panels sculpted in the Chinese Ming manner (as at the Tōshōgū in Nikkō) and painted in bright colors. Sculpture having lost its religious utility, as the triumphant Zen sects did not favor veneration of images, it became the sphere of artisans, with soulless repetition of old works. Sculptors became ceramists, landscape architects, architects. Several artists tried to revive sculpture, such as the monk Enkū (seventeenth century), but they were isolated artists who did not form schools. Sculpture did have a revival among commoners in the eighteenth century with the invention of netsuke, and artists achieved great virtuosity linked to extreme creativity. Their art, sometimes disparaged as minor, in fact displayed beautiful sculptural creativity. After 1868, modern sculpture followed Western styles, and Japan, which had never raised statues to its eminent citizens, began timidly to erect some in bronze or, more rarely, in stone. They were not very original and mirrored trends in international schools.

Se. Ancient unit of area, equivalent to about 100 m². *See* TSUBO.

Sebald, William Joseph. American diplomat (1901 –80), born in Baltimore. From 1947 to 1952, he was the head of the diplomatic section of S.C.A.P. and a political adviser to General MacArthur. He then held various ambassadorial posts, including in Burma and Australia. He was decorated with the Order of the Rising Sun.

Sechi-e. Official and imperial ceremony. *See* GO-SECHI-E, SECHIE-ZUMŌ.

• **Sechie-zumō.** During the Nara period, major sumo tournaments that took place in the presence of the emperor within the walls of Shinto shrines, with musical accompaniment and sacred dances (Kagura); their goal was to obtain good harvests and social peace from the *kami*. They generally began on July 7. In 719, Empress Genshō created an official position, *nukide no tsukasa,* charged with recruiting wrestlers. One of these, Shiga Seirin, codified the 48 authorized holds in 740. *Sechie-zumō* was assimilated with military arts in 868, but another, exclusively religious form of sumo, *shinji-sumo,* developed. Special sumo tournaments, called *kanjin-sumo,* were sometimes organized to raise funds for the construction of Buddhist temples or Shinto shrines. The first *kanjin-sumo* took place in

Kyoto in 1596 and 1615, and began to be held in Osaka and Edo in 1620. Today's sumo evolved from the mixture of these various sorts of sumo in the seventeenth century. *See* SUMO.

Sedōka. Minor form of song in fashion mainly in the seventh and eighth centuries, composed of two tercets of 5, 7, and 7 syllables. Sixty-three Sedōka were included in the *Man'yōshū. See* WAKA.

Segawa Jōkō. Family of Kabuki actors and playwrights, founded by Segawa Jōkō I (1739–94), specializing in playing *onnagata* roles and writing *jōruri: Yowa-nasake ukina no yokogushi,* among others. The other members of this family were Segawa Jōkō II (1757–1833), author of many plays that are still performed, such as *Kashima odori* (1813) and *Kakubei* (1828); Segawa Jōkō III (1806–80), author of *Konoshita soga megumi no masagoji* (Goemon the Pirate Boiled Alive, 1851) and *Higashiyama nasake ukina no yokogushi* (1853); Segawa Jōkō IV (1857–1938); and Segawa Jōkō V (1888–1957).

• **Segawa Kikunojō.** Family of Kabuki dancers and actors: Segawa Kikunojō I (1693–1749), *onnagata* roles; Segawa Kikunojō III (1750–1801).

Seibi-kan. School for foreign languages (French, English, Russian, Dutch, and Chinese), founded in Edo in 1863 and based on a *hankō* of the same type in Mino. This school was transferred to Ogaki (Mino province) in 1868 and renamed Tengaku-ryō.

Seibo. Custom consisting of offering gifts to relatives and friends at the end of the year in thanks for services rendered. *See* GIFTS.

Seibu Hyakkaten. Chain of department stores in Tokyo (in Ikebukuro) and Kanto, founded in 1940 under the name Musashino Depatō by the railroad company Musashino Tetsudō. After the Second World War, the group quickly expanded throughout Japan and into other countries, taking over a large number of similar companies. Head office in Tokyo. Also known as Seiyū (for its supermarkets). *See* SEIYŪ, TSUTSUMI YASUJIRŌ.

Seichō no Ie Kyōdan. A modern religion, created in 1930 by Taniguchi Masaharu (1893–1985) in Kobe. Its headquarters was transferred to Tokyo in 1934. It is a syncretic religion mixing Christianity, Buddhism, and Shinto, in which man is considered the son of God. This sect, which encouraged the imperial cult during the Second World War, quickly expanded and now has 2–3 million followers.

Seidan. "Discourse on the Government." A political treatise written by Ogyū Sorai from 1716 to 1728 and presented to shogun Tokugawa Yoshimune, recommending a restructuring of the shogunal government, the promotion of talented people without regard to their origin, and the sending of samurai to the countryside.

Seidō. Temple-museum created in Edo in honor of Confucius in 1690.
• "Western Hall," a name for the monks of the Zen sect, after the district where they usually lived. This term was also used for monks of a temple that was established within another one and who lived in its "western hall." It is now the title given to an old monk supervising novices.

Seigai. Painter (Sakurama Shin; *azana:* Zentotsu; *gō:* Utei, Seigai, 1786–1851) of the Nanga (Bunjinga) school. He studied with Katagiri Tōin and Kazan in Edo.

Seigan. Painter (Yanagawa Mōi; *mei:* Shinjūrō; *azana:* Kōto, Mushō; *gō:* Tenkoku, Hyakuhō, Rōryūan, Osek-shōin, Seigan, 1789–1858), of the Nanga school, and poet, known mainly for his poems written in Chinese *(kanshi)* in the style of Chinese poets of the Tang dynasty. A Confucianist, he followed the way of Wang Yangming *(Jap.:* Ō-Yōmei). His wife, Kōran, was also an accomplished *kanshi* poet.

Seigan-ji. Title of a Noh play: the spirit of the poet Izumi appears on her tomb at the Seigan-ji temple (Kyoto) and dances for a man and woman who are paying tribute to her.

Seiganto-ji. Buddhist temple in Nachi (Wakayama prefecture), one of the 33 temples dedicated to Kannon Bosatsu (*see* SANJŪSAN-SHO). *Hondō* reconstructed in 1590.

Seihakuji. Term sometimes used for porcelain pieces with a bluish-white glaze and for those called *sometsuke.* Porcelain under a milky glaze is called *hakuji.*

Seihin. Concept of frugality, anchored in tradition, often advocated by Japanese monks, which often returns to fashion in periods of austerity.

Sei-i-tai-shōgun. "Commander-in-chief against the barbarians," a title for great military chiefs, at first (eighth century) those who went to northern Honshu to fight the Ezo tribes; later, the heads of warrior clans. This title, abridged to *shōgun,* became hereditary upon the death of Minamoto no Yoritomo, who had received it in 1192. It could be conferred only by the emperor. *See* SHŌGUN.

Seiji. Name in Japan for "celadon" ceramics. *See* CERAMICS.

Seiji-shōsetsu. "Political novels," a genre of novels with a political theme in style in the 1880s and 1890s, consisting either of original works (such as those by Tsubouchi Shōyō and Yano Ryūtei) or of translations of Western works, such as those by Disraeli. *See* SHŌSETSU.

Seikadō Bunko. Large private library founded in Setagaya-ku (Tokyo) in 1892 by Iwasaki Yanosuke (1851–1908), son of the founder of Mitsubishi. The library houses more than 200,000 works and more than 5,000 objets d'art relating to Japan and all Asian countries; there is also a small museum.

Seikan. Railroad and road tunnel linking Aomori (northern Honshu) to Hakodate (Hokkaido) under Tsugaru Strait. Dug from 1964 to 1985, it is 58.85 km long (of which 23.3 km are under the sea), with a maximum depth of 240 m under sea level. Opened to traffic in 1988, it is the longest underwater tunnel in the world. *See* AOMORI, TSUGARU KAIKYŌ.

Seiken-ji. Zen Buddhist temple belonging to the Rinzai-shū sect, founded in Okitsu (Shizuoka prefecture) in 1572 and rebuilt by Tokugawa Ieyasu in the late sixteenth century. A number of rooms were added in 1865.

Seiki. Painter (Yokoyama Kizō, Yokoyama Seiki; *mei:* Shōsuke, Shume; *azana:* Seibun; *gō:* Gogaku, Kibun, Kajō, Seiki, 1792–1864) of the Shijō school, Keibun's student in Kyoto.
→ *See* KURODA KIYOTERU.
→ *See* YOKOSUKA.

Seikisan Myōjin. Shinto *kami* who appeared to the monk Ennin (794–864) when he returned from China. Its image sometimes replaces that of the Yadaijin at the entrance to Shinto shrines.

Seiko. Sculptor of netsuke (Matsuura Seiko, early twentieth century) in Osaka.

→ *See* OKUHARA SEIKO.

Seikō. Era of Emperor Montoku: Nov. 854–Feb. 857. *See* NENGŌ.

• **Seikō (watchmaker).** *See* HATTORI KINTARŌ, YA-MAMOTO HŌSUI.

• **Seikō-kai.** Episcopalian Anglican church, founded in Japan by American missionaries (in 1859) and English missionaries (in 1869 and 1873), who joined together in 1887 to form the Nihon Seikō-kai. This Protestant Christian religious society has about 60,000 members. It operates Rikkyō (St. Paul) University in Tokyo and Momoyama Gakuin University in Osaka, as well as various hospitals and charitable institutions.

Seikyō-sha. "Society for Political Education," formed in 1888 to oppose the government's foreign policy and demand revision of the "Unequal Treaties" (*see* JŌYAKU KAISEI). It published a magazine, *Nihonjin* (The Japanese), but its activities were very limited. Reorganized in 1923, it became increasingly nationalist. It was dissolved in 1945.

• *Seikyō Shimbun.* Daily newspaper of the Sōka Gakkai, founded in 1951 by Josei Toda, second president of this religious society. Since 1971, it has been published in a 12-page format, and it has a print run of about 5.5 million. It is printed in 28 cities in Japan and has correspondents in many parts of the world. Aside from describing the Soka Gakkai's activities, it contains news of the world and in-depth articles on various topics.

• *Seikyō yōroku.* "Summary of Sacred Teachings,"a work written by Yamaga Sokō (1622–85) criticizing the official teachings of Confucian Shushi (*Chin:* Zhu Xi) philosophy, which he considered too theoretical and not applicable in practice. Yamaga Sokō was temporarily banished from Edo and sent to Akō province (Hyōgo prefecture).

Seimei. In the old Japanese agricultural calendar, the period of "clear weather," March 5–20. *Chin.:* Qingming. *See* NIJŪSHI-SETSU.
→ *See* ABE NO SEMEI, TAN-YŪ.

Seimin. Bronze foundryman and sculptor in metal (mid-eighteenth century), famous for his sculptures of tortoises and his cast incense holders and burners.

• Sculptor of netsuke (late nineteenth century) in Tokyo.

Seimu Tennō. Thirteenth emperor (Prince Waka-tarashi-hiko, traditionally 83<131–ca. 191>), son of and successor to Keikō Tennō. Chūai succeeded him.

Seinan no Eki. "Military Campaign in the Southeast," a rebellion by the samurai of Satsuma led by Saigō Takamori from January to September 1877. *See* SAIGŌ TAKAMORI. Also called Seinan Sensō.

Seinei Tennō. Twenty-second emperor (Prince Shiragatake Hirokuni Oshiwaka Yamato-neko, traditionally 444<480–84>), son of and successor to Yūryaku Tennō. When he died, Iitoyo Ao no Kōjo was appointed regent until Kensō succeeded Seimei Tennō in 485.

Seiryōden. The emperor's private apartments in the imperial palace *(kinri, dairi, gosho).*

Seiryō-ji. Buddhist temple in Kyoto, which contains a statue of the Buddha (in the Shaka-dō) in the Indian *gupta* style, probably imported from China in 987. The *Seiryō-ji engi*, an *emakimono* of the Muromachi period (sixteenth century), describes the temple's foundation.

Seiryō-ki. Warrior-chronicle (*see* GUNKI-MONO-GATARI) on the life and exploits of Doi Seiryō (Doi Kiyoyoshi, 1546–1629), daimyo of the Ōmori castle in Iyo province, written between 1624 and 1681 by an unknown author, perhaps one of his agricultural experts. This 36-volume work (30 volumes in some editions) also discusses agricultural techniques.

Seiryū Gongen. Shinto *kami,* poorly characterized, who may have been a temporary incarnation *(gongen)* of the Buddhist divinity Nyoirin Kannon *(Skt.:* Chintāmanichakra).

• **Seiryū-un.** *See* ROSHŪ.

Seisen-in. Painter (Kanō Yōshin; *mei:* Shōzaburō; *gō:* Kaishinsai, Gyokusen, Seisen-in, 1796–1846) of the Kanō school, son and student of Isen (Eishin) in Kobikichō (Edo).

Seisen-tanzaku-shiki. Ceremony of presentation of poems to the emperor, traditionally held on the fifth day of the fifth month. The thousands of poems submitted are screened, and the best are kept to be read on this day by the emperor or empress.

Seisho. Japanese name for the Bible.

Sei Shōnagon. Writer (Kiyohara Akiko, b. ca. 965), lady-in-waiting to Empress Fujiwara no Sadako (977–100); little is known about her life. It is thought that she was the daughter of Kiyohara Motosuke (908–90), one of the poets who helped compile the *Gosen-shū* anthology in 951. She had a well-known relationship with Murasaki Shikibu, who was not much in love with her, if her diary is to be believed. It is thought that she was married to (or lived with) Tachibana no Norimitsu (b. 965), with whom she had a son, Tachibana no Norinaga (982–1034), and tradition has it that she was also married to Fujiwara no Muneyo, with whom she had a daughter, Koma no Myōbu, or to Fujiwara no Sanekata (?–998). In any case, Sei Shōnagon is the author of the unforgettable *Makura no sōshi* (The Pillow Book of Sei Shōnagon) and a collection of poems, *Sei Shōnagon-shū.* Her "pillow book" inaugurated a new literary form called *zuihitsu;* in it, she used remarkably pure language to give innumerable details on life in the Heian court, court customs, and events that took place while she was in the empress's service. She became a Buddhist nun when Fujiwara no Sadako died.

Seitai no Eki. Punitive military expedition sent by the Japanese government against the aboriginal people of Taiwan, on the pretext of avenging the death of 54 sailors from the Ryukyu Islands who were shipwrecked on Taiwan's coast and massacred in 1871. In May 1874, about 3,000 soldiers under the command of Saigō Tsugumichi debarked on the southern coast of Taiwan, but the aboriginals defended themselves with such ferocity that the Japanese were forced to withdraw. Faced with this deployment of forces, China (which had sovereignty over the island) agreed to pay an indemnity of 500,000 taëls and to recognize Japan's implicit authority over the Ryukyu Islands. This was more a political operation than a military one. Also called Taiwan-shuppei.

Seitei. Painter (Watanabe Yoshimata; *mei:* Ryōsuke; *gō:* Seitei, 1851–1918), Kikuchi Yōsai's student in Tokyo.

• **Seitei Tennō.** *See* IITOYO AO NO KŌJO.

Sei-tō. Political party created in the early nineteenth century to support the idea of restoration of imperial power and to resist the intrusion of foreigners. It was opposed to the Kan-tō party. →*See* KAN-TŌ.

Seitoku. Painter of ukiyo-e prints (Izutsuya Tokuemon; *gō:* Gi-on Seitoku, Seitoku, 1781–1829) and print collector in Kyoto.

• **Seitoku-kan.** School of Western medicine founded by Matsumoto Ryōjun in Nagasaki in 1861. It used only foreign professors.

Seitō-sha. "Bluestocking Society," a women's liberation movement active from 1911 to 1916, marking the inception of feminism in Japan. It was launched by Hiratsuka Raichō (1886–1971), following in the footsteps of women activists such as Kishida Toshiko and Fukuda Hideko. The society published a literary magazine, *Seitō* (Bluestocking), containing exclusively works by women (among them Yosano Akiko). The movement was weakened by several scandals provoked by women who were too "liberated," and the magazine stopped publishing in February 1916.

Sei'un Hōshinnō. Imperial prince, son of Emperor Kameyama (<1260–1305>) and head of the Buddhist monks at the Daigo-ji temple.

Seiwa Tennō. Fifty-sixth emperor (Prince Korehito, 850<859–76>880), son of and successor to Montoku Tennō. He abdicated in favor of his brother Yōzei. He received the posthumous name Minoo no Mikado.

• **Seiwa-genji.** Branch of the Minamoto family directly descended from Emperor Seiwa. *See* MINAMOTO.

Seiyaku-in Zensō. Buddhist monk (late sixteenth century) of the Tendai-shū on Mt. Hiei, adviser to Toyotomi Hideyoshi. He apparently persuaded Hideyoshi of the need to persecute Christian missionaries. Called Jacuin by European Jesuits. → *See* HIDEN'IN.

Seiyō kibun. "Notes on Western Countries" by Arai Hakuseki (1657–1725), recounting the story of the Sicilian Jesuit G. Battista Sidotti (1668–1715), who debarked at night on Yakushima in 1708, was arrested, and died in prison in 1714. *See* SIDOTTI.

• *Seiyō-dōchū hizakurige.* Account of a trip to London in the style of Jippensha Ikku's *Tōkai-dōchū hizakurige.*

• *Seiyō jijō.* "Conditions in the West." A three-volume work by Fukuzawa Yukichi, published in 1866, 1868, and 1870, telling of his experiences in Europe and America and providing valuable information on governments, mores, and scientific progress. This very successful work enabled the Japanese to become familiar with the West and to accept westernization of their country.

• *Seiyō tetsugaku-shi.* "Story of Western Philosophy," a famous work by Onishi Hajime (1864–1900), the first of its type in Japan.

Seiyū. Department-store chain founded by the Seibu company in 1956 to distribute its merchandise. It is now one of the three largest chains in Tokyo and has subsidiaries in the United States, Hong Kong, London, Paris, and Beijing. *See* SEIBU.

Seiyū Hontō. "True Seiyū party," a conservative political party founded in June 1924 by Tokonami Takeijirō and other politicians belonging to the Rikken Seiyūkai (Friends of Constitutional Government party). After gaining a majority in the Diet, it rapidly lost its seats in 1926 as many of its members rejoined the Seiyūkai to support the policies of Tanaka Giichi, that party's new leader. The remaining members joined the Kenseikai (Constitutional Association party) and then formed the Rikken Minseitō (Constitutional Democratic party). *See* RIKKEN SEIYŪKAI.

Seiyūkai. *See* RIKKEN SEIYŪKAI.

Seizan. Branch of the Buddhist Jōdo-shū sect founded by the monk Shōkū (or Shōtatsu), a disciple of Zennebō, in the thirteenth century. It was later divided into four sub-branches.

Sekai. "The World." A general-interest monthly magazine published since 1946 by the Iwanami Shoten publishing house. Many of its articles, written by Japanese and foreign authors, are ideological in content. It has gained a large readership among intellectuals. *Circulation:* about 130,000.

• *Sekai fujin.* "Women of the World." A socialist women's magazine, published from 1907 to 1909 by Fukuda Hideko, and featuring articles with a socialist slant on politics and women's conditions.

• **Sekai Kyūsei-kyo.** "Religion for the Salvation of the World," a religious sect founded in 1933 by Okada Mikochi (1882–1954), who presented himself as the Messiah that the entire world was awaiting. This sect, whose doctrine was updated in 1950, was related to Christian Science and embraced some of its principles, such as the refusal of any but natural medicines. It drew many followers from the Omote-kyō sect, but after Okada died and was replaced by his wife, then his daughter, Okada Itsuki (b. 1927), divergences of views, mainly about the use of modern medicines, led to a number of schisms. The sect nevertheless claimed to have 300,000 followers in the 1970s. Also called Meshiya-kyō (Universal Messianic Church).

• **Sekai Shindō-kyo.** Subsect of the Tenryū-kyō sect, founded in 1945 by Aida Hide (b. 1898).

Seki. Old unit of volume, equivalent to about 0.018 liter. Also called *shaka. See* GO, KOKU.
• Former toll gate between provinces. *See* SEKISEN, SEKISHO.

Sekibō. Stones carved into a phallic shape, often more than a meter high, and sometimes engraved with designs, grouped into ceremonial sites and sometimes found inside houses. *Sekibō* from the Middle and Final Jōmon periods were found in Kinsei (Yamanashi prefecture) and Matsuida (Gumma prefecture). In December 1992, more than 800 *sekibō* were found, in all stages of manufacture, in a stone-carving workshop in the Kinsei-jinja in Miyagawa-mura (Gifu prefecture), and it is likely that most *sekibō* found in the surrounding area were made there.

Sekidera komachi. Title of a Noh play: the poetess Ono no Komachi teaches the principles of poetry to Buddhist monks and dances for them.

Seki-en. Painter of ukiyo-e prints (Sano Toyofusa; *gō*: Toriyama Seki-en, Reiryō, Seki-en, 1712–88), Kanō Gyokuen's student in Edo. He also painted *e-ma* and made book illustrations.

Seki-ga. In Japanese art, a quick sketch of a subject, as opposed to a finished drawing, or *ryaku-ga.*

Sekigahara no Tatakai. "Battle of Sekigahara." A major battle that took place near Sekigahara (Gifu prefecture) in 1600, between Tokugawa Ieyasu and his allies and troops faithful to Toyotomi Hideyori, led by Ishida Mitsunari. Ieyasu's troops were commanded by his son, Yūki Hideyasu (1574–1607), and Date Masamune; his main allies were Tokugawa Hidetada (his third son), Sanada Yukimura, Kuroda Nagamasa, Mastudaira Tadayoshi, Honda Tadakatsu, Ii Naomasa, Ikeda Terumasa, Yamanouchi Kazutora, and Tōdō Takatora, each of whom commanded an army. Ishida Mitsunari's forces were supported by those of Konishi Yukinaga, Ankokuji Ekei, Wakizaka Yasuharu (1554–1626), Kobayakawa Hideaki, and the armies of the large Mōri, Ukita, and Shimazu families. The main battle took place in the rain on October 20, 1600 (old calendar, Keichō 5.9.14, corresponding to September 15), and continued the following day. More than 210,000 soldiers were involved. On the afternoon of October 21, Kobayakawa and several other daimyo lined up behind Tokugawa Ieyasu, and the battle, up to then undecided, turned in Ieyasu's favor. The battle marked the beginning of a new era and hastened Ieyasu's accession to power.

Sekigun-ha. "Red Army Faction," a group of dissident students from the Nihon Kyōsantō (Japan Communist party) advocating revolution through violence, formed in 1969. These extremists performed numerous violent acts, including attacking police stations and hijacking airplanes. The police arrested 54 of Sekigun-ha's members and besieged its headquarters in Karuizawa in 1972. One of its leaders, Shigenobu Fusako, went to Europe and then to Lebanon. There, she reorganized the Japanese Red Army (Nihon-sekigun) to succeed the Unified Red Army (Rengō-sekigun), and launched attacks on Israel (in concert with the Palestine Liberation Front), hijacked airplanes, attacked embassies in The Hague and Kuala Lumpur, and committed various acts of sabotage all over the world. Finally, Sekigun-ha's leaders were arrested and the movement dissolved.

Sekihan. Cooked rice mixed with red peas *(azuki).* Once reserved for important occasions, it is now a more common but still a highly esteemed dish. *See* CUISINE.

Sekihara yoichi. Title of a Noh play based on an episode in the life of Ushiwaka (the young Minamoto no Yoshitsune) on Mt. Kurama, including a duel with an opponent.

Sekiho. Painter (Okano Tōru; *azana:* Genshin; *gō:* Unshin, Sekiho, late eighteenth century) of the Nanga school in Kyoto about 1768. He painted mainly landscapes and apparently wrote several books, now lost. *See* KANRIN, OKUHARA SEIKO.

Sekino Tadashi. Architect (1867–1935) known mainly for his research on ancient architecture, for which he frequently traveled to Korea.

Sekiran. Sculptor (mid-nineteenth century) who worked in Mito. He made netsuke and sculptures for Shinto shrines.

Sekirankai. "Society of the Red Wave," a socialist feminist group founded in 1921 by Yamakawa Kikue, Itō Noe, and several other women to support the activities of the Nihon Shakai Shugi Dōmei (Japan Socialist League). This group demanded the abolition of capitalism, which it claimed was responsible for the miserable condition of women. It was broken up by the police in 1923.

Sekisen. Sculptor and ceramist (nineteenth century) from Gifu, known for his ceramic netsuke.
• "Toll currency," payment, in rice or cash, required of travelers and merchants at the many barriers *(sekisho)* erected along the main roads by lords of *shōen* and landowning nobles, then, in the Edo period, by daimyo and the shogunate. The very large number of *sekisho* and the tolls demanded by local authorities were a severe impediment to trade, and they were abolished by Oda Nobunaga and Toyotomi Hideyoshi. *See* SEKISHO.

• **Sekisho.** "Barriers" set up on roads or in mountain passes to control travel and exact a toll payment *(sekisen).* This custom started in the seventh century, and military posts set up at each *sekisho* enabled the court, then local lords, to protect the territories they controlled. The first three were at Suzuka, Fuwa, and Arachi (called the *sankan,* "three gates"). During the Heian period, as *shōen* were formed, lords erected a proliferation of *sekisho* to collect a sort of tax on merchandise transiting through their land; during the Kamakura period, they were used as a means of controlling warriors' movements. Because they were a severe impediment to trade, they were abolished by Oda Nobunaga and Toyotomi Hideyoshi. During the Edo period, the shogunate restored *sekisho* at some fifty points on major arteries *(go-kaidō)* throughout Japan in order to regulate the movements of the daimyo (thus reinforcing the *sankin-kōtai* system), survey troop movements, and oversee the arms trade. The main ones were at Hakone, Imagire, Usui, and Kobo-tōge, on roads leading to Edo. These barriers were finally abolished in 1869. *See also* SEKISEN, SHUKU-EKI.

Sekitai. Leather belt decorated with precious stones that was part of the *sokutai* court costume. Also called *ishi no obi* (belt of stones). *See* OBI.

Seki Takakazu. Mathematician (Seki Kowa, 1642–1708) who invented a new method of algebraic computation in 1674 (one year before it was invented by Bernouilli) and described it in *Katsuyō sampo* (1712). He founded a school of mathematics; his most brilliant student was Takebe Katahiro.

Sekkan-seiji. In ancient Japan, the term for regency by a *sesshō* or *kampaku,* a regime established in 858 and in effect until the late eleventh century. *See* FUJI-WARA.

Sekkei. Painter (Yamaguchi Sōsetsu; *gō*: Baian, Hakuin, Sekkei, 1644–1732) who studied with Sesshū and Mokkei.
→ *See* SHISEKI, SHŌKEI.

Sekki. General term for ceramics (stoneware) fired at very high temperatures (over 1200°C), made mainly in Bizen and Shigaraki.
→ *See* ICHIKAWA SHŌICHI, NIJŪSHI-SETSU.

Sekki no Ichi. *See* TOSHI NO ICHI.

Sekku. Seasonal festivals during which offerings *(ku)* of food were made to the divinities to mark the change of seasons *(sechi)*. In the Edo period, five of these festival days *(harebi)* were made official: January 7 (Jinjitsu no Sekku, Nanakusa no Sekku), March 3 (Jōshi no Sekku, Momo no Sekku), May 5 (Tango no Sekku, Shōbu no Sekku), July 7 (Tanabata no Sekku), September 9 (Kiku no Sekku). They are still faithfully celebrated today.

Sekkyō-jōruri. Type of *jōruri* used in the seventeenth century by Buddhist monks to teach and explain the religious doctrines. *See* JŌRURI.

Semimaru. Legendary blind *biwa* player who was probably in the employ of imperial prince Atsuzane Shinnō (897–966), the eighth son of Emperor Uda. One of his poems, composed during his passage through the tollgate *(sekisho)* at Ausaka (Ōsaka-yama), located between Heian-kyō and Lake Biwa, is in the *Gosen waka-shū.* The *Konjaku monogatari* cites this poet-bard. A Noh play bearing his name helped spread his popularity: a son of Emperor Uda, born blind, is sent to the Ausaka toll gate to become a Buddhist monk. A man then builds him a hut in which he lives. His sister Sakagami comes to visit him and finds him playing his *biwa,* his only possession; she promises to visit often.

Semmei-reki. Change made in 861 to the calendar *(reki)* that was in use until 1684. This calendar, of Chinese origin (*Chin.*: Xuanming), was corrected by the astronomer Shibukawa Shunkai and his assistant, Shibukawa Kōkyō. Also called Semmyō-reki.

Semmin. Under the *ritsuryō* system (late seventh century), a very lower-class ethnic group that was subordinate to the *ryōmin,* or ordinary people. It was divided into five categories *(gosen): ryōko* (guardians of the imperial tombs), *kanko* (palace servants), *kenin* (servants of noble families), *kunuhi* (slaves serving the bureaucrats), and *shinuhi* (slaves of noble families). The *nuhi* system was abolished in the tenth century. However, Japanese society continued to despise and discriminate against descendants of the *semmin,* called *genin* in the medieval period and *hinin* or *burakumin* today.

Semmyō. Ancient imperial decrees written in Japanese, as opposed to decrees written (starting in the eighth century) in Chinese *(chokusho)*. They were preserved in the *Rikkokushi* (except in the *Nihon shoki,* which gives their Chinese transcription, or *kambun*). Also called *mikotonori*. *See also* MIKO-TONORI, SENJI.
→ *See* SEMMEI-REKI.

Sempai-kōhai. Bonds between young and old that affect human relationships in society, in both families and organizations. Elders naturally owe friendly aid and assistance to their juniors, who, in turn, must show respect and loyalty. In a company, this relationship often determines advancement in the hierarchy, with seniority often counting more than talent. *See also* NENKŌ JORETSU, OYABUN-KOBUN.

Sempū-yō. Type of book binding consisting of folding long sheets of paper *(origon)* in a zigzag and gluing them together on one side.

Sen. Old unit of currency, equivalent to 0.01 *yen*. With inflation, sen became small change, and coins with a face value in sen are no longer in circulation. *See also* MON, YEN.

Senaga Kamejirō. Politician, born 1907 in Okinawa (Ryukyu Islands); vice-president of the Nihon Kyōsantō (Japan Communist party), elected mayor of Naha in 1956, then to the Diet for the Okinawa People's party, which joined the Communist party in 1973.

Sencha. Type of tea (*see* CHA, TEA) with steeped leaves, and type of ceramics for the tea ceremony (*chanoyu*) created in Kyoto by Okuda Eisen and Shimizu Rokubei in the eighteenth century. This style was also produced in Hizen province.

Senchaku hongan nembutsu-shū. "Selection of the *Nembutsu* of the Original Vow [of Amida]." A treatise written by Hōnen in 1198 to expound the fundamental principles of the Jōdo-shū sect. This work became a sacred writing for followers of the Pure Land. Also called *Senchaku-shū.*

Sendai. Chief city of Miyagi prefecture, in northern Honshu, 320 km northeast of Tokyo; major political, cultural, and trade center of Tōhoku. Formerly Mori no Miyako, a fortified post defending against the Ezo in the eighth century, the town developed around the Aoba castle built by Date Masamune in 1601; nothing is left of the castle but the Ote-mon gate, moats, and a *yagura.* Sendai was bombed during the Second World War and was completely reconstructed on a modern plan. It is heavily industrialized (steel mills, textiles, rubber, print shops, petrochemicals plants) and is the home of the Osaki Hachiman-gū Shinto shrine, with a double roof, dating from the Momoyama period and rebuilt in 1604; Tōhoku University, founded in 1907; and an observatory. Every August, the Tanabata Matsuri draws large numbers of visitors. *Pop.:* 670,000.

• *Sendai-hagi.* Title of a Kabuki play, adapted from a puppet play and first produced in 1785: a nurse sacrifices her own son to save the son of her lord, who was attacked by traitors.

Sengai Gibon. Zen Buddhist monk (1750–1837), born in Mino (Gifu prefecture), of the Rinzai-shū sect. He was the 123rd abbot of the Shōkofu-ji temple in the town of Hakata, where he lived from 1770 to 1783 and studied with Gessen Zenji. After 1811, he retired and devoted himself to painting and calligraphy; he painted Zen scenes, often in a humorous style, augmented with poems. Most of his works are currently at the Idemitsu Art Gallery in Tokyo.

Sengaku-ji. Buddhist temple in Tokyo, in Shinagawa, where the tombs of the 47 *rōnin* of Akō (*see* AKŌ-GISHI) are located.

Sengen-jinja. General term for Shinto shrines dedicated to Konohana Sakuya-hime, usually built on the slopes of Mt. Fuji. There were apparently 13,000 of them. Also called Asama-jinja.
• Shinto shrine (former Fujisan Hongū Sengenjinja) in the town of Fujino-miya (Shizuoka prefecture) dedicated to Konohana Sakuya-hime and two other *kami.* It is the main shrine of all religious sects venerating Mt. Fuji, the Fuji-kō. The current shrine was rebuilt in a style peculiar to the Sengen-jinja. It is decorated with paintings by Kanō Yūsen and Kanō Motonobu. Every year in early May, a major *yabusame* contest takes place there. Annual festival on November 4.

• **Sengen Myōjin.** *Kami* of Mt. Fuji and of cherry blossoms, generally portrayed as a very beautiful young woman. Also called Asama, Fuji-hime, Konohana Sakuya-hime.

Sengoku-jidai. "Warring States Period," the period from 1467 (Ōnin War) to 1568, during which Japan's political situation was completely unstable and characterized by internal struggles for supremacy between religious sects, daimyo, and *jitō.* It ended only when Oda Nobunaga entered Kyoto. This period saw the accession to local power of a number of low-ranking warriors and small-scale lords, whence its other name, *gekokujō.* Taking advantage of the weakness of the Ashikaga shoguns and the imperial court after the Ōnin War, which had left the country in disorder, many warriors began to fight each other for territory. Despite the political instability of this Japanese "Hundred Years' War," however, trade and crafts expanded. The daimyo reinforced their armies, built luxurious fortresses, and showed their power by making ostentatious displays of their wealth. Mines were developed to supply the *sengoku-daimyō* with iron, copper, gold, and silver. A cotton industry was developed, and in the cities many retailers and artisans began to cater to the constantly growing demand for goods from daimyo and army troops. It was during this period that trade cities such as Sakai, Hyōgo, and Hakata grew, along with castle towns (*jōka-machi*) and *monzen-machi.* Because of rivalries among traditional Buddhist sects, Zen monks were able to spread their religion among both commoners and the aristocracy. Also at this time, the first Christian missionaries arrived in Japan. The end of this period marked the end of Japan's medieval period.

Sengonkō kofun. Group of five large *kofun* with access corridors built on the slopes of Mt. Gongen (Kumamoto prefecture, Kyushu) with a small raised terrace *(bekku)* where primary burials took place. The *kofun* are roughly oval in shape. Their interior chambers have flat ceilings and painted decorations (quivers, concentric circles) in blue and red. Tomb No. 3 has an engraving portraying a boat.

Sengū-shiki. Official ceremony transferring the old Shinto shrines of Ise to a new site beside the old ones; it takes place every 20 years according to a decree issued by Emperor Temmu. It was done for the first time under Empress Jitō (<686–97>). On this occasion, the *naikū* and *gekū* and their 123 attached structures are destroyed and reconstructed in cypress from the Kiso forest. The last *sengū-shiki* took place in 1993. Also called *shikinen-sengū. See* ISE KŌDAIJINGŪ, ISE TOYOUKE DAIJINGŪ.

Sen-hime. Tokugawa Hidetada's daughter (1597–1666), who married Toyotomi Hideyori on September 4, 1603. She was Tokugawa Ieyasu's granddaughter through her mother, Tatsu Hime. During the attack on the Osaka castle by Tokugawa Ieyasu, Sen-hime tried to intercede with her father to save Hideyori's life, but in vain. In 1617, she married Honda Heihachirō Tadatoki, the daimyo of Kuwana and Himeji; when he died, in 1626, she remained in Edo. She is said to have been saved from the flames of the Osaka castle by a warrior, Sakazaki Naomori, who perished in the battle. Literature and theater have often portrayed Sen-hime as an evil influence. *See* TOYOTOMI HIDEYORI.

Senji. Imperial edicts promulgated after 810 by the Kurōdo-dokoro (Bureau of Archivists), and generally written in Chinese *(kambun). See also* SEMMYŌ.

Senji-masu. System of volume measurements imposed in 1072, whose value was equivalent to 81/100 of the norm. Also called Enkyū Senji-masu.

Senji mon. Japanese title of the Chinese classic "One Thousand Characters" *(Chin.: Qianzi wen). See* KANJI.

Senjinkun. Code of military instructions for soldiers and officers, issued on January 8, 1941. Written by Imamura Hitoshi (1886–1968), assisted by Yoshikawa Eiji and others, the *Senjinkun* em-phasized *kokutai,* Shinto worship, reverence to the emperor, absolute obedience to orders, an interdiction on surrendering to the enemy or retreating, and so on. Each soldier received a copy of these instructions.

Senju-ji. Buddhist temple attached to the Jōdo Shin-shū, founded by Shinran in 1226 in Tsu (Mie prefecture) and rebuilt from 1645 to 1745. It was designated an imperial temple *(chokugan-ji)* in 1477, then a Monzeki-dera in 1574. It is the headquarters of the Takada branch of the Jōdo Shin-shū, with about 300,000 followers.

Senju Kannon Bosatsu. One of the esoteric (Tantric) forms of Kannon Bosatsu *(Skt.:* Avalokiteshvara), portrayed with (theoretically) 1,000 arms; in fact, most portrayals show only 42. It corresponds to the Indian Buddhist divinity Āryāvalokiteshvara or Āryapāla. *Chin.:* Qianshou Qianyan Guanyin. *See* KANNON.

Senka. Painter *(gō:* Sōsetsu-sai, early sixteenth century), of the Muromachi *suiboko* school in Kyoto.

Senkaku. Buddhist monk (1203–ca. 1273) of the Tendai-shū sect, born in Hitachi province, who devoted his life to studying the *Man'yōshū* and created a stream of studies on this anthology. He wrote a long (10-volume) treatise on the subject, *Man'yōshū chūshaku* (also titled *Senga kushō*) in 1269. Sometimes called Sengaku.

Senka Tennō. Twenty-eighth emperor (Prince Takeo-hiro Oshi-tachi, 467<536–39>), Ketai Tennō's son and successor to his brother, Ankan. Kimmei succeeded him when he died.

Senke Motomaro. Poet (1888–1948) of the Shirakaba group. He wrote prolifically, sometimes to the detriment of quality. His main works, *Jibun wa mita* (I Live Myself, 1918) and *Mukashi no ie* (The House of the Past, 1929), are still very popular.

Senke-ryū. School of the tea ceremony *(chanoyu)* created by Sen no Rikyū and still active. Its main masters *(chajin)* were:
—Sen no Rikyū (1522–91)
—Shoan (1547–1615), Sen no Rikyū's son
—Gempaku (1578–1658)
—Koshin (1614–73)
—Zuiryū (1652–92)
—Kakkaku (1679–1730)
—Joshin (1706–51)

—Sottaku (1744–1808)
—Ryoryo (1775–1825)
—Kyuko (1817–60)
—Rokuroku (1847–1910)
—Seisai (1863–1937)
—Sokuchūsai (b. 1901)

Senki. "The Flag." A pro-communist literary movement that split from the Bungei Sensen movement about 1930; also, the title of the magazine it published. Founded in 1928, this magazine was the organ of the Zen Nihon Musansha Geijutsu Remmei (better known as NAPF, "Nippona Artista Proletaria Federacio," in Esperanto). It later abandoned literature for political propaganda, and ceased publication in 1930. *See* BUNGEI SENSEN.

Senkoku. Type of metal engraving *(chōkin)*, also called Kebori, Keribori, Namekuri-bori, Sen-bori, Suji-bori.

Senkyo. Japanese name for an imaginary country traditionally located in China, whose inhabitants have a hole in their chest with a piece of wood going through it, which they use to move around.

Sennimbari. White cloth belts embroidered with "a thousand stitches" in needlework. They were made by soldiers' families and friends and sent to them to provide protection when they were at the front during the Second World War. This custom had been inaugurated during the Sino-Japanese War of 1894–95.

Sennin. Type of ideal man according to Confucian concepts, sometimes a hermit with supernatural powers or an "immortal" Taoist. *Sennin* are often portrayed in paintings, usually accompanied by their favorite animal (toad, deer, turtle, tiger, etc.). Also called *rishi* (from Skt.: *rishi*). Chin.: *xianren*.

• **Sennin-yama.** *See* FUJI-SAN.

Sen no Rikyū. Innovative tea master (Tanaka Yoshirō, Sōeki, 1522–91), born in Sakai to a family of fish merchants. He studied the art of the tea ceremony *(chanoyu)* with Kitamuki Dōchin (1504–62) of the Nōami school, then with Takeno Jōō (1502–55) of Murata Shūko's (1422–1502) school, and Zen Buddhism under Shōrei Shukin at the Daitoku-ji temple in Kyoto. In 1570, he began to work for Oda Nobunaga as tea master *(chajin)*, thanks to the recommendation of two tea masters from Sakai, Imai Sōkyū and Tsuda Sōkyū; he went to serve Toyotomi Hideyoshi, who granted him large estates, in 1573. He presided over the huge tea ceremony organized by Hideyoshi at the Kitano temple in 1587. But he suddenly incurred Hideyoshi's displeasure and was forced to commit suicide on April 21, 1591.

Sen no Rikyū had created for Hideyoshi a particular style of *chanoyu,* using common utensils (*see* RAKU) and a simple tea house *(chashitsu).* The school that he created (*see* SENKE-RYŪ) still has many followers today. Among his main disciples were Nambō Sōkei and Yamanoue Sōji, who wrote treatises on their master's teachings. He also created flower arrangements *(rikyū* style; *see* IKEBANA) and was a popular poet. It has been said that he was forced to commit suicide for refusing to give his daughter in marriage to Hideyoshi, but this may be apocryphal.

Sennyo. Buddhist monk (1581–1636) of the Jōdo Shin-shū at the Higashi Hongan-ji (Kyoto); he founded a number of temples, among them the Daitsū-ji.

Sennyū-ji. Buddhist temple and funerary chapel for emperors in Kyoto. It contains many tombs from the thirteenth and fourteenth century. Its present structures date from 1668. Also called Senyū-ji.
→ *See* SHINGON-SHŪ.

Sen'oku Hakkokan. Major collection of ancient Chinese bronzes and Chinese and Japanese mirrors, amassed by Sumitomo Kichizaemon VII (d. 1926). Since 1970, it has been housed in a museum in Kyoto, where more than 500 objets d'art are on display.

Senryū. Genre of haiku in a satiric mode created by Karai Senryū, consisting of three lines of 5, 7, and 5 syllables. These haiku were collected in an anthology called *Haifū-yanagidaru* in 1765. Also called *maekuzuke. See also* ZAPPAI.
→ *See* KARAI SENRYŪ.

Sensei. "Professor," a title given to all people respected for their knowledge or achievements, as well as to all masters of arts and university professors.

Senshin-kyō. Shinto subsect of the Shinri-kyō, founded by Mabuchi Toshitomo (1856–1918) in 1886. It has about 30,000 followers.

Sentai. "One Thousand Bodies," a term for groups of 1,000 small statues of a buddha (usually Amida) or a bodhisattva (Jizō, Kannon, or another), supposed to have originally represented the thousand buddhas of each *kalpa* (Buddhist eons—of the past, present, and future). The *sentai* are either painted or sculpted, as at the Sanjūsangendō in Kyoto and as in the cases of the innumerable "Jizō *sentai*" found throughout Japan, notably in cemeteries. Also called Sentai Butsu (Thousand Bodies of Buddha).

Senzai kaku. "Verses of a Thousand Years," an anthology of *rō-ei* poems and Chinese verses compiled by Ōe no Koretoki (888–963).

• *Senzai waka-shū.* "Anthology of a Thousand Years," compiled by Fujiwara no Toshinari (Shunzei) in 1188; it was the seventh of the great imperial anthologies (*see* CHOKUSEN WAKA-SHŪ), produced on the order of Retired Emperor Go-Shirakawa. Divided into 20 volumes, it contains 1,285 poems by 383 poets, among them Minamoto no Toshiyori, Fujiwara no Mototoshi, Izumi Shikibu, and, of course, Shunzei. Also called *Senzai-shū.*

Senzan. Painter (Nakamura Kan; *azana*: Saimō; *gō*: Juzan, Senzan, 1820–62) of the Nanga (Bunjinga) school, Kazan's student.

Senzoku kofun. Large *kofun* in Okayama prefecture, decorated with motifs made of *chokkomon* divided into panels.

Seoul, Treaty of (Kanjō Jōyaku). This treaty, signed in January 1885, ratified the reopening of diplomatic relations between Korea and Japan, which had been interrupted by the coup d'état of 1884. In the treaty, Korea apologized to Japan, agreeing to pay an indemnity of 110,000 *yen* and to rebuild Japan's legation in Seoul and ensure its safety, in accord with the Treaty of Chemulpo (Inchŏn) of 1882.

Seppuku. Ritual suicide performed by Japanese warriors by cutting open the stomach, popularly called *hara-kiri* (literally, "cutting the stomach"). This ceremony was performed before a small audience. The person committing suicide, dressed in white, wrote a poem of farewell, then made a shallow cut across the abdominal muscles from left to right then up toward the liver, or a double cross-shaped incision, using a dagger called *kusungobu* ("nine inches and five *bu*," or about 25 cm), thus showing his firm resolution to end his life. Once this incision was made, he bent forward slightly to allow his assistant *(kaishiakunin)* to behead him neatly with one sword blow. Women committed suicide by cutting their jugular vein with a dagger. The first *seppuku* was performed, according to legend, by Minamoto no Tametomo in 1156. After he was captured in battle, his enemies cut the tendons in his arms so that he could no longer use a bow and arrow. He committed suicide soon after by cutting his stomach open so that his soul could escape. *See* JIGAI.

• A famous film, called *Harakiri,* showing this act in all its horror, was made in 1962 by Kobayashi Masaki, starring Nakadai Tatsuya and Mikuni Rentarō. Another movie with the same subject and title was made by Mishima Yukio; he also starred in it, prefiguring his own suicide.

Seriage. In Kabuki theater, the platform on which an actor is raised (or lowered) for an entrance (or exit), through an opening in the stage called *seridashi.* This system was probably invented by Namiki Shōzō (1730–73).

Serizawa Keisuke. Painter and fabric designer (1895–1984), born in Shizuoka. He was inspired by the dyeing techniques used by Okinawan peasant artisans *(bingata).* He was designated a Living National Treasure in 1956, and his works were exhibited in Paris in 1976.

Serizawa Kōjirō. Writer (1897–1993), born in Shizuoka prefecture. He studied economics in France from 1925 to 1929. After a stay in a sanitarium in Switzerland, he began to write novels: *Asu o oute* (1931), *Isu o sagasu* (1932). He resigned from his position as an economics professor at Chūō University to devote himself to literature: *Pari ni shisu* (I Will Die in Paris, 1942), *Hitotsu no sekai* (A Single World, 1953), *Pari fuji* (Madame Aida, 1955), *Ningen no ummei* (The Fate of Humanity, 1968), *Daishizen no yume* (Mother Nature's Dream, 1992). Most of his works were translated into French.

Sesonji-ryū. Calligraphy school founded in Kamakura in the fourteenth century by Sesonji Yukifusa and Fujiwara Yukinari.

Sessai. Painter (Matsuyama Masakata; *azana*: Kunsen; *gō*: Gyoku-en, Kan'en, Setsuryo, Chōshū, Sekiten-dōjin, 1755–1820) of the Nagasaki school, influenced by Nampin's art. Daimyo of Nagashima (now Mie prefecture), he was also a poet and writer. He signed most of his works Sessai.

• Painter of ukiyo-e prints (Tsukioka Shūei; *azana*: Taikei; *gō*: Sessai, d. 1839) who studied with his father, Settei, in Osaka. He received the titles Hokkyō and Hōgen. Better known by his full name, Tsukioka Sessai.

• Sculptor (Shima Sessei, Hokkyō Sessai, 1821–79) of Buddhist images and netsuke in Echizen.

→ *See* AOYAMA NOBUYUKI, TAKII KZŌSAKU.

Sesshō. In the Heian period, the regent for an underage emperor. Starting in 866, this title and function were reserved for members of the Fujiwara family. However, the position had existed previously: Prince Shōtoku Taishi was *sesshō* for Empress Suiko. During much of the Heian period, the Fujiwara *sesshō* retained the regency when emperors became adults (at age 13) and took the title of *kampaku;* they thus held absolute power. More recently, in 1889, it was stipulated that only a member of the imperial family could hold the title of *sesshō* or *kampaku*. Crown Prince Hirohito was thus regent for his ill father, Taishō Tennō, from 1921 to 1926. Since 1947, a *sesshō* can be appointed only if the reigning emperor is under 18 years of age. Also called *shissei, shippei, setsuroku. See also* SHIKKEN.

→ *See* HANABUSA ITCHŌ.

Sesshū. Buddhist monk and painter (*mei:* Sessō, then, after he turned 40, Oda Tōyō; *gō*: Unkoku, Sesshu Tōyō, Sesshū, 1420–1506), Shūbun's student at the Shōkoku-ji temple in Kyoto. He studied the art of China ink washes *(suiboku)*. In 1467, he went to China with a trade delegation sent by the Ōuchi family; there, he visited monasteries, including Tiantong-shan, where he received the rank of *shuso,* and took lessons with painter Li Zai. He returned to Japan in 1469 and lived in Bungo, then Suō. Most of his surviving works are from after his return to Japan. His wash paintings are distinguished from Shūbun's by the vigor of his brush strokes, which sometimes give a jagged look to the rocks and plants in his landscapes. He also painted portraits, and flowers and birds *(kachō-ga)*. Among his disciples were Shūgetsu Tōhaku, Josui Sōen, and Tōshun, and his art profoundly influenced generations of artists, including Hasegawa Tōhaku and Unkoku Tōgan. The latter founded the Unkoku school, which claimed to be directly descended from Sesshū.

Sesson. Painter (Satake? Heizō; *gō*: Shūkyosai, Shūkei, Kakusen-rōjin, Sesson, Sesson Shūkei, ca. 1504–ca. 1589) of the Muromachi *suiboku* school, born in Hitachi province, and Buddhist monk of the Jōdo-shū. He first followed Sesshū's style, but added a very personal note to his rendering of landscapes and birds, portraying them in a more naturalistic manner than did his masters, thus distancing himself from Chinese and Japanese traditions.

Sesson Yūbai. Zen Buddhist monk (1290–1346) of the Rinzai sect, born in Echigo province. In 1307, he went to China, where he was imprisoned by the emperor to avenge Kublai Khan's defeat by Hiradō; he obtained permission to return to Japan only in 1329. He wrote very beautiful poems, which were collected in the anthology *Minga-shū* (Between the Mii River and Mt. E-mei), about his site of exile.

Setaisho. "Book on the Form of Government," or "Constitution of 1868," the first constitution of the Meiji government, published in 1868–69 and announcing, among other measures, the separation of powers into executive and legislative branches. The text mixed Western concepts with Japanese traditions, maintaining the principle of the Dajōkan Council; it remained the supreme agency (under the emperor) until 1885, when the system of ministerial cabinets was adopted.

Setchū-ha. Confucian school founded by the scholars Nakanishi Tan'en (1709–52), Inoue Randai (1705–61), Uno Meika (1698–1745), Inoue Kinga (1733–84), Katayama Kenzan (1730–82), and Hosoi Heishū, mixing the teachings of the three major schools of Confucianism, Shushi (*Chin.*: Zhu Xi), Ō-Yomei (*Chin.*: Wang Yangming), and *kogaku*. Also called Setchūgaku-ha. *See also* KOGAKU.

Setchū-yōshiki. "Composite style" of religious architecture developed during the Muromachi period, incorporating Chinese Song-dynasty architectural elements with the Japanese *wa-yō* style.

Seto. City in Aichi prefecture, northeast of Nagoya, famous for its ceramics industry *(setomono)* since the twelfth century, due to the excellent-quality clay at the foot of the Sanageyama hills. Aichi prefecture has bid to host the World Fair in Seto in 2005 with the theme "Technology, Culture, and Communications." *Pop.*: 120,000.

• **Setoguro.** Type of porcelain with black glaze produced in Seto starting in the sixteenth century, imitating Chinese pieces. *See* SETO-YAKI.

• **Setomono.** General term for ceramic objects, named after the city of Seto.

• **Seto-yaki.** Ceramics produced from the twelfth to the sixteenth century in Seto and environs; the art of applying ash glazes had been imported to Seto from Sanage, east of Nagoya. In the thirteenth century, more than 80 kilns were built at Seto, which produced jars with four small handles at the shoulders, with a stamped or incised (with a comb) design. In the fourteenth century, the number of kilns doubled, and both production and decoration techniques diversified. Ceramics began to be produced with a glaze made with iron oxide, imitating Chinese pieces and *temmoko.* In the following centuries, the Seto kilns produced dark-green pottery for the tea ceremony and for daily use, in new shapes inspired by Chinese porcelain. Around the mid-sixteenth century, production at the Seto kilns dropped off due to competition from the kiln at Mino. The Seto region has maintained the tradition, but production is now relatively low. A ceramics museum was recently opened in Seto. *See also* KI SETO, KO-SETO, SETOGURO.

Setonaikai. "Inland Sea" of Japan, between Honshu, Shikoku, and Kyushu, formed in the Quaternary Era by land subsidence. It is quite shallow and divided into five basins, Harima, Bungo, Aki, Iyo, and Suō, which form distinct "seas." It has more than 3,000 small islands, distributed unequally between Honshu and Shikoku prefectures. Its salinity is low and it has violent currents. The sea opens to the west via Shimonoseki Strait, to the south via Hōyo Strait, and to the east via two straits around the island of Awaji. Its very jagged coasts make for excellent ports. On its western coast, on Honshu, is an almost uninterrupted stretch of cities and industrial facilities that pollute its waters. The Setonaikai has always played an important role in relations between the islands and the mainland. Many national parks have been created to protect its most characteristic sites. *Total length:* about 770 km; *maximum width:* 60 km. *Main islands:* Awaji, Shōdoshima. Also called Setouchi, Seto no Uchi.

Setō Shōji. Engineer (1891–1977) born in Wakayama prefecture; he developed the principle of the electron microscope in Japan during the Second World War. He was decorated with the Order of Culture (Bunka-shō) in 1973.

Setouchi Harumi. Writer, born 1922 in Tokushima prefecture. She specialized in biographies of famous women, including *Tamura Yoshiko* (1960). Although she became a Buddhist nun in 1973, she continued to write: *Natsu no owari* (The End of a Summer, 1962), *Kanoko ryōran* (biography of Okamoto Kanoko, 1971).

Setsubun. *See* ONI-HARAI.

Setsuwa bungaku. Literary genre based on ancient tales and legends, composed of texts written between 800 and 1300. The most famous example of a *setsuwa* is the *Konjaku monogatari.* At one time, legends *(densetsu)* and myths *(shinwa)* were seen as distinct from each other.

Setsuzan. Painter (Koto Setsuzan, sixteenth century), perhaps Sesson's student.
• Calligrapher (Kitajima Sanritsu; *gō:* Kain, Setsuzan, 1636–97) in the Chinese Qing-dynasty style.

Settai. Title of a Noh play: Minamoto Yoshitsune, fleeing from his brother Yoritomo, asks for shelter from the family of a warrior who has remained faithful to him.

Settan. Painter (Hasegawa Sōshū; *mei:* Gotō Moemon; *gō:* Gangakusai, Ichiyōan, Settan, 1778–1843) of ukiyo-e prints in Edo. He mainly illustrated books.

Settei. Painter (Tsukioka Settei, Minamoto Settei; *azana:* Kida Masunobu; *mei:* Tange; *gō:* Daikei, Masunobu, Shintenō, Kindō, Tōki, Rojinsai, Settei, 1710–86) of ukiyo-e prints in Osaka, Takada Keiho's student. He produced mainly erotic prints. He received the title Hokkyō in 1777, then the title Hōgen. Founder of the Settei-ryū school (also called Tsukioka-ryū), stemming from the Unkoku-ryū. His son Sessai was his main disciple.

Settsu. Former province, now included in Osaka and Hyōgo prefectures, where a number of emperors established their palaces before the seventh century. It was the territorial base of the Seiwa-Genji and Minamoto families.

Sewa-mono. Genre of Kabuki plays created by Chikamatsu Monzaemon, in which the action takes place within the merchant class and depicts the customs and mores of the ordinary people. This genre was divided into several others, including the *zangiri-mono,* depicting the customs of the new working class that had adopted the Western hairstyle *(zangiri),* as opposed to those who had retained the old style *(chonmage).* Sometimes called Nibanme-mono (second plays), as opposed to Ichiban-me-mono, or plays with a historical subject.

Seyaku Kannon Bosatsu. One of the 33 forms (*see* SANJŪSAN ŌGESHIN) of Kannon Bosatsu (*Skt.:* Avalokiteshvara), considered a "giver of joy" and portrayed sitting near water, in a pensive attitude, looking at lotus flowers.

Shabaku. Painter (*gō:* Gessen, late sixteenth century) of the Muromachi *suiboko* school, one of Shūbun's students.

Shachi. In castle architecture, decoration of roof corners with sea monsters (or dolphins), generally in gold-leafed metal, supposed to protect the building against fire and evil spirits. Also called *shachi-hoko. See also* SHIBI.

Shadō. Japanese archery *(kyūdō)* viewed from a spiritual (Zen) point of view and practiced as a sort of ceremony; archers wear a costume that leaves the right shoulder bare.

Shakai Minshutō. "Socialist Democratic party," founded in 1901 by Abe Isoo, Katayama Sen, Kōtoku Shūsui, and other socialists, demanding disarmament, abolition of the class system, and nationalization of transportation and land. The party was immediately banned by the government.

• **Shakai Minshūtō.** "Socialist People's party," founded in 1926 by members of the Rōdō Nōmintō (Labor-Farmer paty) and led by Abe Isoo and Katayama Tetsu. This party was anti-communist and advocated a parliamentary system; it was supported by the Japan Federation of Labor (Sōdōmei). In 1931, it backed the government policy of territorial expansion, but many members disapproved of this, so it merged with the Zenkoku Rōnō Taishūtō (National Labor-Farmer party) to form the Shakai Taishūtō (Socialist Masses party).

• **Shakai-shugi-kyōkai.** Name of two socialist Marxist associations, one founded in 1900 and the other in 1951; most of the members were intellectuals of the Rōnō-ha current.

• **Shakai Taishūtō.** "Socialist Masses party," created in 1932 by the merger of the Shakai Minshūtō (Socialist People's party) and the Zenkoku Rōnō Taishūtō (Japan Farmer-Labor party), with Abe Isoo as leader. This moderate party was opposed to communism, fascism, and capitalism; it advocated

international cooperation but declared itself in favor of war against China in 1937. It was dissolved in 1940.

• **Shakaitō.** "Rickshaw party," a political association involving a large number of rickshaw pullers *(jinriksha),* created in 1882 by Ōmiya Takeyuki to oppose the spread of streetcars pulled by horses. It formed a common front with the Jiyūtō (Liberal party), but was dissolved in 1884 after several confrontations with the police.

Shakkū. Pseudonym under which Shinran (and other monks) signed the *Shichikajō kishōmon* manifesto.

Shakkyō. "The Stone Bridge," title of a Noh play: a Buddhist monk must cross a stone bridge to reach the paradise of Monju Bosatsu, but a child warns him that this will be a dangerous enterprise. The lion of Mañjushrī then appears and dances for the monk.

Shaku. Unit of length corresponding to about 0.3 m, divided into 10 *sun.* Formerly called *saka. See also* KOMA-SHAKU, SEKI. *Chin.: chi.*
   • Small wooden plank about one *shaku* long (sometimes made of ivory or lacquered wood), carried by senior court bureaucrats to indicate their rank. On the back of some *shaku* were written the rules of the ceremonies in which the bureaucrats had to take part or other information pertinent to their work. Also called *kotsu. Chin.: gui.*
   • Japanese form of the word *Shakyamuni.*

• **Shaku-buku.** In the Sōka-Gakkai sect, an act in which followers must destroy the *butsudan* in their house and replace it with a small board bearing the title of the *Lotus Sutra (Hokke-kyō).*

• **Shakudō.** Alloy of antimony and copper with about 3% gold. Treated in an acid solution, it took on a smooth dark-blue patina. This alloy was widely used by sculptors and artisans.

• **Shakuhachi.** Straight one-piece bamboo flute, 1 *shaku* and 8 *sun* long (whence its name). The mouthpiece is a simple beveled slot, sometimes reinforced with a piece of buffalo horn. It has four holes on top, equally spaced, and one on the bottom for the thumb. The inside is lacquered. The *shakuhachi* was imported from China, probably in the late seventh century (when it had five holes on top, in the Chinese style), and was used in Gagaku orchestras.

It was popularized in the early sixteenth century by mendicant Buddhist monks *(komusō)* and was called *hito-yogiri.* The *shakuhachi* now has a repertoire of its own and often accompanies the koto or shamisen. It is also used in Noh orchestras and instrumental folk groups.

• **Shakujō.** Stick used by Buddhist monks to warn that they were approaching because certain people believe that seeing them is harmful (because of their association with death, considered by Shinto followers to be a blot). Ordinary monks and pilgrims have *shakujō* with two rings of metal at the top, while high-ranking monks and some divinities, such as Jizō Bosatsu, have a stick decorated with six rings representing the "six destinies of transmigration" *(rokudō).* Also sometimes called *kongō-zue. Skt.: khakhara.*

• *Shaku Nihongi.* Twenty-eight-volume commentary on the *Nihon shoki* written by Urabe Kanekata, a Shinto priest, around 1300. It also contains excerpts from some *fudoki* and ancient chronicles.

Shaku Sōen. Zen Buddhist monk (1859–1919) of the Rinzai sect, born in Wakasa province, appointed abbot of the Engaku-ji in Kamakura in 1892. He traveled in India, Ceylon, and the United States, where he gave a series of lectures on Zen philosophy and gathered disciples. *See* MATSUGAOKA BUNKO.

Shakyō-jo. Official bureau for copying Buddhist texts in the Nara court, created in 727 and responsible for reproduction and translation of religious texts imported from China and Korea. Many of these copies are kept in the Shōsō-in in Nara.

Shami. In Buddhist monastic orders, a novice or lay follower who has taken the ten vows of the novitiate, equivalent to the Sanskrit title *shramanera.* Monks who enter Buddhist orders are called *shamon (Skt.: shramana). See* NYŪDŌ.

Shamisen. Musical instrument: a three-stringed lute with a long neck and a square soundbox covered with cat- or dog-skin. Imported from China to Okinawa in the mid-sixteenth century, it was used in *jōruri,* Kabuki, and other ensembles, and by geisha during the Edo period. The strings are made of silk or (today) nylon. It is played with a large triangular pick, made of hardwood or ivory, called *bachi.* The body of the instrument is made of red sandalwood or other similar wood. There are sev-

eral varieties, including *chosen, taisen,* and *kirisen.* Also called *samisen* (in Kansai), *sangen* (for chamber music), *sanshin,* and *jamisen* (in Okinawa). *Chin.: sanxian.*

Shamo. Ainu word for the majority of Japanese.

Shamu. Former title for administrators of Shinto shrines.
• Japanese name for Thailand (Siam).

Sharaku. Painter (Tōshūsai Sharaku; *mei:* Saitō Jurobei; *gō:* Tōshūsai, active 1794–95 in Osaka) who made ukiyo-e prints portraying Kabuki actors, to be used as posters. Nothing is known about his life, and he seems to have worked (at least under this name) for only six months, producing 145 colored prints, 10 drawings of sumo wrestlers (of which only one has been found), and 8 copies of drawings for book illustrations. He may have been a Noh actor serving a daimyo in Awa province. His works were all published by Tsutaya Juzaburō (who, according to some critics, himself made the prints attributed to Sharaku). Sharaku's prints are characterized by extremely tense faces and attitudes, and are printed on a micaceous background. They had a profound influence on the art of other painters of ukiyo-e prints, including Utagawa Kunimasa and Utagawa Toyokuni.

Sharebon. "Naughty books," a literary genre of novels *(gesaku)* in the Edo period; they appeared about 1755 and described, in plain language, the life of courtesans in Edo and Osaka. Considered obscene by the shogunal authorities, these works were banned in 1790 and replaced in public favor (and that of the authorities) by *ninjōbon* and *kokkeibon.* Noted writers of *sharebon* included Ōta Nampo and Santō Kyōden; lesser-known authors such as Hōraisanjin Kikyō and Tanishi Kingyō also wrote *sharebon* during this period.

Shari. Relics, generally bones or cinders of a holy Buddhist man, sometimes symbolized by small bits of crystal. *Skt.: sharīra.*

• **Shariden.** In Buddhist temples and Shinto shrines, a hall reserved for housing relics *(shari).*

• **Shari-tō.** Buddhist grave-marker in the form of a small pagoda or other object, intended to contain relics *(shari).* Also called *gorin-tō, hōbyō. Kor.: sari-tap; Chin.: shelita.*

Sharp. Manufacturer and distributor of electronic equipment—photocopiers, computers, air conditioners, etc.—and electronic components, founded in 1912 by Hayakawa Tokuji, the inventor of a mechanical pencil called Eversharp. Sharp began to produce radio receivers in Osaka in 1925; televisions, in 1953. It took the name Sharp Corporation in 1970. It currently exports more than 50% of its production and has plants through various companies in seven other countries. Head office in Osaka.

Shaseki-shū. "Collection of Sand and Stones," a collection of stories in the Sewa-mono genre written by the Buddhist monk Mujū Ichien (1226–1312) between 1279 and 1283, expounding Buddhist morals through folk anecdotes.

Shasenbyō. Type of perspective "in oblique lines" used in *emakimono* produced by painters of the imperial court, in which architectural lines are drawn in parallel from upper right to bottom left. This technique was used mainly by painters of the Yamato-e and was used for illustrations in the *Genji monogatari.*

Shasō. Warehouses built in villages during the Edo period to forestall famine, stocked with voluntary grain donations. The *shasō* were created in 1655 and eliminated in 1868. During the same period, the government built other state warehouses, called *gisō*, and distributed their contents free of charge during famines.

Shasui Kannon Bosatsu. One of the 33 forms (Sanjūsan Ōgeshin) of Kannon Bosatsu (*Skt.*: Avalokiteshvara) dedicated to the sprinkling of lustral water and portrayed holding a stick and a bowl.

Shaw, Glenn William. American writer and translator (1886–1961), born in Los Angeles, who worked in Japan from 1916 to 1940 and from 1949 to 1957. He translated works by modern Japanese writers into English and, as historian for the Ministry of Foreign Affairs, made microfilms of official Japanese documents after the Second World War. As cultural officer for the United States in the Tokyo embassy, he received many honorific titles from the American and Japanese governments. Among his most noted works are *Ōsaka Sketches* (1929), *Japanese Scrapbook* (1932), and *Living in Japan* (1936). He also translated works by Kurata Hyakuzō, Futabatei Shimei, Kikuchi Kan, and Akutagawa Ryūnosuke.

Shi. "Four." This number (like the number 13 in the West) is regarded as bad luck in Japan because it is a homophone for the word "death." Thus, the presentation of objects in fours is scrupulously avoided, and room numbers in traditional hospitals and hotels never bear this digit. In conversation, the Japanese pronunciation *yon* is used.

• An alternative pronunciation for the word "*tsukasa,*" designating a government department (or ministry) in the Nara and Heian periods.

Shiatsu. Therapy derived from (or perhaps older than) acupuncture, consisting of applying pressure with the fingers on certain specific points *(tsubo)* of the body and limbs, following "meridians" *(keiraku; Chin.: jing).* *Amma* (massages), sometimes performed with the feet, are now considered to be part of *shiatsu*. In martial arts, *shiatsu* is widely used for resuscitation. *See* KUATSU.

Shibaki Yoshiko. Writer (Oshima Yoshiko, 1914–91), born in Tokyo; she received the Akutagawa Prize in 1941 for her story *Seika no ochi* (The Vegetable Market). Her novels describe life among ordinary people and artisans of the lower town *(shitamachi)* of Tokyo; *Yuba* (1960), *Sumidagawa* (1961), and *Marunouchi hachigōkan* (1962) are autobiographical. In 1981, she received the Japan Art Academy (Nihon Geijutsu-in) Prize, and she was elected a member of the Academy in 1983. In 1984, she published *Sumidagawa boshoku* (Night Scene on the Sumida).

Shiba Kōkan. Engraver and painter (1747–1818), and scholar of "Dutch science" *(rangaku)*; the first to attempt engraving on copper, he hand-colored his prints. He lived in Nagasaki and was interested in astronomy, particularly Copernicus's system, which he expounded in *Kopperu temmon zukai* (Illustrated Explanation of Copernicus's Astronomy, 1808); later, he produced portraits of women using oil paints. He became a student of Suzuki Harunobu, and adopted the name Harushige for his ukiyo-e prints around 1770–75.

Shibano Ritsuzan. Confucian scholar (1736–1807), born in Sanuki province, appointed professor at the Shōheikō in 1788. He was one of the three Kanse no Sansuke (or San-hakase), with Bitō Nishū and Koga Seiri.

Shibaraku. "Wait a Moment!" A classic Kabuki play (one of the Kabuki-jūhachiban) written by Ichikawa Danjūrō I in *aragoto* style about 1697.

This one-act play features an evil daimyo who oppresses the people and is finally killed by a heroic samurai who reestablishes justice in his estates. The phrase said by the hero as he prepares to avenge the people is the play's title.

Shiba Ryōtarō. Writer and journalist, born 1923 in Osaka, author of popular historical novels: *Fukurō no shiro* (Naoki Prize 1959), *Ryōma ga yuku* (1966), *Yo ni sumu hibi* (1970), *Saka no ue no kumo* (1972).

Shibata Katsuie. General (ca. 1522–83) under Oda Nobunaga, for whom he won many battles in Ise and Ōmi, and against the Ikkō-ikki. Oda Nobunaga appointed him governor of Echizen province in 1575. Attacked by Toyotomi Hideyoshi in 1583 at the Battle of Shizugatake, he committed suicide. He was married to Oichi, one of Oda Nobunaga's younger sisters.

Shibata Renzaburō. Writer (1917–78), born in Okayama prefecture, author of many swashbucklers featuring an invulnerable samurai, Nemuri Kyōshirō. He created the *kengō* (swordsman) genre, which he exploited to great popular success, in collaboration with Gomi Yasusuke: *Kyōshirō burai hikae* (starting in 1956), *Akai kagebōshi* (1960).

Shibata Shō. Writer, born 1935 in Tokyo, expert in German literature. He received the Akutagawa Prize in 1964 for his novel *Saredo warera ga hibi,* which was influential among Japanese young people.

Shiba Tatto. Chinese monk who, according to the twelfth-century chronicle *Fudo ryakki* by the Buddhist monk Zenshin, went to Japan in 522 and built a small temple housing an image of the Buddha near Asuka (Nara prefecture). According to the *Nihon shoki,* he was the ancestor of the Kuratsukuribe sculptors. His Chinese name was Sima Dadeng. His three daughters became Buddhist nuns. His son, Tasuna, and grandson, Tori, were also sculptors of Buddhist images. *See* KURATSUKURIBE NO TORI.

Shibata Zeshin. Painter and lacquer artist (1807–91), born in Edo. He studied lacquer decoration at the Koma school (founded by Koma Kitoe), then naturalist painting at the Shijō school with Suzuki Nanrei and Okamoto Toyohiko. From 1886 to 1889, he produced a large number of lacquered panels for the imperial palace.

Shiba Yoshimasa. General (1350–1410) who was opposed to Ashikaga Yoshiakira; he was named *kanrei* in 1379 under the shogunate of Ashikaga Yoshimochi, a position he held for 18 years. He was firmly opposed to the reopening of diplomatic relations with China.

Shiba Zenkō. Writer (ca. 1750–93) of *kusazōshi*-type novels, such as *Ote ryōri oshiru nomi* (The Rooster You Know, 1785).

Shibi. In architecture, a roof ornament, usually in the form of an animal or animal head (horse or dolphin), placed at the ends of the ridge beam. *See also* SHACHI.

Shibue Chūsai. Physician and Confucian scholar (1805–58) born in Edo. As a professor of medicine at the Seijukan school (shogunal school of Chinese medicine), he conducted philological research and compiled a voluminous bibliography of classic Chinese texts, *Keiseki hōko-shi,* still used today. He also republished the *Ishimpō,* a medical treatise from the Heian period. Mori Ōgai wrote a biography of him and his master, Isawa Ranken (1777–1829), in 1916.

Shibui. "Rough or astringent taste," a word explaining the inherent subtle nature of poignant beauty; it can be applied to both things and people, and is used mainly by artists. It is the idea (expressed by the word *shibumi*) of an elegance hidden behind ordinary appearances—an eloquent silence, modesty without prudery. In art, it is a form of *sabi,* denoting a harmonious simplicity. In literature, it is *wabi,* full of active spirit. These concepts have been the ideal of many artists and writers from the Muromachi period to the present. In literature, *shibui* (*shibumi, sabi,* and *wabi*) is called *heitammi* when all affectation and mannerisms are transcended and the true nature of things is only suggested.

Shibuichi. Alloy of copper (75%) and silver (25%). When the proportions of silver and copper are equal, the alloy is called *rogin*. Both alloys were used by jewelers and goldsmiths during the Edo period. *See also* SHAKUDŌ.

Shibukawa Shunkai. Astronomer (Yasui Santetsu, Yasui Shunkai, Yasui, Harumi, Shibukawa Harumi, 1639–1715). He discovered errors in the Sennyō calendar of Chinese origin, which had been in use for eight centuries, and created, in collaboration with Shibukawa Kōkyō, a new calendar, called Tenkyō-*reki,* in 1684. He also drew a new map of the skies, based on the North Star, in 1677, and the following year he calculated the exact latitude of the city of Azabu (Edo) at 35° 38' north; this calculation was off by just one minute. He also wrote *Jōkyō-reki* (or *Jōkyō koyomi*), a treatise on calendars, in 1684.

Shibusawa Eiichi. Senior bureaucrat and industrialist (1840–1931), born in Saitama prefecture, and samurai serving the Hitotsubashi family. He accompanied Tokugawa Akitake to the 1867 World Fair in Paris, and devoted himself to scientific development in Japan. In 1870, Emperor Meiji made him responsible for reorganizing the system of weights and measures. He left this position in 1873 to create the first industrial corporations, helping to found some 500 companies. He was in correspondence with Thomas Edison and tried, through him, to improve relations between the United States and Japan. He also founded many banks and cotton mills in Osaka. His nickname is "the father of Japanese capitalism."

• **Shibusawa Keizō.** Industrialist and banker (1896–1963), born in Tokyo, Shibusawa Eiichi's grandson. He was president of the Bank of Japan in 1944, then minister of finance in Shidehara Kijūrō's cabinet in 1945–46. After the Second World War, he continued his financial activities and began to collect folk art *(mingei),* founding a museum in 1921 that became the Nihon Jōmin Bunka Kenkyūjo (Institute of Ethnological Research) in Tokyo, which stimulated the development of the field of ethnology.

Shibutsu. Painter (Ōkubo, Gyō; *mei:* Ryūtarō; *azana:* Temmin; *gō:* Shiseidō, Kozansho-oku, Shibutsu, 1766–1837) of the Nanga (Bunjinga) school, and poet.

Shibu-uchiwa. Flat fan of the *uchiwa* type, used to fan the embers in fireplaces; it became the symbol of poverty and of the *kami* of poor people, *bimbō-gami. See* ŌGI, UCHIWA.

Shibuya Tengai. Actor and playwright (1906–83), born in Kyoto, son of a comic actor of the same name, and a comic himself. In 1930, he married the actress Naniwa Chieko, whom he divorced in 1950. He played on stage and in movies and was considered the greatest comic actor of his generation.

Shichi. "Seven," in Sino-Japanese reading *(on).* In Japanese reading *(kun),* it is read *nana.*

• "Loan against security," a system instituted in the eighth century by individuals and reorganized during the Edo period, when lenders against security *(shichiya)* were organized into guilds regulated by the daimyo. At first, the word *shichi* meant an indispensable object that was entrusted to a person (or appropriated by someone, legally or illegally). In the Muromachi period, an indebted person often offered himself (or someone in his family) as security. Similarly, a warrior might be held in security for the good conduct (or neutrality) of his family: he was then called a *hitojichi* (security-man). In the Edo period, the only authorized *hitojichi* were members of families of daimyo who were forced, under the *sankin-kōtai,* to live in Edo. The word *shichi* then designated objects given in security against a sum of money obtained from specialized lenders, and the sale of human beings (except for girls) and the taking of hostages was banned by law.

Shichifukujin. "The Seven Gods of Good Fortune," said to bring luck and health. This group was formed, on a Chinese model, in the early seventeenth century and quickly became the object of veneration by the people. It mixes Indian, Chinese, and Japanese divinities symbolizing, for Confucians, the essential human virtues: Longevity, Luck, Popularity, Candor, Kindness, Dignity, and Magnanimity. The Shichifukujin sail together in the "ship of treasures" *(takara-bune),* and their image is considered a powerful charm. They are very often portrayed as a group in paintings and sculpture. These seven propitiatory divinities are Ebisu and Daikoku-ten (of Japanese origin); Bishamon-ten (*Skt.:* Vaishravana), Benzai-ten (*Skt.:* Sarasvatī), and Kichijō-ten (*Skt.:* Shrīmahādevī), of Indian origin; and Jurōjin and Hotei (of Chinese origin). Children place an effigy of the Shichifukujin under their pillow on the night of December 31 to January 1 so that the divinities will ensure them a prosperous and happy year. They are venerated mainly among the merchant classes. They are also sometimes called *fuku no kami,* "the *kami* of happiness." *Chin.:* Qifushen.

Shichigen-kin. Musical instrument, a seven-stringed zither *(koto)* about 1.1 to 1.2 m long and 20 to 25 cm wide, without movable frets. Notes are obtained by pressing the fingers on the strings. This instrument of Chinese origin was imported to Japan in the Nara period and again in the seventeenth century by Zen Buddhist monks of the Sōtō-shū sect. It stopped being used in the late nineteenth century, when it was replaced by the koto. Also called *kin*. Chin.: *qin*.

Shichigosan. "Seven–Five–Three," an annual festival on November 15 during which children who have reached the ages of seven, five, and three are celebrated because an old superstition has it that these ages are critical. Parents drive their children, luxuriously clothed in traditional garb (*kimono* and *hakama*) to the Shinto shrine near their home or to another famous shrine to ask the *kami* to protect them. When they return home, they purchase *chitoseame* (cakes of a thousand years of happiness) to hand out to relatives and friends.

• **Shichigosan-nawa.** *See* SHIMENAWA.

Shichijō-bussho. "Studio of Sculptors of Seventh Street," founded in Kyoto by the Buddhist sculptor Kakujo, Jōchō's son, and his descendants in the eleventh and twelfth centuries:
   —Kōshō, Jōchō (d. 1057), Kakujo (d. 1077)
   —Kakyō, father of Injō (d. 1108), Kōjo
   —Kōjo, father of Kōchō, Kōkei
   —Kōchō, father of Jōchō
   —Kōkei, father of Unkei, Kaikei
   —Unkei, father of Tankei, Kōun, Kōben, Kōshō (father of Kosei), and Koyo, Unga, Unjo (father of Kōyū), and Koshun (father of Kō-i)
   —Injō, father of Inkaku and Inchō
   —Inkaku, father of Inkei and Inson
   —Inson, father of Injitsu, Inhan
   —Inchō, father of Inshō
   —Inshō, father of In-en, Inken (father of Inchū)
→ *See also* BUSSHO, IN-PA, SANJŌ-BUSSHO.

Shichijūichi-ban shokunin uta awase. "Poetry Contest Held in Seventy-One Sessions by the Members of Various Professions." An *emakimono* describing 142 artisans at work, one of the most valuable surviving works on the life and customs of artisans in the Muromachi period (sixteenth century).

Shichikajō kishōmon. "Vow in Seventeen Articles," taken by the Buddhist monk Shinran (under the name Shakkū) and other monks of Mt. Hiei to reassure and calm their community, which had been divided by the new doctrines of the Jōdo Shin-shū.

Shichinin no samurai. "The Seven Samurai," a famous movie produced in 1954 by Kurosawa Akira: a village harassed by bandits hires seven *rōnin* samurai to protect it. This film was artfully transposed

to the American West by John Sturges as *The Magnificent Seven* (1960).

Shichiya. "Seventh night," a family ceremony conducted on the seventh day after the birth of a child, during which the baby is given a name and presented to the family's tutelary *kami*. On this day, birth notices are sent to friends and acquaintances.

Shichō. In the seventh century, a term for men in charge of work parties at the imperial palace and in the court. Villages had to designate one man out of thirty (then out of fifty) to fulfill the domestic tasks required by government departments and for construction of temples.

Shichū. Type of traditional roof with four symmetrical slopes, joined at the summit by a large ridge beam. A variant is called *yosemune*.
→ *See* USHŪ.

Shidehara Kijūrō. Politician (1872–1951), born in Osaka, sent on diplomatic missions to Korea, the United States, and Europe starting in 1896. Ambassador to the United States (1919) and delegate to the Washington Conference (1921–22); minister of foreign affairs in Katō Takkaki's cabinet from 1924 to 1927, then in Tanaka Giichi's cabinet from 1929 to 1931. He became prime minister (October 1945), succeeding Higashikuni Naruhiko, but had to resign when his party, the Nihon Shimpotō (Japan Progressive party), was defeated in the elections of May 1946. He was then reelected to the House of Representatives twice. Throughout his career, he was pro-Western, although he was suspected by the ultranationalists of being anti-imperial. His older brother, Shidehara Taira (1870–1953), was also a scholar and talented administrator of educational institutions.

Shiden. Painter (Kosaka Tamejirō; *azana*: Shijun; *gō*: Kanshōkyo, 1871–1917) of the Nanga (Bunjinga) school, Kodama Kotei's student. He painted mainly landscapes.
   • In the late seventh century, according to the *ritsuryō* code, rice paddies belonging to the government but temporarily ceded to individuals as compensation for their services. Starting in the eighth century, the *shiden* were recognized as definitively belonging to those who were cultivating them. *See also* KŌDEN.

Shido. Small town in Kagawa prefecture (Shikoku), east of Takamatsu, containing a number of important monuments: Shido-ji, a Buddhist temple of the Shingon-shū dating from the seventeenth century; Taima-jinja, a Shinto shrine containing wooden statuettes from the Heian period; Chōko-fuku-ji, a twelfth-century Buddhist temple housing a wooden statue of Yakushi Nyorai from the Heian period, and others.

• Person having taken Buddhist religious ordination without official authorization, at least during the Nara and Heian periods.

Shidō Bunan. Buddhist monk (Shidō the "Non-difficult," 1603–76) of the Zen Rinzai-shū sect established in Mino. He was a disciple of the Zen master Gudō Tōshoku (1579–1661), and his own students were two other famous masters of the Rinzai-shū doctrine, Dōkyō Ekan (Shoju Rōjin, 1642–1721) and Hakuin. His teachings were collected in *Kana hōgo* (1671). Also called Shidō Munan.

Shidō-shōgun. "Generals of the Four Directions," the name given to four generals—Ōhiuto no Mikoto, Takenunakawawake, Kibitsuhiko, and Tamba Michinushi—charged by Emperor Suinin with conquering the peoples not yet pledged to the court. These generals, cited in the *Kojiki,* may be mythical.

Shie. Purple robe symbolizing the highest level in the Buddhist hierarchy, which can be granted only by the court. However, senior court bureaucrats had conferred this honor upon payments of large sums of money, so the Tokugawa shogunate decreed in 1627 that it would from then on be awarded only with its approval, which led to the abdication of Emperor Go-Mizunoo in 1629.

Shigajiku. Paintings portraying artificial landscapes in *suiboku* genre, produced in imitation of similar Chinese paintings by Buddhist monks in the fifteenth century. They were made mainly on *kakemono* and were accompanied by a handwritten poem, in the Song and Yuan styles. Also called *shijiku.*

Shiga-ken. Prefecture in central Honshu, located around Lake Biwa; formerly Ōmi province, of which Ōtsu was a provisional capital in the seventh century. Because it controlled access to Kyoto and was of great strategic importance, this province was the object of many rivalries between the lords. Oda Nobunaga built his castle in Azuchi beside Lake Biwa. Shiga prefecture is surrounded by mountains on all sides: Hira and Nosaka to the west, Ibuki and Suzuka to the east. It is mainly agricultural, with fishing on Lake Biwa. *Main cities:* Ōtso (chief city), Kusatsu, Ōmi Hachiman, Hikoni Nagahama. *Area:* 4,016 km²; *pop.:* 1.1 million.

Shiga Kiyoshi. Bacteriologist (Satō Kiyoshi, 1870–1957), born in Sendai. In 1897, he and Kitazato Shibasaburō discovered the bacillus responsible for dysentery *(Shigella dysenteriae);* he then worked with Paul Erlich in Germany. He was appointed a professor at Keiō University in 1920, then at Keijō University (Seoul) in 1925. He was decorated with the Order of Culture (Bunka-shō) in 1944.

Shiga Naoya. Writer (1883–1971), born in Miyagi prefecture to a former samurai family. Influenced by Uchimura Kanzō, he became a Christian but later renounced that faith. He began to write when he was 21, publishing several stories and then his first major novel, *Nano-hana to komusume* (The Rapeseed Flower and the Little Girl, 1921). Other novels followed, written in the first person *(watakushi-shōsetsu),* and he published a number of short stories in literary magazines such as *Shirakaba*. His major work was a two-volume novel, *An'ya kōro* (In the Black Night, 1921–37). In 1926, he founded a publishing house, and he was elected a member of the Japan Art Academy (Nihon Geijutsu-in) in 1941. Shiga Naoya was known mainly for his many stories, some of which were collected in 1939. A number were adapted to the screen by Itami Mansaku, Shibuya Minoru, Toyoda Shirō (*The Night Pilgrimage,* 1959), and Nakamura Noboru. His very concise and pure style fits with the neo-realist and idealist currents.

Shigaraki. Small town in Shiga prefecture, whose high-quality clay led to the construction of a number of potters' kilns. It was the site of the Shigaraki no Miya, an imperial residence built by Emperor Shōmu in 745, which was abandoned several months later because of forest fires. Shōmu Tennō returned to Heijō-kyō (Nara). *Pop.:* 15,000.

• **Shigaraki-yaki.** Type of stoneware produced in Shigaraki and the surrounding villages in the Kamakura period. They were mainly jars and ordinary mortars shaped "from a lump" and fired in *anagama* kilns, then, in the sixteenth century, in *noborigama,* at temperatures of between 600°C and 1300°C. In the seventeenth century, these kilns produced jars for the tea ceremony, as well as various objects for ornamenting gardens. The brownish pottery was characterized by half-melted bits of white feldspath and quartz, which roughened the surface.

Shiga Shigetaka. Geographer (Shiga Jūkō, 1863–1927), born in Aichi prefecture. Following a trip to the Pacific islands, he published *Nan'yō jiji* (Conditions in the Southern Islands, 1886), in which he tried to convince his contemporaries that because Japan was an island, it was vulnerable to colonialism by European nations, and it was necessary to strengthen the country by intensifying trade and industry. He also wrote a treatise on the geology of Japan, *Nihon fukei-ron* (The Landscapes of Japan, 1894). Following trips to Sakhalin and the Near East, he published *Sekai sansui zusetsu* (Illustrated Geography of the World, 1911).

Shigayama Mansaku. Kabuki actor and dancer (late eighteenth century) in Edo; as founder of the Shigayama-ryū school of dance, the keeper of the oldest traditions. Nakamura Nakazō I (1736–90) became the director of this school in the 1780s. The Shigayama-ryū is now the oldest active dance school in Japan. *See* IEMOTO.

Shiga Yoshio. Politician (1901–89), born in Fukuoka prefecture (Kyushu); he became a member of the Communist party in 1922. He helped reestablish the party in 1926, but was arrested in 1928 and sentenced to 18 years in prison. When he was freed, at the end of the Second World War, he edited the party's newspaper, *Akahata;* he was elected to the Diet in 1946, but was expelled by the Occupation authorities in 1950. Elected to the party's Central Committee in 1955, he was then expelled from the party in 1964 for having accepted ratification of the nuclear test-ban treaty in 1963.

Shige-daruki. In traditional architecture of the *wayō* mode, small props placed at regular intervals under roof overhangs.

Shigehira. Noh play depicting the agony of one of Taira no Kiyomori's sons who had attacked a number of temples in Nara and set fire to the capital, Heian-kyō. This play seems to have been written before 1403, perhaps with the collaboration of Zeami. It was performed only once between 1403 and 1432, and again starting in December 1983, in Tokyo.

Shigekane Yoshiko. Contemporary writer. She received the Akutagawa Prize in 1979 for her novel *Fumée dans le ravin* (Smoke in the Ravine), at the same time Aono Sō received it for his novel *La nuit d'un fou* (The Night of a Madman).

Shigemasa Kitao. Painter (Kitao Shigemasa; *mei:* Kyūgorō; *gō:* Kōsuisai, Karan, Tairei, Ichiyōsai, Kōsuifu, Suihō Itsujin, 1738–1820) of ukiyo-e prints, founder of the Kitao school in Edo. The son of a bookseller, he collaborated with Shunshō to illustrate books such as *Ehon arashiyama* (1760) and *Shashin kachō-zu* (1805) in the old style. He was Masanobu and Shumman's master.

Shigemitsu Mamoru. Politician and diplomat (1887–1957), born in Ōita (Kyushu). He entered the Ministry of Foreign Affairs in 1911 and was a member of several delegations, including the one sent to the peace conference in Paris in 1919. Appointed consul general to Shanghai in 1928, he was injured during an assassination attempt in April 1932. The following year, he became vice-minister of foreign affairs, a position he held until 1936. He was ambassador to the Soviet Union in 1936, to Great Britain in 1938, and to the Wang Jingwei puppet government in China from 1941 to 1943. In 1944–45, he was minister of "Greater Asia" (Daitōa), succeeding Aoki Kazuo, and was replaced by Tōgō Shigenori. As minister of foreign affairs in Higashikuni Naruhiko's cabinet, he represented Japan on board the *Missouri,* General MacArthur's flagship anchored in Tokyo Bay, on September 2, 1945. Sentenced by the Allied court to seven years in prison for war crimes in 1946, he was freed in November 1950. He quickly returned to politics, becoming leader of the Nihon Kaishintō (Japan Reform party) in 1952. He was also minister of foreign affairs in Hatoyama Ichirō's cabinet from 1954 to December 1956, when he was replaced by Ishibashi Tanzan and retired from public life. He wrote a number of books on politics, among them *Shōwa no doran* (1952), *Gaikō kaisō roku* (1953), *Sugamo nikki* (1953), and *Zoku sugamo nikki* (1953).

Shigenaga. Painter (Nishimura Shigenaga; *mei:* Magosaburō, Magojirō; *gō:* Senkadō, Eikadō, Hyakuju, Shigenaga, 1697–1756) of ukiyo-e prints in Edo. He created the first *abuna-e* and *uki-e* prints, producing mainly triptychs. His art was influenced by Kiyonobu and Masanobu. He was Ishikawa Toyonobu and Suzuki Harunobu's master.

Shigeno Sadanushi. Minister (785–852) for emperors Junna and Nimmyō, famous in his time as a writer and jurist. A fervent Buddhist, he founded the Jion-ji.

Shigeno Yasutsugu. Historian (1827–1910), born to a samurai family in Satsuma. He conducted peace talks with the British naval squadron after the bombing of Kagoshima in 1863. In 1868, he worked for the Ministry of Education, compiling historical works such as the *Kōchō seikan;* in 1869, he translated *Wanguo gonfa* (International Laws), written in Chinese by W. A. P. Martin, an American missionary in China, as *Bankoku kōhō.* He went to Tokyo in 1878 and became director of historical research, but he was forced to resign under pressure from Shinto nationalists in 1893, one year after his colleague, Kume Kunitake, because of his desire to separate historical writings from apocryphal texts.

Shigesato Naizen. Painter (1565–1608) of the Kanō school in Kyoto, perhaps the painter of a *namban-byōbu* produced in 1604.

Shigeyoshi. Sculptor (Hasegawa Shigeyoshi, Kyōrinsai, mid-nineteenth century) and lacquer artist.
→ *See* IKKEI.

Shigi-san. Hill in northwest Nara prefecture, famous for its Buddhist Shigisan-ji temple belonging to the Shingon-shū sect of the Kōya-san. This temple, also known as Chōgosonshi-ji and Bishamonten, was probably founded by Prince Shōtoku Taoshi and renovated in the twelfth century by the Buddhist monk Myōren. It was heavily damaged by Oda Nobunaga's troops in 1577 and reconstructed by Toyotomi Hideyori in 1602.

It is famous for the three-scroll *emakimono Shigisan engi emaki,* dating from between 1156 and 1180, telling the history of its foundation. These scrolls, featuring ink drawings with flowing lines, are approximately 8.72 m (No. 1), 12.73 m (No. 2), and 14.16 m (No. 3) long, and have an average width of 31.5 cm. They portray the miracles accomplished by the monk Myōren; among the most famous scenes are "the flying silo," "the exorcism of Emperor Engi," and "the story of Myōren's sister searching for her brother." The lightly colored ink drawings, caricatured treatment of faces, and sense of movement in the scenes are characteristic of illuminated art in the late twelfth century. Author unknown.

• **Shigisan-ji.** *See* CHŌGOSONSHI-JI.

Shigō. Posthumous name *(okurina)* granted to an emperor or important man, Buddhist or other. *See* NAMES.

Shihōhai. Private ceremony held by the emperor on the first day of the year, in the hour of the Tiger (4:00 A.M.), during which he venerates the *kami* of the four directions and prays for peace and prosperity in the country. This ceremony, inaugurated in 890 under the reign of Emperor Uda Tennō, is still celebrated today.

Shihonryū-ji. Buddhist temple built in Nikkō in 766. Its current buildings date from the late thirteenth century, and it has a three-story pagoda *(sanju-no-tō)* dating from about 1200.

Shihōshō. Former Ministry of Justice, created in 1871 to replace the Gyōbushō (Ministry of Punishment) and Danjōdai (Bureau of Censorship). This ministry was called Hōmuchō (Bureau of Justice) in 1948, then Hōmufu, and finally Hōmushō in 1952. *See* MINISTRIES.

Shiina Etsusaburō. Politician (1898–1979) who was vice-minister of trade and industry in Tōjō's cabinet and cabinet chief during Kishi's second mandate, then minister of trade and industry and of foreign affairs. From 1972 to 1977, he was vice-president of the Liberal Democratic party (Jiyū Minshutō).

Shiina Rinzō. Writer (Otsubo Noboru, 1911–73), born in Himeji to a poor family. In his youth, he did a number of odd jobs and avidly studied Marxism; he joined the Communist party, which resulted in his being arrested and imprisoned from 1931 to 1933. When he was freed, he went to Tokyo; after reading Nietzsche, he left the Communist party. He began to write stories in 1939 in the magazine *Sōsaku,* but became known only in 1947, with the publication of *Shin'ya no shuen* (The Midnight Banquet), a work strongly influenced by Dostoyevsky, then *Eien naru joshō* (Eternal Prologue, 1948). His works show a sense of the absurd and the comic that some have called existential: *Akai kodokusha* (Solitary Red, 1951), *Jiyū no kanata* (The Side of Freedom, 1953), and *Utsukushii onna* (The Beautiful Woman, 1955), but with a clear leaning toward Christianity.

Shiitake. Edible mushroom *(Lentinus edodes),* considered an "elixir of long life" in both China and Japan, highly sought after for its scent and taste. It is sometimes astronomically expensive.

Shijō. Former title of a senior bureaucrat assisting provincial governors. Also called *ichibu.*
• District of Kyoto, of the "fourth bridge."
• Name used in the court by Abutsu-ni.
→ *See* IMPO, KINKOKU.

• **Shijō Dainagon.** *See* FUJIWARA NO KINTŌ, MINAMOTO NO SADAMU.

• **Shijō-ha.** School of painting founded in Kyoto by Goshun (1752–1811), a student of Ōkyo. Also called Shijō-ryū. *See* MARUYAMA ŌKYO.

• **Shijō Tennō.** Eighty-seventh emperor (Prince Mitsuhito, 1231<1233–42>), son of and successor to Go-Horikawa Tennō. Go-Saga succeeded him.

Shijūhattai Butsu. Series of 48 statuettes of the Buddha, in various styles, made of bronze or gold-leafed metal, about 0.3 m high, dating from the seventh and eighth centuries, part of a larger collection and now housed in the National Museum. Originally offered to the Hōryū-ji temple in thanksgiving, they were later associated with Amida Buddha's "48 vows," whence their name "Foty-Eight Bodies of the Buddha." It is estimated that there were once more than 100 statuettes.

Shijuku. During the Edo period, private schools run by independent professors in their homes. Many philosophers and thinkers ran such schools, among them Nakae Tōju, Itō Jinsai, Kan Sazan, Motoori Norinaga, Hirata Atsutane, and Yoshida Shōin. Courses were given free of charge and the curriculum was left to the professors' discretion. *See* JUKU.

Shikan. "Bureau of History," founded in the Shō-hei-gakkō in Edo in 1660 on the order of Tokugawa Ietsuna to compile a history of Japan.
• Type of suicide supposed to serve as a warning to other persons. Rarely used.

• **Shikan-gakkō.** First military school, founded in Tokyo in 1870 and directed by French and German officers.

Shika-shū. Personal poetry anthologies, as opposed to imperial anthologies *(Chokusen waka-shū).* Such anthologies, some of which predate the *Kokin-shū,* proliferated after the tenth century. Also called *Ie no shū. See* SHIKA WAKA-SHŪ.

Shikatsube Magao. Poet (Koikawa Sakimachi, 1753–1829) of *kyōka* and author of *kibyōshi* novels, born in Edo to a family of merchants. He wrote a collection of light verse, *Ashiogi-shū* (Collection of Reeds, 1815), also titled *Roteki-shū.*

Shika waka-shū. "Collection of Spoken Flowers," sixth of the major imperial *waka* anthologies (see

CHOKUSEN WAKA-SHŪ), compiled about 1151–52 by Fujiwara no Akisuke, on the order of Retired Emperor Sutoku. This ten-book anthology comprises 411 poems by 192 poets. Also called *Shika-shū.*

Shiki. "Four Seasons," a group of anti-surrealist poets advocating the sensitivity of intellect and poetic style, created about 1935. It published a magazine of the same name.
• In ancient Japan, official profit drawn from taxes on operation of a *shō* or *shōen.* Also, property title to a piece of land. Also called *shi, tsukasa.* Today, this expression also designates any administrative job.
→ *See* KATEI, MASAOKA SHIKI, RITSURYŌ.

• **Shikibu.** *See* SHŌJŌ, MURASAKI SHIKIBU.

• **Shikibu-kyō.** Title of chief of protocol in the imperial court in the Nara and Heian periods. *See* FUJIWARA NO UMAKAI.

• **Shikibushō.** "Ministry of Rites," one of the eight ministries *(hasshō),* renamed Mombushō in 758. It returned to its original name in 764.

• **Shiki-ke.** *See* FUJIWARA NO FUHITO, FUJIWARA NO UMAKAI.

Shikidō ōkagami. "The Great Mirror of the Erotic Path." An exhaustive study of prostitution in the Edo period, published in 1678 by Hakateyama Kizan (Fujimoto Kizan, ca. 1627–1704), a historian and haiku poet born in Kyoto. It is both a guide to the Yoshiwara pleasure quarter and a description of the life and customs of geisha of all ranks and statuses, their ways of expressing themselves, their tastes, their education, and so on. Many writers, including Saikaku Ihara, used it as a source for their novels.

Shiki Masaoka. Buddhist monk and poet (1867–1902), founder of a new school of haiku, the Nippon-ha, taking Bashō's poems as a model. He also wrote a Noh play, *Togan koji.*

Shikimoku. Lists of rules for the composition of *renga* and *haikai* poems.
• Group of laws promulgated by the provincial lords and the shogunal government from the thirteenth to the sixteenth century. They are generally titled for the name of the era in which they took effect. *See* GOSEIBAI SHIKIMOKU.

Shiki no Ōji. Imperial prince (?–716), Emperor Tenji's fourth son. He received the posthumous names Tawara Tennō and Kasuga no Miya no Tennō in 769. A *tanka* poem he wrote was included in the *Man'yōshū*. His cousin, Emperor Temmu's son, had the same name as him, Shiki. Also called Shiki no Miko.

Shikishi. Imperial princess (Shokushi Naishinnō, ?–1201), Emperor Go-Shirakawa's daughter, Shinto high priestess of the Kamo Shrine in Kyoto, and a very talented poet. Nine of her poems were included in the *Senzai waka-shū* anthology. In 1197, she became a Buddhist nun. Her poems show a profound sense of *yūgen* and a certain "evanescent" charm *(yōen)* that gained her consideration as one of the best poets of her time. Forty-nine of her poems are in the *Shin kokin-shū,* and more than 160 appear in various other anthologies. Her personal anthology contains 360 poems.
• Thick paper cut into rectangles of about 15 × 12 cm, sometimes decorated, and used mainly to write poems or make drawings. *See* PAPER, WASHI.

Shikitei Samba. Writer (Shiki Sanjin, Kikuchi Tai-suke, 1776–1822), son of a wood engraver in Edo. He became known for his novels in the *kibyōshi* genre emulating those of Santō Kyōden, such as *Kyan taiheiki mukō hachimaki* (1799) and *Ikazuchi tarō gōaku monogatari* (10 volumes, 1806); his *sharebon, Tatsumi fugen* (1798), *Chūshingura hen-chikiron* (1812); and, especially, his comic novels *(kokkeibon),* such as *Ukiyoburo* (At the Public Baths, 1813), *Ukiyodoko* (At the Barber, 1814), *Namaei katagi* (Portraits of Drunkards, 1806), *Kokkon hyaku baka* (One Hundred Madmen, Past and Present, 1814). He also wrote several literary essays, including *Kusazōshi kojitsuke nendaiki* (Chronology of the Kusazōshi, 1802).

Shikken. Title of regents of the Kamakura shoguns, inaugurated in 1203 by Hōjō Tokimasa, and later reserved for members of the Hōjō family (*see* list at HŌJŌ). The *shikken* effectively governed in the name of the shoguns, and were the heads of the Mandokoro and the Samurai-dokoro. They were sometimes assisted by a co-signatory *(rensho)* starting in 1224. *See also* KAMPAKU, SESSHŌ.

Shikki. General term for all objects decorated with lacquer *(urushi).* Also called *urushi no mono, nuri-mono. See* LACQUER, URUSHI.

Shikō. Painter (Watanabe Shikō; *mei:* Motome, Motoki, 1683–1755) of the Kōrin and Kanō schools in Kyoto. He made mainly colored *suiboku,* influenced by Naonobu's art.
• Japanese name for Chinese Emperor Shihuangdi of the Qin dynasty.
→ *See* CHŌKI, IMAMURA SHIKŌ, IPPŌ, KATEN, MUNAKATA SHIKŌ.

Shikoku. "Four Provinces" (formerly Awa, Sanuki, Tosa, and Oyo), the smallest of Japan's main islands, on the southeast edge of the Inland Sea (Setonaikai). It is divided into four prefectures, Kagawa, Tokushima, Ehime, and Kōchi. A series of mountain ranges crosses the island over a distance of 180 km, culminating in Mt. Ishizuchi-san (1,982 m). Shikoku is covered with forest and has a large karstic plain (between Ehime and Kōchi prefectures) at an altitude of about 400 m. Its rivers are relatively long: Yoshino-gawa (194 km) and Shimanto-gawa (185 km). The island has two distinct climates: temperate on the coast of the Inland Sea, and high precipitation and many typhoons in September and October on the Pacific coast. Shikoku's economy is mainly agricultural, although the part bordering the Inland Sea has been heavily industrialized for several decades. The population is involved in various crafts activities: salt, plant dyes (indigo), hemp, and so on. The coasts have populations of fishers. *Area:* 18,782 km². *Pop.:* 4.2 million.

Shikunshi. "The Four Venerables," subjects of Chinese origin, often portrayed in Japanese art and decorative elements, consisting of plum-tree blossoms, bamboo, orchids, and chrysanthemums. They were often portrayed by painters of the Nanga (Bunjinga) school starting in the seventeenth century.

Shima. Former province now included in Mie prefecture.
• Term for islands. Also called *-jima* (in composition), Tō.

• **Shima no Ko.** *See* URASHIMA TARŌ.

• **Shima Kubō.** Nickname for shogun Ashikaga Yoshitane, who died in exile on Awaji in 1523.
→ *See* ZENSHIN-NI.

Shimabara no Ran. "Shimabara Uprising." Famous popular rebellion that took place on the Shimabara Peninsula, near Nagasaki (Kyushu), and on the islands near Amakusa, in December 1637. The many Christians and peasants in the region were heavily taxed by their daimyo, Matsukura Katsuie (?–1638) and Terazawa Katataka (1609–

47). After the Battle of Sekigahara (1600) and the execution of the Christian daimyo Konishi Yukinaga, the peasants, led by the son of a vassal of Konishi, Amakusa Shirō, revolted in the hope that this young man (whom they called "Heavenly Child" or "Heavenly Master") could convince the authorities to repeal anti-Christian measures and lower the taxes. They were soon joined by many discontented *rōnin* (most of them formerly Konishi's samurai), and their numbers were quickly swelled by landless peasants. They managed to capture the Amakusa Islands and the Shimabara Peninsula, but were soon driven back by 200,000 shogunal troops commanded by Matsudaira Masanobu, assisted by artillery supplied by the Dutch of Dejima. The rebels took refuge in the Hara castle and resisted desperately. Finally, they had to surrender, and 37,000 of them (including women and children) were executed by sword on April 14, 1638, just two days after the castle fell. Amakusa Shirō was killed in combat. Also called Amakusa no Ran. *See also* AMAKUSA SHIRŌ.

Shimadai. Ornamental structure used in marriage ceremonies and decorated with propitiatory symbols: pins *(matsu)*, cranes *(tsuru)*, bamboo *(take)*, tortoises *(kame)*, rocks *(hōrai-zan)*, dorados *(tai)*, and so on.

Shimada Saburō. Politician (1852–1923), born in Edo. He entered the government in 1875 but resigned in 1881, at the same time as Ōkuma Shigenobu. He then helped to found the Rikken Kaishintō (Constitutional Reform party), while continuing to work as a journalist for the *Yokohama Mainichi*. Starting in 1890, he was elected fourteen times in a row to the Diet, where he fought corruption among politicians.

Shimada Shigetarō. Admiral (1883–1976), minister of the navy in Tōjō's cabinet in 1941. He was appointed commander-in-chief of the navy in 1944, then was replaced by Nomura Naokuni. He was sentenced to prison for life by the Allied war-crimes court after the Second World War and was freed on parole in 1955.

Shimada Shizu. Painter, born 1928 in Tokyo. She has lived in Paris since 1958. She signs her works Simada.

Shimai Sōshitsu. *Sake* merchant (1539–1615) and tea connoisseur, born in Hakata (Kyushu). With Kamiya Sōtan, he took part in the reconstruction of Hakata in 1587, then was sent to Korea by Toyotomi Hideyoshi, along with Konishi Yukinaga and Kobayakawa Takakage (1533–97), to plan the invasion of that country. He became famous thanks to the will he left to his son, Shimai Tokuzaemon, in which he expounded the ethical principles of the merchant class.

Shimaji Mokurai. Buddhist monk (1838–1911), born in Suō province. He entered the Jōdo Shin-shū sect at the Nishi Hongan-ji temple in Kyoto. In 1872, he traveled in Europe, the Near East, and India to study the relationships between religion and the state. When he returned, in 1873, he asked the Meiji government to eliminate the Daikyō-in (Bureau of Religions), which was done in 1875; the effect of this was to temper the intolerance of State Shinto (Kokutai Shintō). He founded magazines such as *Shimbun Zasshi* and *Nihonjin* and started a school for girls.

Shimaki Akahiko. Poet (Kubota Toshihiko, Tsukahara Toshihiko, 1876–1926), born in Nagano prefecture, author of modern *waka* with a moralistic leaning: *Taikyo-shū* (1924), *Shiin-shū* (1926). He was a contributor to the literary magazine *Araragi*, of which he became editor in 1914. Also called Shimagi Akahiko.

Shimaki Kensaku. Writer (Asakura Kikuo, 1903–45), born on Hokkaido. He participated in "proletarian" movements and was arrested in 1928. Freed in 1932, he wrote politically tinged novels in which he explained why he had abandoned communism: *Rai* (Leprosy, 1934), *Seiken* (1935), *Seikatsu no tankyū* (1938); he then advocated a return to the land: *Ningen no fukkatsu I, II* (Resurrection of Man, 1940–41), *Chihōsei katsu* (Living in the Provinces, 1942), *Akagaeru* (The Flying Fox, 1944, published 1946), *Kuro neko* (The Black Cat, 1944). He died of tuberculosis, which he had contracted in prison.

Shimamura Hōgetsu. Writer and literary critic (Shimamura Takitarō, Sasayama Takitarō, 1871–1918), born in Shimane prefecture. He studied psychology in England and Germany from 1902 to 1905, then taught European literature at Waseda University. He took part in the movement promoting modern theater, introducing Ibsen's plays to Japan and founding the "school of new drama" *(geijutsu-za)* with the actress Matsui Sumako (1886–1919). Matsui Sumako committed suicide soon after Shimamura's death.

Shimamura Mitsu. Buddhist monk, born 1831 in Nagano prefecture, founder of the Remmon-kyō sect.

Shimane prefecture. Prefecture in southwestern Honshu, on the Sea of Japan (Nihonkai), in Chūgoku. Its territory is largely mountainous (Chūgoku and Iwami Kōgen mountains) and was once divided among Izumo, Iwami, and Ōki provinces. The Ōki Islands are still under its administration. Shimane prefecture is relatively undeveloped and is mainly agricultural. Fishing is a major activity on the coasts. Some textile industries and molybdenum mines. *Chief city:* Matsue. *Other major cities:* Izumo, Yasugi, Gōtsu, Hamada, Masuda. *Area:* 6,627 km². *Pop.:* 800,000.

Shima no Chitōse. Dancer (eleventh–twelfth century). She created *shirabyōshi* dances with Waka no Mei in 1115.

Shimanrokusen-nichi. "Day of the Forty-Six Thousand," a famous pilgrimage to the Kannon-ji temple in the Asakusa district of Tokyo, which, if it is made on July 10, is worth the good works accumulated during 46,000 other pilgrimages.

Shimaoka Tatsuzō. Contemporary ceramist, born 1933 in Tokyo. His works have been exhibited in Japan and in Boston (1976), Hamburg (1977 and 1991), London (1986 and 1991), Munich (1986 and 1989), Mannheim (1987), Los Angeles (1991), and Paris (1994).

Shimao Toshio. Writer (1917–86), born in Yokohama. In 1945, he commanded a kamikaze naval unit. After the Second World War, he began to write war novels, often in a surrealist style: *Shima ni hate* (The End of the Island, 1948), *Shi no toge* (The Sting of Death, 1960), *Shuppatsu wa tsui ni otozurezu* (The Starting Orders Never Came, 1962).

Shimazaki Tōson. Writer (Shimazaki Haruki, 1872–1943), born in Nagano prefecture to a family of wealthy peasants. He studied at the Meiji Gakuin in Tokyo, and converted to Christianity. He then began to write novels, publishing *Hakai* (The Broken Sermon, 1906), then *Ie* (Family, 1910). After his wife died, he lived with his niece, Komako, but his incestuous relationship with her forced him to leave Japan. He went to Paris and Limoges, where he lived until 1916. When he returned to Japan, he found Komako once again and wrote a novel telling her moving story, *Shinsei* (A New Life, 1919). He

remarried in 1928 and wrote stories and novels: *Yoake mae* (Before Dawn, 1932–35), *Tōhō no mon* (The Western Gate, 1943), *Arashi* (Storm), and others. He was elected president of the P.E.N. Club of Japan in 1935 and a member of the Imperial Academy in 1940. He died of a cerebral hemorrhage. A number of his works were adapted for the theater and brought to the screen by Ichikawa Kon and Kinoshita Keisuke (*Hakai,* in 1948 and 1962), Inagaki Hiroshi (*Arashi,* in 1956), and Yoshimura Kōzaburō (*Yoake mae,* in 1953).

Shimazono Junjirō. Physician (1877–1937), born in Wakayama prefecture. In 1926, he received the Japan Academy Prize (Nihon Gakushi-in-shō) for his work on vitamin B1 deficiency, the cause of beriberi, in collaboration with Ogata Tomosaburō.

Shimazu Genzō. Engineer (1869–1951), born in Kyoto. In 1896, he was the first to take X-rays; in 1928, he invented an induction generator.

Shimazu Hisamitsu. Daimyo (Shimazu Saburō, 1817–87) from Satsuma, Shimazu Nariakira's younger brother. He helped his brother in his political struggle to reconcile the shogunate and the imperial court. Thanks to his military strength, he persuaded Tokugawa Yoshinobu to become shogunal regent in Edo; as he was returning to Satsuma, his samurai killed an English merchant, Richardson, which provoked an immediate reply from Great Britain and the bombing of Kagoshima (*see* SATSUEI SENSŌ, NAMAMUGI JIKEN). After the 1868 Restoration, he joined the government, but he was considered too conservative by the Chōshū "clique" *(hambatsu)* and did not play an active role.

• **Shimazu Nariakira.** Daimyo (1809–58) of Satsuma, Shimazu Hisamitsu's older half-brother. He industrialized his estates and formed a European-style army. He also established shipyards and reverberation furnaces *(hansharō)* for casting cannons (1856). He helped his brother pressure the shogunate to accelerate its modernization efforts and supported Tokugawa Yoshinobu in 1858.

• **Shimazu Shigehide.** Daimyo (1745–1833) from Satsuma. He studied Dutch, astronomy, artillery, medicine, and cartography with Western experts and wrote a diary of his activities in romanized Japanese (so that it would remain secret). He built an astronomical observatory in Kagoshima, helped introduce vaccination in Satsuma, and compiled the first Japanese–Dutch dictionary.

• **Shimazu Tadatsune.** Daimyo (Shimazu Iehisa, 1578–1638) of Satsuma and Ōsumi, Shimazu Yoshihiro's son. He consolidated his possessions on Kyushu and conquered the Ryukyu Islands, imprisoning the king (*see* RYŪKYŪ) in 1609.

• **Shimazu Takahisa.** Daimyo (1514–71) of Satsuma, Ōsumi, and Hūga. He received the first firearms imported by the Portuguese who were shipwrecked on Tanegashima in 1543, and welcomed Francis Xavier to Kagoshima in 1549.

• **Shimazu Yoshihiro.** Daimyo (1535–1619) of Satsuma and Ōsumi, Shimazu Takahisa's son. With his brother, Shimazu Yoshihisa (1533–1611), he conquered much of Kyushu from the Ōtomo, Ryūzōji, and Itō families, provoking the invasion of Kyushu in 1587 by Toyotomi Hideyoshi, who was concerned that a too-powerful clan would firmly establish itself on his home front. In defeat, Shimazu Yoshihiro kept only Satsuma and Ōsumi, as Yoshihisa had withdrawn. He became Hideyoshi's vassal and participated in the invasion of Korea; after this, he received a territory worth 560,000 *koku* in Satsuma, Ōsumi, and Hyūga. In 1597, at Hideyoshi's request, he banned Christianity and the Jōdo Shinshū sect. He opposed Tokugawa Ieyasu in the Battle of Sekigahara in 1600, but then fled and kept his provinces, which he passed on to his son, Shimazu Tadatsune (1576–1638), when he retired.

Shimazu Yasujirō. Movie director (1897–1945); he joined the Shōchiku company as assistant to Murata Minoru in 1921. He then directed his own movies. He also wrote screenplays. A number of his students became major directors in their own right, including Gosho Heinosuke, Yoshimura Kōzaburō, and Toyoda Shirō.

Shimbashi. Archeological site in Tokyo, on the north shore of the Nogawa river, excavated by Edward Kidder in 1976. Uncovered were a large number of pre-ceramic lithic tools, divided into a number of levels, as well as stone tools and pottery from the Jōmon era. Level 4 was carbon-dated to 15,000 BC; levels 2 and 1 were dated to between 4500 and 1000 BC.
→ *See* TŌKYŌ.

Shimbetsu. Class of family and noble titles denoting "divine ancestry," such as Fujiwara, Minamoto, Taira, Tachibana; it was divided into *kōbetsu* (descendants of an emperor) and *hambetsu* (descendants of an ancient noble family). The others were in the *shoban* category. An eighth-century directory,

the *Shinsen-shōji-roku,* lists the names and origins of the *shimbetsu. See* KŌBETSU.

Shimbun. Newspaper, daily or other, publishing news, articles, and serials (Shimbun-shōsetsu). *See* PRESS.

• **Shimbun-shōsetsu.** "Serials." In the late nineteenth century, many novels began to appear in serial form in newspapers before being published as books. Most great novelists of the first half of the twentieth century had their works published this way; as this type of publication became more common, they gained an enormous readership. The trend weakened just before the Second World War, but strengthened again afterward, and continues today. Almost all the great writers of the modern period first publish their works in serial form. *See* SHŌSETSU.

Shimbutsu (Shin-butsu). Religious name taken by a governor of Shimotsuke when he retired from his position in favor of his brother in 1225 to become Shinran's disciple. He was the founder of the Takada and Bukkō-ji branches of the Jodō Shin-shū. *See* TAKADA-HA.

Shimbutsu-bunri. "Separation of Buddhism and Shinto" imposed by Emperor Meiji Tennō in 1868. It gave rise to violent anti-Buddhist movements resulting in the destruction of many *jingū-ji,* or Buddhist temples associated with Shinto shrines. The law favored Shinto sects and inaugurated "State Shinto" (*see* KOKUTAI SHINTŌ), abolishing the Shimbutsu-shūgō, which had overseen the fusion of Shinto and Buddhism (Honji-suijaku, Ryōbu Shintō) since the ninth century.

Shimenawa. Sacred cord stretched across a gate *(torii)* at the entrance to a Shinto shrine or circling a rock or tree; it indicates that the territory marked off is the estate of the *kami,* from which all pollution must be excluded, thus forming a sort of religious taboo. The cord is generally made of wisps of rice straw twisted from left to right and is thicker at one end than at the other. *Shimenawa* are often hung from *nusa* (a type of *gohei*) made of folded paper and rice spikes. Also called *shichigosan-nawa. Okinawa: sang, hijainna; Kor.: güm-chul. See* GOHEI.

Shimizu. Branch of the Tokugawa family founded by Tokugawa Shigeyoki (1745–95), one of Tokugawa Ieshige's sons. *See* SANKYŌ, TOKUGAWA.
→ *See* SHOKATSUKAN.

Shimizu Hamaomi. Physician (1776–1824) and *waka* poet, born in Edo, Murata Harumi's student. He conducted philological studies on ancient classic texts. His *waka* collection, *Sazanaminoya-shū,* was published after his death by his son, Shimizu Mitsufusa, in 1829. He also compiled a glossary of poetry in the Heian period, *Gorin ruiyō.*

Shimizu Kensetsu. One of the largest public-works and construction companies in Japan, founded in 1804. Head office in Tokyo.

Shimizu Muneharu. Warrior (d. 1582), lord of the Takamatsu castle in Bitchū province, working for the Mōri family. In 1582, he was attacked by Toyotomi Hideyoshi, then Oda Nobunaga's lieutenant, who flooded the area around his castle. The same day that Oda Nobunaga was assassinated by Akechi Mitsuhide, Shimizu Muneharu embarked on a boat and committed suicide by *seppuku* in exchange for the lives of his followers being spared.

Shimizu no Jirochō. Famous gangster (1820–93) of Shizuoka prefecture, who controlled the merchant-marine and public-works unions in the early Meiji era. He was popular with the public, and his decisions were faithfully followed by other yakuza of his time.

Shimizu Rokubei. Ceramist (nineteenth century) in Kyoto, who produced mainly *sencha* pottery in the Kiyomizu kilns.

• **Shimizu Shichibei.** Ceramist (nineteenth century) in Kyoto, perhaps Shimmizu Rokubei's son.

• **Shimizu Uichi.** Contemporary ceramist, born 1926 in Kyoto. He specialized in pottery with an iron oxide glaze. Named a Living National Treasure in 1985.

Shimizu Tōkoku. Painter and photographer, very popular during the Meiji era. Some of his works, mainly of plants, signed simply Tōkoku, are in the Siebold collection in the Komarov Botanical Institute in St. Petersburg.

Shimmei. Oldest style of Shinto architecture; its most representative building is the main shrine of the *naikū* in Ise. Also, term for a simple type of torii, in its earliest form. *See* AMATERASU-ŌMIKAMI, JINJA, TORII.

• **Shimmei Kyōdan.** Minor Shinto sect affiliated with the Jinja Shinto; it has just 1,000 followers.

Shimmei Masamichi. Sociologist (1898–1984), born in Taiwan, who introduced American sociological theories to Japan. He wrote many works on the subject and compiled a dictionary of social sciences, *Shakaigaku jiten* (1944).

Shimmi Masaoki. Senior bureaucrat (1822–69) in the Edo shogunate and the commissioner of foreign affairs *(gaikoku-bugyō)* who led the Japanese delegation to Washington in 1860. He was made grand chamberlain on his return, but retired from public affairs in 1864.

Shimoda. Town and port in Shizuoka prefecture, on the Izu Peninsula. The Shimoda Jōyaku, or "Japanese-American Friendship Treaty," a nine-article document that opened the ports of Nagasaki, Shimoda, and Hakodate to foreign trade, was signed in Shimoda in 1854. Two years later, an American consul, Townsend Harris, was interned in Shimoda's Buddhist Gyokosen-ji temple. A festival is celebrated each May to commemorate the arrival of Commodore Perry's "black ships" *(kurofune).* *Pop.:* 35,000.

Shimoda Utako. Educator (Hirao Seki, 1854–1936) and talented poet (Emperor Meiji gave her the pseudonym Utako, a tribute to her gifts), born to a family of samurai in Iwamura (now Gifu prefecture). She devoted herself to teaching Chinese and Japanese classics to women of the intelligentsia, opening a school in her house (Tōyō Gakkō, Tōyō Jojuku) in 1881, and a school for the daughters of peers (Kazoku Jogakkō) in 1885. She then traveled in Europe and the United States to study educational systems. With other women, she formed the Teikoku Fujin Kyōkai (Imperial Association of Women) to encourage the education of young women and the creation of charitable works. She also opened other schools (for Chinese women in Japan, for the training of women in manual trades, etc.) and was president of the Aikoku Fujinkai (Women's Patriotic Association) from 1920 to 1931.

Shimogamo-jinja. Shinto shrine founded around 678 in Heian-kyō and dedicated to Tamayori-hime, Jimmu Tennō's mother. It was rebuilt in 1628, and from 1863 to 1868. With the Kamigamo-jinja shrine, it forms a grouping called Kamo-jinja.

Shimokōbe Chōryū. Writer and poet (Shimokōbe Nagaru, Kozaki Tomohira, 1624–1686), born in Yamato, son of a samurai. He conducted research on the *Man'yōshū* and published many *waka* poems, which he collected, with those of other authors, in an anthology called *Rin'yō ruijin-shū* (1670). His other works were published after his death by Keichū.

Shimokōbe Yukihira. Famous archer who taught archery to shogun Minamoto no Yoriie in 1189.

Shimomichi. Ancient unit of length, equivalent to 655 m (6 *chō*), once used in the western provinces. *See* RI.

Shimonaka Yasaburo. Publisher (1878–1961), born in Hyōgo prefecture and self-educated, founder of the Heibonsha publishing house in 1914. *See* HEIBONSHA.

Shimonoseki. City in Yamaguchi prefecture and port on the Kammon Strait (Shimonoseki Strait), former capital of Nagato province, near which a famous battle between the Taira and the Minamoto, Dan no Ura, took place in 1185. The port was bombed (Shimonoseki Jiken) in 1864 by a European fleet in reprisal for attacks on Western ships by the Chōshū clan in June and July 1863, and Allied soldiers destroyed the city's munitions depots and fortifications. A peace was concluded in September 1864, under which the Chōshū clan was to pay the Allies three million Mexican dollars, a sum that the shogunate did not have; the British demanded other trade concessions in compensation. Today, the port flourishes thanks to deep-sea fishing and naval industries. An underwater tunnel (Kammon) and a bridge 1,068 m long link it to Kyushu. Shimonoseki was once called Amagaseki and Bakan. *Pop.*: 280,000.

• **Shimonoseki Jōyaku.** "Treaty of Shimonoseki," signed April 17, 1895, between China (represented by Li Hongzhang) and Japan (represented by Itō Hirobumi), ending the Sino-Japanese War of 1894–95. With this treaty, a conquered China ceded Taiwan, the Pescadores, and the Liaodong Peninsula to Japan and agreed to pay an indemnity of 200 million silver taëls. On the express demand of Western nations (France, Russia, and Germany), the Shimonoseki Jōyaku was modified by the Treaty of Zhifu, signed November 8, 1895, which returned Liaodong to China and, in compensation, increased the indemnity by 30 million taëls. Korea returned to independent status.

Shimōsa. Former province, now divided between Chiba and Ibaraki prefectures, in the Kanto plain.

Shimose Masachika. Military engineer (1859–1911), born in Hiroshima prefecture. He invented Shimose powder, which enabled the cannons of the Japanese fleet to outgun those of the Russian fleet during the Battle of Tsushima in May 1905.

Shimotsuke. Former province, now constituting Tochigi prefecture, in northern Kanto.

Shimotsuki. Formerly, the eleventh month (of the white frost) of the year.

Shimozawa Kan. Writer (Umetani Matsutarō, 1892–1968), born on Hokkaido. He wrote many popular stories set in the late Edo period, known for their historical accuracy and descriptions of life in Edo; *Shinsengumi shimatsuki* (1928), *Kunisada chūji* (1933), and *Oyakodata* (1956) are his best-known works.

Shimpa. "New form" *(shin-pa)* of Kabuki theater, created by Sudō Teiken (Sudō Takanori, 1867–1907) and Kawakami Otojirō in 1891, at first to be used as political propaganda, and later transformed into pure theater. For the first time since the inception of Kabuki, female actors were used. This type of theater formed a sort of juncture between classic Kabuki and Shingeki theater. It became popular in the early twentieth century under the influence of Takata Minoru (1877–1916), Kawai Takeo (1877–1942), and Kitamura Rokurō, and is still widely performed today.

Shimpan. Judge or referee in martial-arts competitions.
 • Ordeal or "heavenly judgment," often using the test of boiling water *(kukatachi)*.

• **Shimpan-daimyō.** Generic term for daimyo of the Tokugawa and Matsudaira families and those of the Mito, Owari, Kii, Echizen, and Aizu families. During the Edo period, these families supplied most of the senior bureaucrats in the army and the administration. Also called San-ke (for Mito, Owari, and Kii). *See also* GOSAN-KYŌ.

Shimpeitai. "Divine soldiers," the name given to a group of conspirators led by the navy commander Yamaguchi Saburō and members of the ultranationalist Dai Nippon Seisantō (Great Japan Production) and Aikoku Kinrōtō (Patriotic Labor) parties. They planned a mass insurrection and tried to enlist several thousand volunteers to assassinate politicians, bomb the Diet, and attack the police headquarters. The police were alerted and the plot was uncovered in July 1933, and aborted. The leaders were convicted in 1937, but they received light sentences and were freed in 1941.

Shimpotō. "Progressive party," founded in 1896 by the merger of the Rikken Kaishintō (Constitutional Reform party) and other minor parties to counterbalance the growing influence of Itō Hirobumi and the Jiyūtō (Liberal party). It merged with the Jiyūtō in 1898 to form the Kenseitō (Constitutional party). Reconstituted in 1945 by Machida, it again joined with the Jiyūtō the following year and was called Minshutō (Democratic party, 1947), Kokumin Minshutō (People's Democratic party, 1951), Kaishintō (Reform party, 1952), then again Minshutō (1954).

Shimura Takashi. Movie actor (Shimazaki Shōji, 1905–82), born in Hyōgo prefecture. He appeared in most of Kurosawa Akira's films, with Mifune Toshirō, including *Rashōmon* (1950) and *Shichinin no samurai* (The Seven Samurai, 1954).

Shin. In art and architecture, a term for classic, conventional styles. *See also* GYŌ, SŌ.
• Japanese name for the Chinese Qin, Jin, and Qing dynasties.
• With different Sino-Japanese *(kanji)* characters, a term for "new," "spirit," "heart," "sentiment," "heaven," "divinity," and other words.

Shinagawa Yajirō. Politician (1843–1900) of the Chōshū clan. After the Meiji Restoration (1868), he was sent to England and Germany to study local systems of government and agricultural cooperatives. He returned in 1876; in 1882, he became vice-minister of agriculture and trade. In 1891, he was minister of the interior in Matsukata Masayoshi's cabinet, but was forced to resign for attempting to interfere in the elections to the Diet in 1892. He then founded the Kokumin Kyōkai (Nationalist Association party) with Saigō Tsugumichi.

Shi-nagon. Name for a group of four poets who lived in the tenth century: Fujiwara no Kintō, Fujiwara no Yukinari, Minamoto no Yoshitaka, and Minamoto no Tsunenobu.

Shinai. Substitute sword used in place of a real one *(katana)* during kendo training and competitions. It has four polished-bamboo blades attached together, the weight and size of which vary depending on the

combatant's age; a leather handle and guard; and a chamois tip. *See* KENDŌ.

Shinano. Former province, now Nagano prefecture.

Shinchō. "New Currents," an important literary magazine founded in 1904 by Satō Giryō (1878–1951) to replace the magazine *Shinsei* (published from 1896 to 1903). A great many major writers have published their work in this monthly, which is very popular in literary circles. Shinchō-sha, the publisher of *Shinchō,* was founded in 1896 as Shinsei-sha and took its current name when it began to publish the magazine.

Shinchō kō ki. "Chronicle of Oda Nobunaga," written about 1610 by Ōta Gyūichi (1527–after 1610), chronicler serving Oda Nobunaga then Toyotomi Hideyoshi. Although it is sometimes inaccurate, this work is indispensable for information on the Azuchi-Momoyama period. Also sometimes called *Nobunaga kō ki.*

Shin chokusen-shū. "New Imperial Collection." A 20-scroll official anthology comprising 1,371 poems, compiled by Fujiwara no Sadaie in 1232. *See* CHOKUSEN WAKA-SHŪ.

Shinden. "Sacred fields," lands (generally rice paddies) owned by major Shinto shrines in the time of the *ritsuryō* system (late seventh century) and exempted from taxation. In the Heian period, many of them became *shōen.* Also called Mitoshiro, Mitoshiroda. *See* KŌDEN.
• "Holy of holies" of a Shinto shrine. Also, main house in a residence in *shinden-zukuri* style.

• **Shinden kaihatsu.** "Development of new fields," the opening of new lands to cultivation and the transformation of others into rice paddies; called *konden* before the Edo period. Most were opened during the Edo period and produced a supplemental harvest of about 1.3 million *koku.* The reclamation of these lands, which had been taken over by forest or marshland, was financed by the daimyo, the shogunate, and sometimes rich urban merchants. The lots were generally rectangular in shape, with their short sides aligned with new roads or streets. Also called *kaikon.*

• **Shinden-zukuri.** In architecture and urban planning, a style of noble residential building, with a main house *(shinden)* surrounded by annex build-

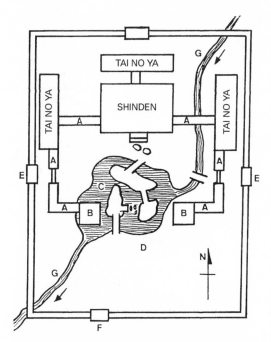

Shinden-zukuri residence. A. Covered corridors. B. Pavilions. C. Lake. D. Garden. E. *Chūmon* (covered door). F. South gate (main entrance). G. River

ings *(tai no ya)* on three sides, which were linked to the central house by raised, sometimes covered passages. In front of the *shinden* was a lake with three small islands linked by bridges. Sometimes, two small pavilions were erected on the edges of the lake. According to laws of geomancy, the lake had to be fed by a stream flowing from northwest to southeast. *Shinden-zukuri* could comprise a fairly large number of buildings and corridors, guard posts, walls pierced with "four-pillar gates" *(yotsuashimon),* coach houses, reception halls, and so on. The grouping was generally on a lot measuring one square *chō* (about 120 m per side). In the Heian period, *shinden-zukuri* were reserved mainly for aristocratic families. No examples remain, though they are portrayed in *emakimono* illustrations. This residential style was gradually abandoned in the Kamakura period for warrior houses *(yashiki);* in the Muromachi period, they were replaced by the *shoin-zukuri* palace style.

Shindō Kaneto. Director, born 1912 in Hiroshima to a family of wealthy farmers. He began to direct movies in 1934 as Mizoguchi Kenji's assistant, and then wrote screenplays for Mizoguchi, Kinoshita

Keisuke, Ichikawa Kon, and other well-known directors. In 1950, he created his own production company and directed films such as *Aisai monogatari* (Tale of a Beloved Woman, 1951). The following year, he made a film about the atom bomb, *Gembaku no ko* (The Children of the Bomb), which was felt not to be critical enough and which led to the making of *Hiroshima* (1953) by Sekigawa Hideo. He is known in the West mainly for *Hadaka no shima* (The Naked Island, 1960) and *Onibaba* (1963). Among his other important films are *Kuroneko* (The Black Cat, 1968), *Kagerō* (1969), and *Kokoro* (The Poor Heart of Men, 1973), an adaptation of a novel by Natsume Sōseki.

Shin Fujin Kyōkai. "New Woman's Association," the first feminist association in Japan, founded in 1920 by Hiratsuka Raichō, Ichikawa Fusae, and Oku Mumeo; its goals were to obtain greater equality between men and women and better protection of mothers and children. It published a magazine, *Josei Dōmei* (The League of Women).

Shinga. Important Buddhist monk (801–79) of the Shingon-shū sect. He received the title Hōkō Daishi posthumously.
→ *See* KAKUMYŌ.

Shingaku. "Teaching of the Heart" (from the Chinese term Xinxue), a Confucian and Shinto philosophy derived from Shushi (*Chin.:* Zhu Xi), advocated by Ishida Baigan and his school of thought starting in 1729. Updated by Teshima Toan (1718–86), it offered a new popular ethic called Sekimon Shingaku, according to which all classes were equal with regard to their respective duties, and demanded the creation of a specific ethic for the merchant class, the lowest of the four recognized classes in the Edo period. This ethic was spread through discourse, or *dōwa* (Shingaku-dōwa), and illustrated posters called *sein.* Ishida Kampei, Teshima Toan, and Nakajima Dōni were its most fervent proponents in the eighteenth century.

Shingeki. Modern theater movement (in the Western style) and a magazine, published starting in 1954 to spread the principles elaborated by Tsubouchi Shōyō, Osanai Kaoru, and other playwrights in 1909. Shingeki involved adaptation of Western plays and was often used as a tool of social criticism. Many modern writers, including Mishima Yukio, Abe Kōbō, and Yamazaki Masakazu, joined the movement, which now seems to have reached maturity.

Shingen Kahō. Collective name of two familial and provincial codes of the Takeda Shingen family, promulgated in 1547 and 1554. Also called *Shingen hatto, Koshū hatto.*

Shingon-shū. Buddhist sect of the "True Speech," introduced from China (Zhenyang-zong sect) in the early ninth century by the monk Kūkai. It belonged to the esoteric current *(mikkyō)* of the Buddhist schools of the North (Mahayana), notably Lamaism, with which it has retained some affinities. Kūkai drew his teachings from those of the Chinese monk Huiguo, whose esoteric interpretation of the two mandalas jointly called *Ryōkai mandara (see* RYŌKAI MANDARA) stated that all things in the universe (and the universe itself) are only emanations (or manifestations) of the Great Sun Buddha Dainichi Nyorai (*Skt.:* Mahāvairochana). This doctrine is founded on two major texts of the Mahayana, the *Mahāvairochana-sūtra (Jap.: Dainichi-kyō)* and the *Vajrashekhara-sūtra (Jap.: Kongō-gyō).* The historical Buddha Shakyamuni (Gautama Siddhārtha; *Jap.:* Shaka) is thus only a manifested form of Dainichi Nyorai. According to Kūkai, it followed that man could obtain identification with the Great Sun Buddha through the grace *(kaji)* that He could confer upon followers through an ascetic practice *(yoga)* that would allow them to attain *samadhi,* and through recitation of mantras *(Jap.: shingon).* There are currently two major divisions in the Shingon-shū, Shingi ("new," founded by Kakuban [Kōkyō Daishi] in 1130) and Kogi ("old"). Its center is on Mt. Kōya, where Kūkai himself founded the temples based on the Kongōbu-ji. The Shingi branch has its headquarters at the Negoro-ji (transferred, after it was destroyed by Toyotomi Hideyoshi in 1585, to the Hase-dera temple) and the Chishaku-in temple. The Shingon-shū is currently divided into 47 subsects, among them Birushana, Busan, Chisan, Daigō, Kokubun-ji, Kōyasan, Nakayama Shingō-shō, Omuro, Sennyū-ji, Shin Bukkyō Kūkai, Shingon-ritsu, Shin Shingon, Shōden, Tō-ji, Yamashina, and Zentsū-ji.

• **Shingon Hasso.** "The Eight Masters of Shingon" (*Chin.:* Zhenyang Bazu): Ryūmo (Nāgārjuna), Ryūchi (Nāgabodhi), Kongōchi (Vajrabodhi, 671–741), Fukū (Bukong, 705–74), Zemmui (Shan Wuwei, 637–735), Ikkō (683–727), Keika (746–805), and Kūkai (774–835).

Shin gosen-shū. "New *Gosen-shū,*" a poetry anthology compiled by Nijō Tameto in 1303, comprising 1,970 poems in 20 scrolls. *See* CHOKUSEN WAKA-SHŪ.

Shin go-shūi-shū. Poetry anthology compiled by Nijō Tameto and supplemented in 1383 by Nijō Tameshige, comprising 1,554 poems in 20 scrolls. *See* CHOKUSEN WAKA-SHŪ.

Shin Ikei. Chinese diplomat (Shen Weijing, d. ca. 1597) who was sent to Korea in 1592 to negotiate the withdrawal of Japanese troops from the peninsula with General Konishi Yukinaga. Shin Ikei went to Japan to continue the talks, but was unsuccessful; he was recalled to China and executed.

Shinja. Noh mask *(nōmen)* representing a horned demon.

Shinjin-kai. "Society of the New Man," a political organization founded in 1918 by a group of law students in Tokyo to promote the ideas of democracy and social reform among the people. The group was dissolved in 1929 under pressure from other groups that were closer to the government and that belonged to an activist right wing.

Shinjō Shinzō. Physicist and astronomer (1873–1938), professor of astrophysics at the University of Tokyo starting in 1918, and president of the University of Kyoto from 1929 to 1933. He directed the Institute of National Sciences in Shanghai from 1935 to his death. He was the best-known expert on Chinese astronomy and calendar sciences.

Shinjū. Double suicide, generally performed by lovers who cannot be together officially, or by a wife who does not want to outlive her husband.

• *Shinjū-ten no amijima.* "Celestial Suicide in Amijima," a three-act tragedy written by Chikamatsu Monzaemon in 1720 for puppet theater *(ayatsuri-shibai)* in the *sewa-mono* genre, based on a news item. *See also* SONEZAKI SHINJŪ.

• *Shinjū-yoi-gōshin.* Three-act *jōruri* play in the *sewa-mono* genre by Chikamatsu Monzaemon, performed in 1722 at the Takemoto-za in Osaka. It relates the story of a double suicide *(shinjū).*

Shinjū-kyō. Ancient mirrors whose backs were ornamented with pictures of animals or divinities. These mirrors, from China (or made in Japan imitating Chinese models), have been found in great numbers in *kofun. See* KAGAMI, KYŌ, MIRRORS.

Shinju-wankōgeki. Name for the surprise attack on Pearl Harbor by Admiral Yamamoto Isoroku in December 1941, which instigated American involvement in the Pacific War.

Shin Kabuki-jūhachiban. List of 18 Kabuki plays established by the successors of actor Ichikawa Danjūrō VII as part of their repertoire. The best known were written by Kawatake Mokuami *(Jishinkato, Momijigari, Ōmori hikoshichi, Sakai no taiko, Funa-benkei, Takatoki, Tsurigitsune, Futaribakama, Suō otoshi)* and Fukuchi Ōchi *(Suō otoshi). See also* KABUKI-JŪHACHIBAN.

Shinkai. Painter (active ca. 1282) and Buddhist monk at the Daigo-ji temple in Kyoto. He painted Buddhist subjects.
• Sword maker (Inoue Shinkai, Kunisada II, d. 1682) in Osaka.

• **Shinkai Taketarō.** Sculptor of wood (1868–1928). He studied in Europe.

• **Shinkaku.** Buddhist monk (d. 1180) and painter of religious subjects.

Shinkan. Ancient Japanese name for the Korean kingdom of Kōryō (Koma).
• Calligraphy executed by an emperor or empress.
→ *See* KANNUSHI.

Shinkankaku-ha. Literary group with modernist leanings founded about 1924, also called the "neo-impressionist school" or "school of the new sensibility," which published the magazine *Bungei Jidai* (The Literary Age, 1924–27). Among its 19 founding members were writers Yokomitsu Riichi, Kawabata Yasunari, and a number of young authors. *See* KATAOKA TEPPEI.

Shinkansen. "New main line," a high-speed-train service following the path of the old Tōkaidō road and linking Morioka to Hakata (Kyushu) via Tokyo, Osaka, and Shimonoseki, built in 1964. New trunk lines were put into service in 1983, linking Tokyo to Morioka (Tōhoku Shinkansen) and Niigata (Jōetsu Shinkansen).

Shinka-seishiki. Code of provincial laws *(bunkoku-hō)* compiled by the Buddhist monks Gen'e and Shin'e in the thirteenth century, and rewritten in the late sixteenth century by Miyoshi Nagaharu.

Shinkei. Buddhist monk (1406–75) at the Jūjūshin (Kiyomizu) temple in Kyoto, who was a *waka* and *renga* poet, Shōtetsu's disciple. He wrote many works of poetry criticism, such as *Sasamegoto* (Whispered Conversations, 1463), *Hitorigoto* (Monologue, 1468), and *Oi no kurigoto* (An Old Man's Drivel, 1471). He followed the aesthetic leanings of Fujiwara Shunzei and Fujiwara no Teika. He was called Shin'e until 1451.

Shinken. Buddhist monk (1179–1261) of the Shingon-shū and painter of Buddhist subjects. He founded the Jizō-in of the Daigo-ji temple in Kyoto.

Shinkō Geijutsu-ha. "School of New Art," a group of writers sharing an admiration for art in all of its forms and rejecting the "proletarian" art advocated by Marxists in the 1920s (*see* NAPF). Due to lack of cohesion, however, its members dispersed in 1931 and 1932. This movement's literature was sometimes called "grotesque" and "erotic."

Shin kokin waka-shū. "New Collection of *Waka* of Ancient and Modern Times," eighth imperial anthology (*see* CHOKUSEN WAKA-SHŪ), compiled by Minamoto no Michitomo (1171–1227), Fujiwara no Ariie (1155–1216), Fujiwara no Sadaie (1162–1241), Fujiwara no Ietaka (1158–1237), Fujiwara no Masatsune (1170–1221), and the Buddhist monk Jakuren between 1201 and 1205 (with later additions). It comprises 1,870 poems in 20 scrolls, from all periods of Japanese poetry up to the late twelfth century. Also abridged to *Shin kokin-shū.*

Shinkokugeki. Type of modern folk theater created by actor Sawada Shōjirō in 1917. Many movie actors trained there; it closed in 1979.

Shin Kokugikan. "New National Sports Stadium," dedicated to sumo, built in 1985 in the Ryūgoku district of Tokyo, with a seating capacity of more than 10,000. This covered stadium can be used for other sports, as the *dohyō* can be stored in the basement. The old Kokugikan was demolished. *See* SUMO.

Shin kokushi. "New National History." Official imperial history compiled by Fujiwara no Saneyori (900–70) and Ōe no Asatsuna (886–957) on the order of Emperor Murakami. This work is now lost.

Shinkō shūkyō. Term for the "new religions" and relatively syncretic sects that were created or developed in Japan starting in the late nineteenth century, such as Tenri-kyō, Konkō-kyō, and Sōka Gakkai.

Shinkyō. "Religion of Spirits," the Japanese name for an ancient Korean religion related to shamanism, in which the spirits of nature are venerated through a sort of priestess called a *mudang (Jap.: miko)* using a ritual borrowed from Buddhism. *Kor.:* Singyo.

• Old wooden bridge over the Daiya River at Nikkō, providing access to the Tōshōgū Shrine. It is 30 m long and lacquered red. It was built in 1636, destroyed in 1902, and rebuilt on the original plan in 1907. Only high-ranking religious people are allowed to use it.

• **Shinkyō-shōsetsu.** *See* SHI-SHŌSETSU, SHŌSETSU.

Shin Nihon Bungaku. "New Japanese Literature," a literary journal founded by the Society for New Japanese Literature (Shin Bungaku-kai) after the Second World War and publishing works by former members of the NAPF (proletarian literature). Although this organ has been attacked numerous times by the Communist party, it is still in existence, publishing works by young authors. It has competition from another "left-wing" magazine, *Jimmin Bungaku* (People's Literature).

Shinnin. "New men," an aristocratic class created in the Meiji era (late nineteenth century) and composed of senior bureaucrats.

Shinnō. Title for imperial princes who were sons and grandsons of an emperor in the direct family line. This title (Shinnō-shōgun) was also given to shoguns of Kamakura from the imperial family. Also called Ryūshū, Take no Sono, Teiyō, Tenshi. *See also* HŌSHINNŌ, NAISHINNŌ.

Shinnyō-dō. Buddhist temple of the Jōdo-shū sect transported to Kyoto from Mt. Hiei in the eleventh century. Its current buildings date from the seventeenth century. A sixteenth-century three-scroll *emakimono (Shinnyō-dō-engi,* kept at the Shinshō Gokuraku-ji in Kyoto) describes its foundation.

Shinoda Masahiro. Movie director, born 1931 in Gifu, leader of the Shōchiku company's "new wave." His films are influenced by Mizoguchi Kinji's and by traditional theater. He is sometimes accused of showing a sado-masochistic tendency (which he describes as typically Japanese) in the screenplays for his films.

Shi-nō-kō-shō. "Warriors-peasants-artisans-merchants," the name for Japanese society of the Edo period, which was divided into four distinct classes (excluding, of course, outcasts such as the *hinin*). This system, based on one in ancient China, came into force in the mid-seventeenth century and was often reinforced by shogunal edicts. In practice, Tokugawa society was divided mainly into samurai and non-samurai, since artisans and merchants were included in the *chōnin* (urban-dwellers) category and peasants were regarded as unimportant. These categories were abolished in 1869 and replaced by three new classes, *kazoku* (nobles), *shizoku* (former samurai), and *heimin* (ordinary people). This system was in turn abolished after the Second World War, when the new Constitution was promulgated.

Shino Shōjin. Master *(chajin)* of the tea ceremony (late sixteenth century) who asked the potters of Seto to make special utensils for the *chanoyu.* They produced pottery with an opaque white glaze with bubbles and cracks, sometimes decorated with iron oxide under a slip (E-shino) or with designs engraved on the clay under a gray slip (Nezumi-iro). Also called Shino Shōshin. *See* SHINO-YAKI.

• **Shino-yaki.** Pottery made in Tajimi, Mino province, on request of Shino Shōjin (late sixteenth century), characterized by a thick white feldspathic glaze; mainly used for implements for the tea ceremony *(chanoyu).* Types include undecorated Muji-shino, decorated E-shino, Oni-ita with a white slip, Nezumi-shino with a partly scratched slip, Aka-shino (red), and Beni-shino (mostly pink). *See also* MINO-YAKI.

Shinra. Japanese name for the Korean Silla (Sinra) dynasty in the sixth century. Also called Shiragi. *See* HACHINOHE.

• **Shinra Myōjin.** *Kam*i analogous to Susanoo no Mikoto, venerated by Genshin (942–1017) as a *gongen* when he returned from the kingdom of Shinra in Korea.

Shinran Shōnin. Buddhist monk (Zenshin, Shakku, 1173–1263); little is known about his life. In 1181, he was a novice at the Enryaku-ji temple (Tendai-shū) on Mt. Hiei, and he became a disciple of Hōnen, of the Jōdo-shū sect, in 1201. He may have been the son of a Fujiwara noble, Hino Arinori, and married Eshin-ni, daughter of *kampaku* Fujiwara no Kanezane (Kanenori). In 1203, he became

Genkū's disciple. He was exiled at the same time as Hōnen, who was sent to Shikoku; Shinran was sent to Niigata, where he was laicized with the name Fujii Zenshin, in 1207. Granted amnesty in 1212, he did not return to Kyoto, because Hōnen had died, but settled in Kanto, where he raised his seven or eight children. Shinran was one of the first Buddhist monks to marry publicly and lead a normal family life, which later became a common practice among Buddhist monks of the Jōdo Shin-shū.

It was while living in Kanto that Shinran wrote his major work, *Kyōgyōshinshō,* in which he departed from Hōnen's thought to teach that a life of rectitude and faith in Amida was sufficient for followers to reach the Western Paradise, on condition that Amida had breathed faith into them. Shinran's arguments were later sung in *wasan,* or religious hymns, which he composed when he returned to Kyoto in 1235. His son, Zenran (1210–92), who had in the meantime assumed leadership of his followers in Kanto without his permission, disavowed him. He then wrote *Jinen hōni shō* (Treatise on the Ultimate Truth of Things). He died in Kyoto in 1263, attended by his daughter Kakushin-ni (1224–83) and his brother Jin'yu, a monk from Mt. Hiei. He was buried in Ōtani, where the Hongan-ji temple now stands. His teachings led to the foundation of a "New Sect of the Pure Land," which expanded greatly in ensuing centuries (*see* JŌDO SHIN-SHŪ). He received the posthumous title Kenshin Daishi. There is only one portrait of him, drawn in pencil in 1242 by a monk named Jōzen, a painter about whom nothing is known, and a sculpture that he apparently made himself, kept in the Higashi Hongan-ji in Kyoto. An *emakimono, Shinran shōnin den-e,* painted in the fourteenth century, gives an embellished account of his life (kept at the Nishi Hongan-ji, Kyoto).

• **Shinren-bō.** One of Shinran Shōnin's sons, born 1211, a Buddhist monk under the name Myōshin.

Shinri-kyō. One of the thirteen sects of Kyōha Shintō (pure Shinto) founded in the late nineteenth century by Sanō Tsunehiko (Kanagibe, 1834–1906) in Fukuoka (Kyushu), stressing a sense of aesthetics. It was divided into four subsects in 1946: Shinri, Sekō, Meisei, and Uchu. It has about 350,000 followers.

Shin Rokkasen. Collective term for six famous poets of the twelfth and thirteenth centuries: Go-Kyōgoku (?–1206), Ji'en (ca. 1155–1225), Shunzei (1114–1204), Fujiwara no Sadaie (1162–1241), Karyū (1158–1237), and Suigyō Hōshi (1118–90).

Shinron. "New Theory." A three-volume political work by Aizawa Seishisai (1782–1863), scholar of the Mito school, in 1825. Aizawa recommended that the shogunate resist the "Western Barbarians," since he felt that Japan was a divine country (*kokutai*) and Westerners should be considered dangerous barbarians. This work was to form the ideological basis of the *sonnō jōi* movement.

Shinsai. Buddhist monk (798–858), Kūkai's disciple and *sōjō* of the Shingon-shū on Mt. Kōya.
→ *See* HOKUSAI.

Shinsambetsu. "National Federation of Industrial Labor Organizations" (Zenkoku Sangyōbetsu Rōdō Kumiai Rengō), created in 1949. It joined the Sōhyō when it was founded in 1950, but separated from it in 1952. It followed a neutral union policy, between those of the Sōhyō and the Dōmei.

Shin sarugaku-ki. Work describing a Sarugaku show written by Fujiwara no Akihira (late Heian period), valuable for its information on this ancient theater form and the crafts that revolved around it.

Shinsei. Buddhist monk (Koizumi Shinsei, 1443–95) of the Tendai-shū, a distant descendant of Ki no Tsurayuki and founder of a school of Buddhist thought (Shinsei-ha) that advocated practice of the *nembutsu;* he preached for many years. Emperor Go-Tsuchimikado conferred the title of Shōnin ("saint") on him.

Shinsen-en. Site of the imperial palace of Heian-kyō in the ninth century, whose garden has recently been renovated. *See* GOSHO.

Shinsen-gumi. A sort of militia composed of samurai, created by the Edo shogunate in 1863 to serve as a police force and protect the shogun when he traveled to Kyoto. At first called *rōshi-gumi,* it was renamed *shinsen-gumi* after a number of internal struggles, and was led by Kondō Isami and Hijikata Toshizō (1835–69). During the Boshin Civil War (1868), the *shinsen-gumi* remained faithful to the shogunate. *See* IKEDAYA JIKEN, MATSUDAIRA KATAMORI.

Shinsen jikyō. Large dictionary of Sino-Japanese characters *(kanji)* compiled in Kyoto around 900 by a Buddhist monk named Shōjū, and comprising about 20,000 characters categorized by their roots and given with their Chinese *(on)* and Japanese *(kun)* pronunciations. It is the oldest dictionary of its type.

• *Shinsen man'yōshū.* Anthology of *tanka* poems, the first part of which was written by Sugawara no Michizane in 893, the second part in 914. Each poem is accompanied by its corresponding version in Chinese.

• *Shinsen shōjiroku.* "New List of Family Names." A genealogical dictionary of the great families of Japan. It was compiled in 799, on the order of Emperor Kammu, by a group of scholars led by Kammu's son Manda (788–830), and supplemented during the reign of Emperor Saga in 815. It lists 1,177 families in Kyoto and surrounding provinces.

• *Shinsen tsukuba-shū.* Anthology of *renga* poems, a sequel to the *Tsukuba-shū,* compiled in 1495 by Sōgi and Inawashiro Kensai. It contains 2,000 verses by 241 poets.

• *Shinsen waka-shū.* Anthology of *waka* poems compiled in 933 by Ki no Tsurayuki.

• *Shin senzai-shū.* "New *Senzai-shū*," a poetry anthology (*see* CHOKUSEN WAKA-SHŪ) compiled in 1359 by Nijō Tamesada. It comprises 2,359 poems in 20 scrolls.

• *Shinsen-zuinō.* Poetics treatise dealing mainly with *waka,* written by Fujiwara no Kintō about 1150.

Shinshichi. Line of Kabuki actors of the Kawatake family.
→ *See* KAWATAKE MOKUAMI.

Shinshichō. "New Thought." A literary magazine founded by Osanai Kaoru and published from 1907 to 1970. It introduced new Western plays and novels and printed translations of works by European authors.

Shinshintō. "New Progress party," political party created in December 1994, bringing together followers of the Renaissance party, the Party of New Japan (Shinseitō), and the Kōmeitō (Clean Government party).

Shinsho. Buddhist monk (ninth century), founder of the Eikan-ji temple in Heian-kyo in 855; this temple later became the main temple of the Seizan branch of the Jōdo-shū.

Shinshō. Buddhist monk (1167–1230) of the Tendai-shū, Prince Mochihito's oldest son; he was appointed *zasu* of the Tendai-shu in 1203.
→ *See* BUSON.

• **Shinshō-ji.** Main Buddhist temple of the Chizan branch of the Shingon-shū sect, founded in Narita (Chiba prefecture) around 950 and rebuilt in 1705. It contains a famous épée made by Amakuni for Emperor Mommu in the seventh century and a statue of Fudō Myō-ō (*Skt.:* Achalanātha), named Namikiri-Fudō, attributed to Kūkai. The statue draws huge numbers of pilgrims each year who go to seek talismans offering protection against accidents. *Hondō* rebuilt in 1857.

Shinshōsetsu. "New Fiction," a literary magazine published irregularly from 1889 to 1926, founded by Aeba Kōson, Sudō Nansui (1857–1920), and Morita Shiken (1861–97) to print excerpts of works in the "new novel" style and to encourage young authors. Among its contributors were Izumi Kyōka, Shimazaki Tōson, Natsume Sōseki, Nagai Kafū, and other writers who later became famous.

Shin shūi-shū. Poetry anthology (*see* CHOKUSEN WAKA-SHŪ) compiled in 1362–64 by Nijō Tamekira and Ton'a. Its 20 scrolls contain 1,919 poems.

Shin Shū-kyō. One of 13 sects of pure Shinto (Kyōha Shintō) founded in 1881 by Yoshimura Masamochi (1839–1916). In 1946, it was divided into five subsects: Shinshū, Meisei, Dainichi, Nikkō, and Shinnō. It emphasizes purification (*misogi, harai*) and ritual and has about 400,000 followers. Headquarters in Tokyo.

• **Shin Shōkyō Remmei.** Association of Shinto sects created in 1951 and grouping together about 700 sects of all denominations.

Shintai. In Shinto, a *kami*'s "body" or "material support." This symbol may be a mirror, a sword, a jewel, or an effigy (often kept secret). *See* GOSHINTAI, HONSHA, MITAMA-SHIRO, SHINTŌ.

Shintaishi. Style of Western-inspired modern poetry created in 1882 by Toyama Masaichi (1848–1900), Inoue Tetsujirō, and Yatabe Ryōkichi

(1851–99). This style featured lines of 17 to 20 syllables grouped in stanzas of 8, 10, or 12 lines. *See* INOUE TETSUJIRŌ.

Shintō. Indigenous shamanic religion of Japan, venerating *kami* (forces of nature, or "superior beings") whose spirits are said to be able to inhabit objects or plants temporarily (*see* SHINTAI). Shintō has a complex mythology, expounded in part in the *Kojiki* and *Nihon shoki,* but no sacred texts.

This ensemble of beliefs and rites based on purification *(harai, misogi)* was elaborated over the centuries in Japan and incorporated (probably after the third century) similar beliefs from the Korean Peninsula and Siberia. The religion has a clearly Altaic origin. It is not certain that it goes back to the Jōmon period, although it is possible that some of its fundamental elements existed then. It was probably in the Yayoi period (ca. 300 BC–ca. AD 300) that its basic precepts were adopted, following population movements that were taking place between the mainland and the islands at the time. The "horsemen-archers" (*see* KIBAMINZOKU) added their own myths and consolidated the various beliefs that had developed in northern Kyushu, Izumo, and other kingdoms (*see* MIYATSUKO). The *dogū* of the Jōmon period, the mirrors and *dōtaku* of the Yayoi period, and the *haniwa* and wall paintings in the tombs of the *kofun* period show that the beliefs of the Japanese coalesced into a religion called Shintō in the seventh century, to distinguish it from the new religion imported from Korea—Bukkyō, or Buddhism.

Quite quickly, Buddhism and Shintō beliefs began to amalgamate in the minds of the Japanese people, who did not see much difference between the respective divinities in the two religions, and to whom Buddhism brought a sort of eschatology absent from Shintō. With the arrival in Japan of Esoteric Buddhist sects (early fourteenth century), many syncretic sects were created. In the Edo period, efforts were made to separate Buddhism and Shintō, but the people did not follow this movement. Only at the beginning of the Meiji era was Shintō made state doctrine and completely separated from Buddhism, which was considered a "foreign" religion. In fact, Shintō is inherent to the Japanese people; it may be said that all Japanese are born Shintō (even if individuals later adopt a different religion) because Shintō, being a religion of the land, attached to its local *kami,* can be neither exported nor proselytized. Shintō is divided into four main types, which developed more or less in different periods: Kōshitsu, or imperial Shintō; Jinja Shintō, or sect Shintō (*see also* KYOKA SHINTŌ);

Kokka (or Kokutai) Shintō, or state Shintō; and Minkan Shintō, or folk Shintō; the latter involves many beliefs borrowed from Buddhism, Taoism, and Confucianism. The number of Shintō sects and subsects is enormous, currently more than 1,000, and followers have borrowed a number of customs from Buddhism, notably that of pilgrimages (*see* KO). Shintō priests (*kannushi* or others) are laypeople, elected by the community, who receive specific training.

Shintō architecture is original and distinct from Buddhist architecture (imported from Korea and China) due to its pillars deeply driven into the ground and its shrines, which followers do not enter, the main structures *(honden)* being intended to shelter the Shintai or *kami.* Followers venerate the *kami* in front of the entrance to the shrine by clapping their hands once or several times, making a small offering (*see* KASHIWADE), and murmuring a prayer or invocation while bowing in a sign of deep respect. Shintō shrines are always built on natural sites renowned for their beauty and simplicity. They are preceded by one or several special porches called *torii* (reminiscent of Chinese *pailou* and Indian *torana*), which indicate the sacred nature of the place. *See* FUKKO SHINTŌ, JINGŪ, JINJA, JINJA SHINTŌ, KAMIDANA, KOKUTAI SHINTŌ, KYOHA SHINTŌ, MITAMA-SHIRO, MIYA, RYŌBU SHINTŌ, SAKAKI, SANNŌ ICHIJITSU SHINTŌ, SHINTAI, SUIKA SHINTŌ, YOSHIDA SHINTŌ.

• Subset of Shintō Taikyō founded in 1950 by Asō Shōi (1881–1953), with about 12,000 followers.

• *Shintō gobushō.* The "Five Books of Shinto." Sacred writings of the Watarai sect, attributed to Yamato-hime no Mikoto, a mythical being said to have founded the Ise shrines in the fourth century, and to the Buddhist monk Gyōgi (Gyōki). In fact, the apocryphal works were likely written in the thirteenth century by Watarai Yukitada and members of the Watarai family, and collected by a priest at the Ise Shrine, Deguchi Nobuyoshi, in the eighteenth century: *Ise futadokoro* (I and II), *Toyouke kōdaijingū, Zō Ise futadokoro,* and *Yamato-hime.* They are a mixture of Shinto, Buddhist, Confucian, and Taoist precepts, long kept secret, and had some influence on the thinking of authors such as Kitabatake Chikafusa and Ichijō Kaneyoshi. *See also* YOSHIDA SHINTŌ.

• **Shintō Honkyoku.** Shintō sect based in Ise, to which the Tenri Kyōkai, Kinkō Kyōkai, and Maruyama Kyōkai branches are attached. *See* TAI-KYŌ.

- **Shintō Kanshin-kyō.** Subsect of Shintō Tai-kyō, founded in 1882 by Takashima Chōhei (1862–1928).

- **Shintō Kotohira-kyō.** Subsect of the Jikkō-kyō, founded in 1946 by Nishiyama Jinnosuke (1895–1962). Also called Shintō-Kompira. *See* JIKKŌ-KYŌ, KOMPIRA-KYŌ.

- **Shintō Kōtoku-kyō.** Shintō sect founded in 1946 by Kurihara Izuhiko (1889–1960). *See* SHINTŌ TAI-KYŌ, TAI-KYŌ.

- **Shintōku-kyōdan.** Subsect of the Mitake-kyō founded in 1950 by Kaminaga Nichirin (1889–1964).

- **Shintō-kyō.** Shintō sect founded in 1947 by Yamaguchi Naosuke.

- **Shintō-kyodan.** Shintō sect founded in 1951 by Obayashi Sugahiko.

- **Shintō Rengō-kai.** Federation of Shintō sects created in 1921, comprising the twelve largest Shinto sects. *See* JINJA HONCHŌ, SHIN SHŪKYŌ REMMEI.

- **Shintō Sempō-kyō.** Shintō sect founded in 1949 in Osaka by Masai Kieki (b. 1907).

- **Shintō Shindō-kyō.** Shintō sect founded by Adachi Tajūrō (1841–95).

- **Shintō Shinkyō.** Shintō sect founded in 1947 by Unigame Itoko (b. 1876).

- *Shintō-shū.* Book on the origins of temples and shrines according to the Honji Suijaku (fourteenth century).

- **Shintō Shūsei-ha.** Shintō-Confucian sect founded in 1873 by Nitta Kuniteru (1829–1902). Also called Shūsei-kosha.

- *Shintō sōshu.* Compilation of historical texts dealing with Shintō beliefs, published in Tokyo in 1896–98.

- *Shintō taii.* "Profound Significance of Shintō," a mythological chronicle by Urabe Kanenao (fourteenth century). Yoshiwara Koretari wrote a commentary on it, *Shintō taii kōdan*, in 1669. Also titled *Banjin kigen* (Origin of All *Kami*).

- **Shintō Taikyō.** Shintō sect with about 1.2 million followers, divided into 15 subsects: Shintō Tenkō-kyō, Kantori Konkō-kyō, Kannagara-kyō, Shintō Kanshin-kyō, Misen-kyō, Tengen-kyō, Shiseima-hashira-kyō, Shinto Inari-kyō, Shintō Shindō-kyō, Shinto Shin-shin-kyō, Ōmiya-kyō, Shizen-sha, Mizuhō-kyō, Tenzen-kyō, Shintō Yamato-kyō.

- **Shintō Tenkyō-kyō.** Subsect of the Shintō Tai-kyō, founded in 1927 by Tomokiyo Yoshizane (1888–1952).

- **Shintō Yamato-kyō.** Subsect of the Shintō Tai-kyō, founded in 1946 by Tatsumi Kōichi (b. 1882) in Ise.

Shin-tō. *See* KATANA.

Shintō Hisashi. Industrialist, born 1910 in Fukuoka (Kyushu), and naval architect. A powerful magnate, he had a great influence on the 1985 government decision to return certain nationalized companies to the private sector.

Shin Yakushi-ji. Buddhist temple of the Kegon-shū sect, founded in Heijō-kyō (Nara) in 747 by Empress Kōmyō to cure her husband, Emperor Shōmu, of an eye disease, and dedicated to the Buddha of medicine, Yakushi Nyorai (*Skt.:* Bhaishajyaguru). Only the Yakushi-dō remains of the original temple, which houses a bronze statue of Yakushi Nyorai 2 m high, and those of eleven (out of twelve) of his "acolytes" *(jūni-shinshō),* dating from 747. The Jizō-dō dates from the Kamakura period. *See also* YAKUSHI-JI.

Shin'yō. Painter (Ba Dōryō; *gō:* Kitayama Shin'yō) of the Nanga school in Edo. Kangan's father (d. 1801).

Shin'yō. Code name for an attack boat used for suicide missions during the Second World War. One-man crew; explosive charge of 2 tonnes of TNT. *Length:* 5.5 m; *Speed:* 30 knots. It also had two 10 cm rocket-launchers at the prow. One thousand *shin'yō* were built, but they proved not very practical.

Shin zoku kokin waka-shū. "New Supplement to the *Kokin waka-shū.*" Twenty-scroll *waka* anthology compiled, on imperial order, by Asuka Masayo (1390–1452) from 1433 to 1439. It contains 2,144 poems and was the last (21st) official anthology (*see* CHOKUSEN WAKA-SHŪ).

Shiogama-jinja. Shinto shrine in the town of Shiogama (Miyagi prefecture), dedicated to the *kami* of the sea, founded before 927. It was honored by the emperors and the daimyo of the Date family in the Edo period. It was expanded in 1874 by the addition of another shrine, the Shiwashiko-jinja, brought from the nearby district of Iwakiri. Annual festival on July 10, with *yabusame* demonstrations.

Shiori Matsusaburō. Engineer and agricultural chemist (1889–1962), born in Nagano prefecture. He conducted important research on soil composition in order to improve agriculture through the use of fertilizers.

Shioki. *See* PUNISHMENTS.

Shiozawa Masasada. Economist (1870–1945), born in Ibaraki prefecture. In 1896, he went to the United States and Germany to study. He began to teach at Waseda University in 1902, and soon became president of the university, succeeding Ōkuma Shigenobu.

Shippi. Technique of working leather by molding or lacquering.

Shippō-ruri. Technique of cloisonné enamel, practiced since the seventh century and revived in Kyoto in 1880. It is now a well-known craft in that city. *See* ENAMEL.

Shirabyōshi. Type of dance performed by women or *chigo* (pages) in some Buddhist temples during Ennen ceremonies. According to tradition, *shirabyōshi* was first produced around 1115 by Waka no Mae and Shima no Chitōse. The dancers, both men and women, dressed in white and used props such as swords, court bonnets, tambourines, cymbals, and fans. Shizuka Gozen was a famous *shirabyōshi* dancer. The dancers themselves were also called *shirabyōshi*. *See* SHIMA NO CHITŌSE.

Shiragi. Old Japanese name for the Korean Silla (Sinla, Sinra, Shinra, Bakan) dynasty.

• **Shiragi-yaki.** Ceramics from the Shiragi period (57 BC–ca. AD 935) in Korea, found in a number of *kofun*. Fired at a high temperature, they were dark gray and resembled *sue-ki* pottery.

Shirai Kyōji. Writer (Inoue Yoshimichi, 1889–1980), born in Kanagawa prefecture. He wrote popular novels, most of which took place in the Edo period: *Kai tenchiku 12-dan gaeshi* (The Mysterious House at No. 12, 1920), *Fuji ni tatsu kage* (The Shadows of Mt. Fuji, 1924–27), *Shimpen foetsuzōshi* (1924), *Shinsen-gumi* (1925), *Bangaku no isshō* (1932).

Shirai Seiichi. Architect (1905–83), born in Kyoto. He received part of his education in Germany. Among his most notable designs: Akinomiya city hall (1949), Matsuida city hall (1955), the Zenshō-ji Buddhist temple at Asakusa (Tokyo, 1958), the Kai-shōkan computer center (Tokyo, 1975).

Shirakaba-ha. "School of the White Birch," a neo-idealist literary group that developed in the 1920s; it was opposed to the naturalist current and inspired by Tolstoy and Walt Whitman. Among the group's main authors, who published their work in the magazine named after it, *Shirakaba*, were Mushanokōji Saneatsu, Shiga Naoya, Arishima Takeo, Satomi Ton, Arishima Ikuma, Nagayo, Yoshirō, Yanagi Muneyoshi, and Kishida Ryūsei. *Shirakaba* published many articles on Western arts and literature and was very influential in literary circles before the Second World War.

Shirakawa Tennō. Seventy-second emperor (Prince Sadahito, 1053<1073–86>1129), successor to his father, Go-Sanjō. He inaugurated the system of "retired emperors" *(insei)* when he abdicated in favor of his son, Horikawa, while holding on to the reins of power, in order to neutralize the ever-growing influence of the Fujiwara family. He became a Buddhist monk with the name Yūkaku.

Shiramoto kofun. Group of twenty megalithic tombs *(kofun)* carved out of the slopes of Mt. Mura, in Kumamoto prefecture (Kyushu). The tombs have domed, vaguely square-shaped funerary chambers, with incised decorations (traces of red paint). Tomb No. 7 has an entrance decorated in Korean style. Formerly called Omura.

Shiranami-mono. In Kabuki theater, plays in which the hero is a pirate.

• **Shiranami gonin-otoko.** "Five Bandits Make a Friendship Pact," a five-act Kabuki play written by Kawatake Mokuami in 1862. Also called *Bentokozō*. A supplement to the play, *Shiranami gonin-onna*, was written in the *sewa-mono* genre.

Shirase Nobu. Geographer (1861–1946) and explorer of Antarctica. He reached 85°05' south latitude in January 1912, after making an attempt (with the ship *Kainan Maru*) via the Ross Sea in 1910. He named the point he reached (longitude 154° west) Yamato Tetsugen.

• In 1982, a Japanese icebreaker 134 m long, 214 m wide, drafting 14.5 m, with a displacement of 11,600 tons, was named *Shirase*. It is powered by a diesel motor developing 30,000 HP. Its first expedition to the Antarctic took place in 1983–84.

Shirashi. Whitish ceramics with a slip made with plant cinders, fired at high temperature, produced mainly in the kilns of the village of Sanage, east of Nagoya, starting in the late eighth century. *See* SANAGE, SUE-KI.

Shirasu. "White-sand beach," a space where commoner defendants were held during a civil or criminal trial; leading citizens sat on the steps of the platform where the judges sat.

Shiratori Kurakichi. Orientalist (1865–1942), born in Chiba prefecture, and professor at the University of Tokyo. A recognized authority on the ethnography and linguistics of the peoples of Central Asia, Mongolia, and Manchuria, he conducted major comparative studies on the ancient peoples of Japan and Korea and their relationships with the Altaic populations. He helped to found the Tōyō Bunko Library.

Shiratori Toshio. Diplomat (1887–1949), ambassador to Scandinavia (1933–36) and Italy (1938).

Shirazaya. Scabbard made of magnolia wood in which samurai kept their sword blade when it was not in use, to keep it in good condition. Also called *shirasaya. See* SAYA.

Shiritaki. Paleolithic site south of Abashiri (Hokkaido), where flint and obsidian blades and shards were found, dated by radiocarbon techniques to 12,850 and 13,850 BC (± 800 years). It is the oldest site discovered to date. Similar sites exist at Okido, Masanru, and Sakkatsu. *See* PREHISTORY.

Shiro. Old unit of area equivalent to about 5 *bu* (about 22.75 m²), with a value varying according to its yield in rice.

• "Castle." Also *jō* (*-jirō* in composition). *See* CASTLES.

• The color white.

• **Shiro-gane.** "White metal," term for silver *(gin)*.

• **Shirojirō.** *See* MASANOBU, MOTONOBU, MUNENOBU, TAN'YŪ, YASUNOBU.

Shiroyama Saburō. Writer (Sugiura Eiichi), born 1927 in Eichi prefecture, and economist. His novels, such as *Shōsetsu Nihon ginkō* (On Banking Circles, 1963), dealt with economic problems. In 1958, he received the Naoki Prize for *Sōkaya kinjō*. He is also known for his biographies: *Rakujitsu moyu* (Life and Death of Hirata Kōki, 1974).

Shiryō. In the tenth century, lands owned by individuals, as opposed to public lands *(kōryō)*. During the Kamakura and Muromachi periods, lands obtained by reclamation or acquisition, as opposed to lands given by the shogunate *(onryō)*. Finally, during the Edo period, lands given to the *hatamoto* and *gokenin. See* DAI NIHON SHIRYŌ.
→ *See* KŌIN.

• *Shiryō taikan.* Collection of 62 "memoranda" dating from the Kamakura and Muromachi periods, published in 1898 by Kurita Hiroshi and his partners.

Shiseidō. Manufacturer of cosmetics and beauty products, founded in Tokyo in 1872. It owns modern laboratories, and its products are distributed by some hundred companies throughout the world under the brand names Shiseidō, Moisture, Mist, Inoui, Zen, and Murasaki. It controls companies in the United States and Italy that make its products. Head office in Tokyo.
→ *See* SHIBUTSU.

Shisei Masahira-kyō. Subsect of the Shinto Taikyō, founded in 1928 by Oshima Yoshitarō. It apparently has about 7,000 followers.

Shiseki. Painter (Kusumoto Shiseki, Sō Shiseki; *azana:* Kunkaku; *gō:* Sekkei, Katei, Sōgaku, Shiseki, 1712–86), of the Nagasaki school, student of the Chinese painter Zi Yan.

Shiseki nempyō. Chronological charts and bibliographies from the beginnings of Japan to 1616, compiled by Ban Nobutomo and published from 1845 to 1883. In 1903, Koizumi Anjirō compiled a supplement for the years 1603–1867.

• *Shiseki shūran.* Compilation of historical texts made by Kondō Heijō and Kondō Keizō from 1881 to 1885, and supplemented by *Zoku shiseki shūran,* compiled from 1893 to 1895. *See* SHIRYŌ TSŪSHIN SŌSHI.

Shisekobo. Ancient tombs, analogous to Western dolmens, mainly from the Yayoi period, common in northern Kyushu. This type of tomb was widespread in northern China and northern Korea.

Shishi. "Lion," a mask portraying a mythical lion, used in Noh theater. Also called *shishiguchi. Chin.: shi. See* KARA-SHISHI.

• **Shishi-kagura.** *See* KAGURA.

• **Shishi-mai.** "Lion dances." *See* AMAGOI, GI-GAKU, JINJI-MAI, KADOZUKE.

• **Shishi Odori.** "Dance of the deer," a folk dance of northern Honshu performed in late summer and autumn by 3, 8, or 12 men wearing deer masks and striking drums to drive away danger.

Shishi Bunroku. Writer and theater director (Iwata Toyoo, 1893–1969), born in Kanagawa prefecture. In 1937, he and several other writers founded the Bungaku-za theater company, where they produced French plays. Many of his novels were best-sellers, including *Etchan* (1937), *Jiyū gakkō* (1950), *Musume to watashi* (My Daughter and Me, 1956), and the historical novel *Kaigun* (The war ship, 1942).

Shishinden. Throne room in the imperial palace. Also sometimes called *nanden, shishiiden, zenden. See also* DAIDAIRI, KINRI.

Shi-sho. Japanese name for the Confucian "Four Books" (*Chin.:* Sishu): Daigaku (*Chin.:* Daxue), Chūyō (*Chin.:* Zhongyong), Mōshi (*Chin.:* Mengzi), and Rongo (*Chin.:* Lunyü).

Shishō. King (<1405–22>), installed as ruler of the Chūsan kingdom in the Ryukyu Islands by his son Shōhashi, who unified the kingdoms of Samboku, Chūsan, and Sannan under his authority. *Chin.:* Sishao.

Shi-shōsetsu. Novel written in the first person (also called *watakushi-shōsetsu*), very often autobiographical, part of the naturalist movement and very much in fashion from the early twentieth century to the 1920s. The originator of this literary genre was Tayama Katei, with his novel *Futon,* published in 1907. Many other authors also wrote in the first person (and sometimes in the third person), includ-

ing Shimazaki Tōson, Shiga Naoya, and Mushanokōji Saneatsu. An offshoot of this "personal" literature, called *shinkyō-shōsetsu,* was a "confessional" genre that was also in fashion at the time and that was taken up again after the Second World War by writers such as Dazai Osamu and Mishima Yukio. The *shi-shōsetsu* genre was revived after the 1960s by a number of authors, including Abe Akira and Shōno Junzō. *See* SHIMBUN-SHŌSETSU, SHŌSETSU.

Shisō. "Thought," a journal of philosophy and ideas published by the firm Iwanami Shoten starting in 1921, and still widely read in intellectual circles.

• **Shisō no Kagaku.** "The Science of Thought," an intellectual movement founded in 1946 to promote Anglo-Saxon currents of thought and philosophies in a Japan that had up to then been Germanophilic. It published a small magazine of the same name, as well as philosophical, and sometimes political, essays.
→*See* KEIBUN.

Shita (-jita). "Under," a word often used in composition.
• "Language."

• **Shita-etsuke.** Technical ceramics term describing decorative painting under a transparent or translucent slip.

• **Shita-gasane.** Long white robe *(kyo)* worn under the garment called *hō* in the *sokutai* costume.

• **Shita-machi.** "Lower town," a term for the part of Tokyo built over marshes or the sea. Also, a term for the commercial districts of ancient Japanese cities.

• **Shita-obi.** *See* FUNDOSHI.

Shitakiri suzume. "The Sparrow with the Cut Tongue," a folk tale telling the story of a sparrow who, having eaten a bit of rice that an old man gives him, has its tongue *(shita)* cut off by the man's wife, a miserly old woman. The old man goes looking for the sparrow and is welcomed by its family. When he leaves, the old man is asked to choose between two boxes. He takes the one that weighs less. When he returns home, he finds that it is full of treasure. His cantankerous wife decides that she wants to profit from this bounty, and she goes to visit the sparrow's family. When she leaves, she chooses the heavier box, but when she opens it, terrible demons and snakes leap out at her. There are many other tales with a similar theme, taken from old legends, with several variants.

Shite. In Noh theater, an actor playing the lead role in a play. He generally wears a mask *(nōmen)* and is sometimes assisted by another unmasked actor called *shite-zure. See* NOH.

Shi-tennō. "Four Heavenly Kings" in Buddhist iconography, the four "guardians" of the horizons and of the Buddhist Law, corresponding to the Chaturmahārāja of India and the Tian Wang of Chinese Buddhism. Portrayed as armored warriors in threatening poses, they are placed at the corners of mandala. They are:
—*To the north:* **Bishamon-ten** *(Skt.:* Vaishravana), who holds a pagoda and a lance or trident with banner.
—*To the west:* **Kōmoku-ten** *(Skt.:* Virūpāksha) or Birubakusha-ten, who holds a scroll of writings and a stick.
—*To the south:* **Jōchō-ten** *(Skt.:* Virūdhāka), or Birurokusha-ten, who holds a sword or a lance.
—*To the east:* **Jikoku-ten** *(Skt.:* Dhritarāshtra), who holds a sword and a trident.
The Shi-tennō are often portrayed trampling on demons (Amanojaku). Also called Shi Dai-tennō, "the Four Great Celestial Sovereigns."

• **Shi Tennō-ji.** Buddhist temple founded in Naniwa (Osaka) in 593 and belonging to the Tendaishū after 1010. According to tradition, it was built by Prince Shōtoku Taishi to thank the Buddha for having permitted him to confound his enemies, notably Mononobe no Moriya. Destroyed a number of times by fires and rebuilt each time, the Shi Tennō-ji was razed during bombing in 1945. Its old foundations have been reconstructed in concrete (the original foundations were made of wood). It is the oldest example of a Buddhist monastery plan in Japan (with the Hōryū-ji); it was built on a north-south axial plan according to a standard brought from Korea (which is why it is sometimes considered to be in the Kudara or Paekche style).

Shito-ga. Painting and decoration technique in which the fingers, the palm of the hand, and the nails are used instead of brushes. It was used mainly by Ike no Taiga and Yanagisawa Kien.

Shitōkan. Generic term for the four highest ranks of bureaucrats during the Nara and Heian periods, according to the Chinese system of the Sui and Tang eras: *kami* (bureau head), *suke* (assistant to the *kami), jō* (archivist), and *sakan* (secretary).

Shitoku. Era of Emperor Go-Komatsu, of the Northern Court (Hokuchō), Feb. 1384–Aug. 1387. *See* NENGŌ.
→ *See* GYOKUSAN, ZAIMEI.

Shitomi. In traditional architecture, a type of outdoor shutter, generally openwork, opening horizontally.

• **Shitomi Tokki.** *See* KANGETSU.

Shittan. Buddhist sacred writing, a variant of Sanskrit *(Skt.:* Siddham, Bīja), in which each phoneme (represented by a syllabic sign) represents a divinity; its repetition was said to have the power to invoke the corresponding divinity. These alphabetic signs are often found on the haloes of Buddhist statues. Also called *bonji* (Brahmanic characters).

Shiwazu. Old name sometimes used for the last month of the year.

Shiyui-in. "Pensive pose," an attitude often portrayed in Buddhist statues of Miroku Bosatsu *(Skt.:* Maitreya), the right hand near the cheek and one leg crossed over the other. This type of portrayal, which came from China via Korea, was common in Japan from the sixth to the ninth century.

Shizan. Painter (Kusumoto Hakkei, Sō Shizan; *azana:* Kunshaku; *gō:* Sekkō, Shizan, 1733–1805) of the Nagasaki school; he studied with his father, Shiseki, in Edo.

Shizen-sha. Subsect of the Shintō-taikyō, founded by Kaneda Tokumitsu (1863–95).

• **Shizen-shindō.** Shinto sect founded by Maeshima Reiki (b. 1893) in 1947.

Shizen-shugi. Naturalist literary current, influenced by the works of Émile Zola and the French symbolists, that emerged in the early twentieth century.

Shizoku. "People descended from warriors," a term for all former samurai in 1869, according to the new designation of social classes dividing the Japanese people into *kōzoku* (imperial family), *shizoku* (former samurai), *kazoku* (former nobles), and *heimin* (commoners). This new class division replaced the *shi-nō-kō-shō* system of the Edo period. The *shizoku* (who comprised about 5% of the population) lost their privileges in the ensuing years, and most of them were forced to enter the administration (army, police force, and other government organizations) to earn a living. In 1876, they lost the right to carry their swords (except for those in the army and the police force) and to wear the *chon-mage,* the distinctive hairstyle of their former class. The *shizoku* class was abolished in 1947, when the new Constitution was promulgated. *See* KAZOKU, SHI-NŌ-KŌ-SHŌ.

Shizugatake no Tatakai. Major battle on June 11, 1583, in northern Ōmi province between the armies of Toyotomi (Hashiba) Hideyoshi and Shibata Katsuie, the daimyo of Echizen and Saga. Hideyoshi's victory reinforced his position as military dictator and unifier of the country and ensured that he would succeed Oda Nobunaga.

Shizuka Gozen. Famous *shirabyōshi* dancer (late twelfth century), best remembered as Minamoto no Yoshitsune's mistress. When Yoshitsune fled to the north in 1185, Shizuka Gozen was left behind in the Yoshino mountains and captured by Buddhist monks faithful to Minamoto no Yoritomo. It is said that Yoritomo forced her to dance for him in the Tsurugaoka Hachiman Shrine in Kamakura. He then freed her, and she returned to Kyoto, where she became a Buddhist nun. However, Yoritomo had her and Yoshitsune's child killed. Her story was the subject of many legends and novels, including the *Gikeiki,* and was portrayed on stage.

Shizuki Tadao. Scholar (Nakano Ryūho, 1760–1806) of "Dutch science" *(rangaku)* and an astronomer, Motoki Yoshinaka's disciple, born in Nagasaki. An interpreter *(tsūki)* by hereditary tradition, he translated many Dutch astronomy works, in particular *Rekishō shinsho* (ca. 1800), expounding the principles *(Principia)* discovered by Newton. Shizuki Tadao also translated Kaempfer's *History of Japan.*

Shizuoka. Chief city of Shizuoka prefecture, on Suruga Bay, west of Izu Peninsula. It developed in the Edo period, around the Sumpu castle built by Tokugawa Ieyasu in 1586, and was a flourishing port and an important post town on the Tōkaidō road. Nearby is the Yayoi Toro site. Shizuoka is a major agricultural and commercial center, famous for its lacquer crafts. The university there was founded in 1949. The city includes ruins of the Sumpu castle, the former Tōshōgū Shrine (1617), a museum of armor of the shoguns (10 km southeast, on the Kunō-zan), and the Taiseki-ji Buddhist temple. *Pop.:* 475,000. *See* SUMPU.

• **Shizuoka-ken.** Shizuoka prefecture, surrounding Suruga Bay and encompassing Izu Peninsula and the eastern part of Mt. Fuji, which marks its border with Yamanashi prefecture. It is irrigated by the Fujikawa, Abekawa, Ōi-gawa, and Tenryū-gawa rivers, which have carved deep gorges into the Akaishi Mountains. The prefecture includes the former Suruga, Tōtōma, and Izu provinces. It is heavily industrialized, especially on the seashore. Izu Peninsula is a major tourist attraction thanks to its natural sites. *Chief city:* Shizuoka. *Main cities:* Shimizu, Fuji, Numazu, Shimoda, Irō, Atami, Yaizu, Fujieda, Shimada, Tenryū, Gotemba. *Area:* 7,772 km². *Pop.:* 3.5 million.

Shizuri. The oldest type of fabric known in Japan, woven with mulberry-bush *(kōzō)* bark fibers and various dyed barks.

Shō. Royal dynasty of the Ryukyu Islands, with its capital in Shuri, before the Japanese conquest. *Chin.:* Shang. The best-known sovereigns of this dynasty are (Japanese names): Shi Shō (<1405–22>); Shō Hashi (<1422–39>); Shō Toku (d. 1469); Shō En (<1470–76>); Shō Shin (<1477–1526>); Shō Rei (<?–1609>); Shō Iku (?<1843>); Shō Tai (<1843–79>1901), last king of the Ryukyu Islands.

• Unit of volume, equivalent to about 1.8 liters or 10 *gō*.

• In ancient Japan, exemption of an estate from taxes granted by the emperor to a noble or a Buddhist monastery. *See* SHŌEN.

• Imperial decree. Formerly called Kami no Ōsegoto, Mikoto, Mikotonori, Ō-Mikoto, Tennō no Ōsegoto.

• Musical instrument: "mouth organ" of Chinese origin *(Chin.: sheng).* Its sound box contains 17 bamboo pipes of different lengths. Two of the pipes are mute and used to evacuate air; the others have vibrating metal reeds that can be silenced by blocking a small orifice just underneath them with the fingers. This instrument (the alto version of which is called *U*) was imported from China in the eighth century and used in Gagaku music. *See also* FLUTES, SHŌKO.

• Japanese name for the Chinese Shang dynasty.

• Buddhist bell, with no clapper. *See* BONSHŌ.

Sho. Character usually written on a painting or ukiyo-e print following the name of the artist, and meaning "painted by." *See* GA, HITSU.

Shōaku. In Buddhist folk mythology, an acolyte of Jizō Bosatsu (*Skt.:* Kshitigarbha) representing man's evil nature (symbolized by a red garment), complementary to Shōzen, the good nature of man (symbolized by a white garment).

Shōan. Painter (*gō:* Baian, fifteenth–sixteenth century) of the Muromachi *suiboku* school, Kei Shoki's student. He was a Zen Buddhist monk.
→ *See* ASADA GŌRYŪ.

Shō-an. Era of Emperor Go-Fushimi: Apr. 1299–Nov. 1302. *See* NENGŌ.

Shoban. In ancient Japan, title of families descended from the clan chiefs, or *miyatsuko. See* SHINSEN SHŌJIROKU.

Shōbi-kan. Private school of painting in the Western style, founded by Harada Naojirō (1863–99) in Tokyo.

Shōbō. Imperial prince and Buddhist monk (832–909) of the Shingon-shū, Shinga's disciple. *Posthumous name:* Rigen Daishi.

• *Shōbō-genzō.* "Treasury of the True Dharma Eye," Dōgen's major work on Zen Buddhism of the Sōtō sect, written from 1231 to 1253 and including his sermons and commentaries on koans. It has 95 chapters and is written in Japanese, which was quite rare in Buddhist writings of the time. This philosophical *summa* is still very widely studied. Complete title: *Shōbō-genzō keisei sanshoku.*

• *Shōbō-genzō zuimon-ki.* Six-scroll collection of Dōgen's sermons and dialogues, written by his disciple Ejō (1198–1280), *zasu* of the Ehei-ji temple.

Shōbu. Type of iris (*Acorus calamus,* var. *asiaticus*) of the araceous family; it is common in Japan and flowers around ponds in June. Formerly called *ayame.* When the irises bloom, people dress in traditional costumes and go to admire them. Because the shape of iris leaves resembles that of sword blades, they are considered symbols of virility and are used to decorate houses during the Boys' Festival (Tango no Sekku) on May 5.

• **Shōbu-gata.** *See* NAGINATA.

Shōbutsu. Buddhist monk of the Tendai-shū, on Mt. Hiei-zan (perhaps sixteenth century); a famous blind *biwa* player, he was, according to tradition, the first *biwa-hōshi* to sing the *Heike monogatari.*

Shōchiku. Movie and show production company, founded in Tokyo in 1902 to promote Kabuki plays; it began to specialize in movie production in 1920. *See* CINEMA.

Shochikubai. Name for three symbols of happiness: pine tree *(matsu),* bamboo *(take),* and plum tree *(ume).*

Shōchō. Era of Emperor Shōkō: Apr. 1428–Sept. 1429. *See* NENGŌ.
→ *See* NAKAMURA SHICHISABURŌ.

Shōchū. Era of Emperor Go-Daigo: Dec. 1324–Apr. 1325. *See* NENGŌ.
→ *See* SAKE.

Shōchū no Hen. Failed coup d'état in 1324, when Emperor Go-Daigo attempted to overthrow the Kamakura shogunate and take back the reins of power with the help of his supporters, Hino Suketomo (1290–1332) and Hino Toshimoto (?–1332), who tried to raise an army. The plot was discovered, but Go-Daigo denied knowing of it and was left free.

Shōda Kenjirō. Mathematician (1902–76), related to the imperial family (Princess Shōda Michiko's uncle), born in Gumma prefecture. He was a professor at, then president of, the universities of Osaka and Musashi. In 1969, he received the Order of Culture (Bunka-shō) for his contribution to the development of theoretical algebra in Japan. His brother, Shōda Hidesaburō (b. 1903), Princess Michiko's father, is a businessman who founded a major flour mill, Nisshin Flour Milling Co., in 1929.

Shōdōshi. Term for people, monks or laypersons, who devote themselves to spreading the teachings of Buddhism among the people.

Shōdō-shōnin. Buddhist monk (735–817), founder of the Shihonryū-ji temple in Nikkō; the temple was renamed Honryū-ji in 808.

Shōei. Painter (Kanō Naonobu; *mei:* Genshichirō, Ōinosuke; *gō:* Shōei, ca. 1520–ca. 1593) and Buddhist monk. He studied with his father, Kanō Motonobu (Munenobu), in Kyoto.

Shōen. Starting in the eighth century, cultivable lands or estates given by the emperor to a high-ranking noble or a religious institution and exempted from taxes. At first conceded for a specific length of time, *shōen* (or *shō*) became hereditary starting in 743, and therefore constituted estates effectively independent from the central power.

At first, *shōen* were usually small in size, but in the tenth century, notably under the Fujiwara, they became much larger. When the owner was a noble residing in Kyoto, the *shōen* was administered by an assistant, the *jitō,* and the absent owner was called *shōji* (estate owner). As payment, the *jitō* received one eleventh of the reported value of the estate, at least in theory. They also had the right to levy a military tax *(hyōrōmai)* on the lands they administered equivalent to about 5 *shō* (9 liters) of rice per *tan* (0.12 hectare) under cultivation, so that they could defend, if necessary, the estate for which they were responsible. During the Kamakura period, many *jitō* rose up against their *shōji* and became independent, resorting to arbitration by the *bakufu* if they had to. Other *jitō* negotiated with their *shōji* to pay them a certain sum each year, in place of a salary, for the right to run the *shōen.*

As the *jitō* became, to all intents and purposes, owners of the *shōen,* they began to impose taxes on the peasants *(myōshū)* on their own behalf. During the civil wars of the Muromachi period, they became totally independent (*see* GEKOKUJŌ), and many elevated themselves to military leaders, replacing the *shugo.* But with the political disintegration that followed the Ōnin War, many *shōen* were absorbed by larger ones. By the sixteenth century, the only *shōen* that had survived were those managed by religious institutions, which were defended by "monk-soldiers" *(sōhei).* Oda Nobunaga, then Toyotomi Hideyoshi, as they gained power, put a final end to the *shōen.*

Shō-en. King (<1470–76>) of the Chūsan, on the Ryukyu Islands, successor to Shō Hashi. He was a descendant of Shunten. Shō Shin succeeded him. *See* SHŌ.

Shōen Hōshinnō. Buddhist monk (1292–1347), one of Emperor Go-Uda's sons. He received the posthumous name Nanchi-in.

Shoes. Shoes, generically called *kutsu* (-*gutsu* in composite words) were, in the courts of the Asuka, Nara, and Heian periods, imitations of Chinese slippers, usually made of lacquered papier mâché, with a sole of leather or thick fabric *(asa-gutsu).* At home, people wore embroidered fabric slippers called *kinkai;* on hunting parties or to play *kemari,* they wore boots *(kamo-gutsu).* Peasants went barefoot or wore straw sandals *(waraji)* combined with straw or fabric gaiters *(kyahan),* or wooden clogs *(geta, amageta, ashida, takageta,* etc.). In the winter, they made straw boots *(wara-gutsu).* Upper-class women wore sandals made of fine rice straw *(zōri),* sometimes with slightly thicker soles *(koma-geta, pokkuri).* At first, socks were simply shaped; starting in the Kamakura period, when use of *waraji* became widespread, *tabi,* with separated toes, were used by most people. Men's *tabi* were generally dark colored (with white soles), while women's were always white. During the Edo period, some wealthy people wore deerskin *tabi,* brown for men and red for women. Western-style shoes appeared at the beginning of the Meiji era, but became widespread (except for soldiers) among the general population only in the early twentieth century. *See* GETA, TABI, WARAJI, ZŌRI.

Shōfū. "Bashō's style," a style of haiku poems *(haikai)* developed by Bashō, emphasizing the concept of restraint *(sabi).*

Shōga. Painter (Takuma Shōga, active ca. 1191) of the Takuma-ryū school. He painted mainly Buddhist subjects, such as the Jūni-ten at the Tō-ji in Kyoto, in Yamato-e style.

Shōgaku-in. School for children of the nobility in Heian-kyō, founded by Ariwara Yukihira (Narihira) in 881. The principal of this school held the title of *bettō* and belonged to the Minamoto clan. In the Edo period, the position was taken over by members of the Tokugawa family. Tokugawa Ieyasu held the title *shōgaku-in no bettō.*

Shōgakukan. Publishing house (Kabushiki Gaisha Shōgakukan) founded by Ōga Takeo in Tokyo in 1922, specializing in books for young people, encyclopedias, and dictionaries.

Shōgen. Era of emperors Go-Fukakusa and Kameyama: Mar. 1259–Apr. 1260. *See* NENGŌ.
→ *See* HAKYŌ.

Shōgi. Game similar to chess played on a board with nine squares per side; the flat, wooden pentagonal pieces are engraved with different characters. *Shōgi* was imported from China (*Chin.: xianqi*) and is mentioned for the first time in Japan during the Heian period (it had different names depending on

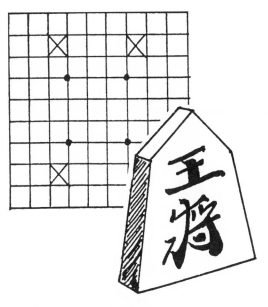

Shōgi board and pawn (king)

the rules used: *shōshōgi, chūshōgi, daidaishōgi,* or *makadaishōgi*). During the Muromachi period, use of the castle and the bishop became widespread (previously, these pieces had been used only in *chūshōgi*).

Each player has 20 pieces *(koma)* arranged on three rows: two lancers *(kyōsha, kyō),* two knights *(keima, uma),* two silver generals *(ginshō, gin),* two gold generals *(kinshō, kin),* and the king *(ōshō, ō)* on the first row; a bishop *(kakugyō, kaku)* and a castle *(hisha)* on the second row; and nine pawns *(fu)* on the third row. The pieces' moves are about the same as those in Western chess, but when some of them are captured, they can be returned with a different value. Also, a piece taken from the adversary can be put back into play by its holder in the opposing camp at certain times. The piece representing the king *(ōshō)* in one camp is called "gem" *(gyokushō)* in the other. There is no queen. Each piece has its name written in black ink on one side and its "returned" value in red on the other side.

Shōgi was very popular during the Edo period and is still played by about 200,000 players in clubs and federations. The best professional players have titles and ranks. Monthly magazines, *Shōgi Sekai* (circulation 120,000) and *Shōgi Magajin* (circulation 40,000), report on the tournaments that take place regularly throughout Japan, and tens of thousands of players, both men and women, attend *shōgi* schools, usually after work. The most coveted title is *eisei-meijin (meijin* for life), conferred on the player who has been *meijin,* national champion, five times. Other players are ranked on nine levels *(dan)* according to skill. The first player to reach the rank of *meijin* since the competitions were reorganized in 1924 was Kimura Yoshio (b. 1905). The second was Ōyama Yasuharu (1923–92), who won the title in 1952 and who was considered the best player in history.

Shōgi-tai. Group of about 500 samurai faithful to the Tokugawa shogunate, especially Tokugawa Yoshinobu, who, after the Battle of Toba in January 1868, gathered groups of supporters (Jinchu-tai, Byakko-tai, Garyū-tai, Manji-tai, Shimboku-tai, and others) to fight the imperial troops at Ueno (Tokyo). This army, about 2,000 soldiers strong, under the command of Shibusawa Kisaku (1838–1912), was soundly defeated on July 4, 1868, by General Ōmura Masujirō. The survivors who escaped then joined the last anti-imperial forces at Hakodate and took part in the Battle of Goryōkaku in 1869.

Shōgo-in. Buddhist temple founded under the name Jōkō-in by the monk Enchin (814–91) in Kyoto, and reestablished in 1090 by the monk Zōyo (1032–1116), of the Mii-dera temple (Onjōji). This temple, a *monzeki-dera* since the late twelfth century, was always directed by a tonsured member of the imperial family. In 1613, it was designated a main temple of the Shugendō belonging to the Tendai-shū, charged with control of the Yamabushi. Destroyed in 1675, it was rebuilt one year later on a different site.

Shōgun. Abridgment of the title *sei-i-tai-shōgun* ("military governor against the barbarians"), conferred by the emperor on leaders in the battle against the Ezo in northern Honshu or those rebelling against the imperial power. In the Kamakura period, this title was granted (still by the emperor) to the most powerful leaders of military clans, including Minamoto no Yoritomo in 1192. During the Muromachi period, it was given to the leaders of the Ashikaga family. In 1603, Tokugawa Ieyasu received the title of *shōgun,* and his descendants retained it until 1868.

In fact, *shōgun* were military dictators governing in place of the emperor who gave them their authority, while the emperor remained the spiritual leader of the Japanese nation. The powers of the *shōgun* varied depending on the era. In the Kamakura period, they directed the *bakufu* with the assistance of three agencies, the Mandokoro, the Samurai-

Shōgun

Kamakura period:

1. Minamoto no Yoritomo (1147<1192–99>)
2. Minamoto no Yoriie (1182<1202–03>1204)
3. Minamoto no Sanetomo (1192<1203–19>)
4. Kujō Yoritsune (1218<1226–44>1256)
5. Kujō Yoritsugu (1239<1244–52>1256)
6. Munetaka (prince, 1242<1252–66>1274)
7. Koreyasu (prince, 1264<1266–89>1326)
8. Hisaaki (prince, 1276<1289–1308>1328)
9. Morikuni (prince, 1301<1308–33>)

Muromachi period (Ashikaga family):

1. Takauji (1305<1338–58>)
2. Yoshiakira (1310<1359–68>)
3. Yoshimitsu (1358<1368–94>1408)
4. Yoshimochi (1386<1395–1423>1428)
5. Yoshikazu (1407<1423–25>)
6. Yoshinori (1394<1429–41>)
7. Yoshikatsu (1434<1442–43>)
8. Yoshimasa (1436<1449–73>1490)
9. Yoshihisa (1465<1474–89>)
10. Yoshitane (1466<1490–93>1523)

11. Yoshizumi (1480<1495–1508>1511)
    Yoshitane (without the title, <1508–21>)
12. Yoshiharu (1511<1522–47>1550)
13. Toshiteru (1536<1547–65>)
14. Yoshihide (1540<1568>)
15. Yoshiaki (1537<1568–82>)

Edo period (Tokugawa family):

1. Ieyasu (1542<1603–05>1616)
2. Hidetada (1579<1605–23>1632)
3. Iemitsu (1604<1623–51>)
4. Ietsuna (1641<1651–80>)
5. Tsunayoshi (1646<1680–1709>)
6. Ienobu (1662<1709–12>)
7. Ietsugu (1709<1713–16>)
8. Yoshimune (1684<1716–45>1751)
9. Ieshige (1711<1745–60>1761)
10. Ieharu (1773<1760–86>)
11. Ienari (1773<1787–1837>1841)
12. Ieyoshi (1793<1837–53>)
13. Iesada (1824<1853–58>)
14. Iemochi (1846<1858–66>)
15. Yoshinobu (Keiki), 1837<1867>1913)

dokoro, and the Monchugo. They had direct authority over the *shugo* and *jitō* of the *shōen,* and they were assisted by regents, the *shikken.* The Ashikaga *shōgun* had similar arrangements (with variants). In the Edo period, the *shōgun* directed the country with the help of a council of *tairō* (elders), which, in its turn, controlled the government through three "agencies": the *metsuke,* the *rōju,* and the *wakadoshiyori.* The *shōgun* himself had direct authority over the *bugyō* and *daimyō,* and his direct vassals, *kenin* and *hatamoto.* At the end of the Edo shogunate, the *shōgun*'s guardian representing him in the imperial court had the title of *shōgun kōken-shoku.*

Shōhaku. Painter (Soga Kiyu; *gō:* Joki, Ranzan, Dasukoren, Kishinsai, Hiran, Shōhaku, died 1781), of the Kanō school, Sesshū's disciple in Kyoto.
• Poet (Botange, Muan, Rōkaken, 1443–1527) of *waka* and *renga,* born to a noble family. During the Ōnin War, he took refuge in Settsu province, where he built a hermitage; he then became a Buddhist monk and settled in Sakai in 1518. He collaborated with Sōgi, Kenzai, and other poets to compile the *Shinsen tsukuba-shū* in 1495. His own poems were included in a voluminous collection

called *Shummusō* (Book of a Summer Night's Dream). Best known as Muan.

Shōhan gakkō. Private schools established for various clans or large daimyo families to educate young samurai in the early Edo period. *See* MEIRIN-DŌ, MEIRIN-KAN, SHŌHEI-KŌ.

Shō Hashi. King (<1422–39>) of the Ryukyu Islands, successor to Murei after having placed his father on the throne of Chūsan. At first *anji* of Soshiki Mairi, he conquered all of Okinawa, amassing under his rule the three kingdoms of Samboku, Chūsan, and Sannan, and established his capital in Shuri. *Chin.:* Shang Bazhi.

Shōhei. Era of emperors Go-Murakami and Chōkei: Dec. 1346–July 1370. *See* NENGŌ.

• **Shōhei-kō.** Official academy *(kangaku)* founded in Edo by Tokugawa Iemitsu in 1630. It was originally called Kōbun-in, then Seidō, and finally Gakumonjo in 1797, and its first director was Hayashi Razan. When the academy was moved to the Kanda district (Edo) by Tokugawa Tsunayoshi, it was renamed Shōhei (*Chin.:* Changping), after Confucius's birthplace. Subjects taught were Confucianism according to the Shushi (*Chin.:* Zhu Xi) school, the Chinese classics, medicine, and the military arts. It closed in 1871.

Shōheki-ga. Painting intended to be hung on a wall, fusuma, screen *(byōbu),* or *tsuitate,* to be used exclusively for interior decoration. Also called *shōhei-ga, shōbyō-ga.*

Shōhin. Painter (Noguchi Chika, 1847–1917) of the Nanga (Bunjinga) school in Tokyo. She studied with Taizan.

Shōhō. Era of Emperor Reigen: Dec. 1644–Feb. 1648. *See* NENGŌ.

Shōin Hōshinnō. Imperial prince (Kajii no Miya, d. 1377) and Buddhist monk, *zasu* of the Tendai-shū.

Shoin-zukuri. Style of noble residence that developed during the Azuchi-Momoyama era in the late sixteenth century; derived from a Chinese style, it became the basis for residential architecture in the Edo period. The *shoin*-style house had a square plan and was oriented north-south. The entrance was on the south side, with a covered door *(chūmon)* giving onto a veranda that ran around three sides of the house. Rooms gave onto the veranda via *shoji* and sliding doors. Two large square rooms, the *naka no ma* and *naijin,* were reserved for everyday use. They were surrounded by other rectangular rooms, one of which, the *jōza no ma,* used for receptions, had a *tokonoma* on the north side. All floors were covered with tatami. This basic plan was repeated in palatial residences such as the Ninomaru of the Nijō castle in Kyoto, which was a true palace with walls and fusuma decorated with paintings *(shōheki-ga).* A room *(sukiya-shoin)* reserved for the tea ceremony *(chanoyu)* was sometimes included in the plan or added on to the main structure. *See* SUKIYA-ZUKURI.

Shōji. In architecture, a sliding door or window with mullions; its open surfaces are covered with white translucent rice paper so that light can enter. *Shōji* are still widely used, and their function is as practical as it is decorative. In modern homes, they are often lined with glass on the outside to protect them.

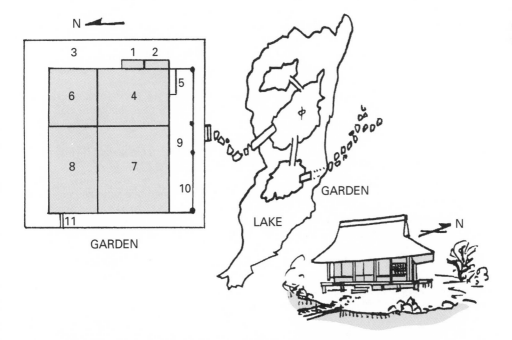

Plan of *shoin-zukuri* residence. 1. *Tokonoma.* 2. *Tokowaki.* 3. Back veranda. 4. *Ichi-no-ma* (main room). 5. *Tsuke-shoin.* 6 and 8. Bedrooms. 7. *Ni-no-ma* (second room). 9. Main veranda. 10. Balustrade. 11. Solid wood door

Shōji. Era of Emperor Tsuchimikado: Apr. 1199–Feb. 1201. *See* NENGŌ.

• **Shōji.** *See* SHŌEN.

• **Shōji-ita.** In the *yoroi* type of samurai armor, part of the helmet *(kabuto)* protecting the back of the neck.

Shōji Kaoru. Writer (Fukuda Shōji), born 1937 in Tokyo. In 1958, he received the *Chūō-kōron* Prize for one of his stories; in 1969, he received the Akutagawa Prize for *Akazukin-chan ki o tsukete* (Watch Out, Little Red Riding Hood!), a novel written in the first person *(shi-shōsetsu)*.

Shōjin. Buddhist monk (Fujiwara no Mototada, fourteenth century) of the Shingon-shū, son of *kampaku* Fujiwara Takatsukasa. He helped Emperor Go-Daigo flee and was exiled by the Kamakura *bakufu* to Shimōsa, then returned to the Todai-ji in Kyoto in 1333. He was appointed *ajari,* then *dai-sojō.*

Shōjō. Painter (Nakamura Shōjō; *mei:* Shikibu; *gō:* Seisei-ō, Shōkadō, 1584–1639), and Buddhist monk of the Shingon-shū. He painted in the style of Chinese painters of the Song and Yuan periods. Also a renowned poet and calligrapher, one of the Sampitsu (Three Brushes) of the Kan'ei period, and master of the tea ceremony *(chajin).*
• In legend, sea spirit that loves *sake.* This being is portrayed as a human being with long red hair and is sometimes confused with Umi-bozu.

• *Shōjo.* Title of a Noh play drawn from an ancient Chinese legend told by Kōfū: a man named Gao Feng, who has made his fortune selling rice, sees a *shōjo* come out of the sea and dance for him after having drunk *sake.* In another version, a *shōjo* shows him how to get rich. Another Noh play on the same subject, in which a Midare-style dance is performed instead of the Chō no Mai dance, is called *Midare;* another variant is called *Taihei shōjo.*

Shōjō-bukkyō. Buddhism of the Hīnayana (Small Vehicle), as opposed to Daijō-bukkyō, or Mahayana (Great Vehicle).

• **Shōjōkō-ji.** Buddhist temple founded in 1325 in Fujisawa (Kanagawa prefecture) by Donkai (1265–1327), the fourth leader of the Ji-shū sect, to be its headquarters. Destroyed several times by fire, in-cluding in 1911 and 1923, it was rebuilt and still has some vestiges from the fourteenth and fifteenth centuries. Now called Yugyo-ji.

Shōju. Sculptor (Ō-Kano Shōju, sixteenth century?). All his descendants adopted the same name. Among the best known are Shōju IX (1725–95), who made dolls (Nara-*ningyō,* for Noh) and netsuke, and Shōju X (Hokyū, 1768–1825).

Shojū. Former social category of persons reduced to a state of slavery, who served infantry soldiers *(zusa, ashigaru)* in wartime.

Shōka. Era of Emperor Go-Fukakusa: Mar. 1257–Mar. 1259. *See* NENGŌ.
• Painter (Naka-e Tochō; *azana:* Chōkō; *gō:* Katei-dōjin, Goteki, early eighteenth century) of the Nanga (Bunjinga) school; Kyūjo's student. He also engraved seals, wrote poems, and was a calligrapher and famous koto player. He painted mainly landscapes.
• Painter (Watanabe Kai; *azana:* Shōkei, 1835–87) of the Nanga school; Kazan's student in Tokyo.

Shokaku. Heavy aircraft carrier; it and the *Zuikaku* formed the fifth aircraft-carrier squadron during the Second World War. Built in 1939, it had a bulb keel and displaced 26,675 tons. *Length:* 281 m; *width:* 28.5 m; *draft:* 9.6 m; *speed:* 34 knots; *crew:* 1,660; *weapons:* 16 125 mm cannons, 36 anti-aircraft cannons; *payload:* 24 planes on board.

Shōkan. Division of the agricultural year corresponding to the "slight cold" and lasting about 15 days starting on January 6. *Chin.:* Xiaohan. *See* NIJŪSHI-SETSU.
• Buddhist monk (d. 1137), *ajari,* then *tandai* in 1105.
• General title for various bureaucrats of the *shōen* charged with collecting taxes and protecting assets. They had various names depending on their tasks and the region. Their duties were taken over by the *jitō* during the Kamakura period.

Shokatsukan. Painter (Shimizu Matashirō; *azana:* Shibun; *gō:* Seisai, Kogadō, Shokatgsukan, 1719–90) in Edo. He belonged to no particular school.

Shōkei. Painter (Kenkō Shōkei; *mei:* Sekkei, Keishoki; *gō:* Hinrakusai, Shōkei, late fifteenth–early sixteenth century) of the Muromachi *suiboku* school. His life is known only through his inscriptions on his paintings. He studied with Gei-ami and

Chūan Shinkō in Kyoto and was a Zen Buddhist monk in Kamakura. He made excellent copies of Chinese paintings of the Nan Song and Yuan periods, and painted landscapes in the style of the Chinese painter Xia Gui (late twelfth–early thirteenth century).

Shokei (or Shōkyō). Era of Emperor Kōgon of the Northern Court (Hokuchō): Apr. 1332–Apr. 1334. *See* NENGŌ.
• Painter (fourteenth century) of the Muromachi *suiboku* school. Nothing is known about his life; he may be the same person as Eiga.

Shōki. Mythical being of Japanese and Chinese legend *(Chin.: zhonggui)*, enemy of the demons *(oni)*, whom he constantly tormented. First mentioned in Japan in the twelfth-century *emakimono* titled *Jigoku-zōshi*, Shōki was later a favorite subject of painters. He is portrayed as a bearded and booted Chinese man with a black scholar's hat, brandishing a sword. Pictures of him are attached to walls of houses to chase away evil genies. His hat had the power to make him invisible. Also written Shō Ki.

Shokkō Giyūkai. "Fraternal Society of Workers," the first modern union, founded in 1897, organized on the model of American unions by Takano Fusatarō when he returned from San Francisco. Katayama Sen and Shimada Saburō joined its ranks. A few months after it was founded, the union's name was changed to Rōdō Kumiai Kiseikai; it published a magazine, *Rōdō Sekai* (The World of Labor). It was dissolved in 1901.

• *Shokkō jijō.* "Workers' Conditions." A five-volume report on working conditions in factories, published by the Ministry of Commerce and Industry in 1903. It became a classic work for the study of working conditions in the Meiji era.

Shōko. Large gong hung from a tripod, used in Gagaku orchestras. Also called *tataki-shō, shō, daishōkō*. A smaller gong, hung from a pole carried on the shoulders of two men during some processions, is called *ni-shōkō*.
→ *See* SHŌSEN-IN.

Shōkōkan. Office created in 1657 by Tokugawa Mitsukuni, daimyo of Mito, in his Edo residence for scholars who were writing the *Dai Nihon shi* (History of Great Japan), a work to which some 60 people contributed from 1657 to 1909. The Shōkōkan

was later transferred to Mito, and it was converted into a library in 1907.

Shōkoku-ji. Zen Buddhist temple of the Rinzai-shū sect built in 1383 by the monk Gidō Shūshin in Kyoto, under the auspices of shogun Ashikaga Yoshimitsu, who asked the daimyo to contribute to its construction. The monk Shun'oku Kyōha (1311–88), a disciple of Musō Soseki, was its first abbot; he was decreed the second *gozan* of Kyoto in 1386. Destroyed by fire in 1394, the temple was soon rebuilt; it sustained other damage in 1425, 1467, 1551, 1620, and 1788, and was restored each time. Its *hondō* was reconstructed in *kara-yō* style by Toyotomi Hideyori in 1605.

Shōkō-shōnin. Buddhist monk (thirteenth century), founder of the Chinzei branch of the Jōdo-shū.

Shōkō Tennō. Hundred and fifth emperor (Prince Mihoto, 1401<1413–28>), son of and successor to Go-Komatsu. He died without an heir, so he was replaced by his cousin, Go-Hanazono.

Shokugen-shō. Two-volume work by Kitabatake Chikafusa (1293–1354), describing the imperial administration, intended to educate the young Emperor Go-Murakami about his future duties. It is the oldest history of governmental institutions in Japan.

Shokuhō seiken. "Oda-Toyotomi regime," the name of the period from 1568 to 1600 that saw Oda Nobunaga's and Toyotomi Hideyoshi's authority extend almost throughout Japan; it coincided with the historical and aristocratic era called Azuchi-Momoyama.

Shōkun. Title of a Noh play: every day, a magical mirror owned by an aged couple reflects the image of their daughter, who was offered in marriage to a Barbarian king, and of the king, who is ashamed of his ugliness. From a Chinese legend.

Shoku Nihongi. "Continuation of the *Nihon shoki (Nihongi)*," the second work of the *Rikkokushi*, covering the period from 697 to 791 and containing the texts of 62 imperial edicts in Japanese. It was compiled in 797 by Sugeno Mamichi and his collaborators.

• *Shoku Nihon kōki.* "Continuation of the *Nihon kōki*," the fourth work of the *Rikkokushi*, covering the period from 832 to 850. Its 20 volumes were compiled by Fujiwara no Yoshifusa, Haruzumi no Yoshitada, Fujiwara no Yoshisuke, Ban Yoshio, and Agatatainukai no O-Sukune Sadamori.

Shokunin. Former term for all classes of artisans, peddlers, and traveling artists. The term is now used only for artisans.

• **Shokunin-zukushi-e.** Genre paintings showing artisans and workers. These paintings were in fashion starting in the Heian period and became very popular in the Kamakura period.

Shōku-shōnin. Buddhist monk (twelfth century), founder of the Seizan branch of the Jōdo-shū.

Shōkyō. Japanese name for the Chinese "Book of Documents" *(Shujing)* or "Annals," the oldest piece of Chinese literature, dating from the Qian Han period. It is one of the *Gokyō (Chin.: Wujing)* and one of the Confucian *Shikyō (Chin.: Sijing)*.

Shōkyō Kannon Bosatsu. One of the 33 forms *(see* SANJŪSAN ŌGESHIN) of Kannon Bosatsu *(Skt.:* Avalokiteshvara), corresponding to Nilakanthī, "Blue-Necked Avalokiteshvara," probably a Buddhist extrapolation of Shiva that is said to chase away evil and bad luck. He (or she) is portrayed sitting on a rock or a lotus, sometimes with a vase placed beside him (or her). There are several representations, one of them perhaps associated with Marishi-ten. Also called Seitsu Kannon Bosatsu.

Shōman. Former division of the agricultural year, corresponding to the period of "forming of seeds," beginning May 21 and lasting 15 days. *Chin.:* Xiaoman. *See* NIJŪSHI-SETTSU.
• Posthumous name conferred on Emperor Shōmu by Gyōki in 748.

Shōmei Jiken. "Shōmei Incident" or "Incident of Inscription of the Bell," which began the hostilities between Toyotomi Hideyori and Tokugawa Ieyasu. Hideyori had dedicated a bell in the Hōkō-ji in Kyoto by having written on it a poem, several verses of which said, essentially, "were Toyotomi your lord, your prosperity would be assured." Ieyasu, seeking a pretext for getting rid of Hideyori, saw fit to consider this an insult; in 1614, he began the conflict that ended in 1615 with the fall of the castle of Osaka and the destruction of the Toyotomi family.

Shōmen Kongō. Syncretic divinity, an aspect of the "descent" *(gongen)* of Gundari Myō-ō or Daigensui Myō-ō in the guise of a "wrathful" divinity *(funnu)*. It is the main divinity of the Kōshin Shinkō, sometimes called Kōshin. It is also sometimes considered an aspect of the *kami* Saruta-hiko, with the three monkeys *(sambiki-zaru)* as its "messengers."

• **Shōmen-zuri.** Technique of burnishing the paper of an ukiyo-e print with agate to make the colors brighter. The technique was invented in the eighteenth century. Also called *tsuya-zuri*.

Shōmon-ki. "Chronicle of Masakado." The first warrior chronicle *(gunki-monogatari)*, written by an unknown author soon after 940 and telling of Taira no Masakado's rebellions. Two versions of this work are known: one, dated 1099, is kept at the Shimpuku-ji temple in Nagoya, and the other is in a private collection in Tokyo. Also titled *Masakado-ki*.

Shōmono. Works in the form of commentaries (at first simple copies of texts), written by monks starting in the fifteenth century to explain Buddhist texts and Chinese classics. They were written in kana mixed with kanji, in a style called Kana-majiri-bun, and thus provide valuable evidence of the spoken language of the time.

Shōmu Tennō. Forty-fifth emperor (Prince Ame Shirushi Kuni Oshi Haruki Toyo Sakura-hiko, 699<724–49>756), successor to his aunt, Genshō. He abdicated in favor of his daughter, Kōken, and became a Buddhist monk with the name Shōman. Shōmu was related to the Fujiwara family through his mother, Kyūshi, a daughter of Fujiwara no Fuhito. His wife, Empress Kōmyō, was also one of Fuhito's daughters. He changed capitals several times during his reign, going from Heijō-kyō to Kuni no Miya, Naniwa, and Shigara-kyō, then returning to Heijō-kyō in 745. He ordered the erection of *kokubun-ji* temples in each province, and he had the Tōdai-ji built and the large statue of Daibutsu in Nara cast. When he died, his personal possessions were stored in the Shōsō-in in Nara, where they are today.

Shōmyō. Buddhist chants of Chinese origin. *See* MYŌDEN.

• **Shōmyō-ji.** Buddhist temple founded in Kanazawa by Hōjō Sanetoki (1225–76) to house the Kanagawa library.

Shōnagon. Former title for bureaucrats of the Da-jōkan; in the Heian period, generally conferred on three fifth-rank nobles, who were responsible for reading ordinary reports and taking care of imperial travel.

Shōnan-tō. Japanese name for Singapore in 1942, when Japan captured the city.

Shōnen. Painter (Suzuki Matsutoshi; *gō:* Shōnen, 1849–1918), Hyakunen's student.
→ *See* TAIZAN.

• *Shōnen.* "The Boy," title of a famous movie, directed by Oshima Nagisa in 1969, telling the story of a child trained by his parents to simulate automobile accidents in order to extort money from insurance companies and drivers. It mixes color and black-and-white images.

• *Shōnen Jump.* Weekly magazine for young people, created to replace *Shōnin Kurabu* about 1970; published by the Shueisha publishing house, it has a circulation of about 6 million. It publishes mainly comics *(manga)* and is supported by cartoons, television spots, and advertising.

• *Shōnen Kurabu.* "Boy's Club," a magazine for young people, created in 1914 by the Kōdansha publishing house, which was extraordinarily popular until the Second World War. With competition from comic books *(manga),* it folded in 1962 and was later replaced by *Shōnen Jump.*

Shōni. Family of warriors in northern Kyushu, who became known mainly during the attempts to invade the island by Korean and Mongolian forces in 1274 and 1281. They drew their family name from their position *(shōni)* of vice-governor of Da-zaifu. Shōni Tsunesuke (1226–89) and his brother, Shōni Kagesuke (?–1285) commanded the Japanese armies that opposed the Mongols. Their descendants formed an alliance with Ashikaga Takauji to battle the armies of the Southern Court (Nanchō), but they lost their territories to the Ōuchi family in the fourteenth and fifteenth centuries. They were annihilated by the Ryūzōji family in 1590.

Shōnin. "Saint," or "Reverend," a title given to very high-ranking Buddhist monks. The first to hold this title was the monk Kūya (903–72).

Shōno Junzō. Writer, born 1921 in Osaka. In 1954, he received the Akutagawa Prize for one of his sto-

ries. Most of his novels are written in auto-biographical style *(shi-shōsetsu): Yūbe no kumo* won the *Yomiuri* Prize in 1965; *E-awase,* the Noma Prize in 1971.

Shonsui Gorōdayu. Potter (late sixteenth century) who learned how to make porcelain in China. When he returned to Arita, he established kilns where he made "white and blue" porcelain with elaborate decorations, imitating Chinese production of the same type from the late Ming dynasty. He transmitted his techniques to his students, Gorō-shichi and Gorōhachi. Also called Gorōdayu, Shon-zui. Porcelain in this style imported from China was called *sometsuke* and *ko-sometsuke.*

Shōnyo. Buddhist monk (Kōsen, 1517–54) of the Jōdo-shū, tenth head *(hossu)* of the Hongan-ji in Kyoto. *See* HONGAN-JI.

Shō-ō. Era of Emperor Go-Uda: Apr. 1288–Aug. 1293. *See* NENGŌ.
→ *See* RYŪHO.

Shō Rei. Last king of the Shō dynasty on the Ryu-kyu Islands, taken prisoner in 1609 by the Japanese of Satsuma and deported to Edo. Okinawa was then declared a vassal state of Japan and the Amami Islands were annexed. *Chin.:* Shang Ning. *See* SHŌ.

Shōren-in. Former residence of the *zasu* of the Tendai-shū in Kyoto. The current buildings date from 1895. Paintings on fusuma by artists of the Tosa and Kanō schools. The picture of the "Blue Fudō" (Aoi-Fudō) is kept there; the gardens were designed by Sōami and Kobori Enshū. The first owner of this royal residence was Prince Kakukai (1134–81), seventh son of Emperor Toba Tennō. Succeeding him at the head of the Shōren-in was the monk Zi-en, author of *Gukansho;* he was followed by other famous monks, including Son-en (1298–1356), who introduced the new styles of calligraphy called *jubo-kudō* and *oie-ryū,* used for official documents. At the entrance to the temple are four huge camphor trees said to have been planted by Shinran (1173–1263).

Shōrinji-kempō. Particular style of karate created by Zen Buddhist monks to complement their *zazen* exercises. The name is a Japanization of that of the Chinese Shaolin-si monastery. *Shōrinji-kempō* techniques include certain movements from Chinese boxing *(Chin.: taiqi-chuan).* The "sport" was introduced and codified by the monk Sō Doshin (Nakano Michiomi, b. 1911) after the Second World War. It is more a religious discipline than a true martial art. Its main temple is in Tadatsu, Kagawa prefecture (Shikoku). Practitioners wear the same costumes as *jūdōka,* but with a swastika *(Jap.: manji)* embroidered on the chest.

Shōro. In Buddhist temples and monasteries, a special structure housing a large bell with no clapper *(shō),* which was once used to mark the hours and announce prayer and ceremony times. Also called *shurō.*

Shōrui Awaremi no Rei. "Edicts of Compassion for Living Beings." A series of edicts promulgated in 1685 by shogun Tokugawa Tsunayoshi, forbidding all acts of cruelty toward animals. In 1687, similar edicts issued banned the capture, hunting, and slaughter of all animals. In 1695, Tokugawa Tsunayoshi had huge kennels built in Edo to house stray dogs. These extravagant measures earned him the nickname Inu-kubō ("shogun of dogs"). The edicts were withdrawn by Tokugawa Ienobu in 1709.

Shōryaku. Era of Emperor Ichijō: Nov. 990–Feb. 995. *See* NENGŌ.

Shōryō. Old coin *(ryō)* equivalent, in the Edo period, to 4 *bu* or 24 *shu. See* RYŪ, SHU.

Shōryō-shū. "Collection of Henjō's Spirit," a collection of essays and poems by Henjō (Kūkai), written in *kambun* by Shinzei (800–60), a disciple of the master of the Shingon-shū. Complete title: *Henjō hakki seirei-shu.*

Shosa. Category of Kabuki plays composed exclusively of dances with shamisen accompaniment. These plays were called *gengemono* (with three to five dances) or *matsubamemono* (with dances adapted from Noh plays).

• **Shosagoto.** Old type of Kabuki plays composed of dances and drama, usually in a single act, as opposed to the more recent and realistic style called *jigei.* Also called *furigoto. See* KABUKI.

Shōsai. Sculptor (Tsuda Shōsai, 1879–1928) and engraver, maker of netsuke in Osaka.
• Lacquer artist (Shirayama Fukumatsu; *gō:* Fukumatsu, 1853–1923) who received the title of Teishitsu Gigei-in (Artist of the Imperial Household).
→ *See* HOKUJU, SAITŌ BISHU.

Shosai-ga. Style of *suiboko* painting, portraying a landscape with a small hut. Also called *shosai-zu.*

Shōsei-in. Residence of the abbots *(hossu)* of the Higashi Hongan-ji in Kyoto. Gardens by Ishikawa Jōzan and Kobori Enshū. Also called Kikokutei.

Shōsen. Painter (Soga Shōsen, early sixteenth century) of the Muromachi *suiboku* school; he studied with his father, Sōyo (Dasoku).
• Buddhist monk of the Jōdo Shin-shu, founder of the Gōshō-ji branch in Echizen province in the fourteenth century.

• **Shōsen-in.** Painter (Kampo Shōsen, Kanō Masanobu; *gō:* Soshōsei, Shōko, Shōsen-in, 1823–80) of the Kanō school of Kobikichō in Edo. He studied with his father, Kanō Seisen (Yōshin).

Shōsetsu. Ancient division of the agricultural year corresponding to "little snow," beginning around November 22 and lasting 15 days. *Chin.:* Xiaoxue. *See* NIJŪSHI-SETSU.
• General term for all literary works of fiction, including novels. *See* SHI-SHŌSETSU, SHIMBUN-SHŌSETSU.

• *Shōsetsu shinzui.* "Essence of the Novel," a work published in 1885 by Tsubouchi Shōyō (1859–1935) announcing the birth of modern Japanese literature and defining what he means by a "novel" and the goals to be pursued in it.

Shoshi. In old families, a general term for younger sons or the offspring of concubines, who were not in line for the family inheritance.

Shoshidai. Title of the leader of the Samurai-dokoro in Kyoto, where he represented (starting in the sixteenth century) the shogun at the imperial court. The position and title were created by Oda Nobunaga. *See* NAIRAN.

Shoshi-hatto. Laws promulgated in 1632 by the Edo shogunate to regulate the rights and duties of the direct vassals of the shoguns, the *hatamoto* and *gokenin.* Amended in 1663 and comprising 23 articles, the *Shoshi-hatto* were abrogated by Tokugawa Tsunayoshi.

Shō Shin. King (<1477–1526>) of the Ryukyu Islands, succeeding Shō Toku. He abolished feudalism in his states, imposed Confucianism, and had all arms owned by non-warriors confiscated, then forced the *anji* to live permanently in his capital, Shuri. *See* SHŌ.

Shōshin. Buddhist monk (thirteenth century), founder of the Kibe-ha branch of the Jōdo Shin-shū.

• *Shōshin nembutsu-ge.* Buddhist chant composed in Chinese verses by Shinran and expounding the principles of the Jōdo Shin-shū. Also abridged to *Shōshin-ge.*

Shosho. Ancient imperial decrees concerning important events, as opposed to *chokusho,* which dealt with minor matters.
• Ancient division "of the warm period" of the agricultural year, beginning around July 7 and lasting 15 days. *Chin.*: Xiaoshu. *See* NIJŪSHI-SETSU.

Shosho. Ancient division "of the hot period" of the agricultural year, beginning around August 23 and lasting 15 days. *Chin.*: Chushu. *See* NIJUSHI-SETSU.

Shōshō. In the Meiji era, a military grade corresponding to captain.
→ *See* AKAMATSU YOSHINORI.

Shōshō Hakkei. "Eight Views of the Xiao and Xiang Rivers." A subject often painted by Chinese and Japanese artists, more or less copying eight works by the Chinese painter Song Di (ca. 1015–80) portraying the shores of Lake Dongting in China. Painters of the Muromachi *suiboku* school were able to view these works in collections of Chinese paintings that had been collected by the shoguns Ashikaga Yoshimitsu and Ashikaga Yoshinori (fourteenth–fifteenth centuries).

Shōsō-in. Granary *(kura)* made of cypress wood in the *azekura-zukuri* style, built on the property of the Tōdai-ji temple in Nara about 760. This rectangular structure, supported on 40 pilings 2.4 m high, is in three parts: the ends, in pure *azekura* style (built with triangular beams), are joined by a part made of planks juxtaposed on edge. The *yosemune*-type roof has slightly up-curved corners and is covered with tiles. The specific mode of construction preserves a constant level of hygrometry in the interior, with the triangular beams shrinking slightly in dry times to let air pass through and becoming hermetically sealed in humid times. This structure, built to store rice, was used in the eighth century to store more than 3,000 objects from the collections amassed by Emperor Shōmu and Empress Kōken: musical instruments, paintings, calligraphy, various ornaments, weapons and armor, dance costumes, sculpture, perfumes and medicinal plants, lacquered objects and objects in ceramics, metal, leather, glass, and so on. Some of these objects were made in Japan, while others had been brought from China and Central Asia by ambassadors; the most valuable and fragile were kept in wooden boxes. This collection constitutes the oldest museum in the world and provides an invaluable source of information on the necessities of life in Japan and Central Asia in the eighth century. The Shōsō-in was restored in 1883, and the objects it contained were transferred in 1953 and 1962 into new buildings made of reinforced concrete, for fear that fire would destroy them. The treasures of the Shōsō-in are open to the public for only a few days at the beginning of October each year.

• *Shōsō-in monjo.* More than 10,000 documents dating from the Nara period, kept in the Shōsō-in.

• *Shōsō-in sansai.* Type of ceramics fired at low temperature and covered with green, brown, and white glazes, produced during the Nara period (645–794) on the model of Chinese ceramics of the Tang dynasty called Tō-sansai (*Chin.*: Tang *sancai*), or "three colors." Fifty-seven pieces of this type are housed in the Shōsō-in.

Shōsoku-gyō. Buddhist sutras *(kyō)* decorated with paintings produced during the Heian and Kamakura periods. They are a specific type of *emakimono.*

Shōtai. Era of Emperor Daigo: Apr. 898–July 901. *See* NENGŌ.

Shō Tai. Last king (?<1843–79>1901) of the Ryukyu Islands, successor to Shō Iku, vassal of the Satsuma clan and China. Attacked by the latter and defeated in 1879, he took refuge in Japan, where he received a noble title. The Ryukyu Islands were then annexed by Japan.

Shotai. Styles of calligraphy using Sino-Japanese characters *(kanji).* There are three *(santai)* or five *(gotai)* styles, depending on the era; their names are adapted from the Chinese ones. The three major styles are *kaisho,* angular, official; *gyōsho,* semicursive; and *shōsho,* "unripe" cursive. To these are added *tensho* writing, of ancient origin, used for seals, and *reisho,* used by scribes. The *kaisho* style is now the most used. *See* CALLIGRAPHY.

Shōtatsu. Buddhist monk (thirteenth century), Zennobō's disciple and founder of the Seizan branch of the Jōdo-shū.

Shōtei. *See* HOKUJŪ.

Shōtetsu. Buddhist monk (Ki Seigen, 1381–1459) of the Tōfuku-ji in Kyoto and *waka* poet in the style of Fujiwara no Teika. He wrote a work of poetics criticism, *Shōtetsu monogatari,* and a collection containing more than 20,000 poems, *Sōkon-shū* (Collection of Roots and Plants). However, despite his fame, none of his poems was included in the last of the imperial anthologies (*see* CHOKUSEN WAKA-SHŪ), *Shin zoku kokin-shū* (1439).

Shō Toku. King (d. 1499) of the Ryukyu Islands, of the Shō dynasty, descended from Shun Ten. Shō En succeeded him in 1470. *Chin.:* Shang De Wang.

Shōtoku. Era of Emperor Nakamikado: Apr. 1711 –June 1716. *See* NENGŌ.

• Shōtoku-in. *See* TOKUGAWA IEMOCHI.

• Shōtoku-kingin. Gold and silver coins of the Edo period, issued during the Shōtoku era.

• Shōtoku Taishi. Imperial prince (Umayado no Ōji, Toyosatomimi no Ōji, Jōgū Taishi, 574–622), Emperor Yōmei's son and regent for Empress Suiko. He held de facto power; a fervent Buddhist, he undertook to spread Buddhist doctrine among the nobility and violently opposed the holders of traditional Shinto beliefs led by Momonobe no Moriya. When Emperor Yōmei died in 587, he battled the Soga family (whose leader was the minister Soga no Umako) for the right to choose his successor. Soga no Umako finally prevailed by enthroning Emperor Sushun; when Sushun was assassinated in 592, he put his niece, Suiko, Emperor Bidatsu's widow, on the throne. Because Soga no Umako favored the adoption of Buddhism, he had Prince Shōtoku's support.

Following a war resulting in the death of Momonobe no Moriya, Shōtoku Taishi became regent in 593; in 604, he installed a new system of ranks in the court (designated by the color of headwear), following a Chinese style, in order to gain support among the leaders of the great families and clans *(miyatsuko).* The same year, he is said to have promulgated his Seventeen-Article Constitution (*see* JŪSHICHIJŌ NO KEMPŌ), which was to have an immense influence on later governments

and on the social behavior of the Japanese people. Having proclaimed Buddhism the state religion in 594, he had temples built, such as the Shintennō-ji in Naniwa and the Hōkō-ji (Asuka-dera) in Asuka, and contributed to the building of the Hōryū-ji. A disciple of the Korean Buddhist monk Eji, he studied the *Sangyō gishō,* three major Buddhist texts, and wrote three commentaries on them. He is also credited with writing two historical works, the *Tennō-ki* and the *Koku-ki (Kokki),* now lost. Also in 604, he adopted the Chinese calendar (with the system of eras, *nengō*). In 600, he sent the first official Japanese delegation to China, followed by a second one in 607 under Ono no Imoko. Shōtoku Taishi died in his palace in Ikaruga in 622.

Shōtoku Taishi's Seventeen-Article Constitution probably was not promulgated until after his death. The Buddhists made him a divinity and an incarnation of Kannon Bosatsu. He is sometimes also called Yatsumimi no Ōji. A portrait of him, accompanied by two young princes in Central Asian costume, in color on paper, has survived and is kept in the agency of the imperial family. *See* I, SHIGI-SAN.

• Shōtoku Tennō. Forty-eighth sovereign (Princess Abe Naishinnō, 718<765–70>), Shōmu Tennō's daughter; she succeeded Junnin Tennō. This was her second reign, the first having been under the name Kōken, when she succeeded her father (from 749 to 758). Between her two reigns, she used the name Takano Tennō. Her capitals were established successively at Kuni, Shigaraki, and Yugi, in Yamato. She was very pious and had printed (in xylography) almost 1 million copies of Buddhist invocations *(Skt.: dhāranī). See* KŌKEN TENNŌ.

Shō-un. Painter (Iwamoto Suenobu; *mei:* Ichiemon; *gō:* Kanō Shō-un, Chōshinsai, Shō-un, 1637–1702) of the Kanō school, Yasunobu's student in Edo.

→ *See* GION NANKAI.

• Shōun Genkei. Sculptor (1648–1710) and Zen Buddhist monk *(zenji),* who made a group of the Five Hundred Arhats *(gohyaku-rakan).*

Shōwa. Era of Emperor Hanazono: Mar. 1312–Feb. 1317. *See* NENGŌ.
• Era of Emperor Hirohito: Dec. 25, 1926–Dec. 31, 1989.
• Research station in the Antarctic, on the Prince Harald coast (69°S, 39°35'E), opened in 1937. It was closed in 1958, then reopened from 1962 to 1965.

- **Shōwa Genroku.** *See* GENROKU-JIDAI.

- **Shōwa Kyōkō.** Major financial depression that affected the Japanese economy in the 1930s, following the depression that started in the United States in 1929. The recession started in early 1930 and ended only in late 1935. It led to the incident of February 1936 (*see* NINIROKU JIKEN), in which most of the officers who revolted came from the countryside, where the crisis had been particularly devastating.

- **Shōwa Tennō.** Name given to Emperor Hirohito in 1990, after the name of his era *(nengō)*. He had the longest reign in Japanese history (65 years, plus 4 years as regent for his father, Taishō Tennō). *See* HIROHITO.

Shōya. During the Edo period, the term for village chiefs in Kansai; they were called *nanushi* in Kanto and *kimoiri* in northern Honshu. They assisted local representatives of the shogunate with its estates. At first, their position was hereditary, but in the eighteenth century they were elected in some regions.

Shōyu. Soy sauce, a basic ingredient in Japanese cuisine, composed of fermented soybeans, salt, water, and wheat. There are many sorts, depending on age, degree of fermentation, and what is added to them, such as sweet *sake*. Each region has its *shōyu* specialty. *Tōnyu* is a sort of milk made from filtered pressed soybeans and water, and *tofu* is a soybean cake made from *tōnyū* solidified with a gelling agent. Tofu can be consumed raw or grilled. Soy derivatives are very rich in protein and are consumed in great quantities in various forms. These products make a healthy vegetarian diet possible for monks.

Shōyū-ki. Journal of daily notes by minister Fujiwara no Sanesuke (957–1046) covering the years 977 to 1032, and telling about life in the court.

Shōzei. Tax in rice collected by the government starting in the late seventh century, and stored in provincial granaries called *shōsō.* The rice was controlled by provincial governors *(kokushi),* who often redistributed it to peasants in the form of loans against interest *(suiko).* Also called *ōchikara.*

Shōzen. In Japanese folk Buddhist iconography, an acolyte of Jizō Bosatsu (*Skt.:* Kshitigarbha) symbolizing the good nature of human beings. He is characterized by a white garment (or piece of fabric) and is opposed to Shōaku, who represents the evil nature of humanity.

Shōzuka no Baba. In Buddhist folk legends, a witch who undresses dead children on the bank of the river *(sozu-gawa)* that separates the mortal world from Hell (the Buddhist River Styx). The children are then consoled by Jizō Bosatsu.

Shu. Ancient coin, worth one sixth of a *bu* in the Edo period; 72 *bu* made one *dairyō,* and 24 *shu* were equivalent to 1 *shōryō* (or *ryō*). *Shu* and *bu* were silver coins.

Shū. "Religious sect."
- "Poetry collection."
- Japanese term for the Chinese Zhou dynasty.

Shūbun. Autumn equinox, around September 23, and, in general, any change in season. *Chin.:* Qiu-fen. *See* NIJŪSHI-SETSU.
- Painter (*azana:* Tenshō; *gō:* Ekkei, Shūbun, ?–1460) and Zen Buddhist monk at the Shōkoku-ji temple in Kyoto, considered to be the founder of the Chinese style *(karayō)* of *suiboku.* He studied with Josetsu. He decorated the fusuma in the residence of imperial prince Fushima Sadashige. In addition, he sculpted Buddhist images. He apparently went to Korea in 1424–25 to look for a Korean edition of the Tripitaka (Buddhist writings). Sesshū Tōyō was his main disciple.
- Painter (fourteenth–fifteenth century) in the style of Chinese artists, who was nicknamed Tō no Shūbun. Because he married a woman from the Soga family, he was also called Soga Shūbun.
- Painter (mid-sixteenth century); nothing is known about his life. He painted in the Muromachi *suiboku-ga* style.

Shuchō. Era of Emperor Temmu: June 686–Sept. 686. *See* NENGŌ.

Shūchō. Painter (Tamagawa Shūchō, late eighteenth century) of ukiyo-e prints, Bunchō's (Ippitsu-sai) disciple. He made prints in the Utamaro style.

Shūei. Buddhist monk (d. 884) of the Shingon-shū, Enchin's disciple. He was in China from 862 to 866, then was appointed *chōja* of the Tōdai-ji temple in Heian-kyō.

Shufu no Tomo. "The Housewife's Friend," first women's magazine published in Japan, founded by Ishikawa Takeyoshi in 1917. It is still widely read.

Also, the name of a major Japanese publishing house.

• **Shufuren.** "Association of Japanese House-wives" (Shufu Rengōkai), founded in 1948 by Oku Mumeo to improve the quality of life of women in the home. It became a major political organization and served as a guide for consumers and an adviser on environmental problems.

Shūgaishō. "Collection of Dust," a three-volume encyclopedia classifying subjects in 99 categories, compiled in the Kamakura period by one or several unknown authors, perhaps Tōin Kinkata. It is a valuable source of information on life in the imperial court in the late twelfth century.

Shugaku-in Rikyū. "Shugakuin Detached Palace." Imperial villa and gardens constructed from 1656 to 1659 by Emperor Go-Mizunoo at the foot of Mt. Hiei, northeast of Kyoto, including a "high villa" and a "low villa." After 1680, Go-Mizunoo's daughter, Ake no Miya, added a monastery for Buddhist nuns, the Rinkyū-ji. Most of the pavilions in the grouping are in the *suki-ya* style and are sparsely decorated. The Rokushiken is decorated with paintings by Sumiyoshi Gukei (1631–1705) and Maruyama Ōkyo. The gardens, in rustic style *(shakkei),* were designed to look completely natural. They belong to the imperial family and can be visited only with permission.

Shugei Shuchi-in. Private school founded by Kūkai in 828 in Heian-kyō to teach Buddhism and Confucianism to children of commoners. It was closed when Kūkai died in 835 because no one wanted to be responsible for it. *See also* DAIGAKURYŌ, KOKUGAKU.

Shugendō. Group of more or less syncretic cults belonging to the Tendai-shū and the Shingon-shū, and combining the teachings of these sects with folk beliefs mixed with Taoism. Created, according to legend, by En no Gyōja (sixth century), the Shugendō movement developed mainly in the twelfth century, drawing many *hijiri* and Yamabushi who worshiped in the mountains and who had been organized into groups since the Heian period under the authority of a type of priest called *sendatsu.*

Members of Shugendō practice various forms of asceticism—such as climbing mountains (*nyūbu* or *mineiri*) and praying under cold waterfalls—which are intended to reveal to them their true inner nature and make them similar to a buddha. Many also practice a sort of witchcraft and use magical-religious practices, including mudras (*i-zō,* hand gestures), to obtain "powers." The main centers of worship are the Kimbusen-ji on Mt. Ōmine, the Kongō-san, the Kumano and Dewa Sanzan shrines, and others. The practices were originally kept secret: they were made public in the seventeenth century. Because the Shugendō sects were affiliated with the Shingon-shū or the Tendai-shū and were not recognized independently by the 1873 law, they were effectively banned. They were revived in 1946, and have expanded somewhat since. Also called Sangaku-bukkyō ("mountain Buddhism"). *See* YAMABUSHI.

• **Shugendō-kyo.** Subsect of the Taisei-kyō, founded in 1946 by Kawashima Tetsuzō (1897–1956).

• **Shugen-ichijitsu Shintō.** *See* REISO SHINTŌ.

• **Shugenja.** *See* YAMABUSHI.
→ *See* ARAGYŌ.

Shūgetsu. Painter (Shūgetsu Tōkan, Tōkan; *mei:* Takashiro Gon no Kami, Taki Kantō, Takagi Gon no Kami, ca. 1427–ca. 1510); he became a Buddhist monk in 1462. He studied *suiboku* under Sesshū, then worked for the Shimazu family in Satsuma. After living in China from 1494 to 1497, he returned to his monastery, the Fukushō-ji, in Satsuma. He painted landscapes in the Chinese style *(kara-yō)* with the *haboku* technique, portraits in the Yamato-e style, and pictures of flowers and birds.

• Painter (Hara Shūgetsu, mid-eighteenth century) and sculptor of netsuke in Osaka and Edo. His descendants also signed their netsuke with the *go* Shūgetsu.

Shūgi-bukuro. Decorated envelope, used mainly to present cash in a way that it is hidden from view, to avoid offending the recipient. According to this ancient custom, still in use, the envelope is adorned with a *noshi.* All celebratory festivals, as well as the gifts given on these occasions, are called *shūgi;* at funerals, these gifts are called *bu-shūgi* or *kōden.* The wages of geisha and tips are also called *shūgi.* *See* GIFTS.

Shūgi-in. "House of Representatives," constituting, with the House of Peers (Kizoku-in), the Imperial Parliament starting in 1889. Since 1946, it and the Chamber of Councillors (Sangi-in) have been part of the National Diet (Kokkai). Its members are elected for four years. Unlike the Chamber of Councillors, however, it cannot be dissolved. It currently has about 511 representatives.

Shugo. During the Kamakura period, military governor of a *shōen* or a province, representing the shogun. The *shugo* had limited authority and were required to defer to the *bakufu* or the shogun himself on serious or important issues. The *shugo* assisted the *kokushi* appointed by the emperor and were specifically in charge of recruiting soldiers and maintaining public order. Only warriors from Kanto could become *shugo*.

• **Shugo-daimyō.** In the Muromachi period, provincial lords who had been made *shugo* by the Ashikaga shogunate and who expanded their territorial possessions and power to the point that they were considered daimyo. Many of them took advantage of the disorder of the Sengoku period to become quasi-independent, as many *jitō* and owners of *shōen* sought their protection. Among the most important *shugo-daimyō* at the time were the Hosokawa, Shiba, Katakeyama, Ōuchi, Imagawa Takeda, Yamana, and Ōtomo. Those who were defeated during the Sengoku disappeared, leaving room for larger-scale daimyo, called Sengoku-*daimyō*. *See also* DAIKAN, GEKOKUJŌ.

Shugo-kokkai-shō. "Writings for Protection of the Kingdom," a theoretical religious text written by Saichō (Dengyō Daishi) in 818. In this three-section work, Saichō refuted the arguments advanced by the Hossō-shū school.

Shūhō. Zen Buddhist monk (Myōchō, Sōhō Myōchō, Kōzen, Daitō Kokushi, 1282–1337) and famous calligrapher, founder of the Daitoku-ji temple of the Rinzai sect. He was the disciple of Nampo Shōmyō (1235–1308), a student of Rankei Dōryū.
• Painter (Ishida Shūhō, nineteenth century), born in Ōmi, Kayō's student.

Shūhō Kannon. One of the 33 forms (*see* SANJŪSAN ŌGESHIN) of Kannon Bosatsu, said to have given treasures to his followers.

Shūhō-sha. Special pavilion to which emperors withdrew during storms and typhoons. Also called Kaminari no Tsubo.

Shūi. Painter (*gō*: Mutō, active ca. 1349) of the Muromachi *suiboku* school, Musō Kokushi's disci-

ple. A Zen monk, he painted mainly portraits of monks.

Shuinsen bōeki. From 1590 to 1635, trading ships that had permission (*shuinjō*), symbolized by a "vermilion seal" (*shuin*), to trade between Japanese ports and those in Southeast Asia and the Philippines. This control over trade enabled Hideyoshi and the Tokugawa to eliminate pirates (*wakō*). There were about 350 licenses of this type granted to merchants of the shogunate, to other merchants sponsored by daimyo, and sometimes to Europeans. The ships made a large number of trips: 73 to Cochin-China, 47 to Annam, 44 to Cambodia, 55 to Siam, 54 to Luzon (Philippines), and 36 to Taiwan. Merchandise exported consisted mainly of silver, copper, iron, sulfur, and Japanese crafts (swords). The ships returned to Japan with silk, spices, medicinal plants, and some objets d'art and various crafts. *See* CHAYA SHIROJIRŌ.

Shūi waka-shū. Third imperial anthology (*see* CHOKUSEN WAKA-SHŪ), compiled between 995 and 998 by Fujiwara no Kintō (and perhaps also by Retired Emperor Kazan) and supplemented around 1007. It contains 1,351 *waka* poems in 20 scrolls. Also called *Shūi-shū.*

Shūkei. Painter (Watanabe Kiyoshi; *mei*: Daisuke; *gō*: Setchōsai, Shūkei, 1778–1861) of the Fukko Yamato-e school; he studied with Hidenobu, Mitsusada, and Totsugen in Nagoya.

Shūki. *See* OKAMOTO SHŪKI.

Shukke. Type of Buddhist painting portraying Prince Siddhartha Gautama (the future Shakyamuni Buddha) leaving his family to go in search of Truth. *See* ZAIKE.

Shukkō. System under which employees in a company can be transferred to a secondary firm or a subsidiary during a recession or as a promotion or punishment. Such transfers also take place when an employee needs additional training. In recessions, employees are not laid off and remain with the company, even though their salary drops. When conditions have returned to normal, the company offers a salary compensation.

Shuko. Painter (*mei*: Murata Mokichi; *gō*: Kōrakuan, Nansei, Dokuryoken, Shuko, 1422–1502) of the Muromachi *suiboku* school, Gei-ami's student.

He was also a master *(chajin)* of the tea ceremony *(chanoyu)* at the Daitoku-ji temple in Kyoto.

Shuku-eki. "Post towns" established on the main roads in the Edo period, comprising an inn, a teahouse, and a horse-relay point. Peasants in nearby villages were responsible for maintaining the *shuku-eki.* Often, a guard post was added to control travelers and the merchandise they were transporting. Many of today's cities developed around these post towns, which played an important role in communications. Also called *shukuba. See* GO-KAIDŌ, SEKISHO, SUKEGO.

Shukushin. Japanese name for a group of pirates on the northeast coast of China. In 660, Empress Seimei launched an expedition against them, led by Abe no Hirafu. *See* MISHIHASE, WAKŌ.

Shumboku. *See* ŌOKA SHUNBOKU.

Shumbun. Spring equinox, around March 21, formerly called Chū-nichi Ō-Higan, Ō-Higan. *Chin.:* Chunfen. *See* NIJŪSHI-SETSU.

Shūmin. Sculptor (Hara Shūmin, late eighteenth century) of Noh masks *(nōmen)* and netsuke; Shuzan's student.
• Netsuke sculptor (mid-nineteenth century), Shūgetsu III's student.

Shumman. Painter (Kubota Yasubei; *gō:* Kubo Shumman, Issetsu Senjō, Kōzandō, Nandaka-shiran, Shōsadō, Sashōdō, Shiokarabō, 1757–1820) of ukiyo-e prints; studied with Nahiko and Shigemasa in Edo. He made many prints in the *beni-girai* and *surimono* genres, and illustrated *kyōka.* He was also a *kyōka* poet.

Shummei. Painter (Igarashi Shummei; *azana:* Hō-toku; *gō:* Kohō, Chikuken, Bokuō, Shummei, 1700–81) who studied with Ryoshin and was influenced by Chinese painters. He worked in Niigata and Kyoto.

Shūmon aratame. In the Edo period, a type of religious inquisition aimed at extirpating Christianity from Japan. When people suspected of being Christian were discovered, they were forced to apostasize on pain of death. To facilitate the search for Christians, the Japanese population was forced to sign registers *(Shūmon nimbetsu aratame-chō)* kept in Buddhist temples, even if they did not belong to a sect; the temples then became guarantors *(terauke)* of their good faith. Sometimes, suspects were forced to step on an image of the Virgin Mary or a cross *(fumi-e)* to show that they were not Christian. These measures were used most frequently on Kyushu, where conversions had been very numerous in the late sixteenth century, especially in Nagasaki. They were not completely effective, however, since many Christians (Kakure Kirishitan) continued to worship in secrecy. The persecution stopped only in 1873.

Shunchō. Painter of ukiyo-e prints (Katsukawa Shunchō; *mei:* Kichizaemon; *gō:* Yūbundō, Shien, Kissadō, Kichisadō, Tōshien, Chūrinsha, Yūshidō, active 1780–90), Shunshō's student. He painted mainly landscapes and beautiful women *(bijin).* He also wrote several stories.
→ *See* KOIKAWA HARUMACHI, SHUNSHŌ.

Shun'e. Buddhist monk (1113–ca. 1190) at the Tō-dai-ji temple in Nara and poet; Minamoto no Toshi-yori's son. He was the master of Fujiwara no To-shinari (Shunzei) and Kamo no Chōmei. His poems, profoundly influenced by a sense of *yūgen,* were preserved in a collection that he compiled in 1178, *Rin'yō-shū* (Collection of Leaves from the Forest), and 84 other poems are in various imperial anthologies (*see* CHOKUSEN WAKA-SHŪ).

Shun'ei. Painter (Isoda Kyūjirō; *gō:* Katsukawa Shun'ei, Kyūtokusai, Shun'ei, 1762–1819) of ukiyo-e prints, Shunshō's student in Edo. He painted portraits of Kabuki actors, theater scenes, and sumo wrestlers.

• *Shun'ei.* Noh play: two brothers captured in battle are to be beheaded. But one of them, to save the other, claims that they are not related. Both are pardoned.

Shunga. Buddhist monk (thirteenth century), painter of Buddhist images at the Jingo-ji and Kōzan-ji in Kyoto.
• "Images of spring," a poetic term for erotic paintings (which are now usually called *higa,* "secret images"). The Japanese, who feel that sexual relations are as normal a part of everyday life as eating and drinking, have never had taboos about sex, and it has been a common subject for painters. Illustrated books on various sexual practices were published during the Nara period, to be used both by individuals and by physicians, and are now called *osokuzu no e* (pictures of positions). A famous picture book *(emakimono)* of erotic images by Toba

Sōjō, *Yōbutsu kurabe* (Contest of the Phalluses), showing the intimate frolics of nobles in the imperial court, and the late-twelfth-century *Koshibagaki-zōshi* are among the first well-known *emakimono* in the genre. The oldest *shunga* that has survived to the present is *Chigo no sōshi*, dating from 1321 (now kept in the Sambō-in of the Daigo-ji temple in Kyoto). Erotic art took on a new dimension with the advent of ukiyo-e prints in the Edo period, and many major artists produced series of erotic (sometimes frankly pornographic) images after 1660. Moronobu, Torii Kiyonaga, Okumura Masanobu, Ippitsusai Bunchō, and especially Utamaro and Utagawa Kuniyoshi were renowned for their *ukiyo-e shunga*. Painters from other schools also painted *shunga*. In modern times, under the influence of Anglo-Saxon Puritanism, the art of *shunga* has disappeared, replaced by pornographic photography.

Shungyōsai. Painter (Hayami Tsuneaki; *mei:* Genzaburō, ?–1823) of ukiyo-e prints and book illustrator in Osaka. He illustrated the *Shagaku seisō*, a translation from Chinese of *Shexue zhengzong*, the standard book on archery by Gao Yingshu (ca. 1061). Recommended by Ogyū Sorai, it became the bedside book for all archers in Japan starting in the eighteenth century.

Shunjō. Buddhist monk (1166–1227) of the Shingon and Jōdo sects. He was in China from 1199 to 1211; when he returned, he preached the doctrines of the Ritsu-shū. *Posthumous name:* Getsurin Daishi.
→ *See* SHUNSHŌ.

• **Shunjōbō Jūgen.** Buddhist monk (?–1206) of the Shingon-shū, Genkū's disciple. He left for China in 1167 and returned the following year with Eisai. In 1203, he rebuilt the Tōdai-ji in Nara, and he founded other temples dedicated to the worship of Amida.

Shunkan. Buddhist monk (ca. 1142–1179?) of the Shingon sect and *bettō* (administrator) of the Hosshō-ji in Shirakawa (Kyoto). A member of the Minamoto family, he plotted with Retired Emperor Go-Shirakawa to drive Taira no Kiyomori from Kyoto. The plot was discovered, and Shunkan was exiled to an island in Kagoshima Bay in 1177. The other conspirators were granted amnesty the following year, but not Shunkan. This episode was the subject of a Noh play called *Shunkan* or *Kikai ga shima,* by Zeami Motokiyo (1363–1443), and of a

novel *(Shunkan sōzu shima monogatari)* by Kyokutei Bakin.

Shunkei-nuri. Decoration technique consisting of applying translucent lacquer to a base of stained wood. Also called *noshiro-nuri. See* TAKAYAMA.

Shunkin. Painter (Uragami Ken; *azana:* Hakukyo; *gō:* Suian, Bunkyōtei, Shunkin, 1779–1846) of the Nanga (Bunjinga) school, who studied with his father, Gyokudō.

Shunkō. Painter (Katsukawa Shunkō; *gō;* Sahitsuan, d. ca. 1827) of ukiyo-e prints, Shunshō's student in Edo.
• Painter (Kiyokawa Denjirō, 1743–1812) of ukiyo-e prints, Shunshō's student. He painted with his left hand after 1788, making mainly portraits.

Shunkyo. Painter (Yamamoto Kin'emon, 1871–1933) who studied with Nomura Bunkyo and Kansai in Kyoto.

Shun'oku Myōka. Zen Buddhist monk (ca. 1311–88) of the Rinzai sect, member of the Taira family, from Kai province. He was one of Musō Kokushi's collaborators and a leader of the *gozan.*

Shunsa. Painter (Tachihara Kuri; *azana:* Sasa, 1818–58) of the Nanga (Bunjinga) school; she studied with her father, Kyōsho, and with Kazana in Kaga.

Shunshō. Painter (Katsumiyagawa, Katsukawa Shunshō; *mei:* Yūsuke; *gō:* Jūgasei, Ririn, Yūji, Kyokurōsei, Rokurokuan, 1726–92) who studied with Mitagawa Chōshun and Shunsui in Edo. A designer of ukiyo-e prints of the Torii school, he later renounced this style and painted portraits of Kabuki actors, sumo wrestlers, and beautiful women *(bijin)* in a very long, narrow format *(hashira-e).* In his youth, he signed his work with a stamp in the shape of a gourd enclosing the character for "forest"; later, he signed his various names. He had a great number of students, among them Shunkō, Shun'ei, Shunjō, Shundō, Shunchō, Shunzan, Hokusai, and Harunobu.

Shunshoku ume-goyomi. Four-volume novel in the *ninjō-bon* genre by Tamenaga Shunsui, published in 1832–33. It describes the customs of Yoshiwara, the pleasure district of Edo, and the love life of the city's middle class.

Shunsui. Painter (Katsukawa Shunsui, Miyagawa Shunsui; *mei:* Tōshirō, late eighteenth century) of ukiyo-e prints; he studied with his father, Chōshun.

Shuntei. Painter (Katsukawa Shuntei, 1770–1820) of ukiyo-e prints, Shun'ei's disciple.

Shunten. Japanese name for one of the first sovereigns of the Ryukyu Islands, who ruled in the 36th generation after Tenson; perhaps, according to tradition, one of Minamoto no Tametomo's sons. Also known by the name Tenson. *Chin.:* Shuntian. *See* RIYŪ, RYŪKYŪ.

Shun'yō-kai. Art society created in 1922 by non-academic painters (according to the standards of the time) who rejected the Nihonga style, especially followers of Yōga. Among its most famous members were Kosugi Misei (1881–1964), Morita Tsunetomo (1881–1933), Adachi Gen'ichirō (1889–1973), Hasegawa Noboru (1886–1973), Kurata Hakuyō (1881–1938), Yamamoto Kanae (1882–1946), and painters of various other schools, such as Ishii Tsuruzō (1887–1973), Kishida Ryūsei (1891–1929), and Umehara Ryūzaburō (1888–1986), all of whom claimed complete creative freedom and painted in oils.

Shunzan. Painter (Katsukawa Shunzan, active 1781–1800) of ukiyo-e prints, Shunsō's student.

Shura. In Buddhist mythology, the world of the Titans or asuras, one of the *rokudō* (six worlds that were the destinations of transmigration).

Shuraku. Metal engraver and sculptor of netsuke (early nineteenth century).
• Sculptor of netsuke and *okimono* (Kawamoto, late nineteenth century) in wood and ivory.

Shuramono. Type of Noh play featuring warriors and describing a battle in which the role of the oldest warrior is played by the *shite*.

Shuri. Capital of the *anji* and kings of Okinawa and the Ryukyu Islands, east of the city of Naha, starting in the fifteenth century. Ruins of a castle probably built soon after 1422 by King Shō Hashi of Chūsan, and expanded during the eras of kings Shō Shin and Shō Sei in the sixteenth century. The castle (called Gusuku in Okinawa) was destroyed during the Second World War. The site is now considered a national shrine. Formerly called Sukuri.
→ *See* SANRAKU.

Shuriken. Throwing weapons used in Japan since at least the eleventh century, and by *ninja* in the Edo period. They were steel blades about 20 cm long *(bō-shuriken)* whose shape differed depending on the martial-arts school; some were shaped like a star with four (or more) sharp points *(shaken)*. *Shuriken* were generally thrown in bunches. Other types, resembling needles *(fumibari),* were hidden in the mouth and then spit into the face of an adversary. *Shuriken* sometimes had a hole in the center so that they could be attached to each other *(semban-shuriken)*. They were used mainly in the Aizu, Mito, and Sendai regions, where special schools (Tagyū, Tsugawa, Shirai) taught how to throw them. *See* NINJA.

Shurin. Japanese term for the typhoon season, with abundant rain, beginning in mid-September and ending in late October.

Shurō. In Buddhist temples and monasteries, a structure that shelters a bell with no clapper *(shō)*. Also called *shōrō*.

Shūsei-kyō. During the Meiji era, one of the 13 official Shinto sects influenced by Confucianism, whose members included about 45,000 ultranationalist followers before the Second World War. Headquarters in Tokyo.

• **Shūsei-sha.** Syncretic Shinto sect founded in 1873 by Nitta Kunimitsu.

Shūseki. Painter (Watanabe Shūseki; *azana:* Genshō; *gō:* Jinjusai, Randōjin, Enka, Chikyū, Shūseki, 1639–1707) of the Nanga (Bunjinga) school, Itsunen's student in Nagasaki. He painted mainly landscapes.

Shushi. Shinto priest responsible for exorcisms. Some *shushi* dances inspired those in Noh theater. *See* KANNUSHI.
• Japanese name for the Confucian philosopher Xhuxi (1130–1200).

• **Shushi-gaku.** Philosophical school based on the neo-Confucian teachings of Zhu Xi *(Jap.:* Shushi) and his concept of the duality of *ri (Chin.: li)* and *ki (Chin.: qi)*. *Ri* is considered to be the immutable principle of everything (and thus cannot create), and *ki* is another active principle, which, by its movement and union with *ri*, produces the interactions of Yin and Yang *(Jap.:* In and Yō) that determine the shape and nature of everything that exists in the world. This doctrine was introduced to Japan during the Kamakura period and studied by Zen monks of the *gozan,* who transformed it somewhat by considering that *ri* and *ki* formed an indissoluble whole. This theory was officially adopted by philosophers of the Edo shogunate, including Yamazaki Anzan and Asami Keisai. It emphasized loyalty *(chū)* and filial piety *(kō)* and facilitated a sort of syncretism between Shinto and Confucianism.

Shūshin. Painter (seventeenth century) of the Kanō school, Eisen's master and father. He belonged to the Kobikichō branch of the Kanō school in Edo.
• Concept drawn from Confucius's *Analects* requiring that each individual control his or her conduct. Taught in schools in 1890, it led to an education based on fidelity, friendship, and hard work. It was then taken up by nationalist military officers to exalt civic and military virtues.

Shu Shunsui. Chinese scholar (Zhu Shunshui, 1600–82) who, having remained faithful to the Ming dynasty, expatriated himself to Japan in 1644 and settled in Nagasaki. Invited to Mito by Tokugawa Mitsukuni, he taught Confucianism and many Chinese techniques there.

Shussan no Shaka. In Buddhist iconography, an image showing the Buddha "leaving the mountain"— that is, abandoning his ascetic practices to adopt a middle path of deliverance. Also called Shussanbutsu, Shutsuzan.

Shusse Kagekiyo. Playwright (seventeenth century) who wrote *jōruri.* His works had a great influence on Chikamatsu Monzaemon.

Shutamba. In Kabuki theater, a scene during which two characters separate.

Shūto (or shuto). In ancient Japan, low-ranking Buddhist monks, generally used as temple guardians and, by extension, as warriors. Also called *sōhei.*

Shūtoku. *See* IKEI SHŪTOKU.

Shūzan. Painter (Yoshimura Shūzan, d. 1776) from Osaka, Kanō Tan'yū's student, and a sculptor of netsuke.
• Sculptor of netsuke (eighteenth–nineteenth century), the above Shūzan's student.
• Name of a number of sculptors of netsuke from Osaka and Niigata.

• Japanese name of a Chinese Chan monk (926–93) who went to Japan to teach.

Shuzen-ji. Small town in Shizuoka prefecture, on the Kanō-gawa river, and a well-known hot spring since the Edo period. Shogun Minamoto no Yoriie was assassinated at the Buddhist temple of the same name in 1204.

• *Shuzenji monogatari.* Title of a famous Kabuki play by Okamoto Kidō (1872–1939) in the *jidai-mono* genre, produced for the first time in 1911, telling of the events that took place at the Shuzen-ji temple.

Sidotti, Giovanni Battista. Sicilian Catholic priest (1668–1714) who, defying the ban by the Edo shogunate, landed on the island of Yakushima (Ryukyu Islands) in 1708 from the Philippines. Soon captured, he was sent to Nagasaki, then to Edo, and questioned by Arai Hakuseki. Imprisoned in the Kirishitan Yashiki, he managed to convert two of his jailers. He was then placed in a hole in the ground so that he could not communicate with the outside world. He died on November 28, 1714.

Siebold, Philipp Franz von. German physician (1796–1866), born in Würtzburg. As an employee of the Dutch East India Company, he was sent to Dejima (Nagasaki) in 1923, where he opened a school of "Dutch science" *(rangaku)* in Narutaki, near Nagasaki, and began to collect Japanese objects, which he received in payment for his teaching. He went to Edo in 1826 to meet the shogun and became friends with astronomers Takahashi Kageyasu, Inō Tadataka, and Mogami Tokunai, who gave him information on Hokkaido and the Ainu. Accused of spying for Russia and of having illegally procured a map of Japan, he was expelled in December 1829; leaving his Japanese mistress, Kasumoto Sonogi, and his daughter, Ine (1827–1903), in Japan, he returned to Batavia and the Netherlands. He was then ennobled by the court. In 1859, he returned to Japan with his son, Alexander (having in the meantime married a German woman), and lived there until 1863. His collections were bought by the Dutch government, and he introduced to the Netherlands more than a thousand plants harvested in Japan. He wrote a number of books on his time in Japan and his research there, among them *Fauna Japonica* (5 vols., 1833–50) and *Nippon, Archiv zur Beschreibung von Japan* (published 1938–58).

Sima Dadeng. *Chin.:* Szu-ma Ta-teng. *See* KURA-TSUKURIBE NO TORI, SHIBA TATTO.

Sino-Japanese wars. The first of these wars (Imjin no Ran) took place following Toyotomi Hideyoshi's invasion of Korea in 1592. *See* TOYOTOMI HIDE-YOSHI.

The purpose of the second (Nisshin Sensō) was to take control of the Korean Peninsula. It took place in 1894–95 and was ended by the Treaty of Shimonoseki.

The third, and longest, was started by the incident on the Marco Polo Bridge (July 7, 1937), though war was never officially declared. The Japanese captured Shanghai in the fall of 1937, reached Yanzi-jiang in November, and took Nanjing in December. Canton and Hangzhou fell in October 1938. But the Eighth Chinese Army, led by Mao Zedong, halted the Japanese advance in late 1938. Japan occupied eastern China until 1945, even though its forces were defeated in July 1942, by Mao Zedong in Jianxi. The end of the Second World War also saw the end of the Sino-Japanese War and the complete withdrawal of imperial troops.

Sladen, Douglas Brooke Wheelton. English writer (1856–1947), born in London. He visited Japan in 1889–90 and wrote an account of his trip, *The Japs at Home* (1892), and some articles on Japan.

Smedley, John. Australian architect and painter (1841–1903), born in Sydney; William Dexter's student. He worked as an architect in Hong Kong, then went to Japan in 1869, visiting Yokohama, Kobe, and Tokyo. From 1872 to 1876, he designed many buildings in Yokohama. When he returned to Japan, from 1877 to 1880, he designed the buildings of the Russian legation; in 1878–79, he also taught architecture at the University of Tokyo. He returned to Japan yet again in 1891 and painted a number of watercolors. He died in Hankou, China.

Sō. During the Muromachi period, an administrative unit corresponding to a village, often independent of the *shōen*, and organized by *myōshū* and *hyakushō.* Also called *sōchu, sōshō, sōmura.*
• Unconventional art style, opposed to the more formal style called *shin. See* GYŌ, SHIN.
• Japanese name for the Chinese Song dynasty (Nansō: Nan-Song; Sō: Bei Song).
• Family of *shugo* (military governors) of the island of Tushima (Nagasaki prefecture) in the Kamakura period. They fought against the Korean Mon-

gols (Mōkō) in 1274 and 1281, then the pirates *(wakō)* in 1419. Having helped Toyotomi Hideyoshi with his invasion of Korea in 1592, they received large estates and were elevated to the rank of daimyo. They were the natural intermediaries between Korea and Japan throughout the Edo period.

Sō-ami. Painter (Shinsō; *gō:* Kangaku, ca. 1455–1525), Gei-ami's son and Nō-ami's grandson (*see* AMI-HA), employed as archives curator for shogun Ashikaga Yoshimasa. He painted landscapes in the *suiboku* style and designed many gardens, including those at the Ryō'an-ji and Daitoku-ji in Kyoto. He also painted in the Mokkei (*Chin.:* Muqi) style and in the "flowers and birds" genre, thus inaugurating the Bunjinga school in Japan. Much admired by his contemporaries, he was a master *(chajin)* of the tea ceremony and the art of flower arranging *(ikebana).* He also dabbled in poetry, and wrote a sort of critical catalogue of the shogun's collection, *Kundaikan sō choki* (1511); a work on decoration, *Goshoku-ki;* and a document on exhibiting objects, *Okazari-ki* (1524).

Sōban. In architecture, a base made of wood or stone supporting a structure's pillars. *Chin.: zhu-chu.*

Soba-yōnin. Grand chamberlain responsible for transmitting messages between the Edo shogun and the *rōjū;* this position was created in 1681.

Sobokai-yaki. Type of ceramics made in Owari under the auspices of daimyo Tokugawa Mitsutomo, around 1630, by a potter named Katō Kagamasa (or Katō Tōzaburō). This pottery resembles biscuit with a grayish-white varnish.

Sōchō. Zen Buddhist monk (Sōkan, 1448–1532) from Suruga province, who in 1476 became Ikkyū's disciple at the Daitoku temple in Kyoto, then Sōgi's disciple. He was known mainly for his *renga* poems; he helped Sōgi compile the *Shinsen tsukuba-shū* (1495). His own *renga* collections are titled *Kabe-kusa* (Grass on the Wall, 1512), *Nachigomori* (Retreat to Nachi, 1517), and *Oi no mimi* (An Old Man's Ear, 1526). He is also credited with compiling an anthology of songs called *Kangin-shū* (Collection of Airs for the Hours of Leisure).

Society and religion. The Japanese have always been influenced by religious beliefs, both indigenous ones such as Shinto and those imported from

Korea and China, such as Buddhism, Taoism, and Confucianism.

Shinto is the "natural" religion of Japan, with its origins in shamanic beliefs brought by groups of horsemen from Siberia, via Korea, in the late third century. These beliefs were mixed with what were probably animist beliefs of the earliest inhabitants of the islands of Japan, which consisted of veneration of *kami,* or forces of nature, representing life in all of its forms, and which placed great importance on the "impurities" of lack of respect for nature and death. Shinto (religion of spirits) does not conceive of life after death; when Buddhism was imported, about 538, it complemented Shinto by contributing metaphysics and a sense of the impermanence of all things. From a mixture of these beliefs arose an ethic of individualistic thought, to which Confucianism (the first elements of which arrived in Japan well before Buddhism) added an ethic of social and political conduct. Aspects of Taoism that came along at the same time influenced popular beliefs but had no real influence on society.

At first an aristocratic religion, Buddhism, as it was spread among the common people, became associated with Shinto in a sort of folk syncretism. While Shinto strongly encouraged the Japanese to practice a "moral" pragmatism, Buddhism, through simplified doctrines, brought a hope for life after death that tended to provide comfort in the face of life's misfortunes. From this came two paths of moral conduct: the relatively materialistic one of Shinto, and one of passive acceptance of human destiny. From then on, Japanese society constantly wavered between one pole and the other, each Japanese person being in essence (and by the very fact of having been born in Japan, land of the *kami*) Shinto, while also being Buddhist, or sometimes Christian. Confucianism "framed" the various beliefs of the population and enabled leaders to create the hierarchies that remain one of the characteristics of Japanese society today. It is this religious synthesis that has given the Japanese their multifaceted character and that has enabled them to overcome social and political crises.

Sōda Kiichirō. Economist (1881–1927), born in Yokohama. He studied neo-Kantian philosophy in Germany and created a philosophy of economics named after him (Sōda philosophy), which he expounded in his works *Geld und Wert* (Money and Values, 1909) and *Keizai tetsugaku no shomondai* (Problems in Philosophy of Economics, 1917). He was elected a member of the House of Peers in 1925.

Sōdei-sha. Art movement started in 1944 to revive the art of ceramics, succeeding the Mingei Undō movement.

Sōdoku. Skin disease, common in China and Japan, caused by a spirochete transferred to humans by rat bites.

Sōdōmei. Abridgment of Nihon Rōdō Sōdōmei (Japanese Federation of Labor), a union federation founded in 1912 as Yūaikai (Friendship Association) and reorganized in 1919 and 1921, then in 1946 by Nishio Suehirō, after having been dissolved in 1940. It was divided into several factions in 1950 and dissolved in 1964 because most of its members had joined Dōmei (Japanese Confederation of Labor).

Sō Doshin. Zen Buddhist monk (Nakano Michiomi, b. 1911), creator in Kobe of a style of martial arts, *Shōrinji-kempō,* inspired by Chinese techniques. Also called Kanchō-sensei.

Soejima. Name sometimes used for the Soga family in the sixth and seventh centuries.

• **Soejima Sōkai.** Poet (1827–1907) from Kyushu, writing in Chinese, and calligrapher.

• **Soejima Taneomi.** Politician (1828–1905), born on the Saga estate, and leader of the anti-shogunal movement in Saga province. In 1868, he was appointed a councillor *(san'yo)* and wrote, with Fukuoka Takachika, the first Constitution *(Setaisho)* of the Meiji era. He was minister of foreign affairs while Iwakura was on his mission and was made ambassador to Beijing in 1873. Having subscribed to Saigō Takamori's views on Korea, he resigned from the government and formed the Aikoku party with Itagaki Taisuke. He was briefly minister of the interior in Matsukata Masayoshi's cabinet in 1892.

Sōen. Buddhist monk (Josui Sōen, active ca. 1495–99) and painter in Sesshū's style in Kamakura, where he was *zōsu* of the Engaku-ji temple.

Sōfuku-ji. Buddhist temple built in Nagasaki (Kyushu) in 1629 for the Obaku sect, in the Chinese Ming-dynasty style. Also called "Nanjing temple."

Soga. Powerful clan in the sixth and seventh centuries. In opposition to the Mononobe and Nakatomi families, the Soga clan wanted to impose Buddhism as a state religion. Many of its members were ministers; the most famous was Soga no Iname. However, they were supplanted by the Fujiwara (Tachibana) family after the assassination of Soga no Umako's sons and the Battle of Shigisan in 587. Also called Soejima.

- **Soga brothers.** *See* SOGA SUKENARI.

- **Soga no Emishi.** *See* SOGA NO IRUKA.

- **Soga no Iname.** Minister (?–570) under emperors Senka and Kimmei. Having received Buddhist statues from Korea, he built the first Buddhist temple in Japan, the Kōgen-ji, in his house. He was given the title Ō-ōmi ("master of clan leaders").

- **Soga no Iruka.** Senior bureaucrat (?–645), Soga no Emishi's (d. 645) son. He supported Prince Tamura's candidacy for the throne in 628, against Prince Shōtoku, who proposed his own son, Yamashiro no Ōe. Soga no Iruka then installed Emperor Jōmei's widow, Kōgyoku, as empress, and forced Yamashiro no Ōe to commit suicide in 643. But Prince Naka no Ōe conspired with Nakatomi no Kamatari against Soga no Iruka and his father Soga no Emishi, and had Soga no Iruka assassinated. Soga no Emishi committed suicide and Empress Kōgyoku was deposed. Naka no Ōe became Emperor Tenji.

- **Soga no Umako.** Minister (d. 626), Soga no Iname's son. In 587, he fought the Mononobe family, which opposed the introduction of Buddhism, and he had Emperor Sushun assassinated in 592 in order to place his niece, Empress Suiko, on the throne. He collaborated effectively with the government of Shōtoku Taishi. The Ishibutai *kofun* in Asuka (Nara prefecture) is probably his tomb.

Soga-ha. School of painting founded by Soga Chokuan (*see* NICHOKUAN), a branch of the Muromachi *suiboku* school active from the fifteenth to the eighteenth century. Most painters of this school were Zen Buddhist monks of the Daitoku-ji temple in Kyoto. Its most famous artists were Chokuan and his son, Nichokuan.

Soga Jasoku. *See* JASOKU.

Sō-gaku. School of Chinese thought of the Song era, based on the neo-Confucian teachings of Zhu Xi (*Jap.*: Shushi). Also called Shushi-gaku.

Soganoya Gorō. Comic actor and playwright (Wada Hisakazu, 1877–1948), born in Sakai; he

and another Kabuki actor, Ōmatsu Fukumatsu (1869–1925), created a modern theater form. Soganoya Gorō wrote (under the pseudonym Ikkai Gyojin) more than 1,000 short comedies. Ōmatsu Fukumatsu (also called Soganoya Jūrō, in tribute to the Soga brothers; *see* SOGA SUKENARI) also wrote a large number.

Soga Shōhaku. Painter (Miura Shōhaku, 1730–81), perhaps born in Kyoto to a merchant family. He studied painting with Takada Keiho (1674–1755), who did not belong to any one school, and painted monochrome works (although he sometimes used color) in the style of Soga Dasoku (*see* DASOKU). His works are notable for the spontaneity of the brushstrokes.

Soga Sukenari. Warrior (Jurō, 1172–93), Itō Sukeyasu's son; his brother was Soga Tokimune (Gorō, 1174–93). Itō Sukeyasu had been assassinated by General Kudō Suketsune in 1177, and the brothers decided to avenge his death; they found the right moment 17 years later. Assisted by their faithful vassals, the Oniodoza brothers, they killed their enemy in Minamoto no Yoritomo's camp, then committed ritual suicide by *seppuku* on May 28, 1193. Their story has been told in novels and in Kabuki and Noh plays. *See also* KASAYAKI.

- *Soga monogatari.* Fourteenth-century epic novel telling of the vengeance of the Soga brothers. *See* SOGA SUKENARI.

Sogen Mugaku. Zen Buddhist monk from China (Zuyuan, 1226–86), who arrived in Japan in 1280. He was appointed abbot of the temple of the Rinzai Engaku-ji temple in Kamakura in 1282. *Posthumous name*: Bukkō Zenji.

Sōgetsu. Modern school of flower arranging (*ikebana*) founded by Teshigahara Sōfu in Tokyo in 1927. It is characterized by the use of a variety of materials and bark mixed with dried flowers. *See* TESHIGAHARA SŌFU.

Sōgi. Buddhist monk (Iio Sōgi, 1421–1502) and *renga* poet; not much is known about his life. He may have been the son of a Gigaku dancer in Ōmi province. He became a monk at the Shōkoku-ji Zen temple (Rinza-shū) in Kyoto and studied under Shinkei, Senjun, Sōzei, and Ichijō Kaneyoshi, all well-known *renga* poets. A protégé of the Ashikaga shogun, he traveled extensively on the Tōkaidō road and wrote many *renga* that were admired by his contemporaries. He often organized poetry contests and compiled, with his most faithful disciple, Sochō, the anthology *Shinsen tsukuba-shū* (1495). Among his other works are *Azuma-mondo,* a treatise on *renga* (1470); *Wasure-gusa* (ca. 1473); *Tuskushi no michi no ki* (A Voyage to Kyushu, 1480); *Minase sangin hyaku-in,* a sequence of 100 famous lines (1491); *Yuyama sangin hyaku-in* (1494), another collection of 100-line *renga.*

Sōgō. "Supervisors of the Buddhist Community," a corps of bureaucrats formed during the Nara period to oversee the activities of the temples.

• **Sōgō.** Department-store chain founded in Osaka about 1830, now with branches in all of Japan's main cities. Head office in Osaka.

Sōgyō-hachiman. Portrayal of the *kami* Hachiman as a Buddhist monk, common in the Heian and Kamakura periods in sects following the Honji-suijaku.

Sōhei. Painter (Takahashi U, 1804–34), Chikuden's student.
• Low-ranking monks employed by the large Buddhist temples and monasteries as guardians and, later, soldiers. Also called *shūto* (or *shuto*). See DŌSHŪ.

Sō-hitta. Technique of weaving and dyeing fabrics for kimonos in which the free threads formed the design of the fabric; each knot was attached to a silver needle and cut with tiny scissors *(hasami).* This very time-consuming and laborious procedure was banned in 1683 by the shogunate, which wanted to restrict purchases of luxurious clothing.

Sōhyō. Abridgment of Nihon Rōdō Kumiai Sō Hyōgikai (General Council of Trade Unions of Japan), a large labor federation with socialist leanings, founded in 1950 as an umbrella organization for office workers' unions. It has more than 4.5 million members belonging to more than 50 unions.

Sōji-ji. Zen Buddhist temple (Sōtō-shū sect), founded in Ishikawa by Keizan Jōkin (1268–1325) in 1321 and transported to Tsurumi, near Yokohama, in 1911. It and the Eihei-ji are the main temples of the Zen Sōtō sect.

Sō Jiseki. Painter (1712–86) in the Hokusō-ga style.

Sōjō. Former Buddhist title for abbots of many temples. See SŌ-KAN.

Sōjōbō. In Japanese legends, king of the *tengu* who gave swordfighting lessons to the young Minamoto no Yoshitsune on Mt. Kurama. He is portrayed with a long crow's beak and wings. Also called Dai Tengu Sōjōbō. See TENGU.

Sō-jutsu. Art of fighting with a lance *(yari),* still taught in some martial-arts schools attached to the *kobudō.* See KINOSHITA TOSHIMASA, YARI.

Sōka Gakkai. "Value-Creating Educational Society," a religious movement following the thought of Nichiren Shōshū, based on mutual assistance and devotion to the title of the *Lotus Sutra (Hokke-kyō).* It was founded in 1930 by Makiguchi Jōzaburō (Tsunasaburō), a teacher, who became its first president. Its main temple (Taiseki-ji) was established in Fujinomiya (Shizuoka prefecture).

At first called Sōka Kyōku Gakkai, the movement recruited its followers mainly from among teachers who were interested in Makiguchi's theories. In 1943, Makiguchi, his partner, Toda Jōsei, and some of their followers were thrown in prison for having preached non-veneration of the Shinto shrines and *kami.* Makiguchi died in prison on November 18, 1944; Toda Jōsei, freed in June 1945, began to reorganize Sōka Gakkai as its second president. When he died, in 1958, the movement had more than 1 million followers. The highly structured sect at first used "forced conversion" *(shakubuku),* with each member required to recruit another follower to faith in Nichiren. Claiming only to provide for the immediate well-being of its members, the sect conducted an intense propaganda campaign in Japan. Ikeda Daisaku succeeded Toda Jōsei, becoming the third president of Sōka Gakkai in May 1960, and worked to expand and gain an international audience, militating against war and advocating international cooperation in his books and through personal contacts with various notables in the worlds of the arts, literature, and politics. He resigned in 1979 to devote himself to his mission and was replaced by Hōjō Hiroshi (1923–81), then by Einosuke Akiya (b. 1930).

Sōka Gakkai supports many educational organizations and is constantly founding temples in Japan; it maintains a university with an international reputation (founded in 1971) and publishes works on Buddhism and pacifism and a daily newspaper, *Seikyō Shimbun,* with a print run of almost 5 million. From 1964 to 1970, it also supported a political party, the Kōmeitō (Clean Government party). Since 1972, it has held part ownership in the daily newspaper *Asahi Shimbun,* and it publishes several magazines, including *Seikyo Graphics* (weekly) and *Daibyaku Renge* (monthly). Sōka Gakkai now claims to have more than 20 million followers in Japan. It separated from the Nichiren-Shoshu sect in 1989. It proselytizes in foreign countries and has had its works, mainly those by Ikeda Daisaku, translated. A monthly newsletter keeps Japanese and foreign followers up-to-date on its activities.

Sō-kan. Buddhist hierarchical titles and categories. There are 10, comprising three ranks followed by a fourth, *sō-i.* They are:
　—**Dai-sōjō** (first rank)
　—**Sōjō** (first rank)
　—**Gon-sōjō** (first rank); these three titles are abridged to *sōjō*
　—**Dai-sōzu** (second rank)
　—**Gon-dai-sōzu** (second rank)
　—**Shō-sōzu** (second rank)
　—**Gon Shō-sōzu** (second rank); these four titles are abridged to *sōzu*
　—**Dai-risshi** (third rank)
　—**Chū-risshi** (third rank)
　—**Gon-risshi** (third rank); theses titles are abridged to *risshi*
Then come the following titles *(sō-i):*
　—**Hōkyō** (Bridge of the Law)
　—**Hō-in** (Seal of the Law)
　—**Hōgen** (Eye of the Law)
　—**Ajari** (Spiritual master)
　—**Zasu** (Master of the seat, head of the temple)
　—**Shūza** (Senior master)
• Buddhist name of warrior Imagawa Ujizane (1538–1614).
→ *See also* YAMAZAKI SŌKAN.

Soken. *See* YAMAGUCHI SOKEN.

Sōkō. In the old agricultural calendar, 15-day season "of the beginning of the white frost," starting around October 23. *Chin.:* Shuangjiang. *See* NIJŪ-SHI-SETSU.
• Sculptor of netsuke (Toshiyama Sōkō, 1868–1935) in Osaka.
• Sculptor of netsuke (Morita Sōkō, b. 1879) in Tokyo.

Sōkon-shū. Collection of about 20,000 poems by Shōtetsu (1381–1459), with a preface by Ichijō Kaneyoshi. *See* SHŌTETSU.

Sokotsushi. Type of suicide committed to expiate a fault committed by clumsiness or lack of attention.

Sokuchi-in. In Buddhist iconography, the Buddha in a sitting position, his right hand touching the ground near the knee (corresponding to the Sanskrit *bhūmishparshamudrā*), a gesture made to take the Earth as witness to the merits he acquired in the course of his previous lives.

Sokuhi. Japanese name taken by the Chinese painter Ji Fei (1616–71) when he became a Japanese citizen. A Zen Buddhist monk, he painted in the Song (Sō) style. He was an excellent calligrapher and one of the Sampitsu (Three Brushes) of the Ōbaku-shū sect. *See* MAMPUKU-JI, ŌBAKU-SHŪ.

Sokushin jōbutsu. "Buddhahood in this very body," a belief of the Shingon sect that it is possible, in one's lifetime, to become a buddha and train oneself to attain spiritual awakening. This doctrine, expounded by Kūkai, was decisive in the concept, developed later, that each individual possesses buddha-nature; in this sense, *sokushin jōbutsu* resembles the Zen doctrines of the Rinzai-shū sect and some Hindu beliefs *(Skt.: Jīvan mukta). See* YO-DONO-SHŪ.

Sokutai. "Knotted Belt," a ceremonial costume for the emperor, grand nobles, officers of the Imperial Guard, and senior bureaucrats in the court, designed in the twelfth century on the model of the ordinary garb of nobles of the Nara period. It was composed of a *kammuri* (bonnet with horsehair "ears"), a *hō (hōeki-hō)* robe, a decorated leather belt *(sekitai),* very long pants *(hakama-sekitai),* an undergarment *(hirao shita-gasane, kyo),* and shoes called *asa-gutsu.* The under-robe was shorter than before *(ketteki-hō).* The *hakama* were tucked into wide, high boots *(kamokutsu)* when the people wearing the costume had to leave the palace. Also called Hi no Shōzoku.

Sōkyoku. Style of instrumental music for koto created in the seventeenth century by Yatsuhashi Kengyō (1614–85), composed of airs such as the *kumi-uta* and *dammono. See also* JI-UTA.

Sōkyū. Sculptor of netsuke (Negoro Sōkyō, mid-eighteenth century) in Osaka.

Sōma. City in Fukushima prefecture on the Pacific coast, castle town *(jōka-machi)* that developed around the Sōma family's fortress. Sōma Nomaoi

Matsuri, featuring traditional horse races, takes place every July 23–25.

• Family of daimyo of southern Mutsu province (northern Honshu), descended from Taira no Masakado. Its members helped Minamoto no Yoritomo conquer the province, but they came into conflict with the Date family during the Sengoku period (1467–1568). Since they had refused to fight on Tokugawa Ieyasu's side at Sekigahara (1600), their land was confiscated, but it was returned to them in 1604 when a general amnesty was proclaimed.

• **Sōma Daisaku.** Warrior (Shimodomai Hidenoshin, 1789–1822) of the Nambu fief and master of martial arts. He became a *rōnin* and was implicated in an assassination attempt, so he took the name Sōma Daisaku and fled to Edo. He was found and executed.

• **Sōma-yaki.** Ceramics produced in Sōma and Namie (Fukushima prefecture), in the kilns at Nakamura and Ōbori, respectively. These kilns, built about 1630 by a potter from Kyoto, Tashiro Gengoemon (Nonomura Ninsei's student), produced painted ceramics under a honey-colored slip, with a drawing of a galloping or jumping horse. The Nakamura kiln is one of the oldest that is still active. The Ōbori kiln was founded later, about 1680. It produces a wide variety of ceramics.

Sōma Kokkō. Businesswoman (Hoshi Ryō, 1876–1955), Sasaki Toyoju's niece, born in Sendai. She opened a chain of restaurants in Tokyo; after she made her fortune, she began to sponsor artists and writers. She hid the Indian political leader Rashbehārī Bose, whom her daughter Toshiko married in 1918. She wrote her memoirs, *Mokui* (Silent Transition, 1934).

Somegami. Dyed paper, popular in the Heian period for writing love letters and poems. *See also* PAPER, WASHI.

Sōmen. Mask *(men)* covering the warrior's face in armor and complementing the helmet *(kabuto)*. *See also* HŌATE, MEMPŌ.

Some-nishikite. Type of Kakiemon porcelain produced in Kyoto in the eighteenth century, with a brocade decoration under a slip, made with cobalt oxidized in a decoction of boiled green tea. *See* SOMETSUKE.

• **Sometsuke.** Type of porcelain decorated with indigo blue (cobalt oxide, *gosu*) or purple under a slip, with a technique similar to the one called *qinghua* in China. This method was used in Japan starting in the early seventeenth century by Korean potters at Arita and by Okuda Eisen in the Seto kilns. The blue color was obtained by mixing cobalt with boiled green tea. These ceramics were used mainly for *sencha*. An older variety was called *ko-sometsuke*. *See* AKAE, SHONSUI GORŌDAYU.

Sōmin. Buddhist monk (Min, Bin, Sōbin, d. 653) who accompanied a mission sent by the Yamato court to Sui-dynasty China (*see* KENTŌSHI) led by Ono no Imoko. When he returned, Sōmin helped Prince Naka no Ōe (the future Emperor Tenji) prepare the Taika Reform (645).

• Sculptor and engraver of *tsuba* and netsuke (Yokoyama Sōmin, 1651/1669–1717/1733) in Edo. *See* GOTŌ.

Somin shōrai. Wooden talisman shaped like a short octagonal column, topped with a pointed capital, also octagonal; somewhat similar to ancient Hindu *lingam,* reputed to be the supreme protection against misfortune. The words *somin* and *shōrai* are inscribed on its faces. According to legend, this good-luck charm was given by Susanoo no Mikoto to a peasant in Izumo in gratitude for sheltering him during a storm. Some authors theorize that it gave rise to *kokeshi* dolls.

Sompi bummyaku. "Genealogical Lines, Great and Humble." A 14-scroll group of genealogical tables of emperors, noble families, and traditions, begun in the late fourteenth century by Tōin Kinsada (1340–99) and continued by his descendants, Tōin Mitsusue and Tōin Sanehiro (1409–57).

Sonchō Hōshinnō. *See* MUNENAGA SHINNŌ, MORINAGA SON'UN.

Son'en Hōshinnō. Buddhist monk (Morihiko, 1298–1356), Emperor Fushimi's sixth son, appointed *zasu* of the Tendai-shū. He was a famous calligrapher in the Seson-ji and Jōdai-hō styles and founder of the Onke-ryū school of calligraphy.

• **Son'en-ryū.** *See* O-IE-RYŪ.

Sone no Yoshitada. Poet (So-Tango, So-Tan, active ca. 985), nonclassical and somewhat eccentric, using folk language. Although he was not very popular in his own time, his work had a great impact on poetry in ensuing centuries. Nine of his poems appear in the imperial anthology (*see* CHOKUSEN WAKA-SHŪ) *Shui waka-shū* (1007) and 89 in other anthologies. His personal collection, *Sotan-shū,* contains 625 poems.

Sonezaki shinjū. "Double Suicide in Sonezaki." A three-act puppet play by Chikamatsu Monzaemon, premiered at the Takemoto-za in Osaka in 1703. This play, in the *sewa-mono* genre, describes a current event of the time. It is still performed today. *See also* SHINJŪ-TEN NO AMIJIMA.

Sonjo Hōshinnō. Buddhist monk (Shōren no Miya, d. 1290) and Emperor Tsuchimikado's son. He was appointed *zasu* of the Tendai-shū.

Sonkeikaku Bunko. Maeda family library (Maeda Ikutoku Kai Sonkeikaku Bunko) in Tokyo, founded by Maeda Toshiie (ca. 1538–99) and maintained by his descendants. It contains many Chinese and Japanese works, as well as objets d'art from the Ming dynasty and some old and rare Japanese manuscripts. This library has been classified a National Treasure. Part of its collection is now in the public library in Kanazawa. *See* KANAZAWA BUNKO.

Sonkoroku-yaki. Japanese name for Siamese ceramics from Sawankhalōk, imported to Japan and imitated (celadons) in the sixteenth and seventeenth centuries. *See also* TEMMOKU.

Sonnō jōi. "Venerate the emperor, expel the barbarians," an anti-shogunal movement and slogan launched in the late Edo period by members of the Mito philosophical and historical school and expressed in 1838 in the *Kōdōkan-ki,* a political work written by Fujita Tōko on request of daimyo Tokugawa Nariaki. The movement advocated both restoration of imperial power and proscription of the barbarians—in other words, Christians. This idea was born in 1825 in a work called *Shinron* by Aizawa Seishisai, a scholar of the Mito school, who stated that it was the will of the people to achieve national union under the authority of the highest spiritual figure in the country, the emperor. This movement resulted in the Meiji Restoration of 1868.

Sonnyo Shōnin. Buddhist monk (active ca. 1400) of the Jōdo Shin-shū, Rennyo Shōnin's father. Also called Enken Hōshi.

Sono Ayako. Writer (Miura Chizuko, Machida Chizuko), born 1931 in Tokyo; she married the writer Miura Shumon in 1953. A convert to Catholicism, she analyzes Japanese society from a Christian viewpoint in her stories and novels: *Tamayura* (One Moment, 1959), *Rio Gurande* (Rio Grande, 1961), *Ikenie no shima* (The Island of Sacrifice, 1970).

Sonoda Sunao. Politician (b. 1913) of the Liberal Democratic party (Jiyū Minshutō); minister of health and welfare (1967–68), then of foreign affairs (1977). He played an important role in the normalization of relations between China and Japan and represented Japan at the signature of the Sino-Japanese treaty of Beijing in 1978.

Sonsai. Painter (Kimura Sonsai, Kimura Kōkyō; *azana:* Seishuku; *gō:* Kenkadō, Sonsai, 1736–1802) of the Nanga (Bunjinga) school in Osaka. He painted landscapes.

Sonshō Hōshinnō. Buddhist monk (?–1239), Emperor Go-Takakura's second son. He was *kura-in,* then *zasu* of the Tendai-shū.

Sonshō-ō. Buddhist divinity, a form of Myōdo Bosatsu, identified in Shinto-Buddhist syncretism with the white horse that is the messenger of the *kami,* and sometimes with the North Star (*Skt.:* Sudrishti). Also called Myōjin, Myōken, Sozen.

Son'un Hōshinnō. *See* MORINAGA SHINNŌ.

Sony. Company that invents and manufactures electronic and audiovisual equipment, founded in 1946 by Ibuka Masaru and Morita Akio as Tokyo Tsushin Kōgyō (Corporation of Telecommunications Engineering). It took its current name in 1958. Its engineers invented the first tape recorders and transistor radios, as well as the first transistorized television, the Trinitron, which was imitated by other companies throughout the world. Sony also created a video-recording format, Betamax; in spite of its superior quality, this format was supplanted by the VHS system. In collaboration with Philips, Sony produced 3.5-inch computer diskettes and the first compact disks. It is known for its innovation and for the extreme miniaturization and reliability of its products. It has many production subsidiaries abroad, including in California, Great Britain, the Netherlands, and Hong Kong. It exports more than 70% of its production. Head office in Tokyo. *See* IBUKA MASARU, MORITA AKIO.

Sophia University (Jōchi Daigaku). A private Catholic university founded in Tokyo in 1913 by the German Herman Hoffman as Jōchi Gakuen; it obtained university status in 1928. It has many faculties and is famous for the quality of its foreign-language instruction. Enrollment about 10,000 students, both Japanese and foreign.

Sorge, Richard. German agent in the employ of the Soviet secret service, arrested in October 1941 by the Tokyo police along with several other agents—Branco Vukelic, a Yugoslav working for a French press agency; Max Klausen, a German businessman; and two Japanese. At their trial, which took place in September 1943, it was revealed that Sorge had been spying for the USSR since 1939 and had been in close contact with German Ambassador Eugen Ott, who believed he was a Nazi, since that time. The entire affair came to light only when it was made public in 1945. Sorge and Ozaki were sentenced to death and hanged on November 7, 1944; Vukelic and Klausen were sentenced to life in prison. Klausen was freed in October 1945, and returned to East Germany; Vukelic had died in prison a few months earlier. Although the USSR denied any knowledge of this affair, it finally publicly honored Sorge as a hero in November 1964, and issued a postage stamp bearing his portrait in 1965. Sorge's tomb is in the Tama Cemetery (Tokyo). The "Sorge affair" was later taken up in books and movies, but it has never been completely explained.

Sōri. Painter (Tawaraya Sōri; *mei:* Mototomo; *gō:* Ryūryūkyo Hyakurin, late eighteenth century) of the Kōrin school, Sumiyoshi Hiromori's student.
→ *See* HOKUSAI.

Sōrin. Bronze mast on top of some Buddhist pagodas. It is generally composed of several elements, from top to bottom: *hōshu* (small ball), *ryūsha* (another bronze ball), *suien* (decoration in découpé bronze), *kyūrin* (series of nine rings symbolizing the *chattra,* or parasols, decorating the top of Indian *stūpa*), and the base, composed of an *ukebana,* a *fukubashi,* and a *fukuban. See also* SŌRINTŌ.
→ *See* ŌTOMO YOSHISHIGE.

• **Sōrintō.** A *sōrin* constituting a monument in itself. The best example is the *sōrintō* erected in Nikkō, a bronze column 14 m high, built by Tenkai (1536–1643) in 1643, similar to the one erected in the Enryaku-ji temple on Mt. Hiei. *Sōrintō* are the equivalent of Buddhist pagodas.

Sōritsu. Painter (Oguri Sōritsu, sixteenth century) of the Muromachi *suiboku* school who studied with his father, Sōtan. He painted mainly animals.

Soroban. Abacus with four beads on the lower part and one on the upper part, used daily for most calculations; its operation is taught in elementary school. *Soroban* are usually made of wood, but also of plastic. The *soroban* is an improvement on the Chinese abacus of the same type (which has two beads on the upper part and five on the lower part), in use in Japan since 1612. A book by mathematician Yoshida Mitsuyoshi, *Jinkō-ki* (1627), popularized its use. The current *soroban* was introduced to Japan in 1891 by Irie Garyū. Special schools *(juku)* provide advanced instruction in calculating with the *soroban,* which is still widely used today despite the increasing prevalence of electronic calculators. *See* IRIE GARYŪ.

• **Soroban-bashi.** *See* KINTAI-BASHI.

Sōrōbun. Classic "epistolary style," using, among other particular formulas, the auxiliary verb *sōrō* (to be, to be used) instead of the normal verbal ending *matsu.* The epistolary style used by women is called *mairase sōrōbun.*

Sorori Shinzaemon. Buddhist monk (Sōyū, ?–1603), famous armor maker, poet, and master *(chajin)* of the tea ceremony *(chanoyu).* He was a favorite of Toyotomi Hideyoshi.

Sōryo. Former term designating Buddhist monks. Also called Sōto.
• Title given to the main heir in a warrior family.

Sōsaku hanga. "Creative prints," modern school (twentieth century) of ukiyo-e prints, exemplified by Munakata Shikō, Saitō Kiyoshi, Azechi Umetarō, Hagiwara Yoshida, Ikeda Masuo, Izumi Shigeru, Hara Takeshi, Shima Kuniichi, Takamatsu Jirō, and Inui Toshiaki.

Sosei. Buddhist monk (Yoshimine no Harutoshi, Yoshiyori no Ason, ca. 859–923), son of poet Henjō (Yoshimine no Munesada) and a *waka* poet himself, one of the Sanjūrokkasen. Thirty-six of his poems were included in the *Kokin-shū,* and 25 are in various other imperial anthologies (*see* CHOKUSEN WAKA-SHŪ). His personal collection, *Sosei-shū,* contains about 65 poems.

Sosen. *See* MORI SOSEN.

Sōsen. "Song currency," coins issued in Song-dynasty China (960–1279) and imported to Japan in large quantities in the thirteenth century. They were widely used, as were the Chinese coins *kōbusen* and *eirakusen*, until the late sixteenth century.

Sō Senshun. Naturalist (Sō Shōkei, Sō Han, 1757–1834) and prolific writer.

Sōsetsu. Painter (Kitagawa Sōsetsu, active ca. mid-seventeenth century), Sōtatsu's student.
• Painter (Nonomura Sōsetsu; *gō*: Inen), perhaps the same as the above. *See also* SŌTATSU.

Sōshi. In the late nineteenth century, a category of urban youths with no defined principles who rented themselves out to politicians to help them get elected.

Sōshi (-zōshi). "Stories."

• *Sōshi-arai komachi.* Noh play: during a poetry contest held by the emperor, between Ono no Komachi and the poet Kuronushi, the latter falsely accuses the former of having copied his poem in the *Man'yōshū*. The error is discovered and Ono no Komachi dances in honor of poetry.

Sōshin-in. School for women of the Fujiwara family, founded in Kyoto in 860 by *sadaijin* Fujiwara no Yoshisuke.

Sōshū. Painter (Kanō Suenobu; *mei*: Jinnosuke, 1551–1601) of the Kanō school; he studied with his father, Shōei, and his older brother, Eitoku, in Kyoto.

Sōshū-mono. School of blacksmiths who made sword blades in Sagami province. In the Kamakura period, its most famous members were Bizen Suke-zane, Kunimune, Awataguchi Kunitsuna, Shintōgo Kunimitsu, Yukimitsu (active 1318–35), his son Sadamune, Hiromitsu, and Akimitsu (fourteenth century).

Sōtatsu. Painter (Tawaraya Sōtatsu, Nomomura Sōtatsu; *gō*: Inen, Taiseiken, died ca. 1643), founder of the Sōtatsu-ha school of Yamato-e in Kyoto, also called the Rimpa school. He decorated fusuma with a gold background (at the Kennin-ji, Kyoto) and illustrated several *emakimono*, including the *Saigyō monogatari emaki* (1630). He may have been related by marriage to Hon'ami Kōetsu. In his ink paintings *(sumi-e)*, he adopted the technique of the Zen Buddhist monks. His constant use of inks and colors and his choice of mythological subjects had a profound influence on later styles of painting and were probably at the origin of the "Japanese" style (Nihonga) that developed in the late nineteenth century.

• **Sōtatsu-ha.** School of painting in the traditional Yamato-e style, but with a decorative tendency, making great use of ink tracings and colors, inaugurated by Sōtatsu in the seventeenth century. *See also* RIMPA.

Sōtei. Painter (Kanda Sōtei, Kanda Nobusada, Kanda Munenobu; *mei*: Shōshichi, 1590–1662) of Buddhist subjects. His disciples and descendants signed their works with his *gō* of Sōtei.

Sōten. Armor maker (Niudo Soheishi Sōten, seventeenth century) and chiseler of *tsuba* in Hikone; his son had the same name and profession. They founded a school bearing their name.

Sotoba. Wood or stone pillars, generally topped with a *gorintō*, erected at crossroads or in cemeteries. Also called *toba*, a corruption of the Sanskrit *stūpa*.

• *Sotoba komachi.* "Komachi in the Temple," one of the oldest Noh plays, written by Kan'ami Kiyotsugu (1333–84): the spirit of the poet Ono no Komachi alights on a *sotoba* on Mt. Kōya-san and discusses religion with the monks who gather around her. Then, the spirit of one of her rejected lovers, Fukakusa no Shōshō, appears.

Sotōri-hime. Fifth-century imperial princess famous for her beauty, Emperor Inkyō's daughter-in-law. He was in love with her, and made her a gift of the Fujiwara palace in Yamato and a special guard. Also known by the name Oto-hime.

Sōtō-shū. Zen (*Chin.*: Chan) Buddhist sect imported from China to Echizen by Dōgen in 1227; it complemented the Rinzai sect, introduced several years before by Eisai. The Sōtō sect was popularized by Keizan Jōkin, its fourth "patriarch." Since the early seventeenth century, its main temples have been the Eihei-ji and the Sōji-jhi. The essential difference between the Rinzai and Sōtō doctrines is that the former advocates active meditation *(kannazen)*, whereas the latter emphasizes silent meditation *(mokushō-zen)* and does not make much use of *kōan* to awaken the spirit of disciples. The Sōtō-shū sect has more than 14,000 temples in Japan, and about 7 million followers.

Sotsuzoku. Class of persons claiming a warrior ancestry, created in 1869 and eliminated in 1872, when its members were integrated into the *shizoku* class.

Sōun. Painter (Tazaki Un, 1815–98) of the Nanga (Bunjinga) school who studied with Kanai Ushū, Haruki Nammei, and Tani Bunchō. He painted mainly landscapes.
→ *See* HŌJŌ SŌUN.

• **Sōun-ji.** Buddhist temple founded by Hōjō Sōun (1432–1519) in Hakone for the Zen Buddhist Rinzai-shū sect. It was partly destroyed in 1590, but the tombs of the members of the Hōjō family were preserved.

• *Sōun-ji dono nijūikkajō.* "The Twenty-One Articles of Sōun," a series of familial precepts attributed to Hōjō Sōun, giving instructions to members of the family and its vassal samurai.

Sōya-kaikyō. Japanese name for La Perouse Strait, between Cape Sōyamisaki (northern tip of Hokkaido) and Sakhalin (Karafutō), linking the Sea of Okhotsk and the Sea of Japan (Nihonkai). Maximum width: 43 km, average depth, about 50 m.

Sōyama Sachihiko. Painter (Ono Sachihiko, 1859–92) in the Western style, a student of the Italian painter San Giovanni. He painted landscapes in watercolors and oils.

Soyo. Blacksmith, maker of sword blades and *tsuba* for the Edo shogunate, active in the seventeenth century, and founder of a school called Yokoya.

So, yō, chō. Taxation system in use after promulgation of the *ritsuryō* code in the seventh century and comprising three types of taxes: the *so,* payable in rice and about 4% of the annual harvest; the *yō* (also called *chikarashiro*), payable in craft products such as silk, and replacing work parties; and the *chō* (also called *mitsugi*), payable in local products directly to the court. These taxes replaced those that had existed previously, payable in rice *(tachikara),* local products *(mitsugi),* and work parties *(edachi).* These various taxes were a very heavy burden; in the tenth century, owners or operators of *shōen* or their deputies began to collect them for their own profit.

Sōyū. Painter (sixteenth century) of the Kanō school, perhaps the same person as Gyokuraku.

Sōyū-kan. Military school *(shohan-gakkō)* founded in Kumazawa in 1792.

Sozen. Zen Buddhist monk (Jōzan, 1293–1375) of the Rinzai-shū, sent into exile in 1368.
→ *See* YAMANA SOZEN.
• Syncretic form of the Buddhist divinity Myōdo Bosatsu *(Skt.:* Sudrishti), symbolizing the South Star and considered the protector of horses and wild animals.

Sozō. Sculptures in dried clay, a technique used mainly during the Nara period to make Buddhist images. The clay, to which a sort of plant lime was added, was modeled on a wooden framework surrounded with rice straw. Once dry, the sculpture was coated with a slip made of light clay, then painted or lacquered; mica flakes were applied to the surface of the completed statue so that the colors would adhere better.

Sōzu. Title given to high-ranking Buddhist monks, heads of temples or monasteries. There were four classes: *Dai sōzu, Gondai sōzu, Shō sōzu,* and *Gonshō sōzu. See* SŌJŌ, SŌ-KAN.

Sōzudai. Prehistoric site in Ōita prefecture, northeast Kyushu, which revealed an industry of the early paleolithic period *(mudōki bunka),* somewhat similar to that found in the Zhoukoudian cave in China. Its dating, however, remains conjectural. *See* JŌMON, NYŪ.

Sozu-gawa. In Buddhist legends, a river in Hell *(jigoku)* that is guarded by a sort of witch called Shōzuka no Baba who steals the clothing of dead children. It is equivalent to the River Styx of Greek legend.

Speck, Jacques. First Dutch director of the Hirado trading post. He arrived in Japan in 1609 and returned to Holland in 1627, where he was appointed governor-general of Batavia.

Sports. There are two categories of sports in Japan: the traditional ones, such as *sumo, judō (aikidō* and other related sports), *karate,* the art of wielding the *naginata, kendō, kyūdō,* and so on *(see these entries);* and those imported from the West. The latter are very popular and practiced assiduously by a wide variety of people.
—**Track and field** debuted in its Western form at the University of Tokyo in 1883, thanks to an English athlete, F. W. Strange, and stadiums with cinder tracks were built that very year. Japanese athletes

went to the Olympic Games for the first time in Stockholm in 1912. In the following years, many more stadiums were built. In 1951, five years after the reopening of playing fields, Japanese athletes dominated the first Asian Games in New Delhi and Tanaka Shigeki won the fifty-ninth Boston Marathon. Japanese athletes have proved to be particularly adept at the marathon and the triple jump.

—**Swimming**, though long practiced in Japan, where it was considered a warrior art, became popular in 1898, when Japanese swimmers competed against foreign members of the Yokohama Amateur Rowing Club. They participated in the Olympic Games for the first time in Anvers in 1920; at the Amsterdam Games in 1928, Tsuruta won a bronze medal in the 200 m breaststroke. In Los Angeles in 1932, Japanese swimmers broke records in all disciplines; they repeated the feat in Berlin in 1936, where a young swimmer, Maehata Hideko, won the 200 m breaststroke. Thereafter, Japanese swimmers won a large number of medals, including at the Melbourne Olympics in 1956. **Diving** was less popular, as it began to be practiced only in 1924 among students at Keiō University and the University of Tokyo. **Water polo** was first played in Japan in Kobe and Yokohama about 1898, but the country had no international-level teams. **Rowing**, with two or more rowers, was introduced by foreigners to Yokohama at the beginning of the Meiji era, but the first club was founded in Tokyo in 1877. Japanese rowers participated in the 1928 Olympic Games in Amsterdam and ensuing Games.

—**Tennis** was introduced in 1878 by an American, G. E. Leland. It quickly caught on with young people; by about 1910, it was the most popular sport among students. But it was only in 1913 that the Japanese adopted regular balls to replace the rubber balls they had been using. Tennis is still popular, but it is relatively costly because there is little space in Japan for courts.

—**Rugby** debuted at Keiō University in Tokyo, introduced by a Professor Clark, who had played at Cambridge; the Japanese Rugby Association was established in 1928. There are currently about 2,000 rugby teams.

—**Soccer** was introduced to Japan in 1878, and the Dai Nippon Soccer Association was founded in 1922. Japan currently has about 2,000 teams; the best known are the Red Diamonds (Urawa) Verdi Yomjiuri (Kawasaki), the Grampus Eight (Nagoya), Hiroshima F. C. (Hiroshima), the Kashima Antlers (Kashima), Ichihara Jef United, AS Flügels (Yokohama), S-Pulse (Shimizu), Marinos (Yokohama), and Gamba (Osaka). Previously not widely played,

soccer suddenly became very popular among young people when the first national championship was held, on May 15, 1992, and games broadcast on television have a huge viewership, equal to that for baseball.

—**Table tennis** was introduced in 1902 by Tsuboi Gendō and regulated by an official sports federation in 1921. The Japanese quickly became experts at table tennis, winning an international championship in 1926. They also won the international championship in Bombay in 1952 and in London in 1954, then in Utrecht in 1955 and Tokyo in 1956. Since then, victories by both men and women have been numerous. Their fiercest rivals are the Chinese and, now, the Koreans.

—**Volleyball** was imported from the United States in 1914. It is well established and played mainly in schools and commercial and industrial firms.

—**Basketball** was introduced at the same time as volleyball and developed similarly, with Japanese teams winning a number of international meets. However, the players are generally "handicapped" (as are volleyball players) by their relatively small size, compared to the very tall players on the teams of some Western nations.

—**Handball** was introduced to Tokyo by Ōtani Takeichi in 1922. The first tournament took place in 1937 in Tokyo; the following year, the Japanese handball federation joined the international organization.

—The first **freestyle wrestling** match took place in 1931 at Waseda University, and Japanese wrestlers were very successful at the Olympic Games in Helsinki and Melbourne (1956).

—**Boxing,** adopted by students at Keiō and Meiji universities in Tokyo in 1927, was long an amateur sport, and some Japanese boxers competed at various Olympic games. But amateurism was overshadowed by professional bouts, where Japanese featherweights were very successful.

—**Weightlifting** was inaugurated in Japan by Kanō Jigorō, the founder of *judō* techniques, in 1922.

—**Downhill skiing** won acceptance in Japan as far back as 1895, and teams were sent to international competitions starting in 1928. After the Second World War, skiing expanded spectacularly, with a large number of ski resorts opening (*see* SAPPORO). However, Japanese skiers are rarely on the podium at world-class competitions. Other winter sports, such as **skating** (inaugurated in Sapporo in 1877) and **ice hockey,** are not widely practiced, although the top skaters and teams have taken part in various Olympic Games.

Although all modern sports are actively practiced on various scales in Japan, such as **equitation** (*see* HORSES), the most popular are undeniably **baseball** and **golf** *(see these entries). See also* GETOBŌRU.

Subaru. "The Pleiades." A literary magazine published in Tokyo from January 1909 to December 1913, succeeding the defunct *Myōjō,* by Mori Ōgai and several other writers. It published mainly poetry *(tanka)* and translations of foreign works in an anti-naturalist style. Yosano Akiko, Nagai Kafū, Ueda Bin, and Tanizaki Jun'ichirō were contributors.
→ *See* FUJI JŪKYŌGYŌ.

Submarines. During the Second World War (in 1941), Japan had 18 K6–class submarines, with a displacement of 11,000 tons; they were armed with four torpedo tubes and had a range of 11,000 nautical miles and a top speed of 12 knots. Almost all were sunk between 1942 and 1945. Japan then built mid-class submarines (KS type displacing 600 tons) and giant submarines (classes I and L) that could carry an airplane *(range:* 20,000 nautical miles; *surface tonnage:* about 3,000 tons). The D1 type of the I class *(range:* 15,000 miles) was used as a mothership. The last submarine of this type was the STO (I/400 class), armed with eight tubes for 530 mm torpedoes, a snorkel, and a rubber skin (surface displacement 5,300 tons, with one 140 mm cannon and ten anti-aircraft 25 mm cannons). In the I/70 class, submarines had a range of 14,000 nautical miles and a surface displacement of 1,785 tons; they were armed with six tubes for 530 mm torpedoes and one anti-aircraft 100 mm cannon; their speed was 23 knots on the surface and 8 knots underwater. *See* KAIRYŪ, KAITEN, KŌRYŪ.

Sūden. *See* KONCHI-IN SŪDEN.

Sue-bizen. Group of blacksmiths who made sword blades during the Muromachi period; the best known were Sukesada and Katsumitsu. *See* OSAFUNE KAJI.

Sue Harukata. Warrior (1521–55), a vassal of Ōuchi Yoshitaka, who fomented a coup d'état in 1551, forcing his suzerain to commit suicide. He was defeated during a revolt at Itsukushima and committed suicide.

Suehiro. *See* ŌGI.

Suehiro Tetchō. Politician and writer (Suehiro Shigeyasu, 1849–96), born on Shikoku. In 1881, he helped to found the Jiyūtō (Liberal party). He wrote politically tinged novels: *Nijūsannen miraiki* (1886) and *Setchūbai* (1886). He was elected to the Diet for the Rikken Kaishintō (Constitutional Reform party) in 1890.

Sue-ki. Ceramics made of coiled clay and fired at high temperature, introduced to Japan in the fifth century by Korean potters, and also called *iwaibe-doki* and *Chōsen-doki.* These ceramics, reduction-fired in *anagama*-type kilns, were made of gray clay, and some had a bright glaze (produced by cinders). *Sue* pottery consisted of jars, decorated vases on a perforated pedestal, used mainly to contain funerary offerings placed in tombs, and were characterized by a wide mouth and decorations added on the shoulders (small vases, people, animals, and so on). These ceramics became widespread in the seventh century and were used for daily purposes. Also called *sue no utsuwa. See* CERAMICS, SHIRAKI-YAKI.

Suematsu Kenchō. Politician (1855–1920), born in northern Kyushu. He married one of Itō Hirobumi's daughters and went to Great Britain in 1878. When he returned in 1886, he entered politics; elected to the Diet in 1890, he was minister of communications and of the interior in Itō Hirobumi's cabinets in 1898 and 1900. He was the first to translate the *Genji monogatari* into English, and he was elected a member of the Imperial Academy (Teikoku Gakushi-in).

Suetsugu Heizō. Shipowner (?–1630) in Hakata and Nagasaki. He obtained a *shuin-jō* (red seal) from the shogunate, and sent his ships to trade at Luzon, the Philippines, and Siam. One of his captains, Hamada Yahyōe, was forced to fight the Dutch at Taiwan, which interrupted relations between the shogunate and Dutch merchants for some time. Suetsugu's grandson was found guilty of having secret trade relations with Cambodia in 1676, and his entire family was forced to cease its activities. *See* SUEYOSHI MAGOZAEMON.

Suetsugu Nobumasa. Navy officer (1881–1944), appointed admiral in 1937, and minister of the interior.

Sueyoshi Magozaemon. Merchant and shipowner (Sueyoshi Yoshiyasu, 1570–1617). He helped his father establish the Mint *(ginza)* in Edo and built Tokugawa Ieyasu's general quarters during the siege of Osaka. Having received a *shuin-jō,* he sent three-masted merchant ships (Sueyoshi-bune) to trade in the Philippines and Vietnam. His descendants retained this privilege until 1635. *See* SUETSUGU HEIZŌ.

Sugae Masumi. Writer (Shirai Hideo, 1754–1829) and ethnologist. He traveled extensively in Honshu to find and describe folk customs and to make geographic descriptions of the provinces (notably Dewa). His studies were published only in 1966–71, under the title *Sugae masumi yūranki* (13 volumes).

Sugai Kumi. Painter (1919–96), born in Kobe to a family of Malaysian origins. He studied in Osaka from 1927 to 1932, then moved to Paris in 1952. He was part of the "October" group founded by Charles Estienne and had exhibitions in various countries. His paintings are inspired by Japanese calligraphy.

Sugawara. Noble family descended from the leaders of the *hajibe* guild, who abandoned their professions of ceramist and potter in 781 and took the name Sugawara.

• *Sugawara denju tenarai kagami.* Title of a *ningyō-jōruri* play in the *jidai-mono* genre on an episode from Sugawara no Michizane's life, written by Takeda Izumo, his son Takeda Koizumo, Namiki Senryū, and Miyoshi Shōraku.

• **Sugawara no Kiyogimi.** Statesman (770–842) and minister. After a trip to China, he suppressed the custom of corporal punishment, advocated a Chinese-type administration, and reformed the *daigaku* of Heian-kyō. *See* RYŌUN-SHŪ.

• **Sugawara no Koreyoshi.** Scholar (812–80), Sugawara no Kiyogimi's son, imperial tutor and rector of the *daigaku* in Heian-kyō. He was one of the compilers of the *Montoku jitsuroku.*

• **Sugawara no Michizane.** Statesman (845–903), Sugawara no Koreyoshi's son and one of the compilers of the *Sandai jitsuroku.* A historian and poet, he became famous for his knowledge of the Chinese classics. In 877, he was appointed a professor of Chinese literature; in 866, he became governor of Sanuki province on Shikoku, a position he held for four years. In 899, Emperor Uda appointed him minister of the right *(udaijin),* but in 901 the Fujiwara, jealous of his influence in the court, accused

him of plotting against Emperor Daigo, and he was sent to govern Dazaifu on Kyushu. He died there in 903, still proclaiming his innocence. During his mandate as minister, he had suggested that the delegations regularly sent to China be stopped because of political instability in that country, a proposal that was accepted in 894. After his death, various unfortunate events occurred in the court, and it was believed that Michizane's spirit was taking its revenge. To appease it, he was officially rehabilitated and posthumously given the highest honors. Commoners divinized him, making him a sort of *kami* of literature, and shrines were erected in his memory in Kyoto (Kitano Tenjin) and Dazaifu. Thus deified, Michizane received the names Tenjin Sama, Karai Tenji, Kan Shōjō, Temmangu, and others. In most of the shrines dedicated to him, there is a statue of a reposing steer (alluding to the buffalo of the Chinese wise man Laozi), to which people attribute the power to cure diseases. Students are in the habit of rubbing the statue before taking examinations in the hope of improving their calligraphy and getting better marks.

• **Sugawara no Motomichi.** *See* HAKURYŪ.

• **Sugawara no Takasue.** Scholar (eleventh–twelfth century). Nothing is known about his life, but his daughter (Sugawara no Takasue no Musume, b. 1008) was a famous writer, author of *Sarashina nikki.* She is also credited with writing *Hamamatsu chūnagon monogatari* and *Yoru no nezame.* She lost her husband, Tachibana no Toshimichi, in 1059, and probably died after 1067.

• **Sugawara no Tamenaga.** Writer (1158–1246) credited with writing the *Jikken-shō.*

Sugihara Chiune. Diplomat (Sugihara Senpo, ?–1986). As Japan's vice-consul in Kaunas, Lithuania, in 1940, he saved the lives of thousands of Jews by illegally providing visas to those who wanted to transit through Japan to escape persecution. The refugees were greeted in Kobe by Kotsuji Seiyū, who was sympathetic to their cause. When he returned to Japan in 1947, Sugihara Chiune was forced to resign. A street in Kaunas bears his name, and Israel has honored him. His wife, Sugihara Yukiko, wrote a book about his activities, *6000 Nin no inochino bisa* (Visas for Six Thousand Lives).

Sugi Kuhei. Famous Kabuki actor in Kyoto, who created the role of *kashagata,* or old woman, about 1670–80.

Sugimura Jihei. Painter (active between 1680 and 1703) of ukiyo-e prints in the style of Hishikawa Moronobu. He illustrated many books (most of them erotic; *see* SHUNGA) in *sumizuri-e*. In his paintings, he hid his signature in the folds of the women's clothing.

Sugita Gempaku. Physician (Sugita Tasuku, Sugita Shiho, Kyūkō, 1733–1817) and scholar in "Dutch science" *(rangaku)*. In 1771, he attended the dissection of the corpse of a woman criminal; this led him to translate the "Anatomical Tables" *(Anatomische Tabellen)* by the German Johhanes Kulmus (1689–1745), which had been translated into Dutch in 1734. He published the book as *Kaitai shinsho* (New Anatomy Book) in 1774, in collaboration with Maeno Ryōtaku. He also wrote an account of a dissection he performed in 1771 in *Rangaku kotohajime* (1774).

Sugiura Jūgō. Educator and philosopher (Sugiura Shigetake, 1855–1924), born in Ōmi province. After a long stay in Great Britain, he worked in the Ministry of Education and various institutions, then founded his own school, the Shōkōjuku, in Tokyo. He helped found the newspaper *Nihonjin* in 1888, then the *Nippon Shimbun,* in which he advocated nationalist ideals, the following year. From 1914 to 1921, he was tutor to Crown Prince Hirohito and Princess Nagako.

Sugiura Yasuyoshi. Contemporary ceramist, born 1949 in Tokyo; his pottery has certain sculptural aspects.

Sugiyama Hajime. General (Sugiyama Gen, 1880–1945), born in Fukuoka prefecture to a family of former samurai. Minister of the armed forces in Konoe Fumimaro's first cabinet, minister of the War Council in 1935, minister of war (1937–38), chief of general quarters of the armed forces in 1940, then again minister of armed forces in Koiso Kuniaki's cabinet (1944–45), succeeding Tōjō Hideki. On September 12, 1945, after Japan's defeat, he committed suicide using a revolver; his wife, an officer's daughter, committed suicide the same day.

Sugiyama Sampū. Haiku poet (1647–1732), a disciple of Bashō (Bashō Juttetsu). A wealthy fish merchant, he provided financial assistance to his master. His collection of poems was titled *Sampū ku-shū* (1785).

Sugiyama Waichi. Physician (1610–94) for shogun Tokugawa Tsunayoshi, whom he treated with acupuncture. He founded a school to teach his technique in Edo about 1681.

Sugiyama Yasushi. Painter (1909–93) in the Nihonga style, born in Tokyo, Matsuoka Eikyū's student. He traveled in Europe and Egypt and received the Japan Art Academy (Nihon Geijutsu-in) Prize in 1957 and 1966. His oldest daughter, Yōko, married Mishima Yukio.

Sugoroku. Game similar to backgammon, introduced from China around the eighth century. Several varieties existed. *Bansugoroku* (board *surgoroku*), abandoned during the Edo period, was played with 15 pieces and dice. It was replaced by *e-soguroku* (illustrated *soguroku*), played on a sheet of paper decorated with pictures, often Buddhist in inspiration, and divided into squares. *Sugoroku* is still occasionally played, usually on New Year's Day. The board is divided into two rows of twelve squares, and each player has 12 pieces *(ishi)*; the object is to move the pieces onto the opponent's territory, using dice. *Chin.: shuanglu. See* ROKUSAI.

Suian. Painter (Hirafuku Un; *mei:* Junzō; *gō:* Bunchi, Suian, 1844–90) of the Shijō school, Tukemura Bunkai's student in Tokyo. He painted mainly animals.
→ *See* SHUNKIN.

Suiboku. Painting technique (wash) with China ink *(sumi-e)* and light touches of color, following the style of Chinese painters of the Song and Yuan dynasties, whose works were imported to Japan by Zen monks. *Suiboku* paintings *(suiboku-ga)* are often accompanied by a *san,* or inscription in prose or poetry. In the fourteenth and fifteenth centuries, the Muromachi *suiboku* school had the best representatives, including the uncontested master, Sesshū, and there were many branches led by different painters. *Chin.: shuimo.*

• **Suibokusai.** Painter (An'ei, Tōrin, fifteenth century) of the Muromachi *suiboku* school in Kyoto.

• **Suiboku Sanjin.** *See* KŌYŌ.

Suicide. The act of voluntarily killing oneself was never a religious or other taboo in Japan. On the contrary, custom had it that it was the noblest way of begging pardon for an offense or of expiating a crime. It was also used as a sort of protest against certain bans, such as double suicides for love. Suicide was rare among commoners; people tended to kill themselves when they were submitted to extreme psychological or social pressure.

Commoners drowned or hanged themselves, while nobles and warriors preferred to indicate their desire to die by incising the stomach muscles (*harakiri; see* SEPPUKU) and allowing one of their intimates to decapitate them with a sword blow. Women cut open their carotid vein. *See* JIGAI, JŌSHI, MUNEN-BARA, SEPPUKU, SHIKAN, SHINJŪ, SOKOTSUSHI, SONEZAKI SHINJŪ.

Suigetsu Kannon. One of the 33 forms (*see* SAN-JŪSAN ŌGESHIN) of Kannon Bosatsu (*Skt.:* Avalokiteshvara), portrayed sitting on a rock or standing on a lotus leaf floating on the water, and looking at the moon's reflection in the water. Sometimes portrayed with three heads and six arms. *Chin.:* Shuiye Guanyin.

Suijaku-ga. Type of painting in Shinto shrines, showing, mainly in syncretic sects, *kami* in the form of their Buddhist incarnations; this type of painting developed during the Heian and Kamakura periods. Most of them are mandalas depicting a shrine. *Suijaku-ga,* as a Shinto art, generally followed Buddhist styles of painting. *See* HONJI-SUIJAKU.

Suijin. Shinto divinities associated with water. They are very diverse—of the sea, waves, clouds, rivers, ponds, wells, and so on—and very often incarnated by dragons. Mainly on Kyushu, this type of *kami* is represented by *kappa*. In peasant communities, *suijin* (rice paddies) are often associated with *Ta no kami* (the *kami* of the fields), and are venerated as such. Steles are erected for *suijin* near wells and springs.

Suikan. Simple loose blouse (stiffened not with starch but with pure water), drawn in at the waist and the sleeves with cords. Generally worn by peasants, *suikan* were adopted by warriors to wear under their armor during the Kamakura period. In the Edo period, *suikan* were worn exclusively by young men.

Suika Shintō. Shinto sect founded by Yamazaki Ansai (1619–82); it mixed elements borrowed from neo-Confucianism with Shinto beliefs in order to give Shinto a moral content that met the ethical standards of the Tokugawa. According to its doctrine, the emperor belonged to a divine family line and therefore had to be highly venerated. Suika

Shintō was adopted by some scholars of the Mito school, who made it one of their political arguments against the Edo shogunate.

Suiko Tennō. Thirty-third sovereign (Princess Toyomike Kashikiya-hime, 554<593–628>639), Kimmei Tennō's daughter. She succeeded her brother, Sushun, who had been assassinated, and married her half-brother, Emperor Bidatsu, in 576. She made her nephew, Shōtoku Taishi, regent and established her capital at Asuka. After her abdication, Jōmei succeeded her.

Suinin Tennō. Eleventh emperor, according to the traditional genealogy (Prince Ikume-iri Hiko Hisachi, 70 BC<29–70 AD>, but probably around the early second century). He succeeded his father, Sujin Tennō. He is credited with construction of the first shrine in Ise. Keikō Tennō succeeded him.

Suiō. Painter (Tamura Suiō, early eighteenth century) of ukiyo-e prints. He painted mainly beautiful women *(bijin)*.

• **Suiō Eiboku.** Painter (1716–89); studied with Ikeno Taiga and Hakuin. He was a Zen Buddhist monk at the Shōin-ji temple in Suruga province.

Sujin Tennō. Tenth emperor (Prince Mimari-iri Hiko Inie, traditionally 148<97–30 BC>, but probably first century AD). He was the second son of and successor to Kaika Tennō. Tradition has it that he built the first shrine dedicated to Amaterasu-Ōmikami; according to the *Kojiki* and *Nihon shoki,* he developed agriculture and created the first government. He is sometimes confused with Jimmu Tennō, the "first emperor." It is in fact likely that all sovereigns before Sujin Tennō were mythical.

Sukashibori. Decoration technique consisting of working with sheets of metal in repoussé and découpage.

Suke. Title associated with another to indicate a subordinate position. There were two classes of *suke: shō-suke* and *oi-suke* (junior and senior).

Sukegō. In the Edo period, obligatory work parties for peasants who lived close to post towns and major roads, and the villages on which these work parties were imposed. The peasants had to perform maintenance in the post towns *(shuku-eki, shukuba)* and serve as porters for official travelers.

Sukegō were abolished in 1868. *See* BUYAKU, SHUKU-EKI.

Sukehiro. Blacksmith who made sword blades (Tsuda Sukehiro, 1637–1782), Tsuda Ōmi no Kami's father.

Sukehito Shinnō. Imperial prince (1733–94), Emperor Kōkaku's father. In 1884, he received the posthumous title of Kyōkō Tennō, even though he had never reigned.

Sukeroku. Kabuki play, one of the Kabuki-jūhachiban, written by Danjūrō II about 1713: a man called Sukeroku fights a hoodlum who is molesting a courtesan and takes from him a valuable sword, which turns out to belong to his lord. At the end of the play, we discover that Sukeroku is in reality a samurai who was sent to find this sword. This play is still performed today.

Suketada. Painter (Nishikawa Suketada; *mei:* Yūzō; *gō:* Tokuyūsai, Bunseidō, Suketada, active between 1740 and 1760), son and student of Sukenobu (Nishikawa Sukenobu). He mainly illustrated books.

Sukeyasu. Painter (Kaida Sukeyasu; *mei:* Uneme no Suke, active ca. 1500) of the Tosa school. He illustrated the *Saigyō monogatari* (now lost).

Sukezane. Blacksmith, maker of sword blades (Ichimonji Sukezane, b. 1204) from Bizen province.

Sukiyaki. Dish consisting of fine slices of meat, vegetables, and mushrooms with soy sauce *(shōyu),* cooked in a cast-iron platter. Probably imported from Korea, it was first made in the early nineteenth century and became a favorite in the middle of the Meiji era, when commoners began to get accustomed to the taste of meat. Today, high-quality beef is used, cut into very fine slices. There are many ways of preparing *sukiyaki.* This dish has also become popular among foreigners, for whom it is representative of Japanese cooking. *See* CUISINE.

Sukiya-zukuri. Style of luxurious residential architecture in which a room for the tea ceremony *(chanoyu)* is included. This style, very popular in the Muromachi period, at the same time as the *shoin* style, was taken up by the merchant class *(chōnin)* in the Edo period. The most accomplished example of *sukiya-zukuri* style is found in the Katsura-rikyū pavilions in Kyoto.

Sūkoku. Painter (Kō Kazuo; *azana:* Shiei; *gō:* Toryūō, Suiundō, Korensha, Rakushisai, Sūkoku, 1730–1804), Hanabusa Ichō's student. He lived in Edo and painted in the style of the Tosa school.

Sukō Tennō. Third emperor of the Northern Court (Prince Okihito, 1334<1348–51>1398), Kōgon Tennō's son and successor to his uncle, Kōmyō Tennō. He was taken prisoner by the army of the Southern Court (Nanchō) in 1352, and freed in 1357. Gō Kōgon succeeded him in 1352.

Suku. Archeological site from the Yayoi period, located near the town of Kasuga (Fukuoka prefecture, Kyushu). A cemetery was uncovered there in 1899; one of its funerary jars contained mirrors and Chinese objects made of bronze from the Han dynasty, as well as glass *magatama.* Other excavations, made in 1929 and 1962, revealed more jars of the same type. It is thought that this cemetery was for the sovereigns *(miyatsuko)* of the state of Nakoku.

Sukuna-bikona. In Shinto legends, a *kami* who helped Ōkuninushi establish his kingdom in Izumo and who taught humans about medicine and sorcery.

Sukune. Ancient title equivalent to "noble" in the sixth century. *See* YAKUSA NO KABANE.

Suma. District in Kobe, on the coast of the Inland Sea (Setonaikai), once famous for its white-sand beaches and pines; it was often mentioned in the *Man'yōshū,* the *Genji monogatari,* and other works. It was also the site of major battles between the Minamoto and Taira clans from 1180 to 1185.

Sume-mi-oya no Mikoto. Ancient title (before 702) given to the mother of an emperor. It was replaced by the title Kōtaigō. *See* KŌGYOKU TENNŌ.

Sumera. Japanese name for the mythical Mt. Meru, the axis of the world in Hindu Buddhist cosmogony.

• **Sumeragi.** "He Who Reigns under Heaven," a title given to emperors and certain Shinto *kami.* Also called Sumera no Mikoto.

• **Sumera-kyō.** Shinto sect founded in 1946 in Atami by Onikura Taruhiko (1879–1960).

Sumi. "China ink," usually in solid form, in sticks decorated with gold or silver. These sticks are made by mixing a water-soluble glue and pine soot, and perfume is sometimes added. To use *sumi* for calligraphy or painting *(sumi-e)*, the sticks are rubbed on a special ink stone called *suzuri* with a few drops of water.

• **Sumi-e.** *See* SUMI.

• **Suminagashi.** *Sumi-e* painting technique consisting of letting a drop of China ink fall into water to which oil has been added. The ink spreads in various shapes, and paper or fabric is lightly pressed on the spots to absorb the liquid. In ceramic decoration, this procedure is sometimes used to obtain marbling. Paper decorated this way was used for writing poems, love letters, and sometimes Buddhist texts. During the Edo period, red China ink was sometimes added for a different effect. Some families of artisans in Fukui prefecture have preserved the *suminigashi* technique.

• **Sumizuri-e.** The oldest technique of printing ukiyo-e prints, using only black China ink *(sumi)*, with no color added.

Sumida-gawa. Name of the Arakawa river for the 23.5 km of its lower course, where it crosses the north part of Tokyo and drains into Tokyo Bay. In the Edo period, it was lined with holiday cottages and teahouses, and pleasure boats and merchant ships plied its waters. It was often portrayed by painters of ukiyo-e prints.

• *Sumidagawa.* Title of a Noh play: a woman wandering in search of the son she has lost crosses the Sumida River in a boat. The boatman tells her the story of a stolen child who died nearby. The woman realizes that he is talking about her son and has him take her to the tomb, where she prays to Amida. The child's spirit then appears and disappears.
→ *See* AZUMA-MONDO.

Suminokura ryōi. Merchant and shipowner (Yoshida Mitsuyoshi, 1554–1614), born in Kyoto to a family of physicians and money lenders. He obtained a license from Hideyoshi *(shuin-jō)* and sent his ships to trade with Vietnam. Also an engineer and hydraulics expert, he made the Ōi-gawa river navigable by dredging its gorges. His sons, Suminokura Genshi and Suminokura Soan (1571–1632), continued his work, dredging the Fujikawa and Kamo-gawa rivers.

Sumi Taigi. Haiku poet (active ca. 1709), Bashō's disciple.

Sumitomo. Trading house founded in the early seventeenth century that became an important zaibatsu, expanding in the early twentieth century by taking over the Ashio Mines. This industrial firm was founded by Sumitomo Masatomo (1585–1652) and his adoptive son, Sumitomo Tomomochi (Soga Rihei), who used a technique that he had learned from the Europeans at Dejima to extract the silver from copper during the refining process. By 1690, Sumitomo had bought the Besshi Mines (Shikoku) and was the main exporter of silver and supplier of metal to the Edo shogunate. In the Meiji and Taishō eras, the company diversified its activities; before the Second World War, it was the third-largest zaibatsu in Japan (after Mitsui and Mitsubishi), owning banks and insurance companies in addition to its metallurgic plants, for a total of more than 135 companies. The Sumitomo zaibatsu was dismantled in 1948 but re-formed in 1950 as a *keiretsu* and now controls some 80 companies, among them the Sumitomo Bank (Sumitomo-ginkō), the chemical-products company Sumitomo Kagaku Kōgyō, the Sumitomo Semento cement works, a public-works firm (Sumitomo Kensetsu), a general trading company (Sumitomo Shōji), a heavy-industry plant (Sumitomo Jūkikai Kōgyō), lumber operations (Sumitomo Ringyō), mines (Sumitomo Kinzoku Kōzan), an insurance company (Sumitomo Seimei Hoken Sōgo Kaisha), pneumatics plants (Sumitomo Gomu Kōgyō), transportation companies (Sumitomo Sōko), and others.

• **Sumitomo Ginkō.** Bank founded by Sumitomo Kichizaemon in 1895. It has branches in Hawai'i (since 1916), San Francisco (1925), and Brazil (1958). It is the third largest in Japan in terms of investments. Head office in Osaka.

Sūmitsu-in. In the Meiji, Taishō, and Shōwa eras, the emperor's Privy Council, composed of between 12 and 24 members. It was dissolved in 1947 when the new Constitution was promulgated.

Sumi-yagura. In Japanese castle architecture, a corner tower of fortifications used as a lookout and sometimes as lodging for guards or storing of merchandise. *See* CASTLES, YAGURA.

Sumiyaki chōja. "The Millionaire Coal Miner," a folk tale in which a poor coal miner makes a fortune when his wife discovers a gold mine. Variations are called *Imohori chōja* (The Millionaire Potato Gatherer) and *Asahi chōja* (The Morning Millionaire).

Sumiyoshi-ha. Painting school founded by Tosa Hiromichi (Sumiyoshi Jokei) in 1662 as a branch of the Yamato-e school. While painters of the Tosa school worked mainly for the imperial court in Kyoto, those of the Sumiyoshi school worked for the Edo shogunate. The name Sumiyoshi came from the fact that Tosa Hiromichi, Tosa Mitsunori's brother, was appointed *hokkyō* and official painter of the Sumiyoshi shrine in Osaka by Emperor Gosai-in. Having attracted the attention of the shogunate, he was invited to Edo, where he founded his own school of official painters (Goyō-eshi), becoming at the same time the private painter for shogun Tokugawa Tsunayoshi. In the eighteenth century, the Sumiyoshi-ha was divided into two branches, Itaya and Awataguchi. The best-known members of this school were Sumiyoshi Hiromichi (Jokei, 1599–1670), Sumiyoshi Hirozumi (Gukei, 1631–1705), Sumiyoshi Hironatsu (Kakushū, 1644–1735), Sumiyoshi Hiroyasu (1666–1750), Sumiyoshi Hiromori (1705–77), Sumiyoshi Hiroyuki (1754–1811), Sumiyoshi Hironao (1780–1828), and Sumiyoshi Hirotsura (1793–1863).

Sumiyoshi mode. Title of a Noh play: Prince Genji meets Lady Akoshi, who consoles him during his exile at the Sumiyoshi shrine.

Sumiyoshi monogatari. Tale written by an anonymous author in the Kamakura period, a sort of Japanese version of "Cinderella," perhaps a revision of a text dating from the Heian period. It is now lost.

Sumiyoshi Myōjin. Three-person Shinto *kami*: three sons of Susanoo no Mikoto who represent the sea, fish, and shells, respectively. Traditionally considered guardians of seafood vendors, they are venerated at the Sumiyoshi shrines in Osaka, Shimonoseki, and Fukuoka. They are said to have helped Jingū Kōgō conquer Korea.

• **Sumiyoshi-taisha (or -jinja).** Shinto shrine erected in Naniwa (Osaka), according to legend, by Jingū Kōgō when she returned from Korea. It has four buildings dedicated to four *kami*—the "three Sumiyoshi brothers" and Empress Jingū Kōgō, deified with the name Okina-gatarashi-hime no Mikoto. Built in the *sumiyoshi-zukuri* style, the buildings are considered National Treasures. It includes an arch bridge from about 1600. Most of the other structures were reconstructed in 1708 using the old plans. The annual festival takes place on July 31. There are many other Sumiyoshi shrines throughout the country; the best known are in Fukuoka and Shimonoseki and on the island of Iki. Also sometimes called Suminoe-jinja. *See* JINJA.

Summers, James. English scholar (1828–91), born in Ritchfield, who studied a number of Chinese dialects while teaching English literature in Hong Kong. When he returned to London, he learned Jap-

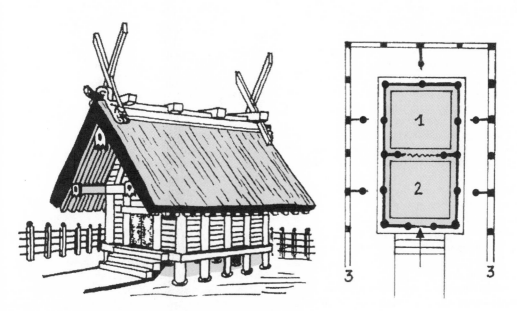

Plan of a *sumiyoshi*-style shrine. 1. Shrine. 2. Antechamber. 3. Fence

anese with E. Satow, then was invited to teach in Japan by the Iwakura mission. He and his family moved to Tokyo in 1873, and he taught English literature at the Kaisei Gakkō, introducing the works of Shakespeare and Milton to his students. He also taught in Niigata (1876) and Sapporo (1878) before settling in Tokyo in 1882 and opening his own school.

Sumo. Ritual wrestling match of shamanic (Shinto) origin, performed between two powerful combatants in the center of a circular arena symbolizing Heaven and bounded by a thick, semi-buried straw cord with four "gates" delineating a square area symbolizing the Earth. The winner is the one who throws his opponent to the ground or makes him step outside the circle. Matches, preceded by a ritual of exorcism and purification (throwing handfuls of salt), are controlled by referees *(gyōji)* dressed in sixteenth-century costumes who indicate the points won with a fan *(gumbai)*.

The ring, or *dohyō*, a square measuring 5.5 m per side, is on a platform about 50 cm high. The circle of combat measures 4.5 m in diameter and is made of clay. In the center are two lines about 1.2 m apart that mark the starting places *(hikirisen)* of the combatants. Above the *dohyō* is a suspended roof imitating that of a Shimmei-style Shinto shrine, on the corners of which are hung pompons *(fusa)* in colors symbolizing the four seasons (green for spring, red for summer, white for autumn, black for winter). Formerly, the roof *(yakata)* was supported by four pillars decorated in the same colors.

Before a tournament, the *sumotori* (wrestlers), divided into two teams (East and West), parade around the arena dressed in their ceremonial aprons *(keshō-mawashi)*, preceded by the *yokozuna* (grand champions), each attended by a herald *(tsuyaharai)* and a sword bearer *(tachimochi)*. They wear a wide twisted belt *(tsuna)* made of white hemp, somewhat similar to the *shimenawa* of Shinto shrines, because their function is sacred. After observing each other from their marks *(shikiri)*, pairs of *sumotori* confront each other: they launch themselves toward each other, and the fight is very short. They must use only 48 codified "holds"; punches and kicks are forbidden, but they may pull an adversary's belt *(mawashi)* to unbalance him. They must not grab the adversary's codpiece *(maetate-mitsu)*. Fights are overseen by head referees *(tate-gyōji)*, assisted by judge-referees *(gyōji)*.

According to legend, *sumo* wrestling originates with a fight that took place between two *kami* for possession of the country. In fact, it commemorates

a fight that took place, in the early centuries AD, between two enemy chiefs, one probably Korean (from Izumo) and the other Japanese (from Yamato). At first, as a shamanic religious manifestation, *sumo* was practiced in villages to win favor with the *kami* and obtain abundant harvests. Some matches took place in the presence of the emperor (*see* SECHIE-ZUMŌ). The rules were very different than they are now. It was only in the Heian period that *sumo* tournaments were organized and held more or less regularly, drawing wrestlers from all parts of Japan. In the Kamakura period, *sumo* became a military art *(jōran-zumō)*. When the rules of *sumo* were clarified, in the Edo period, it took the form that we know today and became popular.

Currently, six major tournaments are held every year: three in Tokyo, and the others in Osaka, Nagoya, and Fukuoka. A tournament lasts 15 days, and each *sumotori* faces a different adversary in each match *(torikumi)*. The winner of the tournament—the one with most victories—receives a trophy from the emperor. The other prizes awarded are the *shukun-shō*, which goes to the *sumotori* who has defeated the greatest number of *yokozuna* and *ōzeki* (*see* SUMOTORI); the *kantō-shō*, to the one who was most combative; and the *ginō-shō*, to the one with the best technique. To receive one of these prizes, a *sumotori* must have won at least 8 victories out of his 15 matches. At the end of each day of a tournament, a low-ranking *sumotori* *(maku-shita)* climbs onto the *dohyō* and performs a dance with a bow *(yumi-shiki)* to thank the *kami* and the audience. *Sumo* tournaments are extremely popular and are broadcast on television in their entirety.

• **Sumotori.** *Sumo* wrestlers, also called *rikishi*. They are organized into a hierarchy based on their victories in tournaments. The highest-level *sumotori (maku-uchi)* are the "grand champions" *(yokozuna)*, "champions" *(ōzeki)*, and three "upper ranks," *sekiwake*, *komosubi*, and *maegashira*, collectively called *sanyaku*. Below the champions come the *jūryō* ("10 *ryō*," fifth rank), the *maku-shita* (fourth rank), *sandamme* (third rank), *jōnidan* (second rank), *jōnokuchi* (first rank), and beginners *(mae-zumō)*. An apprentice *sumotori* can attain the rank of *sekitori* (*maku-uchi* and *jūryō*) only after at least two years of training. All *sumotori* belong to a "stable" *(heya)*, usually directed by a former *yokozuna*, the *toshiyori*. After each match, the names and ranks of the *sumotori*, written with special characters, are posted on placards *(banzuke)* giving their placings. *Rikishi* fight wearing a codpiece *(mae-tate-mitsu)* and a very thick silk belt *(ma-*

Yokozuna (Sumo Grand Champions)

Akashi (sixteenth century)
Maruyama (1712–49)
Ayagawa (b. 1700)
Tanikaze (Kajinosuke, 1750–95)
Onagawa (1758–1805)
Ao no Matsu (1791–1851)
Inazuma (1795–1877)
Shiranui I (1801–54)
Hide no Yama (1808–62)
Unryū (1823–91)
Shiranui II (1825–79)
Jimmaku (1829–1903)
Kimenzan (1826–71)
Sakaigawa (1843–89)
Ume ga Tani I (1845–1928)
Nishi no Umi I (1855–1908)
Konishiki (1867–1914)
Ozutsu (1870–1918)
Hitachiyama (1874–1922)
Ume ga Tani II (1878–1927)
Wakashima (1876–1943)
Tachiyama (1877–1941)
Okidō (1877–1956)
Otori (1887–1956)
Nishi no Umi II (1880–1931)
Onishiki I (Kasugano, 1855–1908)
Tochigiyama (1892–1959)
Onishiki II (1892–1943)
Miyagiyama (1895–1943)
Nishi no Umi III (1890–1933)
Tsune no Hana (Dewa no Umi, 1896–1960)

Tamanishiki (1903–33)
Musashiyama (1909–69)
Minanogawa (1903–71)
Futabayama (Tokisukaze, 1912–68)
Haguroyama (Tatsunami, 1914–69)
Aki no Umi (b. 1914)
Terukuni (Araiso, 1919–77)
Maedayama (Takasago, 1914–71)
Azumafuji (1921–73)
Chiyo no Yama (1926–77)
Kagamisato (b. 1922)
Yoshibayama (1920–77)
Tochinishiki (b. 1925)
Waka no Hana (b. 1928)
Asahi-hō (b. 1929)
Kashiwadō (b. 1938)
Taihō (b. 1940)
Tochi no Umi (b. 1938)
Sadanoyama (b. 1938)
Tama no Umi (b. 1944)
Katinofuji (b. 1942)
Kotozakura (b. 1940)
Wajima (b. 1948)
Kita no Umi (b. 1953)
Wakamisugi (Wakanohana, b. 1953)
Mie no Umi (b. 1948)
Chiyonofuji Mitsugu (*see* entry)
Takanosato (b. 1952)
Futahaguro Koji (b. 1963)
Hokuto-umi (b. 1963)
Onokuni (b. 1962)
Asahifuji (b. 1960)
Akebono (b. 1970)

washi), with naked torso and bare feet. Their hairstyle is traditional, *ō-ichō-mage* or *chon-mage,* depending on their rank. They also have special names *(shikona). Yokozuna* are extremely popular and are idolized by the public, despite the fact that they weigh more than 200 kg; they maintain their bulk thanks to a specially designed diet. There are currently about 700 *sumotori* belonging to about 30 *heya.* The most popular *sumo* stadium in Japan is the Shin Kokugikan in Tokyo, with seating for more than 10,000 spectators; it was built in 1985 to replace the old Kokugikan, which was destroyed during the Second World War. It has a garden and a *sumo* museum.

Sumoto. City on Awaji (Hyōgo prefecture), economic center of the island and site of a castle from the Edo period. Electrical industries. *Pop.*: 45,000.

Sumpu. Former name (before 1869) of the city of Shizuoka (Honshu). Tokugawa Ieyasu retired there in 1605, after leaving his shogunal responsibilities to his son, Hidetada, and died there on June 1, 1616. He was buried on a nearby hill, Kunōzan, and his body was transferred to the Tōshōgū in Nikkō the following year. Castle built by Tokugawa Ieyasu in 1607–08. Also called Fuchū, Funai.

• *Sumpu-ki.* Chronicle covering the period 1611–15, when Tokugawa Ieyasu had retired to his castle in Sumpu, attributed either to Hayashi Razan or to Gotō Mitsutsugu.

Sunagawa. Archeological site in Saitama prefecture, containing many stone tools (backed knives, chisels, blades, various shards) in flint, obsidian, and slate, from the Sendoki period; it may date from about 15,000 to 13,000 BC.

Sunaona. Term for a person who is able to behave normally with no effort—that is, to obey the authorities and follow customs—as opposed to *hinkureta,* a person who is too individualistic and unreliable. *See also* AMAE.

Suntory. Anglicized name of the liquor and beer producer Santorī. Founded in 1899 by Torii Shinjirō, it is famous for its Suntory brand whiskey and is currently the second-largest whiskey producer in the world; it also owns an international chain of Japanese restaurants. It created a foundation for development of the arts and music and an art museum in Tokyo, as well as an annual award for social and humanitarian sciences. Head office in Osaka. *See* SAJI KEIZŌ.

Suō. Former province, also called Suō no Kuni, Bōshū. In 1871, it was merged with Nagato (Chōshū) province to form Yamaguchi prefecture.
• Garment made of hemp once worn by low-ranking warriors, shaped like the *hitatare* worn by noble warriors, but without decorations or *mon.*
→ *See* SETONAIKAI.

Suō Nukina. Confucian philosopher (1778–1863), born in Kyoto, and calligrapher in the styles of the Chinese Jin and Tang dynasties.

Suō otoshi. Title of a Kabuki play adapted from a Kyōgen play by Fukuchi Ochi in 1892. *See* SHIN KABUKI JŪHACHIBAN.

Surimi. Pasta made from fresh sea fish that has been skinned and boned, washed, ground, and flavored, intended to replace fish in the normal diet. All sorts of fish are used to make *surimi*—elver, tuna, whiting, cod, smelts, pollock, haddock, hake, crustaceans, and mollusks. The final product can be frozen; it is tasty, rich in protein, produces no waste, and offers an excellent quality-price ratio. At first made in Japan, *surimi* has become popular in many other countries and is now made all over the world. *See* CUISINE.

Surimono. "Printed items," a type of opulent ukiyo-e prints printed in limited editions, generally to celebrate a birthday, for New Year's gifts, or to announce a birth, marriage, death, or other event. These prints had no standard dimensions and could be anywhere from the size of a visiting card to that of a large sheet of paper. Many *surimono,* which gave rise to calendar pictures, were full of bright colors and gold or silver, and some had embossed designs; some were printed on silk *(suri-e).* An infinite number of subjects were portrayed. The most famous artists who made *surimono* were Kubo Shumman, Gakutei (ca. 1786–1868), Hokusai, and Hokkei (1780–1850).

Suruga. Former province on Suruga Bay; now Shizuoka prefecture.

Surugadai-ha. School of painting, branch of the Kanō school of Edo; it directed the group of painters called *omote-eshi.* Its name came from the name of the district in Edo where it was established.

Susanoo no Mikoto. Important character in Shinto mythology, born from the nose of Izanagi and half-brother to Amaterasu-Ōmikami. This "impetuous *kami*" may symbolize storms and the destructive forces of nature. According to the *Kojiki,* he destroyed his sister's rice paddies and upset weavers in their houses by throwing a horse skinned "backward" into the room where they worked; this infuriated Amaterasu, and she hid in a cave, thus plunging the world into darkness. Expelled from the land of the *kami (takamagahara)* by the other divinities, Susasnoo descended to Earth and settled in Izumo, where, to save a young woman, Kushi Inada-hime, he slew a dragon with eight heads and eight tails, Yamata no Orochi. He pulled from the monster's tail a famous sword, *kusanagi,* which became one of the three treasures of the empire, with the jewels *(magatama)* and the sacred mirror *(yata no kagami).* His main shrine, Izumo-taisha, is in Izumo. The myth of Susanoo may represent the conflict between some Japanese clans and the Koreans. In Kyoto, he is sometimes assimilated with the syncretic *kami* Gozu Tennō and is venerated at the Yasaka-jinja.

Sushi. Typical Japanese dish consisting of small rolls of rice with vinegar or another condiment added, rolled in algae *(nori),* and topped with a small piece of fish or crustacean. It is eaten accompanied by *sake.* There are various types of *sushi.* The most popular are *nigiri-zushi,* hand rolled with *wasabi* (black radish) and *umeboshi* (salted plums); *hako-zushi,* pressed in a wooden mold; *maki-zushi,* the most popular, rolled in a *nori* leaf; *chirashizushi,* in which vinegar rice is mixed with vegetables, egg, and other ingredients. *Sushi* is said to have come from southern China. Each region has its specialty, and many restaurants *(sushi-ya)* serve only *sushi*. *See* CUISINE.

Sushun Tennō. Thirty-second emperor (Prince Hatsusebe Wakasazaki, 523<588–92>), Kimmei Tennō's son and successor to his brother, Yōmei. He was assassinated by Soga no Umako, who placed Empress Suiko on the throne.

Susukida Kyūkin. Poet (Susukida Junsuke, 1877–1945), born in Okayama prefecture. He wrote in symbolist style; *Boteki-shū* (1900), *Yuku haru* (1901), and *Hakuryōkyū* (1906) are his best-known collections. He also wrote several literary essays.

Sutego. In ancient Japan, the ritual practice of abandoning a child that was congenitally deformed or born in a year considered unfavorable in the astrological cycle. The child was left on a riverbank or at a crossroads, where a respectable person *(hiroi-oya),* chosen in advance, usually a Shinto priest or a Buddhist monk, would "find" it and raise it.

Sutoku Tennō. Seventy-fifth emperor (Prince Akihito, 1119<1124–42>1164), son of and successor to Toba Tennō. His mother was Fujiwara Shoko (Taiken Mon'in). Since he was only five years old when he ascended to the throne, Retired Emperor Shirakawa was the de facto ruler. In 1142, Toba Tennō forced Sutoku to abdicate in favor of his half-brother, Konoe. He tried to recapture the throne by force after his father's death, with the help of Fujiwara no Yorinaga (1120–56), but he was defeated by the new emperor, Go-Shirakawa *(see* HŌGEN NO RAN*),* and exiled to Sanuki province, where he died.

Suwa. Former province, now included in Nagano prefecture.

• **Suwa-jinja (or -taisha).** Shinto shrines, one in Nagano *(kami-sha)* and the other about 10 km away, in Shimo Suwa; both are dedicated to three *kami,* Suwa Myōjin (Tate Minakata), Yasakatome, and Kotoshironushi. Every six years (in the years of the Monkey and the Tiger), a strange festival takes place during which hundreds of young men cut down large pine trees and take them to the two shrines, where they replace the sacred pillars *(ombashira).* Annual *matsuri* April 15 and August 1.

Suwa Sōzan. Master ceramist (1852–1922) in Kyoto.

Suzaka no Ōji. In Heian-kyō (Kyoto), a wide avenue running south-north, from the south gate to the entrance to the imperial palace, dividing the city into two equal parts.

Suzaku Tennō. Sixty-first emperor (Prince Yuta-akira, 923<931–46>952), son of and successor to Daigo Tennō. He abdicated in favor of his brother, Murakami.

Suzu. Small bell made of clay or bronze, typical ornament on the costumes of ancient shamans and now in Shinto shrines. *Suzu* are of very ancient origins (Jōmon period); they were used to decorate Shinto sacred objects, such as mirrors and horse harnesses. In Kagura dances, garlands of *suzu* were used to call upon the *kami* to comfort the souls of the deceased. A large *suzu* is often hung in the entrance to Shinto shrines; followers can pull a cord to ring it to summon the *kami* of the site.

Suzuki Akira. Confucian scholar (1764–1837), born in Nagoya; his father was a physician. He studied with Motoori Norinaga and became interested in Japanese grammar, which he set out to define by classifying the language's components. He wrote two short treatises on the subject, *Gengyo shishu-ron* (published in 1824) and *Katsugo danzoku fu* (published after his death), and an essay on the origin of the language, *Gago onjō kō* (1816).

Suzuki Bunji. Christian union leader (1885–1946). After a trip to the United States in 1915, he founded two fraternal organizations that were transformed into labor unions; one, the Yūaikai (1912), became the Dai Nippon Rōdō Sōdōmei Yūaikai in 1919. He was elected to the Diet three times beginning in 1928 for the Shakai Minshūtō (Socialist People's party), then the Shakai Taishūtō (Socialist Masses party). Japan's representative to the International Labor Organization, he wrote several works on the labor movement in Japan.

Suzuki Daisetsu. Philosopher (Suzuki Teitarō, 1870–1966), born in Kanazawa. After receiving Zen Buddhist training at the Engaku-ji temple in Kamakura, he went to the United States, where he stayed from 1897 to 1910, translating various works of Eastern philosophy into English; in 1907, he published *Outlines of Mahāyāna Buddhism*. When he returned to Japan, he became an English professor at the Peers' School (Gakushūin) and married Beatrice Lane, who was his collaborator until his death. In 1921, he became a professor of

Buddhism at Ōtani University in Kyoto and published the magazine *Eastern Buddhist;* he collected the articles into *Essays in Zen Buddhism* (3 vols., 1927, 1933, 1934). He translated various Buddhist texts and published *Zen Buddhism and Its Influence on Japanese Culture* (1938). Elected to the Japan Academy (Nihon Gakushi-in), he received the Order of Culture (Bunka-shō) in 1949. He often traveled abroad to spread the teachings of Zen Buddhism. Among his other books are *Introduction to Zen Buddhism* (1934), *Manual of Zen Buddhism* (1935), and *Studies on the Lankāvatāra-sūtra* (1930). In the West, he was called Daisetz (or D. T.) Suzuki. *See* MATSUGAOKA BUNKO.

Suzuki Eitarō. Sociologist (1894–1966), born in Nagasaki prefecture. He was known for his sociological studies of Japanese villages and cities, about which he wrote a number of important books.

Suzuki Harunobu. *See* HARUNOBU.

Suzuki Jidōsha Kōgyō. Manufacturer of automobiles, minibuses, and motorcycles; along with Honda and Yamaha, the largest in Japan, affiliated with Isuzu and General Motors. It was founded in 1920 in Hamamatsu by Suzuki Michio. Suzuki motorcycles have won many international races. The company currently has assembly plants in Thailand, the Philippines, Indonesia, Pakistan, and other countries. It exports more than 44% of its production. Head office in Hamamatsu (Shizuoka prefecture).

Suzuki Kantarō. Admiral (1867–1948), born in Osaka. He was a personal adviser to the emperor starting in 1929, then prime minister (Apr.–Oct. 1945), succeeding General Koiso Kuniaki. After relieving General Tōjō Hideki of his position, the emperor asked Suzuki Kantarō to seek peace, but he resigned instead. Prince Higashikuni Naruhiko succeeded him as government leader.

Suzuki Kiitsu. Painter (Suzuki Motonaga, 1796–1858) in the Rimpa style, born in Ōmi; Sakai Hōitsu's favorite disciple. He specialized in painting faces, and flowers and birds, and was also an excellent haiku poet. He sometimes signed his works Kiitsu.

Suzuki Kisaburō. Politician (1867–1940), born in Kawasaki. He became a judge; appointed minister of justice in Kiyoura Keigo's cabinet. A member of the Rikken Seiyūkai (Friends of Constitutional

Government party) and minister of the interior in Tanaka Giichi's cabinet in 1927, he was responsible for mass arrests of communists in 1928 and forced to resign. He also resigned as president of the Seiyūkai in 1937.

Suzuki Masaharu. Sculptor and painter (b. 1920 in Aomori) who adorned his birthplace with his works; a small museum is devoted to him in Aomori. He had an exhibit at the Franco-Japanese institute in Tokyo in 1995.

Suzuki Masatsugu. Public-works engineer (1889–1987), born in Nagano; professor at Nihon University. He was decorated with the Order of Culture (Bunka-shō) in 1968. He designed most of the major ports in Japan.

Suzuki Miekichi. Writer of children's stories (1882–1936), born in Hiroshima prefecture. In 1918, he founded a magazine for children, *Akai Tori* (The Red Bird), to which well-known writers, including Akutagawa Ryūnosuke, contributed.

Suzuki Mosaburō. Politician (1893–1970), born in Aichi prefecture. At first a journalist with socialist leanings, he founded a number of "proletarian" parties but was arrested in 1937. After the Second World War, he helped revive the Socialist party, of which he was president in 1951. He was elected to the Diet nine times in a row, starting in 1946, and amassed a large library (Shakai Bunko) of works on socialism in Japan.

Suzuki Osamu. Contemporary ceramist, born 1926 in Kyoto. His works have won many gold medals, including in Prague (1962) and Vallauris (1970), and have been exhibited in Paris in 1986 and 1994, and in Mons, Belgium, in 1989.

Suzuki Shigetane. Scholar (1812–63) of National Learning (Kokugaku), Hirata Atsutane's disciple. Born in Awaji, he lived in Edo. In 1853, he began to write a commentary on the *Nihon shoki (Nihon-shoki den);* this work remained unfinished because he was murdered under mysterious circumstances.

Suzuki Shin'ichi. Musician (1898–1998). After studying the violin in Germany and with Andō Kō (1878–1963) in Japan, he developed a method of teaching the violin that bears his name and that has been used in Japan and abroad by hundreds of thousands of students.

Suzuki Shōsan. Zen Buddhist philosopher (1579–1655), born in Mikawa; he fought under Tokugawa Ieyasu at the Battle of Sekigahara in 1600 as a minor vassal, then took part in the siege of the castle of Osaka in 1614–15. In 1621, he became a Zen Buddhist monk, but he did not accept the principles of the Rinzai-shū or the Sōtō-shū and remained independent. His teachings, in which he recommended making fists and striking a fierce pose in order to frighten evil spirits, were called *niō-zen*. His most important work is a collection of his thought, *Roankyō* (1648). Also known by the names Shōzan, Suzuki Shōzō.

Suzuki Umetarō. Chemist (1874–1943), born in Shizuoka prefecture. He studied at the University of Tokyo and in Germany and conducted interesting research on proteins, vitamin B1, and nutrition. He received the Japan Academy Prize (Nihon Gakushi-in-shō) in 1924 and the Order of Culture (Bunka-shō) in 1943.

Suzuki Zenkō. Politician, born 1911 in Iwate prefecture. An expert in maritime and fishing issues, he was elected to the House of Representatives for the Socialist party in 1947, but he switched parties, joining the Minshu Jiyūtō in 1949. Continually reelected, he was minister of the post office and telecommunications in Ikeda Hayato's first cabinet in 1960 and minister of health in Satō Eisaku's cabinet in 1965. When Prime Minister Ōhira Masyoshi died, in 1980, he succeeded him, but he suddenly resigned in 1982 and was replaced by Nakasone Yasuhiro. He was nicknamed Hotoke Zenkō ("Zenkō the Buddha") by his friends.

Suzuri. Ink stone carved into very fine-grained stone, generally imported from China, on which the painter or calligrapher rubs a *sumi* (solid China ink) stick to make ink, adding a few drops of pure water. Some stones are decorated with fine bas-relief sculptures and are very valuable.

• **Suzuri-bako.** Special box containing writing utensils: *suzuri, mizu-ire* (water flask), *sumi* sticks, and brushes *(fude)*.

Sweet potatoes. Although its proper name is *kansho,* this tuber has many other common names, the most widely used of which are Satsuma-imo and Kara-imo. It is not known exactly when this plant was introduced into Japan. Some say that it arrived in Satsuma from the Ryukyu Islands in 1698; others posit 1705, or even earlier, in the late sixteenth century. It seems that it was cultivated in Satsuma and Nagasaki around 1696. Shogun Tokugawa Yoshimune introduced its cultivation in Kanto. Aoki Kon'yō wrote a treatise on the sweet potato, *Kansho-ki,* and another work on sweet potatoes (called "barbarian potato"), *Bansho-ko.*

Swords (tō). Swords probably evolved from épées imported from the mainland by "horsemen-archers" around the late third or early fourth century. At the time, hand weapons were straight, double-edged épées called *ken* or *tsurugi,* and they remained in use until at least the eighth century, more as a symbol of position among the nobles than as a true combat weapon. The treasures on exhibit in the Shosō-in in Nara include magnificent examples of such épées, probably made in China or Korea.

In the ninth century, Japanese sword makers mastered the art of forging and produced slightly curved, single-edged blades (*see* KATANA) of a constantly improving quality. *Ko-tō* (old swords) date from between 900 and 1530. By the Muromachi period, swords called *shin-tō* (new swords) were being manufactured, with ornamentation on their accessories (*tsuba,* scabbard, decorations); *shin-tō* further evolved during the Edo period, while sword types diversified.

After the wearing of swords was banned early in the Meiji era, manufacture slowed considerably, but swords were passed down as a precious inheritance in samurai families. Until the Second World War, officers wore them proudly. Unfortunately, a great number of these masterpieces of forging were destroyed by American troops, who piled them up and crushed them with tanks to wipe out what they considered to be symbols of the Japanese warrior spirit. They are still used symbolically in the martial arts. *See* AIKUCHI, AMAKUNI, AME NO MURAKUMO, ARAMI MEIZUKUSHI, BOKUTŌ, DAISHŌ, HAMON, HIRU NO OMASHI NO TSURUGI, HISAKUNI, HŌJU, HORIMONO, HŌSHŌ SADAYOSHI, HŌZŌ-IN INEI, KATANA, KŌGAI, KOZUKA, MAMORI-GATANA, MEI, MEKUGI-ANA, SAYA, SHINAI, TACHI, TANTŌ, TSUBA, TSUKA, TSURUGI, UMABARI, WAKIZASHI, YAKIBA.

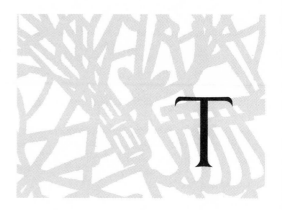

T. This consonant exists only in conjunction with the five vowels *a, i, u, e, o*. However, the sound *ti* does not exist (in current Hepburn transcription) and is replaced by the sound *chi,* which becomes *ji* through "nigorization" (*see* NIGORI). Similarly, the sound *tu* is replaced by *tsu,* which also becomes, through nigorization, the sound *zu. See* NIGORI.

Tabata. Former district of Tokyo, not far from Ueno, completely destroyed by bombing in 1945. Before the Second World War, it was considered the "Montmartre of Japan," and many writers and artists, including Kosugi Hōan, Itaya Hazan, Akutagawa Ryūnosuke, and Kikuchi Kan, lived there.

Tabe. Groups of farmers on the estates *(tadokoro, miyake)* of major families; before the Taika Reform, they were controlled by the state. They were called *kōmin* after 645.

Tabei Junko. Mountain climber, born 1939 in Fukushima prefecture. She climbed Annapurna in 1970. On May 16, 1975, she led a team of 13 Japanese women, accompanied by 23 Sherpas led by Ang Tsering, to the top of Mt. Everest. Her companion, Hisano Eiko, assisted her in this effort.

Tabi. Japanese socks. Once made of deerskin, they were shaped like simple socks; starting in the Kamakura period, because of the growing use of *zōri* sandals, they had a separation for the big toe. They began to be made in cotton in the seventeenth century. Women wear white *tabi,* while men wear maroon; men also sometimes wear white *tabi* during ceremonies. They are often worn with the traditional costume *(kimono)*. Laborers wear *tabi* made of coarse canvas with a thick rubber sole.

Tachi. Samurai sword worn not slid into the belt but hung from it by a chain, with the blade up. This type of sword was used mainly by nobles during the Heian, Kamakura, and Muromachi periods. Longer than *katana* and with a more pronounced curve, *tachi* were mainly ceremonial. In ancient times, only very high-ranking nobles (such as *nagon* and *sangi*) were allowed to wear them. A similar type, called *efu no tachi,* was reserved for high nobles and guards of the imperial palace. *Sayamaki no tachi* had a highly decorated scabbard, and *shirizaya no tachi,* used by high-ranking warriors, had a scabbard made of fur *(saya)*. Ordinary nobles preferred to carry a straight sword *(ken, tsurugi)* or a shorter *tachi,* called *shōzoku-tachi* or *shin no tachi. See* DAISHO, KATANA, KEN, TSURUGI.

Tachibana. Noble family whose origins go back to the Nara period: Agata no Inukai no Michiyo, wife of Prince Minu (a descendant of Emperor Bidatsu), received the family name Tachibana in 708 for services rendered to the court. Her descendants used this name and received the title *ason. See* TAJIMA MORI.

• **Tachibana Akemi.** Poet (Ide Akemi, 1812–68).

• **Tachibana Chikage.** *See* KATŌ CHIKAGE.

• **Tachibana-dera.** Buddhist temple founded in 606 in Takaichi (Asuka, Takechi, Nara) by Shōtoku Taishi, and reconstructed in 1864.

• **Tachibana Eizaburō.** Philosopher (1867–1901) who wrote works on the history of aestheticism and art.

• **Tachibana Hayanari.** Calligrapher (?–842) in "square" style *(reisho; Chin.: lishu)*. He went to China and returned with Kūkai in 806. He was one of the Sanseki of his era, with Saga Tennō and Kūkai. Implicated in a plot, he was banished from Kyoto and died on his way to exile.

• **Tachibana Hiromi.** Scholar (837–90), tutor for Emperor Uda, appointed *sadaiben*. He helped to compile many works, including those written by other members of his family.

• **Tachibana Hokuchi.** Haiku poet (1665–1718), one of the Bashō Juttetsu.

• **Tachibana Kachiko.** Daughter (787–851) of Tachibana Kiyotomo (757–89), Emperor Saga's wife and Emperor Nimmyō's mother. She became a Buddhist nun and built many temples. With the help of her brother, Tachibana Ujikimi, she founded the Gakkan-in school for educating children of the Tachibana family. Also called Danrin Kōgō.

• **Tachibana Kōzaburō.** Politician and social reformer (1893–1974), born in Mito. In 1915, he founded a "fraternal village," Kyōdai Mura, to demonstrate that it was possible to live in a climate of mutual assistance and understanding; in 1929, he created an agricultural cooperative; in 1931, he formed a nationalist movement, Aikyōjuku (*see* AIKYŌJUKU). With some of his disciples and a few officers, he attempted a coup d'état on May 15, 1932 (incident called Goichigo Jiken), in order to "cleanse" the government of the excesses of modern capitalism. During the incidents that followed, Prime Minister Inukai Tsuyoshi was assassinated. Arrested and convicted, Tachibana Kozaburō was sentenced to six years in prison. After the Second World War, he abandoned all political activity and devoted himself to scholarship.

• **Tachibana Moribe.** *Waka* poet (1781–1849), born in Ise. He studied the songs of the *Kojiki* and *Nihon shoki* and conducted major studies on the origin and phonetics of Japanese, publishing more than 50 books on these subjects. He was opposed to the theories of Motoori Norinaga, promoter of National Learning (Kokugaku).

• **Tachibana Morikuni.** Painter and engraver (1679–1748), Tanzan's student in Osaka.

• **Tachibana no Moroe.** Imperial prince (Katsuragi, 684–757), son of Prince Minu and Agata no Inukai no Tachibana. He was appointed *dainagon,* then minister of the right *(udaijin)* in 738 and minister of the left *(sadaijin)* in 743. He put down Fujiwara no Nakamaro's revolt in 740, but was accused of being part of a conspiracy and forced to withdraw from public affairs. His son, Tachibana no Naramaro, was killed in 757 in an attempt to oppose Fujiwara no Nakamoro. Moroe, a fervent Buddhist, built two imperial palaces; he was also a renowned poet, and his poems were included in the *Man'yōshū. See* KUNI-KYŌ.

• **Tachibana no Naramaro.** Son (721–757) of Tachibana no Moroe. He conspired with several other princes against Nakamoro but was arrested before he could take action; it is thought that he died in prison.

• **Tachibana no Narisue.** Writer (thirteenth century), sometimes considered the author of *Jikkinshō*. He wrote *Chomon-jū.*

• **Tachibana Shiraki.** Sinologist (1881–1945), born in Ōita prefecture. He worked in Manchuria and was editor of *Manshū Hyōron* (Manchuria Magazine) in 1931. He wrote various studies on Chinese civilization and Confucianism, the most important of which was *Shina shisō kenkyū* (Studies on Chinese Philosophy), published in 1936.

• **Tachibana no zushi.** *See* NENJI-BUTSU NO ZUSHI.

Tachihara Masaaki. Writer (Yonemoto Masaaki, 1926–80), born in Korea. He received the Naoki Prize in 1965 for his novel *Shiroi keshi* (The White Poppy). Among his other works are *Tsurugigasaki* (The Edge of the Cliff, 1965), *Kinuta* (1972), and *Urushi no hana* (The Lacquer Flower). His Zen-influenced novels deal mainly with the problems of people of mixed blood.

Tachihara Michizō. Poet (1914–39) who wrote lyric sonnets: *Wasure-gusa ni yosu* and *Atsuki no yūbe no shi* (1937).

Tachikawa. City in Tokyo prefecture, located about 27 km south of the capital; its military airports and aeronautics plants have been converted to automobile plants. Pop.: 150,000.

• **Tachikawa K1-74.** Bomber built in 1939 in Tachikawa. American code name: "Patsy." *Maximum speed:* 570 km/h; *range:* 7,000 km; *payload:* 1,000 kg of bombs. Only a small number of this model were built; it was one of the first to have a pressurized cockpit, and it was not part of military operations in the Second World War.

Tachiki Kannon-ji. Buddhist temple built near the Chūzen-ji in Nikkō; it houses a famous wooden statue of Senju Kannon dating from the ninth century.

Tachū-saimon-kyō. Japanese mirrors, decorated on the back with one or several buttons and finely incised zigzags or parallel lines. A large number were found in sites from the Yayoi period in northern Kyushu.

Tadanobu. Noh play: a brave warrior from the Minamoto clan fights to the death to save Minamoto no Yoshitune's life. *See* FUJIWARA NO TADANOBU.

Tadanori. Title of a Noh play: a traveling monk arrives in Ichi no Tani and falls asleep under a cherry tree. He dreams of the poet-warrior Taira no Tadanori, who appears to him and tells him about how he died in battle. The Noh play *Shunzei tadanori* deals with the same subject.

Tadayoshi. Family line of sword makers founded in Hizen province by Tadayoshi I (1572–1632). Also called Kyūshū-mono.
• Maker of swords (Hashimoto Tadayoshi, 1572–1614) in Saga province.
• Sculptor (Hōgen Tadayoshi, mid-nineteenth century) of netsuke and Buddhist images.
→ *See* ASHIKAGA TADAYOSHI.

Tada Yūkei. Writer (1913–80) and haiku poet. He wrote the novels *Chōkō dureta* (The Jiangjing Delta, 1941), *Hebi-shi* (The Snake Charmer), *Shō-setsu bashō* (Bashō's Novel), and others.

Tadokoro. Before the Taika Reform (645), a term for lands belonging to major families or clans.

Tadoshiki-doki bunka. Prehistoric cultures in Kanto and on Kyushu and Hokkaido, characterized by comb-decorated pottery *(Kammkeramik)* similar to that in Siberia. These cultures may have been related to the Yori-ito mondoki bunka and Oshigata mondoki bunka cultures.

Taema. Noh play, a continuation of *Hibariyama*: in a dream, a Buddhist monk sees Amida and Kannon Bosatsu weaving a magnificent tapestry for Chūjō, who then appears and sings and dances. *See* CHŪJŌ-HIME.

Taga-jō. Town in Miyagi prefecture, about 10 km northeast of Sendai, the site of an eighth-century fort (built by Ōno no Azumahito in 724) and former seat of government of Mutsu province, on the Pacific coast. In 1978, a number of documents *(mokkan* and manuscripts) dating from 780 to 822 were found in the ruins of the fort. They are the oldest writings on lacquered paper found to date in Japan. Electrical and electronics plants. *Pop.:* 50,000.

Tagata-jinja. Shinto shrine in the village of Ajioka (Aichi prefecture), founded before the seventh century and dedicated to the *kami* Tagata Tenjin, Tama-hime, Ame no Hohi, and Mitoshi. During fertility rites celebrated there every March 15, an enormous phallus carved from *hinoki* wood is solemnly carried in a procession, then placed in a restaurant and venerated.

Tageta. Very wide wooden clogs used by peasants to keep them from sinking into the mud of rice paddies. This type of footwear was found in the Yoyoi site in Toro. Also called *ōashi*. *See* GETA.

Taguchi Ukichi. Historian (1855–1905), born in Edo. He founded an economics journal, *Tōkyō Keizai Zasshi,* in which he advocated adoption of a liberal economy, and wrote several important works on the history of economic development in Japan. He also wrote several history books, including *Nippon kaika shōshi* (Short History of Japanese Civilization, 1877–87), edited a historical journal, *Shikai* (Ocean of History), and published collections of ancient documents. He was elected to the House of Representatives (Shūgi-in) in 1894.

Tahō-tō. A specific type of Buddhist pagoda used by the Tendai and Shingon sects, with one or two square roofs and a hemispheric "main part" imitating an Indian *stūpa*. The top roof is generally of the *hōgyō* type (*see* ROOFS). This type of pagoda resembles the *shari-tō* type and was probably inspired by the *tabo-tap* in Kyŏng-ju, Korea.

Tai. Fish (dorado family) highly prized in Japan for its flesh and considered a symbol of happiness. This fish is often offered to people as an honor. It is also the emblem of Ebisu, one of the Seven Gods of Good Fortune (Shichifukujin).

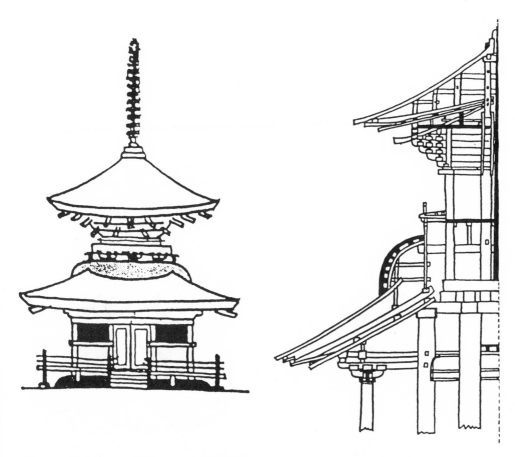

Schematic elevation and cross-section of a *tahō-tō* pagoda

Tai-ei. Era of Emperor Shōkō: Aug. 1521–Aug. 1528. *See* NENGŌ.

Taifu. Title for nobles of the fifth rank (*see* I) in the Nara period. By the Edo period, the term had become an honorific conferred on officers of the estates of daimyo and high-ranking courtesans *(taiyū)*.

Taigan. Painter (*gō*: Unge, Unge-in, Kōsetsu, Sen-kōjin, Taigan, 1773–1850) of the Nanga school and Buddhist monk, professor of Confucianism at the Takakuragakuryō school in Kyoto. He painted mainly bamboo and flowers.

Taigen-shō. Book on music theory written by Toyohara Muneaki (1450–1524) in 1512; its subjects included musical instruments, rhythm, singing, orchestras, and families of musicians. It was one of the Sambusho (Three Musical Treatises), with *Kyō-kun-sho,* by Koma no Chikazane, and *Zoku kyō-kun-shō,* by Koma's grandson.

Taihei-gempō. Term for several silver coins struck starting in 760, at the same time as gold coins called *kaiki-shōhō* (which were worth 10 *taihei-gempō*). No examples of these coins have been found.

Taiheiki. "History of the Great Peace." A fictionalized historical chronicle in 41 volumes by an unknown author, often attributed to the Buddhist monk Kojima (d. 1374) and probably rewritten at a later date. This long chronicle describes the intrigues and battles that took place between 1318 and 1367, the fall of the Kamakura *bakufu,* the war between the two courts (Nambokuchō), and how small-scale lords took over from major ones *(geko-kujō).* Written in a mixed Chinese-Japanese style *(wakan-konkōbun)* and sung by itinerant bards, it was supplemented by Chinese and Buddhist tales. This work spawned many variants and inspired a number of plays and novels. It is also sometimes attributed to the Buddhist monk Gen-e (1269–1352) and his disciples.

Taihei-yō. Japanese name for the Pacific Ocean.

• **Taihei-yō Gakkai.** Association of Japanese painters using a style tending toward the European (Yōga), founded in 1901. Many of its members studied at Académie Julian in Paris and under Jean-Paul Laurens.

• **Taihei-yō Sensō.** "Pacific War" (1941–45) between the Allies and Japan.

Taihō. Era of Emperor Mommu: Mar. 701–May 704. *See* NENGŌ.

• *Taihō ritsuryō.* Legal code *(ritsuryō)* promulgated in 701, modeled on the code of the Chinese Tang dynasty, compiled by a group of scholars of the imperial court, among them Prince Osakabe (?– 705), Fujiwara no Fuhito, and Awata no Mahito. It comprised eight volumes on penal law *(ritsu)* and eleven volumes on laws concerning administration *(ryō)*. This code, revised in 718 as *Shin-ryō*, or *Yōrō ritsuryō*, was in use until 1858 *(see* RITSURYŌ KYAKU-SHIKI). It gave rise to a series of important reforms *(Taihō no kaishin)* aimed at reinforcing the Yamato court's authority and centralizing administrative agencies, following the Chinese model. It definitively replaced the older legal codes, such as the *Asuka no kiyomihara* (689) and the *Ōmi* (668).

Tai-i. Military grade in the Meiji era, equivalent to captain.

Taiji. Era of Emperor Sutoku: Jan. 1126–Jan. 1131. *See* NENGŌ.

Taika. Era of Emperor Kōtoku: Aug. 645–Feb. 650. This was the first imperial era *(nengō)* in Japan, according to the Chinese system of eras (Nianhao).

• *Taika no kaishin.* "Taika Reform." A group of administrative laws based on those of Tang-dynasty China, promulgated in 645, that created court ranks *(see* I), divided up cultivated land, and established a calendar *(reki)* and the use of eras *(see* NENGŌ). These laws were made obsolete by the

Taihō Code (701), although some of its measures were maintained.

Taika Nijūikkajō Yōkyū. "Twenty-One Demands" formulated by the Japanese government in early 1915 for the Chinese government of Yuan Shikai, with the aim of intensifying Japan's political and trade grip on China. The demands were presented to Yuan Shikai by the Japanese ambassador to Beijing, Hioki Eki (1861–1926), and were aimed mainly at ensuring Japanese dominance over Manchuria. They also forbade China from giving territorial or port concessions to any nation but Japan. Finally, they stipulated that Japanese "counselors" would enter the government and that only Japan could supply China with arms; they also demanded rights on the railroads in the Yangzi-jiang region. After long negotiations, the Chinese government agreed to some of these "proposals," which gave rise to a wave of indignant protests and to anti-Japanese sentiment in China, but it rejected most of them, so the Japanese government sent an ultimatum on May 7, 1915. China then agreed to sign an accord, upon the advice of the British, but it did not include the last demands, which were simply "requests" and not requirements.

Taiki. Title of Fujiwara no Yorinaga's (1120–56) personal diary, covering the years 1136–55. This work contains important information on the period of "retired emperors" *(see* INSEI), even though some years have been completely left out. Also titled *Ukaiki.*

Taiko. Period of Japanese mythical history, beginning at the origin of Japan and ending with the ascension of Jimmu Tennō. *See* CHIJIN-GODAI, JINDAI.

Taikō. During the Heian period, a title given to *dajō-daijin* and to *sesshō* and *kampaku.* Toyotomi Hideyoshi was often designated by this title after 1592, when he named his son, Hidetsugu, *kampaku* in his place. It was also used by the Tokugawa shoguns between 1854 and 1867 when they dealt with foreigners. The word "tycoon" is derived from *taikō.* Also sometimes called Taikō-sama, Zenkō. *See* TAIKUN, TOYOTOMI HIDEYOSHI, ZENKŌ.

• **Taikō-kenchi.** Term often used for the general census and surveying operations first ordered by Oda Nobunaga and continued by Toyotomi Hideyoshi.

• *Taikō-ki.* "Biography of Toyotomi Hideyoshi," a work illustrated by Gyokusan (1737–1812). Also, a generic term for all works on Hideyoshi's life. The most famous is *Hoan taikō-ki,* written by Oze Hoan (1564–1640), a Confucian physician, about 1625.

• *Taikō-taigō.* Starting in 702, the title for an emperor's grandmother.

Taikun. Title used by foreigners for shoguns of Japan, starting in 1636, and designating them in diplomatic correspondence until 1868.

Taikyō (Tai-kyō). Major Shinto sect (more than 1 million followers) among the 13 officially designated in the Kyōha Shintō. In 1946, it was divided into nine branches: Tai, Bosei, Hinomoto, Maruyama, Shintō Ishikiri, Shintō Kotodama, Shintō Kotoku, Shintō Seitai, and Tengyō-kyō. Main headquarters in Tokyo. Also sometimes called Shintō Honkyōku.

• *Taikyō sempu.* "Proclamation of the Great Doctrine" made by the Meiji government in 1868 to declare Shinto the national religion; its goal was to unite all Japanese people under the spiritual authority of the emperor, the natural leader of Shinto. In 1869, an Office of Shinto Worship (Jingikan) was established. The doctrine was made public in 1870; the following year, all followers were obliged to register at their local shrine. This was the beginning of State Shinto (Kokutai Shintō), directed in 1871 by the Ministry of Shinto (Jingishō), then in 1872 by the Ministry of Religion (Kyōbushō), which became subordinate to the Ministry of the Interior in 1877.

Taima-dera. Buddhist temple located 10 km from Ōji (Osaka-fu) in Nara; built, according to tradition, in 612 by Prince Maroko, Emperor Yōmei's son. This temple was originally built in Kawachi province as Mampōzō-in and moved to its present site in 682. Its *mandara-dō* (which contains the Taima-mandara) dates in part from the seventh century and in part from about 1242. It is flanked by two pagodas (two and three stories) built in 1180 in the eighth-century style. It has a *kōdō* from 1303, containing a large wooden statue of Amida (4.25 m) dating from the eleventh century; *kondō* from 1184, renovated in 1326, with a statue of Miroku Bosatsu and the Four Guardian Kings (Shi-tennō) dating from the Nara period; and a tea garden from the Edo period. Festival on May 14–15.

Taima-jinja. Shinto shrine founded in Oazataima (Shikoku) in the Heian period. It houses wooden images from the same period portraying the *kami* Ame no Futatama and Hikohodemi-ninigi no Mikoto. *See* SHIDO.

Taima-mandara. Mandala representing Amida's paradise (Gokuraku-jōdo), made in 763. According to one legend, it was made by Chūjō-hime (753–81), one of Fujiwara no Toyonari's daughters, when she was a nun at the temple. Another legend has it that it was made by Amida and Kannon (*see* TAEMA). This image, the oldest portrayal of a mandala in Japan, measures about 1.5 m per side and is in such poor condition that it cannot be determined whether it was painted or woven. It is housed in the *mandara-dō* of the Taima-dera temple. *See* CHŪJŌ-HIME.

• *Taima-mandara emaki.* Two-scroll *emakimono* describing the legend of the weaving of the Taima-mandara, attributed to Sumiyoshi Keion (thirteenth century). It is housed in the Kōmyō-ji temple (Kanagawa prefecture).

Taimitsu. Esoteric part *(mikkyō)* of Buddhism of the Tendai-shū, as opposed to the esoteric doctrines of the Shingon-shū, or Tōmitsu. There are 13 schools of Taimitsu; the first was created by Saichō. The other major schools are the Jikaku-daishi-ryū, founded by Ennin; the Chishō-daishi-ryū, founded by Enchin; the Jien-daishi-ryū (or Kawa no Ryū), founded by Kakuchō; and the Tani-ryū (or Kōke-ryū), founded by Kōke.

Tainichi Rijikai. "Allied Council for Japan." Council established after the Second World War to manage Japan's affairs during the occupation period; its main role was to advise S.C.A.P. It was composed of representatives from the United States, China, the USSR, and Great Britain, it first met on April 5, 1946.

Taira. City in Fukushima prefecture, north of Nikkō, on the Pacific coast. Textile and lumber industries. *Pop.*: 100,000. This city was the site of an incident (Taira Jiken) during which a police station was occupied on June 30, 1949, by members of the Communist party, in a futile gesture. The 150 people arrested were acquitted.
• Powerful warrior clan (also called Heike, Heiji), descended from Prince Takamune, a grandson of Kammu Tennō. Kammu gave Takamune the family name "Taira" in 825. The various Taira fam-

ilies, including the Nimmyō, Heiji, Montoku Heiji, and Kōkō Heiji, were established on the basis of the emperor from whom they were directly descended. The main branch, Kammu Heiji, was descended from Prince Takamochi, a great-grandson of Emperor Kammu who settled in Kazusa province (Chiba prefecture) in the late ninth century. This clan gradually became very powerful in Kanto, and its members, among them Taira no Masakado and Taira no Tadatsune, led major rebellions against the central power in 940 and 1030. Having attained prominence in the court in the twelfth century, the Taira then went to war against a rival clan, the Minamoto (also called Genji), but were ultimately defeated in the Dan no Ura naval battle in 1185, by armies led by Minamoto no Yoritomo and Minamoto no Toshistune. The Taira had numerical superiority and controlled the coasts of the Inland Sea (Setonaikai), but their troops were malnourished due to persistent drought in the region, and they surrendered en masse. The Taira now controlled only the sea, but their ships were pushed by the wind onto the rocks in the Shimonoseki pass; many warriors drowned, as did the young Emperor Antoku, who was with them. This family gave rise to many others that played an important role in Japan's history, including the Chiba, Hatakeyama, Hōjō, Jō, Kajiwara, Miura, Nagao, Ōba, and Sōma.

• **Taira no Atsumori.** Warrior (1168–84), Taira no Tsunemori's (1125–85) son and Taira no Kiyomori's nephew. He died a noble death at the age of 16 in the Ichi no Tani battle against the Minamoto. The conqueror, Kumagai Naozane, became a Buddhist monk after the war in remorse. This episode has been the subject of many novels and plays, among them the Noh play *Atsumori* and the Kabuki play *Kumagai*.

• **Taira no Kagekiyo.** Warrior (?–1185), a son of Fujiwara no Tadakiyo who was adopted by the Taira. He became a general in their army, confirmed the emperor on his throne in 1156, and tried, in vain, to have Minamoto no Yoritomo assassinated. Taken prisoner in the Dan no Ura battle, he starved himself to death.

• **Taira no Kiyomori.** Leader of the Taira clan (1118–81) and son, according to various traditions, of Retired Emperor Shirakawa or of Taira no Tadamori. He obtained preeminence over the Minamoto in the court, accumulated titles, practiced wild nepotism, and finally imposed his will on the emperor. He managed to eliminate the Minamoto clan from

the court and to defeat them militarily in the Heiji no Ran (1160). He was the first in Japanese history to show a determination to exterminate his opponents; he massacred them ruthlessly, sparing only one young boy, Minamoto no Yoritomo. He took the emperor hostage, fought the Buddhist monks of the Onjō-ji temple in Ōtsu who opposed him, and transferred the emperor's court to Fukuhara-kyō (now Kobe); he was forced to retreat to Kyoto six months later. He retired in 1178, taking the religious name Jōkai; three years later, before dying of disease, he placed his grandson Antoku on the throne.

• **Taira no Kiyotsune.** *See* KIYOTSUNE.

• **Taira no Korehira.** Warrior (tenth century), Taira no Sadamori's son. Appointed governor of several eastern provinces, he gained a reputation as an outstanding swordsman.

• **Taira no Koremori.** Grandson (1160–?) of Taira no Kiyomori, chief general of the imperial forces that fought the Minamoto in 1180. Defeated several times, he fled Kyoto and is said to have committed suicide.

• **Taira no Kunika.** Warrior (tenth century), governor of Hitachi province. He was killed by his uncle, Taira no Masakado, in 935.

• **Taira no Masakado.** Warrior (?–940), Taira no Takamochi's grandson and governor of Shimōsa province (Chiba prefecture). In 935, he assassinated his nephew, Kunika, in order to seize his province; winning the support of many warriors, he took control of almost all of Kanto, which he made an autonomous state, and appointed himself emperor. The court sent its army against him, but Taira no Sadamori, a warrior serving Fujiwara no Hidesato, was ahead of them. He killed Masakado in 940, and this ended the rebellion, known in the annals as Tenkei no Ran or Jōkei Tenkei no Ran. Many legends were created around Masakado's life and death. It was said that he had three sons with a heavenly being *(tennin)* who visited him in Shimōsa, and that he was so brave that his enemies facing him in battle believed that he was seven warriors. Folklore attributed him with seven lives, associated with the seven stars of Ursa Major, which is why the Kanda Myōjin shrine in Tokyo was dedicated to him. It is not known where his tomb is, but traditions place it at several sites in Tokyo and Chiba prefectures.

- **Taira no Masako.** *See* HŌJŌ MASAKO.

- **Taira no Masamori.** Warrior (d. ca. 1121), governor of Oki province, then Inaba province. In 1108, he was made responsible for repressing Minamoto no Yoshichika's revolt.

- **Taira no Miyako.** *See* HEIAN-KYŌ, HEIJŌ-KYŌ.

- **Taira no Munemori.** Warrior (1147–85), Taira no Kiyomori's son. He succeeded Kiyomori at the head of the Taira clan in 1181 and continued the war against the Minamoto, who were backed by Emperor Go-Shirakawa, but he was expelled from Kyoto by Minamoto no Yoshinaka in 1183. He fled, taking with him young Emperor Antoku and Taira no Kiyomori's widow, Nii no Ama. Commander of the Taira fleet at Dan no Ura, he was defeated by Minamoto no Yoshitsune's army, and he and his son were taken prisoner. Both were executed on the way to Kyoto, as Minamoto no Yoritomo had refused to meet with them.

- **Taira no Sadamori.** Warrior serving Fujiwara no Hidesato; he fought and killed Taira no Masakada in 940, thus avenging his father, Taira no Kunika, whom Masakada had assassinated.

- **Taira no Sadayoshi.** Warrior (twelfth century) and governor of Higo and Chikugo provinces, the only member of the Taira family spared by the Minamoto after their victory at Dan no Ura in 1185. He became a Buddhist monk with the name Higonyūdō.

- **Taira no Shigehira.** Warrior (1157–85), Taira no Kiyomori's son. He fought Minamoto no Yoritomo's forces in Uji in 1180 for imperial prince Mochihito (1151–80), then attacked the monks at the Onjō-ji temple in Ōtsu. He burned down the temples in Nara, including the large Daibutsu-den of the Tōdai-ji, and razed the Kōfuku-ji. He was taken prisoner at the battle of Ichi no Tani and delivered by the Minamoto to the monks of Nara, who beheaded him.

- **Taira no Shigeko.** Daughter (1142–76) of Taira no Tokinobu (*see* FUJIWARA NO TOKINOBU). She was Emperor Go-Shirakawa's second wife, Emperor Takakura's mother, and Taira no Kiyomori's sister-in-law. Also called Kenshun Mon'in.

- **Taira no Shigemori.** Warrior (1138–79), Taira no Kiyomori's oldest son. He apparently tried to cool his father's ardor for war and his ambitions. However, he seconded Kiyomori in the battles against the Minamoto in 1156 (Hōgen no Ran) and 1160 (Heiji no Ran). In 1177, he was appointed *naidaijin,* but he resigned two years later. He was regarded by many historians as a model of fidelity to the emperor.

- **Taira no Tadamori.** Head of the Taira clan (1096–1153) and Taira no Kiyomori's father. He married Ike no Zenni. Governor of several provinces, he consolidated the position of the Taira at the court and fought for the clan against the monks of Mt. Hiei and of the Nara temples. He also fought the pirates *(wakō)* in 1129 and had the Renge-ō-in temple (Sanjūsangendō) built in Kyoto in 1132. He received the privilege of serving the emperor at the court, an honor that no other warrior had previously attained.

- **Taira no Tadanori.** Warrior (1144–84), Taira no Kiyomori's younger brother, killed at the battle of Ichi no Tani in 1184. He was an excellent *waka* poet, Fujiwara no Toshinari's student. His poems were included in the *Senzai waka-shū* and *Gyokuyō waka-shū* anthologies, but as anonymous works.

- **Taira no Tadatsune.** Governor (967–1031) of Kanto. He killed the governor of neighboring Awa province and took control of Kanto, which he retained for about three years, from 1028 to 1031, because the imperial troops were too weak to intervene effectively. Taira no Naokata attacked him in 1028 but was defeated. Finally, Minamoto no Yorinobu (968–1048) forced him to surrender and took control of Kanto. Taira no Tadatsune died of disease before reaching the capital, where he was being transferred for trial.

- **Taira no Tokitada.** Noble (ca. 1127–1189), grand counselor *(gon-dainagon),* who was spared by the Minamoto after his defeat at Dan no Ura. He then formed an alliance with Minamoto no Yoshitsune; he was exiled to Noto province when Yoshitsune died.

- **Taira no Tokuko.** Daughter (1155–1213) of Taira no Kiyomori; Emperor Takakura's wife in 1171 and Emperor Antoku's mother. In 1181, she took the name Kenrei Mon'in. Taken prisoner at the end of the battle of Dan no Ura in 1185, she became a Buddhist nun in Kyoto.

- **Taira no Tomomori.** Fourth son (1151–85) of Taira no Kiyomori. After battling the Minamoto with some success alongside his father, he was finally defeated at Ichi no Tani in 1184 and at Dan no Ura the following year. Seeing that all hope was lost, he threw himself into the sea and drowned. His sad fate was recounted in Noh and Kabuki plays called *Funa benkei.*

- **Taira no Yorimori.** Warrior (1132–86), Taira no Tadamori's son, called Ike Dainagon. He became a Buddhist monk in 1185 with the name Chōren.

- **Taira no Yoritsuna.** Vassal (?–1293) of the Hōjō family in Kamakura. He plotted against Adachi Yasumori (1231–85), *shikken* Hōjō Sadatoki's father-in-law, and caused the destruction of the Adachi family, but he was killed by Hōjō Sadatoki when he tried to impose his son as regent.

Taira Yoshihisa. Composer, born 1937 in Tokyo. He studied in Tokyo and with André Jolivet, Henri Dutilleux, and Olivier Messiaen at the Conservatoire National Supérieure de Musique in Paris in 1966. He received many contemporary-music prizes, including the UNESCO Prize in 1982 and the Florent-Schmitt Prize from the Académie des Beaux-Arts de Paris in 1985. Professor (1995) at the École normale de musique in Paris.

Tairiku rōnin. In the early twentieth century, a term for Japanese agents based in China and Manchuria who acted as spies or revolutionary agents in support of Japanese imperialism. Most of them were members of extremist organizations such as the Gen'yōsha and the Kokuryūkai. Many were unscrupulous mercenaries who enriched themselves at the expense of mainland populations. Kodama Yoshio was the last of these "mainland *rōnin.*"

Tairō. "Great elders"; during the Tokugawa shogunate, the highest rank among state ministers. From the seventeenth century to 1857, this post fell exclusively to the *fudai-daimyō* of the Ii family in Hikone. Ii Naosuke was the last *tairō*. Also called *ganrō, ōtoshiyori. See* GO-TAIRŌ.
- Painter (Ishikawa Tairō; *mei:* Shichizaemon; *gō:* Kunshōken, early nineteenth century) of the Kanō school.

Tairo Dōshikai. Anti-Russian political organization created in 1903 by Konoe Atsumaro to sway public opinion and pressure the government to declare war on Russia, which had, despite its declarations, maintained important military forces in Manchuria. After the conclusion of peace in 1905, the members of Taira Dōshikai felt that the Treaty of Portsmouth was humiliating for Japan and protested violently (*see* HIBIYA), then joined other groups to create a larger movement called Kōwa Mondai Dōshi Rengōkai (Society of Patriots Active on the Peace Issue).

Tairyōbata. Insignia flag *(mon)* used by owners of fishing ships. *Tairyōbata* were hoisted at the prow of ships when they returned from sea to signal that they had a good catch.

Taisa. In the Meiji era, a military grade equivalent to colonel in the land army.

Taisan-ji. Buddhist temple founded in Kobe in 716, absorbed by the Tendai-shū sect. It has a main hall dating from 1304, and a *Ni-ō mon* from the fourteenth–fifteenth century.

Taisei. In medieval Japan, the leader of a troop of 50 warriors *(gundan).*
→ *See* IKE NO TAIGA.

Taisei-kyō. Syncretic Shinto-Confucian sect founded in 1870 by Hirayama Shōsai (1815–90) and admitted as one of the 13 sects of Kyōha Shintō. It gave rise to the Tenchi-kyō sect in 1928. In 1946, it was divided into three subsects: Taisei, Shugendō, and Daidō. Its teachings are based on Confucianism and on the texts of the *Kojiki* and *Nihon shoki.* It has about 140,000 followers, mainly in the Tokyo region.

- **Taisei Yokusankai.** "Imperial Rule Assistance Association." A political movement advocating a "Sphere of Asian Co-Prosperity" that would involve Japan's economic domination of Asia, launched by Konoe Fumimaro in 1940 to replace all political parties. It particularly favored the military class, and was dismantled in 1945.

Taiseki-ji. Buddhist temple of the Nichiren sect founded in 1290 by Nikkō Shōnin (1246–1333), Nichiren's most direct disciple, at the Minobu temple on the northern slope of Mt. Fuji (Yamanashi prefecture). The Taiseki-ji was re-created south of Mt. Fuji on a plot donated by the region's governor in Ōishihara. The monk Nikkan (1665–1726) made it the headquarters of the Nichiren Shōshū sect. The Sōka Gakkai had a new temple built there in 1945. *See* NANJŌ TOKIMITSU.

Taisha. Name for some major Shinto shrines. *See* JINJA.

• General amnesty *(sha)* granted on certain important occasions, such as the coronation or death of an emperor.

Taishaku-ten. Japanized form of the Buddhist divinity Shakradevendra, who is a Buddhized form of Indra, commanding the eastern regions and considered a defender of the Buddhist Law. Also called Indara, Kōshika, Shakudaikanin.

Taisha-kyō. The largest of the 13 sects of Kyōha Shintō, with about 3.5 million followers. Its headquarters is at the Izumo-taisha in Izumo. Its preferred *kami* is Ōkuninushi no Mikoto.

Taishi. In ancient Japan, the title for the emperor's son who is considered the crown prince. Also sometimes called *kōtaishi. See* KŌTAISHI, SHINNŌ, SHŌTOKU-TAISHI, TAITEI.

Taishō. Title of a general of the armed forces, created in the ninth century for the commander of the Imperial Guard. It became the title of the commander-in-chief of Japan's armies.

• Era of Emperor Yoshihito (1912–26). *See* TAISHŌ TENNŌ.

• Name for several models of machine guns:

—Taishō 3: copy of the Hotchkiss 1914 with a Lewis injection system, used since 1914. *Weight:* 27 kg; *caliber:* 6.5 mm; *initial velocity:* 730 m/sec.; *shooting speed:* 500 per minute.

—Taishō 11: designed in 1922 by Colonel Nambu Kijirō, using Arisaka magazines. *Weight:* 10.5 kg; *caliber:* 6.5 mm; *initial velocity:* 690 m/sec.; *shooting speed:* 450 per minute.

—Taishō 92: called "Woodpecker" by the Allies. *Weight:* 27.5 kg (55 kg with tripod); *caliber:* 7.7 mm; *initial velocity:* 720 m/sec; *shooting speed:* 450 per minute.

—Taishō 96: Taishō 3 modified to imitate the Czech ZB 26 machine gun. *Weight:* 9.5 kg; *initial velocity:* 720 m/sec.; *shooting speed:* 550 per minute.

—Taishō 99: created in 1939. *Weight:* 10.35 kg; *caliber:* 7.7 mm; *initial velocity:* 705 m/sec.; *shooting speed:* 850 per minute. This was the most-used weapon during the Second World War.

• **Taishō Tennō.** Hundred and twenty-third emperor (Prince Yoshihito, Haru no Miya, 1879<1912–26>), Emperor Meiji's third son; his mother was a concubine, Yanagihara Naruko. Yoshihito married Princess Sadako, Prince Kujō's daughter, in 1900, and had four sons with her, but he suffered from meningitis and was little involved with politics. By 1919, in declining health, he could no longer fulfill his functions effectively. In 1921, his son Hirohito was appointed regent. His reign was characterized by a reinforcement of imperialism and a fairly liberal domestic policy. In 1919, he signed a "reform act"; in March 1925, he accepted the principle of universal suffrage. Under his reign, the country underwent great industrial growth but suffered a terrible revolt in Korea and a catastrophic earthquake, in September 1923, that affected all of Kanto and almost completely destroyed Tokyo. When Yoshihito died, in December 1926, his son Hirohito officially succeeded him, becoming the hundred and twenty-fourth emperor. Yoshihito was then called by the name of his era *(nengō)*, Taishō (Great Justice).

Taishū bungaku. Type of commercial literature that developed between 1920 and 1935. It consisted mainly of pseudo-historical, detective, and romantic novels that appeared in serial form in the daily newspapers of the time. A literary magazine, *Taishū-bungei* (Popular Literature), published by Heibonsha in 1926–27, was a 60-volume anthology of *taishū bungaku.*

Taisō. Ancient solemn funerary ceremony for an emperor, organized by the Jibushō and led by a bureaucrat called *hinkyū-taiyū.* Before 701, emperors were buried; after this date, starting with Empress Jitō, they were cremated in Buddhist fashion. The Shinto custom of burial *(kasō)* was reinstated in 1654, when Emperor Go-Kōmyō died. *See* FUNERALS.

Taiso Yoshitoshi. Painter (Tsukioka Kinzaburō, Tsukioka Yoshitoshi, 1839–92), born in Edo, adoptive son of Tsukioka Sessai of the Settei-ryū school of ukiyo-e prints. Utagawa Kuniyoshi's (1797–1861) student, he rapidly became popular for his prints depicting nature in a very realist style, perhaps influenced by Kikuchi Yōsai (1788–1878). He undertook every genre, from newspaper illustrations to paintings of beautiful women *(bijin),* landscapes, humorous drawings, theater scenes, and historical characters. At around age 45, seriously ill, he took the nickname Taiso Hōnen ("Taiso the revived"). He went insane shortly before his death. He had trained at least 80 disciples.

Taitei. In ancient Japan, title for an emperor's brother, when he was destined to succeed that emperor as crown prince. Also called *kōtaitei*. *See* TAISHI.

Taito. Painter (Katsushika Taito; *mei:* Kisaburō; *gō;* Hokusen, Beikasei, Genryū-sai, Taito, early nineteenth century) of ukiyo-e prints, Hokusai's student in Edo and Osaka. Also sometimes called Taito II. *See* HOKUSAI.

Taiwan. This island was colonized by Japan from 1895 to 1945, and was divided into three regions, Taihoku prefecture, Taichi prefecture, and Tainan prefecture, and three prefectures, Giran-chō, Taitō-chō, and Hōko-chō. It was known in Japanese as Takakuni and Takasago. Japanese governors-general of Taiwan:
1. Kabayama Sukenori (<1895–96>), admiral
2. Katsura Tarō (<1896>)
3. Nogi Kiten (<1898>)
4. Kodama Gentarō (<1898–1906>)
5. Sakuma Sabatai (<1906–15>)
6. Antō Sadami (<1915–18>)
7. Akashi Genjirō (<1918–19>)
8. Den Kenjirō (<1919–23>), civil governor
9. Uchida Kaoyoshi (<1923–24>)
10. Izawa Takio (<1924–26>)
11. Ueyama (<1926–28>)
12. Kawamura Takeji (<1928–29>)
13. Ishizuka Eizō (<1929–31>)
14. Oda Masahiro (<1931–32>)
15. Minami Hiro (<1932>)
16. Nakagawa Kenzō (<1932–36>)
17. Kobayashi Tetsuzō (<1936–40>)
18. Hasegawa Kiyoshi (<1940–44>)
19. Andō Rikichi (<1944–45>)
→ *See* SEITAI NO EKI.

Taiyō. "Big Sun," a general-interest magazine published from 1895 to 1928 by the Hakubunkan publishing house in Tokyo; it featured contributions by many writers, including Ueda Bin, Kunikida Doppo, Shimazaki Tōson, and Tayama Katei. Two other magazines with the same title were published by Chikuma Shobō (1957–58) and Heibonsha (1963–present); the latter has a large readership.
→ *See* TŌYŌ.

• **Taiyō-zoku.** Group of young "modern" people rebelling against society; it took its name from a novel by Ishihara Shintarō, *Taiyō no kisetsu* (1955). Between 1956 and 1960, it performed acts of violence against the "establishment."

Taizan. Painter (Hime Morinaga; *azana:* Shōnen; *gō;* Taizan, 1814–69) of the Nanga school in Kyoto, and potter in the style of Awata ceramics. He painted mainly landscapes.
→ *See* HINE TAIZAN, HIROSE TAIZAN.

Tajihi no Agatamori. Diplomat (668–737) who went to the Tang court in China in 717 and was later named a provincial governor. He fought the Ebisu.

• **Tajihi no Kasamaro.** Poet (seventh–eighth century) whose works were included in the *Man'yōshū.*

• **Tajihi no Takanushi.** Poet (eighth century) whose works were included in the *Man'yōshū.*

Tajikara-o no Mikoto. Celestial *kami* of Shinto endowed with great strength. According to the *Kojiki*, he opened the cave in which Amaterasu-Ōmikami had hidden, thus returning light to the world.

Tajima. Former province, one of the eight provinces of San'in-dō, now included in Hyōgo prefecture.

• **Tajima Mori.** Japanese name for a Korean who, according to legend, introduced the cultivation of oranges *(tachibana)* to Japan around the first century AD. He may have been the founding ancestor of the Tachibana family.

Tajima Naoto. Athlete (1912–90), born in Yamaguchi prefecture. He won a gold medal in the triple jump in the Berlin Olympic Games in 1936, establishing a world record of 16 m, and a bronze medal in long jump. He became a member of the Olympic Committee in 1969.

Tajiri Shinkichi. Contemporary sculptor, born 1923 in Los Angeles. His bronze and metal sculptures are inspired by mechanical devices. He has had critically acclaimed exhibitions in Paris (1948) and Amsterdam (1955).

Takaba Ran. Young woman from a samurai family in Fukuoka (Kyushu). In 1866, she founded a school teaching absolute devotion to the emperor. Because of this, she was imprisoned a number of times by the shogunal authorities.

Takabatake Motoyuki. Socialist theoretician (1886 –1928), born in Gumma prefecture, who translated Marx's *Das Kapital,* under the title *Shihonron,* in

1919–24, and took part in many study groups on Marxist thought before gradually turning to nationalism.

Takabori. General term for all relief sculpture. There are several types: *atsuniki-bori* (very high relief), *chūniku-bori* (medium relief), *usuniku-bori* or *shishiai-bori* (low relief). Objects in sculpted lacquer, notably the Kamakura *takabori,* are well known. Also called *niku-bori.*

Takachiho. Small town in Miyazaki prefecture (Kyushu); according to the *Kojiki,* the location of the cave in which Amaterasu-Ōmikami took refuge. A sacred dance, called Yokagura, is performed from time to time in the Shinto shrine of Amano-iwato to celebrate this fact. *Pop.:* 20,000.

• **Takachihonomine.** Volcano dome located between Miyazaki and Kagoshima prefectures (Kyushu), where, according to legend, Ninigi no Mikoto, Amaterasu-Ōmikami's grandson, descended to Earth. *Alt.:* 1,574 m.

Takada. Fief of many *fudai-daimyō,* in Echigo province, south of Niigata.

Takada-ha. Branch of the Jōdo Shin-shū sect, founded in 1226 by the monk Shimbutsu in Ise. It has about 100,000 followers.

Takada Hiroatsu. Contemporary sculptor (1900–87), born in Ishikawa prefecture, Takamura Kōtarō's student. In 1931, he went to Paris, where he became friends with Jean Cocteau, Georges Rouault, and Romain Rolland. He published a Japanese-language newspaper, *Nichifutsu Tsūshin* (Franco-Japanese News), then went to Berlin near the end of the Second World War. He went back to Paris in 1946 as a correspondent for the *Yomiuri Shimbun,* then returned to Japan in 1957. He sculpted mainly busts of his Parisian friends.

Takada Kenzō. Fashion designer, born 1939 in Hyōgo prefecture. He created a special style for youth, which made him famous both in Japan and abroad, called "Kenzo style."

Takada Sanae. Politician and academic (1860–1938) who, with Ōkuma Shigenobu, founded Waseda University in Tokyo. In 1887, he became editor of the newspaper *Yomiuri Shimbun;* after 1891, he was elected to the House of Representatives five times. Minister of education in Ōkuma Shigenobu's second cabinet, from 1914 to 1916. Elected chancellor *(sōchō)* of Waseda University in 1921.

Takadaya Kahei (Kahee). Merchant (1769–1827) taken prisoner by the Russians and sent to Kamchatka in 1812. He was used as a bargaining chip for the sailors of the *Diana,* a Russian ship captured by the Japanese in 1811. When he returned to Japan in 1813, he was able to persuade the authorities to free Golovnin, one of the Russian officers detained. Also called Takataya Kahei.

Takagari. *See* FALCONRY.

Takagi Sōkichi. Vice-admiral of the imperial fleet (1894–1979), who served as intermediary between the authorities concerned when Japan surrendered in 1945. He later wrote a history of the war in the Pacific.

Takagi Teiji. Mathematician (1875–1960), born in Gifu prefecture. After studying in Tokyo, then in Berlin and Göttingen from 1898 to 1901, he became internationally known for his works on Gauss imaginary numbers. A professor at the University of Tokyo from 1904 to 1936, he invented a theory named after him that gave rise to the study of algebraic numbers. He received an honorary doctorate from the University of Oslo in 1929 and was decorated with the Order of Culture (Bunka-shō) in 1940.

Takahama Kyōshi. Haiku poet (Takahama Kiyoshi, 1871–1959), Masaoka Shiki's disciple and publisher of the magazine *Ototogisu.* He studied *waka* under his father in Matsuyama (Shikoku), then moved to Tokyo in 1894. When Masaoki Shiki died, he began to write prose and published several novels, including *Haikaishi* (The Haiku Master, 1908), *Bonjin* (An Ordinary Person, 1909), *Chōsen* (Korea, 1912), *Kaki futatsu* (Two *Kaki* Fruits, 1915), and *Niji* (Rainbow, 1947). He received the Order of Culture (Bunka-shō) in 1954.

• **Takahama Toshio.** Haiku poet (1901–79), publisher of the magazine *Hototogisu* starting in 1951. Takahama Kyōshi's son.

Takahashi Dōhachi. Ceramist (Mitsutoki; *Buddhist name* and *gō:* Ninnami, 1783–1855) and sculptor of netsuke from Kyoto.

• **Takahashi Dōnyū.** Family of ceramists in Kyoto since the nineteenth century. Its members, including

Dōhachi, specialized in production of *unkin* ceramics decorated with cherry blossoms and maple leaves under an enameled slip.

Takahashi Kageyasu. Geographer (1785–1829), born in Osaka, Takahashi Sakuzaemon's son and interpreter from the Dutch, Russian, and Manchu. He produced a map of the world, the most accurate that Japan had at the time, and maps of Japan based on observations by Mamiya Rinzō, Inō Tadataka, and Mogami Tokunai. Having supplied maps of Japan to Franz von Siebold in exchange for several Dutch works when Siebold visited Edo in 1826, he was arrested and sentenced to death, but he died in prison before he was executed.

Takahashi Kazumi. Writer (1931–71), expert in Chinese literature, and professor at the University of Kyoto. Among his best-known works are *Hi no utsuwa* (1962), *Yūutsu naru tōha* (The Sad Sect, 1965), *Jashūmon* (Bad Faith, 1966), and *Waga kaitai* (My Dismemberment, 1971), all rather pessimistic novels. His wife, Takahashi Takako (b. 1932), is also a talented writer.

Takahashi Kenji. Archeologist (1871–1929), born in Miyagi prefecture, famous for his research on the Nara region, especially on *kofun,* ancient customs, bronze weapons, and the mirrors found in the tombs.

Takahashi Korekiyo. Politician (1854–1936), born in Edo to the Kawamura family and adopted by a samurai from Sendai. He went to the United States in 1867 to pursue his studies; the following year, he was accepted by Mori Arinori as a student-servant *(shosei).* After working in several ministries and banks, he became director of the Bank of Tokyo in 1911. He was minister of finance in Yamamoto Gonnohyōe's cabinet in 1913, then in Hara Takashi's cabinet from 1918 to 1921, and succeeded Hara as prime minister in 1921–22. He was prime minister for only seven months because of internal dissension in his party, the Rikken Seiyūkai (Friends of Constitutional Government party), but was elected to the lower chamber of the Diet. In 1924, he was minister of agriculture and commerce in Katō Takaaki's cabinet. The following year, he resigned from the leadership of the Seiyūkai. He was again minister of finance in Tanaka Giichi's cabinets from 1927 to 1929, Inukai Tsuyoshi's cabinets in 1931 and 1932, Saitō Makoto's cabinets from 1932 to 1934, and Okada Keisuke's cabinet from 1934 to 1936. He refused to increase military credit as part of the budget reform, and he was assassinated by an extremist military officer during the riots of February 1936 (*see* NINIROKU JIKEN).

Takahashi Mutsuo. Poet, born 1937 in Fukuoka prefecture (Kyushu), and writer. His best-known poetry collections are *Mino, atashi no ushi* (Mino, My Bull, 1959), *Bara no ki: nise no koibitotachi* (The Rosebush: Imitation of Lovers, 1964), *Jūni no enkei* (Twenty Perspectives, 1970), *Doshi* (Verb, 1974), *Zen no henreki* (A Zen Pilgrimage, 1974). In his works, featuring a strange mix of homoeroticism and Buddhism, he expresses his concerns about the dualism between sexuality and religion.

Takahashi Nobuko. Diplomat, born 1916 in Manchuria. She studied at Waseda University and the Tokyo Christian Women's University. After the Second World War, she was an interpreter for the Allied Occupation forces. She then represented young people at the Ministry of Labor; from 1976 to 1978, she worked at the International Labor Organization in Geneva. She was ambassador to Denmark from 1980 to 1983, the first Japanese woman to hold this position, and wrote two books of memoirs, *Jūnebu nikki* (Geneva Journal, 1979) and *Demmāku nikki* (Denmark Journal, 1985).

Takahashi no Mushimaro. Poet (eighth century) of the *Man'yōshū* and senior bureaucrat in Mutsu around 717–32. He helped to write the *Hitachi fudoki* and wrote tales and legends in the form of *chōka, sedōka,* and *tanka* poems.

• *Takahashi ujibumi.* Collection of documents about the Takahashi family, containing a great number of legends and folk tales, presented to the emperor in 789.

Takahashi Oden. Commoner (1851–79), born in Gumma prefecture. Her husband suffered from leprosy, so she poisoned him; she then led a life of debauchery and crime. Arrested in 1877 for the murder of a clothing merchant, she was sentenced to death and decapitated. Her trial and death were a great shock to public opinion, and a number of novelists, including Kanagaki Robun (*Takahashi Oden yasha monogatari,* 1879), and playwrights, including Kawataki Mokuami (a Kabuki play), made use of her story.

Takahashi Sakuzaemon. *See* TAKAHASHI YOSHITOKI.

Takahashi Satomi. Philosopher (1886–1964) born in Yamagata prefecture. He completed his studies in Germany and France (from 1924 to 1927) after receiving a degree from the University of Tokyo. In his essays, he opposed Nishida Kitarō's theory of "absolute emptiness" and attempted to transcend, in a global philosophy, the theories of Kant, Hegel, Marx, and Buddhism in a sort of "universal dialect" *(hō benshōhōteki zentaisei).*

Takahashi Shinkichi. Poet (1901–87), born in Ehime prefecture (Shikoku), influenced by dadaism, the works of Tristan Tzara, and the Buddhist sense of emptiness. His best-known collections are *Gion matsuri* (1926) and *Nisshoku* (1934).

Takahashi Yoshitoki. Astronomer (Takahashi Sakuzaemon, 1764–1804), born in Osaka. A disciple of Asada Gōryū, he helped reform the calendar in 1795 and translated Joseph Jérôme Lalande's (1732–1807) *Traité d'astronomie* (Astronomy Treatise), from a Dutch translation, as *Rarande rekisho kanken.* His sons, Kageyasu (1785–1829) and Kagesuke (1787–1856), were also well-known astronomers.

Takahashi Yuichi. Painter (*gō:* Ransen, Kainitsujin, 1828–94) in the Western style (Yōga), born in Edo. He studied with Kawakami Tōgai, then, in 1866, with Charles Wirgman. A professor at the Daigaku Nanko (later the University of Tokyo), he founded his own school, Tenkai Gakusha, in 1873. His encounter with Antonio Fonatesi enabled him to deepen his approach to Western techniques. He painted views of Tokyo, portraits, and scenes of daily life in a rather rough, realistic style.

Takahira Kogorō. Diplomat (1854–1926), born in Iwate prefecture, ambassador to the Netherlands (1892), Italy (1894, 1907–08), Austria (1895), and the United States (1900–05, 1908–09). He took part in the negotiations concerning the Treaty of Portsmouth and signed the Takahira-Root Agreement.

• **Takahira–Root.** Pact between the United States and Japan, signed in 1908 by Takahira Kogorō and American Secretary of State Elihu Root, fining the countries' respective zones of influence in the Pacific Ocean and recognizing the status quo. This agreement acknowledged American influence over Hawai'i and the Philippines and ratified Japan's influence over Manchuria.

Takahisa Aigai. Painter (Takahisa Chō; *azana:* Shi'en; *mei:* Akisuke; *gō:* Aigai, Soringaishi, Joshō, Sekisō, 1796–1843) of the Nanga (Bunjinga) school, Tani Bunchō's student. He painted mainly landscapes.

Takaida kofun. Tomb dug into the rock near Kashiwara-machi (Osaka-fu), about 5 m long. Its walls are decorated with engraved images of six soldiers and boats. Date unknown, perhaps fifth century.

Takai Kitō. Poet (1741–89), born in Kyoto, Buson's disciple. He wrote very subtle haiku, collected in *Seika-shū* (1789).

Takakane. Painter (Takashina Takakane, early fourteenth century) of the Yamato-e school, head of the imperial *e-dokoro* (Kyūtei E-dokoro). He painted mainly historical subjects and illustrated the *Kasuga gongen rei-genki,* a 20-scroll *emaki-mono* dating from 1309.

Takakura Ken. Movie actor (Oda Gōichi), born 1931 in Fukuoka prefecture (Kyushu). Starting in 1956, he played yakuza roles in several series of movies for the Toei company and became extremely popular. He was also in the American director Sydney Pollack's movie *The Yakuza,* starring Robert Mitchum, in 1975.

Takakura Tennō. Eightieth emperor (Prince Norihito, 1161<1169–79>1181), uncle of and successor to Rokujō Tennō. Under pressure from the Taira clan, he abdicated in favor of his grandson Antoku in 1179.

Takamagahara. "High Plain of Heaven." The name, in the *Kojiki* and Shinto legends, for the home of the celestial *kami,* where Izanagi, Izanami, and Amaterasu live. This mythical region is the opposite of Ne no Kuni (Place of Death), and the land separating the two is the world of humans, called Ashihara no Nakatsu Kuni (Country of Reeds). Many interpretations are given to this name by different philosophers, but it is currently accepted in Shinto mythology that it represents the inaccessible upper world of the celestial *kami (amatsu-kami).*

Takamatsu. Imperial prince (Nobuhito, 1905–87), Taishō Tennō's third son and younger brother of Emperor Shōwa Tennō (Hirohito). A military attaché during the Second World War, he was pro-

moted to captain in 1942. At the end of the war, he conspired to overthrow Tōjō Hideki.
→ *See* MATSUDAIRA.

• Chief city of Kagawa prefecture (Shikoku), on the north coast, sea port and industrial center (paper products, lacquer, textiles, chemical products). The city developed around the castle built in 1588 by Ikoma Chikamasa called Tamamo no Jō, of which only ruins, the eastern gate, and a *yagura* remain. Garden by Ritsurin (eighteenth century), with six lakes; Buddhist Negoro-ji and Yashimadera temples. Facing the city is the small island of Onigashima (featured in the legend of Momotarō); Yashima, a nearby volcanic island, was the site of a major naval battle between the Minamoto and the Taira in 1185. *Pop.*: 325,000.

Takamatsuzuka kofun. Megalithic tomb *(kofun)* near the village of Asuka, south of Nara, excavated in March 1972. It is small (18 m in diameter and 5 m high) and has a funerary chamber with plastered walls only 2.6 m long, 1 m wide, and 1.1 m high. In the tomb were found the skeleton of a man of about 40 resting in a lacquered-wood casket and various bronze objects of Chinese origin. The inside walls of the tomb have paintings of people: eight women (east wall) and eight men (west wall) in groups of four, separated by portrayals of the Blue Dragon on the east side and the White Tiger on the west side. The snake and tortoise are painted on the north wall. The costumes resemble those worn in seventh-century Korea. Above these paintings, 72 red spots designate the 28 constellations, and there are paintings of different Chinese or Korean objects. The decorations in the tomb are organized similarly to those in tombs in Tonggou, northern Manchuria (then part of the Korean kingdom of Koguryŏ). The paintings have at least 10 colors. According to some archeologists, this tomb belonged to Prince Takechi (654–96), one of Temmu Tennō's sons. If so, it would date from the late seventh century. *See* ASUKA.

Takami Jun. Poet and writer (Takami Yoshio, 1907–65), born in Fukui prefecture. At first a Marxist, he abandoned his convictions after being arrested, which he tells about in *Kokyū wasurerubeki* (Abandoning Old Ideas, 1936). He then began to write partly autobiographical novels and stories. He received the Noma Prize in 1964 for his poetry collection *Shi no fuchi yori* (Near the Abysses of Death). Among his novels: *Ikanaru hoshi no moto ni* (Beyond Which Star? 1940), *Iyana kanji* (Unpleasant Sensation, 1963).

Takamine Hideko. Actor (Matsuyama Hideko), born 1924 in Hakodate (Hokkaido), married to director Matsuyama Zenzō. Working for the Shōchiku company since childhood, she became popular as an adult in starring roles in movies directed by Yamamoto Kajirō and Kinoshita Keisuke (notably *Nijūshi no hitomi,* "The Twenty-Four Eyes," 1954).

Takamine Jōkichi. Chemist and biologist (1854–1922), born in Toyama prefecture. He studied in England (from 1880 to 1883); after working for the Ministry of Agriculture and Commerce, he moved to the United States. He isolated adrenaline in crystalline form in the glands of cattle in 1901 and founded a research laboratory in Clifton, New Jersey. Although he received an Imperial Prize in 1912, he spent most of his life in the United States and died in New York.

Takami Senseki. Samurai (1785–1858) and scholar in "Dutch science" *(rangaku)* from Saga; he served daimyo Doi Toshitsura in Osaka in 1831, then in Edo. He amassed a large collection of maps and advised the shogunal government to invite foreign engineers to Japan and send delegations to Europe and America. Watanabe Kazan, a friend of his, painted an excellent portrait of him (National Museum of Tokyo) when he was 53 years old.

Takamitsu. Painter (Awataguchi Takamitsu, early fifteenth century) of the Yamato-e school. Almost all his works were on Buddhist subjects, and he helped produce the *Yūzū nembutsu engi,* housed in the Seiryō-ji temple in Kyoto.

Takamitsu nikki. "Fujiwara no Takamitsu's Journal," covering the years 961 and 962, also called *Tō no mine shōshō monogatari.* Its true author is not known, and it may be apocryphal. *See* FUJIWARA NO TAKAMITSU.

Takamiyama. Famous *sumotori* (Jessi Kuhaulua, b. 1944), from Hawai'i, now a Japanese citizen. Although he weighed 195 kg and won a large number of tournaments, he never achieved the rank of *yokozuna.* He retired in 1984 and opened a *sumotori* stable *(heya). See* SUMO.

Takamochi. In the Edo period, a term for landowning peasants. Also called *honbyakushō,* as opposed to landless peasants, *mudaka* (also called *mizunomi,* "water drinkers").

Takamori. Prehistoric site in Tsukitate (Miyagi prefecture), discovered in 1988. It contained vestiges of a lithic industry probably belonging to people who lived about 500,000 years ago and who would have been contemporaries of Peking Man.

Takamuko no Kuromaro (no Genri). Noble in the Yamato court (?–654), of Korean ancestry. He was sent with Ono no Imoko to China in 608 and remained there for 32 years. When he returned in 640, he helped write the Taika Reform (645). Sent to Tang-dynasty China as an ambassador *(kentōshi)* in 654, he died when he arrived in Chang'an.

Takamura Kōtarō. Sculptor (1883–1956), Takamura Kōun's son; his works were heavily influenced by Western art. Also a poet, he was a member of the Shirakaba group and wrote collections of verses imbued with idealism: *Dōtei* (1914), *Chieko-shō* (1978).

• **Takamura Kōun.** Sculptor (Nakajima Mitsuzō, 1852–1934), born in Edo; his works were in traditional Buddhist style but were nevertheless very realistic. He made the famous bronze statue of Kusunoki Masashige standing in front of the imperial palace in Tokyo and that of Saigō Takamori in Ueno Park. Takamura Kōtarō's father.

Takamure Itsue. Historian (1894–1964), born in Kumamoto prefecture (Kyushu). After she married Hashimoto Kenzō (1897–1976), she became involved in the feminist movement and specialized research on women's conditions through the ages. In addition to a major history of women in Japan (*Jose no rekishi*, 4 vols., 1954–58), she published studies on matrilineal and matrilocal societies in ancient Japan, *Bokeisei no kunkyū* (1938) and *Shōseikon no kenkyū* (1953), and wrote an autobiography, *Hi no kuni no onna no nikki* (Journal of a Woman in the Country of Fire, 1965).

Takanobu. Painter (Fujiwara no Takanobu, ca. 1142–ca. 1206) of the Yamato-e school, and poet, Fujiwara no Tamataka's son and Tokiwa Mitsunaga's (Kasuga Mitsunaga) student. He is credited with painting portraits of Minamoto no Yoritomo, Taira no Shigemori, and Fujiwara no Mitsuyoshi (1188). In 1201, he became a lay Buddhist monk with the name Hōshōji. He was Fujiwara no Nobuzane's father.
• Painter (Kanō Takanobu; *mei:* Ukon-shōhen, 1571–1618) of the Kanō school, Kanō Eitoku's son and father of Morinobu, Naonobu, and Yasunobu.

Takano Chōei. Physician (1804–50), born in Mutsu province; he studied in Edo with Sugita Gempaku's son, Sugita Hakugen (1763–1833), and Yoshida Chōshuku. He went to Nagasaki in 1820 to study medicine under Franz von Siebold, who conferred the title of doctor on him in 1826. In 1838, he wrote *Bojutsu yume monogatari* (Tale of a Dream), in which he criticized the shogunate's xenophobic policies, and he was arrested and sentenced to prison for life. In 1844, his prison caught fire and he was able to escape and hide, disfiguring himself with acid and using the name Takayanagi Ryūnosuke. Discovered and again imprisoned, he committed suicide. The Meiji government ennobled him posthumously in 1898.

Takano Fusatarō. Union leader (1869–1904), born in Nagasaki. After a stay in the United States, he founded the first union in Japan, the Rōdō Kumiai Kiseikai (Society for Formation of Labor Unions) in 1896–97, then the metallurgists' union. He opposed Katayama Sen and resigned from the leadership of the union to create consumers' and workers' cooperatives. Because the government opposed these movements, he moved to Qingdao, China, where he died.

Takano Sujū. Physician and poet (Takano Yoshimi, 1893–1976), born in Ibaraki prefecture. He published his haiku in the magazine *Hototogisu* and became one of the most highly regarded poets of the Hototogisu group. *Hatsugarasu* (1947) and *Seppen* (1952) are among his best haiku collections.

Takarabe Takeshi. Navy officer and politician (1867–1949), born in Hyūga province. He fought in naval battles during the Sino-Japanese War of 1894–95, studied in England, then took part in the Russo-Japanese naval war of 1904–05. He became a vice-admiral in 1909 and served in the Ministry of the Navy, at the time directed by his father-in-law, Yamamoto Gonnohyōe, then was promoted to admiral in 1919 after commanding the Sasebo naval base. In 1923, he was minister of the navy in Katō Tomosaburō's cabinet, then a delegate to the first naval conference in London in 1929. Upon his return, the ultranationalists blamed him for not attaining the objectives they had sought. He resigned from the Ministry of the Navy after the treaty was ratified, in 1930.

Takarazuka Kagekidan. "Takarazuka Theater Company." A music-hall theater troupe founded in Takarazuka (Hyōgo prefecture) by Kobayashi

Ichizō (1873–1957) in 1914. This troupe, composed exclusively of women singers and dancers (men's roles were played by women), was so successful that it was divided into several groups that performed in specially built theaters, notably in Tokyo (1934). Theater and movie directors often recruited their stars from among the "girls" in these troupes, whose repertoire was very eclectic, ranging from European operettas and American musicals to more traditional "shows." Another Takarazuka group was founded on the same principle, but more for dance than singing, by the Shōchiku movie company in 1922.

Takasago. Ancient Japanese name for Taiwan. Also called Gū.

• *Takasago.* Title of a famous Noh play: two old people reveal to a Buddhist monk that they are the spirits of two ancient pines on the Takasago beach. This play, sometimes titled *Aioi no matsu* (The Pines of a Shared Life), written by Zeami Motokiyo from a poem by Ki no Tsurayuki appearing in his preface to the *Kokin waka-shū,* deals with the fidelity of two old people who have lived together their entire life.

• **Takasago-shōgun.** *See* SAKAI TADAKIYO.

Takase-bune. Flat-bottomed boats once used in rice paddies and to transport merchandise on shallow rivers, notably the Takase-gawa.

Takashima. Small island at the entrance to the port of Nagasaki (Kyushu), where the Japanese repelled an attack by the Korean-Mongolian fleet in 1282. In the early eighteenth century, one of the most important coal mines in Japan was discovered there; it is now run by Mitsubishi.

Takashima Shūhan. Military engineer (Takashima Mochiatsu, Takashima Shirodayū, 1798–1866), born in Nagasaki. He was made responsible for fortifying the island of Dejima in 1814, and used this opportunity to import European cannons and attempt to make copies of them. He demonstrated the efficacy of these weapons for the shogunate in 1841, but he was accused of divulging information, thrown in prison, then banished in 1846. In 1855, however, the shogunate recalled him and made him head artillery instructor. Many daimyo asked him to instruct their soldiers in his techniques, called Takashima-ryū, which he also transmitted to Mito

Nariaki. He is considered the father of Japanese artillery.

Takashimaya. Japanese department store, founded in Tokyo in 1919, based on a fabric shop established in Kyoto in 1831. Takashimaya is known for the quality of its products and now has branches in Osaka, Kyoto, Sakai, Wakayama, and other cities. In 1982, it opened branches in the United States, France, and several other countries. Its art and antiquities department and fashion shows have helped gain it an international reputation. Head office in Osaka.

Takashi Tsujii. Contemporary poet (Tsutsumi Seiji) and businessman, former president of the Saison group (distribution); his father was Tsutsumi Yasujirō, founder of the Seibu railroad company. His poems and novels, which denounce consumer society in a resolutely modern tone, have gained him some recognition: *Futashikana asa* (Uncertain Mornings, 1955), *Ihōjin* (The Foreigner, 1961), *Gunjō, waga mokushi* (Blue Overseas, Revelations, 1992), *Sugiteyuku kōkei* (Scenes Passing By, 1994).

Takasugi Shinsaku. Samurai (1839–67) of the Chōshū clan, born in Hagi. To oppose the shogunate more effectively, he formed a troop of *rōnin* samurai and peasants, called Kiheitai, to which he gave military instruction following European methods. With them, he fought the conservative elements of the Chōshū, becoming leader of the clan with Kido Takayoshi. He fought the shogunal troops sent to do battle with the Chōshū in 1866, but died of tuberculosis one year later.

Takasuke. *See* FUJIWARA NO TAKASUKE.

Takata Moyokiyo. Writer and historian (1783–1847), Murata Harumi's disciple and author of more than 50 literary and historical works.

Takatori-yaki. Ceramics from the Nōgata kilns near Fukuoka (Kyushu), where they have been produced since 1601. These kilns, famous for their utensils for the tea ceremony *(chanoyu),* were built by Korean potters in various places—Takuma, Uchigaiso, Yamada, Sengoku—and run, after 1610, by the Korean ceramist Pal San (*Jap.:* Hachizan, Takatori Hachizō). Takatori ceramics, with their unsophisticated style, somewhat resembled ancient Karatsu pottery, with a thick, opaque grayish or broken-white slip. After 1630, on the instigation of Kobori Enshū, the descendants of Takatori Hachizō produced different ceramics with thinner walls, covered with a coffee-colored glaze. Later, the kilns became specialized, some producing objects for daily use, and others, bowls and vases for the tea ceremony and porcelain (Sarayama kilns). The tradition of Takiyori-*yaki* was revived in the twentieth century by Takatori Seizan (b. 1907).

Takatsukasa-ke. Title of one of the five families (Go-sekke) that traditionally supplied the regents (*sesshō* and *kampaku*) to the imperial court. This family was descended from the northern branch of the Fujiwara.

Takauchi Hidetake. Contemporary ceramist, born 1937 in Tokyo. He received a prize at the exhibition in Vallauris in 1980, and he had exhibitions in Washington and London in 1983 and in Paris in 1994.

Takayama. Town in Gifu prefecture, former castle town (*jōka-machi*) of the Kanamori family (before 1692). It contains houses from the Edo period, most of which have been transformed into museums of folk art (*mengei*) and *shunkei-nuri* lacquer objects. Festival in April, with parades of floats and *mikoshi*. *Pop.*: 70,000.

Takayama Chogyū. Writer (Saitō Rinjirō, 1871–1902), born in Yamagata prefecture. Aside from historical novels such as *Takiguchi nyūdō* (1894), he wrote essays in which he strongly criticized the government's policy and demanded that total nationalism be applied, excluding even Buddhism as a "foreign religion," although he was a fervent admirer of Nichiren. He is best known for his essay on aesthetics, *Kinsei bigaku*.

Takayama Masayuki. Historian and samurai (Takayama Hikokurō, 1747–93) who distinguished himself for his acts of piety toward the emperor, going so far as to whip Ashikaga Takauji's tomb and prostrate himself on Sanjō bridge in Kyoto facing the imperial palace. Expelled by the shogunate, which was embarrassed by his gestures, he took refuge in Kyushu and ultimately committed suicide. He was one of the Three Eccentrics (Sankijin) of the Kansei era, with Hayashi Shihei and Gamō Kumpei. A bronze statue of him was erected at the entrance to the Sanjō bridge in Kyoto. *See* KAINAI SANKIJIN.

Takayama Nagafusa. Samurai (Takayama Ukon, Justo Ukondono, 1553–1615), baptized in 1564. He took over the Tagatsuki estate, having killed his own daimyo, Wata Korenaga, in 1573. He also betrayed his daimyo Araki Murashige for going over to Oda Nobunaga's side, then converted the population of Takatsuki to Christianity by force. After serving Toyotomi Hideyoshi at the Battle of Yamazaki (1582), he was named daimyo of Akashi, in Harima province, in 1585, where he attempted to convert the population. Two years later, however, Hideyoshi dispossessed him because of his misplaced zeal and put him under the control of Maeda Toshiie in Kaga province. Tokugawa Ieyasu banished him in 1614. He fled to Manila, where he died the following year. He had gained great fame as a master (*chajin*) of the tea ceremony following the methods of Sen no Rikyū.

Takayama Sōzei. *Renga* poet (?–1455) who became a Buddhist monk about 1426. Grand master (*sōshō*) of *renga* at the Kitano Shrine in Kyoto, he was considered one of the greatest *renga* poets of his time.

Takayama Tatsuo. Painter in the Nihonga style, born 1912 in Ōita prefecture, Matsuoka Eikyū's (1881–1938) student. Influenced by Gauguin, he mixed that painter's style with Japanese traditional styles to create a new genre. His works were in many Teiten and Nitten exhibitions, and he was elected to the Japan Art Academy (Nihon Geijutsu-in) in 1972. Decorated with the Order of Culture (Bunka-shō) in 1982.

Takayanagi Kenjirō. Electronics engineer (1899–1990), born in Shizuoka prefecture. He made the first television transmission in Japan in 1926 and invented an iconoscope in 1933, shortly before Zvorikin did so in the United States. Director of the NHK laboratory in 1937, he was made head of research at Japan Victor Company (JVC) in 1946.

Takayanagi Kenzō. International jurist (1887–1967), born in Saitama prefecture. After studying in Europe and the United States from 1915 to 1920, he taught at the University of Tokyo until 1948. A member of the House of Peers, he directed revision of the Constitution from 1947 to 1965 as chairman of the commission entrusted with this task.

Takayasu-jō. Ancient castle or fort mentioned in the *Nihon shoki* and the *Shoku Nihongi*. It was constructed in 667 in the country of Wa, with the assistance of refugees from the kingdom of Paekche (Korea) after the Battle of Hakusukinoe (663), in order to prevent a possible attack by forces from

Silla and the Tang. In 1978, the vestiges of this fort were found in the Heguri-chō region (Nara prefecture). It was one in a series of six forts built by Tenji Tennō; the vestiges of the Ōno-jō were found in Fukuoka.

Takayoshi. *See* FUJIWARA NO TAKAYOSHI.

Takayoshi Shinnō. Oldest son (Takanaga, ?–1337) of Emperor Go-Daigo. In 1335, he opposed the armies of the Ashikaga, but he was forced to flee Kyoto and take refuge in the north. Finally defeated, he committed suicide.

Takebe Ayatari. Writer (Kitamura Kingo Hisamura, 1719–74), born in Edo, Daidōji Yūzan's halfbrother. He studied the Nanga painting style and painted several subjects under the *gō* Kan'yōsai. He is better known, however, as the author of novels in the *yomihon* genre in which he defended *wagaku,* or "Japanese science." His best-known novels, *Nishiyama monogatari* (1768) and *Honchō suikoden* (1773), were not very popular during his lifetime. He also wrote *waka* and haiku poems in the old manner *(katauta),* which he signed with the *gō* Ryōtai. He may have been one of Kamo Mabuchi's students.

Takebe Katahiro. Astronomer and mathematician (1664–1739), Seki Takakazu's disciple. He ran the observatory established by shogun Tokugawa Yoshimune in 1720. He discovered the principle of integral calculus *(yenri)* and helped write *Taisei sankyō* (published in 1712), a 20-volume work on Japanese mathematics. *See* WASAN.

Takebe no Kurohito. Senior bureaucrat in the court and poet (active 690–710), author of 19 *tanka* poems annotated in the *Man'yōshū.* His name can also be read Takaichi no Kuroto.

Takechi Makuni. Bronze-foundry worker who, with his brother (or son or father), Takechi Mamaro, worked on casting the large Daibutsu in the Tōdai-ji in Nara from 749 to 752. *See* DAIBUTSU.

Takechi no Ōji. Emperor Temmu's oldest son (654–96); he helped Temmu seize the throne. In 690, he was appointed *dajō-daijin.* He was a renowned poet, and three of his *tanka* are in the *Man'yōshū,* in which Kokinomoto no Hitomaro sings his praises.

Takechi Zuizan. Samurai (1829–65) and master of arms of Tosa province. He opened a *ken-jutsu* (swordfighting) school in Tosa, then went to Edo in 1861, where he joined the emperor's supporters fighting the shogunate. When he returned to Tosa, he organized a small army called Tosa Kinnōtō (Tosa Loyalist party), which made its mark by murdering Yoshida Tōyō in 1862. When the Tosa clan adopted a more moderate attitude, in 1865, Zuizan was arrested with some of his followers and forced to commit suicide.

Takeda Harunobu. Painter (early eighteenth century), member of the Kaigetsudō-ryū group.
→ *See* TAKEDA SHINGEN.

Takeda Izumo no Jō. Family of playwrights and puppet-theater *(ayatsuri-shibai)* directors at the Takemoto-za in Osaka, starting in 1705, succeeding Chikamatsu Monzaemon. The first member of this family, Takeda Izumo I (?–1747), also a puppeteer, established the reputation of the Takemoto-za. His son, Takeda Izumo II (also called Geki, Senzenken, Koizumo I, 1691–1756), was a remarkable playwright who wrote many *jōruri.* In collaboration with Nimiki Senryū and Miyoshi Shoraku, he wrote the plays *Chūshingura, Sugawara denju tenarai kagami* (Secrets of the Calligraphy of Sugawara no Michizane, 1746), *Kanadehon chūshingura* (1748), *Natsumatsuri naniwa kagami* (Mirror of the Naniwa Summer Festival, 1745), and others. His son, Takeda Izumo III (Takeda Koizumo II), continued to direct the Takemoto-za for several years, but left soon after 1767.

Takeda Katsuyori. Daimyo (Takeda Shirō, 1546–82) of Kai, Shinano, Suruga, and Kōzuke provinces, Takeda Shingen's son. He tried to expand his estates by doing battle with Oda Nobunaga and Tokugawa Ieyasu, who defeated him at the Battle of Nagashino in 1581. Abandoned by his allies, who had joined Oda Nobunaga, he was not able to resist attack and was forced to flee. He committed suicide on April 3, 1582, and his death marked the end of the Takeda family.

• **Takeda Shingen.** Daimyo of Kai province (Takeda Harunobu; *religious name:* Shingen, 1521–73), descendant of a long family line of *shugo* of the province since the Kamakura period. In 1541, he succeeded his father, Takeda Nobutora (1498–1574), whom he had expelled, and began an aggressive policy of conquering his neighbors. He overwhelmed the small-scale lords of Shinano (1542);

appointed *shugo* of that province by Ashikaga Yoshiteru, he then attacked Uesugi Kenshin, daimyo of Echigo province, and defeated him after a famous series of battles from 1553 to 1564. He tried to form an alliance with Imagawa Yoshimoto, then with Oda Nobunaga after he defeated Imagawa in Okehazama in 1560. But he then opposed the Hōjō clan of Odawara, which provoked Tokugawa Ieyasu to form an alliance against him with Uesugi Kenshin. Reconciling with the Hōjō, Shingen attempted to attack Uesugi Kenshin again. He defeated Oda Nobunaga and Tokugawa Ieyasu's armies at Mitakagahara in 1573, but died of disease on May 13 of that year. Many legends surround the character of Takeda Shingen, and a movie, *Kagemusha,* was made by Kurosawa Akira in 1980 on his last battle and death. His son, Takeda Katsuyori, succeeded him and tried to continue his work.

Takeda Kinosuke. Puppeteer (1923–59) of the Takeda *ningyō-za* in Osaka. Also known as Okamoto Takao, Kinosuke Ningyō.

Takeda Kōunsai. Samurai (1803–65) of the Mito estate, who helped Tokugawa Nariaki formulate the series of reforms that he demanded from the shogunate. Takeda led the revolt by supporters of the *sonnō jōi* begun by Fujita Tōkō at Mt. Tsukuba in 1864. He tried to lead his troops into Kyoto, but was defeated by the shogunal army after a hard three-month battle. He escaped, but was captured soon after and executed.

Takeda Nobumitsu. Samurai (1162–1248) serving the Hōjō *shikken* of Kamakura. Having fought the Taira and the emperor, he was made *shugo* of Suruga province and governor of Aki. He became a Buddhist monk with the name Kōren. A widely renowned warrior, he revived the Kyūba no Michi techniques and breathed new life into the Genji no Heihō techniques. He was the ancestor and founder of the large Takeda family of Kai (*see* TAKEDA SHINGEN).

Takeda Rintarō. Writer (1904–46), born in Osaka, a member of the movement for proletarian literature (NAPF). His novels dealt mainly with urban life and were virulent critiques of the social conditions of urban workers; *Nihon sammon opera* (Japanese Three-Penny Opera, 1932) and *Ginza hatchō* (1934) are his best-known works.

Takeda Taijun. Writer (1912–76), born in Tokyo to a family of Buddhist monks of the Jōdo-shū. He himself became a monk in 1932 and studied Chinese literature; in 1934, he and several Sinologist friends started a journal of Chinese studies, *Chūgoku Bungaku.* Mobilized to Shanghai in 1937, he continued his studies there. He returned to Japan in 1939 and published *Shiba sen,* a critical biography of the Chinese historian Sima Qian, in 1943. From 1944 to 1946, he directed the Sino-Japanese Cultural Association in Shanghai. In 1947, he published *Shimpan* (The Judgment) and *Mamushi no sue* (Race of Vipers). Thereafter, he wrote constantly: *Ai no katachi* (Faces of Love, 1948), *Igyō no mono* (A Strange Person, 1950), *Fūbaika* (Anemophilous Flowers, 1952), *Hikarigoke* (Luminescent Foam, 1954), *Mori to mizuumi no matsuri* (The Festival of Forests and Lakes, 1955–58, on the gradual extinction of the Ainu), *Fuji* (1969–71), *Keraku* (Ecstasy, 1973, unfinished). His last novel, *Menaimo suru sampo* (The Vertiginous Walk, 1976), was published after his death. He also wrote essays, among them *Ningen bungaku rekishi* (Humanity, Literature, and History, 1954) and *Miru kiku kangaeru* (Seeing, Hearing, and Thinking, 1957). Some of his stories and novels were adapted for the screen by Uchida Tomu (*Moi to mizuumi no matsuri,* in 1958), Ōshima Nagisa (*Hakuchū no tōrima,* "Obsession in Daylight," in 1966), and other directors.

Takeda Takehito. Contemporary ceramist, born 1944 in Niigata. His works were exhibited in Paris in 1994.

Takehara Han. Dancer (Takehara Yukiko; 1903–98), born in Tokushima prefecture. She excelled in *jiuta-mai* and Kabuki, and was elected a member of the Japan Art Academy (Nihon Geijutsu-in) in 1985.

Takehara-zuka kofun. Megalithic tomb *(kofun)* with antechamber in Wakamiya-machi (Fukuoka prefecture, Kyushu), discovered in 1956. It has a high, vaulted funerary chamber, and its walls are magnificently decorated with paintings portraying ceremonial fans, horses and warriors, and ships and waves, in blue and red. It dates from around the seventh century.

Takehashi-sōdō. Military revolt on August 28, 1878, led by two soldiers, Mizoe Unosuke and Nagashima Takeshirō, who were demanding higher salaries and compensation for having put down the Satsuma Rebellion in 1877. More than 260 soldiers followed them, killing their officers and attacking the Ministry of Finance. The revolt was quickly put down and 52 of the soldiers were sentenced to death, while 118 others were banished from Tokyo. General Yamagata Aritomo then strengthened military discipline.

Takehisa Himeji. Painter (Takehisa Shigejirō, 1884–1934), born in Okayama prefecture. He worked at the *Yomiuri Shimbun* as an illustrator, then published a series of prints titled *Haru no maki* in 1909. He also produced portraits in oils of sad women with big eyes, and made watercolors and engravings. He also wrote poems and songs.

Takei Nagoya. Sculptor (1893–1940) with Western leanings, who made realist wood sculptures. He was Bourdelle's student in Paris.

Takeiri Yoshikatsu. Politician, born 1926 in Nagano prefecture, who was affiliated with Sōka Gakkai in 1953. He became one of the most active members of the Kōmei Seiji Remmei, the sect's political wing, and represented the Kōmeitō (Clean Government party) in the Diet starting in 1967.

Takekoshi Yosaburō. Politician (1865–1950) and historian, born in Saitama prefecture. Editor-in-chief of the magazine *Sekai no Nihon* (Japan in the World), founded by Saionji Kimmochi, he was elected to the Diet in 1902 for the Rikken Seiyūkai (Friends of Constitutional Government party), then to the House of Peers in 1923. His main work, *Nihon keizai shi* (Economic History of Japan, 1920), is still a widely used reference. Among his other works are *Shin Nihon shi* (New History of Japan, 1892) and *Nisengohyakunen shi* (Twenty-Five Hundred Years of History, 1896). An expert in German literature, he also published several studies on the subject, including *Doitsu tetsugatsu eika* (1884) and *Shinron kōwa* (1941). Also called Takegoshi Yosiburō.

Take-mikazuchi no Kami. Celestial *kami (amatsu-kami)* who, according to the *Kojiki,* was sent to Earth to obtain the surrender of Ōkuninushi no Mikoto and thus prepare for the arrival of Ninigi no Mikoto. He defeated Take-minaka no Kami, Ōkuninushi's son, in battle and forced him to flee. Take-minaka no Kami was also known as Suwa Myōjin.

Takemitsu Toru. Composer, born 1930 in Tokyo. He began to write jazz-inspired music about 1947, and he composed many scores for movies and orchestras, using electronic instruments. He also up-dated traditional airs for the *shakuhachi* and *biwa.* He wrote more than 75 movie scores, among them *Seppuku, Kaidan,* and *Suna no onna* (The Woman in the Dunes).

Takemoto Gidayū. *Jōruri* singer (Gidayū, Kiyomizu Gorobei, 1651–1714), born in Osaka. He took the name of the theater where he sang to accompany puppet plays *(ayatsuri-shibai),* the Takemoto-za, and collaborated with Chikamatsu Monzaemon, who wrote plays for him. A disciple of Inoue Harima no Jō, he took the name Takemoto Chikugo no Jō in 1701. The songs that he wrote and his style, called Gidayū-busshi, became so popular that *jōruri* came to be called *gidayū.* His son, Takemoto Seidayū, also sang in his style and followed him as director of the Takemoto-za.

• **Takemoto Hinatayū.** Singer (1899–1980) of *gidayū (jōruri)* and Kabuki actor. In 1979, he was designated an Intangible Cultural Treasure.

• **Takemoto-za.** Puppet theater foundeded in Osaka in 1684, where Chikamatsu Monzaemon's plays were performed. It was directed by Takeda Izumo starting in 1705; closed in 1767, it opened some time after and then closed again.

Takemoto Hayata. Ceramist (1848–92) in Kyoto, son of a *hatamoto.* He worked with Ryōkichi in Takada, producing Satsuma-type ceramics.

Takeno Jōō. Master of the tea ceremony (1502–55) in Sakai, and *renga* poet. He was one of the first to use the *wabi* style, invented many utensils for the *chanoyu,* and, with his son-in-law, Imai Sōkyū, was Sen no Rikyū's master.

Takenouchi Shikibu. Confucian scholar (1712 or 1716–1767 or 1771), born in Echigo province; Tamaki Isai's disciple. He founded a school in Kyoto to teach the doctrines of Zhu Xi *(Jap.:* Shushi). Having taught the military arts to nobles of the court *(kuge),* he was imprisoned in 1758, then sentenced to exile.

Takenouchi (Takeshi-uchi) no Sukune. According to the *Kojiki* and *Nihon shoki,* a legendary character who was a general for a number of successive "emperors" and who fought the Ebisu. He may have been one of the generals sent to Korea by Jingū Kōgō. Legend has it that he lived for 244 years. Perhaps the same character as Tamichi; it may also be that this name was used by a number of people in the same family.

Takenouchi Tsuna. Politician (1840–1922), born in Tosa province. He fought with the imperial troops in the Boshin Civil War (1868), but in 1877 he supported Saigō Takamori's rebellion in Tosa. Pardoned, he entered politics, joining the Jiyūtō (Liberal party), and was elected to the Diet in 1890. He was also a powerful businessman. Yoshida Shigeru's father.

Takenouchi Yasunori. *Hatamoto* samurai (1806 –?), born in Edo, appointed *bugyō* in Hakodate in 1854, then commissioner of finances and foreign affairs *(gaikoku-bugyō)* in 1861. In 1862, the shogunate sent him to Europe at the head of an information delegation whose goal was to have the opening of ports called for in the Ansei Treaty delayed until 1868. He was appointed *machi-bugyō* of Osaka and retired in 1864.

Take no yuki. Noh play: a young man, sent to sweep the snow from a bamboo grove, dies of cold. The *kami* of the bamboo grove, moved by his family's pain, brings him back to life.

Takeshi Kaikō. Writer and journalist (b. 1930), famous for his reports written in very classical language. His novel *Hadaka no osama* (The Naked King, 1957) was a best-seller. He received the *Mainichi* Cultural Award in 1978.

Takeshima. Small island in the Sea of Japan (Nihonkai), located midway between Honshu and the Korean Peninsula, discovered in 1849 by Europeans, who called it Liancourt. This uninhabited islet, with an area of only 0.23 km², has been claimed by both Japan and Korea since the Edo period, and the question of its ownership has not yet been resolved. The Koreans call it Tokto.

Takeshita Noboru. Politician, born 1924 in Shimane. In 1986, he became one of Nakasone Yasuhiro's most formidable rivals; he had been Nakasone's minister of finance after creating a study group called Soseikai. A member of the Liberal Democratic party (Jiyū Minshutō), he succeeded Nakasone as prime minister in November 1987.

Taketombo. "Bamboo dragonfly," small toy made by children, with a propeller slipped onto a stick that is spun rapidly between the hands. It is said to have been invented by Hiraga Gennai, but examples dating from the Yayoi period have been found. Also called *mokutombo*.

Taketori no monogatari. "Tale of the Bamboo Cutter." A prose text by an anonymous author dating from between 850 and 950. It tells the story of a lunar princess exiled to Earth and found by chance by a poor woodsman, who names her Kaguyahime, "Bright Princess," and raises her as his own daughter. Courted by princes and then by the emperor, she imposes so many conditions that they are forced to give up on her. She then puts on a robe of feathers and returns to the moon. This tale, a composite of seven Japanese and Chinese folk tales, both Buddhist and Taoist, is written in kana in a simple, unadorned language. The same themes are found in Chinese (Zhu Wang Shen), Southeast Asian, and Indonesian (Buloh Betong) folklore. An *emakimono* with calligraphy by Ki no Tsurayuki and illustrations by Kose Ōmi relates this ancient legend, whose complete title is *Taketori no okina no monogatari*. Also sometimes titled *Kaguya-hime no monogatari*.

Takeuchi Kyūichi. Sculptor (1857–1916), born in Edo. He worked first in ivory, then turned to wood, and attempted to imitate ancient techniques. At the request of Okakura Kokuzō, he reproduced many works from the Nara period. Also called Kyūichi, Takeuchi Hisaichi.

Takeuchi Seihō. Painter (Takeuchi Tsunekichi, 1864–1942), born in Kyoto. He studied with Tsuchida Eirin, then with Kōno Bairei. His early work featured fusuma in the traditional style of the Tosa school, and he proved to be a fine observer of nature. In 1900, he took a study trip to Europe, where he visited museums of painting. The screens that he painted in Western style with Japanese techniques were very remarkable, and his works were exhibited in the Bunten. In 1920, he went to China; after this, he painted landscapes in ink and watercolors. He had exhibitions in Japan and in Paris, where he received the Legion of Honor in 1924. In Japan, he was elected a member of the Imperial Fine Arts Academy (Teikoku Bijutsu-in) and appointed an Artist of the Imperial Household (Teishitsu Gigei-in). *See* SEIHŌ.

Takeyama Michio. Writer (1903–84) and translator of German works. His best-known novel, *Biruma no tategoto* (The Harp of Burma, 1956), was adapted to the screen by Ichikawa in 1956.

Takezaki Suenaga. Samurai (1246–?) from Higo province. His prowess during the resistance to the Korean-Mongolian invasions of 1274 and 1281 was celebrated in a two-scroll *emakimono* called *Mōko shūrai ekotoba* (Account of the Mongolian Invasion, 1293), attributed to Tosa Nagataka (kept at the National Museum of Tokyo). Nothing is known about this hero's life.

Takigawa Kazumasu. Warrior (1525–86) from Ōmi province, serving Oda Nobunaga, who appointed him Kantō-kanrei. When Oda Nobunaga died, Takigawa Kazumasu served Toyotomi Hideyoshi; after being defeated in 1594, he retired and became a Buddhist monk.

Takiguchi. Guard corps formed by Emperor Uda in the late ninth century, responsible for protecting the emperor in his palace and during his travels.

Takiguchi Shūzō. Poet and art critic (1904–79) known for his essays on surrealism and avant-garde art. He wrote many poetry collections, such as *Tezukuri kotowaza* (House Proverbs) and *Yōsei no kyori* (Distance of Nymphs), and essays: *Kyō no bijutsu to ashita no bijutsu* (Art of Today and Art of Tomorrow), *Jūroku no yokogao* (Sixteen Profiles), *Gensō gaka-ron* (Painters of Fantasies), and others.

Takii Kōsaku. Writer and haiku poet (*gō:* Sessai, 1894–1984), born in Gifu prefecture. Shiga Naoya's friend and disciple, he wrote intimist novels describing family conflicts, such as *Mugen hōyō* (1921–24), an autobiographical work, and stories. His modern haiku collections were highly regarded, especially *Sessai kushū* (1931). He was elected a member of the Japan Art Academy (Nihon Geijutsu-in) in 1959.

Takimi Kannon Bosatsu. One of the 33 forms (*see* SANJŪSAN ŌGESHIN) of Kannon Bosatsu, as the Bodhisattva of Infinite Virtue. He is portrayed looking at a waterfall *(taki).*

Taki Motokata. Physician (1695–1766), born in Edo. Along with his descendants, Taki Motonori, Taki Motoyasu, and Taki Motokata, he served the Tokugawa family. He established his own school of medicine in Edo and was considered the best physician of his time.

Taki Rentarō. Musician and composer (1873–1903), born in Tokyo. He studied piano and composition with Raphael von Koeber (1848–1923), a German pianist who went to Japan in 1893. He then went to the Leipzig Conservatory in 1900, but fell ill and was forced to return to Japan in 1902; he died in Ōita the following year. He wrote songs in the Western style, the first of their type in Japan.

Takizawa Bakin. Writer and poet (Takizawa Okikuni, Kyokutei Bakin, Bakin, 1767–1848), born in Edo, a prolific novelist. A disciple of Santō Kyōden, he first published several *kusazōshi,* then turned toward *yomihon,* writing some 30 works in this genre, of which the best known are *Nansō satomi hakkenden* (Satomi and the Eight "Dogs," or Samurai, 1814–42), a long historical novel, and *Chinsetsu yumiharizuri* (The Crescent Moon, Adventures of Tametomo, 1807–11). He also wrote a major work of literary criticism, *Kinsei mono no hon: Edo sakusha burui* (Writers of Edo: Categories of New Novels, 1834), and "journals" such as *Waga hotoke no ki* (Our Family's Lineage, 1822) and *Nochi no tame no ki* (In Order to Survive, 1835), giving accurate descriptions of the customs and ways of Edo. Having lost his sight toward the end of his life, he was assisted by his daughter-in-law starting in 1841. A samurai by birth, he had abandoned his status and privileges, but he tried to have them restored to his son, Sōhaku (1798–1835). Bakin was famous during his lifetime and is still widely read today. Among his other novels are *Sanshi-chi zenden Nanka no yume* (Nanka's Dream, 1808), *Shunkan sōzu-shina monogatari* (The Monk Shunkan on the Island of Spirits, 1808), *Aoto Fujitsuna moryōan* (The Condemnation of Aoto Fujitsuna, 1811), *Shichi-ya no kura* (The Bookmaker's Warehouse), *Heso ga wakasuo saiyu no monogatari* (Funny Stories), *Ume-shibu Yoshibei hosshin ki* (The Story of Yoshibei, 1811), *Tsukai hatashite mibu kyōgen* (The Farce of the Spendthrift, 1791). He signed with a wide variety of names, including Takizawa Kai, Takizawa Sagorō, and Takizawa Toku.

Takizawa Mieko. Writer (b. 1940). She received the Akutagawa Prize in 1990 for her novel *Niko Baba no iru machi de* (In Niko Baba's Town).

Takuan Sōhō. Zen Buddhist monk (Takuan, Takuan Shūō, 1573–1645), born near Hyōgo, active at the Daitoku-ji (Rinzai-shū) temple in Kyoto starting in 1594. He became *dai-sōjo* of the temple about 1608. After several run-ins with the authorities, he left Kyoto and moved to Edo, where the shogun Tokugawa Iemitsu asked him to found the Tōkai-ji temple in Shinagawa in 1638. He was famous as a painter in the tradition of the Zen masters (*see* ZENGA) and as a calligrapher. He was also a poet and master *(chajin)* of the tea ceremony *(chanoyu).*

Takuchi Seiho. Painter (1864–1911) in the Western style, Fenellosa's disciple. He adopted the technique of the European perspective in his "Japanese style" (Nihonga) paintings.

Takuhō. Painter (1652–1714) of the Kanō school, Tan'yū's student. He was a Buddhist monk.

Takuma-ryū. School of Buddhist painting founded in the late tenth century by Takuma Tameuji and his son, Takuma Tamenari (active ca. 1030–51), following the principles of Yamato-e defined by Kose Kanaoka. The most famous painters of this school, aside from Takuma Tameuji and Takuma Tamenari (who decorated the *hōō-dō* of the Byōdō-in in Uji), were Takuma Tametō (ca. 1150), Takuma Tamehisa (ca. 1180), Takuma Ryōga (ca. 1220), Takuma Tameyori (ca. 1230), Takuma Shōga (late twelfth–early thirteenth century), Takuma Tameyuki (ca. 1320), Takuma Ryōson (1265–1327), Takuma Shikibu-tayū (ca. 1330), Takuma Jōkō (ca. 1380), and perhaps Takuma Eiga (late fourteenth century). The relationship between Takuma Eiga and the Takua-ryū school is not clear, because Eiga used many different styles, though always in a Buddhist artistic environment. Little is known about these artists, and many of the paintings with which they are credited have neither signature nor seal, and they can therefore be dated only very approximately. They are notable, however, for a high degree of realism and vigorous brush strokes, somewhat in the manner of Chinese Song-dynasty painters. Most of the painters lived in Nara or Heian-kyō.

Takusai. Sculptor (Tachikawa Takusai, Tomikane Takusai, 1817–88) and maker of netsuke in Nagano.

Tama. In Buddhism, the "jewel" equivalent to the Sanskrit *chintāmani,* the "magical pearl that grants all wishes," also called *hōshu, nyoi-shū.* Artisans *(bumin)* who specialized in making *tama* (jewelry) were grouped in guilds called Tamatsukuri-be. *See* HŌSHU.
   • In Shinto, the *tama* is the equivalent of the *mitama* (somewhat similar to the soul in Western thought), which causes death when it separates from the body. *See* KAMI, MAGATAMA, MITAMA.

• **Tamagushi.** In Shinto, the offering of a *sakaki* branch to a *kami.*

Tama-gawa. River in Kanto, 126 km long, running into the Bay of Tokyo. Its source is in Yamanashi prefecture, and its lower course separates Tokyo and Kanagawa prefectures. A reservoir lake made on its course, Okutama, supplied potable water to the capital via a canal 50 km long, the Tamagawa-jōsui, dug in 1654. It was abandoned only in 1965, in favor of the waters of the Oku-tama and Lake Tama-ko. *See* KANDA-JŌSUI.

Tamagawa Daigaku. Private university in Machida, Setagaya-ku, Tokyo, founded in 1929. It has faculties of literature, engineering, and agriculture; attendance, about 5,500 students.

Tamamushi no zushi. Small portable Buddhist altar *(zushi)* dating from the seventh century (in the Hōryū-ji, Nara), decorated with paintings on lacquer, in Central Asian style, and elytrons of beetles (*Chrysochroa elegans, tamamushi* in Japanese); painted in four colors (yellow, green, red, and brown), it portrays episodes from the Buddha's former lives, guardian kings, and bodhisattvas. This shrine, in the form of a square two-story pagoda on a Mt. Meru–type pedestal, is topped with a representation of a temple roof. The paintings that decorate its lower panels are among the most ancient in Japan. *Total height of the zushi:* 2.4 m. *Size of each lower panel:* approx. 0.65 x 0.35 m. *See* HŌRYŪ-JI.

Tama no Ura. Former name of the port of Nagasaki (Kyushu). Also called Nigitatsu, Fukae no Ura.

Tamatsukuri komachi seisui-sho. "Grandeur and Decadence of Tamatsukuri Komachi," an educational book on the life of poet Ono no Komachi, written by an anonymous Buddhist monk in the eleventh century.

Tamayori-hime. Name by which the mother of the mythical emperor Jimmu Tennō is known. Also sometimes called Mi-Oya no Kami.

Tamba. Former province, now included in Hyōgo and Kyōto prefectures. Also called Tamba no Kuni.

• **Tamba-yaki.** Ceramics produced in Tamba province, notably in Konda (Hyōgo prefecture), starting in the Kamakura period, for the daily needs of peasants. They were fired in *anagama* kilns dug into hillsides. Asymmetrical jars made with rolled clay, with a shallow neck and a cinder glaze, are typical of this manufacture until around 1600. In the seventeenth century, Korean potters moved to Tamba; they introduced potter's wheels *(rokurō)* turned by the feet and built *noborigama* kilns. These kilns produced minimally decorated utilitarian jars, mortars, rice bowls, and *sake* bottles with a floral design, of a type called Tamba-*gama*. After a period of decline in the Meiji era, the Tamba kilns were updated to produce industrial ceramics, mainly in the villages of Shimo Tachikui and Kami Tachikui. However, several "old-style" kilns continue to produce traditional ceramics.

Tamba Yasuyori. Physician (912–95), born in Tamba province, of Chinese origin. He served in the court; his medical treatise titled *Ishimpō* (982), a 30-part medical compendium imitating similar Chinese works of the Sui and Tang periods, is still well known. *See* ISHIMPŌ.

Tambi. Painter (Kanō Moritaka, 1840–93) of the Kanō school, Tan'en's son and student in Kyoto. He painted mainly landscapes.

Tamenaga Shunsui. Writer (Echizen'ya Chōjirō, Tamenaga Shōsuke, Nansenshō Somabito, 1789/1790–ca. 1843) and storyteller *(yose)*, born in Edo. He adopted the name Tamenaga Shunsui in 1829. He studied with Shikitei Samba and wrote novels in the *gesaku* and *ninjō-bon* genres, the best known of which are *Shunshoku umegoyomi* (Almanac of the Plum Trees, 1883) and *Shunshoku tatsumi no sono* (1835). These sentimental and often erotic stories got him arrested by the authorities on the charge of immorality. He probably died in prison.

• **Tamenaga Shunsui II.** Writer (Somezaki Nobufusa, 1823–86) who contributed to the *Iroha bunko*. Perhaps Tamenaga Shunsui's son.

Tamenari. Painter (perhaps a member of the Fujiwara family, eleventh century) credited with making the paintings on the walls and doors of the Byōdō-in in Uji (1053). *See* FUJIWARA NO TAMENARI.

Tameshi-giri. Type of training used by samurai, consisting of testing their technique and their sword blades on cadavers. When no cadavers were available, they used balls of compressed rice straw.

Tametō. Painter (Takuma Tametō; *gō:* Shōchi, mid-twelfth century) of the Yamato-e school, serving Emperor Konoe. He painted Buddhist subjects.

Tamichi. Famous warrior who was said to have been victorious in an expedition to Korea in 365 and to have brought back many Korean artisans who stayed in Japan and became citizens. He was apparently killed while fighting the Ebisu in northern Honshu in 367. He may have been the same person as Takenouchi no Sukune. Also called Kamisukenu Tamichi, Kamitsukenu Katana.

Tamiya Hiroshi. Physiologist and botanist (1903–84), born in Tokyo. Shibata Keita's student, he discovered a new method of growing chlorella algae. He was decorated with the Order of Culture (Bunka-shō) in 1977.

Tamiya Torahiko. Writer (1911–88), born in Tokyo. He wrote many best-selling novels, most of them historical, such as *Kiri no naka* (In the Fog, 1947), *Monogatari no naka* (In the Novel, 1948), *Matsugo no mizu* (Water of the Decline, 1949), *Rakujō* (The Fall, 1949), and *Ashizuri-misaki* (Cape Ashizuri, 1949), and a collection of stories, *Ehon* (Illustrated Book, 1950).

Tamon. In castle architecture, a low tower on a fortification wall, similar to a *yagura*.

• **Tamon'in.** Buddhist temple secondary to the Kōfuku-ji in Nara.

• *Tamon'in nikki.* Journal kept by the monks of the Tamon'in, including the monk Eishun (1518–96), from 1478 to 1618, known only from one eighteenth-century copy. Relatively accurate from the historical point of view, this journal is a valuable source of information for the period it covers.

• **Tamon-ten.** One of the Four Guardian Kings of Buddhist iconography (Shi-tennō), corresponding to the North and to the Sanskrit Vaishravana. Also called Bishamon-ten. He was included in the series of the Seven Gods of Good Fortune (Shichifukujin) in the seventeenth century.

Tamura. Title of a Noh play: an itinerant Buddhist monk arrives at the Kiyomizu-dera temple in Kyoto and asks a novice to tell him the story of the temple. The novice reveals himself to be the spirit of Sakanoue no Tamuramaro, presents himself in a general's uniform, and dances a mime of his military feats against the Ebisu.
→ *See* JOMEI TENNŌ.

Tamura Kōnosuke. Painter (1904–86), specializing in portraits. He also painted landscapes and dolls with characteristic color-rich realism. President of the Nika-kai, a society of painters, he was elected to the Japan Art Academy (Nihon Geijutus-in) and named a "Person of Cultural Merit."

Tamura Ransui. Confucian philosopher (Tamura Gen'yū, 1718–76), Abe Shōō's student and Hiraga Gennai's master. He cultivated ginseng *(Chōsen-ninjin)* in Japan and published a study of this plant's pharmacological properties, *Ninjin kōsakuki* (1747).

Tamura Taijirō. Writer (1911–83), born in Yok-kaichi (Mie prefecture). After contributing to various literary magazines, he published *Nikutai no akuma* (The Demon of the Flesh) in 1946, and *Nikutai no mon* (The Door of Flesh) the following year; the latter novel, describing the lives of prostitutes and war widows during the Second World War, was a best-seller. He continued in this vein, publishing *Shumpu-den* (Chronicle of a Soldier's Girl, 1947), then a series of novels based on carnal desire: *Nikutai no bungaku* (1948), *Nikutai no sakebu koe* (The Cry of the Body, 1949), *Shinsō gonin onna* (Five Women, 1950), *Onna no fukushu* (Woman's Vengeance, 1951), *Teikō suru onnatachi* (Women in the Struggle, 1952), *Sensō no kao* (The Face of War, 1958). He then wrote other war novels, such as *Heishi no monogatari* (Soldier's Story, 1971); an autobiography, *Waga bundan seishun-ki* (My Literary Youth, 1963); and series of stories. Many of his works were adapted for the screen.

Tamura Toshiko. Writer (Satō Toshi, 1884–1945), born in Tokyo; Kōda Rohan's disciple. At first a stage actor, she began to write after marrying the novelist Tamura Shōgyō (1874–1948), publishing *Akirame* (Resignation, 1911), *Miira no kuchibani* (Lipstick for Mummies, 1913), *Onna sakusha* (The Woman Writer, 1913). In 1918, she left her husband to follow a journalist to Canada and lived in Vancouver until 1936. When she returned to Japan, she revived her literary career and published *Yama-michi* (Mountain Road, 1938). She then moved to Shanghai, where she published a women's literary magazine. She died in Shanghai. A literary prize was created in her name in 1960.

Tan. Unit of length for fabrics, equivalent to about 25 or 30 *shaku*. In the Edo period, 2 *tan* were worth 1 *hiki*.

• Unit of area, equivalent to 300 *tsubo* (991 m²), supposed to produce about 170 liters of rice in the Edo period.

Tanabata. "Festival of Stars." Celebrated for the first time in 755, it takes place every year on the seventh day of the seventh month (July 7; sometimes August 7 in some regions) and is one of the five traditional festivals *(gosekku)*. At first called Tanabata-tatsume, this major festival marks, according to a Chinese tradition, the annual encounter of the star Vega (the weaver, Shokujo) and the star Altair (the oxherd, Kengyu), who meet on the Milky Way *(amano-gawa)*—or sometimes on a bridge made of magpies. Its celebration, faithfully observed by young men and women, involves many festivities associated with the Shinto rites of abstinence and ablution (*see* HARAI). Houses are decorated with bamboo poles festooned with colored paper lanterns, large pompons, and bands of paper bearing love poems. When the festival is over, the bamboo poles are thrown into the river or put into rice paddies to serve as scarecrows, in the hope of obtaining good harvests. In the *nemurinagashi* rite, boats made of straw (Tanabata-*bune*) containing dolls also made of straw (Tanabata-*ningyō*) are floated in the rivers. Sendai and Hiratsuka are famous for their opulent celebrations of the Tanabata Festival on August 7. Also called Kikōten, Hoshi Matsuri. *Chin.:* Ji Qiaotian; *Kor.:* Chil-sök; *Viet.:* Tết Thất Tich.

Tanabe Hajime. Buddhist philosopher (1885–1962) who studied in Germany under Edmund Husserl starting in 1922. He opposed German idealism and the theories of Nishida Kitarō; from the religious viewpoint, he stressed the importance of the notion of *tariki* ("the strength of the Other"), often evoked in the Jōdo and Jōdo Shin-shū sects. His 15-volume complete works *(Tanabe Hajime zenshū)* were published in 1963–64.

Tanabe Seiko. Writer, born 1928 in Osaka, using mainly the Osaka dialect. Her novel *Senchimentaru jānī* (Sentimental Journey, 1964) won the Akutagawa Prize. She worked in television and for newspapers, and wrote a fictionalized biography of Yosano Akiko, *Chisuji no kurokami* (A Thousand Black Hairs, 1972).

Tanabe Taichi. Politician and diplomat (1831–1915), born in Edo. In 1864, he accompanied a shogunal delegation to Europe to demand revision of the Ansei treaties, and he was sent to Paris as a delegate to the 1867 World Fair. He traveled to Europe and North America with the Iwakura delegation in 1871–73 as its secretary, then seconded Ōkubo Toshimichi on his mission to Beijing to settle the Taiwan affair in 1874. Elected to the Genrō-in, he helped write the *Bakumatsu gaikōdan* (History of Diplomatic Relations in the Late Edo Period, 1898).

Tanaka Chikao. Theater director and playwright (1905–95), born in Nagasaki, influenced by French existentialism. His one-act play *Ofukuro* was first staged in 1933; another of his plays, *Kyōiku,* received the *Yomiuri* Literary Prize in 1953. Among his other plays are *Kumo no hatake* (1947) and *Maria no kubi* (1959). Elected to the Japan Art Academy (Nihon Geijutsu-in) in 1981. He married Tanaka Sumie in 1935.

Tanakadate Aikitsu. Geophysicist (1856–1952), born in Iwate prefecture. He studied in England and Germany from 1881 to 1891 and taught at the University of Kyoto. His studies on earthquakes gained him the nickname "the father of Japanese seismology." He founded a bureau of astronomy in Mizusawa, advocated adoption of the metric system, and proposed a new system of transliteration of Japanese. He received the Order of Culture (Bunka-shō) when this honorific distinction was created, in 1944.

Tanaka Fujimaro. Politician (1845–1909), born in Owari province. He was a member of the Iwakura delegation to Europe and North America (1871–73) and was appointed vice-minister of education in 1874. In 1876–77, he went to the United States to study the American educational system; when he returned, he advocated many changes based on that system. Minister of justice in 1880, ambassador to Italy (1884) and France (1887), and again minister of justice in 1891–92.

Tanaka Fuyuji. Poet (Tanaka Kichinosuke, 1894–1980), born in Fukushima prefecture. He published his works in the magazine *Shiki* starting in 1933. His collections *Aoi yomichi* (Voyage in the Blue Night, 1929), *Mieru ishidan* (1930), and *Banshun no hi ni* (Late-Spring Days, 1961) received wide critical acclaim.

Tanaka Giichi. Politician (1864–1929), born in Chōshū. A member of the military, he served in Manchuria during the Sino-Japanese War of 1894–95 under Yamagata Aritomo, then was sent to Russia, where he studied the organization of the army from 1898 to 1902. During the Russo-Japanese War of 1904–05, he was Kodama Gentarō's aide-de-camp. After holding a number of important positions, he was promoted to general in 1923 and

was minister of the armed forces in Yamamoto Gonnohyōe's cabinet. He became leader of the Rikken Seiyūkai (Friends of Constitutional Government party) in 1925 and prime minister in 1927; as chief of the secret services in Manchuria, he is said to have presented a detailed plan for Japan's role in Asia (known as the Tanaka Memorandum) to the emperor on July 27, 1927. As a consequence, he sent troops to Shandong to assist the Chinese warlord Zhang Zuolin. After Zhang was assassinated by members of the Guandong army in 1928, Tanaka was forced to resign; Hamaguchi Osachi succeeded him in July 1929. He died soon after. Many Japanese historians deny that the Tanaka Memorandum ever existed and allege that it was fabricated by the Chinese as anti-Japanese propaganda.

Tanaka Hidemitsu. Writer (1913–49), born in Tokyo, Dazai Osamu's disciple. An athlete, he was a member of the rowing team at the Los Angeles Olympic Games in 1932 and wrote two memoirs about this event: *Orimposu no kajitsu* (1940) and *Tantei sōshu* (1944). After the Second World War, he joined the Communist party, but he was soon expelled because of his debauched life style. He published a war memoir, *Yami no yo* (A World of Blackness), in 1947, and committed suicide on Dazai Omasu's tomb.

Tanaka Hisashige. Mechanic and inventor (Tanaka Giemon, 1799–1881), born in Kurume (Fukuoka prefecture), serving the Saga estate. He invented a fire pump, a perpetual clock, and a boiler for steamships; he also cast cannons. The company he founded to exploit his inventions was the forerunner of the Toshiba industrial group.

Tanaka Kakuei. Politician (1918–93), born in Niigata prefecture. A public-works entrepreneur whose company prospered during the Second World War, he entered politics in 1947 in the Japan Progressive party (Nihon Shimpōtō) and was elected to the House of Representatives for the Minshutō (Democratic party). The following year, he joined the Minshu Jiyūtō (Democratic Liberal party, a forerunner of the Jiyū Minshutō, or LDP), and became minister of the post office and communications in Kishi Nobusuke's cabinet. He was then minister of finance in Ikeda Hayato's and Satō Eisaku's cabinets. In 1972, he became leader of the LDP and succeeded Satō Eisaku as prime minister. Implicated in a number of financial scandals, he was forced to resign in 1974; Miki Takeo replaced him.

He was arrested in 1976 for having been the kingpin of the Lockheed scandal, but he continued to influence government policy. He retired in 1990 due to failing health. In 1972, he wrote a book intended to remodel Japan's industrial landscape, *Nihon rettō* (Building a New Japan).

Tanaka Kinuyo. Movie actor (1910–77) and director. Her career began in 1931 under director Gosho Heinosuke. She played memorable roles in Mizoguchi Kenji's films, including *Saikaku ichidai onna* (1952), *Ugetsu monogatari* (1953), and *Sanshō daiyū* (1954). Her directing career began in 1953 with the film *Koibumi* (Love Letter). She also played many roles on television and received the "best actress" award (Kinema Jumpō Award) in 1974.

Tanaka Kōtarō. Jurist (1890–1974), born in Kagoshima prefecture. Minister of education in Yoshida Shigeru's first cabinet in 1946, and member of the Chamber of Councillors (1947–50), then guard of the seals and judge at the International Court of Justice in The Hague (1960–70). He wrote a number of books on jurisprudence, including *Sekaihō no riron* (Theory of International Law, 1932–34), which is still authoritative. He converted to Christianity and was baptized Paul Francis.

Tanaka Ōdō. Journalist and essayist (Tanaka Kiichi, 1867–1932), born in Saitama prefecture, baptized in 1889. In that year, he left for the United States, where he lived for nine years studying philosophy and psychology with John Dewey and G. H. Mead, among others. A professor of philosophy at Waseda University, he wrote a number of essays on the Meiji era.

Tanaka Shōsuke. Kyoto merchant (Don Francisco de Joçuquen-dono, early seventeenth century) who crossed the Pacific Ocean in 1610 to accompany the former viceroy of the Philippines, Vivero de Velasco, who had been shipwrecked on the Kazusa coast in 1609. He also bore gifts from Tokugawa Ieyasu to the viceroy of Mexico, and returned to Japan in 1611 with a Spanish envoy, Sebastian Viscaino. Shōsuke was the first Japanese to go overseas. Called Don Francisco de Velasco by the Spanish.

Tanaka Shōzō. Politician (1841–1913), born in Tochigi province. He was of a deeply humanist and liberal turn of mind, and fought bureaucratic corruption and the damage caused by overindustrial-ization throughout his life, going so far as to submit petitions directly to the emperor, which resulted in his being arrested and considered insane. Elected to the Diet in 1890, he remained there for 10 years, campaigning constantly against pollution. He was then imprisoned several times for disturbing the peace, but persisted in his struggle for improvement in peasants' living conditions.

Tanaka Sumie. Writer (Tsujimura Sumie), born 1908 in Tokyo. She wrote a number of novels and plays, including *Tsuzumi no onna* (The Woman with the Drum, 1958), *Garashiya Hosokawa fujin* (Life of Hosokawa Gracia, 1959), and *Genshi josei wa taiyō de atta* (In the Beginning the Sun Was a Woman, 1971). In 1935, she married the writer Tanaka Chikao.

Tandai. Title of a military and civil deputy of the Kamakura and Muromachi shogunates in Kyoto (Rokuhara-*tandai,* starting in 1221), on Kyushu (Chizai-*tandai,* in 1293), in northern Honshu (Ōshu-*tandai*), and in Chūgoku (Chūgoku-*tandai*).
• Former title for superiors in Buddhist monasteries responsible for supervising the education of novices.
• Term for poems improvised on a theme chosen by chance during a literary meeting.

• *Tandai-shoshin roku.* "Prudent and Imprudent Notes." A major literary-criticism text written by Ueda Akinari in 1808.

Tan-e. Technique of printing ukiyo-e prints in which the lines of the drawing are printed in black, and color (usually vermilion) is then applied with a brush. It was used mainly during the Genroku, Hoei, and Shōtoku eras (1688–1716).

Taneda Santōka. Poet (1882–1940), born in Yamaguchi prefecture. He is known mainly for his haiku written in a simple language, with a lyrical spirit, celebrating wine and nature. His two most famous collections are *Sōmokutō* (Monument to Grass and Trees, 1940) and *Gochū nikki*, a five-volume work about his travels in Japan, published after his death.

Tanegashima. Island about 40 km south of Ōsumi Bay (Kyushu), to which Dutch shipwreck survivors introduced the first harquebuses (*see* TEPPŌ) in 1543. The lord of the island, Tanegashima Tokitada (1528–79), obtained a few and had them copied in great numbers. Use of these weapons spread very rapidly and revolutionized the military tactics of the samurai.

The island, with a relatively small population (about 50,000), has only one town, Nishino-otome, and two villages. A particular breed of cattle, *uchiuma* ("half-horse, half-cow"), is raised there. Recently, a major aerospace base was built there at 30°4′ latitude. It has a number of launch platforms and rocket-assembly plants on the Osaki and Takasaki sites. It is controlled by NASDA, the second-largest Japanese space agency after ISAS. *Area:* 450 km². *See* KAGOSHIMA, SATELLITES.

Tanemaku hito. "The Sower," a socialist literary movement; the magazine of the same name, published from 1921 to 1923, launched the "movement for proletarian literature" (*see* NAPF). Founded in Akita prefecture, the magazine was moved to Tokyo and drew many writers with socialist leanings; Anatole France contributed several articles. The magazine *Bungei Sensen* succeeded *Tanemaku Hito* when it suspended publication after the major earthquake of September 1923.

Tange Kenzō. Architect, born 1913 in Imabari (Shikoku). He worked with Maekawa Kunio; after completing his education, he became a professor at the University of Tokyo. He designed many buildings in Japan, all of them notable for their modernistic plans and use of materials, and gained an international reputation for the impressive Yoyogi sports complex, built for the Tokyo Olympic Games (1964). He also drew up plans for a hypothetical futuristic city on Tokyo Bay. Among his most famous buildings are the Peace Center in Hiroshima (1949); the Shizuoka conference center (1953); the Tokyo prefectural offices (1957); the prefectural buildings in Kurayoshi (1957), Takamatsu (1958), and Kurashiki (1960); and the Japanese pavilions for the Ōsaka World Fair (1970). He helped with reconstruction of the Yugoslav city of Skopje after it was destroyed by an earthquake in 1960. His work inspired architects throughout the world, and he was decorated with the Order of Culture (Bunka-shō) in 1979.

Tangen. Painter (Kimura Takikazu; *mei:* Muraemon, Morihiro; *gō:* Sangyō-an, Daini, Tangen, 1679–1767) of the Kanō school, Tanshin's student in Edo.

Tango. Former province, now included in Kyoto prefecture.

• *Tango fudoki.* Eighth-century provincial chronicle of Tango province. In it is found, among other tales, the legend of the fisherman Urashima.

Tango no Sekku. "Boy's Festival," held each year on the fifth day of the fifth month (May 5). On this occasion, iris and artemisia leaves are hung in the doorways of houses to ward off evil influences, and people eat rice cakes wrapped in oak leaves (*kashiwa*). Parents of boys display replicas of ancient armor (or samurai helmets), and *koi-nobori*, fabric windsocks shaped like carp, are flown on long poles on the roofs of houses to show how many children live there (black carp for boys, smaller red carp for girls). This festival is of Chinese origin, and its counterpart is the "Girls' Festival" (Hina Matsuri, on March 3). Also called Ayama no Sekku, Tango Matsuri, Chōgo, Tan'yō, Kodomo no Hi. *Chin.:* Duanwu; *Viet.:* Tết Doang Ngô.

Tani Bunchō. Painter (1763–1840) and poet. In Nagasaki, he studied Chinese paintings of the Ming and Qing eras and learned about Western painting (Yōga). He painted mainly landscapes, but also several portraits. Among his many disciples were Watanabe Kazan and Takaku Aigai.

Taniguchi Masaharu. Lay religious leader (1893–1985), born in Hyōgo prefecture. After joining the Ōmoto-kyō, he had revelations that led him to found a new religious group, Seichō no Ie, and a magazine of the same name, in 1930. He took the government's side during the Second World War and gained many followers, but he fell into disapproval after Japan's defeat. He then turned to Shinto and advocated a return to traditional morals.

Taniguchi Yoshirō. Architect (1905–79), born in Kanazawa, professor at the Tokyo Institute of Technology. His designs were notable for their audacity and modernism, although they retained some traditional characteristics, as seen in the Okura Hotel in Tokyo (1962). He also designed the Imperial Theater, the Tokyo Kaikan, buildings for Keiō University (1938), the Tōson Memorial (1948), the eastern section of the Tokyo National Museum (1969), the Tōgū palace, and, abroad, the Pagoda of Peace in San Francisco.

Tani Jichū. Confucian philosopher (1598–1649) of the Tosa estate, where he taught Zhu Xi (*Jap.:* Shushi) philosophy after having been a Buddhist monk. His disciples included Yamazaki Ansai.

Tani Jinzan. Neo-Confucian philosopher (1663–1718), born in Tosa; Yamazaki Ansai's student in Kyoto.

Tani Kanjō. Politician (Tani Tateki, 1837–1911), born on the Tosa estate. A member of the military, he defended the Kumamoto castle during the Satsuma Rebellion in 1877, then was promoted to general. As minister of agriculture and commerce in Itō Hirobumi's first cabinet in 1885, he disagreed with the other ministers and resigned. He was elected to the House of Peers in 1890.

Tanikawa Shuntarō. Poet, born 1931 in Tokyo, Tanikawa Tetsuzō's son. He experimented with various poetry styles, researching the rhythms and sounds of Japanese. *Kotoba-asobi uta* (Wordplay Songs, 1972) is his best-known poetry collection.

• **Tanikawa Tetsuzō.** Philosopher and aesthete (1905–98); president of Hosei University from 1962 to 1970. He followed the line of thought of Western philosophers such as Nietzsche and Kierkegaard, and Japanese philosophers such as Watsuji Tetsurō. Abroad, he founded the National Japanese Commission within UNESCO. Tanikawa Shuntarō's father.

Tani Masayuki. Politician and diplomat (1889–1962). He was ambassador to France (1918–23), the United States (1927–30), and Manchukuo (1933–36). In 1942–43, he was minister of foreign affairs.

Tanin no kao. "The Face of Another." A novel by Abe Kōbō, published in 1964, dealing with the taking of a false identity and posing the eternal question "Who am I, really?" Teshigawara Hiroshi made a movie from the book that bore little relation to the novel.

Taniuchi Kōta. Writer (b. 1947) of modern and Christian inspiration. He has written many stories and novels.

Tanizaki Jun'ichirō. Writer (1886–1965), born in Tokyo. His first story, *Shisei* (or *Irezumi,* Tattoos), published in 1910, already showed his tendency toward masochism mixed with a sort of adoration of the female body. His other early stories, *Kirin* (1910), *Shōnen* (1910), *Hōkan* (1911), and *Akuma* (1912), also combined eroticism and a fear of female power, and were very much admired by Nagai Kafū. Very early, Tanizaki joined the Romantic

movement (Rōman-ha). His first marriage, to Chiyoko in 1915, and his relationship with the writer Satō Haruo supplied him with experiences that he attempted to sublimate in novels such as *Otsuya-goroshi* (The Murder of Otsuya, 1915) and stories such as *Shindō* (1916) and *Oni no men* (1916).

It seems that Tanizaki stopped writing for several years, until he published a play, *Aisureba koso* (If One Loves), in 1921. This was followed by an almost uninterrupted series of novels written in very classic language, whose themes appealed to all the resources of the Japanese soul, and in which his slightly morbid romanticism and love of nature were fully revealed: *Kami to hito no aida* (Between the Human and the Divine, 1924), *Chijin no Ai* (The Love of an Idiot, 1924–25). After the earthquake in Tokyo, Tanizaki moved to the Kyoto region, where he immersed himself in traditional culture. He then published *Tade kuu mushi* (Some Prefer Needles, 1928), an exploration of female love; *Manji* (Swastika, 1928); *Bushūkō hiwa* (The Secrets of the Lord of Musashi, 1931); and *Yoshinokuzu* (Roots of Yoshino, 1931), on maternal love.

After divorcing Chiyoko, Tanizaki married Furukawa Tomiko, but he also entered a tumultuous relationship with Morita Matsuko, who later became his third wife. She was born in Osaka and seems to have inspired the novels he wrote after this period of emotional upheaval. He published the stories *Mōmomu monogatari* (The Blind Man's Ditty, 1931), *Ashikari* (A Cut in the Reeds, 1932), *Shunkin-shō* (Shunkin's Story, 1933), and *Inei raisan* (Elegy of Shadow, 1933), then undertook to transpose the *Genji monogatari* into modern Japanese; it was published in 26 volumes in 1939–41. Matsuko left him soon after to marry his best friend, which caused quite a scandal.

After the Second World War, Tanizaki began to write again, publishing a novel that drew very wide attention, *Sasami-yuki* (Fine Snow, 1947), begun in 1943; his subsequent novels were sometimes called "fiendish," such as *Kagi* (The Key, or Indecent Confession, 1956), *Yume no ukihashi* (The Bridge of Dream Boats, 1959), *Fūten rōjin nikki* (The Journal of an Old Madman, 1961). He committed suicide in 1965.

Tanizaki's works were translated into many languages, and some of his stories and novels were made into movies, including *Amachua kurabu* (The Amateurs' Club), *Katsushika sunako, Hinamatsuri no yoru* (The Night of the Girls' Festival), and *Jasei no in* (The Lechery of the Snake), all directed by Kurihara Kisaburō in 1920 and 1921. Among other movie adaptations of his work are *Okoto no sa-suke,* by Kinugasa Teinosuke (1961); *Chijin no ai,* by Kimura Keigo (1949); *Masumura yasuzō* (The Japanese Cat, 1967) and *Sanka* (Ode), by Shindō Kaneto (1972); and *Sasame-yuki,* by Shima Kōji (1959) and Ichikawa Kon (1984). Recently, a new work of Tanizaki's was discovered, *Kozō no yume* (An Apprentice's Dream); it had been published in 1917 in a Fukuoka (Kyushu) newspaper.

Tanjō-butso. *See* KAMBUTSU-E.

Tanka. Buddhist monk (?–824). According to legend, one winter day he burned statues of the Buddha to warm himself, thus showing his disdain for the cult of images.
• "Short poem," a poetic form comprising 31 syllables in five lines of 5, 7, 5, 7, and 7 syllables each. This type of *waka* (Japanese poem) is very old (it appeared in the *Man'yōshū*) and was the first "classic" form of poetry. In the modern era, it was the term for *waka,* to distinguish them from "Chinese-style" poems *(kanshi)* and long poems *(chōka).* Starting in the thirteenth century, the first tercet of *tanka (kami no ku)* was used by poets to compose *haikai,* then, in the seventeenth century, *haiku.* Kor.: Danga. See HAIKU, RENGA, WAKA.

Tankai. Buddhist monk and sculptor (Hōzan Tankai, 1629–1716). A hermit of the Shingon-shū sect, he apparently lived for a number of years in a cave on Mt. Ikoma-yama, near Nara. He founded the Hōzan-ji temple near Nara in 1678. *See* HŌZAN-JI.

Tankei. Sculptor of Buddhist images (1173–1256), Unkei's son and student; his works were often influenced by Kaikei art. He restored the Tōdai-ji and Kōfuku-ji temples and received the titles Hokkyō (1194), Hōgen (1208), and Hōin (1213). He is credited with sculpting the large statue of Senju Kannon Bosatsu at the Sanjūsangendō (Renge-ō-in) in Kyoto (1254).

Tankin. Sculpting technique, consisting of working metal with a hammer and forge. Also called *uchimono.*

Tankō. Type of armor found in *kofun* and dating from the third and fourth centuries, made with plates of iron attached by leather thongs or by rivets, protecting only the upper body. Several *haniwa* illustrate typical *tankō. See* KATCHŪ, KEIKŌ.

Tannishō. "Book About Deplorable Heterodoxies," in 18 chapters, written about 1250 by one of Shinran's disciples at the Jōdo Shin-shū, perhaps Yuien, who collected his master's speeches just before his death. Little known before the late nineteenth century, this work was popularized by Kiyozawa Manshi and is now considered one of the major texts of the Amidist faith according to the Jōdo Shin-shū sect.

Ta no kami. "*Kami* of the fields," the term for a large number of Shinto *kami* said to protect rice paddies and fields and to provide, when they were venerated, abundant harvests. According to ancient legends, the *kami* of the mountains *(Yama no kami)* descended into the fields and villages in early spring and during certain festivals. This belief is probably behind the *dōtaku* and sacred scabbards of the Yayoi period. In early spring, the custom among villagers was to welcome them with songs and dances *(kamiumkae)* and to accompany them back to the hills on the second day of the year or, in certain villages, after the harvest. Also called *sakugami* and *sukurigami. See* DŌTAKU, YAMA NO KAMI.

Tanomoshi. Benevolent associations created within village communities to help the poorest when the need arises.

Tanomura Chokunyū. Painter (1814–1907), born in Bungo province, Tanomura Chikuden's (*see* CHIKUDEN) adoptive son and student. He worked at first in Ōita (Kyushu), then moved to Kyoto in 1868. Like Chikuden, he followed the Nanga (Bunjinga) style and reproduced many Chinese paintings. He was also a calligrapher, poet, and Zen scholar. He was one of the founders of the Nihon Nanga Kyōkai (Japan Literati Painting Association) in 1877.

Tanroku-bon. Books with wood-block prints, published in the early seventeenth century. The illustrations were generally colored with *tan* (orange-red color) and *roku* (mineral green). They illustrated classic texts of the *otogi-zōshi* and *kana-zōshi* genres and *jōruri* librettos.

Tansu. Mirrored chest or commode, usually made of *kiri* wood (*kiri no ki,* paulownia), used to store kimonos. It was customary, until quite recently, to offer such a chest to a bride, made from the wood of a tree planted when she was born. *See* KIMONO, TSUZURA.

Tan Taigi. Poet (1709–71), born in Edo, who became a Buddhist monk at the Daitoku-ji temple in Kyoto in 1751. He wrote a large number of haiku, influenced by Buson, and published an anthology of his works, *Taigi kusen,* in 1770.

Tantō. Short sword or long dagger, less than 30 cm in length, with no *tsuba,* generally worn by samurai in their belt *(sashizoe),* along with a *katana* called *koshigatana.* Buddhist monks sometimes carried a *tantō.* Women used a shorter model, called *futokoro-gatana* or *kaiken,* hidden in their *obi,* for self-defense. *See* AIKUCHI.

• **Tantō-jūtsu.** The art of self-defense with a *tantō.*

Tanuki. Viverrine dog (*Nyctereutes viverrinus* T., or *Nyctereutes procyonides*) of the Canidae genus, originally from Siberia; it plays an important role in Japanese folklore. This omnivorous animal, measuring about 0.6 m from head to tail, hibernates during cold seasons. In recent decades, it has tended to replace foxes in Eastern and Northern Europe, where it fills the same ecological niche. In legends, strange powers are attributed to it, such as the ability to transform itself into a beautiful woman, a Buddhist monk, or a teapot (*see* BUMBUKU-CHA-GAMA), to play tricks on humans. It is said that *tanuki* play the drum by slapping their stomachs on moonlit nights, and that they are particularly fond of rice and *sake.* Effigies of *tanuki* are often found on the counter in bars and at the entrance to geisha houses; they are portrayed standing on their back paws, with a white belly and large genitals. The name is often used as a sobriquet designating a crafty and powerful person: shogun Tokugawa Ieyasu was called *furu-tanuki,* "the old *tanuki.*" This animal was called *mujina* before the thirteenth century. It is often used as a parallel for the fox *(kitsune). See* KACHIKACHI-YAMA.

Tanuma Okitsugu. Politician (Tanuma Mototsugu, 1719–88), from a family of modest means, serving the shoguns Tokugawa Ieshige and Ieharu. He became a page *(koshō)* under Ieshige and remained his confidant when he acceded to power in 1745; he was elevated to the rank of daimyo in 1758, with an income of 10,000 *koku.* Appointed grand chamberlain *(sobayōnin)* in 1767, his allocation was raised to 20,000, then to 57,000 *koku,* and his son, Tanuma Okitomo (1749–84), was appointed *wakadoshiyori* in 1783. When shogun Tokugawa Ienari died, however, he lost his position and part of his revenue to his successor, Matsudaira Sadanobu.

He is known in history as a symbol of poor administration, although he was only partly responsible for the disturbances (peasant uprisings) and financial stagnation that characterized his mandate.

Tan'yū. Painter (Kanō Tan'yū, Kanō Morinobu; *mei:* Shirojirō, Uneme; *gō:* Byakurenshi, Hippōdaikoji, Seimei, Tan'yū, 1602–74) of the Kanō school, founder of the Kajibashi branch of this school in Edo. He was appointed chief of the shogunal *e-dokoro.* He was Kanō Tadanobu's oldest son and studied with Kōi.

Tanzan. Painter (Tsuruzawa Kanenobu; *gō:* Yūsen, Tansen, Tanzan, 1655–1729) of the Kanō school, Tan'yū's student in Kyoto. He received the title Hōgen and was made an official painter of the imperial court.

Taoka Reiun. Literary critic and journalist (Taoka Sayoji, 1870–1912), born in the Tosa estate. He studied at the University of Tokyo; in 1895, he founded a literary magazine, *Seinen-bun* (Literature for Young People), which advocated a new literature based on social criticism. He also worked for other journals and traveled in China, where he joined the revolutionaries. The government censored his writing repeatedly because of his overly strong opposition to the regime of the Meiji era.

Tapukaru. Ainu ritual dance performed in honor of the *kamui* (*see* KAMUI), involving prayers and invocations.

Tarason Kannon Bosatsu. One of the 33 forms (*see* SANJŪSAN ŌGESHIN) of Kannon Bosatsu (*Skt.:* Avalokiteshvara), sometimes identified with the Buddha's mother, Māyā Devī (*Jap.:* Maya Bunin). She was born from the light of Kannon's eyes. In Japan, she is portrayed under two aspects: first, standing on a lotus flower, with three faces, wearing an image of Ashuku Nyorai (*Skt.:* Akshobhya) in her hair, in pale blue, holding a blue lotus flower in her left hand and a pomegranate (or a human skull) in her right hand; second, sitting on a lotus flower, hands in *gasshō-in* (*Skt.:* Añjali-mudrā) holding a lotus flower, or holding it in her left hand with the right hand in the *don* position (*Skt.:* Varada-mudrā). She may symbolize Avalokiteshvara's resolution to save all living beings. This particular form of Kannon Bosatsu was mentioned in the seventh century by the Chinese pilgrim Xuanzang. She may also be one of the forms of Bikuchi Kannon. Also called Tarani Bosatsu (*Skt.:* Tārā).

Tariki. "The strength of the Other," a Buddhist concept specific to Amidist sects, according to which the power (or grace) of Amida (the Other) can save others (or bring them enlightenment). In sects of the Jōdo-shū, it is also the power of the forty-eighth vow that Amida made to save all beings who invoked his name and to bring them to his "paradise" (Gokuraku-jōdo). This concept is opposed to that of *jiriki,* according to which salvation can come only from the efforts of the faithful.

• **Tariki-shū.** "Sect of the Strength of the Other," a name sometimes used for the Jōdo Shin-shū.

Taru. Wooden container with cover, hooped with ropes, once used to transport liquids, oil, or spices. Some *taru* were lacquered. When they were used by temples or shrines, they were called *tsunodaru.* They are now used to transport *sake;* during certain ceremonies, the flat cover *(kagami-ita)* is broken with a mallet to draw the liquor out. *Taru* are very similar to old-style barrels.

• **Taru-kaisen.** During the Edo period, boats that transported barrels of *sake (taru)* between Osaka and Edo. They also carried various other products, such as *shōyu,* paper, and fabrics.

Tarui Tōkichi. Politician (1850–1922), born near Nara. He was a fervent defender of Saigō Takamori; when Saigō rebelled, he tried to raise a supporting army in northern Honshu. In 1882, he founded the Tōyō Shakaitō (Asian Socialist party) in Shimabara (Kyushu), which attracted mainly local peasants hoping to improve their living conditions. This party was almost immediately banned by the government, and Tarui was sentenced to one month in prison in 1883. He was elected to the lower house of the Diet in 1892. In his writings (*Daitō gappō,* 1893), he was the first to advocate a union of all Asian countries under Japan's leadership.

Tasaka Tomotaka. Movie director (1902–74), born in Hiroshima prefecture. He worked for the Nikkatsu company starting in 1924, and made many silent and sound movies. Irradiated during the bombing of Hiroshima, he began to direct again only in 1950, working mainly with the actress Hidari Sachiko.

Tashiro Sanki. Physician (1465–1537), born in Kantō, who studied in China for 12 years and imported techniques of the Jin-yuan school to Japan. He was Manase Dōsan's teacher.

Tashiro Shirō. Chemist and biologist (1883–1963), inventor of a "biometer" designed to measure the quantity of CO_2 in the human body.

Tasuki. Cord used by women wearing kimonos, tied under their arms to hold their sleeves when they have to work. This accessory goes back to the *kofun* period and was portrayed on *haniwa.*

Tatami. Mats made of compressed straw covered with braided straw or grass, used to cover the floors of houses and palaces starting in the seventeenth century. They are derived from platforms (*chōdai*) made in the same way, which were used as daises for lords in palace reception-halls. Before the seventeenth century, commoners sat on straw cushions, called *zabuton,* placed on the floor.

Tatami are placed against each other so that they cover the floor completely. They are generally of a set size, corresponding to one intercolumnation (*ken*) in length—from 1.86 to 1.92 m, depending on the region. In Kanto, they are generally 5 *shaku* and 7 *sun* (or 5 *shaku* and 8 *sun*) and are called Edo-ma or Inaka-ma. *Tatami* from the Kyoto region are the largest, at 6 *shaku* and 3 *sun* long and 3 *shaku* and 1.5 *sun* wide. Those from Owari (Nagoya-ma) are generally 6 *shaku* by 3 *shaku.* The mats are always twice as long as they are wide, and about 2 *sun* thick. Two *tatami* therefore make a square surface, called a *tsubo.* The number of *tatami* determines the size of a room. Border colors (*herinuno*), black or brown, once indicated the social status of the homeowner. A half-*tatami* is called *hanjō,* while a *tatami* that is three-quarters the normal size, used mainly in tea-ceremony houses, is called *daimedatami.* Once made by hand, *tatami* are now machine-made. Even today, they are the obligatory floor covering in a house's reception room and bedrooms. *See* ENZA.

Tatara. Sort of semi-buried cabin, probably used during the Jōmon period. Square or rectangular in shape, *tatara* had a double-sloped roof descending to the ground and triangular gable openings to let smoke out. Also called, in some cases, *tateana-shiki.*

• **Tatara-buki.** Traditional method of casting iron, generally practiced in a *tatara*-style hut. It consisted of blowing air (using foot-activated bellows) into the base of a large tank filled with a mixture of charcoal embers and hot ferriferous sand (found in abundance in the Izumo region, where it seems that this procedure was first used). Several men together could operate bellows with multiple ducts. The tank was made of heat-resistant clay and had an inclined bottom and one or two openings through which the molten iron flowed. In some cases, the contents of the tank were allowed to cool inside it and it was broken to recover the cast iron. This procedure was in use until about 1880.

Tatari. In Shinto rites, a curse or punishment inflicted on the perpetrator of a serious fault *(tsumi)* or on someone who caused an impurity *(negare)*, necessitating purification sessions *(harai)*. These rites may have been inspired by Buddhism. *See* KAMI, KEGARE.

Tatchū. Funerary *stūpa* for an important Buddhist monk. This term was later used for a semi-independent pavilion affiliated with a Zen monastery. In the Meiji era, it was the term for "auxiliary" temples.

Tate. In Kabuki theater, danced simulations of battles. *See* TATE-YAKU.
• Shield used by foot soldiers *(zusa)* during battles and sieges. *Tate* were large and rectangular; several placed together could form a sort of rampart. They were made of thick wood covered with leather and were used mainly to protect archers. *Tate* were propped on the ground and held up by an assistant. Hand shields were not used.

Tateana. Type of semi-buried dwelling *(see* TATARA) used during the pre- and proto-historical periods. This term was also used for stone funerary chambers in certain tumuli during the *kofun* period. *See* YOKOANA.

Tatekawa Yoshitsugu. General (1880–1945), born in Niigata prefecture, hero of the Russo-Japanese War. Sent to Manchuria in 1931 to attempt to temper the ardor of the Guandong army, he ended up supporting the army's young officers. The following year, ironically, he was the delegate to the Conference on Disarmament in Geneva, and he was ambassador to the Soviet Union from 1940 to 1942.

Tatemae. Reasons invoked, as opposed to real intentions or motives *(honne)*. This Japanese concept emanates from a concern for civility, *omote-ura* ("face and back"), implying that one should say (or do) the opposite to what one really thinks. *See* KENCHIKU-GIREI.

Tateminakata. In Shinto mythology, and especially in the *Kojiki,* Ōkuninushi no Mikoto's son and

Kotoshironushi's brother. He was supposedly killed for refusing to surrender to Ninigi no Mikoto.

Tatewaki Sadayo. Politician (1904–90), born in Shimane prefecture, known for her attempts to improve conditions for women industrial workers and her union activities on their behalf. She was imprisoned a number of times for her opinions, including in 1932, 1934, and 1944. She continued her fight after the Second World War and wrote several works defending the rights of women.

Tate-yaku. In Kabuki theater, the role of a brave man, an idealized character according to the standards of his time. *See* TATE.

Tateyama. Group of volcanoes in Toyama prefecture, in the northern part of the Hida Mountains; the highest peak is over 3,000 m. It is one of the most sacred mountains in Japan. The Oyama Shrine, at the summit of the mountain, is visited by several million of the faithful each year.

Tatsuemon. Sculptor (Ishikawa Tatsuemon, Shigemasa, late fifteenth century) of Noh masks, one of the Jissaku.

Tatsugomo. Portable screen, similar to the *kichō,* used before the tenth century.

Tatsuno Kingo. Architect (1854–1919), born in Saga prefecture. He studied in England; when he returned to Japan in 1883, he taught at the University of Tokyo. He formed his own firm in 1902. Among the buildings he designed are the Bank of Japan (1896) and Tokyo's Central Station (1914).

Tatsuta-taisha. Shinto shrine in Ikoma (Nara prefecture), built, according to tradition, by Emperor Sujin to appease the *kami* seen as responsible for agricultural disasters. Its *kami* are invoked against typhoons. Festivals on April 4 and July 4.

Tattoos. The customs of body tattooing *(bunshin),* ritual tattooing *(horimono),* and discriminatory tattooing *(irezumi),* which derive from magical and shamanic concerns, existed in ancient Japan, as evidenced by the portrayal of tattoos on *haniwa* and in the text of *Gishi wajinden.* The *Nihon shoki* also mentions tattooing of criminals' foreheads. Tattooing was abandoned, then taken up again in the Edo period, when warriors and young men took pride in the magnificent colored designs with which they had their bodies decorated, and was outlawed in 1870. In the Ryukyu Islands and among the Ainu, a socio-cultural custom had it that married women had their faces, arms, and forearms tattooed. Although the authorities banned this practice in the Meiji era, the fashion of tattooing spread among certain social classes, especially rickshaw pullers *(jinrikisha)*. The Prince of Wales (the future King George VI) and the tsarevitch (the future Nicholas II of Russia) had themselves tattooed by someone called Hori Chō in Yokohama, and the art of tattooing spread. Today, it is practiced mainly in "shady" circles such as the yakuza. *See* SHIOKI, TANIZAKI JUN'ICHIRŌ.

Ta-ue Odori. "Sowing dances," folk dances performed by village women when the rice seedlings are transplanted, often accompanied by erotic songs and pantomimes evoking fertility *(manzai, ji-kyōgen)*. Also called, depending on the region, *emburi, haruta-uchi,* Saotome Odori, *hayashi-mai,* and other names. *See* DENGAKU, SAOTOME.

• *Ta-ue zōshi.* Cycle of 133 traditional songs sung by women during Ta-ue Odori dances, collected in a book in the late sixteenth century. These songs are categorized into morning, noon, and evening songs.

Taut, Bruno. German architect (1880–1938) who, fleeing the rise of Nazism, took refuge in Japan in 1933. He studied Japanese art, classifying it into "imperial" and "shogunal." In 1936, he moved to Istanbul, where he died.

Tawara. Large rice-straw sacks, in standard sizes, used to transport grain, straw, vegetables, dried seafood products, coal, and other items. Synonym for *hyō* (a measure of rice that fills a *tawara* and equivalent to about 720 liters, or 4 *koku*). Also called *tawaramono.*

Tawara Kuniichi. Metallurgist (1872–1958), born in Shimane prefecture, known for his studies on traditional metallurgy and production of steel for swords. He studied in Germany from 1903 to 1906 and was a professor at the University of Tokyo. He received the Order of Culture (Bunka-shō) in 1946.

Tawara Machi. Contemporary poet (b. 1962). In 1988, she began publishing collections of modern *tanka* using everyday words. *Salad Anniversary* was a best-seller among young people (1 million copies sold in less than three months). Her work immediately inspired innumerable imitations of her style.

Tawara Sunao. Biologist (1873–1952), born in Ōita (Kyushu). In Germany, he and Ludwig Aschoff discovered certain cardiac functions in mammals between 1903 and 1906. He received the Imperial Prize (Gakushi-in Onshi-shō) of the Japan Academy (Nihon Gakushi-in) in 1914.

Tawara Tōda emaki. "Adventures of Tawara Tōda," sixteenth-century illustrated folk tale (one scroll), kept in the Konkai Kōmyō-ji in Kyoto.

Tawaraya Sōtatsu. *See* SŌTATSU.

Tayama Katai. Writer (Tayama Kaki, Tayama Rokuya, 1871–1930), born in Tatebayashi (Gumma prefecture). He first studied traditional *waka;* then, with Ozaki Kōyō's encouragement, he began to publish stories influenced by Turgenev and Zola: *Futon* (The Mattress, 1907), *Ippeisotsu* (The Soldier, 1908). He then turned to writing novels: *Sei* (Life, 1908), *Tsuma* (The Wives, 1909), *Inaka kyōshi* (The Country Teacher, 1909), *Enishi* (Links, 1910), *Zansetsu* (Leftover Snow, 1918), *Momoyo* (The Hundred Nights, 1926), and others. Late in life, he also wrote some historical novels.

Taya no dōmon. Series of artificial caves near the Ofuna train station in Yokohama, apparently made by the Hōjō family (Kamakura period) for the Buddhist monks of the Shingon-shū. In the eighteenth century, their walls were decorated with thousands of sculpted images of Buddhist divinities.

Tayasu. Branch of the Tokugawa family, descended from Tokugawa Munetake (Tayasu Munetake, 1715–71), one of shogun Tokugawa Yoshimune's sons. Munetake was later Kamo no Mabuchi's student and a well-known poet, who wrote *waka* in the style of those in the *Man'yōshū. See* TOKI ZEMMARO.

• **Tayasu Munetake.** Poet (1715–71). *See* MATSUDAIRA SADANOBU.

Tayū. Term for the best *jōruri* singers *(gidayū)* in puppet shows.
• Title for the highest-class geisha. *See* GEISHA, TAIFU.

Tazaki Hirosuke. Painter (1899–1984) in Western style, specializing in landscapes and mountain scenes. He received the Order of Culture (Bunka-shō) in 1975.

TDK (Tōkyō Denki Kagaku Kōgyō). Manufacturer of magnetic products, founded in 1935, known mainly for its magnetic tapes of all kinds, made under license and exported to many countries. Head office in Tokyo.

Tea (cha). Tea plants *(Camellia sinensis),* imported very early from China by Buddhist monks, were first planted in 805, apparently in Uji or Sakamoto, and their introduction is attributed to Saichō. It seems that Kūkai planted several bushes soon after in the Nagasaki region. However, the oldest mention of tea dates from 729, when Emperor Shōmu invited several monks to taste it with him, since some of them had brought tea leaves back from China. For a long time, the beverage was considered a medication and was reserved for a privileged few. Only in the late twelfth century, on the initiative of the Zen monk Eisai, did the use of tea spread in Zen monasteries because it kept the monks awake during their long meditation sessions *(zazen).*

The monk Myō-e planted tea plants in Uji to supply the monasteries. It was the Ashikaga shoguns (notably Ashikaga Yoshimasa, a lover of Zen and things Chinese) who turned their attention to tea and made its tasting a sort of ceremony. Later, its use spread into the well-off military classes, and tea lovers, both monks and laypeople, such as Shuko and Sen no Rikyū, under the aegis of Toyotomi Hideyoshi, elevated the previously informal rite of tea tasting into a true ceremony, which was called *chanoyu,* and a specific art form developed, influencing ceramics, lacquer, architecture, and garden design. In the Edo period, the habit of drinking tea spread among rich urban dwellers *(chōnin),* then among commoners, as tea-plant cultivation had evolved greatly and peasants liked to plant a few shrubs in their gardens. *See* CERAMICS, CHAMESHI, CHA NO MA, CHANOYU, CHASHITSU, CHAWAN, CHA-YA, CHAZUKE, RAKU, SUKIYA-ZUKURI.

Teatoro. Esperanto word for "Theater," the title of a magazine founded in 1934 by Akita Ujaku (1883–1962) and still the most popular of its type in Japan, dealing essentially with Shingeki (New Theater).

Teien. "Art of gardening." *See* GARDENS.

Teika. Noh play based on an episode from the life of Fujiwara no Teika, written by Zeami.

• *Teika jittei.* Poetry anthology compiled by Fujiwara no Teika between 1207 and 1213, comprising 286 poems.

• **Teika-ryū.** Poetry school introduced by Fujiwara no Teika. *See* FUJIWARA NO SADAIE.

Teikei. Japanese name for the son of Koxinga (Kokusen'ya, Tei Seikō; *Chin.*: Zheng Chenggong), a famous Chinese pirate who controlled Taiwan when his father died in 1662. *See* KOKUSEN'YA.

Teiki. "Journal of the Emperors," genealogical list of all emperors up to the sixth century, now lost. This work apparently served as the basis for the *Kojiki* and *Nihon shoki.*

Teiki-ichi. Markets held on a set date; they later became permanent and developed in the fifteenth and sixteenth centuries to form towns called *ichi-machi.*

Teikin-ōrai. "Precepts for Writing Letters," a short work on morals giving models for letters, probably written by the Buddhist monk Gen'e (1279–1350) of the Tendai-shū sect; sometimes also attributed to the monks Ze'en and Shin'e, among others. It remained in use throughout the Edo period, especially in the *terakoya.*

Teikoku. "Imperial," an adjective describing many companies, parties, buildings, organizations, and other entities claiming the emperor's patronage.

• **Teikoku Bijutsu-in.** "Imperial Fine Arts Academy," organized in 1919 and replaced in 1937 by a similar organization, the Teikoku Geijutsu-in.

• **Teikoku daigaku.** "Imperial university"; the title was changed to state university *(koku-daigaku)* in 1947. There were nine:
—Tōkyō (now Tōkyō Daigaku), founded in 1886.
—Kyōto (Kyōto Daigaku), founded in 1897.
—Kyūshū, in Fukuoka, founded in 1910.
—Tōhoku, in Sendai, founded in 1907.
—Ōsaka, in Osaka, founded in 1931.
—Hokkaidō, in Sapporo, founded in 1924.
—Nagoya, in Nagoya, founded in 1939.
—Keisei, in Seoul, Korea, from 1910 to 1945.
—Taihoku, in Taipei, Taiwan, from 1895 to 1945.

• **Teikoku Geijutsu-in.** "Imperial Art Academy." *See* TEIKOKU BIJUTSU-IN.

• **Teikoku-gikai.** Japanese name for the Diet (Parliament) in Tokyo before 1947. The first assembly was held in 1890, following promulgation of the

Constitution (Dai-Nihon Teikoku Kempō). *See* TO-KYO.

• **Teikoku-hōteru.** *See* RAYMOND, WRIGHT.

• **Teikokutō.** "Imperial party." Pro-government political party, found in 1899 by members of the Kokumin Kyōkai (Nationalist Association). It did not win enough seats in the Diet, so it was dissolved and its members joined the Daidō Kurabu in 1905.

Teikyō-reki. Calendar adopted in 1684 and published by Shibukawa Shunkai. Also called *Jōkyō-reki*.

Teimon-ha. Poetry school dedicated to "old-style" haiku, founded by Matsunaga Teitoku (1571–1653). *See* DANRIN-FŪ.

Teinensei. "Age-limit system," instituted around 1920, setting the obligatory retirement age at 55 for all bureaucrats and employees of medium-sized and large enterprises. After the Second World War, the retirement age was raised to 60. When they retire, workers generally receive a sum of money calculated on the basis of their average salary and the number of years they worked. *See* AMAKUDARI, OLD AGE.

Teishitsu Gigei-in. Title of "Artist for the Imperial Household," given to deserving artists during the Meiji era. *See* SHŌSAI.

Teishu-ha. School of Confucianism founded by Hayashi Razan and Fujiwara no Seika in the seventeenth century. *See* TOKUGAWA-JIDAI NO KEIGAKU-HA.

Teiten. "Imperial Exhibition of the School of Fine Arts," inaugurated in 1919, succeeding the exhibitions called Bunten. Abridgment of Teikoku Bijutsu-in Tenrankai. Its first president was Mori Ōgai. *See* BUNTEN.

Tekagami. "Mirror of the Hands," a collection of examples of calligraphy used in the seventeenth century to learn the art of calligraphy. *See* KAGAMI, KYŌ.

Temari. Handball-like game, similar to the game of *kemari*. At first, a ball made of cloth was used; rubber balls began to be used in 1880. While *temari* is played, songs called *temari-uta* are performed.

Tembimbō. Yoke or pole carried over one or both shoulders, used to transport heavy loads.

Tembu (Ten-bu). Minor Buddhist divinities, corresponding to ordinary devas, whose name is always followed by the designation *-ten*, as in Daikoku-ten.

Tembun. Era of Emperor Go-Nara: July 1532–Oct. 1555. Sometimes pronounced Temmon. *See* NENGŌ.

Temiya dōkutsu. Natural cave in Oharu (Hokkaido), discovered in 1866; its walls are covered with enigmatic carved figures, probably related to magical hunting rites. Similar inscriptions were discovered in 1951 in a cave near Fugoppe. Date undetermined.

Temma. Post horses kept at post towns *(shuku-eki)* for official couriers and daimyo.

Temmangū. General term for all Shinto shrines dedicated to Sugawara no Michizane. The main ones are the Kitano Temmangū in Kyoto (dating from 947) and the Dazaifu Temmangū in the Fukuoka region (Kyushu), which apparently dates from 919. *See* SUGAWARA NO MICHIZANE, TENJIN-SAMA.

Temmei. Era of Emperor Kōkaku: Apr. 1781–Jan. 1789. *See* NENGŌ.

• **Temmei no Kikin.** Terrible famine that affected northern Honshu, Kyushu, Shikoku, and Hokkaido from 1782 to 1787. It caused the death of almost 1 million people and led to acts of cannibalism and a great number of peasant uprisings *(hyakushō-ikki)*, especially in northern Honshu.

Temmoku. Ceramics for the tea ceremony, generally in "crow's-wing black," made in Hangzhou, China (*Chin.:* Tienmu), and exported to Japan in the fourteenth and fifteenth centuries. These ceramics, with a dark ferrous oxide slip, can be "oil drop" *(yūteki temmoku)*, iridescent *(yōhen temmoku)*, or with a reddish tint *(kaki temmoku)*. *See* ISHIGURO MUNEMARO, SETO-YAKI, TETSUYŪ TŌKI.

Temmon-dō. "Path of Astronomy," the science of celestial phenomena, somewhat similar to astrology. In the Edo period, the shogunate set up its own bureau, called the Temmon-kata, which was responsible for reforming the calendar.

Temmon Hokke no Ran. Riots that took place in Kyoto during the Tembun (Temmon) era, from 1532 to 1536, provoked by followers of the Nichiren sect who were violently opposed to followers of the Ikkō-ikki and Tendai-shū sects. In 1536, the monk-soldiers *(heisō)* of Mt. Hiei invaded Kyoto, destroying the main temples of the Nichiren sect and the capital's commercial center, and forcing the "Nichirenites" to flee and take refuge in Sakai; they were allowed to return to the capital in 1542.

Temmu Tennō. Fortieth emperor (Prince Ō-ama, Ama no Nunahara-Oki no Mabito, 622<673–86>), Jomei Tennō's son and successor to Kōbun Tennō. He rebelled against Kōbun, defeating him, then moved his capital to Asuka Kiyomihara. He reinforced imperial power, revised the court ranks (see I), had a legal code *(Asuka no kiyomihara risturyō)* written in 681, made agrarian reforms *(jōri* and *tonden* systems), and adopted the Chinese system of administration. Empress Jitō succeeded him.

Tempō. Era of Emperor Ninkō: Dec. 1830–Dec. 1844. *See* NENGŌ.

• **Tempō no Kikin.** Famine that affected Honshu from 1833 to 1836, leading to acts of cannibalism and many revolts by peasants and urban dwellers, notably in Osaka (*see* ŌSHIO HEIHACHIRŌ). After the famine, reforms were made by Mizuno Tadakuni in Edo, as well as in various provinces, aimed at stabilizing the country's finances and improving agricultural production.

• **Tempō-tsūhō.** Oval-shaped copper coins pierced with a square hole, issued in 1835. Similar coins in gold and silver, called Tempō-*kingin,* were issued from 1837 to 1843. *See* CURRENCY.

Tempuku. Era of Emperor Go-Horikawa: Apr. 1233–Nov. 1234. *See* NENGŌ.

Tempura. Seafood and vegetables deep-fried in a light batter, eaten with soy sauce *(shōyu)* and grated radish *(daikon).* The word *tempura* is a corruption of the Portuguese word *tempero* ("kitchen"); the dish was apparently imported to Japan by Portuguese missionaries in the sixteenth century. Since the early nineteenth century, it has become one of the main components of Japanese cuisine. Many restaurants specialize in *tempura,* cooked to taste in front of the customer. *See* CUISINE, MEALS.

Tempyō. Era of Emperor Shōmu: Aug. 729–Apr. 749. *See* NENGŌ.

→ *See* NARA-JIDAI.

• **Tempyō bunka.** "Culture of the Tempyō era," characterized by the importation of objects and customs and, by extension, of Buddhism and literature *(Man'yōshū)* from Tang-dynasty China.

• **Tempyō-Hōji.** Era of Emperor Murakami: Aug. 757–Jan. 765.

• **Tempyō-Jingo.** Era of Empress Shōtoku: Jan. 765–Aug. 767.

• **Tempyō-Kampō.** Era of Emperor Murakami: Apr. 749–July 749.

• **Tempyō-Shōhō.** Era of Emperor Murakami: July 749–Aug. 757.

Tenaga. "Long Arms," a mythical character in folk legends, the almost inseparable companion of Ashinaga, "Long Legs."

Ten'an. Era of Emperor Montoku: Feb. 857–Apr. 859. *See* NENGŌ.

Tenaraiko. Kabuki dance performed in Edo in 1792, under the name Kakitsubata nanae no Someginu, on the subject of the innocence of a young schoolgirl.

Tenazuchi. In legends of Shinto mythology, the young woman who married Susanoo. She gave birth to Kushi Inada-hime during her first marriage to Izumo Ashinazuchi. *See* INADA-HIME, SUSANOO.

Tenchi (Tenji). Name of a number of religious sects. *See* FUSŌ-KYŌ.

• **Tenchi no Daikyō.** Sect founded in 1953 by Okada Matsunosuke (born 1894).

• **Tenchi-kōdō Zenrin-kai.** Sect founded by Tatsusai (b. 1908) on Kyushu in 1947; about 40,000 followers.

• **Tenchi-kyō.** Subsect of the Taisei-kyō, founded by Uozumi Masanobu (d. 1928) in Himeji in 1928 and updated in 1936 by Yamanouchi Sōkei (1895–1959).

• **Tenchi Tennō.** *See* TENJI TENNŌ.

Tenchō. Era of Emperor Junna: Jan. 824–Jan. 834. *See* NENGŌ.

Tenchō-setsu. Festival to celebrate the emperor's birthday. It is an official national holiday *(harebi).* Another festival of the same type, Chikyu-setsu, celebrates the empress's birthday, but it is not a public holiday. Emperor Akihito's birthday is December 23. *See* TENNŌ TANJŌBI.

Tenchū-gumi. "Group of Divine Anger," an association of samurai serving the emperor. In 1863, the Tenchū-gumi fomented a revolt against the shogunate in Yamato province, led by the samurai Shimazu Hisamitsu, Fujimoto Tesseki, Matsumoto Kensaburō, Azumi Gorō, and others. Some peasants, led by a village chief from the Tosa estate, Yoshimura Toratarō (1837–63), joined them, as did a number of local *rōnin* and samurai and a noble from Kyoto, Nakayama Tadamitsu. The shogunal troops reacted quickly and expelled the rebels from Kyoto. Yoshimura was injured and committed suicide; the other leaders of the rebellion fled to Kyushu.

Tendai-shū. Buddhist sect imported from China in 805 by Saichō; its headquarters was established in the Enryaku-ji temple on Mt. Hiei, near Heian-kyō. This sect, also called Hokke-shū ("Sect of the Lotus") because of the importance it accorded to the *Hokke-kyō (Skt.: Saddharmapundarika-sūtra)* and its commentaries, drew its doctrines from the Chinese Tiantai-jiao sect founded by the monk Zhiyi (538–97). Like the rival Shingon-shū sect, it emphasized esoterism *(taimitsu),* and its goal was to provide Japan with a series of religious masters who had been educated for at least 12 years on Mt. Hiei. The sect gave rise to other Buddhist currents, such as Amidism, and later was divided into four major subsects: Ji-mon (80,000 followers), Shinsei (30,000), Shugen (30,000), and Tendai (1.2 million), which has subsidiary branches: Haguro-yama Shugen Honshū and Shugendō. The great masters of the Tendai-shū (Tendai-soshi; *Chin.:* Tiantai zushi) were:
—**Emon** (*Chin.:* Gao Huiwen, ?–ca. 550), founder
—**Echi** (*Chin.:* Huisi, 515–77)
—**Chigi** (*Chin.:* Zhiyi, 538–97)
—**Kanchō** (*Chin.:* Guangding, 561–632)
—**Tannen** (*Chin.:* Ganran, 711–82)
—**Saichō** (766–822)
—**Ennin** (794–864)
—**Enchin** (814–91)

The Tendai-shū now has more than 4,000 temples, about 17,000 monks, and almost 5.5 million followers.

Ten'ei. Era of Emperor Toba: July 1110–July 1113. *See* NENGŌ.

Ten'en. Era of Emperor En'yū: Dec. 973–July 976. *See* NENGŌ.

Tengai. Water mill, of Chinese origin. The technology was imported to Japan in 610 by the Korean monk Donchō.

Tengen. Era of Emperor En'yū: Nov. 987–Apr. 983. *See* NENGŌ.

Tengen-kyō. Subsect of the Shintō-kyō, founded in 1931 by Naniwa Jūichi (b. 1909); it has about 15,000 followers.

Tengi. Era of Emperor Go-Reizei: Jan. 1053–Aug. 1058. *See* NENGŌ.

Tengu. The *yaksha (Jap.: yasha)* of Buddhist legends and Japanese folklore, creatures with a human body and a bird's beak and wings, said to live in the mountains. Some, called *konsha-tengu,* are portrayed with a long, phallus-like nose; the "king" of the *tengu,* Sōjōbo, has a red face and holds a fan made of seven feathers. *Tengu* were said to be omniscient genies and experts in the military arts. According to legend, it was the *tengu* of Mt. Kurama who taught young Ushikawa (Minamoto no Yoshitsune) his combat and strategic techniques. *Tengu* liked to play evil tricks on humans and had winged slaves, called *karasu-tengu* (*tengu*-crows). In folklore, they may symbolize the Yamabushi monks.

• *Tengu-zōshi emaki.* Late-thirteenth-century *emakimono* describing the life of *tengu* and of the Buddhist monks of Nara. It has at least seven scrolls, kept in five temples (Enryaku-ji, Onjō-ji, Mii-dera, Kōfuku-ji, and Tōdai-ji).

Tenji. Era of Emperor Sutoko: Apr. 1124–Jan. 1126. *See* NENGŌ.

Tenjiku. Former Japanese name for India.

• **Tenjiku Tokubei.** Nickname for a Japanese traveler (1618–86) who went to Macao and India. He wrote a book (now lost) on these countries and became a Buddhist monk with the name Sōshin.

• **Tenjiku-yō.** "Indian style," a construction mode for Buddhist temples imported from Southern Song–dynasty China (Nansō) during the Kamakura period by the monk Sunjōbō Chōgen (who had built the Asiwangsi monastery in this style in China). In this type of architecture (exemplified by the *nandaimon* of the Tōdai-ji, 1199), the struts *(hijiki)* supporting the gables *(to-kyō)* cross the main pillars and are called *sashi-hijiki.* The joists supporting the corners of the canopy are arranged in a fan shape *(ōgi-daruki),* and those on the sides are in parallel rows. The pillars do not rest on a base *(soban)* and sometimes are slightly narrower on top. All dados *(to)* supporting the entablatures are the same size. Finally, the stories are all the same size, and the beams called *kōryō* are round in section. This construction technique, featuring standardized elements, allowed for great flexibility and speed in the erection of structures.

Tenjin-sama. Shinto divinization of Sugawara no Michizane (845–903) as the *kami* of calligraphy and literary studies. Also called, depending on the shrine and the period, Kan Shōjo, Temmangū, Gokuraku Go-dō, Shōshaken-butsu, Kaito Tenjin, Temman Tenjin, and other names; according to tradition, he has 63 different names. *See* TEMMANGŪ.

• **Tenjin-shichidai.** In Shinto mythology, the "seven generations of heavenly *kami*" *(amatsu-kami)* who preceded Amaterasu-Ōmikami. These are, according to the *Kojiki,* Kunitoko-tachi no Mikoto, Kunisatscuchi, Toyokunnu, Uijini and Suijini, Ōtonoji and Ōtonabe, Omotaru and Kashikoni, and Izanagi and Izanami no Mikoto. *See* CHIJIN-GODAI.

Tenji Tennō (or Tenchi Tennō). Thirty-eighth emperor (Prince Ame-mikoto Hirakasu-wake, Katsuragi no Ōji, Naka no Ōe, 626<662–72>), Jomei Tennō's son and regent for his uncle, Emperor Kōtoku. He succeeded Empress Saimei. In 663, he sent an army to Korea in support of the state of Paekche, which had been attacked by the armies of Silla and the Chinese Tang dynasty, but it was defeated at the Battle of Hakusukinoe. He transferred his capital from Naniwa to Ōtsu, on Lake Biwa, in 667. Kōbun Tennō succeeded him.

Tenjō. General term for ceilings of traditional structures.

• **Tenjōbito.** Term designating most senior bureaucrats of the court with the right to have imperial audiences in the Seiryōden. Also called *kumo no ue hito,* "those who are above the clouds."

• **Tenjō-ji.** *See* ROKKŌ-SAN.

• **Tenjō-kyō.** Subsect of the Mikate-kosha founded in 1931 by Ishiguro Jō (b. 1908).

Tenju. Era of Emperor Go-Kameyama: May 1375–Feb. 1381. *See* NENGŌ.

Tenjukoku shuchō. Piece of embroidered silk showing the Buddhist paradise, made by ladies-in-waiting in 622 on the order of Tachibana no Ōiratsume, Shōtoku Taishi's wife. This very old piece of embroidery is kept in the Chūgū-ji of the Hōryū-ji temple in Nara. Also called Tenjukoku mandara.

Tenkai. Buddhist monk (1536–1643), famous for his wisdom. He was appointed to the head of a number of temples, including those in Nikkō and Ueno. *Posthumous title:* Jigen-daishi.
→ *See* DAIZŌ-KYŌ, SŌRINTŌ.

• **Tenkai-gakusha.** School of painting created in 1873 by Takahashi Yuichi (*see* TAKAHASHI YUICHI).

• **Tenkai-kutsu.** *See* GANKU.

Tenkan nōryoku. "Capacity for change," an expression designating the capacity of industrial firms in Japan to adapt to modern techniques, a factor essential to their growth in the post–World War II economy.

Tenkei (or Tenkyō). Era of Emperor Shujaku: May 938–Apr. 947. *See* NENGŌ.

• **Tenkei no Ran.** Name sometimes used for Taira no Masakado's insurrection in 940. Also called Tenkyō no Ran.

Tenko. Title of a Noh play: a child receives a magical drum from Heaven. The emperor covets the drum, so he steals it and has the child, Tenko, drowned. But the drum refuses to work except when Tenko's father strikes it. The spirit of the child then leaves the river to play his drum and dance.

Tenna. Era of Emperor Reigen: Sept. 1681–Feb. 1684. Also called Tenwa. *See* NENGŌ.

Tennin. Era of Emperor Toba: Aug. 1108–July 1110. *See* NENGŌ.

• Celestial beings: Buddhist angels, musicians, dancers, and singers. One *tennin* is remarkably portrayed on the eighth-century bronze lantern in front of the Daibutsu-den of the Tōdai-ji in Nara. Also called *tennyo*.

Tennō. Since the eighth century, the title given to all emperors after their death to replace the ancient title Dai-ō or Okimi. Since 1868 (Meiji era), the title of a deceased emperor has been the same as that of his era *(nengō)*. "Tennō" is a Japanization of the Chinese Tian-wang (Celestial King). Also called Tenshi, Mikado.

• *Tennō-ki.* Ancient biographical chronicle of emperors, theoretically compiled in 612 by Shōtoku Taishi and Soga no Umako; now lost, it supposedly served as a basis, along with its corollary, the *Kokki,* for the writing of the *Kojiki* and *Nihon shoki.* It would have been compiled in the time of Empress Suiko, around 620.

• **Tennō no Ōsegoto.** *See* SHŌ.

• **Tennō-sei.** "Constitutional monarchy" (or "emperor's reign"), defined by Emperor Meiji in 1889.

• *Tennō sekkan daijin ei.* "Portraits of Emperors, Regents, and Ministers," thirteenth-century documentary *emakimono* kept in the Imperial Collection in Tokyo.

• **Tennō tanjōbi.** Celebration of an emperor's birthday, currently December 23 (Akihito's birthday), considered a national holiday. *See* TENCHŌ-SETSU.

Tennō-zan. Hill 270 m high in southern Kyoto, at the foot of which Toyotomi Hideyoshi fought the forces of Akechi Mitsuhide, Oda Nobunaga's assassin, in 1582. The tunnel of the Meishin expressway, dug in 1963, runs through it. *See* YAMAZAKI NO TAKAKAI.

Ten'ō. Era of emperors Kōnin and Kammu: Jan. 781–Aug. 872. *See* NENGŌ.

Tenri. Town in Nara prefecture that developed around the Shinto Isonokami shrine; it has become the center of the Tenri-kyō sect. *Pop.:* 70,000.

• **Tenri Chūō Toshokan.** Library founded in 1926 by the Tenri-kyō sect in Tenri, housing about 1.5 million works in many languages. It includes the Wataya Bunko (17,000 poetry works), which came from the private libraries of major families, including the Nakayama; the Kogidō Bunko (7,000 engravings and texts from the school founded by Itō Jinsei); the Yorozuyo Bunko (materials relating to sixteenth- and seventeenth-century Christian missions); and the Lafcadio Hearn Bunko (devoted to the British writer).

• **Tenri Daigaku.** Private university founded in 1925 by the Tenri-kyō sect to teach foreign languages to its missionaries. Faculties: foreign languages, classical studies, physical education; research institutes, including the Oyasato Research Institute. Attendance, about 2,500 students.

• **Tenri-kyō.** "Religion of the Divine Wisdom," founded in 1838 by the peasant Nakayama Miki (1798–1887), who wrote the basic texts of the sect's beliefs, *Mikagura uta* (Songs for the Sacred Dance), *Ofudesaki* (Tip of the Divine Writing Brush), and *Osashizu* (Divine Directions). She also taught particular hand movements *(kagura-zutome)* for ritual dance and designated the sacred place *(jiba)* where the temple was to be erected. According to the Tenri-kyō, the divinity that revealed itself to Miki, Tenri Ō no Mikoto, is the primordial creator *(moto no kami)* and the one "true god" *(jitsu no kami)*. He is assisted by ten *kami (tohashira no kami)* who represent his various activities in relation to humanity. To reach salvation *(tasuke),* the follower must return to an original state of purity and sincerity *(makoto)*.

When Miki died, her most faithful disciple, Iburi Izō (1833–1907), succeeded her at the head of the movement and began an intense propaganda campaign in Japan and, starting in 1896, in the United States, Taiwan, Korea, and China. After the Second World War, the sect was reorganized and continued its efforts; it now claims to have 2.5 million followers in Japan and more than 16,000 shrines throughout the world. In Tenri, it owns huge tracts of land on which temples, a university, sports and recreation facilities, a hospital, a radio station, a library, and a museum have been built. The Tenri-kyō is divided into a number of subsects: Dai-Nihon Daidō-kyō (1911), Shūyōdan Hōsei-kai (1924), Sekai Shindō-kyō (1945), Tenri Hommichi (founded 1946), Seishō-in Kyōdan (1946), Hikawa-kyō (1949), Hinomoto Shinsei-kyō (1950), Taidō-kyō,

Yuishin Remmei, and others. *See* NAKAYAMA MIKI, SHINKŌ SHŪKYŌ.

• **Tenri Kyōkai.** *See* SHINTŌ HONKYOKU.

Tenroku. Era of Emperor En'yū: Mar. 970–Mar. 973. *See* NENGŌ.

Tenryaku. Era of Emperor Murakami: Apr. 947–Oct. 957. *See* NENGŌ.

Tenryō. Name for the territories that belonged directly to the Tokugawa shogunate and had not been conceded to the *hatamoto*. These territories, in Kanto, Kinai, and other parts of Honshu, were producing about 4.25 million *koku* at the end of the shogunate, providing about 40% of the *bakufu*'s total revenue. Also called *bakuryō*.
→ *See* KOKURYŌ.

Tenryū-ji. Buddhist temple in Saga, west of Kyoto, on the site of a former villa of Emperor Go-Saga, founded by Musō Soseki in 1339–42 in memory of Go-Daigo Tennō and to serve as general quarters for the Rinzai-shū sect. This temple, once very prosperous, ordered trade missions to China under Ashikaga Tadayoshi's aegis; its ships, the *Tenryū-ji bune*, carried large numbers of Buddhist monks. The first voyage by the *Tenryū-ji bune* left from Hakata in 1342; its mission was to raise funds for the temple, which was one of the largest in Japan in the late fourteenth century, controlling some 120 secondary temples, and the most important *gozan* in Kyoto. Destroyed a number of times by war and fire, the temple buildings were rebuilt in 1900, and the garden designed by Musō Kokushi was re-created.

Tensho. Stylized signature in the form of a symbol, sometimes used instead of (or with) the seal *(in-kan, han)* in official documents. *See* KAŌ.
→ *See* SHOTAI.

Tensho. Chronological history of Japan, by Fujiwara no Hamanari (771–90).

Tenshō. Era of Emperor Sutoku: Jan. 1131–Aug. 1132. *See* NENGŌ.
• Era of Emperor Reigen: July 1573–Dec. 1592. *See* NENGŌ.
→ *See* SHŪBUN.

• **Tenshō Ken'ō Shisetsu.** The first Japanese mission sent to the West, in the late sixteenth century, by the Christian daimyo Ōtomo Sōrin, Arima Harunobu, and Ōmura Sumitada. It was composed of ambassadors and young people educated at the Arima Seminariyo. This mission was organized on the initiative of A. Valignano, who accompanied it. It left Nagasaki on February 20, 1582, and reached Lisbon on August 10, 1584. Its members were received solemnly by King Philip II of Spain; they then went to Italy and met Pope Gregory XII in Rome on March 23, 1585, and his successor, Sixtus V. The mission returned to Nagasaki on July 28, 1590.

• **Tenshō-kyō.** Religious sect founded in 1946 by Aida Tenshū (1884–1943).

• **Tenshō-tsūhō.** Gold or silver coins issued in 1587. The gold coins (Tenshō-*ōban*), oval in shape, were worth 10 *ryō* and weighed 165 grams. *See* CURRENCY.

Tenshu. Castle keep *(jō, shiro)* used as an observation tower, governor or daimyo's residence, and refuge in the case of siege. It had up to six or seven stories and verandahs. Built in wood on a strong foundation of large stones, its walls were plastered and it was defended by moats and several courtyards *(maru)* protected by walls and narrow entrances. The roofs were covered with tiles and decorated with dolphins or sea monsters in gold-leafed bronze or painted terra-cotta. Also called *tenshukaku*. *See* CASTLES.

Tenshūko Kyōkai. Japanese name for the Roman Catholic church.

Tenshū-kyō. Shinto sect founded in 1941 by Unakami Seihan (1894–1965).

Tenson. Mythical founder of the royal family of the Ryukyu Islands. This lineage was interrupted in the 25th generation (in 1187) by a noble *(anji)* named Riyū. *Chin.:* Tiansun.

Tenugui. Rectangular pieces of cotton, about 35 to 40 cm wide and of varying lengths, used as all-purpose towels. Generally white, *tenugui* are sometimes decorated with the family *mon* or, today, with advertising pictures and texts. They are often used as *hachimaki* tied around the forehead, or as bath towels. *See* HACHIMAKI.

Ten'yō. Era of Emperor Konoe: Feb. 1144–July 1145. *See* NENGŌ.

Traditional Order of Tennō

1. Jimmu (trad. 711<600–585> BC)
2. Suisei (trad. 632<581–49> BC)
3. Annei (trad. 567<549–11> BC)
4. Itoku (trad. 544<510–477> BC)
5. Kōshō (trad. 506<475–393> BC)
6. Kōan (trad. 427<392–291> BC)
7. Kōrei (trad. 342<290–15> BC)
8. Kōgen (trad. 273<214–158> BC)
9. Kaika (trad. 208<157–98> BC)

The dates of the following emperors are more historically accurate, although they should be treated with caution up to Emperor Bidatsu Tennō, the thirtieth on the list.

10. Sujin (trad. 149<97–30 BC>)
11. Suinin (trad. 70 BC<29 BC–ca. AD 70>)
12. Keikō (trad. 12 BC<AD 71–AD 130>)
13. Seimu (trad. 83<131–191>)
14. Chūai (trad. 149<192–200>)
15. Jingō Kōgō (regent, trad. 170<201–69>)
16. Ōjin (trad. 201<201–310?>)
17. Richū (trad. 336<400–05>)
18. Hanshō (trad. 352<406–11>)
19. Inkyō (trad. 374<412–53>)
20. Ankō (trad. 401<454–56>)
21. Yūryaku (trad. 418<457–79>)
22. Seinei (trad. 444<480–84>)
23. Kensō (trad. 440<485–87>)
24. Ninken (trad. 448<488–98>)
25. Buretsu (trad. (489<499–506>)
26. Keitai (trad. 450<507–31>)
27. Ankan (trad. 466<534–35>)
28. Senka (trad. 467<536–39>)
29. Kimmei (trad. 509<540–71>)
30. Bidatsu, or Bitatsu (538<572–85>)
31. Yōmei (540<586–87>)
32. Sushun (523<588–92>)
33. Suiko (empress, 554<593–628>)
34. Jomei (593<629–41>)
35. Kōgyoku (empress, 594<642–45>)
36. Kōtoku (597<645–54>)
37. Saimei (empress, <655–61>)
38. Tenji, or Tenchi (626<662–72>)
39. Kōbun (648<672>)
40. Temmu (622<673–86>)
41. Jitō (empress, 646<686–97>703)
42. Mommu (683<697–707>)
43. Gemmei (empress, 662<708–14>722)
44. Genshō (empress, 681<715–23>748)

45. Shōmu (699<724–48>756)
46. Kōken (empress, 718<749–58>)
47. Junnin (733<759–64>765)
48. Shōtoku (empress, <765–70>)
49. Kōnin (719<770–81>)
50. Kammu (737<782–806>)
51. Heijō (774<806–09>824)
52. Saga (785<810–23>824)
53. Junna (786<824–33>840)
54. Nimmyō (810<834–51>)
55. Montoku (827<851–58>)
56. Seiwa (851<859–76>880)
57. Yōzei (868<877–84>949)
58. Kōkō (830<885–87>)
59. Uda (867<888–97>931)
60. Daigo (855<898–930>)
61. Shujaku (923<931–46>952)
62. Murakami (926<947–67>)
63. Reizei (950>968–69>1011)
64. En'yū (959<970–84>991)
65. Kazan (968<985–86>1008)
66. Ichijō (980<987–1011>)
67. Sanjō (967<1012–16>1017)
68. Go-Ichijō (1008<1017–36>)
69. Go-Shujaku (1009<1037–45>)
70. Go-Reizei (1025<1046–68>)
71. Go-Sanjō (1034<1069–72>1073)
72. Shirakawa (1053<1073–86>1129)
73. Horikawa (1078<1087–1107>)
74. Toba (1103<1108–23>1156)
75. Sutoku (1119<1124–41>1164)
76. Konoe (1139<1142–55>)
77. Go-Shirakawa (1127<1156–58>1192)
78. Nijō (1143<1159–65>)
79. Rokujō (1164<1166–68>1176)
80. Takakura (1161<1169–80>1181)
81. Antoku (1178<1181–83>1185)
82. Go-Toba (1179<1184–98>1239)
83. Tsuchimikado (1195<1199–1210>1231)
84. Juntoko (1197<1211–21>1242)
85. Chūkyō (1218<1221–21>1242)
86. Go-Horikawa (1212<1222–32>1234)
87. Shijō (1231<1233–42>)
88. Go-Saga (1220<1243–46>1272)
89. Go-Fukakusa (1243<1247–59>1304)
90. Kameyama (1249<1260–74>1305)
91. Go-Uda (1267<1275–87>1324)
92. Fushimi (1265<1288–98>1317)
93. Go-Fushimi (1288<1299–1301>1336)
94. Go-Nijō (1285<1302–08>)
95. Hanazono (1297<1308–18>1348)
96. Go-Daigo (1287<1319–38>)

Tenzen-kyō. Subsect of the Shintō-kyō, founded in 1924 by Shiina Ken'ichi (1895–1963). About 10,000 followers.

Teppō. Originally, a term for large explosives used by the Korean and Mongolian forces when they attacked Japan in 1274 and 1281; from the Chinese word *tiepao*. This term was then used for the first harquebuses introduced to Japan on Tanegashima by shipwrecked Portuguese sailors in 1543.

• **Teppō-ashigaru.** "Harquebusiers." *See* ASHIGARU, MAEDA TOSHIIE, NAGASHINO TATAKAI.

• **Teppō-gumi.** *See* KUMI-GASHIRA.

• *Teppō-ki.* A work relating to European harquebuses, written by Nampo Bunshi (1556–1620), a Zen monk from Satsuma, in 1606. It was republished in 1625 and 1650.

• **Teppō-shū.** *See* NAGASAWA SHOGUETSUMA.

Tera. Buddhist temple. This word, often used in composition, takes the form -*dera*. Also called *ji*.

• **Terakoya.** "Temple school," a term used starting in 1716 for schools for commoners' children, in which basic education was given by Buddhist monks, and for shops that offered poor students food and board in exchange for small services. "Temple schools" may have existed as far back as the fourteenth century; the practice was laicized in the Edo period, when many village schools and urban neighborhood schools were founded by literate couples or older people, who charged small fees for teaching, heat, and sometimes lodging. They taught mainly reading and writing. Manuals used for this purpose included the *Teikin-ōrai.* Studies of the *terakoya* show that there were more male students; only one-quarter of the attendees were girls.

• **Tera-machi.** New towns formed around Buddhist temples. *See* JŌKA-MACHI, TEIKI-ICHI.

• **Tera-uke.** System of controlling the population established during the Edo period, implemented by Buddhist temples; its goal was to flush out Christian sympathizers (*see* SHŪMON ARATAME) and members of banned sects (such as the Fuju Fuse). Its only result was a very accurate census of the population.

Terada Torahiko. Physicist (Terada Yabukōji, 1878–1935). He went to Europe in 1909 to study geophysics and seismology, then was appointed a professor at the University of Tokyo in 1916. He was also known as a haiku poet and writer of novels influenced by Natsume Sōseki. He published a large number of scientific articles under the name Yoshimura Fuyuhiko.

Terada Tōru. Literary critic and writer, born 1915 in Kanagawa prefecture, and specialist in French literature. He published many essays on Japanese writers, including Mori Ōgai and Masaoka Shiki, and on French authors (Balzac, Camus, Valéry, etc.).

Terajima Ryōan. Naturalist (seventeenth–eighteenth century), author of *Wakan sansai zue* in 1713.

Terakado Seiken. Writer (1796–1868), born in Hitachi province, who opened a school of Confucianism and Chinese studies in Edo. He wrote series of satirical and humorous stories on life in Edo, such as *Edo hanjō* (1832–36), but these texts were judged irreverent by the shogunate. Exiled to Niigata, he continued to write in the same style on life in that city, as in *Niigata hanjō ki*. He gave himself the derisive nickname Muyō no hito ("the useless man").

Terashima Munenori. Politician and diplomat (1832–93), born in Satsuma, Kagoshima. He studied Western medicine, then accompanied the shogunal delegation to London in 1862. When he returned, the following year, he taught medicine at the Kaiseijo shogunal school, then went back to England in 1865 with the delegation sent by Satsuma. Appointed a councilor *(san'yo)* in the Meiji government in 1868, he became minister of foreign affairs in 1873 and negotiated the Treaty of St. Petersburg with Russia in 1875. Appointed vice-president of the emperor's Privy Council in 1891.

Terauchi Jūichi. Military officer (Terauchi Hisaichi, 1879–1946), born in Yamaguchi prefecture, Terauchi Masaki's son. He was minister of the armed forces in 1936 after the incidents of February 26 (*see* NINIROKU-JIKEN). After being commander-in-chief of the Japanese troops in China in 1937, he was commander-in-chief of the armed forces in the South Pacific and China from 1942 to 1945.

• Terauchi Masaki. Military officer and politician (Terauchi Masatake, Terauchi Seki, 1852–1919), born in the Chōshū estate. He lost his right hand during the Satsuma Rebellion in 1877; appointed inspector-in-chief of military education, then general and minister of armed forces in Katsura Tarō's first cabinet in 1904. Sent to Korea in 1910 as the first governor-general, he was merciless with regard to Koreans opposed to Japanese domination and banned publication of newspapers in Korean. He was appointed prime minister to succeed Ōkuma Shigenobu in 1916, but he was unpopular and forced to resign after the peasant revolts of 1918. Hara Kei succeeded him. Terauchi Jūichi's father.

Terayama Shūji. Poet and playwright (1935–83), born in Aomori prefecture. After a difficult childhood, he began to write *tanka,* such as *Den'en ri shisu* (Dying in the Nation, 1965), then plays, for which he founded a theater company called Tenjō Sajiki (Upper Balcony): *Jashūmon* (The Gate to Hell), *Aomori prefecture no semushi otoko* (The Hunchback of Aomori Prefecture), *Sho o suteyo machi e deyō* (Throw Out Your Books, Go into the Streets, 1971). He then turned to directing, first in the theater, then in movies, making films in which he expressed his youthful revolt against society: *Tomato Kechappu kōtei* (Emperor Tomato Ketchup, 1970). He produced some short films and several feature films while writing screenplays for other directors, including Hani Susumu and Shinoda Masahira, and continuing to direct his theater company.

Terazaki Kōgyō. Painter (Terazaki Chūtarō; *gō:* Shūsai, Shūzan, 1866–1919) in Nihonga style, specializing in landscapes and genre scenes. He worked in several other styles, including Nanga, and began exhibiting in the Bunten in 1907. He was made an Artist of the Imperial Household (Teishitsu Gigei-in) in 1917.

Teriyaki. Dish consisting of meat or fish seasoned with *mirin* (sweet *sake*) and thick soy sauce, roasted on an open fire. Analogous to *yakitori* (pieces of chicken) and *kabayaki* (slices of eel) grilled in the same way. *See* CUISINE.

Teshigahara Hiroshi. Movie director, born 1927 in Tokyo, Teshigahara Sōfū's son. He directed, from screenplays by Abe Kōbō, *Otoshiana* (The Abyss, 1962), *Suna no onna* (Woman in the Dunes, 1964), *Tanin no kao* (The Face of an Other, 1966), and *Moetsukita chizu* (The Map in Ruins, 1968). After the failure of *Natsu no heitai* (Summer Soldiers,

1972), he abandoned movies to devote himself to pottery.

• **Teshigahara Sōfū.** Master (Teshigahara Kōichi, 1901–79) of flower arranging *(ikebana)*, potter, and sculptor. In 1927, he created a new modern school of ikebana in Tokyo, the Sōgetsu school, and he had exhibitions in Europe and the United States. Teshigahara Hiroshi's father.

Teshima Toan. Philosopher (1718–86), born in Kyoto to a family of merchants. He was the disciple of Ishida Baigan, whose works he published. He founded the Shingaku movement and made frequent tours around the country, establishing conference halls in many cities to spread Shingaku thought and attracting large numbers of disciples.

Tessai. Sculptor (Kanō Tessai, 1845–1925) and maker of netsuke, professor at the Academy of Fine Arts in Tokyo and Nara.
→ *See* TOMIOKA TESSAI.

Tesseki. *See* FUMIMOTO TESSEKI.

Tessen. Stiff fan *(uchiwa)* made of iron or wood edged with metal, used by samurai to fan themselves and occasionally as a weapon. *See* GUMPAI-UCHIWA.

Tesshū Tokusai. Buddhist monk (?–1366), Musō Soseki's disciple at the Tenryū-ji temple in Kyoto. He went to China, where he studied calligraphy, painting, and poetry and received the title Entsū-daishi. When he returned to Japan in 1343, he was appointed *shuso* of the Tenryū-ji; in 1347, abbot of the Hodai-ji in Awa and the Zukō-ji in Harima; in 1362, abbot of the Manju-ji in Kyoto. He was a talented painter in the Muromachi *suiboku* style, famous for his portrayals of orchids. He signed his works simply Tesshū.

Tetsu. "Iron." *Chikatetsu:* "Underground railroad," or subway.

• **Tetsudō.** "Railroad." The first line, between Shinagawa (Tokyo) and Yokohama, was inaugurated on October 14, 1872.

• **Tetsu-e.** Ceramic decoration (stoneware and porcelain) painted with iron oxide, over or under a slip. On a white slip, these decorations are sometimes called *e*-Gōrai, *e*-Shino, and *e*-Karatsu.

• **Tetsuyū tōki.** Ceramics with an iron oxide slip that takes on a color ranging from black to brownish red when fired. *See* TEMMOKU.

Tetsugen Dōkō. Zen Buddhist monk (1630–82) of the Ōbaku-shū sect, born in Higo province, disciple of the Chinese master Ingen and of Mokuan at the Mampuku-ji temple in Kyoto. He spent 10 years copying the entire canon of Buddhist writings onto 6,771 planks of engraved wood (kept at the Mampuku-ji), under the title *Daizō-kyō.* His sermons on Zen are still famous. *See* DAIZŌ-KYŌ.

Tetsuō. Painter (Hidaka; *gō:* Somon, Tetsuō, 1791–1871) and Buddhist monk, Ishizaki Yūshi's student in Nagasaki.

Tetsuzan. Painter (Mori Shushin; *azana:* Shigen; *gō:* Tetsuzan, 1775–1841), Maruyama Ōkyo's student in Kyoto. He also painted faces, and flowers and birds in Western style (Yōga).

Tezuka Osamu. Cartoonist (1928–89), born in Osaka prefecture. At first influenced by Walt Disney's work, he developed a unique style. He illustrated many journals of humorous and science-fiction stories, and later adapted these images into cartoons for television. In 1985, he received the city of Tokyo's cultural award.

Theater. Most forms of theater in Japan draw on shamanic dances and mimes, such as Kagura and dances to invoke the *kami* performed during work in the fields (*see* DANCE), which existed well before the introduction of Buddhism in the sixth century AD. Some were adapted in the Nara period, under the influence of danced dramas imported from China and Korea, such as Gigaku, Bugaku, and Sangaku. While Bugaku became an art of the court (it has remained so to the present day as an element of imperial music) and Gigaku faded away, Sangaku gave rise to other types of popular shows during the Heian period, such as Sarugaku (*see* SARUGAKU), which led, in following periods, to Noh and Kyōgen. Sangaku also evolved into puppet shows such as *kugutsu,* which developed, with *ayatsuri-shibai* and *jōruri* shows, into Bunraku in the late nineteenth century in Osaka. From mixtures of Sangaku and Bugaku emerged types of folk theater that culminated, in the late Heian and early Kamakura periods, in *ennen* and *dengaku* dances; the latter was amalgamated with rural *ta-mai* or Ta-ue Odori rites and related dances, which have remained typical of rural festivals to the present day.

Another type of theater emerged in the early seventeenth century from puppet plays and *fūryū* dances, which led, in stages, to classic Kabuki. This theater form evolved during the Meiji era into neo-Kabuki, then merged to a certain extent with folk dances to result in comedy and burlesque theater and Shimpa theater. In the Meiji era, Japanese theater began to undergo major transformations. While classic Kabuki theater continued to be popular among city dwellers, Western influences led actors to turn toward a more realist form of theater, Shingeki (New Theater), first by translating and performing Western plays, then by performing plays written on specifically Japanese subjects. As this new type of theater developed, it influenced productions based on the earlier movements, and, either based on or inspired by Western music, gave rise to Western-style revues and shows mixing acting and dancing. Specialized troupes, such as the Takarazuka, were enormously successful. *See entries cited and* BUDŌ, BUTŌ, CHIKAMATSU MONZAEMON, DANCE, JIYŪ-GEKIJŌ, MUSIC, NEMBUTSU ODORI, SHINKOKU-GEKI, YOSE, ZENSHIN-ZA.

Thunberg, Carl Peter. Swedish botanist (1743–1828), Linnaeus's student in Uppsala, who signed on as a physician on a ship of the Dutch East India Company and debarked in Nagasaki in 1775. He stayed there for one year, during which time he gathered more than 800 plant specimens. He published *Flora Japonica* in 1784.

Tianjin, Convention of. Accord signed in Tianjin, China, in April 1885, between Itō Hirobumi and the Chinese plenipotentiary ambassador Li Hongzhang. Under the accord, Chinese and Japanese troops had to leave Korea, where they had been sent after the Kapsin coup d'état in 1884, within four months.

Titsingh, Izaak. Dutch negotiator (ca. 1744–1812). As head of the Dejima trading post (Nagasaki) in 1779–80, 1781–83, and 1784, he went to Edo on official visits twice. He returned to Holland after long stays in Batavia and Bengal and serving as Dutch ambassador to China (1794). He wrote, in French, two long memoirs on Japan: *Cérémonies usitées au Japon pour les mariages et les funérailles* (Ceremonies Performed at Marriages and Funerals in Japan, 1819) and *Mémoires et anecdotes sur la dynastie régnante des djogouns, souverains du Japon* (Memories of and Anecdotes about the Reigning Dynasty of Shoguns, Sovereigns of Japan, 1820).

To. In traditional architecture, a cubical wooden dado supporting an entablature *(to-kyo)* either on top of a pillar *(dai-to)* or between crossing beams *(hijiki)*. Also sometimes called *masu. See* DAITO-HIJIKI, TO-KYŌ.

• Measure of volume corresponding to 0.1 *koku,* or 10 *shō* (18.03 liters), used mainly for rice.

Tō. Buddhist structure or pagoda, derived from the Indian *stūpa;* the model came to Japan via Korea and China. A three-story "pagoda" is called *sanju-no-tō;* a five-story pagoda, *goju-no-tō.* Japanese pagodas can have as many as 10, 13, or even 15 stories (or false roofs); the Danzan Jinja is an example. A *tahō-tō* is a one- or two-story structure with roofs on a hemispheric body, specific to the Shingon and Tendai-shū sects. *Kor.: tap, tabo-tap. See* SHARI-TŌ, SŌRIN-TŌ.

• Abridged signature of an unknown author (perhaps from the Fujiwara family) who wrote a six-volume collection of tales, *Chirizuka monogatari* (Worthless Tales), about 1552.

• Japanese name for the Chinese Tang dynasty.

• The Sino-Japanese reading for the character "East." Also *nishi, sai.*

Tōa Dōbunkai. "Cultural Society of Eastern Asia," founded in 1898 by Konoe Atsumaro to promote cultural exchanges between China and Japan. It founded a school in Nanjing, China, in 1899 to teach the Chinese language and culture to Japanese students. The Dōbun Shoin was moved to Shanghai in 1901 and renamed Tōa Dōbun Shoin. A similar school was founded in Tokyo.

Tōa Kokunai Kōkū (TKK). Third largest airline in Japan, after Japan Airlines and All Nippon Airways, founded in 1964. It operates on domestic routes and leases helicopters. Head office in Tokyo.

Tōa Remmei. "League of Eastern Asia." An extremist organization founded in 1939 by Ishiwara Kanji to support the expansionist activities of Prime Minister Konoe Fumimaro. Dissolved by Tōjō Hideki in 1942, it was re-formed in 1952 to promote a policy of disarmament and political neutrality.

Tōa Shinchitsujo. "New Order in East Asia," a slogan launched by Konoe Fumimaro in 1938 to announce the inauguration of cooperation between China, Manchukuo, and Japan on the economic, cultural, and military levels. The slogan was intended to explain Japan's goals and encourage the Chinese to collaborate. Only Wang Jingwei joined the movement; he was installed at the head of a "government" in Nanjing by the Japanese in 1940. This movement prefigured the "Greater East Asia Co-Prosperity Sphere" (Daitōa Kyōeiken) that defined Japan's expansionist policy during the Second World War.

Tobacco ("tabako"). Use of tobacco was imported to Japan in the late sixteenth century by Portuguese and Spanish merchants who had come from the Philippines and Macao. The first tobacco plantings took place in Nagasaki in the early seventeenth century. Smoking spread very quickly, in spite of a number of edicts by the shogunate banning it because of fire hazard. Throughout the Edo period, long pipes *(kiseru)* with a small metal bowl were used; this type of bowl seems to have been imported from Southeast Asia (the bamboo tube was called *rao,* the Japanese name for Laos). Smoking kits, called *tabako-bon,* contained pipes, tobacco, embers, pipe cleaners, ashtray, and other items, and netsuke were made in the shape of small shovels to pick up ashes. Cigarettes, imported from the West, began to be used in the Meiji era, and the first cigarette-vending licenses were handed out to merchants in 1875. Tobacco sales became a state monopoly in 1904. Japanese tobacco is made from locally grown leaves often mixed with imported tobacco. There are many local cigarette brands, and Japan imports large quantities of cigarettes, mainly from the United States. Pipe smokers have become a rarity in Japan.

Toba-dono. Villa used by retired emperors, built in 1087 in Fushimi, near Kyoto, and transformed into a Buddhist temple (Anrakuju-in) in 1124. Also called Toba-rikyū.

Toba-Fushimi no Tatakai. Battle that took place at Toba-Fushimi, near Kyoto, on January 27, 1868, during which the shogunal troops were defeated by the pro-imperial forces from Chōshū and Satsuma. The Aizu clan, which supported the shogunate, was able to escape (1,858 survivors) from Kadaura (Wakayama) to Edo by sea, with the help of warriors from the Kishū estate. *See* BOSHIN SENSŌ.

Toba Sōjō. Buddhist monk (Kakuyū, 1053–1140) of the Tendai-shū sect, Minamoto no Takakuni's (Uji Dainagon, 1004–77) son. He entered the order very young and was at first *bettō,* later receiving the titles of *hokkyō, hōgen* (1113), and *hōin* (1121). He was then appointed *sōjō* (1134) and finally *zasu* of the Enryaku-ji, and was later promoted to head

monk of the Hōrin-in of the Miidera in 1135. Independent of his brilliant religious career, he was known for his humorous drawings in which he satirized human beings by portraying them as animals. His collections titled *Chōjū giga* (Three Scrolls) gained international fame, although certain critics claim that he was not the sole author. He also probably painted panels on the gates of the Ninna-ji temple in Kyoto in 1135, but none of the painted works that have survived can be attributed to him with certainty. Also known as Hōrin-in no Sōjō. *See* CHŌJŪ GIGA.

Toba Tennō. Seventy-fourth emperor (Prince Munehito, 1103 < 1107–23 > 1156), son of and successor to Horikawa Tennō. His grandfather, Shirakawa, governed the country in his name as retired emperor. Toba married, in succession, Fujiwara Shoko (Taiken Mon'in), Fujiwara Yasuko (Koyo), and Fujiwara Tokuko (Bifuku-mon'in). Shirakawa forced him to abdicate in favor of his son, Sutoku, in 1123, but he retained power and forced Sutoko to abdicate in 1142, in order to replace him with one of Bifuku-mon'in's sons, who was only two years old; this was one of the causes of the Hōgen Civil War in 1156 (see HŌGEN NO RAN). He acquired an enormous fortune in *shōen* and retired, taking the Buddhist name Kōkaku; he left the throne to another of his sons, Sutoku's brother, Go-Shirakawa.

Tobigumo. Type of handmade paper, similar to *somegami,* in which only certain fibers were dyed. *See* PAPER, WASHI.

Tōboku. Noh play: an itinerant Buddhist monk sits at the very spot where the poetess Izumi had planted a plum tree. Izumi's spirit appears and dances and recites poems.

Tōbun. Painter (Doki Tōbun, sixteenth century) of the Muromachi *suiboku* school, Shūbun's disciple. Perhaps the same artist as Tomikage.

Tochigi prefecture. Tochigi prefecture, between Gumma, Ibaraki, and Saitama prefectures, the former Shimotsuke province. It is mountainous in the west (Mounts Ashio and Taishaku), while its eastern part consists of a large plain irrigated by the Naka-gawa river. *Chief city:* Utsunomiya; *main cities:* Nikkō (national park), Tochigi, Ashikaga, Sano, Oyama, Ōtawara, Imaichi, Kuroiso, Kanuma. *Area:* 6,414 km². *Pop.:* 1.8 million.

Tōdai-ji. Buddhist temple built in Nara from 728 to 749 by the monk-architect Rōben for the Kegon-shū sect on the order of Emperor Shōmu. Construction on the large Daibutsu-den designed to house the statue of Daibutsu Vairochana, cast from 749 to 752, started in 745 (*see* DAIBUTSU). This huge temple was destroyed by fire in 1180 (reconstructed in 1195) and 1567, and was finally rebuilt by Tokugawa Tsunayoshi in 1708 on a somewhat smaller plan. It was restored in 1914 and 1974–80.

The current Daibutsu-den *(kondō)* is the largest wooden structure in the world, measuring 57 × 50 m in area and 47 m in height. It is a double-roofed structure whose upper corners are decorated with gold-leafed *shibi* in the form of stylized horse heads. The building, in the style of the 1195 structure, is in *tenjiku-yō* mode, but the *kara-hafu* over the entrance is typical of seventeenth-century style. Inside, enormous pillars made of several tree trunks attached by iron rings support the colossal weight of the roof: some have a diameter of 1.55 m. The floor is paved with large flagstones. The coffered false ceiling is 28 m high. According to the *Tōdai-ji yō-*

roku (Report on Important Issues Relating to the Tōdai-ji), construction of the buildings constituting the temple required the work of 50,000 carpenters, 370,000 metallurgists, and 2,180,000 other workers, and took 20 years. It was originally flanked by two pagodas with six and eight stories, respectively, no longer in existence. In front of the temple rises a high stone pillar topped with an eighth-century octagonal bronze lantern with découpé panels and cutouts portraying the bodhisattvas and *tennin*. Among the other major structures in the monastic complex are:

—The **nandaimon**, great south gate, built in pure *tenjiku-yō* style in 1199. It is 29 m wide and 11 m deep, with five bays *(ken)* on the wide sides and two on the narrow sides. Inside are two large statues of the Ni-ō sculpted by Unkei and Kaikei.

—The **nigatsu-dō** (hall of the second month), founded in 752, reconstructed in 1669. Every March, a specific ceremony, held since its foundation, perpetuates ancient customs from the Nara period. *See* ŌMIZU-TORI.

—The **shurō** (belfry), covered with an *irimoya* roof, erected in 1239, contains the largest bell (without clapper, *shō*) in Japan.

—The **hokke-dō** (or **sangatsu-dō**, hall of the third month), founded by Rōben in 733, was linked to the *rai-dō* in the Kamakura period. It houses a museum for sculptures from the eighth, ninth, and fourteenth centuries.

—The **kaisan-dō** (founder's hall), built in 1019, was reconstructed in 1250, also in *tenjiku-yō* style. It contains a statue portraying Rōben.

This unique grouping is classified as a National Treasure. *See* DAIBUTSU, SAEKI IMAEMISHI, SHŌSŌ-IN.

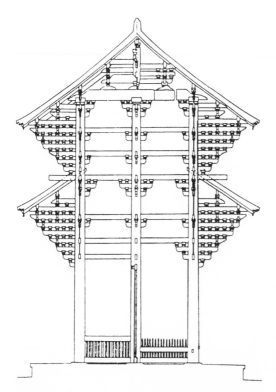

Tōdai-ji in Nara: section drawing of the *nandaimon* (south gate)

Toda Jōsei. Religious reformer (1900–58), born in Kaga. A teacher in Tokyo in 1920, he became the disciple closest to Makiguchi Tsunesaburō, founder of the Sōka Gakkai, and was arrested with him in 1943 for their opposition to State Shinto (Kokutai Shintō). Makiguchi died in prison in 1944; when Toda Jōsei was freed in 1945, he made it his duty to revive Sōka Gakkai. He became president of the movement in 1951, infusing it with great momentum. He wrote many books. Ikeda Daisaku succeeded him.

Toda Mosui. Poet (Toda Yasumitsu, 1629–1706), born in Suruga province. He wrote *waka* and works on poetics; one of his best-known books is *Murasaki no hitomoto* (1682), in which he describes the famous sites of Edo.

Todoroki. Series of waterfalls extending for about 5 km on the Kaifu-gawa river in the southern part of Shikoku, near the town of Kainan. Every autumn, there is a major festival there, including processions and immersion of the *mikoshi* of the local *kami*. Also called Kujūku-taki (Ninety-Nine Waterfalls).

→ *See* JŌMON.

Tōdo Takatora. Warrior (1556–1630), born in Ōmi province. He was employed by Asai Nagamasa, then by Hashiba Hidenaga (1541–91), Toyotomi Hideyoshi's half-brother, and fought in Kyushu and Korea. He allied himself with Tokugawa Ieyasu and assisted him at the Battle of Sekigahara (1600). He was then appointed daimyo of Iyo with a revenue of 300,000 *koku*. He is remembered as a skillful man, a courageous warrior, and an honest administrator.

Tōei. Noh play: the *shikken* Hōjō Tokiyori, traveling incognito, reconciles a man and his nephew, Tōei, who had been arguing.

Tōei Co., Ltd. Acronym of a movie-production company, founded in 1949 in Tokyo as Tōkyō Eiga Haikyū. Since 1951, it has produced many adventure and historical movies, using talented directors such as Uchida Tomu and Imai Tadashi. After 1970, it specialized in production and world distribution of cartoons.

Tōei-zan. Name given by Tokugawa Iemitsu to the Buddhist temple in Ueno (Edo) in 1655.

Tōeki. Painter (Unkoku Motonao, Unkoku II; *gō:* Tōeki, 1591–1644) of the Unkoku school; studied with his father, Tōgan (Unkoku Tōgan). He received the title Hokkyō.
• Painter (Kanō Harunobu; *gō:* Tōeki, d. 1841) of the Kanō school; studied with his father-in-law, Tōhaku. He belonged to the Surugadai branch of the Edo-Kanō.

Toen. Sculptor of netsuke (Morikawa Toen, 1820–94) and doll maker in Nara.

Tōetsu. Painter (late fifteenth century) of the Muromachi *suiboku* school, perhaps Sesshū's student.

Tofu. Soy cake, made by soaking soy beans in water and passing the resulting paste through a fine cloth. The liquid obtained (*tōnyū*) is coagulated to form a soft, white cake with very little taste. There are many ways to make *tofu*, and even more ways to cook it. *Tofu* was invented in China more than 2,000 years ago and imported to Japan around the seventh century. It has various names, according to how it is made: *aburaage, gammodoki, kōridōfu, namaage, yakudōfu, yudōfu*, and so on. It is an indispensable ingredient in Japanese cooking and is a major source of protein. *See* CUISINE, SHŌYU.

Tōfuku-ji. Buddhist temple in Higashiyama-ku, southwest Kyoto, founded by Kujō Michiie as the seat of the Rinzai branch of the Zen-shū sect. It was built from 1236 to 1255 on the site of the ruins of the Hosshō-ji temple, which belonged to the Fujiwara family, and is included in the list of *gozan* of Kyoto. It was destroyed by fire in 1319 and 1334, and partially reconstructed in 1347. The Fujiwara, Hōjō, and Ashikaga clans, Toyotomi Hideyoshi, and Tokugawa Ieyasu added buildings, but another fire destroyed most of it in 1881. The *butsuden* (large hall) was rebuilt in 1932–34; *yuya* from the fifteenth century; *sammon* from 1394 (sculpture of Jōchō and paintings by Minchō); *zen-dō* from 1347; *funda-in* (sand-and-stone garden) designed by Sesshū; *ryū-in* (Zen garden) from 1938; *hōjō* rebuilt in 1890. Many other structures classified as "important cultural properties." The Tōfuku-ji's buildings house many paintings, calligraphies, and sculptures.

Togakure-ryū ninjutsu. School of martial arts using *ninja* techniques, located, according to tradition, in the town of Noda for 34 generations. It developed in the late Heian period in the mountains around Kyoto, then spread among warriors and peasants in Iga, Ise, and Kaga provinces.

Tōgan. Painter (Unkoku Tōgan; Hara Jihei Naoharu; *gō:* Tōgan, 1547–1618), from Bizen, Sesshū's disciple and founder of the Unkoku school. Nothing is known about his life except that he worked for the Mōri family and traveled a great deal in Japan. Some signed works that have survived show that he was as good a painter as Hasegawa Tōhaku and the best painters of the Kanō school.

Togariishi. Archeological site in Nagano prefecture, at the foot of the Yatsugatake volcano, at about 1,000 m altitude, discovered in 1893 and excavated extensively in 1940–42 and 1954. Traces of 33 semi-buried cabins (*tateana-shiki, tatara*) and many stone and terra-cotta objects dating from the Middle Jōmon period (Chūki) were uncovered, similar to those found on the nearby Idojiri site.

Tōgen. Sculptor (Seya Tōgen, 1844–1908) of net-suke and dolls in Nara.

Tōgi Tetteki. Court musician *(gakunin),* actor, and composer (Tōgi Sueharu, 1869–1925); *gakunin* Tōgi Suiyoshi's son. He wrote, among other pieces, the Waseda University students' song.

Tōgō Heihachiro. Admiral (1847–1934), born in Satsuma. He fought in the war between Satsuma and Great Britain in 1863; after supporting the emperor during the Boshin Civil War, he studied naval sciences in England from 1871 to 1878. A captain during the Sino-Japanese War of 1894–95, he was named commandant of the Sasebo naval base, then commander-in-chief of the navy during the Boxer Rebellion in China (1900). He was promoted to admiral in 1904 and commanded the Japanese war fleet at the Battle of the Strait of Tsushima in May 1905, in which the fleet of Russian admiral Rodjestvensky was decisively defeated. Tōgō's flagship was the *Mikasa* (see TSUSHIMA). Named head of the naval general staff in 1906 and councillor to the emperor, he was made responsible for the education of Prince Hirohito from 1914 to 1924. A shrine was built in his memory in the Harajuku district of Tokyo.

Tōgō Seiji. Painter (1898–1978) in the impressionist style, a member of the Nikai-kai group. He painted mainly women.

Tōgō Shigenori. Diplomat and politician (1882–1950), born in Kagoshima prefecture. Ambassador to Germany (1937–39) and the USSR (1941–42); minister of "Greater Asia" (Daitōa) in 1945, succeeding Sagemitsu Mamoru; and minister of foreign affairs in Suzuki Kantarō's cabinet in 1945. In 1940, he had helped to modernize the war navy. Convicted as a war criminal in 1946 by the Allied court, he was sentenced to 20 years in prison. His son-in-law, Tōgō Fumihiko, was appointed ambassador to the United States in 1970.

Tōhaku. *See* HASEGAWA TŌHAKU.

Tōhan. Painter (Unkoku Tōhan, mid-seventeenth century) of the Unkoku school who studied with his father, Tōeki. He was Tōyo's brother. *See* UNKOKU-HA.

Tōhō Gakuen Daigaku. Private music conservatory in Chōfu (Tōkyō-to), founded as Sansui Girls' High School in 1941. The orchestra conductor Ozawa Seiji studied music there. It has about 800 students.

Tōhō Kabushiki Gaisha. Movie-production company, founded in 1937 as Tōhō Eiga Co. In 1943, it merged with Tōkyō Takarazuka Gekijō and took its current name. The actor Mifune Toshirō made his first movie with the company, and it produced films by major directors, such as Kurosawa Akira's *Sugata sanshirō* (1943) and *Kagemusha* (1980). It also produces television series.

Tōhōkai. "Far East Society." A nationalist political group founded in 1936 by Nakano Seigō, a defector from the Kokumin Dōmei (Nationalist League). Inspired by Kita Ikki, the Tōhōkai demanded that reforms be made by the Diet. Arrested in October 1943 for criticizing Tōjō Hideki's policies, Nakano committed suicide; the movement that he had created dissolved.

Tōhoku. Name for the northern region of Honshu, comprising Aomori Iwate, Akita, Miyagi, Yamagata, and Fukushima prefectures. Formerly called Ōu Chihō, Tōsandō.

• **Tōhoku Daigaku.** National university in Sendai (Miyagi prefecture), founded as an imperial university in 1907. It has many faculties—literature, medicine, science, economics, law, dentistry, agriculture, engineering, pharmacology—and various science and research institutes. Attendance, about 10,000 students.

• *Tōhoku-in shokunin uta-awase.* "Poetry Contest Among Members of Various Professions at the Tōhoku-in," on the theme of the moon and love, held in 1215 at the Tōhoku-in temple. This early-fourteenth-century *emakimono* shows men and women doing their normal work, and each image is accompanied by a *waka* poem. Kept in the Tokyo National Museum.

Toi. Korean word designating the Ruzhen (Djurchet) peoples of the Jin dynasty of northern China, who, in 1019, attacked Tsushima, Iki, and the north coast of Kyushu, taking several prisoners. The attackers were repelled, and the Korean state of Koryö, which had rescued about 270 Japanese warriors from the Toi, returned them to Japan. Also called Toi no Zoku.

Toimaru. In the Kamakura period, trade agents working in the ports and responsible for regulating trade in merchandise. These merchants, who became independent in the Muromachi period and were then called *toiya*, moved to Nara and Kyoto to be wholesalers, selling mainly rice and *sake*. They continued their trade throughout the Edo period, organized in guilds called *kabunakama*. Also called On'ya.

Tōin Kinkata. *See* FUJIWARA NO KINKATA.

Toita Yasuji. Writer and theater critic (1916–93), member of the Japan Art Academy (Nihon Geijutsu-in) from 1991. He wrote a best-selling novel, *Danjūrō seppuku jiken* (The Incident of Danjūrō's Suicide), which received the Naoki Prize, and many stories on theater people, including *Chotto ii hanashi* (Intriguing Anecdotes).

Tōji. Winter solstice, starting around December 22. *Chin.*: Dongzhi. *See* NIJŪSHI-SETSU.
→ *See* KYŌŌGOKOKU-JI.
• *Sake* brewers.

• **Tōji Hōmotsuden.** *See* KYOŌ GOKOKU-JI.

• **Tōji-in.** Buddhist temple founded in Kyoto in 1341, rebuilt in 1818. Garden designed by Sōami in 1457.

Tōjin-machi. Term sometimes used for districts inhabited mainly by Chinese or Koreans, especially in Nagasaki, Hakata, Ōita, and other cities. The district in Nagasaki where the Edo government confined them starting in 1689 was called Tōjin-yashiki.

Tōjin Okichi. "Foreigner's Okichi," a young woman (Saitō Kichi, ca. 1841–1890) born in Izu province. She began to work for American consul Townsend Harris soon after he moved to Shimoda in 1857, but was dismissed three days later. Held in disgrace by her contemporaries for having worked in the house of a foreigner, she did odd jobs and finally drowned herself. Her life has been the subject of several novels and plays.

Tōjō Hideki. Politician and military officer (1884–1948), born in Tokyo. He was the military attaché in Switzerland and Germany from 1919 to 1922, and was appointed commander of the infantry in 1929. Promoted to colonel in 1933, after working at general quarters, he was sent to Manchuria to command the military police of the Guandong army. In 1937, he actively supported the military faction demanding that the war against China be expanded, in opposition to Ishawara Kanji, the head of the chiefs of staff. He was minister of the armed forces in Konoe Fumimaro's three cabinets in 1938, 1940, and 1941. Once promoted to general, he forced Konoe Fumimaro to resign, assisted by Matsuoka Yosuke, and replaced him as prime minister in October 1941. It was Tōjō who decided to attack Pearl Harbor on December 7 of that year. In 1942, he created the Council of Greater Asia, then was appointed leader of the general chiefs of staff. He supported the cause of the Indian Subhachandra Bose, had Burma and the Philippines proclaim independence in August and October, 1943, respectively, and directed the military police *(komeitai)*. With the war turning against Japan, the emperor relieved him of his position on July 20, 1944, and replaced him with General Koiso Kuniaki, who brought in Sugiyama Hajimei as minister of war. At the end of the war, Tōjō Hideki tried to commit suicide but failed, and was brought before the Allied war-crimes court and sentenced to death. He was hanged on December 23, 1948. Also called Tōjō Eiki.

Tōjō Misao. Linguist (1884–1966), born in Tokyo, famous for his studies on Japanese dialects, including the *Dai Nihon hōgen chizu* (Atlas of Japanese Dialects, 1927) and *Zenkoku hōgen jiten* (Dictionary of Dialects, 1951).

Tojō Teruo. Businessman and engineer, born 1914 in Tokyo, Tōjō Hideki's son. He was appointed director general of Mitsubishi, then vice-president in 1980, and president of the group in 1981.

Tōka. Ancient folk dances, probably imported from China around the sixth century. They consisted of rhythmically stamping the feet on the ground.

• **Tōka-ebisu.** Festival in honor of Ebisu that takes place in Osaka every year on the tenth day *(tōka)* of the first month.

Tōkai Daigaku. Private university in the Shibuya district of Tokyo. Since 1950, it has had a number of faculties in Japan's main cities. It owns a radio station (Tōkai FM). Its research institutes in oceanography, visual arts, civilizations, and industrial sciences are famous. Attendance, over 30,000 students.

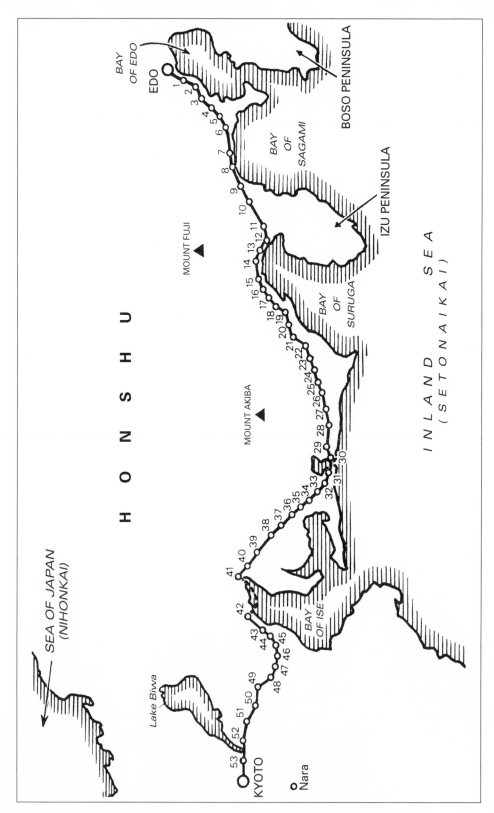

The 53 Stages of the Tōkaidō

Tōkaidō. "Road of the Eastern Sea" linking Kyoto to Edo via Ōtsu, Kuwana, Atsuta, Okazaki, Hamamatsu, Fuchū, and Odawara. It ran for about 500 km (estimates vary from 488 to 514) along the coasts of the Pacific Ocean and the Inland Sea (Setonaikai). Sometimes called Omote-kaidō, "Road of the Place," as opposed to the Tōsandō. It had 53 post towns *(shuku-eki)* between 5 and 20 km apart, which were illustrated in ukiyo-e prints, notably by Hiroshige. This old road was refurbished in 1604, widened by about 10 m, and bordered with cryptomeria. Each *ri* (about 4 km) was marked with a stone marker from the Nihombashi bridge to Edo. This road, used since ancient times, was the one that the Tozama daimyo had to take to obey the *sankin-kōtai* law. Along its length, inns and relays were established that became the nuclei of towns and cities. It was one of the *go-kaidō,* or five great roads of the Edo period, all of which were refurbished in 1604:

—**Nakasendō,** from Kyoto to Edo via Kusatsu, Gifu, Kiso, Karuizawa, and Takasaki.

—**Hokurikudō,** from Maibara to Niigata, via Tsuruga and Fukui.

—**Koshu-kaidō,** going from Edo to join the Nakasendō, going around Mt. Fuji.

—**Ōshu-kaidō,** from Edo to Aomori, via Sendai.

—**Nikkō-kaidō,** branch of the Ōshu-kaido going to Nikkō via Ustunomiya.

See also GO-KAIDŌ, TŌSANDŌ.

• *Tokaidō bunken e-zu.* Series of prints portraying the 53 stages of the Tōkaidō, published in 1690 by Hishikawa Moronobu.

• *Tōkaidōchū hizakurige.* See JIPPENSHA IKKU.

• *Tōkaidō gojūsan tsugi.* "The Fifty-Three Stages of the Tōkaidō," a series of prints produced by Hiroshige in 1832. *See* HIROSHIGE.

• *Tōkaidō yotsuya kaidan.* "Story of the Yotsuya Ghosts on the Tōkaidō." A Kabuki play written by

---

The 53 Stages of the Tōkaidō, from Nihombashi (Edo) to Kyoto

1. Shinagawa (Musashino)	27. Fukuroi (Tōtōmi)
2. Kawasaki (Musashino)	28. Mitsuke (Tōtōmi)
3. Kanagawa (Musashino)	29. Hamamatsu (Tōtōmi)
4. Hodogaya (Musashino)	30. Maisaka (Tōtōmi)
5. Tostuka (Sagami)	31. Arai (Arai)
6. Fujisawa (Sagami)	32. Shirasuka (Tōtōmi)
7. Hiratsuka (Sagami)	33. Futakawa (Mikawa)
8. Ōiso (Sagami)	34. Yoshida (Mikawa)
9. Odawara (Sagami)	35. Goyu (Mikawa)
10. Hakone (Sagami)	36. Akasaka (Mikawa)
11. Mishima (Izu)	37. Fujikawa (Mikawa)
12. Numazu (Suruga)	38. Okazaki (Mikawa)
13. Hara (Suruga)	39. Chiryū (Mikawa)
14. Yoshiwara (Suruga)	40. Narumi (Owari)
15. Kambara (Suruga)	41. Miya (Owari)
16. Yui (Suruga)	42. Kuwana (Ise)
17. Okitsu (Suruga)	43. Yokkaichi (Ise)
18. Ejiri (Suruga)	44. Ishiyakushi (Ise)
19. Fuchū (Suruga)	45. Shōno (Ise)
20. Mariko (Suruga)	46. Kamayama (Ise)
21. Okabe (Suruga)	47. Seki (Ise)
22. Fujieda (Suruga)	48. Sakanoshita (Ise)
23. Shimada (Suruga)	49. Tsuchiyama (Ōmi)
24. Kanaya (Tōtōmi)	50. Minakuchi (Ōmi)
25. Nissaka (Tōtōmi)	51. Ishibe (Ōmi)
26. Kabegawa (Tōtōmi)	52. Kusatsu (Ōmi)
	53. Ōtsu (Ōmi)
	The road ended in Kyoto (Yamashiro).

Tsuruya Namboku in 1825. It is one of the most famous Kabuki ghost plays.

Tokai Ginkō. Major bank in Nagoya, founded in 1877 as Aichi Ginkō. It expanded in 1941 by absorbing other local banks and took its current name. It has many branches in Japan and about 26 others in various countries in Europe, Southeast Asia, and the United States.

Tōkai ichiō-shū. Collection of poems and texts written in Chinese by the Zen monk Chūgan Engetsu (Tōkai Ichiō, 1300–75), part of the "Literature of the Five Mountains" (Gozan Bungaku).

Tōkai-mura. Town in Ibaraki prefecture that expanded starting in 1956, when the Institute of Research on Atomic Energy was established there; since then, several nuclear reactors have been built there. *Pop.*: 30,000.

Tōkai Shanshi. Politician and writer (Shiba Shirō, 1852–1922), born in Kazusa province. He fought for the shogunate in 1868, then went to the United States in 1879, where he studied at Harvard and in Pennsylvania. When he returned to Japan in 1885, he devoted himself to literature, writing a major political and romantic novel, *Kajin no kigū* (Chance Encounters with Beautiful Women, 1886) that was very influential among young people. He became interested in politics, was elected to the Diet, then published *Tōyō no kajin* (A Beauty of the Orient, 1888), *Ejiputo kansei shi* (Modern History of Egypt, 1889), and other novels and political works.

Tōkan. Pottery sarcophaguses sometimes used in *kofun*, and often decorated with bands in relief *(kikkō-gata)* or images of men and animals *(yane-gata)*. *Kikkō-gata* were generally shaped like a tortoise shell, while *yane-gata* were house-shaped. *Tōkan* were often supported on several cylindrical feet.

Tōkan-fu. Organization for political and social control imposed on Korea by Itō Hirobumi in 1905, following Russia's defeat.

Tōkan kikō. "Notes on Travel to the East." Journal of a trip across Japan from Kyoto to Kamakura, written in 1242 by an unknown author. Composed in *wakan-konkō* (Japanese with Chinese words), it is a valuable document on the period and an excellent example of "travel literature" *(kikō)*.

Tōka-shō. Honorific distinction *(kunshō)* of the paulownia *(kiri no ki)*, created in 1876 and again in 1888. It was designed to reward princes and high-ranking persons. Red-and-white sash.

Tōkei-ji. Buddhist temple in Kamakura, of the Zen Rinzai sect, founded in 1285 by Hōjō Tokimune's wife, Kakusan, to serve as an asylum for mistreated women (*see* ENKIRI-DERA). Its main divinity is Suigetsu Kannon Bosatsu, portrayed as a woman (fourteenth-century wooden sculpture).

Toki. Town in Gifu prefecture, known mainly for its varnished ceramics, fired at about 1000°C, including porcelain *(jiki)*, stoneware *(sekki)*, earthenware *(toki)*, and terra-cotta *(doki)*.
• Family of lords of Mino province, descended from Minamoto no Yorimitsu, vassal of Kamakura and the Ashikaga. The family lost its territories after the Ōnin War, but its members remained *hatamoto* serving the Tokugawa.

Tokitsugu kyōki. "Chronicle of Yamashina Tokitsugu" (1507–79), *dainagon* at the court, in 37 volumes, covering the years 1527 to 1576. It is extremely valuable for study of the Sengoku era.

Tokiwa Gozen. Wife (1123–60) of Minamoto no Yoshitomo and mother of Minamoto no Yoshitsune, known for her great beauty. Captured by Taira Kiyomori, she agreed to become his concubine in order to save her mother and children from being massacred. Later, she married Fujiwara no Naganari. Her life is told in the *Heike monogatari*. Also sometimes called Hotoke Gozen.

Tokiwazu-bushi. Type of *jōruri* shamisen music used in Kabuki; it was probably invented by the singers Miyakoji Bungonojō (1660–1740) and Mojidayū (1709–81). This music is derived from the *gidayū-bushi* tradition, and is used mainly to accompany dramatic danced episodes. The current repertoire contains about 70 Tokiwazu-bushi pieces.

Toki Yoriyasu. Warrior (1318–87) of the Toki family, appointed *shugo* of Mino, Owari, and Ise. He fought against the Southern Court (Nanchō) for the Ashikaga and won a reputation as a powerful archer. He was also a poet.

Toki Zemmaro. Poet (*gō*: Toki Aika, 1885–1980), born in Tokyo. He wrote mainly *waka* on everyday subjects in the roman alphabet (*Naki warai*, 1910).

He also wrote several literary studies, including one on the poet Tayasu Munetake, which won the Japan Academy Award (Nihon Gakushi-in-shō) in 1947. In 1939, he and Kita Minoru wrote a modern Noh play, *Yumedono*. He was a well-known expert on the life and works of the Chinese poet Du Fu (712–70).

Tokkō. Abridgment of Tokubetsu Kōtō Keisatsu, a police corps formed around 1910, responsible mainly for surveillance of socialist activities. It quickly became a political police force, and was abolished only in 1945.
• Buddhist monk (seventh century) of the Hossō-shū, Gyōki's master.

Tokko-sho. Object of Esoteric Buddhist worship (Shingon and Tendai sects, mainly) symbolizing the Indian *vajra* (lightning; *Jap.: kongō*). Several forms: with one fork *(tokko-sho)*, three forks *(sanko-sho)*, five forks *(goko-sho)*, or seven or even sometimes nine forks. The most frequently used is the *goko-sho*.

Toko. Dart game of Chinese origin, in which players must shoot their darts (by hand or using a small bow) into a small opening in a vase. Once the prerogative of aristocratic women, *toko* is no longer played.

Tōkō. Painter (Kuroda Bushō; *mei:* Rokunojō; *gō:* Tōyō, Tōkō, 1787–1846), Tōrei's student.
→ *See* AOYA GEN'EMON, ISSHI.

Tokoname. Town in Aichi prefecture, south of Nagoya, specializing in production of ceramics since the twelfth century, thanks to the high-quality clay found in the region. Ceramics museum. *Pop.:* 55,000.

• **Tokoname-yaki.** Type of ceramics produced in Tokoname from the twelfth to the mid-sixteenth century, and still produced in some kilns. They are characterized by jars and bowls, funerary urns, and Buddhist *kyōzutsu* in a fairly rough, partly varnished brown-red clay. They were fired at about 1250°C in *anagama* kilns. A natural glaze, produced by the cinders, partly covers the shoulders of vases and parts of the bowls and urns, giving them a dark-green color. It seems that this technique was brought to Tokoname by potters from Sanage. To date, more than 500 kilns have been found in the Chita Peninsula region, all of which produced this type of ceramics, mainly for everyday use by peasants.

Tokonami Takejirō. Politician (1867–1935), born in Satsuma. Elected to the Diet in 1914 for the Rikken Seiyūkai (Friends of Constitutional Government party), he was minister of the interior in the cabinets of Hara Takashi (1918) and Takahashi Korekiyo (1921). In 1934, he was minister of communications in Okada Keisuke's cabinet, but he was expelled from the Rikken Seiyūkai.

Tokonoma. In traditional sixteenth-century *shoin*-style houses, the largest room contained an alcove with a slightly raised floor (about 0.1 m) about 0.5 m deep, used to display a vase of flowers (*see* IKEBANA) or an art object, as well as a *kakemono* evoking the season. This alcove, or *tokonoma*, was always placed beside the main pillar, called *toko-bashira*, and was often attached to a *tokowaki* or a shelf unit (*chigaidana*). Guests were always placed in such a way that they could see the *tokonoma*, a place of honor in the house. This arrangement, first designed for teahouses (*chashitsu*), was later adopted in palaces, then in commoners' houses in the seventeenth and eighteenth centuries. It is still an integral part of the Japanese house. Called *utuku* in Okinawa.

Tokoyo. Imaginary country beyond the sea, and, according to the *Kojiki*, a land of bliss and immortality. Various tales mention this "paradise," similar to Washington Irving's *Rip Van Winkle* (*see* URASHIMA TARŌ).

Tokuda Kyūichi. Politician (1894–1953), born in Okinawa. He helped found the Japanese Communist party (Nihon Kyōsantō) in 1922, after a short stay in Moscow. His political activities got him arrested in 1928. He was freed only in 1945, and became the secretary-general of the party. He was elected to the House of Representatives three times in a row, but was "purged" in 1950 by the Occupation authorities. He fled to Beijing, where he died.

Tokuda Shūsei. Writer (Tokuda Sueo, 1871–1943) in the naturalist style, born in Kanazawa. His autobiographical novels were marked by a sort of fatalism. Among his most remarkable works are *Arajotai* (The Young Household, 1908), *Kabi* (Humidity, 1911), *Tadare* (Inflammation, 1913), *Kasō jimbutsu* (Masquerades, 1938), and *Shukuzu* (Miniature, 1941); the latter dealt with his tumultuous affairs with geisha and other topics.

Tokuda Yasokichi. Ceramist, born 1933 in Komatsu (Ishikawa prefecture), known mainly for his Kutani-style pottery. Made a Living National Treasure in 1986. His works were exhibited in Egypt, Singapore, Washington, Boston, Bangkok, and Moscow from 1986 to 1991, and at the Mitsukoshi space in Paris in 1994.

Tokugawa. Family of warriors originally from Matsudaira, which began to emerge from obscurity in the fifteenth century and which exercised almost complete domination over Mikawa province (in the area of today's Nagoya) in the sixteenth century. In 1567, the young Matsudaira Takechiyo entered the employ of Oda Nobunaga and took the name Tokugawa Ieyasu. His goal was to become the daimyo of Mikawa; the Matsudaira family did not have the necessary ancestors, while the name Tokugawa could, according to some court genealogists, trace its origins to the Minamoto family through Nitta Yoshishige, a grandson of Minamoto no Yoritomo's who settled in the village of Tokugawa, Kōzuke province, in the thirteenth century.

In the seventeenth and eighteenth centuries, the Tokugawa family was divided into six main branches. Three were descended from Tokugawa Ieyasu (the *gosanke*): the Owari, descendants of Tokugawa Yoshina, Ieyasu's seventh son; the Kii, descendants of Tokugawa Yorinobu, Ieyasu's eighth son; and the Mito, descendants of Tokugawa Yorifusa, Ieyasu's ninth son. The three others (the *gosankyō*) were the Tayasu, descendants of Tokugawa Munetake, a son of Tokugawa Yoshimune; the Hitotsubashi, descendants of Tokugawa Munetada, another of Yoshimune's sons; and the Shimizu, descendants of Tokugawa Shigeyoshi, a son of Tokugawa Ieshige. Minor branches of the Tokugawa, such as the Kōfu (descendants of Tokugawa Tsunashige, Tokugawa Iemitsu's son) and the Tatebayashi (descendants of Tokugawa Tsunayoshi, another of Tokugawa Iemitsu's sons), are considered direct collaterals, as are some Matsudaira (from Echizen, Oshi, and Aizu; *see* MATSUDAIRA).

Fifteen shoguns of Japan came from the Tokugawa family:

1. Tokugawa Ieyasu (1542<1603–05>1616)
2. Tokugawa Hidetada (1579<1605–22>1632)
3. Tokugawa Iemitsu (1604<1623–51>)
4. Tokugawa Ietsuna (1641<1651–80>)
5. Tokugawa Tsunayoshi (1646<1680–1709>)
6. Tokugawa Ienobu (1662<1709–12>)
7. Tokugawa Ietsugu (1709<1713–16>)
8. Tokugawa Yoshimune (1684<1716–45>1751)
9. Tokugawa Ieshige (1711<1745–60>1761)
10. Tokugawa Ieharu (1737<1760–86>)
11. Tokugawa Ienari (1773<1786–1837>1841)
12. Tokugawa Ieyoshi (1793<1837–53>)
13. Tokugawa Iesada (1824<1853–58>)
14. Tokugawa Iemochi (1846<1858–66>)
15. Tokugawa Yoshinobu (Hitotsubashi Keiki, 1837<1867–68>1913)

These shoguns established an era of relative governmental stability commonly called the Edo period, or Tokugawa *bakufu* (or Edo *bakufu*).

• **Tokugawa Akitake.** Daimyo (1853–1919) of the Mito estate, Tokugawa Nariaki's son. He represented the shogun at the Paris World Fair in 1867. Having allied himself with the emperor's supporters, he was appointed governor of Mito in 1868.

• **Tokugawa bakufu gakkō.** Confucian schools established under the patronage of the Tokugawa: Shōhei-hō in Edo (1630), Kiten-kan in Kōfu (ca. 1795), Shūkyō-kan in Sado (ca. 1820), Meirindō in Nagasaki (1845), Meishin-kan in Sumpu (1855), Gakkanjo in Nikkō (1862).

• **Tokugawa Hidetada.** Tokugawa Ieyasu's third son (1579–1632) and second shogun (<1605–22>) of Edo. A general under his father, he fought at the Battle of Sekigahara (1600) and at the siege of Osaka (1615). Although he was appointed shogun to succeed his father in 1605, he had little power until Ieyasu died because Ieyasu continued to govern from his residence in Sumpu. Hidetada's daughter, Kazuko, married Emperor Go-Mizunoo in 1630. He abdicated in favor of his son, Tokugawa Iemitsu. *Posthumous name:* Taitoku.

• **Tokugawa Hideyasu.** *See* TOKUGAWA IEYASU.

• **Tokugawa Ieharu.** Tokugawa Ieshige's oldest son (1737–86) and tenth shogun of Edo (<1760–86>). He ordered foreign books to be translated and promoted "Dutch science" *(rangaku)*. His son, Tokugawa Ienari, succeeded him. *Posthumous name:* Shimmei-in.

• **Tokugawa Iemitsu.** Tokugawa Hidetada's oldest son (1604–51) and third shogun of Edo (<1623–51>), succeeding his father. He closed Japan to foreign relations (1639) and inaugurated the *sankin-kōtai* system, which forced the *tozama-daimyō* to reside in Edo one year out of two. He protected Buddhism and Confucianism while persecuting Christianity (Shimabara Revolt, 1638), and he reinforced the *bakufu*'s power. His oldest son, Tokugawa Ietsuna, succeeded him. He was buried in the Tōshūgū in Nikkō. *Posthumous name:* Taiyū-in.

• **Tokugawa Iemochi.** Nephew (Kii branch, 1846–66) of Tokugawa Ieyoshi and fourteenth shogun of Edo (<1858–66>). The Chōshū incident at Shimonoseki and the bombardment of Kagoshima by the Allies (1863) took place during his reign. He also saw the arrival of Commodore Perry's fleet off Edo and violently opposed the Chōshū in 1866. His son, Tokugawa Yoshinobu, succeeded him when he died. *Posthumous name:* Shōtoku-in.

• **Tokugawa Iemoto.** One of Tokugawa Ieharu's sons (1763–79). *Posthumous name:* Kōkyō-in.

• **Tokugawa Ienari.** Tokugawa Iesada's son (1773–1841), of the Hitotsu-bashi branch; appointed shogun (<1786–1837>) by Tokugawa Ieharu, who had no son to succeed him. The last revolt by the Ainu of Hokkaido took place under Ienari's relatively uneventful reign. He had 40 concubines and fathered 55 children, and his "harem" *(ōoku)* consisted of several hundred women. He married a daughter of the daimyo of Satsuma, Shimazu Shigehide (1745–1833), and it was his policy to form extensive alliances with other daimyo by having them marry his daughters. Tokugawa Ieyoshi succeeded him. *Posthumous name:* Kan'ei-ji.

• **Tokugawa Ienobu.** Son (Tsunatoyo, 1662–1712) of Tokugawa Tsunahige (1644–78); daimyo of Kōfu and nephew of Tokugawa Ietsuna and Tokugawa Tsunayoshi. Adopted by Tokugawa Tsunayoshi, who had no heir, in 1704, Ienobu succeeded him as sixth shogun of Edo (<1709–12>). Arai Hakuseki was his tutor and adviser. He abrogated some of the disastrous laws promulgated by his uncle, Tsunayoshi, and undertook monetary reforms. His son, Tokugawa Ietsugu, succeeded him at the age of four. *Posthumous name:* Bunshō-in.

• **Tokugawa Iesada.** Tokugawa Ieyoshi's son (1824–58) and successor as shogun of Edo (<1853–58>), the thirteenth to hold the title. Under his reign, Commodore Perry returned in 1854, and he opened the ports of Shimoda, Hakodate, and Nagasaki to foreign trade. He welcomed the first foreign consul, Townsend Harris, and, for the first time in the history of the shogunate, consulted the emperor on policy matters. His cousin, Tokugawa Iemochi, succeeded him. *Posthumous name:* Onkyō-in.

• **Tokugawa Iesato.** Statesman (1863–1940), head of the Tokugawa family after the retirement of the last shogun, Yoshinobu. Governor of Shizuoka prefecture, he went to Great Britain in 1877. When he returned in 1882, he was honored with the title of prince. President of the House of Peers from 1903 to 1933, when he retired. He was a delegate to the Washington conference on disarmament (1921), and chairman of the Red Cross and various other organizations.

• **Tokugawa Ieshige.** Tokugawa Yoshimune's oldest son (1711–61) and his successor as ninth shogun of Edo (<1745–60>). His health was delicate and he was not interested in public affairs, so his father, then his chancellor, Ōoka Tadamitsu, governed in his name. His oldest son, Tokugawa Ieharu, succeeded him when he abdicated, soon before his death. *Posthumous name:* Junshin-in.

• **Tokugawa Ietsugu.** Son (1709–16) of and successor to Tokugawa Ienobu, thus becoming the seventh shogun of Edo (<1713–16>). Tokugawa Yoshimune succeeded him. *Posthumous name:* Yūshō-in.

• **Tokugawa Ietsuna.** Oldest son (1641–80) of and successor to Tokugawa Iemitsu, becoming the fourth shogun (<1651–80>) of Edo. His health was precarious, and he let his advisers, Hoshina Masayuki, Sakai Tadakiyo, and Matsudaira Nobutsuma, govern in his name. He banned suicides due to fidelity *(junshi)* in 1663. His brother, Tokugawa Tsunayoshi, succeeded him. *Posthumous name:* Gen'yū-in.

• **Tokugawa Ieyasu.** Warrior (Matsudaira Takechiyo, 1543–1616) and founder of the hereditary dynasty of the Tokugawa shoguns; his father was Matsudaira Hirotada (1526–49), and his mother was Odai no Kata (1528–1602). His father sent him as a hostage to seal his alliance with the Imagawa family, but he was captured en route by enemies and held prisoner for two years in the Oda castle in Nagoya. When the Matsudaira and the Oda made peace, Takechiyo gave himself up to the Imagawa because his father had died in 1549. At the end of his captivity, he changed his name to Matsudaira Motoyasu. He was 18 years old.

Oda Nobunaga killed Imagawa Yoshimoto at the Battle of Okehazama (1560), and the young Motoyasu went to serve the victor in 1561, then set out to conquer the territories of the Imagawa and the other provinces adjacent to his own estates. He was soon master of Mikawa and Tōtōmi provinces. He then changed his first name to Ieyasu and obtained authorization from the emperor to take the family name Tokugawa. As a general under Oda Nobunaga, he seconded him in many battles, while constantly expanding his own lands. He then fought the Takeda family; after Takeda Shingen died, Ieyasu easily defeated his descendants and took over Suruga province.

In 1579, Ieyasu, who had married a woman from the family of a vassal of the Imagawa, was ordered by Oda Nobunaga to put her to death and force his oldest son to commit suicide. But when Oda Nobunaga died, Ieyasu, master of five provinces, became a potential rival for Toyotomi Hideyoshi, who attacked him. Because their battles were not conclusive, the two warlords made peace; Ieyasu sent one of his sons as a hostage, and Hideyoshi gave Ieyasu his sister's hand in marriage; she was 43 at the time, and Hideyoshi had forced her to divorce.

In 1590, Hideyoshi and Ieyasu united their armies to fight the Hōjō of Odawara. In compensation, Hideyoshi gave Kanto to Ieyasu (in exchange for five provinces), which produced a revenue of about 2.5 million *koku*—a considerable income. After the disastrous war in Korea, which weakened him, Hideyoshi appointed Tokugawa Ieyasu and four other generals to be regents *(tairō)* for his son Hideyori.

After Hideyoshi died, Ieyasu opposed the other *tairō*, and there was an armed confrontation with Toyotomi Hideyori's supporters. Ieyasu and his allies defeated his enemies at the Battle of Sekigahara in 1600 and became the most powerful daimyo in Japan. Three years later, Emperor Go-Yōzei conferred upon him the coveted title of *sei-i-tai-shōgun*, which meant that he was now the uncontested master of the entire warrior class (*bushi, samurai,* and others). He established his *bakufu* in Edo; in 1605, at the age of 63, he passed his title of shogun to his third son, Tokugawa Hidetada, and retired to Sumpu, from which he continued to govern.

However, Toyotomi Hideyori's supporters had not disarmed, and they had made Osaka a fortified town. In 1614, Ieyasu decided to attack it. In two campaigns (winter of 1614, Fuyu no Jin, and summer of 1615, Natsu no Jin), he besieged the castle and destroyed its fortifications. Hideyori committed suicide with his son and some of his followers. Ieyasu fell ill a few months later, and died on June 1, 1616. He was buried on the Kunōzan hill; later, his remains were transported to the Tōshōgi in Nikkō. He received the posthumous title Tōshō Daigongen (and was commonly called Gongen-sama, the "pro-

tector of the people"). Because of his character, he was also nicknamed *furu-tanuki,* "the old Tanuki."

In establishing his *bakufu,* Tokugawa Ieyasu founded a dynasty of shoguns that lasted until 1868 in Edo, and set up most of his sons in various provinces (including Owari, Kii, and Mito). He had completed the work started by Oda Nobunaga and Toyotomi Hideyoshi: the unification of Japan and installation of a stable government that inaugurated a long era of peace. He had three daughters and nine sons: Nobuyasu (1559–79), Hideyasu (1574–1607), Hidetada (1579–1632), Tadayoshi (1580–1607), Nobuyoshi (1583–1603), Tadeteru (1593–1683), Yoshinao (1600–50), Yorinobu (1602–71), and Yorifusa (1603–61).

• **Tokugawa Ieyoshi.** Son (1793–1853) of and successor to Tokugawa Ienari, becoming the twelfth shogun of Edo (<1837–53>). Not long before his death, Commodore Perry brought him a letter from the president of the United States, Millard Fillmore, asking him to open Japan's ports to international trade. His son, Tokugawa Iesada, succeeded him. *Posthumous name:* Shintoku-in.

• **Tokugawa-jidai.** Period of the government of the Tokugawa shoguns in Edo, 1603–1868. Also called Edo-jidai.

• **Tokugawa-jidai no keigaku-ha.** Schools of Confucian studies founded during the Edo period: Fukko-ha, Setchū-ha, Teishu-ha, and Yomei-gaku. *See these entries.*

• *Tokugawa jikki.* "Chronicle of the Tokugawa," concerning the first 10 shoguns of Edo, in 516 chapters. Compiled by some 20 historians directed by Hayashi Jussai, including Narushima Shichoku (1778–1862), it was begun in 1809 and completed in 1849. A supplement, *Zoku Tokugawa jikki,* was never finished.

• **Tokugawa Kazuko.** Daughter (1607–78) of Tokugawa Hidetada; in 1620, she married Emperor Go-Mizunoo. She had two sons and five daughters, most of whom died at a young age. The emperor abdicated in favor of Kazuko's oldest daughter, Okiko, who became Empress Meishō. Kazuko was influential in the courts of emperors Go-Kōmyō, Go-Saiin, and Reigen, all of whom were brothers (or half-brothers) of Go-Mizunoo. She generously sponsored arts and Buddhist temples. Also called Tōfuku Mon'in.

- **Tokugawa Keiki.** *See* TOKUGAWA YOSHINOBU.

- *Tokugawa kinrei kō.* Collection of laws and regulations in use during the Edo period, compiled between 1878 and 1890 by the Ministry of Justice; 102 volumes.

- **Tokugawa Mitsukuni.** Grandson (1628–1700) of Tokugawa Ieyasu and second daimyo (<1661–90>) of Mito. A Confucian historian, he gathered 130 other Chinese and Japanese historians in Mito to produce a major historical work, the *Dai Nihon shi.* This work, covering the origins of Japan to the fourteenth century, was completed only in 1906 and comprises 397 volumes. Mitsukuni was the founder of the history school of Mito. Opposed to Buddhism, he supported Shinto and encouraged its revival. Also called Mito Kōmon, Gikō Seizan.

- **Tokugawa Mitsutomo.** *See* SOBOKAI-YAKI.

- **Tokugawa Munetake.** *See* TAYASU MUNETAKE, TOKUGAWA.

- **Tokugawa Nariaki.** Daimyo (1800<1829–60>) of Mito and father of the last shogun, Tokugawa Yoshinobu. He made extensive reforms in his estates, assisted by Fujita Tōko and Aizawa Seishisai, and in 1841 founded a special school, the Kōdōkan, to promote "Dutch science" *(rangaku)* and support the emperor's cause *(sonnō jōi* movement). This angered the Edo shogunate, which fired him from his position of daimyo in 1844, forcing him to cede the Mito estate to his oldest son, Tokugawa Yoshiatsu. After 1853, the shogunate made him responsible for organizing the defense of the coasts. But when shogun Tokugawa Iesada died, he came into conflict with Ii Naosuke over the shogunal succession. He then opposed the Harris Treaty, signed in 1858, and was kept under house arrest until his death. Also called Rekkō.

- **Tokugawa Nobuyasu.** Tokugawa Ieyasu's oldest son (1559–79). He married one of Oda Nobunaga's daughters, but Nobunaga accused him of associating with the enemy Takeda clan and forced him to commit suicide.

- **Tokugawa Shi-tennō.** *See* SAKAKIBARA YASU-MASA.

- **Tokugawa Tadanaga.** Tokugawa Hidetada's son (1605–33) and Tokugawa Iemitsu's brother. Ac-cused of conspiracy, he was forced to commit suicide. Also known as Suruga Dainagon.

- **Tokugawa Tadetaru.** *See* TOKUGAWA IEYASU.

- **Tokugawa Tsunayoshi.** Tokugawa Iemitsu's son (1646–1709); he became the fifth shogun of Edo (<1680–1709>), succeeding his older brother, Tokugawa Ietsuna. At the beginning of his mandate, he governed wisely, protecting the arts and sciences with the assistance of his adviser, Hotta Masayoshi. But after Masayoshi died in 1684, he turned to Yanagisawa Yoshiyasu and was less and less concerned with governing, letting the currency be devalued and taxes *(nengu)* be increased. He then went mad and promulgated "Edicts of Compassion for Living Beings" (Shōrui Awaremi no Rei), particularly dogs, which earned him the sobriquet Inu-kubō ("shogun of dogs"). His wife, Mi-Daidokoro, a daughter of the former *kampaku* Takatsukasa Fusasuke, assassinated him and committed suicide. Because he had no heir, he had adopted his nephew, Tokugawa Tsunatoyo, who succeeded him under the name Tokugawa Ienobu. He was buried in Ueno. *Posthumous name:* Jōken-in.

- **Tokugawa Yoshimune.** Son (1684–1751) of Tokugawa Mitsusada (of the Kii branch), a grandson of Tokugawa Ieyasu through his father, Tokugawa Yoshinobu; he succeeded Tokugawa Ietsugu as eighth shogun of Edo (<1716–45>). In 1721, he inaugurated the custom of placing at the gate to the castle a *meyasu-bako* (suggestion box) to receive complaints and suggestions from commoners. A patron of the arts and literature, he was concerned with the lot of the poorest people, to whom he distributed rice; he stabilized the price of this staple, which earned him the nickname Kome-shōgun ("shogun of rice"). He also enacted sumptuary laws and led a frugal life. Because he was interested in Western sciences, he softened the laws banning the use of foreign books; he himself conducted botanical experiments to try to find new crops that could improve the lot of the peasants. He abdicated in favor of his oldest son, Tokugawa Ieshige. *Posthumous name:* Yūtoku-in.

- **Tokugawa Yoshinobu.** Fifteenth and last shogun of Edo (Tokugawa Keiki, Hitotsubashi Keiki, 1837<1867–68>1913), succeeding Tokugawa Ie-mochi. He was the seventh son of Tokugawa Nari-aki, of the Mito estate. He took up arms against the emperor during the Boshin Civil War, but was defeated and offered his resignation as shogun to Emperor Mutsuhito, then retired to Mito. He returned to Kyoto in 1897 and was ennobled in 1902, but he had no political power.

Tokugawa Musei. Actor (Fukuhara Toshio, 1894–1971), born in Shimane prefecture. At first a narrator for silent films (*see* RAKUGO), he became a stage actor in 1933, founded the Bungaku-za theater company, and appeared in several films. His contributions to radio earned him a number of national awards.

Tokugen. Buddhist religious name of Hatakeyama Motokuni (1352–1406), appointed *kanrei* of Kyoto in 1398.

Tokuhon. Buddhist religious name of Hatakeyama Mochikuni (1397–1455), appointed *kanrei* of Kyoto in 1442.

Tokuji. Era of Emperor Go-Nijō: Dec. 1306–Oct. 1308. *See* NENGŌ.

Tokunaga Sunao. Writer (1899–1958), born in Kumamoto prefecture (Kyushu) to a lowly peasant family. He joined labor movements at a young age, which inspired his first "proletarian" novel, *Taiyō no nai machi* (The City Without Sunshine, 1925), then a number of stories with similar leanings, such as *Hataraku ikka* (The Entire Family Works, 1938) and *Hachinesai* (Eight Years of Studies, 1939). After the Second World War, he joined the Communist party and began to write again, but it seems that his inspiration had faded. Some of his works were adapted into movies in Japan.

Tokuō Kannon. One of the 33 forms (*see* SANJŪSAN ŌGESHIN) of Kannon Bosatsu (*Skt.:* Avalokiteshvara), "the king of virtue," portrayed holding a willow branch. For this reason, he is often confused with Yōryū Kannon.

Tokuoka Shinsen. Painter (Tokuoka Tokijirō), born 1896 in Tokyo; studied with Takeuchi Seihō. He was a member of the Seikō-kai and was elected to the Japan Fine Arts Academy (Nihon Bijutsu-in) in 1957. Decorated with the Order of Culture (Bunka-shō) in 1966.

Tokusei. "Acts of virtue," decrees promulgated by the Ashikaga shoguns forgiving the debts of overly indebted peasants in order to ease their misery and avoid rebellion *(tokusei-ikki)*. The Muromachi shogunate often used the *tokusei* (13 times during the "reign" of Ashikaga Yoshimasa). The Tokugawa shoguns also used this measure, under the name *kienrei* ("forgiving of debts").

Tokushima. City in Tokushima prefecture, on Shikoku, on the coast of the Strait of Kii, at the mouth of the Yoshino-gawa river; former castle town *(jōka-machi)* of the Hachisuka family, who built a fortress there in 1586. It is now an industrial center. Awa Odori dance festival in August. *Pop.*: 250,000.

• **Tokushima prefecture.** Prefecture at the eastern end of Shikoku, separated from Hyōgo prefecture (Honshu) by the Naruto Narrows. It is surrounded by mountains and irrigated by the long Yoshino-gawa river, running from west to east. Formerly Awa province. *Chief city:* Tokushima; *major cities:* Naruto, Anan, Komatsushima. *Area:* 4,145 km². *Pop.*: 850,000.

Tokushin-kyō. Subsect of the Mitakekosha, founded in 1940 by Yoshida Jūjirō (1897–1958).

Tokutomi Roka. Writer (Tokutomi Kinjirō, 1868–1927), born in Higo province. He was of Christian Protestant leanings, and his novels, in a fairly rough but colorful and lively language, were generally based on real events. *Hototogisu* (The Cuckoo, 1899), his first well-known work, dealt with family problems that are usually kept hidden. Then came *Shizen to jinsei* (Nature and Man, 1900) and the enormously successful *Omoide no ki* (Footprints in the Snow, 1901), inspired by Dickens's *David Copperfield*. In 1906, he visited Tolstoy in his home village, Yasanaya Polyana, Russia; following Tolstoy's advice, he tried to live like a peasant in the village of Yotsuya (now a district of Tokyo). He was an unusual—some said eccentric—person. Tokutomi Sohō's younger brother.

Tokutomi Sohō. Writer (Tokutomi Iichirō, 1863–1957), born in Higo province; Tokutomi Roka's older brother. In 1887, he founded the Min'yūsha publishing house, which published the magazines *Kokumin no Tomo* (The Friend of the People), *Katei Zasshi* (The House Diary), *Kokumin Shimbun* (The People's Newspaper), and an English-language version of *Kokumin no Tomo* called *Far East*. A prolific writer, Tokutomi Sohō published about 350 works on a wide variety of subjects, the largest of which is the 100-volume *Kinsei Nihon kokumin shi* (History of Early Modern Japan, 1918–52). Very popular among young people were *Shōrai no*

Nihon (The Future Japan, 1886) and *Shin Nihon no seinen* (Youth of New Japan, 1887), in which he emphasized *heimin shugi,* or "idealistic view of Western industrial democracies." Realizing that his outlook was utopian, he turned to more nationalist and imperialist ideas after 1895, and his early supporters felt that he had betrayed them. He continued to publish until 1929. Considered an ultranationalist by the Allied occupation forces, he was condemned as a war criminal in 1945 and forbidden to publish until 1952. He had amassed an excellent library of ancient Japanese, Chinese, and Korean works, which formed the basis of the Seikidō Bunko (Seikido Library).

Tōkyō. "Eastern Capital," the capital of Japan since 1868, replacing Kyoto. Called Edo before this date, it was the center of the Tokugawa shogunate from 1603 to 1868. Tōkyō is located on the Kanto plain, at the mouth of several rivers (Edo-gawa, Arakawa, Tama-gawa), and spreads around a deep bay on the Pacific Ocean. Because of land subsidence, its lower part is 1 or 2 m below sea level in spots; other districts are raised and on landfill in the bay. The city is centered on the imperial palace and has in recent centuries absorbed many villages around it, which are distinct districts *(ku)* that retain their individual character. The city itself can be divided into two parts: the one by the ocean consists of the port, or "lower city" *(shitamachi);* the one scaling the hills inland, *yamanote* (mountainside), contains essentially business and residential areas. Tōkyō's 23 districts developed around large railroad and subway stations, where commercial activities, hotels, and recreational centers are concentrated. The city is now so large that there is a new term for it, Tōkyō-to, or "urban prefecture of Tōkyō," and the name "Tōkyō" is reserved for the center of the huge metropolis, which has a population of over 10 million.

The city was founded about 1453 by a warrior, Ōta Dōkan, vassal of the Uesugi family, who built a castle there. The castle was expanded by the first Tokugawa shogun in the seventeenth century, and Edo, until then a small town with only strategic importance, grew considerably as the vassals of the Tokugawa and their retinues were forced to live there for at least one year out of two (*see* SANKINKŌTAI), which also caused trade and crafts to develop rapidly. In 1868, when Emperor Meiji moved to the city, he renamed it Tōkyō ("Eastern Capital") as opposed to Kyoto ("Capital City"). The city has few monuments or very old buildings because successive fires (the "blossoms of Edo"),

earthquakes, and bombing during the Second World War destroyed many of them. A curious mixture of ultra-modern structures and more traditional buildings, it is crisscrossed by elevated and underground expressways, and the streets, most of them winding and narrow, are always jammed with dense traffic that grows worse by the day.

The two largest monuments in Tōkyō are the Diet (Kokkai Gijidō), or Parliament, erected in 1936, and the "Tōkyō Tower" (*see* TŌKYŌ TAWĀ). Most of the city was completely rebuilt after the 1923 earthquake (at 8.2 on the Richter scale, it destroyed 575,000 houses and killed 143,000 people), then again hastily after the destruction caused by bombing in 1944 and 1945 (more than 400,000 dead). It is now a very modern city, with old buildings constantly being torn down to make room for new ones. Entire districts have been renovated, such as Shinjuku and Harajuku (where the huge Yoyogi sports complex was built in 1964).

The head offices of most of Japan's large industrial and commercial enterprises are in Tōkyō, and on its periphery are major industrial complexes (mainly the Keihin Industrial Zone in the northeast). It is also home to the large Tōkyō Daigaku university, as well as other universities, such as Keiō, Waseda, Tōkai, and Sophia, and has many museums (National, Nezu, Bridgestone, Western Art, etc.). The original center of the city is near the Nihombashi, an old bridge over a branch of the Sumida River, now covered; all distances from Edo were calculated from this point. Tōkyō is still a major industrial and fishing port, and the large Tsukiji fish market (in Shitamachi) is one of the busiest in the world.

One distinct aspect of Tōkyō is that the streets do not have names. The wards *(ku)* are divided into districts *(chō),* which are, in turn, divided into *chōme,* or "blocks," in which the houses are numbered *(banchi)* according to when they were built. The simplest way to find an address is to go to the police station *(kōban)* on the closest corner, but it is still not always easy. At the beginning of their occupation of Japan, the Americans tried to assign letters and numbers to the main streets of Tōkyō, but these designations were not adopted by the Japanese; they preferred their own system, which relied on an intimate knowledge of the city. Some major avenues *(dōri),* however, do have names, including Aoyama-dorī, Yasukuni-dōri, Sotobori-dōri, Uchibori-dōri, and Ginza, providing some degree of orientation. The districts also have names. The main ones are:

—**Akihabara** (central), stores selling electrical and electronic products.

—**Asakusa,** in the northeast, built around the major temple of Asakusa Kannon.

—**Chūō-ku,** the true heart of the capital, grouping several central neighborhoods and most office buildings.

—**Ginza,** the luxury shopping district in the center of the city; the old Mint is there.

—**Harumi** (in the south), industrial port on the ocean, where the exposition park is.

—**Ikebukuro,** in the northwest, major commercial and railroad center.

—**Kanda** (central), the city's "Latin quarter."

—**Marunouchi,** near the central train station and the imperial palace, center for business, banks, and major hotels.

—**Minato** (near the port), home to many embassies.

—**Shibuya** (central), which developed around a major "train-station store," center for young people.

—**Shimbashi** (west-central), popular shopping district with many restaurants.

—**Shinjuku,** new district established around an ultra-modern train station; recreational center, the "Times Square of Tokyo."

—**Tsukiji** (south-central), major Kabuki theater (Kabuki-za) and the fish market; it was a European concession until 1896.

—**Ueno** (central-north), parks and museums.

Tōkyō has two airports. The national airport, in Haneda, is on the ocean south of the city, to which it is linked by an elevated monorail; the international airport is about 60 km north, in Narita. Japan's economic engine, Tōkyō has about 800,000 businesses employing more than 8 million workers and employees. Its area is 2,145 km² and its population is about 10 million. Tōkyō-to, including the 23 districts of Tōkyō, 26 towns (*machi*, or *shi*), a district (*gun*), four administrative units (*shichō*), and 15 villages (*chō*, *son*), has a population of more than 13 million. Its dependent islands are Izu and Ogasawara.

Given the unbridled growth of the capital, various authorities have been recently been considering the transfer of central and political administrations to another location. Those that have been proposed, in order of probability, are Ise Bay, the Lake Hamana region, the Mt. Fuji region, the Nasu region, and the Abukuma Hills region. But establishing a new capital would take at least 20 years after the ideal site is chosen and construction work contracted.

• **Tōkyō Bijustu Gakkō.** Tokyo School of Fine Arts, founded in 1889; it organizes annual exhibitions *(bunten)*. A department of Western art was added in 1896.

• **Tōkyō Chigaku Kyōkai.** "Geographical Society of Tokyo," founded in 1879; its members are geographers, geophysicists, and geologists. Has published a journal, *Chigaku Zasshi,* since 1889.

• **Tōkyō Daigaku.** National university of Tokyo, former imperial university, founded in 1877, commonly known as Tōdai. It has many faculties and technology institutes (Tōkyō Daigaku Uchūkū Kan Kenkyasho) in Uchinoura and in the university and science town of Tsukuba. It is Japan's best-known university. Attendance, around 20,000 students.

• **Tōkyō Denryoku.** Tokyo's electricity company, the largest in Japan, and the largest private electricity company in the world. Founded in 1883, it now has a capacity of 33 million kilowatts, produced by 28 thermal power plants, 162 hydroelectric power plants, and 1 nuclear power plant.

• **Tōkyō Disneyland.** Large recreational center built in April 1983 in Urayasu (Chiba prefecture), north of Tokyo, on the model of the Disneyland in the United States. It has an area of about 82 hectares.

• **Tōkyō Hōsō.** Commercial radio station and television channel founded in 1951, associated with the newspaper *Mainichi Shimbun* and several banks. It broadcasts throughout Kanto and has agreements with most other broadcasters in Japan.

• **Tōkyō Kokuritsu Hakubutsu-kan.** "National Museum of Tokyo," located in Ueno Park. It has a number of buildings and houses huge collections of Japanese, Chinese, and Western art. It also produces temporary exhibitions of art from private collections, foreign museums, and temples. *See* MUSEUMS.

• *Tōkyō Nichinichi Shimbun.* The first daily newspaper published in Tokyo, founded by Jōno Dempei in 1872. It merged with the *Osaka Mainichi Shimbun* in 1911, and absorbed the *Jiji Shimpō* in 1936. These newspapers took the name *Mainichi Shimbun* in 1943.

• **Tōkyō Orimpiku.** "Tokyo Olympic Games," held October 10–24, 1964, the first to take place in an Asian country. They had been planned for 1940, but were delayed due to the war between Japan and China. Ninety-four countries and 5,500 athletes participated; 47 world records were broken. For the occasion, the Japanese government undertook huge works in Tokyo, building highways, hotels, and modern sports facilities, such as the Yoyogi complex designed by Tange Kenzō. The event marked the beginning of Tokyo's modernization.

• **Tokyo Rose.** Nickname given by American soldiers to Iwa Toguri d'Aquino (Toguri Ikuko), a daughter of Japanese immigrants to Los Angeles, born 1916, who made English-language broadcasts of pro-Japanese propaganda aimed at soldiers in the Pacific during the war of 1941–45. Sentenced to ten years in prison in 1948, she was pardoned in 1977. Also, a general term for Japanese women radio announcers broadcasting in English during the Second World War.

• *Tōkyō Shimbun.* Daily newspaper that began publication in 1942, created by the merger of the *Miyako Shimbun* and the *Kokumin Shimbun.* In 1944, it became an evening newspaper; in 1956, it began to publish a morning edition. It has correspondents in the major Japanese cities and in foreign countries. Its two daily editions have a circulation of about 1.5 million.

• **Tōkyō Tawā.** "Tokyo Tower," large steel tower (4,000 tons) erected in Tokyo in 1957–58 for television broadcasting. It is 333 m high and has two platforms (at 150 and 250 m) accessible to the public by elevator. Between its four feet is the Museum of Modern Sciences, a five-story concrete building. The tower is topped by an antenna that enables broadcasting by 9 television channels, 15 relay stations, and 15 FM radio broadcasters, as well as radar and ham-radio operators.

• **Tōkyō Toritsu Hibiya Toshokan.** "Hibiya Metropolitan Library," the largest prefectural library in Japan, established in 1908 in Hibiya Park, with a capacity of 500,000 books. It has a branch in Azabu district.

• **To-kyō.** In traditional architecture, an overhang made of several stories of "arms" *(hijiki)* placed on dados *(to, masu).* They support the weight of a roof while remaining relatively mobile so that they will not crumble in case of a low-amplitude earthquake. *Chin.: dougong. See* ARCHITECTURE.

Tōkyū. Abridgment of Tōkyō Kyūkō Dentetsu, private transportation company serving southwest Tokyo and the surrounding region, founded in 1922 and uniting about 250 companies. It controls rail-

road and subway lines, the domestic airline Tōa, international hotels, securities and real-estate agencies, and shipping containers. The Tōkyū (for Tōkyō Hyakkaten) chain, founded in 1919, owns department stores, restaurant chains, and pastry shops, and has branches in Japan and Hawai'i. Tōkyū Fudōsan is a major construction company that builds houses, real-estate developments, and recreational centers, and sells land. Head offices in Tokyo.

Tomiharu. Sculptor (Shimizu Tomiharu, Iwao Tomiharu, Seiyodō, 1733–1810) and maker of netsuke; he worked in Izumo, Edo, and Iwami.

Tomikage. Painter (Doki Tomikage, mid-fifteenth century) in the style of the Muromachi *suiboku,* Shūbun's student. He painted mainly birds. Perhaps the same artist as Tōbun.

Tomikuji. Lotteries for commoners in the Edo period, organized mainly to raise money for temples and shrines. They were banned in 1842, when fraudulent practices were uncovered. Also called *tomitsuki, tsukitomi.*

Tomimoto Kenkichi. Ceramist (1886–1963), born in Ando (Nara prefecture), who specialized in pro-

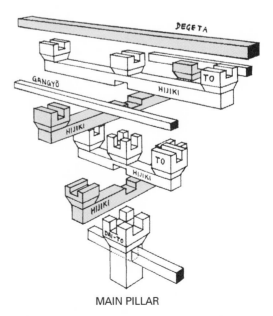

MAIN PILLAR

Exploded view of a type of roof bracket *(mitesaki)* or *to-kyō*

duction of porcelain decorated with flowers in gold and silver under a slip. He also made ceramics decorated with plant motifs in cobalt blue under a slip. He first established kilns in Ando, where he worked from 1915 to 1926, making raku pottery. Later, he abandoned raku for Korean-type earthenware production, then moved to Tokyo, where he began to produce pieces in porcelain, some white with no decoration, others decorated on or under a slip. Toward the end of his life, he moved to Kyoto. He was designated a Living National Treasure in 1955.

Tominaga Heibei. Kabuki actor and playwright (active 1670–1700) in Kyoto and Osaka.

Tominaga Nakamoto. Scholar (Tominaga Kensai, 1715–46), born in Osaka to a merchant family. He became famous for his critical studies of religions (Buddhism, Shinto, and Confucianism), such as *Shutsujō kōgo* (The Buddha's Commentaries After his Meditation, 1745) and *Okina no fumi* (Writings of an Old Man, 1746).

Tomioka Tessai. Painter (Tomioka Yūsuke, Tomioka Hyakuren, 1836–1924), born in Kyoto to a merchant family. Intending to become a Shinto priest, he studied the Japanese classics with Ōkuni Takamasa, then went to Nagasaki, where he studied Nanga (Bunjinga) painting. He traveled throughout Japan, painting landscapes and drawing family scenes and Ainu people, then settled in Kyoto in 1882. He was elected a member of the Imperial Academy in 1919, and appointed an Artist for the Imperial Household (Teihitsu Gigei-in) in 1927. A prolific artist, he produced more than 20,000 drawings and paintings. His works are housed in the Kiyoshi Kōjin Seichō-ji temple, in Takarazuka, and a museum devoted to him, the Tessai Bijutsukan, was built there in 1975. Also sometimes called Tessai.

Tomita Keisen. Painter (Tomita Shizugorō, 1879–1936), born in Fukuoka (Kyushu). He followed the Kanō style at first, but moved to the Maruyama-Shijō school in Kyoto, where he studied with Tsuji Kakō (1870–1931). He was also influenced by the Zen painters and Tomioka Tessai.

Tomita Tsuneo. Writer (1904–67) of best-selling novels such as *Sugata sanshirō* (1942), which was adapted for the screen in 1943 by Kurosawa Akira; *Irezumi* (1947), which won the Naoki Prize; *Men* (1948); *Benkei* (1955); and *Yawara* (1965).

Tōmitsu. Esoteric Buddhism *(mikkyō)* of the Shingon-shū, once taught at the Tō-ji temple in Kyoto, as opposed to Taimitsu, Esoteric Buddhism of the Tendai-shū.

Tomo. Bracelet made of bone, leather, or wood, once worn by archers to protect the arm from being rubbed by the cord of the bow. Some *tomo* made of stone have been found in *kofun*.

Tomoakira. Title of a Noh play: the spirit of Taira no Tomoakira, a twelfth-century warrior, appears to a Buddhist monk and describes his death on the battlefield.

Tomochika. Sculptor (Yamaguchi Tomochika, Chikukyōsai, 1800–73) of netsuke in Edo. His descendants and students also used the name Tomochika to sign their works.

Tomoe Gozen. Concubine (late twelfth century) of Minamoto (Kiso) no Yoshinaka. According to the *Heike monogatari,* she accompanied her husband into battle and was famous for her bravery and strength. She later apparently remarried or became a Buddhist nun. A Noh play, *Tomoe,* attributed to Zeami, tells of her exploits. *See* MINAMOTO NO YOSHINAKA.

Tomonaga Shin'ichirō. Physicist (1906–79), born in Tokyo. He studied atomic physics with Werner Eisenberg in Berlin in 1937; when he returned to Japan in 1939, he elaborated a theory on the meson (discovered in 1935 by Yukawa Hideki) that earned him the Nobel Prize for physics in 1965 (jointly with Americans R. Feynman and J. Schwinger). He also studied quantum electrodynamics. Director of research at the University of Tokyo, he was the university's president from 1956 to 1962; he was decorated with the Order of Culture (Bunka-shō) in 1952. He wrote remarkable works on quantum physics: *Ryōshi rikigaku* (Quantum Mechanics, 1962), *Ryōshi rikigakuteki sekaizō* (The World Seen Through Quantum Physics), *Supin wa meguru* (The Spin Phenomenon, 1974), and others.

Tomo no Yoshio. Minister (*see* BAN DAINAGON) in Emperor Seiwa's court. On March 10, 866, he set fire to the Ōtemmon gate of the imperial palace in Kyoto and accused his political enemy, Minamoto no Makoto, of the misdeed. Discovered, he was sent into exile on Izu Peninsula. This incident was the subject of a famous *emakimono* titled *Ban daina-gon ekotoba. See* ŌTEMMON NO HEN.

Tomoto. Painter (Kobori Tomoto; *mei:* Keizaburō; *gō:* Tsurunoya, 1864–1931) of the Tosa school in Tokyo. He painted historical subjects.

Ton'a. Buddhist monk (Nikaidō Sadamune, 1289/ 1301–72/84) and *waka* poet, Nijō Tameyo's disciple; he belonged to the Tendai-shū sect. He was one of the Waka Shi-tennō (Four Kings of *Waka*) of his time, with Yoshida Kenkō, Keiun, and Jōben. Forty-five of his poems appear in various anthologies, and about 2,000 are in his personal collection, *Sōan-shū.* He also wrote the poetry books *Seiashō* (Notes by a Frog at the Bottom of Its Well, 1360– 64) and *Gumon kenchū* (Wise Answers to Idiotic Questions, 1363) and a journal, *Jūrakuan ki* (Notes from the Retreat of Ten Pleasures, 1364). He is also said to have completed the compilation of the *Shin shūi-shū.*

Tonari-gumi. "Groups of neighbors"; in the Edo period, guilds formed of five to ten families in a town or village district. *Tonari-gumi* were reestablished in 1938, this time composed of 10 to 15 families, charged with fire fighting and patrolling neighborhoods. Although they were abolished in 1947, they still exist unofficially, providing an effective front against thievery and control of social disorder. *See* KUMI.

Tondabayashi. Town in Osaka prefecture, crafts center (bamboo, glass), and headquarters of the P. L. Kyōdan sect (founded in 1954). It also contains the Janai-chō temple of the Jōdo Shin-shū sect (founded in 1560), Shōtoku Taishi's tomb in the Eifuku-ji temple, and remains of a fortress of Kusunoki Masashige, founded in the fourteenth century.

Tonden-hei. Relatively recent type of land-use pattern, applied starting in 1869 for settlement of Hokkaido, in which the land was parceled in straight lines without taking account of the landscape (American system). These new lands were occupied for the most part by former samurai and peasants from the poor regions of Honshu, who were organized into militias charged with defense of the island against a possible invasion by the Aka-Ezo (Russians). The system was abandoned in 1903. The word *tonden* comes from a Chinese agrarian concept called *tuntian. See* KURODA KIYOTAKA.

Tonegawa Susumu. Biologist, born 1939 in Aichi prefecture. He studied in San Diego and became an associate of the immunology laboratory in Basel in 1971. In 1981, he began to teach biology at M.I.T., where he conducted important research on DNA. Decorated with the Order of Culture (Bunka-shō) in 1984, he received the Nobel Prize for medicine in 1987.

Toneri. Title given to many servants in the imperial court before the seventh century. It became the family name of some noble families in the Nara period. *See* HIEDA NO ARE.

• **Toneri Kine.** Poet in the court of Emperor Tenui. She was probably an imperial princess.

• **Toneri Shinnō.** Third son (676–735) of Emperor Temmu and Niitabe, one of Tenji Tennō's daughters. His seventh son, Ōi, became Emperor Junnin in 758. Toneri Shinnō held the highest positions in the imperial administration and was made responsible for compiling the *Nihon shoki* in 720.

Tonfa. Weapon derived from an instrument (a sort of flail) for beating rice, used by peasants in Okinawa to defend against samurai and bandits armed with swords. It consists of a thick plank of wood with a short handle at a right angle. This weapon is now used in training by some martial-arts schools.

Tōnomine. Mountain 620 m high, near Sakurai (Nara prefecture), on the slopes of which Fujiwara no Jōe built a shrine and a Buddhist temple, the Danzan-jinja, in memory of his father, Fujiwara no Kamatari (seventh century). This temple later became a famous pilgrimage destination, and it was the site of several battles during the war of the two courts (Nambokuchō) in the fourteenth century. Also called Tabunomine, Tamunomine. *See* DANZAN-JINJA.

Tōno monogatari. "The Legends of Tōno." A work published in 1910 by Yanagita Kunio, relating a large number of folk legends and peasant customs of the small town of Tōno (Iwate prefecture). It became a classic in Japanese folklore studies.

Tonomura Shigeru. Writer (1902–61), born in Shiga prefecture. A cotton merchant, he left his business to his younger brother to devote himself to his literary career. He was known for his trilogy— *Kusaikada* (1938), *Ikada* (1956, Noma Prize), and *Hanakaida* (1958)—relating the history of a merchant family in the eighteenth and nineteenth centuries. Another of his novels, *Miotsukushi* (1960), received the *Yomiuri* Literary Prize.

Tō no Tsuneyori. Warrior (Tōyashū, 1401–84) and classical *waka* poet, of the Nijō poetry school. Two of his collections are still in existence, containing a total of 565 poems.

Toori Akuma. Demon of folk legend, portrayed as a winged man brandishing a short sword.

Torai Sanna. Writer (1749–1810) of novels in *kibyōshi* and *sharebon* genres; *Tenka ichimen kagami no umebachi* (Fruits of the Mirror of the World, 1789) is his best-known work.

Tora no ko watashi. "Path of children of the tiger," the art of carefully placing selected stones in a garden in such a way as to suggest movement.

Toranomon. Tokyo district and gate to the imperial palace near which, on December 27, 1923, a man named Namba Daisuke (1899–1924) tried to assassinate Regent-Prince Hirohito with a revolver; fortunately, he missed his target. Arrested immediately, Namba claimed that he was a communist and wanted to kill Hirohito to avenge the death of Kōtoku Shūsui. Although the government knew that he had acted deliberately, it declared that he was insane; following a secret trial, he was sentenced to death and executed on November 15, 1924. This incident provoked the fall of Yamamoto Gonnohyōe's cabinet.

Tora-san. Legendary movie character, a sort of "vagabond of the fields" with a heart of gold, portrayed by actor Atsumi Kiyoshi. He became famous in the 1960s, and the series in which he appeared, "It's Hard to Be a Man," was still very popular in 1991.

Tora, tora, tora! "Now, now, now!" The military code designating Japan's planned attack on Pearl Harbor on December 7, 1941; it was confirmed by the message "Niitaka-yama Nobore."

Toraya. Traditional pastry manufacturer, founded, according to tradition, in the eighth century in Heijō-kyō (Nara); supplier to the imperial court since the sixteenth century. It has more than 70 stores in the Kyoto and Tokyo regions and a branch in Paris. It specializes in *yōkan*, a sweet *azuki*-based dough made in Japan since the Kamakura period.

Torazuka. Funerary mound *(kofun)* discovered in Ibaraki prefecture in 1973. Excavation revealed a megalithic funerary chamber with a ceiling painted red and walls with geometric designs (circles, triangles), also in red. This *kofun,* one of the northernmost on Honshu, probably dates from the early seventh century.

Tōrei. *See* HIJIKATA TŌREI.

Tōrei Enki. Zen Buddhist monk (1721–92), *zasu* of the Ryōtaku-ji monastery. He was an excellent painter and Hakuin's disciple.

Tori. *See* KURATSUKURIBE NO TORI.
• In martial arts, a term for "he who throws the adversary," *uke* being the term for one who sustains the attack and is thrown.

Torifunezuka kofun. Large megalithic tomb *(kofun)* in ruins, not far from Fukuoka (Kyushu). Its interior walls are decorated with paintings of boats, birds, concentric circles, épées, and "quivers." Nearby is the Hara tomb, decorated with a painting of a boat in red.

Torii. Portico marking the entrance to a Shinto shrine or proximity to a sacred site. *Torii* can be single, in a row of three (the most common), or in large numbers (as at the Fushimi Inari-jinja in Kyoto). A few are gates (as at the Kasuga Jinja and the Ōmiya-jinja). Some scholars have tried to link their origins to Indian *torana* and Chinese *pailou,* but they are generally felt to be of purely Japanese origins. There are five "major" styles of *torii:*
—The simplest (and oldest) is the **Shimmei** style (also called **Koruki**): it is composed essentially of two pillars joined at the top by two transversal bars, one a crosspiece *(nuki)* and the other hat-shaped *(kasagi).* The pillars have no base and are anchored directly in the ground. In the Ise type, the *kasugi* is pentagonal instead of round in section. The Kashima and Hachiman types belong to this style.
—The **Myōjin** style has two pillars that are slightly inclined at the top. The *nuki* crosses the pillars and sticks out on either side, while the *kasagi* (pentagonal in section), slightly curved, rests on a beam, rectangular in section, called *shimaki;* a vertical piece of wood *(gakuzuka)* links the *numi* and the *shimaki* in the middle. The pillars rest on a base. The Sannō and Nune types belong to this style.
—The **Mihashira** style has three pillars arranged on a triangular base and joined at the top by three crossed beams. It is quite rare.
—The **Miya** style consists of four pillars in a line.
—The **Ryōbu** style (also called **Yotsuashi**) is similar to the Myōjin, but its two main pillars are buttressed by four smaller ones (Itsukushima-jinja type).

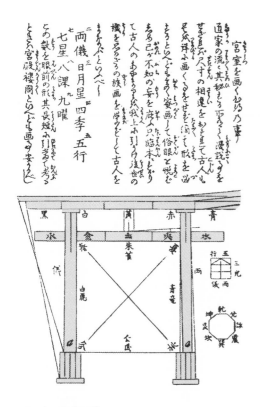

Torii (after Hokusai)

The most widespread style is Myōjin. However, there are many variations, depending on the era and the shrine. Generally made of wood and painted in red and black, *torii* can also be made of stone or bronze, and their size varies considerably. To enter within the outer walls of a shrine, one must pass through *torii,* which symbolize the passage between the earthly and divine realms. On the first *torii,* a sign, often a calligraphy by an emperor bearing the name of the shrine, is often attached to the *gakuzuka.*

• Family of painters of ukiyo-e prints whose members specialized in making Kabuki theater posters in the eighteenth century. The best known are Kiyonobu, Kiyonaga, Kiyohiro, Kiyomasu, Kiyomitsu, Miyoshige, Kiyotada, and Kiyotsune. *See these entries.*

Torii Ryūzō. Archeologist (1870–1953), born in Tokushima prefecture. He led expeditions to Okinawa, Manchuria, China, Mongolia, Taiwan, Korea, and Sakhalin in search of the ancient civilizations of Japan, mainly the Jōmon and Yayoi. He wrote interesting treatises on these periods.

Torii Yōzō. Senior bureaucrat (1804–74) of the Edo shogunate, Hayashi Jussai's son, adopted by the Torii family. Appointed *metsuke* (inspector), then *machi-bugyō* for Edo (1841–44), he was known for having had a large number of *rangaku* ("Dutch science") scholars arrested in 1839 and for mercilessly repressing the rebellion in Ōsaka during the Tempō era. *See* BANSHA.

Torikaebaya monogatari. "Tale of Role Changes." A relatively short text dating from the late Heian period and probably revised during the Kamakura period, by an unknown author, no doubt a lady-in-waiting. In four volumes, it tells the story of two children brought up in a bizarre way, with the parents inverting their roles as boy and girl.

Tori no Ichi. "Fair of the Cock," a Shinto festival taking place on the days of the cock in November in Ōtori-type shrines throughout the country, mainly in Sakai and in the Asakusa district of Tokyo. At this time, the *kami* of these shrines, considered a divinity of luck, is honored, and shops at the gates to the shrines sell rake-shaped talismans to "rake in happiness." Also called Otorisama or Tori no Machi.

Tori oi. Title of a Noh play: a man returning home after a 10-year absence finds that his wife and son have become slaves of the lord of the region, who forces them to serve as scarecrows for sparrows. He wants to avenge them, but his wife begs him to forgive the evil man.

Torishima. Volcanic island at the south end of the Izu-tō archipelago, settled in 1886. Its entire population was killed during an eruption of the volcano in 1902. A meteorological station was set up there, but it was evacuated in 1965, when the volcano threatened to erupt again. Torishima has remained uninhabited since.

Tori uta-awase emaki. "Contest of Poems on Birds," an *emakimono* dating from the Muromachi period (sixteenth century) and kept in Keiō University in Tokyo. Also titled *Suzume no hosshin* (The Sparrows Who Became Buddhist Monks).

Toro iseki. Archeological site from the Yayoi period near Shizuoka, discovered in 1947. It contains the remains of a dozen huts surrounded with wooden palisades, 2 granaries on high pilings, and 40 rice paddies separated by low walls and wooden planks, covering an area of about 1,000 *tsubo* (almost 4 hectares). The houses were about 12 m long, oval in plan, and had a central fireplace. In 1965, vestiges of irrigation canals were also found. Excavations unearthed pottery, plowing instruments, wooden and iron tools, wooden clogs *(tageta),* and other items. Study of this site shed much light on the organization and cultural level of villages in the Yayoi period. *See* KARAKO.

Tōru. Title of a Noh play attributed to Kan'ami (1333–84), Zeami's father, on the life of Prince Tōru, twelfth son of Emperor Saga (d. 895): a man bearing salt seals tells an itinerant Buddhist monk the story of Kawara no In, the magnificent house built by Minamoto no Tōru on the model of the Shiogama beach, and its deterioration after his death. The old man weeps about the past and finally reveals that he is the spirit of Tōru.

Tosa. Former province in southern Shikoku, now Kōchi prefecture. In the Edo period, it produced 250,000 *koku* of rice. The samurai from this province played an important role in the Meiji Restoration of 1868. *See* SATCHŌ-TO-HI.

• **Tosa inu.** Breed of fighting dogs, bred in Tosa province in the early twentieth century from a mixture of indigenous and imported dogs. Massive, with a short, light-brown coat, they are fierce combatants. Dogfights are regularly held during which the dogs are put into categories similar to those for sumo wrestlers. *See* AKITA INU.

• *Tosa nikki.* "Tosa Travel Diary," written in kana by Ki no Tsurayuki in 935, when he was governor of Tosa.

• *Tosa-ryū.* School of painting of the Yamato-e whose members worked mainly for the imperial court from the fifteenth to the late nineteenth century. Most painters of this school had the family name Tosa and first names starting with Mitsu: Mitsuaki, Mitsuatsu, Mitsubumi, Mitsukiyo, Mitsumochi, Mitsumoto (1530–69), Mitsunobu (1434–1525), Mitsunari, Mitsunori (1583–1638), Mitsuoki (1617–91), Mitsusada, Mitsusuke, Mitsutoki, Mitsuyoshi (1539–1613), Mitsuzane. Others, such as Tosa Jōku (1588–1670), Tanaka Totsugen (1768–1813), Reizei Tamechika (1768–1823), Tosa Yoshimitsu, Tosa Yukihide, and Tosa Yukihiro, departed from the tradition. The Tosa school, which was probably founded by Fujiwara Tsunetaka (Yukimitsu), replaced the old Yamato-ryū (also called Kasuga-ryū). It specialized in portrayals of historical subjects and traditional scenes, without any Chinese influence.

Tōsai. Painter (Sugai Gakuho; *gō:* Baikan-sanjin, 1784–1844) of the Nanga (Bunjinga) school; studied with Bunchō and Kō Kahō in Sendai.

Tōsandō. Region composed of nine provinces (Ōmi, Mino, Hida, Shinano, Kōzuke, Musashi, Shimotsuke, Mutsu, and Dewa). The road passing through these mountainous provinces was called Ura-kaidō ("the wrong path"), as opposed to the Tōkaidō, called Omote-kaidō ("the right path"). In 711, Musashi province was incorporated into Tōkaidō.

Tosei e-den. An *emakimono* relating the travels of the Chinese monk Ganjin toward Japan, painted by Rengyō about 1298. Five scrolls. Property of the Tōshōdai-ji in Nara.

Tōsei-ha. "'Control' Faction." A nationalist society composed of officers opposed to the policy of the minister of war, Araki Sadao, from 1931 to 1934. Led by Utagaki Kazushige and officers to whom Araki and the members of the Kōdō-ha ("Imperial Way" faction) had refused promotions, it was dissolved when Araki Sadao was replaced, in 1934.

Tōsenkyō. Pastime practiced during the wet season by nobles of the court in the Heian period, consisting of trying to throw an open fan to land on an object. Also called *ōgi-otoshi. See* TOKO.

Toshiba. Abridgment of Tōkyō Shibaura Denki, large manufacturer of electrical and electronic equipment, founded in 1904 as Shibaura; it formed a partnership with Tōkyō Denki in 1939 to produce light bulbs. In partnership with the Mitsui group and General Electric, it has subsidiaries throughout the world and is second to Hitachi in sales volume. It has diversified its products considerably, from single electrical components to computers, to thermodynamic and nuclear power plants. It exports more than 30% of its production. Head office in Kawasaki (Kanagawa prefecture).

• **Tōshiba Kikai.** Maker of mechanical equipment and machine tools, which separated from Tōshiba Shibaura Denki in 1938, although it is still part of the Tōshiba Shibaura industrial complex, which holds 51% of its shares. It exports to many countries. Head office in Tokyo.

Toshigami. Shinto *kami* of the new year, said to visit all houses to bring them happiness on New Year's Day. A small altar is prepared to welcome him, decorated with pine branches so that he can rest for a moment, and dishes containing *sake* and *mochi* are laid out. The *toshigami* represents the tutelary ancestors of the family. *See* YUKI-ONNA.

Toshigoi no Matsuri. Festival celebrated in some rural areas on the fourth day of the second month, during which prayers are offered to the *kami* to protect the sown seeds.
→ *See* CHŪSHI.

Tōshi Kaden. "Biographies of the Fujiwara family," dating from about 760. The first part was written by Fujiwara no Nakamoro; the second part, by Enkei. Also titled *Kaden*.

Toshikata. *See* MIZUNO TOSHIKATA.

Tō-shikibu. *See* MURASAKI SHIKIBU.

Toshinobu. Painter (Okumura Toshinobu; *gō*: Kakugetsudō, Bunsen, Toshinobu, active 1722–40) of ukiyo-e prints, Okumura Masanobu's brother (or disciple). He made prints mainly in *urushi-e*.

Toshi no Ichi. Fair at which New Year's decorations are sold, traditionally held in late December at the gates to Shinto shrines and Buddhist temples. It takes place at the Kannon temple in Asakusa (Tokyo) on December 17–18, and most stores open a special section for the occasion. Also called Sekki no Ichi.

Tōshirō. Family of potters and ceramists that settled in Seto in the eighth century; starting in 1227, they made porcelain (Tōshirō-*karamono*) using kaolin imported from China by Katō Shirōzaemon.
→ *See* SHUNSUI.

Toshiyori. "Ancients," a term for the oldest people in a given social group, applied to powerful senior warrior bureaucrats in the Muromachi and Edo periods. The title was also given to village leaders. *See* RŌJŪ, WAKADOSHIYORI.

Toshiyori-kuden. Poetry treatise attributed to Minamoto no Toshiyori (early twelfth century). Also known as *Toshiyori zuinō*, *Toshiyori munyōshō*, *Shumpishō*.

Tōshōdai-ji. Buddhist temple founded in 759 in Heijō-kyō (Nara) by the Chinese monk Jianzhen (*Jap.*: Ganjin) for the Ritsu-shū sect and for monas-

tic ordinations. This group of buildings has been relatively well preserved, although only its *hondō* dates from the Nara period (restored in 1323, roof line slightly modified in the Edo period). It is a rectangular structure measuring 28 × 15 m; its single *yosemune*-type roof has greatly overlapping canopies. It houses excellent statues of Rushana Buddha (*Skt.*: Vairochana), Yakushi Nyorai Buddha (*Skt.*: Bhaishaiyaguru), and Senju Kannon (Thousand-Armed Avalokiteshvara), in gold lacquer, dating from the eighth century. The *kōdō*, restored in typical eighth-century style, contains many old sculptures and a portrait of Ganjin made by one of his disciples in 763. Drum tower from 1240; *ridaō* from 1202; *kyōzō* in Azekura style, restored in the thirteenth century; *kaisandō* from the seventeenth century. Every June 6, the anniversary of Ganjin's death is celebrated.

Tōshōgū. Posthumous title conferred on Tokugawa Ieyasu by the imperial court.
• Shinto shrine and mausoleum of the Tokugawa shogun in Nikkō, founded in 1617 in memory of Tokugawa Ieyasu and expanded in 1624 by chief architect Kōra Munehiro. Its very numerous buildings are full of sculpted and painted decorations in the Chinese Ming style. The most remarkable structures are the black-lacquered five-story pagoda (*goju-no-tō*), built by Ōkubo Kiheiji about 1807–15; the *yomei-mon*, or "ivory gate," by Kanō Tan'yū and Kanō Yasunobu, made in 1624 (12 decorated pillars); the *rinzō*, a bronze lantern-tower dating from 1636; the *haiden*, decorated with paintings of the Sanjūrokkasen by Tosa Mitsuoki and calligraphy by Emperor Go-Mizunoo; the *futarasan*, dating from 1617–20, with a bronze lantern dating from the thirteenth century; the bronze *sōrintō* 17 m high, dating from 1642; and the *kagura-den* from the early seventeenth century. All other buildings are from the seventeenth century and richly decorated with brightly colored sculptures and paintings. The grouping is in a magnificent forest of giant cryptomeres. Annual festival with period costumes on May 17.
• Shinto shrine built in 1617 in Ueno (Edo) and expanded in 1651 by the architects Kōra Munehiro and his son, Kōra Munehisa.
• Shinto shrine built in memory of Tokugawa Ieyasu in 1617 on the Kunōzan hill in Shizuoka.
• Shinto shrine built in Nagoya in 1619, destroyed in 1945 by air bombardment and rebuilt after the Second World War.
• More than 100 shrines with the same name, all dedicated to Tokugawa Ieyasu, were built in Japan.

Tōshun. Painter (Kanō Fukunobu; *gō:* Shuseisai, Tōshun, d. 1723) of the Kanō school. He studied with his father-in-law, Tōun, and belonged to the Surugadai branch in Edo.
• Buddhist monk (sixteenth century) and painter, Sesshū's disciple, son of a carpenter in Nara. He studied the style of the Nanga school; he made paintings on several fusuma of the Ryōgen-in in the Daitoku-ji in Kyoto.

Toshun. Painter (Kanō Yoshinobu; *mei:* Sanshiro; *gō:* Toshun, 1747–97) of the Surugadai branch of the Kanō school in Edo.

Tōsu. In the Heian period, an ornamental knife worn in the belt by some nobles during official court ceremonies. Its length was determined by the rank of its owner.

Totoki Baigai. Painter (Totoki Shi; *azana:* Shiu; *gō:* Sekitei, Seimuken, Baigai, Hanzō, 1749–1804), born in Osaka, of the Nanga school; active in Kyoto, Edo, and Nagasaki (after 1790). Most of his works date from after 1792, when he returned to Osaka. He painted landscapes and *shikunshi* in a very spontaneous style, sometimes rough and uneven. Also called Baigai.

Tōtō Kiki. The largest Japanese manufacturer of earthenware and porcelain for sanitary uses, founded in 1917. Factories and head office in Kita Kyūshū, Fukuoka (Kyushu).

Tōtōmi. Former province, now part of Shizuoka prefecture.

• **Tōtōmi-kō.** *See* FUJIWARA NO KANEMICHI.

Totoya Hokkei. Painter (Iwakubo Tatsuyuki, 1780–1850) of ukiyo-e prints, Hokusai's disciple. He was a fish merchant *(totoya)*. Working in Edo, he specialized in production of *surimono* and illustrations of humorous poems *(kyōka)*.

Totsugen. Painter (Tanaka Totsugen, Tanaka Chi, Tanaka Bin; *azana:* Kotō; *gō;* Daikōsai, Chiō, Kahukyūshi, Tokuchū, Kimpei, Kyūmei, Kaison, Totsugen, 1768–1823) of the Fukko Yamato-e school, raised in Kyoto by Ishida Yūtei and Mitsusada. He also worked in Nagoya and Edo, producing mainly historical subjects and scenes. He received the title Hokkyō.

Totsuka Seikai. Physician (1799–1876) who was one of Franz von Siebold's students in Nagasaki.

Tottori. Chief city of Tottori prefecture, in southwest Honshu, on the Sea of Japan (Nihonkai); former castle town *(jōka-machi)* of the Ikeda family in the seventeenth century. An active sea port (fishing and various industries) at the mouth of the Sendaigawa river, Tottori was heavily damaged by an earthquake in 1942 and a giant fire in 1952, and was rebuilt on a modern plan. It is home to the University of Tottori and a private art museum. Nearby is an area of sand dunes (Tottori Sakyū), often portrayed in art and used as a set for movies; many *kofun* located in the Tottori-heiya plain. *Pop.:* 140,000.

• **Tottori prefecture.** Prefecture on the shore of the Sea of Japan (Nihonkai), about 150 km west of Tokyo, in northern Chūgoku. The south part is mountainous, and the coast is generally low and sandy (Tottori-heiya). The region was inhabited in prehistoric times (Jōmon and Yayoi remains). In the seventh century, it comprised Inaba and Hōki provinces. Distant from major industrial centers, it has remained essentially agricultural (fruit, tobacco, rice, cattle). *Chief city:* Tottori; *main cities:* Yonago, Kurayoshi, Sakaminato. *Area:* 3,492 km². *Pop.:* 650,000.

Tōun. Painter (Kanō Masanobu, Kanō Uneme; *gō:* Hakuyūken, Sōshin-dōjin, Shōinshi, Tōun, 1625–94) of the Kanō school who studied with his father-in-law, Kanō Tan'yū, in Edo.
• Sculptor (Ikkōsai, early nineteenth century) of netsuke in Edo.
• Sculptor (Takamura Tōun, 1847–1910) of netsuke and Buddhist images.
• Bronzesmith and metal sculptor (eighteenth century), famous for his jointed animals and dragons made of iron.

Towada-ko. Large lake in Aomori prefecture, about 60 km south of the city of Aomori, formed by an ancient mountain crater. It is the source of the Oirase-gawa river. *Alt.:* 400 m; *area:* 60 km²; *depth:* 320 m.

Towazu-gatari. "Impromptu Confession," an autobiographical journal *(nikki)* by Lady Nijō (Fukakusa-in no Nijō, Nijō no Tsubone, b. 1258). Covering the years 1271–1306, it relates how she became Emperor Go-Fukakusa's concubine, then a Buddhist nun in 1283. A copy of the manuscript was found in the 1940s.

Toyama. Chief city of Toyama prefecture, on the Sea of Japan (Nihonkai), about 180 km north of Nagoya, southeast of Noto Peninsula, at the mouth of the Jinzū-gawa river. It has an old castle and Buddhist temples, chemical and pharmaceutical firms, and a university and a folklore museum. *Pop.:* 310,000.

• **Toyama prefecture.** Toyama prefecture, on Toyama Bay (Sea of Japan), former Etchū province, fief of the Maeda family in the Edo period. The prefecture is mainly agricultural but also has some industries, fed by its many hydroelectric dams. *Chief city:* Toyama; *other major cities:* Takaoka, Shimminato, Uozu, Himi, Kurobe, Tonami. *Area:* 4,252 km². *Pop.:* 1,150,000.

Tōyama Gorō. Painter (1888–1928) in the Western style. He studied at the Académie Julian in Paris.

Tōyama Kagetomo. Politician (Tōyama Kinshirō, d. 1855), Edo-bugyō in 1840, famous for the excellence of his administration. He cleaned up the Shitamachi district by having drainage infrastructure built. In 1850, he retired and became a Buddhist monk.

Toyama Masakazu. Samurai and poet (Toyama Shōichi, Toyama Masasichi, 1848–1900), born in Edo. He studied at the Bansho Shirabesho, then went to Great Britain in 1866 and the United States in 1870. Appointed a professor of philosophy at the University of Tokyo, he became president of the university in 1897 and was minister of education in Itō Hirobumi's third cabinet. He tried to have kanji characters replaced by a romanized alphabet and founded a society for this purpose, the Rōmaji-kai.

Tōyama Mitsuru. Samurai (Tsutsui Mitsuru, 1854–1944), born in Fukuoka, adopted by the Tōyama family. He was imprisoned in 1876 for his anti-government political opinions; when he was freed, in 1878, he and several friends organized a political group, the Kōyōsha, supporting the Jiyū Minken Undō (Freedom and People's Rights Movement). Kōyōsha changed its name to Gen'yōsha and constantly contested government decisions, especially those concerning the policy on China. Tōyama Mitsuru and Uchida Ryōhai were among the founders of the Black Dragon Society (Kokuryūkai), active in China and Manchuria, and began

to promote the nationalist sentiments of the "*rōnin* of the right" (Rōninkai) in 1908.

Tōyo. Painter (Unkoku Tōyo, early seventeenth century) of the Unkoku school who studied with his father, Tōeki.

Tōyō. Painter (Azuma Tōyō; *azana:* Taiyō; *gō:* Gyokuga, Tōyō, 1755–1839) of the Maruyama school; Baishō's student.
→ *See* IIZUKA TŌYŌ, SESSHŪ, TŌKŌ.

Toyo Ashihara no Mizuho no Kuni. "Fertile Country of Many Reeds, Where Rice and the Four Cereals Grow." An ancient poetic name for the islands of Japan. Also called Toyo Akitsu Shima.

Tōyō Bunko. Private library founded in 1917 by Iwasaki Hisaya (1865–1955), Iwasaki Yatarō's son, devoted to works on Asia, containing more than 500,000 titles. Called Morrison Bunko until 1924. Located in the Bunkyō district of Tokyo, it has been part of the Diet National Library since 1948. It publishes magazines on Asian subjects, mostly Japanese, and scholarly books. It is a very popular research center.

Toyoda Sakachi. Industrialist and inventor (1867–1930). The automatic weaving systems that he developed in 1897 and 1926 breathed new life into textile plants. His research led to the creation of textile plants such as the Toyoda Jidō Shokki Seisakusho and the Toyota automobile plants.

Toyoda Shirō. Movie director (1906–77), born in Kyoto. He worked for Nikkatsu, then Shōchiku. In 1923, he began to make movies drawn from literary classics, for which he became famous. He adapted for the screen *Gan* (The Wild Goose, 1953), taken from a story by Mori Ōgai, and *Yukiguni* (The Country of Snow, 1956), from a work by Kawabata Yasunari. He later worked for Tōhō.

Toyoda Soemu. Admiral (ca. 1885–1957) of the Japanese fleet in 1944 and 1945. Found guilty of war crimes by the Allies in 1945, he spent four years in prison (1945–49).

Toyohara Kunichika. Painter (Arakawa Yasoya; *gō:* Ittō Kunichika, Ichiōsai, Kachōrō, Hōshunrō, Sōgenshi, Yone-o, 1835–between 1900 and 1909), born in Edo. A student of Toyohara Chikanobu, he was a member of the Utagawa-ryū school and specialized in *nishiki-e* triptychs. He had an extremely frenetic life, marrying 40 times and changing residence 83 times. Also called Kunichika.

Toyoharu. Painter (Utagawa Toyoharu, Tajimaya Shōjirō, Tajimaya Shin'emon; *gō:* Ichiryūsai, Senryūsai, Sen-ō, Toyoharu, 1735–1814) of ukiyo-e prints; founder of the Utagawa school. Influenced by Harunobu, he began to paint landscapes.

Toyohiko. Painter (Okamoto Toyohiko; *mei:* Shiba, Shume; *azana:* Shigen; *gō:* Kōson, Rikyō, Chōshinsai, Tangaku-sanjin, Toyohiko, 1773–1845) of the Shijō-Maruyama school; studied with Ryōzan and Goshun. He painted mainly landscapes.

Toyohiro. Painter (Utagawa Toyohiro, Okajima Tōjirō; *gō:* Ichiryūsai, 1774–1829) of ukiyo-e prints, Toyoharu's student. He also studied the techniques of the Kanō school and was Hiroshige's master. He illustrated books and made paintings of beautiful women *(bijin).*

Tōyō Jiyū Shimbun. "Newspaper of Freedom in the East," founded in 1881 by Saionji Kimmochi and Nakae Chōmin. Influenced by French liberal ideologies, it was banned on the order of Emperor Meiji.

Tōyō Jiyūtō. "Asian Liberal party," founded in 1892 by Ōi Kentarō and a few politicians from the Jiyū-tō. It published the first union newspaper, *Shin Tōyō* (New East). It demanded an aggressive anti-foreigner policy and organized the Society for Greater Japan (Dai Nihon Kyōkai), which did not survive its internal dissension and dissolved at the end of 1893.

Tōyō-kanji. "Chinese characters for daily use," list of 1,850 Sino-Japanese *(kanji)* characters formulated in 1946 by the Ministry of Education. It was revised in 1981 (Jōyō-kanji) and expanded to 1,945 characters, plus a series of 166 others to be used only for proper nouns. *See* JŌYŌ-KANJI.

Tōyō Keizai Shimpō. "Economic Magazine of the East," economics newspaper founded in 1895 by Machida Chūji (1863–1946). Starting as a biweekly, it went weekly in 1919. In 1945, its title changed to *Shūkan Tōyō Keizai* (Weekly Eastern Economics Magazine).

Tōyō Kisen Kaisha. Shipping company. In the early twentieth century, it specialized in transporting Jap-

anese emigrants to Shin Nihon, a Japanese colony founded in California in the nineteenth century, and to South America.

Toyokuni. Painter (Utagawa Toyokuni; *mei:* Kumakichi, Kurahashi, Kumauemon; *gō:* Ichiyōsai, 1769–1825) of ukiyo-e prints; Toyoharu's student in Edo. He painted pictures of beautiful women and actors. Among his students were Toyokuni II, Toyokuni III, Kunimasa, Kunitora, and Kuniyoshi.

• **Toyokuni II.** Painter (Utagawa Toyokuni; *mei:* Genzō; *gō:* Kunishige, Toyoshige, Ichiryūsai, Kōsotei, Ichieisai, Ichibetsusai, Toyokuni II, 1777–1835); Toyokuni I's student. He was a pottery merchant.

• **Toyokuni III.** *See* KUNISADA.

Toyokuni no Michi no Kuchi. Poetic name of the former Buzen province.

Toyokuni no Michi no Shiri. Poetic name of the former Bungo province.

Toyokuni no Yashiro. Shinto shrine built in Edo in 1599 in memory of Toyotomi Hideyoshi, and rebuilt in 1873. Also called Hōkoku-jinja.

Toyomasa. Sculptor of netsuke and engraver of seals (Naitō Toyomasa, 1773–1856) in Tamba. His son, Toyoyasu (Naitō Toyoyasu, mid-nineteenth century), followed his style.

Toyora-dera. Name of the first Buddhist temple in Japan, built in 553 in Asuka by Soga no Umako. It was destroyed in 645. Also called Kōgen-ji, Katsuragi-dera.

Toyoshima Yoshio. Writer (1890–1955), born in Fukuoka, author of a great number of novels and stories, including *Yamabuki no hana* (1954). He also translated a number of works by Western authors, including Romain Rolland's *Jean Christophe* (in 1910) and "The Thousand and One Nights" from Sir Richard Burton's English translation (in 1950).

Toyota Hokkei. *See* HOKKEI.

Toyota Jidōsha. Manufacturer of motors, automobiles, buses, trucks, and prefabricated houses, the largest in Japan and the second largest in the world in volume of production. In 1933, it was part of the textile firm Toyoda Jidō Shokki, but it became independent in 1937. After the Second World War, it moved to Toyota, in Aicha prefecture, and intensified production, partnering with more than 200 spare-parts makers, and became known throughout the world for the quality of its products. It has 27 foreign facilities, most of them assembly plants, and exports 43% of its production. Among its best-known automobile models are the Corona, the Corolla, and the Celica. The company Toyota Shatai, specializing in bodywork (head office in Kariya, Aichi prefecture), is associated with Toyota Jidōsha.

Toyotake Wakatayū. *Jōruri* singer (1681–1764) in Osaka, founder of a family line of singers.

• **Toyotake Yamashiro no Shōjō.** *Jōruri* singer (Kanasugi Yatarō, 1878–1967), born in Kyoto; Takemoto Tsudayū II's (1839–1912) disciple at the Bunraku-za in Osaka. Prince Chichibu conferred upon him the court title of Yamashiro no Shōjō in 1947.

Toyotake-za. *See* KI NO KAION.

Tōyō Takushoku Kaisha. "Company to Run the Far East," formed in 1908 by the government to develop agricultural land in Korea; this encouraged many Japanese to settle in the peninsula starting in 1910, when Japan annexed Korea. It controlled not only agriculture but also mines, transport, and electricity production. Its head office, originally in Seoul (*Jap.*: Heijō-kyō), was transferred to Tokyo in 1917, and it then expanded its operations into Manchuria, China, and the South Pacific. It was dissolved in 1945.

Toyotomi Hidetsugu. Son (1568–95) of Yoshifusa of Owari and Zuiryū-in, Toyotomi Hideyoshi's half-sister. He changed his name to Miyoshi Hidetsugu, then to Hashiba when Toyotomi Hideyoshi, his adoptive father, was appointed *kampaku*. In 1591, Hideyoshi gave him the title of *kampaku*, taking the title *taikō* for himself, and designated him his successor. Hidetsugu was, it seems, a violent and cruel man. When Yodogimi bore Hideyoshi a son, Hideyori, Hideyoshi turned his hopes to this child and, accusing Hidetsugu of conspiracy, forced him to commit suicide. His children and entire family were exterminated.

• **Toyotomi Hideyori.** Son (Hiroi, 1592–1615) of Toyotomi Hideyoshi and his favorite, Yodogimi. When Toyotomi Hidetsugu died, Hideyori succeeded to the title of *kampaku;* he married Sen-hime, one of Tokugawa Ieyasu's granddaughters, in 1603. Ieyasu had been designated one of the *go-tairō* (five elders) charged with the regency in Hideyori's name, but after the Battle of Sekigahara (1600) and his accession to the shogunate in 1603, Ieyasu became concerned that Hideyori would claim to be his father's heir and isolated him in Osaka castle. During an incident that he provoked (Shōmei Jiken), Ieyasu declared war on Hideyori and besieged him in Osaka during the winter of 1614–15. On June 3, 1615, Sen-hime tried to persuade her grandfather to spare her husband's life. He was unmoved, however, and continued the siege, setting the castle afire. Hideyori and his mother, Yodogimi, committed suicide as the last bastion was about to surrender. His son, Toyotomi Kunimatsu, then aged seven, was taken as a prisoner to Kyoto and executed, and his daughter, aged six, was sent to a Buddhist monastery.

• **Toyotomi Hideyoshi.** Warrior (Kinoshita Hiyoshi, 1536–98), born in Owari; served under Oda Nobunaga with the name Kinoshita Tōkichirō. He took the name Hideyoshi in 1562, although Oda Nobunaga had nicknamed him Saru ("the monkey") because of his ugliness. Known for his military valor, he conquered a fief in the Ōmi region, taking the title Chikuzen no Kami and the family name Hashiba in 1572. As Oda Nobunaga's faithful lieutenant, he seconded him in most of his campaigns and obtained a number of estates and castles. He seized the fief of Himeyama (Himeji) in 1577, then the castle in Tottori (1581) and the one in Takamatsu (1582).

When Oda Nobunaga died, Hideyoshi went to war against Akechi Mitsuhide, defeating him 13 days later at the Battle of Yamazaki (July 2, 1582). He thus became the master of Ōmi, Harima, Yamashiro, Tamba, and Kawachi provinces. Then, after defeating Shibata Katsuie at Shizugatake, he added to his estates Echizen, Kaga, Noto, and Etchū provinces. Tokugawa Ieyasu, another of Oda Nobunaga's generals, opposed his claims for a short time, supporting one of Oda Nobunaga's grandsons, Oda Hidenobu (1580–1605), but soon made peace with him, leaving him free to continue his conquests and his attempt to realize Oda Nobunaga's dream: the unification of Japan. He seized Kii province, overcame the resistance of the monks of the Negoro-ji temple, then attacked the powerful Ikkō-ikki sect in Kii province. Continuing his advance, he defeated the Chōsokabe of Shikoku and, in 1585, received the title of *kampaku* from the court. Only Kyushu and Kanto were still beyond his control. In 1587, he launched a major campaign to defeat the Shimizu family, all-powerful in Kyushu. After two years of combat, he won, reorganized the island, and entrusted the provinces to his most faithful allies, the Ōmoto, and to his generals, Katō Kiyomasa, Konishi Yukinaga, and Kuroda Nagamasa.

In 1587, Hideyoshi banned Christianity, proclaiming that Japan was "the country of *kami*," and took the port of Nagasaki back from the Jesuits (who had held it under Christian daimyo Ōmura Sumitada). In his luxurious Kyoto residence, Jurakutei, and in the Kamo shrines, he had grandiose ceremonies conducted. He then forbade peasants to own weapons and organized a "hunt for swords" *(katana-gari)*, which were then melted down; thus, the peasant class was clearly distinguished from the *bushi*. At the same time, he continued the land census *(taikō prefecturechi)* started by Oda Nobunaga. All that stood in the way of his being the uncontested master of Japan was the conquest of Kanto. In an alliance with Tokugawa Ieyasu, he attacked the Hōjō of Odawara, who surrendered on August 12, 1590. Their castle was razed. Hideyoshi then gave six provinces of Kanto to Ieyasu and launched a campaign to conquer northern Honshu, which took him just over one year. By the end of 1591, he had almost unified Japan, with a good number of the provinces under his own control and the rest ruled by his vassals.

In the meantime, Hideyoshi's favorite, Yodogimi, had borne him a son, Toyotomi Tsurumatsu. When Tsurumatsu died in 1591, Hideyoshi, desperate at not having an heir, appointed his nephew, Hidetsugu, *kampaku* and took the title of *taikō* for himself (February 11, 1592). But Yodogimi bore him another son, Hideyori, and Hidetsugu became a burden. Detested for his bloody-minded character, Hidetsugu was accused of conspiracy and forced to commit suicide in August 1595. Hideyoshi had previously, in 1591, forced his adviser and master of the tea ceremony, Sen no Rikyū, to perform *seppuku* for an unknown reason. Intoxicated by his military successes (and perhaps to get rid of the burdensome samurai, who were always on the verge of revolt), he decided to invade Korea and China. In 1592, his armies crossed the strait and attacked the Korean Peninsula, but they met with fierce resistance and were defeated at sea by the Korean admiral Yi Sun-sin, who was using "turtle-ships" (armored battleships) for the first time. In 1597, Hideyoshi sent a second army, but this one was forced onto the defensive and ceded the territory when Hideyoshi's death was announced, in 1598.

To ensure his succession, Hideyoshi had created a council of five "elders" *(go-tairō)*, among them Tokugawa Ieyasu, to assume the regency in the name of his son, Hideyori. Then, alarmed by the presence of a Spanish ship, the *San Felipe*, in Japanese waters, and sure that the Jesuits were the forerunners of a military expedition, he had 26 priests executed in Nagasaki (*see* MARTYRS). Ill and depressed over the failure of his armies in Korea, Hideyoshi died on September 18, 1598.

An attractive if unpredictable man, Toyotomi Hideyoshi left behind a great many letters to Yodogimi, to his wife Nene (Kita no Mandokoro), to his mother, and to his concubines that reveal his thoughts and show an affable, open man. At the time of his death, Japan was almost unified but still unstable, ready to explode at the slightest spark. It fell to Hideyoshi's general, Tokugawa Ieyasu, to establish peace and realize Oda Nobunaga and Hideyoshi's dream of unification. Hideyoshi received from the emperor the title Toyokuni Daimyōjin.

Toyo-uke-hime no Kami. *Kami* of cereals, Izanagi and Izanami's daughter, sometimes identified with Uga no Mitama, Ukemochi no Kami, Ōketsu-hime, Wakamusubi no Kami, and Inari. The outer shrine *(gegū)* of Ise is dedicated to her.

• *Toyo-uke kōdai-jingū go-chinza hongi.* "Report on the August Consecrations in the Great Toyo-uke Imperial Shrine," one of the *Go-busho* (sacred texts) of Ise, attributed to a *kannushi* (priest) named Asuke, who would have written them in 529. It is definitely an apocryphal text.

Tozama-daimyō. "Vassal daimyo from outside," the term for vassals of the Tokugawa shogunate who received their properties from Oda Nobunaga or Toyotomi Hideyoshi; they were not directly related to the Tokugawa family but were recognized as vassals before or after the Battle of Sekigahara (1600). The main *tozama-daimyō* were those of Satsuma, Chōshu, Tosa, and the Maeda, Shimazu, Date, Hosokawa, Kuroda, and Asano clans. They had to have revenues of more than 500,000 *koku*. Their numbers fell over the years, going from 117 in 1603 to 98 by the late eighteenth century. They were required to stay in Edo one year out of two and to leave their families as hostages with the shogunate (*see* SANKIN-KŌTAI). In the Kamakura and Muromachi periods, vassals who were not directly under members of shogunal families were also called *tozama*. *See* FUDAI-DAIMYŌ, HATAMOTO.

Trade. Since the dawn of Japanese history, there has been steady trade between Japan and the mainland; even after the expulsion of official embassies in the tenth century, merchant guilds *(za)* and major temples continued to trade with Korea, China, and the countries of Southeast Asia. The major export items were silk and weapons (swords), and the main imports were various consumer goods and ores. Trade with China intensified during the Ashikaga period, with Japan importing mainly luxury items; starting in the late sixteenth century, it exported lacquered objects and porcelain to Europe via Dutch training posts (see DEJIMA). After Japan's isolationist decrees were put into effect (1639), only a few merchant ships, armed with the red seal *(see* SHINSEN-BŌEKI), had some freedom to trade with foreign countries.

Imports grew during the Meiji era because Japan needed enormous amounts of raw materials and technology (ore, cotton, machinery) to carry out its policy of forced industrialization, and exports were reduced to a minimum (mainly silk). Thereafter, the balance of trade was at a slight deficit, but it eventually stabilized thanks to the creation of major shipping companies (such as Nippon Yūsen Kaisha) and large banks.

After the Second World War, trade was disorganized; during the Korean War, however, American demand for many products tripled Japanese exports, and Japan's balance of trade quickly turned positive, then rose further in the 1960s. The "Nixon Shock" *(see* NIKUSON SHOKKU) of 1971 considerably slowed trade, although the balance of trade remained stable. Changes in industrial production (ships and cars, mainly) provoked foreign countries (mainly the United States) to demand that Japan open its market more widely to their products. This process is underway, although Japan has placed certain restrictions on imports (notably rice).

The Japanese domestic market is still difficult to penetrate, because its structure forces foreign exporters to use Japanese intermediaries, who generally have their own sales networks. Moreover, to maintain competitiveness in the face of foreign competition, the government attempts to protect its high-technology industries by limiting imports, not officially but through various constraints.

The main importer of Japanese products is still the United States, whose foreign debt with Japan is constantly growing. However, the Japanese economy is becoming oriented toward market globalization, and the increased cost of labor in Japan will compromise its competitiveness on world markets over the longer term. Japan must therefore maintain its position by stressing the originality and quality of its products. *See* BANKS, ECONOMY, JAPAN *(statistics),* MITI, NIKUSON SHOKKU.

Tsu. Chief city of Mie prefecture, on Ise Bay, formerly called Anotsu, relay point on the Tōkaidō road in the Edo period, and castle town *(jōkamachi)* of the Tōdō family. Home to Mie University, and a flourishing agricultural and fishing center. *Pop.:* 150,000. *See* ANOTSU.

• **Tsu-fubito.** *See* FUBITO.

• **Tsu no Kuni.** Poetic name for the former Settsu province.

Tsū. *See* ONO TSŪ.

Tsuba. Sword guard, often in the form of a flat disk about 8 cm in diameter, pierced in the center by an oblong hole *(nakagoana)* for the blade to pass through. Usually made of iron and in various thicknesses, *tsuba* were designed to protect the hand holding the sword and at the same time to balance the blade. Some *tsuba* were made in openwork or decorated with inlays of gold or silver. The decoration often corresponded to the status of the samurai who had ordered the *tsuba* from the goldsmith: although *tsuba* belonging to ordinary samurai were relatively simple, those belonging to high-ranking samurai were decorated luxuriously. Among the most famous makers of *tsuba* were members of the Gotō family. The oldest *tsuba* go back to the Nara period, but they became objets d'art in their own right in the seventeenth century, when swords were no longer used in war but were symbols of the status of their owner. Schools of *tsuba* makers then proliferated, with daimyo and samurai as customers. Among the main schools were:

—**Chōshū,** in the sixteenth century. *Tsuba* only in iron.

—**Gomoku-zōban,** starting in the late sixteenth century.

—**Gotō,** founded by Gotō Yūjō (1453–1512), characterized by a background made of points in relief, and used mainly for ceremonial swords.

—**Heian-jō,** founded in Kyoto in the late sixteenth or early seventeenth century.

—**Higo,** founded in Higo province by Hayashi Matashichi.

—**Hirata,** in Awa (Sengoku-*tsuba*).

—**Hōan,** founded in Owari in the early seventeenth century.

—**Hōju,** old *tsuba* (before the sixth century), imported.

—**Itō Masatsugu,** Umetada's student, who founded his own school about 1600.

—**Jakushi Kisaemon,** in Nagasaki, influenced by Chinese art.

—**Kaga,** founded in Kaga province in the early seventeenth century.

—**Kamakura,** iron *tsuba,* often sculpted and lacquered.

—**Kaneie,** founded in Fushimi, near Kyoto, in the late sixteenth century.

—**Katsushi** and **Kabutsohi,** in the style of the Tosho school.

—**Kinai,** founded in Echizen. Découpé iron.

—**Ko-kinko,** *tsuba* made of soft metal, highly decorated, starting in the late fifteenth century.

—The **Mito** schools (seventeenth century).

—**Myōchin,** founded in the twelfth century, roughly forged iron *tsuba.*

—**Namban,** *tsuba* made with imported iron or decorated with foreign designs, produced mainly in Nagasaki.

—**Nobuie,** founded by Myōchin Nobuie in the sixteenth century.

—**Ōnin,** founded in the sixteenth century, with *tsuba* decorated with appliqué relief.

—**Ōtouki,** founded in Kyoto in the early nineteenth century.

—**Shingen,** founded in the late sixteenth century.

—**Shitogi,** very rare *tsuba,* made from the sixth to the ninth century.

—**Shōami,** founded in Kyoto in the late sixteenth century. Gave rise to many other schools.

—**Sōten,** founded in Hikone by Kitagawa Sōten. Chinese influence.

—**Sukashi,** *tsuba* in découpé iron, from the early seventeenth century.

—**Tachikanagushi,** founded in the sixteenth century. Soft metal with inlays.

—**Tanaka,** founded in the nineteenth century.

—**Tosho,** founded in the sixteenth century for parade swords, in découpé iron.

—**Tsuchiya,** in the school called Yasuchika.

—**Umetada,** founded in Yamashiro by Umetada Myōju (1558–1631), a maker of sword blades.

—**Yokoya.**

The most famous *tsuba* goldsmiths were Shimizu Jingō, Hirata Hikozō, Nara Toshinaga, Omori Teruhide, Tsuchiya Yasuchika, Iwamoto Konkan, Ōtsu Jimpō, Kanō Natsuo, and Shummei Hōgen.

Tsuba were sometimes in other shapes, including square (rarely), serrated, and oval. The central hole, often edged with brass or copper, was usually flanked by two smaller holes used to hold the scabbard's *(saya)* accessories, such as *kōgai* and *kozuka.* They were made with forged iron, but also with alloys such as *shakudō,* bronze, and sometimes silver. They are prized by collectors, and some fetch exorbitant prices. *See* KATANA.

Tsubai Ōtsuka-yama kofun. Large *kofun* (185 × 75 m) in Yamashiro-chō, near Kyoto, in *zempō-kōen* (keyhole) shape, with a *tateana* funerary chamber measuring 9 × 1.2 m. It contained a wooden casket, bronze mirrors made in China, iron épées, and iron and copper lance points and arrows.

Tsubaki Dai-jingū. Shinto shrine about 30 km east of Nagoya, dedicated to Saruta-hiko, considered the *kami* of awareness. This *kami* is portrayed (though rarely) as a wooden statue of a bearded man with a very long nose, holding a lance in his right hand.

• **Tsubaki-hitsu.** *See* CHINZAN.

• **Tsubaki-ichi.** "Camellia market," once located near the town of Sakurai (Nara prefecture). Sei Shōnagon mentioned it in *Makura no sōshi.* Also called *tsuba-ichi.*

Tsubo. Unit of area equivalent to 2 *tatami* or 1 *ken²* (about 3.35 m²), also called *bu:* 30 *tsubo* make 1 *se* (about 100 m²); 10 *se* make 1 *tan,* and 10 *tan* make 1 *chō* (60 × 50 *ken,* about 1 hectare); 36 *chō* make 1 *ri* (about 16 km²). Land is still measured in *tsubo.* *See* KUMI.

• *Tsubo* is also the term used for certain sensitive parts of the body used in acupuncture, *amma, mogusa,* and similar techniques; they are found along the "meridians" *(keiraku). See* ACUPUNCTURE.

• Term for certain ceramic jars designed to contain tea.

Tsuboi Asuka. Ceramist, born 1932 in Osaka. Her works were purchased by the national manufacture in Sèvres, in 1984, and by the Centre National des Arts Plastiques in France in 1985. She has participated in exhibits at the Triennale de Nyon (Switzerland, 1988) and the Mitsukoshi space (Paris, 1994).

Tsuboi Kumezō. Historian (1858–1936), born in Osaka. He studied in Germany and Austria, then returned to teach at the University of Tokyo, introducing German methods of historical research to Japan.

Tsuboi Sakae. Writer (Iwai Sakae, 1900–67), born on Shōdo Island (Kagawa prefecture); she married Tsuboi Shigeji in 1925. She wrote mainly for children. Her novel *Nijūshi no hitomi* (Twenty-Four Eyes, 1952) was adapted for the screen by Kinoshita Keisuke in 1954. Among her best-known works are *Uchikake* (The Dress, 1956) and *Haha no kaiko to kononai haha to* (Child Without Mother and Mother Without Child).

Tsuboi Shigeji. Poet (1898–1975), born in Kagawa prefecture, of proletarian inspiration (*see* NAPF), Tsuboi Sakae's husband. He wrote several literary essays: *Teiko no seishin* (1949) and poetry collections, such as *Atama no naka no heishi* (1956).

Tsuboi Shōgorō. Archeologist (1863–1913), born in Edo, who discovered the first Yayoi pottery near Tokyo in 1884. He studied ethnology in France and Great Britain from 1889 to 1892, then introduced ethnology courses at the University of Tokyo in 1893. He formulated several theories on the origin of the Japanese people, which later turned out to be false, and did interesting excavations of ancient sites, notably *yokoana,* or "tunnel-tombs." *See* KŌGOISHI.

Tsuboiya Kichiemon. *Sake* brewer (1736–1802) in Osaka and painter of landscapes and flowers; Ono Ranzan's student. He also collected rare books.

Tsubota Jōji. Writer (1890–1982), born in Okayama prefecture, a disciple of Ogawa Mimei and a famous author of children's stories, including *Obake no sekai* (The World of Ghosts, 1935), *Kaze no naka no kodomo* (The Child in the Wind, 1936), *Kodomo no shiki* (The Four Seasons of Childhood, 1938). He was elected a member of the Japan Art Academy (Nihon Geijutsu-in) in 1964.

Tsubouchi Shōyō. Writer and literary critic (Tsubouchi Yūzō, 1859–1935), born near Nagoya to a peasant family. After studying at the University of Tokyo, he became a professor at Waseda University in 1883; later, he became dean, a position he held for 40 years. He translated the complete works of Shakespeare between 1883 and 1928, and wrote novels and plays for Kabuki and Shingeki theater starting in 1888. His works, tending toward realism, had a great influence on modern Japanese literature. The best known are *Shōsetsu shinzui* (The Essence of the Novel, 1885), *Tōsei shōsei katagi* (Today's Students, 1886), *Imo to sekagami* (1886), *Matsuo no uchi* (1888), *Saikun* (1888), *Hotogisu,*

Maki no kata, Natsu kyoran, Kiri to ha (Paulownia Leaves, a Kabuki play, 1896). *See* BUNGEI KYŌKAI.

Tsuboya-yaki. Type of ceramics produced in Okinawa prefecture (Ryukyu) since 1682, decorated with floral, animal, or geometric motifs cut into or painted under a red or green slip. These ceramics, cooked at a low temperature in *anagama* or *noborigama* kilns, are earthenware. They are divided into two categories, *jōyaki,* with a feldspar slip, used for dishes, and *arayaki,* without slip or with a manganese-based slip, used for jars (sometimes sculpted funerary urns). The tradition is perpetuated today in 12 kilns built at the site.

Tsuchida Bakusen. Painter (Tsuchida Kinji, 1887–1936), born on Sado, who studied with Suzuki Shōnen and Takeuchi Seihō in the Nihonga style. A Buddhist monk in Kyoto, he abandoned the robe to devote himself to painting and lived in Europe from 1921 to 1923; his works were exhibited in various salons and won many prizes. In 1918, he and Murakami Kagaku had founded a "National Creative Painting Association" (Kokuga Sōsaku Kyōkai). His works, mixing Nihonga traditions with Western techniques, had some influence on modern Japanese painting. He was elected to the Imperial Fine Arts Academy (Teikoku Bijutsu-in) in 1934. He painted mainly screens *(byōbu).*

Tsuchigumo. "Ground spiders," a term used in the *Kojiki* for troglodytic aboriginals (they lived in semi-buried cabins—*tatara, tateana*) who opposed the conquest of the islands by Jimmu Tennō.

• *Tsuchigumo.* Title of a Kabuki play, adopted from a Noh play by Kawatake Mokuami, and performed for the first time in 1881. Raikō falls ill, and a Buddhist monk reveals to him that his illness is caused by a giant spider, a *tsuchigumo.* Raikō, realizing that the spider is none other than the monk, tries to kill him but succeeds only in injuring him. A warrior, Hitorimusha, tracks the monster and kills him after a fierce battle.

• *Tsuchigumo-zōshi.* Painted *emakimono* on the theme of the monstrous spider, a folk tale adapted into a Noh play. National museum, Tokyo.

Tsuchiguruma. Title of a Noh play: a man, desolate over the loss of his wife, abandons his son to become a Buddhist monk. His son and the son's tutor climb into a low vehicle on wheels *(tuschiguruma)* and go to look for him. They finally find him in the Zenkō-ji temple.

Tsuchimikado Tennō. Eighty-third emperor (the Prince Tamehito, 1195<1199–1210>1231), oldest son of and successor to Go-Toba Tennō. He abdicated in favor of his brother, Juntoku, and died in voluntary exile in Awa province.

Tsuchiya Bummei. Poet (1890–1990), born in Gumma prefecture; he wrote *tanka* (*Fuyukasa,* 1925) and was publisher of the poetry magazine *Araragi* in 1930, succeeding Saitō Mokichi. His most highly regarded works are *Ōkanshū* (1930) and *Sankokushū* (1935), collections of traditional *tanka,* and a 20-volume study on the *Man'yōshū, Man'yōshū shichū* (1949–56). He received the Order of Culture (Bunka-shō) in 1986.

Tsuda Juku Daigaku. Private college founded by Tsuda Umeko in 1900 in Kodaira (Tokyo), Chiyoda district, first called Joshi Eigaku Juku, to teach English to young women. It was transferred to its present site in 1930 and expanded to include faculties of literature and science. Attendance, about 2,500 students.

Tsuda Kemmotsu. Ironsmith who, in 1543, studied the harquebuses that had been imported by the Portuguese to Tanegashima in 1542 and established a firearms factory in Sakai, the first of its type in Japan. He formed a school (Tsuda-ryū), and his son, Tsuda Jiūsai, assisted him, then succeeded him.

Tsuda Mamichi. Scholar (1829–1903), born in the Tsuyama estate (Okayama prefecture). He studied Western military techniques with Sakuma Shōzan and taught at the Bansho Shirabesho. The Tokugawa shogunate sent him to Holland in 1862 to continue his studies at the University of Leyde. When he returned in 1865, he became an instructor at the Kaisejo; he wrote the first Japanese work devoted to Western laws, *Taisei kokuhō,* in 1866. He then helped write various legal codes and published a number of articles in *Meiroku Zasshi.*

Tsuda Seifū. Painter (1881–1978), founder of the Nika-kai group. At first a follower of Western oil painting, he changed his style to "Japanese painting" (Nihonga).

Tsuda Sen. Politician (1837–1908) and writer; he accompanied Fukazawa Yukichi to the United States in 1867. An expert in agricultural issues, he published *Nōgyō sanji* (1874), in which he discussed artificial pollination techniques. He was the editor of an agricultural journal, *Nōgyō Zasshi.* Tsuda Umeko's father.

Tsuda Sōgyū. Wealthy merchant (?–1591) in the port of Sakai and master *(chajin)* of the tea ceremony *(chanoyu)* under Oda Nobunaga and Toyotomi Hideyoshi. He and Sen no Rikyū organized the great public tea ceremony held by the Hideyoshi at the Kitano shrine in Kyoto in 1587.

Tsuda Sōkichi. Writer and historian (1873–1961), born in Gifu prefecture. He studied the ancient civilizations of China and Japan and became a professor at Waseda University in 1919. He became famous for showing that most of the legends in the *Kojiki* and *Nihon shoki* did not have a historical basis but were compilations made by courtiers to justify the existence of the imperial court. His works, considered by right-wing extremists to be blasphemous, were banned in 1940, and he and his publisher, Iwanami Shigeo, were sentenced to three months in prison. After the Second World War, he wrote a few works in favor of the imperial family and adopted an anti-communist stance. He received the Medal of Cultural Merit in 1949. His complete works (33 vols.) were published from 1963 to 1965 by Iwanami Shoten.

Tsuda Umeko. Tsuda Sen's daughter (1865–1929), born in Edo. She and four other girls were sent to the United States in 1871 with the Iwakura mission. She was baptized there; when she returned to Japan in 1882, she became the teacher of Itō Hirobumi's children. She lived in the United States from 1889 to 1892, then founded the Tsuda Juku Daigaku in Tokyo and organized the Japanese branch of the YWCA. She went to the United States again in 1907 and 1913 to improve cultural and educational relations with her country.

Tsue. Ancient measure of length, equivalent to 1 *jō* or 10 *shaku. See* GŌ.

Tsugaru Kaikyō. Tsugaru Strait, linking the Sea of Japan (Nihonkai) and the Pacific Ocean between Hokkaido and Honshu. A tunnel (Seikan) was recently dug under the strait to link Cape Tappizaki (Aomori prefecture) to Yoshioka on Hokkaido. *Width:* 20–50 km; *maximum depth:* 450 m. *See* SEIKAN.

Tsugaru-nuri. Lacquered objects made in the twelfth century by Ikeda Gentarō, in which successive layers of colored lacquer were applied in different thicknesses, then polished so that the different colors emerged in irregular designs.

Tsuiji. Wall around a monastery or Buddhist temple.

Tsuina. Title for a Buddhist monk with an official responsibility in a temple or monastery. Also called *ino, ina. See* RISSHI.

Tsuishu Heijūrō. Lacquer artist (late sixteenth–early seventeenth century), creator of the Tsuishu style of sculpted objects in red lacquer, imitating the Chinese Ming style.

Tsuison Tennō. Title for imperial princes who received the posthumous title Tennō but did not reign.

Tsuitachi. Abridgment of "Tsuki-tachi" (new moon), designating the first day of each month in the lunar calendar.

Tsuitate. Movable screen on feet, sometimes decorated with a *shōhei-ga* painting, used to divide a room in the absence of fusuma, or to protect the inhabitants of a house from prying eyes or the wind. *See* BYŌBU, KICHŌ.

Tsūji. Interpreters, generally from Dutch *(oranda-tsūji)* or Chinese *(tō-tsūji),* used by the Edo shogunate to conduct trade relations with foreigners, mainly in Nagasaki and Hirado. The position was hereditary. Among the most famous *tsūji* were Hayashi Dōei, Baba Tadayoshi, and Shizuki Tadao.

Tsujigahana. "Crossed flowers," a decorative design on certain textiles made with the *shibori-zome* dyeing method, used mainly during the Muromachi and early Edo periods to decorate *kosode (see* KIMONO) and temple banners. The technique consisted of painting on silk *(nuishime-shibori),* which was then basted with thread and knotted, dipped into successive dye baths, and rinsed numerous times. Although *tsujigahana* produced sumptuous fabrics, the technique was lost in the early Edo period. It was revived in the 1950s by Kubota Ichiku in Tokyo.

Tsujihara Noboru. Novelist (b. 1956), winner of the Akutagawa Prize (1990) for his book *Mura no namae* (The Name of the Village).

Tsuji Kiyoharu. Ceramist, born 1927 in Tokyo, founder of a ceramics research center (1937). He had exhibitions in Germany, Washington, and London (1983), and at the Kisaragi gallery in Paris (1986), and his works were in the exhibition at the Mitsukoshi space in Paris (1994).

Tsuji Kunio. Writer (1925–99), born in Tokyo, expert in French literature. He lived in France from 1957 to 1961. Among his best-known novels are *Kairō ni te* (1963), *Azuchi ōkan ni* (1968), and *Sagano meigetsu ki* (1971).

Tsuji Masanobu. Politician and military officer (1902–after 1961), born in Ishikawa prefecture. An officer in the Guandong army in Manchuria in the 1930s, he commanded a Japanese army in Thailand in 1943. He escaped from the Occupation authorities and returned to Japan in 1950, then published an account of his adventures, *Senkō sanzenri* (Three Thousand Miles in Hiding). He was elected to the House of Representatives in 1952 and to the House of Peers in 1959. In 1961, he disappeared while visiting Laos as a tourist.

Tsuji Naoshirō. Scholar (1900–79), director of the Center for Cultural Studies of the Far East and director of the Asian Library (Tōyō Bunko). He was named a Person of Cultural Merit in 1978.

Tsuji-ura. Ancient divination procedure *(uranai)* consisting of standing at a crossroads at night and interpreting the words said by passersby. This rite, which is mentioned as far back as the *Man'yōshū* (eighth century), was later associated with the cult of the *Dōsojin, kami* of the roadsides. *See* DIVINATION, URANAI.

Tsuji Zennosuke. Historian (1877–1955), born in Hyōgo prefecture. He studied the history of Buddhism in Japan and received the Japan Academy Prize (Nihon Gakushi-in-shō) in 1921 and the Order of Culture (Bunka-shō) in 1952.

Tsuka. Ancient unit of length, equivalent to the width of four fingers.
• Sword *(katana)* handle, composed of a pommel *(kashira),* fastenings *(tsukaito),* bronze decorations hiding the dowels attaching the tang *(menuki, tsuka-ai),* and the guard *(tsuba). See* KATANA.

Tsukahara Takashi. Contemporary painter, born 1932 in Yokohama. He received the Ōshashi Prize in 1955, then moved to Paris, where he specialized in trompe-l'oeil painting.

Tsukamoto Kunio. Poet, born 1930 in Shiga prefecture, author of many collections of avant-garde *waka* poems, including *Suisō monogatari* (1952), *Sōshoku gakku* (1956), *Nihonjin reika* (1958), *Yūgure no kaichō* (1971), *Saredo yūsei* (1975).

Tuskamoto Saburō. Politician, born 1927 in Aichi prefecture. Elected to the House of Representatives in 1958 for the Socialist party, he was appointed secretary-general of the party in 1974. He became its leader in 1985, succeeding Sasaki Ryōsaku.

Tsukamyōjin kofun. Megalithic tomb excavated in 1984 near Takatori (Nara prefecture), measuring about 18 m in diameter; it may originally have been octagonal in shape. Uncovered was an oblong chamber composed of 400 blocks of cut stone in which was a lacquered-wood casket. Unfortunately, most of the objects it contained had been stolen. It may have been the tomb of Prince Kusakabe (662–89), one of Temmu Tennō's sons.

Tsukemono. Vegetables prepared in brine or with spices or vinegar added. There are an infinite variety of *tsukemono* because each region has its own specialty. It is very popular among Japanese of all ages, and is usually among the gifts brought home from trips or visits. *Umeboshi* are one kind of *tsukemono,* as are *takuan-zuke* (daikon in brine) and *hakusai-zuke* (Chinese cabbage in brine). Also called *kōnomono. See* CUISINE, PICKLES.

Tsukimaro. Painter (Kitagawa Tsukimaro, Kitagawa Jun; *mei:* Rokusaburō; *azana:* Shitatsu; *gō:* Bokutei, Kansetsusai, Kikumaro, Tsukimaro, active 1801–29), in Edo. He made ukiyo-e prints under the direction of Utamaro, and took the name Tuskimaro only in 1804.

Tsukimono. Spirits or disembodied beings said to possess a person's mind under certain conditions, provoking hallucinations or pain. Foxes *(kitsune)* are often accused of being such spirits; in certain regions, they are a sort of dog *(inugami, izuna)* or a snake *(tōbyō). Tsukimono* can also be spirits of the deceased who are unhappy that their memory has been neglected or *kami* wishing to avenge an offense.

Tsukioka Kōgyō. Painter (Hanyū Sadanosuke, Kōgyo, Kohan, 1869–1927), born in Tokyo, adop-

tive son of Tsukioka Yoshitoshi (1839–92). He studied under Matsumoto Fukō (1840–1923), a painter of historical subjects, and Ogata Gekkō. His ukiyo-e prints portrayed Noh and Kyōgen theater scenes.

Tsukuba. New city created in 1979 in Ibaraki prefecture, at the foot of Mt. Tsukuba (*alt.:* 876 m), to become a sort of "science city" (Tsukuba Kenkyū Gakuen Toshi), comprising six villages. It houses a great number of study and research institutes and is affiliated with the University of Tokyo. It can accommodate more than 9,000 students, and the city itself was planned for a population of 120,000. From March 17 to September 16, 1985, it hosted a huge international science and technology exposition, with participation by 48 countries and 37 international organizations. The exposition drew more than 20 million visitors, both Japanese and foreign.

• **Tsukuba Daigaku.** National university of Tsukuba, founded in 1973 on a different model from that of traditional universities, with three campuses and a large number of faculties. Attendance, about 7,000 students.

Tsukuba-shū. Anthology of *renga* poems compiled in 1356 by Nijō Yoshimoto and Gusai, in 20 volumes, featuring the work of 530 poets (more than 2,000 verses arranged in categories such as seasons, travel, and religion). It was the first imperial anthology of *renga. See* SŌGI.

Tsukuchi no Michi no Kuchi. Former name of Chikuzen province.

• **Tsukuchi no Michi no Shiri.** Former name of Chikugo province.

Tsukuri-e. Type of painting in Yamato-e style, characterized by the static attitudes of the people portrayed and by bright colors, very fashionable throughout the Heian period. The term is also used for *emakimono* painted with thick, opaque colors that cover a drawing made in *sumi* (China ink). Also called *kaki-okoshi. See* NEZAME MONOGATARI EMAKI.

Tsukushi. Ancient kingdom in northern Kyushu, near Fukuoka. The name is sometimes used, mainly in literature, to designate Kyushu.

Tsumami. In ancient bronze mirrors, a button pierced with a hole through which a string is passed so that the mirror can be held. *See* KAGAMI.

Tsume. Plectrums made of ivory or shell (now often of plastic) used by koto players. These "fingernails" are usually kept in a special box called a *tsume-bako,* which is also used to store extra strings and frets.

Tsumegome. *See* KAKOIMAI.

Tsume-gumi. *See* KARA-YŌ.

Tsumi. Term describing all infringements on morality or religious ethics, especially Shinto, necessarily involving a state of impurity *(kegare),* which must be erased by an act of purification *(harai, misogi).* It is somewhat similar to the Western notion of sin. There are two kinds of *tsumi: amatsu-tsumi* (criminal acts, violations of taboos), and *kunitsu-tsumi* (murders, diseases, hereditary deformations, incest, and so on). *See* KEGARE.

Tsumugi. Silk pongee, handwoven and quite uneven, generally yellow or brown, used for summer clothes. Sometimes woven with ikat *(Jap.: kasuri)* techniques. All ordinary cotton fabrics are called *tsumugi-momen.*

Tsunami. Tidal waves caused by underwater earthquakes; when they hit the coasts, they ravage everything in their path. The earthquake that struck Kanto on September 1, 1923, was followed by a huge *tsunami* that caused considerable damage. *See* EARTHQUAKES, OKUJIRI.

Tsunemasa. Painter (Kawamata Tsunemasa, 1720–50) of ukiyo-e prints in Edo, Tsuneyuki's student. He painted *bijin* (beautiful women) and genre scenes.

Tsunemasa. Title of a Noh play: the *biwa* belonging to the warrior Tsunemasa, who serves the Heike (Taira), is given to a Buddhist temple. Tsunemasa's spirit then appears and tells the story of the instrument. Although he is invisible, he plays his *biwa* and dances (on stage, only his shadow is seen).

Tsunenobu. Painter (Kanō Tsunenobu; *mei:* Ukon; *gō:* Yōboku, Seihakusai, Kosensō, Kōkansai, Shiniō, Kan'unshi, Bokusai, Kōcho-sanjin, Rōgōken, Sen-oku, Tsunenobu, 1636–1713) of the Kanō school. He studied with his father, Naonobu, in Kobikichō (Edo).
→ *See* MINAMOTO NO TSUNENOBU.

Tsunenori. *See* ASUKABE.

Tsunesada Shinnō. Imperial prince (825–84), Emperor Junna's son, who became a Buddhist monk with the name Kōseki. He was a famous scholar and poet.

Tsuneyuki. Painter (Kawamata Tsuneyuki, 1677–after 1741) in Edo, Tsunemasa's master. Most of his ukiyo-e prints portrayed beautiful women *(bijin).*

Tsunodaru. Special bottle, lacquered in red, in which *sake* is offered at the Shinto shrine during marriages or celebrations *(matsuri).*

Tsuno-kakushi. "Top to hide horns," a piece of white fabric worn by women over their hair during a wedding in traditional costume, supposed to hide the "horns of jealousy." *See* MAGE, MARRIAGE.

Tsurana. Painter (Morizumi Sadateru; *mei:* Tokujirō; *gō:* Shisai, Tsurana, 1809–92) of the Sumiyoshi school; Kōki's student in Osaka. He painted historical subjects.

Tsurayoshi. Painter (Yamana Kangi, 1836–1902) of the Sumiyoshi school in Tokyo. He painted historical subjects.

Tsurezuregusa. "Herbs of Boredom," a collection of philosophical thoughts, in 243 paragraphs, written in 1331 by Kenkō Hōshi (Urabe Kaneyoshi, 1283–1350), in the *zui-hitsu* genre. *See* KENKŌ HŌSHI.

Tsuridono. In traditional *shinden*-style architecture, a small pavilion, usually square in plan, located at the end of a long gallery and overlooking a lake, used for solitary meditation.

Tsuridōrō. In Buddhist temples, a bronze lantern hung on the edge of roof awnings.

Tsurugaoka Hachiman-gū. Shinto shrine in Kamakura, dedicated to the spirits of Emperor Ōjin (deified as Hachiman, Yahata no Kami), tutelary divinity of the Minamoto family; Jingū Kōgō; and Ōjin Tennō's wife, Hime Ōkami (or Himegami). At first a dependency of the Iwashimizu Hachiman-gū shrine in Yuigahama (a nearby site), built in 1063 by the famous archer Minamoto no Yoriyoshi (988–1075), it was transferred to its present site by Minamoto no Yoritomo in 1191. It was destroyed during the fall of the Kamakura *bakufu* in 1333 and rebuilt in 1828 in the style of the Momoyama era (late sixteenth century). Annual festival September 15, during which archery demonstrations *(yabusame)* take place. The shrine has a small museum and a *dōjō* by Kyūdō.

- **Tsurugaoka Itsumin.** *See* KAGEI.

Tsurugi. Double-bladed straight épée, used mainly before the eighth century and preserved as an attribute of some Buddhist divinities, such as Fudō Myō-ō. Also called *ken*.
→ *See* NAKAJIMA KI–115.

- **Tsurugi-in.** *See* GUNDARI-IN.

Tsuru-kame. Collective term for the two symbols of longevity, the crane *(tsuru)* and the tortoise *(kame)*.

Tsurumi Yūsuke. Writer (1885–1973), born in Gumma prefecture, Nitobe Inazō's disciple. A firm believer in liberalism and peaceful cooperation between peoples, he published a newspaper, *Shin Jiyū Shugi* (The New Liberalism), from 1928 to 1935, and organized series of lectures to expound his ideas in both Japan and the United States. He founded an association, Taiheiyō Kyōkai (Pacific Institute) to improve relations with the United States and helped found the Institute of Pacific Relations. His works caused a sensation among young people, especially *Eiyū taibōron* (Waiting for Heroes, 1929) and *Haha* (The Mother, 1932). Elected to the Diet in 1928 and reelected four times, he was minister of welfare in Hatoyama Ichirō's cabinet (1954–55).

Tsurunen Marutei. Lutheran missionary (Martti Turunen), born 1940 in Finland. Principal of an English school, he became a Japanese citizen in 1979 and entered politics. In 1992, he won a seat in the communal assembly of the town of Yugawara (a spa about 100 km from Tokyo), then, in 1995, set his sights on one of the three vacant seats in Kanagawa prefecture, running as an independent candidate. This was an unprecedented act in Japanese politics, up to then the exclusive preserve of Japanese-born citizens.

Tsuru-nyōbō. Folk tale of the "crane wife": a crane, wounded by a hunter's arrow, is rescued by a man. She transforms herself into a beautiful woman and marries her savior. With her feathers, she secretly makes luxurious dresses, which she sells for a very high price, making her husband wealthy. But he surprises her while she is weaving, despite her having forbidden him to watch her work, and she turns back into a crane and leaves him.

Tsuruoka Masao. Painter (1906–79) in avant-garde Western style. In 1930, he founded a group of anti-fascist artists called NOVA.

Tsuruta Kinshi. Musician, born 1911 in Hokkaido to a family of peasants. She became an expert in playing the *biwa* and singing the accompanying songs. She composed, among other pieces, the *biwa* melodies for Kobayashi's movie *Kaidan.*

Tsuruya Namboku. Family of Kabuki actors, founded in Edo in the eighteenth century. The most famous actor and playwright of this family was Tsurya Namboku IV (Ebiya Genzō, 1755–1829), who wrote more than 120 Kabuki plays. He created a new dramatic style called Kizewa-kyōgen, in which satires on the society of the *chōnin* were mixed with a certain moral content, somewhat influenced by Nichiren's Buddhist ethic. Tsuruya Namboku's most famous play is *Tōkaidō Yotsuya kaidan* (The Story of the Ghosts of Tōkaidō Yotsuya, 1825). Among his other plays are *Tenjiku Tokubei* (Tokubei of India, 1804) and *Sakura-hime azuma bunshō* (The Scarlet Princess of Edo, 1817).

Tsushima. Archipelago of five islands (the largest being Kami-Agata and Shimo-Agata) north of Kyushu, between it and the Korean Peninsula, administratively part of Nagasaki prefecture. These islands, with an average altitude of about 400 m, were the fief of the Sō family from the twelfth century to 1868; their main town was Izuhara, on Shimo-Agata. The islands were attacked and sacked by the Mongols in 1274 and 1281. *Area:* Kami-Agata, 255 km², Shimo-Agata, 450 km²; *total pop.:* 50,000. Also called Fuchū.

- **Tsushima, Battle of.** On May 27–28, 1905, a group of Russian warships, on a seven-month voyage from Kronstadt to Vladivostok (with a stopover at Madagascar), carrying reinforcements for the Russian troops in Siberia and Manchuria, met the Japanese fleet, commanded by Admiral Tōgō Heihachirō, off the Tsushima Islands. The Russian squadron, commanded by Vice-Admiral Zinovii Rodjestvensky, was composed of 45 warships from the Baltic fleet. When the battle was over, 34 Russian ships had been sunk by the Japanese fleet, 4,380 Russian sailors had been killed, and 5,917 had been taken prisoner. Only three ships managed to escape the dragnet and reach Vladivostok without damage. The Japanese had lost only three torpedo boats and 110 men. The Japanese ships were using a special cannon powder, invented by Shimose, which gave them an advantage. They were also more modern than their Russian counterparts, and their crews were fresher and better trained. The Battle of Tsushima is known in Japan as Nihonkai Kaisen (Battle of the Sea of Japan). *See* MIKASA.

• **Tsushima Jiken.** In 1861, a Russian warship, the *Posadnik,* stopped at Tsushima, and its sailors began to build an army camp there. They claimed that they were making repairs, but in reality they wanted to capture this strategic base. The shogunate's diplomatic efforts were fruitless, so the British (Sir Rutherford Alcock) sent two warships to the site. The Russians, outnumbered, left after a six-month stay.

• **Tsushima Kaikyō.** Strait separating the Tsushima Islands from the Korean Peninsula, linking the eastern China Sea and the Sea of Japan (Nihonkai). A warm current (Tsushima-kairyū) runs through it from south to north, reaching the Pacific Ocean through the Tsugaru Strait. *Width:* 50 km; *maximum depth:* 130 m.

Tsushima Yūko. Writer (b. 1947), Dazai Osuma's daughter and Ōta Haruko's half-sister. Her works deal mainly with the condition of women in Japan after the Second World War: *Chōji* (Child of Luck, 1978), *Hikari no ryōbun* (The Domain of Light, 1979), *Dammari ichi* (The Silent Stalkers).

Tsūshin-shi. Title for Korean envoys to the court of Japan until about 1450, when relations between the two countries were interrupted. Relations were revived in 1549, then again from 1607 to 1811. The last Korean delegation was received on the island of Tsushima in 1811. Also called Chōsen-shinshi. *Kor.:* Tongsin-sa, Pobing-sa.

Tsutaya Jūzaburō. Publisher of books and prints in Osaka. Around 1794–95, he published Sharaku's ukiyo-e prints. He may have in fact made these prints himself. *See* SHARAKU.

Tsutsui Junkei. Daimyo (1549–84) of Yamato during the Sengoku period. He was allied with Akechi Mitsuhide, but he broke the alliance when he attacked Oda Nobunaga in the Honnō-ji temple in 1582, and formed an alliance with Toyotomi Hideyoshi.

Tsutsumi chūnagon monogatari. "Tale of the Adviser of the Tsutsumi Center." An anonymous collection of ten stories about various events that took place in the imperial court in the late Heian and early Kamakura periods, offering a satiric view of the degradation of customs in the court. This work was probably written between 1055 and 1385, because the first episode takes place in 1055.

Tsutsumi-yaki. Folk pottery made in the Tsutsumi region, near Sendai (Miyagi prefecture), in the late seventeenth century. It consisted of a type of thrown raku in rough brown clay, varnished in black or brown, sometimes with greenish glints. The kilns now produce mainly tiles and drainage pipes.

Tsutsumi Yasujirō. Politician and industrialist (1889–1964), founder of railroads and the Seibu stores. He was elected to the Diet 13 times, starting in 1924. His son, Tsutsumi Seiji, is a well-known writer and poet under the name Takashi Tsujii.

Tsutsumu. Typically Japanese art of wrapping products or packages using rice straw *(komedawara),* or braided-straw cases *(komobukuri)* for *sake* jars. It is also a way of wrapping traditional gifts.

Tsuzumi. Two-faced, hourglass-shaped drum with skins held by cords, played with one or two drumsticks. It is held on the shoulder, and its tone can be varied by pressing on the cords linking the two skins. There are many types of different sizes; most were introduced from China in the seventh century. The *san no tsuzumi* (or *ikko*) was once used in *gagaku* orchestras. Today's *tsuzumi* are the ō-tsuzumi and the *kotsuzumi,* used in Noh and Kabuki performances; the skins are cow or horsehide. *See* TAIKO.

Tsuzura. During the Muromachi period, large rectangular covered baskets used to store clothing. They were often lacquered or covered with waterproofed paper. The most elaborate bore the *mon* of the family to which they belonged. They were very light and easily transportable.

Tsuzure-ori. Brocade fabric imitating tapestry, from a technique imported from China around 1400. It is used mainly to make obi. Silk *tsuzure-ori* is called *tsuzure-nishiki.*

Typhoon (taifū). "Great wind." Meteorological phenomenon common in Japan, especially in September and October, characterized by extremely violent winds that reach a velocity of more than 200 km/h. Typhoons generally originate in the Sea of the Philippines and hit Japan from south to north. The most devastating one was in 1959 (5,000 dead and more than 1,350,000 houses damaged), but typhoons claim many victims each year. They can be predicted with some accuracy thanks to an American satellite called Himawari (Sunflower). *See* KA-MIKAZE, SHURIN, TATSUTA-TAISHA.

U. Third vowel in the Japanese syllabary (*see* GOJŪON-ZU). It is also used, in kana writing, to indicate that a syllable is long when it is placed afterward. For example, "tofu" is written *to + u − hu;* "Tokyo" is written *to + u − ki + yo + u.*

Ubasoku. Lay Buddhist *(Skt.: upāsaka),* or simply someone following Buddhist precepts. This term is rarely used. *See* ZAIKE.

Ubasute. *See* OBASUTE.

Ubayama. Hill in Chiba prefecture, on the slopes of which a *kaizuka* (shell mound) was discovered in 1926. It revealed traces of semi-buried cabins *(tatara, tateana)* of the Middle *(chūki)* and Low *(kōki)* Jōmon periods. The floor of the cabins was about 0.5 m below the surface. They were 6–7 m in diameter, and the roof was supported by four to six pillars with a diameter of about 0.4 m. *See* JŌMON, TSUCHIGUMO.

Ubusunagami. *Kami* who protects the birthplace of an individual, merged with *ujigami.* Also called *chinju no kami.*

Uchida Ginzō. Historian (1872–1919), expert on the Edo period, the first professor of economics at the University of Tokyo. *Keizaishi sōron* (Introduction to the History of Economics, 1912) and *Kinsei no Nihon* (Japan During the Edo Period, 1919) are his two major works.

Uchida Hyakken. Writer (Uchida Eizō, 1889–1971), born in Okayama prefecture. A professor of German, he began to write in 1935, publishing novels and essays in the style of Natsume Sōseki. He also used the *gō* Hyakkien.

Uchida Kōsai. Politician (Uchida Yasuya, 1865–1936), born in Kumamoto (Kyushu). He was ambassador to China from 1901 to 1906, Austria (1906), and the United States (1908–11), and minister of foreign affairs in Saionji Kimmochi's second cabinet (1911–12). In 1914, he was ambassador to Russia, then again minister of foreign affairs under Hara Takashi (1918–21), Takahashi Korekiyo (1921–22), and Katō Tomosaburō (1922–23). Appointed president of the South Manchuria Railroad, he let the Guandong army use the lines. Saitō Makoto asked him to be minister of foreign affairs in his cabinet in 1932, a position he held until 1934; during this time, he demanded recognition of the state of Manchukuo.

Uchida Roan. Writer (Uchida Mitsugu, 1868–1929), born in Tokyo. He translated Dostoyevsky's *Crime and Punishment* and wrote many essays on Western literature, favoring the naturalist style.

Uchida Ryōhei. Politician (1874–1937), born in Fukuoka prefecture. A disciple of Tōyama Mitsuru, he joined the Gen'yōsha and went to Korea and Siberia to propagate the Japanese nationalist ideal *(see* TAIRIKU RŌNIN). When he returned to Japan in 1901, he founded an extremist society, the Kokuryūkai (Black Dragon Society); after the Russo-Japanese War of 1904–05, he demanded that Korea be annexed. Until he died, he was a firm opponent of any attempt at liberalization.

Uchida Shungiku. Dancer, singer, and famous maker of *manga* (cartoons), born 1959 in Nagasaki. In 1984, she gained great popularity with her *manga* series *Shungiku* and with *Minami-kun,* the story of a girl named Chiyomi who was reduced to the size of a doll, which was on television. Uchida Shungiku published more than 60 works, among them translations of literary works, essays, and especially *manga.*

Uchida Tomu. Movie director (1898–1970), born in Okayama. At first a comic actor, he became Kurihara's assistant *(Thomas)* and directed silent films. He became famous for directing *Tsuchi* (The Earth, 1939), a realist film about poor peasants. After the Second World War (he was a prisoner in China until 1954), he worked for Tōei making soap operas. His most critically acclaimed film was *Kiga kaikyō* (The Strait of Hunger), made in 1965.

Uchigatana. Alternate name for the *katana* saber. Some *wakizashi* sabers are also called *uchigatana.* The *uchigatana* has the same features as the *katana* and uses the same kind of scabbard *(saya). See* KATANA, WAKIZASHI.

Uchigiki-shū. Collection of stories and Buddhist legends from Japan, China, and India, written by an unknown author, perhaps in the twelfth century. Only one part has been found.

Uchi-kake. Long overgarment (or coat) once worn by women over their kimonos. In the Heian period, a similar garment, called *uchiki,* was worn by ladies of the court over a red *hakama.*

Uchi-ko Naishinnō. A daughter (807–47) of Emperor Saga, and a talented writer and poet.

Uchimura Kanzō. Writer and Christian philosopher (1861–1930), born in Edo to a family of samurai. He studied at the Sapporo Agricultural College, where he met Nitobe Inazō, and they were baptized together. He then lived in the United States from 1884 to 1888; when he returned to Japan, he became editor of the newspaper *Yorozu Chōhō.* He founded a new church called Mukyōkai (Christianity "Without a Church") and started a magazine, *Seisho no Kenkyū* (Bible Studies), of which he was editor until his death. His many works include autobiographical books: *Kyūanroku* (Search for Peace, 1893), *Kirisuto shinto no nagusame* (Consolations of a Christian, 1893), and *How I Became a Christian* (1895). He wrote other works in English, including *Japan and the Japanese* (1894), and published another Christian magazine, *The Japan Christian Intelligence,* from 1926 to 1928. His es-

says are mainly sermons directed at his fellow believers. His son, Uchimura Yūshi (1898–1980), was a well-known psychiatrist who wrote a number of medical works.

Uchimura Naoya. Playwright (Sugawara Minoru, 1909–89), born in Tokyo; Kishida Kunio's disciple. He also worked for radio and television and wrote treatises on dramaturgy.

Uchi no Ō-ōmi. Ancient title equivalent to *naidajin* ("assistant" minister). Also called *uchi no otodo, naifu, naijin.*

Uchinoura. Village in Kagoshima prefecture (Kyushu), where a large satellite launch base was recently established, along with a technical university, the Daigaku Uchūkūkan Kenkyūsho. It is the seat of the University of Tokyo's Space Center. *Pop.:* 7,000.

Uchiri. Ancient woman's court costume, similar to the *hō* for men, but with long, wide sleeves. *See* SOKUTAI.

Uchiwa. Non-bending fan. May be in various shapes—round, oval, square—and is made of paper or silk glued onto fine blades of bamboo attached to a handle. Most *uchiwa* have poems written or painted on them and are now used as decoration. They were once used (as were *ōgi,* or folding fans) to present an object or a letter to a high-ranking person in a polite manner, and were most often used by women. They were also employed to fan embers. *See also* GUMPAI-UCHIWA, ŌGI, SHIBU-UCHIWA.

• **Uchiwa-daiko.** *See* TAIKO.

Uchū-kyōdan. Religious sect founded in Yokohama in 1946 by Sakai Akiko (b. 1907). *See* SHINRI-KYŌ.

Udagawa Genzui. Physician (Udagawa Genshin, Kai'en, 1755–97) and Confucian philosopher; Ōtsuki Gentaku's student. He introduced to Japan the use of internal medicines and wrote a treatise on this subject, *Seisetsu naika sen'yo* (1793), based on *Gezuiverde Geneeskonst,* published by the Dutchman Johannes de Gorter (1689–1762), in 1744.

• **Udagawa Shinsai.** Confucian scholar (1769–1834), Udagawa Genzui's son and a well-known physician.

• **Udagawa Yōan.** Physician (1798–1846), born in Gifū; Udagawa Shinsai's adoptive son. He studied

Dutch with Baba Sajūrō (1787–1822), as well as Latin, German, and English, and translated European books. He was particularly interested in botany and chemistry and wrote a number of works on these sciences, including *Botanika-kyō* (1922), *Shokubutsu keigen* (1834), and *Shami kaishū* (or *Seimi kaisō,* 1837); the latter was the first treatise on chemistry written in Japan, a translation of a work in English by William Henry.

Uda Tennō. Fifty-ninth emperor (Prince Sadayoshi, 867<887–97>931), Kōkō Tennō's seventh son and successor. He was a patron of Sugawara no Michizane and, on his advice, stopped sending official missions to China in 894. Opposed to the Fujiwara and wanting to reign in spite of them, he abdicated in favor of his son, Daigo, and became a Buddhist monk at the Ninna-ji temple, thus becoming the first of the "retired emperors" (*in, hō-ō; see* INSEI). His descendants constituted a branch of the Minamoto family known as Uda-Genji. He wrote, for Daigo, the *Kampyō goyuikai,* a group of precepts for governing; he also wrote his memoirs, *Kampyō gyoki* (also titled *Uda tennō gyoki),* of which only fragments have survived.

Udo. Archeological site 54 km south of Miyazaki (Kyushu), on the seashore, where Buddhist temples and altars are sculpted into a cliff. A natural cave serves as the main temple. It is painted red, and 300 steps cut into the rock lead to it. Date undetermined, perhaps fifteenth century.

• **Udo-jingū.** Shinto sanctuary in the village of Nichinan (Miyazaki-ken, Kyushu), dedicated to the memory of the father of mythical emperor Jimmu, Ugayafukiaezu no Mikoto; according to legend, he was born there. Founded in the seventh century, the Udo-jingū was transformed into a Buddhist temple, the Ninnō Gokoku-ji, but it was returned to Shinto and took back its original name in 1868. Festival on February 1.

Ueda Akinari. Writer (Ueda Tōsaku, 1734–1809), born in Osaka to an unknown father and adopted by a former samurai who had become a merchant. He married Otama, a servant of his adoptive father, and went into the family business in 1761, while writing haiku poems and stories in *ukiyo-zōshi* style. In 1766, he published two series of short stories with the publisher Hachimonjiya under the *gō* Wayaku Tarō: a group of satires on the *chōnin, Shodō kikimimi sekenzaru* (The Monkey Who Knew All the Arts); and *Seken tekake katagi* (Sketches of Mistresses). He then wrote *yomihon,*

including the famous *Ugetsu monogatari* (Tales of Rain and the Moon, 1776), dealing with supernatural events. After writing collections of *waka* poems, he studied medicine. His various essays were signed Muchō ("crab") because of a partial incapacity of his right hand, contracted in childhood following a bout of smallpox that was not properly treated.

In 1793, Ueda Akinari abandoned medicine and retired to Kyoto, still writing poems. He then started once again to write stories, such as the *Harusame monogatari* (Tales of Spring Rain, 1808, unfinished), and various essays: *Kinsa* (1804), on the poetry in the *Ise monogatari,* and *Tandai-shō-shin roku* (a sort of last testament, 1808), on literature in general. He also wrote a work on tea, *Seifū sagen* (Pure Air, Few Words, 1797), and a major collection of *waka, Tsuzura-bumi* (1806). He is famous for his dispute with Motoori Norinaga; he claimed, in opposition to Motoori, that Japan, being a small country, could not be the source of all civilizations.

Ueda Bin. Poet (1874–1916), born in Tokyo, known mainly for his many translations of French poetry (Verlaine, Baudelaire) and German and English poetry (*Keichōon,* 1905). He also published a novel, *Uzumaki* (1910), and a collection of his own poems, *Bokuyōshin* (1920).

Ueda Mannen. Linguist (Ueda Kazutoshi, 1867–1937), born in Tokyo. After studying in France and Germany from 1890 to 1894, he was a member of the national commission on reforming the language (Kokugo Shingitai). He wrote important works on Japanese linguistics: *Kokugo no tame* (For a Japanese Language, 1903); *Daijiten* (1917), a dictionary of kanji characters; and, in collaboration with Matsui Kanji, the famous *Dai Nihon kokugo jiten* (Dictionary of the Language of Greater Japan, 1919). Father of novelist Enchi Fumiko.

Uehara Yūsaku. General (1856–1933), born in Hyūga province to a family of samurai. After studying in France from 1881 to 1885, he served in both wars in which Japan was involved in the Meiji era, then was minister of the armed forces in 1912. Unable to expand the size of the military, he resigned, which led to the fall of Saionji Kimmochi's government.

Uejima Onitsura. *Haikai* poet (Uejima Munechika, 1661–1738), born in Settsu province; Nishiyama Sōin's disciple. His poems, such as *Taigo monogurui* (1690), are imbued with a sense of *makoto.* He also wrote essays (*Hirigoto,* 1685).

Ueki Emori. Politician (1857–92), son of a samurai in Tosa. He and Itagaki Taisuke became the theoreticians of the Jiyūtō (Liberal party), traveling throughout the country to promote the Freedom and People's Rights Movement (Jiyū Minken Undō). He was the first representative elected to the Diet in 1890.

Uemura Masahisa. Presbyterian pastor (1857–1925), born to a family of *hatamoto* samurai in Edo. He published several Christian magazines (he was baptized in 1873), including *Rikugo Zasshi* (Magazine of the Universe) and *Shinri Ippan* (On the Only Truth), and founded a church, the Fujimichō Kyōkai. He translated part of the Old Testament and helped found Meiji Gaku-in University. He also published some literary magazines, such as the *Nihon Hyōron,* and a weekly Christian magazine, *Fukuin Shimpō.* Uemura Tamaki's father.

• **Uemura Tamaki.** First woman pastor in Japan (1890–1982), Uemura Masahisa's daughter, born in Kyoto and educated in the United States. She taught at Tsuda College (Joshi Eiga Juku), then studied theology in Edinburgh before acquiring her own ministry at the Nihon Kirisuto Kyōkai (Christian Church of Japan, founded 1872).

Uemura Naomi. Mountain climber (1941–84), born in Hyōgo prefecture. He went down the Amazon by boat in 1968, then became known for his solo climbs of Kilimanjaro (1966), Aconcagua (1968), Mont Blanc, Elburz, and Mt. McKinley (1969). From 1974 to 1976, he crossed North America by dogsled from Greenland to Alaska (12,000 km) via the North Pole. He died while trying to climb Mt. McKinley a second time.

Uemura Shōen. Painter (Uemura Tsuneko, 1874–1949), born in Kyoto. She studied painting with Kono Bairei and, after 1895, with Takeuchi Seihō. Her works, in the Nihonga style, earned many prizes in various exhibitions, and she regularly participated in the Bunten starting in 1907, when the salon was inaugurated. Her paintings of women were particularly admired. She was elected a member of the Imperial Fine Arts Academy (Teikoku Bijutsu-in) in 1941, then appointed a Teishitsu Gigei-in (Artist for the Imperial House) in 1944. In 1947, she was the first woman decorated with the Order of Culture (Bunka-shō). Uemura Shōkō's mother.

• **Uemura Shōkō.** Painter (Uemura Shintarō), born 1902 in Kyoto, Uemura Shōen's son. He painted in the Nihonga style, had works in the Teiten and Bunten, and began to teach at the Kyoto Municipal College of Arts (Kyōto Shiritsu Bujutsu Daigaku) in 1953. His paintings of flowers and birds updated the Maruyama-Shijō style. He received many distinctions and, with other painters, founded several art associations. Member of the Japan Art Academy (Nihon Geijutsu-in) in 1981, he was decorated with the Order of Culture (Bunka-shō) in 1984. His son, Uemura Atsushi (b. 1933), more or less followed his style. Both painters had an exhibit at the Mitsukoshi space in Paris from December 1993 to February 1994.

Ueno. Town in Mie prefecture, former castle town of the Tōdō family in the seventeenth century, with ruins of the castle, built about 1570 and renovated in 1593. Birthplace of the poet Bashō. *Pop.:* 60,000.

• **Ueno Kōen.** District *(ku)* and park in Tokyo, opened in 1873; the Tokyo University of Arts and Music, the National Museum, the Tokyo Metropolitan Museum of Art, the Japan Art Academy (Nihon Geijutsu-in), the National Museum of Western Art, the National Science Museum, a zoo, and the Kan'ei-ji temple are located there. The modern buildings in this grouping were designed by Watanabe Hitoshi, Le Corbusier, Sakakura Junzō, and Maekawa Kunio. The zoo, the largest in Japan, was founded in 1882. The park also includes a number of attractions, and is a favorite place for Tokyo inhabitants to take a stroll. Its library is also famous. It was the center of fierce resistance by supporters of the shogunate against imperial troops on July 4, 1868, during which the Kan'ei-ji temple was destroyed (only a small pagoda remains).

Ueshiba Morihei. Athlete and philosopher (Ueshiba Moritaka, 1883–1969), born in Wakayama prefecture; a fervent practitioner of the martial arts. He was sent to Manchuria in 1904; when he returned to civilian life, in 1908, he opened a dojo. With a group of 84 peasants, he went to Hokkaido to found a village. In 1916, he was made a master of ju-jutsu by a famous fighter, Takeda Sōkaku (ca. 1860–1943). He became Deguchi Onisaburō's disciple and went to Mongolia with him; then, after having a vision, he "invented" the techniques of aikido, which he continued to develop, opening a sort of dojo-sanctuary in Tokyo, the Aiki-kai. The emperor decorated him in 1964. *See* AIKIDO.

Uesugi. Family of *shugo* in the Muromachi period, related to the Fujiwara, founded by Shigefusa (d.

1336), who received the Uesugi estate near Kyoto. Its members were appointed Kantō-kanrei and dominated Kanto in the fifteenth and sixteenth centuries. The family line went from Uesugi Norimasa (1523–75) to a warrior from another family, Nagao Kagetora, who took the name Uesugi Kagetora (1530–78), then the name Uesugi Kenshin. Because his adoptive son, Uesugi Kagekatsu, fought Tokugawa Ieyasu at the Battle of Sekigahara (1600), the family's estates were reduced and confined to Yonezawa in Mutsu province, northern Honshu. Among the most famous members of the family were Shigefusa (late thirteenth century), Norifusa (?–1335), Shigeyoshi (?–1349), Akiyoshi (?–1351), Yoshinori (?–1378), Noriharu (?–1379), Norikata (1335–94), Norimoto (1383–1418), Norizane (1410–66), Kiyokata (?–1442), Fusaaki (1432–66), Noritada (1433–54), Akisada (1454–1510), Norimasa (1522–79), Terutora (1530–78), Kagetora (1552–79), Kagekatsu (1555–1623), and Harunori (1751–1822).

• **Uesugi Akiyoshi.** Warrior (?–1351), Uesugi Shigeyoshi's son. He killed Kō Moronao to avenge his father's death and was sent into exile.

• **Uesugi Harunori.** Daimyo (Uesugi Yōzan, 1751–1822) of Yonezawa, in Mutsu, son of a daimyo from Akizuki (Miyazaki-ken), adopted by the Uesugi family; he became daimyo in 1767. He was noted for his excellent administration of the estate, which, due to the measures he took, did not suffer from the famine of the Temmei era.

• **Uesugi Kagekatsu.** Uesugi Kenshin's adoptive son (Nagao Kagekatsu, 1555–1623). He battled against another adoptive son, Uesugi Kagetora, and forced him to commit suicide in 1579, thus taking over the family. He fought Oda Nobunaga, but allied himself with Toyotomi Hideyoshi and received a huge estate in Echigo province (550,000 *koku*). After taking part in all of Hideyoshi's battles and fighting in Korea, he was rewarded with an estate in Wakamatsu (Dewa) with a revenue of 1.2 million *koku,* and was appointed *tairō.* But because he opposed Tokugawa Ieyasu in the Battle of Sekigahara in 1600, his fiefs were confiscated and he had to content himself with the one in Yonezawa, Mutsu province, with a revenue of only about 300,000 *koku.* He nevertheless took part in the attack on the Osaka castle at Ieyasu's side in 1614.

• **Uesugi Kenshin.** *See* UESUGI TERUTORA.

• **Uesugi Kiyoko.** *See* UESUGI NORIFUSA.

• **Uesugi Kiyotaka.** *See* UESUGI NORIZANE.

• **Uesugi Norifusa.** *Shugo* (?–1336), Uesugi Shigafusa's grandson, who served Ashikaga Takauji. His sister, Uesugi Kiyoko, married Ashikaga Sadauji; her sons were Ashikaga Takauji and Ashikaga Tadayoshi. Norifusa was killed during the Battle of Kyoto between the shogunate and supporters of the Southern Court (Nanchō).

• **Uesugi Norizane.** *Shugo* (1410–66) of Awa province, appointed Kantō-kanrei in 1419 as assistant to Ashikaga Mochiuji (1398–1439), then Kamakura-kubō. When Mochiuji rebelled against the shogunate, Norizane took refuge in Kōzuke province; he returned to Kamakura in 1439, after Mochiuji was defeated and forced to commit suicide. But he soon abandoned his position, leaving it to his brother, Uesugi Kiyotaka, and became a Buddhist monk. He had generously sponsored the Ashikaga Gakkō and expanded its library.

• **Uesugi Shigefusa.** Warrior (late thirteenth century) of the Fujiwara family. Having received the Uesugi estate near Kyoto, he created his own family with the family name Uesugi.

• **Uesugi Shigeyoshi.** Warrior (?–1349), Uesugi Norifusa's adoptive son. He was defeated by Kō Moronao, who had him assassinated.

• **Uesugi Terutora.** Daimyo (Nagao Sarumatsumaru, Nagao Terutora, Uesugi Kenshin, 1530–78), son of a vassal of the Uesugi family, Nagao Tamekage (?–1537). Nagao Terutora disputed the succession from his father to his older brother, Nagao Harukage (d. 1553), and took the name and leadership of his family. In 1549, Terutora became lord of the Kasugayama castle, in the town of Takada. Uesugi Norimasa adopted him in 1561 and gave him his title of Kantō-kanrei. He fought Takeda Shingen, then daimyo of Kai, for possession of Kanto, then the Hōjō of clan Odawara and Oda Nobunaga, but without great success. In 1571, he became a Buddhist monk. As he was about to launch a massive attack on Oda Nobunaga, he died. His two sons, Uesugi Kagekatsu and Uesugi Kagetora, fought over his inheritance, but Kagetora committed suicide in 1579 and Kagekatsu was alone at the helm of the Uesugi family. Uesugi Terutora, a monk under the names Kenshin and Shūshinbō, received the *posthumous name* Shinkō.

- **Uesugi Tomomune.** Warrior and statesman (1339–1414), minister for Ashikaga Ujimitsu. He became a Buddhist monk with the name Jōsho.

- **Uesugi Zenshū no Ran.** Rebellion led by Uesugi Zenshū (Uesugi Ujinori) in 1416–17 against Ashikaga Mochiuji, then Kamakura-kubō, who had replaced him as Kantō-kanrei with one of his close friends. Zenshū ejected Mochiuji from Kamakura, but was defeated by the troops of the Muromachi shogunate and committed suicide.

Ugajin. Ancient divinity of water, portrayed as a large white snake, companion to Benten-sama (Benzai-ten). It sometimes takes the form of an old man around which a white serpent called Hakuja is coiled. *See* BENZAI-TEN.

Ugaki Issei. General (Ugaki Kazushige, 1868–1956), born in Okayama prefecture. He was vice-minister of the armed forces under Tanaka Giichi in 1923, then minister of the armed forces under Kiyoura Keigo, Katō Takaaki, and Wakatsuki Reijirō, and then under Hamaguchi Osachi. In 1927, then from 1932 to 1936, he was governor-general of Korea. Appointed prime minister in 1937, he was unable to form a cabinet and resigned in favor of Konoe Fumimaro, returning to the position of minister of the armed forces; he resigned four months later, when his plan for peace with the Chinese Nationalist government failed.

Ugamisā. On Okinawa (Ryukyu), a term for shamans and medicine men.

Ugetsu monogatari. "Tales of Rain and the Moon." A collection of fantasy stories published by Ueda Akinari in 1776, which started the series of works in the *yomihon* genre. It was adapted to the screen in 1953 by Mizoguchi Kenji. *See* UEDA AKINARI.

Ugo. Former province, now included in Akita prefecture (Honshu).

Uguisu-bari. "Nightingale floors," parquet floors on the outside galleries of houses belonging to nobles and samurai, made so that they creaked when people walked on them, thus informing the residents of the presence of an intruder. These types of floors are still found at the Nijō-jō, the Nijō Jin'ya, and the Chion-in, in Kyoto. *See* HIDARI JINGORŌ.

- *Uguisu no ichimon.* *See* MIRUNA NO ZASHIKI.

- **Uguisu-zuka.** *See* WAKAKUSAYAMA.

Uhō Dōji. Shinto *kami (gongen),* said to have the power to fend off bad luck, perhaps a form of Vairochana (Dainichi Nyorai) or Marīchī (Marishiten). It is (very rarely) portrayed as a noble with a small pagoda on his head and a white *tanuki* lying at his feet.

Uijin. Former title of officers of the Imperial Guard.

Uji. City in Kyoto prefecture, on the Uji-gawa river, site of the Byōdō-in temple. The region is famous for the quality of its tea. It also has synthetic textile plants. The Ujibashi bridge over the river, built by Dōchō in 647 and rebuilt in the ninth century (it is now made of cement), was the site of a number of battles because it was the only route from Kyoto to the east. Near the bridge, within the walls of the Hashi-dera temple ("temple of the bridge"), a ninth-century stone monument commemorates its reconstruction. *Pop.:* 160,000.

- **Uji Dainagon.** *See* TOBA SŌJŌ.

- *Uji Dainagon monogatari.* "Account of the Uji State Counselor," a title sometimes used for the *Konjaku monogatari.*

Uji. Before the Nara period, "extended" family groups (including servants) constituting a "family line" similar to a clan. These groups succeeded the older *ujizoku,* which included only families in the direct family line. They were led by an *uji no kami,* their members were called *ujibito,* and those who served them generally constituted *be* (or *kahibe).* The *uji no kami* were responsible for honoring the family's tutelary *kami,* the *ujigami.* From the Yamato court they received hereditary titles *(kabane),* which later became family names. Before the Taika Reform (645), the *uji* (also called *shisei)* system affected the entire organization of the state of Yamato.

- **Ujidera.** Family temple belonging to a clan *(uji).*

- **Ujigami.** Tutelary *kami* of an *uji,* or family clan. Also, title of the leader of an *uji,* also called *uji no kami.*

- **Ujiko.** Followers (parishioners) of a Shinto shrine. Also, a synonym for *ujibito (see* UJI).

Uji Kaganojō. Playwright (Uji Kadayū, 1635–1711), a famous *jōruri* narrator, and Kabuki actor. He worked with Chikamatsu Monzaemon.

Uji no Waki-iratsuko. Emperor Ōjin's son (?–ca. 312) and Nintoku Tennō's brother. He is said to have committed suicide to enable his younger brother to ascend to the throne.

Ujishima Noriyuki. Painter in the Western style, born 1900 in Kumamoto prefecture (Kyushu). He was a member of several artists' groups but left them to work alone, painting simple landscapes with a poetic touch. Member of the Academy of Arts (Bijutsu-in) in 1981; decorated with the Order of Culture (Bunka-shō) in 1983.

Ujishūi monogatari. Collection of tales by an anonymous author (generally attributed, but without certainty, to Minamoto no Takakuni), compiled about 1215. Of its 197 stories, 80 seem to have been taken from the *Konjaku monogatari*. The title of this work is not clear, and a precise translation is not possible, nor has its relationship with the *Konjaku monogatari* been clarified. It is nevertheless a valuable work for its information on the life of commoners in the late Heian period.

Ukei. In Shinto, a vow made by a follower to lead a life of purity of spirit and body, and to make "efforts" *(shoshin)* in this direction.

Ukemi. In martial arts, the art of falling without injuring oneself. With training, one could fall on one's back *(ma-ukemi)*, side *(yoko-ukemi)*, or front *(zempo-ukemi)*.

Uki-e. "Image in relief," a type of ukiyo-e print in which the painter uses the laws of Western perspective.

Ukifune. Title of a Noh play: a woman tells a Buddhist monk the story of a girl called Ukifune who drowned herself in despair because she was unable to choose between two suitors. The monk then meets Ukifune in a village. She tells him how she was saved from death and why she now lives in this isolated place.

Ukigumo. "Floating Couds." A novel written by Futabatei Shimei in 1877, in spoken style, inspired by European novels. It was the precursor of realistic dialogue in Japan.

• Title of a novel by Hayashi Fumio written in 1947.

Ukita Hideie. Daimyo (1573–1655) of Okayama, Bizen province; Ukita Naoie's son. He became Toyotomi Hideyoshi's favorite and married Gō-hime (1574–1634), Maeda Toshiie's daughter, who had been adopted by Hideyoshi. He seconded Hideyoshi in all his campaigns and was general-in-chief *(gensui)* in Korea; Hideyoshi appointed him *tairō* to protect Toyotomi Hideyori (*see* GO-TAIRŌ). He fought Tokugawa Ieyasu at the Battle of Sekigahara in 1600 but was defeated, lost his estates, and fled to Satsuma. In 1603, the Shimazu clan of Satsuma delivered him to Ieyasu, who sent him into exile on Hachijōjima in 1606. He then became a Buddhist monk with the name Raifu.

• **Ukita Ikkei.** *See* IKKEI.

• **Ukita Naoie.** Daimyo (1529–92) of Bitchū province; Ukita Hideie's father.

Ukiyaku. "Fluctuating tax"; in the Edo period, a surtax collected in cash, depending on the shogunate's needs; it could vary over time, by amount, and on the products on which it was charged. Also called *ukimononari, jōmonari*. It was sometimes included in the *komononari (see this entry)*.

Ukiyo-e. "Images of the Floating World," a style of woodblock prints printed on various formats of paper, sold at a low price and reflecting the tastes of the *chōnin* of the Edo period. These prints, which were also used to illustrate books, were invented by Iwasa Matabei in the early seventeenth century. They were sometimes produced in very large print runs.

Some *ukiyo-e* were not prints but painted works, called *nikuhitsu ukiyo-e* (for example, by Miyagawa Chōshun and Kaigetsudo Ando), but these were the exception. The most frequent subjects of *ukiyo-e* prints were portraits (full figure or busts) of beautiful women *(bijin)*, courtesans (who often served as fashion models for *kimono*), Kabuki actors (in regular clothes or costume), and sumo wrestlers. Some painters (including Hiroshige) also produced landscapes, scenes of rural and urban life, and, in the early nineteenth century, pictures of foreigners, in Japan or an imaginary site. Many artists also made "parody" prints *(mitate-e)* in which they took up old literary themes and transposed facts and characters into the styles of their own era. Some eighteenth-century painters made remarkable images of birds, insects, and flowers. In the late nineteenth and early twentieth centuries, many artists made prints of war scenes (in China or against Russia) on sea and land that are magnificent testimonials to military conditions at the time. At first, artists restricted themselves to a relatively short list of subjects, but by the mid-nineteenth century, all subjects were fair game.

The technique was simple. A drawing made on rice paper was glued to the back of a wooden plank (usually cherry wood), then the engraver cut the wood following the drawing. The woodblock was inked using a pad *(baren),* then a sheet of paper was applied and pressed more or less firmly, depending on the desired effect. For images with several colors, a separate woodblock was used for each color, and the paper was positioned accurately thanks to registration marks *(kentō)* on the woodblocks.

Paper formats differed. At first, a large sheet *(ō-ōban)* was divided into several pieces along its length, which provided the *hosoban* format (about 33 × 15 cm). Later, another "large sheet" (53 × 39 cm) was divided in half, giving the most commonly used format, *ōban* (39 × 26.5 cm). Other formats were also used, always based on geometric divisions of the large sheet: *chūban* (26.5 × 19 cm), *ōtanzaku* (39 × 17.5 cm), *chūtanzaku* (39 × 12 cm), and so on. Some artists preferred different formats, such as the *aiban* (33 × 22.7 cm), the *hashira-e* (69/75 × 12/13 cm), the *kakemono-e* (58.4 × 30.4 cm), the *chō-ōban* (52 × 18 cm), the *koban* (23 × 16.5 cm), and so on. These formats were used in "portrait" *(tate-e)* or "landscape" *(yoko-e)* mode.

Printing techniques changed over the years. The oldest, using black only, were called *sumizuri-e;* then came *benizuri-e* with touches of red applied by hand, *tan-e* (with orange highlights), *urushi-e* (with bright, thick inks), *benizuri-e* with touches of red and green, *nishiki-e* (several colors), *murasaki-e* (in purple tones), *aizuri-e* (in indigo monochrome), and others.

Some prints included a poem or a title, in a box or not. They bore the signature of the artist followed by the character *ga* ("painted by") or *hitsu* ("from the brush of"), and sometimes one or several vermilion or black stamps—those of the artist and the publisher (sometimes with a date). Like all publications, *ukiyo-e* prints were subject to censorship and had to bear an official censor's stamp *(kiwami).* After 1840, another censorship stamp, called *aratame* ("approved"), was also placed on prints. Later, collectors' or merchants' stamps were often added.

Ukiyo-e prints were "discovered" by Europeans (such as Titsingh) in 1827. Félix Bracquemont, a French designer, and Théodore Duret circulated them widely among European artists, and they were exhibited for an art-loving public at the world fairs in London in 1862 and Paris in 1867. They had a very enthusiastic reception and gave rise to an art movement called "Japanism" that influenced painters such as Cassatt, Monet, Toulouse-Lautrec, Degas, and Van Gogh, and writers such as the Goncourt brothers and Zola. Art galleries and collectors eagerly sought out the prints. This fashion rebounded to Japan, where the genre had been somewhat scorned by the aristocracy, and the prints were studied and had a major influence on "Japanese" style painting (Nihonga). After the Meiji period, increasing numbers of artists, including Itō Shinsui (1898–1972), updated the genre by producing modern *ukiyo-e* prints. Among the most famous *ukiyo-e* artists were Kiyonaga, Moronobu, Utamaro, Hokusai, Hiroshige, Ichō, Eisen, Eishi, and Sharaku. These painters belonged to various schools (Hishikawa, Kaigetsudō, Torii, Katagawa, etc.), named after their founders or styles, and worked mainly in Edo (Tokyo), Osaka, and Nagasaki. *See* ABUNA-E.

• *Ukiyo-gata rokumai byōbu.* "Six-Panel Screen, Floating Like the World." A six-volume novel by Ryūtei Tanehiko (1821), illustrated with *ukiyo-e* prints by Utagawa Toyokuni (1769–1825).

• **Ukiyo-ningyō.** Dolls made in Edo in the late Edo period, in a very elaborate style, usually portraying beautiful women in formal costume.

• **Ukiyo-zōshi.** "Books of the Floating World," the term for a genre of popular novels published in Edo and Osaka between 1680 and 1770. Its prototype was *Kōshoku ichidai onna,* by Ihara Saikaku, although this type of work was considered a *kana-zōshi* until about 1710. After 1700, most *ukiyo-zōshi* novels were published in Kyoto and called Hachimonjiya-bon, for the name of their main publisher, Hachimonjiya. They often depicted the amorous tribulations of men and women, although they could not be labeled erotic. *Ukiyo-zōshi* stopped being published after 1766, because the main authors of these novels, Eijima Kiseki and the publisher Hachimonjiya Jishō, had died.

Umabari. Small knife with a straight, two-sided blade, sometimes included with the *kogai* and *kozuka* on the scabbard *(saya)* of a *katana* sword. *See* KŌGAI.

Uma-jirushi. Banners used in the sixteenth century by warriors to signal their position to the troops they commanded during a battle. They were carried by samurai on horseback or held in reserve by foot soldiers *(ashigaru)*. *See* ŌGI.

Uma no Naishi. Poet (eleventh century), Akazome Emon's sister and lady-in-waiting to Empress Jōtō Mon'in. She was one of the Chūko no Sanjū-rokkasen.

Umaya. "Relay of (post) horses." Also called *eki, ekiya*.

Umban. Wooden stick used by some Zen monks during *zazen* sessions to awaken, with a blow to the shoulder, monks who tended to fall asleep, and to announce to them that it was time for meals.
• Round metal gong hung from a single point, sometimes used in *mikkyō* (esoteric) ceremonies and rites.

Umeboshi. A type of *tsukemono*, made of sun-dried prunes *(ume)* with *chisō* leaves. It has fungicidal properties and aids digestion. It is a very popular food among Japanese, but Westerners find it unappetizing because of its pronounced acidity. *Umeboshi* often accompany rice-based dishes such as *onigiri* (pressed-rice balls). *See* PICKLES, TSUKEMONO.

Umeda Haruo. Writer (1920–80) who translated Eugène Labiche's plays. In 1949, he received the Minakami Takitarō Prize for his novel *Gogatsu no hana* (May Flowers). Among his other novels are *Michinaru mono* (The Unknown) and *Haha no shōzō* (Portrait of My Mother).

Umeda Umpin (Umbin). Samurai and Confucian scholar (Umeda Genjirō, 1815–59) who opened a school in Kyoto. Having joined the *sonnō jōi* movement with Yanagawa Seigan and Rai Mikasaburō, Rai San'yo's son, he was arrested by the shogunate in 1852 and stripped of his samurai status. He nevertheless continued his pro-imperial activities; he was arrested a second time during the "purge" of the Ansei era (*see* ANSEI NO TAIGOKU) and sentenced to death.

Umehara Ryūzaburō. Painter (1888–1986) in the Western style, born in Kyoto. In 1908, he went to France, where he studied in Paris at the Académie Julian and in Cagne with Renoir. When he returned to Japan in 1913, he had an exhibit that caused a sensation and helped found the Nika-kai painters' group. He went back to France in 1920 and lived there for one year. He was appointed an Artist for the Imperial Household (Teishitsu Gigei-in) in 1944, and a professor at the Tokyo School of Fine Arts (Tokyo Bijutsu Gakkō); decorated with the Order of Culture (Bunka-shō) in 1952. His paintings are characterized by a very rich palette, thanks to a careful mixture of traditional Japanese pigments and Western oil paints. After the Second World War, he went to Europe several times, where he painted mainly landscapes in Cannes and Venice.

Umehara Sueji. Archeologist (1893–1983), born in Osaka. In 1921, he was a member of a commission examining archeological sites in Korea; he then went to Europe, where he studied from 1923 to 1929. He became an archeology professor at the University of Kyoto, his alma mater, in 1939. Umehara's most important work concerns Japanese *kofun* and Korean tombs; his studies on bronze mirrors from the *kofun* period (fourth–seventh century) are still authoritative.

Ume Kenjirō. Jurist (1860–1910), born in Matsue (Shimane prefecture). A professor at the University of Kyoto, he studied in Lyon and Berlin, returning to Japan in 1890. He was one of the principal compilers of the Japanese civil code, promulgated in 1898 (revised in 1947, it is still in use). He also prepared the Japanese commercial code, which came into effect in 1899 and is still in use. His main work, the five-volume *Mimpō yōgi* (Compendium of Civil Laws), published from 1896 to 1900, is still the reference on the subject. Among his other works are *Shōhō-gikei* and *Mimpō-genri*. He founded Hōsei University.

Umesao Tadao. Writer and ethnologist (b. 1920), director of the National Ethnography Museum in Osaka. A political adviser in foreign affairs, he wrote a very interesting work, *Le Japon à l'ère planétaire* (Japan in the Global Era).

Umetada. Family of blacksmiths whose members were famous for their *tsuba* and sword accessories from the fifteenth to the nineteenth century. It was founded by Umetada Ninju, who was the first to decorate *tsuba* using alloys of various colors. *See* MYŌJU SHIGEYOSHI.

Umewaka Rokurō. Noh actor (1908–79) of the Kanze school, specializing in *shite* roles. He was named a Living National Treasure.

Umezaki Haruo. Writer (1915–65), born in Fukuoka. He became known after the Second World War for his war stories, such as *Sakurajima* (1946) and *Hi no hate* (Day's End, 1948), then for somewhat satirical stories, such as *Boroya no shunju,* which won the Naoki Prize in 1954. His novels, in contrast, were partly autobiographical: *Kuruidako* (1963), *Genka* (1965).

Umezawa Hamao. Microbiologist (1914–86), born in Fukui prefecture, internationally known for his contributions to the development of many types of antibiotics. A professor at the University of Tokyo, he received the Order of Culture (Bunka-shō) in 1962.

Umezu Masagake. Samurai (1581–1633) of the Akita estate in Dewa province, serving the Satake family. He was controller-general of mines and *kanjō-bugyō* (commissioner of finances). He wrote a journal, the *Umezu masakage nikki,* that is an unequaled source of information on administration of *han* (provincial estates) in the early Edo period.

Umezu Yoshijirō. General (1882–1949), born near Ōita (Kyushu). He commanded the Japanese forces at Tianjin, China, in 1935 and the Guandong army in 1940. In 1944, he succeeded General Sugiyama Hajime as chief of general quarters, and in this capacity signed the surrender of Japan's armed forces on the *Missouri* on September 2, 1945. Found guilty of war crimes, he was sentenced to prison in 1947. *See also* SHIGEMITSU MAMORU.

Umi-bōzu. "Monk of the Sea," a storm demon feared by sailors, portrayed as a Buddhist monk dressed entirely in black, with a shaved head. Sometimes merged with Shōjō.

Umpo. Painter (Ryōin; *gō:* Umposai, fifteenth century) of the Muromachi *suiboku* school, Shūbun's student. Nothing is known about his life.

• **Umpō.** Painter (Ōoka Seikan, Ōoka Jihei; *azana:* Kōritsu, 1765–1848) of the Nanga (Bunjinga) school in Edo; Fuyō's student.

Unchiki. Painter (Hayashi Kan, Hayashi Hachirōemon; *gō:* Kitamuki Unchiko, Keiō, Gyokurandō, Taikyoan, Unchiku, 1632–1703) of the Nanga (Bunjinga) school in Kyoto. He painted mainly bamboo.

Unebi-yama. Hill in Yamato, 199 m high, where, according to tradition, Jimmu Tennō lived and was buried. A Shinto shrine, the Kashiwabara-jingū, was built on its peak in his honor in 1889. Nearby are tombs supposedly belonging to emperors Annei and Itoku. Also called Jimyō-ji San.

Uneme. In ancient Japan, servants of the emperor chosen from among the daughters and sisters of the Kuni no Miyatsuko, and kept as hostages so that their parents would not revolt. Having *uneme* became an official prerogative of emperors after the Taika Reform (645), and the servants (or ladies-in-waiting) of the emperor and empress continued to be chosen from noble families. This custom continued until 1868.

UNESCO. Japan was admitted into UNESCO in 1951. It is represented at the head office in Paris by a national commission charged with coordinating activities of nongovernmental organizations affiliated with UNESCO, and working in Japan in many cultural and scientific domains. Japan's financial contribution to UNESCO is currently the second largest. A "UNESCO village" has been established in Tokorozawa (Saitama prefecture).

Uniforms (seifuku). The Japanese have always been attracted to uniforms, which distinguish one group from another and thus provide a sense of belonging to a specific group. *Seifuku* were first used when Shōtoku Taishi promulgated a law (604) regulating the hats and colors of the 12 court ranks that he instituted (*see* I). Later, special clothes were used on many occasions, especially official ceremonies. In the modern era, at the same time as uniforms were adopted by the military, standardized clothing was assigned to students in schools and colleges, copied from uniforms worn by German students in the late nineteenth century. Each profession then created its own uniform in Western style, from plant workers (who derive a sense of solidarity from them) to employees in stores, banks, and other types of firms.

Unions. There are a great many labor unions in Japan (more than 70,000 unions with a total membership of about 12.5 million workers). They are grouped into large federations, but their usefulness is often disputed. A company usually has its own union, whose role is to see to the well-being of workers; these unions are affiliated with one or another of the big union federations, such as Sōhyō and Dōmei. *See also* JICHIRŌ, KEIDAN-REN, NIKKEI-REN, SŌDŌMEI, SUZUKI BUNUI, YŪAIKAI.

United Nations. Japan was admitted into the United Nations on December 18, 1956. It had been seeking membership since 1952, but the USSR used its veto then, and again in 1955. Following a joint declaration by the USSR and Japan, the veto was lifted and Japan was admitted. It has a permanent bureau at the headquarters of the United Nations in New York, and a permanent delegation at the Geneva quarters. The Japanese name for the organization is Kokuren or Kokusai-rengō.

Universities. *See* DAIGAKU, EDUCATION, TEIKOKU DAIGAKU.

University degrees (gakui). Since the reform of the educational system (1953), there have been only two degrees recognized in Japan: the master's degree *(shūshi),* and the doctorate *(hakushi).* The level corresponding to a Western bachelor's degree, called *gakushi* (in reality, a diploma for completion of secondary school), is more a title than a true degree. *See* EDUCATION.

Unkei. Sculptor (ca. 1148–1223) of Buddhist images, Kōkei's son and Tankei's father; all of them were sculptors of the Kei school. Unkei worked at the Kōfuku-ji temple in Nara, producing vigorous, realistic works. He received the titles Hō-in and Bitchū-in.
• Painter (fifteenth–sixteenth century) of the Muromachi *suiboku* school. He was a Zen Buddhist monk.
→ *See* DONKYŌ.

Unken. Painting technique originally from China, used mainly during the Nara period, consisting of portraying the contours of figures in tinted colors. In the Heian period, this technique was taken up by fabric designers. Also called *ungen.*

Unkoku-ha. School of painting founded by Unkoku Tōgan (*see* TŌGAN), claiming to represent the art of Sesshū Tōyō (1420–1506) in the Chinese *suiboku* style of the Muromachi period. The best-known artists of this school (also called Unkoku-ryū), apart from Unkoku Tōgan, are his son, Unkoku Tōeki (1591–1644); Unkoku Tōoku (?–ca. 1615), few of whose works are known; and Unkoku Tōhan. *See* TŌEKI, TŌHAN.

Uno Chiyo. Novelist (1897–1996), born in Yamaguchi prefecture. She lived with the writer Ozaki Shirō, then with the painter Tōgō Seiji (1897–1978), and her second marriage was to the writer Kitahara Takeo. Her works, mainly autobiographical, are interesting for their views on female psychology; *Ohan* (1957) and *Aru hitori no onna hanashi* (Story of a Woman, 1971) are her best-known novels.

Uno Kōji. Writer (Uno Kakujirō, 1891–1961), born in Fukuoka. He wrote many stories for various newspapers, mainly the *Chūō Kōron,* in the naturalist style and on personal subjects. His most popular novels were written after the Second World War: *Omoigawa* (The River of Love, 1948), which won the *Yomiuri* Prize in 1951, and *Ku no sekai* (The World of the Conquered, 1949). He also wrote a biography of his friend Akutagawa Ryūnosuke in 1953.

Unō Sōsuke. Contemporary politician, leader of the Jiyū Minshutō (Liberal Democratic party, LDP); he succeeded Takeshita Noboru as prime minister on June 2, 1989.

Unrin-in. Title of a Noh play: to obey a dream, a man goes to the Unrin-in temple, where he meets a woman. The ghost of the poet Ariwara no Narihisa then appears in the middle of flowering cherry trees.

Unshitsu. Painter (Kōzan, Ryōki; *azana:* Gengi, Kōhan, Sekisō, Taishū Sanjin, 1753–1827) of the Nanga (Bunjinga) school in Edo; also, poet and Buddhist monk, abbot of the Kōmyō-ji temple starting in 1792. He painted landscapes in the style of the Chinese painter Yi Fujiu (*Jap.:* I Fukyū) and wrote some works on painting, *Sōshi gaden, Sansui-chō,* and *Unshitsu zuihitsu.* His style was followed by many other painters, all of whose names began with Un:

• **Un'en.** Painter (Anzai Oto, Anzai Toraki-chi; *azana:* San'un; *gō:* Shūsetsu, Un'en, d. 1852); author of *Kinsei shiga-dan,* a work on modern painting.

• **Unpō.** *See* UMPŌ.

• **Unsho.** Painter (Maita Ryō; *azana:* Kōhitsu; *gō:* Unsho, 1812–65) of bamboo.

- **Untan.** Painter (Kaburagi Shōin; *azana:* San-kitsu; *gō:* Shōsasei, Untan, 1782–1852) of land-scapes, Bunchō's student.

- **Unzan.** Painter (Yamazaki Ryūkichi; *azana:* Gensho; *gō:* Bunken, Unzan, 1761–1837) of land-scapes.

- **Unzen.** Painter (Kushiro Shū; *mei:* Bumpei; *azana:* Chūfu; *gō:* Rikuseki, Rairakuji, Unzen, 1759–1811) of landscapes.

Urabe. Guild *(be)* of soothsayers. *See* DIVINATION.

Urabe Kanefumi. Writer and historian (thirteenth century), author of the oldest known commentary on the *Kojiki,* the *Kojiki uragaki,* in 1273. His son, Urabe no Kanekata, followed in his footsteps, writ-ing a commentary on the *Nihongi,* the *Shaku Nihongi.*

- **Urabe Kananao.** Historian (fourteenth century) serving Emperor Go-Daigo; author of *Shintō taii.*

- **Urabe Kaneyoshi, Urabe Kenkō.** *See* KENKŌ HŌSHI.

- **Urabe Yoshida.** Shinto priest (Urabe Kanetomo, 1435–1511), founder of Yoshida Shintō (sometimes called Urabe Shintō), which became the official sect of the Tokugawa family. He wrote the text summa-rizing its doctrine, *Yui-itsu shintō myōba yōshu. See* YOSHIDA SHINTŌ.

Urabon-e. "Celebration of the Souls," a Buddhist festival in honor of souls of the departed that takes place every July 13–15. Introduced from China to the imperial court in 657, Urabon-e was spread among commoners about the tenth century with sermons by monks of the Jōdo-shū. Its origins are in the Indian ceremony and legend of *Ullambana.* Fol-lowers believe that during these three days, the souls (or spirits) of the deceased return to Earth to share life and meals with their families. Lamps are placed on roads leading from cemeteries to houses to show the souls the route to take, and a place and food are set at the family table so that they can rest and eat. On these days, people visit cemeteries and put flowers and water on the tombs, which are cleaned and repaired if necessary. On the evening of July 15, small boats made of paper and bamboo carrying lights are floated in rivers or the sea to wish farewell to the souls that are returning to the Here-

after. In villages, Bon Odori dances are organized. The rites differ by region. Also called Bon, O-Bon.

Uraga. Sea port about 10 km southeast of Yoko-suka (Kanagawa prefecture) at the entrance to To-kyo Bay. In the Edo period, a commissioner (Uraga-*bugyō*) was stationed there to survey the entrance to the bay. It was here (specifically at the place called Kurihama) that Commodore Perry, after crossing Uraga Strait (Uraga-suidō), dropped anchor on July 8, 1853. Uraga has one of the largest shipyards in Japan.

Uragami. In the Muromachi period, a family of *shugo* serving the Akamatsu family in Harima prov-ince. After the Ōnin War (1467–77), Uragami Muramune (?–1531) assassinated Akamatsu Yoshi-mura and thus became daimyo of Harima, Bizen, and Mimasaka. The family was decimated in 1561 by one of its vassals, Ukita Naoie (1529–81).

- **Uragami Gyokudō.** *See* GYOKUDŌ.

- **Uragami Hitsu.** *See* GYOKUDŌ.

- **Uragami Ken.** *See* SHUNKIN.

Urahaku. Technique of painting on gold leaf, using silk gauze as a screen.

Uranai. Soothsaying techniques of Chinese origin, used by various shamans, *miko,* and *eki.* Also called Eikishia, and Uranaisā in Okinawa. *See* DIVINA-TION.

Urashima Tarō. Legendary character, originating in the *Nihon shoki,* who was said to have married the female *kami* of water, Oto-hime, in 478. He saved Oto-hime when she was resting on a beach in the form of a turtle. Transforming herself into a rav-ishing young woman, she took him to her father's underwater palace, where she married him. After three years of happiness, he wanted to return to land. Oto-hime let him go, but gave him a box con-taining the years of his life. When he returned home, Urashima Tarō could not keep himself from open-ing the box. His years quickly fled, and he died in-stantly of old age. In some versions of this tale, Urashima Tarō is called Shima no Ko or Urashima no Ko. It is a Japanese version of "Rip van Winkle," and its adventures were the subject of a Noh play called *Urashima* and many *otogi-zōshi* tales. *See also* TOKOYO.

Urasoe. Town on Okinawa (Ryukyu), capital of the island from the twelfth to the fourteenth century. Tombs of several kings of the Ryukyu Islands are on the site of the former castle. Automobile plants. *Pop.:* 70,000.

Urayama Kirio. Director (1930–85), maker of many movies dealing with social problems, some of which earned prestigious prizes in Japan and at the Moscow Festival (*Hikō shōjo,* "The Delinquent Girl"). He made his last film, *Yumechiyo nikki* (Yumechiyo's Diary), in 1985.

Uriko-hime. "The Melon-Princess." A folk tale similar to that of Momo-tarō, but in which the peach is replaced by a melon and the boy by a girl. She grows more and more beautiful and is betrothed to a prince but, on the wedding day, the demon Amanojaku tries to take his place. The scheme is discovered by a sparrow.

Uroko-gata. Noh play: the Shinto-Buddhist divinity Benten-sama (Benzai-ten) gives a pennant to a warrior who has come to worship him in his shrine on the island of Enoshima.

Urushi. Term for lacquer, material obtained by drying the sap of a type of tree, *Rhus vernicifera* (*urushi no ki,* sumac). Objects made or decorated with lacquer are called *shikki, urushi no mono, nurimono.* Various manufacturing techniques are used, including *nashiji* (pear skin), *fundame* (sprinkled with gold or silver), *tokidashi* (with designs in gold or silver), *maki-e* (in relief), *taka maki-e* (in high relief), *hira maki-e* (in bas relief), *rō-iro* (black and polished to a mirror finish), *chinkin-bori* (engraved), *kirikane* (decorated with small leaves of gold or silver), and *raden* (with various inlays). *Chin.: qishu.*

• **Urushi-e.** Monochrome (or in two or three colors) paintings made mainly during the Nara period. In the Edo period, the number of colors grew, and painters sometimes used them for their brightness, sometimes imitating lacquer. Pigments used were sometimes mixed with real lacquer.
  • Printing technique for ukiyo-e prints, similar to the *beni-e* technique but using bright inks; the colors, mixed with glue, were applied by hand.

Uryū Sotokichi. Vice-admiral (1854–1937); he took part in the Battle of Tsushima in May 1905.

Usa Hachiman-gū. Shinto shrine in Usa (Ōita prefecture, Kyushu), dedicated in the eighth century to the mythical emperor Ōjin, his mother, Empress Jingū Kōgō, and his wife, Hime Ōkami. It is the main shrine controlling about 25,000 temples throughout Japan dedicated to Hachiman. Its architecture is unique. Festivals March 18 and from July 31 to August 2 (Shinkōsai). Also called Usa-jingū.

Usami Sensui. Confucian scholar (1710–76), one of Ogyū Sorai's main disciples.

Usen. *See* OGAWA USEN.

Ushikawa. Prehistoric site in Aichi prefecture, where vestiges of human skeletons seeming to possess Neanderthal features were uncovered.

Ushin. "Sentiment," an aesthetics term coined by Fujiwara no Taika, used during the Kamakura period in *waka* and *renga* poetry. It is based on the musicality of words more than their meaning; its goal is to describe, as subjectively as possible, an ideal world.
  • In Buddhism, a concept describing attachment to life, as opposed to *mushin,* or detachment from the world.

Ushū. Painter (Kanai Jibin, Kanai Tai; *mei:* Sachūta, Hikobei; *azana:* Shichū; *gō:* Ushū, 1796–1857), born in Edo. He painted mainly landscapes.

Usobuki. Masks used in Kyōgen plays, representing spirits, ghosts, or strange things such as mosquitoes, octopuses, or daikon.

Usu. General term for mortars used to grind rice to make *mochi.* There are many types, including single vertical *(tsuki-usu),* with a pestle moved by the foot *(fumi-usu* or *kara-usu),* and mill-shaped (two stones turning against each other, *suri-usu).* These mortars or grinders are made of stone or wood, depending on their use. The pestle is called *kine.* In folklore, mortar and pestle are associated with woman and man and have a sexual connotation, as evidenced during certain fertility festivals.

Usui. Former agrarian division of the year, corresponding to the beginning of the rainy season, beginning about February 19 and lasting 15 days. *Chin.:* Yushui. *See* NIJŪSHI-SETSU.

Usui Yoshimi. Literary critic and writer (1905–87), born in Nagano prefecture; editor-in-chief of *Tembō,* a literary magazine founded after the Second World War and published by Chikuma Shōbō. Author of the novel *Azumino* (1964–74).

Usuki. Town in Ōita prefecture (Kyushu), former castle town *(jōka-machi)* of the Christian daimyo Ōtomo Sōrin, who settled there in 1563. In the environs is a hill sculpted with some 75 faces of the Buddha, most of them dating from the Heian period.

Usuzan. Active volcano with a double caldera, located northeast of Uchiura Bay in western Hokkaido. One of its calderas forms Lake Tōya. It has erupted frequently; the most recent eruptions were in 1663, 1822, 1943, and 1947. The last one gave rise to a volcanic cone called Shōwa Shinzan ("new volcano of the Shōwa era").

Usuzuka kofun. Megalithic tomb located near the town of Yamaga, Kumamoto prefecture (Kyushu), with an antechamber decorated at the entrance with a painted human figure and white triangles on a red background. The cist is decorated with circles and triangles in red, blue, and white. Date not determined, perhaps before the fifth century.

Uta-awase. "Poetry contest," a sort of literary competition in which poets, in groups of two, strove to compose "linked" *waka (renga)*. The poets were judged on their talent and on the sentiments they expressed. These contests were first held in the late ninth century, were very popular among aristocratic and warrior circles in the twelfth and thirteenth centuries, and continued to be held up to the twentieth century. Very precise rules of etiquette ruled the introduction and recitation of poems by the poets, who were chosen long in advance. The poems had to relate to a defined theme. Many *emakimono* were produced to commemorate the most remarkable *uta-awase.*

Uta-e. "Poem-painting," a type of small painting inspired by a poem, sometimes with calligraphy in kana. Most *uta-e* paintings only alluded to a famous poem or to a passage of Buddhist writings, and were composed of symbols, landscapes, clouds, rocks, cranes, Wheels of the Law, and so on, whose "reading" gave them meaning and recalled a poem. This genre was in style mainly in the late Heian period.

Utagaki. "Ballads for dancing," once sung by villagers who gathered to climb a hill and celebrate the beginning of spring or autumn by dancing, singing, eating, or reciting poems that they exchanged with one another. These gatherings, part of the fertility rites, sometimes took place by the sea and gave rise to much free sexual activity. *Utagaki* texts, recorded in the *Man'yōshū* and in *fudoki,* are among the oldest forms of literature in Japan. Also called *kagai.*

Uta-garuta. Game using 200 illustrated cards, on each of which was written half a poem from the *Hyakunin ishhū* series. The goal was to unite the two halves of a poem as quickly as possible from a deck of cards laid out face-up, while a reciter read the verse halves from the second deck of cards. Very popular during the Edo period, this game is now rarely played except by young women during New Year's festivities. *See* KARUTA.

Utagawa-ryū. School of painting and ukiyo-e printing founded by Utagawa Toyoharu (Moronobu, 1735–1814). Many artists of the Utagawa family (or adopted by the family) belonged to this school, including the Hiroshige (I, II, III), Kunimaru, Kunimasa, Kuninao, Kunisada, Kunishige (1777–1835), Kuniyasu (1802–36), Kuniyoshi, Toyoharu, Toyohiro, and the Toyokuni (I, II, III). *See these entries.*

Utakai Hajime. Reading of *waka* poems performed each year at the imperial palace about January 10 to celebrate the New Year. The poems submitted must be on a subject chosen by the emperor. After 1879, the poems could be written by commoners; before this time, only poems written by members of the imperial family or guests were accepted. The poems, which must be submitted to the court before November 10 of the preceding year, are selected by a jury before being presented to the emperor.

Uta-makura. Place names that appear in literature and poetry and that have traditionally, since at least the ninth century, been associated with a sentiment, memory, or poetic image. By the late Heian period, there were catalogues of these places, and it was considered good taste to include them in poems. The list grew longer over the centuries. *Waka* and haiku poets made great use of them to suggest events or sentiments without describing them directly.

Utamaro. Painter (Kitagawa Utamaro, Toriyama Shimbi, Kitagawa Yūsuke, Kitayama Ichitarō; *azana:* Toyoaki, Sekiyō, Entaisai, Murasaki-ya; *gō:* Utamaro, Toyoaki, ca. 1753–1806) of ukiyo-e prints, born in Kawagoe, died in Edo. Perhaps a son and disciple of Toriyama Sekien (1712–88), an

Uzen

artist who was quite independent from the Kanō school. He signed with the name Toyoaki from 1775 to 1780, then adopted the name Utamaro in 1781. At first, he worked in the style of Katsukawa Shunshō, drawing portraits of Kabuki artists; he then developed his own style, making portraits of beautiful women *(bijin)*, which established his reputation, and erotic images, which got him sent to prison in 1804. He also wrote *kyōka* poems under the name Fude no Ayamaru. His prints, often produced in triptychs, were admired by Westerners, who discovered them in the late nineteenth century. He was best known for his bust portraits of women, although he also excelled at portraying them in head-to-toe portraits, usually in groups of three. He attracted many disciples who imitated his style more or less successfully, including Utamaro II, Yukimaro, Tsukimaro, Nikumaro, Shikimaro, and Hidemaro, all of whom used the family name Kitagawa in tribute to their master. It seems, however, that Utamaro's work became overvalued due to the fact that many of his prints went to Europe; his main publisher, Tsutaya Jūzaburō (1750–97), also contributed greatly to his popularity. When Tsutaya died, Utamaro seemed to lose his inspiration, and his late prints were clearly stereotypical; some of them were probably made by his students.

Utaura. Noh play: a boy looking for his father finds a soothsayer, who reveals that he is his father.

Utazawa-bushi. Vocal music with shamisen accompaniment, performed in the late Edo period by Sasamoto Hikotarō (Utazawa Yamato, 1797–1857).

Utokusen. Tax on wealth created on the instigation of the Tōdai-ji temple in Nara in 1304, which made a census of wealthy (*utokunin,* "virtuous") people in order to tax them for the monastery's needs. This taxation policy was continued during the Muromachi period by the shogunate, which also taxed the enormous profits made by moneylenders (*dosō*) and home distillers (*sakaya*).

Utsubo monogatari. "The Tale of the Hollow Tree." A 14-chapter novel by an unknown author (sometimes attributed to Minamoto no Shitagō), written between 960 and 980, making it the oldest novel in the world. Realistic in style, it tells the story of a noble, Kiyowara no Toshikage, and his descendants to the third generation. Toshikage, shipwrecked on the coast of an unknown country, has extraordinary adventures, during which he learns

to play the seven-string koto. His daughter has a son, Nakatada, who falls in love with a beautiful woman called Atemiya, but she marries the crown prince. Various adventures then follow relating to the succession to the throne. The oldest manuscript of this story dates from 1651. The style is varied, as if this novel had several authors. However, a certain continuity of the plot suggests a single author, who might have rewritten it several times, making successive changes. This novel was illustrated in *emakimono,* notably by Asukabe Tsunenori, with calligraphy by Ono Michikaze. Also pronounced *Utsuho-monogatari.*

U-tsuki. Former name for the fourth month of the year, from the name of the flower *u (Deutzia scabra),* which blossoms at that time.

Utsunomiya. Chief city of Tochigi prefecture, at the foot of Mt. Nikkō, about 100 km north of Tokyo; former fief of the Utsonomiya family, *shugo* of the region in the Kamakura and Muromachi periods. It developed in the Edo period around the castle of the Toda family. Airplane and engine plants. *Pop.:* 390,000.
  • Former family of *shugo* and daimyo descended from Fujiwara Michikane.

  • **Utsunomiya Daimyōjin.** *See* FUTARAYAMA-JINJA.

Uwa-etsuke. Technique of painting on a slip, used in ceramics.

Uwai kakuken nikki. "Journal of Uwai Kakuken" (Uwai Satokane, 1545–89), a vassal of the Shimazu in Kyushu. It covers the years 1574 to 1586, with some interruptions, and tells in great detail about the campaigns of the Shimazu to conquer Kyushu. It is a valuable document for study of the period just before Toyotomi Hideyoshi defeated the Shimazu family in 1587.

Uyoku-undō. Extreme-right political movements based on tradition; before the Second World War, they included the many ultranationalist societies that made installation of a militarist regime possible. These movements were dissolved after 1945, but some re-formed, becoming "patriotic movements."

Uzen. Former name of a province now included in Yamagata prefecture.

V. The letter *v* does not exist in Japanese. Most of the time, it is replaced with the sound *b* ("nigorization" of the sound *h*) and is used only for transcription of foreign words with katakana characters.

Vacations. The Western concept of annual vacations is practically unknown in Japan. In recent years, however, a number of Japanese have tried to adapt to the government's decree of an annual holiday period for workers, a measure taken in order to slow production. The French word *vacances (bakansu)* is used to designate the concept. In spite of this, few people take their entire legal vacation at one time, preferring to break it into several smaller periods of a few days each. Schoolchildren and university students have school holidays from mid-July to September 1; they generally use this time to make group "culture" or sports tours, or to study for their entrance exams. Apprentices traditionally have one week of vacation starting on January 15, a holiday called *yabuiri*. In general, most Japanese do not feel the need to "take vacations" because they are better than Westerners at finding time to relax during the day.

Valignano, Alessandro. Italian Jesuit (1539–1606), born in Chieti and ordained as a priest in 1566. Appointed "visitor" to the missions of the Far East, he was in Japan three times, arriving via Macao, from 1579 to 1582, 1590 to 1592, and 1598 to 1603. He was cordially received by Oda Nobunaga and Toyotomi Hideyoshi; Nobunaga gave him permission to preach and to establish a church and school in Azuchi. Valignano wrote many letters about etiquette in Japan, and on the novitiate that he founded in Usuki and the schools for children that he opened in Funai and Azuchi. He died in Macao. *Chinese name:* Fan Li'an.

Vaughn, Miles W. American journalist (1891–1949) who reported on Japanese business; he died in a shipwreck. A prize called Ueda-Vaughn was created in 1950 to reward international reporting.

Verbeck, Guido Herman Fridolin. American missionary (1830–98), born in Holland. Sent to Nagasaki in 1859 by the Dutch Reform Church, he had Itō Hirobumi and Ōkuma Shigenobu, among other statesmen, as students. He arrived in Tokyo in 1869 and was an adviser to the government, then devoted himself to evangelizing in 1877.

Verny, François Léonce. French engineer (1837–1908) asked by the Edo shogunal government in 1865 to build lighthouses and shipyards in Japan. He built a foundry in Yokohama, a shipyard in Yokosuka, and four lighthouses for the Meiji government in Kannonzaki, Nojimazaki, Jōgashima, and Shinagawa; the last is located in Meiji-mura in Kanagawa prefecture. Verny returned to France in 1876, but continued to work for the Japanese government by sending engineers. *See* YOKUSUKA.

Victor Co. Nippon Bikutā. Manufacturer of audiovisual equipment, founded in 1927 as a subsidiary of the American firm Victor Talking Machine Company, and acquired by the Matsushita group in 1945. It has subsidiaries in many countries and distributes its products under the brand name JVC (Japan Victor Company), exporting more than 70% of its production. Head office in Tokyo.

Vining, Elizabeth Gray. American Quaker writer and educator (1902–99), born in Philadelphia. In

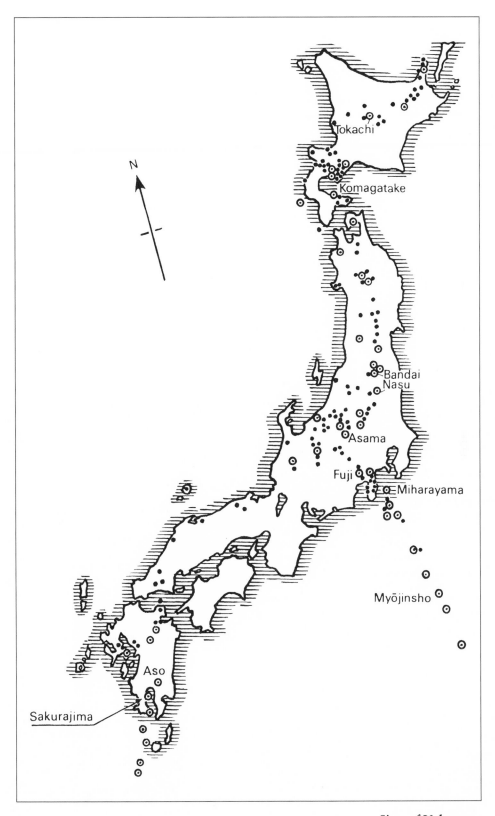

Tokachi

Komagatake

Bandai
Nasu

Asama

Fuji

Miharayama

Myōjinsho

Aso

Sakurajima

Sites of Volcanoes

Major Volcanic Eruptions, 1888–1985

Date	Volcano	Deaths
1888, July 15	Bandai-san (Iwashiro)	461
1902, Aug.–Dec.	Torishima	125
1914, Jan. 12	Sakurajima (Kagoshima)	29
1926, May 24	Tokachi-san	146
1929, June 16–19	Komagatake (Hokkaido)	1
1940, July–Aug.	Miyakejima (Izu-tō)	11
1944, June/1945, Nov.	Mount Usu (new volcano, Hokkaido)	
1950	Mihariyama (Ōshima)	
1953, Apr. 27	Mount Aso (Kyushu)	6
1952, Sept./1953, Sept.	Izu-tō	31
1958, July 24	Mount Aso (Kyushu)	12
1985	Mihariyama (Ōshima)	

1946, she was invited to Japan to be tutor and English teacher to crown prince Akihito. She held this position until 1950, then returned to the United States, where she wrote a book on her experience, *Windows for the Crown Prince*. She also wrote many works for young people.

Viscaino, Don Sebastian. *See* VIVERO Y VELASCO.

Vivero y Velasco, Dom Rodrigo de. Spanish governor of the Philippines (?–1631) in 1608–09. On his way back to Mexico, he was shipwrecked on the coast of Kazusa (Chiba-ken) and stayed in Japan for two months. Having been received by Tokugawa Ieyasu, on the recommendation of Will Adams, he asked for privileges for a naval base, permission to make a map of the coasts, freedom for Spanish missionaries to preach, expulsion of Dutch merchants, and establishment of trade relations between Japan and Spain. He received few positive responses, but Ieyasu allowed him to return to Mexico on a ship built by Will Adams, accompanied by a few Japanese merchants. In 1611, another envoy from Spain, Sebastian Viscaino (ca. 1551–1615), arrived at the port of Uraga; his mission was to thank Tokugawa Ieyasu for the hospitality extended to Vivero y Velasco. He met Ieyasu in Sumpu and shogun Hidetada in Edo, then returned to Mexico in 1613 with the Hasekura Tsunenaga mission.

Volcanoes. Called *kazan* in Japanese, volcanoes are a major feature of the islands of Japan. More than 200, most of them formed in the Quaternary period and are permanently or cyclically active. They are part of the Pacific Ring of Fire and are distributed along the western coasts of two large ocean trenches, the Japan Trench and the Ryukyu Trench, created by the subduction of the Pacific Plate under

the large Eurasian Plate. The Pacific Plate created the volcanoes of the Kuril Islands, Hokkaido, and the northern part of Honshu, while the Ryukyu Trench gave rise to the volcanoes of Chūbu, Kyushu, and the Ryukyu Islands; this latter trench resulted from the sliding of the Philippine Plate under the continental plate. A large number of Japanese volcanoes are stratovolcanic, or cone-shaped; the most perfect example is Mt. Fuji (Fuji-san). The other types are pyroplastic cones and are domed; these are the lower peaks, found mainly on the Izu Peninsula. Volcanic explosions and eruptions can have catastrophic consequences; the eruption of Mt. Bandai in 1888 profoundly changed the geography of its environs, blocking rivers and causing enormous landslides. Many volcanoes have formed calderas, which often become lakes. Volcanoes can cause tidal waves *(tsunami)* when they explode on the ocean floor or on the coasts.

The largest active volcanoes in Japan are Mt. Fuji (3,776 m), Kirishima (1,811 m), Mihari-yama (Ōshima), Sakurajimi (1,192 m), Mt. Aso (1,697 m), Asama-yama (2,710 m), Bandai-san (1,939 m), Chōkai-san (2,378 m), Azuma (2,487 m), Norikura (3,026 m, Nagano-ken), and Chausu-dake (2,044 m).

→ *See also* EARTHQUAKES, GEOGRAPHY, GEOLOGY, MOUNTAINS.

Vories, William Mercel. American educator (1880–1964), born in Kansas; sent to Japan as a missionary in 1905. He started a company in Ōmi Hachiman, Shiga prefecture, and founded churches, schools, and a sanitarium. He married a Japanese woman, Hitotsuyanagi Makiko (1884–1969) in 1917 and became a Japanese citizen in 1941, with the name Hitotsuyanagi Mereru, having been "adopted" by his parents-in-law.

W. In the kana syllabary, the sound *w* is conveyed only by the syllable *wa*. Because the syllables *wi, wu, we,* and *wo* have not been designated a particular character, they have been replaced by the vowels *i, u, e,* and *o*. Only the sound *wa* is normally used.

Wa. "Dwarf," an ancient Chinese and Korean name for Japan (*Chin.:* Wo) as it appeared in the *Hanshu* (first century) and the *Weizhi* (ca. 297). It corresponded to northern Kyushu, which was divided into a large number of small states, including Nanoku and Itokoku, which were apparently unified by Himiko. The word *wa* still designates everything that is typically Japanese, as opposed to what is Chinese *(kan)* or Western *(yō)*.

• **Wabun.** Typical Japanese literature written in classic language, as opposed to *kambun*, or Chinese literature, used sometimes in literature and in ancient official documents.

• **Wa no Nakoku.** *See* NAKOKU.

Wabi. "Languor," an aesthetic and moral concept designating a life of leisure, without mundane, daily concerns, and free of emotion. In the Kamakura period, it became synonymous with solitude and tranquillity in simplicity. It was widely applied by *waka* poets and, later, by aesthetes of the tea ceremony *(chanoyu)*, who advocated isolation from the world and the use of simple, rustic things, seen to represent pure beauty. This concept then became typical of Zen Buddhist and Shinto philosophies that were close to nature. *See also* SABI, SHIBUI, YŪGEN.

Wadachi Kiyoo. Geophysicist (1902–95), born in Aichi prefecture, specializing in earthquakes. He

was director of the Central Meteorological Observatory from 1947 to 1963, director of the National Research Center for the Prevention of Natural Disasters from 1963 to 1966, dean of Saitama University from 1966 to 1972, and director of the Japan Academy from 1974 to 1980. He received the Order of Culture (Bunka-shō) in 1985.

Wada Eisaku. Painter (1874–1959), born in Kagoshima. He studied Western painting in France from 1898 to 1903 under Raphael Collin, and directed the Tokyo University of Fine Arts and Music (Tokyo Geijutsu Daigaku) from 1932 to 1935. His painting was strongly influenced by the Barbizon school. He was decorated with the Order of Culture (Bunka-shō) in 1943.

• **Wada Sanzo.** Painter (1883–?) in Edo and maker of ukiyo-e prints.

Wada Emi. Costume designer for theater and movies. She received an Academy Award in 1986 for her costumes for Kurosawa Akira's movie *Ran*.

Wada Morihiro. Ceramist, born 1944 in Nishinomiya (Hyōgo prefecture). He received the prize of the Association of Ceramics Art of Japan in 1988 and took part in the exhibition in the Mitsukoshi space in Paris in 1994.

Wada Yoshie. Writer (1906–77) in the naturalist style, author of a number of very successful novels, including *Kabutō* (The Fight, 1941), *Ichiyō no nikki* (Ichiyō's Diary, 1956), *Chiri no naka* (Amidst the Rubble, 1964), *Kurai nagare* (The Black River, 1976). In 1976, he received the grand prize of Japanese literature.

Wada Yoshimori. Warrior (1147–1213) from Miura Peninsula, who assisted Minamoto no Yoritomo during his war against the Taira in 1180 and was then appointed *bettō* of the Samurai-dokoro. In 1203, shogun Minamoto no Yoriie ordered him to kill Hōjō Tokimasa, but Yoshimori prevented this, replacing Yoriie with his young brother, Minamoto no Sanetomo. He was defeated and killed in battle by Hōjō Yoshitoki.

Wadō. Era of Empress Gemmei (Gemmyō): Jan. 708–Sept. 715. *See* NENGŌ.

• **Wadō-kaihō.** Coins made of silver, then of pure copper, issued starting in 708 on the order of Empress Gemmei; they remained in circulation until 958. In imitation of Chinese coins, they were round with a square hole in the center, and were inscribed with the four kanji characters for *wa, dō, kai,* and *hō*. There were eight different types, collectively called *jūnezeni* ("the 12 *sen*"). Also called Wadō-*kaichin. See also* CURRENCY, KŌCHŌ-JŪNISEN.

Wafuku. Japanese costume—kimonos and men's clothes—as opposed to *yōfuku,* or Western garb. Uniforms are called *seifuku. See* CLOTHING.

Wagaku-jo. Literary school founded by Hanawa Hokiichi in 1793; at first called Wagaku Kōdansho. Its name was changed in 1805. Also called Wagaku-sho. *See* WAGAKUSHA.

• **Wagakusha.** Scholars and writers who advocated a return to purely Japanese sources, as opposed to Chinese and foreign sources. Motoori Norinaga (1730–1801) and Takebe Ayatari were the best-known representatives of this movement, which gave rise to literary "schools" such as the Wagaku-jo. *See* KOJIKI-DEN.

Wagener, Gottfried. German engineer (1831–92), born in Hanover, and civil servant. He studied in Göttingen and in Paris, where he lived for eight years, then taught in Switzerland. In 1868, he went to Nagasaki on behalf of a Shanghai-based American firm to supervise construction of a soap factory; in 1870, he worked in Arita for a ceramics plant; the following year, he began to teach in Tokyo and to provide industrialists with technical advice. He was actively involved with organizing Japanese participation in the world's fairs in Vienna (1873), Philadelphia (1876), and Japan. He died in Japan. Also sometimes called Gottfried Wagner.

Wagoto. In Kabuki theater, the role of a young man in love (romantic lead), created by Sakata Tōjūrō (1645–1709). Also in Kabuki, a type of play describing melancholy sentiments, as opposed to the *aragoto* and *jitsugoto* genres. Also called *nimaine, nuregoto, yatsushi*.

Waka. "Japanese poetry," in contrast to *kanshi,* or "Chinese poetry." This term applies to all forms of classic poetry and, in a stricter sense, to poems written in Japanese aristocratic circles from the eighth to the twentieth century. More specifically, it designates *tanka* poems consisting of five lines of 5, 7, 5, 7, 7 syllables. In these poems, the top three lines (5, 7, and 5 syllables), called *kami no ku* or *hokku,* gave rise to *haikai* and *haiku*. The bottom two lines (7 syllables each) are called *shimo no ku* or, more commonly, *ageku*.

There are other forms of *waka*. *Chōka* (or *naga-uta*) are long poems consisting of an indeterminate number of verses of two lines of 5 and 7 syllables, finishing with a line of 7 syllables. *Wedōka* were *waka* in sequences of six lines (5, 7, 7, 5, 7, 7 syllables); *katauta,* or half-*sedōka,* were *waka* of only three lines (5, 7, and 7 syllables or, more rarely, 4, 7, and 7 syllables). Another form of *waka, bussoku-seki no uta,* was composed of six lines of 5, 7, 5, 7, 7, 7 syllables. All of these forms disappeared in the ninth century, and only *tanka* and *chōka* continued to be used.

Rhetorical devices, such as *makura no kotoba, jotokotoba, kakekotoba, utamakura,* and *engo-kotoba* were used in *waka;* these devices consisted of associations of images, sounds, and ideas intended to evoke a memory or give the words a double meaning. After the first major anthology, the *Man-yōshū,* emperors had imperial anthologies of *waka* compiled (*see* CHOKUSEN WAKA-SHŪ); every great poet was interested in compiling *waka* anthologies, personal or other. Almost all literate Japanese composed *waka* until the modern era, and a number of societies were founded to perpetuate the genre, although today the preferred style is *haiku,* or "free" poems.
→ *See also* NOH.

• **Waka-dokoro.** "Poetry Bureau," created by the imperial court in 951 for compilation of official anthologies.

• *Waka jittai.* "The Ten Styles of Poetry." A poetics treatise attributed to Mibu no Takamine, written in 945. Also titled *Wakatai-jisshū*.

• *Waka kuhon.* "The Nine Books of Poetry." A poetics treatise attributed to Fujiwara no Kintō, early ninth century.

• **Waka Ni-sei.** Collective name for two poets, Kakinomoto no Hitomaro and Yamabe no Akihito, as Shinto divinities of poetry.

• *Waka rōei-shū.* "Collection of Japanese and Chinese Songs," containing 589 Chinese poems by 30 poets and 216 *waka* poems by 50 poets, compiled by Fujiwara no Kintō (966–1041) about 1013. *See also* SENZAI-KAKU.

• **Waka shisho.** Collective name for four major poetry works: Yamato monogatari, Sumiyoshi monogatari, Taketori monogatari, and Utsubo monogatari.

Wakadoshiyori. "Young elder" or "young Toshiyori." In the Tokugawa shogunate, as assistants to the *rōjū*, their task consisted essentially of surveillance of the *hatamoto* and *gokenin,* with the help of inspectors *(metsuke).* They also supervised the work of artisans, artists, and palace guards. This position was created in 1633. There were generally six *wakadoshiyori,* chosen from among the *fudai-daimyō,* who alternated in the position for one-month periods. Also sometimes called *shōrō* or *sansei. See also* RŌJŪ, TOSHIYORI.

Wakakusa-yama. Hill about 340 m high, located east of Nara, at the top of which is a tomb *(kofun)* called Uguisu-zuka ("nightingale tomb"). Custom has it that the grass growing there is burned every January. A monastery formerly at the Hōryū-ji, the Wakakusa-garan, was built there; the remains were excavated in 1939.

Wakamatsu Shizuko. Writer (1864–96), born in Wakamatsu (Fukushima prefecture). She taught English in Yokohama in 1882 and married Iwamoto Yoshiharu in 1889. She translated works by Tennyson and Longfellow, as well as F. H. Burnett's *Little Lord Fauntleroy,* as *Shōkōshi,* in 1892.

Wakamono-gumi. "Groups *(kumi)* of young men" at least 15 years old, who formed associations in villages responsible for preparing for festivals, helping with public works, and watching for fires. They worked alongside similar groups of young women called *musume-gumi.* Young people were freed from their duties to the *kumi* when they married. In the nineteenth and twentieth centuries, *wakamono-gumi* groups were replaced by analogous associations called *seinenkai* (youth associations), which are still active today in many villages and urban neighborhoods.

Wakan sansai zu-e. "Sino-Japanese Encounter of the Three Components of the Universe." An illustrated encyclopedia in 105 chapters, published in 1712 by Terajima Ryōan, an Osaka physician. The articles were written in *kambun.*

Wakao Ayako. Movie actor, born 1933 in Tokyo. She worked for the Daiei company starting in 1950; one of Mizoguchi Kenzo's favorites, she became a sex symbol in the 1950s and 1960s. After Daiei went bankrupt, she acted in the theater and on television.

Wakasa no Kuni. Former province in Hokurikudō, corresponding to the current Fukui prefecture.

Wakashu. "Young man," "young warrior," and sometimes "homosexual." Kabuki plays performed by adolescents were called Wakashu-kabuki from 1629 to 1652, when they were banned because of the actors' homosexuality.

Wakatsuki Reijirō. Politician (1866–1949), born in Shimane prefecture. He was minister of finance in Katsura Tarō's third cabinet (1912) and Ōkuma Shigenobu's second cabinet. In 1924, he was minister of the interior in Katō Komei's coalition cabinet; when Katō died, he succeeded him as prime minister and leader of the Kenseikai (Constitutional Association party). Tanaka Giichi succeeded him in 1927. In 1930, he was a delegate to the London conference on naval disarmament. As leader of the Rikken Minseitō (Constitutional Democratic party), he was elected prime minister in 1931, succeeding Hamaguchi Osachi, but he resigned a few months later, leaving the position to Inukai. Having always been firmly opposed to Japan's entry into war against the United States, he ceased all political activity in 1940.

Wakayama. Chief city of Wakayama prefecture, on Kii Peninsula, about 50 km south of Osaka; it developed around a castle built by Toyotomi Hideyoshi for Hidetada in 1585. This castle's *donjon,* destroyed by lightning in 1845, was rebuilt in 1850 (its ruins are still visible). Steel mills, chemical and carpentry plants. *Pop.:* 400,000.

• **Wakayama prefecture.** Prefecture in the southwest part of the Kii Peninsula, southwest of Osaka, former Kii province. It is very mountainous and relatively undeveloped, except for the part bordering Osaka prefecture, on a small plain formed by the Kinokawa river. It contains many sacred sites, including Mt. Kōya and the Kumano shrines. Its agricultural production consists mainly of citrus fruits. *Chief city:* Wakayama; *main cities:* Tanabe, Shingū, Kainan, Arida. *Area:* 4,722 km². *Pop.:* 1.1 million.

Wakayama Bokusui. Poet (Wakayama Shigeru, 1885–1928), born in Miyazaki prefecture. He wrote *tanka* (*Betsuri,* 1910) and led an adventurous life, writing poems and travel accounts, such as *Minakami kikō* (1924), in a naturalist style.

Wake. Ancient title for imperial princes, and sometimes conferred upon noble families in the eighth and ninth centuries.

• **Wake no Hiromushi.** Wake no Kiyomaro's older sister (730–99); she became a Buddhist nun with the name Hōki. Famous for her kindness, she followed her brother into exile.

• **Wake no Hiroyo.** Wake no Kiyomaro's brother (eighth–ninth century) and physician, author of the first Japanese botanical treatise, *Yakkyō-taisō.* He and his brother founded a school, the Kōbun-in, and amassed a large library.

• **Wake no Kiyomaro.** Statesman (Iwanasu no Wake no Kimi, 733–99). Serving the imperial court, he suppressed Fujiwara no Nakomaro's rebellion in 764 and received the title Fujino no Mahito. He was promoted to minister by Empress Shōtoku, but opposed the appointment of the scheming Buddhist monk Dōkyō, who had him exiled to Ōsumi province. When Shōtoku died, Emperor Kōnin recalled him to the court and gave him the title of *ason.* In 784, Emperor Kammu appointed him to the head of several ministries; in this capacity, he directed construction of the new capitals of Nagaoka and Heian-kyō. He was the co-founder, with his brother, Wake no Hiroyo, of the Kōbun-in school for educating children of the Wake family. He is often cited in literature as a fervent supporter of the imperial cause.

Wake Kitei. Ceramist (early nineteenth century) who worked in the Kiyomizu kilns in Kyoto and followed Takahashi Dōhachi's style.

Waki. In Noh theater, an actor playing supporting roles to the *shite.* He is never masked. In Kabuki theater, an actor playing a supporting role, who may have one or several assistants called *wakizure.*

Waki-kaidō. In the Edo period, secondary roads, generally linking the five main roads (*go-kaidō*); these included the Hokku-kaidō, Chūgoku-kaidō, Nagasaki-kaidō, Mito-kaidō, Sayaji, Minoji. This term was also used for roads that senior bureaucrats and imperial envoys were required to take: Nikkō Onari-kaidō, Reiheishi-kaidō, and others. Also called *waki-ōkan. See* GO-KAIDŌ, TŌKAIDŌ.

Wakizashi. Sword with a relatively short blade (0.3 to 0.6 m) carried by commoners during the Edo period. When samurai carried this "companion" sword in their belt with the *katana,* the ensemble was called *daisho.*

Wakō. A general term for pirates, Japanese pronunciation of the Chinese *wokou* ("brigand"). Pirates were always numerous off the coasts of China, Korea, and Japan, and their activities have been recorded since the fifth century. The Koreans gave this name to Japanese troops trying to conquer the southern part of the peninsula (fourth–fifth century). It was then applied to bands of pirates, generally Japanese (but with Korean and Chinese accomplices), who lived on Tsushima and Iki and who launched raids on the Japanese, Korean, and Chinese coasts, going as far as Fujian, mainly in the sixteenth century. Toyotomi Hideyoshi put an end to their activities after he conquered Kyushu in 1587. *Kor.: wae-gu.*

Wakon-yōsai. "Japanese spirit, Western knowledge." At the beginning of the Meiji era, an expression advocating acceptance of Western science while maintaining the national "spirit." It was taken from an older expression, *wakon-kansai,* "Japanese spirit, Chinese knowledge," attributed to Sugawara no Michizane.

Wakun no shiori. Major dictionary of Japanese compiled in the late eighteenth century by Tanigawa Kotosuga (1709–76), published in part after his death. The words are classified in the traditional *gojūon* order of the kana syllabary. It was followed by a revised and expanded edition, the *Zōho gorin wakun no shiori,* still used today.

Wakyō. Bronze mirror with a decorated back, made in the mid-Heian period. *See* KAGAMI.

Waley, Arthur David. English Japanologist and Sinologist (1889–1966). He translated a great number of Chinese and Japanese works, thus making a major contribution to the dissemination of East Asian literature in Europe, but he refused to learn to speak Japanese or Chinese and never went to Asia. His translations of the *Genji monogatari,* the poems of the *Man'yōshū,* the *Makura no sōshi,* and Noh plays are often incomplete and sometimes inaccurate in detail.

Wamyō ruiji-sho. "Japanese Words Classified by Category." The oldest Chinese–Japanese dictionary, published in Japan about 934 by Minamoto no Shitagō (911–83) on the request of Princess Noriko, one of Emperor Daigo's daughters. It is a valuable work for study of the usage and pronunciation of Japanese in the tenth century. It uses *man'yō-gana* characters and indicates their "Japanese" spelling *(wamyō)*. Also titled *Wamyō-sho.*

Wani. Korean scholar from Paekche. According to the *Kojiki,* he went to Japan around 400 to be the tutor for one of Emperor Ōjin's sons, and was said to have brought Confucian books with him. He settled in Yamato, perhaps in the Osaka region, and put down roots, becoming the founder of the Kawachi no Fumi family. He was probably the ancestor of the Buddhist monk Gyōki. Also called Wani Kishi. *Chin.:* Wang Yin. *See also* ACHIKI, AYA, KIKAJIN.

Waniguchi. Large metal gong hung at the entrance to Shinto shrines, which is rung by followers to draw the attention of the *kami.* It is often replaced by a large bell *(suzu)*.

Waragutsu. Large straw boots worn by peasants in the winter, especially in northern Honshu and on Hokkaido. Also called *yukigutsu. See* KUTSU.

• **Waraji.** Sandals made of braided straw, generally shorter than the foot, leaving the heel protruding beyond the sole, and attached to the ankle by a cord. Popular belief had it that they repelled snakes. They were once worn by peasants, soldiers, and itinerant monks. *See also* KUTSU, ZŌRI.

Warai-hotoke. "Smiling Buddha," a popular form of Hōtei (*Skt.:* Maitreya) or Fu Daishi-ten, portrayed as a fat, clean-shaven Buddhist monk with long ears, arms raised above his head, and a broad smile.

Warashibe chōja. "The Straw Millionaire." A folk tale in which a poor man, having prayed to Kannon Bosatsu, finds a straw in his path. He trades it for an orange, the orange for a piece of fabric, and so on, each time increasing the value of the object until he obtains a field that, well farmed, brings him wealth. This tale appeared very early in the literature, and was included in the *Konjaku monogatari.*

War crimes. After the Second World War, the Allies created a special court (similar to the one in Germany), the International Military Court of the Far East (Kyokuto Kokusai Gunji Saiban), to try the Japanese whom they considered war criminals. It sat in Tokyo from 1946 to 1948 and heard some 6,000 cases, sentencing 920 people to death, including Doihara Kenji, Hirota Kōki, Itagaki Seishirō, Kimura Heitarō, Matsui Iwane, Mutō Akira, and Tōjō Hideki. Other politicians and military officers, not considered "class-A" criminals but deemed "responsible," were sentenced to prison terms of from 7 years (such as Shigemitsu Mamoru) to 20 years (Tōgō Shigenori) or life. Many of the latter were freed on parole in 1950, 1954, and 1955. The others were freed unconditionally on April 7, 1958.

Warner, Langdon. American expert in Eastern art (1881–1955), director of the collections at the Fogg Museum at Harvard University. In Japan, he was Okakura Kakuzō's student after 1903; in 1912, he was appointed director of the American School of Archeology in Beijing. He led a number of scientific expeditions to Central Asia, and, with Professor Asakawa Kan'ichi of Yale University, was credited with having persuaded President Roosevelt not to order the bombing of Kyoto and Nara because they belonged not only to Japan but to the cultural heritage of all humanity. In reality, it was the American secretary of state for war, Henry L. Stimson, who took this initiative with the assent of President Harry S. Truman. Warner was decorated with the Order of the Sacred Treasure.

Wasa Daihachirō. Samurai (1663–1713) of Kii province, and archer, student of Yoshimi Kyōbu (Yoshimi Daizaemon). During the Sanjūsangendō archery competition (Renge-ō-in) in Kyoto in April 1686, he shot 13,053 arrows, 8,133 of which hit the target about 63 m away, in a 24-hour period. In performing this feat, he dethroned the champion, Hoshino Kanzaemon.

Wasan. Term for higher mathematics, generally considered relatively secret during the Edo period, and expounded in Arima Yoriyuki's *Jūki sampō*. This term was used in contrast to mathematical theories imported from Europe, *yōsan*. Sticks *(sangi)* were still being used in calculations (up to the solving of first-degree algebraic equations), but Seki Takakazu invented a system of algebraic notation enabling the solution of more complicated problems. His research was continued by his disciples, Takebe Katahiro, Kurushima Yoshihiro (?–1757), Matsunaga Yoshisuke (ca. 1690–1744), and Yamaji Nushizumi (1704–72). Arima Yoriyuki (1714–83), then daimyo of Fukuoka, spread the teaching of his precursors. Other *wasan* scholars included Ajima Naonobu (1739–96), Wada Nei (1787–1840), Aida Yasuaki (1747–1817), and Fujita Sadasuke (1734–1807). *Wasan* theories were abandoned in the early Meiji era in favor of European calculation methods. *See* ARIMA YORIYUKI, SANGI, SEKI TAKAKAZU.

Wasan. Buddhist hymns sung in honor of the Buddha or important monks, developed in the tenth century. *Wasan* were composed on a *waka* pattern and often contained many couplets. The most important *wasan* were composed by Shinran and Rennyo to enable followers to remember the teachings of the Jōdo Shin-shū and the Yūzū Nembutsu more easily.

Waseda Daigaku. Private university founded in Tokyo in 1882 by Ōkuma Shigenobu as Tōkyō Semmon Gakkō and renamed Waseda in 1902. It has many faculties and is attended by more than 8,000 foreign students each year. It also gives evening courses, notably in literature. Its campus houses a theater museum (Empaku) founded in 1928 to commemorate Tsubouchi Shōyō's birthday. Attendance, about 40,000 students.

• *Waseda Bungaku.* Literary magazine founded by students at Waseda University and the writer Tsubouchi Shōyō in 1891. It was published in several series: the first from 1891 to 1898, the second from 1906 to 1927, the third from 1934 to 1949, and the following ones at various intervals between 1949 and 1975. The eighth series began in 1976 and is still in publication.

Washi. General term for all types of Japanese paper made by hand with bark from *kōzō* (mulberry bushes, *Broussonetia Kazunoki*), *gampi* (*Wikstroemia Sikokiana*), *mitsumata* (*Edgeworthia papyrifera*), or hemp *(asa, Cannabis sativa)*. The technique for making this type of paper was imported from China and used very early in Japan; more than 200 types were found in the Shōso-in in Nara. In the Heian period, *washi* artisans perfected the process and produced the best types of paper, called, depending on the texture and mode of fabrication, *danshi, hanshi, kujinshi, michinokugami, shukushi, suminagashi, sugiharashi, tobigumo, uchigumori,* and others. Production intensified during the Kamakura and Muromachi periods because of constantly growing demand. The *washi* tradition is preserved in villages in northern Honshu (where there is cold, pure water), and *washi* paper is used not only for decoration but to print luxury books, greeting cards, and other materials. Some sheets of paper are true craft masterpieces, with parts of plants or even butterfly wings in their pulp. Centers currently producing *washi* are concentrated in Ehime, Nagano, Gifu, Fukuoka, Tottori, Yamanashi, Fukui, Kōchi, Saitama, and Shimane prefectures. *See* PAPER.

Washington, Conference of (Washington-kaigi). General conference held in Washington, D.C., from November 1921 to February 1922, between the United States, England, and Japan, with the objective of realigning these countries' naval powers to reflect the new international relations determined by the First World War. The Americans proposed decommissioning 30 warships if Great Britain would decommission 23 and Japan 25, in order to avoid naval conflict. It was finally agreed that the three countries' fleets should have the proportions 10, 10, and 6. The conference also set relations between Japan and China by accepting the status quo in the Pacific, and it resulted in a treaty being signed on February 5, 1922, by the United States, Great Britain, Japan, France, and Italy, for a 15-year term. Japan ratified the treaty on August 5, 1922, and it went into effect on August 17, 1922. The treaty limited shipbuilding in the countries concerned, ended the Anglo-Japanese alliance treaty of 1902, and reaffirmed the sovereignty of China. However, it was a point of bitter controversy in the Japanese government, and it was finally denounced in 1934.

Watanabe Iwao. Painter (Watanabe Nangaku, 1767–1813), born in Kyoto. Maruyama Ōkyo's student, he painted carp and beautiful women *(bijin)* in the style of his school. He taught in Edo, where he introduced the Maruyama-shijō style.

Watanabe Jōtarō. General (1874–1936), born in Aichi prefecture, promoted in 1931. Considered the leader of the Tōseiha military faction, he was assassinated by officers of the rival Kōdōha faction during the incidents of February 26, 1935 (*see* NINI-ROKU JIKEN).

Watanabe Kazan. Painter (Watanabe Sadayasu, 1793–1841) and samurai from Aichi province, Tani Bunchō's student in Bunjinga style. A scholar of "Western sciences" *(rangaku),* he formed a study group called Shōshikai, but because he demanded closer relations with foreigners, he was arrested by the shogunate and sentenced to death in 1839; this sentence was commuted to house arrest on his estate. He committed suicide in 1841 for having embarrassed his daimyo by his presence. Kazan was an eclectic painter who emulated the Chinese style but also worked in a "Western" style. He painted the traditional "flowers and birds" *(gachō)* but also excelled in landscapes and portraits from live models. One of his most famous portraits, of Takami Senseki (1785–1858), is housed in the National Museum of Tokyo.

Watanabe Masanosuke. Laborer (1899–1928), born in Chiba prefecture. He joined the Communist party in 1922, but was arrested the following year. Freed in 1924, he continued his union activities with his wife, Tanno Setsu, but was excluded from the Sōdōmei because of his radicalism. He was elected a member of the party's Central Committee in 1926, then went to Moscow in 1927 and Shanghai in 1928. Knowing that he would be arrested by the police if he attempted to return to Japan, he committed suicide.

Watanabe Michio. Politician (1923–95), minister of foreign affairs and vice-prime minister (1991–93), very influential in political circles, famous for his sometimes tempestuous statements about the annexation of Korea by Japan in 1910.

Watanabe Sadao. Jazz musician, born 1933 in Tochigi; studied in Boston 1962–65. Interested in Latin American and African music, he imported these musical styles to Japan, which earned him the nickname "Nabe Sada" from young people who appreciated his unique style.

Watanabe Shikō. *See* SHIKŌ.

Watarai Shintō. Shinto sect of the Ise shrines, founded by Watarai Yukitada (1236–1305), a priest who saw a need to place the *gegū* shrine on the same level as the *naikū.* Basing his theories on the Ryōbu Shintō, he asserted that the *kami* Toyouke was superior to all other *kami,* even Amaterasu-Ōmikami.

His successors built a complex theology on this foundation, which they expounded in the *Shintō gobushō* (Five Books of Shinto). It stated, among other things, that, contrary to the theories in the *Honji suijaku,* the Buddhist divinities are emanations of the *kami.* Also called Ise Shintō. *See* ISE.

Watari-shima. One of the ancient names for Hokkaido.

Waters, Thomas James. English architect (1830–?) who arrived in Japan about 1868. He built the first Western-style brick buildings and made plans for reconstruction of Tokyo's Ginza, which had been destroyed by a terrible fire in 1872. He also constructed a foundry in Osaka, the Tokyo Museum of Commerce (1871), the British legation (1872), and the Osaka Mint. He left Japan about 1880.

Watsuji Tetsurō. Philosopher and historian (1889–1966), born in Himeji (Hyōgo prefecture), an expert in Western philosophy who wrote studies on Nietzsche and Kierkegaard (1913, 1915). He also concentrated on early Japanese culture and Buddhism. His essays on Dōgen (1923) are considered important for the information they give on the thought of this Zen Buddhist monk. Watsuji Tetsurō was a professor of ethics at Kyoto University and began to write his voluminous treatise on aesthetics, *Rinrigaku,* in 1937. From 1934 to 1949, he taught at the University of Tokyo. His principles of aesthetics posit that Japanese are different from Westerners because they accord more importance to the general concept of humanity *(ningen)* than to individuality. In his studies on ancient Japan, including *Nihon kodai bunka* (Ancient Culture of Japan, 1920), he compared the myths of the *Kojiki* to Greek mythology and tried to demonstrate that Japanese myths are mainly expressions of the people's emotions. His complete works were published in 20 volumes by Iwanami Shoten, from 1961 to 1963.

Wa-yō. "Japanese style." A construction mode imitating those in use in northern China, adopted in Japan during the Nara period. This "traditional" style was called *wa-yō* only in the Kamakura period, to distinguish it from two other styles, Kara-yō and Tenjiku-yō. It is characterized by low-sloping roofs, "cloud-shaped" *to-kyō* (only during the Asuka period), parabolic *hijiki* tips, parallel joists under the awnings, doors in solid wood or formed of butt-jointed planks, square *renji-mado* windows with equally spaced vertical or horizontal mullions, the use of extra awnings to widen the base of structures,

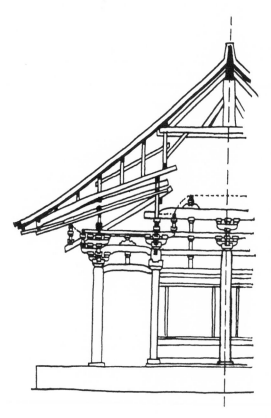

Cross-section of a structure in *wa-yō* style

and simple struts between the beams meeting at the tops of the pillars. All religious buildings were built in this mode (sometimes with variants, as in the Shin Yakushi-ji pagoda) until at least the twelfth century. *See also* KARA-YŌ, KAERUMATA, MADO, TENJIKU-YŌ, TO-KYŌ.

Wazen. *See* EIRAKU WAZEN.

Weights and measures. Since ancient times, Japan has had a relatively standardized system of weights and measures. In the Meiji era, it also adopted the metric system. There are slightly different units of measurement for fabrics and papers. Over all, Japanese units of mass, length, area, and volume follow standards accepted throughout the country, except for minor local differences.

These values varied slightly depending on the era or the region. For fabrics, the units of length *(komashaku)* were greater than normal by about 25%.

See also CURRENCY, KOKU, RYŌ, and the values cited.

Weston, Walter. English mountain climber (1861–1940) who went to Japan as a missionary in 1889. He was the first European to climb Mt. Fuji and other high peaks in the "Japanese Alps." He also helped create the Mountain Climbing Club in Japan in 1905, and published *Mountaineering and Exploration in the Japanese Alps* (London, 1896). He was decorated with the Order of the Sacred Treasure in 1937.

Whales. In ancient Japan, whales and other cetaceans *(kujira)* were considered not mammals but fish; therefore, they were not subject to Buddhist bans, and their flesh could be consumed. However, many fishers avoided killing them, seeing them as divine messengers. In the seventeenth century, whaling *(hogei)* was organized systematically, as an extension of hunting whales that were grounded or that came very close to the coast. The fishers had been using only harpoons, but began to use more modern equipment, following Norwegian methods, about 1897. Becoming bolder, they scoured the seas, hunting large whales for meat and oil. The Japanese whaling fleet was almost completely destroyed during the Second World War, but was reconstructed and considerably expanded in 1952. The Japanese whalers were so successful that international commissions were formed to regulate the whale hunt, forcing Japan to cut back considerably on its whaling campaigns, which became subject to a severe quota.

Williams, Samuel Wells. American Sinologist (1812–84) and missionary who went from Guangzhou, where he edited a newspaper, to Japan on board the *Morrison.* He learned Japanese and was Commodore Perry's official interpreter in 1854–55. He then went back to China. After he returned to the United States in 1876, he was chair of the department of Chinese language and literature at Yale University.

Willis, William. English physician (1837–94), born in Edinburgh. He went to Japan with a British delegation in 1861 and cared for the wounded of the pro-imperial army; in 1868, he was appointed head of the clinic at the Tokyo faculty of medicine (Igakkō). In 1876, he moved to Kagoshima, then to Tokyo; he practiced there until 1881, when he returned to Great Britain.

Wirgman, Charles. English designer (1832–91), sent to Japan in 1861 as a correspondent for the *Illustrated London News.* He fell in love with the

Weights and Measures

Name	Subunits	Metric equivalent
Units of mass		
Bu		0.375 g
Momme	(10 *bu*)	3.750 g
Kin	(160 *momme*)	600 g (variable)
Kan, kamme	(1,000 *momme*)	3,750 g
Units of volume		
Shaku		0.0180 l
Gō	(10 *shaku*)	0.1803 l
Shō	(10 *gō*)	1.8039 l
To	(10 *shō*)	18.039 l
Koku	(10 *to*)	180.39 l
Units of length		
Bu		0.003 m
Sun	(10 *bu*)	0.030 m
Shaku	(10 *sun*)	0.303 m
Ken, hiro	(6 *shaku*)	1.818 m (variable)
Chō	(60 *ken*)	109.09 m (variable)
Kairi (nautical mile)		1,852 m
Ri	(36 *chō*)	3,927 m
Units of area		
Tsubo, bu	(1 *ken*^{2})	3.306 m^2
Se	(30 *tsubo*)	99.175 m^2
Tan	(10 *se*)	990 m^2 (1,190 m^2 before the late 16th century)
Chō, chōbu	(10 *tan*)	9,900 m^2 (3,600 *bu* or 11,901 m^2 before the late 16th century)

country and settled there, drawing many sketches of Japanese life and working with the photographer Felice Beato. They jointly published two works, *Native Types* and *Views of Japan*. Wirgman returned to England only for a brief visit in 1887, then went back to Japan, where he died. He taught his techniques to many Japanese artists, among them Kobayashi Kiyochika and Nozaki Bunzō.

Wrappings (tsutsumu). The Japanese are deservedly famous for the quality of their boxes *(bako)* and wrappings, always executed with extreme care, even for ordinary articles. The presentation of things is very important in Japan because it is seen as a distinctive sign of elegance and of respect for the consumer. *See* GIFTS, TSUTSUMU.

Wright, Frank Lloyd. American architect (1867–1959). He saw the model of the Byōdō-in temple at the Chicago World Fair in 1893, became interested in Japanese art, and went to Japan in 1905 to research ukiyo-e prints. Somewhat inspired by Japanese standards, he then designed his famous Prairie House. In 1922, he designed the Imperial Hotel (Teikoku Hoteru) in Tokyo, using anti-earthquake techniques for the first time; the hotel withstood the 1923 earthquake. Dismantled in 1976, it was reconstructed in Meiji-mura. Wright's other buildings in Tokyo include the Odawara Hotel (1917), a movie theater in the Ginza (1918), and the Yamamura house and the Jiyū Gakuen school (1927). Many Japanese architects emulated him, including his own student, Endō Arata.

Writing. Japanese writing is essentially adapted from Chinese ideogrammatic writing. However, the Japanese and Chinese languages are quite different, and the Japanese modified somewhat the writing of characters *(kanji),* using them either for their phonetic value or for their meaning. Originally, Japanese was polysyllabic, and the Chinese characters adopted at various times came from different regions of China. A number of readings were thus possible: one or several monosyllabic *(on)* "Chinese" readings, and a polysyllabic *(kun)* Japanese reading. The many Japanese grammatical flexional endings were added to the Sino-Japanese characters by transcription, using a syllabic alphabet *(kana, hirigana)* invented in the early ninth century. To distinguish words of a foreign (non-Chinese) origin, and notably for use in telegraphy, another "square" alphabet, *katakana,* was used, the characters in which were simplifications of certain Chinese characters corresponding roughly to their pronunciation. Currently, it is necessary to know 1,945 *kanji* characters (*see* JŌYŌ-KANGI) in order to read a newspaper. Different characters are used to transcribe proper names. *See* CALLIGRAPHY, FURIGANA, GENJI-MON, HIRAGANA, INK, KANA, KANJI, KATA-KANA, KUN, MANA, NIGORI, ON, SHITTAN, TŌYŌ-KANGI.

Xavier, François. Spanish Jesuit (Francisco de Jassu Javier, 1506–52), one of the founders of the Company of Jesus. As apostolic delegate for Asia, he worked in India and in Malacca; there, he met the Japanese fugitive Anjirō, who described Japan to him and urged him to go there. Accompanied by two Jesuit priests and Anjirō, Xavier landed at Kagoshima on August 15, 1549, and began to preach, converting about 100 people relatively easily. He visited Hirado and Yamaguchi and went to Kyoto to meet the emperor, but was not able to obtain an audience. He left Japan in 1551 and died after he reached China, on December 3, 1552. In his letters, he spoke admiringly of the Japanese people, praising their sense of honor and civility.

Y. The consonant-vowel *y* is associated with the vowels *a, u,* and *o* to form the syllables *ya, yu,* and *yo*. In the Hepburn transcription system (used in this book), the older syllables *yi* and *ye* are replaced by the vowels *i* and *e*. The syllables *ya, yu,* and *yo,* placed after certain consonant syllables, such as *ki, shi, chi, hi, mi,* and *ri,* produce composite syllables: *kya = ki + ya; kyu = ki + yu; kyo = ki = yo; sha = shi + ya; shu = shi + yu; sho = shi = yo; hya = hi + ya; hyu = hi + yu; hyo = hi + yo; rya = ri + ya; ryu = ri + yu; ryo = ri + yo; mya = mi + ya; myu = mi + yu; myo = mi + yo; cha = chi + ya; chu = chi + yu; cho = chi + yo; nya = ni + ya; nyu = ni + yu; nyo = ni + yo*. These composite syllables are sometimes "nigorized" into *gya, gyu, gyo; ja, ju, jo; bya, byu, byo; pya, pyu, pyo. See* GOJŪON-ZU, NIGORI.

Ya. "Arrow." Arrows for Japanese bows *(yumi)* are generally very long (about 1 m) and have only two feathers on the heel. The steel tip may be pointed, lanceolate, arced, forked *(karimata),* or armed with a whistle *(kabura-ya)*. The strident-sounding *kabura-ya* were shot before a battle to scare the enemy—and evil spirits. *See* KYŪDŌ, YUMI.

• **Yabusame.** Exercise conducted by warriors and samurai on horseback, consisting of galloping at full speed and shooting arrows at nearby targets set along the route they were taking. Although it seems to have been practiced as early as the eighth century, *yabusame* evolved considerably during the Kamakura period, at the same time as *inu-oi-mono* and *kasagake*. The classic ceremony included between 7 and 36 contestants, but it now features only 3 to 5 horsemen dressed in period costume. The length of the track is about 2 *chō* (240 m), and the three tar-

gets are placed on top of wooden pillars about 1 to 1.5 m high. The event is accompanied by a Shinto ritual during certain *matsuri* and festivals, notably in Tokyo and Kamakura. There are two styles of *yabusame;* in the "classic" style, invented by Minamoto no Yoritomo, the archers are dressed in "hunting costume" *(kariginu)*. The "Edo" style, or *kishahasamimono,* was probably created by shogun Tokugawa Yoshimune in the eighteenth century. The Edo style is displayed each year in early April at the Asakusa shrine in Tokyo. Today, only three families pride themselves on perfect knowledge of the etiquette of *yabusame:* the Miura, the Ogasawara, and the Takeda. The Ogasawara practice a special *yabusame* ceremony at the Tsurugaoka Hachimangū shrine in Kamakura, while the Takeda (represented by the Kaneko family) regularly perform *yabusame* in Kamakura, at the Meiji-jingū in Tokyo, and in Samukawa (Kanagawa prefecture). They also sometimes demonstrate their art in foreign countries. *See* SHIOGAMA JINJA.

• **Yagura.** "Arrow warehouses," turrets built on the walls of a castle and used to store arms, defend access routes, and sometimes lodge certain guests of the castle's governor.
→ *See* YOKOANA.

• *Yagura no oshichi*. Title of a puppet play in *sewa-mono* genre, written by Suga Sensuko, Matsuda Wakichi, and Wakataka Fuemi and first produced in Osaka in 1773 with the title *Date Masamune koi no higanoko*.

• *Ya no ne*. "Arrowhead," a Kabuki play about an episode of vengeance by the Soga brothers: Gorō is busy polishing the tip of a large arrow when his brother Jūrō summons him in a dream. This play, one of the Kabuki-jūhachiban, was first produced by Danjūrō II around 1730.

Yabe Hisakatsu. Geologist (1878–1969), born in Tokyo. He proved that the islands of Japan separated from the mainland about 1 million years ago. He was decorated with the Order of Culture (Bunka-shō) in 1953.

Yabuta Teijirō. Chemist (1888–1977), born in Chiba prefecture, who isolated *Gibberelline,* a plant hormone that accelerates the growth of rice, in 1938. He received the Order of Culture (Bunka-shō) in 1964.

Yaeyama Shotō. Archipelago south of the Ryukyu Islands, part of the Sakishima group; its main islands are Iriomote, Ishigaki, and Taketomi. Tropical crops (pineapple, sugar cane). Area: 584 km². *Pop.:* 50,000.

Yagaku. Secondary schools offering night classes for people who work during the day. Colleges and universities also offer evening courses in programs lasting four to five years. *See* JUKU.

Yagawa Terazaemon. Engineer (nineteenth century) who, with his colleague Takashima Shūhan, was arrested and imprisoned in 1846 by the Edo *bakufu* for having learned about artillery from the Dutch in Nagasaki.

Yagi Hidetsugu. Electronics engineer (1886–1976), born in Kyoto. His research, conducted jointly with Uda Shintarō, resulted in the invention of a type of antenna (called Yagi-Uda) now used universally for television and radio. President of Osaka University and the Tokyo Institute of Technology; decorated with the Order of Culture (Bunka-shō) in 1956.

Yagō. Family name adopted by some people, beyond their family name, to distinguish themselves from others with the same name. It was taken from the name of the house they occupied, their business, or a particular place, spot, village, province, or other geographic entity. During the Edo period, this practice was current among publishers of books and ukiyo-e prints and among Kabuki actors. Also called *iena, kadona. See* GŌ, NAMES.

Yagyū Munenori. Famous master of arms (1571–1646), originally from Nara, who studied with his father, Yagyū Muneyoshi (Yagyū Tajima no Kami, 1527–1606), founder of a swordfighting school, the Yagyū-ryū (renamed Yagyū Shinkage-ryū in 1603). After fighting alongside Tokugawa Ieyasu at the Battle of Sekigahara (1600) and the siege of the castle of Osaka (1615), he became master-at-arms for Tokugawa Hidetada and Tokugawa Iemitsu, then was appointed ō-*metsuke* (inspector general) in 1632. His descendants taught swordfighting to succeeding Tokugawa shoguns. He wrote a few works on his art, including *Heihō kadensho* (Family Traditions on the Warrior Arts) and *Gyokusei-shū.*

Yakiba. Wavy section of dull martensite running along the edge of a saber blade, bordering the surface of the steel tempering. The shape of the *yakiba* was often used to identify the saber maker, or at least the school to which he belonged. The line bordering the *yakiba* is called *yokote. See* KATANA.

Yakko. Before the Nara period, this term was equivalent to "slave" *(nuhi)*. During the Edo period, *yakko* were servants personally attached to a daimyo or *hatamoto*. Those who, for one reason or another, had no master and became *rōnin* formed bands *(machi-yakko)* and sometimes terrorized urban areas. The term *yakko* was also applied to women who had to serve as slaves, either because they had infringed on a shogunal order or because they were the wives of banned people. In the early Meiji era, Westerners used this term for all sorts of indigenous servants—palanquin porters, rickshaw pullers *(jinrikisha)*, and others. *See* SHIOKI, YAKUNIN.

• In Kabuki theater, the role of a foot soldier *(ashigaru, zusa)*, who often executes an acrobatic dance.

Yakoshiso Tamafuru. Astrologer (seventh century) who studied Korean astronomy books brought back to Japan by the Buddhist monk Kanroku in 602. He established a calendar called Genka-*reki* in 604.

Yakubyōgami. *Kami* of Shinto folk beliefs, one of the *goryō,* or evil or avenging spirits, said to provoke epidemics. Also called Ekibyōgami, Eyami no Kami, Ekijin.

Yakudoshi. According to a very widespread belief, crucial years in the live of individuals, said to be hazardous, especially the 25th and 42nd for men, the 19th, 33rd, and 49th for women, and the 61st and 70th for both sexes. In fact, this belief (like many others of the same type) is based only on the fact that words said to bring bad luck and the numbers in the incriminated years are homonyms.

Yakumo mishō. Treatise on classic poetry *(waka),* one of the first of its type, written by Emperor Juntoku when he was in exile on Sado, after 1221.

Yakunin. In the Edo period, low-ranking bureaucrat in charge of the police. Also, a term applied by Westerners to all sorts of low-ranking servants. Also called *yakko. See* MACHI-YAKUNIN.

Yakusa no Kabane. Collective term for eight official titles conferred upon nobles by Emperor Temmu in 684: Mahito, Ason (Asomi), Sukune, Imiki, Michinoshi, Omi, Muraji, and Inagi (Inaki). The titles Mahito and Ason were reserved for members of the imperial family. *See* I, KABANE.

Yakusha-banashi. "Commentaries on the Actors." A collection of advice and Kabuki plays compiled by Sugi Kuhei, Tominaga Heibei, Fukuoka Yagoshirō, Kaneko Kichizaemon, and several other actors about 1776; some parts were written earlier. Also called *Yakusha-rongo.*

Yakushi-in. Mudra (hand gesture; Jap.: *in-zō)* specific to images of the Medicine Buddha, Yakushi Nyorai (*Skt:* Bhaishajyaguru), the right hand being in the "absence of fear" (*Skt.:* Abhaya) position and the left hand holding a jar of medications.

• **Yakushi-ji.** Buddhist temple in Nishinokyō (Nara prefecture), about 3 km southwest of Nara, founded for the Hosshō-shu sect between 680 and 720. Its buildings, dedicated to the Medicine Buddha, Yakushi Nyorai, were often destroyed by war and fire and periodically rebuilt. All that remains from the era of its foundation is the *tō-tō* (eastern pagoda), a unique structure, in that it has three real stories and three *mokoshi* (intermediary stories), so that it appears to have six in all. This pagoda, in pure *wa-yō* style, built in 717 or 729, is 37 m high. It is topped with a bronze *sorin (kyūrin).* All that remains of its counterpart, the western pagoda *(sai-tō),* are the stone bases of the pillars. It has a *tō-in-dō* dating from 1285, and *bussokudō,* structure containing "Buddha's footprints" *(see* BUSSOKU-SEKI), dating from 753. The *kondō,* rebuilt in 1635, houses a bronze triad dating from 719–29, with halos added in the seventeenth century. Every March 3, the temple hosts the Saishō-e ceremony, during which the monks read sutras; in January is the

Kichijō Keka-e (Veneration of Kichijō-ten) ceremony. Nearby is a Shinto shrine dedicated to Hachiman (ninth-century wooden sculptures).

• **Yakushi Nyorai.** Buddhist divinity, the Medicine Buddha (*Skt.:* Bhaishajyguru), sometimes considered a form of (or substitute for) Ashuku Nyorai (*Skt.:* Akshobhya), whose preferred land is also to the east. He is the "doctor of soul and body," often invoked for the purpose of healing. *Chin.:* Yaoshi Fo.

Yakushima. Island south of Tanegashima, in the Ōsumi group. This very mountainous island's highest peak has an altitude of 1,935 m. It has the rainiest climate in Japan, with precipitation of up to 10,000 mm per year. Cedar forests *(yakusugi). Area:* 500 km^2; *pop.:* 50,000.

Yakushin. Buddhist monk (827–906) of the Shingon-shū, *zasu* of the Ninna-ji temple in Heian-kyō. He received the posthumous title Hongaku Daishi.

Yakuza. "Gangster," term for individuals who belong to secret societies and make their living (sometimes a huge income) operating gaming rooms and brothels and conducting all sorts of illegal activities. These gangs, like the Mafia, are highly organized and hierarchical and have their own code of honor. There are currently more than 2,500 *yakuza* societies in Japan, involving more than 100,000 people. Most *yakuza* leaders have strong connections with political and financial circles, which makes their elimination by the police extremely difficult. Some groups have branches as far away as the United States, where they control Japanese communities. The word *yakuza* is apparently derived from a card game favored by young criminals in the Edo period, in which the one who drew an 8 *(ya),* a 9 *(ku),* and a 3 *(san, sa, za)* lost the game, having passed the winning total of 19. After the Second World War, the *yakuza* were often in the headlines, and many movies about their supposed exploits were made in Japan and the United States. However, once the anti-gang law came into effect on March 1, 1992, the police declared *yakuza* societies illegal, and they have diverted their activities into trade and other businesses to cover their illegal activities. *See* TAKA-KURA KEN.

Yama. Japanese reading *(kun)* of the Sino-Japanese *(kanji)* character meaning "mountain." In Chinese reading *(on),* it is pronounced *san.* According to the rules for reading *kanji* characters, *kun* and *on* read-

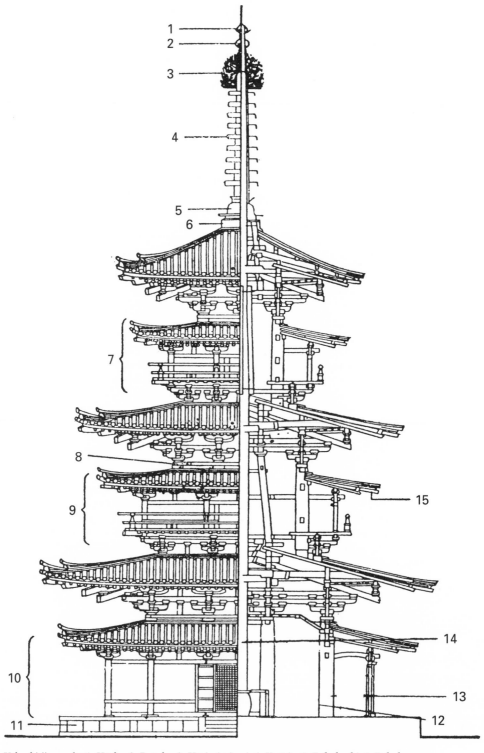

Yakushi-ji pagoda. 1. *Hōshu*. 2. *Ryūsha*. 3. *Hōrin (sui-en)*. 4. *Kyūrin*. 5. *Fukubashi*. 6. *Fukuban*.
7 and 9. *Mokoshi* (awnings). 8. Top of pillar. 10. Base *mokoshi*. 11. *Kidan* (terrace). 12. Outside pillar.
13. *Mokoshi* pillar. 14. Central pillar. 15. *Hien-daruki*

ings cannot be combined in a single word. Therefore, one cannot say Fuji-yama, because "Fuji" is an Ainu word *(on)* and "yama" is a Japanese word *(kun);* one must say Fuji-san. The word *take (-dake* in composite words) is also used to describe a high mountain, a peak, or a summit. A great many Japanese words and nouns have the word "yama" as a component. Yamamoto, for example, means "the origin of the mountain" or "the foot of the mountain." *See* SAN.

• Term for chariots in the procession during the festival of the Gion shrine in Kyoto, because their pointed form evokes a mountain. The largest chariots are called *hoko* (lance) and are mounted on wheels, while *yama* are carried on the shoulders of young men (or sometimes mounted on small wheels). Portable shrines, which are completely different from these chariots, are called Yamaboko Junko ("mountains and lances"). *See also* DASHI.

• General term for coal mines. *See* MINING, COAL.

• **Yama-biraki.** Shinto religious ceremony that opens the season for climbing sacred mountains, especially Mt. Fuji. The ritual is generally conducted by Yamabushi monks.

Yamabe no Akihito. Poet and court noble (?–ca. 736), whose works (37 *tanka* and 13 *chōka)* appear in the *Man'yōshū.* Describing the beauties of nature, they were written during voyages that the author made in the company of Emperor Shōmu between 724 and 736. Yamabe is also credited with other poems (at least 50) included in various anthologies. He received the title of *kasei (see* WAKA NI SEI) and is considered one of the *Man'yō* no Gotaika.

Yamabushi. "Those Who Sleep on the Mountain," ascetics generally belonging to the Buddhist Tendaishū sect (sometimes the Shingon-shū), recognized as followers *(shugenja)* of the Shugendō doctrines. Once hermit-sorcerers, medicine men, and miracle workers, they were divided into many groups and claimed En no Gyōja as the founder of their "order." In the Edo period, they often lived with *miko* in isolated villages. The Yamabushi wear an ancient costume, related to that of Siberian shamans, decorated with pompons and small bells, a black skullcap *(tokin),* wide pants drawn in at the ankle, and a tunic made of pieced-together bits of fabric; they carry a conch shell *(hora),* a pilgrim's stick *(shakujō)* with chiming rings, and a string of holy beads *(nenju).* They let their hair grow freely. In the Meiji

era, they were forced to join recognized Buddhist sects. *See* SHUGENDŌ.

Yama-chawan. Unvarnished tea bowls, in the *sueki* tradition, made of rough earthenware and often twisted in shape. They were produced for daily use in many kilns in the twelfth and thirteenth centuries, and "rediscovered" in the fifteenth century by tea-ceremony aesthetes. In Sanage, the remains of a number of kilns that had produced *yama-chawan* pottery have been found.

Yamada Akiyoshi. General (1844–92) and politician. Appointed minister in 1883, he helped write the legal code of 1883–84.

Yamada Bimyō. Writer and poet (Yamada Taketarō, Bimyōsai, 1868–1910), born in Tokyo, founder with Ozaki Kōyō of the magazine *Garakuta Bunko* in 1885. In 1887, he began to write stories in spoken language, such as *Mushashino,* which were published in a collection titled *Natsuko-dachi* (1888). His best-known novels are *Chōkai shōsetsu tengu* (1887) and *Kochō* (1889). His poems inaugurated the Shintai-shi style in 1882. He also wrote an essay on vernacular style, *Gembun itchiron gairyaku.*

Yamada-dera. Buddhist temple founded in Sakurai (Nara prefecture) in 641 by a member of the powerful Soga family; it was completed in 676. Excavations on the site of this temple between 1976 and 1982 uncovered the foundations of a *kondō* and a pagoda that were originally located at the center of a court surrounded by an open gallery. A large bronze head from a statue of Yakushi Nyorai (probably *jōroku* size), now in the Kōfuku-ji temple in Nara, belonged to the main statue of the Yamada-dera. *See* KAWARA-DERA.

Yamada Hikaru. Ceramist, born 1924 in Gifu. He received many distinctions in Japan, and his works were in the exhibition of Japanese ceramics in Paris in 1994 (Mitsukoshi space).

Yamada Isuzu. Movie actor (Yamada Mitsu), born 1917 in Osaka. She began to work for the Nikkatsu company in 1930, then moved to the Daiichi company in 1934, appearing in a number of films by Mizoguchi Kenji. Then, working for Tōhō, she acted under directors Hasegawa Kazuo, Kinugasa Teinosuke, and Makino Masahiro. She also performed in the theater and formed her own troupe, Gendai Haiyū Kyōkai, in 1954. She received the grand prize of the National Festival of Arts in 1974 for her performance in the film *Tanuki*.

Yamada Kōsaku. Composer and orchestra conductor (1886–1965), born in Tokyo. He studied in Berlin from 1908 to 1914 with Max Bruch and K. L. Wolf, then founded the Tokyo Symphony Orchestra in 1915, conducted the New York Symphony Orchestra at Carnegie Hall in 1917, and founded the Opera of Japan in 1920. One of his operas, *Ayame*, was performed at the Pigalle theater in Paris in 1931. He composed more than 150 songs and other pieces.

Yamada Nagamasa. Adventurer (Yamada Nizaemon-Nikichi, 1578–1630), born in Suruga province. He stowed away in a ship belonging to two merchants, Taki and Ōta, bound for Taiwan, then boarded a Dutch ship in 1611 and went to Siam. He settled in Ayuthyā, working for the king of Siam, Songtham, and fought under him at the head of a company of émigré Japanese. When the king died, in 1628, Yamada formed a troop of 800 Japanese armed in samurai style and helped the Siamese army secure the throne for the crown prince. But the usurper, Prasat Thong, killed both of the king's sons and seized the throne, and Yamada and several hundred of his Japanese soldiers were exiled to Ligor. Wounded in battle, he was poisoned by one of his servants. His son, Yamada A-in, fled to Cambodia, but he also died fighting against the Siamese army. Finally, in 1633, the survivors of Yamada Nagamasa's army were allowed to return to Siam. According to some accounts, King Songtham gave Yamada his daughter in marriage and appointed him regent while his son was a minor (1630). During his stay in Siam, Yamada apparently hosted the merchants Taki and Ōta, who told of his adventures when they returned to Japan and offered gifts in his name to the Sengen-miya shrine. It is not known, however, exactly how much of what has been said about him is true.

Yamada Tomohiko. Writer, born 1936 in Yokohama, author of *Chichi no shanikusai* (The Fathers' Carnival, 1968) and *Jikken shitsu* (The Laboratory, 1972).

Yamada Yōji. Movie director, born 1931 in Tokyo. He went to work at Shōchiku in 1955 as an assistant director for Ōshima Nagisa; in 1963, he began to make his own films, including the very popular *Tora-san* series. He also made many intimist films on the lives of ordinary people, including *Mutsuko*

(The Son, 1991) and *Otoko wa tsurai yō* (It's Hard to Be a Man), and received many awards in Japan, including the prestigious Kinema Jumpō Prize.

Yamada Yoshio. Grammarian (1873–1958), born in Toyama prefecture. He compared the syntax of Japanese to traditional elements of European languages and conducted research on the history of linguistics in Japan. His many works are considered essential for an understanding of Japanese grammar.

Yamaga Sōkō. Samurai (1622–85) of the Aizu clan, Hayashi Razan's disciple. He studied Confucianism, Shinto, and military sciences, then founded his own school (Yamaga-ryū), which taught that samurai, even in times of peace, had to follow certain Confucian ideals and assume entire moral and intellectual responsibility for society. In 1665, he published his concepts of ethics, which were quite distant from those of Zhu Xi (*Jap.*: Shushi) taught by Hayashi Razan and favored by the shogunate, and he was exiled. In *Seikyō yōroku* (Basics of the Sacred Teachings) and his other works, *Buke-jiki* and *Chūchō jijitsu* (a historical work written in 1669), he laid the true foundations of what would soon after become Bushido. He was particularly intolerant of Buddhism and claimed that Shinto was superior to all other religions. His tomb, in the Sōsan-ji temple in Shinjuku (Tokyo), still receives visitors.

Yamagata. Chief city of Yamagata prefecture, on the Mogami-gawa river, about 120 km northeast of Niigata; former castle town (*jōka-machi*) of the Mizuno family; in the Edo period, an important post town (*shuku-eki*) at the crossroads of a number of routes. It is an industrial and commercial center (fruit, silk, petroleum and natural-gas industries, foundries). Annual Hanagasa festival is in August; Buddhist Risshaku-ji temple, founded in the ninth century. *Pop.*: 250,000.

• **Yamagata prefecture.** Prefecture in northern Honshu, bordering the Sea of Japan (Nihonkai), formerly part of Dewa province. Mountainous (Mounts Ōu, Asahi, and Dewa) and irrigated by the Mogami-gawa river, which forms the Shōnai plain. Populated by the Ezo before the seventh century, it was the fief of the Ōshū Fujiwara family in the Heian period. Forests, rice paddies, and orchards are its main resources. *Chief city*: Yamagata; *main cities*: Sakata, Tsuruoka, Kaminoyama, Nan'yō, Yonezawa, Tendo. *Area*: 9,326 km². *Pop.*: 1.3 million.

Yamagata Aritomo. Politician (1838–1922), born in Hagi to a family of samurai from Chōshū. A solid supporter of the pro-imperial *sonnō jōi* movement, he led the small Kiheitai army, which earned him a position as vice-minister of military affairs in 1870, after having been sent to Europe for a year to study military systems. In 1877, he helped suppress the Satsuma Rebellion (*see* SAIGŌ TAKAMORI), and in 1878 he reorganized the army on the Prussian model. He became chief of general quarters, but resigned in 1882 to become president of the Legislative Bureau *(sanjin);* then, as minister of the interior *(naimushō),* he reformed the police and installed a new system of local government. In December 1889, he became prime minister, succeeding Kuroda; Matsukata succeeded him in 1891. As minister of war in 1894–95, he directed the war against China. In 1896, he led a diplomatic mission to Russia and obtained rights equal to Russia's in Korea. Two years later, he was once again prime minister, succeeding Ōkuma, and he was succeeded by Itō Hirobumi in 1900. He supported Katsura Tarō's cabinet in the Anglo-Japanese alliance of 1904–05, and was chief of general quarters. He was appointed president of the State Council in 1905 and received the title of prince *(kōshaku)* from Emperor Meiji in 1907. As *genrō* and president of the Privy Council, he gave well-heeded advice in the choice of prime ministers and was influential in political circles for the rest of his life. He is considered the father of the Japanese army.

Yamagata Bantō. Scholar (Hasegawa Yūkyū, Masuya Kouemon, Yamagata Yoshihide; *gō:* Bantō, 1748–1821), born to a family of wealthy merchants in Osaka; adopted by the family of his uncle, Masuya Kyūbei. He studied "Dutch science" *(rangaku)* under Asada Goryū and Nakai Riken, and attempted to reconcile certain Confucian theories with Western materialist concepts. He began to write a synthesis of his ideas, *Yume no shiro,* in 1802; this voluminous work was completed only in 1820 (six volumes). Fundamentally a materialist, he denied the existence of the soul as such, considered Buddhism simply an amalgam of superstitions, doubted all dogma, and feared the danger represented by the European colonial powers. After studying the *Kojiki,* he declared ancient mythology to be without serious foundation. Although his views on history conformed fully with those of the shogunate, he was an isolated thinker. His ideas had some influence on modern Japanese philosophers, but he was not really "rediscovered" and appreciated until after the Second World War.

Yamagata Daini. Confucian scholar (Yamagata Ryūso, 1725–67), born in Kai province and adopted by a samurai family. He served in the police force, then studied medicine; he began practicing as a physician in Edo in 1752. He wrote a work, *Ryūshi shinron* (1759), in which he advocated armed resistance against the shogunate, which, according to him, was corrupt. Because he had conspired with some of his friends, he was arrested, sentenced to death, and executed.

Yamagata-Lobanov Pact. Accord signed on June 9, 1896, between Yamagata Aritomo and the Russian minister of foreign affairs, Aleksei Lobanov-Rostovski, in St. Petersburg, according to which Russia and Japan recognized that they had equal rights in Korea and declared that they would participate jointly in modernization of that country. This pact, which gave concrete expression to an accord signed several months before between Komura and Weber, was modified in Japan's favor by the accord signed between Nishi and Rosen in April 1898.

Yamagata Masao. Naval architect (1898–1981), born in Tokyo, whose research led to advances in Japanese shipbuilding. He received the Order of Culture (Bunka-shō) in 1967.

Yamagiwa Katsusaburō. Biologist (1863–1930). With Ichikawa Kōichi (1888–1948), he artificially caused cancer in rabbits. He received various honorary distinctions for his work.

Yamaguchi. Chief city of Yamaguchi prefecture, about 50 km northeast of Shimonoseki; castle town *(jōka-machi)* of the Ōuchi family in the fifteenth and sixteenth centuries. In 1555, the Mōri replaced the Ōuchi, who moved to Hagi. The town was built in the fourteenth century on a grid plan similar to that for Kyoto. Francis Xavier founded a Christian mission there in 1550. Buddhist Ruriko-ji temple with a fourteenth-century pagoda and a garden designed by Sesshū. Festival of Yamaguchi Gion at the Yasaka shrine July 20–27; another festival November 23–25. *Pop.:* 120,000.

• **Yamaguchi-ken.** Prefecture in Chūgoku, in extreme southwest Honshu, comprising two former provinces, Nagato and Suō, which formed Chōshū. It has very jagged coasts on both the Sea of Japan (Nihonkai) and the Inland Sea (Setonaikai), which is called "Sea of Suō" in the region. Yamaguchi prefecture is linked to Fukuoka prefecture (Kyushu) by a tunnel and a bridge linking Shimonoseki to Kita

Kyūshū (*see* KAMMON KAIKYŌ). Heavy-industry and chemical plants are found along the south coast, while the interior produces mainly rice and citrus fruit. *Chief city:* Yamaguchi; *main cities:* Shimonoseki, Ube, Hōfu, Hikari, Tokuyama, Iwakuni (on the Sea of Suō), Nagato, Hagi (on the Sea of Japan), Mine, Yuda, Yumoto (spas). *Area:* 6,095 km². *Pop.:* 1.6 million.

Yamaguchi no Atai Ōguchi. Sculptor (seventh century), who worked for Emperor Kōtoku around 650, according to the *Kojiki.* He was said to have sculpted 1,000 images of Buddha (Sentai Butsu). It seems that he also worked for the Hōryū-ji in Nara.

Yamaguchi Hitomi. Writer, born 1926 in Tokyo. In 1962, he received the Naoki Prize for his novel *Eburimanshi ni yūga na seikatsu* (The Days of Mr. Everyman). He also wrote essays—*Danseijishin* (1963)—and other novels dealing with the life of office workers *(sararīman),* including *Majime ningen* (A Serious Person, 1965); he received the Kikuchi Kan Prize for *Ketsuzoka* (Relatives) in 1979.

Yamaguchi Hōshun. Painter (Yamaguchi Saburō, 1893–1971), from Hokkaido. He was a member of the Rokuchō-kai and Saikō-kai and was decorated with the Order of Culture (Bunka-shō) in 1965.

Yamaguchi Kaoru. Painter (1907–68) in Western style, born in Gumma prefecture. He was profoundly influenced by the Paris school, having lived in Europe for three years starting in 1930. He helped to found the Society of Free Artists (Jiyū Bijutsuka Kyōkai), and had works in the Salon de Mai in Paris in 1952; he exhibited widely, including in São Paulo, New York, and Venice. He began to teach at the Tokyo School of Fine Arts (Tokyo Bijutsu Gakkō) in 1953.

Yamaguchi Kayō. Painter (Yamaguchi Yoneijirō, 1899–1984) in "Japanese" style (Nihonga), born in Kyoto; studied with Takeuchi Seihō (1864–1942). He was elected a member of the Japan Art Academy (Nihon Geijutsu-in) in 1971 and decorated with the Order of Culture (Bunka-shō) in 1981. He is known mainly for his paintings of animals.

Yamaguchi Seishi. Modern haiku poet (Yamaguchi Chikahiko, 1902–94), born in Kyoto. He published more than 10,000 poems, in 16 collections, and some of them appeared in *Hototogisu.* He left this circle in 1935 to work with *Ashibi.* His best-known

collections are *Tōkō* (The Frozen Port, 1932), *Wafuku* (1955), and *Kōjitsu* (Red Sun, 1991).

Yamaguchi Sekkei. Painter (Yamaguchi Sōsetsu; *gō:* Baian, Hakuin, 1644/1649–1732) from Kyoto, in Sesshū's style. He may have been Kanō Einō's student, although his style was very different from that of his two masters. He painted fusuma for the Daigo-ji and Myōshin-ji temples in Kyoto.

Yamaguchi Sodō. Poet (Yamaguchi Nobuaki, 1642–1716), born in Kai province; a friend of Bashō. He studied with Hayashi Gahō and worked briefly for the shogunate, but retired to devote himself to poetry and calligraphy. He probably influenced Bashō's art by introducing him to the beautiful Chinese poems by Li Bai and Du Fu. He was also a master *(chajin)* of the tea ceremony *(chanoyu).* His students formed a school called Katsushika, named for the place near Edo where he had retired.

Yamaguchi Soken. Painter (Yamaguchi Takejirō; *azana:* Hakugo; *gō:* Sansai, 1759–1818) from Kyoto, Maruyama Ōkyo's student; he painted beautiful women, and flowers and birds. He also illustrated books and wrote a six-volume work, *Yamato jimbutsu gafu,* describing the customs and ways of Kyoto residents. He also signed his works with the name Soken.

Yamaguchi Susumu. Buddhist monk (1895–1976) of the Jōdo-shū in the Ganshō-ji temple (Kyoto) and famous scholar. He was rector of Ōtani University from 1950 to 1965. He wrote a number of scientific works on Buddhism and translated several works by Western writers.

Yamaguchi Takeo. Painter (b. 1902) in Western style, and sculptor. He lived in Paris from 1928 to 1930 and worked in Zadkine's studio, then had exhibitions in many galleries in the West and Japan. He received a number of prizes, including that of the Ministry of Education in 1962.

Yamaguchi Yoshiko. Movie actress (Ri Kōran), born 1920 in Manchuria; she was very popular before the Second World War, notably in films by Watanabe Kunio. In 1951, she married the sculptor Noguchi Isamu; later, she married a diplomat, Ōtaka Hiroshi. She ran for election in 1974 and was elected to the Upper House of the Diet.

Yamaha Hatsudōki. Manufacturer of engines for motorcycles, boats, generators, and various vehicles, founded in 1955 when it separated from the Nippon Gakki firm. It began to be internationally known for its motorcycles in 1958, when its products won the Catalina race, and they have since been entered in most championships and races. Yamaha exports 70% of its production and has opened subsidiaries and plants in many countries. Head office in Iwata (Shizuoka prefecture).

Yamai no sōshi. Ten-page *emakimono* describing various physicians and illnesses and telling nine tales of Buddhist morals, painted in Yamato-e technique, probably in the late twelfth century, by an unknown author. Sekido Collection, Aichi prefecture.

Yamaji Aizan. Christian writer and journalist (1864–1917), born in Edo; in 1905 he co-founded (with another journalist, Shiba Teikichi, 1869–1939) the National Socialist party (Kokka Shakaitō) to oppose communism. In addition to many nationalist-leaning articles published in various newspapers and magazines, he wrote biographies of Ogyū Sorai (1893) and Ashikaga Takauji (1909) and political works.

Yamaji monogatari. Thirteenth-century novel by an unknown author, intended to be a continuation of the *Genji monogatari;* because it lacks spontaneity and style, however, it does not stand up to its predecessor.

Yamakawa Hitoshi. Marxist theoretician (1880–1958), born in Kurashiki. After studying at the Dōshisha in Kyoto, he and several of his friends were arrested for treason (they had written a pamphlet opposing the marriage of the crown prince); during his four years in prison, he read excerpts of Marx's *Das Kapital.* When he was freed, he embraced the socialist cause, then, influenced by Kōtoku Shūsui, became something of an anarchist. He wrote articles on Marx's work and paraded through the street carrying socialist posters, so he was arrested again and imprisoned from 1908 to 1910. In 1916, he married fellow socialist Aoyama Kikue, continuing to write articles advocating socialism and then, after the Russian Revolution of 1917, communism. In 1922, he was a co-founder of the Japan Communist party (Nihon Kyōsantō), but he left it in 1924, feeling that conditions in Japan were different from those in the USSR. He formed the Rōnō-ha (Labor-Farmer faction) with a few friends, then abandoned all political activity in 1927 to devote himself to writing. He was neverthe-

less arrested for his opinions in 1937 and 1938. After the Second World War, he helped revive the Socialist party.

• **Yamakawa Kikue.** Yamakawa Hitoshi's wife (Aoyama Kikue, 1890–1980). She attended Tsuda University in Tokyo and began to publish feminist articles and translations of foreign works on socialism. In 1921, she helped to found the Sekirankai (Red Wave Society), the first women's socialist organization in Japan. She also helped her husband publish the newspaper *Rōnō.* As a member of the new Japan Socialist party (Nihon Shakaitō) after the Second World War, she fought against prostitution, and she translated August Bebel's *Di Frau und der Sozialismus.* She was the first Japanese woman to demand that women's rights be maintained through the creation of a true social-security system. Her collected works (11 vols.) were published in 1981–82 by the publisher Iwanami Shoten.

Yamamai. Silkworm *(Attacus yamamai)* unique to Japan. The silk from its cocoons is very highly valued.

Yamamba. Female demon living in the mountains with the *Yama no kami.* In most legends, she is portrayed as a stupid being. Also called Yamauba. *See* KINTARŌ, TA NO KAMI.

• *Yamamba.* Title of a Noh play: a strange female boar, the spirit of a mountain, meets a dancer named Hyakuma Yamamba who is traveling to the Zenkō-ji temple; she teaches her the dances of the four seasons.

Yamamoto Baiitsu. Painter (Yamamoto Ryō, Yamamoto Shinryō; *azana:* Meikei; *gō:* Shun-en, Tendō-gaishi, Gyoku-zen Koji, Baika Shujin, Yūchiku-sōkyo, Baiitsu, 1783–1856), born in Nagoya. A student of Kamiya Ten'yū, he first copied the works of painters of the Nanga school, then gradually developed his own style. He was appointed painter of his clan in Nagoya in 1854, which earned him the status of samurai. He painted mainly landscapes, flowers, and birds, and also worked with Chikuto in Kyoto.

Yamamoto Fujiko. Movie actor, born 1931 in Osaka. In 1953, she began to work for the Daiei company, starring in films by Kinugasa Teinosuke and Yoshimura Kōzaburō. Following a contractual dispute with Daiei in 1963, she abandoned her career. This ephemeral star was known for her beauty.

Yamamoto Gonnohyōe. Politician and admiral (Yamamoto Gombei, 1852–1933), born to a samurai family in Satsuma. He fought in the Boshin Civil War (1868) on the imperial side, then, after studying at the naval school, trained on board a German warship from 1878 to 1888. He took part in the Sino-Japanese War of 1894–95, and was promoted to vice-admiral in 1895. Appointed minister of the navy in Yamagata Aritomo's second cabinet in 1898, he kept this position until 1904. In 1913, he became prime minister, succeeding Katsura Tarō, but resigned the following year because of a scandal that tainted the honor of the navy, and retired from this branch of the armed forces. In 1923, he was again prime minister, succeeding Katō Tomosaburō, but he abandoned all political activity following Toranomon's failed assassination attempt. Viscount Kiyoura succeeded him. He was decorated with the Order of the Chrysanthemum (Kiku no Shō).

Yamamoto Hokuzan. Confucian scholar (1752–1812), born in Edo. Refusing any official position, he created a school in his home, where he had collected a large number of books. A poet, he wrote an essay on the poems of Yuan Hongdao (1568–1610), a Chinese anti-conformist who used vernacular language.

Yamamoto Hōsui. Painter (Yamamoto Tamenosuke; *gō:* Hōsui, Seikō, 1850–1906) in the Western style, born in Mino province. He first followed the style of the Nanga (Bunjinga) school, then studied Western painting with Charles Wirgman and Goseda Hōryū (1827–92) and under Antonio Fontanesi. He then went to Paris, where he studied at the school of fine arts as Gérôme's student from 1878 to 1887. When he returned to Japan, he opened a painting academy, the Seikōkan, in Edo, and taught the French style of the Barbizon school.

Yamamoto Isoroku. Admiral (Takano Isoroku, 1884–1943), born in Nagaoka and adopted by the Yamamoto family. As an officer in the Russo-Japanese War of 1904–95, he was wounded at the Battle of Tsushima. In 1919, he was sent to Harvard University, and he was the naval attaché to the Japanese embassy in Washington from 1926 to 1928. Because he was a pilot, he became interested in air combat, and he was appointed vice-minister of the navy in 1936. He unsuccessfully opposed the Tripartite Pact, which, he felt, would inevitably lead to war with the United States. In 1940, he was appointed commander of the combined fleets, and in this capacity, he recommended the attack on Pearl Harbor in December 1941. His plane was shot down by American fighter planes on April 18, 1943, while he was conducting an inspection tour above Kahili, the Solomon Islands. Admiral Kōga Mineichi replaced him. Yamamoto Isoroku was posthumously appointed admiral of the fleet. *See* AGAWA HIROYUKI.

Yamamoto Kajirō. Movie director (1902–73) who first acted and wrote screenplays for the Nikkatsu company and was an assistant to Murata Minoru and Kurosawa Akira. He then made comedies and, during the Second World War, many propaganda films. After the war, he returned to light comedies.

Yamamoto Kanae. Painter (1882–1946) in the Western style, born in Aichi prefecture. He went to France in 1912, then visited Russia before returning to Japan in 1916. He founded an institute for the development of folk art in Nagano prefecture, then became interested in modern-style prints. In 1922, he helped found the Shun'yō-kai and made oil paintings and prints.

Yamamoto Kansai. Fashion designer, born 1944 in Kanagawa prefecture. His avant-garde ("Kansai" style) fashions debuted in London in 1971.

Yamamoto Kenkichi. Writer and literary critic (Ishibashi Teikichi, 1907–88), born in Nagasaki; Ishibashi Ningetsu's son. He became known for his studies on modern writers and authors who use the first person (*see* SHI-SHŌSETSU) in his series of essays titled *Shi-shōsetsu sakkaron* (1943). He received the Japan Art Academy (Nihon Geijutsu-in) Prize 1966. Among his best-known works are a critique of modern authors, *Koten to gendai bungaku* (1955) and a study on the poet Kakinomoto no Hitomaro.

Yamamoto Kyūjin. Painter (Yamamoto Masayoshi, 1900–86) in Nihonga style, born in Tokyo; Matsuoka Eikyū's student. At first, he painted landscapes in Yamato-e style. He organized a few painters' societies and received a number of high distinctions for the quality of his works, including the Japan Art Academy (Nihon Geijutsu-in) Prize in 1964 and the Order of Culture in 1977. Some of his works are on exhibit in the Riccar Museum and the Museum of Modern Art in Tokyo.

Yamamoto Michiko. Novelist and poet (b. 1938). She lived mainly in Australia and the United States. Among her best-known works are *Maho* (Powers),

Betty-san no niwa (Betty-san), which won an award, *Bereji no ame* (Village in the Rain), and *Hito no ki* (The Human Tree).

Yamamoto Morinosuke. Painter (1877–1928) in the Western style who studied with Asai Chū and Hōsui in Tokyo.

Yamamoto Satsuō. Movie director (1910–83), born in Kagoshima. He made many feature films on social subjects, which had a great influence on the Japanese public. After having been Naruse Mikio's assistant at the Sōchiku company, he worked for the Tōhō company. His most important films, most of which denounce the corruption of ministers and bureaucrats, are *"Symphonie pastorale"* (1938), *Senso to heiwa* (War and Peace, 1947), *Boryoku no machi* (District without Sunshine, 1950), *Hakone fu-unkoko* (Storm over Hakone, 1951), *Shinku chitai* (Vacuum Zone, 1952), *Kareinaru ichizoku* (The Family, 1974), *Kinkanshoku* (Solar Eclipse, 1975), and *Fumō chitai* (Barren Zone, 1975).

Yamamoto Senji. Politician (1889–1929), born in Kyoto. A biologist, he advocated birth control, but lost his professorship at the University of Kyoto for having publicly taken a position against government policy. In 1928, he was elected to the Diet for the Rōdō Nōmintō (Labor-Farmer party), and kept his seat after the party was dissolved. He opposed the government's pro-Chinese policy and was assassinated by a member of an extreme-right party.

Yamamoto Shūgorō. Writer (Shimamazu Satomu, 1903–67), born in Yamanashi prefecture. When he moved to Yokohama, he was adopted by a merchant, whose name he took. He worked as a journalist in Osaka, then went to Tokyo in 1926 and began to write novels and stories describing the life of ordinary people. Fundamentally an anarchist, he refused all prizes that his novels won. His novels dealt with injustice, as in *Sabu* (1963) and *Nagai saka* (The Long Slope, 1964); life among disadvantaged classes, as in *Akahige shinryōtan* (The Redbeard Clinic, 1958), adapted for the screen by Kurosawa Akira in 1965; and life among fishers, as in *Aobeka monogatari* (Stories from the Blue Fishing Boat, 1960). The novel *Kisetsu no nai machi* (The Neighborhood with No Seasons, 1962) was also adapted for the screen by Kurosawa as *Dodes'kaden*. Yamamoto also wrote historical works from his particular viewpoint, including *Shōsetsu ki* (History of Yūi Shōsetsu, 1956) and *Momi no ki wa nokotta* (Only the Pine Tree Resisted, 1958), and novels de-

voted to the moral strength of Japanese women, including *Nihon fudōki* (The Path of Womanhood, 1942). His body of work includes some 50 novels, stories, and essays, many of which were adapted for the screen, not only by Kurosawa but also by Nomura Takeshi, Okamoto Kihachi, Kobayashi Masaki, and Kawashima Yūzō, among others.

Yamamoto Tatsuō. Politician (1856–1947), minister of finance in 1911–12, then of commerce (1913–14 and 1918–22). In 1924, he founded the Seiyū Hontō (True Seiyū party), which merged with the Rikken Minseitō (Constitutional Democratic party) in 1927.

Yamamoto Yasue. Stage actress (1902–93), born in Tokyo, one of the founders of the Tsukiji theater (Tsukiji Shōgekijō) in Tokyo in 1924, then of the New Tsukiji theater company Shin Tsukiji Gekidan), with which she performed until 1940. She received the prize of the Ministry of Education in 1951 for her performance of the role of Tsū in Kinoshita Junji's play *Yūzuru* (The Dusk Crane, 1949).

Yamamoto Yōji. Fashion designer (b. 1943) whose styles are inspired by the Japanese kimono; his Western designs are modern, even avant-garde. His collections are shown in Paris and New York as well as Japan.

Yamamoto Yūzō. Author and playwright (1887–1974), born in Tochigi. With Akutagawa Ryūnosuke and Kikuchi Kan, he continued publication of the literary magazine *Shinshi-chō*. He translated Strindberg's plays and wrote several of his own, including *Eijigoroshi* (Story of a Child's Murder, 1920) and *Sakazaki dewa no kami* (The Daimyo of Dewa, 1921); he then turned to novels: *Nami* (Waves, 1928), *Onna no shō* (1933), *Robō no ishi* (Stones in the Road, 1937). Elected to the Chamber of Councillors after the Second World War, he received the Order of Culture (Bunka-shō) in 1965.

Yamamura Bochō. Writer and poet (Tsuchida Hakkujū, 1884–1924), born in Gumma prefecture, who became known for a collection of poems, *Sei sanryō hari* (The Sacred Prism, 1915), composed of impressions with no apparent connection between them. He also wrote several novels, including *Jūjika* (The Cross, 1922), about a plot in Christian circles. His second, and more accessible, poetry collection, *Kuno* (Clouds, 1924), was published after his death.

Yamamura Saisuke. Geographer (Yamamura Masanaga, 1770–1807), born in Hitachi province. He was the disciple of Ōtsuki Gentaku, who rewrote *Sairan igen,* a geography treatise by Arai Hakuseki.

Yamamura Sō. Movie director (Yamamura Satoru, b. 1910), who made *Kankio sen* (The Factory Ship, the Ships of Hell, 1953), *Kuroi oshio* (Black Tide, 1954), and other films.

Yamana. Warrior family of the Muromachi period, descended from the Seiwa Genji branch of the Minamoto, who controlled Kōzuke province (now Gumma prefecture). Ashikaga Takauji gave its members large estates; in 1363, the Yamana were *shugo* of five provinces, and later of eleven. But some members of the family rebelled against the shogun Ashikaga Yoshimitsu in 1391 and the Yamana lost many of their territories, which Yamana Sōzen managed to recover in 1441. The rivalry between the Yamana and the Hosokawa was one of the causes of the Ōnin War (1467–77).

• **Yamana Sōzen.** Warrior (Yamana Mochitoyo, 1404–73), *shugo* of a number of provinces in western Honshu. In 1441, he fought Akamatsu Mitsusuke, who had assassinated shogun Ashikaga Yoshinori; for this feat, he received three of the provinces previously held by Akamatsu Mitsuhide, which somewhat redeemed the honor of his family. Although he became a Buddhist monk in 1450, with the name Sōzen, he continued to be active, taking Ashikaga Yoshihisa's side against Hosokawa Katsumoto in the dispute over the succession to shogun Ashikaga Yoshimasa. The resulting civil war lasted 10 years, during which much of Kyoto was destroyed. *See* ŌNIN NO RAN.

Yamanaka Sadao. Movie director (1909–38) who worked for only about six years, making historical films in which he showed the daily life of samurai and ordinary people in Edo. Among his best-known films are *Ninjō kamifūsen* (Humanity and Paper Balloons, 1937) and *Akinishi kakita,* made just before he died in Hina, where he had been sent as a soldier.

Yamanaka Shikanosuke. Warrior (Yamanaka Yukimori, 1545–78) serving the Amako family of Izumo province. The Amako were dispossessed by the Mōri in 1566, and Yamanaka became a *rōnin,* constantly doing battle with the Mōri to recover Izumo province for the Amako. He supported the cause of Amako Katsuhisa (1553–78) and, assisted

by Oda Nobunaga and Toyotomi Hideyoshi, defended a line of forts built against the Mōri. When they were defeated, Amako Katsuhisa committed suicide; Yamanaka was captured by the Mōri and executed.

Yamanashi-ken. Prefecture in central Honshu, north of Mt. Fuji, formerly Kai province, controlled in succession by the Minamoto, the Takeda, the Asano, and, in the Edo period, directly by the shogunate. It is mountainous, with a small plain surrounding its chief city, Kōfu. Mt. Minobu (with the main temple of the Nichiren sect) and the five lakes of Mt. Fuji are in Yamanashi prefecture. *Main cities:* Ōtsuki, Fuji Yoshida, Tsuru, Yamanashi, Enzan, Uenohara. *Area:* 4,463 km². *Pop.:* 820,000.

Yamanoi Kanae. Neo-Confucian historian (Yamanoi Konron, 1680–1728) who lived in Edo.

Yama no kami. "*Kami* of the mountain" who descends into the fields during the spring planting and becomes a *Ta no kami.* This belief may be related to the Yayoi-period bronze halberds and *dōtaku* found buried in hillsides. Sometimes called *hitosume kozō* because it is portrayed in some regions with one eye and one leg. It also sometimes symbolizes echoes and is then called Yamabiko. *See* TA NO KAMI, YAMAMBA.

Yamanouchi Kazutoyo. Warrior (1545–1605), born in Owari, who began to serve Toyotomi Hideyoshi in 1573 and fought at his side at the Battle of Shizugatake in 1583. He was promoted to daimyo in Wakasa province, then moved to Ōmi province when Hideyoshi appointed him adviser to Toyotomi Hidetsugu. After the siege of the Odawara castle (1590), Hideyoshi assigned him a fief, worth 59,000 *koku,* in Tōtōmi province. After allying himself with Tokugawa Ieyasu in the Battle of Sekigahara (1600), he was made daimyo of an estate worth 200,000 *koku* in Tosa province. Yamanouchi then fought the supporter of the former daimyo, Chōsokabe Morichika (1575–1615), and founded the Tosa clan. It was said that his wife, Kenshō-in (1557–1617), was a great help to him in establishing his hegemony in this province.

Yamanouchi Sugao. Archeologist (1902–70), born in Tokyo, who became famous for his dating of Jōmon pottery and his studies on the making and decoration of this pottery. He taught at several universities, including the University of Tokyo.

Yamanouchi Toyoshige. Daimyo (Yamanouchi Yōdō, 1827–72) of the Tosa estate, which he helped to modernize, with the assistance of Yoshida Tōyō. He opposed the treaties of the Ansei era and the policy of Ii Naosuke and was forced to resign in 1859. He was among those who advised shogun Tokugawa Yoshinobu to return power to the emperor, and later tried in vain to have the former shogun admitted into the Meiji government.

Yamanoue no Okura. Court bureaucrat (660–ca. 773) and poet. He was sent to China from 702 to 707 as the embassy secretary, then was tutor to the crown prince, the future Emperor Shōmu. In 726, he became governor of Chikuzen province. As a poet, he was considered eccentric; he wrote 63 *tanka,* 2 poems in Chinese, and an essay in prose that was included in the *Man'yōshū.* He also compiled *Ruijukarin* (The Forest of Chinese Bamboo), an anthology of poems (between 721 and 733), now lost. It is thought that he was of Korean origin.

Yamanoue Sōji. Tea master (1544–90), Sen no Rikyū's disciple, author of a famous work on the tea ceremony *(chanoyu),* the *Yamanoue sōji-ki,* written while his master was still alive. *See also* NAMBŌ SŌKEI.

Yamaoka Sōhachi. Writer (Fujino Shōzō, 1907–78), born in Niigata prefecture. After writing propaganda during the Second World War, he was banned from publishing until 1950. He made a remarkable return with his biography of Tokugawa Ieyasu (1950–57), an enormous 26-volume work, which received the Yoshikawa Eiji Prize in 1968. He also wrote biographies of Oda Nobunaga (5 vols., 1954–60) and Toyotomi Hideyoshi (6 vols.).

Yamaoka Tesshū. *Hatamoto* samurai (Yamaoka Tetsutarō, 1836–88), born in Edo. In 1868, he played an important role in the restoration of imperial power by negotiating the disarmament of the shogunal troops and the surrender of the Edo castle. He was appointed adviser to the imperial household in 1881, and a senator the following year. A talented calligrapher and well-known fencing master *(ken-jutsu; see* KENDŌ), he also excelled in handling the lance *(yari).* He revived the "swordless" school of combat *(mu-tō),* inspired by the one created by Yagyū Takima (1527–1606), which taught that it is possible to resolve conflicts without using a sword, solely by the strength of a pure spirit sincerely wishing to avoid confrontation.

Yamasaki Minoru. Architect (1912–86) who became an American citizen. He designed the St. Louis International Airport and the World Trade Center in New York (1972).

Yamashiro. Original name of Kyoto (in 784–94) and former province, now Kyoto prefecture (Kyōto-fu).
• Painter (late sixth century) commonly called "the master of Yamashiro." Nothing is known about his life.

Yamashiro no Ōe no Ō. Prince Shōtoku Taishi's oldest son (?–643). He claimed to be Empress Suiko's successor in 628, but he was ousted by Prince Tamura, who, supported by Soga no Emishi, was enthroned as Emperor Jomei in 629. When Soga no Iruka attacked his residence in 643, Yamashiro and his entire family committed suicide. *See* SARUMARU-DAYŪ.

Yamashiro Tomoe. Novelist (Tokumo Tomoe, b. 1912), wife of communist activist Yamshiro Yoshimune (1900–45), who died in prison. She wrote novels based on living conditions of poor rural women: *Fuki no tō* (A Stem of Coltsfoot, 1948), *Niguruma no uta* (Handcart Songs, 1955), *Toraware no onnatachi* (Life of Women in Prison, 1980, 10 vols.).

Yamashita Kyōemon. Kabuki actor (Yamashita Hanzaemon, ca. 1650–1717), who specialized in *tachiyaku* roles. He was *zamoto* (theater director) in Kyoto.

Yamashita Tomoyuki. General (Yamashita Hōbun, 1885–1946), born in Kōchi prefecture. During the Second World War, he commanded the 25th army in Malaysia. In this capacity, he captured Singapore from the British navy on February 15, 1942, and commanded the retreat of the Japanese forces from the Philippines in 1944. Because his soldiers had committed atrocities, he was found guilty of war crimes in Manila and was executed.

Yamatai-koku. In the third-century Chinese chronicles *Sanguozhi* and *Weizhi,* the name of a Japanese state whose location has never been definitely pinpointed, but which is generally thought to have been in northern Kyushu and which probably had its capital in Na(koku). Queen Himiko would have been its leader. There were important trade and diplomatic relations between Yamatai and Wei-dynasty China. Some authors think that Yamatai was in Yamato. The debate is ongoing; an answer would be important because it would provide information about the formation of the Japanese state and its relations with the mainland. *See* YOSHINOGARI.

Yamataka Shigeri. Suffragette (Kaneko Shigeri, 1899–1977), born in Mie prefecture. She was active in the movement for women's voting rights in the 1920s, alongside Ichikawa Fusae, then continued her fight for protection of women and children. She founded a consumers' association (Chifuren) in 1952 and was elected to the Chamber of Councillors in 1962 and 1965.

Yamata no Orochi. In Shinto mythology, according to the *Kojiki,* a legendary dragon with eight heads and eight tails that ravaged Izumo province. Susanoo no Mikoto vanquished it by plying it with *sake.* After killing it, he found in its tail the magical sword Ame no Murakumo no Tsurugi (later called Kusanagi no Tsurugi), which was to become one of the three symbols of the imperial family given by Amaterasu-Ōmikami to Ninigi no Mikoto when he descended to Earth. Some authors think that Yamata no Orochi is symbolic of a river; others, that it represents the eight *kuni* (kingdoms) conquered by Susanoo. *See* INADA-HIME.

Yamate Kiichirō. Writer (Iguchi Chōji, 1899–1978), born in Tochigi prefecture. His best-known novels are *Uguisu-zamurai* (The Nightingale Samurai, 1940) and its supplement, *Momotarō-zamurai* (The Samurai Momotarō, 1940), and *Yumesuke senryō miyage* (1947).

Yamato. Former province, now Nara prefecture. This name is also applied to all of Japan. Also called Yamato-chōtei, "heart of Japan."
• Name of a kingdom in southern Nara before the fifth century, perhaps the same as Yamatai-koku.

• *Yamato.* Name of the largest battleship built during the Second World War, in 1941. *Displacement:* 64,170 tons; *crew:* 3,332; *speed:* 27 knots; *weapons:* nine 450 mm cannons, twelve 155 mm cannons, twenty-four 25 mm cannons, and four 13 mm cannons. It could hold six airplanes. *Range of action:* 7,200 nautical miles; *length:* 250 m; *width:* 39 m. It took part in the battles of Midway, the Philippines, and the Gulf of Leyte. Commanded by Admiral Itō Seichi, it was sunk during the Battle of Okinawa on April 7, 1945, and its demise marked the end of the Japanese naval war effort.

• **Yamato Bunkakan.** Private art, history, and archeology museum, in a modern building located in the countryside near Nara. Its collections (more than 2,000 objects) are featured in a seven-volume catalogue.

• **Yamato-damashii.** "Spirit of Yamato," an expression used mainly before and during the Second World War as a symbol of Japan's strength, spirit, courage, and capacity of devotion to the homeland and the emperor. In literary circles of the medieval period, it meant all that was in essence purely Japanese, as opposed to what had been received from China. It was said that a man had Yamato-damashii when he had accomplished all things.

• **Yamato-e.** Style of painting that developed during the Heian period, named to distinguish it from Chinese Tang painting, Kara-e. The oldest examples of Yamato-e painting seem to have been inspired by the seasons *(shiki-e),* famous sites *(meisho-e),* and agricultural and other activities *(tsukinami-e).* Yamato-e paintings also illustrated *waka* poems, which were often handwritten on the painting itself. These art works were executed on paper *(emakimono),* hanging panels *(kakemono),* or screens *(fusuma, byōbu,* etc.). In the eleventh century, Yamato-e began to be used mainly for *emakimono* illustrations, portraying episodes in great literary works (such as the *Genji monogatari)* and poetry books. The best Yamato-e painters generally belonged to the *e-dokoro* of the imperial court, although many artists worked for *e-dokoro* of temples or noble families.
    Yamato-e painting is characterized by a high-angle view looking down into the interior of houses, as if the roof has been lifted off *(fukinuki-yatai),* and by a simplified treatment of faces: a hooked line for a nose and eyes like commas *(hike-me kagi-hana).* Paintings were first drawn in ink and then colored with bright colors *(tsukuri-e).* The painters of the Tosa family, including Tosa Mitsuyoshi, Tosa Mitsunori, and Sumiyoshi Hiromichi, were attached to this school (also called Yamato-ryū, Kasuga-ryū). Yamato-e was gradually abandoned in the late thirteenth century, but was revived in the late Edo period and called Fukko Yamato-e.

• **Yamato-hime.** Empress, Tenji Tennō's wife. She led the government after her husband died in 671.
    • Legendary princess, Emperor Suinin's daughter, and grand priestess of the Ise shrines. Her life was recounted in a work called *Yamato-hime no mikoto seiki,* considered one of the *Shintō gobushō,*

written by the *kannushi* (priest) Mike and rewritten by someone called Satsukimaro in 768. Modern researchers have identified Yamato-hime with Himiko.

• *Yamato-honzō.* Work on botanical pharmaceuticals, written by Kaibara Ekiken in 1708, published in 1709 (its illustrated part was published in 1715).

• **Yamato-kai.** Subsect (Ōnushi-kyō) of the Jikko-kyō, founded in 1949 by Matsui Shizue (b. 1915).

• **Yamato-mai.** Ancient dance that may have been performed for the first time before Emperor Ōjin (fourth century?) by villagers from the Yamato region and that was adopted by the court for certain ceremonies. *See also* JINJI-MAI.

• **Yamato-mono.** School of blacksmiths who made sword blades in Nara. During the Kamakura period, it split into five subschools attached to Shinto shrines: Senju-in, Tegai, Taema, Hōshō, and Shikkake. One of the best-known blacksmiths of the early period of this school was Amakuni. Also called Goha-mono.

• *Yamato monogatari.* "Tales of Yamato," a collection of 173 short stories, in two scrolls. Each story related to a *waka,* so this work is of the *uta-monogatari* ("novel-poem") genre, as is the *Ise monogatari.* Dating from the late tenth century, and probably written by several authors, it gives many details on life in the court in the ninth and tenth centuries, and inspired many later "novels" and Noh plays.

• **Yamato Nadeshiko.** During the Second World War, a term for women who, according to Japanese authorities, had the "Yamato spirit" (Yamato-damashii)—that is, who were fiercely nationalistic. The others were disdainfully called Kara Nadeshiko, after a wild carnation.

• **Yamato Setsugen.** In 1912, explorer Shirase Nobu gave this name to the part of Antarctica that he had explored.

• **Yamato-takeru no Mikoto.** Legendary hero, supposedly Emperor Keikō's third son (O-usu, Yamato-oguna, second century?), whose story is told in two very different ways in the *Kojiki* and *Nihon shoki.* Yamato-tekaru was said to have fought the Kumaso in southern Kyushu and the Ezo

in Kanto, thus expanding the imperial territories. He died of disease at age 30. His legend, probably drawn from a *fudoki,* was likely written in the fifth or sixth century.

Yamatoya Jimbei. Kabuki actor (active 1650–1704) and *zamoto* in Osaka and Kyoto. He is still famous for his technique in *roppo* (men's dances).

• **Yamatoyama Jinzaemon.** Kabuki actor (Tōjūrō II, Kosakata, 1677–1721) who specialized in *tachiyaku* roles.

Yamawaki Tōyō. Physician (Shimizu Tōyō, 1705–62), born in Kyoto. On March 30, 1754, he performed the first human dissection in Japan, on a cadaver in a prison near Kyoto. Five years later, he published the results of his observations in an illustrated work called *Zōshi* (Entrails). He also had a Chinese medical work from the Tang dynasty reprinted and wrote a number of medical treatises.

Yamazaki Ansai. Neo-Confucian philosopher (1618–82), born in Kyoto to a family of low-ranking samurai serving the daimyo of Himeji. When he was 10 years old, he studied at the Enryaku-ji and became a Buddhist monk of the Tendai-shū affiliated with the Zen Rinzai-shū sect of the Myōshin-ji. He then studied Zhu Xi (*Jap.:* Shushi) Confucianism and abandoned Buddhism to teach neo-Confucianism in Kyoto and Edo, creating a "school" called Kimon. It was very successful and drew students from all parts of Japan, for whom he wrote an excellent short treatise, *Bunka hitsuroku* (Reading Notes). He had also studied Shinto and realized that although Zhu Xi doctrine was perfect for China, the "Way of the *Kami*" was perfect for Japan. He therefore advocated simultaneous study of both doctrines and founded a new sect, Suika Shintō, that mixed the theories of Ise Shinto with neo-Confucian concepts, making it the precursor to the nationalist Kokugaku (National Learning) school of thought.

Yamazaki Masakazu. Playwright (b. 1934); he wrote modern plays that were performed in Japan and the West, including *Zeami* (1963), *Ō Eroizu* (Oh, Heloise, 1972), and *Sanetomo shuppan* (Sanetomo Sets Sail, 1973).

Yamazaki no Tatakai. Battle that took place on July 2, 1582, near Ōyamazaki, northeast of Osaka (*see* HONNŌ-JI), between the armies of Toyotomi Hideyoshi and Akechi Mitsuhide, after Akechi had attacked Oda Nobunaga and forced him to commit suicide. Assisted by Oda Nobutaka, Ikeda Tsuneoki (1536–84), Takayama Ukon, and other daimyo, Hideyoshi attacked Akechi on the slopes of Tennō-zan. Akechi, who had 16,000 soldiers, had to retreat before the 40,000 soldiers commanded by Hideyoshi, and he took refuge in the Shōryū-ji castle. Surrounded, he fled, but was killed by peasants. This battle was the first step taken by Toyotomi Hideyoshi toward unification of Japan.

Yamazaki Ryū. Painter of ukiyo-e prints (active around 1720); daughter of a samurai, Yamazaki Bunzaemon. Her painting style was called O-Ryū-e.

Yamazaki Sōkan. *Renga* poet (ca. 1465–ca. 1553), known mainly for having compiled the first haiku anthology, *Inu tsukuba-shū,* to parody *Tsukuba-shū.* Sōkan was probably a samurai serving Ashikaga Yoshihisa. He likely became a Buddhist monk and retired to Yamazaki, whence the name he was given. *See* INU TSUKUBA-SHŪ.

Yame kofun. Group of megalithic tombs located on a plateau near the town of Yame (Fukuoka prefecture, Kyushu), containing 11 keyhole-shaped tombs and some 60 round tombs. Most of the tombs (among them the Iwatoyama *kofun*) date from the late fifth or early sixth century and have inner chambers decorated with paintings or bas-reliefs. Some of them have sculpted figures. *See* KOFUN.

Yanagawa Shunsan. Scholar and journalist (1832–70), born in Nagoya. In 1867, he published the newspaper *Seiyō Zasshi,* aimed at introducing the West to the Japanese people; in 1868, he published another newspaper, *Chūgai Shimbun,* which ran 86 issues. He also created the *Chūgai Shimbun Gaihen* in 1868, with the assistance of Watanabe Ichirō.

Yanagida Izumi. Translator (1894–1969) of works in English, born in Aomori. He became known for his translations of works by Whitman, Thoreau, and Carlyle, and he published a major 24-volume work on society in the Meiji era, *Meiji bunka zenshū* (1930). He also wrote a number of books on culture in that period.

Yanagihara Mutsuo. Ceramist, born 1934 in Uwajima (Ehime prefecture). He became a professor at the Osaka University of Fine Arts in 1968. His works were in the exhibition "Avant-garde Art of Japan" at the Centre Georges Pompidou in Paris in

1986, and in an exhibition at the Mitsukoshi space in 1994.

Yanagi Keisuke. Portrait painter in the Western style (1881–1923) who worked mainly in the United States and France.

Yanagimachi Mitsuo. Movie director, born 1945 in Ibaraki prefecture. His first film, *God Speed You Black Emperor,* was a success. He also made *Jukyu sai no chizu* (His Nineteen-Year Plan, 1979) and *Saraba itoshiki daichi* (Farewell, Dear Earth, 1982).

Yanagi Muneyoshi. Art historian (Yanagi Sōetsu, 1889–1961). He helped found the magazine *Shirakaba;* in 1924, he founded the art museum in Seoul, Korea, where he had been living since 1916. He studied folk art and coined a new term for it, *mingei.* He gave a number of lectures on this subject overseas, including at Harvard University in 1929 and 1936, and helped found the Komaba Folk-Art Museum in Tokyo. He also made ceramics inspired by folk art, worked with Bernard Leach, and designed clothes. *See* MINGEI UNDŌ.

Yanagisawa Kien. Painter (Yanagisawa Rikyō; *azana:* Kōbi; *tsūshō:* Ryū Rikyō, 1704–58) and samurai serving Kōriyama, the daimyo of Yamato. A student of Ei Genshō (Yoshida Shūsetsu), he followed the Kanō and Nanga styles. He painted birds and flowers, large landscapes, and bamboo in monochrome.

Yanagisawa Yoshiyasu. Samurai (1658–1714), a favorite of shogun Tokugawa Tsunayoshi, who made him daimyo of Sanuki and Kōfu and, in 1701, authorized him to use the name Matsudaira, reserved for the Tokugawa family. He was made responsible for transgressions by the shogun, but in fact he did nothing about the aberrant edicts the shogun promulgated. He promoted both Confucianism and Buddhism and made use of the services of eminent men such as Ogyū Sorai and Hosoi Kōtaku. Also called Dewa no Kami, Mino no Kami.

Yanagita Kunio. Ethnologist and writer (Matsuoka Kunio, 1875–1962), born in Hyōgo prefecture; his father was a Shinto priest and physician. He adopted his wife's family name when he married Yanagita Ko, a daughter of Yanagita Naohei, a judge at the Supreme Court. Secretary of the House of Peers from 1914 to 1924 and observer at the League of Nations in Geneva from 1921 to 1923, he also worked as a correspondent for *Asahi Shimbun* until 1932. He studied folk traditions with Sasaki Kyōseki, and his many writings (more than 100 books and hundreds of articles) described the traces of ancient folklore and vocabularies. Among his major works are *Tōno monogatari* (1910), *Nihon mukashi-banashi-shū* (1930), and *Nihon no densetsu* (1940). He was the true founder of the study of Japanese folklore *(minzoku-gaku).*

Yanagui. Cylindrical *(tsuboyanagui)* or flat *(hirayanagui)* quivers. The latter were used in the sixth century and were portrayed on *haniwa* and in tomb *(kofun)* paintings. They seem to have had a religious significance (now lost), because the arrows they contained had their point up, contrary to custom.

Yanaihara Tadao. Economist (1893–1961), born in Ehime prefecture, who was Uchimura Kanzo's student. A Christian, he was firmly opposed to the war in Manchuria and therefore had to resign from his position as professor at the University of Tokyo in 1937. His most important work is a study on Japanese colonies, *Shokumin oyobi shokumin seisaku* (Colonization and Colonial Policy), published in 1927. He was president of the University of Tokyo from 1951 to 1957.

Yano Ryūkei. Politician and writer (Yano Fumio, 1850–1931), born on Kyushu. He worked with Ōkuma Shigenobu and published a political novel that caused a sensation, *Keikoku bidan* (Beautiful Story of the Classical Countries, 1883–84), on the rivalry between Thebes and Sparta in ancient Greece, extolling the importance of the notions of freedom and independence. While contributing to a number of newspapers, he wrote other novels with a social content, such as *Ukishiro monogatari* (The Floating Fortress, 1890) and *Shin shakai* (The New Society, 1902). *See* KEIKOKU-BIDAN.

Yari. Lances used mainly by Buddhist monks and foot soldiers *(zasu, ashigaru).* There are many sorts, including *te-yari* (or *ko-yari*), small in size; *nagayari,* with a very long shaft; *jomon-yari* and *kagiyari,* with a sort of cross or hook on the iron base; *kama-yari,* with a sickle-shaped blade at the base of the point; and *magari-yari,* in the form of a cross all of whose edges are sharp. The blade is protected by a scabbard, usually made of wood, called *saya.* For training *(yari-dō),* the blades are buttoned. *See also* JITE, NAGINATA.

Yasaka-jinja. Shinto shrine in Kyoto, dedicated to Susanoo no Mikoto, built in the Gion-*zukuri* style from 1654 to 1664 on the site of a former shrine dedicated to Gozu Tennō, a syncretic divinity. The festival there lasts almost the entire month of July. Torii dating from 1646; *rōmon* from the thirteenth century. Also called Gionsha, Gion Tenjin, Kanshinin.

Yasakani no magatama. Necklace made of *magatama,* housed in the Tokyo Imperial Treasury, one of the three jewels (Mi-kusa no Kandakara) symbolizing the emperor's power, along with the sacred mirror *(yata no kagami)* and sword (Ame no Murakumo no Tsurugugi, or, later, Kusanagi no Tsurugi).

Yasaka no Tō. *See* HŌKAN-JI, KENNIN-JI.

Yashao. Famous sculptor of masks who may have made a mask for Minamoto no Yoriie in 1204 that is currently housed in the Shuzen-ji in Izu.

Yashica. Camera manufacturer, founded in 1949, that popularized medium-sized viewfinder cameras, similar to the Rolleiflex, and small-format cameras. It has plants in Hong Kong, Brazil, the United States, Germany, and Canada, and exports more than 60% of its production. Head office in Tokyo.

Yashiki. Formerly, residences and their surrounding land, whose owners were forced to pay taxes in the Edo period.

Yashima. Formerly a small island off the coast of Shikoku, northwest of Takamatsu (Kagawa prefecture), now physically linked to Honshu. It was the site of famous battles between the Taira and the Minamoto in 1185.

• *Yashima.* Title of a Noh play, attributed to Zeami: a fisherman reveals to a Buddhist monk and his servant that he is the ghost of Minamoto no Yoshitsune and tells them about his battle against the Heike (Taira) at Yashima and how he rode his horse into the sea to recover his lost bow.

• *Yashima-dera.* Buddhist temple near Yashima (Shikoku) containing a beautiful statue of Kannon dating from the ninth century.

Yashiro. General term for Shinto shrines. They are divided into *amatsu-yashiro* (simple shrines) and *kuni-yashiro* (national shrines). *See also* JINGŪ, JINJA, MIYA.

Yashiro Hirokata. Confucian scholar (Rinchi, 1758–1841), born in Edo, and follower of National Learning (Kokugaku). A great calligrapher, he was hired by the shogunate as an official scribe *(yūhitsu)*. He wrote a questionnaire and had it sent to all so that he could gather accurate information about customs. He also wrote a sort of encyclopedia on Japan and China and amassed a large collection of works on Chinese and Japanese classics; this library was destroyed during the bombing of Tokyo in 1944.

Yashiro Seiichi. Playwright, born 1927 in Tokyo. He worked for the Bungaku-za theater company founded by Kishida Kunio, and his play *Kiiro to momoiro no yūgata* (1959), on problems faced by young people after the Second World War, was very successful. Among his other plays are *Yoaki ni kieta* (They Disappear at Dawn, 1968) and works on the great painters of ukiyo-e prints, such as *Sharaku-kō* (1972) and *Hokusai manga* (1973).

Yasuchika. Metal engraver (Tsuchiya Yasuchika; *gō:* Tōu, Tōō, 1670–1744), one of the Nara Sansaku.

Yasuda. Major financial institution *(zaibatsu),* formed in 1880 by Yasuda Zenjirō (1838–1921), assassinated by an extremist to whom he had refused a cash donation), that controls many companies, mainly banks and trading firms. It absorbed a number of local banks in 1923. In 1945, Yasuda was dismantled and its components became independent. It has nevertheless remained one of the largest financial institutions in Japan.

• **Yasuda Denki.** *See* DENKI.

Yasuda Yojūrō. Writer and critic (1910–81). In 1935, he wrote *Nihon rōman-ha,* a journal of the modern Romantic school of Japanese literature, in collaboration with Kamei Katsuichirō (1907–66). An anti-modernist and aesthete, he tried to preserve tradition.

Yasuda Yukihiko. Painter (Yasuda Shinzaburō, 1884–1978) in "Japanese" (Nihonga) style, born in Tokyo. He studied the style of the Tosa school, then converted to ukiyo-e style, in which he was noted for the fluidity of his drawn lines and the restraint with which he treated his subjects (most of them historical). Artistic advisor to the imperial household in 1934, he taught at the Tokyo School of Fine Arts (Tokyo Bijutsu Gakkō) from 1944 to 1948 and

received the Order of Culture (Bunka-shō) in 1951. He was elected president of the Japan Art Academy (Nihon Geijutsu-in) in 1958.

Yasui Sōtarō. Painter (1888–1955) in the Western style, born in Kyoto; Asai Chū's student. He lived in Paris from 1907 to 1914 and studied at Académie Julian. His works were strongly influenced by Pissarro and Cézanne. He specialized in portraits, genre scenes, and landscapes. A member of the Nika-kai and the Imperial Fine Arts Academy (Teikoku Bijutsu-in) in 1935, he was decorated with the Order of Culture (Bunka-shō) in 1952. *See* ISSUI-KAI.

Yasui Tetsu. Teacher (1870–1945), born in Tokyo to a family of former samurai. She studied in Great Britain from 1897 to 1900 and taught in Bangkok from 1904 to 1907. When she returned to Japan, she taught at the Peers' School (Gakushūin), then was president of the Christian University of Tokyo from 1924 to 1940.

Yasukuni-jinja. Shinto shrine in Tokyo, founded in 1868 by Prince Arisugawa Taruhito; later dedicated to the memory of the 2.4 million Japanese people killed in war between 1853 and 1945. This shrine, at first called Shōkonsha ("to invite the spirits"), was renamed Yasukuni ("for the peace of the empire") in 1879. Until 1945, it was customary for the emperor to send a representative *(chokushi)* there each year to preside over an official ceremony, but this custom was abolished after the Second World War. Prime Minister Ōhira visited it in 1979; this provoked a number of protests because the gesture was seen as a revival of nationalist sentiment.

Yasumi Toshio. Writer (1903–91), born in Osaka. He wrote scripts for many films directed by Toyoda Shiro, Imai Tadashi, Yamamoto Satsuo, Abe Yutaka, and Gosho Heinosuke.

Yasunobu. Painter (Kanō Yasunobu, Kanō Shirojirō, Kanō Genshirō; *gō:* Eishin, Bokushinsai, Seikanshi, Ryōfusai, Yasunobu, 1613–85) of the Kanō school who studied with his older brother, Tan'yū. He founded the Nakabashi branch of the Kanō school in Edo and directed the shogunal *e-dokoro*. One of his descendants, also a painter, had the same name, Yasunobu (1767–98).

Yasuoka Masahiro. Confucian philosopher (1898–1983) of the Ō-Yōmei (*Chin.:* Wang Yangming) school and theoretician of nationalism before the

Second World War. He had a strong influence on politicians and government bureaucrats, even after 1945, and published the imperial rescript ending the Second World War. He specialized in writing ministerial speeches.

Yasuoka Shōtarō. Writer, born 1920 in Kōchi prefecture, who received the Akutagawa Prize for two stories published in 1953. He also received the Noma Prize for his novel *Umibe no kōkei* (A View by the Sea, 1959), written in a personal style (*see* SHI-SHŌSETSU). Among his other works are *Maku no orita kara* (After the Curtain Falls, 1967), *Shichiya no nyōbō*, and *Amerika kanjō ryokō* (A Sentimental Journey to America, 1962).

Yasurime. Mark made with a file on the tang of a sword: irregular *(sensuki)*, in parallel lines *(kiri)*, oblique to the right *(katte-sagari)*, very oblique *(sujikai)*, herringbone *(takahona)*, or crossed *(higaki)*. These marks often make it possible to identify the school or maker. *See* KATANA.

Yatabe Ryōkichi. Botanist (1851–99), born in Shizuoka prefecture. After studying in the United States, he founded the Tokyo Biological Society, directed the National Museum of Science, and founded the Tokyo Botanical Society. He wrote poetry in the "new style" *(shintaishi)* and was a proponent of adoption of the roman alphabet *(romaji)* to write Japanese.

Yata-garasu. Three-footed crow, a mythical bird of Chinese origin, said to live in the sun. It is often drawn on an image of the sun. *Chin.*: Yangwu.

Yata jizō engi. Early-fourteenth-century two-scroll *emakimono* on the legend of Jizō Bosatsu and the foundation of the Yata-dera temple (*see* KONGŌSEN-JI), kept in the Yata-dera in Kyoto.

Yata no kagami. Flower-shaped bronze mirror with eight petals, one of the three treasures of the imperial dignity (Mi-kusa no Kandakara), kept in the *naigū* of Ise. According to tradition, it was made by Ishikaritome no Mikoto. It symbolizes the sun (Amaterasu-Ōmikami) and purity of spirit. *See also* ISE KŌDAIJINGŪ, KAGAMI, KASHIKO-DOKORO, YASAKANI NO MAGATAMA.

Yatsuhashi Kengyō. Blind musician (1614–85), composer of modern music for koto, including the *dammono* and *rokudan* airs. *See* SŌKYOKU.

Yatsuko. Before 645, a term for commoners. Lower social classes were called *yatsume*.

Yawata (Yahata). "Eight Banners," one of the names given to the *kami* Hachiman (Ōjin).

• **Yawata Seitetsujo.** Industrial combine established in Yawata (a conurbation of Kita-Kyushu) in 1896 with the assistance of German engineers, using funds from the war indemnity received from China in 1895. It is currently the largest steel mill in Japan, using ore imported from India (Goa), China, and Korea. In 1970, it affiliated with Fuji Seitetsu to form the Nippon Steel Corporation.

Yayoi. Period in Japanese history from about 300 BC to about AD 300, succeeding Jōmon culture. It was characterized by the creation of flooded rice paddies, the use of iron and bronze, the use of wheels to make pottery, and the establishment of kingdoms (*see* KUNI, MIYATSUKO) and social classes.

Yayoi civilization began in northern Kyushu and spread rapidly through Honshu, Yamato, and up to Kanto, where the first ceramics belonging to this culture were discovered near Tokyo (on the eponymously named site). It was probably imported from the mainland (perhaps southern China) by small groups of immigrants who dominated the Jōmon peoples and the Ebisu. Typical of Yayoi-culture religion are *dōtaku* and bronze halberds, which have been found shallowly buried on hills overlooking villages. Villages were quite large and contained houses on short pilings and very elevated granaries. Many Chinese bronze mirrors (*see* KAGAMI) dating from this period have been found. Men and women dressed in fabrics made from hemp and mulberry-bush *(kozō)* fibers. The rice paddies were irrigated by canals lined with planks of wood, and the villages were surrounded by moats. The houses had clay walls and thatched roofs.

Yayoi pottery, made on a wheel and not varnished, was first found on the Mikōgaoka *kaizuka* in Tokyo and other sites (*see* KARAKO, TORO). It came in five styles: in the early phases, it was plain, while in the middle phase there were attempts at decoration (sometimes portraying human beings or animals). At the end of the period, jars had parallel horizontal bands, incised or painted—a feature that is found, from region to region, in all Yayoi pottery. In northern Kyushu, large, open-mouthed jars (*see* KAMEKAN), joined in pairs, were sometimes used for burial. The clays used varied in color from ocher to red and gray. They were probably fired in ditches.

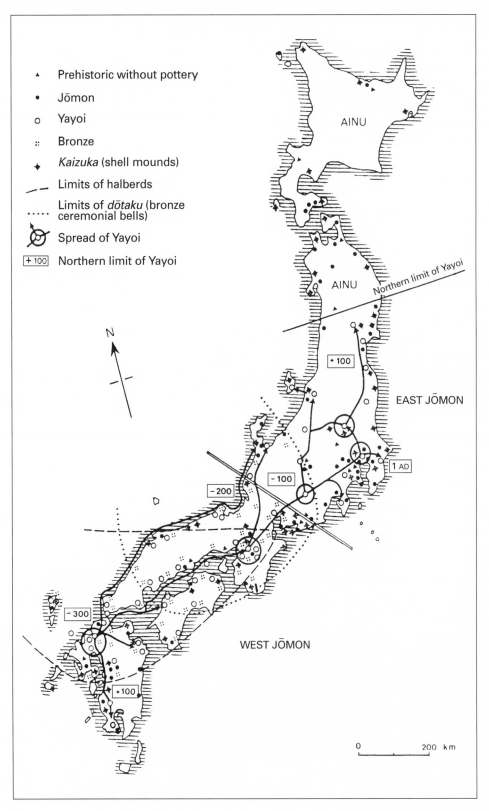

Yayoi Prehistoric Sites

Legend

▲ Prehistoric without pottery

● Jōmon

○ Yayoi

∷ Bronze

✦ *Kaizuka* (shell mounds)

— Limits of halberds

····· Limits of *dōtaku* (bronze ceremonial bells)

⊕ Spread of Yayoi

+ 100 Northern limit of Yayoi

AINU

AINU

Northern limit of Yayoi

+ 100

EAST JŌMON

1 AD

-100

-200

-300

+100

WEST JŌMON

N

0   200 km

The largest sites excavated to date are those in Yūsu, Mikumo, and Yoshinogari, in northern Kyushu, and Karako, Iba, and Toro, on Honshu. The most recently discovered sites, such as those at Inakadate and Tokiwa on Tōhoku, are in the north. This culture was replaced—or covered over—by new arrivals from Korea, who established the *kofun* culture *(kofun-bunka)*.

• "Awakening of nature," the former name for the third month of the year.

• **Yayoi Kusama.** *See* MONO-HA.

Yaze. Archeological site discovered in December 1992, in Gumma prefecture, containing the remains of a village from the Late Jōmon period (ca. 1500/ 1000 BC), including foundations of houses *(tate-ana),* wells, wooden colonnades, and cult sites.

Yen (en; ¥). Japan's monetary unit, divided into 100 *sen* and 1,000 *rin,* created in 1871 to replace the monetary system used during the Edo period. It was based on the gold standard, with the *yen* worth 1.5 g of gold and equivalent to the Mexican dollar (which was in use at the time throughout East Asia), or to 375 g of silver. The newly created Bank of Japan issued one-*yen* bills in 1882, but returned to parity with gold. In 1897, the *yen* was worth 0.75 g of gold. Paper money was issued a second time, and Japan returned to the gold standard only in 1930. After the Second World War, the *yen* was pegged at 360 to one American dollar (1949); as the dollar floated on international money exchanges, the *yen* followed. By 1990, the exchange rate had risen to 130 *yen* to the dollar. There has been discussion of creating a "new *yen*" pegged at 100 or 1,000 *yen,* and to reintroduce the *sen,* which would facilitate calculations in international currency exchanges.

Yobai. Ancient custom in which a man visited his wife (or mistress) at night, while she continued to live with her parents. This custom is still in use in some regions of Japan, but is mainly the object of gossip. Similarly, a woman sometimes went to visit her husband or lover at night. The ancient chronicles, including the *Man'yōshū* and *Genji monogatari,* frequently mention *yobai. See* MARRIAGE, YOMEIRIKON.

Yobikō. Private schools specializing in preparation for university-entrance examinations. These schools also require an entrance examination, and *rōnin* (students not admitted to any university and looking to enter one) are often forced to take *juku* courses in order to enter *yobikō.*

Yobina. In ancient Japan, an assumed name imposed by custom on women serving in the imperial court (mainly in the Heian period) and used instead of their family name. *See* NAMES.

Yoda Yoshikata. Screenwriter (1909–91) who worked mainly for director Mizoguchi Kenji. He started by writing for the Nikkatsu company. He also wrote some novels and essays, the best known of which is *Kyō no ōnna* (Women of Kyoto, 1971).

Yodo-gawa. River about 75 km long, with its source in Lake Biwa and its mouth in Osaka Bay. Its name changes several times along its course; it is called Seta-gawa near its source, Uji-gawa on its middle course, and then Yodo-gawa. It has always been an important travel artery between Lake Biwa, Kyoto, and the Inland Sea (Setonaikai).

Yodogimi. Concubine (Chacha, Yodo no Nyōbō, ca. 1567–1615) of Toyotomi Hideyoshi. She was the daughter of a sister of Oda Nobunaga, Odani no Kata, and daimyo Asai Nagamasa, and was Toyotomi Hideyori's mother. She committed suicide with Hideyori on June 4, 1615, when the Osaka castle, besieged by Tokugawa Ieyasu, fell. *See* ODANI NO KATA, TOYOTOMI HIDEYOSHI.

Yodono-shū. Subsect of the Shugendō; its members practiced a unique rite called "living mummification" so that they could become buddhas in their own bodies *(sokushin-butsu).* They were extremely ascetic; their diet involved no cereals, they took ice-cold baths every day, and after several months of this regime, they reduced their food intake each week, then sat in the lotus position and let themselves die. They were venerated as the "saviors of humanity" *(sokushin-jōbutsu).*

Yodo no tsukai. "System of the four envoys," under which, according to the *ritsuryō* code, local governors sent emissaries to the capital to inform the central government of the real situation in the provinces. At first their numbers varied, but by the early ninth century there were four: *chōshū-shi,* sent to the imperial assembly; *keichō-shi* or *daichō-shi,* charged with population control; *kōchō-shi,* charged with tolls; and *shōzichō-shi,* charged with use of the rice that was collected as tax *(so).* This system apparently disappeared around the mid-tenth century.

Yodoya Tatsugorō. Family of wealthy merchants from Osaka (*real name:* Okamoto), who had the confidence of the Tokugawa shoguns and who amassed an enormous fortune trading in raw silk with China and acting as intermediaries between the daimyo and rice merchants in Osaka. However, family members' luxurious life style clashed with their status as merchants, and the shogunate confiscated their fortune and expelled them from Osaka in 1705.

Yōeki. Obligation to participate in "work parties" imposed on peasants in the seventh and eighth centuries by the government to supply the labor needed for major public works. Peasants were required to participate for a certain number of days per year *(saieki)* or provide various services *(sōyō). Yōeki* were imposed directly by the central government or by provincial governors. The number of days of work varied between 15 and 60 per person aged 17 to 50. When the *shōen* were established, in the tenth and eleventh centuries, the work parties were called *buyaku*. Also called *edachi*.

Yōga. "Western painting," a school founded in Nagasaki by Christian missionaries, who imported the medium of oil paints and introduced the art of copper engraving. In the sixteenth and seventeenth centuries, most Yōga painters were Japanese converts to Christianity who attempted to imitate the works of Western painters. The school disappeared during the period of persecutions, but it was revived in 1857 by Kawakami Tōgai, who, on order of the shogun, studied Western-style drawing and painting techniques. In 1871, Western-style drawing courses became compulsory in all institutes; gradually, painters belonging to other schools, such as the Kanō, came to adopt more or less the styles of European painters who had come to teach art in Japan, such as Wirgman and Fenellosa. The term Yōga was then applied to all works in Western styles and techniques, to distinguish them from "Japanese" paintings, called Nihonga.

• **Yōgaku.** "Western learning," a term sometimes used instead of "Dutch sciences" *(rangaku),* and one that better defined all studies with a basis in Western science.

• **Yōgaku-jo (Yōgakusho).** "School of Western Science," founded in Edo in 1855 to teach Dutch, German, English, and French, in order to train interpreters. *See* BANSHO SHIRABE DOKORO.

Yogoto. Ancient ritual texts (from before the seventh century) somewhat similar to *norito*, but consisting mainly of praise or congratulations.

Yōha no nezame. "Awakening in the Night." An eleventh-century novel by an unknown author, perhaps a daughter (1008–?) of Sugawara no Takasue, telling of the loves of the beautiful Nezame. Only five scrolls have survived. Also titled *Yōwa no nezame. See also* NEZAME MONOGATARI.

Yojirō. Caster of iron objects (Tsuji Yojirō, late sixteenth century) who specialized in making kettles *(chagama)* for the tea ceremony *(chanoyu).* Nishimura Dōjin's student, he worked for Sen no Rikyū.

Yojō. An aesthetic concept that developed in *waka* poetry from the writings of Ki no Tsurayuki, according to which sentiments should not be expressed openly but only be suggested by an allusion—an object, a landscape, and so on. This concept also influenced literature and art (a landscape is better suggested in fog than full sunshine, for example) and was often combined with the concept of *yūgen*.

Yokei. Buddhist monk (ca. 919–991) of the Tendaishū, Myōzen's disciple, appointed *zasu* of the Tendai-shū in 989.
→ *See* CHIKUŌ.

Yōkihi. Japanese name for Yang Guifei (719–56), a famous Chinese imperial concubine of Emperor Xuan Zong of the Tang dynasty, and the title of a Noh play: a medium finds Princess Yang Guifei in the Hereafter on Mt. Hōraizan and visits her. He then tells Emperor Xuan Zong how he met the princess whom the emperor had loved.

Yokoana. "Horizontal hole," a term for tombs with a corridor *(kofun)* dug into the flank of a hill for burial of members of a single family, or located directly underground with access via a shaft. Most *yokoana* date from the *kofun* period, but the custom of digging them continued in some regions until the Muromachi period, when they were called *yagura*. In ancient times, *yokoana* contained the same funerary furnishings as "constructed" *kofun,* whereas *yagura* usually contained funerary urns, statues of Jizō Bosatsu, and stone *gorin-tō*.

Yokohama. Chief city of Kanagawa prefecture, on Tokyo Bay, about 30 km from the capital and linked to it by a large conurbation. It was founded by European merchants in 1859 on the site of a small fishing village, and is now the largest port in the country. The first railroad line in Japan, opened in 1872, linked Yokohama to the Shimbashi district of Tokyo. Almost completely destroyed by the tsunami caused by the 1923 earthquake, then again by American bombing in 1944, Yokohama was completely reconstructed on a modern plan and has become the center of the Keihin Industrial Zone, with a large number of industries of all sorts. Its very active port is a major export center. *Pop.:* 2.8 million.

• **Yokohama-e.** Type of ukiyo-e prints made after foreigners arrived in Yokohama and other Japanese ports in the mid-nineteenth century, and portraying mainly foreigners and their accomplishments. Production reached a peak about 1860, after which their popularity declined. Most Yokohama-e artists belonged to the Utagawa family, including Utagawa Sadahide (1807–ca. 1873), Yoshiiku, Yoshitora, and Kuniyoshi.

• *Yokohama Mainichi Shimbun.* First Japanese daily newspaper, founded in 1871 by Iseki Moriyoshi, then governor of Kanagawa prefecture. It became the political organ of the Jiyū Minken Undō (Freedom and People's Rights Movement), then was purchased by Numa Morikazu in 1879. He transferred it to Tokyo, where it was renamed *Tōkyō-Yokohama Mainichi Shimbun* and had liberal leanings. In 1887, it became *Mainichi Shimbun;* in 1906, *Tōkyō Mainichi Shimbun.* It was absorbed by another newspaper, *Teito Nichinichi Shimbun,* in 1940.

Yokoi Kinkoku. Painter (Yokoi Myōdō, 1761–1832), born in Ōmi province. A rather undisciplined Buddhist monk, he led a dissolute life, living in Edo and Nagoya and practicing various arts. As a painter, he first followed the principles of the Tosa school. He then made landscapes related to the style of the Maruyama Shijō school, and finally, late in life, adopted the Nanga (Bunjinga) style, imitating Yosa Buson's works.

Yokoi Shōnan. Politician (Yokoi Heishirō, 1809–69), born to a samurai family from Kumamoto (Kyushu). He studied the Chinese Confucian philosophers and opened a school, Shōnandō, teaching that it was necessary to observe strict moral principles in politics. Summoned to Edo by Matsudaira Yoshinaka in 1862, he demanded that Japan be opened to international trade, but his status as a samurai was revoked because his ideas were judged

to be dangerous. The new Meiji government nevertheless made him an adviser *(san'yo),* but he was assassinated the following year by samurai who suspected him of being a Christian.

Yokoi Yayū. Samurai (Yokoi Tokitsura, 1702–83), born in Nagoya, and a senior bureaucrat of the Edo shogunate in charge of the castles in Edo, Osaka, and Kyoto. He wrote many essays in *haibun* style, including a work that is typical of the genre, *Uzuragoromo* (The Quail's Coat), published between 1788 and 1823.

Yōkoku. Painter (Katayama Sadao, Katayama Sōma; *gō:* Gazen-kutsu, 1675–1716) and master *(chajin)* of the tea ceremony *(chanoyu).*

Yokomitsu Riichi. Writer (Yokomitsu Toshikazu, 1898–1947), born in Fukushima prefecture. After a chaotic and unproductive period in school, he began to write, encouraged by Kikuchi Kan. He was one of the founders, in 1924, of the neo-impressionist Shinkankaku-ha school; a passionate admirer of James Joyce, he helped Kawabata Yasunari publish the literary magazine *Bungaku-jidai* (Age of Literature). The same year, he made an impression with excerpts from his first novel, *Kanashimi no daika* (The Price of Sadness), which was published in its entirety only in 1955. He then wrote *Nichirin,* a sort of parody of Gustave Flaubert's *Salammbô,* using the shamaness-queen Himiko as his main character. The illness and death of Yokomitsu Riichi's first wife inspired a series of pathetic stories, published from 1925 to 1927. He remarried in 1927 and, after traveling to Shanghai, wrote *Shanhai.* He then abandoned the stylistic principles of Shinkankaku and began to write stories that were long psychological monologues, such as *Kikai* (Machines, 1930) and *Jikan* (Weather, 1931). In his novels, he returned to a more natural style: *Shin'en* (The Imperial Mausoleum, 1932), *Monshō* (The Family Crest, 1934), *Kazoku kaigi* (Family Meeting, 1935). After he went to Berlin for the Olympic Games in 1936, he wrote *Ōshū kikō* (Journal of a Trip to Europe, 1936), then a long novel that he never completed, *Ryoshū* (The Traveler's Sadness). After the Second World War, he published *Yoru no kutsu* (Shoes in the Night, 1947) and a short story, *Bishō* (The Smile), which was published posthumously in 1948.

Yokomizo Seishi. Writer (1902–81), born in Hyōgo prefecture. After studying pharmacology, he began to write, publishing adventure and detective novels with a police officer called Kindaichi Kō-suke as the main character: *Onibi* (1935), *Ningyō sashichi torimono-chō* (1939). After the Second World War, he continued in the same vein, imitating Western detective novels: *Honjin satsujin jiken, chōchō satsujin jiken* (1946), *Akuma ga kitarite fue no fuku* (1953), and *Inugami no ichizoku* (The Inugami Family). He wrote about 40 books, and they are very popular: a total of more than 10 million copies have been printed.

Yokoo Tadanori. Graphic designer, born 1936 in Hyōgo prefecture. He became known for his posters using collage and for his drawings influenced by American pop art. He had a major exhibition at the Museum of Modern Art in New York in 1970.

Yokose Yau. Poet (Yokose Torahisa, Tonemaru, 1878–1934), born in Ibaraki prefecture. He wrote modern lyrical poems, collected in *Yūzuki* (1899), *Hanamori* (1905), and *Nijūhasshuku* (1907).

Yokosuka. Port in Kanagawa prefecture, located at the entrance to Tokyo Bay on Miura Peninsula, and naval base founded by French engineer L. Verny about 1850. The tomb of Will Adams (Miura Anjin) and his wife is located there. In 1871, shipyards began to be built on the site of the old shogunal shipyards called Yokosuka Zōsenjō. The first modern wood-hulled Japanese ship, the *Seiki*, with a displacement of 897 tons, was built there in 1876. *Pop.*: 430,000.
• Name of a number of Second World War planes:
—**Yokosuka D4-Y:** Suisei bomber designed for kamikaze pilots. American code name: "Judy." About 2,300 different models (D4-Y1, D4-Y2) were built. The D4-Y2 had a *range of action* of 2,100 km; *maximum speed:* 540 km/h; *crew:* two; *weapons:* three 7.7 mm machine guns and 500 kg of bombs.
—**Yokosuka MXY-7 and 8:** *See* ŌKA.
—**Yokosuka P1-Y1:** Ginga bomber built in 1944. American code name: "Frances." *Range:* 4,800 km; *speed:* 500 km/h; *weapons:* two 20 mm cannons and two 12.7 mm machine guns.

Yokoyama Gennosuke. Writer (1871–1915), born in Toyama prefecture. He wrote works on social conditions among residents of the urban slums and the most disadvantaged peasants, notably *Nihon no kasō shakai* (The Lower Classes of Japan, 1899).

Yokoyama Matsusaburō. Painter (Yokoyama Bunroku, 1838–84) in the Western style, born in Hokkaido. He studied painting under a Russian artist living in Japan, and photography and lithography with Shimo-oka Renjō. He made mainly portraits.

Yokoyama Taikan. Painter (Sakai Hidemaro, Sakai Hidezō, Sakai Hidematsu, 1868–1958), born to a samurai family in Ibaraki prefecture. He studied the style of the Kanō school with Hashimoto Gahō, then became a fervent disciple of Okakura Kakuzō. With Okakura and several other painters, including Shimamuro Kanzan and Hishida Shunsō, he organized the Japan Fine Arts Academy (Nihon Bijutsu-in). He traveled in India, Europe, the United States, and China, then was sent as an "art ambassador" to Italy in 1930. He was best known for his monochrome paintings. Although he had no disciples, many younger artists revered him as a master. Elected a member of the Imperial Fine Arts Academy (Teikoku Bijutsu-in) in 1931, he was decorated with the Order of Culture (Bunka-shō) in 1937.

Yokoya Soyo. Goldsmith who made sword accessories (Yokoya Moritsugu, active ca. 1640), Gotō Injo's student. He founded a school in Edo.

Yōkyoku. Texts specific to Noh theater, generally recited by a chorus with orchestra accompaniment *(hayashi-kata)*. These texts usually have historical and Buddhist themes and are composed in an archaic style of lines of 5 and 7 syllables. Also called *utai. See* NOH.

Yōmei Bunko. Large library in Kyoto containing works amassed by the Konoe family, established by Konoe Fumimaro in 1938. It holds more than 10,000 rare manuscripts and about 10,000 books. *See* MIDŌ KAMPAKU-KI.

Yōmei-gaku. "School of Wang Yangming," a neo-Confucian philosophical system founded by the Chinese philosopher Wang Yangming (*Jap.*: Ō-Yōmei, 1472–1529), opposed to the Zhu Xi (*Jap.*: Shushi) school; it taught that man is good in nature and must necessarily unite thought and action, and advocated practice over theory.
In Japan, this philosophy was written about by a number of well-known thinkers, including Nakae Tōju (1608–48), Kumazawa Banzan (1619–91), Miwa Shissei, Satō Issai, and Ōshio Heihachirō, who interpreted Wang Yangming's precepts according to their respective temperaments. However, the shogunate was violently opposed to diffusion of this

doctrine, preferring the older Zhu Xi doctrine. Among the other proponents of Yōmei-gaku were Nakae Jōsei (1666–1709) and Nakagawa Gi'emon (1763–1830). Also called Yōmei-ha. *See* JUKYŌ.

Yōmeimon'in. Emperor Sanjō's daughter (Teishi, 1013–94). She married Emperor Go-Sujaku and was Emperor Go-Sanjō's mother. She became a Buddhist nun in 1069.

• **Yōmei Tennō.** Thirty-first emperor (Prince Tachibana no Toyohi, 540<586–87>), brother of and successor to Bidatsu Tennō. He was Prince Shōtoku Taishi's father and embraced Buddhism. Sushun succeeded him.

Yomeirikon. Patrilocal-type marriage, in which the spouses live close to (or in the same house as) the husband's parents, as opposed to matrilocal marriage *(mukoirikon)*. This type of union developed during the Kamakura period (1185–1333) because it was seen to be more likely to ensure the safety of the family in warrior society. *See* MARRIAGE, YOBAI.

Yomihon. "Storybooks"; novels or prose with fantasy or moral content, popular starting about 1744. They told strange stories, usually based on Chinese legends. A *yomihon* consisted of several slim volumes (generally five) and had one or two illustrations in ukiyo-e prints. The authors of the most typical *yomihon* were Takizawa Bakin and Ueda Akinari. The earliest ones were published in Kyoto and Osaka. In the nineteenth century, they were published in Edo and the most popular authors were Takebe Ayatari and Santō Kyōden. Also sometimes called *yomisho*.

Yomi no Kuni. *See* NE NO KUNI, YOMOTSU-KAMI.

Yomiuri Shimbun. Morning daily newspaper founded in 1874; an evening edition was added in 1920. It quickly became one of the most widely read dailies in the Tokyo region. During the Second World War, it merged with another newspaper and was renamed *Yomiuri-Hōchi;* it returned to the name *Yomiuri Shimbun* in 1946. In 1952, it began to publish an Osaka edition, and it was soon distributed throughout the country, including Tokyo, Osaka, and Kita-Kyushu. It now has several other regional bureaus and 20 subsidiaries abroad, where it is linked with Associated Press, Agence France-Presse, and Tass. It also publishes an English-language newspaper, the *Yomiuri Daily*. Its circulation, the highest in the world, is estimated at almost 9 million. In 1958, *Yomiuri Shimbun* opened a commercial television channel, Yomirui Terebi, based in Osaka.

Yomotsu-kami. *Kami* of the Hereafter, ruling the destinies of Yomi no Kuni, the Hades of Shinto mythology. *See* NE NO KUNI.

Yōmyō. Term for a boy before he reaches the age of receiving the "man's hat" *(eboshi)* and his adult name *(eboshi-na)* in the *gempuku* ceremony. Also called *osana-na*.

Yonai Mitsumasa. Admiral and statesman (1880–1948), born in Iwate prefecture. After graduating from naval school, he occupied various ministerial positions; in 1936, he became commander-in-chief of the combined fleets, and he was promoted to admiral in 1937. Minister of the navy in the cabinets of Hayashi Senjūrō, Konoe Fumimaro, and Hiranuma Kiichirō, he was opposed to Japan's alliance with Germany and Italy. He was nevertheless appointed prime minister in 1940, but had to resign six months later. He was then minister of the navy in several cabinets, and again prime minister, succeeding Shimada Shigetarō, in 1944–45.

Yonaoshi ikki. Peasant rebellions that took place, mainly in the shogunate's estates, between 1866 and 1869, in which bands of about 1,000 men attacked the houses of usurers and rich merchants. The uprisings were brutally suppressed by the shogunate, but broke out again from time to time in various places due to the continuing impoverishment of the peasants, whose purchasing power was constantly being eroded. *See also* HYAKUSHŌ IKKI.

Yoneyama Mamako. Dancer and mime, born 1935 in a village west of Mt. Fuji. She went to Tokyo in 1953 and studied at the Eguchi Studio, a dance school following Martha Graham's style, but her art was later very much influenced by the French mime Marcel Marceau. She went to the United States and taught at the University of California. When she returned to Japan in 1972, she opened her own dance and mime school in Tokyo.

Yōnin. Term for provincial governors who lived in the capital, Heian-kyō, keeping their title and privileges but delegating their powers in their estates to deputies called *mokudai*.

• **Yōnin-kokushi.** *See* ZURYŌ.

Yori-ito mondoki bunka. Prehistoric culture (perhaps of Siberian origin) characterized by pottery decorated "with strings." It preceded true Jōmon culture, introducing the Oshigata mondoki bunka culture, typical of the Early Jōmon period.

Yorimasa. Type of Noh mask (*nōmen*) portraying a man in the prime of life playing the role of hero.
→ *See* MINAMOTO NO YORIMASA.

Yoritake. Sculptor (Kawai Yoritake, mid-eighteenth century) of Buddhist images and netsuke, working in Kyoto.

Yōro. Era of Empress Genshō: Nov. 717–Feb. 724. *See* NENGŌ.
• Town in Gifu prefecture, on the Ibi-gawa river, completely protected from floods by raised piers called *wajū. Pop.:* 35,000.

Yoro-boshi. Noh play: a boy, rejected by his father on a false pretext, becomes a blind beggar. As he walks the streets dancing and singing about his miserable fate, his father recognizes him and takes him home.

Yoroi. "Armor," a term adopted in 923 to designate warriors' armor, replacing the older term, *kawara.* A complete set of armor consisted of a helmet (*kabuto*) and mask (*men, hō-ate*), a protector for the nape of the neck (*shikoro*), a throat protector (*nodowa*), a breastplate (*dō*) with shoulder pads (*sode*), sleeves in coat of mail (*kote*), a skirt (*kusazuri,* with four parts in back and three in front), thigh protectors or greaves (*sune-ate*), and shoes (*kohake, ke-gutsu*). A pennant (*sashimono*) was attached to the back. There were various types of *yoroi,* depending on their shape and luxuriousness, including *kisenaga, shikisei-yoroi,* and *ō-yoroi,* and various types of helmets. *See* GUSOKU, KABUTO, KATCHŪ, KUSAZURI, MUSHA ROKUGU, Ō-SODE, SHŌJI-ITA.

• **Yoroi-hitsu.** Special chest for storage of *yoroi* or *gusoku* armor. Also called *gusoku-hitsu.*

Yōrō ritsuryō. "Legal Code of the Yōrō Era." A revision of the Taihō Code (701) presented to the court by Fujiwara no Fuhito in 718, but applied only in 757, thanks to the influence of his grandson, Fujiwara no Nakamoro. This 10-chapter code of administrative, fiscal, and governmental laws has come to us through its main commentary, *Ryō no gige,* and another called *Ryō no shūge,* both dating

from the ninth century. The *Yōrō ritsuryō* remained in use until 1868. *See* RITSURYŌ, TAIHŌ RITSURYŌ.

Yorozu Chōhō. Newspaper founded in 1892 by Kuroiwa Ruikō; it was very popular in the late Meiji era. Pacifist in tone, it published articles by Kōtoku Shūsui, Uchimura Kanzō, and Sakai Toshihiko, among other "socialists." The *Yorozu Chōhō* disappeared in 1940, when it was absorbed by the *Tōkyō Maiyū Shimbun.*

Yorozu Tetsugorō. Painter in the Western style (1885–1927), born in Iwate prefecture. He traveled to the United States in 1906; when he returned to Japan the following year, he produced "avant-garde" works influenced by fauvism. He soon abandoned this style, however, for cubism. In 1919, he returned to the more traditional Nanga (Bunjinga) style.

Yorozuya Kinnosuke. Movie actor (Nakamura Kinnosuke), formerly a Kabuki actor, born 1932 in Tokyo. He first appeared in films for the Tōei company in 1954, then in many movie series, and changed his name in 1972.

Yoryū Kannon. One of the 33 forms of Kannon Bosatsu (*Skt.:* Avalokiteshvara; *see* SANJŪSAN ŌGESHIN), a sort of portrayal of Yaku-ō Bosatsu, the Buddhist divinity of medicine, assistant to Yakushi Nyorai (*Skt.:* Bhaishajyaguru). He is portrayed holding a willow branch.

Yosano Akiko. Poet and writer (Hō Shō, 1878–1942), born in Sakai. In 1901, she married the journalist and writer Yosano Tekkan, then published her first poetry collection, *Midaregami* (Tangled Hair, 1901), containing about 400 love poems; the book was a best-seller. She helped edit the magazine *Myōjō,* published by her husband. Her poetic style, freed from the constraints of *waka,* resolutely modern, was imitated by many young poets. She published some 20 poetry collections, rewrote the *Genji monogatari* in modern style (*Kōgai Genji-monogatari*), and compiled, with several friends, *Shin Man'yōshū* (The New *Man'yōshū,* 1937–39), an anthology containing 26,783 poems by 6,675 poets from the Meiji era on. Also called Ōtori Akiko, Hō Akiko.

Yosano Tekkan. Poet and writer (Yosano Hiroshi, 1873–1935), born in Kyoto. He founded the poetry magazine *Myōjō* in 1899, in which he published Romantic-style poems. In 1901, he married Hō

Shō, who became Yosano Akiko. His body of work, smaller than his wife's, included a collection of his "new *tanka*" poems, *Tōzai-namboku* (1896).

Yose. Vaudeville-type shows produced in the eighteenth century, developed from the art of strolling musicians *(kōshaku)*, who had been performing in the countryside and in towns since the twelfth century, and *rakugo.* Some *rakugoka* abandoned their itinerant life, settled in towns, and presented shows featuring comedy, songs (usually satirical), mimes, acrobatics, and other forms of entertainment. Today, such shows may last five to six hours and are updated three times a month. Modern *yose* include jazz and pop singers, and the actors and singers also perform on television and radio. The different types of *yose* are *manzai, naniwa-bushi* (or *rōkyoku*), and *mandan* (one-man shows). Also called *kōdan. See* RAKUGO.

Yosegi-zukuri. Method of making a wooden sculpture, inaugurated in the eleventh century by Jōchō (d. 1057). It consists of carving a statue in several pieces, which are then assembled, in contrast to *ichiboku-zukuri,* in which the entire statue is carved into a single piece of wood.

Yō-sempō. Traditional musical mode *(ryō-sempō),* based on the scale D, F, G, A, C, D. *See* RYŌ-SEMPŌ.

Yoshida Hiroshi. Painter (Ueda Hiroshi, 1876–1950), born in Fukuoka prefecture, who made oil paintings in the Western style and modern ukiyo-e prints. He went to Paris (1900) and the United States (St. Louis, 1904), where he received awards for his exhibitions.

Yoshida Isoya. Architect (1894–1974) who, after a study trip to the United States in 1925, created a "modern traditional" style that interpreted the ancient *sukiya* style. Among his best-known buildings are the Gotō art museum (1960), the Yamato Bunkakan (1960), the Gyokudō art museum (1961), and the Chūgū-ji temple (1968).

Yoshida Kanetomo. Shinto priest (Urabe Kanetomo, 1435–1511) from a family of soothsayers and monks attached to the imperial court and the Yoshida Shrine in Kyoto, whence the family name, authorized in 1387. He adapted certain Esoteric Buddhist principles to Shinto worship and may have been the initiator of what was later called Yoshida Shintō, for he wrote two works that be-

came its basis, *Shintō taii* and *Yuiitsu shintō myōbō yoshū.*

• **Yoshida Shintō.** Ritualist Shinto school founded by Yoshida Kanetomo and transmitted to the present day by the Yoshida family. It accepts three types of Shinto: Ryōbu Shintō (*see* RYŌBU SHINTŌ), Honjaku Engi Shintō for regional cults, and Gempon Sōgen Shintō (from the "original source") or Yoshida Shintō (also called Urabe Shintō and Yuiitsu Shintō), considered superior to the others. This type of Shintō involves "exoteric" teachings, including study of the myths of the *Kojiki,* and a more or less secret "esoteric" Shinto, somewhat resembling the Esoteric Buddhism *(mikkyō)* of the Shingon-shū.

Yoshida Ken'ichi. Writer (1912–77) and literary critic. An expert in English literature, he translated the works of D. H. Lawrence and published studies on Shakespeare. Yoshida Shigeru's son.

Yoshida Kenkō. *See* KENKŌ HŌSHI.

Yoshida Kōken. Botanist (Takanori, Jakusō, 1805–59) and samurai of the Owari family in Aichi. He collected plants and rocks and made many drawings of them.

Yoshida Mitsuyoshi. Mathematician (1598–1672), born in Kyoto. After translating the mathematics work *Suanfa tongzong* (1593) from the Chinese, he wrote an explanatory treatise on the use of the *soroban, Jinkōki* (Large and Small Numbers, 1627), containing many examples, a number of which were illustrated with color plates. This work was an important factor in spreading use of the abacus in Japan, and in replacing, in part, old Japanese mathematics *(wasan)* and the *sangi* calculation methods. *See* SANGI, SOROBAN, WASAN.

Yoshida Seiichi. Literary critic (1908–84), born in Tokyo. A professor of modern literature at the University of Tokyo, he became known for his scientific studies of texts (for which he received the Japan Art Academy (Nihon Geijutsu-in) Prize in 1958), his critical study of the works of Akutagawa Ryūnosuke (1942), and other works.

Yoshida Shigeru. Politician (Takeuchi Shigeru, 1878–1967), born in Yokohama. As a diplomat, he was attached to the embassies in Mukden (1907–08), London (1908–09), Rome (1909–12), and other cities. He was then consul in the port of Andong and secretary of the general government of

Korea (1913). He was an attaché to the embassy in Washington (1916), consul in Jin'an (1918), took part in the peace conference in Paris (1919), and was first secretary at the embassy in London (1920–22). In 1925, he became consul general in Tianjin; he held this position from 1925 to 1928 in Mukden.

Appointed vice-minister of foreign affairs in Tanaka Giichi's cabinet in 1928, he kept this position until 1931, when he became ambassador to Italy (he resigned in 1932). He then held insignificant positions, for he was opposed to the government's nationalist policy as expressed in the Anti-Comintern Pact of 1936 and the Tripartite Pact of 1940. Because of his opinions and his contribution to the memorandum presented to the emperor by Konoe Fumimaro demanding Japan's surrender, he was arrested in 1945 and detained for two months.

After the Second World War, Yoshida Shigeru succeeded Shigemitsu Mamoru as minister of foreign affairs (in the cabinets of Higashikuni Naruhiko, Sept.–Oct. 1945, and Shidehara Kijūrō, Oct. 1945–May 1946). In April 1946, he succeeded Hatoyama Ichirō as president of the Liberal party (Jiyūtō), which made him leader of the Council (prime minister), a position he occupied until May 1947. He returned to the prime ministership in October 1948, succeeding Ashida Hitoshi, and ran in the general election in January 1949, after which he inaugurated his third cabinet (Feb. 1949–Oct. 1952).

He then fought communism, having more than 20,000 sympathizers arrested, and signed the Treaty of San Francisco (Sept. 1951). He also signed the bilateral security treaty with the United States and strengthened Japan's policing capability, increasing the Territorial Defense Force to about 180,000 officers (the United States wanted 350,000). He received his fourth and fifth mandates in 1952 and 1953, but was deposed as leader of the Liberal party in December 1954, and replaced by Hatoyama Ichirō, the former leader. He retired from politics and wrote his memoirs. In 1964, the emperor decorated him with the Supreme Order of the Chrysanthemum (Daikun'i Kikka-shō). He died honored by all in his estate of Ōiso (Kanagawa prefecture). He was Yoshida Ken'ichi's father.

Yoshida Shōin. Samurai (Norikata Torajirō; *gō*: Shōin, Nijuūikkai Mōshi, 1830–59), born in Hagi and adopted by the Yoshida family. His uncle, Yoshida Daisuke, a descendant of Yamaga Sokō, was a famous master-at-arms. When Daisuke died, in 1836, Shōin became the head of the Yamaga school, and he studied Western and Chinese military strategy and science. In 1848, he was made an instructor at the Meirinkan, the military school of the Chōshū clan. He went to Edo in 1851 and openly supported the emperor (*see* SONNŌ JŌI) against the shogunate. In 1853, he and a friend, Kaneko Jūsuke (1831–55), tried to stow away on Commodore Perry's flagship, the *Powhatan,* anchored off Shimoda, but he was arrested by the shogunal authorities. Under house arrest, he militated in favor of the emperor and, following an attempted rebellion, was executed in Edo.

Robert Louis Stevenson wrote about Yoshida Shōin in *Familiar Studies of Men and Books.* Shōin himself was known for having written a book on the life of a woman samurai, Tōzoku Shimazu, who searched for her husband's assassin for twelve years in order to avenge his death. He also wrote works on government, national defense, foreign countries, and Chinese classics, among them *Kaikoroku* (Accounts of the Past, 1855), *Ryūkonroku* (Story of an Eternal Spirit, 1858), and *Kōkokushi* (A Hero's Hopes, 1858).

Yoshida Tōgo. Geographer and historian (1864–1918), born in Echigo province. A professor at Waseda University, he was known for his study on Japanese place names, *Dai Nihon chimei jisho* (1900–07). He was also an expert on Noh theater.

Yoshida Tomizō. Physician and researcher (1903–73), born in Fukushima prefecture. He studied cancer in Germany from 1935 to 1938; in 1938, he produced "Yoshida's sarcoma" in experiments on rats in the medical laboratory at Nagasaki College. He received the Japan Academy Prize (Nihon Gakushi-in-shō) twice (1936, 1953) and the Order of Culture (Bunka-shō) in 1959.

Yoshida Yoshihiko. Ceramist, born 1936 in Utsunomiya (Tochigi prefecture). He published six volumes on his works and had exhibitions in Tokyo, Portland (1988), Paris (Mitsukoshi space, 1994), and other cities.

Yoshida Yoshishige. Movie director (b. 1933), maker of often inaccessible avant-garde films: *Le Lac d'une femme* (A Woman's Lake, 1966), *Au revoir lumière d'été* (Farewell Summer Light, 1968), *Éros + massacre* (1969), *Eroica* (1970), *Coup d'État* (1973).

Yoshida Zengō. Navy officer (1885–1942), commander-in-chief of the First Squadron (1936–37) and the China Seas Fleet (1942).

Yoshiharu Shikimoku. Code of provincial laws *(bunkoku-hō)* published in 1567 by Rokkaku Yoshiharu (1545–1612), daimyo of Ōmi province. Also known by the name Rokkakushi Shikimoku.

Yoshihito. *See* TAISHŌ TENNŌ.

• **Yoshihito Shinnō.** *See* GO-SUKŌ-IN.

Yoshii Imasu. Poet and playwright (1886–1960), born in Tokyo. He wrote modern *tanka,* which he published in the magazine *Myōjō* (Morning Star). He published the magazine *Subaru,* which succeeded *Myōjō.* Generally considered one of the best "decadent" poets, he also wrote several one-act plays, collected in *Gogo sanji* (1911).

Yoshikawa Eiji. Writer (Yoshikawa Hidetsugu, 1892–1962), born in Yokohama to an impoverished family of former samurai. He earned his living as a journalist at the *Tōkyō Maiyū Shimbun* and wrote his first historical novel, *Shinran-ki* (Shinran's Life) in 1922. He continued in this popular genre with *Ken'nan jonan* (Dangers of Swords and Women, 1926) and *Naruto hichō* (Naruto's Secret Notebook, 1927). He became famous for *Miyamoto Musashi* (published in serial form from 1935 to 1939), in which he masterfully described the life of the celebrated early-seventeenth-century swashbuckler. After the Second World War, he published less "heroic" and more historically satisfying novels, including *Takayama ukon* (1949), a modern adaptation of the *Heike monogatari, Shin Heike monogatari* (1950–57), and *Taikō,* a historical novel about Toyotomi Hideyoshi (published by his wife, Fumiko, in 1967). His works were adapted to the screen many times (more than 230 movies), notably by Takizawa Eisuke, Ozaki Jun, Inagaki Hiroshi, and Uchida Tomu.

Yoshikawa Kōjirō. Historian (1904–81), born in Hyōgo prefecture, and professor at Kyoto University from 1931 to 1967. He translated many ancient Chinese works and wrote interesting studies on Chinese literature, earning the title of Person of Cultural Merit in 1962. His writings and studies were collected in *Yoshikawa Kōjirō zenshū,* published by Chikuma Shobō in 24 volumes from 1973 to 1976.

Yoshikawa Koretari. Shinto philosopher (Yoshikawa Koretaru, Kikkawa Koretari, 1616–94), born in Edo; founder of the Yoshikawa Shintō sect, a divergent branch of Yoshida Shinto, which he had studied in Kyoto under Hagiwara Kaneyori (1588–

1660), then leader of the sect. He added elements of Confucianism from the Zhu Xi (*Jap.:* Shushi) school, and was appointed director of Shinto affairs by Tokugawa Tsunayoshi in 1682, a position that was inherited by members of his family until 1868. He was Yamazaki Ansai's master.

Yoshiki Masao. Naval architect (1908–93), professor at the University of Tokyo starting in 1930, internationally known for his improvements to freight ships and tankers. He received the Order of Culture (Bunka-shō) in 1982.

Yoshimasu Tōdō. Physician (Yoshimasu Shūsuke, Yoshimasu Tamenori, 1702–73), born near Hiroshima. He was one of the first physicians to reject the Chinese theories of Yin and Yang (*see* OMMYŌDŌ) and to advocate diagnosis based on symptoms revealed by auscultation of the abdominal area. He thought that although physicians had the power to heal, only Heaven had the power to cause death. He published his theories and methods in two books, *Idan* (1759) and *Ruijuhō* (1764).

Yoshimidai. A site of the Late Jōmon period, discovered in 1984 in Chiba prefecture. The site includes a very large semi-buried house *(tatara, tateana),* more or less circular, with a diameter ranging from 16.5 to 19 m, perhaps a ceremonial center or meeting hall.

Yoshimi hyakketsu. Group of about 230 *yokoana*-type tombs *(kofun),* hollowed out of the cliffs on the banks of the Ichino-gawa river (Saitama prefecture). They date from the sixth and seventh centuries and were excavated in 1887 by Tsuboi Shōgorō. *Sue* pottery, *haniwa, matagama,* and a few skeletons were found.

Yoshimine no Munesada. Senior bureaucrat (816–90) and poet; several of his poems are in the *Kokinshū.* Ennin's student, he was appointed *henjō-sōjō* in 885.

Yoshimine no Yasuyo. Imperial prince (785–830), Emperor Kammu's son. He helped write the *Nihonkōki* (819), the *Dairi-shiki* (821), and the *Keikoku-shū* (827). He also had irrigation works built in the Heian-kyō region.

Yoshimitsu. Painter (Tosa Yoshimitsu, early fourteenth century) of the Tosa school, head of the imperial *e-dokoro* (Kyūtei E-dokoro).
→ *See* ASHIKAGA YOSHIMITSU, AWATAGUCHI YOSHIMITSU, MINAMOTO NO YOSHIMITSU.

Yoshimoto. Japanese name for a sovereign of the Ryukyu Islands (thirteenth century), grandson of and successor to Shunten. He abdicated in favor of a descendant of the Tenson family, Eisō. *Chin.:* Yiben.

Yoshimoto Banana. Contemporary novelist (b. 1964), whose works, mostly for young people, are best-sellers, including *Kanashii yokan* (Sad Feeling) and *Kitchin* (Kitchen, 1987). Her books have been adapted for the screen by Morita Yoshimitsu and other directors.

Yoshimoto Ryūmei. Literary critic and writer (Yoshimoto Takaaki, b. 1924). He published two major poetry collections, *Koyūji tono taiwa* (1952) and *Ten'i no tame no juppen* (1953), then turned toward criticism, rejecting all institutionalism. He wrote on a wide variety of subjects—psychology, linguistics, religion—and was considered one of the most influential critics of the post–Second World War period.

Yoshimura Junzō. Architect (1908–97), born in Tokyo, professor at the Tokyo School of Fine Arts (Tokyo Bijutsu Gakkō, now the Tokyo Geijutsu Daigaku) from 1945 to 1970. His designs were innovative for their mixture of traditional Japanese architecture and modern techniques. Among his best-known buildings are the Japanese pavilion (1954) at the Museum of Modern Art, New York, and the Nara National Museum (1973), for which he received the Japan Art Academy (Nihon Geijutsu-in) Prize.

Yoshimura Kōzaburō. Movie director, born 1911 in Hiroshima. He worked for the Shōchiku company as Shimazu Yasujirō's assistant, and began to direct films in 1951, mainly for the Daiei company. One of his most popular films is *Bija to kairyū* (The Woman and the Dragon, 1955). An eclectic director, he made films in all genres and excelled in portrayals of women's conditions. One of his best productions is a war film, *Nishizumi senshachō den* (The Story of Tank Commander Nishizumi), made in 1940. Also known as Yoshimura Kimisaburō.

Yoshino. Group of hills south of Nara famous for their flowering cherry trees, and a devotional center for those who venerate the Shinto divinities of the mountains *(Yama no kami).* Yoshino was home to the Nanchō court during the war of the two courts (Nambokuchō, fourteenth century).
→ *See* FUJIWARA NO YOSHINO.

• **Yoshino-jingū.** Shinto shrine in Yoshino (Nara prefecture), with some buildings from the thirteenth and fourteenth centuries.

• **Yoshino Mikumari-jinja.** Shinto shrine in Yoshino, founded in the late sixteenth century and dedicated to a number of *kami,* including Ame no Kumari no Mikoto, Chijihime no Mikoto, Ninigi no Mikoto, Takamusubi, and Sukuna-bikona no Kami.

• *Yoshino shizuka.* Title of a Noh play: Minamoto no Yoshitsune's mistress, Shizuka, helps a warrior of the Minamoto, Tadanobu, protect Yoshitsune's flight north and dances for him.

• *Yoshino-shūi.* Collection of tales and legends from Yoshino, written by an unknown author about 1358.

Yoshinobu. Painter (Kanō Yoshinobu, Kanō Genzaburō, early seventeenth century) of the Kanō school who studied with his father, Eitoku, in Kyoto.
→ *See* TOKUGAWA YOSHINOBU.

Yoshinogari (Yoshinoga-sato). A recently discovered proto-historic site of the Yayoi period, in northern Kyushu between Kanzaki and Mitagawa (Saga prefecture), which was found to have been the capital of a state *(kuni)* of the ancient country of Yamatai. Uncovered were the vestiges of 5,000 houses and granaries and 8,000 "treasuries" containing more than 100,000 articles. The exterior moat, dug in a "V" shape, was 6.5 m wide and 3 m deep. Remains of four bridges were found. North of the moat, an enormous funerary tumulus (47 m in diameter) contained an urn painted red on the inside, which held a bronze épée 0.45 m long with a decorated handle and glass beads. Scattered around the 32 hectares excavated were 2,350 tombs containing 2,000 funerary urns, shells from the Amami Islands, pig bones, and human skeletons with no skulls. *See* YAMATAI.

Yoshino Sakuzō. Historian (1878–1933), professor of political science. He converted to Christianity, then went to China, where he was tutor to Yuan Keming, Yuan Shikai's son, from 1906 to 1909. He compiled a 24-volume collection of documents on the Meiji era, *Meiji bunka zenshū,* which he published from 1927 to 1930.

Yoshioka Kenji. Painter in the Nihonga style, born 1906 in Tokyo. From 1940 to 1942, he copied the paintings from the *kondō* of the Hōryū-ji, which enabled them to be restored after fire destroyed them in 1949. He painted mainly flowers and birds and taught at the Tokyo University of Fine Arts and Music (Tokyo Geijutsu Daigaku) from 1959 to 1969.

Yoshioka Yasunori. Officer (twentieth century). A member of the Sakura-kai and the Kokuryū-kai, he was "attached" to the imperial household of Emperor Kangde (Puyi) in Manchuria, who was the true ruler of Manchukuo in 1932.

Yoshioka Yayoi. Physician and educator (Washiyama Yayoi, 1871–1959). After obtaining her degree in 1892, she married a physician, Yoshioka Arata (1868–1922); they founded a medical school for women (Tōkyō Joigakkō) in 1900, which became the Tōkyō Joshi Igaku Semmon Gakkō (Tokyo Women's Professional Medical School) in 1912. She also founded a hospital. In 1955, she was decorated with the Fujin Bunka-shō, the highest distinction for women.

Yoshio Kogyū. Physician and interpreter (eighteenth century) in Nagasaki. His son, Yoshio Nagayasu, studied English and compiled a Japanese–Dutch–English dictionary about 1800.

Yoshishige. Painter (Yano Yoshishige, Yano Rokubei, seventeenth century) of the Unkoku school. A descendant of samurai, he painted mainly battle scenes.

Yoshitsune. *See* FUJIWARA NO YOSHITSUNE, MINAMOTO NO YOSHITSUNE.

• *Yoshitsune sembon-zakura.* "Yoshitsune with a Thousand Cherry Trees." A five-act Kabuki play in the *jidai-mono* genre, first produced in 1748 by Takeda Izumo, Miyoshi Shōraku, and Namiki Senryū, for the Bunraku theater. This play, portraying an episode from the story of Minamoto no Yoshitsune, is still one of the best known in the Kabuki repertoire.

Yoshiwara. The pleasure quarter of Edo from the beginning of the Edo period until 1958. Located in the Taitō district, this center of legal prostitution (also called Yūkaku, Kuruwa, and Iromachi) was a source of inspiration for poets, writers, musicians, and artists, who drew from it themes based on the beauty, elegance, and love of women.

Courtesans in Yoshiwara came from all parts of Japan, and some of them were highly esteemed for their elegance and their musical and literary talents. The quarter was closed—surrounded by walls and moats. It included not only pleasure houses but inns, tea houses, restaurants, and other establishments.

Yoshiwara ("plain of reeds") was so named because it was first located on a marsh; destroyed by a large fire in 1657, it was rebuilt in the Taitō-ku quarter and called Shin Yoshiwara (New Yoshiwara). It covered almost 8 hectares, and its gridplan streets were bordered with willows (the Chinese symbol for prostitution) and cherry trees. Each pleasure house had a distinct name, and the women who lived there also used this name. Between 2,000 and 3,000 women of all classes lived in the quarter; they spoke a dialect called *kuruwa-kotoba* (or *arinsu-kotoba*).

In the late nineteenth century, the popularity of the women of Yoshiwara began to fade in favor of those in other pleasure quarters, such as Fukugawa; the quarter was demolished in 1958 on the order of the Occupation authorities. There were similar quarters in other large cities: Shimabara in Kyoto, Shimmachi in Osaka, Maruyama in Nagasaki, Kanayama in Sado, Chimori in Sakai, Kitsuji in Ara, Shumokuchō in Fushimi, and so on. In general, these quarters were termed *yūri*. The oldest one was established by Hideyoshi in 1589, in the Rokujō quarter in Kyoto. *See* GEISHA.

Yoshiwara Jirō. Painter (1905–72), born in Osaka to a family of oil manufacturers. He began to paint in oils very young; in 1928, he met Ueyama Jirō, just back from France, who introduced him to Fujita Tsuguji and other known painters. He exhibited with the Nika-kai group in 1937 and received prizes for his works. After the Second World War, he had an exhibit at Carnegie Hall, New York (1952), and at the Salon de Mai in Paris, then founded Gutai, an association of avant-garde painters. In 1958, he had two-man shows with painter Michel Tapie in Paris and New York. He opened an art gallery in Osaka that featured the works of abstract painters, thus helping to spread familiarity with this style in Japan.

Yoshiya Nobuko. Novelist (1896–1973), born in Niigata prefecture. She began to write very young, publishing her first novel, *Hana monogatari* (The Story of the Flowers), from 1916 to 1924. She then published *Chi no hate made* (Toward the End of the Earth, 1920), which received the *Ōsaka Asahi*

Shimbun Prize, and later wrote biographies of women, then *Onna no yūjō* (Female Friendships, 1934), *Otto no teisō* (A Husband's Chastity, 1937), *Onibi* (The Demon's Fire, 1951), *Atakake no hitobito* (The Ataka Family, 1965), *Tokugawa no fujintachi* (The Tokugawa Women, 1966), and others. Her works were very popular among Japanese women.

Yoshiyuki Junnosuke. Writer (1923–94), born in Okayama, the son of a little-known author, Yoshiyuki Eisuke (1906–40). Because he suffered from asthma, he did not serve in the army; he studied literature at the University of Tokyo and published a small magazine called *Ashi* (Reeds). His short stories ("The Rose Seller," 1950; "The Rain Shower," 1954; "The City of Matching Colors," 1956) appeared in somewhat disreputable newspapers. In 1954, he received the Akutagawa Prize for one of his stories, *Shūu* (Sudden Shower). He was an admirer of Henry Miller and translated his works; he then devoted himself exclusively to literature and published *Honoo no naka* (In the Flames, 1956), "Relationships in a Landscape" (1960), *Suna no ue no shokubutsugun* (Plant Kingdom in the Dunes, 1963), *Anshitsu* (The Darkroom, 1969), *Shimetta sora kawaita sora* (Wet Sky, Dry Sky, 1971). He received the Noma Prize in 1978 for the story *Yūgure made* (Until Dusk). He also wrote other works, including "The Show of Dreams: Paul Klee and the Twelve Illusions." His last novel, *Medama* (The Eyes), was never finished. Yoshiyuki's writings are a stunning mix of the avant-garde, sex, and philosophy, written in a forceful first-person style.

Yoshizawa Ayame. Kabuki actor (Yoshizawa Ayanosuke, Tachibanaya Gonshichi, Yoshizawa Gonshichi, 1673–1729) who specialized in *tachiyaku* and *onnagata* roles. He was reputed to be extraordinarily beautiful.

Yoshizawa Kenkichi. Diplomat (1874–1965), born in Niigata prefecture. He was sent to Beijing from 1923 to 1929, then was ambassador to France and the League of Nations. In 1932, he was minister of foreign affairs in Inukai Tsuyoshi's cabinet. During the Second World War, he was ambassador stationed in Hanoi (1941–44), and he was posted to the Republic of China (Taiwan) in 1952.

Yōtesaki. In traditional architecture, a corbel in *wa-yō* style composed of a quadruple *degumi* supporting the main beams of a roof overhang, *gangyō*, or *degeta*. See TO-KYŌ.

Yotsutsuji Yoshinari. Poet (Seikan-ji, Yotsutsuji Sadaijin, 1326–1402) of the imperial family, who received the family name Minamoto in 1356. He was minister of the left *(sadaijin)* in 1395, then retired with the name Jōshō. He wrote a commentary on the *Genji monogatari,* titled *Kakai-shō,* under the pseudonym Minamoto Koreyoshi.

Yotsuya-kaidan. Four-act Kabuki play, first produced in 1825 by Tsuruya Namboku: the spirit of a woman who was abused and killed by her husband avenges her.

Youchi Soga. Noh play: the Soga brothers, Gorō and Jūrō, attack their enemy by night, but find themselves counterattacked by Minamoto no Yoritomo. Gorō is wounded and the brothers must flee, putting off their vengeance until later.

Yōwa. Era of Emperor Antoku: July 1181–May 1182. *See* NENGŌ.

Yōwan. "Bright bowls"; ceramic tea bowls made by Deguchi Onisaburō (1871–1948), in raku style with clay mixed with gold and other bright-colored powders.

Yōyūsai. Lacquer artist (Hara Yōyūsai, 1772–1845) and sculptor of netsuke in Edo.

Yōzei Tennō. Fifty-seventh emperor (Prince Sadaakira, 868<877–84>948), son of and successor to Seiwa Tennō. He was deposed and replaced by his great-uncle, Kōkō.

YS-11. Series name for a medium-range plane with two turboprop engines made after the Second World War by Nihon Aeroplane Manufacturing Co. This plane, the first made in Japan after the war, needed only 1,200 m for take-off and could carry about 60 passengers. Engines and parts imported from the United States and England were used, and about 76 YS-11s were exported to the U.S. and Europe. *See* AERONAUTICS.

Yūaikai. "Friendship Association." The first union organization in Japan, created in 1912 by Suzuki Bunji and several of his friends. This socialist-leaning fraternal society grew rapidly; in 1918, it had more than 30,000 members. In 1919, it took the name Dai Nippon Rōdō Sōdōmei Yūaikai; in 1921, it became Nihon Rōdō Sōdōmei (Japan Federation of Labor). *See* SŌDŌMEI.

Yuasa Hachirō. Christian educator (1890–1981), born in Gumma prefecture. In 1908, he went to the United States, where he studied agriculture and entomology. In 1923, he was appointed to one of the first agricultural chairs at the University of Kyoto; in 1935, he became president of Dōshisha University, but he retired in 1938 and returned to the United States, where he lived throughout the Second World War. When he returned to Japan in 1946, he was once again elected president of Dōshisha University. In 1950, he was among the group that founded the Tokyo International Christian University, of which he was elected president. He also was actively involved with the YMCA and UNESCO in Japan.

Yuasa Jōzan. Confucian writer (1708–81) from Bizen, the well-known author of *Jōzan kidan,* a collection of anecdotes on the famous warriors of the Sengoku period (fifteenth–sixteenth century), published in 1739.

Yuasa Kurahei. Politician (1874–1940), civil administrator of Korea from 1925 to 1929. He was appointed Grand Chancellor in 1936.

Yuasa Toshiko. Physicist (1910–80) specializing in nuclear research. She taught at the Ochanomizu University for Women (Tokyo), then went to Paris, where she worked at the Centre National de la Recherche Scientifique (National Science Research Center). She died in Paris.

Yūchiku. Painter (Kaihō Gantei, Kaihō Doshin; *gō:* Dōkō, 1654–1728) of the Kaihō school who studied with his father, Yūsetsu, in Kyoto. *See* KAIHŌ-HA.
→ *See* MORONOBU.

• **Yūchiku-sōkyō.** *See* YAMAMOTO BAIITSU.

Yudate-kagura. Shinto rites consisting of divinations made on boiling water, practiced mainly in the Kamakura, Nagano, and Shizuoka regions. These rites are part of the Ise tradition and related to the ancient esoteric practices of the *miko* and Yamabushi. *See* DIVINATION, URANAI.

Yū-en. Buddhist monk (active ca. 1384) and painter of Buddhist subjects.

Yūga. Painter (Nemoto, 1824–66) of the Kanō school; Ichiga's student in Tottori.

Yūgao. Name of one of the main characters in the *Genji monogatari,* a woman passionately in love with Prince Genji. A Noh play was written from her story. *See also* HASHITOMI.

Yūge Kannon. One of the 33 forms (*see* SANJŪSAN ŌGESHIN) of Kannon Bosatsu (*Skt.:* Avalokiteshvara), perhaps representing a bodhisattva of joy and portrayed sitting in "royal ease" on a cloud that gives off light rays.

Yūgen. An aesthetic concept designating mystery, elegance, charm, and contained sadness. Codified by Fujiwara no Shunzei (1114–1204), it was cultivated by poets and writers until the sixteenth century. In Buddhism, it is the highest truth that the intellect can comprehend. In *waka* poetry, *yūgen* meant that the deepest sentiments were not expressed but only suggested by allusions, like harmonies *(yojō)* in a melody. In the fourteenth century, this concept evolved to evoke the harmony and innate elegance of things. It has been described as a "somewhat mystical condition that cannot be expressed by forms," a "beauty that is elegant and full of nobility and thought, but not restrictive." It was fully expressed in the fifteenth century in Noh plays. In poetry, it is expressed in *yūgemmi,* the art of suggesting things without describing them. In the Japanese sense, it is the very essence of poetry. *Sabi,* which is also derived from *yūgen,* is symbolized by "a bright point in a colored space." *See* SABI, YOJŌ.

Yūgiri. Courtesan in Osaka (?–1678), famous in her time for her beauty and her talent for music and poetry. Her life and death were the subject of many plays, including *Yūgiri Awa no naruto* (Yūgiri and the Awa Whirlpool), a three-act Bunraku play written by Chikamatsu Monzaemon and first produced at the Takemoto-za in Osaka in 1710, and *Yūgiri nagori no shōgatsu* (Yūgiri's Farewell in January), a Kabuki play first produced in Osaka by Sakata Tōjūrō.

Yugyō-jin. In beliefs related to Ommyōdō, itinerant divinities that at certain moments control the cardinal points. It becomes necessary to avoid them so as not to encounter bad luck, which is why indirect routes *(kata-tagae)* are taken. The divinities are Konjin Ten'ichi, Taihaku, Daishōgun, and Ōso. *See* IMI, KATA-IMI, KATA-TAGAE, ŌSŌ.

• **Yugyō Yanagi.** In Noh theater, the spirit of a weeping willow, portrayed as an old man.

Yūhi. *See* KUMASHIRO YŪHI.

Yuima Koji. Japanese name for the Indian Buddhist saint Vimalakīrti, a lay disciple of the Buddha who, according to tradition, discussed the Buddhist Law (Dharma) with Mañjushrī (*Jap.*: Monju Bosatsu). He is portrayed as a sickly-looking old man.

Yui Shōtetsu. Military tactician (1605–51) from Suruga province who founded a school of martial arts in Edo. Compromised in the plot hatched by Marubashi Chūya against shogun Tokugawa Ietsuna, he was arrested and committed suicide.

Yukaji. Shinto rite of purification *(harai)* during which priests and Yamabushi walk across burning cypress embers after sprinkling themselves with lustral water with a broom made of *sasa* (dwarf bamboo). *Hiwatari* (walking over fire) is traditionally practiced at the Shiofune Kannon-ji temple in Kabe, near Tokyo, every May 3.

Yūkaku. Districts reserved for prostitution; also called Irozato, Yūri, Yūsho. *See* GEISHA, YOSHI-WARA.

Yukara. Traditional Ainu epic ballad, complete recitation of which took three days. Today, no Ainu is capable of reciting it in its entirety. *See* KINDAICHI KYŌSUKE.

Yukata. "Bathrobe"; a kimono made of light cotton for men and women, generally used after the bath *(o-furo)* in summertime, or for relaxing at home. It closes with a narrow belt knotted in the back or on the side. The designs on *yukata,* usually in indigo blue on a white background, are in lines or geometric motifs for men, while those for women have drawings of flowers or waves, sometimes with hints of color. When *yukata* are worn, *geta* are generally worn on the feet. *See* CLOTHING, KIMONO.

Yukawa Hideki. Physicist (1907–81), born in Tokyo, an expert in atomic particles; he discovered the meson in 1935. He was a professor at the University of Tokyo in 1939–40 and was invited to the United States in 1948 by Robert Oppenheimer to teach at Princeton University; a year later, he lectured at Columbia University. In 1949, he received the Nobel Prize for physics. When he returned to Japan in 1953, he worked with Sakata Shōichi and Tomonaga Shin'ichirō, two of the greatest experts in atomic science.

Yūki. Family of warriors and daimyo descended from Fujiwara no Hidesato. It had many illustrious members, including Oyama Tomomitsu (1168–1254), who served Minamoto no Yoritomo and received the fief of Yūki in Shimōsa province. The family was divided into two branches, the Shimōsa Yūki and the Shirakawa Yūki, which were on opposite sides during the Nambokuchō war. The latter branch was decimated by Toyotomi Hideyoshi, while the former prospered until the Edo period. Its most famous members were Yūki Tomohiro, one of Tomomitsu's sons; Munehiro (?–ca. 1340); Chikatomo (?–1347); Chikamitsu (?–1336); Akitomo (?–ca. 1370); Ujitomo (1398–1441); Naritomo (1439–62); Masatomo (1477–1545); Masakatsu (1504–59); and Harutomo (1534–1616).

• *Yūki kassen ekotoba.* "Story of the Battles of the Yūki," a fifteenth-century *emakimono.* Hosomi Collection, Osaka.

• **Yūkike Shin Hattō.** "New Laws of the Yūki Family." Code of provincial laws *(bunkoku-hō)* promulgated by Yūki Masakatsu (1504–59) for his province, Shimōsa, in 1556. It contains 107 articles designed to regulate the behavior of the samurai, who apparently lacked some discipline.

Yukihide. Painter (Tosa Yukihide, early fifteenth century) of the Tosa school who studied with his father, Yukihiro. He was Ashikaga Yoshimitsu's personal painter and made mainly portraits.
　• Sword maker (Sa Yukihide, 1816–85) in Chikuzen and Edo.

Yukihira. Maker of sword blades (Kishin-dayū, 1145–1222) in Bungo. *See* KYŪSHŪ-MONO.
→ *See* ARIWARA NO YUKIHIRA.

Yukihiro. Painter (Tosa Yukihiro, fourteenth–fifteenth century), Yukimitsu's son and Yukihide's father, in Kyoto.

Yukihito. Imperial prince, poet, and painter (Arisugawa no Miya, 1656–99), son of Emperor Go-Sai-in.

Yukimi-dōrō. Stone lantern *(shi-dōrō)* with three feet and a large shade, generally placed near a pond in gardens.

Yukimitsu. Maker of sword blades (Tōsaburō Yukimitsu, 1199–1280) in Kamakura. *See* MASAMUNE, SŌSHŪ-MONO.
→ *See* FUJIWARA NO YUKIMITSU.

Yukinaga. *See* FUJIWARA NO YUKINAGA.

Yukinobu. Painter (Kanō Yukinobu, Kanō Uta-nosuke; *gō:* Mō-in, 1513–75) of the Kanō school who studied with his father, Masanobu, in Kyoto.
• Painter (Kiyohara Yuki, mid-seventeenth century); she followed the Kanō school.

Yuki-onna. "Snow Woman," a character in folk tales, said to appear on snowy nights when the moon is full. Her embrace is fatal to men whom she attracts. Supposedly a divinity of the new year *(toshigami)*, she is often described as a ghost holding a child in her arms, and is also portrayed as a small girl with one leg and one eye. Also called Yuki-jorō.

Yūki Shōji. Writer (Tamura Yukio), born 1927 in Tokyo. He wrote spy and detective novels in an unvarnished style. He received the Naoki Prize in 1970 for his novel *Gunki hatameku moto ni,* which was made into a movie by Shindō Kaneto in 1972.

Yūkoku. Painter (Noguchi Minosuke, 1827–99) of the Nanga (Bunjinga) school; Chinzan's student in Tokyo.

• **Yūkoku-ji.** *See* KUMAGAYA.

Yume. "Dreams"; religious premonitions or visions. Called *imi* in Okinawa.
→ *See* KURASAWA AKIRA.

• *Yumedono.* "Pavilion of Dreams," a one-story octagonal building set on top of a double stone terrace, located in the Tō-in of the Hōryū-ji in Nara. Its octagonal roof is topped with an unusually shaped *roban.* It was probably built by Gyōshin during the Tempyō era (729–48) in memory of Prince Shōtoku Taishi. This structure, 12.8 m high, is enclosed within a square gallery on pillars. *See* IKARUGA NO MIYA.

• *Yume no ki.* "Book of Dreams," a treatise on dream interpretation written about 1220 by the Buddhist monk Kōben. *See* MYŌE.

• *Yume monogatari.* "The Story of Dreams," a work written by Takano Chōei (published in Edo in 1838) describing Western society and criticizing the shogunal government; Takano Chōei was imprisoned for this work.

Yumi. Uniquely Japanese asymmetrical bow, about 2 m long, made of glued bamboo blades held together by rings that are also made of bamboo. This type of bow was created for horsemen, and the handle was about one-third of the way up from the base. Considered sacred, it is said to be able to ward off evil influences when its silk cord is vibrated (*see* AZUSA). It is still used in traditional Japanese archery *(kyūdō)* and for concentration exercises in Zen practice. It is also used in certain dances, including sumo; during religious ceremonies; and during *yabusame.* The arrows, called *ya,* are also made of bamboo. *See* KYŪDO, YA, YABUSAME.

• *Yumi-harizuki.* Novelized biography of the famous archer Minamoto no Tametomo, published by Takezawa Bakin from 1807 to 1811.
→ *See* HACHIRŌ TAMETOMO.

• **Yumi-shiki.** *See* SUMO.

• **Yumi-ya San-ten.** Shinto triple divinity—Benzai-ten, Marishi-ten, and Daikoku-ten—said to protect warriors.

• **Yumi-ya-yari bugyō.** Inspector of shogunal weapons (bows, arrows, lances), a position created in 1637. In 1863, the position was replaced by *bugu-bugyō. See* BUGYŌ.

Yuna. In the Edo period, young women working in public baths, often low-ranking prostitutes. They were also called *saru* (monkeys) or *denju-onna* (traditional women). These women were the subject of many literary works, including one by Ihara Saikaku, and served as models for ukiyo-e painters. Although their activities were banned by shogunal decree in 1648, they continued to work until at least the mid-eighteenth century.

Yuri Kimimasa. Politician (1829–1909), born on the Fukui estate. After the restoration of imperial power, he worked for the Meiji government and issued the first bank bills *(dajōkan-satsu)* in 1868. He was also a member of the Iwakura mission in 1871 and was appointed *genro* in 1875.

Yuriwaka. Title of a popular legend in Yamaguchi prefecture: a noble called Yuriwaka has been away from home for a long time chasing demons, and his family does not recognize him. Finally, after some exploits, he marries the daughter of his lord. This legend may be of foreign origin.

Yūryaku Tennō. Twenty-first emperor (Prince Ō-Hatsuse Wakatake no Mikoto, Waōbu, 418/427<457–479>), successor to his brother, Ankō. He had many artisans brought from Korea (*see* YUZUKI NO KIMI) and developed cultivation of mulberry bushes for silkworms. Some of his poems were included in the *Man'yōshū.* Seinei succeeded him.

Yūsetsu. Painter (Kaihō Dōki; *azana:* Chūzaemon; *gō:* Dōkisai, Yūsetsu, 1598–1677) of the Kaihō-ha school who studied with his father, Yūshō. *See* KAIHŌ-HA.
→ *See* MUNENOBU.

Yūshi. Painter (Ishizaki Yūshi, Ishizaki Keitarō; *azana:* Shisai; *gō:* Hōrei, 1768–1846) of the Yōga school who studied with his father, Gen'yū, and with Gentoku in Nagasaki. He was also a poet and engraver of seals.

Yūshō. Painter (Kaihō Yūshō, Kaihō, Shōeki, 1533–1615), founder of the Kaihō-ha school, following the Ryōkai style. He studied with Kanō Motonobu and decorated the Jurakutei while in Toyotomi Hideyoshi's employ. *See* KAIHŌ-HA.
• Painter (1818–69) of the Kaihō-ha school.

• **Yūshō-in.** *See* TOKUGAWA IETSUGU.

Yūsu. Archeological layer discovered in 1978 in northern Kyushu. It revealed vestiges from the Late Jōmon period, including a spade and a stone urn, perhaps used for growing rice. This culture and its pottery thus would have dated from the very early Yayoi period.

Yūtei. *See* ISHIDA YŪTEI.

Yuya. Title of a Noh play: Taira no Munemori refuses his concubine, Yuya, permission to go to the bedside of her ill mother. The young women prays to Kannon Bosatsu to save her mother and writes a poem that moves Munemori so deeply that he finally allows her to go.

Yuya. In Zen Buddhist monasteries, the monks' bath room.

Yūzen. Painter (Miyazaki Yūan; *gō:* Yūzensai, d. 1758) and fabric designer in Kyoto; about 1700, he invented a dyeing technique named after him: *yūzen-zome.*
→ *See* INAGAKI TOSHIJIRŌ.

• **Yūzen-zome.** Technique for dyeing fabrics in several colors, using a stenciling technique, invented about 1700 by the painter Yūzen. This technique resembles *rōkechi* but uses a glutinous rice paste and soymilk instead of wax. It involved a difficult, long procedure, and was perfected during the Genroku era (1688–1704). For expediency, stencils *(kata-yūzen)* made of waterproofed paper were sometimes used, and the dye was applied with a brush, but the results were inferior.

Yūzon-sha. Secret "Survivors' Society" founded about 1919 by Kita Ikki, Ōkawa Shūmei, and other extremists, including Mitsukawa Kametarō (1888–1936), whose ultranationalist views were expressed by Kita Ikki in the secretly printed *Nihon kaizō hōan taikō* (Basic Plan for a National Reorganization, 1919). However, the Yūzon-sha was not immune to internal tension and dissolved in 1923.

Yuzuki no Kimi. Korean prince, who, according to the *Nihon shoki,* arrived in Japan around 400, bringing with him many artisans, artists, and scholars fleeing their country, which had just been conquered by the kingdom of Silla. These immigrants *(kikajin)* settled in the Nara region, introducing silkworm cultivation and the art of weaving silk. Yuzuki may have been the founding ancestor of the Hata family.

Yūzū Nembutsu. Buddhist religious sect of the Pure Land (Jōdo) school, founded about 1123 by the monk Ryōnin (1072–1132), according to which all that was required for rebirth in Amida's Pure Land was to join with other followers and recite the *nembutsu.* The sect had few followers at first and was revived by its seventh "patriarch," Ryōson (1279–1349). However, its doctrine was systematized only in the seventeenth century, in *Yūzū emmonsho* by the monk Yūkan (1649–1716), the forty-sixth leader of the sect. It has about 100,000 followers.

• *Yūzū nembutsu engi emaki.* An *emakimono* describing the history of the Yūzū Nembutsu sect, with a text attributed to Ryōchin (1147–1251), its sixth "patriarch," illustrated in 1414 by Eishun and Jakusai (1348–1424). It is kept in the Seiryō-ji in Kyoto.

Z. The sounds *za, zu, ze,* and *zo* are produced by "nigorization" (*see* NIGORI) of the syllables *sa, su, se,* and *so.* The syllable *zi* does not exist.

Za. Associations of merchants or artisans (even farmers in some provinces), grouped into guilds. Their goal was to obtain tax exemptions and the right to impose taxes and to preserve a sort of monopoly on the manufacture or sale of certain products. *Za* were active mainly during the Muromachi period, but continued to exist during the Edo period, although many daimyo abolished them in their estates. They were then replaced by other commercial organizations, such as *kabunakama.*
　• Professional associations, notably of Bunraku and Kabuki actors, were also called *za,* as were the theaters in which they performed. *See* ZAMOTO.
　• Generic name for seats. *See* ZABUTON.

• **Zabuton (safuton).** Cushions once used as seats, placed directly on the floor. They were usually square in shape, but there were also round ones, made of braided straw, called *enza.* Use of straw *zabuton* declined in the seventeenth century, when tatami became more popular. They are still used, but now they are made of cotton covered with fabric. *See* TATAMI.

• **Za-tō.** During the Muromachi period, heads of guilds of actors and dancers.
　• Term for blind singers and musicians *(biwa-hōshi)* and for masseurs *(amma).* Blind musicians were called *goze.*

Zaibatsu. "Financial groups," industrial and financial conglomerates created by powerful industrial families, who, through the intermediary of *honsha* (parent companies), controlled a large number of different types of enterprises. Most *zaibatsu* were created during the Meiji and Taishō eras, though some originated in the seventeenth century. Among the largest *zaibatsu* were Mitsui (created in the seventeenth century), Mitsubishi (nineteenth century), Sumitomo (seventeenth century), Yasuda (banks), Asano (cement works), Furikawa, Kawasaki, Nichitsu, Mangyō, Mori, Nissō, Nomura, and Riken. The *zaibatsu* provided financial resources for the militarist government before the Second World War and for the war economy. These oligopolistic "trusts" were abolished by imperial decree on July 23, 1946, and the companies that had formed them became more or less independent. But most *zaibatsu* began to be reconstituted in 1953, for the Japanese economic system is based on hierarchies and relationships (*see* OYABUN-KOBUN) that tie companies to each other. When the *zaibatsu* were dismantled in 1946, they were replaced by *zaikai,* industrial and financial groups based on banks, which formed lobbies that had a major influence on the postwar political balance and that were behind the spectacular development of Japanese industry. *See* BATSU.

Zaichū. Painter (Hara Chi'en; *azana:* Shichō; *gō:* Gayū, Zaichū, 1750–1837), in the Chinese style of the Ming period, working in Kyoto. Zaimei's father.
→ *See* ARAI HAKUSEKI.

Zaikata shōnin. In the late Edo period, peddlers, generally from remote villages, who traveled the countryside selling a wide variety of products, from medications to fabrics to seeds, spices, and consumer goods. They played an extremely important role in the rural economy. They traveled on foot, carrying on their backs large wooden boxes containing their merchandise; few had packhorses. Also called *zaigō shōnin.*

Zaike. Buddhist monks not attached to any temple and living at home, as opposed to monastery monks, *shukke.* The *zaike* of the Jōdo Shin-shū sect, who were the most numerous since they generally married and had families, were called *ubasoku* or *konji.* Nuns of the sect were called *ubai* or *konjin-nyo.* Lay Buddhist organizations are now called *zaike-bukkyō.*
• During the Middle Ages, a term for peasants in *shōen* bound to the land, whose status was equivalent to that of serfs.

Zaimei. Painter (Hara Chikayoshi; *azana:* Shitoku; *gō:* Shashō, 1778–1844) of the Nanga (Bunjinga) school in Kyoto. Zaichū's son and student.

Zainichi. "Sun on the left," a modern elliptical expression mainly designating Koreans living in Japan, who suffer discrimination.

Zamoto. In the seventeenth century, "actors"—in fact, troupe directors—who had obtained a license to sponsor Kabuki shows. Especially in Osaka and Kyoto, they usually represented the actors they hired, and were elected by them for a one-year period.

Zange monogatari. "Tales of confession," a literary genre based on realistic personal accounts. In favor in the fifteenth century, this genre later gave rise to *shi-shōsetsu* novels, written in the first person.

Zangiri-mono. Type of Kabuki play describing the life of commoners after 1868, named for the term for the Western hairstyle adopted by young modernists, *zangiri-atama. See also* HAIRSTYLES, MAGE, SEWA-MONO.

Zaō-dō. *See* KIMUBUSEN-JI.

Zaō Gongen. A "wrathful" syncretic Shinto Buddhist divinity who was created, according to legend, by En-no Gyōja, and who was venerated by warriors in the thirteenth and fourteenth centuries in the form of a *myō-ō (Skt.: vidyārāja).* In mandalas, he is portrayed as a bodhisattva *(Jap.: bosatsu)* and called Kongō-zō; he is thus a fierce emanation of Shaka Nyorai (Shakyamuni Buddha) and Jizō

Bosatsu. Also called Kongō Zaō, Himitsu Kongō, and Tokkyō Kongo (in Ryōbu Shinto).

Zappai. General term for many types of humorous poems. Types of *zappai* were named according to their form, the number of lines, and the sequential arrangement: *kasazuke, kiriku, maekuzuke, oriku, tsukeku,* and so on. The *senryū* belonged to this genre. *See also* KYŌKA, SENRYŪ.

Zashiki-waraji. A folk divinity of the hearth, venerated mainly in northern Honshu, who is portrayed as a young man with long hair and a red face.

Zasu. Title held by the head monk (abbot) of a temple or Buddhist monastery. *See* BETTŌ, JIMU, SŌKAN.

Zazen. "Sitting Zen"; total relaxation, a "non-meditation" designed to clear the mind and spirit in order to attain a sort of enlightening emptiness. In Zen Buddhist monasteries, *zazen* is practiced in a sitting position. The term comes from the Chinese *zuochan,* which has the same meaning. *See* SATORI, ZEAN-SHŪ.

Zeami. Actor and playwright (Seami, Kanze Motokiyo, 1363–1443), born to a family of Shinto priests, Kan'ami's son; he directed a troupe of Sarugaku actors in the Nara region. Noticed as a young man by shogun Ashikaga Yoshimitsu in 1374, he became his protégé. He produced Noh theater, wrote about 90 plays (although only 21 can be attributed to him with certainty) in which he performed, and wrote treatises on the theater arts, the best known of which are *Fūshi kaden* (Transmission of the Flower of the Actor's Art, 1400–18), *Shikadō-sho* (Essay on the Path of the Flower, 1420), *Ka-kyō* (The Mirror of the Flower, 1424), *Kyūi shidai* (The Order of the Nine Degrees), *Sarugaku dangi* (Conversations on Sarugaku, ca. 1430), *Nikyoku santai ezu* (Study of the Two Elements and Three Types), *Yūgaku shūdō kempusho kadensho* (Book on the Study of Musical Shows), and *Kadensho* (Book of the Flower).
Among Zeami's most famous "Sarugaku no Noh" plays, still performed today, are *Hagoromo, Shunkan, Takasago, Tadanori, Kinuta,* and *Izutsu.* Zeami became a Buddhist monk of the Zen Sōtō-shū sect in 1422, and passed the baton to his oldest son, Kanze Motomasa. Motomasa died ten years later, and Zeami's other son, On'ami, then presided over Noh shows. Zeami refused to pass his "secrets" on to On'ami, so he was exiled to the island of Sao by the shogun in 1434. He returned only a

few years before his death, and his son-in-law, Komparu Zenchiku, succeeded him as head of his theater company. Also called Dayū Motokiyo, Yūsakizaemon. *See* ZENCHIKU.

• *Zeami jūroku-bushū.* "Collection of Sixteen Booklets by Zeami." A collection of 23 texts published in 1989 by the philologist Yoshida Tōgo, constituting part of the "secret tradition" *(hiden)* of Noh theater. Some of these texts were rediscovered only in 1932. It is possible that some of them were written not by Zeami, but by Zenchiku.

Zegai. Noh play: a malicious *tengu,* disguised as a Yamabushi, argues about religion with a Buddhist monk, but must admit defeat.

Zekkai Chūshin. Buddhist monk of the Zen Rinzai-shū sect (1336–1405), a member of the Fujiwara family, born in Tosa province. A disciple of Musō Soseki, he was considered one of the best *gozan* poets. He lived in China from 1368 to 1378 and had an audience with Emperor Taizu of the Ming dynasty. His writings were included in a collection titled *Shōkenkō. See* GOZAN.

Zempa (Zen-pa). During the Kamakura period, a school of Buddhist sculpture active in the Nara region, thus named because most of its members had the character "Zen" in their name.

Zempō kōen-fun. A type of keyhole-shaped megalithic burial site *(kofun),* rectangular in the front and round in the back. *See* FUTAGO-ZUKA, KOFUN.

Zenchiku. Actor and playwright (Komparu Zenchiku, 1405–68), Zeami's son-in-law and disciple. He is credited with writing the Noh play *Mutsura. See* KOMPARU, ZEAMI JŪROKU-BUSHŪ.

Zenga. "Zen painting," a term for paintings and calligraphy by Zen monks in the Edo period, and sometimes for works by other monks. The best-known *zenga* masters were Fūgai Ekun and Hakuin.

Zengakuren. "Flowers of All Schools," abbreviation of All-Japan Federation of Student Self-Governing Associations (Zen Nihon Gakusei Jichikai Sōrengō), formed in 1948 and imitated by a number of extreme-left-wing student movements, all of which were called Zengakuren. In the 1960s, these movements incited serious disturbances and clashes with the police. The original Zengakuren was founded by students belonging to the Communist party, but it separated into a number of groups and gave rise to a new left-wing movement in 1960 (called Minsei Zengakuren in 1964), opposed to traditional communist ideology. In 1968, it split into several other factions, the best known of which were Kakumaru and Sampa. However, the faction supported by the Communist party remained the largest.

Zeniya Gohei. Engineer and merchant (1773–1852), born in Kaga province to a family of money changers *(zeniya).* He built for the shogunate a merchant fleet of more than 20 ships with a capacity of about 1,000 *koku* each, and devoted himself to the rice trade, making an immense fortune. He reclaimed the Kahoku-gatu marshes and drained them to make rice paddies, but this project failed and all his goods were seized; he died in prison.

Zenji. In Zen Buddhism (*see* ZEN-SHŪ), the title of "master in satori," given to a monk who has attained this state of enlightenment.

Zenji soga. Title of a Noh play: the brothers Soga, Jūrō, and Gorō seek revenge on Minamoto no Yoritomo. They attack him, but Gorō is wounded and his younger brother, Zenji, is taken prisoner. *See* SOGA.

Zenken kojitsu. "Biographies of Brave and Faithful Men" (in Japanese history), an illustrated 11-volume book, with notes and idealized portraits, by Kikuchi Yōsai (1788–1878). *See* KIKUCHI YŌSAI.

Zenki-zu. Zen poem or religious painting designed to provoke illumination *(satori)* among those who contemplate it. *See* ZEN-SHŪ.

Zenkō. Title given to a *kampaku* who retired from political affairs and became a lay Buddhist. Also called Taikō.
→ *See* SHIBA ZENKŌ.

• **Zenkō-ji.** Buddhist temple belonging to the Jōdo and Tendai-shū sects, founded in Nagano between 664 and 670. It is one of the largest temples in Japan, after the Tōdai-ji, and houses sculptures of Amida that were probably brought from Korea in the seventh century. The Zenkō-ji commands some 60 subsidiary temples *(matsu-ji).* Most of its current structures date from 1726, as it was completely reconstructed in the early eighteenth century. The huge *hondō* (1707) is made of about 60,000 wooden beams. The *honzon* (main image), called Ikkō Sanzon, portrays Amida flanked by two bodhisattvas, all three sharing a single halo *(kōhai)*. Reliquary dating from 1369; *niō-mon* from the late nineteenth century.

Zenkunen no Eki. "Earlier Nine-Years' War." In fact, it lasted from 1051 to 1062 and featured sporadic confrontations between imperial troops and the Abe family in Mutsu province. It started when Abe no Yoritoki refused to pay taxes to the court, which sent Minamoto no Yoriyoshi and his son, Minamoto no Yoshiie, to do battle with him. Yoritoki was killed in 1057; his sons, Abe no Sadatō and Abe no Munetō, continued the struggle but were ultimately defeated. This war was followed by the "Later Three-Years' War" (Gosannen no Eki), waged in the same region between 1083 and 1087, during which Minamoto no Yoshiie defeated the Kiyohara family, thus ensuring the Minamoto family's preeminence in eastern Japan.

Zen Nihon Bukkyō-kai. "Japan Buddhist Federation," created in 1954 when a number of national and local religious agencies merged in order to coordinate Buddhist activities. Its first president was the monk Ōtani Kōchō (b. 1903).

Zennin. Buddhist monk (twelfth century) of the Tendai-shū, Minamoto no Motoyuki's son. He was, in succession, *ajari* (1103), *risshi* (1127), and *daisōzu* (1128) of the Tendai-shū, and received the title Hō-in.

Zenran. One of the sons (1210–92) of the Buddhist monk Shinran. He was disinherited by his father in 1256 for his heretical views of the teachings of the Jōdo Shin-shū. *See* SHINRAN.

Zenrin-ji. Buddhist temple of the Jōdo-shū, founded in Kyoto in 855, destroyed during the Ōnin War (1467–77), and reconstructed in 1497. Also called Eikan-dō.

Zenrō. Board of workers' unions of Japan that broke away from the Sōhyō in 1954. In 1960, it joined Sōdōmei to form Dōmei.

Zensen Dōmei. "Federation of Textile Workers," powerful union formed in 1946, with about 450,000 members. At first affiliated with Sōhyō (from 1950 to 1953), it joined Dōmei in 1964.

Zensetsu. Painter (Tokuriki Yukikatsu, 1591–1680) and Buddhist monk of the Kanzō school. Head of the *e-dokoro* of the Hongan-ji temple in Kyoto.

Zenshin-ni. Chinese Buddhist nun who apparently went to Japan via Korea in 522, bringing with her Buddhist images and sacred texts *(Skt.: sūtra; Jap.: kyō)*. Also called Shima.

Zenshin-za. Company of Kabuki actors formed in 1931 to promote a "modern," progressivist Kabuki theater. Ironically, however, the group had real success only when it performed Kabuki classics.

Zen-shū. Buddhist sect imported from China (*Chin.*: Chan-zong) by Eisai in 1192, then by Dōgen in 1227. Its teachings are transmitted from master to disciple through the use of "paradoxes" *(kōan)*, but there is no rigid doctrine. Zen-shū rejects veneration of images and advocates self-realization through the practice of *zazen,* which enables individuals, through sudden or gradual enlightenment *(satori),* to attain the awareness of the Buddha. It is divided into four main streams: Ōbaku-shū (about 120,000 followers), Rinzai-shū (about 2 million), Sōtō-shū (about 7 million), and Shōbō-shū. The "six masters" (Zenshū-rokusō) of the sect were:
—Eka (Huike, Chinese, 487–593)
—Daruma (Bodai-Daruma, Bodhidharma, Indian, ?–528)
—Dōshin (Daoxin, Chinese, 580–651)
—Sōsan (Sengcan, Chinese, ?–606)
—Kōnin (Hongren, Chinese, 602–75)
—Enō (Huineng, Chinese, 638–713)
Zen was immediately successful among warriors in the Kamakura period, and Buddhist monks spread its doctrines throughout the country. The Japanese mentality adapted very well to Zen, which offered some reconciliation between traditional Buddhism and the sense of integration inherent to Shinto. Zen could be interpreted in different ways and gave rise to particular genres of art and literature in the Kamakura and Muromachi periods. During the Edo period, Zen monks who opposed traditional Buddhism were supported by the shoguns, especially because Zen monasteries advocated the study of Confucian theories.

In the modern era, Zen became popular in the West thanks mainly to the writings of D. T. Suzuki, and was used as a method of reflection even by Christians. Because it is neither philosophy nor religion, Zen can be adapted to all sorts of thought, and that is why it has spread so rapidly. Unfortunately, Western authors have often misinterpreted the Zen doctrines, especially the *kōan* and the practice of *zazen*. *See the cited words,* DŌGEN.

Zentsū-ji. Buddhist temple of the Shingon-shū sect, apparently founded in 806 by Kūkai on a piece of land donated by his father, Saeki Zentsū, in the town of Zentsū-ji (Kagawa-ken, Shikoku). Destroyed by fire several times, and each time rebuilt, it has a five-story pagoda from the ninth century (restored in the nineteenth century). Most of its buildings date from the seventeenth century, except for the Yakushi-dō, which is from the fifteenth century. This temple is one of the three sacred sites of the Shingon-shū, with Mt. Kōya and the Tō-ji in Kyoto, and is the largest of the 88 temples associated with Kūkai on Shikoku. The Zentsū-ji has about 300,000 followers.

Zeshin. *See* SHIBATA ZESHIN.

Zō-ami. Sculptor (Zō-ami Hisatsugu, fourteenth–fifteenth century) of Noh masks *(nōmen)* and a Dengaku dancer. He was one of the Rokusaku.

Zōbiki. "Pulling the Elephant," a Kabuki play, one of the Kabuki-jūhachiban: duel between a hero and a villain. At the end, the hero lures an elephant to him and throws it on his adversary. *Zōbiki* is very rarely performed.

Zōgan. Technique of inlaying metal, ivory, shell, ceramics, wood, or mother-of-pearl on objects, often lacquers.

Zōjō-ji. Buddhist temple of the Jōdo-shū sect, founded in Minato-ku (Tokyo) by Shūei (809–84), a disciple of Kūkai. At first affiliated with the Shingon-shū, it was transferred to the obedience of the Jōdo-shū in 1393 by the monk Shōsō (1366–1440). Tokugawa Ieyasu designated it a family temple of the Tokugawa in 1590. Seriously damaged by the bombing of Tokyo in 1944–45, it was rebuilt in 1974 on a somewhat reduced plan.

Zōkoku. Lacquer artist (Tamakaji Zōkoku, 1806–69), Fujiwara no Uemon's student, serving the Matsudaira family in the Kagawa region. He also sculpted netsuke.

Zoku. Term meaning "continuation," used mainly in literature (also pronounced *shoku*).

• *Zoku gosen-shū.* "Continuation of *Gosen-shū,*" a poetry anthology compiled by Fujiwara no Tameie in 1251. It includes 1,368 poems in 20 scrolls. *See* CHOKUSEN WAKA-SHŪ.

• *Zoku go shūi-shū.* "Continuation of *Go shūi-shū,*" a poetry anthology compiled by Nijō Tamefuji about 1325 and supplemented by Nijō Tamesada. It has 1,343 poems in 20 scrolls. *See* CHOKUSEN WAKA-SHŪ.

• **Zoku gunsho ruijū.** *See* GUNSHO RUIJŪ.

• *Zoku kokin-shū.* "Continuation of *Kokin-shū,*" a poetry anthology compiled by Fujiwara no Yukiie, Fujiwara no Mitsutoshi, and Fujiwara no Ienaga in 1265, with 1,972 poems in 20 scrolls. *See* CHOKUSEN WAKA-SHŪ.

• *Zoku kokushi taikei.* *See* KOKUSHI TAIKEI.

• *Zoku sarumino.* *See* BASHŌ HAIKAI SHICHI-BUSHŪ.

• *Zoku senzai-shū.* "Continuation of *Senzai-shū,*" a poetry anthology compiled by Nijō Tameie in 1320, with 2,120 poems in 20 scrolls. *See* CHOKUSEN WAKA-SHŪ.

• *Zoku shigushō.* Historical work published in 1791, a continuation of *Hyakuren-shō,* by Yanagiwara no Motomisu (1746–1830).

• **Zoku shiseki shūran.** *See* SHISEKI SHŪRAN.

• *Zoku shūi-shū.* "Continuation of *Shūi-shū,*" poetry anthology compiled by Nijō Tameuji in 1278, with 1,600 poems in 20 scrolls. *See* CHOKUSEN WAKA-SHŪ.

Zokumyō. Name given to a boy after the hat-giving ceremony *(gembuku)* marking his passage to adulthood, corresponding to a first name in the West. Also called *tsūshō*. *See* GEMBUKU, NAMES.

Zoku-Shintō. Term coined by Hirata Atsutane to describe syncretic sects mixing Shinto, Buddhism, Taoism, and Confucianism.

Zonkaku. Buddhist monk (Kōgen, 1290–1373) of the Jōdo Shin-shū school, Kakunyo's son. He wrote many works on his sect's doctrine, as well as autobiographical notes, *Zonkaku shōnin ichigo-ki.*

Zoos. There are currently about 70 zoos in Japan, the largest of which is in Ueno Park in Tokyo (founded in 1882); it has more than 900 species. The Nagoya zoo has more than 300. There are also large zoos in Kyoto (founded 1903) and Osaka (1915). The primate zoo in Inuyama (Aichi-ken) is one of the most interesting because of its variety of species. Almost every city has a zoo, public or private, but each is small. The Tama zoo near Tokyo, created in 1958, is famous for its African lions.

Zori. Straw sandals with a thong for the big toe and two straps *(hanao)* to keep them on the foot. *Zori* have been used in Japan since ancient times. There are a number of types, from *ashinaka-zōri* (half-*zori*), once used by soldiers, to wedge-heeled *zori* worn by women with a kimono. They are now made in other materials, such as plastic and rubber, and they are worn all over the world as summer or beach footwear. *See also* SHOES, WARAJI.

Zōshiki. General term applied to all categories of servants and, in the Kamakura period, to the lowest-ranking warriors. In the Muromachi and Edo periods, *zōshiki* were semi-bureaucrats responsible for helping the governor (Kyōto-shoshidai) of the shogunate in Kyoto in the most trivial tasks, such as those delegated to the police.

Zu. Character meaning "image" or "painting," equivalent to "painted by"; it often follows the artist's name on a painting or print. Sometimes replaced by the character *hitsu* ("from the brush of") or *ga*. The character *zu* also designates a map or a book of descriptive drawings.

Zuigan-ji. Buddhist temple founded in 828 in Matsushima and rebuilt in 1609 in the style of the Momoyama era. It is decorated with paintings by artists of the Kanō school.

Zuihitsu. "As the brush paints" or "literary jottings," a literary genre comprising various essays, thoughts, or notes accumulated in no apparent order or simply by association of ideas, and not (at least originally) destined for publication. Very popular in the eleventh and twelfth centuries, *zuihitsu* is typified by *Makura no sōshi,* by Sei Shōnagon, *Hōjōki,* by Kamo no Chōmei, and *Tsurezuregusa.* During the Edo period, many writers tried to revive the genre, including Matsudaira Sadanobu and Motoori Norinaga. Some modern authors also like to write collections of thoughts related to the *zuihitsu* genre.

Zuikei Shūhō. Zen Buddhist monk (Ga-un, 1391–1473) of the Shōkoku-ji temple in Kyoto, famous for his studies of Chinese classics. He wrote a collection of notes, *Ga-un nikkenroku,* valuable for information it gives on the shogun Ashikaga Yoshimasa, whose confidant he was, as well as on Zen temples and the arts of his time. This journal, which covers the years 1446–73, was originally in 74 parts. Only one part has been found, thanks to a copy made in 1562 by Koretaka Myōan.

Zuiryū-in. Religious name of a half-sister (Chieko) of Toyotomi Hideyoshi who married Miyoshi Yoshifusa and who was Toyotomi Hidetsugu's mother. She became a Buddhist nun in 1595.

Zuisen-ji. Buddhist temple founded in Kamakura in 1327 by the monk Musō Soseki for the Engaku-ji branch of the Zen Rinzai-shū sect. It was restored in the fourteenth and fifteenth centuries under the patronage of the Ashikaga shoguns. It has a Zen-style garden attributed to Musō Soseki and a statue of Soseki, sculpted from a single block of wood *(ichi-moku-zukuri),* that dates from the fourteenth century.

Zuishin. Guardian semi-divinities whose images are usually placed at the entrance to Shinto sanctuaries. They are portrayed as Heian-period ministers of the right *(udaijin)* and the left *(sadaijin),* armed with a bow and arrow to chase away evil spirits. Also called Dadaijin, Kado no Osa, Yadaijin, Zuijin.
   • Corps of guards attached to senior court bureaucrats in the Heian and Kamakura periods.

   • *Zuishin teiki emaki.* "*Emakimono* of the Guards," portraying nine members of the Imperial Guard and eight horses, dating from 1247 and attributed to Fujiwara no Nobuzane. One scroll; housed at the Okura Foundation in Tokyo. Also called *Zuijin teiki emaki.*

Zuishō. Sculptor (Hotta Zuichō, 1837–1916) of objects in wood and bamboo, born in Edo.

Zuryō. Assistant administrators in *shōen* for owners residing in the capital *(yōnin-kokushi),* charged with collecting taxes. The *zuryō* became quite wealthy on the backs of the peasants and founded families who hired groups of warriors *(bushidan)* to protect them in the late Heian period. The Kamakura *bakufu* replaced them with official bureaucrats, the *shugo.*

Zushi. Portable Buddhist altar, in the form of a cabinet, holding effigies of divinities. The most famous is the Tamamushi no zushi belonging to Lady Tachibana (seventh century), kept in the Hōryū-ji temple in Nara. *See these entries.*

Zushoryō. "Bureau of Archives" or "Bureau of Books and Charts," the library of archives created by the *ritsuryō* code (701) to preserve the official documents of eight ministries, and attached to the Nakatsukasa-shō (Ministry of Imperial Affairs). It continued to exist over the years and was revived in the Meiji era. Mori Ōgai was its director from 1917 to 1922. It is now part of the Shoryō-ryō (Bureau of Imperial Mausoleums). Also called Toshoryō.

BIBLIOGRAPHY

Revised for this edition by Hiraku Shimoda

General Works

Collcutt, Martin, Marius Jansen, and Isao Kumakura. *Cultural Atlas of Japan.* Oxford, England: Phaidon, 1988.

De Bary, Wm. Theodore, et al., comp. *Sources of Japanese Tradition.* 2nd ed. New York: Columbia University Press, 2001.

De Vos, George A., and Wagatsuma, Hiroshi. *Japan's Invisible Race: Caste in Culture and Personality.* Berkeley: University of California Press, 1966.

Dempster, Prue. *Japan Advances: A Geographical Study.* 2nd ed. London: Methuen, 1969.

Dening, Maberly Esler. *Japan.* London: Benn, 1960.

Embree, John F. *The Japanese Nation: A Social Survey.* Westport, Conn.: Greenwood Press, 1945.

Fairbank, John K., Edwin O. Reischauer, and Albert M. Craig. *East Asia: The Modern Transformation.* Rev. ed. Boston: Houghton Mifflin, 1989.

Fukuzawa, Yukichi. *The Autobiography of Fukuzawa Yukichi.* Tr. Eiichi Kiyooka. Tokyo: The Hokuseido Press, 1934.

Gibney, Frank. *Five Gentlemen of Japan: The Portrait of a Nation's Character.* New York: Farrar, Straus and Young, 1953.

Godement, François. *The New Asian Renaissance: From Colonialism to the Post–Cold War.* Tr. Elizabeth J. Parcell. London and New York: Routledge, 1997.

Goedertier, Joseph M. *A Dictionary of Japanese History.* New York: Walker/Weatherhill, 1968.

Grew, Joseph C. *Report from Tokyo: A Message to the American People.* New York: Simon and Schuster, 1942.

——— *Ten Years in Japan.* New York: Simon and Schuster, 1944.

Grousset, Rene. *The Civilizations of the East.* Tr. Catherine Alison Phillips. New York: Knopf, 1931–34.

Guillain, Robert. *The Japanese Challenge.* Tr. Patrick O'Brian. London: Hamish Hamilton, 1970.

Hall, John Whitney, et al. *Twelve Doors to Japan.* New York: McGraw-Hill, 1965.

Harada, Jirō. *A Glimpse of Japanese Ideals: Lectures on Japanese Art and Culture.* Tokyo: The Society for International Cultural Relations, 1937.

Hearn, Lafcadio. *Glimpses of Unfamiliar Japan.* Boston: Houghton, Mifflin and Company, 1894.

Holtom, Daniel Clarence. *The Japanese Enthronement Ceremonies: With an Account of the Imperial Regalia.* Tokyo: The Kyo Bun Kwan, 1928.

The Japan Biographical Encyclopedia & Who's Who. 1st ed. Tokyo: Japan Biographical Research Dept., Rengo Press, Ltd., 1958.

Japan P.E.N. Club. *Japanese Literature in Foreign Languages, 1945–1990.* Tokyo: Japan Book Publishers Association, 1990.

Japan Travel Bureau. *Japan: The Official Guide.* Tokyo: Japan Travel Bureau, 1952.

Japan Writers Society. *Japan Bibliographic Annual.* Tokyo: Hokuseido Press 1956–57. 2 v.

Japanese National Commission for UNESCO. *Japan: Its Land, People and Culture.* Tokyo: Ministry of Finance, 1958.

Katō, Shūichi. *The Japan-China Phenomenon: Conflict or Compatibility?* Tr. David Chibbett. London: Paul Norbury Publications Ltd., 1974.

Kawai, Kazuo. *Japan's American Interlude*. Chicago: University of Chicago Press, 1960.

Kawasaki, Ichirō. *The Japanese Are Like That*. Tokyo and Rutland, Vt.: Tuttle, 1955.

Keene, Donald. *Living Japan*. Garden City, N.Y.: Doubleday, 1959.

Kirkup, James. *Heaven, Hell and Hara-kiri: The Rise and Fall of the Japanese Superstate*. London: Angus and Robertson, 1974.

Kodansha Encyclopedia of Japan. New York: Kodansha, 1983. 9 vols.

Koestler, Arthur. *The Lotus and the Robot*. London: Hutchinson, 1960.

Kokusai Bunka Shinkōkai. *Catalogue of the K.B.S. Library*. Tokyo: Kokusai Bunka Shinkokai, 1937.

Kōsaka, Masataka. *100 Million Japanese: The Postwar Experience*. Tokyo: Kodansha International, 1972.

Maraini, Fosco. *Japan: Patterns of Continuity*. Tokyo: Kodansha International, 1971.

Michaux, Henri. *A Barbarian in Asia*. Translation by Sylvia Beach. New York: New Directions, 1949.

Motono, Tōru. *Illuminants of Old Japan*. Tokyo, 1929.

Nachod, Oskar. *Bibliography of the Japanese Empire, 1906–1926*. London: E. Goldston, 1928.

Okakura, Kakuzō. *Ideals of the East*. New York: Dutton, 1903.

Papinot, Edmond. *Historical and Geographical Dictionary of Japan*. Tokyo: Sansaisha, 1909.

Sakamaki, Shunzō. *Ryūkyū: A Bibliographical Guide to Okinawan Studies*. Honolulu: University of Hawaii Press, 1963.

Sansom, George Bailey. *The Western World and Japan: A Study in the Interaction of European and Asiatic Cultures*. New York: Knopf, 1950.

Shikaumi, Nobuya. *Cultural Policy in Japan*. Paris: Unesco, 1970.

Shively, Donald H., ed. *Tradition and Modernization in Japanese Culture*. Princeton: Princeton University Press, 1971.

Stoetzel, Jean. *Without the Chrysanthemum and the Sword: A Study of the Attitudes of Youth in Post-war Japan*. New York: Columbia University Press, 1955.

Taeuber, Irene Barnes. *The Population of Japan*. Princeton: Princeton University Press, 1958.

Totman, Conrad D. *A History of Japan*. Malden, Mass.: Blackwell Publishers, 2000.

Wolferen, Karel Van. *The Enigma of Japanese Power: People and Politics in a Stateless Nation*. New York: Knopf, 1989.

Yazaki, Takeo. *Social Change and the City in Japan: From Earliest Times through the Industrial Revolution*. Tr. David L. Swain. Tokyo: Japan Publications Trading Co., 1968.

History

Akamatsu, Paul. *Meiji, 1868: Revolution and Counter-revolution in Japan*. Tr. Miriam Kochan. New York: Harper & Row, 1972.

America-Japan Society. *The First Japanese Embassy to the United States of America*. Tokyo: The America-Japan Society, 1920.

Ball, W. Macmahon. *Japan: Enemy or Ally?* New York: Institute of Pacific Relations, 1949.

Battistini, Lawrence Henry. *Japan and America: From Earliest Times to the Present*. New York: J. Day Co., 1953.

——— *The United States and Asia*. New York: Praeger, 1955.

Beasley, William G. *Great Britain and the Opening of Japan, 1834–1858*. London: Luzac, 1951.

——— *The Meiji Restoration*. Stanford: Stanford University Press, 1972.

Beasley, W. G., and E. G. Pulleyblank, eds. *Historians of China and Japan*. London: Oxford University Press, 1961.

Bisson, T. A. *Japan's War Economy*. New York: Institute of Pacific Relations, 1945.

Bix, Herbert P. *Hirohito and the Making of Modern Japan*. New York: Harper Collins Publishers, 2000.

Black, John R. *Young Japan: Yokohama and Yedo*. London: Trubner & Co., 1880–81.

Bolitho, Harold. *Treasures among Men: The Fudai Daimyo in Tokugawa Japan*. New Haven: Yale University Press, 1974.

Borton, Hugh. *Japan's Modern Century*. New York: Ronald Press, 1955.

Borton, Hugh, ed. *Japan*. Ithaca: Cornell University Press, 1950.

Butow, Robert J. C. *Japan's Decision to Surrender*. Stanford: Stanford University Press, 1954.

Byas, Hugh. *Government by Assassination*. New York: Knopf, 1942.

Clyde, Paul Hibbert. *The Far East: A History of the Impact of the West on Eastern Asia*. New York: Prentice-Hall, 1948.

Cohen, Jerome Bernard. *Japan's Postwar Economy*. Bloomington: Indiana University Press, 1958.

Cooper, Michael, ed. *The Southern Barbarians: The First Europeans in Japan*. Tokyo: Kodansha International, 1971.

Craig, Albert M. *Chōshū in the Meiji Restoration.* Cambridge: Harvard University Press, 1961.

Craig, William. *The Fall of Japan.* New York: Dial Press, 1967.

Crowley, James B. *Japan's Quest for Autonomy: National Security and Foreign Policy, 1930–1938.* Princeton: Princeton University Press, 1966.

De Bary, Wm. Theodore, and Ainslie T. Embree, eds. *Approaches to Asian Civilizations.* New York: Columbia University Press, 1964.

Dore, Ronald Philip. *Land Reform in Japan.* London and New York: Oxford University Press, 1959.

Dore, Ronald Philip, ed. *Aspects of Social Change in Modern Japan.* Princeton: Princeton University Press, 1967.

Dower, John W. *Embracing Defeat : Japan in the Wake of World War II.* New York: W.W. Norton & Co./New Press, 1999.

Dower, John W. *War without Mercy: Race and Power in the Pacific War.* New York: Pantheon, 1986.

Dulles, Foster Rhea. *Forty Years of American-Japanese Relations.* New York and London: Appleton-Century, 1937.

Duus, Peter. *Party Rivalry and Political Change in Taisho Japan.* Cambridge, Mass.: Harvard University Press, 1968.

Elsbree, Willard H. *Japan's Role in Southeast Asian Nationalist Movements, 1940 to 1945.* Cambridge, Mass.: Harvard University Press, 1953.

Eunson, Roby. *100 Years: The Amazing Development of Japan since 1860.* Tokyo: Kodansha International, 1965.

Frédéric, Louis. *Daily Life in Japan at the Time of the Samurai, 1185–1603.* Tr. Eileen M. Lowe. London: Allen and Unwin, 1972.

Frédéric, Louis, and Michel Random. *Japan.* Tr. Alexandra Campbell. Newton Abbot: David & Charles, 1987.

Gordon, Andrew. *Labor and Imperial Democracy in Prewar Japan.* Berkeley: University of California Press, 1991.

Groot, Gerard C. de. *The Prehistory of Japan.* New York: Columbia University Press, 1951.

Hall, John Whitney. *Government and Local Power in Japan, 500 to 1700: A Study Based on Bizen Province.* Princeton: Princeton University Press, 1966.

——— *Japanese History: A Guide to Japanese Reference and Research Materials.* Ann Arbor: University of Michigan Press, 1954.

——— *Japan from Prehistory to Modern Times.* New York: Dell, 1970.

Hall, John Whitney, and Toyoda Takeshi, eds. *Japan in the Muromachi Age.* Berkeley: University of California Press, 1977.

Harris, Townsend. *The Complete Journal of Townsend Harris, First American Consul General and Minister to Japan.* Garden City, N.Y.: Doubleday, 1930.

Harrison, John Armstrong, ed. and tr. *New Light on Early and Medieval Japanese Historiography.* Gainesville: University of Florida Press, 1960.

Howell, David Luke. *Capitalism from Within: Economy, Society, and the State in a Japanese Fishery.* Berkeley: University of California Press, 1995.

Ienaga, Saburō. *History of Japan.* Tokyo: Japan Travel Bureau, 1959.

Ike, Nobutaka. *The Beginnings of Political Democracy in Japan.* Baltimore: The Johns Hopkins Press, 1950.

Ishii, Ryōsuke. *Japanese Legislation in the Meiji Era.* Tr. William J. Chambliss. Tokyo: Pan-Pacific Press, 1958.

Iwao, Seiichi, ed. *Biographical Dictionary of Japanese History.* Tr. Burton Watson. Tokyo: Kodansha International, 1978.

Jansen, Marius B. *The Making of Modern Japan.* Cambridge, Mass.: Belknap Press of Harvard University Press, 2000.

——— *Sakamoto Ryōma and the Meiji Restoration.* Princeton: Princeton University Press, 1961.

Kahn, Herman. *The Emerging Japanese Superstate: Challenge and Response.* Englewood Cliffs, N.J.: Prentice-Hall, 1970.

Kawakami, Kiyoshi Karl. *Japan and World Peace.* New York: Macmillan, 1919.

Keene, Donald. *The Japanese Discovery of Europe: Honda Toshiaki and Other Discoverers, 1720–1798.* London: Routledge and Kegan Paul, 1952.

Kerr, George H. *Okinawa: The History of an Island People.* Rutland, Vt.: Tuttle, 1958.

Kidder, J. Edward. *Japan before Buddhism.* London: Thames and Hudson, 1959.

Kuno, Yoshi Saburō. *Japanese Expansion on the Asiatic Continent.* Berkeley: University of California Press, 1937.

Latourette, Kenneth Scott. *The History of Japan.* New York: Macmillan, 1947.

Lederer, Emil. *Japan in Transition.* New Haven: Yale University Press, 1938.

Lord, Walter. *Incredible Victory.* New York: Harper & Row, 1967.

Mabire, Jean. *The Samurai.* Tr. W. G. Corp. London: Wingate, 1975.

Maki, John McGilvrey. *Government and Politics in Japan: The Road to Democracy.* New York: Praeger, 1962.

Mass, Jeffrey P., and William B. Hauser, eds. *The Bakufu in Japanese History.* Stanford: Stanford University Press, 1985.

Morris, Ivan I. *Nationalism and the Right Wing in Japan: A Study of Post-war Trends.* Westport, Conn.: Greenwood Press, 1960.

—— *The World of the Shining Prince: Court Life in Ancient Japan.* New York: Knopf, 1964.

Morris, Ivan I., ed. *Japan 1931–1945: Militarism, Fascism, Japanism?* Boston: Heath, 1963.

Murdoch, James. *A History of Japan.* London: K. Paul, Trench, Trubner & Co., 1925–26.

Naga, Kalidasa. *Prehistoric Japan.* Tokyo: The Society for International Cultural Relations, 1941.

Najita, Tetsuo. *Hara Kei in the Politics of Compromise, 1905–1915.* Cambridge, Mass.: Harvard University Press, 1967.

Nihongi: Chronicles of Japan from the Earliest Times to A.D. 697. Tr. W. G. Aston. London: Allen & Unwin, 1956.

Noda, Yoshiyuki. *Introduction to Japanese Law.* Tr. Anthony H. Angelo. Tokyo: University of Tokyo Press, 1976.

Onoda, Hiroo. *No Surrender: My Thirty-year War.* Tr. Charles S. Terry. New York: Kodansha International, 1974.

Pacific War Research Society. *The Day Man Lost: Hiroshima, 6 August 1945.* Tokyo and Palo Alto, Calif.: Kodansha International, 1972.

Packard, George R. *Protest in Tokyo: The Security Treaty Crisis of 1960.* Princeton: Princeton University Press, 1966.

Reischauer, Edwin O. *Japan, Past and Present.* New York: Knopf, 1946.

—— *Japan: The Story of a Nation.* New York: Knopf, 1970.

—— *The United States and Japan.* Cambridge, Mass.: Harvard University Press, 1950.

Reischauer, Robert Karl. *Early Japanese History.* Princeton: Princeton University Press, 1937.

Roberts, Luke S. *Mercantilism in a Japanese Domain: The Merchant Origins of Economic Nationalism in 18th-century Tosa.* Cambridge and New York: Cambridge University Press, 1998.

Rodrigues, Joao. *This Island of Japon: Joao Rodrigues' Account of 16th-century Japan.* Tr. Michael Cooper. New York: Kodansha International, 1973.

Sansom, George Bailey. *A History of Japan.* 3 vols. Stanford: Stanford University Press, 1958–63.

—— *Japan: A Short Cultural History.* New York: Century, 1932.

—— *The Western World and Japan: A Study in the Interaction of European and Asiatic Cultures.* New York: Knopf, 1949.

Scalapino, Robert A. *The Japanese Communist Movement: 1920–1965.* Santa Monica, Calif.: Rand Corporation, 1966.

Scalapino, Robert A., ed. *The Foreign Policy of Modern Japan.* Berkeley: University of California Press, 1977.

Scalapino, Robert A., and Masumi Junnosuke. *Parties and Politics in Contemporary Japan.* Berkeley: University of California Press, 1962.

Sheldon, Charles David. *The Rise of the Merchant Class in Tokugawa Japan, 1600–1868: An Introductory Survey.* Locust Valley, N.Y.: Augustin, 1958.

Shinoda, Minoru. *The Founding of the Kamakura Shogunate, 1180–1185, with Selected Translations from the* Azuma kagami. New York: Columbia University Press, 1960.

Statler, Oliver. *Shimoda Story.* New York: Random House, 1969.

Storry, Richard. *The Double Patriots: A Study of Japanese Nationalism.* Boston: Houghton Mifflin, 1957.

—— *A History of Modern Japan.* Baltimore: Penguin Books, 1960.

Suematsu, Kenchō. *The Risen Sun.* London: Archibald Constable, 1905.

—— *Russia and Japan.* Woking, England: The Oriental Institute, 1904.

The Taiheiki: A Chronicle of Medieval Japan. Tr. Helen Craig McCullough. New York: Columbia University Press, 1959.

Takekoshi, Yosaburō. *The Economic Aspects of the History of the Civilization of Japan.* London: Allen & Unwin, 1930.

—— *The Story of the Wakō: Japanese Pioneers in the Southern Regions.* Tr. Hideo Watanabe. Tokyo: Kenkyusha, 1940.

Thayer, Nathaniel Bowman. *How the Conservatives Rule Japan.* Princeton: Princeton University Press, 1969.

Toland, John. *But Not in Shame: The Six Months after Pearl Harbor.* New York: Random House, 1961.

—— *The Rising Sun: The Decline and Fall of the Japanese Empire, 1936–1945.* New York: Random House, 1970.

Totman, Conrad D. *The Collapse of the Tokugawa Bakufu, 1862–1868.* Honolulu: University Press of Hawaii, 1980.

Treat, Payson J. *The Far East: A Political and Diplomatic History.* New York and London: Harper, 1928.

Uenoda, Setsuo. *Calendar of Annual Events in Japan.* Tokyo: Tokyo News Service, 1954.

Van Alstyne, Richard Warner. *The United States and East Asia.* New York: Norton, 1973.

Wang, Yi-tung. *Official Relations between China and Japan, 1368–1549.* Cambridge, Mass.: Harvard University Press, 1953.

Ward, Robert Edward, ed. *Political Development in Modern Japan.* Princeton: Princeton University Press, 1968.

Wigen, Karen. *The Making of a Japanese Periphery, 1750–1920.* Berkeley: University of California Press, 1995.

Williams, Justin. *Japan's Political Revolution under MacArthur: A Participant's Account.* Athens: University of Georgia Press, 1979.

Wilson, Robert Arden. *Genesis of the Meiji Government in Japan, 1868–1871.* Berkeley: University of California Press, 1957.

Wray, Harry, and Hilary Conroy, eds. *Japan Examined: Perspectives on Modern Japanese History.* Honolulu: University Press of Hawaii, 1983.

Yakhontoff, Victor A. *Russia and the Soviet Union in the Far East.* New York: Coward-McCann, 1931.

Yanaga, Chitoshi. *Japan since Perry.* New York: McGraw-Hill, 1949.

Yoshikawa, Eiji. *The Heike Story.* Tr. Fuki Wooyenaka Utamatsu. New York: Knopf, 1956.

Yoshitsune: A Fifteenth-century Japanese Chronicle. Tr. Helen Craig McCullough. Stanford: Stanford University Press, 1966.

Young, John. *The Location of Yamatai: A Case Study in Japanese Historiography, 720–1945.* Baltimore: The Johns Hopkins Press, 1958.

Literature

The Actors' Analects. Tr. Charles J. Dunn and Bunzō Torigoe. New York: Columbia University Press, 1969.

Araki, James T. *The Ballad-drama of Medieval Japan.* Berkeley: University of California Press, 1964.

Aston, William George. *A History of Japanese Literature.* London: Heinemann, 1899.

Beck, L. Adams. *The Ghost Plays of Japan.* New York: The Japan Society, 1933.

Blyth, Reginald Horace. *Haiku.* Tokyo: Kamakura Bunko, 1963–9.

——— *Japanese Humour.* Tokyo: Japan Travel Bureau, 1957.

——— *Oriental Humour.* Tokyo: Hokuseido Press, 1959.

——— *Senryū: Japanese Satirical Verses.* Tokyo: Hokuseido Press, 1949.

——— *Zen in English Literature and Oriental Classics.* Tokyo: Hokuseido Press, 1942.

Bowers, Faubion. *Japanese Theatre.* New York: Hermitage House, 1952.

Brower, Robert H., and Earl Miner. *Japanese Court Poetry.* Stanford: Stanford University Press, 1961.

Clavell, James. *Shōgun: A Novel of Japan.* New York: Atheneum, 1975.

Daniels, Otome. *Dictionary of Japanese Soshō Writing Forms.* London: Lund, Humphries and Co., 1944.

Diaries of Court Ladies of Old Japan. Tr. Annie Shepley Omori. Boston: Houghton Mifflin, 1920.

Ernst, Earle. *The Kabuki Theatre.* New York: Grove Press, 1956.

Gatenby, Edward Vivian. *The Cloud-men of Yamato.* London: Murray, 1929.

Gluck, Jay, ed. *Ukiyo: Stories of "the Floating World" of Postwar Japan.* New York: Universal Library, 1964.

Gunji, Masakatsu. *Kabuki.* Tr. John Bester. Tokyo and Palo Alto: Kodansha International, 1969.

Halford, Aubrey S. *The Kabuki Handbook.* Tokyo and Rutland, Vt.: Tuttle, 1956.

Hearn, Lafcadio. *Earless Hō-ichi: A Classic Japanese Tale of Mystery.* Tokyo: Kodansha International, 1966.

——— *Japanese Goblin Poetry.* Tokyo: Oyama, 1934.

——— *Kokoro: Hints and Echoes of Japanese Inner Life.* Boston: Houghton Mifflin, 1896.

——— *Kwaidan: Stories and Studies of Strange Things.* Boston: Houghton Mifflin, 1904.

——— *On Poetry.* Tokyo: The Hokuseido Press, 1934.

——— *The Romance of the Milky Way and Other Studies and Stories.* Boston: Houghton Mifflin, 1905.

Hibbett, Howard. *The Floating World in Japanese Fiction.* New York: Oxford University Press, 1959.

Hyakunin-isshu: Single Songs of a Hundred Poets. Tr. Clay MacCauley. Tokyo: The Asiatic Society of Japan, 1889.

Karatani, Kōjin. *Origins of Modern Japanese Literature*. Tr. Brett de Bary. Durham, N.C.: Duke University Press, 1993.

Katō, Shūichi. *A History of Japanese Literature*. 3 vols. Tr. David Chibbett. London: Macmillan, 1979–1983.

Kawatake, Shigetoshi. *Kabuki: Japanese Drama*. Tokyo: Foreign Affairs Association of Japan, 1958.

Keene, Donald. *Anthology of Japanese Literature: From the Earliest Era to the Mid-nineteenth Century*. New York: Grove Press, 1955.

—— *Four Major Plays*. New York: Columbia University Press, 1961.

—— *Japanese Literature: An Introduction for Western Readers*. London: Murray, 1953.

—— *Modern Japanese Literature: An Anthology*. New York: Grove Press, 1956.

—— *Nō: The Classical Theatre of Japan*. Tokyo and Palo Alto: Kodansha International, 1966.

Kimura, Ki. *Japanese Literature: Manners and Customs in the Meiji-Taisho Era*. Tr. Philip Yampolsky. Tokyo: Obunsha, 1957.

Kokusai Bunka Shinkōkai. *Introduction to Classic Japanese Literature*. Tokyo: Kokusai Bunka Shinkokai, 1948.

Kōnō, Ichirō. *An Anthology of Modern Japanese Poetry*. Tokyo: Kenkyusha, 1957.

Kusano, Eisaburō. *Stories behind Nōh and Kabuki Plays*. Tokyo: Tokyo News Service, 1962.

The Man'yōshū. Tr. J. L. Pierson, Jr. Leyden: E. J. Brill, 1929.

Michener, James A. *The Floating World*. New York: Random House, 1954.

Miyake, Shūtarō. *Kabuki Drama*. Tokyo: Board of Tourist Industry, 1938.

Miyamori, Asatarō. *Haiku Poems, Ancient and Modern*. Tokyo: Maruzen, 1940.

—— *Masterpieces of Japanese Poetry*. Tokyo: Maruzen, 1936.

Nakamura, Mitsuo. *Modern Japanese Fiction, 1868–1926*. Tokyo: Kokusai Bunka Shinkokai, 1968.

Nogami, Toyoichirō. *Zeami and His Theories on Nōh*. Tr. Ryōzō Matsumoto. Tokyo: Hinoki Shoten, 1955.

Okada, Rokuo. *Japanese Proverbs and Proverbial Phrases*. Tokyo: Japan Travel Bureau, 1958.

Okakura, Kakuzō. *The Book of Tea*. New York: Duffield, 1906.

O'Neill, Patrick Geoffrey. *Early Nō Drama: Its Background, Character, and Development*. London: Lund Humphries, 1958.

The Pillow-book of Sei Shōnagon. Tr. Arthur Waley. London: Allen & Unwin, 1928.

Reischauer, Edwin O., and Joseph K. Yamagiwa. *Translations from Early Japanese Literature*. Cambridge, Mass.: Harvard University Press, 1951.

Scott, Adolphe Clarence. *The Kabuki Theatre of Japan*. London: Allen & Unwin, 1955.

The Tale of Genji. Tr. Arthur Waley. 6 vols. London: Allen & Unwin; Boston: Houghton Mifflin, 1925–1933.

Tales of Times Now Past: Sixty-two Stories from a Medieval Japanese Collection. Tr. Marian Ury. Berkeley: University of California Press, 1979.

Waley, Arthur. *The Nō Plays of Japan*. London: Allen & Unwin, 1921.

Watanabe, Yoshio. *Bunraku: Japanese Puppet Play*. Tokyo: Japan Photo Service, 1939.

Religion

Agency for Cultural Affairs, Japan. *Japanese Religion: A Survey*. Tokyo and Palo Alto: Kodansha International, 1972.

Anesaki, Masaharu. *History of Japanese Religion*. London: K. Paul, Trench, Trubner & Co., 1930.

—— *Religious Life of the Japanese People*. Tokyo: Kokusai Bunka Shinkokai, 1961.

Aston, William George. *Shintō: The Ancient Religion of Japan*. Chicago: Open Court, 1907.

—— *Shintō: The Way of the Gods*. London and New York: Longmans, Green, 1905.

Bandō Shojun, ed. *A Bibliography on Japanese Buddhism*. Tokyo: CHB Press, 1958.

Blyth, Reginald Horace. *Zen and Zen Classics*. 5 vols. Tokyo: Hokuseido Press, 1960–1970.

Bownas, Geoffrey. *Japanese Rainmaking and Other Folk Practices*. London: Allen & Unwin, 1963.

Bunce, William K., ed. *Religions in Japan: Buddhism, Shintō, Christianity*. Rutland, Vt.: Tuttle, 1955.

Cary, Otis. *A History of Christianity in Japan*. New York: Revell, 1909.

Casal, U. A. *The Five Sacred Festivals of Ancient Japan: Their Symbolism and Historical Development*. Tokyo: Tuttle, 1967.

Coomaraswamy, Ananda K. *Elements of Buddhist Iconography*. Cambridge, Mass.: Harvard University Press, 1935.

Creemers, Wilhelmus H. M. *Shrine Shintō after World War II*. Leiden: Brill, 1968.

Czaja, Michael. *Gods of Myth and Stone: Phallicism in Japanese Folk Religion*. New York: Weatherhill, 1974.

Davis, Winston Bradley. *Toward Modernity: A Developmental Typology of Popular Religious*

Affiliations in Japan. Ithaca, N.Y.: China-Japan Program, Cornell University, 1977.

De Bary, Wm. Theodore, ed. *The Buddhist Tradition in India, China and Japan.* New York: Modern Library, 1969.

De Bary, Wm. Theodore, and Irene Bloom, eds. *Principle and Practicality: Essays in Neo-Confucianism and Practical Learning.* New York: Columbia University Press, 1979.

Eliot, Charles. *Japanese Buddhism.* London: Arnold, 1935.

Elison, George. *Deus Destroyed: The Image of Christianity in Early Modern Japan.* Cambridge, Mass.: Harvard University Press, 1973.

Ennin's Diary: The Record of a Pilgrimage to China in Search of the Law. Tr. Edwin O. Reischauer. New York: Ronald Press Co., 1955.

Faure, Bernard. *Chan Insights and Oversights: An Epistemological Critique of the Chan Tradition.* Princeton: Princeton University Press, 1993.

———— *The Red Thread: Buddhist Approaches to Sexuality.* Princeton: Princeton University Press, 1998.

———— *The Rhetoric of Immediacy: A Cultural Critique of Chan/Zen Buddhism.* Princeton: Princeton University Press, 1991.

Foucher, Alfred. *The Life of the Buddha: According to the Ancient Texts and Monuments of India.* Tr. Simone Brangier Boas. Middletown, Conn.: Wesleyan University Press, 1963.

Getty, Alice. *The Gods of Northern Buddhism.* Tr. J. Deniker. Oxford: The Clarendon Press, 1914.

Griffis, William Elliot. *The Religions of Japan: From the Dawn of History to the Era of Meiji.* New York: Scribner, 1895.

Harada, Tasuku. *The Faith of Japan.* New York: Macmillan, 1914.

Hearn, Lafcadio. The Buddhist Writings of Lafcadio Hearn. Santa Barbara, Calif.: Ross-Erikson, 1977.

Hecken, Joseph Leonard van. *The Catholic Church in Japan since 1859.* Tr. John Van Hoydonck. Tokyo: Herder Agency, 1963.

Holtom, Daniel Clarence. *The National Faith of Japan: A Study in Modern Shintō.* London: K. Paul, Trench, Trubner, 1938.

Holtom, Daniel Clarence. *Modern Japan and Shinto Nationalism: A Study of Present-day Trends in Japanese Religions.* Chicago: University of Chicago Press, 1943.

Hori, Ichirō. *Folk Religion in Japan: Continuity and Change.* Chicago: University of Chicago Press, 1968.

Hozumi, Nobushige. *Ancestor-worship and Japanese Law.* Tokyo: Maruya, 1901.

International Congress for the History of Religions. *Basic Terms of Shintō.* Tokyo: Association of Shinto Shrines, 1958.

Jennes, Jozef. *History of the Catholic Church in Japan.* Tokyo: Committee of the Apostolate, 1959.

Kapleau, Philip, ed. and tr. *The Three Pillars of Zen: Teaching, Practice, and Enlightenment.* New York: Harper & Row, 1965.

Kishimoto, Hideo. *Japanese Religion in the Meiji Era.* Tr. John F. Howes. Tokyo: Obunsha, 1956.

Kitagawa, Joseph Mitsuo. *Religion in Japanese History.* New York: Columbia University Press, 1966.

Kiyota, Minoru. *Shingon Buddhism: Theory and Practice.* Los Angeles: Buddhist Books International, 1978.

Kraft, Kenneth, ed. *Zen: Tradition and Transition.* New York: Grove Press, 1988.

Lebra, William P. *Okinawan Religion: Belief, Ritual and Social Structure.* Honolulu: University of Hawaii Press, 1966.

Lubac, Henri de. *Aspects of Buddhism.* Tr. George Lamb. London: Sheed and Ward, 1953.

Moore, Charles A., ed. *The Japanese Mind: Essentials of Japanese Philosophy and Culture.* Honolulu: East-West Center Press, 1967.

Murakami, Shigeyoshi. *Japanese Religion in the Modern Century.* Tr. H. Byron Earhart. Tokyo: University of Tokyo Press, 1980.

Nakamura, Hajime. *A History of the Development of Japanese Thought from A.D. 592 to 1868.* Tokyo: Kokusai Bunka Shinkokai, 1967.

———— *The Ways of Thinking of Eastern Peoples.* Tokyo: Japanese Government Print Bureau, 1960.

Nishida, Kitarō. *A Study of Good .* Tr. V. H Viglielmo. New York: Greenwood Press, 1988.

Ono, Motonori. *Shintō: The Kami Way.* Rutland, Vt.: Tuttle, 1962.

Philosophical Studies of Japan. 11 vols. Tokyo: Japan Society for the Promotion of Science, 1959–1970.

Piovesana, Gino K. *Recent Japanese Philosophical Thought, 1862–1962.* Tokyo: Enderle Bookstore, 1963.

Reischauer, August Karl. *Studies in Japanese Buddhism.* New York: Macmillan, 1917.

Reps, Paul. *Zen Flesh, Zen Bones: A Collection of Zen and Pre-Zen Writings.* Garden City, N.Y.: Anchor Books/Doubleday, 1961.

Reynolds, Frank. *Guide to Buddhist Religion.* Boston: Hall, 1981.

Ross, Floyd Hiatt. *Shintō: The Way of Japan.* Boston: Beacon Press, 1965.

Saunders, E. Dale. *Buddhism in Japan: With an Outline of Its Origins in India.* Philadelphia: University of Pennsylvania Press, 1964.

——— *Mudra: A Study of Symbolic Gestures in Japanese Buddhist Sculpture.* New York: Pantheon Books, 1960.

Shunjo. *Hōnen, the Buddhist Saint: His Life and Teaching.* Tr. Harper Havelock Coates and Ryūgaku Ishizuka. Kyoto: Chionin, 1925.

Smith, Robert John. *Ancestor Worship in Contemporary Japan.* Stanford: Stanford University Press, 1974.

Smith, Warren W. *Confucianism in Modern Japan: A Study of Conservatism in Japanese Intellectual History.* Tokyo: Hokuseido Press, 1959.

Steenstrup, Carl. *A History of Ideas in Japan.* London: Athlone, 1985.

Steinilber-Oberlin, Emile. *The Buddhist Sects of Japan: Their History, Philosophical Doctrines and Sanctuaries.* Tr. Marc Loge. London: Allen & Unwin, 1938.

Suzuki, Daisetz Teitaro. *Essays in Zen Buddhism.* 3rd series. London: Luzac and Co., 1927.

——— *The Essence of Buddhism.* London: Buddhist Society, 1957.

——— *An Introduction to Zen Buddhism.* Kyoto: Eastern Buddhist Society, 1934.

——— *Zen and Japanese Culture.* 2d ed. New York: Pantheon Books, 1959.

Thomsen, Harry. *The New Religions of Japan.* Rutland, Vt.: Tuttle, 1963.

Visser, Marinus Willem de. *Ancient Buddhism in Japan: Sutras and Ceremonies in Use in the Seventh and Eighth Centuries A.D. and Their History in Later Times.* Paris: Geuthner, 1928–35.

——— *The Arhats in China and Japan.* Berlin: Oesterheld, 1923.

——— *The Dragon in China and Japan.* Amsterdam: Muller, 1913.

Waley, Arthur. *Zen Buddhism and Its Relation to Art.* London: Luzac, 1922.

Wheeler, Post. *The Sacred Scriptures of the Japanese.* London: Allen & Unwin, 1952.

White, James W. *The Sōkagakkai and Mass Society.* Stanford: Stanford University Press, 1970.

Wing Tsit-Chen. *The Platform Sutra: Basic Classic of Zen Buddhism.* New York: St. John's University Press, 1963.

Arts

Adachi, Barbara C. *The Living Treasures of Japan.* Tokyo and New York: Kodansha International, 1973.

Akiyama, Aisaburō. *Shintō and Its Architecture.* Kyoto: Japan Welcome Society, 1936.

Akiyama, Terukazu. *Japanese Painting.* Cleveland: World Publishing, 1961.

Alcock, Rutherford. *Art and Art Industries in Japan.* London: Virtue, 1878.

Allen, Maude Rex. *Japanese Art Motives.* Chicago: McClurg, 1917.

Anderson, Joseph L., and Donald Ritchie. *The Japanese Film: Art and Industry.* Tokyo and Rutland, Vt.: Tuttle, 1959.

Anderson, William. *The Pictorial Arts of Japan.* Boston: Houghton Mifflin, 1886.

Architecture and Gardens. Tokyo: Toto Bunka Co., 1954.

Artistic Japan. 6 vols. New York: Artistic Japan, 1888–1891.

Audsley, George Ashdown. *Gems of Japanese Art and Handicraft.* London: Low, Marston, 1913.

——— *The Ornamental Arts of Japan.* London: Sampson Low, Marston, Searle & Rivington, 1882–1884.

Auriti, Giacinto. *On Japanese Art: Comparative Observations on Far-Eastern and Western Art.* Tokyo: Society for International Cultural Relations, 1937.

Awakawa, Yasuichi. *Zen Painting.* Tr. John Bester. Tokyo: Kodansha International, 1970.

Azechi, Umetarō. *Japanese Woodblock Prints: Their Techniques and Appreciation.* Tokyo: Toto Shuppan, 1963.

Ball, Katherine M. *Decorative Motives of Oriental Art.* San Francisco, 1918.

Barnett, Percy Neville. *Hiroshige.* Sydney, 1938.

Barrett, Timothy. *Japanese Papermaking: Traditions, Tools, and Techniques.* New York: Weatherhill, 1983.

Binyon, Laurence. *The Flight of the Dragon: An Essay on the Theory and Practice of Art in China and Japan, Based on Original Sources.* London: Murray, 1911.

——— *Painting in the Far East.* London: Elkin Mathews, 1919.

——— *The Spirit of Man in Asian Art.* New York: Dover, 1935.

Binyon, Laurence, and J. J. O'Brien. *Japanese Colour Prints.* New York: Scribner, 1923.

Blacker, J. F. *The ABC of Japanese Art.* London: S. Paul, 1911.

Blair, Dorothy. *Preliminary Survey of East Asiatic Art in the Museums of Europe.* Ann Arbor, Mich.: Edwards Brothers, 1937.

Blaser, Werner. *Structure and Form in Japan: Architectural Reflections.* Scarsdale, N.Y.: Wittenborn, 1963.

———— *The Temple and Teahouse in Japan.* Tr. D. Q. Stephenson. Basel and Boston: Birkhauser Verlag, 1988.

Bowie, Henry P. *On the Laws of Japanese Painting: An Introduction to the Study of the Art of Japan.* San Francisco: Elder, 1911.

Brockhaus, Albert. *Netsukes.* Tr. M. F. Watty. New York: Duffield, 1924.

Brown, Louise Norton. *Block Printing and Book Illustration in Japan.* Geneva: Minkoff, 1973.

Burch, Noel. *To the Distant Observer: Form and Meaning in the Japanese Cinema.* Rev. and ed. Annette Michelson. Berkeley: University of California Press, 1979.

Bushel, Raymond. *The Wonderful World of Netsuke.* Tokyo, 1964.

Cahill, James. *Scholar Painters of Japan: The Nanga School.* New York: Asia Society, 1972.

Caiger, George. *Dolls on Display: Japan in Miniature, Being an Illustrated Commentary on the Girls' Festival and the Boys' Festival.* Tokyo: Hokuseido Press, 1933.

Carver, Norman F. *Form and Space of Japanese Architecture.* London: Dover, 1954.

Conder, Josiah. *Paintings and Studies by Kawanabe Kyōsai.* Tokyo: Maruzen, 1911.

Cutter, Margot. *Bibliography of Japanese Painting.* New York, 1936.

Dick, Stewart. *Arts and Crafts of Old Japan.* Chicago: McClurg, 1905.

Dotzenko, Grisha F. *Enkū: Master Carver.* Tokyo and New York: Kodansha International, 1976.

Dresser, Christopher. *Japan: Its Architecture, Art, and Art Manufactures.* London: Longmans, Green, 1882.

Drexler, Arthur. *The Architecture of Japan.* New York: Museum of Modern Art, 1955.

Egami, Namio. *The Beginnings of Japanese Art.* Tr. John Bester. New York: Weatherhill, 1973.

Elisséeff, Danielle, and Vadime Elisséeff. *Art of Japan.* Tr. I. Mark Paris. New York: Abrams, 1985.

Engel, David H. *Japanese Gardens for Today.* Tokyo and Rutland, Vt.: Tuttle, 1959.

Feddersen, Martin. *Japanese Decorative Art: A Handbook for Collectors and Connoisseurs.* Tr. Katherine Watson. New York: Yoseloff, 1962.

Fenollosa, Ernest Francisco. *Epochs of Chinese and Japanese Art.* New York: Yamanaka, 1907.

Ficke, Arthur Davison. *Chats on Japanese Prints.* New York: Frederick A. Stoke, 1915.

Frédéric, Louis. *Japan: Art and Civilization.* London: Thames and Hudson, 1971.

Fujikake, Shizuya. *Japanese Woodblock Prints.* 7th ed. Tokyo: Japan Travel Bureau, 1961.

Fukui, Kikusaburō. *Human Elements in Ceramic Art.* Tokyo: Society for International Cultural Relations, 1934.

———— *Japanese Ceramic Art and National Characteristics.* Tokyo, 1926.

Fukukita, Yasunosuke. *Cha-no-yu: Tea Cult of Japan.* Tokyo: Maruzen, 1932.

———— *Tea Cult of Japan: An Aesthetic Pastime.* Tokyo: Board of Tourist Industry, 1935.

Miki, Fumio. *Haniwa: The Clay Sculpture of Protohistoric Japan.* Tr. Roy Andrew Miller. Tokyo and Rutland, Vt.: Tuttle, 1960.

Garner, Harry Mason. *Oriental Blue and White.* London: Faber and Faber, 1954.

Gompertz, Godfrey St. George Montague. *Celadon Wares.* New York: Praeger, 1969.

Gookin, Frederick William. *Japanese Colour-prints and Their Designers.* New York: Japan Society, 1913.

Gorham, Hazel H. *Japanese Netsuke.* Yokohama: Yamagata, 1957.

———— *Japanese and Oriental Pottery.* Yokohama: Yamagata, 1951.

Gropius, Walter, and Tange Kenzō, eds. *Katsura: Tradition and Creation in Japanese Architecture.* New Haven: Yale University Press, 1960.

Gunji, Masakatsu. *Buyō: The Classical Dance.* Tr. Don Kenny. New York: Walker/Weatherhill, 1970.

Happer, John Stewart. *Japanese Sketches and Japanese Prints.* Tokyo: Kairyudo, 1934.

Harada, Jirō. *English Catalogue of Treasures in the Imperial Repository.* Tokyo: Imperial Household Museum, 1932.

———— *The Gardens of Japan.* London: The Studio Limited, 1928.

———— *The Lesson of Japanese Architecture.* London: The Studio Limited, 1936.

Harich-Schneider, Eta. *A History of Japanese Music.* London: Oxford University Press, 1973.

Hartmann, Sadakichi. *Japanese Art.* Boston: Page, 1904.

Havens, Thomas R. H. *Artist and Patron in Postwar Japan: Dance, Music, Theater, and the Visual Arts, 1955–1980.* Princeton: Princeton University Press, 1982.

The Heibonsha Survey of Japanese Art. 30 vols. New York: Weatherhill, 1976.

Henderson, Harold Gould, and Louis V. Ledoux. *The Surviving Works of Sharaku.* New York: Society for Japanese Studies, 1939.

Herberts, Kurt. *Oriental Lacquer: Art and Technique.* Tr. Brian Morgan. London: Thames and Hudson, 1962.

Hikoen. *Album Formerly in the Kuroda Collection,*

Now Belonging to Nakamura Tomijirō. Tokyo: Shimbi Shoin, 1912.

Hillier, Jack Ronald. *Japanese Masters of the Colour Print: A Great Heritage of Oriental Art.* London: Phaidon, 1954.

—— *The Japanese Print: A New Approach.* Rutland, Vt.: Tuttle, 1960.

Hincks, Marcelle Azra. *The Japanese Dance.* London: Heinemann, 1910.

Hisamatsu, Shin'ichi. *Zen and the Fine Arts.* Tokyo: Kodansha, 1958.

History of Japanese Ceramics and Metal Work. Tokyo: Toto Shuppansha, 1953.

Holloway, Owen E. *Graphic Art of Japan: The Classical School.* London: Tiranti, 1957.

Hughes, Sukey. *Washi: The World of Japanese Paper.* Tokyo and New York: Kodansha International, 1978.

Hurtig, Bernard. *The Masterpieces of Netsuke Art.* New York, 1973.

Index of Japanese Painters. Tokyo: The Society of Friends of Eastern Art, 1941.

Ishida, Mosaku. *Japanese Buddhist Prints.* Tr. Charles S. Terry. New York: Abrams, 1964.

Itō, Teiji. *Kura: Design and Tradition of the Japanese Storehouse.* Tr. Charles S. Terry. Tokyo and New York: Kodansha International, 1973.

—— *Minka: Traditional Domestic Architecture of Japan.* Tr. Richard L. Gage. New York: Weatherhill, 1972.

Jahss, M. *Inrō and Other Forms of Japanese Lacquer Art.* London, 1970.

Japanese Arts & Crafts in the Meiji Era. Ed. Uyeno Naoteru. Tr. Richard Lane. Tokyo: Pan-Pacific Press, 1958.

Japanese Gardens and Architecture. Tokyo: Japan Travel Bureau, 1962.

Jenyns, Soame. *Japanese Porcelain.* London: Faber, 1965.

—— *The Polychrome Wares Associated with the Potter Kakiemon.* London: Oriental Ceramics Society, 1937–38.

—— *The Wares of Kutani.* London: Oriental Ceramics Society, 1945–6.

Jonas, Frank Morris. *Netsuke.* London: K. Paul, Trench, Trubner, 1928.

Kawakita, Michiaki. *Modern Currents in Japanese Art.* Tr. Charles S. Terry. New York: Weatherhill, 1974.

Kawazoe, Noboru. *Contemporary Japanese Architecture.* Tokyo: Kokusai Bunka Shinkokai, 1968.

Keene, Donald. *Landscapes and Portraits: Appreciations of Japanese Culture.* Tokyo and New York: Kodansha International, 1971.

Kidder, J. Edward. *The Birth of Japanese Art.* New York: Praeger, 1965.

—— *Prehistoric Japanese Arts: Jōmon Pottery.* Tokyo and Palo Alto: Kodansha International, 1968.

Kishibe, Hideo. *The Traditional Music of Japan.* Tokyo: KBS, 1969.

Kishida, Hideto. *Japanese Architecture.* Tokyo: Maruzen, 1935.

Kobayashi, Katsuhiro, Hiroyuki Suzuki, and Reyner Banham. *Contemporary Architecture of Japan: 1958–1984.* New York: Rizzoli, 1985.

Koehn, Alfred. *Bonkei: Japanese Tray Landscapes.* Tokyo: Foreign Affairs Association of Japan, 1956.

Komiya, Toyotaka. *Japanese Music and Drama in the Meiji Era.* Tr. Edward G. Seidensticker and Donald Keene. Tokyo: Obunsha, 1956.

Konparu, Kunio. *The Nōh Theater: Principles and Perspectives.* New York: Weatherhill/Tankosha, 1983.

Kondō, Ichitarō. *Japanese Genre Painting: The Lively Art of Renaissance Japan.* Tr. Roy Andrew Miller. Tokyo and Rutland, Vt.: Tuttle, 1961.

Kondō, Ichitarō, and Michiaki Kawakita, eds. *Feminine Beauty in Japanese Painting.* Tokyo: Toto Bunka Co., 1955.

Koyama, Fujio, ed. *Japanese Ceramics from Ancient to Modern Times.* Oakland, Calif.: Oakland Art Museum, 1961.

Lane, Richard. *Images from the Floating World: The Japanese Print.* New York: Putnam, 1978.

Leach, Bernard. *Hamada, Potter.* Tokyo: Kodansha International, 1975.

—— *A Potter's Book.* London: Faber and Faber, 1940.

Lee, Sherman E. *Tea Taste in Japanese Art.* New York: Asia Society, 1963.

Lieberman, William Slattery. *The New Japanese Painting and Sculpture.* New York: Museum of Modern Art, 1966.

List of Books on Ukiyo-e. Tokyo: Keiogijuku University Library, 1939.

Maeda, Taiji. *Japanese Decorative Design.* Tokyo: Japan Travel Bureau, 1957.

Malm, William P. *Japanese Music and Musical Instruments.* Tokyo and Rutland, Vt.: Tuttle, 1959.

Masterpieces of Modern Japanese Art. Tokyo: National Museum of Modern Art, 1958.

Meinertzhager, F. *Art of the Netsuke Carver.* London, 1956.

Michener, James A. *Japanese Prints: From the Early Masters to the Modern.* Tokyo and Rutland, Vt.: Tuttle, 1959.

Miller, Roy Andrew. *Japanese Ceramics*. Tokyo: Toto Shuppan Co., 1960.

Minamoto, Hoshū. *An Illustrated History of Japanese Art*. Tr. Harold G. Henderson. Kyoto: K. Hoshino, 1935.

Mitsuoka, Tadanari. *Ceramic Art of Japan*. Tokyo: Japan Travel Bureau, 1949.

Morrison, Arthur. *The Painters of Japan*. 2 vols. London and Edinburgh: T. C. & E. C. Jack, 1911.

Munsterberg, Hugo. *The Ceramic Art of Japan: A Handbook for Collectors*. Rutland, Vt.: Tuttle, 1964.

—— *The Folk Arts of Japan*. Tokyo and Rutland, Vt.: Tuttle, 1958.

—— *The Landscape Painting of China and Japan*. Rutland, Vt.: Tuttle, 1955.

Museums of Japan. Tokyo: Japanese National Commission for UNESCO, 1960.

Naitō, Toichirō. *The Wall-paintings of Hōryūji*. Tr. William Reynolds, Beal Acker, and Benjamin Rowland, Jr. Baltimore: Waverly Press, 1943.

Nakamura, Ichisaburō. *Catalogue of the National Treasures of Paintings and Sculptures in Japan*. Kyoto: Suizando Press, 1915.

Nakamura, Tanio. *Contemporary Japanese-style Painting*. Tr. Mikio Ito. New York: Tudor, 1969.

Narazaki, Muneshige. *The Japanese Print: Its Evolution and Essence*. Tr. C. H. Mitchell. Tokyo and Palo Alto: Kodansha International, 1966.

—— *Masterworks of Ukiyo-e*. 11 vols. Tokyo: Kodansha, 1968–1975.

Newman, Alexander R. *Japanese Art: A Collector's Guide*. London: Bell, 1964.

Nishikawa, Kyōtarō. *The Great Age of Japanese Buddhist Sculpture, A.D. 600–1300*. New York: Japan Society, 1982.

Nogami Toyoichirō. *Nōh Masks*. Tokyo, 1938.

Noguchi, Yone. *Emperor Shōmu and the Shōsōin*. Tokyo: Kyo Bun Kwan, 1941.

—— *The Spirit of Japanese Art*. London: Murray, 1915.

—— *The Ukiyoe Primitives*. Tokyo: Yukio Ogata, 1933.

Noma, Seiroku. *The Arts of Japan: Ancient and Medieval*. Tr. John Rosenfield. Tokyo and New York: Kodansha International, 1966.

—— *Masks*. Tokyo: Tuttle, 1957.

Odakane, Tarō. *Tessai: Master of the Literati Style*. Tr. Money L. Hickman. Tokyo: Kodansha International, 1965.

Okada, Yuzuru. *Netsuke: A Miniature Art of Japan*. Tokyo: JTB, 1962.

Okakura, Kakuzō. *Ideals of the East, with Special Reference to the Art of Japan*. New York: Dutton, 1903.

Okamoto, Yoshitomo. *The* Namban *Art of Japan*. Tr. Ronald K. Jones. New York: Weatherhill/Heibonsha, 1972.

Okudaira, Hideo. *Emaki: Japanese Picture Scrolls*. Rutland, Vt.: Tuttle, 1961.

Pageant of Japanese Art. 6 vols. Tokyo: Toto Bunka Co., 1952–54.

Paine, Robert T., Jr. *Catalogue of a Special Exhibition of Japanese Screen Paintings: Birds, Flowers and Animals*. Boston: Museum of Fine Arts, 1935.

Petit, Gaston. *44 Modern Japanese Print Artists*. 2 vols. Tokyo and New York: Kodansha International, 1973.

Piggott, Francis Taylor. *The Music and Musical Instruments of Japan*. London: Batsford, 1893.

Rambach, Pierre. *The Secret Message of Tantric Buddhism*. Tr. Barbara Bray. New York: Rizzoli, 1979.

Rhodes, Daniel. *Tamba Pottery: The Timeless Art of a Japanese Village*. Tokyo: Kodansha International, 1970.

Riani, Paolo. *Kenzō Tange*. London and New York: Hamlyn, 1970.

Richie, Donald. *The Japanese Movie*. Rev. ed. Tokyo and New York: Kodansha International, 1982.

Rosenfield, John M. *Japanese Arts of the Heian Period, 794–1185*. New York: Asia Society, 1967.

Ryerson, Egerton. *The* Netsuke *of Japan*. London: Bell, 1958.

Sadler, A. L. *Cha-no-yu: The Japanese Tea Ceremony*. London: Kegan Paul, Trench, Trubner, 1934.

—— *A Short History of Japanese Architecture*. Sydney and London: Angus and Robertson, 1941.

Sagara, Tokusō. *Japanese Fine Arts*. Tokyo: JTB, 1962.

Sanders, Herbert H. *The World of Japanese Ceramics*. Tokyo and New York: Kodansha International, 1967.

Satō, Tadao. *Currents in Japanese Cinema: Essays*. Tr. Gregory Barrett. Tokyo: Kodansha International, 1982.

Schodt, Frederik L. *Manga! Manga!: The World of Japanese Comics*. Tokyo and New York: Kodansha International, 1983.

Seckel, Dietrich. *Buddhist Art of East Asia*. Tr. Ulrich Mammitzsch. Bellingham: Western Washington University, 1989.

——— Emakimono: *The Art of the Japanese Painted Hand-scroll*. Tr. J. Maxwell Brownjohn. New York: Pantheon, 1959.

Seike, Kiyoshi, and Charles S. Terry. *Contemporary Japanese Houses*. Tokyo: Kodansha International, 1964.

Sen, Sōshitsu. *Tea Life, Tea Mind*. Tr. Urasenke Foundation. New York: Weatherhill, 1979.

Shaver, Ruth M. *Kabuki Costume*. Rutland, Vt.: Tuttle, 1966.

Siren, Osvald. *Chinese and Japanese Sculptures and Paintings in the National Museum, Stockholm*. London: Goldston, 1931.

Smith, Bradley. *Japan: A History in Art*. New York: Simon & Schuster, 1964.

Snellgrove, David L., ed. *The Image of the Buddha*. Tokyo and New York: Kodansha International, 1978.

Soper, Alexander Coburn. *The Evolution of Buddhist Architecture in Japan*. Princeton: Princeton University Press, 1942.

Statler, Oliver. *Modern Japanese Prints: An Art Reborn*. Rutland, Vt.: Tuttle, 1956.

Stern, Harold P. *Master Prints of Japan: Ukiyo-e Hanga*. New York: Abrams, 1969.

Sunaga, Katsumi. *Japanese Music*. Tokyo: Maruzen Company, 1936.

Swann, Peter C. *Art of China, Korea, and Japan*. New York: Praeger, 1963.

——— *The Art of Japan: From the Jōmon to the Tokugawa Period*. New York: Crown, 1966.

Tajima, Shiichi. *Selected Relics of Japanese Art*. Kyoto: Nippon Bukkyo, 1899.

Tajima, Shiichi, ed. *Masterpieces Selected from the Fine Arts of the Far East*. 15 vols. Tokyo: Shimbi Shoin, 1909–20.

——— *Sesshū Gashū: Paintings by Sesshū*. Tokyo: Shimbi Shoin, 1909.

Takahashi, Seiichirō. *The Evolution of Ukiyoe: The Artistic, Economic and Social Significance of Japanese Wood-block Prints*. Tr. Ryozo Matsumoto. Yokohama: Yamagata, 1955.

Takashina, Shuji, ed. *Art in Japan Today*. Tokyo: Japan Foundation, 1974.

The Tale of Genji Scroll. Tr. Ivan Morris. Tokyo and Palo Alto: Kodansha International, 1971.

Tamba, Akira. *The Musical Structure of Nō*. Tr. Patricia Matore. Tokyo: Tokai University Press, 1981.

Tamburello, Adolfo. *Japan*. London: Cassell, 1975.

Tanabe, Hisao. *Japanese Music*. Tr. Shigeyoshi Sakabe. Tokyo: Society for International Cultural Relations, 1936.

Tange, Kenzō, and Kawazoe Noboru. *Ise: Prototype of Japanese Architecture*. Cambridge: M.I.T. Press, 1965.

Tatsui, Matsunosuke. *Japanese Gardens*. Tokyo: Board of Tourist Industry, 1936.

Tazawa, Yutaka, ed. *Biographical Dictionary of Japanese Art*. Tokyo and New York: Kodansha International, 1981.

Terry, Charles S., ed. *Masterworks of Japanese Art*. Tokyo and Rutland, Vt.: Tuttle, 1960.

Toda, Kenji. *Japanese Scroll Painting*. Chicago: University of Chicago Press, 1935.

Tokyo National Museum. *Pageant of Japanese Art*. 6 vols. Tokyo: Toto Bunka Co., 1952–54.

Ueda, Reikichi. *The Netsuke Handbook*. Tr. Raymond Bushell. Tokyo and Rutland, Vt.: Tuttle, 1961.

UNESCO. *Japan: Ancient Buddhist Paintings*. Greenwich, Conn.: New York Graphic Society, 1959.

Warner, Langdon. *The Enduring Art of Japan*. Cambridge, Mass.: Harvard University Press, 1952.

——— *Japanese Sculpture of the Suiko Period*. New Haven: Yale University Press, 1923.

——— *Japanese Sculpture of the Tempyō Period: Masterpieces of the Eighth Century*. Cambridge, Mass.: Harvard University Press, 1959.

Waterhouse, David B. *Harunobu and His Age: The Development of Colour Printing in Japan*. London: British Museum, 1964.

Watson, W. *Sculptures of Japan from the 5th to the 15th Century*. New York, 1959.

Who's Who among Japanese Artists. Tokyo: Government Printing Bureau, 1961.

Who's Who in the Japanese World of Art. Tokyo: O&M, 1993.

Yamada, Chisaburō, ed. *Decorative Arts of Japan*. Tokyo: Kodansha International, 1964.

——— *Dialogue in Art: Japan and the West*. Tokyo and New York: Kodansha International, 1976.

Yashiro, Yukio. *2000 Years of Japanese Art*. London: Thames and Hudson, 1958.

Yoshida, Hiroshi. *Japanese Wood-block Printing*. Tokyo: Sanseido, 1939.

Yoshikawa, Itsuji. *Major Themes in Japanese Art*. Tr. Armins Nikovskis. New York: Weatherhill, 1976.

Science and Technology

Anderson, Alun M. *Science and Technology in Japan*. Harlow, England: Longman, 1984.

Anderson, L. John. *Japanese Armour*. London: Arms & Armour, 1968.

Anderson, William. *Japanese Wood Engravings: Their History, Technique and Characteristics*. New York: Macmillan, 1895.

Arai, Hakuseki. *The Sword Book in Honcho*. Tr. Henri L. Joly and Inada Hogitaro. London: Joly, 1913.

Averill, Mary. *Japanese Flower Arrangement*. London and New York: John Lane, 1914.

Blair, Dorothy. *A History of Glass in Japan*. New York: Kodansha International, 1973.

Bolton, Sheila. *Some Aspects of Japanese Heraldry and Genealogy, Coat of Arms*. London: Heraldry Society, 1962.

Bowes, James Lord. *Japanese Pottery*. Liverpool: Edward Howell, 1890.

Brockhaus, Albert. *Netsukes*. Tr. M. F. Watty. New York: Duffield, 1924.

Brown, Louise Norton. *Block Printing and Book Illustration in Japan*. Geneva: Minkoff, 1973.

Conder, Josiah. *The Flowers of Japan and the Art of Floral Arrangement*. Tokyo: Kelly and Walsh, 1891.

Dick, Stewart. *Arts and Crafts of Old Japan*. Chicago: McClurg, 1905.

Feddersen, Martin. *Japanese Decorative Art: A Handbook for Collectors and Connoisseurs*. Tr. Katherine Watson. New York: T. Yoseloff, 1962.

Francks, Penelope. *Technology and Agricultural Development in Pre-war Japan*. New Haven: Yale University Press, 1984.

Frédéric, Louis. *A Dictionary of the Martial Arts*. Tr. Paul Crompton. London: Athlone, 1991.

Garner, Harry Mason. *Chinese and Japanese Cloisonné Enamels*. London: Faber and Faber, 1962.

Gunsaulus, Helen C. *Japanese Sword-mounts in the Collections of Field Museum of Natural History*. Chicago: Field Museum of Natural History, 1923.

Hakusui, Inami. *Nippon-tō, the Japanese Sword*. Tokyo: Cosmo, 1948.

Hawley, Willis M. *Japanese Swordsmiths: 13,500 Names Used by About 12,000 Swordsmiths from 700 to 1900 A.D*. Hollywood, Calif., 1964.

Herberts, Kurt. *Oriental Lacquer: Art and Technique*. Tr. Brian Morgan. London: Thames and Hudson, 1962.

Hunter, Janet, ed. *Japanese Women Working*. London and New York: Routledge, 1993.

Ishimoto, Tatsuo. *The Art of Growing Miniature Trees, Plants and Landscapes*. New York: Crown, 1956.

Honma, Junji. *Japanese Sword*. Tokyo: Kogei-sha, 1948.

Jonas, Frank Morris. *Netsuke*. London: K. Paul, Trench, Trubner, 1928.

Koizumi, Gunji. *Lacquer Work*. New York: Pitman, 1925.

Koop, Albert J. *Japanese Names and How to Read Them*. London: Eastern Press, 1923.

Laking, Guy Francis. *Wallace Collection of Oriental Arms and Armour*. London: Clowes, 1964.

Lock, Margaret M. *East Asian Medicine in Urban Japan: Varieties of Medical Experience*. Berkeley: University of California Press, 1980.

Mihori, Fukumensi. *Japanese Game of Go*. Tr. Z. T. Iwado. Tokyo: Board of Tourist Industry, 1939.

Munro, Neil Gordon. *Coins of Japan*. Yokohama: Box of Curios Printing and Publishing, 1904.

Nakayama, Shigeru. *Academic and Scientific Traditions in China, Japan, and the West*. Tr. Jerry Dusenbury. Tokyo: University of Tokyo Press, 1984.

National Research Council of Japan. *Scientific Japan: Past and Present*. Kyoto: National Research Council of Japan, 1926.

Okada, Yuzuru. *Japanese Handicrafts*. Tokyo: Japan Travel Bureau, 1956.

Popov, Konstantin M. *Japan: Essays on National Culture and Scientific Thought*. Trs. B. E. Belitsky and S. M. Chulaki. Moscow: Nauka, 1969.

Salwey, Charlotte Maria Birch. *Fans of Japan*. London: Kegan Paul, Trench, Trubner, 1894.

Sargeant, J. A. *Sumo: The Sport and the Tradition*. Tokyo: Tuttle, 1959.

Smith, David Eugene. *A History of Japanese Mathematics*. Chicago: Drugulin, 1914.

Sollier, Andre. *Japanese Archery: Zen in Action*. New York: Walker/Weatherhill, 1970.

Sugimoto, Masayoshi. *Science and Culture in Traditional Japan, A.D. 600–1854*. Cambridge: MIT Press, 1978.

Tsuchimochi, Gary Hōichi. *Education Reform in Postwar Japan: The 1946 U.S. Education Mission*. Tokyo: University of Tokyo Press, 1993.

Tsuchiya, Keizō. *Productivity and Technological Progress in Japanese Agriculture*. Tokyo: Tokyo University Press, 1961.

Tuge, Hideomi, ed. *Historical Development of Science and Technology in Japan*. Tokyo: Kokusai Bunka Shinkokai, 1961.

Uemura, Rokurō. *Old Art Treasures from Japan's Needles and Looms*. Tr. Shiho Sakanishi. Kyoto: Korinsha, 1949.

Victoria and Albert Museum. *Guide to the Japanese Textiles*. London: H.M. Stationery Office, 1920.

Yamada, Tokuhei. *Japanese Dolls*. Tokyo: JTB, 1955.

Yamagami, Hachirō. *Japan's Ancient Armour*. Tokyo: Board of Tourist Industry, 1940.

Yamamoto, Yukichi. *Japanese Postage Stamps*. Tokyo: Board of Tourist Industry, 1940.

Yanagi, Muneyoshi. *The Unknown Craftsman: A Japanese Insight into Beauty*. Tr. Bernard Leach. Tokyo and Palo Alto: Kodansha International, 1972.

Yoshimura, Yūji. *The Japanese Art of Miniature Trees and Landscapes: Their Creation, Care and Enjoyment*. Rutland, Vt.: Tuttle, 1957.

Yumoto, John M. *The Samurai Sword: A Handbook*. Rutland, Vt.: Tuttle, 1958.

Geography

Bekki, Atsuhiko. *New Geography of Japan*. Tokyo: International Society for Educational Information, 1978.

Brochier, Hubert. *The Climatographic Atlas of Japan*. Tokyo, 1949.

Ishida, Ryujiro. *Geography of Japan*. Tokyo: Kokusai Bunka Shinkokai, 1969.

Macdonald, Don, et al. *Geography of Modern Japan*. Kent, England: Paul Norbury, 1984.

McCune, Shannon. *The Ryūkyū Islands*. Newton Abbot: David and Charles, 1975.

Sugimura, Arata. *Island Arcs: Japan and Its Environs*. New York: Elsevier, 1973.

Takai, Fuyuji, ed. *Geology of Japan*. Berkeley: University of California Press, 1963.

Trewartha, Glenn Thomas. *Japan: A Geography*. Madison: University of Wisconsin Press, 1965.

Ethnography and Sociology

Algarin, Joanne P. *Japanese Folk Literature: A Core Collection and Reference Guide*. New York: Bowker, 1982.

Anesaki, Masaharu. *Art, Life, and Nature in Japan*. Boston: Marshall Jones, 1932

Batchelor, John. *The Ainu and Their Folk-lore*. London: Religious Tract Society, 1901.

Beardsley, Richard K. *Village Japan*. Chicago: University of Chicago Press, 1959.

Bownas, Geoffrey. *Japanese Rainmaking and Other Folk Practices*. London: Allen & Unwin, 1963.

Chamberlain, Basil Hall. *The Language, Mythology, and Geographical Nomenclature of Japan,*

Viewed in the Light of Ainu Studies. Tokyo: Imperial University, 1887.

——— *Things Japanese*. London: Kegan Paul, French, Trubner, 1890.

De Mente, Boye. *Some Prefer Geisha: The Lively Art of Mistress Keeping in Japan*. Rutland, Vt.: Tuttle, 1966.

Dore, Ronald Philip. *City Life in Japan: A Study of a Tokyo Ward*. Berkeley: University of California Press, 1958.

Dorson, Richard Mercer. *Folk Legends of Japan*. Tokyo and Rutland, Vt.: Tuttle, 1961.

Dorson, Richard Mercer. *Studies in Japanese Folklore*. Tr. Yasuyo Ishiwara. Bloomington: Indiana University Press, 1963.

Dunn, Charles James. *Everyday Life in Traditional Japan*. New York: Putnam, 1969.

Embree, John F. *Suye mura, a Japanese Village*. Chicago: University of Chicago Press, 1939.

Etter, Carl. *Ainu Folklore: Traditions and Culture of the Vanishing Aborigines of Japan*. Chicago: Wilcox & Follett, 1949.

Frédéric, Louis. *A Dictionary of the Martial Arts*. Tr. Paul Crompton. London: Athlone, 1991.

Fukutake, Tadashi. *Japanese Rural Society*. Tr. R. P. Dore. Tokyo and New York: Oxford University Press, 1967.

——— *Man and Society in Japan*. Tokyo: University of Tokyo Press, 1962.

Iso, Mutsu. *Kamakura: Facts and Legends*. Tokyo: Tokyo News Service, 1929.

Joly, Henri L. *Legend in Japanese Art: A Description of Historical Episodes, Legendary Characters, Folk-lore, Myths, Religious Symbolism*. London and New York: J. Lane, 1908.

Kato, Hidetoshi, ed. and tr. *Japanese Popular Culture: Studies in Mass Communication and Cultural Change*. Tokyo and Rutland, Vt.: Tuttle, 1959.

Kawakatsu, Kenichi. *Kimono*. Tokyo: Maruzen, 1936.

Koyama, Takashi. *The Changing Social Position of Women in Japan*. Paris: UNESCO, 1961.

Matsumoto, Yoshiharu Scott. *Contemporary Japan: The Individual and the Group*. Philadelphia: American Philosophical Society, 1960.

Menges, Karl H., and Nelly Naumann, eds. *Language and Literature: Japanese and the Other Altaic Languages*. Wiesbaden: Harrassowitz, 1999.

Nakane, Chie. *Japanese Society*. Berkeley: University of California Press, 1970.

——— *Kinship and Economic Organization in Rural Japan*. New York: Humanities Press, 1967.

Nishizawa, Tekiho. *Japanese Folk-toys*. Tr.
S. Sakabe. Tokyo: Board of Tourist Industry,
1939.

Norbeck, Edward. *Takashima: A Japanese Fishing
Community*. Salt Lake City: University of Utah
Press, 1954.

Ōhara, Eiroku. *Japanese Chess: The Game of
Shogi*. Rutland, Vt.: Bridgeway Press, 1958.

Ozawa, Satoko. *Dolls of Japan: Their Creation and
Appreciation*. Tokyo: Toto Shuppansha, 1957.

Pinguet, Maurice. *Voluntary Death in Japan*. Tr.
Rosemary Morris. Cambridge: Polity Press,
1993.

Random, Michel. *Japan: Strategy of the Unseen*.
Tr. Cyprian P. Blamires. Wellingborough,
Northamptonshire: Crucible, 1987.

Seki, Keigo. *Folktales of Japan*. Tr. Robert J. Adams. Chicago: University of Chicago Press,
1963.

Shibusawa, Keizō. *Japanese Life and Culture in the
Meiji Era*. Tr. Charles S. Terry. Tokyo: Obunsha,
1958.

Taut, Bruno. *Houses and People of Japan*. Tokyo:
Sanseido, 1937.

Wolferen, Karel Van. *The Enigma of Japanese
Power: People and Politics in a Stateless Nation*.
New York: Knopf, 1989.

Visser, M. V. de. *The Fox and the Badger in Japanese Folklore*. Yokohama, 1909.

Yanagita, Kunio. *Japanese Folk Tales*. Tr. Fanny
Hagin Mayer. Tokyo: Tokyo News Service,
1966.

——— *Japanese Manners and Customs in the Meiji
Era*. Tr. Charles S. Terry. Tokyo: Toyo Bunko,
1969.

INDEX